Introduction to American History 8E

Volume II ~ since 1865

CARL N. DEGLER
Stanford University

VINCENT P. DE SANTIS
University of Notre Dame

BRIAN FARMER
Amarillo College

BVT
PUBLISHING

BUFFALO BILL'S WILD WEST
AND CONGRESS OF ROUGH RIDERS OF THE WORLD.
A COMPANY OF WILD WEST COWBOYS.

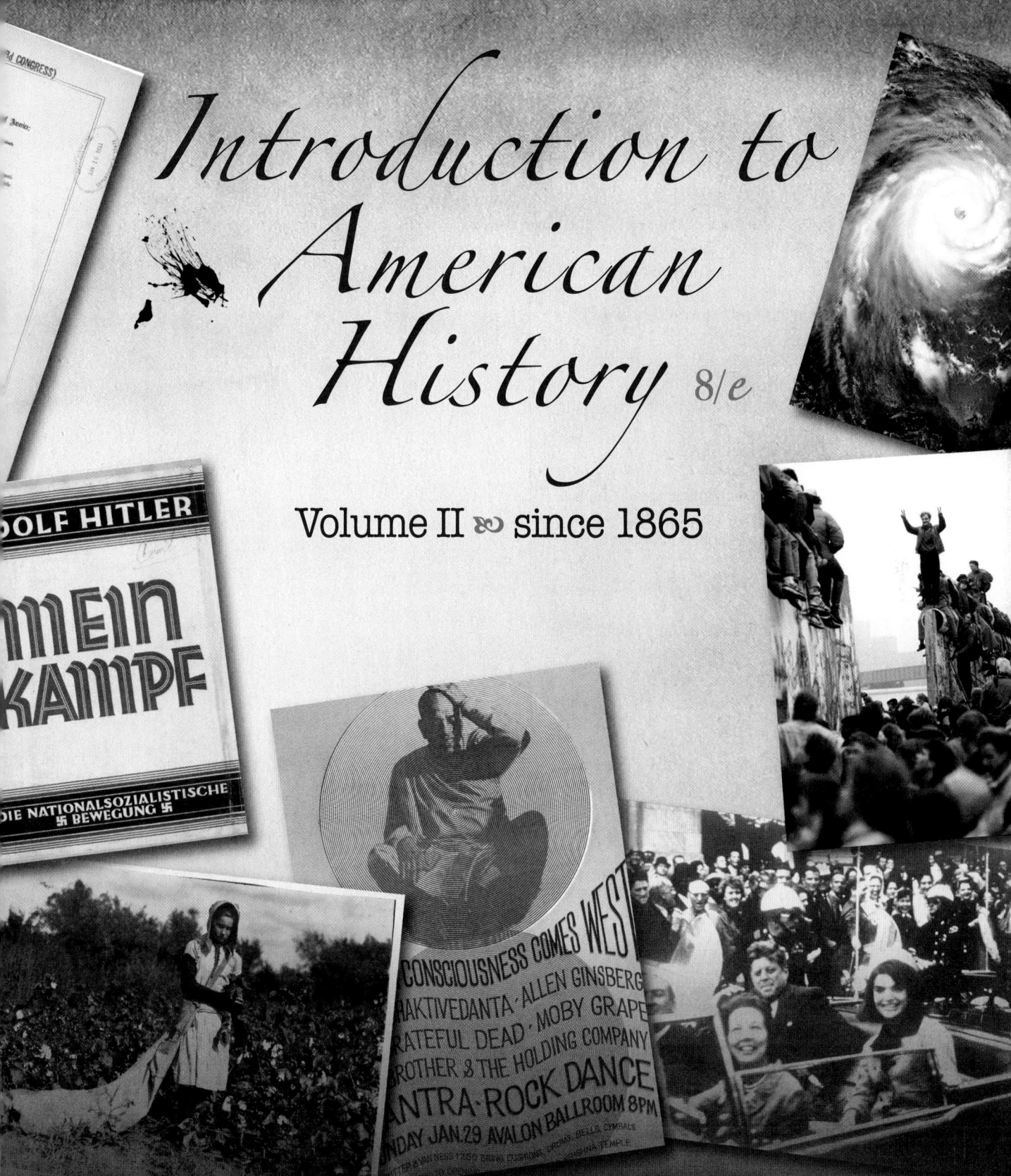

Introduction to American History 8/e

Volume II ∞ since 1865

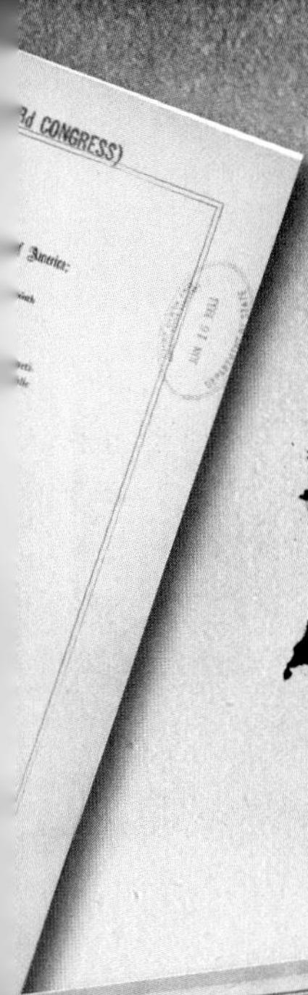

Project Development Manager: Brae Buhnerkemper

Project Development Assistant: Brandi Cornwell

Managing Editor: Joyce Bianchini

Photo Researcher: Michelle Hipkins

Design and Illustrations: Rachel Weathersbee

Typesetter: Dan Harvey

Text and Cover Printing: Quad/Graphics

Sales Manager: Robert Rappeport

Marketing Manager: Richard Schofield

Permissions Coordinator: Suzanne Schmidt

Art Director: Esther Scannell

ISBN: 978-1-60229-876-7

BVT
PUBLISHING

Brief Contents

Table of Contents

AN OFFICE OR YOUR LIFE!

USA
WORK
PROGRAM
WPA

29 The Price of Power, Part II, 1963–1980 661

30 Culture Shift, 1963–1980 731

List of Maps & Charts

Foreword

The opportunity to take a fresh look at the nation's history is always an exciting one. This text represents a solid interpretation of traditional economic and political history, while also including many original insights into social and cultural changes that have influenced and been influenced by economic and political events. Special attention has also been paid to the role of technology. What emerges, in fact, is a vivid picture of the interrelationship of a nation's technology with its culture and its political and economic life. It is hoped that students will gain insights into the ideas and events that inspired this nation's founding and continue to influence its development.

Of special importance are the biographies. The fascinating people profiled range from Phillis Wheatley to W. E. B. DuBois, from Parson Weems to Belva Lockwood, from Dorothea Dix to J. Robert Oppenheimer.

The book that results is an engrossing story of a young nation engaged in what Thomas Paine described as a "bold and sublime experiment" in government. We hope you enjoy the story of the continuing effort to realize the high ideals of this nation's founding.

Special Acknowledgements

In *Introduction to American History's* earlier iteration the textbook had been a collaboration among Carl N. Degler, Thomas C. Cochran, Vincent P. de Santis, Holman Hamilton, William H. Harbaugh, James M. McPherson, Russel B. Nye, and Clarence L. Ver Steeg. These prestigious authors had brought to it many strengths which resulted in a well received and respected textbook for nearly two decades.

We must also extend our appreciation to the many other historians and scholars whose work is reflected in this edition, including Dr. Brian R. Farmer, who provided extensive editing. Special gratitude goes to those teachers and historians who read the manuscript for the previous editions and gave their comments: Frank W. Abbott, University of Houston, Downtown College; Thomas J. Archdeacon, University of Wisconsin at Madison; Morris H. Holman, Eastfield College; Arthur McClure, Central Missouri State University; and Thomas R. Tefft, Citrus College.

Finally, we want to acknowledge the contributions of Dee Andrews of California State University, East Bay, who consulted on early American history, and John Snetsinger of California State Polytechnic University, San Luis Obispo, who consulted about twentieth-century diplomatic history.

The Publisher

Preface

New to this Edition

The *Introduction to American History* text has undergone significant revisions for 2011 in an effort to create both a more comprehensive and readable text for students. A number of chapters have been rearranged so that discussions of culture follow discussions of major events rather than vice versa and some redundancy has been eliminated. New material has been added throughout the text, including new material on the French colonial experience, expanded discussions of slavery and the slave trade, the "New South," the nineteenth century West, the Triangle Shirtwaist Factory fire, the Spanish Flu Pandemic of 1918, crime in the Prohibition era, including Hoover's FBI and Public Enemy #1 John Dillinger, the Baby Boom, and the first year of the Obama administration. The brief biography of Abraham Lincoln and his reelection and assassination are now covered in the chapter on the Civil War so that courses that end with the Civil War, rather than Reconstruction, will have the needed material. Volume II now begins with Reconstruction as "Chapter 15" so as to preserve continuity from Volume I. The discussions of culture in the Gilded Age, Jazz Age, and Cold War eras now follow the discussion of major events and international politics in the Gilded Age, Jazz Age, and Cold War these epochs. Similarly, the culture shift that occurred between 1963 and 1980 now follows the discussion of politics and events for the time period. The final result is a more readable and understandable text that better meets the needs of students in the twenty-first century.

Pedagogical Features

The text contains a number of pedagogical features that are intended to stimulate student interest and enhance learning.

Chapter Openers

Each chapter begins with a **Chapter Opener** that is intended not only to pique the reader's attention, but also preview the topics to be discussed in the chapter and provide insight into the chapter's themes.

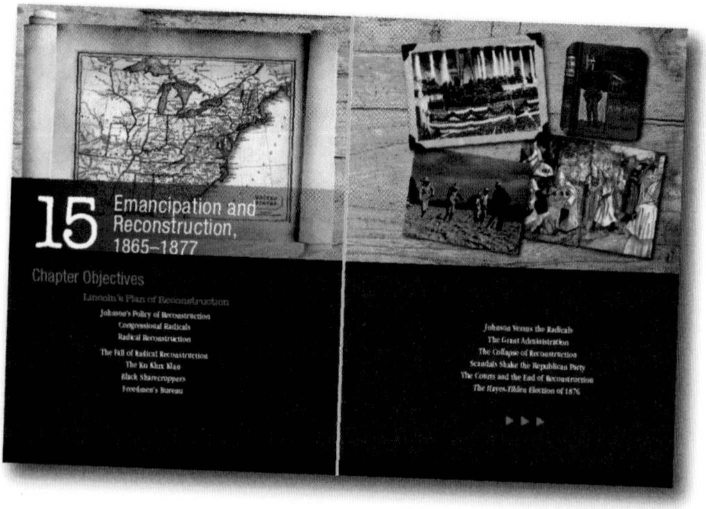

15
Emancipation and Reconstruction, 1865–1877
Chapter Objectives

"People that Made A Difference" Vignettes

Each chapter also contains **"People that Made a Difference" vignettes.** These short biographies not only drive home the fact that people make a difference in history, but also enhance the themes driving the narrative and provide details into the topics being discussed. The fascinating people profiled range from Phillis Wheatley to W. E. B. DuBois, from Parson Weems to Belva Lockwood, from Dorothea Dix to J. Robert Oppenheimer.

People that Made a Difference

Helen Hunt Jackson: Crusader for the Indians

One of the most influential champions of the Indian during the late nineteenth century was the writer Helen Hunt Jackson. Her biting criticism of federal Indian policy in *A Century of Dishonor* (1881) and her sentimental novel *Ramona* (1884) presented the classic statement of American injustice toward the Indian and aroused the national conscience. Described by some of her contemporaries as "the most brilliant, impetuous, and thoroughly individual woman of her time," she is, ironically, almost forgotten today.

She was born Helen Maria Fiske on October 13, 1830, in Amherst, Massachusetts, the daughter of Nathan Welby and Deborah (Vinal) Fiske. A professor of Latin, Greek, and philosophy at Amherst College, her father was also a Congregational minister and author. Her mother, a Bostonian, also wrote. Helen

Helen Hunt Jackson

Chapter Review

At the end of each chapter is a **chapter review** that provides a concise summary of the major events and themes covered in that chapter.

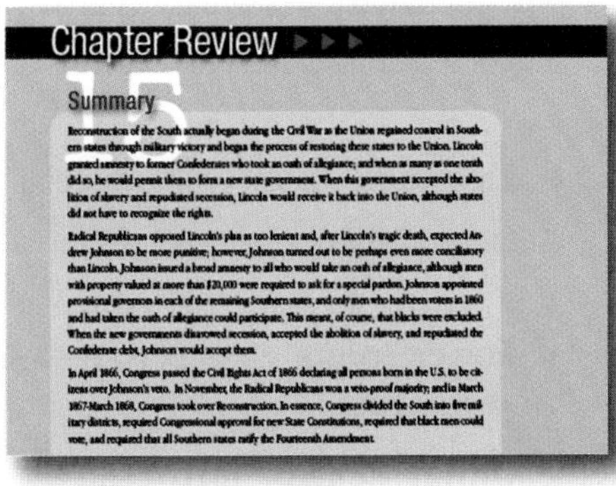

Chapter Review 15

Summary

Reconstruction of the South actually began during the Civil War as the Union regained control in Southern states through military victory and began the process of restoring these states to the Union. Lincoln granted amnesty to former Confederates who took an oath of allegiance; and when as many as one tenth did so, he would permit them to form a new state government. When this government accepted the abolition of slavery and repudiated secession, Lincoln would receive it back into the Union, although states did not have to recognize the rights.

Radical Republicans opposed Lincoln's plan as too lenient and, after Lincoln's tragic death, expected Andrew Johnson to be more punitive; however, Johnson turned out to be perhaps even more conciliatory than Lincoln. Johnson issued a broad amnesty to all who would take an oath of allegiance, although men with property valued at more than $20,000 were required to ask for a special pardon. Johnson appointed provisional governors in each of the remaining Southern states, and only men who had been voters in 1860 and had taken the oath of allegiance could participate. This meant, of course, that blacks were excluded. When the new governments disavowed secession, accepted the abolition of slavery, and repudiated the Confederate debt, Johnson would accept them.

In April 1866, Congress passed the Civil Rights Act of 1866 declaring all persons born in the U.S. to be citizens over Johnson's veto. In November, the Radical Republicans won a veto-proof majority, and in March 1867-March 1868, Congress took over Reconstruction. In essence, Congress divided the South into five military districts, required Congressional approval for new State Constitutions, required that black men could vote, and required that all Southern states ratify the Fourteenth Amendment.

Chronological Timeline

Accompanying the chapter summaries are **timelines** that provide a chronology of the key events covered in each chapter designed to help students place the events in their proper context.

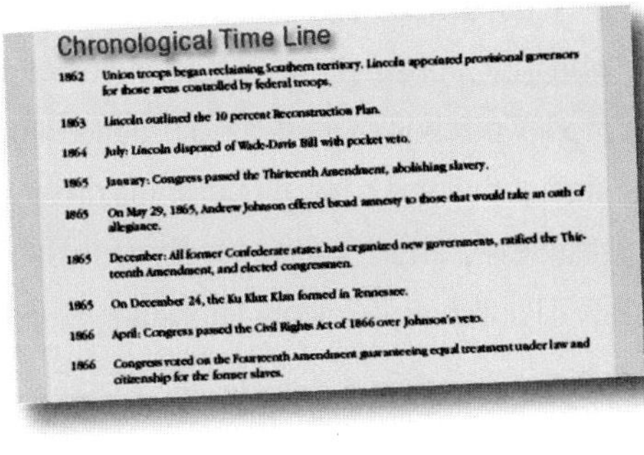

Chronological Time Line

1862	Union troops began reclaiming Southern territory. Lincoln appointed provisional governors for those areas controlled by federal troops.
1863	Lincoln outlined the 10 percent Reconstruction Plan.
1864	July: Lincoln disposed of Wade-Davis Bill with pocket veto.
1865	January: Congress passed the Thirteenth Amendment, abolishing slavery.
1865	On May 29, 1865, Andrew Johnson offered broad amnesty to those that would take an oath of allegiance.
1865	December: All former Confederate states had organized new governments, ratified the Thirteenth Amendment, and elected congressmen.
1865	On December 24, the Ku Klux Klan formed in Tennessee.
1866	April: Congress passed the Civil Rights Act of 1866 over Johnson's veto.
1866	Congress voted on the Fourteenth Amendment guaranteeing equal treatment under law and citizenship for the former slaves.

Key Terms

Each chapter is also followed by a list of **key terms,** each with a concise definition provided to help students understand the important people, places, and events as well as why they are considered important.

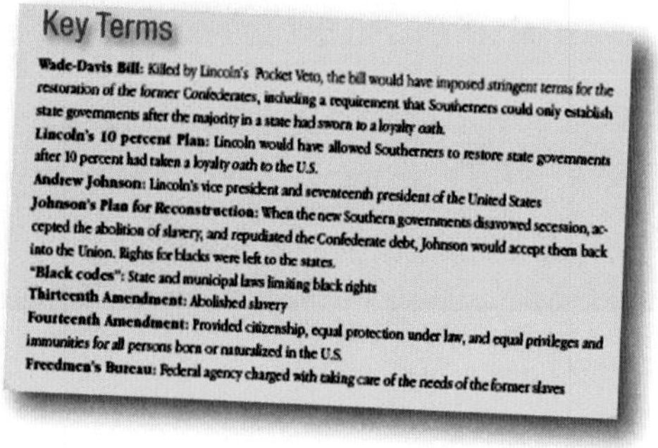
Key Terms

Wade-Davis Bill: Killed by Lincoln's Pocket Veto, the bill would have imposed stringent terms for the restoration of the former Confederates, including a requirement that Southerners could only establish state governments after the majority in a state had sworn to a loyalty oath.
Lincoln's 10 percent Plan: Lincoln would have allowed Southerners to restore state governments after 10 percent had taken a loyalty oath to the U.S.
Andrew Johnson: Lincoln's vice president and seventeenth president of the United States
Johnson's Plan for Reconstruction: When the new Southern governments disavowed secession, accepted the abolition of slavery, and repudiated the Confederate debt, Johnson would accept them back into the Union. Rights for blacks were left to the states.
"Black codes": State and municipal laws limiting black rights
Thirteenth Amendment: Abolished slavery
Fourteenth Amendment: Provided citizenship, equal protection under law, and equal privileges and immunities for all persons born or naturalized in the U.S.
Freedmen's Bureau: Federal agency charged with taking care of the needs of the former slaves

Pop Quiz

Finally, a **pop quiz** is included at the end of each chapter to help students review the material and cognitively assemble the material in a manageable way.

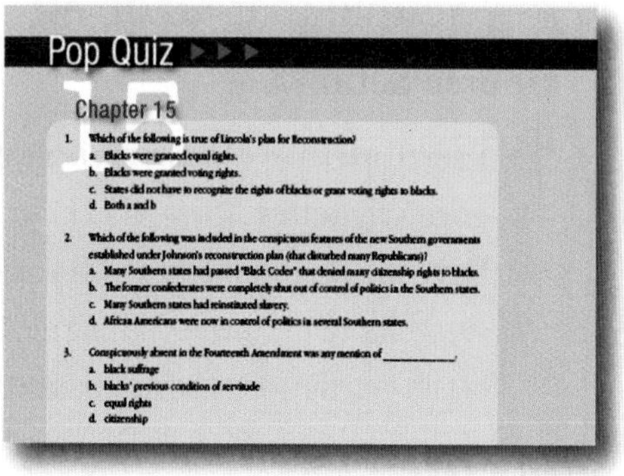
Pop Quiz

Chapter 15

1. Which of the following is true of Lincoln's plan for Reconstruction?
   a. Blacks were granted equal rights.
   b. Blacks were granted voting rights.
   c. States did not have to recognize the rights of blacks or grant voting rights to blacks.
   d. Both a and b

2. Which of the following was included in the conspicuous features of the new Southern governments established under Johnson's reconstruction plan (that disturbed many Republicans)?
   a. Many Southern states had passed "Black Codes" that denied many citizenship rights to blacks.
   b. The former confederates were completely shut out of control of politics in the Southern states.
   c. Many Southern states had reinstituted slavery.
   d. African Americans were now in control of politics in several Southern states.

3. Conspicuously absent in the Fourteenth Amendment was any mention of ___________.
   a. black suffrage
   b. blacks' previous condition of servitude
   c. equal rights
   d. citizenship

Supplements for Instructors

- **Instructor's Manual** The Instructor's Manual for each volume contains material which can be used to prepare lectures and stimulate discussions. The manual includes a brief chapter outline, learning objectives, suggestions for lecture topics, discussion questions, and a list of relevant audio/visual material and WebPages.

- **Test Bank** A test bank is available to instructors in both hard copy and electronic forms. Each chapter consists of a variety of multiple choice, true/false, and essay questions.

- **Power Points** A set of Power Point slides are available to instructors who adopt this book.

- **Online Cement Software** Use our online course management software to create dynamic, randomly-generated tests which can be downloaded directly into your course management software, such as Blackboard, Web CT, Desire 2 Learn, and E Learning.

- **Customize This Book** If you have additional material you'd like to add (handouts, lecture notes, syllabus, etc.) or simply rearrange and delete content, BVT Publishing's Custom Publishing Division can help you modify this book's content to produce a book that satisfies your specific instructional needs. BVT Publishing has the only custom publishing division that puts your material exactly where you want it to go, easily and seamlessly. Please visit **www.bvtpublishing.com** or call us at **1-800-646-7782** for more information on BVT Publishing's Custom Publishing Program.

New to this Edition!

BVT*Lab*

BVT*Lab* —a simple, robust, online lab for college instructors and their students—provides essential teaching, assessment, and communication tools. It is an affordable option for students, with student lab fees costing only $19.99 for a full-semester course. Even if you do not use the lab as your online classroom, your students can still take advantage of the many free student resources.

Course Setup

BVT*Lab* has an easy-to-use, intuitive interface that allows instructors to quickly set up their courses and grade books, and replicate them from section to section and semester to semester. Multiple choice and true/false questions can be delivered online as practice questions, homework assignments, quizzes, and tests—each of which draws from a separate bank of questions. Homework, quizzes, and tests have assigned start and end times; and tests can be proctored in the computer lab or self-proctored for distance learners. Homework and quizzes offer optional hints and instructor tips. In addition, practice questions can be linked to fully worked solutions and multimedia tutorials.Instructors can preview and manually select questions assigned to students, or they can use the "quick-pick" feature in BVTLab to generate sets of questions.

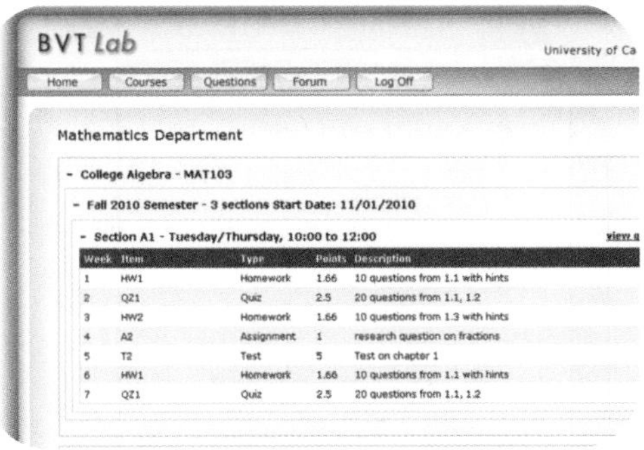

Grade Book

Using an assigned passcode, students register themselves into the grade book. All homework, quizzes, and tests are automatically graded and recorded in the grade book. In addition, instructors can manually enter or modify scores, with provisions for extra credit, attendance, and participation grades. Grade books can be replicated from section to section, semester to semester, and can be easily edited or modified if required.

Communications Tools

Instructors can post discussion threads to a class forum and then monitor and moderate student replies. Important notifications can also be sent directly to each student via email.

www.BVTLab.com

Supplements For Students

Free Student Resources!

BVT*Lab* is a comprehensive online learning environment designed to help students succeed. It provides a complete online classroom, as well as the practice questions, learning aids, and communication tools that students need for success. Even if your instructor does not use the lab as a classroom, you are always welcome to visit as a guest and take advantage of the many free resources.

Practice Questions Students work through hundreds of practice questions online. Questions are multiple choice or true/false and are graded instantly for immediate feedback.

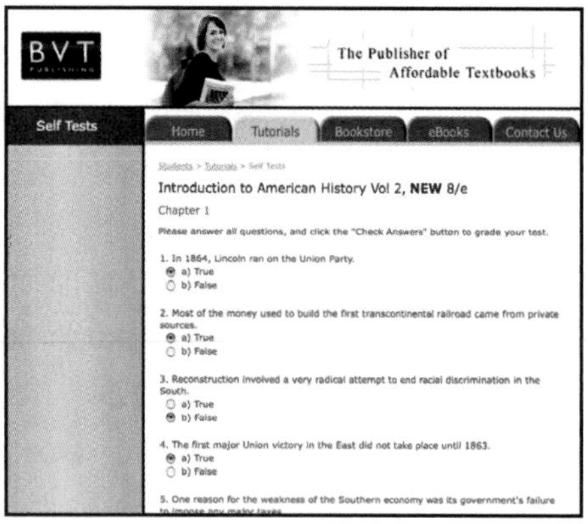

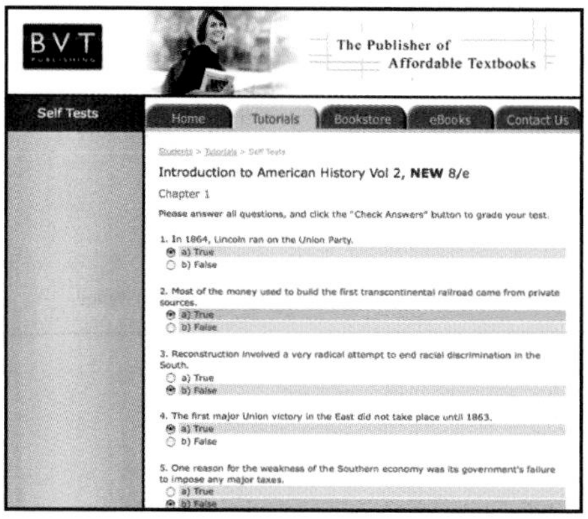

Flashcards **BVT*Lab*** includes sets of flashcards for each chapter that reinforce the key terms and concepts from the textbook.

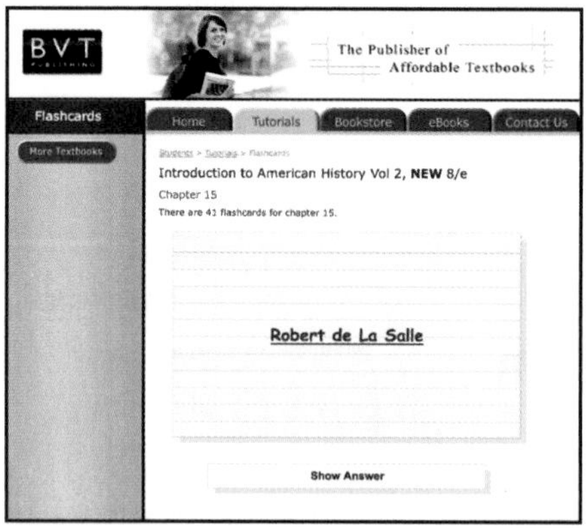

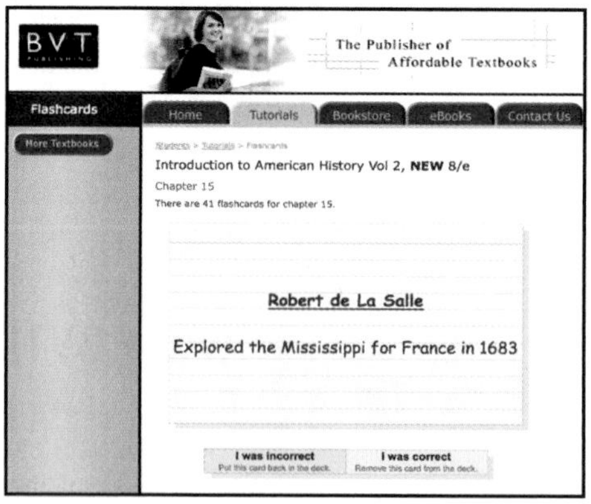

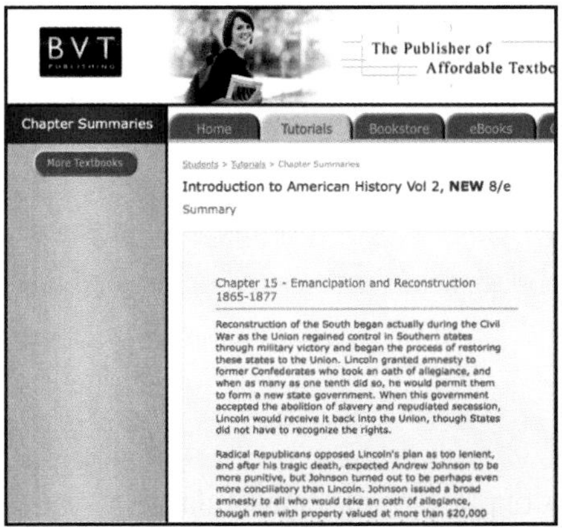

Chapter Summaries A convenient and concise chapter summary is available as a study aid for each chapter.

Discussion Forum An online discussion forum allows students to interact with each other and the instructor to explore challenging concepts and share other resources, while providing an online community for distance learning.

Review For classes taught within the lab, students can view their grades for all completed work and also review prior homework and quizzes to identify areas that require additional study.

www.BVTLab.com

Shop Online

1. Textbook For the student's convenience and pocketbook, students have the added option of purchasing this textbook in the following three formats at **www. bvtstudents.com.**

- **Hard Copy textbook**
- **Loose-Leaf Black & White**
- **eBook Subscription (6 months)**

2. Study Guide Each chapter consists of learning objectives, a chapter summary, matching exercises, true/false statements, multiple choice questions, and review diagrams and charts. Additionally, the study guide contains application exercises which challenge students to apply chapter content to "real life" situations and/or problems, and critical thinking exercises that encourage students to analyze and evaluate psychological research and concepts.

About the Authors

Dr. Brian R. Farmer received his Ph.D. from Texas Tech University in 1996 and has been teaching on the college level since 1991. He is the author of numerous books and articles including *The Question of Dependency and Economic Development* (Lexington Books, 1999), *American Political Ideologies* (McFarland Press, 2005), *American Conservatism: History Theory and Practice* (Cambridge Scholars Press, 2006), *Understanding Radical Islam* (Peter Lang Publishing, 2007), and *Radical Islam in the West* (McFarland Press, 2011). Dr. Farmer is currently Professor of Social Sciences at Amarillo College.

Carl N. Degler was born in Orange, New Jersey in 1921, educated in public schools of New Jersey. He earned his B.A. in history at Upsala College in 1942, and served in the U.S. Army Air Force from 1942–45 and received his M.A. in 1947 and Ph.D. in 1952 from Columbia University. Moving from an Instructor to a Professor at Vassar College (1952–1968), he joined the faculty of Stanford University in 1968 and was named the Margaret Byrne Professor of American History in 1972. He became an emeritus in 1990. Degler also served as Visiting Professor, Columbia University Graduate School (1963–1964) and as Harmsworth Professor of American History, Oxford University, 1973–1974.

Principal Publications: *Out of Our Past: The Forces that Shaped Modern America* (New York, 1959; 2nd revised ed., 1984); *The Age of the Economic Revolution* (Chicago, 1967, rev. ed., 1977); *Affluence and Anxiety* (Chicago, 1968, rev. ed., 1975); *Neither Black Nor White: Slavery and Race Relations in Brazil and the United States* (New York, 1971); *The Other South: Southern Dissenters in the Nineteenth Century* (New York 1974, Gainesville, FL, 2000); *Place Over Time the Continuity of Southern Distinctiveness* (Baton Rouge, LA 1977); *At Odds: Women and the Family from the Revolution to the Present* (New York, 1980); *In Search of Human Nature: the Fall and Revival of Darwinism in American Social Thought* (New York, 1991). Degler has also edited *Pivotal Interpretations in American History* (2 vols., 1966) and *The New Deal* (Chicago, 1970). He wrote an introduction to Charlotte Perkins Gilman, Women and Economics [orig. 1898] in (New York, 1966). Since 1954, he has published seventy-five articles and more than one hundred book reviews.

Neither Black Nor White won the Pulitzer Prize in History, 1972, the Bancroft Prize of Columbia University and the Beveridge Prize of the American Historical Association. *In Search of Human Nature* was awarded the Ralph Waldo Emerson Prize by Phi Beta Kappa in 1991. Degler received the Dean's Award for Teaching in 1979 and honorary degrees from Oxford University, Colgate University, Ripon College, and Upsala College.

Carl Degler has served as President of the Pacific Coast Branch of the American Historical Association (1974–75), President of the Organization of American Historians (1978–79), President of the Southern Historical Association, and President of the American Historical Association (1985–86).

He was a Fellow of the American Council of Learned Societies (1964–1965), the John Simon Guggenheim Foundation (1972–1973), the National Endowment of the Humanities (1976–77 and 1983–1984), the Center for Advanced Studies in the Behavioral Sciences (1979–1980). Degler is an elected member of the American Academy of Arts and Sciences, The American Philosophical Society, The American Antiquarian Society, and the Society of American Historians.

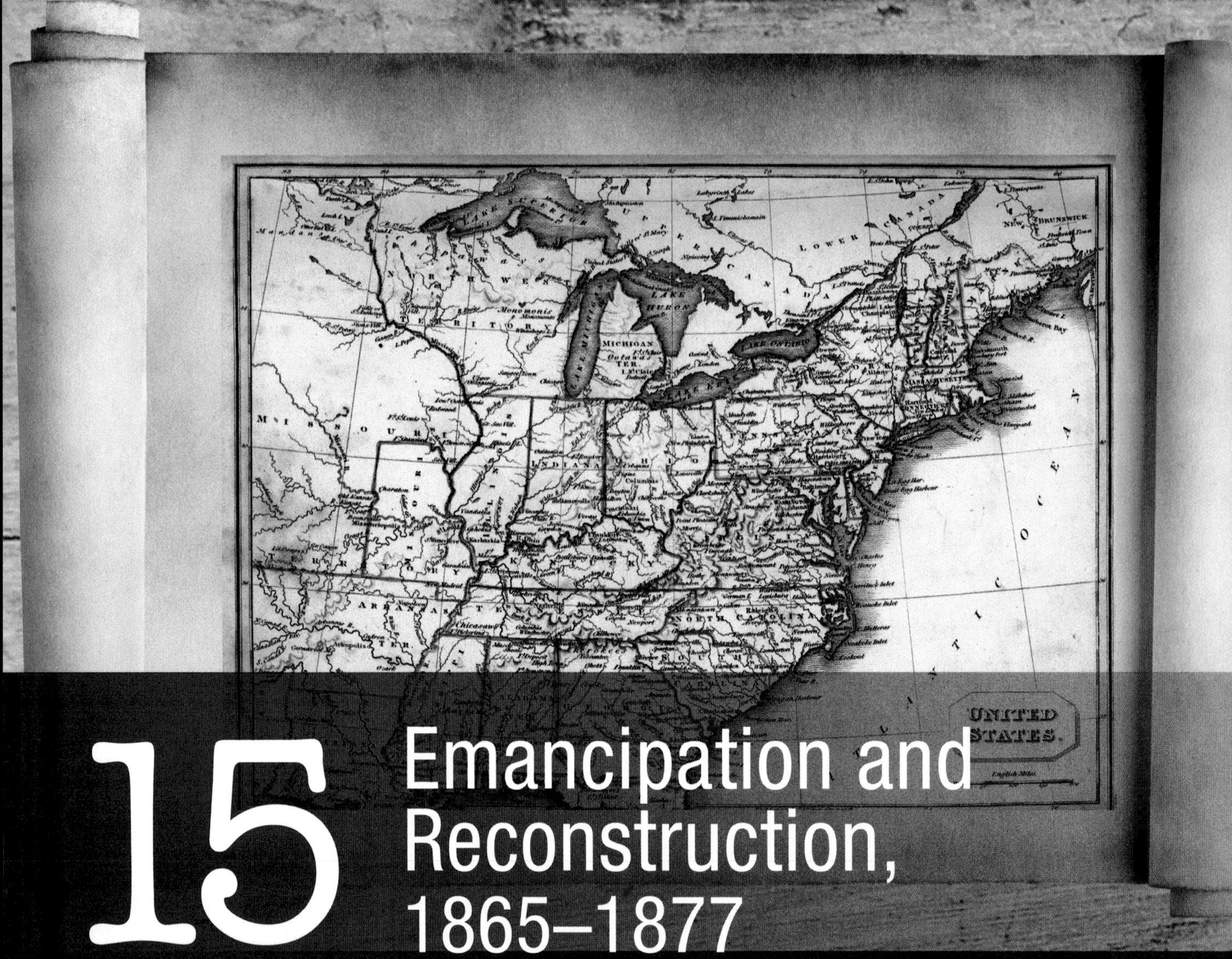

15 Emancipation and Reconstruction, 1865–1877

Chapter Objectives

Lincoln's Plan of Reconstruction

Johnson's Policy of Reconstruction

Congressional Radicals

Radical Reconstruction

The Fall of Radical Reconstruction

The Ku Klux Klan

Black Sharecroppers

Freedmen's Bureau

Johnson Versus the Radicals
The Grant Administration
The Collapse of Reconstruction
Scandals Shake the Republican Party
The Courts and the End of Reconstruction
The Hayes-Tilden Election of 1876

Lincoln's Plan of Reconstruction

The process of readmission to the Union for Southern sates had begun as early as 1862 when Union troops began reclaiming Southern territory. Lincoln then appointed provisional governors for those parts of the Union controlled and occupied by federal troops. Although he had always opposed slavery on moral as well as political grounds, Lincoln was skeptical about the prospects for racial equality in the United States. The legacy of slavery and race prejudice, he believed, would prevent blacks from rising to the level of whites or prevent whites from allowing blacks to change their place in society. This was why Lincoln had supported the colonization abroad of freed slaves as a possible solution of the race problem.

By 1864, however, the president was convinced of the impracticality, if not the injustice, of this policy. The contribution of blacks to the Union war effort and the growing strength of Northern antislavery convictions also made him more hopeful about the chances for eventual black advancement and racial adjustment. On this question, though, Lincoln remained a moderate and a gradualist to the end of his life.

Lincoln and the Northern moderates also believed that victory in war could not really restore the Union. It could only prevent secession. After that, the Union would be restored only if the Southern people again accepted the Union and gave their loyalty to it. To bring them back, Lincoln wanted a conciliatory policy. So when in 1864 Congress adopted a measure known as the Wade-Davis Bill, imposing stringent terms for the restoration of the former Confederates and included a requirement that Southerners could only establish state governments after the majority in a state had sworn to a loyalty oath, Lincoln quickly disposed of the Wade-Davis Bill with the pocket veto. (The president did not sign the bill during the last ten days of a Congressional session, thus killing the bill through his inaction.)

▶Lincoln's tomb in Springfield, Illinois.

When people raised technical questions about the legal status of the Confederate states (Were they still states, or conquered territories? Had they committed "state suicide"?), Lincoln was impatient about such "pernicious abstractions." All that mattered was whether the states could be brought back into their proper relationship with the Union.

By 1864, the Union had regained enough control in Louisiana, Tennessee, and Arkansas to start a process of restoring these states to the Union, and Lincoln laid down generous terms on which this could be done. He would grant amnesty to former Confederates who took an oath of allegiance; and when as many as one-tenth of the number who had been citizens in 1860 did so, he would permit them to form a new state government. When this government accepted the abolition of slavery and repudiated the principle of secession, Lincoln would receive it back into the Union. States did not have to recognize the rights of blacks or give a single black person the vote.

Louisiana was the first state reorganized on this basis. Despite its denial of black suffrage, Lincoln accepted Louisiana, though he did ask the governor "whether some of the colored people may not be let in, as for instance, the very intelligent, and especially those who have fought gallantly in our ranks." In Virginia, Tennessee, and Arkansas, also, Lincoln recognized state governments that did not enfranchise the black Americans.

It was clear, however, that Republicans in Congress were suspicious of these states—more because of their leniency toward the former Confederates than because of their treatment of the blacks. Secondly, the Radical Republicans favored a reconstruction policy that would punish the South; and they, therefore, opposed Lincoln's plan because it was not punitive. Radical Republicans in Congress also disliked Lincoln's conciliatory "10 percent plan" because it allowed the president, rather than Congress, to establish reconstruction policy . It was also clear that Congress might deny the re-established states recognition by refusing to seat their newly elected senators and representatives.

GRAND, NATIONAL UNION BANNER FOR 1864.
LIBERTY, UNION AND VICTORY.

Johnson's Policy of Reconstruction

Although a Southerner, and the only Senator from a Southern state to remain loyal to the Union, Andrew Johnson was expected to be more severe in his Reconstruction policy than Lincoln. Johnson was the son of poor, illiterate parents in Raleigh, North Carolina, who could not afford to send their son to school. Instead, Johnson's mother apprenticed him to a tailor after his father died, and Johnson later worked as a tailor in Tennessee. The ambitious Johnson, who had been illiterate until his wife taught him to write, not only became a successful tailor but also accumulated a fortune in land and at one time even owned five slaves. Johnson was a man of strong emotions. As a Southerner with the roots of a common man, he hated both aristocrats, whom he blamed for secession, and secessionists in general; but when his policy developed, it turned out that he disliked abolitionists and radicals even more. In the end, Johnson proved even more lenient toward former Confederates than Lincoln had been. Johnson was a strong states' rights advocate, who as a Senator had voted against everything that smacked of increased federal power. He even once voted against a bill to pave the streets of Washington, D.C.

Johnson was a defender of slavery and accepted emancipation only grudgingly. Johnson's eventual opposition to slavery developed more out of his dislike for the planter class than out of any moral outrage against slavery or sympathy for blacks. Johnson believed blacks to be intellectually inferior and naturally more suited to manual labor.

On May 29, 1865, he issued a broad amnesty to all who would take an oath of allegiance, including ex-Confederate government officials and military officers, although men with property valued at more than $20,000 (in other words, planters) were required to ask for special pardon, which was freely given. In the six weeks after May 29, he appointed provisional governors in each of the remaining Southern states to reorganize governments for these states. Only men who had been voters in 1860 and who had taken the oath of allegiance could participate in these reorganizations. This meant, of course, that blacks were excluded. When the new governments disavowed secession, accepted the abolition of slavery, and repudiated the Confederate debt, Johnson would accept them. As to what policy should be followed toward the freed men—that was to be determined by the states themselves.

▶ Portrait of Confederate Vice-President Alexander Stephens

The Southern states moved swiftly under this easy formula. Before the end of the year, every state except Texas, which followed soon after, had set up a new government that met the president's terms. Two conspicuous features of these governments, however, were deeply disturbing to many Republicans.

First, these Southern states had adopted a series of laws known as "Black Codes" that denied blacks many of the rights of citizenship—including the right to vote and to serve on juries. Blacks could not testify against whites, and laws were passed against interracial marriage. Of course, blacks were also denied the right to bear arms. Other laws were passed that excluded them from certain types of property ownership and certain occupations. In some cases, black employment was limited to agriculture and domestic servitude. Unemployed Negroes might be arrested as vagrants and bound out to labor in a new form of involuntary servitude. Black workers truant from jobs were forced to do public service until they returned to their former employer to whom they were contractually bound.

Second, the former Confederates were in complete control. By December 1865, all former Confederate states had organized new governments, ratified the Thirteenth Amendment abolishing slavery, and elected Congressmen. Between them, the newly organized states elected to Congress no fewer than nine Confederate congressmen, seven Confederate state officials, four generals, four colonels, and Confederate Vice-President Alexander Stephens.

Congressional Radicals

Presidential Reconstruction, as a *fait accompli,* confronted Congress when it met at the end of 1865. At this point, the Republicans were far from ready for the kind of all-out fight against Johnson that later developed, but they were not willing to accept the reorganized states. They were especially resentful because these states could now claim a larger representation in Congress with the free black population (only three fifths of the blacks had been counted when they were slaves), without actually allowing the blacks any voice in the government. It would be ironic, indeed, if the overthrow of slavery should increase the representation of the South in Congress and if the Rebels should come back into the Union stronger politically than when they seceded.

For some months, the Republicans in Congress moved slowly, unwilling to face a break with a president of their own party and far from ready to make a vigorous stand for the rights of blacks. However, they would not seat the Southern congressmen-elect, and they set up a Joint Committee of the Senate and the House to assert their claim to a voice in the formulation of Reconstruction policy. They also passed a bill to extend the life and increase the activities of the Freedmen's Bureau—an agency created to aid blacks in their transition from slavery to freedom. The new duties Congress wanted to grant to the Freedmen's Bureau were to expand its responsibilities to include federal protection of blacks against white oppression in the South.

Johnson vetoed this measure as an unnecessary and unconstitutional use of the military during peacetime, and he also vetoed a Civil Rights bill that declared blacks to be U.S. citizens and denied Southern states the ability to withhold property rights on the basis of race. Tensions increased; and in April 1866, Congress re-passed the Civil Rights Act of 1866 over Johnson's veto, the first Congressional over-ride of a presidential veto in American history. The over-ride of the president's veto shifted the political upper hand to Congress, which would, henceforth, assume the lead in Reconstruction policy.

In June 1866, Congress voted a proposed Fourteenth Amendment. This amendment clearly asserted the citizenship of blacks by stating, "All persons born or naturalized in the U. S. are citizens", thus effectively overturning the Dred Scott decision that held that blacks were not citizens and did not have standing to sue. It also asserted that blacks were entitled to the "privileges and immunities of citizens," to the "equal protection of the laws," and to protection against being deprived of "life, liberty, and property without due process of law." In effect, the Fourteenth Amendment was designed to overturn the Black Codes.

Lawyers have been kept busy for more than a century determining exactly what these terms meant, but one thing was clear. The amendment did not specify a right of black suffrage. It did, however, provide that states that disfranchised a part of their adult male population would have their representation in Congress proportionately reduced. It almost seemed that Congress was offering the Southerners a choice: They might disfranchise the blacks if they were willing to pay the price of reduced representation, or they might have increased representation if they were willing to pay the price of black suffrage. This might not help the blacks, but it was certain to help the Republicans. It would either reduce the strength of Southern white Democrats or give the Republicans black political allies in the South.

The Fourteenth Amendment, also, provisionally excluded from federal office any person who had held any important public office before the Civil War and had then gone over to the Confederacy. This sweeping move to disqualify almost the entire leadership of the South led the Southern states to make the serious mistake of following President Johnson's advice to reject the amendment. During the latter half of 1866 and the first months of 1867, ten Southern states voted not to ratify the Fourteenth Amendment. By March 1867, Tennessee was the only Southern state that had ratified the Fourteenth Amendment.

Radical Reconstruction

Southern rejection of the Fourteenth Amendment precipitated the bitter fight that had been brewing for almost two years. Congressional elections of 1866, however, gave Radical Republicans a two thirds majority in Congress, thus solidifying their power to over-ride presidential vetoes and take the lead in Reconstruction. Congress now moved to replace the Johnson governments in the South with new governments of its own creation. Between March and July 1867, it adopted a series of Reconstruction Acts that divided ten Southern states into five military districts under five military governors. The governors were vested with "all powers necessary" to protect the civil rights of all persons, maintain order, and supervise the administration of justice. These governors were to hold elections for conventions to frame new state constitutions. In these elections adult males, including blacks, were to vote, but many whites, disqualified by their support of the Confederacy, were not to vote. The constitutions these conventions adopted must establish black suffrage, and the governments they established must ratify the Fourteenth Amendment. Then, and only then, might they be readmitted to the Union.

Congress followed with a second Reconstruction Act that required military authorities in the South to register voters and supervise the election of the delegates to state constitutional conventions. Furthermore, new constitutions had to be ratified by a majority of voters. Thus, two years after the war was over, when the South supposed that the postwar adjustment had been completed, the process of Reconstruction actually began.

MAP 15.1 Reconstruction

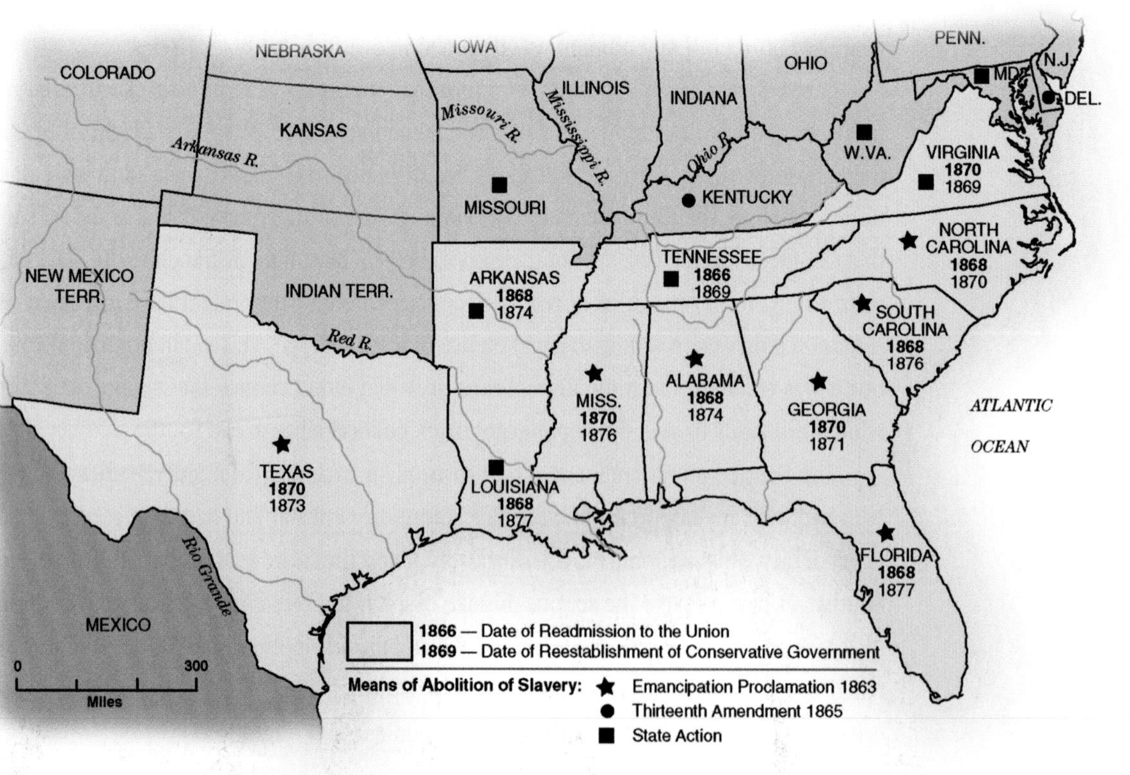

The period that followed has been the subject of more bitter feeling and more controversy than perhaps any other period in American history, and the intensity of the bitterness has made it hard to get at the realities. During 1867 the military governors conducted elections, and in late 1867 and early 1868 the new constitutional conventions met in the Southern states. They complied with the terms that Congress had laid down, including enfranchisement of the black men; however, many Southerners resisted. Military authorities in many places found that they could not get a majority of voters to the polls, as Congress had required. In essence, the former Confederates protested their new constitutions, which they viewed as externally imposed, by staying home and not voting. In March 1868, Congress altered the rules to allow state constitutions to be ratified by the majority of those who voted in an election. Three months later, Arkansas fulfilled the requirements necessary for readmission to the Union; and within a year after the third Reconstruction Act (of July 1867), seven states had adopted new constitutions, organized new governments, ratified the Fourteenth Amendment, and been readmitted to the Union. In Virginia, Mississippi, Georgia, and Texas, however, the process was for one reason or another not completed until 1870. In July 1870, Georgia became the last Southern state to be readmitted to the Union.

All of these new governments, except the one in Virginia, began under Republican control, with more or less black representation in the legislatures. In one state after another, however, the Democrats, supporting a policy of white supremacy, soon gained the ascendancy. Military and "Radical" rule lasted for three years in North Carolina; four years in Tennessee (never under military government) and Georgia; six years in Texas; seven years in Alabama and Arkansas; eight years in Mississippi; and ten years in Florida, Louisiana, and South Carolina.

Historians of the past and those of the present have interpreted the experience of this so-called "carpetbag" rule (so-named in reference to a popular nineteenth-century suitcase literally made from carpet and carried by many Northerners who moved South in search of economic opportunity) in completely different terms. The earlier interpretation reflected the feelings of the Southern whites that resented this regime bitterly, seeing it as one of "military despotism" and "Negro rule." According to this version, later elaborated by a pro-Southern school of historians, the South was at the outset the victim of military occupation in which a brutal soldiery maintained bayonet rule. Then came the "carpetbaggers"—unscrupulous Northern adventurers whose only purpose was to enrich themselves by plundering the prostrate South. Southerners used the term "carpetbagger" disparagingly in reference to Northerners who moved south and became involved in Southern politics.

In the view of Southerners, in order to maintain their ascendancy, the carpetbaggers incited the blacks, who were essentially well disposed, to assert themselves in swaggering insolence. Thereupon, majorities made up of illiterate blacks swarmed into the legislatures, where the carpetbaggers manipulated them. A carnival of riotous corruption and looting followed until at last the outraged whites, excluded from all voice in public affairs, could endure these conditions no longer and arose to drive the vandals away and to redeem their dishonored states.

This picture of Reconstruction has a very real importance because it has undoubtedly influenced subsequent Southern attitudes, but it is an extreme distortion of the realities. Historical treatments since 1950 have presented quite a different version, stressing the brief nature of the military rule and the constructive measures of the "carpetbag" governments. As for bayonet rule, the number of troops in the "Army of Occupation" was absurdly small. In November 1869, there were 1000 federal soldiers scattered over the state of Virginia and 716 over Mississippi with hardly more than a corporal's guard in any one place.

For certain, Southern politics during Reconstruction was fraught with factionalism and corruption, and some of the blame must be placed at the feet of the "carpetbaggers." For example, Illinois native Henry Clay Warmoth was elected governor of Louisiana in 1868 with an annual salary of $8,000. Four years later, Warmoth had a net worth of over $1 million. A full 50 percent of the state budget in Louisiana during Warmoth's tenure went for the salaries and "mileage" of state representatives and their staff members. This, however, was not the only incident of overpaid public officials. One year, South Carolina's legislature voted an additional $1,000 in salary for one member who had recently lost the same amount on a horse race. Inflated and corrupt government contracts were also rampant. For example, the state of Arkansas constructed a bridge one year at a cost of $500 and then repaired the bridge the next year at a cost of $9,000. To be sure, not all of the corruption was due to "carpetbaggers" in government; but for Southerners, the transplanted Northerners made easy targets. Among the American writers who familiarized the country with the looters and scoundrels was Mark Twain, whose fictional writings presented unscrupulous characters with which Southerners became all too familiar.

▶Among the American writers who familiarized the country with the looters and scoundrels known as carpet baggers, was Mark Twain, author of the American classic, *Huckleberry Finn*.

Although there were indeed looters and scoundrels among the carpetbaggers, there were also idealists that did all they could to improve conditions in the South. Many Northern women came to teach the freed slaves. Many men came to develop needed industry, which even if it enriched the Northern carpetbagger in the process, was also good for the South as a whole. Many others worked with integrity and self-sacrifice to find a constructive solution for the problems of a society devastated by war and left with a huge population of former slaves to absorb and support. Many native Southerners, who joined with the "carpetbaggers" in their programs and who were therefore denounced as "scalawags," were equally public-spirited and high-minded.

As for "Negro rule," the fact is that the blacks were in a majority only at the convention and the first three legislatures of South Carolina. Elsewhere they were a minority, even in Mississippi and Louisiana where they constituted a majority of the population. In view of their illiteracy and their political inexperience, the blacks handled their new responsibilities well and they tended to choose educated men for public office. Thus many of the black legislators, congressmen, and state officials they chose were well qualified. They were, on the whole, moderate and self-restrained in their demands; and they gave major support to certain policies of long-range value, including notably the establishment of public school systems, which the South had not had, in any broad sense, before the Civil War.

▶African Americans moved from the plantations to the state legislatures during the Reconstruction of the South. Of the conditions in which the Southern states had to meet in order to be readmitted into the Union, the enfranchisement of black men was one of the most unpopular.

As for the "carnival of corruption," the post-Civil War era was marked by corruption throughout the country. All the Southern states combined did not manage to steal as much money from the public treasury as did the Tweed Ring in New York City, led by William Marcy Tweed, commonly known as "Boss Tweed." New York was also famous for fraudulent elections, and the corruption in government spearheaded by Tweed would become a major issue in national politics in the 1870s. It was true, however, that the impoverished South could ill afford dishonesty in government. Nevertheless, much that was charged to "corruption" really stemmed from increased costs necessary to provide new social services, such as public schools, and to rebuild the Southern economy laid waste by war.

Finally, it should be noted that the Southern whites were never reduced to abject helplessness as is sometimes imagined. From the outset they were present in all of the Reconstruction conventions and legislatures—always vocal, frequently aggressive, and sometimes dominating the proceedings.

The Fall of Radical Reconstruction

For an average of six years, then, the regimes of Radical Republican Reconstruction continued. After that they gave way to the Democratic Redeemers—those who wanted to "redeem" the South to white rule—delaying until the twentieth century further progress toward equal rights for blacks.

When one considers that the South had just been badly defeated in war, that Radical Reconstruction was the policy of the dominant party in Washington, and that black and white Republicans constituted a majority of the voters in a half-dozen Southern states, it is difficult to understand why the Radical regimes were so promptly—almost easily—overthrown. Several contributing factors must be recognized.

First, the former slaves lacked experience in political participation and leadership. Largely illiterate and conditioned for many decades to defer to white people, they grasped the new opportunities with uncertain hands. Very often they seemed to wish, quite realistically, for security of land tenure and for education more than for political rights. At the same time, however, a number of articulate and able blacks, some of them former slaves, came to the fore and might have provided effective leadership for their race if Reconstruction had not been abandoned so soon.

Second, and more importantly, one must recognize the importance of the grim resistance offered by the Southern whites. With their deep belief in the superiority of their own race, these Southerners were convinced that civilization itself was at stake. They fought with proportionate desperation, not hesitating to resort to violence and terror.

The Ku Klux Klan

On Christmas Eve 1865, six Confederate army veterans, who were simply bored and restless after the war and sought something for their own amusement, formed a half-whimsical secret society known as the Ku Klux Klan (KKK) in Tennessee. The name "Ku Klux Klan" was derived from the Greek word "Kuklos," the root of the English word "circle." Since the six founding members were of Scotch-Irish ancestry, they added the word "Klan" and then added the made-up word "Klux" to add "mystery and baffle," as well as something "secret-sounding" and "nonsensically inscrutable." With nothing sinister in mind, Jon C. Lester reportedly said to his other listless, five founding members, "Boys, let's start something to break the monotony and cheer up our mothers and girls. Let's start a club of some kind." The original purpose of the young men, evidently, was merely to play practical jokes and serenade women and had nothing to do with racism or terror.

▶The scare tactics of the Ku Klux Klan eventually escalated to extreme violence.

In furtherance of their playful goals, however, the men donned white regalia and rode through the Tennessee countryside in search of adventure. Accidentally, the men discovered that their midnight marauding frightened the black refugees who were aimlessly wandering the Tennessee countryside in large numbers. The accident then began to take on a more purposeful character, and the Klansmen began a campaign of scare tactics against the wandering black refugees. An unforeseen consequence was that blacks quickly tended to avoid the roadways in the area where Klansmen were playing their games. Word of the KKK fun and games spread across the South. People in surrounding areas contacted the Klan wanting to know how they, too, could set up KKK dens of their own for the express purpose of scaring vagrant blacks away from the roadways. Soon every Southern state had its organization of masked and robed riders, either as part of the Klan or under some other name. Klan tactics quickly escalated from jokes and scare tactics to naked violence, contrary to the original intensions of the Klan's founders. By use of threat, horsewhip, and even rope, gun, and fire, they spread fear not only among blacks but also perhaps, even more so, among the Republican leaders. By 1868, the Klan claimed to have five hundred thousand members, and their expressed purpose had grown from playful mischief to overt resistance to the Congressional Reconstruction Act of 1867.

Klan members were sworn to secrecy and had to swear that they were opposed to negro equality and in favor of a white man's government, including the "restoration of the civil rights to Southern White men." The Klan stated, in its bylaws, a reverence for the "majesty and supremacy of the Divine Being" and recognized the supremacy of the U.S. Constitution. The Klan claimed that it was an institution of chivalry, humanity, mercy, and patriotism that existed to protect the weak, defend the Constitution, and execute all Constitutional laws.

In 1870, KKK violence had increased to such an extent that it drew the attention of the Radical Republicans in Congress, who passed "An Act to Enforce the Provisions of the Fourteenth Amendment to the Constitution of the United States, and for Other Purposes," more generally known as the First Ku Klux Klan Act. The Act imposed heavy penalties for violations of the Fourteenth and Fifteenth Amendments and gave the state governments the authority to take whatever action they deemed necessary against the Klan. In furtherance of the execution of the Act, Union troops and state militiamen arrested Klansmen and tried them for their crimes, sending many to prison. Under this pressure from the federal and state governments, the KKK was no longer a force by the end of 1872.

The dramatic quality of the Klan has given it a prominent place in the public's mental picture of the Reconstruction. Though violence played a prominent role, the white South had other, less spectacular weapons that were no less powerful. Southern whites owned almost all of the land. Whites controlled virtually all employment, and they dominated the small supply of money and credit that was to be found in the South. Also they dominated the legal system. In unspectacular ways they could make life very hard for individuals who did not comply with the system. These factors, perhaps more than the acts of nightriders and violent men, made the pressure against Radical rule almost irresistible.

Another important reason for the downfall of "Radical" Reconstruction was that it was not, really, very radical. It did not confiscate the land of plantation owners and distribute that land

▶The Ku Klux Klan's expressed purpose had grown from playful mischief to overt resistance to the Congressional Reconstruction Act of 1867. Klan members were sworn to secrecy and had to swear that they were opposed to negro equality and in favor of a white man's government, including the "restoration of the civil rights to Southern White men."

among the freed slaves, as radicals and abolitionists such as Thaddeus Stevens and Wendell Phillips had urged. It also did not reduce the former Confederate states to the status of territories for a probationary period as many Radicals also advocated. Furthermore, it did not permanently disfranchise the South's former ruling class, nor did it permanently disqualify more than a handful of ex-Confederate leaders from holding office. It did not enact Charles Sumner's bill to require universal public education in the South and to provide federal aid for schools there; hence, the former slaves were to remain largely uneducated. These would have been genuinely radical measures; but they went beyond what a majority of Northern voters were willing to support; and perhaps these measures would have even risked the renewal of revolt in the South.

Indeed, even the limited radicalism of the Fourteenth Amendment and the Reconstruction Acts strained the convictions of most Northerners to the utmost. The North was not a racially equalitarian society. Black men did not have the right to vote in most Northern states at the time the Reconstruction Acts of 1867 enfranchised them in the South. The enactment of Negro suffrage in the South was accomplished by the Radical Republicans, not because of a widespread conviction that it was right in principle but because it seemed to be the only alternative to Confederate rule.

Later, Republicans found that many Northern voters cared little about black suffrage in the South. They also found that the white South would not consent to a real reunion on this basis and that the restoration of former Confederates to political power did not threaten Northern or national interests. As a result, the Republicans let the existing forces in the South find their own resolution, which was one of white supremacy.

Yet Reconstruction was far from a total failure. It established public schools in the South that gradually brought literacy to the children of freed slaves. By 1900, illiteracy among blacks had dropped from 90 percent after the Civil War to an estimated 48 percent by 1900. It brought abolitionists and missionaries from the North to found such colleges as Howard, Fisk, Morehouse, Talladega, and many others. These colleges trained future generations of black leaders, who in turn led the black protest movements of the twentieth century. Furthermore, though Reconstruction did not confiscate and redistribute land, many freed slaves became landowners through their own hard work and savings. In 1865 scarcely any black farmers owned their farms; by 1880, one fifth of them did.

▶ Sharecropping was a wage-labor system where blacks worked the land for the white owners and paid them a percentage of their harvest. Sharecropping helped open the doors for blacks to finally achieve economic freedom.

Black Sharecroppers

A full 80 percent of black farmers, however, were not landowners, even of small plots; however, they became sharecroppers, often working on the same plantation for the same landowner that had once owned them. Sharecropping was a wage-labor system where blacks worked the land for the white owners and paid them a percentage of their harvest (normally 25 percent of the cotton crop and one third of other crops) for the privilege of working on the owner's land. Planters generally divided their plantations into small twenty-five to thirty acre plots and signed contracts with individual black sharecroppers to work each plot. Landowners supplied the sharecroppers with the necessary mules, seed, plows, and tools, while blacks were responsible for their own food and necessities. A system of credit developed where local merchants would advance goods to black sharecroppers with payment due at the time of harvest.

Sharecropping allowed blacks the beginnings of economic freedom, and also the freedom to decide which family members would work the land, how long they would work each day, and how the labor would be divided. Blacks also typically moved out of the slave cottages and into their own dwellings. On some plantations, however, blacks worked for wages in gangs as they had under slavery, complete with white overseers, and, in some instances, even whippings.

Still, change did come with emancipation in that a full third of the black women that had worked in the fields abandoned fieldwork either to tend to the home and child rearing or for paid domestic servitude. Indoor work, even if it consisted of cleaning and laundry, was much preferable to working in the field in the hot southern sun.

Freedmen's Bureau

Reconstruction also created the Freedmen's Bureau, which was perhaps charged with more responsibility than any federal agency in history. The Freedmen's Bureau was created for the

THE FREEDMEN'S BUREAU.—Drawn by A. R. Waud.—[See Page 467.]

▶ An illustrations from *Harper's Weekly*, 1868; a Bureau agent stands between armed groups of Southern whites and Freedmen. The freedmen's Bureau was created for the purpose of aiding the former slaves in their transition to freedom.

▶ Sojourner Truth and President Abraham Lincoln.

purpose of aiding the former slaves in their transition to freedom. Though woefully undermanned and underfunded, the Freedmen's Bureau provided food, clothing, medical care, and shelter for former slaves. In the first two years after the War, the Freedmen's Bureau issued over $20 million to needy black Americans and treated 450,000 illnesses. The Bureau also constructed forty hospitals across the South to help meet the medical needs of the former slave population.

After the Civil War, the Southern roadways were literally clogged with refugees as Southern plantation owners, who had no money with which to hire their labor, released thousands of free blacks. With nowhere to go, thousands of blacks wandered aimlessly across the South. Many of these refugees would be among those terrorized by the night rides of the KKK since they made easy targets without shelter on the roadways. The Freedmen's Bureau helped transport the dislocated refugees to shelter, helped blacks find family members from whom they had become separated either before or after the War, and performed formal marriage ceremonies for the many blacks who wanted legal sanction for the de facto marriages they had lived within under slavery. In the first two years after the war, the Freedmen's Bureau helped resettled thirty thousand displaced black Americans.

The Freedmen's Bureau also attempted to ensure fair trials for blacks in the South, to provide for black education, and serve as an employment agency for the thousands of unemployed black refugees. In total, the Freedmen's Bureau constructed over 4,300 schools in the first two years following the Civil War.

Finally, Reconstruction also left as a permanent legacy the Fourteenth and Fifteenth Amendments, which formed the constitutional basis for the civil-rights movements of the post-World War II generation.

Johnson Versus the Radicals

The Republicans did not abandon their program all at once. Rather, it faded out gradually although the Radicals remained militant while Johnson remained president. Johnson had used his administrative powers to evade or modify the enforcement of some Republican Reconstruction measures. This convinced most Republicans that his removal was necessary if their policy was to be carried out in the South; and in 1868, they tried to remove him by impeachment. The immediate pretext for impeachment was Johnson's dismissal of Secretary of War Stanton in February 1868.

A year earlier Congress had passed a series of laws designed to strengthen the legislative branch at the expense of the executive. Among these laws was the Tenure of Office Act, which forbade removal of public officials who had been confirmed by the Senate without first obtaining Senate approval. Later, the Supreme Court would deem the Tenure of Office Act unconstitutional. However, at the time that Johnson removed Stanton, who was reporting to the Radicals what went on in administration councils, there had been no judicial ruling; and the House of Representatives voted to impeach Johnson, which meant that he must be tried by the Senate on the articles of impeachment.

The trial was conducted in a tense atmosphere and scarcely in a judicial way. Immense pressure was put on all Republican senators to vote for conviction. When a vote was finally taken on May 16, 1868, conviction failed by one vote of the two-thirds required. Seven Republicans had stood out against their Party. Johnson was permitted to serve out his term, and the balance between executive and legislative power in the American political system, which had almost been destroyed, was preserved. Johnson, however, would fail to win the Democratic Party's nomination for president at their national convention two months later.

▶ The impeachment of Andrew Johnson.

The determination of Republicans to achieve congressional domination of the Reconstruction process also manifested itself in restrictions on the judiciary. When a Mississippi editor named McCardle appealed to the Supreme Court to rule on the constitutionality of one of the Reconstruction acts under which he had been arrested by the military, Congress, in March 1868, passed an act changing the appellate jurisdiction of the Court so that it could not pass judgment on McCardle's case.

The Grant Administration

In 1868 the country faced another election, and the Republicans turned to General Grant as their nominee. He was elected over the Democratic candidate, Governor Horatio Seymour of New York, by a popular majority of only 310,000—a surprisingly close vote. Without the votes of the newly enfranchised blacks in the seven reconstructed Southern states, Grant might have had no edge in popular votes at all. The Radical Republicans were alarmed at their narrow margin of victory and sought to find ways to add more black voters to the ranks. Although the Fourteenth Amendment theoretically forced black suffrage in the South, the issue of suffrage for blacks had been generally ignored in a number of Northern states. Between 1865 and 1869, a number of Northern states had held referendums on black suffrage; and voters in Kansas, Ohio, Michigan, Missouri, Wisconsin, New York, and the District of Columbia voted down black suffrage. The vote in the District of Columbia was an overwhelming 6,521 to 35 against black suffrage. Of the Northern states that held elections on the issue, only Iowa and Minnesota passed laws granting the franchise to blacks. To implant Negro suffrage permanently in the Constitution—for the North as well as the South—Congress, in 1869, passed the Fifteenth Amendment, forbidding the states to deny any citizen his right to vote "on account of race,

▶ President Ulysses S. Grant delivering his inaugural address at the U.S. Capitol on March 4, 1873.

color, or previous condition of servitude." The Amendment was ratified in 1870; it had almost immediate impact as black men, just five years removed from slavery, were elected to public office. Although blacks were still severely under-represented in the 1870s, seventeen black men served in Congress, one served in the U.S. Senate, and one black man served as Chief Justice of the South Carolina Supreme Court. For a brief interlude, blacks even held a majority of the seats in the South Carolina legislature.

President Grant supported the measures of the Radicals and gave his backing to their policies. Like the good military man he was, he believed that wherever violence broke out, it should be put down uncompromisingly. Accordingly, he favored the adoption of Enforcement Acts for the use of federal troops to break up the activities of the Ku Klux Klan. When these laws were passed, he did not hesitate to invoke them; and troops were sent in on a number of occasions.

Fundamentally, however, Grant was not a Radical. He wanted to see tranquility restored, and this meant reuniting North and South on any basis both would be willing to accept. Accordingly, he urged a broader extension of amnesty to all former Confederates, and he grew to resent the frequent appeals of Republican governments in the South for troops to uphold their authority. Though he realized that the tactics of the Redeemers were very bad—"bloodthirsty butchery" and "scarcely a credit to savages"—he became convinced that constant federal military intervention was worse in the long run.

Meanwhile in foreign affairs, Secretary of State Hamilton Fish was busy putting through an important settlement by which Great Britain and the United States adopted the principle of international arbitration as a means of settling American claims that had grown out of the raiding activities of the *Alabama* and other ships, which British shipyards had built for the Confederacy. Though the U.S. did not get the $2 billion in "indirect" damages it sought on the pretense that the British-built Confederate ships extended the war, it did get $15 million in damages from the British for their role in supplying the ships to the Confederacy

The Collapse of Reconstruction

During the eight years of Grant's presidency, Republican governments were overthrown in eight of the Southern states. As Grant's second term neared its end, only three states—Louisiana, Florida, and South Carolina—remained in the Republican ranks. The program of Radical Reconstruction still remained official policy in the Republican Party, but it had lost its steam. The country was concerned about other things.

In financial circles, there was a controversy over what to do about the greenback dollars issued during the war. Since greenbacks were not backed by gold, people had saved the more valuable gold dollars and spent the less valuable greenback dollars, thus driving gold out of circulation. The government was willing to give gold for greenbacks, even though such a policy would tend to increase the value of the dollar. Debtor interests (such as farmers), who wanted a cheap dollar, fought hard against the policy of redemption; but the policy was adopted in 1875. Not only did the policy limit the growth of the money supply and therefore hinder economic recovery in a cash-short economy, the decision weakened the Republicans among farmers in the West.

Scandals Shake the Republican Party

In politics, public confidence in the Republican-led government was shaken by a series of disclosures concerning government corruption. In 1869, investors Jay Gould and Jim Fisk began purchasing gold futures for the purpose of driving up the price of gold, which skyrocketed from four dollars per ounce to twenty-five dollars per ounce. It was expected that at a certain point the U.S. Treasury Department would place U.S. gold reserves on the market in an effort to stabilize the gold market. Grant's brother-in-law in the Treasury Department struck a deal, unknown to Grant, with Gould to inform him in advance when the Treasury Department would release its gold reserves. Gould could then sell before the prices dropped. Grant's brother-in-law dutifully sent Gould a telegraph the morning that the Treasury Department released its gold to the open market, but Gould was out of the office and did not get the message. Prices quickly fell back to the pre-panic price of four dollars per ounce, and Gould's losses were $16 million.

In 1872, it was revealed that several congressmen had accepted gifts of stock in a construction company, the Crédit Mobilier, which was found to be diverting the funds of the Union Pacific Railroad—including the funds the government had granted to it—with the knowledge of the officers of the road. In 1875, Grant's private secretary was implicated in the operations of the "Whiskey Ring," which, by evading taxes, had systematically defrauded the government of millions of dollars. The following year, the Secretary of War was caught selling appointments to Indian posts. Meanwhile, in the New York City government, the Tweed Ring, headed by Tammany boss William Marcy Tweed, was exposed as guilty of graft and thefts that have seldom been equaled in size and have never surpassed in effrontery.

The epidemic of corruption inspired a revolt by reform Republicans, who bolted the party in 1872, organized the Liberal Republican party, and nominated Horace Greeley, editor of the *New York Tribune*, for president. Although the Democrats also nominated Greeley and formed a coalition with the Liberal Republicans, Grant easily won reelection because most Northern voters were not yet prepared to trust the Democrats.

In the economic orbit, the country was trying to weather the financial depression that began with the panic of 1873. With the economic problems experienced between whites in the North, the problems of Southern blacks seemed more and more distant, and less and less important to the people of the North. Moreover, the economic recession weakened the Republican Party even further. In the 1874 mid-term elections, the Democrats won control of the House of Representatives for the first time since 1856. The next year, the Democrat-controlled House threatened to withdraw any appropriations for the Justice Department or the U.S. Army that were intended for use in the South.

In a number of Southern states, white Democrats created paramilitary organizations (the White Leagues, Rifle Clubs, and Red Shirts) that, unlike the Klan, operated openly. In Louisiana, the Democratic paramilitary groups fought battles with Republican militias until President Grant sent the U.S. Army to restore order. Citizens on both sides of the Mason-Dixon line protested what they termed as Grant's "military rule" of Louisiana. Protests grew even louder after the U.S. Army ousted recently elected legislators in the Louisiana legislature due to electoral irregularities.

In Mississippi, in 1875, Democratic Party Rifle Clubs broke up Republican Party rallies, shooting dozens of black Mississippi Republicans. Republican Mississippi Governor (a former Union soldier and native of Maine) called for sending federal troops to Mississippi to restore order. Grant considered sending troops, but refrained when Ohio Republicans warned him that such action could cost him the state of Ohio in the next election. In essence, Mississippians were left to fight out their problems among themselves. Governor Ames attempted to assemble a Republican militia to put down the unrest, but his efforts met with little success; and the Democrats won control of Mississippi in the state election of 1875.

The Courts and the End of Reconstruction

In the companion cases in 1876, *U.S. v. Reese* and *U.S. v. Cruickshank*, the Supreme Court stuck down statutes that had provided for the enforcement of the Fourteenth and Fifteenth Amendments. With these rulings, federal officials could no longer prosecute individuals for violations of the equal rights of black people. Instead, the protection of individual rights was left to the states and the rights of blacks in the South were left in the hands of the white Southerners that were now in control of Southern governments.

MAP 15.2 The Election of 1876

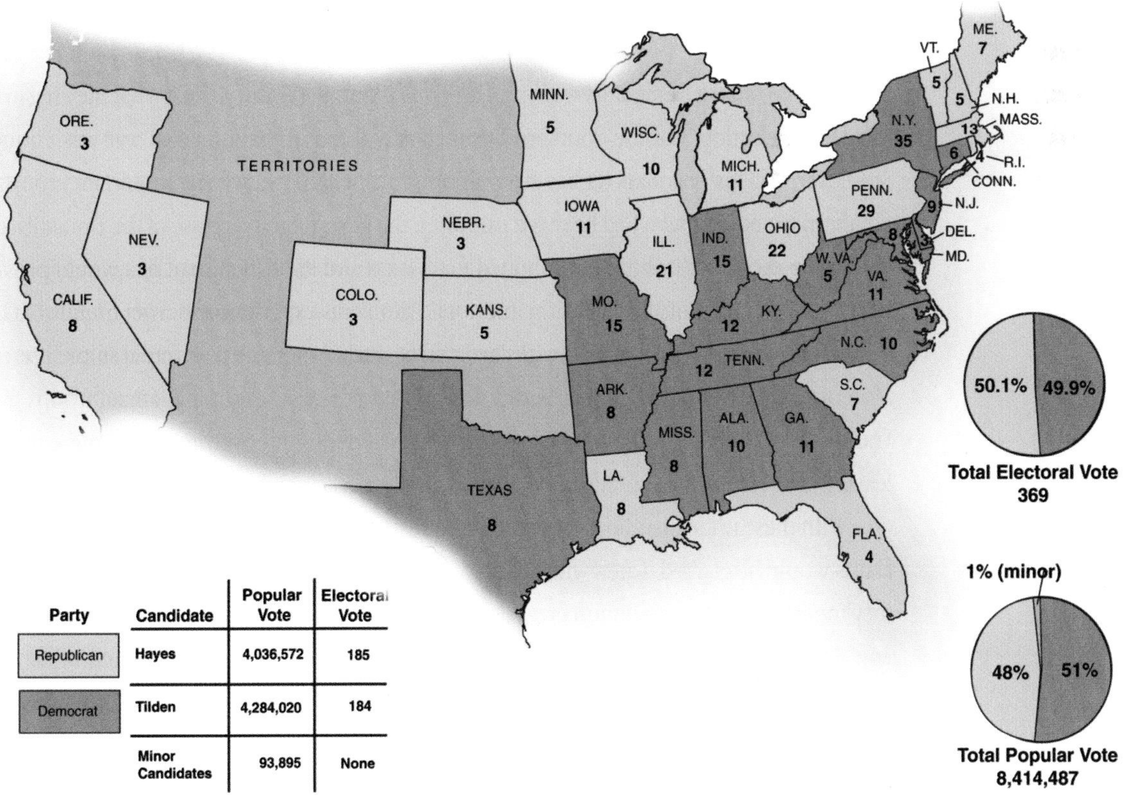

Party	Candidate	Popular Vote	Electoral Vote
Republican	Hayes	4,036,572	185
Democrat	Tilden	4,284,020	184
	Minor Candidates	93,895	None

▶ Rutherford B. Hayes

The Hayes-Tilden Election of 1876

The election of 1876 brought to an end the program of Reconstruction, which probably would have ended soon in any case. In this election the Republicans, who were badly divided, turned to a Civil War veteran and governor of Ohio, Rutherford B. Hayes, as their nominee. Hayes was a conspicuously honest man, and so was his Democratic opponent, Samuel J. Tilden of New York, who owed his reputation to his part in breaking up the Tweed Ring.

When the votes were counted, Tilden had a popular majority (obtained partly by the suppression of black votes in some Southern states) and was within one vote of an electoral majority. However, there were three states—Florida, Louisiana, and South Carolina—in which the result was contested; and rival officials filed two sets of returns, though Tilden had clearly won the popular vote in all three states. To count the votes in such a case, the Constitution calls for a joint session of the Congress; however, the House of Representatives, with a Democratic majority, was in a position to prevent an election by refusing to go into joint session with the Senate. Congress agreed to appoint an Electoral Commission to provide an impartial judgment; but the commission divided along party lines, with eight Republicans and seven Democrats, and voted eight to seven for Hayes. As late as two days before the inauguration it was doubtful whether the Democrats in the House would accept the decision.

Many Northern Democrats were prepared to fight to the finish against what they regarded as a stolen election, but the Southern Democrats had found that one civil war was enough. Moreover, various negotiations had been in progress behind the scenes. Important groups of Southern Democrats who had been left out when the government largesse of the Union Pacific-Central Pacific was distributed now hoped for a Texas and Pacific Railroad that would provide bountiful federal grants for Southern interests. They received assurances from friends of Governor Hayes that he would look with favor upon such programs of internal improvement. Moreover, they were assured that he would withdraw the last remaining federal troops from Louisiana and South Carolina, meaning that their Republican governments would collapse, leaving the score of states: redeemed, eleven and reconstructed, none.

With these understandings, Southern congressmen voted to let the count proceed so that Hayes would be elected. Later, when they were explaining their conduct to their constituents, they thought it best to say quite a great deal about how they had ransomed South Carolina and Louisiana and very little about their hopes for the Texas and Pacific Railroad and other such enterprises. Thus a legend grew up that there had been a "compromise" by which Reconstruction had ended.

▶ Electoral commission of 1877.

What had really happened was that Southern Democrats and Northern Republicans had discovered that there were many features of economic policy on which they were in close harmony. The slaves were emancipated, the Union was restored, and bygones were bygones. The harmony of their views made reconciliation natural and Reconstruction unnecessary. There was still the question of the blacks, but only a few whites had ever supported black suffrage or racial equality for its own sake. It had been an expedient; and now that the expedient was no longer needed, it could be laid aside. Such was the spirit of reconciliation.

Thus, the country ended a period of intense friction and entered upon a long era of sectional harmony and rapid economic growth. However, this was done at the expense of leaving the question of racial relations still unattended to, even though slavery itself had, at immense cost, been removed.

▶ ▶ ▶

Chapter Review 15

Summary

Reconstruction of the South actually began during the Civil War as the Union regained control in Southern states through military victory and began the process of restoring these states to the Union. Lincoln granted amnesty to former Confederates who took an oath of allegiance; and when as many as one tenth did so, he would permit them to form a new state government. When this government accepted the abolition of slavery and repudiated secession, Lincoln would receive it back into the Union, although states did not have to recognize the rights.

Radical Republicans opposed Lincoln's plan as too lenient and, after Lincoln's tragic death, expected Andrew Johnson to be more punitive; however, Johnson turned out to be perhaps even more conciliatory than Lincoln. Johnson issued a broad amnesty to all who would take an oath of allegiance, although men with property valued at more than $20,000 were required to ask for a special pardon. Johnson appointed provisional governors in each of the remaining Southern states, and only men who had been voters in 1860 and had taken the oath of allegiance could participate. This meant, of course, that blacks were excluded. When the new governments disavowed secession, accepted the abolition of slavery, and repudiated the Confederate debt, Johnson would accept them.

In April 1866, Congress passed the Civil Rights Act of 1866 declaring all persons born in the U.S. to be citizens over Johnson's veto. In November, the Radical Republicans won a veto-proof majority; and in March 1867-March 1868, Congress took over Reconstruction. In essence, Congress divided the South into five military districts, required Congressional approval for new State Constitutions, required that black men could vote, and required that all Southern states ratify the Fourteenth Amendment.

Northern opportunists, labeled "carpetbaggers" by Southerners, moved south and exploited the political and economic situation. Some, such as Henry Clay Warmoth, who was elected governor of Louisiana, fleeced the taxpayers for millions. Southerners also objected to "negro rule" as blacks were elected to office on the state and municipal level in the South.

Many blacks, however, became not elected officials but sharecroppers, paying landowners for the privilege of working their land with a percentage of their harvest. The sharecroppers were among the poorest Americans in the late nineteenth century.

Whites reacted against black freedom with the formation of the Ku Klux Klan. Although the Klan was begun as a social organization by young men seeking fun and recreation, it quickly devolved into a terror organization that targeted blacks until it was squelched by federal authorities.

The Freedmen's Bureau was established to assist blacks in their transition to freedom, but the Bureau was understaffed and underfunded considering the scope of the problems for the former slaves. Regardless, until the early 1870s the regimes of Radical Republican Reconstruction continued. After that they gave way to the Democratic Redeemers—those who wanted to "redeem" the South to white rule—delaying until the twentieth century further progress toward equal rights for blacks. Radical Republicans went as far as impeaching Andrew Johnson, but the Senate failed, by one vote, to convict the president.

General Ulysses S. Grant was elected in 1869; however, his administration was fraught with scandals, including the Credit Mobilier scandal in conjunction with the Transcontinental Railroad and the efforts of Jay Gould and Jim Fiske to corner the gold market in 1869.

Reconstruction would finally come to an end with the Compromise of 1877 where the Southern Democrats agreed to accept Rutherford B. Hayes, a Republican who lost the popular vote, as president in exchange for a federal withdrawal from the South. Real equality for black Americans would be an issue for future generations.

Chronological Time Line

1862 Union troops began reclaiming Southern territory. Lincoln appointed provisional governors for those areas controlled by federal troops.

1863 Lincoln outlined the 10 percent Reconstruction Plan.

1864 July: Lincoln disposed of Wade-Davis Bill with pocket veto.

1865 January: Congress passed the Thirteenth Amendment, abolishing slavery.

1865 On May 29, 1865, Andrew Johnson offered broad amnesty to those that would take an oath of allegiance.

1865 December: All former Confederate states had organized new governments, ratified the Thirteenth Amendment, and elected congressmen.

1865 On December 24, the Ku Klux Klan formed in Tennessee.

1866 April: Congress passed the Civil Rights Act of 1866 over Johnson's veto.

1866 Congress voted on the Fourteenth Amendment guaranteeing equal treatment under law and citizenship for the former slaves.

1866 November: Radical Republicans gained a two-thirds majority in Congress.

1867 March: First Reconstruction Act was passed over Johnson's veto.

1868 January–May: House of Representatives impeached President Andrew Johnson, but the Senate failed to convict, by one vote.

1868 November: Ulysses S. Grant was elected president.

Chapter Review (cont'd)

Chronological Time Line (cont'd)

1869 Congress passed the Fifteenth Amendment prohibiting the denial of voting rights based on race.

1869 Jay Gould and Jim Fisk attempted to corner the gold market.

1870 July: Georgia became last Southern state to be admitted to the Union.

1870 The First Ku Klux Klan Act prohibited violations of Fourteenth and Fifteenth Amendments.

1872 Credit Mobilier Scandal

1872 November: President Grant was reelected.

1873 Financial panic plunged the economy into depression.

1876 In *U. S. v. Reese* and *U. S. v. Cruickshank*, the Supreme Court ruled that the Fifteenth Amendment did not confer voting rights.

1876 Rutherford B. Hayes lost the popular vote to Samuel Tilden, but won the electoral vote in a disputed election.

1877 The Compromise of 1877 ended Reconstruction in the South, and the South accepted Hayes as president.

Key Terms

Wade-Davis Bill: Killed by Lincoln's Pocket Veto, the bill would have imposed stringent terms for the restoration of the former Confederates, including a requirement that Southerners could only establish state governments after the majority in a state had sworn to a loyalty oath.

Lincoln's 10 percent Plan: Lincoln would have allowed Southerners to restore state governments after 10 percent had taken a loyalty oath to the U.S.

Andrew Johnson: Lincoln's vice president and seventeenth president of the United States

Johnson's Plan for Reconstruction: When the new Southern governments disavowed secession, accepted the abolition of slavery, and repudiated the Confederate debt, Johnson would accept them back into the Union. Rights for blacks were left to the states.

"Black codes": State and municipal laws limiting black rights

Thirteenth Amendment: Abolished slavery

Fourteenth Amendment: Provided citizenship, equal protection under law, and equal privileges and immunities for all persons born or naturalized in the U.S.

Freedmen's Bureau: Federal agency charged with taking care of the needs of the former slaves

Key Terms (cont'd)

Civil Rights Act of 1866: This act declared that all persons born in the U.S. to be U.S. citizens. The act was passed over Andrew Johnson's veto.

Reconstruction Acts: Four acts of Congress passed between March 1867 and March 1868 that divided the South into five military districts, required Congressional approval for new State constitutions, required that blacks could vote, and required that all Southern states ratify the Fourteenth Amendment

Carpetbaggers: Northerners that moved South after the Civil War seeking economic opportunity

William Marcy "Boss" Tweed: Head of the New York City political machine in the late nineteenth century notorious for fraud

Ku Klux Klan: Secret society that began in the 1870s as a social organization but quickly developed into a terror organization targeting blacks

First Ku Klux Klan Act: The act imposed heavy penalties for violations of the Fourteenth and Fifteenth Amendments and gave the State governments the authority to take whatever action they deemed necessary against the Klan.

Sharecroppers: Farmers that worked the land for landowners and paid a percentage of their harvest to the landowners

Jay Gould: Railroad tycoon and investor that attempted to corner the gold market in 1869

Jim Fisk: Partner with Jay Gould in the gold market scheme of 1869

15th Amendment: Prohibited any voter qualifications that denied voting rights based on race

Tenure of Office Act: Forbade removals of public officials who had been confirmed by the Senate without first obtaining Senate approval

Credit Mobilier: Construction company owned by the major stockholders of the Union Pacific Railroad that was set up to make it appear that the Union Pacific was not profiting from the construction of the Transcontinental Railroad. (Credit Mobilier bribed Congressmen with shares in the company.)

"Liberal" Republicans: Reform Republicans, who bolted the party in 1872 in reaction to scandals in the Grant administration, organized the Liberal Republican Party, and nominated Horace Greeley, editor of the *New York Tribune,* for president

White Leagues, Rifle Clubs, and Red Shirts: Paramilitary groups in the South that fought battles against the Republican state militias during Reconstruction

Election of 1876: Disputed election where Democrat Samuel Tilden won the popular vote but Republican Rutherford B. Hayes won the electoral vote when an electoral commission of eight Republicans and seven Democrats voted 8-7 to give all votes in dispute to Hayes.

U.S. v. Reese, U.S. v. Cruickshank: Supreme Court ruled that the 15th Amendment did not confer voting rights on anyone. Instead, if voting rights are denied, it cannot be on the basis of race.

Rutherford B. Hayes: Republican Elected president in the disputed election of 1876

Samuel Tilden: Democrat that won the popular vote but lost the electoral vote in the disputed election of 1876

Pop Quiz

Chapter 15

1. Which of the following is true of Lincoln's plan for Reconstruction?
   a. Blacks were granted equal rights.
   b. Blacks were granted voting rights.
   c. States did not have to recognize the rights of blacks or grant voting rights to blacks.
   d. Both a and b

2. Which of the following was included in the conspicuous features of the new Southern governments established under Johnson's reconstruction plan (that disturbed many Republicans)?
   a. Many Southern states had passed "Black Codes" that denied many citizenship rights to blacks.
   b. The former confederates were completely shut out of control of politics in the Southern states.
   c. Many Southern states had reinstituted slavery.
   d. African Americans were now in control of politics in several Southern states.

3. Conspicuously absent in the Fourteenth Amendment was any mention of _____________.
   a. black suffrage
   b. blacks' previous condition of servitude
   c. equal rights
   d. citizenship

4. Under Congressional Reconstruction, blacks were the majority in the first three legislatures of________.
   a. South Carolina
   b. Mississippi
   c. Alabama
   d. All of the above

5. What was one factor, even more important than the Klan, that worked to limit black advancement in the South?
   a. Whites owned all of the land.
   b. Whites controlled most of the money and credit.
   c. Whites controlled all of the business and employment.
   d. All of the above.

6. For what was the Freedmen's Bureau responsible?
   a. purchasing the freedom of slaves from their masters
   b. aiding the former slaves in their transition to freedom
   c. propaganda in support of black supremacy
   d. helping slaves escape to freedom via the Underground Railroad

(cont'd)

7. What did the Fifteenth Amendment forbid?
   a. The denial of voting rights based on race, color, or previous condition of servitude
   b. The denial of voting rights based on sex or gender
   c. The denial of voting rights based on illiteracy
   d. All of the above

8. The Hayes-Tilden Election was decided by __________.
   a. the popular vote
   b. the Electoral College
   c. the Supreme Court
   d. an Electoral Commission appointed by Congress.

9. How were Southern Democrats persuaded to accept the results of the election of 1876?
   a. They received assurances that Hayes would oppose any railroad in the South.
   b. They received assurances that Hayes would withdraw the remaining Union troops from the South.
   c. They received assurances that blacks would have equal rights in the South.
   d. They received assurances that all blacks would be removed to the North.

10. The first major Union victory in the East did not take place until 1863. T F

11. In 1864, Lincoln ran on the Union Party. T F

12. Reconstruction involved a very radical attempt to end racial discrimination in the South. T F

13. A person drafted into the Union Army could purchase an __________ for __________.

14. Andrew Johnson was charged with violating the __________ __________ but was not convicted.

15. The Reconstruction Acts abolished __________ and created __________ military districts.

1. C	6. B	11. T	14. Tenure of Office Act
2. A	7. A	12. F	
3. A	8. D	13. Exemption; $300	15. States; Five
4. D	9. B		
5. D	10. T		

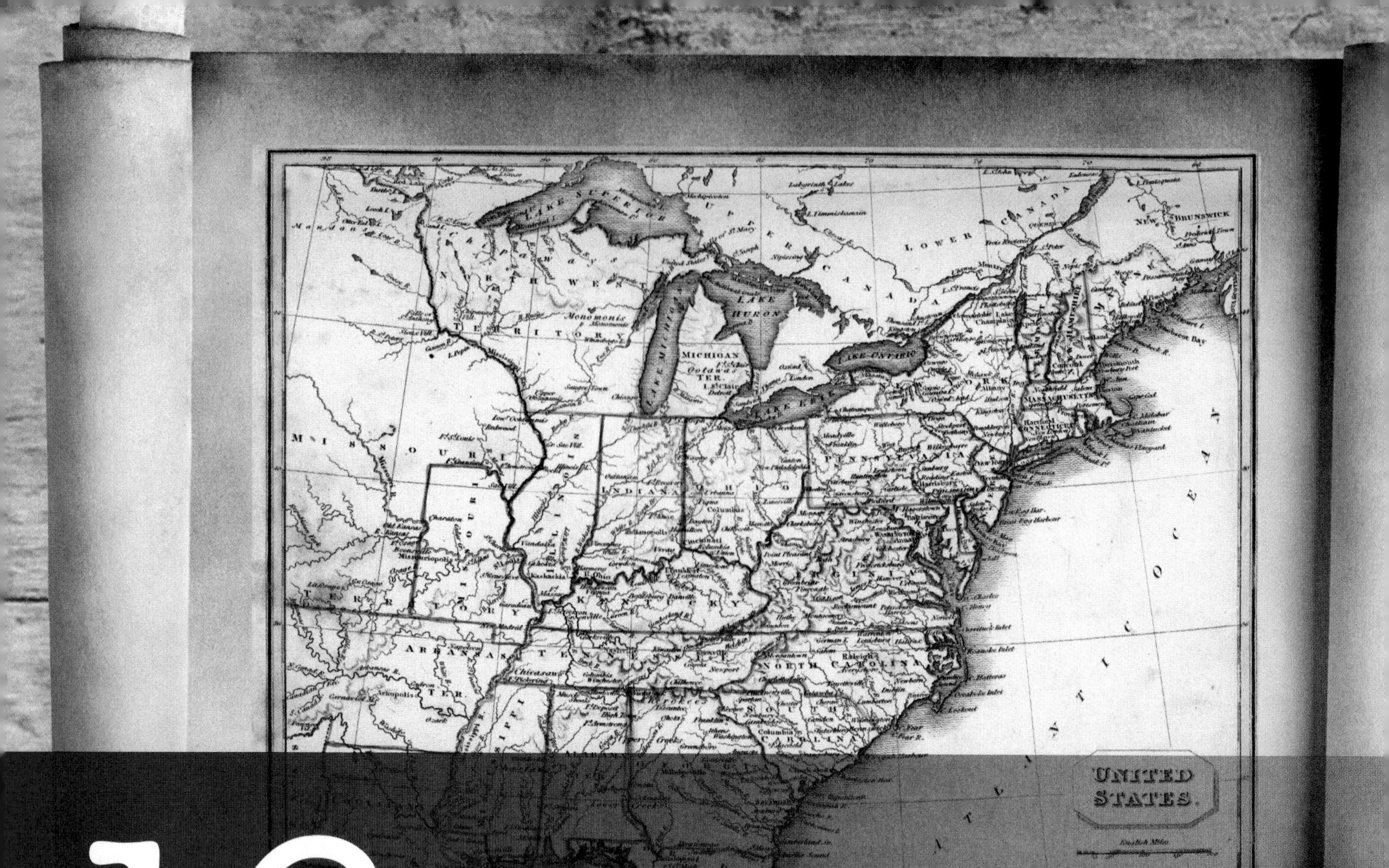

16 The Age of Big Business, 1865–1900

Chapter Objectives

The American Industrial Revolution

- The Effect of the Civil War
- The Post-Civil War Boom
- The Role of Government in Business
- The Role of the Courts

The Railroad Age

The Industrialists

- "Robber Barons" or "Captains of Industry"?
- The Trust
- John D. Rockefeller and the Standard Oil Trust
- Carnegie and Steel
- The Growth of Trusts
- Opposition to the Trusts
- The Interstate Commerce Act
- The Sherman Antitrust Act
- Edison, Electricity, and Inventions
- Alexander Graham Bell and the Telephone
- The Growth of Finance Capitalism

Labor

- The Knights of Labor
- The Rise of the AFL
- Labor Conflict

The Great Railroad Strike of 1877

The Homestead Steel Mill Strike

Unions and the Black Worker

Women and "the Incorporation of America"

The Last Frontier

The West

The Transcontinentals

Governmental Aid to Railroads

Public Benefits

Chinese Labor

The Mining Frontier

Comstock Lode

The Settlers

New Mexico

California

The Ranching Frontier

Trails of the Cattle Drive Era

The New South

Blacks in the New South

The Indian

Last Stands and Massacres

Little Big Horn

Cochise, Geronimo, and the Apaches

Wounded Knee

The White Victory and the Destruction of the Buffalo

A New Ethnic Mix

Klondike Gold Strike

The American Industrial Revolution

The Effect of the Civil War

It has been customary to credit the Civil War with a major role in bringing about the Industrial Revolution through the great impetus that it supposedly gave to the growth of manufacturing in the North. In fact, the Civil War was fought amidst a long-term trend of industrial and technological growth and may have retarded American industrial development because growth rates slowed during the conflict. Between 1839 and 1899, total output for commodities, including agricultural products, increased eleven fold, or at an average rate per decade of slightly less than 50 percent. Growth rates, however, varied widely from decade to decade. The 1840s and 1880s were periods of considerably more rapid advance than those of the 1850s, 1860s, and 1870s; and the lowest level of industrial growth occurred during the decade of the Civil War.

Nevertheless, the government gave strong encouragement to entrepreneurs during the Civil War. The Republican Party, seeking the votes of businessmen in the 1860 campaign, promised them favorable legislation; and once in power, the Republicans carried out their pledges and through tariff, railway, banking, and immigration legislation that created conditions suitable for industrial capitalism.

The Post-Civil War Boom

A number of factors were responsible for the post-Civil War industrial boom. The United States possessed bountiful raw materials, and the government was willing to turn them over to industry for little or no money. Combined with the abundance of natural resources and continuing technological progress was a home market steadily expanding through immigration and a high birthrate. Both capital and labor were plentiful. The increase in trade and manufacturing in the Northeast in the years before the war produced an accumulation of savings while additional millions of dollars came from European investors. Furthermore, from 1860 to 1900, unbroken waves of millions of European immigrants provided American industry with workers as well as with customers.

The Role of Government in Business

One factor in the growth of industrialism was the continuation of the government's friendly attitude toward big business. The protective tariff—beginning with the Morrill Tariff of 1861 and expanded by the McKinley bill of 1890, the Wilson-Gorman law of 1894, and the Dingley Tariff of 1897—allowed American manufacturers to charge high prices without fear of foreign competition. The national banking system adherence to the gold standard and the financial policies pursued by the Treasury Department resulted in a currency deflation that benefited creditors more than debtors. Businesses also received grants of land and of natural resources. While these measures can be considered a sign of governmental favoritism toward business at the expense of farmers and labor unions, they can also be seen as a way to encourage economic growth, a traditional policy of American government since the days of the Federalists. For ex-

MAP 16.1 Territorial Growth (1880)

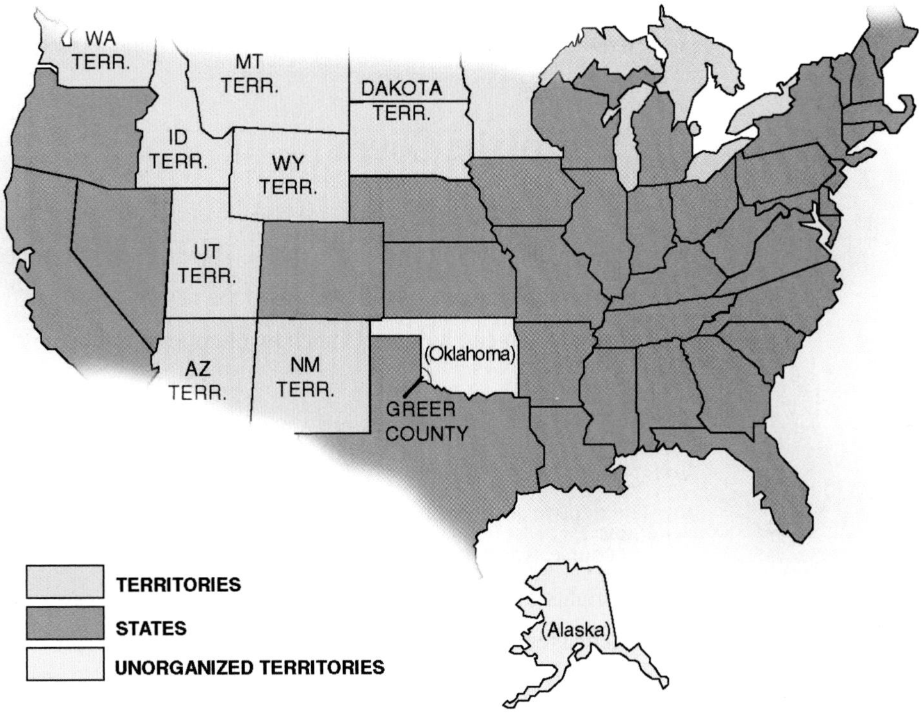

ample, over the years the railroads were granted over 180 million acres of federal land (in other words, an area of acreage larger than the state of Texas). The railroads then reaped huge profits by selling the land to settlers who purchased land in the West along the rail lines.

Equally friendly to the development of business was the lax public control of it. There were few investigations of business practices, no legislation to protect consumers, and few effective regulatory commissions or laws. Businessmen knew that almost any action could be justified by the doctrines of Social Darwinism and laissez-faire; most Americans in the Gilded Age considered governmental regulation of business to be unnecessary, unjust, and even immoral. Even reformers felt that governmental regulation of business should be confined to those cases where it was clearly necessary and where a careful study had been made. With cheerful inconsistency, the business leaders who championed laissez-faire welcomed governmental intervention in the economy in the form of tariffs, grants, and subsidies—measures that clearly violated laissez-faire doctrine. The downside of laissez-faire, however, included corporate corruption, worker exploitation, unsafe consumer products, and rampant degradation of the environment. For example, after the discovery of the Comstock silver mine at Virginia City, Nevada, the mining companies cut down every tree at Lake Tahoe for the timber needed to build mine shafts. Laissez-faire also meant that the inevitable economic recessions were especially harsh since there were no social safety nets such as unemployment insurance or worker's compensation insurance, and the Social Darwinist outlook dictated that efforts to help the poor were doomed to failure because the poverty itself proved that the poor and unemployed were naturally inferior. Any effort to help them was, therefore, akin to "casting pearls before swine."

John D. Rockefeller perhaps best summed up the prevailing Social Darwinist attitude when he told a YMCA group in Cleveland that "the growth of a large business is merely a survival of the fittest" and that, like the growth of a beautiful rose, "the early buds which grow up around it" must be sacrificed. This situation, according to Rockefeller, was not anything to be corrected—"merely the working out of a law of nature and a law of God."

The Role of the Courts

Also beneficial to the growth of business was the protection given by the Supreme Court in its interpretation of the Fourteenth Amendment. This amendment, added to the Constitution in 1868, was presumably designed to safeguard the newly emancipated blacks. The original intent of the amendment, however, somehow disappeared; it became instead a refuge for private enterprise.

In its first section the Fourteenth Amendment declares, "No state shall make or enforce any law which shall abridge the privileges or immunities of citizens of the United States; nor shall any state deprive any person of life, liberty, or property, without due process of law." The purpose, of course, was to overturn the last vestiges of the Dred Scott decision and grant equal citizenship rights to the former slaves. In the first postwar cases involving the question of governmental regulation of business, however, the Court interpreted this "due process" clause in favor of the state governments. In the Slaughterhouse Cases of 1873, involving a Louisiana law that granted a monopoly of the slaughterhouse business in New Orleans to one corporation, the Court declared the law to be a legitimate exercise of the state's police powers to protect its citizens. The Court also significantly weakened the federal government's ability to protect black Americans under the Fourteenth Amendment by making a distinction between national and state citizenship. The Court ruled that the Fourteenth Amendment protected only those rights that stemmed from the federal government under the United States Constitution, such as the right to vote in federal elections. Most rights, however, remained the jurisdiction of the states, thus severely limiting federal protections of the rights of all Americans, but especially those of former slaves.

Even when the Supreme Court ruled against big business, as in *Munn v. Illinois* (1877) where the Court approved an Illinois law that fixed maximum storage rates for grain elevators on the grounds that a state could regulate "a business that is public in nature though privately owned and managed," the power of big business ensured that the ruling would not last long.

The *Munn v. Illinois* decision so alarmed American businessmen that some predicted the end of private property. Others believed that the only remedy lay in a constitutional amendment to protect business against state regulation. Then a change occurred in the make-up of the Court with the appointment of more conservative justices. The *Munn v. Illinois* decision was reversed by the Court, in 1886, in *Wabash v. Illinois,* when the Court ruled that since railroads crossed state boundaries, they fell outside the realm of state jurisdiction and into the federal realm because Congress was granted the exclusive powers to regulate interstate commerce.

The end of the depression years of the mid-80s quieted demands from farmers, who had pushed for federal regulation of railroads and grain elevators; and a series of decisions, beginning in the Santa Clara case of 1886 and culminating in *Smyth v. Ames* in 1898, made the

▶ Shown here, the restored Old Supreme Court Chamber in the United States Capitol. Here, decisions were made that affected the growth and legality of new businesses and regulated business owners and their practices.

Fourteenth Amendment into something quite different. In these cases, the Court greatly broadened the interpretation of the amendment by holding that the word *person* in its first section meant corporations as well as individuals. Thus, corporations became "persons" under the law, endowed with standing to sue while labor unions did not, thus giving corporations an edge in their legal battles with organized labor. The Court also widened the application of the "due process" clause (which had originally been intended only to prohibit confiscation of property or other arbitrary violations of individual rights) to invalidate any regulation that would prohibit a corporation from making a "reasonable" profit on its investment. Finally, the Court held that the courts, and not the states, should decide how much profit was reasonable. Thus it became corporations, rather than the former slaves, whose rights were protected by the Fourteenth Amendment.

With these last cases the Fourteenth Amendment had practically been rewritten. Businessmen who denounced the rule laid down in *Munn v. Illinois* found protection in the later decisions. Lower courts handed down injunctions that tied the hands of regulatory commissions, and the Supreme Court became the stronghold of laissez-faire.

The Railroad Age

The new industrialism could never have been possible without the tremendous expansion of the railroad systems in America. In fact, they played such a dominant role that the period could well be called the railroad age. Between 1831 and 1861, thirty thousand miles of railroad created a network connecting the Atlantic seaboard and the Mississippi valley. The war slowed down construction; but between 1867 and 1873 about thirty thousand miles of railroad were added and during the 1880s a record-breaking seventy-three thousand miles were constructed. In 1900 the American railroad system, extending into every section of the country, measured 193,000 miles. This represented 40 percent of the world's railroad mileage and was more than the mileage of all the European countries combined. Railroad building increased more rapidly than the population. In 1865, there was one mile of track in operation for every 1,150 Americans. Twenty years later there was one mile for every 450. Capital invested in railroads jumped in this period from $2 billion to nearly $10 billion.

After the war, most of the short lines were consolidated into a few large systems. Cornelius Vanderbilt, who had already made a fortune in steamboats, led the way. Before his death in 1877, he had extended the New York Central System to Chicago, offering improved service at reduced rates.

The New York Central's chief competitor for the traffic between the East and the Middle West was the Pennsylvania Railroad, which became the most important railroad and one of the foremost business enterprises in the country. At the end of the nineteenth century, the Pennsylvania had lines tapping the most important Middle Atlantic and North Central industrial centers.

The Erie Railroad was a competitor for much of this traffic; but in the 1860s and 1870s, it suffered from being in the hands of three of the most disreputable railroad manipulators of the era: Daniel Drew, Jay Gould, and Jim Fisk. Through bribery, chicanery, and fraud they made the Erie synonymous with all the vices of the Industrial Revolution. Consolidation enabled the Baltimore and Ohio to push into the Middle West, and the New York, New Haven, and Hartford to fan out into New England. By 1900 railroad consolidation had reached such vast proportions that groups led by Cornelius Vanderbilt, James J. Hill, E. H. Harriman, Jay Gould, John D. Rockefeller, and John Pierpont Morgan controlled more than two-thirds of the railroad mileage of the country.

MAP 16.2 The Railroad Network (1885)

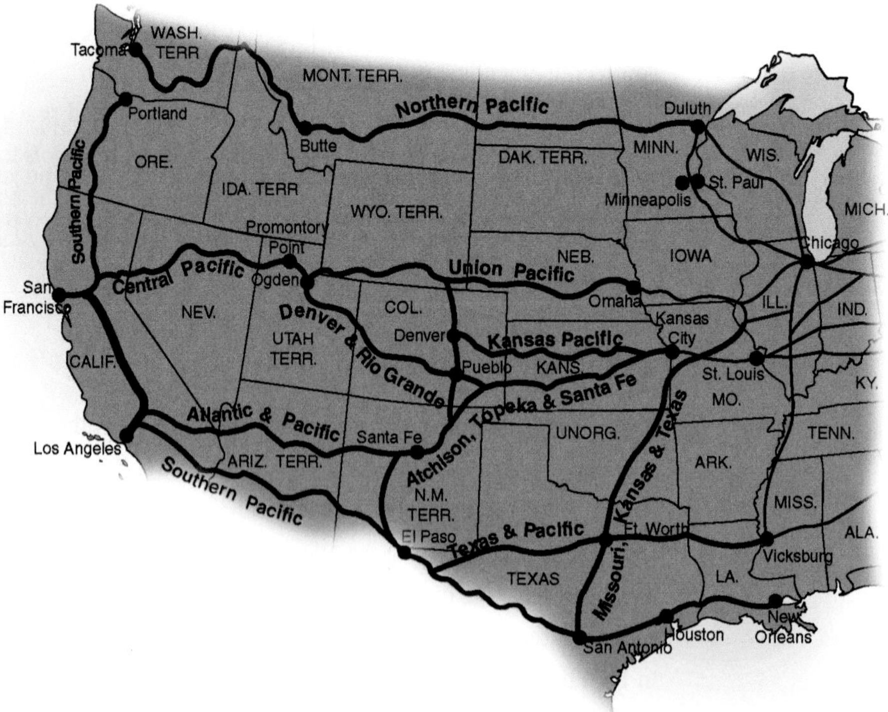

▶ Pennsylvania Railroad in West Philadelphia

Gould was primarily a speculator who invested money in everything from gold, to stocks, to railroads. Gould purchased his first railroad at age twenty-four and then sold it two years later at a profit of $130,000. Bolstered by this success, Gould purchased stock in other railroads, normally buying enough to take control of railroad operations, then dropping his prices to a point where his competitors could not make a profit. Gould would then sell his stock to competitors who desired to rid themselves of their cheap competitor. Though Gould's primary purpose was simply to purchase railroads and sell them at a profit, his methods caused consolidation in the industry and forced his competitors to expand their operations in order to keep pace with Gould's purchases. The result was exponential expansion not only in miles of railroad track but also in the size of corporations. For example, in 1860, the largest textile mill in New England (the center of the American textile industry) employed only eight hundred people. In the 1870s, the Pennsylvania Railroad alone employed over fifty-five thousand workers and had a stock value of over $400 million, making it the largest corporation in the world at the time.

Gould's practices may have made him the "richest man in America" by the time of his death in 1892. Upon his death, newspapers proclaimed that the country had lost the "world's richest man," and his net worth was estimated at over $100 million at a time of no income taxes and an average wage in America of approximately $600 per year. Competitor Cornelius Vanderbilt—who built both the largest house in America, the "Biltmore" near Asheville, North Carolina, and the New York Central Railroad—proclaimed Gould to be the "smartest man in America." Gould himself, however, perhaps put it more accurately shortly before he died when he described himself as "the most hated man in America."

Gould's competitive practices induced other railroads to engage in collusion and set up what were known as "pool" agreements, whereby they essentially divided the map into separate areas for each and promised not to compete in each other's area so that each could set prices high. Pool agreements normally did not hold, however, as competing railroads seeking an edge tended to violate their own agreements and undercut their competition.

The Industrialists

"Robber Barons" or "Captains of Industry"?

It is important to recognize that the foregoing factors were not wholly responsible for the American Industrial Revolution. It required the superb talent found among those Americans who mobilized the nation's productive energies to build the railroads and factories. The new industrialists were ambitious, resourceful, and extremely able. At times, they were ruthless and dishonest but probably no more so than many other Americans of their day. They displayed the vigor, cleverness, and strength of will that have characterized the great entrepreneurs of all epochs of capitalistic expansion. They lived at a time when the highest goal was to acquire wealth and when one's position in society was determined by the amount amassed. In their day they were known as Captains of Industry and praised for the economic growth of modern America. In time, however, they came to be described in many quarters as Robber Barons, who exploited the working class and exacted tribute from the public.

Few of the industrialists were guided by the morality and ethics that had prevailed in business before the Civil War. To eliminate competitors and get around legal and political obstacles, they did not hesitate to use trickery, bribery, and corruption. Their attitude toward complaints about their methods was summed up in William Vanderbilt's famous reply to a reporter's questions about the motives for his management of the railroads: "The public be damned."

If we indict or criticize these industrialists for what they did to attain economic and industrial power, we must remember that they were the products of their time, an era of lax regulation when many of their activities, now judged as unscrupulous, were perfectly legal. Probably even the worst and coarsest of their activities reflected the dominant Social Darwinist mores of American society in the Gilded Age. While they used wasteful and ruthless methods to promote economic development, they also faced such risks as overexpansion and unfair competition. Some now regard these businessmen more as creative agents in economic change whose long-run material contributions to society outweighed their short-run self-serving activities. Of course, historians making such arguments also have been spared the punishment of working 72-hour weeks in nineteenth-century steel mills. Whether "Captains of Industry" or "Robber Barons," they were launching the beginnings of a great economic expansion and economical mass production, Yet they also did it very much on the backs of exploited American workers.

▶ Andrew Carnegie was the epitomie of the 'rags to riches' dream. Carnegie started in the lowly position of immigrant bobbin-boy in a cotton textile mill at the wage of $1.20 a week and worked his way up to be a multimillionaire of the American steel industry.

As already noted, in the Gilded Age there was great faith in the rags-to-riches story. Andrew Carnegie's success in climbing from the lowly position of immigrant bobbin-

▶ A nineteenth century steel mill. Some employees worked 72-hour work weeks in these facilities. Such practices, though unlawful today, were accepted as perfectly legal in the late 1800s.

boy in a cotton textile mill at the wage of $1.20 a week to that of multimillionaire of the American steel industry is the classic American story of the poor boy making good. Carnegie's autobiography and the work of historians helped to keep alive for many years the "rags-to-riches" dream and the belief that the Captains of Industry came from poor, immigrant, rural, uneducated families, without social advantages—that, in fact, they became rich and powerful by pulling themselves up not only by their own bootstraps but also by a strict adherence to the Calvinist ethic of hard work, thrift, chastity, and abstinence. New research, however, has shown that the bulk of the business leaders came from white Anglo-Saxon Protestant, urban, northeastern, educated professional and business families. It seems that the doors of business success were not generally opened to immigrants, farm boys, or youths of poor education and background and that Carnegie was the exception rather than the rule.

While these tycoons accumulated large fortunes, many insisted they were not materialistic. "I know of nothing more despicable and pathetic than a man who devotes all the waking hours of the day to making money for money's sake," wrote John D. Rockefeller in his *Reminiscences*. He maintained it was "the association with interesting and quick-minded men," not money alone, that prompted him to follow his course to success. Critics point out, however, that Rockefeller was less disinterested in profit when the federal government moved to break up his Standard Oil monopoly. Andrew Carnegie expressed a similar view when he said that many of his "clever partners" in the steel business had been his friends from boyhood. He emphasized the joy he found in "manufacturing something and giving employment to many men." While Carnegie may have been speaking the truth, critics argue that he was less caring and sympathetic to his steel mill workers during labor disputes such as the famous Homestead Steel Mill strike.

A number of the new industrialists were of military age during the Civil War, but most of them took advantage of a law that allowed them to hire a substitute or to pay a certain amount of money in lieu of military service. Writing from Pittsburgh in 1863, Thomas Mellon, the founder of an aluminum fortune, declared, "Such opportunities for making money had never existed before in all my former experience." When his son James asked permission to enlist, the elder Mellon wrote, "Don't do it. It is only greenhorns who enlist. Those who are able to pay for substitutes do so, and no discredit attaches." Then he added, "It is not so much the danger as disease and idleness and vicious habits. ... I had hoped my boy was going to make a smart, intelligent businessman and was not such a goose as to be seduced from his duty by the declamations of buncombed speeches."

Simon Cameron, as Secretary of War during the Civil War, handed out war contracts left and right and asked only for production in return. As a result, gigantic frauds and great fortunes resulted from shoddy contracts and shady deals. For example, Cornelius Vanderbilt supplied the government with leaky ships, and J. P. Morgan, twenty-four years old in 1861, purchased five thousand discarded carbines and sold them back to the army for $112,000. These deals of both Morgan and Vanderbilt were exposed, but neither man was punished. Similarly, Jim Fisk went south to smuggle cotton to the North and sell it for large profits. Jay Gould's inside information enabled him to cash in on railroad deals and speculation in gold. Hence, the term "Robber Barons" is, in many cases, at least as accurate as "Captains of Industry."

The Trust

Before the Civil War, American business was highly competitive and consisted of small units—mostly individual enterprises or partnerships. After the war, businessmen sought ways to check increasing competition, which they had come to regard as inefficient, wasteful, and threatening to their profits. They established trade agreements, associations, and pools to limit competition. Because, however, these devices depended upon voluntary cooperation and were not enforceable in the courts, none proved sufficiently reliable. The answer seemed to lie in the formation of industrial trusts, which provided businessmen with more efficient control over the policies of all members within a single industry.

Under the trust system the stock of several competing companies was placed under the control of a group of trustees in exchange for trustee certificates. Ownership remained with the original companies, but management was consolidated in a single board of directors. John D. Rockefeller was by far the most important figure in the trust movement, and the formation of his Standard Oil Trust in 1882 established the trust pattern in the United States. Standard Oil's chief attorney, T. C. Dodd, established a board of nine trustees empowered to "hold, control, and manage" all of Standard Oil's assets. Stockholders in Standard Oil exchanged their Standard Oil stock for trust certificates, essentially stock in the trust, on which dividends were paid. Rockefeller's trustees held stock in numerous oil refinery companies "in trust" for Standard Oil Company stockholders. Rockefeller's trustees coordinated policy among all the refineries, ensuring that they would all follow the same policies and essentially giving Rockefeller controlling interest in virtually all of the oil refineries in America.

Other companies copied the Standard Oil trust structure, and soon trusts existed in the railroad, whiskey, lead, sugar, and other industries. The word "trust" became synonymous with the word "monopoly"; but it must be remembered that Rockefeller had essentially established a monopoly in oil refining in America prior to the reorganization of Standard Oil as a trust.

John D. Rockefeller and the Standard Oil Trust

At age fourteen, John D. Rockefeller received his pay from his first pay period on his first job and gave 10 percent to God, kept 50 percent for himself, and saved 40 percent, a practice he would continue essentially for the rest of his life. By age nineteen, Rockefeller had enough saved that he was able to purchase a produce business in Cleveland, Ohio. Finding success in the produce business, at age twenty-three he decided to enter the oil industry during the Civil War by purchasing an oil refinery in Cleveland. Here he found violence, lawlessness, and waste; and being no exponent of such free enterprise, he took steps to end this competitive strife. Rockefeller considered competition itself to be wasteful and small-scale enterprises to be inefficient. In his view, the wave of the future would be consolidation of small businesses into large corporations. Rockefeller adopted the most efficient methods of production, regularly saved a part of his profits, and surrounded himself with some of the ablest men in the industry. It was said that Rockefeller "could see farther ahead than any of them, and then see around the corner." Rockefeller's mantras were "nothing in haste, nothing ill-done" and "your future hangs on every day that passes." Rockefeller paid attention to minute details, counting rivets in oilcans and stoppers in barrels. In one famous case of efficiency, Rockefeller experimented with exactly how many drops of solder were required on kerosene cans to prevent them from leaking, and he reduced the number of welds through trial and error from forty to thirty-nine. In another instance, Rockefeller found that he could shorten barrel hoops to save metal. Meanwhile, he employed a chemist, Herman Frasch, who made numerous advancements in increasing the efficiency of refining oil. Rockefeller would triumph over his competition by providing better products at lower costs, a sound path to business success if one could accomplish it, even in the twenty-first century.

By 1867 Rockefeller was the largest refiner of oil in Cleveland, and in 1870 he organized the Standard Oil Company of Ohio with a capitalization of $1 million. This was the original *trust,* and the term came to be applied to any large combination with monopolistic powers.

With his trust, Rockefeller soon eliminated his Ohio competitors. He then proceeded to take on refiners in New York, Pittsburgh, and Philadelphia. Those who accepted Rockefeller's terms shared in the large profits. Those who continued to resist him were attacked with every weapon in cutthroat competitive warfare. He usually crushed his competitors with ruthless price-cutting, but he also had an immense competitive advantage in the rebates[1] and drawbacks[2] he received from the railroads. By 1879 Rockefeller controlled about 90 percent of America's refining industry.

Of all the trusts that appeared in the 80s and 90s, none aroused more alarms or pointed up more moral issues than the Standard Oil Trust. Even the means Rockefeller used to gain a mo-

---

[1] Powerful industrial shippers, in a strong bargaining position with railroads, often demanded—and received—secret "rebates," or discounts, from publicly posted shipping rates. Rebates sometimes were given in return for a specified volume of business or in return for the shipper's distributing his traffic in accordance with a pooling agreement made among competing lines.

[2] In exchange for the privilege of transporting the freight of a large shipper (e.g., Standard Oil), railroads agreed to pay the shipper "drawbacks," or subsidies drawn from a percentage of all receipts of its competitors.

▶ Standard Oil Trust Certificate, 1896. Established by John D. Rockefeller, Standard Oil Trust made its CEO the first man in the United States to be worth over a billion dollars.

nopoly in the oil industry produced conflicting opinions. "I ascribe the success of the Standard Oil Company to its consistent policy of making the volume of its business large through the merit and cheapness of its products," declared Rockefeller. However, Senator James K. Jones of Arkansas, however, offered another explanation on the floor of the United States Senate in 1889:

> "The iniquities of the Standard Oil Company have been enumerated and recounted until some of them are familiar to everyone," said Jones, "and the colossal fortunes which have grown from it, which in all their vastness do not represent one dollar of honest toil or one trace of benefit to mankind, nor any addition to the product of human labor, are known everywhere."

Indeed, Rockefeller threatened his competitors and bribed politicians when necessary. He also employed spies to harass the customers of competing refiners. Hence, some writers see the rise of Standard Oil as a dark record of unfair trade practices, railroad favors, bribery and blackmail, and an alliance between the corporation and politics by which legislators, officials, and judges closed their eyes to practices that violated the law. Others have argued that Standard Oil straightened out a disorderly industry by introducing efficiency and competency, lowered prices, and created a great industry. Both sides, however, agree that Standard's methods frequently were ruthless.

Rockefeller had a way of being ahead of the law most of the time. William Vanderbilt, testifying about the leaders of Standard Oil before a congressional committee in 1879, expressed an opinion prevalent in those years: "Yes, they are very shrewd men. I don't believe that by any legislative enactment or anything else, through any of the States or all of the States, you can keep such men down. You can't do it! They will be on top all the time. You see if they are not."

Rockefeller not only had his oil monopoly integrated horizontally (i.e., he took over competing refineries until he completely dominated the oil refining industry) but he also integrated vertically, owning every phase of the oil exploration, production, manufacturing, transportation, and marketing industries. Standard Oil, therefore, not only owned drilling rigs but also timberlands, barrel and chemical plants, refineries, warehouses, pipelines, rail cars,

▶Rockefeller threatened his competitors and bribed politicians when necessary. He also employed spies to harass the customers of competing refiners. Some view the rise of Standard Oil as a rise of unfair trade practices, railroad favors, bribery, and blackmail.

and eventually ocean-going oil tankers. Standard also exported oil across the oceans to Asia, Africa, and South America. Rockefeller retired in 1897 with a fortune approaching one billion dollars. Eventually, it is estimated that Rockefeller would control two percent of the gross domestic product of the United States.

Be that as it may, in 1892 the Supreme Court of Ohio ordered the dissolution of the Standard Oil Trust on the grounds that it was designed to "establish a virtual monopoly" and was "contrary to the policy of our state." This decision, however, did not produce the desired results. The Standard trustees, although they returned the stock to the stockholders, continued to manage the member concerns as "liquidating trustees" until 1897, when the court forced them to abandon this stratagem.

Prior to this, in 1889, New Jersey had changed its corporation laws in such a way as to make legal the formation of a holding company, a company that owned a majority of the stock in a number of subsidiary corporations and was established to unify their control. Put simply, a holding company was a corporation that owned controlling interest in other companies. In 1899, the various subsidiaries of Standard were legally combined through the creation of a giant holding company, the Standard Oil Company of New Jersey, capitalized at $110 million. Standard's control over the refining business continued as complete as ever. In 1911, the United States Supreme Court, after it adopted the "rule of reason" whereby any combination that placed a "reasonable" restraint on trade could be in violation, held that Standard had violated the 1890 Sherman Antitrust Act. However, this decision, like earlier ones in the state courts, had little effect upon the management of Standard's affairs.

Carnegie and Steel

Andrew Carnegie came to America as a Scottish immigrant in 1848, at the age of twelve and quickly went to work in a Pennsylvania cotton mill for $1.20 per week. From there, Carnegie took a job in a telegraph office where he worked until 1852 when he was offered a job by Thomas A. Scott of the Pennsylvania Railroad as Scott's personal telegrapher. Seven years later, Carnegie had risen to become a well-paid divisional superintendent for the railroad at age twenty-four; and by 1868, Carnegie's income was upwards of fifty thousand dollars per year. Over the decade, of the 1860s, Carnegie amassed a fortune of over one million dollars from shrewd investments and had enough to build a steel mill.

Just as Rockefeller captured the refining market from his competitors, so did Andrew Carnegie capture much of the steel market although he never achieved a monopoly. Like Rockefeller, however, Carnegie gained an edge over his competitors by finding a more efficient way to make his product. Upon purchasing his first steel mill, Carnegie was surprised to discover that there was no hard and fast recipe for steel. Consequently, he hired chemists to determine the exact ingredients that would produce the best mix. Carnegie also instituted the Bessemer process, a method of eliminating the impurities in steel developed by Henry Bessemer in 1859. Bessemer discovered that blowing a stream of air into a mass of molten iron caused carbon and other impurities to combine with oxygen and burn off. When measured amounts of carbon, silicon, and manganese were then added to the purified iron, higher quality steel resulted. Soon, Carnegie was producing top quality steel from waste discarded by his competitors. When Carnegie first introduced the Bessemer process into his steel mill in the 1870s, the price of steel dropped 50 percent. As more technological innovations were introduced, the price of steel eventually declined from $100 per ton in the 1870s to $12 per ton by 1890.

As his steel enterprise grew, Carnegie found that he could get ahead of the competition by expanding his business during slow times when purchasing a competing steel mill was less expensive. Given that the steel industry in the late nineteenth century was very prone to boom-bust cycles, Carnegie was able to expand quickly and greatly during the bust cycles when others were selling off their assets.

By 1890, steel had become a cheaper, stronger, and more durable material than iron, and its greater malleability lent the metal to new uses. Railroads converted their rails from iron to steel, and bridges were soon designed with steel cables. Eventually, steel would be used as the frames for high-rise buildings in American cities as well as for all forms of wire, nails, bolts, nuts, and screws.

Like Rockefeller, Carnegie secured rebates from the railroads. He also was aided, materially, by the depression of the seventies. As he said about it afterward, "So many of my friends needed money that they begged me to repay them [for their investments in early Carnegie enterprises]. I did so and bought out five or six of them. That was what gave me my leading interest in this steel business."

From this time on, Carnegie led the field in the steel industry. He bought out and took into his business Henry Clay Frick, who in the seventies had gained control of most of the coke ovens around Pittsburgh. Together they created a great vertical combine of coalfields, coke ovens, limestone deposits, iron mines, ore ships, and railroads. In 1892, the Carnegie Steel Company was formed at a capitalization of $25 million. It controlled all its sources of supply and was soon making one fourth of all unfinished steel in the United States. At the turn of the century, it became a New Jersey corporation with a capitalization of $160 million.

Carnegie was essentially an *industrial capitalist* in that his money came from industry and not from bankers. He put a large part of his profits back into his business, and he did not allow his corporation's stock to be sold to persons outside his organization. He was successful because of his efficient business methods and driving energy and because he skillfully chose partners of almost equal ability, such as Frick and Charles Schwab. However, his labor policy, like that of most of the corporation leaders of this era, was one of long hours, low wages, and hostility to trade unions. Carnegie was willing to make innovations in methods and machinery and ready to discard equipment whenever better came along. He made his improvements in times of depression; and when prosperity returned, he was ready to produce.

Carnegie believed that it was a disgrace to die rich, so he desired to retire and engage in philanthropic work. In 1901, Carnegie essentially sold out to J. P. Morgan. Morgan had reportedly asked Carnegie's associate, Charles M. Schwab, to "go and find his price." Schwab then discussed the matter with Carnegie on the golf course, and the next day Carnegie handed Schwab a note hand-written in pencil asking for almost a half billion dollars. Upon viewing the note, Morgan exclaimed, "I accept this price!" The owners of Carnegie Steel received $492 million, of which $250 million went to Carnegie alone. According to legend, Carnegie later teased Morgan, stating that he should have asked for $100 million more, to which Morgan replied, "You would have got it if you had."

The Growth of Trusts

Soon after Standard Oil Company had set the trust pattern, other business enterprises of this type appeared. The McCormick Harvester Company of Chicago secured almost a monopoly of mechanical farm equipment. James B. Duke's American Tobacco Company, established in 1890, and Henry O. Havemeyer's American Sugar Refining Company, founded in 1891, gained almost complete monopolies, while Philip D. Armour and Gustavus Swift won domination of the meat packing business. The E. C. Knight Company controlled 98 percent of the sugar manufacturing in the United States. Other consumer goods controlled by trusts were salt, whisky, matches, crackers, wire, and nails.

Eventually, prosecution by states or state legislation declaring trusts illegal ended these organizations. Although the original form of trust disappeared, the term trust continued in use and applied to any type of monopoly. Many of the former trusts reorganized themselves into holding companies under the friendly corporate laws of New Jersey. Others became corporate combines created by mergers of separate firms. Fewer combinations occurred during the depression of 1893–1897, but after this they increased at an extraordinary rate.

Opposition to the Trusts

As the American people watched the proliferation of trusts and millionaires, they became convinced that something must be done to restore competition. There arose a popular outcry against monopolies, and by the 1880s public speakers and writers began to condemn them. In 1881, Henry D. Lloyd attacked the Standard Oil Trust in "The Story of a Great Monopoly" in the *Atlantic Monthly*. Similar articles against other examples of big business followed. Edward Bellamy in his "Looking Backward" (1887) assailed economic conditions of the time and pictured a future socialist utopian state where life's necessities and luxuries would be produced by a co-operative society for the benefit of all. Henry George in his "Progress and Poverty" (1879) maintained that the problems of the times were largely the result of a monopoly of land. "All who do not possess land," he argued, "are toiling for those who do, and this is the reason why progress and poverty go hand in hand." George proposed that the unearned increments in land values be confiscated by the government in the form of a single tax on land. This would benefit the whole of society and adjust those economic disparities from which American society was suffering. (The ideas of Bellamy and George were discussed more fully in Chapter 4.)

During the eighties a number of states passed laws prohibiting trusts, but these failed to check the increasing concentration of industry. Some trusts appeared more powerful than the states that attempted to regulate them; and when one device for creating monopoly ran afoul of the law, another was substituted. State legislation also proved ineffective so long as such states as New Jersey, Delaware, and West Virginia placed few restrictions on the chartering corporations and permitted the creation of holding companies.

The Interstate Commerce Act

These frustrations aroused the opponents of monopoly to demand federal action. Between 1873 and 1885 more than thirty measures were introduced in the House of Representatives providing for the regulation of interstate railroads, an economic sector in which there were frequent abuses. Railroads discriminated significantly between the rates they charged on routes where they had competition as opposed to those where they did not. In general, railroads would charge very low rates where they had competition; however, on routes where they had none, the prices they set were exorbitant, placing extreme burdens on farmers and shippers from remote areas. For instance, the dome for the Texas State capitol in Austin was made in Belgium; but it cost more to ship the dome via rail from Houston to Austin, Texas, than it did to transport it from Belgium to Texas via cargo ship. Farmers and shippers in remote areas, along with railroads who faced competition from other railroads that charged low prices in one area to force out competitors while making up for it with the high rates charged elsewhere, pressured Congress to intervene.

The House of Representatives passed some of the measures favored by those who supported federal railroad regulation, only to have them fail in the Senate. Under the pressures of Easterners as well as Westerners, however, the Senate yielded at last and appointed the Cullom Committee to investigate. In 1886 the committee made its report, concluding: "It is the deliberate judgment of the Committee that upon no public question are the people so nearly unanimous as upon the proposition that Congress should undertake in some way the regulation of interstate commerce." This recommendation together with the Supreme Court's Wabash decision in 1886, forbidding the states to continue their regulation of *interstate* railroad traffic, led to the Interstate Commerce Act of 1887.

This law provided that all railway rates "shall be reasonable and just." It prohibited such discriminatory practices as rebates and drawbacks and made illegal some of the long and short haul abuses.[3] It forbade pooling agreements[4] and required that all rates and fares be printed and publicly posted. The act established a five-man Interstate Commerce Commission (ICC), the first federal regulatory agency, with power to investigate the railroads and to require reports from them.

---

[3] The "long and short haul" abuse pointed out the fact that railroads charged rates based not on operating costs but on what the public could be forced to pay. Over "long hauls"—e.g., from Chicago to New York—competition between railroads was keen and freight charges were low (sometimes lower than operating costs); but over "short hauls"—i.e., between local points serviced by only one line—a railroad, in a noncompetitive situation, could charge rates as high as the public could bear, thereby recouping whatever losses it might have suffered on long hauls.

[4] By means of "pooling agreements" competing railroads sometimes agreed to maintain uniformly high rates in a particular locality by apportioning traffic among themselves or dividing accumulated earnings. Pooling was intended to avoid competitive rate wars.

The ICC could hear complaints of violations of the law but could not impose fines, cease and desist orders, or other penalties by itself. Instead, it had to depend upon the courts to enforce its rulings, and the five-member Commission was overwhelmed with thousands of petitions. Thus the ICC did not receive the powers necessary to regulate the transportation system. Also, the commissioners were virtually required by the act to be inexperienced in railroad practices, so they had difficulties fully understanding and acting on the complaints of the shippers.

The chief weakness of the law, however, was its vagueness in not defining "reasonable and just" rates. Such grave defects in the act were recognized even by such a staunch opponent of federal regulation as Senator Nelson W. Aldrich of Rhode Island, who described the new law as a "delusion and a sham, an empty menace to great interests, made to answer the clamor of the ignorant and unreasoning."

The ICC soon discovered that it could not compel witnesses to testify and that appeals to the courts produced endless delays. Even in those cases that reached the Supreme Court, the decisions generally favored the railroads over the Commission. Between 1887 and 1905 the Court heard sixteen cases appealed by the ICC, and in fifteen of those cases, it upheld the railroads.

The Sherman Antitrust Act

Senator John Sherman of Ohio outlined the need for stronger federal control of the trusts when he said in 1890:

> Congress alone can deal with the trusts, and if we are unwilling or unable there will soon be a trust for every production and a master to fix the price for every necessity of life.

In 1890 Congress passed the Sherman Antitrust Act, another departure from laissez-faire policies, by an almost unanimous vote. Although Sherman introduced the act, Senators George F. Edmunds of Vermont and George F. Hoar of Massachusetts, mainly, wrote it. The act declared that "every contract, combination in the form of trust or otherwise, or conspiracy in restraint of trade or commerce" was illegal. It was left to the courts, however, to determine the meaning of the terms and phrases in the law, and it could not be enforced without the cooperation of the Attorney General. Senator Orville Platt of Connecticut, in commenting on the act, stated, "The conduct of the Senate ... has not been in the line of honest preparation of a bill to prohibit and punish trusts. It has been in the line of getting some bill with that title that we might go to the country with." Senator Shelby Cullom of Illinois thought that if the act "were strictly and literally enforced, the business of the country would come to a standstill."

Whether or not Cullom was correct is unknown, however, because the act was not enforced. From 1890 to 1901, the Justice Department instituted only eighteen antitrust suits; and the Supreme Court—in *United States v. E. C. Knight Co.* (1895)—undermined the law by holding that manufacturing, being wholly intrastate in character even though ultimately affecting interstate commerce, was not subject to federal regulation. This limited definition of the "commerce clause" in the Constitution put trusts beyond federal control. Hence, the E. C.

Knight Company, which at the time controlled 98 percent of sugar manufacturing in the United States, could not be broken up as a monopoly by the federal government because "manufacturing" was not "interstate commerce" under the definition of the Supreme Court.

Edison, Electricity, and Inventions

Perhaps the greatest inventor in American history, one who had an almost unparalleled impact on American life with his inventions, was Thomas Edison of Menlo Park, New Jersey. Edison was a tireless worker who slept only three to four hours per night, spending the rest of his time in his laboratory and vowing to produce a "minor invention every ten days and a big thing every six months or so." At the height of his inventing career, Edison employed as many as two hundred chemists, machinists, engineers, and experimenters, averaging a patent every eleven days. He provided the world with the "big" inventions that included not only the electric light bulb but also the phonograph and the motion picture camera, all three of which would eventually change America and the world indelibly. In his lifetime, Edison would own over one thousand patents, including the mimeograph and the electric storage battery. Furthermore, although it was Ben Franklin who discovered that lightning was electricity in the eighteenth century, it was Edison who, along with competitor George Westinghouse, harnessed electricity as a power source to fuel not only electric lights but also factory machinery, urban trolleys, and a host of other items common in urban America at the turn of the century. Edison built his first electric power station in New York in 1882, supplying electric power to eighty-five customers. By 1898, there were over three thousand electric power stations supplying electricity to homes and industry all over the country. Electricity would transform American industry from one that was fueled primarily by water power in 1900, to one that was driven primarily by electricity by 1930.

Edison did not, however, amass the type of fortune that one might imagine from his inventions. Patent laws in the late nineteenth century provided Edison with far less protection than Edison had expected, and he spent the next four decades after the invention of his incandescent bulb in patent lawsuits. In the words of Edison, "My electric light inventions have brought me no profits, only forty years of litigation." Later Edison lamented that "a patent, is simply an invitation to a lawsuit." Nevertheless, in 1892 Edison and his competitor, Thomson-Houston Electric merged to form General Electric, a corporation with an estimated net worth of $35 million. Thereafter, General Electric and Westinghouse would dominate the manufacture of light bulbs and other electrical equipment along with the distribution of electric power to run the new electric inventions.

Alexander Graham Bell and the Telephone

Alexander Graham Bell, like Andrew Carnegie, was a Scottish immigrant who came to America as a young man (age twenty-four in Bell's case) to seek his fortune. Both Bell's wife and his mother were deaf mutes, which gave him a passion for developing a way for the deaf to speak. Instead, what he developed was a way to transmit the human voice over a wire, and his invention became known as the telephone. Bell first demonstrated his invention to the world at the Philadelphia Centennial

▶ The original General Electric logo, circa 1899.

Exposition in 1876, and communications in America has never been the same since. Bell formed his company, American Bell, in 1880. He worked with Theodore N. Vail, who pioneered long telephone lines, and created American Telephone and Telegraph as a subsidiary of Bell. In 1900, the corporation was reorganized with AT&T as the parent company, controlling Bell and Western Electric, which manufactured and installed Bell's telephone equipment. By 1900, there were almost eight hundred thousand telephones in America with people communicating from coast to coast.

Other inventions in the Gilded Age that changed the nature of America included the typewriter (1867), barbed wire (1867), cash register (1879), adding machine (1885), Kodak camera (1888), zipper (1891), safety razor (1895), and tape recorder (1899).

The Growth of Finance Capitalism

During the 1890s, industrial capitalism began to give way to *finance capitalism* as investment bankers became more influential in the development of American industry. The industrial capitalists like Rockefeller and Carnegie were producers who had grown rich with their own industries. Finance capitalists like J. P. Morgan and August Belmont, in contrast, came to power not because they were skilled industrial organizers but because they had enormous sums of money with which they could invest in and purchase control of an industry. A corporation in need of capital could ask a banking house to sell the corporation's securities. In return, the investment banker demanded a share in the management of the corporations in which his customers had invested. Hard-pressed industrialists could not refuse, and gradually the bankers assumed supervision of corporate policies. By the turn of the century, control of a number of corporations had passed from industrialists to bankers.

The leading American finance capitalist was J. P. Morgan, who was also a dominant figure in the national economy. The New York banking houses—August Belmont and Company and Kuhn, and Loeb and Company—and the Boston banking houses—Lee, Higginson, and Company and Kidder Peabody and Company—were also important. Morgan worked to bring about order and stability in one industry after another because he wanted to make sure that dividends would be paid regularly to stockholders. He disliked competition because he felt it would lead to cutthroat price-cutting, which would be bad for business. Instead, he wanted corporations to collude in order to control prices and markets. Morgan's disdain for competitors induced rivals to refer to him as "Jupiter," after the ruler of the Roman gods. Morgan's policies meant more protection to stockholders but higher prices to consumers. Eventually, his domination of American finance was so thorough that critics complained that he controlled a "money trust."

Morgan's finance capital brought a reorganization of American industry as he took over struggling railroads and other businesses and then consolidated them into a larger entity. Eventually, Morgan had nominal control over two-thirds of America's rail lines. Morgan increased his profits from the railroads by issuing more shares of stock than the assets of the companies were worth. Morgan's practices not only set up the stock market for an eventual fall but also saddled the railroads with debt problems that hindered continued investment in research and development. Morgan did not stop with railroads, however; he used the same approach in creating massive corporations in other industries such as General Electric and United States Steel.

Probably the biggest of Morgan's ventures was his launching of the United States Steel Corporation in 1901. He bought out the Carnegie Steel Corporation and combined it with ten other steel companies into one vast corporation capitalized at the unprecedented figure of slightly over $1 billion plus a bonded debt of over $303 million. This made United States Steel America's first billion-dollar company (though the Bureau of Corporations later estimated that the total value of the combined assets of all the merged companies was actually only $676 million). United States Steel controlled 60 percent of America's steel business and employed almost 170,000 people.

With Carnegie's sale to Morgan, the era of industrial capitalism came to a close. Finance capitalism brought even greater economic consolidation. In 1893, there were twelve great companies with an aggregate capital of about $1 billion. By 1904, there were 318 industrial combinations—one of them Morgan's United States Steel Corporation—with a combined capital in excess of $7.25 billion. Together these 318 companies controlled more than 5,000 separate plants. Corporations had become larger and larger, and fewer and fewer companies owned an ever-increasing share of American gross domestic product. In 1870, over eight hundred iron and steel firms competed in the American marketplace, but by 1900, fewer than 10 percent remained. This pattern repeated itself in industry after industry so that by 1900, one percent of American corporations overall controlled over one-third of America's manufacturing.

At the time of Morgan's death in 1913, his estate was estimated at $118 million, including $50 million in art treasures. Though his fortune was much less than that of Carnegie or Rockefeller, he indirectly controlled billions of dollars worth of assets. Morgan's power in the American economy may have been unparalleled.

Labor

Labor had a difficult time in the new industrial age. While businessmen solicited governmental assistance in the form of tariff protection and did not regard this as governmental intervention, they bitterly opposed any attempt to improve the conditions of labor by legislation on the premise that this would be unwarranted interference with the economic system. Most businessmen regarded as absurd the notion that employees had the same right to government protection and aid as had already been afforded business. Instead businessmen believed that they alone had the right to determine the terms and conditions of employment, and they dismissed the idea of collective bargaining.

As business formed ever-larger combinations, however, so did labor. The rise of labor organizations was further boosted by the age of invention itself, as more and more skilled workers found themselves replaced by machinery and unskilled workers who merely tended the machines. Labor discontent was also fueled by the fact that an absence of labor protections, such as worker's compensation insurance, left thousands impoverished after family breadwinners were disabled on the job. The rate of on-the-job injury in the United States during the Gilded Age was the highest in the world.

Among the earliest of the significant labor organizations was the National Labor Union, (NLU) that organized in 1866 and was mainly a reform organization that summed up various grievances labor had had since the 1840s. The NLU argued for an eight-hour day, the abolition of slums, and the establishment of cooperatives. It favored arbitration over strikes in labor disputes, and it frowned, at first, upon independent political action by labor groups. Its most important leader was William Sylvis, who died in 1869 after heading the organization for only a year. Had he lived longer, the union might have played a greater role in the history of labor. After his death, however, it turned more and more to political activity; and in 1873 its trade-union aspect disappeared when it became the National Labor Reform Party. The NLU withered and died amidst an economic recession at the same time. Even so, the National Labor Union prepared the way for more effective labor organizations, such as the Knights of Labor.

The Knights of Labor

The Knights of Labor were organized in 1869 under the leadership of Uriah Stephens. Believing in the solidarity of labor, the Knights admitted almost everyone to membership, excluding only lawyers, bankers, stockbrokers, liquor dealers, and professional gamblers. This meant that for the first time there was a substantially male labor organization that accepted women members—albeit grudgingly at first—and a substantially white labor organization that was not invariably opposed to black members. The Knights announced their primary purpose was "to secure to toilers a proper share of the wealth they create." They hoped to achieve their goals through secrecy, the organization of cooperatives, and education and propaganda.

Secrecy was of prime importance to the members, for their jobs were at stake: Industries locked out workers who belonged to unions. Even the name of the organization was not made public until 1881. Their secrecy, however, caused the Knights trouble with the churches, especially the Catholic Church, which feared the members might be taking a secret oath that was in conflict with their religion. Only the intercession of Cardinal Gibbons of Baltimore kept the Pope from excommunicating the Catholics in the federation.

The Knights were of national importance from 1879 to 1893, while *Terence v. Powderly,* who replaced Uriah Stephens, was their Grand Master Workman. Some denounced Powderly as a revolutionary, and others as a faker who sold out labor. He seldom gave full attention to the union, considering it only a part-time position, and engaged in other activities such as being mayor of Scranton, Pennsylvania, from 1878 to 1884, and a leader of the Irish Land League. His great strength with the workers, however, was his oratorical power. Powderly supported land reform, temperance, and public education. More importantly, Powderly also abandoned Stephens' strategy of secrecy, and the Knights of Labor would recruit members and make their grievances known openly.

The Knights hoped to organize all workers, skilled and unskilled, black and white, into one big union for mutual protection against "the aggression of employers." They worked for the eight-hour day, abolition of child labor, settlement of labor disputes by arbitration rather than by strikes, and encouragement of cooperative stores and factories.

The Knights' official opposition to the use of strikes—like that of unions generally in the 70s—was because most strikes up to this point had been unsuccessful. The depression of the 70s had dealt unions some severe blows. They lost strength, and workers saw wages drop as much as 40 percent in textiles and on the railroads where the strikes led to much turbulence. Moreover, workers faced increasing unemployment, prosecution of strikers, and use of police and private detective agencies as strike breakers. In addition to lockouts (restricting employment to nonunion labor) employers resorted to blacklisting (circulating names of union leaders and members) and to "yellow dog" contracts (pacts whereby employees agreed not to join unions). So the 70s and the depression of that decade were a very difficult time for unions. Only a handful of the national unions pulled through these years.

Although Powderly himself was opposed to use of the strike as a weapon and was willing to come to terms with employers at almost any price, the hard times of the mid-80s led to boycotts and strikes, notably on the Union Pacific in 1884 and Jay Gould's Wabash in 1885. Spontaneous strikes by shop men and trainmen caught the companies off guard and compelled Powderly's support of his followers. These were labor's first major victories, and they forced Gould to negotiate with the Knights. An illusion of easy success arose, and suddenly the Knights were flooded with members. In 1886, their peak year, membership shot up to seven hundred thousand.

Fast on the heels of these successes, however, came the Great Southwestern Strike of 1886 and failure. Powderly had agreed in the Wabash settlement to have no more strikes without notifying the railroads in advance. It was an agreement he could not enforce, however. The strikes that had occurred were not of his making but were strikes of local origin that had drawn him in only after they had begun. In the Southwestern strike, Gould refused to negotiate with the union because the Knights had given no advance notice to the railroad; and the workers were unable to hold out.

Of all the labor upheavals of the period, none was more frightening to men of property and order or did more damage to the prestige of labor than the bombing at Haymarket Square in Chicago in 1886. On May 1, a number of independent trade unions struck for recognition of the eight-hour day at the McCormick Harvester plant in Chicago. Two days later the police shot and clubbed some of the strikers who were beating up strike breakers, and four persons were killed. The violence of the police prompted growls of resentment and threats of retaliation in the labor press. The next day, May 4, a group of anarchists called a protest meeting in Haymarket Square. As the speeches were coming to a close, almost two hundred policemen arrived on the scene and ordered the crowd to go home. Before anyone could move, however, a bomb exploded, killing one policeman outright and fatally wounding several others. Almost immediately the police opened fire on the workers, and soon a riot was in full swing. Ten people were killed, six who were policemen, dozens wounded, and in the confusion and excitement several of the policemen shot each other.

The reaction in Chicago and throughout the nation was one of horror. In the resulting hysteria, hundreds of labor union leaders were arrested, including eight who were anarchists that were indicted for inciting the person who threw the bomb into doing it." They were tried and convicted on what later has come to be seen as flimsy, inconclusive evidence. In fact, witnesses in the trial even testified that none of the eight men on trial actually threw the bomb. In spite of this, the state's prosecutor, Julius S. Grinnell, sought to make examples of the men as a deterrent to others to refrain from violence and union activities, in general. Grinnell argued that the state must "make examples of them, hang them, and save our institutions." Seven of the eight men were sentenced to death—one committed suicide, four were executed and the others sentenced to imprisonment for life—in spite of the fact that the state

▶ This engraving of "The Anarchists of Chicago" was widely circulated among anarchists, socialists, and labor activists following the incident at Haymarket Square in Chicago.

could not link any of the defendants to the Haymarket bomb. Clearly, the men had been arrested and convicted primarily for their political views rather than for the evidence against them. The next year, Illinois governor John Peter Altgeld recognized it as such when he pardoned the three remaining Haymarket convicts at the cost of his own political career. Labor leaders reacted by designating May 1 as an international celebration day of labor in memory of the Haymarket martyrs.

The rest of the nation was not so sympathetic, however. The Haymarket Riot had a disastrous impact on labor unions, in general, as it convinced many Americans that labor unions were dangerous and full of "bomb throwing radicals." Although the Knights of Labor had nothing to do with the Haymarket Riot, they were identified in the public mind with the anarchists; and skilled workers began to desert the Knights in large numbers. From this time on, the Knights declined in influence, and by 1890 the membership had fallen to one hundred thousand. The failure of their cooperatives also contributed to their downfall.

In addition, they were weakened by the same conflict that had earlier rent the National Labor Union. It was the division between a national leadership dedicated to general economic and political reform and the trade unions that preferred to concentrate on the immediate economic betterment of workers. This controversy came to a head, ironically, during 1886, when the Knights had their most spectacular growth, largely as a result of the success of strikes and when Powderly and other union leaders refused to support new strikes. These and other dissensions over immediate strategy and long-range goals led to a loss in the numbers and influence of the Knights.

The Rise of the AFL

While the power and influence of the Knights waned, a new labor organization, the American Federation of Labor (AFL), was created in 1886 under the leadership of Samuel Gompers. The AFL was essentially a federation of autonomous craft unions representing skilled workers. Gompers abandoned the Knights' idea of labor solidarity and, with it, the outreach to women and people of color, except in a few limited cases. Trade unionism was his aim, and his plan was to group workers according to crafts. Thus, the AFL was for "skilled" workers only and closed to the "unskilled." Gompers believed that female and black workers drove down wages for everyone and were more easily manipulated by big business. Nevertheless, the AFL did seek equal pay for women who did work—under the premise that by rais-

ing female wages, the AFL could make women less attractive to employers; in effect, women would be driven from the workforce.

AFL pursued three practical objectives: higher wages, shorter hours, and better working conditions. Gompers opposed direct affiliation of labor unions with political parties. He also, favored cooperation with employers and mediation of labor disputes on the premise that what government gave they could also take away. Therefore, the best route for laborers was to negotiate directly with the employers. Gompers did, however, advocate strikes when necessary to secure better working conditions, including the eight-hour day.

The Knights and the AFL competed for supremacy in American labor unions at the end of the nineteenth century. In 1896, the AFL had only 138,000 members compared to the Knights' 730,000; but by the end of the nineteenth century the AFL had won, and the Knights of Labor would dissipate into existence only in history books.

Labor Conflict

Most labor organizations rejected violence as a weapon in their struggle to improve the conditions of labor, but there were some exceptions. One was the Molly Maguires, an organization active among Pennsylvania coal miners from the mid-sixties to the late seventies that resorted to violence, intimidation, and the destruction of property. Making them more ominous to the public, the Molly Maguires was a predominantly Irish organization that operated within the Ancient Order of Hibernians, an Irish fraternal society about which Americans had little knowledge but much fear. The Molly Maguires threatened mine owners and managers with death and, occasionally, made good on their threats. Mine owners, however, often hired persons to perform dastardly acts for the purpose of blaming the violent acts on the Mollies, thus justifying ruthless suppression of the labor union with public support. Another exception to the nonviolent labor unions was the Anarchists, a small group that supported acts of terror directed at ending capitalism.

The Great Railroad Strike of 1877

There was, however, violence in some of the strikes often, if not invariably, owing to decisions made by employers. The first truly national strike occurred among railroad workers in 1877. In 1873, an economic recession that led to severe declines in wages hit. For example, brakemen in West Virginia had experienced a drop in pay from $70 per month to $30. In the words of one railroad worker, "We eat our hard bread and tainted meat two-days old on the sooty cars up the road, and when we come home, find our children gnawing on bones and our wives complaining that they cannot even buy hominy and molasses." Beginning on the Baltimore & Ohio in response to wage cuts (the Baltimore and Ohio had announced a 10 percent wage cut while simultaneously declaring a 10 percent dividend to stockholders), the Great Railroad Strike of 1877 spread to several other rail lines from coast to coast. An estimated one hundred thousand railroad workers walked off the job; and another half million workers in other industries, most notably steel workers and longshoremen, staged sympathetic strikes. In Pittsburgh and Philadelphia, workers fought militia and also committed property damage, but the Pennsylvania militia made the situation even worse by firing into a crowd of workers and killing twenty people in Pittsburgh. Workers retaliated with even more violence and burned two miles of property along the railroad tracks. The militia responded by shooting another twenty workers before the day was over. Property damage in Pittsburgh was estimated at over $2 million. In Reading, Pennsylvania, the situation was the opposite as militiamen refused to fire on strikers, stating that "we may be militiamen, but we are workers first."

Within a little more than a week, governors of nine states declared a state of insurrection and called for federal troops to put down the strike. President Rutherford B. Hayes sent the United States army to the hot spots; but by the time the troops arrived, the violence had subsided and the United States army did not shoot a single striking worker. The army did, however, protect "scab" workers and get the railroads moving again. In a matter of three weeks, the strike was over; but the bloody violence and slanted journalism against the strikers caused many more Americans to view labor unions as dangerous. *The New York Times* warned Americans about the "dangerous classes," and the *Independent* magazine urged the use of force to put down strikers. In the words of one *Independent* editorialist, "If the club of a policeman, knocking out the brains of the rioter, will answer, then well and good. But if it does not … then bullets and bayonets, canister and grape (shot) … constitutes the one remedy."

▶ The Great Railroad Strike of 1877 occurred after Baltimore and Ohio had announced a 10 percent wage cut while simultaneously declaring a 10 percent dividend to stockholders. In Pittsburgh and Philadelphia, militia were called in to handle the revolting workers.

The Homestead Steel Mill Strike

Another bloody episode occurred in a strike of steelworkers against Carnegie's Homestead plant near Pittsburgh in 1892. Ironically, labor unrest at the Homestead Steel Mill during the 1870s had been one of the factors that had helped Carnegie purchase the mill from his competitors at a low cost. Furthermore, Carnegie fancied himself as a friend of the workers, writing in 1886, "The right of the workingmen to combine and to form trades unions is no less sacred than the right of the manufacturer to enter into associations and conferences with his fellows."

In 1892, however, Carnegie attempted to rid the Homestead Mill of union contracts since most of its workers were non-union employees. Carnegie's manager, Henry Clay Frick erected a fifteen-foot fence around the mill and hired over three hundred Pinkerton detectives to defend scab workers against an expected onslaught from striking employees. On June 28, 1992, Frick locked the regular employees out of the mill. On July 6 at 4:00 a.m., the Pinkertons attempted to sneak into the mill, undetected, via two river barges on the Monongahela River. Union men, who put out a call to all workers, spotted the Pinkertons. A twelve-hour gun battle ensued between the Pinkertons and the union men, and thirty union men were wounded and three killed. In the end, however, the Pinkertons were forced to surrender, and one Pinkerton agent was killed. Another Pinkerton agent had his eye gouged out by an angry woman with an umbrella.

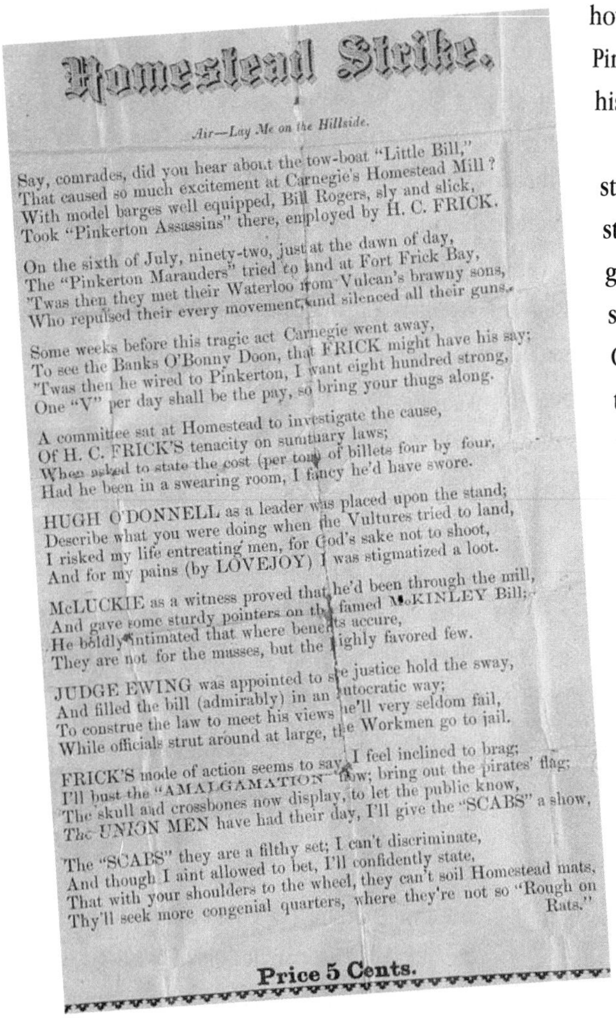

Homestead Strike.

Air—Lay Me on the Hillside.

Say, comrades, did you hear about the tow-boat "Little Bill,"
That caused so much excitement at Carnegie's Homestead Mill?
With model barges well equipped, Bill Rogers, sly and slick,
Took "Pinkerton Assassins" there, employed by H. C. FRICK.

On the sixth of July, ninety-two, just at the dawn of day,
The "Pinkerton Marauders" tried to land at Fort Frick Bay,
'Twas then they met their Waterloo from Vulcan's brawny sons,
Who repulsed their every movement, and silenced all their guns.

Some weeks before this tragic act Carnegie went away,
To see the Banks O'Bonny Doon, that FRICK might have his say;
'Twas then he wired to Pinkerton, I want eight hundred strong,
One "V" per day shall be the pay, so bring your thugs along.

A committee sat at Homestead to investigate the cause,
Of H. C. FRICK'S tenacity on sumtuary laws;
When asked to state the cost (per ton) of billets four by four,
Had he been in a swearing room, I fancy he'd have swore.

HUGH O'DONNELL as a leader was placed upon the stand;
Describe what you were doing when the Vultures tried to land,
I risked my life entreating men, for God's sake not to shoot,
And for my pains (by LOVEJOY) I was stigmatized a loot.

McLUCKIE as a witness proved that he'd been through the mill,
And gave some sturdy pointers on the famed McKINLEY Bill;
He boldly intimated that where benefits accure,
They are not for the masses, but the highly favored few.

JUDGE EWING was appointed to see justice hold the sway,
And filled the bill (admirably) in an autocratic way;
To construe the law to meet his views he'll very seldom fail,
While officials strut around at large, the Workmen go to jail.

FRICK'S mode of action seems to say, I feel inclined to brag;
I'll bust the "AMALGAMATION" now; bring out the pirates' flag;
The skull and crossbones now display, to let the public know,
The UNION MEN have had their day, I'll give the "SCABS" a show.

The "SCABS" they are a filthy set; I can't discriminate,
And though I aint allowed to bet, I'll confidently state,
That with your shoulders to the wheel, they can't soil Homestead mats,
Thy'll seek more congenial quarters, where they're not so "Rough on Rats."

Price 5 Cents.

The union workers temporarily took over the Homestead Steel Mill and elected a council to govern the Homestead community. Four days later, however, Pennsylvania's governor ordered the entire Pennsylvania National Guard, some eight thousand troops, to Homestead to reclaim Carnegie's property. The National Guard troops occupied the mill for three months and ushered scab workers into the mill to take the jobs of the union men. One union man attempted to retaliate by assassinating Frick, whom he shot twice and stabbed with a knife; but Frick, while seated at his desk, had a doctor remove the bullets and tend to his wounds. Unfortunately for the union men, the assassination attempt turned public opinion against the union. The assassin, Alexander Berkman, a Russian immigrant and anarchist, was arrested and sentenced to prison; his ethnicity and political leanings convinced many that unions were violent and filled with dangerous men with foreign ideas.

In the end, the Homestead strike was a major defeat for the unions as the workers gave in after four and a half months and returned to work. Union leaders were blacklisted and could not find work; and the Homestead Steel Mill cut wages, reinstated the twelve-hour day, and cut some five hundred jobs. The Amalgamated Labor Union, which had a membership of twenty-four thousand in 1891, saw its membership decline to less than seven thousand within a decade; and virtually every steel mill in the Northeastern United States broke its relationship with the union.

With the onset of depression in the summer of 1893, however, unrest and dissatisfaction among the working class deepened. Among the most violent of the labor upheavals, which aroused national apprehension, was the Pullman Strike called by the American Railway Union in sympathy for the distress of Pullman workers. The Pullman Palace Car Company made railroad sleeper cars at a factory near Chicago. Pullman constructed a "company town" where employees lived in eighteen hundred company houses, children played in company parks;

and there was a company library and company stores, but no saloon. The Pullman houses were better than those most workers lived in near Chicago; but rent on Pullman houses was 10–20 percent more, and Pullman workers could not own the homes in the company town. Between May and December 1893, as the economic panic hit hard at the Pullman Company, wages at Pullman were cut 28 percent, but rents in the Pullman housing remained the same. Furthermore, the Pullman Company garnished the rents from the employees' wages. Meanwhile, Pullman paid stockholders an 8 percent dividend, and the company showed a $25 million profit. During the spring of 1894, the desperate Pullman workers went on strike; and the American Railway Union (ARU), led by Eugene V. Debs, staged a sympathetic strike and refused to work trains that pulled Pullman cars. By the end of June 1894, some twenty thousand railroad men were on strike in and around Chicago, tying up every midwestern railroad. Debs urged his union men to avoid violence, but the nation's newspapers printed slanted anti-union stories, claiming that there were "Wild Riots" in Chicago.

In retaliation, the railroad companies fired all of the protesting switchmen who refused to work trains that carried Pullman cars. United States Attorney General Richard Olney, who was sympathetic to the railroads, appealed to a federal court for an injunction against the strikers on the basis of the Sherman Antitrust Act, arguing that the unions were combinations in a restraint on trade, such as the act forbade and interfering with the mail. The court issued the injunction, and Olney argued to President Grover Cleveland that federal troops had to intervene to prevent interruption of the mail, which was hauled by rail. Meanwhile, two Chicago judges issued an injunction that prevented ARU leader Debs from speaking in public. Debs defied the injunction and reminded his followers, "Troops cannot move trains."

The railroads made sure that Pullman cars were put on every mail train so that the Union would interrupt the mail. At the same time, violence broke out in Chicago, and President Cleveland (over the protest of Governor Altgeld of Illinois) sent in eight thousand federal soldiers to "protect the mails." Before order was restored, some twenty people were reported killed, sixty more wounded, and two thousand railway cars destroyed, causing over $340,000 in damage. Eugene V. Debs, president of the American Railway Union (ARU), and other labor leaders were arrested, convicted of contempt of court for violating the injunction and sentenced to six months to a year in jail. The conviction of the ARU leaders was upheld by the Supreme Court of the United States, which declared the injunction issued against the union to be a legitimate device for the protection of interstate commerce and the mails. Pullman reopened his factory with scab workers, and sixteen hundred union employees of Pullman suddenly found themselves unemployed.

For thirty years after the Debs' case, a federal court injunction was a potent weapon in the hands of employers threatened with a strike. Although the Clayton Act of 1914 appeared to limit the court's authority to interfere in labor disputes on behalf of employers, many anti-labor injunctions continued to be granted by the federal courts; and it was not until the Norris-La Guardia Anti-Injunction Act was passed in 1932 that labor gained the protection it had long sought against injunctions.

It is noteworthy that in the Homestead and Pullman strikes the companies were run by two of the leading industrialists in the country, who themselves believed that they were among the most enlightened and concerned of American employers—and were so regarded in many quarters. Carnegie had written magazine articles supporting the rights of labor, and George Pullman had built what he considered a "model town" where his employees could live.

We have talked about the labor strife, but a large number of American workers in these years accepted existing working conditions as inevitable and made the best of it. Although they might be discontented, they did not protest. In fact, many industrial workers were influenced by rural values. Many were unskilled, poorly educated, and socially underprivileged. They were also awed by the enormous achievements of the new industry and were proud of being a part of it. Those who were upwardly mobile generally identified with their employers and accepted the values of American capitalism.

Unions and the Black Worker

Unlike the politicians of the day—who managed to evade the race issue—the national labor organizations of the post-Civil War decades had to deal with it. Should they organize black workers? If they did, should they allow black workers to join the same unions as white workers, or should they put them in segregated unions? This was a difficult problem for labor leaders, most of whom shared the prejudicial attitudes of the day, because they also recognized that black workers were potential competitors. The National Labor Union, owing to the wide diversity of opinion among its members, never took any specific action on this matter; however, the Knights of Labor, whose goal was to organize all workers, skilled and unskilled, sought to bring blacks into the labor movement. Thus it organized black as well as mixed locals not only in the North but also in the South, where vigilantes and lynch mobs attacked Knights' organizers. It is not possible to tell from the available records how many blacks became members of the Knights; but at the 1886 convention of the union, the general secretary reported "The colored people of the South are flocking to us, being eager for organization and education . . . ." That same year, the peak year for the Knights, it has been estimated that there were no fewer than sixty thousand blacks in the Knights of Labor.

Since the American Federation of Labor (AFL) was comprised of national craft unions (skilled workers only), it had few black members because few black workers qualified as "skilled workers" and had been admitted to craft unions. Gompers' position on the black worker was made clear in his annual report of 1890 when he emphasized the "necessity of avoiding as far as possible all controversial questions." It would be many years before blacks became "a regular element in the labor force of every basic industry."

Women and "the Incorporation of America"

Women responded to the vast economic transformation, what has been called "the incorporation of America," in multiple ways. During times of labor conflict, such as the railroad strikes of 1877, they comprised a part of the mobs that destroyed property. Because increasing numbers of them were gainfully employed, they sought entrance to unions—successfully during the heyday of the Knights of Labor and less successfully once the AFL became dominant. A few of them did become organizers for the AFL. Many joined the Socialist Party, including middle-class clubwomen and even farm wives. Historian Mari-jo Buhle has written an authoritative account of women and socialism, in which she documents the presence of such seemingly unlikely adherents. Finally, two of the best-known women in the country gained their fame owing to their activism in response to labor conflict: Mother Jones and Emma Goldman.

Mary Harris "Mother" Jones was born in Ireland in 1837, came to the United States, married, and had four children. In 1867, yellow fever took the lives of her entire family. She then made the workers of the whole country into her family, traveling incessantly to places where a strike was in progress and organizing the wives and children of the striking men so as to strengthen support for the strike. Active in the Socialist Party, she was one of the founders of the Industrial Workers of the World in 1905. By the time of her death in 1930, Mother Jones was a living legend, and fifty thousand miners attended a memorial service in her honor.

Emma Goldman, another immigrant like Mother Jones, was born in what is now Lithuania in 1869 and came to this country in 1885, just in time for the Haymarket bombing the next year. When four anarchists were hanged after a trial that seemed a travesty of justice, Goldman became an anarchist herself and spent the rest of her life speaking, writing, and agitating on behalf of various radical causes—including birth control, at the time a very avant-garde position. In 1919, the U.S. by the director of the Radical Division of the Justice Department, J. Edgar Hoover, deported Goldman from the United States after speaking out against military conscription during World War I. Goldman died in Canada in 1940.

The Last Frontier

The West

While industrial expansion was transforming post-Civil War America, there took place another movement of momentous consequence—the settlement of the western half of the country. It

▶ Emma Goldman became an anarchist after the bombing at Haymarket Square. She spent the rest of her life speaking, writing, and agitating on behalf of various radical causes. Here she speaks to a crowd advocating birth control, at the time a very avant-garde position.

was a migration probably unparalleled in the history of the world. In one generation Americans established more than a million farms in this "last West" and occupied more new land than earlier Americans had settled in two and a half centuries. From 1607 to 1870 Americans had occupied 407 million acres and had placed 189 million of them under cultivation. In the last three decades of the nineteenth century, they took up 430 million acres and brought 225 million of them under cultivation.

The Transcontinentals

More spectacular and more important than railroad building in the older sections of the country was the construction of the transcontinental railroads that connected rail lines on the West Coast with the rail lines in the East. Between 1869 and 1893, five transcontinental railroads were built. The first of these was spawned in 1862 when Congress chartered the Union Pacific and the Central Pacific railroads. Upon their completion of the transcontinental line from St. Louis to San Francisco in 1869, with Chinese immigrant labor having done much of the heaviest work, it should be noted that the two railroads had received fifty-four million acres of government land and government loans amounting to about sixty million dollars. In addition the Union Pacific had issued one million shares of stock at $100 a share.

Much of the profiteering that accompanied the building of both roads can be ascribed to the separation of ownership and control in modern corporate enterprise. Managers systematically bled their companies for their own profit. The public first became aware of the large scale of this practice in the Crédit Mobilier scandal of 1872. Officers of the Union Pacific Railroad had used a dummy construction company (the Crédit Mobilier), which they owned, to build the road and had turned over most of the assets of the road, including loans from the government and investments by shareholders, to themselves as constructors, thus paying themselves, by a conservative estimate, $73 million for a $50 million job. Their bribery of congressmen in connection with this deal was only incidental. The concept of "conflict of interest" present in intimate relationships between government officials and business did not yet exist. More fundamental to an understanding of this evil is the fact that executives were placed in a position that gave them constant opportunity to enrich themselves at the expense of the investors and of the enterprise itself.

The Crocker Company, which built the Central Pacific, amassed a profit of about $63 million on an investment of $121 million. Most of this went to the four leading officials of the Central Pacific—Leland Stanford, Collis P. Huntington, Charles Crocker, and Mark Hopkins; each left a fortune of $40 million or more at his death. Critics of the railroad magnates in California referred to their railroad as an "Octopus," with tentacles that controlled San Francisco's financial district, California agriculture, lumber interests, shipping, stage lines, and mining. Frank Norris expanded this theme in 1901 in his best-selling novel, *The Octopus*.

Governmental Aid to Railroads

While individual initiative and enterprise played a large part in the building of America's great railroad empire, it is doubtful if American railroads would have become so highly developed had it not been for the generosity of the federal, state, and local governments. Between 1850 and

1871, the railroads received from the federal government, alone, more than 130 million acres of land—an area as large as the New England states, Pennsylvania, and New York combined—and from the states about forty-nine million acres of land. It is nearly impossible to assess the value of this land, but a conservative estimate (based on $2.00 an acre) would place the value at $360 million. Some estimates have been as high as $2.5 billion.

Because they failed to meet all the conditions under which this land was granted, the railroads were able to retain only about 116 million acres. Even so, at the end of the land-grant era it was discovered that railroads had been granted one-fourth of the entire area of Minnesota and Washington; one-fifth of Wisconsin, Iowa, Kansas, North Dakota, and Montana; one-seventh of Nebraska; one-eighth of California; and one-ninth of Louisiana. At one point (1882) Texas discovered that its donations of land to railroads exceeded by eight million acres the amount remaining in the public domain.

To such grants of land were added loans and subsidies. Towns, cities, and counties gave the railroads about $300 million; and the states, at a conservative estimate, furnished an additional $228 million. The federal government made loans of approximately $65 million, most of which went to the Union and Pacific. A town was at the mercy of a railroad, which could bypass it and thereby cause it to dry up. With this threat the railroads were able to secure cash grants, loans, exemption from taxation, and subscription to their stocks.

Yet many loans were made voluntarily and enthusiastically to get local railroad advantages, because as the governor of Maine asked in 1867, "Why should private individuals be called upon to make a useless sacrifice of their means when railroads can be constructed by the unity of public with private interests, and made profitable to all?" By 1870, according to one estimate, public subsidies plus land grants contributed 60 percent of the costs of all railroad construction. Nevertheless, mileage of rails had increased from just over three thousand at the end of the Civil War to over seventy-two thousand by 1890. Not only had the railroads connected the Midwest with the South and the West Coast, but the railroad infrastructure and railroad land sales spurred settlement and economic development of the Great Plains.

Public Benefits

The national railroad system, no doubt, brought great benefits to the economy. In addition to facilitating the movement of goods, the railroads used enormous amounts of iron and steel, coal, lumber, and other products and provided employment for hundreds of thousands of workers. In the decade of the 1880s, the railroad companies bought nearly fifteen million tons of rails, purchasing in some years over 90 percent of the rolled steel manufactured in the United States.

The railroads were also one of the most active colonizers of the last West. They possessed vast tracts of land grants to sell, and they stood to gain in increased passenger and freight business as settlement expanded. They offered rail tickets at reduced prices to prospective settlers and sometimes even provided free transportation for a settler's furniture. The railroads kept agents at eastern seaports to welcome immigrants and to arrange for their transportation to the West. They even had immigration agencies in Europe to persuade Europeans to come to America.

Chinese Labor

In the three decades following the discovery of gold in California over two hundred thousand Chinese immigrants crossed the Pacific and came to America. By 1880, Chinese immigrants made up approximately 10 percent of the California population. The first Chinese immigrants worked in the gold mines, but in 1852 the California Legislature imposed a tax on "foreign" miners that drove many Chinese immigrants to seek their fortunes elsewhere. Many of these displaced workers found employment in the railroads. For instance, over twelve thousand Chinese immigrants worked on the first transcontinental railroad and approximately 90 percent of the workers for the Central Pacific Railroad were Chinese. The railroads preferred the Chinese workers over others because they had a strong work ethic, would work for lower wages, and were not unionized.

After the first transcontinental railroad was completed, thousands of Chinese workers were suddenly unemployed. Many of these laborers moved to cities, and "Chinatowns" developed in San Francisco and other Western cities. Chinese normally worked in the cities as unskilled laborers, but Chinese entrepreneurs invested in commercial laundries because the capital investment required in the laundry business was low. By the 1890s, two-thirds of the people in California working in commercial laundries were Chinese.

Unfortunately, the Chinese presence in the West spawned anti-Chinese nativism; anti-coolie clubs developed in Western cities, advocating bans on Chinese immigration, employment, and overseas trade. Anti-coolie clubs attacked Chinese people in the streets and burned down factories that employed Chinese workers.

The Mining Frontier

Miners were the first to reveal to the nation the resources and potentialities of the territory between the Missouri River and the Pacific. The discovery of gold in 1848 had lured many miners to California; and later, throughout the 1860s, miners hurried to "strikes" in Colorado, Arizona, Idaho, Montana, and Wyoming. In each case gold attracted the first settlers, the min-

▶ Over twelve thousand Chinese immigrants worked on the first transcontinental railroad. The railroads preferred the Chinese immigrants for labor over others because they had a strong work ethic, would work for lower wages, and were not unionized.

ers. When the pay dirt was exhausted, ranchers and farmers, aided by the government and the railroads, laid the foundations of the territory.

The discovery of gold—in the foothills of the Rocky Mountains close to Pike's Peak, near Lake Tahoe on the eastern slopes of the Sierra Nevada, on the reservation of the Nez Perce Indians in the eastern part of Washington territory, in Last Chance Gulch in Montana, and in the Black Hills region of South Dakota on the reservation of the Sioux Indians— brought thousands upon thousands of persons to these areas. Into them crowded all the elements of a rough and active civilization. A large number of the miners, such as those in Idaho, "were like quicksilver," said H. H. Bancroft, the historian. "A mass of them dropped in any locality, broke up into individual globules, and ran off after any atom of gold in their vicinity. They stayed nowhere longer than the gold attracted them." Others, as in Colorado, stayed on, once the mining boom had spent itself, to farm and to help their area become a territory.

The story of the mining towns is a familiar one in fiction and motion pictures, and their lawlessness has attracted much attention. To be sure, it existed; but it would be a mistake to represent the mining communities as mere nests of lawlessness or to argue, as most Easterners did, that mining camps had abandoned the institutions of civilized society. Mining camps had few churches, schools, newspapers, theaters, and so forth, but they quickly established them. For example, in the town of Deadwood, South Dakota, known as the most lawless place in the country and consisting mainly of two long rows of saloons, a stage company played Gilbert and Sullivan's *Mikado* for a record run of 130 nights.

Each mining camp was a separate administrative and judicial district, having its own governing officials who passed and enforced its own laws. The legal codes and practices of these mining camps were eventually recognized in American courts, and a number of them were incorporated into constitutions and laws of the Western states.

The miners' frontier came to an end in the 1880s. No more important discoveries were made, and the individual prospector was gradually replaced by big corporations, usually run by Eastern financiers. Between 1860 and 1890, $1,242,000,000 in gold and $901,000,000 in silver were taken out of the mines in the West. These amounts enabled the federal government to resume specie payment and helped precipitate the money question, a major political issue during the last quarter of the nineteenth century (see the next chapter).

Comstock Lode

In 1859, silver ore was discovered near Virginia City, Nevada, and quickly became known as the "Comstock Lode," named after prospector Henry Comstock. In the two decades that followed, over $300 million in silver was hauled out of the earth in Nevada. Virginia City became a short-lived industrial center with over three thousand laborers working in the mines and another two thousand working in stamping mills and other silver manufacturing industries. The mines spawned an investment boom in California, which unfortunately led to fraud as unscrupulous businessmen sold more stock in the mines than the silver was worth. The mines spawned new technology, such as pumps to suck water from mine shafts and new ventilators to circulate air in the underground shafts. Due to the labor demands, Comstock miners earned $4 per day, well above the average wage for miners in the West. By 1875, Virginia

▶ Town of Deadwood, South Dakota, circa 1890s.

City had a population of twenty-five thousand people, making it the largest city in Nevada at the time and one of the largest cities between St. Louis and San Francisco.

The Settlers

The opportunities for obtaining cheap or free land induced many settlers to go west. Most of the settlers were Anglo-Americans from the eastern United States, but over two million settlers between 1870 and 1900 were recent immigrants from Europe. The new wave of immigrants to the West did not come from England, but from Ireland, Germany, Scandinavia and Eastern Europe. Some of the settlers were attracted to the gold and silver strikes in California, Nevada, Colorado, and Idaho, but most came seeking land in the vast emptiness that was the American West. They could buy a farm outright from the national government under the terms of the Preemption Act of 1841, which allowed them to obtain a quarter section (160 acres) at the price of $1.25 an acre; or they could purchase their quarter section from one of the land-grant railroads or from one of the states, whose holdings of public domain were greatly increased by the passage of the Morrill Act of 1862. (This act had given every state that established a public, agricultural college thirty thousand acres for each senator and representative then in Congress.) Finally, western settlers could secure their quarter section free of charge under the Homestead Act of 1862. This law made it possible for any American citizen, or any alien who had declared the intention of becoming a citizen, to acquire 160 acres of unoccupied government land by living on it or by cultivating it for five years. A homesteader who wished to gain ownership sooner could, after six months of residence, buy the quarter section at the prevailing minimum price, usually $1.25 an acre. The residence requirement went up to fourteen months in 1891.

The Homestead Act has been called "the greatest democratic measure of all history," but it had a number of faults. The best farming lands east of the 100th meridian (the line approximately bisecting the Dakotas and Nebraska, east and west) were largely taken by 1862; and in the region from the Great Plains to the Pacific, to which the law chiefly applied, small home-

▶The Virginia City Chollar Mine, better known as the Comstock Lode Mine, became a short-lived industrial center with over three thousand laborers working in the mines and another two thousand working in stamping mills and other silver manufacturing industries. Over $300 million in silver was mined within two decades.

steads were inadequate because the climate was too arid and rainfall too unpredictable. Moreover, the Homestead Act did not end land speculation. Individuals made larger purchases than ever. For example, William S. Chapman bought a million acres in California and Nevada, and Francis Palms and Frederick E. Driggs together procured 486,000 acres of timberland in Michigan and Wisconsin. There was also fraudulent administration of the law. False claims were made, and claims were turned over to speculators and to land, mining, and timber companies. In addition, perjury and bribery of land officials were common so that, in practice, the act was a perversion of the land reformers' ideas.

Nevertheless, "sodbusters" moved to the Great Plains of Texas, Kansas, Nebraska, and the Dakotas. The invention of the windmill allowed people to settle in places that were not necessarily next to rivers and other natural water sources. Unusually heavy rainfall in the 1870s (rainfall varies greatly on the Great Plains not only from year to year but also from decade to decade) induced settlers under the mistaken idea that "rain follows the plow." Many settlers erroneously believed that merely breaking the ground somehow increased rainfall. Lacking building materials on the treeless plains, settlers on the Great Plains made building materials out of the sod itself and built houses with cut rectangles of sod. Frugality and ingenuity, however, would not prevent a mass exodus in the 1880s when drought returned and the Great Plains would not produce.

During this period, a generous Congress passed other measures to dispose of the public domain. The Timber Culture Act of 1873 provided free grants of 160 acres in certain regions on condition that the settler plant forty acres (later reduced to ten acres) in trees and keep them growing for ten years. Under the terms of the Desert Act of 1877, the government offered semiarid lands in 640-acre tracts to those who would irrigate them; but since irrigation projects usually required more capital than most settlers had, the law benefited primarily the large-scale grazing companies. The Timber and Stone Act of 1878 permitted the sale of quarter sections of land not suited for agriculture but valuable for timber. Large corporations and speculators employed "dummy" registrants and illegally managed to get possession of more than thirteen million acres of such government lands.

The migration of people created new states in the West in areas that previously had been left to the Native Americans and the buffalo. Kansas was admitted as a state in 1861; Nevada in 1864; Nebraska in 1867; Colorado in 1876; Washington, Montana, and North and South Dakota in 1889; Wyoming and Idaho in 1890; and Utah in 1896. Utah's statehood had been delayed for decades over the polygamy issue, but by 1896 Congress was satisfied that the practice had been officially abandoned. By 1900, only New Mexico, Arizona, and Oklahoma remained territories in the continental U.S. that had not been granted status as states.

New Mexico

When the U.S. gained New Mexico in 1848 in the Treaty of Guadalupe Hidalgo, it gained territory from Mexico with a Spanish heritage that dated back two hundred years. General Stephen Kearney, who commanded U.S. Army troops at Santa Fe, attempted to establish a territorial government; but his appointments were mostly Americans, who were outnumbered in New Mexico by Hispanics by almost a 50:1 margin. Hispanics and the Taos Indians in the region feared that their new rulers would confiscate their lands and destroy their ways of life; consequently, the Taos Indians rebelled. The U.S. army put down the rebellion, but New Mexico remained under military rule until 1850.

The new territorial government established in 1850, however, was corrupt and used its powers to gain control of over two million acres of land from Hispanic landowners by 1870. In the end, the territorial government accomplished exactly what New Mexico's citizens had feared when New Mexico became part of the United States.

California

Like New Mexico, California became part of the Union with the Treaty of Guadalupe Hidalgo and had a long Hispanic heritage and Hispanic population. Spain began settlement of California in the eighteenth century with a series of missions on the Pacific coast. The Spanish attempted to convert the Native Americans, but they also tried to use them as a labor force to take care of livestock owned by the missions. Missions declined in the nineteenth century when Spain required that the missions must be self-supporting. In their place, an agricultural economy based on large estates arose in California's fertile central valleys. After the gold rush brought white American settlers, most of the Hispanic landowners lost their lands to American swindlers and court seizures. The large Hispanic-owned estates became large American-owned estates, and California quickly became the most productive agricultural state in the U.S., to the benefit of the new white landowners.

The Ranching Frontier

Flourishing on the Great Plains for about two decades after the Civil War was an open-range cattle industry, originating with the long drive of cattle from Texas northward to railroads on the Great Plains for shipment eastward to the large cities. The Spanish had introduced longhorn cattle on to the Texas plains in the eighteenth century. With no natural predators, the longhorns multiplied until after the Civil War when some five million head of unowned cattle roamed the plains of Texas. The cattle were worth only $1.00 per head in Texas, but worth $60.00 to $70.00 in Chicago; hence to reap profits, a person had only to round up the cattle in Texas and drive them to rail connections, none of which had yet made it to Texas in 1866.

Trails of the Cattle Drive Era

In 1866, Texas cattlemen drove their cattle to rail connections in Sedalia, Missouri, along what became known as the Sedalia Trail. Some 260,000 head of cattle were driven toward rail connections via the Sedalia Trail, but problems with Indians in Oklahoma and with farmers en route who objected to thousands of cattle traipsing uninvited across their land led cattlemen to search for an alternative route in 1867. That year, rail lines had reached Abilene, Kansas, and cattlemen shifted to the Chisholm Trail from South Texas to Abilene, Kansas. Only thirty-five thousand head of cattle would make it to Abilene in 1867, but over four million head would make it across the Chisholm Trail over the next two decades.

At Abilene, Joseph G. McCoy, an enterprising meat dealer from Illinois, built a hotel and erected barns, stables, pens, and loading chutes. In 1868, Abilene received seventy-five thousand head of cattle; and in 1871, a record year, handled seven hundred thousand head.

The cattle were moved slowly across the plains from Texas to Kansas in herds of two or three thousand head. This procedure required the services of sixteen or eighteen cowboys, a cook with a chuck wagon, and a wrangler with extra cow ponies. It was on the long drive that the cowboy came into his own, as a unique character of the frontier. He was a picturesque figure, usually clothed in a flannel shirt, with a brightly colored handkerchief loosely

▶ The Spanish originally introduced long horn cattle to Texas. Worth only a dollar a head in Texas, the animals had to be driven to rail connections for shipping to places like Chicago, where they were worth sixty dollars a head.

knotted around his neck, high-heeled boots into which his trousers were tucked, a pair of leather chaps—or heavy riding overalls—and a broad-brimmed felt hat. Heavy spurs and a revolver completed his costume. The cowboy's work, however, was hazardous. With only a cow pony, a lasso, and a six-shooter, he and his companions tried to keep several thousand head of cattle under safe control during two months of continuous travel.

There were many risks along the trail: stampedes, set off by a sudden noise or lightning flash, thefts by rustlers, and raids by Indians. One of the veterans of the Long Drive wrote, "It was tiresome grimy business for the attendant punchers who traveled ever in a cloud of dust and heard little but the constant chorus from the crackling of hoofs and of ankle joints, from the bellows, lows, and bleats of the trudging animals."[5] The cowboy's life was also a lonely one. He sang sentimental words to soothe the restless cattle and to cheer himself as he whiled away the lonely hours on the Chisholm Trail. Although fans of Western stories and movies might never suspect the fact, blacks were numerous among the cowboys who drove the herds to market.

As new rail lines opened in Dodge City, Kansas, Ogallala, Nebraska, and Cheyenne, Wyoming, new cattle drive trails would open from Texas toward the rail destinations. Trail-end towns, such as Abilene, Dodge City, Ogallala, Nebraska, and Cheyenne, Wyoming, became raucous centers of drunkenness, gaming, fighting, and prostitution as cowboys weary from the trail quickly spent their earnings on immediate gratification. In Abilene, twenty-four saloons were open 24-hours a day, and the railroads made almost as much money shipping liquor into town as cattle out of it.

The cattle drive reached its peak in the early 1880s, when profits of 40 to 50 percent were common and profits of 10,000 percent were achieved on occasion. Such returns, however, quickly attracted so many prospective ranchers that they overstocked the range. The unfenced plains of the public domain in the 1870s were bountiful and free, and the ranchers made use of this public land. Between 1882 and 1884, they sent as many young steers north to the ranges as they shipped east to the markets. Unfortunately, the two disastrous winters (1885–1886 and 1886–1887) and the blistering summer of 1886, however, destroyed most of the feed and the cattle. The steers that eventually did reach market were so inferior in quality that the bottom fell out of beef prices despite the great shortage. Thus 90 percent of the cattle died, and 90 percent of the cattle ranchers went broke.

At this time, too, large numbers of sheepherders began to cross the plains. The sheep stripped the range of grass; so when the sheep men came to stay, the cattlemen had to fight or leave. Farmers were also homesteading the plains and fencing the open range after the invention of barbed wire made fencing affordable. Many of them, also, turned to raising cattle. Soon they were able to produce beef of higher quality than that found on the open range. With the increase of railroad facilities, including the extension of the railroads to Fort Worth, Texas, the long drive became unnecessary. The erection of barbed wire fences across the plains quickly made cattle drives impossible; gradually this stage of the colorful cattle industry was ending, and with it came an end to the last frontier.

---

[5] Philip Ashton Rollins, *The Cowboy* (New York: Charles Scribner's Sons, 1922), p. 253.

The New South

As the North left the South to its own affairs, blacks were edged out of politics in the South; black participation and representation in the democratic political system was systematically eliminated by 1900. The New South began to flex its political muscle in 1880 when it nominated Union soldier Winfield Scott Hancock for president on the Democratic ticket. Hancock lost the popular vote to James Garfield by only ten thousand votes in the closest popular vote in American history. Hancock won every Southern state, but the Democrats and the South still lost. As a consequence, Southerners focused on rebuilding the South without control of the political system. Partially due to Northern investment, Southerners would build competitive steel mills in Birmingham, Alabama, and textile mills in the Carolinas and Georgia. Although the "New South" would remain much more agricultural than the North, the beginnings of an industrial economy were planted in the South.

Rather than slaves, the industrial economy of the New South was built on the labor of women and children. Some 40 percent of the Southern cotton mill industry workers in the 1880s were women and another 25 percent were children. Wages for Southern women and children in the cotton mills was approximately half the wages in Northern textile mills. The cheap labor gave the South an advantage, and the American textile industry began to move south. In 1880, the South produced only 5 percent of the nation's textiles, but by 1900 it was almost 25 percent. Simultaneously, James E. Duke installed a cigarette-making machine at Durham, North Carolina, in 1885, and the tobacco industry suddenly was transformed to the South. In 1890, Duke created the American Tobacco Company which controlled 90 percent of the American tobacco industry.

Railroads, the economic engine of the Gilded Age, outpaced the national average in terms of percentage increase in the South. In 1886, Southern railroads changed their gauge from five feet to four feet, eight and one half inches so as to integrate with the railroads throughout America. The railroads boosted the Southern iron industry. In 1880, the South produced only 9 percent of America's pig iron; but in just ten years, the South's percentage of iron production doubled to 18 percent. Nevertheless, the combination of low wages in the South and the fact that most of the investment in Southern industry was from Northern sources meant that Southern wages remained only 40 percent of the national average, in spite of the advances in industrialization.

One reason that the South failed to advance more economically after the Civil War was that Southern agriculture stagnated. Monoculture in cotton, overproduction, and declining prices due to America's hard-money policies led to a situation where Southerners produced more and more cotton, but made less and less money. Farmers became indebted to country storekeepers (from whom they bought provisions between planting and harvest) at interest rates of over 50 percent. Simultaneously, cotton prices would decline 50 percent between 1870 and 1890. The result was sharecropper indebtedness and a general debt crisis in Southern agriculture that would persist until the turn of the century when gold finds in Alaska would finally end price deflation.

Blacks in the New South

The Southern white backlash against the former slaves perhaps reached its apex in the 1890s when lynchings averaged near two hundred per year. Anti-black riots erupted in several Southern states and Southern states reduced blacks to second-class citizenship through both formal and informal disenfranchisement. Literacy tests and tests of moral character, along with poll taxes and white primaries, were imposed so as to prevent blacks from voting or running for office. A host of anti-black laws were passed on state and local levels, limiting blacks to employment in agriculture or domestic servitude and imposing zoning laws, curfews, and other restrictions on black rights. Public facilities of all kinds became legally segregated, and the "Separate, but Equal" doctrine was upheld by the Supreme Court in *Plessy v. Ferguson* in 1896. In short, the period following the Civil War replaced slavery with a form of second-class citizenship that included significant impediments to the economic and political advancement of African Americans.

The Indian

An essential step in the conquest of the last West was a solution of the Indian "problem." The Indians of the Great Plains and the Rocky Mountains, about 250,000 in number, actively opposed white settlement in their areas. The land had been theirs for centuries, and they were determined to fight, if necessary, to keep it. The strongest and most warlike were the Sioux, Blackfoot, Crow, Cheyenne, Comanche, and Apache tribes. These nomadic buffalo-hunting tribes clung tenaciously to their land and fought valiantly for it. Mounted on swift horses and armed with bows and arrows, the Indians of the Great Plains were more than a match for the whites until the repeater rifle was perfected.

Until the time of the Civil War, the Plains Indians had been relatively peaceful, but this was largely because whites had avoided the Great Plains as an uninhabitable "Great American Desert." Then the miners invaded the mountains, cattlemen moved into the grasslands, and white settlers followed the railroads across the prairies. The invention of the windmill allowed whites to settle in remote locations far from natural sources of surface water. Wanton destruction of the buffalo by the intruding whites threatened the Indians' very existence because the Indians depended on the animal for food, fuel, clothing, robes, bowstrings, tools, and other essentials. Faced with all these pressures, the tribes became dissatisfied with their treaties with the federal government.

During the quarter-century Indian war that followed the Civil War, whites clashed with the Comanche, Apache and Navaho in the Southwest and with the Sioux, Arapaho, and Cheyenne on the Great Plains; and for the next twenty-five years Indian warfare constantly recurred. In the mountain areas most of the tribes were eventually persuaded to give up their lands and move to reservations, but the tribes on the plains were not willing to abandon their hunting grounds to the encroaching whites.

In 1867, Congress enacted legislation providing for the removal of all Indians to reservations, thereby breaking the promises given to the Plains Indians in the 1820s and 1830s that they could keep their lands forever. The federal government decided to create two

▶ The strongest and most warlike were the Sioux, Blackfoot, Crow, Cheyenne, Comanche, and Apache tribes. These nomadic buffalo-hunting tribes clung tenaciously to their land and fought valiantly for it. Mounted on swift horses and armed with bows and arrows, these were the Great Plains Indians.

reservations for the Plains Indians—one in the Black Hills of Dakota, the other in present-day Oklahoma. Of course, however, difficulties would quickly arise. While the tribal chieftains signed the treaties, individual Indians often refused to be bound by them. General W. T. Sherman wrote, "We have … provided reservations for all, off the great roads. All who cling to their old hunting grounds are hostile and will remain so until killed off. We will have a sort of a predatory war for years—every now and then be shocked by the indiscriminate murder of travelers and settlers; but the country is so large, and the advantage of the Indians so great, that we cannot make a single war to end it." Sherman added that because of the Indians' swiftness and guerrilla tactics, "Fifty Indians could checkmate three thousand United States soldiers." Indeed, the Indians won 90 percent of their encounters with the United States Army during this time period, but due to the sheer numbers of white men the Indians would ultimately lose any war of attrition against a larger population with superior resources and technology.

Sherman's predictions and estimations proved accurate. Between 1869 and 1875, more than two hundred battles between the United States Army and the Indians took place. What went on in these conflicts can be derived from a statement of General Francis A. Walker, Commissioner of Indian Affairs, in 1871: "When dealing with savage men, as with savage beasts, no question of national honor can arise. Whether to fight, to run away, or to employ a ruse is solely a question of expediency." A few years earlier General S. R. Curtis, United States Army commander in the West, had told his subordinate officers: "I want no peace until the Indians suffer more."

The Indians, of course, did suffer. A white trader reported that Cheyenne "were scalped, their brains knocked out; the men used their knives, ripped open women, clubbed little children, knocked them in the head with their guns, beat their brains out, mutilated their bodies in every sense of the word." This barbarity surely raised the question: Who were the savages, the Indians or the whites?

The Indian wars after 1865 cost the federal government millions of dollars and hundreds of lives, yet a solution to the problem seemed to be nowhere in sight. Much of the failure rested with the national government whose officials regarded each tribe as a separate nation. Indians frequently misunderstood the terms of the tribal treaties, and many individual Indians did not feel obligated by them. Moreover, authority over Indian affairs was divided between the Department of the Interior and the War Department, each pursuing different policies and objectives. Finally, frontiersmen, in general, believed that the only good Indian was a dead one; most soldiers agreed.

Easterners, far removed from the scene of strife, had a different attitude. Churchmen and reformers united, there to urge a policy of humanitarianism toward the Indians. As the War Department followed its policy of fighting the Indians, new ideas about the problem began to have influence in Washington. A new civilian Board of Indian Commissioners, created in 1869, attempted to convert the nomadic Plains Indians to agriculture on the reservations and sought to persuade the government to break down tribal autonomy.

In 1871 Congress abolished the policy of dealing with tribes as though they were separate nations. In the 1870s, too, the government began to establish Indian boarding schools removed from the reservations. To give Indians greater incentive, the Indian commissioners recommended individual land holdings and the gradual elimination of the system of reservations. Books on behalf of the Indian began to appear, among them Helen Hunt Jackson's *Century of Dishonor* (1881), which had the greatest influence in stirring up public opinion behind efforts to improve the Indians' lot.

Finally, in 1887, the Dawes Act initiated a new Indian policy that reversed the old military policy of extermination. The act provided for the dissolution of tribal autonomy and the division of tribal lands, with each family head receiving 160 acres. To protect the Indian on his property, the right of disposal was withheld for twenty-five years. At the end of this probationary period the Indian received full rights of ownership and full United States citizenship.

The new policy did not work well, however. In dividing up the reservations, the best tracts were usually sold to white settlers and the worst given to the Indians. Often the Indian owners were disheartened and failed to cultivate, adequately, the land they kept. Furthermore, when individual Indians, without experience as property owners, acquired good land, they were too easily persuaded to sell it. (The Burke Act of 1906 gave the Secretary of the Interior discretionary authority to reduce the probationary period preceding legal sale.) Nor was the policy universally applied. Some tribes, especially in Arizona and New Mexico, retained their tribal organizations and continued to hold their land in tribal fashion. To make matters worse, the Dawes Act actually reduced the total volume of land held by the Indians since the number of Indian "heads of household" times 160 acres did not equal the total amount of land that had been held by the Indians when it was granted to tribes instead of individuals. Furthermore, many whites married Indian widows to get their 160 acres and then divorced them, while all-white juries and judges awarded the land to the white men who had married the Indian women for the sole purpose of getting their land.

Gradually the feeling developed that it had been a mistake to have the Indians abandon their traditional way of life. An effort was made to reverse the policy promoted by the Dawes Act and to allow the tribes to hold their land as communal property. This was to be realized in the Indian Reorganization Act of 1934, but clearly it was too little, too late.

Last Stands and Massacres

The battles between the Indians and the white men were simply too numerous to detail in this limited space, but there are several incidents that stand out as worthy of further attention. Among those was the Sand Creek Massacre in Colorado in 1864. The discovery of gold near Pike's Peak in 1858 had led to a rush of white fortune-seekers to Colorado. Cheyenne and Arapaho Indians were then further concentrated onto reservations in southeastern Colorado. Renegade Indians, resisting further concentration, raided white settlements and stagecoach lines in retaliation. The governor of Colorado responded by urging all friendly Indians to gather at army forts for protection before the government launched a campaign to stop Indian raiders. One group of Cheyenne and Arapaho Indians under the leadership of Black Kettle camped near Fort Lyon on Sand Creek, apparently in response to the governor's urging. On November 29, 1864, Colonel John Chivington, himself a Methodist elder, and the Colorado militia, made up of unemployed miners many of whom were drunk, massacred a village of 133 Indians, 105 of which were unarmed women and children. A Congressional inquiry into the incident resulted in a court martial for Chivington, but this was of little consolation for the slaughtered Indians. Black Kettle escaped, only to be killed four years later near the Texas border in a skirmish with United States troops under General George Armstrong Custer.

Little Big Horn

In 1874, gold was discovered in the Black Hills, leading hordes of whites to encroach on land reserved for the Indians. By 1875, over one thousand whites had arrived in Dakota Territory and the Northern Pacific Railroad planned to build railroad connections. The federal government offered to purchase the Black Hills, but the Indians refused to sell, regarding the area as sacred Indian lands. The United States responded by ordering the Indians to further concentration on the Pine Ridge Reservation southeast of the Black Hills. Many of the Dakota Indians resisted and instead fled to southeastern Montana in the area of the Big Horn River where the Sioux under Chief Red Cloud had waged a guerrilla war against whites encroaching on their land several years before. In June 1876, General George A. Custer led a scouting party of 265 men to find the Indians' camp. Led by Chiefs Crazy Horse and Sitting Bull, an Indian army of some two thousand Sioux warriors surprised Custer and his men, overwhelming the scouting party with superior numbers. Custer and all 265 of his men were killed, and their bodies mutilated. The Indian victory would be short-lived, however; within six years Sitting Bull surrendered, and Crazy Horse had been killed.

Cochise, Geronimo, and the Apaches

During the late 1860s, the Apaches under Chief Cochise waged a war of raids and resistance against the United States Army in New Mexico and Arizona. In 1872, Cochise accepted a peace treaty that included some of the Apaches' tribal lands. Cochise, however, also agreed that the Apaches would follow assimilation policies favored by whites. Cochise died in 1874; and his successor, Chief Geronimo, an Apache shaman or medicine man, rejected white assimilation policies and renewed raids on white settlements and outposts. Geronimo raided isolated ranches and stole food, horses, and ammunition while killing the white ranchers and burning their homesteads. Riding with Geronimo's raiders was Lozen, a female warrior that was armed with a rifle and rode and raided with the men. In 1885, Lozen and Geronimo launched a series of raids over ten months on both sides of the United States/Mexico border. At one time, over two thousand United States troops under General Nelson Miles were involved in searching for Geronimo, but the Indians seemed to always stay one step ahead of the United States Army. Finally, in 1886, Geronimo met with General Miles to negotiate a peace. By the time Geronimo surrendered, his band of raiders numbered only thirty-three and included a good number of women and children. Upon his surrender, Geronimo explained, "We have not slept for six months, and we are worn out."

Geronimo's career as a raider may have been over, but his legend grew over the years to the point that when he appeared at the St. Louis Exposition in 1904, he sold photographs of himself for a quarter each. Geronimo also rode with President Theodore Roosevelt in his inaugural parade in 1905. Geronimo and the Apaches were not allowed, however, to return to their homeland in Arizona. Geronimo was buried in Oklahoma in 1909.

▶ The battle of Little Big Horn, "Custer's Last Stand." General George A. Custer and a band of over 250 scouts were ambushed by some 2,000 Sioux warriors. Overwhelmed, Custer and all his men were killed.

Wounded Knee

In 1889, an Indian religious man known as Wovoka combined elements of Christianity with traditional Indian religious practices into a new religion known as the "Ghost Dance." Wovoka claimed that God spoke through him and promised that all whites would soon be destroyed in an apocalypse, that all Indians slain by whites would be resurrected from the dead, and that the buffalo, which whites had essentially wiped out by 1890, would return in great numbers to roam the plains. Central to the ceremony of Wovoka's new religion was a "ghost dance" where Indians danced in a circle in traditional style, often until some collapsed of exhaustion. As the religion spread, it grew and mutated. Wovoka's Sioux disciples taught that wearing white ghost shirts made them impervious to bullets.

Whites feared the dance as a prelude to an Indian uprising, and the Bureau of Indian Affairs agent at Pine Ridge Indian Reservation in South Dakota asked Republican President Benjamin Harrison for federal troop reinforcements in anticipation of an Indian uprising. In December 1890, Chief Sitting Bull was arrested and then shot and killed by Indian police when he joined the ghost dancers. Sitting Bull's followers fled the scene of his death, but the U. S. Army met them at Wounded Knee Creek. The soldiers of the United States Army opened fire and massacred some two hundred defenseless Indians, many of them women and children, in the snow. An eyewitness to the scene, an Indian named American Horse, described the event thusly:

> They turned their guns, Hotchkiss guns (cannons that fired an explosive shell) upon the women who were in the lodges standing there under a flag of truce, and of course as soon as they were fired upon they fled. ... There was a woman with an infant in her arms who was killed as she almost touched the flag of truce, and the women and children of course were strewn all along

▶ The massacre at Wounded Knee was horrendous.Men, women, and children of the Lakota tribes were brutally shot down with Hotchkiss guns by U.S. troopers and buried in mass graves.

> the circular village until they were dispatched. Right near the flag of truce a mother was shot down with her infant; the child not knowing that its mother was dead was still nursing, and that especially was a very sad sight. The women as they were fleeing with their babes were killed together, shot right through, and the women who were very heavy with child were also killed. . . . After most all of them had been killed a cry was made that all those who were not killed or wounded should come forth and they would be safe. Little boys who were not wounded came out of their places of refuge, and as soon as they came in sight a number of soldiers surrounded them and butchered them right there."

In addition to the obvious tragedy, the Wounded Knee massacre represents an end to the Indian way of life. In the words of the Indian leader Black Elk, "The nation's hoop is broken and scattered. There is no center any longer and the sacred tree is now dead." Similarly, Chief Joseph of the Nez Perce in the Pacific Northwest uttered the following speech after being captured by federal troops forty miles south of his goal of the Canadian border:

> "I am tired of fighting. Our chiefs are killed. . . . It is cold and we have no blankets. The little children are freezing to death. My people, some of them, have run away to the hills, and have no blankets, no food; no one knows where they are—perhaps freezing to death. I want to have time to look for my children and see how many I can find. Maybe I shall find them among the dead. Hear me, my chiefs, I am tired; my heart is sick and sad. From where the sun now stands, I will fight no more forever."

▶ Chief Joseph of the Nez Perce tribe and his family.

The White Victory and the Destruction of the Buffalo

The white victory over the Native Americans can be attributed to numerous factors, including the European diseases that had wiped out over 90 percent of the Indians since the landing of Columbus and the superior technology of the Europeans, as well as the European mastery of the horse that was not present in North America until the arrival of the Spanish. The destruction of the

Plains Indians and the final victory, however, should be attributed to the destruction of the buffalo, which must be listed as another in a long list of American tragedies. At the close of the Civil War, an estimated fifteen million buffalo roamed the Great Plains. By 1900, however, the American bison was in danger of extinction, and only an estimated three hundred remained.

Several factors worked to bring about this waste of life. First, the United States Army well understood that the buffalo were the source of food, shelter, and clothing for the Plains Indians; without the buffalo the Plains Indians would not survive. Therefore, some of the buffalo were methodically shot by the United States Army in an effort to vanquish their foe. Second, given that one buffalo would feed one hundred people, the railroads slaughtered the buffalo to feed their workers as they built the railroad lines across the Great Plains. Third, buffalo rugs became a fashionable item, not only on the east coast of the United States but also in Europe; so thousands of buffalos were killed to provide rugs for the wealthy—both in the United States and in Europe. Fourth, a popular societal myth was that the buffalo tongue was an aphrodisiac; therefore, millions of buffaloes were slaughtered just for the tongue. Dodge City, Kansas, alone shipped some seven million pounds of buffalo tongue. Finally, the railroads sold buffalo hunting expeditions for sport, in spite of the fact that since it had few natural enemies, the buffalo tended not to run when hearing a shot. Although mountain lions could and did kill young buffalo, any animal predators were simply no match for the adult buffaloes due to their size and strength until Europeans arrived with lead and gunpowder.

A New Ethnic Mix

In the first two centuries of American history, the nation's ethnic mix was more or less tripartite: Native American, European, and African American. After the Mexican War and the acquisition of the Southwest, the mix began to include Latinos and among them were mestizos of mixed Spanish and Indian ancestry. After the California gold rush, immigrants began to arrive on the West Coast from China and then from other Asian countries. Sadly, the record of the treatment of the people of color in the American West is a story of virulent prejudice, discriminatory legislation, and ghettoization—patterns that would not really change until World War II. In California, for example, the state legislature enacted the Foreign Miners' Tax in 1850, a measure whereby "foreigners" had to pay an additional $20 in order to mine. What was especially unfortunate was the fact that Latinos, many of whom had been born in Mexican California, were often defined as "foreign," despite the guarantees of protection for the Californios in the Treaty of Guadalupe Hidalgo that ended the Mexican War. Furthermore, we have already discussed the violent reaction to Chinese immigration in San Francisco, followed by Congress's passage of the Chinese Exclusion Act of 1882, which barred entrance of Asian immigrants to the United States.

The new ethnic mix, the voluminous immigration to the East Coast from southern and eastern Europe, the labor turmoil and the exploitation of the vulnerable, the overcrowded cities, the problems for farm families, struggling to market their crops profitably—all these constituted challenges to the nation's political system. In the next chapter, we shall see how well the system responded.

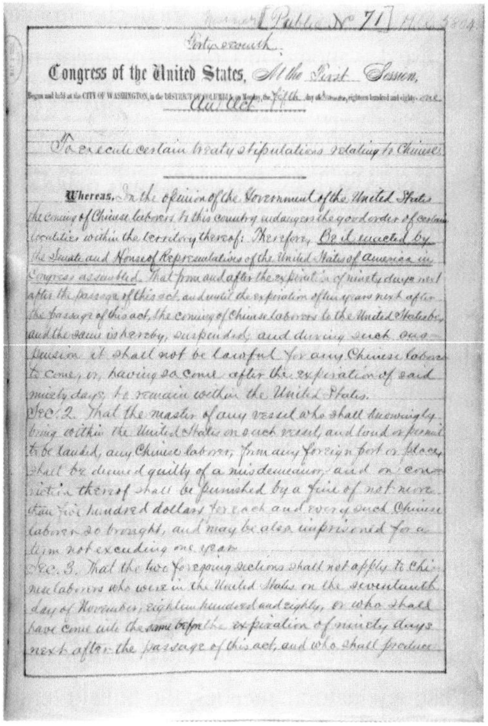

[Public No 71]

Forty-seventh

Congress of the United States, At the First Session,

Begun and held at the CITY OF WASHINGTON, in the DISTRICT OF COLUMBIA, on Monday, the fifth day of December, eighteen hundred and eighty-one.

An Act

To execute certain treaty stipulations relating to Chinese.

Whereas, In the opinion of the Government of the United States the coming of Chinese laborers to this country endangers the good order of certain localities within the territory thereof: Therefore, Be it enacted by the Senate and House of Representatives of the United States of America in Congress assembled, That from and after the expiration of ninety days next after the passage of this act, and until the expiration of ten years next after the passage of this act, the coming of Chinese laborers to the United States be, and the same is hereby, suspended; and during such suspension it shall not be lawful for any Chinese laborer to come, or, having so come after the expiration of said ninety days, to remain within the United States.

Sec. 2. That the master of any vessel who shall knowingly bring within the United States on such vessel, and land or permit to be landed, any Chinese laborer, from any foreign port or place, shall be deemed guilty of a misdemeanor, and on conviction thereof shall be punished by a fine of not more than five hundred dollars for each and every such Chinese laborer so brought, and may be also imprisoned for a term not exceeding one year.

Sec. 3. That the two foregoing sections shall not apply to Chinese laborers who were in the United States on the seventeenth day of November, eighteen hundred and eighty, or who shall have come into the same before the expiration of ninety days next after the passage of this act, and who shall produce

▶The first page of the Chinese Exclusion Act, signed in 1882. The act barred Asian immigrants from entering the United States by penalty of imprisonment and or deportation. The Chinese were tolerated if not welcomed, earlier on during the gold rush as they were needed for labor, but with the post-Civil war economy slump, they were blamed for taking jobs that could have otherwise been held by white citizens.

Klondike Gold Strike

In 1896, the discovery of gold along the valleys of the Yukon and Klondike rivers launched a great stampede of prospectors north to Alaska and the Yukon Territory of Canada. Although gold had been found all across Alaska since the 1870s, it was news of a huge gold strike at Bonanza Creek in August 1896 that launched the frenzy of the last great gold rush. The outside world learned of the riches of the Yukon Valley in the summer of 1897, when two ships arrived in San Francisco and Seattle loaded with approximately $1 million in Alaskan and Canadian gold. By the time winter cut communications, two thousand prospectors had gathered in Canada at the former fishing camp of Dawson, at the head of the Yukon, with several thousand others on their way. By the summer of 1898, Dawson had a population of thirty thousand, making it the largest Canadian city west of Winnipeg.

The Klondike strike was one of the best-publicized events of its time. Because of improved communications linking the Atlantic with the Pacific Coast, the news reached New York and Europe almost as soon as it reached the West Coast. New infrastructure, unavailable in previous gold strikes, such as the transcontinental railroad completed in 1869, quickly helped bring prospectors from all over the world.

Gold prospecting in the far north, however, was harsh. Prospectors landed by ship from Seattle at the Alaskan boomtown of Skagway and then made their way over the Alaskan Rockies to the Yukon and Klondike rivers. The prospectors' journeys began for many when they climbed the mountains over the White Pass above Skagway and onward across the Canadian border to Bennett Lake, or one of its neighboring lakes, where they built barges and floated down the Yukon River to the gold fields around Dawson City. Officials in Canada began requiring that each prospector entering Canada on the north side of the White Pass bring with him one ton of supplies to ensure that they didn't starve during the winter. This placed a large

THE WHITE PASS CHRONICLE

GROWING WITH THE LAST GREAT FRONTIER

NEWS FROM THE KLONDIKE.

GOLD! GOLD! GOLD! GOLD!

Special Tug Chartered To Get The News.

Seattle, July 17, 1897. ON BOARD THE STEAMSHIP PORTLAND, 3:00 A.M. — At 3 o'clock this morning the steamship Portland, from St. Michaels for Seattle, passed up the Sound with more than a ton of solid gold on board and 68 passengers. In the captain's cabin are three chests and a large safe filled with the precious nuggets. The metal is worth nearly $700,000 and most of it was taken from the Klondike district in less than three months last winter. In size the nuggets range from the size of a pea to a guinea hen egg. Of the 68 miners on board hardly a man has less than $7,000, and one or two have more than $100,000 in yellow nuggets.

WHITE HORSE TODAY

BUILDING BOOMING

QUEEN VICTORIA

SKAGWAY AND UP RIVER POINTS

Alex Schwartz and Party Leave Bennett By Boat

The Land Of Gold

Running Dawson Soon

▶ The discovery of gold along the valleys of the Yukon and Klondike rivers launched a great stampede of prospectors north to Alaska. The gold strike at Bonanza Creek was considered the last great gold rush.

burden on the prospectors and the pack animals climbing the steep pass. Thousands of horses froze to death in the unpredictable Alaskan weather where storms seemed to arise out of nowhere. Of the hundred thousand hopeful prospectors who left for the Yukon in 1896–1897, only about thirty thousand were able to complete the journey due to the harsh elements.

The population of the Alaska Panhandle town of Skagway boomed along with that of Dawson. Upon arrival in Skagway, many realized how difficult the trek ahead would be en route to the gold fields, and they chose to stay behind to profit by supplying goods and services to miners. Within weeks after news of the gold strikes in the Yukon, stores, saloons, and offices lined the muddy streets of Skagway. The population was estimated at eight thousand residents during the spring of 1898 with approximately one thousand prospective miners passing through town each week. By June 1898, with a population between eight thousand and ten thousand, Skagway was the largest city in Alaska.

One of the effects of the sudden rush of people was that Skagway became a lawless town, described by one member of the Northwest Mounted Police as "little better than a hell on earth." Fights, prostitutes and liquor were ever-present on Skagway's streets. The most colorful resident of this period was bad man Jefferson Randolph "Soapy" Smith. Smith headed a ring of thieves who swindled prospectors with cards, dice, and shell games. His telegraph office, in 1898, charged five dollars to send a message anywhere in the world, and prospectors sent news to their people back home, not realizing there was no telegraph service to or from Skagway until 1901. Smith also controlled a comprehensive spy network, a private militia called the Skaguay Military Company, the newspaper, the Deputy U.S. Marshall and an array of thieves and con-men who roamed about the town. Smith, however, was killed in a shootout on the streets of Skagway on July 8, 1898.

The Klondike gold rush, like the career of Soapy Smith, would be short-lived. By 1899, the stream of gold-seekers had diminished along with new gold finds, and the economies of Dawson and Skagway began to collapse. By 1900, when the railroad was completed, the gold rush was nearly over and most of the prospectors were absorbed by West Coast cities such as Seattle. The last saga of the American West, it seemed, had come to a close.

▶ ▶ ▶

Chapter Review 16

Summary

The decades following the Civil War were years of economic expansion and industrial revolution in the United States. The U.S. government helped facilitate the boom by granting resources to individuals and industry for economic development and the construction of infrastructure. Coupled with the abundance of natural resources and continuing technological progress was a home market steadily expanding through immigration and a high birth rate. The prevailing attitudes favored free market capitalism and social Darwinism; however, the downside of laissez faire was corporate corruption, worker exploitation, unsafe consumer products, repeated periods of economic panic, and rampant degradation of the environment. The courts contributed to the laissez-faire abuses by weakening the Sherman Act and the Fourteenth Amendment in the Slaughterhouse Cases, *Plessy v. Ferguson*, and *U. S. v. E. C. Knight*.

Railroads were the driving force of the economy, a situation made possible by federal land grants to the railroads. Railroad magnates, such as Jay Gould, became extraordinarily wealthy, but often engaged in graft and corruption along the way and gained notoriety as "Robber Barons" as well as "Captains of Industry." Corporate monopolies developed, led by John D. Rockefeller's Standard Oil Trust, which made Rockefeller the wealthiest man in the world. The people and the government fought back against the power of the trusts with the Interstate Commerce Act, which created the first federal regulatory agency to regulate the railroads, and the Sherman Anti-Trust Act.

Invention also drove the American economy led by Thomas Edison, who not only invented the electric light bulb but also had over one thousand other patents. Alexander Graham Bell's invention of the telephone would be another invention that would help transform America.

The Industrial Revolution also required finance capital. America's leading financier was J. P. Morgan, who branched out from just finance to ownership of railroads, General Electric, and eventually Carnegie's steel empire.

The rise of an industrial economy with poor pay and conditions for workers led to the development of a significant labor movement, at first by the Knights of Labor and later by the American Federation of Labor under the leadership of Samuel Gompers. Although there were some successful strikes, such as the Great Rail Strike of 1877, most major strikes ended in failure for the unions since government intervened on the side of management. Strikes were often violent with scores of workers losing their lives, many at the hands of U.S. government troops.

Settlement of the West was precipitated by a number of factors: the construction of the railroads, the federal Homestead Act which granted land to settlers, and the discovery of precious metals in the West. Gold was discovered in California in 1848, but gold and silver were also discovered in other Western states including Colorado, Idaho, and Nevada. The most important of these finds was the Comstock Lode at Virginia City, Nevada, which was the largest silver strike in American history.

The arrival of railroads in the West precipitated the great cattle drive era in Texas as the five million cattle that roamed Texas unowned after the Civil War were driven to rail connections in Kansas, Nebraska,

(cont'd)

Wyoming, and Missouri. Trail's end towns became raucous centers of violence and debauchery along with the explosion of commerce.

Settlement of the West by whites led to the removal of the Plains Indians to reservations beginning in 1867. The Indians resisted; and a twenty year war ensued where the Natives won 90 percent of the battles, including the massacre of General Custer and 265 men at Little Big Horn. Eventually, however, the destruction of the buffalo by whites left the Natives with no choice but to go to the reservations with their way of life destroyed. In a final sad chapter, the U.S. Army massacred two hundred mostly unarmed Indians at Wounded Knee, South Dakota, in 1890.

A final frontier was opened in the far north in 1896 when gold was discovered in the Yukon Territory of Canada. Skagway, Alaska, became the main port of entry for over one hundred thousand gold prospectors that headed to the Yukon. Like the Trail's End towns of the previous decades, Skagway became a center not only of commerce but also a hotbed of raucous swindling and debauchery. By 1900, however, the gold rush to the Yukon was over; the last saga of the American West had reached its end.

Chronological Time Line

1841	Preemption Act allowed the individual purchase of 160 acres at $1.25 per acre.
1859	"Comstock Lode" silver strike at Virginia City, Nevada
1859	Henry Bessemer invented a process for purifying steel.
1862	Morrill Act granted thirty thousand acres for each member they had in Congress to states for the establishment of agricultural colleges.
1862	Homestead Act granted 160 acres free to settlers in the West.
1864	Sand Creek Massacre in Colorado
1866	The Sedalia Trail began the cattle drive era.
1867	Opening of the Chisholm Trail from South Texas to Abilene, Kansas
1867	Congress provided for the removal of Plains Indians to reservations.
1869	The Knights of Labor was organized.
1869	Completion of the first transcontinental railroad

Chapter Review (cont'd)

Time Line (cont'd)

1873	Slaughterhouse Cases: The Supreme Court limited the Fourteenth Amendment rights of the former slaves, distinguishing between national and state citizenship.
1874	Geronimo revolted against assimilation policies.
1876	Custer's last stand at Little Big Horn
1877	The Great Railroad Strike
1877	*Munn v. Illinois*: Allowed state regulation of railroads and fixed maximum storage rates for grain elevators.
1882	John D. Rockefeller formed his Standard Oil Trust.
1882	Chinese Exclusion Act barred Asian immigration to the U.S.
1885	James E. Duke installed a cigarette making machine in Durham, North Carolina.
1886	*Wabash v. Illinois*: Ruled that since railroads crossed state boundaries, they fell outside the realm of state jurisdiction and into the federal realm because Congress was granted the exclusive powers to regulate interstate commerce
1886	American Federation of Labor was organized.
1886	May 1: Haymarket riot in Chicago
1886	Harsh weather killed 90 percent of the Texas cattle and ended the cattle drive era.
1886	Geronimo surrendered.
1887	Interstate Commerce Act created the Interstate Commerce Commission.
1887	Dawes Act: Native Americans were treated as individuals rather than tribes, and 160 acres was granted to heads of households.
1889	New Jersey allowed the formation of holding companies.
1890	Sherman Anti-Trust Act declared "any combination in restraint of trade" to be illegal.
1890	Massacre at Wounded Knee
1892	Jay Gould died and newspapers proclaimed that America has lost its "richest man."

Time Line (cont'd)

1892 The Ohio Supreme Court ordered the dissolution of the Standard Oil Trust.

1892 Homestead Steel Mill Strike

1893 Panic of 1893

1894 Pullman Strike

1895 *U. S. v. E. C. Knight* limited the Sherman Anti-Trust Act by separating manufacturing from commerce.

1896 Klondike Gold Strike

1896 *Plessy v. Ferguson* validated the "separate but equal" doctrine.

1898 *Smyth v. Ames:* The court ruled that corporations are persons under the law.

1901 Frank Norris published *The Octopus.*

1905 Mary Harris "Mother" Jones helped found the Industrial Workers of the World (IWW).

1911 Supreme Court ruled that the Standard Oil Trust violated the Sherman Anti-Trust Act.

1932 Norris-Laguardia Anti-Injunction Act granted labor unions protection from injunctions.

Key Terms

Slaughterhouse Cases of 1873: Allowed the state to grant a monopoly to a business that is in the public interest and limited the Fourteenth Amendment rights of blacks, distinguishing between national and state citizenship

Munn v. Illinois: Approved an Illinois law that allowed state regulation of railroads and fixed maximum storage rates for grain elevators on the grounds that a state could regulate "a business that is public in nature though privately owned and managed"

Wabash v. Illinois: Ruled that since railroads crossed state boundaries, they fell outside the realm of state jurisdiction and into the federal realm since Congress was granted the exclusive powers to regulate interstate commerce

Social Darwinism: The application of Darwin's principles of natural selection to humans and the idea that some groups of humans are more "evolved" than others

Robber Barons: Capitalists that achieved their success at least partially through graft and corruption

Chapter Review (cont'd)

Key Terms (cont'd)

Jay Gould: Railroad magnate, investor, and "Robber Baron" once proclaimed as the "world's richest man."

Cornelius Vanderbilt: Railroad magnate and owner of the Biltmore, the largest house in America

Captains of Industry: Leading industrial capitalists such as John Rockefeller, Andrew Carnegie, and J.P. Morgan

"The Octopus:" The railroads in California and their economic and political power

John D. Rockefeller: Founder of Standard Oil and the wealthiest man in the world

Trusts: Monopolistic corporate structures that helped monopolistic corporations evade anti-monopoly laws

Horizontal Integration: The domination of one segment of a particular industry by a single company, such as Rockefeller's monopoly on oil refining

Vertical Integration: The domination of all segments of a particular industry, such as Rockefeller's expansion from refining into exploration, transport, and retailing of oil

Andrew Carnegie: Scottish immigrant that became America's #1 manufacturer of steel

Bessemer Process: Henry Bessemer's process of purification of steel by blowing air into the mixture and burning off the impurities

E. C. Knight: Controlled 98 percent of America's sugar manufacturing in 1895

Holding company: Corporations that own other companies

Edward Bellamy: Wrote *Looking Backward* (1887) in which he assailed economic conditions of the time and pictured a future socialist utopian state where life's necessities and luxuries would be produced by a cooperative society for the benefit of all

Henry George: Wrote *Progress and Poverty* (1879) in which he maintained that the problems of the times were largely the result of a monopoly of land

Interstate Commerce Act: Created the first federal regulatory agency in 1887 to regulate the railroads

Sherman Antitrust Act 1890: Designed to combat monopolies, the Act declared that "Any combination in restraint of trade" was illegal.

U. S. v E .C. Knight Co.: Declared that manufacturing was exempt from prosecution under the Sherman Act because manufacturing was not "commerce"

J. P. Morgan: Leading financier and railroad magnate of the Gilded Age

Thomas Edison: Inventor of the electric light bulb, phonograph, and motion pictures with over 1,000 patents

George Westinghouse: Inventor of the air brake

Alexander Graham Bell: Inventor of the telephone

Knights of Labor: Labor Union that was founded in 1869

Uriah Stephens: Original head of the Knights of Labor

Terrence Powderly: Leader of the Knights of Labor that changed the strategy to strikes and the end of secrecy

Key Terms (cont'd)

Haymarket Square Bombing: Explosion at a Labor Rally in Chicago in 1886 that led to the death of seven policemen and execution or imprisonment of seven union men

American Federation of Labor: Skilled labor union founded by Samuel Gompers

Samuel Gompers: Head of the American Federation of Labor

Molly Maguires: Coal mining union famous for violent tactics

Great Railroad Strike of 1877: Successful Railroad Strike that paralyzed the nation's rail system

Homestead Steel Mill Strike: 1892 strike against Andrew Carnegie's steel mill that was put down by the Pennsylvania National Guard

Pinkerton Agency: Detective Agency hired by Management to escort scab workers into the workplace.

Pullman Strike: Strike against the Pullman sleeper car company in 1894 that paralyzed the nation's rail lines and was violently put down by the U.S. army resulting in the deaths of 40 workers

"Mother" Jones: Irish immigrant active in the Socialist Party, Mother Jones was one of the founders of the Industrial Workers of the World in 1905.

Emma Goldman: Lithuanian immigrant, anarchist, and female activist that was deported by the United States in 1919

Anti-Coolie Clubs: Anti-Asian groups that opposed Chinese immigration

Comstock Lode: The nation's largest silver strike at Virginia City, NV

Sodbusters: Plains farmers

Homestead Act: Granted 160 acres of free land to settlers

Great Trail Drives: 1866-1886, the overland drives of cattle from Texas rangeland to rail connections in Kansas, Nebraska, Wyoming, and Missouri

Trail's End: Towns such as Abilene and Dodge City Kansas with rail connections to Chicago where cattle from Texas were driven

Chisholm Trail: Most famous cattle drive trail from Texas to Abilene Kansas

The New South: The Southern economy in the Gilded Age that used sharecropping and wage labor instead of slavery and expanded into manufacturing

Plessy v. Ferguson: 1896 Court case that validated the "separate but equal" doctrine

Helen Hunt Jackson: Author of *Century of Dishonor* (1881), which had the greatest influence in stirring up public opinion behind efforts to improve the Indians' lot

Dawes Act of 1887: Treated the Indians as individuals rather than tribes and granted 160 acres to each head of household

Cochise: Apache chief that accepted assimilation policies in 1872

Geronimo: Apache chief that revolted against assimilation policies 1874–1886

George A. Custer: Led a scouting party of 265 U.S. soldiers that was massacred by a superior force of Indians at Little Big Horn, Montana in 1876

Little Big Horn: Site of the massacre of Custer and his men by Indians in 1876

Chapter Review (cont'd)

Key Terms (cont'd)

Wounded Knee (South Dakota): Site of the massacre of 200 Indians, most unarmed women and children, by the U.S. Army in 1890

Final Solution: A reference to the destruction of the Buffalo as a means to drive the Plains Indians to the Reservations.

Klondike gold strike: Gold strike in the Yukon Territory of Canada in 1896

Jefferson Randolph "Soapy" Smith: Headed a ring of thieves in Skagway that swindled prospectors with gambling and a fake telegraph office

Dawson: Mining town in the Yukon Territory

Skagway: Alaskan port that was the beginning point for the trek from the Ocean to the Yukon gold strike.

Pop Quiz

Chapter 16

1. In the Slaughterhouse Cases, the Court ruled that:
   a. the Fourteenth Amendment protected only those rights that stemmed from the Federal government under the Constitution.
   b. states could not discriminate against blacks because they had equal rights and privileges.
   c. all citizens of American states had the rights under the Fourteenth Amendment.
   d. both b and c.

2. Jay Gould was described as:
   a. the richest man in America.
   b. the smartest man in America.
   c. the most hated man in America.
   d. all of the above.

3. William Vanderbilt's famous reply to a reporter's question about his railroad was:
   a. "it is all for the public."
   b. "I cannot answer that question in the interest of national security."
   c. "I refuse to answer that question under the rights of executive privilege."
   d. "the public be damned."

Pop Quiz (cont'd)

4. Trusts and monopolies were built with all of the following EXCEPT:
   a. cheap labor
   b. high tariffs
   c. low tariffs
   d. efficient business methods

5. Perhaps the greatest magnate of capitalist finance was:
   a. Richard Chase.
   b. J. P. Morgan.
   c. A. G. Edwards.
   d. Charles Schwab.

6. Which union organized only skilled workers?
   a. National Labor Union
   b. Knights of Labor
   c. American Federation of Labor
   d. American Railway Union

7. The "Comstock Lode" was the nation's largest silver strike at:
   a. San Francisco, California.
   b. Deadwood, South Dakota.
   c. Denver, Colorado.
   d. Virginia City, Nevada.

8. General William Tecumseh Sherman argued which of the following?
   a. Fifty Indians can checkmate three thousand U.S. soldiers.
   b. The Indians are terrible fighters and will be easily eradicated.
   c. The Indians can be eradicated by burning a swath sixty miles wide through Texas.
   d. The best approach would be to poison all the Buffalo.

9. Geronimo's revolt was precipitated by:
   a. the failure of the U.S. to grant a reservation on tribal lands.
   b. Geronimo's rejection of assimilationist policies.
   c. Geronimo's belief that he could take over the entire United States.
   d. Geronimo's raid of the U.S. Army saloon at Albuquerque.

Chapter Review (cont'd)

Pop Quiz (cont'd)

10. The Alaska boom town that became the departure point for the Klondike prospectors was:
    a. Sacramento.
    b. Independence
    c. Dawson
    d. Skagway

11. The Knights of Labor was a secret organization of workers. T F

12. Most mining towns had their own laws but were still wild and violent places. T F

13. The Knights of Labor __________ in membership after the bombing at __________ __________ in 1886.

14. A company that owned stock in other companies was called a __________ __________.

15. A court ruling prohibiting a strike was called an __________.

1. A	6. C	11. T	14. Holding Company
2. D	7. D	12. F	15. Injunction
3. D	8. A	13. Declined; Haymarket Square	
4. C	9. B		
5. B	10. D		

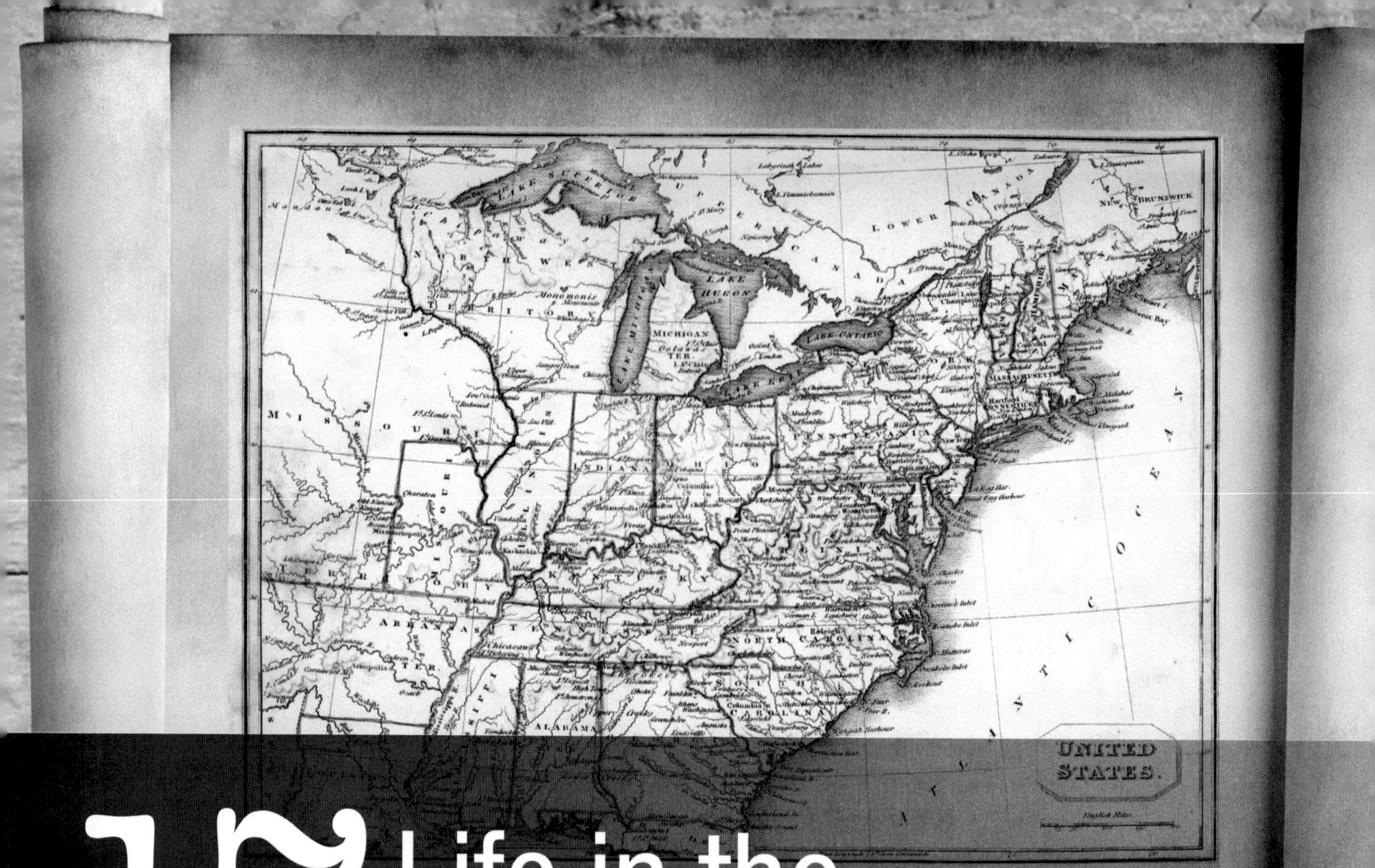

17 Life in the Gilded Age

Chapter Objectives

Economic Advancement

The Growth of Industry

Popular Culture

Recreation and Leisure

The New Rich

The Middle Class

The Worker

The New Immigration

"Survival of the Fittest"

The Shock of Darwinism

Social Darwinism

Laissez-Faire

Industrialism and Religion

Protestantism and Darwinism

The Social Gospel

The Catholic View

Idealism

American Pragmatism

The New Legal Theory

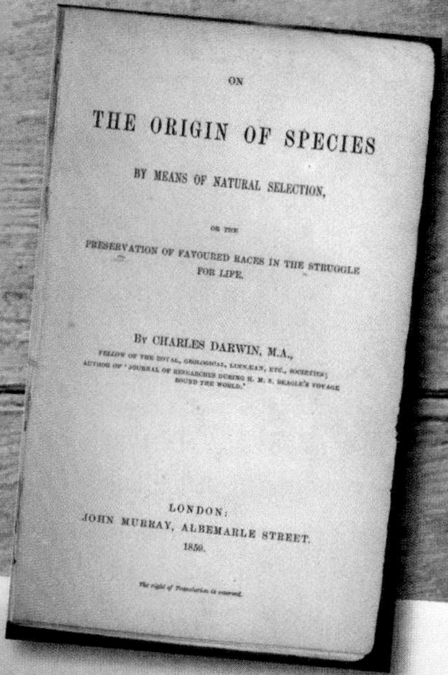

Challenges to Darwinism and Laissez-Faire

Reform Darwinism

The New Economists

Thorstein Veblen

Reformers

Socialism

Achievements of the Gilded Age

Arts and Letters

The Chautauqua Movement

Economic Advancement

After the Civil War and Reconstruction, Americans largely turned their attention from the immense social issues of the day, such as equal rights for African Americans, toward securing economic advancement. After the failures of active government during Reconstruction, Americans, in general, came to favor a laissez faire approach to governing, assuming that the free market and capitalism was, essentially, self-regulating. James Bryce wrote of the situation in the 1880s that politicians were "clinging too long to outworn issues" and "neglecting to discover and work out new principles capable of solving the problems which now perplex the country."

Nevertheless, the era following Reconstruction was one of great invention and economic growth. All, however, did not share in that prosperity equally, and the politics of the era was fraught with corruption. The existence of this situation is what led Mark Twain to label the era as the Gilded Age. In terms of definition, "gilded" is a description of something that has been altered to appear more attractive or valuable than it actually is. In reference to the Gilded Age, Twain described it as "dazzling on the surface, but base metal beneath." The "dazzling" part to which Twain made reference was the robust economic growth and the explosion of invention, along with 75 percent voter turnout, much higher than that in the early twenty-first century. The "base metal beneath," however, was gross income inequality, segregation and legal inequalities for blacks, gender inequality, xenophobia, political corruption, monopolies, worker exploitation, incompetence in government, and the lack of empathy that accompanied Social Darwinism, the application of the "survival of the fittest" approach to the human existence.

The Growth of Industry

The years following the Civil War were a period of rapid and vast economic expansion known as the American Industrial Revolution. No factor fueled this industrial revolution more than the construction of the railroads. Between 1860 and 1900, the total railroad mileage increased from 30,000 to 193,000 while the capital invested in manufacturing jumped from $1 billion to almost $10 billion, the number of workers from 1.3 million to 5.3 million, and the value of the annual product from under $2 million to over $13 billion. The economy absorbed 2.5 million new workers from Europe in the 1870s and another 5 million in the 1880s. Industry had come of age, and the United States had become the greatest industrial nation in the world.

This enormous economic growth not only made the United States potentially the most powerful country in the world but also transformed it from a rural and agrarian nation into an urban and industrial one. By 1890, the value of the country's manufactured goods exceeded that of its agricultural products. Ten years later manufactured products were worth twice as much—this in spite of the fact that agricultural production also increased in the Gilded Age due to a seemingly endless stream of new machines for cultivating and harvesting, and the construction of railroads to get agricultural products to the markets. The advances in agricultural production combined with the industrial revolution to create a boom in commercial packaging of food, including packaged cereals and canning factories.

Big business came to dominate economic life. Antebellum factories and plants—where the relationship between owners and employees was close, the workshop was small, the market local, and the ownership was comprised of an individual or a partnership—gave way to large, impersonal corporations. The demand for immense sums of capital to build railroads and factories led to the rise of the stock market as a way to finance the industrial revolution. The hitherto scattered banking institutions now became concentrated in four or five financial centers, with New York becoming the most important. East of the Mississippi River, factory and foundry workers and their families helped change towns into cities and to create sprawling industrial centers. Into these centers came millions of immigrants who were to alter the racial and ethnic composition of the nation.

Although the Civil War is generally regarded as marking the beginning of the triumph of industrial capitalism, it alone did not produce the Industrial Revolution. Instead, the forces responsible for the rapid postwar expansion of American industry had been developing for more than half a century. In the 1850s, railroads had revolutionized transportation, and many inventions had transformed both industry and agriculture. Then, in the post-Civil War years, major advances in every field of science, especially in chemistry and physics, provided the principles for new technology. Inventions that spurred industrial growth were made in transportation, communications, electrical power, the production of steel, and the use of oil.

Railroad development played a key role in the expansion of industry, the economy, and the nation; and by 1900 the American railroad system extended into every region. Moreover, through the use of standard-gauge track, the rolling stock of railroads could travel over each other's lines all over the country, greatly facilitating the shipment of goods. Equipment improved when steel replaced heavier and more brittle iron in the construction of tracks, locomotives, and freight and passenger cars. Simultaneously, service also improved. The Westinghouse airbrake, the automatic coupler, and the block and signal system increased safety while the Pullman sleeping car, the dining car, and improved lighting offered both comfort and safety.

The telegraph had been widely used before the Civil War, and in the following decades came the submarine cable, the telephone, the stock ticker, the typewriter, and wireless telegraphy. Cyrus W. Field succeeded first in laying a cable across the Atlantic Ocean in 1866, and Alexander Graham Bell and his assistant Thomas A. Watson invented the telephone in 1876. Even more significant was the development, by Italian electrical engineer Guglielmo Marconi in 1901, of wireless telegraphy from which came the radio, television, and radar.

Also vital to industrial growth was the typewriter, the first practical one invented by Charles L. Scholes in 1867. By the mid-1880s, the typewriter was used by most large business concerns. It assisted business by making communication more legible, preserving records, and providing carbon copies of correspondence and other papers. (Parenthetically, it can be noted, it opened up a whole new avenue of employment for women, called, at first, "typewriter girls"). These advances in communications were as essential as those in transportation to the development of business.

The use of electricity also contributed to industrial growth. In 1879, after much trial and error (at one point, Edison stated that he knew one thousand things that did not make a good filament), Thomas Edison invented a practical incandescent light bulb that enabled entire towns, and even large cities, to be illuminated. Another major accomplishment was his development of a system of central power stations for generating the electric current necessary for any extensive lighting system. The opening of the Pearl Street Central Station in New York, in 1882, was considered to be the beginning of the electrical age. Early customers were *The New York Times* and the banking firm of J. P. Morgan and Company. Out of these developments came, in the 1880s, a workable electric railway, a practical dynamo, and electric motor. The use of electric light and power brought a revolution—in the home, in transportation, and in the factory—where electric motors would replace the steam engine.

Of major importance, too, was the development of ways to mass-produce steel. In the 1850s William Kelly of Kentucky and Henry Bessemer, an Englishman, independently invented the open-hearth process of making steel, which came to be known as the Bessemer process. Air was blown through the molten liquid, and the air burned off most of the carbon and other impurities in the iron. When certain amounts of carbon, silicon, and manganese were added, the end product became steel. What had previously been a rare metal could now be mass-produced, and the country's vast supplies of iron ore and coal could be more fully utilized.

In 1870 only 77,000 tons of steel were manufactured, but by 1880 1.39 million tons were produced yearly; by 1900, nearly 11.4 million tons were produced. Historians regard this rapid expansion of the steel industry as one of the most important reasons for the Industrial Revolution of the late nineteenth century. At the same time the petroleum industry expanded from a state of nonexistence before the Civil War to that of about fifty million barrels annually by the early 1890s. Similarly, George B. Eastman created a new industry with his development of mass-produced roll photographic film and the Kodak camera. The Bonsack cigarette-rolling machine essentially created a new industry that ended up changing the habits of millions, eventually "hooking" Americans on cigarettes.

All these inventions increased productivity, but they also offered opportunities for vast wealth to entrepreneurs with drive, initiative, and the courage to compete in a free-enterprise system that accepted graft, corruption, and the worship of material goods. Many took the chance, and some acquired immense fortunes.

At the same time, the new inventions and the vast economic growth created a new social geography of gender. With so many more employment options, women were much less confined to the home than they had been formerly. The burgeoning department stores in cities all over the country now attracted women shoppers "downtown." Dance halls and amusement parks in the growing cities gave young working-class people a place to go where even the women were unsupervised. Finally, for the first time in American history, a small number of single women began to live alone or with other single women.

Popular Culture

Since they shared neither the cultivated tastes of the intellectuals nor the bankrolls of the industrialists and financiers, most Americans sought their own cultural pleasures. In time, catering to this mass audience would create whole new industries.

Most Americans knew no more about the lives of the very rich than what they read in their newspapers and magazines, and these media were developing as never before. The Gilded Age was the age of the warring newspaper barons, Joseph Pulitzer and William Randolph Hearst, of the first major newspaper chains and press services. Magazines were being aimed at particular segments of the public—lowbrow, middlebrow, and highbrow. As circulations mounted, advertising, another whole new industry, began to surge.

Since readers of the time did not know that Mark Twain was a major figure in American literature, they simply enjoyed his books. They also enjoyed the hacks that turned out dime novels and books for boys—the writers of historical romances, sentimental stories, exposés, inspirational works, and love stories. A few are remembered—for instance, Horatio Alger, Jr. and his successful "rags to riches" young heroes, and Lew Wallace and his sensational epic success, *Ben Hur.* There were, also, the popular poets: including James Whitcomb Riley, Eugene Field, and Mrs. Ella Wheeler Wilcox. In at least one way the writers for mass audiences had a kinship with the captains of industry in that they believed in production—poets turned out a daily poem, novelists a hundred novels. With few exceptions what they wrote ignored the real world and offered escape.

Recreation and Leisure

Family fun was largely do-it-yourself. The middle-class family would leave its home—often a wooden "Gothic" structure surrounded by a lawn and shade trees—to have a picnic. After consuming quantities of food, the men and boys might pitch horseshoes. Later on, the women and girls might join them for a game of croquet. Furthermore, in the 1890s every American seemed to want a bicycle.

There were no movies in the Gilded Age, but many towns had theaters where plays, vaudeville, and minstrel shows were performed. Additionally, one of the great thrills of the late nineteenth century was the circus. When the circuses of Barnum and Bailey or the Ringling Brothers or "Buffalo Bill's Wild West Show" came to town, hundreds of patrons bought tickets to get into the big tents. Another attraction was the county fair with its horse racing, sideshows, fireworks, livestock exhibitions, and possibly even a baseball game. At county fairs, families had picnics and reunions with relatives and friends from other towns.

There was growing interest in outdoor sports in the Gilded Age, but it was not until the end of the century that athletic contests began to draw large crowds. In 1869, a professional baseball club, the Cincinnati Red Stockings, was organized. In 1871, the National Association of Professional Baseball Players was created in an effort to deal with abuses then afflicting the game, such as foul language by the players, gambling, and bribing of the players. Then, in 1876, the National Association of Professional Baseball Clubs came into being. Though professional baseball became more respectable, not everyone thought it was proper to attend games, especially those played on Sunday. In some cities—Philadelphia, Cleveland, and Boston—Sunday baseball was prohibited. Baseball in the Gilded Age was a simpler, far less expensive game than it is today. There were no huge salaries for players or imposing grandstands and playing fields, nor did the games receive much space in the newspapers.

Football was played almost entirely at universities and colleges with Harvard, Yale, and Princeton leading the way. The first intercollegiate football game was played in 1869. Virtu-

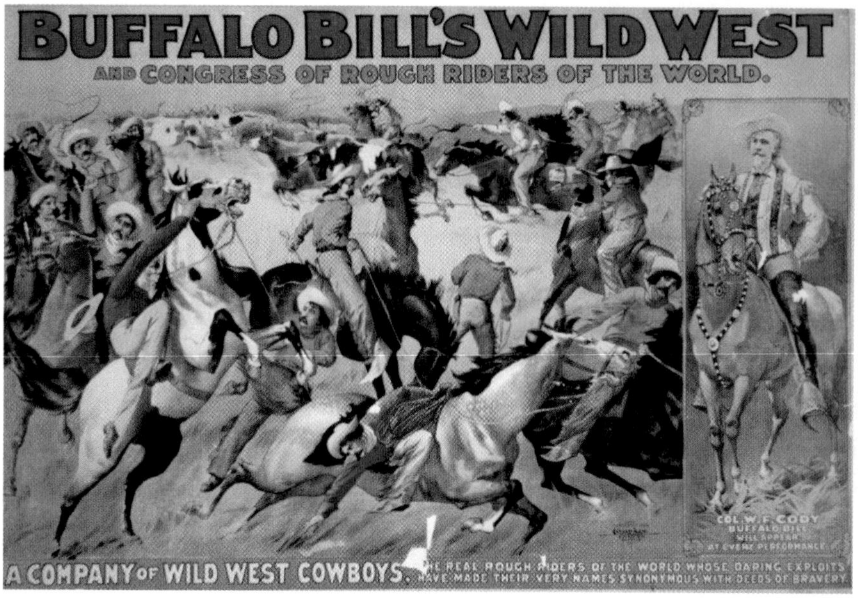

▶ Poster for Buffalo Bill's Wild West show which toured for almost ten years. Attractions of the show included a reenactment of the Pony Express, Indian battles, trick riders, rough riding cowboys, and a parade of people from different horse cultures, such as Turks, Gauchos, Arabs, Mongols, and Georgians.

ally all the players who made Walter Camp's All American Team were from Eastern schools. Little money was budgeted for football; there were no large, high-salaried coaching staffs, huge stadiums, or intersectional games. Even though the railroads had made transcontinental travel possible, it would not be efficient enough for collegiate or professional sports to become intersectional in character until the development of jet travel in the 1950s.

The New Rich

At the top of the social and economic structure in the United States in the Gilded Age were the Captains of Industry, as many contemporaries called them and as they considered themselves to be. They were the new rich—Standard Oil king John D. Rockefeller leading the way with his nearly $900 million. The economic inequality in the country became acute during the Gilded Age. By 1900, it was estimated that one-tenth of the population owned nine-tenths of the wealth in the country, and the few millionaires at the time of the Civil War had increased to thirty-eight hundred. Meanwhile, though there was no government-set poverty line, average wages for American workers hovered around $600 per year, a figure that many economic historians argue would have been approximately equal to the "poverty line" if any such government-set standard had existed.

One of the symbols of the great capitalists' position in society was their style of living, which included palatial mansions and gold-trimmed carriages. Their big houses had libraries, billiard rooms, art galleries, several dining rooms, and even small theaters, and chapels. They lived in brownstone houses in the large cities and in manor houses in the suburbs or in the country. Built in virtually every known style and copied from those of the Europeans and Persians, these residences often showed bad and even vulgar taste. It was a time when the jigsaw, the cupola, the mansard roof with its dormer windows, and an orgy of decoration were in vogue. Historian and socio-literary critic Vernon L. Parrington described it as "flamboyant lines and meaningless detail" with "tawdry decorations" and "a stuffy and fussy riot of fancy."

"The Gilded Age" was a fitting label for the tawdriness characteristic of this period. This term captured the cynical spirit and crudeness of the new age. The United States, wrote E. L.

▶John D. Rockefeller walking with John D. Rockefeller, Jr.

Godkin in *The Nation* in 1866, is a "gaudy stream of bespangled, belaced, and beruffled barbarians. . . . Who knows how to be rich in America? Plenty of people know how to get money; but . . . to be rich properly is, indeed, a fine art." The new rich were unsure of themselves and used gaudy display to impress others. The conspicuous waste of money was the measure of social status. This prompted the craze whereby wealthy Americans went on shopping sprees for European antiques and art collections, launching perhaps the greatest plunder of the European continent since the sacking of Rome.

Though perceptive social critics assailed the new rich for their coarse taste and lack of business ethics, the typical American saw the rich as respected members of society, pillars of the churches, and philanthropists who occupied positions of prestige and power both at home and abroad. Vernon L. Parrington, though sharply critical of the period, was also fascinated. He interpreted the Gilded Age as one in which the energies damned up by the limitations of frontier life and the inhibitions of backwoods religion had been suddenly released.

Economist Thorstein Veblen considered this extravagant and ostentatious living and intentionally conspicuous waste a clear sign of the increasing inequality of wealth. He maintained that ornamentation, too, was a form of conspicuous waste and that buildings, household interiors, and even spoons should be designed simply for use. While working as a forester on Cornelius Vanderbilt's Biltmore estate (near Asheville, North Carolina, the largest house in America, young Gifford Pinchot—later to be a leading Progressive in the country, a governor of Pennsylvania, and eventually head of the federal Forest Service under Theodore Roosevelt—observed about the chateau: "As a feudal castle, it would have been beyond criticism, and perhaps beyond praise. But in the United States of the nineteenth century and among the one-room cabins of the Appalachian mountaineers it did not belong. The contrast was a devastating commentary on the injustice of concentrated wealth."

The Middle Class

More representative of the American lifestyle of these years was that enjoyed by the middle class—the clerks, professionals, shopkeepers, and lower-level executives and their families. For these people, home was a simple house or an apartment (something rather new then) with heavy furniture and draperies, marble-topped tables, and considerable bric-a-brac. Their standard of living was usually better than that of their parents. They could educate their children, and they could hope and work for a better status. The middle-class enjoyed the increased comforts resulting from the inventions of the day: the telephone in the 70s, the electric light in the 80s, and the gas burner after 1890. If they lived in a city, they might enjoy the benefits of electric trolley cars, elevated railways, better sewage disposal, improved water distribution plants and street paving, and more efficient fire departments. They would also suffer, however, the dreadful noise of the "el," the congested traffic of wagons and hacks, and the constant danger of large-scale fires, such as the great Chicago fire of 1871, laying waste to large sections of cities.

Walking city streets could be dangerous, especially at night, and wise citizens stayed at home after darkness came. In the *Centennial Guide to New York City and Its Environs,* published in 1876, travelers were advised to "reach the city in the day-time," to "avoid being too free with strangers," to "avoid all crowds, particularly at night," and, if they were obliged to make inquiries on the street, to "apply to a policeman or go into a respectable place of business." Present-day Americans may find small comfort in the knowledge that the dangers of urban living are nothing new.

In the country, travel was still by horseback, wagons, or buggies and over muddy trails and roads filled with bumps and holes. A trip to the village or to the county seat, accomplished now in a matter of minutes or, at most, an hour or so, was then generally an all-day event. Mail reached post offices only several times a week, and rural free delivery did not come to some areas until the 90s. With no radios and only weekly newspapers in rural areas, the general store was the center for news and gossip, much of it inaccurate.

The Worker

In contrast with the visible wealth and comfort of the new entrepreneurs were the wretched living conditions of the workers, brought in great numbers to the cities by the lure of jobs. Many of them lived in tenements that were cheerless, cold, frequently without running water, and cut off from the sun and air. Tenements were built to crowd as many people as possible into the smallest possible space. For block upon block in the slum areas, these ugly structures were to be found covering every inch of building space. Jacob Riis, the reformer, estimated in 1890 that about 330,000 persons were living in one square mile on the lower East Side of

▶ Raging for two days, the great Chicago fire claimed hundreds of lives and destroyed about four square miles of the city. It was one of the largest U.S. disasters of the nineteenth century.

New York City. Even the stables of the rich cost more and were more comfortable than the tenements of the poor.

Despite these miserable living conditions, the industrial growth of the Gilded Age did bring material benefits for American workers. The technological advances expanded production and thus made higher wages possible. Between 1870 and 1890, both money and real wages increased, the former by more than 10 percent and the latter from 10 to 25 percent. In the same decades the cost of living fell, with the price index (taking 1860 as 100) going down from 141 to 98.

Whether or not the worker received a fair share of the great economic growth of the last quarter of the nineteenth century or not is a debatable matter. With half of the time period being mired in a depression or recession, it is uncertain how many workers shared the benefits; and the benefits were unequal even among those receiving them. Skilled and white-collar workers received the highest wages with adult males receiving about 75 percent more for similar work than women and two to three times as much as children—whose gainful employment was then taken for granted if they had been born to a poor family.

As for the length of the working day and week, there were many variations. By 1890, the typical worker labored ten hours a day, six days a week; but bakers averaged more than sixty-five hours a week, steelworkers over sixty-six, and canners about seventy-seven. In the construction industry the average workweek was slightly more than fifty-five hours.

Although it was commonly believed that workers had unlimited opportunities to advance and thus had much upward economic mobility, studies do not support this assumption. The evidence shows that few unskilled workers went beyond the ranks of the semiskilled and virtually none achieved middle-class status. The myth of upward mobility and limitless opportunity, however, popularized by the stories of Horatio Alger and others,

▶ During the late 1800s, the living conditions for the poor working class were miserable. 330,000 persons could be living in one square mile on the lower East Side of New York City. These slum areas were cold, frequently without running water, and cut off from the sun and air.

persisted; and a number of Americans continued to believe that anyone who worked hard and was thrifty and virtuous could, with some luck, become a millionaire.

The New Immigration

Europeans came to the United States in unprecedented numbers during this period, as did a smaller number of Asians. By the 1890s, New York City had as many Italians as did Naples, as many Germans as Hamburg, and twice as many Irish as Dublin. By 1900, three-fourths of the people of Chicago were foreign-born. In San Francisco, Chinese immigrants flocked to Chinatown—to which they were largely confined by virulent prejudice. By 1900 immigrants were also coming from Japan, Korea, and the Philippines.

The most important thing about this huge movement of peoples was not its size but the immigrants' origins. Previously, nearly all immigrants had come from northern and western Europe—Germany, Ireland, England, and Scandinavia. Now the tide flowed from southern and eastern Europe—particularly from Italy, Austria-Hungary, Poland, and Russia—along with those from Asia who arrived on the West Coast. In the 1860s, southern and eastern Europeans had constituted only 1.4 percent of all immigrants. Their percentage rose to 7.2 in the 1870s, to 18.3 in the 1880s, to 51 percent in the 1890s, and to 70 percent in the first decade or so of the twentieth century. This heavy influx of the "new immigration," brought a variety of ethnic groups who had never existed before in America in appreciable numbers.

Most of the "old" immigrants had been able to read and write; most (except for the Irish) had been Protestants; and most had settled on farms. In contrast, the immigrants from southern and eastern Europe came from "backward" countries, and most were illiterate. Most were Roman Catholic, Greek Orthodox, or Jewish; and most of them turned to industry and settled in the cities. As for the Asian immigrants, their religious and cultural practices struck most Americans as even more exotic.

Promoters of American industry recruiting cheap labor and agents of steamship companies seeking passengers spread the news that America was the land of opportunity and the haven of the oppressed. Their claims were amply substantiated in letters from immigrants already here and in stories told by those who returned to their native lands. Transportation was cheap; and wages, by European standards, were high. Also, there was religious freedom, no compulsory military service, and best of all, the overpowering lure of freedom.

Strangers in a new world and ignorant of its language and customs, immigrants of the same nationality flocked together in the same areas, spoke the same languages, and clung to their own customs and beliefs. Crowding into the large cities, they formed their own communities with newspapers and even theatrical productions in their own languages.

Because the newcomers were so different, older Americans wondered whether these immigrants could ever be assimilated into the mainstream of American life. They also feared that the waves of "racially inferior" immigrants would annihilate the "native" American stock and resented the fact that so many immigrants were Catholics and Jews. Columnist Finley Peter Dunne's "Mr. Dooley" expressed a popular position with the following:

▶ A group of Eastern European immigrants sits on the deck of the S.S. *Amsterdam*. In the late 1800s, immigration to the U.S. shifted from northern and western Europe to southern and eastern Europe.

> As a pilgrim father that missed the' first boats, I must raise me claryon voice again' th' invasion in this fair land by th' paupers an' anychists in effete Europe. Ye bet I must—because I'm here first.

Labor leaders contended that the new workers from abroad were degrading American labor standards by accepting lower wages, working longer hours, and allowing themselves to be used as strike breakers. Labor leaders also found it hard to unionize people who spoke so many strange and different languages.

These hostilities and fears led to anti-immigrant movements that bore various names—the United Order of Deputies, the American League, the Red, White, and Blue, and so on. In San Francisco during the depression of the 1870s, white workingmen organized against the Chinese, and for a brief time mobs ruled the streets. The political pressure exerted convinced Congress to pass the Chinese Exclusion Act in 1882, by which Chinese workingmen were denied entry to the country along with idiots, lunatics, and criminals. Perhaps the most powerful anti-immigrant group, however, was the American Protective Association, organized in 1887 to rally Americans for a fight against Catholicism. It grew with startling rapidity after the onset of the Panic of 1893 and stirred hostilities that would affect American society for decades to come.

This influx of immigrants created acute problems in the cities. Too many people moved in too rapidly, and wretchedness resulted. There were too many to be housed, and too many for water or sewage or transportation facilities to accommodate, too many for the police and fire departments to look after. For employers seeking cheap labor, the situation was splendid, and so it was for the middle-class family looking for servants. An amazing number of ordinary American households had live-in maids and cooks. For others, however, urban living was a horror. In 1890 the immigrant journalist Jacob Riis published his shocking report on New York's slums, *How the Other Half Lives.* It was, in part, upon this "other half" that the vast fortunes of the Gilded Age were built.

"Survival of the Fittest"

The Shock of Darwinism

A very strong influence on Americans in the Gilded Age was the theory of evolution set forth by Charles Darwin in his *Origin of Species,* published in 1859 and soon applied to social and economic life by English philosopher Herbert Spencer. According to Darwin's theory, all complex forms of plant and animal life, including human beings, had evolved over a long period of time from lower organisms. In that process, there had been a natural selection of those individual organisms best adapted to survive in their environment. Thus there was "survival of the fittest," with the strong and hardy surviving and the weak falling by the wayside.

Darwin's theory of evolution directly challenged the Biblical story of creation and, according to Sigmund Freud, severely wounded the self-love of human beings when they learned that the presumed gulf between themselves and lower forms of life did not really exist. The new biology of the nineteenth century, wrote Jacques Barzun, a leading cultural historian, "seemingly made final the separation between man and his soul." Naturally, such a theory and such a trauma provoked considerable debate among Gilded Age Americans, especially scientists, theologians, and clergymen.

Social Darwinism

Spencer's theory, applying Darwin's biological theory to economic and social life, was invaluable to the new industrial order because it seemed to justify the acquisition of wealth and power and gave an explanation of why some became wealthy while others stayed poor. Spencer maintained that evolution was leading inevitably to a society in which people would enjoy "the greatest perfection and the most complete happiness," and that competitive struggle was the natural means whereby this would come about. The weak would fall by the wayside, while the strong and able would push forward.

The new doctrine thus opposed relief for the poor, housing regulations, and public education, while it justified poverty and slums. Any governmental attempt to alter the situation would be interfering with natural law and impeding progress. The poor were poor because they were the "less fit," and any attempt to help them was fighting nature and a waste of time. The Christian equivalent was "casting pearls before swine." Thus, any government efforts to help the poor, in general, or blacks (the poorest), in particular, were doomed to failure because those on the societal "bottom" were there due to natural forces that could not be resisted.

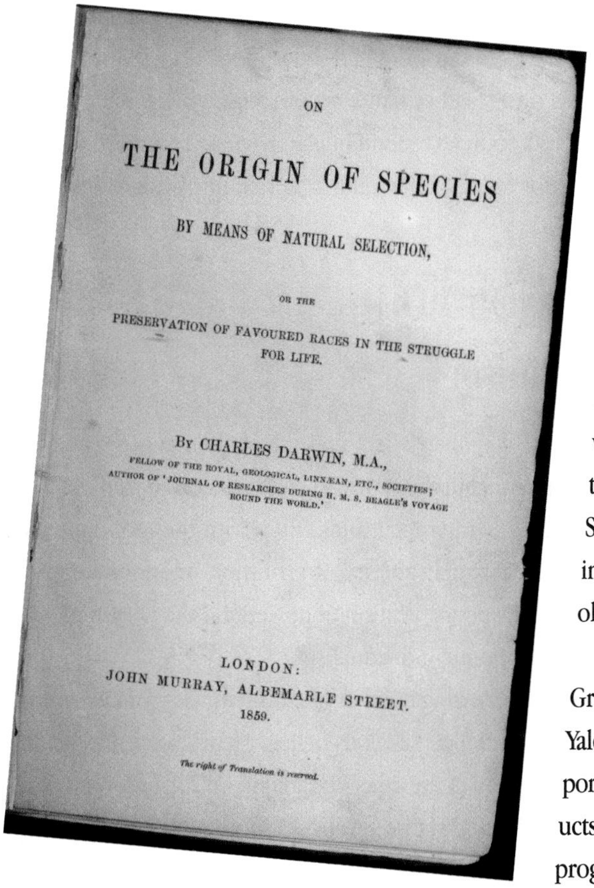
ON

THE ORIGIN OF SPECIES

BY MEANS OF NATURAL SELECTION,

OR THE

PRESERVATION OF FAVOURED RACES IN THE STRUGGLE FOR LIFE.

BY CHARLES DARWIN, M.A.,

FELLOW OF THE ROYAL, GEOLOGICAL, LINNÆAN, ETC., SOCIETIES; AUTHOR OF 'JOURNAL OF RESEARCHES DURING H. M. S. BEAGLE'S VOYAGE ROUND THE WORLD.'

LONDON:
JOHN MURRAY, ALBEMARLE STREET.
1859.

The right of Translation is reserved.

Spencer's ideas were especially attractive to American businessmen, who could thus feel that they themselves were the finest flower of evolution. With his first reading of Spencer, Andrew Carnegie exclaimed, "I remembered that light came in as a flood and all was clear. Not only had I got rid of theology and the supernatural, but I had found the truth of evolution."

Spencer enjoyed a great vogue in the United States from 1870 to 1890. Numbered among his many devoted American followers were Edward Livingston Youmans and John Fiske, who spread the gospel of Social Darwinism all over the country through magazine articles, popular books, and lectures. Such leading universities as Harvard, Johns Hopkins, and Yale included the Spencerian philosophy in courses on religion, biology, and social science.

Spencer's most influential American disciple was William Graham Sumner, who taught sociology and political economy at Yale from 1872 until his death in 1910. Sumner vigorously supported economic individualism and hailed the millionaires as products of natural selection. He scornfully derided reformers and their programs to protect the weak. He ridiculed democracy as the "pet superstition of the age" and repudiated the idea of human equality.

Laissez-Faire

Much of the reasoning of Social Darwinism was found in the other dominant theory of the times, laissez-faire, which included ideas of the classical economists going back as far as Adam Smith's *Wealth of Nations* (1776). Beyond what was necessary to maintain law and order and to protect life and property, the government was not to interfere in the conduct of business or in personal matters. According to this view, those pursuing their business interests free of government meddling would achieve the best possible use of resources, would promote steady economic progress, and would be rewarded— all according to their just desserts. Acquisition of wealth was considered evidence of merit, for did not wealth come as a result of frugality, industriousness, and sagacity? Poverty carried the stigma of worthlessness, for did it not result from idleness and wastefulness? During most of the late nineteenth century, these attitudes prevailed in America and were upheld by prominent educators, editors, clergymen, and economists.

Somewhat paradoxically, philanthropy also was expected to play a part in the behavior of those who were successful in business. They were expected to be humanitarian and to relieve distress, but they were forbidden by the dictates of Social Darwinism from offering any aid that might undermine self-reliance, initiative, and ambition. Andrew Carnegie, in *The Gospel of Wealth* (1889) offered the solution to this dilemma. While asserting that wealth must necessarily be concentrated in the hands of the few, Carnegie also set forth the maxim that the man who dies rich, dies disgraced. The duty of the man of wealth, he maintained, was to administer his surplus funds as a trust to yield the greatest value to the community. Funds should be given, for example, to help found public libraries, improve education, and promote world peace. To support a needy individual, on the other hand, was wrong. Carnegie argued that every person maintained by charity was a source of moral infection to the community. He asserted that of every $1000 spent for poor relief, $950 would better be thrown into the sea.

Industrialism and Religion

Protestantism and Darwinism

The churches had to adapt themselves to industrialism and the challenge of Darwinism. This proved to be difficult for the Protestant churches. Most Protestants considered the Bible to be the supreme authority and had closely identified their ethics with the economic individualism of the middle class, but the Darwinian theory of evolution undermined confidence in the authority of the Bible, and the concentration of power and the wealth of a few weakened the beliefs in the virtues of economic individualism.

In the 1880s and 1890s, however, an increasing number of Protestant clergymen accepted the theory of evolution and reconciled it with their religious beliefs. Henry Ward Beecher, for instance, one of the most celebrated preachers of the time, declared in his *Evolution and Religion* (1885) that evolution was merely "the deciphering of God's thought as revealed in the structure of the world." A few clergymen went beyond this to deny some of the supernatural events in Christianity. This alarmed the Protestant "fundamentalists," who reasserted their literal belief in the supreme authority of the Bible as the only solid foundation for religious faith. A struggle ensued between the fundamentalists and the liberals.

Throughout the Gilded Age most Protestant clergymen believed that the existing economic order was just. For instance, Lyman Beecher, the younger brother of Harriet Beecher Stowe, condemned the eight-hour day (as not enough work), insisted that poverty was a sign of sin, and advocated the use of force, if necessary, to put down strikes. Beecher further argued that poverty was the result of the "improvidence of laborers who squandered their wages on tobacco." Additionally, Beecher contended, "No man in this country suffers from poverty unless it be more than his fault—unless it be his sin." Commenting in 1877 on the sharp wage cuts suffered by railway workers, Beecher concluded the following:

> It is said that a dollar a day is not enough for a wife and five or six children. NO, not if the man smokes or drinks beer. . . . But is not a dollar a day enough to buy bread with? Water costs nothing; and a man who cannot live on bread is not fit to live.

Beecher and other clergymen like him were unconcerned with the social causes of poverty, certain that poverty was an act of God and the result of sin. Perhaps Beecher and other clergymen like him were conservative because wealthy businessmen in their congregations made heavy contributions to church funds. In any case, the conservative sentiments of many of the clergy and their lack of sympathy for the workers' demands coincided with a drop in working-class attendance in the churches.

The Social Gospel

In the 1880s, a few socially conscious Protestant clergymen took issue with Beecher's teachings on current economic questions and began to preach the Social Gospel, which focused on improving living conditions and feeding "God's children" rather than upon saving souls. The basic idea was that tending to the physical needs of the poor was God's work and that sin and decadence in the urban areas could be reduced through meeting the physical needs of the poor. Social Gospel preachers advocated civil service reform and the end of corruption in politics, child labor regulation, regulation of big corporations and monopolies, and graduated income taxes, especially taxes on large inheritances. They insisted that the problems created by industrialism could be solved only by a universal application of the teachings of Christ, and in particular his admonitions to help the poor. Among the chief exponents of the Social Gospel were Josiah Strong, Washington Gladden, Dwight L. Moody, Charles M. Sheldon, and Walter Rauschenbusch. In his writings and sermons, Gladden upheld the right of labor to organize and strike, and he recommended that industrial disputes be eliminated by an "industrial partnership" that would allow workers to receive "a fixed share" of industry's profits. Gladden espoused the idea of government ownership of public utilities and government-imposed factory inspection laws, although he rejected socialism as a system. Other Social Gospel preachers, however, such as William D. P. Bliss of Boston, believed in welfare state capitalism or socialism and government relief programs designed to aid the urban poor. Walter Rauschenbusch, for example, severely censured industrial capitalism as a "mammonistic organization with which Christianity can never be content." Moody evangelized in the urban slums and urged people to cast aside sin in the inner cities. Moody founded schools in the urban slums and provided recreational facilities for the poor in hopes that people would abandon their sinful ways and adopt the ways of Jesus. Charles M. Sheldon, in his novel *In His Steps,* asked the simple question, "What would Jesus do?" before deciding on any course of action. The inference of Sheldon's work, however, was that Jesus would be engaged in helping the less fortunate.

The Catholic View

The position of the Catholic Church on evolution was that the hypothesis had to stop short of human beings. The attitude of the Church toward social reform was more negative than positive, and more tolerating than approving. Only in part was the Catholic hierarchy moved by considerations of justice and charity. James Cardinal Gibbons, Archbishop of Baltimore, insisted that Catholics cultivate a patriotic citizenship in keeping with the nation's civil institutions and customs. Gibbons asserted, "The accusation of being un-American—that is to say, alien to our national spirit—is the most powerful weapon which the enemies of the Church can employ against her." Only in this sense—as an aspect of Americanization—did the Catholic Church display any marked interest in social reform before the second decade of the twentieth century.

Archbishop John Ireland of St. Paul minimized the economic problems of the time and advocated only temperance and conservative trade unionism. In 1903 he said publicly, "I have no fear of greater fortunes in the hands of individuals, nor of vast aggregations of capital in the hands of corporations." Archbishop Ireland's friendship with President McKinley and with James J. Hill, the railroad builder, brought him under the criticism of reformers. Yet he often expressed strong sympathy for organized labor, saying on one occasion, "Until their material condition is improved it is futile to speak to them of spiritual life and duties."

▶Archbishop John Ireland of St. Paul advocated only temperance and conservative trade unionism. Ireland expressed a rare, strong sympathy for organized labor, saying, "Until their material condition is improved it is futile to speak to them of spiritual life and duties."

Through its indifference to social reform, the Church jeopardized its hold on the loyalty of its communicants. Catholics in large numbers lost interest in a church that seemed indifferent, if not hostile, to movements promoting their economic welfare. As the Church began to lose members to Protestantism and socialism, it developed a greater interest in social problems. Finally bringing change to the Church's attitude was Pope Leo XIII's famous encyclical *De Rerum Novarum* (1891), which condemned the exploitation of labor and asserted that it was the duty of the state to bring social justice. The Pope condemned the excesses of capitalism, including what he termed as the "greed of unchecked competition," defended the right of workers to form unions, and stressed the obligation of governments to care for the poor. According to Pope Leo, workers were entitled to wages that would guarantee their families a reasonable, frugal comfort; workers did not sin by seeking government assistance in obtaining a living wage.

Idealism

Perhaps in response to the horrifying bloodshed of the Civil War or perhaps to the stresses and strains of the new urban industrial order—or perhaps due to both—there was an outpouring of creativity among American philosophers in the Gilded Age. From the 1870s forward, probably the most important new influence on philosophy was German idealism, particularly as expressed by Georg Wilhelm Friedrich Hegel (1770–1831). Hegel viewed the whole course of history as the working out of divine purpose by certain general laws of nature, culminating in the achievement of perfect freedom. But Hegelianism, however, rationalized existing conditions, and what Hegel meant by freedom was very different from the traditional American conception. Hegel's philosophy glorified the state and taught that individuals could be free only by subordinating themselves to their national government and to their social institutions—ideas that Adolph Hitler would exploit in Germany several decades later.

The idealist movement was strongest in New England, where its leaders were Josiah Royce of Harvard and C. E. Garman of Amherst; but the idealist awakening was evident also at such universities as California, Columbia, Cornell, Johns Hopkins, Michigan, and Princeton. The idealists believed in the priority of the mind over matter and in the fundamental unity of the universe, but they modified these concepts to support American individualism.

American Pragmatism

Meanwhile a school of philosophy more distinctively American and opposed to idealism was growing in popularity. Pragmatism, unlike most earlier philosophies, did not offer theories about God and the universe. It presented, instead, a way of evaluating acts and ideas in terms of their consequences in concrete experience. Pragmatism says that we cannot reject any hypothesis if consequences useful to life flow from it. The pragmatist's decision regarding the truth or falsity of an idea, then, is based on experiential test: One decides whether an idea is true or false by seeing whether it works. This concept was closely associated with two ideas that had gained wide currency in American thought: the idea of progress through evolution and the idea of truth obtained through scientific investigation. The forerunners of pragmatism were Chauncey Wright and Charles S. Peirce; but two other men, William James and later John Dewey, are credited with developing the philosophy of pragmatism.

William James, philosopher and psychologist at Harvard, rejected Spencerian determinism, which afforded no place for chance or human will. He upheld the independence of the mind and "the right to believe at our own risk any hypothesis that is live enough to tempt our will." At times he was inclined to suggest that if someone felt happier or behaved better as a result of believing some idea, that idea should be regarded as true. While James repudiated absolutes, however, he also spoke out against a skepticism that would inhibit impulsively generous commitment. He distrusted all general laws and abstractions that denied the human capacity for free action. James contended that a person's decisions would influence the course of events and that, in spite of the existence of God, good or evil would result from human device and intelligence.

In his *Principles of Psychology* (1890), James made the first important American contribution to the scientific study of the mind; and in later books he expounded his views on pragmatism. Theories to him were "instruments, not answers to enigmas." James further argued that pragmatism "has no dogmas, and no doctrines save its method," and that was a method for reaching the truth.

"The true is the name of whatever proves to be good in the way of belief," James said, "and good, too, for definite, assignable reasons." Such views were a sharp departure from nearly all the philosophies and religions of the past, and they captivated many Americans; yet they also laid James open to the charge that pragmatism was simply another name for expedience: Anything is good that works.

The New Legal Theory

There was also a revolt against formalism in law. The preceding generation had regarded the law as fixed and unchanging and as a standard measure that the judge simply applied to the question at hand like a yardstick; but a new school of legal theorists arose following the reasoning of Oliver Wendell Holmes, son of the poet of the same name and friend of William James, that law should be based on changing social needs or political policies rather than simply upon logic or precedent. "It is revolting," said Holmes, "to have no better reason for a rule of law than that it was laid down in the time of Henry I. It is still more revolting if the grounds upon which it was laid down have vanished long since, and the rule simply persists from blind imitation of the past." The new school of theorists went on to contend that the meaning of any general legal principle must always be judged by its practical effects.

Challenges to Darwinism and Laissez-Faire

Reform Darwinism

In the 1880s, a number of sociologists and economists revolted against the fatalism and lack of social responsibility of Social Darwinism. These "reform Darwinists" accepted evolution but maintained that societies could command their own destinies and that human intelligence applied to social problems could improve the existing system.

A leader among the dissenters was Lester Ward, a largely self-educated sociologist. He came from a poor family in Illinois, endured privations in his early life, worked in factories, fought in the Civil War, and for many years was a government official. When he was sixty-five, Ward became Professor of Sociology at Brown University, where he taught "A Survey of All Knowledge." His ideas were first presented in his *Dynamic Sociology* (1883) but were more readable in *The Psychic Factors of Civilization* (1893). Ward believed that a laissez-faire economic system did not necessarily advance human progress, and he advocated state management and social planning.

Younger professors of sociology—such as Albion Small of Illinois, Charles Horton Cooley of Michigan, and Edward Allsworth Ross of Wisconsin—seconded Ward's assault on Social Darwinism. Contrary to Spencer's notion that society was composed of separate individuals operating independently of one another, they asserted that social institutions, themselves amenable to social control, shaped each individual personality. In *Sin and Society* (1907) Edward Allsworth Ross argued that in the new industrial society, morality required the impersonal corporation to accept full responsibility for its antisocial acts. Followers of Spencer and Sumner declined in numbers and influence in the universities at the turn of the century as the reform Darwinists ascended. In 1906 the American Sociological Society was founded and Ward was its first president. His ideas on government social planning eventually came to be very influential in American social thinking.

The New Economists

Similarly, the viewpoint of economists changed. In the mid 1880s, a new group of scholars, many of whom had been trained in German universities, began to challenge laissez-faire sentiments. In 1885 they founded the American Economic Association, which boldly declared that the state was "an agency whose positive assistance is one of the indispensable conditions of human progress" and that "the doctrine of laissez-faire is unsafe in politics and unsound in morals." Among the leaders of this revolt were Richard T. Ely of Johns Hopkins University and the University of Wisconsin, Simon Nelsen Patten of the University of Pennsylvania, John R. Commons of the University of Wisconsin, and Wesley C. Mitchell of Columbia University. Although they differed in their economic and political programs, they all dissented from the classical belief in absolute economic laws valid for all societies. They insisted that society, constantly changing, had to be examined in terms of process and growth. Using the historical approach to study economic realities, they discovered that there were great differences between what actually had happened and what, according to classical economics, was supposed to have happened. In recent years, it should be noted, there have been challenges to these theorists from conservative economists and social thinkers; but the ideas of these "New Economists" have been somewhat resurrected since the economic meltdown of 2008 resulted in economic intervention by governments on a global scale.

Thorstein Veblen

The leading academic rebel at the turn of the century was Thorstein Veblen. Born in Wisconsin of Norwegian immigrants and educated at Yale and Johns Hopkins, he taught at Chicago, Stanford, and Missouri. Veblen bitterly assailed what he called the "kept classes" and their "pecuniary" society. He derided the ideas that the wealthy leisure class was the most biologically fit and millionaires were a product of natural selection. Veblen argued that the millionaire was not responsible for the creation of the industrial technology but rather had taken possession of the wealth produced by the skill and labor of other people. In his most widely read book, *The Theory of the Leisure Class* (1899), and a number of other volumes Veblen analyzed the role of the upper class in American society. Although he had little popular appeal, he wielded a great deal of influence among subsequent intellectuals, particularly after the Great Depression that began in 1929.

Reformers

Outside of academic circles, increasing numbers of radical reformers began to attack the existing social and economic system and to propose new plans for economic organization. They, too, rejected Spencer's fatalism and the idea that progress resulted from the struggle for existence and the consequent removal of the unfit.

The most important of these reformers was Henry George. Born in Philadelphia, he moved to San Francisco as a young man and for twenty years watched a frontier society become transformed into a wealthy and class-stratified society. What was the cause of the imbalance that deepened the poverty of the masses and increased the wealth of a few? George believed the explanation lay in the inequities of private land ownership that allowed landowners to enrich themselves solely through the rise of real-estate values. Land took on value not because of anything the owner did but because people lived on it. George maintained that the unearned increment, instead of going to private individuals, ought to be taken by the government in the form of a "single tax" on land values. This would make other taxes and other forms of government intervention unnecessary, leave individual enterprise otherwise free, and promote "the Golden Age of which poets have sung and high-raised seers have told us in metaphor!"

George set forth his theories in *Progress and Poverty* (1879) and found a wide audience both in the United States and abroad. He spent the rest of his life working for the single tax program and continued to develop his theme in subsequent books. In addition, he edited a newspaper, gave many speeches, and came close to being elected mayor of New York City in 1886. George's ideas influenced virtually every reformer for years to come, and they still have appeal as a practical way to change the social system.

▶ Birthplace of reformer Henry George in Philadelphia.

Somewhat more radical than George's program was that of his contemporary Edward Bellamy. Rejecting both classical economics and the fatalism of the Social Darwinists, Bellamy concentrated his attack on the free-enterprise system itself. He attacked excessive individualism, private monopoly, and competition, characterizing the latter as "sheer madness, a scene from bedlam" and the price system as "an education in self-seeking at the expense of others." He assailed the "imbecility of the system of private enterprise" and the callousness of industrialists, who "maim and slaughter [their] workers by thousands."

In his utopian novel *Looking Backward* (1888), Bellamy portrayed an ideal community in the year 2000 whose beauty and tranquility contrasted sharply with the ugly industrial towns of his day. In this utopia the government owned all the means of production, and everyone shared equally the material rewards. At least five hundred thousand copies of the book were sold. Bellamy called his system "Nationalism," and "Nationalist" clubs sprang up to spread the new faith. "Nationalist" magazines advocated public ownership of railroads and utilities, civil service reform, and government aid to education. This served to renew interest in socialism and caused Americans to consider socialist ideas and programs. Both George and Bellamy, however, rejected Marxian socialism.

George regarded Karl Marx as "the prince of muddleheads"; and Bellamy maintained that American Marxists were really in the pay of the "great monopolists," employed by them "to wave the red flag and talk about burning, sacking, and blowing people up, in order, by alarming the timid, to head off any real reforms."

Young social reformers seeking a way to refute Social Darwinism were influenced by the ideas of the reform Darwinists and of reformers like George and Bellamy. They were also influenced by the social-justice movement that had its roots in European, especially English, reform movements. Nearly every leading English reformer had visited the country, and many young American progressives and reformers came under their influence. Implicit in all these new ideas and ferment was the vision of a life of service, thus conducing toward the ideal of social work as a way young reformers could serve society. Jane Addams of Chicago's Hull House became a leading symbol of these social reformers and their work. She had visited Toynbee Hall in the slums of London; and when she returned to the United States in 1889, she established Hull House, a slum-relief center in Chicago. Her experiences at Hull House showed her that people could become stronger and learn to deal with adversity. Thus she began to reject Social Darwinism. Hull House served its immediate neighborhood, but it also became a center of creative thinking about social issues because a number of the most brilliant men and women of the day spent brief periods of time in residence there.

Also involved in the social justice movement was the Salvation Army, which had come from England at the end of the nineteenth century. The Salvation Army offered assistance as well as religion, as did the clergy of various faiths now working in the slums. Joining in the movement, too, were middle-class and upper class women, who had begun to join a variety of socially-oriented organizations. They were pushing not only for the ballot and legal equality for themselves but also for reforms on behalf of children, working women, and Indians. (See *Helen Hunt Jackson: Crusader for the Indian.*)

▶Jane Addams established the Hull House, a slum-relief center in Chicago. Addams became a leading symbol of social reformers and their work. At the Hull House, Addams learned that people could become stronger and learn to deal with adversity.

Socialism

Bellamy and other reformers avoided the word socialism not only because they found it distasteful but also because they realized that in the United States it was often identified with anarchism and communism, labels that frightened most Americans. The first socialist political parties in this country appeared in New York, Philadelphia, Chicago, St. Louis, Milwaukee, and other large cities in the years immediately following the Civil War. In the beginning, most American socialists, like their European counterparts, were followers of Karl Marx. Seeking to develop a revolutionary spirit among American workers, these socialists urged workers to "offer an armed resistance to the invasions by the capitalist class and capitalist legislatures" and exhorted them to overthrow American capitalism by "energetic, relentless, revolutionary and international action."

A National Labor Reform Party was organized in 1868 with a platform declaring that "our government is wholly perverted from its true design.... [The] mass of the people have no supply beyond their daily wants and are compelled

Helen Hunt Jackson: Crusader for the Indians

Helen Hunt Jackson

One of the most influential champions of the Indian during the late nineteenth century was the writer Helen Hunt Jackson. Her biting criticism of federal Indian policy in *A Century of Dishonor* (1881) and her sentimental novel *Ramona* (1884) presented the classic statement of American injustice toward the Indian and aroused the national conscience. Described by some of her contemporaries as "the most brilliant, impetuous, and thoroughly individual woman of her time," she is, ironically, almost forgotten today.

She was born Helen Maria Fiske on October 13, 1830, in Amherst, Massachusetts, the daughter of Nathan Welby and Deborah (Vinal) Fiske. A professor of Latin, Greek, and philosophy at Amherst College, her father was also a Congregational minister and author. Her mother, a Bostonian, also wrote. Helen had two brothers, who died in infancy, and a sister, Anne. Her mother died when she was fourteen and her father three years later, leaving Helen in the care of an aunt. However, her father had given her a good education at the well-known Ipswich (Massachusetts) Female Seminary and the private school of Reverend J. S. C. Abbott in New York City. She was a neighbor and schoolmate of Emily Dickinson, who would become one of America's great poets; and they remained lifelong friends.

In 1852, Helen married Army Captain Edward Bissell Hunt, brother of a former governor of New York. Helen's husband was an accomplished engineer officer and thus held high army rank. For the next eleven years she and her husband led the usual wandering life of a military family.

Then there were tragedies in store for her. Her first child, Murray, died of a brain disease in 1854, when he was only eleven months old. In 1863 her husband suffocated while experimenting with an underwater naval vessel he had designed. Two years later her other son, "Rennie," died of diphtheria. With her parents, husband, and sons dead, she was alone.

Up to this time, Helen Hunt had shown no signs of literary ability. In 1866, she returned to Newport, Rhode Island, where she and her husband had once been stationed. For a while, she was interested in spiritualism and clairvoyance. After spending some time with Emily Dickinson and coming to know Thomas Wentworth Higginson, well-known author, soldier, and reformer, she decided to turn to a writing career.

She began to write travel sketches, children's stories, novels, poems, and essays under the pseudonyms "H. H." and "Saxe Holm," eventually writing over thirty books and hundreds of articles. The pseudonyms kept her from becoming more prominent. It was still the convention for women writers to conceal their authorship because respectable women were not supposed to play any public role. Only after she began to write her books about Indians did she use her full name. By that time she was perhaps the most productive woman writer in the country. In 1874 Ralph Waldo Emerson rated her "the greatest American woman poet" and placed her poetry above that of almost all American men.

In May 1872, Helen Hunt took a trip to California, and then, because of bronchial trouble, spent the winter of 1873–1874 at Colorado Springs, Colorado. There she met Pennsylvania Quaker William Sharpless Jackson, a wealthy banker and railroad manager, whom she married on October 22, 1875. Relieved of her financial concerns, she moved to Colorado. From that time on, the West and its Indians took up more and more of her attention.

During an 1879 visit to Boston, Helen Hunt Jackson heard a lecture by the Ponca chief, Standing Bear, about the sufferings of the dispossessed Plains Indians. This was a turning point in her life, and she began to champion the cause of Indians almost at once. Not only did she expose the government's mistreatment of Indians in her writings, but she also sent out petitions, wrote letters to newspapers, and endeavored to awaken public opinion on behalf of the Indians. Soon she was a reformer at war with government officials over their Indian policy.

Her book, *A Century of Dishonor*, published in 1881, is a powerful story of dispossession, broken treaties, crooked dealings, unfulfilled promises, and the federal government's inhumane treatment of the Indian tribes who were its powerless wards. The book caused a national sensation. An emotional and partisan book, it is not a balanced history but rather is an impassioned plea on behalf of the Indian. At her own expense, she sent a copy to every member of Congress with the following words printed in red on the cover: "Look upon your hands! They are stained with the blood of your relations."

The impact of this book was so great that it has been called the *Uncle Tom's Cabin* of the Indian cause. Helen Hunt Jackson regarded herself as an "Indian Harriet Beecher Stowe," saying "If I can do one-hundredth for the Indians as Mrs. Stowe did for the Negro, I will be thankful." Within a year of her book's publication, the strong Indian Rights Association was created. In 1883 President Chester Arthur appointed Mrs. Jackson a Commissioner of Indian Affairs; and in 1887 the first comprehensive reform legislation for Indians was enacted in the Dawes Act (subsequent opinion has been very critical of this legislation, to be discussed more fully later).

Helen Hunt Jackson continued her fight for the Indian and also continued to be a prolific writer of poetry, novels, and essays until her death. Probably her best-known fictional work is *Ramona* (1884), an idyllic account of the Indian past, which is set in California. In 1886, the North American Review called this book "unquestionably the best novel yet produced by an American woman," ranking it with *Uncle Tom's Cabin* as one of the two famous ethical novels of the century. Since then it has gone through hundreds of printings and countless stage and screen showings. Written as an act of conscience, it proved a boon to tourism in the Golden State since hordes of people wanted to see Ramona's supposed home.

Helen Hunt Jackson: Crusader for the Indians (Continued)

Jackson also continued to have personal tragedy in her life. In June 1884, she suffered a severe fracture of her leg and she was transferred to a place in California that proved to be malarial. While confined there, a cancer developed. During this period, "her sunny elasticity never failed," wrote one of her closest friends; "and within a fortnight of her death she wrote long letters, in clear and vigorous hand, expressing only cheerful hopes for the future." On August 12, 1885, she died and was interred temporarily in San Francisco. Later she was buried near the summit of Mount Jackson, Colorado, one of the Cheyenne peaks named in her honor, about four miles from Colorado Springs. Still later, to escape commercialism and the possible vandalism of the spot, her body was taken to Evergreen Cemetery at Colorado Springs, where it remains.

. . . to become paupers and vagrants." These appeals were too radical for the masses of wage earners and found only a small receptive audience among them. The National Labor Reform Party's presidential candidate in 1868 polled fewer than thirty thousand votes.

In 1877, a Socialist Labor Party was formed. Marxian doctrines were the basis of its program, and recent European immigrants provided most of its members. The party's purpose was not to reform but to revolutionize the industrial order. It blamed the plight of the masses on the concentration of economic power in private hands, and it advocated having all the basic means of production run by the government in democratic association with the workers. For some years the Socialist Labor Party avoided regular political activities and instead attempted to bore its way into control of the labor federations, but the leaders of post-Civil War unionism, however, successfully opposed the efforts of socialists to control labor and rejected their radical solutions to economic and social problems.

Eventually, in the 1890s, the splintered factions of the Socialist Labor Party united under the leadership of Daniel De Leon, who became known as "the socialist pope." Born on the island of Curacao and educated in Germany, De Leon had come to the United States, where he studied law and taught for a short time at Columbia College. A brilliant orator and pamphleteer, he became a champion of Marxism and took a militant stand against traditional trade unionism. He derided the American Federation of Labor as "a cross between a windbag and a rope of sand" and called its founder, Samuel Gompers, "a labor faker" and "a greasy tool of Wall Street."

De Leon urged all workers to join an independent political movement that would win control of the government and establish "a socialist or co-operative commonwealth, whereby the instruments of production shall be made the property of the whole people." In 1892, however, the Socialist Labor presidential ticket polled only twenty-two thousand votes and in the next election only thirty-four thousand. The party was too foreign in its makeup and too radical in its program to attract wide support. To offset some of this deficiency, a rival organization, the Social Democratic Party, was organized in 1896 by Eugene V. Debs, president of the American Railway Union. In 1901 the anti-De Leon group in the Socialist Labor Party joined Debs to form the Socialist Party of America. In its heyday it won allegiance from hundreds of thousands of Americans, including those in the rural heartland as well as in the cities.

Achievements of the Gilded Age

Despite the obvious cultural excesses and the long list of social problems, intellectual and artistic developments of the Gilded Age were impressive. The original and creative thinkers of the 80s and the 90s made these decades one of the most intellectually fertile periods in the whole of American history. In scholarship, the age saw the birth of two new social sciences. Lewis Henry Morgan founded anthropology, and Lester Ward fathered American sociology. The period also witnessed a revolution in higher education. Until this time, colleges and universities had concentrated on training ministers and lawyers; but now learning began to shake off its fetters and to range freely in the physical, natural, and social sciences, the arts, and the humanities.

The most famous of the daring new university presidents were Charles W. Eliot of Harvard and Daniel Coit Gilman of Johns Hopkins. At Harvard, Eliot greatly expanded the curriculum and sponsored the elective system, which had originated at the University of Virginia at the time of its founding. He also drastically reformed Harvard's medical and law schools and gave them true professional status. At Johns Hopkins, Gilman built the first great graduate school in America. The graduate school and the seminar method were introduced from Germany in the 1870s, and some graduate work was done at Harvard and Yale in that decade. It was Johns Hopkins, however, designed primarily as a center for graduate work at its founding in 1876, that took the lead in this field and held it for the next quarter of a century. At that time, also, professional schools got under way—the Columbia School of Mines (1864), the Massachusetts Institute of Technology (1865), Stevens Institute (1871), and the Johns Hopkins Medical School (1893).

Arts and Letters

During the two or three decades following the Civil War, there developed a new realism in American literature, stimulated by Darwinism, the influence of European writers, a reaction against the sentimentality, and the women writers that had come to dominate the sales of fiction. An early manifestation of the trend was the regional short story. Bret Harte in the West, Hamlin Garland in the Midwest, George Washington Cable and Joel Chandler Harris in the South, and Sarah Orne Jewett in New England—all gave readers a fresh and exciting view of regional America.

In his own day, Mark Twain (Samuel L. Clemens) was considered a regional author; but his novels, essays, and sketches have made a lasting reputation for him as a major figure in

American literature. The materials for Twain's best narratives—*The Adventures of Tom Sawyer* (1876), *Life on the Mississippi* (1883), and *Adventures of Huckleberry Finn* (1884)—were his boyhood home, Hannibal, Missouri, and the great Mississippi River that rolled before it. Along with many other writers of the period, he deplored the evils of crass materialism and ridiculed the get-rich-quick schemes of his money-mad countrymen. In *The Gilded Age:A Tale For Today* for example, Twain and Charles Dudley Warner pointed out that sober industry and contentment with a modest income honestly earned are infinitely preferable to frantic moneymaking schemes. Yet Twain tirelessly sought ways to increase his own wealth.

The growing social ills of the Gilded Age called forth specific indictments that became increasingly prominent in the realistic literature of the late nineteenth and early twentieth centuries. William Dean Howells, who by 1900 was considered by many young writers to be the dean of American letters, exhibited the grime and squalor of New York City in *A Hazard of New Fortunes* (1890). Stephen Crane's *Maggie: A Girl of the Streets* (1893) exposed the ugly life of New York's Bowery. Hamlin Garland in *Main-Traveled Roads* (1891) described the hardships and injustices suffered by farmers in Iowa and Wisconsin. While they emphasized the abuses of the new industrial order, writers were, however, comparatively gentle in their treatment of the captains of industry. In Howells' *The Rise of Silas Lapham* (1884), for example, the author implied that the great majority of American financiers were honest—that "robber barons" were the exception, not the rule.

▶ Mark Twain (Samuel Langhorne Clemens) authored American classics, *The Adventures of Tom Sawyer* (1876), *Life on the Mississippi* (1883), and *Adventures of Huckleberry Finn.* (1884)

Even the much more subtle and sensitive novelist and literary critic, Henry James (brother of psychologist William James), who lived abroad most of his life, presented American financiers as men of integrity and charm in several of his books. James' particular interest was the interaction of men and women—American and European—in sophisticated international society. *The American* (1877), *The Portrait of a Lady* (1881), and *The Ambassadors* (1903)—all present Americans that are morally superior to their more cultured European counterparts.

Because many poets—Bryant, Longfellow, Holmes, Lowell, Emerson, and Whittier—whose careers had begun in an earlier period continued to satisfy tastes after the war, much of American poetry showed remarkably few effects of the changing intellectual climate. By the end of the century, however, American poets and prose writers were feeling its impact. For example, much of Stephen Crane's poetry inferred from the biological struggle for survival and the astronomical immensity of the universe that the individual is unimportant, a grim attitude congruent with European naturalism:

A man said to the universe

"Sir, I exist!"

"However," replied the universe,

"The fact has not created in me

A sense of obligation."

The Gilded Age knew nothing of Emily Dickinson because only seven of her poems were published during her lifetime (1830–1886), but she is today considered one of the leading poets of the post-Civil War period. She began to write poetry in the mid-50s and continued until her death, but she spent the last half of her life as a recluse in Amherst, Massachusetts. Spare and unsentimental, her poems constituted a new voice in American literature.

In striking contrast was Walt Whitman, whose revolutionary volume of poetry, *Leaves of Grass,* had been published in three editions before the Civil War and who continued to be an important figure in American poetry of the postwar period. Although many critics objected to his departures from the conventions of versification and to his frankness about sex, he became for many others the very voice of America—enthusiastic, optimistic, energetic, and free. His Quaker inheritance contributed to the independence, love and peace, and sense of brotherhood celebrated in so many of his works—among them *Drum Taps* (1866), a volume of poems recounting the experiences and suffering shared by both North and South, and the richest account of the Civil War to be found in American poetry.

Increasing wealth and leisure time after the Civil War contributed to a new awareness of art among Americans. The work of the artists George Inness, Thomas Eakins, Winslow Homer, and Albert Pinkham Ryder was of such high caliber that some might call the Gilded Age the most important era in American painting. Inness pioneered a new landscape school, and Homer and Eakins were the leading American representatives of the naturalistic movement in painting. Homer grounded his art in direct observation of nature, while Eakins depicted ordinary middle-class city life of the United States in the late nineteenth century. Ryder, haunted throughout his life by the sea, was the most original romantic of his time. Two American expatriates, James McNeill Whistler and John Singer Sargent, both of whom lived most of their lives in London, enjoyed international reputations—Whistler for his muted, poetic compositions and Sargent as the most sought-after portraitist of the Anglo-Saxon world. A third expatriate artist, Mary Cassatt, the sister of a railroad executive, settled in Paris and exhibited with the great French Impressionists.

Although in architecture the Gilded Age has been said to mark the low point in taste, fine and outstanding architects did exist. Henry Hobson Richardson and Louis H. Sullivan were the first major architects to meet the demands of industrialism upon their art. To these men, buildings had a sociological function as well as an artistic one. In his *Autobiography of an Idea,* Sullivan wrote, "Masonry construction was a thing of the past ... [and] the old ideas of

▶ Walt Whitman's revolutionary volume of poetry, *Leaves of Grass*, had been published in three editions before the Civil War. Though criticized for his departures from the conventions of versification and to his frankness about sex, he became for many others the very voice of America—enthusiastic, optimistic, energetic, and free.

superimposition must give way before a sense of vertical continuity." For a number of architects it was a golden age. The rich commissioned them to design giant urban residences, baronial country homes, and great stone "cottages" on the shore. The imitation French chateaus and Italian palaces were sometimes ugly and often absurd, but gifted and imaginative architects like Richard Morris Hunt put the limitless funds of their patrons to good use.

The Chautauqua Movement

There was a mass desire for knowledge in the Gilded Age, and various efforts were made to meet the demand. Most successful of these ventures was the Chautauqua movement, founded in 1874 by Lewis Miller, an Ohio businessman, and John H. Vincent, a Methodist minister. The two-week summer course they organized for a few Sunday-school teachers at Lake Chautauqua in New York proved to be such an enjoyable experience for those who attended that the word spread, and within a few years thousands from all parts of the country were coming to Lake Chautauqua. Consequently, the Chautauqua movement, like the earlier Lyceum movement, expanded its activities. The founders broadened their range of instruction to include such subjects as economics, government, science, and literature. During the years of Chautauqua's greatest popularity, eminent authorities, including some of the presidents of the period, gave talks to open-air audiences on every subject conceivable. In addition, the Chautauqua Literary and Scientific Reading Circle was organized and became a national society. This organization provided correspondence courses leading to a diploma. Textbooks were written for the program, and a monthly magazine, the *Chautauquan*, was published. According to the Reverend Vincent, the program was formulated to give "the college outlook" to those who did not have a higher education.

▶There was a mass desire for knowledge in the Gilded Age and the Chautauqua movement met this demand. The program was a two-week summer course, held at the Chautauqua House in New York, (shown above) formulated to give "the college outlook" to those who did not have a higher education.

Because the Chautauqua movement was so successful, various imitators appeared. By 1900 there were about two hundred Chautauqua-type organizations. Most were of a more commercial character but were designed to satisfy the same craving for self-culture. They furnished a varied fare of music, humor, and inspirational lectures and probably provided more entertainment than enlightenment for those who attended.

The Chautauqua movement and its imitators helped popularize information that earlier had been the property of experts only. Also, thousands of Americans who sought cultural and intellectual improvement probably felt rewarded by many of the programs, and perhaps their interests were broadened.

From all contemporary accounts, Americans of the Gilded Age pursued diverse cultural interests. They listened to lectures, went to museums, plays, and circuses, sought more education at Chautauqua institutes, sat through religious revival meetings, and began to watch new phenomena such as baseball and football. In all this, they had a sense of assurance and optimism that would begin to decline as the Gilded Age neared its close. We now turn to an account, in more depth, of the era's big business.

Chapter Review 17

Summary

During the Gilded Age, so labeled by Mark Twain because of its rapid economic growth that obscured the corruption and inequality beneath, Americans largely turned their attention away from the immense social issues of the day, such as equal rights for African Americans, toward securing economic advancement. Americans, in general, came to favor a laissez faire approach to governing, and the Social Darwinist ideas that dominated the time period taught that government efforts to alleviate the plight of the poor were doomed to failure.

Major advances in virtually every field of science, especially in chemistry and physics, provided the principles for new technology. Inventions that spurred industrial growth were made in transportation, communications, electrical power, the production of steel, and the use of oil—with the railroads as the principal engine of growth. All these inventions increased productivity, but they also offered opportunities for vast wealth to entrepreneurs in a free-enterprise system that accepted graft, corruption, and the worship of material goods.

The new wealth brought with it new leisure activities, including the beginnings of football and baseball, bicycles, and the circus. The economic growth spawned a class of new rich that built ostentatious mansions and went on spending sprees. Meanwhile, the middle class lived in simple houses and apartments, but their standard of living was usually better than that of their parents. They could educate their children, and they could hope and work for a better status. They enjoyed the increased comforts resulting from the inventions of the day, including the telephone, the electric light, and the gas burner. Life in the cities included electric trolley cars, elevated railways, better sewage disposal, improved water distribution plants, street paving, and more efficient fire departments. The working class, however, remained in squalid conditions, crowded into tenements and worked long hours—even though actual worker compensation did increase during the Gilded Age. Much of the working class was composed of the "new immigrants" from southern and eastern Europe, as well as Asia. This new wave of immigration spawned nativism in the U.S. since the new immigrants were predominantly non-Protestants and did not speak English.

The Gilded Age was profoundly affected by the Social Darwinist ideas of Herbert Spencer and the ideas of laissez-faire. As a consequence, the excesses of capitalism—including inequality, poverty, and corruption—were largely left unchecked. However, the excesses also spawned a Social Gospel movement in which people sought to use government and other human organizations to do God's good work. Even the Catholic Church, as of 1891 with Pope Leo XIII's encyclical, *De Rerum Novarum,* became involved in using human organizations to promote social justice.

Gradually, intellectuals and reformers began to chip away at laissez-faire as insufficient to meet human needs. Idealists, inspired by Hegel, sought freedom through subordination to the state while pragmatists judged policies based on whether or not they achieved the desired results. Oliver Wendell Holmes espoused a new pragmatic legal theory where judges could abandon legal precedents if the social situation called for it. New economists argued that laissez-faire was insufficient to meet societal needs and that intervention of the state was necessary for progress. Intellectuals such as Thorstein Veblen assailed the ostentatious living

(cont'd)

of the wealthy while social reformers, such as Henry George, sought ways of redistributing income. Eventually, a significant socialist movement developed including a Socialist Party under Eugene V. Debs.

Finally, the Gilded Age produced significant contributions in academics as academia moved away from the focus on theology toward an emphasis on professional schools, led by the medical school at Johns Hopkins University. New academic disciplines in sociology and economics were forged; and there were also significant contributions in arts and literature from Mark Twain, Walt Whitman, and Emily Dickinson that remain American classics through the present. The new intellectualism in turn spawned the Chautauqua movement designed to give "the college outlook" to those who did not have a higher education. The new intellectualism provided a basis for optimism as the nineteenth century came to a close.

Chronological Time Line

1859 Henry Bessemer invented a process for purifying steel.

1859 Charles Darwin published ***Origin of the Species.***

1865 The Massachusetts Institute of Technology was founded.

1867 Charles L. Scholes invented the typewriter.

1868 The National Labor Reform Party was founded.

1869 The Cincinnati Red Stockings professional baseball team was formed.

1869 The first intercollegiate football game was played.

1871 The Great Chicago Fire

1874 Chautauqua movement was founded by Lewis Miller and John H. Vincent.

1876 Johns Hopkins was founded as a research institution.

1876 Alexander Graham Bell invested the telephone.

1876 The National Association of Professional Baseball Clubs was organized.

Chapter Review (cont'd)

Time Line (cont'd)

1876	Mark Twain published *The Adventures of Tom Sawyer.*
1877	The Socialist Labor Party was founded.
1879	Thomas Edison invented the light bulb.
1879	Henry George, in *Progress and Poverty,* argued for a "single tax" on land values.
1882	The opening of the Pearl Street Central Station in New York signaled the beginning of the electrical age.
1882	The Chinese Exclusion Act prohibited Asian immigration.
1884	Mark Twain published *The Adventures of Huckleberry Finn.*
1885	The American Economic Association was founded and denounced laissez-faire.
1887	The American Protective Association was formed in opposition to immigration.
1888	Edward Bellamy published the utopian novel, *Looking Backward.*
1889	Jane Addams established Hull House in Chicago.
1890	Jacob Riis published *How the Other Half Lives.*
1890	William James published *Principles of Psychology.*
1891	Pope Leo XIII's *De Rerum Novarum* denounced worker exploitation.
1893	Johns Hopkins School of Medicine is founded.
1893	Lester Ward published *The Psychic Factors of Civilization.*
1896	The Social Democratic Party was organized by Eugene V. Debs.
1899	Thorstein Veblen published *Theory of the Leisure Class.*

Time Line (cont'd)

1901 The Socialist Party of America was organized.

1906 The American Sociological Society was founded.

Key Terms

Gilded Age: Term given to the era by Mark Twain because of the prosperity of the time period obscured the corruption, inequality, and exploitation of workers that was also present.

The "new immigration": Immigrants arrived in large numbers from southern and eastern Europe, along with those from Asia that had never before immigrated in large numbers

Social Darwinism: The idea that Darwin's theory of natural selection should be applied to humans, thus explaining the social strata as survival of the fittest

Hebert Spencer: Applied Darwin's theory of natural selection to human social and economic phenomena

Laissez-faire: The idea that the government should take a "hands off" approach to economics and social problems and allow free market forces to work

Social Gospel: The idea that government and other human organizations can be used to do God's good works

Charles M. Sheldon: A proponent of the Social Gospel who in his novel, *In His Steps*, asked the question, "What Would Jesus Do?"

De Rerum Novarum: Pope Leo XIII's famous encyclical which condemned the exploitation of labor and asserted that it was the duty of the state to bring social justice

Pragmatism: The idea that one decides whether an idea is true or false by seeing whether it works

William James: Credited with developing the philosophy of pragmatism

Henry Ward Beecher: Argued that evolution was not inconsistent with religion and could be incorporated into Christian thought

Oliver Wendell Holmes: Judge who argued that law should be based on changing social needs or political policies rather than simply upon logic or precedent

Lester Ward: Argued that a laissez-faire economic system did not necessarily advance human progress, and advocated state management and social planning

George B. Eastman: Created a new industry with his development of mass-produced roll photographic film and the Kodak camera

Thorstein Veblen: As the economist who derided the idea that the wealthy leisure class was the most biologically fit and were a product of natural selection, Veblen condemned inequality and ostentatious wealth.

Henry George: Reformer that sought to remedy the income inequality with a single tax on land values

Chapter Review (cont'd)

Key Terms (cont'd)

Edward Bellamy: Condemned the free market for its inequities and harshness and favored government ownership of production

Jane Addams: Founded Hull House, a slum relief center in Chicago

Socialism: The idea that advocates public ownership of the means of production

Helen Hunt Jackson: Writer and most influential advocate for the Native Americans in the late nineteenth century

Chautauqua Movement: An educational outreach program formulated to give "the college outlook" to those who did not have a higher education

Pop Quiz

Chapter 17

1. Which of the following is true: In spite of the fact that agricultural production increased during the Gilded Age?
   a. Manufacturing increased as a percentage of GNP.
   b. Hunting and gathering increased as a percentage of GNP.
   c. America became a decidedly socialist society.
   d. All of the above

2. George B. Eastman created a new industry with his _________
   a. Process for making steel
   b. Electric light bulb
   c. Air brake
   d. Mass-produced roll photographic film

3. One negative social and economic factor in the Gilded Age was _________
   a. A significant socialist and communist movement
   b. Massive income redistribution plans
   c. Great income inequality
   d. While there was a wealthier class, none could be considered "super-rich."

Pop Quiz (cont'd)

4. Which of the following is true of the Gilded Age?
   a. Men received about 75 percent more than women for similar work.
   b. Men received about two to three times as much as children for similar work.
   c. The typical laborer worked ten hours a day, six days a week.
   d. All of the above

5. Social Darwinists opposed which of the following?
   a. poor relief
   b. public education
   c. the conspicuous wealth of the Gilded Age millionaires
   d. Both a and b

6. On what did Henry Ward Beecher blame poverty?
   a. the fact that some men had not evolved beyond the status of apes
   b. worker exploitation by the ruling classes and the bourgeoisie
   c. the sins of the poor people themselves
   d. God's plan to keep people in humility

7. Pragmatists tended to test ideas against _________
   a. the Bible
   b. common sense
   c. whether or not they worked
   d. laissez-faire free market capitalism

8. Thorstein Veblen argued which of the following?
   a. The leisure class is the most biologically fit.
   b. Millionaires were a product of natural selection.
   c. Millionaires were responsible for the creation of industrial technology.
   d. Millionaires had taken possession of the wealth produced by the labor and skills of others.

9. How could the Chautauqua movement best be described?
   a. an attempt to "Frenchify" America
   b. a movement to instruct the masses in government, economics, science, literature, and culture
   c. a movement that predicted the second coming of Jesus and the "end times"
   d. a movement for the enrichment of the founders based on the sale of "snake oil" elixirs

Chapter Review (cont'd)

Pop Quiz (cont'd)

10. Most Protestant churches taught the Social Gospel. T F

11. Lester Ward and Reform Darwinists challenged the idea of "survival of the fittest." T F

12. Thorstein Veblen accepted the principles of laissez-faire economics. T F

13. Reform Darwinists attacked government for interfering in the economy. T F

14. __________ __________ was the first president of the American Federation of Labor.

15. Henry George believed that land was valuable because __________ lived on it, not because the __________ did anything.

1. A	6. C	11. T	15. People;
2. D	7. C	12. F	Owner
3. C	8. D	13. F	(landlord)
4. D	9. B	14. Samuel	
5. D	10. F	Gompers	

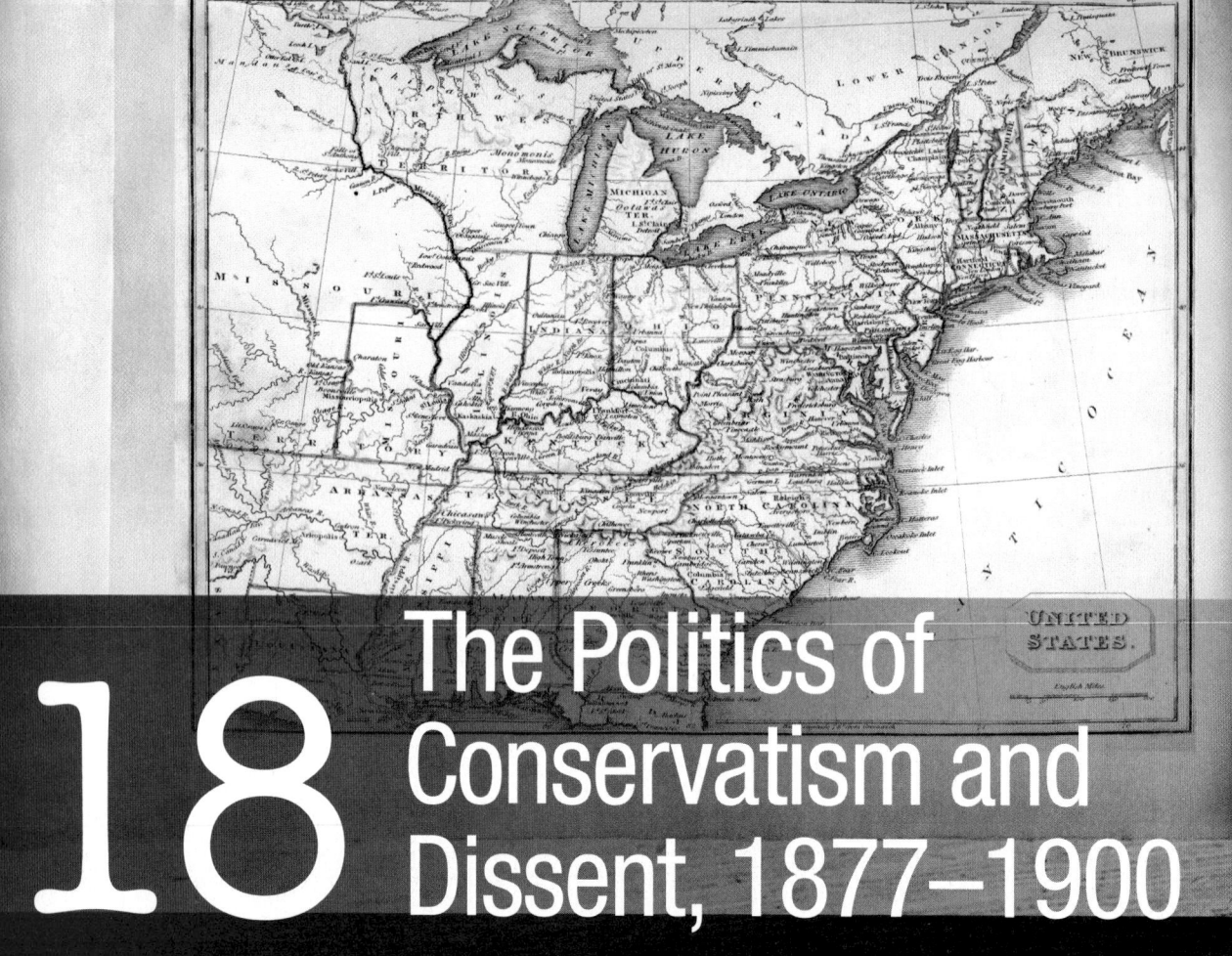

18 The Politics of Conservatism and Dissent, 1877–1900

Chapter Objectives

Political Doldrums

Critics of the Gilded Age
Two Empty Bottles
The Pull of Sectionalism
The Disabled Presidency
The Party Bosses
Upper-Class Reformers
The Voters

The Fight for Rights

The Abandonment of the Blacks
New Achievements for Women

From Hayes to Harrison

Hayes and the Presidency
Hayes Withdraws Troops from the South
Depression and the Silver Question
The Election of 1880
Garfield and Arthur
The Civil Service Act
The Election of 1884

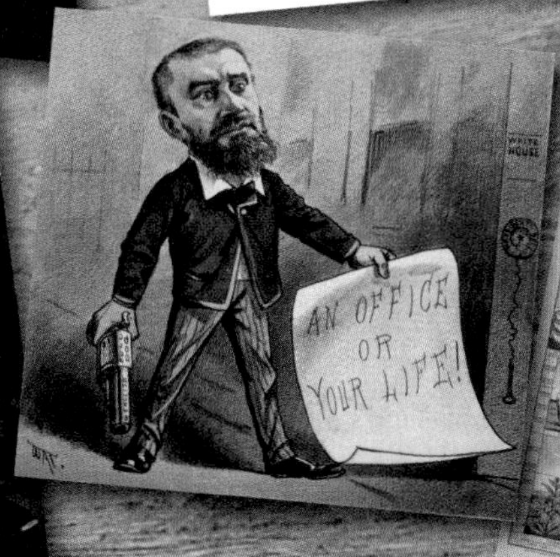

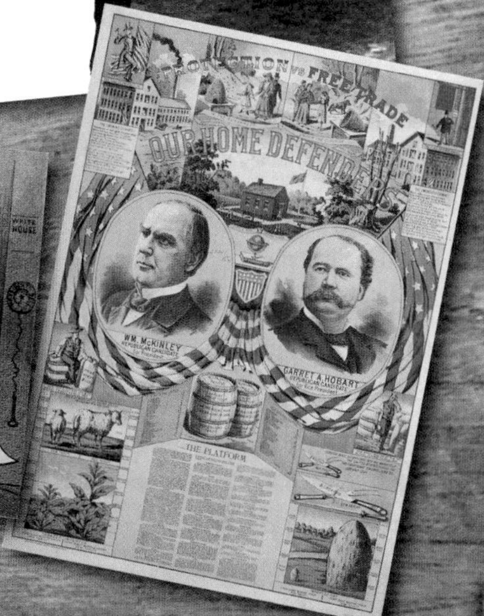

Cleveland and the Presidency

The Tariff Issue

The Election of 1888

Harrison and the Republicans

The Agrarian Revolt

The Plight of the Farmer

The Granger Movement

The Greenback Movement

The Farmers' Alliance

The Emergence of Populism

Populist Ideology

The Election of 1892

Cleveland and the Depression of 1893

The Election of 1896

The Populists in Perspective

McKinley and the End of an Era

Political Doldrums

Critics of the Gilded Age

In contrast to the dramatic industrial and economic progress in the post-Reconstruction years—to say nothing of the vibrant intellectual life we have explored—the political activity of the United States in the Gilded Age seemed to lack the vitality and productivity of earlier periods. The presidents had executive ability and high principles; but they, like most of the important men in Congress, proved to be mediocre and uninspiring leaders. "No period so thoroughly ordinary has been known in American politics since Christopher Columbus first disturbed the balance of power in American society," wrote Henry Adams, that biting commentator of the Gilded Age. "One might search the whole list of Congress, Judiciary, and Executive during the twenty-five years 1870 to 1895 and find little but damaged reputation. The period was poor in purpose and barren in results."

This era in American politics has been kicked and scuffed by historians until little remains of its reputation. Most critics believe that at no other time in American history was the moral and intellectual tone of political life so uniformly low and political contests so preoccupied with political gain and patronage. "Even among the most powerful men of that generation," said Henry Adams, speaking of the politicians, there were "none who had a good word for it." It has become a historical convention to censure the politicians of these years for degenerating into a group of spoilsmen who served the business community, as they were themselves served by it.

The most serious charge leveled against the major parties was that they failed to meet the problems generated by the Industrial Revolution and the anguish being endured by African Americans in the post-Reconstruction South. Far-reaching economic changes necessitated extensive social readjustments; and problems arising from recurrent industrial crises and depressions demanded vigorous governmental action, as did the intransigence of the white South. A variety of factors, however, dissipated the political energies that might have been directed at these social problems.

Two Empty Bottles

The common explanation for this failure is that there were no important differences on major issues between Democrats and Republicans. "Neither party has any principles, any distinctive tenets," wrote James Bryce, a contemporary English observer of the American party system. "The two major parties in this period," concluded Bryce, "were like two bottles. Each bore a label denoting the kind of liquor it contained, but each was empty." Historians have called the period the "age of negation" and its politics "the politics of dead center."

The Republican Party was a loose combination of Northeastern business groups and upper Midwestern farming groups—an alliance that had been formed in 1860 and had fought and won the Civil War. In much of the North and West, Republicans were the party of wealth and respectability.

Two other large groups attached to the Republican Party were blacks and Union army veterans. The blacks, loyal to the party of emancipation, had been able to elect a few congressmen from the South; but after the Republicans abandoned them in 1877, they became more openly critical of the Republican Party and rapidly lost what little political power they had previously enjoyed. War veterans, on the other hand, increased their political importance by organizing the Grand Army of the Republic in 1866 and pressuring Congress into voting for generous pension laws.

Sharply divergent views between Northeastern businessmen and Western farmers occasionally threatened party unity, but Republican orators tried to sidestep their differences by "waving the bloody shirt"—equating party loyalty with national patriotism and charging the Democrats with having fought under the Confederate flag.

The bloody shirt itself was a reference by Northerners to the continued Southern defiance and rebellion. Radical Republican leader Charles Sumner had once waved, on the floor of the U.S. Senate, a bloody shirt that had been worn by a Northern resident who moved South seeking his fortune and was subsequently flogged in Mississippi. To Northerners, the bloody shirt was, in this instance, a negative symbol; but to Southerners, the bloody shirt was a positive symbol of the Southern spirit. Though the South had been crushed militarily in the Civil War, the spirit of the South had risen again; and no northerner in his right mind would entertain the notion of moving south with a carpetbag lest he be flogged as well.

The Democratic Party, known in the South as the "Southern White Man's Party," was a more regional coalition than the Republicans. Its support came chiefly from the "solid South" and the city machines of the Northeast, but it also had some support from the industrial workers of the big cities and from those Northeastern bankers and merchants—"sound money" men—who opposed protective tariffs and government subsidies to special interests and who favored contraction of the currency. The Democrats also made inroads in the Gilded Age among Western farmers who were experiencing falling agricultural prices combined with arbitrary high shipping charges from railroads and high interest rates charged by banks due to the shortage of currency.

▶Radical Republican leader Charles Sumner waved a bloody shirt on the floor of the U.S. Senate. The shirt had been worn by a Northern resident who moved South and was subsequently flogged in Mississippi. The bloodied shirt was a symbol of the Southern spirit, which was still alive and well.

In the South, the Democrats were the party of white supremacy. Southern Democratic leaders, often of Whig background, called themselves "Conservatives" and were frequently labeled "Bourbons" (after the discredited French monarchs) by their opponents. They had much in common with Democratic leaders in the Midwest, who shared their conservative economic views and were also known as "Bourbons." In large northern cities the Democratic Party had the allegiance of most immigrants, who were attracted by the party's name and its sympathy toward labor unions, and whose leaders had sometimes risen to places of influence in the party. The rank-and-file Democrats—farmers, industrial workers, and small businessmen—were often restive under the conservative leaders; but those leaders prevailed until the mid-1890s.

In the early twenty-first century, the big cities of the country will usually vote Democratic, but in the Gilded Age, most of the large urban centers outside the South were more likely to be Republican than Democratic. New York and Boston ordinarily went Democratic due to large Catholic populations; however, in the three presidential elections of the 1880s, for example, a majority of the cities of over fifty thousand outside the South went Republican. The Republican Party in these years was able to appeal successfully to urban voters and many immigrants as the party of prosperity and economic growth. In contrast, the Democrats appeared as the more conservative and frugality-minded party of the South and did not have the same appeal.

To account for the seeming impotence of political parties during the era, it must be remembered that a generally held opinion in America, in line with laissez-faire, was that government should "let well enough alone." Consequently, government rarely concerned itself with economic and social problems.

There were, however, other deterrents to governmental action. Probably most important of these was the sharp contest between the parties and the failure of either to control the national government for any appreciable length of time. Contrary to popular belief, the years of the Gilded Age were not years of Republican supremacy. Rather, they were a period of party stalemate and equilibrium.

In the six presidential elections from 1876 to 1896, the Republicans, while winning four, gained a majority of the popular vote in only one (1896) and a plurality in only one (1880)—and even that plurality was less than one-tenth of one percent. In three of these elections the difference between the popular vote for the two major party candidates was less than one percent although electoral vote majorities ranged from one in 1876 to 132 in 1892. The Democrats—while electing a president twice, in both 1884 and 1892 when they elected Grover Cleveland—won a majority of the popular vote in 1876 and a plurality in 1884, 1888, and 1892. Each party managed to control the presidency and Congress at the same time for only two years—Republicans from 1889 to 1891 and the Democrats from 1893 to 1895.

In recent years, the two major parties in the Gilded Age have received much attention from historians. One might have expected the parties to show increasing centralization and bureaucracy, paralleling the centralization then going on in American business, with the national committees rising to a position of power over the state organizations. Instead, the parties revealed decentralization—a lack of continuity between campaigns, weak national administrations, and even weaker national party committees.

In place of increasing professionalism, political adventurers—businessmen without firm state party bases—almost invariably beat the pros in presidential politics. Political coalitions were formed to serve during approaching elections and then fell apart soon afterwards, only to be rebuilt, many times, in different forms. In general, the increased bureaucratization and centralization of American life were largely thwarted in political life.

The two major parties had few if any national leaders. Of course, there were Democratic and Republican officeholders, and some of these people were well known to voters beyond their immediate constituencies; but public office and a degree of popularity seldom transferred themselves into effective power. Leaders of both parties worked to keep abreast of the changes in the public mood but did not often try to change that mood. The greatest strength of the party system was its ability to reflect the diversity and diffuseness of the American electorate. Finding an issue to appeal to a broad cross-section of the party's voters or office-holders in a country so large and diverse was a formidable task in the late nineteenth century and one rarely undertaken successfully. Politicians acted less to address the national problems arising from industrialism and more to satisfy newly created sectional interests.

The Pull of Sectionalism

Sectional interests resulting from the growth of industry and the expansion of the West served to dissipate and disrupt legislative activity during the 70s and 80s. The leading issues of the country, as indicated by party platforms and congressional action, were currency and banking, tariffs, public lands, internal improvements, railroad and trust regulation, immigration, issues involving blacks in the South, and the "bloody shirt" or continued Southern defiance and rebellion. While all of these produced strong sectional feelings, they generally had one common feature—opposition in the agricultural regions to politics of the industrial centers of the nation. One result was that political personalities seemed to play a subordinate role in determining the outcome of votes on national policies while efforts to find adjustments between sectional interests and party allegiances took priority.

Because the Industrial Revolution had made businessmen the new ruling class in the country, they could obtain political favors, supplanting the Southern planters and Northeastern merchants in the seats of power. The usual explanation for this alliance between business and politics is that the politicians were the hirelings of the business community. "Business ran politics, and politics was a branch of business," writes one historian.

Despite its favored position, business did not control American politics without opposition. Businessmen had to pay heavily for political favors, and often they were blackmailed by threats of regulation or of withdrawal of government assistance. Businessmen complained that politicians treated them simply as customers, compelling them to pay for protection, selling political benefits to the highest bidders, and refusing to do "the proper thing" (in the eyes of the businessmen) without pay. As we shall see, farmers and workers, too, were able to win political favors once they became organized and began to put pressure on politicians. Democracy, it seemed, was open to the highest bidder.

Voters, for their part, did more sectional voting during depressions and showed more party loyalty in times of prosperity. Those sections hardest hit in a depression broke party ranks and combined with other distressed areas to attempt to do something about their grievances. The vagueness of party platforms until 1888 also stimulated sectional divisions since it allowed representatives from discontented sections to interpret the planks to suit their own interests. In Congress, sectional voting was more pronounced when the control of the houses was divided between the two parties than in those instances when one party was in control. This was equally true for depression and prosperity years in the seventies and eighties. Thus presidents had to deal not only with divided Congresses but also with Congresses in which their own party members did more sectional than party voting.

The Disabled Presidency

The president might have been expected to mediate sectional interests, but the office of the presidency was at low ebb in power and prestige during this period. National political power was vested chiefly in Congress. Congressional leaders almost overthrew Andrew

Johnson, gained nearly complete control of Grant, and had tried to put subsequent presidents in the Gilded Age at their mercy. Senator John Sherman, Republican leader of Ohio and a perpetual aspirant to the office, wrote: "The executive department of a republic like ours should be subordinate to the legislative department. The president should [merely] obey and enforce the laws." presidents in the Gilded Age, such as Grover Cleveland and Benjamin Harrison, tended to agree.

Congressional leaders acted accordingly. "The most eminent Senators," observed George F. Hoar, Republican of Massachusetts, about his colleagues in the Senate, "would have received as a personal affront a private message from the White House expressing a desire that they should adopt any course in the discharge of their legislative duties that they did not approve. If they visited the White House, it was to give, not to receive advice."

The Party Bosses

The political rulers of the day were not the titular leaders but the political party bosses, many of them United States senators, who headed powerful state machines and rewarded their followers with public offices. Among the important bosses were Senators James G. Blaine of Maine, Roscoe Conkling of New York, Zachariah Chandler of Michigan, and John A. Logan of Illinois—all Republicans—and Arthur P. Gorman of Maryland, a Democrat. Before 1883, these party bosses had at their disposal an enormous amount of spoils in the form of federal, state, and local offices, as well as government contracts. They controlled a hierarchy of workers down to the ward heelers, to whom they gave offices in return for faithful service. The assessment of officeholders and the sale of nominations and offices tightened the bosses' grips on local machines.

▶ George F. Hoar, Republican Senator from Massachusetts

When the Civil Service Reform Act of 1883 (to be discussed later in this chapter) began to remove these powers by eliminating the federal spoils that produced them, politicians turned increasingly to businessmen for money and support. A new type of political boss appeared—a business type who resembled and worked closely with corporation executives, made few speeches, and conducted his activities in anterooms, caucuses, and committees. Matthew S. Quay of Pennsylvania, Leland Stanford of California, Philetus Sawyer of Wisconsin, Thomas Platt of New York, and Nelson W. Aldrich of Rhode Island were bosses of the new type. Some had been prosperous bankers and businessmen and had entered the Senate to protect their interests. In 1889 journalist William Allen White could say: "A United States Senator ... represented something more than a state, more even than a region. He represented principalities and powers in business." According to White, one senator "represented the Union Pacific Railway System, another the New York Central. ... Coal and iron owned a coterie from the Middle and Eastern seaport states. Cotton had half a dozen senators. And so it went." Many labeled this imposing body the "Millionaires' Club." Senator George Hearst of California, one of the group, echoed Darwinian theory when he said, "I do not know much about books; ...but I have traveled a good deal and have observed men and things and I have made up my mind after my experiences that the members of the Senate are the survivors of the fittest."

Besides these prominent establishment bosses, there were the backroom bosses, that often ruled without ever holding elective office. The principal effect of the spoils system was to transfer party control from publicly elected leaders to "inside" rulers. The most flagrant examples of "invisible government" occurred in the cities, many of which were run by corrupt political party machines. Whether Democratic like Tammany Hall in New York led by William Marcy "Boss" Tweed, or Republican like the Gas Ring in Philadelphia, their methods were the same. James Bryce expressed the opinion that municipal government was "the one conspicuous failure of the United States." Similarly, Andrew D. White in an article in *Forum* in 1890 stated that "with very few exceptions, the city governments of the United States are the worst in Christendom—the most expensive, the most inefficient, and the most corrupt."

New York City furnished the country its most notorious example of a municipal machine. Tammany Hall, an organization dating back to the eighteenth century, controlled the Democratic Party and the local government. William Marcy Tweed and his followers—A. Oakey Hall, the mayor; Peter B. Sweeney, county and city treasurer; and Richard B. Connally, the city controller—ran Tammany Hall and plundered the city. With every type of embezzlement this repulsive crew robbed the city treasury year after year until, at the height of their power, they were splitting among themselves 85 percent of the total expenditures made by the city and county.

▶ As politicians began turning to businessmen for money and support, a new type of political boss appeared—a business type who resembled corporation executives, made few speeches, and conducted activities in anterooms, caucuses, and committees. Leland Stanford (above) was just such a political boss.

Their technique was simple. Everyone who had a bill against the city was instructed to pad it—at first by 10 percent, later 66 percent, and finally by 85 percent. Tweed's gang received the padding. For example, the courthouse, originally estimated at $3 million cost the taxpayers $11 million. The plastering bill alone amounted to $2.87 million and the carpeting to $350,000, "enough to cover the whole City Park three times." The loot taken by the Tweed Ring has been variously estimated at from $45 million to $100 million.

Although respectable citizens protested, they were powerless for several years to move against Tweed because he controlled every arm of the government. Finally, courageous editorials in *The New York Times* and the cartoons of Thomas Nast in *Harper's Weekly* exposed the corruption of the Tweed Ring and aroused the general public. His own followers, Tweed said, could not read, but they could "look at the damn pictures." Tweed offered George Jones, owner of *The New York Times*, $1,000,000 to quiet his paper and Nast $500,000 to study art in Europe, but they refused. A citizens' committee headed by Samuel J. Tilden and Charles O'-Conor launched an investigation that was able, by the end of 1872, to drive every member of the Tweed Ring out of office; Tweed himself died in jail.

Yet the traditional view of the boss as nothing but a corrupting force in American politics needs to be modified. Studies of Boss Tweed and of the Cox machine in Cincinnati show that these political organizations furnished some element of order and stability in a rapidly expanding and disordered society. They point out that the boss provided a valuable service in giving services to many people—especially immigrants—who had no other institutional or social order to which to appeal. The political party machines essentially ran informal welfare systems, providing food and necessities, housing, and employment to immigrants and the working classes in the nation's urban centers in exchange for political support. The result was very high (75 percent) voter turnout since more people had a vested interest in whether their preferred party remained in office.

Moreover, not all bosses used politics to advance their material interest. Common as the various forms of graft and corruption were in the Gilded Age, not all bosses sought material profit. Boies Penrose, Republican boss of Pennsylvania, apparently never made a dollar out of politics; and according to Theodore Roosevelt, "Senator Platt [Republican boss of New York state] did not use his political position to advance his private fortunes—therein differing from many other political bosses. He lived in hotels and had few extravagant tastes."

Upper-Class Reformers

In this age of corruption, voices such as those of the "single-tax" advocate Henry George and the socialist Edward Bellamy were calling for reform, and Jane Addams and her colleagues in the settlement house movement were reaching out to new immigrants. Into this mix, there were also reformers with an upper-class orientation. Probably the most respectable of all the reformers were the "mugwumps," as their opponents called them. The term was first used politically in 1884 to describe the independent Republicans who refused to support presidential candidate James G. Blaine, due to his reputation for political corruption. Mugwumps generally were newspapermen, scholars, and intellectuals—earnest men of high ideals and prominent social position, of conservative economic views, and usually of Republican background. Foremost among them were George William Curtis, editor of *Harper's Weekly*; E. L. Godkin, editor of *The Nation*; Carl Schurz; William Cullen Bryant; Whitelaw Reid; and Samuel Bowles. They lashed out against the spoils system and worked to purify politics through civil service reform. Since they believed in laissez-faire, however, they restricted their economic program to tariff reform and sound money.

The mugwumps spoke in moralistic terms, rather than in economic ones. They appealed primarily to the educated upper classes and seldom identified themselves with the interests of the masses, whom they viewed with an aristocratic disdain. They regarded the reform movements of labor and farmers as radical and dangerous and had little use for other reform movements of the period; but this was characteristic of most of their contemporary reform movements which tended to have little in common and had great difficulty in understanding one another. Divided and mutually suspicious, the reformers thus exerted little influence.

Historians, who have generally accepted the mugwumps' censure of the Gilded Age, have long praised them; but recent studies of these reformers challenge both the indictment of that period and mugwump beliefs. It will be difficult for future writers to extol these "independents," who condemned corruption, without recognizing that they too were elitists who opposed the democratizing direction of their time. The mugwumps "seemed to dislike thinking about the workingman as such," writes Geoffrey Blodgett. "They had no solution for the poor," doubting in fact that there *was* a solution because poverty "resulted from the poor people spending too much money." Furthermore, unlike the Progressives of the succeeding generation, they "made no real effort to break the control of the elective process enjoyed by party professionals."

These liberal reformers of the Gilded Age believed that political independence helped to purify politics, but they also had a price for their reforms. They wanted a small, efficient government run by themselves or by men like themselves—reducing property taxes, encouraging individual effort, and cutting back public services. "Unable to come to terms with his age, the liberal reformer exaggerated its defects and overrated the past," observes John G. Sproat. "Everything considered—this campaign to reform postwar society was a pathetic failure." Liberal reformers of the Gilded Age are now found wanting almost as much as the Gilded Age was found wanting by them.

The Voters

There were limits to what could be done about relieving social and economic discontent, and mainly the voters themselves imposed these limits. For one thing, those interested in reform did not give consistent support to either party. Victory in national elections depended on heavily populated "doubtful" states, which had enough shifting voters to swing the results either way. These were Connecticut, New York, and New Jersey in the East, and Ohio, Indiana, and Illinois in the Midwest. These states, especially New York and the three Midwestern ones, enjoyed strong bargaining power with which they secured favorable posts for their politicians and obtained most of the funds from the campaign treasuries at election time. The doubtful states were wedded to neither party, but courted by both. The parties chose presidential and vice-presidential candidates from these areas and awarded their congressmen important committee assignments.

"Not the Republican politician but the voting public failed reform in the early years of the Gilded Age," writes La Wanda Cox about New York. "Civic improvement did not win the anticipated votes from New York City's Democratic faithful, and Republican support for equal suffrage [for African Americans] brought political disaster. The hopeful union of idealism and practical politics within the state Republican Party could not be consummated in the face of public repudiation at the polls."

In the Northeast, and in Massachusetts in particular, according to Blodgett, the political leaders were all acting in an essentially conservative manner because of these restraints. They realized that the country was changing, and they were willing to make adjustments; however, their constituents—native born Americans and immigrants alike—opposed basic change because to them perpetuating their community was more important than improving it. As a result, the Democratic Party in Massachusetts did not rise to the occasion and by the end of the nineteenth century could no longer be considered an effective instrument of social and economic change.

It is important to remember that some pieces of major legislation were passed during this period, despite the limitations imposed by voters and the politicians' reluctance to address the issues. The abiding belief that this was a period in which issues were steadfastly ignored is testimony to the lasting quality of the progressive-liberal historians' interpretation of the Gilded Age, which is echoed even by modern historians. The assumptions of the early historians also overlooked the fact that there was proportionately a heavier turnout of voters in the Gilded Age than in the twentieth century, evidence of voter concern with politics and partisanship.

Both voter behavior and party alignment revolved primarily around ethno-cultural issues and responses, mostly religious and sectarian in nature. The expansion in the Catholic population in the country in the last third of the nineteenth century by the flood of immigrants from Europe greatly strengthened the Democratic Party, which has traditionally been identified with Catholic voters. Then, in the 1880s, there was a revival of anti-immigrant activism that was supported by many Republican Protestants. The very moralistic Protestants sharply assailed the drinking habits and the easy Sunday recreational activities of the immigrants, especially the Germans and the Irish Catholics. These Republicans wanted prohibition and Sunday laws, demands that angered many Americans who believed their personal liberties were in danger. German Lutherans and Irish and Polish Catholics were alarmed that the Republicans would also attempt to eliminate their parochial schools, which they considered essential for maintaining their religion and their culture; thus, they gave their support to the Democratic Party.

The Fight for Rights

The Abandonment of the Blacks

The failure of Americans in the Gilded Age to deal adequately with the pressing issues of the day can be clearly seen in the way they handled their greatest and most tragic problem—the plight of American blacks, who comprised one-tenth of the population. Though the Civil War had settled the question of human slavery, it did not settle the problem of securing for all Americans the inalienable rights set forth in the Declaration of Independence; nor did it alter the fact that white supremacy was generally taken for granted. During Reconstruction significant constitutional and legislative steps—the Thirteenth, Fourteenth, and Fifteenth Amendments and the passage of civil rights legislation in 1866 and 1875—were taken to insure the freedpeople's political and civil rights; but developments during the last quarter of the nineteenth century virtually destroyed these political gains.

When President Hayes removed the last of the federal troops and federal control from the South in April 1877, he left Southern blacks in the custody of Southern whites. Governor Wade Hampton of South Carolina had promised, "We ... will secure to every citizen, the lowest as well as the highest, black as well as white, full and equal protection in the enjoyment of all his rights under the Constitution." Because of such promises Hayes believed that a new "era of good feeling" between the two races was developing in the South. Even before 1877 was over, he learned differently. "By state legislation, by frauds, by intimidation, and by violence of the most atrocious character, colored citizens have been deprived of the right of suffrage," he wrote in his diary; however, he did practically nothing to correct the situation as he had earlier said he would, partially because he believed that Congress—rather than the president—should assume policy leadership, and partially because Hayes was never viewed as a legitimate ruler in the South due to the fraudulent election of 1876. Hayes's successor, James Garfield, was no more proactive, stating only, "Time is the only cure."

The Republican Party had emerged from the Civil War as the champion and protector of the Southern blacks. It had emancipated and enfranchised them and had provided them with the same political and civil rights as whites. In their platforms from 1876 to 1896, the Republicans solemnly pledged themselves to enforce the Fourteenth and Fifteenth Amendments, to secure to "every American citizen of whatever race and color complete liberty and exact equality in the exercise of all civil, political, and public rights," protect "honest voters" against terrorism, violence and fraud, and never to relax their efforts "until the integrity of the ballot and purity of elections ... be fully guaranteed in every state." In Congress, they sponsored investigations of fraud and violence in elections in the South, accused Southern Democrats of holding their seats illegally and of exercising a disproportionate voting influence, and focused attention upon indiscreet statements by Southern leaders and the press. Unfortunately, while Republicans talked much, they took few steps to remedy the desperate situation of African Americans or to meet their obligations to the freedmen.

Actually, throughout most of the last quarter of the nineteenth century, the Republicans were in no position in Congress to enforce the Fourteenth and Fifteenth Amendments, but their abandonment of blacks was also part of a well-planned policy. Their new plans called for a shift in Republican appeals in the South from blacks to whites. They wanted to maintain and even increase their black support, but that was subsidiary to their main aim: swelling their ranks with Southern whites.

Thus, Hayes abandoned the Southern blacks when he removed the Union troops from the South in the hope of reconciling North and South, conciliating Southern whites and ingratiating the Republican Party with them. President Chester Arthur deserted the blacks when he chose to work with Independents in the South in the belief that it was necessary to subordinate the freedmen to exploit the Democratic cleavages in the South, which he had concluded was the only path to Republican success there. Furthermore, in 1890, when Republicans had control of the presidency and the Congress at the same time for the only period in these years, they again forsook blacks when they failed to pass the Federal Elections or "Force" Bill, providing for national supervision of federal elections as a way of protecting the rights of Southern blacks to vote. They did so because they had a greater interest in the tariff and silver measures, but also because there was considerable opposition to the elections legislation in party ranks.

The Republican abandonment of the blacks was also a part of a general abandonment by all Northerners. By the end of Reconstruction, most Northerners probably agreed with Southern whites that the blacks were not prepared for equality and that the South should be allowed to deal with them in its own way. Northerners had also come to believe that the elimination of the issue of blacks from politics was necessary for a return to national solidarity and a development of trade relations between the North and South.

To make matters worse, the courts also abandoned the blacks. After 1877, practically every Supreme Court decision affecting blacks nullified their rights or curtailed them somehow. The Court drastically limited the powers of the federal government to intervene in the states to protect the rights of blacks. For all intents and purposes, it invalidated the Fourteenth and Fifteenth Amendments as effective safeguards for black people. When, in 1883, the Court set aside the Civil Rights Act of 1875 on the ground that the Fourteenth Amendment was binding on states but not individuals, it ended federal attempts to protect blacks against discrimination by private persons. There would be no federal civil rights legislation thereafter until 1957. In the 1870s, when the Court held in *United States v. Reese* and *United States v. Cruickshank* that the Fifteenth Amendment did not confer the right to vote upon anyone and that Congress did not have the authority to protect the right to vote generally, sections of the Enforcement Act of 1870 were declared unconstitutional because they provided penalties for hindering a person in voting. In 1894, Congress repealed the entire law. Again, there was no further legislation on the subject until 1957.

Finally, in two decisions in the 1890s, the Court paved the way for additional curtailment of the rights of blacks. In *Plessy v. Ferguson* (1896), the Court laid down the "separate but equal" rule in defense of segregation. Reflecting adherence to Social Darwinism, the Court ruled that "if one race be inferior to another," it was not the role of the Court to place them "on the same plane." The "separate but equal doctrine" became the law of the land until 1954. Then, in *William v. Mississippi* (1898), the Court opened the road to legal disfranchisement by approving Southern plans for depriving blacks of the vote.

Blacks had continued to vote, though in reduced numbers, after the return of white supremacy in the South. In some parts of the South they were prevented from voting by threats or intimidation, and in other parts their vote was nullified by artful means such as the use of tissue ballots and a complicated system of ballot boxes. In the 1890s, however, the Southern states proceeded with plans to disfranchise them with laws. Within two decades practically all black voters had been disfranchised by means of poll taxes, white primaries, tests of "moral character," and literacy or property qualifications that were enforced against blacks but not against whites. Illiterate whites were generally exempt from literacy tests by so-called "Grandfather Clauses" that stated that persons were exempt from the tests if their grandfather voted. For African Americans, none could be exempt under the Grandfather Clauses because none of the grandfathers were allowed to vote during the days before emancipation. "White Primaries" disfranchised blacks by preventing them from voting in party primaries. Since in the South the only real question in any election was who would win the Democratic nomination for any particular position in the primary—because voting Republican was considered "unsouthern" and "dishonored the confederate dead"—blacks were allowed to vote in the general election in some counties after the Democratic Party nominee had already been chosen by whites only. The Democratic nominee would then defeat the Republican in the general election in a landslide, thus cutting blacks out of the "real decision" that had been made at the primary level.

In the same years, the Southern states also passed numerous "Jim Crow" laws, segregating blacks in virtually every aspect of public life. State and municipal laws were passed against such crimes as "night-walking," "leering," "lurking," and "misspending one's income." Blacks were denied the right to bear arms, limited by zoning to certain sections of town (normally the east side of town so that they would be downwind from whites rather than vice versa), and even banned from residence in some towns by "sundown laws" that required that no blacks could remain in town after sundown. Economically, laws were passed limiting blacks to employment only in agriculture or domestic servitude.

Most Northerners shared the segregationists' attitudes toward blacks. They deplored agitation on behalf of blacks and were willing to accept the South's racial policies. Even educated, intelligent Northerners believed that black people were racially inferior because most scientists at the time also believed this. Furthermore, most of the Northern press supported the discriminatory decisions in the civil rights cases. As historian Rayford W. Logan has shown, Northern newspapers usually described blacks in a derogatory manner, regardless of the actual circumstances, strengthening a stereotype of the "criminal Negro." The leading literary magazines of the North such as *Harper's, Scribner's* and the *Atlantic Monthly*, mirroring the refined tastes of the upper classes, regularly used derisive terms when they referred to blacks.

Most Americans did not especially wish blacks ill. Writes John A. Garraty, a leading historian of the Gilded Age. "... They simply refused to consider them quite human and consigned them complacently to oblivion, along with the Indians."

The position of black leader Booker T. Washington among his race may have also contributed to the assault upon the rights of blacks. Washington, founder and principal of Tuskegee Institute in Alabama was, according to Louis R. Harlan, a biographer, a "white man's black man" and a "safe, sane Negro" to Southern whites. In the Northern white world, Washington was "deferential but dignified," drawing philanthropy from such men as Carnegie. Among Southern whites, says Harlan, Washington made a point of not crossing the color line and sought to reduce social friction. He believed that, for the time being, blacks should forgo agitation for the vote and social equality and devote their efforts to achieving economic security and independence. "In all things that are purely social," he said in 1895, "we can be as separate as the fingers, yet one as the hand in all things for mutual progress."

"Washington unmistakably accepted a subordinate position for Southern Negroes," writes Rayford Logan. "This position was far different from the unequivocal standard for equal citizenship advanced by [Frederick] Douglass in 1889. He definitely renounced social equality. ... In return he asked for a chance to gain a decent livelihood. Washington was convinced, and rightly so," continues Logan, "that it would have been folly to ask in 1895 for equal rights for Negroes." Washington's position won the enthusiastic support of the white community and had much to do with fixing the pattern of race relations in the country for most of the remainder of his lifetime. Most blacks of that time probably accepted Washington's view. Supporters of Washington, however, argue that the attitudes of whites were so racist and that blacks were so out-

▶ Instead of purely pushing for racial equality and rights for blacks, Booker T. Washington encouraged blacks to devote their efforts to achieving economic security and independence. Washington was a respected leader in the black community for twenty-five years.

numbered, impoverished, and without political power that Washington was simply a realist who adopted the only practical approach. Washington was famous for the statement "Cast down your bucket where you are," which was a janitorial reference imploring blacks to work for economic success within the segregated system imposed by whites. If all whites would allow blacks to do was be janitors, Washington was essentially saying that blacks should do their very best at being janitors and their hard work would eventually pay off. Washington is also known for what is termed as the "Atlanta Compromise," whereby Washington urged blacks to accept segregation in return for white support of black educational and economic success.

As for black people in "the New South" (the way that many of its white businessmen advocates chose to bill it), their plight was desperate in the years after Reconstruction ended. They faced disfranchisement, discrimination, physical intimidation and the ultimate penalty, lynching. In the 1890s, the numbers of lynching in the South rose precipitously with 161 black people being lynched in the peak year of 1892—and these are only the victims who show up in the public record—and they do not include hundreds of other beatings, castrations, and other forms of non-lethal intimidation. Black men, in particular, might be lynched on the mere suspicion of a sexual assault on a white woman. Moreover, the vast majority of African Americans lived in a state of peonage, because they were sharecroppers with little ability to get ahead. They were the poorest of the poor in a poor region—despite the trumpeting of change by New South boosters.

Even in this dark time, with Booker T. Washington preaching accommodation, there was one African American who fought lynching publicly, Ida B. Wells-Barnett. Born to slave parents in the waning days of the Confederacy, Wells-Barnett became a newspaper editor in Memphis. In March 1892, a mob lynched three black men whom she knew and admired; and she wrote an editorial denouncing this event. She had to leave the South to continue her crusade against lynching, eventually settling in Chicago. In 1895, she published *The Red Record*, her account of lynching in the South over a three-year period. Similarly, other black leaders, such as Harvard and Berlin University-educated William E. B. DuBois and T. Thomas Fortune, argued that blacks should accept nothing short of full citizenship rights.

Many scholars have explored the way that the black churches offered both leadership and comfort, as the clergy and the laity struggled to deal with an impossible situation. Prior to the Civil War, blacks in the South had attended white-dominated churches where they were taught that God sanctioned slavery and that slaves were to submit to their masters. After the Civil War, blacks in the South generally abandoned the white-dominated churches and established their own. These black churches became the center of the black community in the South, providing not only community leadership but also often meeting the basic needs of food and shelter for the most impoverished. It should also be noted that these tragic years were the seedtime for cultural developments within the African American community that would be of enormous consequence in the twentieth century, both at home and abroad. The segregated society also spawned a limited level of black entrepreneurship as blacks, who were denied service at whites-only businesses, were forced to establish their own in order to meet the black community's needs.

New Achievements for Women

While blacks were slowly losing their rights, women in the Gilded Age were struggling for more rights, opportunities, and privileges and for a more equal place with men in the participation in and conduct of American affairs. Much of this activity centered on the effort to win the vote.

The battle for women's suffrage had been renewed with fresh vigor after the end of the Civil War partially because the discussion over broadening the franchise to include African Americans gave suffragists hope that women might be included in any new legislation or Constitutional amendments. This did not prove to be the case, and the result was a schism within the ranks of suffragists. One group, led by Lucy Stone, accepted the Reconstruction amendments, even though they did not include women; another, led by Elizabeth Cady Stanton and Susan B. Anthony, opposed them.

Indeed, there was considerable opposition to women's claim of equal political rights with men in this period. Gilded Age politicians insisted that the political arena was a male preserve, that politics itself was masculine, and that any effort to change that situation was contrary to human nature. Politicians, however, were not alone in holding this view. Francis Parkman, one of the era's most prominent historians, thought women's suffrage would leap over "Nature's limitations," disrupt the home, and give women excitement and cares "too much for their strength." Publicly he wrote that especially in the "crowded cities" women's suffrage would be "madness" and would certainly make bad governments worse. Similarly, many Protestant fundamentalists argued that women's suffrage violated the natural place in society designed by God for women. Some even argued that women's suffrage would lead to "divorce and destruction of the family" since many suffragettes, such as Emma Goldman, argued for less restrictive divorce laws.

▶ Lucy Stone was an American suffragist who advocated for women's rights and protested against slavery.

A number of supporters of women's rights, including Wendell Phillips, a leading social reformer of the day, vigorously disagreed. "One of two things is true," declared Phillips. "Either woman is like man—and if she is, then a ballot based on brains belongs to her as well as to him; or she is different, and then man does not know how to vote for her as well as she herself does."

The major political parties, however, generally either ignored or opposed the demand for women's suffrage; many women—although probably not a majority—decided to take action themselves. Under the leadership of Susan B. Anthony and Elizabeth Cady Stanton, there was agitation for women's suffrage from the 1870s until women finally secured the right to vote in 1920. Then some women's groups, such as the Equal Rights Party, took direct political action by nominating women for president of the United States—Victoria Claflin Woodhull in 1872 and Belva Ann Bennett Lockwood in 1884 and 1888.

Other women worked to unite the two disputing groups. By 1890, the two principal competing groups fighting for women's suffrage had merged into the National American Women's Suffrage Association, which sought to win support for the cause from Congress and the state legislatures. In the last third of the nineteenth century, there was a great battle for women's suffrage in the nation's magazines, public meetings, legislative assemblies, and state constitutional conventions. As Thomas Wentworth Higginson, a Civil War commander of a black regiment and a well-known reformer and feminist of these years pointed out, "Mrs. [Harriet Beecher] Stowe helps to free Uncle Tom in his cabin, and then strikes for the freedom of women in her own 'Hearth and Home.' Mrs. [Julia Ward] Howe writes the 'Battle Hymn of the Republic,' and keeps on writing more battle hymns in behalf of her own sex. Miss [Louisa May] Alcott not only delineates 'Little Women,' but wishes to emancipate them." Other prominent persons such as George William Curtis, civil service reformer, and John Greenleaf Whittier, poet and abolitionist, as well as the two most important labor organizations of the day, the Knights of Labor and the American Federation of Labor, supported the movement for women's suffrage.

Women tried unsuccessfully to win the vote through the Fifteenth Amendment, which the denial of voting rights based on race, but not gender. At first, the suffragettes failed in efforts in the states when seven states turned down women's suffrage proposals between 1867 and 1877. They also suffered a serious legal setback when the Supreme Court in *Minor v. Happersett* (1875) refused to accept the argument that women could vote because they were citizens and unanimously ruled that the Fourteenth Amendment had not conferred the vote upon women. When some state laws barred women from the legal profession, the Supreme Court upheld such laws, with one justice saying, "The natural and proper timidity and delicacy which belongs to the female sex, unfits it for many … occupations." Women, he said, should stay with "the noble and benign offices of wife and mother."

In 1878, Senator Aaron Augustus Sargent of California introduced into Congress an equal suffrage amendment. During the remaining years of the century, Senate committees reported five times and House committees twice in favor of the amendment, but Congress never took action on it. Despite considerable effort by the suffragists, the increasing militancy of the women's suffrage movement, and a growing sympathy and backing for it generally, only four states at the close of the nineteenth century had given the vote to women—Wyoming (1869), Colorado (1893), Utah (1896), and Idaho (1896).

Women made more progress in some other aspects of American life than they did politically. More women were working outside their homes and going to college than had been the case in earlier periods of American history, for example. The old prejudice against self-support for women was beginning to weaken, and at the same time colleges and universities were preparing increasing numbers of women for positions previously held mainly by men. "We have reached a new era," asserted *Harper's Bazaar*, a leading woman's magazine in 1883. "Slowly as woman has come to her inheritance, it stretches before her now into illimitable distance; and the question of the hour is rather whether she is ready for her trust than whether that trust is hampered by conditions."

As Arthur M. Schlesinger, Sr., one of America's most distinguished historians, pointed out two generations ago, "Women who would have shrunk from factory work and domestic service or even from teaching trooped forth with a sense of adventure to become typists, telephone girls, typesetters, bookkeepers, nurses, librarians, journalists, lecturers, social workers, doctors, lawyers, artists. Even in the realm of mechanical invention, a time-honored monopoly of men," added Schlesinger, "they were displaying surprising capacity in a variety of fields."

▶ Although they still struggled to gain the right to vote, women in the late 1800s were increasingly working outside the home.

▶A section on hair styles in *Harper's Bazar*, a popular women's magazine in 1880. *Harper's Bazar* ran an article stating "We have reached a new era, slowly as woman has come to her inheritance, it stretches before her now into illimitable distance; and the question of the hour is rather whether she is ready for her trust than whether that trust is hampered by conditions."

According to Emily Faithfull, an English social worker and observer of American life in the late nineteenth century, in 1882 there were, in Massachusetts alone, almost three hundred branches of industry and business where women could earn from $100 to $3,000 a year.

Though there had long been a large number of women who worked for a living outside the home, the great economic expansion of the late nineteenth century brought increasing numbers into the work force. From 1880 to 1890, the number of women workers went up from 2.5 million to more than 4 million, about one-sixth of the total work force, and by 1900, to 5.3 million. Unfortunately, this was counterbalanced by the fact that women usually filled the lowest-paid jobs and received unequal pay in virtually every position they held for work equal to that performed by men.

Since unions did not pay much attention to working conditions for women, not much was done to correct the injustice of the unequal wage scale. One gain was made when Congress, in 1872, enacted the Arnell Bill, giving female government employees equal pay with men for equal work. Belva Ann Bennett Lockwood had much to do with the passage of this act. She drafted the measure, and a petition she circulated at the meetings of the National and American Women's Suffrage Associations in New York in 1870 hastened its passage. (See *"Belva Ann Bennett Lockwood: A Campaigning Woman."*) Another gain was that legislatures in the industrial states began in the 1880s to consider legislation regulating working conditions of women in factories.

Women also made progress in education in these years despite the fact that they were up against a generally held view, expressed by a minister in 1880, that women's emotional nature "painfully disqualifies" them from the effort to be educated. By this time women had been accepted in colleges for about twenty years. In fact, by 1870 one-third of American colleges were coeducational. Probably the greatest educational opportunities for women occurred in the Middle West and in the South where the new state universities began to admit women as well as men. President James B. Angell of the University of Michigan told a visitor to the campus in 1883 that while coeducation was still an experiment in the East it was definitely settled in the West, adding, "none of the ladies had found the curriculum too heavy for their physical endurance."

Angell's concern about women's physical stamina for the rigors of study was shared by a number of Americans, both women and men. M. Carey Thomas, a graduate of Cornell in 1877 and the first president of Bryn Mawr, expressed this concern when she said, "The passionate desire of the women of my generation for higher education was accompanied ... by the awful doubt, felt by women themselves as well as by men, as to whether women as a sex were physically and mentally fit for it."

Women clearly demonstrated their fitness for college, and coeducation grew rapidly in these years. Between 1880 and 1898, the proportion of coeducational colleges increased from 51 percent to 70 percent and the number of female students from 2,750 to more than 25,000. At the same time some women's colleges on a level with the top ones for men were established—Vassar (1861), Wellesley (1870), Smith (1871), and Bryn Mawr (1885). Mount Holyoke, a girl's seminary begun in 1836, became a college in 1893. Also, two of the country's leading universities, Harvard and Columbia, added women's colleges—Radcliffe in 1879 and Barnard in 1889. By the end of the nineteenth century, four out of every five colleges, universities, and professional schools in the country admitted women.

Women, especially of the upper middle class, also turned their attention to club activities and joined in large numbers the women's organizations springing up all over the country. "We have art clubs, book clubs, dramatic clubs, pottery clubs," wrote one woman in 1880 in the *Atlantic Monthly*. "We have sewing circles, philanthropic associations, scientific, literary, religious, athletic, musical, and decorative art societies." These various associations provided a good way for women to find out about the world in which they were now playing a larger role. They also furnished good training for many women who became active civic and humanitarian leaders in their communities. In one decade, 1888–1897, four important groups were formed that placed more women in public affairs: the National Council of Women, the General Federation of Women's Clubs, the National Association of Colored Women's Clubs, and the National Congress of Parents and Teachers. By the close of the nineteenth century, the General Federation of Women's Clubs (which did not then admit black

▶Mount. Holyoke College postcard. Mount Holyoke, a girl's seminary, begun in 1836, became a college in 1893.

Belva Ann Bennett Lockwood: A Campaigning Woman

▶ Belva Ann Bennett Lockwood

Few American have achieved as much prominence and subsequently been so forgotten as Belva Ann Bennett Lockwood, who was twice nominated for president. Until she died at the age of eighty-seven, she spent more than fifty years of tireless work expanding the opportunities, privileges, and human rights of her sex. She never doubted that women would eventually have an equal place with men in the conduct of American affairs.

Belva Ann Bennett was born October 24, 1830, on her parents' farm in Royalton, New York. She attended country schools and in later years recalled the hard benches of the one-room schools and the white line painted on the floor where she had to "toe the mark" when reciting. "I always wanted an education, even when a girl," she said, "and when I was fourteen I had enough money to attend the Royalton Academy a year." Belva gave great credit to her mother for both moral and financial support. However, at fifteen, a lack of funds and her father's opposition compelled her to give up her education and teach in various area country schools. Her pay was ten shillings a week and "boarding around." Even in those early years, Belva was vexed that men teachers were paid more for the same work.

Belva was first married on November 8, 1848, shortly after she became eighteen, to a young neighbor farmer, Uriah H. McNall. They had a daughter Lura in 1849 before her husband died of a foot injury in 1853. The young widow sold the farm, sent Lura to her grandparents, and went back to school: first a year at the nearby Gasport (N.Y.) Academy and then to Genesee Wesleyan Seminary and Genesee College (later Syracuse University). In her last year at school, Belva heard and met Susan B. Anthony, who also resented the inferior position of women in American life. This meeting increased Belva's determination to work for women's rights.

After graduating from Genesee in 1857 with honors and a B.S., Belva was elected preceptress (principal) of the Lockport (N.Y.) Union School. For the next four years she supervised the small staff, taught, and, despite some disapproval, promoted gymnastics, public speaking, nature walks, and skating. The school code allowed her assistant men teachers to receive nearly twice the salary she was paid. When she protested this injustice, she was told by the minister's wife, "You can't help yourself; it is the way of the world." So she resigned. As she reported later, "Those words opened my eyes and raised my dander."

In 1866 Belva moved to Washington, D.C., opened a successful private school, and in 1868 married Dr. Ezekiel Lockwood, a former Baptist minister and dentist twenty-seven years her senior. He ran the school until it was closed because of his ill health. He died in 1877, again leaving Belva a widow. Their only child, Jesse, had died in infancy.

With her husband's encouragement, Belva had begun reading law. Her application to the law school of Columbia College was turned down on the traditional ground that her presence would distract the young men. After being rejected at Georgetown and Howard Universities as well, Belva, along with fourteen other women, gained admission to the newly established National University Law School in 1871. Only she and one other woman finished the course.

Even then, because of prejudice against women in the professions, the Law School finally refused to grant them diplomas; but after Belva wrote a spirited letter to President Grant, who was ex-officio president of the Law School, she received her diploma, signed by Grant himself. In September 1873, she was admitted to the District of Columbia bar, after overcoming the objection that she was a woman—and, in addition, a married woman.

In her law training, Lockwood had specialized in claims cases against the government; but because she was a woman, both the Court of Claims (1874) and the United States Supreme Court (1876) refused her admission. Undaunted, Lockwood pushed for the passage of legislation that would remove this restriction. In 1879, after her persistent lobbying, Congress enacted the "Lockwood Act" allowing women lawyers to practice before both the Supreme Court and the Court of Claims.

Some of the highlights of Lockwood's career include her successful efforts to obtain equal pay for women government workers (1872) and to secure equal property rights and equal guardianship of children for women in Washington, D.C. (1896). She also worked, unsuccessfully (1903), to include women's suffrage clauses in the statehood bills for Oklahoma, Arizona, and New Mexico. In 1906, she represented the Eastern Cherokee Indians, who were awarded $5 million in land claims against the government.

By the 1880s Lockwood was widely known for her work in the women's rights movement. She decided it was time for women to take political action and be nominated for public office. She contended that, while women could not vote, they could legally receive votes and, if elected, hold office. In 1884 the National Equal Rights Party nominated Belva Lockwood for president and Mrs. Marietta L. B. Stow for vice-president.

Lockwood's nomination was a daring act, designed to revive interest in women's rights. Her platform embraced all her interests—equal rights for all, including blacks, Indians, and immigrants; uniform marriage and divorce laws; reduction of the liquor traffic; and universal peace. The two most important leaders of women's suffrage, Susan B. Anthony and Elizabeth Cady Stanton, who supported James G. Blaine, the Republican nominee, opposed her campaign, which many ridiculed. Nevertheless, Lockwood ran a strong campaign, received 4,149 votes in six states, and claimed she was defrauded of more. She ran again in 1888 with less impressive results.

Belva Ann Bennett Lockwood: A Campaigning Woman (Continued)

Disappointed with politics and estranged from the major women's suffrage groups, Lockwood worked for international peace, attending nearly every major peace conference from 1890 to 1914 and serving on the nominating committee for the Nobel Peace Prize. She also lectured and was prominent both nationally and internationally in promoting women's rights, temperance, peace, and arbitration.

Lockwood lived her last years in severe financial difficulty. Her lucrative law practice faded, and irregularity in the Cherokee claims case forced her to return half of her legal fee. Most of her remaining money was lost when she entrusted it to an unscrupulous male admirer. Evicted from her large Washington home at the age of eighty-four, she lived on a pension provided by Andrew Carnegie. After a period of declining health, she died in Washington on May 19, 1917, and was buried in the Congressional Cemetery. Belva Lockwood had several lives and careers—teacher, lawyer, public speaker, wife, and mother—and her contribution to the cause of women's rights did not end with her death. She deserves to be remembered.

women) claimed a membership of 150,000 and was supporting such reforms as child welfare, education, and sanitation.

Of course, as we have seen, the participation of women in reforms was not new to the Gilded Age. Women had taken an active role in reform movements before the Civil War, and this momentum continued. Probably the strongest women's reform group of this era was the Woman's Christian Temperance Union (W.C.T.U.), formed in Cleveland in 1874 to fight the saloons and to promote prohibition of alcohol. The movement for prohibition had begun in the first half of the nineteenth century. By the time of the Gilded Age four states—Maine, New Hampshire, Vermont, and Kansas—had prohibition laws. The United States Supreme Court upheld such laws in 1847, but reversed itself in 1888 on the grounds that the interstate control of liquor belonged to Congress.

Frances E. Willard became the head of the W.C.T.U. in 1879 and began to campaign for legislation for the outright banning of strong drink. She also worked through schools and churches to arouse public opinion against liquor. Under her vigorous leadership the W.C.T.U. became the leading force in the prohibition movement. A generation of scholarship in women's history has demonstrated how inclusive Willard was in her political imagination. She convinced her organization to endorse women's suffrage; worked with other Gilded Age reformers on a broad array of issues; became a Socialist (though not of the Marxist variety); and galvanized grass roots, female political energy as did no other nineteenth-century woman leader.

In 1893, the Anti-Saloon League, comprised of both women and men, joined the antiliquor crusade. With pressure from the W.C.T.U., all states but two added the requirement of "scientific temperance instruction" to the school curriculum between 1882 and 1898. Many women who saw the saloon as an implacable foe were also aware of a number of other social problems—such as child labor, unsanitary housing, lack of public-health measures, and penal conditions that needed their support for reform—with prompting from Willard herself. Not all women, however, agreed that the increased activities of women meant progress. "What is this curious product of today, the American girl or woman?" asked a woman writer in 1880 in the *Atlantic Monthly*. "... Is it possible for any novel, within the next fifty years, truly to depict her as a finality, when she is still emerging from new conditions..., when she does not yet understand herself...?" She added, "The face of today is stamped with restlessness, wandering purpose, and self-consciousness."

▶ Frances E. Willard campaigned for legislation for the outright banning of strong drink. She also worked through schools and churches to arouse public opinion against alcohol.

Thus, by the end of the nineteenth century, increasing economic independence and more educational opportunities for women had enlarged their social freedom and widened their range of activity. They had gone far, but they had much farther to go.

From Hayes to Harrison

Hayes and the Presidency

An Electoral Commission chose Rutherford B. Hayes for president, and historians have portrayed him as a respectable mediocrity with an average capacity and an impeccable public and private life. True, there was no dramatic flair in his personality, and he lacked brilliance; however, he was a man of integrity and honest intentions, and his determination and steadfastness of purpose eventually frustrated even his bitterest foes. Hayes' presidency is an excellent illustration of how political party stalemate and equilibrium can hamper effective executive leadership. Hayes worked under severe handicaps that have not been fully appreciated.

His right to the office had been disputed, and Republicans and Democrats alike referred to him as "the *de facto* president" and "His Fraudulency." His programs for the South and for civil service reform, plus his show of independence, caused such a deep split within his own Republican Party that he was nearly read out of it. At one time Hayes had but three supporters in the Senate, one of them a lifelong friend and relative. Moreover, the Democrats controlled the House of Representatives throughout his administration and the Senate the last two years of his term. Under these circumstances, it is amazing that he could accomplish anything.

▶ President Rutherford B. Hayes

Hayes endeavored to reestablish presidential power and prestige and to redress the balance between the executive and legislative branches. He first challenged congressional dominance in the make-up of his cabinet when he picked men who were most unwelcome to the bosses, particularly the liberal Republican Carl Schurz for Secretary of the Interior and the Southern Democrat and former Confederate David M. Key for the important patronage-dispensing position of Postmaster General. At first the Senate balked and refused to confirm the entire cabinet list, but under much public pressure it finally gave in to the president.

Hayes gained another victory over congressional encroachment by refusing to yield the right given him by the Force Acts of 1870–1871 to intervene in federal elections in the states. Democratic majorities in Congress sought to nullify these Reconstruction laws by attaching to army appropriation bills riders aimed at removing federal supervision of elections. Hayes fought these attempts because they would have placed him under the "coercive dictation" of a "bare" majority in Congress and because he wanted to make the executive "an equal and independent branch of the government." He vetoed eight such bills, and Congress lacked enough votes to override him.

Hayes also struck a daring and spectacular blow for reform against the spoils system and its greatest champion, Senator Roscoe Conkling of New York. Hayes had already vexed the bosses with his inaugural statement: "He serves his party best who serves his country best," and he further angered them with his comment, "party leaders should have no more influence in appointments than other equally respectable citizens." He appointed a commission headed by John Jay of New York, grandson of the first Chief Justice, to investigate the largest patronage office in the federal service, the New York Custom House—long an example of the spoils system at its worst. The commission found that most of the employees had been appointed in the interest of the Conkling machine, that 20 percent of them were superfluous, and that the place was ridden with "ignorance, inefficiency, and corruption." When Conkling's lieutenants, Collector of the Port Chester A. Arthur and Naval Officer Alonzo B. Cornell, refused to clean up the corruption or to resign, Hayes boldly removed them and named two others to the posts. On Conkling's insistence the Senate refused to confirm the nominations, but Hayes persisted;within a year his choices were approved. He had won a battle, but he had not routed the spoilsmen.

Hayes Withdraws Troops from the South

Hayes removed the last of the federal troops from the South and ended military Reconstruction, acting to restore harmony between North and South and between whites and blacks. In

▶President Hayes appointed a commission to investigate New York Custom House the largest patronage office in the federal service

doing so, he responded to a general demand for a change in policy in the South. Hayes considered that Reconstruction governments had lost so much support that they had become completely unable to sustain themselves even with the use of force; and he dreamed of building in the South a strong Republican Party—one that would no longer depend upon the blacks for its main strength and that could command the esteem and support of Southern whites.

Hayes became the first Republican president to experiment with the plan of appointing regular Democrats to important posts in the South in the hope of gaining Republican success there. He seldom was credited with any honest motives, however, for the public in 1877—and many years later—believed this was part of the bargain that had made him president. In any case, his experiment was a sharp departure from the strategy of the Radicals during Reconstruction. Had it worked, the "solid South" as a Democratic stronghold might not have developed. As it was, however, the strategy did not work; and black people were left even more vulnerable than they had been previously, as Hayes' Democrat appointees in the South generally remained committed to segregation.

Depression and the Silver Question

When Hayes entered the presidency, the country was experiencing the worst years of a depression that had begun in 1873. Almost immediately he was confronted with the first great industrial conflict in our history—a railroad strike that began on the Baltimore and Ohio and spread through fourteen states, affecting two-thirds of the railroad mileage in the country outside New England and the South. At the request of four state governors, Hayes sent federal troops to intervene in the strike and restore order.

Hayes ran further afoul of labor, however, especially on the West Coast, when he vetoed a bill passed in 1879 to restrict Chinese immigration. He felt the bill violated the Burlingame Treaty of 1868, which had given the Chinese the right of unlimited immigration to the United States. Hayes sent a mission to China to negotiate a new treaty, and the resultant Treaty of 1880 gave the United States the right to regulate or suspend Chinese immigration. The Exclusion Act, passed by Congress in 1882, suspended such immigration for ten years.

President Hayes also took an unpopular stand on the currency question. Discontented agrarians, suffering from falling agricultural prices, wanted "cheap money" and inflationary monetary policies so as to bring about increases in the prices of agricultural products. Consequently, farmers favored the repeal or modification of the Resumption Act of 1875, which obligated the Treasury to redeem greenbacks in specie at full face value on January 1, 1879. Many predicted that such redemption would wreck the monetary system, for everyone would want gold rather than paper notes. Hayes, however, resisted the pressure and aided Secretary of the Treasury John Sherman in accumulating a gold reserve to redeem the currency. Greenback dollars, which were worth only sixty-seven cents in 1865, rose to one hundred cents before the deadline of resumption; and people, realizing this, preferred the notes that were easier to handle. Thus no run on the gold reserve developed.

Inflationists pushed demands for free coinage of silver, meaning that the federal government would purchase all the silver that could be mined and press it into coins, thus devaluing the currency and leading to a rise in agricultural prices. Once again, however, Hayes took the unpopular side. The old ratio between gold and silver had been 16 to 1, with sixteen times as much silver in a silver dollar as there was gold in a gold dollar. When the Gold Rush of 1849 lowered the price of gold, however, an ounce of silver became worth more than one-sixteenth of an ounce of gold; Americans sold their silver on the open market rather than have it coined at a loss. Silver dollars nearly disappeared from circulation, and in 1873 Congress abolished their coinage. The government discontinued the purchase of silver because no one was willing to sell silver to the government at the government-set price that was well below the market price. Farmers and miners, however, believed that the discontinuation of silver purchase by the government was some sort of plot against them and thus referred to the government action as the "Crime of '73." Subsequently, silver mines in Nevada, Arizona, and Colorado produced such large quantities of silver that the market price of silver fell below the government-set price; and miners and agrarians called for a return to the coinage of silver at the old ratio.

Hayes and the Republicans, however, were advocates of the gold standard, and Hayes opposed the resumption of silver coinage. Congress responded by passing over Hayes' veto in 1878 the Bland-Allison Act, authorizing the Treasury to purchase not less than $2 million and not more than $4 million worth of silver each month and coin it into dollars at the former gold/silver price ratio of 16 to 1. The act, however, did not fully meet the demands of the silverites, who demanded the "free and unlimited coinage of silver." Moreover, the Treasury, dominated by gold-advocate Republicans, consistently purchased only the minimum amount of silver required by the act.

The Election of 1880

With virtually no support among Democrats and some opposition from within his own party over Hayes' failure to fully support the spoils system, Hayes did not seek reelection; and the

Republican convention of 1880 was divided in its support. The "Stalwart" faction, which favored continuation of the spoils system, was led by Republican Party boss Roscoe Conkling and sought a third term for Ulysses S. Grant. James G. Blaine of Maine and John Sherman of Ohio, however, also had Republican supporters. Blaine was a leader of the opposing Republican faction in Congress known as the "Half-Breeds" that, at least in rhetoric, favored eliminating the spoils system, though Blaine's own political career appeared just as spoils-oriented as Conkling's when placed under the microscope. When it became clear that none of the three could secure a majority, the delegates nominated Congressman James A. Garfield of Ohio, a "Half-Breed," on the thirty-sixth ballot of the Republican Party Convention.

To appease the Stalwarts, second place on the Republican ticket went to one of Conkling's closest associates, Chester A. Arthur, whom Hayes in 1878 had dismissed as head of the New York Custom House in reaction to a scandal involving Custom House corruption. When Samuel J. Tilden, who had won the popular vote for the Democrats in 1876, declined to run, the Democrats picked General Winfield Scott Hancock, a Pennsylvanian and a Union hero in the Battle of Gettysburg. His running mate was William H. English of Indiana.

The platforms of the two parties revealed few basic differences on policy and no real understanding of the country's problems. Despite the failure of the major parties to discuss the vital issues of the day, less than 4 percent of the electorate voted for a protest party candidate—General James B. Weaver of Iowa of the Greenback Labor Party, which advocated inflationary policies and stricter federal regulation of interstate commerce.

The campaign, which turned largely on personalities and irrelevant issues, produced a great deal of sound and fury but nothing of importance. Five-sixths of the voters turned out, and Garfield won by fewer than forty thousand popular votes, although his electoral vote was 214 as compared to 155 for Hancock. With Garfield's election, the Republicans had retained the White House, but their margin in the popular vote was razor-thin, reflecting

MAP 18.1 Presidential Election of 1880

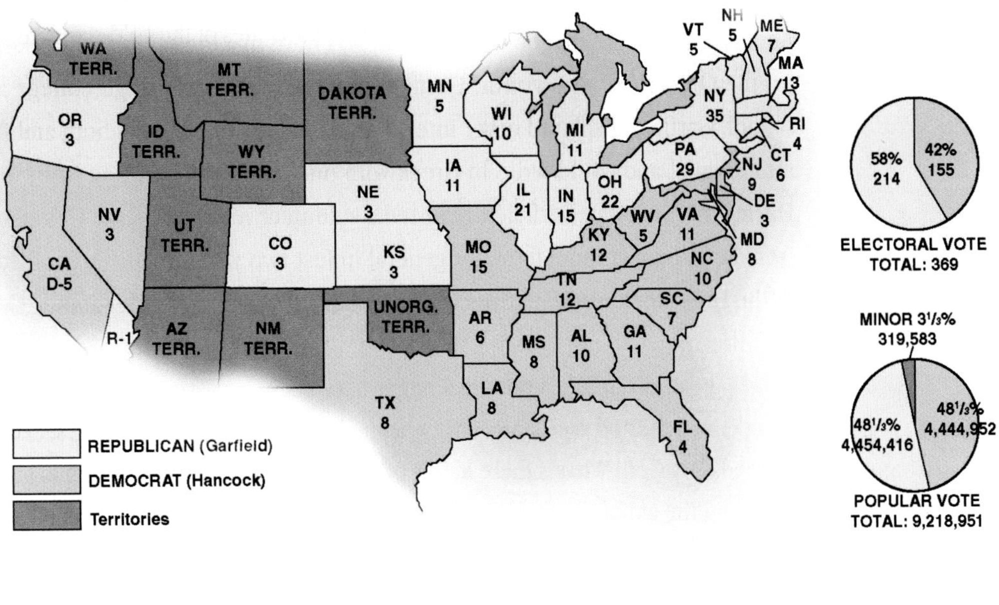

▶James A. Garfield and his family. Garfield was later assassinated by way of a gunshot wound to the belly and died from infection, leaving Chester Arthur to the presidency for the remainder of the term.

the close balance between the two major parties that had been reflected in 1876 and would continue throughout the Gilded Age. The Republican victory also reflected the sectional nature of the parties that had developed in 1860 with the Republicans carrying the northern states, but the Democrats dominating the South. The Republicans, however, won slim majorities in both Houses of Congress, setting them up for what they believed would be a productive four years.

Garfield and Arthur

The new president, James Garfield, had been an effective speaker and an able party leader in the House; many historians argue that if there were a president during the Gilded Age that might have achieved greatness, it was Garfield. Garfield draws many comparisons to Abraham Lincoln in that he, like Lincoln, was born in a log cabin and worked as a laborer on the Ohio canal as a youth. Garfield put himself first through college and then law school. Garfield displayed other interesting talents in that he was both ambidextrous and multilingual and could write in Greek with one hand while writing Latin with the other. During the Civil War, Garfield organized a volunteer regiment of the Union Army and rose from lieutenant colonel to major general in just two years. In 1863, Garfield was elected to the House of Representatives where he quickly became a leader among the Republican Half-Breeds.

As great as Garfield's potential might have been, however, many of his contemporaries found him timid and vacillating. Overwhelmed with the demands of office seekers, he once exclaimed, "My God! What is there in this place that a man should ever want to get into it?" After accepting the aid of the Stalwarts during the campaign and apparently reaching some understanding with them on patronage matters, Garfield antagonized Roscoe Conkling by making

Conkling's great rival, James G. Blaine, Secretary of State and by appointing another Conkling opponent in New York Collector of the Port.

In the ensuing fight between President Garfield and the Stalwarts, Conkling and his colleague from New York, Thomas "Me Too" Platt, resigned their seats in the Senate and were not reelected by the New York legislature. At the height of the conflict, on July 2, 1881, Charles J. Guiteau, a disappointed office seeker who was mentally unbalanced, shot Garfield at a Washington railroad station and shouted, "I am a Stalwart and Arthur is president now." Attending physicians assured Garfield that he would survive, to which Garfield famously replied, "I'm a dead man." Doctors were unable to find the bullet in Garfield's abdomen, and Alexander Graham Bell was even invited in to search for the bullet with his newly invented metal detector. Garfield died of infection from the wound on September 19, and Chester Arthur became president of the United States.

The certifiably insane Guiteau was tried for murder and executed, but not before he revealed his deranged nature at his trial. Guiteau evidently suffered from illusions of grandeur and believed that God had planned for him some special destiny. Guiteau credited himself with Garfield's election; and then, when Garfield refused to appoint him to the position he desired, he viewed Garfield as "blocking his destiny." Guiteau pleaded "insanity by Divine power, " stating that "It was God's act, not mine," and claiming, "God told me to kill." Guiteau's final words at the gallows were reportedly, "I am going to the Lordy."

To many Americans the succession of Arthur was a calamity, for he had the reputation of a New York machine politician. Reformers shuddered at the thought of a spoilsman in the presidency, and there was a widespread feeling that the Stalwarts would take over. In spite of his unsavory reputation and political career as a defender of the spoils system, Arthur was personally honest and did have administrative abilities. The responsibilities and dignity of the high office caused him to rise to the occasion and to give the country a good administration. He did not turn over the patronage to Conkling, as many thought he would. Furthermore, he supported civil service reform, thus abandoning his previous po-

▶ A caricature of Charles J. Guiteau. Guiteau was a mentally unbalanced, disappointed office seeker who shot and killed President Garfield at a Washington railroad station. The assassin claimed God had told him to kill, but was found guilty and executed by hanging.

sition on the issue and alienating the Stalwarts in his own party that had supported his nomination for vice president. Arthur prosecuted frauds in the post office, cleared the way for the construction of a modern navy, and had the Chinese immigration question settled, though in a way that modern Americans find unacceptable. He also tried to bring about a reduction in the tariff and to check federal spending on unnecessary public works by vetoing an $18 million rivers-and-harbors bill, but Congress defeated both efforts.

The Civil Service Act

The most important legislation during Arthur's presidency was the Pendleton Civil Service Act of 1883. Since the end of the Civil War, reformers had been denouncing the spoils system and advocating the establishment of a permanent civil service where government jobs would be awarded based on merit rather than party affiliation. Garfield's murder dramatically advanced their cause by shocking the public into believing there was something dreadfully wrong with the patronage system if crazed office seekers were shooting the president. The Pendleton Act authorized the president to appoint a Civil Service Commission of three members to provide "open competitive examinations for testing the fitness of applicants for the public service now classified or to be classified." In addition, the act forbade the levying of political campaign assessments on federal officeholders and protected them against ouster for failure to make such contributions.

At first the act affected only the lowest offices—about fourteen thousand, or 12 percent of the total number of federal employees—leaving the remainder under the spoils system; but the president was given authority to extend the classified list at his discretion. Arthur demonstrated good faith by making excellent appointments to the Commission. Every subsequent president extended the classified list to protect the jobs of those whom he had appointed to office, and at the end of the century it included 40 percent of all federal positions. By the end of World War II, approximately 90 percent of federal jobs would be Civil Service jobs with political appointees typically occupying only the upper echelon of the federal bureaucracy.

The Election of 1884

In 1884 the Republicans turned their backs on Arthur, who was also ill with a disease (probably cancer) that would take his life two years later, and nominated Half-Breed leader James G. Blaine of Maine for president. The Democrats named Grover Cleveland, a former mayor of Buffalo and governor of New York, their nominee. Cleveland was most famous at the time for vetoing a bill that would have reduced fares charged by the New York City elevated railway. According to Cleveland, the bill was unconstitutional government interference into private business. Cleveland was also viewed as honest, and his popularity soared among conservative Democrats.

Though a Half-Breed and theoretically against the spoils system, Blaine had been connected with the granting of favors to the Little Rock and Fort Smith Railroad, perhaps in exchange for "gifts." Viewing Blaine as an old guard politician inimical to good government, William Curtis, Carl Schurz, and other reformist mugwumps bolted the Republican Party and supported Cleveland. As in 1880, few real issues were discussed, and the campaign degenerated into one of personal abuse and vilification. "The public is angry and abusive," observed Henry Adams. "Everyone takes part. We are all doing our best, and swearing like demons. But the amusing thing is that no one talks about real issues." The Democrats publicized the "Mulligan letters" to prove that Blaine, as Speaker of the House, had been guilty of unethical conduct in connection with land-grant railroads; and the Republicans retaliated with the charge that Cleveland was the father of an illegitimate child. At Cleveland's rallies, Republican hecklers chanted, "Ma, Ma, where's my pa?" Cleveland, however, turned the accusation to his favor by showing that he had supported the child over the years and taken responsibility for his mistakes. In retaliation, Democrats pointed out that Blaine's wife had been pregnant when the two married and that Cleveland had not required a shotgun to stir his conscience. To the chant of "Ma, Ma, where's my pa?" Democrats added, "Gone to the White House, ha, ha, ha!" Cleveland had also twice played the role of hangman as sheriff of Erie County, New York in the 1870s. Cleveland himself had affixed the noose around the neck of the condemned and pulled the lever. The idea of a "hangman president" was unsettling to a few. Blaine, however, had even greater problems within his own party where many Stalwarts refused to support his candidacy. When Stalwart leader Roscoe Conkling was asked if he planned to support his party's nominee, he replied that he would not support Blaine because "I do not engage in criminal activities." Democrats heckled Blaine rallies with chants of "Blaine, Blaine, James G. Blaine, Continental Liar from the state of Maine."

MAP 18.2 Presidential Election of 1884

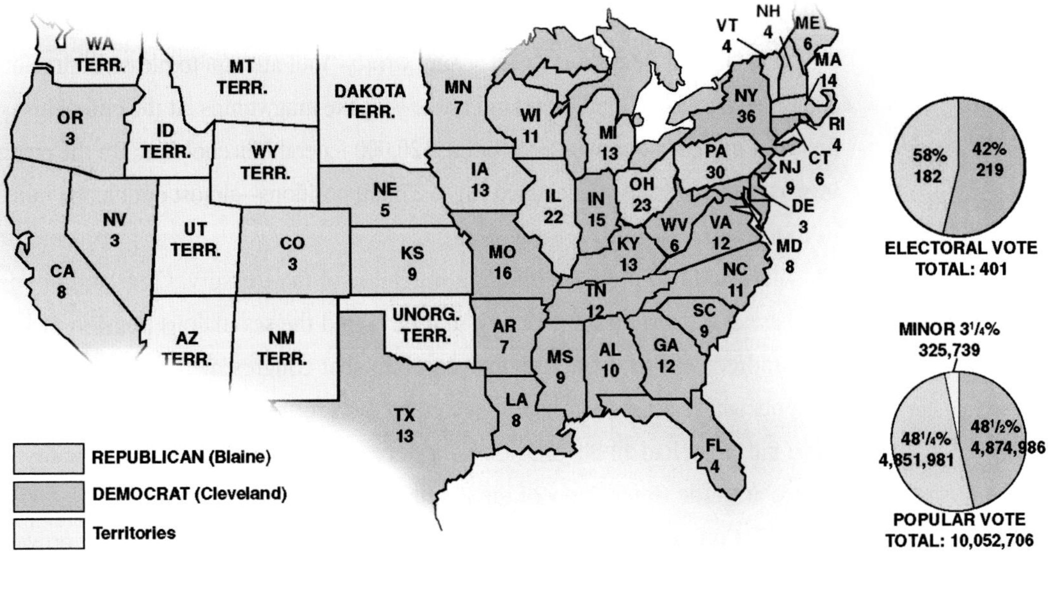

Overall, the decision in 1884 was even closer than in 1880. Cleveland's plurality in popular votes was only 29,000 and his electoral vote was 219 to Blaine's 182. So narrow was the margin of victory for Cleveland that he carried the pivotal state of New York by a mere 1,149 votes. Two weeks prior to the election, a Protestant Blaine campaign worker in New York City referred to the Democrats as the party of "Rum, Romanism, and Rebellion." Many viewed this, of course, as a slur against the Catholic Church, and New York City, in particular, had a large Catholic population. Whether or not that slur cost Blaine the votes needed in New York City to win the state of New York cannot be known, but less than six hundred votes cast the other direction in New York would have given Blaine the victory. It is at least possible that without that speech, James G. Blaine would have been president of the United States. It was said that no candidate could slur the Catholic Church and expect to win New York.

Cleveland and the Presidency

Cleveland, a strapping figure of well over two hundred pounds, came to the White House in 1885 with a reputation as a reformer and a man of courage, integrity, and prodigious work habits. Actually he was unimaginative, stolid, obdurate, and brutally candid; and he lacked a sense of timing. He was also a thoroughgoing conservative, a believer in sound money, and a defender of property rights. In his inaugural he promised to adhere to "business principles," and his cabinet included conservatives and business-minded Democrats of the East and South. His administration signified no break with his Republican predecessors on fundamental issues. A statement that Cleveland made when vetoing $10,000 in federal drought relief for farmers best sums up his philosophy of government: "People should support the Government. The Government should not support the people."

Cleveland faced the task of pleasing both the mugwumps and the hungry spoilsmen of his own party, who had been cut off from federal patronage for twenty-four years. At first he refused to yield to the bosses on appointments and, thereby, won the acclaim of reformers; but faced with a revolt within his own party, Cleveland gave in to the spoilsmen and replaced Republicans with "honest Democrats." Carl Schurz wrote, "Your attempt to please both reformers and spoilsmen has failed," and Cleveland broke with the mugwumps. At the end of his presidency he had removed about two-thirds of the 120,000 federal officeholders. On the credit side, he increased the civil service classified list to 27,380 positions—almost double the number when he took office.

Cleveland had more success as a watchdog of the treasury. Cleveland opposed silver purchase as a drain on the treasury, and he halted the scandalous pension racket by vetoing hundreds of private military pension bills that congressmen pushed through for constituents whose claims had been rejected by the Pension Office. Cleveland signed more of these bills than had all his predecessors since Johnson, but he was also the first president to veto any. The Grand Army of the Republic (G.A.R.) screamed at the vetoes; and in January 1887, Congress responded by passing a Dependent Pension Bill, which provided a pen-

▶ The Grand Army of the Republic (GAR) was an organization made up of discharged disabled veterans of the Union army who served in the Civil War.

sion for all honorably discharged disabled veterans who had served as little as three months in the Union army, irrespective of how they had become disabled. Cleveland vetoed it and thus angered the G.A.R.

Aside from the Interstate Commerce Act, for which Cleveland deserves no credit and which he signed with reluctance and "with reservations," little significant legislation was enacted during his term. He did not compel railroad, lumber, and cattle companies to give up 81 million acres of public land that they had fraudulently occupied. In Cleveland's view, Congress was the legislative branch and, therefore, should lead in policy while the president's job, as chief executive, was to carry out policy made elsewhere. In 1886 Congress passed a presidential Succession Law: after the vice-president, the succession should pass to the members of the cabinet, beginning with the secretary of state, in the order of the creation of their departments. In 1887 the Dawes Act was passed, initiating a new Indian policy, but Cleveland did not take the lead in Indian policy either.

The Tariff Issue

Cleveland devoted his entire annual message of December 1887 to the tariff question, advocating a drastic reduction in duties. The federal government at the time enjoyed a surplus, and Cleveland viewed the government surplus largely as an invitation for Congress to waste money. The Democratic-controlled House responded with a low tariff measure; but the Republican-dominated Senate turned it down and passed a highly protective bill that the House would not accept. This led to a deadlock and the injection of the tariff question into the 1888 election. For the first time in that era, both major parties were forced to take a position on the tariff issue. Northern Republicans, typically, supported high tariffs as a measure to support Northern manufacturing against foreign competition, while Southerners tended to favor lower tariffs in an effort to induce Europeans to lower tariffs as well and, thus, boost Southern agricultural exports to Europe.

The Election of 1888

The Democrats renominated President Cleveland and chose the elderly ex-Senator Allen G. Thurman of Ohio as his running mate. The Republicans nominated Senator Benjamin Harrison of Indiana, the grandson of former president and hero of Tippecanoe, William Henry Harrison, for president, and Levi P. Morton, a wealthy New York banker, for vice-president. Harrison had run unsuccessfully for the governorship of Indiana in 1876, but he was elected to the United States Senate in 1880. Harrison had fought for the Union under General Sherman and gained a reputation as a stern military disciplinarian. Two labor parties, voicing the industrial unrest of the period, entered the campaign. Union Labor and United Labor condemned the major parties for being under the control of monopolies and for being indifferent to the welfare of workers.

The campaign was waged largely on the tariff issue, with Republicans defending protection and Democrats advocating a reduction of duties. The Republicans appealed to the manufacturing interests, who would profit from a high tariff, and to veterans, who were promised generous pension legislation. The Republican candidate Harrison, announced that he was opposed to reducing the tariffs because he was opposed to "cheaper costs" and that "cheaper costs" necessarily led to a "cheaper man and woman under the coat." Both parties used money freely as throughout the country voters were bribed in one of the most corrupt presidential elections in our history. Although Cleveland had a plurality of more than 90,000 popular votes, Harrison carried the crucial states of Indiana, New York, and Ohio and gained 233 electoral votes to Cleveland's 168. The decisive factors were probably the efficiency of the Republican organization and the purchase of the floating vote in the doubtful states.

MAP 18.3 Presidential Election of 1888

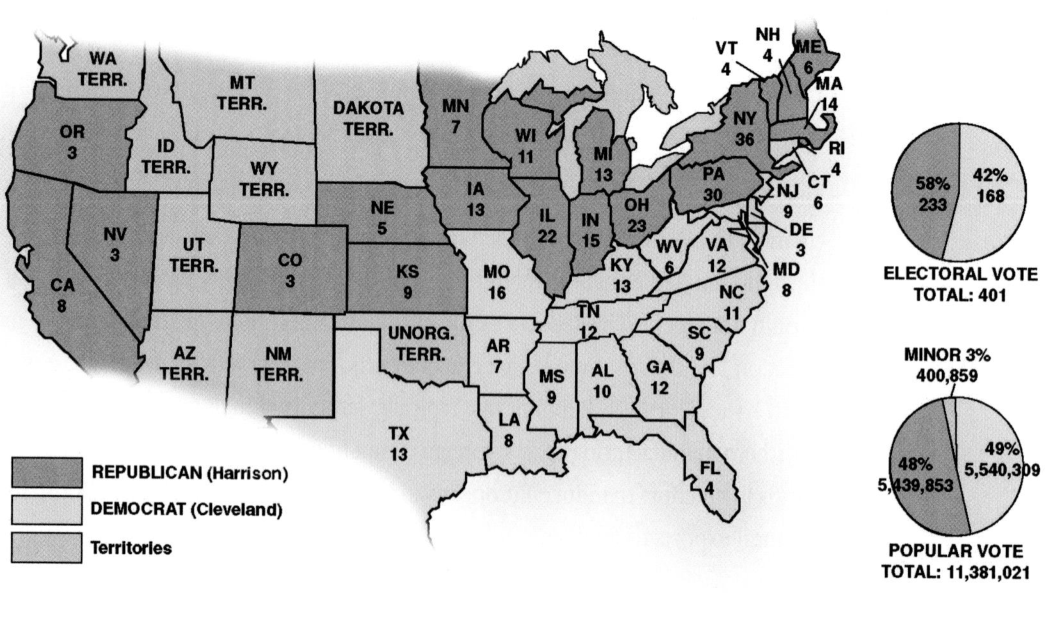

Harrison and the Republicans

Harrison possessed intellectual and oratorical gifts, but he was very cold in his personal relationships. "Harrison sweats ice water" became a popular phrase. One of his close associates remarked, "Harrison can make a speech to ten thousand men and every man of them will go away his friend. Let him meet the same ten thousand in private, and every one will go away his enemy." Harrison's unflattering nickname on Capitol Hill became "the human iceberg." Theodore Roosevelt, whom Harrison appointed to the Civil Service Commission, referred to Harrison as a "cold-blooded, narrow-minded, prejudiced, obstinate, timid old psalm-singing Indianapolis politician."

Although Harrison had ability, he lacked forcefulness; the leadership passed largely to the Republican leaders in Congress, especially to Senator Nelson W. Aldrich of Rhode Island and Speaker of the House Thomas B. Reed of Maine. Reed pushed, through the House, a revision of the rules that gave him almost dictatorial powers over proceedings and earned him the title of "czar."

▶ Congress earned itself the label "the Billion Dollar Congress" by handing out so much money that by 1894 the Treasury surplus was gone. The United States has never had a surplus since.

For the first time since 1875, the Republicans had the presidency and a majority in both houses of Congress, and they began to pay off their political debts. The McKinley Tariff of 1890 raised rates to a higher level and protected more products than any previous tariff in American history. In the same year the Dependent Pension Act, substantially the same measure vetoed by Cleveland, granted pensions to all G.A.R. veterans that suffered from any disability, acquired in war service or not, and to their widows and children. In the same year, to meet the demands of the silverites, the Sherman Silver Purchase Act increased the amount of silver to be purchased by the Treasury to 4.5 million ounces a month. To appease the popular clamor against monopolies, the Sherman Antitrust Act was also passed in 1890.

This same Congress earned itself the label "the Billion Dollar Congress." By distributing subsidies to steamship lines, passing extravagant rivers-and-harbors bills, offering large premiums to government bondholders, and returning federal taxes paid by Northern states during the Civil War, it handed out so much money that by 1894 the Treasury surplus was gone. The United States has never had a surplus since.

Instead of the widespread support that such policies were expected to bring, the public reaction was one of hostility; and in the congressional elections of 1890, the Republicans were severely rebuked. They retained only 88 of the 332 seats in the House and had their majority in the Senate reduced from 14 to 6. The appearance of nine new congressmen representing farm interests and not associated with either of the major parties indicated that a third-party revolt was shaping up. A new phase in American politics was under way.

The Agrarian Revolt

The Plight of the Farmer

The third-party revolt took the form of an agrarian insurgency in the West and South, that had been coming on since the Civil War and reached its culmination in the 1890s. There were a number of causes for agrarian discontent. The conversion of American agriculture to a commercial basis made the farmer a specialist whose role was to produce a surplus by which the United States could adjust an unfavorable balance of trade. Unlike the manufacturer, however, the farmer had no control over his market or his prices. He worked alone and competed with other farmers, American and foreign. Instead of benefiting from the new order of things, he was one of its victims.

Prices for agricultural products had declined. Between 1870 and 1897, wheat prices dropped from $1.06 to 63.6 cents a bushel, corn from 43.1 to 29.7 cents a bushel, and cotton from 15.1 to 5.8 cents a pound. These were the market prices after warehouse and transportation charges had been added. The net prices paid to the farmer were even lower. Farmers of the "old" Northwest received only 42 cents a bushel for wheat that government economists estimated cost 45.1 cents a bushel to produce. In Kansas, in 1889, corn sold for 10 cents a bushel and was commonly used for fuel, and in 1890 a farmer in Nebraska shot his hogs because he could neither sell nor give them away.

Rural and Urban Population Trends, 1860–1940

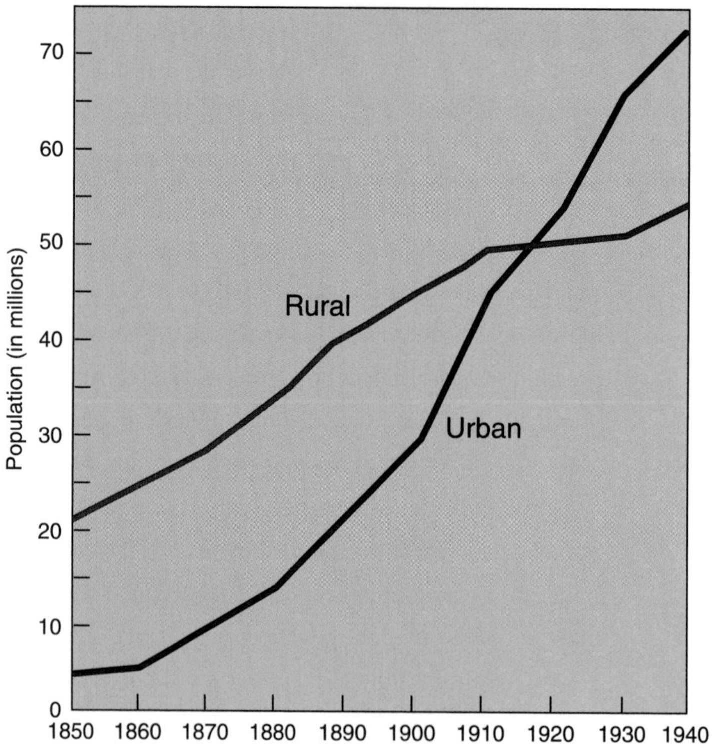

Farmers increasingly were shackled with debts and loss of proprietorship over their land. In 1900, nearly one-third of the country's farms were mortgaged. In the Middle West the percentages were highest—45 percent in Wisconsin, 48 percent in Michigan, and 53 percent in Iowa. Mortgages were few in the South because of the crop-lien system, by which local merchants advanced seed, equipment, and personal necessities to planters in return for a first lien on the planter's future cotton crop. Throughout the country, the number of tenant farmers increased from 25.9 percent of all the farms in 1880 to 29.4 percent in 1890 and to 35.3 percent in 1900. In Kansas, in the 1880s, wagons were seen moving east with the signs, "In God we trusted, but in Kansas we busted."

The basic cause of the farmer's misfortune was an overexpansion in agricultural production. In addition to the continuing increase in agricultural production, the number of farmers also kept going up. Between 1860 and 1890, the number of farms increased from 2 million to 4.5 million, the wheat crop from 173 million bushels to 449 million, and the cotton from 5.3 million bales to 8.5 million. Supply was outrunning demand, and the farmers were falling behind in the economic race. To make matters worse, total economic growth in the United States exceeded the growth of the money supply, thus inflating the value of the American dollar but causing price deflation in agricultural goods.

The farmers blamed, most particularly, the railroads, the middlemen, and the banks. Most vociferously, they resented railroad rate differentials and discriminations against them. On through routes and long hauls, rates were low, because the railroads competed with one another; but on local or short hauls where there was little or no competition, rates were high. Sometimes the Western local rate was four times that charged for the same distance and commodity in the East where rail lines were more numerous. Farmers paid more to ship their grain from Minnesota towns to St. Paul or Minneapolis than a shipper in Minneapolis had to pay for a haul to New York. In addition, farmers resented the way railroads favored shippers and dominated state politics.

The farmers also believed themselves to be at the mercy of the middlemen—local merchants, grain dealers, brokers, and speculators. The national banks' rules precluded loans on real estate and farm property, and the banks did not respond to the farmers' seasonal needs for money. Due to the currency shortage that plagued the Gilded Age, interest rates soared to as high as 36 percent due to the demand for money that exceeded supply. Farmers, however, ignorant of the market forces around them, viewed the high interest rates as a plot by bankers to take their farms.

The farmers also complained that they bore the brunt of the tax burden. The merchants could underestimate the value of their stock, householders might exclude some of their property, and the owners of securities could conceal them; but the farmers could not hide their land. Finally, the protective tariff hurt the farmers because they purchased manufactured goods in a highly protected market and sold their crops in an unprotected one. They shared none of the benefits of protection and withstood all of the liabilities. Instead, in their view, they contributed heavily to the subsidization of business. This injustice was all the more difficult to bear in view of their belief that the tariff was "the mother of trusts."

The Granger Movement

Feeling that they were being left behind and believing that politicians were indifferent and even hostile to their interests, farmers decided to organize and protest against their condition. In 1867 Oliver Hudson Kelley, a government clerk, founded National Grange of the Patrons of Husbandry, which became better known as the Grange. Kelley began the organization as a social organization that farmers could use to share information about new technology and common problems; however, the farmers quickly saw in the Grange a weapon with which to fight their foes. By 1874, its peak year, the Grange had an estimated membership of 1.5 million. The Grangers established a number of cooperatives in an effort to eliminate the profits of the middleman, but mismanagement and business opposition doomed most of them.

▶Farmers felt they were being left behind and believed politicians to be unsupportive of their interests and decided to organize and protest. Oliver Hudson Kelley, a government clerk, founded National Grange of the Patrons of Husbandry, (the Grange) in order to protect the farmers' way of life.

Although the Grange officially declared itself "nonpolitical," individual members joined various agrarian third parties organized in the Midwest. In coalition with either the Democrats or the Republicans, these third parties gained control of several state legislatures and enacted granger laws to regulate the rates charged by grain elevators and railroads. The new regulations favored by the Grangers were challenged in the courts; but in *Munn v. Illinois* in 1877, the most important of these cases, the Supreme Court upheld the "police power" of the state regulation.

After 1875, Grange membership decreased rapidly. Out of the twenty thousand local granges extant in 1874, only four thousand remained in 1880. Many farmers had been attracted by the novelty and vogue of the Grange, and others had believed it would provide a panacea for all their ills. They left when they found there was not immediate and universal success.

The Greenback Movement

Farmers next were attracted to the Greenback movement, which advocated the circulation of paper money. From 1867 to 1872, Eastern labor dominated the movement, and its primary objectives then were to lower the interest rate on money and to reduce taxation. After 1873, farmers favored an expansion of the currency in the hope that it would bring higher prices for their products. When the panic of 1873 intensified the agricultural depression and the Granger movement failed to relieve the situation, farmers took over the Greenback movement. Its high-water mark was the election of fifteen congressmen in 1878; but with the resumption of specie payment in 1879 and with the rise of the price of corn in 1880, farmers lost interest in Greenbackism, and its support rapidly declined. In the presidential election of 1880 the Greenback candidate, James B. Weaver of Iowa, received only 300,000 votes, about three percent of the total. By 1888 the Greenback Party was dead.

The Farmers' Alliance

With the decline of the Grange and the disappearance of Greenbackism, a new set of farm groups appeared. Most important were the Farmers' Alliances, two distinct organizations of different origins. Milton George in Chicago organized the Northwestern Alliance in 1880, while the Southern Alliance was formed in 1875 in a frontier county of Texas for protection against horse thieves and land sharks. It remained small until 1886, when it expanded throughout the South under the vigorous leadership of C. W. Macune and absorbed rival farmers' organizations. For blacks, there was a Farmers' National Alliance and Cooperative Union.

The Alliances experimented with cooperatives more than the Grange had, but with no greater success. A merger of the Northwestern and the Southern Alliance was unsuccessfully attempted in a meeting at St. Louis in 1889. The Southern Alliance insisted upon the retention of its secret rituals and the exclusion of blacks, at least from the national body. The Northwestern Alliance wanted a federation in which each organization would keep its identity.

Then, the Southern Alliance changed its name to the National Farmers' Alliance and Industrial Union and induced the three strongest state alliances of the Northwestern Alliance, those of Kansas and North and South Dakota, to join. Due to its support for urban workers, the National Farmers' Alliance then gained the endorsement of the Knights of Labor.

The Emergence of Populism

Though the Alliances proclaimed themselves nonpolitical organizations, they issued demands each year that could be realized only by political means. For example, the Ocala, Florida, platform of 1890 called for the abolition of national banks, establishment of sub-treasuries, a graduated income tax, direct election of United States senators, lower tariffs, federal grain warehouses, and government control of communication and transportation facilities.

By 1890, the Northwestern Alliance concluded that nonpartisan activities were a failure and, therefore, decided to enter electoral politics. Kansas led the way by organizing the People's (Populist) Party in June 1890, and Alliancemen in other Western states set up independent parties under other names. Suddenly, the West was in the throes of a mighty political party upheaval. A later commentator called it "a pentecost of politics in which a tongue of flame sat upon every man and each spoke as the spirit gave him utterance."

"Sockless" Jerry Simpson, Ignatius Donnelly, Mary Elizabeth Lease, Annie L. Diggs, and General James B. Weaver were among the leaders of Western Populism. That party, though hastily constructed, was successful in three states. In Kansas it elected five congressmen and one senator in the 1890 elections. In Nebraska, it gained control of both houses of the legislature and elected two congressmen, and in South Dakota it elected a senator.

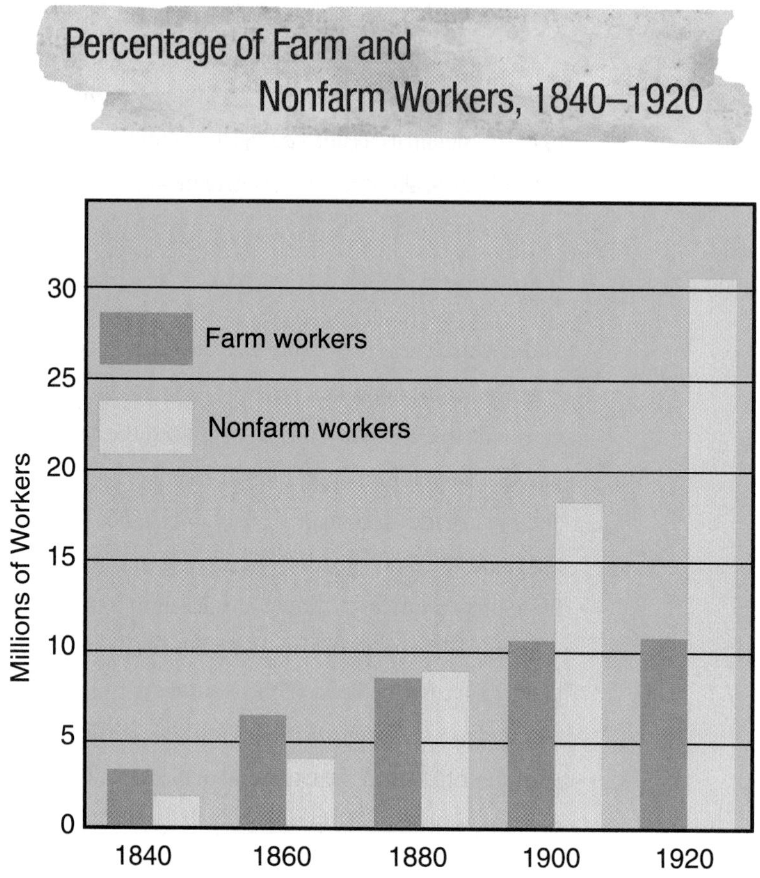

In the South, the Alliance feared that the establishment of a third political party might split the white vote and bring the Republicans and their black supporters into power again. At first the Alliance tried to gain control of the Democratic Party machinery. It attacked the industrial and urban leadership of the Democrats and endorsed candidates who pledged themselves to the Ocala platform. The Alliance appeared to have captured the Democratic Party in the elections of 1890 when four governors, eight state legislatures, forty-four congressmen, and three senators promised to support Alliance demands; but after the election nearly all these elected officials reverted to Democratic orthodoxy once in office. This disillusioning experience, plus the prospects of Cleveland's renomination by the Democratic Party, stimulated Southern Alliancemen to become Populists. In July 1892 the national People's Party was formally organized in Omaha.

Populist Ideology

Populist ideology of the nineteenth century was a combination of anti-elitism, plot mentality, paranoia, and elements of rational reform. Populists viewed American society as corrupt and in decay and believed in the myth of a better vantage time from a bygone era to which they desired to return. The Populists believed that they could redirect society to the just and stable course that would benefit the common people, whom they viewed as the moral backbone of America. The Populists harbored animosity toward intellectuals—in the form of scientists, economists, and the media—and hysterically denounced their political enemies—

the railroads, bankers, grain elevators, intellectuals, scientists, and middlemen of all forms as plotting against them. The Populists also viewed themselves as putting the power back into the hands of the common people; and their means of doing so was through the implementation of direct primaries, ballot initiatives and referendums, and direct election of United States senators, whom they viewed as elites out of touch with the common man. The Populists also favored free silver, the inclusion of blacks in the political process, the eight-hour day, and the elimination of the Pinkertons detective agency, which they viewed as a tool of elites to oppress the common man. The Populist goal was to build a coalition of farmers, miners, urban workers, and blacks who would overthrow the rule of elites in favor of rule by the common man.

The Election of 1892

The Populist platform of 1892 restated earlier Alliance demands, including the free and unlimited coinage of silver at the ratio of 16 to 1; government ownership and operation of railroads and the telephone, telegraph, and postal systems; prohibition of alien ownership of land; restriction of immigration; and a graduated income tax. The death of L. L. Polk of North Carolina, just before the convention met in Omaha on July 4, probably deprived the Populists of their strongest candidate. They nominated General James B. Weaver of Iowa for president and General James G. Field of Virginia for vice-president. Both Cleveland and Harrison were renominated by the major parties. Their running mates were Adlai E. Stevenson of Illinois and Whitelaw Reid, editor of the New York *Tribune*.

The free silver plank was the only exciting issue in the campaign, and Weaver polled 1,040,000 popular votes and 22 electoral votes. Populists became the first third party since the Civil War to break into the Electoral College—winning the states of Kansas, Colorado, Idaho, and Nevada. Furthermore, Populist governors were elected in Kansas and North Dakota. They also elected ten representatives, five senators, three governors, and fifteen hundred members of state legislatures. Populists were unsuccessful, however, in their attempt to lure urban workers who feared job competition from black workers. In the end, it is evident that the appeal of the Populists was strongest among miners who favored free silver. In terms of the major parties. Cleveland defeated Harrison with 277 to 145 electoral votes and 5,555,426 to 5,182,690 popular votes. Cleveland won his second term in office as president, but he had won the popular vote for the presidency for the third straight time.

Cleveland and the Depression of 1893

Shortly after Cleveland assumed the presidency in 1893, the country began to experience the worst financial panic in years. Following the failure of a number of prominent firms, most notably the Philadelphia and Reading Railroad and the National Cordage Company, the stock market suddenly collapsed. Banks, which had invested heavily in the stock market, called in their loans; and credit evaporated. Consequently, businesses failed daily; runs on banks followed; and before the year was out, five hundred banks, including Baring Brothers of London, and nearly sixteen thousand businesses had gone into bankruptcy. This included over one

MAP 18.4 Populist Strength (1892)

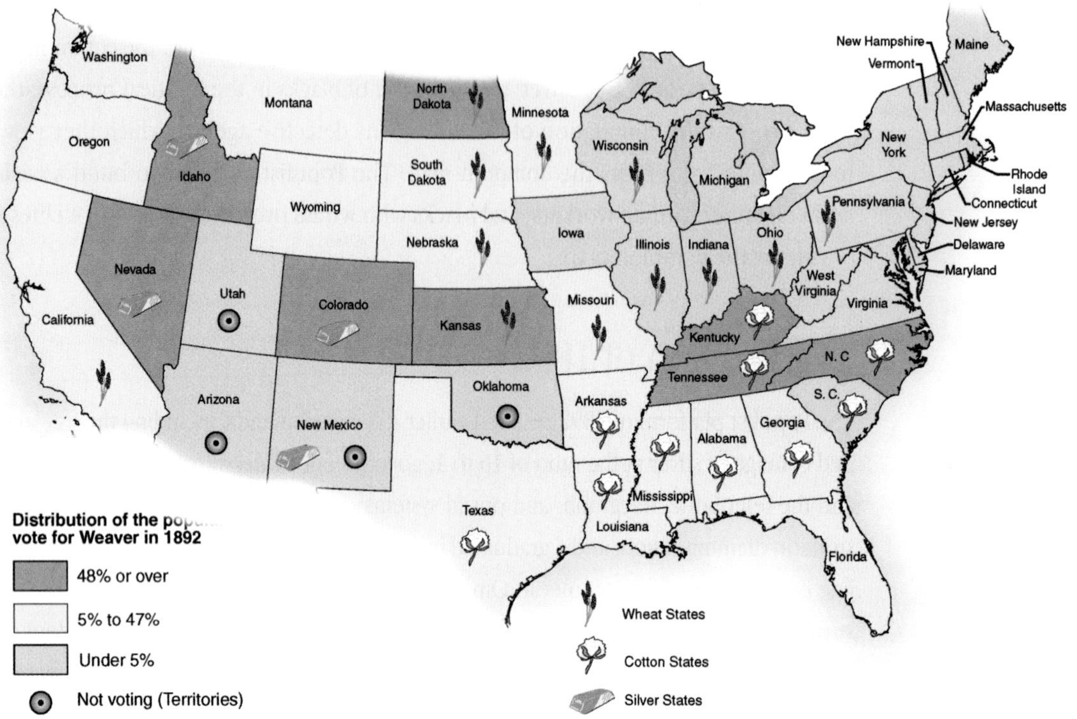

hundred fifty railroads. An estimated one million workers became unemployed, approximately 20 percent of the workforce. The bank collapses produced a capital shortage in the economy, and corporations could not find the loans necessary to operate. According to the *Commercial and Financial Chronicle*, never before had there been such a sudden and striking cessation of industrial activity, and no part of the nation escaped it. Everywhere mills, factories, furnaces, and mines closed down in large numbers, and hundreds of thousands of workers lost their jobs. By the fall of 1893, the *Banker's Magazine* of London reported the American people to be "in the throes of a fiasco unprecedented even in their broad experience" and declared, "ruin and disaster run riot over the land."

The panic developed into a major depression, but there was no agreement at the time as to its causes. Conservative business leaders attributed it to the Sherman Silver Purchase Act and to radical attacks on property. Labor leaders and agrarians blamed it on the capitalists, the Democrats blamed the Republicans, and the Republicans accused the Democrats.

There had been periodic panics followed by depressions ever since the end of the Civil War, and in each instance, reckless speculation over-inflated stock market values. The over-inflated market was then followed by a collapse in confidence, with attendant business failures and unemployment. The primary cause for the debacle of 1893 was the overexpansion of transportation facilities and industrial production, accompanied by stock manipulation and reckless speculation. Following the pattern of previous recessions, it had been preceded by a similar depression abroad.

Like his predecessors in office, Cleveland believed it was not the duty of the federal government to alleviate suffering in a depression. As he complacently stated in his second inaugural, "... while the people should patriotically and cheerfully support their Government, its functions do not include the support of the people." In his view, the Sherman Silver Purchase Act had caused the depression by depleting the Treasury, and his proposed remedy was to repeal the act and maintain the gold standard. The silverites, however, disagreed. They contended that the cure lay in the free and unlimited coinage of silver at a ratio of 16 to 1 of gold and that the Sherman Act, though a step in the right direction, had provided inadequate relief; many debtor agrarians agreed.

Cleveland, however, was convinced that the silver certificates issued under the Sherman Act and redeemed in gold were responsible for the drain on the gold reserve that was in the process of being lowered to the established minimum of $100 million. This was an oversimplification, for there were several causes for the drain on the nation's gold, most certainly including a decline in revenues from import tariffs due to the severe economic recession. However, Cleveland summoned Congress into special session in 1893, and through a combination of Gold Democrats and Republicans had the Sherman Silver Purchase Act repealed. Most Western and Southern Democrats in Congress voted against the Democratic administration, widening the split within the party on the currency issue.

Repeal of the Sherman Silver Purchase Act, of course, failed to restore prosperity, and the Treasury's gold reserve continued to fall. To keep the country on the gold standard, Cleveland had the Treasury sell government bonds for gold. A group of bankers headed by J. P. Morgan absorbed three bond issues in 1894 and 1895; but it was not until 1897, when the depression had finally run its course, that the Treasury crisis ended. Although the gold purchases enabled the Treasury to meet its obligations, the bond sales intensified the silverites' hatred of the president. Meanwhile, many Americans became alarmed over the government's dependence upon a syndicate of New York bankers. As the economy improved in the late 1890s, gold standard advocates felt vindicated; but the fact of the matter was that new gold finds in Alaska and the Yukon territory had flooded the cash-short economy with new currency and thus remedied the currency shortage that had been endemic in the Panic of 1893. Good fortune in gold prospecting, rather than monetary responsibility in adherence to the gold standard, had ended the panic and the price deflation that had plagued the Gilded Age since the 1870s.

Cleveland himself, however, failed to bring about any substantial reduction of the tariff. In the House the Democrats, fulfilling their campaign promises, had passed a tariff bill drawn up by William L. Wilson of West Virginia that provided for a modest reduction in rates. In the Senate, though, a group of protectionists from both parties led by Senator Arthur Gorman, an influential Democrat from Maryland, attacked the bill with more than six hundred amendments, restoring some old rates and raising others. The resultant Wilson-Gorman Tariff of 1894, which Cleveland denounced as "party perfidy and party dishonor" and which became law without his signature, was a far cry from reform. It did provide for a small income tax of two percent on incomes over $4,000, but the Supreme Court, as unpopular as Cleveland, held the tax to be unconstitutional.

For the remainder of his presidency, Cleveland confined his role to that of protector of the status quo. He vetoed the Seigniorage bill, which would have increased the supply of the currency. Through subordinates he rudely rejected the petitions of "Coxey's Army," as it was

▶ "Coxey's Army," was a group of some five hundred men who marched from Ohio to Washington to protest unemployment, lobby for the government to create jobs, and for government funds to be used for public works such as building roads.

called, was a group of some five hundred men who marched from Ohio to Washington to demand free coinage of silver and the establishment of a $500 million federal public works program to provide jobs for the unemployed. Cleveland, however, did not view a public works program as within the proper role of government and did not view Coxey's protest as legal. Consequently, when Coxey's Army arrived at the Capitol, they found themselves barred from entry by armed police. Coxey and two others were arrested and convicted of trespassing (for walking on the grass), and police dispersed the rest of Coxey's followers. In the same year, Cleveland sent federal troops to crush the Pullman strike. The combination of the force used in the Pullman strike with Cleveland's manhandling of Coxey's Army, along with Cleveland's unwillingness to introduce a major program to combat the recession, convinced Americans that Cleveland neither understood nor cared about their plight. On a personal note, Cleveland suffered from serious health problems and had a secret operation aboard an offshore yacht to remove a cancerous upper jaw. Things could hardly have been worse for Cleveland in his second term.

Three Supreme Court decisions in 1895 added to the general discontent in the country. The Court in a 5–4 decision in *Pollock v. Farmers' Loan and Trust Company* invalidated the income tax clause of the Wilson-Gorman Tariff on the ground that it was a direct tax. Therefore, according to the Constitution, it had to be apportioned among the states on the basis of population. Moreover, Justice Stephen J. Field had earlier called the income tax "an assault upon capital" and a "stepping stone to others, larger and more sweeping, till our political contests ... become a war of the poor against the rich."

Shortly after this, the Court, in the case of *in re Debs*, unanimously upheld the injunction sending American socialist leader and labor activist Eugene V. Debs to prison at the time of the Pullman strike. At the same time, the Court in an 8–1 decision in *United States v. E. C. Knight Company*, in the first United States Supreme Court case involving the Sherman Antitrust Act of 1890, distinguished manufacturing from commerce and held that the Sherman Act did not apply to manufacturing combinations within states because manufacturing itself was not commerce that could be regulated by Congress. This decision seriously weakened the enforcement of the antitrust laws, and for some time, placed most monopolies beyond the reach of federal regulation. Thus, the E. C. Knight Company, which controlled 98 percent of the sugar manufacturing in the U.S., could not be broken up as a monopoly under the Sherman Anti-Trust Act. Partially due to these elitist Supreme Court decisions, there was a widespread feeling in the country during the mid-nineties that there was a war on between the rich and the poor and that the president, the Supreme Court, and Congress were on the side of the rich.

The Election of 1896

The Republicans met in St. Louis, in June 1896, and nominated William McKinley of Ohio for president and Garret A. Hobart, a corporation lawyer of New Jersey, for vice-president. Marcus Alonzo Hanna, a wealthy Ohio industrialist, was largely responsible for McKinley's nomination. Hanna was a good example of the new kind of political boss then emerging—the businessman holding office and actually running the party instead of remaining in the background and paying out political favors. As a leader of the Republican Party in Ohio and soon to become Republican national chairman, Hanna gathered the necessary delegate votes for McKinley's nomination and financed and managed his preconvention campaign.

On the preeminent question of the day, the monetary question, McKinley's record was not consistent. He had voted for both the Bland-Allison Act and the Sherman Silver Purchase Act. Yet in 1891, in running for governor, he had condemned the free coinage of silver and advocated international bimetallism. Hanna had already decided upon a gold standard plank, but at the convention he gave the impression he had to be "persuaded" by the Eastern delegates that "the existing gold standard must be maintained." After a gold plank was adopted at the Republican Convention, a small group of silver advocates, led by Senator Henry M. Teller of Colorado, left the hall and organized the Silver Republican Party.

Similarly, the Democrats were torn by bitter strife when they met in Chicago in July. The agrarians looked upon their own president, Grover Cleveland, as an enemy. He personified the Northeastern conservatism against which they were in revolt. Consequently, within the Democratic Party, insurgency was rampant. In the elections of 1894, the Democrats had barely retained control of the Senate and had lost the House.

Insurgent Democrats prepared to outdo the silverites in denouncing Cleveland and in advocating free silver. In short, they hoped to win back the Populists and take over the Democratic Party. Their work was so effective that by the summer of 1896 they had gained control of every state Democratic organization south of the Potomac and west of the Alleghenies—except South Dakota, Minnesota, and Wisconsin.

The silverites dominated the convention, and Cleveland was denounced in Democratic Party resolutions and speeches. The Democratic Party platform of 1896 repudiated the Cleveland program and attacked the protective tariff, national banks, trusts, and the Supreme Court. It, also, called for an income tax and the free coinage of silver at the ratio of 16 to 1. The leading contender for the nomination was Congressman Richard P. ("Silver Dick") Bland of Missouri, who had fought for free silver since the seventies; but the convention passed him by and on the fifth ballot nominated William Jennings Bryan, "the silver-tongued orator

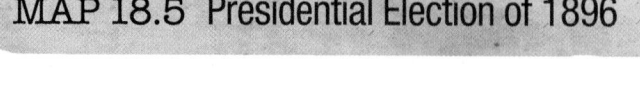

MAP 18.5 Presidential Election of 1896

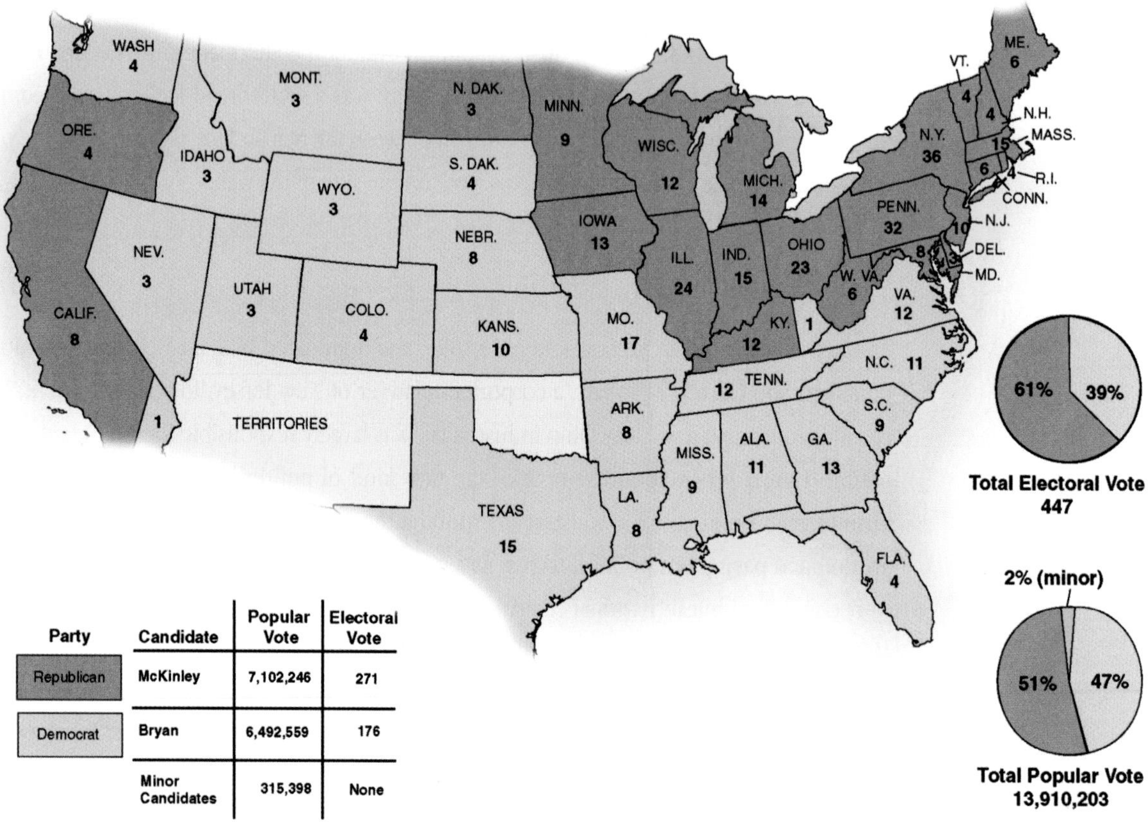

Party	Candidate	Popular Vote	Electoral Vote
Republican	McKinley	7,102,246	271
Democrat	Bryan	6,492,559	176
	Minor Candidates	315,398	None

from Nebraska." He had captivated the silver delegates with a speech that rose to a stirring peroration. "You shall not press down upon the brow of labor this crown of thorns, you shall not crucify mankind upon a cross of gold," at which point the demonstrative Bryan spread out his arms and mimicked a crucifixion. The delegates roared in approval, but some viewed Bryan's antics as more bluster than substance. For example, Congressman Joseph Foraker once commented, "Boy Orator of the Platte" was an apt name for Bryan since like the Platte, Bryan was about "six inches deep and a mile wide at the mouth."

Bryan, only thirty-six at the time, seemed to have been nominated by the accident of a spontaneous speech. He had, however, been rounding up support for several years and had presented his ideas many times to other audiences; his convention speech was simply the last step. As a recent biography by Michael Kazin demonstrates, Bryan had an exceptional ability to connect with audiences with his use of rhetoric, speaking in political terms in the style of a Protestant evangelist. Bryan's running mate was Arthur Sewall of Maine, a wealthy shipbuilder, banker, and protectionist, but an advocate of free silver.

The Populists faced a dilemma when their convention met in St. Louis in July. If they nominated their own candidate, they feared they would split the reform vote and permit the Republican William McKinley to win. If they endorsed Bryan, they would surrender their identity to the Democrats and sacrifice their broad program of reform for one that placed a disproportionate emphasis on the silver question. Western Populists were eager to nominate Bryan, but Southern Populists wanted a separate party ticket.

▶ William Jennings Bryan (left) and William McKinley (right), opponents in the fiercely fought election of 1896

The Populists finally were induced to nominate Bryan through trickery. Senator William V. Allen of Nebraska, chairman of the convention, told the Southerners that the Democrats had promised to withdraw Sewall and accept Thomas E. Watson, Populist leader of Georgia, as their vice presidential candidate—if the Populists would nominate Bryan. Watson's decision to accept this compromise persuaded Southern opponents of "fusion," whereby Populists would "fuse" with the Democrats to vote for Bryan's nomination. This would have created a true Democratic-Populist partnership, but the Democrats refused to withdraw Sewall. Henry Demarest Lloyd watched the convention with great disgust and finally concluded, "The People's Party has been betrayed . . . but after all it is its own fault." Similarly, Populist candidate for vice-president Tom Watson proclaimed, "Fusion means that we play Jonah while they play whale," fully understanding that "fusion between the Populists and the Democrats" would mean the end of the Populist Party and its absorption by the Democrats.

The campaign of 1896 was a highly emotional and dramatic one. In spite of the fact that Bryan was a very large man who weighed over three hundred pounds, he possessed tremendous energy and spoke in twenty-one states, traveled eighteen thousand miles on his "whistle-stop" railroad tour, and addressed some five million people in more than six hundred speeches, an unprecedented achievement.

William McKinley, in contrast, was a rather poor speaker, and Hanna's strategy was, therefore, to shield him from the public. Hanna's strategy called for a "front porch" campaign where McKinley remained at his home in Canton and read well-prepared speeches from his front porch to carefully coached delegations that visited him. Ostensibly, the candidate had to remain at home because his mother's health was failing, his wife suffered from seizures, and both needed his care. Exactly how McKinley planned to carry out the affairs of state while playing nursemaid to the invalid women in his life was not explained. Furthermore, there is some evidence that McKinley's wife and mother could hardly have suffered through worse care. William Howard Taft later told a story of attending a dinner function with President McKinley and his wife where Mrs. McKinley suffered an epileptic seizure. McKinley's response was simply to place a white dinner napkin over his wife's face to shield others from having to watch her convulsions and then continue with his dinner discussion virtually uninterrupted.

▶ This 1896 pro McKinley poster was meant to show the beneficial aspects of the Republican Party's protectionist policy compared to the negative consequences that would develop from adopting the Democratic Party's free trade policy.

Whether the reasons McKinley stayed home were a farce or not, Hanna's strategy worked. The railroads brought staunch Republican partisans from all over the country to McKinley's home in Canton to witness the charade. The speeches were carefully choreographed by Hanna, complete with places where the crowd would drown out the candidate with seemingly spontaneous applause. Pro-Republican newspapers then reported the daily speeches with high praise for McKinley and details of the crowd's enthusiasm.

The powerful response to Bryan's appeal frightened Eastern conservatives, and Hanna took advantage of their panic to collect campaign funds. From trusts, banks, railroads, and tycoons he raised a sum estimated at between $3.5 million and $15 million against a bare $300,000 for Bryan. John D. Rockefeller, alone, contributed $300,000 to the Republican cause, a sum equal to what Bryan and the Democrats were able to garner in total.

Hanna used the money lavishly, but wisely. The Republicans printed 250 million pieces of campaign literature, printed in twelve languages so as not to miss new immigrants. Some fifteen hundred professional speakers were paid to go into closely contested districts and stump for McKinley. The Republicans also received great assistance from the press, which heaped all kinds of abuse upon Bryan with slanted journalism. *The Louisville Courier Journal* called him "a dishonest dodger ... a daring adventurer ... a political faker," and the New York *Tribune* referred to him as a "wretched, rattle-pated boy." The Philadelphia *Press* described the "Jacobins" of the Democratic convention as "hideous and repulsive vipers," and Theodore Roosevelt was reported as saying that the silver men might well "be stood up against the wall and shot." John Hay, writing to Henry Adams in London, said of Bryan, "The Boy Orator makes only one speech—but he makes it twice a day. There is no fun in it. He simply reiterates the unquestionable truths that every man who has a clean shirt is a thief and should be hanged, and there is no goodness or wisdom except among the illiterates and criminal classes." Bryan's Protestant fundamentalist-style speeches also tended to alienate Catholics, a group whose vote would be critical to winning a number of states in the North and East. In addition, there were dire warnings that Bryan's victory would bring disaster. Farmers were told that mortgages would not be renewed, and workers were informed that factories would be closed or wages cut.

Out of almost fourteen million popular votes cast, McKinley won with a margin of over a half million and with 271 electoral votes to 176 for Bryan. Bryan failed to carry a single industrial and urban state and did not win a single state north of the Potomac and east of the Mississippi. Despite the widespread unrest among labor, he failed to elicit its support. This failure was one of the principal reasons for his defeat; but, also, he had nowhere near the material resources backing McKinley. He represented the party blamed for the depression. The election was a sound defeat for the Democrats overall as the Republicans also gained a majority in both houses of Congress.

McKinley lost all the mining states and the wheat-growing states of South Dakota, Nebraska, and Kansas where Republicans had always been strong; but he held onto the corn-producing states of the Middle West, where the farmers were better off than those on the Plains. He also gained an ascendancy in the Northeast such as no previous Republican president had had. From Maine south to Virginia and from the Great Lakes to Tennessee, he carried every state. While the margin by which he carried some was narrow, McKinley had a majority of the popular vote in the nation. The Republicans continued to hold the bulk of the Northern farmers and had gained new strength among the commercial and industrial interests of the North and the Upper South. For the first time since 1872, New England and the Middle Atlantic, Central, and North Central states were solidly Republican; and these sections were strong enough, if united, to control the Electoral College and, thereby, the presidency itself.

Historians are generally agreed that the election of 1896 was the most important one since 1860, and they have regarded it as a turning point in American history. For one thing, it gave the Republicans a clear majority of the popular vote in the country as a whole for the first time since Reconstruction. For another, it ushered in a series of Republican triumphs and a period of Republican supremacy in the national government that was to last until 1932, interrupted only by Woodrow Wilson's two terms. McKinley's victory also marked a triumph for conservatism and industrialism, and the backbone of agrarian resurgence was broken in 1896.

In the mourning for Bryan, the fate of Populism was largely forgotten. Its passing seemed to be the concern of few, yet it was one of the most significant results of the election of 1896. Fusion with the Democrats and the abandonment of a broad program of reform for the sake of silver had all but destroyed the Populist Party on the national level. It was Populism, not Bryanism, that furnished the backbone of agrarian resurgence; and when that backbone was broken in 1896, it meant that agrarian radicalism had made its last aggressive political stand.

The Populists in Perspective

Despite their defeat in 1896 and their disappearance from the political scene, the Populists have an important, albeit a controversial, place in American history. For quite a number of years historians portrayed the Populists as the champions of the common man and as the makers of modern reform in the country. John D. Hicks put forth the favorable and traditional point of view about the Populists in *The Populist Revolt* in 1931, and this remained the standard general account for many years. According to Hicks, Populism represented "the last phase of a long and perhaps a losing struggle—the struggle to save agricultural America from the devouring jaws of industrial America." Hicks wrote in the tradition of the Progressive historians, who were very critical of American industrial society and who regarded the older agrarian America as having many virtues.

This favorable view of the Populists came under attack in the 1950s when critics like Richard Hofstadter and Victor C. Ferkiss charged them with all kinds of mischief—including racism, anti-Semitism, jingoism, nativism, anti-intellectualism, xenophobia, and even being the forerunners of American fascism. Though the critics agreed that Populism was the first modern political movement of practical importance in the United States to insist that the federal government had some responsibility for the commonwealth, they also believed that the Populist leaders were haunted by nonexistent conspiracies and frequently were given to scapegoating rather than to rational analysis.

The 1960s witnessed another turnabout. A more favorable view of Populism reappeared. C. Vann Woodward and William P. Tucker, while conceding some of the points scored by the critics of Populism, found that the negative and unlovely characteristics of the Populists were not peculiar to them and that the irrational and illiberal side of Populism was no reason to repudiate its heritage.

Thereafter, some of the new writers saw the Populists as hoping to transform the American social system by putting forth a logical and reasonable analysis of industrial America, including the rejection of laissez-faire capitalism, Social Darwinism, and the success ethic. Others showed that Populism, at least in Kansas—the most Populist of the western states, was not hostile "to things non-American" but instead was a rational, legitimate political response to economic distress. Still others reported that the Populists in Alabama, at least, were neither revolutionaries nor reformers but repeatedly even voted against reforms to which they were pledged.

Then, in 1976, Lawrence Goodwyn published the first scholarly, general study of the Populist movement on a national scale since that of Hicks. In *Democratic Promise: The Populist Moment in America*, Goodwyn contended that Hicks had missed the essential dynamics of Populism, thereby opening the way for the later distortions and misinterpretations. He accused Hicks of mistaking "the shadow movement" accompanying Populism for the real thing. The real thing, argued Goodwyn, was the political revolt growing out of the cooperative movement of the Alliance and the elaborate program of structural economic and political reforms developed in that struggle getting under way in the 1880s. The shadow movement was the effort to substitute for that entire program and the reform spirit behind it the single demand for the free coinage of silver. Even more recently, Michael Kazin has written a book, *The Populist Persuasion*, in which he not only evaluates the Populists of the Gilded Age (mostly favorably) but also looks at their heirs, in some cases evaluating these not so favorably.

Despite the extensive literature on Populism, it remains difficult to assess its place in American history, though in general scholars are far more positive than they were a few decades ago. In any case, it is generally acknowledged that the Populists pioneered many measures that would eventually be enacted in the twentieth century, during either the Progressive period or the New Deal.

McKinley and the End of an Era

The McKinley administration was ushered in under highly favorable circumstances. Businessmen knew that their interests would be safeguarded for four years. There was a return to prosperity, which was to continue for several years although many long-term structural problems remained, especially where workers were concerned. Farmers largely dropped politics—though in some parts of the country they continued to be unhappy with the status quo and even voted for the Socialist Party. Politicians were happy and looked forward to a long period of abundance. McKinley, well aware of the economic distress that had affected Americans, promised in his first inaugural that this would be his chief concern. To maintain recovery he advocated two principal measures: a higher tariff and a gold standard act, the latter having been the panacea of Cleveland. Congress responded with the Dingley Tariff of 1897, which raised duties to an average of 52 percent, the highest in our history, and the Gold Standard Act of 1900, which declared the gold dollar from that time on would be the sole standard of currency.

▶The Gold Standard Act of 1900 declared that the sole standard of currency from that time on would be the gold dollar. The act's passage proved the McKinley administration was following through on its campaign promises.

With these two laws, the McKinley administration made good its campaign promises. Beyond this, neither the president nor Congress intended to interfere with the economy. They planned to let it alone and to allow business to create prosperity in good laissez-faire fashion. The attitude was perhaps best summed up by Marcus Hanna, who stated, "A man had a right to do what he pleased with his own." McKinley's inauguration marked the beginning of the greatest consolidation movement in American industry (1897–1904). This, coupled with the Spanish-American War, produced golden years of prosperity for business. The McKinley years would be less "golden," however, for African Americans. On the subject of black rights, McKinley essentially chose the same path that had been chosen by all his predecessors throughout the Gilded Age and did nothing, in spite of an upsurge in racial violence in the 1890s. When a riot in Wilmington, North Carolina, resulted in the death of eleven blacks, McKinley had little to say about the matter and did even less. T. Thomas Fortune spoke for many blacks when he described McKinley as "a man of jelly, who would turn us loose to the mob and not say a word."

Nevertheless, McKinley's presidency marked the beginning of a new era not only in national politics but also in the running of the national government. According to historian Lewis Gould, William McKinley was the first modern president, for reasons such as his appointing a de facto chief of staff, creating a war room, and, in general, skillfully employing bureaucratic means to advance his agenda. McKinley would also be the last of the Union Civil War officers to become president. We now turn to the new century, over which he would preside, if only briefly.

Chapter Review 18

Summary

The Gilded Age was a time of political patronage and corruption where both parties were often concerned more with the political spoils than with good governance. It was the era of the urban political machines, where patronage jobs and inflated government contracts were exchanged by politicians with their political supporters in return for their support. The party machines provided informal welfare and immigration services in the urban centers in efforts to co-opt the voters. The efforts were largely successful since voter turnout was as high as 80 percent; however, but voter fraud, corruption, and incompetence in government were the norm.

The two parties were closely balanced throughout the Gilded Age, and electoral victories on the national level tended to be narrow. Twice, in 1876 and 1888, the winner of the popular vote lost the presidential election. Politics was divided primarily between Northern and Southern sections of the country since the parties were similar in terms of their policies, with both generally laissez-faire, although Republicans favored higher tariffs to protect American manufacturing and Democrats favored lower tariffs to promote Southern agricultural exports. Farmers everywhere favored loose monetary policies in an effort to end the price deflation that plagued the time period. Farmers also favored regulation of railroads, banks, and grain elevators—entities they viewed as unscrupulously sapping the farmers' profits.

The plight of African Americans took a turn for the worse as Northern Republicans withdrew from the South and allowed Southerners to do as they pleased with blacks in the interest of gaining Southern acceptance of Republican President Rutherford B. Hayes after the disputed election of 1876. The Supreme Court further eroded rights for blacks with several decisions that essentially removed the protections of citizenship and voting rights that the Fourteenth and Fifteenth Amendments had been intended to provide. With its ruling in *Plessy v. Ferguson* in 1896, the Court validated the Separate but Equal Doctrine and helped entrench the segregated society that would dominate the African-American experience for the next seventy years.

The Gilded Age also experienced the stirrings of the Prohibition movement, with the Women's Christian Temperance Union, the Anti-Saloon League, and the formation of women's suffrage groups. Wyoming became the first territory to allow female suffrage in 1869, and Colorado became the first state to do so in 1893. Other gains for women included equal pay for equal work in government employment in 1872, and the establishment of Vassar as a college for women in 1861 and Harvard's establishment of Radcliffe as a college for women in 1879.

The Republican Party was divided between Stalwarts, led by Roscoe Conkling, that favored patronage, and Half-Breeds, led by James G. Blaine, that favored civil service, at least in rhetoric. In 1880, the Republicans attempted to unite the party with the nomination of the Half-Breed James Garfield with a Stalwart running mate, Chester Arthur. The assassination of President James Garfield in 1881 by a deranged job-seeker induced Chester Arthur into supporting the passage of the Pendleton Act of 1883 that began federal civil service.

Chapter Review (cont'd)

Summary (cont'd)

In 1884, the Republicans ran Half-Breed leader James G. Blaine against Democrat Grover Cleveland, but Blaine narrowly lost the election after one of his campaign workers slandered the Catholic Church in New York City. Cleveland would lose four years later to Benjamin Harrison in spite of winning the popular vote by one hundred thousand and then defeat Harrison to gain a second (nonconsecutive) term in 1892.

The 1892 election would also witness the formation of the Populist Party, which did well in the Western agricultural and mining states. The Populists would fuse with the Democrats in 1896 and back the "Boy Orator of the Platte" William Jennings Bryan for president on a Populist platform against Republican William McKinley. While Bryan campaigned eighteen thousand miles across the country via rail, Republican strategist Marcus Alonzo Hanna kept William McKinley at home for a "front porch campaign" so as to mask his poor oratory skills. McKinley spoke at his home, in choreographed speeches, in front of friendly Republican audiences and enjoyed favorable press coverage. Big business supported McKinley, who outspent Bryan 20 to 1 and won the election. Historians argue that this was not only a "modern" presidential campaign but also McKinley's presidency would be the first "modern" presidency, with his de facto Chief of Staff, "War Room," and use of the bureaucracy to achieve his objectives. McKinley would also be the last Civil War veteran to be president and usher the country into the next century.

Chronological Time Line

1861 Vassar was established as a college for women.

1866 Civil War veterans formed the Grand Army of the Republic.

1867 The National Grange of the Patrons of Husbandry was founded by Oliver Kelley.

1869 The Territory of Wyoming allowed women to vote.

1872 The passage of the Arnell Bill gave female government employees equal pay with men for equal work.

1872 The Equal Rights Party nominated Victoria Claflin Woodhull for president.

1873 In what farmers and miners referred to as the "Crime of '73," the government discontinued silver coinage.

Time Line (cont'd)

1873 The Panic of 1873 sent the country into economic recession.

1874 The Woman's Christian Temperance Union formed in Cleveland.

1875 *Minor v. Happersett* (1875) rejected the argument that women could vote because they were citizens and ruled that the Fourteenth Amendment had not conferred the vote upon women.

1875 The Specie Resumption Act obligated the government to redeem Greenbacks at face value.

1875 The Southern Alliance was formed in Texas.

1876 Rutherford B. Hayes was elected president in a disputed election where he lost the popular vote.

1876 In *U.S. v. Reese* and *U.S. v. Cruickshank,* the Court ruled that the Fifteenth Amendment did not confer voting rights on anyone.

1877 The Socialist Labor Party was founded.

1878 Senator Aaron Augustus Sargent introduced into Congress an equal suffrage amendment.

1878 The Bland-Allison Act authorized government purchase of $2 million to $4 million worth of silver each month and coined it into dollars at the former gold/silver price ratio of 16 to 1.

1879 Harvard University established Radcliffe as a college for women.

1880 The Northwestern Alliance was formed in Chicago.

1880 James Garfield was elected president.

1881 James Garfield was assassinated, and Chester Arthur became president.

1882 The Chinese Exclusion Act banned Asian immigration.

1883 In the Civil Rights cases of 1883, the Supreme Court upheld discrimination by private individuals and applied the Fourteenth Amendment protections only to states.

Chapter Review (cont'd)

Time Line (cont'd)

1883 The Civil Service Reform Act (Pendleton Act) began federal civil service.

1884 Grover Cleveland narrowly defeated James G. Blaine for the presidency.

1886 Presidential Succession Law provided that after the vice-president, the succession should pass to the members of the cabinet, beginning with the Secretary of State, in the order of the creation of their departments.

1887 The Dawes Act ended the policy of treating the Indians as separate tribes.

1888 Benjamin Harrison lost the popular vote but won the electoral vote to defeat Grover Cleveland for the presidency.

1890 The National American Women's Suffrage Association was formed from the merger of competing suffrage groups.

1890 Populist Party was founded in Kansas.

1890 Sherman Anti-Trust Act

1890 McKinley Tariff Act

1892 The National People's Party or Populist Party was organized in Omaha.

1892 Grover Cleveland defeated Benjamin Harrison for his second (nonconsecutive) term in the White House.

1893 The Anti-Saloon League was founded.

1893 The Panic of 1893 sent the economy into severe recession.

1893 The Sherman Silver Purchase Act was discontinued.

1893 Colorado became the first state to allow women's suffrage.

Time Line (cont'd)

1894 The Wilson-Gorman Tariff Act included an income tax.

1894 Coxey's Army was dispersed in D.C. by police at the order of Grover Cleveland.

1895 *Pollock v. Farmers' Loan and Trust Company* invalidated the income tax.

1895 Ida Wells-Barnett published *The Red Record.*

1895 In *U.S. v. E. C. Knight,* the Court ruled that manufacturing was not commerce and did not fall within the Sherman Anti-Trust Act.

1896 *Plessy v. Ferguson* upheld the "Separate but Equal" doctrine.

1896 William McKinley defeated populist Democrat William Jennings Bryan for the presidency in one of the most colorful campaigns in history.

1897 The Dingley Tariff raised tariffs to an all-time high.

1898 In *William v. Mississippi* (1898), the Court opened the road to legal disfranchisement by approving Southern plans for depriving blacks of the vote.

1901 The Socialist Party of America was organized.

Key Terms

"Waving the bloody shirt": Euphemism for fanning the flames of sectionalism

"Two Empty Bottles": James Bryce's description of the two political parties, both of which lacked ideas and principles

"Southern White Man's Party": The Democratic Party in the "Solid South"

Political machines: Political party organizations, primarily in urban centers, that were built on patronage and corruption

Mugwumps: Generally they were newspapermen, scholars, and intellectuals, earnest men of high ideals and prominent social position, of conservative economic views, and usually of Republican background and opposed to patronage and corruption

Prohibition: The movement to prohibit the sale and consumption of alcohol

Chapter Review (cont'd)

Key Terms (cont'd)

***Plessy v. Ferguson*:** Landmark case that validated the "separate but equal" doctrine

Jim Crow laws: Social and legal restrictions that were placed on blacks by states and municipalities

"Grandfather Clause": Clauses in the voting laws in Southern states that exempted whites from taking literacy tests for voting if their "Grandfathers" had voted

White Primaries: Primary elections that excluded blacks

Booker T. Washington: African American leader that is credited with founding Tuskegee Institute

"Atlanta Compromise": Booker T. Washington's assertion that blacks would accept segregation in return for white support of black educational and economic success

W.E.B. DuBois: Black intellectual who argued that blacks should accept nothing short of equal rights

Lucy Stone: Leader of a women's suffrage group that accepted the Reconstruction Amendments, even though they did not include women

Elizabeth Cady Stanton: Leader of a women's suffrage group that opposed the Reconstruction Amendments because they did not include women

WCTU: Women's Christian Temperance Union that opposed consumption of alcohol

Frances Willard: Head of the WCTU in 1879 that favored a prohibition of alcohol

Belva Ann Bennett Lockwood: Presidential candidate for the Equal Rights Party in 1884 and 1888

Rutherford B. Hayes: Republican president in 1877 that lost the popular vote in the disputed election of 1876

James Garfield: Republican president that was assassinated by a deranged job-seeker in 1881

Chester A. Arthur: Vice president for James Garfield that assumed the presidency after Garfield's assassination

Civil Service Act: Also known as the Pendleton Act of 1883 that created federal civil service

Grover Cleveland: The only Democratic president in the Gilded Age who served two nonconsecutive terms and won the popular vote three straight times

The Tariff Issue: Republicans favored higher tariffs to protect northern manufacturing while the Democrats favored lower tariffs in an effort to boost southern agricultural exports.

Benjamin Harrison: Grandson of William Henry Harrison and defeated Grover Cleveland for president in 1888 despite narrowly losing the popular vote

Stalwarts: Faction of the Republican Party that favored continuation of the patronage system

Half-Breeds: Faction of the Republican Party that favored civil service, at least in rhetoric

"Crime of '73": The reference by farmers and miners to the discontinuation of silver coinage by the federal government in 1873

Granger Movement: Began as a social and educational organization to benefit farmers, but evolved into a political pressure group and eventually became the Populist Party

Key Terms (cont'd)

Greenback Movement: Advocated inflationary monetary policies so as to benefit farmers

Farmers' Alliance: Agricultural political pressure groups that favored inflationary monetary policies and federal regulation of railroads, banks, and grain elevators

Sectionalism: The political divisions between the Northern and Southern sections of the country that tended to dominate politics in the Gilded Age

Charles J. Guiteau: Deranged government job-seeker that assassinated James Garfield

Rum, Romanism, and Rebellion: A reference by a supporter of James G. Blaine in the election of 1884 to the Democratic Party, the statement was viewed as a slur against the Catholic Church and may have contributed to Blaine's defeat.

Grand Army of the Republic: Civil War veterans' pressure group

Populist Party: Formed in 1892 as a coalition of farmers and miners in Western states that favored inflationary monetary policies and more government controls of railroads and big business

Fusion: The merger of the Populist Party with the Democrats in 1896 that effectively ended the Populist Party

***Pollock v. Farmer's Loan and Trust*:** 1895 case that invalidated the income tax

***U. S. versus E. C. Knight*:** Landmark case in which the Court ruled that manufacturing is not commerce and does not fall within the Sherman Anti-Trust Act

Depression of 1893: Economic panic precipitated by a stock market crash and financial collapse that dominated the mid-1990s

Jacob Coxey: Led a group of unemployed men to Washington demanding public works spending only to be arrested upon arrival in D.C.

William McKinley: Republican president who defeated William Jennings Bryan with his "front porch campaign" in 1896

William Jennings Bryan: Populist Democrat and gifted orator that lost the 1896 presidential election to William McKinley in spite of his eighteen thousand mile whistle-stop tour

Marcus Alonzo Hanna: Republican political strategist that orchestrated McKinley's winning front porch campaign

Bland-Allison Act: Authorized the government purchase of $2 million to $4 million worth of silver each month to coin it into dollars at the former gold/silver price ratio of 16 to 1

Front Porch Campaign: William McKinley's presidential campaign that was designed to hide his poor oratory skills by having him speak only to friendly audiences in well-choreographed events at his home

Whistle-Stop Tour: William Jennings Bryan's eighteen thousand mile speaking tour via rail where he spoke to an estimated 5 million people

Pop Quiz

Chapter 18

1. Which of the following characterized politics in the Gilded Age?
   a. close balance between the political parties
   b. sectionalism
   c. patronage and corruption
   d. all of the above

2. Which of the following is true of the plight of African Americans in the Gilded Age?
   a. Presidents, such as James Garfield and Rutherford B. Hayes, did much to alleviate black suffering.
   b. Republicans talked much about black rights, but did little.
   c. Black men achieved equal rights, but black women did not.
   d. Southerners, such as Tom Watson, favored black rights as a way to limit the power of Jews in America.

3. Which of the following did William E. B. Dubois and T. Thomas Fortune argue?
   a. Blacks should accept segregation in return for white support of black economic success.
   b. Blacks should wage a nonviolent strategy of resistance to whites.
   c. Blacks should accept nothing less than full equality.
   d. Black men should be equal with whites, but black women should be subordinate to both whites and black men.

4. The first state to allow women to vote was __________.
   a. Wyoming in 1869
   b. Nebraska in 1898
   c. Massachusetts in 1910
   d. California in 1918

5. The "Crime of '73" is a reference by __________.
   a. blacks to the *Plessy v. Ferguson* decision in 1873
   b. agriculturalists to the government discontinuation of silver purchase in 1873
   c. Southerners to the election of Rutherford B. Hayes in 1873
   d. Half-Breeds to the New York Custom House Scandal in 1873

Pop Quiz (cont'd)

6. How are the elections of 1888 and 1876 similar?
   a. The winner of the popular vote lost both elections.
   b. The Republican candidate won both elections.
   c. Both elections should be considered landslides.
   d. Both a and b

7. Populists supported all of the following reforms EXCEPT __________.
   a. a graduated income tax
   b. a higher tariff
   c. government control of public transportation
   d. direct election of U.S. senators

8. Why was the Election of 1896 considered a turning-point in American history?
   a. It was a victory for Populism.
   b. It was a victory for big business.
   c. The party that spent the least amount of money finally won an election.
   d. Conservatives finally lost control of the White House.

9. Which of the following is true of William Jennings Bryan?
   a. atheist
   b. physically fit exercise and diet enthusiast
   c. considered to be a gifted speaker in his time
   d. avoided trains when campaigning

10. Which president signed the highest tariff in American history into law?
   a. Grover Cleveland
   b. William McKinley
   c. Benjamin Harrison
   d. Rutherford B. Hayes

Chapter Review (cont'd)

Pop Quiz (cont'd)

11. Mugwumps were corrupt machine politicians. T F

12. Booker T. Washington accepted inequality in exchange for security. T F

13. The Populists had little impact on twentieth century America. T F

14. The Gilded Age was a period of political ____________

15. In 1879, Rutherford B. Hayes ____________ a Chinese immigration bill.

1. D	5. B	9. C	13. T
2. B	6. D	10. B	14. Stalemate
3. C	7. B	11. F	15. Vetoed
4. A	8. B	12. T	

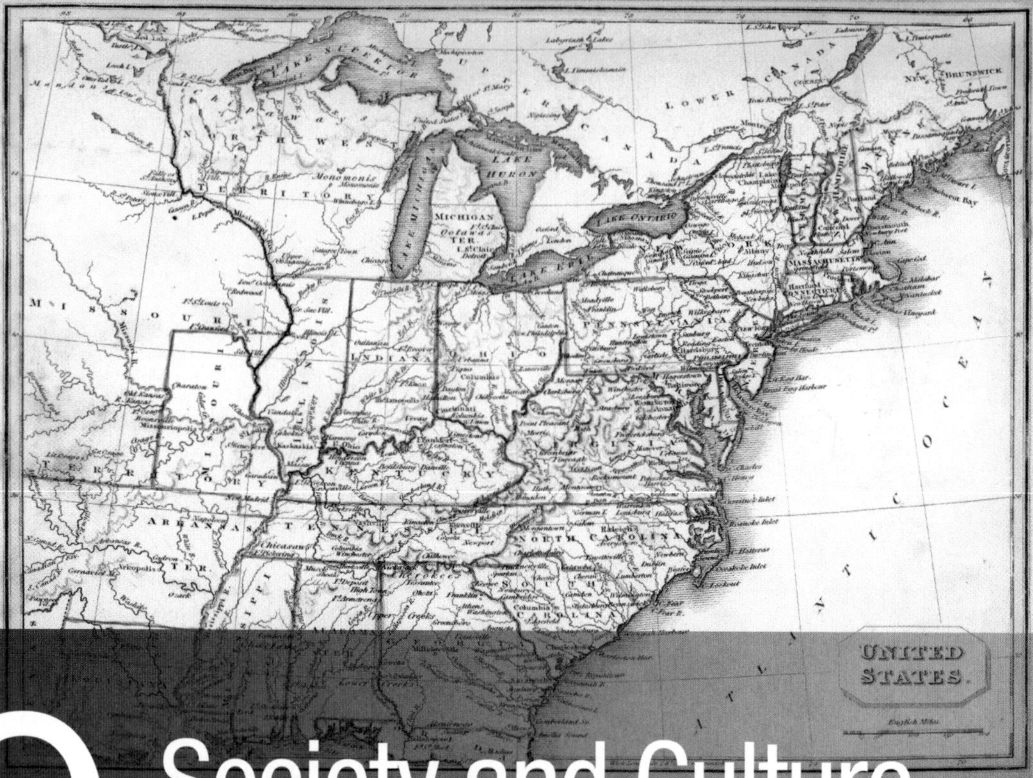

19 Society and Culture in the Progressive Era

Chapter Objectives

Progressivism

The Growth of Cities

The Flight from the Farm

The New Immigrants: Problems and Achievements

The Leo Frank Case

Education and Social Mobility

The Modern City

The Rise of Mass Culture

The Growth of Spectator Sports

Motion Pictures

Popular Reading

Music

Journalism

Muckraking

Architecture, Painting, and Literature

Architecture

Painting

The Novel

Poetry

Two Milestones

Women and Women's Suffrage

Margaret Sanger and Birth Control

The Triumph of National Prohibition

The Institutions of Change

Technology and Business

Modernizing the Government

The Social Sciences

Psychology and Economics

The New History

Progressive Education

Public Education

Higher Education

Church and Society

Protestantism

Catholicism

Judaism

Political Main Currents

Political Thought

Known as "the Progressive Era," the period lasting roughly from 1900 until American entry into World War I was replete with changes in public policy, innovative reforms on many fronts, breakthroughs in technology, and exciting cultural developments. There were also changes in American foreign policy that foreshadowed the subsequent course of the twentieth century. The Progressives, drawn from both Republican and Democratic ranks, had a belief both in the power of human intelligence and in the power of government to deal with social problems. We turn first to a discussion of Progressivism and then to culture and to the intense speed-up in urbanization that underlay much of the Progressive Era cultural transformation.

Progressivism

Progressivism was essentially the popular response to the excesses of the Industrial Age from the late nineteenth century through World War I. Progressivism was based on a number of basic assumptions, one of which was that society was capable of improvement—morally, socially, and politically, and economically and technologically, as well. The Progressives believed that order is essential to progress. Hence, growth should not be allowed to occur recklessly as it had in the laissez faire nineteenth century. Instead, growth should be controlled through societal institutions, including government, which Progressives viewed as a legitimate tool for improving society. Progressives argued that the natural laws of the marketplace, laissez faire, and Social Darwinism were insufficient means to promote progress, justice, and the greater good; hence, direct, purposeful intervention into human affairs was essential to creating a better society. The Progressive vision essentially rested on the idea of the good of the whole; and Progressives argued that individuals had a responsibility to the whole, and the whole had a responsibility to the individual. As such, laissez faire economics that allowed unsafe workplaces, child labor, low wages, and monopolies were rejected as bad both for individuals and the whole. The breakup of corporate monopolies, even if they had done nothing wrong or illegal, but had just played the free market game better than competitors, was justified in the interest of the good of the whole.

▶ The Progressive way of thinking rejected laissez faire economics that allowed unsafe workplaces, child labor, low wages, and monopolies as they were bad both for individuals and the whole.

The Growth of Cities

The Flight from the Farm

The population of the cities increased sevenfold between 1860 and 1910. About 30 percent of this increase reflected a movement of native whites, and to a much lesser extent blacks, out of rural areas and into the cities as mechanization of agriculture reduced the need for labor and increased agricultural productivity while continued industrialization produced higher paying jobs in the urban centers. Although farm prices rose so high during the Progressive Era that the years 1909–1914 are known as "The Golden Age of Agriculture," the exodus continued through World War I. (It should be noted, however, that these high prices were an average and that many pockets of desperate poverty remained). By 1920, well under a third of all Americans still lived on farms and less than half in rural areas.

Several interrelated factors worked together to produce this migration to the cities. Rural births exceeded deaths, output per farmer increased, and the quality of rural life suffered a relative decline. Just before the Civil War, it took thirty-nine man-hours to produce forty bushels of corn. By 1894, improved farm machinery had reduced that number to fifteen. The increase in the efficiency of wheat production was even more dramatic. In 1896, with full mechanization, a wheat farmer could harvest eighteen times more crop than in 1830. This increase in output per farmer, together with a relatively high rural birthrate and a shortage of good new land, created a surplus of agricultural workers. The rise in output and increase in farm prices also drove up land values disproportionately. These same factors further contributed to a growth in tenancy from 25 percent of all farmers in 1880 to 37 percent in 1910. Partly because of the extraordinarily high incidence of black tenants, South Carolina, Georgia, Alabama, and Mississippi led the nation at between 60 and 70 percent; even in Illinois the rate stood at 44 percent.

For the more substantial farmers, rural life remained moderately rewarding; but for those on the margins of existence, it became more depressing. Tens of thousands of farm families lived without church, school, or society. Thousands of mothers died in childbirth, and more thousands of children died from privation and inadequate medical care. Most farms, especially in the South, remained without electricity until after the Great Depression.

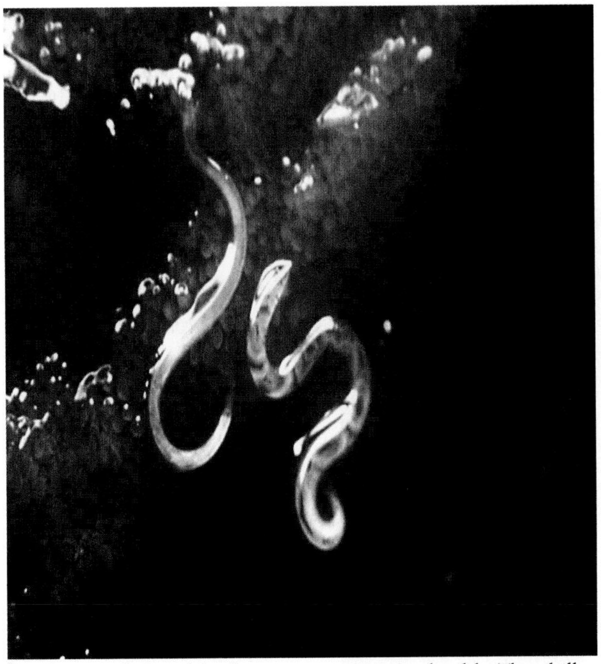

▶ Most southern white farmers were in poor health. The chills and fever of malaria were accepted as hazards of the trade and at least half a million whites were infected with hookworm (shown above) due to living in unsanitary conditions.

Southern farmers typically fared the worst. Both blacks and whites in the South accepted the recurring fevers and chills of malaria as facts of life; and at least a half million whites were infected, through ignorance of elementary sanitation, with the debilitating hookworm disease (an intestinal parasite that sucks blood voraciously and causes anemia). As a distraught southern physician wrote to Theodore Roosevelt, "I would prefer to see my own daughter, nine years old, at work in a cotton mill than have her live as a tenant on the average southern, one-horse, tenant farm."

In 1909, the privately financed Rockefeller Sanitary Commission opened a campaign that eventually wiped out the hookworm disease, and in 1912 the United States Public Health Service began a prolonged assault on malaria. By then, however, a generation or more of afflicted Southerners had lost all opportunity for normal development.

The New Immigrants: Problems and Achievements

The wave of "new immigrants," discussed in a previous chapter, continued to rise until the outbreak of World War I. Between 1901 and 1914 some 3 million Italians, 1.5 million Jews, and 4 million Slavs poured into the United States. The relatively high literacy rate of male Jews and the skills they had learned in eastern European villages enabled them to adapt quite readily to urban economic and social life. Most other new immigrants, however, came from rural European peasant backgrounds and were ill-prepared for city life. A small number of Poles, Bohemians, and Italians settled on run-down farms, which their superior diligence and use of women and children in the fields made into productive units. The lack of transferable skills, however, forced most to take menial jobs in overcrowded cities or grime-ridden industrial and mining towns. On the other hand, the Italians who found their way to the West, especially to California, fared considerably better than this dismal picture would suggest because they were able to establish a toehold in the burgeoning fruit industry.

No society could have absorbed so many disparate people without social tension, nor could any society have been expected to adequately house such vast numbers upon arrival. One result—and the one most often emphasized—was a pronounced increase in social and economic discrimination. Among the new arrivals, perhaps those from Asia suffered most; but all immigrants—including the Germans, Scandinavians, and Irish, who still came in large, though sharply reduced numbers—suffered in degree. This was in spite of the ideal personified by the inscription plaque placed on the Statue of Liberty in 1903: "Give us your tired, your poor, your huddled masses yearning to breathe free."

Much of the social tension was rooted in class and economic rivalries. Old-stock employers, for example, often used the most recent immigrants as strikebreakers. They also kept certain ethnic groups from management positions in many industries. Conversely, members of a particular ethnic group would establish themselves in a certain occupation and close out other ethnic strains. In fact, virtually every ethnic group discriminated to some degree against each

▶ Waves of immigrants poured into the country during the early 1900s. Many came through ports in New York City and those coming from peasant backgrounds were unprepared for the culture shock of city life.

other. German Jews discriminated against east European Jews, Germans against Slavs, Norwegians against Swedes, and Irish against Italians, Slavs, Jews, and even French-Canadians.

Much of the tension was also religious, and as such, it long antedated the American experience. Anti-Catholicism was particularly acute. For example, in 1910, former Populist candidate Tom Watson denounced the Catholic hierarchy as "the deadliest menace to our liberties and our civilization." Watson also wrote a book entitled *Maria Monk and Her Revelation of Convent Crimes* where he argued that there were murders of infants in Catholic convents. Watson even argued that the Pope had secretly organized and armed the Knights of Columbus for a takeover of the United States.

Conflict between Catholics and Protestants dated back to the Reformation, and that between Christians and Jews, to the Roman Empire. Thus most of the Jews who came to the United States during this period were fleeing systematic discrimination and even outright persecution—both official and unofficial—by Rumanians, Russians, Ukrainians, and Poles. Just as many Irish had earlier fled Ireland because of their long economic repression by the English. It is a tribute to the openness of American society and its institutions, including the absence of a state church, that discrimination proved mild on balance, at least by the standards of most of the rest of the world. This does not, however, mean that the United States was void of more severe cases of overt bigotry. The bigotry at times proved violent—as the Leo Frank case in 1914 demonstrated.

The Leo Frank Case

Leo Frank was a Jewish manager of a pencil factory in Georgia who was accused of murdering a fourteen year-old girl, Mary Phagan. Her body had been found in the cellar of the factory; she had been raped and strangled. However, before she expired, she had managed to scribble a note accusing an unnamed black man of the crime. In spite of the note, Frank was charged with the crime and convicted based on the testimony of a black man who had been in the factory at the time of the murder. Prominent lawyers throughout the country pointed out the obvious—

MAP 19.1 Sources of Immigrants (1900–1920)

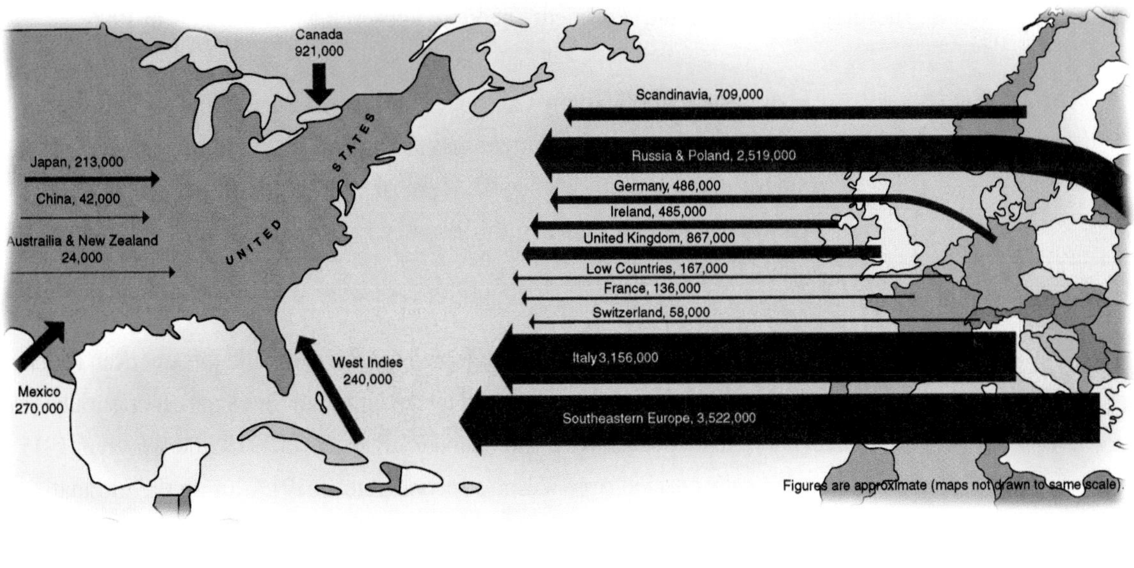

that most likely the black man that testified against Frank was the real culprit. Frank was sentenced to death, but his sentence was later commuted, causing outrage among Georgian nativists. Frank was eventually lynched in 1915 by a Georgia mob, an action that Tom Watson defended as just—while he further argued that it would be prudent to reorganize the Ku Klux Klan. Watson also published his own magazine where he continually railed against Catholics and Jews and accused them of working together to undermine American society. Watson would ride his anti-Semitism and anti-Catholicism to a seat in the United States Senate in 1920.

Meanwhile the rise of racist theory in Europe, much of it popularized in the United States, gave a pseudo-intellectual cast to the notion that the old immigrants from northwestern Europe were inherently superior and that the new immigrants should be refused entry. Nativists in America argued that the new immigrants were somehow diluting the pure American race. Madison Grant, in *The Passing of the Great Race,* argued that immigration would lead to a "mongrelization" of America and that in cases of intermarriage between persons of different races, the children of the union tended to go to the "lower case."

Even John R. Commons—a progressive economist, Christian layman, and zealous friend of labor—favored immigration restrictions on genetic grounds. Markedly higher scores by northern Europeans on the crude intelligence tests then coming into use gave a further veneer of scientific truth to these views. Not until after the new immigration had ended, did more sophisticated research indicate that cultural and environmental factors such as urban or rural origin, family occupational and educational background, command of the English language, and quality of schooling figured crucially in intelligence test scores.

Actually, the heavy environmental emphasis of reform Darwinism led many Progressives to remain skeptical of the more sweeping racist theories. Unlike conservatives, they equated race more with culture than genetics. However, they also believed that excessive immigration enabled employers to hold down wages and feared that immigrants from non-democratic countries would not readily be assimilated, partly because many constituted a kind of migrant work force. In 1908, more Italians and Hungarians returned to their homelands than entered the United States.

Progressives strove, nevertheless, to "Americanize" those who were here and to give them a measure of political representation. "I grow extremely indignant at the attitude of coarse hostility to the immigrant," President Theodore Roosevelt wrote privately in 1906:

> I have one Catholic in my Cabinet ... and I now have a Jew ... and part of my object in each appointment was to implant in the minds of our fellow Americans of Catholic or Jewish faith, or of foreign ancestry or birth, the knowledge that they have in this country just the same rights and opportunities as every one else.

Yet probably a majority of progressives joined conservatives and the American Federation of Labor in supporting a literacy test designed to curtail the new immigration drastically. Passed four times and vetoed four times—by Cleveland in 1896, Taft in 1913, and Wilson in 1915 and 1917—it was finally enacted over Wilson's second veto in 1917 during the ultranationalist frenzy that accompanied World War I.

▶ Immigrants arriving by sea at Ellis Island in New York. Between 1901 and 1914 some 3 million Italians, 1.5 million Jews, and 4 million Slavs poured into the United States, hoping to build a new life for themselves and their families.

Most new immigrants tended to enter lower-class occupations, obscuring another development of great importance. They, or at least their children, moved from unskilled to skilled jobs with the same or higher frequency as old-stock whites of the same economic class. Many also became homeowners with somewhat greater frequency, though Jews invested much more heavily in education than housing. Regardless, whether as owners or renters, most immigrants gravitated toward the familiar. Virtually every large American city developed neighborhood pieces of Europe—"Little Italy," "Little Polonia," and so forth. Through foods, music, customs, and their ways of looking at life, these distinctive settlements enriched American culture as a whole and helped transform the United States into a pluralistic society.

Education and Social Mobility

Public education served as the broadest avenue of upward mobility in American society. For cultural and economic reasons, not all ethnic groups took that route in the same proportions. For the same reasons, most old-stock whites in the South and many in rural areas elsewhere did not take it either. For those who did, however, including numerous sons and daughters of substantial Mid-western farmers and rural and small-town clergymen, it opened new social and economic opportunities.

Urban Jews made the most notable advances. Despite the impoverishment of many of their immigrant parents, Jewish youngsters—especially males—graduated from high school in much higher proportions than the offspring of most other ethnic groups. One result was a lower delinquency rate and another, adequate preparation for college. In 1908, at a time when Jews made up about 2 percent of the population, male Jews of the first and second generations comprised 8.5 percent of the male student bodies at seventy-seven major colleges and universities. By the next generation they constituted a disproportionately high percentage of physicians and lawyers in the larger cities. This led to the institution of quotas at many private colleges—though not public ones—and a drive by the American Bar Association to eliminate night law schools, where Jewish males were able to gain ready access.

The teaching profession also became an agency of upward mobility for rural whites and blacks, for small-town Americans of older stock, and for urban Jews and Irish, especially in New York and New England. Teaching in grammar and secondary schools was one of the few careers open to women, and the proportion of female teachers rose from 70 percent in 1900 to 85 percent in 1920—though males maintained a firm hold on higher-paying administrative positions. In the colleges and universities, it should be said, women who were not enrolled in a "female" course of study—such as teaching, nursing, or librarianship—were probably subjected to even greater discrimination than were Jews.

The Modern City

If one word were to characterize the new urban society, it would be mass—mass transit, mass entertainment, mass circulation of written matter, mass education, mass production, and mass distribution. In transit, the electric streetcar and the commuter train hastened the breakup of mixed residential sections in or near the city's core. The upper classes moved out first, but in time even clerks and factory workers bought or rented bungalows and flats in three-story frame houses far removed from offices and plants. Most new neighborhoods and suburbs had discrete ethnic and religious identities, but they tended to be more socially stratified than the old ones. No longer, for example, did workers, managers, and professionals reside on the same block although all might live, say, in the new Irish or Jewish neighborhood. Meanwhile, the vacated residences were replaced by new stores and plants or occupied by the latest immigrants and newly arrived rural families, both white and black.

Not until after World War I would the outlines of the modern city's central problem—loss of industry, tax base, and gainfully employed residents—become perceptible. During the Progressive Era many cities retained administrative cohesiveness by annexing suburbs while the growth of small businesses, great department stores, and white-collar industries like insurance and banking actually increased city tax bases. New civic leaders emerged among the offspring of the immigrants and the rural old stock and, especially, from the ranks of professional men, usually lawyers. Through much of the period America enjoyed an urban renaissance, characterized by beautifying movements, administrative reforms, a new level of public responsibility for health, improved schools, and new or expanded parks, playgrounds, libraries, museums, and zoos.

The Rise of Mass Culture

The Growth of Spectator Sports

The city further stimulated interest in mass spectator sports—football, boxing, and baseball. By the turn of the century, the Yale-Princeton football game was drawing between thirty and forty thousand fans, the Army-Navy game had become a national event, and Walter Camp's "All-America" selections were an annual feature of the sports pages. The winning of the heavyweight boxing championship in 1909 by a black man, Jack Johnson, induced race riots. His defeat in 1915 by a white, Jess Willard, brought a kind of national celebration. Six years later, a new champion, Jack Dempsey, drew eighty thousand fans and the first million-dollar gate in

▶ With the rise of spectator sports, major league baseball became a national pastime. Record setting sports stars emerged such as Ty Cobb whose lifetime batting average has never been rivaled, and Walter Johnson, whose record setting career is still admired today.

a bout in Jersey City. In the early twentieth century, however, it was baseball, not football or boxing, which came closest to being the national pastime.

Major league attendance climbed from 4.75 million in 1903 to 9 million in 1920. Through most of the period it was, in fact, the game of both the classes and the masses. Participation in the major leagues, though hardly the minor ones because they did not pay enough, also enabled a few old-stock, small-town boys and Irish and German urban youths to escape dreary lives in the mills or factories. Significantly, throughout these years blacks were barred from organized baseball, as the white leagues were known.

The greatest "stars" of the era included Ty Cobb, a fiery Georgian whose lifetime .367 career batting average is still unequaled; Honus Wagner, one of the finest all-round players ever; Walter Johnson, whose 413 pitching victories, 110 shutouts, and 3,499 strike-outs set impressive records; and gentlemanly Christy Mathewson, who won more than thirty games in three separate seasons and pitched three shutouts in the World Series of 1905. So attached to the game was the American male that the revelation that the Chicago White Sox had "thrown" the 1919 World Series drove the Red Scare and anti-communist paranoia that gripped the nation that same year off the front pages. A year later, "Babe" Ruth, formerly a superb pitcher for the Boston Red Sox, transformed the game by hitting fifty-four home runs for the New York Yankees.

Motion Pictures

Movies were one of the rare popular amusements to come up from the masses rather than down through the classes. They began in the 1890s as extra attractions in cheap variety houses, and in 1905 found their own home in nickelodeons. The working class—both native-born and immigrant—embraced the new medium. When subtitles flashed on the screen, those in the audience who could read English often read them aloud to their neighbors. For many of the foreign-born, the movies offered a course in Americanization.

By 1910, motion pictures were playing to a weekly audience of ten million in ten thousand theaters across the nation. With few exceptions, American movie-makers fixed their sights firmly on the mass market, turning out films that delivered a good laugh or a good cry, some hair-raising excitement, or steamy passion (then seen as an un-American phenomenon portrayed by exotics like Theda Bara and Rudolph Valentino). American directors displayed an early awareness of the medium's technical potential; and beginning with D. W. Griffith's *The Birth of a Nation* in 1915—as brilliant in technique as it was obnoxious in content, owing to its virulent racism—they created some great spectacles.

America's silent movies celebrated traditional moral values in sentimental and melodramatic cliches, but they also revealed a good-humored, street-smart cynicism. Besides seeing virtue triumph, movie fans could see the police portrayed as bumbling idiots (the Keystone Kops) and the high and mighty brought low by the plucky urchin (Mary Pickford) or the cheeky rogue (Douglas Fairbanks). Master of this subversive theme was the comic genius, Charlie Chaplin, one of the few silent stars who appealed to both sophisticated and unsophisticated tastes, as did another comic genius, Buster Keaton.

Popular Reading

Taste in reading matter was much like that in movies, although popular literature lacked the movies' cynical strain. Russel Nye writes of the pulp magazines, which replaced the dime novel by 1910: "Pulp stories were frankly mass-produced items, written to a rather rigid formula, never realistic, never disturbing, never disappointing. War could never be grim, a hero must never show fear, airplanes could never have accidents ... courtship must end in marriage." By 1915 pulp magazines, led by *Argosy*, were enjoying monthly sales in the millions.

On a somewhat higher plane stood the better Western novels. Foremost among their authors was the dentist from Zanesville, Ohio, Zane Grey. In 1912 he published his first success, *Riders of the Purple Sage*, in 1912, and then went on to write seventy more. Among mystery writers, Mary Roberts Rinehart was queen. Influenced by the domestic novel and the Gothic tale, as well as by both the stories of Edgar Allen Poe and Sir Arthur Conan Doyle, she added a parallel love story (always with a happy ending) to the crime story. The most successful popular novelists of the time were Gene Stratton-Porter, whose sentimental stories sold millions of copies, and Harold Bell Wright, who offered action and inspiration as well as sentiment. The most widely read poet of the era, the unassuming Detroit newspaperman Edgar A. Guest, was really a versifier whose talent lay in the expression of commonplace emotions and experiences in colloquial rhymes.

Even more than the movie fare of that period, the most popular reading matter seems singularly innocent and unsophisticated by today's standards. Ordinary Americans were beginning to have some leisure time; and their quest for diversion in reading led them to romance, moral uplift, and happy endings. Their tastes were not unremittingly mediocre, however. They also read with enthusiasm the books of Jack London and other authors whom the critics praised.

Music

Technology, mass distribution, and increases in per capita income also affected America's musical patterns. As early as the 1890s, mass-production techniques made pianos available to people of moderate means, and the sale of sheet music consequently soared. In 1909, five million copies of "Meet Me Tonight in Dreamland" were sold and the following year eight million of "Let Me Call You Sweetheart." Yet even as more and more Americans gathered around the

▶Jack London, author of American classics *White Fang* and *Call of the Wild,* in his office.

piano in the parlor, Thomas Edison's recently developed phonograph was sounding the comparative decline of this homemade music making. When given the choice, most people chose to listen rather than play or sing; and by the outbreak of World War I sales of phonograph records had skyrocketed while those of pianos and sheet music had plummeted. The decline in participation in music making, however, was partly, perhaps largely, offset by the dance craze sparked by the glamorous husband-and-wife team, Vernon and Irene Castle, who came to New York in 1912. Soon almost every good restaurant had an orchestra and a dance floor, and every middle-class party had a phonograph and dance records.

Some of the new music was indigenous, and much of it was of high quality. The first important development was highly syncopated ragtime, which crossed the color line late in the 1890s. Shelton Brooks wrote ragtime's most famous song, "The Darktown Strutter's Ball," and Scott Joplin, a Texas-born African American, emerged as its finest composer. Hardly had ragtime captured the popular imagination when the blues, which evolved from black Southern folk music and became popular in white circles following the issuance of W. C. Handy's "Memphis Blues" in 1913, challenged it. A black minister's son from Alabama, Handy composed several other classics, including "Beale Street Blues" and that perennial favorite, "St. Louis Blues." By the 1920s jazz, having been born in the red-light district of New Orleans and then having traveled up the river to Chicago and other points north, was in full flower.

Journalism

Another aspect of the new urban culture was yellow, or "people's," journalism. It began with the purchase of the *New York World* in 1883 by Joseph Pulitzer. Sports coverage was greatly

▶ Vernon and Irene Castle sparked the new dancing craze when they came to New York in 1912.

expanded, comic pages were introduced, murders and sex crimes were reported in gruesome detail, and scandals of all sorts were given featured treatment. Within fifteen years the *World's* circulation increased from 15,000 to 1.5 million. During the Progressive Era, Pulitzer and the *World* turned responsible, though the paper continued to be lively and popularly written. Meanwhile, Pulitzer's archrival, young William Randolph Hearst, perfected the new sensationalism in a nationwide chain of newspapers and magazines. The most demagogic of the mass-circulation publishers, Hearst forced his editors to promote his political ambitions and to propagandize his shifting political views. He was especially adept at catering to the passions and prejudices—religious, political, and even ethnic—of his largely lower-middle-class urban readers.

Concurrently, Adolph Ochs, scion of a Southern German-Jewish family, was transforming the *New York Times* from a partisan editorial sheet to "a newspaper of record." Under Ochs' aegis, the *Times* focused on non-sensational news in commerce, education, the arts, government, and foreign events. Its circulation remained small, for its stodgy make-up appealed only to the better educated. Nonetheless, editors and publishers the nation over subscribed to the *Times*, and its broad coverage and high reportorial standards had a pronounced effect upon the more highly principled of them.

Muckraking

Of more direct relevance to the emerging Progressive movement was the rise of investigative reporting. In 1902 a group of journalists, later dubbed "muckrakers" by Theodore Roosevelt because in his view all they did was "rake up the muck," began to publish articles about social, economic, and political problems that appeared in such middle-class magazines as *McClure's*, *Collier's*, *Everybody's*, and *Cosmopolitan*. The muckrakers' subject matter ranged from the traffic in prostitutes to the perversion of democracy in city halls, statehouses, and the United States Senate. Their output varied greatly in quality. Some writers, like Ida M. Tarbell, who carefully documented the impersonal ruthlessness of John D. Rockefeller and his associates in the *History of the Standard Oil Company* (1904), established standards of research and reporting that few journalists have ever surpassed. Others resembled David Graham Phillips, author of *The Treason of the Senate* (1906), whose innuendo and misrepresentation obscured much of the real truth that underlay his work.

One muckraker, Lincoln Steffens, brought to his work extraordinary insight into contemporary practices of American politicians, businessmen, and ordinary citizens. His two chief contributions were *The Shame of the Cities* (1904) and *The Struggle for Self-Government* (1906). Steffens was neither unaware of the defects of character that made public officials accept bribes nor indifferent to the moral lassitude that made average citizens indulgent of bad government, but he was much more interested in the bribe givers than in the bribe takers. Refusing to cater to anti-immigrant biases, he revealed that in Rhode Island the rural Yankee legislators, not urban Italians, had sold out to the streetcar and other interests. He described how the Pennsylvania Railroad in New Jersey and the Public Service Corporation of that state had contrived to have the New Jersey legislature perpetuate low taxes and other special privileges for railroads and public service corporations.

The muckrakers' analysis of business and political corruption confirmed progressive leaders' belief that the American republic must be reformed or become a businessman's oligarchy, and the widespread circulation of their articles helped to create the support necessary for successful progressive political action.

Architecture, Painting, and Literature

Architecture

The two most innovative architects of this period, Louis Sullivan and Frank Lloyd Wright, were perhaps too sophisticated for popular taste, but their work has stood the test of time and is still studied by students of architecture in the twenty-first century. Although Sullivan continued to do distinguished work until after World War I, his commissions became more and more infrequent. Meanwhile, a number of talented designer-engineers built functional and often esthetically inspiring bridges and factories of steel and reinforced concrete, but most architects and their businessmen-clients, however, emphasized form rather than function. The overwhelming majority of the buildings of the era were more banal than creative, more pretentious than graceful. The same held for private houses. Sullivan, Wright, and a few others did imaginative work; but most new construction was eclectic. When historical styles such as Cape Cod, Georgian, or Greek revival were used, the end product almost invariably violated the lines and proportions that had given the originals their distinction.

Sullivan attributed this failure of taste to the appeal of the Roman façades, false monumentalism, and harmonious lagoons of the Great White City fashioned for Chicago's Columbian Exposition of 1893. "The damage ... has penetrated deep into the ... American mind," he wrote, "effecting there lesions of dementia." More likely, however, the Exposition's imperial style touched the same impulses for grandeur that ordained the acquisition of an empire after the war with Spain in 1898.

Frank Lloyd Wright, Sullivan's student, also failed to exercise much immediate influence on the American skyline. "Early in life," Wright once wrote, "I had to choose between honest arrogance and hypocritical humility. I chose honest arrogance." Wright further developed Sullivan's concept of "organic" architecture. Professing a regional style (he was in fact influenced by the Japanese), he designed from the inside out, always emphasizing the unique texture of his materials. He used native woods, horizontal planes, and deep overhangs and often succeeded brilliantly in harmonizing his buildings with their natural surroundings. As early as 1900, the *Architectural Review* recognized Wright's genius; and by 1905 his work had deeply affected the modern movement in Germany, Holland, and France. Only as Europeans like Walter Gropius brought his ideas back to the United States, however, did Wright make a vigorous imprint on American architecture. Meanwhile, the skilled traditionalists Stanford White, Ralph Adams Cram, and their disciples, continued both to form and to reflect the widespread preference for Roman and Gothic.

Ironically, the maligned Columbian Exposition had a much greater impact on progressive public policy than did the works of Sullivan and Wright, the true intellectual progressives. Its classic spaciousness sparked a nationwide movement to beautify American cities. Uncounted urban open spaces were converted into parks, and sums commensurate with the nation's wealth were poured into public buildings. Unfortunately, little attention was given to the flow of traffic, and even less to the needs, interests, and habits of pedestrians. Almost always, moreover, the buildings erected were more derivative than original in design.

Painting

"There is a state of unrest all over the world in art as in all other things," the director of the Metropolitan Museum complained in 1908. "It is the same in literature, as in music, in painting, and in sculpture." This was the year that eight young painters, spearheaded by the realists Robert Henri, George B. Luks, and John Sloan, protested against the National Academy's near blackout of their work and staged a private show in New York. They rebelled not against the old painting techniques—they never mastered the new ones—but against the class bias that failed to see reality in all human activity, including the seamy. Their work of social protest grew more out of the political ferment of the era than the revolution in art forms that had already swept Europe. Inevitably, Victorian-minded critics dismissed them as "apostles of ugliness," "the revolutionary gang," "the black gang," and, most often, "the ashcan school."

▶ Robert Henri's painting *Salome*, 1909.

Meanwhile, more creative European currents were beginning to affect American artists. By 1912, the work of the Postimpressionists was familiar to sophisticated habitués of the New York gallery of the revolutionary camera artist Alfred Stieglitz. The next year sixteen hundred paintings, drawings, prints, and pieces of sculpture representing almost every mode in modern art appeared in a spectacular show at the New York Armory. Picasso, Matisse, Brancusi, Duchamp, Kandinsky, Cezanne, Van Gogh, Gauguin, and others had their work displayed, to the extreme discomfort of conservative critics. The *New York Times* labeled the show "pathological." *Art and Progress* compared many of its artists to "anarchists, bomb-throwers, lunatics, and depravers." An official of the Chicago Law and Order League demanded that the exhibition be banned from his city because the "idea that people can gaze at this sort of thing without it hurting them is all bosh."

New York was the venue for introducing the new work, but it played another role, too, in the transition to modern art. In *The Great American Thing,* art historian Wanda Corn demonstrates how much creative energy flowed from various artists' encounters with New York City itself in these years—the city then being a place where new urban forms were being pioneered. For perhaps the first time, avant-garde sensibilities were being shaped on this side of the Atlantic, as well as in Europe.

In hindsight, it is possible to conclude that the vehemence of conservative criticism and the desperation of these critics' counterattack served only to underscore their artistic bankruptcy. As the art historian Sam Hunter writes, "They were soon unable to pose with real conviction or enthusiasm a possible alternative, since even the art they defended was becoming a retarded and diluted academic derivative of some form of modernism." Nevertheless, the public proved as slow to accept the highly individualized abstractionism of the new painters (including the Americans Max Weber and John Mann) as it did the architecture of Sullivan and Wright.

The Novel

The trend toward realism in literature, begun in part by Henry James, continued in his own late works and in the novels of Willa Cather, author of *O Pioneers!* (1913) and *My Antonia* (1918), and Edith Wharton's novels of manners—including *Ethan Frome* (1911) and *The Age of Innocence* (1920), a story of New York high society.

Meanwhile, Jack London and Frank Norris were writing the survival-of-the-fittest doctrine into a host of brutal novels ranging in subject from the individual's struggle against the elements to the battle with the trusts. It was in the writings of Theodore Dreiser, however, that naturalism—as literary determinism was called—proved most profound. The son of German Catholic immigrants who settled in Indiana, Dreiser early disavowed belief in religion and conventional morality. "Man was a mechanism," he wrote, "undevised and uncreated, and a badly and carelessly driven one at that." Yet Dreiser, no less than his predecessors, was a moralist at heart. All his work was charged by a tension between determinism and its antithesis. In the very act of denying free will and the importance of man, he affirmed them. "To have accepted America as he has accepted it, to immerse oneself in something one can neither escape nor relinquish, to yield to what has been true and to yearn over what has seemed inexorable," this, concluded critic Alfred Kazin, "has been Dreiser's fate and the secret of his victory."

Dreiser's publisher withdrew his first novel, *Sister Carrie* (1900), because of its harsh reception. Critics, many of whom objected to the novel's sympathetic treatment of a "fallen woman," failed to see that its account of the purposelessness of life was counterbalanced by its emphasis on life's sheer vitality. His second book, *Jennie Gerhardt* (1911), like *Sister Carrie* the story of an otherwise virtuous "kept woman," struck at the failure of the conventional moral code to correspond to reality. Similar themes pervaded *The Financier* (1912) and *The Titan* (1914), though they were widely regarded as Progressive indictments of the "robber barons."

Poetry

The years before World War I also witnessed a remarkable renaissance in poetry. Perhaps the most powerful voice was that of Edwin Arlington Robinson, a traditionalist who dealt with the abiding theme of the individual's search for God and truth amidst darkness and suffering.

Robinson failed in his quest. Life and human destiny remained mysterious, yet in the "black and awful chaos of the night" he felt "the coming glory of the Light." Rescued from obscurity by Theodore Roosevelt, who gave him a government sinecure after reading his *Children of the Night* (1897), Robinson failed, nevertheless to receive full recognition until after the war.

In 1912, Harriet Monroe established the magazine *Poetry* in Chicago, and renaissance was at hand. Vachel Lindsay, now remembered more for his jazz-like odes than his sensitive lyrics, published his "General William Booth Enters into Heaven" in the first issue of *Poetry*, and then went on to exalt the common people in numerous other works. Edgar Lee Masters, Clarence Darrow's law partner, startled traditionalists with his masterpiece, *Spoon River Anthology* in 1915. There he laid bare the sham and moral shabbiness of small-town America in a brilliant combination of irony, sadness, and humor that closed, paradoxically, on an affirmative note. A year later, Carl Sandburg's first important volume appeared. A Whitmanesque romantic who employed free verse, Sandburg glorified Chicago as the roaring, brawling butcher and steel-maker to the world. During these same years, Robert Frost was writing deceptively simple verse against a rural New England backdrop that masked his passionate, almost terrifying, life force.

At the same time, another revolt against the genteel tradition was brewing among a group of American and English poets in London, the so-called imagists. Led by Ezra Pound and Amy Lowell, they asserted that the poet should re-create impressions caught in the fleeting image. Holding that meter and rhyme made the creation of a pure image difficult, if not impossible, they rejected these confining conventions. They also dismissed Romanticism as being the literary expression of a decadent humanistic culture. They were soon joined by T. S. Eliot, whose now classic "The Love Song of J. Alfred Prufrock" met a hostile reception when first published in *Poetry* in 1915.

▶ American poet, Robert Frost received four Pulitzer Prizes throughout his lifetime for his work.

Both the novels and the poetry by these early twentieth-century writers reflected a new aesthetic, one that critics have called "modernism." Rejecting the sentimentalism of many nineteenth-century writers, the new voices constituted a definitive break with the past.

Two Milestones

Women and Women's Suffrage

The modest changes in the status of women, which had brought coeducational education to two-thirds of the nation's colleges and universities by the 1890s, continued through the Progressive Era. The revolution in morals commonly ascribed to the 1920s had actually become a subject of social commentary well before World War I. Divorce became much more common; and though divorcees remained "tainted," by 1916 one marriage in nine was ending in divorce, as compared to one in twenty-one in 1880. Meanwhile, working-class men, especially Irish, were deserting their families in appalling numbers. By 1920, despite religious scruples and high legal costs, the working-class divorce rate equaled that of the middle class.

Concurrently, the percentage of married women employed outside the home rose to 10.7 percent by 1910, as the number of working women passed six million. The concept of "equal pay for equal work" even received a brief trial during World War I, though the hostility of unions and the widespread belief that women's employment should be regarded as temporary or supplementary soon restored the old order.

Intellectually, Charlotte Perkins Gilman of the famous Beecher family leveled the era's most penetrating attack on prevailing sexual and familial arrangements. A woman's survival, wrote Gilman, depended on her ability to seduce and hold a husband: "Men worked to live . . ., while, women mated to live." Among many other solutions, Gilman proposed complete emancipation of women from domestic duties through the establishment of day nurseries and communal kitchens—though who would staff them remained somewhat murky.

Most working women labored out of economic necessity, and their particular concerns were addressed by the most celebrated feminists of the era—Jane Addams, Lillian Wald, Florence Kelley—and by thousands of less well-known figures. (See *"Florence Kelley: Social Reformer."*) Often working out of Chicago's Hull House, New York's Henry Street Settlement, and other settlement houses, they strove to help immigrant women adjust to American life while encouraging the immigrants to preserve the best of their own cultures.

More importantly—for the settlement movement reached only a comparative few—the social reformers in the broader circle both inspired and did much of the tedious research behind hundreds of state and federal laws prescribing working conditions for women, children, and even men. Time and again their testimony before state and congressional legislative committees tipped

▶ Women suffragists marching on Pennsylvania Avenue in Washington.

▶ Suffrage parade in New York City on October 23, 1915

the balance. "If I wanted to put a measure through—no matter how silly or outrageous—," grumbled an arch conservative West Virginia assemblyman, "I would simply get a handsome woman—with a sort of cheerful ring in her voice—to come down here and lobby for it." Historian Robyn Muncy has referred to this social reform-oriented feminist network and the various agencies the reformers either ran or influenced as the "female dominion."

Meanwhile the long struggle for women's suffrage was drawing to a successful conclusion, with two discrete organizations each making its own unique contribution. A new voice came into the suffrage battle when, in 1909, Pennsylvania-born Alice Paul returned from studying in England at the height of the suffrage struggle there. Having observed the militant tactics employed by British suffragists, Paul joined the National American Woman Suffrage Association (NAWSA), but quickly became unhappy with what she saw as too tame an approach. She then organized a group of like-minded women into what would eventually become the National Woman's Party in 1917. Paul and her colleagues began picketing the White House in 1913 during Woodrow Wilson's first term in office. Arrested for picketing, they then went on a hunger strike, the same tactics used by British suffragists. It is difficult to parse how much the eventual victory owed to Paul and her group; however, at the very least President Wilson, who long opposed suffrage, began to find NAWSA more attractive when he considered the alternative.

As for NAWSA, its fortunes improved under the leadership of Carrie Chapman Catt. A superb organizer and skilled politician with broad social concerns, Catt had served from 1900 to 1904 as Susan B. Anthony's successor as NAWSA's president. She then put her unflagging energies into mobilizing suffrage sentiment in the states and, in 1915, to helping Jane Addams organize the Woman's Peace Party. Catt returned to the presidency of NAWSA the following year to combat what she saw as the divisive tactics of Alice Paul's group and to confront the mounting opposition of conventional women to the movement for suffrage.

MAP 19.2 Women's Suffrage Before the Nineteenth Amendment

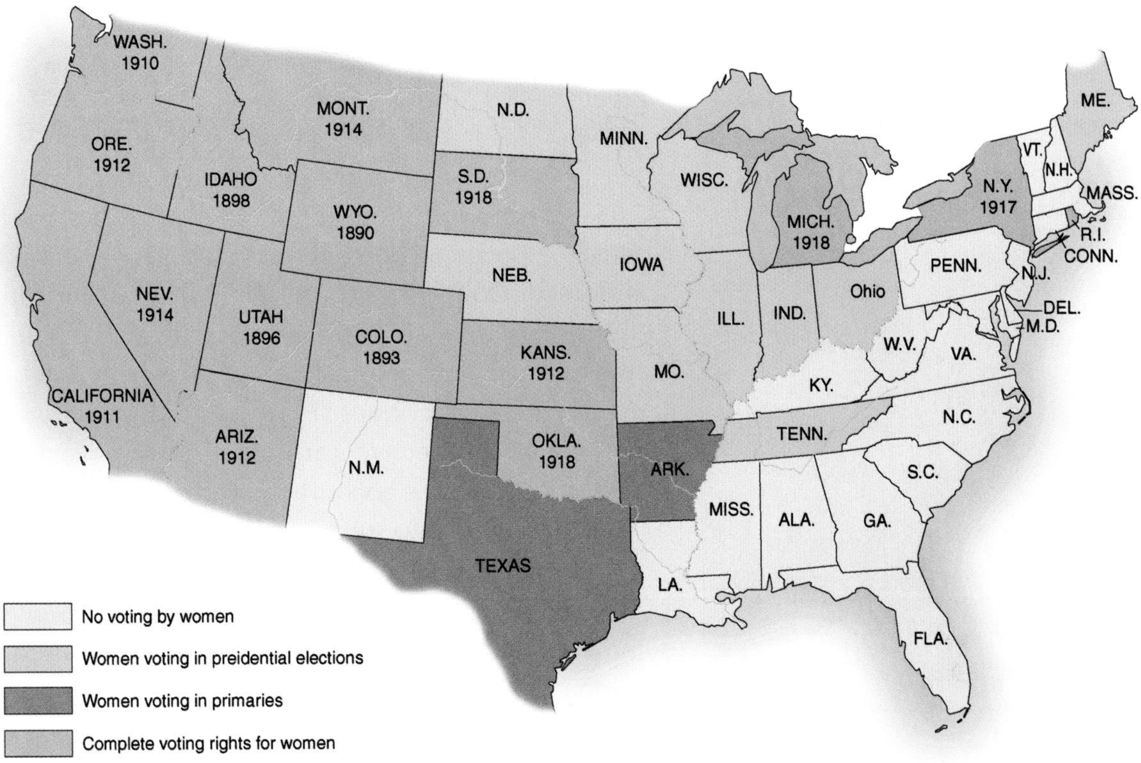

Publicly, at least, the suffragists justified the vote for women in terms of broad social and political policy. Their arguments frequently overlapped, and their emphasis shifted with time and place; in general, however, several distinct approaches emerged. The social-reformer feminists contended that suffrage would produce a more just and compassionate society and even eliminate war. As Addams said, a woman cannot care properly for her family if she has no voice in making the laws and electing the officials who determine whether her home has pure water, fresh food, proper sanitation, and adequate police protection. Others, more politically conservative and probably more representative of suffragists as a whole, argued that suffrage would reestablish Anglo-Saxon domination of urban politics and clean out corruption. Professional women tended to put the case almost solely in terms of career discrimination. Protestant churchwomen, and most social reformers as well, argued that the women's vote would assure national prohibition legislation. Only a small minority of fervent radicals boldly declared that suffrage would enable women to free themselves of male domination within marriage.

Opposition to women's suffrage came from some Protestant fundamentalists, however, who argued that God had created for women a separate, exclusively female role in society and that women did not belong outside of this female "sphere" of "wifery" and childbearing. In this mind-set, suffrage was, therefore, viewed as a threat to the "God-ordained" natural order of society where women were assigned a subservient place as "man's helper." Both Protestant fundamentalists and traditional Catholics also opposed women's suffrage as a measure linked to the movement for birth control—which they equated with promiscuity, loose morals, and the erosion of family values.

People that Made a Difference

▶ Florence Kelly: Social Reformer

▶ Florence Kelley

Of Florence Kelley it was said that she projected so much energy and courage that when she came into a room, "Everyone was brave." Born in Philadelphia in 1859, she was a descendant of Quaker botanist John Bartram. Her father, Congressman William D. Kelley, was a former Jacksonian Democrat who left the party over slavery in 1854 and later earned the sobriquet "Pig Iron" for his vigorous defense of the protective tariff. An early advocate of woman's suffrage, he encouraged Florence, the only one of his six daughters to survive infancy, to attend Cornell.

Although Florence's senior thesis on the legal status of children was published in the *International Review* the summer of her graduation in 1882, she was refused admission to the University of Pennsylvania Graduate School because of her sex. She then enrolled at the University of Zurich, the first European university to admit women. There she became a socialist in the belief that Marxism explained both the cruel treatment of children, which she had earlier observed in England, and American slavery, as her Quaker relatives had described it to her. She also entered into correspondence with Marx's collaborator, Friedrich Engles, and later translated his *The Condition of the Working Class in England* in 1844.

While in Zurich, Florence married a Russian socialist medical student, Lazare Wischnewetsky, and bore the first of three children. In 1886 the couple went to New York and Wischnewetsky tried, with mediocre results, to establish a medical practice. They joined the Socialist Labor Party, but the Europeans who dominated the local group mistrusted her and soon expelled both of them, perhaps because Florence could be as explosive and hot-tempered as she was dedicated and nondoctrinaire. Meanwhile she bore two more children. Then, following several years of estrangement from her husband, she moved to Illinois to obtain a divorce under that state's more permissive laws. At first she lived in Jane Addams' Hull House while the children lived at the home of the reformer Henry Demarest Lloyd in Winnetka. After the divorce, Florence resumed her maiden name and reunited the family in an apartment near Hull House.

Kelley's energy, incisiveness, and wit won her quick entry into Hull House's inner circle. As Addams wrote, she "galvanized us all into more intelligent interest in industrial conditions about us." In 1893, largely as a consequence of Kelley's lobbying, the state legislature enacted a statute to limit hours of work for women, prohibit child labor, and control tenement sweatshops. Appointed Chief Factory Inspector by Governor John Peter Altgeld, Kelley braved a smallpox epidemic to inspect sweatshops and once received a warning shot outside a factory.

Although her annual reports kept conditions before the public, prosecution of violators proved so difficult that she took a law degree in the evening division of the Northwestern University Law School in 1894. Three years later Altgeld's conservative successor dismissed her. Kelley continued to work out of Hull House for two more years, supporting her family by working evenings at the John Crerar Library. Then in 1899, she and the children moved to Lillian Wald's Henry Street Settlement in New York, and Kelley became executive secretary of the newly formed National Consumer's League.

The League strove to persuade consumers to press for improved working conditions, and under Kelley's forceful leadership it became one of the most effective reform agencies of the Progressive Era. At its height it had sixty leagues in twenty states. "No gentle saint," in the words of one of her intimates, Kelley gave her opponents no quarter. She favored "direct assault" but was not averse to "guerilla" tactics. Legislators shrank under the fury of her scorn and the power of her magnificent presence. "She had the voice and presence of a great actress," noted Frances Perkins, "though she was far from theatrical in her intentions."

By 1913, mainly because of Kelley's efforts, nine states had adopted minimum wage legislation for women. Meanwhile she had assembled much of the medical and sociological data on the differences between men and women that Louis D. Brandeis incorporated in his defense of Oregon's ten-hour-day law for women in Muller v. Oregon (1908). (It should be noted that the new feminists of the 1970s repudiated much of this logic—that is, that the differences between men and women are so vast as to warrant special treatment for women workers).

The death of Kelley's only daughter from heart disease in 1905 seemed to give a special urgency to her abiding interest in the welfare of children. She played an important role in marshalling support for a federal children's bureau in 1912, the child labor bill of 1916, and the Sheppard-Towner maternity-aid measure of 1921. Irritated by Samuel Gompers' lack of interest in social legislation, she wrote him off as an "aged Dodo." Nor could she contain herself when the Supreme Court struck down state minimum wage legislation and the second child labor act early in the 1920s. Why, she asked, are "seals, bears, reindeer, fish, wild game in the national parks, buffalo, migratory birds, all found suitable for federal protection; but not the children of our race and their mothers?"

Kelley long served as vice-president of the National Woman Suffrage Association, partly in the conviction that municipal government and services would not be cleaned up until women got the vote. She had felt since 1885, however, that the suffrage movement was preoccupied with problems of the middle-class women, and she feared that the proposed Equal Rights Amendment of the twenties would wipe out the hard-won protective legislation for lower-class working women by eliminating laws based on the physical differences between men and women. "How cruel ...," she wrote, "is the pretension of certain organizations of professional and business women to decide for the wage-earners ... what statutory safeguards they are henceforth to do without."

Florence Kelly: Social Reformer

(Continued)

Kelley was equally scornful of the new Woman's Party's refusal to fight against the disfranchisement of blacks in the South. "An inglorious ideal of equality this!" she expostulated. "Acquiescence in the disfranchisement of millions of women, provided only that the men of their race also are deprived of their constitutional rights."

Kelley continued her leadership of the National Consumers' League and her campaign for social justice until her death. She maintained a nominal socialist affiliation over the years, prompting one conservative United States senator to declare in the 1920s that her proposed child labor amendment "derived straight from the communist manifesto of 1848." Yet, partly because of her Quaker heritage, she lacked the requisite temperament to be doctrinaire on anything but pacifism. More an activist than a theoretician, she believed that the moral sensibilities of the middle classes—especially women—would eventually bring the reforms she sought. She died from anemia in 1932, too early to see the partial harvest that came with the New Deal.

Nevertheless, by 1917, Catt's tactics had already won substantial support in the states, and the suffragists were urgently pressing most of the suffragettes' considerations on Congress. Many congressmen—probably most—were privately unsympathetic; but by mounting pressure on these congressmen from within their home districts, however, shrewdly aligning themselves with the prohibitionists, and capitalizing on the Wilson administration's desire for wartime unity, Catt's forces persuaded the House to approve a federal suffrage amendment in January 1918. Eighteen months later a lobby-wearied Senate also submitted and within fifteen months three-fourths of the states had ratified the Nineteenth Amendment. In simple declarative language it stated that the right to vote should not be abridged "on account of sex." Women would then vote for the first time in the federal elections of 1920, and their presence in the electorate was part of the reason that the Republicans nominated Warren G. Harding that year on the belief that he was physically attractive to women. The overall impact of women in the electorate was less than some expected, however, because women did not vote as a cohesive group and had just as many political divisions among them as men.

Margaret Sanger and Birth Control

The swirling cross currents of the turbulent women's movement engulfed the movement for birth control. In 1873, Congress passed what became known as the "Comstock Law," which banned the sending of obscene materials through the mail. A special postal agent named Anthony Comstock determined, at his discretion, what did or did not violate the law; as a result, contraceptives and information concerning contraception or any anatomical drawings and many medical terms were deemed to be obscene and subject to seizure by the United States Postal Service. Until well into the Progressive Era, Protestants and Catholics alike had regarded artificial contraception as a violation of the law of God; and by 1914 twenty-two states had anti-birth control statutes on their books. By then the shift to an industrial society had made large families an economic liability, especially in towns and cities. This latter reality had already induced a decline in the birth rate, notably among old-stock urban whites in the middle and upper classes. For the most part, however, this decline reflected natural controls.

So strong was the consensus against contraceptives at this time that Congress banned the dissemination of birth control information in interstate commerce in 1914. This ban provoked a bitter reaction, in particular among younger radical feminists and political leftists—for different reasons. The feminists saw contraception as a form of emancipation, or as a means to reduce men's sexual exploitation of women. Those on the political left believed that capitalists wanted more births in order to create a surplus of labor and thus keep down wages. The views of these two groups fused in the early career of Margaret Sanger, who for forty years served as the knife's edge of the movement for birth control.

Sanger was the daughter of an Irish-born workingman, an all-round iconoclast who had renounced his Catholicism and her mother who bore eleven children. Sanger became a nurse with a practice in New York. In 1912, following the death of a working girl from a self-induced abortion, Sanger stripped off her nurse's uniform and emerged as *l'enfant terrible* of the birth-control campaign. Inspired at first by the anarchist Emma Goldman, she was also encouraged by William D. "Big Bill" Haywood of the left-leaning Industrial Workers of the World, Eugene V. Debs of the Socialist Party, and women's liberation groups.

Concluding that the marriage bed was "the most degenerating influence in the social order" because it made sex-chattels of wives, Sanger declared that women "are determined to decide for themselves whether they shall become mothers, under what conditions, and when." Soon she was urging women to stop producing children "who will become slaves to feed, fight and toil for the enemy—Capitalism." Then, in 1916, she defied the law by opening a birth-control clinic in New York. Tried and found guilty, she won a partial victory on appeal, in 1918, when the court's opinion gave physicians somewhat greater latitude to prescribe contraception (a battle that would not be fully won until 1965).

Sanger's agitation broadened the movement's base. Partly in the conviction that smaller families would raise the standard of living of the poor, middle-class reformers organized the National Birth Control League in 1915. Two years later, the philosopher John Dewey drafted a measure that would have made contraceptives freely available in New York. The New York State legislature, however, refused to give the measure serious consideration.

▶ Advertisement in the magazine *Science & Invention* for Margaret Sanger's book, "*Woman and the New Race,*" January 1922, showing Sanger with her two young sons.

Meanwhile, eugenicists took up the cause in the belief that mental defectiveness was transmitted through the genes and could be greatly reduced through birth control. The ranks of these eugenicists included some of the most blatant racists and conservative elitists in the country—as well as people with a genuine concern about hereditary disease. Buoyed by the support of these and other respectable figures, Sanger began to abandon her socialist rationale for birth control. "More children from the fit, less from the unfit—that is the chief issue," she announced in 1919. Marxism, she contemptuously asserted in 1922, is "purely masculine reasoning."

Nevertheless, religious opposition to contraception remained vigorous—and among the lower classes, effective—through the 1920s. The Catholic Church became increasingly militant in its defense of the Papacy's standing disapproval of contraception, and it was not until 1931 that a major Protestant body—the Federal Council of Churches of Christ—formally endorsed birth control. Long before then, however, large numbers of Protestant clergymen had become silent converts to the movement. By the mid-20s the use of contraceptives was commonplace among middle-class Protestants, Jews, and non-church people. Old-line radical feminists like Charlotte Perkins Gilman were continuing to hold that only procreation justified intercourse, but there was wide acceptance among non-Catholics of the newer generation's contention that it should also be indulged in simply for reasons of pleasure.

The Triumph of National Prohibition

The informal alliance of the suffragists and prohibitionists arose out of considerably more than convenience. As Norman H. Clark observes in his perceptive revisionist synthesis, *Deliver Us from Evil*, the prohibition movement aimed to "protect the values sheltered by the American nuclear family" at a time when it seemed that its security was more urgent to society's well-being than were the rights of individuals. Alcoholism had been a "WASP" (White Anglo-Saxon Protestant) problem since the founding of Jamestown, and Southern Baptist and Northern Methodist women had long been in the vanguard of the movement to restrict the indiscriminate use of liquor. By 1900, thirty-seven mainly rural Protestant states had enacted local option laws where local governments could prohibit alcohol, often by popular vote. In 1907, Oklahoma, an old-stock territory with a minuscule foreign population came into the union with a completely dry constitution; and by 1919 ten of the twelve states in which women could vote had outlawed the saloon.

These facts suggest that Prohibition's much remarked anti-ethnic and anti-Catholic thrust was more incidental than causal. Only because many Germans happened to be heavy beer drinkers and many Irish heavy whisky drinkers did the movement become identified as a "nativist" crusade. It should be mentioned, however, that the *Baptist Standard* in 1917 proclaimed, "Prohibition is an issue of Anglo-Saxon culture versus the inferior civilization of niggers in the cities." Therefore, nativism and racism were most certainly present in the movement.

Nevertheless, pietist immigrants from Sweden supported prohibition vigorously, as did many Reformed and other non-Lutheran Germans. A group of priests organized the Catholic Clergy Prohibition League, and Father J. J. Curran served twenty-five years as a national vice-president of the Anti-Saloon League. The bishop of Montana, a state where hard drinking was notorious among Irish miners, even observed that prohibition would contribute to the "spiritual progress of the Catholic Church" in America.

Neither was prohibition an essentially rural phenomenon, despite its successes in rural states. Most sponsors of local option laws were town or city people, and most members of the W.C.T.U. and the Anti-Saloon League were urban. As Clark writes, "Behind them in solid support were the deep ranks of urban business leaders, labor leaders, attorneys, physicians, teachers—both Catholic and Protestant." They stood behind prohibition because they perceived alcoholism to be a grave social problem, as did their counterparts in Finland, Scandinavia, Germany, Britain, France, and the province of Quebec—all of which had serious temperance movements. They realized, of course, that saloons served as workingmen's clubs, but they also saw that many embodied the worst features of urban industrial culture: "blatantly and aggressively masculine to the mood of a sneering *machismo*, linked sordidly to organized crime, organized prostitution, and the organized herding of mercenary voters." Hardly a social reformer with first-hand knowledge of the saloon's impact on family life and urban politics failed to support prohibition, probably with the silent support of hundreds of thousands of workingmen's wives.

Women tended to favor prohibition because, for many women, their husbands were their sole source of financial support for them and their children. Alcoholic husbands were less likely to remain employed, thus threatening the well being of the wife and her children. Thus, women allied with big business owners who favored prohibition for the creation of a sober and, therefore, more productive workforce. Additionally, it was well understood that some men have a tendency to become abusive when under the influence of alcohol, and the women who were the victims of that abuse sought a remedy through prohibition.

Protestant fundamentalists tended to favor prohibition as well, not only as an anti-Catholic measure but also due to strict interpretations of the Bible that viewed the consumption of alcohol, especially to excess, as sinful. An alcohol-free society in their view would, therefore, be a more Godly society.

New scientific evidence on the linkage between alcoholism and brain damage further strengthened the prohibition movement in business and professional circles. Physicians prescribed alcohol less frequently, and in 1914 a national meeting of psychiatrists and neurologists actually pronounced it a poison. At the same time, numerous investigations by social scientists revealed relationships between alcohol and crime, prostitution, and poverty. By 1916, as Clark concludes, science, no less than organized religion, had prepared the way for total abstinence.

The entry of the United States into World War I also produced a general moral crusade linked to the moralistic views of President Woodrow Wilson. Many Americans viewed the American role in World War I as one of bringing the superior "American way" and democracy to the rest of the world. If the United States were to embark on a moral crusade, it would be a contradiction to do it while drunk.

Nevertheless, the moderate prohibitionists would probably have settled for a ban on hard liquor; but the so-called wets, who were liberally financed by the hard liquor industry as well as by German-American beer interests, stiffened dry lines by refusing to compromise. Soon after the United States entered the Great War, the War Department gave the prohibitionists an important victory by banning the sale of alcoholic beverages near army camps. When the Eighteenth Amendment—banning the manufacture, sale, and transportation of intoxicating liquor—still left it to Congress to define what was "intoxicating," prohibitionists won inclusion of beer and wines by playing up the need to conserve grain. The amendment, adopted by Congress in December 1917, went into effect in January 1920.

The Institutions of Change

Technology and Business

Chief among the many forces that made the Progressive Era a period of extraordinarily rapid change were technology and scientific management. In manufacturing, mechanization and time-and-motion-saving techniques pioneered by Frederick Winslow Taylor helped production to increase 76 percent between 1899 and 1909, while the labor force expanded only 40 percent. In organization and distribution, managerial innovations created nationwide markets.

By the early 1900s, the internal combustion automobile, powered by gasoline, had won the day over steam or electric-powered vehicles. In the automotive industry that soon developed, assembly-line production enabled Henry Ford to cut the price of his Model T from $950

▶An American family poses with their newly purchased new car, a Model T Ford, 1920

in 1912 to $290 by 1924. Ford also pioneered "just-in-time" technology where he synchronized with his suppliers just how much of each item he needed at what time so that he could have tires delivered the day he needed them for his cars, etc. Ford standardized and simplified as much as he could so as to keep down costs, with the result that every Ford Model T looked just like every other Model T so that the running joke was that Model T buyers could have "any color they wanted, as long as it was black." Ford also pioneered the idea of paying his employees more than the going rate, "$5 per day," so that they could actually purchase one of the cars they built. In so doing, Ford essentially created his own market for his cars. By 1917, almost 5 million vehicles were clogging a partially macadamized highway system. In addition, the automobile industry produced huge spin-offs, thus boosting the iron, steel, oil, paint, glass, copper, textile, and rubber industries as well as a host of others.

Automobiles, however, were not the only technological innovation driving economic growth. Orville and Wilber Wright launched their successful airplane flight at Kitty Hawk, North Carolina, in 1903; the aviation industry was born. By the time of the American entry into World War I, a seven million telephone network had wrought a revolution in communication by the time of the American entry into World War I, and some fifty corporate research laboratories were forging another revolution in product development. Meanwhile, the use of electricity grew so fast that by the end of World War I it powered more than half of American industry—whereas only 2 percent of American industrial power had been supplied by electricity at the turn of the century. Electricity, in turn, had spawned a booming home appliance industry. Among the most important new electrical powered items was the radio—which brought mass culture, national advertising, and national news. By 1920, Americans owned ten million radios, and the number was growing rapidly.

Not all the effects proved salutary. Skilled workers were downgraded in older industries like steel and textiles; and the dehumanizing efficiencies of the assembly lines and of Taylorism, where workers were viewed as "interchangeable cogs," made virtual automatons of everyone but supervisors in many of the newer industries. On the other hand, real

▶ When Orville and Wilber Wright successfully launched their airplane into flight in 1903, the aviation industry was born.

wages in manufacturing rose 37 percent from 1897 to 1914, and rose again during the war. Outside the factories, moreover, the number of skilled workers—electricians, plumbers, carpenters, toolmakers, automobile mechanics, and heavy equipment operators—grew greatly. An increase in the clerical and sales work force from 3 percent in 1880 to 8 percent by 1910 also raised the number of reasonably challenging jobs. Increased wages, together with the spread of truck gardening, the rise of the citrus industry, and increased use of refrigerated railroad cars, produced a marked improvement in diet. By the early 1900s, the average American worker and his family were consuming twice as much meat as their British counterparts, in addition to increasing amounts of citrus fruits.

Modernizing the Government

Years before the Progressive Era began, thoughtful observers of the American scene agreed that the art of government had not kept pace with the science of industry. Progressives proposed, consequently, to apply the techniques of business management to the bewildering complexities of the new urban and industrial society. With remarkable unanimity, they turned to experts—scientists, engineers, economists, physicians, political scientists, and social workers—for information, political support, and personnel to staff new or enlarged departments and regulatory commissions.

By the end of the era much of American government had become thoroughly modernized and professionalized. Graduate engineers were planning and operating municipal sewer and water systems. Trained medical personnel were combating disease by enforcing public health measures. Experts with Ph.D.s in agronomy, chemistry, and other sciences were engaged in research sponsored by the Department of Agriculture at land-grant universities and experimental stations. Even police and fire department recruits, traditionally trained on the job, were attending newly founded academies.

Politically, the modernization of government increased the distance between the average citizen and the decision-makers, and the move to a more merit-oriented civil service system of government recruitment diminished the "spoils" associated with politics and, therefore, direct vested interests of many in political outcomes. Progressives viewed party reforms as crucial since the primary tool of reform used by progressives was government. It was assumed by progressives that government would not be a good tool for reform if the political party system remained based on patronage and corruption. This doubtless contributed to a decline in voter turnout, one of the most pronounced trends of modern times, but the social benefits were almost incalculable.

Among the political reforms that progressives championed was a shift to secret ballots so as to minimize coercion at the polls. Prior to the introduction of the secret ballot, violence and intimidation of voters were rampant since others knew how one voted at the polling place. The secret ballot was initiated on a state-by-state basis beginning as early as the 1880s.

In reaction to the corruption in government at local levels, such as the famous political machine of Boss Tweed, progressives reformed local government structures to decentralize power away from the mayor's office. Stanton, Virginia, introduced the council-manager format, where an elected city council performed legislative duties, in 1908 but executive powers were vested in an appointed professional city manager that was responsible to the council, thus separating legislative and executive powers at the local government level and introducing professionalism to local government. Some cities made local elections nonpartisan so as to diminish political party influences and further hinder the building of corrupt political party machines.

Other democratic reforms included the provisions of ballot initiatives whereby citizens could, through petition, place items on the ballot for public referendum (vote). Nineteen states had provisions for ballot initiative and referendum by 1918. Some states also implemented recall elections whereby citizens could, through petition, force an elected official to face an electoral challenge before the end of a prescribed term. Twelve states also passed restrictions on lobbyists, twenty-two banned corporate political contributions, and twenty-four states banned free passes on railroads for politicians.

Progress was also being made in the areas of health and sanitation. Louis Pasteur developed his germ theory of disease in 1869, and the discovery eventually led to a revolution in health and sanitation. In 1900, 50 percent of Americans did not live beyond the age of five due to poor sanitation and infectious diseases. In American factories, the drinking supply was often an open water barrel where all employees would simply dip their cups until the water was gone. Employees were sometimes told to dig their own latrines with no instruction and without pay. In the twenty years before the United States entered the Great War, advances in medical science and sanitation based on Pasteur's germ theory combined with improvements in diet to reduce the death rate from 17 to 12.2 per thousand, and to increase life expectancy from forty-nine to fifty-six years.

▶ In a time in which 50 percent of Americans did not live beyond the age of five due to poor sanitation and infectious diseases, Louis Pasteur's (shown above) research and discoveries were revolutionary for health and sanitation.

The Social Sciences

Psychology and Economics

The psychology of the period between the turn of the century and the Great War powerfully influenced progressive thought and attitudes. Freed from its old metaphysical and theological commitment by the Darwinian revolution, psychology had begun to explore the whole range of human activity; and by World War I, two definite schools—the instinct and the behaviorist—had emerged. Both were European in origin, and both found a receptive audience in the United States.

The founder of the instinct school in America, William McDougall, felt strongly that psychology should concern itself with social behavior. He contended that humans were ruled by deep-seated instincts rather than by rational or moral considerations; and his charge that classical economic theory was "a tissue of false conclusions drawn from false psychological assumptions" reinforced the insights Thorstein Veblen had already written into his *Theory of the Leisure Class* (1899). In *The Instinct of Workmanship and the State of the Industrial Arts* (1914), Veblen echoed Mc-

Dougall's strictures against the inadequate psychological base of classical economics. He especially charged that modern industrial institutions had failed to play upon people's constructive instincts. F. W. Taussig argued in *Inventors and Money-Makers* (1915) that the instinct of contrivance, or workmanship, did not depend necessarily on prospective gain, as the defenders of the profit-making system contended, but rather on the satisfaction of making something. Nevertheless, however much instinct psychology undermined classical economic thought, it produced no systematic theory of its own as a substitute.

The behaviorist psychology of the Russian Ivan Pavlov and the Americans E. L. Thorndike and John B. Watson proved both more receptive to, and more reflective of, progressive thought because it supported an environmentalist interpretation of society. Passing over everything that could not be verified by direct observation, the behaviorists sought to measure all human behavior in terms of stimulus and response. "It is the business of behavioristic psychology," wrote Watson, "to be able to predict and control human activity." Since consciousness was not observable, it should not be studied; thought was to be treated as latent speech.

Behaviorism offered too restricted and shocking a view of human nature to win universal acceptance, and humanists rejected it angrily. Nevertheless, it sired a school of psychology and markedly influenced all subsequent social science. It also contributed enormously to both the hard and soft sides of progressivism, to the production efficiencies of Taylorism—and to the reformers' belief that the poor were the victims of their environment. Behaviorism further contributed to the rise of the consumer society by giving an intellectual base to the manipulative skills of advertisers.

The New History

The writing of history proved no more immune to progressive currents than did other disciplines, nor did it escape their paradoxes. The influence of German methodology, first felt at Johns Hopkins, continued as historians now severed their ties with literature almost completely. Seeking scientific truth by the use of rigorously exact techniques, they destroyed hallowed beliefs, stripped history of its individual drama and romance, and lost their popular audience. Yet they added immeasurably to the general body of knowledge and contributed important new insights about the forces that had molded America.

One of the foremost characteristics of the new history was present-mindedness. As James Harvey Robinson and Charles A. Beard confessed in their path finding *The Development of Modern Europe* (1907), they had "consistently subordinated the past to the present" in the "ever-conscious aim to enable the reader to catch up with his own times." Implicit in this approach was a belief in laws of behavior as formulated by social scientists. The insights of philosophers, poets, and observers no longer sufficed. Implicit, also, was a desire to use history to create a better future. This last idea was not new. From the ancient Greek historian Thucydides to the twentieth century, historians had concerned themselves with the usable past. By Robinson and Beard's time, however, probably a majority of America's professional historians had conceived their task as being merely descriptive. It was against them and their failure to search for causal explanations that might indirectly bear on the present—to be, in the new view, truly scientific—that Robinson and Beard revolted.

As an example of the new work, Beard authored one book that is still being debated. "The Constitution," he wrote in *An Economic Interpretation of the Constitution* (1913), "was essentially an economic document based upon the concept that the fundamental private rights of property are anterior to government and morally beyond the reach of popular majorities." He then set forth data to substantiate his contention that through their interest in public securities, money, manufacturing, trade, and shipping, the framers of the Constitution had stood to gain directly from the establishment of the new government.

Beard insisted that his work was American-inspired, rather than inspired by the economic determinism of Karl Marx. James Madison, he repeatedly pointed out, had offered "one of the earliest, and certainly one of the clearest" statements of economic determinism. Morton G. White, however, argued that Beard's *An Economic Interpretation of the Constitution* actually reflected the worst, or at least the simplest, aspects of thought by both Marx and Madison. According to White, Marx neither denied man's capacity for high-minded action nor accepted the idea that every political action derived directly from an economic interest. Conversely, Madison believed with Aristotle that factions and interests were rooted in human nature—not, as Marx contended, in economic systems. In Beard's analysis, the framers had been moved by a narrow Marxist view of the deterministic force of economic systems and a similarly narrow Madisonian view of a direct relationship between self-interest and action. Recent scholarship has seriously challenged the evidence on which Beard based his economic thesis.

Beard always denied that he had written a tract for the times. "I simply sought to bring back into the mental picture of the Constitution," he said, "those realistic features of economic conflict, stress and strain, which my masters had, for some reason, left out of it, or thrust far into the background as incidental rather than fundamental."

Progressive Education

Public Education

Inevitably, the higher educational level required for entry into business and government inevitably transformed the public school system. Every strand of progressivism—from the quest for order, through the cult of efficiency, to the belief in equal opportunity—entered into the transformation. By the end of the era, the foundations and much of the superstructure of modern education had been firmly established.

In 1900, the upper classes sent their children to private schools or had them tutored; and except for a few middle-class sections of large cities, the public school system was in deplorable condition. Politics, corruption, and incompetence were rife; rote instruction, oversized classes, and an out-of-date curriculum were the norm. Teachers were often poorly prepared and even more poorly paid, averaging $42.15 a month—less than the wages of a day laborer. In the South, three years schooling was the norm for the region's schoolteachers; in the North, the norm was seven years. Southern states spent $9.72 per pupil each year on primary and secondary education and the Northern states spent $20.85.

The most pronounced changes occurred in the South, which experienced an educational revival comparable to the one that had swept the North before the Civil War, though mainly for white children only. Between 1900 and 1910, school budgets doubled, the enrollment of white children raised almost a third, and the school term had lengthened from five to six months. White illiteracy had also declined from 11.8 to 7.7 percent.

Nowhere, however, did the increase in expenditures affect all social and economic classes equally. Even in the richest states of the North, dependence on local taxation produced wide disparities between rural, small-town, suburban, and metropolitan appropriations. Old-stock whites in the remote areas of upper New England and western New York frequently fared worse than immigrants in the large cities. Within the urban systems, the middle-class composition of school boards also produced inequities. Almost invariably, facilities tended to be poorer and student-teacher ratios higher in lower class and ethnic neighborhoods.

Discrimination fell heaviest, of course, on blacks. Although they managed to decrease their illiteracy rate from 44.5 percent to 30.1 percent during the first decade of the century, no Southern state (and no Northern one either) made a conscientious effort to give black people equal facilities. By 1910, only 8,251 black youths were attending high school in the entire Southeast. As late as 1915 South Carolina was spending $13.98 annually for each white child and only $1.13 for each black child.

Meanwhile, an exceptionally high dropout rate, especially among immigrants' children, prompted a wave of compulsory attendance laws and curriculum changes. Some progressives believed that early employment deprived children of their birthright. Others feared that lack of schooling would create a permanent urban proletariat.

Virtually all recognized that the technological society required greater education for everyone. Vocational and commercial high schools were established in the larger cities with strong business support and, after 1917, federal subsidization. In single high school-towns, manual training and commercial courses were offered. For numerous reasons, including the failure of equipment and instruction to keep abreast of developments in industry, the vocational schools never flowered; but for years thereafter, the commercial courses produced a steady flow of male bookkeepers and female typists and stenographers.

In keeping with the spirit of the times, basic changes in the aims and methods of teaching accompanied the upgrading of physical facilities in the public schools. The most distinguished educational theorist of this period was philosopher John Dewey. Born in 1859 in Vermont, Dewey taught at the Universities of Michigan, Chicago, and Columbia and remained an influential and active force in American thought until his death in 1952.

To Dewey, valid thinking and understanding had to be based on one's own experience. Thus he abandoned authoritarian teaching methods and the use of rote practice. Subject matter, he felt, should be adapted to the needs and capabilities of children, and learning processes should be centered on their own experience and discovery. They should "learn by doing," inquiring and drawing their own generalizations instead of memorizing someone else's.

To foster such learning, he wrote in *School and Society* (1899), "means to make each one of our schools an embryonic community life, active with types of occupations that reflect the life of the larger society, and permeated throughout with the spirit of art, history, and science."

▶ A class photo of a 1915 class at the Geyer School in Ohio. Schools were better run and maintained in the North than the South, but schools everywhere were generally in poor condition. Classes were oversized, teacher-to-student ratios were unbalanced, curriculum quality was poor, salaries for teachers were miniscule, and there was little funding to support the students themselves.

Such schooling, he believed, would advance democracy and develop intelligence as a tool for social reform. The development of vocational education was in keeping with Dewey's interest in practical education.

Against the sustained opposition of traditionalists, Dewey and his followers accomplished one of the major cultural revolutions of the century. By the end of World War I, the Teachers College of Columbia University was well on the way to inculcating a new generation of teachers with a potentially creative approach to teaching. Dewey's most influential work, *Democracy and Education*, appeared in 1916. Three years later the Progressive Education Association was organized to advance the dynamic new program.

As in most creative changes, the costs proved high. Traditionalists within the universities failed, at first, to grasp the intellectual foundation of the reconstruction of primary and secondary education, thus forcing departments and colleges of education to organize without the help of the liberal arts faculties, who might have exercised a leavening influence on the new education curricula. At the same time, state teachers' colleges began to supplant the two-year normal schools. Directed by professional educators, they offered so many overlapping education courses as to make a mockery of the word *education*. On no level—B.S., M.S., or Ph.D.—did the quality of an education degree compare favorably with that of a degree in one of the traditional disciplines.

Higher Education

Colleges and universities were favorably influenced by the deepening of knowledge, the specialization induced by the new technology, and their own growing commitment to excellence during the Progressive Era. Concurrently, the quality of graduate and professional study rose notably. States greatly expanded their aid to higher education; municipal colleges and universities multiplied. Major strides also occurred in adult education; and between 1900, when the Association of American Universities was founded, and 1914, when the Great War broke out in Europe, the total enrollment in colleges and universities nearly doubled—increasing from 109,929 to 216,493. Concurrently, the status and salaries of college professors rose, and the percentage earning Ph.D.s increased.

The principle of academic freedom was also receiving wider and wider acceptance, except for some notorious violations during World War I. The improvements reflected, in part, the influence of the American Association of University Professors, organized in 1915; however, in the main, they simply marked the coming of age of American higher education.

Increased specialization, expanded research opportunities, and freedom to create led to great contributions to almost all areas of knowledge. By the end of the Progressive Era, American scholarship had surpassed European scholarship in some fields and equaled it in many others. Once again, however, the cost proved high. The social sciences developed their own vocabularies, often unnecessarily; and scientists, physicians, and engineers lost contact with the humanities and social sciences because of their need to specialize early in their undergraduate careers.

Legal education was beset by the same paradoxes. Pre-law training was steadily upgraded so that by World War I two years of undergraduate work was a common requirement for admission to reputable law schools. Except for in a handful of schools attached to the nation's most prestigious universities, however, the nature and theory of law were largely neglected. Even though a law degree became a virtual prerequisite for election to public office, most law schools turned out little more than competently trained technicians.

Medical education, which had become a national scandal, underwent a dramatic upgrading following publication of Abraham Flexner's searching report for the Carnegie Endowment in 1910. Medical care, however, was a different matter. For a few years, progressive elements of the medical profession showed interest in institutionalizing medical service to the poor. By 1919, however, entrepreneurial attitudes had become dominant within the already powerful American Medical Association (AMA). Proposals for the mildest forms of socialized medicine (Medicare) were fiercely repelled, and the United States' record of health care for the poor, both black and white, became one of the worst in the Western world. Conversely, advances in medical science, education, and technology, including an enormous hospital-construction program, put American care of the middle and upper-middle classes among the world's best.

In agriculture, federal grants-in-aid to land grant colleges underwrote invaluable research in crops, soil properties, and conservation practices. County agents and farmers' institutes sponsored by university extension services also brought scientific knowledge to farmers themselves, though the more poorly educated and less prosperous farmers generally resisted it. In the long term, these developments sharply increased the quality and quantity of agricultural production, but they also spurred the growth of commercial farming and the increase in tenancy.

Church and Society

Protestantism

The social and intellectual ferment of the Progressive Era affected religion and its institutions in profound and sometimes paradoxical ways. Organizations like the Young Men's Christian Association (YMCA), the International Sunday Schools Association, and the

American Bible Society blurred denominational lines, while fundamentalism, modernism (the attempt to reconcile contemporary scientific thought and traditional religion), and the Social Gospel cut across them. After 1908, the formation of the Federal Council of Churches of Christ in America by thirty-three evangelical bodies created a loose unity among their seventeen million members.

Simultaneously however, the Northern Presbyterian Church preserved the purity of its doctrines only by expelling several of its most distinguished ministers and losing control of its leading seminary, Union, in New York to the modernists. Modernist clergymen also captured many Northern Baptist, Congregational, and Methodist congregations, while perhaps a majority of intellectuals left the church in spirit.

Rural migrants to the city decisively rejected modernism. Uncomfortable in sophisticated urban congregations and uninterested in theological subtleties, they throve on the thundering fundamentalism of the Reverend Billy Sunday and a wave of revivalism that swept the established evangelical churches. Sunday, a former major league baseball player, attracted the largest crowds of any evangelist before the advent of electronic sound systems. Sunday also blended his religion with politics and openly campaigned for the Republican Party and Prohibition, as well as the American entry into the Great War.

Protestant fundamentalism further fragmented, however, as many became enthusiastic converts to Pentecostalism, to Holiness churches, and to the Jehovah's Witnesses. Many also responded to exhortations by spellbinders, like the Baptist Russell Conwell, to accept the prevailing social and economic order. In a thousand sermons the country over, Conwell affirmed the virtue of getting rich—"to make money honestly is to preach the gospel."

Conversely, a small but growing minority of urban ministers and laymen transformed the Social Gospel into a powerful progressive force during the prewar years. In general, supporters of the Social Gospel believed that churches should become more involved in alleviating societal suffering. Consequently, they offered political support to progressive programs aimed at curbing social injustices and developed essentially social welfare functions of their own. They agreed with the Congregational clergyman George Herron that the dualism of contemporary life was intolerable:

> A corporation, greedy, godless, vicious in many of its operations, consists of men famous for their piety and benevolence. A nation governed by men of eminent Christian character goes mad with the spoils of unrighteousness. . . . A church containing many sincere, teachable, self-sacrificing Christians is as powerless a moral institution in the community as the town pump.

In 1908, one year after the publication of Walter Rauschenbusch's most important work, *Christianity and the Social Crisis*, the Methodist Episcopal Church supported abolition of child labor and a host of other reforms. Though Methodists rejected Rauschenbusch's Christian Socialism, they accepted his graphic analysis of the brutalizing impact of the new industrial order. In that same year, the newly organized Federal Council of Churches of Christ called for the end of exploitative capitalism by a program of social-welfare legislation.

The Social Gospel movement quickened many lay consciences and raised profound questions about business ethics and the morality of the laws of the marketplace. Thus, it broadened and strengthened the moral foundations of the progressive movement. Other volunteer organizations also arose with goals of alleviating the plight of the poor. Perhaps the most well known and most successful of these is the Salvation Army, which grew to twenty-three thousand members by 1920. Nevertheless, the counter-truth remains: Evangelical Protestants spent more energy campaigning for prohibition and against parochial schools than they did in fighting exploitation of their fellow men and women.

Catholicism

Partly because of the Roman Catholic church's authoritarian structure and partly because of the still low educational level of most of its members, the Catholic church in America remained clear of the conflict over modernism that rocked Protestantism. For millions of immigrants, it was the one familiar institution in an alien culture. Despite the drop in membership during the Gilded Age, Poles and other workers supported the Catholic Church with much greater zeal than was being shown in Europe.

Assuredly, Catholicism was beset by other problems, including divisions within the American Catholic Church. A group of dissident Poles founded the National Polish Catholic Church in 1907. Italian American males gave the church only nominal support and broadly refused to send their children to parochial schools. As a consequence of the rapid development of new immigrant populations and internal divisions, there developed an acute shortage of priests of the same ethnic background as their parishioners. Then, after that problem began to be resolved, conflict ensued over whether instruction in the parochial schools should be in English or in the language of ethnic origin.

New immigrants also resented bitterly the reluctance of the Irish to share their domination of the church hierarchy. Finally, public support of parochial education was resisted by non-Catholics and not sanctioned by American legal institutions, subjecting many Catholics to a heavy financial burden. In spite of these difficulties, however, church membership and parochial education grew rapidly throughout the entire Progressive Era.

Although Catholic working people gave greater support than Protestants to the welfare aspects of progressivism, the Social Gospel movement had slight impact on the Catholic Church as an organization. The Paulist priest, economist, and political scientist, John A. Ryan, did emerge as one of the era's more influential reformers following publication of his *A Living Wage: Its Ethical and Economic Aspects* in 1906. Moreover, Pope Leo XIII's charge in *De Rerum Novarum* (1891) that "a small number of very rich men have been able to lay upon the masses of the poor a yoke little better than slavery itself," also spurred uncounted parish priests to compassionate works. The hierarchy's militant philosophic and theological conservatism, however, and especially its sharp perception of the church's need for acceptance by the conservative Protestant business establishment, caused most bishops to continue to ignore the encyclical.

Judaism

Some developments within the Jewish community paralleled those within Protestantism and Catholicism. By 1900, the mainly German-Jewish immigrants of earlier years had risen in extraordinary numbers into the middle, upper-middle, and professional classes. Fearful that the great influx of Jews from Eastern Europe would compromise their own hard-won social position, they were repelled by the political radicalism of many of the newcomers combined with what they regarded as the newcomers' "crude" religious orthodoxy. They turned first to immigration restriction, then to paternalistic programs of uplift. Although tension persisted into the next generation and beyond, modifications in orthodox practices, as the east Europeans became Americanized and educated, eased that tension. Late in the period, moreover, many of the more successful Orthodox Jews moved to the suburbs and joined conservative congregations in a blend of orthodoxy and German Reform Judaism. Furthermore, large proportions of highly educated Jews—even more than Protestants—abandoned religion in all but name.

No comparable Social Gospel-type movement emerged within Judaism in America, partly because Jews came to the United States with a more refined sense of community than most old-stock Americans. Proudly, the German-Jewish social agency, the United Hebrew Charities, reported in 1900 that it had taken care of almost every poverty-stricken Jew it had found. Just as Jews made a disproportionately large contribution to the nation's cultural and intellectual life, they also supported the humanitarian aspects of progressivism with an intensity and strength out of all proportion to their numbers.

Political Main Currents

Political Thought

While Dewey, Pound, and Beard were reconstructing education, law, and history, Herbert Croly, later one of the founders of the progressive weekly, *The New Republic*, was calling for a reconstitution of politics. He charged that the existing system was geared to the interests of the wealthy minority. The remedy, he concluded, was to infuse the political order with the new social and psychological concepts.

In *The Promise of American Life* (1909), Croly accepted the charges of Veblen and the instinct psychologists that industrialism had repressed the finer human instincts. He directed his fire, accordingly, at laissez-faire capitalism's basic precept—the belief that freedom to pursue individual gain leads inevitably to social progress. In words that came close to paraphrasing Theodore Roosevelt's presidential messages of 1907 and 1908, Croly called for the replacement of individualism by social togetherness. By the exercise of self-discipline, said Croly, people must create a community loyal to an ideal—a nation-state that would fulfill humanity's great promise.

Believing in big business' potential for good and despairing of the Democrats' devotion to states' rights, Croly at first fastened on the Republican Party as the vehicle to achieve his purposes. He considered Roosevelt almost the ideal statesman: "The whole tendency of his programme is to give a democratic meaning and purpose to Hamiltonian tradition and method. He proposes to use the power and resources of the Federal government for the purpose of making his country a more complete democracy in organization and practice." Like Roosevelt, however, Croly finally concluded that Republican nationalism served big business interests almost exclusively.

By the end of the Progressive Era, most of these social, intellectual, and economic currents were influencing Washington in greater or lesser degree. Moving upward from the unions in some cases, downward from business in others, and in from the universities in almost all, they usually affected local and state politics first. Often, as in education and birth control, local and state influences remained strongest. On other matters, notably regulation of national corporations, Congress became preeminent; but in most instances, local, state, and federal governments divided responsibilities. We will now explore in more depth the new style of governance then being constructed.

▶ ▶ ▶

Chapter Review

Summary

The Progressive Era, in the first two decades of the twentieth century, was replete with changes in public policy and innovative reforms on many fronts. The Progressives shared a belief both in the power of human reasoning and in the use of government as a tool to deal with social problems. At the heart of Progressivism was the belief that the free market was exceedingly harsh and left many problems unsolved.

The Progressive Era was an era of urbanization as mechanization of agriculture reduced the need for human labor on the farm while it increased farm production. Another factor that contributed to urban growth was a new wave of immigration, primarily from southern and eastern Europe. The new immigrants, who were predominantly Catholic, generally arrived without English language skills and settled in the urban areas. In reaction, a new wave of nativism and anti-Catholicism swept over America, culminating in the passage of a literacy test for immigrants in 1917.

Education provided social mobility in an urbanizing society with mass education, mass transit, mass production and distribution, mass entertainment, and mass culture. Sports for the masses developed, especially baseball, boxing, and football; and movies became the most popular form of mass entertainment. Mass produced pulp magazines, and Western novels emerged to dominate popular literature while mass production pianos and sheet music expanded the American music scene. In journalism, Joseph Pulitzer and William Randolph Hearst incorporated sensationalism into their news reporting, and investigative journalists known as "muckrakers" exposed government and business improprieties.

Louis Sullivan and Frank Lloyd Wright emerged as America's premier architects although their work was too sophisticated for popular tastes, at the time. Simultaneously, modern artists, disparagingly labeled the "ashcan school" by conservatives, shook up the art world by deviating from previous norms. Novels of the time by Theodore Dreiser, Jack London, and Willa Cather were dominated by realism and naturalism.

Reforms during the Gilded Age were plentiful, but perhaps none were larger than prohibition of alcohol (the Eighteenth Amendment to the Constitution), and women's suffrage (the Nineteenth Amendment), both of which went into effect in 1920. Meanwhile, business was revolutionized with Frederick Taylor's scientific management and Henry Ford's "just-in-time technology" that brought greater productivity and efficiency. Progressives reformed local government with the council-manager format, introduced the secret ballot, and introduced provisions for initiative, referendum, and recall. Louis Pasteur's germ theory of disease brought about a sanitation revolution in the American workplace that increased life expectancy from forty-nine to fifty-six years.

In academia, the social sciences witnessed advancement in psychology, with behaviorism, and economics with the abandonment of the doctrine of laissez-faire. Historians also adopted scientific methodology and purged history of the romanticism that had dominated previously. Simultaneously, both public education and higher education expanded and advanced.

Chapter Review (cont'd)

(cont'd)

America's three great monotheistic religions—Protestantism, Catholicism, and Judaism—all moved in the direction of the Social Gospel, advocating the use of government to remedy social injustice. The political thought of those that favored the Social Gospel was epitomized by Herbert Croly who called for the replacement of individualism with social togetherness. Croly believed that laissez-faire served the interests only of big business rather than society as a whole, and his ideas epitomized Progressivism as a whole.

Chronological Time Line

1869 Louis Pasteur developed the germ theory of disease.

1873 Congress passed the Comstock Law, banning the sending of obscene material through the mail.

1883 Joseph Pulitzer bought the *New York World*.

1897 Edward Arlington Robinson published *Children of the Night*.

1899 John Dewey published *School and Society*.

1900 Theodore Dreiser published his first novel, *Sister Carrie*.

1903 Orville and Wilber Wright completed the first successful human flight at Kitty Hawk, North Carolina.

1903 An inscription plaque was placed on the Statue of Liberty with a pro-immigration message.

1906 John Ryan published *A Living Wage: Its Ethical and Economic Aspects* in 1906.

1907 Walter Rauschenbusch published *Christianity and the Social Crisis.*

1907 James Harvey Robinson and Charles A. Beard published *The Development of Modern Europe*.

1907 Oklahoma came into the Union with a "dry" Constitution.

1908 Stanton, Virginia, introduced the council-manager format for municipal government.

Time Line (cont'd)

1909 Five million copies of piano sheet music for "Meet Me Tonight in Dreamland" were sold.

1909 Jack Johnson became the nation's first black heavyweight boxing champion.

1909 Herbert Croly published *The Promise of American Life*.

1909 Rockefeller Sanitary Commission campaigned against the hookworm disease.

1909–1914 The "Golden Age of Agriculture"

1910 Motion pictures play to a weekly audience of ten million.

1910 Former Populist candidate Tom Watson denounced the Catholic Church.

1912 Harriet Monroe established the magazine, *Poetry*.

1912 Zane Grey published *Riders of the Purple Sage*.

1912 United States Public Health Service began a long campaign against malaria.

1913 Willa Cather published *O Pioneers!*

1913 Charles Beard published *An Economic Interpretation of the Constitution*.

1913 Alice Paul and Suffragettes were arrested for picketing the White House.

1914 The Leo Frank Case

1914 Congress banned the dissemination of birth control information in interstate commerce.

1914 A national meeting of psychologists and neurologists pronounced alcohol to be a poison.

1914 The Great War broke out in Europe in August.

1915 The National Birth Control League was founded.

Chapter Review (cont'd)

Time Line (cont'd)

1915 Carrie Chapman Catt and Jane Addams founded the Woman's Peace Party.

1915 T. S. Eliot published "The Love Song of J. Alfred Prufrock."

1916 Margaret Sanger opened a birth control clinic in New York, defying federal law.

1916 John Dewey published *Democracy and Education*.

1917 A literacy test for immigrants was passed over Woodrow Wilson's second veto.

1917 National Women's Party was founded by Alice Paul.

1919 Members of the Chicago White Sox were accused of "throwing" the World Series.

1919 Nineteenth Amendment was ratified guaranteeing women's suffrage.

1920 Prohibition of alcohol went into effect in January.

1920 Edith Wharton published *The Age of Innocence*.

Key Terms

Progressivism: The idea that the free market leaves numerous problems unsolved in society and government is the tool to correct the problems left unsolved by the free market

New immigrants: The wave of immigrants from southern and eastern Europe (most of whom were Catholic) along with immigration from Asia

Racist theories: The ideas that White Anglo-Saxon Protestants were somehow superior to other people

Leo Frank: Jewish factory manager in Georgia who was falsely accused of murder and lynched by a mob

Zane Grey: Ohio dentist who wrote *Riders of the Purple Sage* and seventy other novels

Scott Joplin: Texas-born African-American recognized as the finest composer of ragtime music

Muckraking: Investigative reporting that focused on government and business improprieties

Louis Sullivan: Leading architect of the Progressive Era and mentor to Frank Lloyd Wright

Frank Lloyd Wright: Architect of the Progressive Era whose work was admired more later

Ashcan school: Modern artists that were disparaged by the conservative art world

Key Terms (cont'd)

Willa Cather: Popular author of frontier novels
Edith Wharton: Published novels of manners and New York high society
Jack London: Published critically acclaimed novels of nature
Theodore Dreiser: Wrote novels that portrayed the conventional moral code as out of step with reality
Edwin Arlington Robinson: A traditionalist writer, endorsed by Theodore Roosevelt, and who dealt with the abiding theme of the individual's search for God and truth amidst darkness and suffering, Robinson failed in his quest. Life and human destiny remained mysterious.
Alice Paul: Suffragette that suffered arrest and hunger strike
Carrie Chapman Catt: NAWSA's president who put her unflagging energies into mobilizing suffrage sentiment in the U. S. and, in 1915, to helping Jane Addams organize the Woman's Peace Party
Margaret Sanger: Suffragette and prime advocate of birth control
Comstock Law: 1873 law that prohibited the sending of obscene material in the mail
Prohibition: Eighteenth Amendment to the Constitution that prohibited alcohol
John Dewey: Influential figure in education in the Progressive Era who favored learning by doing
Fundamentalism: The idea that every word of the Bible is the literal, inerrant word of God
Just-in-time technology: Henry Ford's idea that goods needed for manufacturing should arrive at the factory "just in time" to go on to the item being manufactured
Kitty Hawk: Site of the first human flight by Orville and Wilbur Wright
Ballot initiatives: The practice that people could place items on the election ballot, by petition
Referendum: Practice where people vote directly on laws
Recall: By petition, requires individuals to face reelection before the end of their term
Louis Pasteur: Developed the germ theory of disease in 1869
Social Gospel: The idea that government and other human organizations should do God's good works
Salvation Army: Leading Social Gospel organization spawned during the Gilded Age
Herbert Croly: Progressive and founder of the New Republic who favored government intervention to remedy social ills

Pop Quiz

19

Chapter 19

1. Where did rural areas decline in population between 1860 and 1910?
   a. Farmers' productivity and efficiency increased due to mechanization.
   b. Farmers could not find workers to harvest their crops.
   c. Farmers' grew too much and prices declined.
   d. Railroads refused to carry farmer's produce to market.

2. Much of the tension concerning new immigrants was rooted in ____________.
   a. religion and anti-Catholicism
   b. economics and competition for jobs
   c. fear that the immigrants would bring European socialism
   d. both a and b

3. The broadest avenue of upward mobility in American society in the Progressive Era was through ____________,
   a. graft and corruption in local government
   b. working in American factories in the Northeast and Midwest
   c. joining labor unions
   d. public education

4. The most successful novelists of the Progressive Era were ____________.
   a. Gene Stratton-Porter and Harold Bell Wright
   b. Joseph Strauss and Frank Lloyd Wright
   c. James Fennimore Cooper and Herman Melville
   d. J. K. Rowling and C. S. Lewis

5. Two of the most innovative architects of the Progressive Era were ____________.
   a. Louis Sullivan and Frank Lloyd Wright
   b. Leon Alberti and Marcus Agrippa
   c. Joseph Pulitzer and William Randolph Hearst
   d. Jack Johnson and Ty Cobb

Pop Quiz (cont'd)

6. Giving women the right to vote would accomplish all the following, according to its supporters, EXCEPT ____________.
   a. end racial prejudice
   b. assure prohibition
   c. create a more compassionate society
   d. take corruption out of government

7. Political reforms favored by Progressives included ____________.
   a. the secret ballot
   b. civil service
   c. patronage
   d. Both a and b

8. Which of the following is true of higher education in the Progressive Era?
   a. Legal studies were upgraded.
   b. Medical studies were upgraded.
   c. Agricultural research was increased.
   d. All of the above

9. What was the "counter truth" to the Social Gospel?
   a. Lazy people in search of a free ride flocked to the churches for assistance.
   b. Left-wing radicals duped the churches into furthering their socialist agenda.
   c. The Social Gospel was revealed to be a covert effort by the Church of Satan.
   d. Evangelical Protestants expended more energy campaigning for prohibition and against parochial schools than they did fighting exploitation of fellow men and women.

10. Herbert Croly argued that the political system was geared to favor ____________.
    a. the poor
    b. African-Americans
    c. Illegal immigrants
    d. the wealthy

Chapter Review (cont'd)

Pop Quiz (cont'd)

11. Enrollment in higher education declined in the Progressive Era. T F

12. Most Protestant churches taught the Social Gospel. T F

13. Hookworm infected more than ___________ whites in the South.

14. Scott Joplin and Sheldon Brooks wrote ___________ music.

15. The leading author of Western novels was ___________ ___________.

1. B	5. B	9. D	13. 500,000
2. C	6. A	10. D	14. Ragtime
3. A	7. C	11. F	15. Zane Grey
4. D	8. B	12. F	

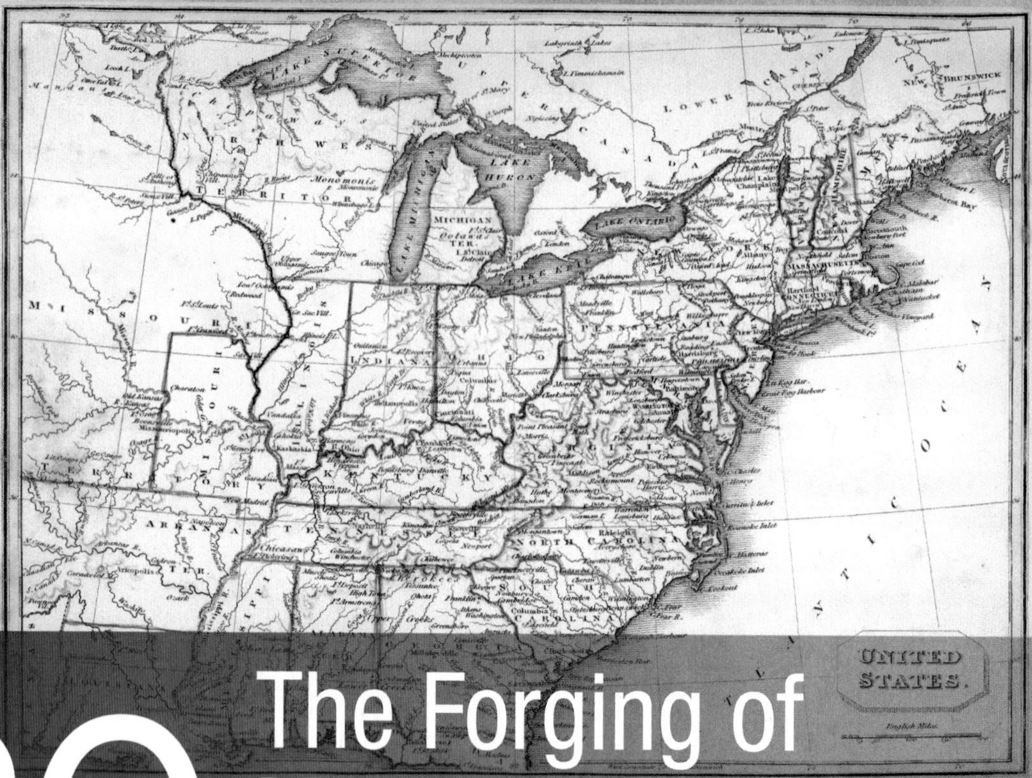

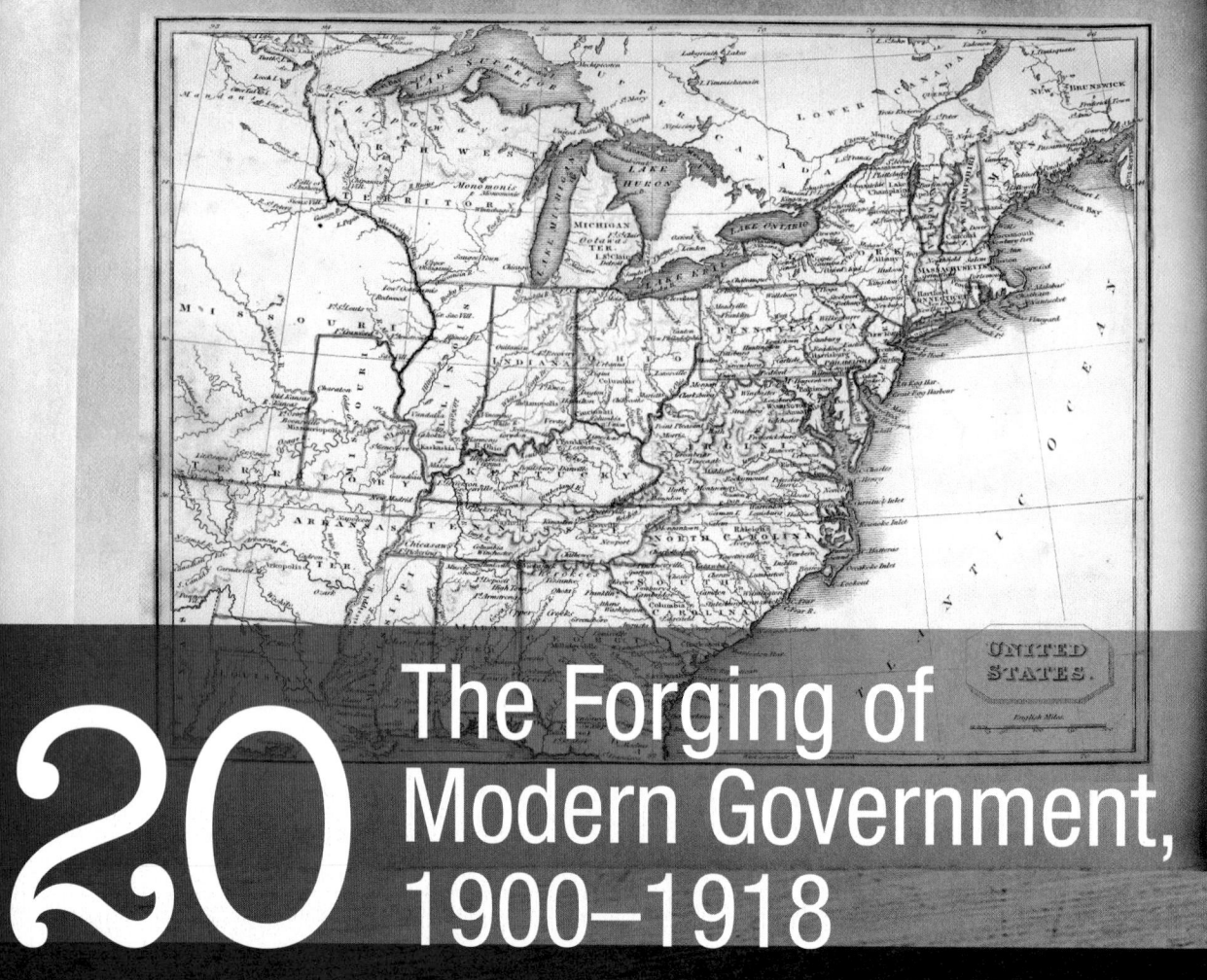

20 The Forging of Modern Government, 1900–1918

Chapter Objectives

Prologue to Change

Enter Theodore Roosevelt

Presidential Initiative

The Revolt of the Middle Classes

The New Consensus

Social Problems

The Power of Business

Stranglehold on Government

Thunder in the

Origins of Urban Reform

State Reforms

Progressivism Moves to Washington

The Party Structure

Railroad Regulation

Public Health Controls

For Generations Yet Unborn

Variations in Antitrust Policy

Trouble on the Labor Front

The Triangle Shirtwaist Factory Fire

Forecasts of the Welfare State

The Disruption of the G.O.P.

Taft's Background

The Tariff Fiasco

The Rise of Insurgency

Roosevelt Challenges Taft

The "Bull Moose" Party

Ironies of American Socialism

The Triumph of Progressivism

Wilson's Background

The New Freedom Program

Tariff and Banking Reform

Moving Toward the New Nationalism

"We Are Also Progressives"

Politics and Blacks

The Progressive Era in Retrospect

Prologue to Change

Enter Theodore Roosevelt

On a September afternoon in 1901, at the Pan-American Exposition in Buffalo, New York, a young anarchist named Leon Czolgosz, proclaiming that he was killing an "enemy of the people," shot President William McKinley at close range while in a receiving line. Eight days later the president died of gangrene. Vice-president Theodore Roosevelt took the presidential oath, and the old order began to give way to the Progressive Era. It was symbolized at first by Roosevelt, at forty-one the youngest man to occupy the White House, and then by Senator Robert M. La Follette of Wisconsin and President Woodrow Wilson.

The Republican Party had not planned for it to be this way. Roosevelt had been elected governor of New York in 1898 following his heroism in the Spanish-American War. Republican Party leaders in the important state of New York viewed Roosevelt as a meddlesome loose cannon and desired to remove him from the office of the governor. However, his popularity, resulting from his war hero status, dictated that he could remain governor of New York as long as he desired. As a consequence, New York Republican Party leaders had urged William McKinley to make Roosevelt his running mate in 1900, thus removing Roosevelt from New York and placing him in a position from which he could do no harm.

▶ Vice-President Theodore Roosevelt was sworn into office after President William McKinley was assassinated.

Republican Party leader Mark Hanna opposed Roosevelt's selection as vice president because he feared that Roosevelt could use the office as a stepping-stone to the presidency. Upon McKinley's untimely death, Hanna reportedly exclaimed, "I told William McKinley that it was a mistake to nominate that wild man at Philadelphia. I asked him if he realized what would happen if he should die. Now look—that damned cowboy is in the White House!"

Roosevelt, however, was much more than a "cowboy." While it is true that Roosevelt had spent time in the Dakotas as a rancher in the 1880s in an effort to recover from the sudden death of his young wife, and it is also true that he fought in the Spanish American War with the "Rough Riders" at San Juan Hill, Roosevelt was born into a wealthy New York family. Roosevelt should also be considered one of America's "scholar-presidents." since he was a reader of thousands of books, as well a writer of several. Roosevelt dedicated himself to both physical and academic pursuits with equal vigor. As a child, Roosevelt had been sickly, asthmatic, and weak, and had poor eyesight; however as an adult, Roosevelt made up for lost time as an avid swimmer, cowpuncher, military man, and big-game hunter. Essentially, Roosevelt glorified warfare, and what he termed as the "strenuous life,"—a route to true "manhood." In an 1899 essay entitled "The Strenuous Life," Roosevelt urged Americans to extinguish "the soft spirit of the cloistered life" and "boldly face the life of strife." Roosevelt advocated enjoying the outdoors and exercising, but he also advocated competitive athletics. Roosevelt's boisterous personality excited the American public, and he eventually became the only twentieth century president immortalized on Mount Rushmore.

Though Roosevelt was viewed by conservative Republicans as a radical and a loose cannon, in reality, Roosevelt was a conservative at heart and viewed reform less as a vehicle for remaking society and more as a means of protecting society against more radical changes. Nevertheless, Roosevelt would bring about numerous reforms during his presidency and gain the reputation as a Progressive. Two and a half months after being sworn in, President Roosevelt sounded the dominant note of twentieth-century American politics: The old system, he said in his first annual message to Congress, must be changed to meet new social and economic problems.

> "When the Constitution was adopted, at the end of the eighteenth century, no human wisdom could foretell the sweeping changes ... which were to take place by the beginning of the twentieth century. At that time it was accepted as a matter of course that the several States were the proper authorities to regulate, so far as was then necessary, the comparatively insignificant and strictly localized corporate bodies of the day. The conditions are now wholly different and wholly different action is called for."

Presidential Initiative

Action soon followed Roosevelt's words. On February 14, 1902, Roosevelt invoked the Sherman Antitrust Act against the Northern Securities Company, a mammoth railroad holding corporation controlled by the bankers J. P. Morgan and Company and Kuhn, Loeb and Company, and the railroad magnates, James J. Hill and Edward H. Harriman.

Morgan was stunned. He exclaimed that Roosevelt had not acted like a "gentleman" and later tried to treat the president like a rival operator. Hill was even more embittered. "It really seems hard," he complained, "that we should be compelled to fight for our lives against the political adventurers who have never done anything but pose and draw a salary." In spite of these complaints, however, the proceedings continued. Two years later the Supreme Court, in a five to four decision, ordered the Northern Securities Company to dissolve.

By the time the Northern Securities case was settled, Roosevelt had added another dimension to presidential leadership. In May 1902, John Mitchell, the moderate leader of the United Mine Workers (UMW), had called anthracite miners of northeastern Pennsylvania out on strike. The strikers demanded an eight-hour day, wage increases, and recognition of their union. The eight railroad companies that dominated the industry would neither recognize the

United Mine Workers nor mitigate the workers' near subhuman conditions of life. "[The miners] don't suffer," the management's chief spokesman expostulated at one point. "Why, they can't even speak English!" Accustomed to getting their way in labor disputes, often with government intervention on their side, the owners refused to budge; and the strike continued through the summer and into the fall.

Fearful of a coal shortage and infuriated by the operators' arrogance, Roosevelt considered filing an antitrust suit against the coal combine; but when the Attorney General advised that it would fail for lack of evidence, Roosevelt decided to invite the contesting parties to the White House. The operators deeply resented this implied recognition of the UMW and vehemently refused to make any concessions at the ensuing conference in October. In contrast, the UMW was more open to Roosevelt's mediation because the union was used to the federal government immediately taking the side of the mine owners rather than taking the middle ground.

Roosevelt was so determined to end the strike in the interest of the American economy that he issued secret orders to the army to prepare to seize the mines. He then warned prominent business leaders on Wall Street of his intent. These measures sufficed, and the mine operators agreed to accept the recommendations of an independent arbitration committee appointed by the president; consequently, their plan to crush the UMW had failed. "This is the great distinguishing fact," the *Springfield Republican* proclaimed at the time, "for while the operators still nominally refuse to recognize the mine workers' union, that union nevertheless is a party to the president's plan of arbitration and is so recognized by him."

The political importance of both the Northern Securities Company suit and the president's intervention in the coal strike far transcended their immediate economic significance. By striking out boldly on his own, Roosevelt had asserted his independence of big business, revitalized the executive office, and helped prepare the way for the Progressive movement to reach the national level. He had also given meaning to the Sherman Antitrust Act and had created the impression that the Republican Party could become a viable instrument of Progressive reform.

▶Theodore Roosevelt giving an election speech in Wyoming, 1903.

The Revolt of the Middle Classes

The New Consensus

The program that Theodore Roosevelt and Woodrow Wilson pressed on Congress and the nation from 1905 to 1916 was neither revolutionary nor original since many reforms of the Progressive Era had been spelled out initially in the Populist Party platform of 1892. Theodore Roosevelt campaigned for re-election in 1904, offering every American what he termed as a "square deal." The slogan and Roosevelt's personality resonated

MAP 20.1 Presidential Election of 1904

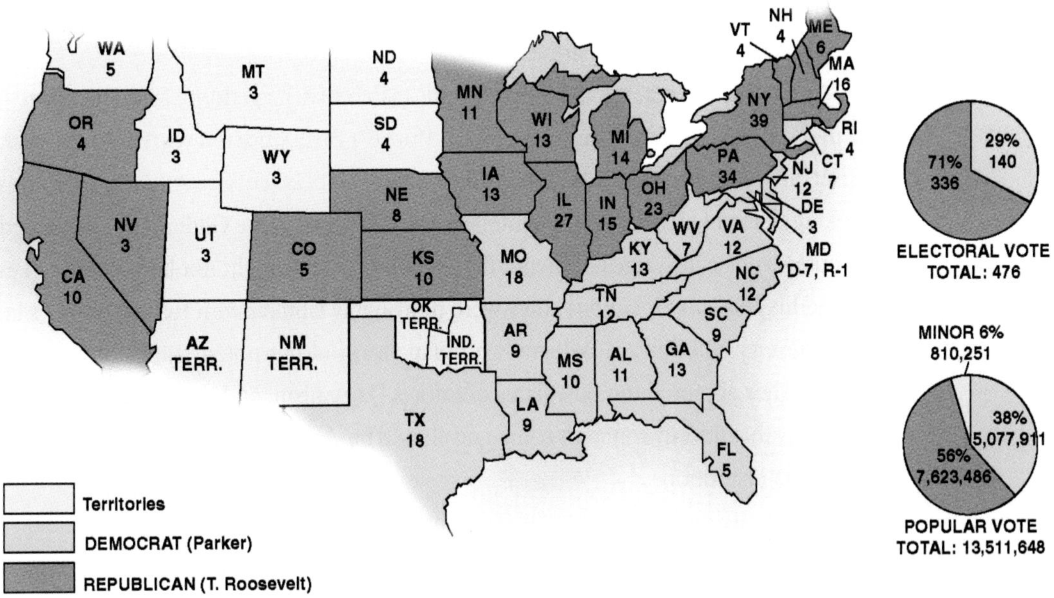

enough with voters that he won a record 57 percent of the vote in 1904 over Democratic candidate Alton B. Parker; however, many Republican backers of Roosevelt did not realize that they had just re-elected a Progressive reformer. Populist Democrat William Jennings Bryan had suggested, earlier, almost every major measure that Roosevelt and his successors would sign into law. Even the attack on the Northern Securities Company was based on a law (the Sherman Anti-Trust Act) enacted twelve years before. Why, then, did Progressivism succeed when Populism and Bryanism had failed?

Many historians argue that the middle-class character of Progressivism's constituency and leadership made the crucial difference. Populism, despite its attempt to win labor support, had been essentially a movement of rural protest. Bryan's Populism had been broadly based, but Bryan's identification with prohibition and evangelical Protestantism had alienated many normally Democratic Catholic and Jewish workers. In 1896, Bryan had generally failed, moreover, to win middle-class support, even among well-to-do farmers.

Middle-class voters had been frightened mainly by Bryan's allegedly "wild" financial ideas. "How intellectually snobbish I was about 'sound economics,' " the editor William Allen White wrote later. ". . . It seemed to me that rude hands were trying to tear down the tabernacle of our national life."

Progressivism triumphed because tens of thousands of civic-minded Americans who shared White's virtues and prejudices were drawn into the environment of change. "Populism shaved its whiskers, put on a derby, and moved into the middle of the class—the upper middle class," White wrote. That, of course, was poetic license; however, Progressivism did appeal more to educated, prosperous farmers than to uneducated, unsuccessful ones. It also exerted a powerful pull on skilled laborers, however. Urban blue-collar workers of old stock or of northern European origins gave it disproportionate support, especially on economic issues. Even in the Middle West, Progressivism's voter strength lay more in cities and medium-size towns than in the countryside.

Assuredly, most first-echelon Progressive leaders came from the old-stock middle or upper-middle classes. The secondary leadership was of similar background although it contained some minor union officials, some old-line politicians, and a number of Jewish professionals. It was augmented, moreover, by the female social reformers—voteless (except in certain states) until 1920, but extraordinarily influential nonetheless.

On the average, the men who would "march to Armageddon" with Theodore Roosevelt in 1912 and form the Progressive ("Bull Moose") Party were ten years younger than the conservatives who remained with the G.O.P. They had been college students or impressionable young men of affairs when the intellectual revolution of the Gilded Age challenged the economic and social values of their fathers. Although they might not have heard of Lester Ward and his *Dynamic Sociology*, they were thoroughly familiar with Henry George's indictment of poverty and Edward Bellamy's utopian vision of the potentialities of the new technology. They accepted the postulates of reform Darwinism, and they believed with varying intensity that the environment could and should be shaped to bring out the best in humankind and its institutions.

Despite their broad identity of background, few Progressives thought alike on all issues. As we have already seen, the Progressive movement was at once positive and negative, liberal and conservative, democratic and elitist. It possessed both a soft side and a hard side, and both a social justice wing and a business wing; thus, many of the urban businessmen—who joined early citizen's movements for local control, city manager government, and efficient administration—had scant sympathy for much of the social justice Progressives' economic program. They had no desire to reform the tax structure or create a welfare policy through minimum wage laws, workmen's compensation, and health insurance systems. Neither did rural and small town Progressives evince much concern for social justice. In Connecticut, for example, small town state legislators voted down workmen's compensation in the same session in which they enacted a strong measure to regulate public utilities. In Congress, as well, rural Progressives gave considerably more support to measures regulating business than to those affecting workers.

Even the urban, middle-class professionals who comprised the heart of the Progressive movement had divided allegiances. The narrower moralists among them wanted mainly to clean up politics by destroying "bossism" and its attendant evils. They believed that the Australian (secret) ballot, the direct primary, and numerous other procedural reforms would shift power from the boss-manipulated masses to themselves and people like themselves. They fumed over soaring tax rates and the gas, electric, and streetcar monopolies. They also, mistakenly, attributed the increasingly high cost of government to corruption rather than to the root cause, expanding services; and they blamed rising prices on the "trusts" rather than on market forces.

The moralists also feared the aggrandizement of power by organized labor, though they sympathized with individual, working men and women. Many felt that they were being squeezed between the upper and nether elements of society. A few of the aristocrats among them may even have been moved by desire to regain a status and prestige lost to the new business leaders, those *nouveaux riches* that one critic described as being "without restraints of culture, experience, the pride, or even the inherited caution of class or rank."

Yet to view progressivism through one or another of its constituent parts would be to miss the thrust of the movement as a whole. All but the most opportunistic Progressives shared a vision of society that impelled them, within limits, to put what they saw as the public good above their private interest. Whatever their personal ambitions—even the purest idealists among them possessed normal drives for prestige and power—their breadth of outlook enabled them to transcend short-range economic and social considerations in pursuit of long-range civic goals.

As political activists, they forged a series of shifting political coalitions based on the mainly material concerns of labor, farmers, white-collar workers, and businessmen. As educated and highly informed citizens, they based their program on the ostensibly objective findings of social scientists. As pragmatic idealists, they gave their designs unity and purpose by evoking the moral impulses roused by the Social Gospel and by the muckrakers' exposures of corruption and exploitation. In short, despite their differences and inconsistencies, they mobilized the new public interest philosophy in three areas of American life: social, economic, and governmental.

Social Problems

Everywhere that Progressives looked they saw poverty, injustice, and political corruption in the midst of growing abundance and seemingly limitless opportunity. One percent of the nation's families owned seven-eighths of its wealth, and ten million Americans lived in abject circumstances. Many workers still toiled sixty hours a week, and almost two million children worked in the fields or in factories, frequently on night shifts. Thousands of workers were killed annually on the railroads alone—by one estimate over seven thousand. As late as 1913, industrial accidents caused twenty-five thousand deaths a year.

Nor did there seem to be much hope that employers would or could cope with these problems. Wages were fixed by supply and demand; and in the absence of a strong labor movement

▶ In the early 1900s almost two million children born into poverty worked in the fields or in factories to help support their families.

or minimum wage laws, even those manufacturers who wished to be humane were forced to keep wages at the subsistence level in order to survive competition. Thus Massachusetts, which had pioneered in strong child labor laws, steadily lost textile mills to the South where child labor helped keep production costs low.

Labor's attempts to organize and strike for higher wages and shorter hours had been systematically weakened by injunctions and, more importantly, by management's use of immigrants as strike breakers. There was no pension system, no automatic compensation for injuries or death sustained on the job. In such an environment, the widow who received $250 from her late husband's employer could consider herself blessed. Relief, when available, came largely from private sources.

The Power of Business

The consolidation of several firms into large industrial combines threatened to make conditions worse rather than better. By 1904, combinations of one form or another controlled two-fifths of all manufacturing in the United States. Six great financial groups dominated about 95 percent of the railroads, and some 1,320 utilities companies were organized under a handful of giant holding companies. As early as 1902, the United States Industrial Commission reported, "In most cases the combination has exerted an appreciable power over prices, and in practically all cases it has increased the margin between raw materials and finished products." The Commission added that the cost of production had probably decreased and that profits had doubtlessly increased. A subsequent report revealed that the cost of living actually increased 35 percent between 1897 and 1913.

As we have seen, efficiency was the economic justification for these developments; but the consolidation movement, like the protective tariff movement, was based primarily on fear of competition and its attendant instability. No one, not even J. Pierpont Morgan, whose very gaze "forced the complex of inferiority ... upon all around him," was immune. Fear of competition had driven him and his associates to buy out Andrew Carnegie and organize the United States Steel Corporation in 1901. The desire for stability and assured profits had also prompted Morgan to organize the Northern Securities Company with James J. Hill in 1901.

The consolidation movement both tended to destroy competition and, more importantly, made it difficult for the nation to solve its festering social and political problems. Great corporations not only had the power to prevent labor from organizing basic industries but also used this power ruthlessly. They transformed economic power into political influence in various ways. If railroad, sugar, oil, and steel interests could not "buy" state legislatures as openly as they had twenty-five years earlier, and if they could no longer send as many hand-picked men to Congress as they once had done, they nevertheless exerted great influence over both elections and legislative decisions. They made huge contributions to the Republican Party, controlled countless newspaper editors and publishers, and kept lobbies in Washington and in state capitals.

Small industrialists, organized in 1895 as the National Association of Manufacturers (NAM), also fought social and economic change. They and other comparatively small businessmen and real estate promoters shared responsibility with big business for the already widespread pollution of America's cities and desecration of the countryside. Small industry fought minimum wage, child labor, and factory safety bills; and small businessmen lobbied most vigorously for low local and state taxes, and, thus for inadequate schools and social services.

Stranglehold on Government

The obstructionist role of small business should not obscure the major issue that Roosevelt and Progressives faced on the national level. The inescapable fact was that big business, in 1901, constituted the most potent threat to American democracy. The post-Civil War shift of power from Washington to Wall Street had accelerated under President McKinley. By Roosevelt's ascension, the presidency had become a kind of branch brokerage office, with the president himself little more than the Washington director of a nationwide financial operation. There was nothing particularly sinister or even secret about the system. Republican politicians, such as McKinley and his friend Mark Hanna believed that national welfare depended upon cooperation between business and government.

In such an environment, no national Progressive movement could gain political power until the reign of big business was effectively challenged. This was why Roosevelt's action against the Northern Securities Company had such great symbolic importance. Progressives continued to emphasize direct democracy—the primary, initiative, referendum, recall of judicial decisions, and, above all, direct election of senators (United States Senators were elected by State Legislatures until the passage of the Seventeenth Amendment). These devices, they believed, would enable them to introduce bills in boss-dominated legislatures, undo the work of conservative legislatures and judges, and replace business-oriented senators with people more representative of the general citizenry.

Thunder in the Cities and States

Origins of Urban Reform

One of the catalysts behind the shifting coalitions that formed the Progressive movement was the prolonged depression of the 1890s. A business editor wrote at the time:

> It is probably safe to say that in no civilized country in this century, not actually in the throes of war or open insurrection, has society been so disorganized as it was in the United States during the first half of 1894; never was human life held so cheap, never did the constituted authorities appear so incompetent to endorse respect for the law.

Appalled by the people's hardships and fearful of their social implications, the middle and upper-middle classes had begun to become politically active in large numbers for the first time. As we have seen, clergymen were trying earnestly to apply the Social Gospel, women's literary societies

MAP 20.2 Map of Cities with at Least 2,500 People (1903)

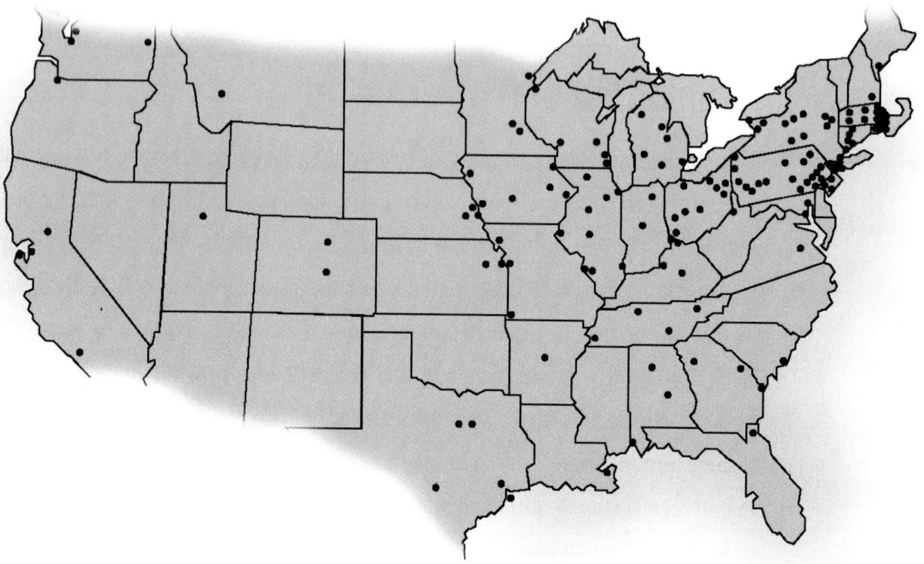

developed an interest in social and economic problems, and men's civic clubs turned their sights on public utility monopolies. Furthermore, untried reform politicians challenged conservative business leaders; and most important of all, farmers' organizations, labor unions, church clubs, and other civic groups formed common fronts. In so doing, they regularly crossed—though they rarely severed—the class, ethnic, and religious lines that had heretofore separated social units.

Between 1894 and 1897, municipal reform movements erupted across the nation. In city after city during the next decade, reform candidates—both Republican and Democratic—campaigned successfully for commission or city manager government, for local control, and for honest elections. Invariably, they found that the trail of privilege and corruption led from the city hall to the statehouse and thence to powerful business interests. Government, they gradually—and often reluctantly—concluded, must be transformed from a negative to a positive force. Only then could insurance and utility companies be brought under control, exploitation of men, women, and children stopped, and the power of the bosses destroyed.

State Reforms

As governor of New York in 1899, Theodore Roosevelt pushed through a corporation tax, strengthened factory and tenement inspection laws, and flouted business interests on so many other counts that the GOP machine eased him out of the state and into the vice-presidential nomination in 1900. In the same year, Robert M. La Follette of Wisconsin abandoned Republican orthodoxy and won the governorship in that state. Much of his program had developed piecemeal in the East, especially in Massachusetts and New York; but La Follette, drawing on a general shift of Progressive support from the countryside to urban centers, implemented his program so imaginatively that it became a model and gained renown as the "Wisconsin Idea." There and

▶ Robert M. La Follette, former governor of Wisconsin, worked for state policy reforms, and Samuel Gompers helped form the National Civic Federation to promote settlement of labor disputes.

elsewhere, Progressives won the direct primary, the short ballot, the initiative and referendum, and the recall of elected officials.

Progressives in state legislatures strengthened child labor laws, created commissions to regulate utilities and railroad rates, and began to impose inheritance, corporation, and graduated income taxes. They also made increasingly large appropriations for schools, state universities, mental and penal institutions, and welfare programs in general. Maryland enacted the first workmen's compensation law in 1902, protecting workers against on-the-job injuries. In the next year Oregon limited women workers to a ten-hour day, in 1911 Illinois established a public assistance program for mothers with dependent children, and in 1912 Massachusetts created a commission to fix wages for women and children. By the end of the Progressive Era, the number of students in high schools had almost doubled, most of the great industrial states had workmen's compensation laws, and the number of industrial accidents had been dramatically reduced by the forced or voluntary adoption of safety procedures. The epilogue that Senator La Follette wrote in his autobiography in 1913 was in reality a prologue:

> It has been a fight supremely worth making, and I want it to be judged … by results actually attained. If it can be shown that Wisconsin is a happier and better state to live in, that its institutions are more democratic, that the opportunities of all its people are more equal, that social justice more nearly prevails, that human life is safer and sweeter—then I shall rest content in the feeling that the Progressive movement has been successful.

Progressivism Moves to Washington

By 1904 President Roosevelt was girding for a mighty struggle with conservatives in his own party. He had come into office well aware that his party was a hostage to business and its spokesmen in Congress and that this situation placed limits on his ability to act. As he explained to intimates, he could do something about either the tariff or the trusts, but not both. He had opted for trust reform—the more popular issue, the issue less offensive to Congress, and the issue more vulnerable to executive leverage.

On the legislative side, the record of his first administration had been modest. A Democratic-sponsored reclamation measure, The Newlands Act, which provided federal funds for the construction of dams and canals in the West and for the construction of hydroelectric power plants, had been passed in 1902 with the president's support. The Elkins Act to prohibit railroad rebates had gone through in 1903 because the railroads favored it; and a Department of Commerce and Labor, including a Bureau of Corporations with investigatory powers, had been created the same year. A handful of conservatives, however, called Old Guardsmen—Nelson W. Aldrich of Rhode Island, William B. Allison of Iowa, Marcus A. Hanna of Ohio, Orville H. Platt of Connecticut, and John C. Spooner of New York—had otherwise kept the legislative hatches closed.

Wealthy, able, and intelligent, these senators were also arrogant and dogmatic. Only Mark Hanna had sought to make peace with labor in 1900 by joining Samuel Gompers in forming the National Civic Federation to promote settlement of labor disputes. Other senators were insensitive to social and economic injustice. They supported governmental subsidies and other favors to business, while invoking the principle of laissez-faire to prevent even the mildest reforms. They did not want Roosevelt to run for a full term in 1904. After Roosevelt captured the party machinery, however, they (and the financial and business interests) helped him win a rousing victory over the conservative Democratic candidate, Judge Alton B. Parker of New York, who actually believed that the trust problem should be left to the states. As the New York *Sun* put it, better to have "the impulsive candidate of the party of conservatism than the conservative candidate of the party which the business interests regard as permanently and dangerously impulsive." Significantly, not even Roosevelt's extraordinary popularity reversed the downward trend in voter turnout, which had started in 1900 and would continue until 1928. This decline was strong in the North as well as in the South, especially among workers and marginal farmers.

The Party Structure

The key to the conservative domination of the Republican delegation in Congress was malapportionment in the states and the election of United States senators by their legislatures. In every state east of the Mississippi, the small towns and rural areas had become grossly overrepresented as the cities grew. Districts were not, generally, equal in population; and rural districts with much smaller populations would have the same representation as urban districts with many more people, especially in state legislatures. In almost every state, a handful of entrenched leaders with close ties to an intricate network of business lobbyists dictated the selection of senatorial candidates; by gerrymandering congressional districts, they assured the election of conservative Republicans to the House. Only in the northwest central states and on the Pacific Coast did Progressive Republicans control the selection of senators and representatives with any consistency.

At no time, therefore—not even during the height of Progressive Republican insurgency between 1910 and 1912—was as much as a fourth of the Republican delegation in Congress Progressive, yet neither was this dominant conservatism truly representative of rank and file Republicanism. "If I thought the Republican organization under the dome of the Capitol represented the Republican Party of the country," a Wisconsin Progressive protested in 1909, "I would be ashamed of being a Republican."

Roosevelt could find little support for his legislative program by turning to the Democrats, however. Most Southern state legislatures were gerrymandered in favor of rural "Tories" and conservative ideologically, but members of the Democratic Party due to the sectionalism that followed the Civil War and continued into the mid-twentieth century. Thus, Progressive thought was far weaker in Congress than outside it; and though Southern Democrats willingly abandoned states' rights on issues that redounded to the South's advantage, they remained basically unsympathetic to Roosevelt's centralizing tendencies. Furthermore, the Democrats' strength in the Senate was too slight for Roosevelt to have forged a viable coalition between them and the small minority of Progressive Republicans. Roosevelt had no choice, therefore, but to work through those who controlled the party—the conservative Republican leaders.

Still, there were offsetting factors. The president controlled the patronage, and he could enforce acts of Congress vigorously or indifferently. He could also appoint fact-finding commissions, and he could use the vast moral force of his office to influence public opinion and thus, indirectly, the Congress. Reinforced by his understanding of these powers and emboldened by his popular mandate and the angry excitement whipped up by the muckrakers, Roosevelt prepared, in December 1904, to present a full program of reform to Congress.

Railroad Regulation

His first major achievement was the Hepburn Act to strengthen the ratemaking power of the Interstate Commerce Commission (ICC). Following publication in *McClure's* of a devastating account of railroad malpractices, a concerted demand for action arose in the Middle West and the South. It came not only from farmers but also from merchants, manufacturers, and civic leaders, whose national organizations protested less against high rates than against the discrepancies between charges for long and short hauls, the curtailment of services induced by the consolidation of lines, and similar abuses.

These powerful pressures drove a number of conservative Republican Senators toward Roosevelt's side. Spurred by brilliant presidential maneuvering, a coalition then passed a compromise measure in 1906. Although La Follette cried "betrayal" because the bill failed to authorize evaluation of a railroad's worth in determining rates, the Hepburn Act had many Progressive features, including extension of the Interstate Commerce Commission's jurisdiction to oil pipeline, sleeping-car, and express companies. In addition, that Act strengthened the regulatory authority of the ICC over railroads, enabling the ICC to set rates and inspect the books, and ended free railroad passes to politicians.

Public Health Controls

Shortly after adoption of the Hepburn Act, the president signed two other significant measures—the Pure Food and Drug Act and the Meat Inspection Amendment to the Agricultural Appropriations Act. Each was necessitated by the callous disregard for the public's health by the industries concerned. Each reflected a growing conviction that only federal regulation could safeguard the people's health against avaricious business.

The Pure Food and Drug Act was a testament both to the new scientism and to the single-minded dedication of the Department of Agriculture's chief chemist, Dr. Harvey W. Wiley, "a very mountain among men, a lion among fighters." Wiley had long been pressing for a law to prevent the manufacture and sale of adulterated, misbranded, or poisonous foods and drugs. With powerful help from President Roosevelt, the American Medical Association, and muckraker Samuel Hopkins Adams, his bill finally came to the floor of the Senate in the spring of 1906. Sneering openly at chemists in the Department of Agriculture, Senator Nelson W. Aldrich said that "the liberty of all the people" was at stake, but Senator Porter J. McCumber of North Dakota rejoined that the real issue was the public's right to receive what it asked for and "not some poisonous substance in lieu thereof." An imperfect but pioneering pure-food-and-drug measure became law on June 30, 1906.

The fight for the Meat Inspection Amendment offered an even more penetrating insight into the business mind. Upton Sinclair's muckraking novel, *The Jungle* (1906), graphically exposed conditions in the meat-packing industry:

> There was never the least attention paid to what was cut up for sausage, there would come all the way back from Europe old sausage that had been rejected, and that was moldy and white—it would be doused with borax and glycerine, and dumped into the hoppers, and made over again for home consumption. There would be meat that had tumbled out on the floor, in the dirt and sawdust, where the workers had tramped and spit uncounted millions of germs. ... [A] man could run his hand over these piles of meat and sweep off handfuls of the dried dung of rats.

After reading *The Jungle*, according to Finley Peter Dunne's humorous character "Mr. Dooley," Roosevelt rose from his breakfast table crying, "I'm pizened" and threw his sausages out the window. Actually, the president ordered an immediate investigation. Meanwhile, lobbyists for the meat-packing industry charged that an inspection measure drawn by Senator Albert J. Beveridge of Indiana was "unconstitutional" and "socialistic." When European sales dropped precipitously, however, the meat packers abruptly reversed themselves. They demanded, in the words of Mark Sullivan, "an inspection law ... strong enough to still public clamor, while not so drastic as to inconvenience them too greatly." The result was compromise in the Roosevelt pattern.

▶ Chicago meat inspectors in a meat-packing facility after the first pure-food-and-drug measure became law in 1906.

For Generations Yet Unborn

By then the president was also deep in a bitter struggle for rational control and development of the nation's natural resources. On his side stood a great host of governmental scientists and experts headed by Gifford Pinchot, uncounted public-spirited citizens from all over the nation (but especially from the East), numerous homesteaders, and the great lumber corporations. Arrayed against him were small lumber companies, grazing, mining, and power interests of all types, most Western state governments, and, in the end, a decisive majority in Congress.

The issues were simple in some instances and complex in others. Should homesteaders be sacrificed to big cattle and sheep men for reasons of efficiency? Should giant lumber corporations, which had the means to pursue scientific forestry, be favored over small companies, which did not? Should the moralistic and scientific assumptions of Roosevelt and his supporters prevail? Those assumptions were that the country's natural resources belong to the people as a whole; that "the fundamental idea of forestry is the perpetuation of forests by use"; that the federal government should reclaim arid lands; that "every stream is a unit from its source to its mouth, and all its uses are interdependent"; and that the electric monopoly is "the most threatening which has ever appeared."

Early in his administration, in the 1930s, Roosevelt saved what would become the heart of the Tennessee Valley Authority by vetoing a bill that would have opened Muscle Shoals on the Tennessee River to haphazard development by private interests. He then set aside governmental reserves in Nebraska for a tree-planting experiment that would serve as a model for a more comprehensive program under the New Deal. In 1905, he rehabilitated the Bureau of Forestry, renamed it the Forest Service, and appointed Gifford Pinchot as its chief.

A small revolution followed. Trained and dedicated foresters staffed the new agency. Enlightened controls directed the development of waterpower sites by corporations, and the president vetoed numerous bills injurious to the public interest. More than 2,500 potential dam sites were temporarily withdrawn from entry in order to assure orderly and constructive development. In addition, 150 million acres were added to the national forests, and half as many acres with coal and mineral deposits were transferred to the public domain. Most large lumber corporations (though not the small ones) were persuaded to adopt selective-cutting techniques, which alone assured the perpetuation of timber resources.

Western congressmen beholden to private interests responded with near-hysterical charges of "executive usurpation" and destruction of states' rights, but Roosevelt remained undaunted. He skirmished for the preservation of the country's natural monuments, even as Congress passed laws depriving him of authority to create new national forests. Before he left office in March 1909, the number of national parks had doubled. Sixteen national monuments, like California's Muir Woods and Washington's Mount Olympus, had been created, and fifty-one wildlife refuges established. "Is there any law that will prevent me from declaring Pelican Island a Federal Bird Reservation?" Roosevelt asked. "Very well, then I so declare it."

The president also appointed a commission to investigate and make recommendations for multipurpose river valley developments such as the Tennessee Valley Authority later became. Then, in May 1908, he urged the first conference of governors to implement the conservation movement in their states. No governor espoused the movement with Roosevelt's zeal and understanding, but spadework for moderate state programs had, nevertheless, begun. "When the historian ... shall speak of Theodore Roosevelt," Senator La Follette later wrote, "he is likely to say ... that his greatest work was inspiring and actually beginning a world movement for ... saving for the human race the things on which alone a peaceful, Progressive, and happy life can be founded."

Variations in Antitrust Policy

Neither La Follette nor most other Progressives were altogether enthusiastic about Roosevelt's attitude toward big business later in his term. The president had followed up action against the Northern Securities Company with a spate of anti-trust suits, and by the end of his second term twenty-five indictments had been obtained and eighteen proceedings in equity had been instituted. His successor, William Howard Taft, intensified the pace, bringing forty-three indictments in four years, far exceeding Roosevelt's "trust-busting." Unlike Roosevelt, who merely wanted to regulate the trusts for the purpose of staving off revolutionary reform, Taft was a legalist who viewed the trusts as in violation of the Sherman Act and, therefore, illegal. In 1911 the Supreme Court implicitly reversed the Knight decision of 1895 in two verdicts, decreeing dissolutions of the Standard Oil Company and the American Tobacco Company. These decisions made it clear that manufacturing combinations were not exempt from the Sherman Antitrust Act, even though the Court qualified its position somewhat with the so-called rule of reason, which acknowledged that bigness per se was no crime.

"The example of these basic decisions served as a powerful negative factor in business affairs," concludes one recent scholar. "Certain lines of development were denied to ambitious men." Yet the decisions wrought few basic changes in the American economy. Price leadership continued as the producers in an industry followed the lead of a few dominant corporations. Moreover, control over credit remained highly concentrated in Wall Street.

▶ William Howard Taft, twenty-seventh president of the United States.

As his administration progressed, Roosevelt himself experienced a metamorphosis in his attitude toward the "trusts." Because he appreciated the advantages of large-scale production and distribution, he sought to distinguish between "good" and "bad" trusts. Putting his faith primarily in regulation, he repeatedly called on Congress to strengthen and expand the regulatory Bureau of Corporations. Then, after he left office, he came out openly for government price-fixing in basic industries.

Otherwise, from this time on Roosevelt maintained cordial relations with the Morgan-U.S. Steel axis. In order to prevent the spread of a severe financial panic that struck New York in 1907, he went to the aid of the banks and acquiesced to U.S. Steel's absorption, financed by J. P. Morgan, of a Southern competitor, the Tennessee Coal and Iron Company. Then, in the next year, he accepted without protest the inadequate Aldrich-Vreeland banking bill, which Progressives and agrarians bitterly opposed as banker-oriented.

Trouble on the Labor Front

Labor continued to make modest advances during the Roosevelt and Taft administrations, mainly because of the Progressives' work in the states. The American Federation of Labor (AFL) grew in fits and starts, and the standard of living of its highly skilled members rose appreciably. In manufacturing, we have seen, wages increased while the average workweek declined from sixty to fifty hours.

The AFL failed, however, to organize basic industry, mainly because of the massive counteroffensive by employers, spearheaded by the National Association of Manufacturers (NAM). To prevent labor from organizing, the NAM resorted to weapons ranging from propaganda to violence. Its most effective tactic was maintenance of the open shop (a shop in which union membership is not a precondition of employment), and its most important ally was the middle class. The employers might have understood that, in practice, an open shop meant a nonunion shop, but middle-class Progressives often did not. Even when they saw the point, a lingering devotion to natural law and individual rights made it difficult for them to accept the idea of the closed shop. Roosevelt was unsure on the issue, and men like Woodrow Wilson, then president of Princeton, and Charles W. Eliot, president of Harvard, were adamant in their opposition to the closed shop. Eliot actually acclaimed the strikebreaker as "a very good type of modern hero." In consequence, labor received virtually no support during the Progressive Era for the one measure that would have assured it success—active governmental support of the organizing process.

To compound labor's difficulties, the basic right to strike was often grossly impaired by management's private police forces, the actions of corporation-dominated state governments, and the indiscriminate issuance of injunctions by judges who cared more for property than for human rights. In speech after speech from 1905 to 1912, Roosevelt inveighed mightily against the abuse of the injunction (six special messages to Congress between 1905 and 1908); however, the NAM was so influential in Republican councils that he failed even to get an anti-injunction plank in the party platform in 1908.

Meanwhile, campaigns to organize the steel industry suffered a series of setbacks and finally collapsed altogether. The United Mine Workers were successful in the East, but they failed in two bloody efforts in Colorado. The first, in 1903–1904, ended in a rout climaxed by the deportation of strikers to the desert. The second, in 1913–1914, ended in tragedy when National Guardsmen burned a strikers' tent colony at Ludlow on April 20, 1914, accidentally killing eleven women and two children.

In 1905, against this background, the formation of the freewheeling and sometimes violent (especially in rhetoric) Industrial Workers of the World ("Wobblies") was almost predictable. Concentrated in the West, the IWW fought the battles of frontier miners, lumberjacks, and migrant workers with a leftist political bent.

The Triangle Shirtwaist Factory Fire

On March 25, 1911, one of the largest industrial disasters in the history of the United States occurred in New York City at the Triangle Shirtwaist Factory where 146 workers, almost all of them women, perished either in the fire or by leaping to their death from the ninth and tenth floors of the factory. The fire blocked one stairway, and the other stairway was locked because

▶ Members of the Industrial Workers of the World union

the factory managers would lock the doors to the stairwells and exits to keep the workers from taking cigarette breaks during their shifts. The exterior fire escape was in disrepair and collapsed as too many people climbed onto its rickety structures at once, sending those on the fire escape to their death on the concrete one hundred feet below. Several people escaped via the elevator, but a number of people jumped to their death down the elevator shaft, landing on the top of the elevator car; the elevator could not make another attempt due to the weight. New Yorkers on the street watched in horror as sixty-two people, some engulfed in flames and falling as human torches, jumped from windows on the south side of the building to their death. One man was seen kissing a young woman at the window before they both jumped to become bloody pulps on the street. Two people were discovered to be still alive an hour later after falling one hundred feet and smashing onto the concrete.

The fire led to legislation requiring improved factory safety standards and helped spur the growth of the International Ladies' Garment Workers' Union, which fought for better and safer working conditions for sweatshop workers in that industry. In October of that year, the American Society of Safety Engineers was founded in New York City.

Forecasts of the Welfare State

By 1907, the Republican majority in Congress had had their fill of Theodore Roosevelt. They approved no major domestic legislation during his last two years in office and repudiated him openly on several occasions. Nevertheless, the executive power under Roosevelt continued to expand. The president appointed numerous investigatory commissions, and he made further advances in conservation. Furthermore, he repeatedly lectured Congress and the people on the need to mitigate the harsh inequities of capitalism by welfare measures. The Supreme

▶ In the Triangle Shirtwaist Factory fire 146 workers perished. Due to a fire escape in disrepair and a malfunctioning elevator, they had been trapped. The tragedy of the fire led to legislation requiring improved factory safety standards and the International Ladies' Garment Workers' Union, which fought for better and safer working conditions.

Court's ruling in *Lochner v. New York* (1905), which held a maximum-hours law for bakers to be unconstitutional on the grounds that it was an unreasonable interference with the right of free contract and an unreasonable use of the state's police power, outraged him. After a New York tenement law was invalidated and a workmen's compensation law declared unconstitutional, Roosevelt wrote Justice William R. Day that, unless the judiciary's spirit changed, "we should not only have a revolution, but it would be absolutely necessary to have a revolution, because the condition of the worker would become intolerable."

On January 31, 1908, Roosevelt sent Congress the most radical presidential message to that time. He charged that businessmen had revived the doctrine of states' rights in order to avoid all meaningful regulation. Furthermore, he observed that there was "no moral difference between gambling at cards . . . and gambling in the stock market." He called for stringent regulation of securities, imprisonment of businessmen who flouted the law, and a comprehensive program of business regulation. In addition, he upbraided "decent citizens" for permitting "those rich men whose lives are evil and corrupt" to control the nation's destiny. He lashed the judiciary for "abusing" the writ of injunction in labor disputes; and he contemptuously dismissed editors, lawyers, and politicians who had been "purchased by the corporations" as "puppets who move as the strings are pulled." Moreover, Roosevelt came out for workmen's compensation, compulsory arbitration of labor disputes, and acceptance of big unionism as a countervailing power to big business.

In doing so, Roosevelt lost the support of big business conservatives that was needed if he were to secure the Republican nomination in 1908. Laissez faire conservatives also erroneously believed that the Panic of 1907 was a result of Roosevelt's meddling in the economy. Finally, Roosevelt was limited by his own words—he had promised in 1904 that he would only run for one term since he had served most of William McKinley's term as well as his own. Consequently, to run again in 1908 would mean going back on his word, which Roosevelt was loathe to do. Consequently, at age fifty, Roosevelt decided that he could not run again in 1908 and briefly retired from public life. Nevertheless, in 1908, the crowd at the Republican National Convention chanted "Four More Years" for forty-nine minutes until Henry Cabot Lodge finally came forward and announced that the president's decision was irrevocable.

The Disruption of the G.O.P.

Taft's Background

Roosevelt's chosen successor, William Howard Taft, unfortunately lacked the energy, conviction, and political skill to carry on Roosevelt's policies. He seemed to be sympathetic to Roosevelt's Progressive views, but he had marked limitations. He believed implicitly in natural law, and he was a good but painfully conventional lawyer. Furthermore, he had no zest for the give-and-take of politics; and although he possessed a strain of courage, he lacked political boldness and energy.

Big and small business heartily concurred in Taft's nomination in 1908. Taft handily defeated William Jennings Bryan's third unsuccessful bid for the presidency by 321 to 162 electoral votes in what was billed as the "fattest election in history" since both candidates probably weighed well over three hundred pounds, giving America a solid "third of a ton" of presidential candidates. A story surfaced from when Taft had been governor of the Philippines in 1902: Taft had sent a cable to Elihu Root from Manila, stating, "Took a long horseback ride—feeling fine," to which Root had reportedly replied, "How is the horse?"

At any rate, no sooner were the election returns in than Taft's troubles began. Taft's personality was a great contrast with that of the energetic Roosevelt, whose popularity may have exceeded any president's since George Washington. Teddy bears, Teddy glasses, and Teddy stories permeated American life; any person following Roosevelt may have found the shoes difficult to fill. For Taft, however, the contrasts were even greater. While Roosevelt had been energetic and athletic, Taft was sedentary and obese. He received much bad press when a wall had to be knocked down at the White House to install a special, oversized bathtub for his oversized body. Taft was also prone to falling asleep at inopportune times; once he dozed off in an open car while campaigning in New York; and on another occasion Taft nodded off at a State funeral.

Politically, Taft conceived his mission as one to consolidate the Roosevelt reforms (giving them the "sanction of law," as he privately phrased it), not to embark on new ventures. Actually, he was too steeped in legal traditionalism to accept Roosevelt's dynamic conception of the Constitution; and he, therefore, failed to seize the executive reins. Taft believed that the counsel of lawyers was superior to that of scientists and other experts, and he deplored Roosevelt's reliance on investigatory commissions. Taft also tended to adhere strictly to the letter of the law and preferred not to see gray areas where Roosevelt had done so, including in the areas of anti-trust and separation of powers.

The Tariff Fiasco

By 1908 so many Midwesterners were blaming rising prices on the high schedules of the Dingly Tariff (1897) that Taft implied, during the campaign, that his administration would revise the tariff downward. Faithfully, he called a special session of Congress for the spring of 1909; but instead of lowering the duties, Old Guardsmen in the Senate raised them. This forced the president to accept a compromise (the Payne-Aldrich Tariff) that left the old schedules more or less intact. Then, to the disgust of Progressive Republicans in the Midwest, he defended the measure as "the best bill that the Republican Party ever passed." Two years later he negotiated a reciprocity agreement with Canada that the Canadians subsequently rejected because of loose talk that it presaged annexation of their country.

The Rise of Insurgency

Meanwhile, Taft was besieged with troubles on other fronts. In 1910 a group of Progressive Republicans in the House, led by George W. Norris of Nebraska, stripped Speaker Joseph G. Cannon of his arbitrary and partisan control over legislation and committee appointments. Taft was secretly pleased, but both the insurgents and the public continued to link the president with the uncouth and reactionary Speaker.

Taft's rather curious stand on conservation led to even worse difficulties. He believed in conservation, but he abhorred the freewheeling methods that Roosevelt had used to achieve his objective. Taft replaced Roosevelt's Secretary of the Interior James R. Garfield with Richard A. Ballinger, an honest conservative who had earlier resigned from the Land Office because he disagreed with Roosevelt's view that the public's interest in natural resources should be given priority over that of entrepreneurs. Construing the law rigidly when government interests were at stake and loosely when private interests were at issue, Ballinger soon provoked Gifford Pinchot, Chief of the United States Forest Service, to charge a "giveaway" of Alaskan mineral lands to the Guggenheims, the great mining industrialists. Ballinger had removed approximately one million acres of forests from public land reserves created by Theodore Roosevelt. Interior department investigator Lewis Glavis charged that Ballinger had engaged in a plan to turn over public coal reserves in Alaska to private investors for profit. Glavis took his evidence to Roosevelt's ally Gifford Pinchot, who was still head of the forest service. Pinchot presented the evidence to Taft, who also heard Ballinger's rebuttal and announced that the charges were groundless. Pinchot then leaked the story to the press and to Congress. An enraged Taft dismissed Pinchot for insubordination. In the end, Taft alienated Progressives and Roosevelt supporters who viewed Pinchot as a defender of the public interests against greedy industrialists.

▶ George W. Norris

Ballinger was eventually exonerated, but President Taft was fatally stamped as anti-conservationist since he had fired Roosevelt's man, Gifford Pinchot. The characterization was not wholly unfair. Although Taft withdrew more lands from public entry (closing them to exploitation by private individuals and corporations) than Roosevelt and put millions of acres of forest lands into new reserves, he never did grasp the Roosevelt-Pinchot concepts of controlled development or of multipurpose river valley projects.

Roosevelt Challenges Taft

Characteristically, Roosevelt had gone big-game hunting in Africa, but he returned from abroad in 1910, in high indignation over Taft's ineptitude and the implied repudiation of his conservation policies. At Osawatomie, Kansas, on September 1, the former president developed further the social welfare program he had set forth in his memorable messages of 1908, calling it the "New Nationalism" because it put the national need "before sectional or personal advantage." Roosevelt quoted Lincoln's assertion: "Labor is prior to, and independent of, capital." He asserted that the judiciary's primary obligation was to protect "human welfare rather than ... property." He also called for graduated income and inheritance taxes, workmen's compensation legislation, a federal child labor law, tariff revision, government health insurance, and more stringent regulation of corporations. Furthermore, Roosevelt turned against his handpicked successor Taft for "completely twisting around the policies I have advocated and acted upon."

The congressional elections in the fall of 1910 produced the most sweeping changes since the great realignment of the mid-90s. From East to West, stand-pat Republicans were turned out of office as the G.O.P. lost fifty-eight seats in the House, ten in the Senate, and a total of seven governorships. Furthermore, Progressive Republican candidates ousted conservatives in forty districts, creating a majority Progressive House. At the time most observers blamed the tariff and Taft's failure to project a dynamic Progressive image; but recent scholars suggest that resentment among normally Republican German-Americans against the increasingly fervent support of prohibition by other Republicans figured importantly, and perhaps decisively.

Taft attempted to pacify Progressives with vigorous anti-trust legislation; and in October 1911, he filed an anti-trust suit against U.S. Steel, alleging that the 1907 acquisition of Tennessee Iron and Coal that had been facilitated by Theodore Roosevelt violated the Sherman Act. Roosevelt was incensed since the suit essentially inferred that Roosevelt's approval of the purchase back in 1907 was improper. Roosevelt followed by announcing his candidacy for the presidency in February 1912.

The "Bull Moose" Party

Early in 1911, Republican Progressives began to call for the nomination of Robert La Follette or Roosevelt in 1912. The Wisconsin senator made an early and earnest bid and then refused to bow out gracefully after his most devoted followers concluded that he could not win. Roosevelt's entry into the race, in February 1912, precipitated one of the most bitter, preconvention campaigns in Republican history. The primary election system was relatively new, and only thirteen states held Republican primaries. Roosevelt outpolled Taft two to one in the thirteen states that held primaries, and won all thirteen states; but the Old Guard Republicans refused to let him have the nomination, awarding 90 percent of the unassigned delegates at the Convention to Taft. "We can't elect Taft," a Kansas regular confessed, "but we are going to hold on to this organization and when we get back four years from now, we will have it and not those d----- insurgents."

Faced with these attitudes, more than three hundred Roosevelt delegates stormed out of the convention hall in Chicago in a dispute over the seating of delegates. Six weeks later they returned to form the Progressive or "Bull Moose" Party (so named because Roosevelt proclaimed himself as fit as a bull moose), to nominate their hero, and to synthesize their program for a just society.

Roosevelt's following included Social Gospel clergymen and laymen, college presidents and professors, liberal businessmen and editors, Gifford Pinchot and his fellow conservationists, and social workers by the hundreds. (Jane Addams gave one of the speeches seconding his nomination.) However, when the Democrats nominated a moderate Progressive, Governor Woodrow Wilson of New Jersey, Roosevelt and his party were doomed. Wilson's platform differed from Roosevelt's only in that Wilson opposed the "largeness" of big business, in and of itself, and favored complete destruction of the trusts, rather than merely regulating them as Roosevelt proposed.

The election of 1912 has been described as a three-candidate election, but only a two-candidate campaign, as Taft quickly recognized that he had no chance of winning and essentially did not even try. When asked why he was not campaigning like the other two candidates, Taft's response was, "There are so many people in the country that do not like me." In the election that autumn, Wilson won forty states and 42 percent of the popular vote while Roosevelt ran second with 27 percent and Taft a poor third with 23 percent of the popular vote. It was the largest defeat of a sitting president in United States history, with Taft winning only eight electoral votes.

Actually, by the time Taft left office in March 1913, his administration had compiled an impressive legislative record. It included safety regulations for miners, an Employers' Liability Act for work done under government contract, and a measure to establish a Children's Bureau. The Interstate Commerce Commission's authority had been extended to telephone, telegraph, cable, and wireless companies; and a postal savings system had been established to serve farmers and others in remote rural areas. Congress had also adopted two of the Progressive movement's most cherished proposals—the Sixteenth Amendment, giving Congress the power to levy an income tax, and the Seventeenth Amendment, providing for direct election of senators. Taft himself had given warm support to some of these measures, perfunctory support to others, and little beyond his signature to one or two. All owed their passage more to a coalition of Democrats and Progressive Republicans than to the regular Republican majority.

Ironies of American Socialism

The election of 1912 also drew the largest Socialist vote to that time although not wholly for reasons of ideology. Probably half the nine hundred thousand voters who cast their ballots for the charismatic Socialist Party candidate, Eugene V. Debs, were simply disaffected by the middle-class character of the Bull Moose leadership and, especially, by the unofficial commitment of the three major parties to prohibition.

The Socialist Party was hardly more radical in practice than the Progressive Party was in theory. Socialist leaders believed firmly in evolution, not revolution; and most of the twelve hundred party members who held office in railroad, mining, and industrial towns during that era pushed Progressive-type programs, including efficiency and economy. Furthermore, the conservative German contingent headed by Victor Berger of Milwaukee was avowedly

MAP 20.3 Presidential Election of 1912

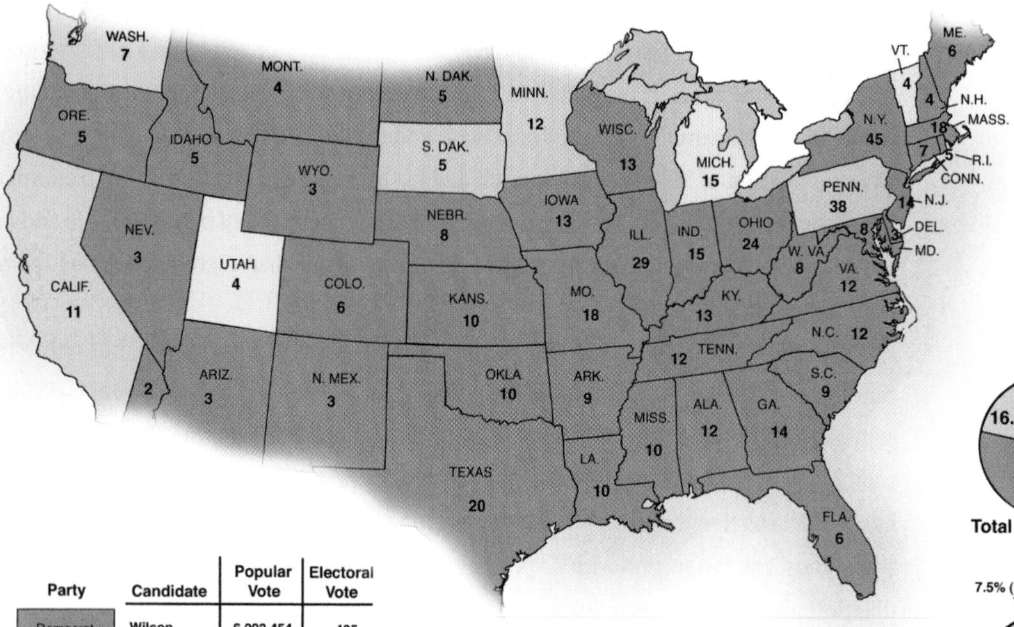

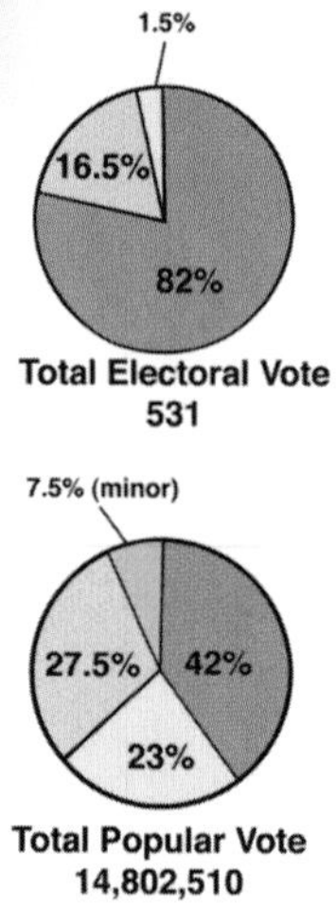

Party	Candidate	Popular Vote	Electoral Vote
Democrat	Wilson	6,293,454	435
Progressive	T. Roosevelt	4,119,538	88
Republican	Taft	3,484,980	8
Minor Candidates	E. V. Debs	900,672	None

racist. Not until after the northward trek of blacks at the end of World War I made it politically expedient to appeal to them, did the party do so, although Debs and many others had long been sympathetic.

Conservative Socialists also differed little from organized labor and the major parties on immigration. "Slavonians, Italians, Russians, and Armenians," said Berger before a House committee in 1911, were the "modern white coolies" of the steel industry and had "crowded out the Americans, Germans, Englishmen, and Irishmen." Even Morris Hillquit, leader of the Party's strongly Jewish eastern wing, favored selective restriction of immigration. More ironic still, the dirt and tenant farmers of Oklahoma and Texas, who constituted the Party's largest faction stood strongly for individual rather than communal ownership of land.

Yet, for all its internal inconsistencies, socialism made a significant impress on American life. As the memoirs of numerous Progressives attest, socialist values influenced the social justice wings of the Republican, Democratic, and Progressive parties alike. They also served as a central inspiration to Jane Addams, Florence Kelley, and many of the other great reformers.

The Triumph of Progressivism

Wilson's Background

Woodrow Wilson was born in a Presbyterian manse in Virginia in 1856 and reared in a South (Georgia) convulsed by Civil War and Reconstruction. Wilson, like Roosevelt, would grow to be one of America's scholar-presidents as he graduated from Princeton in 1879 and went on to obtain a law degree and practiced law in Atlanta. Wilson became dissatisfied with the legal profession and returned to school to earn a Ph.D. in political science from Johns Hopkins University. As a doctorial candidate at Johns Hopkins, he argued in a brilliant dissertation, "Congressional Government" (1885), that the basic weakness in the American political system was its separation of executive from legislative leadership. Wilson obtained a spot on the faculty at Princeton and following a distinguished tenure as a professor, worked his way up to be president of Princeton University in 1902. Wilson gained a reputation for Progressive academic reforms at Princeton and used that reputation to propel himself to the New Jersey governor's office in 1910. As governor, Wilson shifted from being an academic conservative into a practical Progressive. He boldly seized control of the Democratic state machine, pushed a comprehensive reform program through a divided legislature, and gave eloquent voice to high ideals and moderately Progressive aspirations.

Wilson was the first Southerner elected to the White House since 1844 and the only Democrat, other than Grover Cleveland, elected to the White House since Reconstruction. Wilson was a moralist and a teetotaler who called for a day of prayer after his inauguration. His keen intellect and excellent education combined with a strict religious upbringing resulted in Wilson's strong political convictions that were rarely open to compromise.

Wilson was also a single man for a portion of his presidency and courted his second wife, Edith Gault, while in office, creating a tabloid media circus. Love letters from the president to Edith, in which the president proclaimed, "You are my ideal companion, my perfect playmate, with whom everything is gay," and "How deep I have drunk of the sweet fountains that are in you, eventually were published. One Secret Service agent reported that after seeing Mrs. Gault one night, the president skipped down the street singing, "Oh, you beautiful doll." It is perhaps little wonder then that the *Washington Post,* after the president spent an evening on the town with his "perfect playmate," printed the famous gaffe, "The president spent much of the evening entering Mrs. Gault."

After the two married, Edith remained at the president's side at all times, evidently viewing herself as a true partner in all things, even the presidency. When Wilson traveled to Europe to sign the Versailles Treaty after World War I, Edith Wilson was by his side. This brought out Wilson's critics in full force. In the early part of the twentieth century, it was not customary for a First Lady to take an active role in a president's official duties.

In contrast, Edith Wilson believed that being with her husband at all times, to counsel him and give him support and advice, was her right as his wife; and she therefore ignored the critics. Similarly, it appears that President Wilson felt comfortable consulting with his wife on the issues of the day, and it appears that she was his confidant, and that he respected her opinion as much as that of most of his other advisors.

The New Freedom Program

The program Wilson called the New Freedom was grounded in the theory that no group should receive special privileges. It differed from Roosevelt's New Nationalism in two essentials. First, New Freedom advocated regulated competition rather than regulated monopoly. Second, it turned most of the social programs of progressivism back to the states and municipalities. The

▶ Woodrow Wilson on his daily ride in the outskirts of Washington

first goal was to be achieved by downward revision of the tariff, strengthening and relentlessly enforcing the antitrust laws, and freeing the banks from dependence on Wall Street.

Tariff and Banking Reform

Wilson aimed to destroy the Republican system of special privileges for industry and for the producers of raw materials by reducing tariff protection and, thereby, increasing competition. He used patronage to hold wavering Democrats in line; and he marshaled opinion against the G.O.P. Old Guard by charging publicly that Washington had seldom seen "so numerous, so industrious or so insidious a lobby" as had invaded the Capitol. This masterful exertion of leadership resulted in the first substantial reduction of the tariff since before the Civil War.

Wilson began auspiciously by calling a special session of Congress the day of his inauguration and then addressing a joint meeting of the Senate and House in person. In doing so, Wilson became the first president since Thomas Jefferson to make an appearance before Congress in a situation that was neither mandated by the Constitution nor an emergency, but simply to argue for the passage of particular policies. Again, being a major fan of the British Parliamentary system, Wilson desired to approach Congress much as a prime minister would in England and take the lead in legislation. Wilson's first action as president was, therefore, to appear before Congress and argue for a reduction of the tariff. Congress, with a Democratic majority, passed the lower tariff.

After the ratification of the Sixteenth Amendment, Congress under Wilson also passed a modest income tax (1 percent on income over $20,000 and 6 percent on income over $500,000) along with the lower tariff. In October 1913, however, Wilson was embroiled in conflict over banking legislation. Conservative Republicans wanted a single central bank controlled by private bankers, while conservative Democrats insisted on a decentralized reserve system under private control. Bryan Democrats and Progressive Republicans called for a reserve system and a currency supply owned and controlled by the government. (The latter were

▶ Edith Wilson believed that being with her husband at all times, to counsel him and give him support and advice, was her right as his wife and President Wilson consulted with his wife on the issues of the day. She was his confidant, and he respected her opinion.

roused especially by sensational revelations of Wall Street's influence over the nation's financial and investment system.) Finally, in December 1913, after consultations with Louis D. Brandeis, his most influential adviser on domestic matters, Wilson worked out a series of constructive compromises that were adopted as the Federal Reserve Act.

The measure created twelve Federal Reserve Banks, each to be owned and controlled by the individual private banks in its district but responsible to a seven-member central Federal Reserve Board appointed by the president. The Federal Reserve Banks would hold a percentage of the assets of their member banks in reserve and use those reserves to support loans to banks at a discount rate. Federal Reserve Banks could also issue Federal Reserve Notes and shift them to imperiled banks to provide them with the funds necessary to meet loan demands in times of currency shortages. Provision was also made to meet the seasonal needs of agriculture. The Federal Reserve System was not intended to destroy private ownership and initiative in banking, but it did create new centers of financial power to offset the overweening influence of New York bankers.

Wilson planned to round out his program by revising the antitrust laws. There were to be no special benefits to labor, no aid to agriculture, and no such conservation program as Roosevelt had envisaged. Child labor, woman suffrage, workmen's compensation, and all the rest would have to come, if they came at all, by haphazard state action. Indeed, when a bill sponsored by the National Child Labor Committee passed the House in 1914 over the protests of states' rights Southerners, Wilson refused to promote it in the Senate.

Moving Toward the New Nationalism

By 1914, the Progressive movement had gathered too much momentum to be long halted by presidential indifference. While the child labor forces were regrouping for a second assault, new pressures were bearing so heavily on the White House that Wilson had either to accommodate them or risk loss of his office in 1916.

These pressures were first felt when the administration introduced its program, New Freedom, in 1914. Wilson's original measures included legislation to outlaw specific, unfair trade practices and to create a federal trade commission with only fact-finding powers. Progressives in both parties thought little of the former and refused to support the latter because it did not grant the commission power to act on its findings.

Finally, Brandeis and others persuaded Wilson that it was impossible to outlaw every conceivable unfair trade practice and that something like Roosevelt's proposal for continuous regulation was the only workable alternative. Wilson, therefore, signed the Clayton Antitrust Bill despite its ambiguities and qualifications; but he put his energy and influence into Brandeis' measure to create a federal regulatory agency empowered, in effect, to define unfair trade practices on its own terms and to suppress them on its own findings, subject to broad court review. As a consequence, the final component of Wilson's New Freedom was the passage of the Federal Trade Commission Act, which created the Federal Trade Commission (FTC), a new federal regulatory agency that was given the authority to prosecute business for unfair trade practices and the investigative authority necessary to carry out such prosecution. After the creation of the Federal Reserve banking system and the FTC, Wilson considered his New Freedom complete.

Meanwhile, Wilson engaged in a bitter quarrel with organized labor over the Clayton Antitrust Bill. Samuel Gompers and the AFL hierarchy demanded provisions to exempt labor unions from prosecution for the secondary boycott, the blacklist, and other weapons the Supreme Court had declared in violation of the Sherman Antitrust Act. In effect, labor wanted special privileges to offset management's power.

Wilson held rigidly to the New Freedom line against special privilege for any group, but he did accept an affirmation of rights that labor already possessed in law, if not always in fact, and a few other moderate provisions. His adherence to the New Freedom program on this one point did not signify that he was ordinarily unsympathetic to labor. On the contrary, the AFL lobby spoke with greater effect in Washington during Wilson's administration than did the National Association of Manufacturers.

"We Are Also Progressives"

As Wilson's tenure lengthened, it became evident that the New Freedom's opposition to special privilege and commitment to states' rights made it too confining to permit fulfillment of the president's own expanding concept of social justice. For example, Wilson opposed an amendment to impose women's suffrage on the states because of states' rights. It also became clear that the Democrats would have to attract a substantial portion of Roosevelt's disintegrating "Bull Moose" Party to retain the presidency in 1916. Against this background, Wilson again became more Progressive. He began by signing the La Follette Seaman's Act of 1915, which freed sailors from bondage to labor contracts. Then, early in 1916, he nominated Louis Brandeis to the Supreme Court over bitter opposition by Old Guard Republicans and leaders of the legal profession. (Brandeis, a Kentucky-born Jew known as the "people's lawyer," had broken legal tradition in 1908 by presenting a mass of sociological data—with help from Florence Kelley and her colleagues—to the Court in his defense of an Oregon bill establishing maximum working hours for women.)

Next, the president came out in support of a languishing rural-credits bill that he had condemned as class legislation two years before. Wilson also won approval of a model federal workmen's compensation bill. In addition, he successfully urged creation of a tariff commission because he feared that surplus European goods would be dumped in America at the end of World War I. The president also threw strong support behind the Child Labor Bill and won its adoption. Enacted in the summer of 1916, the bill made it illegal to transport goods

▶ Samuel Gompers fought for provisions to exempt labor unions from prosecution for the secondary boycott, the blacklist, and other weapons that had been declared in violation of the Sherman Antitrust Act. All in all, the work force wanted special privileges to offset management's power.

manufactured by child labor across state lines. Two years later, however, the U.S. Supreme Court in *Hammer v. Dagenhart* declared the Act unconstitutional. The Court ruled that though child labor may be an evil, but the goods produced by that labor were not; and Congress, therefore, had no power to restrict their shipment across state lines under its powers to regulate interstate commerce.

The flow of legislation continued until the very eve of the election. A measure to extend federal assistance to the states for highway construction rolled through Congress; and the Revenue Act, adopted late in the summer of 1916, increased income taxes sharply and imposed a new estate tax. In September, the president personally drove through Congress the Adamson bill to establish the eight-hour day for railroad workers; and finally, during his second administration, Wilson signed both the prohibition and woman suffrage amendments, though his heart was in neither.

Altogether, Wilson's first administration embodied an imposing and important program of reform legislation. Wilson could truthfully claim, as he did during the presidential campaign of 1916, that he and his party had put a large part of the Progressive Party's platform of 1912 onto the federal statute books.

Politics and Blacks

For the vast majority of African Americans, progressivism proved more an illusion than a reality, regardless of who occupied the White House. Violence or the threat of violence continued to be the ultimate means of race control. Although the total number of lynchings decreased nationwide because of a sharp decline in lynchings in the North, the number simultaneously increased in the South. As often as not, moreover, the burnings and hangings were for imaginary or concocted offenses. In 1906 twelve persons were slaughtered in a race riot in Atlanta. Similarly, two years later an anti-black riot occurred a half mile from Abraham Lincoln's home in Springfield, Illinois. Meanwhile, Southern orators, like South Carolina's "Pitchfork Ben" Tillman, carried the message of white supremacy to receptive Northern audiences. The production

▶Louis Brandeis often called, the "people's lawyer," had broken legal tradition in 1908 by collaborating with Florence Kelley and her colleagues and established a bill stating the maximum working hours for women.

in 1915 of *The Birth of a Nation*, which was based on Thomas Dixon's blatantly racist book, *The Clansman*, brought more violence.

Roosevelt had been moderately sympathetic to blacks. His original objective had been a biracial Southern Republican party led by patrician whites and educated blacks—his immediate end, the securing of his own nomination in 1904 through control of the Southern delegations. He had maintained close relations with Booker T. Washington, head of the Tuskegee Institute, and, unlike McKinley, appointed eminently qualified blacks to federal offices in the South. He had also denounced lynching and ordered legal action against peonage, in which a worker, usually black, was forced to pay off a debt through the court-rigged assignment of that debt to a private employer.

By 1904, these actions by Roosevelt had produced a vicious reaction in the South. With the tacit acquiescence of Bryan, Southern editors and politicians inflamed the region over "Roosevelt Republicanism" and, thereby, forced enlightened white Southerners on the defensive. After Roosevelt entertained Booker T. Washington at the White House, newspaper headlines included: "Roosevelt Dines a Darky" and "Our Coon Flavored President." Nor was the situation much better in the North, where "scientific" racial theories that taught the innate inferiority of blacks had penetrated even the universities.

Against this background, Roosevelt equivocated. He appointed a few more African Americans to medium-level offices and continued to denounce lynching; however, during the race riot in Atlanta in 1906, he provided no moral leadership. Then in the aftermath of an affray at Brownsville, Texas, erroneously thought to involve blacks, he arbitrarily discharged three companies of black soldiers from the U.S. Army. By the end of his presidency, he had concluded that the hope of a viable biracial Republican Party in the South was an idle dream. Unfortunately, Roosevelt found that attitudes toward blacks in the North were no better. As he sadly reflected, "the North and the South act in just the same way toward the Negro."

His successor, William Howard Taft, had no interest whatever in solving the race problem or in helping black people. "I will not be swerved one iota from my policy to the South ...," Taft snapped. "I shall not appoint Negroes to office in the South. ... I shall not relinquish my hope to build up a decent white man's Party there."

In 1912 many Northern blacks went over to Woodrow Wilson and the Democratic Party, but they were soon disillusioned. Under Wilson, blacks were segregated in some federal departments, and virtually no blacks were appointed to any but the lowest-level offices in either the South or the North. Wilson also reversed Roosevelt's integrationist policies in the United States armed forces and favored the continued segregation of railroad cars. Never in his memory, wrote Booker T. Washington, had he seen his people so "discouraged and bitter." During World War I, discrimination became so extreme in the military service that the Federal Council of Churches of Christ established a commission to investigate.

A few small advances—most of them with greater long-range than short-run significance—punctuated this otherwise dreary record. A handful of Northern philanthropists expanded their support of black colleges, and a small number of Northern Progressives—many the descendants of abolitionists—also formed a common front with blacks. On Lincoln's birthday in 1909, a group of white educators, clergymen, editors, and social workers joined a group of black intellectuals in forming the National Association for the Advancement of Colored People (NAACP). They dedicated the organization to the abolition of all forced segregation and to the promotion of equal justice and enlarged educational opportunities for blacks. However, for tactical reasons, only one black, W. E. B. DuBois, served as an official during the NAACP's early years. (See *William E. Burghardt DuBois: Black Intellectual.*)

Two years after the founding of the NAACP, another group of black intellectuals founded the National Urban League. Neither organization made much headway at first, but they were gathering expertise and resources that would permit a frontal assault on Jim Crow after World War II.

On the legal front, the Supreme Court struck down peonage in separate decisions during the Taft and Wilson administrations though the system actually continued with modifications into the late 1920s. It also overturned an amendment to the Oklahoma Constitution, the so-called Grandfather Clause, which allowed certain illiterate whites, but not illiterate blacks, to vote without first taking a literacy test.

The Progressive Era in Retrospect

Neither the impressive achievements of the Roosevelt, Taft, and Wilson administrations, nor the remarkable flow of legislation in the states fulfilled the best hopes of the social justice Progressives. In 1920, the distribution of wealth was roughly the same as it had been in 1900, the social and economic status of African Americans was only marginally better, and that of women only modestly so. Basic industry remained unorganized, and thousands of steelworkers labored twelve hours a day, seven days a week. Farm tenancy was continuing to rise, and most farm youths still lacked access to secondary schools. The calls of Progressives for social security and unemployment insurance systems were as yet unheeded, and good medical care, like good legal service, remained more a function of the marketplace than a fundamental right.

Civil liberties were no less subject to the whim of the crowd, the local authority, or the business-oriented judge than they had been twenty years earlier. City manager and city coun-

W. E. B DuBois: Black Intellectual

W. E. B. DuBois

The most intensely intellectual black spokesman of the first half of the twentieth century was W. E. B. DuBois, whose greatest achievement, perhaps, was to awaken interest in the black past, both African and American. He was born in Great Barrington, Massachusetts, with, as he phrased it, "a flood of Negro blood, a string of French, a bit of Dutch, but thank God! no Anglo-Saxon." His paternal grandfather, a restless and embittered man, had been the offspring of a wealthy French Huguenot American and a Bahamian mulatto slave. His father, no less restless and embittered, had married Mary Burghardt, whose partly Dutch family was among Great Barrington's earliest settlers; he left her permanently soon after their child was born.

Short and bronze-skinned, with sharp features and an aloof personality that gave him an aristocratic mien, DuBois in his teens was hardly aware that he was "different" until he offered his calling card to a white girl and was rejected "peremptorily, with a glance." Feeling that a "vast veil" had shut him out, he knew "days of secret tears" thereafter. The black man, he wrote in 1903, "feels his two-ness—an American, a Negro, two souls, two thoughts, two unreconciled strivings, two warring ideals in one dark body."

DuBois began to develop an interest in racial matters while still in high school, and at the age of fifteen he became the local correspondent of the black *New York Globe*. His principal, Frank A. Hosmer, recognized his precocity and encouraged him to prepare for college. (DuBois often wondered, he later said, what his fate would have been had Hosmer been "born with no faith in 'darkies.') Financed by local white church goers, DuBois went to Fisk University, an all-black college in Tennessee in 1885. He completed his degree in three years and entered Harvard with Junior standing as a scholarship student. There, as one of his biographers writes, he came to think of the institution "as a library and a faculty, nothing more." Contemptuous of the lack of purpose of most of Harvard's white students, DuBois took an active part in black affairs in Boston during his first years. His aloof personality caused resentment, however, and in time he withdrew into himself. Meanwhile, he was awarded a fellowship to the University of Berlin.

Study in Germany strengthened DuBois' interests in scientific social and historical research, though he had done brilliantly in the natural sciences as an undergraduate. Never—not even after he renounced his American citizenship late in life—did he lose faith that social science would some day triumph over the mythology of racism and the pathology of discrimination.

After two years in Germany, DuBois returned to complete a degree in history under Albert Bushnell Hart (one of the leading figures in sociologically-informed history) in 1895 and to become Harvard's first black Ph.D. Forced to accept a teaching position at Wilberforce College in Ohio, a black institution with a strongly religious orientation, he deplored "the wild screams, cries, groans, and shrieks" of the revival meetings. Only his marriage to Nina Gomer of Cedar Rapids, Iowa, brightened his life. Then, following a temporary appointment in sociology at the University of Pennsylvania, he published one of his finest works, the pioneering *Philadelphia Negro* (1889). It marked the founding of black sociology.

DuBois differed radically from pragmatic Booker T. Washington, who was tied to Southern roots. Harvard and European educated, living in two worlds yet belonging to neither, DuBois believed fervently in the immediate need to prepare the "Talented Tenth" of blacks for the professions and general leadership. "The Negro race," he wrote, "is going to be saved by its exceptional men." From his new urban base at Atlanta University, the faculty he joined in 1897, he came to deplore Washington's emphasis on vocational and industrial education. In 1903, in a moving and at times poetic book of essays entitled *The Souls of Black Folks*, DuBois criticized Washington as a compromiser whose ideology "practically accepts the alleged inferiority of the Negro." Not only does Washington apologize for injustice, DuBois wrote, "He belittles the emasculating effect of caste distinctions, and opposes the higher training and ambition of our brightest minds." Negroes should realize, he also said, that "Beauty is black."

Two years later DuBois invited a select group of black intellectuals to meet at Fort Erie, Ontario, where they formed the Niagara Movement. Condemning racism as "unreasoning human savagery," they called for federal aid to education, and denounced the discriminatory politics of employers and labor unions alike. They also demanded suffrage for blacks on the same basis as whites. The organization was short-lived. DuBois then played a role in founding the interracial National Association for the Advancement of Colored People, the most important civil rights organization of the twentieth century.

Subsequently, as editor for twenty-two years of the NAACP's monthly magazine, *The Crisis*, DuBois explored a whole range of racial issues and personalities. "He does do dangerous things," wrote Mary Ovington, his most loyal white supporter on the NAACP board. "He strikes at people with a harshness and directness that appalls me, but the blow is often deserved and it is never below the belt." Meanwhile DuBois became increasingly frustrated by his inability to resolve the paradox of Negro life in the United States: Should blacks regard themselves as Americans or as Afro-Americans? Should they strive for complete integration or for separatism? Incremental reforms or fundamental changes?

In 1912 DuBois had resigned from the Socialist Party, partly in disgust over its racism but mainly in the vain hope that the election of Woodrow Wilson would bring modest gains to his people. When the country entered World War I, DuBois suffered the contempt of radical black integrationists for urging creation of a separate Negro Officer Candidate's School. Dur-

W. E. B. DuBois: Black Intellectual

(Continued)

ing the 1920s, he charged Robert M. La Follette's Progressive presidential campaign with "deliberately dodging" the black question, and he fought with Communist Party leaders for the same reason.

DuBois resigned his editorship of *The Crisis* in 1932 after a series of policy disputes and returned to Atlanta University. There he edited the *Encyclopedia of the Negro* (1933–1945) and in 1935 published *Black Reconstruction in America*. This brilliant work did much to wrench white historians from the pro-South bias that marred most histories of Reconstruction until that time.

In 1961, angered by the Cold War and the government's harassment of him for his opposition to it, DuBois joined the Communist Party. But by then he had already committed his mind and heart to Africa—"the Spiritual Frontier of humankind," as he called it. He accepted an invitation from the government of Ghana to supervise compilation of the *Encyclopedia Africana* and died in Accra in 1963 at the age of 95. He had become a Ghanian citizen just a few months before his death.

In the early twenty-first century, the outstanding African American scholar Henry Louis Gates, Jr. holds the W. E. B. DuBois Chair of Humanities at Harvard University, a concrete example of the way in which DuBois's stature has grown since his death.

cil forms of government had altered little more than the face of urban politics, and no perceptible change in the quality of candidates had been wrought by the direct election of United States senators. Neither had the conservation movement halted the abuse of privately owned natural resources or the despoliation of the countryside by individuals and businesses, both large and small.

Despite the highly publicized attacks on trusts, corporations were larger and monopoly or near-monopoly was more widespread at the end of each presidential administration than at its beginning. Many of the regulatory agencies had already become virtual captives of the industries they were supposed to regulate, and, close ties had developed in other agencies between the experts who ran them and the interests that sought their favors. By any reasonable measure, America in 1920, like all other advanced technological nations, had become a partially formed bureaucratic, corporate society.

Nevertheless, as we have seen, the majority of people led somewhat more comfortable and more interesting lives in 1920 than they had in 1900; and their opportunities for self-fulfillment were also much greater. Technology relieved some of the drudgery of housework, and the increase in leisure time that resulted from the rise in productivity was generating new forms of entertainment and diversion. Government regulations had reduced the industrial accident rate and eased slightly the severity of labor in factories and mines. Modernization of municipal government made cities more manageable, and advances in public health made them more livable.

The growth of urban colleges and evening courses had opened professional careers to thousands of ethnic youths, and the parallel expansion of state colleges and universities was putting higher education within the reach of small town youngsters and the sons and daughters of well-to-do farmers. More important still, the explosion of knowledge sparked by the development of graduate education was creating an almost entirely new professional class and giving both business and government their guiding intelligence.

Philosophically, progressivism raised the level of political discourse far above that of the late nineteenth century and probably to the highest level since the time of the Founding Fathers. Educationally, it inculcated the belief that advanced training was both a societal need and a public responsibility. Sociologically, it put into the political realm an environmental and behaviorist interpretation of society that, for all its oversimplifications, was and remains the moral rationale for social reform. Psychologically, it changed the perception of government from a negative to a positive force—a view that prevailed for many decades until the advent of Ronald Reagan as a force in American politics—and promoted the view that the federal government should serve as a countervailing power to the large business corporation. Administratively, progressivism demonstrated both the government's dependence on experts and the apparent impossibility of completely insulating them from the influence of powerful private interests. Constitutionally, it raised important, and partly effective, challenges to the concept of state's rights and to the prerogatives of manufacturers engaged in interstate commerce. Economically, it established a revenue base for the society's current and future needs by winning broad acceptance of the general principle of graduated corporation, income, and inheritance taxes.

Just as important, perhaps, progressivism greatly stimulated rising expectations and a dependence on government for the solutions of social and economic problems; These years in which modern governance was being invented, however, were also years of transformation in American foreign policy. As we shall soon learn, both Roosevelt and Wilson left their mark in this arena in ways that few other presidents have had the opportunity so to do.

▶ ▶ ▶

Chapter Review 20

Summary

The assassination of William McKinley in 1901 brought to the presidency Theodore Roosevelt, a man with the popularity, energy, drive, intellect, and will to bring about Progressive change in America, much to the chagrin of conservative Republicans. Roosevelt began his reforms with an anti-trust suit against the Northern Securities Company of J. P. Morgan, E. H. Harriman, and James J. Hill. Later that year he broke with thirty years of federal precedent when he took the middle road instead of backing mine owners in a United Mine Workers' strike. Middle class voters supported Roosevelt's Progressivism in a manner that they had not supported the Populism of William Jennings Bryan in the previous decade, although most of the ideas of the Progressives in the early twentieth century were first proposed by the Populists in the previous century.

Progressives were united by the idea that the public good should take precedent over individual interests. Concerns of the Progressives were directed primarily at the excesses of capitalism that included child labor and worker exploitation, environmental degradation, and corruption. Progressives believed that big business had grown too powerful and influential in government; consequently, the power of business had to be curbed in order to correct all of the other social injustices. Another catalyst for the Progressive movement was the Panic of 1893 and the suffering that followed in the 1890s. Progressives viewed government as a tool that could be used to help alleviate such suffering. Progressive reforms began on the municipal and state level before Theodore Roosevelt arrived in the White House to usher them in on the federal level.

Reforms under Roosevelt included not only trust-busting but also greater federal regulation of railroads, federal regulation of food and drugs, federal meat inspection, and conservation of federal lands and natural resources. Trust-busting would be continued and expanded under Roosevelt's successor, William Howard Taft. Tragedy also played a role in bringing about reforms as the Triangle Shirtwaist Factory fire led to new factory safety standards.

In spite of his trust-busting, William Howard Taft's presidency lost the support of Progressives when he fired Theodore Roosevelt's head of the Forest Service, Gifford Pinchot, for insubordination. Conservatives, however, still supported Taft and viewed Roosevelt as a dangerous loose cannon. When conservatives at the Republican Convention in 1912 nominated Taft, Roosevelt and his supporters withdrew from the party and nominated Theodore Roosevelt for president as the candidate of the Bull-Moose Party. Roosevelt, however, along with Taft would lose the three candidate election to Democratic governor of New Jersey, Woodrow Wilson.

Wilson, a PhD from Princeton and Christian moralist, courted his second wife, Edith Gault, while in office. Aside from that spectacle, Americans were treated to more Progressivism with the passage of the Sixteenth Amendment that provided for a federal income tax, the creation of the Federal Reserve Banking system, the creation of the Federal Trade Commission to enforce fair trade practices, and the institution of child labor laws.

For African-Americans, however, Progressivism brought little progress outside of Theodore Roosevelt's symbolic dinner with Booker T. Washington. President Taft essentially ignored the concerns of blacks, and President Wilson even reversed integrationist policies Roosevelt had prescribed for the U.S. military. The

(cont'd)

NAACP was formed, and W. E. B. DuBois and others clamored for black rights—but they would not be forthcoming.

In spite of all the changes during the Progressive Era, at the end of the era big business remained dominant, blacks remained repressed, income inequality remained approximately what it had been before the Progressive Era, and women achieved suffrage, but the balance of their lives was primarily unchanged. Progressivism did, however, stimulate intellectual discussion and permanently establish the idea that government may be used as a tool for solving societal problems.

Chronological Time Line

1898 Theodore Roosevelt was elected governor of New York after the Spanish-American War.

1900 Mark Hanna joined with Samuel Gompers in forming the National Civic Federation to promote settlement of labor disputes.

1900 William McKinley was reelected president with Theodore Roosevelt as his vice presidential running mate.

1900 Robert La Follette was elected governor of Wisconsin on a Progressive platform.

1901 William McKinley was assassinated by Leon Czolgosz, and Theodore Roosevelt assumed the presidency.

1902 The Newlands Act provided federal funds for the construction of dams, canals, and hydroelectric power plants in the West.

1902 Roosevelt invoked the Sherman Anti-Trust Act against the Northern Securities Company.

1902 Roosevelt offered arbitration and then threatened a federal takeover of the coal mines to end the United Mine Workers' strike.

1902 Maryland enacted the first workers' compensation law.

1903 The Department of Commerce and Labor was created, including a Bureau of Corporations with investigatory powers.

Chapter Review (cont'd)

Time Line (cont'd)

1903	The Elkins Act prohibited railroad rebates.
1904	The United Mine Workers' strike in Colorado ended in a rout, climaxed by the deportation of strikers to the desert.
1904	Theodore Roosevelt defeated Alton Parker for his second term in the White House.
1905	Theodore Roosevelt created the Forest Service, headed by Gifford Pinchot.
1905	*Lochner v. New York* held a maximum-hours law for bakers to be unconstitutional.
1905	The Industrial Workers of the World was founded.
1906	A race riot in Atlanta led to twelve deaths.
1906	The Hepburn Act strengthened the regulatory authority of the ICC over railroads, enabling the ICC to set rates and inspect the books.
1906	The Pure Food and Drug Act forbade the sale and manufacture of adulterated food products and poisonous patent medicines.
1906	The Meat Inspection Amendment provided for federal inspection of meat.
1907	Panic of 1907 was thwarted when Roosevelt negotiated the purchase of Tennessee Iron and Coal by U.S. Steel, financed by J. P. Morgan.
1908	William Howard Taft defeated William Jennings Bryan in the presidential election.
1909	The National Association for the Advancement of Colored People (NAACP) was formed.
1910	A group of Progressive Republicans in the House, led by George W. Norris of Nebraska, stripped Speaker Joseph G. Cannon of his arbitrary and partisan control over legislation and committee appointments.
1910	Theodore Roosevelt returned to politics.

Time Line (cont'd)

1911 Illinois established a public assistance program for mothers with dependent children.

1911 Supreme Court reversed the decision in *United States v. E. C. Knight* and broke up the Standard Oil and American Tobacco monopolies.

1911 The Triangle Shirtwaist Factory fire in New York City led to the death of 146 people, mostly women, 62 of whom leaped to their deaths from the ninth and tenth floors of the building.

1911 Taft filed an anti-trust suit against U.S. Steel, alleging that the 1907 acquisition of Tennessee Iron and Coal facilitated by Theodore Roosevelt violated the Sherman Act.

1912 Massachusetts created a commission to fix wages for women and children.

1912 Republicans nominated William Howard Taft and Theodore Roosevelt and his supporters form the Bull Moose Party.

1912 Democrat Woodrow Wilson defeated Theodore Roosevelt and William Howard Taft in a three way presidential race.

1913 The Sixteenth Amendment allowed restoration of the federal income tax.

1913 Federal Reserve Act created the Federal Reserve Banking System.

1914 The Federal Trade Commission was established.

1914 At the end of a United Mine Workers' strike, National Guardsmen burned a strikers' tent colony at Ludlow, Colorado, killing eleven women and two children.

1915 Seaman's Act released commercial sailors from bondage to labor contracts.

1916 Woodrow Wilson was reelected.

1918 *Hammer v. Dagenhart* struck down the child labor law that prohibited interstate shipment of goods produced with child labor.

Chapter Review (cont'd)

Key Terms

Leon Czolgosz: Assassinated William McKinley in 1901

Mark Hanna: Republican Party strategist that opposed McKinley's selection of Theodore Roosevelt as his running mate

Rough Riders: Soldiers led by Theodore Roosevelt in the Spanish-American War

Square Deal: Theodore Roosevelt's campaign slogan and program in 1904

Northern Securities Company: Railroad trust of J. P. Morgan, E. H. Harriman, and James J. Hill that was broken up by Theodore Roosevelt

Robert La Follette: Progressive Senator from Wisconsin

The "Wisconsin Idea": Robert LaFollette's Progressive program that included the direct primary, the short ballot, the initiative and referendum, and the recall of elected officials

Alton B. Parker: Democratic candidate for president in 1904

Hepburn Act: The act strengthened federal regulatory authority over railroads including the authority to set rates and inspect books, and also ended free railroad passes for politicians.

Pure Food and Drug Act: Forbade the sale and manufacture of adulterated food products and patent medicines

Ballinger-Pinchot Fight: Pinchot believed that Interior Secretary Richard Ballinger had improperly released protected forests for economic development. President Taft disagreed; and when Pinchot took his complaints to the press, Taft fired him for insubordination.

Upton Sinclair: Author of the influential novel on the American meat packing industry, *The Jungle*

The "rule of reason": The Supreme Court's assertion that the "largeness" of big business itself was not a crime

National Association of Manufacturers: An organization of small industrialists that opposed regulation of business and Progressive changes

Industrial Workers of the World: Also known as the "Wobblies," a leftist labor union that sought to unite all the workers of the world to overthrow the ruling class

Lochner v. New York: The Court held a maximum-hours law for bakers to be unconstitutional on the grounds that it was an unreasonable interference with the right of free contract and an unreasonable use of the state's police power.

Triangle Shirtwaist Factory Fire: The fire at the Triangle Shirtwaist Factory in a tall building in New York City led to the death of 146 people, most of whom were women, and 62 of whom leaped to their deaths from the ninth and tenth floors.

William Howard Taft: Theodore Roosevelt's hand-picked successor, who won the presidency in 1908

Key Terms (cont'd)

Old Guard Republicans: Conservative Republicans that opposed Theodore Roosevelt's progressivism and supported William Howard Taft for the Republican nomination in 1912

Panic of 1907: Economic panic precipitated by the rumored bankruptcy of Tennessee Iron and Coal, which led to a stock market crash

The Insurgency: The Progressive Republican challenge to Republican Party leadership 1910–1912

New Nationalism: Theodore Roosevelt's reference to his own Progressive platform in 1910

Bull Moose Party: Independent party that formed around Theodore Roosevelt and ran him for the presidency after he was denied the Republican nomination at the 1912 Republican Convention

Eugene Debs: Union leader and head of the American Socialist Party.

Woodrow Wilson: President of Princeton and governor of New Jersey who won the presidency for the Democrats in 1912

Edith Gault: Dated and married Woodrow Wilson during his presidency

New Freedom: Wilson's economic program in 1913 that included the creation of the Federal Reserve Banking System and the Federal Trade Commission

NAACP: National Association for the Advancement of Colored People that was founded in 1909 to lobby for rights for African-Americans

Federal Reserve Act: Created the Federal Reserve Banking System

Clayton Antitrust Act: Specified particular conduct that would be prohibited as in violation of fair trade practices.

Federal Trade Commission (FTC): Federal regulatory agency that was given the authority to prosecute business for unfair trade practices and the investigative authority necessary to carry out such prosecution

Louis Brandeis: A Kentucky-born Jew known as the "people's lawyer," who had broke legal tradition in 1908 by presenting a mass of sociological data to the Court in his defense of an Oregon bill establishing maximum working hours for women. Brandeis became Woodrow Wilson's most trusted advisor on domestic matters and was appointed to the Supreme Court by Wilson.

Hammer v. Dagenhart: The 1918 Supreme Court ruling that struck down Wilson's child labor regulations that had prohibited the interstate shipment of goods made with the use of child labor

Adamson Bill: Established an eight-hour-day for railroad workers

W. E. B. DuBois: First African-American to earn a PhD from Harvard and activist for rights for African-Americans

Brownsville Incident: Theodore Roosevelt ordered the dishonorable discharge of 160 black soldiers after they were accused of shooting and killing a white man in Brownsville, Texas.

Pop Quiz

Chapter 20

1. Which of the following is true of Theodore Roosevelt?
   a. a great athlete in his youth
   b. sickly and sedentary as an adult
   c. glorified warfare
   d. warned against physical over-exertion

2. The supporters of Theodore Roosevelt and the Bull Moose Party in 1912 were typically ________.
   a. ten years younger than conservatives in the Republican Party
   b. ten years older than conservatives in the Republican Party
   c. ten times more educated that conservatives in the Republican Party
   d. ten points smarter on the available IQ tests in 1912

3. The catalyst behind the shifting coalitions that formed the Progressive movement was ________.
   a. Bolshevism
   b. Feminism
   c. Patriotism
   d. the prolonged economic depression of the 1890s

4. Who were the rural Tories in the Southern states?
   a. persons still loyal to England
   b. conservatives ideologically, but members of the Democratic Party due to sectionalism
   c. liberal supporters of Progressivism in the South
   d. Southern feminists that supported Progressivism

5. Which of the following is true of William Howard Taft and the trusts?
   a. Taft viewed the trusts as illegal.
   b. Taft's trust-busting exceeded that of Roosevelt.
   c. Taft did not break up any trusts.
   d. Both a and b

6. What happened in the Triangle Shirtwaist Factory Fire of 1911?
   a. Ladder trucks saved 146 people.
   b. Dozens of women jumped to their death from the ninth floor .

Pop Quiz (cont'd)

c. Firemen saved 146 people with hand-held landing pads.
d. By using the fire escape in a scandal , 146 people were saved.

7. In a scandal involving Interior Secretary Richard Ballinger, investigator Lewis Glavis charged that Ballinger ___________.
   a. engaged in a plan to turn over public coal reserves in Alaska to private investors for profit
   b. engaged in sexual relations with a young female intern
   c. leaked the name of a CIA agent to the press
   d. engaged in a plan to drill for oil in the Alaska National Wildlife Reserve

8. Theodore Roosevelt ran for president in 1912 as the nominee of the ___________ Party.
   a. Republican
   b. Democratic
   c. Bull Moose
   d. Progressive

9. All of the following reforms were accomplished during Wilson's first term EXCEPT ___________.
   a. reduction in tariffs
   b. the Federal Reserve System
   c. minimum wage for workers
   d. strengthened antitrust law

10. In *Hammer v. Dagenhart*, the Supreme Court ___________.
    a. upheld restrictions on child labor
    b. struck down new restrictions on child labor
    c. ruled that children under ten were too small to work with hammers
    d. ruled that child labor should be left to the discretion of the child

11. Woodrow Wilson discharged three companies of black soldiers as a result of the Brownsville incident. T F

12. The Supreme Court found a child labor law unconstitutional. T F

Chapter Review (cont'd)

Pop Quiz (cont'd)

13. __________ Americans lived in absolute poverty in the Progressive Era.

14. Theodore Roosevelt distinguished between __________ trusts and __________ trusts.

15. Taft's record on reform was __________.

1. C	5. D	9. C	13. Ten Million
2. A	6. B	10. B	14. Good; Bad
3. D	7. A	11. F	15. Impressive
4. B	8. C	12. T	

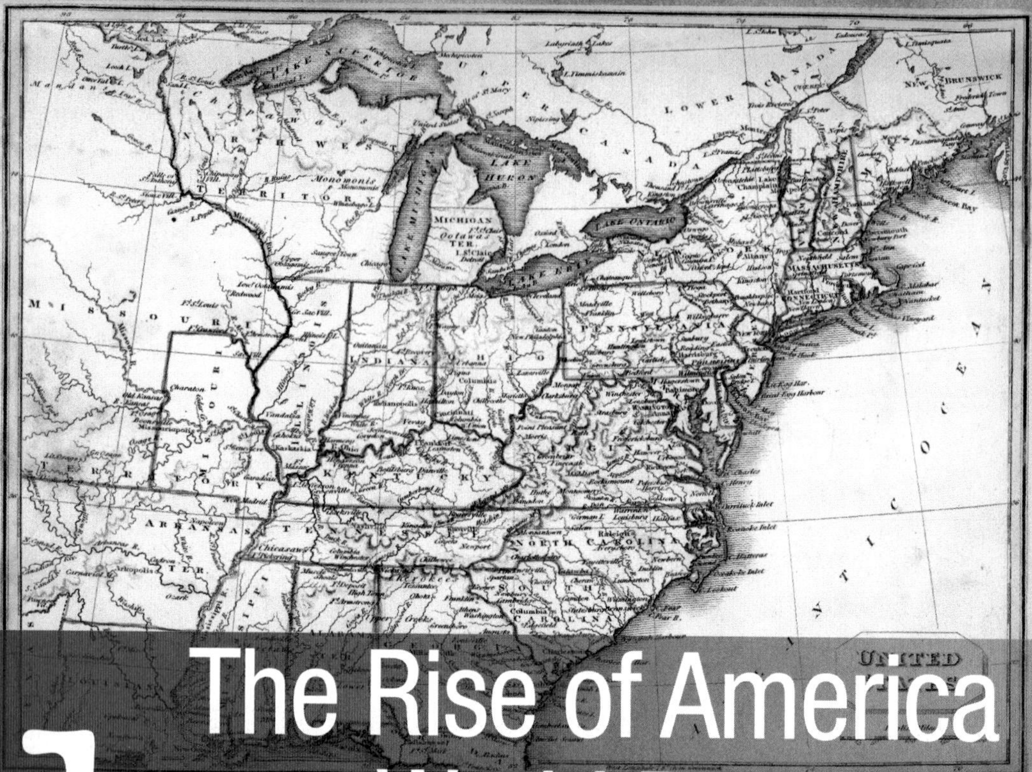

21 The Rise of America as a World Power, 1898–1919

Chapter Objectives

Another Frontier

Samoa

Hawaii

Venezuela and the Monroe Doctrine

The Great Departure

Trouble in Cuba

Escalation of Conflict with Spain

The Spanish-American War

Justification for Imperialism

The Treaty of Paris

The Aftermath of Conquest

The Far East

The Open Door

Boxer Rebellion

Roosevelt's Policy

Panama

The Roosevelt Corollary

Dollar Diplomacy

Another Frontier

Several decades before the historian Frederick Jackson Turner proclaimed in 1893 that the Western frontier had closed, an influential minority of Americans was straining to extend the nation's power and influence to the remote reaches of the globe. Their motives and emphases varied. Some feared that Europe's penetration of South America threatened the United States' security, while others felt that it was the manifest destiny of a "superior" people to extend their influences. Still others believed that expansion would divert the people's attention from slavery or pressing industrial problems; but, in almost all cases, there were the underlying convictions that having assured access to the markets of the world was essential to long-term prosperity and that the possession of outlying territories was one of the hallmarks of greatness.

"Rome expanded and passed away," wrote Theodore Roosevelt, "but all western Europe, both Americas, Australia and large parts of Asia and Africa to this day continue the history of Rome. ... Spain expanded and fell, but a whole continent to this day speaks Spanish and is covered with commonwealths of the Spanish tongue and culture. ... England expanded and England will fall. But think of what she will leave behind her. ..."

The foremost early expansionist was William H. Seward, Secretary of State under Abraham Lincoln and Andrew Johnson. "Give me ... fifty, forty, thirty more years of life," he declared in Boston in 1867, "and I will give you possession of the American continent and control of the world." Two months later the United States took over the unoccupied Midway Islands far out in the Pacific; and then, in April 1867, the Senate ratified a treaty with Russia, negotiated by Seward, for the purchase of Alaska for $7,200,000. Most Americans, however, were still too anti-imperialistic to give Seward his rein; and he went out of office in 1869 with his major objectives unfulfilled—annexation by one means or another of Hawaii, Cuba, Puerto Rico, the Danish West Indies (now the Virgin Islands), St. Bartholomew's Island (now St. Barthélemy), Greenland, Iceland, and Canada.

Nevertheless, the expansionist impulse continued to grow. Under President Grant, an annexation treaty with Santo Domingo was signed, but then rejected by the Senate, 24 to 24; and only the consummate diplomacy of Seward's successor, Hamilton Fish, prevented the United States from becoming embroiled in Cuba where a rebellion against Spain broke out in 1868. Meanwhile the expansionist minority was formulating the intellectual underpinning of its case. As early as 1847 the *New York Sun* had begun to argue that annexation of Cuba would be commercially advantageous, and many Americans subscribed to these sentiments.

More significant in the long run, however, was the growing rapport between naval officers, congressmen, intellectuals, and businessmen. During the 1870s American exports exceeded its imports for the first time, and in the 1880s the aforementioned groups combined forces to promote the revitalization of the navy. Again and again, congressmen justified requests for naval construction in commercial or expansionist terms. "The time has come ...," Senator John F. Miller of California declared in 1884, "when manufactures are springing up all over the land, when new markets are necessary to be found in order to keep our factories running." Congressmen also deferred to the professional officers' expertise. "We assembled at the Navy Department," the chairman of the House Naval Affairs Committee explained, "and listened to the advice of naval officers, and our bill was changed in obedience to their views." Finally, in 1890, Captain Alfred T. Mahan published *The Influence of Sea Power upon History*. A brilliant synthesis of ideas, current in naval circles for 10 years or more, it argued that only a large navy could protect the trade that would be the lifeblood of the new American empire.

Many businessmen agreed. *The National Association of Manufacturers* devoted much of its initial program to promoting expansion of the merchant marine, the navy, and foreign trade, and expansionist intellectuals and politicians continued to trumpet for territorial acquisitions. In 1885, the Reverend Josiah Strong in *Our Country* equated Christianity with those "peculiarly aggressive traits" that would impose Anglo-Saxon civilization "upon Mexico, down upon Central and South America, out upon the islands of the seas, over upon Africa and beyond." That same year John Fiske, the most persuasive of the Social Darwinists, predicted that "every land on the earth's surface that is not already the seat of an old civilization shall become English in its language, in its religion, in its political habits." A decade later, Henry Cabot Lodge, a disciple of Captain Mahan, put forth the commercial rationale for naval expansion in categorical terms:

> Commerce follows the flag. The great nations are rapidly absorbing for their future expansion and their present defense all the waste places of the earth. . . . The United States must not fall out of the line of march.

Samoa

Hard on the completion of the first transcontinental railroad in 1869, American business and naval groups arranged a treaty for a naval station and commercial coaling rights in Samoa in expectation of a quickening of the Asian trade. A decade of jockeying for control of Samoa by Germany, Great Britain, and the United States followed. Open conflict was narrowly avoided in 1889. The German government proposed that the islands be divided; at the United States' insistence, however, they agreed instead to establish a tripartite protectorate. Rivalry continued, and in 1899 the fiction of Samoan independence ended. Germany and the United States divided the Samoan Islands, and Great Britain took the Gilbert and Solomon Islands in compensation.

Hawaii

By the mid-nineteenth century, American investors in Hawaii had developed a prosperous American-owned sugar industry on the Islands. In 1875, the United States signed a Reciprocity Treaty with Hawaii that essentially created exclusive free trade between Hawaii and the United States on sugar. Then in 1887, Hawaii granted exclusive use of Pearl Harbor to the United States Navy. In 1890, however, the McKinely Tariff Act removed the American tariff on all foreign raw sugar, thus opening the United States sugar market to Hawaii's competitors and destroying the advantage enjoyed by Hawaiians since the Reciprocity Treaty. Simultaneously, the McKinley Tariff Act also granted American sugar producers a two-cent per pound bounty on sugar. American sugar growers in Hawaii called for annexation to the United States since annexation would award Hawaiian sugar growers the same two-cent per pound bounty enjoyed by American sugar growers.

Hawaiian Queen Liliuokalani was a Hawaiian nationalist who desired to sever the United States relationship and, therefore, opposed annexation. A group of American naval officers conspired with Hawaiian-American business interests to depose the obstructive queen. American Minister to Hawaii John L. Stevens ordered 160 marines from the U.S.S. *Boston* in Pearl Harbor to help the rebels depose the queen in a near bloodless coup, giving the United States sugar growers control of Hawaii. Stevens immediately recognized the new Hawaiian government controlled by American sugar growers, and the new government sent a mission to Washington to negotiate a treaty of annexation. President Benjamin Harrison signed the Treaty of Annexation in February 1893, but the Senate refused to ratify the treaty on the grounds that the new government did not really represent the Hawaiian people. When new President Grover Cleveland took office, he sent a fact-finding mission to Hawaii that determined that most of the Hawaiian public supported Queen Liliuokalani. Cleveland, therefore, withdrew the treaty on the grounds that the provisional government in Hawaii did not represent the Hawaiian people. Cleveland desired to restore Queen Liliuokalani to the throne; but to do so he would have had to use the same American troops, which had ousted her, against the American sugar growers in Hawaii. Cleveland well understood that using American troops against American citizens in Hawaii would be bad politics; so he instead extended recognition to the Republic of Hawaii in 1894, and Congress passed a new tariff law that restored Hawaii's favored position.

▶ Queen Liliuokalani, the last monarch of the Hawaiian Islands.

This, however, did not produce a final resolution to the Hawaii question. Instead, President Cleveland's refusal to approve the Annexation Treaty set off a four-year debate. American strategists contended that possession of Hawaii would give naval protection to the Pacific Coast, prevent annexation by Japan, and enable the United States to penetrate the Far East commercially and militarily. Annexation, in their view, was part of a "Large Policy" embracing construction of a Nicaraguan canal and acquisition of Canada. Meanwhile, a puppet government ruled Hawaii for white, American businessmen.

President McKinley announced upon taking office that he opposed all acquisition of territory, but he soon changed his mind. Three months after his inauguration he submitted to the Senate a new treaty of annexation, but that treaty was rejected. Later, after naval operations in the Pacific during the Spanish-American War dramatized Hawaii's usefulness as a naval base, Congress annexed the islands by joint resolution in July 1898, ostensibly to prevent Spain from capturing the islands—though Spain in reality had no such plans. "As I look back upon the first steps in this miserable business and as I contemplate the outrage," ex-President Cleveland wrote to his former Secretary of State Richard Olney, "I am ashamed of the whole affair."

Venezuela and the Monroe Doctrine

Yet Cleveland himself had contributed to the jingoism that made the imperialists' triumph possible. Angered by Great Britain's refusal in 1895 to accept American arbitration of a boundary dispute between British Guiana and Venezuela, Secretary of State Olney had bluntly informed the British Foreign Secretary that "... the United States is practically sovereign on this continent, and its fiat is law." The British testily replied that the Monroe Doctrine was not recognized in international law and did not apply to boundary disputes in any event. Cleveland then warned that failure to accept the findings of an American investigation would constitute "a willful aggression." Four years later an international commission fixed the boundary largely in accord with Britain's original claims.

Cleveland's rude threat of force had ironic implications. Until then, enforcement of the Monroe Doctrine had actually been dependent on the might of the Royal Navy. The British had tacitly enforced the Monroe Doctrine because they opposed any new wave of European colonialism in Latin America almost as much as the Americans did. Now, however, the Doctrine became an instrument of American initiative. More ironic still, the president's action prompted Great Britain to reappraise its relations with the United States in the context of Germany's rise as a world power. This was to lead, in time, to a decision of momentous importance—agreement during the administration of Theodore Roosevelt on a kind of unofficial naval alliance between the United States and Great Britain.

The Great Departure

Trouble in Cuba

In spite of the increasingly strong thrust of the imperialists, American foreign policy until 1898 had been generally grounded on a realistic appraisal of the national interest—one that reflected a sharp awareness of both the possibilities and the limitations of American power. The festering crisis in Cuba during the 1890s precipitated the first fateful departure from this policy.

Cubans had always resented Spain's misrule of their island. When their sugar economy collapsed under the weight of European competition, the international depression of 1893, and the restrictive duties of the Wilson-Gorman Tariff of 1894, their smoldering hostilities flamed into a full-scale revolt. Determined to suppress it, Spain sent over its ablest general, Valeriano "Butcher" Weyler, who attempted to put down the insurgency by removing the civilian population, in sectors that had been fraught with guerrilla activity, into concentration camps. Weyler understood that the rebels lived within the civilian population, but it was impossible to know which citizens were rebels and which ones were not. The idea was that if all of the civilians in an area racked with guerrilla activity were removed to the camps, then the rebels would be among those removed and the guerrilla activity in that area would therefore cease. Weyler implemented the policy, but the process of removal and unsanitary conditions at the camps resulted in an estimated cost of two hundred thousand Cuban lives.

An outpouring of propaganda from a revolutionary junta in New York and by the yellow journalism of the *New York World* and *New York Journal* intensified the American people's sympathies for the Cuban people. William Randolph Hearst sent artist Frederick Remington to Cuba to draw pictures of the atrocities in Cuba. When Remington reported back to Hearst that he could find no atrocities to portray, Hearst replied, "You furnish the pictures, and I'll furnish the war." It was the press as a whole, however, feeding voraciously on the junta's releases and reprinting indiscriminately the *World's* and the *Journal's* atrocity stories, that incited the nationwide hysteria.

Genuine sympathy for the Cubans combined with less altruistic attitudes to create growing demand for a war to liberate the Cubans. Conservative Republicans and Democrats hoped that a war would divert attention from liberal or populist issues such as free silver. Others saw commercial benefits. "Free Cuba would mean a great market to the United States" and "an opportunity for American capital," Senator Lodge asserted. Protestant clergymen felt that American intervention would alleviate suffering and, incidentally, open Cuba to Protestantism. Ultranationalists saw war as a means of testing the nation's military might, uniting the North and South, and even resolving the unemployment problem. As one Atlantan wrote the president, "The South dearly loves a fighter; if you will show yourself strong and courageous in defense of Cuba, you will have a solid South at your call. ... Strengthen the Army and Navy of this country and in this way give employment to the thousands of idle men who need it." Furthermore, by 1896, Cuban rebels under Maximo Gomez controlled two-thirds of Cuba and had destroyed millions of dollars worth of American property in the process. American business, with some $50 million in Cuban assets, favored intervention to protect their investments.

▶General Maximo Gomez. Cuban rebels under Gomez controlled two-thirds of Cuba and destroyed millions of dollars worth of American property. American business, which had $50 million wrapped up in Cuban assets, wanted to intervene to protect their investments.

President Grover Cleveland, however, had a different conception of his duty. Convinced that the Cuban insurrectionists were as barbarous as the Spaniards, Cleveland did not favor war with Spain and announced that he would not send the United States to Cuba to fight the Spanish if Congress declared war. Cleveland left office in March 1897 without having yielded to the passions of the times.

Escalation of Conflict with Spain

Cleveland's successor, William McKinley, had won the presidency in 1896 with New Manifest Destiny as part of his foreign policy platform, but McKinley lacked Cleveland's stubborn courage and iron principles. Neither McKinley nor his industrialist and banker friends wanted war, but McKinley's minister to Spain, Stewart Woodford, was nevertheless instructed to demand Spanish withdrawal from Cuba. Under such American pressure, Spain recalled General Weyler in the summer of 1897 and promised a cease-fire. The Spanish government also promised to abolish the concentration camps and to grant Cuba autonomy, similar to that of Canada (then a member of the British Commonwealth). Nevertheless, McKinley gradually locked himself into a policy of full independence for Cuba because he understood that the Cuban rebels would not accept some form of home rule and remained determined to fight for full independence.

The war fever mounted in early February 1898, when the Hearst press published a stolen letter written by the Spanish Minister Dupuy de Lome to a friend in Spain, that called McKinley a "peanut politician" and a "bidder for the admiration of the crowd." The New York Journal called the letter the "worst insult to the United States in its history," in spite of the fact that in democratic politics pretty much all elected officials could be called "bidders for the admiration of the crowds" and Theodore Roosevelt had once described McKinley as "having no more backbone than a chocolate éclair." Nevertheless, western Republicans responded by introducing three separate resolutions to give the Cuban insurrectionists the status of a warring power, and McKinley dispatched the battleship U.S.S. *Maine* to Havana in a gesture designed to display the American government's resolve to force a settlement.

On February 15, an explosion destroyed the U.S.S. *Maine* in Havana Harbor, killing 260 Americans. The cause was never determined with certainty, but the Hearst papers, the New York *Tribune* and a few others blamed the disaster on Spain and called for war. The navy originally concluded that the ship had hit a mine, but this conclusion makes little sense because Spain would

▶ The wreck of the U.S.S. *Maine* in 1898 in Havana Harbor killed 260 Americans. Though the exact cause was never determined, newspapers in the United States called for war with Spain.

be unlikely to mine a harbor it used. The most usual purpose of mining harbors was to disrupt the trade of an enemy, not disrupt the trade of one's own country. Later reconstruction of the event suggested a coal explosion in the engine room, boiler explosion, or explosion of the ship's magazine would have been much more likely causes. Regardless, American newspapers exclaimed, "Remember the *Maine*, to Hell with Spain," and politicians such as Henry Cabot Lodge and Senator Albert J. Beveridge of Indiana joined them in a pro-war chorus. The *Maine* "was sunk by an act of dirty treachery on the part of the Spaniards," then Assistant Secretary of the Navy Theodore Roosevelt charged. However, President McKinley was not yet so moved, and he along with much of the financial establishment still hoped for peace. The president's more cautious response was to appoint a commission of inquiry and resume negotiations with Spain.

As passions mounted, administration circles began to fear that McKinley could not be reelected if he refused to submit to the war cries. Reluctantly, important business and financial leaders that had little interest in expansion and none whatever in liberating the Cubans or avenging the destruction of the *Maine,* now joined the war hawks. Thus presidential adviser Elihu Root warned, "Fruitless attempts to hold back or retard the enormous momentum of the people bent upon war would result in the destruction of the president's power and influence, in depriving the country of its natural leader, in the elevation of the Silver Democracy to power." Under the weight of such counsels McKinley lost the will to resist. "I think … possibly the president could have worked out the business without war," one of his intimates later wrote, "but the current was too strong, the demagogues too numerous, the fall elections too near."

On March 27, 1898, the United States sent an ultimatum to Spain demanding an immediate armistice, closing of the concentration camps, and Cuban independence if the United States decided it was advisable. McKinley also sent a note to Spain offering to arbitrate a settlement in Cuba; but before Spain could respond, the president began to compose his war message. On March 31, Spain ordered the end of its "reconcentration policy," agreed to an armistice if the rebels made the request, and agreed to submit the *Maine* issue to international arbitration. Spain did not, however, offer full independence for Cuba. On April 9, Spain announced a unilateral cease-fire.

On April 11, two days after Spain had offered a unilateral armistice, McKinley sent his unrevised war message to Congress, adding only that Spain had agreed to an armistice. On April 19, Congress enthusiastically passed, and the president then signed, a joint resolution authorizing use of force to compel the Spaniards to evacuate and secure Cuban independence. Neither McKinley nor Congress considered the Spanish offer of a unilateral armistice to be sufficient since they believed that the rebels would not cease hostilities with anything less than full independence. Senator Henry Teller of Colorado attached the "Teller Amendment" to the Resolution whereby the United States forever renounced any future annexation of Cuba. The spirit of the Teller Amendment was to demonstrate that the United States was not going to war out of self-aggrandizement or an imperialistic desire to acquire territory through military conquest, but for the liberation of the oppressed Cuban people.

Spain responded by breaking diplomatic relations with the United States on April 21, 1898, and William McKinley then gave Spain three days to withdraw from Cuba before it would be forcibly removed. Spain declared war on the United States on April 24, and the United States declared war on Spain the following day. Although it is clear that Spain could not have avoided military hostilities with the United States without withdrawal from Cuba, the Spanish war declaration proved to be an error since it allowed the United States to attack Spanish possessions throughout the world. Without a declaration of war, it is possible that the war could have been limited to Cuba; with the War Declaration, the war would become much more costly to the Spanish than they had envisioned.

The Spanish-American War

Due to Assistant Secretary of the Navy Theodore Roosevelt's advanced planning, only the American navy was prepared for hostilities in April of 1898. When Spain declared war, the United States army had only twenty-eight thousand men—enough to put down Native American uprisings, but insufficient for fighting a foreign war away from American soil. Modernization and expansion of the American naval fleet, however, had roughly paralleled the rise of interest in the Far East; and by 1898 the United States navy was the fifth largest in the world and the Asiatic squadron was especially strong. Ten days before the destruction of the *Maine*, in accordance with standing plans put in place by the Assistant Secretary of the Navy Theodore Roosevelt, Commodore George Dewey was ordered to prepare to attack the Philippines in the event of war with Spain.

On May 1, in less than seven hours, Dewey destroyed an antiquated Spanish fleet in Manila Bay and changed the course of history as he sunk the entire Spanish fleet in Manila without losing a single American ship. The U.S. would then dispatch eleven thousand U.S. troops to the Philippines in an attempt to gain control of the islands. Six weeks later seventeen thousand regular army troops and volunteers, including Theodore Roosevelt's "Rough Riders," landed in Cuba amidst incredible confusion. They were short of every basic supply from arms to medicine, but the Spanish army essentially had to wait for orders from Spain and did not engage the American troops during their five day disorganized landing at Daquiri. The American forces drove forward toward Santiago, winning a fierce engagement at El Caney and a major battle at San Juan Hill. San Juan Hill would become famous as the battle where future President Theodore Roosevelt and his "Rough Riders" took out a Spanish garrison. The strategic value of the assault on San Juan Hill by the Rough Riders is questionable, but the courage of Theordore Roosevelt during the battle was not. To his dying day Roosevelt would refer to the battle of San Juan Hill as, "that great day in my life."

At any rate, after the American victories at El Caney and San Juan Hill, they besieged Santiago. Out of these engagements emerged the usual complement of heroes, but none so dramatic as Colonel Roosevelt. "The instant I received the order I sprang on my horse," he wrote, "and then my 'crowded hour' began."

The end of the war swiftly followed. On July 3 an American squadron commanded by Rear Admiral William T. Sampson destroyed the inferior Spanish fleet (without losing a single American ship) after it emerged from Santiago Harbor under orders from Spain. Back in the

▶San Juan Hill would become famous as the battle where future President Theodore Roosevelt and his "Rough Riders" (at left) took out a Spanish garrison. Roosevelt referred to the battle as "That great day in my life".

Pacific, American forces took Wake Island the following day. On July 17, the Spanish ground force in Santiago was surrounded, and eight days later American troops occupied Puerto Rico with little opposition. An armistice ended further hostilities on August 12. In the Armistice, Spain agreed to cede Puerto Rico and Guam to the United States and withdraw from Cuba, thus giving the Cubans their independence and eliminating the primary reason America had to wage war with Spain. In September, the United States sent a delegation to Paris to negotiate with Spain the fate of Cuba and the Philippines.

All told, the United States lost 379 men in battle and 5,462 from disease and other causes. "It has been a splendid little war," Secretary of State John Hay remarked. Most Americans agreed, but at least 5,462 found it not so "splendid." American soldiers were sent into sub-tropical warfare with blue flannel clothing and rations that included "embalmed beef" and canned salt pork left over from the Civil War that had ended thirty-three years earlier. Antibiotics had not yet been invented; minor war wounds became life-threatening infections overnight, and amputations of infected limbs were frequent. The most common cause of death, however, due both to sub-tropical microbes and rancid food rations, was diarrhea.

Justification for Imperialism

The self-denying Teller Amendment had reflected the American people's humanitarian strain as distinct from their romantic imperialist impulses, but expansionist sentiment had grown to gale-like proportions during the war. The Hawaiian annexation resolution rolled through Congress three months after hostilities began. Soon afterward the president also decided that Puerto Rico and Guam should be ceded to the United States.

The acquisitions quickly presented the American public with the question of what to do with the new possessions. In general, Americans were divided between imperialists,

MAP 21.1 The United States in the Pacific

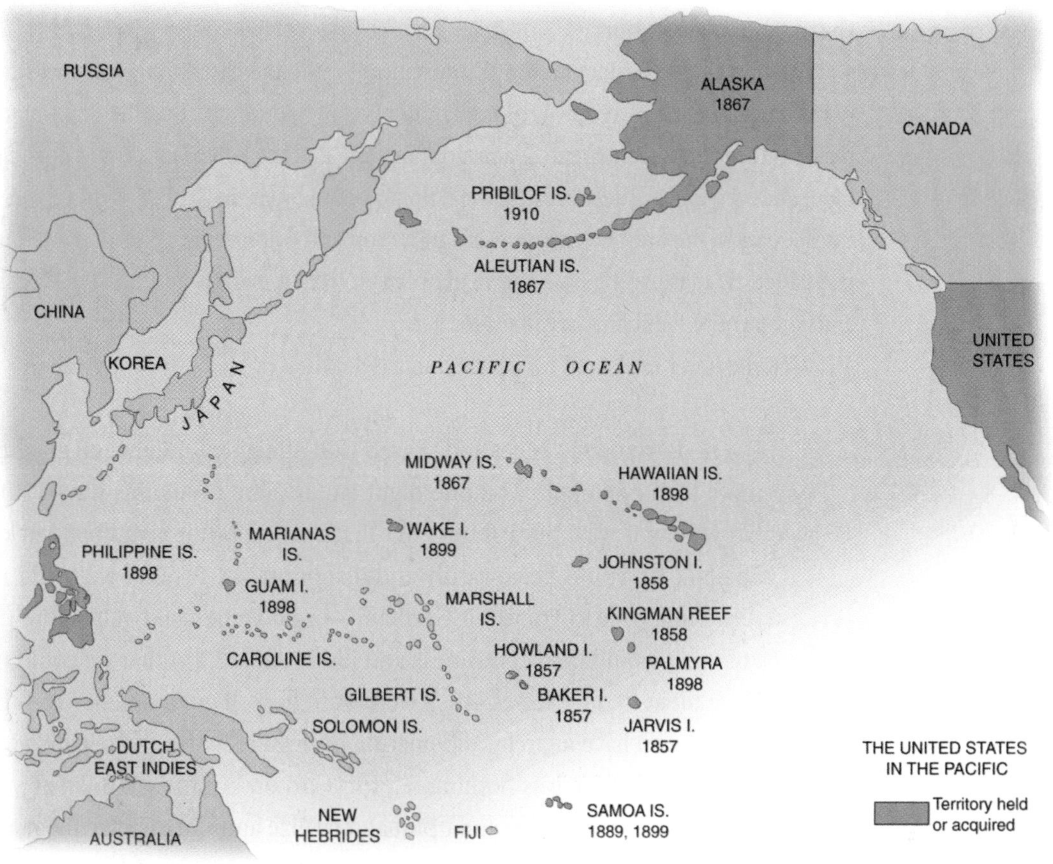

who desired American colonization and control of the newly acquired territories, and isolationists, that wanted to keep the United States out of the "trappings of empire." In the case of Cuba, the Teller Amendment prevented the United States from directly annexing the island. In the case of Puerto Rico, there was little opposition to making it an American colony due to its close proximity to the United States, and most Americans viewed its annexation as "natural." There was also little opposition to the annexation of Guam, which was generally viewed as an insignificant and distant coaling station for the United States navy. The Philippines, however, became a major subject of debate, and significant opposition developed against bringing the Philippines into the United States as an American colony.

Anti-imperialists argued that the logic and spirit of the Teller Amendment was that the United States did not take foreign territory by force; and for the same reasons that the United States relinquished any claim to Cuba, it should also absolve any claim to the Philippines. In addition, anti-imperialists argued that the annexation violated the U.S. Constitution, which did not authorize expansion by military conquest. Furthermore, the colonization of the Philippines was said to violate the spirit of the Declaration of Independence since there was not talk of the Philippines ever becoming an American state, and the U.S. would then be governing the Philippines without the consent of the governed. Nativists opposed annexation of the Philippines for xenophobic reasons, arguing that no nation of non-whites should be placed under the American flag or the American race would surely be mongrelized. Finally, labor unions opposed annexation out of fear of cheap labor competition.

In contrast, big business favored annexation for the increased trade and investment opportunities. The main argument of the imperialists, however, was that the Philippines could not be returned to Spain due to Spanish oppression, and the Philippines could not be granted independence immediately because the Filipino people were incapable of ruling themselves. Consequently, the only alternative was annexation and colonization. President McKinley was persuaded by these arguments and made plans to retain Manila, and he finally deciding to annex the entire Philippine archipelago.

McKinley later explained his decision to a delegation of Methodist clergymen:

> I went down on my knees and prayed God Almighty for light and guidance more than one night. And one night late it came to me this way—I don't know how it was, but it came: (1) that we could not give them back to Spain—that would be cowardly and dishonorable; (2) that we could not turn them over to France or Germany—our commercial rivals in the Orient—that would be bad business and discreditable; (3) that we could not leave them to themselves—they were unfit for self-government—and they would soon have anarchy and misrule over there worse than Spain's was; and (4) that there was nothing left for us to do but to take them all, and to educate the Filipinos, and uplift and civilize and Christianize them, and by God's grace do the very best we could by them, as our fellow men for whom Christ also died. And then I went to bed and went to sleep and slept soundly.

Evidently, McKinley was convinced that "Christianization" of the islands had not occurred under the rule of Catholic Spain. McKinley's most fundamental reason, however, was the third: desire for a commercial outpost in the Far East. As Mark Hanna declared, "If it is commercialism to want the possession of a strategic point giving the American people an opportunity to maintain a foothold in the markets of ... China, for God's sake let us have commercialism."

All through the summer and autumn of 1898, newspapers, religious publications, and civic leaders called for retention of the Philippines for the same reasons the president gave the Methodist clergymen. McKinley sensed the force of this opinion, but he wanted to be certain that the people as a whole would approve such a radical break with tradition. So in October, with a stenographer at his side to time the applause given his various soundings, he toured the Middle West. Convinced finally that national sentiment favored annexation, he cabled his peace commissioners in Paris to demand cession of the entire Philippine archipelago. In December, the American delegates signed the Treaty of Paris, officially ending hostilities.

The Treaty of Paris

By the terms of the treaty signed on December 10, 1898, Spain ceded the Philippines to the United States for $20 million. Spain also acknowledged Cuban independence and ceded Puerto Rico and Guam outright to the United States. Spain also agreed to the assumption of some $400 million in Cuban debt, much of which was owed to Spanish companies. Inhabitants of all the territories were ensured religious freedom, and Congress would determine the civil rights of all citizens in all the territories. Two months later the Senate ratified the treaty. It would probably have been defeated had not a substantial number of anti-imperialist Republicans put party loyalty above conscience. It would also have been defeated if Bryan had not influenced a handful of Democrats to support it in the hope that imperialism would then become the dominant issue in the presidential campaign of 1900.

The Aftermath of Conquest

The ramifications of the Spanish-American War were that the United States had suddenly become recognized internationally as a world power. In the words of the French Foreign Minister, "The United States is now seated at the table where the great game is played and cannot leave it." For the first time in American history, the United States had acquired colonies in the form of Guam, Puerto Rico, and the Philippines.

By 1900, however, the United States tasted the first bitter fruits of imperialism. Filipino partisans had begun a fierce fight for independence from Spain before the Americans arrived. They turned against their new American masters in 1899 and inflicted losses, heavier than those suffered in the war with Spain, on the American occupation troops. Filipino rebels had fought with the Americans against Spain during the Spanish-American War

▶John Hay signing the Treaty of Paris, December 10, 1898. With the signing of the treaty, the United States acquired the Philippines from Spain for $20 million.

and felt betrayed by the American refusal to withdraw and the failure of the United States to grant Filipinos their independence. What resulted is perhaps one of the least remembered, but seriously deadly, wars in American history. The war to subdue the Filipino uprising involved two hundred thousand U.S. troops (only seventeen thousand Americans landed on Cuba), and cost the lives of forty-three hundred U.S. soldiers, more than ten times the battle deaths in the Spanish-American War. The war against Spain had lasted only three months, but the war in the Philippines would last from late 1898 into 1902; and an estimated two hundred thousand Filipinos killed.

Americans at first believed that the rebel faction under Emilio Aguinaldo was a minority renegade faction; but by 1900, General Arthur MacArthur wrote, "I have been reluctantly compelled to believe that the Filipino masses are loyal to Aguinaldo." The rebels did not confront the superior American force head on and, instead, used guerrilla tactics. The United States army viewed such tactics not as warfare, but as murder, and their enemy not as an army, but as murderers. Consequently, captured Filipino rebels were tried by the United States army in military tribunals and executed. American soldiers, in general, viewed the "little brown men" as subhuman and unworthy of mercy. General Arthur MacArthur perpetuated these sentiments with orders to United States soldiers to "Kill and burn, the more you kill and burn, the better it will please me. Shoot everyone over age ten." Not until the Americans resorted to methods as ruthless as those used by the Spanish in Cuba were the Filipinos finally defeated formally in 1902. Finally, Emilio Aguinaldo was captured in 1901 and forced to issue a call to the rebels to put down their arms in exchange for his life. Governor William Howard Taft implemented some home rule reforms; the guerilla warfare slowly dissipated, though some activities continued through 1906.

Partial restitution followed. McKinley, and especially Theodore Roosevelt, took literally the poet's charge to "Take up the White Man's burden—Send forth the best ye breed." McKinley instituted, and Roosevelt greatly strengthened, a political system designed to prepare the Filipinos for self-government. Schools were built, small farmers were installed on lands purchased from the Catholic Church, and numerous other reforms were instituted.

Major criticisms of the American activities in the Philippines, however, were widespread. Mark Twain suggested painting black over the stars and stripes and adding skull and crossbones. Yale professor William Graham Sumner stated, "We talk of civilizing lower races, but we have never done it yet. Instead, we have exterminated them." *The New York World* printed the poignant short political poem with the lines, "We've taken up the white man's burden of ebony and brown; Now will you kindly tell us, Rudyard, how we may put it down."

Meanwhile, the United States observed the form of the Teller Amendment by granting nominal independence to Cuba, though that independence involved temporary rule by the United States military. Certain benefits to the Cuban people followed, above all in security and public health; but the U.S. also insisted that Cuba accept the Platt Amendment, passed by Congress in 1901 and attached to the Cuban Constitution. The amendment forbade Cuba from signing foreign treaties or borrowing money without approval from the U.S. and also

▶ After having resisted American occupation for years, Emilio Aguinaldo, first president of the Philippines, was captured in 1901. Aguinaldo was forced to issue a call to the rebels to put down their arms in exchange for his life.

allowed the United States to intervene militarily, at any time, to preserve order or property. As a consequence, the United States would intervene militarily in Cuba four times by 1921, including America's assuming control of the government from 1906–1909. The United States was also granted a permanent naval base in Cuba at Guantanamo Bay. In May 1902, American forces withdrew, but the United States retained the naval base at Guantanamo Bay under what became a permanent lease.

Anti-imperialists in the United States condemned the new Cuban Constitution and the Platt Amendment, but President Theodore Roosevelt denounced the opposition as "unhung traitors, liars, slanderers, and scandal mongers."

In 1902, an American Reciprocity Treaty with Cuba lowered duties on Cuban exports to the United States, and United States trade with Cuba quadrupled by 1913. The economic advantages accrued the United States from its new island possessions were offset, somewhat, in the long run by vast American expenditures for civic and social improvement. From the outset, moreover, the Philippines were a military liability—"our heel of Achilles," as Roosevelt was calling them by 1907, because of the difficulty America would have defending the islands if they were attacked across the Pacific by their much closer and powerful neighbor, Japan.

Although the United States slowly instituted democratic forms of government on those islands it owned outright, it remains an open question whether native peoples fared better or worse under American rule. Hawaii prospered, but largely as the virtual fief of a half-dozen giant American corporations. Puerto Rico, short of natural resources, suffered from absentee ownership and overpopulation induced by American public health measures, and the Philippines concentrated too much on the production of raw materials for the American market. Everywhere, to be sure, the material standard of living improved considerably; yet the old social structures and extremes of wealth and poverty persisted, while much of the islanders' cultural integrity disintegrated.

The Far East

The Open Door

The quest for trade together with missionary zeal soon drove the United States into the vortex of Far Eastern affairs. Senator Albert J. Beveridge summed it all up in January 1900:

> The Philippines are ours forever. ... And just beyond ... are China's illimitable markets. We will not retreat from either ... will not renounce our part in the mission of our race, trustees under God, of the civilization of the world. ... The power that rules the Pacific is the power that rules the world.

Yet, in another sense, American policy was grounded more on fear than on the aggressive territorial designs of businessmen and romantics. All the great powers—Japan, Russia, France, Britain, and Germany—and two of the smaller ones, Belgium and Holland, were more stridently imperialistic than the United States during this period. Virtually all Africa had already been taken over by Europeans with an agreement dividing Africa between the powers of Europe at the Conference of Berlin in 1884. Southeast Asia had become the province of the British, the Dutch, and the French. Japan was bursting to take over Korea, and Germany aspired to whatever was available in the Far East, North Africa, or South America. However great the ultimate tragedy of the United States' acquisition of the Philippines, McKinley had correctly assayed French and German designs in making his decision to acquire them.

Alone among the great powers, the United States did not have a colony in Africa, nor did it have a "sphere of influence" in China where the great powers had been carving out spheres of influence (in effect, economic colonial enclaves) over several years in that unhappy land. The U. S. feared that it could be denied commercial opportunities, both in the realms of trade and in natural resource extraction in any country's sphere of influence. In 1899, the British began to evade payment of the Chinese tariff, the Chinese government's main source of revenue. Such action, if adopted by the French, Germans, Russians, and Japanese (Italy also sought, but failed to get, a sphere of influence), would have forced the collapse of the Beijing government and the dismemberment of all China into defacto European colonies. Concerned by the implications to American business and persuaded, in any event, that freedom to trade was in the interest of everyone, Secretary of State John Hay sent a round of "Open Door" notes to the powers in 1899 and 1900. The notes proposed, in summary, that Chinese officials continue to collect tariffs and that all nations be guaranteed equal trade rights throughout China. Although most of the powers simply ignored Hay's note, and Russia outright rejected it, Hay unwisely announced their unanimous acceptance.

Boxer Rebellion

The European attitudes toward the Open Door principle would change in 1900 when a Chinese revolutionary group known as I Ho Chuan (Righteous and Harmonious Fists) or "Boxers" staged a rebellion against foreigners in China. The Boxers' goal was to expel all of the foreign influences from China. The Boxers declared, "The will of heaven is that the telegraph

▶ In 1900 the Boxers staged a rebellion against foreigners in China. The Boxers' dangerous goal was to expel all of the foreign influences from China.

wires be cut first, the railways torn up, and then shall the foreign devils be decapitated." The Boxers seized the British Embassy in Beijing and captured the entire diplomatic corps, not only of Great Britain but also of the U.S., Japan, Russia, and France.

The U.S., France, Russia, Germany, and England responded by sending an international expeditionary force of twenty thousand soldiers (five thousand of whom were American) to China to put down the rebellion. In August 1900, the international force defeated the Boxers, and the diplomatic hostages were rescued. Following this successful international cooperation among the great powers during the Boxer Rebellion, both England and Germany agreed to the Open Door principle. While each country favored their own access and special privileges in China, all feared most the dominance of China by any one power. Consequently, the Open Door principle worked because it was consistent with the balance of power game that the great powers were engaged in.

The weakness of the Open Door notes was less one of principle than of power. As Admiral Mahan pointed out at this time, the United States lacked the will and the military strength to enforce them. Nevertheless, they marked a heady triumph for the proponents of the "Large Policy," commanding, in the words of one historian, "a measure of interest and support over the years second only to that accorded the Monroe Doctrine." In particular, they led to deep and continuing involvement in the Far East by the United States and, ultimately, to conflict with Japan.

Roosevelt's Policy

More than any other twentieth-century American president, Theodore Roosevelt viewed the Open Door policy with a measure of realism. He felt that the United States could maintain a legitimate interest in the Far East only by recognizing Japan's need for raw materials and markets. He also believed—even more strongly—that Japan was a natural counterpoise to Russia, whose failure to withdraw from southern Manchuria until 1907, he termed, was an act of "well-nigh incredible mendacity." Thus he approved the Japanese-British naval alliance of 1902, and he privately accepted Japanese suzerainty in Korea in 1905.

By then Roosevelt was mediating the Russo-Japanese War of 1904–1905 at the request of the victorious but nearly insolvent Japanese. In 1895, Russia had played a role in preventing the lease of a port on the Liaodong Biao (Liaotung Peninsula) in southern Manchuria from China to Japan and had also left its troops in Manchuria after the Boxer Rebellion. Since Japan desired control of Manchuria, it attempted, unsuccessfully, to negotiate a settlement with Russia that would secure Japanese interests. In 1904, Japan launched a surprise attack on the Russian Pacific Fleet and sunk it in the Harbor of Port Arthur (Dandong) in Southern Manchuria at Korea Bay. Japan then launched a ground

▶ Russian soldiers looking down upon a mass grave during the Russo-Japanese War, 1904–1905.

war, attacking the Russian troops that were stationed in Korea and Manchuria. Both sides rushed massive armies to the area, and soon a full scale ground war developed with over four hundred thousand troops involved on each side. Nevertheless, the Japanese pushed the Russians out of Korea and captured Mukden (Shenyang), the principal city in Manchuria. In May 1905, the Russian Baltic Fleet, the pride of Russia, arrived from Europe, but the superior Japanese navy sunk it upon arrival in the Korean Strait.

Though Japan had won most of the battles and accomplished most of their objectives, it found itself embroiled in an expensive ground war with Russia and sought a negotiated settlement. Consequently, the Japanese Minister to the U.S., Kogoro Takahira, asked Roosevelt to intervene and mediate a peace settlement.

The American position had been basically neutral; but, in reality, Theodore Roosevelt had originally favored Japan because the Russians had refused to accept the Open Door, and he believed that Japan would do so. Roosevelt was heard to exclaim that it was "Bully the way the Japs started that war," and he referred to the Russian Czar Nicholas II as a "preposterous little creature."

Peace talks were held at Portsmouth, New Hampshire, in August of 1905, with Theodore Roosevelt as the mediator. Basically, he sought to preserve the balance of power and to protect the Open Door, but he also deemed it his moral duty to end the carnage as soon as possible. He further hoped to cement Japanese-American relations. Roosevelt decided to divide the disputed Sakhalin Island (North of Japan and East of the Russian Pacific coast) between Russia and Japan, and both countries accepted the solution. As the victors in the conflict, Japan demanded $600 million in war reparations from the Russians, but the Russians refused. Japan finally relented on the reparations issue essentially to cut their losses and prevent spending more on the costly ground war. Japan did, however, gain the Liaotung Peninsula, and Russia agreed to recognize Japanese interests in Korea. Manchuria was returned to China, and both Russia and Japan were to withdraw their troops from Manchuria.

Roosevelt's mediation fulfilled the first three of his goals—ending the war, preserving the balance of power, and protecting the Open Door in China. However, mediation failed in his fourth goal of improving American-Japanese relations because the Japanese blamed him for Russia's refusal to pay a war indemnity or to cede all of Sakhalin Island to Japan. Japan viewed the results as unfair because Japan had taken all of Sakhalin Island in the war; and as the victors, they believed they were due reparations. Japan did, however, emerge from the conflict as the dominant power in Asia; but the relations between both Japan and Russia and the United States worsened, with both Japan and Russia discontent with the results of the Treaty of Portsmouth. America was their scapegoat.

A decision by the San Francisco Board of Education to segregate the ninety-three Japanese students in the city's public schools, noting the "yellow peril," dealt Japanese-American relations a more serious blow in October 1906. Roosevelt labeled the segregation order "a crime against a friendly nation" and threatened to use "all the forces, civil and military," at his command to rectify it. He then called the board members to the White House. They agreed to reverse the order if Japan would curb the emigration of peasants and laborers. A "Gentlemen's Agreement" to that effect was arranged in 1907. Japan agreed to voluntarily prohibit issuing passports to persons seeking to come to the United States for employment, but this provided the Japanese yet another reason for animosity against the U.S..

Having thus deferred to Japanese sensibilities, in 1907 Roosevelt characteristically decided to flaunt American strength by sending the battle fleet on a world cruise. Roosevelt perceived that the United States could not successfully defend the Philippines in case of a Japanese attack; therefore, he pushed Congress unsuccessfully to grant Philippine independence as quickly as possible. At the same time, Roosevelt desired to show Japan that the U.S. had the power to hold on to its possessions. The United States had embarked on a naval building program (as had Japan) during Roosevelt's presidency. Persuaded by the arguments of Alfred Thayer Mahan that naval power was most important, the United States Navy budget increased from $56 million in 1900 to $117 million in 1905.

To impress the Japanese, Roosevelt had the navy painted white, to make it appear more impressive; and he ordered the fleet to sail around the world, especially to Japan along the way, in a show of strength. Congress refused to fund the expedition as both wasteful and provocative, but Roosevelt ordered the fleet to Japan anyway. Roosevelt stated that he had enough funding to get the navy half way around the world, so Congress could worry about getting them back. Before the fleet returned, however, the president made another realistic concession to Japan. With the Root-Takahira Agreement of November 1908, the United States probably, though not certainly, recognized Japan's economic ascendancy in Manchuria in return for a reaffirmation of the status quo in the Pacific and the Open Door in China.

The sail of the "Great White Fleet" also violated Roosevelt's own policy of "Speak softly, but carry a big stick." The show of force certainly was "big stick," but it hardly qualified as "speaking softly." Roosevelt was also fond of saying, "Don't flourish a revolver unless you intend to shoot." The sail of the "Great White Fleet" appears to be a violation of his own advice.

New Far Eastern Policies

Neither Taft nor Wilson shared Roosevelt's view that the United States should accept Japanese preeminence in East Asia. As early as 1910, Roosevelt warned Taft that China was "weak and unreliable" and "that the United States should abandon its commercial aspirations in Manchuria." Taft, however, believed too strongly in the fiction of Chinese independence and was too enamored with trade possibilities to agree. He followed, instead, a policy of "active intervention to secure for our merchandise and our capitalists opportunity for profitable investment." He permitted his Secretary of State, Philander C. Knox, to demand American participation in an international bankers' consortium to build a network of railways in China. Taft also allowed Knox, who was alarmed by the consolidation of Japanese and Russian influence in Manchuria, to propose internationalization of that province's railways.

President Wilson proved no less determined than Taft to maintain the Open Door. "Our industries have expanded to such a point that they will burst their jackets if they cannot find a free outlet to the markets of the world," he declared in 1912. "Our domestic markets no longer suffice. We need foreign markets." Essentially, however, he conceived of China, which had been penetrated by Christian missionaries, in moralistic terms. He opposed the bankers' consortium because he feared that it would result in European domination, not because he intended to withdraw from the Far East. The United States, he declared at the time, intends "to participate, and participate very generously, in the opening to the Chinese and to the use of the world the almost untouched and perhaps unlimited resources of China." He then urged American bankers to act independently.

▶ Philander C. Knox

Wilson perceived that the outbreak of World War I in 1914 created a power vacuum in China because of the great powers' involvement in Europe. When Japan tried to make China into a satellite by imposing twenty-one far-reaching demands in 1915, the president vigorously defended Chinese integrity and independence. To forestall Japanese economic domination of China, Wilson and Secretary of State Robert Lansing proposed formation of a new four-power consortium to supply China with private capital. With Wilson's approval, Lansing also rejected Tokyo's demand that the United States recognize Japan's paramount interest in China, just as Japan had recognized

America's in Mexico. Finally, after America's entry into the Great War, with Japan also entering the War on the side of the Allies, they arranged a *modus vivendi*—the Lansing-Ishii Agreement of November 1917. By this document the United States recognized Japan's special interests in China while Japan reaffirmed its support of the Open Door and agreed not to use the war situation to seek new privileges in China.

The Caribbean

Panama

President Roosevelt's Caribbean diplomacy aimed to establish stability, security, and U.S. supremacy in the area. Soon after taking office he arranged negotiation of the second Hay-Pauncefote Treaty (1901), by which Great Britain granted the United States the right to build and defend a canal across Central America. Early American planning envisioned a Nicaraguan route, but volcanic activity near the proposed Nicaraguan canal zone, combined with a drop in price from the bankrupt French New Panama Canal Company from $110 million to $40 million caused Roosevelt to seize the opportunity to buy the French company's rights to a canal route through Panama. The president also had Secretary of State Hay draw up a treaty to grant $10 million plus $250,000 annual rental for one hundred years on the proposed six-mile wide

MAP 21.2 The United States and Latin America

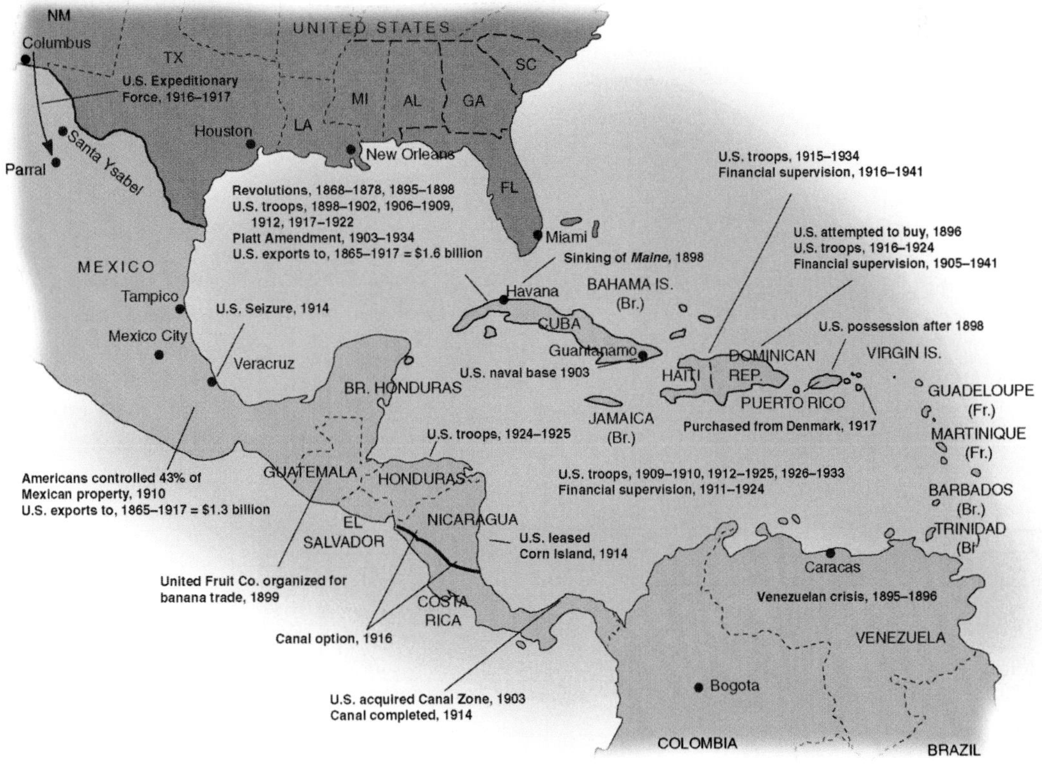

canal zone to Colombia, which possessed the isthmus of Panama. The United States would also pay $40 million to the French New Panama Canal Company, which had begun excavations, for their assets.

After signing the treaty, Colombia's foreign minister was told to delay signing until he received further instruction. It was too late, however; the Treaty had been signed, and the U.S. Senate quickly ratified it. Colombia's Senate, however, rejected the Treaty and demanded $15 million up front instead of the $10 million in the Treaty's provisions; and they also demanded $10 million of the $40 million that was earmarked for the New Panama Canal Company. The Colombian Senate's indignant rejection of the negotiated arrangement infuriated Roosevelt. Privately castigating the Colombians as "Dagos" and "inefficient bandits," he tacitly encouraged agents of the French company to stimulate a Panamanian revolution against Colombia. The Panamanians quickly reasoned that they could become independent and then reap the benefits of the canal for themselves, separate from Colombia. When the revolution broke out on November 3, 1903, Roosevelt sent an American warship to the scene and instituted a blockade of Panama under conditions that assured the revolutionaries' success. In a near bloodless coup (two deaths: a man and a donkey), the Panamanian rebels took over the government by bribing Colombian military and government officials that had been in charge of Panama. A five-hundred-man Colombian army sent to Panama to put down the insurrection never made it to Panama City because the Panama Canal Company, suspiciously, had no railroad cars available to transport them and travel through the Panamanian rain forest was virtually impossible without the railway. Three days later Roosevelt recognized the new Republic of Panama and approved a treaty, negotiated by Panama's new minister (Philippe Vunau-Varilla, an agent of the French company), authorizing the United States to build the canal in the new nation of Panama. The treaty was similar to the original Canal Treaty with Colombia ex-

▶ Construction of the Panama Canal. United States assumed all rights, power, and authority within the zone to the exclusion of Panama.

cept that the United States Canal Zone was widened from six miles to ten, and the United States assumed all rights, power and authority within the zone to the exclusion of Panama. The United States also guaranteed the independence of Panama, thus making Panama a United States "protectorate."

Roosevelt later claimed that "our course was straightforward and in absolute accord with the highest standards of international morality." However, in 1911, he blurted, "I took the Canal Zone and let Congress debate; and while the debate goes on, the canal also does." Ten years after that confession, the United States agreed to pay Colombia $25 million. By then Roosevelt was dead, but the memory of his high-handedness lived on.

Meanwhile, the first great government corporation in American history overcame extraordinary health and engineering problems to complete construction of the Panama Canal. It was opened to the commerce of the world on August 15, 1914, on equal terms to all nations—but only because President Wilson had persuaded Congress to repeal an act of 1912 that exempted American coastwise traffic from payment of tolls. The Panama Canal was completed at a cost of $352 million. While constructing the canal, fifty-six hundred people died, most from malaria or yellow fever.

The Roosevelt Corollary

The need to defend the Panama Canal soon drew the United States deeply into the affairs of the Caribbean, a situation neither Roosevelt nor his successors wanted. As the president said of the Dominican Republic, he had "about the same desire to annex it as a gorged boa constrictor might have to swallow a porcupine wrong-end-to." The poverty, instability, and corruption of the Caribbean countries invited European penetration, however, and even such an apostle of peace as was William Jennings Bryan saw no recourse but to make the Caribbean Sea an American lake.

The first serious incident occurred in December 1902, when the Germans, cooperating with the British in a blockade of Venezuela, bombarded a port town and threatened to take control of Venezuelan customs in order to force payment of debts owed their citizens. Roosevelt and the American people reacted militantly, viewing the German action as a violation of the Monroe Doctrine. Theodore Roosevelt, however, also had little sympathy for Venezuela, referring to Venezuelan leader Cipriano Castro as "an unspeakable villainous little monkey." Roosevelt, however, opposed European intervention in any affairs in the Western Hemisphere. Consequently, Roosevelt offered arbitration of the dispute, which both Venezuela and Germany rejected until Roosevelt threatened to send the United States Navy to Venezuela.

Kaiser Wilhelm II, with a navy inferior to the American's and reluctant to add the United States to the growing list of nations hostile to Germany, eventually accepted Roosevelt's suggestion for mediation, as did Britain. The Hague Tribunal settled the dispute in 1904, ruling against Venezuela. Latin Americans feared the consequences of the Hague decision because they feared it would encourage the use of force in international disputes and increase the likelihood that European powers would, therefore, resort to force to achieve their goals in Latin America.

By 1904 the Dominican Republic had been forced by the German, Italian, and Spanish governments to sign protocols for the payment of debts, totaling $32 million, owed to the European powers. Fearing European military action to ensure payment of the debts, the Dominicans requested Roosevelt "to establish some kind of protectorate over the islands," as the president phrased it. Roosevelt recognized that the Europeans could be expected to intervene militarily as they had done successfully in the Venezuelan crisis. In 1905, the United States assumed control of Dominican customs so that funds could be allotted to the European creditors. The United States collected the customs duties for the Dominican Republic, using 55 percent of the duties collected to pay debts and leaving the remaining 45 percent for the government of the Dominican Republic.

To preclude future intervention in the Caribbean by Europeans, Roosevelt also declared that the United States was empowered to serve as an international police force in the event of "chronic wrongdoing, or an impotence which results in a general loosening of the ties of civilized society." This so-called Roosevelt Corollary to the Monroe Doctrine transformed the original doctrine from an external protective device to a justification for internal intervention by the United States. Two years later, the president sent American troops into Cuba to avert a revolution. Then, in 1911, when the president of the Dominican Republic was assassinated, and rebels from neighboring Haiti were pillaging the country, the United States had to shut down the customs houses until September 1912, when United States marines arrived to restore order. The United States would militarily occupy the Dominican Republic until 1920.

Also in 1911, the Nicaraguan government threatened to cancel mine concessions to the United States and executed two Americans. President William Howard Taft sent twenty-five hundred United States marines to Nicaragua to depose the government and help establish the Samoza regime that would be friendlier to the United States. The United States signed a treaty with Nicaragua, similar to the one with the Dominican Republic, which would have placed the United States government in charge of the Nicaraguan customs house. The United States Senate, however, rejected the Nicaraguan treaty along with a similar one with Honduras, but the State Department helped private New York banks take over the Customs House of Nicaragua in 1912. In 1912, the United States sent another two thousand troops to put down another Nicaraguan revolt, and United States troops would stay in Nicaragua until 1933.

Dollar Diplomacy

President Taft expanded upon Roosevelt's imperialistic foreign policies in Latin America, devising a program called "dollar diplomacy"—use of private American capital, often against both the desire and the judgment of the bankers concerned—to displace European bondholders and concessionaires in Latin America. The idea of dollar diplomacy was to wield influence in Latin America through trade and investment rather than direct military control. Taft, like Roosevelt, strove to achieve stability in Latin America and to ensure the security of the Panama Canal. Over the years, this drive for stability and protection of the Panama Canal resulted in a clear pattern of American support of ultraconservative and often dictatorial governments in much of Central America and the Caribbean.

Wilson's Mission: Ideal and Reality

Woodrow Wilson's vision in foreign policy was to create a progressive world built on capitalism, free trade, and moralism. Wilson's foreign policy was, in part, a reflection of his own, personal, inflexible moralism. Wilson referred to his foreign policy as "releasing the intelligence of America for the service of mankind." Like those before him, however, Wilson pushed for the Open Door in China and sought to resist Japanese expansion in Asia. Wilson denounced both Roosevelt's "big stick" and Taft's "dollar diplomacy." However, Wilson was not averse to using dollar diplomacy when circumstances seemed to require it, and in practice he displayed a propensity to resort to the "big stick" just as quickly as Roosevelt. Wilson and Secretary of State William Jennings Bryan also conceived that they had a mission to democratize the corrupt and revolution-ridden Caribbean republics. "We can have no sympathy with those who seek to seize the power of government to advance their own personal interests or ambition," Wilson warned in a public statement on March 11, 1913. "As friends, therefore, we shall prefer those who act in the interest of peace and honor, who protect private rights and respect the restraints of constitutional provision."

Wilson, therefore, simultaneously adhered to the Monroe Doctrine and the Roosevelt Corollary, a path that produced policy decisions that would be every bit as "big stick" as Roosevelt but one linked to Wilson's own sense of moral idealism. Unparalleled diplomatic and military intervention in the Caribbean and Mexico followed. The Wilson administration regularized the occupation of Nicaragua, which remained occupied by United States marines until 1933. Wilson sent marines to Haiti and, by imposing a puppet but nominally democratic regime in 1915,

THE BIG STICK IN THE CARIBBEAN SEA

▶ Cartoon of Roosevelt's "big stick", (the idea of negotiating peacefully while simultaneously threatening with the "big stick", or the military) in Panama.

made that state a virtual protectorate of the United States. It dispatched marines to the Dominican Republic in 1916 and there governed it directly through military officers. Reflecting Wilson's moral idealism, however, military governance also fostered road building, school construction, and public health projects. In 1913, the Wilson administration attempted to make amends to Colombia for the Panama affair and signed a treaty whereby the United States agreed to pay Colombia $5 million in damages. The Senate, however, was less apologetic and voted down Wilson's treaty of apology.

Triumph and Tragedy in Mexico

Meanwhile, Wilson embarked on a bold new policy toward Mexico where the classic Latin American alliance of dictator, church, and foreign investors had provoked a convulsive political upheaval. By 1911, more than half of Mexico's oil, two-thirds of its railroads, and three-fourths of its mines and smelters were owned by Americans. Much of the remaining oil was British-owned. The Catholic Church was the largest landowner although William Randolph Hearst and other Americans also had huge holdings. The average Mexican peon or industrial worker lived in abject poverty.

Against this background, a revolution erupted in 1910. The dictator Porfirio Díaz, who had ruled Mexico for forty years, was finally driven out in May 1911, by a group of middle-class intellectuals headed by a constitutionalist named Francisco Madero. Madero promised to bring democracy to Mexico, but American conservatives opposed Madero because he had brought instability that threatened American investments in Mexico. Americans owned 40 percent of the property in Mexico at the time, more than was owned by the people of Mexico. Less than a year later, and one month before the inauguration of Woodrow Wilson, the United States Ambassador to Mexico Henry Lane Wilson (no relation to Woodrow) gave support to a conservative military general Victoriano Huerta, who planned to oust Madero in a coup. Huerta asked Ambassador Wilson what he (Huerta) should do with Madero after he ousted him from the seat of government. Wilson replied, "Take whatever steps are necessary to bring peace." Men working for Huerta subsequently executed Madero, shooting him as he was "trying to escape" on the way to prison.

Wilson's first break with tradition came when he withheld recognition from Huerta on the grounds that the United States should henceforth cooperate only with governments based on the unquestioned consent of the governed. Unaware of America's tacit approval of Huerta's execution of Madero, Wilson referred to the Huerta government as a "government of butchers." Wilson announced that the United States would extend recognition only to those governments built on "orderly processes of just government based on law, not upon arbitrary or irregular force." This marked the first time in American history that human rights influenced the recognition of a foreign government. In the words of Wilson, "morality, not material interest, must guide United States foreign policy." Wilson denounced Huerta as a "drunken brute" and publicly called for his resignation; and he persuaded the British, also, to withdraw their support from Huerta. Wilson informed the British foreign minister that the United States intended to not only depose Huerta but also to "exert every influence it can to secure Mexico a better government under which all contracts and business concessions will be safer than ever." Wilson pressured other European governments to denounce and sanction the Huerta government; but the Europeans refused, viewing Huerta as another Diaz who would bring stability to Mexico.

In the meantime, Wilson sought a means by which he could depose Huerta militarily. Then he brought his new policy to fruition by offering to aid Huerta's chief antagonist, the constitutional reformer Venustiano Carranza, in an effort to oust the Huerta government. On February 3, 1914, Wilson lifted an arms embargo to Mexico that had been instituted by Taft.

Nevertheless, Huerta's strength continued to increase, partly as a result of resentment over United States interference. Consequently, Wilson's sense of frustration became more acute. Wilson finally seized opportunity with a trivial incident at Tampico, where several United States naval officers from the *U.S.S. Dolphin* were arrested by Mexican authorities for selling fuel to enemies of the Huerta government. Seeking to avoid a confrontation with the United States, the Mexicans at Tampico quickly released the U.S. soldiers, and the Mexican officer in command personally apologized; but the commander of the U.S.S. *Dolphin* demanded a twenty-one-gun salute as an official apology. When Mexico refused the twenty-one-gun salute apology, Wilson used the opportunity to order a blockade of Vera Cruz on the Southeast Mexican coast to prevent Germany's arms shipments from reaching Huerta's army. Wilson asked Congress for authority to move against the Mexican dictator. Congress had not responded by April 21, 1914, when Wilson ordered the American fleet to occupy Vera Cruz to prevent a German ship from unloading ammunition. In the resultant blockade and invasion of Veracruz, eight hundred United States troops engaged Huerta's Mexican federal troops, and nineteen Americans and 126 Mexicans were killed. Over three thousand more Americans landed on April 22, and over seven thousand United States troops eventually occupied Veracruz to take control of the city. United States troops would remain in Vera Cruz until November 1914.

▶ Several United States naval officers from the U.S.S. *Dolphin* were arrested by Mexican authorities for selling fuel to enemies of the Huerta government.

Simultaneously, Wilson was supplying arms to the opposition rebels of Venustiano Carranza. Wilson offered Carranza the use of American troops to oust Huerta, but Carranza refused them, knowing he could never have popular support in Mexico if he appeared to be a puppet of Wilson and the United States.

The president's militant action horrified peace-loving Americans and provoked even Carranza to threaten full-scale resistance should American troops march on Mexico City. Abandoned by the liberals of both Mexico and the United States, Wilson resolved his dilemma by agreeing to mediation by the "ABC powers"—Argentina, Brazil, and Chile. Huerta eventually resigned in favor of Carranza, who became *de facto* president of Mexico on August 20, 1914, and fled to Germany.

With Huerta gone, Wilson continued to press Carranza to accept his guidance, pushing for democratic reforms. He warned against mass executions and made it clear that he would oppose expropriation of the vast holdings of Americans and other foreigners. Carranza delayed the implementation of democratic reforms, however, arguing that the rebellions of Pancho Villa and Emiliano Zapata continued unabated against the government and putting down these revolts took precedent. Wilson became disenchanted with Carranza over his failure to quickly implement reforms. Then putting much faith in the unpredictable Pancho Villa, about whose role in history debate still rages. Wilson began to support him against Carranza. Armed with Wilson's weapons and provisions, at one point Villa captured Mexico City and ousted the Carranza government. Villa also was slow to implement democratic reforms, however, causing Wilson to once again aid Carranza. Thereupon, Carranza broadened his own reform program while his leading general, Alvaro Obregon, crushed Villa's armies in the field and restored Carranza's government.

Back in Washington, American conservatives put the president under tremendous pressure to mount a full-scale invasion of Mexico. The Catholic hierarchy, the Hearst press, oil and other corporate interests, and ultranationalists like Theodore Roosevelt—all urged him to act; but Wilson held firm and in October 1915 extended *de facto* recognition, but not full recognition, to the Carranza regime.

Reduced to banditry and feeling betrayed by Wilson, Villa strove to regain his power by inciting the United States to war. Early in 1916, he murdered eighteen American engineers in northern Mexico when he stopped a train carrying the American citizens. Then, in a bold sortie into New Mexico, Villa killed seventeen more Americans when he crossed the border into the United States and burned the town of Columbus, New Mexico.

The president ordered Brigadier General John J. Pershing and a United States expeditionary force of seven thousand troops to pursue Villa into Mexico. Villa fled south and evaded the pursuing United States army, which penetrated some three hundred miles south into Mexico. Though the United States army never did find Villa, they engaged Carranza's regular Mexican troops on several occasions, killing forty federal troops at Parral in April 1916. In late June, Carranza's troops killed twelve Americans and captured twenty-three in a skirmish at Carrizal. More incidents followed, and conservatives and ultranationalists called angrily for an all-out American invasion of Mexico.

Wilson responded by mobilizing the National Guard along the Mexican border, but he refused to change the expedition's limited objective. Carranza accused Wilson of secretly planning to occupy northern Mexico and wrote a letter to Wilson threatening war if Wilson did not withdraw. Wilson at first refused; but finally, in late January 1917, he ordered the withdrawal of what was now called the "perishing expedition" in the media because of the escalating problems surrounding World War I in Europe and what appeared to be impending conflict with Germany. In March 1917, one month before the United States entered World War I, Wilson granted full recognition to the Carranza government. The move was perhaps an indicator of the direction that Wilson intended to lead America as he became convinced that America could no longer remain neutral in the Great War. The instability in Mexico would have to be ignored so that Wilson could turn his attention to the larger problem looming in Europe.

▶ ▶ ▶

Chapter Review 21

Summary

Even several decades before Frederick Jackson Turner proclaimed the American Western frontier to be "closed," many Americans were clamoring for the expansion of America beyond its continental borders, either for reasons of security or out of a belief in "Manifest Destiny." In some cases Americans favored expansion simply as a way to divert attention away from domestic problems; however, expansion was viewed as a sign of greatness, and America should expand as other great empires had expanded before her.

The United States under expansionist Secretary of State William H. Seward added the Midway Islands and Alaska in 1867, and there was talk of Cuba, Greenland, Puerto Rico, and other islands becoming American possessions. A Treaty of Annexation of Santo Domingo was actually signed during the Grant administration, but failed to get the necessary two-thirds vote in the Senate. America divided possession of Samoa with Germany in 1899 and annexed Hawaii during the Spanish-American War, under the pretext that annexation was necessary to keep the islands out of the clutches of Spain.

The age of America as a great power had begun in earnest in the Spanish American War when the U.S. ended up not only defeating a declining European power and expelling it from their colony in the Western Hemisphere but also annexing Puerto Rico, Guam, and the Philippines. However, the U.S. renounced any claim to Cuba as a show to the world that the war was not for imperialistic reasons.

This, in fact, was only partially true. American business interests had pushed for Cuban intervention to protect their assets and Assistant Secretary of the Navy Theodore Roosevelt had formulated plans to wrestle the Philippines from Spain prior to the war. William Randolph Hearst's media empire sold the war to Americans with yellow journalism, playing up and even inventing Spanish atrocities in Cuba. After the explosion of the battleship *Maine* in Havana harbor, which the Hearst newspapers blamed on Spain, President McKinley asked Congress to authorize force to expel the Spanish in Cuba to end the atrocities in Cuba.

The "splendid little war" began with an uncoordinated invasion of Cuba in May and ended in Cuba with the capitulation of the Spanish forces at Santiago on July 17. Meanwhile, the U.S. Navy under Commodore Dewey carried out Roosevelt's plans and destroyed the Spanish fleet in Manila, and then U.S. marines invaded and secured the islands by August 13.

A debate ensued over the annexation of the Philippines, and President McKinley pushed for their annexation after he had prayed to God and concluded that God wanted the U.S. to annex the Philippines so as to Christianize them. Meanwhile, Filipino rebels under Emilio Aguinaldo launched a four year rebellion that led to the death of forty-three hundred American soldiers and two hundred thousand Filipinos. The U.S. did not recognize the rebels as a legitimate army and executed fifty thousand Filipino POWs as murderers.

In Cuba, as in the Philippines, the U.S. installed temporary rule by the U.S. military. The U.S. added the Platt Amendment to the Cuban Constitution. That eroded Cuban sovereignty and established a permanent American naval base at Guantanamo Bay.

In the Far East, the U.S. pushed for the "Open Door" in China and sent troops to join an international force that put down the Boxer Rebellion when Chinese nationalists took over the foreign embassy in Beijing. Theodore Roosevelt simultaneously sought to limit Japanese power in the Pacific so as to ensure the security of the Philippines. Roosevelt mediated the conclusion of the Russo-Japanese War in 1905 with a settlement that the Japanese viewed as unfavorable to Japan. Roosevelt then sent the Great White Fleet to Japan in 1907 in a show of force.

The Spanish-American War illuminated the need for a canal in Central America, and Theodore Roosevelt negotiated the rights to build a canal with Colombia. However, when Colombia's Senate rejected the treaty, Roosevelt supported a Panamanian rebellion. He then negotiated a treaty with the new nation of Panama, which he had helped create, and declared a U.S. protectorate. The canal was completed in 1914 at a cost of $352 million, over ten times the original estimates.

In 1902, after England and Germany intervened in Venezuela, Theodore Roosevelt issued his Corollary to the Monroe Doctrine whereby the U.S. assumed international police power in the Western Hemisphere in an effort to prevent European intervention in Latin America. Under Roosevelt's Corrollary, the U.S. under Roosevelt, Taft, and Woodrow Wilson would invade Haiti, the Dominican Republic, and Nicaragua to restore order, protect American business interests, and ensure payment of foreign debts.

In 1911, Democratic Reformer Francisco Madero ousted right-wing Mexican dictator Porfirio Diaz. Conservative business interests in the United States feared instability in Mexico and assisted General Victoriano Huerta in ousting Madero. Huerta had Madero and his vice president executed, causing the new President Woodrow Wilson to denounce Huerta's "Government of Butchers" and a support rebel faction under Venustiano Carranza. Wilson sent the U.S. marines to invade Veracruz in 1914 and cut off Huerta's flow of weapons from Germany. With American aid, Carranza's forces were able to oust Huerta, only to be ousted themselves by Pancho Villa after Wilson temporarily supported Villa. Wilson quickly soured on Villa, however, and again supported Carranza, who deposed Villa. Villa retaliated against Wilson with a massacre of American engineers on a train in northern Mexico and an invasion into New Mexico where he killed seventeen Americans at Columbus, New Mexico.

Wilson then sent an expeditionary force under General John J. Pershing into Mexico to apprehend Villa. Although Pershing invaded three hundred miles into Mexico, he never found Villa but did twice engage Mexican federal troops. Carranza, who had at first welcomed the invasion to rid him of his enemy Villa, threatened war with the United States if Wilson did not withdraw. Wilson withdrew the troops because it was growing clear that American intervention in the Great War in Europe was imminent, and Wilson wanted to avoid simultaneous wars in Europe and Mexico.

Chapter Review (cont'd)

Chronological Time Line

1847 *The New York Sun* argued for the annexation of Cuba.

1867 The U.S. took over the unoccupied Midway Islands in the Pacific.

1867 The U.S. purchased Alaska from Russia for $7.2 million.

1868 Cubans revolted against Spanish rule.

1875 The Reciprocity Treaty with Hawaii granted Hawaii free trade with the U.S. on sugar.

1884 The Conference of Berlin divided Africa between the European powers.

1885 Reverend Josiah Strong in *Our Country* equated Christianity with the aggressive traits of imperialism.

1887 The U.S. gained exclusive rights to a naval base at Pearl Harbor.

1890 Captain Alfred Thayer Mahan published *The Influence of Sea Power on History.*

1890 The McKinley Tariff Act ended the Hawaiian advantage in sugar trade with the U.S.

1893 Historian Frederick Jackson Turner proclaimed the western frontier to be closed.

1893 American sugar growers overthrew Queen Liliuokalani and petitioned the U.S. for annexation.

1893 The U.S. Senate rejected Hawaiian Treaty of Annexation.

1893 Cubans revolted against Spain.

1894 President Grover Cleveland extended recognition to the new Republic of Hawaii.

1895 Great Britain rejected an American offer of arbitration in a border dispute between British Guiana and Venezuela.

1896 William McKinley was elected president on an expansionist platform.

Time Line (cont'd)

1898 The Battleship *Maine* exploded in Havana Harbor on February 15.

1898 On April 19, Congress authorized use of force to expel Spain from Cuba.

1898 On April 24, Spain declared war on the U.S.

1898 On May 1, the U.S. Navy under Commodore George Dewey sank the Spanish fleet at Manila.

1898 On July 17, Spanish forces surrendered in Santiago.

1898 The U.S. annexed Hawaii during the Spanish-American War under the pretense that it prevented a Spanish takeover of the islands.

1898 On August 12, Armistice was signed between the U.S. and Spain, ending the Spanish-American War.

1898 December 10, Spain ceded the Philippines, Puerto Rico, and Guam to the U.S. in the Treaty of Paris.

1898–1902 The Filipino Rebellion led to the death of forty-three hundre American soldiers and two hundred thousand Filipinos.

1899–1900 John Hay sent Open Door notes to the Great Powers.

1900 Boxer Rebellion in China

1901 The Platt Amendment was added to the Cuban Constitution infringing on Cuban sovereignty.

1901 The Second Hay-Pauncefote Treaty, England granted the U.S. rights to build a canal in Central America.

1902 Venezuela Crisis

1902 Reciprocity Treaty with Cuba.

1905 Russo-Japanese War

Chapter Review (cont'd)

Time Line (cont'd)

1903 Theodore Roosevelt aided the Panamanian rebellion and then made the canal treaty with Panama.

1905 Dominican crisis and Roosevelt's Corollary to the Monroe Doctrine

1906 San Francisco segregated Japanese children.

1907 The sail of the Great White Fleet

1911 Democratic Reformer Francisco Madero ousted Mexican dictator Porfirio Diaz.

1911 U.S. marines were sent to the Dominican Republic to restore order.

1911 President Taft sent the U.S. marines to Nicaragua and installed the Samoza regime.

1914 Wilson ordered the military occupation of Veracruz.

1914 World War I broke out in Europe.

1914 August 20, Valeriano Huerta fled to Germany, and Venustiano Carranza became president of Mexico with American support.

1915 Woodrow Wilson sent the U.S. marines to Haiti and effectively made Haiti a U.S. protectorate.

1916 Woodrow Wilson sent marines to the Dominican Republic to restore order.

1916 Pancho Villa invades into the U.S. at Columbus, New Mexico, and killed seventeen Americans.

1916 Woodrow Wilson sent U.S. troops under General John J. Pershing into Mexico after Pancho Villa.

1917 In March, Wilson granted full recognition to Carranza's government in Mexico.

1917 In the Lansing-Ishii Agreement the United States recognized Japan's special interests in China while Japan reaffirmed its support of the Open Door and agreed not to use the war situation to seek new privileges in China.

Key Terms

Frederick Jackson Turner: Historian that declared in 1893 that the western frontier was now closed
Alfred T. Mahan: Author of *The Influence of Sea Power* upon History in which he argued that only a large navy could protect the trade that would be the lifeblood of the new American empire
Reverend Josiah Strong: Equated Christianity with the traits of imperialism
McKinley Tariff Act: Eliminated the Hawaiian advantage on sugar and provided a two-cent per pound bounty to domestic sugar growers
John L. Stevens: American ambassador to Hawaii that ordered the U.S. marines to help depose Queen Liliuokalani
Hawaiian annexation: Accomplished by William McKinley during the Spanish-American War ostensibly to prevent a Spanish takeover of Hawaii
Valeriano Weyler: Spanish general demonized in the American Press because he instituted a concentration camp policy in Cuba
William Randolph Hearst: Owner of a vast media empire that engaged in slanted journalism in support of American military intervention in Cuba
Dupuy de Lome: Spanish Ambassador to the U.S. that sent a letter to a friend in Spain describing McKinley as weak and a bidder for the admiration of the crowds
"Reconcentration Policy": General Valeriano Weyler's concentration camp approach to the Cuban rebellion
U.S.S. *Maine*: American battleship that exploded in Havana Harbor in February 1898, and helped precipitate the war between the U.S. and Spain
William McKinley: America's imperialistic president during the Spanish-American War
Teller Amendment: Renounced any American claims to Cuba
Imperialism: The idea and practice of a great power, such as the United States, expanding itself through conquest
Splendid Little War: Secretary of State John Hay's description of the Spanish-American War, which was a quick American victory with limited casualties
San Juan Hill: Most famous battle of the Spanish-American War involving Teddy Roosevelt and the Rough Riders
Rough Riders: Soldiers that fought under the command of Theodore Roosevelt
Commodore George Dewey: American sea commander that sunk the Spanish fleet at Manila during the Spanish-American War
Treaty of Paris, 1898: Treaty officially ending the Spanish-American War and granting Guam, Puerto Rico, and the Philippines to the U.S.
Platt Amendment: Amendment to the Cuban Constitution limiting Cuban sovereignty and granting a permanent American base at Guantanamo Bay
Emilio Aguinaldo: Leader of the Filipino Rebellion

Chapter Review (cont'd)

Key Terms (cont'd)

Arthur MacArthur: American General in the Philippines during the Filipino Rebellion and known for his policy of No Quarter

Open Door notes: Notes sent by Secretary of State John Hay to the Great Powers calling for equal access to trade and natural resources in China for all the Great Powers

Boxer Rebellion: Rebellion of Chinese nationalists that took over the foreign diplomatic corps in Beijing but were put down by an international force that included Americans.

Russo-Japanese War: War between Japan and Russia in 1905 over control of Manchuria, won by Japan

Treaty of Portsmouth: Treaty negotiated by Theodore Roosevelt ending the Russo-Japanese War

The Great White Fleet: Theodore Roosevelt's show of force to Japan when he painted the American Navy white and sent it around the world

New Panama Canal Company: French company that sold its assets to the U.S. in the Panama Canal Treaty

Panama Canal Treaty: Granted the U.S. a 100-year-lease of a ten-mile-wide zone in Panama at an annual rent of $250,000

Venezuela Crisis: In 1902, Venezuela defaulted on loans, resulting in invasions by Germany and Britain that violated the Monroe Doctrine.

Roosevelt Corollary: Roosevelt proclaimed that in cases of "chronic wrongdoing" in Latin America, the United States must exercise international police power because the Monroe Doctrine prevented the Europeans from doing so.

Dollar Diplomacy: William Howard Taft's policy of wielding influence in Latin America through investment and trade

Wilson's moral idealism: Wilson ties human rights to American foreign policy

"Big Stick": Roosevelt's use of the military to achieve American foreign policy goals

Mexican intervention: Woodrow Wilson's support for the forces of Venustiano Carranza against Valeriano Huerta, including invasions of Mexico at Veracruz and in the north in the hunt for Pancho Villa

Porfirio Diaz: Long-term dictator of Mexico that was ousted by Madero in 1911

Francisco Madero: Democratic Reformer that assumed the Mexican presidency in 1911 only to be executed on the orders of General Victoriano Huerta

Venustiano Carranza: Woodrow Wilson's chosen successor in Mexico

Pancho Villa: Mexican rebel that invaded the United States and killed seventeen people at Columbus, New Mexico.

Tampico: Site of a dispute between the U.S. Navy and Mexican military over the Mexican arrest of U.S. sailors for selling fuel to Mexican rebels

Veracruz: Mexican Atlantic port city invaded by the U.S. military on the orders of President Wilson in 1914

Columbus, New Mexico: Site of Pancho Villa's invasion of the U.S. and killing of seventeen Americans

Pershing Expedition: General John J. Pershing's futile search for Pancho Villa in Mexico on the orders of President Wilson.

Pop Quiz

Chapter 21

1. Alaska was purchased by the United States from __________.
   a. Japan
   b. Germany
   c. France
   d. Russia

2. Reverend Josiah Strong equated Christianity with __________.
   a. peace, love, and understanding
   b. "peculiarly aggressive traits" that would extend Anglo-Saxon culture upon Latin America, islands of the seas, and Africa
   c. passivity
   d. tolerance for diversity

3. In 1895, what caused President Grover Cleveland to threaten the use of force against England?
   a. the Monroe Doctrine and its application to a boundary dispute between Venezuela and British Guiana
   b. the British practice of impressment
   c. the failure of the British to limit German power in Latin America
   d. the failure of the British to relinquish Canada to the U.S.

4. Why did McKinley reject the Spanish offers of unilateral cease-fire and home rule for Cuba?
   a. McKinley was a warmonger.
   b. McKinley believed that the rebels would not stop short of full independence.
   c. McKinley believed the Spanish to be disingenuous.
   d. McKinley thought a communist Cuba would be better than a Spanish one.

5. At Manila on May 1, 1898, which of the following die Commodore George Dewey and the U.S. Navy do?
   a. imposed the Dewey decimal system on Filipino libraries
   b. sunk the entire Spanish fleet in the Philippines without losing a single U.S. ship
   c. took the Philippines for the U.S. without any resistance from Spain
   d. proclaimed the establishment of Christianity in the Philippines

6. Problems for the Americans in the Spanish-American War included __________.
   a. rancid rations
   b. inadequate medical supplies, technology, and techniques

Chapter Review (cont'd)

Pop Quiz (cont'd)

c. illness
d. all of the above

7. Under the Treaty of Paris of 1898 the United States gained control of all of the following Spanish territories EXCEPT __________.
   a. the Philippines
   b. Hawaii
   c. Guam
   d. Puerto Rico

8. Theodore Roosevelt described critics of the Platt Amendment as __________.
   a. "unhung traitors, liars, slanderers, and scandal mongers."
   b. free Americans exercising their rights to free speech
   c. the champions of democracy
   d. ultra left-wing ideologues

9. Which of the following is true of the Treaty of Portsmouth?
   a. Japan gained all of Sakhalin Island.
   b. Japan received $600 million in reparations from Russia.
   c. Russia gained the Liaotung Peninsula.
   d. Japan was unhappy with the settlement and blamed the U.S.

10. Which of the following did the Roosevelt Corollary to the Monroe Doctrine essentially state?
    a. The U.S. will not use its military in Latin America.
    b. Europeans may invade Latin American countries only in cases of "chronic wrongdoing."
    c. The U.S. will attempt to wield influence in Latin America through trade and investment instead of direct political control.
    d. In cases of "chronic wrongdoing" in Latin America, the U.S. must intervene and exercise international police power.

11. Woodrow Wilson's foreign policy could best be described as __________.
    a. liberal pacifism
    b. isolationism
    c. moral idealism
    d. dollar diplomacy only

12. Which of the following is true of Wilson's policy toward the government of Victoriano Huerta?
    a. It was the first time that the U.S. government had supported "a government of butchers."
    b. It was the first time that human rights had influenced American recognition of a foreign government.
    c. It was the first time that the U.S. had ever sent American troops into Mexico.
    d. It was the first time America had supported right-wing dictators instead of Democratic reformers.

13. Grover Cleveland invoked the __________ __________ in a failed attempt to settle a boundary dispute between Venezuela and Britain.

14. Spain put more than two hundred thousand Cubans in __________ __________ before American intervention.

15. In 1902, the United States leased __________ __________ from Cuba to use as a naval base.

1. D	6. D	11. C	14. Concentration Camps
2. B	7. B	12. B	15. Guantanamo Bay
3. A	8. A	13. Monroe Doctrine	
4. B	9. D		
5. B	10. D		

22 America and the Great War, 1914–1918

Chapter Objectives

World War I

Europe Before the War

Outbreak of Hostilities

German Submarine Warfare

Steps Toward United States Preparedness

The Election of 1916

The Failure of Mediation

The Carnage and Stalemate of World War I

A People at War

Mobilization for Victory

The War on Land

SOCIOLOGY

EIGHTH EDITION

John J. Macionis

Kenyon College

Prentice Hall

Upper Saddle River, New Jersey 07458

Library of Congress Cataloging-in-Publication Data

Macionis, John J.
Sociology / John J. Macionis.—8th ed.
p. cm.
Includes bibliographical references and index.
ISBN 0-13-018495-0
1. Sociology. I. Title
HM586 .M33 2000
301—dc21 00-038562

Senior Acquisitions Editor: Christopher De John
Publisher: Nancy Roberts
VP, Editorial Director: Laura Pearson
Editor in Chief of Development: Susanna Lesan
Development Editor: Harriett Prentiss
AVP, Director of Production and Manufacturing: Barbara Kittle
Production Editor: Barbara Reilly
Copyeditors: Amy Macionis, Mary Louise Byrd
Proofreaders: Karen Bosch, Marianne Peters Riordan
Editorial Assistant: Christina Scalia
Production Assistant: Meredith Gnerre
Prepress and Manufacturing Manager: Nick Sklitsis
Prepress and Manufacturing Buyer: Mary Ann Gloriande
Director of Marketing: Beth Gillett Mejia
Marketing Assistant: Judie Lamb
Creative Design Director: Leslie Osher
Art Director: Carole Anson
Interior and Cover Designer: Kenny Beck
Line Art Manager: Guy Ruggiero
Line Art Illustrations: Lithokraft II
Maps: Carto-Graphics
Director, Image Resource Center: Melinda Reo
Image Specialist: Beth Boyd
Manager, Rights and Permissions: Kay Dellosa
Permissions Coordinator: Debra Hewitson
Photo Researcher: Francelle Carapetyan
Cover Coordinator: Karen Sanatar
Cover Art: Roger Bissiere, *The Forest,* 1955. Collection du Centre Georges Pompidou/Musée National d'Art Moderne, Paris.
Senior Media Editor: John Jordan
Media Production Manager: Mike D'Angelo
Media Production Project Manager: Maurice Murdock
Media Producer: Matthew Krack
Media Buyer: Lynn Pearlman

This book was set in 10/11 Janson by Lithokraft II, and was printed and bound by Courier Companies, Inc. The cover was printed by The Lehigh Press, Inc.

Prentice Hall

A Division of Pearson Education
Upper Saddle River, New Jersey 07458

Printed in the United States of America
10 9 8 7 6 5 4 3 2

ISBN 0-13-018495-0

Prentice-Hall International (UK) Limited, *London*
Prentice-Hall of Australia Pty. Limited, *Sydney*
Prentice-Hall Canada Inc., *Toronto*
Prentice-Hall Hispanoamericana, S. A., *Mexico*
Prentice-Hall of India Private Limited, *New Delhi*
Prentice-Hall of Japan, Inc., *Tokyo*
Pearson Education Asia Pte. Ltd., *Singapore*
Editora Prentice-Hall do Brasil, Ltda., *Rio de Janeiro*

Printed on Recycled Paper

BRIEF CONTENTS

CONTENTS

PART II
THE FOUNDATIONS OF SOCIETY

PART III
SOCIAL INEQUALITY

PART IV
SOCIAL INSTITUTIONS

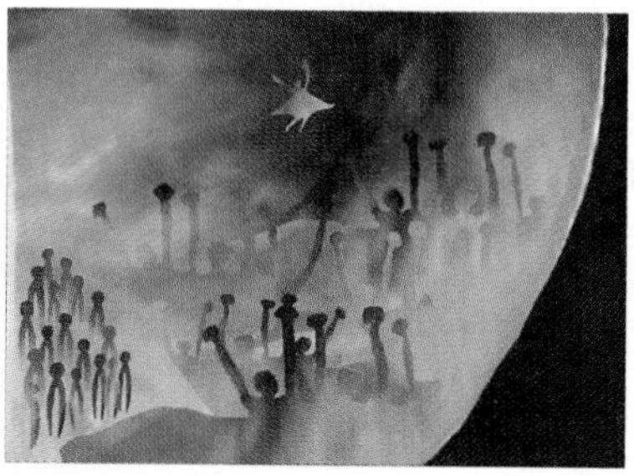

PART V
SOCIAL CHANGE

MAPS

GLOBAL MAPS: WINDOW ON THE WORLD

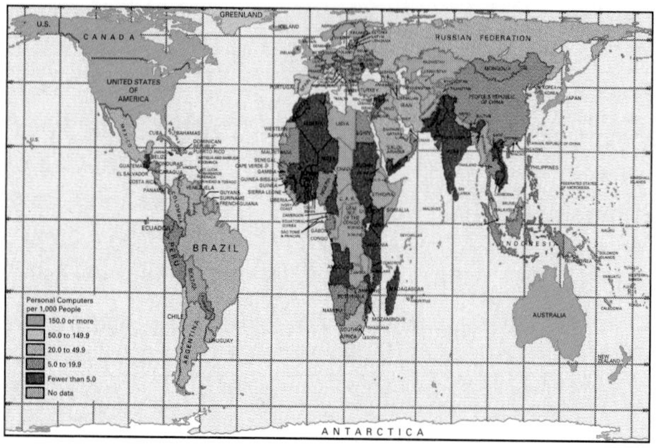

NATIONAL MAPS: SEEING OURSELVES

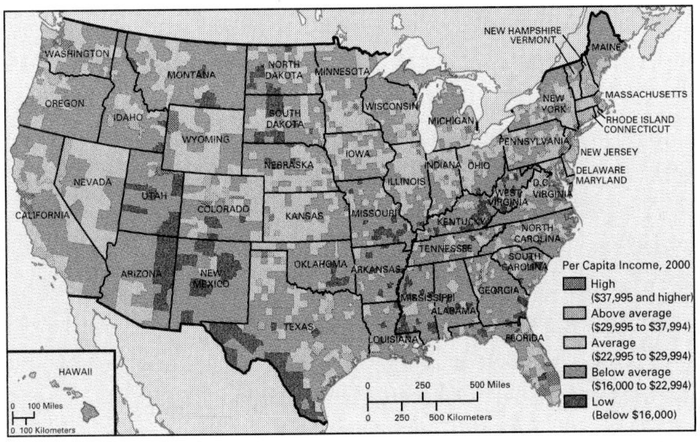

BOXES

APPLYING SOCIOLOGY

CRITICAL THINKING

GLOBAL SOCIOLOGY

SOCIAL DIVERSITY

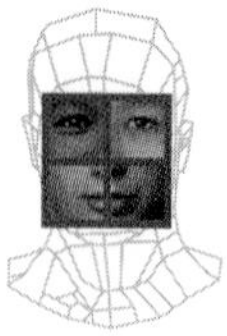

CONTROVERSY & DEBATE

FEATURE ESSAYS

NEW INFORMATION TECHNOLOGY AND SOCIETY

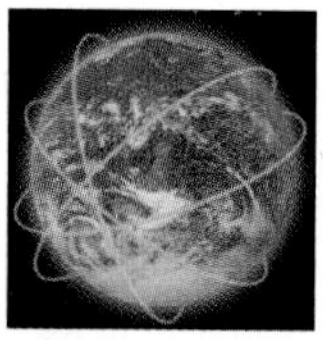

cyber.scope

PREFACE

It was just five or six years ago that people were beginning to talk about the Internet and the Information Revolution. Today, computers and other new technology already play a part in how people entertain themselves, stay in touch with others, shop for everything from gadgets to groceries, teach classes, and study for exams. One can only imagine the extent of the transformation that will unfold over the course of this new century.

Yet there remains a contradiction in calling this the "information age." No one doubts that students have more information available to them than ever before. But who can deny that students (especially young people just out of high school) still know little about their own society and even less about the larger world? It is here that old-fashioned sociology has a crucial part to play. By developing their sociological imagination, we help students see the shape of the society that guides their lives, as well as appreciate ever-present forces of change. This same imagination also lets them place this society in a global context, highlighting the worldwide structures and systems that affect us all.

The daily e-mail I receive from students in the United States and around the world stands as testimony to the power of sociology to transform people's lives. All instructors know the deep satisfaction of making a difference in the lives of our students. Indeed, there is no greater reward for our work, and, in my case, nothing is a better reason for reaching ever further with each new edition of the text. Therefore, I am delighted to offer this revision of *Sociology*, the discipline's most popular text, and a book that never stands still. In the eighth edition, *Sociology* is now better than ever, and includes an unmatched high-technology learning package.

The heart of this package is, of course, the book. As in the past, this eighth edition of *Sociology* is authoritative, comprehensive, stimulating, and—as students' daily e-mail messages testify—plain fun to read. This major revision elevates sociology's most popular text to a still higher standard of excellence, and offers an unparalleled resource to today's students as they learn about both our diverse society and the changing world.

But the book is only one part of a complete learning package. Found in the back of every new copy of *Sociology, Eighth Edition*, is a CD-ROM, included *at no additional cost to the student*. This CD-ROM is the best of its kind—not only does it contain a full study guide and approximately 80 percent of the textbook, but it also includes fully interactive study features such as author's tip videos, multimedia chapter introductions, interactive maps, video applications, a full glossary, and hundreds of links to Web sites around the world. Simply put, no other CD-ROM offers as much that is as good as this one.

A major innovation in the way students learn in sociology will be our new *Sociology Place* Web site at http://www.sociologyplace.com Produced by Peregrine Publishers and Prentice Hall, it is a new supersite for the discipline of sociology and is free to each student who buys a new copy of the textbook. The site has thousands of study questions, video clips, animations, news articles, a career center, a writing center, and a link library. It is updated weekly by our board of editors who are consistently contributing content to make this site a dynamic entity from which students will gain a clearer understanding of the sociological perspective.

In addition, also at no cost to them, students using *Sociology, Eighth Edition*, can log on to a full-featured Web site at http://www.prenhall.com/macionis From the main page, simply click on the cover of the text to access this learning site, which includes chapter overviews and learning objectives, suggested essay questions, and paper topics, as well as multiple-choice and true-false questions that the server will grade, chapter-relevant Web destinations with learning questions, and a chat room where students can share experiences and opinions with others taking the course. Faculty will find a full complement of resources as well, including the syllabus manager system that allows posting a course syllabus to the Internet without having to learn hypertext markup language (HTML); the Prentice Hall server does the work for you.

Textbook, CD-ROM, and Web sites: A three-part, multimedia package that is the foundation for sound learning in this new information age. We invite you to examine all three!

ORGANIZATION OF THIS TEXT

Part I of the textbook and the CD introduces the foundations of sociology. Underlying the discipline is the *sociological perspective*—the focus of Chapter 1, which explains how this invigorating point of view brings the world to life in a new and instructive way. Chapter 2 spotlights *sociological investigation*, or the "doing of sociology." This heavily revised chapter explains the scientific, interpretive, and critical orientations of the discipline, and illustrates research strategies with well-known examples of sociological work. Learning how sociologists see the world and carry out research, students are no longer passive but become active participants exploring the discipline's issues, debates, and controversies.

Part II surveys the foundations of social life. Chapter 3 focuses on the central concept of *culture*, emphasizing the cultural diversity that makes up our society and our world. The focus of Chapter 4 is the concept of *society*, presenting four time-honored models for understanding the structure and dynamics of social organization. This unique chapter provides introductory students with the background to understand the ideas of important thinkers—including Emile Durkheim, Karl Marx, Max Weber, and Gerhard Lenski—that appear in subsequent chapters. Alternatively, instructors may assign any of the chapter's four parts at any point in the course. Chapter 5 turns to *socialization*, exploring how we gain our humanity as we learn to participate in society. Chapter 6 provides a micro-level look at the patterns of *social interaction* that make up our everyday lives. Chapter 7 offers full-chapter coverage of *groups and organizations*, two additional and vital elements of social structure. This chapter, heavily revised this time around, provides a thorough investigation of the large organizations that have come to dominate our way of life. Chapter 8 explains how the operation of society generates both *deviance and conformity*, and also surveys the operation of the criminal justice system. Chapter 9, new to this edition, explains the social foundations of human sexuality. This chapter surveys sexual patterns in the United States and also explores variations in sexual practices through history and around the world today.

Part III offers unparalleled discussion of social inequality, beginning with three chapters on *social stratification*. Chapter 10 introduces major concepts and presents theoretical explanations of social inequality. This chapter richly illustrates historical changes in stratification, and how patterns of inequality vary in today's world. Chapter 11 surveys *social inequality in the United States*, confronting common perceptions of inequality and assessing how well they square with research findings. Chapter 12 extends the analysis with a look at *global stratification*, revealing the gaps in wealth and power that separate rich and poor nations. Both Chapters 11 and 12 pay special attention to how global developments affect stratification in the United States, just as they explore our society's role in global inequality. Chapter 13, *gender stratification*, explains how gender is a central element in social stratification in the United States, as it is worldwide. *Race and ethnicity*, additional important dimensions of social inequality both in North America and the rest of the world, are detailed in Chapter 14. *Aging and the elderly*, a topic of increasing concern to "graying" societies such as our own, is addressed in Chapter 15.

Part IV includes a full chapter on each social institution. Leading off is Chapter 16, *the economy and work*, because most sociologists recognize the economy as having the greatest impact on all other institutions. This chapter traces the rise and fall of industrial production in the United States and the emergence of a global economy, and explains what such transformations mean for the U.S. labor force. Chapter 17, *politics and government*, analyzes the distribution of power in U.S. society, as well as surveying political systems around the world. In addition, this chapter includes discussion of the U.S. military, the threat of war, and the search for peace. Chapter 18, *family*, explains the central importance of families to social organization, and underscores the diversity of family life both here and in other societies. Chapter 19, *religion*, addresses the timeless human search for ultimate purpose and meaning, introduces major world religions, and explains how religious beliefs are linked to other dimensions of social life. Chapter 20, *education*, analyzes the expansion of schooling in industrial societies. Here again, schooling in the United States comes to life through contrasts with educational patterns in many other countries. Chapter 21, *health and medicine*, reveals health to be a social issue just as much as it is a matter of biological processes. This chapter traces the historical emergence of medicine, analyzes current medical issues, and compares U.S. patterns to those found in other countries.

Part V examines important dimensions of global social change. Chapter 22 is a new chapter that highlights the powerful impact of *population growth* and *urbanization* in the United States and throughout the world with special attention to the *natural environment*. Chapter 23 explores forms of *collective behavior* and explains how people seek or resist social change by joining *social movements*. Chapter 24 concludes the text with an overview of *social change* that contrasts *traditional, modern, and postmodern societies*. This chapter rounds out the text, explaining how and why world societies change, and critically analyzing the benefits and liabilities of traditional, modern, and postmodern ways of life.

CONTINUITY: ESTABLISHED FEATURES OF *SOCIOLOGY*

Everyone knows that introductory sociology texts have much in common; but differences run deep. The extraordinary success of *Sociology* and the brief version, *Society: The Basics*, which are far and away the most widely adopted texts in the discipline, results from a combination of the following distinctive features.

The best writing style. Most important, this text offers a writing style widely praised by students and faculty alike as elegant and inviting. *Sociology* is an enjoyable text that encourages students to read—even beyond their assignments. No one says it better than the students themselves, whose recent e-mail includes comments like these:

> Thanks for writing such a brilliant book. It has sparked my sociological imagination. This was the first textbook that I have ever read completely and enjoyed. From the moment that I picked the book up I started reading nonstop.
>
> I have read four chapters ahead; it's like a good novel I can't put down! I just wanted to say thank you.
>
> I am taking a Sociology 101 class using *Sociology, Seventh Edition,* a book that I have told my professor is the best textbook that I have ever seen, bar none. I've told her as well that I will be more than happy to take more sociology classes as long as there is a Macionis text to go with them.

A global perspective. *Sociology* has taken a leading role in expanding the horizons of our discipline beyond the United States. *Sociology* was the first text to mainstream global content, introduce global maps, and offer whole chapters on global topics like stratification and the environment. No wonder this text has been adapted and translated in many languages for use around the world. Each chapter explores the social diversity of the entire world as well as explaining why social trends in the United States—from musical tastes, to the price of wheat, to the growing disparity of income—are influenced by what happens elsewhere. Just as important, students will learn ways in which social patterns and policies in the United States affect poor nations around the world.

A celebration of social diversity. *Sociology* invites students from all social backgrounds to discover a fresh and exciting way to see the world and understand themselves. Readers will discover in this text the diversity of U.S. society—people of African, Asian, European, and Latino ancestry, as well as women and men of various class positions, in all parts of the country, and at all points in the life course. A recent, independent survey of all introductory books gave this text top marks for mainstreaming race and ethnicity (Stone, 1996).

Emphasis on critical thinking. Critical-thinking skills include the ability to challenge common assumptions by formulating questions, to identify and weigh appropriate evidence, and to reach reasoned conclusions. This text not only teaches but encourages students to discover on their own.

The broadest coverage so instructors can choose. No other text matches *Sociology*'s twenty-four-chapter coverage of the field. We offer such breadth—at no greater cost—knowing that few instructors will assign every chapter, but with the goal of supporting instructors as they choose exactly what they wish to teach.

Engaging and instructive chapter openings. One of the most popular features of earlier editions of *Sociology* has been the engaging vignettes that begin each chapter. These openings—for instance, using the tragic sinking of the *Titanic* to illustrate the life and death consequences of social inequality, or telling the story of Linda Brown to explore racial inequality in the United States, or describing textile sweatshops on U.S.-controlled Pacific islands to examine the global economy—spark the interest of readers as they introduce important themes. This revision retains eight of the best chapter-opening vignettes found in earlier editions and offers sixteen new ones as well.

Inclusive focus on women and men. Beyond devoting two full chapters to the important concepts of sex and gender, *Sociology* mainstreams gender into *every* chapter, showing how the topic at hand affects women and men differently, and explaining how gender operates as a basic dimension of social organization.

Theoretically clear and balanced. *Sociology, Eighth Edition,* makes theory easy. Chapter 1 introduces the discipline's major theoretical approaches, which systematically reappear in the chapters that follow. The text highlights not only the social-conflict, structural-functional, and symbolic-interaction paradigms, but incorporates feminist theory, social-exchange analysis, ethnomethodology, cultural ecology, and sociobiology.

Chapter 4—unique to this text—provides students with an easy-to-understand introduction to important social theorists *before* they encounter their work in later chapters. The ideas of Max Weber, Karl Marx, and Emile Durkheim, as well as Gerhard Lenski's historical overview of human societies, appear in distinct sections that instructors may assign together or refer to separately at different points in the course.

Recent research and the latest data. *Sociology, Eighth Edition,* blends classic sociological statements with the latest research as reported in the leading publications in the field. Some 250 new studies inform this revision, and most of the 1500 pieces of research cited throughout the book were published since 1990. From chapter to chapter, the text's statistical data are the most recent available.

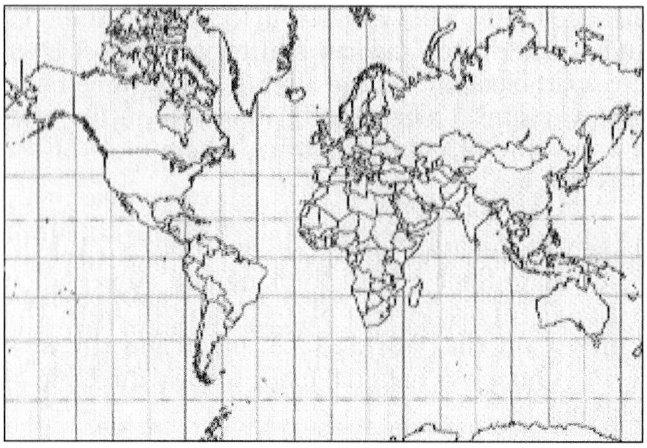 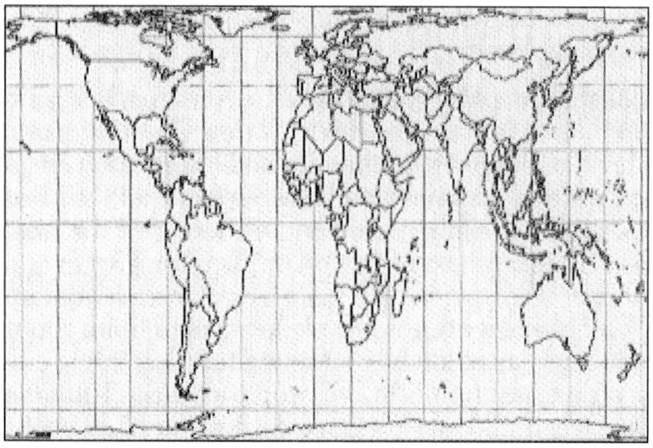

All maps distort reality, since they portray a three-dimensional world in two dimensions. Most of us are familiar with the Mercator projection (devised by the Flemish mapmaker Gerhardus Mercator, 1512–1594), which accurately presents the shape of countries (a vital concern to early seafaring navigators). But Mercator maps, like the one at left, distort the size of the land masses (more so the farther they lie from the equator), thereby exaggerating the dimensions of Europe and North America. The Peters projection, at right, is used in this text because it accurately displays the size of all nations.

Learning aids. This text has many features to help students learn. In each chapter, **Key Concepts** are identified by boldfaced type, and following each appears *a precise, italicized definition.* A listing of key concepts with their definitions appears at the end of each chapter, and a complete **Glossary** is found at the end of the book. Each chapter also contains a numbered **Summary** and four **Critical-Thinking Questions** that help students review material and assess their understanding. Following these are a number of **Applications and Exercises**, which provide students with activities to do on or near the campus. Finally, each chapter ends with an annotated listing of worthwhile **Sites to See** on the Internet.

Outstanding images: photography and fine art. This book offers the finest and most extensive program of photography and artwork available in any sociology textbook. The eighth edition of *Sociology* displays more than 100 examples of fine art as well more than 300 color photographs—more than ever before. Each of these images is carefully selected by the author and appears with an insightful caption. Moreover, both photographs and artwork present people of various social backgrounds and historical periods. For example, alongside art by well-known Europeans such as Vincent Van Gogh and U.S. artists including George Tooker, this edition has paintings by celebrated African American artists Jacob Lawrence and Henry Ossawa Tanner, outstanding Latino artists Frank Romero and Diego Rivera, and the engaging Australian painter and feminist Sally Swain.

Thought-provoking theme boxes. Although boxed material is common to introductory texts, *Sociology, Eighth Edition*, provides a wealth of uncommonly good boxes. Each chapter typically contains four boxes, which fall into five types that amplify central themes of the text. **Global Sociology** boxes provoke readers to think about their own way of life by examining the fascinating social diversity that characterizes our world. **Social Diversity** boxes focus on multicultural issues and amplify the voices of women and people of color. **Applying Sociology** boxes, new to this edition, show the value of applying the sociological perspective to the world around us—especially the work we do. **Critical Thinking** boxes teach students to ask sociological questions about their surroundings, and help them evaluate important, controversial issues. Each Critical-Thinking box is followed by three "What do you think?" questions. **Controversy & Debate** boxes conclude each chapter by presenting several points of view on an issue of contemporary importance. Three "Continue the debate" questions, which follow each box, are sure to stimulate spirited class discussion.

Sociology, Eighth Edition, contains ninety-three boxes in all. Fourteen are new and many more are revised and updated in this revision. A complete listing of this text's boxes appears after the table of contents.

An unparalleled program of sixty-seven global and national maps. One of the most popular features of *Sociology, Eighth Edition*, is the program of global and national maps. Windows on the World Global Maps—thirty in all and many updated for this edition—are truly sociological maps offering a comparative look at income disparity, favored languages and religions, the extent of prostitution, permitted marriage forms, the degree of political freedom, the incidence of HIV infection, and a host of other issues. The Global Maps use the non-Eurocentric projection devised by cartographer Arno Peters that accurately portrays the relative size of all the continents. A complete listing of the Windows on the World Global Maps follows the table of contents.

Seeing Ourselves National Maps—thirty-seven in all, with twelve new to this edition—help to illuminate the social diversity of the United States. Most of these maps offer a close-up look at all 3,014 U.S. counties, highlighting suicide rates, per capita income, labor force participation, college attendance, divorce rates, teen pregnancy rates, most widespread religious affiliation, political apathy, and, as measures of popular culture, where baseball fans live or where households drink more wine or beer. Each National Map includes an explanatory caption that poses several questions to stimulate students' thinking about social forces. A complete listing of the Seeing Ourselves National Maps follows the table of contents.

INNOVATION: CHANGES IN THE EIGHTH EDITION

Each new edition of *Sociology* has broken new ground, one reason that more than 2 million students have learned from this sociological best-seller. A revision raises high expectations, but, after several years of planning and hard work, we are pleased to offer a major revision that makes the text better than ever. Here is a brief overview of the innovations that define *Sociology, Eighth Edition*:

New technology that keeps getting better! Last time around, we offered the first complete high-tech learning package, combining a text, CD-ROM, and Companion Website™. New to this edition is a supersite for sociology called *Sociology Place*. Put the text, the CD-ROM, and the Web sites together for more information *and more ways to learn* than ever before. For additional details on all our textbooks as well as quick links to dozens of sociology sites, visit the author's personal Web site at http://www.thesociologypage.com or http://www.macionis.com

A new chapter on sexuality. The eighth edition has a new chapter. Chapter 9 ("Sexuality") is a sociological look at a central dimension of human existence. The chapter begins by explaining the biological and cultural foundations of sexuality, surveys changing sexual attitudes in the United States, explores the myths and realities surrounding sexual orientation, and then explores sexual controversies including teen pregnancy, pornography, prostitution, and sexual violence. The chapter concludes with various theoretical analyses of sexuality.

A new synthesis: population, urbanization, and the environment. This revision draws three closely related issues together into a new combined chapter. Chapter 22 begins by outlining the study of population, moves to the steady rise in the share of humanity residing in cities, and then links both topics to the state of the physical environment.

A greater focus on applications. This text helps students apply the power of sociology to their present lives and future careers. We've added a set of Applying Sociology theme boxes (nineteen in all). Moreover, at the end of each chapter is a listing of Applications and Exercises that suggests ways students can apply lessons to their campus and community. Finally, many chapters in the new edition have major sections that apply the power of sociology to a wide range of current issues.

Sites to See. Another new feature to the eighth edition is a listing of worthwhile Internet sites. Placed at the end of each chapter along with explanatory annotations, these sites will introduce students to a wide range of organizations involved in relevant research or social action.

Major reworking of two chapters. Chapter 2 ("Sociological Investigation") and Chapter 7 ("Groups and Organizations") are both heavily revised to reflect recent changes in these important areas of study.

More maps! The only way to improve on our colorful maps is to provide more of them. This edition adds seven maps for a total of sixty-seven: thirty Window on the World global maps and thirty-seven Seeing Ourselves national maps. Fourteen of these maps are new to this edition.

New chapter-opening vignettes. This revision keeps the best of the popular chapter-opening vignettes and adds sixteen new ones; overall, two-thirds of the openings are new to this edition.

Many new boxes. A total of ninety-three boxes supports five themes of the text: Global Sociology, Social Diversity, Critical Thinking, Applying Sociology, and, focusing on social policy, Controversy & Debate. Many boxes are revised and updated; fourteen boxes are new to this edition.

The latest statistical data. Instructors count on this text for including the very latest statistical data. The eighth edition comes through again, making use of data from the Internet as well as conventional bound publications of various government agencies and private organizations. The author and Carol A. Singer, a professional government documents librarian at Bowling Green State University (Ohio), have worked together to ensure that the newest statistics are used throughout the text—in many cases for 1998, and even for 1999 and 2000. In addition, the author regularly reviews more than one dozen journals as well as media publications. The result: Readers will find 250 new research citations as well as references to many familiar current events.

New topics. The eighth edition of *Sociology* is completely updated with new and expanded discussions in every chapter. Here is a partial listing, by chapter:

- **Chapter 1 The Sociological Perspective**: A new chapter opening contrasts the rich and poor in Boston, Massachusetts; the applied material includes three Applying Sociology boxes; there are updates of suicide patterns in the United States and around the world; the discussion of social change and the emergence of sociology has been reorganized; find an update on women in professional sports as well as a new Diversity Snapshot figure on racial stereotyping and football; the chapter concludes with an updated and expanded listing of Applications and Exercises as well as new Sites to See.

- **Chapter 2 Sociological Investigation**: With a major rewrite, the discussion now contrasts scientific sociology, interpretive sociology, and critical sociology to better reflect the multimethodological character of the discipline today; a new Applying Sociology box shows how small changes in wording affect responses to survey questions; the chapter ends with an updated and expanded list of Applications and Exercises as well as new Sites to See.

- **Chapter 3 Culture**: A new chapter opening traces the rise of hip-hop culture; new national maps showing beer and wine consumption illustrate high and popular culture; many updated examples and illustrations are found throughout the chapter; the chapter ends with an updated and expanded list of Applications and Exercises as well as new Sites to See.

- **Chapter 4 Society**: The chapter opening includes an update on Africa's Tuareg nomads; a new global map shows computer use around the world; several new Applications and Exercises as well as new Sites to See are found at the end of the chapter.

- **Chapter 5 Socialization**: This chapter includes an update on U.S. television watching, a new National Map on newspaper readership across the United States, and recent research on television and violence; a new figure highlights young people's trust in parents; expanded and updated Applications and Exercises are included as well as numerous new Sites to See.

- **Chapter 6 Social Interaction in Everyday Life**: This chapter now has more emphasis on applications throughout; a new Applying Sociology box asks if we can detect when someone is lying and features photos that compare real and false expressions; an expanded Applications and Exercises section includes new on-campus activities; there are also several new Web destinations in the Sites to See.

- **Chapter 7 Groups and Organizations**: A major reorganization of this chapter adds discussion of early scientific management and traces the evolution of organizations toward a flatter, flexible, "intelligent" form; the chapter also contrasts the rise of intelligent organizations doing highly skilled postindustrial work with the countertrend toward low-skill service work often called "McJobs."

- **Chapter 8 Deviance**: A new chapter opening points out weaknesses in the criminal justice system; there are new sections on corporate crime and organized crime; all crime statistics are updated; there is a new Applying Sociology box explaining the recent decline in violent crime; the chapter ends with new Applications and Exercises as well as new Sites to See.

- **Chapter 9 Sexuality**: This new chapter highlights the socially constructed character of human sexuality; the chapter takes a global view of sexuality and also surveys a number of sexuality issues, from sexual orientation to sexual violence; there are several new boxes, a new national map on births to teenage women, and new Applications and Exercises as well as new Sites to See.

• **Chapter 10 Social Stratification**: This chapter has a reorganized discussion of caste and class; recent changes in the British aristocracy are noted; also updated is discussion of the salaries of corporate CEOs in the United States; new Applications and Exercises and new Sites to See conclude the chapter.

• **Chapter 11 Social Class in the United States**: A new opening contrasts California's Silicon Valley wealth with New York's Lower East Side poverty; find updates on income and wealth disparity in the United States; there are new data tracking rising African American affluence; the chapter concludes with new Applications and Exercises and new Sites to See.

• **Chapter 12 Global Stratification**: A new opening profiles wage slavery in the sweatshops of a Pacific territory controlled by the United States; a dramatic new box describes the culture of slavery in North Africa; the chapter includes updates on global wealth and well-being; several new Sites to See direct students to sources of global data and further study.

• **Chapter 13 Gender Stratification**: A new chapter opening highlights the 1848 Seneca Falls convention and the women's movement it began; a new box investigates female circumcision; the chapter includes statistical updates on women's pay, schooling, and jobs; a new Diversity Snapshot figure details who does the housework in the United States; many of the Applications and Exercises as well as Sites to See are new.

• **Chapter 14 Race and Ethnicity**: A new Social Diversity box highlights the role played by immigrants in the U.S. economy; the chapter adds a new National Map showing the lands controlled by Native Americans at four points over the last two hundred years; updated statistics reflect the social standings of all racial and ethnic categories in the United States; several new Applications and Exercises as well as new Sites to See end the chapter.

• **Chapter 15 Aging and the Elderly**: A new chapter opening highlights the changing (and younger) face of the elderly in the United States; a new section examines the expansion of caregiving in an aging society; there are data updates on the social standing of the elderly throughout the chapter; the entire discussion now offers a more positive take on the aging process.

• **Chapter 16 The Economy and Work**: There is a new chapter opening on the trend toward using temporary workers; find updated statistics on the U.S. labor force—including unemployment rates and the gender, racial, and ethnic composition of the labor force; a new Applying Sociology box highlights corporate welfare; we've added another National Map showing where jobs will be a decade from now; several new Applications and Exercises as well as Sites to See complete the chapter.

• **Chapter 17 Politics and Government**: The chapter includes an update on political freedom around the world; a Global Sociology box provides an update on the politics of Singapore; a new National Map shows where young adults do and do not vote in the United States; there is an update on nuclear proliferation worldwide; the new Sites to See includes Web pages of several organizations concerned with human rights around the world.

• **Chapter 18 Family**: A new chapter opening presents a "family values" court case in Pakistan that pitted young lovers against traditional parents; a research update reports on the causes and consequences of cohabiting; a new Critical Thinking box evaluates the covenant marriage law in Louisiana; there are statistical updates on all the trends regarding family life as well as new Exercises and Applications and Sites to See.

• **Chapter 19 Religion**: A new chapter opening profiles the rising number of Muslims in the United States; a new Critical Thinking box looks at the resurgence of prayer in school; find many statistical updates on various measures of religiosity; a new National Map shows membership in religious organizations across the United States; a number of new Sites to See explore the role of religion in addressing social problems.

• **Chapter 20 Education**: A new chapter opening looks at a controversial school-funding law in Vermont; a new National Map shows the high school dropout rate across the country; a new Social Diversity box explores the "savage inequalities" of U.S. education; statistical updates are included for all measures of educational achievement; the chapter reports on recent trends in the school choice debate.

• **Chapter 21 Health and Medicine**: A new chapter opening describes what happened to women on the island of Fiji after the arrival of television in 1995; a new Global Sociology box describes the free-fall in life expectancy among men following the collapse of the former Soviet Union; the chapter updates all health statistics; listed among the Sites to See are three Web destinations exploring how socially conscious doctors are combating poverty and disease around the world.

• **Chapter 22 Population, Urbanization, and Environment**: This chapter is a new combination of population, urbanization, and environment; a new chapter opening reports on the rapid urban development in Atlanta; find the latest global population figures as well as new demographic data for the United States; there is an update on the development of urban regions and urban sprawl; throughout the chapter the focus is on the interplay of population, urbanization, and the physical environment; many new Applications and Exercises as well as Sites to See complete the chapter.

• **Chapter 23 Collective Behavior and Social Movements**: A new chapter-opening vignette illustrates the mobilization of a social movement across the Internet; expanded coverage of the theories of social movements includes a new discussion of culture theory; several new Applications and Exercises as well as new Sites to See close the chapter.

• **Chapter 24 Social Change: Traditional, Modern, and Postmodern Societies**: A new chapter-opening vignette illustrates the extent of social change over the course of the twentieth century; a new Critical Thinking box evaluates the changing quality of life in the United States; there are many Applications and Exercises as well as new Sites to See.

A WORD ABOUT LANGUAGE

This text's commitment to representing the social diversity of the United States and the world carries with it the responsibility to use language thoughtfully. In most cases, we prefer the terms *African American* and *person of color* to the word *black*. We use the terms *Hispanic* and *Latino* to refer to people of Spanish descent. Most tables and figures refer to "Hispanics" because this is the term the Census Bureau uses when collecting statistical data about our population. Students should realize, however, that many individuals do not describe themselves using these terms. Although the term "Hispanic" is commonly used in the eastern part of the United States, and "Latino" and the feminine form "Latina" are widely heard in the West, across the United States people of Spanish descent identify with a particular ancestral nation, whether it be Argentina, Mexico, some other Latin American country, or Spain or Portugal in Europe.

The same holds for Asian Americans. Although this term is a useful shorthand in sociological analysis, most people of Asian descent think of themselves in terms of a specific country of origin (say, Japan, the Philippines, Taiwan, or Vietnam).

In this text, the term "Native American" refers to all the inhabitants of the Americas (including the Hawaiian Islands) whose ancestors lived here prior to the arrival of Europeans. Here again, however, most people in this broad category identify with their historical society (for example, Cherokee, Hopi, or Zuni). The term "American Indian" designates only those Native Americans who live in the continental United States, not including Native peoples living in Alaska or Hawaii.

Learning to think globally also leads us to use language carefully. This text avoids the word "American"—which literally designates two continents—to refer to just the United States. For example, when referring to this country, the term "U.S. economy" is more correct than the "American economy." This convention may seem a small point, but it implies the significant recognition that we in this country represent only one society (albeit a very important one) in the Americas.

A WORD ABOUT WEB SITES

Because of the increasing importance of the Internet, each chapter of this new edition of *Sociology* ends with a listing of Sites to See. The goal is to provide sites that are current, informative, and, above all, relevant to the sociological discussion at hand. However, students should be mindful of several potential problems.

First, Web sites change all the time. Prior to publication, we made every effort to ensure that the sites listed meet our standards. But readers may find that some sites have changed substantially or have gone away entirely. Obviously, this is a problem beyond our control.

Second, sites have been selected with the goal of providing different perspectives on various issues. The listing of a site does not imply that the author or publisher agrees with everything—or even anything—on the site. Indeed, we urge students to examine all sites critically.

Third, many of the Web sites listed in this text are popular. Because many people visit them, the sites may be slow in responding. Please be patient or, if a site is too busy, simply move on.

Finally, we welcome students and faculty to suggest sites to be included in future editions. You can send e-mail to the author at macionis@kenyon.edu

SUPPLEMENTS

Sociology, Eighth Edition, is the heart of an unprecedented multimedia learning package that includes a wide range of proven instructional aids as well as several new ones. As the author of the text, I maintain a keen interest in all the supplements to ensure their quality and integration with the text. The supplements for this revision have been thoroughly updated, improved, and expanded.

FOR THE INSTRUCTOR

Annotated Instructor's Edition. The AIE is a complete student text annotated by the author on every page. Annotations—which have been thoroughly revised for this edition—have won praise from instructors for enriching class presentations. Margin notes include summaries of research findings, statistics from the United States or other nations, insightful quotations, information highlighting patterns of social diversity in the United States, and high-quality survey data from the National Opinion Research Center (NORC) *General Social Survey* and the Inter-university Consortium for Political and Social Research (CPSR) *World Values Survey.*

Data File. This is the "instructor's manual" that is of interest even to those who have never used one before. The *Data File* provides far more than detailed chapter outlines and discussion questions; it contains statistical profiles of the United States and other nations, summaries of important developments and significant research, and supplemental lecture material for every chapter of the text. The *Data File* is available in Windows format, as well as the traditional print version.

Test Item File. A revised test item file is available in both printed and computerized forms. The file contains 2400 items—100 per chapter—in multiple-choice, true-false, and essay formats. Questions are identified as simple "recall" items or more complex inferential issues, and the answers to all questions are page referenced to the text. Prentice Hall Custom Test is a test generator designed to allow the creation of personalized exams. It is available in DOS, Windows, and Macintosh formats. Prentice Hall also provides a test preparation service to users of this text that is as easy as a call to our toll-free 800 number. Please contact your local Prentice Hall representative for this number.

Core Test Item File, Second Edition. This general test item file consists of over 350 additional test questions appropriate for introductory sociology courses. All of the questions have been class tested, and an item analysis is available for every question.

Film/Video Guide: Prentice Hall Introductory Sociology, Sixth Edition. Keyed to the chapters of this text, this guide describes more than 300 films and videos appropriate for classroom viewing. It also provides summaries, discussion questions, and rental sources for each film and video.

ABCNEWS **ABC News/Prentice Hall Video Library for Sociology.** Few will dispute that video is the most dynamic supplement you can use to enhance a class. However, the quality of the video material and how well it relates to your course still make all the difference. Prentice Hall and ABC News are working together to bring to you the best and most comprehensive video ancillaries available in the college market.

Through its wide variety of award-winning programs—*Nightline, Business World, On Business, This Week, World News Tonight, 20/20,* and *The Health Show*—ABC offers a resource for feature and documentary-style videos related to the chapters in *Sociology, Eighth Edition.* The programs have high production quality, present substantial content, and are hosted by well-versed, well-known anchors.

The authors and editors of Prentice Hall have carefully selected videos on topics that complement *Sociology, Eighth Edition,* and included notes on how to use them in the classroom. An excellent video guide in the *Data File* carefully and completely integrates the videos into your lecture. The guide has a synopsis of each video showing its relation to the chapter and discussion questions to help students focus on how concepts and theories apply to real-life situations.

Volume I—Social Stratification
Volume II—Marriage/Families
Volume III—Race/Ethnic Relations
Volume IV—Criminology
Volume V—Social Problems
Volume VI—Intro to Sociology I
Volume VII—Intro to Sociology II
Volume VIII—Intro to Sociology III
Volume IX—Social Problems II
Volume X—Marriage/Families II
Volume XI—Race and Ethnic Relations II
Volume XII—Institutions
Volume XIII—Introductory Sociology IV
Volume XIV—Introductory Sociology V

Prentice Hall Introductory Sociology PowerPoint™ Transparencies. Created by Roger J. Eich of Hawkeye Community College, this PowerPoint slide set combines graphics and text in a colorful format to help you convey sociological principles in a new and exciting way. Created in PowerPoint, an easy-to-use, widely available software program, this set contains over 300 slides keyed to each chapter in the text.

Prentice Hall Color Transparencies: Sociology Series VI. Full-color illustrations, charts, and other visual materials from the text as well as outside sources have been selected to make up this useful in-class tool.

Instructor's Guide to Prentice Hall Color Transparencies: Sociology Series VI. This guide offers suggestions for using each transparency in the classroom.

MEDIA SUPPLEMENTS

Companion Website™. In tandem with the text, students and professors can now take full advantage of the Internet to enrich their study of sociology. The Macionis Companion Website™ continues to lead the way in providing students with avenues for delving deeper into the topics covered in the text. Features of the Web site include chapter objectives, study questions, faculty resources, as well as links to interesting material and information from other sites on the Web that will reinforce and enhance the content of each chapter. Visit the site at http://www.prenhall.com/macionis and click on the cover of the Eighth Edition.

Online Learning Solutions. Prentice Hall is committed to providing the growing number of courses being delivered over the Internet by developing relationships with the leading vendors—Blackboard, Web CT, and ecollege.com, as well as our own course management system, Pearson CMS. Through these relationships, we provide premium, book-specific content in the delivery method of your choice. Please contact your local Prentice Hall representative to find out more about our solutions in this area.

Sociology on the Internet: Evaluating Online Resources. This guide focuses on developing the critical-thinking skills necessary to evaluate and use online sources. The guide also provides a brief introduction to navigating the Internet, along with complete references related specifically to the discipline of sociology and how to use the companion Web sites for *Sociology, Eighth Edition.* This supplementary book is free to students when shrinkwrapped as a package with *Sociology, Eighth Edition.* Please contact your local Prentice Hall representative for your packaging options.

Sociology: Interactive Edition. Believing strongly that equal access to learning resources is as important as ever, *Sociology: Interactive Edition* offers students review and study material in a rich multimedia environment. The CD-ROM includes chapter-opening introductions, video application exercises, interactive U.S. and global maps, substantial portions of the text, review questions, chapter summaries, and text-specific Web links. The CD-ROM is free to each student with the purchase of a new textbook.

FOR THE STUDENT

Study Guide. This complete guide helps students to review and reflect on the material presented in *Sociology, Eighth Edition.* Each of the twenty-four chapters in the Study Guide provides an overview of the corresponding chapter in the student text, summarizes its major topics and concepts, offers applied exercises, and features end-of-chapter tests with solutions.

***The New York Times* Supplement, *Themes of the Times*, for Introductory Sociology.** *The New York Times* and Prentice Hall are sponsoring *Themes of the Times*, a program designed to enhance student access to current information relevant to the classroom. Through this program, the core subject matter provided in this text is supplemented by a collection of timely articles from one of the world's most distinguished newspapers, *The New York Times.* These articles demonstrate the vital, ongoing connection between what is learned in the classroom and what is happening in the world around us.

To enjoy the wealth of information of *The New York Times* daily, a reduced subscription rate is available. For information, call toll-free 1-800-631-1222.

Prentice Hall and *The New York Times* are proud to co-sponsor *Themes of the Times.* We hope it will make the reading of both textbooks and newspapers a more dynamic and involving process.

Critical Thinking Audiocassette Tape. In keeping with the text's critical-thinking approach, a sixty-minute audio tape is available to help students think and read critically.

IN APPRECIATION

The conventional practice of designating a single author obscures the efforts of dozens of women and men that have resulted in *Sociology, Eighth Edition.* I would like to express my thanks to the Prentice Hall editorial team, including Phil Miller, division president, Laura Pearson, editorial director, Nancy Roberts, publisher, and Chris DeJohn, senior editor in sociology, for their steady enthusiasm and for supporting our pursuit of innovation and excellence. Day-to-day work on the book is shared by the author and the production team. Susanna Lesan, developmental editor-in-chief at Prentice Hall, has played a vital role in the development of all my texts for more than fifteen years, coordinating and supervising the editorial process. Barbara Reilly, production editor at Prentice Hall, is another key member of the team. Barbara deserves much of the credit for the attractive page layout of the book; indeed, if anyone "sweats the details" more than the author, it is Barbara! Amy Marsh Macionis, the text's "in house" editor, checks virtually everything, untangling awkward phrases and eliminating errors and inconsistencies in all the statistical data. Amy is relentless in her pursuit of quality.

I also have a large debt to the members of the Prentice Hall sales staff, the men and women who have given this text such remarkable support over the years. Thanks, especially, to Beth Gillett Mejia and Judie Lamb who have directed our marketing campaign.

Thanks, too, to Kenny Beck for providing the interior design of the book, which was coordinated in-house by art director Carole Anson. Developmental and copy editing of the manuscript was provided by Harriett Prentiss, Mary Louise Byrd, and Amy Marsh Macionis. Francelle Carapetyan did the research for this edition's new photographs and fine art.

It goes without saying that every colleague knows more about some topics covered in this book than the author does. For that reason, I am grateful to the hundreds of faculty and students who have written to me to offer comments and suggestions. More formally, I am grateful to the following people who have reviewed some or all of this manuscript:

Richard Alford, East Central University
Sally Archer, The College of New Jersey
Patricia S. Astry, SUNY College at Fredonia
Judith Barker, Ithaca College
Paul J. Becker, Morehead State University
Jane Bock, University of Wisconsin—Green Bay
Brent Bruton, Iowa State University
Karen A. Callaghan, Barry University
Lois Easterom, Onondaga Community College
John Ehle, Northern Virginia Community College
Jerry Flattum, University of Minnesota
Dona Fletcher, Sinclair Community College
Abby Foster, University of Colorado at Colorado Springs
Mary Theresa Bonhage Freund, Alma College
Patricia Gagné, University of Louisville
Timothy J. Gallagher, Kent State University
Roma Stouall Hanks, University of South Alabama
Mike Hart, Broward County Community College
Christine L. Himes, Syracuse University
G. David Johnson, University of South Alabama
Edward L. Kain, Southwestern University
N. Jane McCandless, State University of West Georgia
Marguerite Martin, Gonzaga University
Michael Miller, University of Texas at San Antonio
Daniel J. Monti, Boston University
David Naylor, Charleston Southern University
Robert Shelly, Ohio University
Blasco Sobrinho, University of Cincinnati
Dee Southard, Central Washington University
Steven Spitzer, Suffolk University
Leslie Stanley-Stevens, Tarleton University
Larry Stern, Collin County Community College
Jan Thomas, Kenyon College
Tim Tuinstra, Kalamazoo Valley Community College
Rhys H. Williams, Southern Illinois University—Carbondale

I also wish to thank the following colleagues for sharing their wisdom in ways that have improved this book:

Doug Adams (The Ohio State University), Peter Adler (University of Denver), Peter K. Angstadt (Wesley College), Kip Armstrong (Bloomsburg University), Rose Arnault (Fort Hays State University), Grace Auyang (University of Cincinnati, RWC), Paula Barfield (Southwest Texas State University), Scott Beck (Eastern Tennessee State University), Lois Benjamin (Hampton University), Philip Berg (University of Wisconsin, La Crosse), Charlotte Brauchle (Southwest Texas Junior College), Bill Brindle (Monroe Community College), John R. Brouillette (Colorado State University), Valerie Brown (Cuyahoga Community College), Cathryn Brubaker (Georgia Perimeter College), Brent Bruton (Iowa State University), Richard Bucher (Baltimore City Community College), Karen Campbell (Vanderbilt University), Stanley Capela (St. Francis College), Joseph Carroll (Colby-Sawyer College), Lynn Chamberlain (Scott Community College), Robert E. Clark (Midwestern State University), William T. Clute (University of Nebraska at Omaha), Karen Conner (Drake University), Harold Conway (Blinn College), Gerry Cox (Fort Hays State University), Lovberta Cross (Shelby State Community College), Robert Daniels (Mount Vernon Nazarene College), James A. Davis (Harvard University), Nanette J. Davis (Chapman University), Sumati Devadutt (Monroe Community College), Michael Donnelly (University of New Hampshire), Keith Doubt (Northeast Missouri State University), Denny Dubbs (Harrisburg Area Community College), Travis Eaton (Northeast Louisiana State University), Helen Rose Fuchs Ebaugh (University of Houston), John Ehle (Northern Virginia Community College), Roger Eich (Hawkeye Community College), Ivan T. Evens (University of California at San Diego), Heather Fitz Gibbon (The College of Wooster), Kevin Fitzpatrick (University of Alabama-Birmingham), Dona C. Fletcher (Sinclair Community College), Julie Ford (Long Island University), Robin Franck (Southwestern College), Charles Frazier (University of Florida), Karen Lynch Frederick (St. Anselm College), Patricia Gagné (University of Louisville), Pam Gaiter (Collin County Community College), Jarvis Gamble (Owen's Technical College), Steven Goldberg (City College, City University of New York), Charlotte Gotwald (York College of Pennsylvania), Norma B. Gray (Bishop State

Community College), Rhoda Greenstone (DeVry Institute), Jeffrey Hahn (Mount Union College), Harry Hale (Northeast Louisiana State University), Dean Haledjian (Northern Virginia Community College), Dick Haltin (Jefferson Community College), Marvin Hannah (Milwaukee Area Technical College), Melissa Hardy (Florida State University), Charles Harper (Creighton University), Darnell Hawkins (University of Illinois), Phyllis Hay (Alvernia College), Gary Hodge (Collin County Community College), Elizabeth A. Hoisington (Heartland Community College), Sara Horsfall (Stephen F. Austin State University), Peter Hruschka (Ohio Northern University), Alicia Hughes-Jones (Tabor College), Glenna Huls (Camden County College), Jeanne Humble (Lexington Community College), Harry Humphries (Pittsburg State University), Cynthia Imanaka (Seattle Central Community College), Patricia Johnson (Houston Community College), Ed Kain (Southwestern University), Paul Kamolnick (Eastern Tennessee State University), Irwin Kantor (Middlesex County College), Michael Kleiman (University of South Florida), Thomas Korllos (Kent State University), Bonnie Korn Ach (Chapman University), Rita Krasnow (Virginia Western Community College), Donald Kraybill (Elizabethtown College), Michael Lacy (Colorado State University), Michael Levine (Kenyon College), George Lowe (Texas Tech University), Don Luidens (Hope College), Dale A. Lund (University of Utah), Richard J. Lundman (Ohio State University), Larry Lyon (Baylor University), Li-Chen Ma (Lamar University), Setma Maddox (Texas Wesleyan University), Errol Magidson (Richard J. Daley College), Mary Ann Maguire (Tulane University), Garth Massey (University of Wyoming), Allan Mazur (Syracuse University), Karen E. B. McCue (University of New Mexico, Albuquerque), Meredith McGuire (Trinity College), Patrick McGuire (University of Toledo), Jack Melhorn (Emporia State University), Antonio V. Menendez-Alercon (Butler University), George Miller (University of Utah), Ken Miller (Drake University), Michael V. Miller (University of Texas at San Antonio), Richard Miller (Navarro College), Neville M. Morgan (Kentucky State University), Joe Morolla (Virginia Commonwealth University), Craig Nauman (Madison Area Technical College), Toby Parcel (The Ohio State University), Anne Peterson (Columbus State Community College), Marvin Pippert (Roanoke College), C. Leon Pitt (Community College of Beaver County), Lauren Pivnik (Monroe Community College), Scott B. Potter (Marion Technical College), Daniel Quinn (Adrian College), Nevel Razak (Fort Hays State College), Jim Rebstock (Broward Community College), George Reim (Cheltenham High School), Virginia Reynolds (Indiana University of Pennsylvania), Laurel Richardson (The Ohio State University), Keith Roberts (Hanover College), Ellen Rosengarten (Sinclair Community College), Robert A. Rothman (University of Delaware), Howard Schneiderman (Lafayette College), Anne Schulte (Des Moines Area Community College), Ray Scupin (Linderwood College), Steve Severin (Kellogg Community College), Harry Sherer (Irvine Valley College), Walt Shirley (Sinclair Community College), Anson Shupe (Indiana University-Purdue University at Fort Wayne), Ree Simpkins (Missouri Southern State University), Glen Sims (Glendale Community College), John Skvoretz (University of South Carolina), Nancy Sonleitner (University of Oklahoma), Edward J. Steffes (Salisbury State University), Larry Stern (Collin County Community College), George F. Stine (Millersville University), Randy Ston (Oakland Community College), Verta Taylor (The Ohio State University), Vickie H. Taylor (Danville Community College), Mark J. Thomas (Madison Area Technical College), William Tolone (Illinois State University), Len Tompos (Lorain County Community College), Wen-hui Tsai (Indiana University-Purdue University at Fort Wayne), Ronnie E. Turner (Colorado State University), Christopher Vanderpool (Michigan State University), Glenna Van Metre (Wichita State University), Phyllis Watts (Tiffin University), Murray Webster (University of North Carolina, Charlotte), Amy Wharton (Washington State University), Debbie White (Collin County Community College), Marilyn Wilmeth (Iowa University), John Wilson (Duke University), Stuart Wright (Lamar University), William Yoels (University of Alabama, Birmingham), Dan Yutze (Taylor University), Wayne Zapatek (Tarrant County Community College), and Frank Zulke (Harold Washington College).

Finally, I would like to dedicate this book to my wife, Amy, who has recently passed that marker on life's highway that we refer to gently as the Big-Four-Oh. Amy is the kindest and most caring person I know, a loving member of her family and an active and giving person in her community. She contributes much to these books but, more important to me, I am a far better person for our life together.

John J. Macionis

ABOUT THE AUTHOR

John J. Macionis (pronounced ma-SHOW-nis) was born and raised in Philadelphia, Pennsylvania. He received his bachelor's degree from Cornell University and his doctorate in sociology from the University of Pennsylvania. His publications are wide-ranging, focusing on community life in the United States, interpersonal intimacy in families, effective teaching, humor, new information technology, and the importance of global education. He and Nijole V. Benokraitis have edited the companion volume to this text, *Seeing Ourselves: Classic, Contemporary, and Cross-Cultural Readings in Sociology.* Macionis has also authored *Society: The Basics*, the leading brief text in the field, and he collaborates on international editions of the texts: *Sociology: Canadian Edition* (with Linda M. Gerber, from Prentice Hall Canada), *Society: The Basics, Canadian Edition* (with Cecelia Benoit and Mikael Jansson, also from Prentice Hall Canada), and *Sociology: A Global Introduction* (with Ken Plummer, published by Prentice Hall Europe). *Sociology* is also available in various international and foreign language editions. In addition, Macionis and Vincent Parrillo have written the urban studies text, *Cities and Urban Life* (Prentice Hall). The latest on all the Macionis textbooks, as well as news, information, and dozens of Internet links of interest to students and faculty in sociology, can be found at the author's personal Web site, http://www.macionis.com or http://thesociologypage.com Additional information, as well as online study guides for the texts, is available at the Prentice Hall site, http://www.prenhall.com/macionis

John Macionis is Professor and Distinguished Scholar of Sociology at Kenyon College in Gambier, Ohio. During a career of almost twenty-five years at Kenyon, he has chaired the Anthropology-Sociology Department, directed the college's multidisciplinary program in humane studies, and presided over the campus senate and also the college's faculty.

In 1998, the North Central Sociological Association named Macionis recipient of the Award for Distinguished Contribution to Teaching, citing his work with textbooks and his pioneering use of new technology in sociology.

Professor Macionis has been active in academic programs in other countries, having traveled to some fifty nations. In the fall of 1994, he directed the global education course for the University of Pittsburgh's Semester at Sea program, teaching 400 students on a floating campus that visited twelve countries as it circled the globe.

Macionis writes, "I am an ambitious traveler, eager to learn and, through the texts, to share much of what I discover with students, many of whom know so little about the rest of the world. For me, traveling and writing are all dimensions of teaching. First and foremost, I am a teacher—a passion for teaching animates everything I do." At Kenyon, Macionis offers a wide range of upper-level courses, but his favorite course is Introduction to Sociology, which he schedules every semester. He enjoys extensive contact with students and each term invites his students to enjoy a home-cooked meal.

The Macionis family—John, Amy, and children McLean and Whitney—live on a farm in rural Ohio. Their home serves as a popular bed and breakfast where they enjoy visiting with old friends and making new ones. In his free time, John enjoys bicycling through the Ohio countryside, swimming, sailing, and playing oldies rock and roll on his guitar. He is currently learning to play the Scottish bagpipes.

Professor Macionis welcomes (and responds to) comments and suggestions about this book from faculty and students. Write to the Sociology Department, Palme House, Kenyon College, Gambier, Ohio 43022, or direct e-mail to MACIONIS@KENYON.EDU

CHAPTER 1

Jonathan Green
The Spirit, 1944

Oil on canvas, 72 in. × 55 in.
 Collection of Jill Farwell. Photograph by Tim Stamm.

THE SOCIOLOGICAL PERSPECTIVE

On June 17, 1999, friends and family gathered to celebrate two graduations in the city of Boston. One was at a school you probably have heard of—Harvard—which dates back to 1636 and today is a leading university that attracts many of the most capable men and women from across the United States and around the world. The other was a school you probably have not heard of—the Pine Street Inn—a homeless shelter and job-training center.

The two schools are close to each other in a physical sense, standing on opposite sides of the Charles River and separated by just a fifteen-minute ride on the Boston subway. But in a social sense, they are worlds apart.

Sarah Martin is typical of the Harvard graduates: This bright, twenty-two-year-old woman completed high school at the top of her class and was voted "Most Likely to Succeed" by her classmates. At Harvard, she continued to earn high grades and went on to win a spot at Harvard Law School, where she will enroll next fall. After that, she hopes to land a job at one of Boston's top law firms. Chances are, she will.

Fred McLemore is typical of the Pine Street Inn graduates. Now thirty-four, he dropped out of school during the eighth grade and lived for years on the streets as a homeless crack addict. Two years ago, he walked into the shelter, determined to turn his life around. Now trained to process business accounts on a computer, he is about to begin an internship with a local company. If it works out, his boss promises that in several months he will have a regular job (adapted from Edwards, 1999).

The sharp differences in the lives of Harvard and Pine Street graduates catch our attention and lead us to wonder why people's lives take such different courses. The answer is that our lives do not unfold according to sheer chance; nor do we decide for ourselves how to live, creating our biographies with what philosophers call "free will." We do make many important decisions every day, of course, but always within a larger arena called "society"—a family, a campus, a city, a nation, an entire world. The essential wisdom of sociology is that our social world guides our actions and life choices in much the same way that the seasons influence our clothing and activities.

THE SOCIOLOGICAL PERSPECTIVE

Sociology is *the systematic study of human society*. At the heart of sociology is a distinctive point of view called "the sociological perspective."

SEEING THE GENERAL IN THE PARTICULAR

Peter Berger (1963) described the sociological perspective as *seeing the general in the particular*. By this, he meant that sociologists identify general patterns in the behavior of particular people. Although every individual is

We can easily grasp the power of society over the individual by imagining how different our world would be had we been born in place of any of these children from, respectively, Bolivia, Sri Lanka, Ethiopia, Botswana, the People's Republic of China, and El Salvador.

unique, society acts differently on various *categories* of people (say, children compared to adults, women versus men, the rich as opposed to the poor). We begin to think sociologically by realizing how the general categories into which we fall shape our particular life experiences.

This text explores the power of society to shape our thoughts, feelings, and actions. The Harvard graduates mentioned in the opening to this chapter, for example, come from more privileged social backgrounds than the graduates of Pine Street Inn. In general, the more privileged people's social background, the more confident and optimistic they are about their own lives. And with good reason, as they are likely to have more opportunities as well as the training and skills to take advantage of them.

Seeing the world sociologically also makes us aware of the importance of gender. As Chapter 13 ("Gender Stratification") describes, every society attaches meaning to being either female or male and gives women and men different kinds of work and family responsibilities. Here, again, society influences us throughout the course of our lives as we encounter advantages and opportunities depending on our sex.

SEEING THE STRANGE IN THE FAMILIAR

At first, using the sociological perspective amounts to *seeing the strange in the familiar.* This does not mean that sociologists focus on the bizarre elements of society. Rather, looking at the world sociologically means giving

Whenever we come upon people whose habits differ from our own, we become more aware of social patterns. This is why travel is an excellent way to stimulate the sociological perspective. But even within the United States there is striking cultural diversity, which prompts us to become conscious of our social surroundings.

up the familiar idea that human behavior is simply a matter of what people *decide* to do, in favor of the initially strange notion that society has a hand in shaping our lives.

For individualistic North Americans, learning to "see" how society affects us may take a bit of practice. Say someone asked you why you "chose" to enroll at your particular college. In response, you might offer any of the following particular reasons:

"I wanted to stay close to home."

"I got a basketball scholarship."

"With a journalism degree from this university, I can get a good job."

"My girlfriend goes to school here."

"I didn't get in to the school I *really* wanted to attend."

Such responses may well be true. But do they tell the whole story?

Thinking sociologically about going to college, we might first realize that, around the world, perhaps one person in one hundred ever gets a college degree. Even in the United States, had we lived a century ago, the "choice" of going to college probably never would have been an option. Today, a look around the classroom shows that social forces still have much to do with college attendance. Typically, college students are relatively young—generally between eighteen and twenty-four. Why? Because in our society, attending college is linked to this period of life. But more than age is involved, since fewer than half of all young men and women actually end up on campus.

Another factor is cost. Because higher education is so expensive, college students tend to come from families with above-average incomes. As Chapter 20 ("Education") explains, if you are lucky enough to belong to a family earning more than $75,000, you are almost three times as likely to go to college as someone whose family earns less than $20,000 each year. Also, because both race and ethnicity are linked to income, a greater share of white people (68 percent) end up "choosing" to go to college than African Americans (60 percent) and Hispanics[1] (66 percent). Figure 1–1, on page 5, illustrates this social pattern.

[1]Hispanics or Latinos may be of any race; about 85 percent state their race as white. (See "A Word about Language" in the Preface.)

APPLYING SOCIOLOGY

What's in a Name? How Social Forces Affect Personal Choices

Have you ever read "Dear Abby" or "Ann Landers"? These two advice columns have been popular in the United States for decades. Not everyone knows that these women are sisters (twins, actually), nor that they both changed their names: Abby was born Pauline Friedman and Ann was born Esther Friedman.

These two women are among tens of thousands of people in our society who change their names to advance their careers. At first glance, changing one's name seems to be just a matter of personal preference. But take a closer look, from a sociological point of view, at the following list:

1. William Claude Dukenfield
2. Cherilyn Sarkisian
3. Wynona Horowitz
4. Robert Allen Zimmerman
5. Larry Zeigler
6. Frederick Austerlitz
7. Paul Rubenfeld
8. George Kyriakou Panayiotou
9. Annie Mae Bullock
10. Joan Molinsky
11. Malden Sekulovich
12. Jerome Silberman
13. Milton Supman
14. Karen Ziegler
15. Ramon Estevez
16. Henry John Deutschendorf, Jr.
17. Allen Stewart Konigsberg
18. Raquel Tejada
19. Jacob Cohen
20. Lee Yuen Kam

Do you see the pattern? In the past, celebrities of various national backgrounds adopted *English-sounding* names. Why? Because our society accords high social prestige to an Anglo-Saxon background. Once again, we see personal choices guided by social forces.

Today, some young actors still adopt English-sounding names—Thomas Mapother, for example, changed his name to Tom Cruise. But the pattern is changing as more of today's film stars are keeping their non–English-sounding names. Consider Janeane Garofalo, Gary Sinise, Salma Hayek, Maria Bello, Cameron Diaz, John Malkovich, and Leonardo DiCaprio. Why the new pattern? Probably because we all have become more accepting of the multicultural mix of our society.

1. W. C. Fields; 2. Cher; 3. Wynona Ryder; 4. Bob Dylan; 5. Larry King; 6. Fred Astaire; 7. Pee Wee Herman; 8. George Michael; 9. Tina Turner; 10. Joan Rivers; 11. Karl Malden; 12. Gene Wilder; 13. Soupy Sales; 14. Karen Black; 15. Martin Sheen; 16. John Denver; 17. Woody Allen; 18. Raquel Welch; 19. Rodney Dangerfield; 20. Bruce Lee

So it is easy to show that society affects the most personal elements of our lives. The box illustrates how society can influence even how comfortable we feel about our own names.

INDIVIDUALITY IN SOCIAL CONTEXT

Evidence of how social forces affect human behavior comes from the study of suicide. What could be a more "personal" choice than taking one's own life? But Emile Durkheim (1858–1917), one of sociology's pioneers, showed that social forces are at work even in the apparently isolated act of self-destruction.

Examining official records in his native France, Durkheim found that some categories of people were more likely than others to take their own lives. He found that men, Protestants, wealthy people, and the unmarried each had significantly higher suicide rates than did women, Catholics and Jews, the poor, and married people. Durkheim explained the differences in terms of *social integration:* Categories of people with strong social ties had low suicide rates, whereas more individualistic people had high suicide rates.

In the male-dominated society studied by Durkheim, men certainly had more freedom than women. But despite its advantages, freedom also contributes to social isolation and a higher suicide rate. Likewise, individualistic Protestants were more prone to suicide than traditional Catholics and Jews, whose rituals foster stronger social ties. The wealthy have much more economic and personal freedom than the poor but, once again, at the cost of a higher suicide rate. Finally, can you see why single people, compared to married people, are also at greater risk?

A century later, Durkheim's analysis still holds true (Thorlindsson & Bjarnason, 1998). Figure 1–2 shows suicide rates for four categories of people in the United States. In 1997, there were 12.4 recorded suicides for every 100,000 white people, which is twice the rate for African Americans (6.2). For both races, suicide was more common among men than among women. White men (20.2) were more than four times as likely as white women (4.9) to take their own lives. Among African Americans, the rate for men (10.9) was nearly six times higher than for women (1.9). Following Durkheim's logic, the higher suicide rate among white people and men reflects their greater wealth and freedom. On the other hand, the lower rate among women and people of color follows from their limited social choices. Just as in Durkheim's day, then, we can see general sociological patterns in the personal actions of particular individuals.

DIVERSITY SNAPSHOT

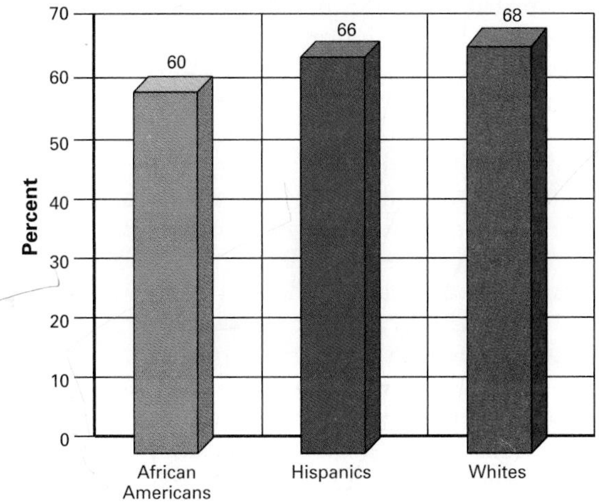

FIGURE 1–1 Share of 1997 High School Graduates Entering College the Following Fall

Source: U.S. National Center for Education Statistics (1999).

DIVERSITY SNAPSHOT

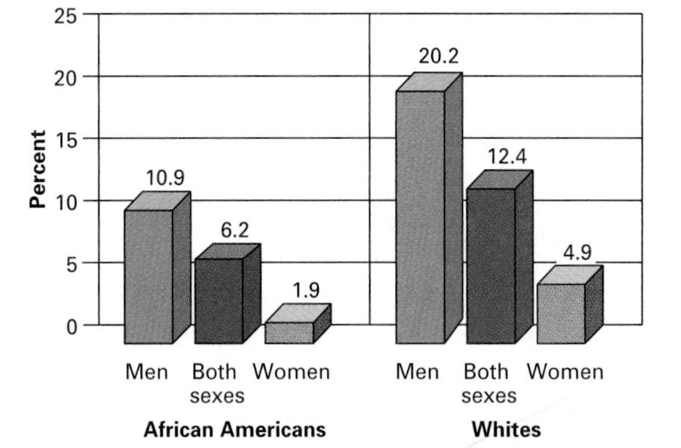

FIGURE 1–2 Rate of Death by Suicide, by Race and Sex, for the United States

Rates indicate the number of deaths by suicide for every 100,000 people in each category for 1997.

Source: U.S. National Center for Health Statistics (1999).

THE IMPORTANCE OF GLOBAL PERSPECTIVE

December 10, 1994, Fez, Morocco. This medieval city—a web of narrow streets and alleyways—is alive with the laughter of playing children, the silence of veiled women, and the steady gaze of men leading donkeys laden with goods. Fez has changed little over the centuries. Here, in northwest Africa, we are just a few hundred miles from the more familiar rhythms of Europe. Yet this place seems a thousand years away. Never have we had such an adventure! Never have we thought so much about home!

As new information technology draws even the farthest reaches of the earth closer to each other, many academic disciplines take a **global perspective,** *the study of the larger world and our society's place in it.* What is the importance of a global perspective for sociology?

First, global awareness is a logical extension of the sociological perspective. Sociology shows us that our place in society profoundly affects our life experiences. It stands to reason, then, that the position of our society in the larger world system affects everyone in the

GLOBAL SOCIOLOGY

The Global Village: A Social Snapshot of Our World

The earth is home to 6.1 billion people who live in the cities and villages of 191 nations. To grasp the social shape of the world, imagine for a moment that the planet's population is reduced to a single settlement of 1,000 people. In this "global village," more than half (610) of the inhabitants are Asian, including 210 citizens of the People's Republic of China. Next, in terms of numbers, we would find 130 Africans, 120 Europeans, 85 from Latin America and the Caribbean, 5 from Australia and the South Pacific, and just 50 North Americans, including 45 of "us" from the United States.

A study of the settlement would reveal some startling facts: The village is a rich place, with a seemingly endless array of goods and services for sale. Yet most people only dream about such treasures, since 80 percent of the village's total income is earned by just 200 people.

For the majority, the greatest problem is getting enough food. Every year, village workers produce more than enough to feed everyone; even so, half the village's people—including most of the children—do not get enough to eat, and many fall asleep hungry. The worst-off 200 residents (who, together, have less money than the richest person in the village) lack both safe drinking water and secure shelter. They are weak and unable to work; every day some of them fall victim to life-threatening diseases.

Villagers boast of their community's many schools, including colleges and universities. About 75 inhabitants have completed a college degree, but almost half of the village's people can neither read nor write.

We in the United States, on average, would be among the richest people in this global village. Although we tend to credit ourselves for living well, the sociological perspective reminds us that our achievements are largely products of the privileged position our nation has in the worldwide social system.

Source: Calculations by the author based on data from United Nations and Population Reference Bureau publications.

United States. The box describes a "global village" to show the social shape of the world and the place of the United States within it.

Global Map 1–1 provides a visual guide to the relative economic development of the world's countries. **High-income countries** are *industrialized nations in which most people have relatively high incomes.*[2] High-income countries include the United States and Canada, most of Western Europe, Israel, Japan, and Australia. Taken together, these forty nations produce most of the world's goods and services and control most of the wealth. On average, individuals in these countries live well, not because they are smarter than anyone else, but because they had the good fortune to be born in an affluent region of the world.

The world's **middle-income countries** are *nations with limited industrialization and moderate personal income.* Individuals living in any of these roughly ninety nations—the countries of Eastern Europe, some of southern Africa, and almost all of Latin America—are more likely to live in rural villages than in cities, to walk or ride tractors, scooters, bicycles, or animals rather than drive automobiles, and to receive only a few years of schooling. Most middle-income countries also have marked social inequality, so that while some people are extremely rich (the sheiks of oil-producing nations in the Middle East, for example), many more lack safe housing and adequate nutrition.

Finally, about half of the world's people live in the sixty **low-income countries,** *nations with little industrialization in which most people are poor.* As Global Map 1–1 shows, most of the poorest countries in the world are in Africa and Asia. Here, again, a few people are very rich, but the majority struggle to get by with poor housing, unsafe water, too little food, limited sanitation, and, perhaps most seriously of all, little chance to improve their lives.

Chapter 12 ("Global Stratification") details the causes and consequences of global wealth and poverty. But every chapter of this text highlights life in the world beyond our own borders for three reasons:

[2]The text favors this terminology over the traditional, but outdated, "First World," "Second World," and "Third World." See Chapter 12 ("Global Stratification") for a full discussion.

One important reason to gain a global understanding is that, living in a high-income society, we scarcely can appreciate the suffering that goes on in much of the world. The life of this Rwandan boy has been shredded by civil war. But even in more peaceful nations of Africa, children have less than a fifty-fifty chance to grow to adulthood.

1. **Societies the world over are increasingly interconnected.** Historically the United States has taken only passing note of the countries beyond its own borders. In recent decades, however, the United States and the rest of the world have become linked as never before. Electronic technology now transmits sounds, pictures, and written documents around the globe in seconds.

   One consequence of new technology, as later chapters explain, is that people all over the world now share many tastes in music, clothing, and food. With their economic clout, high-income countries such as the United States influence other nations, whose people eagerly gobble up our hamburgers, dance to our music, and, more and more, speak the English language.

   We are spreading our way of life around the world; but the larger world, too, has an impact on us. About 1 million documented immigrants entered the United States annually during the 1990s, and we have been quick to adopt many of their fashions and foods as our own, which greatly enhances the racial and cultural diversity of this country.

   Commerce across national boundaries has also created a global economy. Large corporations make and market goods worldwide, and financial markets linked by satellite communication operate around the clock. Stock traders in New York follow the financial markets in Tokyo and Hong Kong, even as wheat farmers in Iowa watch the price of grain in the former Soviet republic of Georgia. With eight out of ten new U.S. jobs involving international trade, global understanding has never been more important.
2. **Many problems that we face in the United States are far more serious elsewhere.** Poverty is a serious problem in this country. But, as Chapter 12 ("Global Stratification") explains, poverty in Latin America, Africa, and Asia is both more common and more serious. Similarly, although women have lower social standing than men in the United States, inequality is much greater in poor countries of the world.
3. **Thinking globally is a good way to learn more about ourselves.** We cannot walk the streets of a distant city without becoming keenly aware of what it means to live in the United States. Making global comparisons also leads to unexpected lessons. For instance, in Chapter 12, we visit a squatter settlement in Madras, India. There, despite a desperate lack of basic material goods, people thrive in the love and support of family members. Why, then, is poverty in the United States associated with isolation and anger? Are material comforts—so crucial to our definition of a "rich" life—the best way to gauge human well-being?

In sum, in an increasingly interconnected world, we can understand ourselves only to the extent that we comprehend others (Macionis, 1993).

WINDOW ON THE WORLD

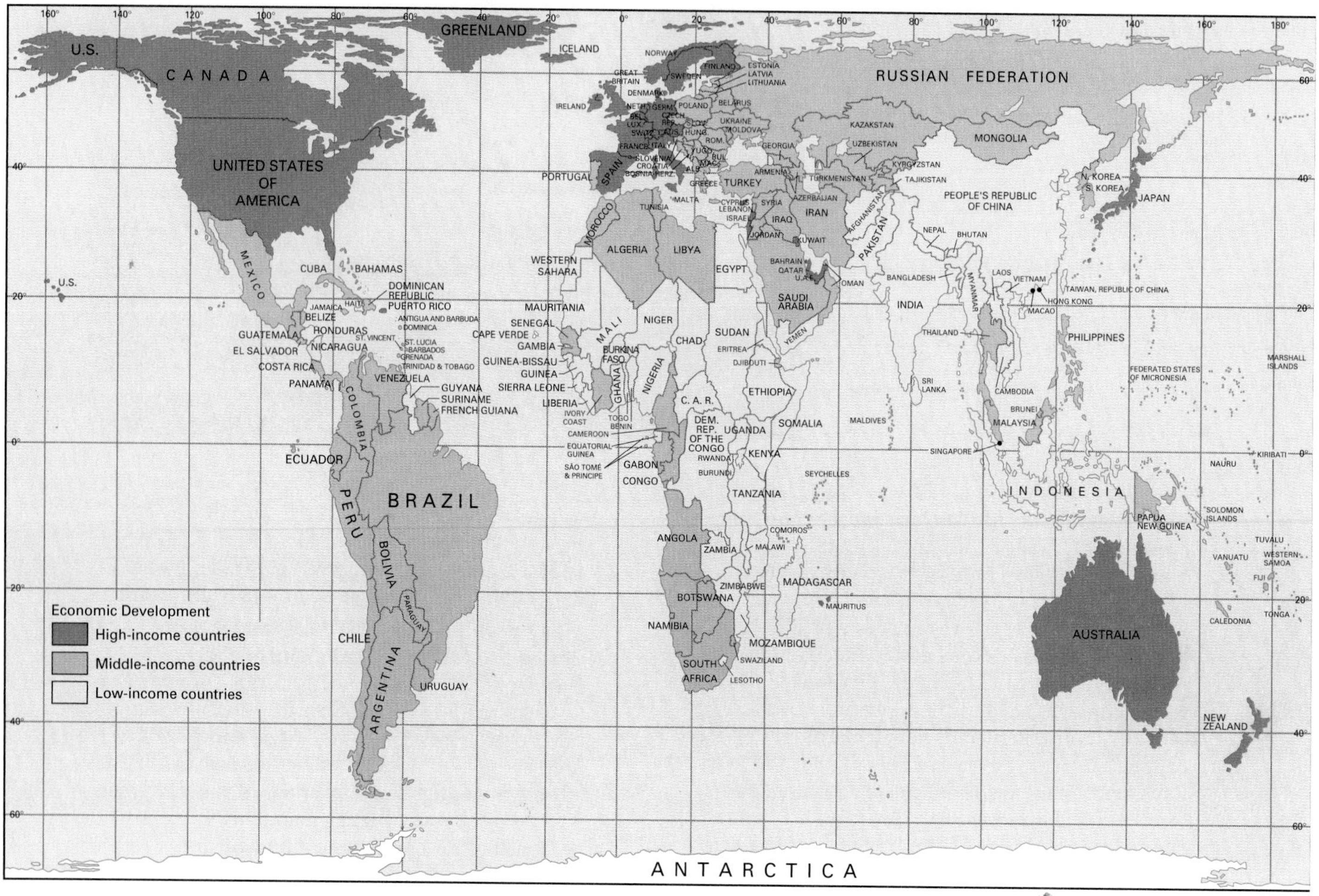

GLOBAL MAP 1–1 Economic Development in Global Perspective

In high-income countries—the United States, Canada, most of the nations of Western Europe, Israel, Australia, and Japan—industrial technology provides people, on average, with material plenty. Middle-income countries—found throughout Latin America and including the nations of Eastern Europe—have limited industrial capacity. Their people have a standard of living about average for the world as a whole but far below that of most people in the United States. These nations also have a significant share of poor people who barely scrape by with meager housing and diet. In the low-income countries of the world, poverty is severe and extensive. Although small numbers of elites live very well in the poorest nations, most people struggle to survive on a small fraction of the income common in the United States.

Note: Data for this map are provided by the World Bank and the United Nations. High-income countries have a per capita gross domestic product (GDP) of at least $10,000. Many are far richer than this, however; the figure for the United States exceeds $29,000. Middle-income countries have a per capita GDP ranging from $2,500 to $10,000. Low-income countries have a per capita GDP below $2,500. Figures used here reflect the new United Nations "purchasing power parities" system. Rather than directly converting income figures into U.S. dollars, this calculation estimates the local purchasing power of each domestic currency.

Sources: Prepared by the author using data from United Nations Development Programme (1995) and The World Bank (1995). Map projection from *Peters Atlas of the World* (1990).

APPLYING THE SOCIOLOGICAL PERSPECTIVE

It is easy to apply the sociological perspective when we encounter people who differ from ourselves—whether around the world or in our own hometowns—because they remind us that society shapes individual lives. But two other kinds of situations help us to see the world sociologically, even before we take a first course in sociology.

SOCIOLOGY AND SOCIAL MARGINALITY

From time to time, we are all "outsiders." For some categories of people, however, being an *outsider*—not part of the dominant group—is part of daily living. The greater people's social marginality, the better able they are to use the sociological perspective.

No African American, for example, grows up in the United States without learning how much race affects personal experience. But white people, as the dominant majority, think less often about race and believe it affects only people of color, not themselves. Women, gay people, individuals with disabilities, and the very old are also, to some degree, "outsiders." People at the margins of social life are aware of social patterns that others rarely think about. To become better at using the sociological perspective, therefore, we must step back from our familiar routines and look at our lives with new awareness and curiosity.

SOCIOLOGY AND SOCIAL CRISIS

Periods of change or crisis make everyone feel a little off balance and prompt us to use the sociological perspective. U.S. sociologist C. Wright Mills (1959) illustrated this idea with the Great Depression of the 1930s. As the unemployment rate soared to 25 percent, people out of work could not help but see general social forces at work in their particular lives. Rather than saying, "Something is wrong with me; I can't find a job," they took a sociological approach and realized, "The economy has collapsed; there are no jobs to be found!"

Just as social change fosters sociological thinking, so sociological thinking can bring about social change. The more we learn how "the system" operates, the more we may wish to change it in some way. Becoming aware of the power of gender, for example, many women and men have actively tried to reduce their traditional differences.

In short, an introduction to sociology is an invitation to learn a new way of looking at familiar patterns of social life. But is this invitation worth accepting? In other words, what are the benefits of applying the sociological perspective?

BENEFITS OF THE SOCIOLOGICAL PERSPECTIVE

Applying the sociological perspective to our daily lives benefits us in four ways:

1. **The sociological perspective helps us assess the truth of "common sense."** Ideas we take for granted are not always true. One good example, noted earlier, is the notion that we are free individuals who are personally responsible for our own lives. If we think people decide their own fate, we may be quick to praise particularly successful people as superior and consider others with more modest achievements personally deficient. A sociological approach, by contrast, encourages us to ask whether commonly held beliefs are actually true and, to the extent that they are not, why they are so widely held.
2. **The sociological perspective helps us assess both opportunities and constraints in our lives.** Sociological thinking leads us to see that, in the game of life, we have a say in how to play our cards, but it is society that deals us the hand. The more we understand the game, the better players we will be. Sociology helps us "size up" our world so we can pursue our goals more effectively.
3. **The sociological perspective empowers us to be active participants in our society.** The more we understand about how society works, the more active citizens we become. For some, this may mean supporting society as it is; others, however, may attempt nothing less than changing the entire world in some way. Evaluating any aspect of social life—whatever your goal—requires identifying social forces and assessing their consequences. In the box, C. Wright Mills describes the power of using the sociological perspective.
4. **The sociological perspective helps us live in a diverse world.** North Americans represent just 5 percent of the world's people, and, as the remaining chapters of this book explain, much of the other 95 percent lead lives that differ dramatically from our own. Still, like people everywhere, we tend to define our own way of

APPLYING SOCIOLOGY

The Sociological Imagination: Turning Personal Problems into Public Issues

The power of the sociological perspective lies not just in changing individual lives but in transforming society. As C. Wright Mills saw it, society, not people's personal failings, is the cause of poverty and other social problems. Using the sociological imagination, then, brings people together by turning personal *problems* into public *issues.*

In the following excerpt* Mills explains the need for a sociological imagination:

> When a society becomes industrialized, a peasant becomes a worker; a feudal lord is liquidated or becomes a businessman. When classes rise or fall, a man is employed or unemployed; when the rate of investment goes up or down, a man takes new heart or goes broke. When wars happen, an insurance salesman becomes a rocket launcher; a store clerk, a radar man; a wife lives alone; a child grows up without a father. Neither the life of an individual nor the history of a society can be understood without understanding both.
>
> Yet men do not usually define the troubles they endure in terms of historical change. . . . The well-being they enjoy, they do not usually impute to the big ups and downs of the society in which they live. Seldom aware of the intricate connection between the patterns of their own lives and the course of world history, ordinary men do not usually know what this connection means for the kind of men they are becoming and for the kinds of history-making in which they might take part. They do not possess the quality of mind essential to grasp the interplay of men and society, of biography and history, of self and world. . . .
>
> What they need . . . is a quality of mind that will help them to [see] . . . what is going on in the world and . . . what may be happening within themselves. It is this quality . . . that . . . may be called the sociological imagination.

*In this excerpt, C. Wright Mills uses "man" and male pronouns to apply to all people. Note that even an outspoken critic of society such as Mills reflected the conventional writing practices of his time as far as gender was concerned.

Source: Mills (1959:3–5).

life as "right," "natural," and "better." The sociological perspective encourages us to think critically about the relative strengths and weaknesses of all ways of life—including our own.

SOCIOLOGY, POLICY, AND CAREERS

The benefits of sociology go well beyond personal growth. Sociologists have helped shape public policy and law in countless ways, involving school desegregation, school busing, pornography, and social welfare. The work that Lenore Weitzman (1985) did on the financial hardships facing women after divorce, for example, "had a real impact on public policy and resulted in the passage of fourteen new laws in California" (1996:538).

A background in sociology is also good preparation for the working world. According to the American Sociological Association, sociologists are hired for literally hundreds of jobs in fields such as advertising, banking, criminal justice, education, government, health care, public relations, and research (Billson & Huber, 1993).

Most men and women who continue beyond a bachelor's degree to earn advanced training in sociology go on to careers in teaching and research. But an increasing number of professional sociologists work in all sorts of applied fields. Clinical sociologists, for example, work with troubled clients much as clinical psychologists do. A basic difference, however, is that, while psychologists focus on the individual, sociologists locate difficulties in a person's web of social relationships. Another type of applied sociology is evaluation research. In today's cost-conscious political climate, administrators must evaluate the effectiveness of virtually every kind of program and policy. Sociologists—especially those with advanced research skills—are in high demand for this kind of work.

The birth of sociology was prompted by rapid social change. The discipline developed in those regions of Europe where the Industrial Revolution most disrupted traditional ways of life, drawing people from isolated villages to rapidly growing industrial cities.

THE ORIGINS OF SOCIOLOGY

Like the "choices" made by individuals, major historical events rarely just happen. So it was that the birth of sociology resulted from powerful social forces.

SOCIAL CHANGE AND SOCIOLOGY

Striking transformations during the eighteenth and nineteenth centuries greatly changed European society. Three changes are especially important to the development of sociology: the rise of a factory-based industrial economy, the explosive growth of cities, and new ideas about democracy and political rights.

A New Industrial Economy

During the European Middle Ages, most people tilled fields near their homes or engaged in small-scale *manufacturing* (a word derived from Latin words meaning "to make by hand"). But by the end of the eighteenth century, inventors had used new sources of energy—the power of moving water and then steam—to operate large machines in mills and factories. Now, instead of laboring at home or in tightly knit groups, workers became part of a large and anonymous labor force, toiling for strangers who owned the factories. This change in the system of production separated families and weakened the traditions that had governed community life for centuries.

The Growth of Cities

Across Europe, factories drew people in need of work. Along with this "pull" came the "push" of the "enclosure movement." Landowners fenced off more and more ground, turning farms into grazing land for sheep—the source of wool for the thriving textile mills. Without land, countless tenant farmers left the countryside in search of work in the new factories.

Cities grew to unprecedented size. The new urban dwellers contended with mounting social problems, including pollution, crime, and homelessness. Living on streets crowded with strangers, they adapted to the new, impersonal social environment.

Political Change

During the Middle Ages, when people viewed society as an expression of God's will, royalty claimed to rule by "divine right," and each person up and down the social ladder played a part in the holy plan. This theological

Here we see Copernicus, the sixteenth-century astronomer, taking careful measurements of the world. Just as Copernicus challenged the common sense of his day, sociologists such as Auguste Comte later argued that society is neither fixed by God's will nor set by human nature. On the contrary, Comte claimed, society is a system we can study scientifically, and, based on what we learn, we can act intentionally to improve our lives.

view of society is captured in lines from the old Anglican hymn "All Things Bright and Beautiful":

> The rich man in his castle,
> The poor man at his gate,
> God made them high and lowly
> And ordered their estate.

But economic development and the rapid growth of cities soon brought new political ideas. By about 1600, tradition was under spirited attack. In the writings of Thomas Hobbes (1588–1679), John Locke (1632–1704), and Adam Smith (1723–1790), we see a shift in focus from people's moral obligations to God and their rulers to the idea that people should pursue their own self-interests. In the new political climate philosophers spoke of *individual liberty* and *individual rights*. Echoing Locke, our own Declaration of Independence asserts that every individual has "certain unalienable rights," including "life, liberty, and the pursuit of happiness."

The French Revolution that began in 1789 symbolized this dramatic break with political and social tradition. The French social analyst Alexis de Tocqueville (1805–1859) declared that the changes in society brought about by the French Revolution amounted to "nothing short of the regeneration of the whole human race" (1955:13; orig. 1856).

A New Awareness of Society

Huge factories, exploding cities, a new spirit of individualism—these changes combined to make people aware of their surroundings. As the social ground trembled under people's feet, the new discipline of sociology was born in England, France, and Germany—precisely where the changes were greatest.

SCIENCE AND SOCIOLOGY

The nature of society fascinated the brilliant thinkers of the ancient world, including the Chinese philosopher K'ung Fu-tzu, or Confucius, (551–479 B.C.E.) and the Greek philosophers Plato (c. 427–347 B.C.E.) and Aristotle (384–322 B.C.E.).[3] Later, the Roman emperor Marcus Aurelius (121–180), the medieval thinkers St. Thomas Aquinas (c. 1225–1274) and Christine de Pizan (c. 1363–1431), and the great English playwright William Shakespeare (1564–1616) took up the question.

Yet these thinkers were more interested in envisioning the ideal society than in analyzing society as it really was. In creating their new discipline, sociology's pioneers certainly cared how society could be improved, but their major goal was to understand society as it actually operates. It was the French social thinker Auguste Comte (1798–1857) who coined the term *sociology* in 1838 to describe this new way of thinking. Thus, sociology is among the youngest academic disciplines—far newer than history, physics, or economics, for example.

Comte (1975; orig. 1851–54) saw sociology as the product of a three-stage historical development.

---

[3]Throughout this text, the abbreviation B.C.E. designates "before the common era." We use this terminology in place of the traditional B.C. ("before Christ") in recognition of the religious plurality of our society. Similarly, in place of the traditional A.D. (*anno Domini*, or "in the year of our Lord"), we employ the abbreviation C.E. ("common era").

We can use the sociological perspective to look at sociology itself. All of the most widely recognized pioneers of the discipline were men. This is because, in the nineteenth century, it was all but unheard of for women to be college professors, and few women took a central role in public life. But women, such as Harriet Martineau in England and Jane Addams in the United States, made contributions to sociology that we now recognize as important and lasting.

During the earliest *theological stage*, from the beginning of human history to the end of the European Middle Ages about 1350 C.E., people took a religious view of society, seeing it as an expression of God's will.

With the Renaissance, the theological approach gave way to what Comte called the *metaphysical stage*. During this period, people understood society as a natural rather than a supernatural phenomenon. Thomas Hobbes (1588–1679), for example, thought that society reflected not the perfection of God so much as the failings of a selfish human nature.

What Comte called the *scientific stage* of history began with the work of early scientists such as the Polish astronomer Copernicus (1473–1543), the Italian astronomer and physicist Galileo (1564–1642), and the English physicist and mathematician Isaac Newton (1642–1727). Comte's contribution came in applying the scientific approach, which was first used to study the physical world, to the study of society.[4]

Comte thus favored **positivism,** defined as *a way of understanding based on science.* As a positivist, Comte believed that society conforms to invariable laws, much as the physical world operates according to gravity and other laws of nature.

At the beginning of the twentieth century, sociology emerged as an academic discipline in the United States, strongly influenced by Comte's ideas. Today, most sociologists still consider science a crucial part of sociology. But, as Chapter 2 ("Sociological Investigation") explains, we now realize that human behavior is far more complex than the movement of planets or even the actions of other living things. This is because humans are creatures of imagination and spontaneity, so that our behavior can never be fully explained by any rigid "laws of society." In addition, early sociologists like Karl Marx (1818–1883), whose ideas are discussed in Chapter 4 ("Society"), were deeply troubled by the striking inequality of the new industrial society. Marx wanted the new discipline of sociology not just to understand society but to bring about change toward social justice.

[4]Illustrating Comte's stages, the ancient Greeks and Romans viewed the planets as gods; Renaissance metaphysical thinkers saw them as astral influences (giving rise to astrology); by the time of Galileo, scientists understood planets as natural objects behaving in orderly ways.

MARGINAL VOICES

Auguste Comte and Karl Marx stand among the giants of sociology. In recent years, though, we have come to see the important contribution that others—pushed to the margins of society because of gender or race—have made.

Harriet Martineau (1802–1876), born to a wealthy English family, first made her mark in 1853 by translating the writings of Auguste Comte from French into English. Subsequently, she became a noted scholar in her own right, revealing the evils of slavery and arguing for laws to protect factory workers and to advance the standing of women.

In the United States, Jane Addams (1860–1935) was a sociological pioneer. Trained as a social worker, Addams spoke out on behalf of immigrants who were entering the nation at the rate of 1 million per year. In 1889, Addams founded Hull House, a settlement house in Chicago that provided assistance to immigrant families.

SEEING OURSELVES

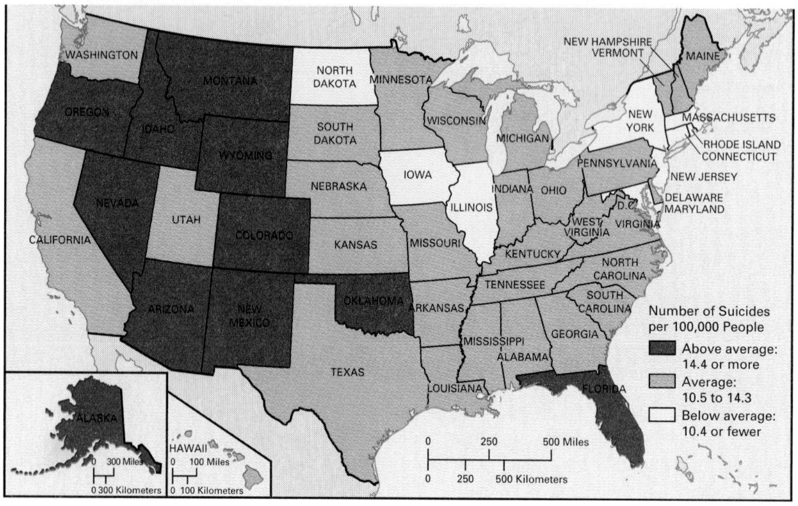

NATIONAL MAP 1–1
Suicide Rates across the United States

This map shows which states have high, average, and low suicide rates. Look for patterns. By and large, high suicide rates occur where people live far apart from one another. More densely populated states, on the other hand, have low suicide rates. Do these data support or contradict Durkheim's theory of suicide? Why?

Source: U.S. National Center for Health Statistics (1999).

She also gathered sociologists and politicians to discuss the urban problems of the day. For her work on behalf of immigrants, Addams received the Nobel Peace Prize in 1931.

An important contribution to understanding race in the United States was made by another sociological pioneer, William Edward Burghardt Du Bois (1868–1963). Born to a poor Massachusetts family, Du Bois enrolled in Fisk University in Nashville, Tennessee, and then Harvard University, where he earned the first doctorate awarded by that university to a person of color. Like Martineau and Addams, Du Bois believed sociologists should try to solve social problems. He therefore studied the black community (1899), spoke out against racial inequality, and served as a founding member of the National Association for the Advancement of Colored People (NAACP).

Widespread belief in the inferiority of women and African Americans kept Martineau, Addams, and Du Bois at the margins of sociology. Looking back with a sociological eye, we can see how the forces of society were at work shaping even the history of sociology itself.

SOCIOLOGICAL THEORY

Weaving observations into understanding brings us to another aspect of sociology: theory. A **theory** is *a statement of how and why specific facts are related.* More to the point, the job of sociological theory is to explain social behavior in the real world.

Recall Emile Durkheim's theory that categories of people with low social integration (men, Protestants, the wealthy, and the unmarried) are especially prone to suicide. As Durkheim pondered the issue of suicide, he considered any number of possible theories. But which one was correct?

To evaluate a theory, as the next chapter explains, sociologists gather evidence using various methods of scientific research. Facts allow sociologists to confirm some theories while rejecting or modifying others. Thus, Durkheim collected data that revealed patterns showing certain categories of people are more likely to commit suicide. These data allowed Durkheim to settle on a theory that best squared with all available evidence. National Map 1–1 displays the suicide rate for each of the fifty states and gives you a chance to do some theorizing of your own.

In building theory, sociologists face two basic questions: What issues should we study? How should we connect the facts? How they answer these questions depends on their theoretical "road map" or paradigm (Kuhn, 1970). A **theoretical paradigm** is *a basic image of society that guides thinking and research.* The three major paradigms in sociology are the structural-functional paradigm, the social-conflict paradigm, and the symbolic-interaction paradigm.

The approach of the structural-functional paradigm is conveyed by the painting St. Regis Indian Reservation *by Amy Jones (1937). Here we see society composed of major rounds of life, each serving a particular purpose that contributes to the operation of the entire system.*

Amy Jones, *St. Regis Indian Reservation*, 1937. Photo courtesy Janet Marqusee Fine Arts Ltd.

THE STRUCTURAL-FUNCTIONAL PARADIGM

The **structural-functional paradigm** is *a framework for building theory that sees society as a complex system whose parts work together to promote solidarity and stability.* As its name suggests, this paradigm points to **social structure,** meaning *any relatively stable pattern of social behavior.* Social structure gives our lives shape, whether it be in families, the workplace, or the classroom. Second, this paradigm looks for a structure's **social functions,** or *consequences for the operation of society as a whole.* All social structure—from a simple handshake to complex religious rituals—functions to keep society going, at least in its present form.

The structural-functional paradigm owes much to Auguste Comte, who pointed out the need for social integration during a time of rapid change. Emile Durkheim, who helped establish sociology in French universities, also based his work on this approach. A third structural-functional pioneer was the English sociologist Herbert Spencer (1820–1903). Spencer compared society to the human body. Just as the structural parts of the human body—the skeleton, muscles, and various internal organs—function interdependently to help the entire organism survive, social structures work together to preserve society. The structural-functional paradigm, then, organizes sociological observations by identifying various structures of society and investigating their functions.

As sociology developed in the United States, many of the ideas of Comte, Spencer, and Durkheim were carried forward by Talcott Parsons (1902–1979), the major U.S. proponent of the structural-functional paradigm. Parsons treated society as a system and sought to identify the basic tasks that any and all societies must perform to survive and the ways they accomplish these tasks.

Contemporary U.S. sociologist Robert K. Merton critically expanded our understanding of the concept of social function. Merton (1968) explains, first, that people rarely perceive all the functions of social structure. He describes as **manifest functions** *the recognized and intended consequences of any social pattern.* By contrast, **latent functions** are *consequences that are largely unrecognized and unintended.* To illustrate, the obvious functions of our nation's system of higher education include providing young people with the information and skills they need to perform jobs. Perhaps just as important, although less often acknowledged, is college's function as a "marriage broker," bringing together people of similar social backgrounds. Another latent function of higher education is keeping millions of young people out of the labor market where, presumably, many of them would not find jobs.

Second, Merton explains, social patterns affect various members of a society differently. For example, conventional families may provide a good setting for rearing children, but they also confer privileges on men while limiting the opportunities of women.

Merton makes a third important point: Social structure is not always useful. **Social dysfunctions** are *a social pattern's undesirable consequences for the operation of society.* People usually disagree about what is useful or harmful. What is functional for one category of people (say, factory owners or landlords) may well be dysfunctional for another category of people (factory workers or tenants).

The painting Furnishings, *by Paul Marcus, presents the essential wisdom of social-conflict theory: Society operates in a way that conveys wealth, power, and privilege to some at the expense of others. Looking at the painting, what are most of the people doing? What do you make of the head hanging on the wall? The classical scene between the drapes? What categories of people does the artist suggest are disadvantaged?*

Critical evaluation. The chief characteristic of the structural-functional paradigm is its vision of society as stable and orderly. The main goal of sociologists who use this approach, then, is to figure out "what makes society tick."

In the mid-1900s, most sociologists favored the structural-functional paradigm. In recent decades, however, its influence has declined. By focusing on social stability and unity, critics point out, structural-functionalism ignores inequalities of social class, race, and gender, which can generate considerable tension and conflict. In general, focusing on stability at the expense of conflict makes this paradigm somewhat conservative. As a critical response to this approach, sociologists developed another theoretical orientation: the social-conflict paradigm.

THE SOCIAL-CONFLICT PARADIGM

The **social-conflict paradigm** is *a framework for building theory that sees society as an arena of inequality that generates conflict and change.* Unlike the structural-functional emphasis on solidarity, this approach highlights inequality. Sociologists guided by this paradigm investigate how factors such as social class, race, ethnicity, gender, and age are linked to the unequal distribution of money, power, education, and social prestige. A conflict analysis rejects the idea that social structure promotes the operation of society as a whole, pointing out instead how social patterns benefit some people while depriving others. The box highlights a key contribution regarding race made by W. E. B. Du Bois.

Sociologists using the social-conflict paradigm look at ongoing conflict between dominant and disadvantaged categories of people—the rich in relation to the poor, white people in relation to people of color, and men in relation to women. Typically, people on top strive to protect their privileges, while the disadvantaged try to gain more for themselves.

A conflict analysis of our educational system shows how schooling reproduces class inequality in every new generation. For example, secondary schools assign students to either college-preparatory or vocational-training programs. From a structural-functional point of view, such "tracking" benefits everyone by providing schooling that fits students' abilities. But conflict analysis counters that tracking often has less to do with talent than with social background, so that well-to-do students are placed in higher tracks while poor children end up in the lower tracks.

In this way, young people from privileged families receive the best schooling, which serves as a springboard to high-income careers later in life. The children of poor families, on the other hand, are not prepared for college and, like their parents before them, typically enter low-paying jobs. In both cases, the social standing of one generation is passed on to another, with schools justifying the practice in terms of individual merit (Bowles & Gintis, 1976; Oakes, 1982, 1985).

Social conflict in the United States extends well beyond schools. Later chapters of this book explain how inequality based on class, gender, and race is rooted in the organization of society itself.

Many sociologists use the social-conflict paradigm not just to understand society but to reduce inequality. This was the goal of W. E. B. Du Bois and also Karl Marx, whose writing was especially important in the development of the social-conflict paradigm. Marx had little patience with those who sought only to analyze

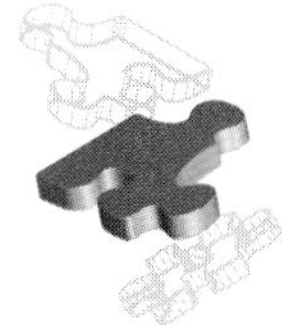

APPLYING SOCIOLOGY

Sociology at Work: Understanding the Issue of Race

One of sociology's pioneers in the United States, William Edward Burghardt Du Bois did not consider sociology a dry, academic discipline. On the contrary, he wanted to apply sociology to solving the pressing problems of his time, especially racial inequality.

Du Bois spoke out against racial separation and served as a founding member of the National Association for the Advancement of Colored People (NAACP). He helped his colleagues in sociology—and people everywhere—to see the deep racial divisions in the United States. White people can simply be "Americans," Du Bois pointed out; African Americans, however, have a "double consciousness," reflecting their status as citizens who are never able to escape identification based on the color of their skin.

In his sociological classic, *The Philadelphia Negro: A Social Study* (1899), Du Bois studied Philadelphia's African American community, identifying both the strengths and weaknesses of people wrestling with overwhelming social problems. He challenged the widespread belief in black inferiority, attributing the problems of African Americans to white prejudice. His criticism extended also to successful people of color for being so eager to win white acceptance that they gave up all ties with the black community, which needed their help.

Early in his career, Du Bois was optimistic about overcoming racial divisions. By the end of his life, however, he had grown bitter, believing that little had changed. At the age of ninety-three, Du Bois left the United States for Ghana, where he died two years later. The problems of race remain with us to this day.

Sources: Based, in part, on Baltzell (1967) and Du Bois (1967; orig. 1899).

society. In a well-known declaration (inscribed on his monument in London's Highgate Cemetery), Marx asserted: "The philosophers have only interpreted the world, in various ways; the point, however, is to change it."

Critical evaluation. The social-conflict paradigm has gained a large following in recent decades. Yet, like other approaches, it has come in for its share of criticism. Because the paradigm focuses on inequality, it largely ignores how shared values and mutual interdependence unify members of a society. In addition, say critics, to the extent that this paradigm pursues political goals, it cannot claim scientific objectivity. As Chapter 2 ("Sociological Investigation") explains, however, conflict theorists counter that *all* theoretical approaches have political consequences, albeit different ones.

A final criticism of both the structural-functional and social-conflict paradigms is that they paint society in broad strokes—in terms of "family," "social class," "race," and so on. A third theoretical paradigm depicts society less in terms of broad social structures and more as everyday experiences.

THE SYMBOLIC-INTERACTION PARADIGM

The structural-functional and social-conflict paradigms share a **macro-level orientation,** meaning *a broad focus on social structures that shape society as a whole.* Macro-level sociology takes in the big picture, rather like observing a city from high above in a helicopter and seeing how highways help people move from place to place or how housing differs in rich and poor neighborhoods. Sociology also has a **micro-level orientation,** *a close-up focus on social interaction in specific situations.* Exploring urban life in this way occurs at street level, perhaps observing how children interact on a school playground

To understand how the social-interaction paradigm views society, consider Emit Bisttram's painting, Domingo Chorus. *Society is never at rest; it is an ongoing process by which interacting individuals define and redefine reality.*

Emil Bisttram, American (1895–1976). *Domingo Chorus,* 1936, gouache and pencil on paper, 57.8 × 43.5 cm. Christie's Images/The Bridgeman Art Library.

or how pedestrians respond to homeless people. The **symbolic-interaction paradigm,** then, is *a framework for building theory that sees society as the product of the everyday interactions of individuals.*

How does "society" result from the ongoing experiences of tens of millions of people? One answer, explained in Chapter 6 ("Social Interaction in Everyday Life"), is that "society" amounts to the shared reality that people construct as they interact with one another. That is, human beings are creatures who live in a world of symbols, attaching *meaning* to virtually everything. "Reality," therefore, is simply how we define our surroundings, our obligations toward others, even our own identities.

Of course, this process of definition is subjective and varies from person to person. For example, one person may define a homeless man as "just a bum looking for a handout" and ignore him, but another might see the man as a "fellow human being in need" and offer help. In the same way, one individual may feel a sense of security passing by a police officer walking the beat, while another may be seized by nervous anxiety. Sociologists who take a symbolic-interaction approach, therefore, view society as a complex, ever-changing mosaic of subjective meanings.

The symbolic-interaction paradigm has roots in the thinking of Max Weber (1864–1920), a German sociologist who emphasized the need to understand a setting from the point of view of the people in it. Weber's approach is discussed in Chapter 4 ("Society").

Since Weber's time, sociologists have taken micro-level sociology in a number of directions. Chapter 5 ("Socialization") discusses the ideas of George Herbert Mead (1863–1931), who explored how we build our personalities from social experience. Chapter 6 ("Social Interaction in Everyday Life") presents the work of Erving Goffman (1922–1982), whose *dramaturgical analysis* describes how we resemble actors on a stage as we play out our various roles. Other contemporary sociologists, including George Homans and Peter Blau, have developed *social-exchange analysis.* In their view, social interaction is guided by what each person stands to gain and lose from others (Molm, 1997; Mulford et al., 1998). In the ritual of courtship, for example, people seek mates who offer at least as much—in terms of physical attractiveness, intelligence, and social background—as they offer in return.

Critical evaluation. The social-interaction paradigm corrects some of the bias found in macro-level approaches to society. Without denying the existence of macro-level social structures such as "the family" and "social class," the symbolic-interaction paradigm reminds us that society basically amounts to *people interacting.* That is, micro-level sociology tries to convey how individuals actually experience society. The other side of the coin is that, by focusing on day-to-day interactions, the symbolic-interaction paradigm ignores larger social structures, effects of culture, and factors such as class, gender, and race.

Table 1–1 summarizes the main characteristics of the structural-functional paradigm, the social-conflict paradigm, and the symbolic-interaction paradigm. Each paradigm is helpful in answering particular kinds of questions. However, the fullest understanding of society comes from using the sociological perspective with all three, as we show with the following analysis of sports in the United States.

TABLE 1-1 The Three Major Theoretical Paradigms: A Summary

Theoretical Paradigm	Orientation	Image of Society	Core Questions
Structural-functional	Macro-level	A system of interrelated parts that is relatively stable because of widespread agreement on what is morally desirable; each part has a particular function in society as a whole.	How is society integrated? What are the major parts of society? How are these parts interrelated? What are the consequences of each part for the overall operation of society?
Social-conflict	Macro-level	A system based on social inequality; each part of society benefits some categories of people more than others; social inequality leads to conflict which, in turn, leads to social change.	How is society divided? What are the major patterns of social inequality? How do some categories of people try to protect their privileges? How do other categories of people challenge the status quo?
Symbolic-interaction	Micro-level	An ongoing process of social interaction in specific settings based on symbolic communication; individual perceptions of reality are variable and changing.	How is society experienced? How do human beings interact to create, maintain, and change social patterns? How do individuals try to shape the reality that others perceive? How does individual behavior change from one situation to another?

APPLYING THE PERSPECTIVES: THE SOCIOLOGY OF SPORT

People in the United States love sports. Soccer moms (and dads) drive their eight-year-olds to practice, and teens play pick-up basketball after school. Weekend television is filled with sporting events. A large share of the daily news covers recent games and the latest on sports stars like Mark McGuire (baseball), Shaquille O'Neal (basketball), and Mia Hamm (soccer). Overall, sports in the United States are a multibillion-dollar industry. What sociological insights can the three theoretical paradigms give us about this familiar part of everyday life?

The Functions of Sports

A structural-functional approach directs attention to the ways sports help society to operate. Their manifest functions include providing recreation, physical conditioning, and a relatively harmless way to "let off steam." Sports have important latent functions as well, from fostering social relationships to generating tens of thousands of jobs. Perhaps most important, sports encourage competition and the pursuit of success, both of which are central to our way of life.

Sports also have dysfunctional consequences. For example, colleges and universities intent on fielding winning teams sometimes recruit students for their athletic ability rather than their academic aptitude. Not only does this practice pull down the academic standards of a school, it shortchanges athletes who devote little time to academic work.

Sports and Conflict

A social-conflict analysis begins by pointing out that sports are closely linked to social inequality. Some sports—including tennis, swimming, golf, and skiing—are expensive, so participation is largely limited to the well-to-do. Football, baseball, and basketball, however, are accessible to people of all income levels. In short, the games people play are not simply a matter of choice but also reflect social standing.

Throughout history, sports have been oriented primarily toward males. For example, the first modern Olympic Games, held in 1896, barred women from competition; in the United States, until recently even Little League teams in most parts of the country did not let girls play. Such exclusion has been defended by unfounded notions that girls and women lack the strength and stamina to play sports or that women lose their femininity when they do. Thus, our society encourages men to be athletes while expecting women to be attentive observers and cheerleaders. Today, more

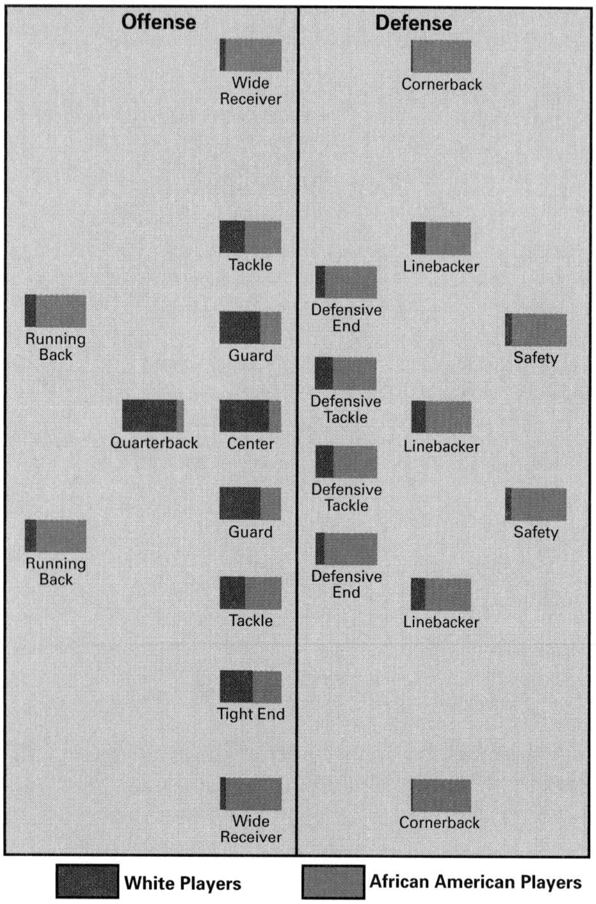

FIGURE 1–3 Race and Sport: "Stacking" in Professional Football

Source: Center for the Study of Sport in Society (2000).

women play professional sports than ever before, yet they continue to take a back seat to men, particularly in sports with the most earnings and social prestige.

Although our society long excluded people of color from big league sports, the opportunity to earn high incomes in professional sports has expanded in recent decades. Major League Baseball first admitted African American players when Jackie Robinson broke the color line and joined the Brooklyn Dodgers in 1947. Fifty years later, in 1997, when professional baseball retired the legendary Robinson's number 42 on *all* teams, African Americans (13 percent of the U.S. population) accounted for 15 percent of Major League Baseball players, 65 percent of National Football League (NFL) players, and 77 percent of National Basketball Association (NBA) players (Center for the Study of Sport in Society, 2000).

One reason for the increasing proportion of people of African descent in professional sports is that athletic performance—in terms of batting average or number of points scored per game—can be precisely measured, regardless of any white prejudice. It is also true that some people of color make a particular effort to excel in athletics, where they perceive greater opportunity than in other careers (Steele, 1990; Hoberman, 1997, 1998). In recent years, in fact, African American athletes have earned higher salaries, on average, than white players.

But racial discrimination still taints professional sports in the United States. For one thing, race is linked to the *positions* athletes play on the field in a pattern called "stacking." Figure 1–3 shows the result of a study of race in football. Notice that white players dominate in offense and also play the central positions on both sides of the line. More broadly, African Americans figure prominently in only five sports: football, basketball, baseball, boxing, and track. Across all of professional sports, the vast majority of managers, head coaches, and owners of sports teams are white (Gnida, 1995; Smith & Leonard, 1997).

We might ask who benefits the most from professional sports. Although individual players may get astronomical salaries, and millions of fans enjoy following their teams, at bottom, sports are big business—generating property for a small number of people (predominantly white men). In sum, sports in the United States are bound up with inequalities based on gender, race, and economic power.

Sports as Interaction

At a micro-level, a sporting event is a complex drama of face-to-face interaction. In part, play is guided by the players' assigned positions and the rules of the game. But players are also spontaneous and unpredictable. Informed by the symbolic-interaction paradigm, then, we see sports less as a system than as an ongoing process.

From this point of view, too, we expect each player to understand the game a little differently. Some thrive in a setting of stiff competition, whereas for others, love of the game may be greater than the need to win.[5]

[5]The ancient Romans recognized this fact, evident in our word "amateur," literally, "lover," which designates someone who engages in some activity for the sheer love of it.

CONTROVERSY & DEBATE

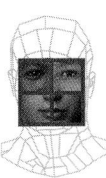

Is Sociology Nothing More than Stereotypes?

"Protestants are the ones who kill themselves!"

"People in the United States? They're rich, they love to marry, and they love to divorce!"

"Everybody knows that you have to be black to play professional basketball!"

Everyone, including sociologists, loves to generalize. But beginning students of sociology may wonder how generalizations differ from stereotypes. For example, are the statements above sound generalizations or simple stereotypes?

The three statements at the top of this column are **stereotypes,** *exaggerated descriptions applied to every person in some category.* First, rather than describing averages, each statement paints every individual in a category with the same brush; second, each ignores facts and distorts reality (even though many stereotypes do contain an element of truth); third, a stereotype sounds more like a "put-down" than a fair-minded assertion.

Good sociology, by contrast, involves making generalizations, but with three important conditions. *First, sociologists do not indiscriminately apply any generalization to all individuals; second, sociologists are careful that a generalization squares with available facts; third, sociologists offer generalizations fair-mindedly, with an interest in getting at the truth.*

Earlier in this chapter, we noted that the suicide rate among Protestants is higher than among Catholics or Jews. However, the statement—"Protestants are the ones who kill themselves"—is not a reasonable generalization, since the vast majority of Protestants do no such thing. Moreover, it would be just as wrong-headed to assume a particular friend, because he is a Protestant male, is on the verge of self-destruction. (Imagine refusing to lend money to a roommate who happens to be a Baptist, explaining, "Well, given your risk of suicide, I might never get paid back!")

Second, sociologists shape their generalizations to available facts. A more factual version of the second statement is that, on average and by world standards, the U.S. population has a very high standard of living. It is also true that our marriage rate is one of the highest in the world. And, although few people take pleasure in divorcing, so is our divorce rate.

Third, sociologists strive to be fair-minded; that is, they are motivated by a passion for truth. The third statement about African Americans and basketball is not good sociology for two reasons. First, it is simply not true, and, second, it seems motivated by bias rather than truth-seeking.

Good sociology, then, stands apart from harmful stereotyping. But a sociology course is an excellent setting for talking over common stereotypes. The classroom encourages discussion and offers the factual information you need to decide if a particular assertion is valid or just a stereotype.

Continue the debate . . .

1. *Do people in the United States have stereotypes of sociologists? What are they? Are they valid?*
2. *Do you think taking a sociology course dispels people's stereotypes? Why or why not?*
3. *Can you cite a stereotype of your own that sociology challenges?*

Beyond different attitudes toward competition, team members also shape their particular realities according to the various prejudices, jealousies, and ambitions they bring to the game. Then, too, the behavior of any single player also changes over time. A rookie in professional baseball, for example, may feel self-conscious during the first few games in the big leagues. In time, however, most players fit in comfortably with the team. Coming to feel at home on the field was slow and painful for Jackie Robinson—the first African American to play in the major leagues, beginning in 1947—who knew that many white players, and millions of white fans, resented his presence. In time, however, his outstanding ability and his confident and cooperative manner won him the respect of the entire nation.

The three theoretical paradigms—structural-functional, social-conflict, and symbolic-interaction—provide different insights, but none is more correct than the others. Applied to any issue, each paradigm generates its own interpretations so that, to appreciate fully the power of the sociological perspective, you should become familiar with all three. Together, they stimulate debates and controversies. In the final box, we review many of the ideas presented in this chapter by asking how sociological generalizations differ from common stereotypes.

SUMMARY

1. The sociological perspective shows "the general in the particular," or the power of society to shape our individual lives.
2. Because our culture emphasizes individual choice, seeing the power of society in our lives may seem, at first, like "seeing the strange in the familiar."
3. Emile Durkheim's research on suicide rates among some categories of people shows that society affects even our most personal actions.
4. Global awareness is a key part of the sociological perspective because, first, societies of the world are becoming increasingly interconnected; second, many social problems are most serious beyond the borders of the United States; and, third, global awareness helps us better understand ourselves.
5. Socially marginal people are more likely than others to see the power of society. For everyone, periods of social crisis foster sociological thinking.
6. There are four general benefits to using the sociological perspective. First, it helps us assess common-sense beliefs. Second, it helps us appreciate the opportunities and limits in our lives. Third, it encourages more active participation in society. Fourth, it increases our awareness of social diversity in the world around us.
7. Sociology arose in response to vast changes in Europe during the eighteenth and nineteenth centuries. Three changes—the rise of an industrial economy, the explosive growth of cities, and the emergence of new political ideas—focused people's attention on how society operates.
8. Auguste Comte gave sociology its name in 1838. Earlier social thinkers focused on what society ought to be, but Comte's new discipline used scientific methods to understand society as it is.
9. A theory weaves observations into insight and understanding. Sociologists use various theoretical paradigms to construct theories.
10. The structural-functional paradigm focuses on how patterns of behavior contribute to the operation of society. This approach highlights stability and integration while minimizing inequality and conflict.
11. While emphasizing inequality, conflict, and change, the social-conflict paradigm downplays a society's integration and stability.
12. In contrast to these broad, macro-level approaches, the symbolic-interaction paradigm is a micro-level framework that focuses on face-to-face interaction in specific settings.
13. Because each paradigm highlights different dimensions of any social issue, the richest sociological understanding is derived from applying all three.
14. Sociological thinking involves generalizations. But, unlike a stereotype, a sociological statement is (1) not applied indiscriminately to everyone in some category, (2) supported by facts, and (3) put forward in the fair-minded pursuit of truth.

KEY CONCEPTS

sociology (p. 1) the systematic study of human society

global perspective (p. 5) the study of the larger world and our society's place in it

high-income countries (p. 6) industrialized nations in which most people have relatively high incomes

middle-income countries (p. 6) nations with limited industrialization and moderate personal income

low-income countries (p. 6) nations with little industrialization in which most people are poor

positivism (p. 13) a way of understanding based on science

theory (p. 14) a statement of how and why specific facts are related

theoretical paradigm (p. 14) a basic image of society that guides thinking and research

structural-functional paradigm (p. 15) a framework for building theory that sees society as a complex system whose parts work together to promote solidarity and stability

social structure (p. 15) any relatively stable pattern of social behavior

social function (p. 15) the consequences of any social pattern for the operation of society as a whole

manifest functions (p. 15) the recognized and intended consequences of any social pattern

latent functions (p. 15) the unrecognized and unintended consequences of any social pattern

social dysfunction (p. 15) the undesirable consequences of any social pattern for the operation of society

social-conflict paradigm (p. 16) a framework for building theory that sees society as an arena of inequality that generates conflict and change

macro-level orientation (p. 17) a broad focus on social structures that shape society as a whole

micro-level orientation (p. 17) a close-up focus on social interaction in specific situations

symbolic-interaction paradigm (p. 18) a framework for building theory that sees society as the product of the everyday interactions of individuals

stereotype (p. 21) an exaggerated description applied to every person in some category

CRITICAL-THINKING QUESTIONS

1. In what ways does using the sociological perspective make us seem less in control of our lives? How does it give us greater power over our surroundings?
2. Consider the following argument: Sociology would not have arisen if human behavior were biologically programmed (as with, say, the behavior of ants); nor could sociology exist if human behavior were random or chaotic. Sociology exists because humans live in a middle ground: both spontaneous and guided by social structure.
3. What factors help explain why sociology developed where and when it did?
4. Guided by the discipline's three major theoretical paradigms, what kinds of questions might you ask about (a) television, (b) war, (c) humor, and (d) colleges and universities?

APPLICATIONS AND EXERCISES

1. Packaged in the back of this new textbook is an interactive CD-ROM that offers a variety of study, review, and applications exercises intended to help you better understand the material covered in this chapter. The CD includes an author's tip video for this chapter, interactive maps, video application exercises, Web links, and study questions.
2. Spend several hours exploring your local community and draw a map of the kinds of people and types of buildings found in various places (for example, "big single-family homes," "run-down business area," "new office buildings," "student apartments," and so on). What patterns do you see?
3. Look ahead to Figure 18–3, which shows the U.S. divorce rate over the last century. Try to identify societal factors that pushed the divorce rate down after 1930, up again after 1940, down in the 1950s, and up again after 1960.
4. During a class, carefully observe the behavior of the instructor and other students. What patterns do you see in who speaks? What about how people use space? What categories of people are taking the class in the first place?

SITES TO SEE

http://www.prenhall.com/macionis

The author and publisher of this book invite you to visit the interactive Web site that accompanies this text. Begin by clicking on the cover of your book. You will find a chapter-by-chapter study guide, practice tests, chat room, and many suggested Web links.

http://www.macionis.com
(or **http://www.thesociologypage.com**)

You can find dozens of additional links to Internet sites, as well as information—including short videos—about the discipline of sociology, at the author's home page. Bookmark this page as your doorway to the discipline.

http://www.sociologyplace.com

You can access a wealth of additional study resources and links to career, writing, and review tools relating to your Intro to Sociology course. Your new textbook includes a passcode you can use to enter this site. With a used textbook, you can purchase a subscription on this site.

CHAPTER 2

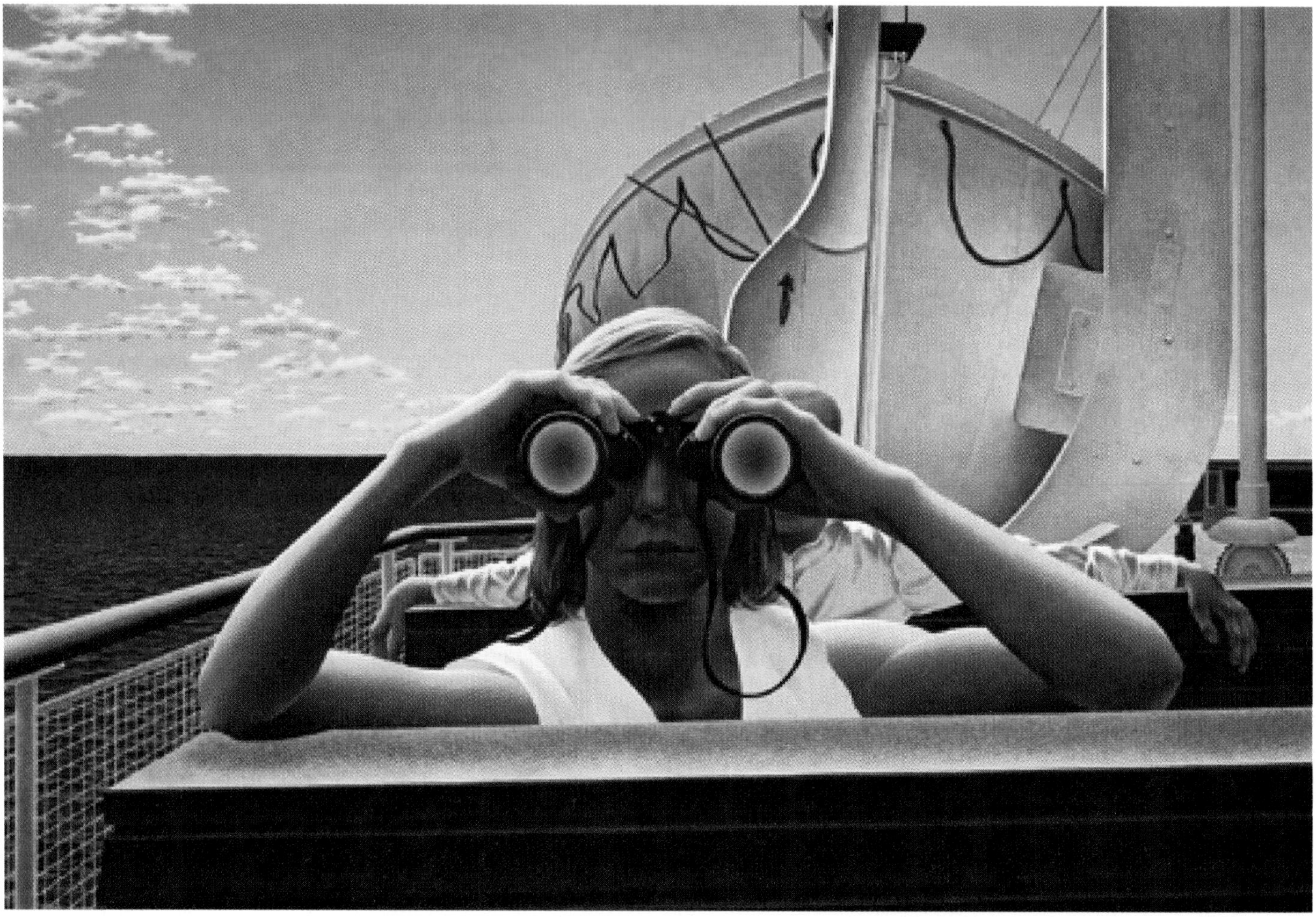

Alex Colville (1920–)
To Prince Edward Island, 1965

Acrylic emulsion on masonite, 61.9 × 92.5 cm. National Gallery of Canada, Ottawa. ©NGC/MBAC.

SOCIOLOGICAL INVESTIGATION

While on a visit to Atlanta during the winter holiday season, sociologist Lois Benjamin (1991) called on the mother of an old friend from college. Benjamin was anxious to learn about her friend, Sheba, a woman who shared her own dream of earning a graduate degree, landing a teaching job, and writing books. Proudly, Benjamin had fulfilled her dream. But as she soon found out, Sheba had fallen disastrously short of her goal.

There had been early signs of trouble, Benjamin recalled. After college, Sheba began graduate work at a university in Canada. But in her letters to Benjamin, Sheba became more and more critical of the world and seemed to be cutting herself off from others. The problem, as Sheba saw it, was racism. As an African American woman, she claimed, she felt she was the target of racial hostility. Before long, she flunked out of school, blaming her white professors for her failure. At this point, she left North America, finally earning a Ph.D. in England and then settling in Nigeria. Since then, Benjamin had not heard a word from her long-time friend.

Benjamin was happy to learn that Sheba had returned to Atlanta. But her delight dissolved into shock when she saw Sheba and realized that her friend, suffering a mental breakdown, was barely responsive to anyone.

For months after, Sheba's emotional collapse troubled Benjamin. She knew that many factors combine to cause such personal tragedy. But having experienced the sting of racism herself, Benjamin believed it had played a major role in Sheba's story. Partly as a tribute to her old friend, Benjamin set out to explore the effects of race in the lives of bright and well-educated people of color in the United States.

Benjamin realized she was challenging the conventional wisdom that race poses less of a barrier today than in previous generations, especially to talented African Americans (W. J. Wilson, 1978). But her own experiences—and, she believed, Sheba's, too—seemed to contradict such thinking.

To test her ideas, Benjamin spent the next two years asking one hundred successful African Americans across the country how race affected their lives. In the words of these "Talented One Hundred"[1] men and women, she found evidence that, even among privileged African Americans, racism remains a heavy burden.

[1]Benjamin derived her concept from the term "Talented Tenth" used by W. E. B. Du Bois (1899) to describe African American leaders in his day.

Later in this chapter, we will take a closer look at Lois Benjamin's research. For the moment, notice how the sociological perspective helped her to spot broad social patterns operating in the lives of individuals. Just as important, Benjamin's work demonstrates the *doing* of sociology, the process of *sociological investigation.*

Many people think that scientists work only in laboratories, carefully taking measurements using complex equipment. But, as this chapter explains, while some sociologists do conduct scientific research in laboratories, most work on neighborhood streets, in homes and workplaces, in schools and hospitals, in bars and prisons—in short, wherever people can be found.

This chapter examines the methods that sociologists use to conduct research. Along the way, we shall see that research involves not just procedures for gathering information but controversies about values: Should research strive to be objective? Or should it point to the need for change? Certainly, for example, Lois Benjamin did not undertake her study simply to show that racism exists; she wanted to bring racism out in the open as a way to challenge it. We shall tackle questions of values after addressing the basics of sociological investigation.

THE BASICS OF SOCIOLOGICAL INVESTIGATION

Sociological investigation starts with two simple requirements. The first was the focus of Chapter 1: *Use the sociological perspective.* This point of view reveals curious patterns of behavior all around us that call for further study. It was Lois Benjamin's sociological imagination that prompted her to wonder how race affects the lives of talented African Americans.

This brings us to the second requirement of sociological investigation: *Be curious and ask questions.* Benjamin sought to learn more about how race affects people with significant personal achievements. She asked questions: Who are the leaders of this nation's black community? What effect does being part of a racial minority have on their self-identity? On the way white people perceive them and their work?

Seeing the world sociologically and asking questions are fundamental to sociological investigation. Yet they are only the beginning. They spark our curiosity, but then we face the task of finding answers to our questions. To understand the kind of insights sociology offers, we need to realize that there are various kinds of "truth."

SCIENCE AS ONE FORM OF "TRUTH"

When we say we "know" something, we can mean many things. Most members of our society, for instance, claim to believe in the existence of God. Few would claim to have direct contact with God, but they say they believe all the same. We call this kind of knowing "belief" or "faith."

A second kind of truth rests on the pronouncement of some recognized expert. Parents with questions about raising their children, for example, may read books by an "expert" or consult a child psychologist.

A third type of truth is based on simple agreement among ordinary people. We come to "know" that, say, sexual intercourse among young children is wrong because just about everyone says it is wrong.

People's "truths" differ the world over, and we often encounter "facts" at odds with our own. Imagine being a Peace Corps volunteer who has just arrived in a small, traditional village in Latin America. Your job is to help local people increase their crop yield. On your first day in the fields, you observe a curious practice: After planting the seeds, the farmers lay a dead fish on top of the soil. In response to your question, they reply that the fish is a gift to the god of the harvest. A village elder adds sternly that the harvest was poor one year when no fish were offered.

From that society's point of view, using fish as gifts to the harvest god makes sense. The people believe in it, their experts endorse it, and everyone seems to agree that the system works. But, with scientific training in agriculture, you have to shake your head and wonder. The scientific "truth" in this situation is something entirely different: The decomposing fish fertilize the ground, producing a better crop.

Science represents a fourth way of knowing. **Science** is *a logical system that bases knowledge on direct, systematic observation.* **Scientific sociology,** then, is *the study of society based on systematic observation of social behavior.* Standing apart from faith, the wisdom of "experts," and general agreement, scientific knowledge rests on **empirical evidence,** that is, *information we can verify with our senses.*

Our Peace Corps example does not mean, of course, that people in traditional villages ignore what their senses tell them, or that members of technologically advanced societies reject nonscientific ways of knowing. A medical researcher using science to develop a new drug for treating cancer, for example, may still practice her religion as a matter of faith; she may turn to experts when making financial decisions; and she may derive political opinions from family and friends. In short, we all hold various kinds of truths at the same time.

Myths as well as scientific facts are an important dimension of human existence. In his painting, The Creation of the Earth, *Mexican painter Diego Rivera (1886–1957) offers a mythic account of human origins. A myth (from the Greek, meaning "story" or "word") may or may not be factual in the literal sense. Yet, it conveys some basic truth about the meaning and purpose of life. Indeed, it is science, rather than art, that has no power to address such questions of meaning.*

Diego Rivera, Mexican (1886–1957). *The Creation of the Earth* page from *Popol Vuh*, watercolor on paper. Museo Casa Diego Rivera (INBA), Guanajuato, Mexico. Index/The Bridgeman Art Library.

COMMON SENSE VERSUS SCIENTIFIC EVIDENCE

Scientific evidence sometimes challenges our common sense. Here are six statements that many North Americans assume are "true":

1. **Poor people are far more likely than rich people to break the law.** Watching a television show like "Cops," one might well conclude that police arrest only people from "bad" neighborhoods. Chapter 8 ("Deviance") explains that poor people do stand out in the official arrest statistics. But research also shows that police and prosecutors are more likely to respond leniently to apparent wrongdoing by well-to-do people. Further, some laws themselves are written in a way that criminalizes poor people more and affluent people less.
2. **The United States is a middle-class society in which most people are more or less equal.** Data presented in Chapter 11 ("Social Class in the United States") show that the richest 5 percent of our people control half the nation's total wealth. If people are equal, then some are much "more equal" than others.
3. **Most poor people don't want to work.** Research described in Chapter 11 indicates that this statement is true of some but not most poor people. In fact, about half of poor individuals in the United States are children and elderly people whom no one would expect to work.
4. **Differences in the behavior of females and males reflect "human nature."** Much of what we call "human nature" is constructed by the society in which we are raised, as Chapter 3 ("Culture") explains. Further, as Chapter 13 ("Gender Stratification") argues, some societies define "feminine" and "masculine" very differently from the way we do.
5. **People change as they grow old, losing many interests as they focus on their health.** Chapter 15 ("Aging and the Elderly") reports that aging changes our personalities very little. Problems of health increase in old age but, by and large, elderly people keep their distinctive personalities.
6. **Most people marry because they are in love.** To members of our society, few statements are so self-evident. Surprisingly, however, in many societies marriage has little to do with love. Chapter 18 ("Family") explains why.

These examples confirm the old saying that "It's not what we don't know that gets us into trouble as much as things we *do* know that just aren't so." We have all been brought up believing conventional truths, being bombarded by expert advice, and being pressured to

Common sense suggests that, in a world of possibilities, people fall in love with that "special someone." Sociological research reveals that the vast majority of people select partners who are very similar in social background to themselves.

accept the opinions of people around us. As adults, we need to evaluate critically what we see, read, and hear. Sociology can help us to do just that.

SCIENCE: BASIC ELEMENTS AND LIMITATIONS

In Chapter 1, we explained how early sociologists such as Auguste Comte and Emile Durkheim applied science to the study of society just as natural scientists investigate the physical world. This approach to knowing, called *positivism*, assumes that an objective reality exists "out there." The job of the scientist is to discover this reality by gathering empirical evidence—facts we can verify with our senses.

In this chapter, we begin by introducing the major elements of scientific sociology. Then we shall discuss some limitations of scientific (or positivist) sociology and present alternative approaches to positivism.

CONCEPTS, VARIABLES, AND MEASUREMENT

A basic element of science is the **concept,** *a mental construct that represents some part of the world, inevitably in a simplified form.* "Society" is itself a concept, as are the structural parts of societies, such as "the family" and "the economy." Sociologists also use concepts to describe individuals, as when we speak of "race" or "social class."

A **variable** is *a concept whose value changes from case to case.* The familiar variable "price," for example, changes from item to item in a supermarket. Similarly, we use the concept "social class" to identify people as "upper class," "middle class," "working class," or "lower class."

The use of variables depends on **measurement,** *the process of determining the value of a variable in a specific case.* Some variables are easy to measure, as when the checkout clerk adds up the cost of our groceries. But measuring sociological variables can be far more difficult. For example, how would you measure a person's "social class"? You might look at clothing, listen to patterns of speech, or note a home address. Or, trying to be more precise, you might ask about income, occupation, and education.

Because almost any variable can be measured in more than one way, sociologists often have to make a judgment about which factors to consider. For example, having a very high income might qualify a person as "upper class." But what if the income comes from selling automobiles, an occupation most people think of as "middle class"? Would having only an eighth-grade education make the person "lower class"? In this case, sociologists sensibly (but arbitrarily) combine these three measures—income, occupation, and education—to assign social class, as described in Chapter 10 ("Social Stratification") and Chapter 11 ("Social Class in the United States").

Sociologists face another interesting problem in measuring variables: dealing with vast numbers of people. How, for instance, do you describe income for thousands or even millions of people? Reporting streams of numbers carries little meaning and tells us nothing about the people as a whole. Thus sociologists use *statistical measures* to describe people. The box explains how.

Defining Concepts

Measurement is always somewhat arbitrary because the value of any variable partly depends on how it is defined. In addition, deciding what abstract concepts such as

APPLYING SOCIOLOGY

Three Useful (and Simple) Statistical Measures

We all talk about "averages," whether it is the average price of a gallon of gasoline or the average salary for new college graduates. Sociologists, too, are interested in averages, and they use three different statistical measures to describe what is typical.

Assume that we wish to describe the salaries paid to seven members of a sociology department at a local college:

\$35,000 \$43,000 \$41,700 \$42,000
\$35,000 \$78,295 \$35,000

The simplest statistical measure is the *mode,* the value that occurs most often in a series of numbers. In this example, the mode is \$35,000, since that value occurs three times, and each of the others occurs only once. If all the values were to occur only once, there would be no mode; if two values occurred three times (or twice), there would be two modes. Although easy to identify, sociologists rarely use the mode because it is a very crude measure of the "average."

A more common statistical measure, the *mean,* refers to the arithmetic average of a series of numbers, calculated by adding all the values together and dividing by the number of cases. The sum of the seven incomes is \$309,995; dividing by seven yields a mean income of \$44,285. But notice that the mean is actually higher than the income of six of the seven sociologists. Because the mean is "pulled" up or down by an especially high or low value (in this case, the \$78,295 paid to one sociologist, who also serves as a dean), it has the drawback of giving a distorted picture of any distribution with extreme scores.

The *median* is the middle case: the value that occurs midway in a series of numbers arranged from lowest to highest. Here the median income for the seven people is \$41,700, since three incomes are higher and three are lower. (With an even number of cases, the median is halfway between the two middle cases.) Because a median is unaffected by an extreme score, it gives a better picture of what is "average" than the mean does.

"love," "family," or "intelligence" mean in real life can lead to lengthy debates before any attempt is made to measure them as variables.

Good research, therefore, requires that sociologists **operationalize a variable,** which means *specifying exactly what one is to measure before assigning a value to a variable.* Before measuring the concept of social class, for example, we would have to decide exactly what we were going to measure: say, income level, years of schooling, occupational prestige. Sometimes sociologists measure several of these things; in such cases, they need to specify exactly how they plan to combine these variables into one overall score. When reading about research, always notice the way researchers operationalize each variable. How they define terms can greatly affect the results.

When deciding how to operationalize variables, sociologists may take into account the opinions of the people they study. Since 1977, for example, researchers at the U.S. Census Bureau have defined race and ethnicity as white, black, Hispanic, Asian or Pacific Islander, and American Indian or Alaskan Native. One problem with this list is that someone can be *both* Hispanic and white or black; similarly, people of Arab ancestry might not identify with *any* of these choices. Just as important, an increasing number of people in the United States are *multiracial.* As a result of such problems, the census in the year 2000 allowed people, if they wish, to describe their race and ethnicity by selecting more than one category (Cose, 1997; O'Hare, 1998).

Reliability and Validity

For a measurement to be useful, it must be reliable and valid. **Reliability** refers to *consistency in measurement.* In other words, the process must yield the same result if repeated time after time. But consistency is no guarantee of **validity,** which means *precision in measuring exactly what one intends to measure.* Valid measurement, in other words, means more than hitting the same spot on a target again and again; it means hitting the bull's-eye.

Valid measurement is more difficult than it may at first seem. Say, for example, you want to study how religious people are. A reasonable strategy might be to ask how often respondents attend religious services. But is going to a church or temple really the same thing as

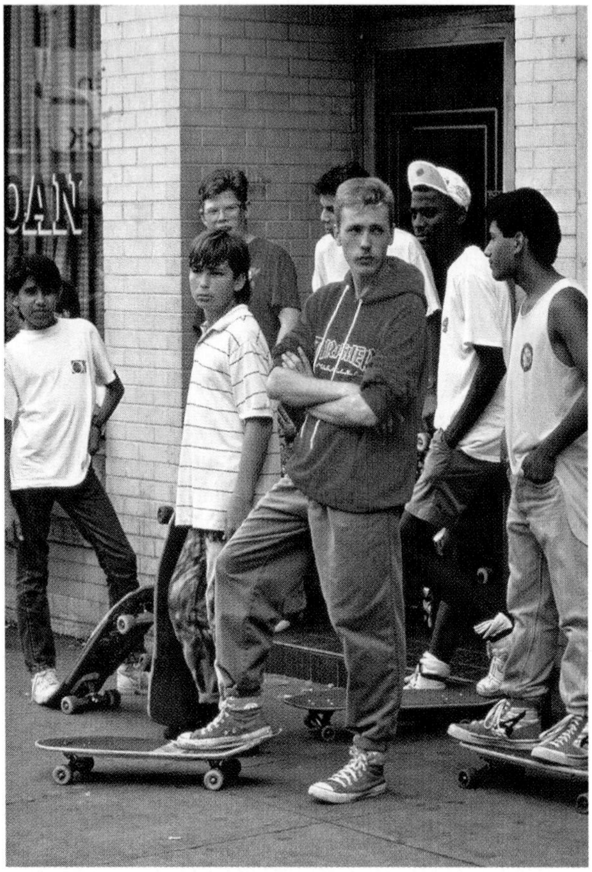

Young people who live in the crowded inner city are more likely than those who live in the spacious suburbs to have trouble with the police. But does this mean that crowding causes delinquency? Researchers know that crowding and arrest rates do vary together, but they have demonstrated that the connection is spurious: Both factors rise in relation to a third factor—declining income.

being religious? It may be that religious people do attend services more frequently, but people also join in religious rituals out of habit or because someone else wants them to. Moreover, some devout believers avoid organized religion altogether. Thus, even when a measurement yields consistent results (making it reliable), it can still miss the real, intended target (and lack validity). Later on, in Chapter 19 ("Religion"), we suggest that measuring religiosity should take account of not only church attendance but also a person's beliefs and the degree to which a person lives by religious convictions. In sum, careful measurement is vital to sociological research and often a challenge.

Relationships among Variables

Once measurements are made, investigators can pursue the real payoff: seeing how variables are related. The scientific ideal is **cause and effect,** *a relationship in which we know that change in one variable causes change in another.* Cause-and-effect relationships occur around us every day, as when studying for an exam results in a high grade. *The variable that causes the change* (in this case, studying) is called the **independent variable.** *The variable that changes* (the exam grade) is called the **dependent variable.** The value of one variable, in other words, depends on the value of another. Why is linking variables in terms of cause and effect important? Because this kind of relationship allows us to *predict* how one pattern of behavior will produce another.

But just because two variables change together does not mean that they are linked by a cause-and-effect relationship. Consider, for instance, that the marriage rate in the United States falls to its lowest point in January, exactly the same month that our national death rate peaks. This hardly means that people die because they fail to marry (or that they don't marry because they die). In fact, it is the dreary weather in much of the nation during January (and maybe also the post-holiday blahs) that causes both a low marriage rate and a high death rate. The flip side holds as well: The warmer and sunnier summer months have the highest marriage rates as well as the lowest death rates. Thus researchers must look below the surface to untangle cause-and-effect relationships.

To take a second case, sociologists have long recognized that juvenile delinquency is more common among young people who live in crowded housing. Say we operationalize the variable "juvenile delinquency" as the number of times (if any) a person under the age of eighteen has been arrested, and define "crowded housing" to mean a home's amount of square feet of living space per person. We would find the variables related; that is, delinquency rates are, indeed, high in densely populated neighborhoods. But should we conclude that crowding in the home (in this case, the independent variable) is what causes delinquency (the dependent variable)?

Not necessarily. **Correlation** is *a relationship by which two (or more) variables change together.* We know that density and delinquency are correlated because they change together, as shown in part (a) of Figure 2–1. This relationship *may* mean that crowding causes misconduct, but it could also mean that some third factor is at work causing change in *both* of the variables under observation. To identify a third variable, think what kind of people live in crowded housing: people with less money and few choices—the poor. Poor children are also more likely to end up with police records. Thus, crowded housing and juvenile delinquency are found together because *both* are caused by a third factor—poverty—as shown in part (b) of Figure 2–1. In short, the apparent connection between crowding and delinquency is "explained away" by a third variable—low income—that causes them both to change. So our original connection turns out to be a **spurious correlation,** *an apparent, although false, relationship between two (or more) variables caused by some other variable.*

Unmasking a correlation as spurious requires a bit of detective work, assisted by a technique called **control,** *holding constant all variables except one in order to see clearly the effect of that variable.* In the example above, we suspect that income level may be causing a spurious link between housing density and delinquency. To check, we control for income (that is, we hold income constant by looking at only young people of one income level) and see if a correlation between density and delinquency remains. If the correlation between density and delinquency is still there despite the control (that is, if young people living in more crowded housing show higher rates of delinquency than young people in less crowded housing, all with the same family income), we have more reason to think that crowding does, in fact, cause delinquency. But if the relationship disappears when we control for income, as shown in part (c) of the figure, we then know we have a spurious correlation. In fact, research shows that the correlation between crowding and delinquency just about disappears if income is controlled (Fischer, 1984). So we have now sorted out the relationship among the three variables, as illustrated in part (d) of the figure. Housing density and juvenile delinquency have a spurious correlation; evidence shows that both variables rise or fall according to people's income.

To sum up, correlation means only that two (or more) variables change together. Cause and effect rests on three conditions: (1) demonstrated correlation, (2) an independent (or causal) variable that precedes the dependent variable in time, and (3) no evidence that a third variable could be causing a spurious correlation between the two.

Natural scientists have an easier time than social scientists identifying cause-and-effect relationships because they can control many variables in a laboratory. Carrying out research in a workplace or on the streets, however, is a more difficult task, and sociologists must often be satisfied with demonstrating only correlation. Moreover, human behavior is highly complex, involving dozens of causal variables at any one time, so establishing all the cause-and-effect relationships in any situation is extremely difficult.

FIGURE 2–1 Correlation and Cause: An Example

(a)

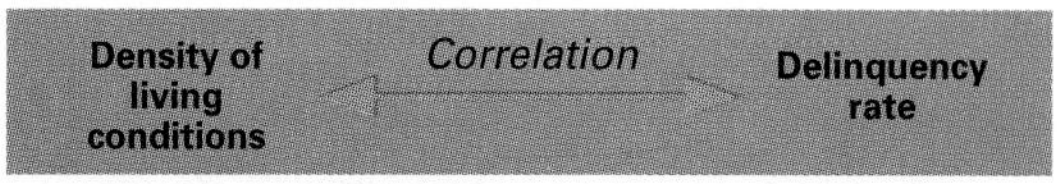

If two variables vary together, they are said to be correlated. In this example, density of living conditions and juvenile delinquency increase and decrease together.

(b)

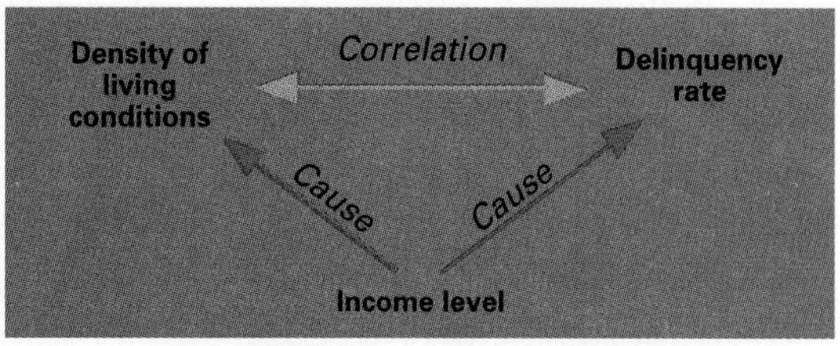

Here we consider the effect of a third variable: income level. Low income level may cause *both* high-density living conditions *and* a high delinquency rate. In other words, as income level decreases, both density of living conditions and the delinquency rate increase.

(c)

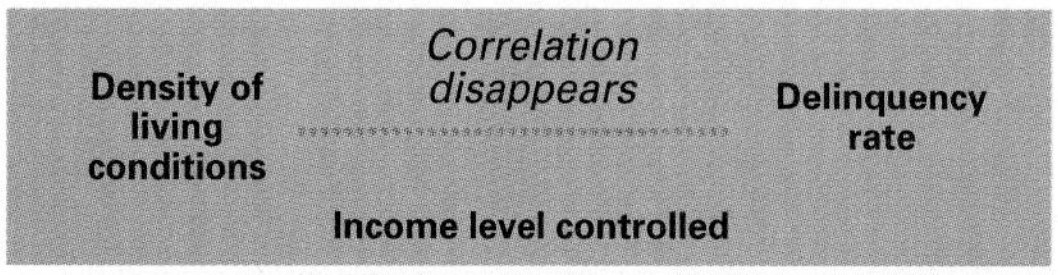

If we control income level — that is, examine only cases with the same income level — do those with higher-density living conditions still have a higher delinquency rate? The answer is *no.* There is no longer a correlation between these two variables.

(d)

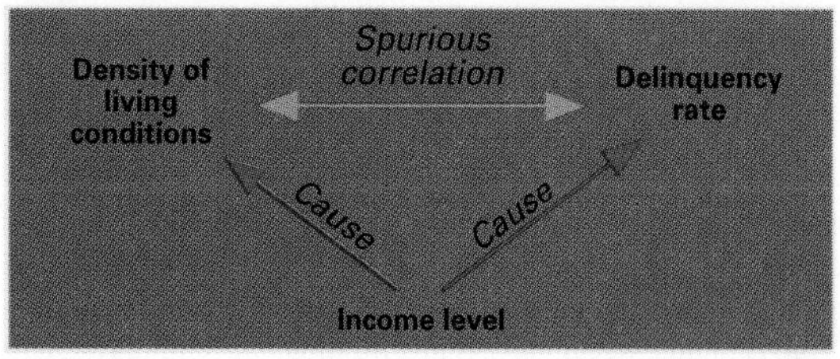

This finding leads us to conclude that income level is a cause of both density of living conditions and delinquency rate. The original two variables (density of living conditions and delinquency rate) are thus correlated, but neither one causes the other. Their correlation is therefore *spurious.*

One principle of scientific research is that sociologists and other investigators should strive to be objective in their work, so that their personal values and beliefs do not distort their findings. But such an aloof attitude may discourage the relationship needed in order for people to open up and share information. Thus, as sociologists study human relationships, they have to be especially mindful of their own—when it comes to their subjects.

THE IDEAL OF OBJECTIVITY

Assume that ten people who work for a magazine in Miami, Florida, are collaborating on a story about that city's best restaurants. With the magazine picking up the tab, they head out on the town for a week of fine dining. Later, they get together to compare notes. Do you think one restaurant will be everyone's clear favorite? That hardly seems likely.

In scientific terms, each of the ten probably operationalizes the concept "best restaurant" differently. For one, it might be a place that serves delicious steaks at reasonable prices; for another, the choice might turn on a menu keyed to nutrition and health; for still another, stunning decor and attentive service might be the deciding factors. Like so many other things in life, the best restaurant turns out to be mostly a matter of individual taste.

Personal values are fine when it comes to restaurants, but they pose a challenge to scientific research. Remember, science assumes reality is "out there." Scientists, then, need to study this reality without changing it in any way. Science, therefore, demands that researchers strive for **objectivity,** *a state of personal neutrality in conducting research.* Objectivity means that researchers carefully hold to scientific procedures while reining in their own attitudes and beliefs in order not to bias the results.

Scientific objectivity is an ideal rather than a reality, of course, since no one can be completely neutral about anything. Even the subject a researcher chooses to study reflects a personal interest of one sort or another, as Lois Benjamin's research on race attests. But the scientific ideal is to keep a professional sense of detachment from how the results turn out. Holding to this ideal, we do our best to see that conscious or unconscious biases do not distort research. As an extra precaution, many researchers inform their readers about their personal leanings so that their conclusions are taken in the proper context.

Max Weber: Value-Free Research

The influential German sociologist Max Weber expected that people would select their research topics according to their personal beliefs and interests. Why else, after all, would one person study world hunger, another the effects of racism, and still another how children fare in one-parent families? Knowing that people select topics that are *value-relevant,* Weber cautioned researchers to be *value-free* in their investigations. Only by being dispassionate (as we expect any professionals to be) can researchers study the world *as it is* rather than tell how they think *it should be.* This detachment, for Weber, is a crucial element of science that sets it apart from politics. Politicians, in other words, are committed to particular outcomes; scientists try to maintain an open-minded readiness to accept the results of their investigations, whatever they may be.

Weber's argument still carries much weight in sociology, although most sociologists concede that we can never be completely value-free or even aware of all our biases (Demerath, 1996). Moreover, sociologists are not "average" people: Most are white people who are highly educated and more politically liberal than the population as a whole (Wilson, 1979). Sociologists need to remember that they, too, are influenced by their own social backgrounds.

A basic lesson of social research is that being observed affects how people behave. Researchers can never be certain precisely how this will occur; while some people resent public attention, others become highly animated when they think they have an audience.

One way to limit distortion caused by personal values is **replication,** *repetition of research by other investigators.* If other researchers repeat a study using the same procedures and obtain the same results, we gain confidence that the results are accurate. The need for replication in scientific investigation probably explains why the search for knowledge is called *re*-search in the first place.

In any case, keep in mind that the logic of science does not guarantee objective, absolute truth. What science offers is an approach to knowledge that is *self-correcting* so that, in the long run, researchers stand the best chance of overcoming their own biases. Objectivity and truth lie, then, not in any particular research, but in the scientific process itself.

SOME LIMITATIONS OF SCIENTIFIC SOCIOLOGY

Science is one important way of knowing. Yet, applied to social life, science has several important limitations:

1. **Human behavior is too complex for sociologists to predict precisely any individual's actions.** Astronomers calculate the movement of objects in the heavens with remarkable precision, but comets and planets are unthinking objects. Humans have minds of their own, so no two people react to any event in exactly the same way. Sociologists, therefore, must be satisfied with showing that *categories* of people typically act in one way or another. This is not a failing of sociology. It is simply the result of what we do: study creative, spontaneous people.
2. **Because humans respond to their surroundings, the mere presence of a researcher may affect the behavior being studied.** An astronomer gazing at a comet has no effect whatever on it. But most people react to being observed. Some become anxious, angry, or defensive; others try to "help" by doing what they think the researcher expects of them.
3. **Social patterns change; what is true in one time or place may not hold true in another.** The laws of physics apply tomorrow as well as today; they hold true all around the world. But human behavior is so variable there are no unchanging sociological laws.
4. **Because sociologists are part of the social world they study, being value-free when conducting social research is difficult.** Barring a laboratory mishap, chemists are rarely personally affected by what goes on in test tubes. But sociologists live in their "test tube"—the society they study. Therefore, social scientists face a greater challenge in controlling, or even recognizing, personal values that may distort their work.

Feminist research is a form of critical sociology. It is concerned not simply with studying the social standing of women, but also transforms research, putting the investigator on a more equal footing with subjects so that they can work together to solve their common problems.

A SECOND FRAMEWORK: INTERPRETIVE SOCIOLOGY

All sociologists agree that studying social behavior scientifically presents some real challenges. But some sociologists go further, suggesting that science as it is used to study the natural world misses a vital part of the social world: *meaning*.

Human beings do not simply act; we engage in *meaningful* action. Max Weber, who pioneered this framework, argued that the proper focus of sociology, therefore, is *interpretation*—or understanding the meanings involved in everyday life. **Interpretive sociology** is *the study of society that focuses on the meanings people attach to their social world.*

Interpretive sociology differs from scientific, or positivist, sociology in three ways. First, scientific sociology focuses on action, what people do; interpretive sociology, by contrast, focuses on the meaning people attach to behavior. Second, while scientific sociology sees an objective reality "out there," interpretive sociology sees reality constructed by people themselves in the course of their everyday lives. Third, while scientific sociology tends to favor *quantitative* data—that is, numerical measurements of social behavior—interpretive sociology favors *qualitative* data—researchers' perceptions of how people understand their surroundings.

In sum, the scientific approach is well suited for research in a laboratory, where investigators stand back and take careful measurements. The interpretive approach is better suited for research in a natural setting where investigators interact with people, learning how they make sense of their everyday lives.

Weber believed the key to interpretive sociology lay in *Verstehen*, the German word for "understanding." It is the interpretive sociologist's job not just to observe *what* people do but to share in their world of meaning and come to appreciate *why* they act as they do. Subjective thoughts and feelings—which science tends to dismiss as "bias"—now become the center of the researcher's attention (Berger & Kellner, 1981; Neuman, 1997).

A THIRD FRAMEWORK: CRITICAL SOCIOLOGY

There is a third methodological approach in sociology. Like the interpretive approach, critical sociology developed in reaction to scientific research. This time, however, the issue was the scientific goal of objectivity.

Scientific sociology holds that reality is "out there" and the researcher's task is to study and document this reality. But Karl Marx, who founded the critical approach, rejected the idea that society exists as a "natural" system with a fixed order. To assume this, he claimed, amounts to saying that society cannot be changed. Scientific sociology, then, ends up supporting the status quo.

Critical sociology, by contrast, is *the study of society that focuses on the need for social change.* Rather than asking the scientific question "How does society work?", critical sociologists ask moral and political questions, especially "Should society exist in its present form?" Their answer, typically, is that it should not. The point, said Marx (1972:109; orig. 1845), is not merely to study the world as it is but to *change* it. In making value judgments

TABLE 2–1 Three Methodological Approaches in Sociology

	Scientific	Interpretive	Critical
What Is Reality?	Society is an orderly system; reality is "out there."	Society is ongoing interaction; reality is socially constructed meanings.	Society is patterns of inequality; reality is that some dominate others.
How Do We Conduct Research?	Gather empirical data—ideally, quantitative; researcher tries to be an objective observer.	Develop a qualitative account of the subjective sense people make of their world; researcher is a participant.	Research is a strategy to bring about desired change; researcher is an activist.
Corresponding Theoretical Paradigm	Structural-functional paradigm	Symbolic-interaction paradigm	Social-conflict paradigm

about how society should be improved, critical sociology rejects Weber's goal that researchers be value-free.

Sociologists using the critical approach seek to change not only society but the character of research itself. They consider their research subjects as equals and encourage their participation in deciding what to study and how to do the work. Often, researchers and subjects use their findings to provide a voice for less powerful people and advance the political goal of a more equal society (Nielsen, 1990; Stanley, 1990; Reinharz, 1992; Wolf, 1996; Hess, 1999).

Scientific sociologists object to taking sides in this way, charging that critical sociology (whether feminist, Marxist, or some other critical approach) is political and gives up any claim to objectivity. Critical sociologists respond that all research is political in that either it calls for change or it does not. Sociologists thus have no choice about their work being political, but they can choose *which* positions to support. Critical sociology, therefore, is an activist approach tying knowledge to action—seeking not just to understand the world but also to improve it. Generally speaking, scientific sociology tends to appeal to researchers with more conservative political views; critical sociology appeals to those with liberal and radical-left politics.

What about the link between methodological approaches and theory? In general, each of the three methodological approaches is related to one of the theoretical paradigms presented in Chapter 1 ("The Sociological Perspective"). The scientific approach corresponds to the structural-functional paradigm, the interpretive approach to the symbolic-interaction paradigm, and the critical approach to the social-conflict paradigm. Table 2–1 summarizes the differences among the three methodological approaches. Sociologists often favor one approach over another; however, most make use of all three (Gamson, 1999).

GENDER AND RESEARCH

In recent years, sociologists have become aware that research is affected by **gender,** *the personal traits and social positions that members of a society attach to being female or male.* Margrit Eichler (1988) identifies five ways in which gender can shape research.

1. **Androcentricity.** Androcentricity (*andro* is the Greek word for "male"; *centricity* means "being centered on") refers to approaching an issue from a male perspective. Sometimes researchers act as if only men's activities are important, ignoring what women do. For years researchers studying occupations focused on the paid work of men and overlooked the housework and child care traditionally performed by women (Counts, 1925; Hodge, Treiman, & Rossi, 1966). Clearly, research that seeks to understand human behavior cannot ignore half of humanity.

   Gynocentricity—seeing the world from a female perspective—is equally limiting to sociological investigation. However, in our male-dominated society, this problem arises less frequently.
2. **Overgeneralizing.** This problem occurs when researchers use data drawn from only people of one sex to support conclusions about "humanity" or "society." Gathering information about a community from a handful of male public officials and then drawing conclusions about the

entire community illustrates the problem of overgeneralizing. In another case, studying child-rearing practices by collecting data only from women would allow researchers to draw conclusions about "motherhood" but not about the more general issue of "parenthood."

3. **Gender blindness.** Failing to consider the variable of gender at all is called "gender blindness." As is evident throughout this book, the lives of men and women differ in countless ways. A study of growing old in the United States would be flawed by gender blindness if it overlooked the fact that most elderly men live with spouses while elderly women typically live alone.
4. **Double standards.** Researchers must be careful not to distort what they study by judging men and women differently. For example, a family researcher who labels a couple as "man and wife" may define the man as the "head of household" and treat him accordingly, while assuming that the woman simply engages in family "support work."
5. **Interference.** Gender distorts a study if a subject reacts to the sex of the researcher and thereby interferes with the research operation. While studying a small community in Sicily, for instance, Maureen Giovannini (1992) found many men responding to her as a woman rather than as a researcher. Gender dynamics precluded her from certain activities, such as private conversations with men, that were considered inappropriate for single women. Local residents also denied Giovannini access to places they considered off-limits to women.

There is nothing wrong with focusing research on one sex or the other. But all sociologists, as well as people who read their work, should be aware that gender can affect an investigation.

RESEARCH ETHICS

Like all researchers, sociologists must be mindful that research can harm as well as help subjects or communities. For this reason, the American Sociological Association (ASA)—the major professional association of sociologists in North America—has established formal guidelines for conducting research (1997).

Sociologists must strive to be both technically competent and fair-minded in their work. Sociologists must disclose all research findings, without omitting significant data. They are ethically bound to make their results available to other sociologists, especially those who wish to replicate a study.

Sociologists must also ensure the safety of subjects taking part in a research project. Should research develop in a manner that threatens the well-being of participants, investigators must stop their work immediately. Researchers must also protect the privacy of anyone involved in a research project. This last promise can be difficult to keep, since researchers sometimes come under pressure (even from the police or courts) to disclose information. Therefore, researchers must think carefully about their responsibility to protect subjects, and they should discuss this issue with participants. In fact, ethical research requires the *informed consent* of participants, which means that subjects understand the responsibilities and risks that the research involves and agree—before the work begins—to take part.

Another important guideline concerns funding. Sociologists must include in their published results the sources of all financial support. They must also avoid conflicts of interest that may compromise the integrity of their work. For example, researchers must never accept funding from an organization that seeks to influence the research results for its own purposes.

There are additional ethical concerns that sociologists face as teachers, college administrators, and in clinical practice. Readers may review the current code of ethics by visiting the American Sociological Association home page on the Internet: http:www.asanet.org

Finally, there are global dimensions to research ethics. Before beginning research in other countries, investigators must become familiar enough with that society to understand what people *there* are likely to perceive as a violation of privacy or a source of personal danger. In a multicultural society such as the United States, the same rule applies to studying people whose cultural background differs from one's own. The box offers some tips about how outsiders can effectively and sensitively study Hispanic communities.

THE METHODS OF SOCIOLOGICAL RESEARCH

A **research method** is *a systematic plan for conducting research.* The remainder of this chapter introduces four commonly used methods of sociological investigation. None is inherently better or worse than any other. Rather, in the same way that a carpenter selects a particular tool for a specific task, researchers choose a method according to who they wish to study and what they wish to learn.

SOCIAL DIVERSITY

Conducting Research with Hispanics

In a society as racially, ethnically, and religiously diverse as the United States, sociologists are always studying people who differ from themselves. Learning—in advance—some of the distinctive traits of any category of people can ease the research process and ensure that no hard feelings are left when the work is finished.

Gerardo Marín and Barbara VanOss Marín have identified five areas of concern in conducting research with Hispanics:

1. **Terminology.** The Maríns point out that the term "Hispanic" is a label of convenience used by the Census Bureau. Few people of Spanish descent think of themselves as "Hispanic" or "Latino"; most identify with a particular country (generally, with a Latin American nation such as Mexico or Argentina, or with Spain).
2. **Cultural values.** By and large, the United States is a nation of individualistic, competitive people. Many Hispanics, by contrast, have a more collective orientation. An outsider, therefore, may judge the behavior of a Hispanic subject as conformist or overly trusting when, in fact, the person is simply trying to be courteous. Researchers should also realize that Hispanic respondents might agree with a particular statement out of politeness rather than conviction.
3. **Family dynamics.** Generally speaking, Hispanic cultures have strong family loyalties. Asking subjects to reveal information about another family member may make them uncomfortable, and they may even refuse. The Maríns add that, in the home, a researcher's request to speak privately with a Hispanic woman may provoke suspicion or outright disapproval from her husband or father.
4. **Time and efficiency.** Spanish cultures, the Maríns explain, tend to be more concerned with the quality of relationships than with simply getting a job done. A non-Hispanic researcher who tries to hurry an interview with a Hispanic family, perhaps wishing not to delay the family's dinner, may be considered rude for not proceeding at a more sociable and relaxed pace.
5. **Personal space.** Finally, as the Maríns point out, people of Spanish descent typically maintain closer physical contact than many non-Hispanics. Consequently, researchers who seat themselves across the room from their subjects may appear "standoffish." Conversely, researchers may inaccurately label Hispanics "pushy" when they move closer than the non-Hispanic researcher finds comfortable.

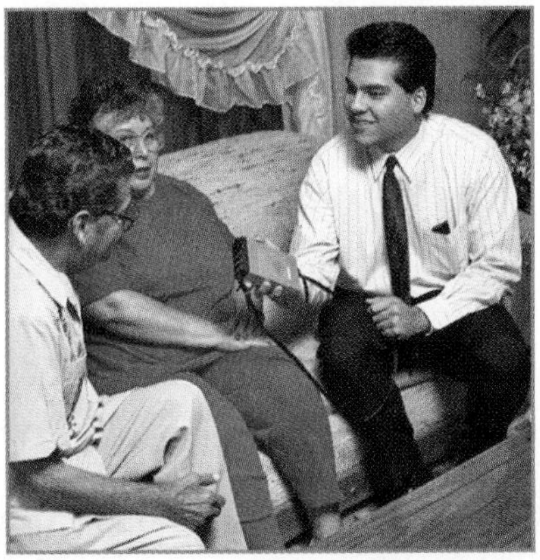

Of course, Hispanics differ among themselves just like people in every other category, and these generalizations apply to some more than to others. But the challenge of being culturally aware is especially great in the United States, where hundreds of categories of people make up our multicultural society.

Source: Marín & Marín (1991).

TESTING A HYPOTHESIS: THE EXPERIMENT

The logic of science is most clearly expressed in the **experiment,** *a research method for investigating cause and effect under highly controlled conditions.* Experimental research is *explanatory*, meaning that it asks not just what happens but why. Typically, researchers turn to an experiment to test a **hypothesis,** *an unverified statement of a relationship between variables.*

The ideal experiment consists of three steps. First, the experimenter measures the dependent variable (the "effect"); second, the investigator exposes the dependent variable to the independent variable (the "cause" or "treatment"); and third, the researcher again measures the dependent variable to see if the predicted

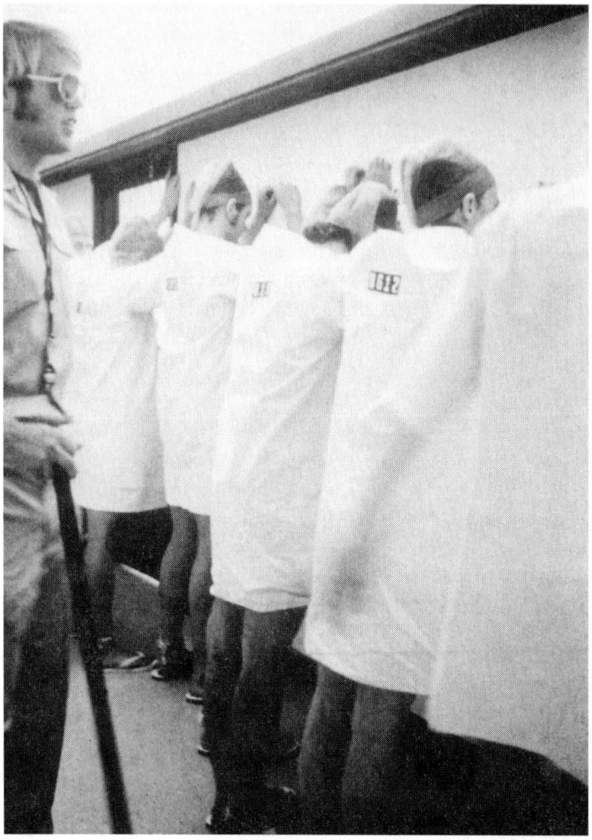

Philip Zimbardo's research helps to explain why violence is a common element in our society's prisons. At the same time, his work demonstrates the dangers that sociological investigation poses for subjects and the need for investigators to observe ethical standards that protect the welfare of people who participate in research.

change took place. If the expected change did occur, the experiment supports the hypothesis; if not, the hypothesis must be modified.

But a change in the dependent variable could be due to something other than the supposed cause. To be certain that they identify the correct cause, researchers carefully control other factors that might intrude into the experiment and affect the outcome. Such control is most easily accomplished in a laboratory, a setting specially constructed for research purposes. Another strategy for neutralizing outside influences is dividing subjects into an *experimental group* and a *control group.* Early in the study, the researcher measures the dependent variable for subjects in both groups but later exposes only the experimental group to the independent variable or treatment. (The control group typically gets a "placebo," a treatment that seems to be the same but really has no effect on the experiment.) Then the investigator measures the subjects in both groups again. Any factor occurring during the course of the research that influences people in the experimental group (say, a news event) would do the same to those in the control group, thus "washing out" the factor. By comparing the before and after measurements of the two groups, a researcher can assess how much of the change is due to the independent variable.

The Hawthorne Effect

Another concern of experimenters is that subjects may change their behavior simply because they are getting special attention, as one classic experiment revealed. In the late 1930s, the Western Electric Company hired researchers to investigate worker productivity in its Hawthorne factory near Chicago (Roethlisberger & Dickson, 1939). One experiment tested the hypothesis that increasing the available lighting would raise worker output. First, researchers measured worker productivity (the dependent variable). Then they increased the lighting (the independent variable) and measured output a second time. Productivity increased, supporting the hypothesis. But when the research team later turned the lighting back down, productivity increased again. What was going on? In time, the researchers realized that the employees were working harder (even if they could not see as well) simply because people were paying attention to them. From this research, social scientists coined the term **Hawthorne effect** to refer to *a change in a subject's behavior caused simply by the awareness of being studied.*

An Illustration: The Stanford County Prison

Prisons are often violent settings, but is this due to the "bad" people who end up there? Or, as Philip Zimbardo suspected, does the prison itself somehow lead to violent behavior? This question led Zimbardo to devise a fascinating experiment (Zimbardo, 1972; Haney, Banks, & Zimbardo, 1973).

Zimbardo contended that, once inside a prison, even emotionally healthy people are prone to violence. Thus, Zimbardo treated the *prison setting* as the independent variable capable of causing *violence,* the dependent variable.

To test this hypothesis, Zimbardo's research team first constructed a realistic-looking "prison" in the basement of the psychology building on the campus of Stanford University. Then they placed an ad in a Palo Alto newspaper, offering to pay young men to help with a two-week research project. To each of the seventy who responded they administered a series of physical and psychological tests, and then selected the healthiest twenty-four.

The next step was to assign randomly half the men to be "prisoners" and half to be "guards." The plan called for the guards and prisoners to spend the next two weeks in the "Stanford County Prison." The prisoners began their part of the experiment soon afterward when the Palo Alto police "arrested" them at their homes. After searching and handcuffing the men, the police took them to the local police station to be fingerprinted. Then they transported their captives to the Stanford prison where the guards put them behind bars. Zimbardo then sat back with a video camera to see what would happen.

The experiment soon turned into more than anyone had bargained for. Both guards and prisoners soon became embittered and hostile toward one another. Guards humiliated the prisoners by assigning them tasks such as cleaning out toilets with their bare hands. The prisoners, for their part, resisted and insulted the guards. Within four days, the researchers removed five prisoners who displayed "extreme emotional depression, crying, rage and acute anxiety" (1973:81). Before the end of the first week, the situation had become so bad that the researchers had to cancel the experiment. Zimbardo explains (1972:4): "The ugliest, most base, pathological side of human nature surfaced. We were horrified because we saw some boys (guards) treat others as if they were despicable animals, taking pleasure in cruelty, while other boys (prisoners) became servile, dehumanized robots who thought only of escape, of their own individual survival and of their mounting hatred for the guards."

The events that unfolded at the "Stanford County Prison" supported Zimbardo's hypothesis that prison violence is rooted in the social character of jails themselves, not in the personalities of guards and prisoners. This finding raises questions about our society's prisons, suggesting the need for basic reform. But also note how this experiment reveals the potential of research to threaten the physical and mental well-being of subjects. Such dangers are not always as obvious as they were in this case. Therefore, researchers must consider carefully the potential harm to subjects at all stages of their work and end any study, as Zimbardo did, if subjects may suffer harm of any kind.

ASKING QUESTIONS: SURVEY RESEARCH

A **survey** is *a research method in which subjects respond to a series of statements or questions in a questionnaire or an interview.* The most widely used of all research methods, surveys are particularly well suited to studying attitudes—such as beliefs about politics, religion, or race—since there is no way to observe directly what people think. Sometimes surveys provide clues about cause and effect, but typically they yield *descriptive* findings, painting a picture of people's views on some issue.

Population and Sample

A survey targets some **population,** *the people who are the focus of research.* In her study of racism, described at the beginning of this chapter, Lois Benjamin's population was talented African Americans. At the broadest level, political pollsters predict election returns using surveys that treat every adult in the country as the population.

Obviously, contacting millions of people would overwhelm even the most well-funded and patient researcher. Fortunately, there is an easier way that yields accurate results: Researchers collect data from a **sample,** *a part of a population that represents the whole.* Everyone uses the logic of sampling all the time. If you look around the classroom and notice five or six heads nodding off, you might conclude that the class finds the day's lecture dull. In reaching this conclusion, you are making a judgment about *all* the people (the "population") from observing *some* of the people (the "sample"). But how can we know if a sample actually represents the entire population?

One way to do this is to use *random sampling,* in which researchers draw a sample from the population randomly so that every element in the population has an equal chance to be selected. The mathematical laws of probability dictate that a random sample will, in most cases, represent the population.

Beginning researchers sometimes make the mistake of assuming that "randomly" walking up to people on a street produces a sample that is representative of the entire city. Unfortunately, such a strategy does not give every person an equal chance to be included in the sample. For one thing, any street, whether in a rich neighborhood or a college town, contains more of some kinds of people than others. For another, any researcher is apt to find some people more approachable than others, again introducing a bias.

Although good sampling is no simple task, it offers a considerable savings in time and expense. We are spared the tedious work of contacting everyone in a population, yet we can obtain essentially the same results.

APPLYING SOCIOLOGY

Survey Questions: A Word or Two Makes All the Difference

Do people approve of their president? During the Clinton years, approval ratings rose or fell depending on a few small words. A majority of adults, surveys showed, had a favorable opinion of Mr. Clinton as president. But if researchers asked people their opinion of Mr. Clinton *as a person*, his approval ratings typically tumbled 20 percent.

Clearly, how researchers word questions affects how the public responds. In 1998, *Newsweek* magazine hired a team of researchers to measure public attitudes toward abortion. The results of this national survey showed once again just how important a few words can be in shaping public response. One question put it this way: *Do you personally believe that abortion is wrong?* In this case, 57 percent of respondents said "yes," while 36 percent said "no" (the rest either were not sure or did not answer). Looking at these results, one might well conclude that a majority of people are pro-life. Yet, another question was worded this way: *Whatever your own personal view of abortion, do you favor or oppose a woman in this country having the choice to have an abortion with the advice of her doctor?* Now 69 percent favored available abortion, and just 24 percent opposed it—clear support for the pro-choice side of the debate.

Are people of two minds on the abortion question? More likely, most people are listening carefully to the wording of the questions. While a slight majority *personally* consider abortion wrong, a larger majority believe that women, after seeking the advice of a doctor, can have an abortion if they decide to.

One final example. Look at the wording in these questions: The first is *"Do you think that the police force is doing a good job?"* The second is *"Do you agree that the police force is doing a good job?"* Which one is more likely to show stronger support for the police? Why?

Source: Data from Witt (1999).

Questionnaires and Interviews

Selecting subjects is only the first step in carrying out a survey. Also needed is a plan for asking questions and recording answers. Most surveys use a questionnaire or an interview.

A **questionnaire** is *a series of written questions a researcher presents to subjects.* One type of questionnaire provides not only the questions but a series of fixed responses (similar to a multiple-choice examination). This *closed-ended format* makes it relatively easy to analyze the results, but by narrowing the range of responses, it can also distort the findings. For example, Frederick Lorenz and Brent Bruton (1996) found that how many hours per week students say they study for a college course depends on the options offered to them. When the researchers presented students with options ranging from one hour or less to nine hours or more, 75 percent said that they studied four hours or less per week. But when a comparable group was given choices ranging from four hours or less to twelve hours or longer (which suggests that they should be studying more), they suddenly became more studious, with only 34 percent reporting that they studied four hours or less each week.

A second type of questionnaire, using an *open-ended format*, allows subjects to respond freely, expressing various shades of opinion. The drawback of this approach is that the researcher has to make sense out of what can be a bewildering array of answers.

The researcher must also decide how to present questions to subjects. Most often, researchers use a *self-administered survey*, mailing or e-mailing questionnaires to respondents and asking them to complete the form and send it back. Since no researcher is present when subjects read the questionnaire, it must be both inviting and clearly written. *Pretesting* a self-administered questionnaire with a small number of people before sending it to the entire sample can avoid the costly problem of finding out—too late—that instructions or questions were confusing.

Using the mail or e-mail allows a researcher to contact a large number of people over a wide geographic area at minimal expense. But many people treat such questionnaires as junk mail, so that typically no more than half are completed and returned. Researchers often send follow-up mailings to coax reluctant subjects to respond.

Finally, keep in mind that many people are not capable of completing a questionnaire on their own. Young children obviously cannot, nor can many hospital patients or a surprising number of adults who simply lack the required reading and writing skills.

An **interview** is *a series of questions a researcher administers in person to respondents.* In a closed-format design, researchers read a question or statement and then ask the subject to select a response from several alternatives. Generally, interviews are open-ended so that subjects can respond as they choose and researchers can probe with follow-up questions. However, the researcher must guard against influencing a subject, which is as easy as raising an eyebrow when a person begins to answer.

Although subjects are more likely to complete a survey if contacted personally by the researcher, interviews have some disadvantages: Tracking people down is costly and time-consuming, especially if subjects do not live in the same area. Telephone interviews allow far greater "reach," but the impersonality of cold calls by telephone can lower the response rate.

In both questionnaires and interviews, how a question is worded greatly affects how people answer. An example: When asked if they object to homosexuals serving in the military, most adults in the United States say "yes." Yet, ask them if the government should exempt homosexuals from military service and most say "no" (NORC, 1999). Emotionally loaded language can also sway subjects. For instance, using the term "welfare mothers" rather than "women who receive public assistance" adds an emotional element to a question that encourages people to answer negatively. The box takes a closer look at the importance of wording in conducting public opinion polls.

Finally, researchers may confuse respondents by asking a double question, like "Do you think that the government should reduce the deficit by cutting spending and raising taxes?" The problem here is that a subject could very well agree with one part of the question but reject the other, so that forcing a subject to say *yes* or *no* distorts the actual opinion the researcher is trying to measure.

These African American women and men are members of the Congressional Black Caucus; they are movers and shakers on the national scene. But, according to Lois Benjamin, who conducted interviews with one hundred highly successful African Americans, "making it" does not eliminate the sting of racial prejudice. On the contrary, she found, even the highest achievers still have to contend with barriers based on skin color.

An Illustration: Studying the African American Elite

We opened this chapter by recounting how Lois Benjamin came to investigate the effects of racism on talented African American men and women. Benjamin suspected that personal achievement did not prevent hostility based on color. She based this view on her own experiences as the only black professor in the history of the University of Tampa. But was she the exception or the rule? To answer this question, Benjamin set out to discover whether—and how—racism had plagued others like herself.

TABLE 2–2 The Talented One Hundred: Lois Benjamin's African American Elite

Sex	Age	Childhood Racial Setting	Childhood Region	Highest Educational Degree	Occupational Sector	Income	Political Orientation
Male 63%	35 or Younger 6%	Mostly black 71%	West 6%	Doctorate 32%	College/ University 35%	More than $50,000 64%	Radical 13%
Female 37%	36 to 54 68%	Mostly white 15%	North/ Central 32%	Medical/Law 17%	Private, profit 17%	$35,000 to $50,000 18%	Liberal 38%
	55 or Older 26%	Racially mixed 14%	South 38%	Master's 27%	Private, nonprofit 9%	$20,000 to $34,999 12%	Moderate 28%
			Northeast 12%	Bachelor's 13%	Government 22%	Less than $20,000 6%	Conservative 5%
			Other 12%	Less 11%	Self-employed 14%		Depends on issue 14%
					Retired 3%		Unknown 2%
100%	100%	100%	100%	100%	100%	100%	100%

Source: Adapted from Lois Benjamin, *The Black Elite: Facing the Color Line in the Twilight of the Twentieth Century* (Chicago: Nelson-Hall, 1991), p. 276.

Opting to conduct a survey, Benjamin chose to interview subjects rather than distribute a questionnaire because, first, she wanted to enter into a conversation with her subjects, to ask follow-up questions, and to pursue topics that she could not anticipate. A second reason Benjamin favored interviews over questionnaires is that racism is a sensitive topic. A supportive investigator can make it easier for subjects to respond to painful questions (Bergen, 1993).

Choosing to conduct interviews made it necessary to limit the number of people in the study. Benjamin settled for one hundred men and women. Even this small number kept Benjamin busy for more than two years scheduling, traveling, and meeting with respondents. She spent two more years transcribing the tapes of her interviews, sorting out what the hours and hours of talk told her about racism, and writing up her results.

In selecting a sample, Benjamin first considered using all the people listed in *Who's Who in Black America.* But she rejected this idea in favor of starting out with people she knew and asking them to suggest others. This strategy is called *snowball sampling* because the number of individuals included grows rapidly over time.

Snowball sampling is appealing because it is an easy way to do research—we begin with familiar people who provide introductions to their friends and colleagues. The drawback, however, is that snowball sampling rarely produces a sample that is representative of the larger population. Benjamin's sample probably contained many like-minded individuals, and it was certainly biased toward people willing to talk openly about race. She understood these problems and did try to make her sample as varied as she could in terms of sex, age, and region of the country. Table 2–2 presents a statistical profile of Benjamin's respondents; the box provides some tips on how to read tables.

Benjamin based all her interviews on a series of questions with an open-ended format so that her subjects could say whatever they wished. As usually happens, the interviews took place in a wide range of settings. She met subjects in offices (hers or theirs), in hotel rooms, and in cars. In each case, Benjamin tape-recorded the conversation, which lasted from two-and-one-half to three hours, so she would not be distracted by having to take notes.

As research ethics demand, Benjamin offered full anonymity to participants. Even so, many—including notables such as Vernon E. Jordan, Jr. (former president of the National Urban League) and Yvonne Walker-Taylor (first woman president of Wilberforce

APPLYING SOCIOLOGY

Reading Tables: An Important Skill

A table provides a lot of information in a small amount of space, so learning to read tables can increase your reading efficiency. When you spot a table, look first at the title to see what information it contains. The title of Table 2–2 tells us that the table presents a profile of the one hundred subjects participating in Lois Benjamin's research. Across the top of the table, you will see eight variables that define these men and women. Reading down each column, note the categories within each variable; the percentages in each column add up to one hundred.

Starting at the top left, we see that Benjamin's sample was mostly men (63 percent versus 37 percent women). In terms of age, most of the respondents (68 percent) were in the middle stage of life, and most grew up in a predominantly black community in the South or the North/Central regions of the United States.

These individuals are, indeed, a professional elite. Notice that half have earned either a doctorate (32 percent) or a medical or law degree (17 percent). Given their extensive education (and Benjamin's own position as a professor), we should not be surprised that the largest share (35 percent) work in academic institutions. In terms of income, these are affluent individuals, with most (64 percent) earning more than $50,000 annually (a salary that only 25 percent of all U.S. workers currently make).

Finally, we see that these one hundred individuals are generally left-of-center in their political orientation. In part, this reflects their extensive schooling (which encourages progressive thinking) and the tendency of academics to fall on the liberal side of the political spectrum.

University)—were accustomed to being in the public eye and permitted Benjamin to use their names.

What surprised Benjamin most about her research was how eagerly many informants responded to her request for an interview. These normally busy men and women appeared to go out of their way to contribute to her project. Furthermore, once the interviews were underway, many became very emotional. Benjamin reports that, at some point in the conversation, about forty of her one hundred subjects cried. For them, apparently, the research provided an opportunity to release feelings and share experiences never revealed before. How did Benjamin, herself, respond to such sentiments? She reports that she laughed and cried along with her respondents.

Benjamin's research is less scientific and more interpretive sociology (she wanted to find out how her subjects understood the concept of race) and critical sociology (she undertook the study partly to document that racial prejudice still exists). Indeed, many subjects reported fearing that race might someday undermine their success, and others spoke of a race-based "glass ceiling" preventing them from reaching the highest positions in our society. Summarizing her findings, Benjamin concluded that, despite the improving social standing of African Americans, black people in the United States still feel the sting of racial hostility.

IN THE FIELD: PARTICIPANT OBSERVATION

Lois Benjamin's research demonstrates that sociological investigation takes place not only in laboratories but "in the field," that is, where people carry on their everyday lives. The most widely used strategy for field study is **participant observation,** *a research method by which investigators systematically observe people while joining in their routine activities.*

Participant observation allows researchers an inside look at social life in settings ranging from nightclubs to religious seminaries. Cultural anthropologists commonly employ participant observation (which they call *fieldwork*) to study communities in other societies. They term their descriptions of unfamiliar cultures *ethnographies*. Sociologists prefer to call their accounts of people in particular settings *case studies*.

At the outset of a field study, most investigators do not have a specific hypothesis in mind. In fact, they may not even know what the important questions will turn out to be. Thus, most field research is *exploratory* and *descriptive*.

As its name suggests, participant observation has two sides. On the one hand, getting an "insider's" look depends on becoming a participant in the setting—"hanging out" with others, trying to act, think, and even

Anthropologists and photographers Angela Fisher and Carol Beckwith have documented fascinating rituals around the world. As part of their fieldwork, they lived for months with the Himba in Namibia, in order to gain their acceptance and trust. During this time, a village man was killed by a lion. Later, his wives fell under the control of a lion spirit, apparently sent by the husband to bring these women to him in the afterlife. In the ritual shown above, photographed by Fisher and Beckwith, the women seek to rid themselves of the curse.

feel the way they do. Compared to experiments and survey research, then, participant observation has fewer hard-and-fast rules. But it is precisely this flexibility that allows investigators to explore the unfamiliar and adapt to the unexpected.

Unlike other research methods, participant observation requires that the researcher become immersed in the setting, not for a week or two but for months or even years. At the same time, however, the researcher must maintain some distance as an "observer," mentally stepping back to record field notes and, eventually, to interpret them. Because the investigator must both "play the participant" to win acceptance and gain access to people's lives and "play the observer" to maintain the distance needed for thoughtful analysis, there is an inherent tension in this method. Carrying out the twin roles of insider participant and outsider observer often comes down to a series of careful compromises.

Most sociologists carry out participant observation alone, so they—and we—must remember that the results depend on the work of a single individual. Participant observation usually falls within interpretive sociology, yielding mostly qualitative data—impressions and understandings—although researchers sometimes collect some quantitative (numerical) data. From a scientific point of view, participant observation is a "soft" method that relies heavily on personal judgment and lacks scientific rigor. Yet, its personal approach is also a strength: Whereas a highly visible team of sociologists attempting to administer, say, formal surveys would disrupt many social settings, a sensitive participant-observer can often gain considerable insight into people's natural behavior.

An Illustration: Street Corner Society

In the late 1930s, a young graduate student at Harvard University named William Foote Whyte was fascinated by the lively street life of a nearby, rather rundown section of Boston. His curiosity ultimately led him to carry out four years of participant observation in this neighborhood, which he called "Cornerville," producing a sociological classic in the process.

At the time, Cornerville was home to first- and second-generation Italian immigrants. Many were poor, and popular wisdom in Boston considered Cornerville a place to avoid: a poor, chaotic slum inhabited by racketeers. Unwilling to accept easy stereotypes, Whyte set out to discover for himself exactly what kind of life went on inside this community. His celebrated book, *Street Corner Society* (1981; orig. 1943), describes Cornerville as a highly organized community with a distinctive code of values, complex social patterns, and particular social conflicts.

In beginning his investigation, Whyte considered a range of research methods. He could have taken questionnaires to one of Cornerville's community centers and asked local people to fill them out. Or he could have invited members of the community to come to his Harvard office for interviews. But it is easy to see that such formal strategies would have prompted little cooperation from the local people and yielded few insights. Whyte decided, therefore, to ease into Cornerville life and patiently build an understanding of this rather mysterious place.

Soon enough, Whyte discovered the challenges of even getting started in field research. After all, an upper-middle-class WASPy graduate student from Harvard did not exactly fit into Cornerville life. He soon found out, for example, that even an outsider's friendly overture could seem pushy and rude. Early on, Whyte dropped in at a local bar, hoping to buy a woman a drink and encourage her to talk about Cornerville. But looking around the room, he could find no woman alone. Presently, he thought he might have an opportunity when a fellow sat down with two women. He gamely asked, "Pardon me. Would you mind if I joined you?" Instantly, he realized his mistake:

> There was a moment of silence while the man stared at me. Then he offered to throw me down the stairs. I assured him that this would not be necessary, and demonstrated as much by walking right out of there without any assistance. (1981:289)

As this incident suggests, gaining entry to a community is the crucial (and sometimes hazardous) first step in field research. "Breaking in" requires patience, ingenuity, and a little luck. Whyte's big break came in the form of a young man named "Doc," whom he met in a local social service agency. Listening to Whyte's account of his bungled efforts to make friends in Cornerville, Doc was sympathetic and decided to take Whyte under his wing and introduce him to others in the community. With Doc's help, Whyte soon became a neighborhood regular.

Whyte's friendship with Doc illustrates the importance of a *key informant* in field research. Such people not only introduce a researcher to a community but often remain a source of information and help. But using a key informant also has its risks. Because any person has a particular circle of friends, a key informant's guidance is certain to "spin" the study in one way or another. Moreover, in the eyes of others, the reputation of the key informant—for better or worse—usually rubs off on the investigator. In sum, a key informant is helpful at the outset, but a participant-observer soon must seek a broad range of contacts.

Having entered the Cornerville world, Whyte began his work in earnest. But he soon realized that a field researcher needs to know when to speak up and when simply to listen, look, and learn. One evening, he joined a group discussing neighborhood gambling. Wanting to get the facts straight, Whyte asked innocently, "I suppose the cops were all paid off?" In a heartbeat,

> The gambler's jaw dropped. He glared at me. Then he denied vehemently that any policeman had been paid off and immediately switched the conversation to another subject. For the rest of that evening I felt very uncomfortable.

The next day, Doc offered some sound advice:

> "Go easy on that 'who,' 'what,' 'why,' 'when,' 'where' stuff, Bill. You ask those questions and people will clam up on you. If people accept you, you can just hang around, and you'll learn the answers in the long run without even having to ask the questions." (1981:303)

In the months and years that followed, Whyte became familiar with life in Cornerville, and even married a local woman. In the process, he learned that this neighborhood was hardly the stereotypical slum. On the contrary, most immigrants worked hard, many were quite successful, and some even boasted of sending children to college. In short, Whyte's book makes for fascinating reading about the deeds, dreams, and disappointments of one ethnic community, and it contains a richness of detail that can only come from long-term participant observation.

Whyte's work shows that participant observation is a method rife with tensions and contrasts. Its flexibility allows a researcher to respond to the unexpected, but makes replication difficult. Participation means getting close to people, but observation depends on keeping some distance. Little expense is involved since no elaborate equipment or laboratory is needed, but most studies take a year or more. This long-term commitment may explain why participant observation is used less often than the other methods described in this chapter. Yet, the depth of understanding gained through interpretive research of this kind greatly enriches our knowledge of many types of human communities.

SEEING OURSELVES

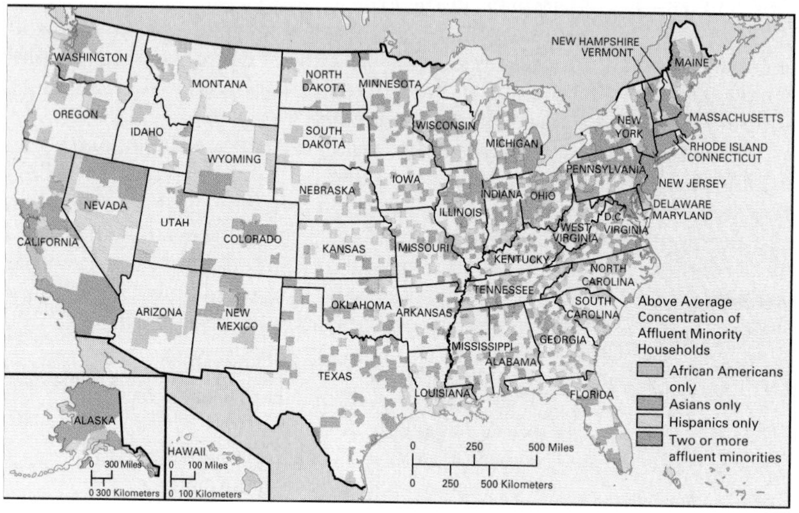

Adapted from *American Demographics* magazine, December 1992, pp. 34–35. Reprinted with permission. © 1992, *American Demographics* magazine, Ithaca, New York. Data from the 1990 decennial census.

NATIONAL MAP 2–1
Affluent Minorities across the United States

Based on 1990 census data, this map identifies the counties of the United States with an above-average share of affluent minority households—people earning at least $50,000 annually. (For the entire country, 28 percent of African American families, 26 percent of Hispanic families, and 53 percent of Asian families fall into this category.) Where in the United States do affluent members of each minority category live? Do members of one category tend to live where members of another category predominate? Can you explain this pattern?

USING AVAILABLE DATA: SECONDARY AND HISTORICAL ANALYSIS

Not all research requires investigators to collect their own data. Sometimes sociologists conduct **secondary analysis,** *a research method in which a researcher uses data collected by others.*

The most widely used statistics in social science are gathered by government agencies (for easy access to many data links, visit http://www.thesociologypage.com). The Census Bureau continuously updates information on the U.S. population. Comparable data on Canada are available from Statistics Canada, a branch of that nation's government. For international data, consult various publications of the United Nations and the World Bank. In short, a wide range of data about the whole world is as close as your library or the Internet.

Using available data—whether government statistics or the findings of individual researchers—saves time and money. This approach, therefore, has special appeal to sociologists with low budgets. Even more important, government data are generally better than what even well-funded researchers could hope to obtain on their own.

Still, secondary analysis has inherent problems. For one thing, available data may not exist in precisely the form needed. Further, there are always questions about the meaning and accuracy of work done by others. For example, in his classic study of suicide, Emile Durkheim acknowledged that there was no way to know whether a death classified as a suicide was really an accident, and vice versa. In addition, various agencies use different procedures and categories in collecting data, making comparisons difficult. In the end, then, using secondhand data is a little like shopping for a used car: Bargains are plentiful, but you have to shop carefully to avoid ending up with a "lemon."

To illustrate, let's assume that reading about Lois Benjamin's account of African American elites sparks our interest in this country's affluent minorities. How many such people are there? Where do they live? National Map 2–1 graphically displays Census Bureau data that address these questions. These statistics are the best available, and at no cost. Yet to use them means accepting the Census Bureau's racial and ethnic categories (until 2000, for example, people could check only one racial category). It also means accepting people's self-reported income on government questionnaires as accurate. Further, if you were to use this map for your own purposes, you would also have to accept the given definitions of "affluent" and "above average," even though they may not exactly fit your purpose.

An Illustration: A Tale of Two Cities

To people trapped in the present, secondary analysis offers a key to unlocking secrets of the past. The award-winning study *Puritan Boston and Quaker Philadelphia*, by E. Digby Baltzell (1979b), exemplifies a researcher's power to analyze the past using historical sources.

A chance visit to Bowdoin College in Maine prompted Baltzell to begin his investigation. Entering the college library, he gazed upon portraits of the celebrated author Nathaniel Hawthorne, the eminent poet Henry Wadsworth Longfellow, and Franklin Pierce, our nation's fourteenth president. He was startled to learn that all three of these great men were members of a single class at Bowdoin, graduating in 1825. How could it be, Baltzell mused, that this small college had graduated more famous people in a single year than his own, much bigger University of Pennsylvania had graduated in its entire history? To answer this question, Baltzell was soon poring over historical documents to see if New England indeed produced more famous individuals than his native Pennsylvania.

For data, Baltzell turned to the *Dictionary of American Biography*, twenty volumes profiling more than 13,000 outstanding men and women in fields such as politics, law, and the arts. The *Dictionary* told Baltzell *who* was great; but he also wanted some way to measure *how* great people were. He decided to base his ranking on the *Dictionary*'s note that, the more impressive the person's achievements, the longer the biography. So counting the number of lines in a biography yielded a reasonable measure of "greatness."

By the time Baltzell had identified the seventy-five individuals with the longest biographies, he saw a striking pattern. Massachusetts had the most, with twenty-one of the seventy-five top achievers. The New England states, combined, claimed thirty-one of the entries. By contrast, Pennsylvania could boast of only two, and the entire Middle Atlantic region had just twelve. Looking more closely, Baltzell discovered that most of New England's great achievers had grown up in and around the city of Boston. Again, in stark contrast, almost no one of comparable standing came from his own Philadelphia, a city with many more people than Boston.

What could explain this remarkable pattern? Baltzell drew inspiration from the German sociologist Max Weber (1958; orig. 1904–5), who argued that a region's record of achievement was largely a result of its predominant religious beliefs (see Chapter 4, "Society"). In the religious differences that set Boston apart from Philadelphia, Baltzell found the answer to his puzzle. Boston was a Puritan settlement, founded by people who were determined in their pursuit of excellence and public achievement. Philadelphia, by contrast, was settled by Quakers, who were equally determined to shun any sort of public notice.

Both the Puritans and the Quakers were fleeing religious persecution in England, but the two religious beliefs produced quite different cultural patterns. Convinced of humanity's innate sinfulness, Boston Puritans built a rigid society in which family, church, and school regulated people's behavior. They celebrated hard work as a means of glorifying God, and viewed public success as a reassuring sign of God's blessing. In other words, Puritanism fostered a disciplined life in which people both sought and respected achievement.

Philadelphia's Quakers, on the other hand, built their way of life on the belief that all human beings are basically good. They saw little need for strong social institutions to "save" individuals from sinfulness. They believed in equality, so that even people who became rich considered everyone else a social equal. Thus, rich and poor alike lived modestly and discouraged one other from standing out by seeking fame or even public office.

In Baltzell's sociological imagination, Boston and Philadelphia took the form of two social "test tubes": Puritanism was poured into one, Quakerism into the other. Centuries later, we can see that different "chemical reactions" occurred in each case. The two belief systems apparently led to different attitudes toward personal achievement, which, in turn, shaped the history of each region. Moreover, we can see the results of these cultural differences even today. Boston's Kennedy family (despite being Catholic) still exemplifies the Puritan pursuit of recognition and leadership, but there has *never* been a family with such public stature in the entire history of Philadelphia.

Baltzell's study uses scientific logic, but it also illustrates the interpretive approach. His research reminds us that sociological investigation often involves various methodological approaches and, of course, a lively sociological imagination.

Table 2–3 summarizes the four major methods of sociological investigation. We now turn to our final consideration: the link between research results and sociological theory.

THE INTERPLAY OF THEORY AND METHOD

No matter how they gather data, sociologists have to turn facts into meaning by building theory. They do this in two ways: inductive logical thought and deductive logical thought.

TABLE 2–3 Four Research Methods: A Summary			
Method	**Application**	**Advantages**	**Limitations**
Experiment	For explanatory research that specifies relationships among variables; generates quantitative data	Provides the greatest opportunity to specify cause-and-effect relationships; replication of research is relatively easy	Laboratory settings have an artificial quality; unless the research environment is carefully controlled, results may be biased
Survey	For gathering information about issues that cannot be directly observed, such as attitudes and values; useful for descriptive and explanatory research; generates quantitative or qualitative data	Sampling allows surveys of large populations using questionnaires; interviews provide in-depth responses	Questionnaires must be carefully prepared and may yield a low return rate; interviews are expensive and time-consuming
Participant observation	For exploratory and descriptive study of people in a "natural" setting; generates qualitative data	Allows study of "natural" behavior; usually inexpensive	Time-consuming; replication of research is difficult; researcher must balance roles of participant and observer
Secondary analysis	For exploratory, descriptive, or explanatory research whenever suitable data are available	Saves time and expense of data collection; makes historical research possible	Researcher has no control over possible biases in data; data may only partially fit current research needs

Inductive logical thought is *reasoning that transforms specific observations into general theory.* In this mode, a researcher's thinking runs from the specific to the general and goes something like this: "I have some interesting data here; I wonder what they mean?" E. Digby Baltzell's research illustrates the inductive logical model. His data showed that one region of the country (the Boston area) had produced many more high achievers than another (the Philadelphia region). He worked "upward" from ground-level observations to the high-flying theory that religious values were a key factor that shaped people's attitude toward achievement.

A second type of logical thought moves "downward," in the opposite direction. **Deductive logical thought** is *reasoning that transforms general theory into specific hypotheses suitable for testing.* The researcher's thinking runs from the general to the specific: "I have this hunch about human behavior; let's collect some data and put them to the test." Working deductively, the researcher first states the theory in the form of a hypothesis and then selects a method by which to test it. To the extent that the data support the hypothesis, we conclude that the theory is correct; data that refute the hypothesis tell us that the theory should be revised or perhaps rejected entirely.

Philip Zimbardo's Stanford County Prison experiment illustrates deductive logic. Zimbardo began with the general idea that prisons change human behavior. He then developed a specific, testable hypothesis: Placed in a prison setting, even emotionally well-balanced young men will behave violently. The violence that erupted soon after his experiment began supported Zimbardo's hypothesis. Had his experiment produced friendly behavior between prisoners and guards, his original theory clearly would have required reformulation.

Just as researchers often employ several methods over the course of one study, they typically make use of *both* kinds of logical thought. Figure 2–2 illustrates both types of reasoning: inductively building theory from observations and deductively making observations to test a theory.

Finally, turning facts into meaning usually involves statistical data. Precisely how sociologists present their numbers affects the conclusions their readers draw. In other words, all research offers the chance to interpret reality in one way or another.

Often, we conclude that an argument must be true simply because there are statistics to back it up. However, we must look at statistics with a cautious eye. After all, researchers choose what data to present, they attach meaning to their statistics, and they may use tables and graphs to steer readers toward particular conclusions. The final box, on pages 50–51, takes a closer look at this important issue.

PUTTING IT ALL TOGETHER: TEN STEPS IN SOCIOLOGICAL INVESTIGATION

We can draw the material in this chapter together by outlining ten steps in the process of carrying out sociological investigation. Each step is represented by an important question:

1. **What is your topic?** Being curious and using the sociological perspective can generate ideas for social research any time and any place. The issue you choose for study is likely to have some personal significance.
2. **What have others already learned?** You are probably not the first person with an interest in some issue. Visit the library to see what theories and methods other researchers have applied to your topic. In reviewing the existing research, note problems that have come up.
3. **What, exactly, are your questions?** Are you seeking to explore an unfamiliar social setting? To describe some category of people? To investigate cause and effect among variables? If your study is exploratory or descriptive, identify *who* you wish to study, *where* the research will take place, and *what* kinds of issues you want to explore. If it is explanatory, you also must formulate the hypothesis to be tested and operationalize each variable.
4. **What will you need to carry out research?** How much time and money are available to you? Are special equipment or skills necessary? Can you do the work yourself? You should answer all these questions as you plan the research project.
5. **Are there ethical concerns?** Not all research raises serious ethical questions, but you must be sensitive to the possibility. Can the research cause harm or threaten anyone's privacy? How might you design the study to minimize the chances for injury? Will you promise anonymity to the subjects? If so, how will you ensure that anonymity is maintained?
6. **What method will you use?** Consider all major research strategies, as well as combinations of approaches. Keep in mind that the appropriate method depends on the kind of questions you are asking as well as the resources available to you.
7. **How will you record the data?** The research method you choose is the system for data collection. Record all information accurately and in a way that will make sense later (it may be some time before you actually write up the results of your work). Be alert for any bias that may creep into the research.
8. **What do the data tell you?** Study the data in terms of your initial questions and decide how to interpret the data. If your study involves a specific hypothesis, you must decide whether to confirm, reject, or modify the hypothesis. Keep in mind that there may be several ways to look at your data, depending on which theoretical paradigm you apply, and you should consider all interpretations.
9. **What are your conclusions?** Prepare a final report stating your conclusions. How does your work advance sociological theory? Improve research methods? Does your study have policy implications? What would the general public find interesting in your work? Finally, evaluate your own work, noting problems that arose and questions left unanswered.
10. **How can you share what you've learned?** Consider sending your research paper to a campus newspaper or magazine or making a presentation to a class, campus gathering, or perhaps a meeting of professional sociologists. The point is to share what you have learned with others and to let them respond to your work.

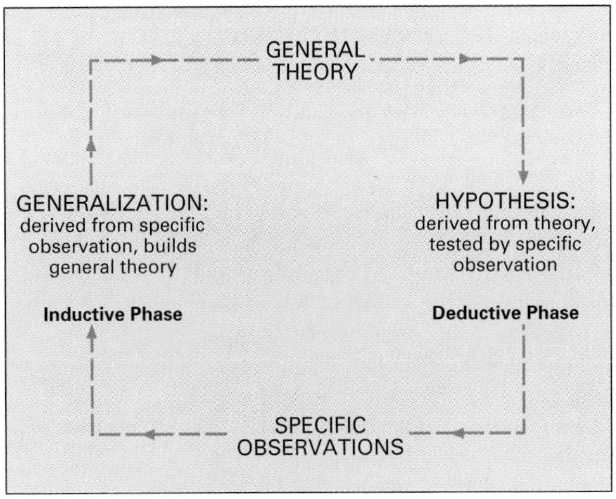

FIGURE 2–2 **Deductive and Inductive Logical Thought**

CONTROVERSY & DEBATE

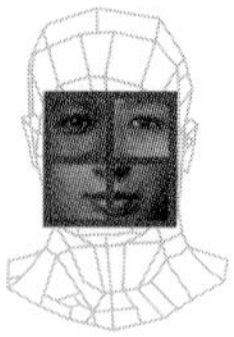

Can People Lie with Statistics?

Is research—especially research involving numbers—always as "factual" as we think? Not according to the great English politician Benjamin Disraeli, who once remarked, "There are three kinds of lies: lies, damned lies, and statistics!" In a world that bombards us with numbers—often described as "scientific facts" or "official figures"—it is worth pausing to consider that "statistical evidence" is not necessarily the same as truth. For one thing, any researcher can make mistakes. For another, because data do not speak for themselves, someone has to interpret what they mean. Sometimes, people (even sociologists) "dress up" their data almost the way politicians deliver campaign speeches—with an eye more to winning you over than getting at the truth.

The best way not to fall prey to statistical manipulation is to understand how people can mislead with statistics.

1. **People select their data.** Many times, the data presented are not wrong, but they are not the whole story. Let's say someone who thinks that television is ruining our way of life presents statistics indicating that we watch more TV today than a generation ago. Moreover, during the same period, College Board scores have fallen. Both sets of data may be correct, but the suggestion that television is lowering test scores is unproven. Moreover, a person more favorable to television might counter with the additional "fact" that our country spends much more on books today than a generation ago, suggesting that television creates new intellectual interests. In sum, people can find statistics that seem to support just about any political argument.

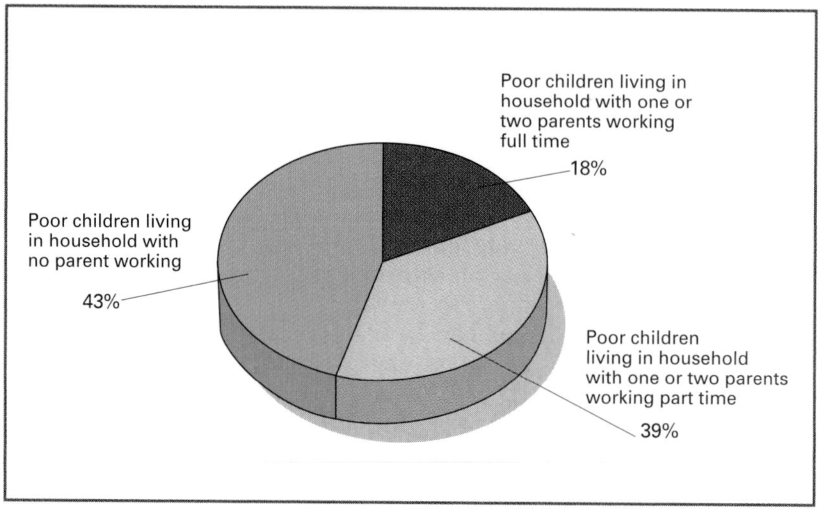

2. **People interpret their data.** Another way people manipulate statistics is to "package" them with a ready-made interpretation, as if numbers can mean only one thing. One publication, for example, presented the results of a study of U.S. children living in poverty

SUMMARY

1. Two basic requirements for sociological investigation are (1) using the sociological perspective and (2) being curious and asking questions about the world around us.
2. Scientific sociology studies society by systematically observing social behavior. This methodological approach requires carefully operationalizing concepts and ensuring that measurement is both reliable (consistent) and valid (precise).
3. A goal of science is to discover how variables are related. Correlation means that two or more variables change value together. A cause-and-effect relationship means that change in one variable actually causes the change in another variable. When a cause-and-effect relationship exists, a researcher who knows the value of an independent variable can predict the value of some dependent variable.

(National Center for Children in Poverty, cited in *Population Today*, 1995). As the figure shows, the researchers reported that 43 percent of these children lived in a household with no working parent, 39 percent lived in a household with one or two parents employed part time, and 18 percent lived in a household with one or two parents working full time. The researchers labeled this figure "Majority of Children in Poverty Live with Parents Who Work." Do you think this interpretation is accurate or misleading?

3. **People use graphs to "spin" the truth.** Especially in newspapers and other popular media, we find statistics in the form of charts and graphs. Graphs help explain data, showing, for example, an upward or downward trend. But they also give people the opportunity to "spin" data in various ways. What trend we think we see depends, in part, on the time frame used in a graph. Looking at just the last few years, for instance, we would see the U.S. crime rate going downward. But, looking at the last few decades, we would see an opposite trend: The crime rate pushes sharply upward.

    The scale used to draw a graph is also important because it lets a researcher "inflate" or "deflate" a trend. Both graphs below present identical data for College Board SAT scores between 1967 and 1995. But the left-hand graph stretches the scale to show a downward trend; the right-hand graph compresses the scale, making the trend disappear. So, understanding what statistics *really* mean depends on being a careful reader!

Continue the debate . . .

1. *Why do you think people are so quick to accept "statistics" as true?*
2. *From a scientific point of view, is spinning the truth acceptable? What about from a critical approach trying to advance social change?*
3. *Can you find a news story on some social issue that you think presents biased data or conclusions? What are the biases?*

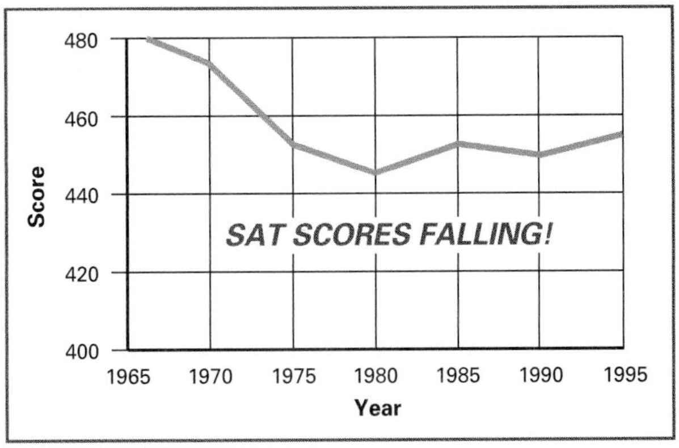

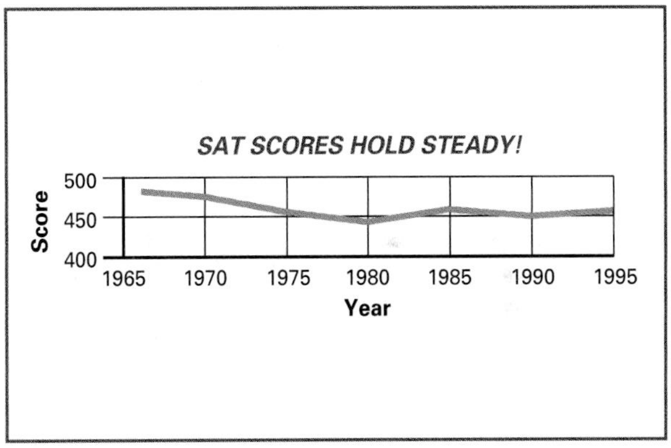

4. Although investigators select topics according to their personal interests, the scientific ideal of objectivity demands that they try to suspend personal values and biases as they conduct research.
5. A limitation of scientific sociology is that human beings, as creative creatures, do not act according to any rigid laws of behavior.
6. Interpretive sociology is a methodological approach that focuses on the meaning that people attach to their behavior. Reality is not "out there" but is constructed by people in their everyday interaction.
7. Critical sociology is a methodological approach that uses research as a means of social change. It rejects the scientific principle of objectivity, claiming that all research has a political character.
8. Because their work has the potential to cause discomfort or harm to subjects, professional sociologists are bound by ethical guidelines.
9. The logic of science is most clearly expressed in the experiment, which is performed under controlled conditions and tries to specify causal relationships between two (or more) variables.

10. Surveys measure people's attitudes or behavior using questionnaires or interviews.
11. Participant observation is a method by which a researcher directly observes a social setting while participating in it for an extended period of time.
12. Secondary analysis is making use of existing data. This method is easier and often more efficient than collecting data firsthand, and allows the study of historical issues.
13. Theory and research are linked in two ways. Deductive logical thought starts with general theories and generates specific hypotheses suitable for testing. Inductive logical thought starts with specific observations and builds general theories.

KEY CONCEPTS

science (p. 26) a logical system that bases knowledge on direct, systematic observation

scientific sociology (p. 26) the study of society based on systematic observation of social behavior

empirical evidence (p. 26) information we can verify with our senses

concept (p. 28) a mental construct that represents some part of the world, inevitably in a simplified form

variable (p. 28) a concept whose value changes from case to case

measurement (p. 28) the process of determining the value of a variable in a specific case

operationalizing a variable (p. 29) specifying exactly what one is to measure before assigning a value to a variable

reliability (p. 29) consistency in measurement

validity (p. 29) precision in measuring exactly what one intends to measure

cause and effect (p. 30) a relationship in which change in one variable (the independent variable) causes change in another (the dependent variable)

independent variable (p. 30) a variable that causes change in another (dependent) variable

dependent variable (p. 30) a variable that is changed by another (independent) variable

correlation (p. 30) a relationship by which two (or more) variables change together

spurious correlation (p. 31) an apparent, although false, relationship between two (or more) variables caused by some other variable

control (p. 31) holding constant all variables except one in order to see clearly the effect of that variable

objectivity (p. 32) a state of personal neutrality in conducting research

replication (p. 33) repetition of research by other investigators

interpretive sociology (p. 34) the study of society that focuses on the meanings people attach to their social world

critical sociology (p. 34) the study of society that focuses on the need for social change

gender (p. 35) the personal traits and social positions that members of a society attach to being female or male

research method (p. 36) a systematic plan for conducting research

experiment (p. 37) a research method for investigating cause and effect under highly controlled conditions

hypothesis (p. 37) an unverified statement of a relationship between variables

Hawthorne effect (p. 38) a change in a subject's behavior caused simply by the awareness of being studied

survey (p. 39) a research method in which subjects respond to a series of statements or questions in a questionnaire or an interview

population (p. 39) the people who are the focus of research

sample (p. 39) a part of a population that represents the whole

questionnaire (p. 40) a series of written questions a researcher presents to subjects

interview (p. 41) a series of questions a researcher administers in person to respondents

participant observation (p. 43) a research method in which investigators systematically observe people while joining in their routine activities

secondary analysis (p. 46) a research method in which a researcher uses data collected by others

inductive logical thought (p. 48) reasoning that transforms specific observations into general theory

deductive logical thought (p. 48) reasoning that transforms general theory into specific hypotheses suitable for testing

CRITICAL-THINKING QUESTIONS

1. What does it mean to say that there are various kinds of truth? What are the advantages of science as a way of knowing? What are the limitations of this approach?
2. How does interpretive sociology differ from scientific sociology? What about critical sociology? Which approach best describes the work of Emile Durkheim, Max Weber, and Karl Marx?
3. Why do some sociologists argue that objectivity is essential to sound research? Why do other sociologists disagree?
4. What are some differences between "hard" research (such as scientific experiments) and "soft" research (such as participant observation)?

APPLICATIONS AND EXERCISES

1. Imagine that you are observing your instructor in an effort to assess his or her skills as a teacher. Operationalize the concept "good teaching." What specific traits might you identify as relevant evidence? Do you think students are always good judges of strong teaching?
2. Drop by to see at least three sociology instructors (or other social science instructors) during their office hours. Ask each the extent to which sociology is an objective science. Do they agree about the character of their discipline? Why or why not?
3. Conduct a practice interview with a roommate or friend on the general topic of "What is the value of a college education?" Before the actual interview, prepare a list of specific questions or issues you think are relevant. Afterward, give some thought to why carrying out an effective interview is much harder than it initially may seem.
4. You can have your sociological imagination working even when watching television. For example, national surveys suggest television sitcom watchers tend to be young, single, and politically liberal while network news watchers are older, married, and more conservative. Watch both kinds of television and pay particular attention to the commercial advertising: Does it seem to be geared, in each case, toward the type of audience just described? Before you begin, decide what exactly you will be looking for, and, based on what you have learned in this chapter, sketch out a research plan.
5. Install the CD-ROM packaged in the back of this new textbook to access a variety of study, review, and applications exercises designed to help you better understand the material covered in this chapter. The CD includes an author's tip video, as well as interactive maps, video application exercises, Web links, and study questions.

SITES TO SEE

http://www.prenhall.com/macionis
Visit the interactive Web site that accompanies this text. Begin by clicking on the cover of your book. You will find a chapter-by-chapter study guide, practice tests, chat room, and many suggested Web links.

http://www.macionis.com
(or **http://www.thesociologypage.com**)
You can find dozens of Web links to important sources of sociological data at the author's Web page.

http://www.census.gov/datamap/www
Data for any county in the United States are available from the U.S. Census Bureau at this Web site. Visit this site and prepare a sociological profile of your local area.

http://www.asanet.org
Read the code of ethics of the American Sociological Association, available on the organization's Web site. Summarize the code's principles by writing a description of a "professional sociologist."

cyber.scope

PART I
Welcome to the Information Revolution!

Now that we have begun the new century—and a new millennium—we are witnessing astounding changes brought on by a new kind of technology. For the last two centuries, the Industrial Revolution has shaped our society, dictating the kind of work people do and how we think about the world. But now another transformation is underway—dubbed the Information Revolution—that is already redefining our world in novel ways.

At the end of each of the five parts of this text, we present a special section called "cyber.scope." These features highlight how computers and new information technology affect the issues raised in the preceding chapters. In this first cyber.scope, we extend our discussion of the sociological perspective (Chapter 1) and sociological research (Chapter 2) to explain what the Information Revolution is all about.

The Age of Machines: Industrial Society

The time line found inside the front cover of this book places the onset of the "modern era" about 250 years ago, the dawn of the Industrial Revolution. At that time—first in England then soon after in the United States—new sources of energy led imaginative people to create new products in new ways. First rivers and then steam generated by coal furnaces provided the power to operate large machines. Soon afterward, the Industrial Revolution was changing all aspects of social life, drawing people away from home to work in the new factories and demanding that they learn the skills needed to operate machinery. As time went on, the increasing size and number of factories encouraged migration from the countryside to rapidly growing cities where most people experienced a faster-paced, more impersonal way of life and, in time, came to enjoy a higher material standard of living. As we have noted, these changes sparked people's interest in studying society and played a key role in the birth of sociology.

Familiarity with computers is far more common among younger members of our society than older generations. Today's young people, who will live out their lives during the twenty-first century, will find computers a natural and indispensable part of day-to-day living.

The Age of Computers: Information Society

The final decades of the twentieth century witnessed the unfolding of another technological transformation—the Information Revolution—which promises to change our world once again. The technology that will define the twenty-first century is based on *information:* the computer and related technology, including the Internet, facsimile machines, modems, and cellular telephones, as well as fiber optics and satellite communications. The fact that we already have shorthand names for such devices—the "Net," "fax," "cell phone," and "dish"—suggests how quickly they have become an established part of our lives.

The age of the computer began in 1946 when U.S. engineers in a Philadelphia laboratory switched on a room-sized machine stuffed with wires and vacuum tubes. Despite its giant size, this "mother of all computers" could do no more than today's ten-dollar hand-held calculator. No wonder Thomas Watson, head of IBM, thought his company would end up selling "maybe five computers." Thirty years later, Ken

Olson, founder of Digital Equipment Corporation, was just as skeptical, stating that "There is no reason anyone would want a computer in the home" (quoted in Lunsford, 1996).

For better or worse, these two men were quite wrong. In the final decades of the twentieth century, increasingly sophisticated computers quickly became a basic element of our lives. We now find microprocessors at work in virtually all new vehicles as well as in the vast majority of U.S. businesses and households. Surveys show that, in 2000, about half of U.S. households had at least one personal computer, with half of these connected to the Internet. As computers become more numerous—as well as more powerful, smaller, and portable—they will rewrite the rules of social life in the twenty-first century just as monstrous machines defined the industrial era now coming to a close.

The earliest computers, including the 1946 ENIAC (Electronic Numerical Integrator and Computer) were monstrous contraptions that filled an entire room. (In fact, in 1949, Popular Mechanics *magazine confidently predicted that computers in the future would weigh no more than 1.5 tons!) It wasn't until the development of small, personal computers in the 1980s that the Information Revolution began to change the everyday lives of most people in the United States.*

What's different about new information technology? Most basically, the change involves the kind of work people do. Yesterday's industrial technology empowered people to create more and more *things;* information technology leads us to work with *ideas*, creating and manipulating symbols. The industrial age was represented by the factory's assembly line, with workers toiling to make steel or to assemble cars. But the typical worker in the information age peers at a computer screen, entering data, writing, calculating, composing, drawing, or designing.

A second key change brought about by the Information Revolution is a declining importance to distance and physical space. Just as industrial technology demands that people work in centralized factories (where the machinery and energy sources are located), information technology allows people to work almost anywhere that they can carry a computer or flip on a cell phone. Note, too, that when we use this technology to communicate with others, we often have no idea where they are. The term *cyberspace* even suggests that our emerging world is less and less bounded by physical dimensions.

Of course, just as we gauge the output of industrial engines with an antiquated reference to the "horsepower" they made obsolete, so we now cling to older, physical images in describing new cyberrealities: We talk about the "information superhighway,"[1] read "bulletin boards," and enter "chat rooms." Yet these "places" are a "virtual reality," meaning that they are computer simulations that we see and interact with, but they have no physical existence at all. In fact, they exist only in the flow of electrons that illuminates our computer, electrons that can circle the world at the speed of light.

As later chapters of the text explain, this new technology is changing virtually every dimension of our lives: reshaping culture and how we learn about the world, connecting us to people in new ways, generating new kinds of crime as well as new ways of pursuing criminals, and even altering patterns of social inequality. There is little doubt that, as we move through the new century, we will see more changes that will spark people's sociological interest in the surrounding world.

New Information Technology: Thoughts on Theory

Chapter 1 ("The Sociological Perspective") discusses sociology's three major theoretical paradigms. What insights do these paradigms give us into new information technology?

[1]The rapidly increasing number of people logging on the Internet has overwhelmed existing telephone lines and sometimes results in long delays in transmitting and receiving information. For a while, at least, the "information superhighway" may remain more of a "dirt road."

SEEING OURSELVES

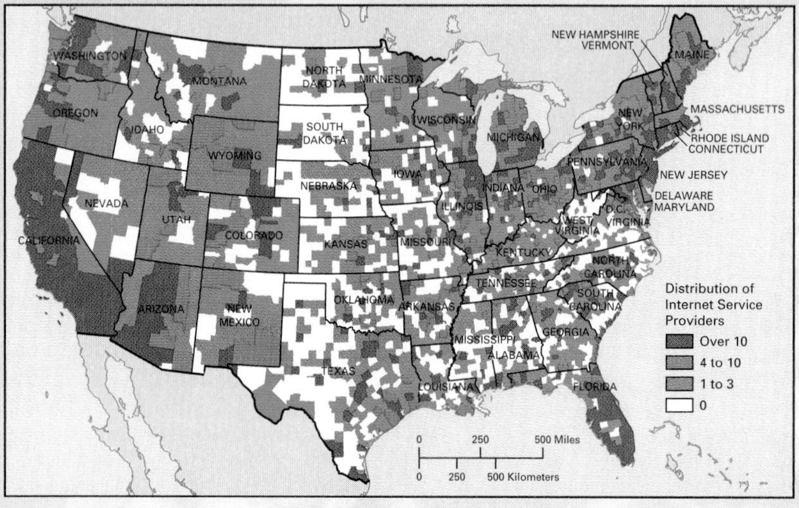

NATIONAL MAP Cyber I–1
Available Internet Service across the United States

The counties that have the most Internet service providers are those with high population densities and, thus, large markets. These same counties also have a large number of affluent people who can afford to log on to the Information Revolution. Thus, while high technology is transforming the United States, the pace of change is faster in urban than rural areas.

Source: *Time*, March 22, 1999. Copyright © 1999, *Time*, Inc. Reprinted by permission.

A structural-functional analysis would point up the fact that, because society is a system of countless interdependent elements, a new form of technology is likely to affect virtually all aspects of our lives. Since the invention of television in 1939, more than 2 billion TV sets have been built (and their numbers are rising faster than global population). Television has altered what we know, how we learn, patterns of recreation, and even the ways family members interact. The computer will almost certainly change our lives even more. Its manifest (that is, intended and expected) effects will range from decentralizing the workplace to encouraging entire cities to spread outward, since talking to or working with others no longer requires being physically with them. The latent (that is, unintended) effects are certainly harder to foresee, but they may well include new kinds of human communities as people pay less attention to their physical neighbors and spend more time communicating online with like-minded others.

A social-conflict analysis of the rise of new information technology offers other, contrasting insights, especially regarding social inequality. Here, we might note that the spread of new information technology has been rapid among affluent people and those living in densely populated urban areas, but far less among the poor and rural people—a pattern illustrated in National Map Cyber I–1. There is already evidence that the information age will be marked by two distinct classes: educated people with sophisticated symbolic skills (who are likely to prosper) and people without symbolic skills (who are likely to remain in low-income jobs). Statistical comparisons show that, among workers in the same job, those able to use a computer earn 15 percent more than those who cannot (Ratan, 1995).

Finally, the symbolic-interaction paradigm asks questions at the micro-level of analysis. How, for example, does communication via electronic mail differ from face-to-face interaction? Obviously, lacking facial expression or tone of voice, electronic communication cannot convey emotion very well. For this reason, as shown in Figure Cyber I–1, people have creatively turned the characters found on their keyboards into new symbols, generating a new cyber-language.

New Information Technology: What about Research?

How is new information technology changing sociological research, the focus of Chapter 2? A generation of sociologists has now been trained to use computers to select random samples, to perform complex statistical analysis, and to prepare written reports efficiently. Electronic mail enables researchers to "travel" almost anywhere instantly and with minimal cost. In the coming years, more and more surveys will take place online. Electronic surveys raise some interesting questions: Will this technology improve survey response rates or be discarded as electronic junk mail? Will cyber-surveys end up protecting respondents' anonymity or threatening their privacy?

What seems sure is that new information technology will greatly enhance communication among researchers throughout the world. The Internet, which is highlighted in the next cyber.scope on pages 244–45, now links at least 150 million people in 175 countries. It gives sociologists a powerful tool for building networks, sharing information, and joining together to conduct research. Just as important, faculty and students alike now have ready access to a rapidly increasing amount of statistical information. For example, the U.S. Census Bureau (see its Web site at http://www.census.gov) publishes reports of all kinds online, and will respond to questions from individuals doing research of their own.

Visit Us Online!

Please accept our invitation to visit the Web site that accompanies this text. Travel to the author's home page, which can be found at http://www.thesociologypage.com (or http://www.macionis.com) to review our family of textbooks, read sociological news, view videos, and find a library of links to a wide range of interesting organizations. The author and publisher have prepared an interactive Web site that serves as a study guide to help you throughout this course. Visit it at http://www.prenhall.com/macionis and click on the cover of this book. There you will find learning objectives for each text chapter, self-scoring practice tests, a chat room where you can share ideas and opinions with others, and links to other instructive Web sites. These sites, along with the CD-ROM that is included with your new textbook, are our invitation to you to join the Information Revolution. Welcome, and enjoy!

FIGURE Cyber I–1: Cyber-Symbols: An Emerging Language

It all started with the "smiley" figure that shows one is happy or telling a joke. Now a new language of gestures is emerging as creative people use computer keystrokes to create emoticons, symbols that convey thoughts and emotions. Here is a sampling of the new cyber-language. (Rotate this page 90° to the right to appreciate the emoticon faces.)

: -) I'm smiling at you.

: `-) I'm so happy (laughing so hard) that I'm starting to cry.

: - O Wow!

: - x My lips are sealed!

: -|| I'm angry with you!

: - P I'm sticking my tongue out at you!

: - (I feel sad.

: - | Things look grim . . . .

% -} I think I've had too much to drink . . . .

-:(Somebody cut my hair into a mohawk!

+O:-) I've just been elected Pope!

@}——>——— Here's a rose for you!

Computers are as popular in Japan as they are in the United States. The Japanese have their own emoticons:

(^_^) I'm smiling at you.

(*^o^*) This is exciting!

(^o^) I am happy.

\(^o^)/ Banzai! This is wonderful!

How far will this new keyboard language go? If you're creative enough, anything is possible. Here's a routine that has been making the rounds on the Internet. It's called "Mr. Asciihead learns the Macarena"! To see Mr. Asciihead in action, go to the link at http://www.thesociologypage.com

```
 o     o     o    o    o    <o    <o>    o>    o
.|.   \|.   \|/   //   X     \     |    <|   <|>
/\    >\    /<    >\   /<   >\    /<    >\    /<
```

Sources: Pollack (1996) and Krantz (1997). "Mr. Asciihead" is the creation of Leow Yee Ling.

CHAPTER 3

Jonathan Green
Decoration Day, 1992

Oil on canvas, 48 in. × 78 in. © Jonathan Green, Naples, Florida. Collection of Chuma Nwokike.

CULTURE

It all began back in 1971 when Cindy Campbell, a young teen in New York's Bronx, needed some back-to-school money. Cindy had an idea. She asked her big brother Clive to throw a party. In Jamaica, where the two had grown up, Clive had been fascinated by the happy crowds that filled dance halls.

Their plan went beautifully: The party was a smash, lasting until 4:00 in the morning. Clive handled the music. Cindy worked the door, collecting 25 cents from each girl and 50 cents from each boy. The two made far more money than they expected. But Cindy's idea led to more than raising money: She started a musical revolution that ended up changing our way of life more than she could have imagined.

In the months after the event, Clive got invitations to do other parties. By 1973, he had taken the name Kool Herc, and was hosting events that attracted thousands of people. As the country's first break-beat deejay, he delighted listeners by reciting rhymes over the records he played. Clive had created a new form of music—what we now call rap.

The whole scene caught on. By the end of the 1970s, deejays everywhere were spinning disks, reciting rhymes, and mixing in a distinctive "scratching" sound. In 1979, the Sugarhill Gang recorded "Rapper's Delight"—rap's first national hit. Rap had arrived coast to coast. Soon after, performers like RUN-D.M.C., Beastie Boys, 2 Live Crew, Sister Souljah, and Snoop Doggy Dogg took up the musical revolution.

How big is rap music today? In 1998, for the first time, the most popular music in the United States (based on record sales) was no longer rock and roll or country; it was rap.[1] Indeed, the entire hip-hop culture—not only music, but fashion and films as well—is now a familiar part of life for most young people.

[1]Opening adapted from Farley (1999).

The United States is clearly a nation with many ways of life. Understanding what we mean by "culture" and how we became a multicultural society is the focus of this chapter. In global perspective, of course, ways of life differ even more. The 6.1 billion people living on the earth are all members of a single biological species: *Homo sapiens*. Even so, differences among people within the United States, and more so around the world, can delight, puzzle, disturb, and sometimes overwhelm us.

Many differences in lifestyle barely matter. Australians, for example, flip switches "down" to put lights "on"; North Americans flip them "up." The Australians, British, and Japanese drive on the left side of the road; we drive on the right. Some differences are charming. Take the practice of kissing: Most people in the United States kiss in public, but the Chinese kiss only in private. The French kiss publicly twice (once on each cheek), and Belgians kiss three times (starting on either

Human beings around the globe create diverse ways of life. Such differences begin with outward appearance: Contrast the women shown here from Brazil, Kenya, New Guinea, and Morocco, and the men from Taiwan (Republic of China), India, Peru, and New Guinea. Less obvious, but of even greater importance, are internal differences, since culture also shapes our goals in life, our sense of justice, and even our innermost personal feelings.

cheek). The New Zealand Maoris rub noses, and, for their part, most Nigerians don't kiss at all. In a marriage ceremony, U.S. couples kiss, Koreans bow, and a Cambodian groom touches his nose to the bride's cheek.

Some cultural differences, however, are more profound. The world over, people have many or few children, honor or push aside the elderly, are peaceful or warlike, embrace different religious beliefs, and enjoy different kinds of art and music. In short, although we are the same creatures biologically, human beings have very different ideas about what is pleasant and repulsive, polite and rude, beautiful and ugly, right and wrong. This capacity for difference is expressed through culture.

WHAT IS CULTURE?

Sociologists define **culture** as *the values, beliefs, behavior, and material objects that, together, form a people's way of life.* Culture includes what we think, how we act, and what we own. Culture is both a bridge to our past and a guide to the future (Soyinka, 1991).

To begin to understand all that culture entails, it is helpful to distinguish between thoughts and things. What sociologists call **nonmaterial culture** is *the intangible world of ideas created by members of a society,* ideas that range from altruism to zen. **Material culture,** on the other hand, refers to *the tangible things created by members of a society,* everything from armaments to zippers.

Not only does culture shape what we do; it also helps form our personalities—what we commonly, but inaccurately, describe as "human nature." The warlike Yąnomamö of the Brazilian rain forest think aggression is natural, whereas, halfway around the world, the Semai of Malaysia live in peace and cooperation. The cultures of the United States and Japan both stress achievement and hard work, but members of our society value individualism more than the Japanese, who are more traditional and group-oriented.

Given the extent of cultural differences in the world, and people's tendency to view their own way of life as "better" or "natural," it is no wonder that travelers often feel **culture shock,** *personal disorientation when experiencing an unfamiliar way of life.* The box on page 62 presents one researcher's encounter with culture shock.

December 1, 1994, Istanbul, Turkey. Harbors everywhere, it seems, have two things in common: ships and cats. Istanbul, the tenth port on our voyage, is awash with felines, prowling about in search of an easy meal. People certainly change from place to place—but not cats.

Like so many elements of our lives, notions about kissing vary from place to place. People in the United States kiss in public; the Chinese do so only in private; moreover, while we touch lips, the French kiss on each cheek, and New Zealand's Maoris, shown above, rub noses.

No way of life is "natural" to humanity, even though most people around the world view their own behavior that way. What is natural to our species is the capacity to create culture. Every other form of life—from ants to zebras—behaves in uniform, species-specific ways. To a traveler, the enormous diversity of human life stands out in contrast to the behavior of, say, cats, which is the same everywhere. This uniformity follows from the fact that most living creatures are guided by *instincts,* biological programming over which animals have no control. A few animals—notably chimpanzees and related primates—have the capacity for limited culture, as researchers have noted by observing them use tools and teach simple skills to their offspring. But the creative power of humans far exceeds that of any other form of life. In short, *only humans rely on culture rather than instinct to ensure the survival of their kind* (Harris, 1987).

To understand how human culture came to be, we need to look back at the history of our species.

CULTURE AND HUMAN INTELLIGENCE

In a universe some 15 billion years old, our planet is a much younger 4.5 billion years of age (see the time lines inside the front cover of this text). Not for a billion years

GLOBAL SOCIOLOGY

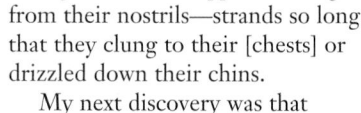

Confronting the Yąnomamö: The Experience of Culture Shock

A small aluminum motorboat chugged steadily along the muddy Orinoco River, deep within South America's vast tropical rain forest. Anthropologist Napoleon Chagnon was nearing the end of a three-day journey to the home territory of the Yąnomamö, one of the most technologically simple societies on earth.

Some 12,000 Yąnomamö live in villages scattered along the border of Venezuela and Brazil. Their way of life could hardly be more different from our own. The Yąnomamö wear little clothing and live without electricity, automobiles, or other familiar conveniences. Their traditional weapon, used for hunting and warfare, is the bow and arrow. Most of the Yąnomamö have had little contact with the outside world, so Chagnon would be as strange to them as they would be to him.

By 2:00 in the afternoon, Chagnon had almost reached his destination. The hot sun and the humid air were almost unbearable. He was soaked with perspiration, and his face and hands swelled from the bites of gnats swarming around him. But he scarcely noticed, so excited was he that in just a few moments he would be face to face with people unlike any he had ever known.

Chagnon's heart pounded as the boat slid onto the riverbank. Chagnon and his guide climbed from the boat and headed toward the sounds of a nearby village, pushing their way through the dense undergrowth. Chagnon describes what happened next.

> I looked up and gasped when I saw a dozen burly, naked, sweaty, hideous men staring at us down the shafts of their drawn arrows! Immense wads of green tobacco were stuck between their lower teeth and lips making them look even more hideous, and strands of dark green slime dripped or hung from their nostrils—strands so long that they clung to their [chests] or drizzled down their chins.
>
> My next discovery was that there were a dozen or so vicious, underfed dogs snapping at my legs, circling me as if I were to be their next meal. I just stood there holding my notebook, helpless and pathetic. Then the stench of the decaying vegetation and filth hit me and I almost got sick. I was horrified. What kind of welcome was this for the person who came here to live with you and learn your way of life, to become friends with you? (1992:11–12)

Fortunately for Chagnon, the Yąnomamö villagers recognized his guide and lowered their weapons. Though reassured that he would survive the afternoon, Chagnon was still shaken by his inability to make any sense of the people surrounding him. And this was to be his home for a year and a half! He wondered why he had forsaken physics to study human culture in the first place.

Source: Chagnon (1992).

after the earth was formed did life appear. Several billion more years went by before dinosaurs ruled the earth, only to vanish. It was then—some 65 million years ago—that our history took a crucial turn with the appearance of the creatures we call primates.

What sets primates apart is their intelligence. They have the largest brains, in relation to body size, of all living creatures. About 12 million years ago, primates began to evolve along two different lines, setting humans apart from the great apes, our closest relatives. But our common lineage is evident in the traits that humans share with chimpanzees, gorillas, and orangutans: great sociability, affectionate and long-lasting bonds for child rearing and mutual protection, the ability to walk upright (normal in humans, less common among other primates), and hands that manipulate objects with great precision.

Fossil records show that some 3 million years ago our distant human ancestors grasped cultural fundamentals such as the use of fire, tools, and weapons, and were able to create simple shelters and basic clothing.

These Stone Age achievements may seem modest, but they mark the point at which our ancestors set off on a distinct evolutionary course, making culture their main strategy for survival.

To see how new we human beings are in the larger scheme of things, the U.S. astronomer Carl Sagan (1977) superimposed the 15-billion-year history of our universe on a single calendar year. The life-giving atmosphere of the earth did not develop until the autumn, and the earliest beings who resembled humans did not appear until December 31—the last day of the year—at 10:30 at night! Just mere minutes before midnight (250,000 years ago), our own species finally emerged. These *Homo sapiens* (derived from the Latin meaning "thinking person") continued to evolve so that, about 40,000 years ago, humans who looked more or less like ourselves roamed the earth. With larger brains, these "modern" *Homo sapiens* rapidly developed culture, as the wide range of tools and cave art from this period suggests.

The road to "civilization," based on permanent settlements and specialized occupations, began in the Middle East (in what is today Iraq and Egypt) only about 12,000 years ago. In terms of Sagan's "year," this cultural flowering occurred during the final *seconds* before midnight on New Year's Eve. And what of our modern, industrial way of life? Appearing only 300 years ago, in Sagan's scheme it amounts to a mere millisecond flash.

Culture, then, is very recent and was a long time in the making. As culture became a strategy for survival, our forebears descended from the trees to the tall grasses of central Africa. There, walking upright, they learned the advantages of hunting in groups. As mental capacity expanded, we became the only species that names itself, and the biological forces we call instincts gave way to a more efficient survival scheme: *fashioning the environment for ourselves.* Ever since, humans have made and remade their worlds in countless ways, which explains today's fascinating cultural diversity.

CULTURE, NATION, AND SOCIETY

Three similar terms—"culture," "nation," and "society"—have slightly different meanings. *Culture* refers to a shared way of life. A *nation* is a political entity, that is, a territory with specific borders, such as the United States, Canada, Argentina, or Zimbabwe. *Society*, the topic of the next chapter, is the organized interaction of people in a nation or within some other boundary.

The United States, then, is both a nation and a society. But many societies, including the United States, are *multicultural*, meaning that their people follow various ways of life that blend (and sometimes clash).

In the United States, how many cultures are there? One clue is that the Census Bureau lists hundreds of languages spoken by this country's people, many brought by immigrants from around the world. Globally, experts have documented more than 5,000 languages, suggesting that at least this many cultures have existed at various times (Durning, 1993; Crispell, 1997a). Fewer cultures exist today, however, because of high-technology communication, increasing international migration, and an expanding global economy. Even so, as the chapter-opening story of the rise of hip-hop suggests, people develop new cultural forms all the time.

And what of world nations? The tally goes up or down as a result of political events. The dissolution of the former Soviet Union and the former Yugoslavia, for example, added nineteen nations to the count. In 1999, there were 191 politically independent nations in the world.

THE COMPONENTS OF CULTURE

Although cultures vary greatly, they all have five common components: symbols, language, values and beliefs, norms, and material culture and technology. We begin with the one that underlies all the others: symbols.

SYMBOLS

Like all creatures, humans sense the surrounding world, but unlike others, we also create a reality of *meaning*. Humans transform elements of the world into **symbols,** *anything that carries a particular meaning recognized by people who share culture.* A word, a wall of graffiti, a flashing red light, a raised fist—all serve as symbols. We can see the human capacity to create and manipulate symbols reflected in the very different meanings associated with the simple act of winking the eye, which can convey interest, understanding, or insult.

We are so dependent on our culture's symbols that we take them for granted. Sometimes, however, we become keenly aware of a symbol when someone uses it in an unconventional way, as when a person burns a U.S. flag during a political demonstration. Entering an unfamiliar culture also reminds us of the power of symbols; culture shock is really the inability to "read" meaning in new surroundings. Not understanding the symbols of a culture leaves a person feeling lost and isolated, unsure of how to act, and sometimes frightened.

Culture shock is a two-way process. On the one hand, travelers *experience* culture shock when encountering

Behavior people in one society consider routine can be chilling to members of another culture. In the Russian city of St. Petersburg, this young mother and her six-week-old son brave the 17°F temperatures for a dip in a nearby lake. To Russians, this is something of a national pastime. To some members of our society, however, this practice may seem cruel or even dangerous.

people whose way of life is different. For example, North Americans who consider dogs beloved household pets might be put off by the Masai of eastern Africa, who ignore and never feed them. The same travelers might be horrified to find that in parts of Indonesia and in the northern regions of the People's Republic of China, people *roast* dogs for dinner.

On the other hand, a traveler *inflicts* culture shock by acting in ways that offend others. A North American who asks for a cheeseburger in an Indian restaurant offends Hindus, who consider cows sacred and never to be eaten.

Global travel provides almost endless opportunities for misunderstanding. In unfamiliar settings, we need to remember that even behavior that seems innocent and normal to us can offend others, as the photos on page 65 suggest.

Then, too, symbolic meanings also vary within a single society. A fur coat may represent a prized symbol of success or the inhumane treatment of animals. Similarly, a Confederate flag embodies regional pride for one person but is a symbol of racial oppression to someone else (cf. Reingold & Wike, 1998).

LANGUAGE

In infancy, an illness left Helen Keller (1880–1968) blind and deaf. Without these two senses, she was cut off from the symbolic world, which greatly limited her social development. Only when her teacher, Anne Mansfield Sullivan, broke through Keller's isolation using sign language did Helen Keller begin to realize her human potential. This remarkable woman, who later became a renowned educator herself, recalls the moment she grasped the concept of language.

> We walked down the path to the well-house, attracted by the smell of honeysuckle with which it was covered. Someone was drawing water, and my teacher placed my hand under the spout. As the cool stream gushed over one hand, she spelled into the other the word *water*, first slowly, then rapidly. I stood still, my whole attention fixed upon the motions of her fingers. Suddenly I felt a misty consciousness as of something forgotten—a thrill of returning thought; and somehow the mystery of language was revealed to me. I knew then that "w-a-t-e-r" meant the wonderful cool something that was flowing over my hand. That living word awakened my soul; gave it light, hope, joy, set it free! (1903:21–24)

Language, the key to the world of culture, is *a system of symbols that allows people to communicate with one another*. Humans have created hundreds of alphabets, and even conventions for writing differ. Most people in Western societies write from left to right, but people in northern Africa and western Asia write right to left, and people in eastern Asia write from top to bottom. Global Map 3–1, on page 66, shows where one finds the three most widely spoken languages.

Language not only allows communication, it ensures the continuity of culture. Language is a cultural heritage, and the key to **cultural transmission**—*the process by which one generation passes culture to the next.* Just as our bodies contain the genes of our ancestors, so our culture contains countless symbols of those who came before us. Language is the key that unlocks centuries of accumulated wisdom.

Every society transmits culture through speech, a process sociologists call the *oral cultural tradition.* Some 5,000 years ago, however, humans invented writing, although just a favored few ever learned to read and write. Not until the twentieth century did rich nations boast of nearly universal literacy. Still, at least 10 percent of U.S. adults (some 20 million people) are functionally illiterate, unable to read and write in a society

People throughout the world communicate not just with spoken words but also with bodily gestures, which vary from culture to culture. To most North Americans, there is nothing unusual about the young woman shown in the left-hand photo. But to people living in Muslim societies—who typically use the left hand for bathroom hygiene—eating this way is disturbing, to say the least! Similarly, the familiar "A-OK" gesture, by which we express approval and pleasure, is likely to insult a French person, who "reads" the message as "You're worth zero." Finally, even the commonplace "thumbs up" gesture we take to mean "Good job!" can get you into trouble in Australia, where people take it to mean "Up yours!"

that increasingly demands symbolic skills. In low-income countries of the world, about one-third of men and almost two-thirds of women are illiterate (United Nations Development Programme, 1999).

Language may link us with the past, but it also sets free the human imagination. Connecting symbols in new ways, we can conceive of an almost limitless range of future possibilities. Language sets humans apart as the only creatures who are self-conscious, aware of our limitations and ultimate mortality, yet able to dream and hope for a future better than the present.

Language: Only for Humans?

Creatures great and small direct sounds, smells, and gestures toward one another. In most cases, these signals are instinctive. But some animals have at least some ability to use symbols to communicate with one another and with humans.

Consider the remarkable achievement of a twelve-year-old pygmy chimp named Kanzi. Chimpanzees lack the physical ability to mimic human speech. But researcher E. Sue Savage-Rumbaugh discovered that Kanzi could learn language by listening and observing people. Under Savage-Rumbaugh's supervision, Kanzi has developed a vocabulary of several hundred words, and he has learned to "speak" by pointing to pictures on a special keyboard. He can respond to requests like "Will you get a diaper for your sister?" or "Put the melon in the potty." Kanzi's abilities go beyond mere rote learning because he can respond to requests he has not heard before. In short, Kanzi has the language ability of a human child of two-and-one-half years (Linden, 1993).

Still, the language skills of chimps, dolphins, and a few other animals are limited. Even specially trained animals cannot, on their own, pass on language skills to others of their kind. But the achievements of Kanzi and others caution us against assuming that humans alone can lay claim to culture.

Does Language Shape Reality?

Do the Chinese, who think using one language, experience the world differently from North Americans who think in, say, English or Spanish? The answer is yes, since each language has its own distinctive symbols that serve as the building blocks of reality.

Edward Sapir and Benjamin Whorf proposed that languages are not just different sets of labels for the same reality (Sapir, 1929, 1949; Whorf, 1956). Rather, each symbolic system has at least some unique words or expressions. In addition, all languages fuse symbols with distinctive emotions. Thus, as multilingual people can

WINDOW ON THE WORLD

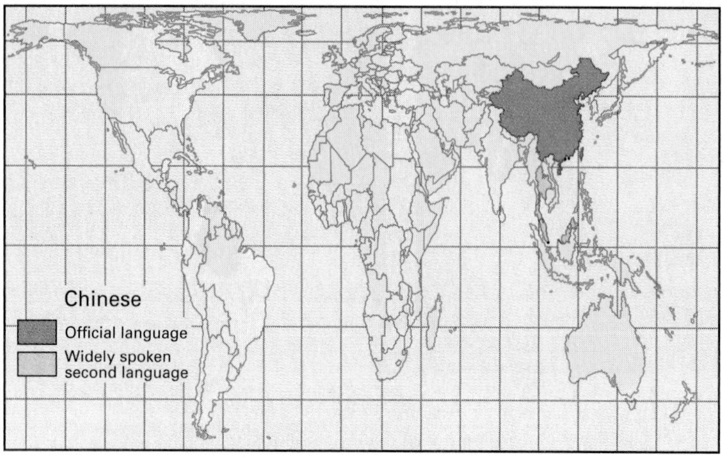

GLOBAL MAP 3–1
Language in Global Perspective

Chinese (including Mandarin, Cantonese, and dozens of other dialects) is the native tongue of one-fifth of the world's people, almost all of whom live in Asia. Although all Chinese people read and write with the same characters, they use several dozen dialects. The "official" dialect, taught in schools throughout the People's Republic of China and the Republic of Taiwan, is Mandarin (the dialect of Beijing, China's historic capital city). Cantonese, the language of Canton, is the second most common Chinese dialect; it differs in sound from Mandarin roughly the way French differs from Spanish.

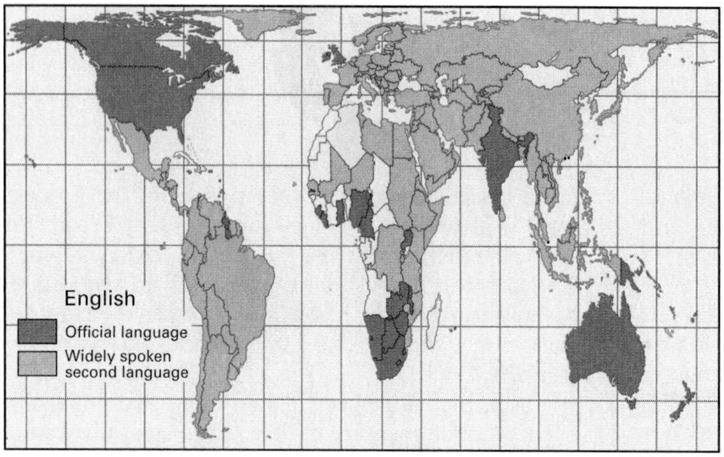

English is the native tongue or official language in several world regions (spoken by 10 percent of humanity) and has become the preferred second language in most of the world.

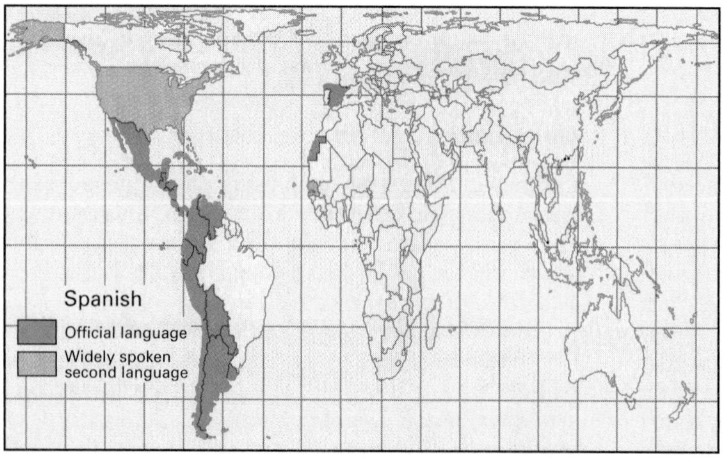

The largest concentration of Spanish speakers is in Latin America and, of course, Spain. Spanish is also the preferred second language of the United States.

Source: *Peters Atlas of the World* (1990).

attest, a single idea may "feel" different when spoken in Spanish rather than in English or Chinese (Falk, 1987). The **Sapir-Whorf thesis** states that *people perceive the world through the cultural lens of language.*

VALUES AND BELIEFS

What accounts for the popularity of film characters such as James Bond, Dirty Harry, Rambo, and Thelma and Louise? Each is ruggedly individualistic, relying on personal skill and savvy to challenge "the system." In applauding such characters, we are endorsing certain **values,** *culturally defined standards by which people assess desirability, goodness, and beauty, and which serve as broad guidelines for social living.* Values are statements, from the standpoint of a culture, of what ought to be.

Values are broad principles that underlie **beliefs,** *specific statements that people hold to be true.* In other words, values are abstract standards of goodness, and beliefs are particular matters that individuals consider true or false. For example, because most U.S. adults share the value of providing equal opportunities for all, they believe a qualified woman could serve as president of the United States (NORC, 1999).

Cultural values and beliefs not only affect how we perceive our surroundings, they also form the core of our personalities. We learn from families, friends, schools, and religious organizations to think and act according to approved principles, to pursue worthy goals, and to believe a host of cultural truths. Particular values and beliefs thus operate as a form of "cultural capital," giving some people the confidence and determination to pursue success and leaving others with a sense of hopelessness that little will ever change (Sowell, 1996).

In a nation as large and diverse as the United States, few cultural values and beliefs are shared by everyone. Our long history of immigration has made the United States a cultural mosaic. In this regard, we stand apart from many nations—especially China and Japan—which are more culturally homogeneous.

Key Values of U.S. Culture

Nonetheless, Robin Williams (1970) has identified ten values that are central to our way of life:

1. **Equal opportunity.** People in the United States endorse not *equality of condition* but *equality of opportunity.* This means that society should provide everyone with the chance to get ahead according to individual talents and efforts.
2. **Achievement and success.** Our way of life encourages competition so that each person's rewards should reflect personal merit. Moreover, greater success confers worthiness on a person—the mantle of being a "winner."
3. **Material comfort.** Success generally means making money and enjoying what it will buy. Although people often remark, "money won't buy happiness," most pursue wealth all the same.
4. **Activity and work.** Popular U.S. heroes, from film's famed archaeologist Indiana Jones to golf champion Tiger Woods, are "doers" who get the job done. Our culture values *action* over *reflection* and controlling events over passively accepting one's fate.
5. **Practicality and efficiency.** People in the United States value the practical over the theoretical—

Australian feminist artist Sally Swain alters a famous artist's painting to make fun of our culture's tendency to ignore the everyday lives of women. This spoof is entitled Mrs. Picasso Dusts the Mantlepiece.

CRITICAL THINKING

Don't Blame Me! The New "Culture of Victimization"

A University of North Carolina law student walked down the street, took aim with an M-1 rifle, and killed two men he never met. Later, from a psychiatric hospital, he sued his therapist for not doing enough to prevent his actions. A jury awarded him $500,000. In Washington, D.C., after realizing that he had been videotaped smoking crack cocaine in a hotel room, the city's mayor blamed his woman companion for "setting him up" and suggested that the police were racially motivated in arresting him. After more than a dozen women accused an Oregon senator of sexual harassment, he claimed his behavior was caused by his problem with alcohol. In the most celebrated case of its kind, a former city politician gunned down the mayor of San Francisco and a city council member, blaming his violence on insanity caused by eating too much junk food (the so-called "Twinkie defense").

In each of these cases, someone denied personal responsibility for an action, claiming instead to be a victim. Examples such as these prompted Irving Horowitz (1993) to declare that our way of life is becoming a "culture of victimization" in which "everyone is a victim" and "no one accepts responsibility for anything."

One indication of this victimization trend is the proliferation of "addictions," a term once associated only with uncontrollable drug use. We now hear about gambling addicts, compulsive overeaters, sex addicts, and even people who excuse runaway credit-card debt as a shopping addiction. Bookstores overflow with manuals to help people deal with numerous new medical or psychological conditions, ranging from the "Cinderella complex" to the "Casanova complex" and even "soap opera syndrome." And U.S. courts are clogged by lawsuits blaming someone for misfortunes that we used to accept as part of life.

What's going on here? Is U.S. culture changing? Historically, our cultural ideal was "rugged individualism," the idea that people are responsible for whatever triumph or tragedy befalls them. But this value has been eroded in a number of ways. First, everyone is more aware (partly through the work of sociologists) of how society shapes our lives. Thus, categories of people well beyond those who have suffered real historical disadvantages (such as Native Americans, African Americans, and women) now say they are victims. The latest victims include white males who claim that "everybody gets special treatment but us."

Second, many lawyers encourage a sense of injustice among clients they hope to represent in court. The number of million-dollar lawsuit awards has risen more than twenty-five-fold in the last twenty-five years.

Finally, a proliferation of "rights groups" promotes what Amitai Etzioni calls "rights inflation." Beyond the traditional constitutional liberties are many newly claimed rights: those of hunters (as well as animals), the rights of smokers (and nonsmokers), the right of women to control their bodies (and the rights of the unborn), the right to own a gun (and the right to be safe from violence). Expanding claims for unmet rights create victims (and victimizers) on all sides.

Does this shift toward victimization signal a change in our individualistic culture? Perhaps. Claims to victimization have always depended on the longstanding belief that everyone has the right to life, liberty, and the pursuit of happiness. What is new, however, is that the explosion of "rights" now does more than alert us to clear cases of injustice: It lessens our responsibility for our own lives.

Since the 1980s, "tell all" television programs have reinforced the emerging "culture of victimization."

What do you think?

1. *Do you think our cultural emphasis on individualism is less strong today than in the past? Why?*
2. *What social factors do you think have encouraged so much talk about "victimization"?*
3. *Does using the sociological perspective encourage us to view people as victims? Why or why not?*

Sources: Based on Etzioni (1991), Taylor (1991), and Hollander (1995).

"doing" over "dreaming." Activity has value to the extent that it earns money.

6. **Progress.** We are an optimistic people who, despite waves of nostalgia, believe that the present is better than the past. We celebrate progress, equating the "latest" with the "best."
7. **Science.** We expect scientists to solve problems and improve our lives. We believe we are rational people, which probably explains our cultural tendency (especially among men) to devalue emotion and intuition as sources of knowledge.
8. **Democracy and free enterprise.** Members of our society recognize individual rights that cannot be overridden by government. We believe that our political system is based on free elections in which adults select their leaders and that our economy responds to the choices of individual consumers.
9. **Freedom.** Our cultural value of freedom means that we favor individual initiative over collective conformity. We believe that people should be free to pursue personal goals with minimal interference from anyone else.
10. **Racism and group superiority.** Despite strong notions about individualism and freedom, most people still evaluate individuals according to gender, race, ethnicity, and social class. Our society values males above females, whites above people of color, people with northwest European backgrounds above those whose ancestors came from other lands, and rich people above poor. Although we like to describe ourselves as a nation of equals, there is little doubt that some of us rank as "more equal than others."

Values: Sometimes in Conflict

Looking at the list of values, we see that some can be inconsistent and even opposed to one another (Lynd, 1967; Bellah et al., 1985; Ray, 1997). For example, people may believe in equality of opportunity, yet they may also degrade others because of their race or sex.

Conflict between values reflects the cultural diversity of U.S. society and also cultural change by which new trends develop alongside older traditions. Recently, for example, what some observers call a "culture of victimization" has arisen to challenge our society's long-time belief in individual responsibility (Best, 1997; Furedi, 1998). The box takes a closer look.

Value conflict leads to awkward balancing acts in our beliefs. Sometimes we decide one value is more important than another by, for example, supporting equal opportunity while opposing the acceptance of gays in the U.S. military. In other cases, we simply learn to live with the contradictions.

Standards of beauty—including the color and design of everyday surroundings—vary significantly from one culture to another. These two Nankani women put the finishing touches on their lavishly decorated homes. Members of North American and European societies, by contrast, make far less use of bright colors and intricate detail so that their housing appears much more subdued.

NORMS

Most people in the United States are eager to gossip about "who's hot and who's not." Members of many Native American societies, however, condemn such behavior as rude and divisive. Both patterns illustrate the operation of **norms,** *rules and expectations by which a society guides the behavior of its members.* Some norms are *proscriptive*, stating what we should *not* do, as when health officials warn us to avoid casual sex. *Prescriptive* norms, on the other hand, state what we *should* do, as when U.S. schools teach "safe sex" practices.

Most important norms in a culture apply everywhere and at all times. For example, parents expect obedience

GLOBAL SNAPSHOT

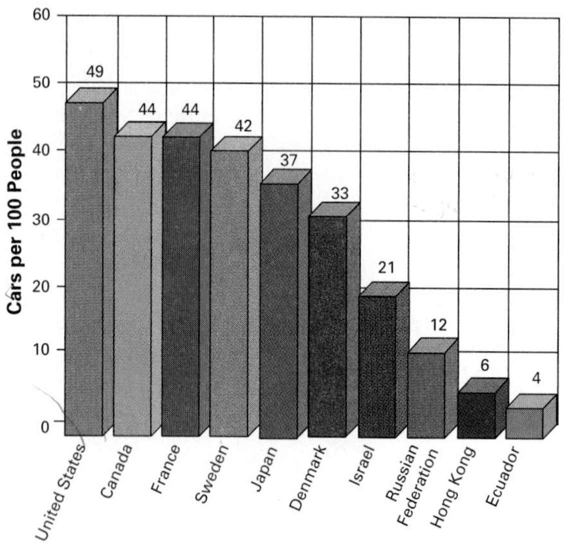

FIGURE 3–1 Car Ownership in Global Perspective
Source: The World Bank (1999).

from young children regardless of the setting. Other norms depend on the situation. In the United States, we expect the audience to applaud after a musical performance; we may applaud (although it is not expected) at the end of a classroom lecture; we do not applaud when a priest or rabbi finishes a sermon.

Mores and Folkways

William Graham Sumner (1959; orig. 1906), an early U.S. sociologist, recognized that some norms are more important to our lives than others. Sumner coined the term **mores** (pronounced MORE-ays) to refer to *norms that are widely observed and have great moral significance.* Mores, or *taboos*, include our society's prohibition against adults engaging in sexual relations with children.

People pay less attention to **folkways,** *norms for routine, casual interaction.* Examples include ideas about appropriate greetings and proper dress. In short, mores distinguish between right and wrong, whereas folkways draw a line between right and *rude.* A man who does not wear a tie to a formal dinner party may raise eyebrows for violating folkways. If, however, he were to arrive at the party wearing *only* a tie, he would violate cultural mores and invite more serious sanctions.

Social Control

Mores and folkways are the basic rules of everyday life. Although we sometimes bristle when others pressure us to conform, we all can see that norms make our dealings with others more orderly and predictable. Observing or breaking the rules of social life prompts a response from others, in the form of reward or punishment. Sanctions—whether an approving smile or a raised eyebrow—operate as a system of **social control,** *various means by which members of society encourage conformity to norms.*

As we learn cultural norms, we acquire the capacity to evaluate our own behavior. Doing wrong (say, downloading a term paper from the Internet) can cause not only *shame*—the painful sense that others disapprove of our actions—but *guilt*—a negative judgment we make of ourselves. Only cultural creatures can experience shame and guilt. This is probably what Mark Twain had in mind when he remarked that people "are the only animals that blush . . . or need to."

"IDEAL" AND "REAL" CULTURE

Values and norms do not describe actual behavior so much as they suggest how we *should* behave. We must remember that *ideal* culture always differs from *real* culture—what actually occurs in everyday life. To illustrate, most women and men agree on the importance of sexual fidelity in marriage. Even so, in a recent study, about 25 percent of married men and 10 percent of married women reported being sexually unfaithful to their spouses at some point in their marriage (Laumann et al., 1994). But a culture's moral prodding is important all the same, calling to mind the old saying "Do as I say, not as I do."

MATERIAL CULTURE AND TECHNOLOGY

In addition to intangible elements such as values and norms, every culture includes a wide range of tangible (from the Latin meaning "touchable") human creations, which sociologists call *artifacts.* The Chinese eat with chopsticks rather than knives and forks, the Japanese put mats rather than rugs on the floor, many men and women in India prefer flowing robes to the close-fitting clothing common in the United States. The material culture of a people may seem as strange to outsiders as their language, values, and norms.

A society's artifacts partly reflect underlying cultural values. The warlike Yąnomamö carefully craft their weapons and prize the poison tips on their arrows. By

CRITICAL THINKING

Virtual Culture: Is It Good for Us?

The Information Revolution is generating symbols—words, sounds, and images—faster than ever before and spreading these symbols across the nation and around the world. What does this new information technology mean for our way of life?

In centuries past, culture was transmitted from generation to generation. It was a heritage—a society's collective memory—that was authentically our own because it belonged to our ancestors (Schwartz, 1996). But in the emerging cyber-society, more and more cultural symbols are new, intentionally *created* by a small cultural elite of composers, writers, filmmakers, and others who work in the expanding information economy.

To illustrate, consider the changing character of cultural heroes, people who represent cultural ideals and serve as role models. A century ago, our heroes were real men and women who made a difference in the life of this nation—George Washington, Abigail Adams, Betsy Ross, Davy Crockett, Daniel Boone, Paul Bunyon, Abraham Lincoln, and Harriet Tubman. Of course, when we make a hero of someone (almost always well after the person has died), we "clean up" the person's biography, highlighting the successes and overlooking the shortcomings. Even so, these people were authentic parts of our history.

Today's youngsters, by contrast, are fed a steady diet of *virtual culture*, images that spring from the minds of contemporary culture-makers and that reach them via a screen: on television, in the movies, or through computer cyberspace. Today's "heroes" are Power Rangers, Rug Rats, Pokémon, Batman, Barbie, and Barney, a continuous flow of Disney characters, and the ever-smiling Ronald McDonald. Some of these cultural icons embody values that shape our way of life. But few of them have any historical reality and almost all have come into being for a single purpose: to make money.

What do you think?

1. *As the Information Revolution proceeds, do you think virtual culture will become increasingly important? Why or why not?*
2. *Does virtual culture erode or enhance our cultural traditions? Is that good or bad?*
3. *What image of this country do U.S. movies and television shows give to people abroad?*

Source: Thanks to Roland Johnson (1996) for the basic idea for this box.

contrast, our society's emphasis on individualism and independence goes a long way toward explaining our high regard for the automobile: We own more than 200 million motor vehicles, one for every licensed driver. Figure 3–1 shows that, even compared to other rich societies, the United States stands out as a car-loving nation.

In addition to reflecting values, material culture also reflects a society's **technology**, *knowledge that people apply to the task of living in their surroundings.* The more complex a society's technology, the more its members are able (for better or worse) to shape the world for themselves.

Because we attach great importance to science and praise sophisticated technology, people in our society tend to judge cultures with simpler technology as less advanced. Some facts support such an assessment. For example, life expectancy for children born in the United States now exceeds seventy-five years; the lifespan of the Yąnomamö is only about forty years.

However, we must be careful not to make self-serving judgments about other cultures. Although many Yąnomamö are eager to acquire modern technology (such as steel tools and shotguns), they are generally well fed by world standards and most are very satisfied with their lives (Chagnon, 1992). Remember, too, that while our powerful and complex technology has produced work-reducing devices and seemingly miraculous medical treatments, it has also contributed to unhealthy levels of stress, eroded the natural environment, and created weapons capable of destroying in a blinding flash everything that humankind has achieved.

DIVERSITY SNAPSHOT

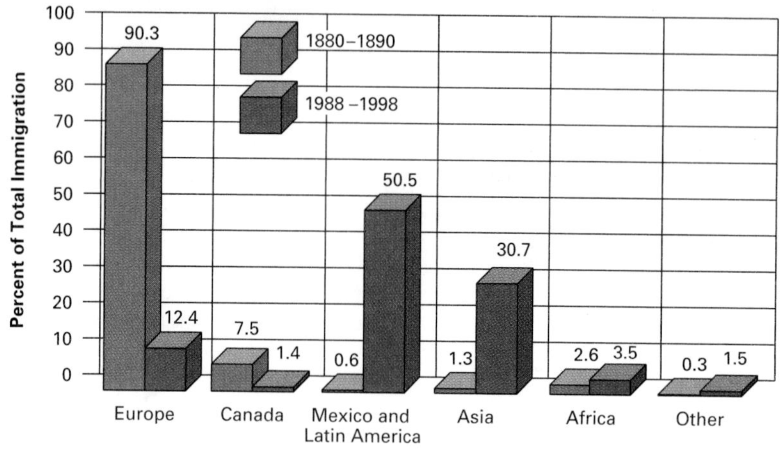

FIGURE 3–2
Recorded Immigration to the United States, by Region of Birth, 1880–1890 and 1988–1998

Sources: U.S. Immigration and Naturalization Service (1996, 1999).

Finally, technology is not equally distributed within our population. Although many of us cannot imagine life without personal computers, televisions, and CD players, many members of our society cannot afford these luxuries. Others, including the Amish, reject them on principle. These "Plain People," who live in small farming communities across Pennsylvania, Ohio, and Indiana, shun most modern conveniences on religious grounds. With their traditional black garb and horse-drawn buggies, the Amish may seem like a curious relic of the past. Yet their communities flourish, grounded in strong families that give everyone a sense of identity and purpose. To the Amish, no doubt, their communities are "islands of sanity in a culture gripped by commercialism and technology run wild" (Hostetler, 1980:4; Kraybill, 1994:28).

NEW INFORMATION TECHNOLOGY AND CULTURE

Many rich nations, including the United States, have entered a postindustrial phase based on computers and new information technology. While industrial production is centered on factories and machinery generating material goods, postindustrial production is based on computers and other electronic devices that create, process, store, and apply information.

In an information economy, workers need symbolic skills in place of the mechanical skills of the industrial age. Symbolic skills include the ability to speak, write, compute, design, and create images in art, advertising, and entertainment. New information technology also enables us to *generate culture* on an unprecedented scale. The box on page 71 takes a closer look.

CULTURAL DIVERSITY: MANY WAYS OF LIFE IN ONE WORLD

As the chapter-opening story about the rise of hip-hop suggests, our nation is becoming more aware of the extent of cultural diversity within our borders. Moreover, our cultural diversity continues to increase as each year almost 1 million people from other lands come to our shores. Over the centuries, heavy immigration has made the United States the most *multicultural* of all industrial countries. By contrast, historic isolation has made Japan the most *monocultural* of all industrial nations.

Between 1820 (when the government began keeping track of immigration) and 2000, more than 60 million people have added to the U.S. cultural mix. A century ago, as shown in Figure 3–2, almost all immigrants hailed from Europe; today, most newcomers arrive from Latin America and Asia.

We are aware of our cultural variety when we hear the distinctive accents of people from New England, the Midwest, or the South. Ours is also a nation of religious pluralism, a land of class differences, and a home to individualists who try to be like no one else. To understand the reality of life in the United States, then, we must move beyond broad cultural patterns and shared values to consider cultural diversity.

SEEING OURSELVES

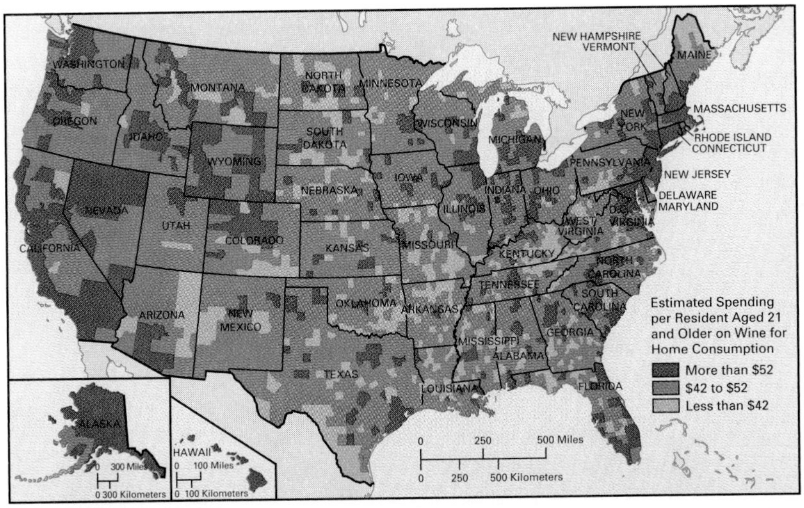

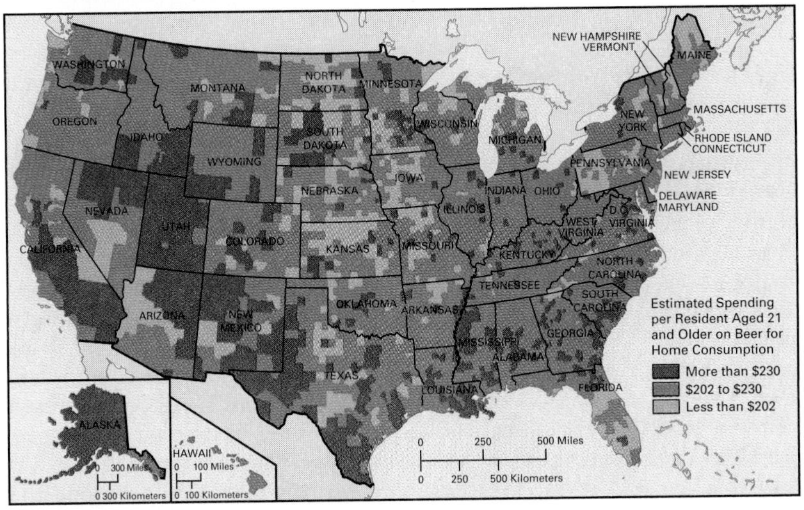

NATIONAL MAP 3–1
What'll Ya Have? Popular Beverages across the United States

What people consume is one mark of their status as a "highbrow" or "lowbrow." Drinking wine at home is an indicator of highbrow standing. These more well-to-do people not only enjoy a glass of wine with dinner, but drink water from bottles rather than the tap, prefer Grey Poupon to Gulden's mustard, and favor Häagen-Daz over the local Tastee-Freeze. Drinking beer, on the other hand, marks a person as a "lowbrow." Such a person has a low to moderate income, consumes a good deal of snack foods, and frequents fast-food restaurants. Looking at the maps, where have the "highbrows" and the "lowbrows" created centers of "high culture" and "popular culture"?

Source: *American Demographics* magazine, March 1998, p. 19. Reprinted with permission. © 1998, *American Demographics* magazine, Ithaca, New York.

HIGH CULTURE AND POPULAR CULTURE

Cultural diversity can involve social class. In fact, in everyday talk, we usually use the term "culture" to mean art forms such as classical literature, music, dance, and painting. We describe people who regularly go to the opera or the theater as "cultured," because we think they appreciate the "finer things in life."

We speak less generously of ordinary people, assuming that everyday culture is somehow less worthy. We are tempted to judge the music of Beethoven as "more cultured" than the blues, couscous as better than cornbread, and polo as more polished than Ping-Pong.

Such judgments imply that many cultural patterns are readily accessible to only some members of a society (Hall & Neitz, 1993). Sociologists use the term **high culture**[2] to refer to *cultural patterns that distinguish a society's elite*; **popular culture** designates *cultural patterns that are widespread among a society's population.* National

[2]The term "high culture" is derived from the term "highbrow." A century ago, people influenced by phrenology—the bogus nineteenth-century theory that personality was affected by the shape of the human skull—praised the tastes of those they termed "highbrows" while dismissing the appetites of "lowbrows."

Whether visual expression in lines and color is revered as "art" or dismissed as "graffiti" or even condemned as "vandalism" depends on the social standing of the creator. How would you characterize images such as this one, common in low-income neighborhoods of U.S. cities? Is this art? Why or why not?

Map 3–1 looks at preferred alcoholic beverages to show the distribution of high and popular culture across the United States.

Common sense may suggest that high culture is superior to popular culture. But we should resist such quick judgments, for two reasons. First, neither elites nor ordinary people share all the same tastes and interests; people in both categories differ in numerous ways. Second, do we praise high culture because it is inherently better than popular culture, or simply because its supporters have more money, power, and prestige? For example, there is no difference between a violin and a fiddle; however, we name the instrument one way when it is used to produce music typically enjoyed by a person of higher position, and the other way when the musician plays works appreciated by individuals with lower social standing. Sociologists, therefore, are uneasy with distinctions between high and popular culture, preferring the term "culture" to refer to *all* elements of a society's way of life, including patterns of rich and poor alike.

SUBCULTURE

The term **subculture** refers to *cultural patterns that set apart some segment of a society's population.* Young people who enjoy hip-hop music and fashion, as well as Polish Americans, frequent-flyer executives, New England "Yankees," Colorado cowboys, the southern California "beach crowd," jazz musicians, campus poets, computer "nerds," and wilderness campers—all display subcultural patterns.

It is easy, but often inaccurate, to place people in some subcultural category, because almost everyone participates in many subcultures without necessarily having much commitment to any of them. In some cases, however, ethnicity and religion do set people apart from one another, sometimes with tragic results. Consider the former nation of Yugoslavia in southeastern Europe. The recent Balkan war is only the latest chapter in a long history of hatred based on cultural differences. Before its breakup, this *one* small country used *two* alphabets, professed *three* religions, spoke *four* languages, was home to *five* major nationalities, was divided into *six* political republics, and absorbed the cultural influences of *seven* surrounding countries. Clearly, subcultures are a source not only of pleasing variety but also of tension and outright violence (cf. Sekulic, Massey, & Hodson, 1994).

Historically, we have viewed the United States as a "melting pot" where many nationalities blend into a single "American" culture. But, given our cultural diversity, how accurate is the "melting pot" image? For one thing, subcultures involve not just *difference* but *hierarchy*. Too often, what we view as "dominant" or "mainstream" culture are patterns favored by powerful segments of the population, while we view the lives of disadvantaged people as "subculture." Some sociologists, therefore, prefer to level the playing field of society by emphasizing multiculturalism.

SEEING OURSELVES

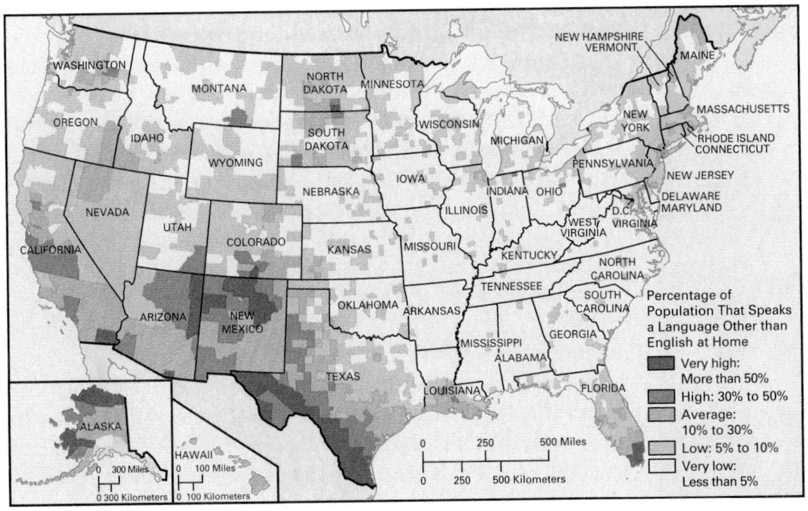

Source: *Time*, January 30, 1995. Copyright © 1995 *Time*, Inc. Reprinted by permission.

NATIONAL MAP 3–2
Language Diversity across the United States

Of 230 million people over the age of five in the United States, the 1990 census reports that 32 million (14 percent) typically speak a language other than English at home. Of these people, 54 percent speak Spanish, 14 percent use an Asian language, and the remaining 32 percent communicate with some other tongue (the Census Bureau lists 25 languages, each of which is favored by more than 100,000 people in the United States). The map shows that non-English speakers are concentrated in certain regions of the country. Which ones? What do you think accounts for this pattern?

MULTICULTURALISM

Multiculturalism is *an educational program recognizing the cultural diversity of the United States and promoting the equality of all cultural traditions.* Multiculturalism is a sharp turn away from the past, when our society downplayed cultural diversity and defined itself primarily in terms of its European (and especially English) immigrants. Today, a spirited debate asks whether we should continue to stress these historical traditions or highlight our cultural diversity (Orwin, 1996; Rabkin, 1996).

E pluribus unum, the familiar Latin phrase that appears on all U.S. coins, means "out of many, one." This motto not only symbolizes our national political union, but also the idea that immigrants from around the world have come together to form a new way of life.

But from the outset, the many cultures did not melt together as much as harden into a hierarchy. At the top were the English, who formed a majority early in U.S. history and established English as the nation's dominant language. Further down, people of other backgrounds were advised to model themselves after "their betters." In practice, then, "melting" was really a process of Anglicization—adoption of English ways. As multiculturalists see it, early in our history, this society set up the English way of life as an ideal to which all should aspire and by which all should be judged.

Ever since, historians have reported events from the point of view of the English and other people of European ancestry, paying little attention to the perspectives and accomplishments of Native Americans and people of African and Asian descent. Multiculturalists call this view **Eurocentrism**, *the dominance of European (especially English) cultural patterns.* Molefi Kete Asante, an advocate of multiculturalism, argues that, like "the fifteenth-century Europeans who could not cease believing that the earth was the center of the universe, many today find it difficult to cease viewing European culture as the center of the social universe" (1988:7).

One contested issue involves language. Some people believe English should be the official language of the United States. By 1999, legislatures in twenty-five states had enacted such laws. But some 30 million men and women—more than one in six—speak a language other than English at home. Spanish is the second most commonly spoken language, and several hundred other tongues are also heard across the country, including Italian, German, French, Filipino, Japanese, Korean, Vietnamese, and a host of Native American languages. National Map 3–2 shows where in the United States large numbers of people speak a language other than English at home.

Proponents also paint multiculturalism as a way of coming to terms with our country's increasing social

Any society is actually made up of countless, different cultural patterns, some of which may seem strange, indeed, to most people. What cultural values are evident in the pierced noses and tattoos of these two men? Are these values completely at odds with our individualistic way of life?

diversity. With the Asian and Hispanic populations of this country increasing rapidly, some analysts predict that children born after 1990 will live to see people of African, Asian, and Hispanic ancestry become a *majority* of this country's population.

Proponents also claim that multiculturalism strengthens the academic achievement of African American children. To offset Eurocentrism, some multicultural educators are calling for **Afrocentrism**, *the dominance of African cultural patterns,* which they see as a corrective for centuries of minimizing or altogether ignoring the cultural achievements of African societies and African Americans.

Although multiculturalism has found favor in recent years, it has provoked its share of criticism as well. Opponents say it encourages divisiveness rather than unity, urging people to identify with their own category rather than with the nation as a whole. Instead of recognizing any common standards of truth, say critics, multiculturalism maintains that we should evaluate ideas according to the race (and sex) of those who present them. Our common humanity thus dissolves into an "African experience," an "Asian experience," and so on.

The bottom line, say critics, is that multiculturalism does not help minorities, as its supporters claim. Some multicultural policies (from African American studies to all-black dorms) seem to endorse the same racial segregation that our nation has struggled so long to end. Then, too, in the early grades, an Afrocentric curriculum may deny children a wide range of important knowledge and skills by forcing them to study only certain topics from a single point of view. The historian Arthur Schlesinger, Jr. (1991:21), puts the matter bluntly: "If a Kleagle of the Ku Klux Klan wanted to use the schools to handicap black Americans, he could hardly come up with anything more effective than the 'Afrocentric' curriculum."

Is there any common ground in this debate? Almost everyone agrees that we need greater appreciation of our cultural diversity. But precisely where the balance is to be struck—between the *pluribus* and the *unum*—is likely to remain an issue for some time to come.

COUNTERCULTURE

Cultural diversity also includes outright rejection of conventional ideas or behavior. **Counterculture** refers to *cultural patterns that strongly oppose those widely accepted within a society.*

In many societies, counterculture is linked to youth (Spates, 1976, 1983; Spates & Perkins, 1982). The youth-oriented counterculture of the 1960s, for example, rejected mainstream culture as overly competitive, self-centered, and materialistic. Instead, hippies and other counterculturalists favored a cooperative lifestyle in which "being" took precedence over "doing" and the capacity for personal growth—or "expanded consciousness"—was prized over material possessions like homes and cars. Such differences led some people to "drop out" of the larger society.

Countercultures are still flourishing. In the 1990s, militaristic bands of men and women, deeply suspicious of the federal government, advocated dropping out of the political system. Countercultural extremism of this kind led to the bombing of the Oklahoma City federal building in 1995, killing 168 people.

CULTURAL CHANGE

Perhaps the most basic human truth of this world is "All things shall pass." Even the dinosaurs, which thrived on this planet for 160 million years (see the time line), remain today only as fossils. Will humanity survive for millions of years to come? All we can say with certainty is that—given our reliance on culture—for as long as we survive, the human record will be one of continuous change.

Table 3–1 shows changes in student attitudes between 1968 (the height of the 1960s counterculture) and 1999. Some attitudes have changed only slightly: Today, as a generation ago, most men and women look forward to raising a family. But today's students are much more interested in making money than in developing a philosophy of life.

Change in one dimension of a culture usually sparks changes in others. For example, women's increased participation in the labor force parallels many changing family patterns, including first marriages at a later age and a rising divorce rate. Such patterns illustrate **cultural integration,** *the close relationship among various elements of a cultural system.*

TABLE 3–1 Attitudes among Students Entering U.S. Colleges, 1968 and 1999

		1968*	1999	Change
Life Objectives (Essential or Very Important)				
Develop a philosophy of life	Men	79%	40%	–39%
	Women	87	39	–48
Keep up with political affairs	Men	52	30	–22
	Women	52	23	–29
Help others in difficulty	Men	50	51	+ 1
	Women	71	66	– 5
Raise a family	Men	64	70	+ 6
	Women	72	72	0
Be successful in my own business	Men	55	44	–11
	Women	32	34	+ 2
Be well off financially	Men	51	76	+25
	Women	27	72	+45

*To allow comparisons, data from the early 1970s rather than 1968 are used for some items.

Sources: Richard G. Braungart and Margaret M. Braungart, "From Yippies to Yuppies: Twenty Years of Freshmen Attitudes," *Public Opinion,* vol. 11, no. 3 (September–October 1988): 53–56; Linda J. Sax, Alexander W. Astin, William S. Korn, and Kathryn M. Mahoney, *The American Freshman: National Norms for Fall 1999* (Los Angeles: UCLA Higher Education Research Institute, 1999).

Cultural Lag

Some elements of culture change faster than others. William Ogburn (1964) observed that technology moves quickly, generating new elements of material culture (like test-tube babies) faster than nonmaterial culture (such as ideas about parenthood) can keep up with them. Ogburn called this inconsistency **cultural lag,** *the fact that some cultural elements change more quickly than others, which may disrupt a cultural system.* How are we to apply traditional notions about motherhood and fatherhood when one woman can give birth to a child using another woman's egg, which has been fertilized in a laboratory with the sperm of a total stranger?

Causes of Cultural Change

Cultural changes are set in motion in three ways. The first is *invention,* the process of creating new cultural elements. Invention has given us the telephone (1876), the airplane (1903), and the computer (the late 1940s), each of which has had a tremendous impact on our way of life. The process of invention goes on constantly, as indicated by the thousands of applications submitted annually to the U.S. Patent Office. (Take a look at the time line inside the front cover of this book to note other inventions that have spurred cultural change.)

Discovery, a second cause of cultural change, involves recognizing and better understanding something already in existence—from a distant star, to the foods of another culture, to the athletic prowess of women. Many discoveries result from painstaking scientific research, and others by a stroke of luck, as when Marie Curie left a rock on a piece of photographic paper in 1898 and thus discovered radium.

The third cause of cultural change is *diffusion,* the spread of cultural traits from one society to another. Because new information technology sends information around the globe in seconds, cultural diffusion has never been greater than it is today.

Certainly our own society has contributed many significant cultural elements to the world, ranging from computers to jazz music. Of course, diffusion works the other way, too, so that much of what we assume to be "American" actually comes from elsewhere. Most clothing, furniture, clocks, newspapers, money, and even the English language are derived from other cultures (Linton, 1937a).

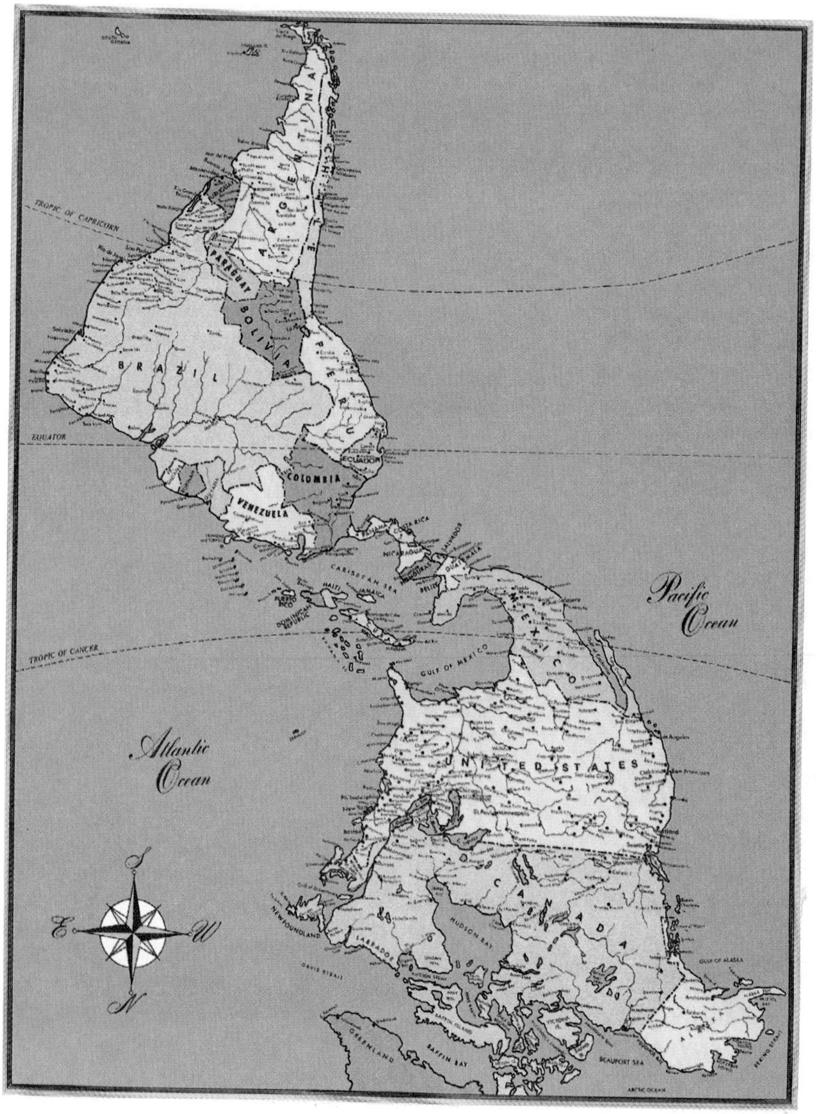

The View from "Down Under"

North America should be "up" and South America "down," or so we think. But, because we live on a globe, such notions are conventions rather than absolutes. The reason that this map of the Western Hemisphere looks wrong to us is not that it is geographically inaccurate; it simply violates our ethnocentric assumption that the United States should be "above" the rest of the Americas.

ETHNOCENTRISM AND CULTURAL RELATIVITY

December 10, 1994, a small village in rural Morocco. Watching many of our shipmates browsing through a tiny ceramic factory, there is little doubt that North Americans are among the world's greatest shoppers. We delight in surveying hand-woven carpets in China or India, inspecting finely crafted metals in Turkey, or collecting the beautifully colored porcelain tiles we find here in Morocco. And, of course, all these items are wonderful bargains. But one major reason for the low prices is unsettling: Many products from the world's low- and middle-income countries are produced by children—some as young as five or six—who work long days for extremely low wages.

We think of childhood as a time of innocence and freedom from adult burdens like regular work. In poor countries throughout the world, however, families depend on income earned by children. So what people in one society think of as right and natural, people elsewhere find puzzling and even immoral. Perhaps the Chinese philosopher Confucius had it right when he noted that "All people are the same; it's only their habits that are different."

Just about every imaginable idea or behavior is commonplace somewhere in the world, and this cultural variation causes travelers equal measures of excitement and distress. The tradition in Japan is to name intersections rather than streets, a practice that regularly confuses North Americans, who do the opposite; Egyptians move very close to others in conversation, which irritates North Americans, used to maintaining several feet of "personal space." Bathrooms lack toilet paper in much of rural Morocco, causing considerable consternation among Westerners unaccustomed to using the left hand for bathroom hygiene.

Given that a particular culture is the basis for everyone's reality, it is no wonder that people everywhere exhibit **ethnocentrism,** *the practice of judging another culture by the standards of one's own culture*. Some ethnocentrism is necessary for people to be emotionally attached to their way of life. But ethnocentrism also generates misunderstanding and sometimes conflict.

Even our language is culturally biased. Centuries ago, people in Europe and North America referred to China as the "Far East." But this term, unknown to the Chinese, is an ethnocentric expression for a region that is far east *of us*. The Chinese name for their country translates as "Central Kingdom," suggesting that they—like us—see their own society as the center of the world. The map shows ethnocentrism at work in a "down under" view of the Western Hemisphere.

The logical alternative to ethnocentrism is **cultural relativism,** *the practice of evaluating a culture by its own standards*. Cultural relativism is a difficult attitude to adopt: It requires understanding unfamiliar values and norms as well as suspending cultural standards we have known all our lives. At the same time, as people of the world come into increasing contact with one another, the importance of understanding other cultures becomes even greater.

United States business is learning that success in the global economy depends on cultural awareness. General Motors, for example, learned the hard way that its Nova wasn't selling well in Spanish-speaking nations because the name in Spanish means "No Go." Coors' phrase "Turn It Loose" startled customers by proclaiming that the beer would cause diarrhea. Braniff Airlines turned "Fly in Leather" into clumsy Spanish reading "Fly Naked." Eastern Airlines transformed its slogan "We Earn Our Wings Daily" into "We Fly Every Day to Heaven." Even Frank Purdue fell victim to poor marketing when his pitch "It Takes a Tough Man to Make a Tender Chicken" ended up in Spanish words reading "A Sexually Excited Man Will Make a Chicken Affectionate" (Helin, 1992).

Most people in the affluent United States take for granted that childhood should be a carefree time of life devoted to learning and play. In low-income societies of the world, however, poor families depend on the income earned by children, some of whom perform long days of heavy physical labor. We may not want to accept all cultural practices as "natural" just because they exist. But what universal standards can be used to judge social patterns as either right or wrong?

But cultural relativity introduces problems of its own. If almost any kind of behavior is normative

For more than a century, the culture of Japan has been strongly influenced by Western ways of life. Perhaps this explains the widespread use of Western-looking models in Japanese advertising for various products.

somewhere in the world, does that mean everything is equally right? Does the fact that some Indian and Moroccan families benefit from having their children work long hours justify child labor?

Since we all are members of a single species, surely there must be some universal standards of proper conduct. But what are they? And, in trying to develop them, how can we avoid imposing our own standards of fair play on others? There are no simple answers. But when confronting an unfamiliar cultural practice, resist making judgments before grasping what "they" think of the issue. Remember, also, to think about your own way of life as others might see it. After all, what we gain most from studying others is better insight into ourselves.

A GLOBAL CULTURE?

Today, more than ever before, we can observe many of the same cultural practices the world over. Walking the streets of Seoul (South Korea), Kuala Lumpur (Malaysia), Madras (India), Cairo (Egypt), and Casablanca (Morocco), we find jeans, hear familiar pop music, and see advertising for many of the same products we use at home. Recall, too, from Global Map 3–1, that English is rapidly emerging as the preferred second language of most of the world. Are we witnessing the birth of a single global culture?

It is true that societies around the world now have more contact with one another than ever before, involving the flow of goods, information, and people.

1. **The global economy: the flow of goods.** There has never been more international trade. The global economy has spread many of the same consumer goods (from cars and TV shows to music and fashions) throughout the world.
2. **Global communications: the flow of information.** Satellite-based communications enable people to experience the sights and sounds of events taking place thousands of miles away—often as they happen.
3. **Global migration: the flow of people.** Knowing about the rest of the world motivates people to move where they imagine life will be better. Moreover, today's transportation technology, especially air travel, makes relocating easier than ever before. As a result, in most countries, significant numbers of people were born elsewhere (including some 30 million people in the United States, about 11 percent of the population).

These global links make the cultures of the world more similar. But there are three important limitations to the global culture thesis. First, the global flow of goods, information, and people is uneven. Generally speaking, urban areas (centers of commerce, communication, and people) have stronger ties to one another, and rural villages remain isolated. Then, too, the greater economic and military power of North America and Western Europe means that these regions influence the rest of the world more than happens the other way around.

Following the structural-functional paradigm, what do you make of the Amish practice of "barn raising," by which everyone in a community joins together to raise a family's new barn in a day? Why is such a ritual almost unknown in rural areas outside of Amish communities?

Second, the global culture thesis assumes that people everywhere are able to afford various new goods and services. As Chapter 12 ("Global Stratification") explains, desperate poverty in much of the world deprives people of even the basic necessities of a safe and secure life.

Third, although many cultural practices are now found throughout the world, people everywhere do not attach the same meanings to them. Do teenagers in Tokyo understand hip-hop the way their counterparts in New York or Los Angeles do? Similarly, we enjoy foods from around the world while knowing little about the lives of the people who created them. In short, people everywhere look at the world through their own cultural lenses (Featherstone, 1990; Hall & Neitz, 1993).

THEORETICAL ANALYSIS OF CULTURE

Culture helps us make sense of ourselves and the surrounding world. Sociologists, however, have the special task of comprehending culture. They use several theoretical approaches.

STRUCTURAL-FUNCTIONAL ANALYSIS

The structural-functional paradigm depicts culture as a complex strategy for meeting human needs. Borrowing from the philosophical doctrine of *idealism*, this approach considers values the core of a culture (Parsons, 1966; Williams, 1970). Cultural values, in other words, give meaning to life and bind people together. Countless other cultural traits have various functions that support a way of life.

Thinking functionally helps us understand an unfamiliar way of life. Take, for example, the Amish farmer plowing hundreds of acres of an Ohio farm with a team of horses. His farming methods may violate our cultural value of efficiency but, from the Amish point of view, hard work functions to develop the discipline necessary for a highly religious way of life. Long days of working together not only make the Amish self-sufficient but unify families and local communities.

Of course, Amish practices have dysfunctions as well. The hard work and strict religious discipline are too demanding for some, who end up leaving the community. Then, too, religious devotion sometimes prevents compromise, resulting in lasting divisions within the Amish world (Hostetler, 1980; Kraybill, 1989; Kraybill & Olshan, 1994).

If cultures are strategies for meeting human needs, we would expect to find many common patterns around the world. The term **cultural universals** refers to *traits that are part of every known culture*. Comparing hundreds of cultures, George Murdock (1945) identified dozens of cultural universals. One common element is the family, which functions everywhere to control sexual reproduction and to oversee the care of children. Funeral rites, too, are found everywhere, because all human communities cope with the reality of death. Jokes are another cultural universal, serving as a safe means of releasing social tensions.

Critical evaluation. The strength of the structural-functional paradigm is showing how culture operates to meet human needs. Yet, by emphasizing a society's dominant cultural patterns, this approach largely ignores cultural diversity. Moreover, because this approach emphasizes cultural stability, it downplays the importance of change. In short, cultural systems are not as stable or a matter of as much agreement as structural functionalism leads us to believe.

SOCIAL-CONFLICT ANALYSIS

The social-conflict paradigm stresses the link between culture and inequality. Any cultural trait, from this point of view, benefits some members of society at the expense of others.

We might well begin a conflict analysis by asking why certain values dominate a society in the first place. Many conflict theorists, especially Marxists, argue that culture is shaped by a society's system of economic production. "It is not the consciousness of men that determines their being," Marx proclaimed, "it is their social being that determines their consciousness" (Marx & Engels, 1978:4; orig. 1859). Social-conflict theory, then, is rooted in the philosophical doctrine of *materialism*, which holds that a society's system of material production (such as our own industrial-capitalist economy) has a powerful effect on the rest of a culture. This materialist approach contrasts with the idealist leanings of structural functionalism.

Social-conflict analysis ties our competitive values to our society's capitalist economy, which serves the interests of our nation's wealthy elite. The culture of capitalism further teaches us to think that rich and powerful people have more energy and talent than others and therefore deserve their wealth and privileges. Viewing capitalism as somehow "natural" also discourages efforts to reduce economic disparity.

Eventually, however, the strains of inequality erupt into movements for social change. Two recent examples in the United States are the civil rights movement and the women's movement. Both seek greater equality and both, too, encounter opposition from defenders of the status quo.

Critical evaluation. The social-conflict paradigm suggests that cultural systems do not address human needs equally, allowing some people to dominate others. This inequity, in turn, generates pressure toward change.

Yet, by stressing the divisiveness of culture, this paradigm understates the ways that cultural patterns integrate members of society. Thus, we should consider both positions—social conflict and structural functionalism—to gain a fuller understanding of culture.

SOCIOBIOLOGY

We know culture is a human creation, but does human biology influence how this process unfolds? A third multidisciplinary paradigm, standing with one leg in biology and one in sociology, is **sociobiology**, *a theoretical paradigm that explores ways in which human biology affects how we create culture.*

Sociobiology rests on the theory of evolution proposed by Charles Darwin (1859) in his book *On the Origin of Species*. Darwin asserted that living organisms change over long periods of time as a result of *natural selection*, which is a matter of four simple principles. First, all living things live to reproduce themselves. Second, the blueprint for reproduction is in the genes, the basic units of life that carry traits of one generation into the next. Third, some random variation in genes allows a species to "try out" new life patterns in a particular environment. This variation allows some organisms to survive better than others and to pass on their advantageous genes to their offspring. Finally, over thousands of generations, the genetic patterns that promote reproduction survive and become dominant. In this way, as biologists say, a species *adapts* to its environment, and dominant traits emerge as the "nature" of the organism.

Sociobiologists claim that the large number of cultural universals reflects the fact that all humans are members of a single biological species. It is our common biology that underlies, for example, the apparently universal "double standard" of sexual behavior. As sex researcher Alfred Kinsey put it, "Among all people everywhere in the world, the male is more likely than the female to desire sex with a variety of partners" (quoted in Barash, 1981:49). But why?

We all know that children result from joining a woman's egg with a man's sperm. But the biological importance of a single sperm and of a single egg are quite different. For healthy men, sperm represent a "renewable resource" produced by the testes throughout most of the life course. A man releases hundreds of

Using an evolutionary perspective, sociobiologists point to a double standard by which men treat women as sexual objects more than women treat men that way. While this may be so, many sociologists counter that behavior—such as that shown in Ruth Orkin's photograph, American Girl in Paris*—is more correctly understood as resulting from a culture of male domination.*

millions of sperm in a single ejaculation—technically, enough to fertilize every woman in North America (Barash, 1981:47). A newborn female's ovaries, however, contain her entire lifetime allotment of follicles, or immature eggs. A woman generally releases a single egg cell from her ovaries each month. So, whereas a man is biologically capable of fathering thousands of offspring, a woman is able to bear only a relatively small number of children.

Given this biological difference, men reproduce their genes most efficiently by being promiscuous—readily engaging in sex. This scheme, however, opposes the reproductive interests of women. Each of a woman's relatively few pregnancies demands that she carry the child for nine months, give birth, and provide care for some time afterward. Thus, efficient reproduction on the part of the woman depends on carefully selecting a mate whose qualities (beginning with the likelihood that he will simply stay around) will contribute to their child's survival and, later, successful reproduction (Remoff, 1984).

The "double standard" certainly involves more than biology and is tangled up with the historical domination of women by men (Barry, 1983). But sociobiology suggests that this cultural pattern, like many others, has an underlying bio-logic. Simply put, the double standard exists around the world because women and men everywhere tend toward distinctive reproductive strategies.

Critical evaluation. Sociobiology has generated intriguing theories about the biological roots of some cultural patterns. But the approach remains controversial for several reasons.

First, some critics fear that sociobiology may revive biological arguments from a century ago that touted the superiority of one race or sex. But defenders counter that sociobiology rejects the past pseudoscience of racial superiority. In fact, sociobiology unites all of humanity because all people share a single evolutionary history. Sociobiology does assert that men and women differ biologically in some ways that culture cannot overcome. But, far from asserting that males are somehow more important than females, sociobiology emphasizes that both sexes are vital to human reproduction.

Second, say the critics, sociobiologists have little evidence to support their theories. Research to date suggests that biological forces do not determine human behavior in any rigid sense. Rather, humans *learn* behavior within a cultural system. The contribution of sociobiology, then, lies in explaining why some cultural patterns seem "easier to learn" than others (Barash, 1981).

CONTROVERSY & DEBATE

What Are the "Culture Wars"?

"Hi, there, this is WYMI's 'Open Line' talk show. This afternoon, we are debating the question 'Should gay partners be permitted by law to marry?' I have Rhonda from the East Side on the line; Rhonda, what do you think? . . ."

The easy rhythm of radio talk is familiar to just about everyone all across the country. But there is nothing easy about the questions being asked and, more often than not, little agreement on the answers. Indeed, on a host of issues—gay rights, gender equality, welfare, abortion, single parenting, prayer in schools, multiculturalism, government funding to the arts, and more—there now seems to be a wide and angry gulf in U.S. society. On both sides, people are thoughtful, committed to their principles, and concerned about the future of their country. They are fighting what sociologists call the "culture wars."

Today's culture wars are this nation's latest round of **cultural conflict,** *political differences, often expressed with hostility, based on disagreement over cultural values.* There is nothing novel about cultural conflict. Throughout much of the nineteenth century, for example, Protestants and Catholics clashed over the direction of change in U.S. society. Many issues at the core of today's culture wars are new, of course, but as sociologist James Davison Hunter explains, this conflict remains a heated struggle to define our country's way of life.

Hunter offers several insights into our current cultural conflict. First, he notes that people's positions on various issues tend to be consistent. That is, knowing someone's view on one issue usually enables us to predict the person's view on another. This connection stems from the fact that most individuals in U.S. society fall into one of two major camps—"traditionalists" and "progressives"—that have different cultural orientations.

Traditionalists, explains Hunter, see the world as a moral system. That is, they recognize "an external, definable, and transcendent authority" that clearly defines right and wrong and to whom everyone is responsible. For many—whether they are Christians, Jews, or Muslims—God is this authority. For others, this authority is the cultural heritage of self-reliance, strong families, and local communities that has guided this country for centuries. Traditionalists, then, are conservatives who tend to be patriotic, religious, and believe in "old-fashioned family values." Thus, traditionalists oppose gay rights, condemn abortion, and think that public schools have abandoned traditional moral standards in favor of teaching our children tolerance of virtually every imaginable lifestyle. From this point of view, the growing tide of violence, divorce, and illegitimate births stems from each of us having too little moral responsibility and too much personal freedom.

To progressives, on the other hand, people are thoughtful and able to make their own choices. Progressives see no clear line between right and wrong. Indeed, they believe that our country deliberately removed religion from public life, making it a matter of individual belief. Certainly, some progressives are religious, but they tend to see the Bible and other religious texts as sources of historical wisdom that people interpret for themselves in light of their own lives today. Thus, progressives oppose prejudice against gay people, support a woman's right to choose an abortion, and see no place for religious observance in public schools. From this point of view, social problems like poverty and racial discrimination are best remedied not by providing people with greater moral discipline but by making everyone more equal.

One reason that this country's culture wars generate so much heat, claims Hunter, is that media coverage focuses on people taking extreme positions on one side or the other of various issues. In addition, many people find compromise difficult not just because they hold deep beliefs but because what one side sees as the "solution," the other sees as the "problem."

Continue the debate . . .

1. *Do you agree that most people find it hard to compromise on important issues such as gay rights and abortion? Why?*
2. *Are the culture wars evident on your campus? If so, how?*
3. *In your opinion, which side of the culture wars has the upper hand? Why?*

Sources: Adapted in part from Hunter (1991); see also Davis & Robinson (1996), DiMaggio, Evans, & Bryson (1996), Nolan (1996), and Evans (1997).

CULTURE AND HUMAN FREEDOM

Underlying the discussion throughout this chapter is an important question: To what extent are human beings, as cultural creatures, free? Does culture bind us to each other and constrain us to the past? Or does culture enhance our capacity for individual thought and independent choices?

CULTURE AS CONSTRAINT

Humans cannot live without culture. But the capacity for culture does have some drawbacks. We may be the only animals able to name ourselves, but living in a symbolic world means that we are also the only creatures who experience alienation. Moreover, culture is largely a matter of habit, limiting our choices and driving us to repeat troubling patterns, such as racial prejudice and gender discrimination, in each new generation. In addition, in this age of new information technology and virtual reality, we may wonder at the extent to which business-dominated media manipulate our culture in pursuit of profits.

Moreover, our society's emphasis on competitive achievement urges us toward excellence, yet this same pattern also isolates us from one another. Material things comfort us in some ways but divert us from the security and satisfaction that come from close relationships and spiritual strength.

CULTURE AS FREEDOM

For better or worse, human beings are cultural creatures, just as ants and bees are prisoners of their biology. But there is a crucial difference. Biological instincts create a ready-made world; culture, by contrast, forces us to choose as we make and remake a world for ourselves. No better evidence of this freedom exists than the cultural diversity of our own society and the even greater human diversity around the world.

Furthermore, culture is ever-changing as the result of human imagination. For this reason, as the box explains, members of our society hotly debate the future direction of our way of life. But, whatever one's politics, the better we understand the workings of our culture, the better prepared we are to use the freedom it offers us.

SUMMARY

1. Culture is a way of life shared by members of a society. Several species display limited capacity for culture, but only human beings rely on culture for survival.
2. As the human brain evolved, the first elements of culture appeared some 3 million years ago; culture replaced biological instincts as our species' primary strategy for survival.
3. Culture relies on symbols. Language is the symbolic system by which one generation transmits culture to the next.
4. Values are culturally defined standards of what ought to be; beliefs are statements that people who share a culture hold to be true.
5. Cultural norms, which guide human behavior, are of two kinds: Mores have great moral significance, whereas folkways are everyday matters of politeness.
6. High culture refers to patterns that distinguish a society's elite; popular culture refers to widespread social patterns.
7. The United States stands among the most culturally diverse societies in the world. Subculture refers to distinctive cultural patterns supported by some part of a population, and counterculture to patterns strongly at odds with a conventional way of life. Multiculturalism represents educational efforts to enhance awareness and appreciation of cultural diversity.
8. Invention, discovery, and diffusion all generate cultural change. Cultural lag results as some parts of a cultural system change faster than others.
9. Ethnocentrism involves judging others by the standards of one's own culture. By contrast, cultural relativism means evaluating another culture according to its own standards.
10. Global cultural patterns result from the worldwide flow of goods, information, and people.
11. Structural-functional analysis views culture as a relatively stable system built on core values. Cultural patterns function to maintain the overall system.

12. The social-conflict paradigm envisions culture as a dynamic arena of inequality and conflict. Cultural patterns benefit some categories of people more than others.
13. Sociobiology studies how humanity's evolutionary past shapes human culture.
14. The concept of cultural conflict refers to political debate ("culture wars") on the direction of cultural change in the United States.
15. Culture can constrain social possibilities; yet, as cultural creatures, we have the capacity to shape and reshape our world to meet our needs and pursue our dreams.

KEY CONCEPTS

culture (p. 61) the values, beliefs, behavior, and material objects that, together, form a people's way of life

nonmaterial culture (p. 61) the intangible world of ideas created by members of a society

material culture (p. 61) the tangible things created by members of a society

culture shock (p. 61) personal disorientation when experiencing an unfamiliar way of life

symbols (p. 63) anything that carries a particular meaning recognized by people who share culture

language (p. 64) a system of symbols that allows people to communicate with one another

cultural transmission (p. 64) the process by which one generation passes culture to the next

Sapir-Whorf thesis (p. 67) the thesis that people perceive the world through the cultural lens of language

values (p. 67) culturally defined standards by which people assess desirability, goodness, and beauty, and which serve as broad guidelines for social living

beliefs (p. 67) specific statements that people hold to be true

norms (p. 69) rules and expectations by which a society guides the behavior of its members

mores (p. 70) norms that are widely observed and have great moral significance

folkways (p. 70) norms for routine, casual interaction

social control (p. 70) various means by which members of a society encourage conformity to norms

technology (p. 71) knowledge that people apply to the task of living in their surroundings

high culture (p. 73) cultural patterns that distinguish a society's elite

popular culture (p. 73) cultural patterns that are widespread among a society's population

subculture (p. 74) cultural patterns that set apart some segment of a society's population

multiculturalism (p. 75) an educational program recognizing the cultural diversity of the United States and promoting the equality of all cultural traditions

Eurocentrism (p. 75) the dominance of European (especially English) cultural patterns

Afrocentrism (p. 76) the dominance of African cultural patterns

counterculture (p. 76) cultural patterns that strongly oppose those widely accepted within a society

cultural integration (p. 77) the close relationship among various elements of a cultural system

cultural lag (p. 77) the fact that some cultural elements change more quickly than others, which may disrupt a cultural system

ethnocentrism (p. 79) the practice of judging another culture by the standards of one's own culture

cultural relativism (p. 79) the practice of evaluating a culture by its own standards

cultural universals (p. 81) traits that are part of every known culture

sociobiology (p. 82) a theoretical paradigm that explores ways in which human biology affects how we create culture

cultural conflict (p. 84) political differences, often expressed with hostility, based on disagreement over cultural values

CRITICAL-THINKING QUESTIONS

1. Hot dogs and hamburgers have long been considered national favorites. What cultural patterns help explain our love for these kinds of foods?
2. What cultural lessons do games like King of the Mountain, Tag, or Keep Away teach our children? What about a schoolroom spelling bee? What cultural values are expressed by children's stories such as *The Little Engine that Could* and popular board games such as "Chutes and Ladders," "Monopoly," and "Risk"?
3. Do you think U.S. cultural values are changing? If so, how and why?
4. Have you ever identified with one or more subcultures? If so, which? How do their values differ from "mainstream" U.S. values?

APPLICATIONS AND EXERCISES

1. Try to find someone on campus who has lived in another country. Ask for a chance to discuss how the culture of that society differs from the way of life here. Does the other person see U.S. culture differently from most of us?
2. Make a list of words with the prefix "self" (self-service, self-image, self-esteem, self-destructive, and so on); there are many of them. What does this high number suggest about our way of life?
3. An easy way to study popular culture is to pick up a number of super-hero comic books. Examine them to see why some people are defined as heroes and others as villains. Does gender figure in this process? (Cf. Hall & Lucal, 1999.)
4. Watch a Disney film like *The Little Mermaid*, *Aladdin*, *Pocahontas*, or *Mulan*. All of these films share cultural themes, which explains their popularity. According to the films, how should young people behave toward their parents? What makes these films especially "American"?
5. Install the CD-ROM packaged in the back of this new textbook to access a variety of study, review, and applications exercises designed to help you better understand the material covered in this chapter. The CD includes an author's tip video, as well as interactive maps, video application exercises, Web links, and study questions.

SITES TO SEE

http://www.prenhall.com/macionis

Visit the interactive Web site that accompanies this text. Begin by clicking on the cover of your book. You will find a chapter-by-chapter study guide, practice tests, chat room, and many suggested Web links.

http://www.macionis.com
(or **http://www.thesociologypage.com**)

Visit the author's Web page to view short videos on the lessons and challenges of traveling in an unfamiliar setting.

http://www.nationalgeographic.com

Visit the Web site for the National Geographic Society. This site offers information on world cultures, including search engines, and a library of maps.

http://www.gorilla.org

The Gorilla Foundation operates a Web site where one can follow the progress that researchers are making in teaching a 450-pound gorilla named Koko to use sign language.

CHAPTER 4

Marc Chagall (1887–1985)
Le Cirque au Village

SOCIETY

Sididi Ag Inaka has never used a computer, sent a fax, or spoken on a cell phone. In today's high-technology world, these facts may seem strange enough. But how about this: Neither Inaka nor anyone in his family has ever seen a television or even read a newspaper.

Are these people visitors from another planet? Prisoners on some remote island? Not at all. They are Tuareg nomads who wander the vastness of the Sahara in western Africa, north of the city of Timbuktu in the nation we know as Mali. Known as the "blue men of the desert," for the flowing blue robes worn by both men and women, the Tuareg herd camels, goats, and sheep and live in camps where the sand blows and the daytime temperature often reaches 120 degrees. Life is hard, but most try to hold onto traditional ways. With a look of determination, Inaka says, "My father was a nomad, his father was a nomad, I am a nomad, my children will be nomads."

The Tuaregs are among the poorest people of the world, living a simple and difficult existence. When the rains fail to come, they and their animals risk losing their lives. Inaka and his people are a society set apart, isolated from the rest of humanity and virtually untouched by modern ideas and advanced technology. To many, no doubt, they seem a curious throwback to the past. But Inaka does not complain: "This is the life of my ancestors. This is the life that we know" (Buckley, 1996; Matloff, 1997; Lovgren, 1998).

Many kinds of human societies have existed in history, and we still find remarkable diversity today. But what is a society, in the first place? How and why have societies changed over the course of human history?

Society refers to *people who interact in a defined territory and share culture*. In this chapter, we shall examine this deceptively simple term from four different angles. We begin with **Gerhard Lenski** and **Jean Lenski,** who describe the changing character of human societies over the last 10,000 years. They explain the importance of *technology*, and how new technology can have revolutionary consequences for social life. Then we turn to three of sociology's founders. **Karl Marx,** like the Lenskis, understood human history as a long and complex process. For Marx, however, the story of society spins around *social conflict* that arises from how people produce material goods. **Max Weber** took another approach, showing that the power of *ideas* also shapes society. Weber contrasted the traditional thinking of simple societies with the rational thought that dominates our modern way of life. Finally, **Emile Durkheim** helped us to see the different ways that traditional and modern societies hang together.

All four visions of society answer key questions: What makes simple people, such as the Tuareg of the Sahara, so different from the society familiar to us? How and why do all societies change? What forces divide a society? What forces hold it together? And, after looking at the trends over time, we might well ask whether societies are getting better or worse.

In technologically simple societies, successful hunting wins men great praise. However, the gathering of vegetation by women is a more dependable and easily available source of nutrition.

GERHARD LENSKI AND JEAN LENSKI: SOCIETY AND TECHNOLOGY

Members of our society, who take telephones and television as well as schools and hospitals for granted, must wonder at the nomads of the Sahara, who live the same simple life their ancestors did centuries ago. The work of Gerhard Lenski and Jean Lenski (Lenski, Nolan, & Lenski, 1995) helps us understand the great differences among societies that have flourished and declined throughout human history.

The Lenskis use the term **sociocultural evolution** to refer to *the changes that occur as a society acquires new technology.* Societies with simple technology, such as the Tuareg, have little control over nature, so they can support only a small number of people. Technologically complex societies, while not necessarily "better," support large numbers of people who live highly specialized lives.

In addition, the more technological information a society has, the faster it changes. Technologically simple societies change very slowly; Sididi Ag Inaka says he "lives the life of his ancestors." Modern, high-technology societies, on the other hand, change so quickly that dramatic transformations can occur during a single lifetime. Imagine how someone who lived just a few generations ago would react to beepers, phone sex, artificial hearts, test-tube babies, genetic engineering, e-mail, smart bombs, space shuttles, the threat of nuclear holocaust, transsexualism, and "tell all" talk shows.

In short, new technology sends ripples of change through a society's way of life. When our ancestors first discovered how to harness the power of the wind using a sail, they set the stage for building sailing ships, which took them to new lands, stimulated trade, and increased their military might. Consider, as a more recent example, how our lives are being changed by the spread of computer technology.

Drawing on the Lenskis' work, we will describe five types of societies according to their technology: hunting and gathering societies, horticultural and pastoral societies, agrarian societies, industrial societies, and postindustrial societies.

HUNTING AND GATHERING SOCIETIES

The simplest of all kinds of societies live by **hunting and gathering,** *the use of simple tools to hunt animals and gather vegetation.* From the emergence of our species 3 million years ago until just 12,000 years before the present, all humans were hunters and gatherers. Even in 1800, there were many hunting and gathering societies in the world. Today, however, just a few remain, including the Aka and Pygmies of central Africa, the Bushmen of southwestern Africa, the Aborigines of Australia, the Kaska Indians of northwest Canada, and the Batek and Semai of Malaysia (Endicott, 1992; Hewlett, 1992).

With little control over their environment, hunters and gatherers spend most of their time searching for game and collecting edible plants. Only in lush areas where food is plentiful do hunters and gatherers have leisure time. Moreover, it takes a lot of land to support even a few people, so hunting and gathering societies are small bands with a few dozen members. They must also be nomadic, moving on as they deplete vegetation in an area or follow migratory animals. Although periodically returning to favored sites, they rarely form permanent settlements.

Hunting and gathering societies are built on kinship. The family obtains and distributes food, protects its members, and teaches the children. Everyone's life is much the same, and is focused on getting their next meal. There is some specialization related to age and gender. The very young and the very old contribute only

Pastoralism historically has flourished in regions of the world where arid soil does not support crops. Pastoral people still thrive in northern Africa, living today much as they did a thousand years ago.

what they can, while healthy adults secure most of the food. Women gather vegetation—the more reliable food source—while men take on the less certain task of hunting. Although men and women perform different tasks, most hunters and gatherers probably saw the sexes as having about the same social importance (Leacock, 1978).

Hunting and gathering societies have few formal leaders. Most recognize a *shaman*, or spiritual leader, who enjoys high prestige but receives no greater material rewards and must work to find food like everyone else. In short, hunting and gathering societies are egalitarian.

Hunters and gatherers employ simple weapons—the spear, bow and arrow, and stone knife—but rarely to wage war. They are much more likely to fall victim to the forces of nature. Storms and droughts can destroy their food supply, and there is little they can do in the event of accident or illness. Such vulnerability encourages cooperation and sharing, raising everyone's odds of survival. Nonetheless, many die in childhood, and no more than half reach the age of twenty (Lenski, Nolan, & Lenski, 1995:104).

During the twentieth century, technologically complex societies slowly closed in on the few remaining hunters and gatherers, reducing their food supply. The Lenskis claim that at this point, we may well have witnessed the end of hunting and gathering societies on earth. Fortunately, study of this way of life has produced valuable information about human history and our fundamental ties to the natural world.

HORTICULTURAL AND PASTORAL SOCIETIES

Ten to twelve thousand years ago, a new technology began to change the lives of human beings (see the time line inside the front cover). People discovered **horticulture,** *the use of hand tools to raise crops.* Using a hoe to work the soil and a digging stick to punch holes in the ground to plant seeds may seem simple and obvious, but horticulture allowed people to give up gathering in favor of "growing their own." Humans first planted gardens in the fertile regions of the Middle East and then in Latin America and Asia. Within some 5,000 years, cultural diffusion spread knowledge of horticulture throughout most of the world.

Not all societies abandoned hunting and gathering in favor of horticulture. Hunters and gatherers living amid plentiful vegetation and game probably took little note of the new technology (Fisher, 1979). Then, too, people inhabiting arid regions (such as the Middle East or the Sahara in western Africa) or mountainous areas found horticulture of little value. Such people (including the Tuareg) turned to **pastoralism,** *the domestication of animals.* Today, societies that mix horticulture and pastoralism thrive in South America, Africa, and Asia.

Of Egypt's 130 pyramids, the Great Pyramids at Giza are the largest. Each of the three major structures stands more than forty stories high and is composed of 3 million massive stone blocks. Some 4,500 years ago, tens of thousands of people labored to construct these pyramids so that one man, the pharaoh, might have a godlike monument for his tomb. Clearly social inequality in this agrarian society was striking.

Domesticating plants and animals greatly increased food production, so societies could support not dozens but hundreds of people. Pastoralists remained nomadic, leading their herds to fresh grazing lands. Horticulturalists, by contrast, formed settlements, moving on only when they depleted the soil. Joined by trade, these settlements formed societies with populations climbing into the thousands.

Once a society is capable of producing *a material surplus*—more resources than needed to support day-to-day living—not everyone has to secure food. Some make crafts, engage in trade, cut hair, apply tattoos, or serve as priests. Compared to hunting and gathering societies, then, horticultural and pastoral societies are more specialized and complex.

Hunters and gatherers believe many spirits inhabit the world. Horticulturalists, however, practice ancestor worship and conceive of God as Creator. Pastoral societies carry this belief further, seeing God directly involved in the well-being of the entire world. This view of God ("The Lord is my shepherd, . . ." Psalm 23) is widespread among members of our own society because Christianity, Islam, and Judaism all began as Middle Eastern pastoral religions.

Expanding productive technology creates social inequality. As some families produce more food than others, they assume positions of relative power and privilege. Forging alliances with other elite families allows social advantages to endure over generations. Along with social hierarchy, simple government, backed by military force, emerges to shore up the dominance of elites. However, without the ability to communicate or to travel over large distances, a ruler can control only a small number of people, so there is little empire-building.

Domestication of plants and animals made simpler societies more productive. But advancing technology is never entirely beneficial. The Lenskis point out that, compared to hunters and gatherers, horticulturalists and pastoralists have more social inequality and, in many cases, engage in slavery, protracted warfare, and even cannibalism.

AGRARIAN SOCIETIES

About 5,000 years ago, another technological revolution was underway in the Middle East and would eventually transform most of the world. This was the discovery of **agriculture,** *large-scale cultivation using plows harnessed to animals or more powerful energy sources*. So great was the social significance of the animal-drawn plow and other technological innovations of the period—including irrigation, the wheel, writing, numbers, and various metals—that this era qualifies as "the dawn of civilization" (Lenski, Nolan, & Lenski, 1995:177).

Using animal-drawn plows, farmers could cultivate fields vastly larger than the garden-sized plots worked by horticulturalists. Plows have the additional advantage of turning and aerating the soil to increase fertility. As a result, farmers work the same land for generations, which, in turn, encourages permanent settlements. Large

SOCIAL DIVERSITY

Technology and the Changing Status of Women

In the earliest human societies, women produced more food than men did. Hunters and gatherers valued meat highly, but men's hunting was not a dependable source of nourishment. Thus, vegetation gathered by women was the primary means of ensuring survival. Similarly, it was women who took charge of the tools and seeds used in horticulture. For their part, men engaged in trade and tended herds of animals. Only at harvest time did men and women work side by side.

Then, about 5,000 years ago, humans discovered how to mold metals. This technology spread by cultural diffusion, primarily along male-dominated trade networks. Thus, it was men who developed the metal plow and, because they already managed animals, thought to hitch the implement to a cow.

The metal plow marked the beginning of agriculture, and for the first time, men took over the dominant role in food production. Elise Boulding explains how this technological breakthrough undermined the social standing of women:

> The shift of the status of the woman farmer may have happened quite rapidly, once there were two male specializations relating to agriculture: plowing and the care of cattle. This situation left women with all the subsidiary tasks, including weeding and carrying water to the fields. The new fields were larger, so women had to work just as many hours as they did before, but now they worked at more secondary tasks. . . . This would contribute further to the erosion of the status of women.

Sources: Based on Boulding (1976) and Fisher (1979).

food surpluses, transported on animal-powered wagons, allow agrarian societies to expand greatly their land area and population. About 100 C.E., for example, the agrarian Roman Empire boasted a population of 70 million spread over some 2 million square miles (Stavrianos, 1983; Lenski, Nolan, & Lenski, 1995).

As always, increasing production meant more specialization. Tasks once performed by everyone, such as clearing land and securing food, became distinct occupations. Specialization also made the early barter system obsolete and money became the standard of exchange. Because money made trade easier, cities grew and their populations soared into the millions.

Agrarian societies exhibit dramatic social inequality. In many cases, including the United States early in its history, peasants or slaves represent a significant share of the population. Freed from manual work, elites can then engage in the study of philosophy, art, and literature. This explains the historical link between "high culture" and social privilege noted in Chapter 3 ("Culture").

Among hunters and gatherers and also among horticulturists, women are the primary providers of food. Agriculture, however, propels men into a position of social dominance (Boulding, 1976; Fisher, 1979). The box looks more closely at the declining position of women at this point in the course of sociocultural evolution.

In many societies, religion reinforces the power of agricultural elites by defining work as a moral obligation. Many of the "Wonders of the Ancient World," such as the Great Wall of China and the Great Pyramids of Egypt, were possible only because emperors and pharaohs wielded absolute power, commanding their people to a lifetime of labor without wages.

In agrarian societies, then, elites acquire unparalleled power. To maintain control of large empires, leaders require the services of a wide range of administrators. Thus, along with the growing economy, the political system emerges as a distinct sphere of life.

Of the societies described so far, agrarian societies have the greatest specialization and the most social inequality. Agrarian technology also gives people a greater range of life choices, which is why agrarian societies differ more from one another than horticultural and pastoral societies do.

INDUSTRIAL SOCIETIES

Industrialism, as found in the United States, Canada, and other rich nations of the world, is *the production*

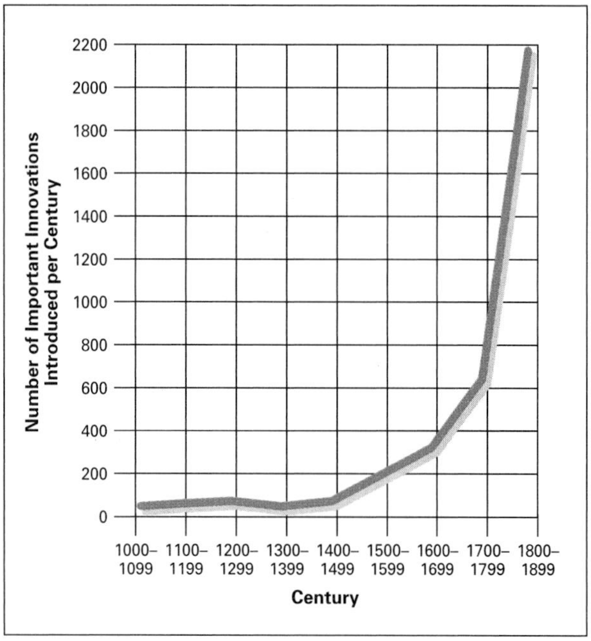

FIGURE 4–1 The Increasing Number of Technological Innovations

This figure illustrates the dramatic change in the number of technological innovations in Western Europe after the beginning of the Industrial Revolution in the mid-eighteenth century. Technological innovation occurs at an accelerating rate because each innovation combines with existing cultural elements to produce many additional innovations.

Source: Lenski, Nolan, & Lenski (1995).

of goods using advanced sources of energy to drive large machinery. Until the industrial era, the major source of energy was the muscles of humans and other animals. But about 1750, mills and factories began to use water and then steam boilers to power ever-larger machinery.

With industrial technology, societies began to change faster, as shown in Figure 4–1. Industrial societies transformed themselves more in one century than they had during the past thousand years. As explained in Chapter 1 ("The Sociological Perspective"), this stunning change prompted the birth of sociology itself. During the nineteenth century, railroads and steamships revolutionized transportation, and steel-framed skyscrapers dwarfed the cathedrals that symbolized an earlier age.

In the twentieth century, automobiles further changed Western societies, and electricity powered modern conveniences such as lighting, refrigerators, and washing machines. Electronic communication, including the telephone, radio, and television, soon followed, making the world seem smaller and smaller. During the last generation, computers have dramatically increased our ability to process information.

Work, too, has changed. In agrarian societies, most men and women work in or near the home. Industrialization, however, creates factories filled with machinery and situated near energy sources. People may travel great distances to their jobs in the factories. Lost in the process are close working relationships, strong kinship ties, and many of the traditional values, beliefs, and customs that guide agrarian life.

Occupational specialization has become more pronounced than ever. In fact, industrial people often size up one another in terms of their jobs rather than according to their kinship ties (as nonindustrial people do). Rapid change and movement from place to place also generate anonymity, cultural diversity, and numerous subcultures and countercultures, as described in Chapter 3 ("Culture").

Industrial technology recasts the family, too, lessening its traditional significance as the center of social life. No longer does the family serve as the primary setting for economic production, learning, and religious worship. And, as Chapter 18 ("Family") explains, technological change also underlies the trend away from traditional families to greater numbers of single people, divorced people, single-parent families, and stepfamilies.

The Lenskis point out that, early in the industrialization process, only a small segment of the population enjoys the benefits that advancing technology brings. In time, however, wealth spreads and more people live longer and more comfortably. Though poverty remains a serious problem in industrial societies, the standard of living has risen fivefold over the course of the last century, and social inequality has declined. Some social leveling, described in Chapter 10 ("Social Stratification"), occurs because industrial societies require an educated and skilled labor force. While the majority of people in nonindustrial societies are illiterate, industrial societies provide state-funded schooling and confer numerous political rights on almost everyone. Industrialization, in fact, intensifies popular demands for a political voice, as seen most recently in South Korea, Taiwan, the People's Republic of China, the nations of Eastern Europe, and the former Soviet Union.

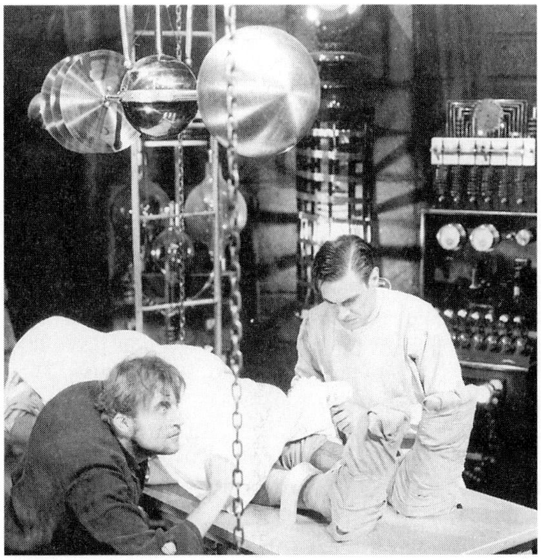

Does advancing technology make society better? In some ways, perhaps. However, many films—including Frankenstein *(1931) and* Jurassic Park *(1993)—have expressed the concern that new technology not only solves old problems but creates new ones. All the sociological theorists discussed in this chapter shared this ambivalent view of the modern world.*

POSTINDUSTRIAL SOCIETIES

Many industrial societies, including the United States, have now entered yet another phase of technological development, and we can extend the Lenskis' analysis to take account of recent trends. A generation ago, sociologist Daniel Bell (1973) coined the term **postindustrialism** to refer to *technology that supports an information-based economy*. Whereas production in industrial societies centers on factories and machinery generating material goods, postindustrial production is based on computers and other electronic devices that create, process, store, and apply information. Thus, members of industrial societies learn and apply mechanical skills, and people in postindustrial societies develop information-based skills for working with computers and other forms of high-technology communication.

With this shift in key skills, the emergence of postindustrialism dramatically changes a society's occupational structure. Chapter 16 ("The Economy and Work") explains that a postindustrial society uses less and less of its labor force for industrial production. At the same time, the ranks of clerical workers, managers, and other people who process information (in fields ranging from academia and advertising to marketing and public relations) swell.

The Information Revolution is most pronounced in rich nations, yet the new technology affects the entire world. As discussed in Chapter 3 ("Culture"), a new, worldwide flow of goods, people, and information ties societies together and fosters a global culture. And, just as industrial technology joined local communities to create a national economy, so postindustrial technology joins nations to build a global economy.

Table 4–1 summarizes how technology shapes societies at different stages of sociocultural evolution.

THE LIMITS OF TECHNOLOGY

Technology remedies many human problems by raising productivity, reducing infectious disease, and sometimes simply relieving boredom. But it provides no quick fix for social problems. Poverty, for example, remains the plight of millions of women and men in the United States (detailed in Chapter 11, "Social Class in the United States") and 1 billion people worldwide (see Chapter 12, "Global Stratification"). Moreover, technology creates new problems that our ancestors (and people like the opening vignette's Sididi Ag Inaka today) hardly could imagine. Industrial societies provide more personal freedom, but often at the cost of the sense of community that characterized preindustrial life.

TABLE 4–1 Sociological Evolution: A Summary

Type of Society	Historical Period	Productive Technology	Population Size
Hunting and Gathering Societies	Only type of society until about 12,000 years ago; still common several centuries ago; the few examples remaining today are threatened with extinction	Primitive weapons	25–40 people
Horticultural and Pastoral Societies	From about 12,000 years ago, with decreasing numbers after about 3000 B.C.E.	Horticultural societies use hand tools for cultivating plants; pastoral societies are based on the domestication of animals	Settlements of several hundred people, connected through trading ties to form societies of several thousand people
Agrarian Societies	From about 5,000 years ago, with large but decreasing numbers today	Animal-drawn plow	Millions of people
Industrial Societies	From about 1750 to the present	Advanced sources of energy; mechanized production	Millions of people
Postindustrial Societies	Emerging in recent decades	Computers that support an information-based economy	Millions of people

Further, although the most powerful nations in the world today rarely engage in all-out warfare, they have stockpiles of nuclear weapons that could return us to a technologically primitive state if, indeed, we survived at all.

Advancing technology has also contributed to a major social problem involving the environment. Each stage in sociocultural evolution has introduced more powerful sources of energy and increased our appetite for the earth's resources. An issue of vital concern, discussed in Chapter 22 ("Population, Urbanization, and Environment"), is whether humanity can continue to pursue material prosperity without permanently damaging our planet.

In some respects, then, technological advances have improved life and brought the world's people closer into a "global village." But establishing peace, ensuring justice, and sustaining a safe environment are problems that technology alone cannot solve.

KARL MARX: SOCIETY AND CONFLICT

The first of our classic visions of society comes from Karl Marx (1818–1883), an early giant in the field of sociology. A keen observer of the industrial transformation of Europe, Marx spent most of his adult life in London, then the capital of the vast British Empire. He was awed by the productive power of the new factories. Great Britain was producing more goods than ever before, with resources from around the world funneling into its factories at a dizzying rate.

What astounded and disturbed Marx was that industry's riches were concentrated in the hands of a few. A walk around London revealed striking contrasts of splendid affluence and wretched squalor. A handful of aristocrats and industrialists lived in fabulous mansions staffed by servants, where they enjoyed luxury and privilege.

Type of Society	Settlement Pattern	Social Organization	Examples
Hunting and Gathering Societies	Nomadic	Family centered; specialization limited to age and sex; little social inequality	Pygmies of central Africa Bushmen of southwestern Africa Aborigines of Australia Semai of Malaysia Kaska Indians of Canada
Horticultural and Pastoral Societies	Horticulturalists form relatively small permanent settlements; pastoralists are nomadic	Family centered; religious system begins to develop; moderate specialization; increased social inequality	Middle Eastern societies about 5000 B.C.E. Various societies today in New Guinea and other Pacific islands Yąnomamö today in South America
Agrarian Societies	Cities become common, though they generally contain only a small proportion of the population	Family loses significance as distinct religious, political, and economic systems emerge; extensive specialization; increased social inequality	Egypt during construction of the Great Pyramids Medieval Europe Numerous nonindustrial societies of the world today
Industrial Societies	Cities contain most of the population	Distinct religious, political, economic, educational, and family systems; highly specialized; marked social inequality persists, diminishing somewhat over time	Most societies today in Europe and North America, Australia, and Japan generate most of the world's industrial production
Postindustrial Societies	Population remains concentrated in cities	Similar to industrial societies with information processing and other service work gradually replacing industrial production	Industrial societies noted above are now entering postindustrial stage

Most people, though, labored long hours for low wages and lived in slums or even slept in the streets, where many eventually died from disease or poor nutrition.

Marx wrestled with a basic contradiction: In a society so rich, how could so many be so poor? Just as important, Marx asked, how can this situation be changed? Many people think Karl Marx set out to tear societies apart. But he was motivated by compassion and sought to help a badly divided society forge a new and just social order.

The key to Marx's thinking is the idea of **social conflict**, *struggle between segments of society over valued resources*. Social conflict can, of course, take many forms: Individuals may quarrel, some colleges have long-standing sports rivalries, and nations sometimes go to war. For Marx, however, the most significant form of social conflict was class conflict arising from the way a society produces material goods.

SOCIETY AND PRODUCTION

Living in the nineteenth century, Marx observed the early stage of industrial capitalism in Europe. This economic system, Marx noted, turned a small part of the population into **capitalists**, *people who own and operate factories and other businesses in pursuit of profits*. A capitalist seeks profit by selling a product for more than it costs to produce. Capitalism transforms most of the population into industrial workers, whom Marx called the **proletarians**—*people who sell their productive labor for wages*. To Marx, conflict between capitalists and workers is inevitable in a system of capitalist production. To keep profits high, capitalists keep wages low. Workers, naturally, want higher wages. Since profits and wages come from the same pool of funds, conflict results. Marx argued that this conflict could end only when people changed capitalism itself.

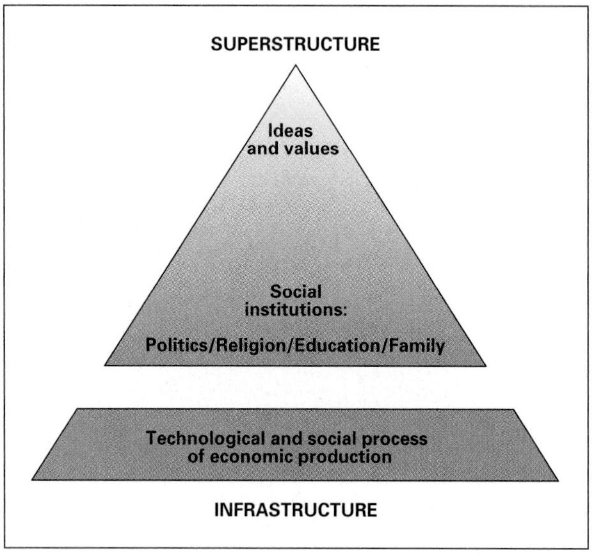

FIGURE 4–2 Karl Marx's Model of Society

This diagram illustrates Marx's materialist view that economic production underlies and shapes the entire society. Economic production involves both technology (industry, in the case of capitalism) and social relationships (for capitalism, the relationship between the capitalists, who control economic production, and the workers, who are simply a source of labor). Upon this infrastructure, or foundation, rests society's superstructure, which includes its major social institutions as well as core cultural values and ideas. Marx maintained that every part of a society supports the economic system.

All societies are composed of **social institutions,** defined as *the major spheres of social life, or societal subsystems, organized to meet human needs*. In his analysis of society, Marx argued that one institution—the economy—dominates all the others and defines the character of a society. Drawing on the philosophical doctrine of *materialism*, which says that how humans produce material goods shapes their experiences, Marx believed that the political system, family, religion, and education generally operate to support a society's economy. Just as the Lenskis argue that technology molds a society, Marx argued that the economy is a society's "real foundation" (1959:43; orig. 1859).

Marx viewed the economic system as society's *infrastructure* (*infra* is Latin, meaning "below"). Other social institutions, including the family, the political system, and religion, are built on this foundation, forming society's *superstructure*. These institutions apply economic principles to other areas of life, as illustrated in Figure 4–2. In practical terms, social institutions maintain capitalists' dominant position by legally protecting their wealth and transmitting property from one generation to the next through the family.

Generally speaking, members of industrial-capitalist societies do not view their legal or family systems as hotbeds of social conflict. On the contrary, individuals come to see their right to private property as "natural." People in the United States find it easy to think that affluent people have earned their wealth, and those who are poor or out of work lack skills or motivation. Marx rejected this reasoning, arguing that grand wealth clashing with grinding poverty is merely one set of human possibilities—the one generated by capitalism (Cuff & Payne, 1979).

Marx rejected capitalist common sense, therefore, as **false consciousness,** *explanations of social problems as the shortcomings of individuals rather than the flaws of society*. Marx was saying, in effect, that industrial capitalism itself is responsible for many social problems. False consciousness, he continued, victimizes people by hiding the real cause of their problems.

CONFLICT AND HISTORY

Marx believed that most societies evolve gradually over time. But, sometimes, they erupt in rapid, revolutionary change. Marx observed (as do the Lenskis) that change is partly caused by technological advance. But most change, he maintained, results from social conflict.

To put the Lenskis' analysis in Marxist terms, early hunters and gatherers formed primitive communist societies. *Communism* is a system by which people share more or less equally in the production of food and other material goods. Although resources were meager, they were shared by all rather than privately owned. In addition, everyone did much the same work, so there was little chance for social conflict.

Horticulture, Marx noted, introduced social inequality. Among horticultural, pastoral, and early agrarian societies—which Marx lumped together as the "ancient world"—warfare was frequent and the victors made their captives slaves. A small elite (the "masters") and their slaves were locked into an irreconcilable pattern of social conflict (Zeitlin, 1981).

Agriculture brought still more wealth to members of the elite, fueling further social conflict. Agrarian serfs, occupying the lowest reaches of European feudalism from about the twelfth to the eighteenth centuries, were only slightly better off than slaves. In Marx's view, both the church and the state defended the feudal system as God's will. Thus, to Marx, feudalism amounted to little more than "exploitation, veiled by religious and political illusions" (Marx & Engels, 1972:337; orig. 1848).

Gradually, new productive forces eroded the feudal order. As trade steadily increased, the merchants and skilled craftsworkers in cities formed a class, the *bourgeoisie* (a French word meaning "of the town"). Expanding trade made the bourgeoisie richer and richer. After about 1800, the bourgeoisie also controlled factories, becoming true capitalists with power that soon rivaled that of the ancient, landed nobility. For their part, the nobility looked down their noses at this upstart "commercial" class; but, in time, it was the capitalists who gained control of European societies. To Marx's way of thinking, then, new technology was only part of the Industrial Revolution. It was also a class revolution by which capitalists overthrew the old, agrarian elite.

Industrialization also led to the growth of the proletariat. English landowners converted fields once tilled by serfs into grazing land for sheep to produce wool for the textile mills. Forced from the land, serfs migrated to cities to work in factories. Marx envisioned these workers one day joining together to form a unified class and thus setting the stage for an historic confrontation. This time, the class revolution would lift the exploited workers over the oppressing capitalists.

Karl Marx, shown here at work on the Manifesto of the Communist Party *with his friend, benefactor, and collaborator Friedrich Engels, was surely the pioneering sociologist who had the greatest influence on the world as a whole. Through the second half of the last century, 1 billion people—nearly one-fifth of humanity—lived in societies organized on Marxist principles.*

CAPITALISM AND CLASS CONFLICT

"The history of all hitherto existing society is the history of class struggles." With these words, Marx and his collaborator Friedrich Engels began their best-known statement, the *Manifesto of the Communist Party* (1972:335; orig. 1848). Industrial capitalism, like earlier types of society, contains two major social classes—the ruling class and the oppressed—reflecting the two basic positions in the productive system. Like masters and slaves in the ancient world, and nobles and serfs in feudal systems, capitalists and proletarians are engaged in class conflict now. Today, as in the past, one class controls the other as productive property. Marx used the term **class conflict** (and sometimes *class struggle*) to refer to *conflict between entire classes over the distribution of a society's wealth and power.*

Class conflict, then, is nothing new. What distinguishes the conflict in capitalist society, Marx pointed out, is how out in the open it is. Agrarian nobles and serfs, for all their differences, were bound together by long-standing traditions and mutual obligations. Industrial capitalism dissolved those ties so that pride and honor were replaced by "naked self-interest." With no personal ties to their oppressors, Marx saw no reason for the proletarians to put up with their situation.

Though industrial capitalism brought class conflict out in the open, Marx realized that revolution would not quickly follow. First, workers must *become aware* of their oppression and see capitalism as its true cause. Second, they must *organize and act* to address their problems. This means workers must replace false consciousness with **class consciousness,** *workers' recognition of themselves as a class united in opposition to capitalists and,*

Norbert Goeneutte's painting Pauper's Meal on a Winter's Day in Paris *suggests the numbing poverty common to migrants drawn to cities as the Industrial Revolution was getting underway. Karl Marx saw in such suffering a fundamental contradiction of modern society: Industrial technology promises material plenty for all, but capitalism concentrates wealth in the hands of a few.*

ultimately, to capitalism itself. Because the inhumanity of early capitalism was plain for him to see, Marx concluded that industrial workers would soon rise up to destroy capitalism.

And what of the capitalists? The capitalists' vast wealth made them strong, indeed. But Marx saw a weakness in the capitalist armor. Motivated by a desire for personal gain, capitalists fear competition with other capitalists. Marx, therefore, thought that capitalists would be slow to band together, even though they, too, share common interests. Furthermore, he reasoned, because capitalists keep employees' wages low in order to maximize profits, the workers' resolve grows ever stronger. In the long run, Marx believed, capitalists contribute to their own undoing.

CAPITALISM AND ALIENATION

Marx also condemned capitalism for producing **alienation**, *the experience of isolation and misery resulting from powerlessness.* Dominated by capitalists, workers are nothing more than a commodity—a source of labor—hired and fired at will. Dehumanized by their jobs (especially monotonous, repetitive factory work), workers find little satisfaction and feel unable to improve their situation. Here we see another contradiction of capitalist society: As people develop technology to gain power over the world, the capitalist economy gains more control over people.

Marx cited four ways in which capitalism alienates workers:

1. **Alienation from the act of working.** Ideally, people work to meet immediate needs and to develop their personal potential. Capitalism, however, denies workers a say in what they make or how they produce it. Further, much work is tedious, a constant repetition of routine tasks. The fact that we replace workers with machines whenever possible would not have surprised Marx. As far as he was concerned, capitalism had turned human beings into machines long ago.
2. **Alienation from the products of work.** The product of work belongs not to workers but to capitalists, who sell it for profit. Thus, Marx reasoned, the more workers invest of themselves in their work, the more they lose.
3. **Alienation from other workers.** Through work, Marx claimed, people build bonds of community. Industrial capitalism, however, makes work competitive rather than cooperative. As the box illustrates, factory work provides little chance for human companionship.
4. **Alienation from human potential.** Industrial capitalism alienates workers from their human potential. Marx argued that a worker "does not fulfill himself in his work but denies himself, has a feeling of misery rather than well-being, does not freely develop his physical and mental energies, but is physically exhausted and mentally debased. The worker, therefore, feels himself to be at home only during his leisure time, whereas at work he feels homeless" (1964a:124–25; orig. 1844). In short, industrial capitalism distorts an activity that should express the best qualities in human beings into a dull and dehumanizing experience.

APPLYING SOCIOLOGY

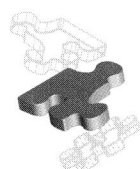

Alienation and Industrial Capitalism

These excerpts from the book *Working* by Studs Terkel illustrate how dull, repetitive jobs can alienate men and women.

Phil Stallings is a twenty-seven-year-old auto worker in a Ford assembly plant in Chicago:

> I start the automobile, the first welds. From there it goes to another line, where the floor's put on, the roof, the trunk, the hood, the doors. Then it's put on a frame. There is hundreds of lines. . . . I stand in one spot, about two- or three-feet area, all night. The only time a person stops is when the line stops. We do about thirty-two jobs per car, per unit. Forty-eight units an hour, eight hours a day. Thirty-two times forty-eight times eight. Figure it out. That's how many times I push that button.
>
> The noise, oh it's tremendous. You open your mouth and you're liable to get a mouthful of sparks. [Shows his arms.] That's a burn, these are burns. You don't compete against the noise. You go to yell and at the same time you're straining to maneuver the gun to where you have to weld.
>
> You got some guys that are uptight, and they're not sociable. It's too rough. You pretty much stay to yourself. You get involved with yourself. You dream, you think of things you've done. I drift back continuously to when I was a kid and what me and my brothers did. The things you love most are what you drift back into.
>
> It don't stop. It just goes and goes and goes. I bet there's men who have lived and died out there, never seen the end of the line. And they never will—because it's endless. It's like a serpent. It's just all body, no tail. It can do things to you. . . .

Twenty-four-year-old Sharon Atkins is a college graduate working as a telephone receptionist for a large midwestern business:

> I don't have much contact with people. You can't see them. You don't know if they're laughing, if they're being satirical or being kind. So your conversations become very abrupt. I notice that in talking to people. My conversation would be very short and clipped, in short sentences, the way I talk to people all day on the telephone. . . .
>
> You try to fill up your time with trying to think about other things: what you're going to do on the weekend or about your family. You have to use your imagination. If you don't have a very good one and you bore easily, you're in trouble. Just to fill in time, I write real bad poetry or letters to myself and to other people and never mail them. The letters are fantasies, sort of rambling, how I feel, how depressed I am.
>
> . . . I never answer the phone at home.

Source: Terkel (1974).

Marx viewed alienation, in its various forms, as a barrier to social change. But he hoped that industrial workers would overcome their alienation by uniting into a true social class, aware of the cause of their problems and ready to transform society.

REVOLUTION

The only way out of the trap of capitalism, argued Marx, is to remake society. He envisioned a more humane productive system, one where people would be equals. He called this system *socialism*. Although Marx knew well the obstacles to a socialist revolution, even so, he was disappointed that he never lived to see workers in England rise up. Still, convinced of the immorality of capitalism, he was sure that, in time, the working majority would realize they hold the key to a better future. This change would certainly be revolutionary, and perhaps even violent. In the end, Marx believed, a socialist society could meet the needs of all.

Chapter 10 ("Social Stratification") explains more about changes that have occurred in industrial-capitalist societies since Marx's time and why the revolution he hoped for never took place. But, in his own time, Marx looked toward the future with optimism (Marx & Engels, 1972:362; orig. 1848): "The proletarians have nothing to lose but their chains. They have a world to win."

For years, the conventional wisdom in the United States was that, once established, socialism stifled its opposition, rendering government immune to overthrow. But that notion collapsed along with the socialist regimes of Eastern Europe and the Soviet Union. The political transformation of this world region during the 1990s was symbolized, in city after city, by the removal of statues of Vladimir Lenin (1870–1924), architect of Soviet Marxism.

MAX WEBER: THE RATIONALIZATION OF SOCIETY

With knowledge of law, economics, religion, and history, Max Weber (1864–1920) produced what many regard as the greatest individual contribution to sociology. This scholar, born to a prosperous family in Germany, generated ideas so wide ranging that, here, we can deal only with his vision of how modern society differs from earlier types of social organization.

In line with the philosophical approach called *idealism*, Weber emphasized how human ideas shape society. He understood the power of technology, and he shared many of Marx's ideas about social conflict. But he countered Marx's materialist analysis by arguing that societies differ mainly in terms of how their members think about the world. For Weber, then, ideas, especially beliefs and values, are the key to understanding society. Weber saw modern society as the product, not just of new technology and capitalism, but of a new way of thinking. This emphasis on ideas, in contrast with Marx's focus on production, leads scholars to describe Weber's work as "a debate with the ghost of Karl Marx" (Cuff & Payne, 1979:73–74).

Weber compared social patterns in different times and places. To make the comparisons, he relied on the **ideal type,** *an abstract statement of the essential characteristics of any social phenomenon*. He explored religion by contrasting the ideal "Protestant" with the ideal "Jew," "Hindu," and "Buddhist," knowing that these models precisely described no actual individuals. Note that Weber's use of the word *ideal* does not mean that something is "good" or "the best." We can analyze "criminals" as well as "priests" in ideal terms. We have already used ideal types, of course, in comparing "hunting and gathering societies" with "industrial societies" and "capitalism" with "socialism."

TWO WORLD VIEWS: TRADITION AND RATIONALITY

Rather than categorizing societies by their technology or productive systems, Max Weber focused on ways people view the world. In simple terms, Weber said, members of preindustrial societies are *traditional*,whereas people in industrial-capitalist societies are *rational*.

By **tradition,** Weber meant *sentiments and beliefs passed from generation to generation*. In other words, traditional people are guided by the past. They consider particular actions as right and proper solely because they have been accepted for so long.

But, argued Weber, people in modern societies favor **rationality,** *deliberate, matter-of-fact calculation of the most efficient means to accomplish a particular task*. Sentiment has no place in a rational world view, which treats tradition simply as one kind of information. Typically, modern people choose to think and act on the basis of present and future consequences—evaluating jobs, schooling, and even relationships in terms of what they put into them and what they expect to receive in return.

Weber viewed both the Industrial Revolution and capitalism as evidence of a surge of rationality. He used the phrase **rationalization of society** to mean *the historical change from tradition to rationality as the dominant mode of human thought*. He went on to say that modern society has been "disenchanted," as scientific thinking has swept away sentimental ties to the past.

The willingness to adopt the latest technology, then, is one strong indicator of how rationalized a society is. To illustrate the global pattern of rationalization, Global Map 4–1 shows where in the world personal computers are found. In general, the high-income

WINDOW ON THE WORLD

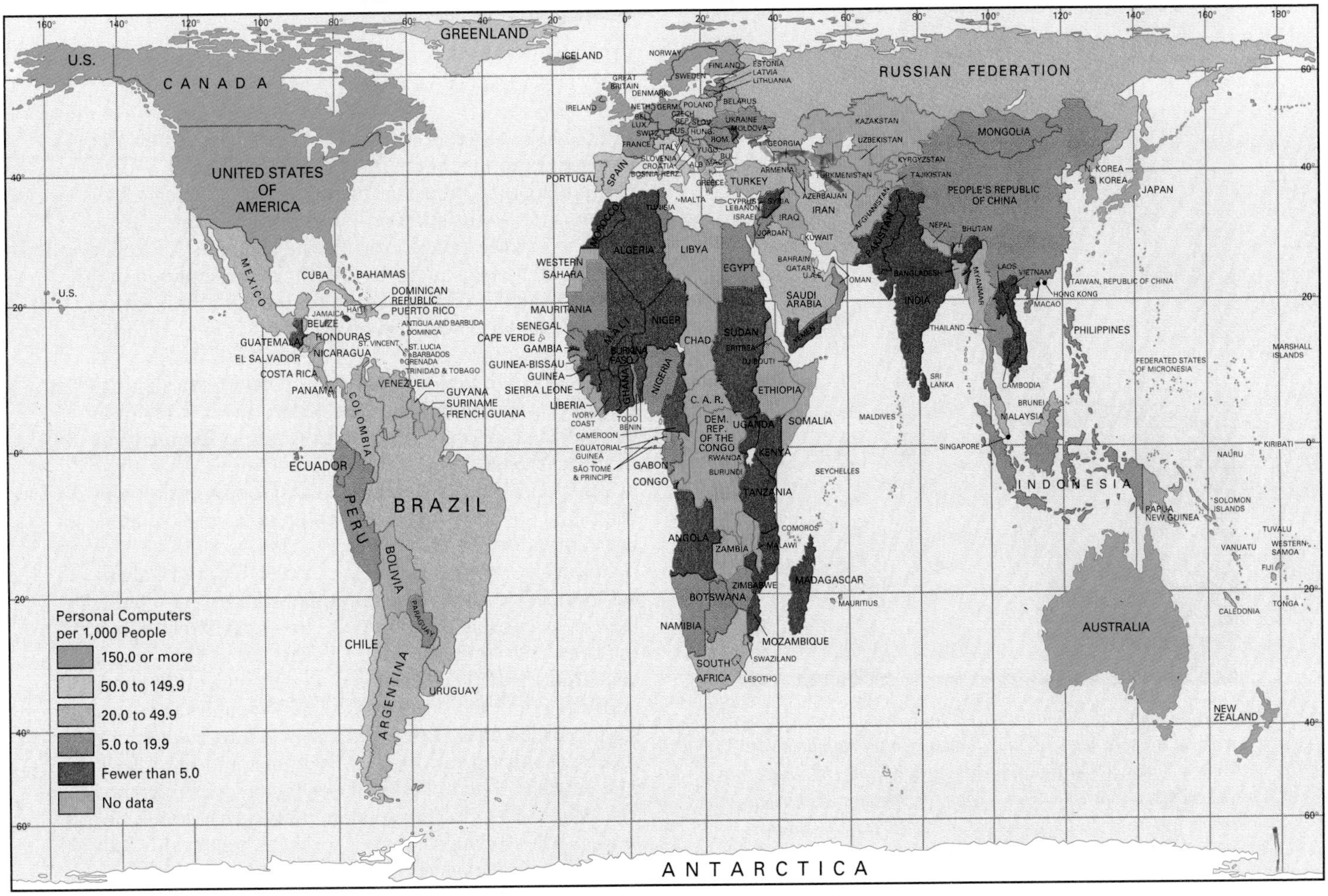

GLOBAL MAP 4–1 High Technology in Global Perspective

Countries with traditional cultures either cannot afford, ignore, or sometimes even resist technological innovation; nations with highly rationalized ways of life quickly embrace such changes. Personal computers, a central form of today's high technology, are numerous in high-income countries such as the United States. In low-income nations, by contrast, they are unknown to most people.

Source: The World Bank (1999).

countries of North America and Europe use personal computers the most, whereas in low-income nations, they are rare.

Using Weber's comparative perspective—and the data found in the map—we can say that various societies value technological advance differently. What one society might consider a breakthrough, another might deem unimportant, and a third might strongly oppose as a threat to tradition. The Tuareg nomads, described at the beginning of this chapter, shrug off the notion of using telephones: Why would anyone want such a thing on the desert? In the United States, the Amish refuse to have telephones in their homes on religious grounds.

A key element of U.S. culture has long been a "work ethic," with its roots in the Calvinist thinking that fascinated Max Weber. This Currier and Ives lithograph from 1875 makes a statement that people should shun the stock market, race track, lotteries, and even labor strikes as ways to improve their lives in favor of climbing the "Ladder of Fortune" based on personal virtue and individual effort.

In Weber's view, then, the extent of technological innovation in a society depends on how people understand their world. Many people throughout history have had the opportunity to adopt new technology, but only in the rational cultural climate of Western Europe did people exploit scientific discoveries to spark the Industrial Revolution (1958; orig. 1904–5).

IS CAPITALISM RATIONAL?

Is industrial capitalism a rational economic system? Here, again, Weber and Marx came down on opposite sides. Weber considered industrial capitalism the essence of rationality, since capitalists pursue profit in whatever ways they can. Marx, however, believed capitalism was irrational because it failed to meet the basic needs of most of the people (Gerth & Mills, 1946:49).

WEBER'S GREAT THESIS: PROTESTANTISM AND CAPITALISM

But, to look more closely at Weber's analysis, how did industrial capitalism emerge in the first place? Weber contended that industrial capitalism is the legacy of Calvinism—a Christian religious movement that arose from the Protestant Reformation. Calvinists, Weber explained, approached life in a highly disciplined and rational way. Moreover, central to the religious doctrine of John Calvin (1509–1564) was *predestination*, the idea that an all-knowing and all-powerful God has predestined some people for salvation and others for damnation. With everyone's fate set before birth, Calvinists believed that people could do nothing to change their destiny. Worse, they did not even know what their destiny was. Thus, Calvinists swung between hopeful visions of spiritual salvation and anxious fears of eternal damnation.

Not knowing one's fate was intolerable, and Calvinists gradually came to a resolution of sorts. Why shouldn't those chosen for glory in the next world, they reasoned, see signs of divine favor in *this* world? Such a conclusion prompted Calvinists to interpret worldly prosperity as a sign of God's grace. Eager to acquire this reassurance, Calvinists threw themselves into a quest for success, applying rationality, discipline, and hard work to their tasks. Their pursuit of wealth was not for its own sake, since self-indulgent spending was clearly sinful. But neither were Calvinists moved to share their wealth with the poor, since poverty was a sign of God's rejection. Their duty was to carry forward what they held to be a personal *calling* from God: reinvesting their profits for still greater success. Calvinists thus built the foundation of capitalism. With religious conviction, they used wealth to create more wealth, saved their money, and eagerly adopted new technology that helped their efforts.

The pursuit of wealth distinguished Calvinism from other world religions. For example, Catholicism, the traditional religion in most of Europe, gave rise to a passive, "otherworldly" view: Good deeds performed humbly on earth would bring rewards in heaven. For Catholics, material wealth had none of the spiritual significance that motivated Calvinists. And so it was, Weber concluded, that industrial capitalism developed primarily in areas of Europe where Calvinism was strong.

Weber's study of Calvinism provides striking evidence of the power of ideas to shape society (versus

Marx's contention that ideas merely reflect the process of economic production). But Weber was not one to accept simple explanations; he knew that industrial capitalism has many causes. In fact, one purpose of Weber's research was to counter Marx's narrow, strictly economic explanation of modern society.

Although later generations of Calvinists were less religious, their success-seeking and personal discipline remained, and a *religious* ethic became simply a *work* ethic. In other words, industrial capitalism can be seen as "disenchanted" religion, with wealth now valued for its own sake. It is revealing that the practice of "accounting," which to early Calvinists meant keeping a daily record of moral deeds, before long was simply a matter of keeping track of money.

RATIONAL SOCIAL ORGANIZATION

According to Weber, then, rationality gave rise to the Industrial Revolution and capitalism and thereby defined modern society. Weber went on to identify seven characteristics of rational social organization:

1. **Distinctive social institutions.** Among hunters and gatherers, the family is the center of all activity. Gradually, however, other social institutions, including religious, political, and economic systems, become separate from family life. In modern societies, new institutions—education and health care—also appear. The separation of social institutions is a rational way to meet human needs efficiently.
2. **Large-scale organizations.** Modern rationality is clearly evident in the spread of large-scale organizations. As early as the horticultural era, political officials oversaw religious observances, public works, and warfare. In medieval Europe, the Catholic church grew into a huge organization with thousands of officials. In our modern, rational society, the federal government employs millions, and most people work for large organizations.
3. **Specialized tasks.** Unlike members of traditional societies, individuals in modern societies perform a wide range of specialized jobs. Flipping through any city's "Yellow Pages" telephone directory shows just how many different occupations there are today.
4. **Personal discipline.** Modern society puts a premium on self-discipline. For early Calvinists, discipline was rooted in religious belief. Although now distanced from its religious origins, discipline is still encouraged by cultural values such as achievement, success, and efficiency.
5. **Awareness of time.** In traditional societies, people measure time according to the rhythm of sun and seasons. Modern people, by contrast, schedule events precisely by the hour and even the minute. Interestingly, clocks began appearing in European cities some 500 years ago, about the time commerce began to expand. Soon, people began to think (to borrow Benjamin Franklin's phrase) that "time is money."
6. **Technical competence.** Members of traditional societies size up one another on the basis of *who* they are—how they are joined to others in the web of kinship. Modern rationality prompts us to judge people according to *what* they are—that is, with an eye toward their skills and abilities.
7. **Impersonality.** Finally, in a rational society technical competence takes priority over close relationships, making the world impersonal. People interact as specialists concerned with particular tasks, rather than as individuals broadly concerned with one another. And because feelings are difficult to control, modern people tend to devalue emotion.

Rationality and Bureaucracy

The medieval church grew large, Weber explained, but it remained basically traditional and resisted change. Truly rational organizations that are both efficient and open to change appeared only in the last few centuries. The kind of organization Weber termed *bureaucracy* arose along with capitalism as an expression of the rationality that shapes modern society. Indeed, Weber explained, bureaucracy and capitalism have much in common:

> Today, it is primarily the capitalist market economy which demands that the official business of public administration be discharged precisely, unambiguously, continuously, and with as much speed as possible. Normally, the very large capitalist enterprises are themselves unequaled models of strict bureaucratic organization. (1978:974; orig. 1921)

As Chapter 7 ("Groups and Organizations") explains, we find aspects of bureaucracy in today's businesses, government agencies, labor unions, and

Max Weber agreed with Karl Marx that modern society is alienating to the individual, but the two thinkers identified different causes of this estrangement. For Marx, economic inequality is the culprit; for Weber, the issue is pervasive and dehumanizing bureaucracy. George Tooker's painting Landscape with Figures *echoes Weber's sentiments.*

George Tooker, *Landscape with Figures*, 1963, egg tempera on gesso panel, 26 x 30 in. Private collection.

universities. Weber considered bureaucracy highly rational because its elements—offices, duties, and policies—help achieve specific goals as efficiently as possible. Thus, Weber concluded, the defining elements of modern society—capitalism, bureaucracy, and science—are all expressions of the same underlying factor: rationality.

Rationality and Alienation

Max Weber joined with Karl Marx in recognizing the efficiency of industrial capitalism. Weber also agreed that modern society generates widespread alienation, although he offered different reasons. Whereas Marx thought alienation was caused by economic inequality, Weber blamed the stifling effect of bureaucracy's countless rules and regulations.

Bureaucracies, Weber warned, treat people as a series of cases rather than as unique individuals. In addition, working for large organizations demands highly specialized and often tedious routines. In the end, Weber envisioned modern society as a vast and growing system of rules seeking to regulate everything and threatening to crush the human spirit.

Like Marx, too, Weber found it ironic that modern society—meant to serve humanity—turns on its creators and enslaves them. Just as Marx described the human toll of industrial capitalism, Weber portrayed the modern individual as "only a small cog in a ceaselessly moving mechanism that prescribes to him an endlessly fixed routine of march" (1978:988; orig. 1921). Although Weber could see the advantages of modern society, he was deeply pessimistic about the future. He feared that, in the end, the rationalization of society would reduce human beings to robots.

EMILE DURKHEIM: SOCIETY AND FUNCTION

"To love society is to love something beyond us and something in ourselves." These are the words of Emile Durkheim (1858–1917), another of sociology's founders. In this curious statement (1974:55; orig. 1924), we find one more influential vision of human society.

STRUCTURE: SOCIETY BEYOND OURSELVES

Emile Durkheim's great insight was recognizing that society exists beyond ourselves. Society is more than the individuals who compose it; society has a life of its own that stretches beyond our personal experiences. Society is here long before we are born, it shapes us while we live, and it will remain long after we are gone. Patterns of human behavior—cultural norms, values, and

Durkheim's observation that people with weak social bonds are prone to self-destructive behavior stands as stark evidence of the power of society to shape individual lives. When rock-and-roll singers become famous, they are wrenched out of familiar life patterns and existing relationships, sometimes with deadly results. The history of rock and roll contains many tragic stories of this kind, including (from left) Janis Joplin's and Jimi Hendrix's deaths by drug overdose (both 1970) and Jim Morrison's (1971) and Kurt Cobain's (1994) suicides.

beliefs—exist as established structures and thus are *social facts* that have an objective reality beyond the lives of individuals.

Because society looms larger than any one of us, it has the *power* to guide our thoughts and actions. This is why studying individuals alone (as psychologists or biologists do) can never capture the essence of the human experience. Society is more than the sum of its parts; it exists as a complex organism rooted in our collective life. A classroom of third graders, a family sharing a meal, people in a hospital waiting room—all are examples of the countless situations that have an organization apart from any particular individual who participates in them.

Once created by people, then, society takes on a life of its own and demands a measure of obedience from its creators. We experience the reality of society in the order of our lives or as we face temptation and feel the tug of morality.

FUNCTION: SOCIETY AS SYSTEM

Having established that society has structure, Durkheim turned to the concept of *function.* The significance of any social fact, he explained, is more than what individuals see in our immediate lives; social facts help society as a whole to operate.

To illustrate, consider crime. Of course, individuals experience pain and loss as a result of crime. But, taking a broader view, Durkheim saw that crime is vital to the ongoing life of society itself. As Chapter 8 ("Deviance") explains, only by defining acts as criminal do people construct and defend morality, which gives purpose and meaning to our collective life. For this reason, Durkheim rejected the common view of crime as "pathological." On the contrary, he concluded, crime is "normal" for the most basic of reasons: A society could not exist without it (1964a, orig. 1895; 1964b, orig. 1893).

PERSONALITY: SOCIETY IN OURSELVES

Durkheim contended that society is not only "beyond ourselves"; it is also "in ourselves." Each of us, in other words, builds a personality by internalizing social facts. How we act, think, and feel—our essential humanity—is drawn from the society that nurtures us. Moreover, society regulates our behavior through moral discipline. Durkheim held that human beings are naturally insatiable and in constant danger of being overpowered by their own desires. That is, "the more one has, the more one wants, since satisfactions received only stimulate instead of filling needs" (1966:248; orig. 1897). Having given us life, then, society must also rein us in.

Nowhere is the need for societal regulation better illustrated than in Durkheim's study of suicide (1966; orig. 1897), described in Chapter 1 ("The Sociological Perspective"). Why is it that rock stars—from Janis Joplin to Kurt Cobain—seem so prone to self-destruction? Durkheim had the answer long before anyone made electric music: A century ago just as today,

APPLYING SOCIOLOGY

The Information Revolution: What Would Durkheim (and Others) Have Thought?

New technology is rapidly reshaping our society. Were they alive today, the founding sociologists discussed in this chapter would be eager observers of the current scene. Let's imagine for a moment the kinds of questions Emile Durkheim, Max Weber, and Karl Marx might ask about the effects of computer technology on society.

Emile Durkheim, who emphasized the increasing division of labor in modern society, probably would wonder if new information technology is pushing specialization even further. There is good reason to think that it is. Because electronic communication (say, a Web site home page) gives anyone a vast market (already, some 200 million individuals access the Internet), people can specialize far more than if they were confined to a limited geographic area. For example, while most small-town lawyers have a general practice, an information-age attorney (living anywhere) could become a specialist in, say, prenuptial agreements or electronic copyright law. Indeed, as we move into the electronic age, the number of highly specialized micro-businesses in all fields—some of which end up becoming very large—is rapidly increasing.

Max Weber believed that modern societies are distinctive because their members share a rational world view, and, of course, nothing illustrates this better than bureaucracy. But will bureaucracy continue to dominate the social scene in the new century? Here is one reason to think it may not: While it may make sense for organizations to regulate workers performing the kinds of routine tasks that were common in the industrial era, much work in the postindustrial era involves imagination. Think, for instance, of such "new age" work as designing homes, composing music, and writing software. The creativity involved cannot be regulated in the same way as, say, assembling automobiles on an assembly line. Perhaps this is why many high-technology companies have done away with dress codes and time clocks.

Finally, what might Karl Marx make of the Information Revolution? Since Marx considered the earlier Industrial Revolution a *class* revolution that allowed the owners of industry to dominate society, he might wonder whether a new symbolic elite is gaining power over us. Some analysts point out, for example, that film and television writers, producers, and performers now enjoy vast wealth, international prestige, and power (Lichter, Rothman, & Lichter, 1990). Similarly, just as people without industrial skills stayed at the bottom of the class system in past decades, so people without symbolic skills are likely to become the "underclass" of the new century.

Durkheim, Weber, and Marx greatly improved our understanding of industrial societies. As we continue into the postindustrial age, there is plenty of room for new generations of sociologists to carry on.

---

the *least* regulated categories of people suffer the *highest* rates of suicide. The enormous freedom of the young, rich, and famous exacts a high price in terms of the risk of suicide.

MODERNITY AND ANOMIE

Compared to traditional societies, modern societies impose fewer restrictions on everyone. Durkheim acknowledged the advantages of modern-day freedom, but he warned of increased **anomie,** *a condition in which society provides little moral guidance to individuals*. What so many celebrities describe as "almost being destroyed by fame" is a prime example of the destructive effects of anomie. Sudden fame tears people from their families and familiar routines; it disrupts society's support and regulation of an individual, sometimes with fatal results. Thus, Durkheim explains, an individual's desires must be balanced by the claims and guidance of society—a balance that is sometimes difficult in the modern world.

EVOLVING SOCIETIES: THE DIVISION OF LABOR

Like Marx and Weber, Durkheim saw firsthand the rapid social transformation of Europe during the nineteenth century. But Durkheim made his own sense of this change.

In preindustrial societies, explained Durkheim, tradition operates as the social cement that binds people together. In fact, what he termed the *collective conscience*

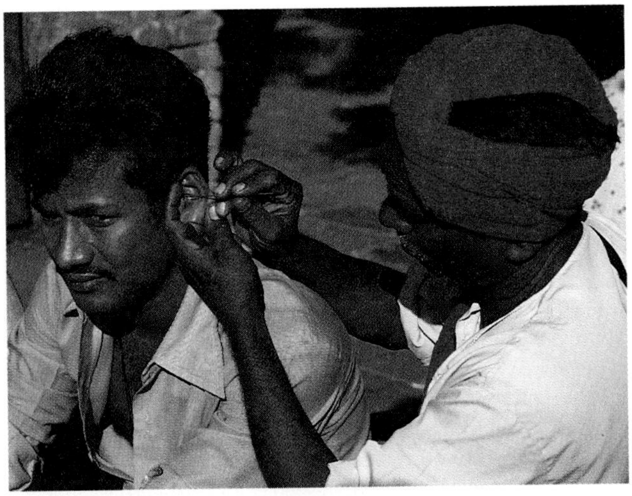

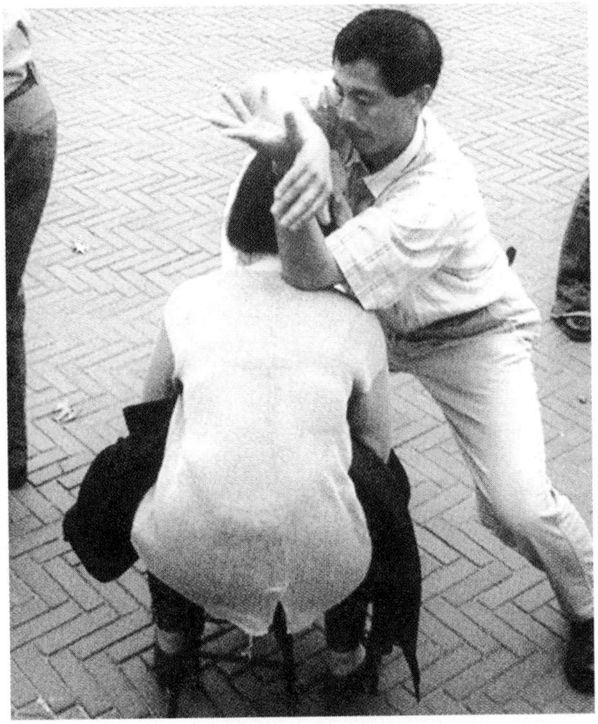

Historically, members of human societies engaged in many of the same activities: searching out food and securing shelter. Modern societies, explained Durkheim, display a rapidly expanding division of labor. Increasing specialization is evident in the streets of countries in the process of industrialization: On a Bombay street, a man earns a small fee for cleaning ears; in a Beijing park, another provides healthful physical therapy.

is so strong that the community moves quickly to punish anyone who dares to challenge conventional ways of life. Durkheim used the term **mechanical solidarity** to refer to *social bonds, based on common sentiments and shared moral values, that are strong among members of preindustrial societies.* In practice, mechanical solidarity springs from *likeness*. Durkheim called these bonds "mechanical" because people feel a more or less automatic sense of belonging together.

With industrialization, Durkheim continued, mechanical solidarity becomes weaker and weaker, and people cease to be bound by tradition. But this does not mean that society dissolves. Modern life generates a new type of solidarity. Durkheim called this new social integration **organic solidarity**, defined as *social bonds, based on specialization and interdependence, that are strong among members of industrial societies.* Where solidarity was once rooted in likeness, it is now based on *differences* among people who find that their specialized work—as plumbers, consultants, midwives, or sociology instructors—make them rely on one another for many of their daily needs.

For Durkheim, then, the key to change in a society is an expanding **division of labor,** or *specialized economic activity.* Max Weber said that modern societies specialize in order to become more efficient, and Durkheim filled out the picture by showing that members of modern societies count on tens of thousands of others—most of them strangers—for the goods and services needed every day. That is, as members of modern societies, we depend more and more on people we trust less and less. Why do we look to people we hardly know and whose beliefs may well differ from our own? Durkheim's answer is, "Because we can't live without them."

So modernity rests far less on *moral consensus* and far more on *functional interdependence*. Herein lies what we might call "Durkheim's dilemma": The technological power and greater personal freedom of modern society come at the cost of declining morality and the rising risk of anomie.

Like Marx and Weber, Durkheim worried about the direction society was taking. But of the three, Durkheim was the most optimistic. He praised our greater freedom and privacy while hoping we could create laws to regulate our behavior.

Finally, can we apply Durkheim's views to the Information Revolution? The box suggests that he and the other theorists we have considered in this chapter would have had much to say about new computer technology.

CONTROVERSY & DEBATE

Is Society Getting Better or Worse?

Optimism has been a defining trait of U.S. culture; as time goes on, we tend to think, life gets better. But these days, our historic optimism may be on the decline. Consider that a recent national survey found 67 percent of U.S. adults agreeing that life for the average person is getting worse, not better (30 percent disagreed, and 3 percent offered no opinion; NORC, 1999:204).

What's going on here? To begin, there are reasons for our society's long-time belief in progress. Since the beginning of the twentieth century, for example, we have seen a tenfold increase in the share of college graduates among U.S. adults. Moreover, even taking inflation into account, the average U.S. income is up fourfold.

Back in 1900, it was the rare home that had a telephone and, outside of large cities, none had electricity. No one had even heard of television, and cars were still on the drawing board. Today, almost every home has at least one telephone, a host of electric appliances, television sets, and videocassette recorders; most are equipped with cable TV and air conditioning, and about half have at least one home computer. Indeed, life is not only better, there is more of it: People born in 1900 lived an average of just forty-seven years; children born today can look forward to reaching age eighty.

But some trends, especially during the last twenty-five years, have been troubling. Members of our society have been losing confidence that hard work pays off: Despite an increasing share of two-income couples, average family earnings have risen only slightly. At the same time, the divorce rate has soared, and there is four times as much violent crime as in 1960. Our relative affluence, coupled with our capacity to move farther and faster than ever before, seems to have unleashed a wave of individualism that sometimes turns into pure selfishness. As a result, not only is pessimism on the rise, but a majority of U.S. adults report thinking that "they can't be too careful in dealing with people" (NORC, 1999:173).

So, which is it? Is society getting better or worse?

The theorists whose ideas we have examined in this chapter shed some light on this issue. It is easy to equate "high tech" with "progress." But, say the Lenskis, history shows us that, although advancing technology does offer real advantages, it is no guarantee of a better life. Marx, Weber, and Durkheim also acknowledged the growing wealth of societies over time; yet all criticized modern society for a dangerous tendency toward individualism. For Marx, capitalism is the culprit, elevating money to a godlike status and fostering a culture of selfishness and materialism. In Weber's analysis, the modern spirit of rationality erodes traditional ties of kinship and neighborhood while expanding bureaucracy, which, he warned, manipulates and isolates people. For Durkheim, members of modern societies may need one another, but they have little moral framework by which to judge right and wrong.

In the end, what societies gain through technological advances may be offset, to some extent, by the loss of human community.

CRITICAL EVALUATION: FOUR VISIONS OF SOCIETY

This chapter opened with several important questions about society. We will conclude by summarizing how each of the four visions of society answers these questions.

What Holds Societies Together?

How is something as complex as society possible in the first place? The Lenskis claim that members of a society are united by a shared culture, although cultural patterns vary according to a society's level of technological development. They also point out that as technology becomes more complex, inequality divides a society more and more, although industrialization brings something of a turnaround, reducing inequality somewhat.

Marx saw not unity but social division based on class position. From his point of view, elites may force an uneasy peace, but true social unity will occur only if production becomes a cooperative endeavor.

To Weber, members of a society share a world view. Just as tradition joined people together in the past, so modern societies have created rational, large-scale organizations that connect people's lives.

Finally, Durkheim made solidarity the focus of his work. He contrasted the mechanical solidarity of preindustrial societies, which is based on shared morality, with modern society's organic solidarity, which is based on specialization.

How Have Societies Changed?

According to the Lenskis' model of sociocultural evolution, societies differ primarily in terms of increasing levels of technology. Modern society stands out in this regard with its enormous productive power. Marx also stressed historical differences in productive systems, yet pointed to the persistence of social conflict throughout all (except perhaps among simple hunters and gatherers). For Marx, modern society is distinctive only because it brings that social conflict out in the open. Weber considered the question of change from the perspective of how people look at the world. Members of preindustrial societies have a traditional outlook, he claimed, while we moderns take a rational world view. Finally, in Durkheim's analysis, traditional societies are characterized by mechanical solidarity based on moral likeness. In industrial societies, mechanical solidarity gives way to organic solidarity based on productive specialization.

Why Do Societies Change?

As the Lenskis see it, social change is first and foremost a matter of technological innovation that, over time transforms an entire society. Marx's materialist approach highlights the struggle between classes as the "engine of history," pushing societies toward revolutionary reorganization. Weber, on the other hand, points up how ideas contribute to social change. He demonstrated how a particular world view—Calvinism—advanced the Industrial Revolution, which, in turn, reshaped just about all of society. Finally, Durkheim pointed to an expanding division of labor as the key dimension of social change.

The fact that these four approaches are so different does not mean that any one of them is, in an absolute sense, right or wrong. Society is exceedingly complex, and we benefit from using all four visions, as shown in the final box.

SUMMARY

Gerhard Lenski and Jean Lenski

1. Sociocultural evolution explores the effects of technological advances on societies.
2. The earliest hunting and gathering societies were composed of a small number of family-centered nomads. Such societies have all but vanished from today's world.
3. Horticulture began some 10,000 years ago as people created hand tools for cultivation. Pastoral societies domesticate animals and trade extensively.
4. Agriculture, about 5,000 years old, is large-scale cultivation using animal-drawn plows. This technology allows societies to expand into vast empires, with greater productivity, more specialization, and increasing inequality.
5. Industrialization began 250 years ago in Europe as people used new energy sources to operate large machinery.
6. In postindustrial societies, production shifts away from the use of heavy machinery to make material things and toward the use of computers and related technology to process information.

Karl Marx

7. Marx's materialist analysis points up conflict between social classes.
8. Conflict in "ancient" societies involved masters and slaves; in agrarian societies, nobles oppose serfs; in industrial-capitalist societies, capitalists oppose the proletariat.
9. Industrial capitalism alienates workers in four ways: from the act of working, from the products of work, from other workers, and from human potential.
10. Marx believed that once workers overcame their false consciousness, they would overthrow the industrial-capitalist system.

Max Weber

11. Weber's idealist approach argues that ideas have a powerful effect on society.
12. Weber contrasted the tradition of preindustrial societies with the rationality of modern, industrial societies.
13. Weber feared that rationality, especially in efficient bureaucratic organizations, would stifle human creativity.

Emile Durkheim

14. Durkheim explained that society has an objective existence apart from individuals.
15. Durkheim relates social elements to the larger society through their functions.
16. Societies require solidarity. Traditional societies have mechanical solidarity, which is based on moral likeness; modern societies depend on organic solidarity, which is based on the division of labor.

KEY CONCEPTS

society (p. 89) people who interact in a defined territory and share culture

sociocultural evolution (p. 90) the Lenskis' term for the changes that occur as a society acquires new technology

hunting and gathering (p. 90) the use of simple tools to hunt animals and gather vegetation

horticulture (p. 91) the use of hand tools to raise crops

pastoralism (p. 91) the domestication of animals

agriculture (p. 92) large-scale cultivation using plows harnessed to animals or more powerful energy sources

industrialism (p. 93) the production of goods using advanced sources of energy to drive large machinery

postindustrialism (p. 95) technology that supports an information-based economy

social conflict (p. 97) struggle between segments of society over valued resources

capitalists (p. 97) people who own and operate factories and other businesses in pursuit of profits

proletarians (p. 97) people who sell their productive labor for wages

social institution (p. 98) a major sphere of social life, or societal subsystem, organized to meet human needs

false consciousness (p. 98) Marx's term for explanations of social problems as the shortcomings of individuals rather than the flaws of society

class conflict (p. 99) conflict between entire classes over the distribution of a society's wealth and power

class consciousness (p. 99) Marx's term for workers' recognition of themselves as a class united in opposition to capitalists and, ultimately, to capitalism itself

alienation (p. 100) the experience of isolation and misery resulting from powerlessness

ideal type (p. 102) an abstract statement of the essential characteristics of any social phenomenon

tradition (p. 102) sentiments and beliefs passed from generation to generation

rationality (p. 102) deliberate, matter-of-fact calculation of the most efficient means to accomplish a particular task

rationalization of society (p. 102) Weber's term for the historical change from tradition to rationality as the dominant mode of human thought

anomie (p. 108) Durkheim's designation of a condition in which society provides little moral guidance to individuals

mechanical solidarity (p. 109) Durkheim's term for social bonds, based on common sentiments and shared moral values, that are strong among members of preindustrial societies

organic solidarity (p. 109) Durkheim's term for social bonds, based on specialization and interdependence, that are strong among members of industrial societies

division of labor (p. 109) specialized economic activity

CRITICAL-THINKING QUESTIONS

1. Would you say that development of new technology is the same as "progress"? Why or why not?
2. Explain how Marx, as a materialist, took a different view of society than did Weber, an idealist.
3. Both Marx and Weber were concerned that modern society alienated people. How are their approaches different? How do their concepts of alienation compare to Durkheim's concept of anomie?
4. Apply the visions of society discussed in this chapter to the changing status of women. How might each theorist explain increasing gender equality? Can you criticize these theories from a feminist perspective?

APPLICATIONS AND EXERCISES

1. Hunting and gathering people mused over stars, and we still know the constellations in terms they used—mostly the names of animals and hunters. As a way of revealing what's important to *our* way of life, write a short paper imagining the meanings we would give clusters of stars if we were starting from scratch.
2. Spend an hour in your home trying to identify every device that has a computer chip in it. How many did you find? Were you surprised by the number?
3. Watch an old Tarzan movie or another film about technologically simpler people. How are they portrayed in the film?
4. Install the CD-ROM packaged in the back of this new textbook to access a variety of study, review, and applications exercises designed to help you better understand the material covered in this chapter. The CD includes an author's tip video, as well as interactive maps, video application exercises, Web links, and study questions.

SITES TO SEE

http://www.prenhall.com/macionis

Visit the interactive Web site that accompanies this text. Begin by clicking on the cover of your book. You will find a chapter-by-chapter study guide, practice tests, chat room, and many suggested Web links.

http://www.macionis.com
(or **http://www.thesociologypage.com**)

Biographical sketches of Marx, Weber, and Durkheim (as well as other social thinkers) are found at the author's Web site.

http://www.runet.edu/~lridener/DSS/DEADSOC.HTML

Visit the the Dead Sociologists' Society to learn more about Marx, Weber, and Durkheim, as well as other sociologists.

http://eddie.cso.uiuc.edu/Durkheim
http://csf.colorado.edu:80/psn/marx/index.html

These two sites provide a close-up look at the work of two great sociologists.

http://www.gwu.edu/~ccps

Visit the Web site for the Communitarian Network, an organization concerned with balancing modern individuality with traditional social responsibility.

CHAPTER 5

Andrew Macara
Footballers, Kos 1993

Oil on canvas, 63.5 × 76.2 cm.
Private Collection/
The Bridgeman Art Library.

SOCIALIZATION

On a cold winter day in 1938, a social worker walked quickly to the door of a rural Pennsylvania farmhouse. Investigating a case of possible child abuse, the social worker entered the home and soon discovered a five-year-old girl hidden in a second-floor storage room. The child, whose name was Anna, was wedged into an old chair with her arms tied above her head so that she couldn't move. She was wearing filthy clothes, and her arms and legs were as thin as matchsticks (Davis, 1940).

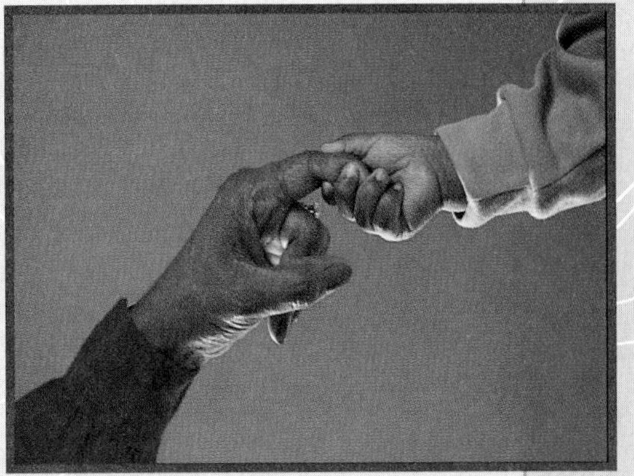

Anna's situation can only be called tragic. She was born in 1932 to an unmarried and mentally impaired woman of twenty-six who lived with her strict father. Enraged by his daughter's "illegitimate" motherhood, the grandfather did not even want the child in his house. For her first six months, therefore, Anna was shuttled among various welfare agencies. But when her mother was no longer able to pay for her care, Anna returned to the hostile home of her grandfather.

To lessen the grandfather's anger, Anna's mother moved Anna to the storage room, and gave her just enough milk to keep her alive. There she stayed—day after day, month after month, with almost no human contact—for five long years.

Learning of the discovery of Anna, sociologist Kingsley Davis (1940) immediately went to see her. He found her with local authorities at a county home. Davis was appalled by the emaciated child, who could not laugh, speak, or even smile. Anna was completely unresponsive, as if alone in an empty world.

SOCIAL EXPERIENCE: THE KEY TO OUR HUMANITY

Here is a terrible case of a child deprived of social contact. Although physically alive, Anna hardly seemed human. Her plight reveals that, without social experience, a child is incapable of thought, emotion, or meaningful action—more an *object* than a *person*.

Sociologists use the term **socialization** to refer to *the lifelong social experience by which individuals develop their human potential and learn culture*. Unlike other living species, whose behavior is biologically set, humans need social experience to learn their culture and survive. Social experience is also the foundation of **personality,** *a person's fairly consistent patterns of acting, thinking, and feeling*. We build a personality by internalizing—or taking in—our surroundings. But without social experience, as Anna's case shows, personality does not develop at all.

HUMAN DEVELOPMENT: NATURE AND NURTURE

Helpless at birth, the human infant depends on others to provide nourishment and care. Anna's case makes these facts clear. But a century ago, most people

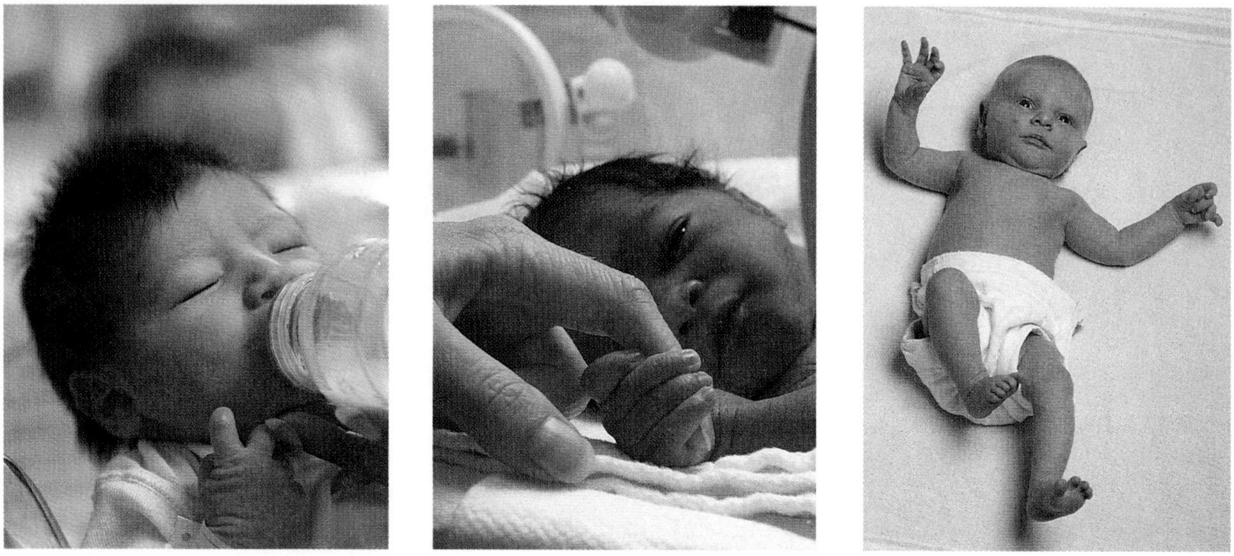

Human infants display various reflexes—biologically based behavior patterns that enhance survival. The sucking reflex, which actually begins before birth, enables the infant to obtain nourishment. The grasping reflex, triggered by placing a finger on the infant's palm causing the hand to close, helps the infant to maintain contact with a parent and, later on, to grasp objects. The Moro reflex, activated by startling the infant, has the infant swinging both arms outward and then bringing them together across the chest. This action, which disappears after several months of life, probably developed among our evolutionary ancestors so that a falling infant could grasp the body hair of a parent.

mistakenly believed that human behavior was the product of our biology.

Charles Darwin: The Role of Nature

Charles Darwin's groundbreaking study of evolution, described in Chapter 3 ("Culture"), explained that each species evolves over thousands of generations as genetic variations improve its ability to survive and reproduce. Traits that enhance survival emerge as a species' "nature." For this reason, people once assumed that humans, like other life forms, had an instinctive "human nature." Given our tendency to see our own way of life as "natural," people argued that our economic system reflects "instinctive human competitiveness," that some people are "born criminals," or that women are "naturally" emotional while men are "innately" rational (Witkin-Lanoil, 1984).

People trying to understand cultural diversity also misunderstood Darwin's thinking. From centuries of world exploration, Western Europeans knew that people around the world behaved quite differently from each other. But Europeans linked these differences to biology rather than culture. It was an easy, although very damaging, next step to claim that members of technologically simple societies were biologically less evolved and, thus, less human. This ethnocentric view helped justify colonialism: Why not exploit others if they are not human in the same sense that you are?

The Social Sciences: The Role of Nurture

In the twentieth century, biological explanations of human behavior came under fire. Psychologist John B. Watson (1878–1958) developed a theory called *behaviorism*, which held that behavior is not instinctive but learned. Thus, people everywhere are equally human, differing only in their cultural patterns. Watson, in short, rooted human behavior not in nature but in *nurture*.

Today, social scientists are cautious about describing *any* human behavior as instinctive. This does not mean that biology plays *no* part in human behavior. Human life, after all, depends on the functioning of the body. We also know that children often share biological traits (like height and hair color) with their parents and that heredity plays a part in intelligence, musical and artistic aptitude, and personality (such as how one reacts to frustration). However, whether a person *realizes* an inherited potential depends on having an opportunity to develop it. In fact, unless children use their brains early in life, the brain itself does not fully develop (Plomin & Foch, 1980; Goldsmith, 1983; Begley, 1995).

Without denying the importance of nature, then, nurture matters more in shaping human behavior. More precisely, as cultural creatures, *nurture is our nature.*

SOCIAL ISOLATION

Of course, researchers cannot isolate human beings in experiments. But, in the past, they did study the effects of social isolation on nonhuman primates.

Studies of Nonhuman Primates

Psychologists Harry Harlow and Margaret Harlow (1962) placed rhesus monkeys—whose behavior is in some ways surprisingly similar to human behavior—in various conditions of social isolation. They found that complete isolation (with adequate nutrition) for even six months seriously disturbed the monkeys' development. When returned to their group, these monkeys were passive, anxious, and fearful.

The Harlows then placed infant rhesus monkeys in cages with an artificial "mother" made of wire mesh with a wooden head and the nipple of a feeding tube where the breast would be. These monkeys, too, were later unable to interact with others.

But when the researchers covered the artificial "mother" with soft terry cloth, the infant monkeys would cling to it. The monkeys benefited from this closeness, the Harlows concluded, because they showed less developmental damage than earlier monkeys. The experiment confirmed how important it is that adults cradle infants affectionately.

Finally, the Harlows discovered that infant monkeys could recover from about three months of isolation. But by about six months, isolation caused irreversible emotional and behavioral damage.

Studies of Isolated Children

Tragic cases of children isolated by abusive family members show the damage caused by depriving human beings of social experience. We will review three such cases.

Anna: the rest of the story. The rest of Anna's story squares with the Harlows' findings. After her discovery,

Early in the twentieth century, most people in the United States thought biology shaped human behavior. The discipline of anthropology helped demonstrate the primary importance of environment on human development. The best known of all anthropologists is Margaret Mead, shown here with a mother and child during a 1953 research project on the Admiralty Islands near New Guinea in the South Pacific.

Anna received extensive attention and soon showed improvement. When Kingsley Davis visited her after ten days, he found her more alert and even smiling with obvious pleasure. Over the next year, Anna made steady progress, showing more interest in other people and gradually learning to walk. After a year and a half, she could feed herself and play with toys.

As the Harlows might have predicted, however, Anna's five years of social isolation had caused permanent damage. At age eight, her mental development was less than a two-year-old's. Not until she was almost ten did she begin to use words. Since Anna's mother was mentally retarded, perhaps Anna was similarly challenged. The riddle was never solved, because Anna died at age ten from a blood disorder, possibly related to years of abuse (Davis, 1940, 1947).

Another case: Isabelle. A second case involves another girl, found at about the same time as Anna and under much the same circumstances. After more than six years of virtual isolation, this girl—known as Isabelle—displayed the same lack of responsiveness as Anna. Unlike Anna, though, Isabelle benefited from a special learning program directed by psychologists. Within a week, Isabelle was attempting to speak and, a year and a half later, she knew some 2,000 words. The psychologists

The personalities we develop depend largely on the environment in which we live. When a child's world is shredded by violence, the damage can be profound and lasting. This drawing, titled Memories from L.A. Riot, *was made by nine-year-old Abdullah Abbas. What are the likely effects of such experiences on a young person's self-confidence and capacity to form trusting ties with others?*

concluded that intensive effort had propelled Isabelle through six years of normal development in only two years. By the time she was fourteen, Isabelle was attending sixth-grade classes, damaged by her early ordeal but on her way to a somewhat normal life (Davis, 1947).

A third case: Genie. A more recent case of childhood isolation involves a California girl abused by her parents (Curtiss, 1977; Pines, 1981; Rymer, 1994). From age two, Genie was tied to a potty chair in a dark garage. In 1970, when she was found at age thirteen, Genie weighed only fifty-nine pounds and had the mental development of a one-year-old. With intensive treatment, she became physically healthy, but her language ability remains that of a young child. Genie lives today in a home for developmentally disabled adults.

Conclusion. All the evidence points to the crucial role of social experience in forming personality. Human beings can sometimes recover from abuse and isolation. But there is a point—precisely when is unclear from the small number of cases studied—at which isolation in infancy causes permanent developmental damage.

UNDERSTANDING SOCIALIZATION

Socialization is a complex, lifelong process. The following sections highlight the work of six researchers who made lasting contributions to our understanding of human development.

SIGMUND FREUD: THE ELEMENTS OF PERSONALITY

Sigmund Freud (1856–1939) lived in Vienna at a time when most Europeans considered human behavior biologically fixed. Trained as a physician, Freud gradually turned to the study of personality and eventually developed the celebrated theory of psychoanalysis.

Basic Human Needs

Freud believed that biology plays a major part in human development, although not in terms of specific instincts, as in other species. He theorized that humans have two basic needs. First is a need for bonding, which Freud called the life instinct, or *eros* (from the Greek god of love). Second, we also have an aggressive drive he called the death instinct, or *thanatos* (from the Greek meaning "death"). These opposing forces operate at an unconscious level, and generate deep inner tension.

Freud's Model of Personality

Freud joined basic needs with the influence of society to form a model of personality with three parts: id, ego, and superego. The **id** (the Latin word for "it") represents *the human being's basic drives*, which are unconscious and demand immediate satisfaction. Rooted in biology, the id is present at birth, making a newborn baby a bundle of demands for attention, touching, and food. But society opposes the self-centered id, which is why one of the first words a young child learns is "no."

To avoid frustration, a child must learn to approach the world realistically. This is done through the **ego** (Latin for "I"), which is *a person's conscious efforts to balance innate pleasure-seeking drives with the demands of society*. The ego develops as we become aware of ourselves but also realize that we cannot have everything we want.

Finally, the human personality develops the **superego** (Latin meaning "above" or "beyond" the ego), which is *the operation of culture within the individual.* The superego operates as our conscience, telling us *why* we cannot have everything we want. The superego begins to form as a child becomes aware of parental control and matures as the child comes to understand that everyone's behavior must take into account cultural norms.

Personality Development

To the id-centered child, the world is a bewildering array of physical sensations that bring either pleasure or pain. As the superego develops, however, the child learns the moral concepts of right and wrong. Initially, in other words, children can feel good only in a physical way; but, after three or four years, they feel good or bad according to how they judge their behavior against cultural norms.

The id and superego remain in conflict, but, in a well-adjusted person, the ego manages these two opposing forces. When conflicts are not resolved during childhood, they may surface as personality disorders later on.

Culture, in the form of superego, serves to *repress* selfish demands, forcing people to look beyond themselves. Often, the competing demands of self and society result in a compromise that Freud called *sublimation*. Sublimation redirects selfish drives into socially acceptable behavior. Sexual urges, for example, may lead to marriage, just as aggression gives rise to competitive sports.

Critical evaluation. Freud's work was controversial in his own time. More recently, critics charge that his work presents humans in male terms and devalues women (Donovan & Littenberg, 1982). But Freud influenced everyone who later studied the human personality. Of special importance to sociology is his notion that we internalize social norms and that childhood experiences have a lasting impact on our personalities.

From a Freudian point of view, weak moral regulation opens the door for the pleasure-seeking drives of the id to express themselves. Such behavior sometimes turns ugly, as it did at the 1999 Woodstock Arts and Music Festival, where intoxicated revelers ended up setting fire to buildings on the site in Rome, New York.

JEAN PIAGET: COGNITIVE DEVELOPMENT

Swiss psychologist Jean Piaget (1896–1980) studied human *cognition*—how people think. As Piaget watched his own three children, he wondered not just *what* they knew but *how* they made sense of the world. Piaget went on to identify four stages of cognitive development.

The Sensorimotor Stage

Stage one is the **sensorimotor stage,** *the level of human development at which individuals experience the world only through their senses.* For about the first two years of life, the infant knows the world only through the five senses: touching, tasting, smelling, looking, and listening. "Knowing" to young children amounts to direct, sensory experience.

In a well-known experiment, Jean Piaget demonstrated that children over the age of seven had entered the concrete operational stage of development because they could recognize that the quantity of liquid remained the same when poured from a wide beaker into a tall one.

The Preoperational Stage

About age two, children enter the **preoperational stage,** *the level of human development at which individuals first use language and other symbols.* Now children begin to think about the world mentally and with imagination. But "pre-op" children between about two and six still attach meaning only to specific experiences and objects. They can identify a favorite toy, but not explain what *kinds* of toys they like.

Lacking abstract concepts, a child also cannot judge size, weight, or volume. In one of his best-known experiments, Piaget placed two identical glasses containing equal amounts of water on a table. He asked several children ages five and six if the amount in each glass was the same. They nodded that it was. The children then watched Piaget take one of the glasses and pour its contents into a taller, narrower glass, raising the level of the water. He asked again if each glass held the same amount. The typical five- and six-year-old now insisted that the taller glass held more water. By about age seven, children are able to think abstractly and realize that the amount of water stayed the same.

The Concrete Operational Stage

Next comes the **concrete operational stage,** *the level of development at which individuals first perceive causal connections in their surroundings.* Between ages seven and eleven, children focus on how and why things happen. In addition, children now attach more than one symbol to a particular event or object. If, for example, you say to a child of five, "Today is Wednesday," she might respond, "No, it's my birthday!" indicating that she can use just one symbol at a time. But a ten-year-old at the concrete operational stage would be able to respond, "Yes, and this Wednesday is my birthday!"

The Formal Operational Stage

The last stage in Piaget's model is the **formal operational stage,** *the level of human development at which individuals think abstractly and critically.* At about age twelve, young people begin to reason abstractly rather than thinking only of concrete situations. If, for example, you were to ask a child of seven, "What would you like to be when you grow up?" you might receive a concrete response such as "a teacher." But most teenagers can think more abstractly, and might reply, "I would like a job that helps others." This capacity for abstract thought also lets young people understand metaphors. Hearing the phrase "A penny for your thoughts" might lead a child to ask for a coin, but the adolescent will recognize a gentle invitation to intimacy.

Critical evaluation. While Freud saw human beings torn by opposing forces of biology and culture, Piaget saw the mind as active and creative. He saw an ability to engage the world unfolding in stages as the result of both biological maturation and social experience.

But do people in all societies pass through all four of Piaget's stages? Living in a traditional society that changes slowly limits the capacity for abstract and critical thought. Even in our own society, perhaps 30 percent of people never reach the formal operational stage (Kohlberg & Gilligan, 1971).

LAWRENCE KOHLBERG: MORAL DEVELOPMENT

Lawrence Kohlberg (1981) built on Piaget's work in studying *moral reasoning*—how individuals judge situations as right or wrong. Here, again, development occurs in stages.

Young children who experience the world in terms of pain and pleasure (Piaget's sensorimotor stage) are at the *preconventional* level of moral development. At this early stage, in other words, "rightness" amounts to "what feels good to me."

CRITICAL THINKING

The Importance of Gender in Research

Carol Gilligan, an educational psychologist at Harvard University, has shown how gender guides social behavior. Her early work exposed the gender bias in studies by Kohlberg and others who had used only male subjects. But as her research progressed, Gilligan made a major discovery: Boys and girls actually employ different strategies in making moral decisions. Thus, by ignoring gender, we end up with an incomplete view of human behavior.

More recently, Gilligan has looked at the effect of gender on self-esteem. Her research team interviewed more than 2,000 girls, ages six to eighteen, over a five-year period. She found a clear pattern: Young girls start out eager and confident, but their self-esteem slips away as they pass through adolescence.

Why? Gilligan claims that the answer lies in the way our culture defines females. In our society, the ideal woman is calm, controlled, and eager to please. Then, too, as girls move from the elementary grades to secondary school, they encounter fewer women teachers and find that most authority figures are men. As a result, by their late teens, girls must struggle to regain the personal strength they had a decade before.

Ironically, when Gilligan and her colleagues returned to a private school—one site of their research—to present their findings, they found further evidence of their theory. Most younger girls who had been interviewed were eager to have their names appear in the forthcoming book, but the older girls were hesitant: Many were fearful that they would be talked about.

What do you think?

1. *How does Gilligan's research show the importance of gender to understanding society?*
2. *How does her work show that socialization may not be a direct and linear progression?*
3. *Do you think boys are subject to some of the same pressures and difficulties as girls? How?*

Sources: Gilligan (1990) and Winkler (1990).

The *conventional* level, Kohlberg's second stage, appears by the teen years (corresponding to Piaget's final, formal operational stage). At this point, young people lose some of their selfishness as they learn to define right and wrong in terms of what pleases parents and is consistent with broader cultural norms. Individuals at this stage also try to assess intention in reaching moral judgments instead of simply observing what others do.

In Kohlberg's final stage of moral development, the *postconventional* level, individuals move beyond their society's norms to consider abstract ethical principles. Now they think about liberty, freedom, or justice, perhaps arguing that what is legal still may not be right.

Critical evaluation. Like the work of Piaget, Kohlberg's model presents moral development in distinct stages. But, here again, whether this model applies to people in all societies remains unclear. Then, too, many people in the United States apparently never reach the postconventional level of moral reasoning, although exactly why is still an open question.

Another problem with Kohlberg's research is that his subjects were all boys. Kohlberg commits the research error, described in Chapter 2 ("Sociological Investigation"), of generalizing the results of male subjects to all people. This problem led a colleague, Carol Gilligan, to investigate how gender affects moral reasoning.

CAROL GILLIGAN: BRINGING IN GENDER

Carol Gilligan, whose approach is highlighted in the box, compared the moral development of girls and boys and concluded that the two sexes use different standards

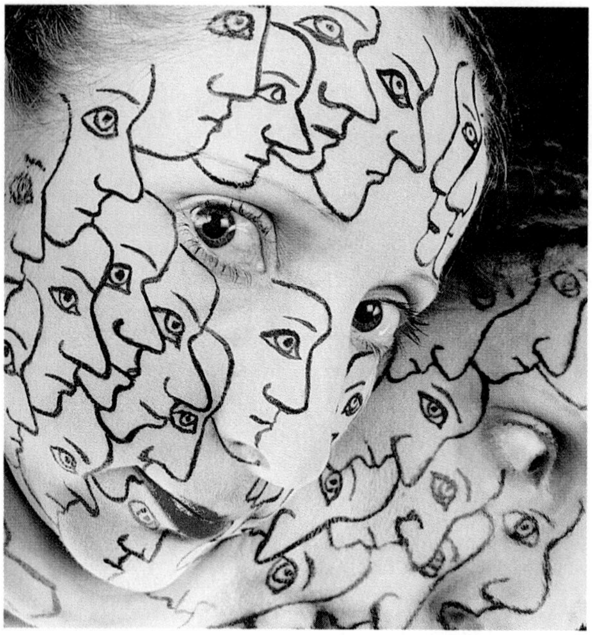

George Herbert Mead wrote: "No hard-and-fast line can be drawn between our own selves and the selves of others." The painting Manyness *by Rimma Gerlovina and Valeriy Gerlovin conveys this important truth. Although we tend to think of ourselves as unique individuals, each person's characteristics develop in an ongoing process of interaction with others.*

Rimma Gerlovina & Valeriy Gerlovin, *Manyness*, 1990. © the artists, Pomona, N.Y.

of rightness. Gilligan (1982, 1990) claims that males have a *justice perspective*, relying on formal rules to define right and wrong. Girls, on the other hand, have a *care and responsibility perspective*, judging a situation with an eye toward personal relationships and loyalties. For example, as boys see it, stealing is wrong because it breaks the law and goes against common morality. Girls are more likely to wonder why someone would steal, and to be sympathetic toward a person who steals to, say, feed a hungry child.

Kohlberg considers rule-based male reasoning superior to the person-based female approach. But Gilligan notes that impersonal rules have long governed men's lives in the workplace, whereas personal relationships are more relevant to women's lives as wives, mothers, and caregivers. Why, then, Gilligan asks, should we set up male standards as the norms by which to judge everyone?

Critical evaluation. Gilligan's work sharpens our understanding of human development and gender issues in research. Yet, what accounts for the differences she documents between females and males? Is it nature or nurture? In Gilligan's view, cultural conditioning is at work. Thus, as more women organize their lives around the workplace, the moral reasoning of women and men will become more similar.

GEORGE HERBERT MEAD: THE SOCIAL SELF

George Herbert Mead (1863–1931) developed a theory of *social behaviorism* to explain how social experience creates individual personality (1962; orig. 1934). His approach calls to mind the behaviorism of psychologist John B. Watson, described earlier. Both saw the power of environment to shape behavior. But whereas Watson focused on outward behavior, Mead studied inward *thinking*, humanity's defining trait.

The Self

Mead's central concept is the **self,** *that part of an individual's personality composed of self-awareness and self-image.* Mead's genius was in seeing the self as the product of social experience.

First, said Mead, *the self develops only with social experience.* The self is not part of the body, and it does not exist at birth. Mead rejected the position that personality is guided by biological drives (as Freud asserted) or biological maturation (as Piaget claimed). For Mead, self develops only as the individual interacts with others. In the absence of interaction, as we see from cases of isolated children, the body grows, but no self emerges.

Second, Mead explained, *social experience is the exchange of symbols.* Only people use words, a wave of the hand, or a smile to create meaning. We can train a dog using reward and punishment, but the dog attaches no meaning to its actions. Human beings, by contrast, find meaning in action by imagining people's underlying intentions. In short, a dog responds to *what you do*; a human responds to *what you have in mind* as you do it. Thus, you can train a dog to go to the hallway and bring back an umbrella. But, without understanding intention, if the dog cannot find the umbrella, it is incapable of the *human* response: to look for a raincoat instead.

Third, Mead continues, *understanding intention requires imagining the situation from the other's point of view.*

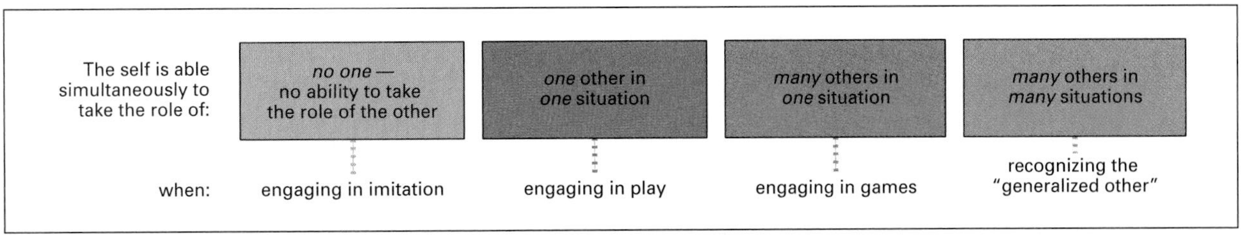

FIGURE 5–1 Building on Social Experience

George Herbert Mead described the development of the self as a process of gaining social experience. That is, the self develops as we expand our capacity to take the role of the other.

Using symbols, we imagine ourselves "in another person's shoes" and see ourselves as that person does. We can, therefore, anticipate how others will respond to us even before we act. A simple toss of a ball requires stepping outside ourselves to imagine how another will catch our throw. Social interaction, then, involves seeing ourselves as others see us—a process that Mead termed *taking the role of the other*.

The Looking-Glass Self

In effect, others represent a mirror (which people used to call a "looking glass") in which we can see ourselves. What we think of ourselves, then, depends on what we think others think of us. For example, if we think others see us as clever, we will think of ourselves in the same way. But if we feel they think of us as clumsy, then that is how we will see ourselves. Charles Horton Cooley (1864–1929) used the phrase **looking-glass self** to mean *a self-image based on how we think others see us* (1964; orig. 1902).

The I and the Me

Mead's fourth point is that *by taking the role of the other, we become self-aware*. The self, then, has two parts. As subject, the self is active and spontaneous. Mead called the active side of the self the *I* (the subjective form of the personal pronoun). But the self is also an object, as we imagine ourselves as others see us. Mead called the objective side of the self the *me* (the objective form of the personal pronoun). All social experience, he claimed, has both components: We initiate an action (the I-phase of self) and then we continue the action based on how others respond to us (the me-phase of self).

Development of the Self

The key to developing the self, then, is learning to take the role of the other. With limited social experience, infants can do this only through *imitation*. That is, they mimic behavior without understanding underlying intentions and, so, have no self.

As children learn to use language and other symbols, the self emerges through *play*, which involves taking the roles of significant others, especially parents. Playing "mommy and daddy" (often putting themselves, literally, "in the shoes" of a parent) helps young children imagine the world from a parent's point of view.

Gradually, children learn to take the roles of several others at once. Now they can move from simple play (say, playing catch) involving one other to complex *games* (like baseball) involving many others. By about age seven, most children have the social experience needed to engage in team sports.

Figure 5–1 charts the progression from imitation to play to games. But a final stage in the development of self remains. A game involves taking the role of others in just one situation, but social life demands that we see ourselves in terms of cultural norms as *anyone* else might. Mead used the term **generalized other** to refer to *widespread cultural norms and values we use as a reference in evaluating ourselves*.

As life goes on, the self continues to change along with our social experiences. But no matter how much events and circumstances affect us, we always remain creative beings. Thus, Mead concluded, we play a key role in our own socialization.

Critical evaluation. Mead's work explores the character of social experience itself. In symbolic interaction, he found the root of both self and society.

Some critics say Mead's view is completely social, allowing no biological element at all. In this, Mead stands apart from Freud (who identified general drives within the organism) and Piaget (whose stages of development are tied to biological maturity).

Be careful not to confuse Mead's concepts of the I and the me with Freud's id and superego. For Freud, the id originates in our biology, while Mead rejected any biological element of self (although he never specified the origin of the I). Moreover, while the id and superego are locked in continual combat, the I and the me work cooperatively together (Meltzer, 1978).

ERIK H. ERIKSON: EIGHT STAGES OF DEVELOPMENT

All of the thinkers discussed so far point to childhood as the crucial time when personality takes shape. Erik H. Erikson (1902–1994) took a broader view of socialization. He explained that we face challenges throughout the life course (1963; orig. 1950).

Stage 1—Infancy: the challenge of trust (versus mistrust). Between birth and about eighteen months, infants face the first of life's challenges: to establish a sense of trust that their world is a safe place. Family members play a key role in how the child meets this challenge.

Stage 2—Toddlerhood: the challenge of autonomy (versus doubt and shame). The next challenge, up to age three, is to learn skills to cope with the world in a confident way. Failing to gain self-control leads children to doubt their abilities.

Stage 3—Preschool: the challenge of initiative (versus guilt). Four- and five-year-olds must learn to engage their surroundings—including people outside the family—or experience guilt at failing to meet the expectations of parents and others.

Stage 4—Preadolescence: the challenge of industriousness (versus inferiority). Between ages six and thirteen, children enter school, make friends, and strike out on their own more and more. They feel proud of their accomplishments, or fear that they do not measure up.

Stage 5—Adolescence: the challenge of gaining identity (versus confusion). During the teen years, young people struggle to establish their own identity. In part, teenagers identify with others, but they also want to be unique. Almost all teens experience some confusion as they struggle to establish an identity.

Stage 6—Young adulthood: the challenge of intimacy (versus isolation). The challenge for young adults is to form and maintain intimate relationships with others. Falling in love (as well as making close friends) involves balancing the need to bond with the need to have a separate identity.

Stage 7—Middle adulthood: the challenge of making a difference (versus self-absorption). The challenge of middle age is contributing to the lives of others in the family, at work, and in the larger world. Failing at this, people become stagnant, caught up in their own limited concerns (think of Scrooge in Dickens's classic *A Christmas Carol*).

Stage 8—Old age: the challenge of integrity (versus despair). Near the end of our lives, Erikson explains, people hope to look back on what they have accomplished with a sense of integrity and satisfaction. For those who have been self-absorbed, old age brings only a sense of despair over missed opportunities.

Critical evaluation. Erikson's theory views personality formation as a lifelong process. Further, success at one stage (say, an infant gaining trust) prepares us for meeting the next challenge.

One problem with this model is that not everyone confronts these challenges in the exact order presented by Erikson. Nor is it clear that failure to meet the challenge of one stage of life means that a person is doomed to fail later on. A broader question, raised earlier in our discussion of Piaget's ideas, is whether people in other cultures and in other times in history would define a successful life in the same terms as Erikson.

In sum, Erikson's model helps us make sense of socialization and points out how the family, the school, and other settings shape us. We turn now to take a close look at these agents of socialization.

AGENTS OF SOCIALIZATION

Every social experience we have affects us in at least a small way. However, several familiar settings have special importance in the socialization process. These include the family, school, peer group, and the mass media.

THE FAMILY

The family has the greatest impact on socialization. Infants are totally dependent on others, and the responsibility typically falls on parents and other family members. At least until children begin school, the family also has the job of teaching children skills, values, and beliefs.

Not all family learning is intentional. Children also learn from the kind of environment that adults create. Whether children learn to see themselves as strong or weak, smart or stupid, loved or simply tolerated, and, as Erik Erikson suggests, whether they see the world as trustworthy or dangerous, largely depends on their surroundings.

The family also gives children a social position in terms of race, religion, ethnicity, and class. In time, all these elements become part of a child's self-concept.

Research shows that the class position of parents affects how they raise their children (Ellison, Bartkowski, & Segal, 1996). Class position shapes not just how much money parents have to spend, but what they expect of their children. Surveys show that, when asked to pick from a list of traits that are most desirable in a child, lower-class people in the United States favor obedience and conformity. Well-to-do people, by contrast, choose good judgment and being creative (NORC, 1999). Why the difference? Melvin Kohn (1977) explains that people of lower social standing usually have limited education and perform routine jobs under close supervision. Expecting that their children will hold similar positions, they encourage obedience and may even use physical punishment like spanking to get it. Well-off parents, with more schooling, usually have jobs that demand imagination and provide more personal freedom. These parents, therefore, try to inspire the same qualities in their children. All parents, then, act in ways that encourage their children to follow in their footsteps.

Sociological research indicates that affluent parents tend to encourage creativity in their children while poor parents tend to foster conformity. While this general difference may be valid, parents at all class levels can and do provide loving support and guidance by simply involving themselves in their children's lives. Henry Ossawa Tanner's painting The Banjo Lesson *stands as a lasting testament to this process.*

Henry Ossawa Tanner, *The Banjo Lesson*, 1893. Oil on canvas. Hampton University Museum, Hampton, Virginia.

THE SCHOOL

Schooling enlarges children's social worlds to include people with backgrounds different from their own. In the process, they learn the importance that society attaches to race and gender. Studies confirm that children tend to cluster in play groups made up of one race and gender (Lever, 1978; Finkelstein & Haskins, 1983).

Schools teach children a wide range of knowledge and skills. But schools informally convey other lessons, which might be called the *hidden curriculum*. Activities such as spelling bees and sports foster the value of competition and showcase success. Children also receive countless informal lessons that their society's way of life is morally good.

School is also most children's first experience with bureaucracy. The school day runs on impersonal rules and a strict time schedule. Not surprisingly, these are the hallmarks of the many organizations that will employ them later in life.

Finally, schools socialize children into gender roles. Raphaela Best (1983) notes that in the early grades, boys

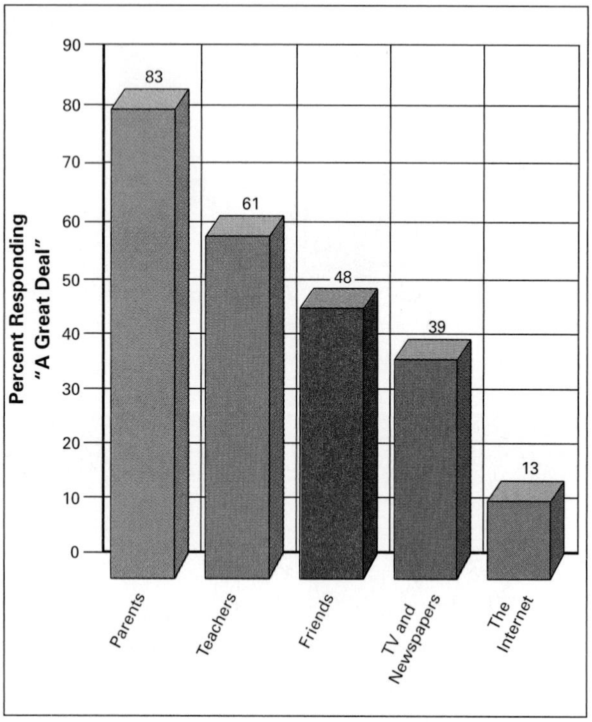

FIGURE 5–2 Whom Do You Trust?

Survey Question: "How much do you trust the information you get from . . . ?"

Sample = 409 U.S. teens, ages 13 to 17, 341 (83%) responding using the Internet. Survey taken April 1999 by Yankelovich Partners, Inc.

Source: Data from Okrent (1999).

engage in more physical activities and spend more time outdoors, while girls often volunteer to help teachers with various housekeeping chores in the classroom. Gender differences continue in college, as women tend toward majoring in the arts or humanities, while men lean in the direction of economics, the physical sciences, and computing.

PEER GROUPS

By the time they enter school, children have discovered the **peer group,** *a social group whose members have interests, social position, and age in common.* Unlike the family and school, the peer group lets children escape the direct supervision of adults. Among their peers, children learn how to form relationships on their own. Peer groups also offer the chance to discuss interests that adults may not share (such as clothing and popular music) or tolerate (such as drugs and sex).

Not surprisingly, then, parents express concern about who their children's friends are. In a rapidly changing society, peer groups have great influence, and the attitudes of young and old may differ because of a "generation gap." The importance of peer groups typically peaks during adolescence when young people begin to break away from their families and think of themselves as adults.

Even during adolescence, however, parental influence on children remains strong. Peers may affect short-term interests such as music or films, but parents retain greater sway over long-term goals, such as going to college (Davies & Kandel, 1981). Figure 5–2 shows the results of a recent survey of teenagers confirming that teens still place their greatest trust in their parents.

Finally, any neighborhood or school is a social mosaic of many peer groups. As Chapter 7 ("Groups and Organizations") explains, individuals tend to view their own group in positive terms and discredit others. Moreover, people are influenced by peer groups they would like to join, a process sociologists call **anticipatory socialization,** *learning that helps a person achieve a desired position.* In school, for example, young people may mimic the styles and slang of the group they hope to join. Or, at a later point in life, a young lawyer who hopes to become a partner in her law firm may conform to the attitudes and behavior of the firm's partners in order to be accepted.

THE MASS MEDIA

<u>September 29, 1994, the Pacific Ocean, nearing Japan.</u> We have been out of sight of land for two weeks now, which makes this ship our entire social world. But more than land, many of the students miss television! Tapes of "Beverly Hills 90210" are a hot item.

The **mass media** are *impersonal communications aimed at a vast audience.* The term "media" comes from Latin meaning "middle," suggesting that media serve to connect people. *Mass media* arise as communications technology (first newspapers and then radio and television) spread information on a mass scale.

In the United States today, the mass media have an enormous effect on our attitudes and behavior. Television, introduced in 1939, soon became the dominant medium, and 98 percent of U.S. households have at least one set (just 94 percent of all households have telephones). Two out of three households also have cable television. As Figure 5–3 shows, the United States has the highest rate of television ownership in the world.

Just how "glued to the tube" are we? Survey data show that the average household has at least one set turned on for seven hours each day, and people spend almost half their free time watching television (Nielsen, 1997; Seplow & Storm, 1997). National Map 5–1 on page 128 shows where in the United States people are more likely to be television watchers and where they are more likely to spend their leisure time reading newspapers.

Years before children learn to read, television watching is a regular routine. In fact, children grow up spending as many hours in front of a television as they do in school or interacting with their parents. This is so despite research that suggests television makes children more passive and less likely to use their imagination (Singer & Singer, 1983; APA, 1993; Fellman, 1995).

Comedian Fred Allen once quipped that we call television a "medium" because it is rarely well done. For a variety of reasons, television (as well as other mass media) provokes plenty of criticism. Some liberal critics argue that television shows mirror our society's patterns of inequality and rarely challenge the status quo. Most programs involve men in positions of power over women. Moreover, although racial and ethnic minorities watch about 40 percent more television than white people, they are largely absent from television programming (Gans, 1980; Cantor & Pingree, 1983; Ang, 1985; Parenti, 1986; Brown, 1990). The box on page 129 provides a closer look at how the U.S. entertainment industry characterizes minorities.

On the other side of the fence, conservative critics charge that the television and film industries are led by a liberal "cultural elite." In recent years, they claim, "politically correct" media have advanced liberal causes, including feminism and gay rights (Lichter, Rothman, & Rothman, 1986; Woodward, 1992b; Prindle, 1993; Prindle & Endersby, 1993; Rothman, Powers, & Rothman, 1993).

A final concern involves the mass media and violence. In 1996, the American Medical Association (AMA) declared that violence in the mass media, especially television and films, had reached levels that were a hazard to the well-being of this country's people. The AMA's research found widespread agreement on this matter: Three-fourths of U.S. adults reported having walked out of a movie or having turned off a television show due to high levels of violence. A more recent national study found that almost two-thirds of television programs contain violence and that, in most violent scenes, characters show no remorse and are not punished (Wilson, 1998).

GLOBAL SNAPSHOT

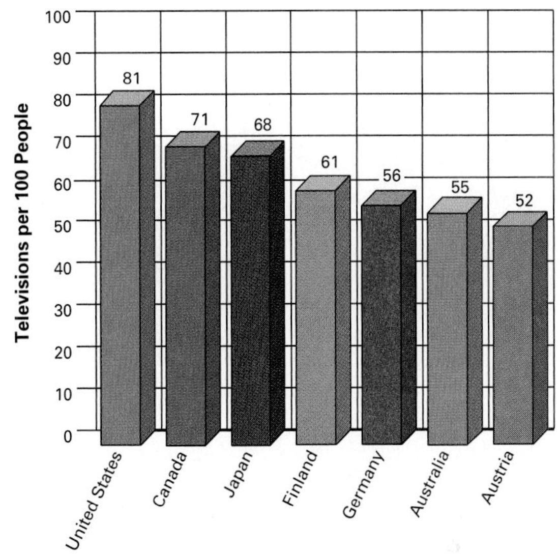

FIGURE 5–3 Television Ownership in Global Perspective

Source: U.S. Census Bureau (1999).

In 1997, the television industry adopted a rating system for shows. But larger questions remain: Does watching sexual or violent programming harm people as much as critics say it does? More important, why do the mass media contain so much sex and violence in the first place?

In sum, television and the other mass media enrich our lives with entertaining and educational programming. The media also increase our exposure to diverse cultures and provoke discussion of current issues. At the same time, the power of the media, especially television, to shape how we think remains highly controversial.

Finally, other spheres of life beyond those just described also play a part in social learning. For most people in the United States, these include religious organizations, the workplace, the military, and social clubs. As a result, socialization involves inconsistencies as we simultaneously absorb different information from different sources. In the end, socialization proves to be not a simple learning process but a complex balancing

SEEING OURSELVES

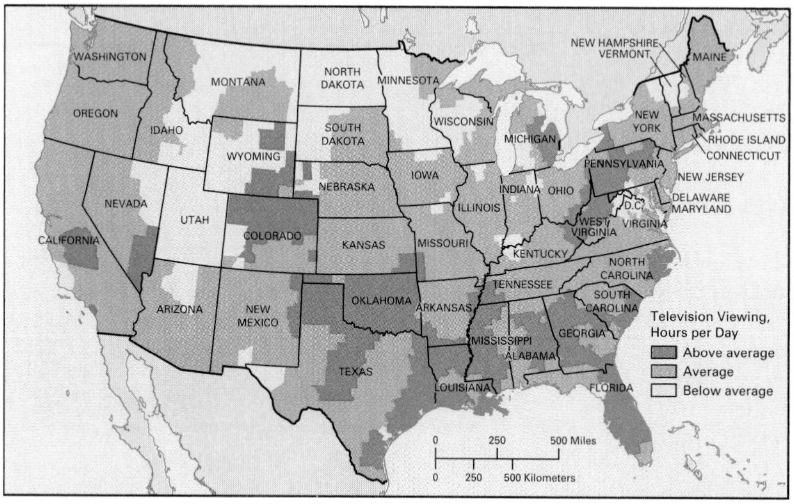

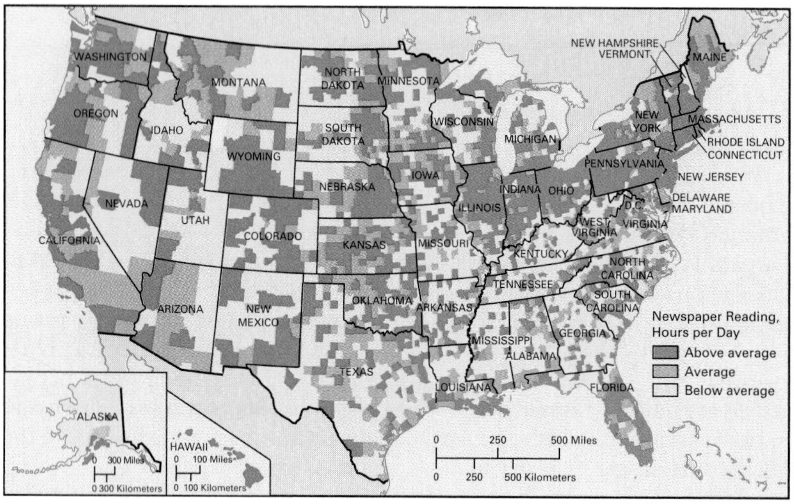

NATIONAL MAP 5–1
Television Viewing and Newspaper Reading across the United States

The map on the left identifies U.S. counties where television watching is above average, average, and below average. The map below provides comparable information for time devoted to reading newspapers. What do you think accounts for the high level of television viewing across much of the South and in rural West Virginia? Does your theory also account for patterns of newspaper reading?

Source: *American Demographics* magazine, August 1993, p. 64; *American Demographics* magazine, November 1998, p. 46. Reprinted with permission. © 1993, 1998 *American Demographics* magazine, Ithaca, New York.

act. As we sort and weigh all the information we encounter, we form our own distinctive personalities and world views.

SOCIALIZATION AND THE LIFE COURSE

Although childhood has special importance in the socialization process, learning continues throughout our lives. An overview of the life course reveals that our society organizes human experience according to age—childhood, adolescence, adulthood, and, finally, old age.

CHILDHOOD

A few years ago, basketball superstar Michael Jordan came under fire for endorsing Nike athletic shoes, because the popular footwear was made in Taiwan and Indonesia by children who work in factories instead of going to school. Some 200 million of the world's

SOCIAL DIVERSITY

How Should the Media Portray Minorities?

On an old "Saturday Night Live" sketch, Ron Howard tells comedian Eddie Murphy about a new film, *Night Shift*, in which two mortuary workers decide to open their own sideline business—a prostitution ring. Murphy asks if there are any black actors in the film; Howard shakes his head "no." Murphy then thunders, "A story about two pimps and there wasn't no brothers in it? I don't know whether to thank you or punch you in the mouth, man!"

Murphy's response points to twin criticisms of the U.S. mass media: Films and television either portray minorities in stereotypical fashion or ignore them altogether (Press, 1993:219). Back in the 1950s, minorities were all but absent from television and films. Even the wildly successful comedy "I Love Lucy" was initially turned down by major television studios because it featured Desi Arnaz—a Cuban—in a starring role. Since then, the media have steadily included more minorities. But, despite top-rated programs like "The Cosby Show" in the 1980s, *visibility* remains an issue: The 1990s came to an end with just a handful of African American stars on prime time television.

Does a television show like "The Hughleys," which depicts a successful family, improve popular perceptions among whites of African Americans, or does it hide the real problems many black families face?

But what about *how* the media portray minorities? The few African Americans who managed to break into television in the 1950s (for example, "Amos 'n' Andy" and Jack Benny's butler "Rochester") were stereotypical low- status characters. Today, more television shows feature African American stars, but most are situation comedies ("sitcoms") that feature crude humor and bumbling characters.

Certainly, the image of minorities in the mass media is better than it used to be. But how minorities should be portrayed on television is still a matter of debate (MacDonald, 1992). Should television portray minorities *as they are*, which risks perpetuating stereotypes? Should shows present minorities *as they should be*, which risks being unrealistic about our nation's problems? Or should the television industry be guided only by ratings, giving the public "what sells"?

children work full time, for about fifty cents an hour (Gibbs, 1996). Global Map 5–1 on page 130 shows that child labor is most common in the nations of Africa and Asia.

Jordan was criticized because North Americans think of *childhood*—roughly the first twelve years of life—as a carefree time for learning and play. In fact, explains historian Philippe Ariès (1965), the whole idea of "childhood" is fairly new. During the Middle Ages, children of four or five were treated like adults and expected to fend for themselves. Even a century ago, children in North America and Europe had much the same life as children in poor countries today: Many worked long hours, often under dangerous conditions, for little pay.

We may be tempted to defend our idea of childhood because youngsters are biologically immature. But a look back in time and around the world shows that the concept of "childhood" is grounded in culture. In rich countries, not everyone has to work, so childhood can be extended to allow time for young people to learn the skills they will need in a high-technology workplace.

Given this extended childhood, it is no surprise that many people worry about children growing up too fast. Today's ten- to twelve-year-olds, says one executive of a children's television channel, have many of the same interests and experiences that were typical of twelve- to fourteen-year-olds a generation ago (Hymowitz, 1998). In part, this "hurried child" syndrome results

WINDOW ON THE WORLD

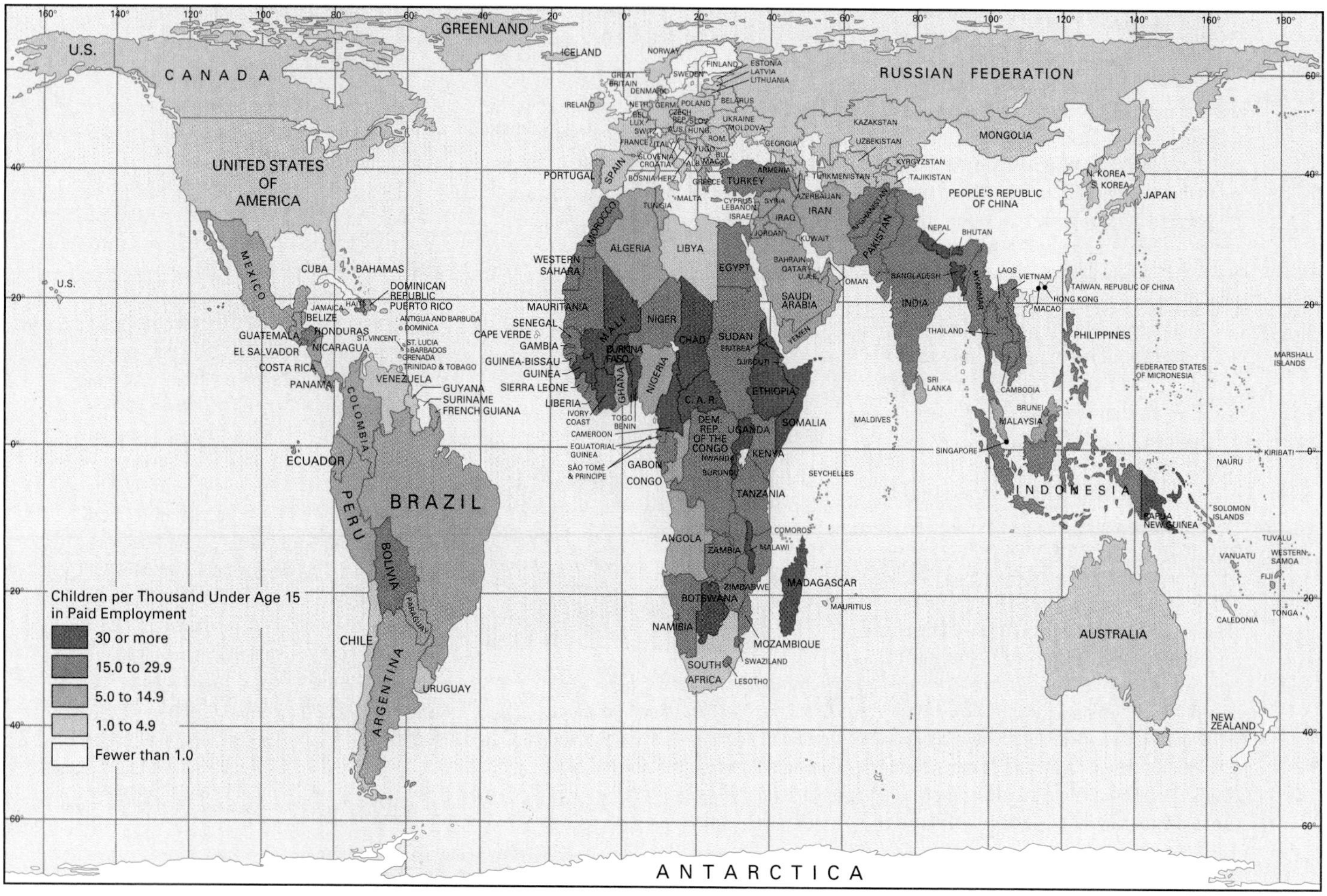

GLOBAL MAP 5–1 Child Labor in Global Perspective

Industrialization prolongs childhood and discourages children from work and other activities deemed suitable only for adults. Thus, child labor is relatively uncommon in the United States and other industrial societies. In less industrialized nations of the world, however, children are a vital economic asset, and they typically begin working as soon as they are able.
Source: *Peters Atlas of the World* (1990).

from dramatic changes in the family—including rising divorce rates and the entry of both parents into the labor force—that leave children with less supervision at home. Then, too, "adult" programming on television (not to mention films and the Internet) carries grown-up concerns such as sex, drugs, and violence into young people's lives.

ADOLESCENCE

Just as industrialization created childhood as a distinct stage of life, adolescence emerged as a buffer between childhood and adulthood. We generally link adolescence, or the teenage years, to emotional and social turmoil as parents spar with young people who are trying to

There is no better example of how parents can "hurry" their children into adulthood than beauty pageants for young girls. In this scene from a Georgia "baby beauty pageant," we see a girl, not even old enough for school, straining to embody traits usually associated with grown-up women. What are these traits? Would you want your daughter to compete in such pageants? Why or why not?

develop their own identities. Here, again, we are tempted to attribute teenage turbulence to the biological changes of puberty. But this turmoil more correctly reflects cultural inconsistency. For example, the mass media glorify sex, and schools hand out condoms, while, at the same time, parents urge restraint. Consider, too, that an eighteen-year-old male may face the adult duty of going to war, but he lacks the adult right to drink alcohol. In short, adolescence is a time of social contradictions when people are no longer children but not yet adults.

As is true of all stages of life, adolescence varies according to social background. Most young people from working-class families move directly from high school into the adult world of work and parenting. Wealthier teens, however, have the resources to attend college and perhaps graduate school, thereby stretching adolescence into the late twenties and even the thirties.

ADULTHOOD

Adulthood, which begins between the late teens and early thirties, depending on social background, is a time of accomplishment. Having completed their schooling, people embark on careers and raise families of their own. Personalities are now largely formed, although a marked change in a person's environment—such as unemployment, divorce, or serious illness—may cause significant change in the self.

Early Adulthood

During early adulthood—until about age forty—young adults learn to manage day-to-day affairs for themselves, often juggling conflicting priorities: parents, partner, children, schooling, and work (Levinson et al., 1978). Women, especially, often try to "do it all," since our culture gives them major responsibility for child rearing and housework, even if they have demanding jobs outside the home (Hochschild, 1989).

Middle Adulthood

In middle adulthood—roughly ages forty to sixty—people sense that their life circumstances are pretty well set. They also become more aware of the fragility of health, which the young typically take for granted. Women who have spent many years raising a family find middle adulthood especially trying. Children grow up and require less attention, and husbands become absorbed in their careers, leaving some women with spaces in their lives that are difficult to fill. Many women who divorce also face serious financial problems (Weitzman, 1985, 1996). For all these reasons, an increasing number of women in middle adulthood return to school and seek new careers.

For everyone, growing older means facing physical decline, a prospect our culture makes more painful for women. Because good looks are defined as more important for women, wrinkles, added weight, and graying

Various categories of people experience the stages of the life course in distinctive ways. Most men, for example, pass through old age with the support of a partner. Women, who typically outlive men, endure much of their old age alone, a reality poignantly captured in G. G. Kopliak's painting Still Life.

hair can be traumatic. Men, of course, have their own difficulties as they get older. Some must admit that they are never going to reach their career goals. Others realize that the price of their career success has been neglect of family or personal health (Farrell & Rosenberg, 1981; Wolf, 1990).

OLD AGE

Old age—the later years of adulthood and the final stage of life itself—begins about the mid-sixties. Again, societies attach different meanings to this stage of life. As explained in Chapter 15 ("Aging and the Elderly"), traditional societies often give older people control over most of the land and other wealth. Also, since traditional societies change slowly, older people amass great wisdom during their lifetime, which earns them much respect (Sheehan, 1976; Hareven, 1982).

In industrial societies, however, most younger people work apart from their families, becoming independent of their elders. Rapid change in a society fosters a youth orientation that leads us to define what is old as unimportant or even obsolete. To younger people, the elderly appear unaware of new trends and fashions, and their knowledge and experience may seem of little value.

No doubt, however, our society's anti-elderly bias will diminish as the share of older people steadily increases. The percentage of our population over age sixty-five has almost tripled since the beginning of the twentieth century, so that today there are more seniors than teenagers. Moreover, life expectancy is still increasing, so that most men and women in their mid-sixties (the "young elderly") can look forward to decades more of life. In the twenty-first century, the Census Bureau (1999) predicts, the fastest-growing segment of our population will be those over eighty-five, whose numbers will soar nearly fivefold.

Old age differs in an important way from earlier stages in the life course. Growing up typically means entering new roles and assuming new responsibilities; growing old, by contrast, is the opposite experience —leaving roles that provided both satisfaction and social identity. Retirement can be a period of restful activity, or it can mean the loss of valued routines and sometimes outright boredom. Like any life transition, retirement demands learning new, different patterns while at the same time *un*learning familiar habits from the past. A nonworking wife or husband who must now accommodate a partner at home has an equally difficult transition to make.

DYING

Through most of human history, low living standards and simple medical technology meant that death, caused by disease or accident, came at any stage of life. Today, however, more than 85 percent of people in the United States die after the age of fifty-five (U.S. National Center for Health Statistics, 1999).

After observing many dying people, Elisabeth Kübler-Ross (1969) described death as an orderly transition involving five distinct responses. A person's first reaction to the prospect of dying is usually *denial*, since our culture tends to ignore the reality of death. The second phase is *anger*, when a person facing death views it as a gross injustice. Third, anger gives way to *negotiation* as the person imagines avoiding death by striking a bargain with God. The fourth response, *resignation*, is often accompanied by psychological depression. Finally, adjustment to death is completed in the fifth stage, *acceptance*. Rather than being paralyzed by fear and anxiety, the person whose life is ending now sets out to make the most of whatever time remains.

As the share of women and men in old age increases, we can expect our culture to become more comfortable with the idea of death. In recent years, for example, people in the United States and elsewhere discuss death more openly, and the trend is to view dying as preferable to painful or prolonged suffering. Moreover, more married couples now prepare for death with legal and financial planning. This openness may ease somewhat the pain of the surviving spouse, a consideration for women who, more often than not, outlive their husbands.

THE LIFE COURSE: AN OVERVIEW

This survey of the life course leads us to two major conclusions. First, although each stage of life is linked to the biological process of aging, the life course is largely a social construction. For this reason, people in other societies may experience a stage of life quite differently or, for that matter, not at all. Second, in any society, the stages of the life course present characteristic problems and transitions that involve learning something new and, in many cases, unlearning familiar routines.

Note, too, that while societies organize the life course according to age, other forces, such as class, race, ethnicity, and gender, also shape people's lives. Thus, the general patterns we have described apply somewhat differently to various categories of people (cf. Duncan et al., 1998).

Finally, people's life experiences also vary according to when, in the history of the society, they are born. A **cohort** is *a category of people who share some trait, usually their age*. Age-cohorts are likely to be influenced by the same economic and cultural trends, so that members have similar attitudes and values (Riley, Foner, & Waring, 1988). Women and men born in the 1940s and 1950s, for example, grew up during a time of economic expansion that gave them a sense of optimism. Today's college students, who have grown up in an age of economic uncertainty, are less confident of the future.

Each of us lives within an age cohort, and common historical experiences frame our way of looking at the world. Here sixth graders from a suburban New York school visit the Franklin Delano Roosevelt Memorial in Washington, D.C. How well do you think they appreciate the significance of this bread line statue that recalls the joblessness and hunger that wracked the United States during the 1930s?

RESOCIALIZATION: TOTAL INSTITUTIONS

A final type of socialization, currently experienced by almost 2 million people in the United States, involves being confined—often against their will—in prisons or mental hospitals. This is the special world of the **total institution,** *a setting in which people are isolated from the rest of society and manipulated by an administrative staff.*

According to Erving Goffman (1961), total institutions have three distinctive characteristics. First, staff members supervise all spheres of daily life, including where residents (often called "inmates") eat, sleep, and work. Second, the environment of a total institution is highly standardized, with institutional food, uniforms, and one set of activities for everyone. Third, formal rules and daily schedules dictate when, where, and how inmates perform their daily routines.

Total institutions impose such regimentation for one reason: **resocialization,** *radically changing an inmate's personality through carefully controlling the environment.* Prisons and mental hospitals physically isolate inmates behind fences, barred windows, and locked doors, and control their access to the telephone, mail, and visitors. Cut off in this way, the institution is the inmate's entire world, making it easier for the staff to produce long-term change—or at least short-term compliance—in the inmate.

Resocialization is a two-part process. First, the staff breaks down the new inmate's existing identity, using what Goffman describes as "abasements, degradations, humiliations, and profanations of self"

The penal system's requirement that new inmates suffer the indignity of having their heads shaved is more than a matter of hair style; such a degrading ritual is also the first stage in the process by which a total institution attempts to break down an individual's established social identity.

(1961:14). For example, an inmate must give up personal possessions, including clothing and grooming articles used to maintain a distinctive appearance. Instead, the staff provides standard-issue clothes so everyone looks alike. The staff subjects new inmates to "mortifications of self," including searches, head-shaving, medical examinations, fingerprinting, and then assigns each a serial number. Once inside the walls, individuals also give up their privacy, as guards routinely monitor their living quarters.

In the second part of the resocialization process, the staff tries to build a new self in the inmate through a system of rewards and punishments. Having a book to read, watching television, or making a telephone call may seem trivial to outsiders, but in the rigid environment of the total institution, these simple privileges can be powerful motivations to conform. In the end, the length of confinement typically depends on how well the inmate cooperates with the staff.

Resocialization can bring about considerable change in an inmate, but total institutions affect different people in different ways. While some inmates are considered "rehabilitated" or "recovered," others may change little, and still others may become hostile and bitter. Furthermore, over a long period of time, the rigidly controlled environment can leave some *institutionalized*, without the capacity for independent living.

But what about the rest of us? Does socialization crush our individuality or empower us? The final box takes a closer look at this important question.

SUMMARY

1. Socialization is the way individuals develop their humanity and particular identities.
2. A century ago, people thought most human behavior was guided by biological instinct. Today, we recognize that human behavior is mostly a result of nurture rather than nature.
3. The permanently damaging effects of social isolation reveal that social experience is essential to human development.
4. Sigmund Freud's model of the human personality has three parts: The id represents innate human drives (the life and death instincts); the superego is internalized cultural values and norms; the ego resolves competition between the demands of the id and the restraints of the superego.
5. Jean Piaget believed that human development reflects both biological maturation and an individual's increasing social experience. He identified

CONTROVERSY & DEBATE

Are We Free within Society?

Throughout this chapter, we have stressed one key theme: Society shapes how we think, feel, and act. If this is so, then in what sense are we free? To answer this important question, consider the Muppets, puppet stars of television and film. Watching the antics of Kermit the Frog, Miss Piggy, and the rest of the troupe, we almost believe they are real rather than objects animated from backstage. Similarly, as the sociological perspective points out, human beings are like puppets in that we, too, respond to backstage forces. Society, after all, gives us a culture and shapes our lives according to class, race, and gender. In the face of such social forces, can we really claim to be free?

Sociologists speak with many voices when addressing this question. One response, with politically liberal overtones, is that individuals are *not* free of society—in fact, as social creatures, we never could be. But if we are constrained to life within society, it is important to make our home as just as possible. That is, we should work to lessen class differences and other barriers to opportunity for minorities, including women.

Another approach, this time with conservative overtones, is that we *are* free because society can never dictate our dreams. Our history as a nation, right from the revolutionary act that led to its founding, is one story after another of individuals pursuing personal goals in spite of great odds.

We find both attitudes in George Herbert Mead's analysis of socialization. Mead recognized that society makes demands on us and sometimes limits us. But he also saw that human beings are spontaneous and creative, capable of continually acting back—individually and collectively—on society. Thus Mead noted the power of society while still affirming the human capacity to evaluate, criticize, and, ultimately, to choose and to change.

In the end, then, we may resemble puppets, but only on the surface. A crucial difference—one that gives us a large measure of freedom—is that we can stop, look up at the "strings" that animate much of our action, and even yank on them defiantly (Berger, 1963:176). If our pull is persistent enough, we can do more than we might think. As Margaret Mead once mused, "Do not make the mistake of thinking that concerned people cannot change the world; it's the only thing that ever has."

Continue the debate . . .

1. *Do you think our society affords more freedom to males than to females? Why or why not?*
2. *What about modern, industrial countries compared to traditional, agrarian nations: Are some of the world's people more free than others?*
3. *Does an understanding of sociology increase your freedom? Why?*

four stages of cognitive development: sensorimotor, preoperational, concrete operational, and formal operational.

6. Lawrence Kohlberg applied Piaget's approach to moral development. Individuals first judge rightness in preconventional terms, according to their individual needs. Next, conventional moral reasoning takes account of parental attitudes and cultural norms. Finally, postconventional reasoning allows people to criticize society itself.
7. In response to Kohlberg's use of only male subjects, Carol Gilligan discovered that while males rely on abstract standards of rightness, females look at the effect of decisions on interpersonal relationships.
8. To George Herbert Mead, social experience generates the self, which he described as partly autonomous (the I) and partly guided by society (the me). Although infants engage in imitation, the self develops through play and games and eventually includes the "generalized other."
9. Charles Horton Cooley used the term "looking-glass self" to explain that we see ourselves as we imagine others see us.
10. Erik H. Erikson identified characteristic challenges that individuals face at each stage of life from infancy to old age.
11. Usually the first setting of socialization, the family has the greatest influence on a child's attitudes and behavior.

12. Schools expose children to greater social diversity and introduce them to impersonal performance evaluations.
13. Peer groups free children from adult supervision and take on great significance during adolescence.
14. The mass media, especially television, have a considerable impact on the socialization process. The average U.S. child spends as much time watching television as attending school or interacting with parents.
15. Each stage of the life course—childhood, adolescence, adulthood, and old age—is socially constructed in ways that vary from society to society.
16. People in high-income countries typically fend off death until old age. Accepting death is part of socialization for the elderly.
17. Total institutions, such as prisons and mental hospitals, try to resocialize inmates—that is, to radically change their personalities.
18. Socialization shows the power of society to shape our thoughts, feelings, and actions. Yet, as humans, we have the ability to act back, shaping both ourselves and our social world.

KEY CONCEPTS

socialization (p. 115) the lifelong social experience by which individuals develop their human potential and learn culture

personality (p. 115) a person's fairly consistent patterns of acting, thinking, and feeling

id (p. 118) Freud's designation for the human being's basic drives

ego (p. 119) Freud's designation for a person's conscious efforts to balance innate pleasure-seeking drives with the demands of society

superego (p. 119) Freud's designation for the operation of culture within the individual in the form of internalized values and norms

sensorimotor stage (p. 119) Piaget's term for the level of human development at which individuals experience the world only through their senses

preoperational stage (p. 120) Piaget's term for the level of human development at which individuals first use language and other symbols

concrete operational stage (p. 120) Piaget's term for the level of human development at which individuals first perceive causal connections in their surroundings

formal operational stage (p. 120) Piaget's term for the level of human development at which individuals think abstractly and critically

self (p. 122) George Herbert Mead's term for that part of an individual's personality composed of self-awareness and self-image

looking-glass self (p. 123) Cooley's term for a self-image based on how we think others see us

generalized other (p. 123) George Herbert Mead's term for widespread cultural norms and values we use as a reference in evaluating ourselves

peer group (p. 126) a social group whose members have interests, social position, and age in common

anticipatory socialization (p. 126) learning that helps a person achieve a desired position

mass media (p. 126) impersonal communications aimed at a vast audience

cohort (p. 133) a category of people who share some trait, usually their age

total institution (p. 133) a setting in which people are isolated from the rest of society and manipulated by an administrative staff

resocialization (p. 133) radically changing an inmate's personality through carefully controlling the environment

CRITICAL-THINKING QUESTIONS

1. What do cases of social isolation teach us about the importance of social experience to human beings?
2. State the two sides of the nature-nurture debate. In what sense are human nature and nurture not opposed to one another?
3. We have all seen young children place their hands in front of their faces and exclaim, "You can't see me!" They assume that if they cannot see you, then you cannot see them. What does this behavior suggest about a young child's ability to "take the role of the other"? Can a parent expect a young child to "see things from *my* point of view"?
4. What are the common themes in the ideas of Freud, Piaget, Kohlberg, Gilligan, Mead, and Erikson? In what ways do their theories differ?

APPLICATIONS AND EXERCISES

1. Work with several members of your sociology class to gather data on socialization. Each person should ask several friends and classmates to name traits that are elements of "human nature." Then compare notes and discuss the extent to which these traits are the product of nature or nurture.
2. Find a copy of the video *Lord of the Flies*, a tale by William Golding based on a Freudian model of personality. Jack (and his hunters) represent the power of the id; Piggy consistently opposes them as the superego; Ralph stands between the two as the ego, the voice of reason. Golding wrote the book after taking part in the bloody D-Day landing in France during World War II. Do you agree with his belief that violence is part of human nature?
3. Make a list of personality traits that characterize you. If you have the courage, ask several others who know you well what they think. Can you explain where these traits came from?
4. Watch several hours of prime time programming on network or cable television. Keep track of every time any element of violence is shown. For fun, assign each program a "YIP rating," for the number of Years In Prison a person would serve for committing all the violent acts you witness (Fobes, 1996). On the basis of observing this small (and unrepresentative) sample of programs, what are your conclusions?
5. Install the CD-ROM packaged in the back of this new textbook to access a variety of study, review, and applications exercises designed to help you better understand the material covered in this chapter. The CD includes an author's tip video, as well as interactive maps, video application exercises, Web links, and study questions.

SITES TO SEE

http://www.prenhall.com/macionis
Visit the interactive Web site that accompanies this text. Begin by clicking on the cover of your book. You will find a chapter-by-chapter study guide, practice tests, chat room, and many suggested Web links.

http://www.macionis.com
(or **http://www.thesociologypage.com**)
At the author's Web site, you can find brief biographies of George Herbert Mead and Charles Horton Cooley, as well as other sociologists discussed in this chapter.

http://www.plaza.interport.net/nypsan
Learn more about Sigmund Freud and his work at the *FreudNet* site.

http://www.piaget.org/
The Jean Piaget Society hosts this Web site, which presents the work of this celebrated social psychologist.

http://www.nd.edu/~rbarger/kohlberg.html
This Web site is dedicated to the ideas and research of Lawrence Kohlberg.

CHAPTER 6

Bernard Stanley Hoyes
Card Players Revelling

Oil on paper 11 × 12 in. Painted at Desert Hot Springs Studio, 1994. Original oil on paper in the collection of the artist. © Caribbean Arts, Inc.

SOCIAL INTERACTION IN EVERYDAY LIFE

Harold and Sybil are on their way to another couple's home in an unfamiliar section of Minneapolis, Minnesota. They are late because, for the last twenty minutes, they have traveled in circles looking for Royal Oak Drive. Harold, gripping the wheel ever more tightly, is doing a slow burn. Sybil, sitting next to him, looks straight ahead, afraid to utter a word. Both realize the evening is off to a bad start (Tannen, 1990:62).

Harold and Sybil are lost in more ways than one: They are unable to grasp why they are growing more and more enraged at their situation and at each other. Consider their plight from Harold's point of view. Like most men, Harold hates getting lost. The longer he drives around, the more incompetent he feels. Sybil, on the other hand, cannot understand why Harold does not pull over and ask someone where Royal Oak Drive is. If she were driving, she fumes to herself, they already would have arrived and would now be comfortably settled with drink in hand.

Why don't men like to ask for directions? Because men value their independence, they are uncomfortable asking for help (and also reluctant to accept it). To men, asking for assistance is the same as saying, "You know something I don't." If it takes Harold a few more minutes to find the address on his own—and keep his self-respect in the process—he thinks it's a good bargain.

If men value self-sufficiency and are sensitive to hierarchy, women are more attuned to others and strive for connectedness. From Sybil's point of view, asking for help is right because sharing information reinforces social bonds. Asking for directions seems as natural to her as searching on his own is to Harold. Obviously, getting lost is sure to generate conflict as long as neither one understands the other's point of view.

Such everyday experiences are the focus of this chapter. We begin by presenting the building blocks of common experience and then explore the almost magical way that face-to-face interaction generates reality. The central concept is **social interaction,** *the process by which people act and react in relation to others.* Through social interaction, we create the reality in which we live. Social structure, in turn, guides our interaction.

SOCIAL STRUCTURE: A GUIDE TO EVERYDAY LIVING

October 21, 1994, Ho Chi Minh City, Vietnam. This morning we leave the ship and make our way along the docks toward the center of Ho Chi Minh City, known to an

In any rigidly ranked setting, no interaction can proceed until people assess each other's social standing. Thus, military personnel wear clear insignia to designate their level of authority. Don't we size up one another in much the same way in routine interactions, noting a person's rough age, quality of clothing, and manner for clues about social position?

earlier generation as Saigon. The government security officers wave us through the heavy metal gates. Pressed against the fence surrounding the port are dozens of men who operate cyclos (bicycles with a small carriage attached to the front), the Vietnamese equivalent of taxicabs. We wave them off, but spend the next twenty minutes shaking our heads at several drivers who pedal alongside pleading for our business. The pressure is uncomfortable. We decide to cross the street, but realize suddenly that there are no stop signs or signal lights—and the street is an unbroken stream of bicycles, cyclos, motorbikes, and small trucks. What to do? The locals don't bat an eye; they just walk at a steady pace across the street, parting waves of vehicles that close in again immediately behind them. Walk right into traffic? With our small children on our backs? Yup, we did it; that's the way it works in Vietnam.

Members of every society rely on social structure to make sense out of everyday situations. As one family's introduction to the streets of Vietnam suggests, the world can be disorienting—even frightening—when cultural norms are not what we expect. So what, then, are the building blocks of our daily lives?

STATUS

One building block of social structure is **status,** *a social position that an individual occupies.* Sociologists do not use the term "status" in its everyday meaning of "prestige," as when a bank president has more "status" than a bank teller. Rather, both "president" and "teller" are statuses within the bank organization.

Every status is part of our social identity and helps define our relationship to others. As Georg Simmel (1950:307), one of the founders of sociology, put it, "The first condition of having to deal with somebody . . . is knowing with *whom* one has to deal."

STATUS SET

Everyone occupies many statuses at once. The term **status set** refers to *all the statuses a person holds at a given time.* A teenage girl is a *daughter* to her parents, a *sister* to her brother, a *friend* to members of her social circle, and a *goalie* to others on her soccer team. Just as status sets branch out in many directions, they also change over the life course. A child grows into a parent, a student becomes a lawyer, and people marry to become husbands and wives, sometimes becoming single again as a result of divorce or death. Joining an organization or finding a job enlarges our status set; withdrawing from activities makes it smaller. Over a lifetime, individuals gain and lose dozens of statuses.

ASCRIBED AND ACHIEVED STATUS

Sociologists classify statuses in terms of how people obtain them. An **ascribed status** is *a social position a person receives at birth or assumes involuntarily later in life.* Examples of ascribed statuses include being a daughter, a Cuban, a

Role models teach us that any one person can truly make a difference for our world. In December, 1955, the driver of a city bus in Montgomery, Alabama, asked passenger Rosa Parks to give up her seat, as required by law, so a white man could sit down. She refused and was arrested, fingerprinted, and later fined $14 for the offense. This courageous act prompted Birmingham's African American population to boycott city buses, leading to the repeal of the bus-segregation law.

teenager, or a widower. Ascribed statuses are matters about which people have little or no choice.

By contrast, an **achieved status** refers to *a social position a person assumes voluntarily and that reflects personal ability and effort.* Among achieved statuses in the United States are being an honors student, an Olympic athlete, a spouse, a computer programmer, or a thief.

In practice, most statuses involve some combination of ascription and achievement. That is, people's ascribed statuses influence the statuses they achieve. People who achieve the status of lawyer, for example, are likely to share the ascribed trait of being born into relatively well-off families. By the same token, many less desirable statuses, such as criminal or drug addict or being out of work, are more easily achieved by people born into poverty.

MASTER STATUS

Some statuses matter more than others. A **master status** is *a status that has special importance for social identity, often shaping a person's entire life.* For most people, one's occupation is a master status because it conveys a great deal about social background, education, and income. In a few cases, being "a Kennedy" or "a Rockefeller" is enough by itself to push an individual into the limelight.

In a negative sense, serious illness also operates as a master status. Sometimes even lifelong friends avoid cancer patients or people with acquired immune deficiency syndrome (AIDS), simply because of their illness. Most societies of the world also limit the opportunities of women, whatever their abilities, making gender a master status (cf. Webster & Hysom, 1998).

Sometimes a physical disability serves as a master status to the point that we dehumanize people by perceiving them only in terms of their disability. In the box, two people with disabilities describe the problem.

ROLE

A second component of social interaction is **role**, *behavior expected of someone who holds a particular status.* People *hold* a status and *perform* a role (Linton, 1937b). Holding the status of student, for example, means one will attend classes, complete assignments, and, more broadly, devote a lot of time to personal enrichment through academic study.

Both statuses and roles vary by culture. In the United States, the status "uncle" refers to a sibling of either mother or father. In Vietnam, however, the word for "uncle" is different on the mother's and father's sides of the family, and the two men have different responsibilities. Of course, in every society, actual role performance varies according to an individual's unique personality, although some societies permit more individual expression than others.

SOCIAL DIVERSITY

Physical Disability as Master Status

In the following interviews, two women explain how a physical disability can become a master status, defining an individual. The first voice is twenty-nine-year-old Donna Finch, who holds a master's degree in social work and lives with her husband and son in Muskogee, Oklahoma. She is also blind.

> Most people don't expect handicapped people to grow up, they are always supposed to be children. . . . You aren't supposed to date, you aren't supposed to have a job, somehow you're just supposed to disappear. I'm not saying this is true of anyone else, but in my own case I think I was more intellectually mature than most children, and more emotionally immature. I'd say that not until the last four or five years have I felt really whole.

Rose Helman is an elderly woman living near New York City. She suffers from spinal meningitis and is also blind.

> You ask me if people are really different today than in the '20s and '30s. Not too much. They are still fearful of the handicapped. I don't know if fearful is the right word, but uncomfortable at least. But I can understand it somewhat; it happened to me. I once asked a man to tell me which staircase to use to get from the subway out to the street. He started giving me directions that were confusing, and I said, "Do you mind taking me?" He said, "Not at all." He grabbed me on the side with my dog on it, so I asked him to take my other arm. And he said, "I'm sorry, I have no other arm." And I said, "That's all right, I'll hold onto the jacket." It felt funny hanging onto the sleeve without the arm in it.

Source: Orlansky and Heward (1981).

ROLE SET

Because we occupy many statuses at once—a status set—everyday life is a mix of multiple roles. Robert Merton (1968) introduced the term **role set** to identify *a number of roles attached to a single status.*

Figure 6–1 shows four statuses of one individual, each status linked to a different role set. First, the woman occupies the status of "wife," with a conjugal role (such as confidante and sexual partner) towards her husband, with whom she shares a domestic role toward the household. Second, she holds the status of "mother," with routine responsibilities for her children (the maternal role), as well as their school and other organizations (the civic role). Third, as a professor, she interacts with students (the teacher role) and with other academics (the colleague role). Fourth, in her work as a researcher, she gathers data (the laboratory role) that she uses in her publications (the author role).

ROLE CONFLICT AND ROLE STRAIN

Most people in industrial societies juggle a host of responsibilities demanded by their various statuses and roles. As many mothers can testify, parenting as well as working outside the home can be both physically and emotionally draining. Sociologists thus recognize **role conflict** as *conflict among roles corresponding to two or more statuses.*

We experience role conflict when we find ourselves pulled in various directions while trying to respond to the many statuses we hold. Sometimes we decide that "something has to go." A governor, for example, may decide not to run for national office because the demands of a campaign would interfere with family life. In other cases, some people wait to have children in order to stay on the "fast track" for career success.

Even roles linked to a single status may make competing demands on us. **Role strain** refers to *tension among roles connected to a single status*. A plant supervisor may enjoy being friendly with other workers. At the same time, however, the supervisor has production goals and must maintain the personal distance needed to evaluate employees. In short, although not all cases of role strain present serious problems, performing the various roles attached to even one status can be something of a balancing act (Gigliotti & Huff, 1995).

One strategy for minimizing role conflict is to "compartmentalize" our lives so that we perform roles linked to one status at one time and place and carry out roles linked to another status in a completely different setting. A familiar example of this scheme is deciding to "leave the job at work" before heading home to one's family.

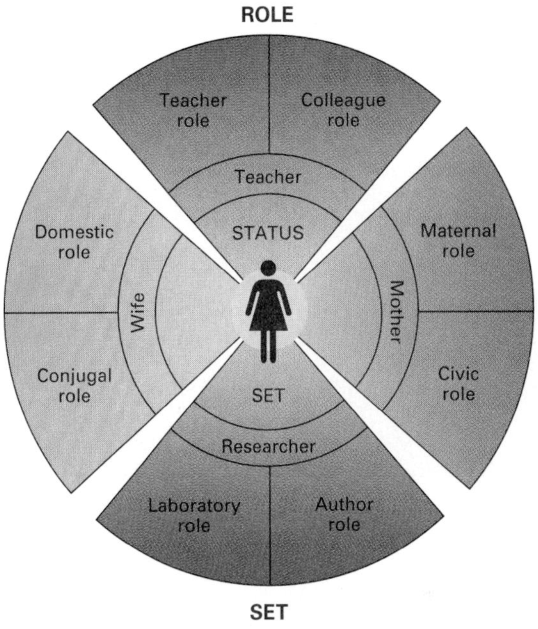

FIGURE 6–1 Status Set and Role Set

ROLE EXIT

After she herself left the life of a Catholic nun to become a university sociologist, Helen Rose Fuchs Ebaugh (1988) began to study *role exit*, the process by which people disengage from important social roles. Studying a range of "exes," including ex-nuns, ex-doctors, ex-husbands, and ex-alcoholics, Ebaugh identified elements common to the process of "becoming an ex."

According to Ebaugh, the process begins as people come to doubt their ability to continue in a certain role. As they imagine alternative roles, they ultimately reach a tipping point when they decide to pursue a new life. Even at this point, however, a past role can continue to influence our lives. "Exes" carry away a self-image shaped by an earlier role, which can interfere with building a new sense of self. An ex-nun, for example, may hesitate to wear stylish clothing and makeup.

"Exes" must also rebuild relationships with people who knew them in their "earlier life." Learning new social skills is another challenge. For example, Ebaugh reports, nuns who begin dating after decades in the church are often startled to learn that sexual norms are now very different from those they knew as teenagers.

THE SOCIAL CONSTRUCTION OF REALITY

More than sixty years ago, the Italian playwright Luigi Pirandello wrote the play *The Pleasure of Honesty*. The main character is Angelo Baldovino—a brilliant man with a checkered past. Baldovino enters the fashionable home of the Renni family and introduces himself in a most peculiar way:

> Inevitably we construct ourselves. Let me explain. I enter this house and immediately I become what I have to become, what I can become: I construct myself. That is, I present myself to you in a form suitable to the relationship I wish to achieve with you. And, of course, you do the same with me. (1962:157–58)

Baldovino's introduction suggests that, while behavior is guided by status and role, we also have the ability to shape what happens moment to moment. "Reality," in other words, is not as fixed as we may think.

The phrase **social construction of reality** describes *the process by which people creatively shape reality through social interaction*. This idea is the familiar foundation of the symbolic-interaction paradigm, described in earlier chapters. As Angelo Baldovino's remark suggests, quite a bit of "reality" remains unclear in everyone's mind, especially in unfamiliar situations. So we "present ourselves" in terms that suit the setting and our purposes, and, as others do the same, reality emerges.

Flirting is an everyday experience in reality construction. Each person offers information to the other, and hints at romantic interest. Yet the interaction proceeds with a tentative and often humorous air so that either individual can withdraw at any time without further obligation.

Social interaction, then, amounts to a complex negotiation. Most everyday situations involve at least some agreement about what's going on, but participants hold different perceptions of events to the extent that they have different interests and intentions. Our very choice of words is one way we put a "spin" on events. The box applies this idea to the language used by the military to create (or conceal?) reality.

"STREET SMARTS"

What people commonly call "street smarts" really amounts to constructing reality. In his biography *Down These Mean Streets*, Piri Thomas recalls moving to an apartment in Spanish Harlem. Returning home one evening, young Piri found himself cut off by Waneko, the leader of the local street gang, who was flanked by a dozen others.

> "Whatta ya say, Mr. Johnny Gringo," drawled Waneko.
>
> *Think man*, I told myself, *think your way out of a stomping. Make it good.* "I hear you 104th Street coolies are supposed to have heart," I said. "I don't know this for sure. You know there's a lot of streets where a whole 'click' is made out of punks who can't fight one guy unless they all jump him for the stomp." I hoped this would push Waneko into giving me a fair one. His expression didn't change.
>
> "Maybe we don't look at it that way."
>
> *Crazy, man*, I cheer inwardly, *the* cabron *is falling into my setup*. . . . "I wasn't talking to you," I said. "Where I come from, the pres is president 'cause he got heart when it comes to dealing."
>
> Waneko was starting to look uneasy. He had bit on my worm and felt like a sucker fish. His boys were now light on me. They were no longer so much interested in stomping me as seeing the outcome between Waneko and me. "Yeah," was his reply. . . .
>
> I knew I'd won. Sure, I'd have to fight; but one guy, not ten or fifteen. If I lost, I might still get stomped, and if I won I might get stomped. I took care of this with my next sentence. "I don't know you or your boys," I said, "but they look cool to me. They don't feature as punks."
>
> I had left him out purposely when I said "they." Now his boys were in a separate class. I had cut him off. He would have to fight me on his own, to prove his heart to himself, to his boys, and most important, to his turf. He got away from the stoop and asked, "Fair one, Gringo?" (1967:56–57)

This situation reveals the drama—sometimes subtle, sometimes savage—by which human beings creatively build reality. But, of course, not everyone enters a situation with equal power to affect the outcome. Should a police officer have come upon the fight between Piri and Waneko, both young men might well have ended up in jail.

APPLYING SOCIOLOGY

The "Spin" Game: Choosing Our Words Carefully

Military organizations choose their words carefully in order to "sanitize" the horror of war and make military action seem necessary and good. William Lutz, an English professor at Rutgers University, collected examples of language used by U.S. military officers in the Persian Gulf War. Read the following military terminology and the straight-talk translations. Do these military terms convey a reality or do they try to alter it?

Military language	Everyday meaning
Incontinent ordinance	Bombs or shells that miss their targets and hit civilians
Area denial weapons	Cluster bombs that kill and destroy anything within a particular area
Coercive potential	The capacity of bombs and shells to kill and injure the enemy
Suppressing assets	Reducing the enemy's ability to fight by killing people and destroying equipment
Ballistically induced aperture	Bullet hole
Scenario dependent, post-crisis environment	Whether we win or lose

THE THOMAS THEOREM

By displaying his wits and fighting with Waneko until they both tired, Piri Thomas won acceptance and became one of the gang. What took place that evening in Spanish Harlem is an example of the **Thomas theorem,** named after W. I. Thomas (1966:301; orig. 1931): *Situations that are defined as real are real in their consequences.*

Applied to social interaction, the Thomas theorem means that although reality is initially "soft" as it is fashioned, it can become "hard" in its effects. In the case we have described, local gang members saw Piri Thomas act in a worthy way, so, in their eyes, he *became* worthy.

ETHNOMETHODOLOGY

Rather than assume that reality is something "out there," the symbolic-interaction paradigm states that people create reality in everyday encounters. But how, exactly, do we define reality for ourselves? Answering this question is the objective of *ethnomethodology*, a specialized approach within the symbolic-interaction paradigm.

The term itself has two parts: The Greek *ethno* refers to people and how they understand their surroundings; "methodology" designates a set of methods or principles. Combining the two makes **ethnomethodology,** *the study of the way people make sense of their everyday surroundings.*

Ethnomethodology is largely the creation of Harold Garfinkel (1967), who challenged the then-dominant view of society as a broad, abstract "system" (recall the structural-functional approach of Emile Durkheim, described in Chapter 4, "Society"). Garfinkel wanted to explore how we make sense of countless familiar situations. Our talk and behavior, explained Garfinkel, rest on deeper assumptions about the world that, typically, we take for granted.

Think for a moment about what we assume in asking someone the simple question, "How are you?" Do we mean physically? Mentally? Spiritually? Financially? Do we even want an answer, or are we "just being polite"?

Ethnomethodology, then, explores the process of making sense of social encounters. Garfinkel argues that the only way to discover how we make sense of events is to purposely *break the rules*. By deliberately ignoring conventional rules and observing how people respond, we "tease out" how people build a reality. Thus, Garfinkel directed his students to refuse to "play the game" in a wide range of situations. Some students living with their parents started acting as if they were

SEEING OURSELVES

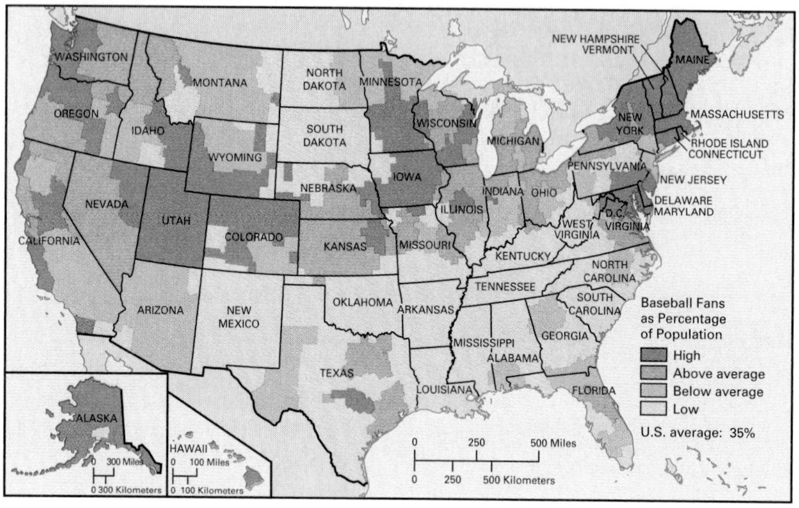

NATIONAL MAP 6–1
Baseball Fans across the United States

One in three U.S. adults claims to follow baseball. The map shows that fans are concentrated in the northern tier of states from New England to the Pacific Northwest. Why? What categories of people have a world view that celebrates this kind of activity? (*Hint:* Baseball is more likely to appeal to white males over forty years of age who were born in the United States.)

Source: From Michael J. Weiss, *Latitudes & Attitudes: An Atlas of American Tastes, Trends, Politics, and Passions*. Copyright © 1994 by Michael J. Weiss. Reprinted by permission of the author.

boarders rather than children; others entered stores and insisted on bargaining for items; others recruited people into simple games (like tic-tac-toe) only to intentionally flout the rules; still others initiated conversations while slowly moving closer and closer to the other person.

The students then reported on people's reactions. Typically, the "victims" became annoyed, suggesting how important our everyday reality is to us. Trying to identify exactly *why* people were disturbed led students to consider the unspoken agreements that underlie family life, shopping, fair play, and the like.

Some sociologists view ethnomethodology as less-than-serious research because it focuses on commonplace experiences and employs unusual, even bizarre, methods. Still, ethnomethodology heightens our awareness of the unnoticed patterns of everyday life.

REALITY BUILDING: CLASS AND CULTURE

People do not build everyday experience out of thin air. In part, how we act or what we see in our surroundings depends on our interests. Scanning the night sky, for example, lovers discover romance, while scientists view the same stars as hydrogen atoms fusing into helium. Social background also directs our perceptions, so that residents of, say, Spanish Harlem experience the world somewhat differently than those living on Manhattan's affluent East Side.

In truth, there is a lot of diversity in the reality construction that goes on across the United States. Take baseball, the activity long described as our national pastime. Only about one-third of U.S. adults describe themselves as fans and, as National Map 6–1 indicates, they are concentrated in particular regions of the country.

In global perspective, reality construction varies even more. Consider these everyday situations: People waiting for a bus in London typically "queue up" in a straight line; people in New York rarely are so orderly. The law forbids women in Saudi Arabia to drive cars, a ban unheard of in the United States. Fear of crime in our big cities is much greater than it is elsewhere—including London, Paris, Rome, Calcutta, and Hong Kong—and this sense of public danger shapes the daily realities of tens of millions of our citizens.

The general conclusion is that people build reality from the surrounding culture. Chapter 3 ("Culture") explains how people the world over find different meanings in specific gestures, so that sometimes travelers find themselves building a most unexpected reality. Similarly, what we "see" in a book or a film also depends on the assumptions we make about the world. In a study of popular culture, JoEllen Shively (1992) showed western films to men of European descent and to Native American men. Both categories claimed to enjoy the films but for different reasons. White men interpreted the films as praising rugged people striking out for the West to impose their will on nature. Native American men, by

When we enter the presence of others, we "construct" ourselves and begin a "presentation of self" that has much in common with a dramatic performance. The ancient Greeks, who understood the element of acting in everyday life, used the same word for "person" and "mask." The painting Mask with False Noses, *by Paul Cadmus, raises questions about the various ways people try to foster impressions in the minds of their audience.*

Paul Cadmus (b. 1904), *Mask with False Noses: An Allegory on Promiscuity*, 1955. Pen and ink and egg tempera on paper. 19 1/4 × 12 inches. Private collection, courtesy DC Moore Gallery, NYC. © Christie's Images.

contrast, saw in the same films a celebration of land and nature apart from any human ambitions.

If people the world over inhabit different realities, what about the full range of human emotions? Are emotions simply human, and thus much the same everywhere? Or do we draw our feelings from our culture? Cross-cultural research, described in the box on pages 148–49, indicates that emotions are rooted in both biology and culture.

DRAMATURGICAL ANALYSIS: "THE PRESENTATION OF SELF"

Erving Goffman (1922–1982) spent much of his life explaining how people in their everyday behavior are very much like actors performing on a stage. If we imagine ourselves as directors observing what goes on in some situational "theater," we can understand Goffman's **dramaturgical analysis**—*the study of social interaction in terms of theatrical performance.*

Dramaturgical analysis offers a fresh look at the concepts of status and role. A status is like a part in a play, and a role serves as a script, supplying dialogue and action for the characters. Goffman described each individual's "performance" as the **presentation of self,** *an individual's efforts to create specific impressions in the minds of others.* This process, sometimes called *impression management*, has several distinctive elements (Goffman, 1959, 1967).

PERFORMANCES

As we present ourselves in everyday situations, we convey information—consciously and unconsciously—to others. An individual's performance includes dress (costume), objects carried along (props), and tone of voice and particular gestures (manner). In addition, people craft their performance according to the setting (stage). We may joke loudly in a restaurant, for example, but lower our voices when entering a church. Individuals design settings, such as homes or offices, to bring about desired reactions in others.

An Application: The Doctor's Office

Consider how a physician uses an office to convey particular information to the audience of patients. Physicians enjoy high prestige and power in the United States, a fact evident upon entering a doctor's office. First, the physician is nowhere to be seen. Instead, in what Goffman describes as the "front region" of the setting, the patient encounters a receptionist who serves as a gatekeeper, deciding if and when the patient can meet the doctor. Who waits to see whom is, of course, a power game. And a simple survey of the doctor's waiting room, with patients (often impatiently) waiting to gain entry to the inner sanctum, leaves little doubt that the physician controls events.

The physician's private office and examination room are the "back region" of the setting. Here, the patient

GLOBAL SOCIOLOGY

The Sociology of Emotions: Do People Everywhere Feel the Same?

On a busy New York City sidewalk, a woman reacts angrily to an in-line skater who zooms past her. Her facial expression, together with a few choice words, broadcasts a strong emotion that North Americans easily recognize. But would an observer from Nigeria, Nicaragua, or New Guinea interpret her emotion the same way? In other words, do all people share similar feelings, and do they express them in the same way?

Paul Ekman and his colleagues studied people's emotions in many countries, including a small society in New Guinea. From this research, they concluded that people the world over share six basic emotions: anger, fear, disgust, happiness, surprise, and sadness. Moreover, people everywhere display these feelings using the same distinctive facial gestures. To Ekman, this commonality is evidence that much of our emotional life is universal rather than culturally variable, and that the display of emotion is biologically programmed in our facial features, muscles, and central nervous system.

But Ekman notes three ways in which emotional life does differ according to culture. First, *what triggers an emotion differs from one society to another*. Whether people define a particular situation as an insult (causing anger), a loss (calling forth sadness), or a mystical event (provoking surprise and awe) depends on culture. In other words, people in various societies react differently to the same event.

Second, *people display emotions according to the norms of their culture*. Every society has rules about when, where, and to whom an individual may exhibit certain emotions. Members of our own society, for example, typically express emotions more freely at home among family members than in the workplace among colleagues. Similarly, we expect children to express emotions to parents, although parents are taught to guard their emotions in front of their children.

Third, *societies differ in terms of how people cope with emotions*. Some societies encourage the expression of feelings, while others belittle emotions and expect members to suppress their feelings. Societies also display significant gender differences in this regard. Our culture labels emotional expression as feminine, expected of women but a sign of weakness among men. In other societies, however, this gender pattern is less pronounced or even reversed.

In sum, people everywhere experience the same basic emotions. But what sparks a particular emotion, how and where a person expresses it, and how people define emotions in general all vary as matters of culture.

Sources: Ekman (1980a; 1980b), Lutz & White (1986), and Lutz (1988).

confronts a wide range of props, such as medical books and framed degrees, that reinforce the impression that the physician has the specialized knowledge necessary to call the shots. In the office, the physician usually remains seated behind a desk—the larger and grander the desk, the greater the statement of power—while the patient is provided with only a chair.

The physician's appearance and manner convey still more information. The usual costume of white lab coat may have the practical function of keeping clothes from becoming soiled, but its social function is to let others know at a glance the physician's status. A stethoscope around the neck or a black medical bag in hand has the same purpose. A doctor's highly technical language, frequently mystifying, is also a statement of power. Finally, patients use the title "doctor," but they, in turn, are frequently addressed by their first names, which further underscores the physician's dominant position. The overall message of a doctor's performance is clear: "I will help you, but you must allow me to take charge."

NONVERBAL COMMUNICATION

Novelist William Sansom describes a fictional Mr. Preedy, an English vacationer on a beach in Spain:

> He took care to avoid catching anyone's eye. First, he had to make it clear to those potential companions of his holiday that they were of no concern to him whatsoever. He stared through them, round them, over them—eyes lost in space.

To most people in the United States, these expressions convey anger, fear, disgust, happiness, surprise, and sadness. But do people elsewhere in the world define them in the same way? Research suggests that all human beings experience the same basic emotions and display them to others in the same basic ways. But culture plays a part by specifying the situations that trigger one emotion or another.

> The beach might have been empty. If by chance a ball was thrown his way, he looked surprised; then let a smile of amusement light his face (Kindly Preedy), looked around dazed to see that there were people on the beach, tossed it back with a smile to himself and not a smile *at* the people. . . .
>
> [He] then gathered together his beach-wrap and bag into a neat sand-resistant pile (Methodical and Sensible Preedy), rose slowly to stretch his huge frame (Big-Cat Preedy), and tossed aside his sandals (Carefree Preedy, after all). (1956; quoted in Goffman, 1959:4–5)

Without uttering a single word, Mr. Preedy offers a great deal of information about himself to anyone observing him. This illustrates the process of **nonverbal communication,** *communication using body movements, gestures, and facial expressions rather than speech.*

People use many parts of the body to generate *body language*, that is, to convey information to others. As explained in the Global Sociology box, people the world over use facial expressions as the most significant form of body language. Smiling, for instance, conveys pleasure, although we distinguish among the deliberate smile of Kindly Preedy on the beach, the spontaneous smile of joy at seeing a friend, the pained smile of embarrassment, and the full, unrestrained smile of self-satisfaction we often associate with the "cat who ate the canary."

Eye contact is another crucial element of nonverbal communication. Generally, we use eye contact to invite social interaction. Someone across the room "catches

APPLYING SOCIOLOGY

Hide Those Lyin' Eyes: Can You Do It?

Poker players and police officers have long realized that a good liar has a real advantage. Deception is a familiar element of everyday interaction, if only because common politeness sometimes demands that we not say what we really think.

Can you tell when another person is trying to deceive you? Paul Ekman suggests paying close attention to four elements of a performance—words, voice, body language, and facial expression.

1. **Words.** Good liars mentally rehearse their lines, but they cannot always avoid a simple slip of the tongue—something the performer did not mean to say in quite that way. For example, a young man who is deceiving his parents by claiming that his roommate is a male friend rather than a female lover might mistakenly use the word "she" rather than "he" in conversation. The more complicated the deception, the more likely a performer is to make a revealing mistake.
2. **Voice.** Tone and patterns of speech contain clues to deception because they are hard to control. Especially when trying to hide a powerful emotion, a person cannot easily prevent the voice from trembling or breaking. Similarly, the individual may speak more quickly (suggesting anger) or slowly (indicating sadness). Nervous laughter, inappropriate pauses between words, or nonwords, such as "ah" and "ummm," also hint at discomfort.
3. **Body language.** A "leak" from body language may tip off an observer to deception as well. Subtle body movements, for example, give the impression of nervousness, as does sudden swallowing or rapid breathing. These are especially good clues to deception because few people can control them. Sometimes, *not* using the body in the expected way—as when a person's body fails to confirm words that suggest excitement—also suggests deception.
4. **Facial expressions.** Because facial expressions, too, are hard to control, they give away many phony performances. Have you picked the lying face? It's the one on the left. While a real smile usually has a relaxed expression and lots of "laugh lines" around the eyes, a phony smile seems forced and unnatural, with fewer wrinkles around the eyes.

Sources: Based on Ekman (1985) and Golden (1999b).

our eye," sparking a conversation. Avoiding another's eyes, by contrast, discourages communication. Hands, too, speak for us. Common hand gestures in our society convey, among other things, an insult, a request for a ride, an invitation for someone to join us, or a demand that others stop in their tracks. Gestures also supplement spoken words. Pointing in a menacing way at someone gives greater emphasis to a word of warning, just as shrugging the shoulders adds an air of indifference to the phrase "I don't know," and rapidly waving the arms lends urgency to the single word "Hurry!"

Body Language and Deception

As any actor knows, it is very difficult to pull off a perfect performance. In everyday performances, unintended body language can contradict our planned meaning. A teenage boy offers an explanation for getting home late, for example, but his mother doubts his words because

Near the end of his life, Erving Goffman (1979) studied the place of gender in advertising—that is, how advertising portrays the relative social position of men and women. Look at this Pepsi ad from an earlier era: What messages does it convey about women and men? Do you think today's advertising is different in this regard?

he avoids looking her in the eye. The movie star on a television talk show claims that her recent flop at the box office is "no big deal," but the nervous swing of her leg suggests otherwise. In practical terms, careful observation of nonverbal communication (most of which is not easily controlled) provides clues to deception, in much the same way that a lie detector records telltale changes in breathing, pulse rate, perspiration, and blood pressure.

Look at the two facial photographs in the box at the left. Can you tell which one is an honest smile and which one is a deception? Detecting phony performances is difficult, because no bodily gesture directly indicates that one is lying. Even so, because any performance involves so many expressions, few people can lie without making a slip and raising the suspicions of a careful observer. Therefore, the key to detecting deceit is to scan the whole performance with an eye for inconsistencies. The box provides a closer look at everyday lie detection.

GENDER AND PERSONAL PERFORMANCES

Because women are socialized to be less assertive than males, they tend to be more sensitive to nonverbal communication. Moreover, gender plays an important part in personal performances. Based on the work of Nancy Henley, Mykol Hamilton, and Barrie Thorne (1992), we can extend the present discussion of personal performances to spotlight the importance of gender.

Demeanor

Demeanor—general conduct or deportment—is a clue to personal power. Simply put, powerful people enjoy more freedom in how they act; subordinates act more formally and self-consciously. Off-color remarks, swearing, or putting one's feet on the desk may be acceptable for the boss, but not for a secretary. Similarly, powerful people can interrupt others whenever they wish, whereas subordinates are expected to display deference through silence (Smith-Lovin & Brody, 1989; Henley, Hamilton, & Thorne, 1992; Johnson, 1994).

Since women generally occupy positions of lesser power, demeanor is a gender issue as well. As Chapter 13 ("Gender Stratification") explains, about half of all working women in the United States hold clerical or service jobs that place them under the control of supervisors, who are usually men. Women, then, craft their personal performances more carefully than men and defer more often in everyday interaction.

Use of Space

How much space does a personal performance require? Power plays a key role because using more space is a sign of personal importance. Thus, men typically command more space than women, whether pacing back and forth before an audience or casually lounging on a beach. Why? Our culture traditionally has measured femininity by how *little* space women occupy (the standard of "daintiness") and masculinity by how *much* territory a man controls (the standard of "turf").

For both sexes, the concept of **personal space** refers to *the surrounding area over which a person makes some claim to privacy*. In the United States, people typically position themselves several feet apart when speaking; throughout the Middle East, by contrast, people stand much closer. But just about everywhere, men often intrude into women's personal space. A woman's encroachment into a man's personal space, however, is often seen as a sexual overture. Here, again, women have less power in everyday interaction than men.

Staring, Smiling, and Touching

Eye contact encourages interaction. Women more than men work to sustain eye contact. But men have their own distinctive brand of eye contact: *staring*. As Henley, Hamilton, and Thorne see it, men staring at women are claiming dominance and defining women as sexual objects.

Although frequently conveying pleasure, *smiling* can also be a sign of appeasement or submission. In a male-dominated world, therefore, women smile more than men.

Finally, mutual *touching* conveys intimacy and caring. Apart from close relationships, however, touching is generally something men do to women (and rarely, in our culture, to other men). A male physician touches the shoulder of his female nurse as they examine a report, a young man touches the back of his woman friend as he guides her across the street, or a male skiing instructor touches young women as he teaches them to ski. In such examples, the touching may evoke little response, but it amounts to a subtle ritual by which men claim dominance over women.

IDEALIZATION

Complex motives underlie human behavior. Even so, Goffman suggests, we construct performances to *idealize* our intentions. That is, we try to convince others (and perhaps ourselves) that what we do reflects ideal cultural standards rather than selfish motives.

Idealization is easily illustrated in the world of physicians and patients. In a hospital, physicians engage in a performance commonly described as "making rounds." Entering the room of a patient, the physician usually stops at the foot of the bed and silently examines the patient's medical chart. Afterward, physician and patient converse briefly. In ideal terms, this routine involves a physician making a personal visit to inquire about a patient's condition.

In reality, the picture is not so perfect. A physician may see several dozen patients a day and remember little about many of them, so that reading the chart is a chance to recall the patient's name and medical problems. Revealing the impersonality of much medical care would undermine the cultural ideal of the physician as one who is deeply concerned about the welfare of others.

Physicians, college professors, and other professionals typically idealize their motives for entering their chosen careers. They describe their work as "making a contribution to science," "helping others," "serving the community," and even "answering a calling from God." Rarely do they concede the less honorable, although common, motives of seeking the income, power, prestige, and leisure these occupations provide.

More generally, idealization is part of civility. Smiling and speaking politely to people we do not like are little lies that ease our way through social interactions. Even when we suspect that others are putting on an act, we are unlikely to challenge their performances, for reasons we explain next.

EMBARRASSMENT AND TACT

The famous professor mispronounces the dean's name; the visiting lecturer rises from the table to speak, unaware of the napkin that still hangs from her neck; the president becomes ill at a state dinner. As carefully as individuals may craft their performances, slip-ups of all kinds occur. The result is *embarrassment*, or discomfort following a spoiled performance. Goffman describes embarrassment simply as "losing face."

Embarrassment is an ever-present danger because, first, all performances typically contain some deception. And, second, most performances involve many elements that, in a thoughtless moment, can shatter the intended impression.

A curious fact is that an audience usually overlooks flaws in a performance, allowing an actor to avoid embarrassment. If we do point out a misstep ("Excuse me, but did you know your fly is open?"), we do it quietly and only to help someone avoid even greater loss of face. In Hans Christian Andersen's classic fable "The Emperor's New Clothes," the child who blurts out that the emperor is parading about naked tells the truth but is scolded for being rude.

Often, too, members of an audience actually help the performer recover a flawed performance. *Tact*, then,

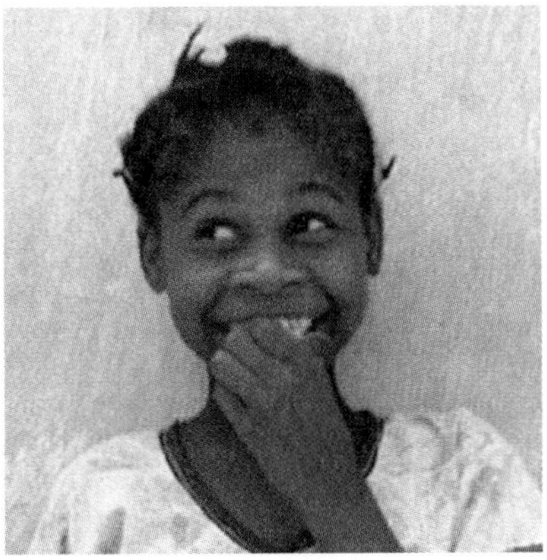

Hand gestures vary widely from one culture to another. Yet people everywhere define a chuckle, grin, or smirk in response to someone's performance as an indication that one does not take another person seriously. Therefore, the world over, people who cannot restrain their mirth tactfully cover their faces.

amounts to helping someone "save face." After hearing a supposed expert make an embarrassingly inaccurate remark, for example, people may tactfully ignore the comment as if it had never been spoken. Or mild laughter may indicate that they wish to treat what was said as a joke. Or a listener may simply respond, "I'm sure you didn't mean that," noting the statement but not allowing it to destroy the actor's performance.

Why is tact so common? Because embarrassment provokes discomfort not simply for the actor but for *everyone*. Just as a theater audience feels uneasy when an actor forgets a line, people who observe someone else's awkward behavior are reminded of how fragile their own performances are. Socially constructed reality thus works like a dam holding back a sea of chaos. Should one person's performance spring a leak, others tactfully help make repairs. Everyone, after all, lends a hand in building reality, and no one wants to see it suddenly swept away.

In sum, Goffman's research shows that, although behavior is spontaneous in some respects, it is more patterned than we like to think. Almost 400 years ago, William Shakespeare captured this idea in memorable lines that still ring true:

> All the world's a stage,
> And all the men and women merely players:
> They have their exits and their entrances;
> And one man in his time plays many parts.
> (*As You Like It*, II)

INTERACTION IN EVERYDAY LIFE: TWO APPLICATIONS

We have examined the major elements of social interaction. The final sections of this chapter apply these lessons to two important, yet very different, aspects of everyday life: language and humor.

LANGUAGE: THE GENDER ISSUE

As Chapter 3 ("Culture") explains, language is the thread that joins members of a society into the symbolic web we call culture. Language conveys not only a surface meaning but also deeper levels of meaning. One level involves gender. Language defines men and women differently in at least three ways, involving control, value, and attention.[1]

Language and Power

A young man proudly astride his new motorcycle rolls up his friend's driveway and eagerly asks, "Isn't she a beauty?" On the surface, the question has little to do with gender. Yet, why does he use the pronoun "she" rather than "he" or "it" to refer to his prized possession? The answer is that men often use language to

[1]The following sections draw primarily on Henley, Hamilton, & Thorne (1992). Additional material comes from Thorne, Kramarae, & Henley (1983).

APPLYING SOCIOLOGY

Gender and Language: "You Just Don't Understand!"

In the story that opened this chapter, a couple faces a situation that rings all too true to many people: When lost, men grumble to themselves, perhaps blame their partners, but avoid asking others for directions. For their part, women can't seem to understand such behavior.

Deborah Tannen, who has conducted extensive research on the linguistic differences that separate the sexes, explains. Men, she claims, see most daily encounters as competitive situations, so getting lost is bad enough without asking for help and thereby letting someone else get "one up" on them. By contrast, because women in the United States hold a generally subordinate position, they are socialized to ask for help. Sometimes, Tannen points out, women will ask for assistance even when they don't need it.

A similar gender-linked problem common to couples involves what men call "nagging." Consider the following exchange (Adler, 1990:74):

SYBIL: What's wrong, honey?

HAROLD: Nothing . . .

SYBIL: Something is bothering you; I can tell.

HAROLD: I told you nothing is bothering me. Leave me alone.

SYBIL: But I can see that something is wrong.

HAROLD: OK. Just why do you think something is bothering me?

SYBIL: Well, for one thing, you're bleeding all over your shirt.

HAROLD [*now irritated*]: It doesn't bother me.

SYBIL [*losing her temper*]: WELL, IT SURE IS BOTHERING ME!

HAROLD: I'll go change my shirt.

The problem couples face in communicating is that what one partner *intends* by a comment is not always what the other *hears* in the words. To Sybil, her opening question is an attempt at cooperative problem solving. She can see that something is wrong with Harold (who has cut himself while doing yard work), and she wants to help him. But Harold interprets her pointing out his problem as belittling, and tries to close off the discussion. Sybil, confident that Harold needs just to understand that she only wants to be helpful, repeats herself. This reaction sets in motion a vicious circle in which Harold, thinking his wife is nagging because she thinks he cannot take care of himself, responds by digging in his heels. His response, in turn, makes Sybil all the more sure that she needs to do something. And round it goes until somebody gets angry.

In the end, Harold gives in only to the extent that he agrees to change his shirt. But notice he still refuses to discuss the original problem. Misunderstanding his wife's motives, Harold just wants Sybil to leave him alone. Likewise, Sybil fails to understand her husband's view of the situation and walks away thinking that he is a stubborn grouch.

Sources: Adler (1990) and Tannen (1990).

establish control over their surroundings. That is, a man attaches a female pronoun to a motorcycle (or car, boat, or other object) because it reflects the power of *ownership*.

Another control function of language relates to people's names. Traditionally in the United States and in many other parts of the world, a woman takes the family name of the man she marries. While few people in this country consider this an explicit statement of a man's ownership of a woman, many think it reflects male dominance. For this reason, an increasing share of married women (almost 15 percent) have kept their own name or merged the two family names.

Language and Value

The English language usually treats as masculine whatever has greater value, force, or significance. For instance, the adjective "virtuous," meaning "morally worthy" or "excellent," is derived from the Latin word *vir*, meaning "man." By contrast, the disparaging adjective "hysterical" is derived from the Greek word *hyster*, meaning "uterus."

In many familiar ways, language also confers different value on the two sexes. Traditional masculine terms such as "king" and "lord" have retained their positive meaning, while comparable terms, such as "queen," "madam," and "dame" have acquired negative connotations in contemporary usage. Language thus both mirrors social attitudes and helps to perpetuate them.

Similarly, use of the suffixes "ette" and "ess" to denote femininity usually devalues the words to which they are added. For example, a "major" has higher standing than a "majorette," as does a "host" in relation to a "hostess." And, certainly, men's groups with names such as the St. Louis Rams carry more stature than women's groups with names like the Radio City Music Hall Rockettes.

Why do we associate ownership with men and characterize what is owned as feminine? How easily can you imagine renaming this boat with the gender reversed?

Language and Attention

Language also shapes reality by directing greater attention to masculine activity. In the English language, the plural pronoun "they" is gender-neutral. But the corresponding singular pronouns "he" and "she" specify gender. According to traditional grammatical practice, we use "he," along with the possessive "his" and objective "him," to refer to *all* people. Thus, we assume that the bit of wisdom "He who hesitates is lost" refers to women as well as to men. But this practice also reflects the cultural pattern of neglecting the existence of women.

The English language has no gender-neutral, third-person singular personal pronoun. In recent years, however, the plural pronouns "they" and "them" increasingly have gained currency as a singular pronoun ("A person should do as they please"). This usage violates grammatical rules, yet there is no doubt that English is changing to accept such gender-neutral constructions.

Grammar aside, the mix of gender and language is likely to remain a source of miscommunication between women and men. In the box, Harold and Sybil, whose misadventures in trying to find a friend's home opened this chapter, return to illustrate how the two sexes often seem to be speaking different languages.

HUMOR: PLAYING WITH REALITY

Humor is an important part of everyday life. But, while everyone laughs at a joke, few people think about what makes something funny or why humor is a part of every culture in the world. We can apply many of the ideas developed in this chapter to explore the character of humor.[2]

The Foundation of Humor

Humor is a product of reality construction; specifically, it stems from the contrast between two different realities. Generally, one reality is *conventional*, that is, what

[2]The ideas discussed here are those of the author (1987), except as otherwise noted. The general approach draws on work discussed in this chapter, especially on the ideas of Erving Goffman.

CRITICAL THINKING

Double Take: Real Headlines That Make People Laugh

Humor is generated by mixing two distinct and opposing realities. Here are several real headlines from recent newspapers. Read each one and identify the conventional meaning intended by the writer as well as the unconventional interpretation that generates humor.

"Police Begin Campaign to Run Down Jaywalkers"

"Drunk Gets Nine Months in Violin Case"

"Survivor of Siamese Twins Joins Parents"

"Iraqi Head Seeks Arms"

"Stud Tires Out"

"Prostitutes Appeal to Pope"

"Panda Mating Fails: Veterinarian Takes Over"

"Soviet Virgin Lands Short of Goal Again"

"Teacher Strikes Idle Kids"

"Squad Helps Dog Bite Victim"

"Miners Refuse to Work after Death"

"Killer Sentenced to Die for Second Time in Ten Years"

"War Dims Hope for Peace"

"British Left Waffles on Falkland Islands"

"Stolen Painting Found by Tree"

What do you think?

1. *For each headline, do you see the "expected" and "unexpected" meanings?*
2. *Which headlines are most funny? Why?*
3. *Can you think of other everyday examples of humor?*

Source: Thanks to Kay Fletcher.

people expect in a specific situation. The other reality is *unconventional*, an unexpected violation of cultural patterns. Humor, therefore, arises from contradiction, ambiguity, and double meanings found in differing definitions of the same situation. Note how this principle works in the newspaper headlines in the box.

There are countless ways to mix realities and thereby generate humor. Contrasting realities emerge from statements that contradict themselves, like "Nostalgia is not what it used to be." Switching words can create humor, as in Oscar Wilde's line: "Work is the curse of the drinking class." Even reordering syllables does the trick, as in the case of the (probably fictitious) country song, "I'd rather have a bottle in front of me than a frontal lobotomy."

Of course, a joke can be built the other way around, so that the comic leads the audience to *expect* an unconventional answer and then delivers a very ordinary one. When a reporter asked the famous desperado Willy Sutton why he robbed banks, for example, he replied dryly: "Because that's where the money is." However a joke is constructed, the greater the opposition or incongruity between the two definitions of reality, the greater the humor.

When telling jokes, the comedian can strengthen this opposition in various ways. One common technique is for the comic to present the first, or conventional, remark in conversation with another actor, then to turn toward the audience to deliver the second, unexpected line. In a Marx Brothers film, Groucho swaggers in front of a young woman and brags, "This morning I shot a lion in my pajamas!" Then, dropping his voice and turning to the camera, he adds, "What the lion was doing in my pajamas *I'll never know*." Such "changing channels" underscores the incongruity of the two parts. Following the same logic, stand-up comics may "reset" the audience to conventional expectations by interjecting "But, seriously, folks . . ." after one joke and before the next one.

To construct the strongest contrast in meaning, comedians pay careful attention to their performances—the precise words they use and the split-second timing of their delivery. A joke is "well told" if the comic creates the sharpest possible opposition between the realities, just as humor falls flat in a careless performance. Since the key to humor lies in the opposition of realities, we can see why the climax of a joke is called the "*punch* line."

Because humor involves challenging established social conventions, most U.S. comedians—including the comedian Chris Rock—have been social "outsiders," members of racial and ethnic minorities.

The Dynamics of Humor: "Getting It"

Someone who does not understand both the conventional and unconventional realities in a joke may complain, "I don't get it." To "get" humor, the audience must understand the two realities involved well enough to appreciate their difference.

But comics may make getting the joke harder still by leaving out some important piece of information. The audience, therefore, must pay attention to the *stated* elements of the joke and then fill in the missing pieces on their own. As a simple case, consider the reflection of movie producer Hal Roach upon reaching his one hundredth birthday:

> "If I had known I would live to be one hundred, I would have taken better care of myself!"

Here, getting the joke depends on realizing that Roach must have taken pretty good care of himself since he lived to be one hundred in the first place. Or take one of W. C. Fields's lines:

> "Some weasel took the cork out of my lunch."

"Some lunch!" we think to ourselves to "finish" the joke.

Here is an even more complex joke, found on the wall of a college rest room:

> Dyslexics of the World, Untie!

To get this one, you must know, first, that dyslexia causes a person to reverse letters in words; second, one must recognize the line as a play on Karl Marx's call to the world's workers to unite; third, one must recognize "untie" as an anagram of "unite," as a disgruntled dyslexic person might write it.

Why would an audience be required to make this sort of effort in order to understand a joke? Simply because our enjoyment of a joke is heightened by the pleasure of having completed the puzzle necessary to "get it." In addition, getting the joke also confers a favored insider status. We can also understand the frustration of *not* getting a joke: fear of being judged stupid coupled with being excluded from a pleasure shared by others. Not surprisingly, outsiders in such a situation sometimes fake getting the joke, or someone may tactfully explain the joke so the other person doesn't feel left out.

But, as the old saying goes, if a joke has to be explained, it won't be very funny. Besides taking the edge off the language and timing on which the *punch* depends, an explanation removes the mental involvement and greatly reduces the listener's pleasure.

The Topics of Humor

People throughout the world smile and laugh, making humor a universal human trait. But the world's people differ in what they find funny, so humor rarely travels well.

October 1, 1994, Kobe, Japan. Can you share a joke with people who live halfway around the world? At dinner, I ask two Japanese college women to tell me a joke. "You know 'crayon'?" Asako asks. I nod.

There are two sides to humor. On the one hand, people use humor as a safety valve to express potentially disruptive sentiments with little harm. On the other hand, people also make fun of others, elevating themselves at the expense of someone else.

"How do you ask for a crayon in Japanese?" I respond that I have no idea. She laughs out loud as she says what sounds like "crayon crayon." Her companion Mayumi laughs, too. My wife and I sit awkwardly, straight-faced. Asako relieves some of our embarrassment by explaining that the Japanese word for "give me" is kureyo, which sounds like "crayon." I force a smile.

What is humorous to the Japanese, then, may be lost on the Chinese, Iraqis, or people in the United States. To some degree, too, the social diversity of our own country means that different types of people will find humor in different situations. New Englanders, southerners, and westerners have their own brands of humor, as do Latinos and Anglos, fifteen- and forty-year-olds, Wall Street bankers and southwestern rodeo riders.

But, for everyone, humor deals with topics that lend themselves to double meanings or *controversy*. For example, the first jokes many of us learned as children were about culturally taboo bodily functions. The mere mention of "unmentionable acts" or even certain parts of the body can dissolve young faces in laughter.

Are there jokes that do break through the culture barrier? Yes, but they must touch upon universal human experiences such as, say, turning on a friend.

I think of a number of jokes, but none seems likely to work. Understanding jokes about the United States is difficult for people who have never been there. Is there something more universal? Inspiration: "Two fellows are walking in the woods and come upon a huge bear. One guy leans over and tightens up the laces on his running shoes. 'Jake,' says the other, 'what are you doing? You can't outrun this bear!' 'I don't have to outrun the bear,' responds Jake, 'I just have to outrun you!'" Smiles all around.

Humor and health have always been related. During the Middle Ages, people used the word *humors* (derived from the Latin *humidus*, meaning "moist") to mean a balance of bodily fluids that regulate a person's well-being. Researchers today document the power of humor to reduce stress and improve health, confirming the old saying that "Laughter is the best medicine" (Robinson, 1983; Haig, 1988). But, at the extreme, people who always take conventional reality lightly risk being defined as deviant or even mentally ill (a common stereotype depicts insane people as laughing uncontrollably, and we have long dubbed mental hospitals "funny farms").

Then, too, every social group considers certain topics too sensitive for humorous treatment. One can joke about such things, but doing so may bring criticism for telling a "sick" joke (and, therefore, *being* sick). People's religious beliefs, tragic accidents, or appalling crimes are the stuff of "sick" jokes.

The Functions of Humor

Humor is found everywhere because it works as a safety valve that vents potentially disruptive sentiments with little harm. That is, humor provides a way to express an opinion on a sensitive topic without being serious. Having said something controversial, a person can also use humor to diffuse the situation by simply stating, "I didn't mean anything by what I said; it was just a joke!"

Similarly, people use humor to relieve tension in uncomfortable situations. One study of medical examinations found most patients begin to joke with doctors to ease their own nervousness (Baker et al., 1997).

Humor and Conflict

If humor holds the potential to comfort those who laugh, it can also be used to harm others. Men who tell jokes about women, for example, typically are voicing some measure of hostility toward them (Powell & Paton, 1988; Benokraitis & Feagin, 1995). Similarly, jokes at the expense of gay people reveal the tensions surrounding sexual orientation in the United States. Humor is often a sign of real conflict in situations where one or both parties choose not to bring the conflict out into the open (Primeggia & Varacalli, 1990).

"Put-down" jokes function to make one category of people feel good at the expense of another. After collecting and analyzing jokes from many societies, Christie Davies (1990) concluded that conflict among ethnic groups is one driving force behind humor almost everywhere. The typical ethnic joke makes fun of some disadvantaged category of people, thereby making the jokester and the audience superior. Given the Anglo-Saxon traditions of U.S. society, Poles and other ethnic and racial minorities have long been the butt of jokes, as have Newfoundlanders ("Newfies") in eastern Canada, the Irish in Scotland, Sikhs in India, Turks in Germany, Hausas in Nigeria, Tasmanians in Australia, and Kurds in Iraq.

Disadvantaged people, of course, also make fun of the powerful, although usually with some care. Women in the United States joke about men, just as African Americans find humor in white people's ways, and poor people poke fun at the rich. Throughout the world, people target their leaders with humor, and officials in some countries take such jokes seriously enough to suppress them (cf. Speier, 1998).

In sum, the significance of humor is much greater than we may think. Humor is a means of mental escape from a conventional world that is never entirely to our liking (Flaherty, 1984, 1990; Yoels & Clair, 1995). Indeed, this fact explains why so many of our nation's comedians come from among the ranks of historically oppressed peoples, including Jews and African Americans. As long as we maintain a sense of humor, we assert our freedom and are not prisoners of reality. By putting a smile on our faces, we change ourselves and the world just a little.

SUMMARY

1. Social structure provides guidelines for behavior, making everyday life understandable and predictable.
2. A major component of social structure is status. Within an entire status set, a master status has special significance for a person's identity.
3. Ascribed statuses are involuntary, whereas achieved statuses are earned. In practice, most statuses are both ascribed and achieved.
4. Role is the dynamic expression of a status. Incompatible roles linked to two or more statuses generate role conflict; likewise, incompatible roles linked to a single status cause role strain.
5. "The social construction of reality" refers to the idea that we build the social world through our interactions with others.
6. The Thomas theorem states, "Situations defined as real become real in their consequences."
7. Ethnomethodology reveals the assumptions and understandings people have of their social world.
8. Dramaturgical analysis views everyday life as theatrical performance, as people do what they can to create particular impressions in the minds of others.
9. Social power affects performances, which is one reason that men's behavior typically differs from women's.
10. Everyday behavior carries the ever-present danger of embarrassment, or "loss of face." People use tact to prevent others' performances from breaking down.
11. Language is vital to the process of socially constructing reality. In various ways, language defines women and men differently, generally to the advantage of men.
12. Humor stems from the difference between conventional and unconventional definitions of a situation. Because humor is an element of culture, people throughout the world find different situations funny.

KEY CONCEPTS

social interaction (p. 139) the process by which people act and react in relation to others

status (p. 140) a social position that an individual occupies

status set (p. 140) all the statuses a person holds at a given time

ascribed status (p. 140) a social position a person receives at birth or assumes involuntarily later in life

achieved status (p. 141) a social position a person assumes voluntarily and that reflects personal ability and effort

master status (p. 141) a status that has special importance for social identity, often shaping a person's entire life

role (p. 141) behavior expected of someone who holds a particular status

role set (p. 142) a number of roles attached to a single status

role conflict (p. 142) conflict among the roles corresponding to two or more statuses

role strain (p. 143) tension among roles connected to a single status

social construction of reality (p. 143) the process by which people creatively shape reality through social interaction

Thomas theorem (p. 145) W. I. Thomas's assertion that situations that are defined as real are real in their consequences

ethnomethodology (p. 145) Harold Garfinkel's term for the study of the way people make sense of their everyday surroundings

dramaturgical analysis (p. 147) Erving Goffman's term for the study of social interaction in terms of theatrical performance

presentation of self (p. 147) an individual's efforts to create specific impressions in the minds of others

nonverbal communication (p. 149) communication using body movements, gestures, and facial expressions rather than speech

personal space (p. 152) the surrounding area over which a person makes some claim to privacy

CRITICAL-THINKING QUESTIONS

1. Consider ways in which a physical disability can serve as a master status. What assumptions do people commonly make about the mental ability of someone with a physical disability such as cerebral palsy? What assumptions are made about the person's sexuality?
2. How do people on a first date present themselves to each other and, in the process, construct reality? What kind of information does each offer? Why do people in such a situation often begin with "small talk"?
3. George Jean Nathan once quipped, "I only drink to make other people interesting." What does this mean in terms of reality construction? Can you identify the elements of humor in this statement?
4. Here is a joke about sociologists: "Question—How many sociologists does it take to change a light bulb? Answer—None, because there is nothing wrong with the light bulb; it's *the system* that needs to be changed!" What makes this joke funny? What sort of people are likely to get it? What kind of people probably won't? Why?

APPLICATIONS AND EXERCISES

1. Write down as many of your own statuses as you can. Do you consider any statuses to be a master status? To what extent are each of your statuses ascribed and achieved?
2. During the next twenty-four hours, every time people ask "How are you?" stop and actually give a truthful answer. What happens when you respond to a "polite" question in an unexpected way? (Watch people's body language as well as note what they say.) What does this experiment suggest about everyday interactions?
3. This chapter illustrated Erving Goffman's ideas with a description of a physician's office. Investigate the offices of several professors in the same way. What furniture is there, and how is it arranged? What "props" do professors use? How are the offices of physicians and professors different? Why?
4. Spend an hour or two walking around the businesses of your town (or shops at a local mall). Observe the presence of women and men at each location. Based on your observations, would you conclude that physical space is "gendered"?
5. Install the CD-ROM packaged in the back of this new textbook to access a variety of study, review, and applications exercises designed to help you better understand the material covered in this chapter. The CD includes an author's tip video, as well as interactive maps, video application exercises, Web links, and study questions.

SITES TO SEE

http://www.prenhall.com/macionis

Visit the interactive Web site that accompanies this text. Begin by clicking on the cover of your book. You will find a chapter-by-chapter study guide, practice tests, chat room, and many suggested Web links.

http://www.census.gov/genealogy/www/namesearch.html

Many interesting patterns of everyday life involve names. This Census Bureau Web site has a search engine for names. Study the frequency of different last names (or investigate first names) in the U.S. population. What patterns can you find? How many others share your own name?

http://www.ai.mit.edu/projects/kismet

Is it possible to build a machine capable of human interaction? That is the goal of robotics engineers at the Massachusetts Institute of Technology. Their Web site provides details and photographs. Look over their work and think about issues raised in this chapter. In what ways are machines able, and unable, to mimic human behavior?

http://www.sociologyplace.com

You can access a wealth of additional study resources and links to career, writing, and review tools dealing with your Intro to Sociology course. Your new textbook includes a passcode that you can use to enter this site. With a used textbook, you can purchase a subscription on this site.

CHAPTER 7

Pablo Picasso (1881–1973)
The Three Dancers, 1925

GROUPS AND ORGANIZATIONS

Back in 1948, people in Pasadena, California, paid little attention to the opening of a new restaurant. Yet one small business—owned by brothers Maurice and Richard McDonald—would transform not only the entire restaurant industry but introduce a new organizational model copied by countless businesses of all kinds.

The McDonald brothers' basic concept—which we now call "fast food"—was to serve meals quickly and cheaply to large numbers of people. The brothers trained employees to perform highly specialized jobs, so that one person grilled hamburgers while others "dressed" them, made french fries, whipped up milkshakes, and presented the food to the customers in assembly-line fashion.

As the years went by, the McDonald brothers prospered, and they decided to move their single restaurant from Pasadena to San Bernardino. It was there, in 1954, that Ray Kroc, a traveling blender and mixer merchant, paid them a visit.

Kroc was fascinated by the efficiency of the brothers' system and saw the potential for a whole chain of fast-food restaurants. The three launched the plan as partners. Soon, however, Kroc bought out the McDonalds and went on to become one of the greatest success stories of all time. Today, more than 20,000 McDonald's restaurants serve people throughout the United States and around the world.

The success of McDonald's is evidence of more than just the popularity of hamburgers. The larger importance of McDonald's lies in the extent to which the principles that guide this company are coming to dominate social life in the United States and elsewhere (Ritzer, 1993, 1998).

We begin with an examination of *social groups*, the clusters of people with whom we interact in much of our daily lives. As we shall see, the scope of group life expanded greatly during the twentieth century. From a world of families, local neighborhoods, and small businesses, our society now turns on the operation of huge businesses and other bureaucracies that sociologists describe as *formal organizations*. Understanding how this expanding scale of life came to be, and what it means for us as individuals, are this chapter's main objectives.

SOCIAL GROUPS

Almost everyone seeks a sense of belonging, which is the experience of group life. A **social group** refers to *two or more people who identify and interact with one another.* Human beings come together in couples, families, circles of friends, churches, clubs, businesses, neighborhoods, and large organizations. Whatever its form, a group is made up of people with shared experiences, loyalties, and interests. In short, while keeping their individuality, members of social groups also think of themselves as a special "we."

Not every collection of individuals can be called a group. People with a status in common, such as women, homeowners, soldiers, millionaires, and Roman Catholics, are not a group but a *category*. Though they know

As human beings, we live our lives as members of groups. Such groups may be large or small, temporary or long-lasting. The United States is regarded as a country where people are especially likely to form groups based on kinship, heritage, or some shared interest.

others who hold the same status, the vast majority are strangers to one another.

What about students sitting together in a lecture hall or bathers enjoying a day at the beach? Some people in such settings may interact, but not very much. These temporary, loosely formed collections of people are better termed a *crowd*. In general, crowds are too anonymous and transitory to qualify as groups.

The right circumstances, however, can turn a crowd into a group. People riding in an elevator that stalls between floors generally recognize their common plight and turn to each other for help. Sometimes out of accidents and disasters, people form lasting relationships.

PRIMARY AND SECONDARY GROUPS

Acquaintances commonly greet one another with a smile and a "Hi! How are you?" The response is usually, "Just fine, thanks. How about you?" This answer, of course, is often more scripted than truthful. In most cases, providing a detailed account of how you are *really* doing would make most people feel so awkward they would beat a hasty retreat.

Sociologists designate two types of social groups, depending on the degree of genuine personal concern that members show for one another. According to Charles Horton Cooley (1864–1929), a **primary group** is *a small social group whose members share personal and enduring relationships.* Bound by *primary relationships,* people typically spend a great deal of time together, engage in a wide range of activities, and feel that they know one another well. Although not without conflict from time to time, members of primary groups display real concern for each other's welfare. The family is every society's most important primary group.

Cooley called these personal and tightly integrated groups *primary* because they are among the first groups we experience in life. In addition, the family and early play groups hold primary importance in the socialization process, shaping attitudes, behavior, and social identity.

Primary relationships give people a comforting sense of security. In the familiar social circle of family or friends, people feel they can "be themselves" without worrying about the impression they are making.

Members of primary groups help one another in many ways, but they generally think of their group as an end in itself rather than as a means to other ends. In other words, we prefer to think that kinship and friendship link people who "belong together." Moreover, members of a primary group tend to view each other as unique and irreplaceable. Especially in the family, we are bound to others by emotion and loyalty. Brothers and sisters may not always get along, but they always remain siblings.

In contrast to the primary group, the **secondary group** is *a large and impersonal social group whose members pursue a specific goal or activity.* In most respects, secondary groups have precisely the opposite characteristics of primary groups. *Secondary relationships* involve weak emotional ties and little personal knowledge of one another. Most secondary groups are short term, beginning and ending without particular significance. Students in a college course, for instance, who may or may not see each other after the semester ends, exemplify the secondary group.

Secondary groups include many more people than primary groups. For example, dozens or even hundreds of people may work together in the same office, yet most of them pay only passing attention to one another. In some cases, time may transform a group from secondary to primary, as with co-workers who share an office for many years. But, generally, members of a secondary group do not think of themselves as "we."

Whereas members of primary groups display a *personal orientation*, people in secondary groups have a *goal orientation*. Secondary ties need not be hostile or cold, of course. Interaction among students, co-workers, and business associates is often pleasant even if it is impersonal. But while primary group members define themselves according to *who* they are in terms of kinship or personal qualities, people in secondary groups look to one another for *what* they are or what they can do for each other. In secondary groups, we tend to "keep score," mindful of what we give others and what we receive in return. This goal orientation means that secondary group members usually remain formal and polite. In a secondary relationship, therefore, we ask the question "How are you?" without expecting a truthful answer.

Table 7–1 summarizes the characteristics that distinguish primary and secondary groups. Keep in mind that these traits define two types of groups in ideal terms; many real groups contain elements of both. But putting these concepts at opposite ends of a continuum helps us describe and analyze group life.

Many people think that small towns and rural areas have mostly primary relationships and that large cities are characterized by more secondary ties. This generalization holds much truth, but some urban neighborhoods—especially those populated by people of a single ethnic or religious category—are very tightly knit. National Map 7–1 on page 166 presents one state-by-state indicator of primary or secondary social ties, namely, how likely people are to resolve disputes personally or to seek redress formally in court.

TABLE 7–1 Primary Groups and Secondary Groups: A Summary

	Primary Group ⟷	Secondary Group
Quality of Relationships	Personal orientation	Goal orientation
Duration of Relationships	Usually long term	Variable; often short term
Breadth of Relationships	Broad; usually involving many activities	Narrow; usually involving few activities
Subjective Perception of Relationships	As ends in themselves	As means to an end
Typical Examples	Families; circles of friends	Co-workers; political organizations

GROUP LEADERSHIP

How do groups operate? One important element of group dynamics is leadership. Though a small circle of friends may have no leader at all, most large secondary groups have a formal chain of command.

Two Leadership Roles

Groups typically benefit from two kinds of leadership. **Instrumental leadership** refers to *group direction that emphasizes the completion of tasks.* Members look to instrumental leaders to "get things done." **Expressive leadership,** on the other hand, *focuses on collective well-being.* Expressive leaders take less of an interest in achieving goals than in raising group morale and minimizing tension and conflict among members.

Because they concentrate on performance, instrumental leaders usually have formal, secondary relations with other group members. Instrumental leaders give orders and reward or punish members according to their contribution to the group's efforts. Expressive leaders, however, build more personal, primary ties. They offer sympathy to a member going through a tough time, keep the group united, and lighten serious moments with humor. Whereas successful instrumental leaders enjoy more *respect* from members, expressive leaders generally receive more personal *affection.*

In the traditional North American family, the two types of leadership are linked to gender. Historically, cultural norms bestowed instrumental leadership on men, who, as fathers and husbands, assumed primary responsibility for earning income and making major family decisions. Expressive leadership traditionally belonged to women: Mothers and wives encouraged supportive and peaceful relationships among family members. One result of this division of labor was that

SEEING OURSELVES

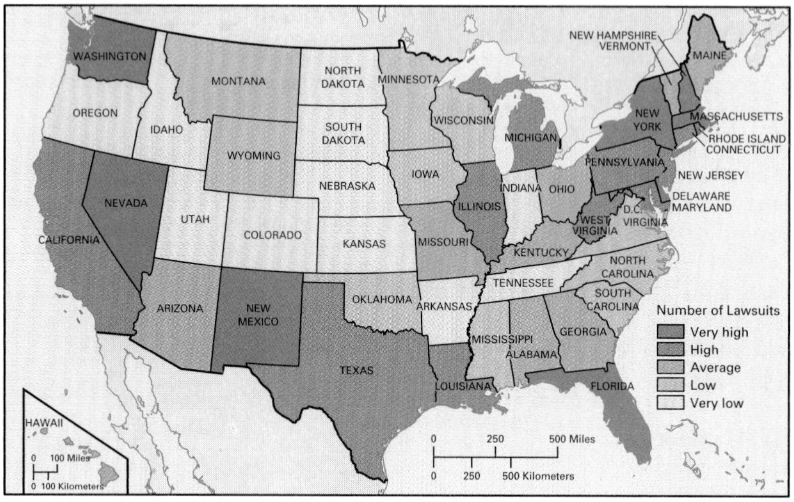

NATIONAL MAP 7–1
The Quality of Relationships: Lawsuits across the United States

Social conflicts are found everywhere, but whether people tend to resolve them informally or resort to legal action varies from state to state. It stands to reason that, in regions of the country where litigation is least common, people's social ties are typically more primary. By contrast, where people are most likely to turn to lawyers, social ties would seem to be more secondary. Looking at the map, what do the states with high levels of litigation have in common? What traits mark the states where people are reluctant to sue each other?

Source: Prepared by the author using data from Frum & Wolfe (1994).

many children had greater respect for their fathers but closer personal ties with their mothers (Parsons & Bales, 1955; Macionis, 1978a).

Greater equality between men and women has blurred this gender-based distinction between instrumental and expressive leadership. In most group settings, women and men now assume both leadership roles.

Three Leadership Styles

Sociologists also characterize leadership in terms of decision-making style. *Authoritarian leadership* focuses on instrumental concerns, takes personal charge of decision making, and demands strict compliance from subordinates. Although this leadership style may win little affection from the group, a fast-acting authoritarian leader is appreciated in a crisis.

Democratic leadership is more expressive and makes a point of including everyone in the decision-making process. Although less successful when crises leave little time for discussion, democratic leaders generally draw on the ideas of all members to develop creative solutions to problems.

Laissez-faire leadership (a French phrase roughly meaning "to leave alone") allows the group to function more or less on its own. This style typically is the least effective in promoting group goals (White & Lippitt, 1953; Ridgeway, 1983).

GROUP CONFORMITY

Groups influence the behavior of members and promote conformity. "Fitting in" provides a secure feeling of belonging, but, at the extreme, group pressure can be unpleasant and, at times, dangerous. Moreover, even strangers can foster conformity, as experiments by Solomon Asch and Stanley Milgram showed.

Asch's Research

Solomon Asch (1952) conducted a classic experiment that showed the power of groups to generate conformity. Asch recruited students allegedly for a study of visual perception. Before the experiment began, he explained to all but one member in a small group that their real purpose was to put pressure on the remaining person. Arranging six to eight students around a table, Asch showed them a "standard" line, as drawn on Card 1 in Figure 7–1, and asked them to match it to one of three lines on Card 2.

Anyone with normal vision could easily see that the line marked "A" on Card 2 is the correct choice. Initially, as planned, everyone made the matches correctly. But then Asch's secret accomplices began answering incorrectly, leaving the naive subject (seated at the table in order to answer next to last) bewildered and uncomfortable.

What happened? Asch found that one-third of all subjects conformed to the others by answering incorrectly. Apparently, many of us are willing to compromise our own judgment to avoid being different, even from people we do not know.

Milgram's Research

Stanley Milgram, a former student of Solomon Asch, conducted conformity experiments of his own. In Milgram's controversial study (1963, 1965; Miller, 1986), a researcher explained to male recruits that they would be taking part in a study of how punishment affects learning. One by one, he assigned subjects to the role of "teacher" and placed another individual—actually an accomplice of Milgram's—in a connecting room to pose as a "learner."

The teacher watched as the learner was seated in a contraption that looked like an electric chair. The researcher applied electrode paste to one of the learner's wrists, explaining that this would "prevent blisters and burns." The researcher then attached an electrode to the wrist and secured the leather straps, explaining that these would "prevent excessive movement while the learner was being shocked." Although the shocks would be painful, the researcher assured the teacher that they would cause "no permanent tissue damage."

The researcher then led the teacher back to the next room, explaining that the "electric chair" was connected to a "shock generator," a phony but realistic-looking piece of equipment with a label that read "Shock Generator, Type ZLB, Dyson Instrument Company, Waltham, Mass." On the front was a dial that supposedly regulated electric current from 15 volts (labeled "slight shock") to 300 volts (marked "intense shock") to 450 volts (marked "Danger: Severe Shock").

Seated in front of the "shock generator," the teacher was told to read aloud pairs of words. Then, the teacher was to repeat the first word of each pair and wait for the learner to recall the second word. Whenever the learner failed to answer correctly, the teacher was told to apply an electric shock.

The researcher directed the teacher to begin at the lowest level (15 volts) and to increase the shock by 15 volts every time the learner made a mistake. And so they did. At 75, 90, and 105 volts, the teacher heard moans from the learner; at 120 volts, shouts of pain; at 270 volts, screams; at 315 volts, pounding on the wall; after that, deadly silence. None of forty subjects assigned to the role of teacher during the initial research even questioned the procedure before reaching 300 volts, and twenty-six of the subjects—almost two-thirds—went all the way to 450 volts. Even Milgram was surprised at how readily people obeyed authority figures.

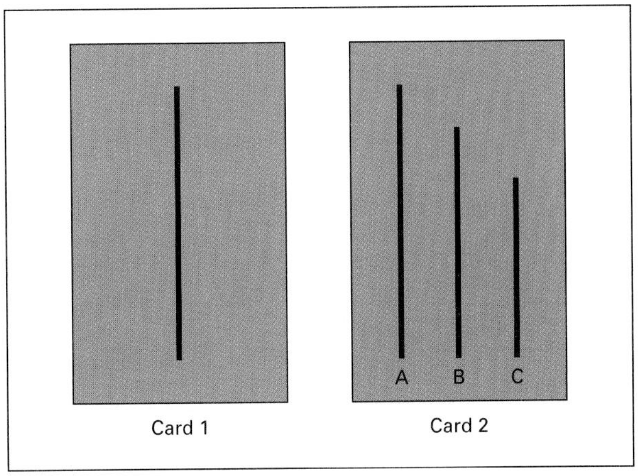

FIGURE 7–1 Cards Used in Asch's Experiment in Group Conformity

Source: Asch (1952).

Milgram (1964) then modified his research to see if Solomon Asch had documented such a high degree of group conformity only because the task he used to measure group conformity—matching lines—was trivial. Could groups of ordinary people—not authority figures—also pressure people to administer electrical shocks?

This time, Milgram formed a group of three teachers, two of whom were his accomplices. Each of the three teachers was to suggest a shock level when the learner made an error; the group would then administer the *lowest* of the three suggestions. This arrangement gave the naive subject the power to deliver a lesser shock regardless of what the others proposed.

The accomplices suggested increasing the shock level with each error, putting pressure on the third member to do the same. And, in fact, they succeeded. The subjects applied voltages three to four times higher than subjects who acted alone in control conditions. Thus Milgram's research suggests that people are likely to follow directions from not only "legitimate authority figures" but also from groups of ordinary individuals, even when it means inflicting harm on another person.

Janis's Research

Experts, too, cave in to group pressure, says Irving L. Janis (1972, 1989). Janis contends that a number of U.S. foreign policy errors, including the failure to foresee the Japanese attack on Pearl Harbor during World War II

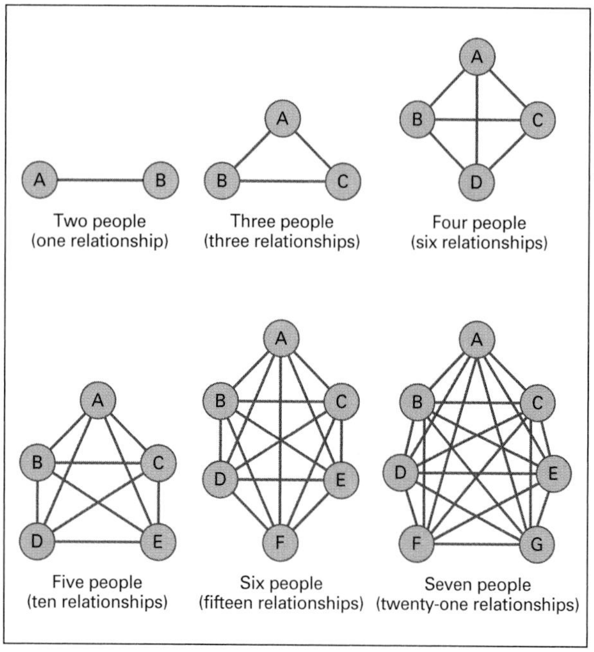

FIGURE 7–2 **Group Size and Relationships**

and the ill-fated Vietnam War, resulted from group conformity among our highest-ranking political leaders.

Common sense tells us that group discussion improves decision making. Janis counters that group members often seek consensus that closes off other points of view. Janis called this process **groupthink,** *the tendency of group members to conform, resulting in a narrow view of some issue.*

A classic example of groupthink led to the disastrous 1961 invasion of the Bay of Pigs in Cuba. Looking back, Arthur Schlesinger, Jr., an advisor to President Kennedy, confessed to feeling guilty for "having kept so quiet during those crucial discussions in the Cabinet Room," adding that the group discouraged anyone from challenging what, in hindsight, Schlesinger considered "nonsense" (quoted in Janis, 1972:30, 40).

REFERENCE GROUPS

How do we assess our own attitudes and behavior? Frequently, we use a **reference group,** *a social group that serves as a point of reference in making evaluations and decisions.*

A young man who imagines his family's response to a woman he is dating is using his family as a reference group. Similarly, a supervisor who tries to gauge her employees' reactions to a new vacation policy is using them as a standard of reference. As these examples suggest, reference groups can be primary or secondary. In either case, our need to conform means that others' attitudes greatly affect us.

We also use groups that we do *not* belong to for reference. Being well prepared for a job interview means showing up dressed the way people in that company dress for work. Conforming to groups we do not belong to is a strategy to win acceptance and illustrates the process of *anticipatory socialization*, described in Chapter 5 ("Socialization").

Stouffer's Research

Samuel A. Stouffer (1949) conducted a classic study of reference group dynamics during World War II. Researchers asked soldiers to rate their own or any competent soldier's chances of promotion in their army unit. One might guess that soldiers serving in outfits with a high promotion rate would be optimistic about their own advancement. Yet Stouffer's research pointed to the opposite conclusion: Soldiers in army units with low promotion rates were actually more positive about their chances to move ahead.

The key to understanding Stouffer's results lies in the groups against which soldiers measured themselves. Those having assignments with lower promotion rates looked around them and saw people making no more headway than they were. That is, although they had not been promoted, neither had many others, so they did not feel deprived. Soldiers in units with a higher promotion rate, however, could easily think of people who had been promoted sooner or more often than they had. With such people in mind, even soldiers who had been promoted were likely to feel shortchanged.

The lesson is that we do not make judgments about ourselves in isolation, nor do we compare ourselves with just anyone. Regardless of our situation in *absolute* terms, we form a subjective sense of our well-being by looking at ourselves in relation to specific reference groups (Merton, 1968; Mirowsky, 1987).

INGROUPS AND OUTGROUPS

Everyone favors some groups over others, whether because of political outlook, social prestige, or just manner of dress. On the college campus, for example, left-leaning student activists may look down on fraternity members, whom they consider conservative; the Greeks, in turn, may snub the computer "nerds" and "grinds," who work too hard. Virtually every social landscape has a comparable mix of positive and negative evaluations.

Such judgments illustrate another important element of group dynamics: the opposition of ingroups and outgroups. An **ingroup** is *a social group commanding a member's esteem and loyalty*. An ingroup exists in relation to an **outgroup,** *a social group toward which one feels competition or opposition*. Ingroups and outgroups are based on the idea that "we" have valued traits that "they" lack.

Tensions among groups sharpen their boundaries and give people a clearer social identity. At the same time, these tensions can distort reality. Specifically, members of ingroups generally hold overly positive views of themselves and unfairly negative views of various outgroups (Tajfel, 1982).

Power also shapes intergroup relations. A powerful ingroup can define others as a lower-status outgroup. Historically, for example, white people have viewed people of color as an outgroup and subordinated them socially, politically, and economically. Internalizing these attitudes, minorities struggle to overcome negative self-images. In short, ingroups and outgroups foster loyalty but also generate conflict (Bobo & Hutchings, 1996).

GROUP SIZE

If you are the first person to arrive at a party, you are in a position to watch some fascinating group dynamics. Until about six people enter the room, everyone usually shares a single conversation. But as more people arrive, the group divides into two or more clusters. Size plays an important role in how group members interact.

To understand the effects of group size, consider the mathematical number of relationships among two to seven people. As Figure 7–2 shows, two people form a single relationship; adding a third person results in three relationships; adding a fourth person yields six. Increasing the number of people one at a time, then, expands the number of relationships much more rapidly since every new individual can interact with everyone already there. Thus, by the time seven people join one conversation, twenty-one "channels" connect them. With so many open channels at this point, the group usually divides.

The Dyad

German sociologist Georg Simmel (1858–1918) studied the social dynamics in the smallest groups. Simmel (1950; orig. 1902) used the term **dyad** to designate *a social group with two members.*

Simmel explained that social interaction in a dyad is typically more intense than in larger groups because neither member shares the other's attention with anyone else. In the United States, love affairs, marriages, and the closest friendships are dyadic.

The triad, illustrated by Jonathan Green's painting Friends, *includes three people. A triad is more stable than a dyad because conflict between any two persons can be mediated by the third member. Even so, should the relationship between any two become more intense in a positive sense, those two are likely to exclude the third.*

Jonathan Green, *Friends*, 1992. Oil on masonite, 14 in. × 11 in. © Jonathan Green, Naples, Florida. Collection of Patric McCoy.

But, like a stool with only two legs, dyads are unstable. Both members of a dyad must work to keep the relationship going; if either withdraws, the group collapses. Because the stability of marriages is important to society, the marital dyad is supported with legal, economic, and often religious ties.

The Triad

Simmel also studied the **triad,** *a social group with three members*. A triad contains three relationships, each joining two of the three people. A triad is more stable than

Today's college campuses value social diversity. One of the challenges of this movement is ensuring that all categories of students are fully integrated into campus life. This is not always easy. Following Blau's theory of group dynamics, as the number of minority students increases, these men and women are able to form a group unto themselves, perhaps interacting less with others.

a dyad because one member can act as a mediator should the relationship between the other two become strained. Such group dynamics help explain why members of a dyad (say, a married couple) often seek out a third person (counselor) to air tensions between them.

On the other hand, two of the three can pair up to press their views on the third, or two may intensify their relationship, leaving the other feeling left out. For example, when two of the three develop a romantic interest in each other, they will understand the old saying, "Two's company, three's a crowd."

As groups grow beyond three people, they become more stable and capable of withstanding the loss of even several members. At the same time, increases in group size reduce the intense personal interaction possible only in the smallest groups. Larger groups are thus based less on personal attachment and more on formal rules and regulations. Such formality helps a group persist over time, though the group is not immune to change. After all, their numerous members give large groups more contact with the outside world, opening the door to new attitudes and behavior (Carley, 1991).

SOCIAL DIVERSITY

Race, ethnicity, and gender also affect group dynamics. Peter Blau (1977; Blau, Blum, & Schwartz, 1982; South & Messner, 1986) points out four ways in which social diversity influences intergroup contact:

1. **Large groups turn inward.** Blau explains that the larger a group, the more likely its members will have relationships just among themselves. Say a college is trying to enhance social diversity by increasing the number of international students. These students may add a dimension of difference, but, as their numbers rise, they become more likely to form their own social group. Thus, efforts to promote social diversity may have the unintended effect of promoting separatism.
2. **Heterogeneous groups turn outward.** The more internally diverse a group is, the more likely its members are to interact with outsiders. Campus groups that recruit people of both sexes and various social backgrounds typically have broader social contact than those with members of one social type.
3. **Social equality promotes contact.** To the extent that all groups have the same social standing, members of all the groups will interact. Thus, whether groups keep to themselves or not depends on how much the groups form a social hierarchy.
4. **Physical boundaries create social boundaries.** To the extent that a social group is physically segregated from others (by having its own dorm or dining area, for example), its members are less likely to associate with other people.

NETWORKS

A **network** is *a web of weak social ties.* Think of a network as a "fuzzy" group containing people who come into occasional contact but who lack a sense of boundaries and belonging. If we think of a group as a "circle of friends," then, we might describe a network as a "social web" expanding outward, often reaching great distances and including large numbers of people.

Some networks are close to being groups, as is the case with college friends who stay in touch after graduation by e-mail and telephone. More commonly, however, a network includes people we *know of*—or who *know of us*—but with whom we interact rarely, if at all. As one woman with a widespread reputation as a community organizer explains, "I get calls at home, someone says,

GLOBAL SOCIOLOGY

The Internet: A Global Network

Its origins seem right out of the 1960s' cold war film *Dr. Strangelove.* Three decades ago, government officials and scientists were trying to figure out how to run the country after an atomic attack, which, they assumed, would knock out telephones and television. The brilliant solution was to devise a communication system with no central headquarters, no one in charge, and no main power switch—in short, an electronic web that would link the country in one vast network.

By 1985, a web of high-speed data lines was in place and the Internet was about to be born. Today, thousands of colleges and universities, as well as tens of thousands of government offices, are joined by the Internet and share in the cost of its operation. Tens of millions of businesses and individuals at home also connect to this "information superhighway" using a telephone-line modem and a subscription to a commercial Internet "gateway."

How many people use the Internet? A rough estimate is that, in 2001, between 175 and 200 million individuals in 180 (of 191) countries around the world are connected by the largest network in history.

What does the network offer to individuals? Popular "search engines" such as YAHOO! (type in its address, http://www.yahoo.com) provide site listings for just about any topic you can imagine. Other popular activities include electronic mail (start a cyber-romance with a pen pal, write to your textbook author [macionis@kenyon.edu], or even send a message to the president of the United States [president@whitehouse.gov]). Through the Internet, you can also join discussion groups, visit museums for "virtual tours," locate data from government agencies (a good starting point is http://www.census.gov), explore Web pages of sociological interest (try the author's Web site, at http://www.TheSociologyPage.com), or review for exams in this course (http://www.prenhall.com/macionis). With no formal rules for its use, the Internet's potential is limited only by our imagination.

Ironically, perhaps, it is precisely this freedom that disturbs some people. Critics claim that "electronic democracy" threatens our political system, parents fear that their children will access sexually explicit "adult sites," and purists bristle as the Internet becomes ever more flooded with advertising.

In its "anything goes" character, of course, the Internet is like the real world. Not surprisingly, therefore, a recent trend is that more and more users now employ passwords, fees, and other "gates" to create restricted subnetworks limited to people like themselves. From one vast network, then, is emerging a host of social groups.

Sources: Based, in part, on Elmer-DeWitt (1993, 1994b), Hafner (1994), and O'Connor (1997).

'Are you Roseann Navarro? Somebody told me to call you. I have this problem . . .'" (quoted in Kaminer, 1984:94).

Network ties may be weak, but they can be a powerful resource. For immigrants seeking to become established in a new community, businesspeople seeking to expand their operations, or anyone looking for a job, *who you know* is often just as important as *what you know* (cf. Luo, 1997; Hagan, 1998).

Networks are based on people's colleges, clubs, neighborhoods, political parties, and personal interests. Obviously, some networks contain people with considerably more wealth, power, and prestige than others, which is what the expression "well connected" means. Some people also have denser networks than others—that is, they are connected to more people. Typically, the most extensive social networks include people who are young, well educated, and living in large cities (Markovsky et al., 1993; Kadushin, 1995; O'Brien, Hassinger, & Dershem, 1996; Fernandez & Weinberg, 1997; Podolny & Baron, 1997).

Gender, too, shapes networks. Although the networks of men and women are typically the same size, women include more relatives (and women) in their networks, whereas those of men include more coworkers (and men). Women's ties, therefore, may not carry quite the same clout as "old boy" networks. Even so, research suggests that as gender equality increases in the United States, the networks of women and men are becoming more alike (Moore, 1991, 1992; Wright, 1995).

Finally, new information technology has generated a global network of unprecedented size in the form of the Internet. The box takes a closer look at this twenty-first-century form of communication, and Global Map 7–1 shows access to the Internet around the world.

WINDOW ON THE WORLD

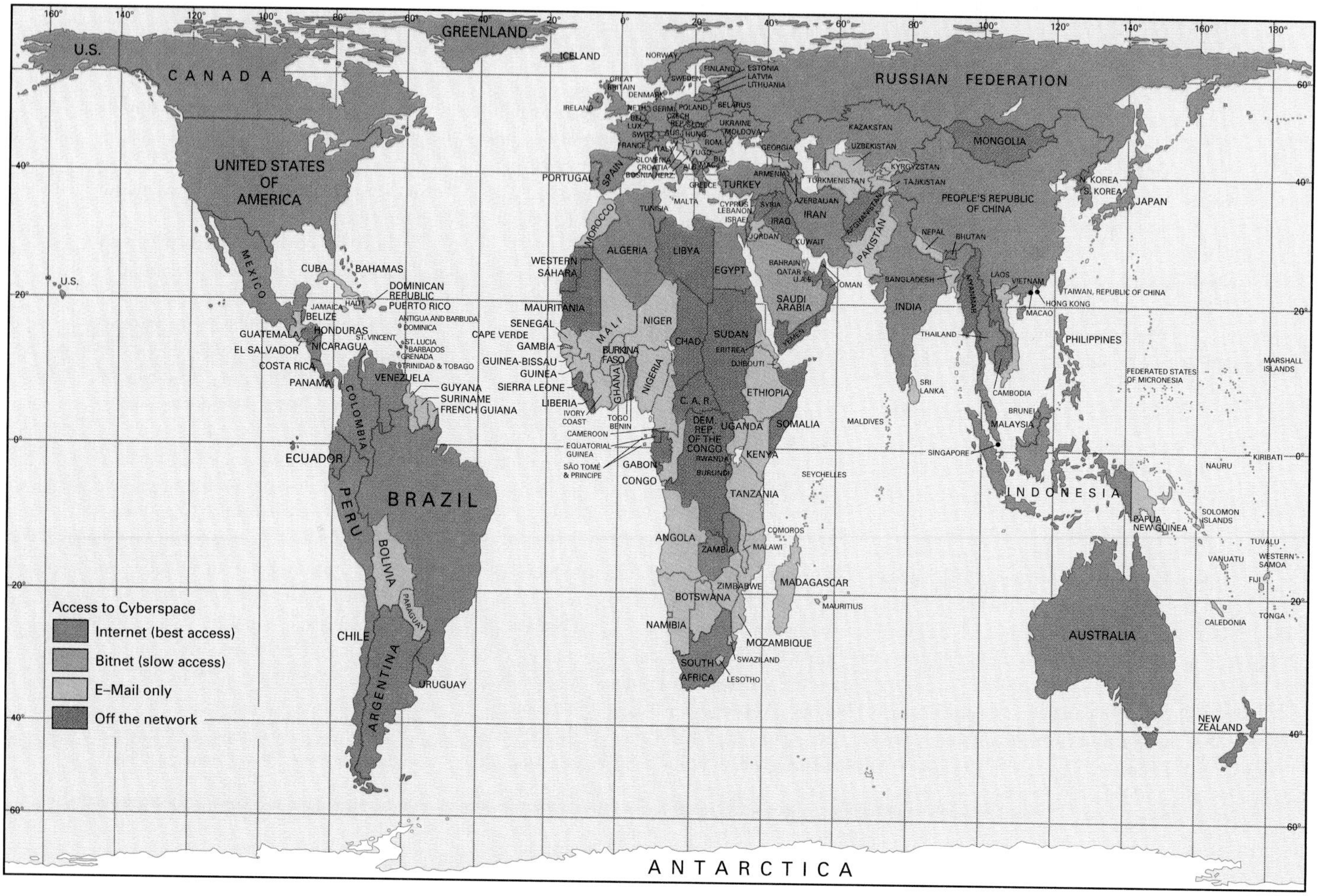

GLOBAL MAP 7–1 Cyberspace: A Global Network

While 180 of the world's 191 nations are connected to the Internet, a majority of the world's people have no access to this valuable resource. For one thing, computers are expensive, well out of the reach of ordinary people in low-income countries, especially in Africa. The vast majority of Internet sites are in the United States, Canada, Western Europe, and Australia. Another barrier to global communication is language: Developed in the United States, the Internet's available software demands that users read and write in the Latin alphabet using English. But, with computer use expanding rapidly, experts around the world are at work developing keyboards and interface programs that will link people using various other languages. Perhaps, in the near future, the Internet may be as multicultural as the world it connects.

Source: Copyright © 1997 by The New York Times Co. Reprinted by permission.

FORMAL ORGANIZATIONS

A century ago, most people lived in small groups of family, friends, and neighbors. Today, our lives revolve more and more around **formal organizations,** *large secondary groups that are organized to achieve their goals efficiently.*

Formal organizations, such as business corporations and government agencies, differ from families and neighborhoods. Their greater size makes social relations less personal and fosters a formal, planned atmosphere. In other words, formal organizations operate in a deliberate way, not to meet personal needs but to accomplish complex jobs.

When you think about it, organizing some 275 million members of our society is remarkable, involving countless jobs, from collecting taxes to delivering the mail. To carry out most of these tasks, we rely upon large, formal organizations. The U.S. government, the nation's largest formal organization, employs more than 5 million people in hundreds of agencies and the armed forces. Large, formal organizations develop lives and cultures of their own so that, as members come and go, the statuses they fill and the roles they perform remain unchanged over the years.

GLOBAL SNAPSHOT

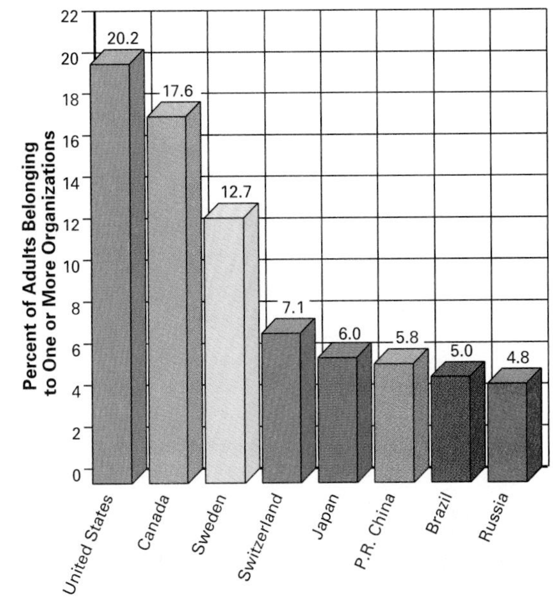

FIGURE 7–3 Membership in Cultural or Educational Organizations

Source: *World Values Survey* (1994).

TYPES OF FORMAL ORGANIZATIONS

Amitai Etzioni (1975) identified three types of formal organizations, distinguished by the reasons people participate—utilitarian organizations, normative organizations, and coercive organizations.

Utilitarian Organizations

Just about everyone who works for income belongs to a *utilitarian organization,* one that pays people for their efforts. Large businesses, for example, generate profits for their owners and income for their employees. Joining utilitarian organizations is usually a matter of individual choice, although, obviously, most people must join one or another utilitarian organization to make a living.

Normative Organizations

People join *normative organizations* not for income but to pursue some goal they think is morally worthwhile. Sometimes called *voluntary associations,* these include community service groups (such as the PTA, the Lions Club, the League of Women Voters, and the Red Cross), as well as political parties and religious organizations. In global perspective, people in the United States tend to join voluntary associations (Curtis, Grabb, & Baer, 1992). Figure 7–3 provides a comparative glance at membership in cultural or educational organizations for selected countries.

Coercive Organizations

Coercive organizations have an involuntary membership. That is, people are forced to join these organizations as a form of punishment (prisons) or treatment (psychiatric hospitals). Coercive organizations have special physical features, such as locked doors and barred windows, and are supervised by security personnel. They isolate people as "inmates" or "patients" for a period of time, seeking to change radically attitudes and behavior. Recall from Chapter 5 ("Socialization") the power of *total institutions* to transform a human being's overall sense of self.

From differing vantage points, any particular organization may fall into *all* of these categories. A psychiatric hospital, for example, serves as a coercive organization for a patient, a utilitarian organization for a

Although formal organization is vital to modern, industrial societies, it is far from new. Twenty-five centuries ago, the Chinese philosopher and teacher K'ung Fu-Tzu (known to Westerners as Confucius) endorsed the idea that government offices should be filled by the most talented young men. This led to what was probably the world's first system of civil service examinations. Here, would-be bureaucrats compose essays to demonstrate their knowledge of Confucian texts.

psychiatrist, and a normative organization for a part-time hospital volunteer.

ORIGINS OF BUREAUCRACY

Formal organizations date back thousands of years. Elites who controlled early empires relied on officials to collect taxes, undertake military campaigns, and construct monumental structures, from the Great Wall of China to the pyramids of Egypt.

These early organizations had two limitations, however. First, they lacked the technology to communicate quickly, to travel over large distances, and to collect and store information. Second, tradition is strong in preindustrial societies, so organizational goals were to preserve cultural systems, not to change them. But, during the last few centuries, what Max Weber called a "rational world view" emerged in parts of the world, a process described in Chapter 4 ("Society"). In Europe and North America, the Industrial Revolution ushered in a new organizational structure concerned with efficiency, what Weber called *bureaucracy*.

CHARACTERISTICS OF BUREAUCRACY

Bureaucracy is *an organizational model rationally designed to perform tasks efficiently.* Bureaucratic officials deliberately enact and revise policy to increase efficiency. To appreciate the power and scope of bureaucratic organization, consider this: Any one of nearly 300 million phones in the United States can connect you, within seconds, to any other phone—in homes, businesses, automobiles, or even a hiker's backpack on an Adirondack mountain trail. Such instant communication was beyond the imagination of people who lived in the ancient world.

Of course, the telephone system depends on technology such as electricity, fiber optics, and computers. But neither could the system exist without the organizational ability to keep track of every telephone call—noting which phone called which other phone, when, and for how long—and then present this information to more than 100 million telephone users in the form of monthly bills.

What specific traits promote organizational efficiency? Max Weber (1978; orig. 1921) identified six key elements of the ideal bureaucratic organization.

1. **Specialization.** Our ancestors spent most of their time looking for food and shelter. Bureaucracy, by contrast, assigns individuals highly specialized duties.
2. **Hierarchy of offices.** Bureaucracies arrange personnel in a vertical ranking of offices. Each person is supervised by "higher-ups" in the organization while, in turn, supervising others in lower positions. Usually, with few people at the top and many at the bottom, bureaucratic organizations take the form of a pyramid.
3. **Rules and regulations.** Cultural tradition counts for little in a bureaucracy. Instead, rationally enacted rules and regulations guide a bureaucracy's operation. Ideally, a bureaucracy seeks to operate in a completely predictable way.
4. **Technical competence.** Bureaucratic officials and staff have the technical competence to carry out their duties. Bureaucracies typically recruit new members according to set criteria and regularly monitor their performance. Such impersonal evaluation contrasts sharply with the ancient custom of favoring relatives, whatever their talents, over strangers.
5. **Impersonality.** Bureaucracy puts rules ahead of personal whim so that clients as well as workers are all treated uniformly. From this detached approach stems the notion of the "faceless bureaucrat."
6. **Formal, written communications.** According to an old saying, the heart of bureaucracy is not people but paperwork. Rather than casual, face-to-face talk, bureaucracy relies on formal, written memos and reports, which accumulate in vast *files* and guide the operation of the organization.

Bureaucratic organization promotes efficiency by carefully recruiting personnel and limiting the unpredictable effects of personal taste and opinion. Table 7–2 summarizes the differences between small social groups and large formal organizations.

TABLE 7–2 Small Groups and Formal Organizations: A Comparison

	Small Groups	Formal Organizations
Activities	Members typically engage in many of the same activities	Members typically engage in distinct, highly specialized activities
Hierarchy	Often informal or nonexistent	Clearly defined, corresponding to offices
Norms	Informal application of general norms	Clearly defined rules and regulations
Criteria for Membership	Variable, often based on personal affection or kinship	Technical competence to carry out assigned tasks
Relationships	Variable; typically primary	Typically secondary, with selective primary ties
Communications	Typically casual and face to face	Typically formal and in writing
Focus	Person-oriented	Task-oriented

ORGANIZATIONAL ENVIRONMENT

No organization operates in a vacuum. How any organization performs depends not only on its own goals and policies but also on the **organizational environment,** *a range of factors outside the organization that affects its operation.* These factors include technology, economic and political trends, the available work force, and other organizations.

Modern organizations are shaped by the *technology* of computers, telephone systems, and copiers. Computers give employees access to more information and people than ever before. At the same time, computer technology allows managers to monitor closely the activities of workers (Markoff, 1991).

Economic and political trends affect organizations. All organizations are helped or hindered by periodic economic growth or recession. Most industries also face competition from abroad, as well as changes in law—such as new environmental standards—at home.

According to Max Weber, bureaucracy is an organizational strategy that promotes efficiency. Impersonality, however, also fosters alienation among employees, who may become indifferent to the formal goals of the organization. The behavior of this municipal employee in Bombay, India, is understandable to members of formal organizations almost anywhere in the world.

Population patterns, such as the size and composition of the surrounding populace, also affect organizations. The average age, typical education, and social diversity of a local community determine the available work force and, sometimes, the market for an organization's products or services.

Other organizations also contribute to the organizational environment. To be competitive, a hospital must be responsive to the insurance industry and organizations representing doctors, nurses, and other workers. It must also keep abreast of the equipment and procedures available at nearby facilities, as well as their prices.

THE INFORMAL SIDE OF BUREAUCRACY

Weber's ideal bureaucracy deliberately regulates every activity. In actual organizations, however, human beings are creative (and stubborn) enough to resist bureaucratic blueprints. Informality may amount to simply cutting corners in one's job, but it can also provide needed flexibility (Scott, 1981).

Informality partly comes from the personalities of organizational leaders. Studies of U.S. corporations document that the qualities and quirks of individuals—including personal charisma and interpersonal skills—greatly affect organizational outcomes (Halberstam, 1986).

Authoritarian, democratic, and laissez-faire types of leadership (described earlier in this chapter) reflect individual personality as much as any organizational plan. Then, too, in the real world of organizations, leaders and their cronies sometimes seek to benefit personally by abusing organizational power. Perhaps even more commonly, leaders take credit for the efforts of their subordinates. Many secretaries, for example, have far more authority and responsibility than their official job titles and salaries suggest.

Communication offers another example of informality within large organizations. Memos and other written communications are the formal way to spread information through the organization. Typically, however, individuals create informal networks, or "grapevines," that spread information quickly, if not always accurately. Grapevines, using both word-of-mouth and e-mail, are particularly important to subordinates because higher-ups may try to keep important information from them.

The spread of e-mail has "flattened" organizations somewhat, allowing even the lowest-ranking employee to bypass immediate superiors and communicate directly with the organization's leader or all fellow employees at once. Some organizations object to "open-channel" communication and limit the use of e-mail. Microsoft Corporation (whose founder, Bill Gates, has an unlisted address yet still receives hundreds of e-mail messages a day) has developed "screens" that allow messages from only approved people to reach a particular computer terminal (Gwynne & Dickerson, 1997).

Using new information technology as well as age-old human ingenuity, members of organizations try to personalize their procedures and surroundings. Such efforts suggest that we now take a closer look at some of the problems of bureaucracy.

PROBLEMS OF BUREAUCRACY

We rely on bureaucracy to manage countless dimensions of everyday life, but many people are, at best, uneasy about large organizations. Bureaucracy can dehumanize and

George Tooker's painting Government Bureau *is a powerful statement about the human costs of bureaucracy. The artist depicts members of the public in monotonous similitude—reduced from human beings to mere "cases" to be disposed of as quickly as possible. Set apart from others by their positions, officials are "faceless bureaucrats" concerned more with numbers than with providing genuine assistance (notice that the artist places the fingers of the officials on calculators).*

George Tooker, *Government Bureau*, 1956. Egg tempera on gesso panel, 19⅝ x 29⅝ inches. The Metropolitan Museum of Art, George A. Hearn Fund, 1956 (56.78). Photograph © 1984 The Metropolitan Museum of Art.

manipulate us, and some say it poses a threat to political democracy.

Bureaucratic Alienation

Max Weber touted bureaucracy as a model of productivity. Nonetheless, Weber was keenly aware of bureaucracy's ability to *dehumanize* the people it is supposed to serve. The same impersonality that fosters efficiency also keeps officials and clients from responding to each other's unique, personal needs. On the contrary, officials must treat each client impersonally—as a standard "case."

Formal organizations create *alienation*, according to Weber, by reducing the human being to "a small cog in a ceaselessly moving mechanism" (1978:988; orig. 1921). Although formal organizations are intended to benefit humanity, Weber feared that people could well end up serving formal organizations.

Bureaucratic Inefficiency and Ritualism

Inefficiency, the failure of an organization to carry out the work that it exists to perform, is a familiar problem. According to one report, the General Services Administration, the government agency that buys equipment for federal workers, takes up to three years to process a request for a new computer. This delay ensures that by the time the computer arrives, it is already out of date (Gwynne & Dickerson, 1997).

The problem of inefficiency is captured in the concept of *red tape* (a phrase derived from the red tape used by eighteenth-century English administrators to wrap official parcels and records; Shipley, 1985). Red tape refers to a tedious preoccupation with organizational routine and procedures. Robert Merton (1968) points out that red tape amounts to a new twist to the already-familiar concept of group conformity. He coined the term **bureaucratic ritualism** to designate *a preoccupation with rules and regulations to the point of thwarting an organization's goals.*

Ritualism stifles individual creativity and strangles organizational performance. In part, ritualism arises from the fact that organizations, which pay modest, fixed salaries, give officials little financial stake in performing efficiently. Then, too, bureaucratic ritualism stands as another form of alienation that Weber feared would arise from bureaucratic rigidity (Whyte, 1957; Merton, 1968; Coleman, 1990; Kiser & Schneider, 1994).

Bureaucratic Inertia

Although bureaucrats sometimes have little motivation to be efficient, they have every reason to protect their jobs. Officials may even strive to keep an organization going when its purpose has been realized. As Weber put it, "once fully established, bureaucracy is among the social structures which are hardest to destroy" (1978:987; orig. 1921).

Bureaucratic inertia refers to *the tendency of bureaucratic organizations to perpetuate themselves.* Formal

DIVERSITY SNAPSHOT

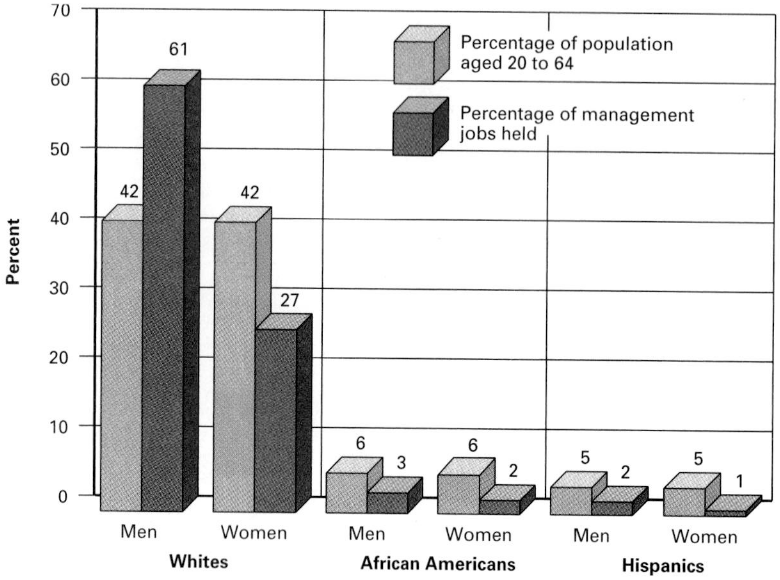

FIGURE 7–4
U.S. Managers by Race, Sex, and Ethnicity, 1996

Source: U.S. Equal Employment Opportunity Commission (1997).

organizations tend to take on a life of their own beyond their formal objectives. For example, the U.S. Department of Agriculture has offices in almost all U.S. counties, even though only one county in seven has working farms (Littman, 1992).

Usually, an organization stays in business by redefining its goals. The Agriculture Department, for example, now performs a number of tasks not directly related to farming, including nutritional and environmental research.

OLIGARCHY

Early in this century, Robert Michels (1876–1936) pointed out the link between bureaucracy and political **oligarchy,** *the rule of the many by the few* (1949; orig. 1911). According to what Michels called "the iron law of oligarchy," the pyramid shape of bureaucracy places a few leaders in charge of organizational resources.

Max Weber credited a strict hierarchy of responsibility with high organizational efficiency. But Michels countered that this hierarchical structure also concentrates power and thus endangers democracy because officials can—and often do—use their access to information, resources, and the media to promote their personal interests.

Furthermore, bureaucracy also insulates officials from the public, as in the case of the corporate president or public official who is "unavailable for comment" to the local press, or the U.S. president who withholds documents from Congress claiming "executive privilege." Oligarchy, then, thrives in the hierarchical structure of bureaucracy and reduces the accountability of leaders to the people (Tolson, 1995).

Political competition, term limits, and a system of checks and balances prevent the U.S. government from becoming an out-and-out oligarchy. Even so, incumbents enjoy a significant advantage in U.S. politics. In the 1998 congressional elections, only 13 of 433 congressional officeholders running for reelection were defeated by their challengers.

THE EVOLUTION OF FORMAL ORGANIZATIONS

The problems of bureaucracy—especially the alienation it produces and its tendency toward oligarchy—stem from two organizational traits: hierarchy and rigidity. To Weber, bureaucracy was a top-down system: Rules and regulations made at the top guide every facet of people's lives down the chain of command. A century ago in the United States, Weber's ideas took hold in an organizational model called "scientific management." We begin with a look at this model, and then describe three challenges over the course of the twentieth century that gradually led to a new model—the "flexible organization."

SCIENTIFIC MANAGEMENT

Frederick Winslow Taylor (1911) had a simple message: Most businesses in the United States were sadly inefficient. Managers had little idea of how to increase their business's output, and workers relied on the same tired skills of earlier generations.

To increase efficiency, Taylor explained, business should apply the principles of science. **Scientific management,** then, is *the application of scientific principles to the operation of a business or other large organization.*

Scientific management involves three steps. First, managers carefully observe the task performed by each worker, identifying all the operations involved and measuring the time needed for each. Second, managers then analyze their data, trying to discover ways for workers to perform each task more efficiently. Managers, for example, might decide to provide workers with different tools, or reposition various work operations within the factory. Third, management provides guidance and incentives for workers to do their jobs more efficiently. If a factory worker moves twenty tons of pig iron in one day, for example, management should show the worker how to do the job more efficiently, and then provide higher wages for the worker's higher productivity. Applying scientific principles in this way, Taylor concluded, companies become more profitable, workers earn higher wages, and, in the end, consumers end up paying lower prices.

In the early 1900s, many businesses followed Taylor's lead and improved their efficiency. As time went on, however, formal organizations faced three new challenges involving race and gender, rising competition from abroad, and changes in work itself. We look briefly at each in turn.

THE FIRST CHALLENGE: RACE AND GENDER

During the 1960s, critics pointed out that big businesses and other organizations were inefficient—and also unfair—in their hiring practices. Rather than hiring on the basis of competence, as Weber had proposed, they excluded women and other minorities. As a result, the vast majority of managers were white men.

During the last fifty years in the United States, women have moved into management positions throughout the corporate world. While some men initially opposed women's presence in the executive office, it is now clear that women bring particular strengths to the job, including leadership flexibility and communication skills. Thus, some analysts speak of women offering a "female advantage."

Patterns of Exclusion

Even by the end of the twentieth century, as shown in Figure 7–4, white men in the United States—42 percent of the working-age population—still held 61 percent of management jobs. White women made up about the same share of the population, but they held just 27 percent of managerial positions (U.S. Equal Employment Opportunity Commission, 1997). The members of other minorities lagged further behind.

According to Rosabeth Moss Kanter (1977; Kanter & Stein, 1979), excluding women and minorities from the workplace ignores the talents of more than half the population. Furthermore, underrepresented people in an organization often feel like socially isolated outgroups—uncomfortably visible, taken less seriously, and given fewer chances for promotion.

"Opening up" an organization, Kanter claims, improves everyone's on-the-job performance by motivating employees to become "fast-trackers" who work

During the 1980s, U.S. corporations turned their eyes to Japan, where competition from Japanese corporations was becoming intense. Japanese organizations are characterized by a collective orientation. Here, employees at the Texas Instruments plant in Kyushu participate in sports day, a company strategy to build work-team morale.

harder and are more committed to the company. By contrast, an organization with many "dead-end" jobs turns workers into unproductive "zombies." An open organization also encourages leaders to seek out the input of everyone, which benefits the organization. It is officials in rigid organizations—those who have little reason themselves to be creative—who jealously guard their privileges and ride herd over their employees.

The "Female Advantage"

Some organizational researchers argue that including more women brings special management skills that strengthen an organization. Deborah Tannen (1994) claims, for example, that women have a greater "information focus," and more readily ask questions in order to understand an issue. Men, on the other hand, have an "image focus" that makes them wonder how asking questions in a particular situation will affect their reputation.

In another study of women executives, Sally Helgesen (1990) found three other gender-linked patterns. First, women place greater value on communication skills and share information more than men do. Second, women are more flexible leaders who typically give their employees greater autonomy. Third, compared to men, women tend to emphasize the interconnectedness of all organizational operations. Thus, women bring a "female advantage" to companies striving to be more flexible and democratic.

In sum, one challenge to conventional bureaucracy is to become more open and flexible in order to take advantage of everyone's experience, ideas, and creativity. The result goes right to the bottom line: greater profits.

THE SECOND CHALLENGE: THE JAPANESE ORGANIZATION

In 1980, the corporate world in the United States was shaken to discover that the most popular automobile model sold in this country was not a Chevrolet, Ford, or Plymouth but the Honda Accord, made in Japan. To people old enough to remember the 1950s, the words "made in Japan" generally meant a cheap, poorly made product. But times had changed. The success of the Japanese auto industry (and, soon after, companies making electronics, cameras, and other products) soon had analysts buzzing about the "Japanese organization." How else could so small a country challenge the world's economic powerhouse?

Japanese organizations reflect that nation's strong collective spirit. That is, while most members of our society prize rugged individualism, the Japanese value

GLOBAL SOCIOLOGY

The Japanese Model: Will It Work in the United States?

What the company wants is for us to work like the Japanese. Everybody go out and do jumping jacks in the morning and kiss each other when they go home at night. You work as a team, rat on each other, and lose control of your destiny. That's not going to work in this country.

John Brodie
President, United Paperworkers
Local 448
Chester, Pennsylvania

Competition—from Asia and, increasingly, from Europe—is forcing U.S. companies to rethink how corporate organizations should operate in a global marketplace. Business leaders are looking, for example, at the Japanese manufacturing plants built here in the United States. These "transplant organizations," operated in the United States by Honda, Nissan, and Toyota, have adapted well to a new environment, achieving the same level of efficiency and quality that won these companies praise in Japan. They have also provided more than 250,000 jobs for U.S. workers.

Yet, some voices in this country—from the ranks of workers, union leaders, and managers—speak as bitterly about importing Japanese organizational techniques as they do about importing Japanese cars. Our corporate culture still favors hierarchy, praises individualism, and remembers its long history of labor-management conflict. As a result, workers and managers are wary of traditional Japanese practices, such as worker participation.

Some employees in the United States think worker participation ends up increasing their workload. While still responsible for building cars, for instance, workers also have to worry about quality control, unit costs, and overall efficiency—concerns usually shouldered by management. Moreover, some employees see the broad training favored by the Japanese as endlessly moving from job to job, always having to learn new skills. Many union leaders fear that any alliance of workers and managers undermines union strength. Some managers, too, look warily on worker participation programs. Sharing the power to set production goals or schedule vacations does not come easily in light of past practices. Finally, U.S. corporations have a short-term outlook on profits, which discourages investing time and money in organizational restructuring.

But the pressure of rising global competition is slowly changing U.S. organizations. The government reports that 70 percent of large businesses have begun at least some reforms of this kind. The fact is that productivity and profits are usually higher when workers have a say in decision making. Moreover, most employees in worker participation programs—even those who may not want to sign up for morning jumping jacks—seem happier about their jobs. Workers who have long used only their bodies are now enjoying the opportunity to use their minds as well.

From Japanese organizations, U.S. companies have learned the value of building team spirit.

Sources: Hoerr (1989) and Florida & Kenney (1991).

cooperation. In effect, then, formal organizations in Japan are like very large primary groups. William Ouchi (1981) highlights five differences between formal organizations in Japan and in the United States:

1. **Hiring and advancement.** U.S. organizations hold out promotions and raises in salary as prizes to be won through individual competition. In Japanese organizations, however, companies hire

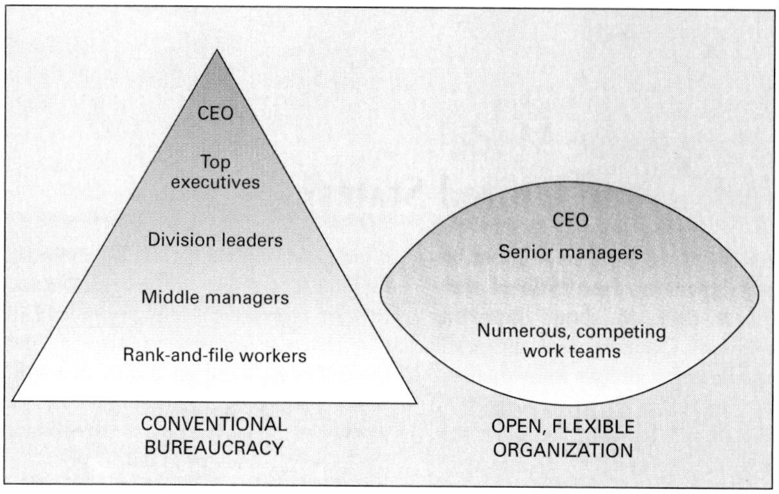

Source: Created by the author.

FIGURE 7–5 Two Organizational Models

The conventional model of bureaucratic organizations has a pyramid shape, with a clear chain of command. Directives flow from the top down, while reports of performance flow from the bottom up. Such organizations have extensive rules and regulations, and their workers have highly specialized jobs. More open and flexible organizations have a flatter shape, more like a football. With fewer levels in the hierarchy, responsibility for generating ideas and making decisions is shared throughout the organization. Many workers do their jobs in teams and have a broad knowledge of the entire organization's operation.

new school graduates together, and all employees in the group receive the same salary and responsibilities. Only after several years is anyone likely to be singled out for special advancement.

2. **Lifetime security.** Employees in the United States expect to move from one company to another to advance their careers. U.S. companies are also quick to lay off employees during an economic setback. By contrast, most Japanese firms hire workers for life, fostering strong, mutual loyalties. If jobs become obsolete, Japanese companies avoid layoffs by retraining workers for new positions.
3. **Holistic involvement.** While we tend to see the home and the workplace as distinct spheres, Japanese companies play a much larger role in workers' lives. They provide home mortgages, sponsor recreational activities, and schedule social events. Such interaction beyond the workplace strengthens collective identity and offers the respectful Japanese employees a chance to voice suggestions and criticisms informally.
4. **Broad-based training.** U.S. workers are highly specialized, and many spend an entire career doing one thing. But a Japanese organization trains workers in all phases of its operation, again with the idea that employees will remain with the company for life.
5. **Collective decision making.** In the United States, key executives make the important decisions. Although Japanese leaders also take responsibility for their organization's performance, they involve workers in "quality circles" to discuss decisions that affect them. A closer working relationship is also encouraged by Japan's lower salary difference between executives and workers—about half of what is typical in the United States.

These characteristics give the Japanese a strong sense of organizational loyalty. Because their personal interests are tied to company interests, workers realize their ambitions through the organization. Japanese *groupism* is thus the cultural equivalent of our society's emphasis on *individual* achievement.

Many U.S. companies have been influenced by Japanese organizations. But transplanting an organizational system from one culture to another is not easy, as the box on page 181 explains.

THE THIRD CHALLENGE: THE CHANGING NATURE OF WORK

Beyond rising global competition, pressure to modify conventional organizations is also coming from changes in the nature of work itself. Chapter 4 ("Society") described the shift from industrial to postindustrial production. Rather than working in factories using heavy machinery to make *things*, more and more people are using computers and other electronic technology to create or process *information*. The postindustrial society, then, is characterized by information-based organizations.

Frederick Taylor developed his concept of scientific management at a time when jobs involved tasks that, while often backbreaking, were routine. Workers shoveled coal, poured liquid iron into molds, attached body panels to automobiles on an assembly line, or shot hot rivets into steel girders to build skyscrapers. In addition, a large part of the U.S. labor force in Taylor's day was immigrants, most of whom had little schooling and many of whom knew little English. The routine nature of industrial jobs coupled with the limited skills of the labor force led Taylor to treat work as a series of fixed tasks, set down by management and followed by employees.

Many of today's information-age jobs are very different: The work of designers, artists, writers, composers, programmers, business owners, and others now demands creativity and imagination. What does this mean for formal organizations? Here are several ways in which today's organizations differ from those of a century ago:

1. **Creative autonomy.** Organizations know that employees with information-age skills are a vital resource. Executives can set production goals but cannot dictate how to accomplish tasks involving imagination and discovery. Thus, highly skilled workers have *creative autonomy*, which means they have little day-to-day supervision as long as they generate good ideas in the long run.
2. **Competitive work teams.** Many organizations give several groups of employees the freedom to work on a problem, offering the greatest rewards to those who come up with the best solution. Competitive work teams, a strategy first used by Japanese organizations, draw out the creative contributions of everyone and, at the same time, reduce the alienation often found in conventional organizations (Yeatts, 1991, 1994; Maddox, 1994).
3. **A flatter organization.** By spreading responsibility for creative problem solving throughout the work force, organizations take on a flatter shape. That is, the pyramid shape of conventional bureaucracy is replaced by a organizational form with fewer levels in the chain of command, as shown in Figure 7–5.
4. **Greater flexibility.** The typical industrial-age organization was a rigid structure guided from the top. Such organizations may accomplish a good deal of work, but they are not especially creative, nor are they able to respond quickly to changes in their larger environment. The ideal model in the information age is a *flexible* organization, one that both generates new ideas and, in a rapidly changing global marketplace, adapts quickly.

The recent trend is toward breaking down the rigid structure of conventional bureaucracy. One example of more flexible organizational form is the self-managed work team, whose members have the skills to carry out their tasks creatively and with minimal supervision.

As important as these changes are, bear in mind that many of today's jobs *do not* involve creative work at all. On the contrary, the postindustrial economy has created two very different types of work: highly skilled creative work and low-skilled service work. Work in the fast-food industry, for example, is routine and highly supervised, and thus has much more in common with

Is McDonaldization becoming a global trend? Yes and no. The spread of McDonald's around the world has been dramatic, and the company now earns most of its revenues from operations outside the United States. But, in some nations, McDonald's has altered its menu to take account of local cultural norms. When McDonald's opened a restaurant in New Delhi, India, Hindu people were not about to begin eating beef. Thus, this restaurant company promotes "vegetable burgers" (with fries, of course).

factory work of a century ago than with the work of teams in information organizations. Therefore, at the same time that some organizations have taken on a flexible, flatter form, others continue to use the rigid chain of command, as we now explain.

THE "MCDONALDIZATION" OF SOCIETY[1]

As noted in the opening to this chapter, McDonald's has enjoyed enormous success, now operating more than 20,000 restaurants in the United States and around the world. In Japan alone, there are more than 850 Golden Arches, and the world's largest McDonald's recently opened in China's capital city of Beijing.

October 9, 1994, Macau. Here we are, halfway around the world, in the Portuguese colony of Macau—a little nub jutting from the Chinese coast. Few people here speak English, and life on the streets seems a world apart from the urban rhythms of New York, Chicago, or Los Angeles. Then I turn the corner and stand face to face with (who else?) Ronald McDonald! After eating who-knows-what for so long, forgive me for giving in to the lure of the Big Mac. But the most amazing thing is that the food—the burger, fries, and drink—looks, smells, and tastes exactly the same as it does back home, 10,000 miles away!

McDonald's may be found almost everywhere these days but, in the United States, it is more than a restaurant—it is a symbol of our way of life. Not only do people around the world associate McDonald's with the United States, but, here at home, one poll found that 98 percent of schoolchildren could identify Ronald McDonald, making him as well known as Santa Claus.

Even more important, the organizational principles that underlie McDonald's are coming to dominate our entire society. Our culture is becoming "McDonaldized," an awkward way of saying that we model many aspects of life on this restaurant chain: Parents buy toys at worldwide chain stores like Toys 'Я' Us; we drive to Jiffy Lube for a ten-minute oil change; face-to-face communication is sliding more and more toward voice mail, e-mail, and junk mail; more vacations take the form of resort and tour packages; television presents news in the

[1]Much of the material in this section is based on Ritzer (1993, 1998).

form of ten-second sound bites; college admissions officers size up students they have never met by their GPA and SAT scores; and professors assign ghost-written textbooks[2] and evaluate students with tests mass-produced for them by publishing companies. The list goes on and on.

McDonaldization: Four Principles

What do all such developments have in common? According to George Ritzer (1993), the McDonaldization of society involves four basic organizational principles:

1. **Efficiency.** Ray Kroc, the marketing genius behind the expansion of McDonald's, set out to serve a hamburger, French fries, and milkshake to a customer in fifty seconds. Today, one of the company's most popular items is the Egg McMuffin, an entire breakfast in a single sandwich. In the restaurant, customers bus their own trays or, better still, drive away from the pickup window taking the packaging and whatever mess they make with them.

   Efficiency is now central to our way of life. We tend to think that anything done quickly is, for that reason alone, good.

2. **Calculability.** The first McDonald's operating manual set the weight of a regular raw hamburger at 1.6 ounces, its size at 3.875 inches across, and its fat content at 19 percent. A slice of cheese weighs exactly half an ounce. Fries are cut precisely 9/32 of an inch thick.

   Think about how many objects around your home, the workplace, and campus are designed and mass-produced according to a uniform plan. Not just our environment but our life experiences—from traveling the nation's interstates to sitting at home viewing television—are more standardized than ever before.

3. **Uniformity and predictability.** An individual can walk into a McDonald's restaurant almost anywhere and receive the same sandwiches, drinks, and desserts prepared in precisely the same way.[3] Predictability, of course, is the result of a highly rational system that specifies every course of action and leaves nothing to chance.

4. **Control through automation.** The most unreliable element in the McDonald's system is human beings. People, after all, have good and bad days, sometimes let their minds wander, or simply decide to try something a different way. To minimize the unpredictable human element, McDonald's has automated its equipment to cook food at fixed temperatures for set lengths of time. Even the cash register at a McDonald's is little more than pictures of the items, so that ringing up a customer's order is as simple as possible.

Similarly, automatic teller machines are replacing banks, highly automated bakeries now produce bread with scarcely any human intervention, and chickens and eggs (or is it eggs and chickens?) emerge from automated hatcheries. In supermarkets, laser scanners are phasing out checking groceries by hand. We do most of our shopping in malls, where everything—from temperature and humidity to the kinds of stores and products—is carefully controlled and supervised (Ide & Cordell, 1994).

Can Rationality Be Irrational?

There can be no argument about the popularity or efficiency of McDonald's. But there is another side to the story.

Max Weber observed the expansion of formal organizations with alarm, fearing that they would cage the imagination and crush the human spirit. As Weber saw it, rational systems were efficient but dehumanizing, and McDonaldization bears him out. Each of the four principles just discussed limits human creativity, choice, and freedom. Echoing Weber, Ritzer states that "the ultimate irrationality of McDonaldization is that people

---

[2]Half a dozen popular sociology texts were not authored by the person or persons whose names appear on the cover. This book is not one of them.

[3]As McDonald's has "gone global," some products have been added or modified according to local tastes. For example, in Uruguay, customers enjoy the McHuevo (hamburger with poached egg on top); Norwegians can buy McLaks (grilled salmon sandwiches); the Dutch favor Groenteburger (vegetable burger); in Thailand, McDonald's serves Samurai pork burgers (pork burgers with teriyaki sauce); the Japanese can purchase Chicken Tatsuta Sandwich (chicken seasoned with soy and ginger); Filipinos eat McSpaghetti (spaghetti with tomato sauce and bits of hot dogs); and in India, where Hindus eat no beef, McDonald's sells a vegetarian Maharaja Mac (Sullivan, 1995).

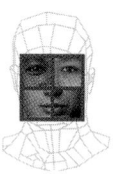

CONTROVERSY & DEBATE

Are Large Organizations a Threat to Personal Privacy?

Joe finishes dressing and calls an 800 number to check the pollen count. As he listens to a recorded message, a Caller ID computer identifies Joe, records the call, and pulls up Joe's profile from a public records database. The profile, which now includes the fact that Joe suffers from allergies, is sold to a drug company, which sends Joe a free sample of a new allergy medication.

At a local department store, Nina uses her American Express card to buy an expensive new watch and some sleepwear. The store's computer adds Nina's name to its database of "buyers of expensive jewelry" and "buyers of sexy lingerie." The store trades its database with other companies, and within a month Nina receives four jewelry catalogues and an adult video brochure (Bernstein, 1997).

Are these organizations providing consumers with interesting products, or are they violating people's privacy? The answer is both: The same systems that help organizations operate efficiently also let them invade our lives and manipulate us. So as large organizations have expanded in the United States, privacy has declined.

Small-town life in the past, of course, gave people little privacy. But at least if people knew something about you, you were just as likely to know something about them. Today, unknown people "out there" can access information about any of us at any time.

Our loss of privacy reflects the number and size of formal organizations, their tendency to treat people impersonally, and their appetite for information. In recent decades, the danger to privacy has increased as organizations have gone online, using computers to store and share information.

Consider some of the obvious ways in which organizations gather personal information. As state agencies issue driver's licenses, for example, they generate files they can dispatch at the touch of a button to other organizations, including police. Similarly, the Internal Revenue Service, the Social Security Administration, and government agencies that benefit veterans, students, the unemployed, and the poor all collect extensive information.

Business organizations now do much the same thing although, as these examples show, people may not be aware that their choices and activities end up in a company's database. Most people find credit cards a great convenience—the U.S. population now holds more than 1 billion of them, averaging more than five per adult—but few people stop to think that credit-card purchases automatically generate records that can end up almost anywhere. Our privacy is also endangered by the surveillance cameras that monitor more and more public places—along main street, in shopping malls, parks, and even across college campuses.

could lose control over the system and it would come to control us" (1993:145).

THE FUTURE OF ORGANIZATIONS: OPPOSING TRENDS

Early in the twentieth century, ever-larger organizations arose in the United States, most taking on the bureaucratic form described by Max Weber. In many respects, these organizations resembled armies led by powerful generals who issued orders to their captains and lieutenants. Foot soldiers—working in the factories—did what they were told.

With the emergence of a postindustrial economy after mid-century, as well as rising competition from abroad, many organizations have evolved toward a flatter, more flexible model that prizes communication and creativity. Such "intelligent organizations" (Pinchot & Pinchot, 1993) have become more productive than ever. Just as important, for highly skilled people whose information-age work demands "creative autonomy," these organizations create less of the alienation that so worried Max Weber.

But this is only half the story. Though the postindustrial economy has created many highly skilled jobs, it has created even more routine service jobs, as exemplified by McDonald's, which has employed one in eight

Concern about the erosion of privacy in the United States runs high. In response, many states have enacted laws giving citizens the right to examine records about themselves kept by employers, banks, and credit bureaus. The U.S. Privacy Act of 1974 also limits the exchange of personal information among government agencies and permits citizens to examine and correct most government files. But the fact is that so many organizations now have information about us—experts estimate that 90 percent of U.S. households are profiled in databases somewhere—that current laws simply cannot address the full scope of the problem.

Across the United States, who is most concerned about the growing assault on privacy? National Map 7–2 provides some insights.

SEEING OURSELVES

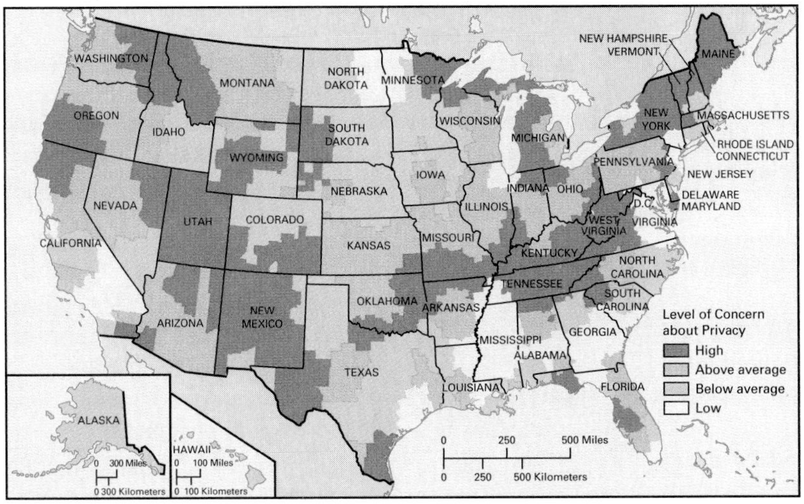

NATIONAL MAP 7–2 Concerns about Privacy across the United States

Source: *Business Geographics* © 1994 GIS World, Inc., 2101 S. Arlington Heights Boulevard, Arlington Heights, Ill., 60005-4185.

Continue the debate . . .

1. *Look over National Map 7–2. Where are people most concerned about losing their privacy? Can you explain this pattern?*
2. *Internet search engines such as YAHOO! [http://www.yahoo.com] have "people search" programs that let you locate almost anyone. Do you think such programs, on balance, help or harm the public?*
3. *In our current age of large organizations and expanding computer technology, do you think the privacy problem will get better or worse? Why?*

Sources: Dunn (1991), Miller (1991), Bernstein (1997), and Wright (1998).

adults in the United States (Ritzer, 1998). Work of this kind, which Ritzer terms "McJobs," offers few of the benefits that today's highly skilled workers enjoy. On the contrary, the automated routines that define work in the fast-food industry, telemarketing, and similar fields are very much the same as Frederick Taylor described a century ago.

Moreover, the organizational "flexibility" that gives better-off workers more autonomy carries the ever-present threat of "downsizing" for rank-and-file employees (Sennett, 1998). That is, organizations facing global competition are eager to have creative employees, but they are just as eager to cut costs by eliminating as many routine jobs as possible. The net result is that some people are better off than ever while others worry about holding their jobs and struggle to make ends meet—a trend that Chapter 11 ("Social Class in the United States") explores in detail.

In sum, many analysts conclude that U.S. organizations remain the envy of the world for their productive efficiency. Indeed, there are few places on earth where the mail arrives as quickly and dependably as it does in the United States (J. Wilson, 1991). But we should remember that the future is far brighter for some than for others. In addition, as the final box explains, organizations pose an increasing threat to our privacy—something to keep in mind as we envision our organizational future.

SUMMARY

1. Social groups are building blocks of society that join members as well as perform various tasks.
2. Primary groups tend to be small and person-oriented; secondary groups are typically large and goal-oriented.
3. Instrumental leadership is concerned with realizing a group's goals; expressive leadership focuses on members' morale and well-being.
4. Because group members often seek consensus, groups may pressure members toward conformity.
5. Individuals use reference groups—both ingroups and outgroups—to form attitudes and make evaluations.
6. Georg Simmel characterized the dyad relationship as intense but unstable; a triad, he added, can easily dissolve into a dyad by excluding one member.
7. Peter Blau explored how group size, homogeneity, and social standing and physical segregation of groups all affect members' behavior.
8. Social networks are relational webs that link people with little common identity and limited interaction. The Internet is a vast electronic network linking millions of people worldwide.
9. Formal organizations are large secondary groups that seek to perform complex tasks efficiently. They are classified as utilitarian, normative, or coercive, based on their members' reasons for joining.
10. Bureaucratic organization expands in modern societies to perform tasks efficiently. Bureaucracy is based on specialization, hierarchy, rules and regulations, technical competence, impersonal interaction, and formal, written communications.
11. Technology, political and economic trends, population patterns, and other organizations all combine to form the environment in which a particular business or agency must operate.
12. Ideally, bureaucracy promotes efficiency, but it can also lead to alienation and oligarchy and contributes to the erosion of personal privacy.
13. Frederick Taylor's scientific management shaped U.S. organizations a century ago. Since then, organizations have evolved toward a more open and flexible form as they have (a) included a larger share of women and other minorities, (b) responded to global competition, especially from Japan, and (c) shifted their focus from industrial production to postindustrial information processing.
14. Reflecting the collective spirit of Japanese culture, formal organizations in Japan are based more on personal ties than their U.S. counterparts.
15. The "McDonaldization" of society involves increasing automation and impersonality.
16. The future of organizations will likely involve opposing trends: toward more creative autonomy for highly skilled information workers and toward supervision and discipline for less skilled service workers.

KEY CONCEPTS

social group (p. 163) two or more people who identify and interact with one another

primary group (p. 164) a small social group whose members share personal and enduring relationships

secondary group (p. 164) a large and impersonal social group whose members pursue a specific goal or activity

instrumental leadership (p. 165) group direction that emphasizes the completion of tasks

expressive leadership (p. 165) group direction that focuses on collective well-being

groupthink (p. 168) the tendency of group members to conform, resulting in a narrow view of some issue

reference group (p. 168) a social group that serves as a point of reference in making evaluations and decisions

ingroup (p. 169) a social group commanding a member's esteem and loyalty

outgroup (p. 169) a social group toward which one feels competition or opposition

dyad (p. 169) a social group with two members

triad (p. 169) a social group with three members

network (p. 170) a web of weak social ties

formal organization (p. 173) a large secondary group organized to achieve its goals efficiently

bureaucracy (p. 174) an organizational model rationally designed to perform tasks efficiently

organizational environment (p. 175) a range of factors outside an organization that affects its operation

bureaucratic ritualism (p. 177) a preoccupation with rules and regulations to the point of thwarting an organization's goals

bureaucratic inertia (p. 177) the tendency of bureaucratic organizations to perpetuate themselves

oligarchy (p. 178) the rule of the many by the few

scientific management (p. 179) Frederick Taylor's term for the application of scientific principles to the operation of a business or other large organization

CRITICAL-THINKING QUESTIONS

1. What are the key differences between primary and secondary groups? Identify examples of each in your own life.
2. According to Max Weber, what are the six characteristic traits of bureaucracy? In what ways do new, "flexible" organizations differ?
3. George Ritzer (1996:1), a critic of the process he calls "McDonaldization," suggests that fast-food restaurants carry the following label: *Sociologists warn us that habitual use of McDonald's systems are destructive to our physical and psychological well-being as well as to society as a whole.* Do you agree? Why or why not?
4. The twentieth century was the first one with the widespread use of initials, such as IRS, IRA, IMF, IBM, CIA, WPA, PLO, NATO, CNN, CDC, and so on. What does this suggest about social trends?

APPLICATIONS AND EXERCISES

1. Spend several hours observing customers at a fast-food restaurant. Think about ways in which not just employees but also *customers* are trained to behave in certain ways. For example, customer norms include lining up to order and finding their own table. What other norms are at work?
2. Make a list of ingroups and outgroups on your campus. What traits account for groups falling into each category? Ask several people to comment on your list to see if they agree with your classification.
3. Using available publications (and some assistance from an instructor), try to draw an organizational pyramid for your college or university showing the key offices and how they supervise and report to each other.
4. Install the CD-ROM packaged in the back of this new textbook to access a variety of study, review, and applications exercises designed to help you better understand the material covered in this chapter. The CD includes an author's tip video, as well as interactive maps, video application exercises, Web links, and study questions.

SITES TO SEE

http://www.prenhall.com/macionis

Visit the interactive Web site that accompanies this text. Begin by clicking on the cover of your book. You will find a chapter-by-chapter study guide, practice tests, chat room, and many suggested Web links.

http://www.saturn.com

Visit the Saturn car company Web site to read about Saturn's "flatter" organizational structure.

http://www.mte.com/webcam

This Web site uses a camera placed at New York City's Fifth Avenue at Forty-fifth Street. Do you think Internet technology of this kind threatens people's privacy? Why or why not?

CHAPTER 8

Emil Kazaz
Saratoga, 1998

Oil on linen, 60 in. × 72 in. Collection of Rafael and Marina Akopian. Courtesy of Noah's Ark Fine Art.

DEVIANCE

Dear Family,

For some reason, I've sat here and prayed to the Lord for answers on why this is happening. Since Ms. Babin took the stand, I knew I was gonna get found guilty. Down in my heart, I truly believe the Gerardi family knew I didn't do it, and I know I didn't do it, the Lord knows, y'all know, my defense team knows, the State knows, and everyone else. But that's not the answer. We will never get an answer as to why this is happening to us.

Shareef Cousin wrote this letter to his family from prison.

The incident that sparked the case against him began about 10:30 P.M. on May 2, 1995, when Michael Gerardi and Connie Babin were leaving a restaurant in the French Quarter of New Orleans. Three young men approached the couple on the street as they were about to enter their car. Sensing an attack, Gerardi told Babin to run. As she turned to flee, she saw one of the young men walk up to Gerardi and shoot him in the face, killing him.

Charged with the crime, Cousin sat in the courtroom as Babin testified he was the one who fired the gun. The jury convicted Cousin of murder, and the court handed down the death sentence. At age sixteen, Cousin found himself at the Louisiana State Prison at Angola, one of the youngest people in the United States locked up on death row.

Cousin continued to declare his innocence. A year later, during the appeals process, sufficient doubt was raised about his guilt that the murder conviction was set aside. As part of the deal, however, Cousin agreed that he took part in the robbery. At first elated to be off death row, he soon realized he would still spend years behind bars. Cousin continues to maintain his innocence, but he is bitter and depressed (Farley & Willwerth, 1997; Shareef-Cousin.com, 1999).

This chapter explores the problem of violent crime and other offenses, profiles offenders, and looks at the criminal justice system. First, however, we tackle the broader issue of why societies develop standards of right and wrong in the first place. As we shall see, law is simply one part of a complex system of social control: Society teaches us all to conform, at least most of the time, to countless rules. We begin our investigation by defining several basic concepts.

WHAT IS DEVIANCE?

Deviance is *the recognized violation of cultural norms.* Because norms guide almost all human activities, the concept of deviance is quite broad. One category of deviance is **crime,** *the violation of society's formally enacted criminal law.* Even criminal deviance spans a wide range of behavior, from minor traffic violations to sexual assault to murder.

The kind of deviance people create reflects the moral values they embrace. The Berkeley campus of the University of California has long celebrated its open-minded tolerance of sexual diversity. Thus, in 1992, when Andrew Martinez decided to attend classes wearing virtually nothing, people were reluctant to accuse "The Naked Guy" of immoral conduct. However, in Berkeley's politically correct atmosphere, it was not long before school officials banned Martinez from campus—charging that his nudity constituted a form of sexual harassment.

Not all deviance involves action or even choice. The very existence of some categories of individuals can be troublesome to others. To the young, elderly people may seem hopelessly "out of it"; and to some whites, the mere presence of people of color causes discomfort. Able-bodied people often view people with disabilities as an outgroup, just as affluent people may shun the poor for falling short of their standards.

Most examples of nonconformity that come readily to mind are negative instances of rule breaking, such as stealing from a convenience store, abusing a child, or driving while intoxicated. But we also define especially righteous people—students who speak up too much in class or people who are overly enthusiastic about new computer technology—as deviant, even if we accord them a measure of respect (Huls, 1987). What deviant actions or attitudes—whether negative or positive—have in common is some element of *difference* that causes us to regard another person as an "outsider" (Becker, 1966).

SOCIAL CONTROL

All of us are subject to **social control,** *attempts by society to regulate people's thought and behavior.* Often, this process is informal, as when parents praise or scold their children or friends make fun of someone's musical taste. Serious deviance, however, may involve the **criminal justice system,** *a formal response by police, courts, and prison officials to alleged violations of the law.*

In sum, deviance is much more than a matter of individual choice or personal failing. *How* a society defines deviance, *who* is branded as deviant, and *what* people decide to do about deviance are all issues of social organization. Only gradually, however, have people recognized this fact, as we shall now explain.

THE BIOLOGICAL CONTEXT

Chapter 5 ("Socialization") explained that people a century ago understood—or, more correctly, misunderstood—human behavior as an expression of biological instincts. Early interest in criminality thus emphasized biological causes. In 1876, Caesare Lombroso (1835–1909), an Italian physician who worked in prisons, proposed that criminals stand out physically—with low foreheads, prominent jaws and cheekbones, big ears, hairiness, and unusually long arms. All in all, Lombroso's profile of a criminal resembled the apelike ancestors of human beings.

But the physical features that Lombroso attributed to prisoners could be found throughout the entire population. We now know that no physical attributes, of the kind described by Lombroso, set off criminals from noncriminals (Goring, 1972; orig. 1913).

At mid-century, William Sheldon (Sheldon, Hartl, & McDermott, 1949) took a different tack, suggesting that body shape predicted criminality. He cross-checked hundreds of young men for body type and criminal history, and concluded that criminality was most likely among boys with muscular, athletic builds. Sheldon Glueck and Eleanor Glueck (1950) confirmed Sheldon's conclusion, but cautioned that a powerful build does not necessarily cause criminality. Parents, they suggested, tend to be somewhat distant from powerfully built sons, who, in turn, grow up to show less sensitivity toward others. Moreover, in a self-fulfilling prophecy, people who expect muscular boys to act like bullies may provoke such aggressive behavior.

Today, genetics research seeks possible links between biology and crime. Though no conclusive evidence connects criminality to any specific genetic trait, people's overall genetic make-up, in combination with social influences, probably accounts for some tendency toward criminality. In other words, biological factors may have a real, but modest, effect on whether or not an individual becomes a criminal (Rowe, 1983; Rowe & Osgood, 1984; Wilson & Herrnstein, 1985; Jencks, 1987; Pallone & Hennessy, 1998).

Critical evaluation. At best, biological theories that try to explain crime in terms of rare physical traits explain only a small proportion of all crimes. Recent sociobiological research—noting, for example, that violent crime is overwhelmingly committed by males and that adults are more likely to abuse foster children than natural children—is promising, but we know too little about the links between genes and human behavior to draw firm conclusions (Daly & Wilson, 1988).

Then, too, because a biological approach looks at the individual, it offers no insight as to how some kinds of behaviors come to be defined as deviant in the first place. Therefore, although there is much to be learned about how human biology may affect behavior, research currently puts far greater emphasis on social influences (Gibbons & Krohn, 1986; Liska, 1991).

PERSONALITY FACTORS

Like biological theories, psychological explanations of deviance focus on individual abnormality. Some personality traits are hereditary, but most psychologists think that personality is shaped primarily by social experience. Deviance, then, is viewed as the product of "unsuccessful" socialization.

Research by Walter Reckless and Simon Dinitz (1967) illustrates the psychological approach. Reckless and Dinitz asked a number of teachers to categorize twelve-year-old male students as either likely or unlikely to get into trouble with the law. They then interviewed both the boys and their mothers to assess each boy's self-concept and how he related to others. Analyzing their results, Reckless and Dinitz found that the "good boys" displayed a stronger conscience (or superego, in Sigmund Freud's terminology), could handle frustration, and identified with cultural norms and values. The "bad boys," by contrast, had a weaker conscience, displayed little tolerance for frustration, and felt out of step with conventional culture.

As we might expect, the "good boys" had fewer run-ins with the police than the "bad boys." Since all the boys lived in an area where delinquency was widespread, Reckless and Dinitz attributed staying out of trouble to a personality that reined in deviant impulses—an idea they call *containment theory.*

Critical evaluation. Psychologists have shown that personality patterns have some connection to deviance. However, the fact is that most serious crimes are committed by people whose psychological profiles are *normal.*

Overall, both biological and psychological research view deviance as an individual trait, without exploring how conceptions of right and wrong initially arise, why people define some rule breakers—but not others—as deviant, or what role power plays in shaping a society's system of social control. To explore these issues, we now turn to a sociological analysis of deviance.

THE SOCIAL FOUNDATIONS OF DEVIANCE

Although we tend to view deviance in terms of the free choice or personal failings of individuals, all behavior—deviance as well as conformity—is shaped by society. Three social foundations of deviance are identified below and explained in more detail in later sections of the chapter:

1. **Deviance varies according to cultural norms.** No thought or action is inherently deviant; it becomes deviant only in relation to particular norms. Norms, of course, vary from place to place, so deviance also varies. In certain places Nevada permits prostitution, a practice outlawed in all other states. Casinos in Atlantic City, Las Vegas, and on Mississippi riverboats and numerous Indian reservations beckon high rollers, but everywhere else in the United States gambling is illegal. Further, most cities and towns have at least one unique statute. For example, South Padre Island, Texas, bans wearing ties; Mount Prospect, Illinois, has a law against keeping pigeons or bees; Los Angeles bans the use of gas-powered leaf blowers; and Beverly Hills regulates the number of tennis balls allowed on the court at one time (Sanders & Horn, 1998).

Artists have an important function in any society: to explore alternatives to conventional notions about how to live. For this reason, while we celebrate artists' creativity, we also accord them a mildly deviant identity. In today's more conservative political climate, some government officials have objected to art that seems to challenge traditional morality. For their part, some artists have found expressive ways to show their displeasure with such thinking.

Around the world, what is considered deviant is even more diverse. Albania outlaws any public display of religious faith, such as "crossing" oneself; Cuba and Vietnam can prosecute their citizens for "consorting with foreigners"; Singapore bans the sale of chewing gum; police in Iran can arrest a woman for wearing makeup; and U.S. citizens risk arrest by traveling to Libya or Iraq.

2. **People become deviant as others define them that way.** Everyone violates cultural norms, sometimes to the extent of breaking the law. For example, most of us sometimes walk around talking to ourselves or occasionally "borrow" a pen from our workplace. Whether such behavior defines us as mentally ill or criminal depends on how others perceive, define, and respond to our behavior.
3. **Both rule-making and rule-breaking involve social power.** The law, claimed Karl Marx, is the means by which powerful people protect their interests. A homeless person who stands on a street corner denouncing the government risks arrest for disturbing the peace; a mayoral candidate during an election campaign does exactly the same thing and receives police protection. In short, norms and how we apply them reflect social inequality.

STRUCTURAL-FUNCTIONAL ANALYSIS

The key insight of the structural-functional paradigm is that deviance is a necessary part of social organization. This point was made a century ago by Emile Durkheim.

EMILE DURKHEIM: THE FUNCTIONS OF DEVIANCE

In his pioneering study of deviance, Emile Durkheim (1964a, orig. 1895; 1964b, orig. 1893) made the surprising statement that there is nothing abnormal about deviance. In fact, it fulfills four essential functions:

1. **Deviance affirms cultural values and norms.** As moral creatures, people must prefer some attitudes and behaviors to others. But any conception of virtue rests on an opposing notion of vice: There can be no good without evil, and no justice without crime. Deviance, then, is needed to define and sustain morality.
2. **Responding to deviance clarifies moral boundaries.** By defining some people as deviant, society draws a boundary between right and wrong. For example, a college marks the line between academic honesty and cheating by punishing students who plagiarize.

3. **Responding to deviance promotes social unity.** People typically react to serious deviance with collective outrage. In this way, Durkheim explained, they reaffirm the moral ties that bind them. For example, after the Columbine High School shootings in 1999, feelings of anguish and outrage brought together not just that community but the entire nation.
4. **Deviance encourages social change.** Deviant people push a society's moral boundaries, suggesting alternatives to the status quo and encouraging change. Today's deviance, declared Durkheim, can become tomorrow's morality (1964a:71). Look, for example, how rock and roll—condemned as morally degenerate in the 1950s—became a multibillion-dollar industry just a few years later.

An Illustration: The Puritans of Massachusetts Bay

Kai Erikson's (1966) study of the Puritans of Massachusetts Bay brings Durkheim's theory to life. Erikson shows that even the Puritans—a disciplined and highly religious group—created deviance to clarify their moral boundaries. In fact, Durkheim might well have had the Puritans in mind when he wrote:

> Imagine a society of saints, a perfect cloister of exemplary individuals. Crimes, properly so called, will there be unknown; but faults which appear [insignificant] to the layman will create there the same scandal that the ordinary offense does in ordinary consciousness. . . . For the same reason, the perfect and upright man judges his smallest failings with a severity that the majority reserve for acts more truly in the nature of an offense. (1964a:68–69)

Deviance, in short, is not a matter of a few "bad apples"; it is a necessary condition of "good" social living.

Deviance may be universal, but the *kind* of deviance people generate depends on the moral issues they seek to clarify. The Puritans, for example, experienced a number of "crime waves." With each response, the Puritans sharpened their views on crucial moral issues. They answered questions about the range of proper beliefs by celebrating some of their members and condemning others as deviant.

Perhaps most fascinating of all, Erikson discovered that even though the offenses changed, the proportion of deviant Puritans remained steady over time. This stability, concludes Erikson, confirms Durkheim's contention that deviants serve to mark a society's changing moral boundaries. In other words, by constantly defining a small number of people as deviant, the Puritans maintained a moral "shape" to their society.

Emile Durkheim's important insight is that no society can exist without deviance. Thus, after arriving in New England in the early seventeenth century, the very religious Puritans soon found themselves accusing some of their members of serious wrongdoing. The best known Puritan "crime wave" climaxed in the Salem witch trials of 1692, which led to two dozen executions of women and men thought to be doing the work of the devil.

MERTON'S STRAIN THEORY

Some deviance may be necessary for a society to function, but Robert Merton (1938, 1968) argued that excessive deviance results from particular social arrangements. Specifically, the extent and kind of deviance depend on whether a society provides the *means* (such as schooling and job opportunities) to achieve cultural *goals* (such as financial success).

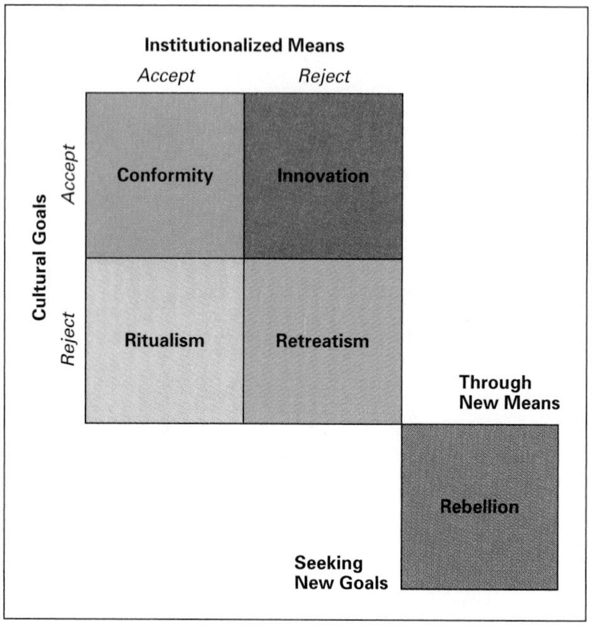

FIGURE 8–1 Merton's Strain Theory of Deviance

Source: Merton (1968).

Conformity, says Merton, lies in pursuing conventional goals through approved means. Thus, our "success stories" celebrate people who acquire wealth and prestige through talent and hard work. But not everyone who seeks conventional success has the opportunity to attain it. People raised in poverty, for example, may see little chance of becoming successful if they play by the rules. As a result, they may try to make money through crime—say, by dealing cocaine. Merton called this type of deviance *innovation*—using unconventional means (drug sales) to achieve a culturally approved goal (wealth). Figure 8–1 shows innovation as accepting the cultural goal (financial success) while rejecting the conventional means (hard work).

According to Merton, the "strain" between our culture's emphasis on wealth and the limited opportunity to get rich gives rise, especially among the poor, to theft and the sale of drugs or other street crime. In some respects, at least, a notorious gangster like Al Capone was quite conventional—he pursued the fame and fortune at the heart of the "American Dream." But, like many minorities who find the doors to "legitimate" success hard to open, Capone blazed his own trail to the top. As one analyst put it:

> The typical criminal of the Capone era was a boy who had . . . seen what was rated as success in the society he had been thrust into—the Cadillac, the big bankroll, the elegant apartment. How could he acquire that kind of recognizable status? He was almost always a boy of outstanding initiative, imagination, and ability; he was the kind of boy who, under different conditions, would have been a captain of industry or a key political figure of his time. But he hadn't the opportunity of going to Yale and becoming a banker or broker; there was no passage for him to a law degree from Harvard. There was, however, a relatively easy way of acquiring these goods that he was incessantly told were available to him as an American citizen, and without which he had begun to feel he could not properly count himself as an American citizen. He could become a gangster. (Allsop, 1961:236)

Perhaps we should not be surprised at the fact that Capone, with little chance of attending Yale or Harvard, landed his first job with a gangster who called himself Mr. Frankie Yale and owned a nightclub named the "Harvard Inn."

The inability to become successful by normative means may also lead to another type of deviance that Merton calls *ritualism* (see Figure 8–1). Low-level bureaucrats, for example, knowing they will achieve only limited financial success, stick closely to the rules in order to feel and appear "respectable."

A third response to the inability to succeed is *retreatism*—the rejection of both cultural goals and means—so that one, in effect, "drops out." Some alcoholics, drug addicts, and street people are retreatists. The deviance of retreatists lies in their unconventional lifestyle and, perhaps more seriously, in their choosing to live this way.

The fourth response to failure is *rebellion.* Like retreatists, rebels reject both the cultural definition of success and the normative means of achieving it. Rebels—such as radical "survivalists"—go one step further by forming a counterculture and advocating alternatives to the existing social order.

DEVIANT SUBCULTURES

Richard Cloward and Lloyd Ohlin (1966) extended Merton's theory, proposing that crime results not just from limited legitimate (legal) opportunity but also from readily accessible illegitimate (illegal) opportunity. In short, deviance or conformity arises from the *relative opportunity structure* that frames a person's life.

The life of Al Capone shows how an ambitious person denied legitimate opportunity could take advantage

In the Kosovo region of Serbia, as in the United States, young people (especially males) cut off from legitimate opportunity may form deviant subcultures as a strategy to gain the prestige denied them by the larger society.

of an illegal opportunity—supplying alcohol during Prohibition (1920–1933). In other words, illegal opportunities foster the development of *criminal subcultures* that provide people with the knowledge, skills, and other resources to succeed in unconventional ways. Capone, for example, built a criminal empire. Indeed, gangs may specialize in one or another form of criminality according to available opportunities and resources (Sheley et al., 1995).

But what happens when people cannot identify *any* kind of opportunity, legal or illegal? Then, deviance often surfaces in the form of *conflict subcultures* (such as armed street gangs), where violence is ignited by frustration and a desire for respect. Alternatively, those who fail to succeed, even using criminal means, may fall into *retreatist subcultures*, dropping out through alcohol or other drug abuse.

Albert Cohen (1971; orig. 1955) suggests that delinquency is most pronounced among lower-class youths because they have the least opportunity to achieve conventional success. Neglected by society, they seek self-respect by creating a delinquent subculture that "defines as meritorious the characteristics they *do* possess, the kinds of conduct of which they *are* capable" (1971:66). Being feared on the street, for example, may win few points with society as a whole, but it may satisfy a youth's desire to "be somebody" in the local neighborhood.

Walter Miller (1970) adds that delinquent subcultures are characterized by (1) *trouble*, arising from frequent conflict with teachers and police; (2) *toughness*, the value placed on physical size and strength, especially among males; (3) *smartness*, the ability to succeed on the streets, to outsmart or "con" others, and to avoid being similarly taken advantage of; (4) *a need for excitement*, the search for thrills, risk, or danger; (5) *a belief in fate*, a sense that people lack control over their own lives; and (6) *a desire for freedom*, often expressed as hostility toward figures of authority.

Finally, Elijah Anderson (1994) explains that the majority of people in poor, urban neighborhoods conform to conventional ("decent") values. Some young men, however, faced with neighborhood crime and violence, hostility from police, and sometimes even neglect from their own parents, adopt a "street code." To show that he can take care of himself and thus survive on the street, a young man displays "nerve," a willingness to stand up to any threat. According to this code, explains Anderson, even a violent death is better than being "dissed" (disrespected) by others. Some manage to escape the dangers, but the risk of ending up in jail—or worse—is very high for these young men pushed to the margins of our society.

Critical evaluation. Durkheim made an important contribution by pointing out the functions of deviance.

The world is full of people who are unusual in one way or another. This Indian man grew the fingernails on one hand for more than thirty years just to do something that no one else had ever done. Should we define such behavior as harmless eccentricity or as evidence of mental illness?

However, evidence shows that a community does not always come together in reaction to crime; sometimes fear of crime drives people to withdraw from public life (Liska & Warner, 1991).

Merton's strain theory has been criticized for explaining some kinds of deviance (theft, for example) far better than others (such as crimes of passion or mental illness). Moreover, not everyone seeks success in conventional terms of wealth, as strain theory implies.

The general argument of Cloward and Ohlin, Cohen, Miller, and Anderson—that deviance reflects the opportunity structure of society—has been confirmed by subsequent research (cf. Allan & Steffensmeier, 1989; Uggen, 1999). However, these theories, too, fall short in assuming that everyone shares the same cultural standards for judging right and wrong. Moreover, we must be careful not to define deviance in ways that unfairly target poor people. If we define crime to include stock fraud as well as street theft, then more affluent people will be counted among criminals. Finally, all structural-functional theories imply that everyone who breaks the rules is labeled deviant. Becoming deviant, however, is actually a highly complex process, as the next section explains.

SYMBOLIC-INTERACTION ANALYSIS

The symbolic-interaction paradigm explains how people define deviance in everyday situations. From this point of view, definitions of deviance and conformity are surprisingly flexible.

LABELING THEORY

The central contribution of symbolic-interaction analysis is **labeling theory,** *the idea that deviance and conformity result not only from what people do but from how others respond to those actions.* Labeling theory stresses the relativity of deviance, meaning that people may define the same behavior in any number of ways. Thus, deviance is nothing more than behavior that people define as deviant (Becker, 1966).

Consider these situations: A woman takes an article of clothing from a roommate; a married man at a convention has sex with a prostitute; a mayor gives a big city contract to a major campaign contributor. In each case, "reality" depends on the response of others. Is the first situation a matter of borrowing or theft? The consequences of the second case depend largely on whether the man's behavior becomes known back home. In the third situation, is the official choosing a good contractor or paying off a political debt? The social construction of reality, then, is a highly variable process of detection, definition, and response.

More broadly, since "reality" depends on time and place, it is no surprise that one society's conformity may be another's deviance. The box describes cockfighting. Is this sport an important cultural ritual or a vicious abuse of animals?

Primary and Secondary Deviance

Edwin Lemert (1951, 1972) observed that some episodes of norm violation—say, skipping school or underage drinking—provoke slight reaction from others and have little effect on a person's self-concept. Lemert calls such passing episodes *primary deviance.*

But what happens if other people notice someone's deviance and make something of it? If, for example,

GLOBAL SOCIOLOGY

Cockfighting: Cultural Ritual or Abuse of Animals?

You won't see it on television, but one of the world's most popular sports—from North America to Europe to Asia—is cockfighting. It is legal in parts of Louisiana, Texas, New Mexico, and Arizona, big business in Mexico, and something of a national pastime in the Philippines. There, the local cock pit is as important as the town square in the U.S. Midwest: Every village has one, and it draws a crowd on weekends and fiesta days.

On the surface, cockfights are about gambling. An afternoon or evening event might include ten fights. A fight begins with the cock owners displaying their birds to one another, calling out for bets as to the stronger bird. Members of the audience weigh in with cash. Keeping track of the bets is the *cristo,* someone who stands, arms extended, taking money.

With the odds set and the money on the table, the actual combat begins. Each rooster is outfitted with a small, sharp blade strapped to the rear of the left leg. The cocks need little encouragement to fight, but the owners do a bit of strutting themselves, swinging their birds in front of each other before dropping them on lines drawn in the pit sand. Upon hitting the ground, the birds fly at one another, merging in a blur of legs and feathers.

Within a few minutes, one bird may collapse from exhaustion; the owner steps in to revive his cock and the process is repeated. Before long, however, a blade finds its mark. The victor, the bird that will live to fight another day, perches on the vanquished, which will not.

In many parts of the world, cockfighting is an important male ritual. Men raise their roosters for about two years, often at considerable expense, and care for them like sons. In the ritual of the cockfight itself, men test their own claims to manhood, establish their standing in the community's pecking order, and pass on to their sons lessons about honor, competition, and masculinity.

Many outside observers are repulsed by the spectacle. But cockfighting is obviously important to insiders. Should one condemn it as brutality or respect it as ceremony?

Sources: Based on *The Economist* (1994), Harris (1994), and the author's research in the Philippines.

people begin to describe a young man as a "boozer" and evict him from their social circle, he may become embittered, drink even more, and seek the company of others who approve of his behavior. In this way, the response to initial deviance sets in motion *secondary deviance,* by which an individual repeatedly violates a norm and begins to take on a deviant identity. The development of secondary deviance is one application of the Thomas theorem (discussed in Chapter 6, "Social Interaction in Everyday Life"), which states that "situations defined as real become real in their consequences."

Stigma

Secondary deviance marks the start of what Erving Goffman (1963) calls a *deviant career.* As individuals develop a stronger commitment to deviant behavior, they typically acquire a **stigma,** *a powerfully negative label that greatly changes a person's self-concept and social identity.*

Stigma operates as a master status (see Chapter 6), overpowering other aspects of social identity so that a person is discredited in the minds of others, becoming socially isolated. Sometimes an entire community formally stigmatizes an individual through what Harold Garfinkel (1956) calls a *degradation ceremony.* A criminal prosecution is one example, operating much like a high school graduation in reverse: A person stands before the community to be labeled in a negative rather than a positive way.

Retrospective and Projective Labeling

Once people stigmatize an individual, they may engage in *retrospective labeling*, interpreting someone's past in light of some present deviance (Scheff, 1984). For example, after discovering that a priest has sexually molested a child, others rethink his past, perhaps musing, "He always did want to be around young children." Retrospective labeling distorts a person's biography by being highly selective and helps deepen a deviant identity.

Similarly, people may engage in *projective labeling* of a stigmatized person. That is, they use a deviant identity to predict future action. People might say of the priest, for example, "He's just going to keep at it until he gets caught." The more others think such things, of course, the greater the chance that they will come true.

Labeling and Mental Illness

Is a woman who believes that Jesus rides the bus to work with her every day mentally ill or just expressing her strong religious faith? Is a homeless man who refuses to allow police to take him to a city shelter on a cold night mentally ill or simply trying to live independently?

The psychiatrist Thomas Szasz charges that people apply the label of "insanity" to what is only "difference." Therefore, he concludes, we should abandon the concept of mental illness entirely (1961, 1970, 1994, 1995). Illness, Szasz continues, is physical, and afflicts only the body; "mental" illness, then, is a myth. The world is full of people whose "differences" in thought or action may irritate us, but such differences are no grounds for defining someone as mentally ill. Such labeling, Szasz claims, simply enforces conformity to the standards of people powerful enough to impose their will on others.

Most health care professionals reject the notion that all mental illness is a fiction. But some hail Szasz's work for pointing out the danger of using medicine to promote conformity. Most of us, after all, experience periods of extreme stress or other mental instability from time to time. Such episodes, although upsetting, are usually of passing importance. If, however, others respond with negative labeling, the long-term result may be further deviance as a self-fulfilling prophecy (Scheff, 1984; Rosenfeld, 1997).

THE MEDICALIZATION OF DEVIANCE

Labeling theory, particularly the ideas of Szasz and Goffman, helps explain an important shift in the way our society understands deviance. Over the last fifty years, the growing influence of psychiatry and medicine in the United States has encouraged the **medicalization of deviance,** *the transformation of moral and legal deviance into a medical condition.*

Medicalization amounts to swapping one set of labels for another. In moral terms, we evaluate people or their behavior as "bad" or "good." However, the scientific objectivity of modern medicine passes no moral judgment, instead using clinical diagnoses such as "sick" or "well."

To illustrate, until the middle of this century, people generally viewed alcoholics as morally weak and easily tempted by the pleasure of drink. Gradually, however, medical specialists redefined alcoholism so that most people now consider alcoholism a disease, making individuals "sick" rather than "bad." Similarly, obesity, drug addiction, child abuse, sexual promiscuity, and other behaviors that used to be moral matters are widely defined today as illnesses for which people need help rather than punishment. National Map 8–1 suggests where in the United States this transformation has been most pronounced.

The Difference Labels Make

Whether we define deviance as a moral or medical issue has three consequences. First, it affects *who responds* to deviance. An offense against common morality usually brings about a reaction from members of the community or the police. A medical label, however, places the situation under the control of clinical specialists, including counselors, psychiatrists, and physicians.

A second difference is *how people respond* to deviance. A moral approach defines the deviant as an "offender" subject to punishment. Medically, however, "patients" need treatment (for their own good, of course). Therefore, whereas punishment is designed to fit the crime, treatment programs are tailored to the patient and may involve virtually any therapy that a specialist thinks will prevent future illness (von Hirsh, 1986).

Third, and most important, the two labels differ on *the personal competence of the deviant person.* Morally speaking, whether we are right or wrong, at least we take

SEEING OURSELVES

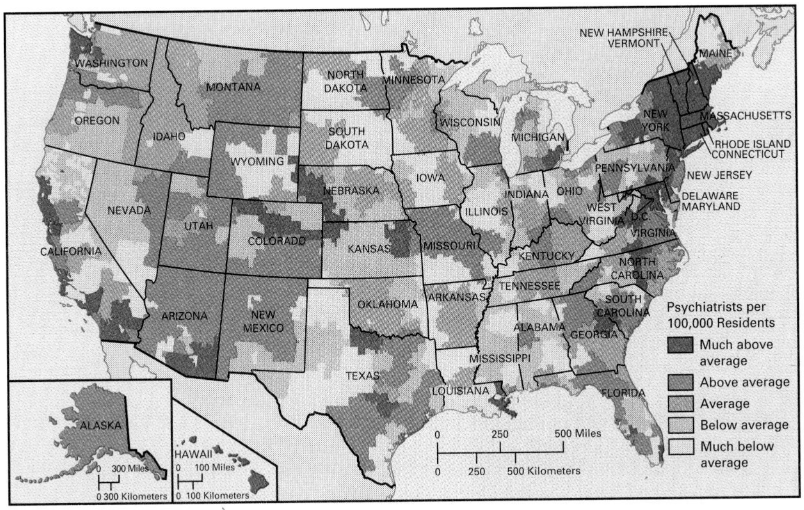

NATIONAL MAP 8–1
Where Psychiatrists Practice across the United States

In general, psychiatrists are found in cities and are heavily concentrated along the East and West coasts of the United States. By contrast, few psychiatrists work in the Plains states in the central region of the country. To some extent, these doctors work where the people are. But what other factors may explain this pattern?

Source: From *The Dartmouth Atlas of Health Care.* Copyright ©1996 by the Trustees of Dartmouth College. Reprinted with permission.

responsibility for our own behavior. Once defined as sick, however, we are seen as lacking the capacity to control (or, if "mentally ill," even understand) our actions. People who are incompetent are, in turn, subject to treatment against their will. For this reason alone, attempts to define deviance in medical terms should be made only with extreme caution.

SUTHERLAND'S DIFFERENTIAL ASSOCIATION THEORY

Learning any behavioral patterns—whether conforming or deviant—is a social process that takes place in groups. Therefore, according to Edwin Sutherland (1940), a person's tendency toward conformity or deviance depends on the amount of contact with others who encourage—or reject—conventional behavior. This is Sutherland's theory of *differential association.*

We can illustrate Sutherland's theory with a study of drug and alcohol use among young adults in the United States (Akers et al., 1979). Questionnaires completed by juniors and seniors in high school showed a close connection between the extent of alcohol and drug use and the degree to which peer groups encouraged such activity. The researchers concluded that young people accept delinquent patterns insofar as they receive praise and other rewards for defining deviance—rather than conformity—in positive terms.

HIRSCHI'S CONTROL THEORY

The sociologist Travis Hirschi (1969; Gottfredson & Hirschi, 1995) developed *control theory,* which states that social control depends on imagining the consequences of one's behavior. Hirschi assumes that everyone finds at least some deviance tempting. But imagining the reaction of family and friends deters most people; for others, the thought of a ruined career is enough. On the other hand, individuals who feel they have little to lose from deviance are likely to become rule-breakers.

Specifically, Hirschi continues, there are four types of social control:

1. **Attachment.** Strong social attachments encourage conformity; weak relationships in the family, peer group, and school leave people freer to engage in deviance.
2. **Commitment.** The greater a person's commitment to legitimate opportunity, the greater the advantages of conformity. By contrast, someone with little confidence in future success is more likely to drift toward deviance.
3. **Involvement.** Extensive involvement in legitimate activities—such as holding a job, going to school, and playing sports—inhibits deviance. People who simply "hang out," waiting for

Artist Frank Romero was one of the founders of the Chicano movement in the late 1960s. Drawing on his own childhood in East Los Angeles, his art depicts the importance of cars, gangs, and violence in young people's efforts to gain a sense of importance and belonging in a society that has pushed them to its margins.

Frank Romero, *Freeway Wars*, 1990, Serigraph, 31½ × 38 inches. © Frank Romero.
Nicolas and Cristina Hernandez Trust Collection, Pasadena, California.

something to happen, have time and energy for deviant activity.

4. **Belief.** Strong belief in conventional morality and respect for authority figures control tendencies toward deviance. People with a weak conscience, and who are left unsupervised, are more vulnerable to temptation (Osgood et al., 1996).

Hirschi's analysis draws together a number of earlier ideas about the causes of deviant behavior. Note that a person's relative social privilege and strength of moral character give the individual a stake in conforming to conventional norms (Wiatrowski, Griswold, & Roberts, 1981; Sampson & Laub, 1990; Free, 1992).

Critical evaluation. The various symbolic-interaction theories see deviance as process. Labeling theory links deviance not to *action* but to the *reaction* of others. Thus, some people come to be defined as deviant while others who think or behave in the same way are not. The concepts of secondary deviance, deviant careers, and stigma demonstrate how being labeled deviant can become a lasting self-concept.

Yet labeling theory has several limitations. First, this theory's highly relative view of deviance ignores the fact that some kinds of behavior, such as murder, are condemned just about everywhere (Wellford, 1980). Labeling theory thus works best in the case of less serious deviance, such as using illegal drugs or mental illness. Second, research on the consequences of deviant labeling has yet to answer a basic question: Does deviant labeling produce further deviance or discourage it (Smith & Gartin, 1989; Sherman & Smith, 1992)? Third, not everyone resists being labeled as deviant; some people actually seek it out (Vold & Bernard, 1986). For example, people take part in civil disobedience and willingly subject themselves to arrest in order to call attention to social injustice.

Both Sutherland's differential association theory and Hirschi's control theory have had considerable influence in sociology. But they provide little insight into why a society's norms and laws define certain kinds of activities as deviant in the first place. This important question is addressed by social-conflict analysis, the focus of the next section.

SOCIAL-CONFLICT ANALYSIS

The social-conflict paradigm demonstrates how deviance reflects social inequality. This approach holds that who or what is labeled "deviant" depends on which categories of people hold power in a society.

DEVIANCE AND POWER

Alexander Liazos (1972) points out that the people we commonly consider deviants—"nuts, sluts, and 'preverts'"—are people who share the trait of powerlessness. That is, bag ladies (not corporate polluters) and unemployed men on street corners (not arms dealers) carry the stigma of deviance.

Social-conflict theory explains this pattern in three ways: First, the norms—and especially laws—of any society generally reflect the interests of the rich and powerful. People who threaten the wealthy, either by taking their property or by advocating a more egalitarian society, are defined as "common thieves" or "political radicals." As noted in Chapter 4 ("Society"), Karl Marx argued that the law (and all social institutions) supports the interests of the rich. Or, as Richard Quinney puts it: "Capitalist justice is by the capitalist class, for the capitalist class, and against the working class" (1977:3).

Second, even if their behavior is called into question, the powerful have the resources to resist deviant labels. Corporate executives who order the dumping of hazardous wastes are rarely held personally accountable. Moreover, as the O. J. Simpson trial made clear, even when charged with violent crimes, the rich have the resources to resist being labeled as criminal.

Third, the widespread belief that norms and laws are natural and good masks their political character. For this reason, we may condemn the *unequal application* of the law but give little thought to whether the *laws themselves* are inherently fair (Quinney, 1977).

DEVIANCE AND CAPITALISM

In the Marxist tradition, Steven Spitzer (1980) argues that deviant labels are applied to people who interfere with the operation of capitalism. First, because capitalism is based on private control of wealth, people who threaten the property of others—especially the poor who steal from the rich—are prime candidates for being labeled deviant. Conversely, the rich who exploit the poor are unlikely to be defined as deviant. Landlords, for example, who charge poor tenants high rents and evict anyone who cannot pay are not considered a threat to society; they are simply "doing business."

Second, because capitalism depends on productive labor, people who cannot or will not work risk being labeled deviant. Many members of our society think people who are out of work—even through no fault of their own—are somehow deviant.

Third, capitalism depends on respect for authority figures, so people who resist authority are labeled deviant. Examples are children who skip school or talk back to parents and teachers and adults who do not cooperate with employers or police.

Fourth, anyone who directly challenges the capitalist status quo is likely to be defined as deviant. In this category are antiwar activists, radical environmentalists, and labor organizers.

To turn the argument around, society positively labels whatever promotes the capitalist system. Winning athletes, for example, enjoy celebrity status because they express the values of individual achievement and competition that are vital to capitalism. Moreover, Spitzer notes, we condemn using drugs of escape (marijuana, psychedelics, heroin, and crack) as deviant, but endorse drugs that promote adjustment to the status quo (alcohol and caffeine).

The capitalist system also strives to control people who don't fit into the system. The elderly, people with mental or physical disabilities, as well as Robert Merton's retreatists (people addicted to alcohol or other drugs) are a "costly yet relatively harmless burden" on society. Such people, claims Spitzer, are subject to control by social welfare agencies. But people who openly challenge the capitalist system, including the inner-city underclass and revolutionaries—Merton's innovators and rebels—are controlled by the criminal justice system and, in times of crisis, military forces such as the National Guard.

Notice that both the social welfare and criminal justice systems blame individuals—not the system—for social problems. Welfare recipients are deemed unworthy freeloaders; poor people who vent their rage are labeled rioters; anyone who challenges the government is branded a radical or a Communist; and those who attempt to acquire illegally what they cannot obtain otherwise are rounded up as common criminals.

WHITE-COLLAR CRIME

In 1987, a Wall Street stockbroker named Michael Milken made headlines for becoming the highest paid U.S. worker in half a century. His yearly salary and bonuses totaled $550 million—*about $1.5 million a day.* Such a sum placed Milken right behind Al Capone, whose earnings in 1927 reportedly reached $600 million in current dollars (Swartz, 1989). Milken had something else in common with Capone: He was jailed—in his case, for business fraud.

Milken committed a **white-collar crime,** defined by Edwin Sutherland (1940) as *crime committed by people of high social position in the course of their occupations* (Sutherland & Cressey, 1978). As the Milken case

Laws regulate the operation of businesses just as they direct the actions of individuals. But, as social-conflict analysis points out, powerful corporate leaders who face allegations of wrongdoing are rarely thought of as "criminals," and rarely are they subject to the punishment accorded to ordinary people.

indicates, white-collar crimes do not involve violence and rarely bring police, guns drawn, to the scene. Rather, white-collar criminals use their powerful occupational positions to enrich themselves and others, often causing significant public harm in the process (Hagan & Parker, 1985; Vold & Bernard, 1986). For this reason, sociologists sometimes call white-collar offenses that occur in government offices and corporate board rooms *crime in the suites* as opposed to *crime in the streets*.

The most common white-collar crimes are bank embezzlement, business fraud, bribery, and antitrust violations. Certainly, some white-collar crime causes little harm. But many cases—like the savings and loan scandal a few years ago—attract a great deal of attention and cause great loss to the public (Weisburd et al., 1991). The government program to bail out the savings and loan industry ended up costing U.S. taxpayers $600 billion—$2,500 apiece.

Sutherland (1940) explains that white-collar offenses typically end up in a civil hearing rather than a criminal courtroom. *Civil law* regulates business dealings between private parties, while *criminal law* defines the individual's moral responsibilities to society. In practice, then, someone who loses a civil case pays for damage or injury but is not labeled a criminal. Furthermore, corporate officials are protected by the fact that most charges of white-collar crime target the organization rather than individuals.

In the rare cases that white-collar criminals are charged and convicted, the odds are almost fifty-fifty that they will not go to jail. One accounting shows that only 55 percent of the embezzlers convicted in the U.S. federal courts served prison sentences; the rest were put on probation. Not surprisingly, then, most people think white-collar criminals are treated too leniently, especially when their crimes harm others (Grabosky, Braithewaite, & Wilson, 1987; Hans, 1992; U.S. Bureau of Justice Statistics, 1999).

CORPORATE CRIME

Sometimes whole companies, rather than individuals, break the law. **Corporate crime** refers to *the illegal actions of a corporation or people acting on its behalf.*

Corporate crime ranges from knowingly selling faulty or dangerous products to deliberately polluting the environment (Benson & Cullen, 1998). As is the case with white-collar crime, most cases go unpunished, and many never become part of the public record. But the cost of corporate crime goes beyond dollars to human lives. For example, for decades, coal mining companies put miners at risk from inhaling coal dust, so that hundreds of people die annually from "black lung" disease. The death toll from all job-related hazards that are *known to companies* probably exceeds 100,000 annually (Reiman, 1998; Carroll, 1999; Jones, 1999b).

When corporations are accused of wrongdoing, they have the resources to fight back. In 1998, for example, the U.S. government charged software giant Microsoft with antitrust violations, meaning that the corporation knowingly sought control of a market in order to set its own prices. Microsoft is vigorously defending itself, however, and the civil proceedings will continue for years (Nocera, 1999). Whatever the outcome, the company as a whole is on trial; individuals who lead the corporation are not subject to criminal prosecution.

ORGANIZED CRIME

Organized crime is *a business supplying illegal goods or services*. Sometimes organized crime forces people to do business with them, as when a gang extorts money from shopkeepers for "protection." In most cases, however, organized crime involves selling illegal goods and services—including sex, drugs, and gambling—to a willing public.

For more than a century, organized crime has flourished in the United States. Its operations expanded as waves of immigrants found that this society was not willing to share its opportunities. Thus, some ambitious minorities (such as Al Capone, described earlier) made their own success, especially when Prohibition banned alcohol coast to coast from 1920 to 1933. Note, too, that because many people associated beer and liquor with immigrants, Prohibition itself was an anti-immigrant movement (Pleck, 1987; Unrau, 1996).

The Italian Mafia is a well-known example of organized crime. But other criminal organizations involve African Americans, Chinese, Colombians, Cubans, Haitians, Russians, and almost every other racial and ethnic category. Moreover, today's organized crime involves a wide range of activities, from selling illegal drugs to prostitution to credit-card fraud to marketing false identification papers to illegal immigrants (Valdez, 1997).

Critical evaluation. According to social-conflict theory, inequality in wealth and power guides the creation and application of laws and other norms. The criminal justice and social welfare systems thus act as political agents, controlling categories of people who threaten the capitalist system.

As with approaches to deviance, however, social-conflict theory has its critics. First, this approach implies that laws and other cultural norms are created directly by the rich and powerful. At the very least, this is an oversimplification, as laws also protect workers, consumers, and the environment, sometimes opposing the interests of the rich.

Second, social-conflict analysis implies that criminality springs up only to the extent that a society treats its members unequally. However, as Durkheim noted, deviance exists in all societies, whatever the economic system.

The sociological explanations for crime and other types of deviance that we have discussed are summarized in Table 8–1.

TABLE 8–1 Sociological Explanations of Deviance: A Summary

Theoretical Paradigm	Major Contributions
Structural-functional analysis	What is deviant may vary, but deviance is found in all societies; deviance and the social response it provokes sustain the moral foundation of society; deviance may also guide social change.
Symbolic-interaction analysis	Nothing is inherently deviant but may become defined as such through the response of others; the reactions of others are highly variable; labeling someone deviant may lead to the development of secondary deviance and deviant careers.
Social-conflict analysis	Laws and other norms reflect the interests of powerful members of society; those who threaten the status quo generally are defined as deviant; social injury caused by powerful people is less likely to be considered criminal than is social injury caused by people who have little social power.

DEVIANCE AND SOCIAL DIVERSITY

What people consider deviant has much to do with the relative power and privilege of different categories of people. The following sections offer two examples: how gender is linked to deviance, and how racial and ethnic hostility motivate hate crimes.

DEVIANCE AND GENDER

Almost every society in the world applies more stringent normative controls to women than to men. Historically, our society has centered the lives of women in the home. Even today, in the United States women's opportunities in the workplace, in politics, in athletics, and in the military are limited. Elsewhere in the world, women face even greater barriers. In Saudi Arabia, women cannot vote or legally operate motor vehicles; in Iran, women who dare to expose their hair or wear makeup in public can be whipped.

Gender also figures in the theories of deviance noted earlier. Robert Merton's strain theory, for example, seems masculine in that it defines cultural goals in terms of financial success. Traditionally at least, accumulating wealth has more to do with the lives of men, while women are socialized to define success in terms of relationships, particularly marriage and motherhood (Leonard, 1982). A more woman-focused theory might recognize the strain that results from the cultural ideal of equality clashing with the reality of gender-based inequality.

In labeling theory, too, gender influences how we define deviance because people commonly use different standards to judge the behavior of females as opposed to males. Further, because society puts men in positions of power over women, men often escape direct responsibility for actions that victimize women. In the past, at least, men who sexually harassed or assaulted women were labeled only mildly deviant, if they were punished at all.

On the other hand, women who are victimized may have to convince an unsympathetic audience that they did not bring sexual harassment on themselves. Research confirms an important truth: Whether people define a situation as deviance—and, if so, whose deviance it is—depends on the sex of both the audience and the actors (King & Clayson, 1988).

Finally, social-conflict analysis, despite its focus on social inequality, neglects the importance of gender. If, as social-conflict theory suggests, economic disadvantage is a primary cause of crime, why do women (whose economic position is much worse than men's) commit far fewer crimes than men do? The section on crime, beginning on this page, addresses this question.

HATE CRIMES

The term **hate crime** refers to *a criminal act against a person or person's property by an offender motivated by racial or other bias.* In other words, hate crime expresses hostility toward someone's race, religion, ancestry, sexual orientation, or physical disability.

Most people were stunned by the brutal killing in 1998 of Matthew Shepard—a gay student at the University of Wyoming—by two men filled with hate toward homosexuals. The National Gay and Lesbian Task Force reports that one in five lesbians and gay men is physically assaulted and more than 90 percent verbally abused because of sexual orientation (cited in Berrill, 1992:19–20). Victims of hate-motivated violence are especially likely to be people who contend with multiple stigmas, such as gay men of color. Approximately 7,800 hate crimes are recorded each year by the federal government.

By 1998, forty states and the federal government had enacted legislation that increased penalties for crimes motivated by hatred. Supporters are gratified, but opponents say such laws punish thoughts, not actions. The box takes a sociological look at this issue.

CRIME

Crime is the violation of statutes enacted into criminal law by a locality, state, or the federal government. Technically, all crimes are composed of two elements: the *act* itself (or, in some cases, the failure to do what the law requires) and *criminal intent* (in legal terminology, *mens rea*, or "guilty mind"). Intent is a matter of degree, ranging from willful conduct to negligence. Someone who is negligent does not deliberately set out to hurt anyone but acts (or fails to act) in a way that might reasonably cause harm to another. Prosecutors weigh the degree of intent in deciding whether, for example, to charge someone with first-degree murder, second-degree murder, or negligent manslaughter. Alternatively, there may be no prosecution if officials consider a killing justifiable, as in the case of self-defense.

TYPES OF CRIME

In the United States, the Federal Bureau of Investigation gathers information on criminal offenses and regularly reports the results in a publication called *Crime in the United States.* Two major types of crime make up the FBI "crime index."

Crimes against the person are *crimes that direct violence or the threat of violence against others.* Such violent crimes include murder and manslaughter (legally defined as "the willful killing of one human being by another"), aggravated assault ("an unlawful attack by one person upon another for the purpose of inflicting severe or aggravated bodily injury"), forcible rape ("the carnal knowledge of a female forcibly and against her will"), and robbery ("taking or attempting to take anything of value from the care, custody, or control of a person or persons by force or threat of force or violence and/or putting the victim in fear").

Crimes against property encompass *crimes that involve theft of property belonging to others.* Property crimes include burglary ("the unlawful entry of a structure to commit a [serious crime] or a theft"), larceny-theft ("the unlawful taking, carrying, leading, or riding away of property from the possession of another"), auto theft ("the theft or attempted theft of a motor vehicle"), and arson ("any willful or malicious burning or attempt to burn the personal property of another").

A third category of offenses, not included in major crime indexes, is **victimless crimes,** *violations of law in which there are no readily apparent victims.* Illegal drug use, prostitution, and gambling are examples. The term "victimless crime" is misleading, however. How victimless is a crime when young people have to steal to support a drug habit? What about a young pregnant woman who smokes crack and permanently harms her baby? Perhaps it is more correct to say that people who commit such crimes are both offenders and victims.

CRITICAL THINKING

Hate-Crime Laws: Do They Punish Actions or Attitudes?

On a cool October evening, Todd Mitchell, an African American teenager, was standing with some friends in front of their apartment complex in Kenosha, Wisconsin. They had just seen the film *Mississippi Burning* and were fuming over a scene showing a white man beating a young black boy who is kneeling in prayer.

"Do you feel hyped up to move on some white people?" asked Mitchell. Minutes later, they saw a young white boy walking toward them on the other side of the street. Mitchell commanded: "There goes a white boy; go get him!" The group swarmed around the youngster, beating him bloody and leaving him on the ground in a coma. The attackers took the boy's tennis shoes as a trophy.

Police soon arrested the boys and charged them with the beating. Todd Mitchell went to trial as the ringleader, where the jury found him guilty of aggravated battery *motivated by racial hatred*. Instead of the usual two-year prison sentence, Mitchell went to jail for four years.

As this case illustrates, hate-crime laws punish a crime more severely if the offender is motivated by bias against some category of people. Supporters make three arguments in favor of hate-crime legislation. First, the offender's intentions are always central to criminal cases, so considering hatred as an intention is nothing new. Second, crimes motivated by racial or other bias inflame the public mood more than crimes carried out, say, for monetary gain. Third, victims of hate crimes typically suffer greater injury than victims of crimes with other motives.

Critics counter that while some hate-crime cases involve hard-core racism, most are impulsive acts by young people. Even more important, critics maintain, hate-crime laws are a threat to First Amendment guarantees of free speech. Hate-crime laws allow courts to sentence offenders not just for actions but for their attitudes. As Harvard law professor Alan Dershowitz cautions, "As much as I hate bigotry, I fear much more the Court attempting to control the minds of its citizens." In short, according to critics, hate-crime statutes open the door to punishing beliefs rather than behavior.

In 1993, the U.S. Supreme Court upheld the sentence handed down to Todd Mitchell. In a unanimous decision, the justices stated that the government did not intend to punish an individual's beliefs. But, they reasoned, a belief is no longer protected when it becomes the motive for a crime.

In 1999, Ricky Byrdsong, former basketball coach at Northwestern University near Chicago, was walking on the street with his two sons when he was killed by a drive-by shooter simply because he was African American. Afterward, his neighbors gathered nightly to walk through their community showing opposition to such hate crimes.

What do you think?

1. *Do you think crimes motivated by hate are more harmful than those motivated by, say, greed? Why or why not?*
2. *On balance, do you favor or oppose hate-crime laws? Why?*
3. *Do you think minorities such as African Americans should be subject to hate-crime laws just as white people are? Why or why not?*

Sources: Greenhouse (1993), Jacobs (1993), and Terry (1993).

Because public views of victimless crimes vary so much, laws differ from place to place. In the United States, gambling is legal only in a few locations within twenty-three states (in Nevada, on some Indian reservations, and on riverboats in some areas); prostitution is lawful only in one (part of Nevada). Yet both activities are commonplace across the country. Homosexual (and some heterosexual) behavior among consenting adults is legally restricted in about half the states. Where such laws exist, enforcement is light and selective.

Common sense suggests that the people we define as "criminal" are simply those who have broken the law. But the sociological perspective reveals that some categories of people are more likely than others to become entangled in the criminal justice system. As you read the remainder of this chapter, consider how our society places men, young people, and minorities at greater risk of becoming both offenders and victims of crime.

CRIMINAL STATISTICS

Statistics gathered by the Federal Bureau of Investigation show crime rising between 1960 and 1990 but declining over the last decade. Even so, police tally more than 12 million serious crimes each year. Figure 8–2 shows the trends for various serious crimes.

Read crime statistics with caution, however; they include only crimes known to the police. Almost all homicides are reported, but assaults—especially among people who know each other—often are not. Police records include an even smaller share of property crimes, especially when the losses are small.

Researchers check official crime statistics using *victimization surveys*, in which they ask a representative sample of people about their experience with crime. According to these surveys, the crime rate is two to four times higher than what official reports indicate (Russell, 1995b).

THE "STREET" CRIMINAL: A PROFILE

Government crime reports paint a broad-brush picture of people arrested for violent and property crimes. We now break down these arrest statistics by age, gender, social class, race, and ethnicity.

Age

Official crime rates rise sharply during adolescence and peak in the late teens, falling thereafter. People between the ages of fifteen and twenty-four represent just 14 percent of the U.S. population, but they accounted for 39.2 percent of all arrests for violent crimes and 45.7 percent for property crimes in 1998.

A disturbing trend is that young people are responsible for more and more serious crimes. In the 1990s, arrests of juveniles for violent crime rose dramatically (U.S. Federal Bureau of Investigation, 1999).

Gender

Although each sex constitutes roughly half the population, police collared males in 71.1 percent of all property crime arrests in 1998. In other words, men are arrested three times as often as women for property crimes. In the case of violent crimes, the disparity is even greater: 83.1 percent of arrests were males, but just 16.9 percent were females (a five-to-one ratio).

One reason for the difference is that law enforcement officers are reluctant to define women as criminals. Even so, the difference in arrest rates for women and men is narrowing, which probably reflects increasing sexual equality in our society. Between 1989 and 1998, the *increase* in arrests of women was much greater (28 percent) than that for men (2 percent) (U.S. Federal Bureau of Investigation, 1999). This pattern holds globally, with the greatest gender difference in crime rates in societies that most limit the opportunities of women.

Social Class

The FBI does not assess the social class of arrested persons, so no statistical data are available. But research confirms that street crime is more widespread among people of lower social position. Yet the link between class and crime is more complicated than it appears on the surface

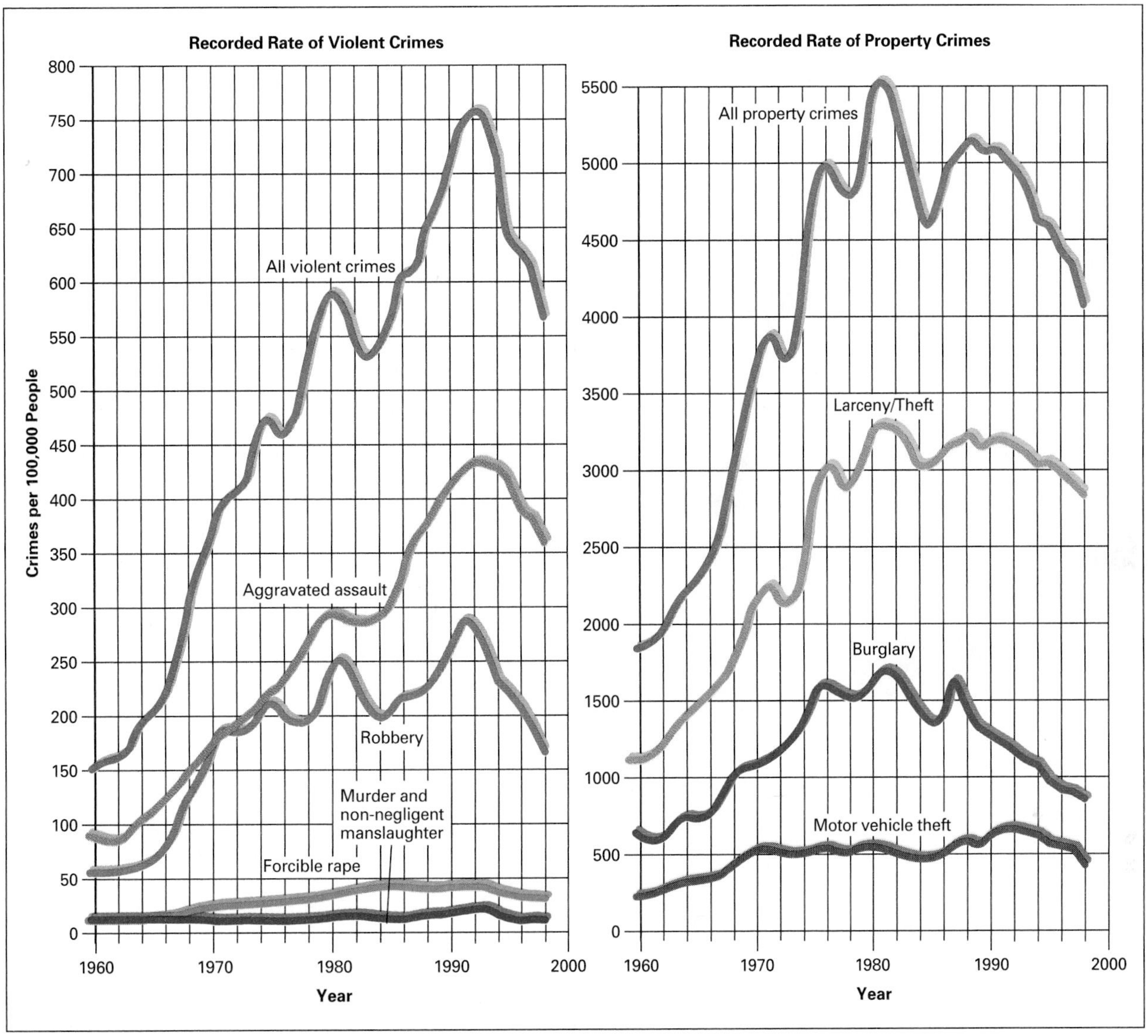

FIGURE 8–2 Crime Rates in the United States, 1960–1998

The graphs represent crime rates for various violent crimes and property crimes during recent decades.

Source: U.S. Federal Bureau of Investigation (1999).

(Wolfgang, Figlio, & Sellin, 1972; Clinard & Abbott, 1973; Braithwaite, 1981; Thornberry & Farnsworth, 1982; Wolfgang, Thornberry, & Figlio, 1987).

Historically, members of our society have viewed poor people as less worthy than people whose wealth and power confer "respectability" (Tittle & Villemez, 1977; Tittle, Villemez, & Smith, 1978; Elias, 1986). But while crime, especially violent crime, is a serious problem in the poorest inner-city neighborhoods, most of these crimes are committed by a few hard-core offenders; the majority of the people who live in poor communities have no criminal records (Wolfgang, Figlio, & Sellin, 1972; Elliott & Ageton, 1980; Harries, 1990).

In the United States, African Americans contend with higher rates of poverty, which goes a long way to explaining their proportionately higher involvement in crime—as victims as well as offenders. Especially in inner cities, where there is little available work, young people can be consumed by despair and anger, perhaps turning to crime or drugs. Paul Marcus captures one man's self-defeating efforts to escape his situation in the painting Cracked-up.

© Paul Marcus, *Cracked-up*, oil on panel, 24 in. × 30 in. Studio SPM Inc.

Moreover, the connection between social standing and criminality depends on what kind of crime one is talking about (Braithwaite, 1981). If we expand our definition of crime beyond street offenses to include white-collar crime and corporate crime, the "common criminal" suddenly looks much more affluent.

Race and Ethnicity

Both race and ethnicity are strongly correlated to crime rates, although the reasons are many and complex. Official statistics show that 68 percent of arrests for index crimes in 1998 involved white people. However, arrests of African Americans were higher than for whites in proportion to their numbers. African Americans represent 12.7 percent of the population and 31.9 percent of arrests for property crimes (versus 65.3 percent for whites) and 40.2 percent of arrests for violent crimes (57.7 percent for whites) (U.S. Federal Bureau of Investigation, 1999).

What accounts for the higher arrest rate among African Americans? First, to the degree that prejudice related to color or class encourages white police to arrest black people or citizens to report African Americans to police as potential offenders, people of color are overly criminalized (Liska & Tausig, 1979; Unnever, Frazier, & Henretta, 1980; Smith & Visher, 1981; Holmes et al., 1993; Covington, 1995).

Second, race in the United States closely relates to social standing, which, as we have already explained, affects the likelihood of engaging in street crimes. Many poor people living in the midst of affluence come to perceive society as unjust and, thus, are more likely to turn to crime (Blau & Blau, 1982; Anderson, 1994).

Third, black and white family patterns differ: Two-thirds of black children (compared to one-fifth of white children) are born to single mothers. In general, single-parenting means children grow up with less supervision and at high risk for being poor. With more than one-third of black children growing up in poverty (twice the rate of white children), no one should be surprised at proportionately higher crime rates for African Americans (Sampson, 1987; Courtwright, 1996; Jacobs & Helms, 1996; U.S. Census Bureau, 1999).

Fourth, remember that the official crime index excludes arrests for offenses ranging from drunk driving to white-collar violations. This omission contributes to the view of the typical criminal as a person of color. If we broaden our definition of crime to include driving while intoxicated, business fraud, embezzlement, and cheating on income tax returns, the proportion of white criminals rises dramatically.

Finally, some categories of the population have unusually low rates of arrest. People of Asian descent, who account for about 4 percent of the population, figure in only 1.1 percent of all arrests. As Chapter 14 ("Race and Ethnicity") documents, Asian Americans enjoy higher than average educational achievement and income. Moreover, Asian American culture emphasizes family solidarity and discipline, both of which keep criminality down.

CRIME IN GLOBAL PERSPECTIVE

By world standards, the crime rate in the United States is high. Although recent crime trends are downward, there were 16,914 murders in the United States in 1998, about forty-six every day. In large cities such as New York, rarely does a day pass with no murder; in fact, more New Yorkers are hit with stray bullets than people deliberately gunned down in most large cities in the world.

Overall, the U.S. violent crime rate is about five times greater than Europe's; the U.S. property crime rate is twice as high. The contrast is even greater between our society and the nations of Asia, including India and Japan, where rates of violent and property crime are among the lowest in the world.

Elliott Currie (1985) suggests that crime stems from our culture's emphasis on individual economic success, frequently at the expense of strong families and neighborhoods. The United States also has extraordinary cultural diversity, resulting from centuries of immigration. Moreover, economic inequality is higher in this country than in most other industrial societies. Thus, our society's relatively weak social fabric, combined with considerable frustration among the have-nots, generates widespread criminal behavior.

Another contributing factor to violence in the United States is extensive private ownership of guns. About two-thirds of murder victims in the United States die from shootings. Since the early 1990s, in Texas and several other southern states, shooting deaths have exceeded automobile-related fatalities. As Figure 8–3 shows, the United States is the runaway leader in handgun deaths among industrial nations.

Surveys suggest that almost half of U.S. households own at least one gun (Gallup, 1993; Wright, 1995; NORC, 1999). Put differently, there are as many guns as there are adults in this country, and one-third of these weapons are handguns that figure in violent crime. In large part, gun ownership reflects people's fear of crime; yet easy availability of guns in this country also makes crime more deadly.

But, as critics of gun control point out, waiting periods and background checks at retail gun stores (mandated by the 1993 "Brady bill") do not keep guns out of the hands of criminals, who almost always obtain guns illegally (Wright, 1995). Moreover, we should be cautious about seeing gun control as the magic bullet in the war on crime. Elliott Currie (1985) notes, for example, that the number of Californians killed each year by knives alone has exceeded the number of Canadians killed by weapons of all kinds. Most experts do think, however, that gun control would lower the level of deadly violence.

Crime rates are soaring in some of the largest cities of the world, including Manila in the Philippines, and São Paulo, Brazil, where rapid population growth has produced millions of desperately poor people. Outside of such cities, however, the traditional character of low-income societies and their strong family structure allow local communities to control crime informally (Clinard & Abbott, 1973; *Der Spiegel*, 1989).

Some kinds of crime have always been multinational, such as terrorism, espionage, and arms dealing (Martin & Romano, 1992). But, today, the "globalization" we are experiencing on many fronts also extends to crime. A recent case in point is the illegal drug trade. In part, the problem of illegal drugs in the United States is a "demand" issue. That is, there is a high demand for cocaine and other drugs in this country, and legions of young people risk arrest or even violent death to enter the lucrative drug trade. But the "supply" side of the issue is just as important. In the South American nation of Colombia, at least 20 percent of the people depend on cocaine production for their livelihood. Furthermore, not only is cocaine Colombia's most profitable export, but it outsells all other exports—including coffee—

GLOBAL SNAPSHOT

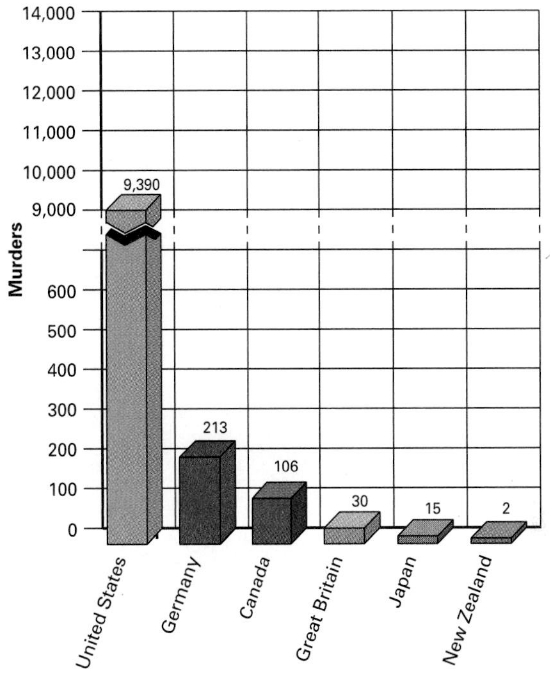

FIGURE 8–3 Number of Murders by Handguns, 1996

Source: Handgun Control, Inc. (1998).

WINDOW ON THE WORLD

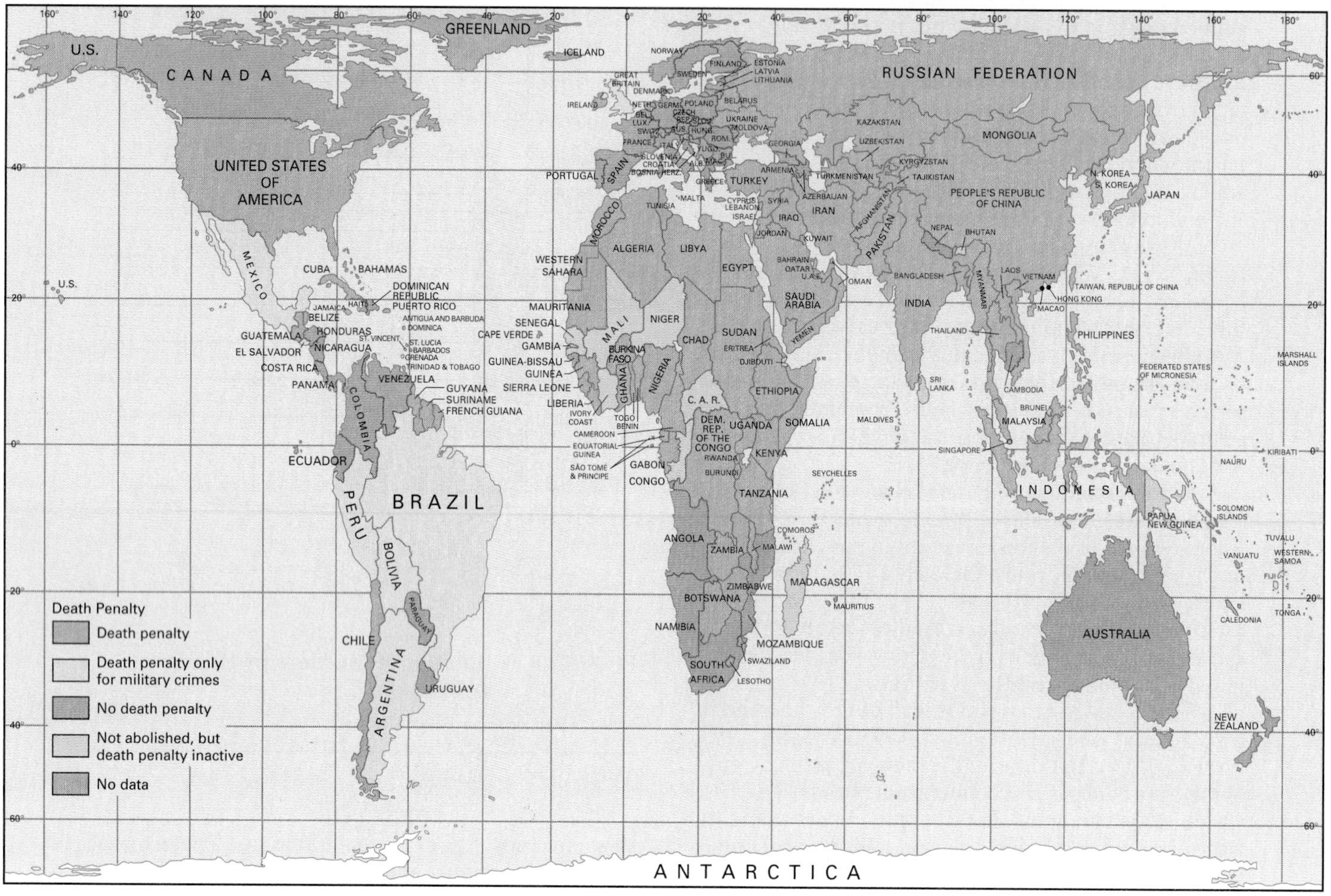

GLOBAL MAP 8–1 Capital Punishment in Global Perspective

The map identifies ninety-one countries and territories in which the law provides for the death penalty for ordinary crimes; in fourteen more, the death penalty is reserved for exceptional crimes under military law or during times of war. The death penalty does not exist in sixty-seven countries and territories; in twenty-three more, although the death penalty remains in law, no execution has taken place in more than a decade. Compare rich and poor nations: What general pattern do you see? In what way do the United States and Japan stand out?

Source: Amnesty International, "The Death Penalty: List of Abolitionist and Retentionist Countries," February 1999, http://www.amnesty.org/ailib/intcam/dp/abrelist.htm

combined. Clearly, then, understanding global crime such as drug dealing means understanding social and economic conditions both in this country and elsewhere.

Countries have different strategies for dealing with crime. The use of the death penalty provides a case in point. Global Map 8–1 identifies countries that employ capital punishment in response to crime and those that do not. The global trend is toward abolition of the death penalty: According to Amnesty International (2000), since 1980 more than thirty nations have ended this practice.

During the last decade, our nation has been building prisons at an unprecedented rate. There are now twice as many people incarcerated (almost 2 million) than in 1990. Even so, as this "tent city" prison in Arizona attests, the number of cells is not keeping up with the number of new offenders.

THE CRIMINAL JUSTICE SYSTEM

December 10, 1994, Casablanca, Morocco. Casablanca! An exciting mix of African, European, and Middle Eastern cultures. Returning from a stroll through the medina, the medieval section of this coastal, North African city, we confront lines of police along a boulevard, standing between us and our ship in the harbor. The police are providing security for many important leaders attending an Islamic conference in a nearby hotel. Are the streets closed? No one asks; people seem to observe an invisible line some fifty feet from the police officers. I play the brash urbanite and start across the street to inquire (in broken French) if we can pass by; but I stop cold as several officers draw a bead on me with their eyes. Their fingers nervously tap at the grips on their automatic weapons. This is no time to strike up a conversation.

The criminal justice system is a society's formal system of social control. In some of the world's countries, military police keep a tight rein on people's behavior; in others, including the United States, police have more limited powers and only respond to specific violations of criminal law. We shall briefly introduce the major components of the criminal justice system: police, the courts, and the punishment of convicted offenders.

POLICE

The police serve as the primary point of contact between the population and the criminal justice system. In the United States, unlike many other countries, police are responsive and accountable to citizens (Bayley, 1998). Of course, there is only so much the 641,208 full-time police officers in the United States (in 1998) can do to monitor the activities of 275 million people. As a result, the police exercise considerable discretion about which situations warrant their attention and how to handle them.

How, then, do police carry out their duties? In a study of police behavior in five cities, Douglas Smith and Christy Visher (1981; Smith, 1987) concluded that, because they must respond swiftly, police quickly size up a situation in terms of six factors. First, *how serious is the alleged crime?* The more serious police consider the situation, the more likely they are to make an arrest. Second, *what is the victim's preference?* Generally, if a victim demands that police make an arrest, they are likely to do so. Third, *is the suspect cooperative or not?* Resisting the police increases a suspect's chances of arrest. Fourth, *have they arrested the suspect before?* Police are more likely to take into custody someone they have arrested before, presumably because previous arrest suggests guilt. Fifth, *are bystanders present?* Smith

GLOBAL SNAPSHOT

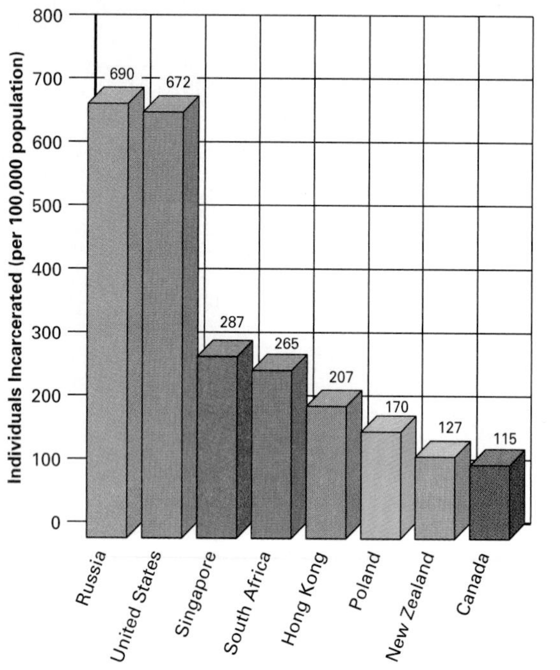

FIGURE 8–4 **Incarceration Rates, 1995**

Source: Mauer (2000).

and Visher claim the presence of observers prompts police to take stronger control of a situation, if only to move the encounter from the street (the suspect's turf) to the police department (where law officers have the edge). Sixth, *what is the suspect's race?* All else being equal, Smith and Visher contend, police are more likely to arrest people of color than whites, perceiving suspects of African or Hispanic descent as either more dangerous or more likely to be guilty.

COURTS

After arrest, a court determines a suspect's guilt or innocence. In principle, our courts rely on an adversarial process involving attorneys—one representing the defendant and another the state—in the presence of a judge, who monitors legal procedures. In practice, however, about 90 percent of criminal cases are resolved prior to court appearance through **plea bargaining,** *a legal negotiation in which a prosecutor reduces a charge in exchange for a defendant's guilty plea.* For example, the state may offer a defendant charged with burglary a lesser charge of possessing burglary tools in exchange for a guilty plea.

Plea bargaining is widespread because it spares the state the time and expense of court trials. A trial is unnecessary if there is little disagreement as to the facts of the case. Moreover, since the annual number of cases entering the system has doubled over the last decade, prosecutors could not possibly bring every case to trial. By quickly resolving most of their work, then, the courts channel their resources into the most important cases (Reid, 1991).

But plea bargaining pressures defendants (who are presumed innocent) to plead guilty. A person can exercise the right to a trial, but only at the risk of receiving a more severe sentence if found guilty. Furthermore, low-income defendants enter the process with the guidance of a public defender—an attorney, often underpaid, who may devote little time to even a serious case (Novak, 1999). Overall, plea bargaining may be efficient but at the cost of undercutting the adversarial process as well as the rights of defendants.

PUNISHMENT

When a young man is shot dead on the street after leaving a restaurant—as in the case of Michael Gerardi featured in the opening to this chapter—some people may wonder why, but almost everyone believes that someone should have to "pay" for the crime. Indeed, sometimes the desire to punish an offender is so great that justice may be lost.

Such cases force us to ask *why* a society should punish its wrongdoers. Over many years, scholars have pointed to four basic reasons to punish: retribution, deterrence, rehabilitation, and societal protection.

Retribution

The oldest justification for punishment is the public's craving for revenge. Knowing the power of this passion, the U.S. Supreme Court justice Oliver Wendell Holmes stated that "the law has no choice but to satisfy [that] craving" (quoted in Carlson, 1976).

The first reason to punish, then, is to satisfy a society's need for **retribution,** *an act of moral vengeance by which society inflicts suffering on the offender comparable to that caused by the offense.* Retribution rests on a view of society as a moral balance. When criminality upsets this balance, punishment exacted in comparable measure restores the moral order, as suggested in the biblical dictum "An eye for an eye."

During the Middle Ages, most people viewed crime as sin—an offense against God as well as society—that warranted a harsh response. Today, although critics point out that retribution does little to reform the offender, many people consider vengeance reason enough for punishment.

Deterrence

A second justification for punishment is **deterrence,** *the attempt to discourage criminality through punishment.* Deterrence is based on the eighteenth-century Enlightenment idea that humans are calculating and rational creatures who will not break the law if they think that the pain of punishment will outweigh the pleasure of crime.

Deterrence emerged as reform in response to the harsh punishments based on retribution. Why put someone to death for stealing, reformists reasoned, if theft can be discouraged with a prison sentence? As the concept of deterrence gained widespread acceptance, execution and physical mutilation of criminals in most industrial societies were replaced by milder forms of punishment such as imprisonment.

Punishment can deter in two ways. *Specific deterrence* convinces an individual offender that crime does not pay. Through *general deterrence,* the punishment of one person serves as an example to others.

Rehabilitation

The third justification for punishment is **rehabilitation,** *a program for reforming the offender to prevent subsequent offenses.* Rehabilitation arose along with the social sciences in the nineteenth century. Sociologists of that time (and also since) saw crime and other deviance springing from a social environment marked by poverty or a lack of parental supervision. Logically, then, if offenders learn to be deviant, they can also learn to obey the rules; the key is controlling the environment. *Reformatories* or *houses of correction* provided controlled settings where people could learn proper behavior (recall the description of total institutions in Chapter 5, "Socialization").

Like deterrence, rehabilitation motivates the offender to conform. But rehabilitation emphasizes constructive improvement, whereas deterrence and retribution make the offender suffer. In addition, where retribution demands that the punishment fit the crime, rehabilitation tailors treatment to each offender. Thus, identical crimes would prompt similar acts of retribution but might call for different rehabilitation programs.

TABLE 8–2 Four Justifications for Punishment: A Summary

Retribution	The oldest justification for punishment that still holds sway today. Punishment is atonement for a moral wrong; in principle, punishment should be comparable in severity to the deviance itself.
Deterrence	An early modern approach. Deviance is considered social disruption, which society acts to control. People are viewed as rational and self-interested; deterrence works because the pains of punishment outweigh the pleasures of deviance.
Rehabilitation	A modern strategy linked to the development of social sciences. Deviance is viewed as the product of social problems (such as poverty) or personal problems (such as mental illness). Social conditions are improved; treatment is tailored to the offender's condition.
Societal Protection	A modern approach easier to implement than rehabilitation. If society is unable or unwilling to rehabilitate offenders or reform social conditions, people are protected by incarcerating or executing the offender.

Societal Protection

A final justification for punishment is **societal protection,** *a means by which society renders an offender incapable of further offenses temporarily through incarceration or permanently by execution.* Like deterrence, societal protection is a rational approach to punishment and seeks to protect society from crime.

Currently, almost 2 million people are incarcerated in the United States, and another 4 million are on parole or probation. In response to tougher public attitudes and an increasing number of drug-related arrests, the U.S. prison population has tripled since 1980. As Figure 8–4 shows, the United States incarcerates a larger share of its population than most other countries in the world.

Critical evaluation. Table 8–2 summarizes the four justifications for punishment. Assessing the actual consequences of punishment, however, is no simple task.

The value of retribution lies in Durkheim's contention that punishing the deviant person increases people's moral awareness. Appropriately, then, punishment was traditionally a public event. Although the last public execution in the United States took place in Kentucky in 1937, today's mass media ensure public

SEEING OURSELVES

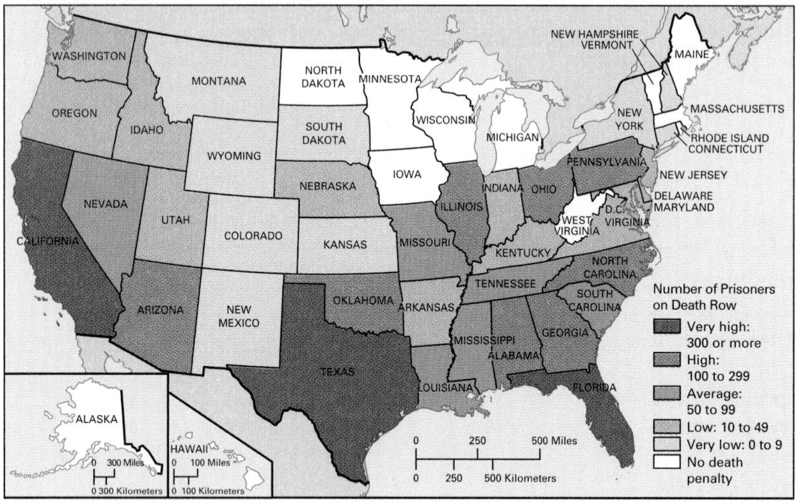

NATIONAL MAP 8–2
Capital Punishment across the United States

The United States and Japan are the only industrial nations in which the government imposes the death penalty. Yet, within the United States, the fifty states have broadly divergent capital punishment laws: Half of the roughly 3,000 prisoners on death row are in five states. What regional pattern do you see in the map? Can you account for this pattern?

Sources: Data from Death Penalty Information Center, as cited in *Time*, "Death or Life," vol. 149, no. 24 (June 16, 1997):34–35; updates U.S. Bureau of Justice Statistics (1999).

awareness of executions carried out inside prison walls (Kittrie, 1971).

Certainly, punishment deters some crime. Yet our society also has a high rate of **criminal recidivism,** *subsequent offenses by people previously convicted of crimes.* About three-fourths of state prisoners have been jailed before, and, once released, about half are back in prison after a few years (McNulty, 1994; Petersilia, 1997). In light of this pattern, we may wonder about the extent to which punishment really deters crime. Then, too, only about one-third of all crimes are known to police, and, of these, only about one in five results in an arrest. The adage "Crime doesn't pay" rings rather hollow when we consider that only a small share of offenses are ever punished.

General deterrence is even harder to investigate scientifically, since we have no way of knowing how people might act if they were unaware of punishments given to others. In the debate over capital punishment, opponents point to research suggesting that the death penalty has limited value as a general deterrent. Moreover, the United States is the only Western, industrial society that routinely executes serious offenders. Even more troubling is the fact that at least some death sentences turn out to be flawed. The case of Shareef Cousin is just one example: Between 1973 and 1998, in fact, seventy-five people have been released from death row, indicating that punishment itself is sometimes unjust (Sellin, 1980; van den Haag & Conrad, 1983; Archer & Gartner, 1987; Lester, 1987; Bailey & Peterson, 1989; Bailey, 1990; Bohm, 1991; Tanber, 1998). National Map 8–2 identifies the thirty-eight states that have the death penalty, and shows that half the prisoners on death row are in just five of these states.

Prisons provide short-term societal protection by keeping offenders off the streets, but they do little to reshape attitudes or behavior in the long term (Carlson, 1976; Wright, 1994). Perhaps rehabilitation is an unrealistic expectation, since according to Sutherland's theory of differential association, locking up criminals together for years probably strengthens criminal attitudes and skills. And because incarceration breaks whatever social ties inmates may have in the outside world, they may be more prone to break the law upon their release, which fits with Hirschi's control theory.

Finally, the stigma of being an ex-convict can be a powerful barrier to building a new life. A classic study of young offenders in Philadelphia found that boys who were sentenced to long prison terms—and thus were likely to acquire a criminal stigma—went on to commit both more crimes and more serious ones when released (Wolfgang, Figlio, & Sellin, 1972).

Ultimately, we should never assume that the criminal justice system can eliminate crime. As the final box explains, police, courts, and prisons have played a part in the recent downturn in crime rates. But more is involved. As this chapter has described, crime and other deviance results not just from the acts of "bad people" but from the operation of society itself.

APPLYING SOCIOLOGY

Violent Crime Is Down—But Why?

During the 1980s, crime rates shot up rapidly. Just about everyone was afraid of violent crime and, in many larger cities, the numbers killed and wounded turned whole neighborhoods into war zones. There seemed to be no solution to the problem.

Then, in the 1990s, something good and unexpected happened—serious crime rates began to fall and by 1999, reached levels not seen in more than a generation. Why? By applying the perspectives and theories presented in this chapter, we can find several reasons.

1. **Changes in policing.** Much of the drop in crime (and the earlier rise in crime) has taken place in large cities. New York City, where the number of murders fell from 2,245 in 1990 to 655 in 1998, has adopted a policy of *community policing*, which means that police are concerned not just with making arrests but in preventing crime before it happens. Officers get to know the areas they patrol and stop young men for jaywalking or other minor infractions in order to check them for concealed weapons (the word is getting around that you risk arrest for carrying a gun). Moreover, there are *more* police at work in large cities. Los Angeles, for example, added more than 2,000 police during the 1990s, and it, too, has seen its violent crime rate fall.
2. **More prisons.** From 1985 until 1998, the number of inmates in U.S. jails and prisons soared from 750,000 to more than 1.7 million. The main reason for this increase is tough laws that demand prison time for many crimes, especially drug offenses. As one analyst put it, "When you lock up an extra million people, it's got to have some effect on the crime rate" (Zimring, cited in Witkin, 1998:31).
3. **A better economy.** The U.S. economy has boomed during the last ten years. With unemployment down, more people are working, which reduces the likelihood that some will turn to crime out of economic desperation. The logic here is simple: More jobs, fewer crimes.
4. **The declining drug trade.** Many analysts agree that the most important factor in reducing rates of violent crime is the decline of crack cocaine. Crack came on the scene about 1985, and violence spread as young people—especially in the inner cities and increasingly armed with guns—became part of a booming drug trade. With legitimate job opportunities low and growing opportunities to make money illegally, a generation of young people became part of a wave of violence. Widespread crack cocaine use also explains the trend, noted earlier, of the younger age of violent criminals.

   By the early 1990s, however, crack became less popular as people saw the damage it was causing to entire communities. This realization, coupled with steady improvement in the economy and stiffer sentences for drug offenses, brought the turnaround in violent crime.

Keep in mind that the current picture looks better *relative* to what it was a decade ago. The crime problem, says one researcher, "looks better, but only because the early 1990s were so bad. So let's not fool ourselves into thinking everything is resolved. It's not."

Sources: Based on Boggess & Bound (1997), Blumstein & Rosenfeld (1998), Fagan, Zimring, & Kim (1998), and Witkin (1998).

SUMMARY

1. Deviance refers to norm violations ranging from mild breaches of etiquette to serious violence.
2. Biological research, from Caesare Lombroso's nineteenth-century observations of convicts to recent research in human genetics, has yet to offer much insight into the causes of deviance.
3. Psychological study links deviance to abnormal personality resulting from either biological or environmental causes. Psychological theories help explain some kinds of deviance.
4. Deviance has societal rather than individual roots because it (a) varies according to cultural norms, (b) is socially defined, and (c) reflects patterns of social power.
5. Using the structural-functional paradigm, Durkheim explained that deviance serves to affirm norms

and values, clarify moral boundaries, promote social unity, and encourage social change.

6. The symbolic-interaction paradigm is the basis of labeling theory, which holds that deviance lies in people's reaction to a person's behavior, not in the behavior itself. Acquiring a stigma of deviance can lead to secondary deviance and a deviant career.
7. Based on Karl Marx's ideas, social-conflict theory holds that laws and other norms reflect the interests of powerful members of society. Although white-collar and corporate crime cause extensive social harm, offenders are rarely branded as criminals.
8. Official statistics indicate that arrest rates peak in late adolescence, then drop steadily with advancing age. Nearly three-fourths of those arrested for property crimes and 83 percent of those arrested for violent crimes are males.
9. People of lower social position commit more street crime than people with greater social privilege. When white-collar and corporate crimes are included among criminal offenses, however, the disparity in overall criminal activity goes down.
10. More whites than African Americans are arrested for street crimes. However, African Americans are arrested more often than whites in proportion to their respective populations. Asian Americans have lower-than-average rates of arrest.
11. Police exercise considerable discretion in their work. Arrest is more likely if the offense is serious, bystanders are present, or the accused is African American.
12. Most prosecutions of criminal cases never go to trial but are resolved through plea bargaining. While efficient, this method puts less powerful people at a disadvantage.
13. Justifications of punishment include retribution, deterrence, rehabilitation, and societal protection. Because its consequences are difficult to evaluate scientifically, punishment sparks controversy among sociologists and the public as a whole.

KEY CONCEPTS

deviance (p. 191) the recognized violation of cultural norms

crime (p. 191) the violation of society's formally enacted criminal law

social control (p. 192) attempts by society to regulate people's thought and behavior

criminal justice system (p. 192) a formal response by police, courts, and prison officials to alleged violations of the law

labeling theory (p. 198) the idea that deviance and conformity result not only from what people do but from how others respond to those actions

stigma (p. 199) a powerfully negative label that greatly changes a person's self-concept and social identity

medicalization of deviance (p. 200) the transformation of moral and legal deviance into a medical condition

white-collar crime (p. 203) crime committed by people of high social position in the course of their occupations

corporate crime (p. 204) the illegal actions of a corporation or people acting on its behalf

organized crime (p. 204) a business supplying illegal goods or services

hate crime (p. 206) a criminal act against a person or person's property by an offender motivated by racial or other bias

crimes against the person (p. 206) (violent crimes) crimes that direct violence or the threat of violence against others

crimes against property (p. 206) (property crimes) crimes that involve theft of property belonging to others

victimless crimes (p. 206) violations of law in which there are no readily apparent victims

plea bargaining (p. 214) a legal negotiation in which a prosecutor reduces a charge in exchange for a defendant's guilty plea

retribution (p. 214) an act of moral vengeance by which society inflicts suffering on the offender comparable to that caused by the offense

deterrence (p. 215) the attempt to discourage criminality through punishment

rehabilitation (p. 215) a program for reforming the offender to prevent subsequent offenses

societal protection (p. 215) a means by which society renders an offender incapable of further offenses temporarily through incarceration or permanently by execution

criminal recidivism (p. 216) subsequent offenses by people previously convicted of crimes

CRITICAL-THINKING QUESTIONS

1. How does a sociological view of deviance differ from the common-sense notion that bad people do bad things?
2. List Durkheim's functions of deviance. From his point of view, can society ever be free from deviance? Why or why not?
3. An old saying is that "Sticks and stones can break my bones, but names can never hurt me." Explain why advocates of labeling theory disagree with this statement.
4. A recent study found that one in three black men between the ages of twenty and twenty-nine is in jail, on probation, or on parole (Mauer, 2000). Based on the material in this chapter, what factors help explain this pattern?

APPLICATIONS AND EXERCISES

1. Research computer crime. What new kinds of crime are emerging in the information age? Is computer technology also generating new ways of tracking lawbreakers?
2. Rent a wheelchair (check with a local pharmacy or medical supply store), and use it as much as possible for a day or two. Not only will you gain a first-hand understanding of the physical barriers to getting around, but you will also discover that people respond to you in many new ways.
3. Watch an episode of the real-action police show "COPS." Based on this program, how would you profile the people who commit crimes?
4. Install the CD-ROM packaged in the back of this new textbook to access a variety of study, review, and applications exercises designed to help you better understand the material covered in this chapter. The CD includes an author's tip video, as well as interactive maps, video application exercises, Web links, and study questions.

SITES TO SEE

http://www.prenhall.com/macionis

Visit the interactive Web site that accompanies this text. Begin by clicking on the cover of your book. You will find a chapter-by-chapter study guide, practice tests, chat room, and many suggested Web links.

http://www.Nashville.Net/~police/risk/

Visit this site, run by the Nashville Police Department, that rates your chances of becoming a victim of a serious crime.

http://www.civilrights.org/

The Leadership Conference on Civil Rights maintains this site dealing with hate crimes and other issues of civil rights.

http://www.igc.apc.org/spr/

The organization "Stop Prisoner Rape" hosts this site dealing with the problem of rape in U.S. prisons.

http://www.ncadp.org
http://www.uaa.alaska.edu/just/death/intl.html

These sites provide information on the death penalty. The first presents the views of the National Coalition to Abolish the Death Penalty. The second provides data on the death penalty in global perspective.

http://www.cybercrime.gov

This site, operated by the U.S. Department of Justice, provides a great deal of information on computer crime and issues surrounding intellectual property.

CHAPTER 9

Andy Warhol
Marilyn, 1967

SEXUALITY

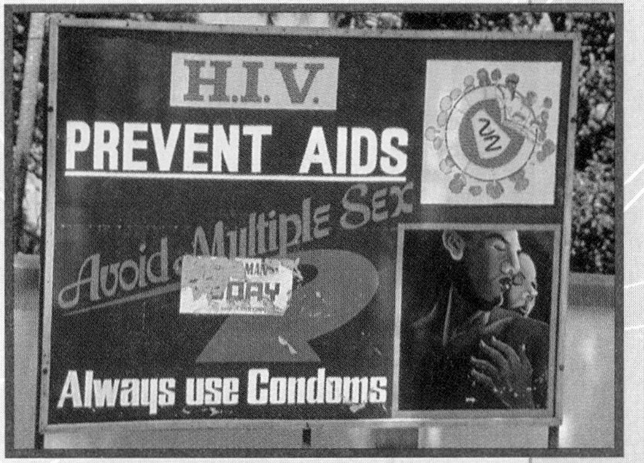

As the old saying goes, birds do it and so do bees. So do frogs, chimps, and even the great elephants. Indeed, biologists tell us that the animal world contains countless fascinating mating rituals. Take, for example, scorpions: The couple engages in a deadly dance, round and round, locked face to face with their mouths and claws. As the mating proceeds, the male repeatedly stings the female. In the end, however, it is the larger female that prevails. Once fertilized, she turns on her mate and in a burst of strength and ferocity devours him.

Nature offers many strange stories about animal mating. However, the most fascinating of all must be about human beings. Humans—most people, at least—like to "do it," too. But as the only creatures who attach meaning to all behavior, what humans "do" when it comes to sex varies quite a bit from culture to culture, as it does over time. Moreover, we humans are the only species whose members think about the purpose of sex, encourage some forms of sex while outlawing others, and, in an effort to learn more, even conduct research about our own sexuality.

This chapter presents some of what we have learned about human sexuality. From a sociological point of view, the main question is how society shapes our sexuality.

UNDERSTANDING SEXUALITY

How much of the day goes by without your giving any thought at all to sexuality? If you are like most people, the answer is "not very much." That is because sexuality is not just about "having sex." Sexuality is a theme found throughout society, apparent on campus, in the workplace, and especially in the mass media. In addition, the sex industry—including pornography and prostitution—is a multibillion-dollar business in its own right. Then, too, sexuality is an important part of how we think about ourselves as well as how we evaluate others. In truth, there are few areas of life in which sexuality does *not* play some part.

But, in spite of its significance in life, few people understand sexuality. Through much of our history, sex has been a cultural taboo so that, at least in polite conversation, people do not talk about it. As a result, while sex can produce much pleasure, it also causes confusion, anxiety, and sometimes outright fear. Even scientists long considered sex off limits for research. It was not until the middle of the twentieth century that researchers turned attention to this pervasive dimension of social life. Since then, as this chapter reports, we have learned a great deal about human sexuality.

SEX: A BIOLOGICAL ISSUE

Sex refers to *the biological distinction between females and males.* From a biological point of view, sex is the means by which humans reproduce. A female ovum and a male sperm, each containing twenty-three chromosomes (biological

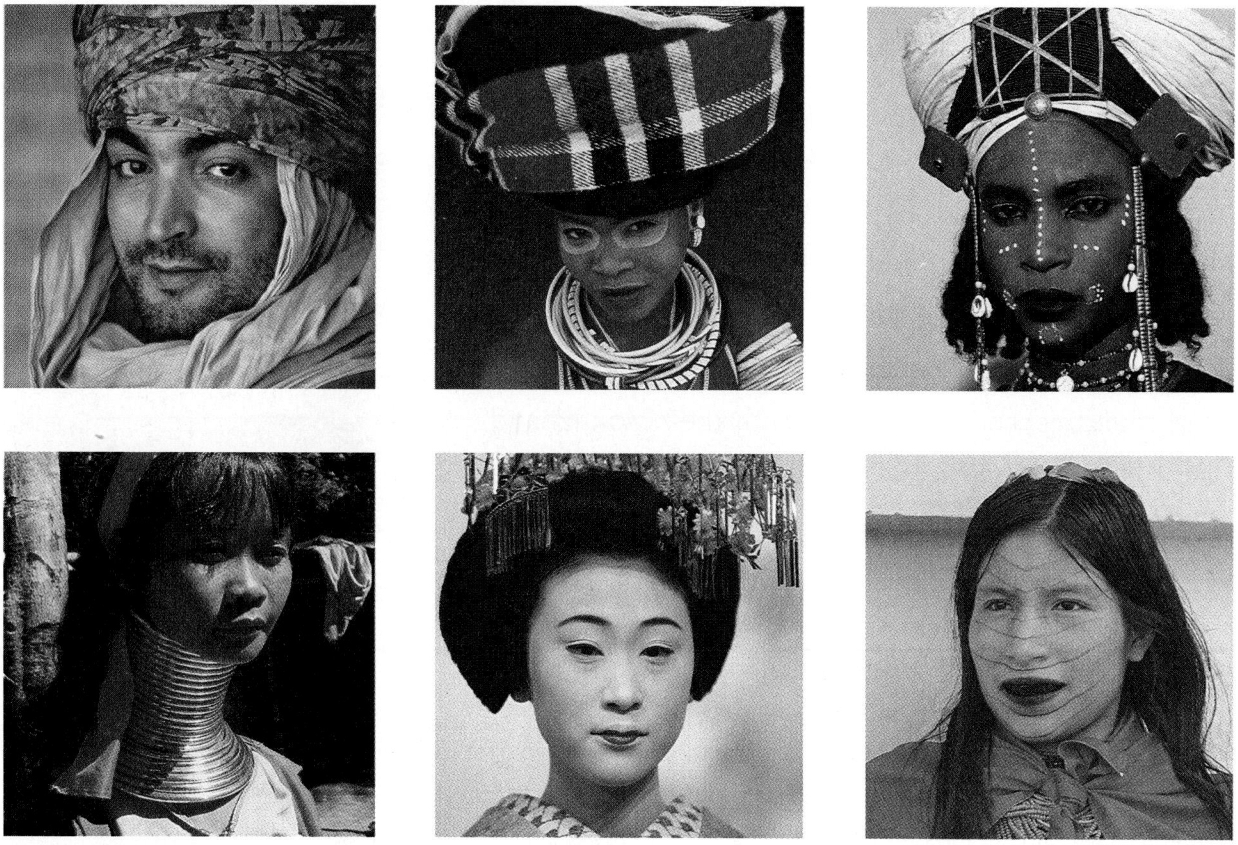

We claim that beauty is in the eye of the beholder, which suggests the importance of culture in setting standards of attractiveness. All of the people pictured here—from Morocco, South Africa, Nigeria, Myanmar (Burma), Japan, and Ecuador—are beautiful to members of their own society. At the same time, sociobiologists point out that, in every society on earth, people are attracted to youthfulness. The reason is that, as sociobiologists see it, attractiveness underlies our choices about reproduction, which is most readily accomplished in early adulthood.

codes that guide physical development), combine to form a fertilized embryo. One of these chromosome pairs determines the child's sex. To this pair the mother contributes an X chromosome and the father contributes either an X or a Y. A second X from the father produces a female (XX) embryo; a Y from the father produces a male (XY) embryo. A child's sex, then, is determined at conception.

Within weeks, the sex of an embryo starts to guide its development. If the embryo is male, testicular tissue starts to produce testosterone, a hormone that triggers the development of male genitals. If no testosterone is present, the embryo develops female genitals. In the United States, about 105 boys are born for every 100 girls, but a higher death rate among males makes females a slight majority by the time people reach their mid-twenties (U.S. Census Bureau, 1999; U.S. National Center for Health Statistics, 1999).

SEX AND THE BODY

What sets females and males apart are differences in the body. Right from birth, the two sexes have different **primary sex characteristics**, namely, *the genitals, organs used for reproduction.* At puberty, as individuals reach sexual maturity, additional sex differentiation takes place. At this point, individuals develop **secondary sex characteristics,** *bodily differences, apart from the genitals, that distinguish biologically mature females and males.* To allow for pregnancy, giving birth, and nurturing

Transsexuals who alter their sex surgically provoke controversy because they challenge conventional norms about what is feminine and masculine. Here, high school students demonstrate in support of Dana Rivers (formerly David Warfield), a teacher who was suspended from her duties after she underwent medical procedures to become a woman.

infants, mature females have wider hips, breasts, and soft fatty tissue that provides a reserve supply of nutrition for pregnancy and breast-feeding. Mature males, on the other hand, typically develop more muscle in the upper body, more extensive body hair, and deeper voices. Of course, these are general differences, since some males are smaller and have less body hair and higher voices than some females.

Hermaphrodites

Sex is not always as clear-cut as we have just described. In rare cases, a hormone imbalance before birth produces a **hermaphrodite** (a word derived from Hermaphroditus, the offspring of the mythological Greek gods Hermes and Aphrodite, who embodied both sexes), *a human being with some combination of female and male genitalia*.

Because our culture is uneasy about sexual ambiguity, some people respond to hermaphrodites with confusion or even disgust. But other cultures lead people to respond quite differently: The Pokot of eastern Africa, for example, pay little attention to what they consider a simple biological error, and the Navajo look on hermaphrodites with awe, seeing in them the full potential of both the female and the male (Geertz, 1975).

Transsexuals

Some hermaphrodites undergo genital surgery to appear (and occasionally function as) a sexually normal female or male. Other people, however, deliberately change their sex: **Transsexuals** are *people who feel they are one sex even though biologically they are the other*. Tens of thousands of transsexuals in the United States have surgically changed their genitals because they feel "trapped in the wrong body" (Restak, 1979, cited in Offir, 1982:146; Gagné, Tewksbury, & McGaughey, 1997).

SEX: A CULTURAL ISSUE

Sexuality has a biological foundation. But, like all dimensions of human behavior, sexuality is also very much a cultural issue. Biology is sufficient to explain the strange mating ritual of scorpions, described in the opening to this chapter, but humans have no similar biological program. Though there is a biological "sex drive" in the sense that people find sex pleasurable and may want to engage in sexual activity, our biology does not dictate any specific ways of being sexual any more than our desire to eat dictates any particular foods or table manners.

One sign of the growing openness about sexuality in the United States after World War II was the 1953 publication of the first issue of Playboy. *Back then, it was conservatives who objected to the magazine on moral grounds; by the 1970s, many liberals also opposed such publications as demeaning to women.*

Cultural Variation

Almost any sexual practice shows considerable variation from one society to another. In his pioneering study of sexuality in the United States, Alfred Kinsey (1948) found that most couples reported having intercourse face to face, with the woman on the bottom and the man on top. Halfway around the world, in the South Seas, most couples *never* have sex in this way. In fact, when people there learned of this practice from missionaries, they poked fun at it as the strange "missionary position."

As noted in Chapter 3 ("Culture"), even the practice of showing affection has extensive cultural variation. While most people in the United States readily kiss in public, the Chinese kiss only in private. The French kiss publicly, often twice (once on each cheek), while Belgians go them one better, kissing three times (starting on either cheek). The Maoris of New Zealand rub noses, and most people in Nigeria don't kiss at all.

Modesty, too, is a culturally variable matter. If a woman entering a bath is disturbed, what body parts does she cover? Helen Colton (1983) reports that an Islamic woman covers her face, a Laotian woman covers her breasts, a Samoan woman her navel, a Sumatran woman her knees, and a European woman covers her breasts with one hand and her genital area with the other.

Around the world, some societies tend to restrict sexuality, while others are more permissive. In China, for example, norms closely regulate sexuality so that few people have sexual intercourse before they marry. In the United States, however—at least in recent decades—intercourse prior to marriage has become the norm, and people may choose to have sex even when there is no strong commitment between them.

THE INCEST TABOO

Are any cultural views of sex the same everywhere? The answer is yes. One cultural universal—an element found in every society the world over—is the **incest taboo,** *a norm forbidding sexual relations or marriage between certain relatives.* In the United States, the law as well as cultural mores prohibit close relatives (including brothers and sisters, parents and children) from having sex or marrying. But exactly which family members are included in a society's incest taboo varies from one place to another. Some societies (such as the North American Navajo) apply incest taboos to the mother and others on her side of the family. There are also societies (including ancient Peru and Egypt) on record that have approved brother-sister marriages among the nobility (Murdock, 1965).

Why does the incest taboo exist everywhere? Biology is part of the reason: Reproduction between close relatives of any species risks offspring with mental or physical problems. But this fact does not explain why, of all living species, only humans observe an incest taboo. In other words, controlling sexuality among close relatives seems a necessary element of social organization. For one thing, the incest taboo limits sexual competition in families by restricting sex to spouses (ruling out, for example, sex between parent and child). Second, since family ties define people's rights and obligations toward each other, reproduction among close relatives would hopelessly confuse kinship (if a mother and son had a daughter, for example, what would the child's relation be to her parents?). Third, by requiring people to marry outside their immediate families, the incest taboo integrates the larger society as people look widely for partners to form new families.

The incest taboo has been an enduring sexual norm in the United States and elsewhere. But in this country, many sexual norms have changed over time. During the twentieth century, as we now explain, our society experienced both a sexual revolution and, later, a sexual counterrevolution.

SEXUAL ATTITUDES IN THE UNITED STATES

What do people in the United States think about sex? Our cultural orientation toward sexuality has always been inconsistent. On the one hand, most of the Europeans who came to this continent held rigid notions about "correct" sexuality, which, ideally, meant that sex was only for the purpose of reproduction within marriage. As explained in Chapter 8 ("Deviance"), the Puritan settlers of New England demanded conformity in all attitudes and behavior, and they imposed severe penalties for any misconduct—even if the sexual "misconduct" took place in the privacy of one's home. Efforts to regulate sexuality continued well into the twentieth century. As late as the 1960s, for example, some states legally banned the sale of condoms in stores. Even today, in a number of states, laws banning homosexuality, and various "unnatural" acts, are still on the books.

But this is just one side of the story of sexuality in the United States. As Chapter 3 ("Culture") explains, our culture is also individualistic, and many believe in giving people freedom to do pretty much as they wish, as long as they cause no direct harm to others. Such thinking—that what people do in the privacy of their own home is *their* business—makes sex a matter of individual freedom and personal choice.

So which is it? Is the United States a restrictive or a permissive society when it comes to sexuality? The answer is that we are both. On the one hand, many people in the United States still view sexual conduct as an important indicator of personal morality. On the other, sex is exploited and glorified everywhere in our culture—and strongly promoted by the mass media—as if to say that "anything goes."

Within this general framework, we turn now to changes in sexual attitudes and behavior over the course of the twentieth century.

THE SEXUAL REVOLUTION

During the last century, people witnessed profound changes in sexual attitudes and practices. The first indications of this change occurred in the 1920s, as millions from farms and small towns migrated to the rapidly growing cities. Living apart from their families and meeting in the workplace, young men and women enjoyed considerable sexual freedom. Indeed, this is one reason the decade became known as the "Roaring Twenties."

In the early 1970s, hardcore sex came to the suburban cinema in the form of the film Deep Throat, *which won no critical acclaim but attracted large audiences. Since then, the invention of VCRs and the spread of the Internet have made watching sexually explicit images a more private matter.*

In the 1930s and 1940s, the Great Depression and World War II slowed the rate of change. But in the postwar period, after 1945, Alfred Kinsey set the stage for what later came to be known as the *sexual revolution*. Kinsey and his colleagues published their first study of sexuality in the United States in 1948, and it raised eyebrows everywhere. It was not so much what Kinsey said about sexual behavior—although he did present some surprising results—but simply the fact that scientists were studying *sex* that set off a national conversation. At that time, after all, many people were uneasy talking about sex even privately at home.

DIVERSITY SNAPSHOT

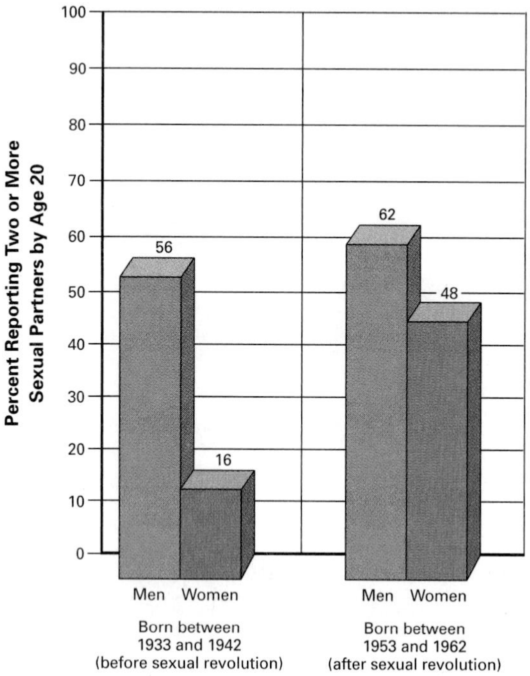

FIGURE 9–1 The Sexual Revolution: Closing the Double Standard

But Kinsey's two books (1948 and 1953) became best-sellers because they revealed that people in the United States, on average, were far less conventional in sexual matters than most had thought. Thus, these books fostered a new openness toward sexuality, which helped move along the sexual revolution.

In the late 1960s, the sexual revolution truly came of age. Youth culture dominated public life, and expressions like "if it feels good, do it" and "sex, drugs, and rock and roll" summed up a new freedom about sexuality. Some people were turned off by the idea of "turning on," of course, but the baby boom generation born between 1945 and 1960 became the first cohort in U.S. history to grow up with the idea that sex was part of everyone's life, married or not.

Technology, too, played a part in the sexual revolution. "The pill," introduced in 1960, not only prevented pregnancy, it made sex more convenient. Unlike a condom or diaphragm, which has to be used at the time of intercourse, the pill could be taken any time during the day. Now women as well as men could engage in sex without any special preparation.

The sexual revolution had special significance for women because, historically, women were subject to greater sexual regulation than men. According to the so-called "double standard," society allows (and even encourages) men to be sexually active, while expecting women to remain chaste before marriage and faithful to their husbands afterwards. The survey data shown in Figure 9–1 support this conclusion. Among people born in the United States between 1933 and 1942 (that is, people in their mid-fifties to mid-sixties today), 56 percent of men but just 16 percent of women report having had two or more sexual partners by the time they were age twenty. Compare this wide gap to the pattern among the baby boomers born between 1953 and 1962 (people now in their forties), who came of age after the sexual revolution. In this category, 62 percent of men and 48 percent of women say they had two or more sexual partners by age twenty (Laumann et al., 1994:198). Thus, while the sexual revolution increased sexual activity overall, it changed behavior among women more than among men.

THE SEXUAL COUNTERREVOLUTION

The sexual revolution made sex a topic of everyday discussion and sexual activity more a matter of individual choice. But given that U.S. society has always had two minds about sex, the sexual revolution was also controversial. By 1980, the climate of sexual freedom that had marked the late 1960s and 1970s was criticized by some as evidence of our country's moral decline. Thus the *sexual counterrevolution* began.

Politically speaking, the sexual counterrevolution was a conservative call for a return to "family values" by which sexual freedom was to be replaced by sexual responsibility. In practice, this meant moving sex back within marriage. Critics objected not just to the idea of "free love" but to trends such as cohabitation (living together) and having children out of wedlock.

Looking back, we can see that the sexual counterrevolution did not greatly change the idea that individuals should decide for themselves when and with whom to have a sexual relationship. What did happen, however, is that more people began choosing to limit their number of sexual partners or to abstain from sex entirely. In many cases, such decisions are made on moral grounds. For others, however, the decision to limit sexual activity reflects a fear of sexually transmitted diseases (STDs). As Chapter 21 ("Health and Medicine") explains, although rates of most infectious diseases fell

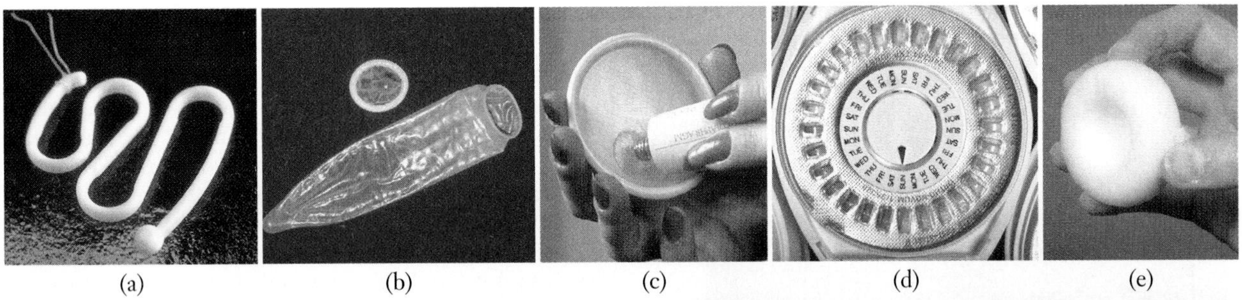

Contraception has a long history, beginning with the intrauterine device or IUD (a) in ancient times (originally, stones were used); by 1500, men employed condoms (b), more to prevent disease than pregnancy; the early 1600s saw the invention of the diaphragm (c), later used with spermicidal jelly; the birth control pill (d) came on the scene in 1960; sponges (e) were first licensed in 1983; the Norplant skin implant (f) debuted in 1990, followed by the female condom (g) in 1993.

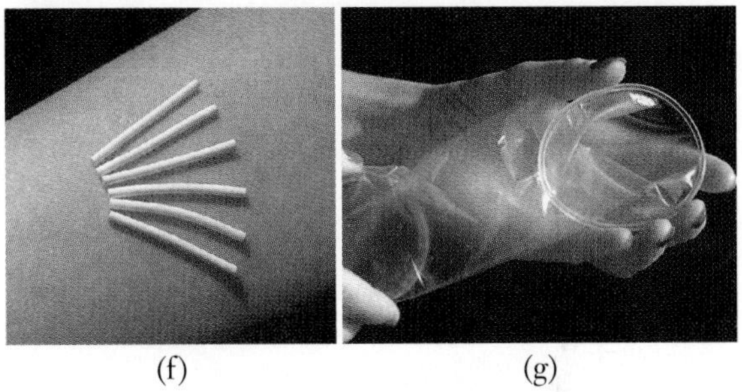

after 1960, rates of STDs rose sharply. Moreover, the fact that some STDs (such as genital herpes) are incurable and others (AIDS) are deadly has given individuals good reason to consider carefully their sexual choices.

PREMARITAL SEX

In light of the sexual revolution and the sexual counterrevolution, how much has sexual behavior in the United States really changed? One interesting trend involves premarital sex—that is, the likelihood that young people will have sexual intercourse before marriage.

Consider, first, what U.S. adults *say* about premarital intercourse. Table 9–1 shows that about 35 percent characterize sexual relations before marriage as "always wrong" or "almost always wrong." Another 20 percent consider premarital sex "wrong only sometimes," while more than 40 percent say premarital sex is "not wrong at all." Public opinion is more accepting of premarital sex today than a generation ago but, even so, our society remains divided on this issue.

Now consider what young people *do* regarding premarital intercourse. For women, there has been marked change over time. The Kinsey studies (1948, 1953; see also Laumann et al., 1994) reported that for people born in the early 1900s, about 50 percent of men but just 6 percent of women had premarital sexual intercourse before age nineteen. Studies of baby boomers born after World War II show a slight increase in premarital intercourse among men but a large increase—to about one-third—among women. The most recent studies, targeting men and women born in the 1970s, show that 76 percent of men and 66 percent of women had premarital sexual intercourse by their senior year in high school (Laumann et al., 1994:323–24). Thus, although general public attitudes remain divided on premarital sex, this behavior is broadly accepted among young people.

TABLE 9–1 How We View Premarital and Extramarital Sex

Survey Question: "There's been a lot of discussion about the way morals and attitudes about sex are changing in this country. If a man and a woman have sex relations before marriage, do you think it is always wrong, almost always wrong, wrong only sometimes, or not wrong at all? What about a married person having sexual relations with someone other than the marriage partner?"

	Premarital Sex	Extramarital Sex
"Always wrong"	25.4%	77.9%
"Almost always wrong"	8.9	12.3
"Wrong only sometimes"	20.2	5.7
"Not wrong at all"	41.9	2.3
"Don't know"/No answer	3.6	1.8

Source: *General Social Surveys, 1972–1998: Cumulative Codebook* (Chicago: National Opinion Research Center, 1999), p. 235.

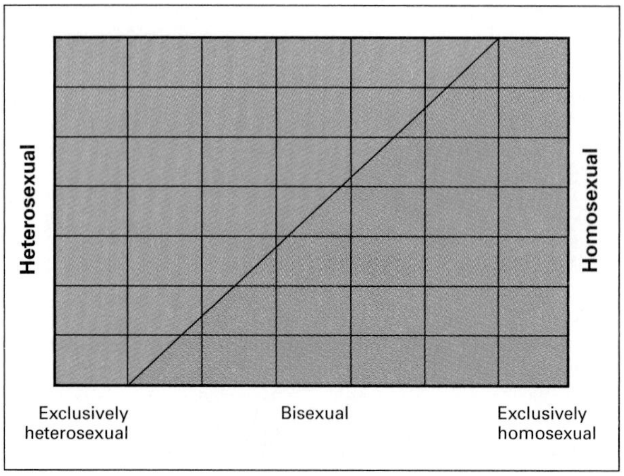

FIGURE 9–2 The Sexual Orientation Continuum

Source: Adapted from Kinsey et al. (1948).

SEX AMONG ADULTS

To hear the mass media tell it, people in the United States are very active sexually. But do popular images exaggerate reality? The Laumann study (1994) found that frequency of sexual activity varied widely in the U.S. population. The pattern breaks down like this: One-third of adults report having sex with a partner a few times a year or not at all; another one-third have sex once or several times a month; the remaining one-third have sex with a partner two or more times a week. In short, no single stereotype accurately describes sexual activity in the United States.

Moreover, despite the widespread image of "swinging singles," it is married people who have sex with partners the most. In addition, married people report the highest level of satisfaction—both emotional and physical—with their partners (Laumann et al., 1994).

EXTRAMARITAL SEX

What about married people having sex with someone other than their marriage partner? What people commonly call "adultery" (sociologists prefer a more neutral-sounding term like "extramarital sex") is widely condemned. Table 9–1 shows that more than 90 percent of U.S. adults consider a married person having sex with someone other than the marital partner to be "always wrong" or "almost always wrong." The norm of sexual fidelity within marriage has been and remains a strong element of U.S. culture.

But, in terms of behavior, the cultural ideal often differs from real life. It probably comes as no surprise that extramarital sexual activity is more common than people say it should be. At the same time, extramarital sex is not as frequent as many believe. The Laumann study reports that about 25 percent of married men and 10 percent of married women have had at least one extramarital sexual experience. Or, the other way around, 75 percent of men and 90 percent of women remain sexually faithful to their partners throughout their married lives (Laumann et al., 1994:214; NORC, 1999:996).

SEXUAL ORIENTATION

Over recent decades, public opinion about sexual orientation has changed remarkably. **Sexual orientation** refers to *a person's preference in terms of sexual partners: same sex, other sex, either sex, neither sex* (Lips, 1993). The norm in all human societies is **heterosexuality** (*hetero* is a Greek word meaning "the other of two"), meaning *sexual attraction to someone of the other sex*. Yet, in every society a significant share of people favor **homosexuality** (*homo* is the Greek word for "the same"), *sexual attraction to someone of the same sex*. When thinking about these categories, keep in mind that homosexuality and heterosexuality are not mutually exclusive. That is, people do not necessarily fall into one category or the other, but may have both sexual orientations to varying degrees. Figure 9–2 presents these two sexual orientations as a continuum, indicating that most people actually experience at least some degree of sexual attraction to people of both sexes.

The fact that sexual orientation is often not clear-cut points to the importance of a third category: **bisexuality,** which refers to *sexual attraction to people of both sexes*. Some bisexual people are equally attracted to males and females; many others, however, are more attracted to one sex over the other. Finally, one additional sexual orientation is **asexuality,** meaning *no sexual attraction to people of either sex*.

It is also important to note that sexual *attraction* is not the same thing as sexual *behavior*. Many people, no doubt, have experienced some attraction to someone of the same sex, but fewer ever experience same-sex behavior. This is in large part because of cultural constraints on our actions.

Cultural systems do not accept all sexual orientations equally. In the United States and around the world, heterosexuality is the norm because, biologically speaking, heterosexual relations permit human reproduction. Even so, most societies tolerate homosexuality. In fact, among the ancient Greeks, upper-class men considered homosexuality the highest form of relationship, partly because they looked down on women as intellectually inferior. As men saw it, heterosexuality was necessary only so they could have children, and "real" men preferred homosexual relations (Kluckhohn, 1948; Ford & Beach, 1951; Greenberg, 1988).

WHAT GIVES US A SEXUAL ORIENTATION?

The question of *how* people come to have a sexual orientation in the first place is vigorously debated. But the arguments cluster into two general positions: first, that sexual orientation is a product of society, and second, that sexual orientation is a product of biology.

Sexual Orientation: A Product of Society

This approach argues that people in any society construct a set of meanings that lets them make sense of sexuality. Understandings of sexuality, therefore, differ from place to place and over time. For example, Michel Foucault (1990) points out that there was no distinct category of people called "homosexuals" until a century ago when scientists and, eventually, the public as a whole began labeling people that way. Through most of history, in other words, some people no doubt had what we would call "homosexual experiences." But neither they nor others saw in this behavior the basis for any special identity.

Anthropologists provide further evidence that sexual orientation is socially constructed. Studies show that various kinds of homosexuality exist in different societies. In Siberia, for example, the Chukchee Eskimo have a ritual practice by which one man dresses like a female and does a woman's work. The Sambia, who dwell in the Eastern Highlands of New Guinea, have a ritual in which young boys perform oral sex on older men in the belief that ingesting semen will enhance their masculinity (Herdt, 1993). Such diverse patterns seem to indicate that sexual orientation and sexual expression have much to do with society itself.

Sexual Orientation: A Product of Biology

The other view is that sexual orientation is innate, that is, rooted in human biology. Arguing this position, Simon LeVay (1993) links sexual orientation to the structure of the human brain. LeVay studied the brains of both homosexual and heterosexual men and found a small but important difference in the size of the hypothalamus, a part of the brain that regulates hormones. Such an

This gathering took place on June 27, 1999, at New York's Stonewall Inn to celebrate the thirtieth anniversary of the so-called "Stonewall Riot" in 1969, when gay people first fought back against harassment by the police, sparking the gay rights movement.

anatomical difference, some claim, plays a part in shaping sexual orientation.

Genetics, too, may influence sexual orientation. One study of forty-four pairs of brothers—all homosexual—found that thirty-three pairs had a distinctive genetic pattern involving the X chromosome. Moreover, the gay brothers had an unusually high number of gay male relatives—but only on their mother's side, the source of the X chromosome. Such evidence leads some researchers to think there may be a "gay gene" (Hamer & Copeland, 1994).

Critical evaluation. The best guess at present is that sexual orientation is derived from *both* society and biology (Gladue, Green, & Hellman, 1984; Weinrich,

FIGURE 9–3 **Sexual Orientation in the United States: Survey Data**

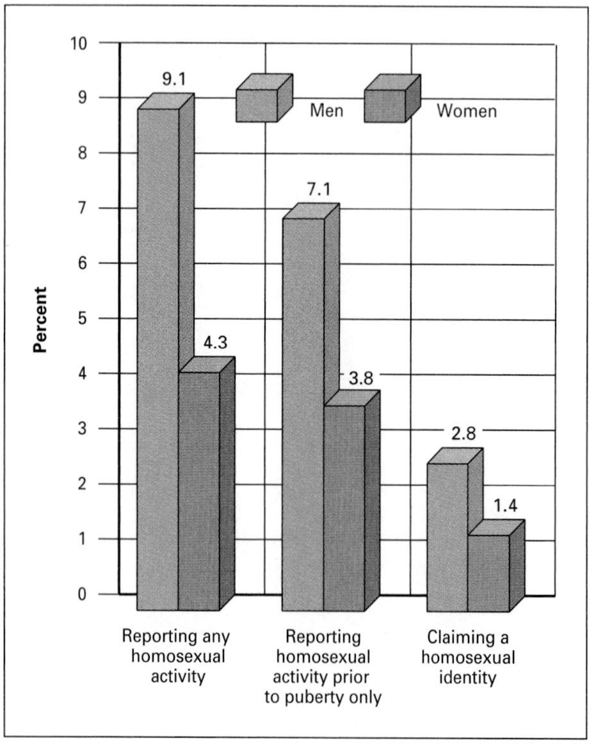

(a) How Many Gay People?

Source: Adapted from Laumann et al. (1994).

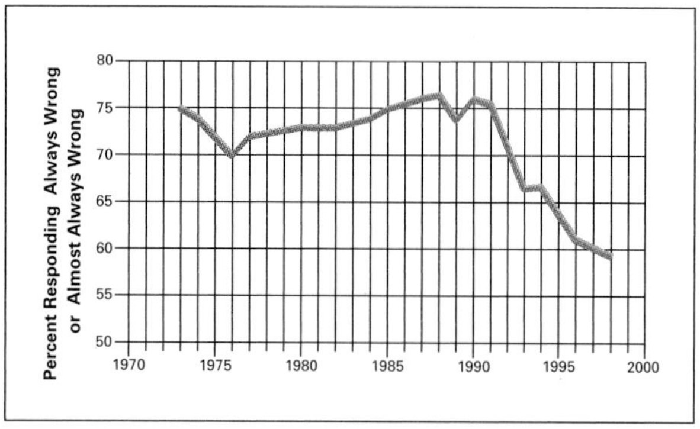

(b) Attitudes toward Homosexual Relations, 1973–1998

Survey Question: "What about sexual relations between two adults of the same sex—do you think it is always wrong, almost always wrong, wrong only sometimes, or not wrong at all?"

Source: NORC (1999).

1987; Troiden, 1988; Isay, 1989; Puterbaugh, 1990; Angier, 1992; Gelman, 1992). But we need to bear in mind that sexual orientation is not a matter of neat categories. That is, most people who think of themselves as homosexual have had some heterosexual experiences, just as many people who think of themselves as heterosexual have had some homosexual experiences. Thus, the task of explaining sexual orientation is extremely complex.

There is also a political issue here with great importance for gay men and lesbians. To the extent that sexual orientation is based in biology, homosexuality is not a matter of choice any more than, say, skin color. If this is so, shouldn't gay men and lesbians expect the same legal protection from discrimination as African Americans? (Herek, 1991)

HOW MANY GAY PEOPLE?

What share of our population is gay? This is a difficult question to answer because, as we have explained, sexual orientation is not a matter of neat categories. Moreover, people are not always willing to reveal their sexuality to strangers or even to family members. Pioneering sex researcher Alfred Kinsey (1948, 1953) estimated that about 4 percent of males and 2 percent of females have an exclusively same-sex orientation, although he thought that at least one-third of men and one-eighth of women have at least one homosexual experience leading to orgasm.

In light of the Kinsey studies, many social scientists put the gay share of the population at 10 percent. But a more recent national survey of sexuality in the United States indicates that how one operationalizes "homosexuality" makes a big difference in the results (Laumann et al., 1994). As Part (a) of Figure 9–3 shows, about 9 percent of U.S. men and about 4 percent of U.S. women aged between eighteen and fifty-nine reported homosexual activity *at some time* in their lives. The second set of numbers shows that a significant share of men (less so women) have a homosexual experience during childhood but not after puberty. And 2.8 percent of men and 1.4 percent of women define themselves as partly or entirely homosexual.

Finally, Kinsey treated sexual orientation as an "either/or" trait: To be more homosexual was, by definition, to be less heterosexual. But same-sex and other-sex attractions can operate independently. At one extreme, then, bisexual people feel strong attraction to people of both sexes; at the other, asexual people experience little sexual attraction to people of either sex.

In the national survey noted above, less than 1 percent of adults described themselves as bisexual. But bisexual experiences appear to be fairly common (at least for a time) among younger people, especially on college campuses (Laumann et al., 1994; Leland, 1995). Many bisexuals, then, do not think of themselves as either gay or straight, and their behavior reflects elements of both gay and straight living.

THE GAY RIGHTS MOVEMENT

In recent decades, the public attitude toward homosexuality has been moving toward greater acceptance. In 1973, as shown in Part (b) of Figure 9–3, about three-fourths of U.S. adults claimed homosexual relations were "always wrong" or "almost always wrong." While that percentage changed little during the 1970s and 1980s, by 1998 it dropped to less than 60 percent (NORC, 1999:236).

In large measure, this change came about through the gay rights movement that arose in the middle of the twentieth century (Chauncey, 1994). At that time, most people did not discuss homosexuality, and it was common for companies (including the federal government and the armed forces) to fire anyone who was thought to be gay. Mental health professionals, too, took a hard line, describing homosexuals as "sick," and sometimes placing them in mental hospitals where, presumably, they might be cured.

In this climate of intolerance, most lesbians and gay men remained "in the closet"—closely guarding the secret of their sexual orientation. But the gay rights movement gained strength during the 1960s. One early milestone occurred in 1973, when the American Psychological Association declared that homosexuality was not an illness but simply "a form of sexual behavior."

The gay rights movement also began using the term **homophobia** to describe *the dread of close personal interaction with people thought to be gay, lesbian, or bisexual* (Weinberg, 1973). The concept of homophobia (literally, "fear of sameness") turns the tables on society: Instead of asking "What's wrong with gay people?" the question becomes "What's wrong with people who can't accept a different sexual orientation?"

SEXUAL CONTROVERSIES

Sexuality lies at the heart of a number of controversies in the United States. Here we take a look at four issues: teen pregnancy, pornography, prostitution, and sexual violence.

GLOBAL SNAPSHOT

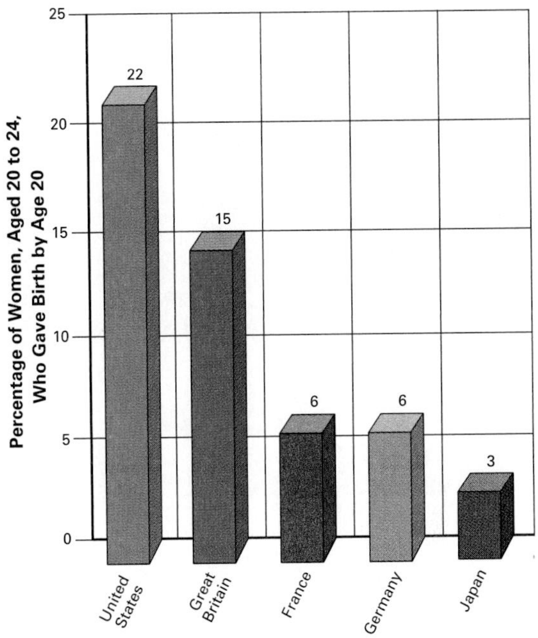

FIGURE 9–4 Births to Teenage Women

Source: The Alan Guttmacher Institute (2000).

TEEN PREGNANCY

Being sexually active—especially having intercourse—demands a high level of responsibility, since pregnancy can result. Teenagers may be biologically mature, but many are not socially mature and may not appreciate all the consequences of their actions. Indeed, surveys indicate that while 1 million U.S. teens become pregnant each year, most did not intend to. Not only does pregnancy mean that many young women (and sometimes young fathers-to-be) cannot finish school, but they are at high risk of poverty. Figure 9–4 shows that this country's rate of births among teens is higher than that of other industrial countries.

Did the sexual revolution raise the level of teenage pregnancy? Surprisingly, perhaps, the answer is no. The rate in 1950 was actually higher than the rate today, but this is because people married younger at the time. Also, many pregnancies led to quick marriages. As a result, there were many pregnant teenagers, but most were married women. Today, by contrast, most teenagers who

SEEING OURSELVES

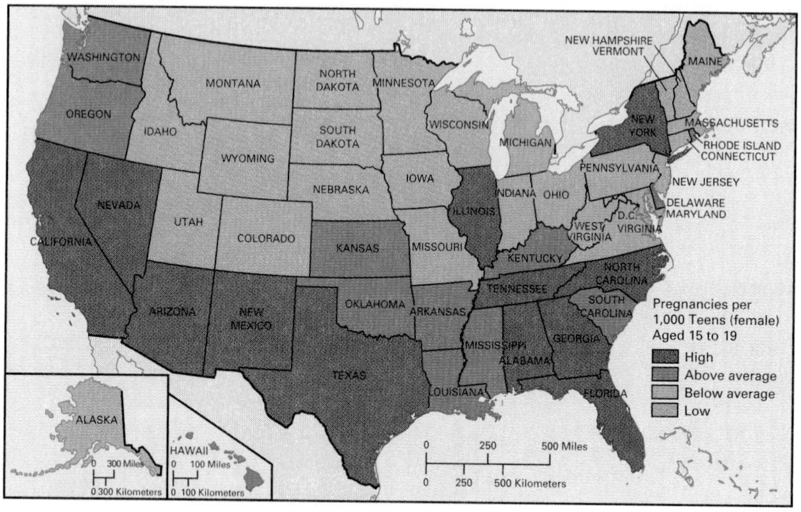

NATIONAL MAP 9–1
Teenage Pregnancy Rates across the United States

The map shows pregnancy rates for women aged fifteen to nineteen for the mid-1990s. In what regions of the country are rates high? Where are they low? What explanation can you offer for these patterns?

Source: *Morbidity and Mortality Weekly Report* (*MMWR*), June 26, 1998. U.S. Centers for Disease Control and Prevention, Atlanta, Georgia.

become pregnant are not married. In about half of all cases, these women have abortions; in the other half, they keep their babies (Voydanoff & Donnelly, 1990; Holmes, 1996a). National Map 9–1 shows the distribution of births to females between the ages of fifteen and nineteen in the United States.

Concern about the high rate of teenage pregnancy has led to sex education programs in schools. But such programs are controversial, as the box explains.

PORNOGRAPHY

In general terms, **pornography** refers to *sexually explicit material that causes sexual arousal.* But what, exactly, is or is not pornographic has long been a matter of debate. Recognizing that people view the portrayal of sexuality differently, the U.S. Supreme Court gives local communities the power to decide for themselves what violates "community standards" of decency and lacks any redeeming social value.

Definitions aside, pornography is surely popular in the United States: X-rated videos, 1-900 telephone numbers for sexual conversations, and a host of sexually explicit movies and magazines together constitute roughly a $10-billion-a-year industry. The figure is rising as people buy more and more pornography from thousands of sites on the Web.

Traditionally, people have criticized pornography on *moral* grounds. As national surveys confirm, 60 percent of U.S. adults are concerned that "sexual materials lead to a breakdown of morals" (NORC, 1999:237). Today, however, pornography is also seen as a *power* issue because it depicts women as the sexual playthings of men.

Some critics also see pornography as a cause of violence against women. While it is difficult to document a scientific cause-and-effect relationship between what people view and how they act, research does support the idea that pornography makes men think of women as objects rather than as people. The public shares a concern about pornography and violence, with almost half of adults holding the opinion that pornography encourages people to commit rape (NORC, 1999:237).

Though people everywhere object to sexual material they find offensive, many also value free speech and want to protect artistic expression. Nevertheless, pressure to restrict pornography is building from an unlikely coalition of conservatives (who oppose pornography on moral grounds) and progressives (who condemn it for political reasons).

CRITICAL THINKING

Sex Education: Problem or Solution?

Most schools today have sex education programs that teach the basics of sexuality. Instructors explain to young people how their bodies grow and change, how reproduction occurs, and how to avoid pregnancy by using birth control or abstaining from sex.

Because half of U.S. teenage boys report having sex by the time they reach sixteen, and half of girls report doing so by seventeen, "sex ed" programs seem to make sense. But critics point out that as the number of sex education programs has expanded, the level of teenage sexual activity has actually gone *up*. This trend seems to suggest that sex education may not be discouraging sex among youngsters and, maybe, that learning more about sex encourages young people to become sexually active sooner. Critics also say that it is parents who should be instructing their children about sex, since, unlike teachers, parents can also teach their beliefs about what is right and wrong.

But supporters of sex education counter that it is unrealistic to expect that in a culture that celebrates sexuality, children will not become sexually active. If this is the case, the sensible strategy is to ensure that they understand what they are doing and take reasonable precautions to protect themselves from unwanted pregnancy and sexually transmitted diseases.

What do you think?

1. *Schools can teach the facts about sexuality. But do you think they can address the emotional issues that often accompany sex? What about the moral issues? Why or why not?*
2. *What about parents? Are they doing their job as far as instructing children about sex? Ask members of your class how many received instruction in sexual matters from their parents.*
3. *Overall, do you think young people know too little about sexuality? Do you think they know too much? What specific changes would you suggest?*

Sources: Gibbs (1993) and Stodghill (1998).

PROSTITUTION

Prostitution is *the selling of sexual services*. Often called "the world's oldest profession," prostitution has always been widespread, and about one in five adult men in the United States reports having paid for sex on at least one occasion (NORC, 1999:996). Even so, to the extent that people think of sex as an expression of interpersonal intimacy, they find the idea of sex performed for money disturbing. As a result, prostitution is against the law everywhere in the United States, except for parts of Nevada.

Around the world, prostitution is greatest in poor countries where patriarchy is strong and traditional cultural norms limit women's ability to earn a living. Global Map 9–1 on page 234 shows where in the world prostitution is most widespread.

Types of Prostitution

Most—but not all—prostitutes are women. Prostitutes (many prefer the morally neutral term "sex workers") fall into different categories. *Call girls* are elite prostitutes, typically women who are young, attractive, well educated, and arrange their own "dates" with clients by telephone. The classified pages of any large city newspaper contain numerous ads for "escort services," by which women (and sometimes men) offer both companionship and sex for a fee.

Members of a middle category of prostitutes work in "massage parlors" or brothels under the control of managers. These sex workers have less choice about their clients, receive less money for their services, and get to keep no more than half of what they make.

At the bottom of the sex-worker hierarchy are *street walkers*, women and men who "work the streets" of large cities. Female street walkers are often under the control of male pimps who take most of their earnings. Many street walkers fall victim to violence from pimps and clients (Gordon & Snyder, 1989).

Most, but not all, prostitutes offer heterosexual services. Gay prostitutes, too, trade sex for money. Researchers report that many gay prostitutes have suffered rejection by family and friends because of their sexual orientation (Weisberg, 1985; Boyer, 1989; Kruks, 1991).

WINDOW ON THE WORLD

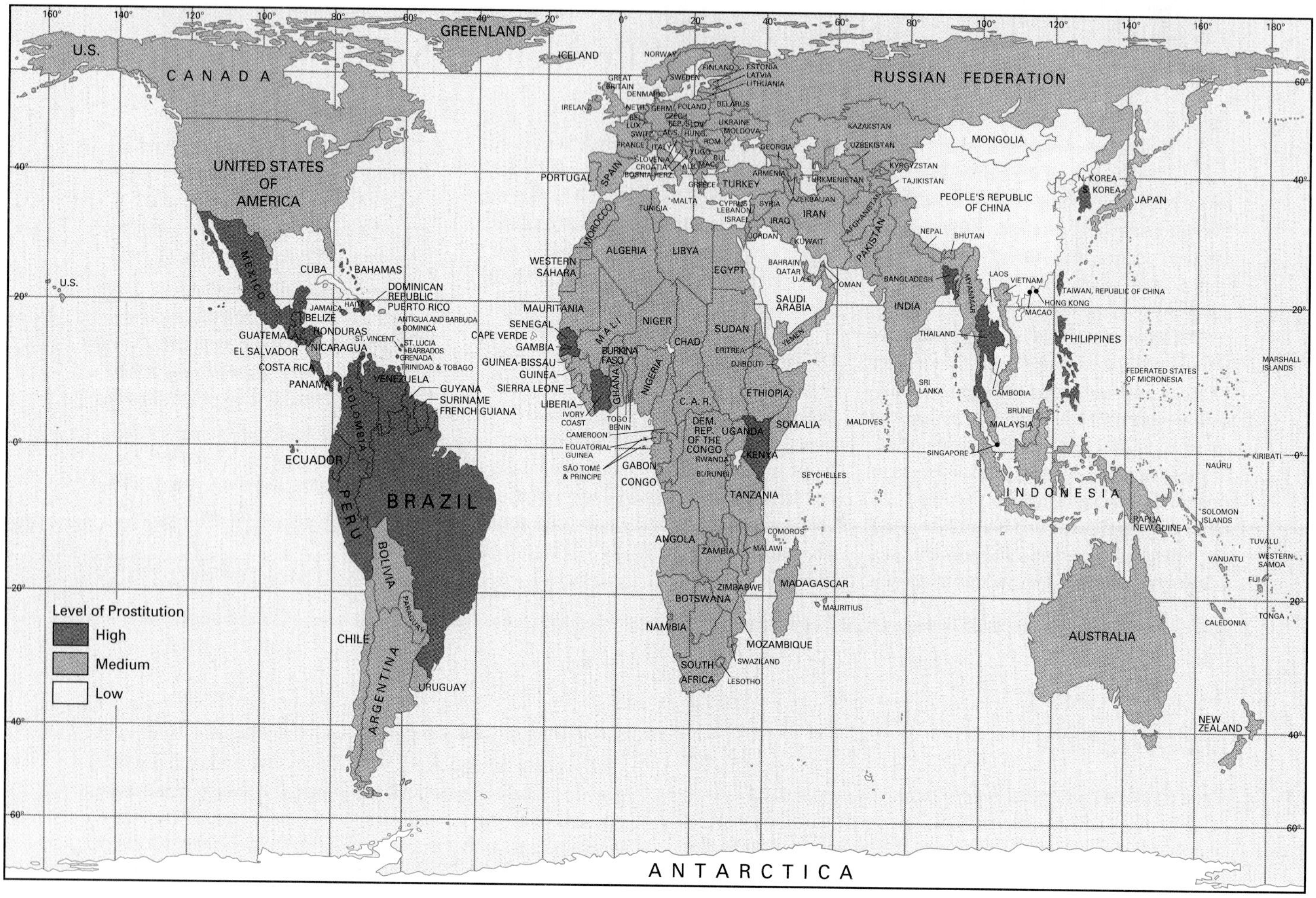

GLOBAL MAP 9–1 Prostitution in Global Perspective

Generally speaking, prostitution is widespread in societies of the world where women have low standing in relation to men. Officially, at least, the now-defunct socialist regimes in Eastern Europe and the former Soviet Union, as well as the People's Republic of China, boast of gender equality, including the elimination of "vice," such as prostitution, which oppresses women. By contrast, in much of Latin America, a region of pronounced patriarchy, prostitution is commonplace. In many Islamic societies patriarchy is also strong, but religion is a counterbalance so prostitution is limited. Western, industrial societies display a moderate amount of prostitution.

Source: *Peters Atlas of the World* (1990); updated by the author.

A Victimless Crime?

Prostitution is against the law almost everywhere in the United States, but many people consider it a victimless crime (see Chapter 8, "Deviance"). Thus, instead of enforcing prostitution laws all the time, police stage occasional crackdowns. Our society seems to want to control prostitution while assuming that nothing will eliminate it.

Is selling sex a victimless crime that hurts no one? Certainly, many people who take a "live and let live" attitude about prostitution would say it is. But this view

GLOBAL SOCIOLOGY

Sexual Slavery: A Report from Thailand

Around the world, poverty forces many women and children into prostitution as a way to survive. Nowhere is this trend more evident than in Southeast Asia. Recent decades have witnessed an explosion of what amounts to sexual slavery that exploits women and attracts men from rich nations as "sex tourists."

Sex-tourism districts can be found in many large cities throughout Africa, Eastern Europe, and, especially, Southeast Asia. Bangkok, Thailand—called the sex-tourism capital of the world—receives tens of thousands of visitors from Japan, Western Europe, and North America each year. Thailand has some 2 million prostitutes, with 10 percent of the female Thai population now working in the sex industry.

Almost all of these women are poor, and many come from rural regions where people struggle to survive. Some girls who see little future in a rural village make their own way to the city, hoping to find work. Without skills and naive about the dangers they face, most fall under the control of pimps and end up in brothels, soliciting in bars, or performing in sex shows. In some cases, desperate parents sell their female infants to agents who promise to see that the girls get work in the city. The agents take the girls, pay others to raise them, and then "harvest their crop" years later when the girls are old enough (sometimes just twelve or thirteen) to work the sex trade. In fact, given fears of sexually transmitted diseases among sex tourists, prostitutes are getting younger and younger, and it is the youngest girls who earn the most money.

Young girls await customers in a Bangkok brothel.

Once they work in the sex industry, the future for women is bleak. Pimps provide girls with clothes and housing, but at a cost that exceeds the girls' salaries. The result is a system of debt bondage that keeps these women virtual prisoners. To make matters worse, most sex workers suffer from a host of diseases brought on by abuse and neglect. Worst of all, estimates suggest that 40 percent are now infected with the virus that causes AIDS.

Sources: Based, in part, on Santoli (1994) and Remy (1996).

---

overlooks the fact that prostitution subjects many women to abuse and outright violence and plays a part in spreading sexually transmitted diseases, including AIDS. In addition, many poor women become trapped in a life of selling sex, generally to the benefit of others, while they put their own lives at risk. This is especially true in Southeast Asia, where the sex trade flourishes. The box offers a closer look.

SEXUAL VIOLENCE AND ABUSE

While sexual activity often occurs within a loving relationship, sex can be twisted by hate and violence. Sexual violence, which ranges from verbal abuse to rape and assault, is widespread in the United States.

Rape

Although some people think rape is a form of sex, it is actually an expression of power—a violent act that uses sex to hurt, humiliate, or control another person. The U.S. Department of Justice reports that about 100,000 women are raped each year, although this number reflects only the reported cases. The actual number of rapes is several times this number (McCormick, 1994; U.S. Bureau of Justice Statistics, 1999).

The official definition of rape, according to the federal government, is "the carnal knowledge of a female forcibly and against her will." Thus, official rape statistics include only victims who are women. But men, too, are raped—in perhaps 10 percent of all cases. Most men who rape men are not homosexual. They are heterosexuals who are motivated by a desire not for sex but to dominate another person (Groth & Birnbaum, 1979; Gibbs, 1991a).

Date Rape

A common myth is that rape involves strangers. In reality, however, most rapes involve people who know one

CRITICAL THINKING

Date Rape: Exposing Dangerous Myths

April Sanders was beside herself with excitement: She had a date with Bob McMahon, a senior she had admired all semester. On Saturday night, she met Bob at 10 o'clock at the south end of the Arts Quad, and they talked easily as they walked across campus to a party. The more Bob talked, the more April liked him.

The music was loud as they joined the crowd at a favorite campus hangout, and beer was flowing freely. They had a few beers and danced. Then they joined Bob's friends at a table where everyone was downing shots of hard liquor. Bob handed April a glass. She paused, but then smiled and drank it down. He kept refilling her glass and soon April's head was spinning. She knew she had drunk too much and had to lie down. Embarrassed, she announced she had better go back to her dorm room. "No problem," Bob responded, insisting on walking her home.

When they reached her room, April let Bob come in while she looked for some aspirin. They were sitting on her couch talking, when Bob tried to kiss her. At that point, he seemed to change, forcefully pushing April into having sex. "Bob, no!" April pleaded, overcome with fear. But Bob was determined as well as strong, and she simply could not stop him.

Ten minutes later, the attack was over, and Bob got up and left. April's first reaction was to take a shower. "I felt so filthy," she recalled later. "I washed myself over and over." For hours, she sat crying, trying to make sense of a night that had gone terribly wrong. "Was I raped?" she asked herself. "I told him 'no,' I tried to stop him." But she also worried, "Who will believe me? We were out drinking together. . . . I let him into my room. . . ."

In the morning, April Sanders went to the dean's office to report the attack. Later that day, she spoke with two city police officers. The police conducted an investigation, but they were reluctant to act since Bob claimed the sex was consensual and there was no other evidence such as bruises, a medical examination, or torn clothes to back up April's story.

This case is typical. In fact, at least half of all victims of sexual attack make no report to police. One reason is that many women and men do not understand what rape is. Three wrong ideas about rape are so common that they might be called "rape myths."

Myth #1: Rape involves strangers. A sexual attack brings to mind a strange man lurking in the shadows who suddenly springs on his victim. In four out of five rapes, however, the victim knows the offender, which is why people speak of *acquaintance rape* or *date rape*.

Myth #2: Women provoke their attackers. Many people think a woman who has been raped must have done *something* to make the man think she wanted to have sex. In April Sanders's

another, and they usually take place in familiar surroundings—especially the home. For this reason, the term *date rape* or *acquaintance rape* refers to forcible sexual violence against women by men they know.

Many victims of date rape do not report the crime. Some believe that because they know the offender, an attack could not have been rape. But the tide is turning, with more and more women speaking out. The box takes a closer look.

THEORETICAL ANALYSIS OF SEXUALITY

We can better understand human sexuality by using sociology's various theoretical paradigms. In the following sections, we apply the three major paradigms in turn.

STRUCTURAL-FUNCTIONAL ANALYSIS

The structural-functional approach highlights the contribution of any social pattern to the overall operation of society. Because sexuality is an important dimension of social life, society regulates sexual behavior.

The Need to Regulate Sexuality

From a biological point of view, sex allows our species to reproduce. But culture and social institutions regulate *with whom* and *when* people reproduce. For example, most societies condemn married people for having sex with someone other than their spouse. To do otherwise—to give the forces of sexual passion free reign—would threaten family life and, especially, the raising of children.

case, didn't she agree to go drinking? Didn't she let Bob into her room late at night? Self-doubt can paralyze victims. But inviting a man into a room is not consent to have sex with him any more than it would be consent to have him beat her with a club.

Myth #3: Rape is simply sex. If there is no knife held to a woman's throat or if she is not bound and gagged, what's the crime? The answer is that, under the law, forcing a woman to have sex without her consent is a *violent crime*. "Having sex" implies intimacy, caring, and, most important of all, consent—none of which is present in rape. Beyond the brutality of being physically violated, rape by an acquaintance also undermines a victim's sense of trust. Psychological scars are especially serious among the half of rape victims who are under eighteen; one-third of these young victims are attacked by their own fathers or stepfathers (Greenfield, 1996).

Is a person who drinks alcohol to excess capable of making a responsible decision about having sex? What role does alcohol play in date rape on the campus?

The ancient Babylonians stoned married women who were raped, convinced that they had committed adultery. Ideas about rape have changed little over thousands of years, which helps explain why—even today—only about one in twenty rapes results in an offender being sent to jail.

Nowhere has the issue of date rape been more widely discussed than on campuses. The collegiate environment promotes easy friendships and encourages trust. At the same time, many young students have much to learn about relationships and about themselves. So while college life encourages communication, it also invites sexual violence.

To counter the problem, many schools now actively address myths about rape and the place of alcohol in campus life. College men and women alike need to understand two simple truths: Sex without a woman's consent is rape, and when a woman says "no," she means just that.

What do you think?

1. *Why, in your opinion, are myths about rape so widespread?*
2. *What programs or policies exist on your campus to address sexual assault?*
3. *What else needs to be done?*

Sources: Gibbs (1991a, 1991b) and Gilbert (1992).

Another example, discussed earlier in this chapter, is the incest taboo. The fact that this norm exists everywhere shows clearly that no society is willing to permit completely free choice in sexual partners. Reproduction by family members other than married partners would break down the system of kinship and muddle relationships among people.

Historically, the social control of sexuality was strong, mostly because sex commonly led to childbirth. Moreover, offspring, as well as parents, were subject to these controls. We see this in the traditional distinction between "legitimate" reproduction (within marriage) and "illegitimate" reproduction (outside of marriage). But once a society can effectively control births, its norms become more permissive. This occurred in the United States where, over the course of the twentieth century, sex moved beyond its basic reproductive function and became accepted as a form of intimacy and even recreation (Giddens, 1992).

Latent Functions: The Case of Prostitution

It is easy to see that prostitution is harmful because it spreads disease and exploits women. But are there latent functions that help explain why prostitution is widespread despite society's attempts to limit it? Definitely, explains Kingsley Davis (1971): Prostitution performs several useful functions. It is one way to meet the sexual needs of a large number of people who do not have ready access to sex, including soldiers, travelers, and people who are not physically attractive, or who have trouble establishing relationships. Moreover, adds Davis, the availability of sex without commitment may even help to stabilize some loveless marriages that might otherwise collapse.

Europeans developed the concept of virginity during the Middle Ages with the rise of feudal estates. With property and titles to pass on, males needed to be certain of their heirs and, thus, desired to marry a woman who had never had sex to ensure she was not pregnant with another man's child. The loss of virginity became a significant life-course event for women, a fact captured in Jean-Baptiste Greuze's painting, The Broken Jug *(1773).*

Jean-Baptiste Greuze (1725–1805), *The Broken Jug* 1772–1773 (La cruche cassée). Rococo painting, canvas, 85 × 86.5 cm. Louvre, Dpt. des Peintures, Paris, France. © Photograph by Erich Lessing/Art Resource, N.Y.

Critical evaluation. The structural-functional paradigm helps us to appreciate the role sexuality plays in how society is organized. With the incest taboo and other cultural norms, society pays attention to who has sex with whom and, especially, who reproduces with whom.

At the same time, this approach pays little attention to the great diversity of sexual ideas and practices found within every society. Moreover, sexual patterns change over time, just as they differ in remarkable ways around the world. To appreciate the varied and changeable character of sexuality, we turn to the symbolic-interaction paradigm.

SYMBOLIC-INTERACTION ANALYSIS

The symbolic-interaction paradigm highlights how, as people interact, they construct everyday reality. As Chapter 6 ("Social Interaction in Everyday Life") explains, the process of reality construction is highly variable, so that one group's or society's views of sexuality may well differ from another's. In the same way, how people understand sexuality can and does change over time.

The Social Construction of Sexuality

Almost all social patterns involving sexuality have seen considerable change over the course of the twentieth century. One good illustration is the changing importance of virginity. A century ago, our society's norm—for women, at least—was virginity before marriage. This norm was strong because there was no effective birth control, and virginity was the only assurance a man had that his bride-to-be was not carrying another man's child. Today, however, we have gone a long way toward separating sex from reproduction, and the virginity norm has weakened. In the United States, among those born between 1963 and 1974, just 16.3 percent of men and 20.1 percent of women report being virgins at first marriage (Laumann et al., 1994:503).

Another example of our society's construction of sexuality involves young people. A century ago, childhood was a time of innocence in sexual matters. In recent decades, however, our thinking has changed. Though we expect children not to be sexually active, most people believe children should be educated about sex so that they can make intelligent choices about their own behavior as they grow older.

Global Comparisons

The broader our view, the more variation we see in the meanings people attach to sexuality. In global perspective, differences can be striking, indeed. Anthropologists report that some cultures are far more accepting of childhood sexuality than people in the United States. Studying the Melanesian people of southeast New Guinea, anthropologist Ruth Benedict (1938) concluded that adults paid little attention when young children engaged in sexual experimentation with one another. Parents in Melanesia shrugged off such activity because, before puberty, sex cannot lead to reproduction.

Critical evaluation. The strength of the symbolic-interaction paradigm lies in revealing the constructed character of familiar social patterns. Understanding that people "construct" sexuality, we can better appreciate the variety of sexual practices found over the course of history and around the world.

One limitation of this approach, however, is that not everything is so variable. Throughout our own history—and around the world—men are more likely to see women in sexual terms than the other way around. If this pattern is widespread, some broader social structure must be at work, as we shall see in the next section.

SOCIAL-CONFLICT ANALYSIS

The social-conflict paradigm highlights dimensions of inequality. This approach, therefore, shows how sexuality both reflects patterns of social inequality and also helps create them.

Sexuality: Reflecting Social Inequality

Recall our discussion of prostitution, a practice outlawed almost everywhere. Even so, enforcement is uneven at best, especially when it comes to who is and is not likely to be arrested. Although two parties are involved, the record shows that police are far more likely to arrest (less powerful) female prostitutes than (more powerful) male clients. Similarly, of all women engaged in prostitution, it is street walkers—women with the least income and those most likely to be minorities—who face the highest risk of arrest (COYOTE, 2000). Then, too, we might wonder if so many women would be involved in prostitution at all if they had economic opportunities equal to those of men.

Sexuality: Creating Social Inequality

Social-conflict theorists, especially feminists, point to sexuality as being at the root of inequality between women and men. How can this be? Defining women in sexual terms amounts to devaluing them from full human beings into objects of men's interest and attention. Is it any wonder that the word "pornography" comes from the Greek word *porne*, meaning "a man's sexual slave"?

If men define women in sexual terms, it is easy to see why many people consider pornography—almost all of which is consumed by males—a power issue. Since most pornography depicts women seeking to please men, it supports the idea that men have power over women.

Some more radical critics doubt that this element of power can ever be removed from heterosexual relations (Dworkin, 1987). While most social-conflict theorists do not reject heterosexuality entirely, they do agree that sexuality can and does degrade women. Further, critics point out that our culture often depicts sexuality in terms of sport (men "scoring" with women) and also violence ("slamming," "banging," and "hitting on," for example, are verbs used for both fighting and sex).

Prostitution involves two people, but far more female prostitutes than male "Johns" face arrest for this crime. Moreover, of all categories of prostitutes, low-income street walkers are at the highest risk of arrest, disease, and violence.

Queer Theory

Finally, social-conflict theory has taken aim not only at men dominating women but also at heterosexuals dominating homosexuals. In recent years, just as many lesbians and gay men have come out in search of public acceptance, so have some sociologists tried to add a gay voice to their discipline. The term **queer theory** refers to *a growing body of knowledge that challenges an allegedly heterosexual bias in sociology.*

Queer theory begins with the assertion that our society is characterized by **heterosexism,** *a view stigmatizing anyone who is not heterosexual as "queer."* Our heterosexual culture victimizes a wide range of people, including gay men, lesbians, bisexuals, transsexuals, and even asexual people. Further, although most people agree that bias against women (sexism) and people of color (racism) is wrong, heterosexism is widely tolerated and sometimes well within the law. This country's military forces, for example, cannot legally discharge a female soldier for "acting like a woman," because that would be a clear case of gender discrimination. But the

CONTROVERSY & DEBATE

The Abortion Controversy

A black van pulls up in front of the storefront in a busy section of the city. Two women get out of the front seat and cautiously scan the sidewalk. After a moment, one nods to the other and they open the rear door to let a third woman out of the van. Standing to the right and left of their charge, the two quickly whisk her inside the building.

Is this a description of two federal marshals escorting a convict to a police station? It might be. But it is actually an account of two clinic workers escorting a woman who has decided to have an abortion. Why should they be so cautious? Anyone who has read the papers in recent years knows about the heated confrontations at abortion clinics across North America. In fact, some opponents have even targeted and killed several doctors who perform abortions. Overall, the 1.3 million abortions performed each year make this probably the most hotly contested issue in the United States today.

Abortion has not always been so controversial. During the colonial era, midwives and other healers performed abortions with little community opposition and with full approval of the law. But controversy arose about 1850, when early medical doctors sought to eliminate the competition they faced from midwives and other traditional health providers, whose income was derived largely from terminating pregnancies. By 1900, medical doctors succeeded in getting every state to pass a law banning abortion.

Such laws did not end abortion, but they greatly reduced the numbers. In addition, these laws drove abortion "underground," so that many women—especially those who were poor—had little choice but to seek help from unlicensed "back alley" abortionists, sometimes with tragic results.

By the 1960s, opposition to abortion laws was rising. In 1973, the U.S. Supreme Court rendered a landmark decision (in the cases of *Roe* v. *Wade* and *Doe* v. *Bolton*), striking down all state laws banning abortion. In effect, this action by the High Court established a woman's legal access to abortion.

In the wake of the Court's decision, the abortion controversy has grown. On one side of the issue are people who describe themselves as "pro-choice," supporting a woman's right to choose abortion. On the other side are those who call themselves "pro-life," opposing abortion as morally wrong; these people would like to see the Supreme Court reverse its 1973 decision.

How strong is the support for each side of the abortion controversy? A recent national survey asked a sample of adults the question: "Should it be possible for a pregnant woman to obtain a legal abortion if the woman wants it for any reason?" In response, 42.6 percent said "yes" (placing them in the pro-choice camp) and 52.1 percent said "no" (the pro-life position); the remaining 5.3 percent offered no opinion (NORC, 1999:209).

A closer look, however, shows that particular circumstances make a big difference in how people see this issue. The figure shows that a large majority of U.S. adults favor legal abortion if a pregnancy seriously threatens a woman's health, if

---

military forces can discharge her for homosexuality if she is a sexually active lesbian.

Heterosexism also exists at a more subtle level in our everyday understanding of the world. When we describe something as "sexy," for example, don't we really mean attractive to *heterosexuals?*

Critical evaluation. Applying the social-conflict paradigm shows how sexuality is both a cause and effect of inequality. In particular, this paradigm helps us understand men's power over women and heterosexual people's domination of homosexual people.

At the same time, this approach overlooks the fact that sexuality is not a power issue for everyone: Many couples enjoy a vital sexual relationship that deepens their commitment to one another. In addition, the social-conflict paradigm pays little attention to strides our society has made toward eliminating injustice. Men, in public at least, are less likely to describe women as sex objects than a few decades ago; moreover, public concern about sexual harassment (see Chapter 13, "Gender Stratification") has had some effect in reducing sexuality in the workplace. Likewise, there is ample evidence that the gay rights movement has secured greater opportunities and social acceptance for gay people.

We bring this chapter to a close with a look at what is perhaps the most divisive sexuality issue of all: **abortion,** *the deliberate termination of a pregnancy.* This issue cuts to the heart of almost everyone's sense of justice, as described in the box.

she became pregnant as a result of rape, or if a fetus is very likely to have a serious defect. The bottom line, then, looks like this: About 40 percent support access to abortion under *any* circumstances, but about 80 percent support access to abortion under *some* circumstances.

Many pro-life people feel strongly that abortion is nothing more than killing unborn children. To them, people never have the right to end an innocent life in this way. But pro-choice people are no less committed to their position. As they see it, the abortion debate is really about the standing of women in society.

Why? For the simple reason that women must have control over their own sexuality. If pregnancy dictates the course of women's lives, women will never be able to compete with men on equal terms, whether it is on campus or in the workplace. Thus, the pro-choice position concludes, women must have access to legal, safe abortion as a necessary condition to full participation in society.

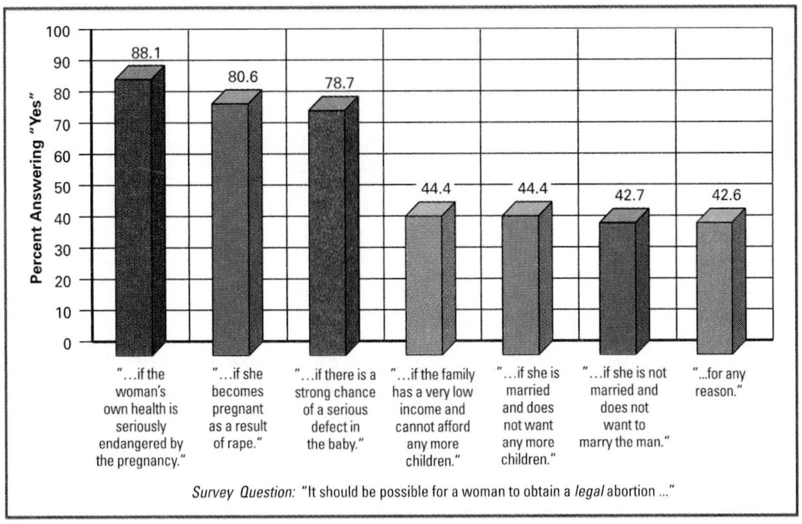

When Should the Law Allow a Woman to Choose Abortion?

Source: NORC (1999).

Continue the debate . . .

1. *The more conservative pro-life people see abortion as a moral issue, while more liberal pro-choice people see abortion as a power issue. Can you see a parallel to how conservatives and liberals view the issue of pornography?*
2. *Surveys show that men and women have almost the same opinions about abortion. Does this surprise you? Why?*
3. *Why do you think the abortion controversy is often so bitter? Why has our nation been unable to find a middle ground on which all can agree?*

Sources: Based, in part, on Luker (1984), Tannahill (1992), and various news reports.

SUMMARY

1. U.S. culture has long defined sex as a taboo topic. The Kinsey studies (1948, 1953) were among the first publications by social scientists on human sexuality.
2. Sex refers to the biological distinction between females and males, which is determined at conception as a male sperm joins a female ovum.
3. Males and females are distinguished not only by their genitals (primary sex characteristics) but also by bodily development as they mature (secondary sex characteristics). Hermaphrodites have some combination of both male and female genitalia. Transsexuals are people who feel they are one sex, although, biologically, they are the other.
4. For most species, sex is rigidly directed by biology; for human beings, sex is a matter of cultural definition as well as personal choice. Patterns of kissing, modesty, and beauty vary around the world, revealing the cultural foundation of sexual practices.
5. Historically, our society has held rigid attitudes toward sexuality, although these attitudes have become more permissive over time.
6. The sexual revolution, which came of age in the 1960s and 1970s, brought a far greater openness

in matters of sexuality. By 1980, a sexual counter-revolution was taking form, condemning permissiveness and urging a return to more conservative "family values."

7. The share of people in the United States who have premarital sexual intercourse increased over the last century. Research shows that three-fourths of young men and two-thirds of young women do so by their senior year in high school.
8. The level of sexual activity varies within the population of U.S. adults: One-third report having sex with a partner a few times a year or not at all; another one-third have sex once or several times a month; the remaining one-third have sex with a partner two or more times a week.
9. Although extramarital sex is widely condemned, about 25 percent of married men and 10 percent of married women report being sexually unfaithful to their spouses at some time.
10. Sexual orientation refers to people's preference in terms of sexual partners. Four major orientations are heterosexuality, homosexuality, bisexuality, and asexuality. Sexual orientation is caused by some combination of biological factors, cultural factors, and human choice.
11. The share of the population that is homosexual depends on how researchers define "homosexuality." About 9 percent of adult men and 4 percent of adult women report having some homosexual experience, compared with 2.8 percent of men and 1.4 percent of women who say they have a homosexual identity.
12. The gay rights movement has worked to gain greater acceptance for gay people. Largely due to this movement, the share of the U.S. population condemning homosexuality as morally wrong has steadily decreased and stands now at about half.
13. Some 1 million U.S. teenagers become pregnant each year. The rate of teenage pregnancy has dropped since 1950, when many teens married and had children. Today, however, most pregnant teens are unmarried and, especially if they drop out of school, are at high risk of poverty.
14. With no universal definition of pornography, the law allows local communities to set standards of decency. Conservatives condemn pornography as immoral; liberals, by contrast, condemn it as demeaning to women.
15. Prostitution, the selling of sexual services, is illegal almost everywhere in the United States. Although many people think of prostitution as a victimless crime, it victimizes women and spreads sexually transmitted diseases.
16. Some 100,000 rapes are reported each year, but the actual number is several times greater. Although many people think of rape as a sexual act, rape is really a violent expression of power. Most rapes involve people who know one another.
17. Structural-functional theory highlights society's need to regulate sexual activity. A universal norm in this regard is the incest taboo that keeps kinship relations clear.
18. The symbolic-interaction paradigm points up how people attach various meanings to sexuality. Thus, societies differ from one another in terms of sexual attitudes and practices; similarly, sexual patterns change within any one society over time.
19. Social-conflict theory links sexuality to inequality. From this point of view, men dominate women in part by devaluing them as sexual objects.

KEY CONCEPTS

sex (p. 221) the biological distinction between females and males

primary sex characteristics (p. 222) the genitals, organs used for reproduction

secondary sex characteristics (p. 222) bodily differences, apart from the genitals, that distinguish biologically mature females and males

hermaphrodite (p. 223) a human being with some combination of female and male genitalia

transsexuals (p. 223) people who feel they are one sex even though biologically they are the other

incest taboo (p. 224) a norm forbidding sexual relations or marriage between certain relatives

sexual orientation (p. 228) a person's preference in terms of sexual partners: same sex, other sex, either sex, neither sex

heterosexuality (p. 228) a sexual orientation in which a person is sexually attracted to someone of the other sex

homosexuality (p. 228) a sexual orientation in which a person is sexually attracted to someone of the same sex

bisexuality (p. 228) a sexual orientation in which a person is sexually attracted to people of both sexes

asexuality (p. 228) a sexual orientation in which a person is not sexually attracted to people of either sex

homophobia (p. 231) the dread of close personal interaction with people thought to be gay, lesbian, or bisexual

pornography (p. 232) sexually explicit material that causes sexual arousal

prostitution (p. 233) the selling of sexual services

queer theory (p. 239) a growing body of knowledge that challenges an allegedly heterosexual bias in sociology

heterosexism (p. 239) a view stigmatizing anyone who is not heterosexual as "queer"

abortion (p. 240) the deliberate termination of a pregnancy

CRITICAL-THINKING QUESTIONS

1. What do sociologists mean by the *sexual revolution?* What did the sexual revolution change? Can you suggest some of the reasons that these changes occurred?
2. What is sexual orientation? Why is this characteristic difficult for researchers to measure?
3. Do you think laws should regulate the portrayal of sex in books, films, or on the Internet? Why or why not?
4. In what ways do societies regulate sexuality? In what ways does sexuality play a part in social inequality?

APPLICATIONS AND EXERCISES

1. The most complete study of sexual patterns in the United States to date is *The Social Organization of Sexuality: Sexual Practices in the United States* by Edward Laumann et al. You can find this book in your campus or community library. Get a copy and browse through some of the chapters most interesting to you. Afterwards, think about the value of doing sociological research on sexuality.
2. Contact your school's student services office, and ask for information about the extent of sexual violence on your campus. Do people report such crimes? What policies and procedures does your school have to respond to sexual violence?
3. In the past, state and local laws permitted prostitution much more widely than they do today. Do some research on the history of prostitution laws in your state or community.
4. Install the CD-ROM packaged in the back of this new textbook to access a variety of study, review, and applications exercises designed to help you better understand the material covered in this chapter. The CD includes an author's tip video, as well as interactive maps, video application exercises, Web links, and study questions.

SITES TO SEE

http://www.prenhall.com/macionis

Visit the interactive Web site that accompanies this text. Begin by clicking on the cover of your book. You will find a chapter-by-chapter study guide, practice tests, chat room, and many suggested Web links.

http://www.teenpregnancy.org

Visit the Web site of the National Campaign to Prevent Teen Pregnancy, an organization formed to guide teens toward responsible sexual behavior. You can find data for your state at this site. What are the key parts of this organization's program? How effective would you imagine it is? Why?

http://www.qrd.org

This Web site, the Queer Resource Directory, looks at a wide range of issues—including family, religion, education, and health—from a "queer theory" perspective. Visit this site to see in what ways various social institutions can be considered "heterosexist." Do you agree? Why?

http://www.gay.com

This is a search engine for all sorts of information on issues involving homosexuality.

cyber.scope

PART II

HOW NEW TECHNOLOGY IS CHANGING OUR WAY OF LIFE

Marshall McLuhan (1969) summed up his pioneering research in the study of communications this way: "Any new technology tends to create a new human environment." In other words, technology affects not just how we work, but it shapes and colors our entire way of life. In this second cyber.scope, we pause to reflect on some of the ways the Information Revolution is changing our culture and society.

The Information Revolution and Cultural Values

Chapter 3 ("Culture") noted the importance members of our society attach to material comfort. Throughout our history, many people have defined "success" to mean earning a good income and enjoying the things money will buy, including a home, car, and fashionable clothing.

But there are signs that, as we move through this new century, our values may shift from a single-minded focus on the accumulation of "things" (the products of industrial technology) to an appreciation of "ideas" (the product of information technology). Such "new age" ideas range from experiences, including both travel and countless experiences with virtual reality,[1] to well-being, including the self-actualization that has become popular in recent decades.

Socialization in the Computer Age

Half a century ago, television rewrote the rules for socialization in the United States and, as Chapter 5 ("Socialization") explained, young people now spend more time watching TV than talking to their parents. Today, in the new information society, screens are not just for television; they are our windows into a cyber-world in which we look to computers to link, entertain, and educate us. But this trend toward cyber-socialization raises several important questions.

First, will the spread of computer-based information erode the regional diversity that has marked this country's history, setting off New England from the Deep South and the Midwest from the West Coast? We know that new information technology is linking our nation and the world, so that we might well expect to see a more national culture emerge and, with time, a more global culture as well.

Second, how will this cyber-culture affect our children? Is having computers at the center of their lives good for them? For most children, at least, computer-based images and information play a significant role in teaching them about themselves and the world. Is this trend reducing the importance of parents in children's lives, as

Almost unlimited access to information can be a mixed blessing, as parents can well understand. How can we prevent children from gaining access to pornography or other objectionable material on the Internet? Or, should we?

[1]For example, "travel" to an Adirondack mountaintop and enjoy the view (http://www.adirondack.net/adnet/bluemt/bluemt1.html), or wander through the Tower of London (http://www.toweroflondontour.com).

television did? Cyber-socialization can certainly entertain and instruct, but can it meet the emotional needs of children? Will it contribute to their moral development? After all, there is nothing more important to a child—and more *low tech*—than a warm hug.

Third, who will control cyber-socialization? Just as parents have long expressed concerns about what their children watch on television, they now worry about what kids encounter as they "surf the Net." To date, the federal courts have taken the position that the Internet should operate with minimal government interference. Do we—as citizens and as parents—have expectations for the content of virtual culture? Should the information industry operate for profit? With standards to ensure some measure of educational content? Who should decide?

The Cyber-Self

A person using the name "VegDiet" enters one of thousands of chat rooms found on the Internet, the vast global network described in Chapter 7 ("Groups and Organizations"). Within a few seconds, "VegDiet" is actively debating the state of the world with three other people: "MrMaine," "Ferret," and "RedWine."

The growing popularity of computer-chat gives us a chance to highlight ways in which online interaction differs from more conventional modes of interaction. After studying online interaction, Dennis Waskul (1997) described the self we transmit via a computer as "disembodied." Using Erving Goffman's dramaturgical approach (see Chapter 6), Waskul notes that computer technology screens out a host of "cues" about people's identities—where they are, what they look like, how they dress, and their age and sex—and conveys only the identities they choose to present.

Cyberspace thus affords us great freedom to "try on" identities with few, if any, lasting consequences. As one chat-room participant explained, "Online is a game. . . . Only here, I play with who I am" (Waskul, 1997:21).

But Wait A Minute . . . The Neo-Luddites

In the eighteenth century, groups of English weavers who opposed the Industrial Revolution traveled about demolishing new machinery whenever they could gain access to a factory. The Luddites (named after Ned Ludd, their leader) were convinced that the new technology of their day would end up eliminating jobs and, generally, make life worse (Zachary, 1997).

Although the Luddites lost their battle to stem the tide of change, their spirit lives on today in people opposed to the Information Revolution. These neo-Luddites, as they are called, speak with many voices. But they agree that we should not race headlong into a cyber-future without thinking critically about how new technology is likely to make our lives better and worse.

The neo-Luddites remind us, first, that technology is never socially neutral. That is, technology does not simply exist *in* the world, it *changes* the world, pushing human lives in one direction while closing off other alternatives. By venerating technology as good in and of itself, Theodore Roszak (1986) points out, we give up the power to decide for ourselves how we should live. Is putting computers in the classroom a substitute for good teaching? We might well remember that no computer ever created a painting, penned a poem, or composed a symphony. Perhaps most important, computers have no capacity to address ethical questions about right and wrong.

Living in a forward-looking culture, we easily imagine the benefits of new technology. But we need to remember that, just as technology can serve us, it also can diminish us and even destroy us. After all, the Luddites were not anti-technology; they simply wanted to be sure that technology responded to human needs—and not the other way around.

"On the Internet, nobody knows you're a dog."

CHAPTER 10

Paul Marcus
The New Nanny

SOCIAL STRATIFICATION

On April 10, 1912, the ocean liner *Titanic* slipped away from the docks of Southampton, England, on its maiden voyage across the North Atlantic to New York. A proud symbol of the new industrial age, the towering ship carried 2,300 men, women, and children, some enjoying more luxury than most travelers today could imagine. Poor people, however, crowded the lower decks, journeying to what they hoped would be a better life in the United States.

Two days out, the crew received radio warnings of icebergs in the area, but paid little notice. Then, near midnight, as the ship steamed swiftly westward, a lookout was stunned to see a massive shape rising out of the calm ocean directly ahead. Moments later, the *Titanic* collided with a huge iceberg, as tall as the ship itself, which split open its side as if the grand vessel were just a giant tin can.

Seawater flooded into the ship's lower levels pulling the ship down by the bow. Within twenty-five minutes of impact, people were rushing for the lifeboats. By 2:00 A.M., the bow was completely submerged and the stern high above the water. Within minutes, all lights went out. Clinging to the deck, in silence and darkness, hundreds of helpless passengers and crew passed their final minutes before the ship disappeared into the frigid Atlantic (Lord, 1976).

The tragic loss of more than 1,600 lives made news around the world. Looking back dispassionately at this terrible accident with a sociological eye, however, we note that some categories of passengers had much better odds of survival than others. In an age of conventional gallantry, women and children boarded the lifeboats first, so that 80 percent of the casualties were men. Class, too, was at work. More than 60 percent of people holding first-class tickets were saved because they were on the upper decks where warnings were sounded first and lifeboats were accessible. Only 36 percent of the second-class passengers survived, and of the third-class passengers on the lower decks, only 24 percent escaped drowning. On board the *Titanic*, class turned out to mean much more than the quality of one's cabin. Class was a matter of life or death.

The fate of those aboard the *Titanic* dramatically illustrates how social inequality affects the way people live—and sometimes whether they live at all. This chapter explores the important concept of social stratification. Chapter 11 delves further into the issue by examining social inequality in the United States, and Chapter 12 examines how our country fits into a global system of wealth and poverty.

WHAT IS SOCIAL STRATIFICATION?

For tens of thousands of years, humans the world over lived in small hunting and gathering societies. Although members of these bands might single out one person as being swifter, stronger, or particularly skillful in

The personal experience of poverty is captured in Sebastiao Salgado's haunting photograph, which stands as a universal portrait of human suffering. The essential sociological insight is that, however strongly individuals feel its effects, our social standing is largely a consequence of the way in which a society (or a world of societies) structures opportunity and reward. To the core of our being, then, we are all the products of social stratification.

collecting food, everyone had more or less the same social standing. As societies became more complex—a process detailed in Chapter 4 ("Society")—a major change came about. Societies began to elevate some categories of people above others, giving segments of the population more money, power, and prestige than others.

Social stratification refers to *a system by which a society ranks categories of people in a hierarchy*. Social stratification is a matter of four basic principles:

1. **Social stratification is a trait of society, not simply a reflection of individual differences.** Many of us think of social standing in terms of personal talent and effort. But we exaggerate the extent to which we control our own fate. Did a higher percentage of the first-class passengers on the *Titanic* survive because they were smarter or better swimmers than second- and third-class passengers? Hardly. They fared better because of the system of privilege at work on the ship. Similarly, children born into wealthy families are more likely than children born into poverty to enjoy good health, achieve academically, succeed in their life's work, and live a long life. Neither the rich nor the poor people are responsible for creating social stratification, yet this system shapes the lives of us all.
2. **Social stratification persists over generations.** To see that stratification is a trait of societies rather than individuals, we need only look at how inequality persists across generations. In all societies, parents pass their social position on to their children.

   In most industrial societies, however, some individuals experience **social mobility,** *change in one's position in the social hierarchy*. Social mobility may be upward or downward. We celebrate the achievements of a Roseanne or a Michael Jordan, both of whom rose from modest beginnings to fame and fortune. But people also move downward because of business setbacks, unemployment, or illness. More often, people move *horizontally*, that is, they switch one job for another at about the same social level. For most people, social standing remains much the same over a lifetime.
3. **Social stratification is universal but variable.** Social stratification is found everywhere. Yet, *what* is unequal and *how* unequal it is vary from one society to another. In some societies, inequality is mostly a matter of prestige; in others, wealth or power is the key dimension of difference. Moreover, some societies display more inequality and others less.
4. **Social stratification involves not just inequality but beliefs.** Any system of inequality not only gives some people more than others, it defines these arrangements as fair. Just as *what* is unequal differs from society to society, so does the explanation of *why* people should be unequal.

CASTE AND CLASS SYSTEMS

Sociologists distinguish between "closed" systems, which allow for little change in social position, and "open" systems, which permit considerable social mobility (Tumin, 1985).

THE CASTE SYSTEM

A **caste system** is *social stratification based on ascription*. A pure caste system is closed because birth alone determines one's destiny with little or no opportunity for social mobility based on individual effort. Caste systems, then, rank people in rigid categories, where they live out their lives.

The traditional caste system still guides people's choice of work, especially in rural areas. Below the four basic castes are the Harijans, people defined as "outcasts" or "untouchables." These people perform jobs, such as turning leather into shoes, defined as unclean for others of higher social position.

Two Illustrations: India and South Africa

Many of the world's societies, most of them agrarian, approximate caste systems. One example is India, or at least India's traditional villages, where most of the people still live. The Indian system of castes (or *varna*, a Sanskrit word that means "color") is composed of four categories: Brahmin, Kshatriya, Vaishya, and Shudra. On the local level, however, each of these is composed of hundreds of subcaste (or *jati*) groups.

Caste has also played an important role in the history of South Africa. Until recently, this nation's policy of apartheid gave the 5 million South Africans of European ancestry a commanding share of wealth and power, dominating some 30 million black South Africans. In a middle position were another 3 million mixed-race people, known as "coloreds," and about 1 million Asians. The box on pages 250–51 describes the current state of South Africa's racial caste system.

In a caste system, birth shapes people's lives in four ways. First, traditional caste groups have specific occupations, so that generations of a family perform the same type of work. In rural India, although some occupations (such as farming) are open to all, castes are identified with the work their members do (as priests, barbers, leather workers, sweepers, and so on). In South Africa, whites still hold most of the desirable jobs, while most blacks perform manual labor and other low-level service work.

Second, maintaining a rigid social hierarchy depends on people marrying within their own categories; "mixed" marriages would blur the ranking of children. Caste systems, therefore, demand that people marry others like themselves. Sociologists call this pattern *endogamous* marriage (*endo* stems from the Greek, meaning "within"). Traditionally, Indian parents select their children's marriage partners, often before the children reach their teens. Before 1985, South Africa outlawed marriage (and even sex) between the races; today, interracial couples are legal but rare since blacks and whites still live in separate areas.

Third, caste norms guide people to stay in the company of "their own kind." Hindus in India support this segregation, believing that a ritually "pure" person of a higher caste will be "polluted" by contact with someone of lower standing. Apartheid in South Africa operated in much the same way.

Fourth, and finally, caste systems rest on powerful cultural beliefs. Indian culture is built on Hindu moral belief in accepting one's life work, whatever it may be. In South Africa, although apartheid is no longer law, most people still distinguish "white jobs" from "black jobs."

Caste and Agrarian Life

Caste systems exist in agrarian societies because the lifelong routines of agriculture depend on a rigid sense of duty and discipline. Thus, caste persists in rural India,

GLOBAL SOCIOLOGY

Race as Caste: A Report from South Africa

At the southern tip of the African continent lies South Africa, a country about the size of Alaska and with a population of about 43 million in 1999. Long inhabited by black people, the region attracted white Dutch traders and farmers in the mid-seventeenth century. Early in the nineteenth century, a second wave of colonization saw British immigrants push the Dutch inland. By the early 1900s, the British had taken over the country, proclaiming it the Union of South Africa. In 1961, the United Kingdom gave up control and recognized the independence of the Republic of South Africa.

But freedom was a reality only for the white minority. Years before, to ensure their political control over the black majority, whites had instituted a policy of *apartheid*, or racial separation. Apartheid was made law in 1948, denying blacks national citizenship, ownership of land, and any formal voice in the government. In effect, black South Africans became a lower caste, receiving little schooling and performing menial, low-paying jobs. Under this system, even "middle-class" white households had at least one black household servant.

The prosperous white minority defended apartheid, claiming that blacks threatened their cultural traditions or, more simply, were inferior beings. But resistance to apartheid rose steadily, prompting whites to resort to brutal military repression to maintain their power.

Steady resistance—especially from younger blacks, impatient for a political voice and economic opportunity—gradually forced change. Adding to the pressure was criticism from most other industrial nations, including the United States. By the mid-1980s, the tide began to turn as the South African government granted limited political rights to people of mixed race and Asian ancestry. Then came the right for all people to form labor unions, to enter occupations once restricted to whites,

more than sixty years after being formally outlawed and even as its grip has relaxed in big cities, where people exercise greater choice in their work and marriage partners. Similarly, the rapid industrialization of South Africa made personal choice and individual rights more important, so that the abolition of apartheid was only a matter of time. In mature industrial nations such as the United States, some caste elements survive, but treating people categorically on the basis of race or sex now invites charges of racism and sexism.

Note that the erosion of caste does not signal the end of social stratification. On the contrary, it simply marks a change in its character, as the next sections explain.

THE CLASS SYSTEM

Farming demands the lifelong discipline created by caste systems. But industrial production depends on developing people's talents, giving rise to a **class system,** *social stratification based on both birth and individual achievement.*

A class system is more open, so that individuals who acquire schooling and skills may be socially mobile in relation to their parents and siblings. Such mobility, in turn, blurs class distinctions, so that even blood relatives may have different social standings. Social boundaries also break down as people immigrate from abroad or move from the countryside to the city, lured by greater opportunity for education and work (Lipset & Bendix, 1967; Cutright, 1968; Treiman, 1970). Typically, newcomers take low-paying jobs, and, in the process, push others up the social ladder (Tyree, Semyonov, & Hodge, 1979).

Categorizing people according to their color, sex, or social background has come to be seen as wrong in industrial societies, as all people acquire political rights and roughly equal standing before the law. Moreover, in industrial societies, work is not fixed at birth but involves some personal choice. Greater individualism also translates into more freedom in selecting a marriage partner.

Meritocracy

Compared to agrarian societies where caste is the rule, industrial societies move towards **meritocracy,** *social stratification based on personal merit.* Because industrial societies need to develop a broad range of capabilities (beyond farming), stratification is not based solely on the accident of one's birth but also on "merit," by which we mean the job one does and how well one does it.

and to own property. Officials also began to dismantle the system of laws that separated the races in public places.

The rate of change increased in 1990 with Nelson Mandela's release from prison. In 1994, the first national election open to all people of all races elected Mandela the president, ending centuries of white minority rule.

Despite this dramatic political change, however, social stratification in South Africa is still based on race. Even with the right to own property, one-third of black South Africans have no jobs, and the majority remain dirt poor. The worst off are some 7 million *ukuhlele-leka*, which means "marginal people" in the Xhosa language. Soweto-by-the-Sea may sound like a summer getaway, but it is home to thousands of *ukuhleleleka* who live crammed into shacks made of packing cases, corrugated metal, cardboard, and other discarded materials. There is no electricity for lights or refrigeration. Without plumbing, people use buckets to haul sewage; women line up to take a turn at a single water tap that serves more than 1,000 people. Any job is hard to come by, and those who do find work are lucky to earn $200 a month.

South Africa's new president, Thabo Mbeki, elected in 1999, leads a nation still twisted by centuries of racial caste. Tourism is up and holds out promise of an economic boom in years to come. But the country can only shed its past by providing all its people with real opportunity.

Sources: Fredrickson (1981), Wren (1991), Hawthorne (1999), and Mabry & Masland (1999).

To advance meritocracy, industrial societies expand equality of opportunity, although people expect inequality of outcomes.

In a pure meritocracy, social position would depend entirely on a person's ability and effort. Such a system would have ongoing social mobility, blurring social categories as individuals continuously move up or down in the system depending on their latest performance. In caste societies, "merit" (from the Latin, meaning "worthy of praise") means persisting in low-skill jobs such as farming. Caste systems honor those who do their work dutifully and remain "in their place."

Caste systems waste human potential, of course, but they are very orderly. And herein lies the answer to an important question: Why do industrial societies keep castelike qualities (such as letting wealth pass from generation to generation) rather than becoming complete meritocracies? Simply because a pure meritocracy diminishes the importance of families and other social groupings. Economic performance is not *everything*, after all. Would we want to evaluate our family members solely on their jobs? Probably not. Therefore, class systems in industrial societies move toward meritocracy to promote productivity and efficiency but retain caste elements to maintain order and social cohesion.

Status Consistency

Status consistency refers to *the degree of consistency in a person's social standing across various dimensions of social inequality*. A caste system has limited social mobility and high status consistency, so that the typical person has the same relative ranking with regard to wealth, power, and prestige. The greater mobility of class systems, however, produces less status consistency. In the United States, then, a college professor with an advanced degree might enjoy high social prestige but earn a moderate income. Low status consistency means that *classes* are less well defined than *castes*.

BIRTH AND ACHIEVEMENT: THE UNITED KINGDOM

The mix of caste and meritocracy in class systems is well illustrated by the United Kingdom (composed of England, Wales, Scotland, and Northern Ireland), an industrial nation with a long agrarian history.

The Estate System

In the Middle Ages, England had a castelike system of three estates. The *first estate* was a hereditary nobility composed of barely 5 percent of the population; they controlled most of the land—the chief form of wealth (Laslett, 1984). Most nobles had no occupation, since they deemed engaging in trade or any other work for income beneath them. Well tended by servants, nobles used their leisure time to cultivate refined tastes in art, music, and literature.

To prevent vast landholdings from being divided by heirs, the law of *primogeniture* (from the Latin, meaning "first born") demanded that all landholdings pass to the oldest son or other male relation. Younger sons had to find other means of support. Some entered the clergy—often termed the *second estate*—where their spiritual power was upheld by the church's extensive landholdings. Other young men of high birth became military officers or lawyers, or took up other professions considered honorable for gentlemen. In an age when no woman could inherit her father's property and few women had the opportunity to earn a living on their own, a noble daughter depended for her security on marrying well.

Below the nobility and the clergy, the vast majority of men and women formed the *third estate*, or commoners. Most commoners were serfs working land owned by nobles. With little education, most were illiterate.

As the Industrial Revolution expanded England's economy, some commoners living in cities made enough money to challenge the nobility. Greater emphasis on meritocracy, the growing importance of money, and extension of schooling and legal rights to more people eventually blurred social rankings and gave rise to a class system.

Perhaps it is a sign of the times that, these days, traditional titles are put up for sale by nobles who simply need the money. In 1996, for example, the title "Lord of Wimbledon" was put on the block by the Earl Spencer—Princess Diana's brother—to raise the $300,000 he needed to redo the plumbing in one of his large homes (McKee, 1996).

The United Kingdom Today

Today, the United Kingdom has a class system, though it retains the mark of a long, feudal past. A small cluster of British families owns inherited estates, attends expensive schools, and exercises considerable political influence. A traditional monarch, Queen Elizabeth II, stands as the United Kingdom's head of state, and Parliament's House of Lords is composed of peers, about half of noble birth. Control of the government, however, has passed to the House of Commons, where the prime minister and other commoners typically reach their position by achievement—winning an election—rather than by birth.

Further down, roughly one-fourth of the British people form the "middle class." Many earn comfortable incomes from professions and business and are likely to own some stocks and bonds.

Below the middle class, about half of all Britons think of themselves as "working class," earning modest incomes through manual work. In recent decades, the decline of British industries such as coal mining and steel production has led to high unemployment among working-class families. Some have slipped into poverty, joining the remaining one-fourth of Britons who are socially and economically deprived. Lower-class people—or, more simply, the poor—are heavily concentrated in northern and western regions of the United Kingdom, which are plagued by economic decay.

Today's British class system mixes caste elements and meritocracy, producing a highly stratified society in which people move both upward and downward. However, one legacy of the historical estate system is that social mobility occurs less frequently in the United Kingdom than in the United States (Kerckhoff, Campbell, & Winfield-Laird, 1985). The more rigid stratification in the United Kingdom is reflected in the importance attached to accent. Distinctive patterns of speech develop in any society when people are separated from one another over many generations. Whereas people in the United States treat accent as a clue to where one lives (there is little mistaking a midwestern "twang" or a southern "drawl"), Britons use accent as a mark of social class, distinguishing elites, who speak the "King's English," from all others. So different are these two accents that the British seem to be, as the saying goes, a single people divided by a common language.

ANOTHER EXAMPLE: JAPAN

Social stratification in Japan also mixes caste and meritocracy. Japan is at once the world's oldest, continuously operating monarchy and a modern society where wealth follows individual achievement.

Feudal Japan

By the fifth century C.E., Japan was an agrarian society with a rigid caste system composed of nobles and commoners and ruled by an imperial family. The emperor ruled by divine right, and his military leader (or *shogun*) oversaw a number of regional warlords.

The traditional caste system, with its concern for people's different social rankings, is still evident in Japan today. Here the women who work at a Japanese inn bow as a sign of respect to a male guest as he departs (in a vintage U.S. automobile that looks to be a 1957 Plymouth).

Below the nobility were the *samurai*, a warrior caste whose name means "to serve." This second rank of Japanese society was made up of soldiers who learned martial skills and whose code of honor was based on absolute loyalty to their leaders.

As in Great Britain, most people in Japan at this time in history were commoners who labored to scrape out a bare subsistence. Unlike their European counterparts, however, Japanese commoners were not lowest in rank. At the bottom were the *burakumin*, or "outcasts," shunned by lord and commoner alike. Much as the lowest caste groups in India, these outcasts lived apart from others, performed the most distasteful work, and, like everyone else, could not change their standing.

Japan Today

By the 1860s (the time of the Civil War in the United States), the nobles realized that Japan could not enter the modern, industrial era with its traditional caste system. Besides, as in Britain, some nobles were happy to have their children marry wealthy commoners who had more money than they did. As Japan opened up to the larger world, the traditional caste system weakened. In 1871, the Japanese legally banned the social category of "outcast," although even today people look down on descendants of this rank. After Japan's defeat in World War II, the nobility, too, lost legal standing, and the emperor remains only as a symbol of Japan with little real power.

Social stratification in Japan is a far cry from the rigid caste system of centuries ago. Today, Japanese society consists of "upper," "upper-middle," "lower-middle," and "lower" classes. But no firm boundaries exist and people move between classes over time. In addition, because Japanese people revere tradition, so family background is never far from the surface in sizing up someone's social standing. Officially, everyone has equal standing before the law, but, in practice, many people still look at one another through the centuries-old lens of caste (Hiroshi, 1974; Norbeck, 1983).

Finally, traditional ideas about gender continue to shape Japanese society. Legally, the two sexes are equal, but men dominate women in many ways. Japanese parents are more likely to send sons rather than daughters to college, so a significant gender gap exists in education (Brinton, 1988). Consequently, most women who work have lower-level support positions in the corporate world, only rarely assuming leadership roles. Thus, individual achievement in Japan's modern class system operates in the shadow of centuries of traditional male privileges.

THE FORMER SOVIET UNION

The former Union of Soviet Socialist Republics (U.S.S.R.), which rivaled the United States as a military

During the last decade, the former Soviet Union has moved towards a market economy. This process has made some people quite wealthy, while others have lost their jobs as old, inefficient factories closed. As a result, the problem of poverty is on the rise. This young woman was photographed begging for money in Moscow's Red Square.

superpower during much of this century, was born out of revolution in 1917. The Russian Revolution ended the feudal estate system ruled by a hereditary nobility, and transferred farms, factories, and other productive property from private ownership to state control.

A Classless Society?

The Russian Revolution was guided by the ideas of Karl Marx, who wrote that private ownership of productive property is the basis of social classes (see Chapter 4, "Society"). When the state took control of the economy, Soviet officials boasted that they had engineered the first classless society.

Outside of the Soviet Union, however, analysts were skeptical of this claim (Lane, 1984). They pointed out that the jobs people held actually fell into four unequal categories. At the top were high government officials, or *apparatchiks*. Next came the Soviet intelligentsia, including lower government officials, college professors, scientists, physicians, and engineers. Below them were manual workers and, at the lowest level, the rural peasantry.

These categories enjoyed very different living standards, so the former Soviet Union was not really classless at all. But putting factories, farms, colleges, and hospitals under state control did limit economic inequality (although doing so probably increased differences of power) compared to capitalist societies such as the United States.

The Second Russian Revolution

After decades of organizing Soviet society according to the ideas of Karl Marx (and revolutionary leader Vladimir Lenin), the Soviet Union shook with change after Mikhail Gorbachev became president in 1985. Gorbachev introduced a program popularly known as *perestroika*, meaning "restructuring." He saw that, while the Soviet system had reduced economic inequality, nearly everyone was poor, and living standards lagged far behind those of industrial nations in the West. Gorbachev sought to generate economic expansion by reducing inefficient centralized control of the Soviet economy.

Gorbachev's economic reforms turned into one of the most dramatic social movements in history. Throughout Eastern Europe, socialist governments toppled and, in 1991, the Soviet Union itself collapsed. People blamed their poverty and their lack of basic freedoms on a repressive ruling class of Communist party officials. In the Soviet Union, for example, just 6 percent of the population formed the Communist party, which ran the entire country.

The Soviet story shows that social inequality involves more than economic resources. Soviet society may not have had the extremes of wealth and poverty found in Great Britain, Japan, and the United States. But an elite class existed all the same, one based on power rather than wealth. Thus, despite the fact that both Mikhail Gorbachev and his successor Boris Yeltsin earned far less than a U.S. president, they wielded awesome power.

What about social mobility in the Soviet Union? During the twentieth century there was as much upward social mobility in the Soviet Union as in Great Britain, Japan, and even the United States. Rapidly expanding industry and government drew many poor rural peasants to factories and offices (Dobson, 1977; Lane, 1984; Shipler, 1984). This trend illustrates what sociologists call **structural social mobility,** *a shift in the social position of large numbers of people due more to changes in society itself than to individual efforts.*

November 24, 1994, Odessa, Ukraine. The first snow of our voyage flies over the decks as our ship puts in at Odessa, the former Soviet Union's southernmost port on the Black Sea. A short distance from the dock, we gaze up the Potemkin Steps—the steep stairway leading to the city proper where the first shots of the Russian Revolution rang out. It has been six years since our last visit and much has changed; indeed, the Soviet Union itself has collapsed. Has life improved? For some people, certainly: There are now chic boutiques where well-dressed shoppers buy fine wines, designer clothes, and imported perfumes. Outside, shiny new Volvos, Mercedes, and even a few Cadillacs stand next to the small Ladas from the "old days." But for most, life seems much worse. Flea markets line the curbs as families sell home furnishings. Many are desperate in a town where meat sells for $4 a pound and the average person earns about $30 a month. Even the city has to save money by shutting off street lights at eight o'clock. The spirits of most people seem as dim as Odessa's city streets.

During the 1990s structural social mobility in the Russian Federation took a downturn. In fact, between 1990 and 1998, living standards fell to the point that the average life span for Russian men dropped by eight years, and for women, two years (Róna-Tas, 1994; Specter, 1997b; Bohlen, 1998; Gerber & Hout, 1998).

In the long run, closing inefficient state industries may improve the nation's economic performance. In the short run, however, most citizens face hard times as living standards fall. Moreover, as businesses become privately owned, the gulf between rich and poor grows, a trend reflected in Figure 10–1. Thus, while some praise the recent changes, others hang on, hoping for a higher living standard.

GLOBAL SNAPSHOT

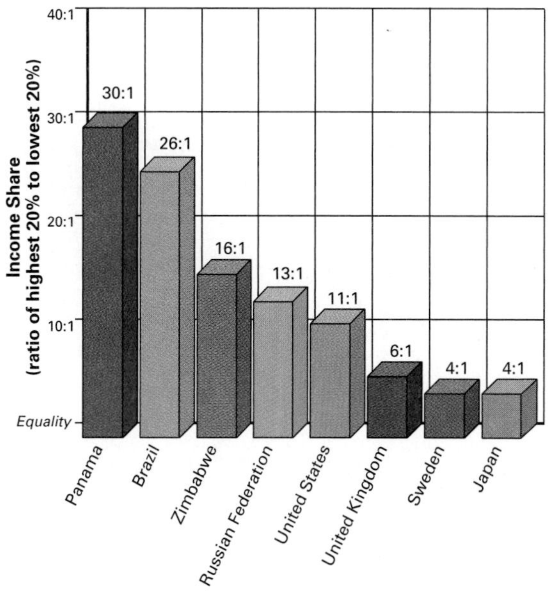

FIGURE 10–1 Economic Inequality in Selected Countries, 1980–1996

These data are the most recent available, representing income share for various years between 1980 and 1996.

Source: The World Bank (2000).

IDEOLOGY: THE POWER BEHIND STRATIFICATION

Noting the extent of social inequality around the world, we might wonder how societies persist without sharing resources more equally. Castelike systems in Great Britain and Japan lasted for centuries, placing land and power

Medieval Europeans accepted rigid social differences as part of a divine plan for the world. This fifteenth-century painting by the Limbourg brothers shows peasants toiling in the fields while the nobles, who are not to be seen, reside in the castle well-attended by servants.

September: Harvesting Grapes, by the Limbourg Brothers. *Tres riches heures du duc de Berry* (early 15th century). Victoria and Albert Museum, London, UK. The Bridgeman Art Library.

in the hands of several hundred families. For 2,000 years, people in India have accepted the idea that they should be privileged or poor because of the accident of birth.

A major reason that social hierarchies endure is **ideology,** *cultural beliefs that justify social stratification.* A belief—for example, the idea that the rich are smart and the poor are lazy—is ideological to the extent that it defines the wealthy as worthy and suggests that poor people deserve their plight.

Plato and Marx on Ideology

The ancient Greek philosopher Plato (427–347 B.C.E.) defined *justice* as agreement about who should have what. Every culture, Plato explained, considers some type of inequality "fair." Karl Marx, too, understood this fact, although he was far more critical of inequality than Plato. Marx took capitalist societies to task for channeling wealth and power to a few and defending the process as "a law of the marketplace." Capitalist law, Marx continued, defines the right to own property, and inheritance ensures that money stays within the same families from one generation to the next. In short, Marx concluded, culture and institutions combine to shore up a society's elite, which is why established hierarchies last a long time.

Historical Patterns of Ideology

Ideology changes as a society's economy and technology change. Because agrarian societies depend on the faithful daily labor of their people, they develop caste systems that define performing the duties of one's "station" a moral responsibility within a natural order. With the rise of industrial capitalism, personal initiative gains value and an ideology of meritocracy develops. Wealth and power become prizes won by those who perform the best. Under industrial capitalism, the poor, who were the object of charity under feudalism, are scorned as personally undeserving. This harsh view is expressed in the work of Herbert Spencer, as explained in the box.

History shows how difficult it is to change social stratification. However, challenges to the status quo always arise. Traditional notions of a "woman's place," for example, are giving way to economic opportunity for women. The continuing progress toward racial equality in South Africa also exemplifies widespread rejection of the ideology of apartheid.

THE FUNCTIONS OF SOCIAL STRATIFICATION

Why are societies stratified at all? One answer, consistent with the structural-functional paradigm, is that social inequality plays a vital part in the operation of society. This influential—and controversial—argument was set forth some fifty years ago by Kingsley Davis and Wilbert Moore (1945).

CRITICAL THINKING

Is Getting Rich "The Survival of the Fittest"?

"The survival of the fittest"—we have all heard these words used to describe society as a competitive jungle. The phrase was coined by one of sociology's pioneers, Herbert Spencer (1820–1903), whose ideas about social inequality are still widespread today.

Spencer, who lived in England, eagerly followed the work of the natural scientist Charles Darwin (1809–1882). Darwin's theory of biological evolution holds that a species changes physically over many generations as it adapts to the natural environment. Spencer, however, distorted Darwin's theory, applying it to the operation of society: Society became the "jungle," with the "fittest" people rising to wealth and the weak gradually sinking into miserable poverty.

It is no surprise that Spencer's distorted views were popular among U.S. industrialists of that time. John D. Rockefeller (1839–1937), who made a vast fortune building the oil industry, recited Spencer's "social gospel" to young children in Sunday school. As Rockefeller saw it, the growth of giant corporations—and the astounding wealth of their owners—was merely "the survival of the fittest," a basic fact of nature. Neither Spencer nor Rockefeller had much sympathy for the poor, seeing poverty as evidence of not measuring up in a competitive world. Spencer opposed social welfare programs for penalizing society's "best" members (through taxes) and rewarding society's "worst" members (through welfare benefits).

Today, sociologists are quick to point out that social standing is not a simple matter of personal effort, as Spencer contended. Moreover, it is not the case that companies or people who generate more money necessarily benefit society. Yet Spencer's view that people get more or less what they deserve in life remains part of our individualistic culture.

What do you think?

1. *What did Herbert Spencer mean when he said society encourages "the survival of the fittest"?*
2. *Does Spencer's idea square with the fact that about half of rich people gain their wealth mostly through inheritance?*
3. *In what sense do highly paid people benefit society? In what ways do they not?*

THE DAVIS-MOORE THESIS

The **Davis-Moore thesis** states that *social stratification has beneficial consequences for the operation of a society*. How else, ask Davis and Moore, can we explain the fact that some form of social stratification has been found in every known society?

Davis and Moore note that modern societies have hundreds of occupational positions of varying importance. Certain jobs—say, washing windows or answering a telephone—are fairly easy and can be performed by almost anyone. Other jobs—such as designing new generations of computers or transplanting human organs—are difficult and demand the scarce talents of people with extensive (and expensive) training.

Therefore, Davis and Moore explain, the greater the functional importance of a position, the more rewards a society attaches to it. This strategy promotes productivity and efficiency, since rewarding important work with income, prestige, power, and leisure encourages people to do these jobs and to work better, longer, and harder. Unequal rewards benefit some individuals, then, and a system of unequal rewards (which is what social stratification is) benefits society as a whole.

Davis and Moore concede that any society can be egalitarian, but only to the extent that people are willing to let *anyone* perform *any* job. Equality also demands that someone who carries out a job poorly be rewarded the same as someone who performs well. Such a system clearly offers little incentive for people to try their best, and thereby reduces a society's productive efficiency.

The Davis-Moore thesis suggests why *some* form of stratification exists everywhere; it does not state precisely what rewards a society should give to any occupational position, or how unequal rewards should be. Davis and Moore merely point out that positions a society considers very important must carry enough reward to draw talent away from less important work.

CRITICAL THINKING

Big Bucks: Are the Rich Worth What They Earn?

For an hour of work, a Los Angeles priest earns about $5, a hotel maid in New Orleans about $7, a bus driver in San Francisco about $15, a Phoenix bartender about $20, and a Detroit autoworker roughly $25. These wages shrink in comparison to the $40,000 that Barry Bonds earns per hour playing baseball for the San Francisco Giants. And what about the $100,000 that actor Jim Carrey makes for every hour he spends making a movie? Or the $200,000 Oprah Winfrey collects for each hour she chats with guests before the television cameras? Or the $1 million Tim Allen earned for filming each episode of the sitcom "Home Improvement"?

The Davis-Moore thesis suggests that rewards reflect an occupation's value to society. But are the talents of Michael Jordan, who earned $33 million in 1998 playing basketball (more than all the other Chicago Bulls combined) worth more than the efforts of all 100 U.S. senators or 1,000 police officers? In short, do earnings really reflect people's social importance?

In industrial-capitalist societies such as the United States, salaries reflect the market forces of supply and demand. In simple terms, if you can do something better than others, and people are willing to pay for it, you can command more reward. According to this view, movie and television stars, top athletes, skilled professionals, and many business executives have rare talents that are much in demand; thus, they earn many times more than the typical worker in the United States.

But critics of the Davis-Moore thesis question whether the market is really a good evaluator of occupational importance. First, they say, the U.S. economy is dominated by a small proportion of people who manipulate the system for their own benefit. Corporate executives, for example, pay themselves multimillion-dollar salaries and bonuses whether their companies do well or not. Gilbert Amelio spent seventeen months as CEO of Apple Computer corporation, during which time the

Critical evaluation. The Davis-Moore thesis is an important contribution to sociological analysis. Yet, Melvin Tumin (1953) asks, does functional importance really explain the high rewards that some people enjoy? Other than by counting rewards, how can we even measure functional importance? Perhaps the high rewards our society gives to, say, physicians, partly results from deliberate efforts by the medical profession to limit the supply of physicians and thereby increase the demand for their services.

Moreover, do rewards really reflect the contribution someone makes to society? With an income approaching $100 million per year, television personality Oprah Winfrey earns more in two days than the president of the United States earns all year. Would anyone argue that hosting a talk show is more important than leading the country? The box takes a critical look at the link between pay and societal importance.

Second, Tumin claims that the Davis-Moore thesis ignores the ways in which social stratification can *prevent* the development of individual talent. Born to privilege, rich children may develop their abilities, something many gifted poor children may never do.

Third, by suggesting that social stratification benefits all of society, the Davis-Moore thesis ignores how social inequality promotes conflict and even outright revolution. This criticism leads us to the social-conflict paradigm, which provides a very different explanation for social hierarchy.

STRATIFICATION AND CONFLICT

Social-conflict analysis argues that, rather than benefiting society as a whole, social stratification provides some people with advantages over others. This analysis draws heavily on the ideas of Karl Marx, with contributions from Max Weber.

KARL MARX: CLASS AND CONFLICT

Karl Marx, whose ideas are discussed fully in Chapter 4 ("Society"), explained that most people had one of two basic relationships to the means of production: They could either (1) own productive property or (2) labor company lost $2 billion. The board of directors fired him, but only after agreeing to pay him $6.7 million in severance pay—in addition to his $2 million salary and bonus for the year (Lublin, 1998).

Moreover, say the critics, many people who make very real contributions to society get little reward in return. The average teacher would have to work more than 250 years to earn Amelio's 1998 income or some 22,500 years to equal the $750 million received by the highest-paid U.S. CEO, Michael Eisner, of the Disney corporation (whose company has also fallen on hard times).

Equating social worth and income, then, is risky business. Those who defend the market as a measure of occupational worth ask, what would be better? But, as critics see it, our economic system amounts to a closed game in which only a handful of people have the money to play.

Actor Jim Carrey, who grew up in a poor family, went on to success as a film star earning $20 million for making a movie.

What do you think?

1. *Do you think that highly paid entertainers like Jim Carrey deserve a thousand times more than an average worker? Why or why not?*
2. *We would all agree that parents perform a vital task as they raise children. Why is parenting unpaid work?*
3. *What about the argument that higher pay would improve the quality and performance of teachers? Do you agree? Why or why not?*

for others. This productive role is the basis of social class. In medieval Europe, the nobility and church officials owned the productive land; peasants toiled as farmers. Similarly, in industrial class systems, the capitalists (or the bourgeoisie) control factories, which use the labor of workers (the proletariat).

Marx saw great inequality in wealth and power arising from capitalism, which, he argued, made class conflict inevitable. In time, he believed, oppression and misery would drive the working majority to organize and ultimately overthrow capitalism.

Marx lived at a time when great industrialists were amassing their fortunes. Andrew Carnegie, J. P. Morgan, John D. Rockefeller, and John Jacob Astor (one of the few very rich passengers to perish on the *Titanic*) lived in fabulous mansions adorned with priceless art and staffed by dozens of servants. Their wealth was staggering: Andrew Carnegie, founder of U.S. Steel, reportedly earned some $20 million a year at the beginning of the twentieth century (more than $100 million in today's dollars), at a time when the average worker earned roughly $500 a year (Baltzell, 1964; Pessen, 1990).

But, according to Marx, the capitalist elite draws strength not just from the operation of the economy. Through the family, opportunity and wealth are passed down from generation to generation. Moreover, the legal system defends private property and inheritance. Finally, elite children mix at exclusive schools, forging social ties that will benefit them throughout their lives. In short, from Marx's point of view, capitalist society *reproduces the class structure in each new generation.*

Critical evaluation. Marx's analysis of how capitalism creates conflict between classes has greatly influenced sociological thinking. But, because it is revolutionary—calling for the overthrow of capitalist society—Marxism is also highly controversial.

One of the strongest criticisms of Marxism is that it denies a central tenet of the Davis-Moore thesis: that motivating people to perform various social roles requires some system of unequal rewards. Marx separated reward from performance, endorsing a more or less equal system based on the principle of "from each according to his ability; to each according to his needs" (1972:388).

This cartoon, titled "Capital and Labour," appeared in the English press in 1843, when the ideas of Karl Marx were first gaining attention. It links the plight of that country's coal miners to the privileges enjoyed by those who owned coal-fired factories.

Critics argue that severing rewards from performance is exactly what caused low productivity in the former Soviet Union and other socialist economies around the world.

Defenders of Marx counter that there is considerable evidence supporting Marx's view of humanity as inherently social rather than selfish (Clark, 1991; Fiske, 1991). We should not assume, therefore, that individual rewards (much less, money alone) are the only way to motivate people to perform their social roles.

A second problem is that the revolutionary developments Marx considered inevitable within capitalist societies have, by and large, failed to happen. The next section explores why the socialist revolution Marx predicted and promoted has not occurred, at least in advanced capitalist societies.

WHY NO MARXIST REVOLUTION?

Despite Marx's prediction, capitalism is still thriving. Why have workers in the United States and other industrial societies not overthrown capitalism? Ralf Dahrendorf (1959) suggests four reasons:

1. **The fragmentation of the capitalist class.** Today, millions of stockholders, rather than single families, own most large companies. Moreover, day-to-day operation of large corporations is now in the hands of a managerial class, whose members may or may not be major stockholders. With stock widely held—by the late 1990s, about 40 percent of U.S. adults were in the market—more and more people have a direct stake in preserving the capitalist system.
2. **A higher standard of living.** As Chapter 16 ("The Economy and Work") explains, a century ago most workers were in factories or on farms performing **blue-collar occupations,** *lower-prestige work that involves mostly manual labor.* Today, most workers hold **white-collar occupations,** *higher-prestige work that involves mostly mental activity.* These jobs are in sales, management, and other service fields. Most of today's white-collar workers do not think of themselves as an "industrial proletariat." Just as important, the average U.S. worker's income rose almost tenfold over the course of the twentieth century, even allowing for inflation, and the workweek decreased. As a result, most workers consider themselves better off than their parents and grandparents—a case of structural mobility encouraging people to accept the present system (Edwards, 1979; Gagliani, 1981; Wright & Martin, 1987).

TABLE 10–1 Two Explanations of Social Stratification: A Summary

Structural-Functional Paradigm	Social-Conflict Paradigm
Social stratification keeps society operating. Linking greater rewards to more important social positions benefits society as a whole.	Social stratification is the result of social conflict. Differences in social resources serve the interests of some and harm others.
Social stratification matches talents and abilities to appropriate occupational positions.	Social stratification ensures that much talent and ability in society will not be developed at all.
Social stratification is both useful and inevitable.	Social stratification is useful only to some people; it is not inevitable.
The values and beliefs that legitimize social inequality are widely shared throughout society.	Values and beliefs tend to be ideological; they reflect the interests of the more powerful members of society.
Because systems of social stratification are useful to society as a whole and are supported by cultural values and beliefs, they are usually stable over time.	Because systems of social stratification reflect the interests of only part of society, they are unlikely to remain stable over time.

Source: Adapted, in part, from Arthur L. Stinchcombe, "Some Empirical Consequences of the Davis-Moore Theory of Stratification," *American Sociological Review*, Vol. 28, No. 5 (October 1963):808.

3. **More worker organizations.** Workers have organizational clout that they lacked a century ago. With the right to organize into labor unions, workers make demands of management backed up by threats of work slowdowns and strikes. In other words, worker-management disputes are settled without threatening the capitalist system.

4. **More extensive legal protections.** During the twentieth century, the government passed laws to make the workplace safer, and developed programs, such as unemployment insurance, disability protection, and Social Security, to provide workers with greater financial security.

A Counterpoint

These developments suggest that society has smoothed many of capitalism's rough edges. Yet many claim that Marx's analysis of capitalism is still largely valid (Miliband, 1969; Edwards, 1979; Giddens, 1982; Domhoff, 1983; Stephens, 1986; Boswell & Dixon, 1993; Hout, Brooks, & Manza, 1993). First, wealth remains highly concentrated, with about half of all privately owned corporate stock in the hands of just 1 percent of our population. Second, many of today's white-collar jobs offer no more income, security, or satisfaction than factory work did a century ago. Third, many benefits enjoyed by today's workers came about through the class conflict Marx described, and workers still struggle to hold on to what they have. Fourth, while workers have gained legal protections, the law still protects the private property of the rich. Therefore, social-conflict theorists conclude, the absence of a socialist revolution in the United States does not negate Marx's analysis of capitalism.

Table 10–1 summarizes the contributions of the two contrasting sociological approaches to understanding social stratification.

MAX WEBER: CLASS, STATUS, AND POWER

Max Weber, whose approach to social analysis is described in Chapter 4 ("Society"), agreed with Karl Marx that social stratification causes social conflict, but he considered Marx's two-class model simplistic. Instead, he thought social stratification involves three distinct dimensions of inequality.

The first dimension is economic inequality—the issue so vital to Marx—which Weber termed *class* position. Weber did not think of "classes" as crude categories but as a continuum ranging from high to low. Weber's second dimension of social stratification is *status*, or social prestige, and the third is *power*.

The Socioeconomic Status Hierarchy

Marx viewed social prestige and power as simple reflections of economic position, and did not treat them as distinct dimensions of inequality. But Weber noted that status consistency in modern societies is often quite low: A local government official, say, might wield considerable power yet have little wealth or social prestige.

The extent of social inequality in agrarian systems is greater than that found in industrial societies. One indication of the unchallenged power of rulers is the monumental structures built over years with the unpaid labor of common people. Although the Taj Mahal in India is among the world's most beautiful buildings, it is merely a tomb for a single individual.

Weber's contribution, then, is portraying social stratification in industrial societies as a multidimensional ranking rather than a hierarchy of clearly defined classes. In line with Weber's thinking, sociologists use the term **socioeconomic status (SES)** to refer to *a composite ranking based on various dimensions of social inequality*.

Because people vary on the three dimensions of class, status, and power, Weber saw society not in terms of distinct classes, as Marx did, but as a broad range of self-interested social categories. Social conflict, for Weber, is therefore both variable and complex.

Inequality in History

Weber noted that each of his three dimensions of social inequality stands out at different points in the evolution of human societies. Agrarian societies emphasize status or social prestige, typically in the form of honor. Members of these societies gain status by conforming to cultural norms that correspond to their rank.

Industrialization and the development of capitalism level traditional rankings based on birth but generate striking financial inequality. Thus, Weber argued, the crucial difference among people in industrial societies is the economic dimension of class.

Over time, industrial societies witness the growth of a bureaucratic state. Bigger government, and the spread of all kinds of other organizations, make power more important in the stratification system. Especially in socialist societies, because government regulates many aspects of life, high-ranking officials become the new elite.

Historical analysis points to a final difference between Weber and Marx. Marx thought societies could eliminate social stratification by abolishing private ownership of productive property. Weber doubted that overthrowing capitalism would significantly diminish social stratification. It might lessen economic disparity, he reasoned, but socialism would simultaneously increase inequality by expanding government and concentrating power in the hands of a political elite. Recent popular uprisings against entrenched bureaucracies in Eastern Europe and the former Soviet Union support Weber's position.

Critical evaluation. Weber's multidimensional view of social stratification has enormously influenced sociologists. But critics (particularly those who favor Marx's ideas) argue that, although social class boundaries may have blurred, all industrial nations still show striking patterns of social inequality.

Moreover, as we shall see in Chapter 11 ("Social Class in the United States"), income inequality has increased in recent years. In light of this trend, while some people favor Weber's multidimensional hierarchy, others think Marx's view of the rich versus the poor is closer to the mark.

STRATIFICATION AND TECHNOLOGY: A GLOBAL PERSPECTIVE

We can weave together a number of observations made in this chapter by considering the relationship between a society's technology and its type of social stratification. This analysis draws on Gerhard Lenski and Jean Lenski's model of sociocultural evolution, detailed in Chapter 4 ("Society").

HUNTING AND GATHERING SOCIETIES

With simple technology, hunters and gatherers produce only what is necessary for day-to-day living. Some people may produce more than others, but the group's survival depends on all members of society sharing what they have. Thus, no categories of people emerge as better off than others.

HORTICULTURAL, PASTORAL, AND AGRARIAN SOCIETIES

As technological advances create a surplus, social inequality increases. In horticultural and pastoral societies, a small elite controls most of the surplus. Large-scale agriculture is more productive still, and marked inequality—as great as any time in human history—means that various categories of people lead strikingly different lives. Agrarian nobility typically exercises godlike power over the masses.

INDUSTRIAL SOCIETIES

Industrialization turns the tide, lessening inequality. Prompted by the need to develop individual talents, meritocracy takes hold and erodes the power of traditional elites. Industrial productivity also raises the standard of living of the historically poor majority. Furthermore, specialized work demands schooling for all, sharply reducing illiteracy. A literate population, in turn, presses for a greater voice in political decision making, further diminishing social inequality and reducing male domination of women.

Over time, even wealth becomes somewhat less concentrated (countering the trend predicted by Marx). The proportion of all wealth controlled by the richest 1 percent of U.S. families, which peaked at about 36 percent just before the stock market crash in 1929, fell to 30 percent by 1990 (Williamson & Lindert, 1980; Beeghley, 1989; *1991 Green Book*). Such trends help explain why Marxist revolutions occurred in *agrarian* societies—such as the former Soviet Union (1917), Cuba (1959), and Nicaragua (1979)—where social inequality is most pronounced, rather than in industrial societies, as Marx predicted.

THE KUZNETS CURVE

In human history, then, technological progress first increases but then moderates the extent of social stratification. Greater inequality is functional for agrarian societies, but industrial societies benefit from a more egalitarian climate. This historical trend, recognized by the Nobel Prize–winning economist Simon Kuznets (1955, 1966), is illustrated by the Kuznets curve, shown in Figure 10–2.

Patterns of social inequality around the world today generally square with the Kuznets curve. Global Map 10–1 shows that industrial societies have somewhat less income inequality than predominantly agrarian countries (common in Latin America and Africa). Of

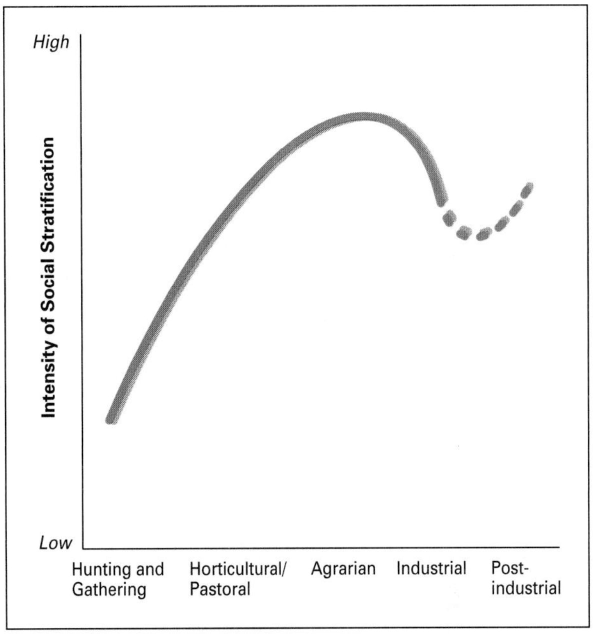

FIGURE 10–2 Social Stratification and Technological Development: The Kuznets Curve

The Kuznets curve shows that greater technological sophistication is generally accompanied by more pronounced social stratification. The trend reverses itself, however, as industrial societies gradually become more egalitarian. Rigid castelike distinctions are relaxed in favor of greater opportunity and equality under the law. Political rights are more widely extended, and there is even some leveling of economic differences. The Kuznets curve may also be usefully applied to the relative social standing of the two sexes. The emergence of postindustrial society may signal greater social inequality, as indicated by the broken line.

Source: Created by the author, based on Kuznets (1955).

WINDOW ON THE WORLD

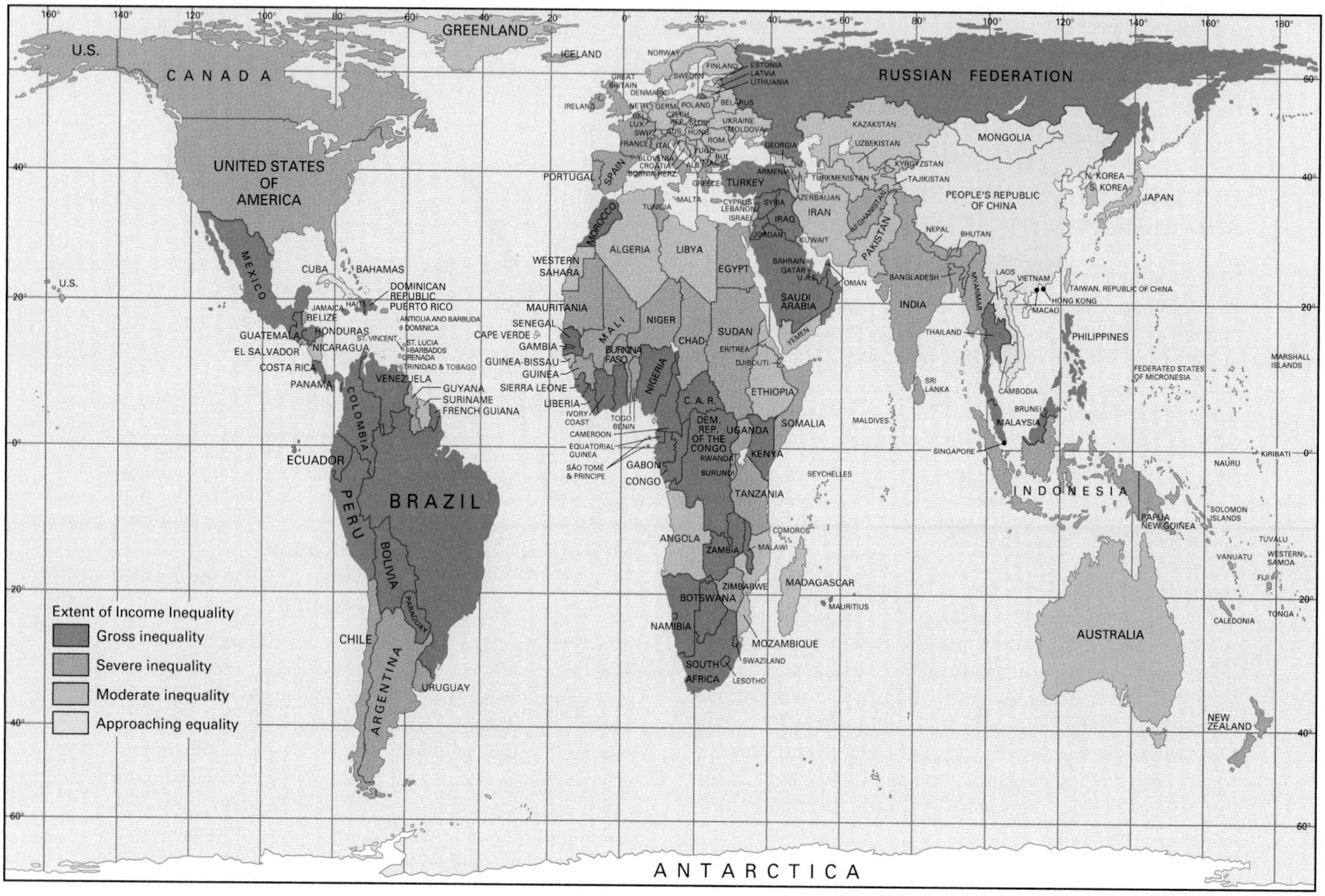

GLOBAL MAP 10–1 Income Disparity in Global Perspective

Societies throughout the world differ in the rigidity and extent of social stratification as well as in overall standard of living. This map highlights income inequality. Generally speaking, countries that have centralized, socialist economies (including the People's Republic of China and Cuba) display the least income inequality, although their standard of living is relatively low. Industrial societies with predominantly capitalist economies, including the United States and most of Western Europe, have higher overall living standards, accompanied by severe income disparity. The low-income countries of Latin America and Africa (including Mexico, Brazil, and the Democratic Republic of the Congo), as well as the Russian Federation, exhibit the most pronounced inequality of income.

Sources: *Peters Atlas of the World* (1990); updates by the author from United Nations Development Programme (1999).

The early industrial era, according to Simon Kuznets, is marked by extreme social inequality that affords aristocratic people a life of leisure while others toil at manual labor for pennies a day. U.S. artist Ford Maddox Brown (1821–1893) captures such class distinctions in his painting, Work. *Today, more than a century after Brown lived, do you think class differences in the United States have become smaller or greater? Why?*

Ford Maddox Brown (1821–1893), *Work.*

course, income disparity reflects not just technology but also political and economic priorities. Societies that have had socialist economic systems (including the People's Republic of China) display relatively less income inequality, albeit with a relatively low standard of living. They also have pronounced inequality in noneconomic areas, such as political power.

And what of the future? Notice that in Figure 10–2 we extend the trend described by Kuznets to the postindustrial era (the broken line) to show increased social inequality. That is, as the Information Revolution moves ahead, we are experiencing some economic polarization (discussed in the next chapter), suggesting that the long-term trend may differ from what Kuznets observed half a century ago (Nielsen & Alderson, 1997).

SOCIAL STRATIFICATION: FACTS AND VALUES

> The year was 2081 and everybody was finally equal. They weren't only equal before God and the law. They were equal every which way. Nobody was smarter than anybody else. Nobody was better looking than anybody else. Nobody was stronger or quicker than anybody else. All this equality was due to the 211th, 212th, and 213th Amendments to the Constitution and the unceasing vigilance of agents of the Handicapper General.

With these words, novelist Kurt Vonnegut, Jr. (1961) begins the story of "Harrison Bergeron," an imaginary account of a future United States in which all social inequality has been abolished. Vonnegut warns that, although it may seem appealing in principle, equality can be a dangerous concept in practice. His story describes a nightmare of social engineering in which every individual talent that makes one person different from another is systematically neutralized by the government.

To eradicate differences that make one person "better" than another, Vonnegut's state requires that physically attractive people wear masks that make them average looking, that intelligent people wear earphones that generate distracting noise, and that the best athletes and dancers be fitted with weights to make them as clumsy as everyone else. In short, although we may imagine that social equality would liberate people to make the most of their talents, Vonnegut concludes that an

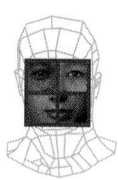

CONTROVERSY & DEBATE

The Bell Curve Debate: Are Rich People Really Smarter?

It is rare when a social science book captures the attention of people across the country. But *The Bell Curve: Intelligence and Class Structure in American Life* by Richard J. Herrnstein and Charles Murray did that and more. The book ignited a firestorm of controversy over why social stratification divides our society and, just as important, what should be done about it.

The Bell Curve is a long book (800 pages) that addresses many complex issues, but at bottom it puts forth eight propositions:

1. There exists something we can describe as "general intelligence"; people with more of it tend to be more successful in their careers than those with less.
2. At least half the variation in human intelligence is transmitted genetically from one generation to another; the remaining variability is due to environmental factors.
3. Over the course of this century—and especially since the Information Revolution began several decades ago—intelligence has become more necessary in our society's most important jobs.
4. At the same time, the best U.S. colleges and universities have shifted their admissions policies away from favoring children of inherited wealth to admitting young people who perform best on standardized tests, such as the Scholastic Assessment Test (SAT), American College Testing Program (ACT), and Graduate Record Examination (GRE).
5. As a result of these changes in the workplace and higher education, our society is coming to be dominated by a "cognitive elite," who are, on average, not only better trained than most people but actually more intelligent.
6. Intelligent people are socially segregated on the campus and in the workplace, raising the odds that they will pair up, marry, and have intelligent children, extending the "cognitive elite" into another generation.
7. The same process is at work at the other end of the social ladder: Poor people, socially segregated, have lower intelligence on average, and tend to pass along their modest abilities to their children.

Thus, Herrnstein and Murray conclude:

8. To the extent that membership in the affluent elite or the impoverished underclass is rooted

---

egalitarian society could exist only by reducing everyone to the lowest common denominator.

Like Vonnegut's story, all of this chapter's explanations of social stratification involve value judgments. The Davis-Moore thesis states not only that social stratification is universal but that it is actually necessary to efficient social organization. Class differences in U.S. society, then, reflect both variation in human abilities and the relative importance of different jobs. From this point of view, equality is undesirable because it could be achieved only through oppressive measures to impose uniformity on the population.

Social-conflict analysis, advocated by Karl Marx, reflects egalitarian values. Marx considered inequality dysfunctional to societies, causing both suffering and conflict. As he saw it, social stratification springs from injustice and greed. Thus, he advocated sharing resources equally. Marx believed that equality would not diminish but enhance human well-being.

The final box addresses the connection between intelligence and social class. This issue—also a mix of fact and value—is among the most troublesome in social science, partly because of the difficulty in defining and measuring "intelligence," but also because the very idea that elites are somehow "better" than others challenges our democratic culture.

The next chapter ("Social Class in the United States") examines inequality in our own nation, highlighting recent economic polarization. Then, in Chapter 12 ("Global Stratification"), we survey the entire world, explaining why some nations have so much more wealth than others. At all levels, as we shall see, the study of social stratification involves a mix of facts and values about the shape of a just society.

in intelligence and determined mostly by genetic inheritance, programs to help the poor (including, say, Head Start and Affirmative Action) will have few practical results.

Within weeks of *The Bell Curve's* publication, analysts pro and con were trading charges on television shows and across the pages of practically every news magazine in the country. Evaluating Herrnstein and Murray's claims must begin with a hard look at the concept of intelligence. Critics of the book argue that it is all but impossible to separate innate ability from the effects of socialization. Intelligence tests, in other words, may not measure cognitive *ability* as much as they measure cognitive *performance*. If this is so, we might well expect rich children to perform better on such tests because, after all, they have had the best schooling. At the very least, we should not think of "intelligence" as biologically fixed because research shows that mental abilities and life experiences *interact*, each affecting the other.

Most researchers who study intelligence agree that genetics plays a part in children's intelligence, but the consensus is that no more than 25 to 40 percent is inherited—less than what Herrnstein and Murray claim. Therefore, *The Bell Curve* misleads readers into thinking that social stratification is both natural and inevitable. In fact, say critics, this book amounts to a new version of the social Darwinism popular a century ago, which justified the great wealth of industrial tycoons as "the survival of the fittest."

Perhaps the more society seems like a jungle, the more people think of stratification as a matter of blood rather than upbringing. But, despite any flaws, *The Bell Curve* raises issues we cannot easily ignore. If some people are, indeed, smarter than others, shouldn't we expect that most will end up in higher social positions? Is that fair or not? Are there advantages to our society's leaders being at least a little smarter than the rest of us? Are there also dangers? Is it true that our society's elites live apart from the problems—including crime, homelessness, and poor schools—that plague most of the population? Finally, what can our society do to ensure that all people have the opportunity to develop their abilities as fully as possible?

Continue the debate . . .

1. *Do you think there is such a thing as "general intelligence"? Why or why not?*
2. *Do you think that well-off people, on average, are more intelligent than people of low social position? If so, how do we know which factor is causing the other?*
3. *Do you think social scientists should study controversial issues such as differences in human intelligence? Why or why not?*

Sources: Herrnstein & Murray (1994), Jacoby & Glauberman (1995), and Kohn (1996).

SUMMARY

1. Social stratification refers to categories of people ranked in a hierarchy. Stratification (a) is a trait of society, not just a result of individual differences; (b) endures over many generations; (c) is universal, yet variable in form; and (d) is supported by cultural beliefs.
2. Caste systems, common in agrarian societies, are based on ascription (birth), permit little social mobility, and shape a person's entire life, including occupation and marriage.
3. Class systems, with an element of meritocracy, are found in industrial societies and allow social mobility based on individual achievement.
4. With public ownership of productive property, socialist societies claim to be classless. While socialist societies usually exhibit less economic inequality than their capitalist counterparts, highly centralized government means that there is much greater inequality in power.
5. Social stratification is difficult to change because it is supported by various social institutions and because cultural values and beliefs—ideology—define certain kinds of inequality as both natural and just.
6. The Davis-Moore thesis states that social stratification is universal because it promotes economic

productivity in a society. In class systems, unequal rewards—in effect, the cause of social stratification—attract the most able people to the most important jobs.

7. Critics of the Davis-Moore thesis challenge the idea that social stratification is functional for a society. They argue that (a) it is difficult to assess objectively the functional importance of any job; (b) stratification prevents many people from developing their abilities; and (c) social stratification benefits some at the expense of others, causing social conflict.
8. For Karl Marx, main architect of social-conflict analysis, conflict in industrial societies places the capitalists (bourgeoisie), who own the means of production and seek profits, in opposition to the proletariat, who provide labor in exchange for wages.
9. The socialist revolution that Marx predicted has not occurred in industrial societies such as the United States. Some sociologists consider this fact to be evidence that Marx's analysis was flawed; others, however, point out that our society is marked by pronounced social inequality and substantial class conflict, which is consistent with Marx's analysis.
10. Max Weber identified three dimensions of social inequality: economic class, social status or prestige, and power. Because people's standing on the three dimensions may differ, stratification takes the form of a multidimensional hierarchy rather than distinct classes.
11. Historically, say Gerhard Lenski and Jean Lenski, technological advances have made societies more unequal. Some reversal of this trend occurs in industrial societies, as shown by the Kuznets curve. The new postindustrial economy in the United States, however, shows some increase in economic inequality.
12. The study of social inequality deals not only with facts but also with politics and values concerning how a society should be organized. In short, issues involving social stratification are almost always controversial.

KEY CONCEPTS

social stratification (p. 248) a system by which a society ranks categories of people in a hierarchy

social mobility (p. 248) change in one's position in the social hierarchy

caste system (p. 248) social stratification based on ascription

class system (p. 250) social stratification based on both birth and individual achievement

meritocracy (p. 250) social stratification based on personal merit

status consistency (p. 251) the degree of consistency in a person's social standing across various dimensions of social inequality

structural social mobility (p. 255) a shift in the social position of large numbers of people due more to changes in society itself than to individual efforts

ideology (p. 256) cultural beliefs that justify social stratification

Davis-Moore thesis (p. 257) the assertion that social stratification is a universal pattern because it benefits the operation of a society

blue-collar occupations (p. 260) lower-prestige work that involves mostly manual labor

white-collar occupations (p. 260) higher-prestige work that involves mostly mental activity

socioeconomic status (SES) (p. 262) a composite ranking based on various dimensions of social inequality

CRITICAL-THINKING QUESTIONS

1. How is social stratification a creation of society rather than simply a reflection of individual differences?
2. How do caste and class systems differ? What do they have in common? Why does industrialization introduce a measure of meritocracy to social stratification?
3. According to the Davis-Moore thesis, why should a college president be paid more than a professor or a secretary? What would happen if these college employees switched jobs?
4. In what respects have Karl Marx's predictions about capitalism failed? In what respects are they correct?

APPLICATIONS AND EXERCISES

1. Is social stratification evident on your college campus? What categories of people are unequal? In what ways are they unequal?
2. Sit down with parents, grandparents, or other relatives and assess how your family's lifestyle has changed over the last three generations. Has social mobility taken place? If so, describe the change. Was it caused by the efforts of individuals or changes in society itself?
3. What are the "seven deadly sins," the human failings recognized by the medieval church? These traits may be deadly to the agrarian caste system, but what about the modern, capitalist class system?
4. Install the CD-ROM packaged in the back of this new textbook to access a variety of study, review, and applications exercises designed to help you better understand the material covered in this chapter. The CD includes an author's tip video, as well as interactive maps, video application exercises, Web links, and study questions.

SITES TO SEE

http://www.prenhall.com/macionis

Visit the interactive Web site that accompanies this text. Begin by clicking on the cover of your book. You will find a chapter-by-chapter study guide, practice tests, chat room, and many suggested Web links.

http://www.macionis.com
(or **http://www.thesociologypage.com**)

You can find a number of additional links that deal with social stratification at the author's home page.

http://www.bea.doc.gov

This Web site is run by the government's Bureau of Economic Analysis. Here you will find income data by county and many other statistics about social inequality. See what you can learn about stratification in your part of the country.

http://www.cbpp.org

This site, developed by the Center on Budget and Policy Priorities, has data and analysis of issues involving social inequality.

http://www.federalreserve.gov

Access this site to learn more about Federal Reserve research on the distribution of income and wealth in the United States.

CHAPTER 11

Jacob Lawrence (b. 1917)
New Jersey, 1946

Watercolor wash and pencil on paper, 61.2 x 50.9 cm. National Museum of American Art, Smithsonian Institution, Washington, DC/Art Resource, NY. © Jacob Lawrence. By permission of DC Moore Gallery, New York.

SOCIAL CLASS IN THE UNITED STATES

On one side of the United States, about thirty miles south of San Francisco, stands Silicon Valley, a cluster of towns called home by many leaders of the high-tech computer revolution. In places like Woodside, the average house sells for almost $2 million. Most properties have electric driveway gates, as well as pools, tennis courts, and guest cottages; some even have helicopter pads.

There are probably as many horses as people living there, and the local deli sells not just ham and cheese but $18-a-pound ostrich salami. People say Silicon Valley is home to 250,000 millionaires, a number that rises every day. But some are far richer than that: Woodside resident Gordon Moore, a founder of Intel Corporation, is worth $10 billion, more or less. If Silicon Valley were a country, it would be the twelfth richest nation in the world (Kaplan, 1999).

On the other side of the United States, on the Lower East Side of Manhattan, is an immigrant neighborhood built around the intersection of Clinton and Delancey streets. No one knows for sure how many people live there, and the housing is a far cry from the mansions of Silicon Valley. Up the stairs, between the pawn shop and the Dominican restaurant, a single ten-by-twelve-foot room rents for $350 a month. Ana Nuñez and her three children live here. The two oldest have bunk beds against one wall, and Ms. Nuñez and her youngest share a single bed. They have only a small gas stove for cooking and heat. The room has no windows, but there are plenty of mice. The family shares a tiny bathroom down the hall with five other people (Sontag, 1996).

The people who live in Silicon Valley and Manhattan's Lower East Side seem to have almost nothing in common. They all live in the same country, but their society is divided by a powerful system of social inequality. This chapter explores social stratification in the United States. We shall see what separates us, how different we are, and why the differences are getting greater.

DIMENSIONS OF SOCIAL INEQUALITY

Many people think of the United States as a more or less equal society. Unlike countries in Europe, this nation never had a nobility. With the significant exception of our racial history, we have never known a caste system that rigidly ranks categories of people.

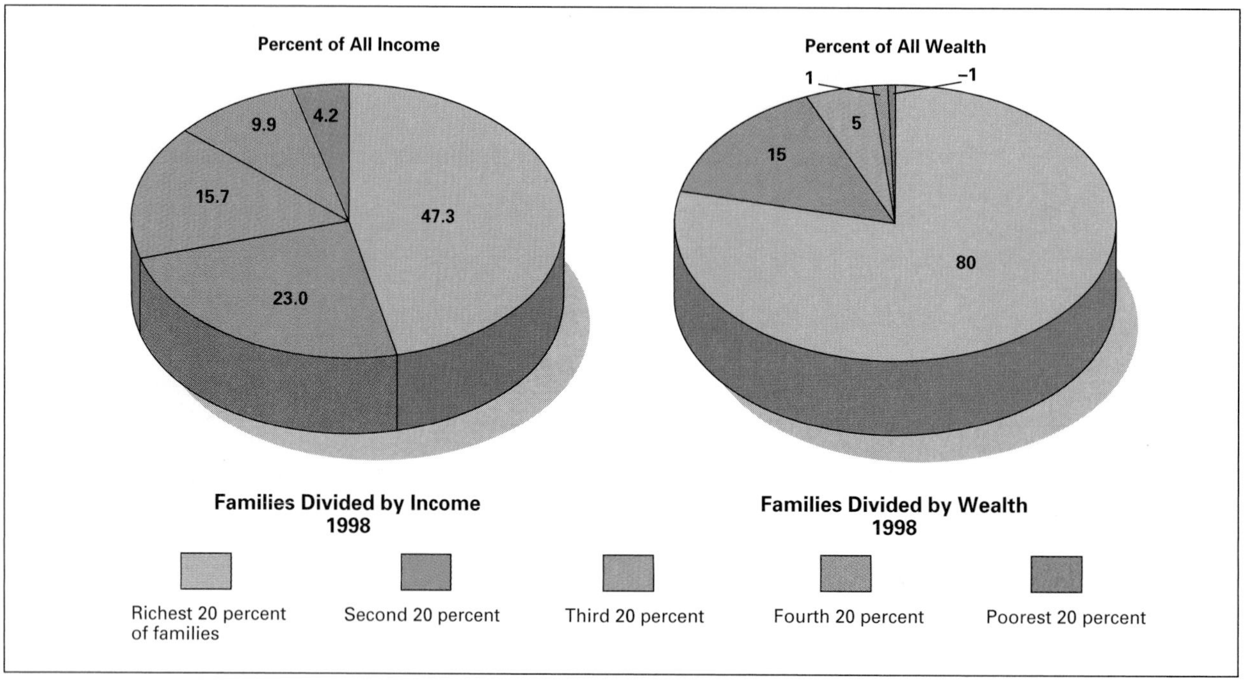

FIGURE 11–1 Distribution of Income and Wealth in the United States

Sources: Income data from U.S. Census Bureau (2000); wealth data are author estimates based on Kennickell & Shack-Marquez (1992) and Russell & Mogelonsky (2000).

Even so, U.S. society is highly stratified. Not only do the rich have most of the money, they also receive more schooling, enjoy better health, and consume the lion's share of goods and services. Such privileges contrast sharply with the poverty of millions of women and men in this same country who worry about paying next month's rent or a doctor's bill when a child becomes ill.

So why do we think of the United States as a middle-class society? We underestimate the extent of social inequality for many reasons. For one thing, our legal system declares that everyone stands equal before the law. Second, our culture celebrates individual effort and downplays the importance of birth in our lives. Third, most of us do not know people like the Silicon Valley multimillionaires or poor immigrants on New York's Lower East Side; we interact mostly with people like ourselves (Kelley & Evans, 1995). Finally, because the United States is such a rich country, it seems that everyone is at least pretty well off.

When people do face up to social inequality, they often speak of a "ladder of social class," as if inequality were a matter of a single factor such as money. But social class in the United States has several dimensions. Socioeconomic status (SES), as discussed in Chapter 10 ("Social Stratification"), reflects not just money (income and wealth and the power they provide) but also occupational prestige and schooling.

INCOME

One important dimension of inequality is **income,** *wages or salary from work and earnings from investments.* The Census Bureau reports that the median U.S. family income in 1998 was $47,467. The first part of Figure 11–1 illustrates the distribution of income among all U.S. families.[1] The richest 20 percent of families

[1]The Census Bureau reports both mean and median income for families ("two or more persons related by blood, marriage or adoption") and households ("two or more persons sharing a living unit"). In 1998, mean family income was $59,589, higher than the median because high-income families pull up the mean, but not the median. For households, the figures are somewhat lower—a mean of $51,855 and a median of $38,885—mostly because families average 3.2 persons, whereas households average 2.6.

(earning at least $83,700 annually, with a mean of $140,846) received 47.3 percent of all income, while the bottom 20 percent (earning less than $21,600, with a mean of $12,526) received only 4.2 percent.

Table 11–1 provides a closer look at income distribution. In 1998, the highest-paid 5 percent of U.S. families earned six-figure annual incomes (averaging $246,520), or 20.7 percent of all income, more than the earnings of the lowest-paid 40 percent. At the very top of the income pyramid, the richest half of 1 percent earned at least $1.375 million. In short, while a small number of people earn very high incomes, the majority make do with far less.

Chapter 10 ("Social Stratification") explained that social inequality declines as industrialization increases (illustrated by the Kuznets curve, Figure 10–2). Thus, the United States has less income inequality than, say, Venezuela (in South America), Kenya (Africa), or Sri Lanka (Asia). However, as Figure 11–2 indicates, the United States has more income inequality than most other industrial societies.

GLOBAL SNAPSHOT

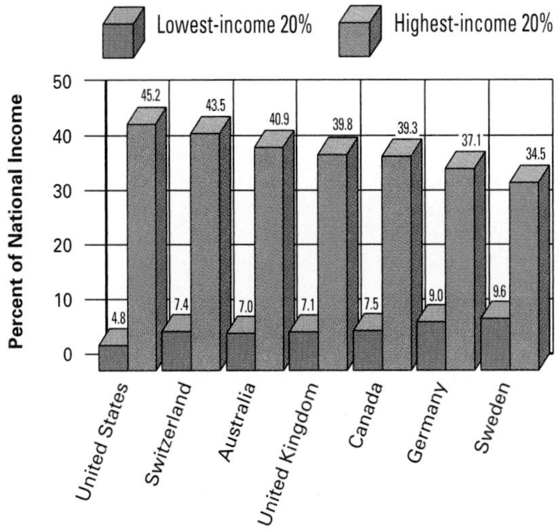

FIGURE 11–2 Income Disparities for Selected Industrial Countries

Source: The World Bank (2000).

WEALTH

Income is only one part of a person or family's **wealth,** *the total value of money and other assets, minus outstanding debts.* Wealth—including stocks, bonds, and real estate—is distributed even less equally than income.

The second part of Figure 11–1 shows the distribution of privately owned wealth in the United States. The richest 20 percent of U.S. families own roughly 80 percent of the country's entire wealth. High up in this privileged category are the wealthiest 5 percent of families—the "very rich"—who own more than half of all private property. Richer still—with wealth into the tens of millions—are the 1 percent of U.S. households that qualify as "super-rich" and possess one-third of the nation's privately held resources. Capping the wealth pyramid, the one dozen richest families in the United States have a combined net worth exceeding $300 billion. This equals the total property of half a million average families, including enough people to fill the cities of Anchorage, Alaska; Alexandria, Virginia; Allentown, Pennsylvania; and Amarillo, Texas (*Forbes,* 1999).

Recent government calculations put the wealth of the average U.S. household at about $71,600. This reflects the value of homes, cars, investments, insurance policies, retirement pensions, furniture, clothing, and all other personal property, minus home mortgages and other debts. The wealth of average people is not only less than that of the rich, however, it is also different in kind. While most people's wealth centers on a home and a car—that is, property that generates no income—the wealth of the rich is mostly in the form of stocks and other income-producing investments.

TABLE 11–1 U.S. Family Income, 1998

Highest paid . . .	Annually earns at least . . .
0.5%	$1,375,000
1	300,000
5	145,200
10	100,000
20	83,700
30	67,000
40	56,000
50	47,500
60	37,700
70	27,000
80	21,600
90	9,000

Sources: Kennickell, Starr-McCluer, & Surette (2000), U.S. Census Bureau (2000), and author calculations.

TABLE 11–2 The Relative Social Prestige of Selected Occupations in the United States

White-collar Occupations	Prestige Score	Blue-collar Occupations
Physician	86	
Lawyer	75	
College/university professor	74	
Architect	73	
Chemist	73	
Physicist/astronomer	73	
Aerospace engineer	72	
Dentist	72	
Member of the clergy	69	
Psychologist	69	
Pharmacist	68	
Optometrist	67	
Registered nurse	66	
Secondary-school teacher	66	
Accountant	65	
Athlete	65	
Electrical engineer	64	
Elementary-school teacher	64	
Economist	63	
Veterinarian	62	
Airplane pilot	61	
Computer programmer	61	
Sociologist	61	
Editor/reporter	60	
	60	Police officer
Actor	58	
Radio/TV announcer	55	
Librarian	54	
	53	Aircraft mechanic
	53	Firefighter
Dental hygienist	52	
Painter/sculptor	52	
Social worker	52	
	51	Electrician
Computer operator	50	
Funeral director	49	
Realtor	49	
Bookkeeper	47	
	47	Machinist
	47	Mail carrier
Musician/composer	47	
	46	Secretary
Photographer	45	
Bank teller	43	
	42	Tailor
	42	Welder
	40	Farmer
	40	Telephone operator
	39	Carpenter
	36	Brick/stone mason
	36	Child-care worker
File clerk	36	
	36	Hairdresser
	35	Baker
	34	Bulldozer operator
	31	Auto body repairperson
Retail apparel salesperson	30	
	30	Truck driver
Cashier	29	
	28	Elevator operator
	28	Garbage collector
	28	Taxi driver
	28	Waiter/waitress
	27	Bellhop
	25	Bartender
	23	Farm laborer
	23	Household laborer
	22	Door-to-door salesperson
	22	Janitor
	09	Shoe shiner

Source: Adapted from *General Social Surveys 1972–1998: Cumulative Codebook* (Chicago: National Opinion Research Center, 1999), pp. 1223–41.

When financial assets are balanced against debits, the lowest-ranking 40 percent of U.S. families have virtually no wealth at all. The negative percentage shown in Figure 11–1 for the poorest 20 percent of the population means that these families are actually in debt.

POWER

In the United States, wealth is an important source of power. Therefore, the small share of families that controls most of the nation's wealth also shapes the agenda of an entire society. Thomas Jefferson (1953; orig. 1785), the third U.S. president and a wealthy man himself, cautioned that a true democracy could not exist if property remained in the hands of a small number of families.

Chapter 17 ("Politics and Government") presents the debate surrounding wealth and power. Some analysts argue that while the rich have certain advantages, they do not dominate the political process. Others counter that the political system mostly serves the interests of the super-rich families.

OCCUPATIONAL PRESTIGE

In addition to being a source of income, work also provides social prestige. We commonly evaluate each other according to the kind of work we do, respecting those who hold high-prestige jobs and looking down on others whose work we consider low prestige.

Sociologists monitor the relative prestige of various occupations (Counts, 1925; Hodge, Treiman, & Rossi, 1966; NORC, 1999). Table 11–2 shows that people accord high prestige to occupations—such as physicians, lawyers, and engineers—that require extensive training and generate high income. On the other hand, less prestigious work—a waitress or janitor, for example—not only pays less but usually requires less ability and schooling.

Researchers have found that occupational prestige rankings are much the same in all industrial societies (Ma, 1987; Lin & Xie, 1988). Almost everywhere, white-collar work that involves mental activity with little or no direct supervision carries greater prestige than blue-collar work that involves supervised, often repetitive manual labor.

In any society, high-prestige occupations go to privileged categories of people. In Table 11–2, for example, the highest ranking occupations are dominated by men. Thirteen jobs down the list we find "registered nurse," where most workers are women. Similarly, many of the lowest-prestige jobs are commonly performed by people of color.

SCHOOLING

Industrial societies make schooling widely available to prepare workers for specialized tasks. Table 11–3 shows the level of schooling in 1998 for U.S. women and men aged twenty-five and older. While more than 80 percent completed high school, close to 25 percent earned college degrees.

Nevertheless, dimensions of inequality are once again linked. Schooling affects both occupation and income, since most (but not all) of the better paying white-collar jobs shown in Table 11–2 require a college degree or other advanced study. Most blue-collar jobs, which bring lower income and social prestige, require less schooling.

SOCIAL STRATIFICATION AND BIRTH

As we discussed in the last chapter, the class system in the United States is, to some extent, a meritocracy—that is, social position reflects individual talent and effort. But birth also plays a big part in shaping what we become later in life.

TABLE 11–3 Schooling of U.S. Adults, 1998 (aged 25 and over)

	Women	Men
Not a high school graduate	**17.1%**	**17.2%**
8 years or less	7.4	7.5
9–11 years	9.7	9.7
High school graduate	**82.9**	**82.8**
High school only	35.2	32.3
1–3 years college	25.3	24.0
College graduate or more	22.4	26.5

Source: U.S. Census Bureau (2000).

ANCESTRY

Nothing affects social standing in the United States as much as being born into a particular family. Family is our point of entry into the social system and has a strong bearing on schooling, occupation, and income. Research suggests that at least half our country's richest individuals—those worth hundreds of millions of dollars—derived their fortunes mostly from inheritance (Thurow, 1987; Queenan, 1989). By the same token, "inherited" poverty just as surely shapes the future of others.

GENDER

Of course, both men and women are found in families at every class level. Yet, on average, women have less income, wealth, and occupational prestige than men. Moreover, households headed by women are nearly three times more likely to be poor than households headed by men. Chapter 13 ("Gender Stratification") examines the connection between gender and social stratification.

RACE AND ETHNICITY

Race is closely linked to social position in the United States. White people receive more schooling and have higher overall occupational standing than African Americans. Thus, the median African American family's income was $30,636 in 1998, just 62 percent of the $49,781 earned by white families. As you can imagine, this disparity makes a huge difference in people's lives. White families, for example, are more likely to own their homes (70 percent do) than black families (46 percent) (U.S. Census Bureau, 2000).

DIVERSITY SNAPSHOT

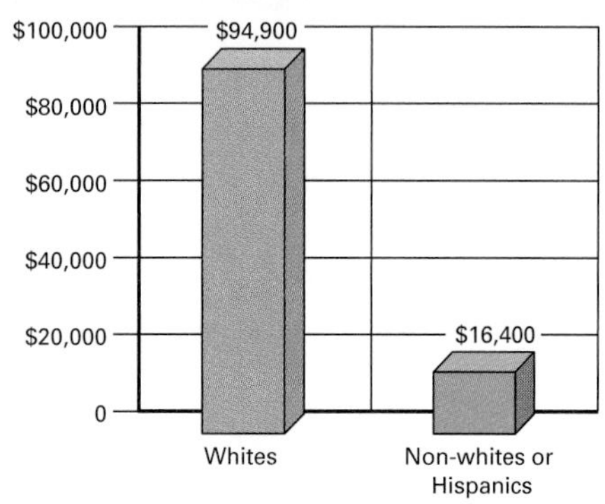

FIGURE 11–3 Average Wealth for Whites and Non-white or Hispanic Minorities, 1998

Source: Kennickell, Starr-McCluer, & Surette (2000).

Much of the disparity in income is due to the larger share of single-parent families among African Americans. Comparing only families headed by married couples, African Americans earned 87 percent as much as whites.

Over time, as Figure 11–3 shows, the income differential creates a considerable "wealth gap." A recent survey of U.S. households by the Federal Reserve found that median wealth for minority families, including African Americans, Hispanics, and Asian Americans ($16,400), is just 17 percent of that ($94,900) for white families. Race is significant even among affluent families, as the box explains.

Social ranking involves ethnicity, as well. Historically, people of English ancestry have enjoyed the most wealth and wielded the greatest power in the United States. The rapidly growing Latino population, by contrast, has long been disadvantaged. In 1998, median income among Hispanic families was $29,608, 60 percent of the comparable figure for all white families. A detailed examination of how race and ethnicity affect social standing is presented in Chapter 14 ("Race and Ethnicity").

RELIGION

Religion, too, has a bearing on social standing in the United States. Among Protestant denominations, with which almost two-thirds of individuals identify, Episcopalians and Presbyterians have significantly higher social standing, on average, than Lutherans and Baptists. Jews, too, have high social standing; Roman Catholics hold a more modest position (Roof, 1979; Davidson, Pyle, & Reyes, 1995).

Even John F. Kennedy—a member of one of this country's wealthiest and most powerful families, had to overcome religious opposition to become our first Catholic president in 1960. Understandably, then, throughout our history, upward mobility has sometimes meant converting to a higher-ranking religion (Baltzell, 1979b).

SOCIAL CLASSES IN THE UNITED STATES

As Chapter 10 ("Social Stratification") explained, rankings in a caste system are rigid and obvious to all. Defining social categories in a more fluid class system, however, is not so easy.

Consider the joke about a couple who orders a pizza, asking that it be cut into six slices because they aren't hungry enough to eat eight. All sociologists agree that social inequality exists in the United States; they just can't agree on how to divide up the population. Followers of Karl Marx see two major classes, capitalists and proletariat; other sociologists find as many as six classes (Warner & Lunt, 1941) or even seven (Coleman & Rainwater, 1978). Still others side with Max Weber, favoring not clear-cut classes but a multidimensional status hierarchy.

Defining classes in U.S. society is difficult because of our relatively low level of status consistency. Especially near the middle of the hierarchy, standing on one dimension often contradicts standing on another. A government official, for example, may have the power to administer a multimillion-dollar budget yet earn a modest personal income. Similarly, members of the clergy enjoy great prestige but moderate power and low pay. Or consider a lucky day trader on the stock market who wins no special respect but makes a lot of money.

Finally, the social mobility typical of class systems—again, most pronounced at the middle—means that social position may change during a person's lifetime, further blurring class lines. With these reservations in mind, we can describe four general social classes in the United States: the upper class, the middle class, the working class, and the lower class.

THE UPPER CLASS

Families in the upper class—5 percent of the U.S. population—earn at least $145,200 annually and may earn ten times that much. As a general rule, the more a

SOCIAL DIVERSITY

The Color of Money: Being Rich in Black and White

African American families earn 62 cents for every dollar a white family earns, which helps explain why black families are two-and-one-half times as likely to be poor. But there is another side to black America—an affluent side—that has expanded dramatically in recent decades.

The number of affluent families—those with annual incomes over $50,000—is increasing faster among African Americans than among whites. In 1998, 2.4 million African American families (28 percent) were financially privileged, one-and-one-half times the number in 1990 and ten times the number in 1970, taking inflation into account. About 26 percent of Latino families also rank as well-off, along with 49 percent of white families and 53 percent of Asian families.

The color of money is the same for everyone, but black and white affluence differs in several ways. First, well-off people of African descent are not *as rich* as their white counterparts. About half of affluent white families (27 percent of all white families) earn more than $75,000 a year, compared to 44 percent of affluent African American families (12 percent of all black families).

Second, African Americans are more likely than white people to achieve affluence through multiple incomes. From another angle, 22.8 percent of white men and 7.7 percent of white women earn more than $50,000, compared to just 10.1 percent of black men and 4.9 percent of black women. Rich black families, then, are more likely to contain two, and perhaps more, working people.

Rich people come in all colors. But are they all the same?

Third, affluent African Americans are more likely to derive their income from salaries rather than from investments. Three-fourths of affluent white families have investment income, compared to just half of affluent African American families.

Beyond differences in income, affluent people of color contend with social barriers that do not limit whites. Even African Americans with the money to purchase a home, for example, may find they are unwelcome as neighbors. This is one reason that a smaller share of well-off African American families (40 percent) live in the suburbs (the richest areas of the country) than affluent white families (61 percent).

Affluent Americans come in all colors. Yet race has a powerful effect on the lives of rich people, just as it does on the lives of us all.

Sources: O'Hare (1989), Weicher (1995), Lach (1999), and U.S. Census Bureau (1999).

family's income comes from inherited wealth in the form of stocks and bonds, real estate, and other investments, the stronger a family's claim to being upper class.

Every year, *Forbes* magazine profiles the richest 400 people in the United States. In 1999, these richest individuals had a *minimum* net worth of $625 million and included 267 billionaires. Their combined wealth was $1 trillion, greater than the GDP of China. The upper class are Karl Marx's "capitalists"—those who own the means of production, and, thus, most of the nation's private wealth. Many members of the upper class work as top corporate executives or senior government officials. Historically, though less so today, the upper class has been composed of white Anglo-Saxon Protestants (WASPs) (Baltzell, 1964, 1976, 1988).

Upper-Uppers

The *upper-upper class*, sometimes called "blue bloods" or simply "society," includes less than 1 percent of the

CRITICAL THINKING

Caste and Class: The *Social Register* and *Who's Who*

Small and exclusive, the upper-upper class comes closest to being a true social group. There is even a listing of these privileged families: the *Social Register*, first published in 1887 as fortunes grew along with the industrial economy. Today, some 40,000 families are included in this inventory of our society's "blue bloods."

Because membership is typically based on birth, the upper-upper class operates much like a caste: You are either "in" or "out." Traditional upper-upper parents urge their children to seek out partners of their own kind, sustaining the class into another generation. Family is thus crucial to the upper-upper class, as it is to all caste groups. This is why the *Social Register* lists *families*, not *individuals*.

The listing for David Rockefeller, a member of one of the most socially prominent families in the United States, indicates (1) his family's address and home telephone number; (2) Mrs. Rockefeller's maiden name; (3) the names of the Rockefeller children along with the boarding schools and colleges they are attending; and (4) exclusive social clubs to which the family belongs. Since achievement is not the issue, the *Social Register* never mentions anyone's occupation or place of business.

The lower-upper class, by contrast, is an achievement elite. This larger category of "new rich" individuals has no clear boundaries, and its members do not engage in formal rituals (like debutante parties) the way many "old money" families do.

There is also a listing, roughly speaking, of people at this class level: the national edition of *Who's Who in America*. Here, instead of established families, we find individuals distinguished for excellence: outstanding athletes, highly successful business people, college presidents, Nobel Prize winners, and famous entertainers.

Who's Who contains a few people, including David Rockefeller, who are also listed in the *Social Register*, but the information provided is quite different. David Rockefeller's entry in *Who's Who* includes a brief biography (date of birth, schooling, and honorary degrees), a list of accomplishments (military decorations, government service, books authored), and—most important—his position as board chair of Chase Manhattan Bank. The address provided in *Who's Who* is his place of business.

These two publications show that there are two kinds of elites in the United States. The castelike *Social Register* lists high-prestige families according to *who they are*. The more classlike *Who's Who* lists individuals on the basis of *what they have done*. But, as the dual listings for David Rockefeller suggest, social privilege and personal achievement sometimes go together.

Two books: One lists "upper-uppers," the other, "lower-uppers."

What do you think?

1. *In what sense are the rich* not *all the same?*
2. *Why are "old money" families more a caste, and "new money" families more a class?*
3. *With time, of course, "new money" becomes "old money." How did the ancestors of some of today's "old money" families (including the Rockefellers or the Kennedys) get their start?*

U.S. population (Warner & Lunt, 1941; Coleman & Neugarten, 1971; Baltzell, 1995). Membership in this elite group almost always comes at birth, as suggested by the quip that the easiest way to become an upper-upper is to be born one. Most of these families possess enormous wealth, primarily inherited. For this reason, members of the upper-upper class are said to have "old money."

Set apart by their wealth, upper-uppers live in old, exclusive neighborhoods, such as Beacon Hill in Boston, Rittenhouse Square or the Main Line in Philadelphia, the Gold Coast of Chicago, and Nob Hill

People often distinguish between the "new rich" and those with "old money." Men and women who suddenly begin to earn high incomes tend to spend their money on "status symbols" because they enjoy the new thrill of high-roller living and they want others to know of their success. Those who grow up surrounded by wealth, on the other hand, are used to a privileged way of life and are more quiet about it. Thus, the "conspicuous consumption" of the lower-upper class (left) can differ dramatically from the more private pursuits and understatement of the upper-upper class (right).

in San Francisco. Their children typically attend private schools with others of similar background and go on to high-prestige colleges and universities. In the tradition of European aristocrats, they study liberal arts rather than vocational skills.

Women of the upper-upper class often maintain a full schedule of volunteer work for charitable organizations. While helping the larger community, such charitable activities also build networks that broaden this elite's power (Ostrander, 1980, 1984).

Lower-Uppers

Most upper-class people actually fall into the *lower-upper class*. To most of us, these people seem every bit as privileged as the upper-upper class. The major difference, however, is that lower-uppers are the "working rich"; earnings rather than inherited wealth are the primary source of their income. Although these "new rich" families generally live in exclusive communities such as Silicon Valley, as profiled in the chapter opening, most do not gain entry to the clubs and associations of "old-money" families.

Historically, the American Dream has been to earn enough to join the ranks of the lower-upper class. The athlete who signs a million-dollar contract, the actress who lands a starring role in a Hollywood film, the computer whiz who becomes an Internet entrepreneur—these are the talented and lucky achievers who reach the lower-upper class. The box sharpens the distinction between "society" and the high achievers of the lower-upper class, people very much like the rest of us—except that they make a lot of money.

THE MIDDLE CLASS

Including 40 to 45 percent of the U.S. population, the large middle class has a tremendous influence on our culture. Television programs and movies usually depict middle-class people, and most commercial advertising is directed toward these "average" consumers. The middle class contains far more racial and ethnic diversity than the upper class.

Upper-Middles

The top half of this category is termed the *upper-middle class*, based on above-average income in the range of $50,000 to $100,000 a year. Such income allows upper-middle-class families to accumulate considerable property—a comfortable house in a fairly expensive area, several automobiles, and investments. Two-thirds of upper-middle-class children receive college educations, and postgraduate degrees are common. Many go on to

Sometimes whole neighborhoods rise or fall due to a changing economy. The photo on the left, taken in 1979, shows Fern Street in Camden, New Jersey, as a stable though modest urban neighborhood. A decade later after several major industries closed their doors, the same neighborhood has the look of a ghost town.

high-prestige careers as physicians, engineers, lawyers, accountants, and business executives. Lacking the power of the richest people to influence national or international events, upper-middles often play an important role in local political affairs.

Average-Middles

The rest of the middle class falls near the center of the U.S. class structure. *Average-middles* typically work in less prestigious white-collar occupations (middle managers, high school teachers, and sales clerks) or in highly skilled blue-collar jobs (say, as building contractors). Household income is between $35,000 and $50,000 a year, which is roughly the national average.

Middle-class people accumulate a small amount of wealth over the course of their working lives, mostly in the form of a house and money in a retirement account. Middle-class men and women are likely to be high school graduates, but the odds are just fifty-fifty that they will complete a college degree, generally at a less expensive state-supported school.

THE WORKING CLASS

About one-third of the population is working class (sometimes called the *lower-middle class*). In Marxist terms, the working class forms the core of the industrial proletariat. Their blue-collar jobs usually yield a family income between $20,000 and $40,000 a year, somewhat below the national average, and they have little or no wealth. Working-class families are thus vulnerable to financial problems caused by unemployment or illness.

Many working-class jobs provide little personal satisfaction—requiring discipline but rarely imagination—and subject workers to continual supervision. These jobs also offer fewer benefits, such as medical insurance and pension plans. About half of working-class families own their own homes, usually in lower-cost neighborhoods. College is a goal that only about one-third of working-class children realize.

THE LOWER CLASS

The remaining 20 percent of our population constitute the lower class. Low income makes their lives unstable and insecure. In 1998, the federal government classified 34.5 million people (12.7 percent of the population) as poor. Millions more—called the "working poor"—are just barely better off, holding low-prestige jobs that provide not only little satisfaction but close to minimum wage. Barely half manage to complete high school, and only one in four reaches college.

Society segregates the lower class, especially when the poor are racial or ethnic minorities. About 40 percent of lower-class families own their own homes, typically in the least desirable neighborhoods. Although poor neighborhoods are usually found in our inner cities, lower-class families also live in rural communities, especially across the South.

THE DIFFERENCE CLASS MAKES

September 2, 1995, Mount Vernon, Ohio. My bike leans right, leaving the trail for the rest station that offers a stretch and a drink of water. Here I encounter Linda, a thirty-something woman having trouble with her roller blades. Eye contact and a perplexed look are a call for help, so I walk over to see what I might do. Several of her boot buckles require adjustment. Close up, she doesn't look well. "Are you OK?" I gently ask. "Very tired," Linda responds, and goes on to explain why. Now divorced, she cannot pay off her debts with one low-income job. So she works an 11 A.M. to 7 P.M. shift as a computer clerk at a bank in town, catches four hours of sleep, and then drives an hour to Columbus, where she sits at another computer, processing catalog orders from 2 A.M. until 10 A.M. That leaves just enough time to drive back to Mount Vernon to start all over again at the bank.

Social stratification affects nearly every dimension of our lives. We will briefly examine some of the ways social standing is linked to our health, values, politics, and family life.

HEALTH

Health is closely related to social standing. Children born into poor families are three times more likely to die from disease, neglect, accidents, or violence during their first years of life than children born to rich families. Among adults, people with above-average incomes are twice as likely as low-income people to describe their health as excellent. Moreover, richer people live, on average, seven years longer because they eat more nutritious food, live in safer and less stressful environments, and receive better medical care (U.S. National Center for Health Statistics, 1999).

Compared to high-income people, low-income people are half as likely to report good health and, on average, live about seven fewer years. The toll of low income—played out in inadequate nutrition, little medical care, and high stress—is easy to see on the faces of the poor, who look old before their time.

VALUES

Cultural values, too, vary from class to class. The "old rich" have an unusually strong sense of family history since their social position is based on wealth passed down from generation to generation (Baltzell, 1979b). With their birthright privileges, upper-uppers also favor understated manners and tastes, while many "new rich" practice *conspicuous consumption,* buying things they know others will notice. They use clothes, homes, cars, and even airplanes to make a statement about their social position.

Affluent people with greater education and financial security also are more tolerant of controversial behavior such as homosexuality. Working-class people, who grow up in an atmosphere of greater supervision and discipline and are less likely to attend college, tend to be less tolerant (Kohn, 1977; NORC, 1999).

Industrial class systems provide the opportunity for social mobility—both upward and downward. Typically, social mobility is modest and gradual. Sociologists track this change by comparing the social standing of people in different generations of the same family—for example, in the achievement of a son that makes his father proud.

POLITICS

Political affiliations flow along class lines. By and large, more privileged people support the Republican party, while people with fewer advantages favor the Democrats.

But issue by issue, the pattern is more complex. A desire to protect their wealth prompts well-off people to be more conservative on *economic* issues, favoring, for example, lower taxes. But on *social* issues, such as abortion and other feminist concerns, highly educated, affluent people are more liberal. People of lower social standing, on the other hand, tend to be economic liberals, favoring expanded government social programs, but support a more conservative social agenda (Erikson, Luttbeg, & Tedin, 1980; Syzmanski, 1983; NORC, 1999).

Another clear pattern emerges when it comes to political involvement. Higher-income people, who are better served by the system, are more likely to vote and to join political organizations than people in the lower class (Hyman & Wright, 1971; Wolfinger & Rosenstone, 1980).

FAMILY AND GENDER

Social class also shapes family life. Most lower-class families are somewhat larger than middle-class families because of earlier marriage and less use of birth control. In addition, working-class parents encourage children to conform to conventional norms and respect authority figures. Parents of higher social standing, however, transmit a different "cultural capital" to their children, teaching them to express their individuality and imagination. In both cases, parents are looking to the future: The odds are that less privileged children will take jobs that require they closely follow rules, while more advantaged children will enter fields that require more creativity (Kohn, 1977; McLeod, 1995).

Of course, the more money a family has, the better parents can develop their children's talents and abilities. For example, an affluent family earning $90,700 a year will spend $228,690 raising a child born in 1998 to the age of eighteen. Middle-class people, with income of $47,900 a year, will spend $156,690, and families earning $36,000 will spend $115,020 (Lino, 1999). Privilege, then, tends to beget privilege as family life reproduces the class structure in each generation.

Class also shapes our world of relationships. Elizabeth Bott (1971) found that most working-class couples divide their responsibilities according to gender; middle-class couples, by contrast, are more egalitarian, sharing more activities and expressing greater intimacy. More recently, Karen Walker (1995) discovered that working-class friendships typically provide material assistance; middle-class friendships, however, are likely to involve shared interests and leisure pursuits.

SOCIAL MOBILITY

Ours is a dynamic society marked by significant social movement. Earning a college degree, landing a higher-paying job, or marrying someone who earns a high income contributes to *upward social mobility;* dropping out of school, losing a job, or divorce (especially for women) may signal *downward social mobility.*

Over the long term, though, social mobility is not so much a matter of individual changes as changes in society itself. During the first half of the twentieth century, for example, industrialization expanded the U.S. economy, pushing up living standards. Even without being very good swimmers, so to speak, people rode a rising tide of prosperity. More recently, *structural social mobility* in a downward direction has dealt many people economic setbacks.

Sociologists distinguish between shorter- and longer-term changes in social position. **Intragenerational social mobility** refers to *a change in social position occurring during a person's lifetime.* **Intergenerational social mobility,** *upward or downward social mobility of children in relation to their parents,* is important because it usually reveals long-term changes in society that affect almost everyone.

MYTH VERSUS REALITY

In few societies do people think about "getting ahead" as much as in the United States. Moving up, after all, is the American Dream. But is there as much social mobility as we like to think?

Studies of intergenerational mobility (almost all of which, unfortunately, have focused exclusively on men) show that almost 40 percent of the sons of blue-collar workers attain white-collar jobs and almost 30 percent of sons born into white-collar families end up doing blue-collar work. *Horizontal mobility*—a change of occupation at one class level—is even more common, so that about 80 percent of sons show at least some type of social mobility in relation to their fathers (Blau & Duncan, 1967; Featherman & Hauser, 1978; Hout, 1998).

Research points to four general conclusions about social mobility in the United States:

1. **Social mobility, at least among men, has been fairly high.** The widespread belief that the United States allows considerable social mobility is true. Mobility is what we would expect in an industrial class system.
2. **The long-term trend in social mobility has been upward.** Industrialization, which greatly expanded the U.S. economy, and the growth of white-collar work over the course of the twentieth century have boosted living standards.
3. **Within a single generation, social mobility is usually small.** Most young families increase their income over time (Duncan et al., 1998). Yet only a very few people move "from rags to riches." While sharp rises or falls in individual fortunes may attract the media, social mobility usually involves limited movement *within* one class level rather than striking moves *between* classes.
4. **Social mobility since the 1970s has been uneven.** Real income (that is, adjusted for inflation) rose steadily during the twentieth century until the 1970s, when it hit a plateau. During the 1980s, real income changed little for many people, rising slowly again by the end of the 1990s.

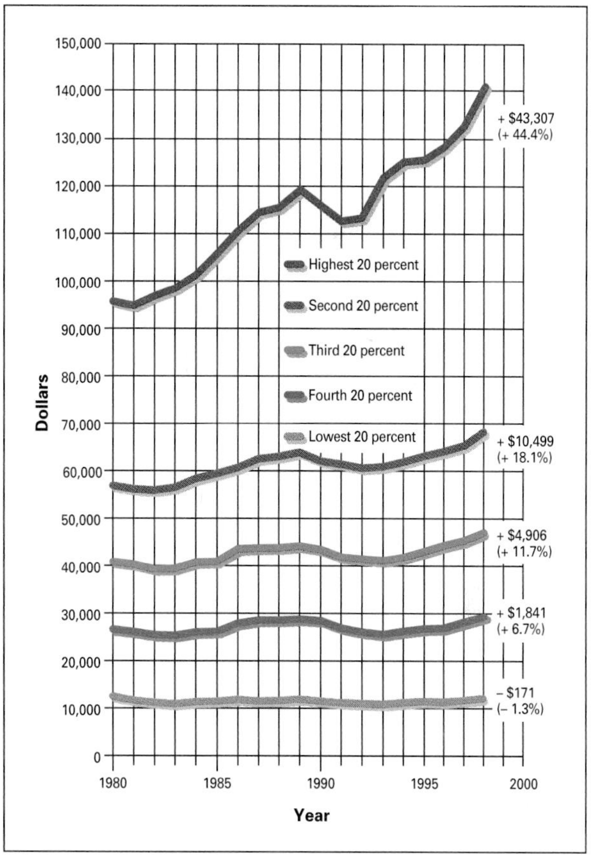

FIGURE 11–4 Mean Income, U.S. Families, 1980–1998 (in 1998 dollars, adjusted for inflation)

Source: U.S. Census Bureau (2000).

MOBILITY BY INCOME LEVEL

General trends often mask the experiences of different categories of people. Figure 11–4 shows how U.S. families at different income levels fared between 1980 and 1998. Well-to-do families (the highest 20 percent, but

SEEING OURSELVES

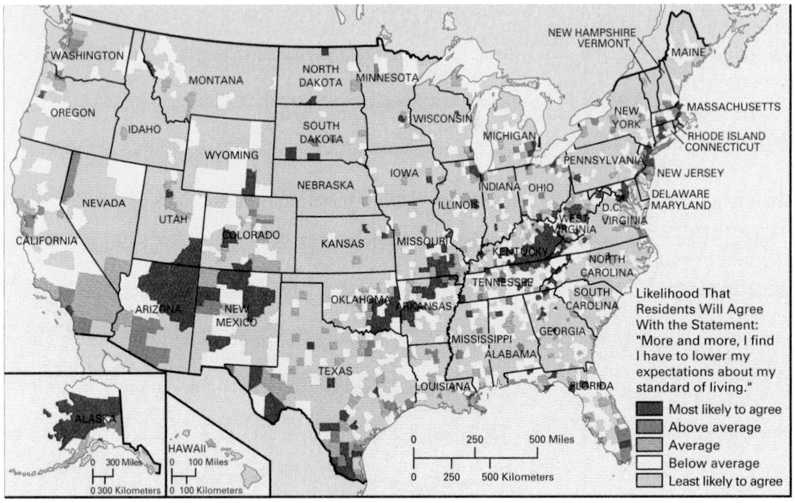

NATIONAL MAP 11–1
"Fear of Falling" across the United States

This map shows, by county, how likely people are to agree with the statement "More and more, I find I have to lower my expectations about my standard of living." What characterizes regions (including Appalachia in Kentucky and West Virginia) where pessimism is high? But pessimism is pronounced not only in poor rural areas. In rich cities, including New York, Chicago, and Los Angeles, people are also afraid of losing their jobs.

Source: *American Demographics* magazine, February 1994, p. 60. Reprinted with permission. ©1994 *American Demographics* magazine, Ithaca, New York. Data from Yankelovich *Monitor* and Clarita's *Prizm* system.

not all the same families over the entire period) saw their incomes jump 44 percent, from an average $97,539 in 1980 to $140,846 in 1998. People in the middle of the population saw small gains during this time, while the lowest-income 20 percent suffered a 1.3 percent loss in earnings.

For families at the top of the income scale (the highest 1 percent), the last fifteen years have been a windfall. These families, with an average income of $132,451 in 1980, were averaging about $500,000 in 1998, almost four times as much (Edmondson, 1995; Nielsen & Alderson, 1997; U.S. Census Bureau, 2000).

MOBILITY: RACE, ETHNICITY, AND GENDER

White people, in a more privileged position to begin with, have been more upwardly mobile in recent decades than people of African or Hispanic ancestry. Through the economic expansion of the 1980s and 1990s, many more African Americans entered the ranks of the wealthy. But the real income of African Americans, overall, has changed little in two decades. African Americans earned nearly the same percentage of white family income in 1998 (62 percent) as in 1970. Compared to white families, Latinos lost ground between 1975 (67 percent) and 1998 (60 percent) (Featherman & Hauser, 1978; Pomer, 1986; U.S. Census Bureau, 1999).

Historically, women have had less opportunity for upward mobility than men, since most working women hold clerical jobs (such as secretary) and service positions (like waitress) that offer few promotions. In addition, when marriages end in divorce (as almost half do), women commonly experience downward social mobility; they lose not only income but a host of benefits, including health care and insurance coverage (Weitzman, 1996).

Over time, however, the earnings gap between women and men has been narrowing. Women working full time in 1980 earned 60 percent as much as men working full time; by 1998, women earned 74 percent as much. Unfortunately, much of the change was due to a *drop* in men's earnings through the 1980s while women's income remained about the same (U.S. Census Bureau, 1999).

THE AMERICAN DREAM: STILL A REALITY?

The expectation of upward social mobility is deeply rooted in our culture. Through most of our history, economic expansion fulfilled this promise by raising living standards. But, about 1970, this upward trend leveled off, starting a period of "income stagnation" for many families that has shaken our national confidence. Note these recent trends:

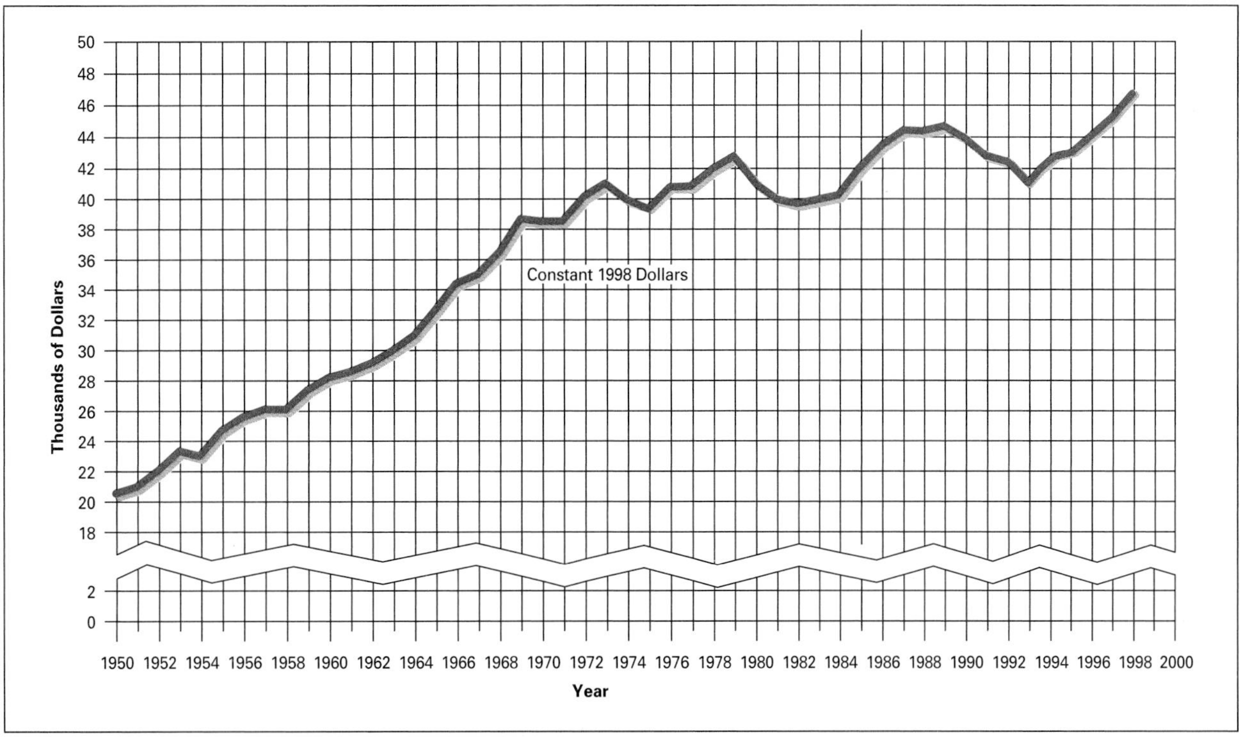

FIGURE 11–5 Median Income, U.S. Families, 1950–1998

Source: U.S. Census Bureau (2000).

1. **For many workers, earnings have stalled.** The annual income of a fifty-year-old man working full time rose 50 percent between 1958 and 1973 (from $21,000 to $32,000 in constant 1990 dollars). Between 1973 and 1998, however, his income remained flat, even as the number of hours worked increased and the cost of necessities like housing, education, and medical care went up (Russell, 1995a; U.S. Census Bureau, 1999).
2. **Multiple job-holding is up.** According to the Bureau of Labor Statistics, 4.7 percent of the U.S. labor force worked at two or more jobs in 1975; by 1998, the share had risen to 6.0 percent.
3. **More jobs offer little income.** In 1979, the Census Bureau classified 12 percent of full-time workers as "low-income earners" because they made less than $6,905; by 1998, this segment increased to 15.4 percent, earning less than the comparable figure of $15,208.
4. **Young people are remaining at home.** Fully 53 percent of young people aged eighteen to twenty-four, unable to afford an apartment or home of their own, are now living with their parents. Since 1975, the average age at marriage has moved upward three years (to 25 years for women and 26.7 years for men).

In sum, over the last generation, the rich have become richer. Moreover, the number of rich people has also increased, to at least 5 million millionaires in the United States, four times the number a decade ago (D'Souza, 1999). So, for some at least, the American Dream is alive and well. But most are less optimistic about the future, and a significant share worry that the chance for a middle-class life is slipping away (Kerckhoff, Campbell, & Winfield-Laird, 1985; Newman, 1993). National Map 11–1 shows where in the United States pessimism about the future is most widespread.

Dubbed the *middle-class slide*, this downward structural mobility came about as more jobs offered low pay. As Figure 11–5 shows, although median family income grew by almost 65 percent between 1950 and 1973, it has moved up only slightly since then (U.S. Census Bureau, 2000).

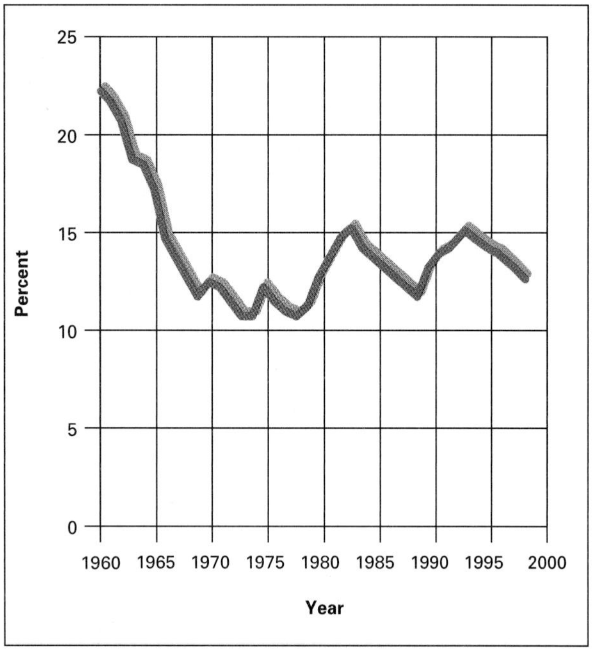

FIGURE 11–6 The Poverty Rate in the United States, 1960–1998

Source: U.S. Census Bureau (1999).

THE GLOBAL ECONOMY AND U.S. CLASS STRUCTURE

Underlying the recent shifts in U.S. class structure is global economic change. Much of the industrial production that gave U.S. workers high-paying jobs a generation ago has moved overseas. With less industry at home, the United States now serves as a vast market for industrial goods such as cars and popular items like stereos, cameras, and computers made in Japan, Korea, and elsewhere.

High-paying jobs in manufacturing, held by 26 percent of the U.S. labor force in 1960, support 16 percent of workers today. In their place, the economy now offers "service work," which often pays far less. A traditionally high-paying corporation like USX (formerly United States Steel) now employs fewer people than McDonald's. Meanwhile, McDonald's continues to expand, and fast-food clerks make only a fraction of what steel workers earn.

The global reorganization of work is not bad news for everyone. On the contrary, the global economy creates upward social mobility for educated people who specialize in areas such as law, finance, marketing, and computer technology. Moreover, global economic expansion has helped push up the stock market tenfold between 1980 and 2000, reaping profits for families with money to invest.

But the same trend has hurt many "average" workers who have seen their factory jobs disappear. Moreover, many companies have "downsized"—cut the ranks of their work force, blue-collar and white-collar alike—to become competitive in world markets. As a result, although half of all households contain two or more workers—double the share in 1950—many people are working harder simply to hold on to what they have (Reich, 1989, 1991; Nelson, 1998; Schlesinger, 1998; Sennett, 1998).

POVERTY IN THE UNITED STATES

Social stratification creates both "haves" and "have-nots." All systems of social inequality create poverty—or at least **relative poverty,** *the deprivation of some people in relation to those who have more.* A more serious but preventable problem is **absolute poverty,** *a deprivation of resources that is life threatening.*

As the next chapter ("Global Stratification") explains, at least 800 million human beings—one in seven—are at risk of absolute poverty. Even in the affluent United States, families go hungry, live in inadequate housing, and suffer poor health because of wrenching poverty.

THE EXTENT OF U.S. POVERTY

In 1964, the federal government established an official *poverty line,* and began counting the poor and offering certain benefits. The idea was to identify people living close to absolute poverty. Mollie Orshansky, the architect of the poverty line, described it as the income needed "to purchase a nutritionally adequate diet on the assumption that no more than a third of the family income is used for food" (1969:38). In other words, the poverty threshold is three times what the government estimates people must spend to eat. The government sets the exact dollar amount according to family size with annual adjustments to reflect the changing cost of living.

Figure 11–6 shows the official poverty rate as calculated annually since 1960. During the 1960s, poverty fell sharply, but there has been little overall change in the rate since. In 1998, the government tallied 34.5

In the 1952 painting The Laundress, *U.S. artist George Tooker captures the humanity and humility of impoverished people. This message—that the poor are human beings, most doing the best they can to get by—is important to remember in a society that tends to define poor people as morally unworthy and deserving of their bitter plight.*

George Tooker (b. 1920), *Laundress*, 1952. Oil on masonite, 23 1/2 × 24 in. (59.7 × 61 cm.) Christies Images, NY. © George Tooker.

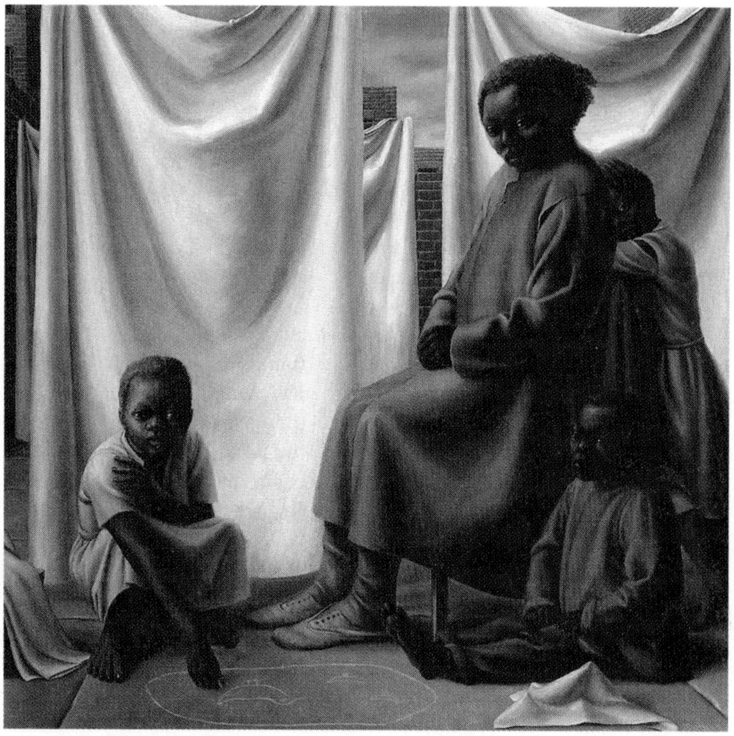

million men, women, and children—12.7 percent of the U.S. population—as poor. Another 12 million people—the *marginally poor*—lived on income no greater than 125 percent of the poverty threshold.

For an urban family of four, the 1998 poverty line was set at $16,660. But the income of the average poor family was much lower—just $10,040. This means that half of poor families must get by on less than poverty-line income (U.S. Census Bureau, 1999).

People like Ana Nuñez, described at the beginning of this chapter, know very well the consequences of living on the edge—not being able to afford the jackets or expensive sneakers their children want so badly and, worse, worrying about what will happen if one of the family becomes injured or ill. In short, poverty means a life of daily stress, insecurity, and—for about half the poor adults and children in the United States—hunger (Schwartz-Nobel, 1981; Physicians' Task Force on Hunger in America, 1987).

WHO ARE THE POOR?

Although the poor fit no single stereotype, certain categories of our population are at high risk of poverty. Where these categories overlap, the problem is especially serious.

Age

A generation ago, it was the elderly who were at greatest risk for poverty, but no longer. From 30 percent in 1967, the poverty rate for seniors over the age of sixty-five fell to 10.5 percent in 1998, or 3.4 million elderly poor. The elderly now have a poverty rate below the national average due to better retirement programs from private employers as well as more extensive government benefits. Even so, with the number of older people steadily increasing, 9.8 percent of the poor are elderly people.

Today, the burden of poverty falls most heavily on children. In 1998, 18.9 percent of people under age eighteen (13.5 million children) were poor. Tallied another way, four in ten of the U.S. poor are children under the age of eighteen. The poverty problem contributes to the high U.S. infant mortality rate, a measure of how likely children are to survive their first year of life. Despite being the richest country in the world, the United States has one of the highest infant mortality

CRITICAL THINKING

U.S. Children: Bearing the Burden of Poverty

We cringe at the sight of starving children in Somalia, the war-torn African nation where the average person struggles to live on less than $200 per year. But child poverty in the United States may be an even greater tragedy, since ours is such a rich nation with more than 100 times the per capita income of Somalia. Applying the sociological perspective, what can we learn about child poverty in the United States?

To begin, nearly one in five U.S. children under the age of eighteen is poor—13.5 million boys and girls. This is the same number of poor children as there were almost forty years ago when the government began its "war on poverty." National Map 11–2 shows that the problem of child poverty is greatest across the South and Southwest.

Like poverty in general, the risk of child poverty varies within our population. In 1998, for the country as a whole, 19 percent of boys and girls under the age of eighteen were counted among the poor. But while 15 percent of white children were poor, 34 percent of Latino and 37 percent of African American youngsters were poor.

From another angle, 63 percent of poor children are white, while 31 percent are African American and 4 percent are Asian; 28 percent of poor children are culturally Hispanic. But while poor children are a diverse lot, they share one trait: They all live in households with low income.

To explain the problem of child poverty, researchers point to the rising share of single-parent households in the United States. Today, about six in ten poor children live in a household with a single mother. In the same share of cases, this household has no full-time worker.

The reasons for poverty are complex and controversial. But everyone agrees that children are not to blame. Tragically, however, this is precisely where the burden of poverty falls. Practically speaking, reducing child poverty is certainly cheaper than dealing with its later effects, including lower achievement in school and higher risk of drug use and crime. Whether we look at this issue from a moral or practical standpoint, can we permit our society's most vulnerable members to suffer this way?

What do you think?

1. *National Map 11–2 shows that the problem of child poverty is greatest across the southern and southwestern United States. Why do you think this is the case?*
2. *More than twice as many poor children are white as are black. Does this surprise you? Why or why not?*
3. *Why, in your opinion, does the United States have such a high level of child poverty? What do you think U.S. society could do to address this problem?*

Sources: Eggebeen & Lichter (1991), Children's Defense Fund (1995), Duncan et al. (1998), and U.S. Census Bureau (1999).

SEEING OURSELVES

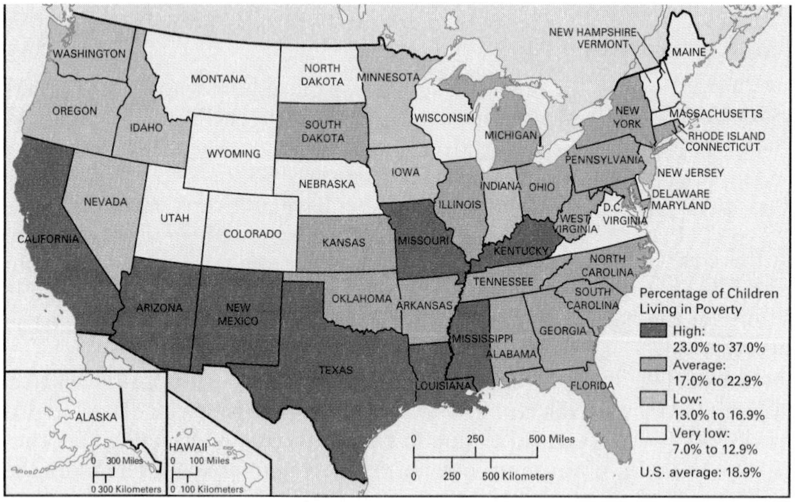

NATIONAL MAP 11–2 Child Poverty across the United States

Source: U.S. Bureau of the Census (1998).

SEEING OURSELVES

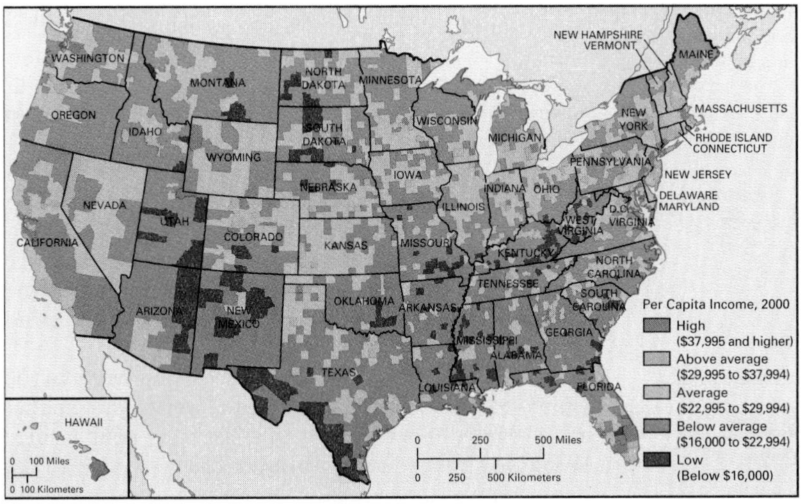

Source: *American Demographics*, April 2000, p. 42–43. © 2000 *American Demographics* magazine.

NATIONAL MAP 11–3
Per Capita Income across the United States, 2000

This map shows the median per-person income (that is, how much money, on average, a person has to spend) for the more than 3,000 counties that make up the United States for the year 2000. The fifty richest counties, shown in dark green, are not spread randomly across the country. Nor are the poorest U.S. counties, which are shown in dark red. Looking at the map, what patterns do you see in the distribution of wealth and poverty across the United States? Do these patterns support our assertion linking affluence to urban living and poverty to rural places?

rates among industrial nations. The box takes a closer look at child poverty in the United States.

Race and Ethnicity

Two-thirds of all poor people are white; 26 percent are African Americans. But in relation to their overall numbers, African Americans are nearly three times as likely as whites to be poor. In 1998, 26.1 percent of African Americans (9.1 million people) lived in poverty, compared to 25.6 percent of Latinos (8.1 million), 12.5 percent of Asians and Pacific Islanders (1.4 million), and 8.2 percent of non-Latino white people (15.8 million). The poverty gap between whites and minorities has changed little since 1975 (U.S. Census Bureau, 1999).

Gender and Family Patterns

Of all poor people eighteen and older, 62 percent are women and 38 percent are men. This disparity reflects the fact that women who head households bear the brunt of poverty. Of all poor families, 53 percent are headed by women with no husband present, while just 7 percent of poor families are headed by single men.

The term **feminization of poverty** describes *the trend by which women represent an increasing proportion of the poor.* In 1960, 25 percent of all poor households were headed by women; the majority of poor families had both wives and husbands in the home. By 1998, however, the share of poor households headed by a single woman had more than doubled to 53 percent.

The feminization of poverty is thus part of a larger change: the rapidly increasing number of households—at all class levels—headed by single women. This trend, coupled with the fact that households headed by women are at high risk of poverty, is why women (and their children) make up an increasing share of the U.S. poor.

Urban and Rural Poverty

The greatest concentration of poverty in this country is found in central cities, where the 1998 poverty rate stood at 18.5 percent. Suburbs, too, have destitute people, but their poverty rate is just 8.7 percent. Thus, the poverty rate for urban areas as a whole is 12.3 percent—lower than the 14.4 percent found in rural areas. National Map 11–3 presents income levels across the United States, and shows where low income is most pronounced.

Survey Question: Some people think that the government in Washington should do everything possible to improve the living standards of all poor Americans [they are at point 1 below]. Other people think it is not the government s responsibility, and that each person should take care of himself [they are at point 5 below]. Where would you place yourself on this scale, or haven t you made up your mind on this?

1	2	3	4	5	*Don t know/ no answer*
12.5%	12.6%	42.8%	16.5%	12.0%	*3.6%*

I strongly agree the government should improve living standards — I agree with both answers — I strongly agree that people should take care of themselves

FIGURE 11–7 Government or Individuals: Who Is Responsible for Poverty?

Source: NORC (1999).

EXPLAINING POVERTY

For the richest nation on earth to have tens of millions of poor people raises serious questions. It is true, as some analysts remind us, that many of the people counted among the officially poor in the United States are better off than the poor in other countries—41 percent of U.S. poor families own their home, for example, 70 percent own a car, and only a few percent report often going without food (Rector, 1998). Nevertheless, poverty harms the overall health of millions of people in this country.

Figure 11–7 shows that the public is divided over what to do about poverty. One-fourth of respondents to this national survey look to the government to help poor people; just slightly more think people must take responsibility for themselves. Almost 43 percent, however, straddle the fence, thinking both government and individuals share this responsibility.

We now focus on two different explanations for poverty. Together, they lead to a lively and important political debate.

One View: Blame the Poor

One approach holds that *the poor are mostly responsible for their own poverty.* Throughout our history, people in the United States have valued self-reliance and have believed that social standing is mostly a matter of individual talent and effort. This view sees society offering plenty of opportunity to anyone able and willing to take advantage of it. Thus, anyone who is poor either cannot or will not work. These are people with few skills, little schooling, and little motivation. This argument represents the right side of the continuum in Figure 11–7.

In a study of Latin American cities, the anthropologist Oscar Lewis (1961) concluded that the poor become trapped in a *culture of poverty,* a lower-class subculture that can destroy people's ambition to improve their lives. Socialized in poor families, children become resigned to their plight, producing a self-perpetuating cycle of poverty.

In 1996, hoping to break the cycle of poverty in the United States, Congress changed the welfare system that had provided federal funds to assist poor people since 1935. Now the federal government sends money to the states to give to needy people; but benefits carry strict time limits: in most cases, no more than two years at a stretch and a total of five years if an individual moves in and out of the welfare system. The objective is to move people from depending on the government to supporting themselves.

Counterpoint: Blame Society

Another position, argued by William Julius Wilson (1996a,b) holds that *society is primarily responsible for poverty.* Wilson points to the loss of jobs in the inner cities as the primary cause of poverty, claiming that there is simply not enough work to support families. Thus, Wilson sees any lack of trying on the part of poor people as a *result of little opportunity* rather than a *cause of poverty.* From this point of view, then, Oscar Lewis's analysis amounts to "blaming the victims" for their own suffering (Ryan, 1976). The view that looks to government to overcome poverty is at the left side of the continuum in Figure 11–7. The box provides a closer look at Wilson's argument and how it would shape public policy.

Weighing the Evidence

What evidence supports one side or the other of the poverty controversy? Government statistics show that 47 percent of the heads of poor households did not work at all during 1998, and an additional 35 percent worked only part time (U.S. Census Bureau, 1999). Such facts

CRITICAL THINKING

When Work Disappears: The Result Is Poverty

> The economy has churned out tens of millions of new jobs in the last two decades. In that same period, joblessness among inner-city blacks has reached catastrophic proportions. Yet in this Presidential election year [1996], the disappearance of work in the ghetto is not on either the Democratic or the Republican agenda. There is harsh talk about work instead of welfare but no talk about where to find it. (Wilson, 1996b:27)

William Julius Wilson points out that, despite the rising number of rich black families, a minority of African Americans who live in the inner city face impossible economic barriers.

Here is the problem: For the first time, a large majority of the adults in our inner cities are not working. Studying the Washington Park area of Chicago, Wilson found a troubling trend. Back in 1950, most adults in the African American community had jobs, but by the 1990s, two-thirds did not. As one elderly woman who moved to the neighborhood in 1953 explains:

> When I moved in, the neighborhood was intact. It was intact with homes, beautiful homes, mini-mansions, with stores, laundromats, with Chinese cleaners. We had drugstores. We had hotels. We had doctors over on 39th Street. We had doctors' offices in the neighborhood. We had the middle class and the upper-middle class. It has gone from affluent to where it is today. (1996b:28)

But *why* has this neighborhood declined? Wilson's eight years of research point to one answer: There are barely any jobs. It is the loss of work that has pushed people into desperate poverty, weakened families, and made people turn to welfare. In nearby Woodlawn, Wilson identified more than 800 businesses that operated in 1950; today, just 100 remain. Moreover, a number of major employers a generation ago—including Western Electric and International Harvester—closed their plant doors in the late 1960s. The inner cities have fallen victim to economic change, including downsizing and jobs being moved overseas.

Wilson paints a grim picture. But he also believes there is an answer: Create jobs. Wilson proposes attacking the problem in stages. First, the government could hire people to do all kinds of work, including clearing slums and putting up new housing. Such a program, modeled on the Works Progress Administration (WPA) enacted in 1935 during the Great Depression, would move people from welfare to work and, in the process, create much-needed hope. In addition, federal and state governments must improve schools by enacting performance standards and providing more funding. Of special importance is teaching children language skills and computer skills to prepare them for the jobs being created by the Information Revolution. Improved regional public transportation would connect cities (where people need jobs) and suburbs (where most jobs now are). In addition, more child-care programs would help single mothers and fathers balance the responsibilities of parenting and work.

Wilson claims that his proposals are well grounded in research. But he knows politics revolves around other considerations as well. For one thing, to the extent that the public *thinks* there are plenty of jobs, they will conclude that the poor are simply avoiding work, making any change unlikely. Moreover, he concedes that his proposals, at least in the short term, are more expensive than continuing to funnel welfare assistance to jobless communities.

But, for the long term, he asks, what are the costs of allowing our cities to decay while suburbs prosper? Of allowing a new generation of preschoolers to join the ranks of the restless and often angry people for whom there is no work? What would be the benefits of affording everyone the hope and satisfaction that are supposed to define our way of life?

What do you think?

1. *According to Wilson, why are many of this country's inner-city neighborhoods so poor?*
2. *What does he think we can do to address this problem?*
3. *Do you agree with his analysis of poverty? Why or why not?*

Sources: Based on Wilson (1996a, b).

About 3 million people in the United States work full time yet do not earn enough to escape poverty. These laundry workers in San Francisco's Chinatown earn $7 per hour, about $14,500 per year, in one of the most expensive cities in the country.

seem to support the "blame the poor" side, since one major cause of poverty is *not holding a job.*

But the *reasons* that people do not work seem more consistent with the "blame society" position. Middle-class women may be able to combine working and child rearing, but this is much harder for poor women who cannot afford child care—and few employers provide child-care programs for their employees. Moreover, as William Julius Wilson explains, many people are idle not because they are avoiding work but because there are not enough jobs. In short, most poor people in the United States find few options and alternatives (Popkin, 1990; Schiller, 1994; Edin & Lein, 1996; Wilson, 1996a; Pease & Martin, 1997).

The Working Poor

But not all poor people are jobless, and the *working poor* command the sympathy and support of people on both sides of the poverty debate (Schwarz & Volgy, 1992). In 1998, 18 percent of poor heads of households (containing 1.4 million people) worked at least fifty weeks of the year and yet could not escape poverty. Another 35 percent of these heads of households (totaling 2 million people) remained poor despite part-time employment by the head of the family. In other words, 2.9 percent of full-time workers earn so little that they remain poor (U.S. Census Bureau, 1999). A key cause of working poverty is that a full-time worker making $5.15 per hour—the minimum wage—cannot lift a family above the poverty line.

To sum up, individual ability and personal initiative do play a part in shaping everyone's social position. However, the weight of sociological evidence points to society—not individual character traits—as the primary cause of poverty. Society must be at fault because the poor are *categories* of people—women heads of families, people of color, people isolated from the larger society in inner-city areas—who face special barriers and limited opportunities.

HOMELESSNESS

Many low-income people in the United States cannot afford even basic housing. Despite enormous wealth and a commitment to providing opportunity for everyone, the United States has not effectively responded to homelessness, a scar on our society (Schutt, 1989).

Counting the Homeless

There is no precise count of homeless people. Fanning out across the cities of the United States on the night of March 20, 1991, Census Bureau officials tallied 178,828 people at shelters and 49,793 on the streets of neighborhoods where homeless people are known to congregate. But experts agree that a full count of the homeless might reach 500,000 *on any given night,* with as many as three times that number—1.5 million people—homeless *at some time during the course of a year* (Kozol, 1988; Wright, 1989).

Causes of Homelessness

The familiar stereotypes of homeless people—men sleeping in doorways and women carrying everything they own in a shopping bag—have been replaced by the "new

Social scientists debate the causes of poverty. Some cite the failings of individuals, such as lack of initiative or drug abuse, and others point to flaws of society, including a minimum wage that does not allow a full-time worker to support a family. Whatever side one takes in this controversy, it is impossible to turn away from the drama of children born into poor families. Here, members of a homeless family spend an afternoon at their living site near Austin, Texas.

homeless": people thrown out of work because of plant closings, those forced out of apartments by rent increases or condominium conversions, and others unable to meet mortgage or rent payments because of low wages or no work at all. Today, no stereotype paints a complete picture of the homeless.

But just about all homeless people have one thing in common: *poverty*. For that reason, the explanations of poverty already offered also apply to homelessness. Some blame the *personal traits* of the homeless themselves. One-third of homeless people are substance abusers and one-fourth are mentally ill. More broadly, it should not be surprising that a fraction of 1 percent of our population, for one reason or another, is unable to cope with our complex and highly competitive society (Bassuk, 1984; Whitman, 1989).

Others, however, see homelessness resulting from *societal factors*, including low wages and a lack of low-income housing (Kozol, 1988; Schutt, 1989; Bohannan, 1991). Supporters of this position point out that one-third of all homeless people are entire families, and children are the fastest growing category of the homeless. A minister in a Pennsylvania town that has lost hundreds of industrial jobs due to plant closings describes the real-life effects of economic recession:

> Yes, there are new jobs. There's a new McDonald's and a Burger King. You can take home $450 in a month from jobs like that. That might barely pay the rent. What do you do if someone gets sick? What do you do for food and clothes? These may be good jobs for a teenager. Can you ask a thirty-year-old man who's worked for GM since he was eighteen to keep his wife and kids alive on jobs like that? There are jobs cleaning rooms in the hotel. . . . Can you expect a single mother with three kids to hold her life together with that kind of work? (Kozol, 1988:6)

No one disputes that a large proportion of homeless people are personally impaired to some degree, but how much is cause and how much is effect is difficult to untangle. Structural changes in the U.S. economy coupled with reduced aid to low-income people and a real estate market that puts housing out of reach of the poorest members of our society all contribute to homelessness (Ratnesar, 1999).

We close this chapter with a look at "welfare," a topic that focuses our thinking about how to respond to issues such as poverty and homelessness.

Finally, social stratification extends far beyond the borders of the United States. In fact, the most striking social inequality is found not within any one nation but in the different living standards among nations of the world. In Chapter 12, we broaden our investigation of social stratification by looking at global inequality.

CONTROVERSY & DEBATE

The Welfare Dilemma

In 1996, Congress ended the federal public assistance that guaranteed some income to all poor people. Now state-run programs require that people receiving aid enroll in job-training programs or find work—or have their benefits cut off.

Almost no one likes "welfare." Liberals criticize welfare for doing too little to help the poor; conservatives charge that it hurts the people it is supposed to help; and the poor themselves find welfare a complex and often degrading program.

So what, exactly, *is* welfare? The term "welfare" refers to a host of policies and programs designed to improve the well-being of the U.S. population. Until the welfare reform of 1996, most people used the term to refer to one part of the overall system—Aid for Dependent Children (AFDC), a program of monthly financial support to parents (mostly single women) to care for themselves and their children. In 1996, some 5 million households received AFDC for some part of the year.

Did AFDC help or hurt the poor? There are two sides to the debate. Conservative critics argue that rather than reducing child poverty, AFDC actually made the problem worse for two reasons. First, this form of welfare weakened families by subsidizing living single as an alternative to marriage. For years, poor mothers received benefits *only if no husband lived in the home*. As conservatives see it, AFDC was an economic incentive to women to have children outside of marriage: one reason for the increase in out-of-wedlock births among poor people. Conservatives see a clear connection between being poor and not being married: Fewer than one in ten married-couple families were poor; more than nine in ten AFDC families were headed by an unmarried woman.

Second, conservatives also believe that welfare made poor people dependent—taking government handouts rather than working to support themselves. This, they say, is the main reason that eight of ten poor heads of households did not have steady, full-time jobs. Furthermore, more than half of nonpoor, single mothers worked full time, compared to only 5 percent of single mothers receiving AFDC. Conservatives sum up by concluding that welfare strayed from its original purpose of giving temporary help to women with children (typically, after divorce or death of a husband) until they could find work. Instead, welfare became a way of life. Once trapped in dependency, poor women are likely to raise children who will, themselves, be poor as adults.

Do welfare programs such as food stamps do too much, or too little, to help the poor?

Liberals charge that their opponents use a double standard in evaluating government programs. Why, they ask, do people object to government money going to poor mothers and children when most "welfare" actually goes to relatively rich people? The AFDC budget was $25 billion annually—no small sum, to be sure—but just half of the $50 billion in home mortgage deductions that homeowners pocket each year. And it pales in comparison to the $300 billion in annual Social Security benefits Uncle Sam provides to senior citizens, most of whom are well-off. And what about "corporate welfare" to big companies? Their tax write-offs and other benefits amount to hundreds of billions of dollars a year. As liberals see it, "wealthfare" is far greater than "welfare."

Second, liberals claim that conservatives have a distorted picture of public assistance. The popular image of do-nothing "welfare queens" masks the fact that most poor families who turn to public assistance are truly needy. Moreover, the typical household receiving AFDC received barely $400 per month, hardly enough to attract people to a "life of welfare dependency." And, in constant dollars, AFDC payments actually declined over recent decades. In fact, liberals fault public assistance as a "Band-Aid approach" to the serious social problems of too few jobs and too much income inequality in the United States.

As for the charge that public assistance weakens families,

liberals concede that the proportion of single- parent families has risen, but they doubt AFDC was to blame. Rather, single parenting is a broad cultural trend found at all class levels in many countries.

Thus, liberals conclude, AFDC was not attacked because it failed but, rather, because it benefited a part of the population that many consider undeserving. Our cultural tradition of equating wealth with virtue and poverty with vice allows rich people to display privilege as a badge of ability, while poverty is a sign of personal failure. According to Richard Sennett and Jonathan Cobb (1973), the negative stigma of poverty is the "hidden injury of class."

The figure shows that people in the United States, more than people in other industrial societies, tend to see poverty as a mark of laziness and personal failure. This perception suggests why the U.S. public offers limited support for social programs to assist the poor. It should not be surprising, then, that Congress replaced the federal AFDC program with state-run programs called Temporary Assistance for Needy Families (TANF). The federal government provides funding, and states can set their own qualifications and benefits, but they must limit assistance to two consecutive years (with a lifetime limit of five years).

By 2002, TANF expects to move half of single parents on welfare into jobs or job training. By 1999, three years after the welfare reform bill took effect, the welfare rolls had shrunk by more than 40 percent (the number of people receiving benefits dropped from 14 million to 8 million). Half of those people have found jobs; others are in school or job-training programs. Supporters declare the reform successful. Opponents, however, fear that many families will end up worse off than before.

Continue the debate . . .

1. *How does our cultural emphasis on self-reliance help explain the controversy surrounding public assistance? Why, then, do people not criticize benefits (like home mortgage deductions) for more well-off people?*
2. *Do you think public assistance has become a way of life and eroded the family? Why or why not?*
3. *Do you approve of the benefit time limits built into the new TANF program? Why or why not?*

GLOBAL SNAPSHOT

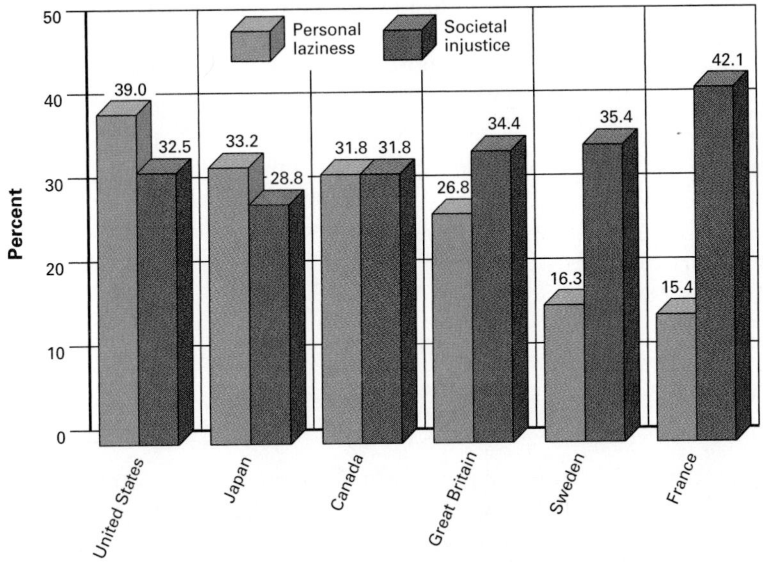

FIGURE 11–8 Assessing the Causes of Poverty

Survey Question: "Why are there people in this country who live in need?" Percentages reflect respondents' identification of either "personal laziness" or "societal injustice" as the primary cause of poverty.

Percentages for each country do not add up to 100 because less frequently identified causes of poverty were omitted from this figure.

Source: *World Values Survey* (1994).

Sources: Katz (1986), Weidenbaum (1991), Jensen, Eggebeen, & Lichter (1993), Shapiro (1995), Church (1996), Murray (1996), Broder (1997), Dervarics (1998), and Jones (1999a).

SUMMARY

1. Social stratification in the United States involves inequality of many kinds, including income, wealth, and power.
2. White-collar jobs generally offer greater income and prestige than blue-collar work. Many of the jobs typically held by women offer little social prestige or income.
3. Schooling is also a resource that is distributed unequally. More than 80 percent of people over age twenty-five complete high school, but only one-quarter are college graduates.
4. From birth, family ancestry, race and ethnicity, gender, and religion all affect a person's social position.
5. The upper class (5 percent of the population) includes the richest and most powerful families. Most members of the upper-upper class, or the old rich, inherit their wealth; the lower-upper class, or the new rich, amass wealth from high incomes.
6. The middle class (40 to 45 percent) enjoys financial security, but only some of these people (the upper-middle class) have substantial wealth.
7. With below-average incomes, most members of the working class or lower-middle class (33 percent) have blue-collar jobs, and only one-third of their children reach college.
8. About one-fifth of the U.S. population belongs to the lower class: people living at or below the government's poverty threshold. People of African and Hispanic descent, as well as women, are disproportionately represented in the lower class.
9. Social class shapes our lives, including health, attitudes, and patterns of family living.
10. Some social mobility is common in the United States, as it is in other industrial societies; typically, however, only small changes occur from one generation to the next.
11. The growing global economy has increased the wealth of rich families in the United States, but stalled or even lowered the standard of living of low-income families.
12. The government classifies 34.5 million people as poor. About 40 percent of the poor are children under the age of eighteen. Two-thirds of the poor are white, but African Americans and Hispanics are disproportionately represented among people with low income. The feminization of poverty means more poor families are headed by women.
13. The culture of poverty thesis suggests that poverty is caused by shortcomings in the poor themselves. Others believe that poverty is caused by society's unequal distribution of jobs and wealth.
14. Our cultural emphasis on individual responsibility helps explain why public assistance for the poor has long been controversial.

KEY CONCEPTS

income (p. 272) wages or salary from work and earnings from investments

wealth (p. 273) the total value of money and other assets, minus outstanding debts

intragenerational social mobility (p. 283) a change in social position occurring during a person's lifetime

intergenerational social mobility (p. 283) upward or downward social mobility of children in relation to their parents

relative poverty (p. 286) the deprivation of some people in relation to those who have more

absolute poverty (p. 286) a deprivation of resources that is life threatening

feminization of poverty (p. 289) the trend by which women represent an increasing proportion of the poor

CRITICAL-THINKING QUESTIONS

1. Assess your own social class. Does your family have the same standing on various dimensions of social stratification (such as income, education, and occupational prestige)?
2. Why do you think many people in the United States find talking about their own social position awkward?
3. Would you be in favor of class-based affirmative action? That is, should our society give people born to lower-class families an edge in college admission and company hiring? Why or why not?
4. Our society is always ready to assist the "worthy" poor, including elderly people, who we do not expect to fend for themselves. At the same time, we have been less generous toward the "unworthy poor," able-bodied people who, we think, could take care of themselves but do not. If this is so, why do you think we have not done more to reduce poverty among children, who surely fall into the "worthy" category?

APPLICATIONS AND EXERCISES

1. Develop several simple questions that, taken together, would let you measure someone's social class position. The trick is to decide exactly what you think social class really means. Then try your questions on several adults, refining the questions as you proceed.
2. During an evening of television viewing, assess the social class level of the characters you see in various shows. In each case, explain why you place someone in a particular social position. What patterns do you find?
3. Visit the social services office that oversees financial assistance to people with low incomes in your community. See what you can learn about the effect of the 1996 welfare reforms.
4. Install the CD-ROM packaged in the back of this new textbook to access a variety of study, review, and applications exercises designed to help you better understand the material covered in this chapter. The CD includes an author's tip video, as well as interactive maps, video application exercises, Web links, and study questions.

SITES TO SEE

http://www.prenhall.com/macionis

Visit the interactive Web site that accompanies this text. Begin by clicking on the cover of your book. You will find a chapter-by-chapter study guide, practice tests, chat room, and many suggested Web links.

http://www.census.gov/datamap/www/
http://www.bea.doc.gov

These two government sites, the first run by the Census Bureau and the second by the Bureau of Economic Analysis, provide state-by-state and county-by-county income data. Visit these sites and see what you can learn about the social standing in your part of the country.

http://www.ssc.wisc.edu/irp
http://www.jcpr.org
http://www.nber.org

Here are three Web sites that are worth a visit to learn more about poverty in the United States. The first is operated by the Institute for Research on Poverty; the second by the Joint Center for Poverty Research; and the third by the National Bureau of Economic Research.

http://www.researchforum.org
http://www.childrensdefense.org/states/data.html

In the United States, children are at a high risk of poverty. The two sites noted above introduce you to the National Center on Children in Poverty and the Children's Defense Fund, both of which are concerned with child poverty.

http://www.iwpr.org

The Institute for Women's Policy Research investigates the interplay of gender and poverty.

CHAPTER 12

Juan O'Gorman (1905–1982)
The March of Loyalty
(*La marcha de la lealdad*)

Detail, mural, Museo Nacional de Historia, Castillo de Chapultepec, Mexico City, Mexico. Schalkwij/Art Resource, NY. © Juan O'Gorman. Kindly lent by Americo Arte Editores.

GLOBAL STRATIFICATION

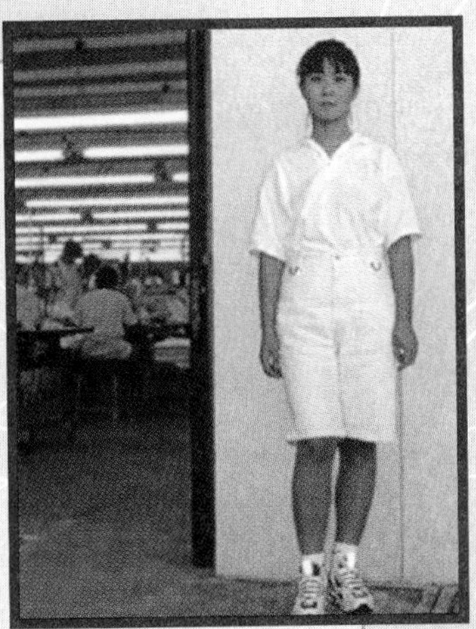

"I am going to America!" Twenty-six-year-old Li Li was elated. It was the chance of a lifetime—to leave the poverty of China and start a new life in the United States. A Chinese clothing company had promised Li Li a job if she would agree to pay a $2,800 "recruitment fee" to cover her transportation to "American soil."

Amid great excitement, Li Li and hundreds of other poor people sailed from China. But two days later, the ship docked and Li Li stepped off not in California but Saipan, the largest of the Northern Mariana Islands, some 1,500 miles southeast of her homeland. Technically speaking, Saipan is "American soil" because the islands are a U.S. territory. Li Li's dream soon became a nightmare. The company put her to work for eighteen hours a day cutting fabric in their clothing factory. At night, she and 700 other workers were herded into the company's rat-infested barracks where they shared just twelve toilets. Guards patrolled the borders of the camp, giving people only one hour of freedom on Sundays.

At about two dollars an hour, Li Li soon realized that she would have to work many months under these terrible conditions just to pay off her "loan." This system of "indentured service," common in poor countries around the world, comes very close to out-and-out slavery.

How did such a system come into existence in a place that flies the flag of the United States of America? In 1975, the United States granted the Northern Marianas control of their labor practices because local officials claimed only their direct control would keep out low-wage foreign workers. But the opposite happened, and today 40,000 workers imported from China, South Korea, the Philippines, and Bangladesh make up 90 percent of the islands' labor force. The Chinese and South Korean factories that operate there make millions of dollars exporting clothing to retail stores here in the states—familiar brands with a "MADE IN THE USA" label. For Li Li and thousands of workers like her, this story has no happy ending (adapted from McCarthy, 1998).

The fact is that billions of people in the world who work hard every day are miserably poor. As this chapter explains, although poverty is a reality in the United States, the problem is both more severe and more widespread in the poor countries of the world.

GLOBAL STRATIFICATION: AN OVERVIEW

Chapter 11 ("Social Class in the United States") described social inequality in the United States. In global perspective, however, social stratification is far more pronounced.

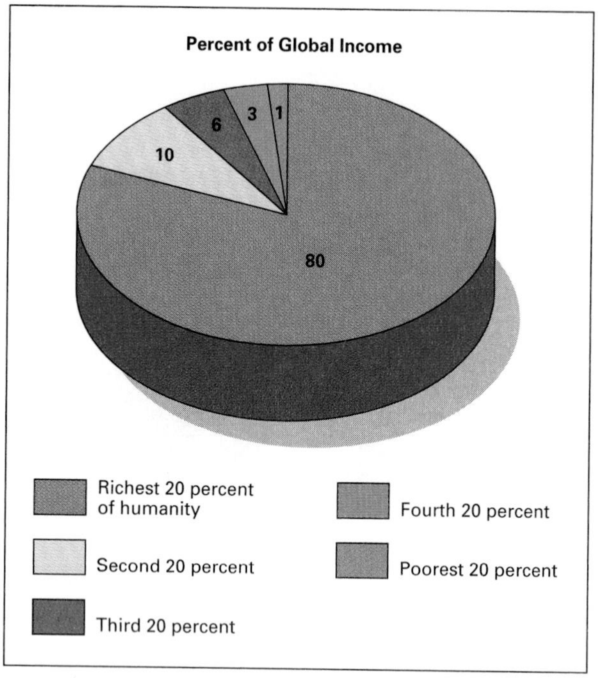

FIGURE 12–1 Distribution of World Income

Source: United Nations Development Programme (1998).

Figure 12–1 divides the world's total income by fifths of the population. Recall that the richest 20 percent of the U.S. population earns about 47 percent of the national income (see Figure 11–1). The richest 20 percent of global population, however, receives about 80 percent of world income. At the other extreme, the poorest 20 percent of the U.S. population earns 4 percent of our national income, but the poorest fifth of the world's people struggles to survive on just 1 percent of global income.

Because global income is so concentrated, even people in the United States with incomes below the government's poverty line live far better than the majority of the earth's people. The average person living in a rich nation such as the United States is quite well-off by world standards. At the very top of the pyramid, the wealth of the world's three richest *individuals* roughly equals the annual economic output of the world's forty-eight poorest *countries* (Annan, 1998).

A WORD ABOUT TERMINOLOGY

A familiar model for describing global stratification, developed after World War II, labeled rich, industrial countries the "First World," less industrialized, socialist countries the "Second World," and nonindustrialized, poor countries the "Third World." Today, however, the "Three Worlds" model is less useful. For one thing, it was a product of cold war politics by which the capitalist West (the First World) faced off against the socialist East (the Second World), while other nations (the Third World) remained more or less on the sidelines. But the sweeping changes in Eastern Europe and the collapse of the former Soviet Union mean that a distinctive Second World no longer exists.

A second problem is that the "Three Worlds" model lumped together more than 100 countries as the Third World. In reality, some relatively better-off nations of the Third World (such as Chile in South America) have fifteen times the per-person productivity of the poorest countries of the world (including Ethiopia in East Africa).

These facts call for a modestly revised system of classification. Here, we define *high-income countries* as the richest forty nations with the highest overall standard of living. The world's ninety *middle-income countries* are somewhat poorer, with economic development more or less typical of the world as a whole. The remaining sixty *low-income countries* have the lowest productivity and the most severe and extensive poverty.

This new model has two advantages over the older "Three Worlds" system. First, it focuses on economic development rather than whether societies are capitalist or socialist. Second, it gives a better picture of the relative economic development of various countries because it does not lump together all less industrialized nations into a single "Third World."

Still, classifying the 191 nations on earth into any three categories ignores many striking differences. These nations have rich and varied histories, speak different languages, and take pride in their distinctive cultures.

Keep in mind, too, that every country is also internally stratified. Thus, the extent of global inequality is actually greater than national comparisons suggest, since the most well-off people in rich countries (such as the United States) live worlds apart from the poorest people in low-income countries (such as Haiti, Sudan, and India).

HIGH-INCOME COUNTRIES

High-income nations are rich because they were the first to be transformed by the Industrial Revolution more than two centuries ago. To understand the power of industrialization, consider that the small European nation of Holland is more productive than the vast continent of Africa south of the Sahara Desert; likewise, tiny Belgium outproduces all of India.

When natural disasters strike high-income countries, such as Hurricane Andrew that devasted much of southern Florida in 1992, property loss is great but the loss of life is low. In low-income countries, by contrast, the converse is true; the death toll from Hurricane Mitch's rampage through Honduras in 1998 reached 5,000.

A look back at Global Map 1–1 on page 8 identifies the forty high-income countries of the world. They include the United States and Canada, most of the nations of Western Europe, Japan, Singapore, Hong Kong (now part of the People's Republic of China), Australia, and New Zealand.

Taken together, countries with the most developed economies cover roughly 25 percent of the earth's land area—including parts of five continents—and lie mostly in the Northern Hemisphere. In 2000, the population of these nations was slightly more than 900 million, or 15 percent of the earth's people. About three-fourths of the people in high-income countries live in or near cities.

Significant cultural differences exist among high-income countries—the nations of Europe, for example, recognize more than thirty official languages. But these societies share an industrial capacity that generates, on average, a rich material life for their people. Per capita income ranges from about \$11,000 annually (in Argentina and Slovenia) to more than \$25,000 annually (in the United States and Switzerland).[1] In fact, people in high-income countries enjoy more than half the world's total income.

Production in rich nations is capital-intensive, that is, it is based on factories, big machinery, and advanced technology. High-income countries also stand at the forefront of the Information Revolution, with most of the largest corporations that design and market computers, as well as most computer users. In addition, high-income countries control the world's financial markets, so that daily events on the financial exchanges of New York, London, and Tokyo affect people throughout the world.

MIDDLE-INCOME COUNTRIES

In middle-income countries, per capita income ranges between \$2,500 and \$10,000, roughly the median for the world's *nations* (but above that for the world's *people*, since most people live in the poorest countries). Industrialization is limited and exists mostly in cities. About half the people still live in rural areas and work in agriculture. Especially in the countryside, schooling, medical care, adequate housing, and even safe water are hard to come by.

Looking back at Global Map 1–1 (on page 8), we see that about ninety of the world's nations fall into the middle-income category. At the high end are Venezuela (Latin America), Slovakia (Europe), and Malaysia (Asia), where annual income is about \$8,500. At the low

[1]High-income countries have per capita annual income of at least \$10,000. For middle- and low-income countries, the comparable figures are \$2,500 to \$10,000 and \$2,500 and less. All data reflect the United Nations' concept of "purchasing power parities," which avoids distortion caused by exchange rates when converting currencies to U.S. dollars. Instead, the data represent the local purchasing power of each nation's currency.

Japan represents the world's high-income countries, in which industrial technology and economic expansion have produced material prosperity. The presence of market forces is evident in this view of downtown Tokyo (above, left). The Russian Federation represents the middle-income countries of the world. Industrial development and economic performance were sluggish under socialism; as a result, Moscow residents had to wait in long lines for their daily needs (above, right). The hope is that the introduction of a market system will raise living standards, although in the short run, Russian citizens must adjust to increasing economic disparity. Bangladesh (left) represents the world's low-income countries. As the photograph suggests, these nations have limited economic development and rapidly increasing populations. The result is widespread poverty.

end are Guyana (Latin America), Latvia (Europe), Swaziland (Africa), and China (Asia) with roughly $3,000 annually in per capita income.

One cluster of middle-income countries includes the former Soviet Union and the nations of Eastern Europe (in the past, known as the Second World). These countries had mostly socialist economies until popular revolts between 1989 and 1991 swept aside their governments. Since then, these nations have begun to introduce market systems, but so far, the results have been uneven. Some (including Slovakia) have improving economies, while living standards in others (including Russia) have actually fallen.

A second category of less developed countries are the oil-producing nations of the Middle East (or, less ethnocentrically, western Asia). These nations—including Saudi Arabia, Oman, and Iran—are very rich, but their wealth is so concentrated that most people do not benefit and remain poor.

The third, and largest, category of middle-income nations includes Venezuela and Brazil in South America and Algeria and Botswana in Africa. Although South Africa's white minority lives as well as people in the United States, the country is considered less developed because its majority black population has far less income.

Taken together, middle-income countries span roughly 40 percent of the earth's land area and include upwards of 2 billion people, or one-third of humanity. Some countries (like El Salvador) are far more crowded than others (like Russia), but compared to high-income countries, these societies are densely populated.

LOW-INCOME COUNTRIES

Low-income countries, where most people are very poor, are primarily agrarian societies with little industry. Most of these sixty nations, identified in Global Map 1–1, are found in Central and East Africa as well

By and large, rich nations such as the United States wrestle with the problem of relative poverty, meaning that poor people get by with less than we think they should have. In poor countries such as Ethiopia, absolute poverty means that people lack what they need to survive. What kind of diet, medical care, and access to clean water do you think families like this one have?

as Asia. Low-income countries cover 35 percent of the planet's land area but are home to half its people. Population density is, therefore, generally high, although greater in Asian countries (such as Bangladesh and India) than in Central African nations (like Chad and the Democratic Republic of the Congo).

In poor countries, barely 25 percent of the people live in cities; most inhabit villages and farms, as their families have for centuries. In fact, half the world's people are peasants, and by and large, they closely follow the folkways of their ancestors. Without industrial technology, peasants are not very productive, one reason many endure severe poverty. Hunger, disease, and unsafe housing frame the lives of the world's poorest people.

People living in affluent nations such as the United States find it hard to grasp the scope of human want in much of the world. From time to time, televised pictures of famine in very poor countries such as Ethiopia and Bangladesh give us a shocking glimpse of the poverty that makes every day a life-and-death struggle. Behind these images lie cultural, historical, and economic forces that we shall explore in the remainder of this chapter.

GLOBAL WEALTH AND POVERTY

October 14, 1994, Manila, the Philippines. What caught my eye was how clean she was—a girl no more than seven or eight years old. She was wearing a freshly laundered dress, and her hair was carefully combed. She followed us with her eyes: Camera-toting Americans stand out in this neighborhood, one of the poorest in the entire world.

Fed by methane from decomposing garbage, the fires never go out on Smokey Mountain, the vast garbage dump on the north side of Manila. Smoke envelopes the hills of refuse like a thick fog. But Smokey Mountain is more than a dump; it is a neighborhood that is home to thousands of people. The residents of Smokey Mountain are the poorest of the poor. It is hard to imagine a setting more hostile to human life. Amid the smoke and the squalor, men and women do what they can to survive. They pick plastic bags from the garbage and wash them in the river and collect cardboard boxes or anything else they can sell. And all over Smokey Mountain are children who must already sense the enormous odds against them. What chance do they have, living in families that earn scarcely a few hundred dollars a year? With barely any opportunity for schooling? Year after year, breathing this air?

TABLE 12–1 Wealth and Well-Being in Global Perspective, 1997

Country	Gross Domestic Product ($ billion)	GDP per Capita (PPP$)*	Quality of Life Index
High Income			
Canada	608	22,480	.932
Norway	153	24,450	.927
United States	7,834	29,010	.927
Japan	4,190	24,070	.924
Sweden	228	19,790	.923
Australia	394	20,210	.922
France	1,393	22,030	.918
United Kingdom	1,287	20,730	.918
South Korea	443	13,590	.852
Middle Income			
Eastern Europe			
Poland	136	6,520	.802
Hungary	46	7,200	.795
Lithuania	10	4,220	.761
Russian Federation	447	4,370	.747
Latin America			
Venezuela	88	8,860	.792
Mexico	403	8,370	.786
Brazil	820	6,480	.739
Asia			
Malaysia	99	8,140	.768
Thailand	154	6,690	.753
China, P.R.	902	3,130	.701
Middle East			
Oman	...	9,960	.725
Iran	...	5,817	.715
Africa			
Algeria	47	4,460	.665
Botswana	5	7,690	.609
Low Income			
Latin America			
Honduras	5	2,220	.641
Haiti	3	1,270	.430
Asia			
India	382	1,670	.545
Bangladesh	41	1,050	.440
Africa			
Democratic Republic of the Congo	6	880	.479
Guinea	4	1,880	.398
Ethiopia	6	510	.298
Sierra Leone	1	410	.254

* These data are the United Nations' new "purchasing power parity" calculations that avoid currency rate distortion by showing the local purchasing power of each domestic currency.

Source: United Nations Development Programme, *Human Development Report, 1999* (New York: Oxford University Press, 1999).

Against this backdrop of human tragedy, one lovely little girl has put on a fresh dress and gone out to play. . . .

Now our taxi driver threads his way through heavy traffic as we head for the other side of Manila. The change is amazing: The smoke and smell of the dump give way to neighborhoods that could be in Miami or Los Angeles. On the bay in the distance floats a cluster of yachts. No more rutted streets; now we glide quietly along wide boulevards lined with trees and filled with expensive Japanese cars. We pass shopping plazas, upscale hotels, and high-rise office buildings. Every block or so we see the gated entrance to an exclusive residential enclave with security guards standing watch. Here, in large, air-conditioned homes, the rich of Manila live and many of the poor work.

Low-income nations are home to some rich and many poor people. For most, incomes of barely several hundred dollars a year mean the burden of poverty is far greater than among the poor of the United States. This does not mean that poverty here at home is a minor problem. In so rich a country, too little food, substandard housing, and no medical care for tens of millions of people—almost half of them children—amount to a national tragedy. Yet poverty in poor countries is both *more severe* and *more extensive* than in the United States.

THE SEVERITY OF POVERTY

Poverty in poor countries is more severe than it is in rich countries. The data in Table 12–1 show why. The first column of figures gives gross domestic product (GDP) for representative high-, middle-, and low-income countries.[2] A large, industrial nation like the United States

[2]Gross domestic product (GDP) includes all the goods and services on record as produced by a country's economy in a given year, excluding income earned outside the country by individuals or corporations. Gross national product (GNP) adds in the foreign earnings. For countries that invest heavily abroad (Kuwait, for example), GDP is much smaller than GNP; for countries in which other nations invest heavily (Hong Kong), GDP is much greater than GNP. For countries that both invest heavily abroad and have high foreign investment at home (including the United States), the two measures are about the same.

had a 1997 GDP of nearly $8 trillion; Japan's GDP was about $4 trillion. Comparing GDP figures shows that the world's richest nations are thousands of times more productive than the poorest countries.

The second column of figures in Table 12–1 indicates per capita GDP in terms of what the United Nations (1995) calls "purchasing power parities"—what people can buy using their income in the local economy. The per capita GDP for rich countries like the United States, France, and Canada is very high—exceeding $20,000. For middle-income countries, such as Brazil and Poland, the figures are much lower—in the $6,500 range. In the world's low-income countries, per capita annual income is just a few hundred dollars. In the Democratic Republic of the Congo or Ethiopia, for example, a typical person labors all year to make what the average worker in the United States earns in several days.

The last column of Table 12–1 measures quality of life in these nations. This index, calculated by the United Nations, is based on income, education (extent of adult literacy and average years of schooling), and longevity (how long people typically live). Index values are decimals that fall between hypothetical extremes of 1 (highest) and zero (lowest). By this calculation, Canadians enjoy the highest quality of life (.932), with residents of the United States close behind (.927). At the other extreme, people in the African nations of Ethiopia and Sierra Leone have the lowest quality of life (.298 and .254, respectively).

A key reason that quality of life differs so much around the world is that economic productivity is lowest in precisely the regions of the globe where population growth is highest. Figure 12–2 shows the division of global population and global income for countries at each level of economic development. High-income countries are by far the most advantaged, with 55 percent of global income supporting just 15 percent of humanity. In middle-income nations, 33 percent of the world's people earn 37 percent of global income. This leaves half of the planet's population with just 8 percent of global income. In short, for every dollar received by individuals in a low-income country, someone in a high-income nation takes home $28.

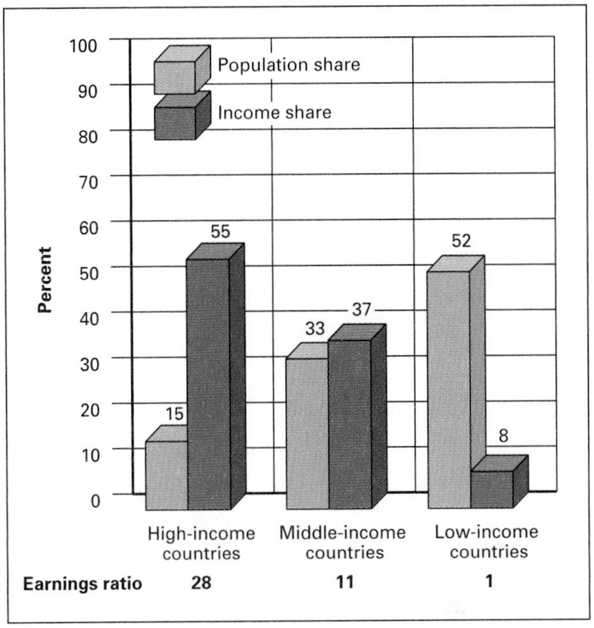

FIGURE 12–2 **The Relative Share of Income and Population by Level of Economic Development**

Relative versus Absolute Poverty

The distinction between relative and absolute poverty, made in the last chapter, has an important application to global inequality. People living in rich countries generally focus on *relative poverty*, meaning that some people lack resources that are taken for granted by others. Relative poverty, by definition, cuts across every society, rich or poor.

More important in global perspective, however, is *absolute poverty*, a lack of resources that is life threatening. Human beings in absolute poverty lack the nutrition necessary for health and long-term survival. To be sure, some absolute poverty exists in the United States. But such immediately life-threatening poverty strikes only a small proportion of the U.S. population; in low-income countries, by contrast, one-third or more of the people are in desperate need.

Since absolute poverty is deadly, one global indicator of this problem is median age at death. Global Map 12–1 on page 306 identifies the age by which half of all people born in a nation die. In rich societies, most people die after the age of seventy-five; in poor countries, half of all deaths occur among children under the age of ten.

THE EXTENT OF POVERTY

Poverty in poor countries is more extensive than it is in rich nations such as the United States. Chapter 11 ("Social Class in the United States") indicated that the U.S.

WINDOW ON THE WORLD

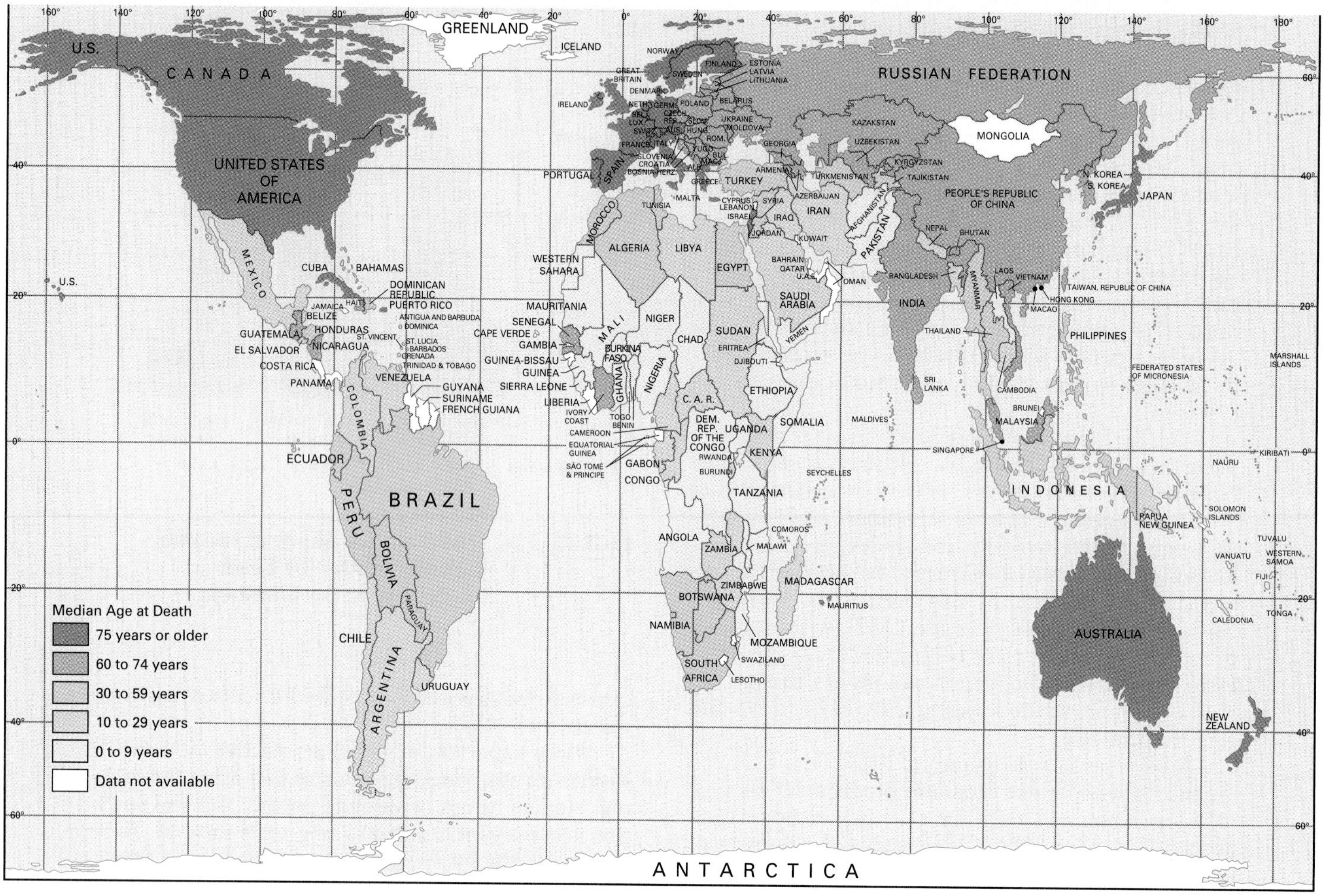

GLOBAL MAP 12–1 Median Age at Death in Global Perspective

This map identifies the age below which half of all deaths occur in any year. In the high-income countries of the world, including the United States, it is mostly the elderly who face death—that is, people age seventy-five or older. In middle-income countries, including most of Latin America, most people die years or even decades earlier. In low-income countries, especially in Africa and parts of Asia, it is children who die, half of them never reaching their tenth birthday.

Sources: The World Bank (1993); map projection from *Peters Atlas of the World* (1990).

government officially classifies about 13 percent of the population as poor. In low-income countries, however, most people live no better than the poor in the United States, and many are far worse off. As Global Map 12–1 shows, the high death rates among children in Africa indicate that absolute poverty is greatest there, where half the population is malnourished. In the world as a whole, at any given time, 15 percent of the people (about 1 billion) suffer from chronic hunger, which leaves them less able to work and puts them at high risk of disease (Kates, 1996; United Nations Development Programme, 1999).

Brazil's Rio de Janeiro is known the world over as a spectacular resort city. The other side of Rio is poverty, which forces thousands of children and young people to live on the streets. These young people are vulnerable to hunger, disease, and violence. Here a seventeen-year-old victim of a gunshot lies dead in the streets in the Lapa district near the center of Rio.

The typical adult in a rich nation, such as the United States, consumes about 3,500 calories a day, an excess that contributes to obesity and related health problems. The typical adult in a low-income country not only does more physical labor but consumes just 2,000 calories a day. The result is undernourishment: too little food or not enough of the right kinds of food.

In the ten minutes it takes to read this section of the chapter, about 300 people in the world who are sick and weakened from hunger will die. This amounts to about 40,000 people a day, or 15 million people each year. Clearly, easing world hunger is one of the most serious responsibilities facing humanity today.

POVERTY AND CHILDREN

Death comes early in poor societies, where families lack adequate food, safe water, secure housing, and access to medical care. Organizations combating child poverty estimate that at least 100 million city children in poor countries beg, steal, sell sex, or work for drug gangs to provide income for their families. Such a life almost always means dropping out of school and puts children at high risk of disease and violence. Many girls, with little or no access to medical assistance, become pregnant: a case of children, who cannot support themselves, being forced to have still more children.

About 100 million of the world's children leave their families altogether, sleeping and living on the streets as best they can. Nearly half of all street children are found in Latin America (One World, 1998). Some 10,000 homeless children roam throughout Mexico City alone (Ross, 1996). In Brazil, millions of street children live in makeshift huts, under bridges, or in alleyways. In Rio de Janeiro, known to many in the United States as Brazil's seaside resort, police try to keep the numbers of street children in check; at times, death squads may sweep through a neighborhood in a bloody ritual of "urban cleansing." Several hundred street children are murdered in that city each year (Larmer, 1992; U.S. House of Representatives, 1992).

POVERTY AND WOMEN

In rich societies, the work women do is typically unrecognized, undervalued, and underpaid. In poor societies, this is even more the case. Workers in the sweatshops found in poor countries—including Li Li, whose eighteen-hour days were described in the opening to this chapter—are mostly women.

Families in poor societies depend on women's income. At the same time, tradition bars many women from attending school, and gives them primary responsibility for child rearing and maintaining the household. The United Nations estimates that, in poor countries, men own 90 percent of the land, a far greater gender disparity in wealth than that in industrial nations. Thus, about 70 percent of the world's 1 billion

GLOBAL SNAPSHOT

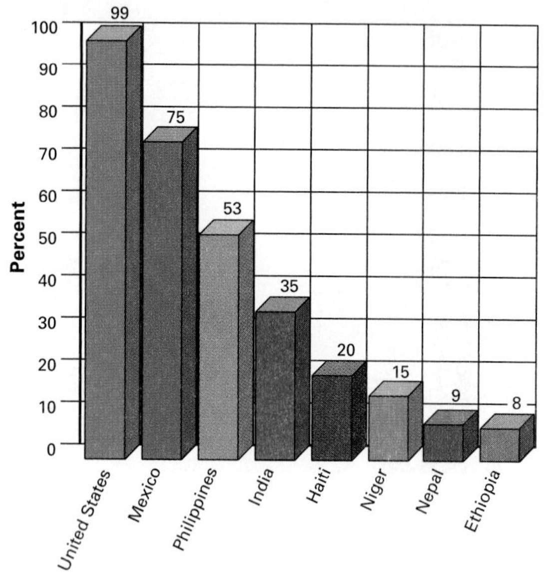

FIGURE 12–3 Percentage of Births Attended by Trained Health Personnel

Source: The World Bank (1999).

people living near absolute poverty are women (Hymowitz, 1995).

Women in poor countries have limited access to birth control (which raises the birth rate), and they typically give birth without the assistance of any trained health personnel. Figure 12–3 draws a stark contrast between high- and low-income countries in this regard.

SLAVERY

Poor societies are vulnerable to many problems: hunger, illiteracy, warfare, and slavery. The British Empire banned slavery in 1833; the United States followed suit in 1865. But, according to Anti-Slavery International (ASI), as many as 400 million men, women, and children (almost 7 percent of humanity) live today in conditions that amount to slavery (Janus, 1996).

ASI distinguishes four types of slavery. In *chattel slavery*, one person owns another. The number of chattel slaves is difficult to estimate because this practice is against the law almost everywhere. Nevertheless, the buying and selling of slaves still takes place in many countries in Asia, the Middle East, and, especially, in Africa. The box describes the reality of one slave's life in the African nation of Mauritania.

A second, more common form of bondage is *child slavery*. Desperately poor families let their children take to the streets to fend for themselves. Perhaps 100 million children—many in poor countries of Latin America—fall into this category.

Third, *debt bondage* refers to the practice by which employers hold workers by paying them too little to cover their debts. In this case, workers receive wages, but not enough to cover the food and housing provided by an employer. Thus, for practical purposes, they are enslaved. The story of Li Li working in Saipan, which opened this chapter, is an example of debt bondage.

Fourth, *servile forms of marriage* may also amount to slavery. In India, Thailand, and some African nations, families marry off women against their will. Many end up as slaves working for their husband's family; some are forced into prostitution.

In 1948, the United Nations issued its Universal Declaration of Human Rights, which states: "No one shall be held in slavery or servitude; slavery and the slave trade shall be prohibited in all their forms." Unfortunately, more than fifty years later, this social evil persists.

CORRELATES OF GLOBAL POVERTY

What accounts for severe and extensive poverty throughout much of the world? The rest of this chapter weaves together explanations from the following facts about poor societies.

1. **Technology.** Almost two-thirds of people in low-income countries farm the land using human muscle or beasts of burden. Since these energy sources fall far short of the force of steam, oil, or nuclear power, there is little use of complex machinery.
2. **Population growth.** As Chapter 22 ("Population, Urbanization, and Environment") explains, the poorest countries have the world's highest birth rates. Despite the death toll from poverty, the populations of poor countries in Africa, for example, double every twenty-five years. In these countries, half the people are teenagers or younger. With such numbers entering their childbearing years, a wave of population growth will roll into the future. In recent years, for example, the population of Swaziland swelled by

GLOBAL SOCIOLOGY

"God Made Me to Be a Slave"

Fatma Mint Mamadou is a young woman living in North Africa's Islamic Republic of Mauritania. Asked her age, she pauses and smiles. She has no idea when she was born. Nor can she read or write. What she knows is tending camels, herding sheep, hauling bags of water, sweeping, and serving tea to her owners. This young woman is one of perhaps 90,000 slaves in Mauritania.

In the central region of this nation, having dark brown skin almost always means being a slave to an Arab owner. Fatma accepts her situation; she has known nothing else. She explains in a matter-of-fact voice that she is a slave as was her mother before her. And her grandmother before that. "Just as God created a camel to be a camel," she shrugs, "he created me to be a slave."

Fatma, her mother, and her brothers and sisters live in a squatter settlement on the edge of Nauakchott, Mauritania's capital city. Their home is a nine-by-twelve-foot hut that they built from wood scraps and other materials taken from construction sites. The roof is nothing more than a piece of cloth; there is no plumbing, not even any furniture. The nearest water comes from a well a mile down the road.

In this region, slavery began 500 years ago, about the time Columbus sailed west toward the New World. Then, as Arab and Berber tribes moved across the region spreading Islam, they raided local villages and made slaves of the people. So it has been for dozens of generations ever since. In 1905, the French colonial rulers of Mauritania banned slavery. After the nation gained independence in 1961, the new government banned slavery once again. But such proclamations have done little to change strong traditions. Indeed, people like Fatma have no idea what freedom to choose means.

The next question is more personal: "Are you and other girls ever raped?" Again, Fatma hesitates. With no hint of emotion, she responds, "Of course, in the night the men come to breed us. Is that what you mean by rape?"

Human slavery continues to exist in the twenty-first century.

Source: Based on Burkett (1997).

3.2 percent annually, so that even with economic development living standards have fallen.

3. **Cultural patterns.** Poor societies are usually traditional. Adhering to long-established ways of life, people resist innovations—even those that promise a richer material life. The box on page 310 explains why traditional people in India respond to their poverty differently than poor people in the United States.
4. **Social stratification.** Low-income societies distribute their wealth very unequally. Chapter 10 ("Social Stratification") explained that social inequality is more pronounced in agrarian societies than in industrial societies. In Brazil, for example, half of all farmland is owned by just 1 percent of the people (Bergamo & Camarotti, 1996).
5. **Gender inequality.** Extreme gender inequality in poor societies deprives women of opportunities, which typically means they have many children. An expanding population, in turn, slows economic development. Thus, many analysts conclude, raising living standards in much of the world depends on improving the social standing of women.
6. **Global power relationships.** A final cause of global poverty lies in the relationships among the nations of the world. Historically, wealth flowed from poor societies to rich nations through **colonialism,** *the process by which some nations enrich themselves through political and economic control of other nations.* The countries of Western Europe colonized much of Latin America and Africa beginning roughly 500 years ago. Such

GLOBAL SOCIOLOGY

A Different Kind of Poverty: A Report from India

Most North Americans know that India is one of the poorest nations on earth. A vast country with per capita gross domestic product (GDP) of only $1,670 a year (see Table 12–1), India is home to one-third of all the world's hungry people.

But most North Americans do not readily understand the reality of poverty in India. Most of the country's 1 billion people live in conditions far worse than those our society labels "poor." A traveler's first experience of Indian life can be shocking. Madras, for example, one of India's largest cities with 7 million inhabitants, seems chaotic to an outsider—streets choked by motorbikes, trucks, carts pulled by oxen, and waves of people. Along the roadway, vendors sit on burlap cloth and hawk fruits, vegetables, and cooked food while people nearby work, talk, bathe, and sleep.

Madras is dotted with thousands of shanty settlements, home to half a million people from rural villages who have come in search of a better life. Shantytowns are clusters of huts built with branches, leaves, and pieces of discarded cardboard and tin. These dwellings offer little privacy and lack refrigeration, running water, and bathrooms. A visitor from the United States may feel uneasy in such an area, knowing that the poorest sections of our own inner cities seethe with frustration and sometimes explode with violence.

But India's people understand poverty differently than we do. No restless young men hang out on corners, no drug dealers work the streets, and there is little danger of violence. In the United States, poverty often means anger and isolation; in India, even shanty towns are organized around strong families—children, parents, and often grandparents—who offer a smile and a welcome to a stranger.

For traditional people in India, life is shaped by *dharma*, the Hindu concept of duty and destiny that teaches people to accept their fate, whatever it may be. Mother Teresa, who worked among the poorest of India's people, went to the heart of the cultural differences: "Americans have angry poverty," she explained. "In India, there is worse poverty, but it is a happy poverty."

Perhaps we should not describe anyone who clings to the edge of survival as happy. But poverty in India is eased by the strength and support of families and communities, a sense that existence has a purpose, and a world view that encourages each person to accept whatever life offers. As a result, a visitor may well come away from a first encounter with Indian poverty in confusion: "How can people be so poor, and yet apparently content, active, and *joyful*?"

Source: Based on the author's research in Madras, India, November 1988.

global exploitation of resources allowed some nations to develop economically at the expense of other nations.

Although 130 former colonies gained their independence during the twentieth century, exploitation continues through **neocolonialism** (*neo* is the Greek word for "new"), *a new form of global power relationships that involves not direct political control but economic exploitation by multinational corporations.* **Multinational corporations**—*huge businesses that operate in many countries*—wield tremendous economic power. Corporate decision makers can impose their will on countries where they do business to create favorable economic conditions, just as colonizers did in the past.

In rich nations such as the United States, most parents expect their children to enjoy years of childhood, largely free from the responsibilities of adult life. This is not the case in poor nations across Latin America, Africa, and Asia. Poor families depend on whatever income their children can earn, and many children as young as six or seven work full days weaving or performing other kinds of manual labor. Child labor lies behind the low prices of many products imported for sale in this country.

GLOBAL STRATIFICATION: THEORETICAL ANALYSIS

There are two major explanations for the unequal distribution of the world's wealth and power—*modernization theory* and *dependency theory*. Each theory suggests a different path toward relieving the suffering of hungry people in much of the world.

MODERNIZATION THEORY

Modernization theory is *a model of economic and social development that explains global inequality in terms of technological and cultural differences among societies*. Modernization theory emerged in the 1950s, a time when U.S. society was fascinated with new technology and many people in poor countries were hostile toward the United States. With the socialist Soviet Union gaining influence abroad, U.S. policy makers drafted a foreign policy that was pro-market and has been with us ever since.[3]

Historical Perspective

Modernization theorists point out that as recently as several centuries ago, the entire world was poor. Because poverty is the norm throughout human history, it is *affluence* that demands an explanation.

Affluence came within reach of a growing share of people in Western Europe during the late Middle Ages as world exploration and trade expanded. Soon, the Industrial Revolution was underway, transforming first Western Europe and then North America. Industrial technology coupled with the spirit of capitalism created new wealth on an unprecedented scale. At the outset, this new wealth benefited only a few. But industrial technology was so productive that gradually the living standard of even the poorest people began to improve. The specter of absolute poverty, which had cast a menacing shadow over humanity, was finally being routed.

During the twentieth century, the standard of living in high-income countries, where the Industrial Revolution began, jumped at least fourfold. Many middle-income nations in Asia and Latin America are now industrializing, and they, too, are becoming richer. But, without industrial technology, low-income countries have changed little.

The Importance of Culture

Why didn't the Industrial Revolution sweep away poverty the world over? Modernization theory points out that not every society has been eager to seek out new technology. Doing so requires a cultural environment that emphasizes the benefits of materialism and innovation.

Modernization theory thus identifies *tradition* as the greatest barrier to economic development. In societies with strong family systems and a reverence for the past, "cultural inertia" discourages people from adopting new

[3]The following discussion of modernization theory draws primarily on Rostow (1960, 1978), Bauer (1981), and Berger (1986); see also Firebaugh (1996) and Firebaugh & Sandu (1998).

technologies that would raise their living standards. Even today, many people—from the North American Amish to Islamic people of Iran to the Semai of Malaysia—oppose technological advances as a threat to their family relationships, customs, and religious beliefs.

As Max Weber (1958; orig. 1904–5) explained, at the end of the Middle Ages, the cultural environment of Western Europe favored change. As discussed in Chapter 4 ("Society"), the Protestant Reformation had reshaped traditional Catholicism to generate a progress-oriented way of life. Wealth—regarded with suspicion by the Catholic church—became a sign of personal virtue, and the growing importance of individualism steadily replaced the traditional emphasis on kinship and community. Taken together, these new cultural patterns nurtured the Industrial Revolution, which propelled one segment of humanity from poverty to prosperity.

Rostow's Stages of Modernization

Modernization theory holds that the door to affluence is open to all. Indeed, as technological advances diffuse around the world, all societies should gradually industrialize. According to W. W. Rostow (1960, 1978), modernization occurs in four stages:

1. **Traditional stage.** Socialized to venerate the past, people in traditional societies cannot easily imagine how life could be different. Therefore, they build their lives around families and local communities and follow well-worn paths that allow for little individual freedom or change. Life is often spiritually rich but lacking in material abundance.

   A century ago, much of the world was in this initial stage of economic development. Nations such as Bangladesh, Niger, and Somalia are still at the traditional stage and remain impoverished.

2. **Take-off stage.** As a society shakes off the grip of tradition, people start to use their talents and imagination, sparking economic growth. A market emerges as people produce goods not just for their own consumption but in order to trade with others for profit. Greater individualism, a willingness to take risks, and a desire for material goods also take hold, often at the expense of family ties and time-honored norms and values.

   Great Britain reached take-off by about 1800, the United States by 1820. Thailand, a middle-income country in eastern Asia, is now at this stage. Rich nations can help poor countries reach take-off by supplying foreign aid, advanced technology, investment capital, and opportunities for schooling abroad.

3. **Drive to technological maturity.** During this stage, "growth" is a widely accepted concept that fuels a society's pursuit of higher living standards. A diversified economy drives a population eager to enjoy the benefits of industrial technology. At the same time, however, people begin to realize (and sometimes lament) that industrialization is eroding traditional family and local community life. Great Britain reached this point by about 1840, the United States by 1860. Today, Mexico, the U.S. territory of Puerto Rico, and South Korea are among the nations driving to technological maturity.

   Societies in stage three have greatly reduced absolute poverty. Cities swell with people who leave rural villages in search of economic opportunity; occupational specialization makes relationships less personal, and heightened individualism generates social movements demanding greater political rights. Societies approaching technological maturity also provide basic schooling for all their people and advanced training for some. The newly educated consider tradition "backward," opening the door to further change. The social position of women steadily becomes more equal to that of men. Even so, in the short term, the process of development may subject women to unexpected problems, as the box explains.

4. **High mass consumption.** Economic development steadily raises living standards, as industrial production stimulates mass consumption. Simply put, people soon learn to "need" the expanding array of goods that their society produces.

   The United States, Japan, and other rich nations moved into this stage by 1900. Now entering this level of economic development are two former British colonies that are prosperous small societies of eastern Asia: Hong Kong (part of the People's Republic of China) and Singapore (independent since 1965).

The Role of Rich Nations

Modernization theory claims that high-income countries play four important roles in global economic development:

GLOBAL SOCIOLOGY

Modernization and Women: A Report from Rural Bangladesh

In global perspective, gender inequality is greatest where people are poorest. Economic development, then, depends on giving women opportunities for schooling and work outside the home. In the process, birth rates decline and traditional male domination weakens.

But modernization also poses dangers for women. Investigating the lives of women in a poor, rural district of Bangladesh, Sultana Alam (1985) reports several hazards.

First, as economic opportunity draws men from rural areas to cities in search of work, women and children must fend for themselves. Some men sell their land and simply abandon their wives, who are left with nothing but their children.

Second, the diminishing strength of the family and neighborhood leaves women who are deserted by their husbands with little assistance. The same holds true for women who become single through divorce or the death of a spouse. In the past, Alam reports, kin or neighbors readily took in a Bangladeshi woman who found herself alone. Today, as Bangladesh struggles to advance economically, the number of households headed by women is increasing, and most are poor. Thus, rather than enhancing women's autonomy, Alam argues, a new spirit of individualism has lowered the social standing of women.

Third, economic development, as well as the growing influence of Western movies and mass media, undermine women's traditional roles as wives, sisters, and mothers, defining them instead as objects of sexual attention. A new cultural emphasis on sexuality now encourages men in poor countries to abandon their aging spouses for younger, more physically attractive partners. The same emphasis contributes to the world's rising level of prostitution.

Modernization, then, does not affect men and women in the same ways. In the long run, the evidence suggests, modernization gives the sexes more equal standing. In the short run, however, many women suffer economic setbacks as they face new problems virtually unknown in traditional societies.

In Rajshahi, Bangladesh, women meet to address their common problems.

Sources: Based on Alam (1985) and Mink (1989).

1. **Helping control population.** Since population growth is greatest in the poorest societies, rising population can overtake economic advances. Rich nations can help limit population growth by exporting birth control technology and promoting its use. Once economic development is underway, birth rates should decline, as they have in industrialized nations, because children are no longer an economic asset.
2. **Increasing food production.** Rich nations can export "high-tech" farming methods to poor nations and thus raise agricultural yields. Such techniques—collectively referred to as the "Green Revolution"—involve new hybrid seeds, modern irrigation methods, chemical fertilizers, and pesticides for insect control.
3. **Introducing industrial technology.** Rich nations can accelerate economic growth in poor societies by introducing machinery and information technology, which raise productivity. Industrialization also shifts the labor force from farming to skilled industrial and service jobs.

4. **Providing foreign aid.** Investment capital from rich nations can boost the prospects of poor societies striving to reach Rostow's "take-off" stage. Foreign aid can purchase fertilizer and fund irrigation projects, which increase agricultural productivity. Financial and technical assistance can also build power plants and factories to improve industrial output.

Critical evaluation. Modernization theory has many influential supporters among social scientists (Parsons, 1966; W. Moore, 1977, 1979; Bauer, 1981; Berger, 1986; Firebaugh & Beck, 1994; Firebaugh, 1996, 1999; Firebaugh & Sandu, 1998). Moreover, for decades it has shaped the foreign policy of the United States and other rich nations. Proponents point to rapid economic development in Asia—including South Korea, Taiwan, Singapore, and Hong Kong—as proof that the affluence that accompanied industrialization in Western Europe and North America is within reach of all countries.

But modernization theory comes under fire from socialist countries (and left-leaning analysts in the West) as a thinly veiled defense of capitalism. Its most serious flaw, according to critics, is that modernization simply has not occurred in many poor countries. The United Nations recently reported that living standards in a number of nations, including Haiti and Nicaragua in Latin America, and Sudan, Ghana, and Rwanda in Africa, are actually lower than in 1960 (United Nations Development Programme, 1996).

A second criticism of modernization theory is that it fails to recognize how rich nations, which benefit from the status quo, often block paths to development for poor countries. Centuries ago, critics charge, rich countries industrialized from a position of global *strength*. Can we expect poor countries today to do so from a position of global *weakness?*

Third, critics continue, modernization theory treats rich and poor societies as separate worlds, ignoring how international relations affect all nations. To begin with, it was colonization that boosted the fortunes of Europe. This economic windfall has left countries in Latin America and Asia reeling to this day.

Fourth, critics contend that modernization theory holds up the world's most developed countries as the standard for judging the rest of humanity, thus revealing an ethnocentric bias. We should remember that our Western conception of "progress" led us to degrade the physical environment throughout the world and to rush headlong into a competitive, materialistic way of life.

Fifth, and finally, modernization theory draws criticism for suggesting that the causes of global poverty lie almost entirely in the poor societies themselves. Critics see this analysis as little more than "blaming the victims" for their own plight. Instead, they argue, an analysis of global inequality should focus as much on the behavior of *rich* nations as poor nations (Wiarda, 1987).

Such concerns reflect a second major approach to understanding global inequality. This is dependency theory.

DEPENDENCY THEORY

Dependency theory is *a model of economic and social development that explains global inequality in terms of the historical exploitation of poor societies by rich ones.* This analysis puts primary responsibility for global poverty on rich nations. It holds that rich countries have systematically impoverished low-income countries, making poor nations *dependent* on rich ones. This destructive process extends back for centuries and persists today.

Historical Perspective

Everyone agrees that before the Industrial Revolution there was little affluence in the world. Dependency theory asserts, however, that people living in poor countries were actually better off economically in the past than their descendants are now. André Gunder Frank (1975), a noted proponent of this theory, argues that the colonial process that helped develop rich nations also *underdeveloped* poor societies.

Dependency theory is based on the idea that the economic positions of rich and poor nations of the world are linked and cannot be understood in isolation from one another. Poor nations are not simply lagging behind rich ones on the "path of progress"; rather, the prosperity of the most developed countries came largely at the expense of less developed nations. In short, then, some nations became rich only because other nations became poor. Both are products of the global commerce that began five centuries ago.

The Importance of Colonialism

Late in the fifteenth century, Europeans began surveying the Americas to the west, Africa to the south, and Asia to the east in order to establish colonies. They were so successful that a century ago Great Britain controlled about one-fourth of the world's land, boasting that "the sun never sets on the British Empire." The United States, itself originally thirteen small British colonies on the eastern seaboard, soon pushed across the North

Was the arrival of Europeans in the Western Hemisphere a tale of brave explorers or greedy conquerors? The painting Colonial Domination, *a mural by Mexican artist Diego Rivera, clearly presents the artist's point of view.*

Diego Rivera, *Colonial Domination.* The Granger Collection. © Banco de Mexico Diego Rivera Museums Trust.

American continent, purchased Alaska, and gained control of Haiti, Puerto Rico, Guam, the Philippines, the Hawaiian Islands, and part of Cuba.

Meanwhile, Europeans and Africans engaged in a brutal form of human exploitation—the slave trade—from about 1500 until 1850. But, then, even as the world was rejecting slavery, Europeans took control of Africa itself. As Figure 12–4 on page 316 shows, European powers dominated most of the African continent until the early 1960s.

Formal colonialism has almost disappeared from the world. However, according to dependency theory, political liberation has not translated into economic autonomy. Far from it: The economic relationship between poor and rich nations perpetuates the colonial pattern of domination. This neocolonialism is the essence of the capitalist world economy.

Wallerstein's Capitalist World Economy

Immanuel Wallerstein (1974, 1979, 1983, 1984) explains global stratification using a model of the "capitalist world economy." The term *world economy* suggests that the prosperity or poverty of any country is the product of a global economic system. According to Wallerstein, today's global economy is rooted in the colonization that began 500 years ago when Europeans first saw the wealth of the rest of the world. Since the world economy is based in the high-income countries, it is capitalist in character.[4]

Wallerstein calls the rich nations the *core* of the world economy. Colonialism enriched this core by funneling raw materials from around the world to Western Europe, where they fueled the Industrial Revolution. Today, multinational corporations operate profitably worldwide, channeling wealth to North America, Western Europe, Australia, and Japan.

Low-income countries, on the other hand, represent the *periphery* of the world economy. Drawn into the world economy by colonial exploitation, poor nations continue to support rich ones by providing inexpensive labor and a vast market for industrial products. The remaining countries are considered the *semiperiphery* of the world economy. They include prospering countries like Portugal and South Korea that have closer ties to the global economic core.

[4]While based on Wallerstein's ideas, this section also reflects the work of Frank (1980, 1981), Delacroix & Ragin (1981), Bergesen (1983), Dixon & Boswell (1996), and Kentor (1998).

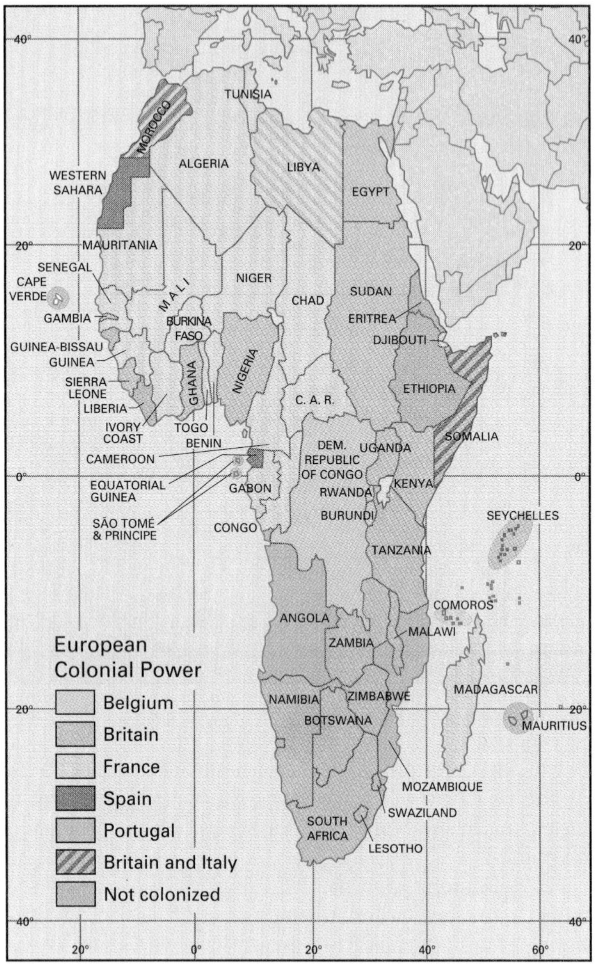

FIGURE 12–4 Africa's Colonial History

According to Wallerstein, the world economy benefits rich societies (by generating profits) and harms the rest of the world (by perpetuating poverty). The world economy thus makes poor nations dependent on rich ones. This dependency involves three factors:

1. **Narrow, export-oriented economies.** Poor nations produce only a few crops for export to rich countries. Examples include coffee and fruit from Latin American nations, oil from Nigeria, hardwoods from the Philippines, and palm oil from Malaysia.

   Today's multinational corporations purchase raw materials cheaply in poor societies and transport them to core nations where factories process them for profitable sale. This practice discourages poor nations from developing industries of their own, and also from trading with one another.

2. **Lack of industrial capacity.** Without an industrial base, poor societies face a double bind: They count on selling inexpensive raw materials to rich nations, and then they buy from the rich nations whatever expensive manufactured goods they can afford. In a classic example of this dependency, British colonialists encouraged the people of India to raise cotton, but prohibited them from weaving their own cloth. Instead, the British shipped Indian cotton to English textile mills in Birmingham and Manchester, manufactured the cloth, and shipped finished goods back to India for profitable sale.

   Dependency theorists claim the Green Revolution, widely praised by modernization theorists, works the same way. Poor countries sell cheap raw materials to rich nations, and then try to buy expensive fertilizers, pesticides, and machinery in return. Typically, rich countries profit from this exchange more than poor nations.

3. **Foreign debt.** Unequal trade patterns have plunged poor countries into debt to the core nations. Collectively, the poor nations of the world owe rich countries more than $1 trillion, including hundreds of billions of dollars to the United States. Such staggering debt paralyzes a country with high unemployment and rampant inflation (Walton & Ragin, 1990; The World Bank, 1999).

The Role of Rich Nations

Nowhere is the difference between modernization theory and dependency theory drawn more sharply than in the role each assigns to rich nations. Modernization theory maintains that rich societies *produce wealth* through capital investment and technological innovation. Accordingly, as poor nations adopt pro-growth policies and more productive technology, they, too, will prosper. By contrast, dependency theory views global inequality in terms of how countries *distribute wealth*, arguing that rich nations have *over*developed themselves as they have *under*developed the rest of the world.

Dependency theorists dismiss the idea that programs developed by rich countries to control population and boost agricultural and industrial output raise living

In the United States, most affluent people manage to distance themselves from the struggles of the poor. This is far more difficult to do in low-income countries, if only because there are so many more poor people. In the cities in India, for example, people routinely approach foreigners traveling by car in the hopes of receiving money in return.

standards in poor countries. Instead, they contend, such programs actually benefit rich nations and the ruling elites, not the poor majority, in low-income countries (Lappé, Collins, & Kinley, 1981).

Hunger activists Frances Moore Lappé and Joseph Collins (1986) maintain that the capitalist culture of the United States encourages people to think of poverty as somehow inevitable. Following this line of reasoning, poverty results from "natural" processes, including having too many children, and natural disasters such as droughts. But global poverty is far from inevitable; it results from deliberate policies. Lappé and Collins point out that the world already produces enough food to allow every person on the planet to become fat. Moreover, India and most of Africa actually *export* food, even though many of their own people go hungry.

According to Lappé and Collins, the contradiction of poverty amid plenty stems from the rich-nation policy of producing food for profits, not for people. That is, corporations in rich nations cooperate with elites in poor countries to grow and export profitable crops such as coffee, which means using land that could otherwise produce staples such as beans and corn for local families. Governments of poor countries support the practice of "growing for export" because they need food profits to repay massive foreign debt. At the core of this vicious cycle, according to Lappé and Collins, is the capitalist corporate structure of the global economy.

Critical evaluation. The main idea of dependency theory is that no country develops (or fails to develop) in isolation, because the global economy shapes the destiny of all nations. Citing Latin America and other poor regions of the world, dependency theorists claim that development simply cannot proceed under the constraints presently imposed by rich countries. Rather, they call for radical reform of the entire world economy so that it operates in the interests of the majority of people.

Critics, however, charge that dependency theory wrongly treats wealth as a zero-sum commodity, as if no one gets richer without someone else getting poorer. Not so, critics continue, since corporations, small business owners, and farmers can and do create new wealth through their drive and imaginative use of new technology. After all, they point out, the entire world's wealth has swelled sixfold since 1950.

Second, critics continue, dependency theory is wrong in blaming rich nations for global poverty because many of the world's poorest countries (like Ethiopia) have had little contact with rich nations. On the contrary, a long history of trade with rich countries has dramatically improved the economies of nations, including Sri Lanka, Singapore, and Hong Kong (all former British colonies), as well as South Korea and Japan. In short, say the critics, most evidence shows that foreign investment by rich nations fosters economic growth, as modernization theory claims, not economic decline, as dependency theorists assert (Vogel, 1991; Firebaugh, 1992).

Third, critics contend that dependency theory is simplistic for pointing the finger at a single factor—world capitalism—as the cause of global inequality (Worsley, 1990). Dependency theory thereby casts poor societies

TABLE 12–2 Modernization Theory and Dependency Theory: A Summary

	Modernization Theory	Dependency Theory
Historical Pattern	The entire world was poor just two centuries ago; the Industrial Revolution brought affluence to high-income countries; as industrialization gradually transforms poor societies, all nations are likely to become more equal and alike.	Global parity was disrupted by colonialism, which made some countries rich while simultaneously making others poor; barring radical change in the world capitalist system, rich nations will grow richer and poor nations will become poorer.
Primary Causes of Global Poverty	Characteristics of poor societies cause their poverty, including lack of industrial technology, traditional cultural patterns that discourage innovation, and rapid population growth.	Global economic relations—historical colonialism and now multinational corporations—have enriched high-income countries while making low-income nations economically dependent.
Role of Rich Nations	Rich countries can and do assist poor nations through population control programs, technology transfers that increase food production and stimulate industrial development, and capital investment in the form of foreign aid.	Rich countries have concentrated global resources, conferring advantages on themselves while generating massive foreign debt in low-income countries; rich nations impede the economic development of poor nations.

as passive victims and ignores factors inside these countries that contribute to their economic plight. Sociologists have long recognized the vital role of culture in shaping people's willingness to embrace or resist change. Iran's brand of fundamentalist Islam, for example, has deliberately discouraged economic ties with other countries. Capitalist societies, then, need hardly accept the blame for Iran's economic stagnation.

Neither should rich societies be saddled with responsibility for the reckless behavior of foreign leaders whose corruption and militaristic campaigns impoverish their countries (examples include the regimes of Ferdinand Marcos in the Philippines, François Duvalier in Haiti, Manuel Noriega in Panama, Mobutu Sese Seko in Zaire, and Saddam Hussein in Iraq). Governments may even use food supplies as a weapon in internal political struggles, a strategy that left the masses starving in the African nations of Ethiopia, Sudan, and Somalia. Other regimes throughout the world have done little to improve the status of women or control population growth.

Fourth, critics chide dependency theorists for downplaying the economic dependency fostered by the former Soviet Union. The Soviet army seized control of most of Eastern Europe during World War II and then politically and economically dominated those countries. Many see the uprisings between 1989 and 1991 as a wholesale rejection of the Soviet Union's socialist colonial system.

Fifth, critics fault this approach for offering only vague solutions to global poverty. Most dependency theorists urge poor nations to end all contact with rich countries, and some call for nationalizing foreign-owned industries. In other words, dependency theory amounts to a thinly disguised call for some sort of world socialism. In light of the difficulties socialist societies have had in meeting the needs of their own people, critics ask, should we really expect such a system to rescue the entire world from poverty?

GLOBAL STRATIFICATION: LOOKING AHEAD

Among the most important trends in recent decades is the development of a global economy. In the United States, rising production and sales abroad have brought record profits to many corporations and their stockholders, especially those who already have substantial wealth. At the same time, the global economy has cut factory jobs in this country, hurting many average workers. The net result: economic polarization in the United States.

As this chapter has noted, however, social inequality is far more striking in global context. The concentration of wealth among high-income countries, coupled with the grinding poverty of low-income nations, may well be the biggest problem facing humanity in the twenty-first century.

Finding answers to questions about global poverty, therefore, takes on some urgency. Which theory is right—modernization theory or dependency theory? In fact, both have their merits and their limitations. Table 12–2 summarizes the main arguments of each approach.

WINDOW ON THE WORLD

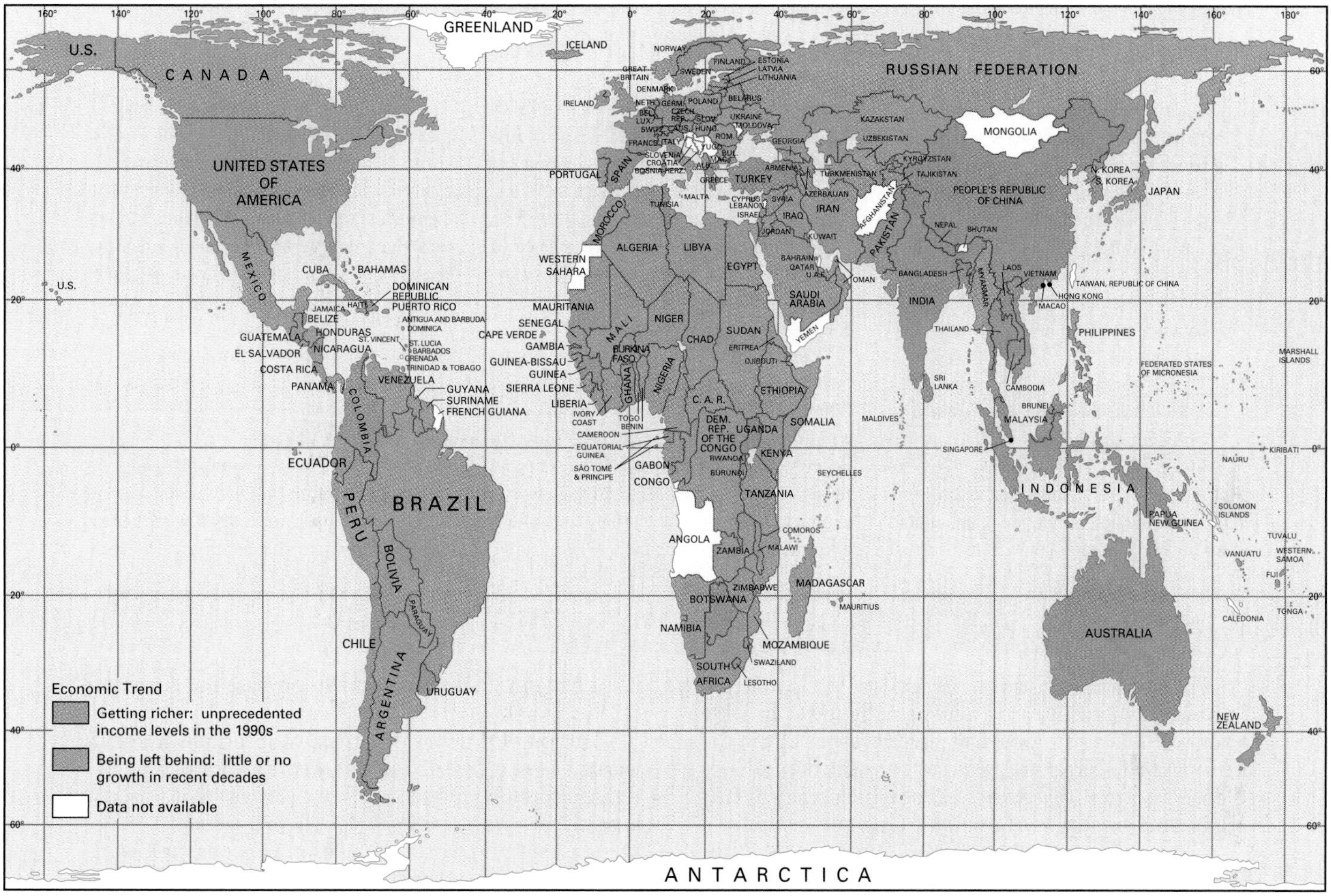

GLOBAL MAP 12–2 Prosperity and Stagnation in Global Perspective

In about sixty nations of the world, people are enjoying a higher standard of living than ever before. These prospering countries include some rich nations (such as the United States) and some poor nations (especially in Asia). For most countries, however, living standards have remained steady or even slipped in recent decades. Especially in Eastern Europe and the Middle East, some nations have experienced economic setbacks since the 1980s. And in sub-Saharan Africa, some nations are no better off than they were in 1960. The overall pattern is economic polarization, with an increasing gap between rich and poor nations.

Source: United Nations Development Programme (1996); updates by the author.

In searching for truth, we must consider empirical evidence. According to a recent world survey conducted by the United Nations (1996), people in about one-third of the world's countries are living better than they have in the past. These nations, identified in Global Map 12–2, include most of the high-income countries but also dozens of poorer countries, especially in Asia. These prospering nations are evidence that the market forces endorsed by modernization theory can raise living standards.

CONTROVERSY & DEBATE

Will the World Starve?

The animals' feet leave their prints
on the desert's face.
Hunger is so real, so very real,
that it can make you walk around
a barren tree looking for
nourishment.
Not once,
Not twice,
Not thrice . . .

These lines, by Indian poet Amit Jayaram, describe the appalling hunger found in Rajasthan, in northwest India. As this chapter has explained, however, hunger casts its menacing shadow not only over Asia but also over much of Africa, as well as parts of Latin America, Asia, and even North America. Throughout the world, hundreds of millions of adults do not eat enough food to enable them to work. And, most tragically, some 10 million children die each year as a result of hunger. As we begin the twenty-first century, what are the prospects for ending the wretched misery of daily hunger?

Pessimists point out that the population of poor countries is increasing by 70 million people annually—equivalent to adding another Egypt to the world every year. Poor countries can scarcely feed the people they have now; how will they ever feed *twice* as many people a generation in the future?

In addition, hunger forces poor people to exploit the earth's resources by using short-term strategies for food production that lead to long-term disaster. For example, farmers are cutting rain forests in order to increase their farmland. But, without the protective canopy of trees, it is only a matter of time before much of this land turns to desert. Taken together, rising populations and short-sighted policies raise the specter of unprecedented hunger, human misery, and political calamity.

But there are also some grounds for optimism. Thanks to the Green Revolution, food production the world over is up sharply over the last fifty years, well

In another one-third of the world's countries, however, living standards were actually lower in 1996 than in 1980. A rising wave of poverty, especially in the nations of sub-Saharan Africa, supports the dependency theory assertion that current economic arrangements are leaving hundreds of millions of people behind.

This evidence calls into question both modernization and dependency theories, and both camps are revising their views of proper "paths to development." On the one hand, few societies seeking economic growth favor a market economy completely free of government control, which challenges orthodox modernization theory and its free-market approach to development. On the other hand, recent upheavals in the former Soviet Union and Eastern Europe demonstrate that a global reevaluation of socialism is underway. Since these uprisings follow decades of poor economic performance and political repression, many poor societies are reluctant to consider a wholly government-controlled path to development. Because dependency theory has historically supported socialist economic systems, changes in world socialism will generate new thinking here as well.

Perhaps the basic problem caused by poverty is hunger. As the final box explains, many analysts wonder if we have the determination to provide for everyone on the planet.

Although the world's future is uncertain, we have learned a great deal about global stratification. One insight, offered by modernization theory, is that poverty is partly a *problem of technology*. A higher standard of living for a surging world population depends on raising agricultural and industrial productivity. A second insight, derived from dependency theory, is that global inequality is also a *political issue*. Even with higher productivity, the human community must address crucial questions concerning how resources are distributed—both within societies and around the globe.

Note, too, that while economic development increases living standards, it also places greater strains on the natural environment. Imagine, for example, if the 1 billion people in India were suddenly to become middle class, with automobiles guzzling gasoline and spewing hydrocarbons into the atmosphere.

Finally, the vast gulf that separates the world's richest and poorest people puts everyone at greater risk of war, as the most impoverished people challenge the social arrangements that threaten their lives. In the long run, we can achieve peace on this planet only by ensuring that all people live with dignity and security.

outpacing the growth in population. The world's economic productivity has risen steadily, so that the average person on the planet now has more income to purchase food and other necessities than ever before. This economic growth has increased daily calorie intake, life expectancy, access to safe water, and adult literacy, while, around the world, infant mortality is half of what it was in 1960.

So what are the prospects for eradicating world hunger? Overall, we see less hunger in both rich and poor countries, and a smaller *share* of the world's people are hungry now than in 1960. But as global population increases, with 90 percent of children born in middle- and low-income countries, the *number* of lives at risk is as great today as ever before. Thus, many low-income countries have made solid gains, but many more are stagnating or even losing ground.

The "best case" region of the world is eastern Asia, where incomes controlled for inflation have tripled over the last generation. It is to Asia that optimists in the global hunger debate point for evidence that poor countries can and do raise living standards and reduce hunger. The "worst case" region of the world is sub-Saharan Africa, where living standards have fallen over the last decade. It is here that high technology is least evident and birth rates are highest. Pessimists typically look to Africa when they argue that poor countries are losing ground in the struggle to feed their people.

Television brings home the tragedy of hunger when news cameras focus on starving people in places like Ethiopia and Somalia. But hunger—and early death from illness—is the plight of millions year-round. The world has the technical means to feed everyone; the question is, do we have the moral determination?

Continue the debate . . .

1. *In your opinion, what are the primary causes of global hunger?*
2. *Do you place more responsibility for solving this problem on poor countries or rich ones? Why?*
3. *Do you consider yourself an optimist or a pessimist about the problem of global hunger? Why?*

Sources: United Nations Development Programme (1994, 1995, 1996, 1997, 1998, 1999).

SUMMARY

1. Around the world, social stratification is more pronounced than in the United States. About 15 percent of the world's people live in industrialized, high-income countries such as the United States and receive 55 percent of all income. Another one-third of humanity lives in middle-income countries with limited industrialization and receives about 37 percent of all income. Half of the world's population lives in low-income countries that have yet to industrialize; residents of these nations earn only 8 percent of global income.
2. While relative poverty is found everywhere, poor societies grapple with widespread, absolute poverty. Worldwide, the lives of some 1 billion people are at risk due to poor nutrition. About 15 million people, most of them children, die annually from various causes because they lack adequate nourishment.
3. Women are more likely than men to be poor nearly everywhere in the world. Gender bias against women is greatest in poor, agrarian societies.
4. The poverty found in much of the world is a complex problem reflecting limited industrial technology, rapid population growth, traditional cultural patterns, internal social stratification, male domination, and global power relationships.
5. Modernization theory maintains that successful development hinges on a nation's ability to break out of traditional cultural patterns to acquire advanced technology.
6. Modernization theorist W. W. Rostow identifies four stages of development: traditional, take-off, drive to technological maturity, and high mass consumption.
7. Arguing that rich societies hold the keys to creating wealth, modernization theory claims rich nations can assist poor nations by providing (a) population control programs; (b) agricultural technology such as hybrid seeds and fertilizers to increase food production; (c) industrial technology, including machinery and information technology; and (d) foreign aid to help pay for power plants and factories.

8. Critics of modernization theory say that this approach has produced limited economic development in the world. Further, they claim, poor nations cannot follow the same path to development taken by rich nations centuries ago.
9. Dependency theory claims global wealth and poverty are the historical products of the capitalist world economy, first because of colonialism and, more recently, because of multinational corporations.
10. Immanuel Wallerstein views the high-income countries as the advantaged "core" of the capitalist world economy; middle-income nations are the "semiperiphery," and poor societies form the global "periphery."
11. Three key factors—export-oriented economies, a lack of industrial capacity, and foreign debt—perpetuate poor countries' dependency on rich nations.
12. Critics of dependency theory argue that this approach overlooks the sixfold increase in the world's wealth since 1950. Furthermore, the world's poorest societies are not those with the strongest ties to rich countries.
13. Both modernization and dependency theories offer useful insights into global inequality. Some evidence supports each view. Less controversial is the urgent need to address the various problems caused by worldwide poverty.

KEY CONCEPTS

colonialism (p. 309) the process by which some nations enrich themselves through political and economic control of other nations

neocolonialism (p. 310) a new form of global power relationships that involves not direct political control but economic exploitation by multinational corporations

multinational corporation (p. 310) a large business that operates in many countries

modernization theory (p. 311) a model of economic and social development that explains global inequality in terms of technological and cultural differences among societies

dependency theory (p. 314) a model of economic development that explains global inequality in terms of the historical exploitation of poor societies by rich ones

CRITICAL-THINKING QUESTIONS

1. Based on what you have read here and elsewhere, what is your prediction about the extent of global hunger fifty years from now? Will the problem be more or less serious? Why?
2. What is the difference between relative and absolute poverty? Use these two concepts to describe social stratification in the United States and around the world.
3. Why do many analysts argue that economic development in low-income countries depends on raising the social standing of women?
4. State the basic tenets of modernization theory and dependency theory. Spell out several criticisms of each approach.

APPLICATIONS AND EXERCISES

1. Keep a log of mass media advertising mentioning low-income countries (selling, say, coffee from Colombia or exotic vacations to India). What image of life in low-income countries does the advertising present? In light of this chapter, do you think this image is accurate?
2. Millions of students from abroad study on U.S. campuses. See if you can identify a woman and a man on your campus who were raised in a poor country. Approach them, explain that you have been studying global stratification, and ask if they are willing to share what life is like in their country. You may be able to learn quite a bit from them.
3. Look over the Global Maps in this text (or the animated maps on the CD-ROM). Comparing the maps, identify social traits associated with the world's richest and poorest nations. Try to use both modernization theory and dependency theory to build theoretical explanations of the various patterns you find.
4. Install the CD-ROM packaged in the back of this new textbook to access a variety of study, review, and applications exercises designed to help you better understand the material covered in this chapter. The CD includes an author's tip video, as well as interactive maps, video application exercises, Web links, and study questions.

SITES TO SEE

http://www.prenhall.com/macionis

Visit the interactive Web site that accompanies this text. Begin by clicking on the cover of your book. You will find a chapter-by-chapter study guide, practice tests, chat room, and many suggested Web links.

http://members.aol.com/casmasalc/

This is the Web site for the Coalition against Slavery in Mauritania and Sudan. This site provides information about the problem of slavery as well as links to similar oranizations.

http://www.oneworld.net

This worthwhile site highlights a variety of global issues and controversies.

http://www.fh.org
http://www.worldconcern.org
http://www.worldvision.org
http://www.care.org

Here are a number of additional Web sites that address global inequality. The first is operated by Food for the Hungry International; the second takes you to the home page for World Concern; the third organization is World Vision; the fourth is CARE. Visit them all and watch for differences in the focus and strategies of the various organizations.

http://www.census.gov/ipc/www/
http://www.prb.org/index.html

These two sites—operated by the U.S. Census Bureau and the Population Reference Bureau—offer a statistical profile of world nations.

http://www.fao.org/NEWS/1999/img/SOFI99-E.PDF

Read a United Nations report titled *The State of Food Insecurity in the World 1999*, which surveys the extent of poverty in high-, middle-, and low-income regions of the globe.

http://www.worldbank.org/poverty/data/index.htm

This site, operated by The World Bank, also provides data and analysis of global poverty.

http://www.globalexchange.org/education/speakers/CarmencitaAbad.html

At this site, read about a woman who spent six years working in a sweatshop in Saipan producing clothing for sale by Gap in the United States.

http://www.un.org/rights/50/decla.htm

Fifty years ago, the United Nations published the Universal Declaration of Human Rights. Read the document and consider how well these principles apply to today's world.

CHAPTER 13

Ernst Ludwig Kirchner (1880–1938)
Self Portrait with a Model, 1907

Oil on canvas, 150.5 × 100 cm. Kunsthalle, Hamburg, Germany. The Bridgeman Art Library International Ltd.

GENDER STRATIFICATION

At first we traveled quite alone . . . but before we had gone many miles, we came on other wagon-loads of women, bound in the same direction. As we reached different cross-roads, we saw wagons coming from every part of the country and, long before we reached Seneca Falls, *we were a procession.*

So wrote Charlotte Woodward in her journal as she made her way along the rutted dirt roads to Seneca Falls, a small town in upstate New York. The year was 1848, a time when slavery was legal in much of the United States, and the social standing of all women—regardless of color—was subordinate in every way to that of men. Back then, in much of the United States, women could not own property or keep their wages if they were married; women could not draft a will; women were barred from filing lawsuits in court, including suits seeking custody of their children; women could not attend college; and husbands could legally beat their wives as long as the stick they used was no thicker than a thumb (the origin of today's phrase "the rule of thumb").

Nor could women express their disapproval of such conditions. In this "land of the free," more than seventy years would pass before women gained the right to vote.

At Wesleyan Chapel in Seneca Falls, some 300 women gathered to challenge their second-class citizenship. They listened as their leader, Elizabeth Cady Stanton, called for expanding women's rights and opportunities, including the right to vote. To many, such a proposal seemed absurd and outrageous; even many attending the conference were shocked by the idea. Stanton's husband, Henry, rode out of town in protest.[1]

[1]This material is drawn from Gurnett (1998).

Much has changed in the century and a half since the Seneca Falls convention, and many of Stanton's proposals are now accepted as a matter of basic fairness. But, as this chapter explains, women and men still lead different lives in the United States and elsewhere around the world, and, in most respects, men still dominate. This chapter explores the importance of gender and explains how, like class position, gender is a major dimension of social stratification.

GENDER AND INEQUALITY

Chapter 9 ("Sexuality") discussed the biological differences that divide the human population into categories of female and male. **Gender** refers to *the personal traits and social positions that members of a society attach to being female and male.* Gender, then, is a dimension of social organization, shaping how we interact with others and how we think about ourselves. Even more

Sex is a biological distinction that develops prior to birth. Gender is the meaning that a society attaches to being female or male. Gender differences are a matter of power, as what is masculine typically has social priority over what is feminine. The importance of gender is not evident among infants, of course, but the ways in which we think of boys and girls set in motion patterns that will continue for a lifetime.

important, gender involves *hierarchy*, ranking men and women differently in terms of power, wealth, and other resources. This is why sociologists speak of **gender stratification,** *the unequal distribution of wealth, power, and privilege between men and women.* Gender, in short, affects the opportunities and constraints each of us encounters throughout our lives (Ferree & Hall, 1996; Riley, 1997).

MALE-FEMALE DIFFERENCES

Many people think there is something "natural" about gender distinctions; after all, there are biological differences between the sexes. But we must be careful not to think of social differences in biological terms. In 1848, for example, women were denied the vote because many people assumed that they "naturally" lacked sufficient intelligence and political interest. But such attitudes had nothing to do with biology. Rather, they reflected the *cultural conventions* of that time and place.

Figure 13–1 presents another example of women's "natural" inferiority—athletics. In 1925, most people would have doubted that the best women runners could ever finish a marathon in anywhere near the time that men could. Yet, today, as the figure shows, the best women routinely post better times than the fastest men of decades past, and the performance gap between the sexes has greatly narrowed. Here, again, most of the differences between men and women turn out to be socially created.

There are some physical differences between the sexes. On average, males are 10 percent taller, 20 percent heavier, and 30 percent stronger, especially in their upper bodies (Ehrenreich, 1999). On the other hand, women outperform men in the ultimate game of life itself: Whereas life expectancy for men is 73.9 years, women can expect to live 79.4 years (U.S. National Center for Health Statistics, 1999).

In adolescence, males show greater mathematical ability, and females excel in verbal skills, a difference that reflects both biology and the socialization process (Maccoby & Jacklin, 1974; Baker et al., 1980; Lengermann & Wallace, 1985). However, research points to no overall differences in intelligence between males and females.

Biologically, then, men and women differ in limited ways, with neither one naturally superior. But culture can define the two sexes very differently, as the global study of gender shows.

GENDER IN GLOBAL PERSPECTIVE

The best way to see the cultural foundation of gender is by making global comparisons. Here, we review three studies that highlight how different the ideas of "masculine" and "feminine" can be.

The Israeli Kibbutzim

In Israel, collective Jewish settlements are called *kibbutzim.* The *kibbutz* (singular form) is especially important for gender research because gender equality is one of its goals, with men and women sharing in both work and decision making.

Members of kibbutzim consider sex irrelevant to most of everyday life. Both men and women take care of children, cook and clean, repair buildings, and make decisions about the day-to-day operation of the kibbutz. Girls and boys are raised in the same way, and, from the first weeks of life, children live together in dormitories. Women and men in kibbutzim have achieved remarkable (although not complete) social equality. Thus, kibbutzim are evidence of the wide latitude cultures have in defining what is feminine and what is masculine.

Margaret Mead's Research

Anthropologist Margaret Mead carried out groundbreaking research on gender. To the extent that gender reflects biological facts of sex, she reasoned, people everywhere should define "feminine" and "masculine" in the same way; if gender is cultural, the two concepts should vary.

Mead studied three societies in New Guinea (1963; orig. 1935). In the mountainous home of the Arapesh, Mead observed men and women with remarkably similar attitudes and behavior. Both sexes, she reported, were cooperative and sensitive to others—in short, what our culture would label "feminine."

Moving south, Mead then studied the Mundugumor, head-hunters and cannibals who stood in striking contrast to the gentle Arapesh. In this culture, both sexes were typically selfish and aggressive, traits we define as more "masculine."

Finally, traveling west to the land of the Tchambuli, Mead discovered a culture that, like our own, defined females and males differently. But, Mead reported, the Tchambuli *reversed* many of our notions of gender: Females were dominant and rational, and males were submissive, emotional, and nurturing toward children. Based on her observations, Mead concluded that culture is the key to gender: What one culture defines as masculine, another may consider feminine.

Some critics view Mead's findings as "too neat," as if she saw in these three societies just the patterns she was looking for. Deborah Gewertz (1981) challenged Mead's "reversal hypothesis," claiming that Tchambuli males are really more aggressive and Tchambuli females more submissive than Mead said they were. Gewertz explains that Mead visited the Tchambuli (who actually call themselves the Chambri) during the 1930s, after they had lost much of their property in tribal wars. Men working in the home, she claims, was a temporary domestic role for Chambri men.

George Murdock's Research

In a broader study of more than 200 preindustrial societies, George Murdock (1937) found some global agreement about which tasks are feminine and which masculine. Hunting and warfare generally fall to men,

DIVERSITY SNAPSHOT

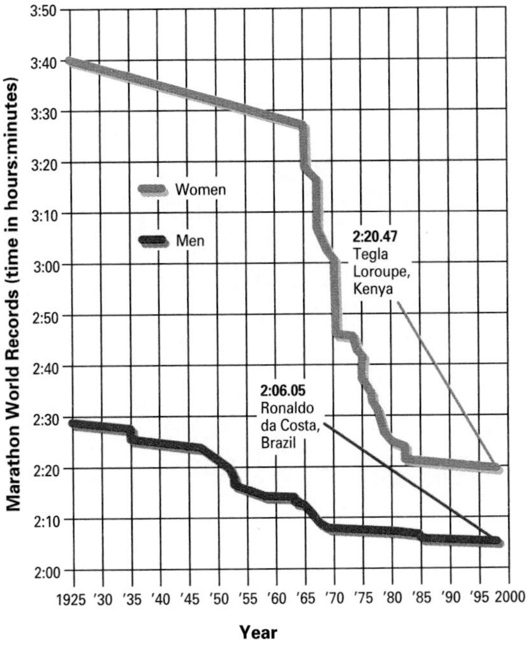

FIGURE 13–1 Men's and Women's Athletic Performance

Do men naturally outperform women in athletic competition? The answer is not obvious. Early in this century, men outdistanced women by many miles in marathon races. But as opportunities for women in athletics increased, women have been closing the performance gap. Less than fifteen minutes separate the current world marathon records for women and for men (both set in 1998).

Sources: *The Christian Science Monitor* (1995) and cnnsi.com (1998). Reprinted with permission of *The Christian Science Monitor*.

In every society, people assume certain jobs, patterns of behavior, and ways of dressing are "naturally" feminine while others are just as obviously masculine. But, in global perspective, we see remarkable variety in such social definitions. These men, Wodaabe pastoral nomads who live in the African nation of Niger, are proud to engage in a display of beauty most people in our society would consider feminine.

while home-centered tasks such as cooking and child care tend to be women's work. With their simple technology, preindustrial societies apparently assign roles reflecting men's and women's physical attributes. With greater size and strength, men hunt game and protect the group; because women bear children, they assume domestic duties.

But beyond this general pattern, Murdock found significant variation. Consider agriculture: Women did the farming in about the same number of societies as men; however, in most societies, the two sexes divided this work. When it came to many other tasks—from building shelters to tattooing the body—Murdock found societies of the world were as likely to turn to one sex as the other.

In Sum: Gender and Culture

Global comparisons show us that, by and large, societies do not consistently define most tasks as either feminine or masculine. As societies industrialize, moreover, the importance of muscle power declines, giving people even more options and further reducing the extent of gender differences (Lenski, Nolan, & Lenski, 1995). Thus, gender is simply too variable across cultures to be considered a simple expression of biology. Instead, as with many other elements of culture, what it means to be either female or male is mostly a creation of society.

PATRIARCHY AND SEXISM

Although conceptions of gender vary, everywhere in the world we find some degree of **patriarchy** (literally, "the rule of fathers"), *a form of social organization in which males dominate females*. Despite mythical tales of societies dominated by female "Amazons," **matriarchy**, *a form of social organization in which females dominate males*, has never been documented in human history (Gough, 1971; Harris, 1977; Lengermann & Wallace, 1985).

But while some degree of patriarchy may be universal, Global Map 13–1 shows significant variation in the relative power and privilege of females and males around the world. According to the United Nations, three Scandinavian countries—Norway, Sweden, and Finland—afford women the highest social standing; by contrast, women in the Asian nations of Pakistan and Afghanistan and the East African nation of Djibouti have the lowest social standing compared to men. Of 116 countries in the United Nations study, the United States ranked eighth in terms of gender equality (United Nations, 1995).

Sexism, *the belief that one sex is innately superior to the other*, is the ideological basis of patriarchy. Sexism is not just a matter of individual attitudes; it is built into the institutions of our society. *Institutional sexism* is part of the economy, for example, so that women are highly concentrated in low-paying jobs. Similarly, the legal system has long excused violence against women, especially

WINDOW ON THE WORLD

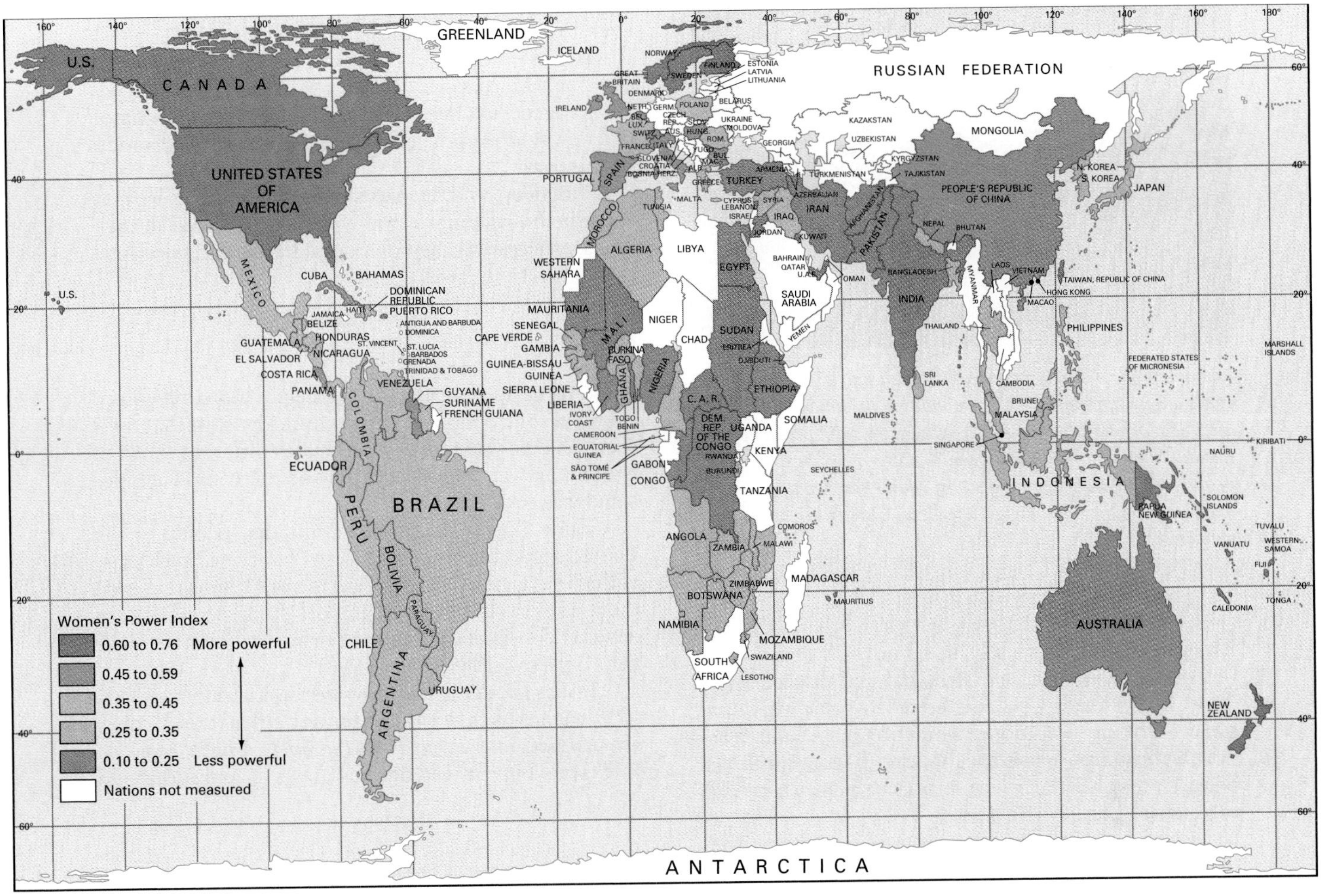

GLOBAL MAP 13–1 Women's Power in Global Perspective

A recent United Nations study ranked 116 nations on a scale of 0 (women have no power) to 1 (women have as much power as men). In general, women fare better in rich nations than in poor countries. Yet some countries stand out: Scandinavian societies lead the world in promoting women's power.

Source: *The Christian Science Monitor* (1995). Reprinted with permission of *The Christian Science Monitor.*

on the part of boyfriends, husbands, and fathers (Landers, 1990).

The Cost of Sexism

Sexism stunts the talents and limits the ambitions of women, who make up half the population. Although men benefit in some respects from sexism, their privilege comes at a high price. Masculinity in our culture calls for men to engage in many high-risk behaviors, including using tobacco and alcohol, participating in physically dangerous sports, and even driving recklessly, so that motor-vehicle accidents are the leading cause of death among young males. Moreover, as Marilyn French (1985) argues, patriarchy compels men to seek control—not only of women but of themselves and their world.

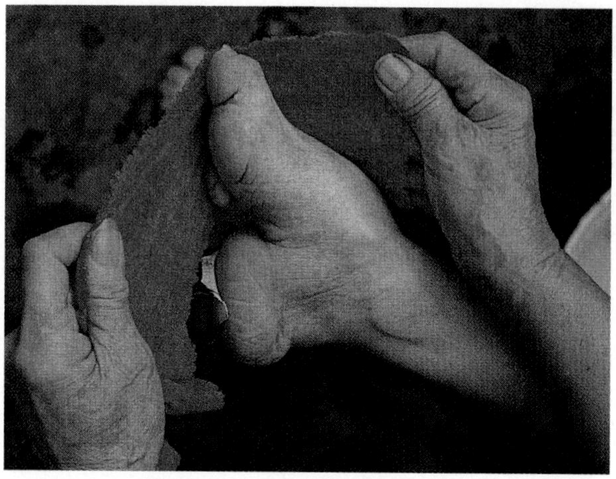

Among the most striking consequences of patriarchy in China is the ancient practice of "foot-binding," by which young girls' feet are tightly wrapped as they grow, with predictable results. Although this practice—now rare—produces what people deem "dainty" proportions, what effect would you imagine this deformity has on the physical mobility of women?

Thus, masculinity is closely linked not only to accidents but suicide, violence, and stress-related diseases. The Type A personality—characterized by chronic impatience, driving ambition, competitiveness, and free-floating hostility—is a recipe for heart disease and almost perfectly matches the behavior that our culture considers masculine (Ehrenreich, 1983).

Finally, insofar as men seek control over others, they lose opportunities for intimacy and trust. As one analyst put it, competition is supposed to separate "the men from the boys." In practice, however, it separates men from men and everyone else (Raphael, 1988).

Is Patriarchy Inevitable?

In preindustrial societies, women have little say over pregnancy and childbirth, which limits the scope of their lives. At the same time, men's greater height and physical strength are highly valued resources. But industrialization—including birth control technology—gives people choices about how to live. Today, then, in societies like our own, biological differences offer little justification for patriarchy.

But, legitimate or not, male dominance remains in the United States and elsewhere. Does this mean that patriarchy is inevitable? Some sociologists claim that biological factors "wire" the sexes with different motivations and behaviors—especially more aggressiveness in males—making patriarchy difficult, perhaps even impossible, to eliminate (Goldberg, 1974, 1987; Rossi, 1985; Popenoe, 1993b). Most sociologists, however, believe that gender is a social construct that *can* be changed. Just because no society has yet eliminated patriarchy does not mean that we must be prisoners of the past.

To understand the persistence of patriarchy, we now examine how gender is rooted and reproduced in society, a process that begins in childhood and continues throughout our lives.

GENDER AND SOCIALIZATION

From birth until death, gender shapes human feelings, thoughts, and actions. Children quickly learn that their society considers females and males different kinds of people; by about age three, they begin to apply gender standards to themselves.

Table 13–1 presents the traits that people in the United States traditionally link to "feminine" and "masculine" behavior. Note the pattern of opposites, even though research suggests that most young people do not develop consistently feminine or masculine personalities (Bernard, 1980; Bem, 1993).

Just as gender affects how we think about ourselves, so it teaches us how to *act.* **Gender roles** (or sex roles) are *attitudes and activities that a society links to each sex.* Insofar as our culture defines males as ambitious and

TABLE 13–1 Traditional Notions of Gender Identity

Feminine Traits	Masculine Traits
Submissive	Dominant
Dependent	Independent
Unintelligent and incapable	Intelligent and competent
Emotional	Rational
Receptive	Assertive
Intuitive	Analytical
Weak	Strong
Timid	Brave
Content	Ambitious
Passive	Active
Cooperative	Competitive
Sensitive	Insensitive
Sex object	Sexually aggressive
Attractive because of physical appearance	Attractive because of achievement

APPLYING SOCIOLOGY

Masculinity as Contest

By the time I was ten, the central fact in my life was the demand that I become a man. By then, the most important relationships by which I was taught to define myself were those I had with other boys. I already knew that I must see every encounter with another boy as a contest in which I must win or at least hold my own. . . . The same lesson continued [in school], after school, even in Sunday School. My parents, relatives, teachers, the books I read, movies I saw, all taught me that my self-worth depended on my manliness, my willingness to stand up to the other boys. This usually didn't mean a physical fight, though the willingness to stand up and "fight like a man" always remained a final test. But the relationships between us usually had the character of an armed truce. Girls weren't part of this social world at all yet, just because they weren't part of this contest. They didn't have to be bluffed, no credit was gained by cowing them, so they were more or less ignored. Sometimes when there were no grownups around we would let each other know that we liked each other, but most of the time we did as we were taught.

Source: Silverstein (1977).

competitive, we expect them to participate in team sports and aspire to positions of leadership. Similarly, to the extent that we define females as deferential and emotional, we expect them to be supportive helpers and quick to cry.

GENDER AND THE FAMILY

The first question people usually ask about a newborn—"Is it a boy or a girl?"—looms large because the answer involves not just sex but the likely direction of the child's entire life.

In fact, gender is at work even before the birth of a child, since most parents hope to start their family with a boy rather than a girl. Soon after birth, family members usher infants into the "pink world" of girls or the "blue world" of boys (Bernard, 1981). Parents even send gender messages in the way they handle daughters and sons. One researcher at an English university presented an infant dressed as either a boy or a girl to a number of women. Her subjects handled the "female" child tenderly, with frequent hugs and caresses; by contrast, they treated the "male" child more aggressively, often lifting him high in the air or bouncing him on the knee (Bonner, 1984). The lesson is clear: The female world revolves around passivity and emotion, while the male world puts a premium on independence and action.

GENDER AND THE PEER GROUP

About the time they enter school, children move outside the family and make friends with others of the same age. Peer groups teach additional lessons about gender. The box explains how play groups shaped one young boy's sense of himself as masculine.

After spending a year watching children at play, Janet Lever (1978) concluded that boys favor team sports with complex rules and clear objectives, such as scoring a run or making a touchdown. Such games nearly always have winners and losers, which reinforces masculine traits of aggression and control.

Girls, too, play team sports. But, Lever explains, girls also play hopscotch, jump rope, or simply talk, sing, or dance. These activities have few rules, and rarely is "victory" the ultimate goal. Instead of teaching girls to be competitive, Lever explains, female peer groups promote interpersonal skills of communication and cooperation—presumably the basis for girls' future roles as wives and mothers.

Lever's observations recall Carol Gilligan's (1982) gender-based theory of moral reasoning, discussed in Chapter 5 ("Socialization"). Boys, Gilligan contends, reason according to abstract principles. For them, "rightness" amounts to "playing by the rules." Girls, on the other hand, consider morality a matter of social responsibility to others. Thus, the games we play have serious implications for our later lives.

CRITICAL THINKING

Pretty Is as Pretty Does: The Beauty Myth

The Duchess of Windsor once quipped, "A woman cannot be too rich or too thin." The first half of her observation might apply to men as well, but certainly not the second. It is no surprise that the vast majority of ads placed by the $20-billion-a-year cosmetics industry and the $40-billion diet industry target women.

According to Naomi Wolf (1990), our culture promotes a "beauty myth" that is damaging to women. The beauty myth arises, first, because society teaches women to measure themselves in terms of physical appearance (Backman & Adams, 1991). Yet the standards of beauty (such as the *Playboy* centerfold or the one-hundred-pound New York fashion model) are unattainable for most women.

The beauty myth also teaches women to prize relationships with men and to use beauty to attract men. Striving for beauty drives women to be superficial and forces them to be highly attuned and responsive to men. Beauty-minded women, in short, try to please men and avoid challenging male power.

The beauty myth affects males, as well: Men should want to possess beautiful women. Thus, our ideas about beauty reduce women to objects and motivate men to possess women as if they were dolls rather than human beings.

Wolf stresses that beauty is not so much about appearance as about behavior. It should not be surprising, therefore, that the beauty myth was strongest during the 1890s, the 1920s, and the 1980s—all decades of heightened debate about the social standing of women.

What do you think?

1. *We might be tempted to say that physical attraction is simply a biological issue. How does Wolf's argument make beauty a social issue?*
2. *Do you think the beauty myth is still strong today? What messages about beauty and women does advertising send?*
3. *Are men harmed by the beauty myth? In what ways?*

Source: Based on Wolf (1990).

GENDER AND SCHOOLING

In high school, more girls than boys learn secretarial skills and take vocational classes such as cosmetology and food services. Classes in woodworking and auto mechanics, conversely, attract mostly young men.

In college, the pattern continues, with men disproportionately represented in mathematics and the sciences, including physics, chemistry, and biology. Women cluster in the humanities (such as English), the fine arts (painting, music, dance, and drama), and the social sciences (including anthropology and sociology). New areas of study are also likely to be gender-typed. Computer science, for example, enrolls mostly men, whereas courses in gender studies tend to enroll more women.

GENDER AND THE MASS MEDIA

Since television first captured the public imagination in the 1950s, white males have held center stage, and racial and ethnic minorities were all but absent from prominent television roles until the early 1970s. Even when both sexes appear on camera, men generally play the brilliant detectives, fearless explorers, and skilled surgeons. Women, meanwhile, play the less capable or

DIVERSITY SNAPSHOT

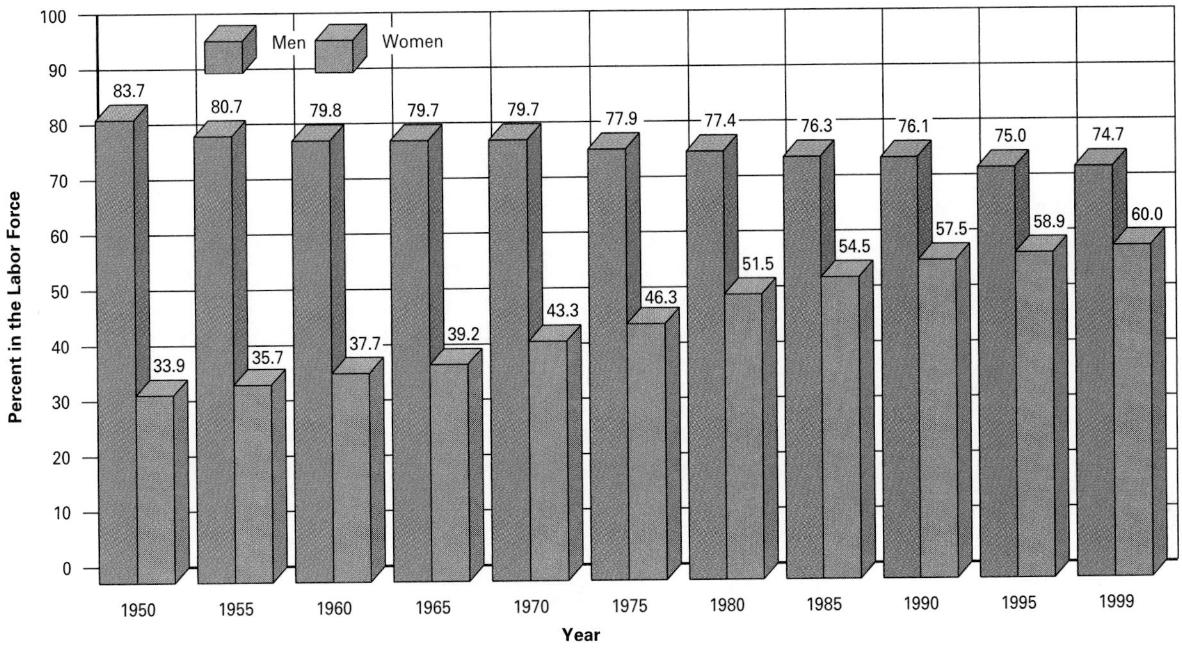

FIGURE 13–2 Men and Women in the U.S. Labor Force
Source: U.S. Department of Labor (2000).

unnecessary characters, except for the sexual interest they add to the story.

Historically, advertisements have presented women in the home, happily using cleaning products, serving food, trying out appliances, and modeling clothes. Men, on the other hand, predominate in ads for cars, travel, banking services, industrial companies, and alcoholic beverages. The authoritative "voice-over"—the faceless voice that describes a product on television and radio—is almost always male (Courtney & Whipple, 1983; Davis, 1993).

In studying magazine and newspaper ads, Erving Goffman (1979) discovered that men usually appear taller than women, implying male superiority. Women are more frequently presented lying down (on sofas and beds) or, like children, seated on the floor. Men's facial expressions exude competence and authority, whereas women often appear demure or even childlike. While men focus on the products being advertised, women focus on the men, playing a supportive and submissive role.

Advertising also actively perpetuates what Naomi Wolf calls the "beauty myth." The box takes a closer look at how this myth affects women.

GENDER AND SOCIAL STRATIFICATION

Gender implies more than how people think and act. It is also about social hierarchy. The reality of gender stratification can be seen, first, in the world of work.

WORKING WOMEN AND MEN

In 1998, almost 70 percent of people in the United States aged sixteen and over were working for income: 74.7 percent of men and 60 percent of women, as shown in Figure 13–2 (U.S. Department of Labor, 2000). This represents a dramatic change from 1900, when only about one-fifth of women were in the labor force (and

WINDOW ON THE WORLD

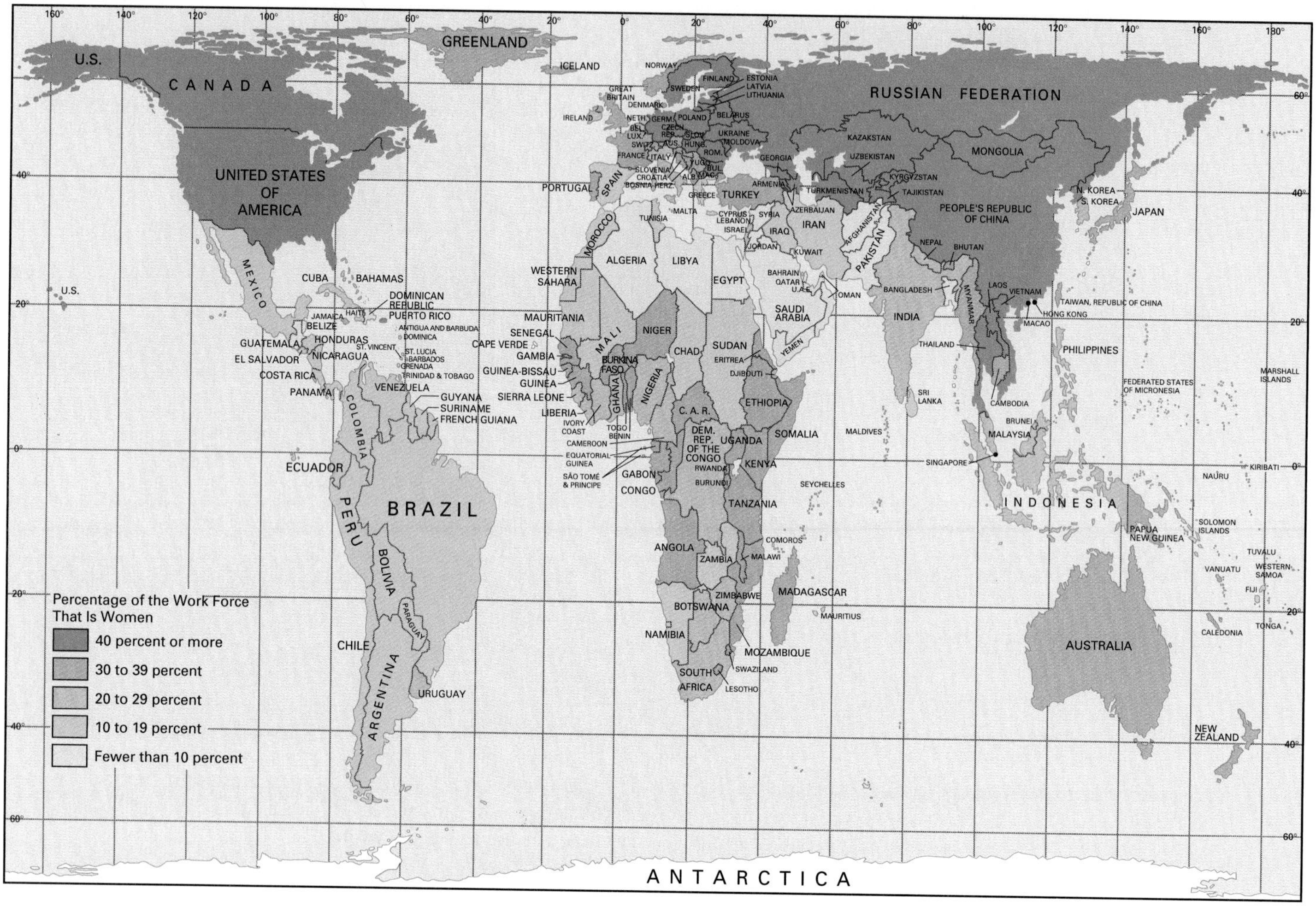

GLOBAL MAP 13–2 Women's Paid Employment in Global Perspective

This map shows, for the world's nations, the percentage of the labor force made up of women. A country's level of technological development plays an important part here. In 1999, women were 47 percent of the labor force in the United States—up almost 10 percent over the last generation. Throughout the industrialized world, at least one-third of the labor force is made up of women. In poor societies, however, women work even harder than in this country, but they are less likely to be paid for their efforts. In Latin America, for example, women represent only about 15 percent of the paid labor force; in Islamic societies of northern Africa and the Middle East, the figure is even lower.

Source: *Peters Atlas of the World* (1990); updated by the author.

these were typically poor women, who have always needed to work). Moreover, three-fourths of women in the labor force now work full time. So, the traditional view that earning an income is exclusively a "man's role" no longer holds true.

Factors changing the U.S. labor force include the decline of farming, the growth of cities, shrinking family size, and a rising divorce rate. In the United States and other industrial societies, women working for income is now the rule rather than the exception. In fact, 60 percent of U.S. married couples depend on two incomes. As Global Map 13–2 shows, women represent almost half of the work force in the United States; this is not the case, however, in many of the poorer nations of the world.

In past generations, many women in the U.S. labor force were childless. But today, 64 percent of married women with children under age six work for income, as do 73 percent of married women with children between six and seventeen years of age. For divorced women with children, the comparable figures are 73 percent of women with younger children and 83 percent of women with older children (U.S. Census Bureau, 1999).

Gender and Occupations

While the shares of men and women in the labor force have been converging, the work they do remains different. The U.S. Department of Labor (2000) reports that nearly half of working women hold one of two types of jobs. Administrative support work draws 23 percent of working women, most of whom are secretaries, typists, or stenographers. Often, these are called "pink-collar" jobs because 79 percent are filled by women. Another 17 percent of employed women do service work. Most of these jobs are in food service industries and in child care and health care.

Table 13–2 shows the ten occupations with the highest concentrations of women. Overall, although more women now work for pay, they remain segregated in jobs at the low end of the pay scale, with limited opportunities for advancement and usually supervised by men (Charles, 1992; Bianchi & Spain, 1996; U.S. Department of Labor, 2000).

Men dominate most other job categories, including the building trades, where 99 percent of brick and stone masons, structural metalworkers, and heavy equipment mechanics are men. Likewise, 89 percent of engineers, 75 percent of physicians, 70 percent of judges and lawyers, and 55 percent of corporate managers are men.

TABLE 13–2 Jobs with the Highest Concentrations of Women, 1999

Occupation	Number of Women Employed	Percent in Occupation Who Are Women
1. Dental hygienist	106,000	99.1%
2. Secretary	2,781,000	98.6
3. Prekindergarten and kindergarten teacher	600,000	98.4
4. Family child-care provider	469,000	98.0
5. Private household child-care worker	295,000	97.4
6. Dental assistant	213,000	96.1
7. Typist	556,000	95.5
8. Receptionist	1,091,000	95.4
9. Early childhood teacher's assistant	509,000	95.4
10. Licensed practical nurse	357,000	95.1

Source: U.S. Department of Labor, Bureau of Labor Statistics, *Employment and Earnings*, vol. 47, no. 1, January 2000, pp. 178–83.

At the top of the business world, men hold 95 percent of senior management jobs in this country's 1,000 largest companies. Just five of these largest U.S. corporations have a woman as their chief executive officer (Catalyst, 2000).

Gender stratification in the workplace is easy to see: Female nurses assist male physicians, female secretaries serve male executives, and female flight attendants are under the command of male airplane pilots. Moreover, in any field, the greater the income and prestige associated with a job, the more likely it is held by a man. For example, women represent 98 percent of kindergarten teachers, 84 percent of elementary school teachers, 58 percent of secondary school teachers, 42 percent of college and university professors, and 16 percent of college and university presidents (U.S. Department of Labor, 2000).

But an important challenge to male domination in the workplace now comes from women who are entrepreneurs. Women now own more than 8 million small businesses in the United States—double the number just a decade ago and more than one-third of the total. Although 86 percent of these businesses are one-person operations, women have shown that they can make opportunities for themselves outside of larger, male-dominated companies (Ando, 1990; O'Hare & Larson, 1991; Mergenhagen, 1996c; Winters, 1999; U.S. Department of Labor, 2000).

WINDOW ON THE WORLD

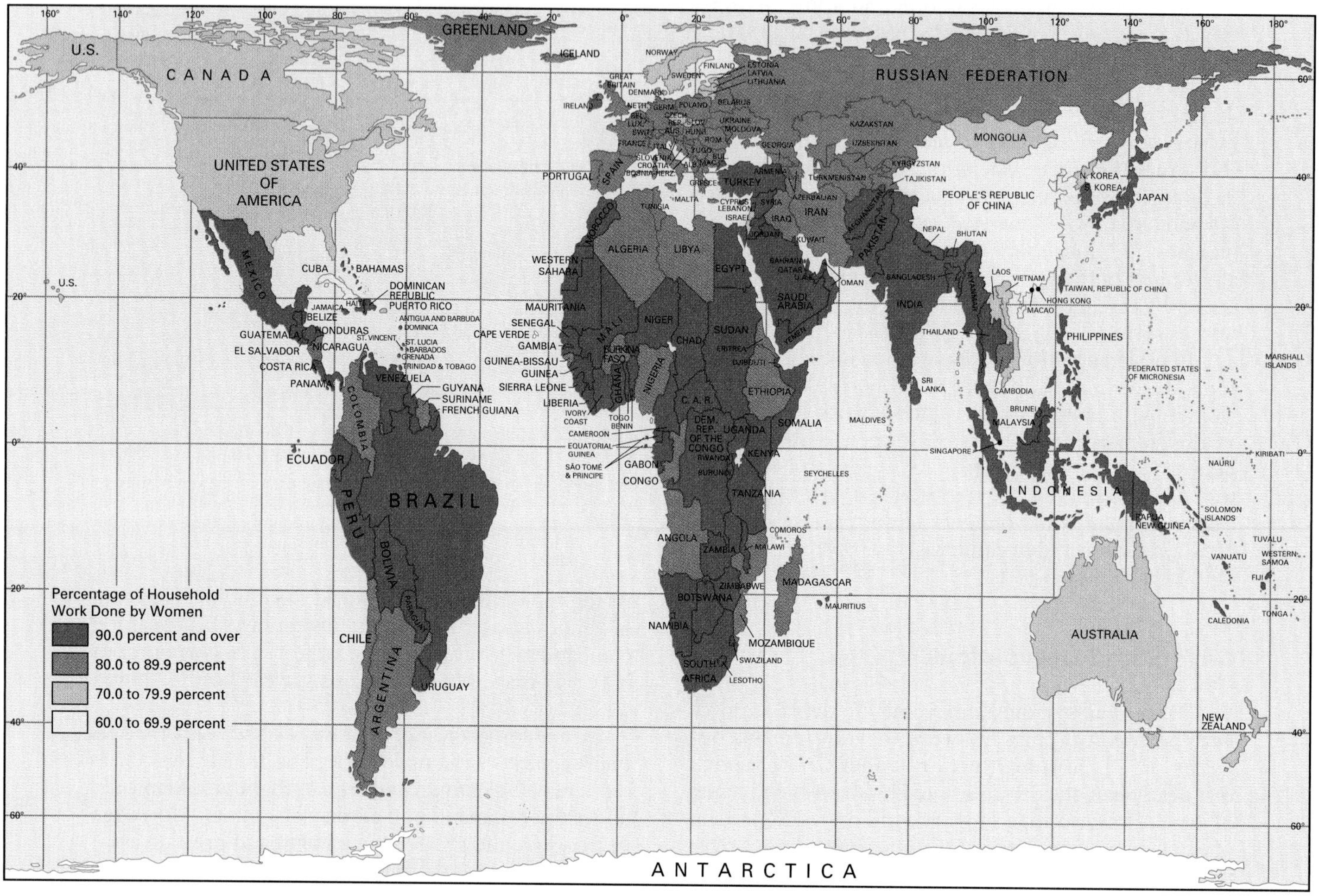

GLOBAL MAP 13–3 Housework in Global Perspective

Throughout the world, housework is a major component of women's daily routines and identities. This is especially true in poor societies of Latin America, Africa, and Asia, where women are not generally in the paid labor force. But our society also defines housework and child care as "feminine" activities, even though a majority of U.S. women work outside the home.

Source: *Peters Atlas of the World* (1990); updated by the author.

HOUSEWORK

Global Map 13–3 shows another indicator of patriarchy—the extent to which housework, including cleaning, cooking, and caring for children—is done by women. In the United States, housework has always been a cultural contradiction: We claim it is essential for family life, but give housework little prestige or other reward (Bernard, 1981).

With women's entry into the labor force, the amount of housework performed by women has declined, but the *share* women do has stayed about the

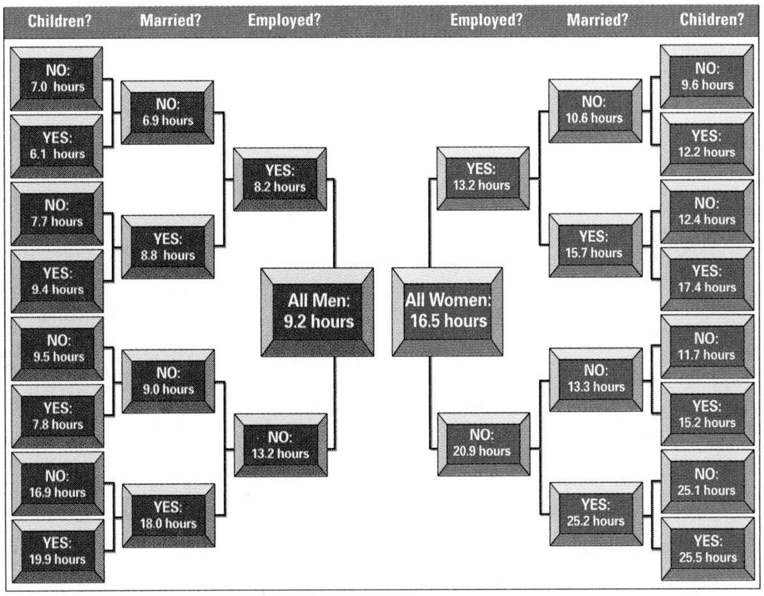

FIGURE 13–3 Housework: Who Does How Much?

Overall, women average 16.5 hours of housework per week, compared to 9.2 hours for men. This pattern holds whether people are employed or not, married or not, and parenting or not.

Source: Adapted from Stapinski (1998).

same. Figure 13–3 shows that, overall, women average 16.5 hours a week of housework, compared to 9.2 hours for men. Among all categories of people, the figure shows, women do significantly more housework than men (Stapinski, 1998).

In sum, men support the idea of women entering the labor force, and most count on the money women earn. But most, although not all, men resist taking on a more equal share of household duties (Komarovsky, 1973; Cowan, 1992; Robinson & Spitze, 1992; Lennon & Rosenfeld, 1994; Heath & Bourne, 1995; Harpster & Monk-Turner, 1998).

GENDER, INCOME, AND WEALTH

In 1998, the median earnings for women working full time were $26,855, while men working full time earned $36,252. This means that, for every dollar earned by men, women earned about 74 cents.

Among full-time workers, 44 percent of women earned less than $25,000 in 1998, compared to 28 percent of comparable men. At the upper end of the income scale, men were three times more likely than women (13.0 percent versus 4.3 percent) to earn more than $75,000 (U.S. Census Bureau, 1999).

The main reason women earn less is the *kind* of work they do: largely clerical and service jobs. In effect, jobs and gender interact. People still perceive jobs with less clout as "women's work," just as people devalue certain jobs simply because they are performed by women (Parcel, Mueller, & Cuvelier, 1986; Blum, 1991; England, 1992; Bellas, 1994; Huffman, Velasco, & Bielby, 1996).

During the 1980s, proponents of gender equality proposed a policy of "comparable worth." That is, people should be paid, not according to the historical double standard, but based on the worth of what they actually do. Several nations, including Great Britain and Australia, have adopted comparable worth policies, but not the United States. As a result, women in this country lose as much as $1 billion annually.

A second cause of gender-based income disparity has to do with the family. Both men and women have children, of course, but our culture defines parenting as more a woman's duty than a man's. Pregnancy and raising small children keep many younger women out of the labor force at a time when their male peers are making significant career gains. As a result, women workers have less job seniority than their male counterparts (Fuchs, 1986; Stier, 1996; Waldfogel, 1997).

Moreover, women who choose to have children may be reluctant or unable to maintain fast-paced jobs that tie up their evenings and weekends. To avoid role strain, they may take jobs that offer a shorter commuting distance, more flexible hours or employer child-care services. Women pursuing both a career and a family are often torn between their dual responsibilities in ways that men are not. Consider this: At age forty, 90 percent of men—but only 35 percent of

TABLE 13–3 Earnings of Full-Time U.S. Workers,* by Sex, 1998

Selected Occupational Categories	Median Income Men	Median Income Women	Women's Income as a Percentage of Men's
Executives, administrators, and managers	$51,351	$34,755	68%
Professional specialties	51,654	36,261	70
Technical workers	40,546	27,849	69
Sales	37,248	23,197	62
Clerical and other administrative support workers	31,153	23,835	77
Precision production, craft, and repair workers	31,631	23,907	76
Machine operators, assemblers, and inspectors	27,890	19,015	68
Transportation and material movers	30,422	21,449	71
Handlers, equipment cleaners, helpers, and laborers	21,871	16,550	76
Service workers	22,515	15,647	69
Farming, forestry, and fishing workers	18,855	15,865	84
All occupations listed above	34,949	25,862	74

*Workers aged 15 and over.

Source: U.S. Bureau of the Census, *Money Income in the United States: 1998*, Current Population Reports, ser. P-60, no. 206 (Washington, D.C.: U.S. Government Printing Office, 1999).

women—in executive positions have at least one child (F. Schwartz, 1989).

These two factors—type of work and family responsibilities—account for about two-thirds of the earnings disparity between women and men. A third factor—discrimination against women—accounts for most of the remainder (Pear, 1987; Fuller & Schoenberger, 1991).

Because discrimination is illegal, it is practiced in subtle ways. Corporate women often encounter a *glass ceiling*, a barrier that is invisible because it is denied by company officials even though it effectively prevents women from rising above middle management (Benokraitis & Feagin, 1995; Yamagata et al., 1997).

For all these reasons, then, women earn less than men in all major occupational categories. As shown in Table 13–3, this disparity varies from job to job, but in only four of the major job classifications do women earn more than 75 percent as much as men.

Finally, perhaps because women typically outlive men, many people think that women own most of this country's wealth. Government statistics tell a different story: Fifty-three percent of individuals with $1 million or more in assets are men, although widows are highly represented in this millionaires' club (U.S. Internal Revenue Service, 1993). Just 12 percent of the individuals identified in *Forbes* magazine as the richest people in the United States are women.

GENDER AND EDUCATION

In the past, women received little schooling because their lives revolved around the home. But times have changed. By 1980, women earned a majority of all associate's and bachelor's degrees; in 1996, that proportion stood at 55 percent (U.S. National Center for Education Statistics, 1999). As college doors have opened to women, differences in men's and women's majors are becoming smaller. In 1970, for example, women earned just 17 percent of bachelors degrees in the natural sciences, computer science, and engineering; by 1995, that proportion had increased to 31 percent.

In 1993, for the first time, women also earned a majority of postgraduate degrees, often a springboard to high-prestige jobs. For all areas of study in 1996, women earned 56 percent of master's degrees and 40 percent of doctorates (including 53 percent of all Ph.D.s in sociology). Women have also broken into many graduate fields that used to be almost all male. For example, in 1970 only a few hundred women received a master's of business administration (M.B.A.) degree, compared to more than 35,000 in 1996 (38 percent of all such degrees) (U.S. National Center for Education Statistics, 1999).

Some professional fields, however, remain predominantly male. In 1996, men received 57 percent of law degrees (LL.B. and J.D.), 59 percent of medical degrees (M.D.), and 64 percent of dental degrees (D.D.S. and D.M.D.) (U.S. National Center for Education Statistics, 1999). Our society still defines high-paying professions (and the drive and competitiveness needed to succeed in them) as masculine; this fact helps to explain why an equal number of women and men begin most professional graduate programs, but women are less likely to complete their degrees (Fiorentine, 1987;

Fiorentine & Cole, 1992). Nonetheless, the proportion of women in all these professions is steadily rising.

GENDER AND POLITICS

A century ago, almost no women held elected office in the United States. In fact, despite the Seneca Falls convention and suffrage movement, women were legally barred from voting in national elections until passage of the Nineteenth Amendment to the Constitution in 1920. A few women, however, were candidates for political office even before they could vote. The Equal Rights party supported Victoria Woodhull for the U.S. presidency in 1872 (perhaps it was a sign of the times that she spent election day in a New York City jail). Table 13–4 identifies later milestones in women's gradual movement into political life.

Today, thousands of women serve as mayors of cities and towns across the United States, and tens of thousands hold responsible administrative posts in the federal government. At the state level, 22 percent of legislators in 1998 were women (up from just 6 percent in 1970). National Map 13–1 on page 340 shows where in the United States women have made the greatest political gains.

Less change has occurred at the highest levels of politics, although a majority of U.S. adults claim they would support a qualified woman for any office, including the presidency. After the 1998 national elections, 3 of the 50 state governors were women (6 percent), and, in Congress, women held 56 of 435 seats in the House of Representatives (13 percent), and 9 of 100 seats (9 percent) in the Senate.

A recent global survey found that, although women are half the earth's population, they hold just 11.7 percent of seats in the world's 179 parliaments. While this represents a rise from 3 percent fifty years ago, only in the Scandinavian nations (Norway, Sweden, Finland, and Denmark) and the Netherlands does the share of parliamentary seats held by women (36.4 percent) even approach their share of the population (Inter-Parliamentary Union, 1997).

TABLE 13–4 Significant "Firsts" for Women in U.S. Politics

1869	Law allows women to vote in Wyoming territory; Utah follows suit in 1870.
1872	First woman to run for the presidency (Victoria Woodhull) represents the Equal Rights party.
1917	First woman elected to the House of Representatives (Jeannette Rankin of Montana).
1924	First women elected state governors (Nellie Taylor Ross of Wyoming and Miriam ["Ma"] Ferguson of Texas); both followed their husbands into office. First woman to have her name placed in nomination for vice-presidency at the convention of a major political party (Lena Jones Springs).
1931	First woman to serve in the Senate (Hattie Caraway of Arkansas); completed the term of her husband upon his death and won reelection in 1932.
1932	First woman appointed to the presidential cabinet (Frances Perkins, secretary of labor in the cabinet of President Franklin D. Roosevelt).
1964	First woman to have her name placed in nomination for the presidency at the convention of a major political party (Margaret Chase Smith, a Republican).
1972	First African American woman to have her name placed in nomination for the presidency at the convention of a major political party (Shirley Chisholm, a Democrat).
1981	First woman appointed to the U.S. Supreme Court (Sandra Day O'Connor).
1984	First woman to be successfully nominated for the vice-presidency (Geraldine Ferraro, a Democrat).
1988	First woman chief executive to be elected to a consecutive third term (Madeleine Kunin, governor of Vermont).
1992	Political "Year of the Woman" yields record number of women in the Senate (six) and the House (forty-eight), as well as (1) first African American woman to win election to U.S. Senate (Carol Moseley-Braun of Illinois); (2) first state (California) to be served by two women senators (Barbara Boxer and Dianne Feinstein); (3) first woman of Puerto Rican descent elected to the House (Nydia Valasquez of New York).
1996	First woman appointed secretary of state (Madeleine Albright).
1998	Record number of women in the Senate (nine) and the House (fifty-six).

Sources: Based on data compiled from Sandra Salmans, "Women Ran for Office before They Could Vote," *New York Times*, July 13, 1984, p. A11, and news reports.

GENDER AND THE MILITARY

Since colonial times, women have served in the armed forces. Yet, in 1940, at the outset of World War II, just 2 percent of armed forces personnel were women. By the 1991 Persian Gulf War, 35,000 women represented 6.5 percent of a total deployment of 540,000 U.S. troops. Five of the 148 Gulf War casualties were women.

In 1998, women represented 15 percent of all armed forces personnel. Only the Coast Guard makes all assignments available to women; at the other extreme, the Marine Corps denies women access to two-thirds of its jobs. Those who defend limited roles for women in the military claim that, on average, women lack the

SEEING OURSELVES

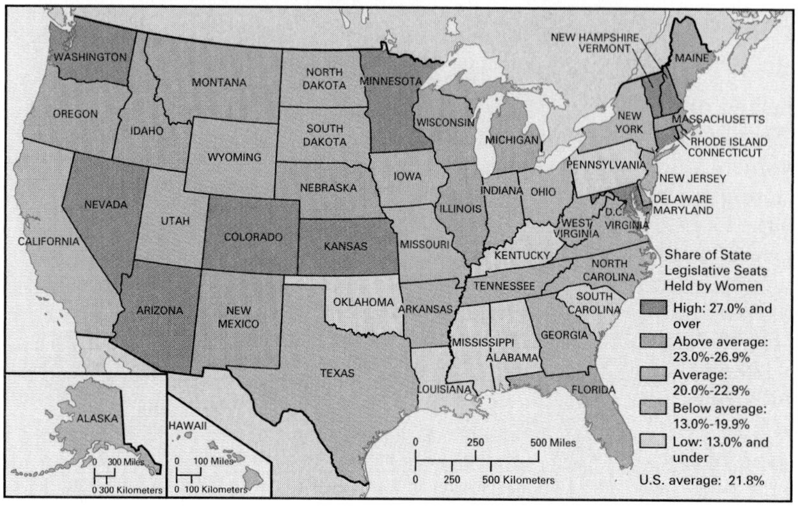

NATIONAL MAP 13–1
Women in State Government across the United States

Although women represent half of U.S. adults, just 22 percent of seats in state legislatures are held by women. Look at the state-by-state variation in the map. In which regions of the country have women gained the greatest political power? What factors do you think account for this pattern?

Source: Center for the American Woman and Politics (CAWP), Eagleton Institute of Politics, Rutgers University, "Women in State Legislatures 1998." [Online] Available http://www.rci.rutgers.edu/~cawp/stleg98.html, January 4, 1999.

physical strength of men. Critics counter that military women are better educated and score higher on intelligence tests than their male counterparts. But the heart of the issue is our society's deeply held view of women as *nurturers*—people who give life and help others—which clashes intolerably with the image of women trained to kill.

Although incorporating women into military culture has been difficult, women in all branches of the armed forces are taking on more and more military assignments. One reason is that high technology blurs the distinction between combat and noncombat personnel. A combat pilot can fire missiles at a radar-screen target miles away, while nonfighting medical evacuation teams go to the battle site (McNeil, Jr., 1991; May, 1991; Segal & Hansen, 1992; Wilcox, 1992; Kaminer, 1997).

ARE WOMEN A MINORITY?

A **minority**[2] is *any category of people, distinguished by physical or cultural difference, that a society sets apart and subordinates.* Given the clear economic disadvantage that our society imposes on women, it seems reasonable to say that U.S. women are a minority.

[2]We use the term "minority" instead of "minority group" because, as explained in Chapter 7 ("Groups and Organizations"), a minority is a category, not a group.

Subjectively speaking, however, most white women do *not* think of themselves this way (Hacker, 1951; Lengermann & Wallace, 1985). This is partly because, unlike racial minorities (including African Americans) and ethnic minorities (say, Hispanics), white women are well represented at all levels of the class structure, including the very top.

Bear in mind, however, that at every class level, women typically have less income, wealth, education, and power than men. In fact, patriarchy makes women dependent for much of their social standing on men—first their fathers and later their husbands (Bernard, 1981).

MINORITY WOMEN

If women are defined as a minority, what about minority women? Are they doubly handicapped? Generally speaking, the answer is yes, as we can show with some income comparisons. Looking first at race and ethnicity, the median income in 1998 for African American women working full time was $23,864, which is 87 percent as much as the $27,304 earned by white women; Hispanic women earned $19,817—just 73 percent as much as their white counterparts. Looking at gender, African American women earned 87 percent as much as African American men, while Hispanic women earned 88 percent as much as Hispanic men.

Combining these disadvantages, African American women earned 64 percent as much as white men, and

Many private companies and public organizations have adopted policies to discourage forms of behavior that might create a "hostile or intimidating environment." In practice, such policies seek to remove sexuality from the workplace so that employees can do their jobs while steering clear of traditional notions about female and male relationships. The hope is that sexual harassment policies will develop a comfortable informal atmosphere in which people can interact freely and easily.

Hispanic women earned 53 percent as much (U.S. Census Bureau, 1999). These disparities reflect minority women's lower positions in the occupational and educational hierarchies compared to white women (Bonilla-Santiago, 1990). Furthermore, whenever the economy sags, minority women are especially at risk for unemployment.

In short, gender has a powerful effect on our lives, but it never operates alone. Class position, race and ethnicity, and gender form a multilayered system of disadvantage for some and privilege for others (Ginsburg & Tsing, 1990; St. Jean & Feagin, 1998).

VIOLENCE AGAINST WOMEN

As noted in the opening to this chapter, the phrase "rule of thumb" entered our language about 150 years ago when common decency prevented a man from beating his wife with a stick thicker than his thumb. Even today, a great deal of "manly" violence is directed at women. A government report estimates 430,000 sexual assaults against women annually, including 316,000 rapes or attempted rapes. To this number can be added perhaps 2 million physical assaults (U.S. Bureau of Justice Statistics, 1996; Goetting, 1999).

Most gender-linked violence occurs where men and women interact most—in the home. Richard Gelles (cited in Roesch, 1984) argues that, with the exception of the police and the military, the family is the most violent organization in the United States. Both sexes suffer from family violence, although, by and large, women sustain more serious injuries than men (Straus & Gelles, 1986; Schwartz, 1987; Shupe, Stacey, & Hazlewood, 1987; Gelles & Cornell, 1990; Smolowe, 1994).

Violence against women also occurs in casual relationships. As noted in Chapter 8 ("Deviance"), most rapes involve not strangers but men known, and often trusted, by the victim. Dianne Herman (2001) claims that abuse of women is built into our way of life. All forms of violence against women—from the wolf whistles that intimidate women on city streets to a pinch in a crowded subway to physical assaults that occur at home—express what she calls a "rape culture" of men trying to dominate women. Sexual violence, she explains, is fundamentally about *power*, not sex, and therefore should be understood as a dimension of gender stratification.

In global perspective, violence against women is built into culture in other ways. One case in point is the practice of female genital mutilation, found in some forty countries—and known to occur in the United States. The box on page 342 explains.

Sexual Harassment

Sexual harassment refers to *comments, gestures, or physical contact of a sexual nature that are deliberate, repeated, and unwelcome.* During the 1990s, sexual harassment became an issue of national importance that rewrote the rules for workplace interaction.

Most victims of sexual harassment are women. This is because, first, our culture encourages men to be

GLOBAL SOCIOLOGY

Female Genital Mutilation: Violence in the Name of Morality

Meserak Ramsey, a woman born in Ethiopia and now working as a nurse in California, paid a visit to a friend's home. Soon after arriving, she noticed her friend's eighteen-month-old daughter huddled in the corner of a room in obvious distress. "What's wrong?" she asked.

Ramsey was shocked when the woman said her daughter recently had a clitoridectomy, or female circumcision, whereby the clitoris is surgically removed. This procedure—performed by a midwife, a tribal practitioner, or a doctor and typically without anesthesia—is common in Nigeria, Togo, Somalia, Egypt, and three dozen other nations in Africa and the Middle East.

In these highly patriarchal societies, husbands demand that their wives be virgins at marriage and remain sexually faithful thereafter. The point of genital mutilation is to eliminate sexual sensation, which, people assume, makes the girl less likely to violate sexual norms and thus more desirable to men. In about one-fifth of all cases, an even more severe procedure, called infibulation, is performed, in which the entire external genital area is removed and the surfaces are stitched together, leaving only a small hole for urination. Before marriage, a husband retains the right to open the wound and ensure himself of his bride's virginity.

How many women have undergone genital mutilation? Worldwide, estimates place the number at more than 100 million. In the United States, hundreds and probably thousands of such procedures are performed every year. In most cases, immigrant mothers and grandmothers who have themselves been mutilated insist that young girls in their family follow their example. Indeed, many immigrant women demand the procedure *because* their daughters now live in the United States, where sexual mores are more lax. "I don't have to worry about her now," one California parent explained to Meserak Ramsey. "She'll be a good girl."

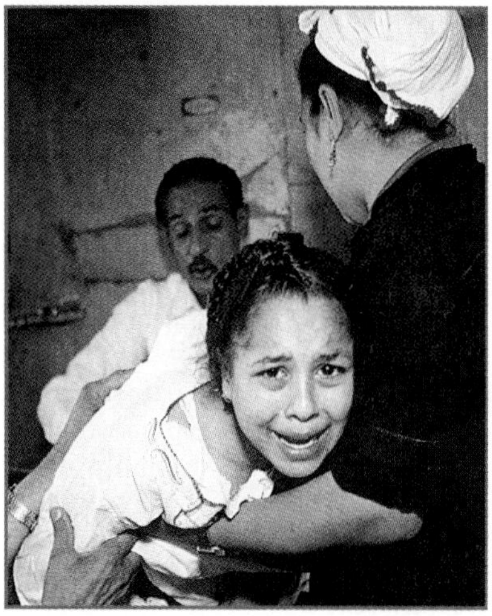

Medically, the consequences of genital mutilation include more than loss of sexual pleasure. Pain is intense and can persist for years. There is also danger of infection, infertility, and even death. Meserak Ramsey herself underwent genital mutilation as a young girl. She is one of the lucky ones who has had few medical problems since. But the extent of her suffering is suggested by this story: She had invited a young U.S. couple to stay at her home. Late at night, she heard the woman's cries and burst into their room to investigate, only to learn that the couple was making love and the woman had just had an orgasm. "I didn't understand," Ramsey recalls. "I thought that there must be something wrong with American girls. But now I know that there is something wrong with me." Or with a system that inflicts such injury in the name of traditional morality.

Source: Based on Crossette (1995).

sexually assertive and to perceive women in sexual terms. As a result, social interaction in the workplace, on campus, and elsewhere can readily take on sexual overtones. Second, most individuals in positions of power—including business executives, physicians, assembly line supervisors, professors, and military officers—are men who oversee the work of women. In surveys carried out in widely different work settings, half of women respondents report receiving unwanted sexual attention (Loy & Stewart, 1984; Paul, 1991; NORC, 1999).

Sexual harassment is sometimes blatant and direct: A supervisor solicits sexual favors from a subordinate by threatening reprisal if the advances are refused. Courts have declared such *quid pro quo* sexual harassment (the Latin phrase means "one thing in return for another") a violation of civil rights.

More often, however, sexual harassment involves subtle behavior—sexual teasing, off-color jokes, pinups displayed in the workplace—that may not even be *intended* to harass anyone. But, using the *effect* standard favored by many feminists, such actions amount to creating a *hostile environment* (Cohen, 1991; Paul, 1991). Incidents of this kind are far more complex because they involve different perceptions of the same behavior. For example, a man may think that complimenting a co-worker on her appearance is simply a friendly gesture; she, on the other hand, may feel his behavior hinders her job performance.

Pornography

A precise definition of *pornography* has long eluded scholars and lawmakers. Unable to set specific standards that distinguish what is from what is not pornographic, the Supreme Court has ruled that local communities should decide for themselves what violates "community standards" of decency and lacks any redeeming social value.

People disagree on precisely where to draw the line setting off pornography from what is merely "erotic." But no one doubts that, in the United States, pornography is big business. Taken together, sexually explicit videos, movies, magazines, telephone chat, and Internet sites represent more than $10 billion in sales each year.

Traditionally, society has cast pornography as a *moral* issue. In fact, national survey data show that 60 percent of U.S. adults express concern that "sexual materials lead to a breakdown of morals" (NORC, 1999:237). A more recent view focuses on pornography as demeaning to women. That is, pornography is really a *power* issue because it implies that men should control both sexuality and women. Pornography also conributes to male dominance in the United States because it dehumanizes women as the subservient playthings of men. It is worth noting, too, that the word *pornography* comes from the Greek word *porne*, meaning a harlot or sexual slave.

Another way pornography involves male power, according to many analysts, is by promoting violence against women. Depicting women as merely the sexual playthings of men amounts to defining women as weak and deserving of little respect. Men may show contempt for women defined this way by striking out against them. Surveys show that about half of U.S. adults think that pornography encourages men to commit rape (NORC, 1999:237).

Like sexual harassment, pornography raises complex and conflicting issues. While everyone objects to offensive material, many also think we must protect free speech and artistic expression. Nevertheless, public support to restrict pornography has increased in recent decades, both from more conservative people who oppose pornography on moral grounds and from more liberal people who oppose it as demeaning and threatening to women.

THEORETICAL ANALYSIS OF GENDER

Each of sociology's major theoretical paradigms addresses the significance of gender in social organization.

STRUCTURAL-FUNCTIONAL ANALYSIS

The structural-functional paradigm views society as a complex system of many separate but integrated parts. From this point of view, gender functions to organize social life.

As Chapter 4 ("Society") explained, members of hunting and gathering societies had little power over the forces of biology. Lacking birth control, women were frequently pregnant, and the responsibilities of child care kept them close to home. At the same time, men's greater strength made them more suited for warfare and hunting game. Over the centuries, this sexual division of labor became institutionalized and largely taken for granted (Lengermann & Wallace, 1985).

Industrial technology, however, opens up vastly greater cultural possibilities. Because human muscles are no longer the main energy source, the physical strength of men becomes less significant. In addition, reproductive technology gives women more control over bearing children and, hence, greater choice in shaping their lives. Modern societies come to see that traditional gender roles waste an enormous amount of human talent; yet change comes slowly, because gender is deeply embedded in culture.

Talcott Parsons: Gender and Complementarity

As Talcott Parsons (1942, 1951, 1954) observed, gender helps to integrate society—at least in its traditional form. Gender, Parsons noted, forms a *complementary* set of roles that links men and women into family units for carrying out various important tasks. Women take primary responsibility for managing the household and raising children. Men connect the family to the larger world as they participate in the labor force.

Parsons further argued that socialization teaches the two sexes appropriate gender identity and skills needed for adult life. Thus, society teaches boys—presumably destined for the labor force—to be rational, competitive, and self-assured. This complex of traits Parsons termed *instrumental.* To prepare girls for child rearing, their socialization stresses what Parsons called *expressive* qualities, such as emotional responsiveness and sensitivity to others.

Society, explained Parsons, promotes gender conformity by instilling in men and women a fear that straying too far from accepted standards courts rejection by the opposite sex. In simple terms, women learn to view nonmasculine men as sexually unattractive, and men learn to shun unfeminine women.

Critical evaluation. Structural functionalism puts forward a theory of complementarity by which gender integrates society both structurally (in terms of what people do) and morally (in terms of what they believe). Influential at midcentury, this approach has lost much of its standing today.

For one thing, functionalism assumes a singular vision of society that is not shared by everyone. For example, many women have always worked outside the home because of economic necessity, a fact not reflected in Parsons's conventional, middle-class view of family life. Second, Parsons's analysis ignores the personal strains and social costs of rigid, traditional gender roles (Giele, 1988). Third, for those who seek sexual equality, what Parsons describes as gender "complementarity" amounts to little more than male domination.

SOCIAL-CONFLICT ANALYSIS

From a social-conflict point of view, gender involves not just differences in behavior but in power. Consider the striking parallel between the way ideas about gender have benefited men and the way oppression of racial and ethnic minorities has benefited whites (Hacker, 1951, 1974; Collins, 1971; Lengermann & Wallace, 1985). That is, conventional ideas about gender promote not cohesion but division and tension, with men seeking to protect their privileges as women challenge the status quo.

As earlier chapters explain, the social-conflict paradigm draws heavily on the ideas of Karl Marx. Yet Marx was a product of his time insofar as his writings focused almost exclusively on men. His friend and collaborator Friedrich Engels, however, did develop a theory of gender stratification (1902; orig. 1884).

Friedrich Engels: Gender and Class

Looking back through history, Engels noted that in hunting and gathering societies, the activities of women and men, while different, were of comparable importance. A successful hunt brought men great prestige, but the vegetation gathered by women provided most of a group's food supply. As technological advances led to a productive surplus, however, social equality and communal sharing gave way to private property and, ultimately, a class hierarchy. At this time, men gained pronounced power over women. With surplus wealth to pass on to heirs, upper-class men wanted to be sure of paternity which led them to control women's sexuality. In other words, the desire to control property led to the creation of monogamous marriage and the family. Women were then taught to remain virgins until marriage, to stay faithful to their husbands thereafter, and to build their lives around bearing and raising one man's children.

Furthermore, said Engels, capitalism intensifies this male domination. First, capitalism creates more wealth, which confers greater power on men as owners of property and primary wage earners. Second, an expanding capitalist economy depends on turning people—especially women—into consumers who seek personal fulfillment through buying and using products. Third, to free men to work in factories, society assigns women the task of maintaining the home. The double exploitation of capitalism, as Engels saw it, lies in paying low wages for male labor and no wages for female work (Eisenstein, 1979; Barry, 1983; Jagger, 1983; Vogel, 1983).

Critical evaluation. Social-conflict analysis highlights how society places the two sexes in unequal positions of wealth, power, and privilege. It is, as a result, decidedly critical of conventional ideas about gender, claiming that society would be better off if we minimized or even eliminated this dimension of social structure.

But social-conflict analysis, too, has its critics. One problem is that this approach sees conventional families—defended by traditionalists as morally positive—as a social evil. Second, from a more practical point of view, social-conflict analysis minimizes the extent to which women and men live together cooperatively, and often happily, in families. A third problem lies in the assertion that capitalism is the basis of gender stratification. In fact, agrarian countries are typically more patriarchal than industrial-capitalist societies, and socialist nations—including the People's Republic of China and Cuba—are strongly patriarchal (Moore, 1992; Rosendahl, 1997).

These three women made enormous contributions to the women's movement during the twentieth century. Margaret Higgins Sanger (1883–1966) was a pioneer activist in the crusade for women's reproductive rights. Margaret Mead (1901–1978), probably the best known anthropologist of all time, showed how definitions of femininity and masculinity are rooted in culture rather than biology. In 1949, Simone De Beauvoir (1908–1986) published The Second Sex, *one of the first books to explore systematically the importance of gender to social life.*

FEMINISM

Feminism is *the advocacy of social equality for men and women, in opposition to patriarchy and sexism.* The first wave of the feminist movement in the United States began in the 1840s as women who were opposed to slavery, including Elizabeth Cady Stanton and Lucretia Mott, drew parallels between the oppression of African Americans and the oppression of women. The Seneca Falls convention, described in this chapter's opening vignette, began the social movement by which women finally won the right to vote in 1920. But women continued to endure other disadvantages, and a second wave of feminism arose in the 1960s and continues today.

BASIC FEMINIST IDEAS

Feminism views the personal experiences of women and men through the lens of gender. How we think of ourselves (gender identity), how we act (gender roles), and our sex's social standing (gender stratification) are all rooted in the operation of our society.

Although people who consider themselves feminists disagree about many issues, most support five general principles:

1. **The importance of change.** Feminist thinking is decidedly political, linking ideas to action. Feminism is critical of the status quo and advocates change toward social equality for women and men.
2. **Expansion of human choice.** Feminists maintain that cultural conceptions of gender divide the full range of human qualities into two opposing and limited spheres: the female world of emotions and cooperation and the male world of rationality and competition. As an alternative, feminists propose a "reintegration of humanity" by which each person develops *all* human traits (French, 1985).
3. **Elimination of gender stratification.** Feminism opposes laws and cultural norms that limit the education, income, and job opportunities of women. For this reason, feminists advocate passage of the Equal Rights Amendment (ERA) to the U.S. Constitution, which states:

   > Equality of rights under the law shall not be denied or abridged by the United States or any State on account of sex.

   The ERA, first proposed in Congress in 1923, has the support of two-thirds of U.S. adults (NORC, 1999:258). Even so, it has yet to become law, which probably reflects the fact that most of the men who dominate state legislatures oppose the amendment.
4. **An end to sexual violence.** Today's women's movement seeks to eliminate sexual violence.

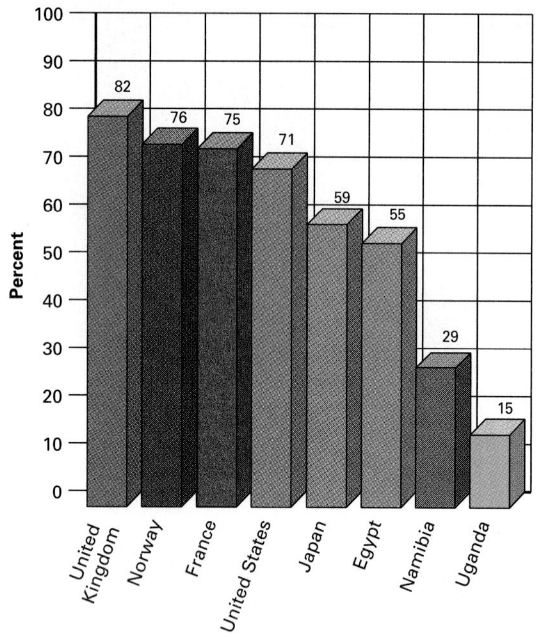

FIGURE 13–4 Use of Contraception by Women of Childbearing Age

Source: United Nations Development Programme (1999).

Feminists argue that patriarchy distorts the relationships between women and men, encouraging violence against women in the form of rape, domestic abuse, sexual harassment, and pornography (Millet, 1970; Bernard, 1982, orig. 1973; Dworkin, 1987).

5. **Sexual autonomy.** Finally, feminism advocates women's control of their sexuality and reproduction. Feminists support the free availability of birth control information. As Figure 13–4 shows, contraceptives are much less available in most of the world than they are in the United States. Most feminists also support a woman's right to choose whether to bear a child or terminate a pregnancy, rather than allowing men—as husbands, physicians, and legislators—to control their reproduction. Finally, many feminists also support gay people's efforts to overcome the many barriers they face in a predominantly heterosexual culture (Deckard, 1979; Barry, 1983; Jagger, 1983).

TYPES OF FEMINISM

Although feminists agree on the importance of gender equality, they disagree on how to achieve it—through liberal feminism, socialist feminism, or radical feminism (Barry, 1983; Jagger, 1983; Stacey, 1983; Vogel, 1983).

Liberal Feminism

Liberal feminism is based on classic liberal thinking that individuals should be free to develop their own talents and pursue their own interests. Liberal feminists accept the basic organization of our society but seek to expand the rights and opportunities of women, in part by passing the Equal Rights Amendment.

Liberal feminists also endorse reproductive freedom for all women. They respect the family as a social institution but seek changes, including more widely available maternity leave and child care for mothers who wish to work.

Given their belief in the rights of individuals, liberal feminists do not think that all women need to work together collectively. Both women and men, through their individual achievement, are capable of improving their lives—as long as society removes legal and cultural barriers.

Socialist Feminism

Socialist feminism evolved from the ideas of Karl Marx and Friedrich Engels, in part as a critical response to Marx's inattention to gender (Philipson & Hansen, 1992). From this point of view, capitalism increases patriarchy by concentrating wealth and power in the hands of a small number of men.

Socialist feminists do not think the reforms sought by liberal feminism go far enough. They argue that the bourgeois family fostered by capitalism amounts to "domestic slavery" and should be replaced by some collective means of carrying out housework and child care. Moreover, replacing the traditional family can come about only through a socialist revolution that creates a state-centered economy to meet the needs of all. Such a basic transformation of society requires that women and men pursue their personal liberation not individually, as liberal feminists propose, but collectively.

Radical Feminism

Radical feminism, too, finds liberal feminism inadequate. Moreover, radical feminists claim that even a socialist

As a general rule, patriarchy is strongest in nations with traditional cultures and less economic development. Here we see a husband dragging his wife through the streets of Dhaka, Bangladesh, reportedly because she did not do the cooking on time. But, while violence against women in the United States may not be so public, it remains a serious problem linked to women's subordination here as well.

revolution would not end patriarchy. Instead, to attain equality, society must eliminate gender itself.

One way to achieve this goal is to use new reproductive technology (see Chapter 18, "Family") to separate women's bodies from the process of childbearing. With an end to motherhood, radical feminists reason, society could leave behind the entire family system, liberating women, men, and children from the tyranny of family, gender, and sex itself (Dworkin, 1987). Thus, radical feminism envisions an egalitarian and gender-free society—a revolution more radical than the one sought by Marx.

OPPOSITION TO FEMINISM

Feminism provokes criticism and resistance from both men and women who hold conventional ideas about gender. Some men oppose sexual equality for the same reasons that many white people have historically opposed social equality for people of color: They want to preserve their own privileges. Other men and women, including those who are neither rich nor powerful, distrust a social movement (especially its more radical expressions) that attacks the traditional family and rejects centuries-old patterns of male-female relationships.

For some men, feminism threatens the basis of their status and self-respect: their masculinity. Men who have been socialized to value strength and dominance feel uneasy about feminist ideas of men as gentle and warm (Doyle, 1983). Similarly, many women whose lives center on their husbands and children think feminism disparages the social roles that give meaning to their lives (Marshall, 1985).

Resistance to feminism also comes from academic circles. Some sociologists charge that feminism willfully ignores a growing body of evidence that men and women do think and act in somewhat different ways, which would make gender equality impossible. Furthermore, say critics, with its drive to enhance women's presence in the workplace, feminism belittles the crucial and unique contribution women make to the development of children—especially in the first years of life (Baydar & Brooks-Gunn, 1991; Popenoe, 1993b).

Finally, there is the question of *how* women should go about improving their social standing. A large majority of U.S. adults believe women should have equal rights, but 70 percent also say that women should advance individually, according to their abilities; only 10 percent favor women's rights groups or collective action (NORC, 1999:355).

In sum, opposition to feminism is primarily directed at its socialist and radical forms, while support for liberal feminism is widespread. Moreover, we are seeing an unmistakable trend toward greater gender equality. In 1977, 65 percent of all adults endorsed the statement "It is much better for everyone involved if the man is the achiever outside the home and the woman takes care of the home and family." By 1999, however, support for this statement had dropped sharply, to 34 percent (NORC, 1999:257).

CONTROVERSY & DEBATE

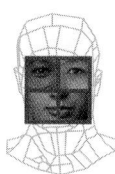

Men's Rights! Are Men *Really* So Privileged?

Anti-male discrimination has become far greater in scope, in degree, and in damage than any which may exist against women.

—*Men's rights advocate Richard F. Doyle*

It is men, this chapter argues, who dominate society. Men enjoy higher earnings, control more wealth, exercise more power, do less housework, and get more respect than women. The quotation above, however, sums up an important counterpoint advanced by the "men's rights movement"—that the male world is not nearly so privileged as some people think.

If men are so privileged in our society, why do they turn to crime more often than women? Moreover, the criminal justice system does not give men any special privileges. Few people are surprised to learn that many police are reluctant to arrest a woman, especially if she has children. This fact helps explain why 78 percent of arrests for serious crime put the handcuffs on a man. Neither do men get a break from the courts, since they make up 94 percent of the U.S. prison population. And, even though women can and do kill, all but two of the almost 400 offenders executed during the last several decades have been male.

Culture is not always generous to men, either. Real men work and play hard; they typically drink and smoke and speed on the highways. Given this view of maleness, is it any wonder that men are twice as likely as women to suffer serious assault, three times more likely to fall victim to homicide, and four times more likely to commit suicide? In light of such statistics, how do we explain our national preoccupation with violence against *women?* Perhaps, critics suggest, we are in the grip of a cultural double standard: We accept harm that comes to males

LOOKING AHEAD: GENDER IN THE TWENTY-FIRST CENTURY

At best, predictions about the future are informed speculation. So just as economists disagree about what the inflation rate will be a year from now, so sociologists can offer only general observations about the likely future state of society and the roles women and men will play in it.

To begin, change so far has been remarkable. A century and a half ago, women occupied a position of striking subordination. Husbands controlled property in marriage, and laws barred women from most jobs, from holding office, and from voting. Although women today remain socially disadvantaged, the movement toward equality has surged ahead. Two-thirds of people entering the work force during the 1990s were women, and the economy of the new century *depends* on the earnings of women.

Many factors have contributed to this transformation. Perhaps most important, industrialization has both broadened the range of human activity and shifted the nature of work from the physically demanding tasks that favored male strength to jobs that require more human thought and imagination. In this respect, women and men are on an even footing. Additionally, since technology has given us greater control over reproduction, women's lives are less constrained by unwanted pregnancies.

Many women and men have also deliberately pursued social equality. Sexual harassment complaints, for example, now are taken much more seriously in the workplace. Further, as more women assume positions of power in the corporate and political worlds, social changes in the new century may be as great as those we have already witnessed.

Gender is an important part of personal identity and family life, and it is deeply woven into the moral fabric of our society. Therefore, efforts to change social patterns involving gender will continue to provoke opposition, as the final box illustrates. On balance, however, while changes may be incremental, we are seeing movement toward a society in which women and men enjoy equal rights and opportunities.

while showing sympathy in the far fewer cases in which violence victimizes women. It is this same double standard, the argument continues, that moves women and children out of harm's way and expects men to "go down with the ship" or to die defending their country on the battlefield.

In school, it is boys more than girls who flunk out, drop out, or are kicked out. Boys are also several times more likely than girls to be diagnosed with a learning disability. Boys are less likely than girls to go to college and those who do earn lower grades.

Child custody is another sore point from the perspective of many men. Despite decades of consciousness-raising for gender fairness, and clear evidence that men earn more than women, courts across the United States routinely award primary care of children to mothers. And, to make matters worse, men separated from their children by the courts are often stigmatized as "runaway fathers" or "dead-beat dads," even though government studies show that *women* are more likely to refuse to pay court-ordered child support (37 percent of cases) than men (24 percent of cases).

Finally, male advocates point out that affirmative action laws now cover three-fourths of the population but notably exclude white males. Therefore, in today's affirmative action climate, women have the inside track to college (where they now outnumber men) as well as the work force (where businesses expect to be called to account for hiring practices).

Even nature seems to plot against men, as, on average, women live nearly six years longer. The controversial question is this: When society plays favorites, who is favored?

Continue the debate . . .

1. *Do you think police are more likely to ticket men than women for traffic violations? Why?*
2. *On your campus, do men's organizations (such as fraternities and athletic teams) enjoy special privileges? What about women's organizations?*
3. *On balance, do you agree or disagree with the "men's rights" perspective? Which specific points do you find convincing or wrong? Why?*

Source: Based on Doyle (1980), Scanlon (1992), Rosenfeld (1998), and Kleinfeld (1999).

SUMMARY

1. Gender refers to the meaning a culture attaches to being female or male. Because society gives men more power and other resources than women, gender is an important dimension of social stratification.
2. Although some degree of patriarchy exists everywhere, gender varies throughout history and across cultures.
3. Through the socialization process, people incorporate gender into their personalities as well as their actions (gender roles). The major agents of socialization—family, peer groups, schools, and the mass media—reinforce cultural definitions of what is feminine and masculine.
4. Gender stratification shapes the workplace. Although a majority of women are now in the paid labor force, most hold clerical or service jobs. Unpaid housework remains a task performed mostly by women, whether or not they hold jobs outside the home.
5. On average, women earn 74 percent as much as men. This disparity stems from differences in jobs and family responsibilities, as well as discrimination.
6. Women now earn a slight majority of all bachelor's and master's degrees. Men still receive a majority of all doctorates and professional degrees.
7. The number of women in politics has increased sharply in recent decades. Still, the vast majority of elected officials, especially at the national level, are men. Moreover, women make up only 15 percent of U.S. military personnel.
8. Because women have a distinctive social identity and are disadvantaged, they are a minority, although most white women do not think of themselves that way. Minority women encounter greater social disadvantages than white women. Overall, minority women earn only about 60 percent as much as white men.
9. Violence against women is a widespread problem in the United States. Our society is also

grappling with the issues of sexual harassment and pornography.

10. Structural-functional analysis suggests that, in preindustrial societies, distinctive roles for males and females reflect biological differences between the sexes. In industrial societies, marked gender inequality becomes dysfunctional and gradually decreases. Talcott Parsons claimed that complementary gender roles promote the social integration of families and society as a whole.
11. Social-conflict analysis views gender as a dimension of social inequality and conflict. Friedrich Engels tied gender stratification to the development of private property.
12. Feminism endorses the social equality of the sexes and opposes patriarchy and sexism. Feminism also seeks to eliminate violence against women and give women control over their sexuality.
13. There are three variants of feminist thinking: Liberal feminism seeks equal opportunity for both sexes within current social arrangements; socialist feminism advocates abolishing private property as the means to social equality; radical feminism seeks to create a gender-free society.
14. Although two-thirds of adults in the United States support the Equal Rights Amendment, this legislation—first proposed in Congress in 1923—has yet to become part of the U.S. Constitution.

KEY CONCEPTS

gender (p. 325) the personal traits and social positions that members of a society attach to being female and male

gender stratification (p. 326) the unequal distribution of wealth, power, and privilege between men and women

patriarchy (p. 328) a form of social organization in which males dominate females

matriarchy (p. 328) a form of social organization in which females dominate males

sexism (p. 328) the belief that one sex is innately superior to the other

gender roles (p. 330) (sex roles) attitudes and activities that a society links to each sex

minority (p. 340) any category of people, distinguished by physical or cultural difference, that a society sets apart and subordinates

sexual harassment (p. 341) comments, gestures, or physical contact of a sexual nature that are deliberate, repeated, and unwelcome

feminism (p. 345) the advocacy of social equality for men and women, in opposition to patriarchy and sexism

CRITICAL-THINKING QUESTIONS

1. In what ways are sex and gender related? In what respects are they distinct?
2. What techniques do the mass media employ in order to "sell" conventional ideas about gender to women and men?
3. What makes gender a dimension of social stratification? How does gender interact with inequality based on class, race, and ethnicity?
4. What are the key assertions of feminism? How do liberal, socialist, and radical feminism differ from one another?
5. In 1997, the British government doubled its number of women in Parliament after the Labor party decided to set a quota ensuring at least 25 percent of all candidates are women. Denmark, Finland, Norway, and Sweden have similar systems. Since just 13 percent of members of the U.S. Congress are women, should the United States do likewise?

APPLICATIONS AND EXERCISES

1. Take a walk through a business area of your local community. Which businesses are frequented almost entirely by women? By men? By both men and women? Try to explain the patterns you find.
2. Watch several hours of children's television programming on a Saturday morning. Notice the advertising, which mostly sells toys (and breakfast cereal). Keep track of what share of toys are "gendered," that is, aimed at one sex or the other. What traits do you associate with toys intended for boys and those intended for girls?
3. Do some research on the history of women's issues in your state. When was the first woman sent to Congress? What laws once existed that restricted the work women could do? Are there any such laws today? Did your state support the passage of the Equal Rights Amendment? What share of political officials today are women?
4. Install the CD-ROM packaged in the back of this new textbook to access a variety of study, review, and applications exercises designed to help you better understand the material covered in this chapter. The CD includes an author's tip video, as well as interactive maps, video application exercises, Web links, and study questions.

SITES TO SEE

http://www.prenhall.com/macionis

Visit the interactive Web site that accompanies this text. Begin by clicking on the cover of your book. You will find a chapter-by-chapter study guide, practice tests, chat room, and many suggested Web links.

http://www.macionis.com
(or **http://www.thesociologypage.com**)

The author's Web site contains a Links Library that includes dozens of sites providing information about women and women's issues from various positions on the political spectrum.

http://www.now.org

Visit the Web site for the National Organization of Women to discover the goals and strategies of this organization.

http://www.iwpr.org

Another informative site is run by the Institute for Women's Policy Research. Identify the issues this organization finds most important. Would you characterize this site as feminist? Why or why not?

http://www.wwwomen.com/

This site provides a search engine to locate all sorts of information concerning women.

http://www.educationindex.com/women/

This site provides numerous and widely varied links to sites concerned with women's issues.

http://www.feminist.org

This site, the home page of the Feminist Majority Foundation Online, offers news and information about issues and political actions.

http://www.catalystwomen.org

This site includes research on the social standing of women in business in the United States, as well as links to additional Web sites of interest to professional women.

CHAPTER 14

© Paul Marcus
Dreaming of Fred and Ginger

Oil painting on wood, 24 × 28 in. Studio SPM Inc.

RACE AND ETHNICITY

On a bright, fall day almost fifty years ago, in the city of Topeka, Kansas, a minister and his nine-year-old daughter walked hand in hand to the public elementary school four blocks from their home. But school officials refused to admit Linda Brown. Instead, they required that she attend another school two miles away, which meant a daily six-block walk to a bus stop where she sometimes waited half an hour for the bus. In bad weather, the child could be soaking wet by the time the bus came; one day she was so cold at the bus stop that she walked back home. Why, she asked her parents, could she not attend the school that was close by?

The answer—difficult for loving parents to give their child—was Linda Brown's introduction to a harsh fact: Skin color made her a second-class citizen in the United States. The injustice of separate schools for black and white children led the Browns and others to file a lawsuit on behalf of Linda Brown and other children, and, in 1954, Linda's question was put to the Supreme Court of the United States. In *Brown* v. *the Board of Education of Topeka*, the Supreme Court ruled unanimously that racially segregated schools provide African Americans with inferior schooling, thus striking down the practice, dating back to 1896, of "separate but equal" education for the two races.

Many greeted the Supreme Court's decision as a turning point in U.S. education. Yet, as the new century begins, most children in the United States still attend racially imbalanced schools. Although our society is officially committed to the principle that all people are created equal, race and ethnicity continue to guide the lives of men, women, and children in all sorts of ways.

The pattern of inequality and conflict based on color and culture is even more pronounced in other parts of the world. Since the fall of the former Soviet empire, Ukrainians, Moldavians, Azerbaijanis, and a host of other ethnic peoples in Eastern Europe are struggling to recover their cultural identity. In the Middle East, Arabs and Jews are trying to overcome deep-rooted tensions, as are Protestants and Catholics in Northern Ireland. In dozens of the world's nations, color and culture often flare in violent confrontation.

The range of biological variation in human beings is far greater than any system of racial classification allows. This fact is made obvious by trying to place all of the people pictured here into simple racial categories.

An irony of the human condition is that color and culture—a source of great pride—also cause us to degrade ourselves with hatred and violence. This chapter examines the meaning of race and ethnicity, explains how these social constructs have shaped our history, and suggests why they continue to play such a central part—for better or worse—in the world today.

THE SOCIAL MEANING OF RACE AND ETHNICITY

People frequently confuse "race" and "ethnicity." For this reason, we begin by defining these important terms.

RACE

A **race** is *a socially constructed category composed of people who share biologically transmitted traits that members of a society consider important.* People may classify each other racially based on physical characteristics such as skin color, facial features, hair texture, and body shape.

Physical diversity appeared among our human ancestors as the result of living in different geographical regions of the world. In regions of intense heat, for example, humans developed darker skin (from the natural pigment melanin) as protection from the sun; in regions with moderate climates, people have lighter skin. Such differences are, literally, only skin deep because *every* human being the world over is a member of a single biological species.

The variety of physical traits found today is also the product of migration, in that genetic characteristics once common to a single place are now found in many lands. Especially distinctive is the racial mix found in the Middle East (that is, western Asia), historically a crossroads of human migration. Greater racial uniformity, by contrast, characterizes more isolated people, such as the island-dwelling Japanese. But every population has some genetic mixture, and increasing contact among the world's people ensures even more racial blending in the future.

Although racial categories point to some biological elements, race is a socially constructed concept. This means that racial categories only come into being because a society considers some physical traits important. Around the world, societies show considerable variation in this regard: Typically, people in the United States attach more meaning to skin color than, say, people in Brazil. In addition, definitions and meanings concerning race change over time. Recently, for example, the U.S. Census Bureau has allowed people to describe themselves using more than one racial category, thus recognizing people as multiracial.

Racial Typology

Race came into being as a social category as nineteenth-century biologists tried to organize the world's physical diversity by constructing three racial types. They defined people with relatively light skin and fine hair *Caucasoid;* they called people with darker skin and coarse hair *Negroid;* and they labeled people with yellow or brown skin and distinctive folds on the eyelids *Mongoloid.*

Sociologists consider such terms misleading, at best, and harmful at worst. For one thing, no society contains biologically "pure" people. The skin color of people we might call "Caucasoid" (or "Indo-European," "Caucasian," or, more commonly, "white" people) ranges from very light (typical in Scandinavia) to very dark (in southern India). The same variation exists among so-called "Negroids" ("Africans," or more commonly, "black" people) and "Mongoloids" (that is "Asians"). In fact, many "white" people (say, in southern India) actually have darker skin than many "black" people (like the Negroid Aborigines of Australia).

The population of the United States, too, is quite mixed. Over many generations and throughout the Americas, the genetic traits of Negroid Africans, Caucasoid Europeans, and Mongoloid Native Americans (whose ancestors came from Asia) have intermingled. Many "black" people, therefore, have a significant Caucasoid ancestry, and many "white" people have some Negroid genes. In short, whatever people may think, race is no black-and-white issue.

Why, then, do people construct these racial categories in the first place? The reason is that such categories allow societies to rank people in a hierarchy, claiming some are inherently "better" than others, although no sound scientific research supports such beliefs. But because so much is at stake, societies may construct racial categories in ways that may seem extreme. Through much of the twentieth century, for example, many southern states labeled as "colored" anyone with as little as one thirty-second African ancestry (that is, one African American great-great-great-grandparent). Today, the law allows parents to declare the race of a child as they may wish. Even so, most members of our society are still very sensitive to people's racial background.

Fifty years ago, in some states, multiracial couples violated the law. The number of multiracial couples has risen steadily, and since the mid-1980s, the number of recorded interracial births has doubled. The result is that more and more people consider themselves to be multiracial. What effect will this trend have on the use of traditional racial categories?

A Trend toward Mixture

The number of officially recorded interracial births in the United States has doubled in the last fifteen years to 150,000 annually, accounting for 4 percent of all births. Moreover, when completing their 1990 census forms, almost 10 million people described themselves by checking more than a single racial category. Although members of our society attach considerable social importance to race, biologically speaking, race has less and less meaning in the United States.

ETHNICITY

Ethnicity is *a shared cultural heritage.* People define themselves—or others—as members of an *ethnic category* based on having common ancestors, language, or

TABLE 14–1 Racial and Ethnic Categories in the United States, 1990

Racial or Ethnic Classification	Approximate U.S. Population	Percent of Total Population
African descent	**29,986,060**	**12.1%**
Hispanic descent*	**22,354,059**	**9.0**
Mexican	13,495,938	5.4
Puerto Rican	2,727,754	1.1
Cuban	1,043,932	0.4
Other Hispanic	5,086,435	2.1
Native American descent	**1,959,234**	**0.8**
American Indian	1,878,285	0.8
Eskimo	57,152	<
Aleut	23,797	<
Asian or Pacific Islander descent	**7,273,662**	**2.9**
Chinese	1,645,472	0.7
Filipino	1,406,770	0.6
Japanese	847,562	0.3
Asian Indian	815,447	0.3
Korean	798,849	0.3
Vietnamese	614,547	0.2
Hawaiian	211,014	<
Samoan	62,964	<
Guamanian	49,345	<
Other Asian or Pacific Islander	821,692	0.3
European descent	**200,000,000**	**80.0**
German	57,947,000	23.3
Irish	38,736,000	15.6
English	32,652,000	13.1
Italian	14,665,000	5.9
French	10,321,000	4.1
Polish	9,366,000	3.8
Dutch	6,227,000	2.5
Scotch-Irish	5,618,000	2.3
Scottish	5,314,000	2.1
Swedish	4,681,000	1.9
Norwegian	3,869,000	1.6
Russian	2,953,000	1.2
Welsh	2,034,000	0.8
Danish	1,635,000	0.6
Hungarian	1,582,000	0.6

*People of Hispanic descent may be of any race. Many people also identify with more than one ethnic category. Thus, figures total more than 100 percent. White people represent 80 percent of the U.S. population.

< Indicates less than 1/10 of 1 percent.

Source: U.S. Census Bureau (1999).

religion that confer a distinctive social identity. The United States is a multiethnic society that favors the English language; even so, some 30 million people speak Spanish, Italian, German, French, or some other tongue in their homes. Similarly, the United States is a predominantly Protestant nation, but most people of Spanish, Italian, and Polish descent are Roman Catholic, while many of Greek, Ukranian, and Russian descent belong to the Eastern Orthodox church. More than 6 million Jewish Americans (with ancestral ties to various nations) share a religious history. Similarly, more than 7 million men and women are Muslim, and they now outnumber Episcopalians (Blank, 1998).

Race and ethnicity, then, are quite different: One involves traits that are biological; the other, cultural. But the two may go hand in hand. Japanese Americans, for example, have distinctive physical traits and—for those who maintain a traditional way of life—a distinctive culture as well. Table 14–1 presents the broad sweep of racial and ethnic diversity in the United States, as recorded by the 1990 census.

People can fairly easily modify their ethnicity: Immigrants may discard their cultural traditions over time or, like many people of Native American descent in recent years, try to revive their heritage (Nagel, 1994; Spencer, 1994). Assuming people mate with others like themselves, however, racial distinctiveness persists over generations.

Finally, ethnicity involves even more variability and mixture than race, because most people identify with more than one ethnic background. Golf star Tiger Woods, for example, describes himself as one-eighth white, one-eighth American Indian, one-fourth black, one-fourth Thai, and one-fourth Chinese (White, 1997).

MINORITIES

As Chapter 13 ("Gender Stratification") described, a *minority* is a category of people distinguished by physical or cultural traits and socially disadvantaged. Distinct from the dominant majority, in other words, a society sets apart minorities and subordinates them.

Both race and ethnicity are the basis for minority standing. As shown in Table 14–1, white people of non-Hispanic background (80 percent of the total) continue to predominate numerically. But the absolute numbers and share of population for virtually every minority are growing rapidly, so that, within a century, minorities, taken together, will likely form a majority of the U.S. population. National Map 14–1 shows where a minority-majority already exists.

Minorities have two major characteristics. First, they share a *distinctive identity*. Because societies attach importance to race, and these physical traits are virtually impossible for a person to change, most minority men and women are keenly aware of their physical appearance. The significance of ethnicity (which people *can* change)

SEEING OURSELVES

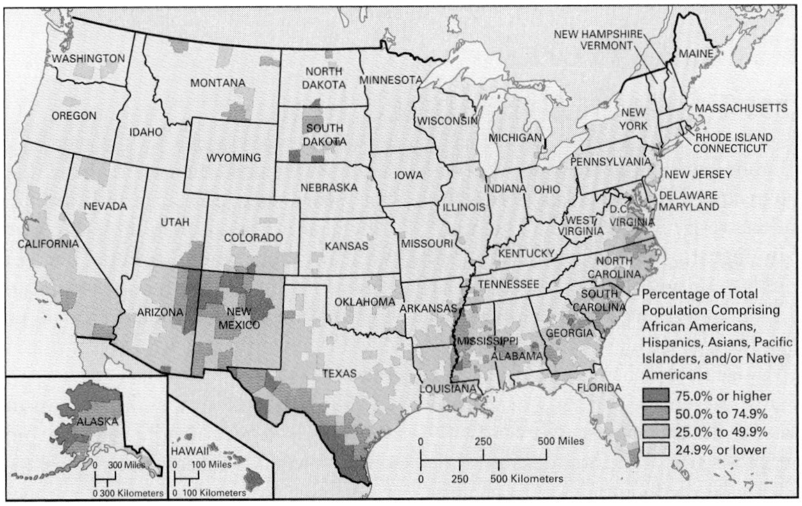

NATIONAL MAP 14–1
Where the Minority-Majority Already Exists

As recorded by the 1990 census, minorities predominate in 186 counties (out of 3,014). That is, the total number of African Americans, Asian Americans, Hispanics, and other minorities exceeds 50 percent of the population. The map also identifies some 40 counties where minorities together exceed 75 percent of the population and more than 200 counties where minority population surpasses the 25 percent mark. Why do you think most of these counties are in the South and Southwest?

Source: *Time*, July 12, 1993, p. 15. Copyright © 1993 Time Inc. Reprinted by permisson. Data from the 1990 decennial census.

is more variable. Throughout U.S. history, some people (such as Reform Jews) have downplayed their historic ethnicity, while others (including many Orthodox Jews) have maintained distinctive cultural traditions and even formed their own neighborhoods.

A second characteristic of minorities is *subordination*. As the remainder of this chapter shows, U.S. minorities typically have lower income, lower occupational prestige, and limited schooling. These facts mean that class, race, and ethnicity, as well as gender, are overlapping and reinforcing dimensions of social stratification. The box on page 358 profiles the struggles of Latin Americans who are recent immigrants to the United States.

Of course, not all members of any minority category are disadvantaged. Some Latinos, for example, are very wealthy, certain Chinese Americans are celebrated business leaders, and African Americans are included among our nation's leading scholars. But even the greatest success rarely allows individuals to rise fully above their minority standing (Benjamin, 1991). That is, race or ethnicity often serves as a *master status* (described in Chapter 6, "Social Interaction in Everyday Life") that overshadows personal accomplishments.

The term *minority* suggests that these categories of people constitute a small proportion of a society's population. But not always. For example, black South Africans are disadvantaged even though they are a numerical majority in their country. In the United States, women represent slightly more than half the population but are still struggling for the opportunities and privileges enjoyed by men.

PREJUDICE

November 19, 1994, Jerusalem, Israel. We are driving along the outskirts of this historic city—a holy place to Jews, Christians, and Muslims—when Razi, our taxi driver, spots a small group of fellasha—Ethiopian Jews—on a streetcorner. "Those people," he begins, "they are different. They don't drive cars. They don't want to improve themselves. Even when our country offers them schooling, they don't take it." He shakes his head and pronounces the Ethiopians "socially incorrigible."

Prejudice is *a rigid and irrational generalization about an entire category of people*. Prejudice is irrational insofar as people hold inflexible attitudes supported by

SOCIAL DIVERSITY

Hard Work: The Immigrant Life in the United States

Early in the morning, it is already hot in Houston as a line of pickup trucks snakes slowly into a dusty yard, where 200 laborers have been gathering since dawn, hoping for a day's work. The driver of the first truck opens his window and tells the foreman that he is looking for a crew to spread boiling tar on a roof. The foreman turns to the crowd and, after a few minutes, three workers step forward and climb into the back of the truck. The next driver is looking for two experienced house painters. The scene is repeated over and over, as men and a few women leave to dig ditches, spread cement, hang drywall, open clogged septic tanks, and even crawl under houses to poison rats.

To each driver who enters, Abdonel Cespedes, the foreman, asks "How much?" Most of the people in the trucks offer five dollars an hour. Cespedes automatically responds, "Six-fifty; the going rate is $6.50 for an hour's hard work." Sometimes he convinces people to pay that much, but usually not. The workers, who come from Mexico, El Salvador, and Guatemala, know that dozens of them will end up with no work at all this day. Most jump at the offer of five dollars an hour because they know, when the day is over, they will have fifty dollars in their pocket.

Labor markets like this one are common in large cities, especially across the southwestern United States. The surge in immigration in recent years has brought millions of people in search of work, and most have little schooling and speak little English.

Manuel Barrera has taken a day's work moving the entire contents of a store to a storage site as part of a repossession. He arrives at the boarded-up store and gazes at the mountains of heavy furniture that he must carry out to a moving van, drive across town, and then carry again. He sighs when he realizes that the store has no air conditioning. There is no break for lunch. No one says anything about toilets. Barrera shakes his head, "I will do this kind of work because it puts food on the table. But I did not foresee it would turn out like this."

The hard truth is that immigrants to the United States do the jobs that no one else wants. Indeed, immigrants represent the bottom level of the national economy, working in restaurants and hotels, on construction crews, and in private homes cooking, cleaning, and caring for children. Many well-off families take the labor of immigrants as much for granted as their sport utility vehicles and cell phones. Few immigrants make much more than minimum wage ($5.15 per hour), and rarely do immigrant workers receive health or pension benefits. Across the United States, about half of all housekeepers, household cooks, tailors, and restaurant waiters are men or women born abroad. In sum, much low-paying service work is performed by immigrants who are, literally, "at your service."

Source: Based on Booth (1998).

little or no direct evidence. Further, prejudice leads people to characterize all members of an entire category, the vast majority of whom they have never even met. Prejudice may target people of a particular social class, sex, sexual orientation, age, political affiliation, physical disability, race, or ethnicity.

Prejudices are *prejudgments* and they may be positive or negative. Our positive prejudices tend to exaggerate the virtues of people like ourselves, while our negative prejudices condemn those who differ from us. Because attitudes are rooted in culture, everyone has at least some measure of prejudice.

STEREOTYPES

Prejudice often takes the form of **stereotypes** (*stereo* is derived from Greek meaning "hard" or "solid"), *an exaggerated description applied to every person in some category.* Many white people hold stereotypical views of minorities. But minorities, too, use stereotypes, sometimes of whites and sometimes of other minorities, including themselves. Some Koreans, for example, portray African Americans as dishonest. Some African Americans, in turn, express the same attitude toward Jewish people (Smith, 1996; Cummings & Lambert, 1997).

RACISM

A powerful and destructive form of prejudice, **racism** refers to *the belief that one racial category is innately superior or inferior to another*. Racism has pervaded world history. The ancient Greeks, the peoples of India, and the Chinese were all quick to consider people unlike themselves as inferior.

Racism has also been widespread in the United States, where notions about racial inferiority supported slavery. Today, overt racism in this country has subsided because our more egalitarian culture urges us to evaluate people, in Dr. Martin Luther King's words, "not by the color of their skin but the content of their character."

Even so, racism—in thought and deed—remains a serious problem everywhere, and people still contend that some racial and ethnic categories are "better" than others. As the box on pages 360–61 explains, however, racial differences in mental abilities are due to environment rather than biology.

Racial and ethnic stereotypes are deeply embedded in our culture and language. Many people speak of someone "gypping" another without realizing that this word insults European Gypsies, a category of people long pushed to the margins of European societies. What about terms such as "Dutch treat," "French kiss," or "Indian giver"?

THEORIES OF PREJUDICE

What are the origins of prejudice? Social scientists have suggested various answers to this vexing question, focusing on frustration, personality, culture, and social conflict.

Scapegoat Theory

Scapegoat theory holds that prejudice springs from frustration among people who are themselves disadvantaged (Dollard, 1939). Take the case of a white woman frustrated by the low wages she earns working in a textile factory. Directing hostility at the powerful people who operate the factory carries obvious risk; therefore, she may attribute her low pay to the presence of minority co-workers. Her prejudice does not improve her situation, but it serves as a relatively safe way to vent anger, and it may give her the comforting feeling that at least she is superior to someone.

A **scapegoat**, then, is *a person or category of people, typically with little power, whom people unfairly blame for their own troubles*. Because they are usually "safe targets," minorities are often scapegoats.

Authoritarian Personality Theory

According to T. W. Adorno et al. (1950), extreme prejudice is a personality trait in certain individuals. This conclusion is supported by research showing that people who display strong prejudice toward one minority are usually intolerant of all minorities. These *authoritarian personalities* rigidly conform to conventional

CRITICAL THINKING

Does Race Affect Intelligence?

Are Asian Americans smarter than white people? Is the typical white person more intelligent than the average African American? Throughout the history of the United States, many people have painted one category of people as more intellectually gifted than another. Moreover, people have used such thinking to justify the privileges of an allegedly superior category or to bar supposedly inferior people from entering this country.

Scientists know that the distribution of human intelligence forms a "bell curve," as shown in the figure at the right. By convention, average intelligence is defined as an intelligence quotient (IQ) score of 100 (technically, an IQ score is mental age, as measured by a test, divided by age in years, with the result multiplied by 100; thus, an eight-year-old who performs like a ten-year-old has an IQ of 10/8 = 1.25 × 100 = 125).

In a controversial study of intelligence and social inequality, Richard Herrnstein and Charles Murray (1994) claim that overwhelming research shows that race is related to intelligence. Specifically, they report that the average IQ of people with European ancestry is 100, of people with East Asian ancestry is 103, and of people of African descent is 90.

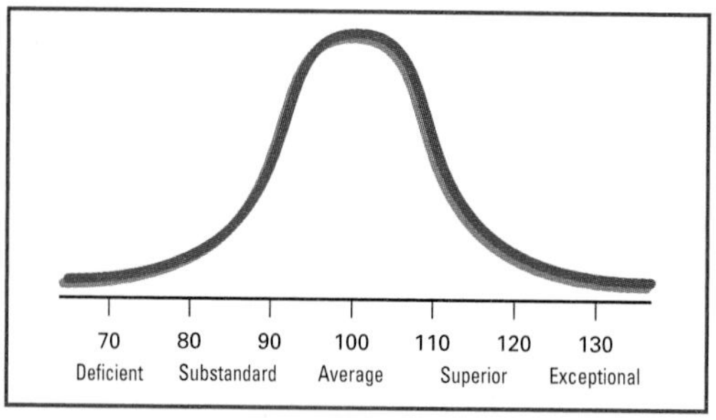

IQ: The Distribution of Intelligence

Of course, assertions of this kind are explosive because they fly in the face of our democratic and egalitarian sentiments, which say no racial type is inherently "better" than another. Some critics of Herrnstein and Murray charge that intelligence tests are flawed, and others question whether what we call "intelligence" has much real meaning at all.

Most social scientists acknowledge that IQ tests do measure something important that we think of as "intelligence, " and they agree that *individuals* vary in intellectual aptitude. But they reject the idea that any *category* of people, on average, is "smarter" than any other. That is, categories of people may show

cultural values and see moral issues as clear-cut matters of right and wrong. People with authoritarian personalities also look upon society as naturally competitive and hierarchical, with "better" people (like themselves) inevitably dominating those who are weaker.

Adorno also found that people tolerant toward one minority are likely to be accepting of all. These people tend to be more flexible in their moral judgments and treat all people as equals.

Adorno thought that people with little education who are raised by cold and demanding parents tend to develop authoritarian personalities. Filled with anger and anxiety as children, they grow into hostile, aggressive adults, seeking scapegoats whom they consider inferior.

Culture Theory

A third theory contends that, while extreme prejudice may be characteristic of certain people, some prejudice is found in everyone because it is embedded in a society's culture. Emory Bogardus (1968) studied the effects of culturally rooted prejudices for more than forty years. He developed the concept of *social distance* to gauge how close or how distant people feel toward others in various racial and ethnic categories. Bogardus found that most people in the United States feel closest to people of English, Canadian, and Scottish background, even welcoming marriage with them. Attitudes are less favorable toward the French, Germans, Swedes, and Dutch, with most people feeling greater social distance from them. Finally, the most negative prejudices target people of African and Asian descent.

According to Bogardus, prejudice is so widespread in the United States that we cannot explain intolerance as simply a trait of "authoritarian personalities," as Adorno suggests. Rather, Bogardus concludes, almost everyone in this society expresses some degree of bigotry because we live in a "culture of prejudice" that has taught us to view certain categories of people as inferior to others.

small differences on intelligence tests, but the crucial question is *why*.

Thomas Sowell explains that most of the documented racial differences in intelligence are not due to biology but to environment. In some skillful sociological detective work, Sowell traced IQ scores for various racial and ethnic categories from the early twentieth century. He found that, on average, immigrants from European nations such as Poland, Lithuania, Italy, and Greece, as well as Asian countries including China and Japan, scored ten to fifteen points below the U.S. average. But *today* people in these same categories have IQ scores that are average or above average. Among Italian Americans, for example, average IQ jumped almost ten points in fifty years; among Polish and Chinese Americans, the increase was almost twenty points.

Because genetic changes occur over thousands of years and these people largely intermarried among themselves, biological factors cannot explain the higher IQ scores. The only plausible explanation is changing cultural patterns. The descendants of early immigrants improved their intellectual performance as their living conditions improved and their opportunity for schooling increased.

Sowell found that a similar pattern applies to African Americans. Historically, the average IQ test score of African Americans living in the North is about ten points higher than the average score of those living in the South. And among descendants of African Americans who migrated from the South to the North after 1940, IQ scores went up just as they did with descendants of earlier immigrants. Thus, if environmental factors are the same for various categories of people, racial IQ differences largely disappear.

What IQ test score disparities do tell us, according to Sowell, is that *cultural patterns* matter. If Asians, on average, score high on tests, it is because they have been raised to value learning and pursue excellence, not because all Asians are smart. For their part, African Americans are no less intelligent than anyone else, but they carry a legacy of disadvantage that can undermine self-confidence and discourage achievement.

What do you think?

1. *Do measures of intelligence always reflect people's environment? To what extent are IQ scores valid measures?*
2. *Why, according to Thomas Sowell, do some racial and ethnic categories show dramatic, short-term changes in average IQ scores?*
3. *What could schools do to raise the IQ scores of children, especially those from disadvantaged backgrounds?*

Sources: Herrnstein & Murray (1994) and Sowell (1994, 1995).

Conflict Theory

A fourth explanation proposes that powerful people use prejudice to justify their oppression of others. To the extent that Anglos look down on illegal Latino immigrants in the Southwest, for example, the well-off among them can get away with paying the immigrants low wages for hard work. Similarly, all elites benefit when prejudice divides workers along racial and ethnic lines and discourages them from working together to advance their common interests (Geschwender, 1978; Olzak, 1989).

Another conflict-based argument, advanced by Shelby Steele (1990), is that minorities themselves cultivate a climate of *race consciousness* in order to win greater power and privileges. In promoting race consciousness, Steele explains, minorities claim that they are victims entitled to special consideration based on their race. While this strategy may yield short-term gains, such thinking can spark a backlash from white people or others who oppose "special treatment" for anyone on the basis of race or ethnicity.

DISCRIMINATION

Closely related to prejudice is **discrimination**, *treating various categories of people unequally*. While prejudice refers to attitudes, discrimination is a matter of action. Like prejudice, discrimination can be either positive (providing special advantages) or negative (subjecting people to obstacles). Discrimination also ranges from subtle to blatant.

Prejudice and discrimination often occur together: A prejudiced personnel manager, for example, may refuse to hire minorities. Robert Merton (1976) describes such a person as an *active bigot* (see Figure 14–1a). But prejudice and discrimination do not always occur together, as in the case of the prejudiced personnel manager who, out of fear of lawsuits, *does* hire minorities. Merton calls this person a *timid bigot*. People who are tolerant of

FIGURE 14–1 **Patterns of Prejudice and Discrimination**

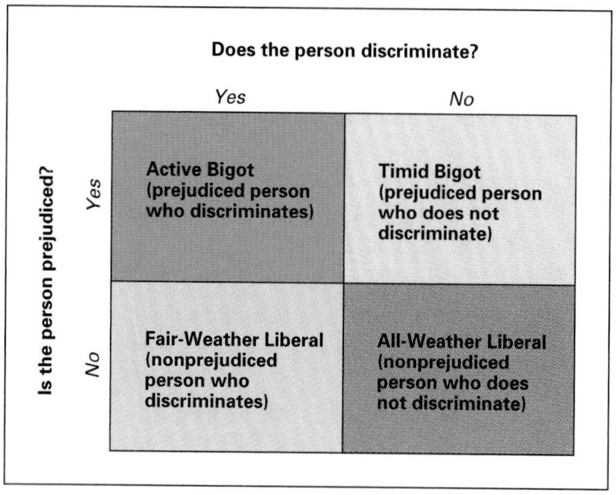

(a) Prejudice and Discrimination: Various Combinations

Source: Merton (1976).

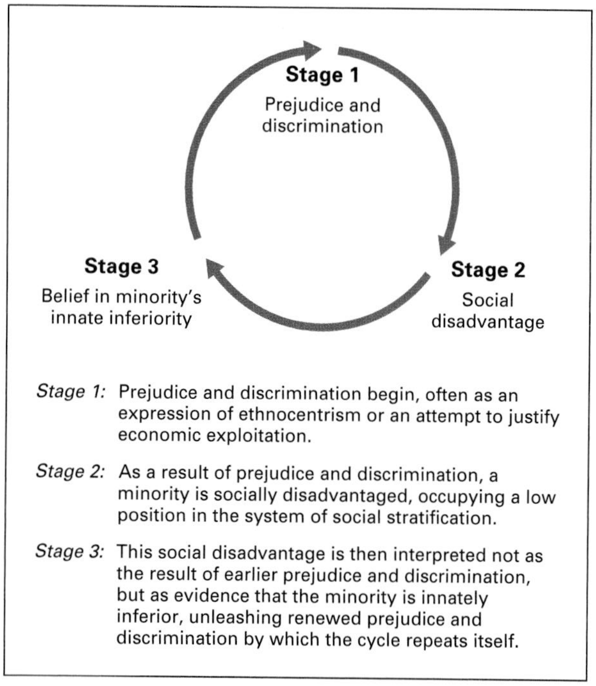

(b) The Vicious Cycle

Prejudice and discrimination can form a vicious cycle, perpetuating themselves.

minorities yet discriminate when it is to their advantage are *fair-weather liberals*. Finally, Merton's *all-weather liberal* is free of prejudice and discrimination.

INSTITUTIONAL PREJUDICE AND DISCRIMINATION

We typically think of prejudice and discrimination as the hateful ideas or actions of specific people. But thirty years ago, Stokely Carmichael and Charles Hamilton (1967) pointed out that far greater harm results from **institutional prejudice and discrimination**, *bias inherent in the operation of society's institutions*, including schools, banks, police, and the workplace. For example, researchers have shown that banks reject home mortgage applications from minorities at a higher rate than those from white people, even when income and quality of neighborhood are held constant (Gotham, 1998).

According to Carmichael and Hamilton, the white majority is slow to condemn or even to recognize institutional prejudice and discrimination because they often involve respected public officials and long-established traditions. A case in point is the Supreme Court's Brown decision in 1954, described in the opening to this chapter. The principle of "separate but equal" had been the law of the land, upholding institutional racism in the form of an educational caste system. Today, half a century later, the law may have changed, but most U.S. students still attend schools that are overwhelmingly one race or the other. Indeed, in 1991, the courts declared that neighborhood schools will never provide equal education as long as our population is divided into racially segregated neighborhoods, with most African Americans living in central cities and most white people (and Asian Americans) living in politically separate suburbs.

PREJUDICE AND DISCRIMINATION: THE VICIOUS CYCLE

Prejudice and discrimination reinforce each other. The Thomas theorem, discussed in Chapter 6 ("Social Interaction in Everyday Life"), offers a simple explanation of this fact: *Situations defined as real become real in their consequences* (Thomas, 1966:301; orig. 1931).

As W. I. Thomas recognized, stereotypes become real to those who believe them, sometimes even to those who are victimized by them. Power also plays a role here, since some categories of people can enforce their prejudices to the detriment of others. Prejudice on the part of whites toward people of color, for example, does not produce *innate* inferiority but it can

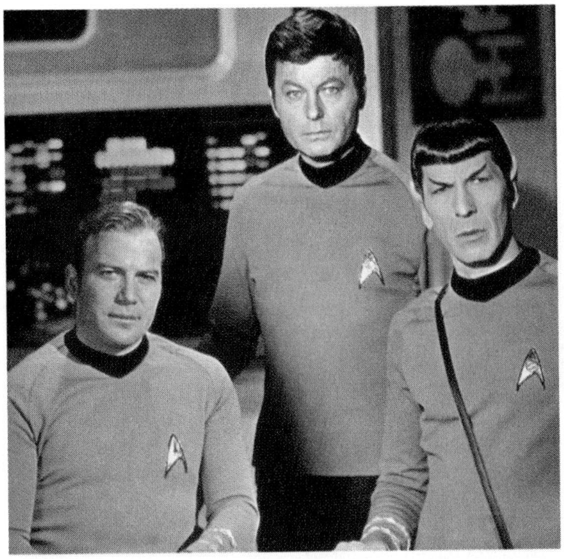

"Star Trek" has been a television favorite for more than thirty years. Compare the cast of the original show, which first aired in 1966, to the crew of the most recent "Star Trek: Voyager." What does the difference in casting suggest about our society's changing view of women? Of racial and ethnic minorities?

produce *social* inferiority, pushing minorities into low-paying jobs, inferior schools, and racially segregated housing. Then, if white people interpret social disadvantage as evidence that minorities do not measure up to their standards, they unleash a new round of prejudice and discrimination, giving rise to a *vicious cycle* (see Figure 14–1b).

MAJORITY AND MINORITY: PATTERNS OF INTERACTION

Social scientists describe patterns of interaction among racial and ethnic categories in terms of four models: pluralism, assimilation, segregation, and genocide.

PLURALISM

Pluralism is *a state in which racial and ethnic minorities are distinct but have social parity*. In other words, categories of people are socially different, but they all share resources more or less equally.

The United States is pluralistic to the extent that our society promises equal standing under the law. Moreover, large cities contain countless "ethnic villages," where people proudly display the traditions of their immigrant ancestors. In New York these include Spanish Harlem, Little Italy, and Chinatown; in Philadelphia, Italian South Philly; in Miami, Little Havana; in Chicago, Little Saigon; and Latino East Los Angeles.

But the United States is not really pluralistic, for three reasons. First, while many people value their cultural heritage, only a small proportion want to live apart from others and exclusively with their "own kind" (NORC, 1999). Second, our tolerance for social diversity is limited. One reaction to the rising proportion of minorities in the United States, for example, is a social movement to establish English as this nation's official language. Third, as we shall see later in this chapter, it is simply a fact that people of various colors and cultures have unequal social standing.

ASSIMILATION

Assimilation is *the process by which minorities gradually adopt patterns of the dominant culture*. Assimilation involves changing modes of dress, attitudes and values, religion, language, and friends. People assimilate by "remaking" themselves to conform to new cultural patterns.

Many people think of the United States as a "melting pot" where different nationalities blend together.

A milestone in this country's efforts to end a racial caste system was Jackie Robinson's success in breaking the "color line" in 1947 to become the first African American to play in Major League Baseball. Here Robinson slides past Cub catcher Toby Atwell to steal home, displaying the outstanding talent and drive that eventually won the respect of a nation.

This concept was well expressed in a play that was popular in the early 1900s:

> America is God's Crucible, the great melting-pot where all races of Europe are melting and reforming. Here you stand, good folks, think I, when I see them at Ellis Island [historical entry point for many immigrants in New York], here you stand with your fifty groups, with your fifty languages and histories, and your fifty blood-hatreds and rivalries. But you won't be long like that, brothers, for these are the fires of God. . . . Germans and Frenchmen, Irishmen and Englishmen, Jews and Russians, into the Crucible with you all! God is making an American! (Zangwill, 1921:33; orig. 1909)

In truth, however, rather than everyone "melting" into some new cultural pattern, most minorities adopt the dominant culture established by the earliest settlers. Why? Assimilation is both the path to upward social mobility and the way to escape the prejudice and discrimination directed at more visible foreigners (Newman, 1973).

The degree of assimilation varies by category. For example, Germans and Irish have "melted" more than Italians, and the Japanese more than the Chinese or Koreans. Multiculturalists, however, oppose assimilation because it suggests that minorities are "the problem" and defines them (rather than majority people) as the ones who need to do all the changing.

Note, too, that assimilation involves changes in ethnicity but not in race. For example, many descendants of Japanese immigrants discard their traditions but retain their racial identity. Racial traits can diminish over time only through **miscegenation**, *biological reproduction by partners of different racial categories*. Although the rate of interracial marriage is rising, it is still low; only 4 in 100 U.S. births are to parents of different races.

SEGREGATION

Segregation refers to *the physical and social separation of categories of people*. Some minorities, especially religious orders like the Amish, voluntarily segregate themselves. Usually, however, majorities segregate minorities by excluding them. Residential neighborhoods, schools, occupations, hospitals, and even cemeteries can be segregated. While pluralism fosters distinctiveness without disadvantage, segregation enforces separation to the detriment of a minority.

Racial segregation has a long history in the United States, beginning with slavery and evolving into racially separated housing, schools, buses, and trains. Decisions such as the 1954 Brown case have reduced *de jure* (Latin, meaning "by law") discrimination in this country. However, *de facto* ("in fact") segregation continues to this day in the form of countless neighborhoods that are home to people of a single race.

Racial segregation in the United States has declined somewhat during recent decades (Farley, 1997). Yet Douglas Massey and Nancy Denton (1989) have documented the *hypersegregation* of African Americans in some inner cities. These people have little contact of any kind with people in the larger society. Hypersegregation disadvantages about one-fifth of all African Americans but only a few percent of comparably poor whites (Jagarowsky & Bane, 1990; Krivo et al., 1998).

Segregated minorities understandably resent their second-class citizenship, and sometimes the action of even a single person can bring about change. On December 1, 1955, Rosa Parks boarded a bus in Montgomery, Alabama, and sat in the section designated by law for African Americans. When a crowd of white passengers boarded, the driver asked four black people to give up their seats to white people. Three did so, but Rosa Parks refused. The driver left the bus and returned with police, who arrested her for violating the racial segregation laws. A court later convicted Parks and fined her $14. Her stand (or sitting) for justice led the African American community of Montgomery to boycott city buses and ultimately end this form of segregation (King, 1969).

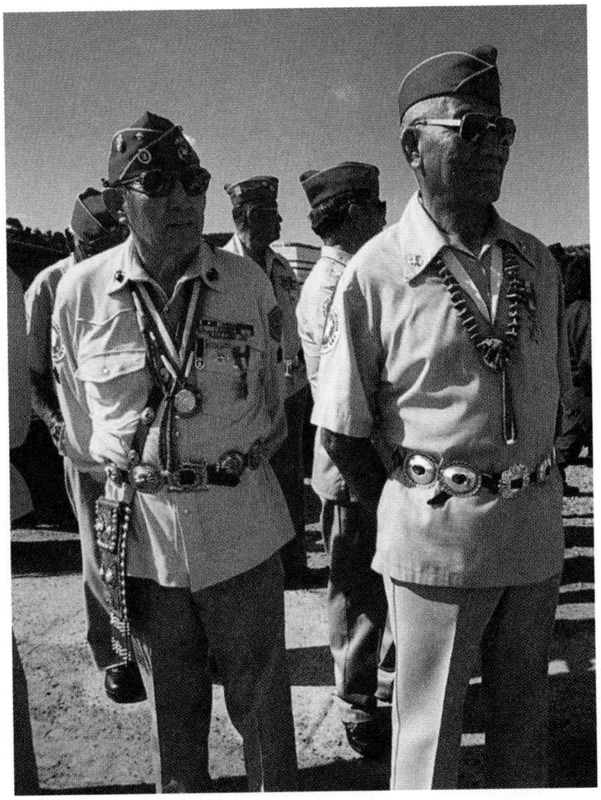

A resurgence of Native American pride is evident in this celebration held in Window Rock, Arizona, in 1991 to honor Navajo soldiers returning from the Persian Gulf War. The older men shown here are World War II veterans—famous Navajo "code talkers"—who fought in the Pacific and devised a code from their native language that the opposing Japanese army was never able to understand.

GENOCIDE

Genocide is *the systematic annihilation of one category of people by another*. Though this deadly form of racism and ethnocentrism violates every moral standard, it has erupted time and again in human history.

Genocide figured prominently in the European conquest of the Americas. From the sixteenth century on, the Spanish, Portuguese, English, French, and Dutch forcefully colonized vast empires. Some native people fell victim to calculated killing, but most succumbed to European diseases, for which they had no natural immunities (Matthiessen, 1984; Sale, 1990).

Genocide also occurred in the twentieth century. Unimaginable horror befell European Jews in the 1930s and 1940s, during the Holocaust, when Hitler's Nazis exterminated more than 6 million Jewish men, women, and children. The Soviet dictator Josef Stalin murdered on an even greater scale, killing perhaps 30 million real and imagined enemies during his violent rule. Between 1975 and 1980, Pol Pot's communist regime in Cambodia butchered all "capitalists," including anyone able to speak a Western language and even people who wore eyeglasses, viewed as an elitist symbol. In all, some 2 million people (one-fourth of the population) perished in the Cambodian "killing fields" (Shawcross, 1979).

Tragically, genocide continues. Recent examples include Hutus killing Tutsis in the African nation of Rwanda, and Serbs killing Bosnians in the Balkans of Eastern Europe.

The four minority-majority patterns just described have all been played out in the United States. While many people proudly point to patterns of pluralism and assimilation, it is also important to recognize the degree to which our society has been built on segregation (of African Americans) and genocide (of Native Americans). The remainder

SEEING OURSELVES

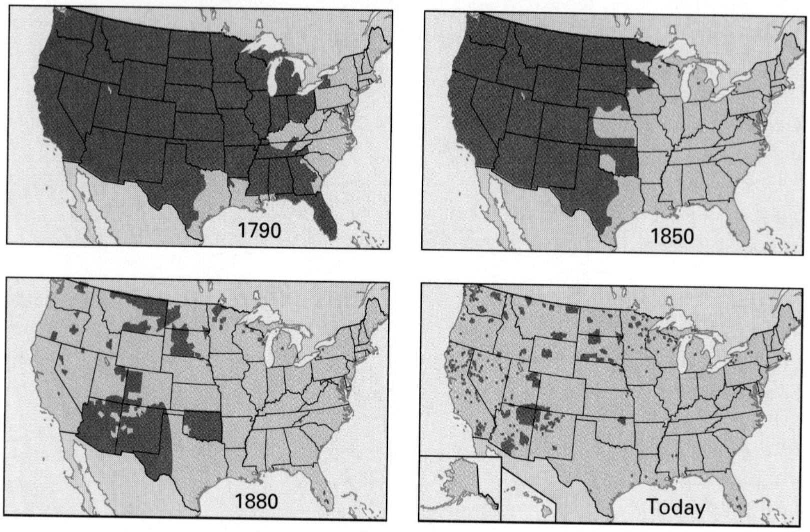

NATIONAL MAP 14–2
Land Controlled by Native Americans, 1790–1998

Two hundred years ago, Native Americans controlled three-fourths of the land that would eventually become today's United States. Today, Native Americans control 314 reservations—scattered across the United States—that, together, account for just 2 percent of the country's land area. How would you characterize these locations?

Source: Copyright © 1998 by The New York Times Co. Reprinted by permission.

of this chapter examines how these four patterns have shaped the history and present social standing of major racial and ethnic categories in the United States.

RACE AND ETHNICITY IN THE UNITED STATES

> Give me your tired, your poor,
> Your huddled masses yearning to breathe free,
> The wretched refuse of your teeming shore,
> Send these, the homeless, tempest-tossed to me:
> I lift my lamp beside the golden door.

These words by Emma Lazarus, inscribed on the Statue of Liberty, express cultural ideals of human dignity, personal freedom, and opportunity. Indeed, the United States has provided more of the "good life" to more immigrants than any other nation. But, as the history of this nation's racial and ethnic minorities reveals, our country's golden door has opened more widely for some than for others.

NATIVE AMERICANS

The term *Native Americans* refers to the societies—including Aleuts, Eskimos, Cherokee, Zuni, Sioux, Mohawk, Aztec, and Inca—who first settled the Western Hemisphere. Some 30,000 years before Christopher Columbus (1446–1506) stumbled on the Americas, migrating peoples crossed a land bridge from Asia to North America where the Bering Strait (off the coast of Alaska) lies today. Gradually, they made their way throughout North and South America.

When the first Europeans arrived late in the fifteenth century, Native Americans numbered in the millions. But by 1900, after relentless subjugation and acts of genocide, the "vanishing Americans" numbered a mere 250,000 (Dobyns, 1966; Tyler, 1973).

It was Christopher Columbus who first referred to Native Americans as *Indians* because he wrongly thought he had reached India. Actually, Columbus had landed in the Bahama Islands in the Caribbean. Columbus found the island people passive and peaceful, a stark contrast to materialistic and competitive Europeans (Matthiessen, 1984; Sale, 1990). Yet early Europeans justified seizing the land by portraying Native Americans as thieves and murderers (Unruh, 1979; Josephy, 1982).

After the Revolutionary War, the new U.S. government took a pluralist approach that recognized Native American societies and sought to gain more land through treaties. Payment for land was far from fair, however, and when Native Americans resisted surrendering their homeland, the U.S. government simply used superior military power to evict them. By the early 1800s, few Native Americans remained east of the Mississippi River.

In 1871, the United States declared Native Americans wards of the government and adopted a strategy of forced assimilation. Now Native Americans continued to lose their land and were well on their way to losing their culture as well. Reservation life fostered dependency, replacing ancestral languages with English and traditional religion with Christianity. Officials of the Bureau of Indian Affairs took children from their parents and put them in boarding schools, where they were resocialized as "Americans." Authorities gave local control of reservation life to the few Native Americans who supported government policies, and distributed reservation land—traditionally held collectively—as the private property of individual families (Tyler, 1973).

Not until 1924 were Native Americans entitled to U.S. citizenship. After that, many migrated from reservations, adopting more mainstream cultural patterns and marrying non–Native Americans. Many large cities have sizable Native American populations. Overall, however, Native Americans control just a small share of land in this country, as shown in National Map 14–2. Table 14–2 reports that the median family income for Native Americans is far below the U.S. average, and relatively few Native Americans earn a college degree.[1]

From in-depth interviews with Native Americans in a western city, Joan Albon (1971) concluded that lower Native American social standing reflects a range of cultural factors, including a non-competitive view of life and a reluctance to pursue higher education. In addition, she noted, many Native Americans have dark skin, which makes them victims of prejudice and discrimination.

Like other racial and ethnic minorities in the United States, Native Americans have recently reasserted pride in their cultural heritage. Native American organizations report a surge in membership, and many children can speak native languages better than their parents (Fost, 1991; Johnson, 1991; Nagel, 1996). Moreover, the legal autonomy of reservations has turned out to be an ace-up-the-sleeve for many tribes, who have built lucrative gaming casinos and now control about 20 percent of all U.S. gambling. But such financial windfalls affect relatively few Native peoples; most endure their disadvantages with a profound sense of the injustice they have suffered at the hands of white people.

TABLE 14–2 The Social Standing of Native Americans, 1990

	Native Americans	Entire United States
Median family income	$21,750	$35,225
Percent in poverty	30.9%	13.1%
Completion of four or more years of college (age 25 and over)	9.3%	20.3%

Source: U.S. Census Bureau (1999).

WHITE ANGLO-SAXON PROTESTANTS

White Anglo-Saxon Protestants (WASPs) were not the first people to inhabit the United States, but they came to dominate this nation once European colonization began. Most WASPs are of English ancestry, but the category also includes Scots and Welsh. At over 50 million people, one in five members of our society claims some WASP background. National Map 14–3 on page 368 shows where in the United States the highest concentrations of WASPs are found.

Historically, WASP immigrants were highly skilled and motivated to achieve by what we now call the Protestant work ethic. Because of their numbers and power, WASPs were not subject to the prejudice and discrimination experienced by other categories of immigrants. In fact, their historical dominance has led others to want to become like them.

WASPs were never one single social group; especially in colonial times, considerable hostility separated English Anglicans and Scotch-Irish Presbyterians (Parrillo, 1994). But during the nineteenth century, most WASPs joined together to bemoan the arrival of "undesirable foreigners"—Germans in the 1840s and Italians in the 1880s. Political movements managed to pass laws that limited the flow of immigrants. Those who could afford it sheltered themselves in exclusive neighborhoods and restrictive clubs. Thus, the 1880s—the decade that saw the Statue of Liberty first welcome immigrants to the United States—also saw the founding of the first country club with only WASP members (Baltzell, 1964).

By about 1950, WASP command of wealth and privileges had peaked, as indicated by the 1960 election of John Fitzgerald Kennedy as the first Irish-Catholic

[1]In making comparisons of education and, especially, income, keep in mind that various categories of the U.S. population have different median ages. The 1999 median age for all U.S. people was 35.6 years. White people have a median age of 36.7 years; for Native Americans, the figure is 27.7 years. Because people's schooling and income increase over time, such an age difference accounts for some of the disparities shown in Table 14–2.

SEEING OURSELVES

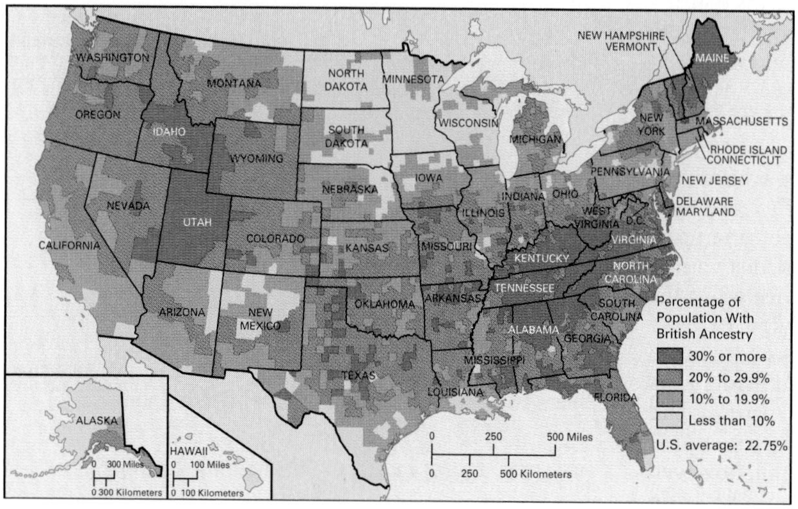

Source: From Rodger Doyle, *Atlas of Contemporary America*. Copyright © 1994 by Rodger Doyle. Reprinted with permission of Facts on file, Inc., New York, N.Y.

NATIONAL MAP 14–3
The Concentration of People of WASP Ancestry across the United States

Many people associate white Anglo-Saxon Protestants with elite communities along the eastern and western seaboards of the United States. But the highest concentrations of WASPs are in Utah (due to migrations of Mormons with English ancestry) and Appalachia and northern New England (due to historic immigration). Overall, however, WASPs form a large share of the U.S. population almost everywhere except Alaska, South Texas, and the upper Great Plains. Do you know why?

president. But the majority of people in the upper-upper class are still WASPs (Baltzell, 1964, 1976, 1979a, 1988). The WASP cultural legacy also remains. English is this country's dominant language and Protestantism, the majority religion. Our legal system, too, reflects its English origins. But the historical dominance of WASPs is most evident in the widespread use of the terms "race" and "ethnicity" to describe everyone but themselves.

AFRICAN AMERICANS

Although African Americans accompanied European explorers to the New World in the fifteenth century, most accounts mark the beginning of black history in the United States as 1619, when a Dutch trading ship brought twenty Africans to Jamestown, Virginia. Whether these people arrived as slaves or indentured servants who paid their passage by performing labor for a specified period, being of African descent on these shores soon became virtually synonymous with being a slave. In 1661, Virginia enacted the first law recognizing slavery (Sowell, 1981).

Slavery was the foundation of the southern colonies' plantation system. White people ran plantations with slave labor, and, until 1808, some were also slave traders. Traders—including Europeans, Africans, and North Americans—forcibly transported some 10 million Africans to various countries in the Americas, including 400,000 to the United States. On board small sailing ships, hundreds of slaves were chained together for the several weeks it took to cross the Atlantic Ocean. Filth and disease killed many and drove others to suicide. Overall, perhaps half died en route (Tannenbaum, 1946; Franklin, 1967; Sowell, 1981).

Surviving the journey was a mixed blessing, since it brought only a life of servitude. Although some slaves worked in cities at various trades, most labored in the fields, often from daybreak until sunset, and even longer during the harvest. The law allowed owners to impose whatever disciplinary measures they deemed necessary to ensure that slaves were obedient and productive. Even killing a slave rarely prompted legal action. Owners often divided slave families at public auctions where human beings were bought and sold as pieces of property. Unschooled and dependent on their owners for all their basic needs, slaves had little control over their destinies (Franklin, 1967; Sowell, 1981).

Some free persons of color lived in both the North and the South, laboring as small-scale farmers, skilled workers, and small-business owners. But the lives of most African Americans stood in glaring contradiction to the principles of equality and freedom on which the United States was founded. The Declaration of Independence states:

> We hold these Truths to be self-evident, that all Men are created equal, that they are endowed by their Creator with certain unalienable Rights, that among these are Life, Liberty, and the Pursuit of Happiness.

Most white people, however, did not apply these ideals to black people. In the Dred Scott case of 1857, the U.S. Supreme Court addressed the question, "Are blacks citizens?" by writing "We think they are not, and that they are not included, and were not intended to be included, under the word 'citizens' in the Constitution, and can therefore claim none of the rights and privileges which that instrument provides for and secures for citizens of the United States" (quoted in Blaustein & Zangrando, 1968:160). Thus arose what Swedish sociologist Gunnar Myrdal (1944) termed the "American dilemma": a democratic society's denial of basic rights and freedoms to an entire category of people. To resolve this dilemma, many white people simply defined black people as innately inferior.

In 1865, the Thirteenth Amendment to the Constitution outlawed slavery. Three years later, the Fourteenth Amendment reversed the Dred Scott ruling, conferring citizenship on all people born in the United States. The Fifteenth Amendment, ratified in 1870, stated that neither race nor previous condition of servitude could deprive anyone of the right to vote. However, so-called Jim Crow laws—classic cases of institutional discrimination—still segregated U.S. society into two racial castes. Especially in the South, white people beat and lynched black people (and some white people) who challenged the racial hierarchy.

The twentieth century brought dramatic changes for African Americans. After World War I, tens of thousands of men, women, and children left the rural South for jobs in northern factories. While most found greater economic opportunity, few escaped the racial prejudice and discrimination that ranked them lower in the class hierarchy than white immigrants arriving from Europe.

In the 1950s and 1960s, a national civil rights movement grew out of landmark judicial decisions that outlawed segregated schools and discrimination in employment and public accommodations. In addition, the "black power" movement gave African Americans a renewed sense of pride and purpose.

Gains notwithstanding, people of African descent continue to occupy a subordinate position in the United States, as shown in Table 14–3. The median income of African American families in 1998 ($30,636) was only 62 percent of white family income ($49,781), a ratio that has not changed in thirty years.[2] Black families remain three times as likely as white families to be poor.

TABLE 14–3 The Social Standing of African Americans, 1998*

	African Americans	Entire United States
Median family income	$30,636	$47,467
Percent in poverty	26.1%	12.7%
Completion of four or more years of college (age 25 and over)	14.7%	24.4%

*For purposes of comparison with other tables in this chapter, 1990 data are as follows: median family income, $21,423; percent in poverty, 31.9%; completion of four or more years of college, 11.3%.

Source: U.S. Census Bureau (1999).

The number of African Americans securely in the middle class rose by more than half between 1980 and 2000; 28 percent earn more than $50,000 a year, and 43 percent earn at least $35,000 annually. But for some African Americans, earnings have slipped during the last fifteen years, as factory jobs—vital to residents of inner cities—have moved to other countries where labor costs are lower. Black unemployment remains twice as high as white unemployment; among African American teenagers in many cities, the figure exceeds 40 percent (Jacob, 1986; Lichter, 1989; U.S. Census Bureau, 1999; U.S. Department of Labor, 2000).

In the last generation African Americans have made remarkable educational progress. The share of adults completing high school rose from half to almost three-fourths, nearly closing the gap between whites and blacks. Between 1980 and 1998, the share of African American adults with at least a college degree rose from 8 to nearly 15 percent. But, as Table 14–3 shows, African Americans are still at half the national standard when it comes to completing four years of college.

The political clout of African Americans has also increased. As a result of black migration to the cities, as well as white movement to the suburbs, half of this country's ten largest cities have elected African American

[2]Here, again, a median age difference (white people, 36.7; black people, 30.2) accounts for some of the income and educational disparities. Disparities also reflect a higher proportion of one-parent families among blacks than whites. Comparing only married-couple families, African Americans (median income $47,383 in 1998) earned 87 percent as much as whites ($54,736).

The efforts of these four women greatly advanced the social standing of African Americans in the United States. Pictured above, from left to right: Sojourner Truth (1797–1883), born a slave, became an influential preacher and outspoken abolitionist who was honored by President Lincoln at the White House. Harriet Tubman (1820–1913), after escaping from slavery herself, masterminded the flight from bondage of hundreds of African American men and women via the "Underground Railroad." Ida Wells-Barnett (1862–1931), born to slave parents, became a partner in a Memphis newspaper and served as a tireless crusader against the terror of lynching. Marian Anderson (1897–1993), an exceptional singer whose early career was restrained by racial prejudice, broke symbolic "color lines" by singing in the White House (1936) and on the steps of the Lincoln Memorial to a crowd of almost 100,000 people (1939).

mayors. At the national level, however, just 1 percent of elected leaders are African Americans. After the 1998 congressional elections, 39 black men and women (of 435) were in the House of Representatives and not one black person (of 100) was in the Senate.

In sum, for more than 350 years, people of African ancestry have struggled for social equality. As a nation, we have come far in this pursuit. Overt discrimination is now illegal, and research documents a long-term decline in prejudice against African Americans (Firebaugh & Davis, 1988; Wilson, 1992; NORC, 1999).

In 1913, fifty years after the abolition of slavery, W. E. B. Du Bois pointed to the extent of black achievement. But Du Bois also cautioned that racial caste remained strong in the United States, and as the twenty-first century begins racial hierarchy continues to persist.

ASIAN AMERICANS

Although Asian Americans share some racial traits, enormous cultural diversity characterizes this category of people with ancestors from dozens of nations. In 1999, the total number of Asian Americans exceeded 11 million—approaching 4 percent of the U.S. population. The largest category of Asian Americans is people of Chinese ancestry (2.2 million), followed by those of Filipino (2.0 million), Asian Indian (1.2 million), Korean (980,000), and Japanese (925,000) descent. The Asian American population doubled between 1980 and 1990 and is expected to double again by 2010 (Lee, 1998). Forty percent of Asian Americans live in California.

Young Asian Americans command respect as high achievers and are disproportionately represented at our country's best colleges and universities. Many of their elders, too, have made economic and social gains; most Asian Americans now live in middle-class suburbs (O'Hare, Frey, & Fost, 1994). Yet, despite (and sometimes because of) their exceptional record of achievement, Asian Americans often find others are aloof or outright hostile toward them.

At the same time, the "model minority" image of Asian Americans obscures the poverty found within their ranks. We now focus on the history and current standing of Chinese Americans and Japanese Americans—the longest-established Asian American minorities—and conclude with a brief look at the most recent arrivals.

Chinese Americans

Chinese immigration to the United States began in 1849 with the economic boom of California's gold rush. New towns and businesses sprang up overnight, and the

TABLE 14–4 The Social Standing of Asian Americans, 1990

	All Asian Americans	Chinese Americans	Japanese Americans	Korean Americans	Filipino Americans	Entire United States
Median family income	$42,240	$41,316	$51,550	$33,909	$46,698	$35,225
Percent in poverty	14.0%	14.0%	7.0%	13.7%	6.4%	13.1%
Completion of four or more years of college (age 25 and over)	37.7%	40.7%	34.5%	34.5%	39.3%	20.3%

Source: U.S. Census Bureau (1999).

demand for cheap labor attracted some 100,000 Chinese immigrants. Most Chinese workers were young men willing to take tough, low-status jobs shunned by whites. But the economy soured in the 1870s, and desperate whites began to compete with the Chinese for whatever work could be found. Suddenly the hard-working Chinese posed a threat. In short, economic hard times led to prejudice and discrimination (Ling, 1971; Boswell, 1986).

Soon, whites acted to bar the Chinese from many occupations. Courts also withdrew legal protection, unleashing vicious campaigns against "the Yellow Peril." Everyone seemed to line up against the Chinese, as expressed in the popular phrase of the time that someone up against great odds didn't have "a Chinaman's chance" (Sung, 1967; Sowell, 1981).

In 1882, the U.S. government passed the first of several laws curbing Chinese immigration. But because Chinese men outnumbered women by almost twenty to one, the sex imbalance limited marriages and sent the Chinese population plummeting to about 60,000 by 1920 (Hsu, 1971; Lai, 1980). Chinese women already living in the United States were in high demand, and they soon shed their traditional submissiveness to men (Sowell, 1981).

Responding to racial hostility, some Chinese moved eastward; many more sought the safety of urban Chinatowns. There, Chinese traditions flourished, and kinship networks, called clans, provided financial help to individuals and represented the interests of all. At the same time, however, Chinatowns discouraged residents from learning the English language, and this limited their job opportunities (Wong, 1971).

A renewed need for labor during World War II prompted President Franklin Roosevelt to end the ban on Chinese immigration in 1943 and to extend the rights of citizenship to Chinese Americans born abroad. Many responded by moving out of Chinatowns and pursuing cultural assimilation. In 1900, for example, 70 percent of Honolulu's Chinese people lived in that city's Chinatown; today, the figure is below 20 percent.

Since 1950, Chinese Americans have made great strides. Today, people of Chinese ancestry are no longer restricted to self-employment in laundries and restaurants; they work in various high-prestige occupations, especially in fields related to science and new information technology.

As shown in Table 14–4, the median family income of Chinese Americans in 1990 ($41,316) stood above the national average ($35,225). The higher income of all Asian Americans reflects, on average, a larger number of family members in the labor force.[3] Chinese Americans also have an enviable record of educational achievement, with twice the national average of college graduates.

Despite their success, many Chinese Americans still grapple with subtle (and sometimes overt) prejudice and discrimination. Such hostility is one reason that poverty among Chinese Americans stands above the national average. Poverty is higher yet among those who remain in the restrictive circle of Chinatowns, working in restaurants or other low-paying jobs. In fact, sociologists debate whether racial and ethnic enclaves help their residents or exploit them (Portes & Jensen, 1989; Zhou & Logan, 1989; Kinkead, 1992; Gilbertson & Gurak, 1993).

[3]Data for 1994 placed the median income for Chinese Americans at $44,456, above the national figure of $36,782. Median age for all Asian Americans in 1999 was 31.7, somewhat below the national median of 35.6 and the white median of 36.7. But specific categories vary considerably in median age: Japanese, 36.1; Chinese, 32.1; Filipino, 31.1; Korean, 29.1; Asian Indian, 28.9; Cambodian, 19.4; Hmong, 12.5 (U.S. Census Bureau, 1995, 2000).

Between 1942 and 1944, more than 100,000 men, women, and children of Japanese ancestry were forcibly removed from their homes and businesses and taken to detention camps. Here, a mother fights back tears as the army prepares to move her and her three small children (note the identification tags) from Bainbridge Island (off the coast of Washington state) to the mainland.

Japanese Americans

Japanese immigration to the United States started slowly in the 1860s, reaching only 3,000 by 1890. Most of these immigrants came to the Hawaiian Islands (annexed by the United States in 1898 and made a state in 1959) as a source of cheap labor. After 1900, however, as the number of Japanese immigrants to California rose and they demanded better pay, white people responded by seeking limits to immigration (Daniels, 1971). In 1907, the United States signed an agreement with Japan curbing the entry of men—the chief economic threat—while allowing women to enter this country to ease the sex ratio imbalance. In the 1920s, state laws in California and elsewhere mandated segregation and banned interracial marriage, virtually ending further Japanese immigration. Not until 1952 did the United States extend citizenship to foreign-born Japanese.

Japanese and Chinese immigrants differed in three ways. First, there were fewer Japanese immigrants, so they escaped some of the hostility directed at the more numerous Chinese. Second, the Japanese knew more about the United States than the Chinese did, which helped them assimilate (Sowell, 1981). Third, Japanese immigrants preferred rural farming to clustering in cities. But many white people objected to Japanese ownership of farmland, so, in 1913, California barred further purchases. Many foreign-born Japanese (called *Issei*) responded by placing farmland in the names of their U.S.-born children (*Nisei*), who were constitutionally entitled to citizenship.

Japanese Americans faced their greatest challenge after December 7, 1941, when Japan bombed the U.S. naval fleet at Hawaii's Pearl Harbor. Rage toward Japan was directed at the Japanese living in the United States, and some feared that Japanese Americans would spy for Japan or otherwise sabotage the U.S. war effort. Within a year, President Franklin Roosevelt signed Executive Order 9066, an unprecedented action that detained people of Japanese descent in military camps. Authorities soon relocated 110,000 people (90 percent of all U.S. Japanese, as well as more than 2,000 Japanese people living in thirteen Latin American nations) to remote inland reservations (Sun, 1998).

While concern about national security always rises in times of war, Japanese internment was sharply criticized. First, it targeted an entire category of people, not one of whom was known to have committed any disloyal act. Second, roughly two-thirds of those imprisoned were *Nisei*, U.S. citizens by birth. Third, although the United States was also at war with Germany and Italy, no such action was taken against people of German or Italian ancestry.

Relocation meant selling homes, furnishings, and businesses on short notice for pennies on the dollar. As a result, almost the entire Japanese American population was economically devastated. In military prisons—surrounded by barbed wire and guarded by armed soldiers—families crowded into single rooms, often in buildings that had previously sheltered livestock (Fujimoto, 1971; Bloom, 1980). The internment ended in 1944, when the Supreme Court declared it unconstitutional. In 1988, Congress awarded $20,000 as token compensation to each victim.

After World War II, Japanese Americans staged a dramatic recovery. Having lost their traditional businesses, they pursued a wide range of new occupations, and because their culture highly values education and hard work, Japanese Americans have enjoyed remarkable success. In 1990, the median income of Japanese American households was almost 50 percent above the national average. The rate of poverty among Japanese Americans was only half the national figure.

Upward social mobility has encouraged cultural assimilation and interracial marriage. The third and fourth generations of Japanese Americans (the *Sansei* and *Yonsei*) rarely live in residential enclaves, as many Chinese Americans still do, and a majority marry non-Japanese. In the process, some have abandoned their traditions, including the Japanese language. A good proportion of Japanese Americans, however, belong to associations as a way of maintaining their ethnic identity (Fugita & O'Brien, 1985). Unfortunately, some appear to be caught between two worlds, no longer culturally Japanese but not completely accepted in the larger society because of racial differences.

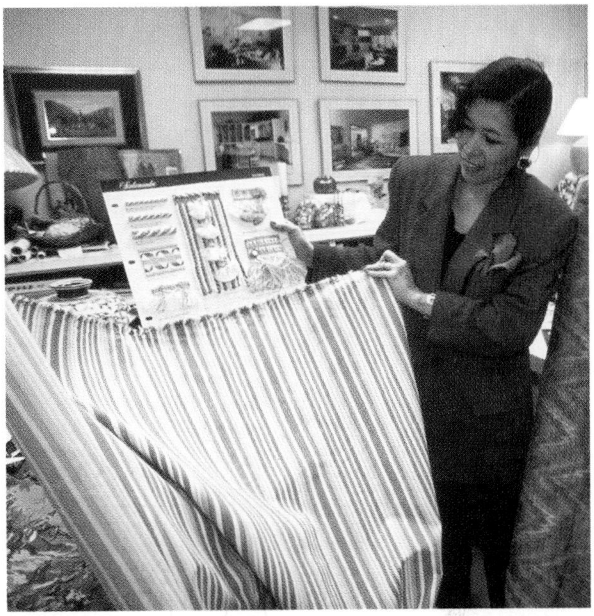

Filipino American women stand out as highly represented in the labor force, and more than 40 percent have completed a four-year college degree. The success of such women goes a long way to explaining why Filipino American families, on average, have one-third more income than the national standard.

Recent Asian Immigrants

More recent immigrants from Asia include Filipinos, Indians, Koreans, Vietnamese, Samoans, and Guamanians. When added to the existing population of Chinese and Japanese descent, Asian Americans are this country's fastest-growing minority, accounting for one-third of all immigration to the United States (U.S. Immigration and Naturalization Service, 1999). A brief look at Koreans and Filipinos—both from countries that have had special ties to the United States—reveals the social diversity of newly arriving people from Asia.

Koreans. Korean immigration to the United States followed the U.S. involvement in the Korean War (1950–53). U.S. troops in South Korea experienced Korean culture firsthand, and some soldiers found Korean spouses. For South Koreans, contact with the troops raised interest in the United States.

The entrepreneurial spirit is strong among Asian immigrants. Asians are slightly more likely than whites, three times more likely than Latinos, and four times more likely than African Americans to own and operate small businesses (U.S. Census Bureau, 1995). Among all Asian Americans, however, Koreans are the most likely to be small business owners. Residents of New York City, for example, know that the majority of grocery stores there are Korean-owned; similarly, Los Angeles residents know that Koreans operate a large share of liquor stores.

Many Koreans work long hours; nonetheless, Korean American family income is slightly below the national average, as shown in Table 14–4. Moreover, Korean Americans face limited social acceptance, even among other Asian American categories.

Filipinos. The large number of immigrants from the Philippines is explained partly by the fact that the United States controlled the Philippine Islands between 1898 (when Spain ceded it as partial settlement of the Spanish-American War) and 1946 (when the Philippines became an independent republic).

The data in Table 14–4 suggest that Filipinos generally have fared well. But a closer look reveals a mixed pattern, with some Filipinos highly successful in the professions (especially in medicine) and others struggling to get by in low-skill jobs (Parrillo, 1994).

For many Filipino families, the key to high income is working women. Almost three-fourths of Filipino American women are in the labor force, compared to just half of Korean American women. Moreover, many of these women are professionals, reflecting the fact that 42 percent of Filipino American women have a

SEEING OURSELVES

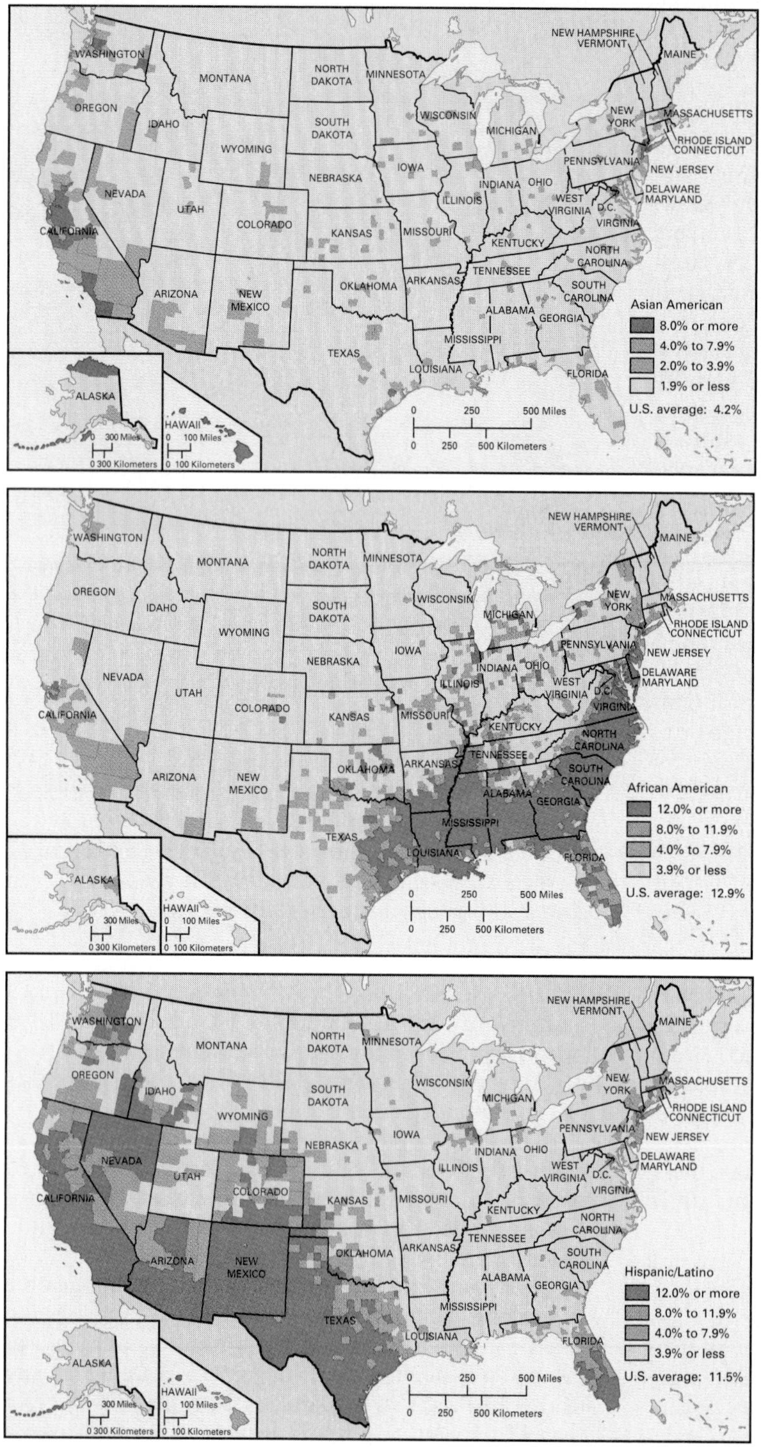

NATIONAL MAP 14–4
The Concentration of Asian Americans, African Americans, and Hispanics/Latinos, by County, Projections for 2001

In 1990, Hispanics represented 9 percent of the U.S. population, compared with 12 percent African Americans and 3 percent people of Asian descent. These three maps show the geographic distribution of these categories of people as projected for 2001. Comparing them, we see that the southern half of the United States is and will be home to far more minorities than the northern half. But do the three concentrate in the same areas? What patterns do the maps reveal?

Source: From *American Demographics* (November 1996, January 1997, and February 1997). Copyright © 1996, 1997 by *American Demographics*. Reprinted with permission.

TABLE 14–5 The Social Standing of Hispanic Americans, 1990

	All Hispanics	Mexican Americans	Puerto Ricans	Cuban Americans	Entire United States
Median family income	$23,431	$23,240	$18,008	$31,439	$35,225
Percent in poverty	25.0%	25.0%	37.5%	13.8%	13.1%
Completion of four or more years of college (age 25 and over)	9.2%	6.2%	10.1%	18.5%	20.3%

Source: U.S. Census Bureau (1999).

four-year college degree, compared to just 26 percent of Korean American women.

In sum, a survey of Asian Americans presents a complex picture. The Japanese come closest to having achieved social acceptance; but, especially for Koreans and the Chinese, economic success has not toppled historical prejudice and discrimination. Although many Asian Americans have prospered, others remain poor. One clear trend is an exceptionally high immigration rate, which means that people of Asian ancestry will play a central role in our society in the twenty-first century (Lee, 1994).

HISPANIC AMERICANS

In 1999, Hispanics numbered nearly 32 million, about 12 percent of the U.S. population. Few people who fall into this category, however, actually describe themselves as "Hispanic" or "Latino." Like Asian Americans, Hispanics are really a cluster of distinct populations, each of which identifies with a particular ancestral nation (Marín & Marín, 1991).

About two out of three Hispanics (20 million) are Mexican Americans, commonly called "Chicanos." Puerto Ricans are next in population size (3 million), followed by Cuban Americans (1.5 million). Many other nations of Latin America are represented by smaller numbers. Because of a high birth rate and significant immigration, analysts predict that Hispanics will surpass African Americans to become this nation's largest racial or ethnic minority by about 2010 (Barone, 1998a; U.S. Census Bureau, 1999).

Most of the U.S. Hispanic population lives in the Southwest. One out of four Californians is a Latino (in greater Los Angeles, almost half the people are Latino). National Map 14–4 locates the Hispanic, African American, and Asian American populations across the United States.

Median family income for all Hispanics—$29,608 in 1998—stands well below the national average.[4] As the following sections discuss, moreover, some categories of Hispanics have fared better than others.

Mexican Americans

Some Chicanos are descendants of people who lived in a part of Mexico annexed by the United States after the Mexican American War (1846–48). Most Mexican Americans, however, are more recent immigrants. In fact, in recent decades, more immigrants have come to the United States from Mexico than from any other country.

Like many other immigrants, many Mexican Americans have worked as low-wage laborers on farms or elsewhere. Table 14–5 shows that the 1990 median family income for Mexican Americans was $23,240, about two-thirds of the national standard. One-fourth of Chicano families are poor, almost twice the national average. And, despite gains since 1980, Mexican Americans still acquire less schooling than U.S. adults as a whole and have a high dropout rate.

Puerto Ricans

Puerto Rico (like the Philippines) came under U.S. control when the Spanish American War ended in 1898. In 1917, Puerto Ricans (but not Filipinos) became U.S. citizens.

New York City is the center of Puerto Rican life in the continental United States, and is home to about 1 million Puerto Ricans. However, one-third of this community is severely disadvantaged. Adjusting to cultural

[4]The 1999 median age of the U.S. Hispanic population was 26.5 years, well below the national median of 35.6 years. This differential accounts for some of the disparity in income and education.

The strength of family bonds and neighborhood ties is evident in this painting of street life in old San Juan, La Vida en Broma, *by Puerto Rican artist Nick Quijano (1988).*

© Nick Quijano 1997. *La Vida en Broma, 1988: Streetlife in Old San Juan.*

patterns on the mainland—including, for many, learning English—is one challenge; also, Puerto Ricans with dark skin encounter especially strong prejudice and discrimination. As a result, about as many people return to Puerto Rico each year as arrive.

This "revolving door" pattern hampers assimilation. Three-fourths of Puerto Rican families in the United States speak Spanish at home, compared to about half of Mexican American families (Sowell, 1981; Stevens & Swicegood, 1987). Speaking only Spanish maintains a strong ethnic identity, but it also limits economic opportunity. Puerto Ricans also have a higher incidence of women-headed households than other Hispanics, a pattern that puts families at greater risk of poverty.

Table 14–5 shows that the 1990 median family income for Puerto Ricans was $18,008, about half the national average. Although long-term mainland residents have made economic gains, more recent immigrants from Puerto Rico struggle to find work. Averaging out the differences, Puerto Ricans remain the most socially disadvantaged Hispanic minority (Rivera-Batiz & Santiago, 1994; Holmes, 1996b).

Cuban Americans

Within a decade after the 1959 Marxist revolution led by Fidel Castro, 400,000 Cubans had immigrated to the United States. Most settled in Miami. Those who fled Castro's Cuba were highly educated business and professional people who wasted little time becoming as successful in the United States as in their homeland (Fallows, 1983; Krafft, 1993).

Table 14–5 shows that the median household income for Cuban Americans in 1990 was $31,439—well above that of other Hispanics, yet still below the national average. The 1 million Cuban Americans living in the United States have managed a delicate balancing act—achieving success in the larger society while retaining much of their traditional culture. Of all Hispanics, Cubans are the most likely to speak Spanish in their homes: Eight out of ten families do. However, their cultural distinctiveness and their highly visible communities, like Miami's Little Havana, provoke hostility from some people.

WHITE ETHNIC AMERICANS

The term *white ethnics* recognizes the ethnic heritage—and social disadvantages—of many white people. White ethnics are non-WASPs whose ancestors lived in Ireland, Poland, Germany, Italy, or other European countries. More than half the U.S. population falls into one or another white ethnic category (Alba, 1990).

Unprecedented emigration from Europe during the nineteenth century first brought Germans and Irish and then Italians and Jews to our shores. Despite cultural differences, all shared the hope that the United States would offer greater political freedom and economic opportunity than their homelands. Most did live better in this country, but the belief that "the streets of America were paved with gold" turned out to be a far cry from reality. Many immigrants found only hard labor for low wages.

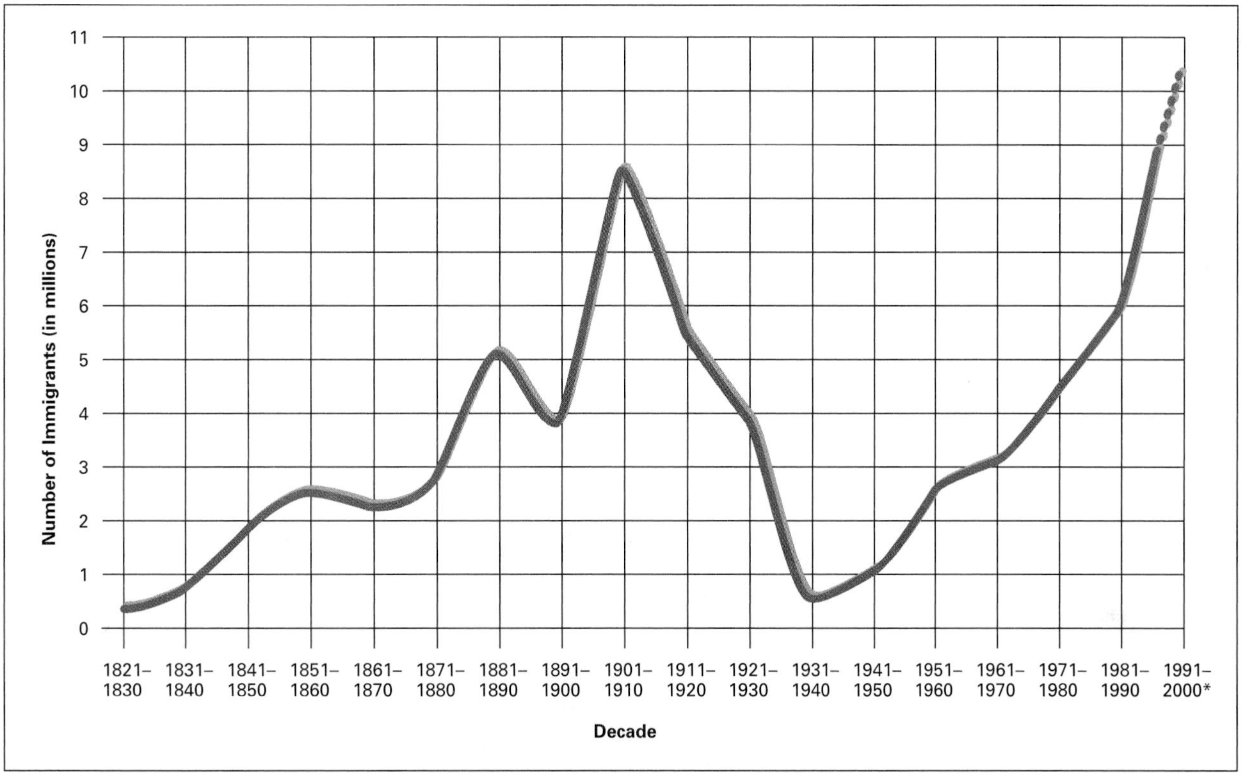

FIGURE 14–2 Immigration to the United States, by Decade

Source: U.S. Immigration and Naturalization Service (1999).

*Projection based on 1991–1998 data.

White ethnics also endured their share of prejudice and discrimination. Nativist organizations opposed the entry of non-WASP Europeans to the United States, and many newspaper ads seeking workers warned new arrivals, "None need apply but Americans" (Handlin, 1941:67).

In 1921, the nativists declared victory when the federal government passed legislation that imposed a quota on immigration. Not until 1968 were restrictions lifted. The most severely targeted were southern and eastern Europeans—people likely to have darker skin and different cultural backgrounds from the dominant WASPs (Fallows, 1983).

In response to widespread bigotry, many white ethnics—like other immigrants—formed supportive residential enclaves. Some also established footholds in certain businesses and trades: Italian Americans entered the construction industry; the Irish worked in construction and in civil service jobs; Jews predominated in the garment industry; many Greeks (like the Chinese) worked in the retail food business (Newman, 1973).

Many working-class people still live in traditional neighborhoods, although those who prospered gradually assimilated. Most descendants of immigrants who labored in sweatshops and lived in overcrowded tenements now lead comfortable lives. As a result, their ethnic heritage is a source of pride.

RACE AND ETHNICITY: LOOKING AHEAD

The United States has been, and will long remain, a land of immigrants. Immigration has brought striking cultural diversity and tales of success, hope, and struggle told in hundreds of tongues.

As Figure 14–2 shows, most immigrants arrived in a great wave that peaked about 1910. The next two generations saw economic gains and some assimilation. The government also extended citizenship to Native Americans (1924), foreign-born Filipinos (1942), Chinese Americans (1943), and Japanese Americans (1952).

CONTROVERSY & DEBATE

Affirmative Action: Problem or Solution?

Adarand Constructors, a white-owned Colorado highway construction company, submitted the low bid for a federal project erecting guard rails. But Adarand did not get the job. Despite having to pay a higher price, the government selected Gonzales Construction, a minority-owned firm. Adarand sued, and a bitter company manager, Randy Perch, explained: "What is prejudice? It's when government makes a decision based on something that doesn't matter, like race or gender."

Should race or ethnicity or gender matter in how we treat people? This question lies at the heart of the affirmative action debate. To begin, what exactly is this controversial policy, and how did it start?

After World War II, the U.S. government funded higher education for veterans of all races. The G.I. Bill held special promise for African Americans, most of whom needed financial assistance to enroll in college. The program was so successful that, by 1960, some 350,000 black men and women were on college campuses with government funding.

But a problem remained: These individuals were not finding the kinds of jobs for which they were qualified. In short, *educational* opportunity was not producing *economic* opportunity.

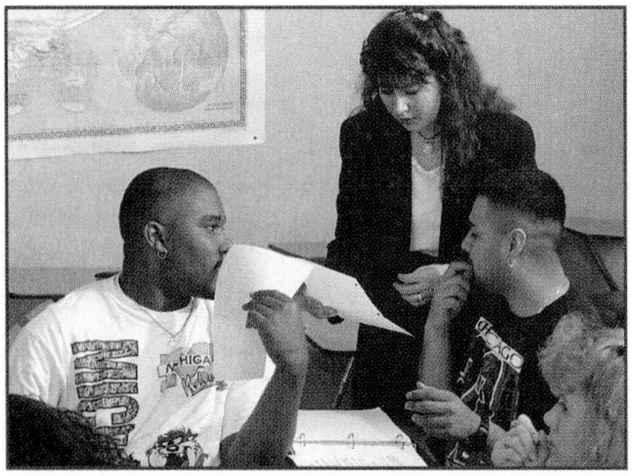
Supporters argue that affirmative action in college admissions is needed to ensure a socially diverse campus.

Thus, in the early 1960s, the Kennedy administration introduced a program called "affirmative action" to provide a broader "net of opportunity" for qualified minorities in the job market. Employers were instructed to monitor hiring, promotion, and admissions policies to eliminate discrimination—even if unintended—against minorities.

Defenders of affirmative action see it, first, as a sensible response to our nation's racial and ethnic history, especially for African Americans, who suffered through two centuries of slavery and a century of segregation under Jim Crow laws. Throughout our history, they claim, being white gave people a big advantage. Thus, minority preference today is a step toward just compensation for unfair majority preference in the past.

Second, given our racial history, the promise of a colorblind society strikes many as hollow. Because prejudice and discrimination are deep in the fabric of U.S. society, simply endorsing the principle of

As the figure on page 377 indicates, another wave of immigration began after World War II and swelled as the government relaxed immigration laws in the 1960s. During the 1990s, about 1 million people came to the United States each year, more than twice the number that arrived during the "Great Immigration" a century ago (although newcomers now enter a country that has five times as many people). Today's immigrants, however, come not from Europe but from Latin America and Asia, with Mexicans, Filipinos, and South Koreans arriving in the largest numbers.

New arrivals face the same kind of prejudice and discrimination experienced by those who came before them. Indeed, recent years have witnessed rising hostility toward foreigners (sometimes termed *xenophobia*, with Greek roots meaning "fear of what is strange"). In 1994, California voters passed Proposition 187, which cut off social services (including schooling) to illegal immigrants. More recently, voters there mandated that all children learn English in school. And, as the final box explains, the debate over affirmative action rages as hotly as ever.

Like their predecessors, many immigrants try to blend into U.S. society without completely giving up their traditional culture. Some have formed racial and ethnic enclaves, so that the Little Havanas and Koreatowns of today stand alongside the Little Italys and Germantowns of the past. New arrivals also share the hope, like those who came before them, that their racial and ethnic identity can be a source of strength and not a badge of inferiority.

colorblindness does not mean everyone will compete fairly.

Third, proponents maintain that affirmative action has worked. Where would minorities be if the government had not enacted this policy three decades ago? Major employers, such as fire and police departments in large cities, began hiring minorities and women for the first time only because of affirmative action. This program has played an important part in expanding the African American middle class. Furthermore, affirmative action on the campus has advanced the careers of a generation of black students and has enhanced interracial interaction (Bowen & Bok, 1999).

But affirmative action has always drawn criticism and, by the mid-1990s, courts began cutbacks in such policies. Critics argue, first, that affirmative action started out as a temporary remedy to ensure fair competition but became a system of "group preferences" and quotas. In other words, the policy did not remain true to the goal of promoting color blindness, as set out in the 1964 Civil Rights Act. Within a decade, it had become "reverse discrimination," favoring people not because of their performance but because of their race, ethnicity, or sex.

Second, critics contend that affirmative action polarizes society. If racial preferences were wrong in the past, they are wrong now. Moreover, why should whites or men today—many of whom are far from privileged—be penalized for past discrimination that was in no way their fault? Our society has undone most of the institutionalized prejudice and discrimination of earlier times, opponents continue, so that minorities can and do enjoy success when they have the talent and make the effort. Giving entire categories of people special treatment inevitably compromises standards of excellence, calls into question the real accomplishments of minorities, and provokes a hostile response from white people.

A third argument against affirmative action is that it benefits those who need it least. Favoring minority-owned corporations or allocating places in law school helps already-privileged people. Affirmative action has done little for the African American underclass that most needs a leg up.

In sum, there are good reasons to argue for and against affirmative action. Indeed, people who believe in a society where no racial or ethnic category dominates fall on both sides of the debate. The disagreement, then, is not whether people of all colors should have equal opportunity, but whether a particular policy—affirmative action—is part of the solution or part of the problem.

Continue the debate . . .

1. *Since, historically, society has favored males over females and whites over people of color, would you agree that white males have received more "affirmative action" than anyone? Why or why not?*
2. *Should affirmative action include only disadvantaged categories of minorities (say, African Americans and Native Americans) and exclude more affluent categories (such as Japanese Americans)? Why or why not?*
3. *What about replacing race-based affirmative action with a class-based policy? Would this help those who need it most?*

Sources: Carr (1995), Cohen (1995), Curry (1996), Bowen & Bok (1999), and NORC (1999).

SUMMARY

1. Races are socially constructed categories that set apart people according to various physical traits. Although a century ago, scientists identified three broad categories—Caucasoids, Mongoloids, and Negroids—there are no pure races. Ethnicity is based not on biology but on shared cultural heritage. Minorities—including people of various racial and ethnic categories—are people society sets apart as both socially distinct and socially disadvantaged.
2. Prejudice is a rigid and biased generalization about a category of people. Racism, a destructive type of prejudice, asserts that one race is innately superior or inferior to another.
3. Discrimination is a pattern of action by which a person treats various categories of people unequally.
4. Pluralism means that racial and ethnic categories, although distinct, have equal social standing. Assimilation is a process by which minorities gradually adopt the patterns of the dominant culture. Segregation is a physical and social separation of categories of people. Genocide is the extermination of a category of people.

5. Native Americans—the earliest human inhabitants of the Americas—have endured genocide, segregation, and forced assimilation. Today, the social standing of Native Americans is well below the national average.
6. WASPs predominated among the original European settlers of the United States, and many continue to enjoy high social position today.
7. African Americans experienced two centuries of slavery. Emancipation in 1865 gave way to segregation by law. Today, despite legal equality, African Americans are still relatively disadvantaged.
8. Chinese and Japanese Americans have suffered both racial and ethnic hostility. Although some prejudice and discrimination continues, both categories now have above-average income and schooling. Recent immigration, especially of Koreans and Filipinos, has made Asian Americans the fastest-growing racial category of the U.S. population.
9. Hispanics include many ethnicities sharing a Spanish heritage. Mexican Americans, the largest Hispanic minority, are concentrated in the Southwest. Puerto Ricans, one-third of whom live in New York, are the poorest Hispanics; Cubans, concentrated in Miami, are the most affluent.
10. White ethnics are non-WASPs of European ancestry. While making gains during this century, many white ethnics still struggle for economic security.
11. Immigration has increased in recent years. No longer primarily from Europe, most immigrants now arrive from Latin America and Asia.

KEY CONCEPTS

race (p. 354) a socially constructed category composed of people who share biologically transmitted traits that members of a society consider important

ethnicity (p. 355) a shared cultural heritage

minority (p. 356) any category of people, distinguished by physical or cultural difference, that a society sets apart and subordinates

prejudice (p. 357) a rigid and irrational generalization about an entire category of people

stereotype (p. 359) an exaggerated description applied to every person in some category

racism (p. 359) the belief that one racial category is innately superior or inferior to another

scapegoat (p. 359) a person or category of people, typically with little power, whom people unfairly blame for their own troubles

discrimination (p. 361) any action that involves treating various categories of people unequally

institutional prejudice and discrimination (p. 362) bias inherent in the operation of society's institutions

pluralism (p. 363) a state in which racial and ethnic minorities are distinct but have social parity

assimilation (p. 363) the process by which minorities gradually adopt patterns of the dominant culture

miscegenation (p. 364) biological reproduction by partners of different racial categories

segregation (p. 364) the physical and social separation of categories of people

genocide (p. 365) the systematic annihilation of one category of people by another

CRITICAL-THINKING QUESTIONS

1. Differentiate between race and ethnicity. Do you think all nonwhite people should be considered minorities, even if they have above-average incomes? Why or why not?
2. In what ways do prejudice and discrimination reinforce each other?
3. Of what significance is the growing influence of Latin music, evident in the popularity of performers such as Gloria and Emilio Estefan and Ricky Martin, to understanding ethnicity in the United States?
4. Do you think U.S. society is becoming more or less colorblind? Is colorblindness a goal worth striving for? Why or why not?

APPLICATIONS AND EXERCISES

1. Does your college or university take account of race and ethnicity in its admissions policies? Ask to speak with an admissions officer to see what you can learn about your school's policies and the reasons for them. Ask, too, if there is a "legacy" policy that favors applicants with a parent who attended the school.
2. Give several of your friends or family members a quick quiz, asking them what share of the U.S. population is white, Hispanic, African American, and Asian (see Table 14–1). If they are like most people, they will exaggerate the share of all minorities and understate the white proportion (Labovitz, 1996). What do you make of the results?
3. There are probably immigrants on your campus or in your local community. Have you ever thought about asking them to tell you about their homeland and their experiences since arriving in the United States? Most immigrants are pleased to be asked, and you can learn a great deal.
4. Install the CD-ROM packaged in the back of this new textbook to access a variety of study, review, and applications exercises designed to help you better understand the material covered in this chapter. The CD includes an author's tip video, as well as interactive maps, video application exercises, Web links, and study questions.

SITES TO SEE

http://www.prenhall.com/macionis

Visit the interactive Web site that accompanies this text. Begin by clicking on the cover of your book. You will find a chapter-by-chapter study guide, practice tests, chat room, and many suggested Web links.

http://www.macionis.com
(or **http://www.thesociologypage.com**)

At the author's home page, you can find additional links to organizations concerned with racial and ethnic inequality.

http://www.naacp.org
http://www.jdl.org
http://www.iprnet.org/IPR/

These three organizations—the National Association for the Advancement of Colored People, the Jewish Defense League, and the Puerto Rican Legal Defense and Education Fund—are concerned with combating prejudice and discrimination and advancing the social standing of minorities in the United States. Determine each organization's strategies and goals.

http://www.access.gpo.gov/eop/ca/index.html

This worthwhile data site, operated by the Council of Economic Advisors, provides an assessment of social and economic well-being of various racial and ethnic categories of this country's population.

CHAPTER 15

Deidre Scherer
Gifts, 1996

From the collection of
St. Mary's Foundation,
Rochester, New York

AGING AND THE ELDERLY

"Great Sex!" read the headline on the magazine cover, which stood out next to the photograph of beautiful Hollywood movie star Susan Sarandon. What's this—another magazine aimed at the twenty-something crowd? Hardly. It's a recent issue of *Modern Maturity*, a publication of AARP,[1] an organization of senior citizens. In the past, AARP covers featured some well-known—but certainly gray-haired—film stars, and its articles focused on financing retirement and staying healthy. But no longer. With features like "The 50 Sexiest People over 50," AARP is refashioning its image with an eye toward the tens of millions of baby boomers who are moving into their fifties.

But the story is bigger than AARP's marketing campaign. There is a revolution going on here. In the United States and other high-income nations, rising living standards, improvements in public health, and new medical technology have boosted the average life span well beyond what was typical a century ago. Moreover, an increasing share of our senior citizens are living active and happy lives that have little in common with yesterday's notions of "growing old" (Toner, 1999).

[1]Until recently known as the American Association of Retired Persons, this organization now calls itself just AARP (rather like Kentucky Fried Chicken becoming just KFC), in an effort to boost its appeal.

This chapter begins by discussing the revolution in aging. Then we turn to the meaning that societies attach to advancing age and explore the transitions that people face as they grow old.

THE GRAYING OF THE UNITED STATES

A quiet but powerful revolution is reshaping the United States. In 1900, the United States was a young nation with half the population under age twenty-three; just 4 percent had reached sixty-five. But the elderly population—that is, women and men aged sixty-five or older—has been increasing twice as fast as the population as a whole. During the last century, the number of seniors increased elevenfold, to 35 million. By 2000, seniors already outnumbered teenagers, and, as shown in Figure 15–1 on page 384, they accounted for about 13 percent of the entire population.

Looking ahead to the year 2050, well within the lifetimes of most readers of this book, projections say the number of seniors will more than double to at least 82 million—20 percent of the population. Then, about *half* this country's people will be over the age of forty (U.S. Census Bureau, 2000).

Global Map 15–1 on page 385 shows that it is the rich nations where the share of elderly people is increasing most rapidly. Typically, two factors combine to drive up the elderly population: low birth rates (meaning that there are fewer children) and increasing longevity (meaning that people typically live longer).

In the United States, another factor will soon swell the ranks of the elderly: the aging of the "baby boomers,"

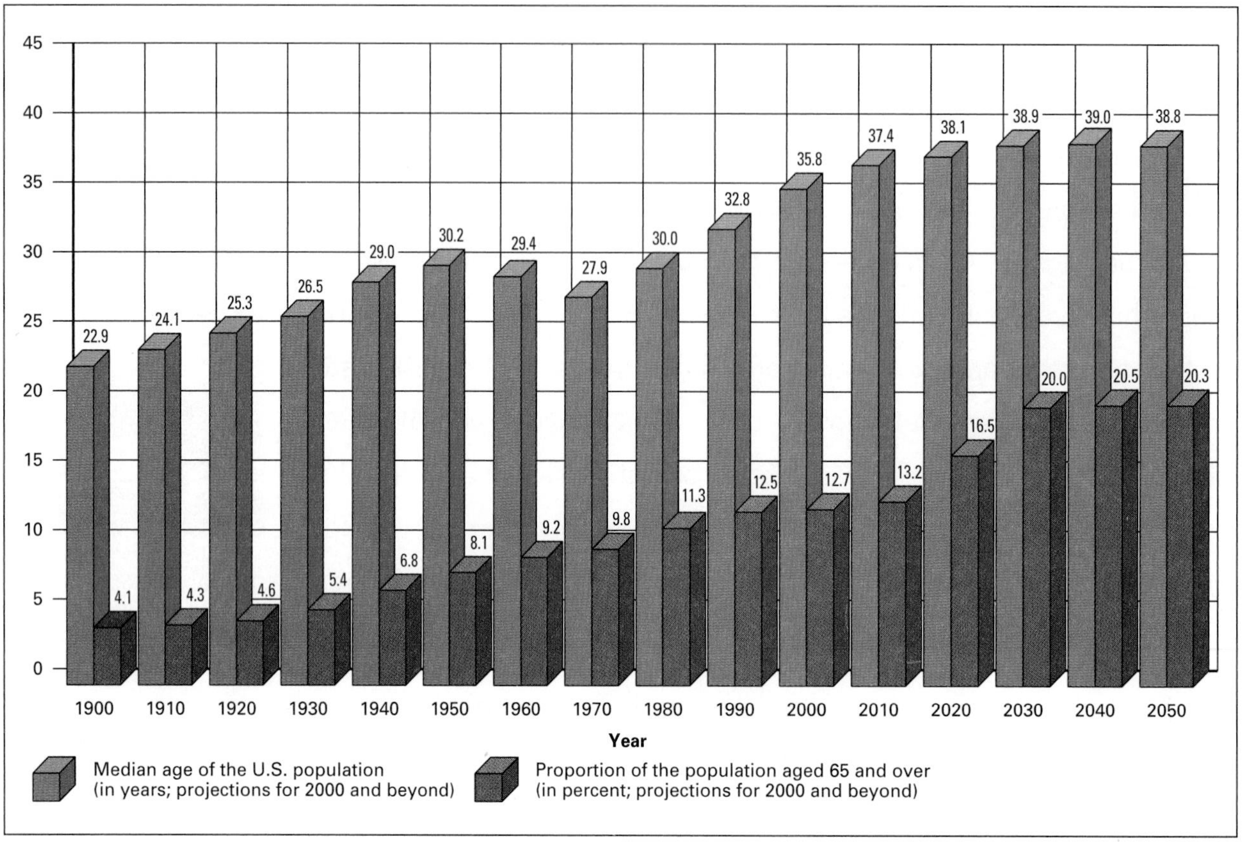

FIGURE 15–1 The Graying of U.S. Society

Source: U.S. Census Bureau (2000).

the 75 million people born soon after the end of World War II. A generation later, after 1965, the birth rate took a sharp turn downward (the so-called "baby bust" era), so that in the twenty-first century, the U.S. population will become more and more "top-heavy."

THE BIRTH RATE: GOING DOWN

The first factor contributing to the graying of our society is a declining birth rate. The birth rate in the United States has been falling for more than a century. One reason is that, as societies industrialize, children are more likely to survive to adulthood, so couples can have fewer to begin with. Another reason is that, although children are an economic asset to farming families, they are an economic liability to families in industrial societies. Put otherwise, children no longer contribute to a family's financial well-being, but are a major expense.

Then, too, as more and more women work outside the home for income, they wish to have fewer children. Advances in birth control technology during the last century have provided the means to avoid unwanted births.

LIFE EXPECTANCY: GOING UP

The second factor contributing to the graying of U.S. society is an increase in life expectancy. It surprises many people to learn that, in 1900, a typical female born in the United States lived just forty-eight years, and a male, forty-six years. By contrast, females born in 1998 can look forward to 79 years, and men, to 74 years (U.S. National Center for Health Statistics, 1999).

A longer life span is a benefit of industrialization. Rising living standards mean that people have better housing and nutrition. At the same time, medical

WINDOW ON THE WORLD

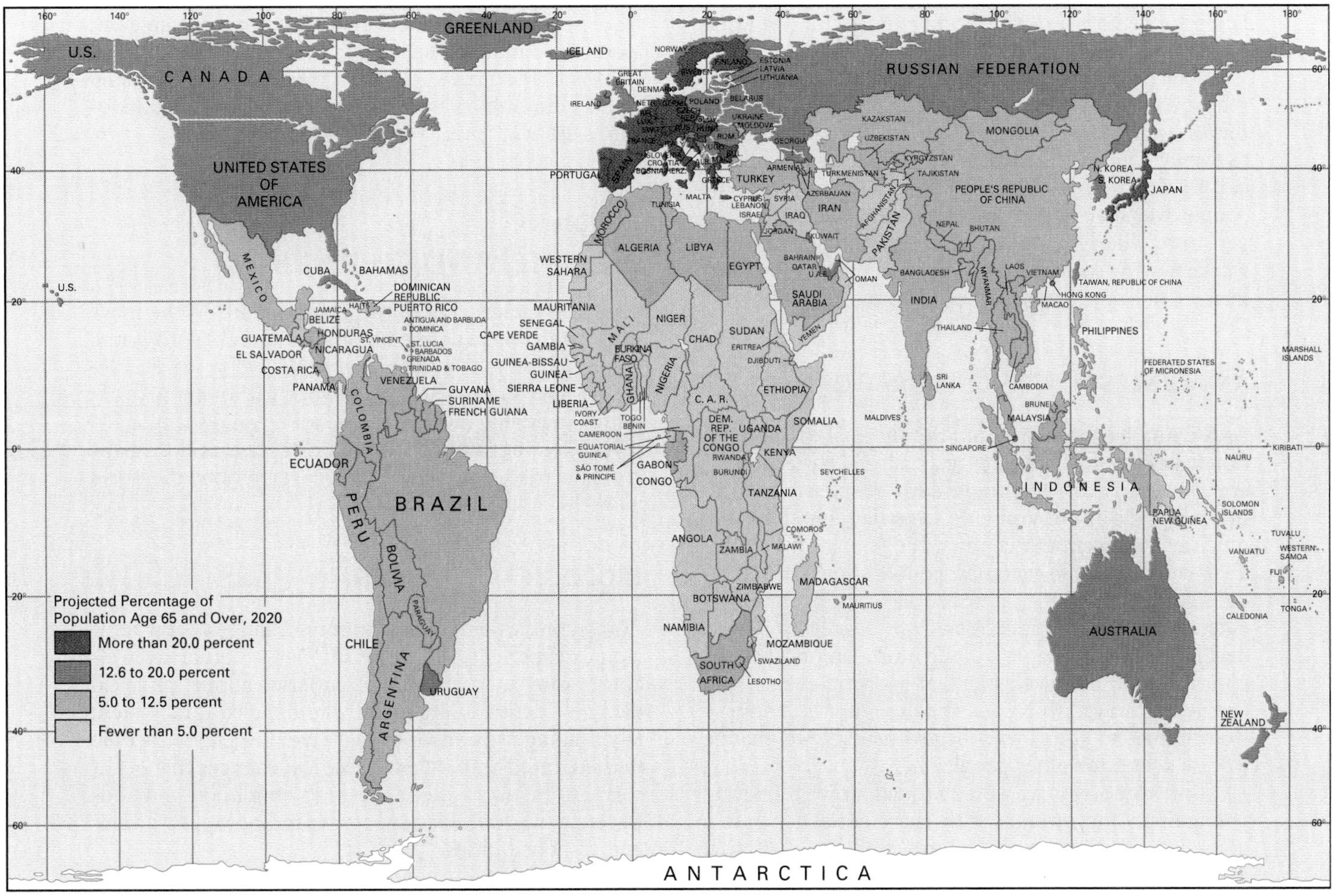

GLOBAL MAP 15–1 The Elderly in Global Perspective, 2020

Here we see projections for the share of population aged sixty-five and older in the year 2020, one generation from now. What relationship do you see between a country's income level and the size of its elderly population?

Source: U.S. Census Bureau (2000).

advances have virtually eliminated infectious diseases such as smallpox, diphtheria, and measles that killed many infants and children a century ago. More recent medical strides fend off cancer and heart disease, which claim most of the U.S. population, but now later in life.

As life becomes longer, the fastest-growing segment of the U.S. population is people over eighty-five, who are already thirty-five times more numerous than they were in 1900. These men and women now number more than 4 million (about 1.6 percent of the total population). Projections put their number at 19 million (about 5 percent of the total) by the year 2050 (U.S. Census Office, 1902; Kaufman, 1990; Harbert & Ginsberg, 1991; U.S. Census Bureau, 2000).

We can only begin to imagine the changes that will accompany this major increase in the elderly population. As the number of older people retiring from the labor force goes up, the proportion of nonworking adults—already about ten times greater than in 1900—will demand more health care and other resources. Thus, the ratio of elderly people to working-age adults, termed the *old-age dependency ratio,* will rise by 2050 (from twenty to twenty-eight elderly people per 100 people aged eighteen to sixty-four). Government spending to support people over sixty-five is already increasing sharply. With yet more elderly people needing support from fewer workers, what security can today's young people expect in their old age? (Treas, 1995; Edmondson, 1996)

AN AGING SOCIETY: CULTURAL CHANGE

As the number of people and the share of the population over sixty-five push upward, cultural patterns, too, are changing. For one thing, elderly people are becoming more and more visible in everyday life. Through much of the twentieth century, the young rarely mingled with the old, so that most people know little about old age. In the twenty-first century, as this country's elderly population increases, age segregation will decline. Younger people will see more seniors at shopping malls, in movie theaters, at sporting events, and on the highways. Moreover, the design of buildings—from homes to stores to colleges—is likely to change to ease access for older people.

But, tomorrow as well as today, how frequently younger people interact with the elderly depends a great deal on where in the country they live. National Map 15–1 looks at residential patterns of people aged sixty-five and older.

A larger share of old people will certainly change our way of life. But it is unlikely that an "elderly culture" (similar to the "youth culture" of the 1960s) will ever emerge. Why not? Because seniors are too diverse. The elderly is an open category in which all of us, if we are lucky, will end up. Thus, elderly people in the United States represent not just men and women but all cultures, social classes, races, and ethnic backgrounds.

THE "YOUNG OLD" AND THE "OLD OLD"

Analysts sometimes distinguish two cohorts of the elderly. The younger elderly are between sixty-five and seventy-five and typically live independently with good health and financial security; they are likely to be living as couples. The older elderly are past age seventy-five and are more likely to have health and money problems and to be dependent on others. Due to their greater longevity, women outnumber men in the elderly population, an imbalance that grows greater with advancing age. Among the "oldest old," those over age eighty-five, about two-thirds are women.

GROWING OLD: BIOLOGY AND CULTURE

Studying the graying of the United States is the focus of **gerontology** (derived from the Greek word *geron,* meaning "an old person"), *the study of aging and the elderly.* Gerontologists—who work within many disciplines, including medicine, psychology, and sociology—investigate not only how people change as they grow old but also the different ways societies around the world view the aging process.

BIOLOGICAL CHANGES

Aging consists of gradual, ongoing changes. How individuals experience life's transitions—whether we welcome our maturity or complain about physical decline—depends largely on whether a cultural system labels aging as positive or negative. In general, people in the United States view biological changes that occur early in life as positive. Through childhood and adolescence, we look forward to expanding opportunities and responsibilities.

But our youth-oriented culture takes a dimmer view of biological changes that develop later in life. Few people receive congratulations for getting old, at least not until they reach eighty-five or ninety. Rather, we commiserate with friends as they turn forty, fifty, or sixty, and make jokes to avoid facing up to the fact that advancing age puts people, sooner or later, on a slippery slope of physical and mental decline. We assume, in short, that by age fifty or sixty, people stop growing *up* and begin growing *down.*

Growing old brings on some predictable changes: gray hair, wrinkles, loss of height and weight, and an overall decline in strength and vitality. After age fifty, bones become more brittle, so that injuries take longer to heal, and the odds of contracting chronic illnesses (such as arthritis and diabetes) and life-threatening conditions (like heart disease and cancer) rise steadily. The sensory abilities—taste, sight, touch, smell, and especially hearing—

SEEING OURSELVES

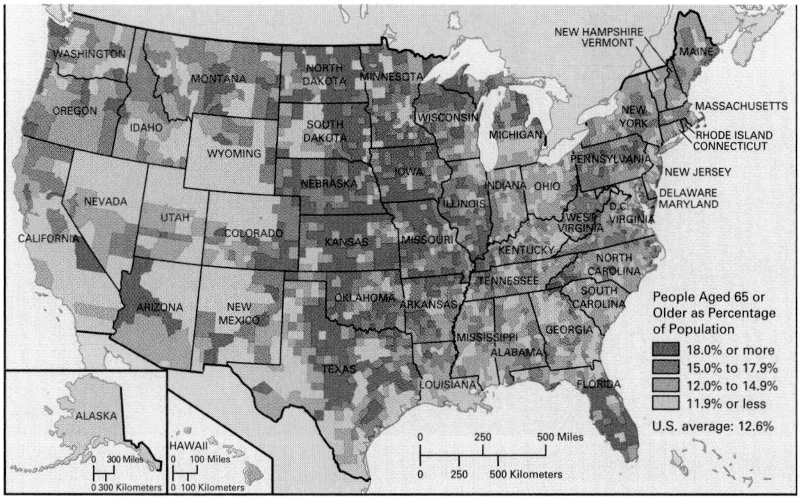

NATIONAL MAP 15–1
The Elderly Population of the United States

Common sense suggests that elderly people live in the Sunbelt, savoring the warmer climate of the South and Southwest. While it is true that Florida has a disproportionate share of people over age sixty-five, it turns out that most counties with high percentages of older people are in the Midwest. What do you think accounts for this pattern? (Hint: Which regions of the United States do *younger* people leave in search of jobs?)

Sources: *American Demographics* magazine, March 1993, p. 34. Reprinted with permission. ©1994, *American Demographics* magazine, Ithaca, New York. Data from the 1990 decennial census.

become less keen with age (Colloway & Dollevoet, 1977; Treas, 1995).

Though health becomes more fragile with advancing age, the vast majority of older people are neither discouraged nor disabled by their physical condition. Only about one in ten seniors reports trouble walking, and fewer than one in twenty requires intensive care in a hospital or nursing home. No more than 1 percent of the elderly are bedridden. Overall, while 27 percent of people over age sixty-five characterize their health as "fair" or "poor," 73 percent consider their overall condition "good" or "excellent." Moreover, the health of seniors, on average, is steadily improving (*Population Today*, 1997; U.S. National Center for Health Statistics, 1999).

Bear in mind, however, that patterns of well-being vary greatly within the elderly population. More health problems beset the "older elderly" past the age of seventy-five. Moreover, because women typically live longer than men, women spend more of their lives suffering from chronic disabilities like arthritis. In addition, well-to-do people live and work in healthful and safe environments and can afford preventive medical care. About 84 percent of elderly people with incomes exceeding $35,000 assess their own health as "excellent" or "good"; that figure drops below 60 percent among people with incomes under $10,000. Lower income and stress linked to prejudice and discrimination also explain why only half of older African Americans assess their health in positive terms, compared to three-fourths of elderly white people (Feagin, 1997; U.S. National Center for Health Statistics, 1999).

PSYCHOLOGICAL CHANGES

Just as we tend to overstate the physical problems of old age, it is easy to exaggerate the psychological changes that accompany growing old. The conventional wisdom about intelligence over the life course can be summed up as "What goes up, must come down" (Baltes & Schaie, 1974).

If we operationalize intelligence to refer to skills like sensorimotor coordination—the ability to arrange objects to match a drawing—we do find a steady decline after midlife. The ability to learn new material and think quickly also declines, although not until around age seventy. But the ability to apply familiar ideas holds steady with advancing age, and some studies actually show improvement in verbal and mathematical skills (Baltes & Schaie, 1974; Schaie, 1980).

We all wonder if we will think or feel differently as we get older. Gerontologists assure us that, for better or worse, the answer is usually no. The only common personality change with advancing age is becoming more introspective. That is, people become more

The reality of growing old is as much a matter of culture as it is of biology. In the United States, being elderly often means being inactive; yet, in rural regions of Iraq and other more traditional societies, old people commonly continue many familiar and productive routines.

engaged with their own thoughts and emotions and less materialistic. Generally, therefore, two elderly people who were childhood friends would recognize in each other the same personality traits that brought them together as youngsters (Neugarten, 1971, 1972, 1977; Wolfe, 1994).

AGING AND CULTURE

November 1, 1994, approaching Kandy, Sri Lanka. Our little van struggles up the steep mountain incline. Breaks in the lush vegetation offer spectacular views that interrupt our conversation about growing old. "Then there are no old age homes in your country?" I ask. "In Colombo and other cities, I am sure," our driver responds, "but not many. We are not like you Americans." "And how is that?" I counter, stiffening a bit. His eyes remain fixed on the road: "We would not leave our fathers and mothers to live alone."

When do people grow old? How do younger people regard society's oldest members? How do elderly people view themselves? The answers to these questions vary from place to place, showing that aging is not only a biological process but a matter of socially constructed meanings. In short, while aging is universal, the significance of growing old varies according to culture.

At one level, how well—and, more basically, how long—people live is closely linked to a society's technology and overall standard of living. Through most of human history, as the English philosopher Thomas Hobbes (1588–1679) put it, people's lives have been "nasty, brutish, and short" (although Hobbes himself lasted to the ripe old age of ninety-one). In his day, most people married and had children while in their teens, became middle-aged in their twenties, and began to succumb to various illnesses in their thirties and forties. Thus, many "greats" of the past never reached what we would call "old age" at all: the English poets Keats and Byron both died at age twenty-six; and Mozart, the Austrian composer, died at thirty-five. Among writers, none of the three Brontë sisters lived to age forty; Edgar Allan Poe died at forty; Henry David Thoreau at forty-five; Oscar Wilde at forty-six; Shakespeare managed to live until fifty-two.

In rich nations, rising living standards and advancing medical technology made living to age fifty common about a century ago. Since then, increasing affluence has added almost thirty more years to life expectancy. But living into what we consider "old age" is not the rule in much of the world. Global Map 15–2 shows that in the world's poorest countries, the average life span is still just fifty years.

WINDOW ON THE WORLD

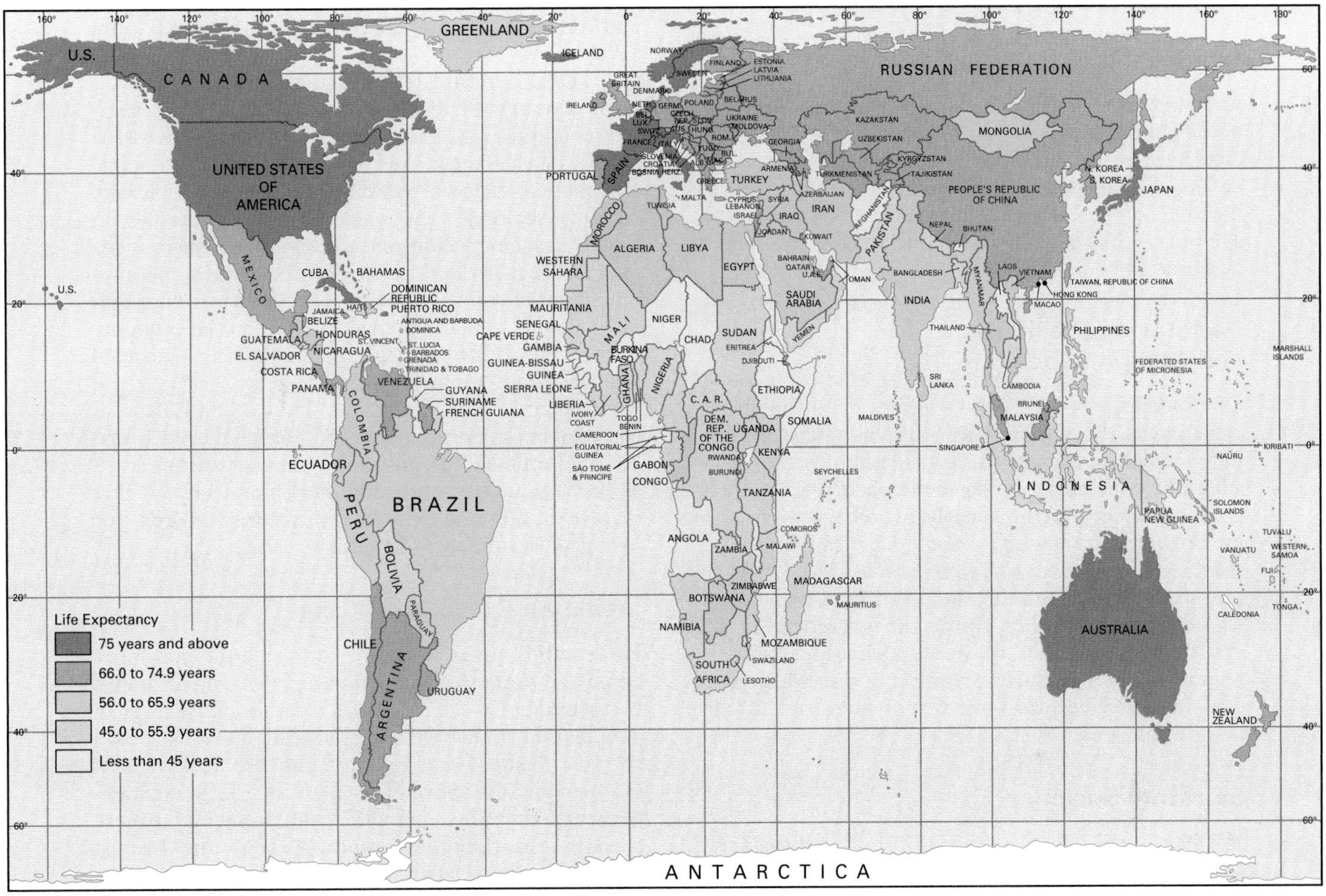

GLOBAL MAP 15–2 Life Expectancy in Global Perspective

Life expectancy has shot upward over the course of this century in industrial countries, including Canada, the United States, Western Europe, Japan, and Australia. A newborn in the United States can expect to live about seventy-seven years, and our life expectancy would be greater still were it not for the high risk of death among infants born into poverty. Since poverty is the rule in much of the world, lives are correspondingly shorter, especially in parts of Africa where life expectancy may be as low as forty years.

Source: *Peters Atlas of the World* (1990).

How long people live, on average, is one vital issue. But just as important as life expectancy is the value societies attach to their senior members. As Chapter 10 ("Social Stratification") explains, all societies distribute basic resources unequally. We now turn to the importance of age in this process.

AGE STRATIFICATION: A GLOBAL ASSESSMENT

Like race, ethnicity, and gender, age is a basis for social ranking. **Age stratification,** then, is *the unequal distribution of wealth, power, and privilege among people at* *different stages of the life course.* As is true of other dimensions of social hierarchy, age stratification varies according to a society's level of technological development.

Hunting and Gathering Societies

As Chapter 4 ("Society") explains, without the technology to produce a surplus of food, hunters and gatherers must be nomadic. Moving about as they do, survival depends on physical strength and stamina. Thus, as members of these societies grow old (in this case, about age thirty) they become less active and are considered an economic burden (Sheehan, 1976).

Pastoral, Horticultural, and Agrarian Societies

Once societies control food supplies by raising crops and animals, they can produce a surplus. Consequently, individuals can accumulate considerable wealth over a lifetime. The most privileged members of these societies are typically the elderly, which gives rise to **gerontocracy,** *a form of social organization in which the elderly have the most wealth, power, and prestige.* Old people, particularly men, are honored (and sometimes feared) by their families, and, as the box reports in the case of the Abkhasians, they are active leaders of society until they die. This veneration of the elderly also explains the widespread practice of ancestor worship in agrarian societies.

Industrial Societies

We have noted that industrialization pushes living standards upward and advances medical technology, which results in increasing life expectancy. But while industrialization adds to the length of life, it does not necessarily improve the *quality* of life for old people. On the contrary, industrial societies give less power and prestige to the elderly. Why? Because the prime source of wealth shifts from land (typically controlled by the oldest members of society) to businesses and other goods (often owned and managed by younger people). For instance, the peak earning years among U.S. workers, on average, occur around age fifty; after that, earnings decline.

Modern living also physically separates the generations as younger people move away to pursue their careers, depending less on their parents and more on their own earning power. Furthermore, because industrial, urban societies change rapidly, the skills, traditions, and life experiences that served the old are not relevant to the young. Finally, the tremendous productivity of industrial nations means that not all members of a society need to work, so most of the very old and the very young play nonproductive roles (Cohn, 1982).

The long-term effect of all these factors transforms *elders* (a term with positive connotations) into *the elderly* (commanding far less prestige). In mature, industrial societies such as the United States and Canada, economic and political leaders are usually middle-aged people who combine seasoned experience and up-to-date skills. In rapidly changing sectors of the economy, especially high-tech fields, many key executives are young, sometimes barely out of college. Industrial societies often consign older people to marginal participation in the economy because they lack the knowledge and training demanded in a fast-changing marketplace.

Certainly some older men and women remain at the helm of businesses, but, more commonly, older people predominate only in traditional occupations (such as barbers, tailors, and shop clerks) and in jobs that involve minimal activity (night security guards, for instance) (Kaufman & Spilerman, 1982).

Japan: An Exceptional Case

Japan stands out as an exception to the rule. Japan has about the same share of seniors as the United States, but its traditional culture reveres older people. Most aged people in Japan live with an adult daughter or son, and they play a significant role in family life. Elderly men in Japan are also more likely than their U.S. counterparts to stay in the labor force, and, in many Japanese corporations, the oldest employees enjoy the greatest respect. But even Japan is steadily becoming more like other industrial societies, where growing old means giving up some measure of social importance (Harlan, 1968; Cowgill & Holmes, 1972; Treas, 1979; Palmore, 1982; Yates, 1986).

TRANSITIONS AND CHALLENGES OF AGING

We confront change at each stage of life. People must unlearn self-concepts and social patterns that no longer apply to their lives and simultaneously learn to cope with new circumstances. Old age has its rewards; but, of all stages of the life course, it presents the greatest challenges.

Physical decline in old age is less serious than most younger people think. But, even so, older people endure more pain, become resigned to limiting their activities,

GLOBAL SOCIOLOGY

Growing (Very) Old: A Report from Abkhasia

The anthropologist Sula Benet was sharing wine and conversation with a man in Tamish, a small village in the Republic of Abkhasia, once part of the Soviet Union. Based on the standards of her own society, she judged the man to be about 70. She raised her glass and offered a toast to his long life. "May you live as long as Moses," she exclaimed. Her gesture of goodwill fell flat: Moses had lived to 120, but Benet's companion was already 119.

In the Caucasus region of the world, surprisingly many people have lived past the age of 100. The *Guinness Book of World Records* lists the world's oldest person as Shirali Muslimov, who died twenty-five years ago at the reputed age of 168. Such reports give outsiders good reason to be skeptical. But government statistics confirm that even if many Abkhasians exaggerate their age, most handily outlive the average North American.

What accounts for the Abkhasians' remarkable life span? The answer certainly is not advanced medical technology, so important to people in the United States; many Abkhasians have never seen a physician or entered a hospital.

The probable explanation for living so long is cultural, including diet and physical activity. Abkhasians eat little saturated fat (which is linked to heart disease), use no sugar, and drink no coffee or tea. Few smoke or chew tobacco. On the other hand, they consume large amounts of healthful fruits and vegetables and drink lots of buttermilk and low-alcohol wine. Abkhasians of all ages also lead active lives based on regular physical work.

Perhaps most important, Abkhasian culture gives everyone a strong feeling of belonging and clear sense of purpose. The elderly are active and valued members of the community, in marked contrast to our own practice of pushing old people to the margins of social life. As Benet explains: "The old [in the United States], when they do not simply vegetate, out of view and out of mind, keep themselves 'busy' with bingo and shuffleboard." The Abkhasians, however, do not even have a word for old people and have no concept of retirement. Furthermore, younger people give senior members of society great prestige and respect since advanced age confers great wisdom. Elders are indispensable guardians of culture who preside at important ceremonial occasions where they transmit their knowledge to the young. In Abkhasia, in short, people look to the old, rather than the young, for decisions and guidance in everyday life.

Given their positive approach to growing old, Abkhasians expect a long and useful life. They feel needed because—in their own minds and everyone else's—they are. Far from being a burden, elders stand at the center of society.

Source: Based on Benet (1971) and Specter (1998).

TABLE 15–1 Living Arrangements of the Elderly, 1998	Men	Women
Living alone	17%	41%
Living with spouse	73	40
Living with other relatives or nonrelatives	9	18
Living in nursing home	1	1

Source: U.S. Census Bureau (1999).

adjust to greater dependence on others, lose dear friends and relatives, and face up to their own mortality. Moreover, because our culture places such high value on youthfulness, aging in the United States often means added fear and self-doubt (Hamel, 1990). As one retired psychologist commented about old age: "Don't let the current hype about the joys of retirement fool you. They are not the best of times. It's just that the alternative is even worse" (Rubenstein, 1991:13).

FINDING MEANING

Recall from Chapter 5 ("Socialization") Erik Erikson's (1963, 1980) theory that elderly people must resolve a tension of "integrity versus despair." No matter how much they still may be learning and achieving, older people recognize that their lives are nearing an end. Thus the elderly spend much time reflecting on their past, including disappointments as well as accomplishments. Integrity, to Erikson, means assessing one's life in a realistic way. Without such honesty, this stage of life may turn into a time of despair—a dead end with little positive meaning.

In a classic study of people in their seventies, Bernice Neugarten (1971) found that some people cope with growing older better than others. Worst off are those who fail to come to terms with aging; they develop *disintegrated and disorganized personalities* marked by despair. Many of these people end up as passive residents of hospitals or nursing homes.

A second segment of Neugarten's subjects, with *passive-dependent personalities*, were only slightly better off. They have little confidence in their abilities to cope with daily events, sometimes seeking help even if they do not actually need it. Always in danger of social withdrawal, their level of life satisfaction is relatively low.

A third category had *defended personalities*, living independently but fearful of aging. They try to shield themselves from the reality of old age by fighting to stay youthful and physically fit. While concerns about health are certainly positive, setting unrealistic standards breeds stress and disappointment.

Most of Neugarten's subjects, however, displayed what she termed *integrated personalities:* They coped well with the challenges of growing old. As Neugarten sees it, the key to successful aging lies in maintaining one's dignity and self-confidence and accepting the inevitability of growing old.

SOCIAL ISOLATION

Being alone can cause anxiety at any age, but isolation is most common among elderly people. Retirement closes off one source of social interaction, and physical problems that limit mobility may prevent them from getting out much. Then, too, negative stereotypes of the elderly as "over the hill" may discourage younger people from close social contact with them.

The greatest cause of social isolation, however, is the inevitable death of significant others. Few human experiences affect people as profoundly as the death of a spouse. One study found that almost three-fourths of widows and widowers cited loneliness as their most serious problem (Lund, 1989). In such cases, people must rebuild their lives in the glaring absence of others with whom, in many cases, they spent most of their adult lives.

The problem of social isolation falls more heavily on women because they typically outlive their husbands. Table 15–1 shows that three-fourths of men aged sixty-five and over live with spouses, compared to only four in ten elderly women. Moreover, 41 percent of older women (especially the "older elderly") live alone, compared to 17 percent of older men. Greater isolation among elderly women in the United States may account for the research finding that their mental health is not as sound as that of elderly men (Chappell & Havens, 1980). Keep in mind, too, that living alone—which many older people value as a sign of independence—presumes the financial means to do so (Mutchler, 1992).

For most older people, families are the major source of social support. The majority of older people have at least one adult child living no more than ten miles way. About half of these nearby children visit their parents at least once a week, although much research confirms that daughters are more likely than sons to visit regularly (Stone, Cafferata, & Sangl, 1987; Lin & Rogerson, 1994).

RETIREMENT

Work not only provides us with earnings, it is also an important part of our personal identity. Thus, retirement means not only a reduction in income but also reduced social prestige and some loss of purpose in life.

Some organizations help ease this transition. Colleges and universities, for example, confer the title "professor emeritus" (from the Latin, meaning "fully earned") on retired faculty members, who are permitted to maintain their library privileges, parking space, and e-mail account.

For many older people, new activities and interests minimize the personal disruption and loss of prestige brought on by retirement. Volunteer work can be very rewarding, allowing individuals to apply their career skills in new settings. AARP, noted at the beginning of this chapter, has more than 15 million members over the age of fifty who engage in a wide range of volunteer activities. Surveys of the oldest baby boomers—those now in their early fifties—suggest that most expect to work at least part-time after they retire (Mergenhagen, 1996b).

Although we take retirement for granted, the concept emerged only within the last century in industrialized countries. Industrial technology reduced the need for everyone to work, just as it placed a premium on up-to-date skills. Retirement permits younger workers, who presumably have the most current knowledge and training, to predominate in the labor force. Then, too, the introduction of private and public pension programs made it financially possible for older people to retire. In poor societies, without pension programs, most people work until they can work no more.

Given how varied the elderly population is, we might wonder exactly when (or even if) we should expect people to retire. In our own history, Congress began phasing out mandatory retirement policies in the 1970s until, by 1987, almost none existed. Even so, the median age at retirement has fallen from sixty-eight in 1950 to sixty-three today. By age sixty-five, then, 83 percent of men and 91 percent of women are not in the paid labor force. Indeed, in recent decades "early retirement" has been gaining in popularity in the United States (Mergenhagen, 1994; U.S. Department of Labor, 2000).

AGING AND POVERTY

By the time they reach age sixty-five, most people have paid off their home mortgages and children's college expenses. But now medical care, household help, and home utility bills typically go up. At the same time, retirement usually means a significant decline in annual income. Seniors in the United States today are more affluent than ever before; nevertheless, many lack sufficient savings or pension benefits to be self-supporting. Social Security is the major source of income for people over sixty-five. Not surprisingly, then, the risk of poverty rises after midlife, as shown in Figure 15–2.

The rate of poverty among the elderly has fallen sharply from about 35 percent in 1960 to 10.5 percent in 1998—below the rate (12.7 percent) for the population as a whole. Moreover, since about 1980, seniors have posted a 28 percent increase in average income (in constant dollars), while income of people under thirty-five has actually declined (U.S. Census Bureau, 2000).

Several factors have caused this financial windfall: Better health now allows people who want to work to remain employed, employer pension programs are more generous, and more couples enjoy double incomes. Government policy, too, has played a part, with programs benefiting the elderly (including Social Security) amounting to almost half of all government spending, even as spending on children has remained more or less flat.

DIVERSITY SNAPSHOT

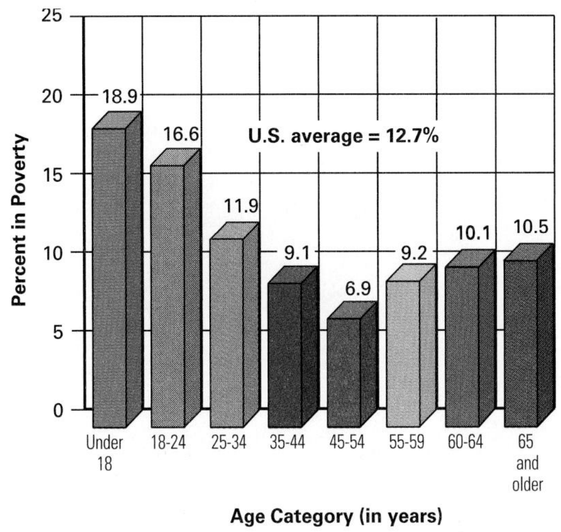

FIGURE 15–2 U.S. Poverty Rates, by Age, 1998
Source: U.S. Census Bureau (1999).

Typically, income drops by the time people pass the age of sixty. Therefore, the risk of poverty rises among the elderly. Research shows that poor elderly people need most of their income just to pay for necessities. For those who fall behind, homelessness can result. It is easy to imagine the struggle of homeless living for those whose desire for independence is offset by waning vitality.

But disadvantages associated with race and ethnicity persist in old age. In fact, income inequality among the elderly is greater than among younger adults. In 1998, the poverty rate among elderly Hispanics (21 percent) and African Americans (26.9 percent) was about three times the rate for their white, non-Hispanic counterparts (8.2 percent).

Gender, too, continues to shape the lives of people as they age. Among full-time workers, women over sixty-five had median earnings of $28,326 in 1998, compared to $43,157 for men over sixty-five. A quick calculation shows that these older full-time working women earn just 66 percent as much as comparable men; thus, the income gap linked to gender is greater among older than younger people (recall that *all* working women earn 74 percent as much as *all* working men). This is because older women typically have much less schooling than men their age and, therefore, they hold lower-paying jobs.

But, of course, the majority of elderly people have retired from the labor force. Thus, a more realistic financial assessment must take account of the entire elderly population, nonworking as well as working. From this point of view, median individual income is far lower: $10,504 for women, which is 58 percent of the $18,166 earned by men.

In the United States, then, although the elderly are faring better than ever, growing old (especially for women and other minorities) still raises the risk of poverty. One recent study, for example, found that poor elderly households typically spend three-fourths of income on basic necessities, which means that these people are just getting by (Koelln, Rubin, & Picard, 1995).

Note, too, that poverty among the elderly is largely hidden from view. Because of personal pride and a desire to remain independent, many elderly people conceal financial problems even from their own families. People who have supported their children for years often find it difficult to admit that they can no longer provide for themselves, even though it may be no fault of their own.

CAREGIVING[2]

In an aging society, the need for caregiving is bound to increase. **Caregiving** refers to *informal and unpaid care provided to a dependent person by family members, other relatives, or friends*. Although parents provide caregiving to children, the term is more often applied to the needs of elderly men and women. Indeed, today's middle-aged adults are called the "sandwich generation" because they may spend as much time caring for their aging parents as for their own children.

[2]This section is based on Lund (1993), as well as helpful personal communication.

Who Are the Caregivers?

Surveys show that 80 percent of caregiving to elders is provided by family members. Most caregivers are nearby, typically living only minutes away from the older person. In addition, 75 percent of all caregiving is provided by women, most often daughters and, next, wives. The gender norm is so strong that daughters-in-law are more likely than sons to care for an aging parent.

About two-thirds of all caregivers are married and one-third are also responsible for young children. When we add the fact that half of all caregivers also work full time or part time, it is clear that caregiving is a responsibility over and above what most people already consider a full day's work. Half of all primary caregivers spend more than twenty hours per week providing elder care.

Elder Abuse

Abuse of older people takes many forms, from passive neglect to active torment; it includes verbal, emotional, financial, and physical harm. Research suggests that 1 million elderly people (3 percent) suffer serious maltreatment each year, and three times as many (about one in ten) suffer abuse at some point. Like other forms of family violence, abuse of the elderly often goes unreported because victims are reluctant to talk about their plight (Bruno, 1985; Clark, 1986; Pillemer, 1988; Holmstrom, 1994; Thompson, 1997, 1998).

Certain factors increase the possibility of elder abuse. Risk is greater if the caregiver (1) works full time, (2) has young children, (3) is poor, (4) feels little affection for the older person, (5) finds the elderly person very difficult, and (6) gets no support or help from others.

Many caregivers contend with fatigue, emotional distress, and guilt over not being able to do more. But there is also a positive side to caregiving: Helping another person is a selfless act of human kindness that affirms the best in us and provides a source of personal enrichment and satisfaction (Lund, 1993).

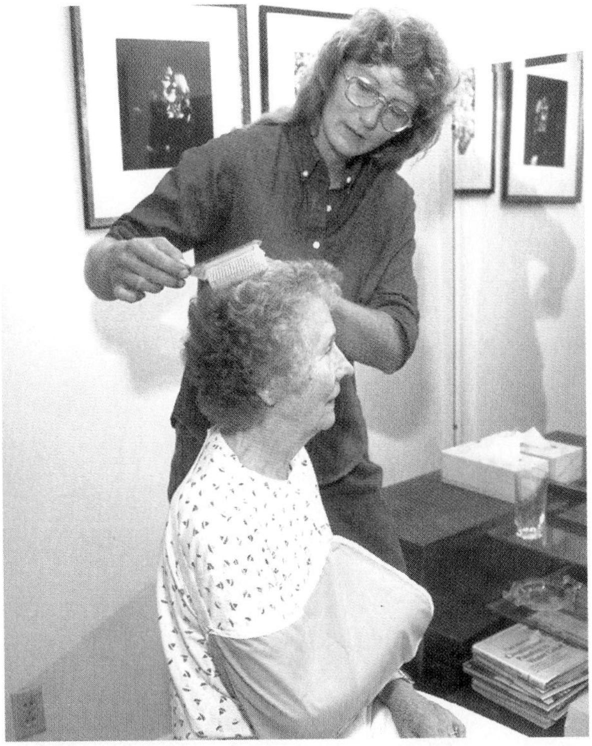

Caregiving is nothing new to most adults who, after all, have spent years providing child care. What is new is that the demands of family life now include elder care. The rapidly increasing number of elderly people, as well as their greater longevity, means that many more middle-aged adults will spend as much time caring for their aging parents as they did raising their children.

AGEISM

In earlier chapters, we explained how ideology—including racism and sexism—serves to justify the social disadvantages of minorities. Sociologists use the parallel term **ageism** for *prejudice and discrimination against the elderly.*

Like racism and sexism, ageism can be blatant (as when a college decides not to hire a sixty-year-old professor because of her age) or subtle (as when a nurse speaks to elderly patients in a condescending tone, as if they were children). Also like racism and sexism, ageism builds physical traits into stereotypes; in the case of the elderly, people consider gray hair, wrinkled skin, and stooped posture signs of personal incompetence. Negative stereotypes portray the aged as helpless, confused, resistant to change, and generally unhappy (Butler, 1975). Even sentimental views of sweet little old ladies and eccentric old gentlemen are stereotypes that gloss over individuality and ignore years of experience and accomplishment.

Sometimes, ageism contains a kernel of truth. Statistically speaking, old people are more likely than young people to be mentally and physically impaired. But we slip into ageism when we make unwarranted generalizations about an entire category of people, most of whom do not conform to the stereotypes.

Women and men experience stages of the life course in different ways. Most men, for example, pass through old age with the support of a partner. Women, who typically outlive men, endure much of their old age alone.

Betty Friedan (1993), a pioneer of today's feminist movement, believes ageism is deeply rooted in our culture. Friedan points out that few elderly people appear in the mass media; only a small percentage of television shows, for example, include main characters over sixty. More generally, when most of us think about older people, it is often in negative terms: This older man *lacks* a job, that older woman has *lost* her vitality, and seniors *look back* to their youth. In short, says Friedan, we often treat being old as if it were a disease—marked by decline and deterioration—for which there is no cure.

Nevertheless, Friedan believes that older women and men in the United States are discovering that they have more to contribute than others give them credit for. Advising small business owners, designing housing for the poor, teaching children to read—there are countless ways in which older people can enhance their own lives and help others.

THE ELDERLY: A MINORITY?

No one doubts that as a category of people in this country, the elderly face distinct social disadvantages. But sociologists disagree as to whether the aged form a minority in the same way as, say, African Americans or women.

According to Leonard Breen (1960), the elderly are a minority because they have a clear social identity based on their age, and they are subject to prejudice and discrimination. But Gordon Streib (1968) counters that minority status is usually both permanent and exclusive. That is, a person is an African American or woman *for life* and can never become part of the dominant category of whites or men. Being elderly, says Streib, is an *open* status because, first, people are elderly for only part of their lives and, second, everyone who has the good fortune to live long enough eventually grows old.

Streib further points out that the social disadvantages faced by the elderly are less substantial than those experienced by true minorities. For example, old people have never been deprived of the right to own property, to vote, or to hold office as African Americans and women have. Some elderly people, of course, do suffer economic disadvantages, but Streib believes the disadvantages are not primarily because of old age. Rather, he says, most of the aged poor fall into categories of people likely to be poor at any age. To Streib, it is not so much that "the old grow poor" as "the poor grow old."

In light of Streib's arguments and the rising economic power of the elderly in recent decades, it seems reasonable to conclude that old people are not a minority in the same sense as other categories are. Instead, perhaps we should describe the elderly as a distinctive segment of our population with characteristic pleasures and challenges.

In sum, growing old involves problems and transitions. Some are brought on by physical decline. But others—including social isolation, adjustment to retirement, and risk of poverty, abuse, and ageism—are products of society. In the next section, we turn to theoretical perspectives for insights into how society shapes the lives of the elderly.

There may be reasons to disengage elderly people from some critical work roles. But research shows that, for most people, satisfaction in old age (or, for that matter, at any age) depends on maintaining a high level of meaningful activity. A rising number of seniors are finding that they have much to contribute to others.

THEORETICAL ANALYSIS OF AGING

Each of sociology's major theoretical paradigms sheds light on the process of aging in the United States. We examine each in turn.

STRUCTURAL-FUNCTIONAL ANALYSIS: AGING AND DISENGAGEMENT

Drawing on the ideas of Talcott Parsons—an architect of the structural-functional paradigm—Elaine Cumming and William Henry (1961) explain that aging threatens to disrupt society as physical decline and death take their toll. In response, society *disengages* the elderly—gradually transferring statuses and roles from the old to the young so that tasks are performed with minimal interruption.

Disengagement is thus a strategy to ensure the orderly operation of society by removing aging people from productive roles while they are still able to perform them. Disengagement has an added benefit in a rapidly changing society, since young workers typically bring the most up-to-date skills and training to their work. Formally, then, **disengagement theory** is *the idea that society enhances its orderly operation by disengaging people from positions of responsibility as they reach old age.*

Disengagement benefits elderly people as well. People with diminishing capacities presumably look forward to relinquishing the pressures of a job in favor of new pursuits of their own choosing (Palmore, 1979a). Finally, we all tend to allow the elderly greater liberties, viewing any unusual behavior on their part as harmless eccentricity rather than dangerous deviance.

Critical evaluation. Disengagement theory explains why rapidly changing industrial societies typically define their oldest members as socially marginal. But there are several limitations to this approach.

First, many workers cannot disengage from paid work because they do not have the financial resources to fall back on. Second, many elderly people—regardless of their financial circumstances—do not wish to disengage from their productive roles. Disengagement, after all, comes at a high personal price, including loss of friends and social prestige. Third, it is far from clear that the societal benefits of disengagement outweigh its social costs, which include the loss of human resources and the need to care for people who might otherwise be able to fend for themselves. Indeed, as the numbers of elderly people swell, finding ways to help seniors remain independent will be a high priority. Fourth, a rigid system of disengagement does not allow for widely differing abilities among the elderly.

SYMBOLIC-INTERACTION ANALYSIS: AGING AND ACTIVITY

Another approach draws heavily on the symbolic-interaction paradigm. **Activity theory** is *the idea that a high level of activity enhances personal satisfaction in old age.*

Because various activities help build social identity, disengagement is bound to reduce satisfaction and meaning in elderly people's lives. What seniors need, in short, is not to be pushed out of roles, but a wider range of productive or recreational activities. The importance of such options increases when we realize that, on average, seniors now have ten hours more leisure time a week than twenty years ago (Robinson, Werner, & Godbey, 1997).

Activity theory does not reject the notion of job disengagement, it simply says that people need to find new roles to replace those they leave behind. Research confirms that elderly people who maintain a high activity level derive the most satisfaction from their lives.

Activity theory also recognizes that the elderly are diverse, with highly variable interests, needs, and physical abilities. Therefore, the activities people pursue and the pace at which they pursue them is always an individual matter (Havighurst, Neugarten, & Tobin, 1968; Neugarten, 1977; Palmore, 1979b; Moen, Dempster-McClain, & Williams, 1992).

Critical evaluation. Activity theory shifts the focus of analysis from the needs of society (as stated in disengagement theory) to the needs of the elderly themselves. It emphasizes the social diversity among elderly people, an important consideration in formulating any government policy.

A limitation of this approach, from a structural-functionalist point of view, is the tendency to exaggerate the well-being and competence of the elderly. Do we really want to depend on elderly people to perform crucial roles? From another perspective, activity theory falls short by ignoring the fact that many problems older people face have more to do with society than with themselves. We turn now to that point of view: social-conflict theory.

SOCIAL-CONFLICT ANALYSIS: AGING AND INEQUALITY

A social-conflict analysis is based on the idea that different age categories have different opportunities and different access to social resources, creating a system of age stratification. By and large, middle-aged people in the United States enjoy the greatest power and the most opportunities and privileges, while the elderly (as well as children) have less power and prestige and a higher risk of poverty. Employers often replace elderly workers with younger men and women as a way of keeping down wages. As a result, older people become second-class citizens (Atchley, 1982; Phillipson, 1982).

To conflict theorists, age-based hierarchy is inherent in an industrial-capitalist society. In line with Marxist thought, Steven Spitzer (1980) points out that a profit-oriented society devalues any category of people that is economically unproductive. To the extent that older people are less productive, then, our society labels them as mildly deviant.

Social-conflict analysis also draws attention to social diversity in the elderly population. Differences of class, race, ethnicity, and gender divide older people, as they do everyone else. Thus, some seniors have far greater economic security, greater access to top-flight medical care, and more options for personal satisfaction in old age than others. Likewise, elderly WASPs typically enjoy many advantages denied to older minorities. And women—an increasing majority as people age—suffer the social and economic disadvantages of both sexism and ageism.

Critical evaluation. Social-conflict theory adds to our understanding of the aging process by underscoring age-based inequality and explaining how capitalism devalues elderly people who are less productive. But it is not capitalism that creates the lower social standing, according to critics; the real culprit is *industrialization.* Thus, the elderly are not better off under a socialist system, as a Marxist analysis claims. Furthermore, the notion that either industrialization or capitalism dooms the elderly to economic distress is challenged by a steady rise in income and well-being among the U.S. elderly in recent decades.

DEATH AND DYING

> To every thing there is a season,
> And a time for every matter under heaven:
> A time to be born and a time to die . . .

These well-known lines from the Bible's Book of Ecclesiastes state two basic truths about human existence: the fact of birth and the inevitability of death. Just as life varies throughout history and around the world, so death, too, has many faces. We conclude this chapter with a brief look at the changing character of death, the final stage in the process of growing old.

HISTORICAL PATTERNS OF DEATH

In the past, confronting death was commonplace. No one assumed that a newborn child would live for long, a fact that led many parents to delay naming children until they were one or two years old. For those fortunate enough to survive infancy, illness, accident, and natural catastrophe made life uncertain, at best.

Sometimes, in fact, food shortages forced societies to protect the majority by sacrificing the least productive members. *Infanticide* is the killing of newborn infants, and *geronticide* is the killing of the elderly.

If death was routine, it was also readily accepted. Medieval Christianity assured believers, for example, that death fit into the divine plan for human existence. Here is how the historian Philippe Ariès describes Sir Lancelot, one of King Arthur's Knights of the Round Table, preparing for death when he thinks he is mortally wounded:

> His gestures were fixed by old customs, ritual gestures which must be carried out when one is about to die. He removed his weapons and lay quietly upon the ground. . . . He spread his arms out, his body forming a cross . . . in such a way that his head faced east toward Jerusalem. (1974:7–8)

As societies gradually learned more about health and medicine, death became less of an everyday experience. Fewer children died at birth, and accidents and disease took a smaller toll among adults. People today view dying as *extra*ordinary, except when it occurs among the very old or is associated with war or catastrophe. Consider that in 1900, about one-third of all deaths in the United States occurred before the age of five, and fully two-thirds before the age of fifty-five. Today, by contrast, 85 percent of our population dies *after* the age of fifty-five. Death and old age have become fused in our culture.

THE MODERN SEPARATION OF LIFE AND DEATH

Now removed from everyday experience, death somehow seems unnatural. If social conditions prepared our ancestors to accept their deaths, modern society, with its youth culture and aggressive medical technology, fosters a desire for eternal youth and immortality. Death has become separated from life.

Death is also *physically* removed from everyday activities. The clearest evidence of this is that many of us have never seen a person die. While our ancestors typically died at home in the presence of family and friends, most deaths today occur in impersonal settings such as hospitals and nursing homes. Even in hospitals, dying patients occupy a special part of the building, and hospital morgues are located well out of sight of patients and visitors alike (Sudnow, 1967; Ariès, 1974).

In many traditional societies, people express great respect not only for elders but also for their ancestors. Dani villagers in New Guinea mummified the body of this elder in a sitting position so that they could continue to honor him and feel his presence in their daily lives.

ETHICAL ISSUES: CONFRONTING DEATH

Moral questions are more pressing than ever now that technological advances give humans the power to prolong life and, therefore, to draw a line separating life from death. We now grapple with how to use these new powers—or whether to use them at all.

When Does Death Occur?

Perhaps the most basic question is the most difficult: Exactly how do we define death? Common sense suggests that life ceases when breathing and heartbeat stop. But our ability to resuscitate someone after a heart attack and artificially sustain breathing makes such definitions of death obsolete. Medical and legal experts in the United States now define death as an *irreversible* state involving no response to stimulation, no movement or breathing, no reflexes, and no indication of brain activity (Ladd, 1979; Wall, 1980).

Our society has long been concerned with the "good life"; more recently, attention has turned to the idea of a good death. The hospice movement is an important part of this trend. In some cases, terminally ill patients move to a hospice facility, where a professional staff provides medical support and emotional comfort. In other cases, hospice workers provide care in the familiar surroundings of a person's home.

The "Right to Die" Debate

Today, many aging people are less afraid of death than the prospect of being kept alive at all costs. In other words, medical technology now threatens personal autonomy by letting doctors rather than the dying person decide when life is to end. In response, many people now seek control over their deaths just as they seek control over their lives.

After deliberation, patients, families, and doctors may decide to forgo "heroic measures" to keep a person alive. *Living wills*—documents stating which medical procedures an individual wants and does not want under specific conditions—are now widespread.

A more difficult issue involves mercy killing, or **euthanasia**—*assisting in the death of a person suffering from an incurable disease.* Euthanasia (from the Greek, meaning "a good death") poses an ethical dilemma because it involves not just refusing life-extending treatment but actively taking steps to end life. In euthanasia, some see an act of kindness, while others find just a form of killing.

Is there a "right to die"? People with incurable diseases can forgo treatment that might prolong their lives. But whether a doctor should be allowed to help bring about death is a matter of debate. In 1994, three states—Washington, California, and Oregon—voted on propositions that physicians should be able to help people who wanted to die. Only in Oregon did voters pass the initiative, and opposition tied up enactment of the law in Oregon's state courts until 1997, when voters again endorsed it. Since then, Oregon doctors have legally assisted in the death of terminally ill patients. Even so, in 1997, the U.S. Supreme Court declared that the U.S. Constitution recognizes no "right to die." Moreover, in 1999, Congress began debating a law that would prohibit states from adopting laws similar to the one in Oregon.

In the Netherlands, we find the most permissive euthanasia law in the world. How does the Dutch system operate? The box takes a closer look.

Should the United States hold the line on euthanasia, or follow the lead of the Dutch? "Right to die" advocates maintain that a person facing unbearable suffering should be able to choose to live or die. And, if death is the choice, medical assistance can help people toward a "good death." Surveys show that a majority of U.S. adults support the option to die with a doctor's help (Rosenbaum, 1997; NORC, 1999).

On the other side of the debate, opponents fear that laws allowing physician-assisted suicide invite abuse. Some point to the Netherlands: In most cases, surveys indicate, the five conditions are not strictly met. In particular, most physicians do not consult with another doctor or even report the euthanasia to authorities. Of greater concern, however, is the fact that in about one-fifth of all doctor-assisted suicides, the patient never explicitly asks to die. This is so even though half of these patients are conscious and capable of making decisions

GLOBAL SOCIOLOGY

Death on Demand: A Report from the Netherlands

Marcus Erich picked up the telephone and dialed his brother Arjen's number. In a quiet voice, thirty-two-year-old Marcus announced, "It's Friday at 5 o'clock." When the time came, Arjen was there, having driven to his brother's farmhouse an hour south of Amsterdam. They said their final goodbyes. Soon afterward, Marcus's physician arrived. Marcus and the doctor spoke for a few moments, and then the doctor prepared a "cocktail" of barbiturates and other drugs. As Marcus drank the mixture, he made a face, joking, "Can't you make this sweeter?"

As the minutes passed, Marcus lay back and his eyes closed. But after half an hour, he was still breathing. At that point, according to their earlier agreement, the doctor administered a lethal injection. In a few minutes, Marcus's life came to an end.

Events like this take us to the heart of the belief that people have a "right to die." Marcus Erich was dying from the virus that causes AIDS. For five years, his body had been wasting away, and he suffered greatly with no hope of recovery. He wanted his doctor to end his life.

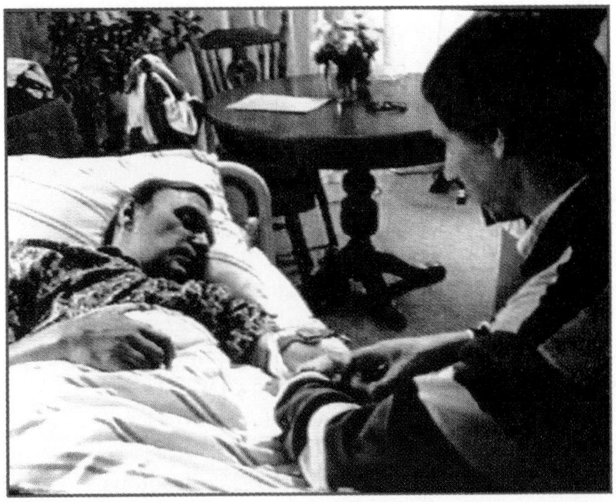

The Netherlands, a small nation in northwestern Europe, has gone further than any other in the world in allowing mercy killing or euthanasia. A 1981 Dutch law allows a physician to assist in a suicide if the following five conditions are met:

1. The patient must make a voluntary, well-considered, and repeated request to the doctor for help in dying.
2. The patient's suffering must be unbearable and without prospect of improvement.
3. The doctor and the patient must discuss alternatives.
4. The doctor must consult with at least one colleague who has access to the patient and the patient's medical records.
5. The assisted suicide must be performed in accordance with sound medical practice.

Official records indicate that doctors end 3,000 to 4,000 lives per year in the Netherlands. But because many cases are never reported, the actual number may well be twice that many.

Sources: Based on della Cava (1997) and Mauro (1997).

for themselves (Gillon, 1999). Opponents, therefore, fear that legalizing doctor-assisted suicide would put our society on a "slippery slope" toward more and more euthanasia. Can anyone deny, they ask, that ill people may be pushed into accepting death by doctors who consider suicide the "right" choice for the terminally ill or by family members who are weary of caring for them or want to avoid the expenses of medical care?

However the debate over the "right to die" turns out in the future, our society has now entered a new era when it comes to dying. Individuals, family members, and medical personnel now must face death not as a medical fact but as a negotiated outcome (Flynn, 1991; Humphrey, 1991; Markson, 1992; Wolfson, 1998).

BEREAVEMENT

Elisabeth Kübler-Ross (1969) found that most people confront their own death in stages (see Chapter 5, "Socialization"). Initially, individuals react with *denial*,

CONTROVERSY & DEBATE

Setting Limits: Must We "Pull the Plug" on Old Age?

Because death struck at any time, often without warning, our ancestors would have found the question, "Can people live *too long*?" absurd. In recent decades, however, as the elderly population soars in the United States, as new technology gives us more power to prolong life, and as life-extending care gets increasingly expensive, many now wonder just how much old age we can afford.

Currently, about half of the average person's lifetime spending for medical care occurs during the final years of life, and the share is rising. Against the spiraling costs of prolonging life, then, we well may ask if what is technically possible is necessarily desirable. During this new century, warns the gerontologist Daniel Callahan, an elderly population ready and eager to extend their lives will eventually force us either to "pull the plug" on old age or shortchange everyone else.

To even raise this issue, Callahan concedes, smacks of a lack of caring. But consider that the bill for the elderly's health topped $200 billion in 2000—more than twice what it cost in 1980. This dramatic increase reflects our current policy of directing more and more medical resources to studying and treating the diseases and disabilities of old age.

So Callahan makes the case for limits. He reasons, first, that to spend more on behalf of the elderly we must spend less on others. But with poverty a growing problem among children, how can we spend more and more on the oldest members of our society?

Second, Callahan reminds us, a *longer* life does not necessarily make for a *better* life. Cost aside, does heart surgery that prolongs the life of an eighty-four-year-old woman a year or two truly improve the quality of her life? Cost considered, would those resources yield more "quality of life" if used, say, to give a ten-year-old child a kidney transplant?

Third, Callahan urges us to reconsider our view of death as an enemy to be conquered at all costs. Rather, he suggests, a more realistic stance for an aging society is to treat death as a natural end to the life course. If we cannot make peace with death for our own well-being, given limited financial resources, we must do it for the benefit of others.

But not everyone agrees. Shouldn't people who have worked all their lives, and made our society what it is, enjoy our generosity in their final years? Moreover, given our cultural values of independence and responsibility, can we deny medical care to aging people able and willing to pay for it?

What is clear is that, in the twenty-first century, we will face questions that few would have imagined even fifty years ago: Is peak longevity good for everyone? Is it even *possible* for everyone?

Continue the debate . . .

1. *Should doctors and hospitals use a double standard, offering more complete care to the youngest people and more limited care to society's oldest members? Why or why not?*
2. *Do you think that a goal of the medical establishment should be to extend life at all costs?*
3. *Is the idea of rationing medical care really new? Hasn't our society always done this since some people have more wealth than others?*

Source: Callahan (1987).

followed by *anger*, then they try to *negotiate* a divine intervention. Gradually, they fall into *resignation* and, finally, reach *acceptance*.

According to some researchers, bereavement follows the same pattern of stages. Those close to a dying person, for instance, may initially deny the reality of impending death, and, with time, gradually reach a point of acceptance. Other investigators, however, question any linear "stage theory," arguing that bereavement is an unpredictable process (Lund, Caserta, & Dimond, 1986; Lund, 1989). Experts do agree, however, that how family and friends view an impending death affects the person who is dying. By accepting an approaching death, others help the dying person do the same; denying death isolates the dying person, who is unable to share feelings and experiences with others.

Many dying people find support in the *hospice movement*. Unlike a hospital that is designed to cure disease, a hospice helps people have a good death. These care centers for dying people try to minimize pain and suffering—either there or at home—and encourage family members to stay close by (Stoddard, 1978).

Even under the most favorable circumstances, though, bereavement may involve profound grief and social disorientation that persist for some time. Research documents that bereavement is less intense for someone who accepts the death of a loved one and feels the relationship with the dying person has reached a satisfactory resolution. Taking the opportunity to put appropriate closure on the relationship with a dying person allows family and friends to better comfort one another after death occurs (Atchley, 1983).

Looking ahead in the twenty-first century, the elderly will represent an increasing share of the U.S. population. How do you think this trend will affect the experiences and attitudes of the young?

LOOKING AHEAD: AGING IN THE TWENTY-FIRST CENTURY

This chapter has explored the "graying" of the United States and other industrial nations. We can predict with confidence that the ranks of the elderly will swell dramatically in the century to come: By 2050, our elderly population will exceed the population of the entire country in 1900. Moreover, one in four of these seniors will be over eighty-five. Within the next fifty years, then, society's oldest members will gain a far greater voice in everyday life. *Gerontology*—the study of the elderly—is also sure to gain in importance.

The reshaping of our society's age structure raises many serious concerns. With more people in their old age (and living longer once they enter old age), will we have the support services to sustain them? Remember that, as the elderly make demands, proportionately fewer younger people will be there to respond. What about the spiraling medical care costs of an aging society? As the baby boomers enter old age, some analysts paint a doomsday picture of the United States as a "twenty-first-century Calcutta," with desperate and dying elderly people everywhere (Longino, 1994:13).

But not all the signs are ominous. For one thing, the health of tomorrow's elderly people (that is, today's young and middle-aged adults) is better than ever: Smoking is way down, and people are eating more healthfully. Such trends probably mean that the elderly of the twenty-first century will be more vigorous and independent than their counterparts today. Moreover, tomorrow's seniors will enjoy the benefits of steadily advancing medical technology, although, as the final box explains, the claim of the old on our nation's resources is already hotly debated.

Another positive sign is the financial strength of the elderly. Though the cost of living is sure to rise, tomorrow's elderly will draw on greater affluence than ever before. Note, too, that the baby boomers will be the first generation of U.S. seniors with women who have been in the labor force most of their lives, a fact reflected in their substantial savings and pensions.

One concern, as we look ahead, is that younger adults will face a mounting responsibility to care for aging parents. Indeed, a falling birth rate coupled with a growing elderly population means caregiving in our society increasingly will include not just the very young but the very old.

More and more people in the United States are learning to care for aging parents. Caregiving includes more than meeting physical needs. Many of us have much to learn about communication, expressing love, and facing up to eventual death. In caring for parents, of course, we will also teach important lessons to our children, including the skills they will need, one day, to care for us.

Finally, an increasingly aging population will almost certainly change the way we view death. In all likelihood, death will become less of a social taboo and people will once again accept it as a natural part of the life course. As this comes to pass, both young and old alike will benefit.

SUMMARY

1. The proportion of elderly people in the U.S. population has risen from 4 percent in 1900 to 13 percent today; by 2050, 20 percent of our people will be elderly.
2. Gerontology, the study of aging and the elderly, focuses on how people change in old age, and how various cultures define aging.
3. Most younger people exaggerate the extent of disability among the elderly. Growing old is accompanied by a rising rate of disease and disability, but most seniors are healthy.
4. Psychological research confirms that growing old does not result in overall loss of intelligence or radical changes in personality.
5. The age at which people are defined as old varies historically: Until several centuries ago, old age began as early as thirty. In poor societies today, where life expectancy is substantially lower than in North America, people become old at fifty or even forty.
6. In global perspective, industrialization fosters a decline in the social standing of elderly people.
7. As people age, they face social isolation brought on by retirement, physical disability, and the death of friends or spouse. Even so, most elderly people enjoy the support of family members.
8. Since 1960, poverty among the elderly has dropped sharply. The aged poor are categories of people—including single women and people of color—who are at high risk of poverty at any age.
9. An increasing elderly population raises the demand for caregiving, most of which is performed by family members, typically women, who are likely to be caring for children as well.
10. Ageism—prejudice and discrimination against old people—is used to justify age stratification.
11. Although many seniors are socially disadvantaged, the elderly encompass men and women of all races, ethnicities, and social classes. Thus, older people do not qualify as a minority.
12. Disengagement theory, based on structural-functional analysis, suggests that society helps the elderly disengage from positions of social responsibility before the onset of disability or death. This process provides for the orderly transfer of statuses and roles from the older to the younger generation.
13. Activity theory, based on symbolic-interaction analysis, claims that a high level of activity affords people personal satisfaction in old age.
14. Age stratification is one focus of social-conflict analysis. Capitalist society's emphasis on economic efficiency leads to devaluing those who are less productive, including the elderly.
15. Modern society has set death apart from everyday life, prompting a cultural denial of human mortality. In part, this attitude is related to the fact that most people now die after reaching old age. Recent trends suggest that people are confronting death more directly and seeking control over the process of dying.

KEY CONCEPTS

gerontology (p. 386) the study of aging and the elderly

age stratification (p. 389) the unequal distribution of wealth, power, and privilege among people at different stages of the life course

gerontocracy (p. 390) a form of social organization in which the elderly have the most wealth, power, and prestige

caregiving (p. 394) informal and unpaid care provided to a dependent person by family members, other relatives, or friends

ageism (p. 395) prejudice and discrimination against the elderly

disengagement theory (p. 397) the idea that society enhances its orderly operation by disengaging people from positions of responsibility as they reach old age

activity theory (p. 397) the idea that a high level of activity enhances personal satisfaction in old age

euthanasia (p. 400) (mercy killing) assisting in the death of a person suffering from an incurable disease

CRITICAL-THINKING QUESTIONS

1. Why are the populations of industrial societies getting older? What are some of the likely consequences of "the graying of rich societies"?
2. Have you ever decided not to take a course because the professor was an older man or woman? Do you think other students consider age in this way?
3. Around the country, more seniors living in retirement communities object to paying taxes to fund public schools. Some want to keep children out of their communities altogether. Should laws permit such options? Why or why not?
4. Political analyst Irving Kristol (1996) praised the elderly as "our most exemplary citizens" because, compared to younger people, they do not kill, steal, use illegal drugs, fall deep into debt, or speak badly of their country. Overall, do you think the elderly receive the respect and social support they deserve? Why or why not?

APPLICATIONS AND EXERCISES

1. What practices and policies does your college or university have for helping older faculty make the transition to retirement? Ask several faculty nearing retirement—and several already retired—for their views. In what ways does retiring from an academic career seem harder or easier than from other kinds of work?
2. Look through an issue of any popular magazine—say, *Time*, *Newsweek*, or *Life*—and note images of men and women featured in stories and pictured in advertising. Are elderly people fairly represented in such publications?
3. Obtain a copy of a living will and try to respond to all the questions it asks. Does filling out such a form help clarify your own thinking about confronting death?
4. The *Journal of Medical Ethics* (Vol. 25, No. 1, February, 1999) has several research articles investigating alleged abuse of euthanasia laws in the Netherlands. Read the articles and decide if you think, on balance, doctor-assisted suicide is a sound or unsound policy.
5. Install the CD-ROM packaged in the back of this new textbook to access a variety of study, review, and applications exercises designed to help you better understand the material covered in this chapter. The CD includes an author's tip video, as well as interactive maps, video application exercises, Web links, and study questions.

SITES TO SEE

http://www.prenhall.com/macionis

Visit the interactive Web site that accompanies this text. Begin by clicking on the cover of your book. You will find a chapter-by-chapter study guide, practice tests, chat room, and many suggested Web links.

http://www.nho.org

Learn about hospices by visiting the Web site for the National Hospice Organization. Then, check your local telephone book to contact people who operate a hospice in your community.

http://www.seniornet.org

This is the site for SeniorNet, a nonprofit organization that is bringing seniors into the age of the Internet. Run by volunteers, SeniorNet offers low-cost computer and Internet instruction to the elderly at several hundred training sites across the United States.

http://www.aoa.gov

This site, operated by the Department of Health and Human Services, provides a look at likely trends involving the elderly over the course of the twenty-first century.

cyber.scope

PART III

NEW INFORMATION TECHNOLOGY AND SOCIAL STRATIFICATION

Change in technology transforms the nature of work. Just as important, such shifts alter the reward structure, reshaping patterns of social inequality. This third cyber.scope considers several ways in which the spread of computer technology is linked to social stratification.

The Information Revolution and U.S. Stratification

Most analysts agree that recent decades have witnessed economic polarization in the United States, with economic growth primarily enriching families that already had high incomes (Persell, 1997). At the outset, at least, technological revolution typically concentrates income and wealth as a small number of people make key discoveries and, with the resulting products and services, establish and expand new markets. Just as John D. Rockefeller and Andrew Carnegie amassed great fortunes a century ago as captains of the Industrial Revolution, the Information Revolution has created a new elite today. For several years, the richest person in the country has been Bill Gates, a founder of Microsoft Corporation that produces, not oil or steel, but the operating systems found in most of today's personal computers. More broadly, it is those with money to invest (many of whom make up what Karl Marx called the capitalist class) who reap most of the profits from successful new industries. During the 1990s, as the Information Revolution rolled ahead, key stock market indicators leaped fivefold, with new technology companies such as Microsoft (software), Intel (computer chips), Dell (personal computers), and Cisco Systems (computer networking) making even more spectacular gains.

But the wave of technological change does not benefit everyone. As companies adopt new technology in their efforts to become more efficient and profitable, some people lose out. In recent decades, for example, tens of millions of jobs in the United States have simply disappeared. For each job lost, a worker—and usually an entire family—suffers.

Both blind and deaf, Georgia Griffith was able to communicate only through conversations traced out on her palms, until specially equipped computers opened up her life. Do you think that, in general, advances in information technology will improve the lives of all persons with disabilities? Or will these people be left behind by the Information Revolution?

Another key link between new information technology and social inequality concerns the unequal spread of computing skills. In 2000, about 35 percent of the U.S. population aged sixteen or older were users of the Internet. Yet these users are not average people; they represent an information elite, privileged in more ways than one. About 95 percent are white (compared to 85 percent of the population), 60 percent are men (versus half the population), and 40 percent are professionals or managers (versus 18 percent of the population). Computer users are, in short, people with above-average incomes. College students stand out among computer users but, even among them, differences emerge. Figure Cyber III–1 shows that students attending private (and more expensive) universities and colleges are more likely to use e-mail frequently than those at public institutions. Similarly, students at two-year colleges and at historically black colleges also make less use of computers.

It is likely that, over time, computer users will come to mirror more closely the population as a whole. But there can be little doubt that, at least for now, new information technology plays a role in rising levels of economic inequality as it creates a cyber-elite and generates a new underclass made up of those without crucial symbolic skills (Wynter, 1995; Edmondson, 1997b).

The Information Revolution: Gender, Race, and Age

The Industrial Revolution ushered in a trend by which women and men are becoming more socially equal. Machinery eroded the link between physical strength and ability to work, and more women entered the labor force as birth control technology helped lower the birth rate by making motherhood a matter of individual choice. The Information Revolution promises to continue this trend. Work in the computer age involves not making or moving *things* but manipulating *ideas*—activity that favors neither men nor women.

Note, too, that communication via computers obscures a person's sex—obvious in face-to-face interaction—placing men and women on more equal footing. The same holds for race and ethnicity, so that the coming cyber-society may well be marked by greater contact among people of all races and cultural backgrounds.

But an important counterpoint involves *access* to computer technology. To date, cultural biases within the new cyber-society have favored males: Most games that introduce children to computers are designed for boys, just as computer science courses in colleges enroll mostly men. Similarly, to the extent that racial and ethnic minorities are economically disadvantaged and have access to inferior schools, this segment of our population will be cut off from owning and operating computers—the key to success in the labor force in this new century.

Finally, the effects of computing on age stratification are likely to be mixed. On the one hand, the fact that computing demands mental more than physical vitality—and allows work to be performed almost anywhere—should expand opportunities for people to continue to work well past the standard of "retirement" that emerged during the industrial era. On the other hand, new technology is almost always age-biased, in that it is readily adopted by the young, but regarded more cautiously by the old whose life experiences have been shaped by earlier ways. Unless our society expands programs of adult education, then, younger people are likely to predominate in, and benefit from, work and other activities that rely heavily on new information technology.

DIVERSITY SNAPSHOT

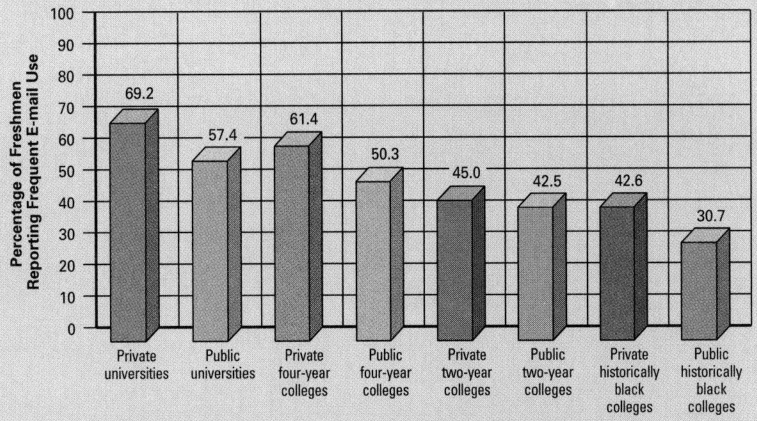

FIGURE Cyber III–1 Percentage of University and College Freshmen Reporting Frequent E-mail Use during the Past Year, 1999

Source: Sax et al. (1999).

The Information Revolution and Global Stratification

Worldwide, the elite pattern we have described holds even more. The Information Revolution directly involves only a tiny share of the planet's people. A look back at Global Map 4–1, on page 103, and Global Map 7–1, on page 172, shows that it is the rich regions of the world where computers and Internet access are readily available, at least to those who can afford it. In most of Africa, by contrast, people are far less likely to have a computer, and, in some countries, there is no network access at all. Moreover, the large number of African languages and alphabets will slow the spread of computing there.

While Internet access is found in most of Asia, at present, a cultural and technical problem limits the spread of computing there: Almost all computer keyboards use the Latin alphabet. In China and other Asian nations, while members of the technical elite are likely to speak and write English, most people utilize complex character sets that have yet to be incorporated into computer technology. Overall, then, the Information Revolution has come to that part of the world already benefiting from industrial technology—yet another case of the rich getting richer.

CHAPTER 16

René Magritte
Le modèle rouge (1898–1967)

THE ECONOMY AND WORK

Some years back, you could spot the office temps in a minute. They were the ones with lots of questions about where everything was. Just about the time they figured it all out, off they went to another company to begin the process all over again.

But in the 1980s, things began to change. Big companies were merging and laying off workers—processes that executives called "restructuring" and "downsizing." Cautious about adding full-time employees, companies began meeting their needs by hiring "temporary" workers until economic trends became clear. But, by the 1990s, temps were becoming permanent fixtures in the office, and their numbers soared from 1.2 million in 1990 to 3 million in 2000. Why? Companies discovered that using temps held down wages and salaries, reduced health care and pension costs (since many temps do not receive such benefits), and allowed firms to let people go at any time.[1]

The college campus, too, is now awash with temporary instructors. By one count, 25 percent of faculty at public institutions and up to 40 percent of faculty at private colleges and universities have temporary contracts (Will, 1999).

Whether in business or academia, some temporary workers are happy to keep their options open. But more have decided they deserve better and are fighting back. In 1999, for example, a court sided with 10,000 former Microsoft temps, saying they should have been allowed to take part in that company's employee stock-purchase plan. Across the country, the "nomads" of the labor force are returning to the old idea that if companies expect loyalty from employees, they have to offer some security in return.

[1]This opening is adapted from Eisenberg (1999).

This chapter examines the economy, widely considered the most influential of all social institutions. (The other major social institutions are examined in subsequent chapters: Chapter 17, "Politics and Government"; Chapter 18, "Family"; Chapter 19, "Religion"; Chapter 20, "Education"; and Chapter 21, "Health and Medicine.") As the chapter-opening story suggests, the economy is changing, and, just as important, it does not operate to the advantage of everyone. Indeed, as we shall see, sociologists debate how the economy ought to work, whose interests it ought to serve, and what companies and workers owe each other.

THE ECONOMY: HISTORICAL OVERVIEW

The **economy** is *the social institution that organizes a society's production, distribution, and consumption of goods and services.* As an institution, the economy operates in a more-or-less predictable manner. *Goods* are commodities ranging from necessities (food, clothing, shelter) to luxury items (cars, swimming pools, yachts). *Services* refer to activities that benefit others (for example, the work of priests, physicians, teachers, and software specialists).

We value goods and services because they ensure survival or because they make life easier, more interesting, or more aesthetically pleasing. Also, what we produce and consume are important to our self-image and social identity. How goods and services are distributed, then, shapes the lives of everyone in a number of basic ways.

The economies of modern industrial societies are the result of centuries of social change. We turn now to three technological revolutions that reorganized production and, in the process, transformed social life.

THE AGRICULTURAL REVOLUTION

Members of the earliest human societies were hunters and gatherers living off the land. In these technologically simple societies, there was no distinct economy. Rather, production, distribution, and consumption were all part of family life.

As Chapter 4 ("Society") explained, the rise of agriculture some 5,000 years ago greatly expanded economic productivity. When people harnessed animals to plows, they produced ten times the yield of hunters and gatherers. This surplus meant that not everyone had to produce food, so many took on specialized work: making tools, raising animals, or building dwellings. Soon towns sprang up, linked by networks of traders dealing in food, animals, and other goods (Jacobs, 1970). These four factors—agricultural technology, job specialization, permanent settlements, and trade—made the economy a distinct social institution.

THE INDUSTRIAL REVOLUTION

By the mid-eighteenth century, a second technological revolution was underway, first in England and then in North America. The development of industry was to bring even greater changes than agriculture had. Industrialization changed the economy in five fundamental ways:

1. **New forms of energy.** Throughout history, "energy" meant the muscle power of people or animals. But in 1765, the English inventor James Watt introduced the steam engine. One hundred times more powerful than muscle power, early steam engines could drive heavy machinery.
2. **Centralization of work in factories.** Steam-powered machines soon moved work out of homes and into factories—centralized and impersonal workplaces housing the machines.
3. **Manufacturing and mass production.** Before the Industrial Revolution, most people grew or gathered raw materials (such as grain, wood, or wool). In an industrial economy, the focus shifted so that most people's workday was spent turning raw materials into a wide range of finished products (like furniture and clothing).
4. **Specialization.** Historically, artisans working at home made products from start to finish. In the factory, a laborer repeated a single task over and over, making only a small contribution to the finished product. Such specialization raised productivity but lowered the skill level of the average worker.
5. **Wage labor.** Instead of working for themselves in a household (called "cottage industry"), factory workers became wage laborers who sold their labor to strangers, who often cared less for them than for the machines they operated.

The Industrial Revolution gradually raised the standard of living as countless new products and services filled an expanding marketplace. Yet the benefits of industrial technology were shared very unequally, especially at the beginning. Some factory owners made vast fortunes, while the majority of industrial workers lived close to poverty. Children, too, worked in factories or in coal mines for pennies a day. Women factory workers, among the lowest paid, endured special problems, as the box explains.

THE INFORMATION REVOLUTION AND THE POSTINDUSTRIAL SOCIETY

By about 1950, the nature of production was changing once again. The United States was creating a **postindustrial economy,** *a productive system based on service work and high technology.* Automated machinery (and,

SOCIAL DIVERSITY

Women in the Mills of Lowell, Massachusetts

Few people paid much attention to Francis Cabot Lowell, ancestor of two prominent Boston families, the Cabots and the Lowells, when he returned from England in 1822. But Lowell carried with him documents that would change the course of the U.S. economy: plans, based on mills operating in England, for this country's first textile factory.

Lowell built his factory beside a waterfall on the Merrimack River in Massachusetts, transforming a farming village into a thriving town. From the outset, 90 percent of the mill workers were women. Factory owners preferred women because they could be paid \$2 to \$3 a week, half the wages men received. (Many immigrant men were willing to work for low wages, but prejudice disqualified "foreigners" from any job at all.)

Recruiters, driving wagons through the small towns of New England, urged parents to send their daughters to the mills, where, they promised, the young women would be properly supervised as they learned skills and discipline. The offer appealed to many parents who could barely provide for their children, and the prospect of getting out on their own surely excited many young women. After all, there were few occupations open to women at that time, and those that were—including teaching and household service—paid even less than factory work.

At the Lowell factory, young women lived in dormitories, paying one-third of their wages for room and board. They were subject to a curfew and, as a condition of employment, regularly attended church. Any morally questionable conduct (such as bringing men to their rooms) brought firm disciplinary action.

Besides fulfilling their promise to parents, factory owners had another motive for their strict rules: They knew that closely supervised women could not organize among themselves. Working twelve or thirteen hours a day, six days a week, the Lowell employees had good reason to seek improvements in their working conditions. Yet any public criticism of the factory, or even possessing "radical" literature, could cost a worker her job.

Sources: Based on Eisler (1977) and Wertheimer (1982).

more recently, robotics) reduced the role of human labor in production while simultaneously expanding the ranks of clerical workers and managers. Service industries—such as public relations, health care, advertising, banking, and sales—now employ most working people in this country. The postindustrial era, then, is distinguished by a shift from industrial work to service work.

Driving this economic change is a third technological breakthrough: the computer. Just as machines did two centuries ago, the Information Revolution has introduced new kinds of products and new forms of communication and has altered the character of work. In general, we see three changes:

1. **From tangible products to ideas.** As we discussed in earlier chapters, the industrial era was defined by the production of goods; in the postindustrial era, work involves manipulating symbols. Computer programmers, writers,

In the United States, only a few percent of the labor force works in agriculture. At the same time, a large share of farm workers are immigrants from low-income countries. These people—new arrivals from Mexico—are harvesting aloe plants in south Texas.

financial analysts, advertising executives, architects, editors, and all sorts of consultants make up the labor force of the information age.

2. **From mechanical skills to literacy skills.** The Industrial Revolution required mechanical skills, but the Information Revolution requires literacy skills—speaking and writing well and, of course, using computers. People able to communicate effectively enjoy new employment opportunities; people with limited skills face declining prospects.
3. **From factories to almost anywhere.** Industrial technology drew workers into factories located near power sources, but computer technology allows workers to be almost anywhere. Laptop computers, cell phones, and portable facsimile (fax) machines now turn the home, car, or even an airplane into a "virtual office." New information technology, in short, blurs the line between work and home life.

SECTORS OF THE ECONOMY

The three revolutions we have just described reflect a shifting balance among the three sectors of a society's economy. The **primary sector** is *the part of the economy that draws raw materials from the natural environment.* The primary sector—agriculture, raising animals, fishing, forestry, and mining—predominates in preindustrial societies. Figure 16–1 shows that 63 percent of the economic output of low-income countries is from the primary sector, compared to 32 percent of economic activity in middle-income nations and just 4 percent in high-income countries like the United States.

The **secondary sector** is *the part of the economy that transforms raw materials into manufactured goods.* This sector grows quickly as societies industrialize. It includes operations such as refining petroleum into gasoline and turning metals into tools and automobiles.

The **tertiary sector** is *the part of the economy involving services rather than goods.* Accounting for just 22 percent of economic output in low-income countries, the tertiary sector grows with industrialization and dominates the economies of high-income, postindustrial nations. Today, about 70 percent of the U.S. labor force is in service work, including secretarial and clerical work and positions in food service, sales, law, advertising, and teaching.

THE GLOBAL ECONOMY

New information technology is drawing people around the world closer together and creating a **global**

economy—*expanding economic activity with little regard for national borders.*

The development of a global economy has four major consequences. First, we see a global division of labor so that different regions of the world specialize in one sector of economic activity. As Global Map 16–1 on page 414 shows, agriculture occupies more than 70 percent of the work force in some low-income countries. Global Map 16–2 indicates that industrial production is concentrated in the middle- and high-income nations of the world. The richest nations, including the United States, now specialize in service-sector activity.

Second, an increasing number of products pass through more than one nation. Look no further than your morning coffee, which may well have been grown in Colombia and transported to New Orleans on a freighter that was registered in Liberia, made in Japan using steel from Korea, and fueled by oil from Venezuela.

A third consequence of the global economy is that national governments no longer control the economic activity that takes place within their borders. In fact, governments cannot even regulate the value of their national currencies, since dollars, pounds sterling, yen, and other currencies are traded around the clock in the financial centers of Tokyo, London, and New York. Global markets are the result of satellite communications that link the world's cities.

A fourth consequence of the global economy is that a small number of businesses, operating internationally, now control a vast share of the world's economic activity. According to one estimate, the 600 largest multinational companies account for half the world's entire economic output (Kidron & Segal, 1991).

The world is still divided into 191 politically distinct nations. But increasing international economic activity makes nationhood less significant.

GLOBAL SNAPSHOT

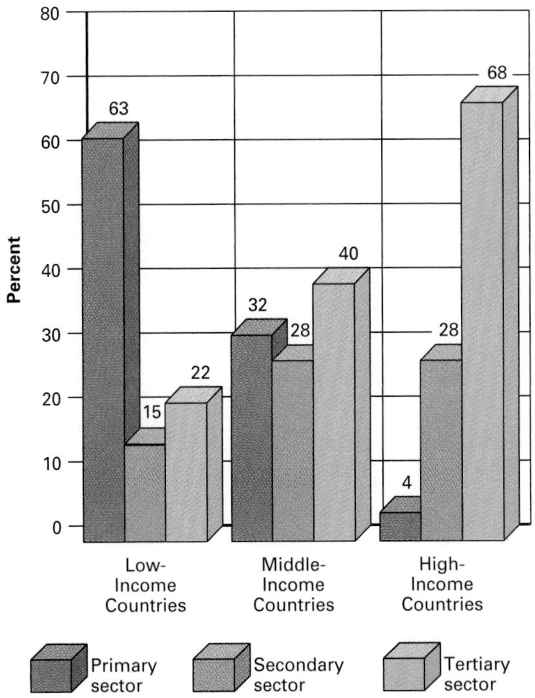

FIGURE 16–1 The Size of Economic Sectors by Income Level of Country

Source: Author estimates based on The World Bank (1995).

ECONOMIC SYSTEMS: PATHS TO JUSTICE

<u>October 20, 1994, Saigon, Vietnam.</u> Sailing up the narrow Saigon River is an unsettling experience for anyone who came of age during the 1960s. We need to remember that Vietnam is a <u>country</u> not a <u>war</u>, and twenty years have passed since the last U.S. helicopter lifted off the rooftop of the U.S. embassy, ending our country's presence there.

Saigon is on the brink of becoming a boom town. Neon signs bathe the city's waterfront in color; hotels, bankrolled by Western corporations, push skyward from a dozen construction sites; taxi meters record fares in U.S. dollars, not Vietnamese dong; Visa and American Express stickers decorate the doors of fashionable shops that cater to shoppers from Japan, France, and (since the U.S. embargo on visiting Vietnam was lifted in 1994) the United States.

There is a heavy irony here: After decades of fighting, the loss of millions of lives on both sides, and the victory

WINDOW ON THE WORLD

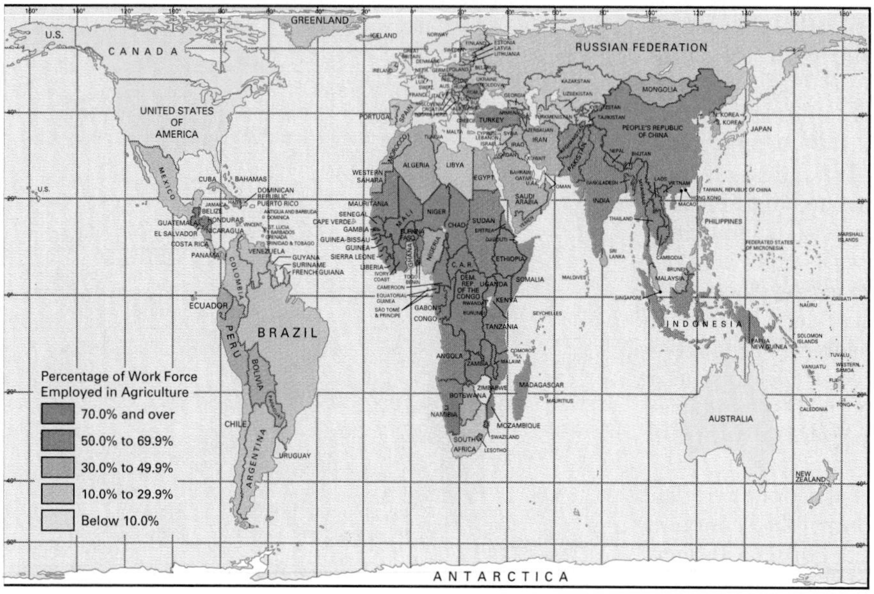

GLOBAL MAP 16–1
Agricultural Employment in Global Perspective

The primary sector of the economy predominates in societies that are least developed. Thus, in the poor countries of Africa and Asia, half, or even three-fourths, of all workers are farmers. This picture is altogether different in the world's most economically developed countries—including the United States, Canada, Great Britain, and Australia—which have less than 10 percent of their work force in agriculture.

Source: *Peters Atlas of the World* (1990).

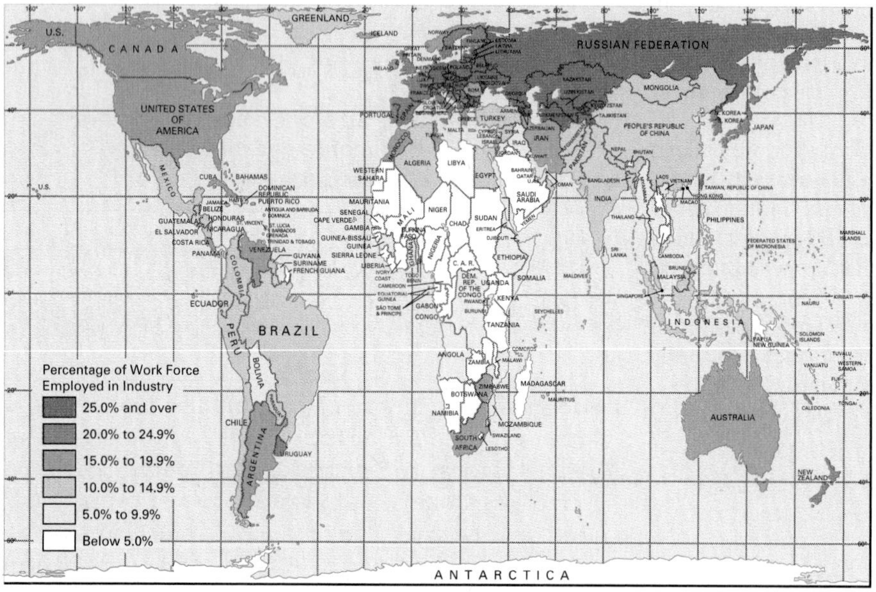

GLOBAL MAP 16–2
Industrial Employment in Global Perspective

Because the world's poor societies, by and large, have yet to industrialize, only a small proportion of their labor force engages in industrial work. The nations of Eastern Europe and the Russian Federation have far more of their workers in industry. In the world's richest societies, we see workers moving from industrial jobs to service work. Thus, the postindustrial economy of the United States now has about the same share of workers in industrial jobs as the much poorer nation of Argentina.

Source: *Peters Atlas of the World* (1990).

of Communist forces, the Vietnamese are doing an about-face and turning toward capitalism. What we see today is what might well have happened had the U.S. forces won the war.

Every society's economic system makes a statement about justice, since the economy broadly determines who gets what. Two general economic models are capitalism and socialism. No society has an economy that is completely one or the other; capitalism and

Capitalism still thrives in Hong Kong (left), evident in streets choked with advertising and shoppers. Socialism is more the rule in China's capital of Beijing (right), a city dominated by government buildings rather than a downtown business district.

socialism represent two ends of a spectrum along which all actual economies can be located. We will look at each type in turn.

CAPITALISM

Capitalism refers to *an economic system in which natural resources and the means of producing goods and services are privately owned.* Ideally, a capitalist economy has three distinctive features:

1. **Private ownership of property.** In a capitalist economy, individuals can own almost anything. The more capitalist an economy is, the more private ownership there is of wealth-producing property such as factories, real estate, and natural resources.
2. **Pursuit of personal profit.** A capitalist society encourages the accumulation of private property and considers the profit motive natural, simply a matter of "doing business." Further, claimed the Scottish philosopher Adam Smith (1723–1790), the individual pursuit of self-interest helps the entire society prosper (1937:508; orig. 1776).
3. **Competition and consumer sovereignty.** A purely capitalist economy is a free-market system with no government interference (sometimes called a *laissez-faire* economy, from the French words meaning "to leave alone"). Adam Smith stated that a freely competitive economy regulates itself by the "invisible hand" of the laws of supply and demand.

   Consumers regulate a free-market economy, Smith explained, by selecting goods and services that offer the greatest value. Producers compete for customers' business by offering the highest quality goods and services at the lowest price possible while still making a profit. As Smith put it, from narrow self-interest comes the "greatest good for the greatest number of people." Government control of the economy, on the other hand, distorts market forces by reducing producer motivation, diminishing quantity and quality of goods, and shortchanging consumers.

"Justice," in a capitalist context, amounts to freedom of the marketplace, where one can produce, invest, and buy according to individual self-interest. The worth of products—or workers—is determined by the dynamic

In the case of Elian Gonzales, the young boy plucked from the Atlantic Ocean after fleeing Cuba with his mother, little of the controversy over where Elian should live focused on what was best for the child. Rather, people used the case to debate the relative merits of life in Cuba's socialist society and the capitalist way of life in the United States.

process of supply and demand. Replacing much of the work force with lower-paid temporary workers, as described in the opening to this chapter, is "just" if it is profitable to the company's stockholders.

The United States is a capitalist nation in that the vast majority of businesses are privately owned. Even so, government plays an extensive role in economic affairs. The government itself owns and operates a number of businesses, including almost all of this country's schools, roads, parks and museums, the U.S. Postal Service, the Amtrak railroad system, and the entire U.S. military. The federal government also had a major part in building the Internet. In addition, governments use taxation and other forms of regulation to influence what companies produce, to control the quality and cost of merchandise, to influence what businesses import and export, and to motivate consumers to conserve natural resources.

Furthermore, government sets minimum wage levels, enforces workplace safety standards, regulates corporate mergers, provides farm price supports, and supplements income in the form of Social Security, public assistance, student loans, and veterans' benefits for a majority of the people in the United States. In fact, local, state, and federal governments together constitute the country's biggest employer, with 14 percent of the labor force on their payrolls (U.S. Census Bureau, 1999).

SOCIALISM

Socialism is *an economic system in which natural resources and the means of producing goods and services are collectively owned.* In its ideal form, a socialist economy is the exact opposite of capitalism:

1. **Collective ownership of property.** A socialist economy limits rights to private property, especially property (such as factories or apartment buildings) used to generate income. Government controls such property and makes housing and other goods available to all, not just to people with the most money.
2. **Pursuit of collective goals.** The individualistic pursuit of profit is also at odds with the collective orientation of socialism. What capitalism celebrates as the "entrepreneurial spirit," socialism condemns as "greed." For this reason, socialist nations outlaw private transactions as "black market" activity.
3. **Government control of the economy.** Socialism rejects capitalism's laissez-faire approach in favor of a *centrally controlled* or *command economy* operated by the government. Socialism also rejects the idea that it is consumers who guide capitalist production, on the grounds that consumers lack the information necessary to evaluate products

and are manipulated by advertising to buy what is profitable for factory owners and other capitalists rather than what they genuinely need. Commercial advertising thus plays little role in socialist economies.

"Justice," in a socialist context, is not freedom to compete and accumulate wealth but, rather, meeting everyone's basic needs in a more or less equal manner. From a socialist point of view, a capitalist practice such as limiting workers' wages and benefits to boost company earnings—as described in the opening to this chapter—is putting profits before people and thus is an injustice.

The People's Republic of China and a number of other societies in Asia and in Africa and Latin America—some two dozen in all—model their economies on socialism, placing almost all wealth-generating property under state control (McColm et al., 1991). The extent of world socialism has declined in recent years as countries in Eastern Europe and the former Soviet Union have restructured their economies toward more of a market system.

Socialism and Communism

Many people equate the terms *socialism* and *communism.* More precisely, **communism** is *a hypothetical economic and political system in which all members of a society are socially equal.* Karl Marx viewed socialism as a transitory stage on the path toward the ideal of a communist society that abolished all class divisions. In many socialist societies today, the dominant political party describes itself as communist, but nowhere has the communist goal been achieved.

Why? For one thing, social stratification involves differences of power as well as wealth. In general, socialist societies have reduced disparities in wealth by expanding government bureaucracies and extensively regulating daily life. In the process, government did not "wither away" as Karl Marx imagined. On the contrary, socialist political officials have enormous power and privilege so that they replace capitalists as a new social elite who dominate society.

Probably Marx would have agreed that a communist society is a *utopia* (from the Greek words meaning "not a place"). Yet Marx considered communism a worthy goal and might well have disparaged reputedly "Marxist" societies such as North Korea, the former Soviet Union, the People's Republic of China, and Cuba for not fulfilling what he saw as the promise of communism.

Global comparisons indicate that socialist economies generate the greatest economic equality although living standards remain relatively low. Capitalist economies, by contrast, engender more income disparity although living standards are typically higher. As the former Soviet Union has moved towards a market system, however, the majority of people have suffered a decline in living standards, while some people have become quite rich.

WELFARE CAPITALISM AND STATE CAPITALISM

Some nations of Western Europe, including Sweden and Italy, have combined a market-based economy with broad social welfare programs. Analysts call this "third way" **welfare capitalism,** *an economic and political system that combines a mostly market-based economy with extensive social welfare programs.*

Under welfare capitalism, the government owns some of the largest industries and services, such as transportation, the mass media, and health care. In Sweden

TABLE 16–1 Participation in the Labor Force by Sex, Race, and Ethnicity, 1999

Category of the Population	In the Labor Force: Number (in millions)	Percentage
Men (aged 16 and over)	**74.5**	**74.7%**
White	63.4	75.6
African American	7.7	68.7
Hispanic	8.5	79.8
Women (aged 16 and over)	**64.9**	**60.0**
White	53.1	59.6
African American	8.7	63.5
Hispanic	6.1	55.9

Source: U.S. Department of Labor, *Employment and Earnings*, vol. 47, no. 1 (January 2000), p. 172.

and Italy, about 12 percent of economic production is "nationalized," or state controlled. That leaves most industry in private hands, although subject to extensive government regulation. High taxation (aimed especially at the rich) funds a wide range of social welfare programs, including universal health care and child care (Olsen, 1996).

Yet another blend of capitalism and socialism is **state capitalism,** *an economic and political system in which companies are privately owned but cooperate closely with the government.* State capitalism is common in the rapidly developing Asian countries along the Pacific Rim. Japan, South Korea, and Singapore, for example, are all capitalist countries, but their governments work in partnership with large companies, supplying financial assistance and controlling foreign imports to help their businesses compete in world markets (Gerlach, 1992).

RELATIVE ADVANTAGES OF CAPITALISM AND SOCIALISM

In practice, which economic system works best? Comparing economic models is difficult because all countries mix capitalism and socialism to varying degrees. Moreover, nations differ in cultural attitudes toward work, available natural resources, levels of technological development, and patterns of trade (Gregory & Stuart, 1985). Despite these complicating factors, some crude comparisons between the two systems are revealing.

Economic Productivity

One key dimension of economic performance is productivity. A commonly used measure of economic output is gross domestic product (GDP), the total value of all goods and services produced annually. "Per capita," or per person, GDP allows us to compare the economic performance of nations of different population sizes.

While the output of mostly capitalist countries at the end of the 1980s varied somewhat, averaging the figures for the United States, Canada, and the nations of Western Europe yields a per capita GDP of about $13,500. The comparable figure for the former Soviet Union and nations of Eastern Europe is about $5,000. In other words, capitalist countries outproduced socialist nations by a ratio of 2.7 to 1 (United Nations Development Programme, 1990).

Economic Equality

How resources are distributed within a society is another important measure of how well an economic system works. A comparative study completed in the mid-1970s looked at income ratios based on the earnings of the richest and poorest 5 percent of the population (Wiles, 1977). The result was that societies with predominantly capitalist economies had an income ratio of about 10 to 1; the figure for socialist countries was 5 to 1. In other words, *capitalist economies support a higher overall standard of living but show greater income disparity.* Or, put another way, *socialist economies create more equality but with lower overall living standards.*

Personal Freedom

One additional consideration in evaluating capitalism and socialism is the personal freedom of its people. Capitalism emphasizes *freedom* to pursue one's self-interest. Capitalism, after all, depends on the freedom of producers and consumers to interact, with little interference from the state. On the other hand, socialism emphasizes *freedom from* basic want. Equality is the goal, which requires state intervention in the economy, which, in turn, limits personal choices for citizens.

No system has yet been able to offer both political freedom and economic equality. In the capitalist United States, the political system guarantees many personal freedoms, but are these freedoms worth as much to a poor person as to a rich one? On the other side of the coin, China has more economic equality but restricts the rights of its people to freely express themselves and move freely inside and outside its borders.

SEEING OURSELVES

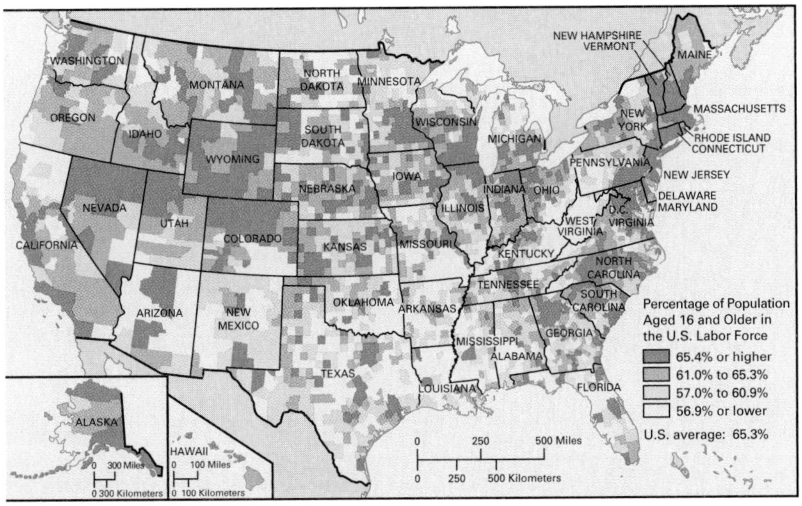

Sources: *American Demographics Desk Reference Series # 4.* Reprinted with permission. ©1992 *American Demographics* magazine, Ithaca, New York. Data from the 1990 decennial census.

NATIONAL MAP 16–1
Labor Force Participation across the United States

Counties with high levels of labor force participation have steady sources of employment, including military bases, recreation areas, and large cities. By contrast, counties with low employment rates generally include a high proportion of elderly people (as well as students). Gender is another important consideration: What do you think is the typical level of employment in regions of the country (stretching from the South up into coal-mining districts of Kentucky and West Virginia) where traditional cultural norms encourage women to remain at home?

CHANGES IN SOCIALIST COUNTRIES

In 1989 and 1990, the nations of Eastern Europe that were seized by the Soviet Union at the end of World War II shook off their socialist regimes. These nations—including the German Democratic Republic, Czechoslovakia, Hungary, Romania, and Bulgaria—have introduced capitalist elements into what were centrally controlled economies. In 1992, the Soviet Union itself formally dissolved and has introduced some free-market principles.

The reasons for these sweeping changes were complex. But two factors stand out: First, the mostly socialist economies grossly underproduced their capitalist counterparts. Though they achieved remarkable economic equality, living standards were low by Western European standards. Second, Soviet socialism was heavy-handed, rigidly controlling the media and restricting individual freedoms. In short, socialism did away with *economic* elites, as Karl Marx predicted, but increased the clout of *political* elites, as Max Weber said it would.

So far, the market reforms in Eastern Europe are proceeding unevenly. Some nations (Czech Republic, Slovakia, Poland, and the Baltic states of Latvia, Estonia, and Lithuania) are faring well, but others (Romania, Bulgaria, and the former Soviet republics) have been buffeted by price increases and falling living standards. Officials hope that expanding production will eventually bring a turnaround. However, there is already evidence that any improvement in living standards will be accompanied by increasing economic disparity (Pohl, 1996; Buraway, 1997; Specter, 1997a).

WORK IN THE POSTINDUSTRIAL ECONOMY

Economic change is occurring not just in the socialist world, but also in the United States. In 1999, the government reports, there were 139 million people in the U.S. labor force, representing two-thirds of the population age sixteen and over. As shown in Table 16–1, a larger proportion of men (74.7 percent) than women (60.0 percent) hold income-producing jobs, although this gap is closing. Among men, 68.7 percent of African Americans are in the labor force, compared to 75.6 percent of white people and 79.8 percent of Hispanics. Among women, 63.5 percent of African Americans are employed, compared to 59.6 percent of white people and 55.9 percent of Hispanics.

National Map 16–1 shows labor force participation across the United States. Since work and income go hand

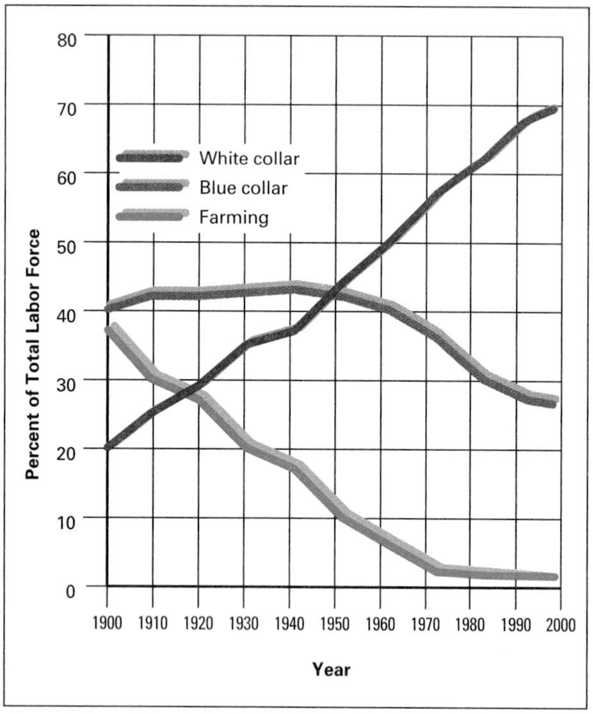

FIGURE 16–2 The Changing Pattern of Work in the United States, 1900–1999

Source: Author estimates based on U.S. Department of Labor (2000).

in hand, regions with greater labor force participation are more affluent.

THE DECLINE OF AGRICULTURAL WORK

In 1900, about 40 percent of the U.S. labor force engaged in farming. In 2000, just 2 percent were in agriculture. Figure 16–2 shows this rapid decline, which reflects the shrinking role of the primary sector in the U.S. economy.

Although farming involves far fewer people today, it is more productive than ever. A century ago, a typical farmer grew food for five people; today, one farmer feeds seventy-five. This dramatic rise in productivity reflects new varieties of crops, pesticides that raise yields, and more efficient farm machinery and farming techniques. The average U.S. farm has also doubled in size since 1950, to about 500 acres.

The family farms of yesterday have been replaced by *corporate agribusinesses*. Agriculture may be more productive, but the transformation has required painful adjustments in farming communities across the country, as a way of life is lost.

FROM FACTORY WORK TO SERVICE WORK

In the early 1900s, industrialization swelled the ranks of blue-collar workers. As shown in Figure 16–2, until about 1960, at least 40 percent of working people had industrial jobs—far more than were in agriculture. By the early 1960s, however, a white-collar revolution had moved a majority of workers into service occupations. By 2000, 90 percent of new jobs were in the service sector, and 70 percent of the entire labor force performed service work.

As Chapter 11 ("Social Class in the United States") explained, the expansion of service work is one reason many people call the United States a middle-class society. But much service work—including sales and clerical positions and jobs in hospitals and restaurants—carries little of the income and prestige of white-collar professions and, at the same time, it offers fewer rewards than factory work. In short, many jobs in this postindustrial era provide only a modest standard of living.

THE DUAL LABOR MARKET

Sociologists see the jobs in today's economy falling into two categories. The **primary labor market** includes *jobs that provide extensive benefits to workers*. This segment of the labor market includes the traditional white-collar professions, such as medicine and law, and upper-management positions. These are jobs that people think of as *careers*, interesting work that provides high income and job security. Such occupations require a broad education rather than specialized training and offer solid opportunity for advancement.

Few of these advantages apply to work in the **secondary labor market,** *jobs that provide minimal benefits to workers*. This segment of the labor force is employed in low-skilled, blue-collar assembly-line operations and low-level service-sector jobs, including clerical positions. Workers in the secondary labor market receive lower income, have less job security, and often feel dissatisfied with their jobs. Women and other minorities are overly represented in the secondary labor market work force (Edwards, 1979; Kohn & Schooler, 1982; Kemp & Coverman, 1989; Hunnicutt, 1990; Greenwald, 1994; Nelson, 1994).

Teaching is one of the most personally rewarding occupations anyone can have. But do all teachers have equal claim to being professionals? Primary school teachers (such as the woman on the left) usually teach a curriculum controlled by the school and state officials. College teachers (such as the man on the right) typically have far more autonomy in deciding what, how, when, and where they teach. What factors account for this difference?

LABOR UNIONS

The changing U.S. economy has seen the role of labor unions greatly diminish. **Labor unions** are *organizations of workers that seek to improve wages and working conditions through various strategies, including negotiations and strikes.* During the Great Depression of the 1930s, union membership increased rapidly until, by 1950, more than one-third of non-farm workers belonged to a union. By 1970, the number of union members peaked at almost 25 million. Since then, union rolls have declined to about 14 percent of non-farm workers, or some 16.5 million men and women.

The pattern of union decline holds in other high-income countries as well. Yet unions claim a far smaller share of workers in the United States than elsewhere. In Canada and Japan, about 33 percent of workers belong to unions; across Europe, about 40 percent; in the Scandinavian countries, the share is 80 percent (Western, 1993, 1995).

The global decline in union membership follows the shrinking industrial sector of the economy. In addition, the newer service jobs are less likely to be unionized. But, as some analysts see it, decreased job security may make unions popular again in years to come. Unions, however, will have to adapt to the new global economy. Union members in the United States, used to seeing foreign workers as "the enemy," will have to build new international alliances (Mabry, 1992; Church, 1994).

PROFESSIONS

All kinds of jobs today are called *professional*—we hear of professional tennis players, professional baby sitters, and even professional exterminators. As distinct from *amateur* (from the Latin for "lover," meaning someone who acts out of love for the activity itself), a professional pursues some task for a living.

A **profession** is *a prestigious, white-collar occupation that requires extensive formal education.* The term "profession" suggests a public declaration to abide by certain principles. Traditional professions include the ministry, medicine, law, academia, and, more recently, architecture, accounting, and social work. Occupations are professions to the extent that they demonstrate the following four characteristics (W. Goode, 1960; Ritzer & Walczak, 1990):

1. **Theoretical knowledge.** Professionals have a theoretical understanding of their field rather than mere technical training. Anyone car first-aid skills, for example, but ph theoretical understanding of h illness.

Jose Clemente Orozco's painting The Unemployed *is a powerful statement of the personal collapse and private despair that afflict men and women who are out of work. How does a sociological perspective help us to understand being out of work as more than a personal problem?*

Jose Clemente Orozco, *The Unemployed*. Photograph © Christie's Images. © Fundacion Jose Clemente Orozco. Reproduction authorized by the Instituto Nacional de Bellas Artes and Literature.

2. **Self-regulating practice.** The typical professional is self-employed, "in practice" rather than working for a company. Professionals oversee their own work and observe a code of ethics.
3. **Authority over clients.** Based on extensive training, professionals advise clients and expect them to follow their direction.
4. **Community orientation rather than self-interest.** The traditional "professing" of duty is a vow to serve the community rather than merely seek income.

Many new occupations in the postindustrial economy seek to *professionalize* their services. Claiming professional standing often begins by renaming the work to imply special, theoretical knowledge, which also distances the field from its previously less distinguished reputation. Stockroom workers, for example, call their work "inventory supply," and exterminators are reborn as "insect control specialists."

Interested parties may also form a professional association to formally attest to their specialized skills. This organization then licenses people who perform the work and writes a code of ethics that emphasizes the occupation's role in the community. In its effort to win public acceptance, a professional association may also establish schools or other training facilities and perhaps start a professional journal (Abbott, 1988). Not all occupations try to claim professional status. Some *paraprofessionals*, including paralegals and medical technicians, possess specialized skills but lack the extensive theoretical education required of full professionals.

SELF-EMPLOYMENT

Self-employment—earning a living without working for an organization—was once common in the United States. About 80 percent of the labor force was self-employed in 1800, compared to 7.6 percent of workers today (8.9 percent of men and 6 percent of women) (U.S. Department of Labor, 2000).

Lawyers, physicians, and other professionals are well represented among the ranks of the self-employed. In addition, the number of people using the Internet to run a small business is growing. But most self-employed workers are small-business owners, plumbers, carpenters, free-lance writers, editors, and artists, and long-distance truck drivers. Overall, the self-employed are more likely to have blue-collar than white-collar jobs.

Finally, a notable trend in the U.S. economy is that women now own about 30 percent of this country's 15 million small businesses, and the share is rising. Moreover, the 5 million firms owned by U.S. women now employ more people than all the Fortune 500 corporations combined (Small Business Administration, 1996).

UNEMPLOYMENT AND UNDEREMPLOYMENT

Every society has some unemployment. Few young people entering the labor force find a job right away; workers may temporarily leave their jobs to seek new work or have children; some may be on strike; others suffer

DIVERSITY SNAPSHOT

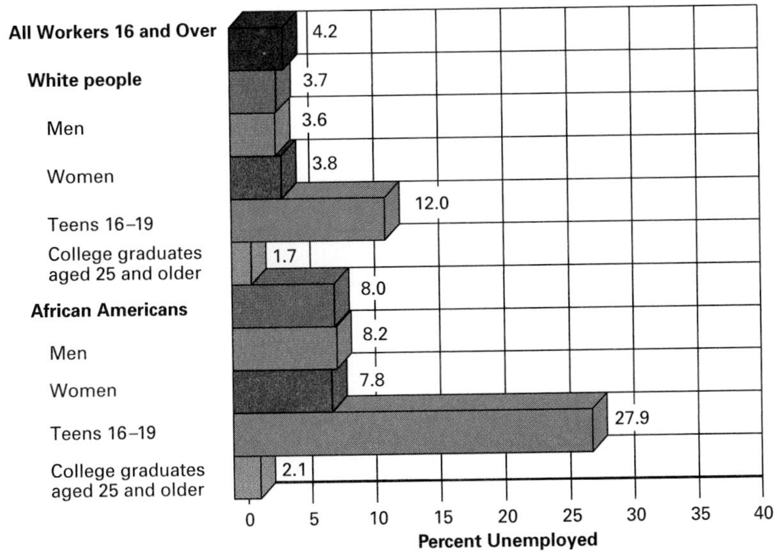

FIGURE 16–3
Official U.S. Unemployment Rate among Various Categories of Adults, 1999

Sources: U.S. Census Bureau (1999) and U.S. Department of Labor (2000).

from long-term illnesses; and still others are illiterate or without the skills to perform useful work.

But unemployment is also caused by the economy itself. Jobs disappear as occupations become obsolete, businesses close in the face of foreign competition or economic recession, and companies downsize to become more profitable. Since 1980, the 500 largest U.S. businesses have eliminated some 5 million jobs—one-fourth of the total.

In 1999, 5.9 million people over the age of sixteen were unemployed, about 4.2 percent of the civilian labor force. As a glance back at National Map 16–1 shows, some regions of the country, including parts of West Virginia and New Mexico, have high unemployment, in some cases twice the national average.

Figure 16–3 shows that unemployment among African Americans (8.0 percent) is more than twice the rate among white people (3.7 percent). For both races, men and women have about the same rates of unemployment.

Underemployment is another serious problem that affects millions of workers. The government reports that more than 30 million people work only part time, meaning no more than thirty-four hours per week. Of these, 80 percent are satisfied with the arrangement; most of the remaining 20 percent (6 million workers) say they want more work but cannot find it (U.S. Department of Labor, 2000).

THE UNDERGROUND ECONOMY

The U.S. government requires individuals and businesses to report their economic activity, especially earnings. Unreported income makes a transaction part of the **underground economy,** *economic activity involving income unreported to the government as required by law.*

On a small scale, most people participate in the underground economy from time to time: A family makes extra money by holding a garage sale, or teenagers babysit for neighbors without reporting the income. Of course, far more of the underground economy is attributable to criminal activity, such as the sale of illegal drugs, prostitution, bribery, theft, illegal gambling, and loan-sharking.

But the single largest segment of contributors to the underground economy is "honest" people who fail to report some or all of their legally obtained income. Self-employed persons such as carpenters, physicians, and owners of small businesses may understate their incomes on tax forms; food servers and other service workers may not report their earnings from tips.

SOCIAL DIVERSITY

Diversity in the New Century: Changes in the Workplace

An upward trend in the U.S. minority population is changing the workplace. As the figure shows, the number of white men in the U.S. labor force is expected to increase by a modest 7 percent between 1998 and 2008. The rate of increase among African American working men will be greater, 18 percent, and among Hispanic men, greater still, 29 percent. Among white women the projected increase is 13 percent, and among African American women, 21 percent. Hispanic women will show the greatest gains, estimated at 49 percent.

The overall result is that, within a decade, non-Hispanic white men will represent less than 38 percent of all workers, and that figure will continue to drop. Therefore, companies that welcome social diversity will tap the largest talent pool and enjoy a competitive advantage.

Welcoming social diversity means, first, recruiting talented workers of both sexes as well as all colors and cultural backgrounds. But developing the potential of all employees requires meeting the needs of women and other minorities, which may not be the same as those of white men. For example, corporations are being pressed to provide child care at the workplace.

Second, businesses must develop effective ways to defuse tensions that arise from social differences. They will have to work harder at treating workers equally and respectfully. Furthermore, no corporate culture can tolerate racial or sexual harassment.

Third, companies will have to rethink current promotion practices. At present, only 5 percent of Fortune 500 top executives are women, and just 1 percent are other minorities. In a broad survey of U.S. companies, the U.S. Equal Employment Opportunity Commission confirmed that white men (42 percent of adults aged twenty to sixty-four) hold 60 percent of management jobs; the comparable figures for white women are 42 and 27 percent; for African Americans, 12 and 6 percent; and for Hispanics, 10 and 4 percent.

In sum, "glass ceilings" that prevent skilled workers from advancing not only discourage effort but deprive companies of their largest source of talent—women and other minorities.

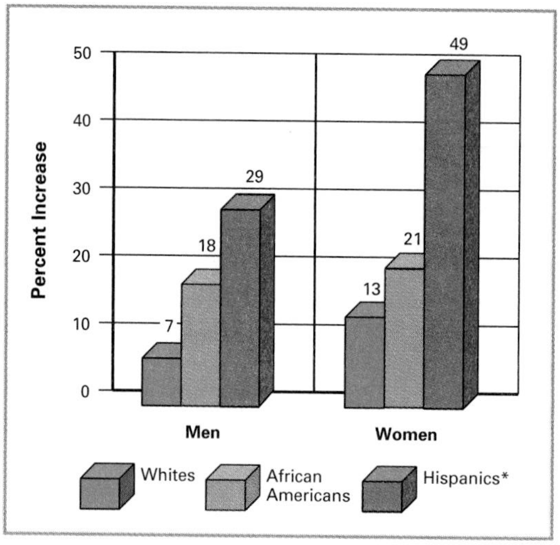

Projected Increase in the Numbers of People in the U.S. Labor Force, 1998–2008

*Hispanics can be of any race.

Source: U.S. Department of Labor (1999).

Sources: U.S. Equal Employment Opportunity Commission (1998), U.S. Department of Labor (1999), and Catalyst (2000).

Individually, the omissions and misrepresentations may be small, but millions of individuals hedging on income tax returns adds up to perhaps $170 billion annually in lost revenues (Speer, 1995).

SOCIAL DIVERSITY IN THE WORKPLACE

Traditionally, white men have been the mainstay of the U.S. labor force. As discussed in Chapter 14 ("Race and Ethnicity"), however, our nation's proportion of minorities is rising rapidly. Between 1990 and 1999, the African American population increased by 14.5 percent, almost twice the 7.7 percent increase for white people. The jump was even greater in the Hispanic (40.8 percent) and Asian American populations (45.8 percent). The prospect of a "minority-majority" in the United States is already having profound consequences. The box takes a closer look at how the increasing social diversity of our society will affect the workplace.

The 1980s and 1990s saw corporations based in high-income countries expanding their reach across the globe. This has altered patterns of consumption almost everywhere, encouraging a homogeneous "corporate culture" that is—for better or worse—undermining countless traditional ways of life.

NEW INFORMATION TECHNOLOGY AND WORK

Another workplace issue is the increasing role of computers and other new information technology. The Information Revolution is changing the kind of work people do and where they do it. Computers are also changing the character of work in more subtle ways (Zuboff, 1982; Rule & Brantley, 1992; Vallas & Beck, 1996):

1. **Computers are deskilling labor.** Just as industrial machinery replaced the master craftsworker of an earlier era, so computers now threaten the skills of managers. More and more business decisions are based not on executive training and experience but on computer modeling. In other words, a machine determines whether to place an order, resupply a client, or approve a loan application.
2. **Computers are making work more abstract.** Most industrial workers have a "hands on" relationship with their product. Postindustrial workers manipulate symbols in pursuit of abstract goals such as making a Web site more attractive, a company more profitable, or software more user-friendly.
3. **Computers limit workplace interaction.** As workers spend more time at computer terminals, they become isolated from one another.
4. **Computers enhance employers' control of workers.** Computers allow supervisors to monitor employees' output precisely and continuously, whether they work at computer terminals or on assembly lines.

Such changes remind us that technology is not socially neutral. Rather, it shapes the way we work and alters the balance of power between employers and employees. Understandably, then, people welcome some aspects of the Information Revolution and oppose others.

CORPORATIONS

At the core of today's capitalist economy lies the **corporation,** *an organization with a legal existence, including rights and liabilities, apart from those of its members.* Incorporating makes an organization a legal entity unto itself, able to enter into contracts and own property. Of some 23 million businesses in the United States, 5 million are incorporated (U.S. Census Bureau, 1999). Incorporating also protects the wealth of owners from lawsuits arising from business debts or as a result of harm to consumers; it may also lower taxes on profits.

ECONOMIC CONCENTRATION

About half of U.S. corporations are small, with assets under $100,000. The largest corporations, however, dominate our country's economy. In 1997, 549 corporations had assets exceeding $1 billion, which represents three-fourths of all corporate assets and profits (U.S. Census Bureau, 1999).

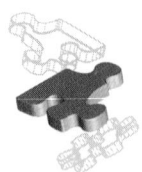

APPLYING SOCIOLOGY

Them That's Got, Gets: The Case of Corporate Welfare

What would you say if the government offered to slash your income taxes and abolish sales tax on your purchases? What if it offered you the money to buy a new house at a below-market interest rate? Would you like the government to hook up all your utilities for free and pay your water and electric bills?

For an ordinary individual, such deals sound too good to be true. But our tax money is doing exactly this—not for individuals, but for big corporations. All a large company has to do is declare a willingness to relocate and then wait for the offers from state and local governments to come pouring in.

Supporters call government aid to corporations "public-private partnerships." They point to the jobs companies create, sometimes in areas hard hit by earlier business closings. For a city or county with a high unemployment rate, the promise of a new factory opening is simply too good to pass up. If some incentives in the form of tax relief or free utilities lure the company away from another possible site, it is considered money well spent.

Critics, however, call these arrangements "corporate welfare." They concede that companies do create new jobs, but they also point out that the corporations get much more than they give. In 1991, for example, the state of Indiana offered $451 million in incentives to lure United Airlines to build an aircraft maintenance facility there. United Airlines built the facility and hired 6,300 people. But some simple math shows that the cost to Indiana came out to be a whopping $72,000 *per job.* Much the same happened in 1993, when Alabama offered $253 million in incentives to Mercedes-Benz to build an automobile assembly plant in Tuscaloosa. The plant opened and 1,500 people were hired—at an average cost of $169,000 for each worker. In 1997, Pennsylvania gave $307 million in incentives to a Norwegian company to reopen part of Philadelphia's naval shipyard. Once the deal was signed, 950 people were hired, at a cost of $323,000 per job. Across the country, the pattern is much the same. Throughout the 1990s, in fact, government support to corporations exceeded $15 billion annually—far more than the "welfare" given to poor people.

In an uncertain economic climate, corporations willing to relocate their facilities attract very generous offers from politicians eager to "create jobs." But, nationwide, while some jobs are created, more are simply moved from one place to another. Nor do many of the jobs pay well. And there is no guarantee that, once settled, a corporation will stay, since businesses are free to try to make a better deal to move somewhere else. In 1993, state and local governments in Kentucky granted General Electric $19 million in tax breaks to build a washing machine factory near Louisville. In 1999, GE announced that most of the 1,500 jobs in this plant would be lost because it was moving to new factories in Georgia and Mexico, where wages were lower.

Source: Adapted from Bartlett & Steele (1998).

The largest U.S. corporation in terms of sales is automaker General Motors, with $257 billion in total assets. GM employs more people than the state governments of California, Oregon, Washington, Alaska, and Hawaii combined. Its sales ($161 billion in 1998) equal the total tax revenues of half the states.

CONGLOMERATES AND CORPORATE LINKAGES

The largest businesses are **conglomerates,** *giant corporations composed of many smaller corporations.* Conglomerates form as corporations enter new markets, spin off new companies, or merge with other companies. For example, RJR-Nabisco is a conglomerate that sells not only cigarettes but dozens of family household products.

Even conglomerates are linked because they own each other's stock, resulting in worldwide corporate alliances of staggering size. General Motors, for example, owns Opel (Germany), Vauxhall (Great Britain), and half of Saab (Sweden) and has partnerships with Suzuki, Isuzu, and Toyota (Japan). Similarly, Ford owns Jaguar and Aston Martin (Great Britain) and a share of Mazda (Japan), Kia (Korea), and Volvo (Sweden).

Corporations are also linked through *interlocking directorates*, networks of people who serve as directors of many corporations (Herman, 1981; Scott & Griff, 1985; Weidenbaum, 1995; Kono et al., 1998). These boardroom connections provide access to valuable information about each other's products and marketing strategies. Beth Mintz and Michael Schwartz (1981) found General Motors linked, through its board members, to 700 other companies. Such linkages do not in themselves run counter to the public interest, but they may encourage illegal activity, such as price-fixing, and they certainly concentrate wealth and power.

CORPORATIONS: ARE THEY COMPETITIVE?

According to the capitalist model, businesses operate independently in a competitive market. But large corporations have extensive linkages, which means they do not operate independently. Moreover, a small number of corporations dominate many large markets. Large corporations are not, therefore, truly competitive.

Law forbids a large company from establishing a **monopoly,** *domination of a market by a single producer,* because a monopoly could simply dictate prices. But **oligopoly,** *domination of a market by a few producers,* is a legal and common practice. Oligopoly arises because the vast investment needed to enter a major market, such as the auto industry, is beyond the reach of all but the biggest companies. Moreover, true competition means risk, which big business tries to avoid.

Corporate power is now so great—and competition among corporations so limited—that government regulation may be the only way to protect the public interest. Yet the government is the corporate world's single biggest customer. The federal government also steps in to support struggling corporations, sometimes with billion-dollar bail-out programs. In addition, as the box explains, state government aid to corporations has drawn fire as "corporate welfare."

GLOBAL SNAPSHOT

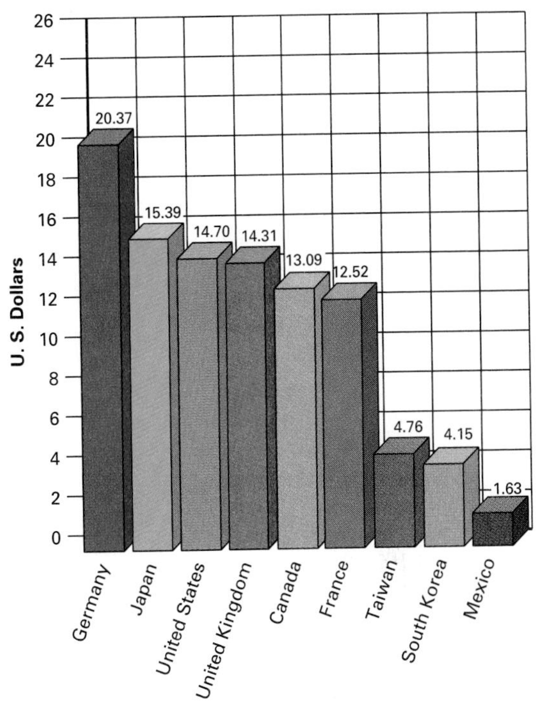

FIGURE 16–4 Average Hourly Wages for Workers in Manufacturing, 1998

Source: Calculations by the author based on U.S. Department of Labor (2000).

CORPORATIONS AND THE GLOBAL ECONOMY

Corporations have grown so big and powerful that they account for most of the world's economic output. The biggest corporations are based in the United States, Japan, and Western Europe, but they consider the entire world one huge marketplace. In fact, many large U.S. companies such as McDonald's generate most of their sales outside the United States.

Poor nations attract the attention of global corporations because most of the world's population and resources are found within their borders. In addition, as shown in Figure 16–4, labor costs are far lower: A factory worker in Mexico, for example, puts in two weeks to earn what a German worker earns in a single day.

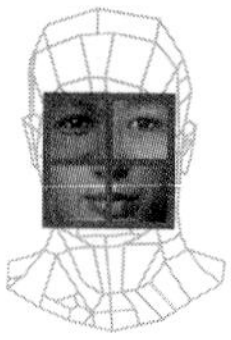

CONTROVERSY & DEBATE

The Market: Does the "Invisible Hand" Look Out for Us or Pick Our Pockets?

"The market" or "government planning"? Each is a means of economic decision making to determine what products and services companies will produce and what people will consume. So important is this process that the degree to which the market or government directs the economy largely determines how nations define themselves, choose their allies, and identify their enemies.

Historically, U.S. society has relied on the market's "invisible hand" for economic decisions. Market dynamics move prices for products up or down according to the supply of products and buyers' demand for the products. The market thus coordinates the efforts of countless people, each of whom—to return to Adam Smith's insight—is motivated only by self-interest.

Defenders of the market system praise it for discouraging some social bad habits, such as racial prejudice. The industrialist J. P. Morgan once commented that he would only sail with a gentleman but he would do business with *anyone*—making the point that market transactions focus on value, not the social traits of traders. Perhaps most important of all, as economists Milton Friedman and Rose Friedman remind us, a more or less freely operating market system has given our society an unprecedented economic standard of living.

J. Pierpont Morgan, railroad tycoon and founder of U.S. Steel (the first $1 billion corporation), symbolized the operation of the market system at a time of little government regulation.

But others point to the contributions government makes to the U.S. economy. First, government must step in to carry out tasks that no one would do, even for profit. Adam Smith, for example, looked to government to defend the country against external enemies. Government also plays a key role in constructing and maintaining public projects, such as roads, utilities, schools, libraries, and museums.

But the Friedmans, as well as other believers in the free-market system, counter that virtually any task the government undertakes is performed inefficiently. The least satisfying goods and services available today—public schools, postal service, and passenger railroad service among them—are government-operated. The products we most enjoy—computers, household appliances, and the myriad offerings of supermarkets and shopping centers—are products of the market. Thus, while some government presence in the economy is necessary, the

The impact of multinationals on poor societies is controversial, as Chapter 12 ("Global Stratification") explains. On one side of the argument, modernization theorists claim that multinationals unleash the great productive power of capitalism to raise living standards in poor nations. Specifically, corporations offer poor societies capital investment, tax revenues, new jobs, and advanced technology that, together, accelerate economic growth (Rostow, 1978; Madsen, 1980; Berger, 1986; Firebaugh & Beck, 1994; Firebaugh & Sandu, 1998).

Dependency theorists, on the other hand, respond that multinationals intensify global inequality. Multinationals, they contend, actually create few jobs because they block the development of local industries and push poor countries to make goods for export rather than food and other products for local consumption. From this standpoint, multinationals make poor societies poorer

Friedmans and other supporters of free markets believe that minimal state regulation best serves the public interest.

But supporters of government intervention in the economy have additional arguments in their arsenal. For one thing, they claim, the market has little incentive to produce anything that is not profitable. This is why few private companies set out to meet the needs of poor people, since, by definition, poor people have little money to spend.

Second, the market has certain self-destructive tendencies that only the government can curb. In 1890, for example, the government passed the Sherman Antitrust Act to break up monopolies that controlled the nation's oil and steel production. Since then—and especially since President Franklin Roosevelt's New Deal of the 1930s—government has taken a strong regulatory role to control inflation (by setting interest rates), enhance the well-being of workers (by imposing workplace safety standards), and benefit consumers (by setting standards for product quality). Despite such interventions, advocates for a stronger government role point out that corporations in U.S. society are so powerful that the government still cannot effectively challenge the capitalist elite.

Third, because the market magnifies social inequality, the government must step in on the side of social justice. Since capitalist economies concentrate income and wealth in the hands of a few, a government system of taxation that applies higher rates to the rich counters this tendency.

Does the market's "invisible hand" look out for us or pick our pockets? While most people in the United States favor a free market, they also support government intervention that benefits the public. Indeed, government assists not only citizens but business itself by providing investment capital, constructing roads and other infrastructure, and shielding companies from foreign competition. Yet, in the United States and around the world, people continue to debate the optimal balance of market forces and government decision making.

Upon his election to the presidency, Franklin Delano Roosevelt announced a "New Deal" that greatly increased the role of government in the economic life of the United States. Here, Roosevelt signs historic Social Security legislation.

Continue the debate . . .

1. *Why do free-market defenders assert that "government is best that governs least"? What do you think?*
2. *What difference does it make if a society's economy is more a market system or more government-centered?*
3. *What is your impression of the successes and failures of socialist economic systems? What about "welfare capitalism" as found in Sweden?*

Sources: Friedman (1980) and Erber (1990).

and increasingly dependent on rich nations (Vaughan, 1978; Wallerstein, 1979; Delacroix & Ragin, 1981; Bergesen, 1983; Walton & Ragin, 1990).

While modernization theory hails the market as the key to progress and affluence for all the world's people, dependency theory calls for replacing market systems with government-based economic policies. The final box takes a closer look at the issue of market versus government economies.

LOOKING AHEAD: THE ECONOMY OF THE TWENTY-FIRST CENTURY

Social institutions are a society's way of meeting people's needs. But, as we have seen, the economy of the United States only partly succeeds in this respect. Although highly productive, our economy provides for some of its people much better than it does for others. Moreover, as we begin the twenty-first century,

SEEING OURSELVES

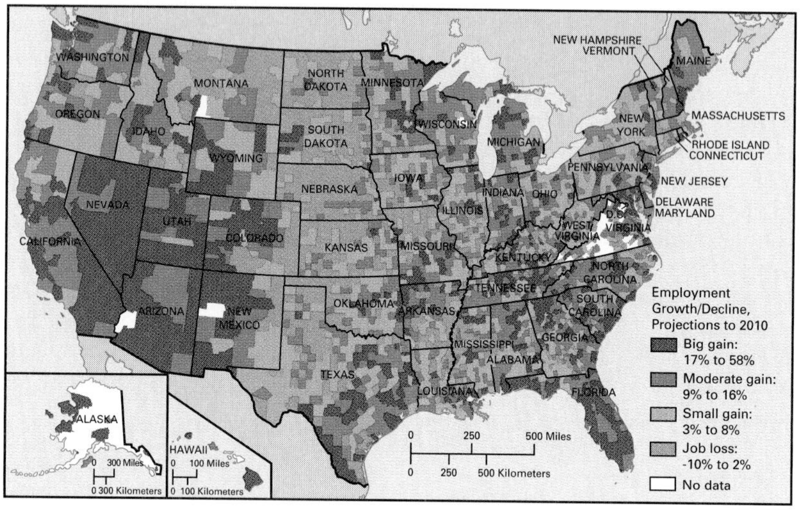

NATIONAL MAP 16–2
Where the Jobs Will Be: Projections to 2010

The economic prospects of counties across the United States are not the same. Much of the mid-section of the country is projected to lose jobs. By contrast, the coastal regions—and most of the West—are rapidly gaining jobs. What factors might account for this pattern?

Source: Used with permission of Woods & Poole Economics, Washington, D.C.

the Information Revolution continues to change our economy. In the postindustrial era, the share of the U.S. labor force employed in manufacturing is half what it was in 1960; service work, especially computer-related jobs, makes up the difference. Therefore, our society must face up to the fact that millions of men and women lack the language and computer skills needed in the new economy. Government, schools, and families need to prepare young people for the kind of work available to them. We must also take into account that some regions of the country are experiencing an economic boom, as shown in National Map 16-2, while other regions are projected to lose jobs in the next decade. Can we afford to consign workers and their families to the margins of society simply because they happen to live in one region of the country rather than another?

In the new century the economy will also become increasingly global. Two centuries ago, the ups and downs of a local economy reflected events and trends in a single town. One century ago, communities were economically linked so that one town's prosperity depended on producing goods demanded by people elsewhere in the country. Today, it makes little sense to speak of a national economy, because what people in a Kansas farm town produce and consume may be affected more by what happens in the wheat-growing region of Russia than by events in their own state capital. In short, U.S. workers and business owners are generating products and services in response to factors and forces that are distant and unseen.

Finally, analysts around the world are rethinking conventional economic models. The global economy shows that socialism is less productive than capitalism, one important reason for the collapse of socialist regimes in Eastern Europe and the former Soviet Union. But capitalism, too, is changing. It now operates with significant government regulation, partly to address the economic inequality generated by market systems.

What are the long-term effects of these changes? Two conclusions seem inescapable. First, the economic future of the United States and other nations will be played out in a global arena. The emergence of the postindustrial economy in the United States is, after all, inseparable from the increasing industrial production of other nations. Second, we must address the related issues of global inequality and population increase (Firebaugh, 1999). Whether the world economy ultimately reduces or deepens the disparity between rich and poor societies may well be what steers our planet toward peace or war.

SUMMARY

1. The economy is the major social institution by which a society produces, distributes, and consumes goods and services.
2. In technologically simple societies, the economy is simply part of family life. Agrarian societies show some productive specialization. Industrialization rapidly expands the economy through greater specialization and new energy sources that power machines in large factories.
3. The postindustrial economy is characterized by a shift from producing goods to services. Just as the Industrial Revolution propelled the industrial economy of the past, the Information Revolution is now advancing the postindustrial economy.
4. The primary sector of the economy, which generates raw materials, dominates in preindustrial societies. The secondary, manufacturing sector prevails in industrial societies. The tertiary, service sector dominates in postindustrial societies.
5. The expanding global economy now produces and consumes products and services with little regard for national boundaries. Today, the 600 largest corporations, operating internationally, account for half the world's economic output.
6. Capitalism is based on private ownership of productive property and the pursuit of profit in a competitive marketplace. Socialism is grounded in collective ownership of productive property through government control of the economy.
7. Although the U.S. economy is predominantly capitalist, government is broadly involved in economic life. Government plays a greater role in the "welfare capitalist" economies of some Western European nations, such as Sweden, and the "state capitalism" of many Asian nations, including Japan.
8. Capitalism is very productive, providing a high average standard of living. A capitalist system allows freedom to act according to one's self-interest. Socialism is less productive but generates greater economic equality. A socialist system offers freedom from basic want.
9. In the United States, agricultural work has declined to just 2 percent of the labor force. Blue-collar jobs have also dwindled, accounting for one-fourth of the labor force. The share of white-collar service occupations, however, has risen to 70 percent of the labor force.
10. While work in the primary labor market provides greater rewards, many new jobs in the United States are service positions in the secondary labor market.
11. A profession is a special category of white-collar work based on theoretical knowledge, occupational autonomy, authority over clients, and a claim to serving the community.
12. Today, 7.6 percent of U.S. workers are self-employed. Although many professionals fall into this category, most self-employed workers have blue-collar occupations.
13. Unemployment has many causes, including the operation of the economy itself; in 1999, 4.2 percent of the U.S. labor force was without work.
14. The underground economy, which includes criminal as well as legal activity, generates income unreported to the government.
15. Women and minorities represent an increasing share of the U.S. labor force. Within a decade, white males, traditionally the backbone of the labor force, will account for less than 38 percent of all workers.
16. New information technology is transforming the kind of work people do, as well as subjecting workers to greater control by supervisors.
17. Corporations form the core of the U.S. economy. The largest corporations, which are conglomerates, account for most corporate assets and profits. Many large corporations operate as multinationals, producing and distributing products in nations around the world.

KEY CONCEPTS

economy (p. 410) the social institution that organizes a society's production, distribution, and consumption of goods and services

postindustrial economy (p. 410) a productive system based on service work and high technology

primary sector (p. 412) the part of the economy that draws raw materials from the natural environment

secondary sector (p. 412) the part of the economy that transforms raw materials into manufactured goods

tertiary sector (p. 412) the part of the economy involving services rather than goods

global economy (p. 412) expanding economic activity with little regard for national borders

capitalism (p. 415) an economic system in which natural resources and the means of producing goods and services are privately owned

socialism (p. 416) an economic system in which natural resources and the means of producing goods and services are collectively owned

communism (p. 417) a hypothetical economic and political system in which all members of a society are socially equal

welfare capitalism (p. 417) an economic and political system that combines a mostly market-based economy with extensive social welfare programs

state capitalism (p. 418) an economic and political system in which companies are privately owned but cooperate closely with the government

primary labor market (p. 420) jobs that provide extensive benefits to workers

secondary labor market (p. 420) jobs that provide minimal benefits to workers

labor unions (p. 421) organizations of workers that seek to improve wages and working conditions through various strategies, including negotiations and strikes

profession (p. 421) a prestigious, white-collar occupation that requires extensive formal education

underground economy (p. 423) economic activity involving income unreported to the government as required by law

corporation (p. 425) an organization with a legal existence, including rights and liabilities, apart from those of its members

conglomerate (p. 426) a giant corporation composed of many smaller corporations

monopoly (p. 427) domination of a market by a single producer

oligopoly (p. 427) domination of a market by a few producers

CRITICAL-THINKING QUESTIONS

1. As a social institution, what is the economy supposed to do? How well do you think our economy does its job?
2. How did the Industrial Revolution alter the economy of the United States? How is the Information Revolution changing the economy once again?
3. What key characteristics distinguish capitalism from socialism? Compare these two systems in terms of productivity, economic inequality, and personal freedoms.
4. What does it mean to say that we now have a global economy? How does the operation of the global economy affect your life?

APPLICATIONS AND EXERCISES

1. The profile of the overall U.S. economy—70 percent of output is in the service sector, 28 percent in the industrial sector, and 4 percent in the primary sector—obscures great variety within this country. Visit the library and locate data that profile your own city, county, or state.
2. Visit a discount store such as Wal-Mart or K-Mart and select an area of the store of interest to you. Do a little "fieldwork," inspecting products to see where they are made. Does your research support the existence of a global economy?
3. What share of the faculty on your campus has temporary teaching contracts? Talk with several tenured faculty, as well as visiting professors: What differences can you discover in their working conditions and their attitude toward their jobs?
4. Install the CD-ROM packaged in the back of this new textbook to access a variety of study, review, and applications exercises designed to help you better understand the material covered in this chapter. The CD includes an author's tip video, as well as interactive maps, video application exercises, Web links, and study questions.

SITES TO SEE

http://www.prenhall.com/macionis

Visit the interactive Web site that accompanies this text. Begin by clicking on the cover of your book. You will find a chapter-by-chapter study guide, practice tests, chat room, and many suggested Web links.

http://stats.bls.gov/blshome.html

Visit this Web site operated by the Bureau of Labor Statistics, where you will find a wide range of interesting data and reports.

http://www.mackinac.org

This is the site for the Mackinac Center for Public Policy, an organization that defends the operation of a market economy.

http://www.kenyon.edu/projects/famfarm/welcome/welcome.htm

Students at Kenyon College, in central Ohio, prepared this Web site to study family farms in the local, rural county.

http://www.fao.org

The Food and Agriculture Organization is a part of the United Nations concerned with how well the global economy meets the needs of the world's people. From their main page, look for their annual report, "State of Food Insecurity in the World."

http://www.corpwatch.org

This site monitors the actions of corporations in the United States.

CHAPTER 17

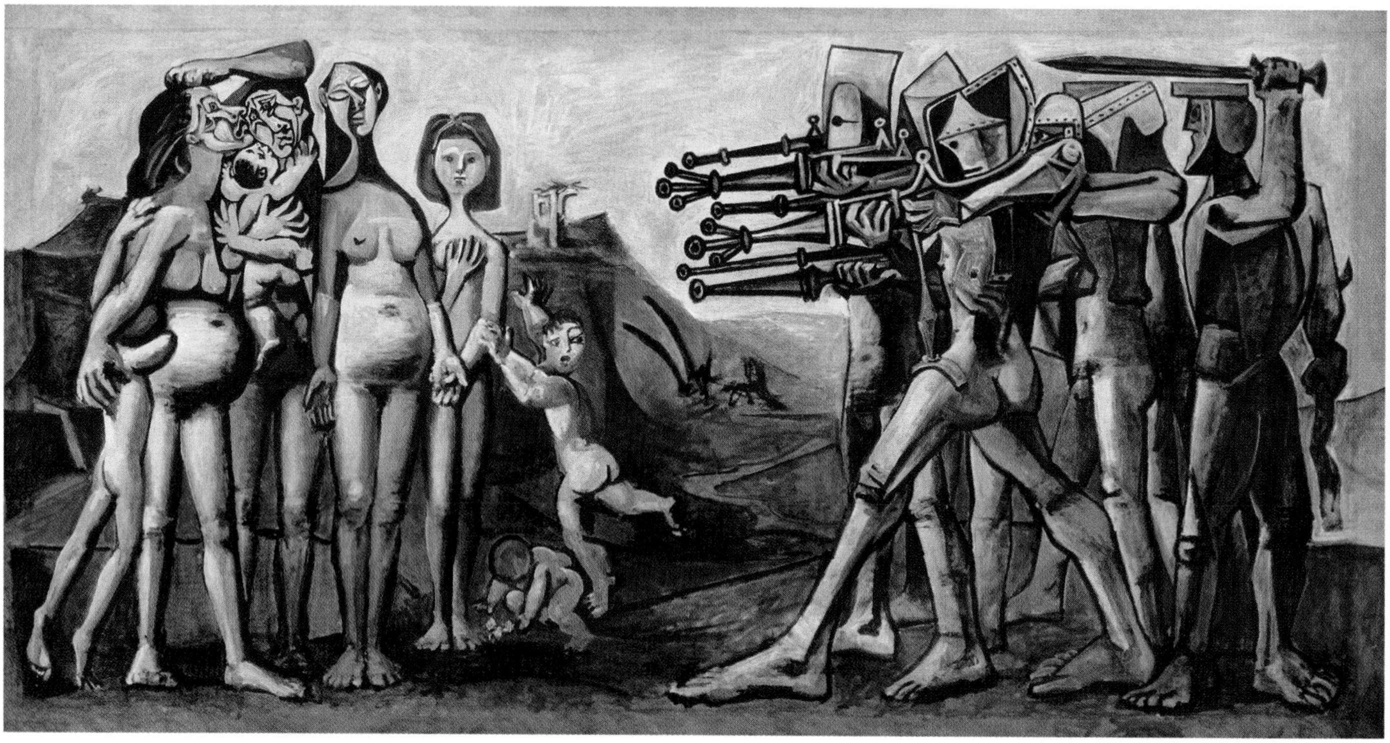

Pablo Picasso (1881–1973)
Massacre in Coree, 1951

Oil on canvas. Musée Picasso, Paris, France. Peter Willi/ The Bridgeman Art Library.

POLITICS AND GOVERNMENT

Charlotte Williams sat straight up in the metal folding chair behind the ballot box, her eyes fixed on the door. It was election day, and she was four hours into her daylong shift overseeing the voting in Washington, D.C.'s Precinct Number 15. To her left, a man of about sixty leaned over a table, completing his ballot. But, except for the man and Williams herself, the large room was empty.

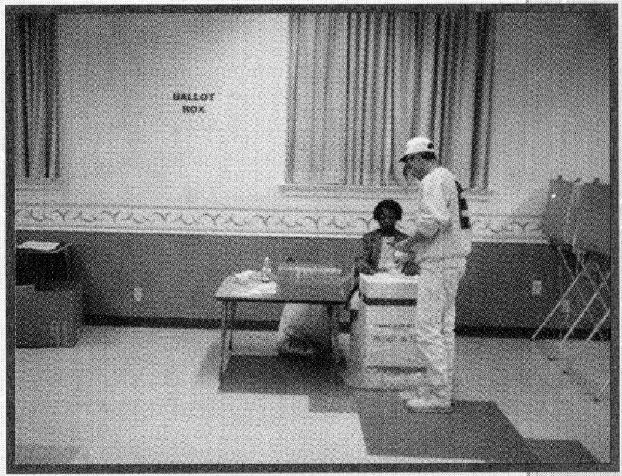

As the man deposited his ballot, he smiled and shrugged his shoulders. "Today we are picking a president," he began, "yet nobody bothers to come out to vote." "Tell me about it," Charlotte Williams responded. "People ought to care, but—you know what—they don't. The welfare system is changing. You know what's happening in our schools. There's way too much crime. I'm sorry, but I can't see it. I just can't see people not caring."

For the 1996 presidential election, less than half the voting age population of the United States bothered to cast a ballot—the lowest level since 1924. And no category of the population is less likely to vote than the poor. In fact, according to government surveys, 80 percent of people earning more than $50,000 a year reported voting in 1996, but only 35 percent of people earning under $10,000 said they went to the polls (Clymer, 1996).

What does this apathy mean? Is our political system failing to meet the needs of the people, especially the poor? Indeed, can we realistically call our nation a "democracy" when most people don't participate in politics—even as once-a-year voters?

This chapter investigates *politics*, the dynamics of power within societies and among nations. Formally, **politics**—or "the polity"—is *the social institution that distributes power, sets a society's agenda, and makes decisions.* But, as the low turnout in many voting precincts suggests, politics may meet the concerns of some far better than others.

POWER AND AUTHORITY

Every society rests on **power,** which Max Weber (1978; orig. 1921) defined as *the ability to achieve desired ends despite resistance from others.* To a large degree, the exercise of power is the business of **government,** *a formal organization that directs the political life of a society.* Yet, as Weber explained, few governments obtain compliance by openly threatening their people. Most of the time, people respect (or, at least, accept) their political system.

Practically speaking, it would be difficult for any large, complex society to persist if power derived *only* from sheer force, and life in such a society would be a nightmare of terror. Social organization, by contrast, depends on some degree of consensus about proper goals (often in the form of cultural values) and suitable means of pursuing them (cultural norms).

Every society, then, seeks to establish its power as legitimate. Weber, therefore, focused on the concept of **authority,** *power that people perceive as legitimate rather* *than coercive.* How is sheer power transformed into stable authority? Weber pointed to three ways, which vary according to a society's level of economic development.

TRADITIONAL AUTHORITY

Preindustrial societies, Weber explained, rely on **traditional authority,** *power legitimized through respect for long-established cultural patterns.* In ideal terms, traditional authority is power woven into a society's collective memory, so that people consider social arrangements almost sacred. Chinese emperors in antiquity were legitimized by tradition, as were nobles in medieval Europe. In both cases, the power of tradition was strong enough that—for better or worse—people typically viewed members of a hereditary ruling family as almost godlike.

But traditional authority declines as societies industrialize. Hannah Arendt (1963) pointed out that traditional authority is compelling only so long as everyone shares the same heritage and world view. This form of authority, then, is undermined by the specialization demanded by industrial production, by modern scientific thinking, and by the social change and cultural diversity that accompany immigration. Thus, no president of today's United States, for example, could ever make the claim of ruling by grace of God. Even so, some well-established upper-class families such as the Kennedys, Roosevelts, and Rockefellers have occupied a privileged position for several generations, so that when one of them enters the political arena, it is with some measure of traditional authority (Baltzell, 1964).

If traditional authority plays only a small part in U.S. national politics, it persists in other aspects of everyday life. *Patriarchy,* the domination of women by men, is a traditional form of power that remains widespread, even though it is increasingly challenged. Less controversial is the traditional authority parents exert over their children. The fact that traditional authority is linked to a person's status as parent is obvious every time a parent answers a doubting child's "Why?" with "Because I said so!" There is no debating the parent's decision because that would defeat traditional authority by putting parent and child on equal footing.

RATIONAL-LEGAL AUTHORITY

Weber defined **rational-legal authority** (sometimes called *bureaucratic authority*) as *power legitimized by legally enacted rules and regulations.* Rational-legal authority, then, is power legitimized in the operation of lawful government.

As Chapter 7 ("Groups and Organizations") explains, Weber viewed bureaucracy as the organizational backbone of rational-thinking, industrial societies. Moreover, just as a rational world view promotes bureaucracy, so it erodes traditional customs and practices. Instead of venerating the past, members of modern societies look to formally enacted rules—especially law—for principles of justice.

Rationally enacted rules also underlie many power relationships in everyday life. The authority of deans and classroom teachers, for example, rests on the offices they hold in bureaucratic colleges and universities. The police, too, are officers, within the bureaucracy of local government. In contrast to traditional authority, rational-legal authority flows not from family background but from one's position in the formal organization of government. Thus, while a traditional monarch rules for life, a modern president accepts and gives up power according to law; presidential authority is in the office, not the person.

CHARISMATIC AUTHORITY

Finally, Weber claimed power could be transformed into authority through charisma. **Charismatic authority** is *power legitimized through extraordinary personal abilities that inspire devotion and obedience.* Unlike tradition and rational law, then, charisma has less to do with social organization and is more a mark of an exceptionally forceful and magnetic personality.

Throughout history, some members of societies have been regarded as charismatic. Charisma enhances the stature of an established leader or strengthens the appeal of a challenger. Charismatics turn an audience into followers, often making their own rules and challenging the status quo: Vladimir Lenin guided the overthrow of feudal monarchy in Russia in 1917; Mahatma Gandhi inspired the struggle to free India from British colonialism after World War II; Martin Luther King, Jr., galvanized the civil rights movement in the United States; and, through her work ministering to the poor in Calcutta, India, Mother Teresa asked the world to confront its stunning poverty.

Because charismatic authority emanates from a single individual, any charismatic movement faces a crisis of survival upon the death of its leader. Thus, Weber explained, the persistence of a charismatic organization depends on the **routinization of charisma,** *the transformation of charismatic authority into some combination of traditional and bureaucratic authority.* Christianity, for example, began as a cult driven by the personal charisma of Jesus of Nazareth. After the death

In 1998, just 28 of the world's 191 nations were political monarchies where single families pass power from generation to generation. The African nation of Swaziland recently celebrated the coronation of a young king.

of Jesus, followers institutionalized his teachings in a church eventually centered in Rome and built on both tradition and bureaucracy. Routinized in this way, the Roman Catholic church has flourished for 2,000 years.

POLITICS IN GLOBAL PERSPECTIVE

Political systems have taken many forms throughout history. The technologically simple hunting and gathering societies that once were found all over the planet operated like one large family. Leadership generally fell to a male with unusual strength, hunting skill, or personal charisma. But these leaders exercised little power, since they lacked the resources to control their own people, much less extend their rule. In the simplest societies, then, leaders were barely discernible from everyone else, and government did not exist as a distinct sphere of life (Lenski, Nolan, & Lenski, 1995).

Larger and more complex agrarian societies are characterized by specialized activity and a material surplus. These societies become hierarchical, with a small elite gaining control of most wealth and power; politics moves outside the family to become a social institution in its own right. Leaders who manage to pass along their power over several generations may acquire traditional authority, perhaps even claiming divine right to govern. Such leaders also may benefit from Weber's rational-legal authority because they are served by a bureaucratic political administration and system of law.

As societies expand, politics eventually takes the form of a national government or *political state.* But the emergence of a political state depends on technology. Just a few centuries ago, armies moved slowly, and communication over even short distances was uncertain. For this reason, the early political empires—such as Mesopotamia in the Middle East, about 5,000 years ago—actually took the form of many small *city-states.*

More complex technology helped the modern world to develop the larger-scale system of *nation-states.* Currently, the world has 191 independent nation-states, each with a somewhat distinctive political system. Generally speaking, however, the world's political systems can be analyzed in terms of four categories: monarchy, democracy, authoritarianism, and totalitarianism.

MONARCHY

Monarchy (with Latin and Greek roots meaning "one ruler") is *a type of political system in which a single family rules from generation to generation.* Monarchy is typical in ancient agrarian societies; the Bible, for example, tells of great kings such as David and Solomon. Today's British monarchy, the Windsor family, traces its lineage back roughly 1,000 years. In Weber's terms, then, monarchy is legitimized by tradition.

During the medieval era, *absolute monarchy,* in which hereditary rulers claimed a monopoly of power based on divine right, flourished from England to China and in parts of the Americas. Monarchs in some nations, including Saudi Arabia, still exercise virtually absolute control over their people.

During the twentieth century, however, a more egalitarian climate gradually weakened monarchs in favor of elected officials. Monarchs remain in several European nations—Great Britain, Spain, Norway, Sweden, Belgium, Denmark, and the Netherlands—but they now preside over *constitutional monarchies.* In other words, they are merely symbolic heads of state, while elected politicians, led by a prime minister, govern according to political principles embodied in a constitution. In these nations, then, the nobility may formally reign, but elected officials actually rule.

DEMOCRACY

The historical trend in the modern world is toward **democracy,** *a type of political system in which power is exercised by the people as a whole.* But members of democratic societies rarely participate directly in decision making; numbers alone make this an impossibility. Instead, a system of *representative democracy* places authority in the hands of elected leaders who are accountable to the people.

Most rich countries of the world claim to be democratic. Economic development and democratic government go together because both depend on a literate populace. Moreover, the traditional legitimization of power in an agrarian monarchy gives way, with the introduction of industrialization, to rational-legal authority. A rational election process puts leaders in offices regulated by law. Thus democracy and rational-legal authority are linked just as monarchy and traditional authority are.

But countries such as the United States are not truly democratic, for two reasons. First, there is the problem of bureaucracy. All democratic political systems rely on large numbers of bureaucratic officials. The federal government of the United States, for example, employs nearly 3 million people (excluding the armed forces), and another 17 million people work in some 87,000 local governments across the country. The vast majority of these bureaucrats are never elected by anyone and are not directly accountable to the people (Scaff, 1981; Edwards, 1985; Etzioni-Halevy, 1985).

The second problem involves economic inequality. In a highly stratified society, the rich will have far more political clout than the poor. One reason George W. Bush got off to such a fast start in the 2000 presidential race was that, as a rich man with many rich friends, he was able to raise more than $50 million in a short time. Magazine magnate Steve Forbes financed his own run for the White House, spending more than $50 million of his own fortune in 1996 and 2000. In short, in the game of politics, few doubt that "money talks." Moreover, given the even greater resources of billion-dollar corporations and labor unions, how can we think our "democratic" system responds to—or even hears—the voices of "ordinary people"?

Democracy and Freedom: Capitalist and Socialist Approaches

Despite the problems we have just described, rich capitalist nations such as the United States claim to operate as democracies. Of course, socialist countries like Cuba and the People's Republic of China make the same claim. This curious fact suggests that we need to look more closely at *political economy:* the interplay of politics and economics.

The political life of the United States, Canada, and the nations of Europe is largely shaped by the economic principles of capitalism. The pursuit of profit within a market system requires that "freedom" be defined in terms of people's rights to act in their own self-interest. Thus, the capitalist approach to political freedom translates into personal liberty—to act in whatever ways maximize profits or other forms of income. From this point of view, moreover, "democracy" means that individuals have the right to select their leaders from among those running for office.

However, as we noted earlier, capitalist societies are marked by a striking inequality of wealth. If everyone acts in a self-interested way, in other words, the inevitable result is that some people accumulate far more wealth and power than others. It is this elite, then, that dominates the economic and political life of the society.

Socialist systems, by contrast, claim they are democratic because their economies meet everyone's basic needs for housing, schooling, work, and medical care. Despite being a much poorer country than the United States, for example, Cuba provides basic medical care to all without regard for people's ability to pay.

But critics of socialism counter that the extensive government regulation of social life in these countries is oppressive. The socialist governments of China and Cuba, for example, do not allow their people to move freely inside or outside their borders and tolerate no organized political opposition.

These contrasting approaches to democracy and freedom raise an important question: Are economic equality and political liberty compatible? To foster economic equality, socialism constrains the choices of individuals. Capitalism, on the other hand, provides broad political liberties, which, in practice, mean little to the poor. A look back at Global Map 10–1, on page 264, shows the extent of income inequality in the world's nations. Global Map 17–1 shows one organization's assessment of the extent of political freedoms around the world.

WINDOW ON THE WORLD

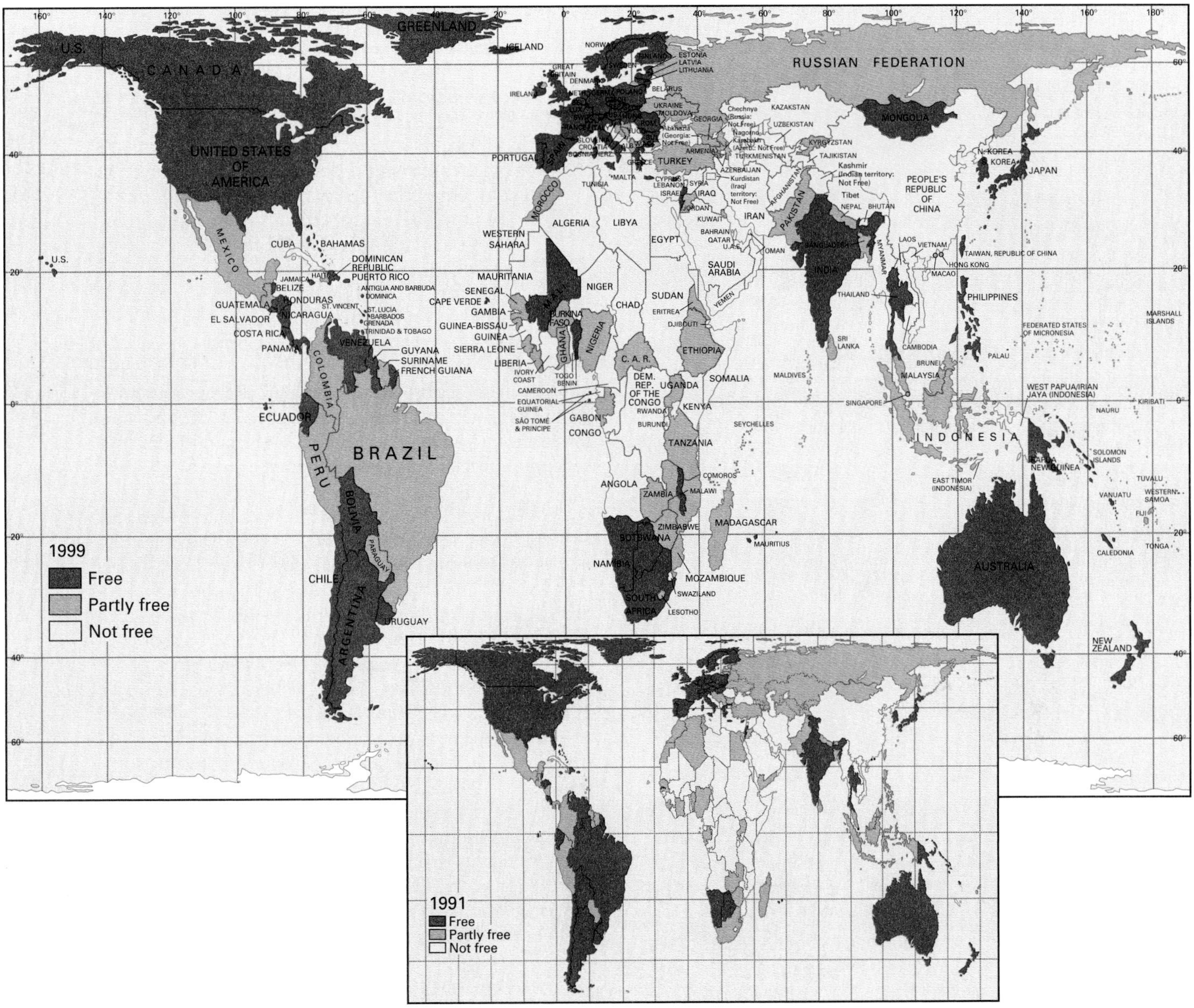

GLOBAL MAP 17–1 Political Freedom in Global Perspective

In 1999, 88 of the world's nations, containing 40 percent of all people, were politically "free"—that is, they offered their citizens extensive political rights and civil liberties. Another 53 countries, which included 27 percent of the world's people, were "partly free," with more limited rights and liberties. The remaining 50 nations, home to 34 percent of humanity, fall into the category of "not free." In these countries, government sharply restricts individual initiative. Between 1980 and 1999 democracy made significant gains, largely in Latin America and Eastern Europe. In Asia, moreover, India (containing nearly 1 billion people) returned to the "free" category in 1999.

Source: Freedom House (1999).

According to Freedom House, a New York–based organization that tracks global political trends, by 1999, 88 of the world's 191 nations (containing 40 percent of global population) were "free," with considerable respect for basic civil liberties. This is the highest number of free nations in history and compares to only 61 nations a decade before (Freedom House, 1999).

AUTHORITARIANISM

As a matter of policy, some nations give their people little voice in politics. **Authoritarianism** refers to *a political system that denies popular participation in government.* An authoritarian government is not only indifferent to people's needs; it lacks the legal means to remove leaders from office and provides people with little or no way even to voice their opinions. The Polish sociologist Wlodzimierz Wesolowski sums up authoritarianism this way: "The authoritarian philosophy argues for the supremacy of the state [over other] organized social activity" (1990:435).

The absolute monarchies in Saudi Arabia and Kuwait are highly authoritarian, as are the military juntas in the Democratic Republic of the Congo and Ethiopia, where political dissatisfaction is widespread. But heavy-handed government does not always breed popular opposition. The box looks at the "soft authoritarianism" that thrives in the small Asian nation of Singapore.

TOTALITARIANISM

October 22, 1994, near Saigon, Vietnam. Six U.S. students on our study-abroad program have been arrested, allegedly for talking to Vietnamese students and taking pictures at the university. The Vietnamese Minister of Education has canceled the reception tonight, claiming that our students meeting their students threatens Vietnam's security.

The most controlling political form is **totalitarianism,** *a political system that extensively regulates people's lives.* Totalitarian governments emerged only during this century, with the development of technological means for rigidly regulating a populace. The Vietnamese government closely monitors the activities of its citizens as well as visitors to the country. Similarly, the government of North Korea uses surveillance equipment and sophisticated computers to store vast amounts of information and thereby manipulate an entire population.

Although some totalitarian governments claim to represent the will of the people, most seek to bend people to the will of the government. As the term itself implies, such governments are *total* concentrations of power, allowing no organized opposition. Denying the populace the right to assemble for political purposes and controlling access to information, these governments thrive in an environment of social atomization and fear. The government of the former Soviet Union, for example, did not permit ordinary citizens to own telephone directories, copying equipment, fax machines, or even accurate city maps.

Socialization in totalitarian societies is intensely political, seeking not just compliance but personal commitment to the system. In North Korea, one of the world's most totalitarian states, pictures of leaders and political messages broadcast over loudspeakers constantly remind citizens that they owe total allegiance to the state. Government-controlled schools and mass media present only official versions of events.

Government indoctrination is especially intense whenever political opposition surfaces in a totalitarian society. After the 1989 pro-democracy movement in the People's Republic of China, for example, officials demanded that citizens report all "unpatriotic" people—even members of their own families—and subjected all the students at Beijing's universities to political "refresher" courses (Arendt, 1958; Kornhauser, 1959; Friedrich & Brzezinski, 1965; Nisbet, 1966; Goldfarb, 1989).

Totalitarian governments span the political spectrum from fascist (including Nazi Germany) to communist (including North Korea). In some totalitarian states, businesses are privately owned (as was the case in Nazi Germany and, more recently, in Chile); in others, businesses are government owned (as in North Korea, Cuba, and the former Soviet Union). In all cases, however, one party claims total control of the society and permits no opposition.

A GLOBAL POLITICAL SYSTEM?

Chapter 16 ("The Economy and Work") described the emergence of a global economy, by which more and more companies operate with little regard to national boundaries. Is there a parallel development of a global political system?

On one level, the answer is no. Although most of the world's economic activity now involves more than one nation, the planet remains divided into nation-states,

GLOBAL SOCIOLOGY

"Soft Authoritarianism" or Planned Prosperity? A Report from Singapore

To many, Singapore, a tiny nation on the tip of the Malay Peninsula with a population of 4 million, seems an Asian paradise. Surrounded by poor societies grappling with rapidly rising populations, squalid, sprawling cities, and rising crime rates, Singapore, with its affluence, cleanliness, and safety, makes North American visitors think more of a theme park than a country.

In fact, since its independence from Malaysia in 1965, Singapore has startled the world with its economic development; its per capita income rivals that of the United States. But, unlike the United States, Singapore has few social problems like crime, slums, unemployment, or children living in poverty. In fact, people in Singapore don't even contend with traffic jams, graffiti on subway cars, or litter in the streets.

The key to Singapore's orderly environment is the ever-present hand of government, which actively promotes traditional morality and regulates just about everything. The state owns and manages most of the country's housing and has a hand in many businesses. It provides tax incentives for family planning and completing additional years of schooling. To keep traffic under control, the government slaps hefty surcharges on cars, pushing the price of a basic sedan up to around $40,000.

Singapore has tough anticrime laws that mandate death by hanging for drug dealing and permit police to detain a person suspected of a crime without charge or trial. The government has outlawed some religious groups (including Jehovah's Witnesses) and bans pornography. To keep the city clean, the state forbids smoking in public and eating on subways, imposes stiff fines for littering, and has even banned the sale of chewing gum.

In economic terms, Singapore defies familiar categories. Government control of scores of businesses, including television stations, telephone service, airlines, and taxis, seems socialist. Yet, unlike most socialist enterprises, these businesses are operated efficiently and very profitably. Moreover, Singapore's capitalist culture applauds economic growth (although the government cautions people against the evils of excessive materialism), and hundreds of multinational corporations are based here.

Singapore's political climate is as unusual as its economy. Freedom House characterizes Singapore as "partly free." The law provides for elections of political leaders, but one party—the People's Action party—dominates the political process and currently controls eighty-one of the eighty-three seats in the country's Parliament. In fact, the People's Action party has ruled Singapore without opposition since its independence thirty years ago. Just as important, members of this society feel the presence of government far more than their counterparts in the United States.

Clearly, Singapore is not a democratic country in the conventional sense. But most people in this prospering nation wholeheartedly endorse their way of life. What Singapore's political system offers is a simple bargain: Government demands unflinching loyalty from the populace; in return, it provides security and prosperity. Critics charge that this system amounts to a "soft authoritarianism" that stifles dissent and controls people's lives. Most of the people of Singapore, however, know the struggles of living elsewhere and, for now at least, consider the trade-off a good one.

Sources: Adapted from Branegan (1993) and Freedom House (1999).

just as it has been for centuries. The United Nations (founded in 1945) might seem a step toward global government, but, to date, its political role has been limited.

On another level, however, politics has become a global process. In the minds of some analysts, multinational corporations represent a new political order, since they have enormous power to shape social life throughout the world. In other words, politics is dissolving into business as corporations grow larger than governments. As one multinational leader declared, "We

GLOBAL SNAPSHOT

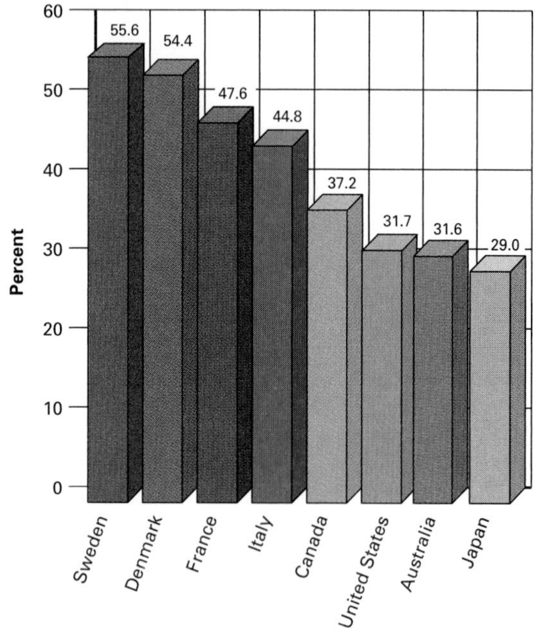

FIGURE 17–1 The Size of Government: Tax Revenues as Share of Gross Domestic Product, 1996

Source: U.S. Bureau of the Census (1998).

are not without cunning. We shall not make Britain's mistake. Too wise to govern the world, we shall simply own it" (quoted in Vaughan, 1978:20).

Then, too, the Information Revolution has put even national politics onto the world stage. Hours before the Chinese government sent troops to Tiananmen Square to crush the 1989 pro-democracy movement, officials "unplugged" the satellite transmitting systems of news agencies to keep the world from watching. Despite their efforts, news of the massacre flashed around the world in minutes via fax machines in universities and private homes.

Finally, several thousand nongovernmental organizations (NGOs) are now in operation, most with global membership and focus. Typically, these organizations seek to advance universal principles, such as human rights (Amnesty International) or an ecologically sustainable world (Greenpeace). In the coming century, NGOs will almost certainly play a key part in forming a global political culture (Boli & Thomas, 1997).

In short, just as the economies of individual nations are linked globally, so are their politics. Today, no nation exists strictly within its own borders.

POLITICS IN THE UNITED STATES

After winning a war against Great Britain to gain political independence, the United States replaced the British monarchy with a democratic political system. Since then, our nation's political development reflects its distinctive history, capitalist economy, and cultural heritage.

U.S. CULTURE AND THE RISE OF THE WELFARE STATE

The political culture of the United States can be summed up in a word: individualism. This emphasis derives from the Bill of Rights, which guarantees freedom from undue government interference. It was this individualism that the nineteenth-century poet and essayist Ralph Waldo Emerson had in mind when he said, "The government that governs best is the government that governs least."

But Emerson's assertion would find little support today among the vast majority of this nation's people, who recognize that government is necessary to maintain national defense, highway systems, schools, and law and order. Moreover, the government has grown into a vast and complex **welfare state**—*a range of government agencies and programs that provides benefits to the population.* Government benefits begin even before birth (through prenatal nutrition programs) and continue into old age (through Social Security and Medicare). Some programs are especially important to the poor, who are not well served by our capitalist economic system; but students, farmers, homeowners, small business operators, veterans, performing artists, and even executives of giant corporations also get subsidies and supports. In fact, a majority of U.S. adults now look to government for at least part of their income (Caplow et al., 1982; Devine, 1985; Bartlett & Steele, 1998).

Today's welfare state is the result of a gradual increase in the size and scope of government. In 1789, when the presence of the federal government amounted to little more than a flag in most communities, the entire federal budget was a mere $4.5 million ($1.50 for every person in the nation). Since then, it has steadily risen, reaching $1.7 trillion in 1999 (a per capita figure of $6,306).

Similarly, when our nation was founded, one government employee served every 1,800 citizens. Today, there is one official to serve every fourteen citizens for

TABLE 17–1 The Political Spectrum: A National Survey, 1998

Survey Question: "We hear a lot of talk these days about liberals and conservatives. I'm going to show you a seven-point scale on which the political views people might hold are arranged from extremely liberal—point 1—to extremely conservative—point 7. Where would you place yourself on this scale?"

1	2	3	4	5	6	7
Extremely liberal	Liberal	Slightly liberal	Middle of the road	Slightly conservative	Conservative	Extremely conservative
2.3 %	12.6%	12.4 %	34.8 %	15.3 %	14.7 %	3.0 %

[*Don't know/no answer* 5.0%]

Source: *General Social Surveys, 1972–1998: Cumulative Codebook* (Chicago: National Opinion Research Center, 1999), p. 91.

a total of 20 million government employees, more than are engaged in manufacturing (U.S. Census Bureau, 1999).

As much as government has expanded in this country, the U.S. welfare state is still smaller than that in many other industrial nations. Figure 17–1 shows that government is larger in most of Europe and especially in Scandinavian countries like Denmark and Sweden.

THE POLITICAL SPECTRUM

Who supports the welfare state? Who would like to see it grow larger? Who wants to cut back on the size of government? Such questions tap attitudes that form the *political spectrum*. Table 17–1 shows how adults in the United States describe their political orientation. Slightly more than one-fourth of the respondents fall on the liberal, or "left," side, while one-third describe themselves as conservative to some degree, placing them on the political "right." The remaining 35 percent claim to be moderates in the political "middle" (NORC, 1999:91).

One reason so many people identify themselves as "moderates" is that most of us are conservative on some issues and liberal on others (Barone & Ujifusa, 1981; McBroom & Reed, 1990). In making sense of people's political attitudes, analysts distinguish two kinds of issues. *Economic issues* focus on economic inequality and the opportunities available for all categories of people. *Social issues* refer to moral concerns about how people ought to live.

Economic Issues

In the second half of the nineteenth century, industrialization generated enormous wealth in the United States, but much of it ended up in the pockets of a small elite. By the time of the Great Depression in 1929, mounting evidence suggested that a market system with little government regulation provided little financial security for much of the population. In response, President Franklin Delano Roosevelt initiated the New Deal programs, greatly expanding government efforts to promote well-being and building the foundation of our current welfare state.

Today, both the Democratic and Republican parties—the two major political organizations in the United States—support the basic outlines of the welfare state, although they disagree about what the government should and should not do. Generally, the Democratic party supports the role of government in U.S. society, including government regulation of the economy. The Republican party, however, has sought to trim the size and scope of government in recent years, especially in the marketplace.

Thus, economic liberals (mostly on the Democratic side of the fence) expect the government to maintain a healthy economy and an adequate supply of jobs. Economic conservatives (likely to be Republicans) counter that government intervention inhibits economic productivity.

Social Issues

Social issues are moral matters, ranging from abortion to the death penalty to gay rights and treatment of minorities. Social liberals are broadly tolerant of social diversity. They endorse equal rights and opportunities for all categories of people, view abortion as a matter of individual choice, and oppose the death penalty because, in their view, it does little to discourage crime and has been unfairly applied to minorities.

On the other side of the political spectrum are social conservatives who advance a "family values" agenda.

Lower-income people have more pressing financial needs and so they tend to focus on economic issues, such as the level of the minimum wage. Higher-income people, by contrast, provide support for many social issues, such as animal rights.

They support traditional gender roles and oppose public acceptance of gay families, affirmative action, and other "special programs" for minorities that, as they see it, recognize group membership rather than reward individual initiative. Social conservatives also condemn abortion and support the death penalty as a just response to heinous crime.

Overall, the Republican party is more conservative on both economic and social issues, while the Democratic party takes a more liberal stand. In practice, then, Republicans endorse traditional values and individual initiative, while Democrats think the government should take an active role in enhancing social well-being and reducing inequality. Yet each party has its own conservative and liberal wings so that there may be little actual difference between a liberal Republican and a conservative Democrat. Furthermore, both Republicans and Democrats favor big government—as long as the government advances their aims. Conservative Republicans (like President Ronald Reagan) have sought to increase military strength by building up this nation's armed forces, for example, while more liberal Democrats (like President Bill Clinton) have tried to expand the government's "social safety net" that, for instance, extends government-regulated health care coverage to all citizens.

Mixed Positions

Pegging the political views of individuals is difficult because most people do not hold the same positions on economic and social issues. Well-to-do men and women tend to be conservative on economic issues (because they have wealth to protect) but liberal on social issues (due, in large part, to higher levels of education). Working-class people display the opposite pattern, combining economic liberalism with social conservatism (Nunn, Crockett, & Williams, 1978; Erikson, Luttbeg, & Tedin, 1980; Syzmanski, 1983).

Race and ethnicity modify these patterns slightly. With significantly less income than white people, African Americans are more liberal on economic issues and, since the New Deal era of the 1930s, have overwhelmingly voted Democratic (in 1996, 84 percent of African American voters supported Democrat Bill Clinton over Republican Bob Dole). On many social issues (including reproductive rights for women), disadvantaged African Americans, like poor white people, tend to be conservative. But when the topic involves race—say, busing schoolchildren or increasing government spending to assist minorities—people of African and Hispanic descent are decidedly liberal, even more so than affluent white people (NORC, 1999).

Party Identification

Because so many people hold mixed political attitudes—espousing liberal views on some issues and taking conservative stands on others—party identification in the United States is weak. In this way, our nation differs from European countries, where most people adhere strongly to one political party. Table 17–2 shows the results of a recent national survey of party identification among U.S. adults (NORC, 1999). Some 47 percent identified themselves—to some degree—as Democrats and about 34 percent as Republicans. Seventeen percent claimed to be independents, voicing no preference for either party. Even though a large majority declare a party preference, their allegiance is weak. Republicans scored a landslide victory in the 1994 congressional elections, for example, while the Democrats held the White House in 1996 and gained ground in Congress in 1996 and 1998.

TABLE 17–2 Political Party Identification in the United States, 1998

Party Identification	Proportion of Respondents
Democrat	**46.5%**
Strong Democrat	13.1
Not very strong Democrat	21.1
Independent, close to Democrat	12.3
Republican	**34.1**
Strong Republican	8.4
Not very strong Republican	17.1
Independent, close to Republican	8.6
Independent	**16.8**
Other party, no response	**2.5**

Source: *General Social Surveys, 1972–1998: Cumulative Codebook* (Chicago: National Opinion Research Center, 1999), p. 83.

SPECIAL-INTEREST GROUPS

In the wake of several recent shootings in public schools, public support for gun control has been rising. The National Rifle Association, representing several million people who are active hunters as well as millions more social conservatives, has steadily worked in opposition to this goal.

The "gun lobby," which has been successful so far in fending off change, is an example of a **special-interest group:** *a political alliance of people interested in some economic or social issue.* Special-interest groups, which include associations of elderly people, tour bus operators, women's organizations, farmers, fireworks producers, and environmentalists, flourish in nations such as the United States, where political parties tend to be weak. Special-interest groups employ *lobbyists* (Washington, D.C., is home to more than 75,000 of them) as their professional advocates in political circles.

One example of a special-interest group concerned with economic issues is the American Federation of Labor–Congress of Industrial Organizations (AFL-CIO), this nation's largest labor union. Special-interest groups lobbying on social issues include not only the conservative National Rifle Association but the liberal American Civil Liberties Union.

Political action committees (PACs) are *organizations formed by special-interest groups, independent of political parties, to pursue political aims by raising and spending money.* Political action committees channel most of their funds directly to candidates likely to support their interests. While legal reforms have limited direct contributions to candidates, since the 1970s the number of PACs has grown rapidly, to 4,600 (U.S. Federal Election Commission, 1999).

Because of the rising costs of campaigns, most candidates eagerly accept support from political action committees. In recent congressional elections, about one-fourth of all funding came from PACs, and two-thirds of all senators seeking reelection received more than $1 million each in PAC contributions. Supporters maintain that PACs represent interests of a vast array of businesses, unions, and church groups, thereby increasing political participation. Critics counter that organizations supplying cash to politicians expect to be treated favorably in return so that, in effect, PACs try to buy political influence (Allen & Broyles, 1991; Cook, 1993; Center for Responsive Politics, 1998).

Whether PACs are good or not, they certainly point up the importance of money in our political system. The rising costs of campaigns is a problem for all candidates, but incumbents have an edge because they have better access to PACs. In the 1996 congressional elections, 66 percent of PAC funds went to those already in office, 94 percent of whom won reelection. No wonder members of Congress—in both major parties—are reluctant to bring about campaign finance reform.

VOTER APATHY

As noted at the beginning of this chapter, a disturbing fact of U.S. political life is that many people seem indifferent to their right to vote. The long-term trend has

SEEING OURSELVES

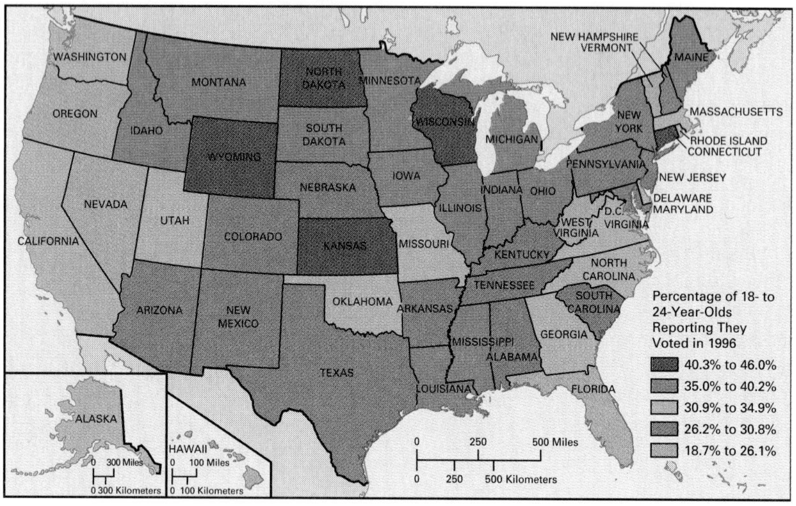

NATIONAL MAP 17–1
Political Apathy among Young People across the United States

Of all age categories, young people are the least likely to vote in national elections. The turnout of young voters at the polls has hit new lows in four of the last six elections: In 1996, just 49 percent of the 25 million eighteen- to twenty-four-year-olds registered to vote and only 32 percent actually cast a ballot. Among all age categories, rates of political participation are higher in the Midwest. Can you figure out why?

Source: *American Demographics* magazine, November 1999, p. 46. Reprinted with permission. © 1999, *American Demographics* magazine, Ithaca, New York.

been for greater *eligibility* to vote—the Fifteenth Amendment, ratified in 1870, enfranchised African American men; the Nineteenth Amendment extended voting rights to women in 1920; in 1971, the Twenty-sixth Amendment lowered the voting age to eighteen years. However, a countertrend shows that, over the last century, a smaller and smaller share of eligible citizens *actually do vote.* In the 1996 presidential election, less than half the registered voters took the time to cast a vote, below the comparable share in almost all other industrialized nations.

Who is and is not likely to vote? Women and men are equally likely to cast a ballot. White people are more likely to vote (64 percent voted in 1996) than African Americans (58 percent), with Hispanics (30 percent) the least likely of all to vote. Generally speaking, people with a bigger stake in society—homeowners, parents with children at home, people with good jobs and extensive schooling—are most likely to vote. Income matters, too: People with incomes in the top 20 percent (73 percent) are twice as likely as people with incomes in the bottom 20 percent (39 percent) to vote (Bennett, 1991; Hackey, 1992; Lewis, McCracken, & Hunt, 1994; DeLuca, 1998; Fetto, 1999).

Age is perhaps the most significant factor of all: People over sixty-five are three times as likely to vote as young adults aged eighteen to twenty-four. In fact, only 49 percent of these young people even bothered to register in 1996. National Map 17–1 shows where in the United States young people were more and less likely to cast a ballot in the 1996 presidential election.

Of course, we should expect some nonvoting, since, at any given time, millions of people are sick or disabled or away from home. Many more people forget to reregister after moving to a new neighborhood. Then, too, registration and voting depend on the ability to read and write, which discourages the tens of millions of U.S. adults who have limited literacy skills.

Conservatives suggest that apathy amounts to an *indifference* to politics. That is, most people who do not vote are reasonably content with their lives. But liberals (and especially political radicals) counter that most nonvoters are *alienated* from politics: Although dissatisfied with the way society operates, they doubt that elections will make any real difference. As Figure 17–2 shows, income is strongly related to whether or not people vote: Most high-income people *do* and most low-income people *don't.* The fact that it is the disadvantaged and powerless people who are least likely to vote suggests that the liberal explanation for apathy is probably closer to the truth.

In the end, apathy probably signifies that people want more of a choice. The two major parties of our political system, after all, have much in common. Perhaps, if additional parties represented a wider spectrum of political opinion—as they do in European countries—

people would have more reason to vote (Zipp & Smith, 1982; Zipp, 1985; Piven & Cloward, 1988; Lewis, McCracken, & Hunt, 1994; Phillips, 1994).

THEORETICAL ANALYSIS OF POWER IN SOCIETY

Sociologists have long debated how power is distributed in the United States. Power is one of the most difficult topics to study scientifically because decision making is complex and takes place behind closed doors. Moreover, it is difficult to separate a theory of power from the theorist's political attitudes and personal values. Nevertheless, three competing models of power in the United States have emerged.

THE PLURALIST MODEL: THE PEOPLE RULE

The **pluralist model** is *an analysis of politics that sees power as dispersed among many competing interest groups.* This approach is closely tied to structural-functional theory.

Pluralists claim, first, that politics is an arena of negotiation. With limited resources, no organization can expect to realize all its goals. Organizations, therefore, operate as *veto groups,* realizing some success but mostly keeping opponents from achieving all their goals. The political process, then, relies heavily on negotiating alliances and compromises among numerous interest groups so that policies gain wide support. In short, pluralists see power as widely dispersed throughout society, with all people having at least some voice in the political system (Dahl, 1961, 1982; Rothman & Black, 1998).

THE POWER-ELITE MODEL: A FEW PEOPLE RULE

The **power-elite model** is *an analysis of politics that sees power as concentrated among the rich.* This second approach is closely allied with the social-conflict paradigm.

The term *power elite* was coined by C. Wright Mills (1956), who argued that a small number of people in the United States effectively control this nation's political system. Mills claimed that the power elite stands atop each of three major sectors of U.S. society—the economy, the government, and the military. Thus, the power elite is made up of the "super-rich" (executives and large stockholders of major corporations), top officials in government (the most powerful figures in Washington, D.C., and state capitals around the country), and the highest-ranking officers in the U.S. military (senior Pentagon officials).

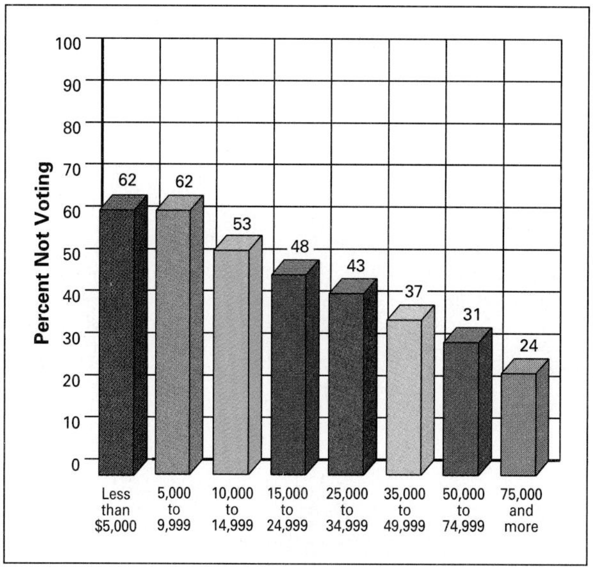

FIGURE 17–2 Political Apathy by Income Level

Percentage of adults who reported not voting in the 1996 presidential election presented according to their annual family income.

Source: U.S. Census Bureau (1998).

Further, Mills explained, these elites move from one sector to another, consolidating their power as they go. Alexander Haig, for example, has served as a top corporate executive, as a member of Ronald Reagan's cabinet (and 1988 presidential candidate), and as a general of the army. Haig is far from the exception: A majority of national political leaders enter government from powerful and highly paid positions—when President Clinton took office and assembled his cabinet, for instance, ten of thirteen members were reputed to be millionaires—and most return to the corporate world later on.

Power-elite theorists challenge the claim that the United States is a political democracy. They maintain that the concentration of wealth and power is simply too great for the average person's voice to be heard. They reject the pluralist idea that various centers of power serve as checks and balances on one another. Instead, the power-elite model holds that people at the top encounter no real opposition.

TABLE 17–3 Three Models of U.S. Politics: A Summary

	Pluralist Model	Power-Elite Model	Marxist Model
How is power distributed in U.S. society?	Highly dispersed	Concentrated	Concentrated
Is the United States basically democratic?	Yes, because voting offers everyone a voice, and no one group or organization dominates society	No, because a small share of the people dominate the economy, government, and military	No, because the bias of the capitalist system is to concentrate both wealth and power
How should we understand voter apathy?	Apathy is indifference; after all, even poor people can organize for a greater voice if they wish	Apathy is understandable, given how difficult it is for ordinary people to oppose the rich and powerful	Apathy is alienation generated by a system that will always leave most people powerless

THE MARXIST MODEL: BIAS IN THE SYSTEM ITSELF

A third approach to understanding U.S. politics is the **Marxist political-economy model,** *an analysis that explains politics in terms of the operation of a society's economic system.* Like the power-elite model, the Marxist model rejects the idea that the United States operates as a political democracy. But, whereas the power-elite model focuses on the disproportionate wealth and power of certain individuals, the Marxist model highlights bias rooted within this nation's institutions, especially its economy. As noted in Chapter 4 ("Society"), Karl Marx claimed that a society's economic system (capitalist or socialist) goes a long way toward shaping how the political system operates. Therefore, the power elites do not simply appear on the scene; they are creations of capitalism itself.

From this point of view, reforming the political system—say, by limiting the amount of money that rich people can contribute to political candidates—is unlikely to bring about true democracy. The problem does not lie in the *people* who exercise great power or the *people* who don't vote, the problem is rooted in the *system* itself, what Marxists term the "political-economy of capitalism." In other words, as long as the United States is a predominantly capitalist economy, just as the majority of people are exploited in the workplace, they will be shut out of politics.

Critical Evaluation

Which of the three different models of the U.S. political system is correct? Over the years, research has provided support for each, suggesting that a case can be made for all three. In the end, how one views this country's political system, and how one thinks it ought to operate, turn out to be as much a matter of political values as scientific fact.

Research by Nelson Polsby (1959) supports the pluralist model. Polsby studied the political scene in New Haven, Connecticut, and concluded that key decisions on various issues—including urban renewal, nominating political candidates, and operating the schools—were made by different groups. He found, too, that few of the upper-class families listed in New Haven's *Social Register* were also economic leaders. Thus, Polsby concluded, no one segment of society rules all the others.

Robert Dahl also investigated New Haven's history, finding that, over time, power had become more and more dispersed. Thus, Dahl's research also supports the pluralist model. As he put it, "No one, and certainly no group of more than a few individuals, is entirely lacking in [power]" (1961:228).

Supporting the power-elite position is research by Robert Lynd and Helen Lynd (1937) in Muncie, Indiana (which they called "Middletown," to suggest that it was a typical city). They documented the fortune amassed by a single family, the Balls, from their business manufacturing glass canning jars, and showed how the Ball family dominated the city's life. If anyone doubted the Balls' prominence, the Lynds explained, there was no need to look further than the local bank, a university, a hospital, and a department store, which all bear the family name. In Muncie, according to the Lynds, the power elite more or less boiled down to a single family.

In a study of Atlanta, Georgia, Floyd Hunter (1963) found further support for the power-elite model. No

The first modern political revolution began in 1789 in France. This engraving, titled To Versailles, To Versailles, *depicts the march of women to the king's palace in Versailles, on the outskirts of Paris, on October 5th, 1789, where they demanded more bread. The day after, the people forcibly led the royal family to Paris. Eventually, in October, 1793, the royal family was executed by guillotine in a crowded public square.*

To Versailles, To Versailles, March of the Women on Versailles, Paris, October 5, 1789, engraving by French School (eighteenth century). Musée Carnavalet, Paris, France. Bulloz/The Bridgeman Art Library.

one family dominated Atlanta, as was the case in Muncie. Yet Hunter found that about forty people held all the top positions in the city's businesses and controlled the city's politics.

From the Marxist perspective, the point is not to look at which individuals make decisions at the local or even the national level. Rather, as Alexander Liazos (1982:13) explains, "The basic tenets of capitalist society shape everyone's life: the inequalities of social classes and the importance of profits over people." As long as the basic institutions of society are organized to meet the needs of the few rather than the many, Liazos concludes, a democratic society will elude us.

Table 17–3 summarizes the three political models. In the end, what are we to make of the U.S. political system? At one level, it affords almost everyone the right to participate in the political process through elections. This is an important opportunity, one that is not enjoyed by a majority of the world's people. At the same time, however, the power-elite and Marxist models point out that, at the very least, the U.S. political system is far less democratic than most people think. Most citizens may have the right to vote, but the major political parties and their candidates typically support only those positions acceptable to the most powerful segments of society and consistent with the operation of our capitalist economy (Bachrach & Baratz, 1970).

Whatever the reasons, many people in the United States do not report having very much confidence in their leaders. More than 80 percent of U.S. adults report having, at best, only "some confidence" that members of Congress and other government officials will do what is best for the country (NORC, 1999:778, 903).

POWER BEYOND THE RULES

Politics always involves disagreement over a society's goals and the means to achieve them. Political systems, therefore, try to resolve controversy within a system of rules. But political activity sometimes exceeds—or tries to do away with—established practices.

REVOLUTION

Political revolution is *the overthrow of one political system in order to establish another.* In contrast to reform, which involves change *within* a system, revolution involves change *of the system itself.* Thus, even one leader deposing another—called a *coup d'état* (in French, literally, "stroke concerning the state")—falls short of revolution since it involves only a change at the top. Moreover, while reform rarely escalates into violence, revolution often does. The revolutions in Eastern Europe beginning in 1989 were surprisingly peaceful, with the exception of Romania, where violence claimed thousands of lives.

No type of political system is immune to revolution; nor does revolution invariably produce any one kind of government. Our country's Revolutionary War transformed colonial rule by the British monarchy into

Not all terrorism is the work of individuals or groups. Since 1950, China has sought to maintain control of Tibet by force. This Tibetan refugee displays instruments of torture used against him by officials of the Chinese government.

democratic government. French revolutionaries in 1789 also overthrew a monarch, only to set the stage for the return of monarchy in the person of Napoleon. In 1917, the Russian Revolution replaced monarchy with a socialist government built on the ideas of Karl Marx. In 1992, the Soviet Union was reborn as the Russian Federation, moving toward a market system and a greater political voice for its people.

Despite their striking variety, revolutions share a number of traits (Tocqueville, 1955, orig. 1856; also Davies, 1962; Brinton, 1965; Skocpol, 1979; Lewis, 1984; Tilly, 1986):

1. **Rising expectations.** Although common sense suggests that revolution would be more likely when people are grossly deprived, history shows that most revolutions occur when people's lives are improving. Rising expectations, rather than bitter resignation, fuel revolutionary fervor.
2. **Unresponsive government.** Revolutionary zeal gains strength when a government is unwilling or unable to reform, especially when such demands are made by powerful segments of society.
3. **Radical leadership by intellectuals.** The English philosopher Thomas Hobbes (1588–1679) observed that intellectuals often provide the justification for revolution, and universities frequently are the center of sweeping political change. During the 1960s in the United States, students were at the forefront of much of the political unrest. Students also played a critical role in China's pro-democracy movement and the uprisings in Eastern Europe.
4. **Establishing a new legitimacy.** Overthrowing a political system is not easy, but more difficult still is ensuring a revolution's long-term success. Some revolutionary movements are unified mostly by hatred of the past regime and fall apart once new leaders are installed. Revolutionaries must also guard against counterrevolutionary drives led by the deposed leaders. This explains the speed and ruthlessness with which victorious revolutionaries dispose of previous rulers.

Scientific analysis cannot declare that a revolution is good or bad. The full consequences of such an upheaval depend on one's values and, in any case, become evident only after many years. In the wake of recent revolution, for example, the future of the former Soviet Union remains unsettled.

TERRORISM

Terrorism constitutes *random acts of violence or the threat of such violence used by an individual or a group as a political strategy.* Like revolution, terrorism is a political act beyond the rules of established political systems. According to Paul Johnson (1981), terrorism has four distinguishing characteristics.

First, terrorists try to paint violence as a legitimate political tactic, despite the fact that such acts are condemned by virtually every nation. Terrorists also bypass (or are excluded from) established channels of political negotiation. Terror is, therefore, a weak organization's strategy to harm a stronger foe. Attacks against U.S. embassies in Tanzania and Kenya in 1998 may have been morally wrong for harming innocent people, but they did raise the profile of organizations with grievances against the United States. Indeed, terrorism has become almost commonplace in international politics, with more than 7,000 attacks directed against U.S. citizens since 1985 resulting in hundreds of deaths.

Second, terrorism is employed not just by groups but also by governments against their own people. *State terrorism* is the use of violence, generally without support of law, by government officials. State terrorism is lawful in some authoritarian and totalitarian states, which survive by inciting fear and intimidation. Saddam Hussein, for example, shores up his power in Iraq through state terrorism.

Third, democratic societies reject terrorism in principle, but they are especially vulnerable to terrorists because they afford extensive civil liberties to their people and have less extensive police networks. In contrast, totalitarian regimes make widespread use of state terrorism, although, at the same time, their extensive police power minimizes opportunities for individual terrorist acts.

Hostage taking and outright killing provoke popular anger, but responding to such acts is difficult. Before taking action, a government must identify those responsible. However, because most terrorist groups are shadowy organizations with no formal connection to any established state, a reprisal may be all but impossible. Yet, as terrorism expert Brian Jenkins warns, the failure to respond "encourages other terrorist groups, who begin to realize that this can be a pretty cheap way to wage war" (quoted in Whitaker, 1985:29). At the same time, a forcible military reaction to terrorism may risk confrontation with other governments.

Fourth, and finally, terrorism is always a matter of definition. Governments claim the right to maintain order, even by force, and may brand opposition groups who use violence as "terrorists." Similarly, political differences may explain why one person's "terrorist" is another's "freedom fighter."

WAR AND PEACE

Perhaps the most critical political issue is **war,** *organized, armed conflict among the people of various societies, directed by their governments.* War is as old as humanity, of course, but understanding it now takes on greater urgency. Because we have the technological capacity to destroy ourselves, war poses unprecedented danger to the entire planet. Most scholarly investigation of war aims to promote peace, meaning the absence of war (but not necessarily the end of all political conflict).

Many people think of war as an extraordinary occurrence; yet, for almost all of the twentieth century, nations somewhere on earth were in violent conflict. In our nation's short history, we have participated in ten large-scale wars, resulting in the deaths of more than 1.3 million U.S. men and women and injury to many

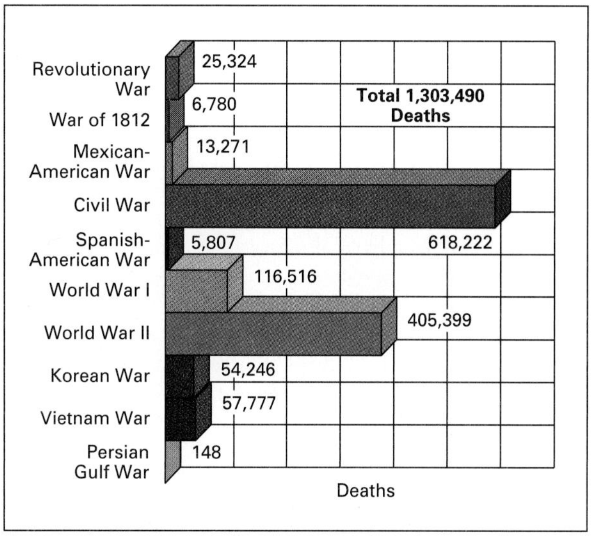

FIGURE 17–3 Death of Americans in Ten U.S. Wars

Sources: Compiled from various sources by Maris A. Vinovskis (1989) and the author.

times that number, as shown in Figure 17–3. Thousands more died in "undeclared wars" and "limited military actions" in the Dominican Republic, Lebanon, Grenada, Panama, and elsewhere.

THE CAUSES OF WAR

The frequency of war in human affairs might imply that there is something natural about armed confrontation. But, whereas many animals are naturally aggressive, research provides no basis for concluding that human beings inevitably wage war under any particular circumstances. Indeed, as Ashley Montagu (1976) observes, governments around the world have to use considerable coercion in order to mobilize their people for war.

Like all forms of social behavior, warfare is a product of *society* that varies in purpose and intensity from place to place. The Semai of Malaysia, among the most peace-loving of the world's people, rarely resort to violence. In contrast, the Yąnomamö, described in Chapter 3 ("Culture"), are quick to wage war.

If society holds the key to war or peace, under what circumstances *do* humans go to battle? Quincy Wright (1987) identifies five factors that promote war:

1. **Perceived threats.** Societies mobilize in response to a perceived threat to their people,

GLOBAL SOCIOLOGY

Violence beyond the Rules: A Report from the Former Yugoslavia

War is violent, but it also has rules. Many of our current rules of warfare were written at the end of World War II, when the victorious Allies, including the United States, charged German and Japanese military officials with war crimes. The United Nations, too, spells out the rules of war in the Geneva Conventions.

One of the most important principles is that whatever violence soldiers inflict upon each other, they cannot imprison, torture, rape, or murder civilians; nor can they deliberately destroy civilian property or wantonly bomb or shell cities. Even so, for years—and especially during the Balkan conflict in 1998—evidence has emerged that Serbs, Croats, and Muslims committed all these war crimes in the former Yugoslavia. Tens of thousands of civilians have been killed, raped, and seriously injured; the loss of property has been enormous. In 1993, a UN tribunal convened in the Netherlands to consider possible responses.

After World War II, the Allies successfully prosecuted (and, in several cases, executed) German officers for their crimes against humanity based on evidence obtained from extensive Nazi records. This time around, however, the task of punishing offenders has turned out to be far more difficult. For one thing, there are few written records of the Balkan conflict; for another, UN officials fear that arrests may upset delicate diplomatic efforts to bring peace to the region.

Even so, since beginning its investigations, the United Nations has indicted dozens of military officers on all sides of the conflict and even Serbian president Slobodan Milosevic. But only a handful of those charged with such crimes have been taken into custody, and it seems more and more likely that, despite a staggering toll in civilian deaths, no one will ever be convicted.

Sources: Adapted from Nelan (1993), Sebastian (1996), Watson (1999), and various news reports.

territory, or culture. The danger of armed conflict between the United States and the former Soviet Union, for example, has diminished as the two nations have become less fearful of each other.

2. **Social problems.** When internal problems generate widespread frustration at home, a society's leaders may divert public attention by attacking an external "enemy" as a form of scapegoating. Some analysts see the lack of economic development in the People's Republic of China as underlying that nation's hostility toward Vietnam, Tibet, and the former Soviet Union.
3. **Political objectives.** Leaders sometimes use war as a political strategy. Poor societies, such as Vietnam, have fought wars to end foreign domination. For powerful societies like the United States, a periodic show of force (recall the recent deployments of troops in Somalia, Haiti, and Bosnia) enhances their global political stature.
4. **Moral objectives.** Rarely do nations claim to fight merely to increase their wealth and power. Leaders infuse military campaigns with moral urgency, rallying their people around visions of "freedom" or the "fatherland." Although few doubted that the 1991 Persian Gulf War was largely about oil, U.S. strategists portrayed the mission as a drive to halt a Hitler-like Saddam Hussein.
5. **The absence of alternatives.** A fifth factor promoting war is the absence of alternatives. Although it is the United Nations' job to maintain international peace, the UN has had

limited success in resolving tensions among self-interested societies.

In short, war is rooted in social dynamics on both national and international levels. Moreover, even combat has rules, and breaking them can lead to charges of *war crimes.* The box takes a closer look.

THE COSTS AND CAUSES OF MILITARISM

The cost of armed conflict extends far beyond battlefield casualties. Together, the world's nations spend some $1 trillion annually ($160 for every person on the planet) for military purposes. Such expenditures, of course, divert resources from the desperate struggle for survival by hundreds of millions of poor people. If the world's nations could muster the will and the political wisdom to redirect their military spending, they could greatly reduce global poverty.

In recent years, defense has been the U.S. government's second largest expenditure (after retirement programs), accounting for 16 percent of all federal spending, or $277 billion in 1999. This huge sum is the legacy of the *arms race*, a mutually reinforcing escalation of military power between the United States and the former Soviet Union that began after World War II.

Today, years after the collapse of the Soviet Union, military expenditures remain high. Thus, analysts who support power-elite theory say that the United States is dominated by a **military-industrial complex,** *the close association of the federal government, the military, and defense industries.* The roots of militarism, then, lie not just in external threats to our security but also within the institutional structures of our own society (Marullo, 1987).

Another reason for persistent militarism in the post–cold war world is regional conflict. During the 1990s, localized wars broke out in Bosnia, Chechnya, and Zambia, and tensions remain high in a host of other areas, including the Middle East, Indonesia, and a divided Korea. Even wars of limited scope have the potential to escalate and involve other countries. In 1998, for example, India and Pakistan exploded atomic bombs, raising fears of nuclear confrontation in that region. As more and more nations acquire nuclear weapons, the risk that regional conflicts will erupt into deadly wars goes up.

NUCLEAR WEAPONS

Despite the easing of superpower tensions, nations still hold almost 25,000 nuclear warheads, a destructive force equivalent to five tons of TNT for every person on the planet. Should even a small fraction of this stockpile

The casualties of war are as likely to be civilians as soldiers. In Leonard Rosoman's 1940 painting, A House Collapsing on Two Firemen, Shoe Lane, London, *we see both the heroism and the horrors of World War II.*

Leonard Rosoman (b. 1913), *A House Collapsing on Two Firemen, Shoe Lane, London*, 1940. Imperial War Museum, London/The Bridgeman Art Library.

be used in war, life as we know it might well cease on much of the earth. Albert Einstein, whose genius contributed to the development of nuclear weapons, reflected: "The unleashed power of the atom has changed everything *save our modes of thinking*, and we thus drift toward unparalleled catastrophe." In short, nuclear weapons make unrestrained war unthinkable in a world not yet capable of peace.

Great Britain, France, and the People's Republic of China all have substantial nuclear capability, but the vast majority of nuclear weapons are based in the United States and the Russian Federation. The two superpowers have agreed to reduce their stockpiles of nuclear warheads by 75 percent by the year 2003. But even if the superpower rivalry winds down, the danger of catastrophic war increases with **nuclear proliferation,** *the acquisition of nuclear-weapons technology by more and more nations.* Israel, India, and Pakistan also possess some nuclear weapons, and other nations (including Iran, Iraq,

In recent years, the world has become aware of the death and mutilation caused by millions of land mines placed in the ground during wartime and left there afterward. Civilians—many of them children—maimed by land mines receive treatment in this Kabul, Afghanistan, clinic.

North Korea, and Libya) are in the process of developing them. While some nations have taken steps to limit the development of nuclear weapons—Argentina and Brazil stopped their work in 1990 and South Africa dismantled its arsenal in 1991—by 2010, as many as fifty nations could have the ability to fight a nuclear war. Such a trend makes any regional conflict much more dangerous (McGeary, 1998).

PURSUING PEACE

How can the world reduce the danger of war? Here are the most recent approaches to peace:

1. **Deterrence.** The logic of the arms race linked security to a "balance of terror" between the superpowers. Based on the principle of *mutually assured destruction (MAD)*—meaning that the side launching a first-strike nuclear attack against the other would sustain massive retaliation—deterrence has kept the peace for more than fifty years. But this strategy has three flaws. First, it has fueled an exorbitantly expensive arms race. Second, as missiles become capable of delivering their warheads more and more quickly, computers are left with less and less time to react to an apparent attack, thereby increasing the risks of unintended war. Third, deterrence cannot control nuclear proliferation, which poses a growing threat to peace.
2. **High-technology defense.** If technology created the weapons, some maintain, it can also deliver us from the threat of war. This is the idea behind the *strategic defense initiative (SDI)* proposed by the Reagan administration in 1981. Under SDI, satellites and ground installations provide a protective shield or umbrella against enemy missiles. In principle, the system would detect enemy missiles soon after launch and destroy them with lasers and particle beams before they could reenter the atmosphere. If perfected, advocates argue, such a "star wars" defense would render nuclear weapons obsolete.

   But critics charge that even years of research costing trillions of dollars would yield at best a leaky umbrella. The collapse of the Soviet Union also calls into question the need for such an extensive and costly defense scheme.

   Worth noting, too, is that sophisticated technology raises not only new possibilities for defense, but also new strategies for waging war. The box takes a closer look at the possibilities for "information warfare."
3. **Diplomacy and disarmament.** Still other analysts point out that the best path to peace is diplomacy rather than technology (Dedrick & Yinger, 1990). Diplomacy can enhance security by reducing, rather than building, weapon stockpiles.

CRITICAL THINKING

Information Warfare: Let Your Fingers Do the Fighting

For decades, scientists and military officials have studied how to use computers to defend against missiles and planes. More recently, however, the military has recognized that new information technology can fundamentally transform warfare itself, replacing rumbling tanks and screaming aircraft with electronic "smart bombs" that would silently penetrate an enemy country's computer system and render it unable to transmit information.

In such "virtual wars," soldiers seated at workstation monitors would dispatch computer viruses to shut down the enemy's communication links, causing telephones to fall silent, air traffic control and railroad switching systems to fail, computer to feed phony orders to field officers, and televisions to broadcast "morphed" news bulletins urging people to turn against their leaders.

Like the venom of a poisonous snake, the weapons of "information warfare" might quickly paralyze an enemy before a conventional attack. Another, more hopeful possibility is that new information technology weaponry might not just precede conventional fighting but might prevent it entirely. If the victims of computer warfare could be limited to a nation's communications links rather than its citizens and cities, wouldn't we all be more secure?

Yet so-called "info-war" also poses new dangers, since, presumably, a few highly skilled operators with sophisticated electronic equipment could also wreak communications havoc on the United States. This country may be militarily without equal in the world, but, given our increasing reliance on high technology, we are also more vulnerable to cyber-attack than any other nation. As a result, in 1996, the Central Intelligence Agency began work on a defensive "cyber-war center" to help prevent what one official termed an "electronic Pearl Harbor."

What do you think?

1. *Do you think it is realistic to expect that virtual warfare will replace conventional battlefield fighting? Why or why not?*
2. *Can you see ways in which new information technology might increase the chances to resolve disputes peacefully?*
3. *Do you think computer technology might increase the dangers of war? If so, how?*

Source: Waller (1995) and Weiner (1996).

But disarmament, too, has limitations. No nation wishes to become vulnerable by reducing its defenses. Successful diplomacy, then, depends not on "soft" concession making or "hard" demands but on everyone sharing responsibility for a common problem (Fisher & Ury, 1988).

While the United States and the former Soviet Union have managed to negotiate arms reduction agreements, the threat from other nations like Libya, North Korea, and Iraq—all of which desire to build nuclear arsenals—remains great.

4. **Resolving underlying conflict.** Perhaps the best way to reduce the danger of nuclear war is to resolve underlying conflicts. Even in the post–cold war era, basic differences between the United States and Russia remain. Moreover, militarism also springs from nationalism, ethnic differences, and class inequality, which have fueled regional conflicts in Latin America, Africa, Asia, and the Middle East. If peace depends on solving international disputes, why do world nations currently spend 3,000 times as much money on militarism as they do on peacekeeping? (Sivard, 1988)

LOOKING AHEAD: POLITICS IN THE TWENTY-FIRST CENTURY

Just as economic systems, the focus of the last chapter, are changing, so are political systems. As we enter the twenty-first century, several problems and trends will likely command widespread attention.

One vexing problem in the United States is the inconsistency between our democratic ideals and low public participation in politics. Perhaps, as the pluralists contend, many people do not bother to vote because

CONTROVERSY & DEBATE

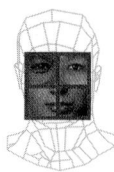

"Online Democracy": Can Computers Increase Political Participation?

How about this as a way to get more people actively involved in politics: Give every home a personal computer and an Internet connection; allow anyone to propose new legislation, and, on the first Saturday of every month, every adult uses a password to vote and make law. What could be easier? Or more truly democratic?

Is it possible, as some predict, that new information technology is about to reverse the trend toward apathy and lead our nation into a new age of democracy? High technology promises to make citizens better informed about the workings of government than ever before by broadcasting government debates live to every home and providing telephone, e-mail, and fax links to all government officials.

Moreover, using computer technology, citizens everywhere could participate in "electronic town meetings," pushing a button on a computer keyboard to help balance the budget, ban handguns, or, perhaps, close our borders to further immigration. In short, as some see it, we are entering the age of a "wired Congress" and "online democracy."

The push for high-tech politics began with the landslide victory in 1994 that gave the Republican party control of both houses of Congress for the first time in more than half a century. Republicans read the victory as evidence that people across the country were fed up with the liberal, big-government politics favored by people "inside the Beltway" (a reference to the interstate that circles our nation's capital). What better way to defeat the government establishment, they reasoned, than to open up debate to the "real" voice of the nation—the people in local towns and neighborhoods from Sarasota to Spokane. Moreover, the Republicans continued, Congress managed to pass a number of unpopular programs over the years only by shutting out the voice of "ordinary people." If the people had been asked in the first place, Republicans suggested, would we have today's high levels of immigration, rigid affirmative action programs, and vast federal

they are basically satisfied with their lives. But perhaps the power-elite theorists are right: People withdraw from a system that concentrates wealth and power in the hands of a few. Or, as Marxist critics contend, perhaps people find our political system gives little real choice, limiting options and policies to what is consistent with our capitalist economic system. In any case, it seems certain that we cannot endure high apathy and low confidence in government without moving toward significant political reforms.

A major trend discussed in this chapter is the expansion of a global political process. The Information Revolution is changing politics, just as it is reformulating the economy (although political change seems to be somewhat slower). Communications technology now allows news and political analysis to flow instantly from one point in the world to another. But will this global avalanche of information expand democracy by empowering individuals? Or will new information technology provide governments with new tools to manipulate their citizens? More basically, perhaps, some critics wonder if we really want to give the average person—who is, after all, no expert—the power to decide important issues. The final box takes a look at two sides of the recent "online democracy" debate.

Another major trend is the global rethinking of political models. The cold war between the United States and the Soviet Union cast political debate in the form of two rigid political alternatives based on capitalism, on the one hand, and socialism, on the other. Today, in the post–cold war era, analysts envision a broader range of political systems, linking government to economic production in various ways. "Welfare capitalism" found in Sweden or "state capitalism" found in Japan and South Korea are just two possibilities.

Fourth, and finally, we still face the danger of war in many parts of the world. Even as tensions between the United States and the former Soviet Union have eased, vast stockpiles of weapons remain, and nuclear technology continues to proliferate around the world. New superpowers may arise (the People's Republic of China is a likely candidate), just as regional conflicts will surely continue to fester. One can only hope that, in the century now begun, a sense of political justice enables us to devise nonviolent solutions to the age-old problems that provoke war.

bureaucracy? As the Republicans see it, much of our law is the creation of liberal, self-righteous politicians who rarely venture outside the Beltway.

But, of course, not everyone agrees with the Republicans. And not everyone is rushing out to "wire" Congress to public opinion. Some people in both major parties counter that using high technology to open up the political process amounts to "hyperdemocracy." Our system of government, they explain, was structured not as a *direct* democracy but as a *representative* democracy. That is, we elect officials to lead rather than follow the whims of the voters. The British philosopher Edmund Burke, himself a conservative, believed that government officials should do more than work hard for their constituents; leaders, he said, owe the people their judgment. In these days of media frenzy and passion-politics, when would-be leaders often seek to inflame public opinion, "online democracy" would result in impulsively passing questionable laws. In the early 1960s, for example, many people across the United States were too racially prejudiced to support the civil rights legislation that Congress enacted. But would we have wanted our representatives to do otherwise?

Like it or not, everyone agrees, new information technology will operate in two directions: It will give people a greater voice in government and also allow elected leaders to present and defend their own thinking to the public. But the question remains: Will this prescription for *more* democracy motivate a larger share of citizens to become politically active? And, more to the point, is a more direct democracy necessarily a *better* democracy?

Continue the debate . . .

1. *Do you think new information technology will give the public a greater voice in government? Why or why not? Could political leaders use new information technology to manipulate the public? How?*
2. *Does technology that would give the public a greater voice necessarily mean that government would make better decisions? Why or why not? Should our leaders consult the people before making decisions, or should they rely mostly on their own judgment?*
3. *Some critics suggest that if we want more democracy, innovations in technology are no substitute for real change in the economic and power structures of this country. Do you agree? Why or why not?*

Sources: Toffler & Toffler (1993), McConnell (1995), Roberts (1995), and R. Wright (1995).

SUMMARY

1. Politics is the major social institution by which a society distributes power and organizes decision making. Max Weber explained that three social contexts transform coercive power into legitimate authority: tradition, rationally enacted rules and regulations, and the personal charisma of a leader.
2. Traditional authority is common to preindustrial societies; industrial societies legitimize power mostly through bureaucratic organizations and law. Charismatic authority, which arises in every society, sustains itself through routinization into traditional or rational-legal authority.
3. Monarchy is based on traditional authority and is common in preindustrial societies. Although constitutional monarchies persist in some industrial nations, industrialization favors democracy based on rational-legal authority and extensive bureaucracy.
4. Authoritarian political regimes deny popular participation in government. Totalitarian political systems go even further, tightly regulating people's everyday lives.
5. The world is divided into 191 politically independent nation-states. One global political trend, however, is the growing wealth and power of multinational corporations. Additionally, new technology associated with the Information Revolution means that national governments can no longer control the flow of information across national boundaries.
6. Government has grown in the United States during the past two centuries and now acts in a wide range of ways to serve the public and regulate the economy. The welfare state in this country, however, is less extensive than in most other industrial nations.
7. Liberals and conservatives take different positions on economic and social issues. Liberals call for government regulation of the economy and action to ensure economic equality; conservatives believe

the government should not interfere in these arenas. Conservatives, however, do support government regulation of moral issues such as abortion, while liberals argue that government should not interfere in matters of conscience.

8. Special-interest groups advance the political aims of specific segments of the population. These groups employ lobbyists and political action committees (PACs) to influence the political process.
9. Many people in the United States do not readily describe themselves in political terms, nor do they strongly identify with either the Democratic or the Republican party. Furthermore, only 48 percent of those eligible to vote actually voted in the 1996 national elections.
10. The pluralist model holds that political power is widely dispersed in the United States; the power-elite model takes an opposing view, arguing that power is concentrated in a small, wealthy segment of the population. The Marxist political-economy view claims that our political agenda is controlled by a capitalist economy.
11. Revolution radically transforms a political system. Terrorism, another unconventional political tactic, employs violence in pursuit of political goals. States as well as individuals engage in terrorism.
12. War is armed conflict directed by governments. The development and proliferation of nuclear weapons have increased the threat of global catastrophe. World peace ultimately depends on resolving the tensions and conflicts that fuel militarism.

KEY CONCEPTS

politics (p. 435) the social institution that distributes power, sets a society's agenda, and makes decisions

power (p. 435) the ability to achieve desired ends despite resistance from others

government (p. 435) a formal organization that directs the political life of a society

authority (p. 435) power that people perceive as legitimate rather than coercive

traditional authority (p. 436) power legitimized through respect for long-established cultural patterns

rational-legal authority (also *bureaucratic authority*) (p. 436) power legitimized by legally enacted rules and regulations

charismatic authority (p. 436) power legitimized through extraordinary personal abilities that inspire devotion and obedience

routinization of charisma (p. 436) the transformation of charismatic authority into some combination of traditional and bureaucratic authority

monarchy (p. 437) a type of political system in which a single family rules from generation to generation

democracy (p. 438) a type of political system in which power is exercised by the people as a whole

authoritarianism (p. 440) a political system that denies popular participation in government

totalitarianism (p. 440) a political system that extensively regulates people's lives

welfare state (p. 442) a range of government agencies and programs that provides benefits to the population

special-interest group (p. 445) a political alliance of people interested in some economic or social issue

political action committee (PAC) (p. 445) an organization formed by a special-interest group, independent of political parties, to pursue political aims by raising and spending money

pluralist model (p. 447) an analysis of politics that sees power as dispersed among many competing interest groups

power-elite model (p. 447) an analysis of politics that sees power as concentrated among the rich

Marxist political-economy model (p. 448) an analysis that explains politics in terms of the operation of a society's economic system

political revolution (p. 449) the overthrow of one political system in order to establish another

terrorism (p. 450) random acts of violence or the threat of such violence used by an individual or group as a political strategy

war (p. 451) organized, armed conflict among the people of various societies, directed by their governments

military-industrial complex (p. 453) the close association of the federal government, the military, and defense industries

nuclear proliferation (p. 453) the acquisition of nuclear-weapons technology by more and more nations

CRITICAL-THINKING QUESTIONS

1. What is the difference between authority and power? What forms of authority characterize preindustrial and industrial societies? Why does democracy gradually replace monarchy as societies industrialize?
2. Using the political spectrum, explain the range of attitudes of the U.S. population. How is class position linked to political opinions?
3. Contrast the pluralist, power-elite, and Marxist models of societal power. Which do you find most convincing?
4. Is danger of war in today's world greater or less than in past generations? Why?

APPLICATIONS AND EXERCISES

1. Immediately after every national election (held the first Tuesday in November), newspapers publish an analysis of who voted and for whom. Visit the library to obtain a "scorecard" for a recent national election (check, for example, *The New York Times* for Wednesday, November 8th, 2000, or Wednesday, November 7th, 2001). To what extent do men and women vote for different presidential candidates? What about people of various racial categories? Ages? Religions? Income levels? Which variables affect political attitudes the most?
2. Along with several other people, make a list of leaders you think are or were charismatic. Discuss why someone is on the list. Do you think personal charisma today is something more than "being good on television"? If so, precisely what?
3. Do a little research to trace the increase in the size of the federal government over the last fifty years. Try to discover how organizations at different points along the political spectrum (from socialist organizations on the left through the Democratic and Republican parties to right-wing militia groups) view the size of the current welfare state.
4. Members of the all-volunteer army are drawn heavily from the working class in the United States. In order to share the burden and danger of defending this country, should the United States reintroduce a lottery system? Why or why not?
5. Freedom House, the organization that studies civil rights and political liberty around the world, publishes an annual report, *Freedom in the World.* Find a copy in the library (or write to the organization at 1319 Eighteenth Street, Washington, D.C., 20036) and examine the trends or political profiles of countries of interest to you.
6. Install the CD-ROM packaged in the back of this new textbook to access a variety of study, review, and applications exercises designed to help you better understand the material covered in this chapter. The CD includes an author's tip video, as well as interactive maps, video application exercises, Web links, and study questions.

SITES TO SEE

http://www.prenhall.com/macionis
Visit the interactive Web site that accompanies this text. Begin by clicking on the cover of your book. You will find a chapter-by-chapter study guide, practice tests, chat room, and many suggested Web links.

http://www.womenconnect.com
The Internet provides enormous organizational potential, linking people who share an interest in some political issue. The goal of this Web site is to increase the political clout of women.

http://www.amnesty.org
Amnesty International operates a Web site that offers information about human rights around the world.

http://www.usis.usemb.se/terror/index.html
This Web site provides information on global terrorism.

http://www.coara.or.jp/~ryoji/abomb/e-index.html
Few of us have firsthand experience of the horrors of war. This Web site provides a personal account of the dropping of the first atomic bomb on the Japanese city of Hiroshima.

CHAPTER 18

John Falter (1910–1982)
July 4th—The Family Portrait

Oil on canvas, 26 × 24 in. (66 × 61 cm). Christie's Images, New York.

FAMILY

Saima Waheed was in love, and she wanted Arshad Ahmed as her husband. Arshad loved her, too. The only problem was that Saima's parents were opposed to the marriage. When the couple went off on their own and secretly married, Saima's parents were furious. Their daughter might be twenty-two, but for a marriage to be legal in Pakistan, the woman's parents must approve.

The parents took their case to the police, and, within days, Arshad was in prison, charged with kidnapping. Saima, meanwhile, fled to a women's shelter. The couple pinned their hopes on the courts, asking just that they be allowed to marry in peace. The legal process took almost a year to unfold, but, in the end, a Pakistani court sided with the young lovers, declaring that a woman was entitled to fall in love and marry—even without her parents' approval.

The story ends happily for this couple, who described their case as "a victory for love and a victory for women's rights." But thousands of Muslims in this traditional society joined Saima's parents in protest against what they saw as a breakdown of "family values." Many insisted that their children were being corrupted by the U.S. television shows, dubbed in the Hindi language, that have become popular in Pakistani homes (Rashid, 1997).

We in the United States may or may not play a part in a debate over marriage and family in Pakistan, but we certainly have plenty of disagreement among ourselves. To hear some people tell it, the family is fast becoming an endangered species. Consider these statistics: The U.S. divorce rate has doubled over the past forty years so that, if the trend holds, almost half of today's marriages will end in divorce. Marital breakdown, coupled with the fact that about one in three children is born to an unmarried woman, means that half the U.S. children born today will live with a single parent at some time before reaching age eighteen. This trend is one reason that the proportion of U.S. children living in poverty has been rising steadily.

Together, these facts point to a basic truth: Families in the United States and many other nations are changing, probably faster than any other social institution (Bianchi & Spain, 1996). Not long ago, the cultural ideal of the family consisted of a working husband, a homemaker wife, and their young children. Today, fewer people have such a singular vision of the family, and, at any given time, only about one in four U.S. households fits that description.

This chapter explores changes in family life, asking why some people call the family the bedrock of social life while others predict—and even encourage—family decline. For better or worse, the family is a topic of controversy almost everywhere.

THE FAMILY: BASIC CONCEPTS

The **family** is *a social institution found in all societies that unites people into cooperative groups to oversee the bearing and raising of children.* Family ties are also called **kinship,** *a social bond based on blood, marriage, or adoption.* Although all societies contain families, just who people call their kin has varied through history, and varies today from one culture to another. In the United States, most people regard a **family unit** as *a social group of two or more people, related by blood, marriage, or adoption, who usually live together.* Initially, individuals are born into a family composed of parents and siblings; this is sometimes called the *family of orientation* because it is central to socialization. In adulthood, people form a *family of procreation* in order to have or adopt children of their own.

Throughout the world, families form around **marriage,** *a legally sanctioned relationship, usually involving economic cooperation as well as sexual activity and childbearing, that people expect to be enduring.* Our cultural belief that marriage is the right setting for procreation explains the historical use of the term *illegitimate* for children born out of wedlock. Moreover, *matrimony,* in Latin, means "the condition of motherhood." The link between childbearing and marriage has weakened, however, as the share of children born to single women (nearing one in three) has increased.

Today, some people object to defining only married couples and children as "families" because it implies a single standard of moral conduct. Many business and government programs use this conventional definition, so that unmarried but committed partners—whether heterosexual or homosexual—are excluded from health care and other benefits. More and more, however, organizations are coming to recognize *families of affinity,* that is, people with or without legal or blood ties who feel they belong together and wish to define themselves as a family.

The U.S. Census Bureau, too, uses the conventional definition of family. Thus, sociologists who use Census Bureau data describing "families" must accept this definition.[1] But the national trend is toward a more inclusive definition of family.

[1]According to the U.S. Census Bureau, there were 102.5 million U.S. households in 1998, of which 70.9 million (69 percent) were family households. The remaining living units contained single people or unrelated individuals living together. In 1960, 85 percent of all households were families.

THE FAMILY: GLOBAL VARIATIONS

In preindustrial societies, people take a broad view of family ties, recognizing the **extended family** as *a family unit that includes parents and children, as well as other kin.* This group is also called the *consanguine family,* meaning it includes everyone with "shared blood." With industrialization, however, increasing social mobility and geographic migration give rise to the **nuclear family,** *a family unit composed of one or two parents and their children.* The nuclear family is also called the *conjugal family,* meaning "based on marriage." Although many members of our society live in extended families, the nuclear family is most common in the United States.

Family change has been greatest in nations that have the most expansive welfare state (see Chapter 17, "Politics and Government"). In the box on pages 464–65, sociologist David Popenoe takes a look at Sweden, which, he claims, has the weakest families in the world.

MARRIAGE PATTERNS

Cultural norms, and often laws, identify people as suitable or unsuitable marriage partners. Some marital norms promote **endogamy,** *marriage between people of the same social category.* Endogamy limits marriage prospects to others of the same age, race, religion, or social class. By contrast, **exogamy** mandates *marriage between people of different social categories.* In rural areas of Pakistan and India, for example, people are expected to marry someone of the same caste (endogamy) but from a different village (exogamy). The logic of endogamy is that people of similar position pass along their standing to offspring, thereby maintaining traditional social patterns. Exogamy, on the other hand, builds alliances and encourages cultural diffusion.

In industrial societies, laws prescribe **monogamy** (from the Greek, meaning "one union"), *marriage uniting two partners.* Our high level of divorce and remarriage, however, suggests that *serial monogamy* might be a more accurate description of this nation's marital practice. Global Map 18–1 on page 466 shows that while monogamy is the rule throughout the Americas and in Europe, many lower-income societies—especially in Africa and southern Asia—permit **polygamy** (from the Greek, meaning "many unions"), *marriage that unites three or more people.* Polygamy takes two forms. By far the more common is **polygyny** (from the Greek, meaning "many women"), *marriage uniting one male and two or more females.* Islamic nations in Africa and southern Asia, for example, permit men up to four wives. Even so, most Islamic families are monogamous

Despite global variations in family form, people everywhere celebrate the ritual of marriage that extends kinship into a new generation. The great attention given to marriage is captured in this painting by Carmen Lomas Garza, titled The Blessing on Wedding Day/La bendición en el dia de la boda.

Carmen Lomas Garza, *The Blessing on Wedding Day/La bendición en el dia de la boda.* Alkyds on canvas, 24 × 32 inches. © 1993 Carmen Lomas Garza (reg. 1994). Photo credit: M. Lee Fatherree. Collection of Smith College Museum, Northampton, Mass.

because few men can afford to support several wives and even more children.

Polyandry (from the Greek, meaning "many men" or "many husbands") is *marriage uniting one female and two or more males.* One case of this rare pattern is in Tibet, a mountainous land where agriculture is difficult. There, polyandry discourages the division of land into parcels too small to support a family and divides the work of farming among many men. Polyandry has also been linked to female infanticide—aborting female fetuses or killing female infants—because a decline in the female population forces men to share women.

Most world societies, at some time, have permitted more than one marital pattern. Even so, as noted, most actual marriages have been monogamous (Murdock, 1965). This cultural preference for monogamy reflects two facts of life: Supporting multiple spouses is a heavy financial burden, and the number of men and women in most societies is roughly the same.

RESIDENTIAL PATTERNS

Just as societies regulate mate selection, so they designate where a couple resides. In preindustrial societies, most newlyweds live with one set of parents who offer them protection and economic assistance. Most common is the norm of **patrilocality** (Greek for "place of the father"), *a residential pattern in which a married couple lives with or near the husband's family.* But some societies (such as the North American Iroquois) favor **matrilocality** (meaning "place of the mother"), *a residential pattern in which a married couple lives with or near the wife's family.* Societies that engage in frequent, local warfare tend toward patrilocality, so sons are close to home to offer protection. Societies that engage in distant warfare may be patrilocal or matrilocal, depending on whether sons or daughters have greater economic value (Ember & Ember, 1971, 1991).

Industrial societies show yet another pattern. Finances permitting, they favor **neolocality** (Greek meaning "new place"), *a residential pattern in which a married couple lives apart from both sets of parents.*

PATTERNS OF DESCENT

Descent refers to *the system by which members of a society trace kinship over generations.* Most preindustrial societies trace kinship through just the father's or mother's side of the family. The more common **patrilineal descent** is *a system tracing kinship through men.* Children are related to others only through their fathers, so that fathers typically pass property on to their sons. Patrilineal descent characterizes most pastoral and

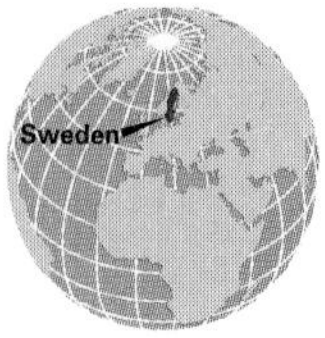

GLOBAL SOCIOLOGY

The Weakest Families on Earth? A Report from Sweden

The Swedes have managed to avoid many of the social problems that plague us in the United States. Swedish cities have little of the violent crime, drug abuse, and grinding poverty that blight whole communities from New York to Los Angeles. Instead, this Scandinavian nation seems to fulfill the promise of the modern welfare state, with an extensive and professional government bureaucracy that sees to virtually all human needs.

But one drawback of an expanding welfare state, according to David Popenoe, is that Sweden has the weakest families on earth. Because people look to the government, not spouses, for economic assistance, Swedes are less likely to marry than members of any other industrialized society. For the same reason, Sweden also has a high share of adults living alone (more than 20 percent, as opposed to 13 percent in the United States). Moreover, a large proportion of couples live outside of marriage (25 percent versus 7 in the United States), and half of all Swedish children (compared to about one in three in the United States) are born to unmarried parents. Average household size in Sweden is also the smallest in the world (2.2 persons versus 2.6 in the United States). Finally, Swedish couples (whether married or not) are more likely to break up than partners in any other country. According to Popenoe, the family "has probably become weaker in Sweden than anywhere else—certainly among advanced Western nations. Individual family members are the

In Sweden, unmarried women bear half of all children, twice the rate of births by single women in the United States.

agrarian societies, in which men produce the most valued resources. Less common is **matrilineal descent,** *a system tracing kinship through women.* Matrilineal descent, through which mothers pass property to their daughters, is found more frequently in horticultural societies, where women are the primary food producers.

Industrial societies with greater gender equality recognize **bilateral descent** ("two-sided descent"), *a system tracing kinship through both men and women.* In this pattern, children recognize people on both the father's side and the mother's side as relatives.

PATTERNS OF AUTHORITY

The predominance of polygyny, patrilocality, and patrilineal descent in the world reflects the universal presence of patriarchy. Wives and mothers exercise considerable power in every society, but, as Chapter 13 ("Gender Stratification") explains, no truly matriarchal society has ever existed.

In industrial societies like the United States, more egalitarian family patterns are evolving, especially as increasing numbers of women enter the labor force. However, even here, men are typically heads of households. Parents in the United States also still prefer boys to girls, and most give children their father's last name.

THEORETICAL ANALYSIS OF THE FAMILY

As in earlier chapters, several theoretical approaches offer a range of insights about the family.

FUNCTIONS OF THE FAMILY: STRUCTURAL-FUNCTIONAL ANALYSIS

According to the structural-functional paradigm, the family performs several vital tasks. In fact, the family operates as "the backbone of society."

most autonomous and least bound by the group . . ." (1991:69).

Popenoe contends that a growing culture of individualism and self-fulfillment, along with the declining influence of religion, began eroding Swedish families in the 1960s. The movement of women into the labor force also played a part. Today, Sweden has the lowest proportion of women who are housewives (10 percent versus about 25 in the United States) and the highest percentage of women in the labor force (77 percent versus 60 in the United States).

But, most important, according to Popenoe, is the expansion of the welfare state. The Swedish government offers its citizens a lifetime of services. Swedes can count on the government to deliver and school their children, provide comprehensive health care, support them when they are out of work, and, when the time comes, pay for their funeral.

Many Swedes supported the growth of welfare, thinking it would *strengthen* families. But with the benefit of hindsight, Popenoe explains, we can see that, with expanding benefits, government actually has been *replacing* families. Take the case of child care: The Swedish government operates public child-care centers, staffed by professionals and available regardless of parents' income. At the same time, however, the government offers no subsidy for parents who desire to care for children in their own home. In effect, then, government benefits operate as incentives for people to let the state do what family members used to do for themselves.

But if Sweden's system has solved so many social problems, why should anyone care about the erosion of family life? For two reasons, says Popenoe. First, it is very expensive for government to provide many "family" services; this is the main reason that Sweden has one of the highest rates of taxation in the world. Second, can government employees in large child-care centers provide children with the level of love and emotional security available from two parents living as a family? Unlikely, says Popenoe, noting that small, intimate groups can accomplish some human tasks much better than large organizations.

Popenoe concludes that the Swedes have gone too far in delegating family responsibilities to government. But, he wonders, have we in the United States gone far enough? With the birth of a child, a Swedish parent may apply for up to eighteen months' leave at 90 percent of regular salary. In the United States, the 1993 Family and Medical Leave Act guarantees workers only ninety days—without pay—to care for newborns or sick family members. Should our society follow Sweden's lead? And if we look to government to help working parents care for children, will it strengthen or weaken families?

Sources: Popenoe (1991, 1994); also Herrstrom (1990).

1. **Socialization.** As explained in Chapter 5 ("Socialization"), the family is the first and most influential setting for socialization. Ideally, parents help children become well-integrated, contributing members of society (Parsons & Bales, 1955). Of course, family socialization continues throughout the life cycle. Adults change within marriage and, as any parent knows, mothers and fathers learn as much from their children as their children learn from them.

2. **Regulation of sexual activity.** Every culture regulates sexual activity in the interest of maintaining kinship organization and property rights. One universal regulation is the **incest taboo,** *a cultural norm forbidding sexual relations or marriage between certain relatives.* Precisely which relatives fall within the incest taboo varies from one culture to another. The matrilineal Navajo, for example, forbid marrying any relative of one's mother. Our bilateral society applies the incest taboo to both sides of the family but limits it to close relatives, including parents, grandparents, siblings, aunts, and uncles. But even brother-sister marriages found approval among the ancient Egyptian, Incan, and Hawaiian nobility (Murdock, 1965; orig. 1949).

   Reproduction between close relatives of any species can mentally and physically harm offspring. Yet only human beings observe an incest taboo, which suggests that the main reason to control incest is social. Why? First, the incest taboo limits sexual competition in families by restricting sexuality to spouses. Second, forcing people to marry outside their immediate families integrates the larger society. Third, because kinship defines people's rights and obligations toward each other, reproduction among close relatives would hopelessly confuse kinship ties and threaten social order.

WINDOW ON THE WORLD

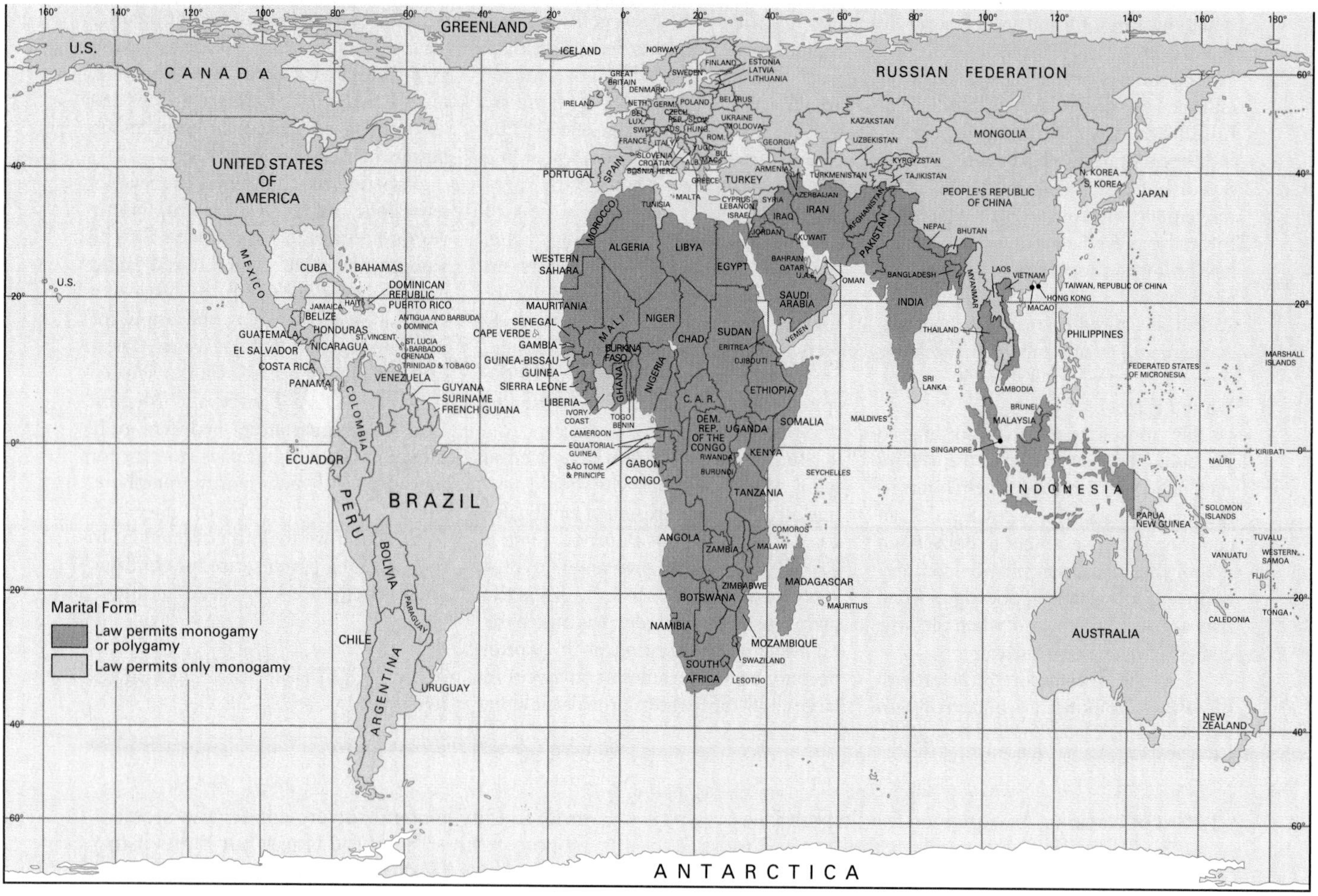

GLOBAL MAP 18–1 Marital Form in Global Perspective

Monogamy is the legally prescribed form of marriage in all industrial societies and throughout the Western Hemisphere. In most African nations and in southern Asia, however, polygamy is permitted by law. In many cases, this practice reflects the historic influence of Islam, a religion that allows a man to have up to four wives. Even so, most marriages in these traditional societies are monogamous, primarily for financial reasons.

Source: *Peters Atlas of the World* (1990).

3. **Social placement.** Families are hardly necessary for people to reproduce, but they help maintain social organization. Parents confer their own social identity—in terms of race, ethnicity, religion, and social class—on children at birth.

4. **Material and emotional security.** Many people view the family as a "haven in a heartless world," looking to kin for physical protection, emotional support, and financial assistance. Thus, people living in families tend to be healthier than people living alone.

The family is a basic building block of society because it performs important functions, such as conferring social position and regulating sexual activity. To most family members, however, the family (at least in ideal terms) is a "haven in a heartless world" in which individuals enjoy the feeling of belonging and find emotional support. Marc Chagall conveyed the promise of marriage in his painting, To My Wife. *Looking at the painting, how does the artist characterize marriage?*

Marc Chagall (1887–1985), *To My Wife*, 1933–44. Georges Pompidou Centre, Paris. The Bridgeman Art Library, London. © 2000 Artists Rights Society (ARS), New York/ADAGP, Paris.

Critical evaluation. Structural-functional analysis explains why society, at least as we know it, depends on families. But this approach glosses over the great diversity of U.S. family life and also ignores how other social institutions (say, government) could meet some of the same human needs. Finally, structural-functionalism overlooks negative aspects of family life, including patriarchy and family violence.

INEQUALITY AND THE FAMILY: SOCIAL-CONFLICT ANALYSIS

The social-conflict paradigm also considers the family central to our way of life. But, rather than focusing on ways that kinship benefits society, conflict theorists point out how the family perpetuates social inequality:

1. **Property and inheritance.** Friedrich Engels (1902; orig. 1884) traced the origin of the family to men's need (especially in the upper classes) to identify heirs so they could transmit property to their sons. Families thus support the concentration of wealth and reproduce the class structure in each succeeding generation (Mare, 1991).
2. **Patriarchy.** To know their heirs, men must control the sexuality of women. Families thus transform women into the sexual and economic property of men. A century ago in the United States, most wives' earnings belonged to their husbands. Today, despite striking economic gains, women still bear most of the responsibility for child rearing and housework (Hochschild, 1989; Presser, 1993; Keith & Schafer, 1994; Benokraitis & Feagin, 1995; Stapinski, 1998).
3. **Race and ethnicity.** Racial and ethnic categories persist over generations only to the degree that people marry others like themselves. Thus endogamous marriage shores up racial and ethnic hierarchies.

Critical evaluation. Social-conflict analysis shows another side of family life: its role in social stratification. Engels criticized the family as part and parcel of capitalism. Yet noncapitalist societies have families (and family problems) all the same. The family may be linked to social inequality, as Engels argued, but the family carries out societal functions not easily accomplished by other means.

CONSTRUCTING FAMILY LIFE: MICRO-LEVEL ANALYSIS

Both structural-functional and social-conflict analyses view the family as a structural system. Micro-level approaches, by contrast, explore how individuals shape and experience family life.

People in every society recognize the reality of physical attraction. But the power of romantic love, captured in Christian Pierre's painting, I Do, *holds surprisingly little importance in traditional societies. In much of the world, it would be less correct to say that individuals marry individuals and more true to say that families marry families. In other words, parents arrange marriages for their children with an eye to the social position of the kin-groups involved.*

Symbolic-Interaction Analysis

Ideally, family living offers an opportunity for intimacy, a word with Latin roots meaning "sharing fear." That is, as family members share activities, they build emotional bonds. Of course, the fact that parents act as authority figures often limits their closeness with children. Only as people reach adulthood do kinship ties "open up" to include confiding in and turning to one another for help with daily tasks and responsibilities (Macionis, 1978a).

Social-Exchange Analysis

Social-exchange analysis, another micro-level approach, depicts courtship and marriage as forms of negotiation (Blau, 1964). Dating allows each person to assess the advantages and disadvantages of taking the other as a spouse, always keeping in mind the value of what one has to offer in return. In essence, exchange analysts suggest, individuals seek to make the best "deal" they can in a partner.

Physical attractiveness is an important dimension of exchange. In patriarchal societies, men bring wealth and power to the marriage marketplace, and women are expected to bring beauty. The importance of physical beauty explains women's traditional concern with their appearance and their sensitivity about revealing their age. But, as women have joined the labor force, they are less dependent on men to support them, which means the terms of exchange are converging for men and women.

Critical evaluation. Micro-level analysis balances structural-functional and social-conflict visions of the family as an institutional system. Both the interaction and exchange viewpoints show how individuals shape the experience of family life for themselves. This approach, however, misses the bigger picture, namely, that family life is similar for people in the same social and economic categories. Families in the United States vary in predictable ways, according to their social class and ethnicity, and, as the next section explains, they typically evolve through distinct stages linked to the life course.

STAGES OF FAMILY LIFE

The family is a dynamic institution, with marked changes across the life course. New families begin with courtship, and evolve as the new partners settle into the realities of married life. Next, for most couples at least, is the years spent raising children, leading to the later years of marriage after children have left home to form families of their own. We will look briefly at each of these four stages.

GLOBAL SOCIOLOGY

Early to Wed: A Report from Rural India

Sumitra Jogi cries as her wedding is about to begin. Are they tears of joy? Not exactly. This "bride" is an eleven-month-old squirming in the arms of her mother. The groom? A boy of six.

In a remote, rural village in India's western state of Rajasthan, two families gather at midnight to celebrate a traditional wedding ritual. It is May 2, in Hindu tradition, an especially good day to marry. Sumitra's father smiles as the ceremony begins; her mother cradles the infant, who has fallen asleep. The groom, dressed in a special costume with a red and gold turban on his head, gently reaches up and grasps the baby's hand. Then, as the ceremony reaches its conclusion, the young boy leads the child and mother around the wedding fire three-and-one-half times, as the audience beams at the couple's first steps together as husband and wife.

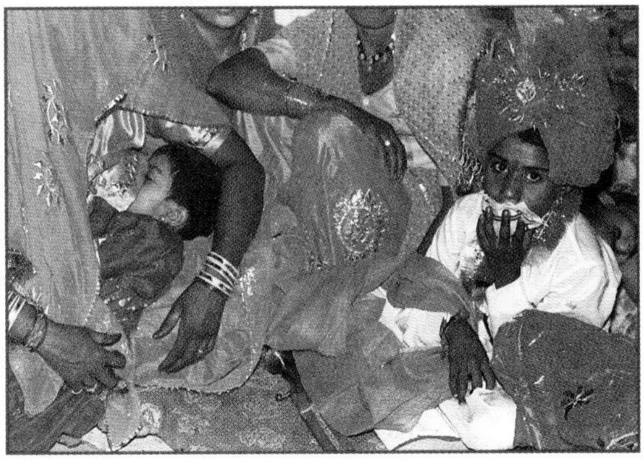

Child weddings are illegal in India, but in the rural regions, traditions are strong and marriage laws are hard to enforce. Thus, experts estimate, thousands of children marry each year. "In rural Rajasthan," explains one social welfare worker, "all the girls are married by age fourteen. These are poor, illiterate families, and they don't want to keep girls past their first menstrual cycle."

For the immediate future, Sumitra Jogi will remain with her parents. But in eight or ten years, a second ceremony will send her to live with her husband's family, and her married life will begin.

If the responsibilities of marriage lie years in the future, why do families push their children to marry at such an early age? Parents of girls know that the younger the bride, the smaller the dowry offered to the groom's family. Then, too, when girls marry this young, there is no question about their virginity, which raises their value on the marriage market. Arranged marriages are an alliance between families. No one thinks about love or the fact that the children are too young to understand what is taking place.

Source: Based on Anderson (1995).

COURTSHIP

November 2, 1994, Kandy, Sri Lanka. Winding through the rain forest of this beautiful island, our van driver, Harry, recounts how he met his wife. Actually, it was more of an arrangement: The two families were both Buddhist and of the same caste. "We got along well, right from the start," recalls Harry. "We had the same background. I suppose she or I could have said 'no.' But 'love marriages' happen in the city, not in the village where I grew up."

In rural Sri Lanka, and in preindustrial societies throughout the world, most people consider the choice of a marriage partner too important to be left to the young (Stone, 1977). Arranged marriages represent an alliance between two extended families of similar social standing and usually involve not just an exchange of children but also wealth and favors. Romantic love has little to do with it, and parents may make such arrangements when their children are very young. A century ago in Sri Lanka and India, for example, half of all girls were married before they reached age fifteen (Mayo, 1927; Mace & Mace, 1960). As the box explains, in some parts of the world, the custom of child marriage persists today.

GLOBAL SNAPSHOT

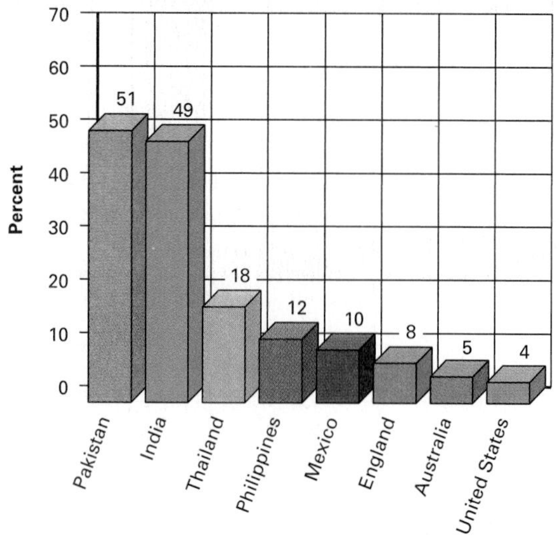

FIGURE 18–1 Percentage of College Students Who Express a Willingness to Marry without Romantic Love

Source: Levine (1993).

Because traditional societies are culturally homogeneous, almost any member of the opposite sex has been suitably socialized to be a good spouse. Thus parents can arrange marriages with little thought to whether or not the two individuals involved are *personally* compatible; they can be confident that virtually any couple will be *culturally* compatible.

Industrialization erodes the importance of extended families as it weakens tradition. Young people choose their own mates and delay marriage until they have financial security and the experience needed to select a suitable partner. Dating sharpens courtship skills and allows sexual experimentation.

Romantic Love

Our culture celebrates *romantic love*—affection and sexual passion for another person—as the basis for marriage. We find it hard to imagine marriage without love; and popular culture—from fairy tales like "Cinderella" to today's romance novels—portrays love as the key to a successful marriage. However, as Figure 18–1 shows, in Pakistan and many other traditional countries, romantic love plays a much smaller role in marriage.

Our society's emphasis on romance motivates young people to "leave the nest" to form new families of their own, and physical passion can help a new couple through difficult adjustments of living together (Goode, 1959). On the other hand, because feelings wax and wane, romantic love is a less stable foundation for marriage than social and economic considerations—one reason that the divorce rate is much higher in the United States than in nations where culture limits choices in partners.

But even here, sociologists point out, society aims Cupid's arrow more than we like to think. Most people fall in love with others of the same race, of comparable age, and similar social class. Our society "arranges" marriages by encouraging **homogamy** (literally, "like marrying like")—*marriage between people with the same social characteristics.*

SETTLING IN: IDEAL AND REAL MARRIAGE

Our culture gives the young an idealized, "happily-ever-after" picture of marriage. Such optimism can lead to disappointment, especially for women, who are taught that marriage is the key to happiness. Then, too, romantic love involves a good deal of fantasy. We fall in love with others, not necessarily as they are but as we want them to be (Berscheid & Hatfield, 1983). Only after marriage do many spouses face up to day-to-day responsibilities and routines.

Sexuality, too, can be a source of disappointment. In the romantic haze of falling in love, people may unrealistically expect marriage to be an endless sexual honeymoon, only to face the sobering realization that sex becomes a less than all-consuming passion. About two in three married people report that they are satisfied with the sexual dimension of their relationship, though marital sex does decline over time.

Many experts agree that couples with the most fulfilling sexual relationships experience the greatest satisfaction in their marriages. This correlation does not mean that sex is the key to marital bliss, but, more often than not, good sex and good relationships go together (Hunt, 1974; Tavris & Sadd, 1977; Blumstein & Schwartz, 1983; Laumann et al., 1994).

Infidelity—sexual activity outside of marriage—is another area where the reality of marriage does not coincide with our cultural ideal. In a recent survey,

90 percent of U.S. adults said sex outside of marriage is "always wrong" or "almost always wrong." Even so, 21 percent of men and 13 percent of women indicated on a private, written questionnaire that they had, at least once, been sexually unfaithful to their partners (NORC, 1999:235, 996).

CHILD REARING

Despite the demands children make on us, adults in the United States overwhelmingly identify raising children as one of life's greatest joys (NORC, 1999:845). Today, however, few people want more than three children, as Table 18–1 documents. This is a change from two centuries ago, when *eight* children was the U.S. average.

Big families pay off in preindustrial societies because children supply needed labor. Thus, people regard having children as a wife's duty, and, without effective birth control, childbearing is a regular event. Of course, a high death rate in preindustrial societies prevents many children from reaching adulthood; as late as 1900, one-third of children born in the United States died by age ten (Wall, 1980).

Industrialization transforms children, economically speaking, from an asset to a liability. It now costs more than $200,000 to raise one child, including college tuition (Lino, 1998). No wonder the size of the U.S. family steadily dropped during the twentieth century to one child per family.[2]

The trend toward smaller families also holds for all industrial nations. But the picture differs in low-income countries in Latin America, Asia, and, especially, Africa, where many women have few alternatives to bearing children. In such societies, four to six children is still the norm.

Parenting is not only expensive, it is a lifetime commitment. As our society has given people greater choice about family life, more U.S. adults have opted to delay childbirth or to remain childless. In 1960, almost 90 percent of women between twenty-five and twenty-nine who had ever married had at least one child; by 1998, this proportion tumbled to 70 percent (U.S. Census Bureau, 1999). About two-thirds of parents in the United States say they would like to devote more of their time to child rearing (Snell, 1990). But unless we accept a lower standard of living, economic realities demand that most parents pursue careers outside the home, even if that means giving less attention to their families.

TABLE 18–1 The Ideal Number of Children for U.S. Adults, 1998

Number of Children	Proportion of Respondents
0	1.3%
1	2.6
2	53.7
3	19.5
4	8.7
5	0.9
6 or more	1.0
As many as you want	8.4
No response	3.8

Source: *General Social Surveys, 1972–1998: Cumulative Codebook* (Chicago: National Opinion Research Center, 1999), p. 231.

Now that most parents with children under eighteen work for income, mothers and fathers have less time for parenting. Children of working parents spend most of the day at school. But after school, some 5 million children between five and fourteen (20 percent of the total) are *latchkey kids* who fend for themselves (Urban Institute, cited in Shellenbarger, 1996). Traditionalists in the "family values" debate charge that many mothers work at the expense of children, who receive too little parenting. Progressives counter that such criticism targets women for wanting the same opportunities that men have long enjoyed.

Congress took a step toward easing the conflict between family and job responsibilities by passing the Family and Medical Leave Act in 1993. This law allows up to ninety days of unpaid leave from work because of a new child or a serious family emergency. Still, most adults in this country have to juggle parental and occupational responsibilities. When mothers work, who cares for the kids? The box on page 472 provides some answers.

THE FAMILY IN LATER LIFE

Increasing life expectancy in the United States means that, barring divorce, couples are likely to remain married for a long time. By about age fifty, most have

[2]According to the U.S. Census Bureau, the median number of children per family was 0.99 in 1998 and holding steady. Among married couples with children, the medians were .89 for whites, 1.15 for African Americans, and 1.53 for Hispanics.

APPLYING SOCIOLOGY

Who's Minding the Kids?

Traditionally, the task of providing daily care for young children fell to mothers. But with a majority of mothers and fathers now in the labor force, finding quality, affordable child care is a high priority for parents.

The figure shows how U.S. children under age five receive care while their mothers work. Most often—in 33 percent of all cases—the child remains at home with the father or another relative. An additional 31 percent of children receive care in another person's home, with relatives, neighbors, or friends looking after them. A small share of children accompany their mothers to work. The remaining 29 percent of children with working mothers attend day care or preschool. The proportion in day-care centers has doubled over the last decade because many parents cannot find in-home care for their children.

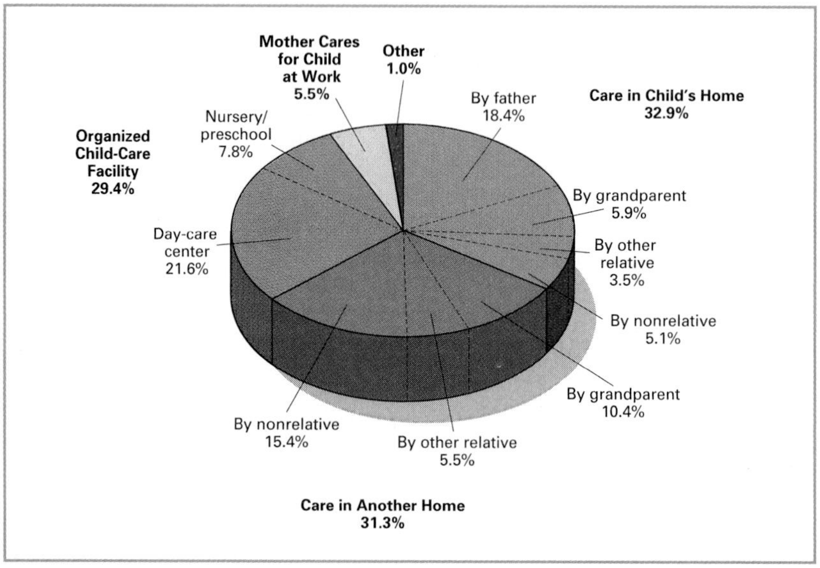

Some day-care centers are so big that they amount to "tot lots" where parents "park" their children for the day. The impersonality of such settings and the rapid turnover in staff prevent the warm and consistent nurturing that young children need in order to develop a sense of trust. Other child-care centers, however, offer a secure and healthful environment. Research suggests that *good* care centers are good for children; *bad* facilities are not.

Source: U.S. Census Bureau (1997).

completed the task of raising children. The remaining years of marriage bring a return to living with only one's spouse.

Like the birth of children, their departure (resulting in the "empty nest") requires adjustments, although a marriage often becomes closer and more satisfying at this stage. Years of living together may diminish a couple's sexual passion for each other, but mutual understanding and companionship often increase as husband and wife reach midlife.

Personal contact with children usually continues, since most older adults live only a short distance from at least one of their children. Moreover, one-third (50 million) of all adults in the United States are grandparents, many of whom help with child care and other household responsibilities. Among African Americans (who have a high rate of single parenting), many grandmothers assume a central position in family life (Cherlin & Furstenberg, 1986; Crispell, 1993; Jarrett, 1994).

The other side of the coin is that more adults in midlife now care for aging parents. The "empty nest" may not be filled by a parent coming to live in the home, but parents reaching age eighty and beyond can be more taxing than raising young children. The oldest of the "baby boomers"—now in their fifties—are called the "sandwich generation" because they (especially women) will spend as many years caring for their aging parents as they did caring for their children (Lund, 1993).

Here is another well-known painting by Carmen Lomas Garza, titled Una tarde *(*An Afternoon*). Garza is illustrating a distinctive quality of Hispanic cultures—the strong involvement of whole families in courtship, especially of a daughter. Young people get to know one another, in short, but only under the watchful eyes of the older generation.*

Carmen Lomas Garza, *Una tarde (An Afternoon)*. Gouache painting, 18 × 25 inches. © 1990 Carmen Lomas Garza. Photo credit: Judy Reed. Collection of Sophie and Daniel Share, Birminham, Michigan.

The final, and surely the most difficult, transition in married life comes with the death of a spouse. Wives typically outlive their husbands because of women's longer life expectancy and the fact that women usually marry men several years older to begin with. Wives can thus expect to spend some years as widows. The challenge of living alone following the death of a spouse is especially great for men, who usually have fewer friends than widows and may lack housekeeping skills.

U.S. FAMILIES: CLASS, RACE, AND GENDER

Dimensions of inequality—social class, ethnicity and race, and gender—are powerful forces that shape marriage and family life. This discussion addresses each factor in turn, but bear in mind that they overlap in our lives.

SOCIAL CLASS

Social class frames a family's financial security and range of opportunities. Interviewing working-class women, Lillian Rubin (1976) found that wives thought a good husband was one who held a steady job, did not drink too much, and was not violent. Rubin's middle-class informants, by contrast, never mentioned such things; these women simply *assumed* a husband would provide a safe and secure home. Their ideal husband was someone they could talk to easily, sharing feelings and experiences.

This difference reflects the fact that people with higher social standing have more schooling and hold jobs that emphasize verbal skills. In addition, middle-class couples share a wide range of activities, while working-class life is more divided along gender lines. As Rubin explains, many working-class men have traditional ideas about masculinity and self-control, and they stifle emotional expressiveness. Women, then, turn to each other as confidants.

Clearly, what women (and men) think they can hope for in marriage—and what they end up with—is linked to their social class. Much the same holds for children; boys and girls lucky enough to be born into more affluent families enjoy better mental and physical health, develop more self-confidence, and go on to greater achievement than children born to poor parents (Komarovsky, 1967; Bott, 1971; Rubin, 1976; Fitzpatrick, 1988; McLeod & Shanahan, 1993; Duncan et al., 1998).

DIVERSITY SNAPSHOT

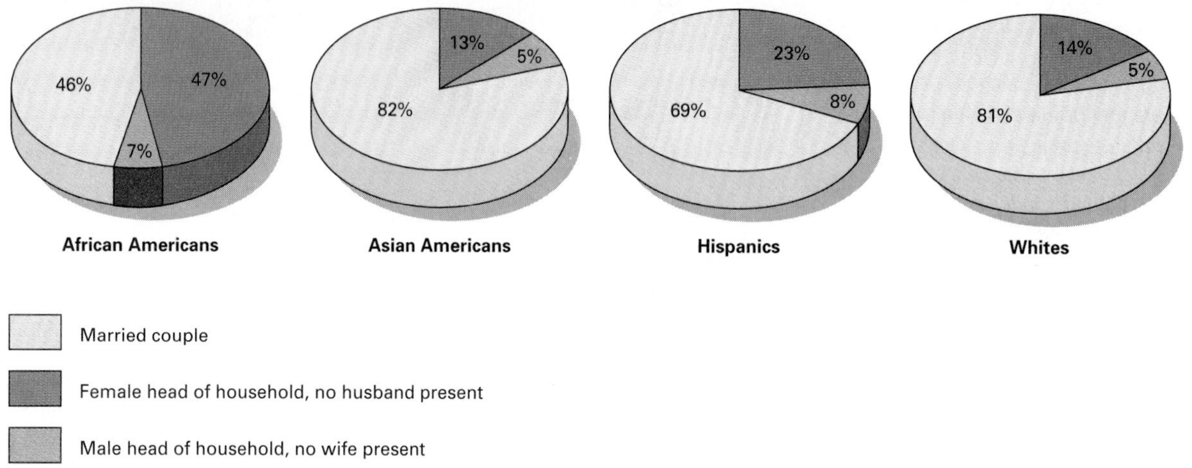

FIGURE 18–2 Family Form in the United States, 1998
Source: U.S. Census Bureau (1998).

ETHNICITY AND RACE

As Chapter 14 ("Race and Ethnicity") discusses, ethnicity and race are powerful social forces, and the effects of both ripple through family life. Keep in mind, however, that like white families, Hispanic, African American, and other categories of families are diverse and conform to no single stereotype (Allen, 1995).

Hispanic Families

Many Hispanics enjoy the loyalty and support of extended families. Traditionally, too, Hispanic parents exercise greater control over children's courtship, considering marriage an alliance of families, not just a union based on romantic love. Some Hispanic families also adhere to conventional gender roles, encouraging machismo—strength, daring, and sexual prowess—among men, while women are both honored and closely supervised.

Assimilation into the larger society, however, is changing these traditional patterns. Many Puerto Ricans who migrate to New York, for example, do not maintain the strong extended families they knew in Puerto Rico. Traditional male authority over women has also diminished, especially among affluent Hispanic families—whose number has tripled in the last twenty years (Moore & Pachon, 1985; Nielsen, 1990; O'Hare, 1990; Lach, 1999).

While some Hispanics have prospered, the overall social standing of this segment of the U.S. population remains below average. The U.S. Census Bureau (1999) reports that the typical Hispanic family had an income of $29,608 in 1998, or 62 percent of the national standard. As a result, many Hispanic families suffer the stress of unemployment and other poverty-related problems.

African American Families

African American families face economic disadvantages: As explained in earlier chapters, the typical African American family earned $30,636 in 1998, or 66 percent of the national standard. People of African ancestry are also two-and-one-half times as likely as whites to be poor, and poverty means families experience unemployment, underemployment, and in some cases, a physical environment of crime and drug abuse.

Under these circumstances, maintaining stable family ties is difficult. For example, 25 percent of African American women in their forties have never married compared to about 10 percent of white women of the same age (Bennett, Bloom, & Craig, 1989). This means that African American women—often with children—are more likely to be single heads of households. As Figure 18–2 shows, women headed 47 percent of all African American families in 1998, compared to 23 percent of Hispanic families, 13 percent of Asian or Pacific Islander families, and 14 percent of white families (U.S. Census Bureau, 1998).

Regardless of race, single-mother families are always at high risk of poverty. Slightly less than one-fourth of families headed by white women are poor, 41 percent of families headed by African American women are in poverty, and the proportion is almost half among women of Hispanic ancestry—good evidence of how class, race, and gender overlap to put women at a disadvantage. African American families with both wife and husband in the home, which represent half the total, are much stronger economically, earning 87 percent as much as comparable white families. But close to 70 percent of African American children are born to single women, and 37 percent of African American boys and girls are growing up poor, meaning that such families carry much of the burden of child poverty in the United States (Hogan & Kitagawa, 1985; U.S. Census Bureau, 1999; U.S. National Center for Health Statistics, 1999).

Mixed Marriages

Many spouses have similar social backgrounds with regard to class, race, and ethnicity. But over the course of the twentieth century, ethnicity mattered less and less. Thus, a woman of German and French ancestry might readily marry a man of Irish and English background without inviting disapproval from their families or from society in general.

Race remains a more formidable consideration, however. Before a 1967 Supreme Court decision (*Loving* v. *Virginia*), interracial marriage was illegal in sixteen states. Today, African, Asian, and Native Americans represent 18 percent of the U.S. population, so we would expect about the same share of marriages to be "mixed" if people ignored race in choosing spouses. The actual proportion of mixed marriages is 2.3 percent, showing that race still matters in social relations. But the number of racially mixed marriages is steadily rising, and most U.S. teens now claim they have dated someone of another race.

Black-white marriages are most numerous, as the large African American population (13 percent of the U.S. total) would lead us to expect. Proportionately, though, most whites involved in racially mixed marriages are likely to have partners of Asian ancestry (U.S. Census Bureau, 1999).

During her long career conducting sociological research, Jessie Bernard provided evidence that marriage is something of a surprise for women. Taught to see marriage as a solution to life's problems, Bernard explained that many women who enter traditional marriages soon face problems they did not expect. Susan Pyzow's painting, Bridal Bouquet, *illustrates the idea.*

GENDER

Regardless of race, Jessie Bernard (1982) says that every marriage is actually *two* different relationships: a woman's marriage and a man's marriage. Today, few marriages are composed of two equal partners. Patriarchy

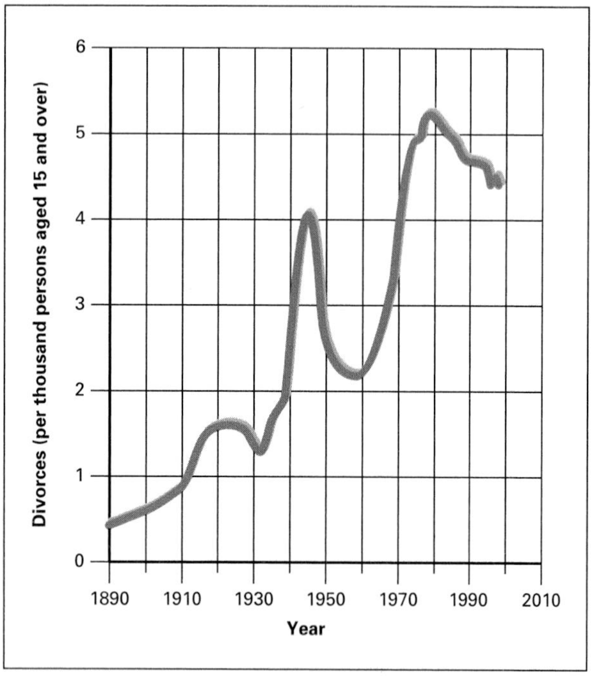

FIGURE 18–3 The Divorce Rate for the United States, 1890–1998

Source: U.S. National Center for Health Statistics (1999).

has weakened, but we still expect men to be older and taller than their wives and to have more prominent careers (McRae, 1986).

Why, then, do many people think that marriage benefits women more than men? (Bernard, 1982) The positive stereotype of the carefree bachelor contrasts sharply with the negative image of the lonely spinster, suggesting that women are fulfilled only through being wives and mothers.

But, Bernard claims, married women actually have poorer mental health, less happiness, and more passive attitudes toward life than single women. Married men, on the other hand, live longer than single men, are mentally better off, and generally report being happier than single men. These differences suggest why, after divorce, men are more eager than women to find a new partner.

Bernard concludes that there is no better guarantor of long life, health, and happiness for a man than a woman well socialized to devote her life to taking care of him and providing the security of a well-ordered home. She is quick to add that marriage *could* be healthful for women if husbands did not dominate wives and expect them to perform virtually all the housework. Indeed, research confirms that husbands and wives with the best mental health share responsibilities for earning income, raising children, and keeping the home (Ross, Mirowsky, & Huber, 1983; Mirowsky & Ross, 1984).

TRANSITIONS AND PROBLEMS IN FAMILY LIFE

Ann Landers (1984), a well-known observer of the U.S. scene, once said that one marriage in twenty is wonderful, five in twenty are good, ten in twenty are tolerable, and the remaining four are "pure hell." Families can be a source of joy, but, for some, the reality falls far short of the ideal.

DIVORCE

Our society strongly supports marriage, and about nine out of ten people at some point "tie the knot." But many of today's marriages unravel. Figure 18–3 shows the tenfold increase in the U.S. divorce rate over the last century. By 1998, more than four in ten marriages were ending in divorce (for African Americans, the rate was about six in ten). Ours is the highest divorce rate in the world: twice as high as that of Canadians, four times as high as that of the Japanese, and ten times higher than in Italy (U.S. Census Bureau, 1998).

The high U.S. divorce rate has many causes (Thornton, 1985; Waite, Haggstrom, & Kanouse, 1985; Weitzman, 1985; Gerstel, 1987; Furstenberg & Cherlin, 1991; Etzioni, 1993):

1. **Individualism is on the rise.** Today's family members spend less time together. We have become more individualistic and more concerned with personal happiness than with the well-being of families and children.
2. **Romantic love often subsides.** Because our culture bases marriage on romantic love, relationships may fail when sexual passion fades. Many people end a marriage in favor of a new relationship that renews excitement and romance.
3. **Women are now less dependent on men.** Increasing participation in the labor force has

Not all marriages thrive "'til death us do part." The United States has the highest divorce rate in the world, with more than four in ten marriages ending because one or both partners want them to. The breakdown of communication that lies at the heart of failing relationships is clearly shown by Edward Hopper in his 1932 painting Room in New York.

Edward Hopper (1882–1967), *Room in New York*, 1932. Oil on canvas. 29 × 36 in. Sheldon Memorial Art Gallery, University of Nebraska–Lincoln. F. M. Hall Collection. 1932. H–166.

reduced wives' financial dependency on husbands. As a practical matter, then, women find it easier to leave unhappy marriages, thinking they have the ability to make it on their own.

4. **Many of today's marriages are stressful.** With both partners working outside the home in most marriages, jobs leave less time and energy for family life. This makes raising children harder than ever. Children stabilize some marriages, but divorce is most common during the early years of marriage, when many couples have young children.
5. **Divorce is socially acceptable.** Divorce no longer carries the powerful stigma it did a century ago. Family and friends are now less likely to try to discourage couples in conflict from divorcing.
6. **Legally, a divorce is easier to get.** In the past, courts required divorcing couples to show that one or both were guilty of behavior such as adultery or physical abuse. Today, all states allow divorce if a couple simply thinks their marriage has failed. Surveys show that more than half of U.S. adults now think that a divorce should be harder to get (NORC, 1999:233). Concern about easy divorce has led some states to consider rewriting their marriage laws. The box on page 478 explains.

Who Divorces?

At greatest risk of divorce are young spouses—especially those who marry after only a brief courtship—with little money, who have yet to mature emotionally. The chance of divorce also rises if the couple marries after an unexpected pregnancy, or if one or both partners are plagued by substance abuse problems. People who are not religious divorce more readily than those who are.

Divorce also is more common when both partners have successful careers, perhaps due to the strains of a two-career marriage but also because financially secure people do not feel compelled to stay in an unhappy home. Finally, men and women who divorce once are more likely to divorce again, presumably because problems follow them from one marriage to another (Booth & White, 1980; Yoder & Nichols, 1980; Glenn

CRITICAL THINKING

Which Will It Be: Real Marriage or Marriage "Lite"?

"'Til death us do part," we say in the marriage vows. In reality, however, divorce is as likely as death to end today's marriages. Part of the reason is the "no-fault" divorce laws that were passed by all the states after the 1960s. Public opinion has now turned, with a slight majority of people wanting to make divorces harder to get. Even so, no state has dropped the no-fault standard. But in 1997, Louisiana began offering not a new kind of divorce but a new kind of marriage (Walker, 1998).

The law in Louisiana, as well as Arizona (twenty other states are considering it), allows couples to choose a regular marriage or a covenant marriage. A *covenant* marriage requires both parties to agree that before they ever seek a divorce, they will turn to marital counseling. They also agree that they will not divorce unless one partner commits adultery, abandons the other for at least a year, becomes a drug or alcohol abuser, assaults the partner or a child, or is sent to prison for a serious crime. What spouses who select a covenant marriage cannot do is walk away from each other simply because they no longer want to stay married (Nock, Wright, & Sanchez, 1999).

Some people defend the covenant marriage law in the belief that it will bring down the high U.S. divorce rate. Maybe, too, the law will make for better marriages: After all, if one partner balks at a covenant marriage, the other may well wonder why and reconsider the marriage.

Critics, however, claim that the new law will simply trap women and children in bad and, perhaps, abusive marriages. Then, too, the courts may end up filled with couples who are trying to escape their covenant bond. They point to early statistics showing that just a few percent of Louisiana's newlyweds are choosing covenant marriage as evidence that most people—even in marriage—want to keep their options open (Whelan, 1998).

What do you think?

1. *Do you think it is too easy for married couples to divorce?*
2. *Do you support Louisiana's covenant marriage law? Why or why not?*
3. *Should society try to keep people married who may not want to be? Why or why not?*

STATE OF LOUISIANA

DECLARATION OF INTENT
COVENANT MARRIAGE
(FOR USE BY COUPLES WHO ARE ALREADY MARRIED)

A COVENANT MARRIAGE

We do solemnly declare that marriage is a covenant between a man and a woman who agree to live together as husband and wife for so long as they both may live. We understand the nature, purpose, and responsibilities of marriage. We have read the Covenant Marriage Act, and we understand that a Covenant Marriage is for life. If we experience marital difficulties, we commit ourselves to take all reasonable efforts to preserve our marriage, including marital counseling.

With full knowledge of what this commitment means, we do hereby declare that our marriage will be bound by Louisiana law on Covenant Marriage, and we renew our promise to love, honor, and care for one another as husband and wife for the rest of our lives.

(Name of the Bride)	(Name of the Groom)
(Signature of the Bride)	(Signature of the Groom)
(Signature Date)	(Signature Date)

SEEING OURSELVES

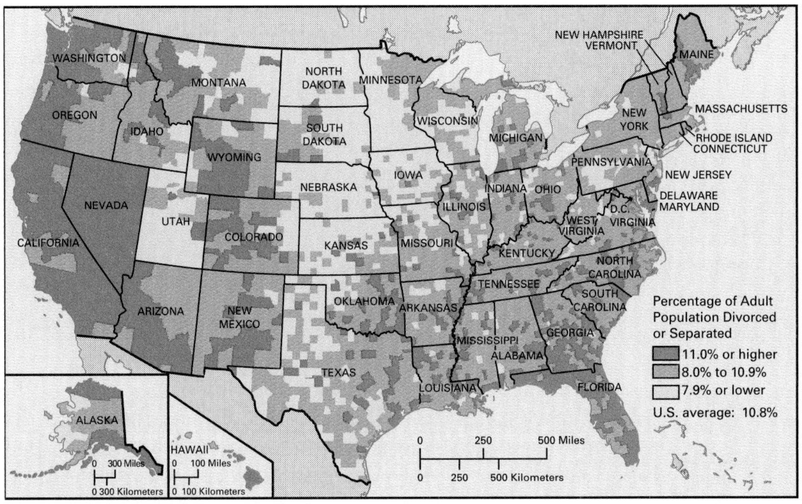

Source: *American Demographics* magazine, October 1992, p. 5. Reprinted with permission. ©1992, *American Demographics* magazine, Ithaca, New York. Data from the 1990 decennial census.

NATIONAL MAP 18–1
Divorced People across the United States

Overall, about 12 percent of the U.S. population aged fifteen and over are divorced or separated. Marriages are most vulnerable to breakup in the Pacific region of the country. Nevada has long been the U.S. divorce capital because of its exceedingly liberal divorce laws. But divorce is also pronounced where religious values are weaker and where people are more likely to move often, thus distancing themselves from a support network of family and friends. How would you characterize the West Coast with regard to these factors?

& Shelton, 1985). National Map 18–1 takes a look at where in the United States the divorced population is greatest.

Because mothers usually secure custody of children but fathers typically earn more income, the well-being of children often depends on fathers making court-ordered child-support payments. As Figure 18–4 on page 480 indicates, courts award child support in 54 percent of all divorces involving children. Yet, in any given year, nearly half the children legally entitled to support receive only partial payments or no payments at all. Because some 2.5 million "dead-beat dads" fail to support their youngsters, federal legislation now mandates that employers withhold money from the earnings of parents who fail to pay up; and in 1998, refusing to make child-support payments or moving to another state to avoid making them became a felony (Waldman, 1992; Graham & Beller, 1996).

Divorce may be hardest on children. Divorce can tear young people from familiar surroundings, entangle them in bitter feuding, and distance them from a parent they love. Most seriously of all, many children blame themselves for their parents' breakup. For many children, divorce changes the course of their entire lives, causing emotional and behavioral problems and raising the risk of dropping out of school and getting into trouble with the law. Many experts counter that divorce is better for children than their staying in a family torn by tension and violence. In any case, parents should remember that when couples think about divorce, more than their own well-being is at stake (Wallerstein & Blakeslee, 1989; Adelson, 1996; Popenoe, 1996; Cherlin, Chase-Lansdale, & McRae, 1998).

REMARRIAGE

Four out of five people who divorce remarry, most within five years. Nationwide, almost half of all marriages are now remarriages for at least one partner. Men, who derive greater benefits from wedlock, are more likely than women to remarry.

Remarriage often creates *blended families*, composed of children and some combination of biological parents and stepparents. Members of blended families thus have to define just who is part of the child's nuclear family. Adjustments are necessary: An only child, for example, may suddenly find she has two older brothers. Nevertheless, blended families offer both young and old the opportunity to relax rigid family roles.

FAMILY VIOLENCE

The ideal family is a source of pleasure and support. However, the disturbing reality of many homes is

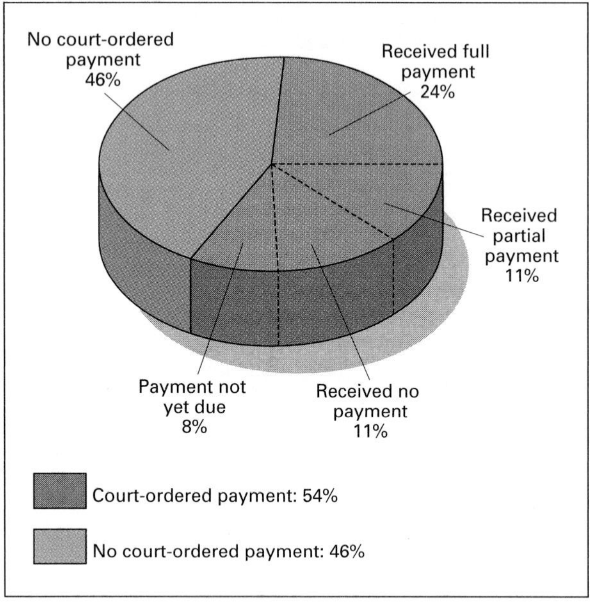

FIGURE 18–4 Payment of Child Support following Divorce

Source: U.S. Census Bureau (1995).

family violence, *emotional, physical, or sexual abuse of one family member by another.* Sociologist Richard J. Gelles calls the family "the most violent group in society with the exception of the police and the military" (quoted in Roesch, 1984:75).

Violence against Women

Family brutality often goes unreported to police, but the U.S. Bureau of Justice Statistics (1998) estimates that at least 840,000 women are victims of domestic violence each year. Twenty percent of women (but just 4 percent of men) who are victims of homicide are killed by spouses or, more often, ex-spouses. Nationwide, the death toll from family violence is 1,300 women each year. Overall, women are more likely to be injured by a family member than to be mugged or raped by a stranger or hurt in an automobile accident (Straus & Gelles, 1986; Schwartz, 1987; Shupe, Stacey, & Hazlewood, 1987; Blankenhorn, 1995).

Historically, the law defined wives as the property of their husbands, so that no man could be charged with raping his wife. Today, however, all states have enacted *marital rape laws.*

In the past, too, the law considered domestic violence a private, family matter, so victims had few options. Now, even without separation or divorce, a woman can obtain court protection from an abusive spouse. Half the states have enacted "stalking laws" that prohibit an ex-partner from following or otherwise threatening someone. Finally, communities across the United States have established shelters to provide counseling and temporary housing for women and children driven from their homes by domestic violence.

Violence against Children

Family violence also victimizes children. Roughly 2 million cases of child abuse and neglect are reported each year, with several thousand cases involving death. Child abuse entails more than physical injury; abusive adults misuse power and trust to damage a child's emotional well-being. Child abuse and neglect are most common among the youngest and most vulnerable children (Van Biema, 1994; Besharov & Laumann, 1996; U.S. National Clearinghouse on Child Abuse and Neglect, 1998).

Although 90 percent of child abusers are men, they conform to no simple stereotype. But most abusers do share one trait: having been abused themselves as children. Research shows that violent behavior in close relationships is learned; in families, then, violence begets violence (Gwartney-Gibbs, Stockard, & Bohmer, 1987; Widom, 1996; Browning & Laumann, 1997).

ALTERNATIVE FAMILY FORMS

Most families in the United States are still composed of a married couple who, at some point, raise children. But in recent decades, our society has displayed greater diversity in family life.

ONE-PARENT FAMILIES

Twenty-three percent of U.S. families with children under eighteen have only one parent in the household, a proportion that more than doubled during the last generation. Put another way, 27 percent of U.S. children now live with only one parent and about half will do so before reaching eighteen. One-parent families—76 percent of which are headed by a single mother—result from divorce, death, or an unmarried woman's decision to have a child. Figure 18–5 compares the share of U.S. births out of wedlock to that of other industrial nations.

Single parenthood increases a woman's risk of poverty because it limits her ability to work and to further her education. The converse is also true: Poverty raises the odds that a young woman will become a single mother (Trent, 1994). But single parenthood goes well beyond the poor, since at least one-third of women in the United States become pregnant as unmarried teenagers, and many decide to raise their children themselves, whether they marry or not. Looking back to Figure 18–2, note that 54 percent of African American families are headed by a single parent. Single parenting is less common among Hispanics (31 percent), Asian Americans (18 percent), and non-Hispanic whites (19 percent). In many single-parent families, mothers turn to their own mothers for support. In the United States, then, the rise in single parenting is tied to a declining role for fathers and the growing importance of grandparenting.

Research shows that growing up in a one-parent family usually disadvantages children. Some studies claim that because a father and mother each make distinctive contributions to a child's social development, it is unrealistic to expect one parent alone to do as good a job. But the most serious problem for one-parent families—especially if that parent is a woman—is poverty. On average, children growing up in a single-parent family start out poorer, get less schooling, and end up with lower incomes as adults. Such children are also more likely to be single parents themselves (Weisner & Eiduson, 1986; Wallerstein & Blakeslee, 1989; Astone & McLanahan, 1991; Li & Wojtkiewicz, 1992; Biblarz & Raftery, 1993; Popenoe, 1993a; Blankenhorn, 1995; Shapiro & Schrof, 1995; Webster, Orbuch, & House, 1995; Wu, 1996; Duncan et al., 1998).

GLOBAL SNAPSHOT

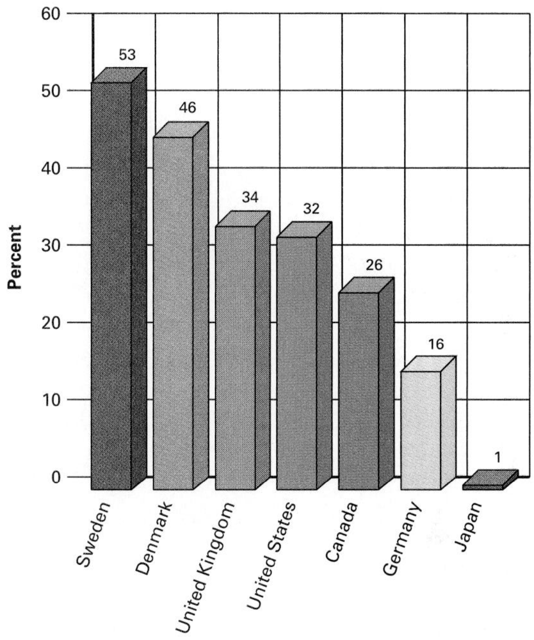

FIGURE 18–5 Percent of Births to Unmarried Women, 1995

Source: U.S. Census Bureau (1998).

COHABITATION

Cohabitation is *the sharing of a household by an unmarried couple.* The number of cohabiting couples in the United States increased from about 500,000 in 1970 to about 5.9 million today (4.2 million heterosexual couples and 1.7 homosexual couples), or 10 percent of all couples (Miller, 1997b; U.S. Census Bureau, 1999).

In global perspective, cohabitation as a long-term form of family life, with or without children, is common in Sweden and other Scandinavian nations. But it is rare in more traditional (and Roman Catholic) nations such as Italy. Cohabitation is gaining in popularity in the United States, with almost half of people between ages twenty-five and forty-four having cohabited at some point. In addition, a rising share of cohabiting couples—already more than one-third—includes children under fifteen (Blumstein & Schwartz, 1983; Macklin, 1983; Gwartney-Gibbs, 1986; Popenoe, 1988, 1991, 1992; Bumpass & Sweet, 1995; Raley, 1996).

Cohabiting tends to appeal to more independent-minded individuals as well as those who favor gender equality (Brines & Joyner, 1999). In the end, most cohabiting couples split up, with just 40 percent eventually marrying. Indeed, mounting evidence suggests that living together actually discourages marriage because partners become used to low-commitment relationships (Popenoe & Whitehead, 1999).

GAY AND LESBIAN COUPLES

In 1989, Denmark became the first country to lift its legal ban on same-sex marriages. This change extended social legitimacy to gay and lesbian couples and equalized advantages in inheritance, taxation, and joint property ownership. Norway (in 1993) and Sweden (in 1995) followed suit. In 1996, however, the U.S. Congress passed

For better or worse, the family is certainly changing. But the fact that young people still find marriage so attractive—even amid the most severe adversity—suggests that families will continue to play a central role in society for centuries to come.

a law banning gay marriage. Homosexual marriage is also illegal in all fifty states, although Hawaii and several cities (including San Francisco and New York) confer limited marital benefits on gay and lesbian couples.

Most of the 1 million U.S. gay couples with children are raising the offspring of previous, heterosexual unions; some couples have adopted children. But many gay parents are quiet about their sexual orientation, not wishing to draw unwelcome attention to their children. Moreover, in several widely publicized cases, courts have removed children from homosexual couples, citing the best interests of the children.

Gay parenting challenges many traditional ideas. But it also confirms that many gay people want to form families just as heterosexuals do (Bell, Weinberg, & Kiefer-Hammersmith, 1981; Gross, 1991; Pressley & Andrews, 1992; Henry, 1993).

SINGLEHOOD

Because nine out of ten people in the United States marry, we tend to see singlehood as a transitory stage of life. In recent decades, however, more people have deliberately chosen to live alone. In 1950, only one household in ten consisted of a single person. By 1999, this proportion had risen to one in four: a total of 25 million single adults.

Most striking is the rising number of single young women. In 1960, 28 percent of U.S. women aged twenty to twenty-four were single; by 1998, the proportion had soared to 76 percent. Underlying this trend is women's greater participation in the labor force. Women who are economically secure consider a husband a matter of choice rather than a financial necessity.

By midlife, however, many unmarried women sense a lack of available men. Because we expect a woman to "marry up," the older a woman is, the more education she has, and the better her job, the more difficulty she has finding a suitable husband (Leslie & Korman, 1989).

NEW REPRODUCTIVE TECHNOLOGY AND THE FAMILY

Recent medical advances involving *new reproductive technology* are changing families, too. A generation ago, England's Louise Brown became the world's first "test-tube baby"; since then, tens of thousands of children have been conceived this way. Within a decade, 2 or 3 percent of the children in industrial societies may be the result of new reproductive technologies.

Test-tube babies are the products of *in vitro fertilization*, whereby doctors unite a woman's egg and a man's sperm "in glass" rather than in a woman's body. When successful, the doctor implants the resulting embryo in the womb of the woman who is to bear the child, or freezes it for use at a later time.

At present, new reproductive technologies help some couples who cannot conceive normally to have children. These techniques eventually may help to reduce the incidence of birth defects, as genetic screening of sperm and eggs allows medical specialists to increase the odds of having a healthy baby. But new reproductive technology also raises fascinating and troubling questions: When one woman carries an embryo made from the egg of another, who is the mother? When a couple divorces, which spouse is entitled to use the frozen embryos? Can one partner later have a child against the will of the other? Such questions remind us that technology changes faster than our capacity to understand its uses and consequences (Thompson, 1994; Cohen, 1998; Nock, Wright, & Sanchez, 1999).

LOOKING AHEAD: THE FAMILY IN THE TWENTY-FIRST CENTURY

Family life in the United States will continue to change—and change, of course, causes controversy. In the case of the family, advocates of "traditional family values" line up against those who support greater personal choice: The final box on pages 484–85 sketches some of the issues. Sociologists cannot predict the outcome of this debate, but we can suggest five likely future trends.

First, divorce rates are likely to remain high, even in the face of evidence that marital breakups harm children. Yet, today's marriages are no less durable than they were a century ago, when many were cut short by death (Kain, 1990). The difference is that more couples now *choose* to end marriages that fail to live up to their expectations. Thus, although the divorce rate has recently stabilized, it is unlikely to return to the low rates that marked the early decades of the twentieth century.

Second, family life in the twenty-first century will be highly variable. Cohabiting couples, one-parent families, gay and lesbian families, and blended families are all on the increase. Most families are still based on marriage, and most married couples still have children. But, taken together, the variety of family forms reveals a trend toward more personal choice.

Third, men will play a limited role in child rearing. In the 1950s, a decade many people see as the "golden age" of families, men began to withdraw from active parenting (Snell, 1990; Stacey, 1990). In recent years, a small countertrend, the "stay-at-home dad," is evident, with some older, highly educated fathers of young children staying at home yet remaining active in their careers thanks to computer technology. But they represent no more than 15 percent of fathers with preschool children (Gardner, 1996). The bigger picture is that with the high U.S. divorce rate and the surge in single motherhood, more children are growing up with weak ties to fathers. At the same time, the evidence is building that the absence of fathers is harmful to children, at the very least because such families are at high risk of being poor.

Fourth, we will continue to feel the effects of economic changes in our families (Hochschild, 1989). In most homes, both household partners work, rendering marriage the interaction of weary men and women who try to squeeze in a little "quality time" for themselves and their children (Dizard & Gadlin, 1990). Two-career couples may advance the goal of gender equality, but the long-term effects on families as we have known them are likely to be mixed.

Fifth and finally, the importance of new reproductive technology will increase. Ethical concerns about whether what *can* be done *should* be done will surely slow these developments, but new forms of reproduction will continue to alter the traditional experience of parenthood.

Despite the changes and controversies that have buffeted the family in the United States, most people still report being happy as partners and parents. Marriage and family life will likely remain a foundation of our society for some time to come.

SUMMARY

1. All societies are built on kinship, although family forms vary across cultures and over time.
2. In industrial societies such as the United States, marriage is monogamous. Many preindustrial societies, however, permit polygamy, of which there are two types: polygyny and polyandry.
3. In global perspective, patrilocality is most common, while industrial societies favor neolocality and a few societies have matrilocal residence. Industrial societies use bilateral descent, while preindustrial societies are either patrilineal or matrilineal.
4. Structural-functional analysis identifies major family functions: socializing the young, regulating sexual activity, social placement, and providing material and emotional support.

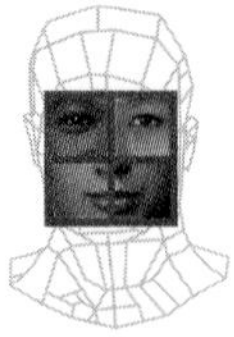

CONTROVERSY & DEBATE

Should We Save the Traditional Family?

What are "traditional families"? Are they vital to our way of life or a barrier to progress? To begin, people use the term *traditional family* to mean a married couple who, at some point in their lives, raise children. But the term is more than description; it is also a moral statement. That is, belief in the traditional family implies putting a high value on becoming and remaining married, placing children ahead of careers, and favoring two-parent families over various "alternative lifestyles."

On one side of the debate, David Popenoe warns that there has been a serious erosion of the traditional family since 1960. Then, married couples with young children accounted for almost half of all households; today, the figure is 26 percent. Singlehood is up, from 10 to 26 percent of present households. The divorce rate has doubled since 1960, so that almost half of today's marriages will end in permanent separation. Moreover, due to both divorce and having children out of wedlock, the share of youngsters who will live with a single parent before age eighteen has quadrupled since 1960, to 50 percent. In other words, just one in four of today's children will grow up with two parents and go on to maintain a stable marriage as an adult.

In light of such data, Popenoe concludes, it may not be an exaggeration to say that the family is falling apart. He sees a fundamental shift from a "culture of marriage" to a "culture of divorce." Traditional vows of marital commitment—"'til death us do part"—now amount to little more than "as long as I am happy." Daniel Yankelovich (1994:20) sums it up this way:

> The quest for greater individual choice clashed directly with the obligations and social norms that held families and communities together in earlier years. People came to feel that questions of how to live and with whom to live were a matter of individual choice not to be governed by restrictive norms. As a nation, we came to experience the bonds of marriage, family, children, job, community, and country as constraints that were no longer necessary. Commitments have loosened.

The negative consequences of the cultural trend toward weaker families, Popenoe continues, are obvious and can be found everywhere: As we pay less and less attention to children, the juvenile crime rate goes up along with a host of other troublesome behaviors like underage smoking and drinking and premarital sex.

As Popenoe sees it, then, we must work hard and act quickly to reverse current trends. Government cannot be the solution and may even be part of the problem: Since 1960, as government spending on social programs has soared fivefold, families have become weaker and weaker. Instead, says Popenoe, we

5. Social-conflict theories explore how the family perpetuates social inequality by transmitting divisions based on class, ethnicity, race, and gender.
6. Micro-level analysis highlights the variety of family life as experienced by various family members.
7. Families originate in the process of courtship. Romantic love is central to mate selection in the United States, but not in much of the world. Even in this country, moreover, romantic love usually joins people with similar social backgrounds.
8. The vast majority of married couples have children, although family size has decreased over time. The main reason for this decline is industrialization, which transforms children into economic liabilities, encourages women to gain an education and join the labor force, and reduces infant mortality.
9. Married life changes as children leave home to form families of their own. Many middle-aged couples, however, care for aging parents, and many older couples are active grandparents. The final transition in marriage begins with the death of one's spouse, usually the husband.
10. Families differ according to class position, race, and ethnicity. Hispanic families, for example, are more likely than others to maintain extended kinship ties. African American families are more

need a cultural turnaround. We must replace our "me-first" attitudes in favor of commitment to our spouse and children. Such a switch, he continues, is entirely possible: Just look at how attitudes toward smoking have changed in recent decades. We can save the traditional family in two steps: first, by publicly affirming the value of staying married and, second, endorsing the two-parent family as best for the wellbeing of children.

But Judith Stacey is unconvinced. She says "good riddance" to the traditional family and provides a counterpoint. To her, the traditional family is more problem than solution. Striking to the heart of the matter, Stacey writes (1990:269):

> The family is not here to stay. Nor should we wish it were. On the contrary, I believe that all democratic people, whatever their kinship preferences, should work to hasten its demise.

The main reason for rejecting the traditional family, Stacey explains, is that it perpetuates social inequality. Families play a key role in maintaining the class hierarchy, transferring wealth as well as "cultural capital" from one generation to another. Moreover, feminists criticize the traditional family's patriarchal form, which subjects women to their husbands' authority and saddles them with most of the responsibility for housework and child care. From a gay rights perspective, she adds, a society that values traditional families inevitably denies homosexual men and women equal participation in social life.

Stacey thus applauds the breakdown of the family as social progress. She does not consider the family a basic social institution but, rather, a political construct that elevates one category of people—affluent white males—at the expense of others, including women, homosexuals, and poor people.

Stacey also claims that the concept of "traditional family" is increasingly irrelevant in a diverse society where both men and women work for income. What our society needs, Stacey concludes, is not a return to some "golden age" of the family but political and economic change, including income parity for women, universal health care and child care, programs to reduce unemployment, and expanded sex education in the schools. Only with such programs can we support our children and ensure that people in diverse family forms receive the respect everyone deserves.

Continue the debate . . .

1. *To strengthen families, David Popenoe suggests that parents put children ahead of their own careers by limiting their joint work week to sixty hours. Do you agree? Why or why not?*
2. *Judith Stacey thinks that marriage is weaker today because women are rejecting patriarchal relationships. Do you agree? Why or why not?*
3. *Do we need to change family patterns for the well-being of our children? As you see it, what specific changes are called for?*

Sources: Popenoe (1993a), Stacey (1990, 1993), and Council on Families in America (1995).

likely than others to be headed by single women. Among all categories of people, well-to-do families enjoy the most options and greatest financial security.

11. Gender affects family dynamics since husbands dominate in most marriages. Research suggests that marriage provides more benefits to men than to women.
12. The divorce rate today is ten times what it was a century ago; at least four in ten current marriages will end in divorce. Most people who divorce—especially men—remarry, often forming blended families that include children from previous marriages.
13. Most family violence victimizes women and children and is far more common than official records indicate. Most adults who abuse family members were themselves abused as children.
14. Our society's family life is becoming more varied. One-parent families, cohabitation, gay and lesbian couples, and singlehood have proliferated in recent years. While the law does not recognize homosexual marriages, many gay men and lesbians form long-lasting relationships and, increasingly, are becoming parents.
15. Although ethically controversial, new reproductive technology is changing conventional ideas of parenthood.

KEY CONCEPTS

family (p. 462) a social institution found in all societies that unites people into cooperative groups to oversee the bearing and raising of children

kinship (p. 462) a social bond based on blood, marriage, or adoption

family unit (p. 462) a social group of two or more people, related by blood, marriage, or adoption, who usually live together

marriage (p. 462) a legally sanctioned relationship, usually involving economic cooperation as well as sexual activity and childbearing, that people expect to be enduring

extended family (consanguine family) (p. 462) a family unit that includes parents and children, as well as other kin

nuclear family (conjugal family) (p. 462) a family unit composed of one or two parents and their children

endogamy (p. 462) marriage between people of the same social category

exogamy (p. 462) marriage between people of different social categories

monogamy (p. 462) marriage uniting two partners

polygamy (p. 462) marriage that unites three or more people

polygyny (p. 462) marriage uniting one male and two or more females

polyandry (p. 463) marriage uniting one female and two or more males

patrilocality (p. 463) a residential pattern in which a married couple lives with or near the husband's family

matrilocality (p. 463) a residential pattern in which a married couple lives with or near the wife's family

neolocality (p. 463) a residential pattern in which a married couple lives apart from both sets of parents

descent (p. 463) the system by which members of a society trace kinship over generations

patrilineal descent (p. 463) a system tracing kinship through men

matrilineal descent (p. 464) a system tracing kinship through women

bilateral descent (p. 464) a system tracing kinship through both men and women

incest taboo (p. 465) a cultural norm forbidding sexual relations or marriage between certain relatives

homogamy (p. 470) marriage between people with the same social characteristics

family violence (p. 480) emotional, physical, or sexual abuse of one family member by another

cohabitation (p. 481) the sharing of a household by an unmarried couple

CRITICAL-THINKING QUESTIONS

1. Identify several changes in the family since 1960. What factors are responsible for these changes?
2. A rising number of companies are extending marital benefits (such as health insurance) to unmarried gay partners. Do you approve of this trend? Why or why not? Should companies also extend benefits to cohabiting heterosexual partners?
3. Do you think that single-parent households do as good a job as two-parent households in raising children? Why or why not?
4. On balance, are families in the United States becoming weaker or simply different? What evidence can you cite?

APPLICATIONS AND EXERCISES

1. Parents and grandparents can be a wonderful source of information about changes in marriage and the family. Spend an hour or two with married people of two different generations and ask about when they married, what their married lives have been like, and what changes in family life today stand out for them.
2. Relationships with various family members differ. With which family member—mother, father, brother, sister—do you most readily and least readily share secrets? Why? Which family member would you turn to first in a crisis? Why?
3. Organize a debate for one class period with one team arguing each side of the "family values controversy." Present arguments for and against the statement: "Resolved: The traditional family is necessary for the survival of our country's way of life."
4. Install the CD-ROM packaged in the back of this new textbook to access a variety of study, review, and applications exercises designed to help you better understand the material covered in this chapter. The CD includes an author's tip video, as well as interactive maps, video application exercises, Web links, and study questions.

SITES TO SEE

http://www.prenhall.com/macionis

Visit the interactive Web site that accompanies this text. Begin by clicking on the cover of your book. You will find a chapter-by-chapter study guide, practice tests, chat room, and many suggested Web links.

http://www.frc.org

This is the Web address for the Family Research Council, a conservative organization supporting what it calls "traditional family values." What does the council consider a "traditional family"? What values does it defend? Why? Are there family problems that it ignores?

http://www.redthreadmag.com

This site provides information about cross-cultural adoptions—specifically, the experiences of people in the United States adopting young girls from China.

http://www.parenttime.com

This site offers parenting advice on any number of topics.

http://www.ronsangels.com

In 1999, the organization named Ron's Angels posted this Web site and began offering the eggs of models for sale to people who, presumably, want to have beautiful children. Who might be interested in "designer children"? What problems do you see with such "brave new families"?

http://www.polyamorysociety.org

Survey the increasing diversity of family life at the Web site for the Polyamory Society. What do you make of the society's views of family life?

CHAPTER 19

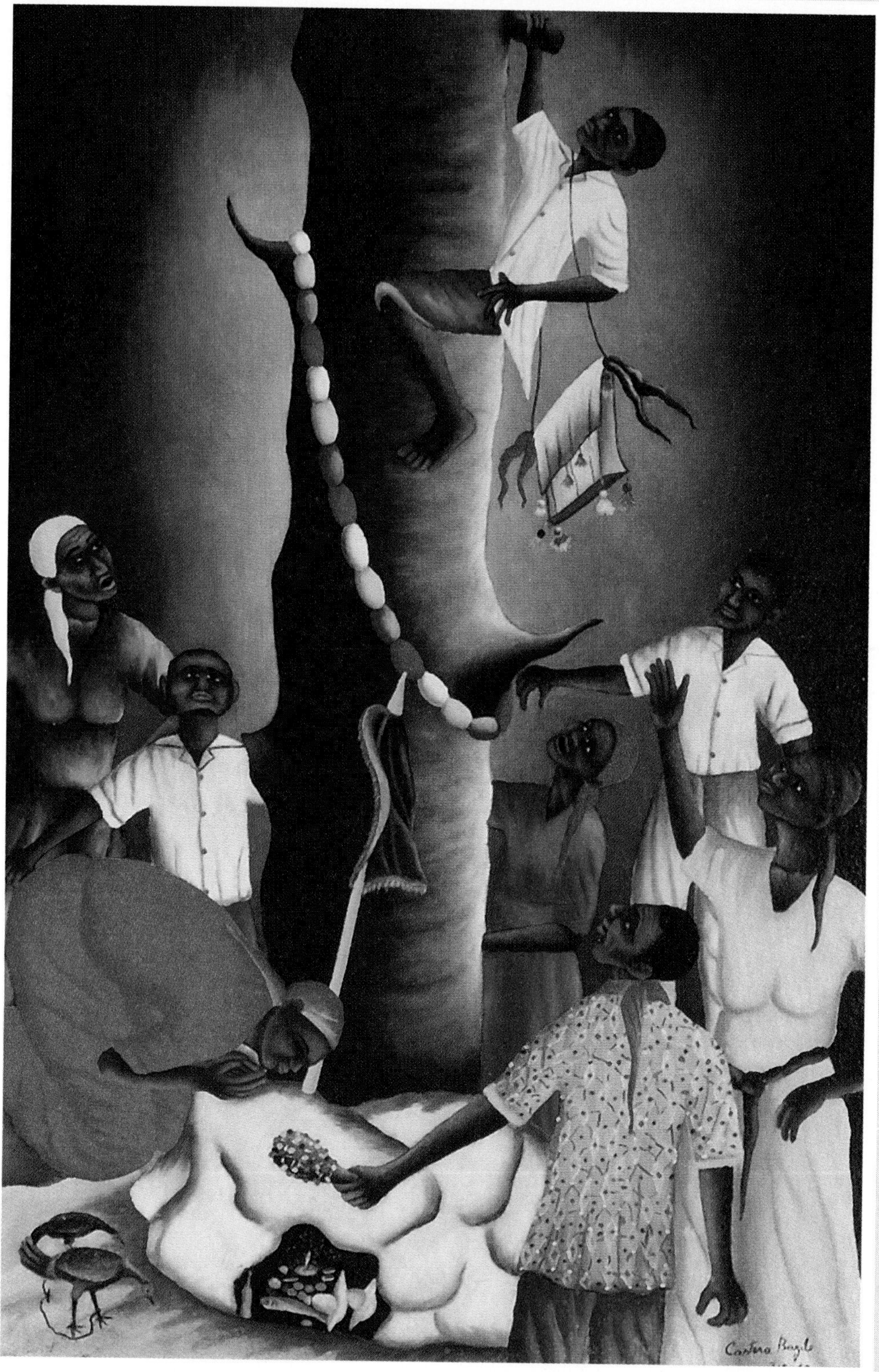

Castera Bazile (1923–1965)
Ceremonie sous mapou, 1962

Oil on masonite. Photo

RELIGION

A warm July wind blows through the open windows of the white-steepled New England church as it has this time of year for three centuries since the original Puritans settled the town of Chelmsford, Massachusetts. Many in the congregation slowly fan themselves with the worship program as they wait for the service to begin. Like Puritans of times past, these are conservative people, men and women who believe in prayer and who follow a strict code of conduct, even abstaining from alcohol. Then their voices rise together, declaring, "God is Great!" But these New Englanders are speaking Arabic: "Allah-u Akhbar!" Muslims make up an increasing share of this Yankee town, as they do in communities across the United States.

There are now between 7 million and 10 million Muslims in the United States, more, in fact, than there are Episcopalians, Presbyterians, or Jews. Indeed, Muslims in this nation now outnumber Mormons, Quakers, Unitarians, Seventh-Day Adventists, Christian Scientists, and Jehovah's Witnesses combined. As some see it, after Christianity, Islam is now this country's second religion.[1]

[1]This opening is adapted from Blank (1998:22).

The names, languages, and rituals may change, but religion has always held a central part in U.S. society. This chapter explains what religion is, explores the changing face of religious belief throughout history and around the world, and examines the vital—yet sometimes controversial—place of religion in today's modern, scientific culture.

RELIGION: BASIC CONCEPTS

The French sociologist Emile Durkheim stated that religion involves "things that surpass the limits of our knowledge" (1965:62; orig. 1915). As human beings, we define most objects, events, or experiences as **profane** (from the Latin, meaning "outside the temple"), *that which is an ordinary element of everyday life*. But we define some things as **sacred,** *that which people set apart as extraordinary, inspiring a sense of awe and reverence*. Distinguishing the sacred from the profane is the essence of all religious belief. **Religion,** then, is *a social institution involving beliefs and practices based on a conception of the sacred*.

A global perspective reveals great variety in matters of faith, with nothing sacred to everyone on earth. Although people regard most books as profane, Jews believe the Torah (the first five books of the Hebrew Bible or Old Testament) is sacred, in the same way that Christians revere the Old and New Testaments of the Bible and Muslims exalt the Qur'an (Koran).

But no matter how a community of believers draws religious lines, Durkheim (1965:62) explained, people understand profane things in terms of their everyday usefulness: We log onto the Web with our computer or turn a key to start our car. What is sacred, however, we reverently set apart from everyday life and denote as "forbidden." Marking the boundary between the sacred and the profane, for example, Muslims remove their shoes before entering a mosque, to avoid

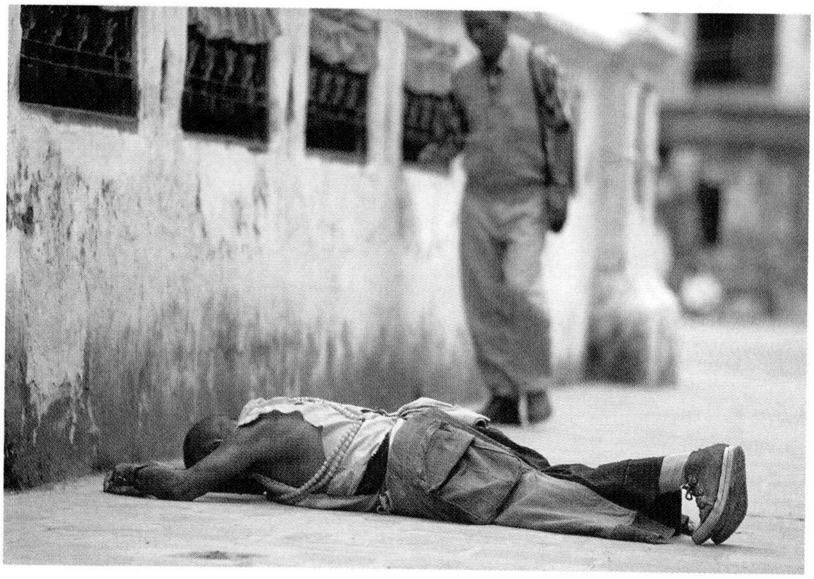

Religion is founded on the concept of the sacred: that which is set apart as extraordinary and which demands our submission. Bowing, kneeling, or prostrating oneself are all ways of symbolically surrendering to a higher power. This monk is performing an act of prostration circumambulation, a complicated way of saying that he falls flat on the ground every few steps as he moves around a holy shrine. In this way, he expresses his complete surrender to his faith.

defiling a sacred place with soles that touch the profane ground outside.

The sacred is embodied in **ritual,** *formal, ceremonial behavior.* Holy communion is the central ritual of Christianity; to the Christian faithful, the wafer and wine consumed during communion are never treated in a profane way as food but as the sacred symbols of the body and blood of Jesus Christ.

RELIGION AND SOCIOLOGY

Because religion deals with ideas that transcend everyday experience, neither sociology nor any other scientific discipline can verify or disprove religious doctrine. Religion is a matter of **faith,** *belief anchored in conviction rather than scientific evidence.* The New Testament of the Bible, for instance, describes faith as "the assurance of things hoped for, the conviction of things not seen" (Heb. 11:1) and exhorts Christians to "walk by faith, not by sight" (2 Cor. 5:7).

Some people with strong faith may be disturbed by the thought of sociologists turning a scientific eye to what they hold sacred. In truth, however, a sociological study of religion is no threat to anyone's faith. Sociologists study religion just as they study the family, to understand religious experiences around the world and how religion is tied to other social institutions. They make no judgments that a specific religion is right or wrong. Rather, scientific sociology takes a more "worldly" approach by delving into why religions take particular forms in one society or another and how religious activity affects society as a whole.

THEORETICAL ANALYSIS OF RELIGION

Sociologists have applied various theoretical paradigms to the study of religion. Each provides distinctive insights about the way religion shapes social life.

FUNCTIONS OF RELIGION: STRUCTURAL-FUNCTIONAL ANALYSIS

According to Durkheim (1965; orig. 1915), society has an existence and power of its own beyond the life of any individual. In other words, society itself is "godlike," surviving the death of its members, whose lives it shapes. Thus, people engage in religious life to celebrate the awesome power of their society.

No wonder, then, that people around the world transform certain everyday objects into sacred symbols of their collective life. Members of technologically simple societies do this with the **totem,** *an object in the natural world collectively defined as sacred.* The totem—perhaps an animal or an elaborate work of art—becomes the centerpiece of ritual, symbolizing the power of collective life over any individual. In our society, the flag

Regularly taking part in religious rituals sharpens the distinction between the sacred and the profane. The wafer used in the Christian ritual of holy communion is never thought of in the everyday sense of food; rather, it is a sacred symbol of the body of Christ.

is a quasi-sacred totem. It is not to be used in a profane manner (say, as clothing) or allowed to touch the ground.

Similarly, putting the inscription "In God We Trust" on all currency (a practice begun in the 1860s at the time of the Civil War) implies our society is bound together with common beliefs. Local communities across the United States also gain a sense of unity through totemic symbolism attached to sports teams: from the New England "Patriots," to the Ohio State University "Buckeyes," to the San Francisco "49ers."

Why is the religious dimension of social life so important? Durkheim pointed out three major functions of religion for the operation of society:

1. **Social cohesion.** Religion unites people through shared symbolism, values, and norms. Religious thought and ritual establish rules of "fair play" that make organized social life possible.
2. **Social control.** Every society uses religious ideas to promote conformity. Societies give many cultural norms—especially mores that deal with marriage and reproduction—religious justification. Religion even legitimizes the political system. Although few of today's politicians claim to rule by divine right (as they did centuries ago), many publicly ask for God's blessing, implying to audiences that their efforts are right and just.
3. **Providing meaning and purpose.** Religious belief offers the comforting sense that our brief lives serve some greater purpose. Strengthened by their faith, people are less likely to despair when one of life's calamities strikes. For this reason, we mark major life-course transitions—including birth, marriage, and death—with religious observances.

Critical evaluation. In Durkheim's structural-functional analysis, religion represents the collective life of society. The major weakness of this approach, however, is that it downplays religion's dysfunctions, especially the fact that strongly held beliefs can generate social conflict. During the early Middle Ages, for example, religious faith was the driving force behind the Crusades—the battles between European Christians and Muslims over the Holy Land, which both religions considered sacred. Conflict among Muslims, Jews, and Christians is still a source of political instability in the Middle East today. Similarly, tensions continue to divide Protestants and Catholics in Northern Ireland, and religious conflict persists in Algeria, India, Sri Lanka, and elsewhere. In short, many nations have marched to war under the banner of their God; few people would dispute that religious beliefs have provoked more violence than differences of social class.

CONSTRUCTING THE SACRED: SYMBOLIC-INTERACTION ANALYSIS

From a symbolic-interaction point of view, religion (like all of society) is socially constructed (although perhaps with divine inspiration). Through various rituals—from daily prayers to annual religious observances like Easter and Passover—individuals sharpen the distinction between the sacred and profane. Further, says Peter Berger (1967:35–36), placing our fallible, brief lives within some "cosmic frame of reference" gives us "the semblance of ultimate security and permanence."

Marriage is a good example. If two people look on marriage as merely a contract, they can end it whenever they want. But defined as holy matrimony, their bond makes far stronger claims on them. This is surely why the divorce rate is lower among people who are religious. More generally, whenever humans confront uncertainty or life-threatening situations—such as illness, war, and natural disaster—we turn to our sacred symbols.

Critical evaluation. Following the symbolic-interaction approach, religion puts everyday life under a "sacred canopy" of meaning (Berger, 1967). Of course, Berger adds, the sacred's ability to give meaning and stabilize society depends on people ignoring its constructed character. After all, how much strength could we derive from beliefs we saw as mere strategies for coping with tragedy? Then, too, this micro-level analysis ignores religion's link to social inequality, to which we now turn.

INEQUALITY AND RELIGION: SOCIAL-CONFLICT ANALYSIS

The social-conflict paradigm highlights religion's support of social hierarchy. Religion, proclaimed Karl Marx, serves ruling elites by legitimizing the status quo and diverting people's attention from social inequities.

Even today, for example, the British monarch is the formal head of the Church of England, showing the close alliance between religious and political elites. In practical terms, working for political change may mean opposing the church and, by implication, God. Religion also encourages people to look hopefully to a "better world to come," minimizing the social problems of *this* world. In a well-known statement, Marx dismissed religion as "the sigh of the oppressed creature, the sentiment of a heartless world, and the soul of soulless conditions. It is the opium of the people" (1964b:27; orig. 1848).

Religion and social inequality are also linked through gender. Virtually all the world's major religions are patriarchal, as the box explains.

For centuries, the powerful Christian nations of Western Europe justified the conquest of Africa, the Americas, and Asia by claiming that they were "converting heathens." In the United States, churches in the South viewed enslaving African Americans as consistent with God's will. Moreover, churches across the country remain segregated to this day. In the words of the African American novelist Maya Angelou, "Sunday at 11:30 A.M., America is more segregated than at any time of the week."

Critical evaluation. Social-conflict analysis reveals the power of religion to legitimize social inequality. Yet religion also promotes change toward equality. Nineteenth-century religious groups in the United States, for example, were at the forefront of the movement to abolish slavery. During the 1950s and 1960s, religious organizations led by the Reverend Martin Luther King, Jr., and others were the core of the civil rights movement. During the 1960s and 1970s, many clergy actively opposed the Vietnam War, and, as will be explained, some support revolutionary change in Latin America and elsewhere.

RELIGION AND SOCIAL CHANGE

Religion is not just the conservative force portrayed by Karl Marx. At some points in history, as Max Weber (1958; orig. 1904–5) pointed out, religion has promoted dramatic social transformation.

MAX WEBER: PROTESTANTISM AND CAPITALISM

Max Weber contended that new ideas are often engines of change. It was the religious doctrine of Calvinism, for example, that sparked the Industrial Revolution in Western Europe.

As Chapter 4 ("Society") explains in detail, John Calvin (1509–1564), a leader in the Protestant Reformation, preached the doctrine of predestination. According to Calvin, an all-powerful and all-knowing God predestined some people for salvation and condemned most to eternal damnation. Each individual's fate, sealed even before birth and known only to God, is either eternal glory or endless hellfire.

Driven by anxiety over their fate, Calvinists understandably sought evidence of God's favor and gradually came to regard prosperity as a sign of divine blessing. Religious conviction and a rigid sense of duty led Calvinists to work all the time, and many amassed great wealth. But money was not for self-indulgent spending or for sharing with the poor, whose plight they saw as a mark

SOCIAL DIVERSITY

Religion and Patriarchy: Does God Favor Males?

Why do two-thirds of U.S. adults envision God as "father" rather than "mother"? (NORC, 1999: 139) Probably because we link "godly" attributes such as wisdom and power to men. Thus, it is hardly surprising that organized religions tend to favor males, a fact evident in passages from the sacred writings of major world religions.

The Qur'an (Koran), the sacred text of Islam, declares that men are to dominate women:

> Men are in charge of women. Hence good women are obedient. As for those whose rebelliousness you fear, admonish them, banish them from your bed, and scourge them. (quoted in Kaufman, 1976:163)

Christianity, the major religion of the Western world, also supports patriarchy. While many Christians revere Mary, the mother of Jesus, the New Testament also includes the following passages:

> A man . . . is the image and glory of God; but woman is the glory of man. For man was not made from woman, but woman from man. Neither was man created for woman, but woman for man. (1 Cor. 11:7–9)

> As in all the churches of the saints, the women should keep silence in the churches. For they are not permitted to speak, but should be subordinate, as even the law says. If there is anything they desire to know, let them ask their husbands at home. For it is shameful for a woman to speak in church. (1 Cor. 14:33–35)

> Wives, be subject to your husbands, as to the Lord. For the husband is the head of the wife as Christ is the head of the church. . . . As the church is subject to Christ, so let wives also be subject in everything to their husbands. (Eph. 5:22–24)

> Let a woman learn in silence with all submissiveness. I permit no woman to teach or to have authority over men; she is to keep silent. For Adam was formed first, then Eve; and Adam was not deceived, but the woman was deceived and became a transgressor. Yet woman will be saved through bearing children, if she continues in faith and love and holiness, with modesty. (1 Tm. 2:11–15)

Judaism, too, traditionally supports patriarchy. Male Orthodox Jews say the following words in daily prayer:

> Blessed art thou, O Lord our God, King of the Universe, that I was not born a gentile.
>
> Blessed art thou, O Lord our God, King of the Universe, that I was not born a slave.
>
> Blessed art thou, O Lord our God, King of the Universe, that I was not born a woman.

Major religions have also been patriarchal by excluding women from the clergy. Even today, Islam and the Roman Catholic church ban women from the priesthood. But a growing number of Protestant denominations, including the Church of England, ordain women, who now represent 10 percent of U.S. clergy. Orthodox Judaism upholds the traditional prohibition against women serving as rabbis, but Reform and Conservative Judaism look to both men and women as spiritual leaders. Across the United States, the proportion of women in seminaries has never been higher (now roughly one-third), further evidence that change is only a matter of time (Chaves, 1996; Nesbitt, 1997).

Challenges to the patriarchal structure of organized religion—from ordaining women to gender-neutral language in hymnals and prayers—has sparked heated controversy between progressives and traditionalists. Propelling these developments is a lively feminism in many religious communities. According to feminist Christians, for example, patriarchy in the church stands in stark contrast to the largely feminine image of Jesus Christ in the Scriptures as "nonaggressive, noncompetitive, meek and humble of heart, a nurturer of the weak and a friend of the outcast" (Sandra Schneiders, quoted in Woodward, 1989:61).

Feminists argue that, unless traditional notions of gender are removed from our understanding of God, women will never be equal to men in the church. The Theologian Mary Daly puts the matter bluntly: "If God is male, then male is God" (quoted in Woodward, 1989:58).

of God's rejection. As agents of God's work on earth, Calvinists believed that they best fulfilled their "calling" by reinvesting profits and reaping ever-greater success in the process.

All the while, Calvinists lived thrifty lives and embraced technological advances, thereby laying the groundwork for the rise of industrial capitalism. In time, the religious fervor that motivated early Calvinists weakened, leaving a profane "Protestant work ethic." To Max Weber, industrial capitalism was a "disenchanted" religion. Weber's analysis clearly shows the power of religious thinking to alter the basic shape of society.

LIBERATION THEOLOGY

Christianity has a long-standing concern for poor and oppressed people, urging all to strengthen their faith in a better life to come. In recent decades, however, some church leaders and theologians have endorsed **liberation theology,** *a fusion of Christian principles with political activism, often Marxist in character.*

This social movement started in the late 1960s in Latin America's Roman Catholic church and continues today with Christian activists helping to liberate people in poor nations from abysmal poverty. The message of liberation theology is simple: Social oppression runs counter to Christian morality, so as a matter of faith and justice, Christians must promote greater social equality.

Despite its Roman Catholic beginnings, Pope John Paul II condemns liberation theology for distorting traditional church doctrine with left-wing politics. But, over the pontiff's objections, the liberation theology movement remains powerful in Latin America, where many people find their Christian faith drives them to improve conditions for the world's poor (Boff, 1984; Neuhouser, 1989).

TYPES OF RELIGIOUS ORGANIZATION

Sociologists categorize the hundreds of different religious organizations found in the United States along a continuum, with *churches* at one end and *sects* at the other. We can describe any actual religious organization, then, in relation to these two ideal types by locating it on the church-sect continuum.

CHURCH

Drawing on the ideas of his teacher Max Weber, Ernst Troeltsch (1931) defined a **church** as *a type of religious organization well integrated into the larger society.* Churchlike organizations usually persist for centuries and include generations of the same families. Churches have well-established rules and regulations and expect their leaders to be formally trained and ordained.

While concerned with the sacred, a church accepts the ways of the profane world, which gives it broad appeal. Church doctrine conceives of God in highly intellectualized terms (say, as a force for good), and favors abstract moral standards ("Do unto others as you would have them do unto you") over specific rules for day-to-day living. By teaching morality in safely abstract terms, church leaders avoid social controversy. For example, many churches that celebrate the unity of all peoples nevertheless have all-white memberships. Such duality minimizes conflict between a church and political life (Troeltsch, 1931).

December 11, 1994, Casablanca, Morocco. The waves of the Atlantic crash along the walls of Casablanca's magnificent coastline mosque, reputedly the largest in the world. From the top of the towering structure, a green laser points eastward to Mecca, the holy city of Islam, toward which the faithful bow in prayer. To pay for this monumental house of worship, King Hassam II, Morocco's head of state and religious leader, levied a tax on every citizen in his realm, all of whom are officially Muslim. This example of "government religion" contrasts sharply with our ideas about the separation of church and state.

A church may operate as an arm of the state. A **state church** is *a church formally allied with the state,* as illustrated by Islam in Morocco. State churches have existed throughout human history; for centuries Roman Catholicism was the official religion of the Roman Empire, as was Confucianism in China until early in the twentieth century. Today, the Anglican church is the official Church of England, as Islam is the official religion of Pakistan and Iran. State churches count everyone in the society as members, a practice that severely limits tolerance of religious difference.

A **denomination,** by contrast, is *a church, independent of the state, that accepts religious pluralism.* Denominations exist in nations such as ours that formally separate church and state. The United States has dozens of Christian denominations—including Catholics, Baptists, Methodists, and Lutherans—as well as various categories of Judaism, Islam, and other traditions. While members of a denomination hold to their own beliefs, they accept the right of others to disagree.

SECT

The second general religious form is the **sect,** *a type of religious organization that stands apart from the larger society.* Sect members have rigid religious convictions and deny the beliefs of others. Generally, to members of a sect, religion is not just one aspect of life, but a firm plan for how to live. In some cases, then, members of a sect may withdraw completely from society in order to practice their religion without interference. The Amish are one example of a North American sect that isolates itself (Kraybill, 1994). Since our culture holds up religious tolerance as a virtue, members of sects are sometimes accused of being narrow-minded in insisting that they alone follow the true religion.

In organizational terms, sects are less formal than churches. Thus, sect members may be highly spontaneous and emotional in worship, while members of churches tend to listen passively to their leader. Sects also reject the intellectualized religion of churches, stressing instead the personal experience of divine power. Rodney Stark (1985:314) contrasts a church's vision of a distant God—"Our Father, who art in Heaven"—with a sect's more immediate God—"Lord, bless this poor sinner kneeling before you now."

A further distinction between church and sect turns on patterns of leadership. The more churchlike an organization, the more likely that its leaders are formally trained and ordained. Sectlike organizations, which celebrate the personal presence of God, expect their leaders to exhibit divine inspiration in the form of **charisma** (from the Greek, meaning "divine favor"), *extraordinary personal qualities that can turn an audience into followers,* infusing them with an emotional experience.

Sects generally form as breakaway groups from established religious organizations (Stark & Bainbridge, 1979). Their psychic intensity and informal structure render them less stable than churches, and many sects blossom only to disappear soon after. The sects that do endure typically become more like churches, losing fervor as they become more bureaucratic and established.

To sustain their membership, many sects actively recruit, or *proselytize,* new members. Sects highly value the experience of *conversion,* a personal transformation or religious rebirth. Members of Jehovah's Witnesses, for example, eagerly share their faith with others in hopes of attracting new members.

In global perspective, the range of religious activity is truly astonishing. Members of this Southeast Asian cult show their devotion to God by suspending themselves in the air using ropes and sharp hooks that pierce their skin.

Finally, churches and sects differ in their social composition. Because they are more closely tied to the world, well-established churches tend to include people of high social standing. Sects, by contrast, attract more disadvantaged people. A sect's openness to new members and its promise of salvation and personal fulfillment appeal to people who may perceive themselves as social outsiders.

CULT

A **cult** is *a religious organization that is largely outside a society's cultural traditions.* Whereas most sects spin off from a conventional religious organization, a cult

Typically, societies with simple technology are animistic, meaning that they recognize divine power in elements of the natural world, such as the sun. This drawing found in the Painted Desert, Arizona, is evidence of the animistic beliefs of early Native Americans.

typically forms around a highly charismatic leader who offers a compelling message of a new and very different way of life. As many as 5,000 cults now exist in the United States (Marquand & Wood, 1997).

Because some cult principles or practices are unconventional, the popular view is that they are deviant or even evil. The suicides of thirty-nine members of California's Heaven's Gate cult in 1997—people who claimed that dying was a doorway to a higher existence, perhaps in the company of aliens from outer space—confirmed the negative image the public holds of most cults. In short, say some scholars, calling any religious community a "cult" amounts to dismissing its members as crazy (Richardson, 1990; Shupe, 1995; Gleick, 1997).

This view of cults is unfortunate because there is nothing intrinsically wrong with this kind of religious organization. Many long-standing religions—Christianity, Islam, and Judaism included—began as cults. Of course, not all or even most cults exist for very long. One reason is that they are even more at odds with the larger society than sects. Many cults demand that members not only accept their doctrine but embrace a radically new lifestyle. Such lifestyle changes sometimes prompt others to accuse cults of brainwashing their members, although research suggests that most people who join cults experience no psychological harm (Barker, 1981; Kilbourne, 1983).

RELIGION IN HISTORY

Religion shapes every society of the world. Like other social institutions, religion shows considerable variation both historically and cross-culturally.

RELIGION IN PREINDUSTRIAL SOCIETIES

Religion is older than written history. Archaeological evidence indicates that our human ancestors performed religious rituals some 40,000 years ago. Early hunters and gatherers embraced **animism** (from the Latin, meaning "the breath of life"), *the belief that elements of the natural world are conscious life forms that affect humanity.* Animistic people view forests, oceans, mountains, even the wind as spiritual forces. Many Native American societies are animistic, which accounts for their historical reverence for the natural environment. While hunters and gatherers might have singled out someone as a *shaman* with special religious skills, there were no full-time religious leaders.

Among pastoral and horticultural people, there arose a belief in a single divine power responsible for creating the world. Our conception of God as a "shepherd" should be no surprise, since Christianity, Judaism, and Islam had their beginnings among pastoral peoples.

In agrarian societies, religion becomes more important, with a specialized priesthood in charge of religious organizations. The centrality of religion is evident in the huge cathedrals that dominated towns in medieval Europe.

RELIGION IN INDUSTRIAL SOCIETIES

The Industrial Revolution ushered in a growing emphasis on science. More and more, people looked to physicians and scientists for the knowledge and comfort they had sought from priests. Even so, religion continues because science is powerless to address issues of ultimate meaning in human life. In other words, learning *how* the world works is a matter for scientists, but *why* we and the rest of the universe exist at all is a question for religion to answer.

WINDOW ON THE WORLD

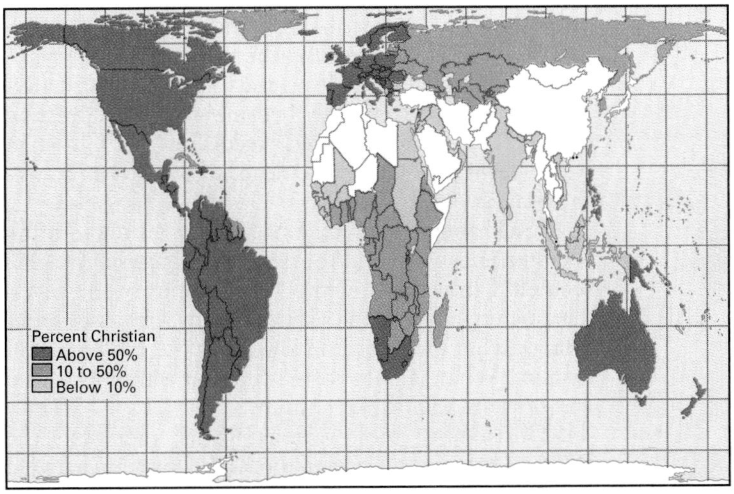

GLOBAL MAP 19–1
Christianity in Global Perspective
Source: *Peters Atlas of the World* (1990).

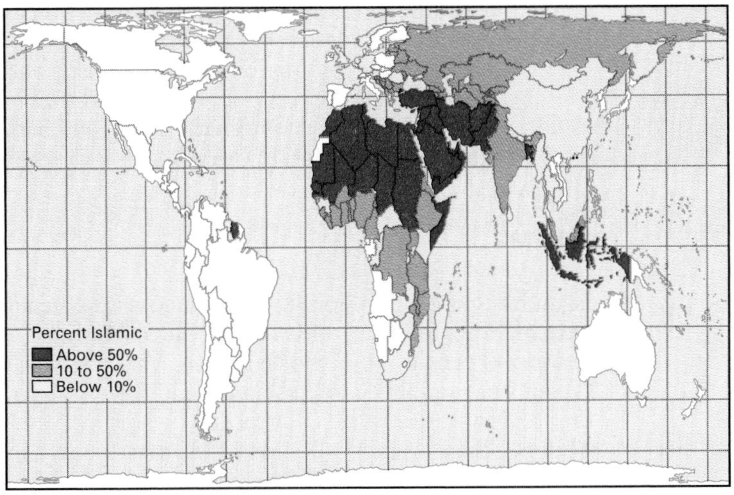

GLOBAL MAP 19–2
Islam in Global Perspective
Source: *Peters Atlas of the World* (1990).

WORLD RELIGIONS

The diversity of religious expression found around the world is almost as wide ranging as the diversity of culture itself. Many of the thousands of different religions are highly localized and have relatively few followers. Those recognized as *world religions*, by contrast, are widely known and have millions of adherents. We shall briefly describe six major world religions, which together claim 4 billion believers—representing fully three-fourths of humanity.

CHRISTIANITY

Christianity is the most widespread religion, with 2 billion followers, roughly one-third of the world's people. Most Christians live in Europe or the Americas; more than 85 percent of the people in the United States and Canada identify with Christianity. Moreover, as shown in Global Map 19–1, people who are at least nominally Christian represent a large share of the population in many other world regions, with the notable exceptions of northern Africa and Asia. European colonization spread Christianity throughout much of the world over the last 500

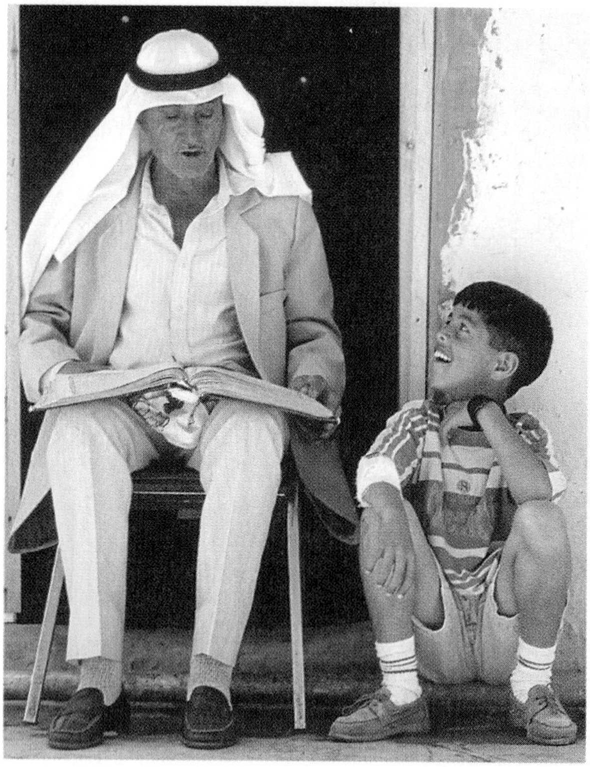

Many religions promote literacy because they demand followers study sacred texts. As part of their upbringing, most Islamic parents teach their children lessons from the Qur'an (Koran); later, the children will do the same to a new generation of believers.

years. Its dominance in the West is shown by the fact that the calendar begins with the birth of Christ.

Christianity originated as a cult, incorporating elements of its much older predecessor, Judaism. Like many cults, Christianity was propelled by the personal charisma of a leader, Jesus of Nazareth, who preached a message of personal salvation. Jesus did not directly challenge the political powers of his day, admonishing his followers to "render therefore to Caesar things that are Caesar's" (Matt. 22:21). But his message was revolutionary, nonetheless, promising that faith and love would triumph over sin and death.

Christianity is one example of **monotheism,** *belief in a single divine power*, and it thus broke with the Roman Empire's traditional **polytheism,** *belief in many gods.* Yet Christianity has a unique vision of the Supreme Being as a sacred Trinity: God the Creator; Jesus Christ, Son of God and Redeemer; and the Holy Spirit, a Christian's personal experience of God's presence.

The claim that Jesus was divine rests on accounts of his final days on earth. Tried and sentenced to death in Jerusalem on charges that he was a threat to established political leaders, Jesus was executed by crucifixion. The cross, therefore, became a sacred Christian symbol. Three days later, according to Christian belief, Jesus arose from the dead, showing that he was the Son of God.

Jesus' apostles spread Christianity throughout the Mediterranean region. At first, the Roman Empire persecuted Christians; by the fourth century, however, Christianity had become a state church—the official religion of what then became known as the Holy Roman Empire. What had begun as a cult four centuries before was now an established church.

Christianity took various forms, including the Roman Catholic church and the Orthodox church, based in Constantinople (now Istanbul, Turkey). Toward the end of the Middle Ages, the Protestant Reformation in Europe created hundreds of new denominations. Dozens of these denominations—the Baptists and Methodists are the two largest—now command sizable followings in the United States (Smart, 1969; Kaufman, 1976; Jacquet & Jones, 1991).

ISLAM

Islam has some 1.2 billion followers (about 20 percent of humanity); followers of Islam are called Muslims. A majority of people in the Middle East are Muslims, which explains our tendency to associate Islam with Arabs in that region of the world. But most Muslims live elsewhere; Global Map 19–2 shows that most people in northern Africa and the Middle East are also Muslims. Moreover, significant concentrations of Muslims are found in Western Asia in Pakistan, India, Bangladesh, Indonesia, and the southern republics of the former Soviet Union. As noted in the opening to this chapter, there are between 7 million and 10 million Muslims in North America, making Islam a significant part of religious life in the United States (Weeks, 1988; University of Akron Research Center, 1993; Blank, 1998).

Islam is the word of God as revealed to Muhammad, who was born in the city of Mecca (now in Saudi Arabia) about the year 570. To Muslims, Muhammad is a prophet, not a divine being as Jesus is to Christians. The Qur'an (Koran), sacred to Muslims, is the word of God (in Arabic, "Allah") as transmitted through Muhammad, God's messenger. In Arabic, the word *Islam* means both "submission" and "peace," and the Qur'an urges submission to Allah as the path to inner peace. Muslims express this personal devotion in a ritual of prayers at five times throughout each day.

Islam spread rapidly after the death of Muhammad, although divisions arose, as they did within Christianity. All Muslims, however, accept the Five Pillars of Islam: (1) recognizing Allah as the one, true God and Muhammad as God's messenger; (2) ritual prayer; (3) giving alms to the poor; (4) fasting during the month of Ramadan; and (5) making a pilgrimage at least once to the Sacred House of Allah in Mecca (Weeks, 1988; El-Attar, 1991). Like Christianity, Islam holds people accountable to God for their deeds on earth. Those who live obediently will be rewarded in heaven, and evil-doers will suffer unending punishment.

Muslims are also obligated to defend their faith, which has led to holy wars against unbelievers (in roughly the same way that medieval Christians fought in the Crusades). Recently, in Afghanistan, Algeria, Egypt, Iran, and elsewhere, some Muslims have sought to rid their society of Western influences that they consider morally wrong (Martin, 1982; Arjomand, 1988).

To many Westerners, Muslim women are among the most socially oppressed people on earth. Muslim women do lack many of the personal freedoms enjoyed by Muslim men, yet many—and perhaps most—accept the mandates of their religion and find security in a system that guides the behavior of both women and men (S. Peterson, 1996). We might also remember that patriarchy was well established in the Middle East long before the birth of Muhammad. Some defenders argue that Islam actually improved the social position of women by requiring that husbands deal justly with their wives. Further, although Islam permits a man to have up to four wives, it admonishes men to have only one wife if having more would cause him to treat any woman unjustly (Qur'an, "The Women," v. 3).

JUDAISM

Simply in terms of numbers, Judaism's 15 million followers worldwide makes it something less than a world religion. Moreover, only in Israel do Jews represent a national majority. But Judaism has special significance to the United States because the largest concentration of Jews (6 million people) is found in North America.

Jews look to the past as a source of guidance in the present and for the future. Judaism has deep historical roots that extend some 4,000 years before the birth of Christ to the ancient cultures of Mesopotamia. At this time, Jews were animistic, but this belief changed after Jacob—grandson of Abraham, the earliest great ancestor—led his people to Egypt.

Jews endured centuries of slavery in Egypt. In the thirteenth century B.C.E., Moses, the adopted son of an Egyptian princess, was called by God to lead the Jews from bondage. This exodus (this word's Latin and Greek roots mean "a marching out") from Egypt is commemorated by Jews today in the annual ritual of Passover. Once liberated, Jews became monotheistic, recognizing a single, all-powerful God.

A distinctive concept of Judaism is the *covenant*, a special relationship with God by which Jews became the "chosen people." The covenant also implies a duty to observe God's law, especially the Ten Commandments as revealed to Moses on Mount Sinai. Jews regard the Old Testament of the Bible as both a record of their history and a statement of the obligations of Jewish life. Of special importance are the Bible's first five books (Genesis, Exodus, Leviticus, Numbers, and Deuteronomy), designated the *Torah* (a word roughly meaning "teaching" and "law"). In contrast to Christianity's central concern with personal salvation, therefore, Judaism emphasizes moral behavior in this world.

Judaism has three main denominations. Orthodox Jews (including more than 1 million people in the United States) strictly observe traditional beliefs and practices, wear traditional dress, segregate men and women at religious services, and eat only kosher foods. Such traditional practices set off Orthodox Jews in the United States as the most sectlike. In the mid-nineteenth century, many Jews sought greater acceptance by the larger society, leading to the formation of more churchlike Reform Judaism (now including more than 1.3 million people in this country). A third segment—Conservative Judaism (with about 2 million adherents)—has since established a middle ground between the other two denominations.

Whatever their denomination, Jews share a cultural history of prejudice and discrimination. A collective memory of centuries of slavery in Egypt, conquest by Rome, and persecution in Europe has shaped Jewish identity. It was Jews in Italy who first lived in an urban ghetto (derived from the Italian word *borghetto*, meaning "settlement outside of the city walls"), and this residential segregation soon spread to other parts of Europe.

Jewish immigration to the United States began in the mid-1600s. Many early immigrants prospered, and many were also assimilated into largely Christian communities. But as larger numbers entered the country toward the end of the nineteenth century, prejudice and discrimination against them—commonly termed

WINDOW ON THE WORLD

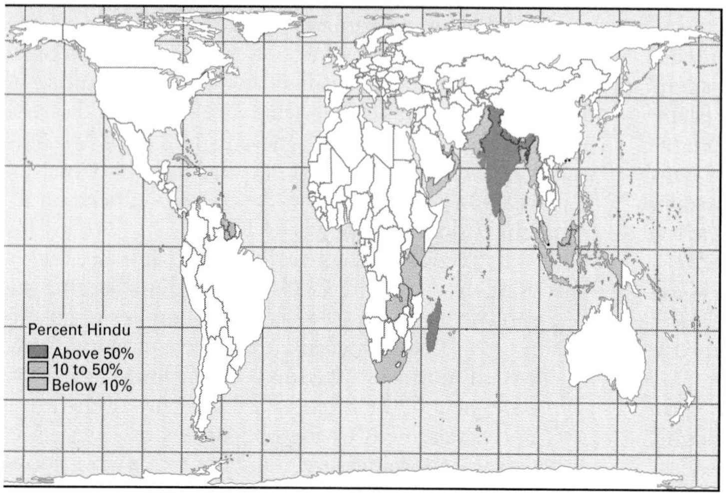

GLOBAL MAP 19–3
Hinduism in Global Perspective
Source: *Peters Atlas of the World* (1990).

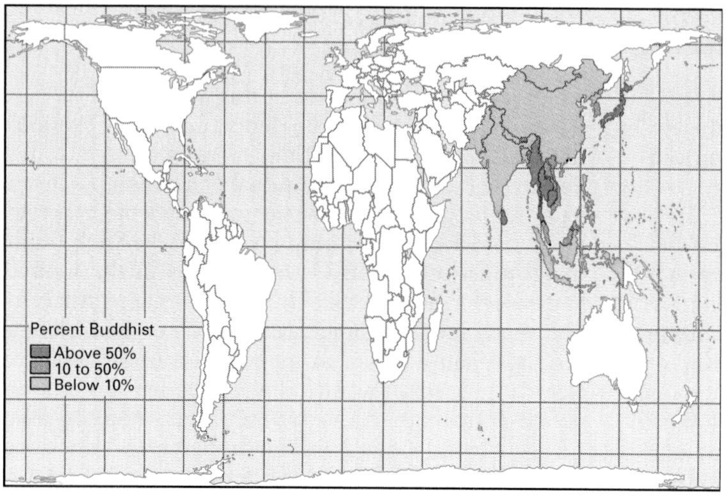

GLOBAL MAP 19–4
Buddhism in Global Perspective
Source: *Peters Atlas of the World* (1990).

anti-Semitism—increased. During World War II, anti-Semitism reached a vicious peak as the Nazi regime in Germany systematically annihilated 6 million Jews.

Today, many Jews are concerned about the future of their religion, but for a different reason: In recent years, more than half of Jews in the United States have married non-Jews. In only a few cases are non-Jewish spouses converting to Judaism. Just as significantly, about half the children raised in Jewish households are not learning Jewish culture and ritual. For the present, such patterns symbolize Jewish success in gaining acceptance into society. At the same time, however, they cast some doubt on the future of Judaism in North America (Bedell, Sandon, & Wellborn, 1975; Holm, 1977; Schmidt, 1980; Seltzer, 1980; B. Wilson, 1982; Eisen, 1983; Dershowitz, 1997; Van Biema, 1997a).

HINDUISM

Hinduism is the oldest of all the world religions, originating in the Indus River valley about 4,500 years ago. Hindus number some 800 million (14 percent of humanity). Global Map 19–3 shows that Hinduism remains an Eastern religion, mostly practiced in India and Pakistan, but with a significant presence in southern Africa and Indonesia.

Over the centuries, Hinduism and the culture of India have become intertwined, so that now one is not easily described apart from the other (although India also has a sizable Muslim population). This connection also explains why Hinduism, unlike Christianity, Islam, and Judaism, has not diffused widely to other nations. Nevertheless, with 1.4 million followers in the United States, Hinduism is a significant part of this country's cultural diversity.

Hinduism differs from most other religions by not being linked to the life of any single person. Hinduism also has no sacred writings comparable to the Bible or the Qur'an. Nor does Hinduism envision God as a specific entity. For this reason, Hinduism—like other Eastern religions, as we shall see—is sometimes described as an "ethical religion." Hindu beliefs and practices vary widely, but all Hindus recognize a moral force in the universe that presents everyone with responsibilities, termed *dharma.* Dharma, for example, calls people to observe the traditional caste system, described in Chapter 10 ("Social Stratification").

Another Hindu principle, *karma,* is a belief in the spiritual progress of the human soul. To a Hindu, all actions have spiritual consequences, and proper living contributes to moral development. Karma works through *reincarnation,* a cycle of death and rebirth, by which the individual is reborn into a spiritual state corresponding to the moral quality of a previous life. Unlike Christianity and Islam, Hinduism proclaims no ultimate judgment at the hands of a supreme god, although in the cycle of rebirth, people reap exactly what they have sown. *Moksha* is the sublime state of spiritual perfection: Only when a soul reaches this level is it no longer reborn.

Hinduism stands as evidence that not all religions can be neatly labeled monotheistic or polytheistic. Hinduism is monotheistic insofar as it envisions the universe as a single moral system; yet Hindus see this moral order at work in every element of nature. Moreover, many Hindus participate in public rituals, such as the *Kumbh Mela,* which every twelve years brings some 20 million pilgrims to the sacred Ganges River to bathe in its purifying waters. At the same time, Hindus practice private devotions, which vary from village to village across the vast nation of India.

While elements of Hindu thought have characterized some cults in the United States over the years, Hinduism is still unfamiliar to most Westerners. But, like religions better known to us, Hinduism is a powerful force offering both explanation and guidance in life (Pitt, 1955; Sen, 1961; Embree, 1972; Kaufman, 1976; Schmidt, 1980).

These South Korean Buddhists gathered in a temple beneath lotus lamps in 1996 to celebrate the 2620th anniversary of Buddha's birth. To millions in South Korea, this annual event is as important as the Christmas celebration is to millions of people in the United States.

BUDDHISM

Twenty-five hundred years ago, the rich culture of India also gave rise to Buddhism. Today some 350 million people (6 percent of humanity) are Buddhists, almost all of whom are Asians. As shown in Global Map 19–4, Buddhists make up more than half the populations of Myanmar (Burma), Thailand, Cambodia, and Japan; Buddhism is also widespread in India and the People's Republic of China. Of the world religions considered so far, Buddhism most resembles Hinduism in doctrine, but, like Christianity, its inspiration stems from the life of one individual.

Siddhartha Gautama was born to a high-caste family in Nepal about 563 B.C.E. As a young man, he

When Western people perform religious rituals they typically do so collectively and formally as members of specific congregations. Eastern people, by contrast, visit shrines individually and informally, without joining a specific congregation. For this reason, Asian temples such as this one in Hong Kong receive a steady flow of people—families praying, individuals engaged in business, and foreign tourists just watching—that seems somehow inappropriate to the Western visitor.

was preoccupied with spiritual matters. At the age of twenty-nine, he underwent a radical personal transformation, and set off for years of travel and meditation. His journey ended when he achieved what Buddhists describe as *bodhi*, or enlightenment. Understanding the essence of life, Gautama became a Buddha.

Energized by his personal charisma, followers spread Buddha's teachings—the *dhamma*—across India. In the third century B.C.E., the ruler of India became a Buddhist and sent missionaries throughout Asia, making Buddhism a world religion.

Buddhists believe that much of life involves suffering. This idea is rooted in the Buddha's own travels in a society where poverty was widespread. But the solution to suffering is not wealth, Buddha claimed; on the contrary, materialism holds back spiritual development. Instead, Buddha taught that we must transcend our selfish concerns and worldly desires through meditation, with the goal of obtaining *nirvana*, a state of spiritual enlightenment and peace.

Buddhism closely parallels Hinduism in recognizing no god of judgment; yet each daily action has spiritual consequences. Another similarity between the two religions is that they share a belief in reincarnation. Here, again, only enlightenment ends the cycle of death and rebirth and finally liberates a person from the suffering of the world (Schumann, 1974; Thomas, 1975; Van Biema, 1997b).

CONFUCIANISM

From about 200 B.C.E. until the beginning of the twentieth century, Confucianism was a state church—the official religion of China. But after the 1949 Revolution, the communist government of the new People's Republic of China vigorously repressed religion. Today, though officials provide no precise count, hundreds of millions of Chinese are still influenced by Confucianism. Almost all Confucianists live in China, although Chinese immigration has spread this religion to other nations in Southeast Asia. Perhaps 100,000 followers of Confucius live in North America.

Confucius or, more properly, K'ung Fu-tzu, lived between 551 and 479 B.C.E. Like Buddha, Confucius was deeply concerned about people's suffering. The Buddha's response was a sectlike spiritual withdrawal from the world; Confucius, by contrast, instructed his followers to engage the world according to a code of moral conduct. Thus it was that Confucianism became fused with the traditional culture of China. Here we see a second example of what might be called a "national religion": As Hinduism has remained largely synonymous with Indian culture, Confucianism is enshrined in the Chinese way of life.

A central concept of Confucianism is *jen*, meaning "humaneness." In practice, this means that we must always subordinate our self-interest to moral principle. In the family, the individual must be loyal and considerate. Likewise, families must remain mindful of their duties toward the larger community. In this way, layer upon layer of moral obligation integrates society as a whole.

Most of all, Confucianism stands out as lacking a clear sense of the sacred. Recalling Durkheim's analysis, we might view Confucianism as the celebration of the sacred character of society itself. Or we might argue that Confucianism is less a religion than a model of disciplined living. Certainly the historical dominance of Confucianism helps explain why Chinese culture is skeptical of the supernatural. But even as a disciplined way of life, Confucianism shares with religion a body of beliefs and practices that have as their goal goodness, concern for others, and social harmony (Kaufman, 1976; Schmidt, 1980; McGuire, 1987).

RELIGION: EAST AND WEST

This overview of world religions points up two general differences between the belief systems of Eastern and Western societies. First, Western religions (Christianity, Islam, Judaism) are typically deity-based, with a clear focus on God. Eastern religions (Hinduism, Buddhism, Confucianism), however, tend to be ethical codes; therefore, they make a less clear-cut distinction between what is sacred and what is profane.

Second, believers in Western religions form congregations. That is, people join an organization and worship formally in groups at a specific time and place. Eastern religious organization, by contrast, is informally fused with culture itself. For this reason, for example, a visitor finds a Japanese temple filled with tourists and worshipers alike, who come and go as they please and pay little attention to those around them.

But these two distinctions do not overshadow the common element of all religions: a conception of a higher moral force or purpose that transcends individualism and the concerns of everyday life. Although they take different paths, all religions give people a spiritual sense that their lives can serve some larger purpose.

GLOBAL SNAPSHOT

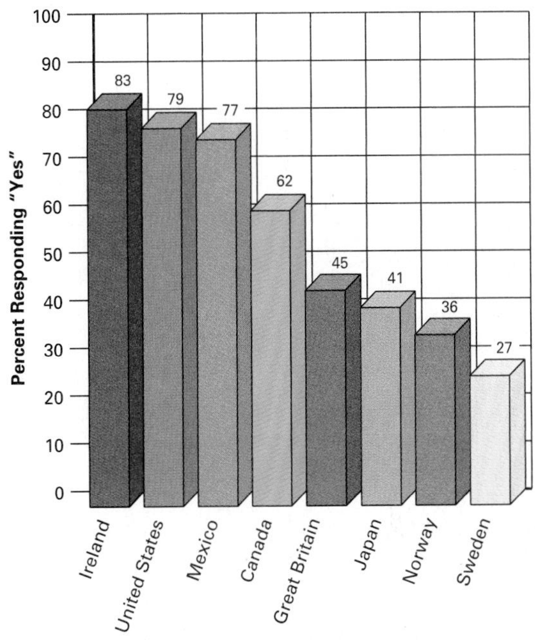

FIGURE 19–1 Religiosity in Global Perspective

Survey Question: "Do you gain comfort and strength from religion?"

Source: *World Values Survey* (1994).

RELIGION IN THE UNITED STATES

In global perspective, the United States is a relatively religious nation. As Figure 19–1 shows, eight in ten members of our society say they gain "comfort and strength from religion," a substantially higher share than in most other industrial countries.

That said, scholars debate exactly how religious this nation is. While some claim that religion remains central to our way of life, others conclude that a decline of the traditional family and the advancing role of science and technology are undermining religious commitment and faith (Collins, 1982; Greeley, 1989; Woodward, 1992a; Hadaway, Marler, & Chaves, 1993).

RELIGIOUS AFFILIATION

The vast majority of people in the United States identify with a religion. On national surveys, 86 percent of U.S. adults claim a religious preference (NORC, 1999:124). Table 19–1 on page 504 shows that more than half of U.S. adults consider themselves Protestants, one-fourth are Catholics, and 2 percent Jews. Significant numbers of people also adhere to dozens of other religions—from animism to Zen Buddhism—making our society as religiously diverse as any on earth.

About 60 percent consider themselves a member of some religious organization, and 90 percent say they

TABLE 19–1 Religious Identification in the United States, 1998

Religion	Proportion Indicating Preference
Protestant denominations	**55.7%**
Baptist	20.7
Methodist	9.1
Lutheran	6.2
Presbyterian	3.2
Episcopalian	2.2
All others or no denomination	14.3
Catholic	**25.7**
Jewish	**1.8**
Other or no answer	**2.3**
No religious preference	**14.5**

Source: *General Social Surveys, 1972–1998: Cumulative Codebook* (Chicago: National Opinion Research Center, 1999), pp. 124–25.

had at least some formal religious instruction when growing up (NORC, 1999:365–66). National Map 19–1 shows the share of people who claim to belong to any church across the United States.

National Map 19–2 takes us one more step, showing that the religion most people identify with varies by region. New England and the Southwest are predominantly Catholic, the South is overwhelmingly Baptist, and in the northern Plains states, Lutherans predominate. In and around Utah, there is a heavy concentration of members of the Church of Jesus Christ of Latter Day Saints (Mormons).

RELIGIOSITY

Religiosity is *the importance of religion in a person's life.* Identifying with a religion is only one measure of religiosity, of course, and a superficial one at that. How religious people turn out to be, therefore, depends on how we operationalize the concept.

Charles Glock (1959, 1962) suggested that we could measure five distinct dimensions of religiosity. *Experiential* religiosity refers to how emotionally tied to a religion someone is. *Ritualistic* religiosity means how often someone prays or goes to church. *Ideological* religiosity describes how much a person believes in religious doctrine. *Consequential* religiosity has to do with how strongly religious beliefs figure in one's daily behavior. Finally, *intellectual* religiosity refers to how much someone knows about the history and doctrines of a religion. Anyone is likely to be more religious on some dimensions and less on others, so that assessing religiosity is a difficult task.

When asked directly, 88 percent of U.S. adults claim to believe in a divine power of some kind, although just 60 percent claim that they "know that God exists and have no doubts about it" (NORC, 1999:367). These measures of experiential religiosity are relatively high.

Measures of ideological religiosity yield lower numbers. About 70 percent of U.S. adults report a belief in life after death. And the numbers for ritualistic religiosity drop further: Just half of adults say they pray at least once a day, and just 31 percent claim to attend religious services on a weekly or almost-weekly basis (NORC, 1999:128, 126, 133).

Clearly, the question "How religious are we?" yields no easy answers. Keep in mind, too, that many people probably claim to be more religious than they really are. For example, a team of researchers posted observers at every place of worship in Ashtabula County, Ohio, and estimated the number of people attending Sunday services; in a subsequent survey of county residents, twice as many people claimed that they attended church that Sunday than really did. The researchers concluded that no more than 20 percent of people attend church regularly (Hadaway, Marler, & Chaves, 1993). Critics charge this study may have underestimated the actual number of people attending religious services. Based on all available evidence, regular church attendance probably characterizes between 25 and 35 percent of the population (Caplow, 1998; Hout & Greeley, 1998; Woodberry, 1998).

Overall, while most people in the United States claim to be at least somewhat religious, probably no more than about one-third actually are. Moreover, religiosity varies among denominations. Members of sects are the most religious of all, followed by Catholics and then "mainstream" Protestants (Stark & Glock, 1968; Hadaway, Marler, & Chaves, 1993).

RELIGION AND SOCIAL STRATIFICATION

Sociologists who study religion have found that religious affiliation is related to other familiar social patterns. We shall consider three: social class, race, and ethnicity.

Social Class

A recent study of *Who's Who in America*, which profiles U.S. high achievers, showed that 33 percent of the people who gave a religious affiliation were Episcopalians, Presbyterians, and United Church of Christ members, denominations that together account for less than 10 percent of the population. Jews, too, enjoy high social position, with this 2 percent of people accounting for 12 percent of listings in *Who's Who.*

SEEING OURSELVES

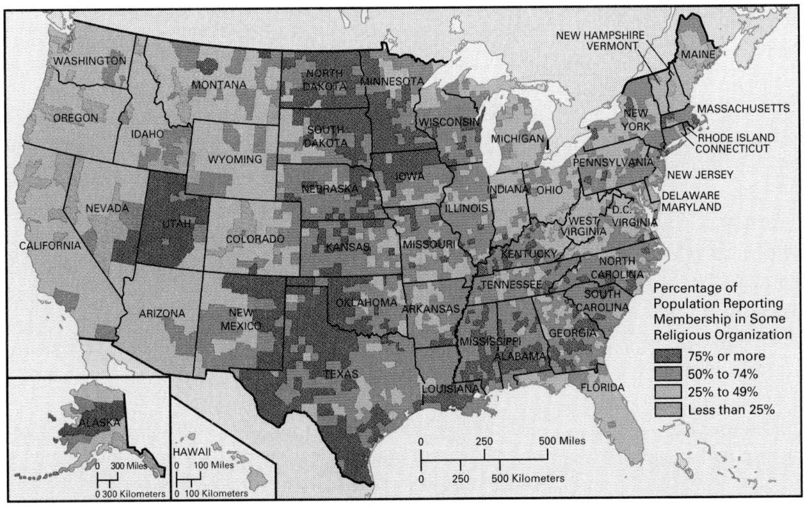

NATIONAL MAP 19–1
Membership in a Religious Organization, by County

In general, people in the United States are more religious than people in other industrial nations (with the exception of Ireland). Yet, membership in a religious organization is more common in some parts of the country than in others. What pattern do you see in the map? Can you explain the pattern?

Source: From Rodger Doyle, *Atlas of Contemporary America*. Copyright © 1994 by Rodger Doyle. Reprinted with the permission of Facts on File, Inc., New York, N.Y.

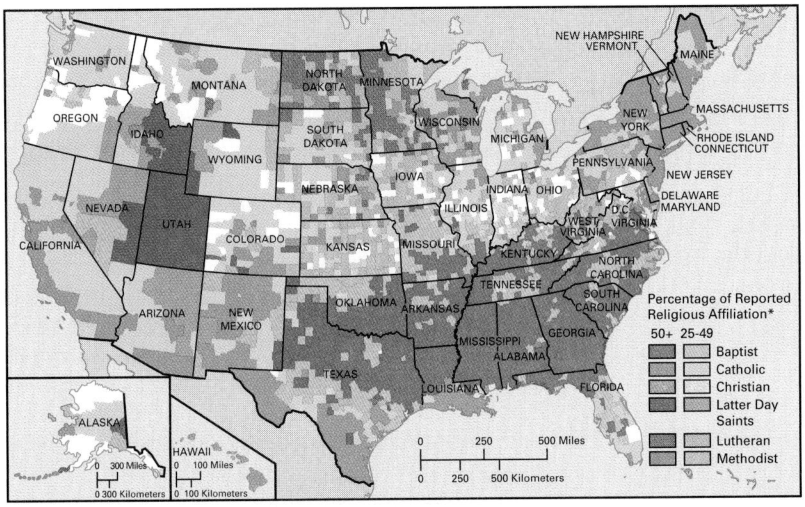

Source: The Glenmary Research Center, Atlanta, Georgia (1990).

NATIONAL MAP 19–2
Religious Diversity across the United States

In the vast majority of counties, at least 25 percent of people who report having an affiliation are members of the same religious organization. Thus, although the United States is religiously diverse at the national level, most people live in communities where one denomination predominates. What historical facts might account for this pattern?

*When two or more churches have 25 to 49 percent of the membership in a county, the largest is shown. When no church has 25 percent of the membership that county is left blank. A few exceptions include Palm Beach County in southern Florida, which is primarily Jewish, and Holmes County in central Ohio, which is largely Amish.

Research shows that other denominations—including Congregationalists, Methodists, and Catholic—have a moderate social position. Lower social standing is typical of Baptists, Lutherans, and members of sects. Within all denominations, of course, there is considerable variation (Roof, 1979; Davidson, Pyle, & Reyes, 1995; Waters, Heath, & Watson, 1995).

By and large, Protestants with high social standing are people whose families came to the United States from Northern Europe at least a century ago. They encountered little prejudice and discrimination and have had the longest time to establish themselves socially. Roman Catholics, more recent immigrants to this country, have faced greater social barriers because of their religion.

Jews command unexpectedly high social standing considering that they often contend with anti-Semitism from the Christian majority. The reason for this achievement is mostly cultural, since Jewish tradition places great value on both education and hard work. Although a large proportion of Jews began life in the United States in poverty, many, although certainly not all, improved their social position in subsequent generations.

Ethnicity and Race

Throughout the world, religion is tied to ethnicity. Many religions predominate in a single nation or geographic region. Islam predominates in the Arab societies of the Middle East; Hinduism is fused with the culture of India; Confucianism runs deep in Chinese society. Christianity and Judaism, however, do not follow this pattern. Whereas these religions are mostly Western, Christians and Jews are found all over the world.

Religion and national identity come together in the United States as well. We have, for example, *Anglo-Saxon* Protestants, *Irish* Catholics, *Russian* Jews, and people who are *Greek* Orthodox. This linking of nation and creed results from the influx of immigrants from nations with a single major religion. Still, nearly every ethnic category displays some religious diversity. People of English ancestry, for instance, may be Protestants, Roman Catholics, Jews, Hindus, Muslims, or followers of other religions.

Historically, the church has been central to the spiritual—and political—lives of African Americans. Transported to the Western Hemisphere in slave ships, most Africans became Christians—the dominant religion in the Americas—but they blended Christian belief with elements of African religions. Guided by this religious mix, Christian people of color, therefore, have developed rituals that are, by European standards, quite spontaneous and emotional (Frazier, 1965; Roberts, 1980).

When African Americans migrated from the rural South to the industrial cities of the North around 1940, the church played a major role in addressing problems of dislocation, poverty, and prejudice (cf. Pattillo-McCoy, 1998). Further, black churches have provided an important avenue of achievement for talented men and women. The Reverends Ralph Abernathy, Martin Luther King, Jr., and Jesse Jackson have all won recognition as national, and even world, leaders.

RELIGION IN A CHANGING SOCIETY

All social institutions evolve over time. Just as the economy, politics, and family have changed over the course of the past century, so has our society's religious life.

SECULARIZATION

Secularization refers to *the historical decline in the importance of the supernatural and the sacred.* For society as a whole, secularization involves a declining influence of religion in everyday life. For religious organizations, becoming more secular means less focus on otherworldly issues (such as life after death) and more on worldly affairs (such as sheltering the homeless and feeding the hungry). Secularization also means that functions once performed by the church (such as charity) are now primarily the responsibility of other, nonreligious organizations, such as the United Way and government.

With Latin roots meaning "the present age," secularization is associated with modern, technologically advanced societies in which science is the dominant mode of understanding. Today, for example, people are more likely to experience the transitions of birth, illness, and death in the presence of physicians (with scientific knowledge) than religious leaders (whose knowledge is based on faith). This shift alone suggests that religion's relevance for our everyday lives has declined. Harvey Cox elaborates:

> The world looks less and less to religious rules and rituals for its morality or its meanings. For some, religion provides a hobby, for others a mark of national or ethnic identification, for still others an aesthetic delight. For fewer and fewer does it provide an inclusive and commanding system of personal and cosmic values and explanations. (1971:3; orig. 1965)

If Cox is right, should we expect religion to disappear someday? The consensus among sociologists is "no." The vast majority of people in the United States still profess a belief in God, and as many people claim to pray each day as vote in national elections. Moreover, religious affiliation today is actually higher than it was in 1850 (Hammond, 1985; Hout & Greeley, 1987; McGuire, 1987). Secularization, then, does not signal the death of religion. More correctly, some dimensions of religiosity (such as belief in life after death) may have declined, but others (such as religious affiliation) have increased.

Our society is of two minds as to whether secularization is good or bad. Conservatives take any weakening of religion as a mark of moral decline. Progressives, however, think secularization liberates people from the all-encompassing beliefs of the past, so people can choose what to believe. Secularization has also brought the practices of many religious organizations (for example, ordaining both men and women) into line with widespread social attitudes.

In 1963, an important event in the secularization trend occurred when the U.S. Supreme Court banned prayer in school as violating the constitutional separation of church and state. In recent years, however, religion has returned to many public schools. The box takes a closer look at this controversial issue.

CRITICAL THINKING

Should Students Pray in School?

It is late afternoon on a cloudy, spring day in Minneapolis, and two dozen teenagers have come together to pray. They share warm smiles as they enter the room. As soon as everyone is seated, the prayers begin, with one voice following another. One girl prays for her brother, a boy prays for the success of an upcoming food drive, another asks God to comfort a favorite teacher who is having a hard time. Then they join their voices to pray for all the teachers at their school who are not Christians. Following the prayers, the young people sing Christian songs, discuss a Scripture lesson, and bring their meeting to a close with a group hug.

What is so unusual about this prayer meeting is that it is taking place in room 133 of Patrick Henry High School, a *public* institution. Indeed, in public schools from coast to coast, something of a religious revival is taking place as more and more students hold meetings like this one.

You would have to be at least in your mid-forties to remember when it was routine for public school students to begin the day with Bible reading and prayer. In 1963, the Supreme Court ruled that the separation of church and state is mandated by the U.S. Constitution, and any religious activity anywhere in public schools is therefore illegal. But right from the outset, critics charged that by supporting other activities and clubs while banning religious activity, schools were really being *anti*religious. In 1990, the Supreme Court handed down a new ruling, stating that religious groups can meet on school property if group membership is voluntary, meetings are held outside of regular class hours, and students rather than adults run them.

Today, student religious groups have formed in perhaps one-fourth of all public schools. Evangelical Christian organizations such as First Priority and National Network of Youth are now using the Internet as well as word of mouth to extend the place of religion in public schools across the country. Opponents of school prayer worry, however, that religious zeal may lead some students to pressure others to join their groups, which ensures that the controversy over prayer in public schools will continue.

What do you think?

1. *Do you think that religious clubs should have the same freedom to operate on school grounds as other organizations? Why or why not?*
2. *The writers of our Constitution stated in the First Amendment that Congress should not establish any official religion or pass laws that would interfere with the free practice of religion. How do you think the First Amendment applies to the issue of prayer in schools?*
3. *In 1995, President Bill Clinton said, "Nothing in the First Amendment converts our public schools into religion-free zones." Do you think schools should support spiritual education and development, be neutral to religious activity, or oppose such activity? Why?*

Sources: Based on Van Biema (1998, 1999).

CIVIL RELIGION

One dimension of secularization is the rise of what Robert Bellah (1975) calls **civil religion,** *a quasi-religious loyalty based on citizenship.* In other words, while some dimensions of religiosity are weakening, citizenship has taken on religious qualities.

Certainly, most people in the United States consider our way of life a force for moral good in the world. Many people also find religious qualities in political movements, whether liberal or conservative (Williams & Demerath, 1991).

Civil religion also involves a range of rituals, from singing the national anthem at sporting events to waving the flag at public parades. At all such events, the U.S. flag serves as a sacred symbol of our national identity, and we expect people to treat it with respect.

Civil religion is not a specific doctrine. It does, however, incorporate many elements of traditional religion into the political system of a secular society.

Fears that the world would come to an end are evident in this thousand-year-old painting in the Abbey of Saint-Sever in Gascony, France. What concerns have you noted in Western societies as we once again approached a new millennium?

Stephanus Garsia. Page with *Flood, Commentary on the Apocalypse*, by Beautus of Liebana, made for the Abbey of Saint-Sever, Gascony, France. 1028–72. Ink and tempera on vellum, 14 1/2 × 11 in. (36.5 × 28 cm). Bibliothèque Nationale, Paris, MS lat. 8878 fol. 85r.

RELIGIOUS REVIVAL

All things considered, religiosity in the United States has been stable in recent decades. But a great deal of change is going on within the world of organized religion. Membership in established, mainstream churches like the Episcopalian and Presbyterian denominations has plummeted by almost 50 percent since 1960. During the same period, affiliation with other religious organizations (including the Mormons, Seventh-Day Adventists, and especially Christian sects) has risen just as dramatically. Secularization itself may be self-limiting so that, as churchlike organizations become more worldly, many people abandon them in favor of more sectlike communities that offer a more intense religious experience (Stark & Bainbridge, 1981; Roof & McKinney, 1987; Jacquet & Jones, 1991; Warner, 1993; Iannaccone, 1994).

Religious Fundamentalism

One of the striking religious trends today is the growth of **fundamentalism,** *a conservative religious doctrine that opposes intellectualism and worldly accommodation in favor of restoring traditional, otherworldly religion.* In the United States, fundamentalism has made the greatest gains among Protestants. Southern Baptists, for example, are the largest religious community in the United States. But fundamentalism has also made gains among Roman Catholics and Jews.

In response to what they see as the growing influence of science and the erosion of the conventional family, religious fundamentalists defend what they call "traditional values." As they see it, liberal churches are simply too open to change. Religious fundamentalism is distinctive in five ways (Hunter, 1983, 1985, 1987):

1. **Fundamentalists interpret sacred texts literally.** Fundamentalists insist on a literal interpretation of the Bible and other sacred texts in order to counter what they consider excessive intellectualism among more liberal religious organizations. Fundamentalist Christians, for example, believe that God created the world precisely as described in Genesis.
2. **Fundamentalists reject religious pluralism.** Fundamentalists believe that tolerance and relativism water down personal faith. They maintain, therefore, that their religious beliefs are true and other beliefs are not.
3. **Fundamentalists pursue the personal experience of God's presence.** In contrast to the worldliness and intellectualism of other religious organizations, fundamentalism seeks a return to "good old-time religion" and spiritual revival. To fundamentalist Christians, being "born again" and having a personal relationship with Jesus Christ should be evident in a person's everyday life.
4. **Fundamentalism opposes "secular humanism."** Fundamentalists think accommodation to the changing world undermines religious conviction. *Secular humanism* is a general term that refers to our society's tendency to look to scientific experts rather than God for guidance about how to live.
5. **Many fundamentalists endorse conservative political goals.** Although fundamentalism tends to back away from worldly concerns, some fundamentalist leaders (including Ralph Reed, Pat Robertson, and Gary Bauer) have entered politics to oppose the "liberal agenda" that includes feminism and gay rights. Fundamentalists oppose abortion, gay marriages, and liberal bias in the media; they support the traditional two-parent

APPLYING SOCIOLOGY

The Cyber-Church: Logging On to Religion

The bumpy red-clay road used to be the only link between the outside world and the Monastery of Christ in the Desert. The monastery, a brown adobe structure hidden away at a remote site in northwestern New Mexico, is twenty miles from the nearest power line and maybe fifty from the closest telephone. Those who make the two-hour auto trek from Albuquerque are greeted by an ancient-looking, hand-carved wooden sign that states simply "Ring this bell."

But in the 1990s, the brothers of the monastery entered the Information Age. On the roof, a dozen solar panels supply power to a personal computer linked to a cellular phone, allowing the monks to spread their message throughout the world on the Benedictine home page.*

What does the sociological perspective tell us about high-tech religion? For one thing, this is not the first time that new technology has changed the face of religion. Six hundred years ago in medieval Europe, face-to-face talk was the way people transmitted religious ideas. Clerics gathered in the universities of the largest cities of the day, and people went to services in churches and other houses of worship across the land. Bibles and other sacred texts were few and far between; monks in monasteries took years to complete the painstaking task of copying them by hand. But religion changed when Johann Gutenberg, a German inventor (in 1999, named by the Biography channel as the most influential person of the last 1,000 years), built a movable-type press and published the first printed book—a Bible—in 1456. Within fifty years, millions of books were in print across Europe, and most of them were about religious matters. It is no coincidence that the spread of printed books was soon followed by a major religious transformation—the Protestant Reformation. An expanding market of religious ideas prompted people to rethink established principles and practices.

In the twentieth century, radio (beginning in the 1920s) and television (after 1950) extended the reach of religious leaders, who founded "media congregations" no longer confined by the walls of a single building. During the 1990s, the Internet accelerated this trend, as hundreds of thousands of Web sites offered messages from established churches, obscure cults, and "New Age" groups.

How will computer technology affect religious life? With more to learn than ever before, some analysts anticipate a new "postdenominational" age in which people's religious ideas are not bound by particular organizations as in the past. New information technology may also usher in an age of "cyber-churches." Television has already shown it can transmit the personal charisma and spiritual message of religious leaders to ever-larger audiences. Perhaps the Internet will lead to "virtual congregations," both larger in number and broader in background than any before.

*Access the monastery's home page at http://www.christdesert.org

Source: Based on Ramo (1996).

family and seek a return of prayer in schools (Hunter, 1983; Speer, 1984; Ellison & Sherkat, 1993; Green, 1993; Manza & Brooks, 1997; Thomma, 1997; Rozell, Wilcox, & Green, 1998).

Opponents regard fundamentalism as rigid and self-righteous. But many find in fundamentalism—with its greater religious certainty and emphasis on the emotional experience of God's presence—an appealing alternative to the more intellectual, tolerant, and worldly "mainstream" denominations (Marquand, 1997).

Which religions are "fundamentalist"? The term is most correctly applied to conservative Christian organizations in the evangelical tradition, including Pentecostals, Southern Baptists, Seventh-Day Adventists, and Assemblies of God. Several national social movements, including Promise Keepers for men and Chosen Women, have a fundamentalist orientation. In national

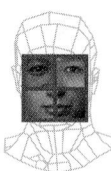

CONTROVERSY & DEBATE

Does Science Threaten Religion?

The Italian physicist and astronomer Galileo (1564–1642) helped start the scientific revolution with a series of startling discoveries. Dropping objects from the Leaning Tower of Pisa, he discovered some of the laws of gravity; fashioning his own telescope, he surveyed the heavens and found that the earth orbited the sun, not the other way around.

For his trouble, Galileo was denounced by the Roman Catholic church, which had preached for centuries that the earth stood motionless at the center of the universe. In response, Galileo only made matters worse by declaring that religious leaders and biblical doctrine had no place in the growing wave of science. Before long, he found his work banned and himself under house arrest.

From its beginnings, science has had an uneasy relationship with religion. In the twentieth century, clashes arose mainly over the issue of creation. Charles Darwin's masterwork, *On the Origin of Species*, theorizes that humanity evolved from lower forms of life over the course of a billion years. Yet the theory of evolution seems to fly in the face of the biblical account of creation found in Genesis, which states that "God created the heavens and the earth," introducing life on the third day and, on the fifth and sixth days animal life, including human beings fashioned in God's own image.

Galileo would certainly have been an eager observer of the famous "Scopes monkey trial." In 1925, the state of Tennessee put a small-town science teacher named John Thomas Scopes on trial for teaching evolution. State law forbade teaching "any theory that denies the story of the Divine Creation of man as taught in the Bible" and especially the idea that "man descended from a lower order of animals." Scopes was found guilty and fined $100. His conviction was reversed on appeal, which prevented the case reaching the U.S. Supreme Court. The Tennessee law stayed on the books until 1967. A year later, the U.S. Supreme Court (*Epperson* v. *Arkansas*) struck down all such laws as an unconstitutional case of government-supported religion.

Today—almost four centuries after Galileo was silenced—many people still

surveys, 31 percent of U.S. adults describe their religious upbringing as "fundamentalist"; 39 percent claim a "moderate" religious background; and 24 percent, a liberal background (NORC, 1999:143).

The Electronic Church

In contrast to small village congregations of years past, some religious organizations, especially fundamentalists, have become electronic churches featuring "prime-time preachers" (Hadden & Swain, 1981). Electronic religion, found only in the United States, propelled Billy Graham, Oral Roberts, Pat Robertson, Robert Schuller, and others to greater prominence than all but a few clergy in the past. About 5 percent of the national television audience (some 10 million people) regularly view religious television, while perhaps 20 percent (about 40 million) watch some religious program every week (NORC, 1999).

Recently, an increasing number of religious organizations are using computer technology to spread their message, a trend that Pope John Paul II has termed the "new evangelism." The box on page 509 offers a sociological look at finding God online.

LOOKING AHEAD: RELIGION IN THE TWENTY-FIRST CENTURY

The popularity of media ministries, the rapid growth of fundamentalism, and the endurance of mainstream churches show that religion will remain a major part of modern society. Moreover, high levels of immigration from many religious countries (in Latin America and elsewhere) will intensify and diversify the religious character of U.S. society in this new century.

The world is becoming more complex, and rapid change seems to outstrip our ability to make sense of it all. But rather than undermining religion, this process fires the religious imagination. Tensions between the spiritual realm of religion and the secular world of science and technology will surely continue; the final box takes a closer look at this dynamic relationship.

Science is unable to provide answers to the most basic questions about the purpose of our lives. Moreover, new technology that can alter, extend, and even create life confronts us with vexing moral dilemmas. Against this backdrop of uncertainty, it is little wonder that many people look to their faith for assurance and hope.

ponder the apparently conflicting claims of science and religion. A third of U.S. adults claim that the Bible is the literal word of God, and many of them reject any scientific findings that run counter to biblical scripture (NORC, 1999:149).

But a middle ground is emerging: Half of U.S. adults (and also many church leaders) say the Bible is a book of truths inspired by God without being correct in a literal, scientific sense. That is, science and religion represent two levels of understanding that respond to different questions. Both Galileo and Darwin devoted their lives to investigating *how* the natural world operates. Yet only religion can address *why* humans and the natural world exist in the first place.

This basic difference between science and religion helps explain why our nation is both the most actively scientific and devoutly religious in the world. Moreover, as one scientist recently noted, the mathematical odds that a cosmic "Big Bang" 12 billion years ago created the universe and led to the formation of life as we know it are utterly infinitesimal—smaller than the chance of winning a state lottery twenty weeks in a row. Doesn't such a scientific fact allow for an intelligent and purposeful power in our creation? Can't one be both a religious believer and a scientific investigator?

In 1992, a Vatican commission created by Pope John Paul II conceded that the church's silencing of Galileo was wrong. Today, most scientific and religious leaders agree that science and religion represent important, but different, truths. Many also believe that, in today's rush to scientific discovery, our world has never been more in need of the moral guidance afforded by religion.

Continue the debate . . .

1. *Why do you think some scientific people reject religious accounts of human creation? Why do some religious people reject scientific accounts?*
2. *Do you think the sociological study of religion challenges anyone's faith? Why or why not?*
3. *Does it surprise you that about half of U.S. adults think science is changing too much of our way of life? Do you agree or not?*

Sources: Based on Gould (1981), Huchingson (1994), and Applebome (1996).

SUMMARY

1. Religion is a major social institution based on distinguishing the sacred from the profane. Religion is a matter of faith, not scientific evidence, which people express through various rituals.
2. Sociology analyzes the consequences of religion for social life, but no scientific research can assess the truth of any religion.
3. Emile Durkheim argued that, through religion, individuals experience the power of their society. His structural-functional analysis suggests that religion promotes social cohesion and conformity and confers meaning and purpose on people's lives.
4. Using the symbolic-interaction paradigm, Peter Berger explains that people construct religious beliefs as a means of responding to life's uncertainties and disruptions.
5. Using the social-conflict paradigm, Karl Marx charged that religion promotes social inequality and the status quo. On the other hand, Max Weber's analysis of Calvinism's contribution to the rise of industrial capitalism demonstrates religion's power to promote social change.
6. Churches, which are religious organizations well integrated into their society, fall into two categories—state churches and denominations.
7. Sects, the result of religious division, are marked by charismatic leadership and suspicion of the larger society.
8. Cults are religious organizations based on new and unconventional beliefs and practices.
9. Technologically simple human societies were generally animistic, with religion incorporated into family life; in more complex societies, religion emerges as a distinct social institution.
10. Followers of six world religions—Christianity, Islam, Judaism, Hinduism, Buddhism, and Confucianism—represent three-fourths of all humanity.

11. In the United States, almost all adults claim a religious preference; 60 percent identify with a religious organization, with the largest number belonging to various Protestant denominations.
12. How religious we conclude our nation is depends on how we operationalize the concept of religiosity. The vast majority of people say they believe in God, but only about 30 percent of the U.S. population attends religious services regularly.
13. Secularization refers to the diminishing importance of the supernatural and the sacred. In the United States, while some indicators of religiosity (like membership in mainstream churches) have declined, others (such as membership in sects) are on the rise. Thus, it is doubtful that secularization will bring on the demise of religion.
14. Civil religion refers to the quasi-religious patriotism that ties people to each other and to their society.
15. Fundamentalism opposes religious accommodation to the world, favoring an otherworldly focus. Fundamentalist Christianity also advocates literal interpretation of the Bible, rejects religious diversity, and pursues the personal experience of God's presence. Some fundamentalist Christian organizations actively support conservative political goals.
16. Some of the continuing appeal of religion lies in the inability of science (including sociology) to address timeless questions about the ultimate meaning of human existence.

KEY CONCEPTS

profane (p. 489) that which people define as an ordinary element of everyday life

sacred (p. 489) that which people set apart as extraordinary, inspiring a sense of awe and reverence

religion (p. 489) a social institution involving beliefs and practices based on a conception of the sacred

ritual (p. 490) formal, ceremonial behavior

faith (p. 490) belief anchored in conviction rather than scientific evidence

totem (p. 490) an object in the natural world collectively defined as sacred

liberation theology (p. 494) a fusion of Christian principles with political activism, often Marxist in character

church (p. 494) a type of religious organization well integrated into the larger society

state church (p. 494) a church formally allied with the state

denomination (p. 494) a church, independent of the state, that accepts religious pluralism

sect (p. 495) a type of religious organization that stands apart from the larger society

charisma (p. 495) extraordinary personal qualities that can turn an audience into followers

cult (p. 495) a religious organization that is largely outside a society's cultural traditions

animism (p. 496) the belief that elements of the natural world are conscious life forms that affect humanity

monotheism (p. 498) belief in a single divine power

polytheism (p. 498) belief in many gods

religiosity (p. 504) the importance of religion in a person's life

secularization (p. 506) the historical decline in the importance of the supernatural and the sacred

civil religion (p. 507) a quasi-religious loyalty based on citizenship

fundamentalism (p. 508) a conservative religious doctrine that opposes intellectualism and worldly accommodation in favor of restoring traditional, otherworldly religion

CRITICAL-THINKING QUESTIONS

1. Explain the basic distinction between the sacred and the profane that underlies all religious belief.
2. Explain Karl Marx's argument that religion supports the status quo. Based on Max Weber's analysis of Calvinism, develop a counterargument that religion can be a major force for social change.
3. Distinguish among churches, sects, and cults. Is one type of religious organization inherently better than another? Why or why not?
4. What evidence suggests that religion is experiencing a decline in importance in the United States? In what ways does religion seem to be getting stronger?

APPLICATIONS AND EXERCISES

1. Some colleges are decidedly religious; others are passionately secular. Investigate the place of religion on your campus. Is your school affiliated with a religious organization? Was it ever? Is there a chaplain or other religious official? See if you can learn from sources on campus what share of students regularly attend any religious service.
2. Assessing people's religious commitment is very difficult. Develop five questions measuring religiosity that might be asked on a questionnaire or in an interview. Present them to several people; how well do they seem to work?
3. Is religion getting weaker? To test the secularization thesis, go the library or local newspaper office and obtain an issue of your local newspaper published fifty years ago and, if possible, one hundred years ago. Compare the attention to religious issues then and now.
4. Install the CD-ROM packaged in the back of this new textbook to access a variety of study, review, and applications exercises designed to help you better understand the material covered in this chapter. The CD includes an author's tip video, as well as interactive maps, video application exercises, Web links, and study questions.

SITES TO SEE

http://www.prenhall.com/macionis

Visit the interactive Web site that accompanies this text. Begin by clicking on the cover of your book. You will find a chapter-by-chapter study guide, practice tests, chat room, and many suggested Web links.

http://www.bwanet.org
http://www.churchworldservice.org
http://www.catholicrelief.org
http://www.jdc.org

A number of religious organizations are involved in addressing hunger and other social problems. These are the Web sites that describe the activities of Baptist World Aid, Church World Service, Catholic Relief Services, and the American Jewish Joint Distribution Committee.

http://www.parishioners.org/

Here is a site offering information on a variety of religious issues, including cults and toleration of religious differences.

http://www.trinityumc.net/youth/cool.htm

This is a Web site just for fun: Check it out!

CHAPTER 20

Jacob Lawrence
The Libraries Are Appreciated, 1943

Gouache and watercolor on paper, 14 1/4 × 21 1/4 in. Louis E. Stern Collection, Philadelphia Museum of Art, Philadelphia, PA, 63-181-40. © Philadelphia Museum of Art/CORBIS. © Jacob Lawrence. By permission of DC Moore Gallery, New York.

EDUCATION

"This is class warfare!" The cry came from the back of the town hall in Dorset, an affluent town in the Vermont countryside. About a hundred of the townspeople had gathered on a warm June evening to discuss their state's new education funding law, and many of them were irate. The well-dressed man in the back continued: "This law attacks a system that works. What the people who are behind it are saying is, 'You have no right to better schools than we have, even if you can afford them.' They want to spend *our* money to educate *their* kids!"

Stirring up the controversy is Vermont's Act 60, a new system of funding public schools that began in 1998. Before Act 60 was passed, communities taxed their own property owners to raise money in order to run the local schools. In practice, rich towns like Dorset could afford excellent schools; but hundreds of less prosperous towns could barely raise enough money to maintain any school, much less a good one. Sensing a crisis in education in the state, the Vermont Supreme Court declared that legislators had to find another means of providing for the poorer districts. The result was Act 60, which equalizes funding across the state, forcing rich towns to share their tax revenues with poorer ones. Supporters like to say that Act 60 "lets Vermonters take care of Vermonters." Opponents, however, are angry that, not only will their taxes continue to rise, but 60 or 70 cents of every tax dollar will leave their communities to educate children elsewhere (Edwards, 1998; Shlaes, 1998).

The same kind of wrangling over school funding is taking place in cities and states across the country. The reason is simple: While many public schools do a good job of teaching children, many others do not, and one reason for this pattern is striking differences in funding.

This chapter focuses on **education,** *the social institution through which society provides its members with important knowledge, including basic facts and job skills as well as cultural norms and values.* In industrial societies such as the United States, education is largely a matter of **schooling,** *formal instruction under the direction of specially trained teachers.*

EDUCATION: A GLOBAL SURVEY

From New England to Hawaii, from Alaska to Texas, people expect children to spend much of their first eighteen years of life in school. A century ago, however, only a small elite in the United States had the privilege of attending school. In poor countries, even

In the past, young children in poor countries such as India were as likely to work as to attend school. In recent decades, however, India has made great strides toward universal schooling. Still, in a nation that is largely rural, about 40 percent of Indian children receive no more than an elementary education.

today, most young people receive only a few years of formal schooling.

SCHOOLING AND ECONOMIC DEVELOPMENT

The extent of schooling in any society is closely tied to its level of economic development. Chapter 4 ("Society") explained that our hunting and gathering ancestors lived a simple life that revolved around their families without institutions such as governments, churches, or schools. For these people, "schooling" amounted to the knowledge and skills parents transmitted directly to their children (Lenski, Nolan, & Lenski, 1995).

In agrarian societies, which make up most of the world today, young people spend several years in school, but their learning is limited mainly to the practical knowledge they need to farm or perform other traditional tasks. The opportunity to study literature, art, history, and science is generally available only to the lucky few whose wealth frees them from the necessity of working. It is no surprise, then, that the word "school" has its roots in the Greek word for "leisure." In ancient Greece, the students of renowned teachers such as Socrates, Plato, and Aristotle were almost all aristocratic young men. The same was true in ancient China, where the famous philosopher K'ung Fu-tzu (Confucius), for example, shared his wisdom with only a select few. And, when the Roman Catholic church founded the first colleges and universities in Europe during the Middle Ages, those institutions admitted only males from privileged families.

Today, schooling in low-income nations is diverse because it reflects the local culture. In Iran, for example, schooling is closely tied to Islam. Similarly, schooling in Bangladesh (Asia), Zimbabwe (Africa), and Nicaragua (Latin America) has been molded by distinctive cultural traditions.

But all low-income countries have one trait in common when it comes to schooling—there is not very much of it. In the world's poorest nations (including several in Central Africa), only half of all elementary-aged children are able to attend school; in the world as a whole, just half of all children reach the secondary grades (Najafizadeh & Mennerick, 1992). As a result, one-fifth of Latin Americans, almost half of Asians, and nearly two-thirds of Africans are illiterate. Global Map 20–1 shows the extent of illiteracy found around the world.

Industrial, high-income societies endorse the idea that everyone should go to school. For one thing, most industrial workers need at least basic reading, writing, and arithmetic skills to perform their jobs. For many industrial nations, literacy is also a necessary condition of political democracy.

The following comparisons of education in India, Japan, Great Britain, and the United States show how schooling is linked to economic development. Notice, too, how even industrial nations differ in their approach to educating their populations.

WINDOW ON THE WORLD

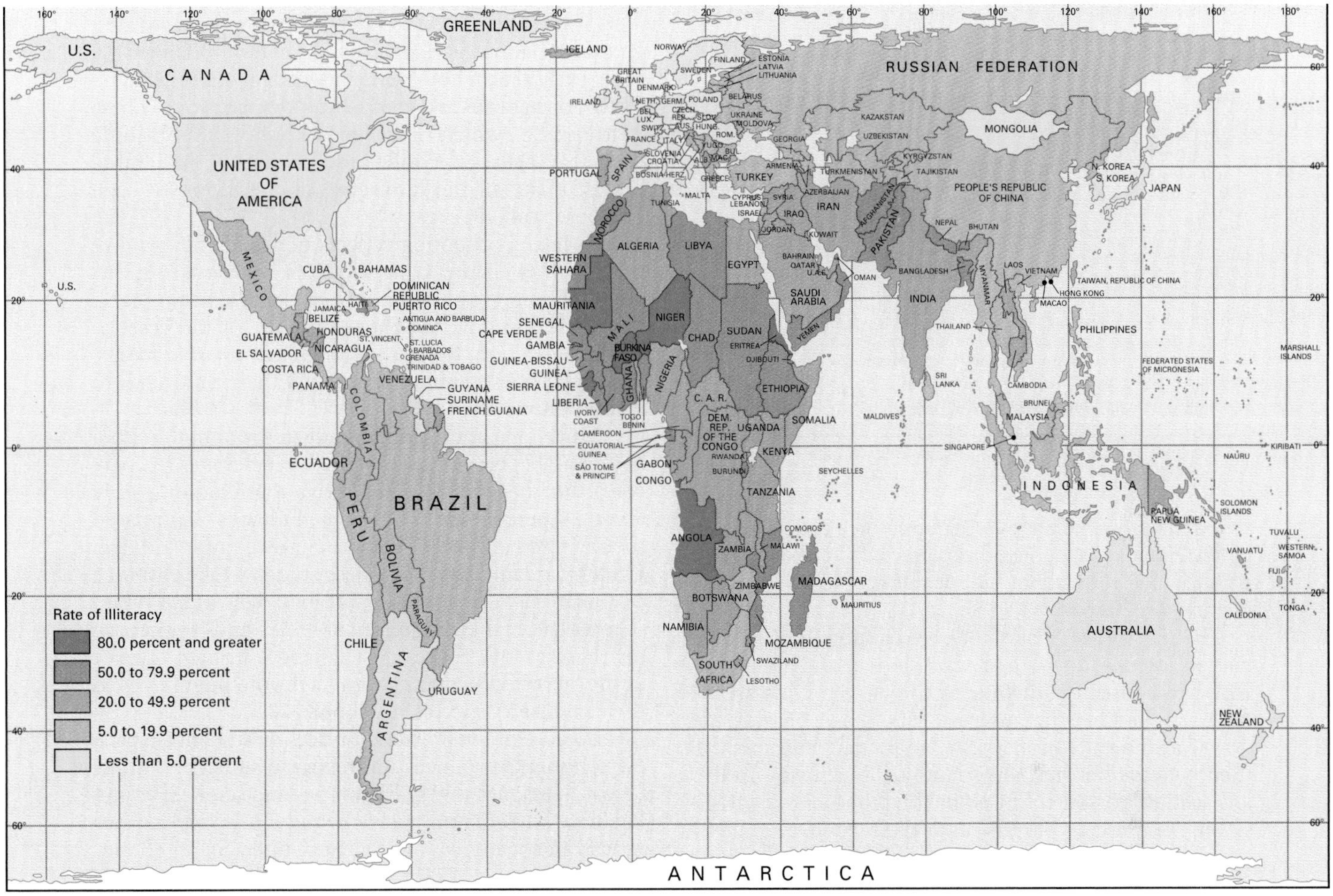

GLOBAL MAP 20–1 Illiteracy in Global Perspective

Reading and writing skills are widespread in every industrial society, with illiteracy rates generally below 5 percent. Throughout Latin America, however, illiteracy is more commonplace—one consequence of limited economic development. In about three dozen nations—many of them in Africa—illiteracy is the rule rather than the exception; there, people rely on "the oral tradition" of face-to-face communication rather than the written word.

Sources: The World Bank (1997); map projection from *Peters Atlas of the World* (1990).

SCHOOLING IN INDIA

India is a poor country. People earn about 5 percent of the income standard in the United States, and poor families often depend on the earnings of children. Thus, even though India has outlawed child labor, many Indian children work in factories—weaving rugs or making handicrafts—up to sixty hours per week, which greatly limits their opportunity for schooling.

In recent decades, schooling in India has increased. Most children now receive some primary education, typically in crowded schoolrooms where one teacher attends to perhaps sixty children (more than twice as many as in the average U.S. classroom). This is all the

TABLE 20–1 Educational Achievement in the United States, 1910–1998*			
Year	High School Graduates	College Graduates	Median Years of Schooling
1910	13.5%	2.7%	8.1
1920	16.4	3.3	8.2
1930	19.1	3.9	8.4
1940	24.1	4.6	8.6
1950	33.4	6.0	9.3
1960	41.1	7.7	10.5
1970	55.2	11.0	12.2
1980	68.7	17.0	12.5
1990	77.6	21.3	12.4
1998	82.8	24.5	12.7

*For persons twenty-five years of age and over. Percentage for high school graduates includes those who go on to college. Percentage of high school dropouts can be calculated by subtracting percentage of high school graduates from 100 percent.

Source: U.S. Census Bureau (1999).

schooling most Indians ever acquire, since less than half enter secondary school and very few go to college. The result is that only about half of the people in this vast country are literate.

Patriarchy also shapes Indian education. Indian parents are joyful at the birth of a boy, since he and his future wife will contribute income to the family. Girls are a financial liability because parents must provide a dowry at the time of marriage, and a daughter's work then benefits her husband's family. Thus, many Indians see less reason to invest in the schooling of girls, so only 30 percent of girls reach the secondary grades compared to 45 percent of boys. The flip side of this pattern is that a large majority of the children working in Indian factories are girls—a family's way of benefiting from their daughters while they can (United Nations Development Programme, 1995).

SCHOOLING IN JAPAN

<u>September 30, 1994, Kobe, Japan.</u> Compared to people in the United States, the Japanese are, above all, orderly. Young boys and girls on their way to school stand out with their uniforms, an armload of books, and a look of seriousness and purpose.

Schooling has not always been part of the Japanese way of life. Before industrialization brought mandatory education in 1872, only a privileged few attended school. Today, Japan's educational system is widely praised for producing some of the world's highest achievers.

The early grades concentrate on transmitting Japanese traditions, especially obligation to family. By their early teens, however, students encounter Japan's system of rigorous and competitive examinations. These written tests, which resemble the Scholastic Aptitude Tests (SATs) used for college admissions in the United States, make all the difference in the future of each Japanese student.

In Japan, schooling reflects personal ability more than it does in the United States, where family income plays a greater part in a student's college plans. The Japanese government pays much of the costs of higher education. But without high examination scores, even the richest families cannot get their children into a good university.

More men and women graduate from high school in Japan (90 percent) than in the United States (83 percent). But because of competitive examinations, only about 44 percent of high school graduates—compared to 67 percent in the United States—enter college. Understandably, then, Japanese students take entrance examinations very seriously, and about half attend "cram schools" after their regular school day ends to prepare for these exams. Since most Japanese women are not in the labor force, many mothers devote themselves to their children's success in school.

Because of the pressure it places on students, Japanese schooling produces impressive results. In a number of fields, notably mathematics and science, young Japanese students outperform students in every other industrial society, including the United States (Benedict, 1974, orig. 1946; Hayneman & Loxley, 1983; Rohlen, 1983; Brinton, 1988; Simons, 1989).

SCHOOLING IN GREAT BRITAIN

During the Middle Ages, schooling was a privilege of the British nobility, who studied classical subjects since they had little interest in the practical skills related to earning a living. But as the Industrial Revolution created a need for an educated labor force, and as working-class people demanded access to schools, a rising share of the population entered the classroom. British law now requires every British child to attend school until age sixteen.

Traditional social distinctions, however, persist in British education. Most wealthy families send their children to what the British call *public schools*, the equivalent of U.S. private boarding schools. These elite schools, which enroll about 7 percent of British students, teach not only academic subjects but also convey to children from wealthy (especially newly rich) families the distinctive patterns of speech, mannerisms, and social graces of the British upper class. These academies are far too expensive for most students, however, who attend state-supported day schools (Ambler & Neathery, 1999).

Since 1960, the British have lessened the influence of social background on schooling by expanding their university system and using competitive entrance examinations. For those who score the highest, the government pays most of college costs. But these exams are less important than those in Japan, since many well-to-do children who do not score well still manage to attend Oxford or Cambridge, the most prestigious British universities on a par with Yale, Harvard, and Princeton in the United States. "Oxbridge" graduates go on to take their place at the center of the British power elite: More than two-thirds of the top members of the British government, for example, have "Oxbridge" degrees (Sampson, 1982; Gamble, Ludlam, & Baker, 1993).

These brief sketches of schooling in India, Japan, and Great Britain show the crucial importance of economic development. In poor countries, many children, especially girls, work rather than go to school. Rich nations adopt mandatory education laws to create an industrial work force as well as to satisfy demands for greater equality. But rich nations vary among themselves, as we see in the intense competition of Japanese schools, the traditional social stratification that shapes schools in Great Britain, and the practical emphasis found in the schools of the United States.

SCHOOLING IN THE UNITED STATES

The United States was among the first countries to set a goal of mass education. By 1850, about half the young people between the ages of five and nineteen were enrolled in school. In 1918, the last of the states passed a *mandatory education law* requiring children to attend school until the age of sixteen or completion of the eighth grade. Table 20–1 shows that a milestone was reached in the mid-1960s, when, for the first time, a majority of U.S. adults had high school diplomas. Today, more than four out of five have a high school education, and almost one in four have a four-year college degree.

The educational system in the United States has been shaped by both our affluence and democratic principles. Thomas Jefferson thought the new nation could become democratic only if people "read and understand what is going on in the world" (quoted in Honeywell, 1931:13). As Figure 20–1 shows, the United States has an outstanding record of higher education for its people: It leads all other nations in the share of the adult population holding a university degree (U.S. Census Bureau, 1999).

Schooling in the United States also tries to promote *equal opportunity*. National surveys show that most people think schooling is crucial to success, and a majority also believe that everyone has the chance to get an education consistent with personal ability and talent (NORC, 1999). In truth, this opinion better expresses our aspirations than our achievement. Earlier in this century, for example, women were all but excluded from higher education, and, even today, most people who attend college come from families with above-average incomes.

In the United States, the educational system stresses the value of *practical* learning, that is, knowledge that has a direct bearing on individuals' work and interests. The educational philosopher John Dewey (1859–1952) championed *progressive education*, constantly updating what our schools teach to make learning relevant to people's lives.

GLOBAL SNAPSHOT

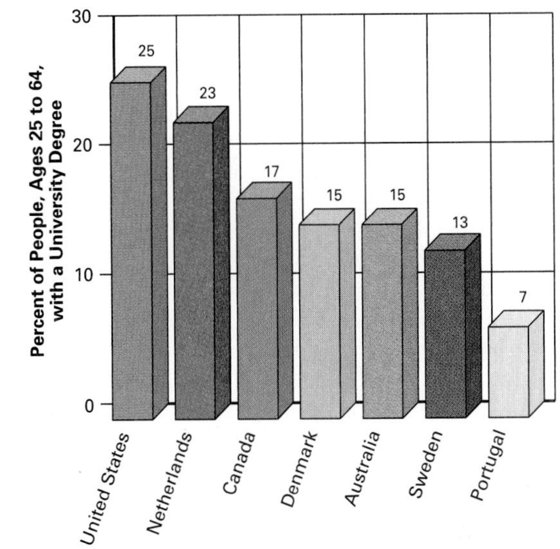

FIGURE 20–1 College Degrees in Global Perspective

Source: U.S. Census Bureau (1999).

APPLYING SOCIOLOGY

Following the Jobs: Trends in Bachelor's Degrees

College attendance in the United States has never been higher, especially among women. Both sexes, however, see college education in *practical* terms and pursue degrees in fields where they think jobs are plentiful.

In our postindustrial economy, the greatest surge in bachelor's degrees is in pre-law, as the figure at the right shows. The number of degrees in the social sciences and education—central to the postindustrial economy—as well as agriculture and natural resources, are also up sharply. On the other hand, students shy away from majors in areas where the demand for workers is slipping. Library science heads the list of fields posting reductions, followed by mathematics, engineering, and physical sciences.

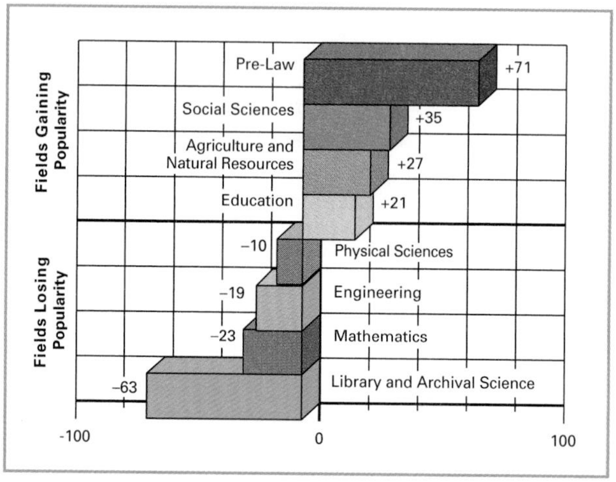

Percentage Changes in Bachelor's Degrees Earned, 1986–1996

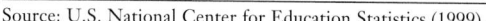

Source: U.S. National Center for Education Statistics (1999).

Reflecting this pragmatism, today's college students select their major area of study with an eye toward future jobs. The box takes a closer look at the changing interests of college students.

THE FUNCTIONS OF SCHOOLING

Structural-functional analysis looks at how formal education contributes to the operation of society. One of the most important functions is socialization. Schooling provides a cultural lifeline that links the generations.

SOCIALIZATION

Technologically simple societies transmit their ways of life informally from parents to children. As societies develop complex technology, however, kin can no longer stay abreast of rapidly expanding information and skills. Thus, schooling gradually emerges as a distinctive social institution employing specially trained personnel to convey the knowledge needed for adult roles.

In primary school, children learn basic language and mathematical skills. Secondary school builds on this foundation, and, for many, college allows further specialization. In addition, schools transmit cultural values and norms. Civics classes, for example, explicitly instruct students in our political way of life. Sometimes the operation of the classroom itself serves to teach important cultural lessons. From the earliest grades, rituals such as saluting the flag and singing "The Star-Spangled Banner" foster patriotism. Likewise, spelling bees and classroom drills develop competitive individualism, respect for authority, and a sense of fair play.

CULTURAL INNOVATION

Education creates as well as transmits culture. Schools stimulate intellectual inquiry and critical thinking, sparking the development of new ideas.

Today, for example, college professors throughout the country are conducting research to expand our knowledge in countless areas. Medical research carried on at major universities over the years has increased life

One of the latent functions of schooling is to care for children. With a majority of both women and men in the labor force, after-school programs that provide additional hours of supervised activities have become more common across the United States.

expectancy, just as research by sociologists and psychologists helps us take advantage of our longevity.

SOCIAL INTEGRATION

Schooling helps forge a mass of people into a unified society. This integrative function is especially important in nations with pronounced social diversity, where various cultures know little about—or may even be hostile to—one another. In the past, the Soviet Union and Yugoslavia relied on schools to unite their disparate peoples—without ultimately succeeding.

Societies in the Americas, Africa, and Asia use schooling to foster social integration. A basic way schools integrate culturally diverse people is by teaching a common language that encourages broad communication and builds a national identity. Of course, some ethnic minorities resist state-sponsored schooling for exactly this reason. In the former Soviet Union, for example, Lithuanians, Ukrainians, and Azerbaijanis objected to learning Russian because they saw it as a threat to their own traditions and emblematic of their domination by others. The Amish, a culturally distinctive people in the United States, historically fought to keep their children out of public schools in order to preserve their cultural traditions.

A century ago, mandatory education laws in the United States coincided with the arrival of millions of European immigrants, helping to integrate society. Today as well, formal education helps integrate large numbers of immigrants from Latin America and Asia, who, in turn, offer their traditions to our ever-changing cultural mix. At the same time, as racial and ethnic minorities have become a numerical majority in many of the largest school districts, the debate over multicultural education has grown (see Chapter 3, "Culture").

SOCIAL PLACEMENT

Formal education helps young people assume culturally approved statuses and perform roles that contribute to the ongoing life of society. Ideally, schools accomplish this by identifying and developing each individual's aptitudes and abilities and then evaluating the student's performance in terms of achievement rather than social background.

In principle, however, teachers encourage the "best and the brightest" to pursue the most challenging and advanced studies, while guiding students with more ordinary ability into educational programs suited to their talents. Schooling, in short, enhances meritocracy by making personal merit a foundation of future social position (Hurn, 1978).

LATENT FUNCTIONS OF SCHOOLING

Besides these manifest functions of formal education, a number of latent functions are less widely recognized. One is child care. As the number of one-parent families and two-career couples rises, schools have become vital to relieving parents of some child-care responsibilities.

For teenagers, too, schooling consumes considerable time and energy, often fostering conformity at a time of life when the risk of unlawful behavior is high. Also, because many students attend school well into their twenties, education engages thousands of young people, especially during times when jobs are not readily available.

Another latent function of schools is establishing relationships and networks. Many people form lifelong friendships, as well as meet their future spouses, in high school and college. Affiliation with a particular school also can create valuable career opportunities.

Critical evaluation. Structural-functional analysis of formal education identifies both manifest and latent contributions of this social institution to an industrial way of life. But it overlooks the core truth noted in the opening to this chapter: The quality of schooling is far greater for some than for others. Indeed, critics of the U.S. educational system maintain that schooling actually reproduces the class structure in each generation. In the next section, social-conflict analysis takes up precisely this issue.

SCHOOLING AND SOCIAL INEQUALITY

Social-conflict analysis counters the functionalist view that schooling is a meritocratic strategy for developing people's talents and abilities. Rather, this approach argues that schools routinely provide learning according to students' social background, thereby perpetuating social inequality.

Many of the world's societies consider schooling more important for males than for females. Although the U.S. education gap between women and men has largely closed in recent decades, many women still study conventionally "feminine" subjects such as literature, while men pursue mathematics and engineering. And by stressing the experiences of some types of people (say, military generals) while ignoring the lives of others (such as farm women), schools reinforce the values and importance of dominant categories of people. Finally, as we shall see later, affluent people have much more educational opportunity than poor people.

SOCIAL CONTROL

Social-conflict analysis suggests that schooling acts as a means of social control, reinforcing acceptance of the status quo. In various, sometimes subtle, ways, schools reproduce the status hierarchy.

Samuel Bowles and Herbert Gintis (1976) point out that the clamor for public education in the late nineteenth century arose at precisely the time that capitalists were seeking a literate, docile, and disciplined work force. Mandatory education laws ensured that schools would teach immigrants not only English but also cultural values that support capitalism. Compliance, punctuality, and discipline were—and still are—part of what conflict theorists call the **hidden curriculum,** *subtle presentations of political or cultural ideas in the classroom.*

STANDARDIZED TESTING

Here is a question of the kind historically used to measure academic ability of school-age children in the United States:

Painter is to painting as _____ is to sonnet.

Answer:	(a) driver	(b) poet
	(c) priest	(d) carpenter

The correct answer is (b) *poet:* A painter creates a painting just as a poet creates a sonnet. This question supposedly measures logical reasoning, but demonstrating this skill depends on knowing what each term means. Unless students are familiar with sonnets as a Western European form of written verse, they are not likely to answer the question correctly.

Educational specialists claim that bias of this kind has been all but eliminated from standardized tests, since testing organizations carefully study response patterns and drop any question that favors one racial or ethnic category over another. Critics, however, maintain that some bias based on class, race, or ethnicity is inherent in any formal testing, because questions inevitably reflect our society's dominant culture and thereby put minorities at a disadvantage (Owen, 1985; Crouse & Trusheim, 1988; Putka, 1990).

SCHOOL TRACKING

Despite continuing controversy over standardized tests, most schools in the United States use them as the basis for **tracking,** *the assignment of students to different types of educational programs.* Tracking is also a common practice in many other industrial societies, including Great Britain, France, and Japan.

The official justification for tracking is to give students the kind of learning that fits their abilities and motivation. Young people have different interests, with some drawn to, say, the study of languages and others

Jonathan Kozol, whose research is described in the box on the next page, has documented how schools in poor communities, such as the one on the left, provide a vastly inferior education compared to schools in more affluent communities. In a nation where people believe in giving everyone a chance to develop individual talents and abilities, should such "savage inequalities" exist?

to art or physical education. Given disparate talents and goals, no single program for all students would serve any of them well.

Critics counter that by tracking students, our schools sort out children as either winners or losers, based as much on their social background as their personal aptitude. Most students from affluent families do well on standardized tests, so schools place them in college-bound tracks; students from modest backgrounds typically do less well on tests and end up in tracks that teach only technical trades. Tracking, therefore, effectively segregates students—academically and socially—into different worlds.

Furthermore, most schools reserve their best teachers for students in the top tracks. These teachers put more effort into teaching, show more respect to students, and expect more from them. By contrast, teachers in low tracks employ more memorization, classroom drill, and other unstimulating techniques. They also emphasize regimentation, punctuality, and respect for authority figures.

In light of these criticisms, schools across the United States are now cautious about making tracking assignments and allow more mobility between tracks. Some schools have even moved away from the practice entirely. While limited tracking seems to be necessary to match instruction with student abilities, rigid tracking has a powerful impact on students' learning and self-concept. Young people who spend years in higher tracks tend to see themselves as bright and able, whereas students in lower tracks have less ambition and low self-esteem (Bowles & Gintis, 1976; Persell, 1977; Davis & Haller, 1981; Oakes, 1982, 1985; Hallinan & Williams, 1989; Kilgore, 1991; Gamoran, 1992; Kozol, 1992).

INEQUALITY AMONG SCHOOLS

Just as students are treated differently within schools, schools themselves differ in fundamental ways. The biggest difference is between public and private schools.

Public and Private Schools

In 1998, 86 percent of the 55 million U.S. school-aged children attended state-funded public schools. The remainder were in private schools.

Most private school students attend one of the 8,000 *parochial schools* (from the Latin, meaning "of the parish") operated by the Roman Catholic church. The Catholic school system grew rapidly a century ago as cities swelled

SOCIAL DIVERSITY

Schooling in the United States: Savage Inequality

"Public School 261? Head down Jerome Avenue and look for the mortician's office." On his way to doing fieldwork for his study of New York City schools, Jonathan Kozol parks his car and walks toward PS 261. Finding PS 261 is not so easy because the school has no sign. In fact, the building is a former roller rink and doesn't look much like a school at all.

Once inside, the principal explains that PS 261 is in a minority area of the North Bronx, so the school population is 90 percent African American and Hispanic. Officially, the school should serve 900 students, but actually enrolls 1,300. The rules say class size should not exceed 32, but later Kozol notes that it sometimes approaches 40. Because of the small cafeteria, the children must eat in three shifts. After lunch, since there is no place to play, students just squirm in their seats until told to return to their classrooms. Only one classroom in the entire school has a window to the world outside.

Toward the end of the day, Kozol asks a teacher about the overcrowding and the poor condition of the building. She sums up her thoughts: "I had an awful room last year. In the winter, it was 56 degrees. In the summer, it was up to 90." "Do the children ever comment on the building?" Kozol asks. "They don't say," she responds, "but they know. All these kids see TV. They know what suburban schools are like. Then they look around them at their school. They don't comment on it, but you see it in their eyes. They understand."

Several months later, Kozol visits PS 24, in the affluent Riverdale section of New York. This school is set back from the road, beyond a lawn planted with magnolia and dogwood trees, which are now in full bloom. On one side of the building is a playground for the youngest children; behind the school are playing fields for the older kids. Many people buy expensive homes in Riverdale because the local schools have an excellent reputation. There are 825 children here; most are white and a few are Asian, Hispanic, or black. The building is in good repair and has a large library and even a planetarium. All the classrooms have windows with bright curtains.

Entering one of the many classes for gifted students, Kozol asks the children what they are doing today. A young girl answers confidently, "My name is Laurie, and we're doing problem solving." A tall, good-natured boy continues: "I'm David. One thing that we do is logical thinking. Some problems, we find, have more than one good answer." Kozol asks if such reasoning is innate or if it is something a child learns. Susan, whose smile reveals her braces, responds: "You know some things to start with when you enter school. But we learn some things that other children don't. We learn certain things that other children don't know because we're *taught* them."

Source: Adapted from Kozol (1992:85–88, 92–96).

with millions of Catholic immigrants and their children. These schools helped the new arrivals maintain their religious heritage in the midst of a predominantly Protestant society. Today, after decades of flight from the city by white people, many parochial schools enroll non-Catholics, including a growing number of African Americans whose families seek an alternative to the local public schools.

Protestants, especially in fundamentalist denominations, also have private schools or Christian academies. These Christian schools are favored by parents who want their children to receive religious instruction or who seek higher academic and disciplinary standards. Some white parents turn to Christian schools to provide a racially homogeneous environment for their children in the face of school desegregation mandates. In recent years, African Americans, too, have sought out Christian schools as an alternative to public education (James, 1989; Dent, 1996).

Some 1,500 nonreligious private schools in the United States also enroll students, mostly from well-to-do families. These prestigious and expensive preparatory schools are especially favored by "newly rich" parents eager for their daughters and sons to rub elbows with children from "old money." These institutions—many modeled on boarding schools in Great Britain—are academically outstanding and send many graduates to equally prestigious and expensive private universities. After learning the mannerisms and social graces of the elite, many "preppies" maintain lifelong school-based networks that provide numerous social advantages.

SEEING OURSELVES

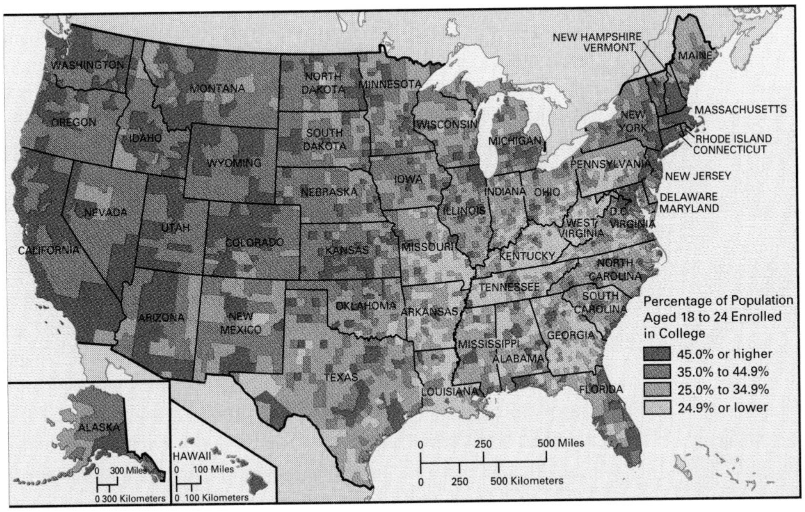

NATIONAL MAP 20–1
College Attendance across the United States

Generally speaking, college attendance is highest among adults along the Northeast and West coasts. By contrast, adults in the Midwest and the South (especially the Appalachian region) are the least likely members of our society to attend college. How would you explain this pattern? (Income is one obvious consideration; would people's ideas about gender equality be another?)

Source: *American Demographics* magazine, April 1993, p. 60. Reprinted with permission. ©1993 *American Demographics* magazine, Ithaca, New York.

Are private schools better than public schools? Research indicates that, given similar backgrounds, students in private schools achieve more than students in public schools. Private schools seem to generate greater interest in learning, probably due to smaller class size and more student-teacher contact. Furthermore, private schools are more academically demanding and enforce stringent disciplinary policies, resulting in a safer, more orderly environment. With everything else equal, graduates of private versus public schools are more likely to complete college and enter high-paying occupations (Coleman, Hoffer, & Kilgore, 1981; Coleman & Hoffer, 1987).

Inequality in Public Schooling

But even the public schools are not all the same. Winnetka, Illinois, one of the richest suburbs in the country, spends more than $8,000 annually per student, compared to less than $3,000 in a poor area like Socorro, Texas. Within states, as the opening to this chapter explained, some school districts have far more money per student to spend than others (Carroll, 1990; Edwards, 1998). The box looks at differences in school quality just within the city of New York.

Beyond the city limits, affluent suburban school districts offer better schooling than less well-funded systems in central cities. This disparity—which benefits whites—led to *busing*, beginning in the 1960s. Busing involves transporting students with the goal of racial balance and equal opportunity in schools. Although only 5 percent of U.S. schoolchildren are bused to schools outside their neighborhoods, this policy has generated heated controversy. Busing advocates claim that the only way government will adequately fund schools in poor, minority neighborhoods is if white children from richer neighborhoods attend them. Critics respond that busing is expensive and undermines the concept of neighborhood schools. But both sides acknowledge that, given the racial imbalance of our nation's urban areas, an effective busing scheme would have to join inner cities and suburbs—a plan that is almost never politically feasible.

A classic report by a research team headed by James Coleman (1966) confirmed that predominantly minority schools suffer more problems, ranging from larger class size to insufficient libraries and fewer science labs. But the Coleman report cautioned that money will not magically improve academic quality. Even more important are the cooperative efforts and enthusiasm of teachers, parents, and the students themselves. In other words, even if school funding were exactly the same everywhere, students whose families value schooling and encourage the development of imagination would still perform better. Thus, we should not expect schools alone to overcome marked social inequality in the United States (Schneider et al., 1998).

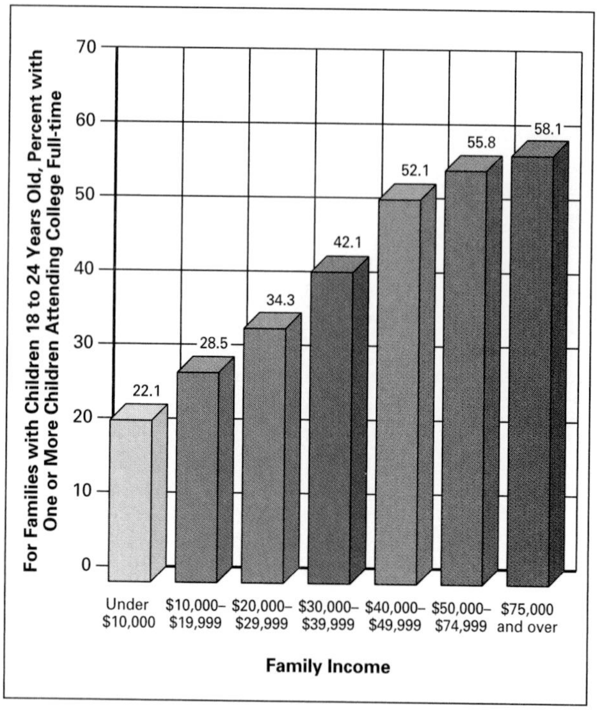

FIGURE 20–2 College Attendance and Family Income, 1998

Source: U.S. Census Bureau (1999).

ACCESS TO HIGHER EDUCATION

In industrial societies, higher education is the main path to occupational achievement. In the United States, 67 percent of high school graduates enroll in college the following fall (U.S. National Center for Education Statistics, 1999). Moreover, among young people eighteen to twenty-four years old, about 37 percent are enrolled in college. National Map 20–1 on page 525 shows where in the United States college attendance is more or less likely.

The most crucial factor affecting access to higher education in the United States is money. College is expensive, and the cost is rising rapidly. Even at state-supported institutions, annual tuition averages about $3,000, and admission to the most exclusive private colleges and universities exceeds $25,000 a year. As shown in Figure 20–2, families with incomes above $75,000 annually (roughly the richest 20 percent of U.S. families, who fall within the upper and upper-middle classes) send about 60 percent of their children to college because they can afford to, while only one-fourth of young people from families earning less than $20,000 each year reach college.

The financial burden of higher education prevents many minorities, typically with below-average incomes, from attending college. As Figure 20–3 shows, whites are more likely than African Americans and Hispanics to complete high school, and this disparity remains with each step up in the educational system. For some, schooling is a path to social mobility, but it has not overcome persistent racial inequality in the United States (Epps, 1995).

Completing college carries numerous rewards, including intellectual and personal growth, as well as higher income. Over an individual's working lifetime, a college degree adds almost $500,000 to personal income (Speer, 1994). Table 20–2 shows why. In 1998, women with less than a ninth-grade education typically earned $14,467; high school graduates averaged $22,780, and college graduates, $36,559. The ratios in parentheses show that a woman with a bachelor's degree earns two-and-one-half times as much as a woman with eight or fewer years of schooling. Across the board, men earn at least 40 percent more than women; moreover, additional years of schooling boost income faster for men than for women. Finally, for both men and women, some of the greater earnings that are associated with more schooling have much to do with social background, since the people with the most schooling are likely to come from relatively affluent families to begin with.

CREDENTIALISM

The sociologist Randall Collins (1979) calls the United States a *credential society* because people regard diplomas and degrees highly. In modern, technologically advanced societies, credentials say "who you are" as much as family background.

Credentialism, then, is *evaluating a person on the basis of educational degrees.* On the one hand, credentialism is simply the way our modern society goes about filling jobs with people well-trained and well-suited for them. On the other hand, Collins explains that credentials often bear little relation to the responsibilities of a specific job. In reality, advanced degrees often are an easy way to sort out the people with the manners, attitudes, and even skin color many employers are looking for. Credentialism is thus a gate-keeping strategy that restricts important occupations to a small segment of the population.

DIVERSITY SNAPSHOT

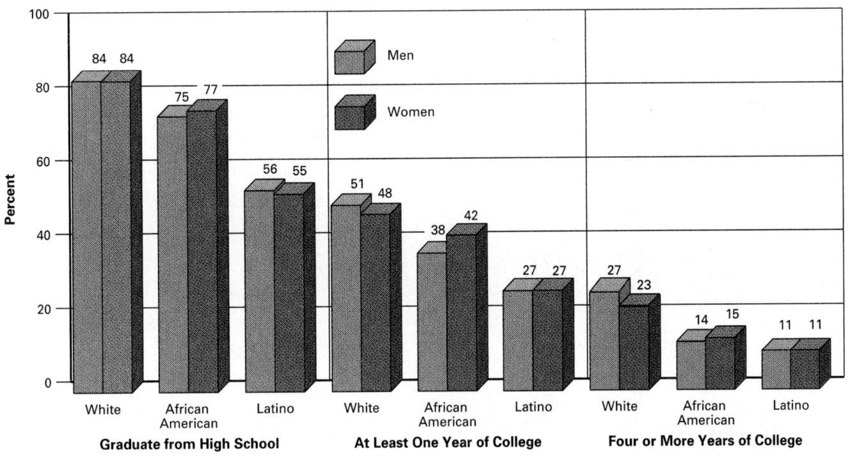

FIGURE 20–3
Educational Achievement for Various Categories of People, Aged 25 Years and over, 1998

Source: U.S. Census Bureau (1998).

PRIVILEGE AND PERSONAL MERIT

If, as social-conflict analysis suggests, attending college is a rite of passage for affluent men and women, then *schooling transforms social privilege into personal merit.* But given our cultural emphasis on individualism, we tend to see credentials as "badges of ability" rather than as symbols of family affluence (Sennett & Cobb, 1973). When we congratulate the new graduate, we rarely recognize the resources—both financial and cultural—that made this achievement possible. Yet the fact is that young people from families with incomes exceeding $100,000 a year average 1,130 on college board exams—more than 200 points higher than young people from families with $15,000 income.

In the same way, we are quick to label the high school dropout as personally deficient, without giving much thought to the social and economic circumstances of that person's life. The box on page 528 illustrates this process with the words of one bright but disillusioned boy.

Critical evaluation. Social-conflict analysis links formal education and social inequality, to show how schooling transforms privilege into personal worthiness, and social disadvantage into personal deficiency. However, critics say that social-conflict analysis minimizes the extent to which schooling provides upward social mobility for talented men and women from all backgrounds. Further, despite the claims that schooling supports the status quo, today's college curricula challenge social inequality on many fronts.

PROBLEMS IN THE SCHOOLS

An intense debate revolves around schooling in the United States today. Perhaps because we expect our schools not only to teach academics but to do so much more—to equalize opportunity, fire the individual imagination, and even instill discipline—that few people think

TABLE 20–2 Median Income by Sex and Educational Attainment*

Education	Men	Women
Professional degree	$94,737 (4.9)	$57,565 (4.0)
Doctorate	75,078 (3.9)	57,776 (4.0)
Master's	62,244 (3.2)	45,283 (3.1)
Bachelor's	51,405 (2.7)	36,559 (2.5)
1–3 years of college	36,934 (1.9)	27,420 (1.6)
4 years of high school	31,477 (1.6)	22,780 (1.6)
9–11 years of school	23,958 (1.2)	16,482 (1.1)
0–8 years of school	19,380 (1.0)	14,467 (1.0)

*Persons aged twenty-five years and over working full time, 1998. The earnings ratio, in parentheses, indicates how many times the lowest income level an individual with additional schooling earns.

Source: U.S. Census Bureau (1999).

SOCIAL DIVERSITY

"Cooling Out" the Poor: Transforming Disadvantage into Deficiency

If schools paint disadvantaged students as "dumb," over time some of them come to believe it. This process of "cooling out" their ambitions sets into motion a self-fulfilling prophecy by which many poor students end up settling for no more than what society handed them when they were born. Eleven-year-old Ollie Taylor describes the experience in these words:

> The only thing that matters in my life is school and there they think I'm dumb and always will be. I'm starting to think they're right. Hell, I know they put all the black kids together in one group if they can, but that doesn't make any difference either. I'm still dumb. Even if I look around and know that I'm the smartest in my group, all that means is that I'm the smartest of the dumbest, so I haven't got anywhere at all, have I? I'm right where I always was. Every word those teachers tell me, even the ones I like most, I can hear in their voice that what they're really saying is "All right you dumb kids. I'll make it as easy as I can, and if you don't get it then, you'll never get it. Ever." That's what I hear every day, man. From every one of them. Even the other kids talk that way to me too.

Source: Cottle (1974): 22–24.

that public schools are doing a good job. Table 20–3 shows that nearly half of all adults give our schools a grade of C or below (Phi Delta Kappa International, 2000).

DISCIPLINE AND VIOLENCE

When today's older teachers think back to their own days as students, school "problems" consisted of students talking out of turn, chewing gum, violating the dress code, and cutting class. But today, schools are grappling with much more serious issues such as drug and alcohol abuse, teenage pregnancy, and—as deadly incidents in a number of schools in recent years illustrate—outright violence. It is little wonder that, while almost everyone agrees that schools should teach personal discipline, few think schools are succeeding (NORC, 1999:758).

In recent years, violence has claimed the lives of students and teachers alike in high schools across the United States. Moreover, in national surveys, about one-fourth of students and 11 percent of teachers report being victims of violence in and around schools in hundreds of thousands of cases that do not capture national headlines (Arnette & Walsleben, 1998).

As most people see it, schools themselves do not create the violence; rather, disorder spills into schools from the surrounding society. But in recent decades, teachers have lost much of their authority in dealing with troublemakers, especially young people who have little interest in school in the first place (Toby, 1998). Nevertheless, schools have it in their power to effect change for the better. The key is to set and enforce firm disciplinary policies, with school personnel supported by parents and, if necessary, police. Violence is a problem deep in society itself, but schools can control violence by forging alliances with parents and community leaders (Gup, 1992).

STUDENT PASSIVITY

If some schools are plagued by violence, many more are afflicted with passive, bored students. Some of the blame for passivity can be placed on television (which now consumes more of young people's time than school), on parents (who are not involved enough with their children), and on the students themselves. But schools, too, play a part, since our educational system itself generates student passivity (Coleman, Hoffer, & Kilgore, 1981).

Bureaucracy

The small, personal schools that served countless local communities a century ago have evolved into huge educational factories. In a study of high schools across the United States, Theodore Sizer (1984) identified five ways in which large, bureaucratic schools undermine education (207–9):

1. **Rigid uniformity.** Bureaucratic schools run by outsider specialists (such as state education officials) generally ignore the cultural character of local communities and the personal needs of their children.
2. **Numerical ratings.** School officials define success in terms of numerical attendance records, dropout rates, and achievement test scores. Therefore, they overlook dimensions of schooling that are difficult to quantify, such as the creativity of students and the energy and enthusiasm of teachers.
3. **Rigid expectations.** Officials expect fifteen-year-olds to be in the tenth grade, and eleventh-graders to score at a certain level on a standardized verbal achievement test. Rarely are exceptionally bright and motivated students permitted to graduate early. Likewise, the system pushes students from grade to grade whether they have learned anything or not.
4. **Specialization.** High school students learn Spanish from one teacher, receive guidance from another, and are coached in sports by still others. Although specialized teachers may know more about their subjects, no school employee comes to know and appreciate the "complete" student. Students experience this division of labor as a continual shuffling from one fifty-minute period to another throughout the school day.
5. **Little individual responsibility.** Highly bureaucratic schools do not empower students to learn on their own. Similarly, teachers have little latitude in what and how they teach their classes; they dare not accelerate learning for fear of disrupting "the system."

TABLE 20-3 Grading Public Schools in the United States, 1999

Rating*	Proportion of Respondents
A	11%
B	38
C	31
D	9
FAIL	5
Don't know	6

*These figures reflect the responses of a national sample of U.S. adults to the question: Students are often given the grades A, B, C, D, and FAIL to denote the quality of their work. Suppose the public schools themselves, in this community, were graded in the same way. What grade would you give the public schools here—A, B, C, D, or FAIL?

Source: Phi Delta Kappa International/Gallup Poll. [Online] Available http://www.pdkintl.org/kappan/kpol9909.htm#1a, February 14, 2000.

Of course, some formal organization in schools is inevitable given the immense size of the task. In 2000, there were some 55 million students nationwide; the number of students in New York City's public schools alone now exceeds the student population of the entire country in 1900. But, Sizer maintains, we can humanize schools to make them more responsive to the students they claim to serve. He recommends eliminating rigid class schedules, reducing class size, and training teachers more broadly to help them become more involved in the lives of their students. Overall, as James Coleman (1993) suggested, schools need to be less "administratively driven" and more "output-driven." Perhaps this transformation could begin by ensuring that graduation from high school depends on what students have learned rather than simply on the number of years spent in the building.

College: The Silent Classroom

Here are the observations of a bright and highly motivated first-year student at a high-quality four-year college. Do they strike a familiar chord?

> I have been disappointed in my first year at college. Too many students do as little work as they can get away with, take courses that are recommended by other students as being "gut" classes, and never challenge themselves past what is absolutely necessary. It's almost like thinking that we don't watch professors but we watch television. (Forrest, 1984:10)

We are all too familiar with the school shootings that have made headlines in recent years. Fear of violence has led many schools to adopt security procedures that seem more appropriate for prisons than places of learning. Here, in the presence of police, officials direct students through a metal detector in an effort to prevent weapons from entering the school.

Passivity is common in colleges and universities. Martha E. Gimenez (1989) describes college as the "silent classroom" because the only voice heard is usually the teacher's. Sociologists tend not to conduct research on the college classroom—a curious fact considering how much time they spend there. An exception is a study at a coeducational university where David Karp and William Yoels (1976) found that, even in small classes, only a handful of students said anything at all during the typical class period. Karp and Yoels concluded that passivity is a classroom norm, and students even become irritated if one of their number is especially talkative.

Students offered Karp and Yoels various explanations for classroom passivity, including not having done the assigned reading or fearing that they might sound unintelligent to teachers and other students. Their reasons suggest that, for the most part, they blame themselves for their passivity. Yet long before they reach college, Karp and Yoels point out, students learn to view instructors as "experts" who serve up "truth." Thus they find little value in classroom discussion and perceive that their proper role is to listen quietly and take notes. As a result, the researchers estimate, just 10 percent of college class time is used for student-led discussion.

Students also realize that instructors generally come to class ready to deliver a prepared lecture. The lecture format allows teachers the opportunity to present a great deal of material in each class, but only to the extent that they avoid being sidetracked by students' questions or comments (Boyer, 1987). Early in each course, most instructors single out a few students who are willing and able to provide the occasional, limited comments they desire. Taken together, such patterns form a recipe for passivity on the part of most college students.

Yet faculty can bring students to life in their classrooms by actively involving them in learning. One recent study of classroom dynamics, for example, linked higher levels of student participation to four teaching strategies: (1) calling on students by name when they volunteer; (2) positively reinforcing student participation; (3) asking analytical rather than factual questions and giving students time to answer; and (4) asking for student opinions even when there are no volunteers (Auster & MacRone, 1994).

DROPPING OUT

If many students are passive in class, others are not there at all. The problem of *dropping out*—quitting school before earning a high school diploma—leaves young people (many of whom are disadvantaged to begin with) ill-equipped for the world of work and at high risk for poverty.

The dropout rate has declined slightly in recent decades; currently about 11 percent of people between

SEEING OURSELVES

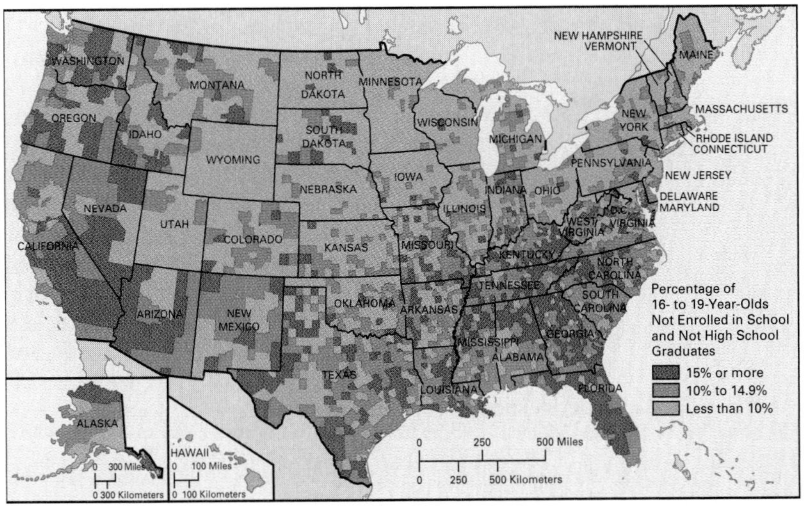

NATIONAL MAP 20–2
High School Dropouts across the United States

Across the United States, the highest dropout rate is found in Holmes County, Ohio, where more than half of young people are not enrolled in school or high school graduates. This county has a largely Amish population, and young people leave school to work on farms. Regionally, dropout rates are high across the South—from West Virginia down to Florida, and from the Carolinas to Louisiana and east Texas. Rates are also high in the Southwest. What factors do you think account for this pattern?

Source: From Rodger Doyle, *Atlas of Contemporary America*. Copyright © 1994 by Rodger Doyle. Reprinted with permission of Facts on File, Inc., New York, N.Y.

the ages of sixteen and twenty-four have dropped out of school, a total of some 3.6 million young women and men. Dropping out is least pronounced among non-Hispanic whites (8 percent), slightly greater among non-Hispanic African Americans (13 percent), and most serious among Hispanics (25 percent) (U.S. National Center for Education Statistics, 1999). National Map 20–2 shows the dropout rate for counties across the United States.

Some students drop out because of problems with the English language or because of pregnancy; others, whose families are poor, must go to work. The dropout rate (12.3 percent) among children growing up in the bottom 20 percent of households is seven times higher than that (1.8 percent) for youngsters whose households fall in the top 20 percent by income (U.S. National Center for Education Statistics, 1999). These data point to the fact that many dropouts are young people whose parents also have little schooling, creating a multigenerational cycle of disadvantage (Pirog & Magee, 1997).

The United States was once the world leader in high school graduation rates. In recent years, however, many other countries have greatly improved their performance, while there has been little change here at home. As a result, this country now ranks twenty-third in high school graduation rate—lagging behind Canada, Japan, and most of the nations of Western Europe (Desruisseaux, 1998).

ACADEMIC STANDARDS

Perhaps the most serious educational issue confronting our society is the quality of schooling. *A Nation at Risk*, a comprehensive report on the quality of U.S. schools published in 1983 by the National Commission on Excellence in Education, begins with this alarming statement:

> If an unfriendly foreign power had attempted to impose on America the mediocre educational performance that exists today, we might well have viewed it as an act of war. As it stands, we have allowed this to happen to ourselves. (1983:5)

Supporting this conclusion, the report notes that "nearly 40 percent of seventeen-year-olds cannot draw inferences from written material; only one-fifth can write a persuasive essay; and only one-third can solve mathematical problems requiring several steps" (1983:9). Furthermore, scores on the Scholastic Aptitude Test (SAT) have declined since the 1960s. In 1967, median scores for students were 516 on the mathematical test and 543 on the verbal test; by 1998, the averages had slipped to 505 and 512, respectively. Nationwide, about one-third of high school students—and more than half in urban schools—fail to master even the basics in reading, math, and science on the National Assessment of Education Progress examination (Sanchez, 1998).

GLOBAL SNAPSHOT

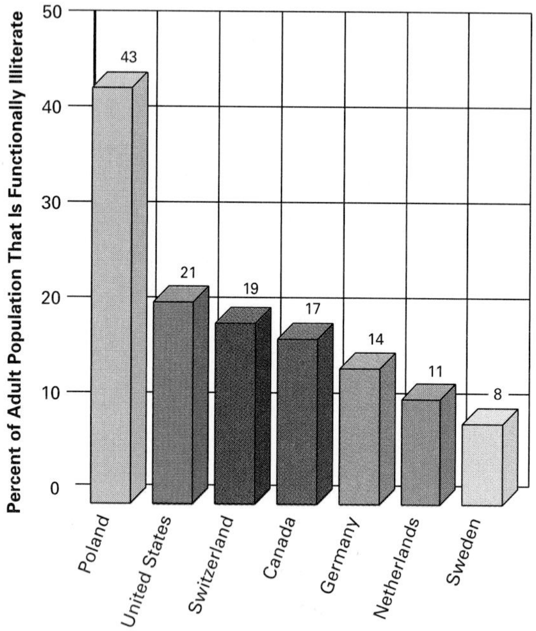

FIGURE 20–4 Functional Illiteracy in Global Perspective

Source: Fiske (1997).

For many, even basic literacy is at issue. **Functional illiteracy,** *a lack of reading and writing skills needed for everyday living,* is a problem for one in eight children who leave secondary schools in the United States. For older people, the problem is even worse, so that, overall, some 40 million U.S. adults (roughly 20 percent of the total) read and write at an eighth-grade level or below. As Figure 20–4 shows, the extent of functional illiteracy in the United States is below that of middle-income nations (such as Poland) but higher than in other rich countries (such as Canada and Sweden).

To improve our educational system, *A Nation at Risk* calls for drastic measures. First, all schools should require students to complete several years of English, mathematics, social studies, general science, and computer science courses. Second, schools should not promote failing students from grade to grade; instead, students should remain in the classroom as long as necessary to learn basic skills. Third, teacher training must improve and teachers' salaries should rise to attract talent into the profession. *A Nation at Risk* concludes that educators must ensure that schools meet public expectations and that citizens must be prepared to bear the costs of good schools.

A final concern is the low performance of U.S. students in a global context. Although per-student spending is greater in this country than almost anywhere else, U.S. eighth graders still place seventeenth in the world in science achievement and twenty-eighth in mathematics (Bennett, 1997; Finn & Walberg, 1998). Cultural values play a big part in international comparisons. For example, U.S. students are generally less motivated than their counterparts in Japan and also do less homework. Moreover, Japanese young people spend sixty more days in school each year than U.S. students. Perhaps one approach to improving schools is simply to have students spend more time there.

RECENT ISSUES IN U.S. EDUCATION

Our society's schools continuously confront new challenges. This final section explores several recent and important educational issues.

SCHOOL CHOICE

Some analysts claim that the reason our schools do not teach very well is that they have no competition. Thus, giving parents options for schooling their children might force all schools to do a better job. This is the essence of a policy called *school choice.*

Proponents of school choice advocate creating a market for schooling, so that parents and students can shop for the best value. According to one proposal, the government would give vouchers to families with school-aged children and allow them to spend that money at public, private, or parochial schools. During the 1990s, Indianapolis, Minneapolis, Milwaukee, Cleveland, and the state of Florida experimented with choice plans aimed at making public schools perform better to win the confidence of families. In addition, the Children's Scholarship Fund, a privately funded charity, has supported 40,000 children who wish to attend nonpublic schools, and has more than 1 million children on its waiting list.

Supporters claim that giving parents a choice about where to enroll their children is the only sure way to improve all schools. But critics (including teachers' unions) charge that school choice has yet to prove itself. Moreover, they see these programs as eroding our

Edison Schools is the country's leading private manager of public schools. Such companies work together with school districts or charter school boards to try to improve learning. Making high technology available to all students is part of the strategy in this charter school in Worcester, Massachusetts.

nation's commitment to public education, especially in the central cities where the need is greatest (Martinez et al., 1995; Godwin et al., 1998; Cohen, 1999; Forstmann, 1999).

A more modest form of school choice involves *magnet schools*, 1,000 of which now exist across the country. To students who qualify, magnet schools offer special facilities and programs to promote educational excellence in a particular area, such as computer science, foreign languages, science and mathematics, or the arts. In school districts with magnet schools, parents can choose the one best suited to their child's particular talents and interests.

Yet another recent development in the school choice movement is *schooling for profit*. Advocates of this plan say school systems can be operated by private profit-making companies more efficiently than by local governments. Private schooling is nothing new; more than 10,000 schools are currently run by private organizations and religious groups. What is new, however, is the idea that private companies can carry out *mass* public education in the United States.

Research confirms that many public school systems suffer from bureaucratic bloat, spending too much and teaching too little. And our society has long looked to competition as a strategy to improve quality. But the results of schooling for profit appear mixed. Several companies claim to have improved student learning, yet some cities have cut back on business-run schools. In 1995, for example, Baltimore canceled the contract of the corporation that had taken over nine of its schools in 1992; school boards in Miami and Hartford, Connecticut, have also canceled contracts. In short, public school systems perform poorly in many cities; but whether private business can improve on their record remains unclear.

Finally, *charter schools*, another recent innovation, have yet to be fully evaluated. These are public schools that operate with less state regulation so that teachers and administrators can try out new teaching strategies. One condition of a "charter" is that the school promises to perform as well or better than other schools in the district. In 1998, some 700 charter schools were operating in about half the states (Putka & Stecklow, 1994; Kanamine, 1995; Ravitch & Viteritti, 1996; Bennett, 1997; Toch, 1998).

SCHOOLING PEOPLE WITH DISABILITIES

Bureaucratic schools do not readily meet the special needs of some people, including many of the 5 million U.S. children with physical impairments. Many children with disabilities have difficulty getting to and from school, and many with crutches or wheelchairs cannot negotiate stairs and other obstacles inside school buildings. Children with developmental disabilities like mental retardation require extensive personal attention from specially trained teachers. As a result, many children with mental and physical disabilities have received a public education only because of persistent efforts by parents and other concerned citizens.

About one-fourth of children with disabilities are schooled in special facilities; the rest attend public

CONTROVERSY & DEBATE

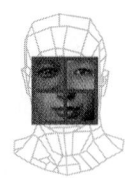

Political Correctness: Improving or Undermining Education?

Are you "P.C."? Is your teacher? What about this textbook? The 1990s witnessed a heightened level of political debate on the college campus. About a decade ago, the term *political correctness* entered our language to refer to thinking and acting in accordance with liberal political principals. To be "politically correct," then, is not so much a matter of being factually correct as expressing sympathy for the "correct" politics. Surveying the campus scene, James Davison Hunter (1991:211) concludes, "The cultural ethos of the modern university clearly favors a progressivist agenda," which includes support for feminism, gay rights, and various other movements that advocate social equality.

But political correctness is controversial. To some people, political correctness threatens the traditional open-mindedness of the university; at its worst, it turns professors into activists and teaching into indoctrination. Moreover, political correctness may have a chilling effect in the classroom, making students afraid to offer opinions on sensitive issues (say, homosexuality or racial issues) for fear of offending others who might, in turn, charge them with homophobia or racism. Professors, too, feel the pressure to be politically correct: Douglas Massey (1995) points out that a number of well-known researchers have been ostracized by their peers for conducting research that is scientifically solid but that advances unpopular notions about race and gender.

But not everyone thinks "P.C." is a problem. Many students and faculty defend a politically engaged campus on moral grounds. As they see it, there is a great deal of injustice in the world that should be addressed. Richard Rorty (1994), for example, applauds the fact that some academic departments have become "sanctuaries for left-wing political views." He believes that activist colleagues do "a great deal of good for people who have gotten a raw deal in our society, namely, women, African Americans, gay men, and lesbians." By focusing on marginalized people, Rorty suggests, the campus "will, in the long run, help to make our country much more decent, more tolerant and more civilized."

Keep in mind, too, that political correctness can be easily exaggerated. While it is probably fair to characterize academia (and sociologists, overall) as politically liberal, virtually every campus includes faculty, administrators, and students representing a wide range of political opinions. Furthermore, charges of political correctness in academia are nothing new. Just sixty years ago, for example, a majority of states sought to keep teachers in check by requiring that they sign loyalty oaths before permitting them to speak in the classroom (Hunter, 1991). Perhaps it is true that the more things change. . . .

Continue the debate . . .

1. *Overall, do you agree that academia has a left-wing political bias? Why or why not?*
2. *Should teachers (or textbooks) take explicit political stands on controversial issues?*
3. *Have you or other students remained silent in class discussion for fear of sounding "politically incorrect"? Has a course ever led you to change attitudes you came to see as narrow-minded?*

schools, many participating in regular classes. Thus, most schools avoid expensive "special education" in favor of **mainstreaming,** *integrating special students into the overall educational program.* Mainstreaming is a form of *inclusive education* that works best for physically impaired students who have no difficulty keeping up with the rest of the class. Moreover, putting children with and without disabilities in the same classroom allows everyone to learn more about interacting with people who differ from themselves.

ADULT EDUCATION

Most schooling involves young people. However, the share of U.S. students aged twenty-five and older has risen sharply in recent years and now accounts for 39 percent of people in the classroom.

By 1998, more than 25 million U.S. adults were enrolled in some type of schooling. These older students range in age from the middle-twenties to the seventies and beyond. Adults in school are twice as likely to be women as men and generally have above-average incomes. Some are part-time students completing college degrees; others already have a college diploma and other advanced degrees (Speer, 1996; Miller, 1997a).

What draws adults back to school? The reasons are as varied as the students, but most return to advance their careers, enrolling in business, engineering, or the health sciences. Others, who study everything from astronomy to Zen, simply enjoy learning.

LOOKING AHEAD: SCHOOLING IN THE TWENTY-FIRST CENTURY

Despite the fact that the United States leads the world in providing a college education to its people, our public school system continues to struggle with serious problems, many of which have their roots in the larger society. Thus, during this new century, we cannot expect schools *by themselves* to improve the quality of education. Schools will only improve to the extent to which students, teachers, parents, and local communities commit to educational excellence. In short, educational dilemmas are *social* problems, and there is no quick fix.

For much of the twentieth century, there were just two models for education in the United States: public schools run by the government and private schools operated by nongovernmental organizations. In the last decade, however, many new ideas about schooling have come on the scene, including schooling for profit and a wide range of "choice" programs (Finn & Gau, 1998). In the decades ahead, we will likely see some significant changes in mass education, guided in part by social science research on the consequences of different strategies.

Whatever decisions are made about who controls education, another factor that will continue to reshape schools is new information technology. Today, 97 percent of conventional primary and secondary schools in the United States have instructional computers. The promise of this new technology goes beyond helping students learn basic skills; computers actually can improve the overall quality of learning. Computers help students be more active learners, and allow them to progress at their own pace. For students with disabilities who cannot write using a pencil, computers permit easier self-expression. For all students, using computers in schools—in some cases, as early as kindergarten—appears to increase significantly how fast students learn and helps prepare them for the workplace of the twenty-first century.

The numerous benefits of computers should not blind us to their limitations, however. Computers will never bring to the educational process the personal insight or imagination of a motivated teacher. Nor can computers tap what one teacher calls the "springs of human identity and creativity" that we discover by exploring literature and language rather than simply manipulating mathematical codes. Indeed, despite their proliferation in the classroom, computers have yet to change teaching and learning in any fundamental sense or even replace the traditional blackboard (Berger, 1991; Elmer-DeWitt, 1991; Skinner, 1997). Thus, we should not look to technology to solve the problems—including violence and rigid bureaucracy—that plague our schools. What we need is a broad plan for social change that refires this country's early ambition to provide quality universal schooling—a goal that has so far eluded us.

SUMMARY

1. Education is the major social institution for transmitting knowledge and skills, as well as teaching cultural norms and values. In preindustrial societies, education occurs informally within the family; industrial societies develop formal systems of schooling.
2. The United States was among the first countries to institute compulsory mass education, reflecting both democratic political ideals and the needs of the industrial-capitalist economy.
3. Structural-functional analysis highlights major functions of schooling, including socialization, cultural innovation, social integration, and placing people in the social hierarchy. Latent functions of schooling include providing child care and building social networks.
4. Social-conflict analysis links schooling to hierarchy involving class, race, and gender. Formal education also serves as a means of generating conformity in order to produce compliant adult workers.
5. Standardized achievement tests are controversial. Some see them as a reasonable measure of academic aptitude and learning, while others say they

are culturally biased tools used to label less privileged students as personally deficient.

6. Tracking, too, is controversial. Some see tracking as the way schools provide appropriate instruction for students with different interests and aptitudes; others say tracking gives privileged youngsters a richer education.
7. The great majority of young people in the United States attend state-funded public schools. Most private schools offer a religious education. A small proportion of students—usually well-to-do—attend elite, private preparatory schools.
8. One-fourth of U.S. adults over the age of twenty-five are now college graduates, marking the emergence of a "credential society." People with college degrees enjoy greatly increased lifetime earnings.
9. Most adults in the United States are critical of public schools. Violence permeates many schools, especially those in poor neighborhoods. The bureaucratic character of schools also fosters high dropout rates and student passivity.
10. Declining academic standards are reflected in today's lower average scores on achievement tests and the functional illiteracy of a significant proportion of high school graduates.
11. The school choice movement seeks to make schools more responsive to the public. Innovative options include magnet schools, schooling for profit, and charter schools, all of which are topics of continuing policy debate.
12. Children with mental or physical disabilities historically have been schooled in special classes or not at all. Mainstreaming affords them broader opportunities.
13. Adults represent a growing proportion of students in the United States. Most older learners are women who are engaged in job-related study.
14. The Information Revolution is changing schooling through increasing use of computers. Although computers permit interactive, self-paced learning, they are not suitable for teaching every subject.

KEY CONCEPTS

education (p. 515) the social institution through which society provides its members with important knowledge, including basic facts, job skills, and cultural norms and values

schooling (p. 515) formal instruction under the direction of specially trained teachers

hidden curriculum (p. 522) subtle presentations of political or cultural ideas in the classroom

tracking (p. 522) the assignment of students to different types of educational programs

credentialism (p. 526) evaluating a person on the basis of educational degrees

functional illiteracy (p. 532) a lack of reading and writing skills needed for everyday living

mainstreaming (p. 534) integrating special students into the overall educational program

CRITICAL-THINKING QUESTIONS

1. Why does industrialization lead societies to expand their system of schooling?
2. In what ways is schooling in the United States shaped by our economic, political, and cultural systems?
3. From a structural-functional perspective, why is schooling important to the operation of society? From a social-conflict point of view, how does formal education reproduce social inequality in each generation?
4. Do you agree with research findings presented in this chapter that, by and large, college students are passive in class? If so, what do you think colleges can do to make everyone more active participants in learning?

APPLICATIONS AND EXERCISES

1. Arrange to visit a secondary school near your college or home. Does it have a tracking policy? If so, find out how it works. How much importance does a student's social background have in making a track assignment?
2. Most people agree that teaching our children is a vital task. Yet most teachers earn relatively low salaries. Check the prestige ranking for teachers in Table 11–2. What can you find out at the library about the average salaries of teachers compared to those of other workers? Can you explain this pattern?
3. Since 1975, the federal government and every state has passed a special education law providing for children with physical disabilities. After the passage of the Americans with Disabilities Act in 1990, schools have sought to "accommodate" students with a broader range of physical and mental disabilities. Do some library research, or contact officials on your campus, to learn how laws of this kind are changing education.
4. Install the CD-ROM packaged in the back of this new textbook to access a variety of study, review, and applications exercises designed to help you better understand the material covered in this chapter. The CD includes an author's tip video, as well as interactive maps, video application exercises, Web links, and study questions.

SITES TO SEE

http://www.prenhall.com/macionis

Visit the interactive Web site that accompanies this text. Begin by clicking on the cover of your book. You will find a chapter-by-chapter study guide, practice tests, chat room, and many suggested Web links.

http://www.acpe.asu.edu/VirtualU/

To explore how new information technology is reshaping education, read about the founding of Western Virtual University, this country's first "cyber-college." Think about the advantages and disadvantages of this type of schooling.

http://www.kenyon.edu/projects/famfarm/welcome/welcome.htm

Visit the Family Farm Web site at Kenyon College. This site was created by students to share what they have learned about farming and rural life in a rural county in central Ohio.

http://www.nces.ed.gov/

The National Center for Education Statistics provides various data about U.S. education, including a profile of college graduates by gender and race.

http://www.nces.ed.gov/pubs98/violence/index.html

The issue of school violence is the focus of this government Web site.

http://www.chronicle.com

This site provides general news and information about higher education.

CHAPTER 21

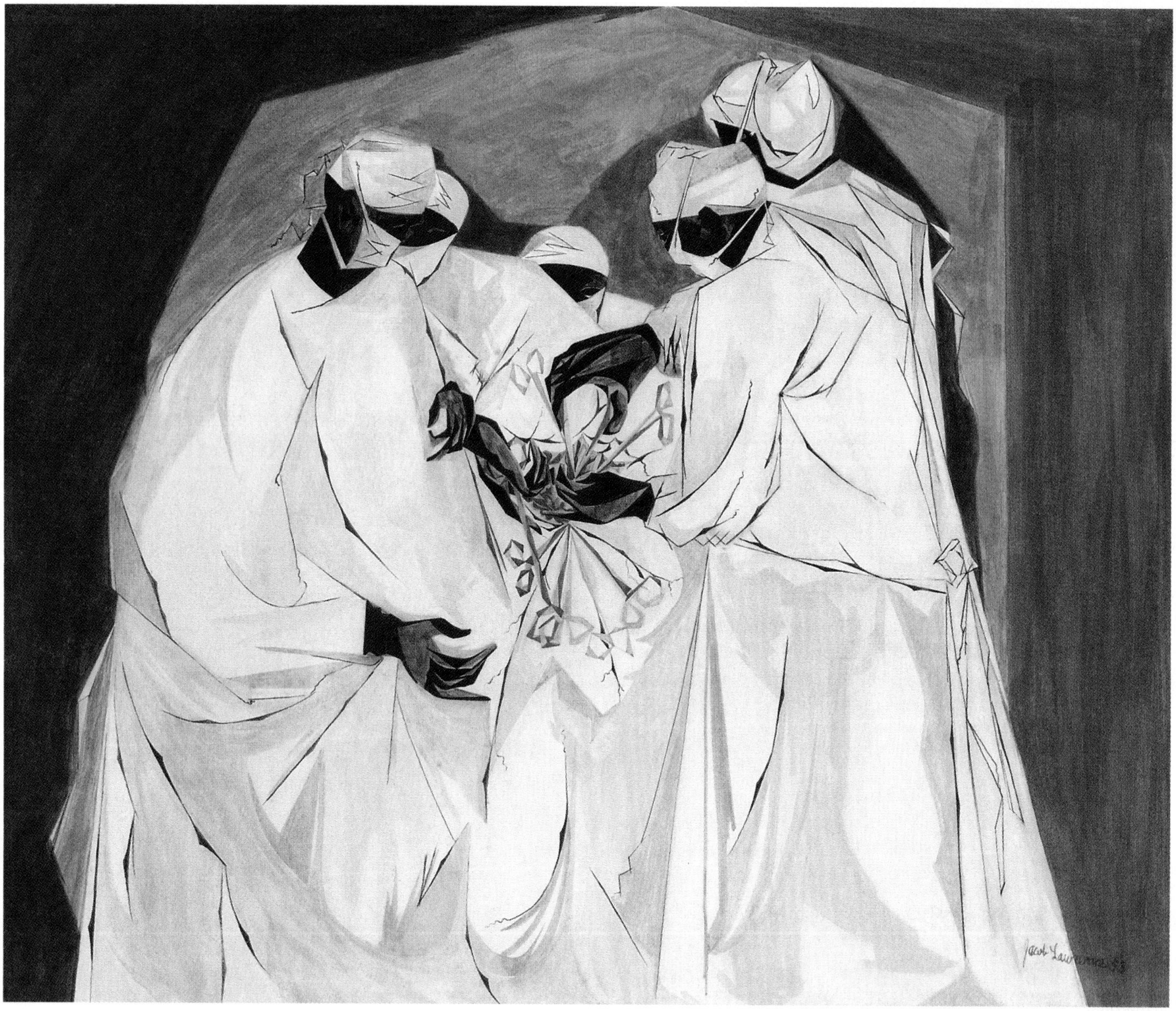

Jacob Lawrence (b. 1917)
Harlem Hospital Surgery, 1953

Tempera on masonite, 20 × 24 in., signed and dated. Courtesy of Michael Rosenfeld Gallery. © Jacob Lawrence. By permission of DC Moore Gallery, New York.

HEALTH AND MEDICINE

In 1995, television came to Fiji, a small island in the South Seas of the Pacific Ocean. A single cable channel carried programming from the United States, Great Britain, and Australia. When Anne Becker, a Harvard researcher specializing in eating disorders, read the news, her sociological imagination led her to wonder what effect watching television would have on young women there.

Becker knew that Fijian culture emphasized good nutrition and looking strong and healthy. Dieting to look very thin had never been common in Fiji. Indeed, in 1995, Becker found, just 3 percent of teenage girls reported ever vomiting to control their weight. By 1998, however, a striking change was evident: Fifteen percent of teenage girls—a fivefold increase—reported this practice. Moreover, Becker found that 62 percent of girls claimed they had dieted during the previous month, and 74 percent reported feeling "too big" or "fat" (Becker, 1999).

The rapid rise in recorded cases of eating disorders in Fiji after television was introduced shows the power of society to shape patterns of health. Eating disorders, including anorexia nervosa (medically, a practice of "severe caloric restriction," commonly understood as compulsive dieting), as well as bulimia (binge eating followed by vomiting) are even more common in the United States, where about half of all college women report engaging in such behavior. This is so in spite of the fact that most of these women, medically speaking, are not overweight.

Consider, too, that 95 percent of people with an eating disorder are female. Why? Because weight control is part of our cultural definition of femininity. As the Duchess of Windsor once put it, "A woman cannot be too rich or too thin." In the United States—and, now, Fiji as well—society teaches young women that they are "never too thin to feel fat" (Wooley, Wooley, & Dyrenforth, 1979; Levine, 1987; Parrott, 1987; Robinson, 1987).

WHAT IS HEALTH?

The World Health Organization defines **health** as *a state of complete physical, mental, and social well-being* (1946:3). This definition underscores the major theme of this chapter: *Health is as much a social as a biological issue, because well-being and illness have their roots in the organization of society.*

HEALTH AND SOCIETY

Society shapes people's health in five major ways:

1. **Cultural patterns define health.** Standards of health vary from society to society. Early in the twentieth century, yaws, a contagious skin disease, was so common in sub-Saharan Africa that people there considered it normal (Dubos, 1980). "Health," therefore, is sometimes a matter of having the same disease as one's neighbors (cf. Pinhey, Rubinstein, & Colfax, 1997).

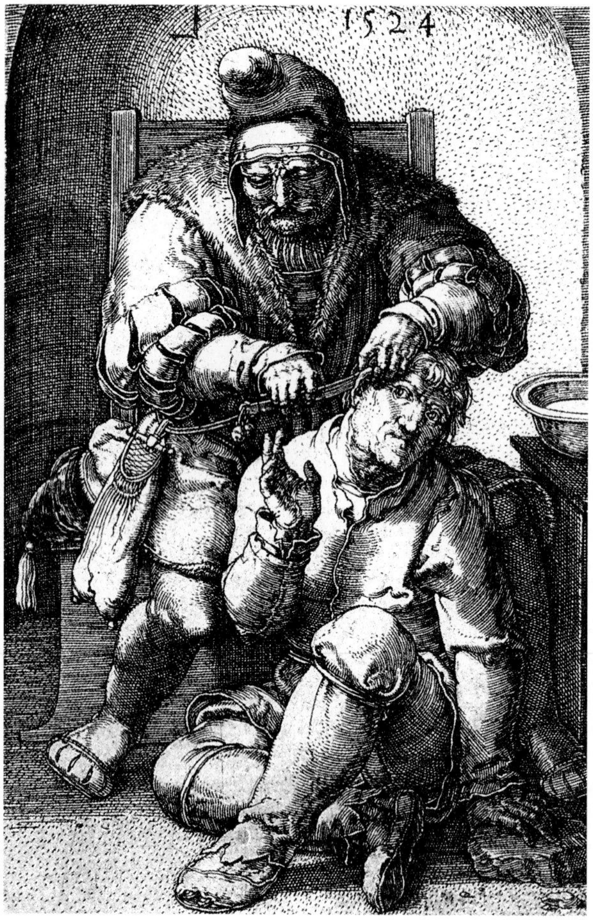

The profession of surgery has existed only for several centuries. Before that, barbers offered their services to the very sick, often cutting the skin to "bleed" a patient. Of course, this "treatment" was rarely effective, but it did produce plenty of bloody bandages, which practitioners hung out to dry. This practice identifies the origin of the red and white barber poles we see today.

Lucas van Leyden, *The Surgeon and the Peasant*, Rijksmuseum, Amsterdam

2. **What is "healthy" is often the same as what people define as morally good.** Members of our society (especially men) think a competitive way of life is "healthy" because it fits our cultural mores. This is so even though stress contributes to heart disease and many other illnesses. On the other hand, some people who object to homosexuality on moral grounds call this sexual orientation "sick," even though it is natural from a biological point of view. Thus, ideas about good health amount to a form of social control that encourages conformity to cultural norms.
3. **Cultural standards of health change over time.** In the early twentieth century, some physicians warned women not to go to college because higher education strained the female brain. Others denounced masturbation as a danger to health. Today, on both counts, we know differently. Fifty years ago, on the other hand, few doctors understood the danger of cigarette smoking, a practice that we now recognize as a serious health risk.
4. **A society's technology affects people's health.** In poor societies, infectious diseases are rampant because of malnutrition and poor sanitation. As industrialization raises living standards, people become more healthy. But industrial technology also creates new threats to health. As Chapter 22 ("Population, Urbanization, and Environment") explains, rich countries threaten human health by overtaxing the world's resources and creating pollution.
5. **Social inequality affects people's health.** All societies distribute resources unequally. Therefore, some people are healthier than others. This pattern starts at birth, with infant mortality highest among the poor. Poor people also live fewer years than rich people.

HEALTH: A GLOBAL SURVEY

Because health is closely linked to social life, we find that humans have fared better and better over the long course of history. For the same reason, we see striking differences in health around the world today.

HEALTH IN HISTORY

With only simple technology, our ancestors could do little to improve health. Hunters and gatherers faced frequent food shortages, which sometimes forced mothers to abandon their children. Those lucky enough to survive infancy were still vulnerable to a host of injuries and illnesses for which there was no treatment. Thus, few people lived to the age of forty, and about half never made it to twenty (Lenski, Nolan, & Lenski, 1995).

With the discovery of agriculture, food became more plentiful. Yet social inequality, too, increased, so

GLOBAL SOCIOLOGY

Killer Poverty: A Report from Africa

The television images of famine in Africa bring home to people in the United States the horror of starving children. Some of the children we see appear bloated, while others seem to have shriveled to little more than skin drawn tightly over bones. Both of these deadly conditions, explains Susan George (1977), are direct results of poverty.

The bloated bodies of some children are caused by protein deficiency. In West Africa this condition is known as *kwashiorkor*, which means literally "one-two." The term comes from the common practice among mothers of abruptly weaning a first child upon the birth of a second. Deprived of mother's milk, a baby may receive no protein at all.

The shriveled bodies of other children come from a lack of both protein and calories. These children have too little food of any kind.

Strictly speaking, only rarely does starvation kill children. Hunger weakens children, leaving them vulnerable to stomach ailments, such as gastroenteritis or diseases like measles. The death rate from measles, for example, is a thousand times greater in parts of Africa than in North America.

Eating just a single food also makes for poor nutrition, providing too little protein, vitamins, and minerals. Millions of people in low-income countries suffer from goiter, a debilitating, diet-related disease of the thyroid gland. Pellagra, common among people who consume mostly corn, is a serious disease that can lead to insanity. Similarly, people who eat only processed rice are prone to beriberi.

Health is obviously a social issue, because diseases that are virtually unknown to the people in rich countries are common in poor nations around the world.

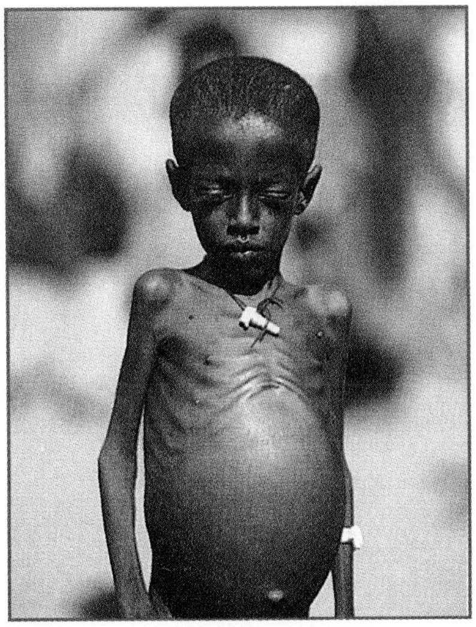

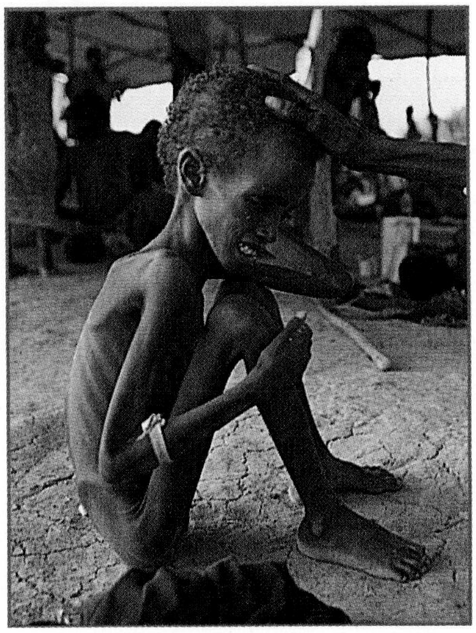

that elites enjoyed better health while peasants and slaves lived in crowded, unsanitary shelters and often went hungry. In the growing cities of medieval Europe, human waste and other refuse piled up in the streets, spreading infectious diseases and plagues that periodically wiped out entire towns (Mumford, 1961).

HEALTH IN LOW-INCOME COUNTRIES

<u>November 1, 1988, central India.</u> Poverty is not just a matter of what you have; it shapes what you are. Probably most of the people we see in the villages here have never had the benefit of a doctor or a dentist. The result is easy to see: People look old before their time.

Severe poverty in much of the world cuts life expectancy far below the seventy or more years typical of rich societies. A look back at Global Map 15–2, on page 389, shows that people in most parts of Africa have a life expectancy of barely fifty, and in the world's poorest nations, such as Ethiopia and Rwanda, the figure falls to forty.

The World Health Organization reports that 1 billion people around the world—one in six—suffer from serious illness due to poverty. Poor sanitation and

WINDOW ON THE WORLD

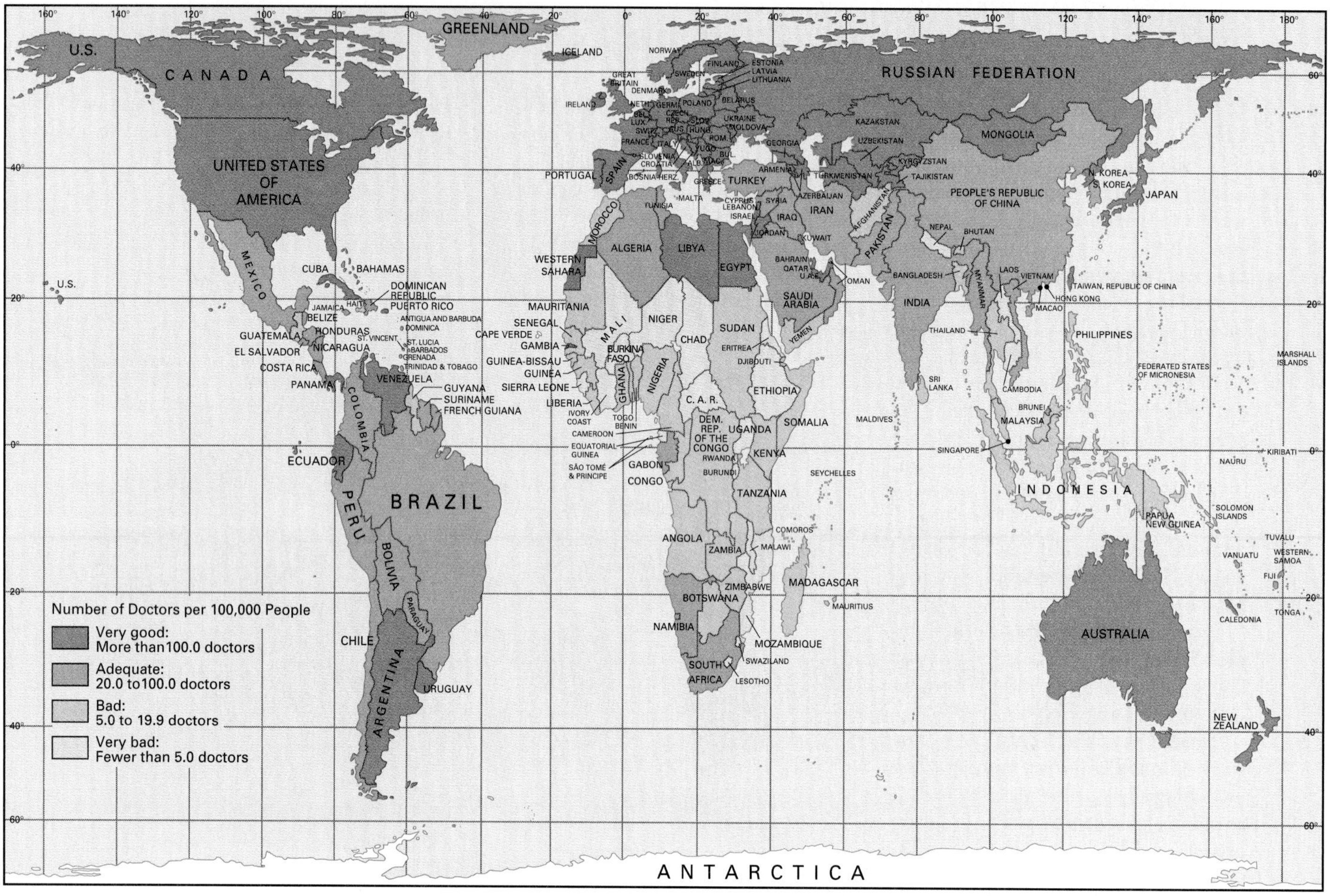

GLOBAL MAP 21–1 The Availability of Physicians in Global Perspective

Medical doctors, widely available to people in rich nations, are perilously scarce in poor societies. While traditional forms of healing do improve health, antibiotics and vaccines—vital for controlling infectious diseases—are often in short supply. In poor countries, therefore, death rates are high, especially among infants.

Source: *Peters Atlas of the World* (1990).

malnutrition kill people of all ages, especially children. Bad health results not just from having too little to eat but also from consuming only one kind of food, as the box on page 541 explains.

In impoverished countries, sanitary drinking water is as hard to come by as a balanced diet. Unsafe water is a major cause of the infectious diseases that imperil both adults and children. The leading causes of death in the United States a century ago, including influenza, pneumonia, and tuberculosis, are widespread killers in poor societies today.

To make matters worse, medical personnel are few and far between, so that the world's poorest people—many of whom live in Central Africa—never see a physician. Global Map 21–1 shows the availability of doctors throughout the world.

In poor nations with minimal medical care, it is no wonder that 10 percent of children die within a year of their birth. In some countries, half the children never reach adulthood—a pattern that parallels the death rates in Europe two centuries ago (George, 1977; Harrison, 1984).

In much of the world, illness and poverty form a vicious circle: Poverty breeds disease, which, in turn, undermines people's ability to work. Moreover, when medical technology does curb infectious disease, the populations of poor nations soar. Without resources to ensure the well-being of the people they have now, poor societies can ill afford large populations. Ultimately, programs to lower death rates in poor countries will succeed only if they are coupled with programs to reduce birth rates as well.

HEALTH IN HIGH-INCOME COUNTRIES

Industrialization dramatically changed patterns of human health in Europe, although, at first, not for the better. By 1800, as the Industrial Revolution took hold, factories offered jobs that drew people from all over the countryside. Cities quickly became overcrowded, creating serious sanitation problems. Moreover, factories fouled the air with smoke, which few saw as a threat to health until well into the twentieth century. And accidents in the workplace were common.

But industrialization gradually improved health in Western Europe and North America as rising living standards translated into better nutrition and safer housing for most people. After 1850, medical advances also improved health, primarily by controlling infectious diseases. In 1854, for example, John Snow mapped the street addresses of London's cholera victims and found they all had drunk contaminated water from the well in Golden Square (Rockett, 1994). Not long afterward, scientists linked cholera to a specific bacterium and developed a vaccine against the deadly disease. Armed with scientific knowledge, early environmentalists campaigned against age-old practices such as discharging raw sewage into rivers used for drinking water. By the early twentieth century, death rates from infectious diseases had fallen sharply.

Over the long term, then, industrialization has dramatically improved human health. In 1900, influenza and pneumonia caused one-fourth of all deaths in the United States. By 1998, these diseases caused fewer than 4 percent of deaths. As Table 21–1 indicates, other infectious diseases that were once major killers now rarely threaten our health.

TABLE 21–1 The Leading Causes of Death in the United States, 1900 and 1998

1900	1998
1. Influenza and pneumonia	1. Heart disease
2. Tuberculosis	2. Cancer
3. Stomach/ intestinal diseases	3. Stroke
4. Heart disease	4. Lung disease (noncancerous)
5. Cerebral hemorrhage	5. Pneumonia and influenza
6. Kidney disease	6. Accidents
7. Accidents	7. Diabetes
8. Cancer	8. Suicide
9. Diseases in early infancy	9. Kidney disease
10. Diphtheria	10. Chronic liver disease and cirrhosis

Sources: Information for 1900 is from William C. Cockerham, *Medical Sociology*, 2d ed. (Englewood Cliffs, N.J.: Prentice Hall, 1986), p. 24; information for 1998 is from U.S. National Center for Health Statistics, *National Vital Statistics Report* (Hyattsville, Md.: The Center, 1999), vol. 47, no. 25 (Oct. 5, 1999).

With infectious diseases less of a threat, it is now chronic illnesses, such as heart disease, cancer, and stroke, that claim most people in the United States. Nothing alters the reality of death, but, by and large, industrial societies manage to delay death until old age (Edmondson, 1997a).

HEALTH IN THE UNITED STATES

In the United States, well-off people are among the healthiest in the world. The poorest, however, are no better off than people living in low-income countries.

SOCIAL EPIDEMIOLOGY: WHO IS HEALTHY?

Social epidemiology is *the study of how health and disease are distributed throughout a society's population.* Just as early social epidemiologists traced the origin and spread of epidemic diseases, researchers today examine the connection between health and our physical and social environments. National Map 21–1 on page 544 surveys the health of women and men across the United States, where there is as much as a twenty-year difference in average life expectancy between the richest and poorest communities. The following sections explain this difference in terms of age and sex, social class, and race.

SEEING OURSELVES

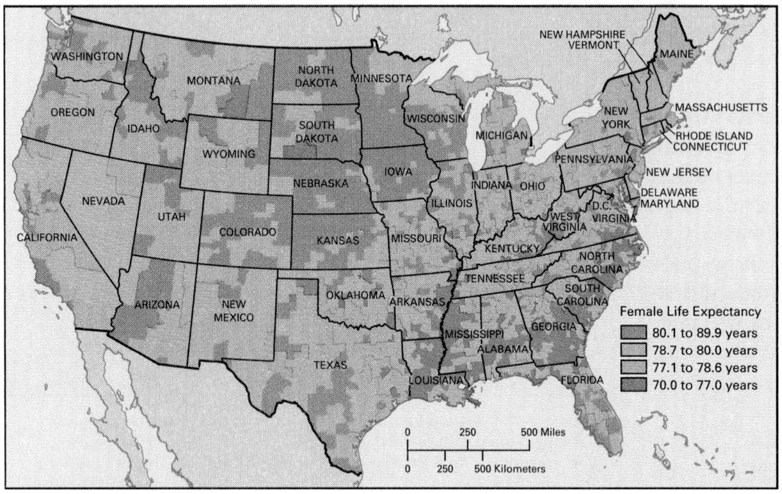

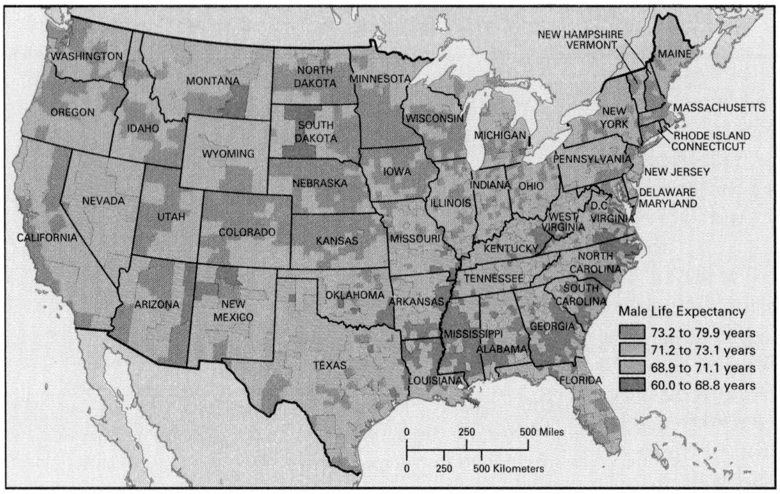

NATIONAL MAP 21–1
Life Expectancy across the United States

These two maps show that, on average, women live longer than men. Yet a gap of roughly twenty years separates people in the healthiest counties of the United States and those in the least healthy counties. Looking over the maps, in which regions of the country is health the best and the worst? Compare these maps with the income distribution shown in National Map 11–3, on page 289, and racial distribution shown in National Map 14–4, on page 374. Can you offer an explanation for the differences in health found here?

Source: C. J. L. Murray, C. M. Michand, M. McKenna, and J. Marks, "U.S. County Patterns of Mortality by Race, 1965–1994" (Boston: Harvard School of Public Health, 1997).

Age and Sex

Death is now rare among young people, with two notable exceptions. Mortality resulting from accidents and, more recently, from acquired immune deficiency syndrome (AIDS) has risen.

Across the life course, women fare better in terms of health than men. Females have a slight biological advantage that renders them less likely than males to die before or immediately after birth. Then, as socialization takes over, males become more aggressive and individualistic, which results in higher rates of accidents, violence, and suicide. Our cultural conception of masculinity also pressures adult men to be more competitive, to repress their emotions, and to take up hazardous behaviors like smoking cigarettes and drinking alcohol to excess. As the box explains, what doctors call "coronary-prone behavior" is really a fairly accurate description of what our culture defines as masculinity.

Social Class and Race

Infant mortality—the death rate among children under one year of age—is twice as high for disadvantaged chil-

APPLYING SOCIOLOGY

Masculinity: A Threat to Health?

Doctors call it "coronary-prone behavior." Psychologists call it the "Type-A personality." Most everyone recognizes it as our culture's concept of masculinity. This pattern of attitudes and behavior—common among men in our society—includes (1) chronic impatience ("C'mon! Go faster or get outta' my way!"), (2) uncontrolled ambition ("I've gotta' have it . . . I need that!"), and (3) free-floating hostility ("Why are so many people *such idiots!?*").

This pattern, although normal from a cultural point of view, is one major reason that men who are driven to succeed are at high risk for heart disease. By acting out the Type-A personality, we may get the job done, but we set in motion complex biochemical processes that are very hard on the human heart.

Here are a few questions to help you assess your own degree of risk (or that of someone important to you):

1. *Do you believe that a person has to be aggressive to succeed? For you, do "nice guys finish last"?* For your heart's sake, try to remove hostility from your life. One starting point: How about eliminating profanity from your speech? Try replacing aggression with compassion, which can be surprisingly effective in dealing with other people. Medically speaking, compassion and humor—rather than irritation and aggravation—will enhance your life.
2. *How well do you handle uncertainty and opposition?* Do you have moments when you fume "Why won't the waiter take my order?" or "Environmentalists are plain nuts!"? We all like to know what's going on and we like others to agree with us. But the world often doesn't work this way. Accepting uncertainty and opposition makes us more mature and certainly healthier.
3. *Are you uneasy showing positive emotion?* Many men think giving and accepting love—from women, from children, and from other men—is a sign of weakness. But the medical truth is that love supports health while hate damages it.

As human beings, we have a great deal of choice about how to live. Think about the choices you make, and reflect on how our society's idea of masculinity often makes us hard on others (including those we love) and—just as important—hard on ourselves.

Sources: Based on Friedman & Rosenman (1974) and Levine (1990).

dren as for children born to privilege. While the health of the richest children in our nation is the best in the world, our poorest children are as vulnerable as those in many poor countries, including Lebanon and Vietnam. Further, research indicates that the negative effects of childhood poverty on well-being continue into adult life (Reynolds & Ross, 1998).

Table 21–2 on page 546 shows that almost 80 percent of adults in families with incomes over $35,000 think their health is very good or excellent, but not quite half of adults in families earning less than $10,000 say the same. Conversely, whereas only about 4 percent of high-income people describe their health as fair or poor, almost one-fourth of low-income people respond this way.

Poverty among African Americans—at two-and-one-half times the rate of whites—helps explain why black people are more likely to die in infancy and, as adults, suffer the effects of violence, drug abuse, and illness. Figure 21–1 shows that life expectancy for white children born in 1998 is six years greater than for African Americans (77.3 years compared to 71.5).

Sex is an even stronger predictor of health than race, since African American females outlive males of either race. From another angle, 79 percent of white men—

TABLE 21-2 Assessment of Personal Health by Income, 1996

Family Income	Excellent	Very Good	Good	Fair	Poor
$35,000 and over	47.2%	30.6%	17.8%	3.5%	0.9%
$20,000–$34,999	34.6	31.2	24.8	7.1	2.4
$10,000–$19,999	27.7	25.7	29.3	12.8	4.6
Under $10,000	24.1	23.9	28.3	16.5	7.2

Source: U.S. National Center for Health Statistics, *Current Estimates from the National Health Interview Survey, 1996*, series 10, no. 200 (Washington, D.C.: U.S. Government Printing Office, 1999).

but just 62 percent of African American men—will live to age sixty-five. The comparable figures for women are 87 percent for whites and 77 percent for African Americans.

Poverty condemns people to crowded, unsanitary living conditions that breed infectious diseases. With a higher risk of poverty, African Americans are three times as likely as whites to die from tuberculosis. Poor people of all races also suffer from nutritional deficiencies. About 20 percent of the U.S. population—more than 50 million people—cannot afford a healthful diet or adequate medical care. As a result, while wealthy people can expect to die in old age of chronic illnesses such as heart disease and cancer, poor people are likely to die younger from infectious diseases such as pneumonia.

Poverty also breeds stress and violence. The leading cause of death among African American men age fifteen to twenty-four—who figure prominently in the urban underclass—is homicide. In 1998 alone, 4,067 African Americans were killed by others of their race—one-third the number of black soldiers killed in the entire Vietnam War.

DIVERSITY SNAPSHOT

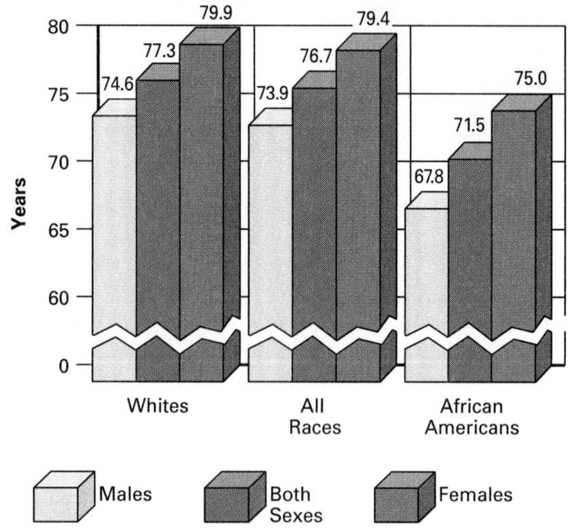

FIGURE 21-1 Life Expectancy for U.S. Children Born in 1998

Source: U.S. National Center for Health Statistics (1999).

CIGARETTE SMOKING

Cigarette smoking, which tops the list of preventable hazards to health, has a definite cultural dimension. Only after World War I did smoking became popular in the United States, and despite growing evidence of its dangers, smoking remained fashionable even a generation ago. Today, however, most adults consider smoking a mild form of social deviance.

The popularity of cigarettes peaked in 1960, when almost 45 percent of U.S. adults smoked. By 1995, only 25 percent were still lighting up (U.S. Centers for Disease Control and Prevention, 1997). Quitting is difficult because cigarette smoke contains nicotine, a physically addictive drug. But people also smoke to cope with stress: Divorced and separated people are likely to smoke, as are the unemployed and people in the armed forces.

Generally speaking, the less schooling people have, the greater their chances of smoking. A slightly larger share of men (28 percent) than women (23 percent) smoke. But cigarettes—the only form of tobacco popular with women—have taken a toll on women's health. By 1990, lung cancer surpassed breast cancer as a cause of death among U.S. women.

Some 430,000 men and women die prematurely each year as a direct result of cigarette smoking, which exceeds the combined death toll from alcohol, cocaine, heroin, homicide, suicide, automobile accidents, and AIDS (Mosley & Cowley, 1991). Smokers also suffer more frequently from minor illnesses such as the flu, and pregnant women who smoke increase the likelihood of spontaneous abortion, prenatal death, and low-birth-weight babies. Even nonsmokers exposed to cigarette smoke have a higher risk of smoking-related diseases.

Tobacco is a $34-billion industry in the United States. In 1997, the tobacco industry conceded that cigarette smoking is harmful to health and agreed to end marketing strategies that targeted young people. But, despite the antismoking trend in the United States, smoking among college students is on the rise, up from 22 percent in 1992 to 29 percent in 1997 (Neergaard, 1998). In addition, the use of chewing tobacco—also a threat to health—is increasing, especially among the young.

Moreover, the tobacco industry is selling more products abroad, especially in low-income societies where there is less regulation of tobacco marketing and sales (Scherer, 1996; Pollack, 1997). Figure 21–2 shows that in many countries, especially in Asia, a large majority of men smoke. Worldwide, more than 1 billion adults (about 30 percent of the total) smoke, consuming some 6 trillion cigarettes annually, and the number is increasing. The good news is that about ten years after quitting, an ex-smoker's health is as good as that of someone who never smoked at all.

GLOBAL SNAPSHOT

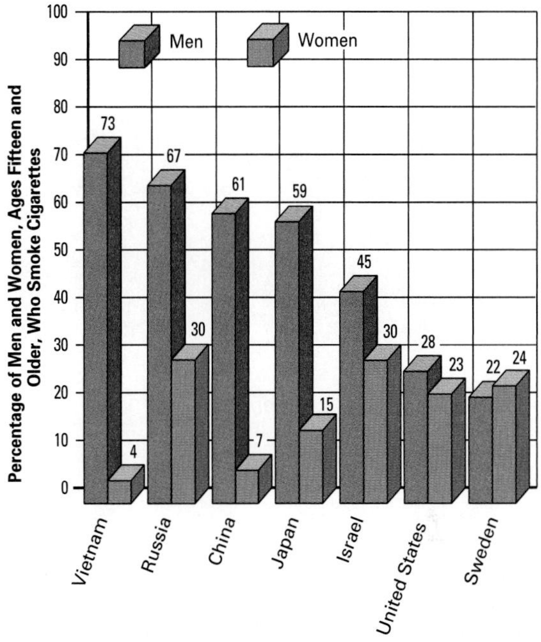

FIGURE 21–2 Cigarette Smoking in Selected Countries

Source: The World Bank (1999).

EATING DISORDERS

An **eating disorder** is *an intense form of dieting or other unhealthy method of weight control driven by the desire to be very thin.* As the opening to this chapter suggests, eating disorders are encouraged by our culture's definition of femininity. Consider, first, that 95 percent of people who suffer from anorexia nervosa or bulimia are women, mostly from white, relatively affluent families. For women, Michael Levine (1987) explains, our culture equates slenderness with success and being attractive to men. On the flip side, we tend to stereotype overweight women (and, to a lesser extent, men) as "lazy," "sloppy," and even "stupid."

Research shows that most college-age women believe (1) "guys like thin girls," (2) being thin is critical to physical attractiveness, and (3) that they are not as thin as men would like. In fact, most college women want to be even thinner than college men say women should be. Most men, on the other hand, think their actual body shape is just about what they want it to be; thus, compared to women, men display little dissatisfaction over body shape (Fallon & Rozin, 1985).

Since few women approach our culture's unrealistic standards of beauty, many women develop a low self-image. Moreover, our idealized image of beauty leads many young women to diet to the point of risking their health.

SEXUALLY TRANSMITTED DISEASES

Sexual activity, though pleasurable and vital to reproducing our species, can transmit more than fifty kinds of infections, or *venereal diseases* (from Venus, the Roman goddess of love). Since our culture associates sex with sin, some people regard venereal diseases not only as illnesses but also as marks of immorality.

Sexually transmitted diseases (STDs) grabbed national attention during the "sexual revolution" of the 1960s when infection rates rose as people began sexual activity earlier and had a greater number of partners. As a result, STDs are an exception to the general decline of infectious diseases during the twentieth century. By

Evidence of the health hazards of smoking cigarettes first appeared in the 1930s. But cigarettes continued to increase in popularity, helped, in part, by celebrity advertising that was, at best, misleading.

the late 1980s, however, the rising dangers of STDs—especially AIDS—generated a sexual counterrevolution that discouraged casual sex (Kain, 1987; Kain & Hart, 1987; Laumann et al., 1994). The following sections briefly describe several common STDs.

Gonorrhea and Syphilis

Gonorrhea and syphilis are caused by microscopic organisms that are almost always transmitted by sexual contact. Untreated, gonorrhea causes sterility; syphilis damages major organs and can result in blindness, mental disorders, and death.

About 356,000 cases of gonorrhea and 38,000 cases of syphilis were recorded in 1998, although the actual numbers may be several times higher. Most cases are contracted by non-Hispanic African Americans (77 percent), with lower numbers among non-Hispanic whites (15 percent), Latinos (6 percent), and Asian Americans and Native Americans (1 percent) (Masters, Johnson, & Kolodny, 1988; Moran et al., 1989; U.S. Centers for Disease Control and Prevention, 1999).

Gonorrhea and syphilis can easily be cured with antibiotics such as penicillin. Thus, neither disease is currently a major health problem in the United States.

Genital Herpes

Genital herpes is a virus that infects 20 to 30 million adults in the United States (one in seven). Though far less dangerous than gonorrhea and syphilis, herpes is incurable. People with genital herpes may exhibit no symptoms or they may experience periodic, painful blisters on the genitals accompanied by fever and headache. Although not fatal to adults, it can be deadly to newborns, and a woman with active genital herpes can transmit the disease to her infant during a vaginal delivery. Such women, therefore, usually give birth by Cesarean section.

AIDS

The most serious of all sexually transmitted diseases is acquired immune deficiency syndrome, or AIDS. Identified in 1981, it is incurable and almost always fatal. AIDS is caused by the human immunodeficiency virus (HIV), which attacks white blood cells, the core of the immune system. AIDS thus renders a person vulnerable to a wide range of other diseases that eventually cause death.

AIDS deaths in the United States dropped to 17,171 in 1998, the lowest number in a decade. But officials recorded some 46,000 new cases in the United States that year, raising the total number of cases on record to more than 711,000. Of these, about 420,000 have died (U.S. Centers for Disease Control and Prevention, 1999).

Globally, HIV infects some 40 million people—half of them under age twenty-five—and the number is rising rapidly. Global Map 21–2 shows that Africa (more specifically, countries south of the Sahara Desert) has the highest HIV infection rate and currently accounts for two-thirds of all world cases. In the cities of central African nations such as Burundi, Rwanda, Uganda, and Kenya, roughly one-fifth of all young adults are infected with HIV (Tofani, 1991; Scommegna, 1996). It is in Asia, however, where the disease is spreading most quickly. North America accounts for less than 5 percent of global HIV cases.

WINDOW ON THE WORLD

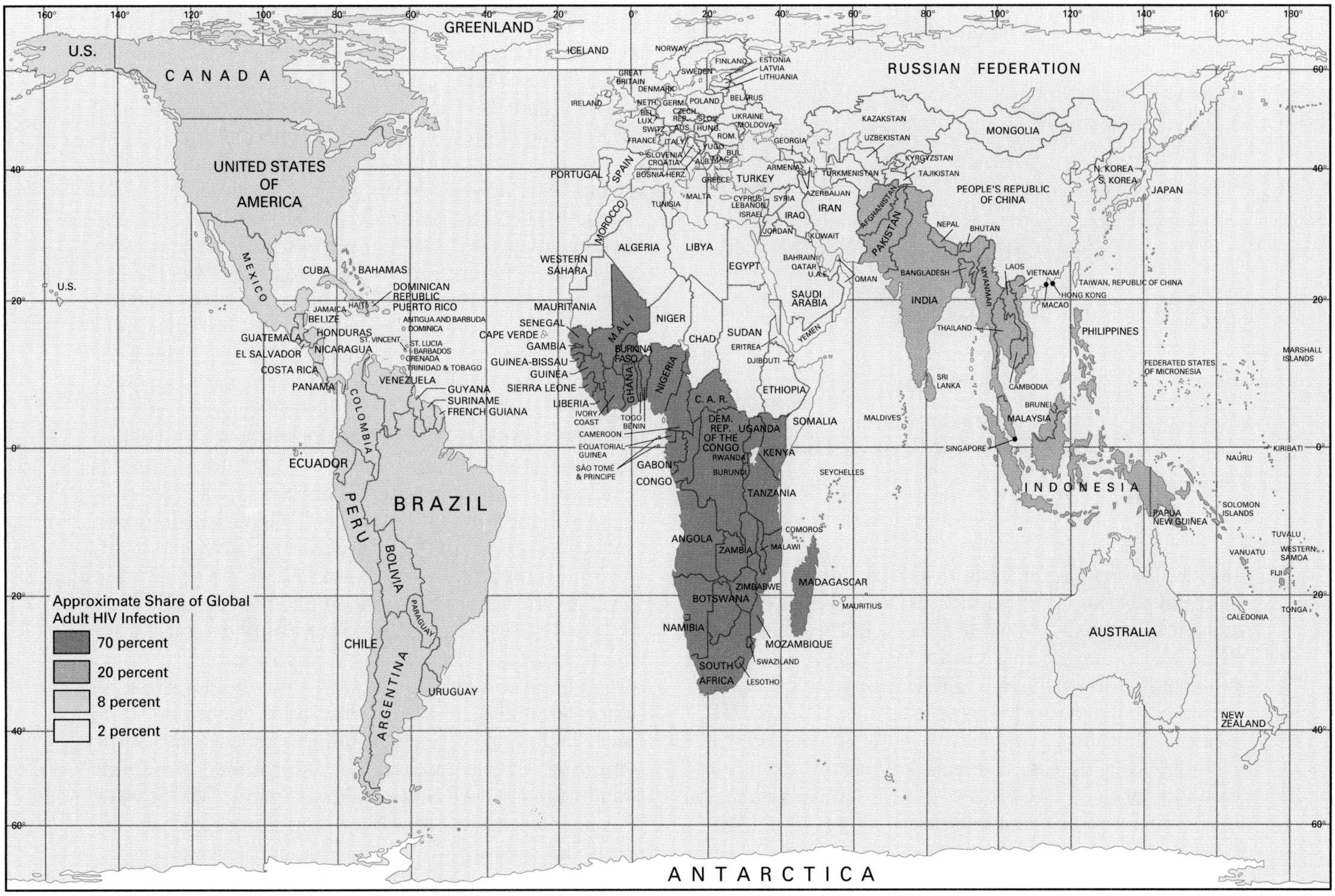

GLOBAL MAP 21–2 HIV Infection of Adults in Global Perspective

Almost 70 percent of all global HIV cases are recorded in sub-Saharan Africa. This high infection rate reflects the prevalence of other sexually transmitted diseases and infrequent use of condoms, factors that promote heterosexual transmission of HIV. Southeast Asia, where HIV is spreading most rapidly, accounts for another 20 percent of infections. South and North America together account for 8 percent of all cases. The incidence of infection is still low in the remaining regions of the world.

Sources: *AIDS* (1997); map projection from *Peters Atlas of the World* (1990).

Upon infection, people with HIV display no symptoms at all, so most are unaware of their condition. Not for a year or longer do symptoms of HIV infection appear. Within five years, one-third of infected people develop full-blown AIDS; half develop AIDS within ten years, and almost all become sick within twenty years.

HIV is infectious but not contagious. In other words, HIV is transmitted from person to person through blood, semen, or breast milk but *not* through casual contact such as shaking hands, hugging, sharing towels or dishes, swimming together, or even by coughing and sneezing. The risk of transmitting the virus through

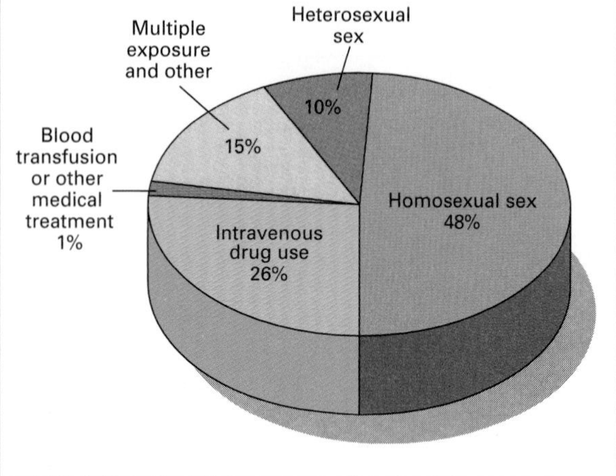

FIGURE 21–3 Types of Transmission for Reported U.S. AIDS Cases, 1999

Source: U.S. Centers for Disease Control and Prevention (1999).

saliva (as in kissing) is extremely low. Moreover, the chance of passing HIV through sexual activity is greatly reduced by the use of latex condoms. But in the age of AIDS, abstinence or an exclusive relationship with an uninfected person is the only sure way to avoid infection.

Specific behaviors put people at high risk for HIV infection. The first is *anal sex*, which can cause rectal bleeding, allowing easy transmission of HIV from one person to another. The practice of anal sex explains why homosexual and bisexual men account for 48 percent of AIDS cases in the United States.

Sharing needles used to inject drugs is a second high-risk behavior. At present, intravenous drug users account for 26 percent of persons with AIDS. Sex with an intravenous drug user is also very risky. Because intravenous drug use is more common among poor people in the United States, AIDS is now becoming a disease of the socially disadvantaged. Although 44 percent of AIDS patients are non-Hispanic white people, African Americans (12 percent of the population) account for 37 percent of people with AIDS. Half of all women with the disease and 58 percent of children are African Americans. Similarly, Latinos (7 percent of the population) represent 18 percent of AIDS cases (and 20 percent of women with AIDS). Asian Americans and Native Americans, however, together account for only 1 percent of people with AIDS (Huber & Schneider, 1992; U.S. Centers for Disease Control and Prevention, 1999).

Using any drug, including alcohol, also increases the risk of HIV infection to the extent that it impairs one's judgment. In other words, even people who understand what places them at risk of infection may act less responsibly if they are under the influence of alcohol, marijuana, or some other drug.

As Figure 21–3 shows, only 10 percent of people with AIDS in the United States became infected through heterosexual contact (although heterosexuals, infected in various ways, account for more than 30 percent of AIDS cases). But heterosexual activity does transmit HIV, and the danger rises with the number of sexual partners, especially if they fall into high-risk categories. Worldwide, heterosexual relations are the primary means of HIV transmission, accounting for two-thirds of all infections.

Treating a single person with AIDS costs hundreds of thousands of dollars, and this figure may rise as new therapies appear. Government health programs, private insurance, and personal savings rarely cover more than a fraction of the cost of treatment. In addition, there is the mounting cost of caring for at least 75,000 U.S. children orphaned by AIDS. Overall, there is little doubt that AIDS represents both a medical and a social problem of monumental proportions.

The government responded slowly to the AIDS crisis, largely because gays and intravenous drug users are widely viewed as deviant. But funds allocated for AIDS research have increased rapidly (now totaling some $7 billion annually), and researchers have identified some drugs, including "protease inhibitors," that suppress the symptoms of the disease. But educational programs remain the most effective weapon against AIDS, since prevention is the only way to stop a disease that currently has no cure.

ETHICAL ISSUES SURROUNDING DEATH

Another social dimension of health and illness involves ethics. Now that technological advances give human beings the power to draw the line separating life and death, we must decide how and when to do so.

When Does Death Occur?

Common sense suggests that life ceases when breathing and heartbeat stop. But the ability to replace a heart and artificially sustain respiration makes such a definition of death obsolete. Medical and legal experts in the United States now define death as an *irreversible* state involving no response to stimulation, no movement or breathing, no reflexes, and no indication of brain activity (Ladd, 1979; Wall, 1980).

Do People Have a Right to Die?

Today, medical personnel, family members, and patients themselves face the agonizing burden of deciding when a terminally ill person should die. Among the most difficult cases are the roughly 10,000 people in the United States in a permanent vegetative state who cannot express their desires about life and death. Generally speaking, the first duty of physicians and hospitals is to protect a patient's life. Even so, a mentally competent person in the process of dying may refuse medical treatment and even nutrition. Moreover, federal law requires hospitals, nursing homes, and other medical facilities to honor such desires of a patient spelled out in advance in a document called a "living will."

What about Mercy Killing?

Mercy killing is the common term for **euthanasia,** *assisting in the death of a person suffering from an incurable disease.* Euthanasia (from the Greek, meaning "a good death") poses an ethical dilemma, being at once an act of kindness and a form of killing.

Whether there is a "right to die" is one of today's most difficult issues. All people with incurable diseases have a right to forgo treatment that might prolong their lives. But whether a doctor should be allowed to help bring about death is the heart of the debate. In 1994, two states—Washington and California—placed before voters propositions that stated physicians should be able to help people who wanted to die; in both cases, the initiatives were defeated. The same year, however, voters in Oregon approved such a measure. This law remained tied up in state court until 1997, when voters again endorsed it. Since then, Oregon doctors have legally assisted in the death of terminally ill patients. In 1997, however, the U.S. Supreme Court decided that, under the U.S. Constitution, there is no "right to die," which has slowed the spread of such laws. Moreover, in 1999, Congress began debating a law that would prohibit states from adopting laws similar to Oregon's.

Supporters of *active* euthanasia—allowing a dying person to enlist the services of a physician to bring on a quick death—argue that there are circumstances (such as when a dying person suffers from great pain) that make death preferable to life. Critics, however, counter that permitting active euthanasia invites abuse (see Chapter 15, "Aging and the Elderly"). They fear that patients will feel pressure to end their lives in order to spare family members the burden of caring for them, as well as the high costs of hospitalization. Further, research in the Netherlands, where physician-assisted suicide is legal, indicates that about one-fifth of all deaths have occurred without a patient explicitly requesting to die (Gillon, 1999).

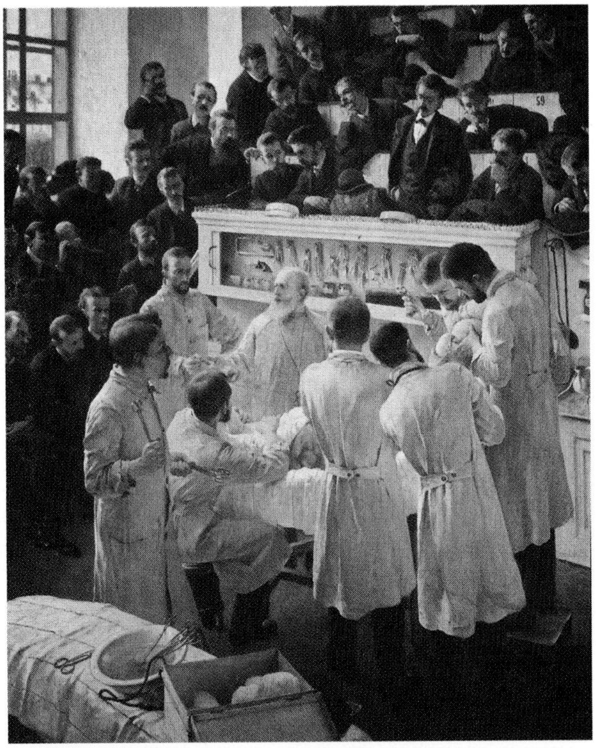

The rise of scientific medicine during the nineteenth century resulted in new skills and technology for treating many common ailments that had afflicted humanity for centuries. At the same time, however, scientific medicine pushed forms of health care involving women to the margins, and placed medicine under the control of men living in cities. We see this pattern in the A. F. Seligmann painting General Hospital, *showing an obviously all-male medical school class in Vienna in 1880.*

In the United States, a majority of adults express support for giving dying people the right to choose to die with a doctor's help (Rosenbaum, 1997; NORC, 1999). Therefore, the "right to die" debate is sure to continue.

THE MEDICAL ESTABLISHMENT

Medicine is *the social institution that focuses on combating disease and improving health.* Through most of human history, health care was entirely the responsibility of individuals and their families. Medicine emerges as a social institution only as societies become more productive and people take on specialized work.

In agrarian societies, health practitioners, including herbalists and acupuncturists, play a central part in improving health. In industrial societies, health falls to specially trained and licensed healers, from anesthesiologists to X-ray technicians. Today's medical establishment in the United States took form over the last 150 years.

THE RISE OF SCIENTIFIC MEDICINE

In colonial times, doctors, herbalists, druggists, midwives, and ministers all engaged in various forms of healing arts. But not all were effective: Unsanitary instruments, no anesthesia, and simple ignorance made surgery a terrible ordeal, and doctors probably killed as many patients as they saved.

But by studying human anatomy and physiology, doctors gradually established themselves as self-regulating professionals with medical degrees. The American Medical Association (AMA) was founded in 1847 and symbolized the growing acceptance of a scientific model of medicine.

Still, traditional approaches to health care, such as a focus on nutrition, had their defenders. The AMA responded boldly—some thought arrogantly—by criticizing these alternative ideas about health. In the early 1900s, state licensing boards agreed to certify only physicians trained in scientific programs approved by the AMA. With control of the certification process, the AMA began closing down schools teaching other healing skills, which limited the practice of medicine to those with an M.D. degree. In the process, both the prestige and income of physicians rose dramatically; today, men and women with M.D. degrees earn, on average, almost $200,000 annually.

Practitioners of other approaches, such as osteopathic physicians, concluded that they had no choice but to fall in line with AMA standards. Thus osteopaths (with D.O. degrees), who originally manipulated the skeleton and muscles, today treat illness with drugs in much the same way as medical doctors (with M.D. degrees). Other practitioners—such as chiropractors, herbal healers, and midwives—have held to traditional roles but at the cost of being relegated to the fringe of the medical profession.

Scientific medicine, taught in expensive, urban medical schools, also changed the social profile of doctors. After the AMA standards were adopted, most physicians came from privileged backgrounds and practiced in cities. Furthermore, women, who had figured in many fields of healing, were scorned by the AMA. Some early medical schools did train women and African Americans, but faced with declining financial resources, most of these schools eventually closed. Only in recent decades has the social diversity of medical doctors increased, with women and African Americans representing 25 percent and 6 percent, respectively, of all physicians (Gordon, 1980; Starr, 1982; Huet-Cox, 1984; U.S. Department of Labor, 2000).

HOLISTIC MEDICINE

The scientific model of medicine has recently been tempered by the more traditional model of **holistic medicine,** *an approach to health care that emphasizes prevention of illness and takes into account the person's entire physical and social environment.*

Holistic practitioners agree on the need for drugs, surgery, artificial organs, and high technology, but they don't want technological advances to turn medicine into narrow specialties concerned with symptoms rather than people and with disease instead of health. Here are three foundations of holistic health care (Duhl, 1980; Ferguson, 1980; Gordon, 1980):

1. **Patients are people.** Holistic practitioners are concerned not only with symptoms but with how people's environment and lifestyle affect health. Holistic practitioners extend the bounds of conventional medicine, taking an active role in combating poverty, environmental pollution, and other dangers to public health.
2. **Responsibility, not dependency.** In the scientific model, patients are dependent on physicians. Holistic medicine tries to shift some responsibility for health from physicians to people themselves by encouraging health-promoting behavior. Holistic medicine thus favors an *active* approach to *health,* rather than a *reactive* approach to *illness.*
3. **Personal treatment.** Conventional medicine locates medical care in impersonal offices and hospitals, which are disease-centered settings. By contrast, holistic practitioners favor, as much as possible, a personal and relaxed environment such as the home.

In sum, holistic care does not oppose scientific medicine but shifts the emphasis from treating disease toward achieving the greatest well-being for everyone. Since the AMA currently recognizes more than fifty medical specialties, there is a need for practitioners who are concerned with the whole patient.

PAYING FOR HEALTH: A GLOBAL SURVEY

As medicine has come to rely on high technology, the costs of health care in industrial societies have skyrocketed. To meet these costs, countries have adopted various strategies.

Medicine in Socialist Societies

In societies with mostly socialist economies, the government provides medical care directly to the people. These nations hold that all citizens have the right to basic medical care. In practice, then, people do not pay physicians and hospitals on their own; instead, the government uses public funds to pay medical costs. The state owns and operates medical facilities and pays salaries to practitioners, who are government employees.

The People's Republic of China. As a poor, agrarian society in the process of industrializing, the People's Republic of China faces the daunting task of providing for the health of more than 1 billion people. China has experimented with private medicine, but the government controls most health care.

China's famed "barefoot doctors," roughly comparable to U.S. paramedics, bring some modern methods of medical care to millions of peasants in remote rural villages. Otherwise, traditional healing arts, including acupuncture and the use of medicinal herbs, are still widely practiced in China. In addition, a holistic concern for the well-being of both mind and body characterizes the Chinese approach to health (Sidel & Sidel, 1982b; Kaptchuk, 1985).

The Russian Federation. The Russian Federation is struggling to transform a state-dominated economy into more of a market system. For this reason, medical care is in transition. Nonetheless, the idea that everyone has a right to basic medical care remains widespread.

As in China, people do not choose a physician but report to a local government-operated health facility. Physicians in the Russian Federation have lower income than their counterparts in the United States, earning about the same salary as skilled industrial workers (compared to roughly a five-to-one ratio in this country). Worth noting, too, is that about 70 percent of physicians in the Russian Federation are women, compared with 25 percent in the United States. As in our society, occupations dominated by women yield fewer financial rewards.

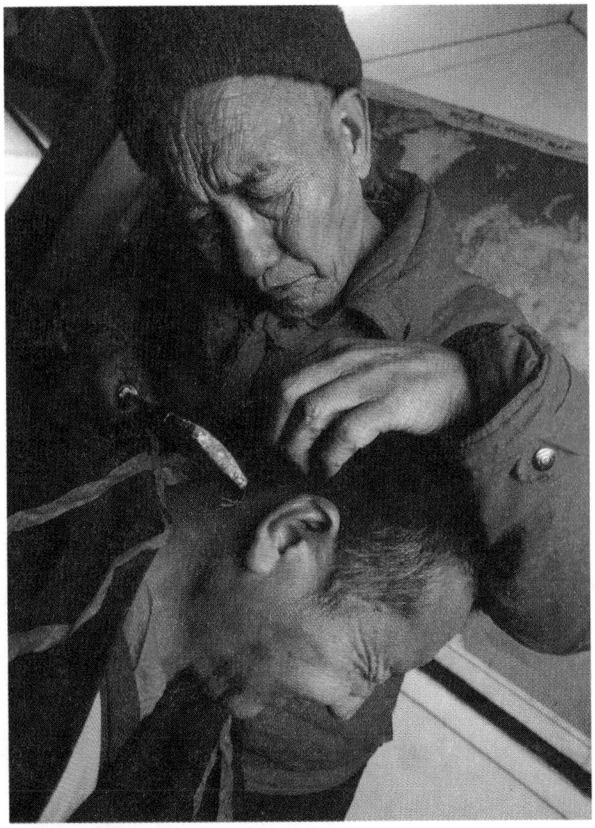

Traditional healers work to improve people's health throughout the world, especially in low-income nations. Here, a Chinese practitioner treats a patient by burning rolled herbs into his scalp.

Funded by government taxes, health care in the Russian Federation has suffered setbacks in recent years, partly because of a falling standard of living, as the box on page 554 explains. Moreover, a rising demand for medical care has strained a bureaucratic system that, at best, provides highly standardized and impersonal care. The optimistic view is that, as market reforms proceed, both living standards and the quality of medical services will improve. In any case, what does seem certain is that disparities in medical care among various segments of the Russian population will increase (Specter, 1995; Landsberg, 1998).

Medicine in Capitalist Societies

People living in nations with mostly capitalist economies usually pay for their own health care. However, because high cost puts medical care beyond the reach

GLOBAL SOCIOLOGY

When Health Fails: A Report from Russia

Night is falling in Pitkyaranta, a small town on the western edge of Russia, near the Finnish border. Andrei, a thirty-year-old man with a round face and a long ponytail, weaves his way through the deepening shadows along a busy street. He has spent much of the afternoon in a bar with friends watching music videos, drinking vodka, and smoking cigarettes. Andrei is a railroad worker, but several months ago he was laid off. "Now," he explains bitterly, "I have nothing to do but drink and smoke." Andrei shrugs off a question about his health. "The only thing I care about is finding a job. I am a grown man. I don't want to be supported by my mother and father." Andrei still thinks of himself as young, yet, according to current health patterns in Russia, for a man of thirty life is more than half over.

After the collapse of the Soviet Union in 1991, living conditions worsened every year. One result, say doctors, is massive stress—especially on men who earn too little to support their families or are out of work entirely. Few people eat well any more, and Russian men now drink and smoke as heavily as people anywhere in the world. The World Health Organization reports that alcohol abuse is Russia's number one killer, with cigarette smoking not far behind.

In towns like Pitkyaranta, the signs of poor health are everywhere: Women no longer breast-feed their babies, adults suffer higher rates of accidents and illness, and people look old before their time. Doctors are struggling to stop the health slide, but, with poorly equipped hospitals, they are simply overwhelmed. Statistically, while life expectancy has dropped several years for women, it has gone into free-fall for men and now stands at just fifty-eight years, about where it was half a century ago. Just 100 miles to the west in Finland—where economic trends are far better—the comparable figure is seventy-two years. In global context, life expectancy for Russian women has fallen below that in rich countries to the West; for Russian men, life expectancy is now the same as in some of the world's lowest-income nations.

A joke is making the rounds among young Russian men like Andrei. Their health may be failing, they say, but this cloud has a silver lining: At least they no longer have to worry about retirement.

Source: Adapted from Landsberg (1998).

of many people, government programs underwrite a considerable share of the expense.

Sweden. In 1891, Sweden instituted a compulsory, comprehensive system of government medical care. Citizens pay for this program with their taxes, which are among the highest in the world. Typically physicians receive salaries from the government rather than fees from patients, and government officials manage most hospitals. Because this medical system resembles that found in socialist societies, it is often described as **socialized medicine,** *a health care system in which the government owns and operates most medical facilities and employs most physicians.*

Great Britain. In 1948, Great Britain, too, established socialized medicine. The British did not do away with private care, however; instead, they created a "dual system" of medical service. All British citizens are entitled to medical care provided by the National Health Service, but those who can afford to may purchase more extensive care from doctors and hospitals that operate privately.

Canada. Canada has a "single payer" model of health care. Like a vast insurance company, the Canadian government pays doctors and hospitals according to a set schedule of fees. But Canada also has a two-tiered system like Great Britain's, with some physicians working outside the government-funded system and setting their own fees.

Canada boasts of providing care for everyone at a lower cost than the (nonuniversal) medical system in the United States. However, the Canadian system uses less state-of-the-art technology and responds slowly to people's needs, so that people may wait months to receive major surgery (Grant, 1984; Vayda & Deber, 1984; Rosenthal, 1991).

Japan. Physicians in Japan have private practices, but a combination of government programs and private insurance pays medical costs. As shown in Figure 21–4, the Japanese approach health care much like the Europeans, with most medical expenses paid through government.

MEDICINE IN THE UNITED STATES

With our primarily private system of medical care, the United States stands alone among industrialized societies in having no government-sponsored medical system that provides care for every citizen. Called a **direct-fee system,** ours is *a medical care system in which patients pay directly for the services of physicians and hospitals.* Thus, while Europeans look to government to fund about 80 percent of their medical costs (paid for through taxation), the U.S. government pays less than half of this country's medical costs (Lohr, 1988; U.S. Census Bureau, 1999).

In the United States, rich people can purchase the best medical care in the world. Yet the poor fare worse than their counterparts in Europe. This disparity explains the relatively high death rates among both infants and adults in the United States compared to many European countries (United Nations Development Programme, 1999).

Why does the United States have no national health care program? First, our society historically has limited government in the interest of greater personal liberty. Second, political support for a national medical program has not been strong, even among labor unions, which have concentrated on winning health care benefits from employers. Third, the AMA and the health insurance industry have strongly and consistently opposed national health care proposals (Starr, 1982).

Expenditures for medical care in the United States have increased dramatically from $12 billion in 1950 to more than $1 trillion in 1998. This amounts to about $3,300 per person, more than any other industrial society spends for medical care. Who pays the medical bills?

GLOBAL SNAPSHOT

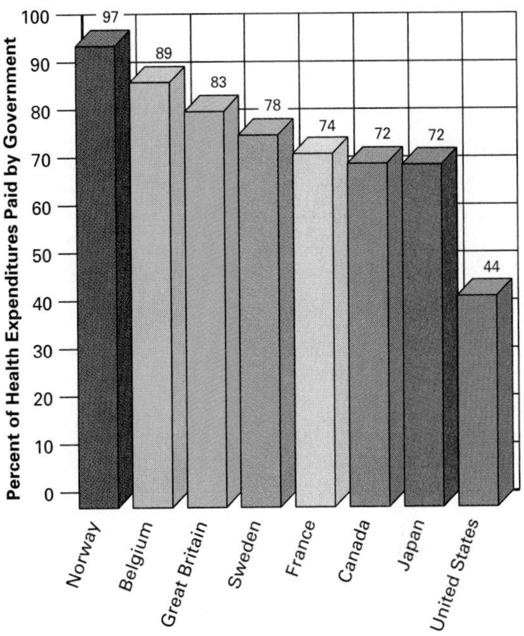

FIGURE 21–4 Extent of "Socialized Medicine" in Selected Countries

Source: United Nations Development Programme (1998).

Private insurance programs. In 1997, 165 million people (61 percent) received some medical care benefits from a family member's employer or labor union. Another 23 million people (9 percent) purchased private coverage on their own. Seventy percent of our population, then, has private insurance (such as Blue Cross and Blue Shield), although few such programs pay all medical costs (U.S. Census Bureau, 1999).

Public insurance programs. In 1965, Congress created Medicare and Medicaid. Medicare pays a portion of the medical costs of men and women over sixty-five; in 1998, it covered 37 million women and men, about 14 percent of the population. During the same year, Medicaid, a medical insurance program for the poor, provided benefits to 34 million people, about 13 percent of the population. An additional 25 million veterans (9 percent of the population) can obtain free care in government-operated hospitals. In all, 36 percent of this country's people enjoy some medical care benefits from the government, but most also have private insurance.

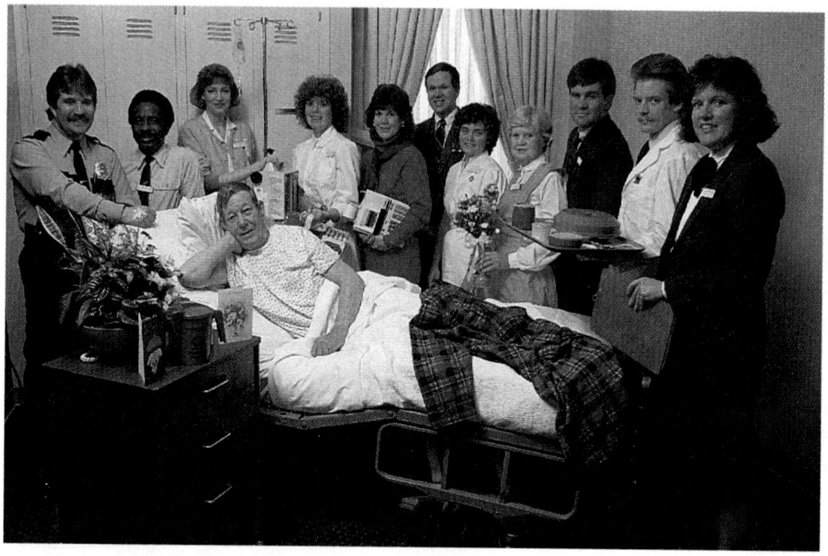

The cost of medical care in the United States has been rising at a dizzying rate. In part, this high rate of increase reflects the fact that hospitals are large, bureaucratic organizations that employ dozens of specialized workers in the treatment of any single patient. Here one man poses for a picture with just the medical staff who directly provide for him.

Health maintenance organizations. About 65 million people (24 percent) in the United States belong to a **health maintenance organization (HMO),** *an organization that provides comprehensive medical care to subscribers for a fixed fee.* HMOs vary in their costs and benefits, and none provides full coverage. But fixed fees make these organizations profitable to the extent that their subscribers stay healthy; therefore, many take a preventive approach to health.

In all, 84 percent of the U.S. population has some medical care coverage, either private or public. But most plans do not provide full coverage, so serious illness threatens even middle-class people with financial hardship. Most programs also exclude certain medical services, such as dental care and treatment for mental health problems. Worse, 44 million people (about 16 percent of the population) have no medical insurance at all. Almost as many lose their medical coverage temporarily each year due to layoffs or job changes. Some of these people choose to forgo medical coverage (especially young people who take good health for granted), but most are part-time or full-time workers who receive no health care benefits. Caught worst in the medical care bind are low- and moderate-income people who cannot afford to become ill but cannot afford to pay for the preventive medical care they need to remain healthy (Altman et al., 1989; Hersch & White-Means, 1993; Smith, 1993; U.S. Census Bureau, 1999).

Recent debate. In 1994, the Clinton administration proposed a sweeping reform of health care called "managed competition." Under the "competition" element of this program, employees would collectively bargain with various medical providers in order to receive the greatest value. The "managed" dimension meant that government would oversee the entire process to ensure that everyone participated.

But after lengthy debate, Congress rejected the Clinton reforms. Still, public concern about health care runs high, so debate over this issue will certainly continue.

THEORETICAL ANALYSIS OF HEALTH AND MEDICINE

Each of the major theoretical paradigms in sociology offers a means of organizing and interpreting the facts and issues presented in this chapter.

STRUCTURAL-FUNCTIONAL ANALYSIS

Talcott Parsons (1964; orig. 1951) viewed medicine as society's strategy to keep its members healthy. In this scheme, illness is dysfunctional because it undermines people's abilities to perform their roles.

The Sick Role

Society responds to sickness, Parsons argued, by providing a **sick role,** *patterns of behavior defined as appropriate for people who are ill.* According to Parsons, the sick role has three characteristics:

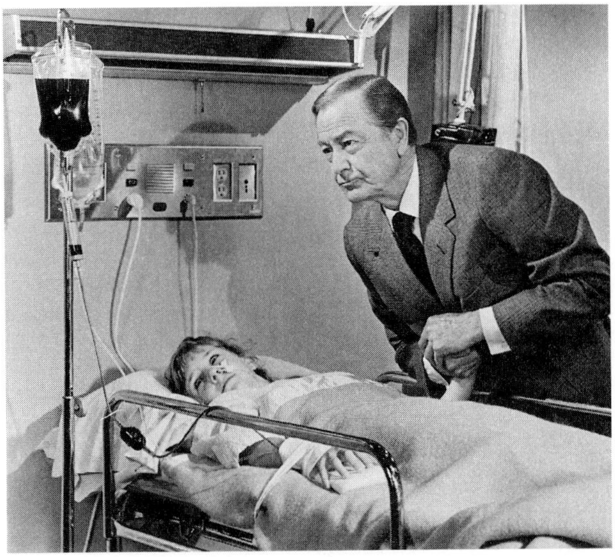

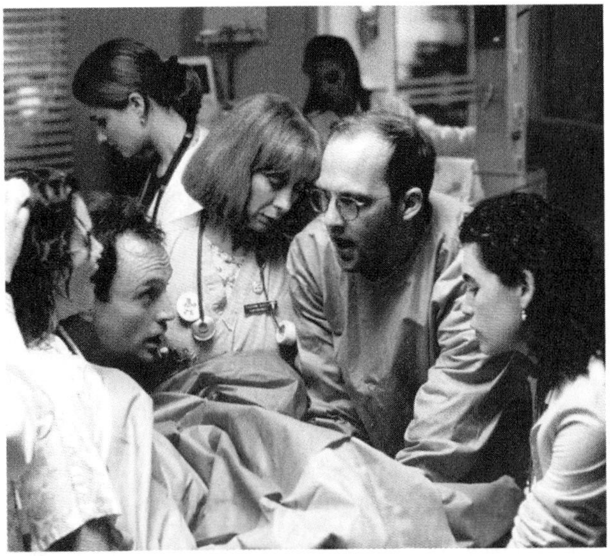

Our national view of medicine has changed during the last several decades. Television viewers in the 1970s watched doctors like Marcus Welby, M.D., confidently take charge of situations in a fatherly—and almost godlike—manner. By the 1990s, programs like "E.R." gave a more realistic view of the limitations of medicine to address illness, as well as the violence that wracks our society.

1. **Illness exempts people from routine responsibilities.** Serious illness relaxes or suspends normal obligations such as going to work or attending school. To prevent abuse of this privilege, however, people do not simply declare themselves ill; they must enlist the support of others—especially a recognized medical expert—before assuming the sick role.
2. **A sick person must want to be well.** We assume that no one wants to be sick, and we withdraw the benefits of the sick role when someone feigns illness in order to avoid responsibility or to get attention.
3. **A sick person must seek competent help.** People who are ill must seek out and cooperate with health care practitioners. By failing to seek medical help or to follow doctor's orders, a person risks losing the benefits of the sick role.

The Physician's Role

Physicians evaluate people's claims of sickness and try to restore the sick to normal routines. To do this, Parsons explained, physicians use their specialized knowledge. Physicians expect patients to provide whatever personal information may assist their efforts and to follow doctor's orders in completing treatment.

Parsons saw the doctor-patient relationship as hierarchical. Yet this pattern varies from society to society. Japanese tradition, for example, gives physicians great authority over their patients. Japanese physicians even take it upon themselves to decide how much information about the seriousness of an illness they will share with the patient (Darnton & Hoshia, 1989). Until about thirty years ago, physicians in the United States similarly made such decisions. But the patient's rights movement embodies the public demand that physicians readily share medical information. A more equal relationship between doctor and patient is developing in Europe, too, and even in Japan.

Critical evaluation. Parsons's analysis links illness and medicine to the broader organization of society. Others have usefully extended the concept of the sick role to some nonillness situations such as pregnancy (Myers & Grasmick, 1989).

One limitation of the sick-role concept is that it applies to acute conditions (like the flu or a broken leg) better than chronic illnesses (like heart disease), which may not be reversible. Moreover, a sick person's ability to regain health depends on available resources. Many poor people simply cannot afford either medical care or taking time off from work.

Finally, critics point out that Parsons's analysis implies that doctors—rather than people themselves—bear the primary responsibility for health. A more prevention-oriented approach makes physicians and patients equal partners in the pursuit of health.

SYMBOLIC-INTERACTION ANALYSIS

According to the symbolic-interaction paradigm, society is less a grand system than a series of complex and changing realities. Health and medical care, therefore, are socially constructed by people in everyday interaction.

The Social Construction of Illness

If we socially construct our ideas of health and illness, it follows that members of a very poor society may view hunger and malnutrition as normal. Similarly, people in rich nations, such as our own, may give little thought to the harmful effects of a rich diet.

How we respond to illness, too, is based on social definitions that may or may not square with medical facts. For instance, people with AIDS contend with fear and sometimes outright bigotry that has no medical basis. Likewise, students may pay no attention to signs of illness on the eve of a vacation, but they dutifully report to the infirmary hours before a midterm examination. Health, in short, is less an objective commodity than a negotiated outcome.

Indeed, how people define a medical situation may actually affect how they feel. Medical experts marvel at *psychosomatic* disorders (a fusion of Greek words for "mind" and "body"), when state of mind guides physical sensations (Hamrick, Anspaugh, & Ezell, 1986). Applying sociologist W. I. Thomas's theorem (1931), we can say that when health or illness is defined as real, it becomes real in its consequences.

The Social Construction of Treatment

In Chapter 6 ("Social Interaction in Everyday Life"), we used Erving Goffman's dramaturgical approach to explain how physicians tailor their physical surroundings ("the office") and their behavior ("the presentation of self") so that others see them as competent and in charge.

Sociologist Joan Emerson (1970) further illustrates this process of constructing reality in her analysis of the gynecological examination carried out by a male doctor. This situation is vulnerable to serious misinterpretation, since a man touching a woman's genitals is conventionally viewed as a sexual act and possibly even an assault.

To ensure that people define the situation as impersonal and professional, the medical staff wear uniforms and furnish the examination room with nothing but medical equipment. The doctor's manner and overall performance are designed to make the patient feel that, to him, examining the genital area is no different from treating any other part of the body. A female nurse is usually present during the examination not only to assist the physician but to dispel any impression that a man and woman are "alone in a room."

Managing situational definitions in this way is only rarely taught in medical schools. The oversight is unfortunate because, as Emerson's analysis shows, understanding how people construct reality in the examination room is as important as mastering the medical skills required for treatment.

Critical evaluation. A strength of the symbolic-interaction paradigm lies in revealing that what people view as healthful or harmful depends on numerous factors, many of which are not, strictly speaking, medical. This approach also shows that in any medical procedure, both patient and medical staff engage in a subtle process of reality construction.

Critics fault this approach, however, for implying that there are no objective standards of well-being. Certain physical conditions do indeed cause definite changes in people, regardless of how we view those conditions. People who lack sufficient nutrition and safe water, for example, suffer from their unhealthy environment, whether they define their surroundings as normal or not.

SOCIAL-CONFLICT ANALYSIS

Social-conflict analysis draws a connection between health and social inequality and, taking a cue from Karl Marx, ties medicine to the operation of capitalism. Researchers have focused on three main issues: access to medical care, the effects of the profit motive, and the politics of medicine.

Access to Care

Personal health is the foundation of social life. Yet, by making health a commodity, capitalist societies allow health to follow wealth. The access problem is more serious in the United States than in other industrialized societies because our country has no universal medical care system.

Conflict theorists concede that capitalism provides excellent health care for the rich, but it does not provide very well for the rest of the population. Most of the 44 million people who lack health care coverage at present have low incomes.

The Profit Motive

Some conflict analysts go further, arguing that the real problem is not access to medical care but the character of capitalist medicine itself. The profit motive turns physicians, hospitals, and the pharmaceutical industry into multibillion-dollar corporations. The quest for higher profits encourages unnecessary tests and surgery as well as an overreliance on drugs (Ehrenreich, 1978; Kaplan et al., 1985).

Of some 25 million surgical operations performed in the United States each year, three-fourths are "elective," meaning that they promote long-term health and are not prompted by a medical emergency. In addition, of course, any medical procedure or use of drugs is risky and harms between 5 and 10 percent of patients. Therefore, social-conflict theorists contend that surgery probably reflects the financial interests of surgeons and hospitals as much as the medical needs of patients (Illich, 1976; Sidel & Sidel, 1982a; Cowley, 1995).

Finally, say social-conflict analysts, our society is all too tolerant of physicians having a direct financial interest in the tests and procedures they order for their patients (Pear & Eckholm, 1991). Health care should be motivated by a concern for people, not profits.

Medicine as Politics

Although science declares itself politically neutral, scientific medicine frequently takes sides on significant social issues. For example, the medical establishment opposes government regulation of fees and services and has always campaigned against proposals for government health care programs. Moreover, the history of medicine itself shows how racial and sexual discrimination has been supported by "scientific" opinions (Leavitt, 1984). Consider the diagnosis of "hysteria," a term that has its origins in the Greek word *hyster*, meaning "uterus." In choosing this word to describe a wild, emotional state, the medical profession suggested that being a woman is somehow the same as being irrational.

Even today, according to conflict theory, scientific medicine explains illness exclusively in terms of bacteria and viruses and ignores the damaging effects of social inequality. From a scientific perspective, in other words, a lack of sanitation and an unhealthy diet make poor people sick; but what about asking why people are poor in the first place? In this way, scientific medicine depoliticizes health by reducing social issues to simple biology.

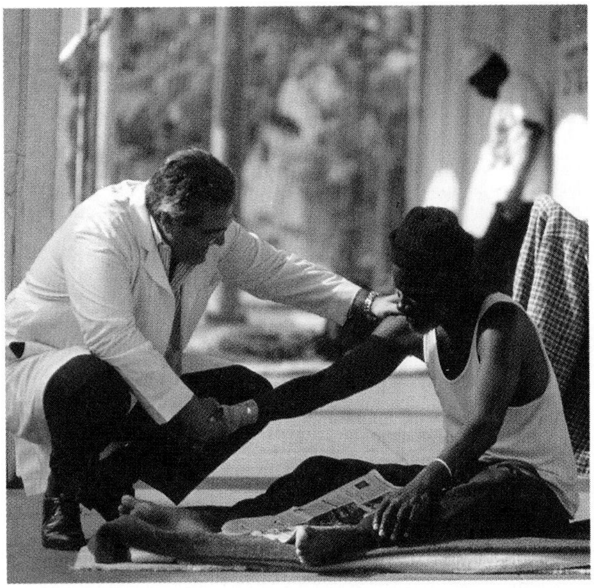

Despite the efforts of exemplary physicians such as Dr. Joe Greer, homeless people throughout the United States have a great need for medical support but receive little health care. In your opinion, what changes are needed to meet the needs of society's most vulnerable members?

Critical evaluation. Social-conflict analysis provides still another view of the relationships among health, medicine, and our society. According to this paradigm, social inequality is the reason some people have better health than others.

The most common objection to the conflict approach is that it minimizes the gains in U.S. health brought about by scientific medicine and higher living standards. Though there is plenty of room for improvement, health indicators for our population as a whole rose steadily over the course of the twentieth century and compare well with those of other industrial societies.

In sum, sociology's three major theoretical paradigms convincingly argue that health and medicine are social issues. Indeed, as the final box explains, advancing technology is making it more and more true as time goes on. The reknowned French scientist Louis Pasteur (1822–1895), who spent much of his life studying how bacteria cause disease, said just before he died that health depends much less on bacteria than on the social

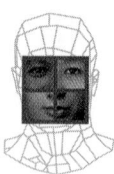

CONTROVERSY & DEBATE

The Genetic Crystal Ball: Do We Really Want to Look?

The liquid in the laboratory test tube seems ordinary enough, rather like a syrupy form of water. But this liquid represents one of the greatest medical breakthroughs of all time; it may even be the key to life itself. The liquid is deoxyribonucleic acid, or DNA, the spiraling molecule found in cells of the human body. DNA contains the blueprint for making each one of us a unique human being.

The human body is composed of some 100 trillion cells, most of which contain a nucleus of twenty-three pairs of chromosomes (one of each pair comes from each parent). Each chromosome is packed with DNA, in segments called genes. Genes guide the production of protein, the building block of the human body.

If genetics sounds complicated (and it is), the social implications of genetic knowledge are even more complex. Scientists discovered DNA in 1952, and now an aggressive program is underway to "map" our genetic landscape. The ultimate goal of the Human Genome Project is to understand how each bit of DNA shapes our being. But do we really want to turn the key to understand life itself?

In the Human Genome Project, many scientists see a completely new approach to medicine that discards treating symptoms and aims to stop illness before it begins. Research, they point out, already has identified genetic abnormalities that cause some forms of cancer, sickle cell anemia, muscular dystrophy, Huntington's disease, cystic fibrosis, and other crippling and deadly afflictions. During this century, genetic screening—a scientific "crystal ball"—could let people know their medical destiny and allow doctors to manipulate segments of DNA to prevent diseases before they appear.

But many people urge caution in such research, warning that genetic information could easily be abused. At its worst, genetic mapping opens the door to Nazi-like efforts to breed a super-race. Indeed, in 1994, the People's Republic of China began to regulate marriage and

environment where the bacteria are found (Gordon, 1980:7). Explaining Pasteur's insight is sociology's contribution to human health.

LOOKING AHEAD: HEALTH AND MEDICINE IN THE TWENTY-FIRST CENTURY

At the beginning of the twentieth century, deaths from infectious diseases like diphtheria and measles were widespread, and scientists had yet to develop penicillin and other antibiotics. Even a simple infection from a minor wound, therefore, was sometimes life-threatening. Today—a century later—most members of our society take good health and long life for granted. It seems reasonable to expect the improvements in U.S. health to continue throughout this new century.

Another encouraging trend is that more people are taking responsibility for their own health (Caplow et al., 1991). Every one of us can live better and longer if we avoid tobacco, eat sensibly and in moderation, and exercise regularly.

Yet health problems will continue to plague U.S. society in the decades to come. The biggest problem, discussed throughout this chapter, is this nation's double standard in health: well-being for the rich but higher rates of disease for the poor. International comparisons reveal that the United States lags in many measures of human health because we neglect those at the margins of our society. An important question for this new century: How can a rich society afford to let millions of people live without the security of medical care?

Finally, repeating a pattern seen in earlier chapters, we find that health problems are far greater in low-income nations than in the United States. The good news is that life expectancy for the world as a whole has been rising—from forty-eight years in 1950 to sixty-six years today—and the biggest gains have been in poor countries (Population Reference Bureau, 1999). But in much of Latin America, Asia, and especially Africa, hundreds of millions of adults and children lack not only medical attention but also adequate food and safe water. Improving the health of the world's poorest people is a critical challenge in the twenty-first century.

childbirth with the purpose of avoiding "new births of inferior quality."

It seems inevitable that some parents will want to use genetic testing to evaluate the health (or even the eye and hair color) of their future child. What if they want to abort a fetus because, while perfectly healthy, it falls short of their expectations? Or, when genetic manipulations eventually become possible, should parents be able to create "designer-children"?

Then there is the issue of "genetic privacy": Can a prospective spouse request a genetic evaluation of her fiancé before agreeing to marry? Can life insurance companies demand genetic testing before issuing policies? Can an employer screen job applicants to weed out those whose future illnesses might drain health care funds? Clearly, what is scientifically possible is not always morally desirable. Society is already grappling with questions about the proper use of our expanding knowledge about human genetics. Such ethical dilemmas will only mount as genetic research moves forward in the years to come.

Scientists are learning more and more about the genetic factors that prompt the eventual development of serious diseases. If offered the opportunity, would you want to undergo a genetic screening that would predict the long-term future of your own health?

Continue the debate . . .

1. *Traditional wedding vows join couples "in sickness and in health." Do you think individuals have a right to know the future health of their potential partner before tying the knot?*
2. *What about the desire of some parents to genetically design their children?*
3. *Is it right that private companies doing genetic research are able to patent their work so that they alone can profit from the results?*

Sources: Elmer-DeWitt (1994a), L. Thompson (1994), Nash (1995), Golden (1999a), and D. Thompson (1999).

SUMMARY

1. Health is a social as well as a biological issue, and well-being depends on the extent and distribution of a society's resources. Culture shapes definitions of health and patterns of health care.
2. Throughout human history, health was poor by today's standards. Health improved dramatically in Western Europe and North America in the nineteenth century, first as industrialization raised living standards and later as medical advances helped control infectious diseases.
3. Health in low-income countries is undermined by inadequate sanitation and hunger. Average life expectancy is about twenty years less than in the United States; in the poorest nations, half the children do not survive to adulthood.
4. Infectious diseases were the major killers at the beginning of the twentieth century. Today most people in the United States die in old age of heart disease, cancer, or stroke.
5. In the United States, more than three-fourths of children born today will live to at least age sixty-five. Throughout the life course, however, people of high social position enjoy better health than the poor.
6. Cigarette smoking increased during this century to become the greatest preventable cause of death in the United States. Now that the health hazards of smoking are known, social tolerance for using tobacco products is declining.
7. The incidence of sexually transmitted diseases has risen since 1960, an exception to the general decline in infectious disease.
8. The ability to prolong the lives of the terminally ill is forcing us to confront a number of ethical issues surrounding death and the rights of the dying.
9. Historically a family concern, health care is now the responsibility of trained specialists. In this country, the dominant model is scientific medicine.

10. Holistic healing encourages people to assume greater responsibility for their own health and well-being, and urges professional healers to get to know patients personally and become familiar with their environment.
11. Socialist societies define medical care as a right that governments offer equally to everyone. Capitalist societies view medical care as a commodity to be purchased, although most capitalist governments support medical care through socialized medicine or national health insurance.
12. The United States, with a direct-fee system, is the only industrialized society with no comprehensive medical care program. Most people have private health insurance, government insurance, or belong to a health maintenance organization. One in six adults in the United States cannot afford to pay for medical care.
13. Structural-functional analysis links health and medicine to other social structures. Central to structural-functional analysis is the concept of the sick role, which excuses the ill person from routine social responsibilities.
14. The symbolic-interaction paradigm investigates how health and medical treatments are largely matters of socially constructed definitions.
15. Social-conflict analysis focuses on the unequal distribution of health and medical care. It criticizes the U.S. medical establishment for overrelying on drugs and surgery, giving free rein to the profit motive in medicine, and overemphasizing the biological rather than the social causes of illness.

KEY CONCEPTS

health (p. 539) a state of complete physical, mental, and social well-being

social epidemiology (p. 543) the study of how health and disease are distributed throughout a society's population

eating disorder (p. 547) an intense form of dieting or other unhealthy method of weight control driven by the desire to be very thin

euthanasia (mercy killing) (p. 551) assisting in the death of a person suffering from an incurable disease

medicine (p. 551) the social institution that focuses on combating disease and improving health

holistic medicine (p. 552) an approach to health care that emphasizes prevention of illness and takes into account the person's entire physical and social environment

socialized medicine (p. 554) a health care system in which the government owns and operates most medical facilities and employs most physicians

direct-fee system (p. 555) a medical care system in which patients pay directly for the services of physicians and hospitals

health maintenance organization (HMO) (p. 556) an organization that provides comprehensive medical care to subscribers for a fixed fee

sick role (p. 556) patterns of behavior defined as appropriate for those who are ill

CRITICAL-THINKING QUESTIONS

1. Why is health as much a social as a biological issue?
2. What are the "diseases of poverty" that kill people in poor countries? What are the "diseases of affluence," the leading killers in rich nations?
3. Can you point to ways in which people can take responsibility for their own health? What about ways in which society affects patterns of health?
4. Should the United States follow the lead of other industrial countries and enact a government program of health care for everyone? Why or why not?

APPLICATIONS AND EXERCISES

1. In most communities, a trip to the local courthouse or city hall is all it takes to find public records showing people's cause of death. Take a look at such records for people a century ago and recently. What patterns emerge in life expectancy? How do causes of death differ?
2. Is there a medical school on or near your campus? If so, obtain a course catalog and see how much (if any) of the medical curriculum involves the social dimensions of health care.
3. Arrange to speak with a midwife (many list their services in the Yellow Pages) about her work helping women bear their babies. How do midwives differ from medical obstetricians in their approach?
4. Install the CD-ROM packaged in the back of this new textbook to access a variety of study, review, and applications exercises designed to help you better understand the material covered in this chapter. The CD includes an author's tip video, as well as interactive maps, video application exercises, Web links, and study questions.

SITES TO SEE

http://www.prenhall.com/macionis

Visit the interactive Web site that accompanies this text. Begin by clicking on the cover of your book. You will find a chapter-by-chapter study guide, practice tests, chat room, and many suggested Web links.

http://www.cdc.gov

Visit the Web site for the Centers for Disease Control and Prevention. Here you will find information about this organization, health news, statistical data, and even travelers' health advisories. This site offers considerable evidence of the social dimensions of health.

http://www.who.int

Visit this Web site, operated by the World Health Organization, to find basic health indicators for many of the world's nations, as well as data profiling the health of the U.S. population.

http://www.unaids.org

Data about the AIDS epidemic around the world can be found at this site, operated by the United Nations.

http://www.doctorsoftheworld.org
http://www.imc-la.org
http://www.dwb.org

Here are Web sites for several organizations of physicians involved in improving health around the world. The first is operated by Doctors of the World, the second presents the International Medical Corps, and the third profiles Doctors without Borders.

PART IV
New Information Technology and Social Institutions

Social institutions change over time for many reasons. One source of change is societal conflict over how social institutions ought to operate. In Chapters 16 through 21, we have highlighted debates about what kind of economy works best, how democratic our political system really is, the meaning of "the family," the role of religion in the modern world, the ways schools go about doing the job of teaching young people, and how nations provide health care to their people.

Another source of change is technology. In the information age, all social institutions are in transition as computers and other communications equipment play a greater role in our lives. This fourth cyber.scope briefly reviews ways in which computer technology is reshaping several of the major social institutions.

The Symbolic Economy

The computer is at the center of the postindustrial economy. As Chapter 16 ("The Economy and Work") noted, work in the postindustrial economy is less likely to involve making *things* and more likely to involve manipulating *symbols*. Thus, gaining literacy skills is as crucial to success in the new century as learning mechanical skills was to workers a century ago.

As the industrial age progressed, machines took over more and more of the manual skills performed by human workers. We might well wonder, then, if computers are destined to replace humans to perform many of the tasks that involve *thinking*. After all, the human brain is capable of only 100 calculations per second; the most powerful computers process information a billion times faster.

Then, too, the expanding array of information available through the Internet to people with computer access may make many traditional jobs obsolete. Will we need as many librarians, when people can browse online catalogs of books? (Indeed, will we even need *libraries* as we have known them in the past?) Will there still be travel agents, when anyone can readily access flight schedules, shop for good fares, and purchase tickets, as well as reserve hotel rooms and rental cars on the Net? Even mall shopping is beginning to lose some of its popularity as consumers purchase more products from online vendors.

Finally, computer technology seems sure to accelerate the expansion of a global economy as the Internet draws together businesses and consumers into a worldwide market. Perhaps, in the computer-based economy of the twenty-first century, we will have to invent a new "virtual currency" to replace the outmoded idea of paper money.

A century ago, shopping meant walking down Main Street, the familiar business district at the center of countless cities and small towns. Fifty years ago, shopping took people to the suburban malls, larger and more impersonal retail centers. Today, commerce is moving to cyberspace, where people can find even more products—but in a totally impersonal environment.

Politics in the Information Age

Cyberspace, by its very nature, is both global and without centralized control. In the emerging information age, it is likely that the current system of dividing humanity into almost 200 distinct nation-states will evolve into a new form. In other words, because the flow of information is unaffected by national boundaries, it makes less and less sense to think of people—who may work, shop, and communicate with others all over the world—as citizens of one geographically bounded nation.

What effect will the global flow of information have on politics itself? By increasing the amount of available information and helping people to communicate more easily, cyber-technology undoubtedly will be a force for political democracy. As long as computer-based communication remains free of government control, at least, how can a totalitarian political order persist?

On the other hand, should governments gain control of computer-based communication, they will have a powerful new tool for spreading propaganda and manipulating their populations. Or, more modestly, governments bent on tyranny may not be able to control the global Internet, but they may try to control access to computer technology within their borders. Such regulation of information would be a blow to democracy, of course. At the same time, however, any nation would pay a high price for isolating itself from the expanding world of computer-based information and trade.

New information technology is spreading ideas and images around the world as never before. These young women live in Malaysia, a relatively traditional society. How do you think the spread of culture via the Internet from the United States and other rich countries will affect the labor force, family patterns, and the desire for education in societies like this one? Will changes be for the better or worse? Why?

Families of the Future

Over the centuries, new technology has shaped and reshaped the family. The Industrial Revolution moved work from farm and home to factories, making "the job" and "the family" separate spheres of life.

More recently, the Information Revolution is creating the opposite effect as new communications technology allows people to work at home (or, with portable computers and telephones, to work anywhere). The trend toward *decentralizing* work means that, for more and more people, the line between "the office" and "the home" is disappearing.

In some respects, this trend should strengthen families, allowing parents, for example, to create more flexible work schedules and placing both fathers and mothers closer to children. Yet, in the cyber age, televisions and computers are playing a larger role in socializing the young. In short, families may be able to spend more time together in this new century, but whether they will choose to do so is less certain.

Medicine and the Pursuit of Health

Just as computer technology is decentralizing work, so it is making medical care more readily available. In the years to come, many routine health checks (pulse rate, blood pressure, heart function) can be performed at home by people with computer access who transmit data via modem to specialists at medical centers.

Around the world, too, new information technology is making better health care available to more people. In the United States, hospitals now rely on Internet sites to match patients and available organs, with the result of saving lives. In villages throughout poor nations, practitioners in clinics now log on to computers to consult with specialists in medical centers in the world's largest cities, gaining the information they need to provide more effective treatments. In 1995, for example, computer links were vital in helping physicians in central Africa share news, skills, and equipment while fighting the outbreak of the deadly Ebola virus.

New information technology is also making an important contribution to the lives of people with mental and physical disabilities. On one level, new computer programs allow officials to determine whether or not plans for new public buildings and private homes will include access to people with disabilities. On another level, specialists at numerous universities and hospitals now use computer simulations to train children to operate wheelchairs and to teach mentally retarded adults to ride the train or bus. More broadly, computers now allow people with physical and mental limitations to enjoy and learn from virtual experiences, including travel, skiing, and even hang gliding, that seemed impossible a generation ago (Briggs, 1996).

Institutions and Technology: Each Shaping the Other

New technology is bringing changes to all aspects of our lives. But although technology is a powerful agent of change, it does not determine the shape of society. On the contrary, technology alters the boundaries of what is possible. Therefore, *how* and even *if* we employ new information technology is an important decision that societies must make. How we decide these questions comes back to our social institutions, which, after all, define *for whom* society should operate in the first place.

CHAPTER 22

Millard Sheets
Tenement Flats (Family Flats),
ca. 1934

National Museum of American Art, Washington, D.C./Art Resource, N.Y.

POPULATION, URBANIZATION, AND ENVIRONMENT

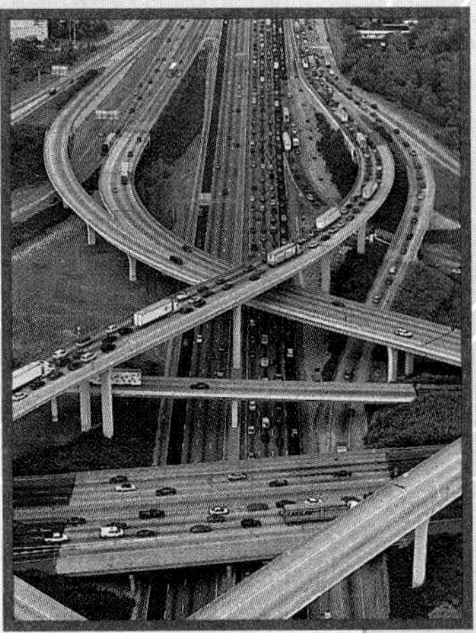

One hundred fifty years ago, northern Georgia was little more than wilderness. Today, the city of Atlanta is 110 miles across and pushing out in all directions as fast as any city in history. In physical size, Atlanta is almost twice as big as it was only twenty years ago, and there is no end in sight. We are witnessing an urban explosion that is consuming 500 acres of fields and farmland every week (Lacayo, 1999).

Growth like this prompted experts to coin the term "urban sprawl." Such uncontrolled growth is the result of more and more people, all of whom want bigger houses and the convenience of nearby superhighways, schools, recreation facilities, and, of course, shopping malls. No doubt, most people in the United States consider growth like this to be good—a sure sign of economic prosperity.

But is it that simple? This chapter examines three closely related topics: population increase, urbanization, and the state of the natural environment. As we shall see, population has soared during the past two centuries—not just in the United States but around the world—and cities everywhere have grown rapidly. We shall consider how these changes have altered the shape of societies and what they mean for the future of the planet. We begin with population.

DEMOGRAPHY: THE STUDY OF POPULATION

From the time people first walked the earth, some 250,000 years ago, until just 250 years ago, the earth's population hovered around 500 million—about the number of people in Europe today. Life was brutal and usually short; people fell victim to countless diseases, frequent injury, and periodic natural disasters.

But about 1750, world population began to spike upward. We now add 77 million people to the planet each year, so that in the fall of 1999, the number of people living on the earth passed the 6 billion mark.

The causes and consequences of this drama are the basis of **demography,** *the study of human population.* Demography (from the Greek, meaning "description of people") is a specialty within sociology that analyzes the size and composition of a population and studies how people move from place to place. Demographers not only collect statistics, they also pose important questions about the effects of population growth and how population might be controlled. The following sections present basic demographic concepts.

FERTILITY

The study of human population begins with how many people are born. **Fertility** is *the incidence of childbearing in a country's population.* During her childbearing years, from the onset of menstruation (typically in the early teens) to menopause (usually in the late forties), a woman is capable of bearing more than twenty children. But *fecundity*, or maximum possible childbearing, is sharply reduced by cultural norms, finances, and personal choice.

Demographers gauge fertility using the **crude birth rate,** *the number of live births in a given year for*

GLOBAL SNAPSHOT

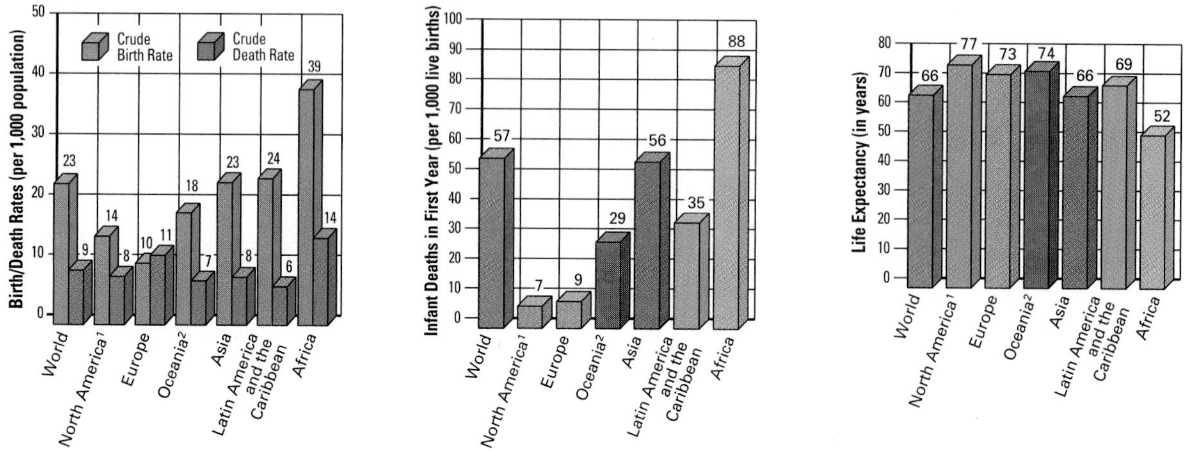

FIGURE 22–1 Crude Birth Rates and Crude Death Rates, Infant Mortality Rates, and Life Expectancy, 1999

[1]United States and Canada

[2]Australia, New Zealand, and South Pacific Islands

Source: Population Reference Bureau (1999).

every thousand people in a population. To calculate a crude birth rate, divide the number of live births in a year by the society's total population and multiply the result by 1,000. In the United States, in 1998, there were 3.9 million live births in a population of 270 million (U.S. National Center for Health Statistics, 1998). That yields a crude birth rate of 14.4.

This birth rate is "crude" because it is based on the entire population, not just women in their child-bearing years. Comparing crude birth rates for various countries can be misleading, then, if one society has a larger share of women of childbearing age than another. A crude birth rate also ignores differences among various racial and ethnic categories. But this statistic is easy to calculate and gives a good measure of a society's overall fertility. Figure 22–1 shows that, in global perspective, the crude birth rate of North Americans is low.

MORTALITY

Population size also reflects **mortality,** *the incidence of death in a country's population.* To measure mortality, demographers use a **crude death rate,** *the number of deaths in a given year for every thousand people in a population.* This time, we take the number of deaths in a particular year, divide that number by the total population, and multiply the result by 1,000. In 1998, there were 2.4 million deaths among the U.S. population of 270 million, which yields a crude death rate of 8.8. Figure 22–1 shows that, in global context, this rate is about average.

A third useful demographic measure is the **infant mortality rate,** *the number of deaths among infants under one year of age for each thousand live births in a given year.* To compute infant mortality, divide the number of deaths of children under one year of age by the number of live births during the same year and multiply the result by 1,000. In 1998, there were 25,000 infant deaths and 3.9 million live births in the United States. Dividing the first number by the second and multiplying the result by 1,000 yields an infant mortality rate of 6.4. The second part of Figure 22–1 indicates that, by world standards, North American infant mortality is low.

But remember the differences among various categories of people. For example, African Americans, with nearly three times the burden of poverty as whites, have

SEEING OURSELVES

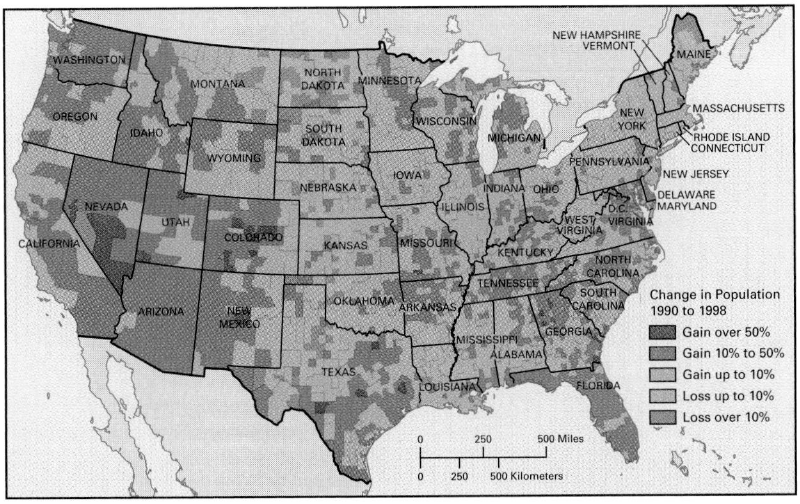

NATIONAL MAP 22–1
Population Change across the United States

In general, population is moving from the heartland of the United States toward the coasts. What do you think is causing this internal migration? Can you offer a demographic profile of the people who remain in counties that are losing population?

Source: U.S. Census Bureau. [Online] Available http://www.census.gov/population/www/estimates/countypop.html, 2000.

an infant mortality rate of 14—more than twice the white rate of 6.

Low infant mortality greatly raises **life expectancy,** *the average life span of a country's population.* U.S. males born in 1998 can expect to live 74 years, and females can look toward 79 years. As the third part of Figure 22–1 shows, life expectancy in North America is twenty-five years greater than in low-income countries of Africa.

MIGRATION

Population size is also affected by **migration,** *the movement of people into and out of a specified territory.* Migration is sometimes involuntary, such as the forcible transport of 10 million Africans to the Western Hemisphere as slaves. Voluntary migration, however, usually results from several "push-pull" factors. Dissatisfaction with life in a poor region may "push" people to move, while the opportunity for a better life may "pull" them to the city.

Movement into a territory—or *immigration*—is measured as an *in-migration rate,* calculated as the number of people entering an area for every thousand people in the population. Movement out of a territory—or *emigration*—is measured in terms of an *out-migration rate,* the number leaving for every thousand people. Both types of migration usually occur at once; the difference is the *net-migration rate.*

All nations also experience internal migration, that is, movement within their borders, from one region to another. National Map 22–1 shows where the U.S. population is moving, and the places left behind.

POPULATION GROWTH

Fertility, mortality, and migration all affect the size of a society's population. In general, rich nations (like the United States) grow almost as much from immigration as natural increase; poor nations (like India) grow almost entirely from natural increase.

To calculate a population's natural growth rate, demographers subtract the crude death rate from the crude birth rate. The natural growth rate of the U.S. population in 1998 was 5.6 per thousand (the crude birth rate of 14.4 minus the crude death rate of 8.8), or about 0.6 percent annual growth.

Global Map 22–1 on page 570 shows that population growth in the United States and other industrialized nations is well below the world average of 1.4 percent. The earth's low-growth continents are Europe (currently posting a slight decline: expressed as –0.1 percent annual growth), North America (0.6 percent), and Oceania (1.1 percent). Close to the global average are Asia (1.5 percent) and Latin America (1.8 percent). The highest growth region in the world is Africa (2.5 percent), where some countries' growth exceeds 3 percent.

WINDOW ON THE WORLD

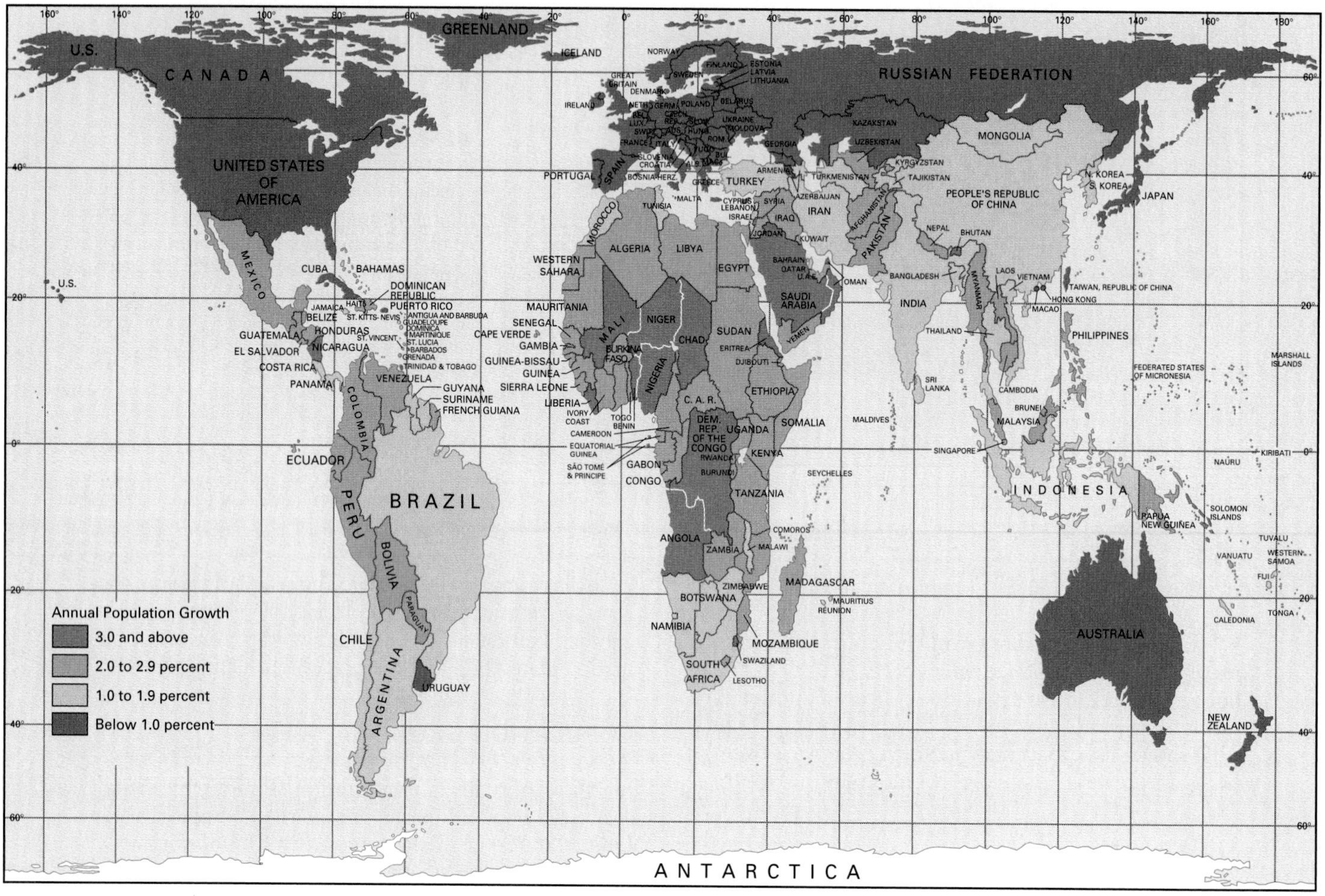

GLOBAL MAP 22–1 Population Growth in Global Perspective

The richest countries of the world—including the United States, Canada, and the nations of Europe—have growth rates below 1 percent. The nations of Latin America and Asia typically have growth rates around 2 percent, which double a population in thirty-five years. Africa has an overall growth rate of 2.5 percent, which cuts the doubling time to twenty-eight years. In global perspective, we see that a society's standard of living is closely related to its rate of population growth: Population is rising fastest in the world regions that can least afford to support more people.

Sources: Peters Atlas of the World (1990); updates by the author from Population Reference Bureau (1999).

A handy rule of thumb for estimating population growth is to divide a society's population growth rate into the number 70 to calculate the *doubling time* in years. Thus, an annual growth of 2 percent (common in Latin America) doubles a population in thirty-five years, and a 3 percent growth rate (found in some of Africa) drops the doubling time to just twenty-four years. The rapid population growth of the poorest countries is deeply troubling because these countries can barely support the populations they have now.

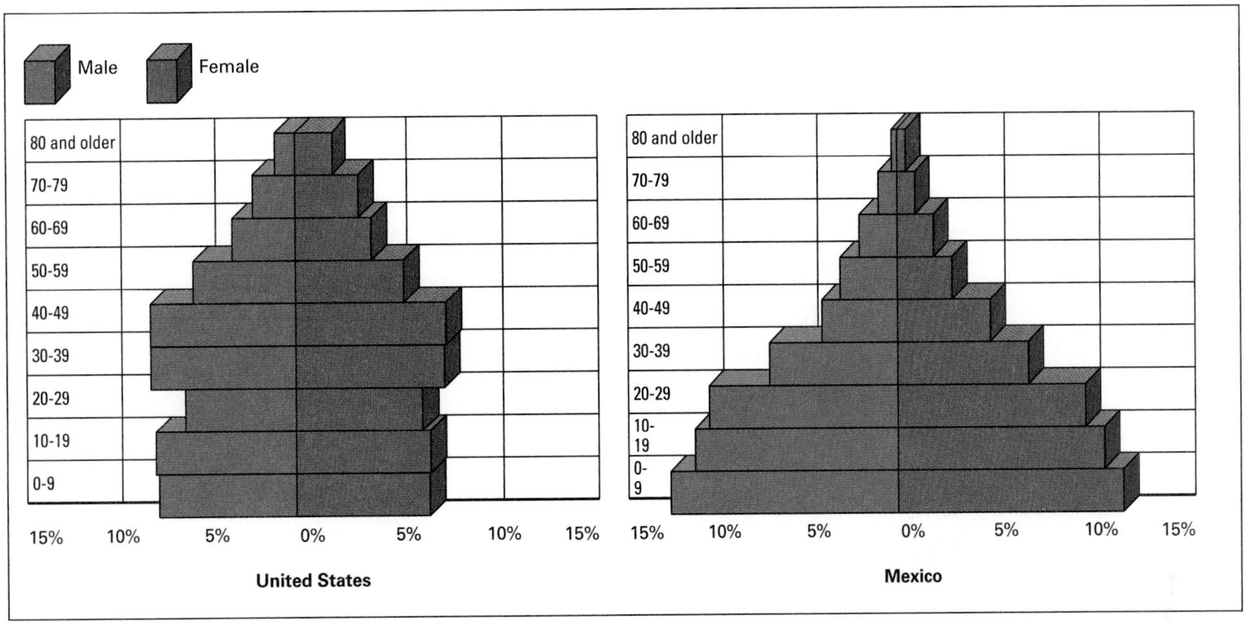

FIGURE 22–2 Age-Sex Population Pyramids for the United States and Mexico, 2000

Source: U.S. Census Bureau (2000).

POPULATION COMPOSITION

Demographers also study the makeup of a society's population at a given point in time. One variable is the **sex ratio,** *the number of males for every hundred females in a nation's population.* In 2000, the sex ratio in the United States was 96, or 96 males for every 100 females. Sex ratios are usually below 100 because, on average, women outlive men. In India, however, the sex ratio is 107, because parents value sons more than daughters and may either abort a female fetus or, after birth, give more care to a male infant, raising the odds that a female child will die.

A more complex measure is the **age-sex pyramid,** *a graphic representation of the age and sex of a population.* Figure 22–2 presents the age-sex pyramids for the populations of the United States and Mexico. Higher mortality with advancing age gives these figures a roughly pyramidal shape. In the U.S. pyramid, the bulge corresponding to ages thirty through the mid-fifties reflects high birth rates during the *baby boom* from the mid-1940s to 1970. The contraction just below—that is, people under thirty—reflects the subsequent *baby bust* as the birth rate dipped from 25.3 in 1957 to a low of 14.4 in 1998.

Comparison of the U.S. and Mexican age-sex pyramids shows different demographic trends. The age-sex pyramid for Mexico, like that of other low-income nations, is wide at the bottom (reflecting higher birth rates) and narrows quickly by what we would term middle age (due to higher mortality). Mexico, in short, is a much younger society with a median age of twenty compared to thirty-five in the United States. With a larger share of females still in their childbearing years, therefore, Mexico's crude birth rate (27) is nearly twice our own (14), and its annual rate of population growth (2.2 percent) is almost four times the U.S. rate (0.6 percent).

HISTORY AND THEORY OF POPULATION GROWTH

Throughout most of human history, people favored large families because human labor was the key to productivity. Moreover, until rubber condoms appeared 150 years ago, the prevention of pregnancy was an uncertain proposition at best. But high death rates from widespread infectious diseases put a constant brake on population growth.

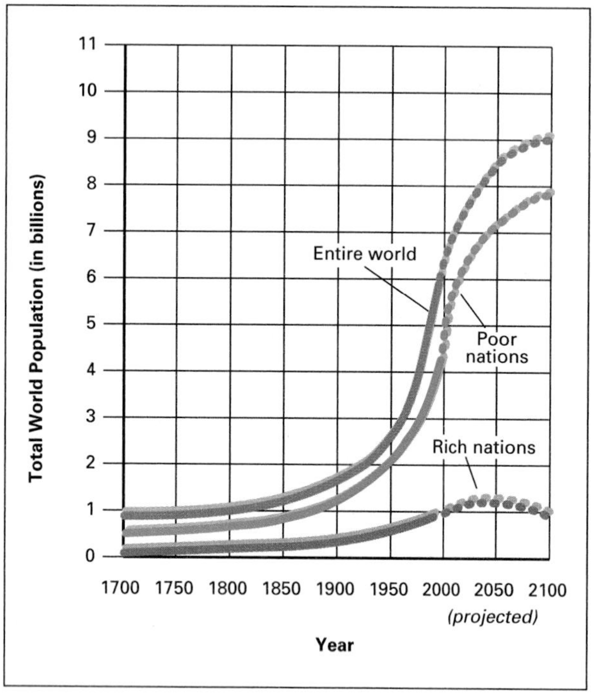

FIGURE 22–3 The Increase in World Population, 1700–2100

However, as shown in Figure 22–3, a major demographic shift began about 1750 as the world's population turned upward, reaching the 1 billion mark by 1800. This milestone (which took all of human history up to this point) was repeated by 1930—barely a century later—when a second billion people were added to the planet. In other words, not only was population increasing but the *rate* of growth was accelerating. Global population reached 3 billion by 1962 (just thirty-two years later) and 4 billion by 1974 (a scant twelve years later). The rate of world population increase has slowed recently, but our planet passed the 5 billion mark in 1987 and the 6 billion mark late in 1999. In no previous century did the world's population even double. In the twentieth century, it increased *fourfold*.

Currently, the world is adding about 77 million people each year, with 96 percent of this increase in poor countries. Experts predict that the earth's population will reach between 8 billion and 9 billion by 2050 (Wattenberg, 1997; Thirunarayanapuram, 1998). Given the world's troubles in feeding the present population, such an increase is a matter of urgent concern.

MALTHUSIAN THEORY

It was the sudden population growth two centuries ago that sparked the development of demography. Thomas Robert Malthus (1766–1834), an English economist and clergyman, warned that population increase would soon lead to social chaos. Malthus (1926; orig. 1798) calculated that population would increase by what mathematicians call a *geometric progression*, illustrated by the series of numbers 2, 4, 8, 16, 32, and so on. At such a rate, Malthus concluded, world population would soon soar out of control.

Food production would also increase, Malthus explained, but only in *arithmetic progression* (as in the series 2, 3, 4, 5, 6) because, even with new agricultural technology, farmland is limited. Thus, Malthus presented a distressing vision of the future: people reproducing beyond what the planet could feed, leading ultimately to widespread starvation.

Malthus recognized that artificial birth control or abstinence might change the equation. But he found one morally wrong and the other quite unlikely. Thus, famine and war stalked humanity in Malthus's scheme, and he was justly known as "the dismal parson."

Critical evaluation. Fortunately, Malthus's prediction was flawed. First, by 1850, the European birth rate began to drop, partly because children were becoming an economic liability rather than an asset, and partly because people began using artificial birth control. Second, Malthus underestimated human ingenuity: Irrigation, fertilizers, and pesticides have increased farm production far more than he imagined.

Some criticized Malthus for ignoring the role of social inequality in world abundance and famine. Karl Marx (1967; orig. 1867), for one, objected to viewing suffering as a "law of nature" rather than the curse of capitalism.

Still, Malthus offered an important lesson. Habitable land, clean water, and fresh air are limited resources, and, as we explain presently, greater economic productivity has taken a heavy toll on the natural environment. In addition, medical advances have lowered death rates, pushing up world population. In principle, of course, no level of population growth can go on forever. Thus, people everywhere must become aware of the dangers of population increase.

DEMOGRAPHIC TRANSITION THEORY

Malthusian theory has been superseded by **demographic transition theory,** *the thesis that population patterns reflect*

FIGURE 22–4
Demographic Transition Theory

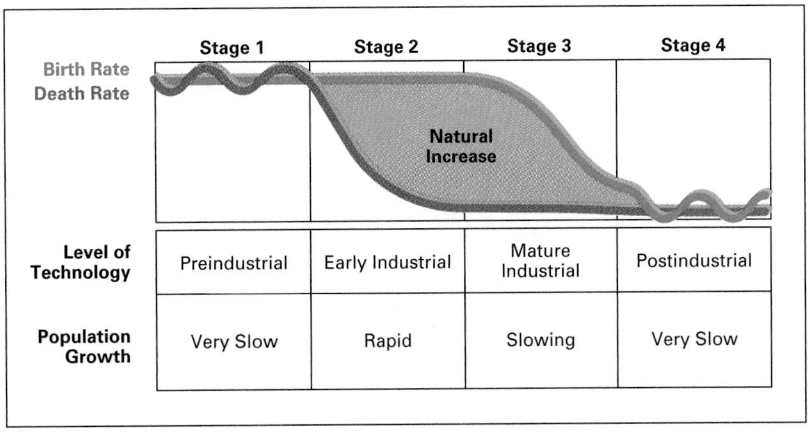

a society's level of technological development. Figure 22–4 shows the demographic consequences at four levels of technological development. Preindustrial, agrarian societies—those at Stage 1—have high birth rates because of the economic value of children and the absence of birth control. Death rates are also high due to low living standards and little medical technology. Outbreaks of disease neutralize births, so population rises and falls with only a modest overall increase. This was the case for thousands of years in Europe before the Industrial Revolution.

Stage 2—the onset of industrialization—brings a demographic transition as death rates fall due to greater food supplies and scientific medicine. But birth rates remain high, resulting in rapid population growth. It was during Europe's Stage 2 that Malthus formulated his ideas, which explains his pessimistic view of the future. The world's poorest countries today are in this high-growth stage.

In Stage 3—a mature industrial economy—the birth rate drops, curbing population growth once again. Fertility falls, first, because most children survive to adulthood and, second, because high living standards make raising children expensive. Affluence, in short, transforms children from economic assets into economic liabilities. Smaller families, made possible by effective birth control, are also favored by women working outside the home. As birth rates follow death rates downward, population growth slows further.

In Stage 4—a postindustrial economy—the demographic transition is complete. The birth rate keeps falling, partly because dual-income couples gradually become the norm and partly because the cost of raising children continues to rise. This trend, coupled with steady death rates, means that, at best, population grows only very slowly or even decreases. This is the case now in Japan, Europe, and the United States.

Critical evaluation. Demographic transition theory suggests that the key to population control lies in technology. Instead of the runaway population increase feared by Malthus, this theory sees technology reining in growth and spreading material plenty.

Demographic transition theory dovetails with modernization theory, one approach to global development discussed in Chapter 12 ("Global Stratification"). Modernization theorists are optimistic that poor countries will solve their population problems as they industrialize. But critics—notably, dependency theorists—strongly disagree. Unless there is a significant redistribution of global resources, they maintain, our planet will become increasingly divided into industrialized "haves," enjoying low population growth, and nonindustrialized "have-nots," struggling in vain to feed more and more people.

GLOBAL POPULATION TODAY: A BRIEF SURVEY

What can we say about population in today's world? Drawing on the discussion so far, we can reach several conclusions.

The Low-Growth North

When the Industrial Revolution began, population growth in Western Europe and North America peaked at 3 percent annually. But in the centuries since, the growth rate steadily declined and, in 1970, fell below 1 percent. As our postindustrial society enters Stage 4,

The Getu family, on the left, lives in the low-income African nation of Ethiopia. The de Frutos family, to the right, lives in the high-income European nation of Spain. Comparing the two photographs, what can you learn about the relationship between a society's level of material affluence and family size? In fact, the fertility rate in Ethiopia is more than five times higher than in Spain. Thus, while population levels are stable or declining in most of the world's richest countries, they are increasing in the world's poorest nations. This is why poor countries now account for 96 percent of global population increase.

the U.S. birth rate is less than the replacement level of 2.1 children per woman, a point demographers term **zero population growth**—*the level of reproduction that maintains population at a steady state.* Some fifty nations, almost all of them rich, have passed the point of zero population growth (Wattenberg, 1997).

Factors holding down population in these postindustrial societies include a high proportion of men and women in the labor force, rising costs of raising children, trends toward later marriage and singlehood, and widespread use of contraceptives and abortion.

In industrial nations, therefore, population increase is not the pressing problem that it is in poor countries. Indeed, some analysts point to a future problem of *underpopulation* in countries such as Japan, Italy, and the United States, where the swelling ranks of the elderly have fewer and fewer young people to look to for support in old age (Chesnais, 1997).

The High-Growth South

Population is a critical problem in poor nations of the Southern Hemisphere. Only a few societies lack industrial technology altogether, placing them in demographic transition theory's Stage 1. But much of Latin America, Africa, and Asia is at Stage 2, with agrarian economies and some industry. Advanced medical technology, supplied by rich societies, has sharply reduced death rates, while birth rates remain high. This is why poor societies now account for two-thirds of the earth's people and 96 percent of global population increase.

In the last decade, the world has made significant progress in lowering fertility. In poor countries throughout the world, birth rates have fallen from an average of about six children per woman in 1950 to about four today. But fertility this high will only intensify global poverty. At a 1994 global population conference in Cairo, delegates from 180 nations agreed that a critical element in controlling world population growth is improving the status of women. The box takes a closer look.

Mortality, too, has fallen significantly over the last several decades. Although few would oppose medical programs that save lives—mostly of children—lower death rates mean rising population. In fact, population growth in most low-income regions of the world is due *mostly* to falling death rates. Around 1920, medical and health advances began spreading from Europe and North America around the world. Since then, inoculations against infectious diseases and the use of antibiotics and

GLOBAL SOCIOLOGY

Empowering Women: The Key to Controlling Population Growth

Sohad Ahmad lives with her husband in a farming village fifty miles south of Cairo, Egypt's capital. Ahmad lives a poor life, like hundreds of millions of other women in the world. Yet her situation differs in an important respect: She has had only two children and will have no more.

Why do Ahmad and her husband reject the conventional wisdom that children are an economic asset? One part of the answer is that Egypt's growing population has already created such a demand for land that Ahmad's family could not afford more even if they had the children to farm it. But the main reason is that she does not want her life defined only by childbearing.

Like Sohad Ahmad, more women in Egypt are taking control of their fertility and seeking more opportunities. Indeed, this country has made great progress in reducing its annual population growth from 3.0 percent just ten years ago to 2.0 percent today.

With its focus on raising the standing of women, the 1994 Cairo conference broke new ground. Past population control programs have simply tried to make birth control technology available to women. This is vital, since only half the world's married women use effective birth control. But even with available birth control, population continues to expand in societies that define women's primary responsibility as raising children.

A simple truth: Women who have more opportunity for schooling and paid work have fewer children. As more women attend school in traditional societies, the fertility rate in these countries is falling.

Dr. Nafis Sadik, an Egyptian woman who heads the United Nations efforts at population control, sums up the new approach to lowering birth rates this way: *Give women more life choices and they will have fewer children.* In other words, women with access to schooling and jobs, who can decide when and if they wish to marry, and who bear children as a matter of choice, will limit their own fertility. Schooling must be available to older women, too, Sadik adds, because they exercise great influence in local communities.

Evidence from countries around the world is that controlling population and raising the social standing of women are one and the same.

Sources: Linden (1994) and Ashford (1995).

insecticides have pushed down death rates with great effectiveness. For example, in Sri Lanka, malaria caused half of all deaths in the 1930s; a decade later, use of insecticides to kill malaria-carrying mosquitoes cut the death toll from this disease in half. Although this is a great medical achievement, Sri Lanka's population began to soar. Similarly, India's infant mortality rate slid from 130 in 1975 to 72 in 1999, boosting that nation's population to almost 1 billion.

In short, in much of the world, mortality is falling, especially among children. Now we must control birth in poor countries as successfully as we are fending off death.

URBANIZATION: THE GROWTH OF CITIES

October 8, 1994, Hong Kong. The cable train grinds to the top of Victoria Peak, where we behold one of the world's most spectacular vistas: the city of Hong Kong at night! A million bright, colorful lights ring the harbor as ships, ferries, and traditional Chinese "junks" churn by. Few places match Hong Kong for sheer energy. This small city is as economically productive as the state of Wisconsin or the nation of Finland. One could sit here for hours entranced by the spectacle of Hong Kong.

For most of human history, the sights and sounds of great cities such as Hong Kong, New York, and Los Angeles were simply unimaginable. Our distant ancestors lived in small, nomadic groups, moving as they depleted vegetation or hunted migratory game. The tiny settlements that marked the emergence of civilization in the Middle East some 12,000 years ago held only a small fraction of the earth's people. Today the largest three or four cities of the world hold as many people as the entire planet did back then.

Urbanization is *the concentration of humanity into cities.* Urbanization redistributes population within a society and transforms many patterns of social life. We will trace these changes in terms of three urban revolutions—the emergence of cities 10,000 years ago, the development of industrial cities after 1750, and the explosive growth of cities in poor countries today.

THE EVOLUTION OF CITIES

Cities are a relatively new development in human history. Only about 12,000 years ago did our ancestors begin founding permanent settlements, launching the *first urban revolution.*

The First Cities

Before humans could build permanent settlements, they had to discover how to domesticate animals and cultivate crops. As explained in Chapter 4 ("Society"), hunting and gathering forced people to move all the time; raising food, however, required people to stay in one place (Lenski, Nolan, & Lenski, 1995). Raising their own food also created a material surplus, which freed some people from food production and allowed them to build shelters, make tools, weave cloth, and take part in religious rituals. The emergence of cities, then, led to specialization and higher living standards.

The first city—Jericho, which lies to the north of the Dead Sea and dates back some 10,000 years—was home to only around 600 people. But, as the century passed, cities grew to tens of thousands of people and became the centers of vast empires. By 3000 B.C.E., Egyptian cities flourished, as did cities in China about 2000 B.C.E. and in Central and South America about 1500 B.C.E. In North America, however, only a few Native American societies formed settlements, so that widespread urbanization had to await the arrival of European settlers in the seventeenth century (Lamberg-Karlovsky & Lamberg-Karlovsky, 1973; Change, 1977; Coe & Diehl, 1980).

Preindustrial European Cities

European cities date back some 5,000 years to the Greeks and, later, the Romans, both of whom created great empires and founded cities across Europe, including Vienna, Paris, and London. With the fall of the Roman Empire, the "Dark Ages" began, as people withdrew within defensive walled settlements and warlords battled for territory. Only in the eleventh century did trade flourish once again, allowing cities to grow.

Medieval cities were very different from today's cities. Beneath towering cathedrals, the narrow and winding streets of London, Brussels, and Florence teemed with merchants, artisans, priests, peddlers, jugglers, nobles, and servants. Occupational groups such as bakers, carpenters, and metalworkers clustered together in distinct sections, or "quarters." Ethnicity also defined communities as residents sought to keep out people who differed from themselves. The term "ghetto" (from the Italian *borghetto*, meaning "outside the city walls") first described the segregation of Jews in Venice.

Industrial European Cities

As the Middle Ages came to a close, steadily increasing commerce enriched a new urban middle class or *bourgeoisie* (French, meaning "of the town"). With more and more money, the bourgeoisie soon rivaled the hereditary nobility.

By about 1750, the Industrial Revolution triggered a *second urban revolution*, first in Europe and then in North America. Factories unleashed tremendous productive power, causing cities to grow to unprecedented size. London, the largest European city, reached 550,000 people by 1700 and exploded to 6.5 million by 1900 (A. Weber, 1963, orig. 1899; Chandler & Fox, 1974).

Cities not only grew but changed shape as well. Older winding streets gave way to broad, straight boulevards that held the flow of commercial traffic and, eventually, motor vehicles. Steam and electric trolleys, too, crisscrossed the expanding cities. Since land was now a commodity to be bought and sold, developers divided cities into regular-sized lots (Mumford, 1961). The center of the city was no longer the cathedral but a bustling central business district, filled with banks, retail stores, and tall office buildings.

With a new focus on business, cities became more crowded and impersonal. Crime rates rose. Especially at the outset, a few industrialists lived in grand style, but most men, women, and children worked in factories for bare subsistence.

Organized efforts by workers to improve their lives eventually brought changes to the workplace, better housing, and the right to vote. Public services such as water, sewage, and electricity further improved urban living. Today, some urbanites still live in poverty, but a rising standard of living has partly fulfilled the city's historical promise of a better life.

THE GROWTH OF U.S. CITIES

Most of the Native Americans who inhabited North America for thousands of years before the arrival of Europeans were migratory people who formed few permanent settlements. The spread of villages and towns, then, came after European colonization.

Colonial Settlement: 1565–1800

In 1565, the Spanish built a settlement at St. Augustine, Florida, and, in 1607, the English founded Jamestown, Virginia. The first lasting settlement, however, came in 1624, when the Dutch established New Amsterdam, later called New York.

New York and Boston (founded by the English in 1630) started out as tiny villages in a vast wilderness. They resembled medieval towns in Europe, with narrow, winding streets, some of which still curve through lower Manhattan and downtown Boston. But economic growth soon transformed these quiet villages into thriving towns with new, wide streets, usually built on a grid pattern. Even so, when the first census was completed in 1790, as Table 22–1 shows, just 5 percent of the nation's people lived in cities.

Urban Expansion: 1800–1860

Early in the nineteenth century, towns sprang up along the transportation routes that opened the American West. By 1860, Buffalo, Cleveland, Detroit, and Chicago were changing the face of the Midwest, and about one-fifth of the U.S. population lived in cities.

Urban expansion was greatest in the northern states; New York City, for example, had ten times the population of Charleston, South Carolina. The division of the United States into the industrial-urban North and the agrarian-rural South was one major cause of the Civil War (Schlesinger, 1969).

TABLE 22–1 The Urban Population of the United States, 1790–1998

Year	Population (in millions)	Percent Urban
1790	3.9	5.1%
1800	5.3	6.1
1820	9.6	7.3
1840	17.1	10.5
1860	31.4	19.7
1880	50.2	28.1
1900	76.0	39.7
1920	105.7	51.3
1940	131.7	56.5
1960	179.3	69.9
1980	226.5	73.7
1990	253.0	75.2
1998	270.3	80.1

Source: U.S. Census Bureau (1999).

The Metropolitan Era: 1860–1950

The Civil War (1861–1865) gave an enormous boost to urbanization, as factories strained to produce weapons. Waves of people deserted the countryside for cities in hopes of obtaining better jobs. Joining them were tens of millions of immigrants, mostly from Europe, forming a culturally diverse urban mix.

In 1900, New York's population soared past the 4 million mark, and Chicago—a city of scarcely 100,000 people in 1860—was closing in on 2 million. Such growth marked the era of the **metropolis** (from Greek words, meaning "mother city"), *a large city that socially and economically dominates an urban area.* Metropolises became the economic centers of the United States. By 1920, cities were home to a majority of the U.S. population as well.

Industrial technology pushed the urban skyline ever higher. In the 1880s, steel girders and mechanical elevators raised structures more than ten stories high. In 1930, New York's Empire State Building became an urban wonder, an early "skyscraper" stretching 102 stories into the clouds.

Urban Decentralization: 1950–Present

The industrial metropolis reached its peak about 1950. Since then, something of a turnaround—termed *urban decentralization*—has occurred as people have deserted downtown areas for outlying **suburbs,** *urban areas beyond the political boundaries of a city.* Thus, the old industrial cities of the Northeast and Midwest stopped growing—and some lost considerable population—in the decades after 1950. The urban landscape of densely packed central cities evolved into sprawling suburban regions, as in the case of Atlanta, described in the opening to this chapter.

SUBURBS AND URBAN DECLINE

Imitating European nobility, some of the rich always lived beyond the city limits or, more precisely, kept both "town" and "country" houses (Baltzell, 1979a). It was not until after World War II that ordinary people found a suburban home within their reach. With more and more cars, new four-lane highways, government-backed mortgages, and inexpensive tract homes, the suburbs grew rapidly. By 1999, most of the U.S. population lived in the suburbs, and they frequented nearby shopping malls rather than the older downtown shopping districts in the cities (Rosenthal, 1974; Tobin, 1976; Geist, 1985; Palen, 1995; Peterson, 1999).

Suburban growth threw many older cities of the Snowbelt—the Northeast and Midwest—into financial crisis. Cities lost affluent taxpayers to the suburbs and were left with the burden of funding expensive social programs for the poor who stayed behind. And so inner-city decay began to scar cities throughout the Northeast and Midwest. Especially to white people, the inner cities became synonymous with slums, crime, drugs, unemployment, the poor, and minorities (Sternlieb & Hughes, 1983; Logan & Schneider, 1984; Stahura, 1986; Galster, 1991).

POSTINDUSTRIAL SUNBELT CITIES

The picture is different in the Sunbelt—the South and West. Gradually, population has shifted to the Sunbelt, where 60 percent of people now live. In 1950, nine of the ten biggest U.S. cities were in the Snowbelt; by 1998, six of the top ten were in the Sunbelt (U.S. Census Bureau, 1999).

Why are Sunbelt cities growing so large? Unlike their colder counterparts, these cities came of age *after* urban decentralization began. So while Snowbelt cities have long been enclosed by a ring of politically independent suburbs, Sunbelt cities have pushed their boundaries outward, along with the population flow. Houston, for example, covers more than 550 square miles, compared to Chicago's 227.

The great sprawl of Sunbelt cities does have drawbacks, however. Many people in cities like Atlanta, Dallas, Phoenix, and Los Angeles argue that the growth follows no plan and ends up with clogged roads leading to slapdash developments. It was a sign of the times that in the 1998 national elections, no fewer than 240 anti-sprawl initiatives were on the ballot across the United States—and voters passed most of them (Lacayo, 1999).

MEGALOPOLIS: REGIONAL CITIES

Another result of urban decentralization is urban regions. The U.S. Census Bureau (1999) recognizes 261 urban regions, which the Bureau calls *metropolitan statistical areas (MSAs)*. Each MSA includes at least one city with 50,000 or more people plus densely populated surrounding counties. Almost all of the fifty fastest-growing MSAs are in the Sunbelt.

The biggest MSAs, containing more than 1 million people, are called *consolidated metropolitan statistical areas (CMSAs)*. In 1999, there were nineteen CMSAs. Heading the list is New York and adjacent urban areas in Long Island, western Connecticut, and northern New Jersey, with a total population of 20 million. Next in size is the CMSA in southern California that includes Los Angeles, Riverside, and Anaheim, with a population of almost 16 million.

As regional cities grow, they begin to overlap each other. For example, along the East Coast a 400-mile supercity stretches all the way from New England to Virginia. In the early 1960s, the French geographer Jean Gottmann (1961) coined the term **megalopolis** to designate *a vast urban region containing a number of cities and their surrounding suburbs.* Other supercities cover the eastern coast of Florida and stretch from Cleveland west to Chicago. More megalopolises will undoubtedly emerge, especially in the fast-growing Sunbelt.

EDGE CITIES

Urban decentralization has also created *edge cities*, business centers some distance from the old downtowns. Edge cities—a mix of corporate office buildings, shopping malls, hotels, and entertainment complexes—differ from suburbs, which contain mostly homes. Thus, while the population of suburbs peaks at night, the population of edge cities peaks during the workday.

As part of expanding urban regions, most edge cities have no clear physical boundaries. Some do have names, including Los Colinas (near the Dallas-Fort Worth

A recent development in the United States is the "edge city," the product of the urban population spreading over a larger and larger area. This is King of Prussia, which lies on the northwestern edge of Philadelphia, about fifteen miles from the downtown center. King of Prussia is best known as a corporate and retail sales area, with one of the country's largest shopping malls.

airport), Tyson's Corner (in Virginia, near Washington, D.C.), and King of Prussia (northwest of Philadelphia). Other edge cities are known only by the major highways that flow through them, including Route 1 in Princeton, New Jersey, and Route 128 near Boston (Garreau, 1991; Macionis & Parrillo, 2001).

URBANISM AS A WAY OF LIFE

Early sociologists in Europe and the United States focused their attention on the rise of cities. We briefly present their accounts of urbanism as a way of life.

FERDINAND TÖNNIES: *GEMEINSCHAFT* AND *GESELLSCHAFT*

In the late nineteenth century, the German sociologist Ferdinand Tönnies (1855–1937) studied how life in the new industrial metropolis differed from life in rural villages. From this contrast, he developed two concepts that have become a lasting part of sociology's terminology.

Tönnies (1963; orig. 1887) used the German word ***Gemeinschaft*** (meaning roughly "community") to refer to *a type of social organization by which people are closely tied by kinship and tradition.* The *Gemeinschaft* of the rural village joins people in what amounts to a single primary group.

By and large, argued Tönnies, *Gemeinschaft* is absent in the modern city. On the contrary, urbanization fosters ***Gesellschaft*** (a German word meaning roughly "association"), *a type of social organization by which people come together only on the basis of individual self-interest.* In the *Gesellschaft* way of life, individuals are motivated by their own needs rather than a drive to enhance the well-being of everyone. City dwellers display little sense of community or common identity and look to others mostly as a means of advancing their individual goals. Thus, Tönnies saw in urbanization the erosion of close, enduring social relations in favor of the fleeting and impersonal ties typical of business.

EMILE DURKHEIM: MECHANICAL AND ORGANIC SOLIDARITY

The French sociologist Emile Durkheim (see Chapter 4, "Society") agreed with much of Tönnies's thinking about cities. But, Durkheim countered, urbanites do not lack social bonds; they simply organize social life differently than rural people.

Durkheim described traditional, rural life as *mechanical solidarity,* social bonds based on common sentiments and shared moral values. With its emphasis on tradition, Durkheim's concept of mechanical solidarity bears a striking similarity to Tönnies's *Gemeinschaft.* Urbanization erodes mechanical solidarity, Durkheim

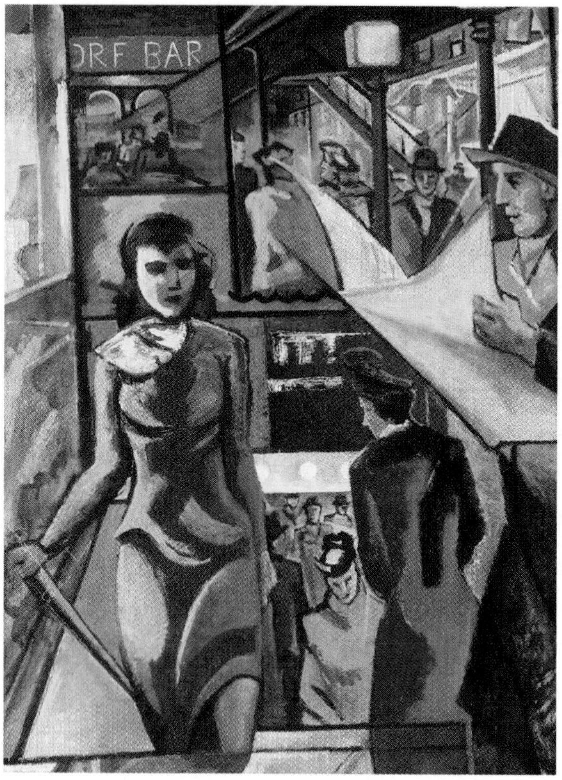

Peasant Dance *(above, c. 1565), by Pieter Breughel the Elder, conveys the essential unity of rural life forged by generations of kinship and neighborhood. By contrast, Ernest Fiene's* Nocturne *(left) communicates the impersonality common to urban areas. Taken together, these paintings capture Tönnies's distinction between* Gemeinschaft *and* Gesellschaft.

Pieter Breughel the Elder (c. 1525/30–1569), *Peasant Dance*, c. 1565, Kunsthistorisches Museum, Vienna/Superstock. Ernest Fiene (1894–1965), *Nocturne*. Photograph © Christie's Images.

explained, but it also generates a new type of bonding, which he termed *organic solidarity*, social bonds based on specialization and interdependence. This concept, which parallels Tönnies's *Gesellschaft*, reveals an important difference between the two thinkers. Both thought the growth of industrial cities undermined tradition, but Durkheim optimistically pointed to a new kind of solidarity. Where societies had been built on *likeness*, Durkheim now saw social life based on *difference*.

For Durkheim, urban society offers more individual choice, moral tolerance, and personal privacy than people find in rural villages. In sum, something is lost in the process of urbanization, but much is gained.

GEORG SIMMEL: THE BLASÉ URBANITE

The German sociologist Georg Simmel (1858–1918) offered a micro-analysis of cities, studying how urban life shapes individual experience. According to Simmel, individuals perceive the city as a crush of people, objects, and events. To prevent being overwhelmed by all this stimulation, urbanites develop a *blasé attitude*, tuning out much of what goes on around them. Such detachment does not mean that city dwellers lack compassion for others; they simply keep their distance as a survival strategy so they can focus their time and energy on those who really matter to them.

THE CHICAGO SCHOOL: ROBERT PARK AND LOUIS WIRTH

Sociologists in the United States soon joined the study of rapidly growing cities. Robert Park, a leader of the first U.S. sociology program at the University of Chicago, sought to add a street-level perspective by getting out and studying real cities. As he said of himself:

> I suspect that I have actually covered more ground, tramping about in cities in different parts of the world, than any other living man. (1950:viii)

Walking the streets, Park found the city to be an organized mosaic of distinctive ethnic communities, commercial centers, and industrial districts. Over time, he observed, these "natural areas" develop and change in relation to each other. To Park, then, the city was a living organism—a human kaleidoscope.

Another major figure in the Chicago School of urban sociology was Louis Wirth (1897–1952). Wirth (1938) is best known for blending the ideas of Tönnies, Durkheim, Simmel, and Park into a comprehensive theory of urban life.

Wirth began by defining the city as a setting with a large, dense, and socially diverse population. These traits result in an impersonal, superficial, and transitory way of life. Living among millions of others, urbanites come into contact with many more people than rural residents. Thus, when city people notice others at all, they usually know them not in terms of *who they are* but *what they do*—as, for instance, the bus driver, florist, or grocery store clerk. Specialized, urban relationships can be pleasant for all concerned. But we should remember that self-interest rather than friendship is the main reason for the interaction.

Finally, limited social involvement coupled with great social diversity make city dwellers more tolerant than rural villagers. Rural communities often jealously enforce their narrow traditions, but the heterogeneous population of a city rarely shares any single code of moral conduct (T. Wilson, 1985, 1995).

Critical evaluation. Both in Europe and in the United States, early sociologists presented a mixed view of urban living. On the one hand, rapid urbanization was troubling. Tönnies and Wirth saw personal ties and traditional morality lost in the anonymous rush of the city. On the other hand, Durkheim and Park emphasized urbanism's positive face, pointing to greater personal autonomy and personal choice.

One problem is that Wirth and others painted urbanism in broad strokes that overlook the effects of class, race, and gender. There are many kinds of urbanites—rich and poor, black and white, Anglo and Latino, women and men—all leading distinctive lives (Gans, 1968). And, in fact, cities can intensify these social differences. That is, we see the extent of social diversity most clearly in cities where various categories can form "critical masses" (Macionis & Parrillo, 2001).

URBAN ECOLOGY

Sociologists (especially members of the Chicago School) also developed **urban ecology,** *the study of the link between the physical and social dimensions of cities.* Consider, for example, why cities are located where they are. The first cities emerged in fertile regions where the ecology favored raising crops. Preindustrial people, concerned with defense, built their cities on mountains (ancient Athens was perched on an outcropping of rock) or in areas surrounded by water (Paris and Mexico City were founded on islands). With the Industrial Revolution, economic considerations situated all the major U.S. cities near rivers and natural harbors that facilitated trade.

Urban ecologists also study the physical design of cities. In 1925, Ernest W. Burgess, a student and colleague of Robert Park, described land use in Chicago in terms of *concentric zones.* City centers, Burgess observed, are business districts bordered by a ring of factories, followed by residential rings with housing that becomes more expensive the farther it is from the noise and pollution of the city's center.

Homer Hoyt (1939) refined Burgess's observations, noting that distinctive districts sometimes form *wedge-shaped sectors.* For example, one fashionable area may develop next to another, or an industrial district may extend outward from a city's center along a train or trolley line.

Chauncy Harris and Edward Ullman (1945) added yet another insight: As cities decentralize, they lose their single-center form in favor of a *multicentered model.* As cities grow, residential areas, industrial parks, and shopping districts typically push away from one another. Few people wish to live close to industrial areas, for example, so the city becomes a mosaic of distinct districts.

Social area analysis investigates what people in particular neighborhoods have in common. Three factors seem to explain most of the variation—family patterns, social class, and race and ethnicity (Shevky & Bell, 1955; Johnston, 1976). Families with children gravitate to areas with large apartments or single-family homes and good schools. The rich seek high-prestige neighborhoods, often in the central city near cultural attractions. People with a common social heritage cluster in distinctive communities.

Finally, Brian Berry and Philip Rees (1969) tie together many of these insights. They explain that distinct family types tend to settle in the concentric zones described by Ernest Burgess. Specifically, households with few children tend to cluster toward the city's center, while those with more children live farther away. Social class differences are primarily responsible for the sector-shaped districts described by Homer Hoyt as, for instance, the rich occupy one "side of the tracks" and the poor, the other. And racial and ethnic neighborhoods are found at various points throughout the city, consistent with Harris and Ullman's multicentered model.

In low-income countries throughout the world, people are migrating from rural areas to cities in hope of a better life. The result is that many cities are overwhelmed with newcomers, who are forced to live wherever they can. Shanty settlements, such as this one in Manila, Philippines, pose obvious dangers to residents (and, especially, children) in terms of accidents and disease. What do you think would happen if heavy rains flooded this neighborhood?

URBAN POLITICAL ECONOMY

After the urban rioting of the 1960s, some analysts turned away from the ecological approach to a social-conflict understanding of city life. The *urban political economy* model applies Karl Marx's analysis of conflict in the workplace to conflict in the city (Lindstrom, 1995).

The ecological approach sees the city as a "natural" organism, with particular districts and neighborhoods developing according to an internal logic. Political economists disagree. They claim that city life is defined by people with power: corporate leaders and political officials. Capitalism, which transforms the city into "real estate" traded for profit and concentrates wealth in the hands of a few, is the key to understanding city life. From this point of view, for example, the decline in industrial, Snowbelt cities after 1950 was the result of deliberate decisions by the corporate elite to move their production facilities to the Sunbelt (where labor is cheaper and less likely to be unionized) or move them out of the country entirely to low-income nations (Harvey, 1976; Molotch, 1976; Castells, 1977, 1983; Feagin, 1983; Lefebvre, 1991).

Critical evaluation. Compared to the older urban ecology approach, the political economy view seems better able to address the fact that many U.S. cities are in *crisis*, with widespread poverty, high crime, and barely functioning schools. But one criticism applies to both approaches: They focus on U.S. cities during a limited period of history. Much of what we know about industrial cities does not apply to preindustrial towns in our own past or the rapidly growing cities in many poor nations today. Therefore, it is unlikely that any single model of cities can account for the full range of urban diversity that we find in the world today.

URBANIZATION IN POOR SOCIETIES

November 16, 1988, Cairo, Egypt. People call the vast Muslim cemetery in Old Cairo The City of the Dead. In truth, it is very much alive: Tens of thousands of squatters have moved into the mausoleums, making this place an eerie mix of life and death. Children run across the stone floors, clotheslines stretch between the monuments, and an occasional television antenna protrudes from a tomb roof. With Cairo gaining 1,000 people a day, families live where they can.

Twice in human history the world has experienced a revolutionary expansion of cities. The first urban revolution began about 8000 B.C.E. with the first urban settlements and continued until permanent settlements were in place on several continents. Then, about 1750, the second urban revolution took off and lasted for two centuries as the Industrial Revolution led to rapid growth of cities in Europe and North America.

A third urban revolution is now underway. Today, 75 percent of people in industrial societies are already city dwellers. But extraordinary urban growth is occurring in poor nations. In 1950, about 25 percent of the people in low-income countries lived in cities; by 2005, the figure will exceed 50 percent. Moreover, in 1950, only seven cities in the world had populations over 5 million, and only two of these were in low-income countries. By 1999, thirty-seven cities had passed this mark, and twenty-six of them were in less developed nations (*World Almanac 2000*, 1999).

A third urban revolution is taking place because many poor nations have entered the high-growth Stage 2 of demographic transition theory. Falling death rates have fueled population increase in Latin America, Asia, and, especially, Africa. For urban areas, the rate of increase is *twice* as high because, in addition to natural increase, millions of people leave the countryside each year in search of jobs, health care, education, and conveniences like running water and electricity.

Cities do offer more opportunities than rural areas, but they provide no quick fix for the massive problems of escalating population and grinding poverty. Many cities in less developed nations—including Mexico City, Egypt's Cairo, India's Calcutta, and Manila in the Philippines—are simply unable to meet the basic needs of much of their population. All these cities are surrounded by wretched shantytowns—settlements of makeshift homes built from discarded materials. As noted in Chapter 12 ("Global Stratification"), even city dumps are home to thousands of poor people, who pick through the waste hoping to find enough to survive for another day.

ENVIRONMENT AND SOCIETY

Our species has prospered, rapidly increasing the population of the planet. Moreover, within the next twenty-five years, most people will live in cities, which offer the promise of a better life than that found in rural villages.

But these advances have come at a high price. Never before in history have human beings placed such demands on the earth. This disturbing development brings us to the final section of this chapter: the interplay between the natural environment and society. Like demography, **ecology** is another cousin of sociology; it is *the study of the interaction of living organisms and the natural environment.* Ecology rests on the research not only of social scientists but natural scientists as well. Here, however, we focus on those aspects of ecology that involve now familiar sociological concepts and issues.

Many environmentalists believe that our planet is in danger. The importance of sociology in understanding environmental issues stems from the fact that problems are not caused by the natural world operating on its own. Rather, they result from the way humans organize social life.

The **natural environment** refers to *the earth's surface and atmosphere, including living organisms as well as the air, water, soil, and other resources necessary to sustain life.* Like every other species, humans depend on the natural environment to live. Yet, with our capacity for culture, humans stand apart from other species. We alone take deliberate action to remake the world according to our own interests and desires—for better *and* for worse.

Why is the environment of interest to sociologists? Simply because environmental problems—from pollution to acid rain to global warming—do not arise from the "natural world" operating on its own. Rather, as we shall explain, such problems result from the specific actions of human beings, making them *social* issues (Marx, 1994).

THE GLOBAL DIMENSION

The study of the natural environment must be approached from a global perspective. The reason is simple: Regardless of political divisions among the world's nations, the planet is a single **ecosystem,** *a system composed of the interaction of all living organisms and their natural environment.*

The Greek meaning of *eco* is "house," reminding us that this planet is our home and that all living things and their natural environment are *interrelated.* In practice, change in any part of the natural environment ripples throughout the entire global ecosystem.

Consider, from an ecological point of view, our national love of eating hamburgers. People in North America (and, increasingly, around the world) have created a huge demand for beef, which has greatly expanded the ranching industry in Brazil, Costa Rica, and other Latin American nations. To produce the lean meat sought by fast-food corporations, cattle in Latin America feed on grass, which uses a great deal of land. Latin American ranchers get the land for grazing by clearing thousands of square miles of forests each year. These tropical forests are vital to maintaining the earth's atmosphere. Deforestation ends up threatening everyone, including people in the United States who enjoy hamburgers without a thought to the environment (Myers, 1984a).

TECHNOLOGY AND THE ENVIRONMENTAL DEFICIT

As humans have developed more powerful technology, we have increasingly remade the world as we choose. Members of societies with simple technology—the hunters and gatherers described in Chapter 4 ("Society")—have scarcely any ability to affect the environment. On the contrary, members of such societies are keenly dependent on nature, so that their lives are defined by the migration of game and the rhythm of the seasons. They are especially vulnerable to natural catastrophes, such as fires, floods, droughts, and storms.

Societies at intermediate stages of sociocultural evolution have a somewhat greater capacity to affect the environment. But the environmental impact of horticulture (small-scale farming), pastoralism (the herding of animals), and even agriculture (the use of animal-drawn plows) is limited because people still rely on muscle power for producing food and other goods.

Human control of the natural environment grew dramatically with the Industrial Revolution. Muscle power gave way to engines that burn fossil fuels: coal at first and then oil. Such machinery affects the environment in two ways: by consuming natural resources and by releasing pollutants into the atmosphere. Even more important, humans armed with industrial technology are able to bend nature to their will, tunneling through mountains, damming rivers, irrigating deserts, and drilling for oil on the ocean floor. This is why people in rich nations, who represent just 15 percent of humanity, use 80 percent of the world's energy (Connett, 1991; Miller, 1992).

The environmental impact of industrial technology goes beyond energy consumption. Just as important is the fact that members of industrial societies produce 100 times more goods than people in agrarian societies. Higher living standards, in turn, increase the problem of solid waste (since people ultimately throw away most of what they produce) and pollution (since industrial production generates smoke and other toxic substances).

From the start, people recognized the material benefits of industrial technology. But only a century later did they begin to see the long-term effects on the natural environment. Indeed, one trait of the recent post-industrial era is a growing concern for environmental quality (Abrahamson, 1997; Kidd & Lee, 1997). Today, we realize that the technological power to make our lives better can also put the lives of future generations in jeopardy (Voight, cited in Bormann & Kellert, 1991:ix–x).

Evidence is mounting that we are running up an **environmental deficit,** *profound and negative long-term harm to the natural environment caused by humanity's focus on short-term material affluence* (Bormann, 1990). The concept of environmental deficit is important for three reasons. First, it reminds us that the state of the environment is a *social issue,* reflecting choices people make about how to live. Second, it suggests that much environmental damage—to the air, land, and water—is *unintended.* By focusing on the short-term benefits of, say, cutting down forests, strip mining, or using throw-away packaging, we fail to see their long-term environmental effects. Third, in some respects, the environmental deficit is *reversible.* Inasmuch as societies have created environmental problems, in other words, societies can undo many of them.

CULTURE: GROWTH AND LIMITS

Whether we recognize environmental dangers and decide to do something about them is a cultural matter. Thus, along with technology, culture has powerful environmental consequences.

The Logic of Growth

Why does our nation set aside specific areas as "parks" and "game preserves"? Doing this seems to indicate that, except for these special areas, people can freely use natural resources for their own purposes (Myers, 1991). This aggressive approach to the natural environment has long been central to our way of life.

Chapter 3 ("Culture") described the core values that underlie social life in the United States. One of these is *material comfort*, the belief that money and the things it buys enrich our lives. We also believe in the idea of *progress*, thinking that the future will be better than the present. Moreover, we look to *science* to make our lives easier and more rewarding. Taken together, such cultural values form the *logic of growth*.

The logic of growth is an optimistic view of the world. It holds that more powerful technology has improved our lives and new discoveries will make the future better still. In simple terms, the logic of growth asserts that "people are clever," "having things is good," and "life gets better." A powerful force throughout the history of the United States and other Western industrial societies, the logic of growth is the driving force behind settling the wilderness, building towns and roads, and pursuing material affluence.

Even so, "progress" can lead to unexpected problems, including harming the environment. The logic of growth responds by arguing that people (especially scientists and other technology experts) will find a way out of any problem that growth places in our path. If, say, one resource becomes inadequate, we will come up with other, new resources that will do the job just as well. For example, by the time the growing number of cars in the world depletes the planet's oil reserves, scientists will have come up with electric, solar, or nuclear engines or some as yet unknown technology to free us from dependence on oil.

But environmentalists counter that the logic of growth is flawed in assuming that natural resources such as oil, clean air, fresh water, and topsoil will always be plentiful. On the contrary, they claim, these are *finite* resources that we can and will exhaust if we continue to pursue growth at any cost. Echoing Malthus, environmentalists warn that if we call on the earth to support increasing numbers of people, we will surely deplete finite resources, destroying the environment—and ourselves—in the process (Milbrath, 1989; Livernash & Rodenburg, 1998).

The Limits to Growth

If we cannot invent our way out of the problems created by the logic of growth, perhaps we need another way of thinking about the world. Environmentalists, therefore, counter that growth must have limits. Stated simply, the *limits to growth thesis* is that humanity must implement policies to control the growth of population, production, and use of resources in order to avoid environmental collapse.

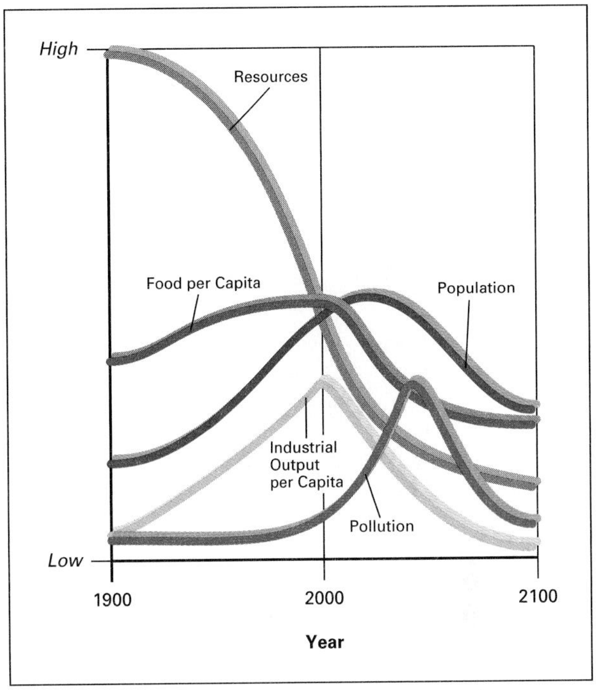

FIGURE 22–5 The Limits to Growth: Projections
Source: Based on Meadows et al. (1972).

In *The Limits to Growth*, a controversial book that was influential in launching the environmental movement, Donella Meadows and her colleagues (1972) used a computer model to calculate the planet's available resources, rates of population growth, amount of land available for cultivation, levels of industrial and food production, and amount of pollutants released into the atmosphere. The model reflects changes that have occurred since 1900, and then projects forward to the end of the twenty-first century. The authors concede that such long-range predictions are speculative, and some critics think they are plain wrong (Simon, 1981). But right or wrong, the general conclusions of the study, shown in Figure 22–5, call for serious consideration.

According to the limits to growth thesis, we are quickly consuming the earth's finite resources. Supplies of oil, natural gas, and other energy sources are already falling sharply and will continue to drop, a little faster

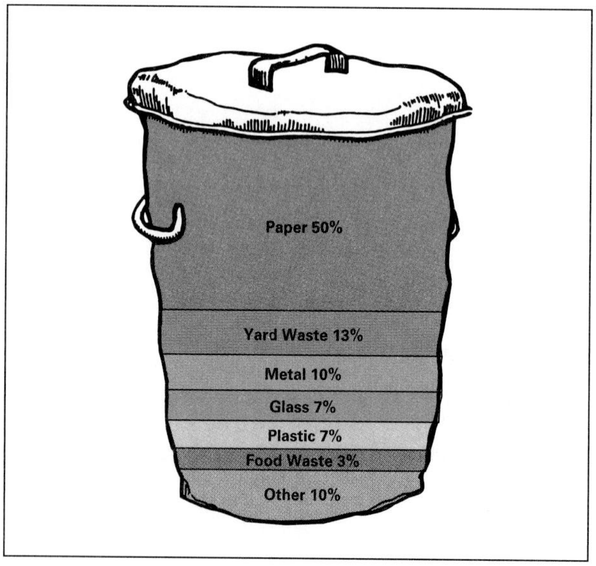

FIGURE 22–6 Composition of Household Trash
Sources: Based on Franklin Associates (1986) and Corley et al. (1993).

or slower depending on conservation policies in rich nations and how fast other nations industrialize. While food production per person will continue to rise during this century, world hunger will persist because existing food supplies are so unequally distributed. By 2050, the model predicts, hunger will reach a crisis level, first stabilizing population and then sending it back downward. Eventually, depleted resources will cripple industrial output as well. Only then will pollution rates fall.

Limits to growth theorists are also known as neo-Malthusians because they share Malthus's pessimism about the future. They doubt that current patterns of life are sustainable for even another century. If so, we face a fundamental choice: Either we make deliberate changes in how we live, or widespread calamity will force change upon us.

SOLID WASTE: THE DISPOSABLE SOCIETY

As an interesting exercise, carry a trash bag around for a single day and collect everything you throw away. Most people are surprised to find that the average person in the United States discards close to five pounds of paper, metal, plastic, and other materials daily (over a lifetime, that's about 50 tons!). For the country as a whole, this amounts to about 1 billion pounds of solid waste *each and every day.* Figure 22–6 shows the composition of a normal household's trash.

As a rich nation of people who value convenience, the United States has become a *disposable society.* We consume more products than virtually any other nation, and many of these products have throw-away packaging. The most familiar case is fast food, served with cardboard, plastic, and Styrofoam containers that we discard within minutes. And countless other products—from film to fishhooks—are elaborately packaged to make the product more attractive to the customer and to discourage tampering and theft.

Consider, too, that manufacturers market soft drinks, beer, and fruit juices in aluminum cans, glass jars, and plastic containers, which not only consume finite resources but also generate mountains of solid waste. Then there are countless items intentionally designed to be disposable: pens, razors, flashlights, batteries, even cameras. Other products—from light bulbs to automobiles—are designed to have a limited useful life and then become unwanted junk. As Paul Connett (1991) points out, even the words we use to describe what we throw away—*waste, litter, trash, refuse, garbage, rubbish*—show how little we value what we cannot immediately use. But this was not always the case, as the box explains.

Living in a rich society, the average person in the United States consumes 50 times more steel, 170 times more newspaper, 250 times more gasoline, and 300 times more plastic each year than the typical individual in India (Miller, 1992). This high level of consumption means that we in the United States not only use a disproportionate share of the planet's natural resources, but also generate most of the world's refuse.

We like to say that we "throw things away." But 80 percent of our solid waste is not burned or recycled and never "goes away." Rather, it ends up in landfills. One problem with landfills is that, across the country, they are filling up. Second, material in landfills can pollute groundwater. Although, in most places, laws now regulate what can be discarded in a landfill, the Environmental Protection Agency has identified 30,000 dump sites across the United States containing hazardous materials that are polluting water both above and below the ground. Third, what goes into landfills all too often stays there—sometimes for centuries. Tens of millions of tires, diapers, and other items that we bury in landfills each year do not decompose and will be an unwelcome legacy for future generations.

Environmentalists argue that we should address the problem of solid waste by doing what many of our

APPLYING SOCIOLOGY

Why Grandmother Had No Trash

Grandma Macionis, we always used to say, never threw away anything. She was born and raised in Lithuania—the "old country"—where life in a poor village shaped her in ways that never changed even after she immigrated to the United States as a young woman.

After opening a birthday present, she would carefully save the box, wrapping paper, and ribbon, which meant as much to her as the gift they contained. Grandma never wore new clothes, her kitchen knives were worn narrow from decades of sharpening, and all her garbage was "recycled" as compost for her vegetable garden.

As strange as Grandma seemed to her grandchildren, she was a product of her culture. A century ago, in fact, there was little "trash." If a pair of socks wore thin, Grandma mended them, probably more than once. When they were beyond repair, she used them as a rag for cleaning, or sewed them (with other old clothing) into a quilt. For her, everything had value—if not in one way, then in another.

During the twentieth century, as women joined men in working outside the home, income went up and families began buying more and more "time-saving" products. Before long, few people cared about the home recycling that Grandma practiced. Soon, cities sent crews from block to block to pick up truckloads of discarded material. The era of "trash" had begun.

grandparents did: Turn waste into a resource. One way to do this is through *recycling*, reusing resources we would otherwise discard. Recycling is an accepted practice in Japan and many other nations, and it is becoming more common in the United States, where we now reuse about 30 percent of waste materials. The share is increasing as laws mandate reuse of certain materials such as glass bottles and aluminum cans. In addition, because our nation has a market-based economy, recycling is bound to increase as it becomes more profitable.

WATER AND AIR

Oceans, lakes, and streams are the lifeblood of the global ecosystem. Humans depend on water for drinking, bathing, cooling, and cooking, for recreation, and for a host of other activities.

According to what scientists call the *hydrological cycle*, the earth naturally recycles water and refreshes the land. The process begins as heat from the sun causes the earth's water, 97 percent of which is in the oceans, to evaporate and form clouds. Because water evaporates at lower temperatures than most pollutants, the water vapor that rises from the seas is relatively pure, leaving various contaminants behind. Water then falls to the earth as rain, which drains into streams and rivers and, finally, returns to the sea. Two major concerns about water, then, are supply and pollution.

Water Supply

For thousands of years, since the time of the ancient civilizations of China, Egypt, and Rome, water rights have figured prominently in codes of law. Today, as Global Map 22–2 on page 588 shows, some regions of the world, especially the tropics, enjoy a plentiful supply of water. But high demand, coupled with modest reserves, makes water supply a matter of concern in much of North America and Asia, where people look to rivers rather than rainfall for their water. In the Middle East, water supply has already reached a critical level. In Egypt, for instance, an arid region of the world, people depend on the Nile River for most of their

WINDOW ON THE WORLD

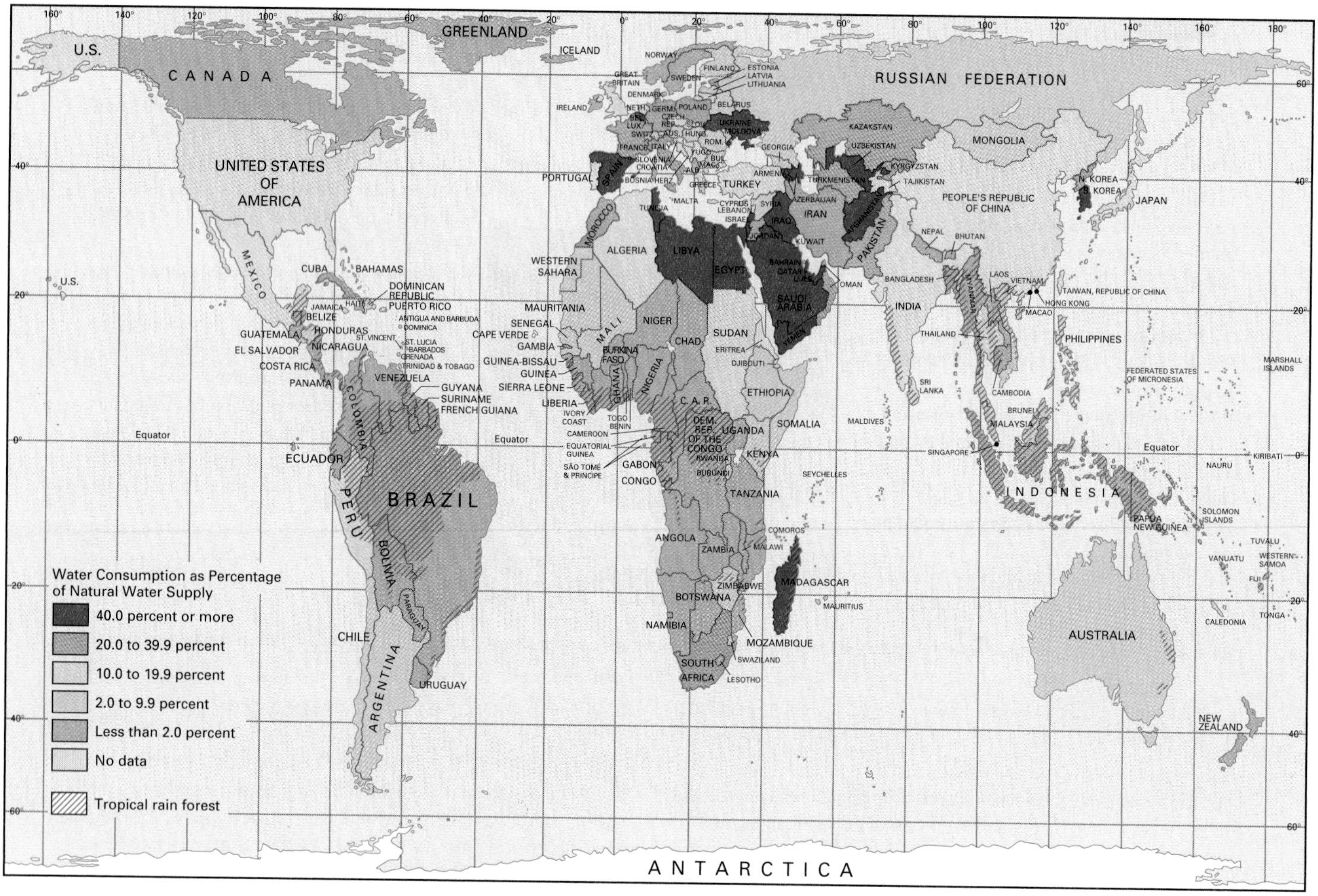

GLOBAL MAP 22–2 Water Consumption in Global Perspective

This map shows each country's water consumption as a percentage of its internal renewable water resources. Nations near the equator consume only a tiny share of their available resources; indeed, as the map shows, much of this region is covered with rain forest. Northern Africa and the Middle East are a different story, however, with dense populations drawing on very limited water resources. As a result, in Libya, Egypt, Saudi Arabia, and other countries, people (especially the poor) do not have as much water as they would like or, often, as they need.

Source: United Nations Development Programme (1995).

water. As the Egyptian population increases, however, shortages are becoming frequent. Egyptians today must make do with one-sixth the amount of water per person from the Nile compared to 1900. Furthermore, experts predict that within thirty years, as many as 1 billion people in northern Africa and the Middle East may lack the water they need for irrigation and drinking (Myers, 1984c; Postel, 1993).

The world over, soaring population and complex technology have greatly increased societies' appetite for water. The global consumption of water (now more than 6 billion cubic feet per year) has tripled since 1950 and is expanding even faster than the world's population. As a result, even in those parts of the world that receive plenty of rainfall, people are using groundwater faster than it can be naturally replenished. In the Tamil Nadu region of southern India, for example, so much groundwater is being used that the water table has fallen 100 feet over the last several decades. Mexico City—which has sprawled to some 1400 square miles—has pumped so much water from its underground aquifer that the city has sunk thirty feet during the last century and is dropping about two inches per year. Farther north, in the United States, the Ogallala aquifer, which lies below seven states and stretches from South Dakota to Texas, is now being pumped so rapidly that some experts fear it could run dry within the next several decades.

In light of such developments, we must face the reality that water is a valuable, finite resource. Greater conservation of water by individuals (the average person consumes 10 million gallons in a lifetime) is part of the answer. However, households around the world account for just 10 percent of water use. We need to curb water consumption by industry, which uses 25 percent of the global total, and farming, which consumes two-thirds of the total for irrigation.

New irrigation technology may reduce the demand for water in the future. But, here again, we see how population increase, as well as economic growth, strains our ecosystem (Myers, 1984a; Goldfarb, 1991; Falkenmark & Widstrand, 1992; Postel, 1993).

In the United States, most of us take safe water for granted. But people, and especially children, in poor countries around the world are at high risk from infectious diseases that are spread by unclean water used for bathing, cooking, and drinking.

Water Pollution

In large cities—from Mexico City to Cairo to Shanghai—many people have no choice but to drink contaminated water. Infectious diseases like typhoid, cholera, and dysentery—all caused by waterborne microorganisms—spread rapidly through these populations (Clarke, 1984b; Falkenmark & Widstrand, 1992). Besides ensuring ample *supplies* of water, then, we must protect the *quality* of water.

Water quality in the United States is generally good by global standards. However, even here the problem of water pollution is steadily growing. According to the Sierra Club, an environmental activist organization, rivers and streams across the United States absorb some 500 million pounds of toxic waste each year. This pollution results not just from intentional dumping but also from the runoff of agricultural fertilizers and lawn chemicals.

A special problem is *acid rain*, rain made acidic by air pollution that destroys plant and animal life. Acid rain (or snow) begins with power plants burning fossil fuels (oil and coal) to generate electricity; this burning releases sulfuric and nitrous oxides into the air. As the wind sweeps these gases into the atmosphere, they react with the air to form sulfuric and nitric acids, which turn atmospheric moisture acidic.

This is a clear case of one type of pollution causing another: Air pollution (from smokestacks) ends up contaminating water (in lakes and streams that collect acid rain). Moreover, acid rain is truly a global phenomenon because the regions that suffer the harmful effects may be thousands of miles from the original pollution. For instance, British power plants have caused acid rain that has devastated forests and fish in Norway and Sweden, up to a thousand miles to the northeast.

The earth's rain forests—vital to the planet's ecology—are now half their original size and become smaller every year. Once the lush vegetation of such forests is lost, the soil is at risk of drying out and turning into a desert. Thus, environmental damage is often irreversible.

In the United States, we see a similar pattern as midwestern smokestacks have harmed the natural environment of New England (Clarke, 1984a).

Air Pollution

Because we are surrounded by air, most people in the United States are more aware of air pollution than contaminated water. One of the unexpected consequences of industrial technology, especially the factory and the motor vehicle, has been a decline in air quality. In 1950, exhaust fumes from automobiles shrouded cities like Los Angeles. In London, factory smokestacks, automobiles, and coal fires used to heat households all added to what was probably the worst urban air quality of the last century. What some British jokingly called "pea soup" was, in reality, a deadly mix of pollution. For five days in 1952, an especially thick haze that hung over London killed 4,000 people (Clarke, 1984a).

Air quality improved in the final decades of the twentieth century. Rich nations passed laws that banned high-pollution heating, including the coal fires that choked London fifty years ago. In addition, scientists devised ways to reduce the noxious output of factories and the growing numbers of automobiles and trucks.

If high-income countries can breathe a bit more easily than they once did, the problem of air pollution in poor societies is becoming more serious. One reason is that people in low-income countries still rely on wood, coal, peat, and other "dirty" fuels for cooking fires and to heat their homes. Moreover, nations eager to encourage short-term industrial development may pay little heed to the longer-term dangers of air pollution. As a result, many cities in Latin America, Eastern Europe, and Asia are plagued by air pollution as bad as London's fifty years ago.

THE RAIN FORESTS

Rain forests are *regions of dense forestation, most of which circle the globe close to the equator.* A glance back at Global Map 22–2, on page 588, shows that the largest tropical rain forests are in South America (notably Brazil), west-central Africa, and Southeast Asia. In all, the world's rain forests cover some 2 billion acres, or 7 percent of the earth's total land surface.

Like other global resources, rain forests are falling victim to the needs and appetites of the surging world population. As noted earlier, to meet the demand for beef, ranchers in Latin America burn forested areas to increase their supply of grazing land. We are also losing rain forests to the hardwood trade. People in rich nations pay high prices for mahogany and other woods because, as environmentalist Norman Myers (1984b:88) puts it, they have "a penchant for parquet floors, fine furniture, fancy paneling, weekend yachts, and high-grade coffins." Under such economic pressure, the world's rain forests are now just half their original size, and they continue to shrink by about 1 percent (65,000 square miles) annually. Unless we stop this loss, the rain forests will vanish before the end of the twenty-first

Members of small, simple societies, such as the Tan't Batu, who thrive in the Philippines, live in harmony with nature; such people do not have the technological means to greatly affect the natural world. Although we in complex societies like to think of ourselves as superior to such people, the truth is that there is much we can—and must—learn from them.

century, and with them will go protection for the earth's biodiversity and climate.

Global Warming

Why are rain forests so important? One reason is that they cleanse the atmosphere of carbon dioxide (CO_2). Since the beginning of the Industrial Revolution, the amount of carbon dioxide produced by humans (mostly from factories and automobiles) has risen tenfold. Much of this carbon dioxide is absorbed by the oceans. But plants take in carbon dioxide and expel oxygen. This is why rain forests are vital to maintaining the chemical balance of the atmosphere.

The problem, then, is that production of carbon dioxide is rising while the amount of plant life on the earth is shrinking. To make matters worse, rain forests are being destroyed mostly by burning, which releases even more carbon dioxide into the atmosphere. Experts estimate the atmospheric concentration of carbon dioxide is now 20 to 30 percent higher than it was 150 years ago.

High above the earth, carbon dioxide acts like the glass roof of a greenhouse, letting heat from the sun pass through to the earth while preventing much of it from radiating away from the planet. The result, say ecologists, is a **greenhouse effect,** *a rise in the earth's average temperature (global warming) due to an increasing concentration of carbon dioxide in the atmosphere.* Over the last century, the global temperature has risen about 1.0° Fahrenheit (to an average of 58° F). And scientists warn that it could rise by 5° to 10° during this century, which would melt vast areas of the polar ice caps and raise the sea level to cover low-lying land around the world. Were this to happen, water would cover all of Bangladesh, for example, and much of the coastal United States, including Washington, D.C., right up to the steps of the White House. On the other hand, the U.S. Midwest, currently one of the most productive agricultural regions in the world, would likely become arid.

Not all scientists share this vision of future global warming. Some point out that global temperature changes have been taking place throughout history, apparently with little or nothing to do with rain forests. Moreover, higher concentrations of carbon dioxide in the atmosphere might speed up plant growth (since plants thrive on this gas), which would correct the imbalance and nudge the earth's temperature downward once again. Still other scientists think global warming might even have benefits, including longer growing seasons and lower food prices (Silverberg, 1991; Moore, 1995; Begley, 1997; McDonald, 1999).

Declining Biodiversity

Clearing rain forests also reduces the earth's *biodiversity.* This is because rain forests are home to almost half of this planet's living species.

On earth, there are as many as 30 million species of animals, plants, and microorganisms. Several dozen unique species of plants and animals cease to exist each day; but, given the vast number of living species, why should we be concerned? Environmentalists give three reasons. First, our planet's biodiversity provides a varied

No one wants to live or work in a dangerous environment. But, in a world of political competition, it is the poor who often end up with the hazards in their backyards. Here, residents of this urban neighborhood protest plans to construct a power plant in the area.

source of human food. Using agricultural high technology, scientists can "splice" familiar crops with more exotic plant life, making food more bountiful as well as more resistant to insects and disease. Thus, biodiversity is needed to feed our planet's rapidly increasing population.

Second, the earth's biodiversity is a vital genetic resource. Medical and pharmaceutical research look to animal and plant biodiversity for new compounds that cure disease and improve our lives. Children in the United States, for example, now have a good chance of surviving leukemia, a disease that was almost a sure killer two generations ago, because of a compound derived from a pretty tropical flower called the rosy periwinkle. The oral birth control pill, used by tens of millions of women in this country, is another product of plant research, this time involving the Mexican forest yam.

Third, with the loss of any species of life—whether it is one variety of ant, the magnificent California condor, or the famed Chinese panda—the beauty and complexity of our natural environment are diminished. And there are clear warning signs of such loss: Three-fourths of the world's 9,000 species of birds are declining in number.

Finally, note that, unlike pollution, the extinction of any species is irreversible and final. An important ethical question, then, is whether we who live today have the right to impoverish the world for those who live tomorrow (Myers, 1984b, 1991; E. Wilson, 1991; Brown et al., 1993).

ENVIRONMENTAL RACISM

Conflict theory has given rise to the concept of **environmental racism,** *the pattern by which environmental hazards are greatest for poor people, especially minorities.* Historically, factories that spew pollution stand near neighborhoods of the poor and people of color. Why? In part, because the poor themselves were drawn to factories in search of work and, once hired, their low incomes often meant they could afford housing only in undesirable neighborhoods. Sometimes the only housing that fit their budgets stood in the very shadow of the plants and mills where they worked.

Nobody wants a factory or dump nearby, but the poor have little power to resist. Through the years, then, the most serious environmental hazards have been located near Newark, New Jersey (not in upscale Bergen County), in Southside Chicago (not wealthy Lake Forest), or on Native American reservations in the West (not in affluent suburbs of Denver or Phoenix) (Perrolle, 1993; Commission for Racial Justice, United Church of Christ, 1994; Szasz, 1994; Pollock & Vittas, 1995).

LOOKING AHEAD: TOWARD A SUSTAINABLE WORLD

The demographic analysis presented in this chapter points to some disturbing trends. We see, first, that earth's population has reached record levels because birth rates remain high in poor nations and death rates have fallen just about everywhere. Lowering fertility will remain a pressing problem throughout this century. Even with some recent decline in population increase, the nightmare Thomas Malthus described is still a real possibility, as the final box explains.

Further, population growth remains greatest in the poorest countries of the world, those without the means to support their present populations, much less their

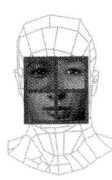

CONTROVERSY & DEBATE

Apocalypse: Will People Overwhelm the Earth?

Are you worried about the world's increasing population? Think about this: By the time you finish reading this box, more than 1,000 people will be added to our planet. By this time tomorrow, global population will rise by 209,000. Currently, as the table shows, there are about four births for every two deaths on the planet, pushing the world's population upward by 77 million annually. Put another way, global population growth amounts to adding another Egypt to the world every year.

Global Population Increase

	Births	Deaths	Net Increase
Per Year	131,577,477	54,998,601	76,577,876
Per Month	10,964,706	4,583,217	6,381,490
Per Day	359,499	150,269	209,229
Per Hour	14,979	6,261	8,718
Per Minute	250	104	145
Per Second	4.2	1.7	2.4

It is no wonder that demographers and environmentalists are deeply concerned about the future. The earth has an unprecedented population: The 2 billion people we have *added* since 1974 alone exceeds the planet's total in 1900. Might Thomas Robert Malthus—who predicted that population would outstrip the earth's resources and plunge humanity into war and suffering—be right after all?

Lester Brown, a population and environmental activist, speaks for the *neo-Malthusians* by predicting an apocalypse if we do not change our ways. Brown concedes that Malthus failed to imagine how much technology (especially fertilizers and altering plant genetics) could boost agricultural output. But he maintains that the earth's rising population is nevertheless rapidly outstripping its finite resources. Families in many poor countries can find little firewood; members of rich societies are depleting the oil reserves; everyone is draining our supply of clean water.

Moreover, according to the neo-Malthusians, we are steadily poisoning the planet with waste. There is a limit to the earth's capacity to absorb pollution, they warn, and as the number of people continues to increase, the quality of life will decline. Some analysts, in fact, argue that we have already passed the earth's "carrying capacity" for population. Holding the line will not be enough; as they see it, we need to *reduce* global population to perhaps half of what it is today (Smail, 1997).

But another camp of analysts, the *anti-Malthusians*, sharply disagrees. Asks Julian Simon, "Why the doom and gloom?" Two centuries ago, he points out, Malthus predicted catastrophe. But today the earth supports almost six times as many people who, on average, live longer, healthier lives than ever before. As Simon sees it, the current state of the planet is cause for celebration.

The mistake of the neo-Malthusians, Simon argues, is assuming the world has finite resources that are spread thinner and thinner as population increases. Rather, people have the ability to control population growth and to improve their lives in many ways. Furthermore, we do not know what number of people the earth can support because humans keep rewriting the rules, in effect, by developing new fertilizers, new crops, and new forms of energy. Simon notes that today's global economy makes available more resources than ever (including energy and consumer goods) at increasingly low prices. He looks optimistically to the future because technology, economic investment, and, above all, human ingenuity have consistently proven the doomsayers wrong. And he is betting they will continue to do so.

Continue the debate . . .

1. *Where do you place your bet? Do you think the earth can support 4, 6, 8, or 10 billion people? Why?*
2. *Ninety-six percent of current population growth is in poor countries. What does this mean for the future of rich nations? For the future of poor ones?*
3. *What should people in rich countries do to ensure our children's future?*

Source: Based, in part, on Brown et al. (1993), Brown (1995), Simon (1995), and Smail (1997).

future ones. Supporting 77 million additional people on our planet each year—almost 74 million of whom are in poor societies—will require a global commitment to provide not only food but housing, schools, and employment. The well-being of the entire world may ultimately depend on resolving the economic and social problems of poor, overly populated countries and bridging the widening gulf between "have" and "have-not" societies.

Urbanization, too, is continuing, especially in poor countries. Throughout human history, people have sought out cities with the hope of finding a better life. But the sheer numbers of people who live in the emerging global supercities—Mexico City, São Paulo (Brazil), Kinshasa (Democratic Republic of the Congo), Bombay (India), Manila (the Philippines)—have created urban problems on a massive scale.

Throughout the entire world, humanity is facing a serious environmental challenge. Part of this problem is population increase, which is greatest in poor societies. But part of the problem is also high levels of consumption, which mark rich nations such as our own. By increasing the planet's environmental deficit, our present way of life is borrowing against the well-being of our children and their children. Globally, members of rich societies, who currently consume so much of the earth's resources, are mortgaging the future security of the poor countries of the world.

The answer, in principle, is to form an **ecologically sustainable culture,** *a way of life that meets the needs of the present generation without threatening the environmental legacy of future generations.* Sustainable living depends on three strategies.

First, the world needs to bring population growth under control. The current population of more than 6 billion is already straining the natural environment. Clearly, the higher the world's population climbs, the more difficult environmental problems will become. Even if the recent slowing of population growth continues, the world will have 8 billion people by 2050. Few analysts think that the earth can support this many people; most argue that we must hold the line at about 7 billion, and some argue that we must *decrease* population in the coming decades.

A second strategy is *conservation of finite resources.* This means meeting our needs with a responsible eye toward the future by using resources efficiently, seeking alternative sources of energy, and, in some cases, learning to live with less.

A third strategy is *reducing waste.* Whenever possible, simply using less is the best solution. But recycling programs, too, are part of the answer.

In the end, making all these strategies work depends on a more basic change in the way we think about ourselves and our world. Our *egocentric* outlook sets our own interests as standards for how to live, but a sustainable environment demands an *ecocentric* outlook that helps us see how the present is tied to the future and why everyone must work together. Most nations in the southern half of the world are *underdeveloped,* unable to meet the basic needs of their people. At the same time, most countries in the northern half of the world are *overdeveloped,* using more resources than the earth can sustain over time. Changes needed to create a sustainable ecosystem will not come easily. But the price of not responding to the growing environmental deficit will certainly be greater (Humphrey & Buttel, 1982; Burke, 1984; Kellert & Bormann, 1991; Brown et al., 1993).

In closing, consider that the great dinosaurs dominated this planet for some 160 million years and then perished forever. Humanity is far younger, having existed for a mere 250,000 years. Compared to the rather dimwitted dinosaurs, our species has the gift of great intelligence. But how will we use this ability? What are the chances that our species will continue to flourish 160 million years—or even 1,000 years—from now? The shape of tomorrow's world depends on the choices we make today.

SUMMARY

Population

1. Fertility and mortality, measured as crude birth rates and crude death rates, are major factors affecting population size.
2. Migration, another key demographic concept, has special importance to the historical growth of the United States and to cities everywhere.
3. Demographers use age-sex pyramids to show graphically the composition of a population and to project population trends. Sex ratio refers to a society's balance of females and males.
4. Historically, world population grew slowly because high birth rates were largely offset by high death rates. About 1750, a demographic

transition began as world population rose sharply, mostly due to falling death rates.

5. Thomas Robert Malthus warned that population growth would outpace food production, resulting in social calamity. Demographic transition theory, however, contends that technological advances gradually slow population increase.
6. World population is expected to reach between 8 billion and 9 billion by 2050. Such an increase will likely overwhelm many poor societies, where most of the increase will take place.

Urbanization

1. The first urban revolution began with the appearance of cities about 8000 B.C.E. By the start of the common era, cities had emerged in most regions of the world except for North America.
2. Preindustrial cities have low-rise buildings, narrow, winding streets, and personal social ties.
3. A second urban revolution began about 1750 as the Industrial Revolution propelled rapid urban growth in Europe. The physical form of cities changed, as planners created wide, regular streets to facilitate trade. The emphasis on commerce, as well as the increasing size of cities, made urban life more anonymous.
4. Urbanism came to North America with Europeans, who settled in a string of colonial towns along the Atlantic coastline. By 1850, hundreds of new cities were founded from coast to coast.
5. By 1920, a majority of the U.S. population lived in urban areas, and the largest metropolises were home to millions of people.
6. About 1950, cities began to decentralize with the growth of suburbs and edge cities. Nationally, Sunbelt cities—but not the older Snowbelt cities—are increasing in size and population.
7. Rapid urbanization in Europe during the nineteenth century led early sociologists to contrast rural and urban life. Ferdinand Tönnies built his analysis on the concepts of *Gemeinschaft* and *Gesellschaft*, and Emile Durkheim proposed parallel concepts of mechanical solidarity and organic solidarity. Georg Simmel claimed that the overstimulation of city life produced a blasé attitude in urbanites.
8. At the University of Chicago, Robert Park believed cities permit greater social freedom. Louis Wirth saw large, dense, heterogeneous populations creating an impersonal and self-interested, though tolerant, way of life. Other researchers have explored urban ecology and urban political economy.
9. A third urban revolution is now occurring in poor countries, where most of the world's largest cities will soon be found.

Environment

1. A key factor affecting the natural environment is how human beings organize social life. Thus, ecologists study how living organisms interact with their environment.
2. Societies increase the environmental deficit by focusing on short-term benefits and ignoring the long-term consequences brought on by their way of life.
3. Our ability to alter the natural world lies in our capacity for culture. Humanity's effect on the environment has increased along with the development of complex technology.
4. The "logic of growth" thesis supports economic development, claiming that people can solve environmental problems as they arise. The opposing "limits to growth" thesis states that societies must curb development to prevent eventual environmental collapse.
5. Environmental issues include disposing of solid waste, as well as protecting the quality of air and water. The supply of clean water is already low in some parts of the world.
6. Rain forests help remove carbon dioxide from the atmosphere and are home to a large share of this planet's living species. Under pressure from commercial interests, the world's rain forests are now half their original size and are shrinking by about 1 percent annually.
7. Environmental racism refers to the pattern by which the poor, especially minorities, suffer most from environmental hazards.
8. To achieve a sustainable environment that does not threaten the well-being of future generations, we must control world population, conserve finite resources, and reduce waste and pollution.

KEY CONCEPTS

Population

demography (p. 567) the study of human population

fertility (p. 567) the incidence of childbearing in a country's population

crude birth rate (p. 567) the number of live births in a given year for every thousand people in a population

mortality (p. 568) the incidence of death in a country's population

crude death rate (p. 568) the number of deaths in a given year for every thousand people in a population

infant mortality rate (p. 568) the number of deaths among infants under one year of age for each thousand live births in a given year

life expectancy (p. 569) the average life span of a country's population

migration (p. 569) the movement of people into and out of a specified territory

sex ratio (p. 571) the number of males for every hundred females in a nation's population

age-sex pyramid (p. 571) a graphic representation of the age and sex of a population

demographic transition theory (p. 572) the thesis that population patterns reflect a society's level of technological development

zero population growth (p. 574) the level of reproduction that maintains population at a steady state

Urbanization

urbanization (p. 576) the concentration of humanity into cities

metropolis (p. 577) a large city that socially and economically dominates an urban area

suburbs (p. 578) urban areas beyond the political boundaries of a city

megalopolis (p. 578) a vast urban region containing a number of cities and their surrounding suburbs

Gemeinschaft (p. 579) a type of social organization by which people are closely tied by kinship and tradition

Gesellschaft (p. 579) a type of social organization by which people come together only on the basis of individual self-interest

urban ecology (p. 581) the study of the link between the physical and social dimensions of cities

Environment

ecology (p. 583) the study of the interaction of living organisms and the natural environment

natural environment (p. 583) the earth's surface and atmosphere, including living organisms as well as the air, water, soil, and other resources necessary to sustain life

ecosystem (p. 584) a system composed of the interaction of all living organisms and their natural environment

environmental deficit (p. 584) profound and long-term harm to the natural environment caused by humanity's focus on short-term material affluence

rain forests (p. 590) regions of dense forestation, most of which circle the globe close to the equator

greenhouse effect (p. 591) a rise in the earth's average temperature (global warming) due to an increasing concentration of carbon dioxide in the atmosphere

environmental racism (p. 592) the pattern by which environmental hazards are greatest for poor people, especially minorities

ecologically sustainable culture (p. 594) a way of life that meets the needs of the present generation without threatening the environmental legacy of future generations

CRITICAL-THINKING QUESTIONS

1. What are fertility and mortality rates? Which one has been more important in increasing global population?
2. How does demographic transition theory explain population patterns in terms of technological development?

3. According to Ferdinand Tönnies, Emile Durkheim, Georg Simmel, and Louis Wirth, what characterizes urbanism as a way of life? Note several differences in the ideas of these thinkers.
4. Evaluate the environmental prediction of Thomas Robert Malthus. On balance, do you think he was more wrong or more right? Why?

APPLICATIONS AND EXERCISES

1. Here is an illustration of the problem of runaway growth (Milbrath, 1989:10): *A pond has a single water lily growing on it. The lily doubles in size each day. In thirty days, it covers the entire pond. On which day does it cover half the pond?* When you realize the answer, discuss the implications of this example for population increase.
2. Draw a mental map of a city familiar to you with as much detail of specific places, districts, roads, and transportation facilities as you can. Compare your map to a real one, or, better yet, a map drawn by someone else. Try to account for the differences.
3. Carry a plastic trash bag around with you for one full day. Put everything you throw away in the bag. Afterward, weigh what you have; multiply this amount by 365 to estimate your yearly "trash factor." Multiply this amount by 275 million to estimate the annual waste of the entire U.S. population.
4. In the Bible, read Genesis, chapter 1, especially verses 28–31. According to this account of creation, are humans empowered to do what we wish to the earth? Or are we charged to care for the earth? For more on this idea, see Wolkomir et al. (1997).
5. Install the CD-ROM packaged in the back of this new textbook to access a variety of study, review, and applications exercises designed to help you better understand the material covered in this chapter. The CD includes an author's tip video, as well as interactive maps, video application exercises, Web links, and study questions.

SITES TO SEE

http://www.prenhall.com/macionis

Visit the interactive Web site that accompanies this text. Begin by clicking on the cover of your book. You will find a chapter-by-chapter study guide, practice tests, chat room, and many suggested Web links.

http://www.eclac.org/Celade-Eng/index.html

This site, created by the Latin American and Caribbean Demographic Center (part of the United Nations), allows country-by-country analysis of population patterns for this region of the world. Most of the site is available in both English and Spanish.

http://www.urban.nyu.edu

New York University's Taub Urban Research Center is on the Internet. Visit this site to survey recent research on urban issues.

http://www.mte.com/webcam/

Watch big-city life from the comfort of your own home: This site uses a cyber-view camera showing the action on New York City's Fifth Avenue and Forty-fifth Street. What can you learn from "people watching" in this way? What does this observation *not* tell you about urban life?

http://www.sierraclub.org
http://www.greenpeace.org

These two environmental sites are maintained by the Sierra Club and Greenpeace. Visit the sites and see how these two organizations are similar to one another and how they are different.

http://www.kenyon.edu/projects/agri/

This site, constructed by college students, investigates how the way we live affects the planet and how the state of our planet affects our lives.

CHAPTER 23

G. Pellizza da Volpedo
The Fourth Estate

Milano, Galleria Civica D'Arte Moderna. © Canali Photobank.

COLLECTIVE BEHAVIOR AND SOCIAL MOVEMENTS

On June 7, 1998, CNN—the Cable News Network—reported that during the Vietnam War, U.S. Marine Green Berets flew a secret mission to drop nerve gas on fellow soldiers in Laos. The victims of the alleged attack, reporters said, were U.S. soldiers who opposed the war; they had fled the fighting and in some cases were helping the North Vietnamese.

Shortly after the story broke, General Colin Powell called CNN to deny the allegations and demand a retraction. But Powell was not the only one taken aback by the damaging charges. Thousands of Vietnam veterans across the country logged on to the Internet to get the facts about the alleged incident and locate the men who had flown the Laos mission. Questions and statements were posted on Web bulletin boards, and within a few weeks, tens of thousands of people were in contact with one another.

Before long, Thomas Stump was identified as a pilot in the Special Forces mission over Laos. Stump confirmed that he had flown the mission, but insisted that the plane never dropped nerve gas. Other pilots came forward with the same statement.

CNN soon backed away from its story and issued an apology, saying its report had been based on insufficient information. As John Plaster, a Vietnam veteran put it, "I was amazed at the speed at which we could find people and gather information." Indeed, in the information age, people have an unprecedented ability to organize for almost any purpose (adapted from McMenamin, 1998).

The groundswell of action among these Vietnam veterans is an example of **collective behavior,** *activity involving a large number of people, often spontaneous and sometimes controversial.* This chapter investigates various forms of collective behavior—including social movements aiming to bring about change, crowds, mobs and riots, rumor and gossip, public opinion, panic and mass hysteria, and fashions and fads.

For much of the last century, sociologists focused on established social patterns like the family and social stratification. They paid less attention to cases of collective behavior, considering most of it trivial, unusual, or even deviant. But numerous social movements characterized the tumultuous 1960s, and many are still changing society today. Thus, in recent decades, sociological interest in all types of collective behavior has increased (Weller & Quarantelli, 1973; G. Marx & Wood, 1975; Aguirre & Quarantelli, 1983; Turner & Killian, 1987; McAdam, McCarthy, & Zald, 1988).

STUDYING COLLECTIVE BEHAVIOR

Despite its importance, collective behavior is difficult for sociologists to study for three main reasons:

1. **Collective behavior is wide ranging.** Collective behavior involves a bewildering array of human action. The traits common to fads, rumors, and mob behavior, for example, are far from obvious.

2. **Collective behavior is complex.** A rumor seems to come out of nowhere and circulates in countless different settings. For no apparent reason, one new form of dress catches on while another does not. Why, over this nation's history, would millions of African Americans endure second-class standing for so long and then begin a civil rights movement in the mid-1950s?
3. **Much collective behavior is transitory.** Sociologists can readily study the family because it is a continuing element of social life. Fashions, rumors, and riots, however, arise and dissipate quickly, making them difficult to study.

Some researchers point out that these problems apply not just to collective behavior but to *most* forms of human behavior (Aguirre & Quarantelli, 1983). Moreover, collective behavior is not always so surprising; anyone can predict that crowds will form at sports events and music festivals, and sociologists can study these gatherings firsthand or later by using videotapes. Researchers can even anticipate natural disasters and study the human responses they provoke. Each year, for example, about sixty major tornadoes occur in particular regions of the United States; sociologists interested in how disasters affect behavior can be prepared to begin research on short notice (Miller, 1985). Researchers can also use historical documents to reconstruct details of a past natural disaster or riot.

Sociologists now know a great deal about collective behavior, but they still have much to learn. The most serious shortcoming, according to Benigno Aguirre and E. L. Quarantelli (1983), is that sociologists have yet to devise a theory that ties together all the different actions termed *collective behavior.*

At the least, all collective behavior involves the action of some **collectivity,** *a large number of people whose minimal interaction occurs in the absence of well-defined and conventional norms.* Collectivities are of two kinds. A *localized collectivity* refers to people in physical proximity to one another; this first type is illustrated by crowds and riots. A *dispersed collectivity*, or *mass behavior*, involves people who influence one another even though they are separated by great distances; examples include the spread of rumors, public opinion, and fashion (Turner & Killian, 1993).

It is important to distinguish collectivities from the already familiar concept of social groups (see Chapter 7, "Groups and Organizations"). Here are three key differences:

1. **Collectivities are based on limited social interaction.** Group members interact frequently and directly. People in mobs or other localized collectivities interact very little. Most people taking part in dispersed collectivities, like a fad, do not interact at all.
2. **Collectivities have no clear social boundaries.** Group members share a sense of identity usually missing among people engaged in collective behavior. Localized crowds may have a common object of attention (such as someone on a ledge threatening to jump), but they show little sense of unity. Individuals involved in dispersed collectivities, such as the "public" that turns out to vote in an election, have almost no awareness of shared membership. Of course, some issues divide the public into well-defined factions, but often it is difficult to say who falls within the ranks of, say, the environmentalist or feminist movement.
3. **Collectivities generate weak and unconventional norms.** Conventional cultural norms usually regulate the behavior of group members. Some collectivities, such as people traveling on an airplane, observe conventional norms, but their interaction is usually limited to polite small talk. Other collectivities—such as excited soccer fans who destroy property as they leave a stadium—spontaneously develop very unconventional norms (Weller & Quarantelli, 1973; Turner & Killian, 1993).

LOCALIZED COLLECTIVITIES: CROWDS

One major form of collective behavior is the **crowd,** *a temporary gathering of people who share a common focus of attention and who influence one another.* Historian Peter Laslett (1984) points out that crowds are a modern development; in medieval Europe, about the only time large numbers of people gathered in one place was when armies faced off on the battlefield. Today, however, crowds of 25,000 or more are common at sporting events, rock concerts, and even the registration halls of large universities.

But all crowds are not alike. Herbert Blumer (1969) identified four categories of crowds. A *casual crowd* is a loose collection of people who interact little, if at all. People at the beach or at the scene of an automobile accident have only a passing awareness of one another.

A *conventional crowd* results from deliberate planning, as illustrated by a country auction, a college lecture, or a family funeral. In each case, interaction conforms to norms appropriate to the situation.

It is easy to understand why ordinary people think they are powerless in the face of entrenched leaders. But, when a sense of injustice is strong and widespread (as among these Chilean people seeking a greater voice in government), protest crowds may be effective in bringing about change.

An *expressive crowd* forms around an event with emotional appeal, such as a religious revival, a World Federation Wrestling match, or a New Year's Eve celebration in New York's Times Square. Excitement is the main reason people join expressive crowds, which makes this experience rather spontaneous and exhilarating for those involved.

An *acting crowd* is a collectivity motivated by an intense, single-minded purpose, such as an audience rushing the doors of a concert hall or fleeing from a burning theater. Acting crowds are ignited by very powerful emotions that can reach feverish intensity and sometimes erupt into mob violence.

Any crowd can change from one type to another. In 1985, a conventional crowd of 60,000 fans filed into a soccer stadium to watch the European Cup Finals between Italy and Great Britain. But once the game started, some drunk British fans began taunting the Italians sitting nearby. At this point, the crowd became expressive. The two sides began to throw bottles at each other; then, in a human wave, the British surged toward the Italians. Some 400 million television viewers watched in horror as what was now an acting crowd trampled hundreds of helpless spectators. In minutes, 38 people were dead and another 400 injured (Lacayo, 1985).

Deliberate action by a crowd is not simply the product of rising emotion. Participants in *protest crowds*—a fifth category we can add to Blumer's list—may stage strikes, boycotts, sit-ins, and marches for political purposes (McPhail & Wohlstein, 1983). For example, students in a protest crowd vary in emotional energy; some display the low-level energy characteristic of a conventional crowd, while others are emotional enough to be in an acting crowd. Sometimes, too, a protest begins peacefully, but people become aggressive when counterdemonstrators appear, as happens when pro-choice and pro-life activists clash.

MOBS AND RIOTS

When an acting crowd turns violent, we may witness the birth of a **mob,** *a highly emotional crowd that pursues a violent or destructive goal.* Despite, or perhaps because of, their intense emotion, mobs tend to dissipate quickly. How long a mob exists often depends on its precise goals and whether its leadership tries to inflame or stabilize the crowd.

Lynching is the most notorious example of mob behavior in the United States. The term is derived from Charles Lynch, a Virginia colonist who sought to maintain law and order in his own way before formal courts were established. The word soon became synonymous with violence and murder outside the law.

Lynching has always been colored by race. After the Civil War, lynch mobs became a terrorist form of social control over emancipated African Americans. African Americans who challenged white superiority risked hanging or being burned alive by hateful whites.

Lynch mobs—typically composed of poor whites threatened by competition from freed slaves—reached

THE RIOTS IN NEW YORK: THE MOB LYNCHING A NEGRO IN CLARKSON-STREET.—SEE PAGE 142.

The greatest urban unrest in U.S. history took place in New York City July 13–16, 1863, during the Civil War. The immediate cause of the rioting was opposition to the military draft, which was strong among poor white immigrants who could not buy their way out of the army. But class differences as well as racial tensions also fueled the rioting. Many frustrated Irish turned their anger on African Americans, burning homes and lynching innocent people. Only the arrival of five units of the U.S. Army—rushed from the battlefield at Gettysburg—ended the violence.

their peak between 1880 and 1930. Police recorded some 5,000 lynchings in that period, though, no doubt, many more occurred. Most of these killings were committed in the Deep South, where a farming economy depended on a cheap and docile labor force. On the western frontier, lynch mobs targeted people of Mexican and Asian descent. In about 25 percent of known cases, whites lynched other whites. Lynching women, however, was rare; only about a hundred such instances are known, almost all involving women of color (White, 1969, orig. 1929; Grant, 1975).

A frenzied crowd without any particular purpose is a **riot,** *a social eruption that is highly emotional, violent, and undirected.* Unlike the action of a mob, a riot usually has no clear goal, except perhaps to express dissatisfaction. Underlying most riots is long-standing anger that is ignited by some relatively minor incident, so that participants soon become violent, destroying property or harming other persons (Smelser, 1962; Rosenfeld, 1997). Whereas a mob action usually ends when a specific violent goal has been achieved (or decisively blocked), a riot tends to disperse only as participants run out of steam or police and community leaders gradually bring them under control.

Throughout our nation's history, riots have erupted as a reaction to social injustice. Industrial workers, for example, rioted to vent rage at their working conditions. In 1886, a bitter struggle by Chicago factory workers for an eight-hour workday led to the explosive Haymarket Riot, which left eleven dead and scores injured. Rioting born of anger and despair also takes place frequently in prisons.

In addition, race riots have occurred in the United States with striking regularity. Early in this century, crowds of whites attacked African Americans in Chicago, Detroit, and other cities. In the 1960s, violent riots rocked numerous inner-city ghettos when seemingly isolated events sparked rage at continuing prejudice and discrimination. In Los Angeles in 1992, the acquittal of police officers involved in the beating of motorist Rodney King set off a deadly riot. Violence and fires killed more than fifty people, injured thousands, and destroyed property worth hundreds of millions of dollars.

Riots are not always fired by hate. They can also begin with very positive feelings. In 1998, for example, the Woodstock II festival brought thousands of people together to share an experience of peace and music; but soon many men began groping women, and the event deteriorated to the point that several buildings went up in flames.

CROWDS, MOBS, AND SOCIAL CHANGE

November 2, 1988, Delhi, India. The sidewalk in front of an office building is blocked by a crowd of people staging some kind of protest. The demonstrators chant

Some have claimed that crowds swell with unrestrained emotion as if they have a mind of their own. But, in most cases, crowds come into being as people with a sense of injustice join together to express their anger and oppose the powers that be. Thus, although some individuals may act in ways that appear irrational, social unrest is usually a matter of broader political issues (in this case, an unpopular tax that brought more than 200,000 Britons into the streets of London in March, 1990).

slogans; anger swirls in the air. From a window several stories above, an older man dressed in a suit glances downward—perhaps he is the target of their attention? His expression of disgust leaves little doubt of what he thinks about his accusers.

Ordinary people typically acquire power only by acting collectively. It is precisely the power of the crowd to effect social change—beginning by disrupting the routine order—that makes crowds controversial. Throughout history, then, elite defenders of the status quo have feared "the mob" as a threat to their power. Of course, the collective action that some people condemn, others support as rightful protest. In 1839, fifty-three Africans rose up and seized the ship *Amistad* off the coast of Cuba to prevent landing in the Americas and being sold into slavery. Were these men a vicious mob? Not according to the U.S. Supreme Court, which, after the ship put in to New York harbor, ruled that the men were fighting for their freedom and were entitled to be released.

Moreover, crowds share no single political cast: Some call for change and some resist it. Judeans rallying to the Sermon on the Mount by Jesus of Nazareth, seventeenth-century weavers destroying industrial machines that threatened their jobs, masses of marchers carrying banners and shouting slogans for or against abortion—these and countless other cases across the centuries show that crowds can challenge their society or support it (Rudé, 1964; Canetti, 1978; Tarrow, 1994).

EXPLAINING CROWD BEHAVIOR

What accounts for the behavior of crowds? Social scientists have developed several different explanations.

Contagion Theory

An early explanation of collective behavior was formulated by the French sociologist Gustave Le Bon (1841–1931). According to Le Bon's *contagion theory*, crowds exert a hypnotic influence over their members (1960; orig. 1895). Shielded by the anonymity afforded by large numbers of people, individuals abandon personal responsibility and surrender to the contagious emotions of the crowd. A crowd thus assumes a life of its own, stirring up emotions and driving people toward irrational, perhaps violent, action.

Critical evaluation. Le Bon's idea that crowds foster anonymity and sometimes generate emotion is surely true. Yet, as Clark McPhail (1991) points out, a considerable body of research shows that "the madding crowd" does not take on a life of its own that is apart from the thoughts and intentions of members. For example, Norris Johnson (1987), investigating panic at a 1979 Who concert in Cincinnati, identified specific factors that led to the deaths of eleven people. They included an inadequate number of entrance doors, an open-seating policy, and too little police supervision. Far from an episode of collective insanity, Johnson concluded, the crowd was composed of many small groups of people mostly trying to help each another.

CRITICAL THINKING

The Rumor Mill: Paul Is Dead!

Everyone knows the Beatles. The music of John Lennon, Paul McCartney, George Harrison, and Ringo Starr caused a cultural revolution in the 1960s. Not everyone today, however, knows the rumor that circulated about Paul McCartney at the height of the group's popularity.

On October 12, 1969, a young man telephoned a Detroit disk jockey to say that he had discovered evidence that Paul McCartney was dead:

1. Filtering out background noise at the end of the song "Strawberry Fields Forever" on the *Magical Mystery Tour* album allows the listener to hear a voice saying, "I buried Paul!"
2. The phrase "Number 9, Number 9, Number 9" from the song "Revolution 9" on the *White Album*, when played backward, seems to intone, "Turn me on, dead man!"

Two days later, the University of Michigan student newspaper ran a story entitled "McCartney Is Dead: Further Clues Found." It sent millions of Beatles fans scurrying for their albums.

3. A picture inside the *Magical Mystery Tour* album shows John, George, and Ringo wearing red carnations, while Paul is wearing a black flower.
4. The cover of the *Sergeant Pepper's Lonely Hearts Club Band* album shows a grave with yellow flowers arranged in the shape of Paul's bass guitar.
5. On the inside of that album, McCartney wears an armpatch with the letters "OPD." Is this the insignia of some police department or confirmation that Paul had been "Officially Pronounced Dead"?
6. On the back cover of the same album, three Beatles are facing forward while McCartney has his back to the camera.
7. On the album cover of *Abbey Road*, John Lennon is clothed as a clergyman, Ringo Starr wears an undertaker's black tie, and George Harrison is clad in workman's

Further, while collective behavior may involve strong emotions, such feelings are not necessarily irrational, as contagion theory suggests. On the contrary, emotions can be the product of a well-developed sense of injustice (Jasper, 1998).

Convergence Theory

Convergence theory holds that crowd behavior is not a product of the crowd itself but is carried into the crowd by particular individuals. Thus, crowds amount to a convergence of like-minded individuals. In other words, while contagion theory states that crowds cause people to act in a certain way, convergence theory says the opposite: that people who wish to act in a certain way come together to form crowds.

From time to time, news stories describe white people banding together to threaten African Americans who try to move into their neighborhood. In such cases, convergence theorists contend, the crowd itself does not generate racial hatred or violence; in all likelihood, hostility has been simmering for some time among many local people. A crowd then arises from a convergence of people who oppose the presence of black neighbors.

Critical evaluation. By linking crowds to broader social forces, convergence theory claims that crowd behavior is not irrational, as Le Bon maintained. Rather, people in crowds express existing beliefs and values (Berk, 1974). But, in fairness to Le Bon, people sometimes do things in a crowd that they would not have the courage to do alone, because crowds can diffuse responsibility. In addition, crowds can intensify a sentiment simply by creating a critical mass of like-minded people.

Emergent-Norm Theory

Ralph Turner and Lewis Killian (1993) developed the *emergent-norm theory* of crowd dynamics. They concede that social behavior is never entirely predictable, but, if similar interests draw people together, distinctive patterns of behavior may emerge in the crowd itself.

According to Turner and Killian, crowds begin as collectivities containing people with mixed interests and motives. Especially in the case of less stable crowds—expressive, acting, and protest crowds—norms may be attire as if ready to dig a grave. For his part, McCartney is barefoot, which is how Tibetan ritual prepares a corpse for burial. Behind Paul, a Volkswagen nearby displays the license plate "28 IF," apparently stating that McCartney would be 28 *if* he were alive.

The rumor explained that McCartney had died of head injuries suffered in an automobile accident in November 1966. After the accident, record company executives had secretly replaced Paul with a double.

Of course, Paul McCartney is very much alive and still jokes about the episode. Few doubt that Paul himself dreamed up some of the details of his "death" with a little help from his friends to encourage the interest of their fans. But the incident has a serious side, showing how quickly rumors can arise and persist in a climate of distrust. In the late 1960s, many disaffected young people were quite ready to believe that the media and other powerful interests were concealing McCartney's death.

In 1969, McCartney himself denied the rumor in a *Life* magazine story. But thousands of suspicious readers noticed that on the other side of the page with McCartney's picture was an ad for an automobile: Holding this page up to the light, the car lay across McCartney's chest and blocked his head. Another clue!

What do you think?

1. *What can we say about the kinds of issues that give rise to rumors?*
2. *Have there been rumors this year on your campus? About what?*
3. *On balance, do you think rumors are helpful or harmful? Why?*

Sources: Based on Rosnow & Fine (1976) and Kapferer (1992).

vague and changing as, say, when one person decides to break a store window and others quickly join in and begin looting merchandise. In short, people in crowds make their own rules as they go along.

Critical evaluation. Emergent-norm theory represents a symbolic-interaction approach to crowd dynamics. Turner and Killian (1972:10) explain that crowd behavior is neither as irrational as contagion theory suggests nor as deliberate as convergence theory implies. Certainly, crowd behavior reflects the desires of participants, but it is also guided by norms that emerge as the situation unfolds.

Decision making, then, plays a major role in crowd behavior, although casual observers of the crowd may not realize it. For example, frightened people clogging the exits of a burning theater may appear to be victims of irrational panic, but, from their point of view, fleeing a life-threatening situation is entirely sensible.

Further, emergent-norm theory points out that people in a crowd take on different roles. Some step forward as leaders, others become lieutenants, rank-and-file followers, inactive bystanders, or even opponents (Weller & Quarantelli, 1973; Zurcher & Snow, 1981).

DISPERSED COLLECTIVITES: MASS BEHAVIOR

It is not just people clustered together in crowds who participate in collective behavior. **Mass behavior** refers to *collective behavior among people dispersed over a wide geographic area.*

RUMOR AND GOSSIP

A common type of mass behavior is **rumor,** *unsubstantiated information people spread informally, often by word of mouth.* People pass along rumors through face-to-face communication, of course, but modern technology—telephones, the mass media, and the Internet—spreads rumors faster and farther than ever before. Rumor has three essential characteristics:

1. **Rumor thrives in a climate of ambiguity.** Rumors arise when people lack definitive information about an important issue. As the new century approached, and people were worried that a "Y2K bug" might shut down computers, all sorts of rumors arose.

2. **Rumor is unstable.** People change a rumor as they pass it along, usually giving it a "spin" that serves their own interests. Before long, many competing versions exist.
3. **Rumor is difficult to stop.** The number of people aware of a rumor increases exponentially as each person spreads information to several others. Rumors dissipate with time; but, in general, the only way to control rumors is for a believable source to issue a clear and convincing statement of the facts.

Rumor can trigger the formation of crowds or other collective behavior. For this reason, officials establish rumor-control centers during a crisis in order to manage information. Yet some rumors persist for years, perhaps just because people enjoy them; the box on pages 604–5 gives one notable example.

Gossip is *rumor about people's personal affairs.* Charles Horton Cooley (1962; orig. 1909) explained that rumor involves an issue of concern to a large audience, but gossip interests only a small circle of people who know a particular person. Rumors, therefore, spread widely, while gossip tends to be more localized.

Communities use gossip as a means of social control, praising or scorning someone to encourage conformity to local norms. Moreover, people gossip about others to raise their own standing as social "insiders" just as more powerful people use gossip to keep those who are socially marginal "in their place" (Baumgartner, 1998). Yet no community wants gossip to get out of control, which may be the reason people who gossip too much are criticized as "busybodies."

PUBLIC OPINION AND PROPAGANDA

Another form of dispersed collective behavior is **public opinion,** *widespread attitudes about controversial issues.* Exactly who is, or is not, included in any "public" depends on the issue involved. Over the years in the United States, "publics" have formed over numerous controversial issues, from water fluoridation, air pollution, and the social standing of women to handguns and health care (Lang & Lang, 1961; Turner & Killian, 1993). More recently, the public has debated affirmative action, welfare reform, and government funding of public radio and television. National Map 23–1 shows where supporters of public broadcasting reside.

On any given issue, anywhere from 2 to 10 percent of people offer no opinion at all because of ignorance or indifference. Moreover, over time, public interest in issues rises and falls. For example, interest in the social position of women in the United States ran high a century ago during the women's suffrage movement but declined after 1920 when women gained the right to vote. Since the 1960s, a second wave of feminism has again created a public with strong opinions on gender-related issues.

Also, keep in mind that on any issue, not everyone's opinion carries the same weight. Some categories of people have more clout because they are better educated, wealthier, or better connected. As Chapter 17 ("Politics and Government") explained, many special-interest groups shape public policy in the United States even though they represent just a small fraction of the population. For example, physicians are a well-organized and well-funded interest group that greatly influences U.S. health care policy.

Special-interest groups and political leaders all try to shape public tastes and attitudes by using **propaganda,** *information presented with the intention of shaping public opinion.* Although the term has negative connotations, propaganda is not necessarily false. A thin line separates information from propaganda; the difference depends mostly on the presenter's intention. We offer *information* to enlighten others; we use *propaganda* to sway an audience toward some viewpoint. Political speeches, commercial advertising, and even some college lectures may disseminate propaganda in an effort to steer people toward thinking or acting in some specific way.

PANIC AND MASS HYSTERIA

A **panic** is *a form of localized collective behavior by which people react to a threat or other stimulus with irrational, frantic, and often self-destructive behavior.* The classic illustration of a panic is people streaming toward exits of a crowded theater after someone yells "Fire!" As they flee, however, they trample one another, blocking exits so that few actually escape.

Closely related to panic is **mass hysteria,** *a form of dispersed collective behavior by which people react to a real or imagined event with irrational, frantic, and often self-destructive behavior.* Whether the cause of the hysteria is real or not, a large number of people certainly take it very seriously. Parents' fears that their children may become infected from a schoolmate who has AIDS may cause as much hysteria in a community as the very real danger of an approaching hurricane. Moreover, people in the grip of mass hysteria sometimes act to make

SEEING OURSELVES

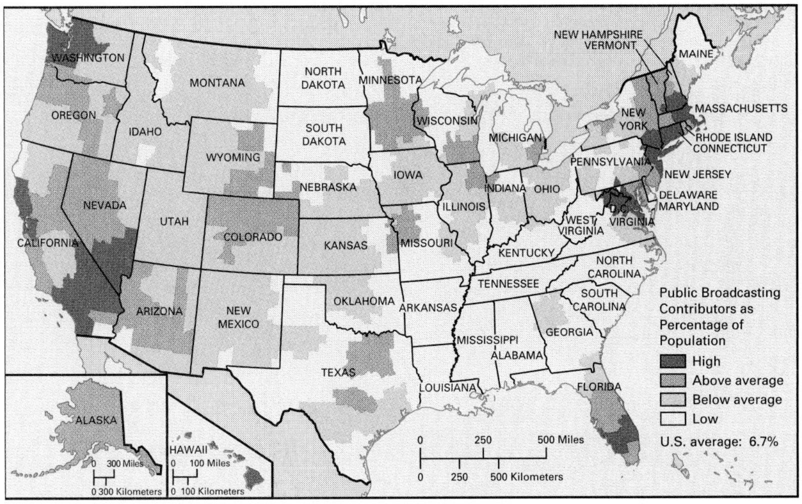

NATIONAL MAP 23–1
Support for Public Broadcasting across the United States

About 7 percent of people in the United States pledge money to support the Public Broadcasting System (PBS). As the map shows, PBS supporters are concentrated in particular regions of the country. What do you think accounts for this pattern?

Source: *Time* (January 16, 1995). Copyright © 1995 Time, Inc. Reprinted by permission.

matters worse. At the extreme, mass hysteria leads to chaotic flight and sends crowds into panic. People who others overcome by fear may become more afraid themselves, as hysteria feeds on itself.

So it was on the night before Halloween in 1938, when CBS radio broadcast a version of H. G. Wells's novel *War of the Worlds* (Cantril, Gaudet, & Herzog, 1947; Koch, 1970). The show started as a program of the day's favorite dance music. Suddenly, a voice interrupted the music with a "special report" of explosions on the surface of the planet Mars and, soon after, the crash landing of a mysterious cylinder near a New Jersey farmhouse. The program then switched to an "on-the-scene reporter" who gave a graphic description of giant monsters equipped with death-ray weapons emerging from a spaceship. An "eminent astronomer" somberly informed the audience that Martians had begun a full-scale invasion of earth. Back then, most people relied on radio for factual news; thus, there was an announcement to clarify that the broadcast was fiction. But about 1 million of the 10 million listeners missed the announcement and actually believed the report.

By the time the show was over, thousands of hysterical people were spilling into the streets with news of the "invasion" and flooding telephone switchboards with warnings to friends and relatives. One college senior and his roommate jumped into their cars and fled:

> My roommate was crying and praying. He was even more excited than I was—or more noisy about it anyway; I guess I took it out in pushing the accelerator to the floor. . . . After it was all over, I started to think about that ride, I was more jittery than when it was happening. The speed was never under 70. I thought I was racing against time. . . . I didn't have any idea exactly what I was fleeing from, and that made me all the more afraid. (Cantril, Gaudet, & Herzog, 1947:52)

FASHIONS AND FADS

Two more kinds of collective behavior—fashions and fads—involve people spread over a large area. A **fashion** is *a social pattern favored by a large number of people.* Some fashions last for years, while others change after just a few months. The arts (including painting, music, drama, and literature), the design of buildings, automobiles, and clothes, our use of language, and public opinion—all change as ideas go in and out of fashion.

Lyn Lofland (1973) explains that in preindustrial societies clothing and personal appearance reflect traditional *style,* which changes very little. Women and men, the rich and the poor, lawyers and carpenters wear distinctive clothes and hairstyles that indicate their occupations and social standing.

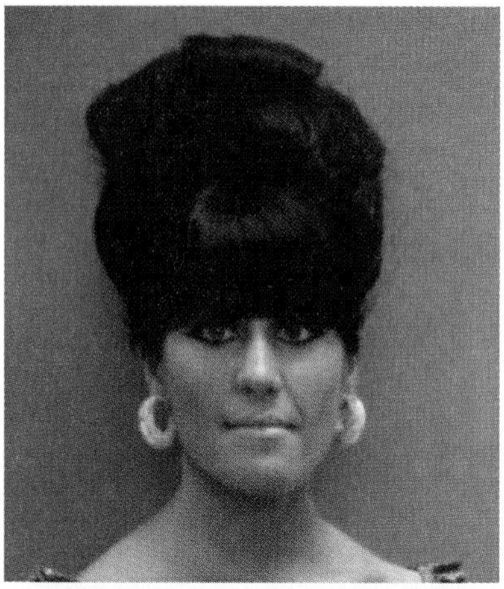
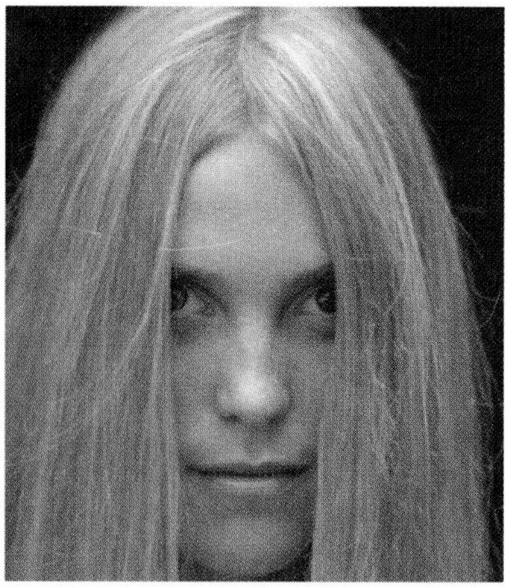

Because change in industrial societies is so rapid, we can see differences in personal appearance—one important kind of fashion—over short periods of time. The five photographs (beginning with the top left) show hair styles commonly worn by women in the 1950s, 1960s, 1970s, 1980s, and 1990s.

In industrial societies, however, established style gives way to changing fashion. For one thing, modern people care less about tradition and generally embrace new ways of living. Then, too, high social mobility means that people use their "looks" to make a statement about themselves. According to the German sociologist Georg Simmel (1971; orig. 1904), affluent people are usually the trendsetters, since people look to them and they have the money to spend on luxuries. Or, as the U.S. sociologist Thorstein Veblen (1953; orig. 1899) observed, fashion involves *conspicuous consumption* because people buy expensive products (from bottled water to Range Rovers) simply to show off their wealth.

Ordinary people who want to appear wealthy often snap up less expensive copies of what the rich make fashionable. In this way, a fashion trickles downward through the class structure. But fashion loses its prestige when too many average people begin to share "the look," so the rich move on to something new. In short, fashions are born along the Fifth Avenues and Rodeo Drives of the rich but reach mass popularity in discount stores across the country.

A reversal of this pattern sometimes occurs when rich people mimic a fashion found among people of lower social position. In the 1960s, for example, affluent college students began buying blue jeans, or dungarees (from a Hindi word for a coarse fabric). For decades, manual laborers have worn blue jeans, but in the era of civil rights and antiwar movements, jeans became the uniform of liberal political activists and were soon popular on college campuses all across the

To pass the time playing alone, a young Japanese boy dreamed up a number of imaginary "pocket monsters." He could hardly have imagined that his creations—eventually marketed around the world as Pokémon—would become one of the biggest crazes among young children. But will Pokémon cards become a mainstay of youth culture (like, say, sports cards) or a short-lived fad that falls from the scene as quickly as it arrived?

country. Author Tom Wolfe (1970) coined the phrase *radical chic* to satirize the desire of the rich to look fashionably poor.

A **fad** is *an unconventional social pattern that people embrace briefly but enthusiastically.* Fads, sometimes called *crazes,* are commonplace in rich industrial societies where many people have the money to spend on amusing, if often frivolous, products. During the 1950s, two young entrepreneurs in California produced a brightly colored plastic version of a popular Australian toy, a three-foot-diameter hoop that could be swung around the waist by gyrating the hips. In no time, the "hula hoop" was a national craze. But in less than a year, hula hoops vanished from the scene.

In the last few years, collecting Pokémon cards and other products has been a fad among young people. But Pokémon's popularity already has begun to fade, suggesting that fads enter and depart from our culture all the time (Aguirre, Quarantelli, & Mendoza, 1988).

How do fads differ from fashions? Fads are passing fancies that capture the mass imagination but quickly burn out and disappear. Fashions, by contrast, reflect basic cultural values like individuality and sexual attractiveness and tend to evolve over time. Therefore, a fashion—but rarely a fad—is incorporated into a society's culture. The fad of streaking, for instance, came out of nowhere and soon vanished; the fashion of wearing blue jeans, on the other hand, originated in the rough mining camps of gold rush California more than a century ago and still influences clothing design today. This "staying power" explains why we are happy to be called "fashionable" but are put off by being called "faddish" (Blumer, 1968; Turner & Killian, 1993).

SOCIAL MOVEMENTS

Social movements refer to *organized activity that encourages or discourages social change.* Social movements are perhaps the most important type of collective behavior, since they are deliberately organized and often have lasting effects on the shape of our society.

Social movements occur more frequently in today's world than in the past. Preindustrial societies are tightly bound by tradition, making social movements extremely rare. Industrial societies, however, foster diverse subcultures and countercultures so that social movements develop around a wide range of public issues. In recent decades, for example, the gay rights movement has won legal victories in numerous cities and several states banning discrimination based on sexual orientation. Like any social movement that seeks change, the gay rights movement has prompted a countermovement made up of traditionalists who want to limit social acceptance of homosexuality. In today's society, almost every important public issue gives rise to a social movement favoring change and an opposing countermovement resisting it (Lo, 1982; Meyer & Staggenborg, 1996).

TYPES OF SOCIAL MOVEMENTS

Sociologists classify social movements according to several variables (Aberle, 1966; Cameron, 1966; Blumer, 1969). One variable asks *who is changed?* Some movements target selected people, while others try to change everyone. A second variable asks *how much change?* Some movements seek only limited change in our lives, while others are radical. Combining these

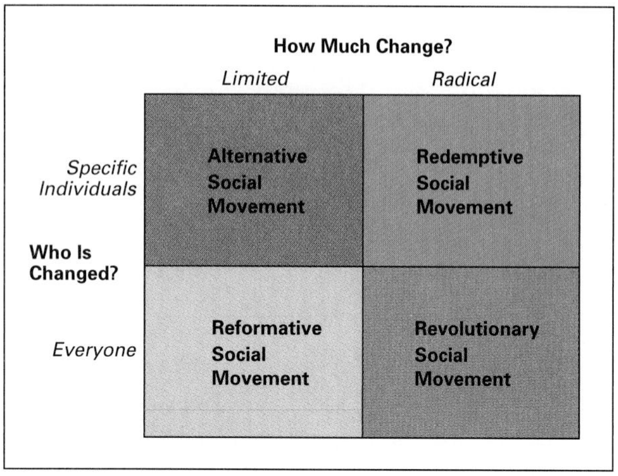

How Much Change?
Limited
Radical
Specific Individuals
Who Is Changed?
Everyone
Alternative Social Movement
Redemptive Social Movement
Reformative Social Movement
Revolutionary Social Movement

FIGURE 23–1 Four Types of Social Movements
Source: Based on Aberle (1966).

variables results in four types of social movements, shown in Figure 23–1.

Alternative social movements are least threatening to the status quo because they seek limited change in only a part of the population. Promise Keepers, one example of an alternative social movement, encourages men to be more spiritual and supportive of their families.

Redemptive social movements also have a selective focus, but they seek radical change in those they engage. For example, Alcoholics Anonymous is an organization that helps alcoholics achieve a sober life.

Reformative social movements aim for only limited social change but target everyone. Multiculturalism, described in Chapter 3 ("Culture"), is an educational and political movement that advocates working toward social equality for people of all races and ethnicities. Reformative social movements generally work inside the existing political system. Some are *progressive* (promoting a new social pattern), while others are *reactionary* (countermovements trying to preserve the status quo or to revive past social patterns). Thus, just as multiculturalists push for greater racial equality, so white supremacist organizations try to maintain the historical dominance of white people.

Revolutionary social movements are the most extreme of all, striving to transform an entire society. Sometimes pursuing specific goals, sometimes spinning utopian dreams, these social movements reject existing social institutions as flawed and promote radically new alternatives. Both the left-wing Communist Party (pushing for government control of the economy) and right-wing militia groups (advocating the destruction of "big government") seek to radically change our way of life.

EXPLAINING SOCIAL MOVEMENTS

Because social movements are intentional and long-lasting, sociologists find this type of collective behavior easier to explain than fleeting incidents of mob behavior or mass hysteria. Several theories have been proposed.

Deprivation Theory

Deprivation theory holds that social movements arise among people who feel deprived. People who feel they lack enough income, safe working conditions, basic political rights, or plain human dignity may organize a social movement to bring about a more just state of affairs (Morrison, 1978; Rose, 1982).

The rise of the Ku Klux Klan and passage of Jim Crow laws by whites intent on enforcing segregation in the South after the Civil War illustrate deprivation theory. With the end of slavery, white people lost a source of free labor and the claim that they were socially superior to African Americans. Many whites reacted to their sense of deprivation by trying to keep all people of color "in their place" (Dollard et al., 1939). African Americans had experienced much greater deprivation, of course, but as slaves they had little opportunity to organize. During the twentieth century, however, African Americans organized successfully in pursuit of racial equality.

As Chapter 7 ("Groups and Organizations") explained, deprivation is a relative concept. Regardless of anyone's absolute amount of money and power, people feel either better or worse off compared to some category of others. **Relative deprivation,** then, is *a perceived disadvantage arising from some specific comparison* (Stouffer et al., 1949; Merton, 1968).

More than a century ago, Alexis de Tocqueville (1955; orig. 1856) studied the French Revolution. Why, he asked, did rebellion occur in progressive France rather than in more traditional Germany, where peasants were, by any objective measure, worse off? Tocqueville's answer was that, as bad as their condition was, German peasants had known nothing but feudal servitude and thus had no basis for feeling deprived. French peasants, on the other hand, had seen improvements in their lives that whetted their appetites for more. Thus the French—not the Germans—felt a keen sense of relative deprivation. The irony, as Tocqueville saw it, was that increasing freedom and prosperity did not satisfy people as much as it stimulated their desire for an even better life.

Closer to home, Tocqueville's analysis helps explain patterns of rioting during the 1960s. Protest riots involving African Americans took place not in the South, where many black people lived in miserable poverty and most were not even registered to vote, but in Detroit, where the auto industry was booming, black unemployment was low, and black home ownership was the highest in the country (Thernstrom & Thernstrom, 1998).

James C. Davies (1962) agrees that as life gets better, people take their rising fortunes for granted and expect even more. But what happens if the standard of living suddenly stops improving or, worse, begins to drop? As Figure 23–2 illustrates, relative deprivation is the result, generating unrest and social movements aimed at change.

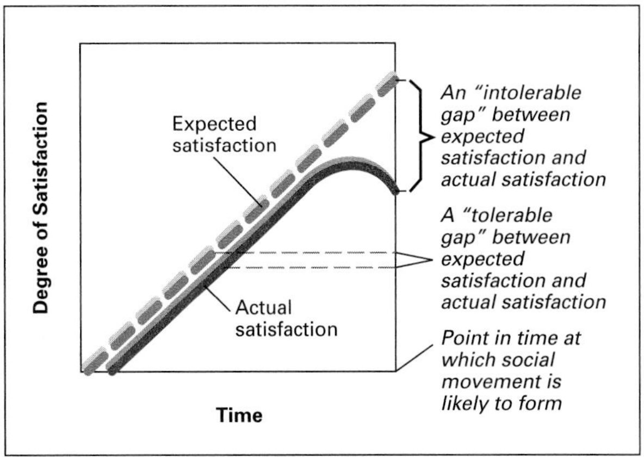

FIGURE 23–2 Relative Deprivation and Social Movements

In this diagram, the solid line represents a rising standard of living over time. The dotted line indicates the expected standard of living, which is typically somewhat higher. James C. Davies describes the difference between the two as "a tolerable gap between what people want and what they get." If the standard of living suddenly drops in the midst of rising expectations, however, the gap becomes intolerable. At this point, we can expect social movements to form.

Source: Davies (1962).

Critical evaluation. Deprivation theory challenges our common-sense assumption that the worst-off people are the most likely to organize for change. People do not organize simply because they suffer in an absolute sense; rather, they form social movements because of *relative* deprivation. Indeed, both Tocqueville and Marx, as different as they were in many ways, agreed on the importance of relative deprivation in the formation of social movements.

But most people experience some discontent all the time, so deprivation theory leaves us wondering why social movements arise among some categories of people and not others. A second problem is that deprivation theory suffers from circular reasoning: We assume that deprivation causes social movements, but often the only evidence of deprivation is the social movement itself (Jenkins & Perrow, 1977). A third limitation of this approach is that it focuses exclusively on the cause of a social movement and tells us little about movements themselves (McAdam, McCarthy, & Zald, 1988). Fourth, some researchers claim that relative deprivation has not turned out to be a very good predictor of emerging social movements (Muller, 1979).

Mass-Society Theory

William Kornhauser's *mass-society theory* (1959) argues that social movements attract socially isolated people who feel personally insignificant. From this point of view, social movements occur in large *mass* societies. Social movements are *personal* as well as *political* in that they offer a sense of purpose and belonging to people otherwise adrift in society (Melucci, 1989).

It follows, says Kornhauser, that categories of people with weak social ties are those who most readily join a social movement. People who are well integrated socially, by contrast, are unlikely to seek membership in a social movement.

Like Gustave Le Bon, discussed earlier, Kornhauser offers a conservative view of social movements. Activists tend to be psychologically vulnerable people who eagerly join groups and can be manipulated by group leaders. Social movements, in Kornhauser's view, are unlikely to be very democratic.

Critical evaluation. To Kornhauser's credit, his theory focuses on both the kind of society that produces social movements and the kinds of people who join them. But one criticism is that if we try to test the idea that mass societies foster social movements, we run up against the problem of having no clear standard for measuring the extent to which we live in a "mass society."

A second criticism is that explaining social movements in terms of people hungry to belong belittles the social justice issues that movements address. Put otherwise, mass-society theory suggests that flawed people—rather than a flawed society—are responsible for social movements.

These people in San Francisco's Marina Park are protesting the 1992 execution of convicted murderer Robert Alton Harris. Many of those shown here went on to take part in similar protests at prison executions in other states. Mass-society theory suggests that people join social movements to gain a sense of meaning and purpose in their lives. How well do you think this theory explains the behavior of such people? Why?

What does research show about mass-society theory? The record is mixed. On the down side, some studies conclude that the Nazi movement in Germany did not draw heavily from socially isolated people (Lipset, 1963; Oberschall, 1973). Similarly, during the 1960s many urban rioters had strong ties to their communities (Sears & McConahay, 1973). Evidence also suggests that most young people who join religious movements have fairly normal family ties (Wright & Piper, 1986). Finally, researchers who have examined the biographies of 1960s political activists find evidence of deep and continuing commitment to political goals rather than isolation from society (McAdam, 1988, 1989; Whalen & Flacks, 1989).

On the up side, research by Frances Piven and Richard Cloward (1977) supports mass-society theory. Piven and Cloward found that a breakdown of routine social patterns encourages poor people to form social movements. Also, in a study of the New Mexico State Penitentiary, Bert Useem (1985) found that when prison programs promoting social ties among inmates were suspended, inmates were more likely to protest their conditions.

Structural-Strain Theory

One of the most influential theories about social movements was developed by Neil Smelser (1962). *Structural-strain theory* identifies six factors that encourage the development of social movements. Smelser's theory also suggests which kinds of situations lead to unorganized mobs or riots and which to highly organized social movements. We will use the prodemocracy movement that transformed Eastern Europe during the late 1980s to illustrate Smelser's theory:

1. **Structural conduciveness.** Social movements arise as people come to believe that their society has some serious problems. In Eastern Europe, these problems included low living standards and political repression.
2. **Structural strain.** People begin to experience relative deprivation when their society fails to meet their expectations. Eastern Europeans joined the prodemocracy movement because they knew their living standards were far lower than living standards in Western Europe and much below what years of socialist propaganda had led them to expect.
3. **Growth and spread of an explanation.** Forming a well-organized social movement requires a clear statement of a problem, its causes, and its solutions. If people are confused about their suffering, they are likely to express their dissatisfaction in an unorganized way, such as rioting. In the case of Eastern Europe, intellectuals played a key role in the prodemocracy movement by pointing out economic and political flaws in the system and proposing strategies to increase democracy.
4. **Precipitating factors.** Discontent frequently festers for a long time only to be transformed into collective action by a specific triggering event. In Eastern Europe, the precipitating event occurred in 1985 when Mikhail Gorbachev came to power in the Soviet Union and introduced *perestroika* (a program for restructuring the government and the economy). As Moscow relaxed its rigid control over Eastern Europe, people there saw a historic opportunity to reorganize political and economic life and claim greater freedom.
5. **Mobilization for action.** Once people share a concern about some public issue, they are ready to take action—to distribute leaflets, stage protest rallies, and build alliances with sympathetic

organizations. The initial success of the Solidarity movement in Poland—covertly aided by the Reagan administration in the United States and by Pope John Paul II in the Vatican—mobilized people throughout Eastern Europe to press for change. The rate of change accelerated as reform movements gained strength: What had taken a decade in Poland required only months in Hungary and weeks in other Eastern European nations.

6. **Lack of social control.** The success of any social movement depends in large part on how political officials, police, and the military respond. Sometimes the state moves swiftly to crush a social movement, as happened with prodemocracy forces in the People's Republic of China. But Gorbachev adopted a policy of nonintervention in Eastern Europe, thereby further opening the door for change. Ironically, the movements that began in Eastern Europe soon spread to the Soviet Union itself, ending the domination of the Communist party and producing a new political confederation in 1992.

Critical evaluation. Smelser's analysis recognizes the complexity of social movements and suggests how various factors encourage or inhibit their development. Structural-strain theory also explains why people may respond to their problems either by forming organized social movements or through spontaneous mob action or rioting.

Yet Smelser's theory contains some of the same circularity of argument found in Kornhauser's analysis. A social movement is caused by strain, says Smelser, but the only evidence of underlying strain appears to be the social movement itself. Finally, structural-strain theory is incomplete, overlooking the important role that resources like the mass media or international alliances play in the success or failure of a social movement (Oberschall, 1973; Jenkins & Perrow, 1977; McCarthy & Zald, 1977; Olzak & West, 1991).

Resource-Mobilization Theory

Resource-mobilization theory points out that no social movement is likely to succeed—or even get off the ground—without substantial resources, including money, human labor, office and communications facilities, access to the mass media, and a positive public image. In short, any social movement rises or falls on its ability to attract resources, mobilize people, and forge alliances. The 1989 prodemocracy movement in

How can we explain a change as monumental as the fall of Soviet-backed governments throughout Eastern Europe at the beginning of the 1990s? At the outset, this movement was simply a strike by shipyard workers, led by Lech Walesa, in the Polish city of Gdansk. But within a decade, discontent and collective action had toppled the Polish government, made Walesa the nation's new president, and spilled throughout the region, ultimately bringing an end to the Soviet Union itself.

China was fueled by students at universities in Beijing, where their proximity to each other allowed them to build networks and recruit new members (Zhao, 1998). Similarly, to challenge socialism in Eastern Europe, Poles and others needed fax machines, copiers, telecommunications gear, money, and moral support provided by other nations.

In other words, according to resource-mobilization theory, outsiders are as important as insiders to the outcome of a social movement. Since socially disadvantaged people, by definition, lack the money, contacts, leadership skills, and organizational know-how that a successful movement requires, sympathetic outsiders fill the resource gap. In our own country, well-to-do white people, including college students, performed a vital

Every social movement gains strength from various resources, including the efforts of committed supporters, money, and publicity. Hollywood celebrities not only lent their prestige to the movement for AIDS awareness, but they provided enormous visibility for the red ribbon that symbolizes this issue. As a result, this social movement has gained strength in recent years.

service to the black civil rights movement in the 1960s, and affluent men have joined women as leaders of the current women's movement (Snow, Zurcher, & Ekland-Olson, 1980; Killian, 1984; Snow et al., 1986; Baron, Mittman, & Newman, 1991; Burstein, 1991; Meyer & Whittier, 1994; Valocchi, 1996).

On the other side of the coin, a lack of resources limits efforts to bring about change. The history of the AIDS epidemic is a case in point. Initially, in the early 1980s, the government ignored the rising incidence of AIDS, leaving gay communities in San Francisco, New York, and other cities to shoulder the responsibility for treatment and educational programs. Gradually, the general public began to grasp the scope of the problem and pressured local, state, and federal governments to allocate more resources for research, education, and treatment. Members of the entertainment industry in particular lent their money, visibility, and prestige to the movement. These resources were crucial in transforming a fledgling social movement into a well-organized, global coalition of political leaders, educators, and medical specialists.

Critical evaluation. Resource-mobilization theory recognizes that resources as well as discontent are necessary to the success of a social movement. Research confirms that forging alliances to acquire resources is especially important and that movements with few resources may, in desperation, turn to violence to call attention to their cause (Grant & Wallace, 1991).

Critics of this theory counter that even relatively powerless segments of a population can promote change if they are able to organize effectively and have strongly committed members (Donnelly & Majka, 1998). Research by Aldon Morris (1981) shows that people of color drew largely on their own skills and resources to fuel the civil rights movement of the 1950s and 1960s. A second problem with this theory is that it overstates the extent to which powerful people are willing to challenge the status quo. Some rich white people did provide valuable resources to the black civil rights movement, but probably more often, elites were indifferent or opposed to significant change (McAdam, 1982, 1983; Pichardo, 1995).

Overall, the success or failure of a social movement is decided by political struggle. A strong and united establishment (perhaps aided by a countermovement) reduces the odds that a social movement will succeed. If, however, the established powers are divided, the movement's chances of success improve.

Culture Theory

In recent years, sociologists have recognized that social movements depend not only on material resources and the structure of political power but also on cultural symbols. That is, people in any particular situation are likely to mobilize to form a social movement only to the extent that they develop "shared understandings of the world that legitimate and motivate collective action" (McAdam, McCarthy, & Zald, 1996:6).

In part, mobilization depends on a sense of injustice, as suggested by deprivation theory. In addition, however, people must come to believe that they cannot effectively respond to their situation by acting individually. Finally, social movements gain strength as they create symbols and a sense of community that generate strong feelings and direct this emotional energy into organized action. News photographs of children harmed by bombing during the Vietnam War, for example, greatly helped the antiwar movement; likewise, visible "protest communities" on college campuses help steer discussion of issues (Morris & Mueller, 1992; Giugni, 1998; Staggenborg, 1998).

Critical evaluation. This approach reminds us that not just material resources but also cultural symbols form the foundation of social movements. At the same time, however, powerful symbols (such as the flag and ideas about patriotism and respect for our leaders) support the status quo. How and when symbols come to turn people from supporting the system toward protest are questions in need of further research.

New Social Movements Theory

A final theoretical approach addresses the changing character of social movements. *New social movements theory* emphasizes the distinctive features of recent social movements in postindustrial societies of North America and Western Europe (Melucci, 1980; McAdam, McCarthy, & Zald, 1988; Kriesi, 1989; Pakulski, 1993).

Most of today's social movements are international, focusing on global ecology, the social standing of women and gay people, animal rights, and reducing the risk of war. As globalization connects the world's nations in more and more ways, in other words, social movements, too, are becoming global.

Second, while traditional social movements such as labor organizations are concerned mostly with economic issues, new social movements tend to focus on cultural change and improving our social and physical surroundings. The international environmental movement, for example, opposes practices that aggravate global warming and other environmental dangers.

Third, whereas most social movements of the past drew strong support from working-class people, new social movements, with their noneconomic agendas, usually draw support from the middle and upper-middle classes. This is because, as discussed in Chapter 17 ("Politics and Government"), affluent people tend to be conservative on economic issues (since they have wealth to protect) but liberal on social issues (partly as a result of extensive education). Furthermore, in the United States and other rich nations, the number of highly educated professionals—the people who most support "new social movements"—is increasing, which suggests that these movements will grow (Jenkins & Wallace, 1996; Rose, 1997).

Critical evaluation. One clear strength of new social movements theory is its recognition that social movements have increased in scale in response to the development of a global economy and international political connections. This theory also highlights the power of the mass media and information technology to unite people around the world in pursuit of political goals.

Critics, however, claim that this approach exaggerates the differences between past and present social movements. The women's movement, for example, focuses on many of the same issues—workplace conditions and pay—that have concerned labor organizations for decades.

One example of a new social movement is the worldwide effort to eliminate land mines. Years after hostilities cease, these mines remain in place and take a staggering toll in civilian lives. At a protest in Berlin, Germany, a mountain of shoes stands as a memorial to the tens of thousands who have been crippled or died as a result of stepping on underground mines.

Each of the six theories we have presented offers some explanation for the emergence of social movements; no single theory can stand alone (Kowalewski & Porter, 1992). Table 23–1 on page 616 summarizes the theories.

GENDER AND SOCIAL MOVEMENTS

Gender figures prominently in the operation of social movements. In keeping with traditional ideas about gender in the United States, men more than women tend to take part in public life—including spearheading social movements.

Investigating "Freedom Summer," a 1964 voter registration project in Mississippi, Doug McAdam (1992) found that most people viewed the job of registering African American voters in the midst of considerable hostility from whites dangerous and, therefore, "men's work," unsuitable for women. He also discovered that project leaders were likely to assign women volunteers to clerical and teaching assignments, leaving the actual

TABLE 23–1 Theories of Social Movements: A Summary

Deprivation Theory	People experiencing relative deprivation begin social movements. The social movement is a means of seeking change that brings participants greater benefits. Social movements are especially likely when rising expectations are frustrated.
Mass-Society Theory	People who lack established social ties are mobilized into social movements. Periods of social breakdown are likely to spawn social movements. The social movement gives members a sense of belonging and social participation.
Structural-Strain Theory	People come together because of their shared concern about the inability of society to operate as they believe it should. The growth of a social movement reflects many factors, including a belief in its legitimacy and some precipitating event that provokes action.
Resource-Mobilization Theory	People may join for all the reasons noted above and also because of social ties to existing members. But the success or failure of a social movement depends largely on the resources available to it. Also important is the extent of opposition within the larger society.
Culture Theory	People are drawn to a social movement by cultural symbols that define some cause as just. The movement itself usually becomes a symbol of power and justice.
New Social Movements Theory	People who become part of social movements are motivated by "quality of life" issues, not necessarily economic concerns. Mobilization is national or international in scope. New social movements arise in response to the expansion of the mass media and new information technology.

field activities to men. This was so even though women who participated in Freedom Summer were more qualified than their male counterparts in terms of years of activism and organizational affiliations. McAdam concluded that only the most committed women were able to overcome the movement's gender barriers. In short, while women have played leading roles in many social movements (including the abolitionist and feminist movements in the United States), male dominance has been the norm even in social movements that otherwise oppose the status quo (Herda-Rapp, 1998).

STAGES IN SOCIAL MOVEMENTS

Despite the many differences that distinguish one social movement from another, all unfold in roughly the same way, as shown in Figure 23–3. Researchers have identified four stages in the life of the typical social movement (Blumer, 1969; Mauss, 1975; Tilly, 1978):

Stage 1: Emergence. Social movements are driven by the perception that all is not well. Some, such as the civil rights and women's movements, are born of widespread dissatisfaction. Others emerge only as a small vanguard group increases public awareness of some issue. Gay activists, for example, initially raised public concern about the threat posed by AIDS.

Stage 2: Coalescence. After emerging, a social movement must define itself and develop a strategy for "going public." Leaders must determine policies, decide on tactics, build morale, and recruit new members. At this stage, the movement may take collective action through rallies or demonstrations that attract media attention and thereby public notice. The movement may also form alliances with other organizations to acquire necessary resources.

Stage 3: Bureaucratization. To become a political force, a social movement must take on bureaucratic traits, described in Chapter 7 ("Groups and Organizations"). Thus, as it becomes established, the social movement depends less on the charisma and talents of a few leaders and more on a capable staff. When social movements do not become established in this way, they risk dissolving. For example, many activist organizations on college campuses during the late 1960s were energized by a single charismatic leader and, consequently, did not last long. On the other hand, the National Organization for Women (NOW), despite its changing leadership, is well established and can be counted on to speak for feminists.

Even so, bureaucratization can sometimes hinder a social movement. In reviewing social movements in U.S. history, Frances Piven and Richard Cloward (1977)

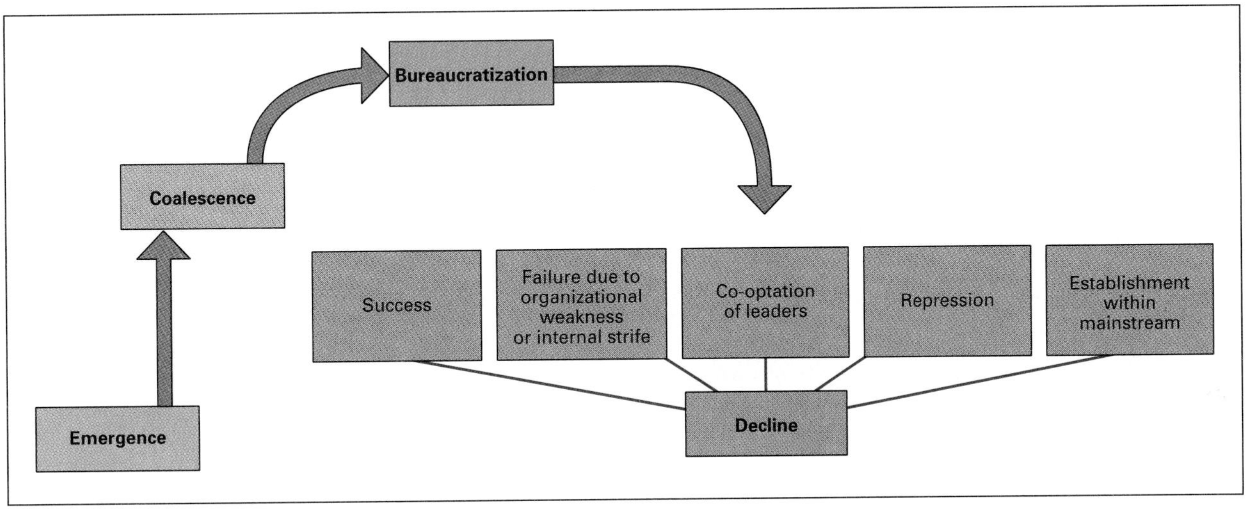

FIGURE 23–3 **Stages in the Lives of Social Movements**

found that leaders can become so engrossed in building an organization that they neglect to keep people "fired up" for change. In such cases, the radical edge of protest is lost.

Stage 4: Decline. Eventually, most social movements lose their vigor. Frederick Miller (1983) suggests four reasons that they decline.

First, if members have met their goals, decline may simply signal success. For example, the women's suffrage movement disbanded after it won women in the United States the right to vote. Such clear-cut successes are rare, however, since few social movements have a single goal. More commonly, winning one victory leads to new campaigns. Because issues related to gender extend far beyond voting, the women's movement has recast itself time and again.

Second, a social movement may fold because of organizational factors, such as poor leadership, loss of interest among members, insufficient funds, or repression by authorities. Some people lose interest when the excitement of early efforts is replaced by day-to-day routine. Fragmentation due to internal conflicts over goals and strategies is another common problem. Students for a Democratic Society (SDS), a student movement promoting participatory democracy and opposing the war in Vietnam, splintered into several small factions by the end of the 1960s, as members disagreed over strategies for social change.

Third, a social movement can fall apart if the established power structure, through offers of money, prestige, and other rewards, diverts leaders from their goals. "Selling out" is one facet of the iron law of oligarchy, discussed in Chapter 7 ("Groups and Organizations"). That is, organizational leaders use their positions to enrich themselves. For example, Vernon Jordan, once head of the National Urban League, which advocated civil rights, became a close adviser to President Clinton—and a rich and powerful Washington "insider." But this process can also work the other way: Some people leave lucrative, high-prestige occupations to become activists. Cat Stevens, a rock star of the 1970s, became a Muslim, changed his name to Yusuf Islam, and now promotes the spread of his religion.

Finally, a social movement can collapse because of repression. Officials may crush a social movement by frightening away participants, discouraging new recruits, and even imprisoning leaders. In general, the more revolutionary the social movement, the more officials try to repress it. Until 1990, the government of South Africa, for example, banned the African National Congress (ANC), a political organization seeking to overthrow the state-supported system of apartheid. Even suspected members of the ANC were subject to arrest. In 1990, the government lifted the decades-old ban and released ANC leader Nelson Mandela from prison; in 1994, the South African people elected Mandela president and began the journey away from apartheid toward democracy.

Beyond the reasons noted by Miller, a fifth cause of decline is that a social movement may "go mainstream." Some movements become an accepted part of

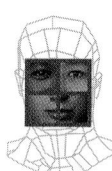

CONTROVERSY & DEBATE

Are You Willing to Take a Stand?

Are you satisfied with our society as it is? Surely, everyone would change some things about our way of life. Indeed, surveys show that if they could, a lot of people would change plenty! There is considerable pessimism about the state of U.S. society: Two-thirds of U.S. adults think that the average person's situation "is getting worse, not better," and three-fourths of respondents think that most government officials are "not interested" in the average person's problems (NORC, 1999:204).

But, even in light of such concerns, few people are willing to work for change. Only 10 percent of U.S. adults have ever picketed during a labor strike; just 5 percent say they have ever taken part in any other kind of demonstration (NORC, 1999:242).

Many college students think age has something to do with our apathy. That is, young people have the interest and idealism to challenge the status quo, but older adults worry only about their families and their jobs. Indeed, one of the popular sayings of the activist 1960s was "You can't trust people over thirty!" But the facts are otherwise: Students entering college in 1999 expressed less interest in political issues than their parents.

Asked to select important goals in life from a list, 26 percent of first-year students included "keeping up with political affairs," but just 21 percent checked off "participating in community action programs." As the figure shows, only a handful of students (20 percent) say they voted in a student election during the past year. An even smaller share (15 percent) claimed to discuss politics frequently in the previous year.

Certainly, people cite good reasons to avoid political controversy. Any time we challenge the system—whether on campus or in the national political arena—we risk making enemies, losing a job, or perhaps even sustaining physical injury.

But the most important reason that people in the United States avoid joining in social movements may have to do with cultural norms about how change should occur. In our individualistic culture, people favor taking personal responsibility over collective action as a means of addressing social problems. For example, when asked about the best way for women or African Americans to improve their social position, most U.S. adults say that individuals should rely on their own efforts, while only a few point to women's groups or civil rights activism as the best way to bring about change (NORC, 1999:220, 353–55). This individualistic orientation explains why U.S. adults are half as likely as their European counterparts to join in lawful demonstrations (*World Values Survey*, 1994).

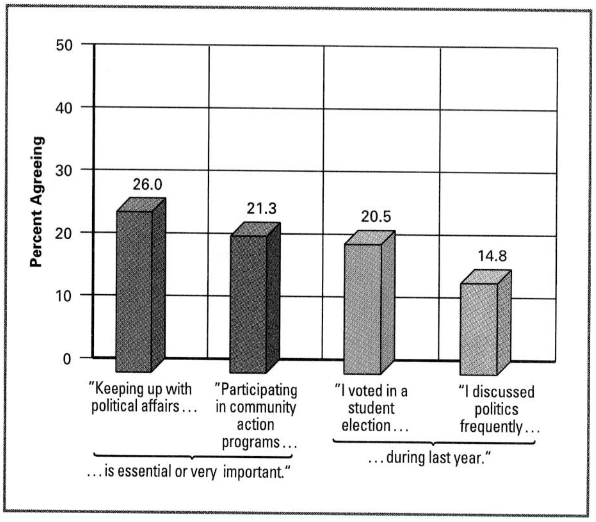

Political Involvement of Students Entering College in 1999: A Survey

Source: Sax et al. (1999).

Sociology, of course, poses a counterpoint to our cultural individualism. As C. Wright Mills (1959) explained decades ago, many of the problems we encounter as individuals are caused by the structure of society. Thus, said Mills, solutions to many of life's problems depend on collective effort—that is, people willing to take a stand for what they believe.

Continue the debate . . .

1. *Do you think the reluctance of people in the United States to address problems through collective action shows that people are basically satisfied with their lives? Or that they think individuals acting together can't make a difference?*
2. *Have you ever participated in a political demonstration? What were its goals? What did it accomplish?*
3. *Identify ways that life today has been affected by people who took a stand in the past (think about race relations, animal rights, the state of the environment, the standing of women, or other issues).*

the system—typically after realizing some of their goals—so that while they continue to flourish, they no longer challenge the status quo. The U.S. labor movement, for example, is now well established; its leaders control vast sums of money and, according to some critics, now have more in common with the business tycoons they opposed in the past than with rank-and-file workers.

SOCIAL MOVEMENTS AND SOCIAL CHANGE

Social movements exist to encourage—or to resist—social change. Whatever the intention, their success varies from case to case. The civil rights movement has certainly pushed this country toward racial equality, despite opposition from a handful of white supremacist countermovements like the Aryan Nation and what's left of the Ku Klux Klan.

Sometimes we overlook the success of past social movements and take for granted the changes that other people struggled so hard to win. Beginning a century ago, workers' movements in the United States fought to end child labor in factories, limit working hours, make the workplace safer, and establish the right to bargain collectively with employers. Laws protecting the environment are another product of successful social movements during the twentieth century. And women today enjoy legal rights and economic opportunities won by earlier generations of women.

Seen one way, major social transformations such as the Industrial Revolution and capitalism give rise to social movements, including those involving workers and women. On the other hand, the efforts of workers, women, racial and ethnic minorities, and gay people have sent ripples of change throughout our society. In short, social change is both the cause and the consequence of social movements.

LOOKING AHEAD: SOCIAL MOVEMENTS IN THE TWENTY-FIRST CENTURY

Especially since the turbulent 1960s—a decade marked by widespread social protests—U.S. society has been pushed and pulled by many social movements and countermovements. Sometimes tension explodes into violence, as with the 1992 Los Angeles riots after the first trial of the police accused of beating motorist Rodney King. In other cases, the struggles are more restrained, as with political debate between congressional Democrats supporting social "safety nets" and Republicans opposed to "big government." Yet people on all sides of controversial issues agree that many of this nation's most pressing problems—racial tension, the size of government, and crime—remain unresolved. In addition, new issues—including the state of the family, funding for political campaigns, and gay rights—have moved to center stage.

Social movements have always been part of U.S. society, although their focus, tactics, and intensity change with time. There is little doubt, therefore, that social movements will continue to shape our way of life during this new century. Indeed, for three reasons, the scope of social movements is likely to increase. First, here at home, protest should increase as women, African Americans, and other historically excluded categories of people gain a greater political voice. Second, at a global level, the technology of the Information Revolution means that anyone with a satellite dish, personal computer, or fax machine can stay abreast of political events, often as they happen. Third, new technology and the emerging global economy mean that social movements are now uniting people throughout the entire world. Moreover, since many problems are global, only international cooperation can solve them.

SUMMARY

1. Collective behavior differs from group behavior in two significant ways: It involves limited social interaction within vague social boundaries, and is characterized by weak and often unconventional norms.
2. Crowds, an important type of collective behavior, take various forms: casual crowds, conventional crowds, expressive crowds, acting crowds, and protest crowds.
3. Crowds that become emotionally intense spawn violence in the form of mobs and riots. Mobs pursue a specific goal; rioting involves undirected destructiveness.
4. Crowds have figured heavily in social change throughout history, although the value of their action depends on one's political outlook.
5. Contagion theory views crowds as anonymous, suggestible, and subject to heightened emotion.

Convergence theory links crowd behavior to the traits of participants. Emergent-norm theory suggests that crowds develop their own behavioral norms.

6. One form of mass behavior is rumor, which thrives in a climate of ambiguity. While rumor involves public issues, gossip deals with personal issues.
7. Public opinion consists of people's positions on important, controversial issues. Public attitudes change, so that, at any time on a given issue, a small share of people holds no opinion at all.
8. A panic (in a local area) and mass hysteria (across an entire society) are types of collective behavior. In both, people respond to a significant event, real or imagined, with irrational, frantic, and often self-destructive behavior.
9. In industrial societies, fashion is a mark of social prestige. A fad is less conventional than a fashion and also of shorter duration.
10. Social movements exist to promote or discourage change. Sociologists classify social movements according to the range of people they seek to involve and the extent of the change they seek.
11. According to deprivation theory, social movements arise as people feel deprived in relation to some standard of well-being.
12. Mass-society theory holds that people join social movements to gain a sense of belonging and moral direction.
13. Structural-strain theory explains the development of a social movement as a cumulative effect of six factors. Well-formulated grievances and goals encourage the formation of social movements; undirected anger, by contrast, promotes rioting.
14. Resource-mobilization theory ties the success or failure of a social movement to the availability of resources, such as money, human labor, and alliances with other organizations.
15. Culture theory links a movement's success to symbols that unite and mobilize individuals.
16. New social movements theory focuses on quality-of-life issues that are usually international in scope.
17. A typical social movement proceeds through consecutive stages: emergence (defining the public issue), coalescence (entering the public arena), bureaucratization (becoming formally organized), and decline (due to failure or, sometimes, success).
18. Past social movements have shaped society in ways that people now take for granted. Just as movements produce change, so change itself cause social movements.

KEY CONCEPTS

collective behavior (p. 599) activity involving a large number of people, often spontaneous and sometimes controversial

collectivity (p. 600) a large number of people whose minimal interaction occurs in the absence of well-defined and conventional norms

crowd (p. 600) a temporary gathering of people who share a common focus of attention and who influence one another

mob (p. 601) a highly emotional crowd that pursues a violent or destructive goal

riot (p. 602) a social eruption that is highly emotional, violent, and undirected

mass behavior (p. 605) collective behavior among people dispersed over a wide geographical area

rumor (p. 605) unsubstantiated information spread informally, often by word of mouth

gossip (p. 606) rumor about people's personal affairs

public opinion (p. 606) widespread attitudes about controversial issues

propaganda (p. 606) information presented with the intention of shaping public opinion

panic (p. 606) a form of localized collective behavior by which people react to a threat or other stimulus with irrational, frantic, and often self-destructive behavior

mass hysteria (p. 606) a form of dispersed collective behavior by which people react to a real or imagined event with irrational, frantic, and often self-destructive behavior

fashion (p. 607) a social pattern favored by a large number of people

fad (p. 609) an unconventional social pattern that people embrace briefly but enthusiastically

social movement (p. 609) organized activity that encourages or discourages social change

relative deprivation (p. 610) a perceived disadvantage arising from a specific comparison

CRITICAL-THINKING QUESTIONS

1. The concept of collective behavior encompasses a broad range of social patterns. List some of these behaviors. What traits do they all have in common?
2. Imagine the aftermath of a football game in which the revelry of college students turns into a destructive rampage. How might contagion theory, convergence theory, and emergent-norm theory explain such behavior?
3. The 1960s were a decade of both great affluence and widespread social protest. What sociological insights help to explain this apparent paradox?
4. In what respects do some recent social movements (those concerned with the environment, animal rights, and gun control) differ from older crusades (focusing on, say, the right of workers to form unions or the right of women to vote)?

APPLICATIONS AND EXERCISES

1. With ten friends, try this experiment: One person writes down a detailed "rumor" about someone important and then whispers it to another person, who whispers it to a third, and so on. The last person to hear the rumor writes it down again. Compare the two versions of the rumor.
2. With other members of the class, identify recent fad products. What makes people want them? Why do they drop from favor so quickly?
3. What social movements are represented by organizations on your campus? Your class might invite several leaders to describe their groups' goals and strategies.
4. In recent years, several plane disasters have occurred on the East Coast: TWA Flight 800 (1996), Swissair Flight 111 (1998), John F. Kennedy, Jr.'s, plane (1999), and Egyptair Flight 990 (1999). None has been fully explained. What rumors have arisen as to how or why these planes crashed? (Paulos, 1999)
5. Install the CD-ROM packaged in the back of this new textbook to access a variety of study, review, and applications exercises designed to help you better understand the material covered in this chapter. The CD includes an author's tip video, as well as interactive maps, video application exercises, Web links, and study questions.

SITES TO SEE

http://www.prenhall.com/macionis

Visit the interactive Web site that accompanies this text. Begin by clicking on the cover of your book. You will find a chapter-by-chapter study guide, practice tests, chat room, and many suggested Web links.

http://www.gallup.com

Tracking trends in public opinion is the job of various pollsters, including the Gallup Organization. Visit this Gallup site to see what they do and read about some of their recent surveys.

http://www.enviroweb.org/cco/

Organizing in support of various social movements has long been a characteristic of college campuses across the United States. This site, operated by the Center for Campus Organizing, provides information on various campus-based social movements.

http://www.natlnorml.org

Visit the Web site for the National Organization for the Reform of Marijuana Laws. What are the goals of this organization? How is it trying to expand the social movement in favor of legalizing marijuana use?

CHAPTER 24

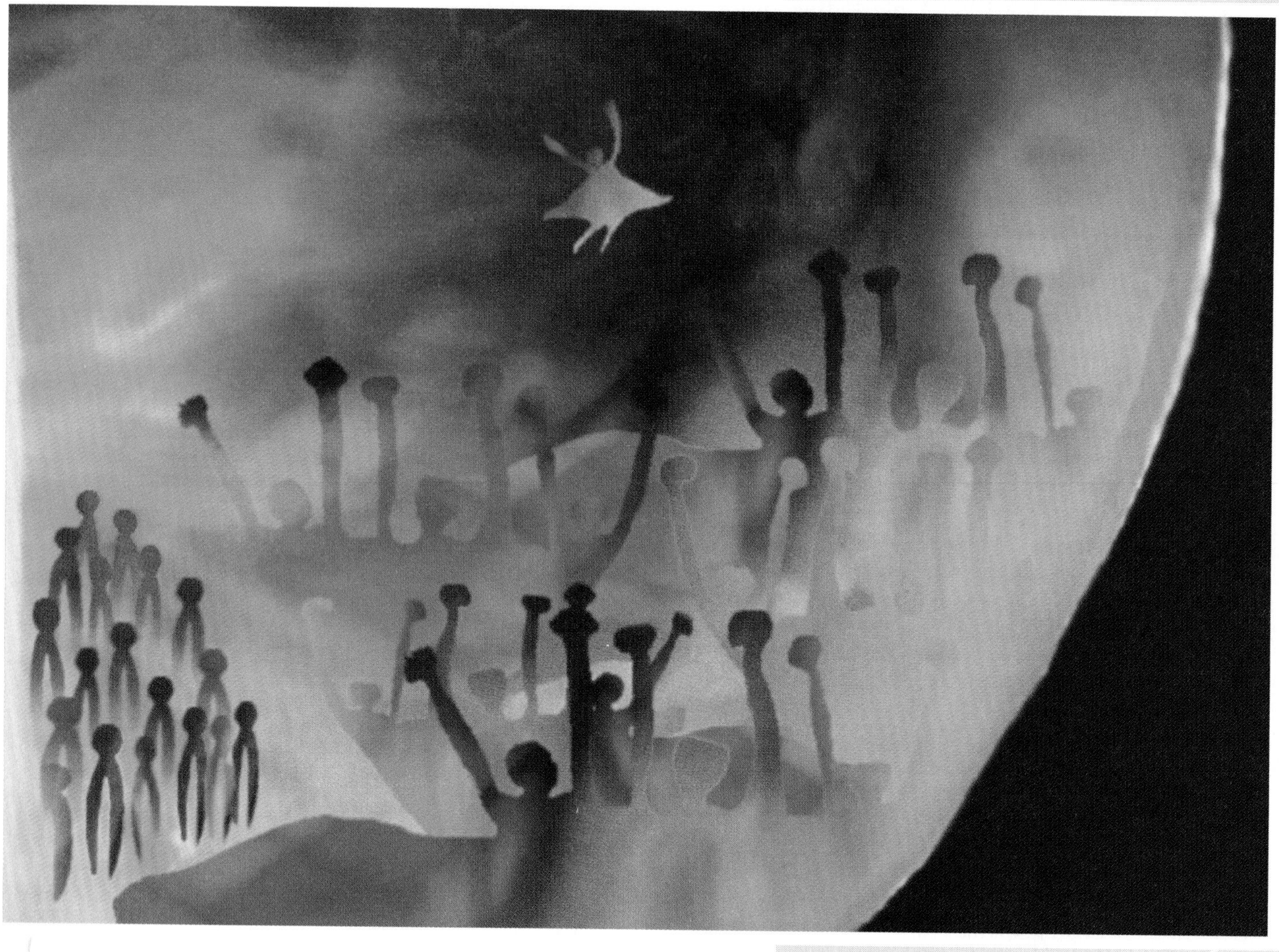

Joan Truckenbrod
Seize Steering, 1995

Iris ink jet, 22 × 38 in.

Represented by The Williams Gallery of Fine Art, Princeton, N.J.

SOCIAL CHANGE: TRADITIONAL, MODERN, AND POSTMODERN SOCIETIES

In 1900, people lined up at the Paris Exposition to see some of the latest inventions, including something called a "voice recorder" and a small camera, called the Brownie, from the Kodak Company. The same year, in Germany, a physicist named Max Planck had just discovered atomic radiation, although he was not sure exactly what it was and had little idea of what people might do with it. Another German, a doctor named Sigmund Freud, published a book on the interpretation of dreams, which few people found very convincing. Also in 1900, farther east in Russia, a young man named Vladimir Lenin published his first newspaper article calling for a people's revolution to overthrow the government. And in China, a rebellion against exploitation by foreign powers started the world thinking about the evils of colonialism.

Across the Atlantic, in the United States, 1900 saw the Wright brothers arrive in Kitty Hawk, North Carolina, with the idea of building a machine that would allow people to fly. Meanwhile, in New York City, J. P. Morgan was already flying high—having just signed a deal to create U.S. Steel, the world's first billion-dollar corporation (Isaacson, 1998).

It is scarcely possible for people today to imagine how different life was a century ago. Most people in the United States still lived in small towns and on farms. They had no computers, televisions, or radios. Most homes did not even have electricity. There were no superhighways—only a few people had ever seen an automobile (known back then as a "horseless carriage"). People traveled around their communities by foot or by horse, and a few went greater distances by railroad, in passenger cars pulled by steam-powered locomotives. Almost all women worked only in the home; none was permitted by law to vote. For both women and men, life was also much shorter: On average, people lived only about fifty years.

It is easy to find ways in which life today seems better than a century ago. We now enjoy countless conveniences, travel farther and faster, and live longer than ever before. Yet, as this chapter explains, social change is a process with negative as well as positive consequences. Indeed, as we shall see, the founding thinkers of sociology were mixed in their assessment of *modernity*, changes brought about by the Industrial Revolution. Likewise, today's sociologists point to both good and bad aspects of *postmodernity*, the recent transformations caused by the Information Revolution and the postindustrial economy. What is clear—for better and worse—is that the rate of change has never been faster than it is now.

WHAT IS SOCIAL CHANGE?

In earlier chapters, we examined relatively *static* social patterns, including status and role, social stratification, and social institutions. The *dynamic* forces that have shaped our way of life range from innovations in technology to the expansion of cities and the growth of bureaucracy. These are all dimensions of **social change,** *the transformation of culture and social institutions over time.* The process of social change has four major characteristics:

1. **Social change is inevitable.** "Nothing is constant except death and taxes" goes the old saying. Yet even our thoughts about death have changed dramatically as life expectancy in the United States has doubled since 1850. Taxes, meanwhile, were unknown through most of human history, instituted only as societies grew in size several thousand years ago. In short, virtually everything is subject to the twists and turns of change.

   Still, some societies change faster than others. As Chapter 4 ("Society") explained, hunting and gathering societies change quite slowly; members of today's rich, complex societies, on the other hand, experience significant change within a single lifetime.

   Moreover, in a given society, some cultural elements change faster than others. William Ogburn's (1964) theory of *cultural lag* (see Chapter 3, "Culture") states that material culture (that is, things) usually changes faster than nonmaterial culture (ideas and attitudes). For example, medical technology that prolongs life has developed more rapidly than ethical standards for deciding when and how to use it.

2. **Social change is sometimes intentional but often unplanned.** Industrial societies actively encourage many kinds of change. For example, scientists seek more efficient forms of energy, and advertisers try to convince us that life is incomplete without this or that new gadget. Yet rarely can anyone envision all the consequences of the changes that are set in motion.

   Early automobile manufacturers understood that cars would allow people to travel in a single day distances that once had required weeks or months. But no one could see how profoundly the mobility provided by automobiles would alter life in the United States, scattering family members, reshaping cities and suburbs, and threatening the natural environment. Neither could automotive pioneers have predicted the more than 43,000 deaths in motor vehicle accidents a year in the United States alone.

3. **Social change is controversial.** The history of the automobile shows that social change brings both good and bad consequences. The Industrial Revolution that led to the invention of the automobile was itself controversial. Capitalists celebrated the new technology that increased productivity and swelled profits. Many workers, however, feared that machines would make their skills obsolete and resisted the push toward "progress."

   Today, as in the past, changing social patterns—between black people and white people, women and men, and homosexuals and heterosexuals—still create controversy as people disagree about how we ought to live.

4. **Some changes matter more than others.** Some changes (such as clothing fads) have only passing significance, whereas others (like computers) last a long time and may end up transforming the entire world. Looking ahead, will the Information Revolution turn out to be as pivotal as the Industrial Revolution? Like the automobile and television, the computer has both positive and negative effects, providing new kinds of jobs while eliminating old ones, isolating people in offices while linking people in global electronic networks, offering vast amounts of information while threatening personal privacy.

CAUSES OF SOCIAL CHANGE

Social change has many causes. Then, too, in a world linked by sophisticated communication and transportation technology, change in one place often begets change elsewhere.

CULTURE AND CHANGE

Chapter 3 ("Culture") identified three important sources of cultural change. First, *invention* produces new objects, ideas, and social patterns. Rocket propulsion research, which began in the 1940s, has produced spacecraft that reach toward the stars. Today we take such technology for granted; during the twenty-first century a significant number of people may well travel in space.

Second, *discovery* occurs when people take note of existing elements of the world. Medical advances, for example, offer a growing understanding of the human body. Beyond the direct effects on human health, medical discoveries have stretched life expectancy, setting in motion the "graying" of our society (see Chapter 15, "Aging and the Elderly").

Third, *diffusion* creates change as products, people, and information spread from one culture to another. Ralph Linton (1937a) recognized that many familiar elements of our culture came from other lands. Cloth (developed in Asia), clocks (invented in Europe), and coins (created in Turkey) are all part of our way of life. In general, material objects diffuse more readily than cultural ideas. That is, new breakthroughs (such as the science of cloning) occur faster than our understanding of when—and even if—they are morally desirable.

Throughout our history, immigrants have brought change to the United States. In recent decades, people from Latin America and Asia have introduced new cultural patterns, clearly evident in the sights, smells, and sounds of cities across the country. Conversely, the global power of the United States ensures that much of our culture—from cheeseburgers to hip-hop to M.B.A. degrees—is being diffused to other societies.

Today, most of the people with access to computers live in rich countries such as the United States. But the number of people in agrarian societies going "online" is on the rise. How do you think the introduction of new information technology will change more traditional societies? Are all the changes likely to be for the good?

CONFLICT AND CHANGE

Tension and conflict in a society also produce change. Karl Marx saw class conflict as the engine that drives societies from one historical era to another (see Chapter 4, "Society," and Chapter 10, "Social Stratification"). In industrial-capitalist societies, he explained, struggle between capitalists and workers propels society toward a socialist system of production.

In the century since Marx's death, this model has proven simplistic. Yet Marx correctly foresaw that social conflict arising from inequality (involving not just class but also race and gender) would force changes in every society, including our own.

IDEAS AND CHANGE

Max Weber also contributed to our understanding of social change. Weber acknowledged that conflict could bring about change, but he traced the roots of most social change to ideas. For example, people with charisma can carry a message that sometimes changes the world.

Weber also highlighted the importance of ideas by showing how the religious beliefs of early Protestants set the stage for the spread of industrial capitalism (see Chapter 4, "Society"). The fact that industrial capitalism developed primarily in areas of Western Europe where the Protestant work ethic was strong proved to Weber the power of ideas to bring about change (1958; orig. 1904–5).

Ideas also direct social movements. Chapter 23 ("Collective Behavior and Social Movements") explained how change comes from the determination of people acting together to, say, clean up the environment or make the world more just by improving the lives of oppressed people. The gay rights movement, for example, draws strength from people who believe that lesbians and gay men should enjoy the same rights and opportunities as the heterosexual majority.

DEMOGRAPHIC CHANGE

Population patterns also transform a society. Profound change is taking place as our population, collectively speaking, grows older. As Chapter 15 ("Aging and the Elderly") explained, 13 percent of the U.S. population was over age sixty-five in 1999, triple the proportion

SEEING OURSELVES

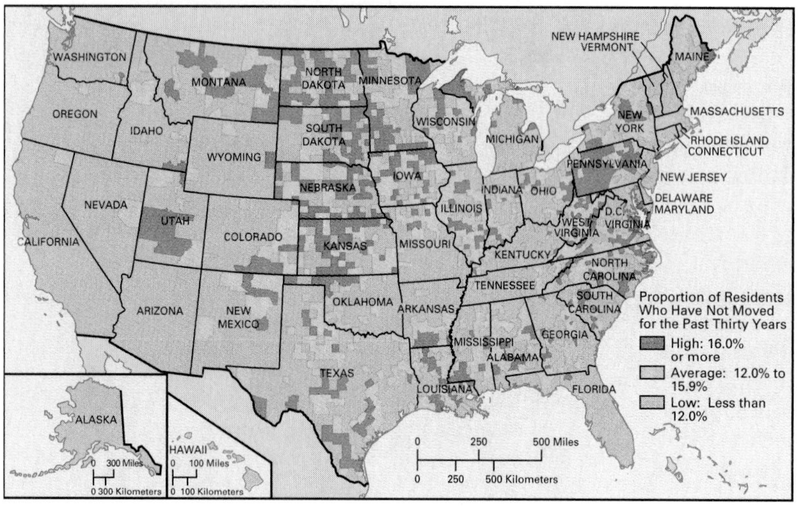

NATIONAL MAP 24–1
Who Stays Put? Residential Stability across the United States

Overall, only about 9 percent of U.S. residents have not moved during the last thirty years. Counties with a higher proportion of "long-termers" typically have experienced less change over recent decades: Many neighborhoods have been in place since before World War II, and many of the same families live in them. Looking at the map, what can you say about these relatively stable areas? Why are most of these counties rural and some distance from the coasts?

Source: U.S. Census Bureau (1996).

back in 1900. By the year 2030, seniors will account for 20 percent of the total (U.S. Census Bureau, 2000). Medical research and health care services already focus extensively on the elderly, and life will change in countless additional ways as homes and household products are redesigned to meet the needs of the growing ranks of older consumers.

Migration within and among societies is another demographic factor that promotes change. Between 1870 and 1930, tens of millions of immigrants entered the industrial cities in the United States. Millions more from rural areas joined the rush. As a result, farm communities declined, cities expanded, and, for the first time, the United States became a predominantly urban nation. Similarly, changes are taking place today as people move from the Snowbelt to the Sunbelt and mix with new immigrants from Latin America and Asia.

Where in the United States have demographic changes been greatest, and which areas have been least affected? National Map 24–1 provides one answer, showing counties where the largest share of people have lived in their present homes for thirty years or more.

MODERNITY

A central concept in the study of social change is **modernity,** *social patterns resulting from industrialization.* In everyday usage, modernity (its Latin root means "lately") designates the present in relation to the past. Sociologists include in this catchall concept the social patterns set in motion by the Industrial Revolution beginning in Western Europe in the mid-eighteenth century. **Modernization,** then, is *the process of social change begun by industrialization.* The time line inside the front cover of the text highlights important events that mark the emergence of modernity.

FOUR DIMENSIONS OF MODERNIZATION

Peter Berger (1977), in his influential study of social change, identified four major characteristics of modernization:

1. **The decline of small, traditional communities.** Modernity involves "the progressive weakening, if not destruction, of the . . . relatively cohesive communities in which human beings have found solidarity and meaning throughout most of history" (Berger 1977:72). For thousands of years, in hunting and gathering camps and the agrarian villages of Europe and North America, people lived in small communities where social life revolved around family and neighborhood. Such traditional worlds gave each person a well-defined place that, although limiting range of choice, offered a strong sense of identity, belonging, and purpose.

In response to the accelerating pace of change in the nineteenth century, Paul Gauguin left his native France for the South Seas where he was captivated by a simpler and seemingly timeless way of life. He romanticized this environment in his painting, Les trois huttes Tahiti.

Paul Gauguin (1848–1903), *Les trois huttes Tahiti.* Photo © Christie's Images.

Small, isolated communities still exist in the United States, of course, but they are home to only a small percentage of our nation's people. And their isolation is little more than geographic: Cars, telephones, television, and, increasingly, computers give rural families the pulse of the larger society and connect them to the entire world.

2. **The expansion of personal choice.** Members of traditional, preindustrial societies view their lives as shaped by forces beyond human control—gods, spirits, or simply fate. But as the power of tradition erodes, people come to see their lives as a series of options, a process Berger calls *individualization.* Many people in the United States, for example, choose a "lifestyle" (sometimes one after another), showing an openness to change. Indeed, a common belief is that people *should* take control of their own lives.
3. **Increasing social diversity.** In preindustrial societies, strong family ties and powerful religious beliefs enforce conformity while discouraging diversity and change. Modernization promotes a more rational, scientific world view as tradition loses its hold and people gain more and more individual choice. The growth of cities, expansion of impersonal bureaucracy, and the social mix of people from various backgrounds combine to foster diverse beliefs and behavior.
4. **Future orientation and growing awareness of time.** While premodern people focus on the past, people in modern societies think more about the future. Modern people are not only forward-looking but optimistic that new inventions and discoveries will improve their lives.

   Modern people also organize their daily routines down to the very minute. With the introduction of clocks in the late Middle Ages, Europeans began to think not in terms of sunlight and seasons but in terms of hours and minutes. Preoccupied with personal gain, modern people demand precise measurement of time and are likely to agree that "Time is money." Berger points out that one good indicator of a society's degree of modernization is the proportion of people who wear wristwatches.

Finally, recall that modernization touched off the development of sociology itself. As Chapter 1 ("The Sociological Perspective") explained, the discipline originated in the wake of the Industrial Revolution in Western Europe, where social change was proceeding most rapidly. Early European and U.S. sociologists set out to analyze the rise of modern society and its consequences—both good and bad—for the lives of human beings.

George Tooker's 1950 painting The Subway *depicts a common problem of modern life: Weakening social ties and eroding traditions create a generic humanity in which everyone is alike yet each person is an anxious stranger in the midst of others.*

George Tooker, *The Subway*, 1950, egg tempera on composition board, 18⅛ x 36⅛", Whitney Museum of American Art, New York. Purchased with funds from the Julianna Force Purchase Award, 50.23. ©2000 Whitney Museum of American Art.

FERDINAND TÖNNIES: THE LOSS OF COMMUNITY

The German sociologist Ferdinand Tönnies (1855–1936) produced a lasting account of modernization in his theory of *Gemeinschaft* and *Gesellschaft* (see Chapter 22, "Population, Urbanization, and Environment"). Like Peter Berger, whose work he influenced, Tönnies (1963; orig. 1887) viewed modernization as the progressive loss of *Gemeinschaft* or human community. As Tönnies saw it, the Industrial Revolution weakened the social fabric of family and tradition by introducing a business-like emphasis on facts, efficiency, and money. European and North American societies gradually became rootless and impersonal as people came to associate mostly on the basis of self-interest—the state Tönnies called *Gesellschaft*.

Early in the twentieth century, at least some areas of the United States approximated Tönnies's concept of *Gemeinschaft*. Families that had lived for generations in small villages and towns were bound together in a hard-working, slow-moving way of life. Telephones (invented in 1876) were rare; it wasn't until 1915 that someone placed the first coast-to-coast call (see the time line inside the front cover of this book). Living without television (introduced in 1939, and not widespread until after 1950), families entertained themselves, often gathering with friends in the evening to share stories, sorrows, or song. Without rapid transportation (although Henry Ford's assembly line began in 1908, cars became commonplace only after World War II), people lived their whole lives in one small town, which was their entire world.

Inevitable tensions and conflicts—sometimes based on race, ethnicity, or religion—divided these small communities. But, according to Tönnies, because of the traditional spirit of *Gemeinschaft*, people were "essentially united in spite of all separating factors" (1963:65; orig. 1887).

Modernity turns societies inside out so that, as Tönnies put it, people are "essentially separated in spite of uniting factors" (1963:65; orig. 1887). This is the world of *Gesellschaft* where, especially in large cities, most people live among strangers and ignore others they pass on the street. Trust is hard to come by in a mobile and anonymous society where people tend to put their personal needs ahead of group loyalty, and a majority of adults believe "you can't be too careful" in dealing with people (NORC, 1999:173). No wonder that millions of men and women attend weekly support groups (also made up of strangers) in order to establish even temporary emotional ties and find someone who is willing simply to *listen* (Leerhsen, 1990).

Critical evaluation. Tönnies's theory of *Gemeinschaft* and *Gesellschaft* is the most widely cited model of modernization. The theory's strength lies in its synthesis of various dimensions of change—growing population, the rise of cities, increasing impersonality in social interaction.

One problem with Tönnies's theory, however, is that modern life, while often impersonal, is not completely devoid of *Gemeinschaft*. Even in a world of strangers, friendships can be strong and lasting. Traditions are especially pronounced in many ethnic neighborhoods where residents maintain close community ties.

Another criticism is that Tönnies said little about which factors (industrialization, urbanization, weakening of families) are cause and which are effect. Some analysts also think that Tönnies favored—perhaps even romanticized—traditional societies while overlooking bonds of family, neighborhood, and friendship in modern societies.

EMILE DURKHEIM: THE DIVISION OF LABOR

The French sociologist Emile Durkheim, whose work is discussed in Chapter 4 ("Society"), shared Tönnies's interest in the profound social changes wrought by the Industrial Revolution. For Durkheim, modernization is defined by an increasing *division of labor*, or specialized economic activity (1964b; orig. 1893). Whereas every member of a traditional society performs more or less the same daily round of activities, modern societies function by having people perform highly specific roles.

Durkheim explained that preindustrial societies are held together by *mechanical solidarity*, or shared moral sentiments. In other words, members of preindustrial societies view everyone as basically alike, doing the same kind of work and belonging together. Durkheim's concept of mechanical solidarity is virtually the same as Tönnies's *Gemeinschaft*.

With modernization, the division of labor becomes more and more pronounced. To Durkheim, this change means *less* mechanical solidarity but *more* of another kind of tie: *organic solidarity*, or the mutual dependency of people engaged in specialized work. Put simply, modern societies are held together not by likeness but by difference: All of us must depend on others to meet most of our needs. Organic solidarity corresponds to Tönnies's concept of *Gesellschaft*.

Despite obvious similarities in their thinking, Durkheim and Tönnies viewed modernity somewhat differently. To Tönnies, the change from *Gemeinschaft* to *Gesellschaft* amounts to the loss of social solidarity, because modern people lose the "natural" and "organic" bonds of the rural village, leaving only the "artificial" and "mechanical" ties of the big city. Durkheim had a different take on modernity, even reversing Tönnies's language to bring home the point. Durkheim labeled modern society "organic," arguing that modern society is no less natural than any other, and he described traditional societies as "mechanical" because they are so regimented. Thus Durkheim viewed modernization not as the loss of community but as a change from community based on bonds of likeness (kinship and neighborhood) to community based on economic interdependence (the division of labor). Durkheim's view of modernity is both more complex and more positive than Tönnies's view.

Critical evaluation. Durkheim's ideas stand alongside those of Tönnies, which they closely resemble, as a highly influential analysis of modernity. Of the two thinkers, Durkheim is the more optimistic; still, he feared that modern societies might become so diverse that they would collapse into a state of *anomie*, a condition in which norms and values are so weak and inconsistent that society provides little moral guidance to individuals. Without strong moral ties to society, modern people become egocentric and find little purpose in life.

The suicide rate—which Durkheim considered a good index of anomie—has, in fact, increased in the United States over this century. Moreover, the vast majority of U.S. adults report that they see moral questions not in clear terms of right and wrong but in confusing "shades of gray" (NORC, 1999:369).

Even so, in modern societies, shared norms and values are still strong enough to give most individuals some sense of meaning and purpose. Moreover, whatever the hazards of anomie, most people seem to value the personal freedom modern society affords.

MAX WEBER: RATIONALIZATION

For Max Weber, whose work is also discussed in Chapter 4 ("Society"), modernity means replacing a traditional world view with a rational way of thinking. In preindustrial societies, tradition acts as a constant brake on change. To traditional people, "truth" is roughly the same as "what has always been" (1978:36; orig. 1921). To modern people, however, "truth" is the result of rational calculation. Because they value efficiency and have little reverence for the past, modern people adopt whatever social patterns allow them to achieve their goals.

Echoing Tönnies and Durkheim, who held that industrialization weakens tradition, Weber declared that modern society is "disenchanted." The unquestioned truths of an earlier time have been challenged by rational, scientific thinking. In short, modern society turns away from the gods. Throughout his life, Weber studied various modern "types"—the capitalist, the scientist, the bureaucrat—all of whom share the rational world view that Weber believed was coming to dominate humanity.

Max Weber maintained that the distinctive character of modern society was its rational world view. Virtually all of Weber's work on modernity centered on types of people he considered typical of their age: the scientist, the capitalist, and the bureaucrat. Each is rational to the core: The scientist is committed to the orderly discovery of truth, the capitalist to the orderly pursuit of profit, and the bureaucrat to orderly conformity to a system of rules.

Critical evaluation. Compared with Tönnies and especially Durkheim, Weber was critical of modern society. He knew that science could produce technological and organizational wonders, but worried that science was turning us away from more basic questions about the meaning and purpose of human existence. Weber feared that rationalization, especially in bureaucracies, would erode the human spirit with endless rules and regulations.

Finally, some of Weber's critics think that the alienation he attributed to bureaucracy actually stemmed from social inequality. That criticism leads us to the ideas of Karl Marx.

KARL MARX: CAPITALISM

For Karl Marx, modern society was synonymous with capitalism; he saw the Industrial Revolution as primarily a *capitalist revolution.* Marx traced the emergence of the bourgeoisie in medieval Europe to the expansion of commerce. The bourgeoisie gradually displaced the feudal aristocracy as the Industrial Revolution placed a powerful new system of production under their control.

Marx agreed that modernity weakened small communities (as described by Tönnies), sharpened the division of labor (as noted by Durkheim), and fostered a rational world view (as Weber claimed). But he saw all these simply as conditions necessary for capitalism to flourish. Capitalism, according to Marx, draws population from farms and small towns into an ever-expanding market system centered in cities; specialization is needed for efficient factories; and rationality is exemplified by the capitalists' relentless pursuit of profit.

Earlier chapters have painted Marx as a spirited critic of capitalist society, but his vision of modernity also has a considerable amount of optimism. Unlike Weber, who viewed modern society as an "iron cage" of bureaucracy, Marx believed that social conflict in capitalist societies would sow seeds of revolutionary change, leading to an egalitarian socialism. Such a society, as he saw it, would harness the wonders of industrial technology to enrich people's lives and also rid the world of social classes, the source of social conflict and dehumanization. Although Marx's evaluation of modern capitalist society was highly negative, he nevertheless imagined a future of human freedom, creativity, and community.

Critical evaluation. Marx's theory of modernization is a complex theory of capitalism. But he underestimated the dominance of bureaucracy in modern societies. In socialist societies, in particular, the stifling effects of bureaucracy turned out to be as bad as, or even worse than, the dehumanizing aspects of capitalism. The recent

TABLE 24–1 Traditional and Modern Societies: The Big Picture

Elements of Society	Traditional Societies	Modern Societies
Cultural Patterns		
Values	Homogeneous; sacred character; few subcultures and countercultures	Heterogeneous; secular character; many subcultures and countercultures
Norms	High moral significance; little tolerance of diversity	Variable moral significance; high tolerance of diversity
Time orientation	Present linked to past	Present linked to future
Technology	Preindustrial; human and animal energy	Industrial; advanced energy sources
Social Structure		
Status and role	Few statuses, most ascribed; few specialized roles	Many statuses, some ascribed and some achieved; many specialized roles
Relationships	Typically primary; little anonymity or privacy	Typically secondary; considerable anonymity and privacy
Communication	Face to face	Face-to-face communication supplemented by mass media
Social control	Informal gossip	Formal police and legal system
Social stratification	Rigid patterns of social inequality; little mobility	Fluid patterns of social inequality; considerable mobility
Gender patterns	Pronounced patriarchy; women's lives centered on the home	Declining patriarchy; increasing number of women in the paid labor force
Economy	Based on agriculture; much manufacturing in the home; little white-collar work	Based on industrial mass production; factories become centers of production; increasing white-collar work
State	Small-scale government; little state intervention in society	Large-scale government; considerable state intervention in society
Family	Extended family as the primary means of socialization and economic production	Nuclear family retains some socialization functions but is more a unit of consumption than of production
Religion	Religion guides world view; little religious pluralism	Religion weakens with the rise of science; extensive religious pluralism
Education	Formal schooling limited to elites	Basic schooling becomes universal, with growing proportion receiving advanced education
Health	High birth and death rates; short life expectancy because of low standard of living and simple medical technology	Low birth and death rates; longer life expectancy because of higher standard of living and sophisticated medical technology
Settlement patterns	Small scale; population typically small and widely dispersed in rural villages and small towns	Large scale; population typically large and concentrated in cities
Social Change	Slow; change evident over many generations	Rapid; change evident within a single generation

upheavals in Eastern Europe and the former Soviet Union reveal the depth of popular opposition to oppressive state bureaucracies.

THEORETICAL ANALYSIS OF MODERNITY

The rise of modernity is a complex process involving many dimensions of change, as described in previous chapters and summarized in Table 24–1. How can we make sense of so many changes going on all at once? Sociologists have developed two broad explanations of modern society, one guided by the structural-functional paradigm and one based on social-conflict theory.

STRUCTURAL-FUNCTIONAL THEORY: MODERNITY AS MASS SOCIETY

One broad approach—drawing on the ideas of Ferdinand Tönnies, Emile Durkheim, and Max Weber—depicts modernization as the emergence of *mass society* (Dahrendorf, 1959; Kornhauser, 1959; Nisbet, 1966,

1969; Stein, 1972; Berger, Berger, & Kellner, 1974; Pearson, 1993). A **mass society** is *a society in which industry and bureaucracy have eroded traditional social ties.* A mass society is marked by weak kinship and impersonal neighborhoods, so individuals are socially isolated. This isolation, in turn, leaves people feeling morally uncertain and personally powerless.

The Mass Scale of Modern Life

Mass-society theory argues, first, that the scale of modern life has greatly increased. Before the Industrial Revolution, Europe and North America formed a mosaic of countless rural villages and small towns. In these small communities, which inspired Tönnies's concept of *Gemeinschaft*, people lived out their lives surrounded by kin and guided by a shared heritage. Gossip was an informal yet highly effective way to ensure conformity to community standards. These small communities, with their strong moral values, tolerated little social diversity—the state of mechanical solidarity described by Durkheim.

For example, before 1690, English law demanded that everyone regularly participate in the Christian ritual of Holy Communion (Laslett, 1984). On this continent, only Rhode Island among the New England colonies tolerated any religious dissent. Because social differences were repressed, subcultures and countercultures rarely arose and change proceeded slowly.

Increasing population, the growth of cities, and specialized economic activity driven by the Industrial Revolution gradually altered this pattern. People came to know one another by their jobs (for example, as "the doctor" or "the bank teller") rather than by their kinship group or hometown. People looked on most others simply as strangers. The face-to-face communication of the village was eventually replaced by the mass media—newspapers, radio, television, and more recently, computer networks—furthering the process of social atomization. Large organizations steadily assumed more and more responsibility for seeing to the daily tasks that had once been carried out by family, friends, and neighbors; public education drew more and more people to schools; police, lawyers, and courts supervised a formal criminal justice system. Even charity became the work of faceless bureaucrats working for various social welfare agencies.

Geographic mobility, mass communications, and exposure to diverse ways of life all erode traditional values. People become more tolerant of social diversity, defending individual rights and freedom of choice. Subcultures and countercultures multiply. Treating people differently—based on their race, sex, or religion—comes to be defined as backward and unjust. In the process, minorities at the margin of society acquire greater power and broader participation in public life. Yet, mass-society theorists fear that transforming people of various backgrounds into a generic mass may end up dehumanizing everyone.

The Ever-Expanding State

In the small-scale, preindustrial societies of Europe, government amounted to little more than a local noble. A royal family formally reigned over an entire nation, but without efficient transportation or communication, the power of even absolute monarchs fell far short of the power wielded by today's political leaders.

As technological innovation allowed government to expand, the centralized state grew in size and importance. At the time the United States gained independence from Great Britain, the federal government was a tiny organization whose prime function was national defense. Since then, government has entered more and more areas of social life—schooling the population, regulating wages and working conditions, establishing standards for products of all sorts, and offering financial assistance to the ill and the unemployed. To pay for such programs, taxes have soared: Today's average worker labors five months each year to pay for the broad array of services that government provides.

In a mass society, power resides in large bureaucracies, leaving people in local communities little control over their lives. For example, state officials mandate that local schools must have a standardized educational program, local products must be government certified, and every citizen must maintain extensive tax records. While such regulations may protect people and advance social equality, they also force us to deal more and more with nameless officials in distant and often unresponsive bureaucracies, and they undermine the autonomy of families and neighborhoods.

Critical evaluation. The theory of mass society concedes that the transformation of small communities has positive aspects, but only at the cost of losing our cultural heritage. Modern societies increase individual rights, tolerate greater social differences, and raise standards of living. But they are prone to what Weber feared most—excessive bureaucracy—as well as Tönnies's self-centeredness and Durkheim's anomie. Their size, complexity, and tolerance of diversity all but doom traditional values and family patterns, leaving individuals isolated, powerless, and materialistic. As Chapter 17

Many people marveled at the industrial technology that was changing the world a century ago. But some critics pointed out that the social consequences of the Industrial Revolution were not all positive. The painting Trabajadores *(*Workers*) by Mirta Cerra portrays the exhausting and mind-numbing routines of manual workers.*

Mirta Cerra (1904–1986), *Trabajadores,* oil on canvas laid down on panel, 46 × 62 in. (107.3 × 157.5 cm). © Christie's Images.

("Politics and Government") noted, voter apathy is a serious problem in the United States. But should we be surprised that individuals in vast, impersonal societies think no one person can make a difference?

Critics, however, contend that mass-society theory romanticizes the past. They remind us that many people in small towns were actually eager to set out for the excitement and higher standard of living found in cities. Moreover, mass-society theory ignores problems of social inequality. Critics say this theory attracts social and economic conservatives who defend conventional morality and are indifferent to the historical plight of women and other minorities.

SOCIAL-CONFLICT THEORY: MODERNITY AS CLASS SOCIETY

The second interpretation of modernity derives largely from the ideas of Karl Marx. From a social-conflict perspective, modernity takes the form of a **class society,** *a capitalist society with pronounced social stratification.* That is, while agreeing that modern societies have expanded to a mass scale, this approach views the heart of modernization as an expanding capitalist economy, rife with inequality (Miliband, 1969; Habermas, 1970; Polenberg, 1980; Blumberg, 1981; Harrington, 1984).

Capitalism

Class-society theory follows Marx in claiming that the increasing scale of social life in modern society results from the insatiable appetite of capitalism. Because a capitalist economy pursues ever-increasing profits, both production and consumption steadily increase.

According to Marx, capitalism rests on "naked self-interest" (Marx & Engels, 1972:337; orig. 1848). This self-centeredness erodes the social ties that once cemented small communities. Capitalism also treats people as commodities: a source of labor and a market for capitalist products.

Capitalism supports science, not just as the key to greater productivity but as an ideology that justifies the status quo. That is, modern societies encourage people to view human well-being as a *technical* puzzle to be solved by engineers and other experts rather than as a moral issue to be realized through the pursuit of *social* justice (Habermas, 1970). A capitalist culture, for example, focuses on improving health through advances in scientific medicine rather than by eliminating poverty, which threatens many people's health in the first place.

Business also raises the banner of scientific logic, trying to increase profits through greater efficiency. As Chapter 16 ("The Economy and Work") explains, today's

TABLE 24–2 Two Interpretations of Modernity: A Summary

	Process of Modernization	Effects of Modernization
Mass-Society Theory	Industrialization; growth of bureaucracy	Increasing scale of life; rise of the state and other formal organizations
Class-Society Theory	Rise of capitalism	Expansion of the capitalist economy; persistence of social inequality

capitalist corporations are enormous and control unimaginable wealth as a result of "going global" and becoming multinationals. From the class-society point of view, then, the expanding scale of life is less a function of *Gesellschaft* than the inevitable and destructive consequence of capitalism.

Persistent Inequality

Modernity has gradually worn away the rigid categories that set nobles apart from commoners in preindustrial societies. But class-society theory maintains that elites persist—albeit now as capitalist millionaires rather than nobles born to wealth and power. In the United States, we may have no hereditary monarchy, but the richest 5 percent of the population nevertheless controls half of all property.

What of the state? Mass-society theorists contend that the state works to increase equality and combat social problems. Marx was skeptical that the state could accomplish more than minor reforms because, as he saw it, the real power lies in the hands of capitalists who control the economy. Other class-society theorists add that, to the extent that working people and minorities do have greater political rights and enjoy a higher standard of living today, these changes are the fruits of political struggle, not expressions of government goodwill. In short, they conclude, despite our pretensions of democracy, most people are all but powerless in the face of wealthy elites.

Critical evaluation. Table 24–2 summarizes the interpretations of modernity offered by mass-society theory and class-society theory. While the former focuses on the increasing scale of life and the growth of government, the latter stresses the expansion of capitalism and the persistence of inequality.

Class-society theory also dismisses Durkheim's argument that people in modern societies suffer from anomie, claiming instead that they suffer from alienation and powerlessness. Not surprisingly, then, the class-society interpretation of modernity enjoys widespread support among liberals (and radicals) who favor greater equality and call for extensive regulation (or abolition) of the capitalist marketplace.

A basic criticism of class-society theory is that it overlooks the many ways that equality in modern societies has increased. For example, discrimination based on race, ethnicity, and gender is now illegal and widely regarded as a social problem. Further, most people in the United States favor unequal rewards, at least insofar as they reflect differences in personal talent and effort.

Moreover, few observers think a centralized economy would cure the ills of modernity in light of socialism's failure to generate a high overall standard of living. Many other problems in the United States—from unemployment, homelessness, and industrial pollution to unresponsive government—are also found in socialist nations such as the former Soviet Union.

MODERNITY AND THE INDIVIDUAL

Both mass- and class-society theories look at the broad societal changes that have taken place since the Industrial Revolution. But from these macro-level approaches we can also draw micro-level insights into how modernity shapes individual lives.

Mass Society: Problems of Identity

Modernity liberated individuals from small, tightly knit communities of the past. Most people in modern societies, therefore, possess privacy and freedom to express their individuality. Mass-society theory suggests, however, that extensive social diversity, isolation, and rapid social change make it difficult for people to establish any coherent identity at all (Wheelis, 1958; Riesman, 1970; Berger, Berger, & Kellner, 1974).

Chapter 5 ("Socialization") explained that people's personalities are largely a product of their social experiences. The small, homogeneous, and slowly changing societies of the past provided a firm (if narrow) foundation for building a meaningful identity. Even today, the Amish communities that flourish in the United States and Canada teach young men and women

Mass-society theory attributes feelings of anxiety, isolation, and lack of meaning in the modern world to rapid social change that washes away tradition. Edvard Munch captured this vision of modern emptiness in his painting The Scream *(left). Class-society theory, by contrast, ties such feelings to social inequality, by which some categories of people are made into second-class citizens (or not made citizens at all). Paul Marcus portrays modern injustice in the painting* Crossing the Rio Grande *(right).*

Edvard Munch, *The Scream*, Oslo, National Gallery. © Paul Marcus, *Crossing the Rio Grande*, 1999, oil painting on canvas, 63 × 72 in. Studio SPM Inc.

"correct" ways to think and behave. Not everyone born into an Amish community can tolerate strict demands for conformity, but most members establish a well-integrated and satisfying personal identity (cf. Hostetler, 1980; Kraybill & Olshan, 1994).

Mass societies, socially diverse and rapidly changing, offer only shifting sands on which to build a personal identity. Left to make many life decisions on our own, many people—especially those with greater affluence—face a bewildering range of options. Choice has little value without standards to guide our selections, and in a tolerant mass society, people may find one path no more compelling than the next. Not surprisingly, many people shuttle from one identity to another, changing their lifestyle, relationships, and even religion in search of an elusive "true self." Beset by the widespread "relativism" of modern societies, people without a moral compass lack the security and certainty once provided by tradition.

To David Riesman (1970; orig. 1950), modernization brings changes in **social character,** *personality patterns common to members of a particular society.* Preindustrial societies foster what Riesman calls **tradition-directedness,** *rigid conformity to time-honored ways of living.* Members of traditional societies model their lives on those of their ancestors, so that "living a good life" amounts to "doing what our people have always done."

Tradition-directedness corresponds to Tönnies's *Gemeinschaft* and Durkheim's mechanical solidarity. Culturally conservative, tradition-directed people think and act alike. Unlike the conformity sometimes found in modern societies, the uniformity of tradition-directedness is not an effort to mimic one another. Instead, people are alike because they all draw on the same solid cultural foundation. Amish women and men exemplify tradition-directedness; in Amish culture, tradition ties everyone to ancestors and descendants in an unbroken chain of righteous living.

Members of diverse and rapidly changing societies consider a tradition-directed personality deviant because it seems so rigid. Modern people, by and large, prize personal flexibility and sensitivity to others, what

GLOBAL SOCIOLOGY

Does "Modern" Mean "Progress"? The Case of Brazil's Kaiapo

The firelight flickers in the gathering darkness. Chief Kanhonk sits, as he has done at the end of the day for many years, ready to begin an evening of animated talk and storytelling (Simons, 2001). This is the hour when the Kaiapo, a small society in Brazil's lush Amazon region, celebrate their heritage. Because the Kaiapo are a traditional people with no written language, the elders rely on evenings by the fire to pass along their culture to their children and grandchildren. In the past, evenings like this have been filled with tales of brave Kaiapo warriors fighting off Portuguese traders in pursuit of slaves and gold.

But as the minutes pass, only a few older villagers assemble for the evening ritual. "It is the Big Ghost," one man grumbles, explaining the poor turnout. The "Big Ghost" has indeed descended upon them; its bluish glow spills from windows throughout the village. The Kaiapo children—and many adults as well—are watching sitcoms on television. The installation of a satellite dish in the village several years ago has had consequences far greater than anyone imagined. In the end, what their enemies failed to do with guns, the Kaiapo may well do to themselves with prime-time programming.

The Kaiapo are among the 230,000 native peoples who inhabit Brazil. They stand out because of their striking body paint and ornate ceremonial dress. During the 1980s, they became rich from gold mining and harvesting mahogany trees. Now they must decide if their newfound fortune is a blessing or a curse.

To some, affluence means the opportunity to learn about the outside world through travel and television. Others, like Chief Kanhonk, are not so sure. Sitting by the fire, he thinks aloud, "I have been saying that people must buy useful things like knives and fishing hooks. Television does not fill the stomach. It only shows our children and grandchildren white people's things." Bebtopup, the oldest priest, nods in agreement: "The night is the time the old people teach the young people. Television has stolen the night" (Simons, 2001:497).

The Kaiapo story shows us that change is not a simple path toward "progress." The Kaiapo are moving toward modernity, but this process will have both positive and negative consequences. On the one hand, they now enjoy a higher standard of living with better shelter, more clothing, and new technology like television to connect to the larger world. On the other hand, this new affluence has greatly weakened Kaiapo traditions, so that many of their number now wonder—and with good reason—who or what they have become. The drama of the Kaiapo is being played out around the world as more and more traditional cultures are being lured away from their heritage by the affluence and materialism of rich societies.

Source: Based on Simons (2001).

Riesman describes as **other-directedness,** *a receptiveness to the latest trends and fashions, often expressed by imitating others.* Because their socialization occurs in societies that are constantly in flux, other-directed people develop fluid identities marked by superficiality, inconsistency, and change. They try on different "selves," almost like so many pieces of new clothing, seek out "role models," and engage in varied "performances" as they move from setting to setting (Goffman, 1959). In a traditional society, such "shiftiness" makes a person untrustworthy, but in a changing, modern society, the chameleon-like ability to fit in virtually anywhere is very useful.

In societies that value the up-to-date rather than the traditional, people anxiously solicit the approval of others, looking to members of their own generation rather than to elders as significant role models. "Peer pressure" can be irresistible to people with no enduring standards to guide them. Our society urges individuals to be true to themselves. But when social surroundings change so rapidly, how can people develop the self to which they should be true? This problem lies at the root of the identity crisis so widespread in industrial societies today. "Who am I?" is a nagging question that many of us struggle to answer. In truth, this problem is not so much psychological as sociological, reflecting the inherent instability of modern mass society.

Class Society: Problems of Powerlessness

Class-society theory paints a different picture of modernity's effects on individuals. This approach maintains that persistent social inequality undermines modern society's promise of individual freedom. For some, modernity serves up great privilege, but for many, everyday life means coping with economic uncertainty and a gnawing sense of powerlessness (Newman, 1993).

For minorities, the problem of relative disadvantage looms even larger. Similarly, although women enjoy increasing participation in modern societies, they continue to run up against traditional barriers of sexism. In short, this approach rejects mass-society theory's claim that people suffer from too much freedom. Instead, class-society theory holds that our society still denies a majority of people full participation in social life.

On a global scale, as Chapter 12 ("Global Stratification") explained, the expanding scope of world capitalism has placed more of the earth's population in the shadow of multinational corporations. As a result, more than half of the world's income is concentrated in the rich, industrial nations, where only 15 percent of its people live. Is it any wonder, class-society theorists ask, that people in poor nations seek greater power to shape their own lives?

The problem of widespread powerlessness led Herbert Marcuse (1964) to challenge Max Weber's statement that modern society is rational. Marcuse condemned modern society as irrational for failing to meet the needs of so many of its people. While modern capitalist societies produce unparalleled wealth, poverty remains the daily plight of more than a billion people. Moreover, Marcuse argues, technological advances further reduce people's control over their own lives. High technology confers great power on a core of specialists—not the majority of people—who now control events and dominate the public agenda, whether the issue is computing, energy production, or health care. Countering the common view that technology *solves* the world's problems, Marcuse believed that science actually *causes* them. In sum, class-society theory claims that people suffer because modern, scientific societies concentrate both wealth and power in the hands of a privileged few.

MODERNITY AND PROGRESS

In modern societies, most people expect, and applaud, social change. We link modernity to the idea of *progress* (from Latin, meaning "moving forward"), a state of continual improvement. At the same time, we see stability as stagnation.

Given our bias in favor of change, members of our society tend to look upon traditional cultures as backward. But change, particularly toward material affluence, is a mixed blessing. As the box shows, social change is too complex to simply equate with progress.

Even getting rich has its advantages and disadvantages, as the case of the Kaiapo shows. Historically, among people in the United States, a rising standard of living made lives longer and, in a material sense, more comfortable. At the same time, many people wonder if today's routines are too stressful, with families often having little time for relaxation or simply spending time together.

Science, too, has its pluses and minuses. As Figure 24–1 on page 638 shows, people in the United States have considerable confidence—more than those in most other industrial societies—that science improves our lives. But surveys also show that many adults in the United States feel that science "makes our way of life change too fast" (NORC, 1999:356).

New technology has always sparked controversy. A century ago, the introduction of automobiles and telephones allowed more rapid transportation and more efficient communication. But, at the same time, such technology weakened people's traditional attachments to their hometowns and even to their families. Today, people might well wonder if computer technology will do the same thing: giving us access to people in distant parts of the world, but shielding us from the community right outside our doors; providing us with more information than ever before but, in the process, threatening our personal privacy. In short, we all realize that social change comes faster all the time, but we may disagree about whether a particular change is progress or a step backwards.

GLOBAL SNAPSHOT

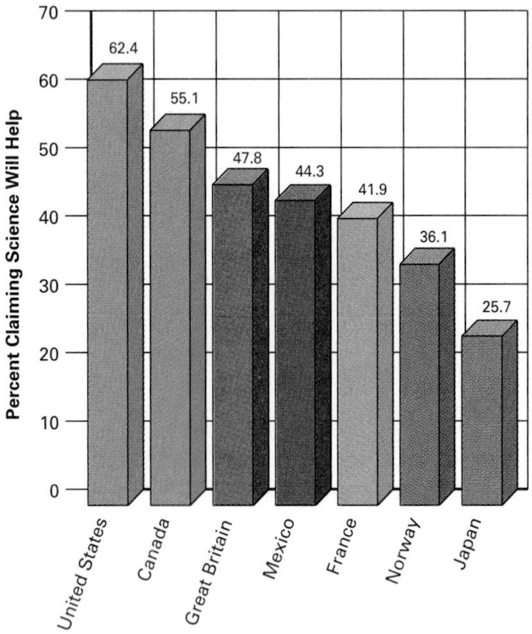

FIGURE 24–1 Support for Science: A Global Survey

Survey Question: "In the long run, do you think the scientific advances we are making will help or harm humankind?"

Source: *World Values Survey* (1994).

MODERNITY: GLOBAL VARIATION

October 1, 1994, Kobe, Japan. Riding the computer-controlled monorail high above the streets of Kobe or the 200-mile-per-hour bullet train to Tokyo, we see Japan as the society of the future, in love with high technology. Yet the Japanese remain strikingly traditional in other respects: Few corporate executives and almost no senior politicians are women; young people still accord their elders considerable respect; and public orderliness contrasts with the turmoil of U.S. cities.

Japan is a nation at once traditional and modern. This contradiction reminds us that, while it is useful to contrast traditional and modern societies, the old and the new often coexist in unexpected ways. In the People's Republic of China, ancient Confucian principles are mixed with contemporary socialist thinking. Similarly, in Mexico and much of Latin America, people observe centuries-old Christian rituals even as they struggle to move ahead economically. In short, combinations of traditional and modern are far from unusual—indeed, they are found throughout the world.

POSTMODERNITY

If modernity was the product of the Industrial Revolution, is the Information Revolution creating a postmodern era? A number of scholars think so, and use the term **postmodernity** to refer to *social patterns characteristic of postindustrial societies.*

Precisely what postmodernism is remains a matter of debate. The term has been used for decades in literary, philosophical, and even architectural circles. It moved into sociology on a wave of social criticism that has been building since the spread of left-leaning politics in the 1960s. Although there are many variants of postmodern thinking, all share the following five themes (Bernstein, 1992; Borgmann, 1992; Crook, Pakulski, & Waters, 1992; Hall & Neitz, 1993; Inglehart, 1997; Rudel & Gerson, 1999):

1. **In important respects, modernity has failed.** The promise of modernity was a life free from want. As postmodernist critics see it, however, the twentieth century was unsuccessful in solving social problems like poverty since many people still lack financial security.
2. **The bright light of "progress" is fading.** Modern people look to the future, expecting that their lives will improve in significant ways. Members (even leaders) of postmodern societies, however, are less confident about what the future holds. Furthermore, the buoyant optimism that carried society into the modern era more than a century ago has given way to stark pessimism; most U.S. adults think life is getting worse (NORC, 1999:204).
3. **Science no longer holds the answers.** The defining trait of the modern era was a scientific outlook and a confident belief that technology would make life better. But postmodern critics

contend that science has not solved many old problems (like poor health) and has even created new problems (such as degrading the environment).

More generally, postmodernist thinkers discredit science as a "metanarrative" that implies a singular truth. On the contrary, they maintain, objective reality and truth do not exist at all. Reality amounts to so much "social construction," they say; moreover, we can "deconstruct" science to see how it has been widely used for political purposes, especially by powerful segments of society.

4. **Cultural debates are intensifying.** Modernity was to be an era of enhanced individuality and expanding tolerance. But it has fallen short here as well. Feminism points out that patriarchy continues to limit the lives of women, and multiculturalism seeks to empower minorities who remain at the margins of social life.

   Moreover, now that more people have all the material things they really need, ideas are taking on more importance. Thus, postmodernity is also a postmaterialist era, in which issues like social justice, as well as the environment and animal rights, command more and more public attention.

5. **Social institutions are changing.** Just as industrialization brought sweeping transformation to social institutions, the rise of a postindustrial society is remaking society all over again. For example, just as the Industrial Revolution placed *material things* at the center of productive life, now the Information Revolution emphasizes *ideas.* Similarly, the postmodern family no longer conforms to any singular pattern; on the contrary, individuals are choosing among many new family forms.

Critical evaluation. Analysts who claim that the United States and other high-income societies are entering a postmodern era criticize modernity for failing to meet human needs. Yet few think that modernity has failed completely; after all, we have seen marked increases in longevity and living standards over the course of this century. Moreover, even if we accept postmodernist views that science is bankrupt and progress is a sham, what are the alternatives?

Finally, many voices offer very different understandings of recent social trends. The box on pages 640–41 provides one case in point.

We tend to view tradition and modernity as opposites—the more of one found in a society, the less there is of the other. In reality, these concepts can operate independently, as we see in Japan, where traditional and modern aspects of life are often seen side by side.

LOOKING AHEAD: MODERNIZATION AND OUR GLOBAL FUTURE

Back in Chapter 1, we imagined the entire world reduced to a village of 1,000 people. About 175 residents of this "global village" come from high-income countries. At the same time, 200 people are so poor that they are at risk for their lives.

The tragic plight of the world's poor shows that some desperately needed change has not yet occurred. Chapter 12 ("Global Stratification") presented two competing views of why 1 billion people around the world are poor. *Modernization theory* claims that in the past the entire world was poor and that technological change, especially the Industrial Revolution, enhanced human productivity and raised living standards in some

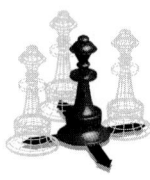

CRITICAL THINKING

Tracking Change: Is Life in the United States Getting Better or Worse?

We began this chapter with a look at what life was like in 1900, more than a century ago. It is easy to see that in many ways life is far better for us than it was for our grandparents and great-grandparents. But especially in recent decades, the indicators are not so clear-cut: Life may be improving in some ways, but in other respects, it is getting worse. Here is a look at some trends shaping the United States since 1970.

First, the good news: By some measures—shown in the first set of figures—life in this country is clearly improving. Infant mortality has fallen steadily, meaning that fewer and fewer children die soon after birth. Moreover, more people are reaching old age, and they are living longer than ever. More good news: The poverty rate among the elderly is well below what it was in 1970. Schooling is another area of improvement: The share of people dropping out of high school is down, while the share completing college is up compared to a generation ago.

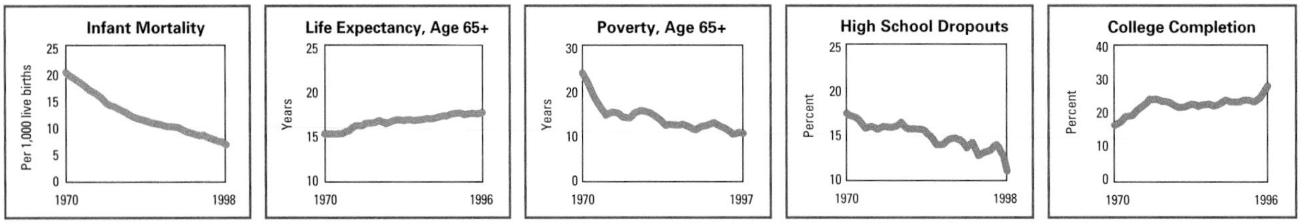

Second, some no-news results: A number of indicators show that life is about the same as it was in 1970. Teenage drug use, for example, was about the same in 1996 as a generation before. Likewise, alcohol-related traffic deaths show only a slight decline. Unemployment has had its ups and downs, but the overall level has stayed about the same. Finally, there was about the same amount of affordable housing in the United States in 1996 as in 1970.

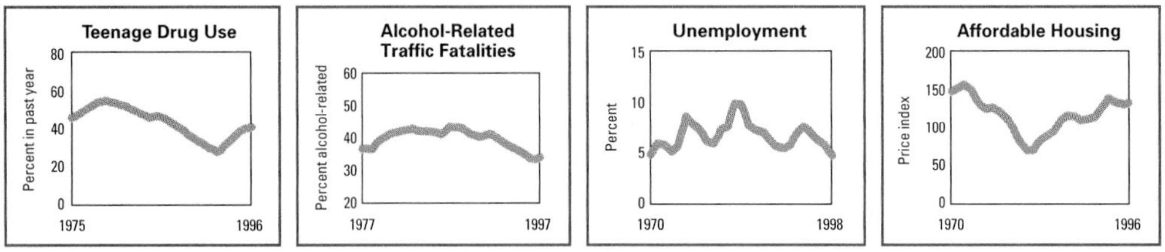

nations. From this point of view, the solution to global poverty is to promote technological development around the world.

For reasons suggested earlier, however, global modernization may be difficult to achieve. Recall that David Riesman portrayed preindustrial people as *tradition-directed* and therefore likely to resist change. So modernization theorists advocate that the world's rich societies help poor countries grow economically. Specifically, industrial nations should export modern technology to poor regions, welcome students from these countries, and provide foreign aid to stimulate economic growth.

The discussion of modernization theory in Chapter 12 points to some success with policies in Latin America, and greater success in the small Asian countries of Taiwan, South Korea, Singapore, and Hong Kong. But jump-starting development in the poorest countries of the world poses greater challenges. And even where dramatic change has occurred, modernization

Third, the bad news: By some measures—several having to do with children—the quality of life in the United States has actually fallen. The official rate of child abuse is up, as are the level of child poverty and the rate of suicide among youths. Although the level of violent crime fell through most of the 1990s, it remains above the level in 1970. Average hourly wages—one measure of economic security—shows a downward trend, so that families have had to rely on two or more earners to maintain family income. The number of people without health insurance is also on the rise. Finally, economic inequality in this country has been increasing.

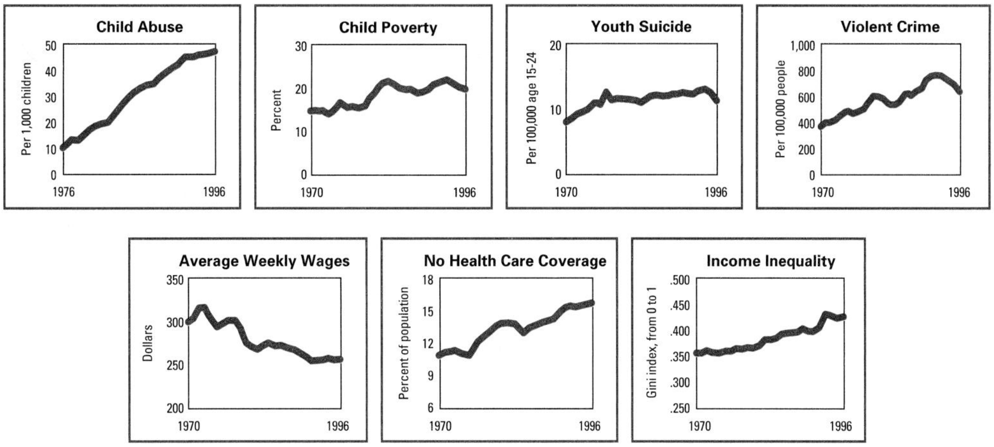

Overall, then, the evidence does not support any simple ideas about "progress over time." Social change has been—and probably will continue to be—a complex process that reflects the kinds of priorities we set for this nation as well as our will to achieve them.

What do you think?

1. *Based on material from earlier chapters, can you explain any of the trends shown here? Which ones?*
2. *Which of the trends do you find most important? Why?*
3. *On balance, do you think the quality of life in the United States is improving or not? Why?*

Source: Miringoff & Miringoff (1999).

entails a tradeoff. Traditional people, such as Brazil's Kaiapo, may acquire wealth through economic development, but they lose their cultural identity and values as they are drawn into global "McCulture," which is based on Western materialism, pop music, trendy clothes, and fast food. One Brazilian anthropologist expressed hope about the future of the Kaiapo: "At least they quickly understood the consequences of watching television. . . . Now [they] can make a choice" (Simons, 2001:497).

But not everyone thinks that modernization is really an option. According to a second approach to global stratification, *dependency theory*, today's poor societies have little ability to modernize, even if they want to. From this point of view, the major barrier to economic development is not traditionalism but the global domination of rich, capitalist societies. Initially, domination took the form of colonialism whereby European societies seized much of Latin America, Africa, and Asia. Trading relationships soon enriched

CONTROVERSY & DEBATE

Personal Freedom and Social Responsibility: Can We Have It Both Ways?

Shortly after midnight on a crisp March evening in 1964, a car pulled to a stop in the parking lot of a New York apartment complex. Kitty Genovese turned off the headlights, locked the doors of her vehicle, and headed across the blacktop toward the entrance to her building. Moments from safety, she was attacked by a man wielding a knife; as she shrieked in terror, he stabbed her repeatedly. Windows opened above, as curious neighbors searched for the cause of the commotion. But the attack continued—for more than thirty minutes—until Genovese lay dead in the doorway. The police never identified her assailant, but they did discover a stunning fact: *Not one of dozens of neighbors who witnessed the attack on Kitty Genovese went to her aid or even called police.*

More than any other event in recent decades, the Genovese tragedy forced people to confront the question of what we owe others. Members of modern societies prize their individual rights and personal privacy, sometimes to the point of withdrawing from public responsibility and turning a cold shoulder to people in need. When a cry for help is met with indifference, have we pushed our modern idea of personal autonomy too far? In a cultural climate of expanding individual rights, can we keep a sense of human community?

These questions point up the tension between traditional and modern social systems, which we can see in the writings of all the sociologists discussed in this chapter. Tönnies, Durkheim, and others concluded that, in some respects, traditional community and modern individualism are incompatible. That is, society can unite its members in a moral community but only to the extent that it limits their range of personal choices about how to live. In short, while we value both community and autonomy, we can't have it both ways.

In recent years, sociologist Amitai Etzioni (1993, 1996) has tried to strike a middle ground. The *communitarian movement* rests on the simple premise that "strong rights presume strong responsibilities." Or, put another way, an individual's pursuit of self-interest must be balanced by a commitment to the larger community.

As Etzioni sees it, modern people have become too concerned with individual rights. That is, people expect the system to work for them, but they are reluctant to support the system. For example, while we believe in the principle of trial by a jury of one's peers, fewer and fewer people today are willing to perform jury duty; similarly, the public is quick to accept government services but reluctant to pay for these services with taxes.

Specifically, the communitarians advance four proposals to balance individual rights and public responsibilities. First, our society should halt the expanding "culture of rights" by which people put their own interests ahead of social responsibility (after all, nothing in the Constitution allows us to do whatever we want to). Second, communitarians remind us, all rights involve responsibilities (we cannot simply take from society without giving something back).

England, Spain, and other colonial powers, and their colonies became poorer and poorer. Almost all societies that were colonized are now politically independent, but colonial-style ties continue in the form of multinational corporations operating throughout the world.

In effect, dependency theory asserts that rich nations achieved their modernization at the expense of poor ones, plundering poor nations' natural resources and exploiting their human labor. Even today, the world's poorest countries remain locked in a disadvantageous economic relationship with rich nations, dependent on wealthy countries to buy their raw materials and in return provide them with whatever manufactured products they can afford. Overall, dependency theorists conclude, ties with rich societies only perpetuate current patterns of global inequality.

Whichever approach one finds more convincing, we can no longer isolate change in the United States from change that is occurring in the rest of the world.

Third, there are certain responsibilities that no one is free to ignore (such as upholding the law and protecting the natural environment). And, fourth, defending some community interests may require limiting individual rights (protecting public safety, for example, might mean subjecting workers to drug tests).

The communitarian movement appeals to many people who, along with Etzioni, seek to balance personal freedom with social responsibility. But critics have attacked this initiative from both sides of the political spectrum. To those on the left, problems such as voter apathy and street crime cannot be solved with some vague notion of "social reintegration." Instead, we need expanded government programs to ensure equality in U.S. society. Specifically, these critics say, we must curb the political influence of the rich and actively combat racism and sexism.

Conservatives on the political right also find fault with Etzioni's proposals, but for different reasons (cf. Pearson, 1995). To these critics, the communitarian movement amounts to little more than a rerun of the 1960s leftist agenda. That is, the communitarian vision of a good society favors liberal goals (such as protecting the environment) but ignores conservative goals such as allowing prayer in school or restoring the strength of traditional families. Moreover, conservatives ask whether a free society should permit the kind of social engineering that Etzioni advocates to build social responsibility (such as institutionalizing antiprejudice programs in schools and requiring people to perform a year of national service).

In a society that stresses individualism and self-interest, how can we encourage people to think of the common good? At his presidential inauguration, John F. Kennedy put it this way, "Ask not what your country can do for you; ask what you can do for your country."

Perhaps, as Etzioni himself has suggested, the fact that both the left and the right find fault with his views shows that he has found a moderate, sensible answer to a serious problem. But it may also be that, in a society as diverse as the United States, people will not readily agree on what they owe to themselves—or each other.

Continue the debate . . .

1. *Have you ever failed to come to the aid of someone in need or danger? Why?*
2. *President Kennedy admonished us to "Ask not what your country can do for you, ask what you can do for your country." Do you think people today support this idea? What makes you think so?*
3. *Do you agree or disagree that our society needs to balance rights with more responsibility? Explain your position.*

At the beginning of the twentieth century, most people in today's high-income countries lived in relatively small settlements with limited awareness of events and trends in the larger world. Now, early in the twenty-first century, the entire world has become one huge village because the lives of all people are increasingly linked.

The twentieth century witnessed unprecedented human achievement. Yet solutions to many problems of human existence—including finding meaning in life, resolving conflicts between nations, and eradicating poverty—have eluded us. To this list of pressing matters new concerns have been added, such as controlling population growth and establishing a sustainable society by living in harmony with the natural environment. In the next hundred years, we must be prepared to tackle such problems with imagination, compassion, and determination. Our unprecedented understanding of human society gives us reason to look to the task ahead with optimism.

SUMMARY

1. Every society changes continuously, although at varying speeds. Social change often generates controversy.
2. Social change results from invention, discovery, and diffusion, as well as social conflict.
3. Modernity refers to the social consequences of industrialization, which, according to Peter Berger, include the erosion of traditional communities, expanding personal choice, increasingly diverse beliefs, and a keen awareness of the future.
4. Ferdinand Tönnies described modernization as the transition from *Gemeinschaft* to *Gesellschaft*, which signifies the progressive loss of community amid growing individualism.
5. Emile Durkheim saw modernization as a function of a society's expanding division of labor. Mechanical solidarity, based on shared activities and beliefs, gradually gives way to organic solidarity, in which specialization makes people interdependent.
6. According to Max Weber, modernity replaces tradition with a rational world view. Weber feared the dehumanizing effects of rational organization.
7. Karl Marx saw modernity as the triumph of capitalism over feudalism. Viewing capitalist societies as fraught with social conflict, Marx advocated revolutionary change to achieve a more egalitarian, socialist society.
8. According to mass-society theory, modernity increases the scale of life, enlarging the role of government and other formal organizations in carrying out tasks previously performed by family members and neighbors. Cultural diversity and rapid social change make it difficult for people in modern societies to develop stable identities and to find meaning in their lives.
9. Class-society theory states that capitalism is central to Western modernization. This approach charges that, by concentrating wealth in the hands of a few, capitalism generates widespread feelings of powerlessness.
10. Social change is too complex and controversial simply to be equated with social progress.
11. Postmodernity refers to cultural traits of postindustrial societies. Postmodern criticism of society centers on the failure of modernity, and specifically science, to fulfill its promise of prosperity and well-being.
12. In a global context, modernization theory links global poverty to the power of tradition. Therefore, some modernization theorists advocate that rich societies intervene to stimulate economic development in poor nations.
13. Dependency theory explains global poverty as the product of the world economic system. The operation of multinational corporations ensures that poor nations will remain economically dependent on rich nations.

KEY CONCEPTS

social change (p. 624) the transformation of culture and social institutions over time

modernity (p. 626) social patterns resulting from industrialization

modernization (p. 626) the process of social change begun by industrialization

mass society (p. 632) a society in which industry and bureaucracy have eroded traditional social ties

class society (p. 633) a capitalist society with pronounced social stratification

social character (p. 635) personality patterns common to members of a particular society

tradition-directedness (p. 635) rigid conformity to time-honored ways of living

other-directedness (p. 636) a receptiveness to the latest trends and fashions, often expressed by imitating others

postmodernity (p. 638) social patterns characteristic of postindustrial societies

CRITICAL-THINKING QUESTIONS

1. How well do you think Tönnies, Durkheim, Weber, and Marx predicted the character of modern society? How are their visions of modernity the same? How do they differ?
2. What traits lead some to call the United States a "mass society"? Why do other analysts describe the United States as a "class society"?
3. What is the difference between *anomie* (a trait of mass society) and *alienation* (a characteristic of class society)? Among which categories of the U.S. population would you expect each to be pronounced?
4. Why do some analysts call the United States a postmodern society? Do you agree?

APPLICATIONS AND EXERCISES

1. Do you have an elderly relative or friend? Most older people will be happy to tell you about the social changes they have seen in their lifetimes.
2. Ask people in your class or friendship group to make five predictions about U.S. society in the year 2050, when today's twenty-year-olds will be senior citizens. Compare notes. On what issues is there agreement?
3. Has the rate of social change been increasing? Do some research about inventions over time and see for yourself. Consider, for example, modes of travel, including walking, riding animals, trains, cars, airplanes, and rockets in space. The first two characterized society for tens of thousands of years; the last four emerged in barely two centuries.
4. Install the CD-ROM packaged in the back of this new textbook to access a variety of study, review, and applications exercises designed to help you better understand the material covered in this chapter. The CD includes an author's tip video, as well as interactive maps, video application exercises, Web links, and study questions.

SITES TO SEE

http://www.prenhall.com/macionis
Visit the interactive Web site that accompanies this text. Begin by clicking on the cover of your book. You will find a chapter-by-chapter study guide, practice tests, chat room, and many suggested Web links.

http://www.gwu.edu/~ccps/
This Web site describes the Communitarian Network, including its goals and how it proposes to achieve them.

http://www.utoronto.ca/utopia/
Deliberate change is sometimes inspired by visions of utopia—ideal societies that exist nowhere. Read about the Society for Utopian Studies at this Web site.

http://www.thesociologypage.com
(or **http://www.macionis.com**)
Finally, on a personal note, I hope this book has helped you and will be a useful resource for courses you take later on. Please visit my Web page, and send an e-mail message (macionis@kenyon.edu) with your thoughts and suggestions. And, yes, I *will* write back!

—*John J. Macionis*

PART V
NEW INFORMATION TECHNOLOGY AND SOCIAL CHANGE

Chapter 3 ("Culture") presented William Ogburn's (1964) concept of *cultural lag*, the pattern by which some elements of culture change faster than others. Usually, Ogburn explained, technology changes quickly; getting used to new technology, on the other hand, takes people much longer. This cultural pattern of "lagging behind" probably explains why we use old terminology to describe new developments, such as measuring the "horsepower" of gasoline engines or, more recently, exploring the "superhighway" of cyberspace.

The fact that developments in science and technology outpace our ability to comprehend them makes many people uneasy about social change. In a national survey, about 40 percent of U.S. adults agreed with the statement: "One trouble with science is that it makes our way of life change too fast" (NORC, 1999:356). But the majority of people are more optimistic, expecting that new technology will improve our lives. This final cyber.scope highlights how the age of computers is altering the shape of cities, forming new kinds of human communities, and bringing people together in new ways to form social movements.

The New Shape of Cities

The metropolis, as Chapter 22 ("Population, Urbanization, and Environment") explains, stands as the greatest monument to the industrial era. A century ago, factories full of huge machines offered jobs that drew people from across the countryside to form cities of unprecedented size. Industrial metropolises such as New York, Chicago, Philadelphia, and Detroit churned with activity, and new buildings of glass, mortar, and steel stretched skyward.

Cities became busier and denser as industrial technology centralized people. Businesses fused into a "central business district," where executives and managers could easily establish face-to-face communication. Factories, too, stood together near rivers and railroads, which brought them fuel and raw materials and took away their finished products.

The industrial cities of the United States reached their peak populations about 1950, just as scientists were building the first computers. Computer technology helped push the economy from industry to service and information work, and this shift spurred the decentralization of cities. Population began radiating farther from the central city so that, by 1970, most city dwellers were actually living in suburbs miles away. Businesses followed suit, deserting the downtowns for industrial parks and outlying shopping malls. Today's urban sprawl is the result.

Why have the old central cities lost much of their attraction? One reason is that, in the business world, having a central city address is no longer so important. That is, with new information technology, people can communicate efficiently without working in the same area. Thus, today's cities are growing "out" more than they are growing "up." The urban scene at the beginning of the twenty-first century shows steady central-city populations surrounded by swelling suburbs and rapidly growing "edge cities"—clusters of office buildings, shopping malls, hotels, and entertainment complexes miles from the old "downtowns."

Change in the shape of cities highlights the fact that physical distance no longer separates people the way it used to. Thus people who work together do not need to share an office building or even live in the same city. The other side of the same coin is that, in the cyber age, we may not pay very much attention to the people who are—physically speaking—all around us. In short, new information technology is forming new kinds of human communities and eroding older ones.

The Rise of Virtual Communities

Consider some dramatic changes taking place at Dartmouth College, in Hanover, New Hampshire, one of the country's most academically competitive schools and a college at the forefront of the Information Revolution. Since wiring all dormitories—sometimes called the "one plug per pillow" model—life on campus has not been the same. In the cyber age, students such as Arthur Desrosiers have discovered that they have fewer and fewer reasons to leave their rooms. Desrosiers, a sophomore, relies on his computer to browse the college library, write papers, ask questions of his professors, send notes to his girlfriend, keep up with old high school friends, and even order pizza while joining in 2:00 A.M. online bull sessions. Perhaps strangest of all, Desrosiers often fires messages back and forth to his two roommates, even though they are silently staring at screens of their own just a few feet away in the same room.

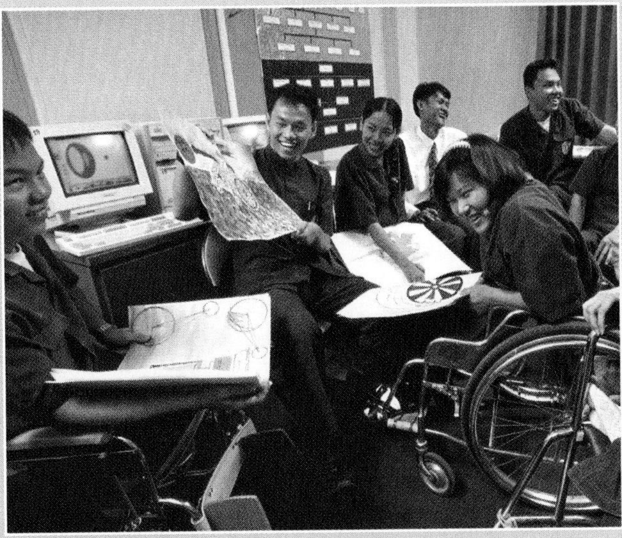

With access to the Internet, these Thai students have joined an international social movement to advance the opportunities of people with disabilities.

It may be a sign of the times that a once-popular restaurant just down the street from dorms that house 3,000 students has closed its doors. Similarly, the student union is far less busy that it was just a few years ago. There, some of the space once used for socializing now accommodates—you guessed it—computer terminals for students who want to check their e-mail between classes.

At Dartmouth, computers have never been more popular. All together, the 8,000 students, faculty, and staff send and receive some 250,000 messages each day. No one doubts that new information technology has expanded the possibilities for accessing more information than ever before and contacting people almost anywhere in the world. But some people are beginning to see that an older form of local community is being lost in the process. Some faculty worry that they see less and less of their students. Some students, too, are beginning to think that they ought to see more of each other. As senior Abigail Butler puts it, "I know people who sit home Friday and Saturday night and e-mail back and forth to people they only know by nicknames, while the rest of the world is going by. After a while it starts to be really unfulfilling. It's easier to just meet someone in person and actually talk" (Gabriel, 1996).

Social Movements: New Ways to Connect

New ways to connect with people means a rising potential for starting and expanding social movements. Today, anyone with an interest in some issue and a computer can make contact, ask questions, and spread ideas—in short, play a role in intentional social change. In addition, computers offer access to the Web pages of countless organizations and individuals with programs for change.

Perhaps most important, computer technology has made it easy to make connections on a global scale. Take the students at the Redemptorist Vocational School in Pattaya, Thailand. These young men and women have physical disabilities, which, before the information age, might have kept them from learning at all. But using their school's computers, the students have established contact with hundreds of other people with disabilities in dozens of countries, including the United States. From these contacts, and from visiting the Web sites of national and international organizations representing people with disabilities, the students have received a rich education indeed. They have been surprised to learn that many countries have laws that protect people with disabilities from discrimination and that mandate access ramps for sidewalks and buildings; they have discovered that cities abroad feature buses that "kneel" to permit entry by people in wheelchairs, as well as public rest rooms designed to accommodate everyone. Armed with their new knowledge, the students at the Redemptorist Vocational School are now taking the lead in their own country, using the Internet to educate people about disabilities and lobbying government officials to make changes in Thailand's laws.

The Internet represents a powerful communication resource for anyone. But it is especially important for people whose ability to make contact with others is otherwise limited, including people with disabilities. As one Thai student reports, "On the Net, I don't feel like a handicapped person" (Smolan & Erwitt, 1996:150). Even though computer access is far from equal around the world, the Internet is providing more and more people in poor countries with the power of a "global reach."

GLOSSARY

abortion the deliberate termination of a pregnancy

absolute poverty a deprivation of resources that is life-threatening

achieved status a social position a person assumes voluntarily and that reflects personal ability and effort

acid rain precipitation, made acidic by air pollution, that destroys plant and animal life

activity theory the idea that a high level of activity enhances personal satisfaction in old age

Afrocentrism the dominance of African cultural patterns

ageism prejudice and discrimination against the elderly

age-sex pyramid a graphic representation of the age and sex of a population

age stratification the unequal distribution of wealth, power, and privilege among people at different stages of the life course

agriculture large-scale cultivation using plows harnessed to animals or more powerful energy sources

alienation the experience of isolation and misery resulting from powerlessness

animism the belief that elements of the natural world are conscious life forms that affect humanity

anomie Durkheim's designation of a condition in which society provides little moral guidance to individuals

anticipatory socialization learning that helps a person achieve a desired position

ascribed status a social position a person receives at birth or assumes involuntarily later in life

asexuality a sexual orientation in which a person is not sexually attracted to people of either sex

assimilation the process by which minorities gradually adopt patterns of the dominant culture

authoritarianism a political system that denies popular participation in government

authority power that people perceive as legitimate rather than coercive

beliefs specific statements that people hold to be true

bilateral descent a system tracing kinship through both men and women

bisexuality a sexual orientation in which a person is sexually attracted to people of both sexes

blue-collar occupations lower-prestige work that involves mostly manual labor

bureaucracy an organizational model rationally designed to perform tasks efficiently

bureaucratic inertia the tendency of bureaucratic organizations to perpetuate themselves

bureaucratic ritualism a preoccupation with rules and regulations to the point of thwarting an organization's goals

capitalism an economic system in which natural resources and the means of producing goods and services are privately owned

capitalists people who own and operate factories and other businesses in pursuit of profits

caregiving informal and unpaid care provided to a dependent person by family members, other relatives, or friends

caste system social stratification based on ascription

cause and effect a relationship in which change in one variable (the independent variable) causes change in another (the dependent variable)

charisma extraordinary personal qualities that can turn an audience into followers

charismatic authority power legitimized through extraordinary personal abilities that inspire devotion and obedience

church a type of religious organization well integrated into the larger society

civil religion a quasi-religious loyalty based on citizenship

class conflict conflict between entire classes over the distribution of a society's wealth and power

class consciousness Marx's term for workers' recognition of themselves as a class united in opposition to capitalists and, ultimately, to capitalism itself

class society a capitalist society with pronounced social stratification

class system social stratification based on both birth and individual achievement

cohabitation the sharing of a household by an unmarried couple

cohort a category of people who share some trait, usually their age

collective behavior activity involving a large number of people, often spontaneous and sometimes controversial

collectivity a large number of people whose minimal interaction occurs in the absence of well-defined and conventional norms

colonialism the process by which some nations enrich themselves through political and economic control of other nations

communism a hypothetical economic and political system in which all members of a society are socially equal

concept a mental construct that represents some part of the world, inevitably in a simplified form

concrete operational stage Piaget's term for the level of human development at which individuals first perceive causal connections in their surroundings

conglomerate a giant corporation composed of many smaller corporations

control holding constant all variables except one in order to see clearly the effect of that variable

corporate crime the illegal actions of a corporation or people acting on its behalf

corporation an organization with a legal existence, including rights and liabilities, apart from those of its members

correlation a relationship by which two (or more) variables change together

counterculture cultural patterns that strongly oppose those widely accepted within a society

credentialism evaluating a person on the basis of educational degrees

crime the violation of society's formally enacted criminal law

crimes against the person (violent crimes) crimes that direct violence or the threat of violence against others

crimes against property (property crimes) crimes that involve theft of property belonging to others

criminal justice system a formal response by police, courts, and prison officials to alleged violations of the law

criminal recidivism subsequent offenses by people previously convicted of crimes

critical sociology the study of society that focuses on the need for social change

crowd a temporary gathering of people who share a common focus of attention and who influence one another

crude birth rate the number of live births in a given year for every thousand people in a population

crude death rate the number of deaths in a given year for every thousand people in a population

cult a religious organization that is largely outside a society's cultural traditions

cultural conflict political differences, often expressed with hostility, based on disagreement over cultural values

cultural ecology a theoretical paradigm that explores the relationship of human culture and the natural environment

cultural integration the close relationship among various elements of a cultural system

cultural lag the fact that some cultural elements change more quickly than others, which may disrupt a cultural system

cultural relativism the practice of evaluating a culture by its own standards

cultural transmission the process by which one generation passes culture to the next

cultural universals traits that are part of every known culture

culture the values, beliefs, behavior, and material objects that, together, form a people's way of life

culture shock personal disorientation when experiencing an unfamiliar way of life

Davis-Moore thesis the assertion that social stratification is a universal pattern because it benefits the operation of a society

deductive logical thought reasoning that transforms general theory into specific hypotheses suitable for testing

democracy a type of political system in which power is exercised by the people as a whole

demographic transition theory the thesis that population patterns reflect a society's level of technological development

demography the study of human population

denomination a church, independent of the state, that accepts religious pluralism

dependency theory a model of economic development that explains global inequality in terms of the historical exploitation of poor societies by rich ones

dependent variable a variable that is changed by another (independent) variable

descent the system by which members of a society trace kinship over generations

deterrence the attempt to discourage criminality through punishment

deviance the recognized violation of cultural norms

direct-fee system a medical care system in which patients pay directly for the services of physicians and hospitals

discrimination any action that involves treating various categories of people unequally

disengagement theory the idea that society enhances its orderly operation by disengaging people from positions of responsibility as they reach old age

division of labor specialized economic activity

dramaturgical analysis Erving Goffman's term for the study of social interaction in terms of theatrical performance

dyad a social group with two members

dysfunction (*see* **social dysfunction**)

eating disorder an intense form of dieting or other unhealthy method of weight control driven by the desire to be very thin

ecologically sustainable culture a way of life that meets the needs of the present generation without threatening the environmental legacy of future generations

ecology the study of the interaction of living organisms and the natural environment

economy the social institution that organizes a society's production, distribution, and consumption of goods and services

ecosystem a system composed of the interaction of all living organisms and their natural environment

education the social institution through which society provides its members with important knowledge, including basic facts, job skills, and cultural norms and values

ego Freud's designation for a person's conscious efforts to balance innate pleasure-seeking drives with the demands of society

empirical evidence information we can verify with our senses

endogamy marriage between people of the same social category

environmental deficit profound and long-term harm to the natural environment caused by humanity's focus on short-term material affluence

environmental racism the pattern by which environmental hazards are greatest for poor people, especially minorities

ethnicity a shared cultural heritage

ethnocentrism the practice of judging another culture by the standards of one's own culture

ethnomethodology Harold Garfinkel's term for the study of the way people make sense of their everyday surroundings

Eurocentrism the dominance of European (especially English) cultural patterns

euthanasia (mercy killing) assisting in the death of a person suffering from an incurable disease

exogamy marriage between people of different social categories

experiment a research method for investigating cause and effect under highly controlled conditions

expressive leadership group direction that focuses on collective well-being

extended family (consanguine family) a family unit that includes parents and children, as well as other kin

fad an unconventional social pattern that people embrace briefly but enthusiastically

faith belief anchored in conviction rather than scientific evidence

false consciousness Marx's term for explanations of social problems as the shortcomings of individuals rather than the flaws of society

family a social institution found in all societies that unites people into cooperative groups to oversee the bearing and raising of children

family unit a social group of two or more people, related by blood, marriage, or adoption, who usually live together

family violence emotional, physical, or sexual abuse of one family member by another

fashion a social pattern favored by a large number of people

feminism the advocacy of social equality for men and women, in opposition to patriarchy and sexism

feminization of poverty the trend by which women represent an increasing proportion of the poor

fertility the incidence of childbearing in a country's population

folkways norms for routine, casual interaction

formal operational stage Piaget's term for the level of human development at which individuals think abstractly and critically

formal organization a large secondary group organized to achieve its goals efficiently

functional illiteracy a lack of reading and writing skills needed for everyday living

fundamentalism a conservative religious doctrine that opposes intellectualism and worldly accommodation in favor of restoring traditional, otherworldly spirituality

Gemeinschaft a type of social organization by which people are closely tied by kinship and tradition

gender the personal traits and social positions that members of a society attach to being female and male

gender roles (sex roles) attitudes and activities that a society links to each sex

gender stratification the unequal distribution of wealth, power, and privilege between men and women

generalized other George Herbert Mead's term for widespread cultural norms and values we use as a reference in evaluating ourselves

genocide the systematic annihilation of one category of people by another

gerontocracy a form of social organization in which the elderly have the most wealth, power, and prestige

gerontology the study of aging and the elderly

Gesellschaft a type of social organization by which people come together only on the basis of individual self-interest

global economy expanding economic activity with little regard for national borders

global perspective the study of the larger world and our society's place in it

gossip rumor about people's personal affairs

government a formal organization that directs the political life of a society

greenhouse effect a rise in the earth's average temperature (global warming) due to an increasing concentration of carbon dioxide in the atmosphere

groupthink the tendency of group members to conform, resulting in a narrow view of some issue

hate crime a criminal act against a person or person's property by an offender motivated by racial or other bias

Hawthorne effect a change in a subject's behavior caused simply by the awareness of being studied

health a state of complete physical, mental, and social well-being

health maintenance organization (HMO) an organization that provides comprehensive medical care to subscribers for a fixed fee

hermaphrodite a human being with some combination of female and male genitalia

heterosexism a view stigmatizing anyone who is not heterosexual as "queer"

heterosexuality a sexual orientation in which a person is sexually attracted to someone of the other sex

hidden curriculum subtle presentations of political or cultural ideas in the classroom

high culture cultural patterns that distinguish a society's elite

high-income countries industrialized nations in which most people have relatively high incomes

holistic medicine an approach to health care that emphasizes prevention of illness and takes into account the person's entire physical and social environment

homogamy marriage between people with the same social characteristics

homophobia the dread of close personal interaction with people thought to be gay, lesbian, or bisexual

homosexuality a sexual orientation in which a person is sexually attracted to someone of the same sex

horticulture the use of hand tools to raise crops

hunting and gathering the use of simple tools to hunt animals and gather vegetation

hypothesis an unverified statement of a relationship between variables

id Freud's designation for the human being's basic drives

ideal type an abstract statement of the essential characteristics of any social phenomenon

ideology cultural beliefs that justify social stratification

incest taboo a cultural norm forbidding sexual relations or marriage between certain relatives

income wages or salary from work and earnings from investments

independent variable a variable that causes change in another (dependent) variable

inductive logical thought reasoning that transforms specific observations into general theory

industrialism the production of goods using advanced sources of energy to drive large machinery

infant mortality rate the number of deaths among infants under one year of age for each thousand live births in a given year

ingroup a social group commanding a member's esteem and loyalty

institutional prejudice and discrimination bias inherent in the operation of society's institutions

instrumental leadership group direction that emphasizes the completion of tasks

intergenerational social mobility upward or downward social mobililty of children in relation to their parents

interpretive sociology the study of society that focuses on the meanings people attach to their social world

interview a series of questions a researcher administers in person to respondents

intragenerational social mobility a change in social position occurring during a person's lifetime

kinship a social bond based on blood, marriage, or adoption

labeling theory the idea that deviance and conformity result not only from what people do but from how others respond to those actions

labor unions organizations of workers that seek to improve wages and working conditions through various strategies, including negotiations and strikes

language a system of symbols that allows people to communicate with one another

latent functions the unrecognized and unintended consequences of any social pattern

liberation theology a fusion of Christian principles with political activism, often Marxist in character

life expectancy the average life span of a country's population

looking-glass self Cooley's term for a self-image based on how we think others see us

low-income countries nations with little industrialization in which most people are poor

macro-level orientation a broad focus on social structures that shape society as a whole

mainstreaming integrating special students into the overall educational program

manifest functions the recognized and intended consequences of any social pattern

marriage a legally sanctioned relationship, usually involving economic cooperation as well as sexual activity and childbearing, that people expect to be enduring

Marxist political-economy model an analysis that explains politics in terms of the operation of a society's economic system

mass behavior collective behavior among people dispersed over a wide geographical area

mass hysteria a form of dispersed collective behavior by which people react to a real or imagined event with irrational, frantic, and often self-destructive behavior

mass media impersonal communications aimed at a vast audience

mass society a society in which industry and bureaucracy have eroded traditional social ties

master status a status that has special importance for social identity, often shaping a person's entire life

material culture the tangible things created by members of a society

matriarchy a form of social organization in which females dominate males

matrilineal descent a system tracing kinship through women

matrilocality a residential pattern in which a married couple lives with or near the wife's family

mean the arithmetic average of a series of numbers

measurement the process of determining the value of a variable in a specific case

mechanical solidarity Durkheim's term for social bonds, based on common sentiments and shared moral values, that are strong among members of preindustrial societies

median the value that occurs midway in a series of numbers arranged in order of magnitude or, simply, the middle case

medicalization of deviance the transformation of moral and legal deviance into a medical condition

medicine the social institution that focuses on combating disease and improving health

megalopolis a vast urban region containing a number of cities and their surrounding suburbs

meritocracy social stratification based on personal merit

metropolis a large city that socially and economically dominates an urban area

micro-level orientation a close-up focus on social interaction in specific situations

middle-income countries nations with limited industrialization and moderate personal income

migration the movement of people into and out of a specified territory

military-industrial complex the close association of the federal government, the military, and defense industries

minority any category of people, distinguished by physical or cultural difference, that a society sets apart and subordinates

miscegenation biological reproduction by partners of different racial categories

mob a highly emotional crowd that pursues a violent or destructive goal

mode the value that occurs most often in a series of numbers

modernity social patterns resulting from industrialization

modernization the process of social change begun by industrialization

modernization theory a model of economic and social development that explains global inequality in terms of technological and cultural differences among societies

monarchy a type of political system in which a single family rules from generation to generation

monogamy marriage uniting two partners

monopoly domination of a market by a single producer

monotheism belief in a single divine power

mores norms that are widely observed and have great moral significance

mortality the incidence of death in a country's population

multiculturalism an educational program recognizing the cultural diversity of the United States and promoting the equality of all cultural traditions

multinational corporation a large business that operates in many countries

natural environment the earth's surface and atmosphere, including living organisms as well as the air, water, soil, and other resources necessary to sustain life

neocolonialism a new form of global power relationships that involves not direct political control but economic exploitation by multinational corporations

neolocality a residential pattern in which a married couple lives apart from both sets of parents

network a web of weak social ties
nonmaterial culture the intangible world of ideas created by members of a society
nonverbal communication communication using body movements, gestures, and facial expressions rather than speech
norms rules and expectations by which a society guides the behavior of its members
nuclear family (conjugal family) a family unit composed of one or two parents and their children
nuclear proliferation the acquisition of nuclear-weapons technology by more and more nations
objectivity a state of personal neutrality in conducting research
oligarchy the rule of the many by the few
oligopoly domination of a market by a few producers
operationalizing a variable specifying exactly what one is to measure in assigning a value to a variable
organic solidarity Durkheim's term for social bonds, based on specialization and interdependence, that are strong among members of industrial societies
organizational environment a range of factors outside an organization that affects its operation
organized crime a business supplying illegal goods or services
other-directedness a receptiveness to the latest trends and fashions, often expressed by imitating others
outgroup a social group toward which one feels competition or opposition
panic a form of localized collective behavior by which people react to a threat or other stimulus with irrational, frantic, and often self-destructive behavior
paradigm (*see* **theoretical paradigm**)
participant observation a method in which investigators systematically observe people while joining in their routine activities
pastoralism the domestication of animals
patriarchy a form of social organization in which males dominate females
patrilineal descent a system tracing kinship through men
patrilocality a residential pattern in which a married couple lives with or near the husband's family
peer group a social group whose members have interests, social position, and age in common
personality a person's fairly consistent patterns of acting, thinking, and feeling
personal space the surrounding area over which a person makes some claim to privacy
plea bargaining a legal negotiation in which a prosecutor reduces a charge in exchange for a defendant's guilty plea
pluralism a state in which racial and ethnic minorities are distinct but have social parity
pluralist model an analysis of politics that sees power as dispersed among many competing interest groups
political action committee (PAC) an organization formed by a special-interest group, independent of political parties, to pursue political aims by raising and spending money
political revolution the overthrow of one political system in order to establish another
politics the social institution that distributes power, sets a society's agenda, and makes decisions
polyandry marriage uniting one female and two or more males
polygamy marriage uniting three or more people
polygyny marriage uniting one male and two or more females
polytheism belief in many gods
popular culture cultural patterns that are widespread among a society's population
population the people who are the focus of research
pornography sexually explicit material that causes sexual arousal
positivism a way of understanding based on science
postindustrial economy a productive system based on service work and high technology
postindustrialism technology that supports an information-based economy
postmodernity social patterns characteristic of postindustrial societies
power the ability to achieve desired ends despite resistance from others
power-elite model an analysis of politics that sees power as concentrated among the rich
prejudice a rigid and irrational generalization about an entire category of people
preoperational stage Piaget's term for the level of human development at which individuals first use language and other symbols
presentation of self an individual's effort to create specific impressions in the minds of others
primary group a small social group whose members share personal and enduring relationships
primary labor market jobs that provide extensive benefits to workers
primary sector the part of the economy that draws raw materials from the natural environment
primary sex characteristics the genitals, organs used for reproduction
profane that which people define as an ordinary element of everyday life
profession a prestigious, white-collar occupation that requires extensive formal education
proletarians people who sell their productive labor for wages
propaganda information presented with the intention of shaping public opinion
prostitution the selling of sexual services
public opinion widespread attitudes about controversial issues
queer theory a growing body of knowledge that challenges an allegedly heterosexual bias in sociology
questionnaire a series of written questions a researcher presents to subjects
race a socially constructed category composed of people who share biologically transmitted traits that members of a society consider important
racism the belief that one racial category is innately superior or inferior to another
rain forests regions of dense forestation, most of which circle the globe close to the equator

rationality deliberate, matter-of-fact calculation of the most efficient means to accomplish a particular task

rationalization of society Weber's term for the historical change from tradition to rationality as the dominant mode of human thought

rational-legal authority (also *bureaucratic authority*) power legitimized by legally enacted rules and regulations

reference group a social group that serves as a point of reference in making evaluations and decisions

rehabilitation a program for reforming the offender to prevent subsequent offenses

relative deprivation a perceived disadvantage arising from a specific comparison

relative poverty the deprivation of some people in relation to those who have more

reliability consistency in measurement

religion a social institution involving beliefs and practices based on a conception of the sacred

religiosity the importance of religion in a person's life

replication repetition of research by other investigators

research method a systematic plan for conducting research

resocialization radically changing an inmate's personality through carefully controlling the environment

retribution an act of moral vengeance by which society inflicts suffering on the offender comparable to that caused by the offense

riot a social eruption that is highly emotional, violent, and undirected

ritual formal, ceremonial behavior

role behavior expected of someone who holds a particular status

role conflict conflict among the roles corresponding to two or more statuses

role set a number of roles attached to a single status

role strain tension among roles connected to a single status

routinization of charisma the transformation of charismatic authority into some combination of traditional and bureaucratic authority

rumor unsubstantiated information spread informally, often by word of mouth

sacred that which people set apart as extraordinary, inspiring a sense of awe and reverence

sample a part of a population that represents the whole

Sapir-Whorf thesis the thesis that people perceive the world through the cultural lens of language

scapegoat a person or category of people, typically with little power, whom people unfairly blame for their own troubles

schooling formal instruction under the direction of specially trained teachers

science a logical system that bases knowledge on direct, systematic observation

scientific management Frederick Taylor's term for the application of scientific principles to the operation of a business or other large organization

scientific sociology the study of society based on systematic observation of social behavior

secondary analysis a research method in which a researcher uses data collected by others

secondary group a large and impersonal social group whose members pursue a specific goal or activity

secondary labor market jobs that provide minimal benefits to workers

secondary sector the part of the economy that transforms raw materials into manufactured goods

secondary sex characteristics bodily differences, apart from the genitals, that distinguish biologically mature females and males

sect a type of religious organization that stands apart from the larger society

secularization the historical decline in the importance of the supernatural and the sacred

segregation the physical and social separation of categories of people

self George Herbert Mead's term for that part of an individual's personality composed of self-awareness and self-image

sensorimotor stage Piaget's term for the level of human development at which individuals experience the world only through their senses

sex the biological distinction between females and males

sexism the belief that one sex is innately superior to the other

sex ratio the number of males for every hundred females in a nation's population

sexual harassment comments, gestures, or physical contact of a sexual nature that are deliberate, repeated, and unwelcome

sexual orientation a person's preference in terms of sexual partners: same sex, other sex, either sex, neither sex

sick role patterns of behavior defined as appropriate for those who are ill

social change the transformation of culture and social institutions over time

social character personality patterns common to members of a particular society

social conflict struggle between segments of society over valued resources

social-conflict paradigm a framework for building theory that sees society as an arena of inequality that generates conflict and change

social construction of reality the process by which people creatively shape reality through social interaction

social control attempts by society to regulate people's thought and behavior

social dysfunction the undesirable consequences of any social pattern for the operation of society

social epidemiology the study of how health and disease are distributed throughout a society's population

social function the consequences of any social pattern for the operation of society as a whole

social group two or more people who identify and interact with one another

social institution a major sphere of social life, or societal subsystem, organized to meet human needs

social interaction the process by which people act and react in relation to others

socialism an economic system in which natural resources and the means of producing goods and services are collectively owned

socialization the lifelong social experience by which individuals develop their human potential and learn culture

socialized medicine a health care system in which the government owns and operates most medical facilities and employs most physicians

social mobility change in one's position in the social hierarchy

social movement organized activity that encourages or discourages social change

social stratification a system by which a society ranks categories of people in a hierarchy

social structure any relatively stable pattern of social behavior

societal protection a means by which society renders an offender incapable of further offenses temporarily through incarceration or permanently by execution

society people who interact in a defined territory and share culture

sociobiology a theoretical paradigm that explores ways in which human biology affects how we create culture

sociocultural evolution the Lenskis' term for the changes that occur as a society acquires new technology

socioeconomic status (SES) a composite ranking based on various dimensions of social inequality

sociology the systematic study of human society

special-interest group a political alliance of people interested in some economic or social issue

spurious correlation an apparent, although false, relationship between two (or more) variables caused by some other variable

state capitalism an economic and political system in which companies are privately owned but cooperate closely with the government

state church a church formally allied with the state

status a social position that an individual occupies

status consistency the degree of consistency in a person's social standing across various dimensions of social inequality

status set all the statuses a person holds at a given time

stereotype an exaggerated description applied to every person in some category

stigma a powerfully negative label that greatly changes a person's self-concept and social identity

structural-functional paradigm a framework for building theory that sees society as a complex system whose parts work together to promote solidarity and stability

structural social mobility a shift in the social position of large numbers of people due more to changes in society itself than to individual efforts

subculture cultural patterns that set apart some segment of a society's population

suburbs urban areas beyond the political boundaries of a city

superego Freud's designation for the operation of culture within the individual in the form of internalized values and norms

survey a research method in which subjects respond to a series of statements or questions in a questionnaire or an interview

symbolic-interaction paradigm a framework for building theory that sees society as the product of the everyday interactions of individuals

symbols anything that carries a particular meaning recognized by people who share culture

technology knowledge that people apply to the task of living in their surroundings

terrorism random acts of violence or the threat of such violence used by an individual or group as a political strategy

tertiary sector the part of the economy involving services rather than goods

theoretical paradigm a basic image of society that guides thinking and research

theory a statement of how and why specific facts are related

Thomas theorem W. I. Thomas's assertion that situations that are defined as real are real in their consequences

total institution a setting in which people are isolated from the rest of society and manipulated by an administrative staff

totalitarianism a political system that extensively regulates people's lives

totem an object in the natural world collectively defined as sacred

tracking the assignment of students to different types of educational programs

tradition sentiments and beliefs passed from generation to generation

traditional authority power legitimized through respect for long-established cultural patterns

tradition-directedness rigid conformity to time-honored ways of living

transsexuals people who feel they are one sex even though biologically they are the other

triad a social group with three members

underground economy economic activity involving income unreported to the government as required by law

urban ecology the study of the link between the physical and social dimensions of cities

urbanization the concentration of humanity into cities

validity precision in measuring exactly what one intends to measure

values culturally defined standards by which people assess desirability, goodness, and beauty, and which serve as broad guidelines for social living

variable a concept whose value changes from case to case

victimless crimes violations of law in which there are no readily apparent victims

war organized, armed conflict among the people of various societies, directed by their governments

wealth the total value of money and other assets, minus outstanding debts

welfare capitalism an economic and political system that combines a mostly market-based economy with extensive social welfare programs

welfare state a range of government agencies and programs that provides benefits to the population

white-collar crime crime committed by people of high social position in the course of their occupations

white-collar occupations higher-prestige work that involves mostly mental activity

zero population growth the level of reproduction that maintains population at a steady state

REFERENCES

ABBOTT, ANDREW. *The System of Professions: An Essay on the Division of Expert Labor*. Chicago: University of Chicago Press, 1988.

ABERLE, DAVID F. *The Peyote Religion among the Navaho*. Chicago: Aldine, 1966.

ABRAHAMSON, PAUL R. "Postmaterialism and Environmentalism: A Comment on an Analysis and a Reappraisal." *Social Science Quarterly*. Vol. 78, No. 1 (March 1997):21–23.

ADELSON, JOSEPH. "Splitting Up." Article on divorce in the Sept 1996 issue of *Commentary*.

ADLER, JERRY. "When Harry Called Sally . . ." *Newsweek* (October 1, 1990):74.

ADORNO, T. W., et al. *The Authoritarian Personality*. New York: Harper & Brothers, 1950.

AGUIRRE, BENIGNO E., and E. L. QUARANTELLI. "Methodological, Ideological, and Conceptual-Theoretical Criticisms of Collective Behavior: A Critical Evaluation and Implications for Future Study." *Sociological Focus*. Vol. 16, No. 3 (August 1983):195–216.

AGUIRRE, BENIGNO E., E. L. QUARANTELLI, and JORGE L. MENDOZA. "The Collective Behavior of Fads: Characteristics, Effects, and Career of Streaking." *American Sociological Review*. Vol. 53, No. 4 (August 1988):569–84.

AIDS (1997). Data cited in Gorman, Christine, "When Did AIDS Begin?" *Time* (February 16, 1998):64.

AKERS, RONALD L., MARVIN D. KROHN, LONN LANZA-KADUCE, and MARCIA RADOSEVICH. "Social Learning and Deviant Behavior." *American Sociological Review*. Vol. 44, No. 4 (August 1979):636–55.

ALAM, SULTANA. "Women and Poverty in Bangladesh." *Women's Studies International Forum*. Vol. 8, No. 4 (1985):361–71.

THE ALAN GUTTMACHER INSTITUTE. *Into a New World: Young Women's Sexual and Reproductive Lives—Executive Summary*. [Online] Available http://www.agi-usa.org/pubs/new_world_engl.html, January 24, 2000.

ALBA, RICHARD D. *Ethnic Identity: The Transformation of White America*. Chicago: University of Chicago Press, 1990.

ALBON, JOAN. "Retention of Cultural Values and Differential Urban Adaptation: Samoans and American Indians in a West Coast City." *Social Forces*. Vol. 49, No. 3 (March 1971):385–93.

ALFORD, RICHARD. "The Structure of Human Experience: Expectancy and Affect; The Case of Humor." Unpublished paper, Department of Sociology, University of Wyoming, 1979.

ALLAN, EMILIE ANDERSEN, and DARRELL J. STEFFENSMEIER. "Youth, Underemployment, and Property Crime: Differential Effects of Job Availability and Job Quality on Juvenile and Young Adult Arrest Rates." *American Sociological Review*. Vol. 54, No. 1 (February 1989):107–23.

ALLEN, MICHAEL PATRICK, and PHILIP BROYLES. "Campaign Finance Reforms and the Presidential Campaign Contributions of Wealthy Capitalist Families." *Social Science Quarterly*. Vol. 72, No. 4 (December 1991):738–50.

ALLEN, WALTER R. "African American Family Life in Social Context: Crisis and Hope." *Sociological Forum*. Vol. 10, No. 4 (December 1995):569–92.

ALLSOP, KENNETH. *The Bootleggers*. London: Hutchinson, 1961.

ALTER, JONATHAN. "Down to Business." *Newsweek* (May 12, 1997):58–60.

ALTMAN, DREW, et al. "Health Care for the Homeless." *Society*. Vol. 26, No. 4 (May–June 1989):4–5.

ALVERSON, HOYT. *Mind in the Heart of Darkness*. New Haven, Conn.: Yale University Press, 1978.

AMBLER, JOHN S., and JODY NEATHERY. "Education Policy and Equality: Some Evidence from Europe." *Social Science Quarterly*. Vol. 80, No. 3 (September 1999):437–56.

American Demographics. Zandi Group survey. Vol. 20 (March 3, 1998):38.

AMERICAN MEDICAL ASSOCIATION (AMA). Executive Summary of Media Violence Survey Analysis. [Online] Available http://www.ama-assn.org/ad-com/releases/1996/mvan1909.htm, 1997.

AMERICAN SOCIOLOGICAL ASSOCIATION. "Code of Ethics." Washington, D.C.: 1997.

AMNESTY INTERNATIONAL. "The Death Penalty: List of Abolitionist and Retentionist Countries." [Online] Available http://www.amnesty.org/ailib/intcam/dp/abrelist.htm, April 3, 2000

ANDERSON, ELIJAH. "The Code of the Streets." *Atlantic Monthly*. Vol. 273 (May 1994):81–94

ANDERSON, JOHN WARD. "Early to Wed: The Child Brides of India." *Washington Post* (May 24, 1995):A27, A30.

ANDO, FAITH H. "Women in Business." In Sara E. Rix, ed., *The American Woman: A Status Report 1990–91*. New York: Norton, 1990:222–30.

ANG, IEN. *Watching Dallas: Soap Opera and the Melodramatic Imagination*. London: Methuen, 1985.

ANGIER, NATALIE. "Scientists, Finding Second Idiosyncracy in Homosexuals' Brains, Suggest Orientation Is Physiological." *New York Times* (August 1, 1992):A7.

ANNAN, KOFI. "Astonishing Facts." *New York Times* (September 27, 1998):16.

APA. *Violence and Youth: Psychology's Response*. Washington, D.C.: American Psychological Association, 1993.

APPLEBOME, PETER. "70 Years after Scopes Trial, Creation Debate Lives." *New York Times* (March 10, 1996):1, 10.

ARCHER, DANE, and ROSEMARY GARTNER. *Violence and Crime in Cross-National Perspective*. New Haven, Conn.: Yale University Press, 1987.

ARENDT, HANNAH. *The Origins of Totalitarianism*. Cleveland, Ohio: Meridian Books, 1958.

———. *Between Past and Future: Six Exercises in Political Thought*. Cleveland, Ohio: Meridian Books, 1963.

ARIÈS, PHILIPPE. *Centuries of Childhood: A Social History of Family Life*. New York: Vintage Books, 1965.

———. *Western Attitudes toward Death: From the Middle Ages to the Present*. Baltimore, Md.: Johns Hopkins University Press, 1974.

ARJOMAND, SAID AMIR. *The Turban for the Crown: The Islamic Revolution in Iran*. New York: Oxford University Press, 1988.

ARNETTE, JUNE L., and MARJORIE C. WALSLEBEN. "Combating Fear and Restoring Safety in Schools." *Juvenile Justice Bulletin* (April 1998). Washington, DC: U.S. Department of Justice.

ASANTE, MOLEFI KETE. *Afrocentricity*. Trenton, N.J.: Africa World Press, 1988.

ASCH, SOLOMON. *Social Psychology*. Englewood Cliffs, N.J.: Prentice Hall, 1952.

ASHFORD, LORI S. "New Perspectives on Population: Lessons from Cairo." *Population Bulletin*. Vol. 50, No. 1 (March 1995).

ASTONE, NAN MARIE, and SARA S. MCLANAHAN. "Family Structure, Parental Practices and High School Completion." *American Sociological Review*. Vol. 56, No. 3 (June 1991):309–20.

ATCHLEY, ROBERT C. "Retirement as a Social Institution." *Annual Review of Sociology*. Vol. 8. Palo Alto, Calif.: Annual Reviews, 1982:263–87.

———. *Aging: Continuity and Change*. Belmont, Calif.: Wadsworth, 1983; 2d ed., 1987.

AUSTER, CAROL J., and MINDY MACRONE. "The Classroom as a Negotiated Social Setting: An Empirical Study of the Effects of Faculty Members' Behavior on Students' Participation." *Teaching Sociology*. Vol. 22, No. 4 (October 1994):289–300.

BACHRACH, PETER, and MORTON S. BARATZ. *Power and Poverty*. New York: Oxford University Press, 1970.

BACKMAN, CARL B., and MURRAY C. ADAMS. "Self-Perceived Physical Attractiveness, Self-Esteem, Race, and Gender." *Sociological Focus*. Vol. 24, No. 4 (October 1991):283–90.

BAILEY, WILLIAM C. "Murder, Capital Punishment, and Television: Execution Publicity and Homicide Rates." *American Sociological Review*. Vol. 55, No. 5 (October 1990):628–33.

BAILEY, WILLIAM C., and RUTH D. PETERSON. "Murder and Capital Punishment: A Monthly Time-Series Analysis of Execution Publicity." *American Sociological Review*. Vol. 54, No. 5 (October 1989):722–43.

BAKER, MARY ANNE, CATHERINE WHITE BERHEIDE, FAY ROSS GRECKEL, LINDA CARSTARPHEN GUGIN, MARCIA J. LIPETZ, and MARCIA TEXLER SEGAL. *Women Today: A Multidisciplinary Approach to Women's Studies*. Monterey, Calif.: Brooks/Cole, 1980.

BAKER, PATRICIA S., WILLIAM C. YOELS, JEFFREY M. CLAIR, and RICHARD M. ALLMAN. "Laughter in the Triadic Geriatric Encounters: A Transcript-Based Analysis." In Rebecca J. Erikson and Beverly Cuthbertson-Johnson, eds., *Social Perspectives on Emotion*. Vol. 4. Greenwich, Conn.: JAI Press, 1997:179–207.

BAKER, ROSS. "Business as Usual." *American Demographics*. Vol. 19, No. 4 (April 1997):28.

BALTES, PAUL B., and K. WARNER SCHAIE. "The Myth of the Twilight Years." *Psychology Today*. Vol. 7, No. 10 (March 1974):35–39.

BALTZELL, E. DIGBY. *The Protestant Establishment: Aristocracy and Caste in America*. New York: Vintage Books, 1964.

———. "Introduction to the 1967 Edition." In W. E. B. Du Bois, *The Philadelphia Negro: A Social Study*. New York: Schocken Books, 1967; orig. 1899.

———. "The Protestant Establishment Revisited." *The American Scholar*. Vol. 45, No. 4 (Autumn 1976):499–518.

———. *Philadelphia Gentlemen: The Making of a National Upper Class*. Philadelphia: University of Pennsylvania Press, 1979a; orig. 1958.

———. *Puritan Boston and Quaker Philadelphia*. New York: Free Press, 1979b.
———. "The WASP's Last Gasp." *Philadelphia Magazine*. Vol. 79 (September 1988):104–7, 184, 186, 188.
———. *Sporting Gentlemen: From the Age of Honor to the Cult of the Superstar.* New York: Free Press, 1995.
BANFIELD, EDWARD C. *The Unheavenly City Revisited*. Boston: Little, Brown, 1974.
BARASH, DAVID. *The Whispering Within*. New York: Penguin Books, 1981.
BARKER, EILEEN. "Who'd Be a Moonie? A Comparative Study of Those Who Join the Unification Church in Britain." In Bryan Wilson, ed., *The Social Impact of New Religious Movements*. New York: Rose of Sharon Press, 1981:59–96.
BARON, JAMES N., BRIAN S. MITTMAN, and ANDREW E. NEWMAN. "Targets of Opportunity: Organizational and Environmental Determinants of Gender Integration within the California Civil Service, 1979–1985." *American Journal of Sociology*. Vol. 96, No. 6 (May 1991): 1362–401.
BARONE, MICHAEL. "How Hispanics Are Americanizing." *Wall Street Journal* (February 6, 1998a):A22.
BARONE, MICHAEL, and GRANT UJIFUSA. *The Almanac of American Politics*. Washington, D.C.: Barone and Co., 1981.
BARRY, KATHLEEN. "Feminist Theory: The Meaning of Women's Liberation." In Barbara Haber, ed., *The Women's Annual 1982–1983*. Boston: G. K. Hall, 1983:35–78.
BARTLETT, DONALD L., and JAMES B. STEELE. "Corporate Welfare." *Time*. Vol. 152, No. 19 (November 9, 1988):36–54.
BASSUK, ELLEN J. "The Homelessness Problem." *Scientific American*. Vol. 251, No. 1 (July 1984):40–45.
BAUER, P. T. *Equality, the Third World, and Economic Delusion*. Cambridge, Mass.: Harvard University Press, 1981.
BAUMGARTNER, M. P. "Introduction: The Moral Voice of the Community." *Sociological Focus*. Vol. 31, No. 2 (May 1998):105–17.
BAYDAR, NAZLI, and JEANNE BROOKS-GUNN. "Effect of Maternal Employment and Child-Care Arrangements on Preschoolers' Cognitive and Behavioral Outcomes: Evidence from Children from the National Longitudinal Survey of Youth." *Developmental Psychology*. Vol. 27 (1991):932–35.
BAYLEY, DAVID H. "Policing in America." *Society*. Vol. 36, No. 1 (November-December 1998):16–19.
BECKER, ANNE. Paper presented at the annual meeting of the American Psychiatric Association, Washington, D.C., May 19, 1999. Reported in "Eating Disorders Jump When Fiji Gets Television." *Toledo Blade* (May 20, 1999):12.
BECKER, HOWARD S. *Outside: Studies in the Sociology of Deviance*. New York: Free Press, 1966.
BEDELL, GEORGE C., LEO SANDON, JR., and CHARLES T. WELLBORN. *Religion in America*. New York: Macmillan, 1975.
BEEGHLEY, LEONARD. *The Structure of Social Stratification in the United States*. Needham Heights, Mass.: Allyn & Bacon, 1989.
BEGLEY, SHARON. "Gray Matters." *Newsweek* (March 7, 1995):48–54.
———. "How to Beat the Heat." *Newsweek* (December 8, 1997):34–38.
BEINS, BARNEY, cited in "Examples of Spuriousness." *Teaching Methods*. No. 2 (Fall 1993):3.
BELL, ALAN P., MARTIN S. WEINBERG, and SUE KIEFER-HAMMERSMITH. *Sexual Preference: Its Development in Men and Women*. Bloomington: Indiana University Press, 1981.
BELL, DANIEL. *The Coming of Post-Industrial Society: A Venture in Social Forecasting*. New York: Basic Books, 1973.
BELLAH, ROBERT N. *The Broken Covenant*. New York: Seabury Press, 1975.
BELLAH, ROBERT N., RICHARD MADSEN, WILLIAM M. SULLIVAN, ANN SWIDLER, and STEVEN M. TIPTON. *Habits of the Heart: Individualism and Commitment in American Life*. New York: Harper & Row, 1985.
BELLAS, MARCIA L. "Comparable Worth in Academia: The Effects on Faculty Salaries of the Sex Composition and Labor-Market Conditions of Academic Disciplines." *American Sociological Review*. Vol. 59, No. 6 (December 1994):807–21.
BELLUCK, PAM. "Black Youths' Rate of Suicide Rising Sharply." *New York Times* (March 20, 1998):A1, A18.
BEM, SANDRA LIPSITZ. *The Lenses of Gender: Transforming the Debate on Sexual Inequality*. New Haven, Conn.: Yale University Press, 1993.
BENEDICT, RUTH. "Continuities and Discontinuities in Cultural Conditioning." *Psychiatry*. Vol. 1 (May 1938):161–67.
———. *The Chrysanthemum and the Sword: Patterns of Japanese Culture*. New York: New American Library, 1974; orig. 1946.
BENET, SULA. "Why They Live to Be 100, or Even Older, in Abkhasia." *New York Times Magazine* (December 26, 1971):3, 28–29, 31–34.
BENJAMIN, LOIS. *The Black Elite: Facing the Color Line in the Twilight of the Twentieth Century*. Chicago: Nelson-Hall, 1991.
BENNETT, NEIL G., DAVID E. BLOOM, and PATRICIA H. CRAIG. "The Divergence of Black and White Marriage Patterns." *American Journal of Sociology*. Vol. 95, No. 3 (November 1989):692–722.
BENNETT, STEPHEN EARL. "Left Behind: Exploring Declining Turnout among Noncollege Young Whites, 1964–1988." *Social Science Quarterly*. Vol. 72, No. 2 (June 1991):314–33.
BENNETT, WILLIAM J. "School Reform: What Remains to Be Done." *Wall Street Journal* (September 2, 1997):A18.
BENOKRAITIS, NIJOLE, and JOE FEAGIN. *Modern Sexism: Blatant, Subtle, and Overt Discrimination*. 2d ed. Englewood Cliffs, N.J.: Prentice Hall, 1995.
BENSON, MICHAEL L., and FRANCIS T. CULLEN. *Combating Corporate Crime*. Boston: Northeastern University Press, 1998.
BERGAMO, MONICA, and GERSON CAMAROTTI. "Brazil's Landless Millions." *World Press Review*. Vol. 43, No. 7 (July 1996):46–47.
BERGEN, RAQUEL KENNEDY. "Interviewing Survivors of Marital Rape: Doing Feminist Research on Sensitive Topics." In Claire M. Renzetti and Raymond M. Lee, eds., *Researching Sensitive Topics*. Thousand Oaks, Calif.: Sage, 1993.
BERGER, PETER L. *Invitation to Sociology*. New York: Anchor Books, 1963.
———. *The Sacred Canopy: Elements of a Sociological Theory of Religion*. Garden City, N.Y.: Doubleday, 1967.
———. *Facing Up to Modernity: Excursions in Society, Politics, and Religion*. New York: Basic Books, 1977.
———. *The Capitalist Revolution: Fifty Propositions about Prosperity, Equality, and Liberty*. New York: Basic Books, 1986.
———. "Sociology: A Disinvitation?" *Society*. Vol. 30, No. 1 (November–December 1992):12–18.
BERGER, PETER, BRIGITTE BERGER, and HANSFRIED KELLNER. *The Homeless Mind: Modernization and Consciousness*. New York: Vintage Books, 1974.
BERGER, PETER L., and HANSFRIED KELLNER. *Sociology Reinterpreted: An Essay on Method and Vocation*. Garden City, N.Y.: Anchor Books, 1981.
BERGESEN, ALBERT, ed. *Crises in the World-System*. Beverly Hills, Calif.: Sage, 1983.
BERK, RICHARD A. *Collective Behavior*. Dubuque, Iowa: Wm. C. Brown, 1974.
BERNARD, JESSIE. *The Female World*. New York: Free Press, 1981.
———. *The Future of Marriage*. New Haven, Conn.: Yale University Press, 1982; orig. 1973.
BERNARD, LARRY CRAIG. "Multivariate Analysis of New Sex Role Formulations and Personality." *Journal of Personality and Social Psychology*. Vol. 38, No. 2 (February 1980):323–36.
BERNSTEIN, NINA. "On Frontier of Cyberspace, Data Is Money, and a Threat." *New York Times* (June 12, 1997):A1, B14–15.
BERNSTEIN, RICHARD J. *The New Constellation: The Ethical-Political Horizons of Modernity/Postmodernity*. Cambridge, Mass.: MIT Press, 1992.
BERRILL, KEVIN T. "Anti-Gay Violence and Victimization in the United States: An Overview." In Gregory M. Herek and Kevin T. Berrill, *Hate Crimes: Confronting Violence against Lesbians and Gay Men*. Newbury Park, Calif.: Sage, 1992:19–45.
BERRY, BRIAN L., and PHILIP H. REES. "The Factorial Ecology of Calcutta." *American Journal of Sociology*. Vol. 74, No. 5 (March 1969):445–91.
BERSCHEID, ELLEN, and ELAINE HATFIELD. *Interpersonal Attraction*. 2d ed. Reading, Mass.: Addison-Wesley, 1983.
BESHAROV, DOUGLAS J., and LISA A. LAUMANN. "Child Abuse Reporting." *Society*. Vol. 34, No. 4 (May/June 1996):40–46.
BESSER, TERRY L. "The Commitment of Japanese Workers and U.S. Workers: A Reassessment of the Literature." *American Sociological Review*. Vol. 58, No. 6 (December 1993):873–81.
BEST, JOEL. "Victimization and the Victim Industry." *Society*. Vol. 34, No. 2 (May/June 1997):9–17.
BEST, RAPHAELA. *We've All Got Scars: What Boys and Girls Learn in Elementary School*. Bloomington: Indiana University Press, 1983.
BEUTEL, ANN M., and MARGARET MOONEY MARINI. "Gender and Values." *American Sociological Review*. Vol. 60 (June 1995):436–48.
BIANCHI, SUZANNE M., and DAPHNE SPAIN. "Women, Work, and Family in America." *Population Bulletin*. Vol. 51, No. 3 (December 1996).
BIBLARZ, TIMOTHY J., and ADRIAN E. RAFTERY. "The Effects of Family Disruption on Social Mobility." *American Sociological Review*. Vol. 58, No. 1 (February 1993):97–109.

Billson, Janet Mancini, and Bettina J. Huber. *Embarking upon a Career with an Undergraduate Degree in Sociology*. 2d ed. Washington, D.C.: American Sociological Association, 1993.

Blank, Jonah. "The Muslim Mainstream." *U.S. News & World Report*. Vol. 125, No. 3 (July 20, 1998):22–25.

Blankenhorn, David. *Fatherless America: Confronting Our Most Urgent Social Problem*. New York: HarperCollins, 1995.

Blau, Judith R., and Peter M. Blau. "The Cost of Inequality: Metropolitan Structure and Violent Crime." *American Sociological Review*. Vol. 47, No. 1 (February 1982):114–29.

Blau, Peter M. *Exchange and Power in Social Life*. New York: Wiley, 1964.

———. *Inequality and Heterogeneity: A Primitive Theory of Social Structure*. New York: Free Press, 1977.

Blau, Peter M., Terry C. Blum, and Joseph E. Schwartz. "Heterogeneity and Intermarriage." *American Sociological Review*. Vol. 47, No. 1 (February 1982):45–62.

Blau, Peter M., and Otis Dudley Duncan. *The American Occupational Structure*. New York: Wiley, 1967.

Blaustein, Albert P., and Robert L. Zangrando. *Civil Rights and the Black American*. New York: Washington Square Press, 1968.

Bloom, Leonard. "Familial Adjustments of Japanese-Americans to Relocation: First Phase." In Thomas F. Pettigrew, ed., *The Sociology of Race Relations*. New York: Free Press, 1980:163–67.

Blum, Linda M. *Between Feminism and Labor: The Significance of the Comparable Worth Movement*. Berkeley: University of California Press, 1991.

Blumberg, Paul. *Inequality in an Age of Decline*. New York: Oxford University Press, 1981.

Blumer, Herbert G. "Fashion." In David L. Sills, ed., *International Encyclopedia of the Social Sciences*. Vol. 5. New York: Macmillan and Free Press, 1968:341–45.

———. "Collective Behavior." In Alfred McClung Lee, ed., *Principles of Sociology*. 3d ed. New York: Barnes & Noble Books, 1969:65–121.

Blumstein, Alfred, and Richard Rosenfeld. "Assessing the Recent Ups and Downs in U.S. Homicide Rates." *National Institute of Justice Journal*. Vol. 237 (October 1998):9–11.

Blumstein, Philip, and Pepper Schwartz. *American Couples*. New York: William Morrow, 1983.

Bobo, Lawrence, and Vincent L. Hutchings. "Perceptions of Racial Group Competition: Extending Blumer's Theory of Group Position to a Multiracial Social Context." *American Sociological Review*. Vol. 61, No. 6 (December 1996):951–72.

Boff, Leonard and Clodovis. *Salvation and Liberation: In Search of a Balance between Faith and Politics*. Maryknoll, N.Y.: Orbis Books, 1984.

Bogardus, Emory S. "Comparing Racial Distance in Ethiopia, South Africa, and the United States." *Sociology and Social Research*. Vol. 52, No. 2 (January 1968):149–56.

Boggess, Scott, and John Bound. "Did Criminal Activity Increase during the 1980s? Comparisons across Data Sources." *Social Science Quarterly*. Vol. 78, No. 3 (September 1997):725–39.

Bohannan, Cecil. "The Economic Correlates of Homelessness in Sixty Cities." *Social Science Quarterly*. Vol. 72, No. 4 (December 1991):817–25.

Bohlen, Celestine. "Facing Oblivion, Rust-Belt Giants Top Russian List of Vexing Crises." *New York Times* (November 8, 1998):1, 6.

Bohm, Robert M. "American Death Penalty Opinion, 1936–1986: A Critical Examination of the Gallup Polls." In Robert M. Bohm, ed., *The Death Penalty in America: Current Research*. Cincinnati: Anderson Publishing Co., 1991:113–45.

Boli, John, and George M. Thomas. "World Culture in the World Polity: A Century of International Non-Governmental Organization." *American Sociological Review*. Vol. 62, No. 2 (April 1997):171–90.

Bonczar, Thomas P., and Allan J. Beck. *Lifetime Likelihood of Going to State or Federal Prison*. Washington, D.C.: U.S. Bureau of Justice Statistics, 1997.

Bonilla-Santiago, Gloria. "A Portrait of Hispanic Women in the United States." In Sara E. Rix, ed., *The American Woman 1990–91: A Status Report*. New York: Norton, 1990:249–57.

Bonner, Jane. Research presented in "The Two Brains." Public Broadcasting System telecast, 1984.

Booth, Alan, and James Dabbs. "Male Hormone Is Linked to Marital Problems." *Wall Street Journal* (August 19, 1992):B1.

Booth, Alan, and Lynn White. "Thinking about Divorce." *Journal of Marriage and the Family*. Vol. 42, No. 3 (August 1980):605–16.

Booth, William. "By the Sweat of Their Brows: A New Economy." *The Washington Post* (July 13, 1998):A1, A10–A11.

Borgmann, Albert. *Crossing the Postmodern Divide*. Chicago: University of Chicago Press, 1992.

Bormann, F. Herbert. "The Global Environmental Deficit." *BioScience*. Vol. 40 (1990):74.

Bormann, F. Herbert, and Stephen R. Kellert. "The Global Environmental Deficit." In Herbert F. Bormann and Stephen R. Kellert, eds., *Ecology, Economics, and Ethics: The Broken Circle*. New Haven, Conn.: Yale University Press, 1991:ix–xviii.

Boswell, Terry E. "A Split Labor Market Analysis of Discrimination against Chinese Immigrants, 1850–1882." *American Sociological Review*. Vol. 51, No. 3 (June 1986):352–71.

Boswell, Terry E., and William J. Dixon. "Marx's Theory of Rebellion: A Cross-National Analysis of Class Exploitation, Economic Development, and Violent Revolt." *American Sociological Review*. Vol. 58, No. 5 (October 1993): 681–702.

Bott, Elizabeth. *Family and Social Network*. New York: Free Press, 1971; orig. 1957.

Boulding, Elise. *The Underside of History*. Boulder, Colo.: Westview Press, 1976.

Bowen, William G., and Derek K. Bok. *The Shape of the River: Long-Term Consequences of Considering Race in College and University Admissions*. Princeton: Princeton University Press, 1999.

Bowles, Samuel, and Herbert Gintis. *Schooling in Capitalist America: Educational Reform and the Contradictions of Economic Life*. New York: Basic Books, 1976.

Boyer, Debra. "Male Prostitution and Homosexual Identity." *Journal of Homosexuality*. Vol. 17, Nos. 1-2 (1989):151–84.

Boyer, Ernest L. *College: The Undergraduate Experience in America*. Prepared by The Carnegie Foundation for the Advancement of Teaching. New York: Harper & Row, 1987.

Braithwaite, John. "The Myth of Social Class and Criminality Reconsidered." *American Sociological Review*. Vol. 46, No. 1 (February 1981):36–57.

Branegan, Jay. "Is Singapore a Model for the West?" *Time*. Vol. 141, No. 3 (January 18, 1993):36–37.

Breen, Leonard Z. "The Aging Individual." In Clark Tibbitts, ed., *Handbook of Social Gerontology*. Chicago: University of Chicago Press, 1960:145–62.

Briggs, John C. "The Promise of Virtual Reality." *The Futurist*. Vol. 30, No. 5 (September–October 1996):13–18.

Brightman, Joan. "Yellow Pages Change with the Times." *American Demographics*. Vol. 17, No. 3 (March 1995):16–18.

Brines, Julie, and Kara Joyner. "The Ties that Bind: Principles of Cohesion in Cohabitation and Marriage." *American Sociological Review*. Vol. 64, No. 3 (June 1999):333–55.

Brinton, Crane. *The Anatomy of Revolution*. New York: Vintage Books, 1965.

Brinton, Mary C. "The Social-Institutional Bases of Gender Stratification: Japan as an Illustrative Case." *American Journal of Sociology*. Vol. 94, No. 2 (September 1988):300–34.

Broder, John M. "Big Social Changes Revive False God of Numbers." *New York Times* (August 17, 1997): section 4, pp. 1, 4.

Brown, Lester R. "Reassessing the Earth's Population." *Society*. Vol. 32, No. 4 (May–June 1995):7–10.

Brown, Lester R., et al., eds. *State of the World 1993: A Worldwatch Institute Report on Progress toward a Sustainable Society*. New York: Norton, 1993.

Brown, Mary Ellen, ed. *Television and Women's Culture: The Politics of the Popular*. Newbury Park, Calif.: Sage, 1990.

Browning, Christopher R., and Edward O. Laumann. "Sexual Contact between Children and Adults: A Life Course Perspective." *American Sociological Review*. Vo. 62, No. 5 (August 1997):540–60.

Bruno, Mary. "Abusing the Elderly." *Newsweek* (September 23, 1985):75–76.

Buckley, Stephen. "A Spare and Separate Way of Life." *Washington Post* (December 18, 1996):A1, A32–33.

Bulletin of the Atomic Scientists. Data on the "doomsday clock." [Online] Available http://www.bullatomsci.org/clock/pressrelease9.html, February 12, 2000.

Bumpass, Larry, and James A. Sweet. *1992–1994 National Survey of Families and Households. Reported in "Report from PPA." Population Today*. Vol. 23, No. 6 (June 1995):3.

Bunzel, John H. "Black and White at Stanford." *The Public Interest*. Vol. 105 (Fall 1991):61–77.

BURAWAY, MICHAEL. "Review Essay: The Soviet Descent into Capitalism." *American Journal of Sociology*. Vol. 102, No. 5 (March 1997):1430–44.

BURCH, ROBERT. Testimony to House of Representatives Hearing in "Review: The World Hunger Problem." October 25, 1983, Serial 98–38.

BURKE, TOM. "The Future." In Sir Edmund Hillary, ed., *Ecology 2000: The Changing Face of the Earth*. New York: Beaufort Books, 1984:227–41.

BURKETT, ELINOR. "God Created Me to Be a Slave." *New York Times* Sunday Magazine (October 12, 1997):56–60.

BURSTEIN, PAUL. "Legal Mobilization as a Social Movement Tactic: The Struggle for Equal Employment Opportunity." *American Journal of Sociology*. Vol. 96, No. 5 (March 1991):1201–25.

BUTLER, ROBERT N. *Why Survive? Being Old in America*. New York: Harper & Row, 1975.

BUTTERFIELD, FOX. "Prison: Where the Money Is." *New York Times* (June 2, 1996):E16.

CALLAHAN, DANIEL. *Setting Limits: Medical Goals in an Aging Society*. New York: Simon & Schuster, 1987.

CAMERON, WILLIAM BRUCE. *Modern Social Movements: A Sociological Outline*. New York: Random House, 1966.

CANETTI, ELIAS. *Crowds and Power*. New York: Seabury Press, 1978.

CANTOR, MURIAL G., and SUZANNE PINGREE. *The Soap Opera*. Beverly Hills, Calif.: Sage, 1983.

CANTRIL, HADLEY, HAZEL GAUDET, and HERTA HERZOG. *Invasion from Mars: A Study in the Psychology of Panic*. Princeton, N.J.: Princeton University Press, 1947.

CAPLOW, THEODORE. "The Case of the Phantom Episcopalians." *American Sociological Review*. Vol. 63, No. 1 (February 1998):112–13.

CAPLOW, THEODORE, et al. *Middletown Families*. Minneapolis: University of Minnesota Press, 1982.

CAPLOW, THEODORE, HOWARD M. BAHR, JOHN MODELL, and BRUCE A. CHADWICK. *Recent Social Trends in the United States, 1960–1990*. Montreal: McGill-Queen's University Press, 1991.

CARLEY, KATHLEEN. "A Theory of Group Stability." *American Sociological Review*. Vol. 56, No. 3 (June 1991):331–54.

CARLSON, NORMAN A. "Corrections in the United States Today: A Balance Has Been Struck." *The American Criminal Law Review*. Vol. 13, No. 4 (Spring 1976):615–47.

CARMICHAEL, STOKELY, and CHARLES V. HAMILTON. *Black Power: The Politics of Liberation in America*. New York: Vintage Books, 1967.

CARR, LESLIE G. "Colorblindness and the New Racism." Paper presented at the annual meeting, American Sociological Association, Washington, D.C., 1995.

CARROLL, GINNY. "Who Foots the Bill?" *Newsweek*. Special Issue (Fall–Winter 1990):81–85.

CARROLL, JAMES R. "Congress Is Told of Coal-Dust Fraud UMW; Senator from Minnesota Rebukes Industry." *Louisville Courier Journal* (Thursday, May 27, 1999):1A.

CASTELLS, MANUEL. *The Urban Question*. Cambridge, Mass.: MIT Press, 1977.

———. *The City and the Grass Roots*. Berkeley: University of California Press, 1983.

CASTRO, JANICE. "Disposable Workers." *Time*. Vol. 131, No. 14 (March 29, 1993):43–47.

CATALYST. *Infobrief: Women CEOs*. [Online] Available http://www.catalystwomen.org/press.html, April 18, 2000.

———. *Infobrief: Women in Corporate Leadership*. [Online] Available http://www.catalystwomen.org/press.html, April 18, 2000.

———. *1999 Catalyst Census of Women Corporate Officers and Top Earners*. [Online] Available http://www.catalystwomen.org/press/factscote99.html, April 18, 2000.

CENTER FOR RESPONSIVE POLITICS. The Big Picture. [Online] Available http://www.crp.org/crpdocs/bigpicture/default.htm, February 12, 1998.

———. The Big Picture: The Money behind the 1998 Elections. [Online] Available http://www.opensecrets.org/pubs/bigpicture2000/index.htm, March 30, 2000.

CENTER FOR THE STUDY OF SPORT IN SOCIETY. *1998 Racial and Gender Report Card*. [Online] Available http://www.sportinsociety.org, February 19, 2000.

CHAGNON, NAPOLEON A. *Yąnomamö: The Fierce People*. 4th ed. New York: Holt, Rinehart & Winston, 1992.

CHANDLER, TERTIUS, and GERALD FOX. *3000 Years of Urban History*. New York: Academic Press, 1974.

CHANDLER, TIMOTHY D., YOSHINORI KAMO, and JAMES D. WERBEL. "Do Delays in Marriage and Childbirth Affect Earnings?" *Social Science Quarterly*. Vol. 75, No. 4 (December 1994):838–53.

CHANGE, KWANG-CHIH. *The Archaeology of Ancient China*. New Haven, Conn.: Yale University Press, 1977.

CHAPPELL, NEENA L., and BETTY HAVENS. "Old and Female: Testing the Double Jeopardy Hypothesis." *The Sociological Quarterly*. Vol. 21, No. 2 (Spring 1980):157–71.

CHARLES, MARIA. "Cross-National Variation in Occupational Segregation." *American Sociological Review*. Vol. 57, No. 4 (August 1992):483–502.

CHAUNCEY, GEORGE. *Gay New York: Gender, Urban Culture, and the Making of the Gay Male World 1890-1940*. New York: Basic Books, 1994.

CHAVES, MARK. "Ordaining Women: The Diffusion of an Organizational Innovation." *American Journal of Sociology*. Vol. 101, No. 4 (January 1996):840–73.

CHERLIN, ANDREW, and FRANK F. FURSTENBERG, JR. *The New American Grandparent: A Place in the Family, A Life Apart*. New York: Basic Books, 1986.

CHERLIN, ANDREW J., P. LINDSAY CHASE-LANSDALE, and CHRISTINE MCRAE. "Effects of Parental Divorce on Mental Health throughout the Life Course." *American Sociological Review*. Vol. 63, No. 2 (April 1998):239–49.

CHESNAIS, JEAN-CLAUDE. "The Demographic Sunset of the West?" *Population Today*. Vol. 25, No. 1 (January 1997):4–5.

CHILDREN'S DEFENSE FUND. *The State of America's Children Yearbook, 1995*. Washington, D.C.: Children's Defense Fund, 1995.

CHOLDIN, HARVEY M. "How Sampling Will Help Defeat the Undercount." *Society*. Vol. 34, No. 3 (March/April 1997):27–30.

CHURCH, GEORGE J. "Unions Arise—with New Tricks." *Time*. Vol. 143, No. 24 (June 13, 1994):56–58.

———. "Ripping Up Welfare." *Time*. Vol. 148, No. 8 (August 12, 1996):18–22.

CLARK, CURTIS B. "Geriatric Abuse: Out of the Closet." In *The Tragedy of Elder Abuse: The Problem and the Response*. Hearings before the Select Committee on Aging, House of Representatives (July 1, 1986):49–50.

CLARK, MARGARET S., ed *Prosocial Behavior*. Newbury Park, Calif.: Sage, 1991.

CLARKE, ROBIN. "Atmospheric Pollution." In Sir Edmund Hillary, ed., *Ecology 2000: The Changing Face of the Earth*. New York: Beaufort Books, 1984a:130–48.

———. "What's Happening to Our Water?" In Sir Edmund Hillary, ed., *Ecology 2000: The Changing Face of the Earth*. New York: Beaufort Books, 1984b:108–29.

CLINARD, MARSHALL, and DANIEL ABBOTT. *Crime in Developing Countries*. New York: Wiley, 1973.

CLOUD, JOHN. "What Can the Schools Do?" *Time*. Vol. 153, No. 17 (May 3, 1999):38–40.

CLOWARD, RICHARD A., and LLOYD E. OHLIN. *Delinquency and Opportunity: A Theory of Delinquent Gangs*. New York: Free Press, 1966.

CLYMER, ADAM. "Class Warfare? The Rich Win by Default." *New York Times* (August 11, 1996): section 4, pp. 1, 14.

COE, MICHAEL D., and RICHARD A. DIEHL. *In the Land of the Olmec*. Austin: University of Texas Press, 1980.

COHEN, ADAM. "A New Push for Blind Justice." *Time*. Vol. 145, No. 7 (February 20, 1995):39–40.

———. "Test-Tube Tug-of-War." *Time*. Vol. 151, No. 13 (April 6, 1998):65.

———. "A First Report Card on Vouchers." *Time*. Vol. 153, No. 16 (April 26, 1999):36–38.

COHEN, ALBERT K. *Delinquent Boys: The Culture of the Gang*. New York: Free Press, 1971; orig. 1955.

COHEN, LLOYD R. "Sexual Harassment and the Law." *Society*. Vol. 28, No. 4 (May–June 1991):8–13.

COHN, RICHARD M. "Economic Development and Status Change of the Aged." *American Journal of Sociology*. Vol. 87, No. 2 (March 1982):1150–61.

COLEMAN, JAMES S. "Rational Organization." *Rationality and Society*. Vol. 2, (1990):94–105.

———. "The Design of Organizations and the Right to Act." *Sociological Forum*. Vol. 8, No. 4 (December 1993):527–46.

COLEMAN, JAMES S., and THOMAS HOFFER. *Public and Private High Schools: The Impact of Communities*. New York: Basic Books, 1987.

COLEMAN, JAMES, THOMAS HOFFER, and SALLY KILGORE. *Public and Private Schools: An Analysis of Public Schools and Beyond*. Washington, D.C.: National Center for Education Statistics, 1981.

Coleman, Richard P., and Bernice L. Neugarten. *Social Status in the City*. San Francisco: Jossey-Bass, 1971.
Coleman, Richard P., and Lee Rainwater. *Social Standing in America*. New York: Basic Books, 1978.
Collins, Randall. "A Conflict Theory of Sexual Stratification." *Social Problems*. Vol. 19, No. 1 (Summer 1971):3–21.
———. *The Credential Society: An Historical Sociology of Education and Stratification*. New York: Academic Press, 1979.
———. *Sociological Insight: An Introduction to Nonobvious Sociology*. New York: Oxford University Press, 1982.
Colloway, N. O., and Paula L. Dollevoet. "Selected Tabular Material on Aging." In Caleb Finch and Leonard Hayflick, eds., *Handbook of the Biology of Aging*. New York: Van Nostrand Reinhold, 1977:666–708.
Colton, Helen. *The Gift of Touch: How Physical Contact Improves Communication, Pleasure, and Health*. New York: Seaview/Putnam, 1983.
Commission for Racial Justice, United Church of Christ. *CRJ Reporter*. New York: Commission for Racial Justice, the United Church of Christ, 1994.
Comte, Auguste. *Auguste Comte and Positivism: The Essential Writings*. Gertrud Lenzer, ed. New York: Harper Torchbooks, 1975.
Connett, Paul H. "The Disposable Society." In F. Herbert Bormann and Stephen R. Kellert, eds., *Ecology, Economics, and Ethics: The Broken Circle*. New Haven, Conn.: Yale University Press, 1991:99–122.
Cook, Rhodes. "House Republicans Scored a Quiet Victory in '92." *Congressional Quarterly Weekly Report*. Vol. 51, No. 16 (April 17, 1993):965–68.
Cooley, Charles Horton. *Social Organization*. New York: Schocken Books, 1962; orig. 1909.
———. *Human Nature and the Social Order*. New York: Schocken Books, 1964; orig. 1902.
Cooney, Mark. "From Warfare to Tyranny: Lethal Conflict and the State." *American Sociological Review*. Vol. 62, No. 2 (April 1997):316–38.
Corley, Robert N., O. Lee Reed, Peter J. Shedd, and Jere W. Morehead. *The Legal and Regulatory Environment of Business*. 9th ed. New York: McGraw-Hill, 1993.
Cose, Ellis. "Census and the Complex Issue of Race." *Society*. Vol. 34, No. 6 (September/October, 1997):9–13.
———. "The Good News about Black America." *Newsweek* (June 7, 1999):28–40.
Coser, Lewis. *The Functions of Social Conflict*. New York: Free Press, 1956.
———. *Masters of Sociological Thought: Ideas in Historical and Social Context*. New York: Harcourt Brace Jovanovich, 1971.
Cottle, Thomas J. "What Tracking Did to Ollie Taylor." *Social Policy*. Vol. 5, No. 2 (July–August 1974):22–24.
Council on Families in America. *Marriage in America: A Report to the Nation*. New York: Institute for American Values, 1995.
Counts, G. S. "The Social Status of Occupations: A Problem in Vocational Guidance." *School Review*. Vol. 33 (January 1925):16–27.
Courtney, Alice E., and Thomas W. Whipple. *Sex Stereotyping in Advertising*. Lexington, Mass.: D. C. Heath, 1983.
Courtwright, David T. *Violent Land: Single Men and Social Disorder from the Frontier to the Inner City*. Cambridge, Mass.: Harvard University Press, 1996.
Covington, Jeanette. "Racial Classification in Criminology: The Reproduction of Racialized Crime." *Sociological Forum*. Vol. 10, No. 4 (December 1995):547–68.
Cowan, Carolyn Pope. *When Partners Become Parents*. New York: Basic Books, 1992.
Cowgill, Donald, and Lowell Holmes. *Aging and Modernization*. New York: Appleton-Century-Crofts, 1972.
Cowley, Geoffrey. "The Prescription That Kills." *Newsweek* (July 17, 1995): 54.
Cox, Harvey. *The Secular City*. Rev. ed. New York: Macmillan, 1971; orig. 1965.
———. "Church and Believers: Always Strangers?" In Thomas Robbins and Dick Anthony, *In Gods We Trust: New Patterns of Religious Pluralism in America*. 2d ed. New Brunswick, N.J.: Transaction, 1990:449–62.
COYOTE (Call Off Your Old Tired Ethics). [Online] Available http://www.freedomusa.org/coyotela/what_is.html, April 2, 2000.
Crispell, Diane. "Grandparents Galore." *American Demographics*. Vol. 15, No. 10 (October 1993):63.
———. "Speaking in Other Tongues." *American Demographics*. Vol. 19, No. 1 (January 1997a):12–15.
———. "Lucky to be Alive." *American Demographics*. Vol. 19, No. 4 (April 1997b):25.
Crook, Stephan, Jan Pakulski, and Malcolm Waters. *Postmodernity: Change in Advanced Society*. Newbury Park, Calif.: Sage, 1992.
Crossen, Cynthia, and Ellen Graham. "Good News—and Bad—about America's Health." *Wall Street Journal* (June 28, 1996):R1.
Crossette, Barbara. "Female Genital Mutilation by Immigrants Is Becoming Cause for Concern in the U.S." *New York Times International* (December 10, 1995):11.
Crouse, James, and Dale Trusheim. *The Case against the SAT*. Chicago: University of Chicago Press, 1988.
Cuff, E. C., and G. C. F. Payne, eds. *Perspectives in Sociology*. London: Allen and Unwin, 1979.
Cumming, Elaine, and William E. Henry. *Growing Old: The Process of Disengagement*. New York: Basic Books, 1961.
Cummings, Scott, and Thomas Lambert. "Anti-Hispanic and Anti-Asian Sentiments among African Americans." *Social Science Quarterly*. Vol. 78, No. 2 (June 1997):338–53.
Currie, Elliott. *Confronting Crime: An American Challenge*. New York: Pantheon Books, 1985.
Curry, George E., ed. *The Affirmative Action Debate*. Reading, Mass.: Addison-Wesley, 1996.
Curtis, James E., Edward G. Grabb, and Douglas Baer. "Voluntary Association Membership in Fifteen Countries: A Comparative Analysis." *American Sociological Review*. Vol. 57, No. 2 (April 1992):139–52.
Curtiss, Susan. *Genie: A Psycholinguistic Study of a Modern-Day "Wild Child."* New York: Academic Press, 1977.
Cutright, Phillip. "Occupational Inheritance: A Cross-National Analysis." *American Journal of Sociology*. Vol. 73, No. 4 (January 1968):400–16.
Dahl, Robert A. *Who Governs?* New Haven, Conn.: Yale University Press, 1961.
———. *Dilemmas of Pluralist Democracy: Autonomy vs. Control*. New Haven, Conn.: Yale University Press, 1982.
Dahrendorf, Ralf. *Class and Class Conflict in Industrial Society*. Stanford, Calif.: Stanford University Press, 1959.
Daly, Martin, and Margo Wilson. *Homicide*. New York: Aldine, 1988.
Daniels, Roger. "The Issei Generation." In Amy Tachiki et al., eds., *Roots: An Asian American Reader*. Los Angeles: UCLA Asian American Studies Center, 1971:138–49.
Darnton, Nina, and Yuriko Hoshia. "Whose Life Is It, Anyway?" *Newsweek*. Vol. 113, No. 4 (January 13, 1989):61.
Davidson, James D., Ralph E. Pyle, and David V. Reyes. "Persistence and Change in the Protestant Establishment, 1930–1992." *Social Forces*. Vol. 74, No. 1 (September 1995):157–75.
Davies, Christie. *Ethnic Humor around the World: A Comparative Analysis*. Bloomington: Indiana University Press, 1990.
Davies, James C. "Toward a Theory of Revolution." *American Sociological Review*. Vol. 27, No. 1 (February 1962):5–19.
Davies, Mark, and Denise B. Kandel. "Parental and Peer Influences on Adolescents' Educational Plans: Some Further Evidence." *American Journal of Sociology*. Vol. 87, No. 2 (September 1981):363–87.
Davis, Byron Bradley. "Sports World." *Christian Science Monitor* (September 9, 1997):11.
Davis, Donald M., cited in "T.V. Is a Blonde, Blonde World." *American Demographics*, special issue: *Women Change Places*. Ithaca, N.Y.: 1993.
Davis, Kingsley. "Extreme Social Isolation of a Child." *American Journal of Sociology*. Vol. 45, No. 4 (January 1940):554–65.
———. "Final Note on a Case of Extreme Isolation." *American Journal of Sociology*. Vol. 52, No. 5 (March 1947):432–37.
———. "The Myth of Functional Analysis as a Special Method in Sociology and Anthropology." *American Sociological Review*. Vol. 24, No. 1 (February 1959):75ff.
———. "Sexual Behavior." In Robert K. Merton and Robert Nisbet, eds., *Contemporary Social Problems*. 3d ed. New York: Harcourt Brace Jovanovich, 1971:313–60.
Davis, Kingsley, and Wilbert Moore. "Some Principles of Stratification." *American Sociological Review*. Vol. 10, No. 2 (April 1945):242–49.
Davis, Nancy, and Robert V. Robinson. "Are the Rumors of War Exaggerated? Religious Orthodoxy and Moral Progressivism in America." *American Journal of Sociology*. Vol. 102, No. 3 (November 1996):756–87.

DAVIS, SHARON A., and EMIL J. HALLER. "Tracking, Ability, and SES: Further Evidence on the 'Revisionist-Meritocratic Debate.'" *American Journal of Education*. Vol. 89 (May 1981):283–304.

DECKARD, BARBARA SINCLAIR. *The Women's Movement: Political, Socioeconomic, and Psychological Issues*. 2d ed. New York: Harper & Row, 1979.

DEDRICK, DENNIS K., and RICHARD E. YINGER. "MAD, SDI, and the Nuclear Arms Race." Manuscript in development. Georgetown, Ky.: Georgetown College, 1990.

DELACROIX, JACQUES, and CHARLES C. RAGIN. "Structural Blockage: A Crossnational Study of Economic Dependency, State Efficacy, and Underdevelopment." *American Journal of Sociology*. Vol. 86, No. 6 (May 1981):1311–47.

DELLA CAVA, MARCO R. "For Dutch, It's as Easy as Asking a Doctor." *USA Today* (January 7, 1997):4A.

DELUCA, TOM. "Joe the Bookie and the Class Voting Gap." *American Demographics*. Vol. 20, No. 11 (November 1998):26–29.

DE MENTE, BOYE. *Japanese Etiquette and Ethics in Business*. 5th ed. Lincolnwood, Ill.: NTC Business Books, 1987.

DEMERATH, N. J., III. "Who Now Debates Functionalism? From *System, Change, and Conflict* to 'Culture, Choice, and Praxis'." *Sociological Forum*. Vol. 11, No. 2 (June 1996):333–45.

DENT, DAVID J. "African-Americans Turning to Christian Academies." *New York Times*, Education Life supplement (August 4, 1996):26–29.

DERSHOWITZ, ALAN. *The Vanishing American Jew*. Boston: Little, Brown, 1997.

Der Spiegel. "Third World Metropolises Are Becoming Monsters; Rural Poverty Drives Millions to the Slums." In *World Press Review* (October 1989).

DERVARICS, CHARLES. "Is Welfare Reform Reforming Welfare?" *Population Today*. Vol. 26, No. 10 (October 1998):1–2.

———. "The Coming Age of Older Women." *Population Today*. Vol. 27, No. 2 (February 1999):2–3.

DESRUISSEAUX, PAUL. "U.S. Trails 22 Nations in High-School Completion." *Chronicle of Higher Education*. Vol. XLV, No. 15 (December 4, 1998):A45.

DE VINCK, CHRISTOPHER. "Why I Read to My Child." *Wall Street Journal* (November 22, 1993):A14.

DEVINE, JOEL A. "State and State Expenditure: Determinants of Social Investment and Social Consumption Spending in the Postwar United States." *American Sociological Review*. Vol. 50, No. 2 (April 1985):150–65.

DIMAGGIO, PAUL, JOHN EVANS, and BETHANY BRYSON. "Have Americans' Social Attitudes Become More Polarized?" *American Journal of Sociology*. Vol. 102, No. 3 (November 1996):690–755.

DIXON, WILLIAM J., and TERRY BOSWELL. "Dependency, Disarticulation, and Denominator Effects: Another Look at Foreign Capital Penetration." *American Journal of Sociology*. Vol. 102, No. 2 (September 1996):543–62.

DIZARD, JAN E., and HOWARD GADLIN. *The Minimal Family*. Amherst: The University of Massachusetts Press, 1990.

DOBSON, RICHARD B. "Mobility and Stratification in the Soviet Union." *Annual Review of Sociology*. Vol. 3. Palo Alto, Calif.: Annual Reviews, 1977:297–329.

DOBYNS, HENRY F. "An Appraisal of Techniques with a New Hemispheric Estimate." *Current Anthropology*. Vol. 7, No. 4 (October 1966):395–446.

DOLLARD, JOHN, et al. *Frustration and Aggression*. New Haven, Conn.: Yale University Press, 1939.

DOMHOFF, G. WILLIAM. *Who Rules America Now? A View of the '80s*. Englewood Cliffs, N.J.: Prentice Hall, 1983.

DONNELLY, PATRICK G., and THEO J. MAJKA. "Residents' Efforts at Neighborhood Stabilization: Facing the Challenges of Inner-City Neighborhoods." *Sociological Forum*. Vol. 13, No. 2 (June 1998):189–213.

DONOVAN, VIRGINIA K., and RONNIE LITTENBERG. "Psychology of Women: Feminist Therapy." In Barbara Haber, ed., *The Women's Annual 1981: The Year in Review*. Boston: G. K. Hall, 1982:211–35.

DOYAL, LESLEY, with IMOGEN PENNELL. *The Political Economy of Health*. London: Pluto Press, 1981.

DOYLE, JAMES A. *The Male Experience*. Dubuque, Iowa: Wm. C. Brown, 1983.

DOYLE, RICHARD F. *A Manifesto of Men's Liberation*. 2d ed. Forest Lake, Minn.: Men's Rights Association, 1980.

D'SOUZA, DINESH. "The Billionaire Next Door." *Forbes*. Vol. 164, No. 9 (October 11, 1999):50–62.

DU BOIS, W. E. B. *The Philadelphia Negro: A Social Study*. New York: Schocken Books, 1967; orig. 1899.

DUBOS, RENÉ. *Man Adapting*. New Haven, Conn.: Yale University Press, 1980; orig. 1965.

DUHL, LEONARD J. "The Social Context of Health." In Arthur C. Hastings et al., eds., *Health for the Whole Person: The Complete Guide to Holistic Medicine*. Boulder, Colo.: Westview Press, 1980:39–48.

DUNBAR, LESLIE. *The Common Interest: How Our Social Welfare Policies Don't Work and What We Can Do about Them*. New York: Pantheon, 1988.

DUNCAN, GREG J., W. JEAN YEUNG, JEANNE BROOKS-GUNN, and JUDITH R. SMITH. "How Much Does Childhood Poverty Affect the Life Chances of Children?" *American Sociological Review*. Vol. 63, No. 3 (June 1998):406–23.

DUNN, ASHLEY. "Ancient Chinese Craft Shifts Building Designs in the U.S." *New York Times* (September 22, 1994):A1, B4.

DUNN, JOHN. "Peddling Big Brother." *Time*. Vol. 137, No. 25 (June 24, 1991):62.

DURKHEIM, EMILE. *Moral Education*. New York: Free Press, 1961; orig. 1902–3.

———. *The Division of Labor in Society*. New York: Free Press, 1964a; orig. 1895.

———. *The Rules of Sociological Method*. New York: Free Press, 1964b; orig. 1893.

———. *Suicide*. New York: Free Press, 1966; orig. 1897.

———. *Sociology and Philosophy*. New York: Free Press, 1974; orig. 1924.

DURNING, ALAN THEIN. "Supporting Indigenous Peoples." In Lester R. Brown et al., eds., *State of the World 1993: A Worldwatch Institute Report on Progress toward a Sustainable Society*. New York: Norton, 1993:80–100.

DWORKIN, ANDREA. *Intercourse*. New York: Free Press, 1987.

EBAUGH, HELEN ROSE FUCHS. *Becoming an EX: The Process of Role Exit*. Chicago: University of Chicago Press, 1988.

———. "Cockfighting: 'Til Death Us Do Part." Vol. 330, No. 7851 (February 19, 1994):30.

EDIN, KATHRYN, and LAURA LEIN. "Work, Welfare, and Single Mothers' Economic Survival Strategies." *American Sociological Review*. Vol. 62, No. 2 (April 1996):253–66.

EDMONDSON, BRAD. "The Great Money Grab." *American Demographics*. Vol. 17, No. 2 (February 1995):2.

———. "Fountains of Youth." *American Demographics*. Vol. 18, No. 7 (July 1996):60.

———. "The Facts of Death." *American Demographics*. Vol. 49, No. 4 (April 1997a):47–53.

———. "The Wired Bunch." *American Demographics*. Vol. 49, No. 6 (June 1997b):10–15.

EDWARDS, DAVID V. *The American Political Experience*. 3d ed. Englewood Cliffs, N.J.: Prentice Hall, 1985.

EDWARDS, RICHARD. *Contested Terrain: The Transformation of the Workplace in the Twentieth Century*. New York: Basic Books, 1979.

EDWARDS, TAMALA M. "Revolt of the Gentry. " *Time*. Vol. 151, No. 23 (June 15, 1998):34–35.

———. "Harvard vs. the School of Hard Knocks." *Time*. Vol. 153, No. 24 (June 21, 1999):8.

EGGEBEEN, DAVID J., and DANIEL T. LICHTER. "Race, Family Structure and Changing Poverty among American Children." *American Sociological Review*. Vol. 56, No. 6 (December 1991):801–17.

EHRENREICH, BARBARA. *The Hearts of Men: American Dreams and the Flight from Commitment*. Garden City, N.Y.: Anchor Books, 1983.

———. "The Real Truth about the Female Body." *Time*. Vol. 153, No. 9 (March 15, 1999):56–65.

EHRENREICH, JOHN. "Introduction." In John Ehrenreich, ed., *The Cultural Crisis of Modern Medicine*. New York: Monthly Review Press, 1978:1–35.

EICHLER, MARGRIT. *Nonsexist Research Methods: A Practical Guide*. Winchester, Mass.: Unwin Hyman, 1988.

EISEN, ARNOLD M. *The Chosen People in America: A Study of Jewish Religious Ideology*. Bloomington: Indiana University Press, 1983.

EISENBERG, DANIEL. "Rise of the Permatemp." *Time*. Vol. 154, No. 2 (July 12, 1999):48.

EISENSTEIN, ZILLAH R., ed. *Capitalist Patriarchy and the Case for Socialist Feminism*. New York: Monthly Review Press, 1979.

EISLER, BENITA. *The Lowell Offering: Writings by New England Mill Women 1840–1845*. Philadelphia: J. B. Lippincott, 1977.

EKMAN, PAUL. "Biological and Cultural Contributions to Body and Facial Movements in the Expression of Emotions." In A. Rorty, ed., *Explaining Emotions*. Berkeley: University of California Press, 1980a:73–101.

———. *Face of Man: Universal Expression in a New Guinea Village*. New York: Garland Press, 1980b.

———. *Telling Lies: Clues to Deceit in the Marketplace, Politics, and Marriage*. New York: Norton, 1985.

El-Attar, Mohamed. Personal communication, 1991.
Elias, Robert. *The Politics of Victimization: Victims, Victimology and Human Rights.* New York: Oxford University Press, 1986.
Elliot, Delbert S., and Suzanne S. Ageton. "Reconciling Race and Class Differences in Self-Reported and Official Estimates of Delinquency." *American Sociological Review.* Vol. 45, No. 1 (February 1980):95–110.
Ellison, Christopher G., John P. Bartkowski, and Michelle L. Segal. "Do Conservative Protestant Parents Spank More Often? Further Evidence from the National Survey of Families and Households." *Social Science Quarterly.* Vol. 77, No. 3 (September 1996):663–73.
Ellison, Christopher G., and Darren E. Sherkat. "Conservative Protestantism and Support for Corporal Punishment." *American Sociological Review.* Vol. 58, No. 1 (February 1993):131–44.
Elmer-DeWitt, Philip. "The Revolution That Fizzled." *Time.* Vol. 137, No. 20 (May 20, 1991):48–49.
———. "First Nation in Cyberspace." *Time.* Vol. 142, No. 24 (December 6, 1993):62–64.
———. "The Genetic Revolution." *Time.* Vol. 143, No. 3 (January 17, 1994a):46–53.
———. "Battle for the Internet." *Time.* Vol. 144, No. 4 (July 25, 1994b):50–56.
———. "Now for the Truth about Americans and Sex." *Time.* Vol. 144, No. 16 (October 17, 1994):62–70.
Ember, Melvin, and Carol R. Ember. "The Conditions Favoring Matrilocal versus Patrilocal Residence." *American Anthropologist.* Vol. 73, No. 3 (June 1971):571–94.
———. *Anthropology.* 6th ed. Englewood Cliffs, N.J.: Prentice Hall, 1991.
Embree, Ainslie T. *The Hindu Tradition.* New York: Vintage Books, 1972.
Emerson, Joan P. "Behavior in Private Places: Sustaining Definitions of Reality in Gynecological Examinations." In H. P. Dreitzel, ed., *Recent Sociology.* Vol. 2. New York: Collier, 1970:74–97.
Endicott, Karen. "Fathering in an Egalitarian Society." In Barry S. Hewlett, ed., *Father-Child Relations: Cultural and Bio-Social Contexts.* New York: Aldine, 1992:281–96.
Engels, Friedrich. *The Origin of the Family.* Chicago: Charles H. Kerr & Company, 1902; orig. 1884.
England, Paula. *Comparable Worth: Theories and Evidence.* Hawthorne, N.Y.: Aldine, 1992.
Epps, Edgar G. "Race, Class, and Educational Opportunity: Trends in the Sociology of Education." *Sociological Forum.* Vol. 10, No. 4 (December 1995):593–608.
Erber, Ernest. "Virtues and Vices of the Market: Balanced Correctives to a Current Craze." *Dissent.* Vol. 37 (Summer 1990):353–60.
Erikson, Erik H. *Childhood and Society.* New York: Norton, 1963; orig. 1950.
———. *Identity and the Life Cycle.* New York: Norton, 1980.
Erikson, Kai T. *Wayward Puritans: A Study in the Sociology of Deviance.* New York: Wiley, 1966.
Erikson, Robert S., Norman R. Luttbeg, and Kent L. Tedin. *American Public Opinion: Its Origins, Content, and Impact.* 2d ed. New York: Wiley, 1980.
Etzioni, Amitai. *A Comparative Analysis of Complex Organization: On Power, Involvement, and Their Correlates.* Rev. and enlarged ed. New York: Free Press, 1975.
———. "Too Many Rights, Too Few Responsibilities." *Society.* Vol. 28, No. 2 (January–February 1991):41–48.
———. "How to Make Marriage Matter." *Time.* Vol. 142, No. 10 (September 6, 1993):76.
———. "The Responsive Community: A Communitarian Perspective." *American Sociological Review.* Vol. 61, No. 1 (February 1996):1–11.
Etzioni-Halevy, Eva. *Bureaucracy and Democracy: A Political Dilemma.* Rev. ed. Boston: Routledge & Kegan Paul, 1985.
Evans, John H. "Worldviews or Social Groups as the Source of Moral Value Attitudes: Implications for the Culture Wars Thesis." *Sociological Forum,* Vol. 12, No. 3 (September 1997):371–404.
Fagan, Jeffrey, Franklin E. Zimring, and June Kim. "Declining Homicide in New York City: A Tale of Two Trends." *National Institute of Justice Journal.* Vol. 237 (October 1998):12–13.
Falk, Gerhard. Personal communication, 1987.
Falkenmark, Malin, and Carl Widstrand. "Population and Water Resources: A Delicate Balance." *Population Bulletin.* Vol. 47, No. 3 (November 1992). Washington, D.C.: Population Reference Bureau.
Fallon, A. E., and P. Rozin. "Sex Differences in Perception of Desirable Body Shape." *Journal of Abnormal Psychology.* Vol. 94, No. 1 (1985):100–5.
Fallows, James. "Immigration: How It's Affecting Us." *The Atlantic Monthly.* Vol. 252 (November 1983):45–52, 55–62, 66–68, 85–90, 94, 96, 99–106.
Farley, Christopher John. "Winning the Right to Fly." *Time.* Vol. 146, No. 9 (August 28, 1995):62–64.
———. "Hip-Hop Nation." *Time.* Vol. 153, No. 5 (February 8, 1999):54–64.
Farley, Christopher John, and James Willwerth. "Dead Teen Walking." *Time.* Vol. 151, No. 2 (January 19, 1998).
Farrell, Michael P., and Stanley D. Rosenberg. *Men at Midlife.* Boston: Auburn House, 1981.
Feagin, Joe. *The Urban Real Estate Game.* Englewood Cliffs, N.J.: Prentice Hall, 1983.
———. "Death By Discrimination?" *Newsletter,* Society for the Study of Social Problems. Vol. 28, No. 1 (Winter 1997):15–16.
Featherman, David L., and Robert M. Hauser. *Opportunity and Change.* New York: Academic Press, 1978.
Featherstone, Mike, ed. *Global Culture: Nationalism, Globalization, and Modernity.* London: Sage, 1990.
Fedarko, Kevin. "Land Mines: Cheap, Deadly, and Cruel." *Time.* Vol. 147, No. 20 (May 13, 1996):54–55.
Fellman, Bruce. "Taking the Measure of Children's T.V." *Yale Alumni Magazine* (April 1995):46–51.
Ferguson, Tom. "Medical Self-Care: Self Responsibility for Health." In Arthur C. Hastings et al., eds., *Health for the Whole Person: The Complete Guide to Holistic Medicine.* Boulder, Colo.: Westview Press, 1980:87–109.
Fernandez, Roberto M., and Nancy Weinberg. "Sifting and Sorting: Personal Contacts and Hiring in a Retail Bank." *American Sociological Review.* Vol. 62, No. 6 (December 1997):883–902.
Ferree, Myra Marx, and Elaine J. Hall. "Rethinking Stratification from a Feminist Perspective: Gender, Race, and Class in Mainstream Textbooks." *American Sociological Review.* Vol. 61, No. 6 (December 1996):929–50.
Fetto, John. "Down for the Count." *American Demographics.* Vol. 21, No. 11 (November 1999):46–47.
Finkelstein, Neal W., and Ron Haskins. "Kindergarten Children Prefer Same-Color Peers." *Child Development.* Vol. 54, No. 2 (April 1983):502–8.
Finn, Chester E., Jr., and Rebecca L. Gau. "New Ways of Education." *The Public Interest.* Vol. 130 (Winter 1998):79–92.
Finn, Chester E., Jr., and Herbert J. Walberg. "The World's Least Efficient Schools." *Wall Street Journal* (June 22, 1998):A22.
Fiorentine, Robert. "Men, Women, and the Premed Persistence Gap: A Normative Alternatives Approach." *American Journal of Sociology.* Vol. 92, No. 5 (March 1987):1118–39.
Fiorentine, Robert, and Stephen Cole. "Why Fewer Women Become Physicians: Explaining the Premed Persistance Gap." *Sociological Forum.* Vol. 7, No. 3 (September 1992):469–96.
Firebaugh, Glenn. "Growth Effects of Foreign and Domestic Investment." *American Journal of Sociology.* Vol. 98, No. 1 (July 1992):105–30.
———. "Does Foreign Capital Harm Poor Nations? New Estimates Based on Dixon and Boswell's Measures of Capital Penetration." *American Journal of Sociology.* Vol. 102, No. 2 (September 1996):563–75.
———. "Empirics of World Income Inequality." *American Journal of Sociology.* Vol. 104, No. 6 (May 1999):1597–1630.
Firebaugh, Glenn, and Frank D. Beck. "Does Economic Growth Benefit the Masses? Growth, Dependence, and Welfare in the Third World." *American Sociological Review.* Vol. 59, No. 5 (October 1994):631–53.
Firebaugh, Glenn, and Kenneth E. Davis. "Trends in Antiblack Prejudice, 1972–1984: Region and Cohort Effects." *American Journal of Sociology.* Vol. 94, No. 2 (September 1988):251–72.
Firebaugh, Glenn, and Dumitru Sandu. "Who Supports Marketization and Democratization in Post-Communist Romania?" *Sociological Forum.* Vol. 13, No. 3 (September 1998):521–41.
Fischer, Claude W. *The Urban Experience.* 2d ed. New York: Harcourt Brace Jovanovich, 1984.
Fisher, Elizabeth. *Woman's Creation: Sexual Evolution and the Shaping of Society.* Garden City, N.Y.: Anchor/Doubleday, 1979.
Fisher, Roger, and William Ury. "Getting to YES." In William M. Evan and Stephen Hilgartner, eds., *The Arms Race and Nuclear War.* Englewood Cliffs, N.J.: Prentice Hall, 1988:261–68.

FISKE, ALAN PAIGE. "The Cultural Relativity of Selfish Individualism: Anthropological Evidence that Humans Are Inherently Sociable." In Margaret S. Clark, ed., *Prosocial Behavior*. Newbury Park, Calif.: Sage, 1991:176–214.
FISKE, EDWARD B. "Adults: The Forgotten Illiterates." *Christian Science Monitor* (May 30, 1997):18.
FITZGERALD, JOAN, and LOUISE SIMMONS. "From Consumption to Production: Labor Participation in Grass-Roots Movements in Pittsburgh and Hartford." *Urban Affairs Quarterly*. Vol. 26 (June 1991):512–31.
FITZPATRICK, MARY ANNE. *Between Husbands and Wives: Communication in Marriage*. Newbury Park, Calif.: Sage, 1988.
FLAHERTY, MICHAEL G. "A Formal Approach to the Study of Amusement in Social Interaction." *Studies in Symbolic Interaction*. Vol. 5. New York: JAI Press, 1984:71–82.
———. "Two Conceptions of the Social Situation: Some Implications of Humor." *The Sociological Quarterly*. Vol. 31, No. 1 (Spring 1990).
FLORIDA, RICHARD, and MARTIN KENNEY. "Transplanted Organizations: The Transfer of Japanese Industrial Organization to the U.S." *American Sociological Review*. Vol. 56, No. 3 (June 1991):381–98.
FLYNN, PATRICIA. "The Disciplinary Emergence of Bioethics and Bioethics Committees: Moral Ordering and its Legitimation." *Sociological Focus*. Vol. 24, No. 2 (May 1991):145–56.
FOBES, RICHARD. "Creative Problem Solving." *The Futurist*. Vol. 30, No. 1 (January–February 1996):19–22.
Forbes. "The Forbes 400: The Ranking." Vol. 164, No. 9 (October 11, 1999):414–18.
FORD, CLELLAN S., and FRANK A. BEACH. *Patterns of Sexual Behavior*. New York: Harper & Row, 1951.
FORREST, HUGH. "They Are Completely Inactive . . ." *The Gambier Journal*. Vol. 3, No. 4 (February 1984):10–11.
FORSTMANN, THEODORE J. "A Competitive Vision for American Education." *Imprimis*. Vol. 28, No. 9 (September 1999):1–4.
FOST, DAN. "American Indians in the 1990s." *American Demographics*. Vol. 13, No. 12 (December 1991):26–34.
FOUCAULT, MICHEL. *The History of Sexuality: An Introduction*. Vol. 1, trans. Robert Hurley. New York: Vintage, 1990; orig. 1978.
FRANK, ANDRÉ GUNDER. *On Capitalist Underdevelopment*. Bombay: Oxford University Press, 1975.
———. *Crisis: In the World Economy*. New York: Holmes & Meier, 1980.
———. *Reflections on the World Economic Crisis*. New York: Monthly Review Press, 1981.
FRANK, JOHN DAVID, JOHN W. MEYER, and DAVID MIYAHARA. "The Individualist Polity and the Prevalence of a Professionalized Psychology: A Cross-National Study." *American Sociological Review*. Vol. 60, No. 3 (June 1995):360–77.
FRANKLIN, JOHN HOPE. *From Slavery to Freedom: A History of Negro Americans*. 3d ed. New York: Vintage Books, 1967.
FRANKLIN ASSOCIATES. *Characterization of Municipal Solid Waste in the United States, 1960–2000*. Prairie Village, Kans.: Franklin Associates, 1986.
FRAZIER, E. FRANKLIN. *Black Bourgeoisie: The Rise of a New Middle Class*. New York: Free Press, 1965.
FREDRICKSON, GEORGE M. *White Supremacy: A Comparative Study in American and South African History*. New York: Oxford University Press, 1981.
FREE, MARVIN D. "Religious Affiliation, Religiosity, and Impulsive and Intentional Deviance." *Sociological Focus*. Vol. 25, No. 1 (February 1992):77–91.
FREEDOM HOUSE. *Freedom in the World 1998–1999*. New York: Freedom House, 1999.
FRENCH, MARILYN. *Beyond Power: On Women, Men, and Morals*. New York: Summit Books, 1985.
FRIEDAN, BETTY. *The Fountain of Age*. New York: Simon and Schuster, 1993.
FRIEDMAN, MEYER, and RAY H. ROSENMAN. *Type A Behavior and Your Heart*. New York: Fawcett Crest, 1974.
FRIEDMAN, MILTON, and ROSE FRIEDMAN. *Free to Choose: A Personal Statement*. New York: Harcourt Brace Jovanovich, 1980.
FRIEDRICH, CARL J., and ZBIGNIEW BRZEZINSKI. *Totalitarian Dictatorship and Autocracy*. 2d ed. Cambridge, Mass.: Harvard University Press, 1965.
FRUM, DAVID, and FRANK WOLFE. "If You Gotta Get Sued, Get Sued in Utah." *Forbes*. Vol. 153, No. 2 (January 1994):70–73.
FUCHS, VICTOR R. "Sex Differences in Economic Well-Being." *Science*. Vol. 232 (April 25, 1986):459–64.
FUGITA, STEPHEN S., and DAVID J. O'BRIEN. "Structural Assimilation, Ethnic Group Membership, and Political Participation among Japanese Americans: A Research Note." *Social Forces*. Vol. 63, No. 4 (June 1985):986–95.
FUJIMOTO, ISAO. "The Failure of Democracy in a Time of Crisis." In Amy Tachiki et al., eds., *Roots: An Asian American Reader*. Los Angeles: UCLA Asian American Studies Center, 1971:207–14.
FULLER, REX, and RICHARD SCHOENBERGER. "The Gender Salary Gap: Do Academic Achievement, Intern Experience, and College Major Make a Difference?" *Social Science Quarterly*. Vol. 72, No. 4 (December 1991):715–26.
FUREDI, FRANK. "New Britain: A Nation of Victims." *Society*. Vol. 35, No. 3 (April 1998):80–84.
FURSTENBERG, FRANK F., JR., and ANDREW CHERLIN. *Divided Families: What Happens to Children When Parents Part*. Cambridge, Mass.: Harvard University Press, 1991.
GABRIEL, TRIP. "Computers Help Unite Campuses but Also Drive Some Students Apart." *New York Times* (November 11, 1996).
GAGLIANI, GIORGIO. "How Many Working Classes?" *American Journal of Sociology*. Vol. 87, No. 2 (September 1981):259–85.
GAGNE, PATRICIA, and RICHARD TEWKSBURY. "Conformity Pressures and Gender Resistence among Transgendered Individuals." *Social Problems*. Vol. 45, No. 1 (February 1998):81–101.
GAGNE, PATRICIA, RICHARD TEWKSBURY, and DEANNA MCGAUGHEY. "Coming Out and Crossing Over: Identity Formation and Proclamation in a Transgender Community." *Gender and Society*. Vol. 11, No. 4 (August 1997):478–508.
GALLUP POLL. *The Gallup Poll Monthly*. December, 1993.
GALSTER, GEORGE. "Black Suburbanization: Has It Changed the Relative Location of Races?" *Urban Affairs Quarterly*. Vol. 26, No. 4 (June 1991):621–28.
GAMBLE, ANDREW, STEVE LUDLAM, and DAVID BAKER. "Britain's Ruling Class." *The Economist*. Vol. 326, No. 7795 (January 23, 1993):10.
GAMORAN, ADAM. "The Variable Effects of High-School Tracking." *American Sociological Review*. Vol. 57, No. 6 (December 1992):812–28.
GAMSON, WILLIAM A. "Beyond the Science-versus-Advocacy Distinction." *Contemporary Sociology*. Vol. 28, No. 1 (January 1999):23–26.
GANS, HERBERT J. *People and Plans: Essays on Urban Problems and Solutions*. New York: Basic Books, 1968.
———. *Deciding What's News: A Study of CBS Evening News, NBC Nightly News, Newsweek and Time*. New York: Vintage Books, 1980.
GARDNER, MARILYN. "At-Home Dads Give Their New Career High Marks." *Christian Science Monitor* (May 30, 1996):1, 12.
GARFINKEL, HAROLD. "Conditions of Successful Degradation Ceremonies." *American Journal of Sociology*. Vol. 61, No. 2 (March 1956):420–24.
———. *Studies in Ethnomethodology*. Cambridge: Polity Press, 1967.
GARREAU, JOEL. *Edge City*. New York: Doubleday, 1991.
GEERTZ, CLIFFORD. "Common Sense as a Cultural System." *The Antioch Review*. Vol. 33, No. 1 (Spring 1975):5–26.
GEIST, WILLIAM. *Toward a Safe and Sane Halloween and Other Tales of Suburbia*. New York: Times Books, 1985.
GELLES, RICHARD J., and CLAIRE PEDRICK CORNELL. *Intimate Violence in Families*. 2d ed. Newbury Park, Calif.: Sage, 1990.
———. "Born or Bred?" *Newsweek* (February 24, 1992):46–53.
GEORGE, SUSAN. *How the Other Half Dies: The Real Reasons for World Hunger*. Totowa, N.J.: Rowman & Allanheld, 1977.
GERBER, THEODORE P., and MICHAEL HOUT. "More Shock than Therapy: Market Transition, Employment, and Income in Russia, 1991–1995." *American Journal of Sociology*. Vol. 104, No. 1 (July 1998):1–50.
GERLACH, MICHAEL L. *The Social Organization of Japanese Business*. Berkeley and Los Angeles: University of California Press, 1992.
GERSTEL, NAOMI. "Divorce and Stigma." *Social Problems*. Vol. 43, No. 2 (April 1987):172–86.
GERTH, H. H., and C. WRIGHT MILLS, eds. *From Max Weber: Essays in Sociology*. New York: Oxford University Press, 1946.
GESCHWENDER, JAMES A. *Racial Stratification in America*. Dubuque, Iowa: Wm. C. Brown, 1978.
GEWERTZ, DEBORAH. "A Historical Reconsideration of Female Dominance among the Chambri of Papua New Guinea." *American Ethnologist*. Vol. 8, No. 1 (1981):94–106.
GIBBONS, DON C., and MARVIN D. KROHN. *Delinquent Behavior*. 4th ed. Englewood Cliffs, N.J.: Prentice Hall, 1986.
GIBBS, NANCY. "When Is It Rape?" *Time*. Vol. 137, No. 22 (June 3, 1991a):48–54.
———. "The Clamor on Campus." *Time*. Vol. 137, No. 22 (June 3, 1991b):54–55.

———. "How Much Should We Teach Our Children about Sex?" *Time*. Vol. 141, No. 21 (May 24, 1993):60–66.
———. "Cause Celeb." *Time*. Vol. 147, No. 25 (June 17, 1996):28–30.
GIDDENS, ANTHONY. *Sociology: A Brief but Critical Introduction*. New York: Harcourt Brace Jovanovich, 1982.
———. *The Transformation of Intimacy*. Cambridge, UK: Polity Press, 1992.
GIELE, JANET Z. "Gender and Sex Roles." In Neil J. Smelser, ed., *Handbook of Sociology*. Newbury Park, Calif.: Sage, 1988:291–323.
GIGLIOTTI, RICHARD J., and HEATHER K. HUFF. "Role Related Conflicts, Strains, and Stresses of Older-Adult College Students." *Sociological Focus*. Vol. 28, No. 3 (August 1995):329–42.
GILBERT, NEIL. "Realities and Mythologies of Rape." *Society*. Vol. 29, No. 4 (May–June 1992):4–10.
GILBERTSON, GRETA A., and DOUGLAS T. GURAK. "Broadening the Enclave Debate: The Dual Labor Market Experiences of Dominican and Colombian Men in New York City." *Sociological Forum*. Vol. 8, No. 2 (June 1993):205–20.
GILL, RICHARD T. "What Happened to the American Way of Death?" *The Public Interest*. Vol. 127 (Spring 1996):105–17.
GILLIARD, DARRELL K., and ALLEN J. BECK. *Prisoners in 1997*. Washington, D.C.: U.S. Bureau of Justice Statistics, 1998.
GILLIGAN, CAROL. *In a Different Voice: Psychological Theory and Women's Development*. Cambridge, Mass.: Harvard University Press, 1982.
———. *Making Connections: The Relational Worlds of Adolescent Girls at Emma Willard School*. Cambridge, Mass.: Harvard University Press, 1990.
GILLON, RAANAN. "Euthanasia in the Netherlands—Down the Slippery Slope?" *Journal of Medical Ethics*. Vol. 25, No. 1 (February 1999):3–4.
GIMENEZ, MARTHA E. "Silence in the Classroom: Some Thoughts about Teaching in the 1980s." *Teaching Sociology*. Vol. 17, No. 2 (April 1989):184–91.
GINSBURG, FAYE, and ANNA LOWENHAUPT TSING, eds. *Uncertain Terms: Negotiating Gender in American Culture*. Boston: Beacon Press, 1990.
GIOVANNINI, MAUREEN. "Female Anthropologist and Male Informant: Gender Conflict in a Sicilian Town." In John J. Macionis and Nijole V. Benokraitis, eds., *Seeing Ourselves: Classic, Contemporary, and Cross-Cultural Readings in Sociology*. 2d ed. Englewood Cliffs, N.J.: Prentice Hall, 1992:27–32.
GIUGNI, MARCO G. "Structure and Culture in Social Movements Theory." *Sociological Forum*. Vol. 13, No. 2 (June 1998):365–75.
GLADUE, BRIAN A., RICHARD GREEN, and RONALD E. HELLMAN. "Neuroendocrine Response to Estrogen and Sexual Orientation." *Science*. Vol. 225, No. 4669 (September 28, 1984):1496–99.
GLEICK, ELIZABETH. "The Marker We've Been Waiting For." *Time*. Vol. 149, No. 14 (April 7, 1997):28–42.
GLENN, NORVAL D., and BETH ANN SHELTON. "Regional Differences in Divorce in the United States." *Journal of Marriage and the Family*. Vol. 47, No. 3 (August 1985):641–52.
GLOCK, CHARLES Y. "The Religious Revival in America." In Jane Zahn, ed., *Religion and the Face of America*. Berkeley: University of California Press, 1959:25–42.
———. "On the Study of Religious Commitment." *Religious Education*. Vol. 62, No. 4 (1962):98–110.
GLUECK, SHELDON, and ELEANOR GLUECK. *Unraveling Juvenile Delinquency*. New York: Commonwealth Fund, 1950.
GNIDA, JOHN J. "Teaching 'Nature versus Nurture': The Case of African American Athletic Success." *Teaching Sociology*. Vol. 23, No. 4 (October 1995):389–95.
GODWIN, KENNETH, FRANK KEMERER, VALERIE MARTINEZ, and RICHARD RUDERMAN. "Liberal Equity in Education: A Comparison of Choice Options." *Social Science Quarterly*. Vol. 79, No. 3 (September 1998):502–22.
GOETTING, ANN. *Getting Out: Life Stories of Women Who Left Abusive Men*. New York: Columbia University Press, 1999.
GOFFMAN, ERVING. *The Presentation of Self in Everyday Life*. Garden City, N.Y.: Anchor Books, 1959.
———. *Asylums: Essays on the Social Situation of Mental Patients and Other Inmates*. Garden City, N.Y.: Anchor Books, 1961.
———. *Stigma: Notes on the Management of Spoiled Identity*. Englewood Cliffs, N.J.: Prentice Hall, 1963.
———. *Interactional Ritual: Essays on Face to Face Behavior*. Garden City, N.Y.: Anchor Books, 1967.
———. *Gender Advertisements*. New York: Harper Colophon, 1979.
GOLDBERG, STEVEN. *The Inevitability of Patriarchy*. New York: William Morrow, 1974.
———. Personal communication, 1987.
GOLDEN, FREDERIC. "Good Eggs, Bad Eggs." *Time*. Vol. 153, No. 1 (January 11, 1999a):56–59.
———. "Lying Faces Unmasked." *Time*. Vol. 153, No. 13 (April 5, 1999b):52.
GOLDFARB, JEFFREY C. *Beyond Glasnost: The Post-Totalitarian Mind*. Chicago: University of Chicago Press, 1989.
GOLDFARB, WILLIAM. "Groundwater: The Buried Life." In F. Herbert Bormann and Stephen R. Kellert, eds., *Ecology, Economics, and Ethics: The Broken Circle*. New Haven, Conn.: Yale University Press, 1991:123–35.
GOLDSMITH, H. H. "Genetic Influences on Personality from Infancy." *Child Development*. Vol. 54, No. 2 (April 1983):331–35.
GOODE, WILLIAM J. "The Theoretical Importance of Love." *American Sociological Review*. Vol. 24, No. 1 (February 1959):38–47.
———. "Encroachment, Charlatanism, and the Emerging Profession: Psychology, Sociology and Medicine." *American Sociological Review*. Vol. 25, No. 6 (December 1960):902–14.
GORDON, JAMES S. "The Paradigm of Holistic Medicine." In Arthur C. Hastings et al., eds., *Health for the Whole Person: The Complete Guide to Holistic Medicine*. Boulder, Colo.: Westview Press, 1980:3–27.
GORDON, SOL, and CRAIG W. SNYDER. *Personal Issues in Human Sexuality: A Guidebook for Better Sexual Health*. 2d ed. Boston: Allyn & Bacon, 1989.
GORING, CHARLES BUCKMAN. *The English Convict: A Statistical Study*. Montclair, N.J.: Patterson Smith, 1972; orig. 1913.
GOTHAM, KEVIN FOX. "Race, Mortgage Lending, and Loan Rejections in a U.S. City." *Sociological Focus*. Vol. 31, No. 4 (October 1998):391–405.
GOTTFREDSON, MICHAEL R., and TRAVIS HIRSCHI. "National Crime Control Policies." *Society*. Vol. 32, No. 2 (January–February 1995):30–36.
GOTTMANN, JEAN. *Megalopolis*. New York: Twentieth Century Fund, 1961.
GOUGH, KATHLEEN. "The Origin of the Family." *Journal of Marriage and the Family*. Vol. 33, No. 4 (November 1971):760–71.
———. "The Origin of the Family." In John J. Macionis and Nijole V. Benokraitis, eds., *Seeing Ourselves: Classic, Contemporary, and Cross-Cultural Readings in Sociology*. Englewood Cliffs, N.J.: Prentice Hall, 1989.
GOULD, STEPHEN J. "Evolution as Fact and Theory." *Discover* (May 1981):35–37.
GOULDNER, ALVIN. *The Coming Crisis of Western Sociology*. New York: Avon Books, 1970.
GRABOSKY, PETER, JOHN BRAITHWAITE, and P. R. WILSON. "The Myth of Community Tolerance toward White-Collar Crime." *Australia and New Zealand Journal of Criminology*. Vol. 20 (1987):34.
GRAHAM, JOHN W., and ANDREA H. BELLER. "Child Support in Black and White: Racial Differentials in the Award and Receipt of Child Support during the 1980s." *Social Science Quarterly*. Vol. 77, No. 3 (September 1996):528–42.
GRANT, DON SHERMAN, II, and MICHAEL WALLACE. "Why Do Strikes Turn Violent?" *American Journal of Sociology*. Vol. 96, No. 5 (March 1991):1117–50.
GRANT, DONALD L. *The Anti-Lynching Movement*. San Francisco: R and E Research Associates, 1975.
GRANT, KAREN R. "The Inverse Care Law in the Context of Universal Free Health Insurance in Canada: Toward Meeting Health Needs through Public Policy." *Sociological Focus*. Vol. 17, No. 2 (April 1984):137–55.
GREELEY, ANDREW M. *Religious Change in America*. Cambridge, Mass.: Harvard University Press, 1989.
GREEN, JOHN C. "Pat Robertson and the Latest Crusade: Resources and the 1988 Presidential Campaign." *Social Sciences Quarterly*. Vol. 74, No. 1 (March 1993):156–68.
GREENBERG, DAVID F. *The Construction of Homosexuality*. Chicago: University of Chicago Press, 1988.
GREENFIELD, LAWRENCE A. *Child Victimizers: Violent Offenders and their Victims*. Washington, D.C.: U.S. Bureau of Justice Statistics, 1996.
GREENHOUSE, LINDA. "Justices Uphold Stiffer Sentences for Hate Crimes." *New York Times* (June 12, 1993):1, 8.
GREENWALD, JOHN. "The New Service Class." *Time*. Vol. 144, No. 20 (November 14, 1994):72–74.
GREGORY, PAUL R., and ROBERT C. STUART. *Comparative Economic Systems*. 2d ed. Boston: Houghton Mifflin, 1985.
GROSS, JANE. "New Challenge of Youth: Growing Up in a Gay Home." *New York Times* (February 11, 1991):A1, B7.
GROTH, NICHOLAS A., and H. JEAN BIRNBAUM. *Men Who Rape: The Psychology of the Offender*. New York: Plenum, 1979.

Gup, Ted. "What Makes This School Work?" *Time.* Vol. 140, No. 25 (December 21, 1992):63–65.
Gurak, Douglas T., and Joseph P. Fitzpatrick. "Intermarriage among Hispanic Ethnic Groups in New York City." *American Journal of Sociology.* Vol. 87, No. 4 (January 1982):921–34.
Gurnett, Kate. "On the Forefront of Feminism." *Albany Times Union* (July 5, 1998):G-1, G-6.
Gwartney-Gibbs, Patricia A. "The Institutionalization of Premarital Cohabitation: Estimates from Marriage License Applications, 1970 and 1980." *Journal of Marriage and the Family.* Vol. 48, No. 2 (May 1986):423–34.
Gwartney-Gibbs, Patricia A., Jean Stockard, and Susanne Bohmer. "Learning Courtship Agression: The Influence of Parents, Peers, and Personal Experiences." *Family Relations.* Vol. 36, No. 3 (July 1987):276–82.
Gwynne, S. C., and John F. Dickerson. "Lost in the E-Mail." *Time.* Vol. 149, No. 15 (April 21, 1997):88–90.
Habermas, Jürgen. *Toward a Rational Society: Student Protest, Science, and Politics.* Jeremy J. Shapiro, trans. Boston: Beacon Press, 1970.
Hacker, Helen Mayer. "Women as a Minority Group." *Social Forces.* Vol. 30 (October 1951):60–69.
———. "Women as a Minority Group: 20 Years Later." In Florence Denmark, ed., *Who Discriminates Against Women?* Beverly Hills, Calif.: Sage, 1974:124–34.
Hackey, Robert B. "Competing Explanations of Voter Turnout among American Blacks." *Social Science Quarterly.* Vol. 73, No. 1 (March 1992):71–89.
Hadaway, C. Kirk, Penny Long Marler, and Mark Chaves. "What the Polls Don't Show: A Closer Look at U.S. Church Attendance." *American Sociological Review.* Vol. 58, No. 6 (December 1993):741–52.
Hadden, Jeffrey K., and Charles E. Swain. *Prime Time Preachers: The Rising Power of Televangelism.* Reading, Mass.: Addison-Wesley, 1981.
Hafner, Katie. "Making Sense of the Internet." *Newsweek* (October 24, 1994):46–48.
Hagan, Jacqueline Maria. "Social Networks, Gender, and Immigrant Incorporation: Resources and Restraints." *American Sociological Review.* Vol. 63, No. 1 (February 1998):55–67.
Hagan, John, and Patricia Parker. "White-Collar Crime and Punishment: The Class Structure and Legal Sanctioning of Securities Violations." *American Sociological Review.* Vol. 50, No. 3 (June 1985):302–16.
Haig, Robin Andrew. *The Anatomy of Humor: Biopsychosocial and Therapeutic Perspectives.* Springfield, Ill.: Charles C. Thomas, 1988.
Halberstam, David. *The Reckoning.* New York: Avon Books, 1986.
Haledjian, Dean. "How to Tell a Businessman from a Businesswoman." Annandale, Va.: Northern Virginia Community College, 1997.
Hall, John R., and Mary Jo Neitz. *Culture: Sociological Perspectives.* Englewood Cliffs, N.J.: Prentice Hall, 1993.
Hall, Kelley J., and Betsy Lucal. "Tapping in Parallel Universes: Using Superhero Comic Books in Sociology Courses." *Teaching Sociology.* Vol. 27, No. 1 (January 1999):60–66.
Hallinan, Maureen T. "The Sociological Study of Social Change." *American Sociological Review.* Vol. 62, No. 1 (February 1997):1–11.
Hallinan, Maureen T., and Richard A. Williams. "Interracial Friendship Choices in Secondary Schools." *American Sociological Review.* Vol. 54, No. 1 (February 1989):67–78.
Hamel, Ruth. "Raging against Aging." *American Demographics.* Vol. 12, No. 3 (March 1990):42–45.
Hamer, Dean, and Peter Copeland. *The Science of Desire: The Search for the Gay Gene and the Biology of Behavior.* New York: Simon & Schuster, 1994.
Hammond, Philip E. "Introduction." In Philip E. Hammond, ed., *The Sacred in a Secular Age: Toward Revision in the Scientific Study of Religion.* Berkeley: University of California Press, 1985:1–6.
Hamrick, Michael H., David J. Anspaugh, and Gene Ezell. *Health.* Columbus, Ohio: Merrill, 1986.
Handgun Control, Inc. [Online] Available http://www.handguncontrol.org/press/archive/march30-98.htm, April 3, 2000.
Handlin, Oscar. *Boston's Immigrants 1790–1865: A Study in Acculturation.* Cambridge, Mass.: Harvard University Press, 1941.
Haney, Craig, Curtis Banks, and Philip Zimbardo. "Interpersonal Dynamics in a Simulated Prison." *International Journal of Criminology and Penology.* Vol. 1 (1973):69–97.
Hans, Valerie P. "Factors Affecting Lay Judgments of Corporate Wrongdoing." Paper presented at the Third European Conference of Law and Psychology. University of Oxford, Oxford, UK, 1992.
Harbert, Anita A., and Leon H. Ginsberg. *Human Services for Older Adults.* Columbia: University of South Carolina Press, 1991.
Hareven, Tamara K. "The Life Course and Aging in Historical Perspective." In Tamara K. Hareven and Kathleen J. Adams, eds., *Aging and Life Course Transitions: An Interdisciplinary Perspective.* New York: Guilford Press, 1982:1–26.
Harlan, William H. "Social Status of the Aged in Three Indian Villages." In Bernice L. Neugarten, ed., *Middle Age and Aging: A Reader in Social Psychology.* Chicago: University of Chicago Press, 1968:469–75.
Harlow, Harry F., and Margaret Kuenne Harlow. "Social Deprivation in Monkeys." *Scientific American.* Vol. 207 (November 1962):137–46.
Harpster, Paula, and Elizabeth Monk-Turner. "Why Men Do Housework: A Test of Gender Production and the Relative Resources Model." *Sociological Focus.* Vol. 31, No. 1 (February 1998):45–59.
Harries, Keith D. *Serious Violence: Patterns of Homicide and Assault in America.* Springfield, Ill.: Charles C. Thomas, 1990.
Harrington, Michael. *The New American Poverty.* New York: Penguin Books, 1984.
Harris, Chauncey D., and Edward L. Ullman. "The Nature of Cities." *The Annals.* Vol. 242 (November 1945):7–17.
Harris, Jack Dash. Lecture on cockfighting in the Philippines. Semester at Sea (October 27, 1994).
Harris, Marvin. "Why Men Dominate Women." *New York Times Magazine* (November 13, 1977):46, 115–23.
———. *Cultural Anthropology.* 1st ed., 1983; 2d ed. New York: Harper & Row, 1987.
Harrison, Paul. *Inside the Third World: The Anatomy of Poverty.* 2d ed. New York: Penguin Books, 1984.
Harvey, David. "Labor, Capital, and Class Struggle around the Built Environment." *Politics and Society.* Vol. 6 (1976):265–95.
Havighurst, Robert J., Bernice L. Neugarten, and Sheldon S. Tobin. "Disengagement and Patterns of Aging." In Bernice L. Neugarten, ed., *Middle Age and Aging: A Reader in Social Psychology.* Chicago: University of Chicago Press, 1968:161–72.
Hawthorne, Peter. "South Africa's Makeover." *Time.* Vol. 154, No. 2 (July 12, 1999).
Hayneman, Stephen P., and William A. Loxley. "The Effect of Primary-School Quality on Academic Achievement across Twenty-nine High- and Low-Income Countries." *American Journal of Sociology.* Vol. 88, No. 6 (May 1983):1162–94.
Heath, Julia A., and W. David Bourne. "Husbands and Housework: Parity or Parody?" *Social Science Quarterly.* Vol. 76, No. 1 (March 1995):195–202.
Helgesen, Sally. *The Female Advantage: Women's Ways of Leadership.* New York: Doubleday, 1990.
Helin, David W. "When Slogans Go Wrong." *American Demographics.* Vol. 14, No. 2 (February 1992):14.
Henley, Nancy, Mykol Hamilton, and Barrie Thorne. "Womanspeak and Manspeak: Sex Differences in Communication, Verbal and Nonverbal." In John J. Macionis and Nijole V. Benokraitis, eds., *Seeing Ourselves: Classic, Contemporary, and Cross-Cultural Readings in Sociology.* 2d ed. Englewood Cliffs, N.J.: Prentice Hall, 1992:10–15.
Henry, William A., III. "Gay Parents: Under Fire and On the Rise." *Time.* Vol. 142, No. 12 (September 20, 1993):66–71.
Herda-Rapp, Ann. "The Power of Informal Leadership: Women Leaders in the Civil Rights Movement." *Sociological Focus.* Vol. 31, No. 4 (October 1998):341–55
Herdt, Gilbert H. "Semen Transactions in Sambian Culture." In David N. Suggs and Andrew W. Miracle, eds., *Culture and Human Sexuality.* Pacific Grove, Calif.: Brooks Cole, 1993:298–327.
Herek, Gregory M. "Myths about Sexual Orientation: A Lawyer's Guide to Social Science Research." *Law and Sexuality.* No. 1 (1991):133–72.
Herman, Dianne. "The Rape Culture." In John J. Macionis and Nijole V. Benokraitis, eds., *Seeing Ourselves: Classic, Contemporary, and Cross-Cultural Readings in Sociology.* 5th ed. Upper Saddle River, N.J.: Prentice Hall, 2001.
Herman, Edward S. *Corporate Control, Corporate Power: A Twentieth Century Fund Study.* New York: Cambridge University Press, 1981.

HERRNSTEIN, RICHARD J., and CHARLES MURRAY. *The Bell Curve: Intelligence and Class Structure in American Life*. New York: Free Press, 1994.
HERRSTROM, STAFFAN. "Sweden: Pro-Choice on Child Care." *New Perspectives Quarterly*. Vol. 7, No. 1 (Winter 1990):27–28.
HERSCH, JONI, and SHELLY WHITE-MEANS. "Employer-Sponsored Health and Pension Benefits and the Gender/Race Wage Gap." *Social Science Quarterly*. Vol. 74, No. 4 (December 1993):850–66.
HESS, BETH B. "Breaking and Entering the Establishment: Committing Social Change and Confronting the Backlash." *Social Problems*. Vol. 46, No. 1 (February 1999):1–12.
HEWLETT, BARRY S. "Husband-Wife Reciprocity and the Father-Infant Relationship among Aka Pygmies." In Barry S. Hewlett, ed., *Father-Child Relations: Cultural and Bio-Social Contexts*. New York: Aldine, 1992:153–76.
HEWLETT, SYLVIA ANN. "The Feminization of the Work Force." *New Perspectives Quarterly*. Vol. 7, No. 1 (Winter 1990):13–15.
HIROSHI, MANNARI. *The Japanese Business Leaders*. Tokyo: University of Tokyo Press, 1974.
HIRSCHI, TRAVIS. *Causes of Delinquency*. Berkeley: University of California Press, 1969.
HOBERMAN, JOHN. *Darwin's Athletes: How Sport Has Damaged Black America and Preserved the Myth of Race*. Boston: Houghton Mifflin, 1997.
———. "Response to Three Reviews of Darwin's Athletes." *Social Science Quarterly*. Vol. 79, No. 4 (December 1998):898–903.
HOCHSCHILD, ARLIE, with ANNE MACHUNG. *The Second Shift: Working Parents and the Revolution at Home*. New York: Viking Books, 1989.
HOCKEY, JENNY, and ALLISON JAMES. *Growing Up and Growing Old: Aging and Dependency in the Life Course*. Newbury Park, Calif.: Sage, 1993.
HODGE, ROBERT W., DONALD J. TREIMAN, and PETER H. ROSSI. "A Comparative Study of Occupational Prestige." In Reinhard Bendix and Seymour Martin Lipset, eds., *Class, Status, and Power: Social Stratification in Comparative Perspective*. 2d ed. New York: Free Press, 1966:309–21.
HOERR, JOHN. "The Payoff from Teamwork." *Business Week*. No. 3114 (July 10, 1989):56–62.
HOGAN, DENNIS P., and EVELYN M. KITAGAWA. "The Impact of Social Status and Neighborhood on the Fertility of Black Adolescents." *American Journal of Sociology*. Vol. 90, No. 4 (January 1985):825–55.
HOGAN, RICHARD, and CAROLYN C. PERRUCCI. "Producing and Reproducing the Class and Status Differences: Racial and Gender Gaps in U.S. Employment and Retirement Income." *Social Problems*. Vol. 45, No. 4 (November 1998):528–49.
HOGGART, RICHARD. "The Abuses of Literacy." *Society*. Vol. 55, No. 3 (March–April 1995):55–62.
HOLLANDER, PAUL. "We Are All (Sniffle, Sniffle) Victims Now." *Wall Street Journal* (January 18, 1995):A14.
HOLM, JEAN. *The Study of Religions*. New York: Seabury Press, 1977.
HOLMES, MALCOLM D., HARMON M. HOSCH, HOWARD C. DAUDISTEL, DOLORES PEREZ, and JOSEPH B. GRAVES. "Judges, Ethnicity and Minority Sentencing: Evidence among Hispanics." *Social Science Quarterly*. Vol. 74, No. 3 (September 1993):496–506.
HOLMES, STEVEN A. "U.S. Reports Drop in Rate of Births to Unwed Women." *New York Times* (October 5, 1996a):1, 9.
———. "For Hispanic Poor, No Silver Lining." *New York Times* (October 13, 1996b): section 4, p. 5.
HOLMES, THOMAS H., and RICHARD H. RAHE. "The Social Readjustment Rating Scale." *Journal of Psychosomatic Research*. Vol. 11 (1967):213–18.
HOLMSTROM, DAVID. "Abuse of Elderly, Even by Adult Children, Gets More Attention and Official Concern." *Christian Science Monitor* (July 28, 1994):1.
HOLTZ, HARVEY, ed. *Education and the American Dream: Conservatives, Liberals, and Radicals Debate the Future of Education*. Granby, Mass.: Bergin & Garvey, 1989.
HONAN, WILLIAM H. "Class Notes: Northwestern University Takes a Lead in Using the Internet to Add Sound and Sight to Courses." *New York Times* (May 28, 1997):B7.
HONEYWELL, ROY J. *The Educational Work of Thomas Jefferson*. Cambridge, Mass.: Harvard University Press, 1931.
HOROWITZ, IRVING LOUIS. *The Decomposition of Sociology*. New York: Oxford University Press, 1993.
HOSTETLER, JOHN A. *Amish Society*. 3d ed. Baltimore: Johns Hopkins University Press, 1980.
HOUT, MICHAEL. "More Universalism, Less Structural Mobility: The American Occupational Structure in the 1980s." *American Journal of Sociology*. Vol. 95, No. 6 (May 1998):1358–1400.
HOUT, MICHAEL, and ANDREW M. GREELEY. "The Center Doesn't Hold: Church Attendance in the United States, 1940–1984." *American Sociological Review*. Vol. 52, No. 3 (June 1987):325–45.
———. "What Church Officials' Reports Don't Show: Another Look at Church Attendance Data." *American Sociological Review*. Vol. 63, No. 1 (February 1998):113–19.
HOUT, MIKE, CLEM BROOKS, and JEFF MANZA. "The Persistence of Classes in Post-Industrial Societies." *International Sociology*. Vol. 8, No. 3 (September 1993):259–77.
HOYT, HOMER. *The Structure and Growth of Residential Neighborhoods in American Cities*. Washington, D.C.: Federal Housing Administration, 1939.
HSU, FRANCIS L. K. *The Challenge of the American Dream: The Chinese in the United States*. Belmont, Calif.: Wadsworth, 1971.
HUBER, JOAN, and BETH E. SCHNEIDER, eds. *The Social Context of AIDS*. Newbury Park, Calif.: Sage, 1992.
HUCHINGSON, JAMES E. "Science and Religion." *The Herald* (Dade County, Florida). December 25, 1994:1M, 6M.
HUET-COX, ROCIO. "Medical Education: New Wine in Old Wine Skins." In Victor W. Sidel and Ruth Sidel, eds., *Reforming Medicine: Lessons of the Last Quarter Century*. New York: Pantheon Books, 1984:129–49.
HUFFMAN, MATT L., STEVEN C. VELASCO, and WILLIAM T. BIELBY. "Where Sex Composition Matters Most: Comparing the Effects of Job versus Occupational Sex Composition of Earnings." *Sociological Focus*. Vol. 29, No. 3 (August 1996):189–207.
HUGHES, MICHAEL, and MELVIN E. THOMAS. "The Continuing Significance of Race Revisted: A Study of Race, Class, and Quality of Life in America, 1972 to 1996." *American Sociological Review*. Vol. 63, No. 6 (December 1998):785–95.
HULS, GLENNA. Personal communication, 1987.
HUMMER, ROBERT A., RICHARD G. ROGERS, CHARLES B. NAM, and FELICIA B. LECLERE. "Race/Ethnicity, Nativity, and U.S. Adult Mortality." *Social Science Quarterly*. Vol. 80, No. 1 (March 1999):136–53.
HUMPHREY, CRAIG R., and FREDERICK R. BUTTEL. *Environment, Energy, and Society*. Belmont, Calif.: Wadsworth, 1982.
HUMPHREY, DEREK. *Final Exit: The Practicalities of Self-Deliverance and Assisted Suicide for the Dying*. Eugene, Ore.: The Hemlock Society, 1991.
HUNNICUT, BENJAMIN K. "Are We All Working Too Hard? No Time for God or Family." *Wall Street Journal* (January 4, 1990).
HUNT, MORTON. *Sexual Behavior in the 1970s*. Chicago: Playboy Press, 1974.
HUNTER, FLOYD. *Community Power Structure*. Garden City, N.Y.: Doubleday, 1963; orig. 1953.
HUNTER, JAMES DAVISON. *American Evangelicalism: Conservative Religion and the Quandary of Modernity*. New Brunswick, N.J.: Rutgers University Press, 1983.
———. "Conservative Protestantism." In Philip E. Hammond, ed., *The Sacred in a Secular Age*. Berkeley: University of California Press, 1985:50–66.
———. *Evangelicalism: The Coming Generation*. Chicago: University of Chicago Press, 1987.
———. *Culture Wars: The Struggle to Define America*. New York: Basic Books, 1991.
HURN, CHRISTOPHER. *The Limits and Possibilities of Schooling*. Needham Heights, Mass.: Allyn & Bacon, 1978.
HYMAN, HERBERT H., and CHARLES R. WRIGHT. "Trends in Voluntary Association Memberships of American Adults: Replication Based on Secondary Analysis of National Sample Survey." *American Sociological Review*. Vol. 36, No. 2 (April 1971):191–206.
HYMOWITZ, CAROL. "World's Poorest Women Advance by Entrepreneurship." *Wall Street Journal* (September 9, 1995):B1.
HYMOWITZ, KAY S. "Kids Today Are Growing Up Way Too Fast." *Wall Street Journal* (October 28, 1998):A22.
IANNACCONE, LAURENCE R. "Why Strict Churches Are Strong." *American Journal of Sociology*. Vol. 99, No. 5 (March 1994):1180–1211.
IDE, THOMAS R., and ARTHUR J. CORDELL. "Automating Work." *Society*. Vol. 31, No. 6 (September–October 1994):65–71.
ILLICH, IVAN. *Medical Nemesis: The Expropriation of Health*. New York: Pantheon Books, 1976.
IMIG, DOUGLAS R., and DAVID S. MEYER. "Privacy and Opportunity and Peace and Justice Advocacy in the 1980s: A Tale of Two Sectors." *Social Science Quarterly*. Vol. 74, No. 4 (December 1993):750–70.

INGLEHART, RONALD. *Modernization and Postmodernization: Cultural, Economic, and Political Change in 43 Societies.* Princeton, N.J.: Princeton University Press, 1997.

INTER-PARLIAMENTARY UNION. *Men and Women in Politics: Democracy in the Making.* Geneva: 1997.

ISAACSON, WALTER. "Our Century . . . and the Next One." *Time 100.* Special Issue. Vol. 151, No. 14 (1998).

ISAY, RICHARD A. *Being Homosexual: Gay Men and Their Development.* New York: Farrar, Straus, & Giroux, 1989.

JACOB, JOHN E. "An Overview of Black America in 1985." In James D. Williams, ed., *The State of Black America 1986.* New York: National Urban League, 1986:i–xi.

JACOBS, DAVID, and RONALD E. HELMS. "Toward a Political Model of Incarceration: A Time-Series Examination of Multiple Explanations for Prison Admission Rates." *American Journal of Sociology.* Vol. 102, No. 2 (September 1996):323–57.

JACOBS, DAVID, and ROBERT M. O'BRIEN. "The Determinants of Deadly Force: A Structural Analysis of Police Violence." *American Journal of Sociology.* Vol. 103, No. 4 (January 1998):837–62.

JACOBS, JAMES B. "Should Hate Be a Crime?" *The Public Interest.* No. 113 (Fall 1993):3–14.

JACOBS, JANE. *The Economy of Cities.* New York: Vintage Books, 1970.

JACOBY, RUSSELL, and NAOMI GLAUBERMAN, eds. *The Bell Curve Debate.* New York: Random House, 1995.

JACQUET, CONSTANT H., and ALICE M. JONES. *Yearbook of American and Canadian Churches 1991.* Nashville, Tenn.: Abingdon Press, 1991.

JAGAROWSKY, PAUL A., and MARY JO BANE. *Neighborhood Poverty: Basic Questions.* Discussion paper series H-90-3. John F. Kennedy School of Government. Cambridge, Mass.: Harvard University Press, 1990.

JAGGER, ALISON. "Political Philosophies of Women's Liberation." In Laurel Richardson and Verta Taylor, eds., *Feminist Frontiers: Rethinking Sex, Gender, and Society.* Reading, Mass.: Addison-Wesley, 1983.

JAMES, DAVID R. "City Limits on Racial Equality: The Effects of City-Suburb Boundaries on Public-School Desegregation, 1968–1976." *American Sociological Review.* Vol. 54, No. 6 (December 1989):963–85.

JANIS, IRVING. *Victims of Groupthink.* Boston: Houghton Mifflin, 1972.

———. *Crucial Decisions: Leadership in Policymaking and Crisis Management.* New York: Free Press, 1989.

JANUS, CHRISTOPHER G. "Slavery Abolished? Only Officially." *Christian Science Monitor* (May 17, 1996):18.

JARRETT, ROBIN L. "Living Poor: Family Life among Single Parent, African-American Women." *Social Problems.* Vol. 41, No. 1 (February 1994):30–49.

JASPER, JAMES M. "The Emotions of Protest: Affective and Reactive Emotions in and around Social Movements." *Sociological Forum.* Vol. 13, No. 3 (September 1998):397–424.

JEFFERSON, THOMAS. Letter to James Madison, October 28, 1785. In Julian P. Boyd, ed., *The Papers of Thomas Jefferson.* Princeton, N.J.: Princeton University Press, 1953:681–83; orig. 1785.

JENCKS, CHRISTOPHER. "Genes and Crime." *The New York Review* (February 12, 1987):33–41.

JENKINS, J. CRAIG, and CHARLES PERROW. "Insurgency of the Powerless: Farm Worker Movements (1946–1972)." *American Sociological Review.* Vol. 42, No. 2 (April 1977):249–68.

JENKINS, J. CRAIG, and MICHAEL WALLACE. "The Generalized Action Potential of Protest Movements: The New Class, Social Trends, and Political Exclusion Explanations." *Sociological Forum.* Vol. 11, No. 2 (June 1996):183–207.

JENSEN, LIEF, DAVID J. EGGEBEEN, and DANIEL T. LICHTER. "Child Policy and the Ameliorative Effects of Public Assistance." *Social Science Quarterly.* Vol. 74, No. 3 (September 1993):542–59.

JOHNSON, CATHRYN. "Gender, Legitimate Authority, and Leader-Subordinate Conversations." *American Sociological Review.* Vol. 59, No. 1 (February 1994):122–35.

JOHNSON, DIRK. "Census Finds Many Claiming New Identity: Indian." *New York Times* (March 5, 1991):A1, A16.

JOHNSON, GEORGE. "It's a Fact: Faith and Theory Collide over Evolution." *New York Times* (August 15, 1999):Sec. 4; 1, 4.

JOHNSON, JEAN. "Americans' Views on Crime and Law Enforcement." *National Institute of Justice Journal.* Issue 233 (September 1997):9–14.

JOHNSON, NORRIS R. "Panic at 'The Who Concert Stampede': An Empirical Assessment." *Social Problems.* Vol. 34, No. 4 (October 1987):362–73.

JOHNSON, PAUL. "The Seven Deadly Sins of Terrorism." In Benjamin Netanyahu, ed., *International Terrorism.* New Brunswick, N.J.: Transaction Books, 1981:12–22.

JOHNSON, ROLAND. [Online] Available http://www.personalwebs.myriad.net/Roland, 1996.

JOHNSTON, DAVID CAY. "Voting, America's Not Keen On. Coffee Is Another Matter." *New York Times* (November 10, 1996): section 4, p. 2.

JOHNSTON, R. J. "Residential Area Characteristics." In D. T. Herbert and R. J. Johnston, eds., *Social Areas in Cities. Vol. 1: Spatial Processes and Form.* New York: Wiley, 1976:193–235.

JONES, ANTHONY. "Soviet Sociology, Past and Present." *Contemporary Sociology.* Vol. 18, No. 3 (May 1989):316–19.

JONES, ARTHUR. "Welfare Reform Makes Children Prime Victims." *National Catholic Reporter* (April 30, 1999a):14–16.

JONES, JUDY. "More Miners Will Be Offered Free X-Rays; Federal Agency Wants to Monitor Black-Lung Cases." *Louisville Courier Journal* (Thursday, May 13, 1999b):1A.

JORDAN, MARY. "New Factors Sustain Age-Old Ritual." *Washington Post* (March 31, 1998):A12.

JOSEPHY, ALVIN M., JR. *Now That the Buffalo's Gone: A Study of Today's American Indians.* New York: Alfred A. Knopf, 1982.

JOYNSON, ROBERT B. "Fallible Judgments." *Society.* Vol. 31, No. 3 (March–April 1994):45–52.

KADUSHIN, CHARLES. "Friendship among the French Financial Elite." *American Sociological Review.* Vol. 60, No. 2 (April 1995):202–21.

KAIN, EDWARD L. "A Note on the Integration of AIDS into the Sociology of Human Sexuality." *Teaching Sociology.* Vol. 15, No. 4 (July 1987):320–23.

———. *The Myth of Family Decline: Understanding Families in a World of Rapid Social Change.* Lexington, Mass.: Lexington Books, 1990.

KAIN, EDWARD L., and SHANNON HART. "AIDS and the Family: A Content Analysis of Media Coverage." Presented to National Council on Family Relations, Atlanta, 1987.

KALLEBERG, ARNE L., and MARK E. VAN BUREN. "Is Bigger Better? Explaining the Relationship between Organization Size and Job Rewards." *American Sociological Review.* Vol. 61, No. 1 (February 1996):47–66.

KAMINER, WENDY. "Volunteers: Who Knows What's in It for Them." *Ms.* (December 1984):93–94, 96, 126–28.

———. "Demasculinizing the Army." *New York Times Review of Books* (June 15, 1997):7.

KANAMINE, LINDA. "School Operation Fails For-Profit Test." *USA Today* (November 24, 1995):6A.

KANN, LAURA, et al. "Youth Risk Behavior Surveillance—United States, 1993." *Morbidity and Mortality Weekly Report.* Vol. 44 (S-1), March 24, 1995.

KANTER, ROSABETH MOSS. *Men and Women of the Corporation.* New York: Basic Books, 1977.

KANTER, ROSABETH MOSS, and BARRY A. STEIN. "The Gender Pioneers: Women in an Industrial Sales Force." In R. M. Kanter and B. A. Stein, eds., *Life in Organizations.* New York: Basic Books, 1979:134–60.

KAPFERER, JEAN-NOEL. "How Rumors Are Born." *Society.* Vol. 29, No. 5 (July–August 1992):53–60.

KAPLAN, DAVID A. *The Silicon Boys.* New York: William Morrow, 1999.

KAPLAN, ELAINE BELL. "Black Teenage Mothers and Their Mothers: The Impact of Adolescent Childbearing on Daughters' Relations with Mothers." *Social Problems.* Vol. 43, No. 4 (November 1996):427–43.

KAPLAN, ERIC B., et al. "The Usefulness of Preoperative Laboratory Screening." *Journal of the American Medical Association.* Vol. 253, No. 24 (June 28, 1985):3576–81.

KAPTCHUK, TED. "The Holistic Logic of Chinese Medicine." In Shepard Bliss et al., eds., *The New Holistic Health Handbook.* Lexington, Mass.: The Steven Greene Press/Penguin Books, 1985:41.

KARP, DAVID A., and WILLIAM C. YOELS. "The College Classroom: Some Observations on the Meaning of Student Participation." *Sociology and Social Research.* Vol. 60, No. 4 (July 1976):421–39.

KATES, ROBERT W. "Ending Hunger: Current Status and Future Prospects." *Consequences.* Vol. 2, No. 2 (1996):3–11.

KATZ, MICHAEL B. *In the Shadow of the Poorhouse.* New York: Basic Books, 1986.

KAUFMAN, MARC. "Becoming 'Old Old'." *Philadelphia Inquirer* (October 28, 1990):1-A, 10-A.

KAUFMAN, ROBERT L., and SEYMOUR SPILERMAN. "The Age Structures of Occupations and Jobs." *American Journal of Sociology.* Vol. 87, No. 4 (January 1982):827–51.

KAUFMAN, WALTER. *Religions in Four Dimensions: Existential, Aesthetic, Historical and Comparative*. New York: Reader's Digest Press, 1976.
KEITH, PAT M., and ROBERT B. SCHAFER. "They Hate to Cook: Patterns of Distress in an Ordinary Role." *Sociological Focus*. Vol. 27, No. 4 (October 1994):289–301.
KELLER, HELEN. *The Story of My Life*. New York: Doubleday, Page, 1903.
KELLERT, STEPHEN R., and F. HERBERT BORMANN. "Closing the Circle: Weaving Strands among Ecology, Economics, and Ethics." In F. Herbert Bormann and Stephen R. Kellert, eds., *Ecology, Economics, and Ethics: The Broken Circle*. New Haven, Conn.: Yale University Press, 1991:205–10.
KELLEY, JONATHAN, and M. D. R. EVANS. "Class and Class Conflict in Six Western Nations." *American Sociological Review*. Vol. 60, No. 2 (April 1995):157–78.
KEMP, ALICE ABEL, and SHELLEY COVERMAN. "Marginal Jobs or Marginal Workers: Identifying Sex Differences in Low-Skill Occupations." *Sociological Focus*. Vol. 22, No. 1 (February 1989):19–37.
KENNICKELL, ARTHUR, and JANICE SHACK-MARQUEZ. "Changes in Family Finances from 1983 to 1989: Evidence From the Survey of Consumer Finances." *Federal Reserve Bulletin* (January 1992):1–18.
KENNICKELL, ARTHUR B., MARTHA STARR-MCCLUER, and BRIAN J. SURETTE. "Recent Changes in U.S. Family Finances: Results from the 1998 Survey of Consumer Finances." [Online] Available http://www.federalreserve.gov/pubs/bulletin/2000/0100lead.pdf, April 7, 2000.
KENTOR, JEFFREY. "The Long-Term Effects of Foreign Investment Dependence on Economic Growth, 1940–1990." *American Journal of Sociology*. Vol. 103, No. 4 (January 1998):1024–46.
KERCKHOFF, ALAN C., RICHARD T. CAMPBELL, and IDEE WINFIELD-LAIRD. "Social Mobility in Great Britain and the United States." *American Journal of Sociology*. Vol. 91, No. 2 (September 1985):281–308.
KIDD, QUENTIN, and AIE-RIE LEE. "Postmaterialist Values and the Environment: A Critique and Reappraisal." *Social Science Quarterly*. Vol. 78, No. 1 (March 1997):1–15.
KIDRON, MICHAEL, and RONALD SEGAL. *The New State of the World Atlas*. New York: Simon & Schuster, 1991.
KILBOURNE, BROCK K. "The Conway and Siegelman Claims against Religious Cults: An Assessment of Their Data." *Journal for the Scientific Study of Religion*. Vol. 22, No. 4 (December 1983):380–85.
KILGORE, SALLY B. "The Organizational Context of Tracking in Schools." *American Sociological Review*. Vol. 56, No. 2 (April 1991):189–203.
KILLIAN, LEWIS M. "Organization, Rationality and Spontaneity in the Civil Rights Movement." *American Sociological Review*. Vol. 49, No. 6 (December 1984):770–83.
KING, KATHLEEN PIKER, and DENNIS E. CLAYSON. "The Differential Perceptions of Male and Female Deviants." *Sociological Focus*. Vol. 21, No. 2 (April 1988):153–64.
KING, MARTIN LUTHER, JR. "The Montgomery Bus Boycott." In Walt Anderson, ed., *The Age of Protest*. Pacific Palisades, Calif.: Goodyear, 1969:81–91.
KINKEAD, GWEN. *Chinatown: A Portrait of a Closed Society*. New York: HarperCollins, 1992.
KINSEY, ALFRED, et al. *Sexual Behavior in the Human Male*. Philadelphia: Saunders, 1948.
———. *Sexual Behavior in the Human Female*. Philadelphia: Saunders, 1953.
KISER, EDGAR, and JOACHIM SCHNEIDER. "Bureaucracy and Efficiency: An Analysis of Taxation in Early Modern Prussia." *American Sociological Review*. Vol. 59, No. 2 (April 1994):187–204.
KITTRIE, NICHOLAS N. *The Right To Be Different: Deviance and Enforced Therapy*. Baltimore: Johns Hopkins University Press, 1971.
KLEIN, J. D. "The National Longitudinal Study on Adolescent Health: Preliminary Results: Great Expectations." *JAMA: The Journal of the American Medical Association*. Vol. 278, No. 10 (1997):864.
KLEINFELD, JUDITH. "Student Performance: Males versus Females." *The Public Interest*. No. 134 (Winter, 1999):3–20.
KLUCKHOHN, CLYDE. "As an Anthropologist Views It." In Albert Deuth, ed., *Sex Habits of American Men*. New York: Prentice Hall, 1948.
KOCH, HOWARD. *The Panic Broadcast: Portrait of an Event*. Boston: Little, Brown, 1970.
KOELLN, KENNETH, ROSE M. RUBIN, and MARION SMITH PICARD. "Vulnerable Elderly Households: Expenditures on Necessities by Older Americans." *Social Science Quarterly*. Vol. 76, No. 3 (September 1995):619–33.
KOHLBERG, LAWRENCE. *The Psychology of Moral Development: The Nature and Validity of Moral Stages*. New York: Harper & Row, 1981.
KOHLBERG, LAWRENCE, and CAROL GILLIGAN. "The Adolescent as Philosopher: The Discovery of Self in a Postconventional World." *Daedalus*. Vol. 100 (Fall 1971):1051–86.
KOHN, MELVIN L. *Class and Conformity: A Study in Values*. 2d ed. Homewood, Ill.: Dorsey Press, 1977.
———. "The 'Bell Curve' from the Perspective of Research on Social Structure and Personality." *Sociological Forum*. Vol. 11, No. 2 (1996):395.
KOHN, MELVIN L., and CARMI SCHOOLER. "Job Conditions and Personality: A Longitudinal Assessment of Their Reciprocal Effects." *American Journal of Sociology*. Vol. 87, No. 6 (May 1982):1257–83.
KOLATA, GINA. "When Grandmother Is the Mother, Until Birth." *New York Times* (August 5, 1991):1, 11.
KOMAROVSKY, MIRRA. *Blue Collar Marriage*. New York: Vintage Books, 1967.
———. "Cultural Contradictions and Sex Roles: The Masculine Case." *American Journal of Sociology*. Vol. 78, No. 4 (January 1973):873–84.
KONO, CLIFFORD, DONALD PALMER, ROGER FRIEDLAND, and MATTHEW ZAFONTE. "Lost in Space: The Geography of Corporate Interlocking Directorates." *American Journal of Sociology*. Vol. 103, No. 4 (January 1998):863–911.
KORNHAUSER, WILLIAM. *The Politics of Mass Society*. New York: Free Press, 1959.
KORPI, WALTER, and JOAKIM PALME. "The Paradox of Redistribution and Strategies of Equality: Welfare State Institutions, Inequality, and Poverty in the Western Countries." *American Sociological Review*. Vol. 65, No. 5 (October 1998):661–87.
KORZENIEWICZ, ROBERTO P., and KIMBERLY AWBREY. "Democratic Transitions and the Semiperiphery of the World Economy." *Sociological Forum*. Vol. 7, No. 4 (December 1992):609–40.
KOSTERS, MARVIN. "Looking for Jobs in All the Wrong Places." *The Public Interest*. Vol. 125 (Fall 1996):125–31.
KOUSHA, MAHNAZ. Review of *Modernizing Women* by Valentine M. Moghadam. In *Gender and Society*. Vol. 8 (December 1994):624–26.
KOWALEWSKI, DAVID, and KAREN L. PORTER. "Ecoprotest: Alienation, Deprivation, or Resources." *Social Sciences Quarterly*. Vol. 73, No. 3 (September 1992):523–34.
KOZOL, JONATHAN. *Rachel and Her Children: Homeless Families in America*. New York: Crown Publishers, 1988.
———. *Savage Inequalities: Children in America's Schools*. New York: Harper Perennial, 1992.
KRAFFT, SUSAN. "¿Quién es Numero Uno?" *American Demographics*. Vol. 15, No. 7 (July 1993):16–17.
KRANTZ, MICHAEL. "Say It with a :-)." *Time*. Vol. 149, No. 15 (1997):29.
KRASKA, PETER B., and VICTOR E. KAPPELER. "Militarizing American Police: The Rise and Normalization of Paramilitary Units." *Social Problems*. Vol. 44, No. 1 (February 1997):1–18.
KRAYBILL, DONALD B. *The Riddle of Amish Culture*. Baltimore: Johns Hopkins University Press, 1989.
———. "The Amish Encounter with Modernity." In Donald B. Kraybill and Marc A. Olshan, eds., *The Amish Struggle with Modernity*. Hanover, N.H.: University Press of New England, 1994:21–33.
KRAYBILL, DONALD B., and MARC A. OLSHAN, eds. *The Amish Struggle with Modernity*. Hanover, N.H.: University Press of New England, 1994.
KRIESI, HANSPETER. "New Social Movements and the New Class in the Netherlands." *American Journal of Sociology*. Vol. 94, No. 5 (March 1989):1078–116.
KRISTOL, IRVING. "Life without Father." *Wall Street Journal* (November 3, 1994):A18.
———. "Age before Politics." *Wall Street Journal* (April 25, 1996):A20.
KRIVO, LAUREN J., RUTH D. PETERSON, HELEN RIZZO, and JOHN R. REYNOLDS. "Race, Segregation, and the Concentration of Disadvantage: 1980–1990." *Social Problems*. Vol. 45, No. 1 (February 1998):61–80.
KRUKS, GABRIEL N. "Gay and Lesbian Homeless/Street Youth: Special Issues and Concerns." *Journal of Adolescent Health*. Special Issue. No. 12 (1991): 515–18.
KÜBLER-ROSS, ELISABETH. *On Death and Dying*. New York: Macmillan, 1969.
KUHN, THOMAS. *The Structure of Scientific Revolutions*. 2d ed. Chicago: University of Chicago Press, 1970.
KUZNETS, SIMON. "Economic Growth and Income Inequality." *The American Economic Review*. Vol. XLV, No. 1 (March 1955):1–28.
———. *Modern Economic Growth: Rate, Structure, and Spread*. New Haven, Conn.: Yale University Press, 1966.
LABOVITZ, PRICISSA. "Immigration—Just the Facts." *New York Times* (March 25, 1996).

LACAYO, RICHARD. "Blood in the Stands." *Time*. Vol. 125, No. 23 (June 10, 1985):38–39, 41.
———. "The Brawl over Sprawl." *Time*. Vol. 153, No. 11 (March 22, 1999): 44–48.
LACH, JENNIFER. "The Color of Money." *American Demographics*. Vol. 21, No 2 (February 1999):59–60.
LADD, JOHN. "The Definition of Death and the Right to Die." In John Ladd, ed., *Ethical Issues Relating to Life and Death*. New York: Oxford University Press, 1979:118–45.
LAI, H. M. "Chinese." In *Harvard Encyclopedia of American Ethnic Groups*. Cambridge, Mass.: Harvard University Press, 1980:217–33.
LAMBERG-KARLOVSKY, C. C., and MARTHA LAMBERG-KARLOVSKY. "An Early City in Iran." In *Cities: Their Origin, Growth, and Human Impact*. San Francisco: Freeman, 1973:28–37.
LANDERS, ANN. Syndicated column: *Dallas Morning News* (July 8, 1984):4F.
LANDERS, RENE M. "Gender, Race, and the State Courts." *Radcliffe Quarterly*. Vol. 76, No. 4 (December 1990):6–9.
LANDSBERG, MITCHELL. "Health Disaster Brings Early Death in Russia." *Washington Times* (March 15, 1998):A8.
LANE, DAVID. "Social Stratification and Class." In Erik P. Hoffman and Robbin F. Laird, eds., *The Soviet Polity in the Modern Era*. New York: Aldine, 1984:563–605.
LANG, KURT, and GLADYS ENGEL LANG. *Collective Dynamics*. New York: Thomas Y. Crowell, 1961.
LAPPÉ, FRANCES MOORE, and JOSEPH COLLINS. *World Hunger: Twelve Myths*. New York: Grove Press/Food First Books, 1986.
LAPPÉ, FRANCES MOORE, JOSEPH COLLINS, and DAVID KINLEY. *Aid as Obstacle: Twenty Questions about Our Foreign Policy and the Hungry*. San Francisco: Institute for Food and Development Policy, 1981.
LARMER, BROOK. "Dead End Kids." *Newsweek* (May 25, 1992):38–40.
LASLETT, BARBARA. "Family Membership, Past and Present." *Social Problems*. Vol. 25, No. 5 (June 1978):476–90.
LASLETT, PETER. *The World We Have Lost: England before the Industrial Age*. 3d ed. New York: Charles Scribner's Sons, 1984.
LAUMANN, EDWARD O., JOHN H. GAGNON, ROBERT T. MICHAEL, and STUART MICHAELS. *The Social Organization of Sexuality: Sexual Practices in the United States*. Chicago: University of Chicago Press, 1994.
LEACOCK, ELEANOR. "Women's Status in Egalitarian Societies: Implications for Social Evolution." *Current Anthropology*. Vol. 19, No. 2 (June 1978):247–75.
LEAVITT, JUDITH WALZER. "Women and Health in America: An Overview." In Judith Walzer Leavitt, ed., *Women and Health in America*. Madison: University of Wisconsin Press, 1984:3–7.
LE BON, GUSTAVE. *The Crowd: A Study of the Popular Mind*. New York: Viking Press, 1960; orig. 1895.
LEE, SHARON M. "Poverty and the U.S. Asian Population." *Social Science Quarterly*. Vol. 75, No. 3 (September 1994):541–59.
———. "Asian Americans: Diverse and Growing." *Population Bulletin*. Vol. 53, No. 2 (June). Washington, D.C.: Population Reference Bureau, 1998.
LEERHSEN, CHARLES. "Unite and Conquer." *Newsweek* (February 5, 1990):50–55.
LEFEBVRE, HENRI. *The Production of Space*. Oxford: Blackwell, 1991.
LELAND, JOHN. "Bisexuality." *Newsweek* (July 17, 1995):44–49.
LEMERT, EDWIN M. *Social Pathology*. New York: McGraw-Hill, 1951.
———. *Human Deviance, Social Problems, and Social Control*. 2d ed. Englewood Cliffs, N.J.: Prentice Hall, 1972.
LENGERMANN, PATRICIA MADOO, and RUTH A. WALLACE. *Gender in America: Social Control and Social Change*. Englewood Cliffs, N.J.: Prentice Hall, 1985.
LENNON, MARY CLARE, and SARAH ROSENFELD. "Relative Fairness and the Doctrine of Housework: The Importance of Options." *American Journal of Sociology*. Vol. 100, No. 2 (September 1994):506–31.
LENSKI, GERHARD, PATRICK NOLAN, and JEAN LENSKI. *Human Societies: An Introduction to Macrosociology*. 7th ed. New York: McGraw-Hill, 1995.
LEONARD, EILEEN B. *Women, Crime, and Society: A Critique of Theoretical Criminology*. New York: Longman, 1982.
LESLIE, GERALD R., and SHEILA K. KORMAN. *The Family in Social Context*. 7th ed. New York: Oxford University Press, 1989.
LESTER, DAVID. *The Death Penalty: Issues and Answers*. Springfield, Ill.: Charles C. Thomas, 1987.
LETSCHER, MARTIN. "Tell Fads from Trends." *American Demographics*. Vol. 16, No.12 (December 1994):38–45.
LEVAY, SIMON. *The Sexual Brain*. Cambridge, Mass.: MIT Press, 1993.
LEVER, JANET. "Sex Differences in the Complexity of Children's Play and Games." *American Sociological Review*. Vol. 43, No. 4 (August 1978):471–83.
LEVIN, JACK, and ARNOLD ARLUKE. *Gossip: The Inside Scoop*. New York: Plenum, 1987.
LEVINE, MICHAEL. "Reducing Hostility Can Prevent Heart Disease." *Mount Vernon News* (August 7, 1990):4A.
LEVINE, MICHAEL P. *Student Eating Disorders: Anorexia Nervosa and Bulimia*. Washington, D.C.: National Educational Association, 1987.
LEVINE, ROBERT V. "Is Love a Luxury?" *American Demographics*. Vol. 15, No. 2 (February 1993):27–28.
LEVINSON, DANIEL J., with CHARLOTTE N. DARROW, EDWARD B. KLEIN, MARIA H. LEVINSON, and BRAXTON MCKEE. *The Seasons of a Man's Life*. New York: Alfred A. Knopf, 1978.
LEWIS, FLORA. "The Roots of Revolution." *New York Times Magazine* (November 11, 1984):70–71, 74, 77–78, 82, 84, 86.
LEWIS, OSCAR. *The Children of Sachez*. New York: Random House, 1961.
LEWIS, PEIRCE, CASEY MCCRACKEN, and ROGER HUNT. "Politics: Who Cares?" *American Demographics*. Vol. 16, No. 10 (October 1994):20–26.
LI, JIANG HONG, and ROGER A. WOJTKIEWICZ. "A New Look at the Effects of Family Structure on Status Attainment." *Social Science Quarterly*. Vol. 73, No. 3 (September 1992):581–95.
LIAZOS, ALEXANDER. "The Poverty of the Sociology of Deviance: Nuts, Sluts and Preverts." *Social Problems*. Vol. 20, No. 1 (Summer 1972):103–20.
———. *People First: An Introduction to Social Problems*. Boston: Allyn and Bacon, 1982.
LICHTER, DANIEL R. "Race, Employment Hardship, and Inequality in the American Nonmetropolitan South." *American Sociological Review*. Vol. 54, No. 3 (June 1989):436–46.
LICHTER, DANIEL T., DIANE K. MCLAUGHLIN, and DAVID C. RIBAR. "Welfare and the Rise in Female-Headed Families." *American Journal of Sociology*. Vol. 103, No. 1 (July 1997):112–43.
LICHTER, S. ROBERT, STANLEY ROTHMAN, and LINDA R. ROTHMAN. *The Media Elite: America's New Powerbrokers*. Bethesda, Md.: Adler & Adler, 1986.
LICHTER, S. ROBERT, STANLEY ROTHMAN, and LINDA S. LICHTER. *The Media Elite: America's New Powerbrokers*. New York: Hastings House, 1990.
LIEBOW, ELLIOT. *Tally's Corner*. Boston: Little, Brown, 1967.
LIN, GE, and PETER ROGERSON. Research reported in Diane Crispell, "Sons and Daughters Who Keep in Touch." *American Demographics*. Vol. 16, No. 8 (August 1994):15–16.
LIN, NAN, and WEN XIE. "Occupational Prestige in Urban China." *American Journal of Sociology*. Vol. 93, No. 4 (January 1988):793–832.
LINDEN, EUGENE. "Can Animals Think?" *Time*. Vol. 141, No. 12 (March 22, 1993):54–61.
———. "More Power to Women, Fewer Mouths to Feed." *Time*. Vol. 144, No. 13 (September 26, 1994):64–65.
LINDSTROM, BONNIE. "Chicago's Post-Industrial Suburbs." *Sociological Focus*. Vol. 28, No. 4 (October 1995):399–412.
LING, PYAU. "Causes of Chinese Emigration." In Amy Tachiki et al., eds., *Roots: An Asian American Reader*. Los Angeles: UCLA Asian American Studies Center, 1971:134–38.
LINN, MICHAEL. Noted in *Cornell Alumni News*. Vol. 99, No. 2 (September 1996):25.
LINO, MARK. "Expenditures on Children by Families: 1997." *Annual Report*. Washington, D.C.: U.S. Department of Agriculture, Center for Nutrition Policy and Promotion, 1998.
———. *Expenditures on Children by Families, 1998 Annual Report*. Washington, D.C.: U.S. Department of Agriculture, Center for Nutrition Policy and Promotion, 1999.
LINTON, RALPH. "One Hundred Percent American." *The American Mercury*. Vol. 40, No. 160 (April 1937a):427–29.
———. *The Study of Man*. New York: D. Appleton-Century, 1937b.
LIPS, HILARY. *Sex and Gender: An Introduction*. 2d ed. Mountain View, Calif.: Mayfield Publishing Co., 1993.
LIPSET, SEYMOUR MARTIN. *Political Man: The Social Bases of Politics*. Garden City, N.Y.: Anchor/Doubleday, 1963.
LIPSET, SEYMOUR MARTIN, and REINHARD BENDIX. *Social Mobility in Industrial Society*. Berkeley: University of California Press, 1967.
LISKA, ALLEN E. *Perspectives on Deviance*. 3d ed. Englewood Cliffs, N.J.: Prentice Hall, 1991.

LISKA, ALLEN E., and MARK TAUSIG. "Theoretical Interpretations of Social Class and Racial Differentials in Legal Decision Making for Juveniles." *Sociological Quarterly*. Vol. 20, No. 2 (Spring 1979):197–207.

LISKA, ALLEN E., and BARBARA D. WARNER. "Functions of Crime: A Paradoxical Process." *American Journal of Sociology*. Vol. 96, No. 6 (May 1991):1441–63.

LITTMAN, DAVID L. "2001: A Farm Odyssey." *Wall Street Journal* (September 14, 1992):A10.

LIVERNASH, ROBERT, and ERIC RODENBURG. "Population Change, Resources, and the Environment." *Population Bulletin*. Vol. 53, No. 1 (March 1998).

LIVINGSTON, KEN. "Politics and Mental Illness." *Public Interest*. Vol. 143 (Winter, 1999):105–9.

LO, CLARENCE Y. H. "Countermovements and Conservative Movements in the Contemporary U.S." *Annual Review of Sociology*. Vol. 8. Palo Alto, Calif.: Annual Reviews, 1982:107–34.

LOFLAND, LYN. *A World of Strangers*. New York: Basic Books, 1973.

LOGAN, JOHN R., and MARK SCHNEIDER. "Racial Segregation and Racial Change in American Suburbs, 1970–1980." *American Journal of Sociology*. Vol. 89, No. 4 (January 1984):874–88.

LOHR, STEVE. "British Health Service Faces a Crisis in Funds and Delays." *New York Times* (August 7, 1988):1, 12.

LONGINO, JR., CHARLES F. "Myths of An Aging America." *American Demographics*. Vol. 16, No. 8 (August 1994):36–42.

LORD, WALTER. *A Night to Remember*. Rev. ed. New York: Holt, Rinehart & Winston, 1976.

LORENZ, FREDERICK O., and BRENT T. BRUTON. "Experiments in Surveys: Linking Mass Class Questionnaires to Introductory Research Methods." *Teaching Sociology*. Vol. 24, No. 3 (July 1996):264–71.

LOVGREN, STEFEN. "Will All the Blue Men End Up in Timbuktu?" *U.S. News & World Report* (December 7, 1998):40.

LOY, PAMELA HEWITT, and LEA P. STEWART. "The Extent and Effects of Sexual Harassment of Working Women." *Sociological Focus*. Vol. 17, No. 1 (January 1984):31–43.

LUBLIN, JOANN S. "Pay for No Performance." *Wall Street Journal* (April 22, 1998):R1.

LUKER, KRISTEN. *Abortion and the Politics of Motherhood*. Berkeley: University of California Press, 1984.

LUND, DALE A. "Conclusions about Bereavement in Later Life and Implications for Interventions and Future Research." In Dale A. Lund, ed., *Older Bereaved Spouses: Research with Practical Applications*. London: Taylor-Francis-Hemisphere, 1989:217–31.

———. "Caregiving." *Encyclopedia of Adult Development*. Phoenix, Ariz.: Oryx Press, 1993:57–63.

LUND, DALE A., MICHAEL S. CASERTA, and MARGARET F. DIMOND. "Gender Differences through Two Years of Bereavement among the Elderly." *The Gerontologist*. Vol. 26, No. 3 (1986):314–20.

LUNDMAN, RICHARD L. Correspondence to author (1999).

LUNSFORD, JACK. Remarks at a meeting of the Arizona Task Force on the Western Virtual University. [Online] Available http://www.acpe.asu.edu/VirtualU/, May 6, 1996.

LUO, JAR-DER. "The Significance of Networks in the Initiation of Small Businesses in Taiwan." *Sociological Focus*. Vol. 12, No. 2 (June 1997):297–317.

LUTZ, CATHERINE A. *Unnatural Emotions: Everyday Sentiments on a Micronesia Atoll and Their Challenge to Western Theory*. Chicago: University of Chicago Press, 1988.

LUTZ, CATHERINE A., and GEOFFREY M. WHITE. "The Anthropology of Emotions." In Bernard J. Siegel, Alan R. Beals, and Stephen A. Tyler, eds., *Annual Review of Anthropology*. Palo Alto, Calif.: Annual Reviews, Vol. 15 (1986):405–36.

LYNCH, MICHAEL, and DAVID BOGEN. "Sociology's Asociological 'Core': An Examination of Textbook Sociology in Light of the Sociology of Scientific Knowledge." *American Sociological Review*. Vol. 62, No. 3 (June 1997):481–93.

LYND, ROBERT S. *Knowledge For What? The Place of Social Science in American Culture*. Princeton, N.J.: Princeton University Press, 1967.

LYND, ROBERT S., and HELEN MERRELL LYND. *Middletown in Transition*. New York: Harcourt, Brace & World, 1937.

LYNOTT, PATRICIA PASSUTH, and BARBARA J. LOGUE. "The 'Hurried Child': The Myth of Lost Childhood on Contemporary American Society." *Sociological Forum*. Vol. 8, No. 3 (September 1993):471–91.

MA, LI-CHEN. Personal communication, 1987.

MABRY, MARCUS. "New Hope for Old Unions?" *Newsweek* (February 24, 1992):39.

MABRY, MARCUS, and TOM MASLAND. "The Man after Mandela." *Newsweek* (June 7, 1999):54–55.

MCADAM, DOUG. *Political Process and the Development of Black Insurgency, 1930–1970*. Chicago: University of Chicago Press, 1982.

———. "Tactical Innovation and the Pace of Insurgency." *American Sociological Review*. Vol. 48, No. 6 (December 1983):735–54.

———. *Freedom Summer*. New York: Oxford University Press, 1988.

———. "The Biographical Consequences of Activism." *American Sociological Review*. Vol. 54, No. 5 (October 1989):744–60.

———. "Gender as a Mediator of the Activist Experience: The Case of Freedom Summer." *American Journal of Sociology*. Vol. 97, No. 5 (March 1992):1211–40.

MCADAM, DOUG, JOHN D. MCCARTHY, and MAYER N. ZALD. "Social Movements." In Neil J. Smelser, ed., *Handbook of Sociology*. Newbury Park, Calif.: Sage, 1988:695–737.

———, eds. *Comparative Perspectives on Social Movements: Political Opportunities, Mobilizing Structures, and Cultural Framings*. Cambridge: Cambridge University Press, 1996.

MCBROOM, WILLIAM H., and FRED W. REED. "Recent Trends in Conservatism: Evidence of Non-Unitary Patterns." *Sociological Focus*. Vol. 23, No. 4 (October 1990):355–65.

MCCARTHY, JOHN D., and MAYER N. ZALD. "Resource Mobilization and Social Movements: A Partial Theory." *American Journal of Sociology*. Vol. 82, No. 6 (May 1977):1212–41.

MCCARTHY, TERRY. "Give Me Your Tired, Your Poor . . ." *Time*. Vol. 151, No. 4 (February 2, 1998):4.

MACCOBY, ELEANOR EMMONS, and CAROL NAGY JACKLIN. *The Psychology of Sex Differences*. Palo Alto, Calif.: Stanford University Press, 1974.

MCCOLM, R. BRUCE, JAMES FINN, DOUGLAS W. PAYNE, JOSEPH E. RYAN, LEONARD R. SUSSMAN, and GEORGE ZARYCKY. *Freedom in the World: Political Rights & Civil Liberties, 1990–1991*. New York: Freedom House, 1991.

MCCONNELL, SCOTT. "New Liberal Fear: Hyperdemocracy." *The New York Post* (January 18, 1995):19.

MCCORMICK, NAOMI. B. *Sexual Salvation*. Westport, Conn.: Praeger, 1994.

MACDONALD, J. FRED. *Blacks and White TV: African Americans in Television since 1948*. Chicago: Nelson-Hall, 1992.

MCDONALD, KIM A. "Debate over How to Gauge Global Warming Heats Up Meeting of Climatologists." *Chronicle of Higher Education*. Vol. XLV, No. 22 (February 5, 1999):A17.

MACE, DAVID, and VERA MACE. *Marriage East and West*. Garden City, N.Y.: Doubleday (Dolphin), 1960.

MCGEARY, JOHANNA. "Nukes . . . They're Back." *Time*. Vol. 151, No. 20 (May 25, 1998):34–42.

MCGUIRE, MEREDITH B. *Religion: The Social Context*. 2d ed. Belmont, Calif.: Wadsworth, 1987.

MCHENRY, SUSAN. "Rosabeth Moss Kanter." In *Ms*. Vol. 13 (January 1985): 62–63, 107–8.

MACIONIS, JOHN J. "Intimacy: Structure and Process in Interpersonal Relationships." *Alternative Lifestyles*. Vol. 1, No. 1 (February 1978a):113–30.

———. "The Search for Community in Modern Society: An Interpretation." *Qualitative Sociology*. Vol. 1, No. 2 (September 1978b):130–43.

———. "A Sociological Analysis of Humor." Presentation to the Texas Junior College Teachers Association, Houston, 1987.

MACIONIS, JOHN J., and VINCENT R. PARRILLO. *Cities and Urban Life*. 2d ed. Upper Saddle River, N.J.: Prentice Hall, 2001.

MCKEE, VICTORIA. "Blue Blood and the Color of Money." *New York Times* (June 9, 1996):49–50.

MACKLIN, ELEANOR D. "Nonmarital Heterosexual Cohabitation: An Overview." In Eleanor D. Macklin and Roger H. Rubin, eds., *Contemporary Families and Alternative Lifestyles: Handbook on Research and Theory*. Beverly Hills, Calif.: Sage, 1983:49–74.

MCLEOD, JANE D., and MICHAEL J. SHANAHAN. "Poverty, Parenting, and Children's Mental Health." *American Sociological Review*. Vol. 58, No. 3 (June 1993):351–66.

MCLEOD, JAY. *Ain't No Makin' It: Aspirations and Attainment in a Low-Income Neighborhood*. Boulder, Colo.: Westview Press, 1995.

MCLUHAN, MARSHALL. *The Gutenberg Galaxy*. New York: New American Library, 1969.

MCMENAMIN, BRIGID. "Humbled by the Internet." [Online] Article circulated on the Internet, available July 17, 1998.

McNeil, Donald G., Jr. "Should Women Be Sent Into Combat?" *New York Times* (July 21, 1991):E3.
McNulty, Paul J. "Who's in Jail and Why They Belong There." *Wall Street Journal* (November 9, 1994):A23.
McPhail, Clark. *The Myth of the Maddening Crowd.* New York: Aldine, 1991.
McPhail, Clark, and Ronald T. Wohlstein. "Individual and Collective Behaviors within Gatherings, Demonstrations, and Riots." *Annual Review of Sociology*. Vol. 9. Palo Alto, Calif.: Annual Reviews, 1983:579–600.
McRae, Susan. *Cross-Class Families: A Study of Wives' Occupational Superiority*. New York: Oxford University Press, 1986.
Maddox, Setma. "Organizational Culture and Leadership Style: Factors Affecting Self-Managed Work Team Performance." Paper presented at the annual meeting of the Southwest Social Science Association, Dallas, February 1994.
Madsen, Axel. *Private Power: Multinational Corporations for the Survival of Our Planet*. New York: William Morrow, 1980.
Malthus, Thomas Robert. *First Essay on Population 1798*. London: Macmillan, 1926; orig. 1798.
Manza, Jeff, and Clem Brooks. "The Religious Factor in U.S. Presidential Elections, 1960-1992." *American Journal of Sociology.* Vol. 103, No. 1 (July 1997):38–81.
———. "The Gender Gap in U.S. Presidential Elections: When? Why? Implications?" *American Journal of Sociology*. Vol. 103, No. 5 (March 1998):1235–66.
Marcuse, Herbert. *One-Dimensional Man*. Boston: Beacon Press, 1964.
Mare, Robert D. "Five Decades of Educational Assortative Mating." *American Sociological Review*. Vol. 56, No. 1 (February 1991):15–32.
Marín, Gerardo, and Barbara Vanoss Marín. *Research with Hispanic Populations*. Newbury Park, Calif.: Sage, 1991.
Marini, Margaret Mooney, and Pi-Ling Fan. "The Gender Gap in Earnings at Career Entry." *American Sociological Review*. Vol. 62, No. 4 (August 1997):588–604.
Markoff, John. "Remember Big Brother? Now He's a Company Man." *New York Times* (March 31, 1991):7.
Markovsky, Barry, John Skvoretz, David Willer, Michael J. Lovaglia, and Jeffrey Erger. "The Seeds of Weak Power: An Extension of Network Exchange Theory." *American Sociological Review*. Vol. 58, No. 2 (April 1993):197–209.
Markson, Elizabeth W. "Moral Dilemmas." *Society*. Vol. 29, No. 5 (July-August 1992):4–6.
Marquand, Robert. "Worship Shift: Americans Seek Feeling of 'Awe'." *Christian Science Monitor* (May 28, 1997):1, 8.
Marquand, Robert, and Daniel B. Wood. "Rise in Cults as Millennium Approaches." *Christian Science Monitor* (March 28, 1997):1, 18.
Marshall, Susan E. "Ladies against Women: Mobilization Dilemmas of Antifeminist Movements." *Social Problems*. Vol. 32, No. 4 (April 1985):348–62.
Martin, John M., and Anne T. Romano. *Multinational Crime: Terrorism, Espionage, Drug and Arms Trafficking*. Newbury Park, Calif.: Sage, 1992.
Martin, Richard C. *Islam: A Cultural Perspective*. Englewood Cliffs, N.J.: Prentice Hall, 1982.
Martinez, Valerie J., R. Kenneth Godwin, Frank R. Kemerer, and Laura Perna. "The Consequences of School Choice: Who Leaves and Who Stays in the Inner City." *Social Science Quarterly*. Vol. 76, No. 1 (September 1995):485–501.
Marullo, Sam. "The Functions and Dysfunctions of Preparations for Fighting Nuclear War." *Sociological Focus*. Vol. 20, No. 2 (April 1987):135–53.
Marx, Gary T., and James L. Wood. "Strands of Theory and Research in Collective Behavior." In Alex Inkeles et al., eds., *Annual Review of Sociology*. Vol. 1. Palo Alto, Calif.: Annual Reviews, 1975:363–428.
Marx, Karl. Excerpt from "A Contribution to the Critique of Political Economy." In Karl Marx and Friedrich Engels, *Marx and Engels: Basic Writings on Politics and Philosophy*, Lewis S. Feurer, ed. Garden City, N.Y.: Anchor Books, 1959:42–46.
———. *Karl Marx: Early Writings*. T. B. Bottomore, ed. New York: McGraw-Hill, 1964a.
———. *Karl Marx: Selected Writings in Sociology and Social Philosophy*. T. B. Bottomore, trans. New York: McGraw-Hill, 1964b.
———. *Capital*. Friedrich Engels, ed. New York: International Publishers, 1967; orig. 1867
———. "Critique of the Gotha Program." In Robert C. Tucker, ed., *The Marx-Engels Reader*. New York: Norton, 1972:388.
———. "Theses on Feuer." In Robert C. Tucker, ed., *The Marx-Engels Reader*. New York: Norton, 1972:107–9; orig. 1845.
Marx, Karl, and Friedrich Engels. "Manifesto of the Communist Party." In Robert C. Tucker, ed., *The Marx-Engels Reader*. New York: Norton, 1972:331–62; orig. 1848.
———. *The Marx-Engels Reader*. 2d ed. Robert C. Tucker, ed. New York: Norton, 1978.
Marx, Leo. "The Environment and the 'Two Cultures' Divide." In James Rodger Fleming and Henry A. Gemery, eds., *Science, Technology, and the Environment: Multidisciplinary Perspectives*. Akron, Ohio: University of Akron Press, 1994:3–21.
Massey, Douglas S. Review of *The Bell Curve: Intelligence and Class Structure in American Life* by Richard J. Herrnstein and Charles Murray. *American Journal of Sociology*. Vol. 101, No. 3 (November 1995):747–53.
Massey, Douglas S., and Nancy A. Denton. "Hypersegregation in U.S. Metropolitan Areas: Black and Hispanic Segregation along Five Dimensions." *Demography*. Vol. 26, No. 3 (August 1989):373–91.
Masters, William H., Virginia E. Johnson, and Robert C. Kolodny. *Human Sexuality*. 3d ed. Glenview, Ill.: Scott, Foresman/Little, Brown, 1988.
Matloff, Judith. "Nomadic 'Blue Men' of the Desert Try to Go Roam Again." *Christian Science Monitor* (September 9, 1997):7.
Matthiessen, Peter. *Indian Country*. New York: Viking Press, 1984.
Mauer, Marc. "Americans behind Bars: U.S. and International Use of Incarceration 1995." [Online] Available http://www.sentencingproject.org/pubs/tsppubs/9030data.html, April 1, 2000.
Mauro, Tony. "Ruling Likely Will Add Fuel to Already Divisive Debate." *USA Today* (January 7, 1997):1A, 2A.
Mauss, Armand L. *Social Problems of Social Movements*. Philadelphia: Lippincott, 1975.
May, Elaine Tyler. "Women in the Wild Blue Yonder." *New York Times* (August 7, 1991):21.
Mayo, Katherine. *Mother India*. New York: Harcourt, Brace, 1927.
Mead, George Herbert. *Mind, Self, and Society*. Charles W. Morris, ed. Chicago: University of Chicago Press, 1962; orig. 1934.
Mead, Margaret. *Sex and Temperament in Three Primitive Societies*. New York: William Morrow, 1963; orig. 1935.
Meadows, Donella H., Dennis L. Meadows, Jorgan Randers, and William W. Behrens, III. *The Limits to Growth: A Report on the Club of Rome's Project on the Predicament of Mankind*. New York: Universe, 1972.
Meltzer, Bernard N. "Mead's Social Psychology." In Jerome G. Manis and Bernard N. Meltzer, eds., *Symbolic Interaction: A Reader in Social Psychology*. 3d ed. Needham Heights, Mass.: Allyn & Bacon, 1978.
Melucci, Alberto. "The New Social Movements: A Theoretical Approach." *Social Science Information*. Vol. 19, No. 2 (May 1980):199–226.
———. *Nomads of the Present: Social Movements and Individual Needs in Contemporary Society*. Philadelphia: Temple University Press, 1989.
Menjivar, Cecilia. "Immigrant Kinship Networks and the Impact of the Receiving Context: Salvadorans in San Francisco in the Early 1990s." *Social Problems*. Vol. 44, No. 1 (February 1997):104–23.
Mergenhagen, Paula. "Rethinking Retirement." *American Demographics*. Vol. 16, No. 6 (June 1994):28–34.
———. "Black-Owned Businesses." *American Demographics*. Vol. 18, No. 6 (June 1996a):24–27, 30–33.
———. "Sun City Gets Boomerized." *American Demographics*. Vol. 18, No. 8 (August 1996b):16–20.
———. "Her Own Boss." *American Demographics*. Vol. 18, No. 12 (December 1996c):37–41.
Merton, Robert K. "Social Structure and Anomie." *American Sociological Review*. Vol. 3, No. 6 (October 1938):672–82.
———. *Social Theory and Social Structure*. New York: Free Press, 1968.
———. "Discrimination and the American Creed." In *Sociological Ambivalence and Other Essays*. New York: Free Press, 1976:189–216.
Meyer, Davis S., and Nancy Whittier. "Social Movement Spillover." *Social Problems*. Vol. 41, No. 2 (May 1994):277–98.
Meyer, David S., and Suzanne Staggenborg. "Movements, Countermovements, and the Structure of Political Opportunity." *American Journal of Sociology*. Vol. 101, No. 6 (May 1996):1628–60.
Michels, Robert. *Political Parties*. Glencoe, Ill.: Free Press, 1949; orig. 1911.
Milbrath, Lester W. *Envisioning A Sustainable Society: Learning Our Way Out*. Albany: State University of New York Press, 1989.

MILGRAM, STANLEY. "Behavioral Study of Obedience." *Journal of Abnormal and Social Psychology*. Vol. 67, No. 4 (1963):371–78.
———. "Group Pressure and Action against a Person." *Journal of Abnormal and Social Psychology*. Vol. 69, No. 2 (August 1964):137–43.
———. "Some Conditions of Obedience and Disobedience to Authority." *Human Relations*. Vol. 18 (February 1965):57–76.
MILIBAND, RALPH. *The State in Capitalist Society*. London: Weidenfield and Nicolson, 1969.
MILLER, ARTHUR G. *The Obedience Experiments: A Case of Controversy in Social Science*. New York: Praeger, 1986.
MILLER, BERNA. "The Quest for Lifelong Learning." *American Demographics*. Vol. 19, No. 3 (March 1997a):20, 22.
———. "Population Update for April." *American Demographics*. Vol. 19, No. 4 (April 1997b):18.
MILLER, DAVID L. *Introduction to Collective Behavior*. Belmont, Calif.: Wadsworth, 1985.
MILLER, FREDERICK D. "The End of SDS and the Emergence of Weatherman: Demise through Success." In Jo Freeman, ed., *Social Movements of the Sixties and Seventies*. New York: Longman, 1983:279–97.
MILLER, G. TYLER, JR. *Living in the Environment: An Introduction to Environmental Science*. Belmont, Calif.: Wadsworth, 1992.
MILLER, MICHAEL. "Lawmakers Begin to Heed Calls to Protect Privacy." *Wall Street Journal* (April 11, 1991):A16.
MILLER, WALTER B. "Lower Class Culture as a Generating Milieu of Gang Delinquency." In Marvin E. Wolfgang, Leonard Savitz, and Norman Johnston, eds., *The Sociology of Crime and Delinquency*. 2d ed. New York: Wiley, 1970:351–63; orig. 1958.
MILLET, KATE. *Sexual Politics*. Garden City, N.Y.: Doubleday, 1970.
MILLS, C. WRIGHT. *The Power Elite*. New York: Oxford University Press, 1956.
———. *The Sociological Imagination*. New York: Oxford University Press, 1959.
MINK, BARBARA. "How Modernization Affects Women." *Cornell Alumni News*. Vol. III, No. 3 (April 1989):10–11.
MINTZ, BETH, and MICHAEL SCHWARTZ. "Interlocking Directorates and Interest Group Formation." *American Sociological Review*. Vol. 46, No. 6 (December 1981):851–69.
MIRINGOFF, MARC, and MARQUE-LUISA MIRINGOFF. "The Social Health of the Nation." *The Economist*. Vol. 352, No. 8128 (July 17, 1999):supp. 6–7.
MIROWSKY, JOHN. "The Psycho-Economics of Feeling Underpaid: Distributive Justice and the Earnings of Husbands and Wives." *American Journal of Sociology*. Vol. 92, No. 6 (May 1987):1404–34.
MIROWSKY, JOHN, and CATHERINE ROSS. "Working Wives and Mental Health." Presentation to the American Association for the Advancement of Science, New York, 1984.
MOEN, PHYLLIS, DONNA DEMPSTER-MCCLAIN, and ROBIN M. WILLIAMS. "Successful Aging: A Life-Course Perspective on Women's Multiple Roles and Health." *American Journal of Sociology*. Vol. 97 (May 1992):1612–38.
MOGELONSKY, MARCIA. "Reconfiguring the American Dream (House)." *American Demographics*. Vol. 19, No. 1 (January 1997):31–35.
MOLM, LINDA D. "Risk and Power Use: Constraints on the Use of Coercion in Exchange." *American Sociological Review*. Vol. 62, No. 1 (February 1997):113–33.
MOLOTCH, HARVEY. "The City as a Growth Machine." *American Journal of Sociology*. Vol. 82, No. 2 (September 1976):309–33.
MONTAGU, ASHLEY. *The Nature of Human Aggression*. New York: Oxford University Press, 1976.
MOORE, GWEN."Structural Determinants of Men's and Women's Personal Networks." *American Sociological Review*. Vol. 55, No. 5 (October 1991):726–35.
———. "Gender and Informal Networks in State Government." *Social Science Quarterly*. Vol. 73, No. 1 (March 1992):46–61.
MOORE, JOAN, and HARRY PACHON. *Hispanics in the United States*. Englewood Cliffs, N.J.: Prentice Hall, 1985.
MOORE, WILBERT E. "Modernization as Rationalization: Processes and Restraints." In Manning Nash, ed., *Essays on Economic Development and Cultural Change in Honor of Bert F. Hoselitz*. Chicago: University of Chicago Press, 1977:29–42.
———. *World Modernization: The Limits of Convergence*. New York: Elsevier, 1979.
MORAN, JOHN S., S. O. ARAL, W. C. JENKINS, T. A. PETERMAN, and E. R. ALEXANDER. "The Impact of Sexually Transmitted Diseases on Minority Populations." *Public Health Reports*. Vol. 104, No. 6 (November-December 1989):560–65.
MORGAN, LAURIE A. "Glass Ceiling or Cohort Effect? A Longitudinal Study of the Gender Earnings Gap for Engineers, 1982 to 1989." *American Sociological Review*. Vol. 63, No. 4 (August 1998):479–93.
MORRIS, ALDON. "Black Southern Sit-in Movement: An Analysis of Internal Organization." *American Sociological Review*. Vol. 46, No. 6 (December 1981):744–67.
MORRISON, DENTON E. "Some Notes toward Theory on Relative Deprivation, Social Movements, and Social Change." In Louis E. Genevie, ed., *Collective Behavior and Social Movements*. Itasca, Ill.: Peacock, 1978:202–9.
MOSLEY, W. HENRY, and PETER COWLEY. "The Challenge of World Health." *Population Bulletin*. Vol. 46, No. 4 (December 1991). Washington, D.C.: Population Reference Bureau.
MOYNIHAN, DANIEL PATRICK. "Toward a New Intolerance." *The Public Interest*. No. 112 (Summer 1993):119–22.
MULFORD, MATTHEW, JOHN ORBELL, CATHERINE SHATTO, and JEAN STOCKARD. "Physical Attractiveness, Opportunity, and Success in Everyday Exchange." *American Journal of Sociology*. Vol. 106, No. 6 (May 1998):1565–92.
MULLER, EDWARD N. *Aggressive Political Participation*. Princeton, N.J.: Princeton University Press, 1979.
MUMFORD, LEWIS. *The City in History: Its Origins, Its Transformations, and Its Prospects*. New York: Harcourt, Brace & World, 1961.
MURDOCK, GEORGE PETER. "Comparative Data on the Division of Labor by Sex." *Social Forces*. Vol. 15, No. 4 (May 1937):551–53.
———. "The Common Denominator of Cultures." In Ralph Linton, ed., *The Science of Man in World Crisis*. New York: Columbia University Press, 1945:123–42.
———. *Social Structure*. New York: Free Press, 1965; orig. 1949.
MURRAY, CHARLES. *Losing Ground: American Social Policy 1950–1980*. New York: Basic Books, 1984.
———. "Keeping Priorities Straight on Welfare Reform." *Society*. Vol. 33, No. 5 (July/August 1996):10–12.
MUTCHLER, JAN E. "Living Arrangements and Household Transitions among the Unmarried in Later Life." *Social Science Quarterly*. Vol. 73 (Spring 1992):565–80.
MYERS, NORMAN. "Humanity's Growth." In Sir Edmund Hillary, ed., *Ecology 2000: The Changing Face of the Earth*. New York: Beaufort Books, 1984a:16–35.
———. "The Mega-Extinction of Animals and Plants." In Sir Edmund Hillary, ed., *Ecology 2000: The Changing Face of the Earth*. New York: Beaufort Books, 1984b:82–107.
———. "Disappearing Cultures." In Sir Edmund Hillary, ed., *Ecology 2000: The Changing Face of the Earth*. New York: Beaufort Books, 1984c:162–69.
———. "Biological Diversity and Global Security." In F. Herbert Bormann and Stephen R. Kellert, eds., *Ecology, Economics, and Ethics: The Broken Circle*. New Haven, Conn.: Yale University Press, 1991:11–25.
MYERS, SHEILA, and HAROLD G. GRASMICK. "The Social Rights and Responsibilities of Pregnant Women: An Application of Parsons' Sick Role Model." Paper presented to the Southwestern Sociological Association, Little Rock, Arkansas, March 1989.
MYERSON, ALLEN R. "This Man Wants to Bury You." *New York Times* (August 1, 1993):section 3, pp. 1, 6.
MYRDAL, GUNNAR. *An American Dilemma: The Negro Problem and Modern Democracy*. New York: Harper & Brothers, 1944.
NAGEL, JOANE. "Constructing Ethnicity: Creating and Recreating Ethnic Identity and Culture." *Social Problems*. Vol. 41, No. 1 (February 1994):152–76.
———. *American Indian Ethnic Renewal: Red Power and the Resurgence of Identity and Culture*. New York: Oxford University Press, 1996.
NAJAFIZADEH, MEHRANGIZ, and LEWIS A. MENNERICK. "Sociology of Education or Sociology of Ethnocentrism: The Portrayal of Education in Introductory Sociology Textbooks." *Teaching Sociology*. Vol. 20, No. 3 (July 1992):215–21.
NASH, J. MADELEINE. "To Know Your Own Fate." *Time*. Vol. 145, No. 14 (April 3, 1995):62.
NATIONAL COMMISSION ON EXCELLENCE IN EDUCATION. *A Nation at Risk*. Washington, D.C.: U.S. Government Printing Office, 1983.
NEERGAARD, LAUREN. "Cigarette Smoking Jumps 28% on Campus." *Bowling Green Sentinel Tribune* (November 18, 1998):9.

NELAN, BRUCE W. "Crimes without Punishment." *Time*. Vol. 141, No. 2 (January 11, 1993):21.
NELSON, AMY L. "The Effect of Economic Restructuring on Family Poverty in the Industrial Heartland, 1970-1990." *Sociological Focus*. Vol. 31 No. 2 (May 1998):201–16.
NELSON, JOEL I. "Work and Benefits: The Multiple Problems of Service Sector Employment." *Social Problems*. Vol. 42, No. 2 (May 1994):240–55.
NESBITT, PAULA D. *Feminization of the Clergy in America: Occupational and Organizational Perspectives*. New York: Oxford University Press, 1997.
NEUGARTEN, BERNICE L. "Grow Old with Me. The Best Is Yet to Be." *Psychology Today*. Vol. 5 (December 1971):45–48, 79, 81.
———. "Personality and the Aging Process." *The Gerontologist*. Vol. 12, No. 1 (Spring 1972):9–15.
———. "Personality and Aging." In James E. Birren and K. Warner Schaie, eds., *Handbook of the Psychology of Aging*. New York: Van Nostrand Reinhold, 1977:626–49.
NEUHOUSER, KEVIN. "The Radicalization of the Brazilian Catholic Church in Comparative Perspective." *American Sociological Review*. Vol. 54, No. 2 (April 1989):233–44.
NEUMAN, W. LAURENCE. *Social Research Methods: Qualitative and Quantitative Approaches*. 3d ed. Boston: Allyn and Bacon, 1997.
NEWMAN, KATHERINE S. *Declining Fortunes: The Withering of the American Dream*. New York: Basic Books, 1993.
NEWMAN, WILLIAM M. *American Pluralism: A Study of Minority Groups and Social Theory*. New York: Harper & Row, 1973.
NIELSEN, A. C. Survey data cited in *Information Please Almanac 1997*. Boston: Houghton Mifflin, 1997.
NIELSEN, FRANCOIS, and ARTHUR S. ALDERSON. "The Kuznets Curve: The Great U-Turn: Income Inequality in U.S. Counties, 1970 to 1990." *American Sociological Review*. Vol. 62, No. 1 (February 1997):12–33.
NIELSEN, JOYCE MCCARL, ed. *Feminist Research Methods: Exemplary Readings in the Social Sciences*. Boulder, Colo.: Westview Press, 1990.
1991 Green Book. U.S. House of Representatives. Washington, D.C.: U.S. Government Printing Office, 1991.
NISBET, ROBERT A. *The Sociological Tradition*. New York: Basic Books, 1966.
———. *The Quest for Community*. New York: Oxford University Press, 1969.
NOCERA, JOSEPH. "Microsoft Tries to Crack AOL's Case." *Fortune*. Vol. 139, No. 12 (June 21, 1999):175–77.
NOCK, STEVEN L., JAMES D. WRIGHT, and LAURA SANCHEZ. "America's Divorce Problem." *Society*. Vol. 36, No. 4 (May/June 1999):43–52.
NOLAN, JAMES L., JR., ed. *The American Culture Wars: Current Contests and Future Prospects*. Charlottesville, Va.: University Press of Virginia, 1996.
NORBECK, EDWARD. "Class Structure." In *Kodansha Encyclopedia of Japan*. Tokyo: Kodansha, 1983:322–25.
NORC. General Social Surveys, 1972–1998: Cumulative Codebook. Chicago: National Opinion Research Center, 1999.
NOVAK, VIVECA. "The Cost of Poor Advice." *Time*. Vol. 154, No. 1 (July 5, 1999):38.
NUNN, CLYDE Z., HARRY J. CROCKETT, JR., and J. ALLEN WILLIAMS, JR. *Tolerance for Nonconformity*. San Francisco: Jossey-Bass, 1978.
OAKES, JEANNIE. "Classroom Social Relationships: Exploring the Bowles and Gintis Hypothesis." *Sociology of Education*. Vol. 55, No. 4 (October 1982):197–212.
———. *Keeping Track: How High Schools Structure Inequality*. New Haven, Conn.: Yale University Press, 1985.
OBERSCHALL, ANTHONY. *Social Conflict and Social Movements*. Englewood Cliffs, N.J.: Prentice Hall, 1973.
O'BRIEN, DAVID J., EDWARD W. HASSINGER, and LARRY DERSHEM. "Size of Place, Residential Stability, and Personal Social Networks." *Sociological Focus*. Vol. 29, No. 1 (February 1996):61–72.
O'CONNOR, RORY J. "Internet Declared Protected Speech." *Post-Star* (Glens Fall, N.Y.: June 27, 1997):A1–A2.
OFFIR, CAROLE WADE. *Human Sexuality*. New York: Harcourt Brace Jovanovich, 1982.
OGBURN, WILLIAM F. *On Culture and Social Change*. Chicago: University of Chicago Press, 1964.
O'HARE, WILLIAM P. "In the Black." *American Demographics*. Vol. 11, No. 11 (November 1989):25–29.
———. "The Rise of Hispanic Affluence." *American Demographics*. Vol. 12, No. 8 (August 1990):40–43.
———. "Managing Multiple-Race Data." *American Demographics*. Vol. 20, No. 4 (April 1998):42–44.
O'HARE, WILLIAM P., WILLIAM H. FREY, and DAN FOST. "Asians in the Suburbs." *American Demographics*. Vol. 16, No. 9 (May 1994):32–38.
O'HARE, WILLIAM P., and JAN LARSON. "Women in Business: Where, What, and Why." *American Demographics*. Vol. 13, No. 7 (July 1991):34–38.
OKRENT, DANIEL. "Raising Kids Online: What Can Parents Do?" *Time*. Vol. 154, No. 18 (May 10, 1999):38–43.
OLSEN, GREGG M. "Re-Modeling Sweden: The Rise and Demise of the Compromise in a Global Economy." *Social Problems*. Vol. 43, No. 1 (February 1996):1–20.
OLZAK, SUSAN. "Labor Unrest, Immigration, and Ethnic Conflict in Urban America, 1880–1914." *American Journal of Sociology*. Vol. 94, No. 6 (May 1989):1303–33.
OLZAK, SUSAN, and ELIZABETH WEST. "Ethnic Conflict and the Rise and Fall of Ethnic Newspapers." *American Sociological Review*. Vol. 56, No. 4 (August 1991):458–74.
ONE WORLD. Data from Web site. [Online] Available http://www.oneworld.org, November 15, 1998.
ORLANSKY, MICHAEL D., and WILLIAM L. HEWARD. *Voices: Interviews with Handicapped People*. Columbus, Ohio: Merrill, 1981:85, 92, 133–34, 172.
ORSHANSKY, MOLLIE. "How Poverty Is Measured." *Monthly Labor Review*. Vol. 92, No. 2 (February 1969):37–41.
ORWIN, CLIFFORD. "All Quiet on the Western Front?" *The Public Interest*. Vol. 123 (Spring 1996): 3–9.
OSGOOD, D. WAYNE, JANET K. WILSON, PATRICK M. O'MALLEY, JERALD G. BACHMAN, and LLOYD D. JOHNSTON. "Routine Activities and Individual Deviant Behavior." *American Sociological Review*. Vol. 61, No. 4 (August 1996):635–55.
OSTRANDER, SUSAN A. "Upper Class Women: The Feminine Side of Privilege." *Qualitative Sociology*. Vol. 3, No. 1 (Spring 1980):23–44.
———. *Women of the Upper Class*. Philadelphia: Temple University Press, 1984.
OUCHI, WILLIAM. *Theory Z: How American Business Can Meet the Japanese Challenge*. Reading, Mass.: Addison-Wesley, 1981.
OWEN, DAVID. *None of the Above: Behind the Myth of Scholastic Aptitude*. Boston: Houghton Mifflin, 1985.
PAKULSKI, JAN. "Mass Social Movements and Social Class." *International Sociology*. Vol. 8, No. 2 (June 1993):131–58.
PALLONE, NATHANIEL J., and JAMES J. HENNESSY. "Brain Dysfunction and Criminal Violence." *Society*. Vol. 35, No. 6 (September–October 1998): 20–27.
PALMORE, ERDMAN. "Advantages of Aging." *The Gerontologist*. Vol. 19, No. 2 (April 1979a):220–23.
———. "Predictors of Successful Aging." *The Gerontologist*. Vol. 19, No. 5 (October 1979b):427–31.
———. "What Can the USA Learn from Japan about Aging?" In Steven H. Zarit, ed., *Readings in Aging and Death: Contemporary Perspectives*. New York: Harper & Row, 1982:166–69.
PARCEL, TOBY L., CHARLES W. MUELLER, and STEVEN CUVELIER. "Comparable Worth and Occupational Labor Market: Explanations of Occupational Earnings Differentials." Paper presented to the American Sociological Association, New York, 1986.
PARENTI, MICHAEL. *Inventing Reality: The Politics of the Mass Media*. New York: St. Martin's Press, 1986.
PARK, ROBERT E. *Race and Culture*. Glencoe, Ill.: Free Press, 1950.
PARRILLO, VINCENT N. "Diversity in America: A Sociohistorical Analysis." *Sociological Forum*. Vol. 9, No. 4 (December 1994):42–45.
PARROTT, JULIE. "The Effects of Culture on Eating Disorders." Paper presented to Southwestern Social Science Association, Dallas, Texas, March 1987.
PARSONS, TALCOTT. "Age and Sex in the Social Structure of the United States." *American Sociological Review*. Vol. 7, No. 4 (August 1942):604–16.
———. *Essays in Sociological Theory*. New York: Free Press, 1954.
———. *The Social System*. New York: Free Press, 1964; orig. 1951.
———. *Societies: Evolutionary and Comparative Perspectives*. Englewood Cliffs, N.J.: Prentice Hall, 1966.
PARSONS, TALCOTT, and ROBERT F. BALES, eds. *Family, Socialization and Interaction Process*. New York: Free Press, 1955.
PATTILLO-MCCOY, MARY. "Church Culture as a Strategy of Action in the Black Community." *American Sociological Review*. Vol. 63, No. 6 (December 1998):767–84.
PAUL, ELLEN FRANKEL. "Bared Buttocks and Federal Cases." *Society*. Vol. 28, No. 4 (May-June, 1991):4–7.

PAULOS, JOHN ALLEN. "After a Crash, Fear Overtakes Logic." *New York Times* (November 2, 1999):A31.
PEAR, ROBERT. "Women Reduce Lag in Earnings, But Disparities with Men Remain." *New York Times* (September 4, 1987):1, 7.
PEAR, ROBERT, with ERIK ECKHOLM. "When Healers Are Entrepreneurs: A Debate over Costs and Ethics." *New York Times* (June 2, 1991):1, 17.
PEARSON, DAVID E. "Post-Mass Culture." *Society*. Vol. 30, No. 5 (July-August 1993):17–22.
———. "Community and Sociology." *Society*. Vol. 32, No. 5 (July-August 1995):44–50.
PEASE, JOHN, and LEE MARTIN. "Want Ads and Jobs for the Poor: A Glaring Mismatch." *Sociological Forum*. Vol. 12. No. 4 (December 1997):545–64.
PERROLLE, JUDITH A. "Comments from the Special Issue Editor: The Emerging Dialogue on Environmental Justice." *Social Problems*. Vol. 40, No. 1 (February 1993):1–4.
PERSELL, CAROLINE HODGES. *Education and Inequality: A Theoretical and Empirical Synthesis*. New York: Free Press, 1977.
———. "The Interdependence of Social Justice and Civil Society." *Sociological Forum*. Vol. 12, No. 2 (June 1997):149–72.
PESSEN, EDWARD. *Riches, Class, and Power: America before the Civil War*. New Brunswick, N.J.: Transaction Books, 1990.
Peters Atlas of the World. New York: Harper & Row, 1990.
PETERSILIA, JOAN. "Probation in the United States: Practices and Challenges." *National Institute of Justice Journal*. No. 233 (September 1997):4.
PETERSON, SCOTT. "Women Live on Own Terms behind the Veil." *Christian Science Monitor* (July 31, 1996):1, 10.
PHELAN, JO, BRUCE G. LINK, ANN STUEVE, and ROBERT E. MOORE. "Education, Social Liberalism, and Economic Conservatism: Attitudes toward Homeless People." *American Sociological Review*. Vol. 60, No. 1 (February 1995):126–40.
PHI DELTA KAPPA INTERNATIONAL. Phi Delta Kappa International/Gallup Poll. [Online] Available http://www.pdkintl.org/kappan/kpol9909.htm#1a, February 14, 2000.
PHILIPSON, ILENE J., and KAREN V. HANSEN. "Women, Class, and the Feminist Imagination." In Karen V. Hansen and Ilene J. Philipson, eds., *Women, Class, and the Feminist Imagination: A Socialist-Feminist Reader*. Philadelphia: Temple University Press, 1992:3–40.
PHILLIPS, KEVIN. *Arrogant Capital: Washington, Wall Street, and the Frustration of American Politics*. Boston: Little, Brown and Company, 1994.
PHILLIPSON, CHRIS. *Capitalism and the Construction of Old Age*. London: Macmillan, 1982.
PHYSICIANS' TASK FORCE ON HUNGER IN AMERICA. "Hunger Reaches Blue-Collar America." Report issued 1987.
PICHARDO, NELSON A. "The Power Elite and Elite-Driven Countermovements: The Associated Farmers of California during the 1930s." *Sociological Forum*. Vol. 10, No. 1 (March 1995):21–49.
PILLEMER, KARL. "Maltreatment of the Elderly at Home and in Institutions: Extent, Risk Factors, and Policy Recommendations." In U.S. Congress. House, Select Committee on Aging and Senate, Special Committee on Aging. *Legislative Agenda for an Aging Society: 1988 and Beyond*. Washington, D.C.: U.S. Government Printing Office, 1988.
PINCHOT, GIFFORD, and ELIZABETH PINCHOT. *The End of Bureaucracy and the Rise of the Intelligent Organization*. San Francisco: Berrett-Koehler, 1993.
PINES, MAYA. "The Civilization of Genie." *Psychology Today*. Vol. 15 (September 1981):28–34.
PINHEY, THOMAS K., DONALD H. RUBINSTEIN, and RICHARD S. COLFAX. "Overweight and Happiness: The Reflected Self-Appraisal Hypothesis Reconsidered." *Social Science Quarterly*. Vol. 78, No. 3 (September 1997):747–55.
PIRANDELLO, LUIGI. "The Pleasure of Honesty." In *To Clothe the Naked and Two Other Plays*. New York: Dutton, 1962:143–98.
PIROG, MAUREEN A., and CHRIS MAGEE. "High School Completion: The Influence of Schools, Families, and Adolescent Parenting." *Social Science Quarterly*. Vol. 78, No. 3 (September 1997):710–24.
PITNEY, JOHN J., JR. "What Scholars Don't Know about Term Limits." *The Chronicle of Higher Education*. Vol. XLI, No. 33 (April 28, 1995):A76.
PITT, MALCOLM. *Introducing Hinduism*. New York: Friendship Press, 1955.
PIVEN, FRANCES FOX, and RICHARD A. CLOWARD. *Poor People's Movements: Why They Succeed, How They Fail*. New York: Pantheon Books, 1977.
———. *Why Americans Don't Vote*. New York: Pantheon Books, 1988.
PLECK, ELIZABETH. *Domestic Tyranny: The Making of Social Policy against Family Violence from Colonial Times to the Present*. New York: Oxford University Press, 1987.
PLOMIN, ROBERT, and TERRYL T. FOCH. "A Twin Study of Objectively Assessed Personality in Childhood." *Journal of Personality and Social Psychology*. Vol. 39, No. 4 (October 1980):680–88.
PODOLNY, JOEL M., and JAMES N. BARON. "Resources and Relationships: Social Networks and Mobility in the Workplace." *American Sociological Review*. Vol. 62, No. 5 (October 1997):673–93.
POHL, RUDIGER. "The Transition from Communism to Capitalism in East Germany." *Society*. Vol. 33, No. 4 (June 1996):62–65.
POLENBERG, RICHARD. *One Nation Divisible: Class, Race, and Ethnicity in the United States since 1938*. New York: Pelican Books, 1980.
POLLACK, ANDREW. "Happy in the East (^-^) or Smiling :-) in the West." *New York Times* (August 12, 1996).
———. "Overseas, Smoking Is One of Life's Small Pleasures." *New York Times* (August 17, 1997):E5.
POLLARD, KELVIN. "Play Ball! Demographics and Major League Baseball." *Population Today*. Vol. 24, No. 4 (April 1996):3.
———. "Speaking Graphically: Per Capita Fresh Water Availability . . ." *Population Today*. Vol. 24, No. 12 (December 1996):6.
POLLOCK, PHILIP H., III, and M. ELLIOT VITTAS. "Who Bears the Burdens of Environmental Pollution: Race, Ethnicity, and Environmental Equity in Florida." *Social Science Quarterly*. Vol. 76, No. 2 (June 1995):294–310.
POLSBY, NELSON W. "Three Problems in the Analysis of Community Power." *American Sociological Review*. Vol. 24, No. 6 (December 1959):796–803.
POMER, MARSHALL I. "Labor Market Structure, Intragenerational Mobility, and Discrimination: Black Male Advancement Out of Low-Paying Occupations, 1962–1973." *American Sociological Review*. Vol. 51, No. 5 (October 1986):650–59.
POPENOE, DAVID. *Disturbing the Nest: Family Change and Decline in Modern Societies*. New York: Aldine, 1988.
———. "Family Decline in the Swedish Welfare State." *The Public Interest*. No. 102 (Winter 1991):65–77.
———. "The Controversial Truth: Two-Parent Families Are Better." *New York Times* (December 26, 1992):21.
———. "American Family Decline, 1960–1990: A Review and Appraisal." *Journal of Marriage and the Family*. Vol. 55, No. 3 (August 1993a):527–55.
———. "Parental Androgyny." *Society*. Vol. 30, No. 6 (September-October 1993b):5–11.
———. "Scandinavian Welfare." *Society*. Vol. 31, No. 6 (September-October, 1994):78–81.
POPENOE, DAVID, and BARBARA DAFOE WHITEHEAD. *Should We Live Together? What Young Adults Need to Know about Cohabitation before Marriage*. New Brunswick, N.J.: The National Marriage Project, 1999.
POPKIN, SUSAN J. "Welfare: Views from the Bottom." *Social Problems*. Vol. 17, No. 1 (February 1990):64–79.
POPULATION REFERENCE BUREAU. *1999 World Population Data Sheet*. Washington, D.C.: Population Reference Bureau, 1999.
Population Today. "Majority of Children in Poverty Live with Parents Who Work." Vol. 23, No. 4 (April 1995):6.
———. "Chronic Disability Declines Dramatically among U.S. Elderly." Vol. 25, No. 9 (September 1997):3.
PORTES, ALEJANDRO, and LEIF JENSEN. "The Enclave and the Entrants: Patterns of Ethnic Enterprise in Miami before and after Mariel." *American Sociological Review*. Vol. 54, No. 6 (December 1989):929–49.
POSTEL, SANDRA. "Facing Water Scarcity." In Lester R. Brown et al., eds., *State of the World 1993: A Worldwatch Institute Report on Progress toward a Sustainable Society*. New York: Norton, 1993:22–41.
POWELL, CHRIS, and GEORGE E. C. PATON, eds. *Humour in Society: Resistance and Control*. New York: St. Martin's Press, 1988.
PRESS, ANDREA L. Review of *Enlightened Racism: "The Cosby Show," Audiences, and the Myth of the American Dream*, by Sut Jhally and Justin Lewis. *American Journal of Sociology*. Vol. 99, No. 1 (July 1993):219–21.
PRESSER, HARRIET B. "The Housework Gender Gap." *Population Today*. Vol. 21, No. 7/8 (July-August 1993):5.
PRESSLEY, SUE ANNE, and NANCY ANDREWS. "For Gay Couples, the Nursery Becomes the New Frontier." *Washington Post* (December 20, 1992):A1, A22–23.
PRESTON, LEE E. "Corporate Boards and Corporate Governance." *Society*. Vol. 32, No. 3 (March–April 1995):17–20.

PRIMEGGIA, SALVATORE, and JOSEPH A. VARACALLI. "Southern Italian Comedy: Old to New World." In Joseph V. Scelsa, Salvatore J. LaGumina, and Lydio Tomasi, eds., *Italian Americans in Transition*. New York: The American Italian Historical Association, 1990:241–52.

PRINDLE, DAVID F. *Risky Business: The Political Economy of Hollywood*. Boulder, Colo.: Westview Press, 1993.

PRINDLE, DAVID F., and JAMES W. ENDERSBY. "Hollywood Liberalism." *Social Science Quarterly*. Vol. 74, No. 1 (March 1993):136–49.

PUTERBAUGH, GEOFF, ed. *Twins and Homosexuality: A Casebook*. New York: Garland, 1990.

PUTKA, GARY. "SAT to Become a Better Gauge." *Wall Street Journal* (November 1, 1990):B1.

PUTKA, GARY, and STEVE STECKLOW. "Do For-Profit Schools Work? These Seem To for One Entrepreneur." *Wall Street Journal* (June 8, 1994):A1, A4.

QUEENAN, JOE. "The Many Paths to Riches." *Forbes*. Vol. 144, No. 9 (October 23, 1989):149.

QUINNEY, RICHARD. *Class, State and Crime: On the Theory and Practice of Criminal Justice*. New York: David McKay, 1977.

RABKIN, JEREMY. "The Supreme Court in the Culture Wars." *The Public Interest*. Vol. 125 (Fall 1996):3–26.

RALEY, R. KELLY. "A Shortage of Marriageable Men? A Note on the Role of Cohabitation in Black-White Differences in Marriage Rates." *American Journal of Sociology*. Vol. 61, No. 6 (December 1996):973–83.

RAMO, JOSHUA COOPER. "Finding God on the Web." *Time* (December 16, 1996):60–67.

RAPHAEL, RAY. *The Men from the Boys: Rites of Passage in Male America*. Lincoln and London: University of Nebraska Press, 1988.

RASHID, AHMED. "Subversive." *New York Times Magazine* (June 8, 1997):78.

RATAN, SUNEEL. "A New Divide between Haves and Have-Nots?" *Time*. Special Issue. Vol. 145, No. 12 (Spring 1995):25–26.

RATNESAR, ROMESH. "Lost in the Middle." *Time*. Vol. 152, No. 17 (September 14, 1998):60–62.

———. "Not Gone, but Forgotten?" *Time*. Vol. 153, No. 15 (February 8, 1999):30–31.

RAVITCH, DIANE, and JOSEPH VITERITTI. "A New Vision for City Schools." *The Public Interest*. Vol. 122 (Winter 1996):3–16.

RAY, PAUL H. "The Emerging Culture." *American Demographics*. Vol. 19, No. 2 (February 1997):29–34, 56.

RECKLESS, WALTER C., and SIMON DINITZ. "Pioneering with Self-Concept as a Vulnerability Factor in Delinquency." *Journal of Criminal Law, Criminology, and Police Science*. Vol. 58, No. 4 (December 1967):515–23.

RECTOR, ROBERT. "America Has the World's Richest Poor People." *Wall Street Journal* (September 24, 1998):A18.

REICH, ROBERT B. "As the World Turns." *The New Republic* (May 1, 1989):23, 26–28.

———. *The Work of Nations: Preparing Ourselves for 21st-Century Capitalism*. New York: Alfred A. Knopf, 1991.

REID, SUE TITUS. *Crime and Criminology*. 6th ed. Fort Worth, Tex.: Holt, Rinehart & Winston, 1991.

REIMAN, JEFFREY. *The Rich Get Richer and the Poor Get Prison: Ideology, Class, and Criminal Justice*. Boston: Allyn and Bacon, 1998.

REINGOLD, BETH, and RICHARD S. WIKE. "Confederate Symbols, Southern Identity, and Racial Attitudes: The Case of the Georgia State Flag." *Social Science Quarterly*. Vol. 79, No. 3 (September 1998):568–80.

REINHARZ, SHULAMIT. *Feminist Methods in Social Research*. New York: Oxford University Press, 1992.

REITZES, DONALD C., ELIZABETH J. MUTRAN, and MARIA E. FERNANDEZ. "The Decision to Retire: A Career Perspective." *Social Science Quarterly*. Vol. 79, No. 3 (September 1998):607–19.

REMOFF, HEATHER TREXLER. *Sexual Choice: A Woman's Decision*. New York: Dutton/Lewis, 1984.

REMY, JACQUELINE. "Interview with Agnes Fournier de Saint-Maur, Interpol Police Lieutenant." For *L'Express*. Reprinted in *World Press Review* (November 1996):7.

REYNOLDS, JOHN R., and CATHERINE E. ROSS. "Social Stratification and Health: Education's Benefit beyond Economic Status and Social Origins." *Social Problems*. Vol. 45, No. 2 (May 1998):221–45.

RHODES, STEVE. "The Luck of the Draw." *Newsweek* (April 26, 1999):41.

RICHARDSON, JAMES T. "Definitions of Cult: From Sociological-Technical to Popular Negative." Paper presented to the American Psychological Association, Boston, August 1990.

RIDDLE, JOHN M., J. WORTH ESTES, and JOSIAH C. RUSSELL. "Ever since Eve . . . Birth Control in the Ancient World." *Archaeology*. Vol. 47, No. 2 (March/April, 1994):29–35.

RIDGEWAY, CECILIA L. *The Dynamics of Small Groups*. New York: St. Martin's Press, 1983.

RIESMAN, DAVID. *The Lonely Crowd: A Study of the Changing American Character*. New Haven, Conn.: Yale University Press, 1970; orig. 1950.

RILEY, MATILDA WHITE, ANNE FONER, and JOAN WARING. "Sociology of Age." In Neil J. Smelser, ed., *Handbook of Sociology*. Newbury Park, Calif.: Sage, 1988:243–90.

RILEY, NANCY E. "Gender, Power, and Population Change." *Population Bulletin*. Vol. 52, No. 1 (May 1997).

RITZER, GEORGE. *The McDonaldization of Society: An Investigation into the Changing Character of Contemporary Social Life*. Thousand Oaks, Calif.: Pine Forge Press, 1993.

———. *The McDonaldization Thesis: Explorations and Extensions*. Thousand Oaks, Calif.: Sage, 1998.

RITZER, GEORGE, and DAVID WALCZAK. *Working: Conflict and Change*. 4th ed. Englewood Cliffs, N.J.: Prentice Hall, 1990.

RIVERA-BATIZ, FRANCISCO L., and CARLOS SANTIAGO, cited in Sam Roberts, "Puerto Ricans on Mainland Making Gains, Study Finds." *New York Times* (October 19, 1994):A20.

ROBERTS, J. DEOTIS. *Roots of a Black Future: Family and Church*. Philadelphia: Westminster Press, 1980.

ROBERTS, STEVEN V. "Open Arms for Online Democracy." *U.S. News & World Report*. Vol. 118, No. 2 (January 16, 1995):10.

ROBINSON, DAWN. "Toward a Synthesis of Sociological and Psychological Theories of Eating Disorders." Paper presented to Southwestern Social Science Association, Dallas, Texas, March 1987.

ROBINSON, JOHN P., PERLA WERNER, and GEOFFREY GODBEY. "Freeing Up the Golden Years." *American Demographics*. Vol. 19, No. 10 (October 1997):20–24.

ROBINSON, JOYCE, and GLENNA SPITZE. "Whistle While You Work? The Effect of Household Task Performance on Women's and Men's Well-Being." *Social Science Quarterly*. Vol. 73, No. 4 (December 1992):844–61.

ROBINSON, VERA M. "Humor and Health." In Paul E. McGhee and Jeffrey H. Goldstein, eds., *Handbook of Humor Research, Vol. II, Applied Studies*. New York: Springer-Verlag, 1983:109–28.

RODGERS, JOAN R. "An Empirical Study of Intergenerational Transmission of Poverty in the United States." *Social Science Quarterly*. Vol. 76, No. 1 (March 1995):178–94.

ROESCH, ROBERTA. "Violent Families." *Parents*. Vol. 59, No. 9 (September 1984):74–76, 150–52.

ROETHLISBERGER, F. J., and WILLIAM J. DICKSON. *Management and the Worker*. Cambridge, Mass.: Harvard University Press, 1939.

ROHLEN, THOMAS P. *Japan's High Schools*. Berkeley: University of California Press, 1983.

RÓNA-TAS, ÁKOS. "The First Shall Be Last? Entrepreneurship and Communist Cadres in the Transition from Socialism." *American Journal of Sociology*. Vol. 100, No. 1 (July 1994):40–69.

ROOF, WADE CLARK. "Socioeconomic Differentials among White Socioreligious Groups in the United States." *Social Forces*. Vol. 58, No. 1 (September 1979):280–89.

ROOF, WADE CLARK, and WILLIAM MCKINNEY. *American Mainline Religion: Its Changing Shape and Future*. New Brunswick, N.J.: Rutgers University Press, 1987.

RORTY, RICHARD. "The Unpatriotic Academy." *New York Times* (February 13, 1994):15.

ROSE, FRED. "Toward a Class-Cultural Theory of Social Movements: Reinterpreting New Social Movements." *Sociological Forum*. Vol. 12, No. 3 (September 1997):461–94.

ROSE, JERRY D. *Outbreaks*. New York: Free Press, 1982.

ROSEN, ELLEN ISRAEL. *Bitter Choices: Blue-Collar Women In and Out of Work*. Chicago: University of Chicago Press, 1987.

ROSENBAUM, DAVID E. "Americans Want a Right to Die. Or So They Think." *New York Times* (June 8, 1997):E3.

ROSENDAHL, MONA. *Inside the Revolution: Everyday Life in Socialist Cuba*. Ithaca, N.Y.: Cornell University Press, 1997.

ROSENFELD, MEGAN. "Little Boys Blue: Reexamining the Plight of Young Males." *Washington Post* (March 26, 1998):A1, A17–A18.

ROSENFELD, MICHAEL J. "Celebration, Politics, and Selective Looting and Riots: A Micro-Level Study of the Bulls Riot of 1992 in Chicago." *Social Problems.* Vol. 44, No. 4 (November 1997):483–502.

ROSENFELD, SARAH. "Labeling Mental Illness: The Effects of Received Services and Perceived Stigma on Life Satisfaction." *American Sociological Review.* Vol. 62, No. 4 (August 1997):660–72.

ROSENTHAL, ELIZABETH. "Canada's National Health Plan Gives Care to All, with Limits." *New York Times* (April 30, 1991):A1, A16.

ROSENTHAL, JACK. "The Rapid Growth of Suburban Employment." In Lois H. Masotti and Jeffrey K. Hadden, eds., *Suburbia in Transition.* New York: New York Times Books, 1974:95–100.

ROSNOW, RALPH L., and GARY ALAN FINE. *Rumor and Gossip: The Social Psychology of Hearsay.* New York: Elsevier, 1976.

ROSS, CATHERINE E., JOHN MIROWSKY, and JOAN HUBER. "Dividing Work, Sharing Work, and In-Between: Marriage Patterns and Depression." *American Sociological Review.* Vol. 48, No. 6 (December 1983):809–23.

ROSS, JOHN. "To Die in the Street: Mexico City's Homeless Population Boom as Economic Crisis Shakes Social Protections." *SSSP Newsletter.* Vol. 27, No. 2 (Summer 1996):14–15.

ROSSI, ALICE S. "Gender and Parenthood." In Alice S. Rossi, ed., *Gender and the Life Course.* New York: Aldine, 1985:161–91.

ROSSI, PETER H. Review of Christopher Jencks, *The Homeless* (Cambridge, Mass.: Harvard University Press). *Society.* Vol. 32, No. 4 (May-June 1995):80–81.

ROSTOW, WALT W. *The Stages of Economic Growth: A Non-Communist Manifesto.* Cambridge: Cambridge University Press, 1960.

———. *The World Economy: History and Prospect.* Austin: University of Texas Press, 1978.

ROSZAK, THEODORE. *The Cult of Information: The Folklore of Computers and the True Art of Thinking.* New York: Pantheon Books, 1986.

ROTHMAN, BARBARA KATZ. "Of Maps and Imaginations: Sociology Confronts the Genome." *Social Problems.* Vol. 42, No. 1 (February 1995):1–10.

ROTHMAN, STANLEY, and AMY E. BLACK. "Who Rules Now? American Elites in the 1990s." *Society.* Vol. 35, No. 6 (September-October 1998):17–20.

ROTHMAN, STANLEY, and S. ROBERT LICHTER. "Social Science and Ideology: A Reply to Prindle, Endersby, and Gans." *Social Science Quarterly.* Vol. 75 (June 1994):455–57.

ROTHMAN, STANLEY, STEPHEN POWERS, and DAVID ROTHMAN. "Feminism in Films." *Society.* Vol. 30, No. 3 (March-April 1993):66–72.

ROWE, DAVID C. "Biometrical Genetic Models of Self-Reported Delinquent Behavior: A Twin Study." *Behavior Genetics.* Vol. 13, No. 5 (1983):473–89.

ROWE, DAVID C., and D. WAYNE OSGOOD. "Heredity and Sociological Theories of Delinquency: A Reconsideration." *American Sociological Review.* Vol. 49, No. 4 (August 1984):526–40.

ROZELL, MARK J., CLYDE WILCOX, and JOHN C. GREEN. "Religious Constituencies and Support for the Christian Right in the 1990s." *Social Science Quarterly.* Vol. 79, No. 4 (December 1998):815–27.

RUBENSTEIN, ELI A. "The Not So Golden Years." *Newsweek* (October 7, 1991):13.

RUBIN, LILLIAN BRESLOW. *Worlds of Pain: Life in the Working-Class Family.* New York: Basic Books, 1976.

RUDÉ, GEORGE. *The Crowd in History: A Study of Popular Disturbances in France and England, 1730–1848.* New York: Wiley, 1964.

RUDEL, THOMAS K., and JUDITH M. GERSON. "Postmodernism, Institutional Change, and Academic Workers: A Sociology of Knowledge." *Social Science Quarterly.* Vol. 80, No. 2 (June 1999):213–28.

RUDOLPH, ELLEN. "Women's Talk: Japanese Women." *New York Times Magazine* (September 1, 1991).

RULE, JAMES, and PETER BRANTLEY. "Computerized Surveillance in the Workplace: Forms and Delusions." *Sociological Forum.* Vol. 7, No. 3 (September 1992):405–23.

RUSSELL, CHERYL. "Are We in the Dumps?" *American Demographics.* Vol. 17, No. 1 (January 1995a):6.

———. "True Crime." *American Demographics.* Vol. 17, No. 8 (August 1995b):22–31.

RUSSELL, CHERYL, and MARCIA MOGELONSKY. "Riding High on the Market." *American Demographics.* Vol. 22, No. 4 (April 2000):44–54.

RUTHERFORD, MEGAN. "Women Run the World." *Time.* Vol. 153, No. 25 (June 28, 1999):72

RYAN, WILLIAM. *Blaming the Victim.* Rev. ed. New York: Vintage Books, 1976.

RYMER, RUSS. *Genie.* New York: HarperPerennial, 1994.

SACHS, JEFFREY. "The Real Causes of Famine." *Time.* Vol. 152, No. 17 (October 26, 1998):69.

SADIK, NAFIS, ed. *Population Policies and Programmes: Lessons Learned from Two Decades of Experience.* New York: New York University Press, 1991.

ST. JEAN, YANICK, and JOE R. FEAGIN. *Double Burden: Black Women and Everyday Racism.* Armonk, N.Y.: M. E. Sharpe, 1998.

SALE, KIRKPATRICK. *The Conquest of Paradise: Christopher Columbus and the Columbian Legacy.* New York: Alfred A. Knopf, 1990.

SAMPSON, ANTHONY. *The Changing Anatomy of Britain.* New York: Random House, 1982.

SAMPSON, ROBERT J. "Urban Black Violence: The Effects of Male Joblessness and Family Disruption." *American Journal of Sociology.* Vol. 93, No. 2 (September 1987):348–82.

SAMPSON, ROBERT J., and JOHN H. LAUB. "Crime and Deviance over the Life Course: The Salience of Adult Social Bonds." *American Sociological Review.* Vol. 55, No. 5 (October 1990):609–27.

SANCHEZ, RENE. "Urban Students Not Making the Mark." *Washington Post* (January 8, 1998):A18.

SANTOLI, AL. "Fighting Child Prostitution." *Freedom Review.* Vol. 25, No. 5 (September-October 1994):5–8.

SAPIR, EDWARD. "The Status of Linguistics as a Science." *Language.* Vol. 5 (1929):207–14.

———. *Selected Writings of Edward Sapir in Language, Culture, and Personality.* David G. Mandelbaum, ed. Berkeley: University of California Press, 1949.

SAX, LINDA J., ALEXANDER W. ASTIN, WILLIAM S. KORN, and KATHRYN M. MAHONEY. *The American Freshman: National Norms for Fall 1999.* Los Angeles: UCLA Higher Education Research Institute, 1999.

SCAFF, LAWRENCE A. "Max Weber and Robert Michels." *American Journal of Sociology.* Vol. 86, No. 6 (May 1981):1269–86.

SCANLON, JAMES P. "The Curious Case of Affirmative Action for Women." *Society.* Vol. 29, No. 2 (January-February 1992):36–42.

SCHAIE, K. WARNER. "Intelligence and Problem Solving." In James E. Birren and R. Bruce Sloane, eds., *Handbook of Mental Health and Aging.* Englewood Cliffs, N.J.: Prentice Hall, 1980:262–84.

SCHEFF, THOMAS J. *Being Mentally Ill: A Sociological Theory.* 2d ed. New York: Aldine, 1984.

SCHERER, RON. "Worldwide Trend: Tobacco Use Grows." *Christian Science Monitor* (July 17, 1996):4, 8.

SCHILLER, BRADLEY. "Who Are the Working Poor?" *The Public Interest.* Vol. 155 (Spring 1994):61–71.

SCHLESINGER, ARTHUR. "The City in American Civilization." In A. B. Callow, Jr., ed., *American Urban History.* New York: Oxford University Press, 1969:25–41.

SCHLESINGER, ARTHUR, JR. "The Cult of Ethnicity: Good and Bad." *Time.* Vol. 137, No. 27 (July 8, 1991):21.

SCHLESINGER, JACOB M. "Finally, U.S. Median Income Approaches Old Heights." *Wall Street Journal* (September 25, 1998):B1.

SCHMIDT, ROGER. *Exploring Religion.* Belmont, Calif.: Wadsworth, 1980.

SCHNEIDER, MARK, MELISSA MARSCHALL, PAUL TESKE, and CHRISTINE ROCH. "School Choice and Culture Wars in the Classroom: What Different Parents Seek from Education." *Social Science Quarterly.* Vol. 79, No. 3 (September 1998):489–501.

SCHOR, JUDITH B. Cited in Cheryl Russell, "Overworked? Overwhelmed?" *American Demographics.* Vol. 17, No. 3 (March 1995):8.

SCHUMANN, HANS WOLFGANG. *Buddhism: An Outline of Its Teachings and Schools.* Wheaton, Ill.: The Theosophical Publishing House/Quest Books, 1974.

SCHUTT, RUSSELL K. "Objectivity versus Outrage." *Society.* Vol. 26, No. 4 (May-June 1989):14–16.

SCHWARTZ, BARRY. "Memory as a Cultural System: Abraham Lincoln in World War II." *American Sociological Review.* Vol. 61, No. 5 (October 1996):908–27.

SCHWARTZ, FELICE N. "Management, Women, and the New Facts of Life." *Harvard Business Review.* Vol. 89, No. 1 (January-February 1989):65–76.

SCHWARTZ, JOE. "Rising Status." *American Demographics.* Vol. 11, No. 1 (January 1989):10.

SCHWARTZ, MARTIN D. "Gender and Injury in Spousal Assault." *Sociological Focus.* Vol. 20, No. 1 (January 1987):61–75.

SCHWARTZ-NOBEL, LORETTA. *Starving in the Shadow of Plenty.* New York: McGraw-Hill, 1981.

SCHWARZ, JOHN E., and THOMAS J. VOLGY. *The Forgotten Americans: Thirty Million Working Poor in the Land of Opportunity.* New York: Norton, 1992.

SCOMMEGNA, PAOLA. "Teens' Risk of AIDS, Unintended Pregnancies Examined." *Population Today*. Vol. 24, No. 8 (August 1996):1–2.
SCOTT, JOHN, and CATHERINE GRIFF. *Directors of Industry: The British Corporate Network, 1904–1976*. New York: Blackwell, 1985.
SCOTT, JOSEPH E., and J. CUVELIER. "Violence in *Playboy* Magazine: A Longitudinal Analysis." *Archives of Sexual Behavior*. Vol. 16 (1987):279–88.
SCOTT, W. RICHARD. *Organizations: Rational, Natural, and Open Systems*. Englewood Cliffs, N.J.: Prentice Hall, 1981.
SEARS, DAVID O., and JOHN B. MCCONAHAY. *The Politics of Violence: The New Urban Blacks and the Watts Riot*. Boston: Houghton Mifflin, 1973.
SEBASTIAN, TIM. "Massacred: 1,000; Tried, 0." *World Press Review* (June 1996):6–10.
SEGAL, MADY WECHSLER, and AMANDA FAITH HANSEN. "Value Rationales in Policy Debates on Women in the Military: A Content Analysis of Congressional Testimony, 1941–1985." *Social Science Quarterly*. Vol. 73, No. 2 (June 1992):296–309.
SEIDMAN, STEVEN. *Queer Theory/Sociology*. Oxford: Blackwell, 1996.
SEKULIC, DUSKO, GARTH MASSEY, and RANDY HODSON. "Who Were the Yugoslavs? Failed Sources of Common Identity in the Former Yugoslavia." *American Sociological Review*. Vol. 59, No. 1 (February 1994):83–97.
SELLIN, THORSTEN. *The Penalty of Death*. Beverly Hills, Calif.: Sage, 1980.
SELTZER, ROBERT M. *Jewish People, Jewish Thought: The Jewish Experience in History*. New York: Macmillan, 1980.
SEN, K. M. *Hinduism*. Baltimore: Penguin Books, 1961.
SENNETT, RICHARD. *The Corrosion of Character: The Personal Consequences of Work in the New Capitalism*. New York: Norton, 1998.
SENNETT, RICHARD, and JONATHAN COBB. *The Hidden Injuries of Class*. New York: Vintage Books, 1973.
SEPLOW, STEPHEN, and JONATHAN STORM. "How TV Defined Our Lives." *Philadelphia Inquirer* (November 30, 1997):A1, A16–17.
SHAPIRO, JOSEPH P. "Welfare: The Myth of Reform." *U.S. News & World Report*. Vol. 188, No. 2 (January 16, 1995):30–40.
SHAPIRO, JOSEPH P., and JOANNIE M. SCHROF. "Honor Thy Children." *U.S. News & World Report*. Vol. 118, No. 8 (February 27, 1995):39–49.
SHAREEF-COUSIN.COM. [Online] Available August, 1999.
SHARPE, ANITA. "The Rich Aren't So Different After All." *Wall Street Journal* (November 12, 1996):B1, B10.
SHAWCROSS, WILLIAM. *Sideshow: Kissinger, Nixon and the Destruction of Cambodia*. New York: Pocket Books, 1979.
SHEEHAN, TOM. "Senior Esteem as a Factor in Socioeconomic Complexity." *The Gerontologist*. Vol. 16, No. 5 (October 1976):433–40.
SHELDON, WILLIAM H., EMIL M. HARTL, and EUGENE MCDERMOTT. *Varieties of Delinquent Youth*. New York: Harper, 1949.
SHELEY, JAMES F., JOSHUA ZHANG, CHARLES J. BRODY, and JAMES D. WRIGHT. "Gang Organization, Gang Criminal Activity, and Individual Gang Members' Criminal Behavior." *Social Science Quarterly*. Vol. 76, No. 1 (March 1995):53–68.
SHELLENBARGER, SUE. "Deciding How Soon to Prepare Your Child to Stay at Home." *Wall Street Journa*l (March 20, 1996):B1.
SHERMAN, LAWRENCE W., and DOUGLAS A. SMITH. "Crime, Punishment, and Stake in Conformity: Legal and Informal Control of Domestic Violence." *American Sociological Review*. Vol. 57, No. 5 (October 1992):680–90.
SHEVKY, ESHREF, and WENDELL BELL. *Social Area Analysis*. Stanford, Calif.: Stanford University Press, 1955.
SHIPLER, DAVID K. *Russia: Broken Idols, Solemn Dreams*. New York: Penguin Books, 1984.
SHIPLEY, JOSEPH T. *Dictionary of Word Origins*. Totowa, N.J.: Roman & Allanheld, 1985.
SHIVELY, JOELLEN. "Cowboys and Indians: Perceptions of Western Films among American Indians and Anglos." *American Sociological Review*. Vol. 57, No. 6 (December 1992):725–34.
SHLAES, AMITY. "Vermont Levels Its Schools." *Wall Street Journal* (April 22, 1998):A22.
SHUPE, ANSON. *In the Name of All That's Holy: A Theory of Clergy Malfeasance*. Westport, Conn.: Praeger, 1995.
SHUPE, ANSON, WILLIAM A. STACEY, and LONNIE R. HAZLEWOOD. *Violent Men, Violent Couples: The Dynamics of Domestic Violence*. Lexington, Mass.: Lexington Books, 1987.
SIDEL, RUTH, and VICTOR W. SIDEL. *A Healthy State: An International Perspective on the Crisis in United States Medical Care*. Rev. ed. New York: Pantheon Books, 1982a.
———. *The Health Care of China*. Boston: Beacon Press, 1982b.
SILVERBERG, ROBERT. "The Greenhouse Effect: Apocalypse Now or Chicken Little?" *Omni* (July 1991):50–54.
SILVERSTEIN, MICHAEL. In Jon Snodgrass, ed., *A Book of Readings for Men against Sexism*. Albion, Calif.: Times Change Press, 1977:178–79.
SIMMEL, GEORG. *The Sociology of Georg Simmel*. Kurt Wolff, ed. New York: Free Press, 1950:118–69; orig. 1902.
———. "Fashion." In Donald N. Levine, ed., *Georg Simmel: On Individuality and Social Forms*. Chicago: University of Chicago Press, 1971; orig. 1904.
SIMON, JULIAN. *The Ultimate Resource*. Princeton, N.J.: Princeton University Press, 1981.
SIMONS, CAROL. "Japan's *Kyoiku* Mamas." In John J. Macionis and Nijole V. Benokraitis, eds., *Seeing Ourselves: Classic, Contemporary, and Cross-Cultural Readings in Sociology*. Englewood Cliffs, N.J.: Prentice Hall, 1989:281–86.
SIMONS, MARLISE. "The Price of Modernization: The Case of Brazil's Kaiapo Indians." In John J. Macionis and Nijole V. Benokraitis, eds., *Seeing Ourselves: Classic, Contemporary, and Cross-Cultural Readings in Sociology*. 5th ed. Upper Saddle River, N.J.: Prentice Hall, 2001:496–502.
SIMPSON, GEORGE EATON, and J. MILTON YINGER. *Racial and Cultural Minorities: An Analysis of Prejudice and Discrimination*. 4th ed. New York: Harper & Row, 1972.
SINGER, JEROME L., and DOROTHY G. SINGER. "Psychologists Look at Television: Cognitive, Developmental, Personality, and Social Policy Implications." *American Psychologist*. Vol. 38, No. 7 (July 1983):826–34.
SIPES, RICHARD G. "War, Sports and Aggression: An Empirical Test of Two Rival Theories." *American Anthropologist*. Vol. 75, No. 1 (January 1973):64–86.
SIVARD, RUTH LEGER. *World Military and Social Expenditures, 1987–88*. 12th ed. Washington, D.C.: World Priorities, 1988.
———. *World Military and Social Expenditures, 1992–93*. 17th ed. Washington, D.C.: World Priorities, 1993.
SIZER, THEODORE R. *Horace's Compromise: The Dilemma of the American High School*. Boston: Houghton Mifflin, 1984.
SKINNER, DAVID. "Computers: Good for Education?" *The Public Interest*. No. 128 (Summer 1997):98–109.
SKOCPOL, THEDA. *States and Social Revolutions: A Comparative Analysis of France, Russia, and China*. Cambridge: Cambridge University Press, 1979.
SMAIL, J. KENNETH. "Beyond Population Stabilization: The Case for Dramatically Reducing Global Human Numbers." Roundtable: World Population Policy commentary and responses. *Politics and the Life Sciences*. Vol. 16, No. 2 (September 1997):183–236.
SMALL BUSINESS ADMINISTRATION. News release on census data for women-owned businesses. January 1996.
SMART, NINIAN. *The Religious Experience of Mankind*. New York: Charles Scribner's Sons, 1969.
SMELSER, NEIL J. *Theory of Collective Behavior*. New York: Free Press, 1962.
SMITH, ADAM. *An Inquiry Into the Nature and Causes of the Wealth of Nations*. New York: The Modern Library, 1937; orig. 1776.
SMITH, DOUGLAS A. "Police Response to Interpersonal Violence: Defining the Parameters of Legal Control." *Social Forces*. Vol. 65, No. 3 (March 1987):767–82.
SMITH, DOUGLAS A., and PATRICK R. GARTIN. "Specifying Specific Deterrence: The Influence of Arrest on Future Criminal Activity." *American Sociological Review*. Vol. 54, No. 1 (February 1989):94–105.
SMITH, DOUGLAS A., and CHRISTY A. VISHER. "Street-Level Justice: Situational Determinants of Police Arrest Decisions." *Social Problems*. Vol. 29, No. 2 (December 1981):167–77.
SMITH, EARL, and WILBERT M. LEONARD II. "Twenty-Five Years of Stacking Research in Major League Baseball: An Attempt at Explaining this Re-Occurring Phenomenon." *Sociological Focus*. Vol. 30, No. 4 (October 1997):321–31.
SMITH, ROBERT B. "Health Care Reform Now." *Society*. Vol. 30, No. 3 (March-April 1993):56–65.
SMITH, TOM W. Research results reported in "Anti-Semitism Decreases But Persists." *Society*. Vol. 33, No. 3 (March/April 1996):2.
SMITH-LOVIN, LYNN, and CHARLES BRODY. "Interruptions in Group Discussions: The Effects of Gender and Group Composition." *American Journal of Sociology*. Vol. 54, No. 3 (June 1989):424–35.
SMOLAN, RICK, and JENNIFER ERWITT. *24 Hours in Cyberspace*. New York: Que* Macmillan Publishing, 1996.
SMOLOWE, JILL. "When Violence Hits Home." *Time*. Vol. 144, No. 1 (July 4, 1994):18–25.

SNELL, MARILYN BERLIN. "The Purge of Nurture." *New Perspectives Quarterly*. Vol. 7, No. 1 (Winter 1990):1–2.

SNOW, DAVID A., E. BURKE ROCHFORD, JR., STEVEN K. WORDEN, and ROBERT D. BENFORD. "Frame Alignment Processes, Micromobilization, and Movement Participation." *American Sociological Review*. Vol. 51, No. 4 (August 1986):464–81.

SNOW, DAVID A., LOUIS A. ZURCHER, JR., and SHELDON EKLAND-OLSON. "Social Networks and Social Movements: A Macrostructural Approach to Differential Recruitment." *American Sociological Review*. Vol. 45, No. 5 (October 1980):787–801.

SONTAG, DEBORAH. "For Poorest, 'Life Trapped in a Cage'." *New York Times* (October 6, 1996):1, 20.

SOUTH, SCOTT J., and KIM L. LLOYD. "Spousal Alternatives and Marital Dissolution." *American Sociological Review*. Vol. 60, No. 1 (February 1995):21–35.

SOUTH, SCOTT J., and STEVEN F. MESSNER. "Structural Determinants of Intergroup Association: Interracial Marriage and Crime." *American Journal of Sociology*. Vol. 91, No. 6 (May 1986):1409–30.

SOUTH, SCOTT J., and GLENNA SPITZE. "Housework in Marital and Nonmarital Households." *American Sociological Review*. Vol. 59, No. 3 (June 1994):327–47.

SOWELL, THOMAS. *Ethnic America*. New York: Basic Books, 1981.

———. *Race and Culture*. New York: Basic Books, 1994.

———. "Ethnicity and IQ." In Steven Fraser, ed., *The Bell Curve Wars: Race, Intelligence and the Future of America*. New York: Basic Books, 1995:70–79.

———. *Migrations and Cultures: A World View*. New York: Basic Books, 1996.

SOYINKA, WOLE. "Africa's Culture Producers." *Society*. Vol. 28, No. 2 (January-February 1991):32–40.

SPATES, JAMES L. "Counterculture and Dominant Culture Values: A Cross-National Analysis of the Underground Press and Dominant Culture Magazines." *American Sociological Review*. Vol. 41, No. 5 (October 1976):868–83.

———. "The Sociology of Values." In Ralph Turner, ed., *Annual Review of Sociology*. Vol. 9. Palo Alto, Calif.: Annual Reviews, 1983:27–49.

SPATES, JAMES L., and H. WESLEY PERKINS. "American and English Student Values." *Comparative Social Research*. Vol. 5. Greenwich, Conn.: JAI Press, 1982:245–68.

SPECTER, MICHAEL. "Plunging Life Expectancy Puzzles Russia." *New York Times* (August 2, 1995):A1, A2.

———. "Deep in the Russian Soul, a Lethal Darkness." *New York Times* (June 8, 1997a): section 4, pp. 1, 5.

———. "Moscow on the Make." *New York Times Magazine* (June 1, 1997b):48–55, 72, 75, 80, 84.

———. "Yogurt? Caucasus Centenarians 'Never Eat It'." *New York Times* (March 14, 1998):A1, A4.

SPEER, JAMES A. "The New Christian Right and Its Parent Company: A Study in Political Contrasts." In David G. Bromley and Anson Shupe, eds., *New Christian Politics*. Macon, Ga.: Mercer University Press, 1984:19–40.

SPEER, TIBBETT L. "Are College Costs Cutting Enrollment?" *American Demographics*. Vol. 16, No. 11 (November 1994):9–10.

———. "Digging Into the Underground Economy." *American Demographics*. Vol. 17, No. 2 (February 1995):15–16.

———. "A Nation of Students." *American Demographics*. Vol. 48, No. 8 (August 1996):32–39.

SPEIER, HANS. "Wit and Politics: An Essay on Laughter and Power." Ed. and trans. by Robert Jackall. *American Journal of Sociology*. Vol. 103, No. 5 (March 1998):1352–1401.

SPENCER, MARTIN E. "Multiculturalism, 'Political Correctness,' and the Politics of Identity." *Sociological Forum*. Vol. 9, No. 4 (December 1994):547–67.

SPITZER, STEVEN. "Toward a Marxian Theory of Deviance." In Delos H. Kelly, ed., *Criminal Behavior: Readings in Criminology*. New York: St. Martin's Press, 1980:175–91.

STACEY, JUDITH. *Patriarchy and Socialist Revolution in China*. Berkeley: University of California Press, 1983.

———. *Brave New Families: Stories of Domestic Upheaval in Late Twentieth-Century America*. New York: Basic Books, 1990.

———. "Good Riddance to 'The Family': A Response to David Popenoe." *Journal of Marriage and the Family*. Vol. 55, No. 3 (August 1993):545–47.

STACK, CAROL B. *All Our Kin: Strategies for Survival in a Black Community*. New York: Harper & Row, 1975.

STAGGENBORG, SUZANNE. "Social Movement Communities and Cycles of Protest: The Emergence and Maintenance of a Local Women's Movement." *Social Problems*. Vol. 45, No. 2 (May 1998):180–204.

STAHURA, JOHN M. "Suburban Development, Black Suburbanization and the Black Civil Rights Movement since World War II." *American Sociological Review*. Vol. 51, No. 1 (February 1986):131–44.

STANLEY, LIZ, ed. *Feminist Praxis: Research, Theory, and Epistemology in Feminist Sociology*. London: Routledge & Kegan Paul, 1990.

STAPINSKI, HELENE. "Let's Talk Dirty." *American Demographics*. Vol. 20, No. 11 (November 1998):50–56.

STARK, RODNEY. *Sociology*. Belmont, Calif.: Wadsworth, 1985.

STARK, RODNEY, and WILLIAM SIMS BAINBRIDGE. "Of Churches, Sects, and Cults: Preliminary Concepts for a Theory of Religious Movements." *Journal for the Scientific Study of Religion*. Vol. 18, No. 2 (June 1979):117–31.

———. "Secularization and Cult Formation in the Jazz Age." *Journal for the Scientific Study of Religion*. Vol. 20, No. 4 (December 1981):360–73.

STARK, RODNEY, and CHARLES Y. GLOCK. *American Piety: The Nature of Religious Commitment*. Berkeley: University of California Press, 1968.

STARR, PAUL. *The Social Transformation of American Medicine*. New York: Basic Books, 1982.

STAVRIANOS, L. S. *A Global History: The Human Heritage*. 3d ed. Englewood Cliffs, N.J.: Prentice Hall, 1983.

STEELE, SHELBY. *The Content of Our Character: A New Vision of Race in America*. New York: St. Martin's Press, 1990.

STEIN, MAURICE R. *The Eclipse of Community: An Interpretation of American Studies*. Princeton, N.J.: Princeton University Press, 1972.

STEINBERG, LAURENCE. "Failure outside the Classroom." *Wall Street Journal* (July 11, 1996):A14.

STEPHENS, JOHN D. *The Transition from Capitalism to Socialism*. Urbana: University of Illinois Press, 1986.

STERNLIEB, GEORGE, and JAMES W. HUGHES. "The Uncertain Future of the Central City." *Urban Affairs Quarterly*. Vol. 18, No. 4 (June 1983):455–72.

STEVENS, GILLIAN, and GRAY SWICEGOOD. "The Linguistic Context of Ethnic Endogamy." *American Sociological Review*. Vol. 52, No. 1 (February 1987):73–82.

STIER, HAYA. "Continuity and Change in Women's Occupations following First Childbirth." *Social Science Quarterly*. Vol. 77, No. 1 (March 1996):60–75.

STODDARD, SANDOL. *The Hospice Movement: A Better Way to Care for the Dying*. Briarcliff Manor, N.Y.: Stein and Day, 1978.

STODGHILL, RON, II. "Where'd You Learn That?" *Time*. Vol. 151, No. 23 (1998).

STOHL, MICHAEL, and GEORGE A. LOPEZ. *The State as Terrorist: The Dynamics of Government Violence and Repression*. Westport, Conn.: Greenwood Press, 1984.

STONE, LAWRENCE. *The Family, Sex and Marriage in England 1500–1800*. New York: Harper & Row, 1977.

STONE, ROBYN, GAIL LEE CAFFERATA, and JUDITH SANGL. *Caregivers of the Frail Elderly: A National Profile*. Washington, D.C.: U.S. Department of Health and Human Services, 1987.

STOUFFER, SAMUEL A., et al. *The American Soldier: Adjustment during Army Life*. Princeton, N.J.: Princeton University Press, 1949.

STRAUS, MURRAY A., and RICHARD J. GELLES. "Societal Change and Change in Family Violence from 1975 to 1985 as Revealed by Two National Surveys." *Journal of Marriage and the Family*. Vol. 48, No. 4 (August 1986):465–79.

STREIB, GORDON F. "Are the Aged a Minority Group?" In Bernice L. Neugarten, ed., *Middle Age and Aging: A Reader in Social Psychology*. Chicago: University of Chicago Press, 1968:35–46.

SUDNOW, DAVID N. *Passing On: The Social Organization of Dying*. Englewood Cliffs, N.J.: Prentice Hall, 1967.

SULLIVAN, BARBARA. "McDonald's Sees India as Golden Opportunity." *Chicago Tribune*. Business section (April 5, 1995):1.

SUMNER, WILLIAM GRAHAM. *Folkways*. New York: Dover, 1959; orig. 1906.

SUN, LENA H. "WWII's Forgotten Internees Await Apology." *The Washington Post* (March 9, 1998):A1, A5, A6.

SUNG, BETTY LEE. *Mountains of Gold: The Story of the Chinese in America*. New York: Macmillan, 1967.

SUTHERLAND, EDWIN H. "White Collar Criminality." *American Sociological Review*. Vol. 5, No. 1 (February 1940):1–12.

SUTHERLAND, EDWIN H., and DONALD R. CRESSEY. *Criminology*. 10th ed. Philadelphia: J.B. Lippincott, 1978.

SWARTZ, STEVE. "Why Michael Milken Stands to Qualify for Guinness Book." *Wall Street Journal*. Vol. LXX, No. 117 (March 31, 1989):1, 4.

SYZMANSKI, ALBERT. *Class Structure: A Critical Perspective*. New York: Praeger, 1983.

SZASZ, THOMAS S. *The Manufacturer of Madness: A Comparative Study of the Inquisition and the Mental Health Movement*. New York: Dell, 1961.

———. *The Myth of Mental Illness: Foundations of a Theory of Personal Conduct*. New York: Harper & Row, 1970; orig. 1961.

———. "Mental Illness Is Still a Myth." *Society*. Vol. 31, No. 4 (May-June 1994):34–39.

———. "Idleness and Lawlessness in the Therapeutic State." *Society*. Vol. 32, No. 4 (May-June 1995):30–35.

TAJFEL, HENRI. "Social Psychology of Intergroup Relations." *Annual Review of Psychology*. Palo Alto, Calif.: Annual Reviews, 1982:1–39.

TANBER, GEORGE J. "Freed from Death Row." *Toledo Blade* (November 22, 1998):B1, B2.

TANNAHILL, REAY. *Sex in History*. Scarborough House Publishers, 1992.

TANNEN, DEBORAH. *You Just Don't Understand: Women and Men in Conversation*. New York: Wm. Morrow, 1990.

———. *Talking from 9 to 5: How Women's and Men's Conversational Styles Affect Who Gets Heard, Who Gets Credit, and What Gets Done at Work*. New York: Wm. Morrow, 1994.

TANNENBAUM, FRANK. *Slave and Citizen: The Negro in the Americas*. New York: Vintage Books, 1946.

TANNER, MICHAEL, and STEPHEN MOORE. "Why Welfare Pays." *Wall Street Journal* (September 28, 1995):A20.

TARROW, SIDNEY. *Social Movements, Collective Action and Politics*. New York: Cambridge University Press, 1994.

TAVRIS, CAROL, and SUSAN SADD. *The Redbook Report on Female Sexuality*. New York: Delacorte Press, 1977.

TAX FOUNDATION. [Online] Available http://www.taxfoundation.org, March 30, 2000.

TAYLOR, FREDERICK WINSLOW. *The Principles of Scientific Management*. *New York:* Harper & Brothers, 1911.

TAYLOR, JOHN. "Don't Blame Me: The New Culture of Victimization." *New York Magazine* (June 3, 1991):26–34.

TERKEL, STUDS. *Working*. New York: Pantheon Books, 1974:1–2, 57–59, 65, 66, 69, 221–22. Copyright © 1974 by Pantheon Books, a division of Random House, Inc.

TERRY, DON. "In Crackdown on Bias, A New Tool." *New York Times* (June 12, 1993):8.

THERNSTROM, ABIGAIL, and STEPHAN THERNSTROM. "American Apartheid? Don't Believe It." *Wall Street Journal* (March 2, 1998):A18.

THIRUNARAYANAPURAM, DESIKAN. "Population Explosion Is Far from Over." *Popline*. Vol. 20 (January-February, 1998):1, 4.

THOMAS, EDWARD J. *The Life of Buddha as Legend and History*. London: Routledge & Kegan Paul, 1975.

THOMAS, PAULETTE. "Success at a Huge Personal Cost." *Wall Street Journal* (July 26, 1995):B1, B6.

THOMAS, PIRI. *Down These Mean Streets*. New York: Signet, 1967.

THOMAS, W. I. "The Relation of Research to the Social Process." In Morris Janowitz, ed., *W. I. Thomas on Social Organization and Social Personality*. Chicago: University of Chicago Press, 1966:289–305; orig. 1931.

THOMMA, STEVEN. "Christian Coalition Demands Action from GOP." *Philadelphia Inquirer* (September 14, 1997):A2.

THOMPSON, DICK. "Gene Maverick." *Time*. Vol. 153, No. 1 (January 11, 1999):54–55.

THOMPSON, LARRY. "Fertility with Less Fuss." *Time*. Vol. 144, No. 20 (November 14, 1994):79.

THOMPSON, MARK. "Fatal Neglect." *Time*. Vol. 150, No. 17 (October 27, 1997):34–38.

———. "Shining a Light on Abuse." *Time*. Vol. 152, No. 5 (August 3, 1998): 42–43.

THORLINDSSON, THOROLFUR, and THORODDUR BJARNASON. "Modeling Durkheim on the Micro Level: A Study of Youth Suicidality." *American Sociological Review*. Vol. 63, No. 1 (February 1998):94–110.

THORNBERRY, TERRANCE, and MARGARET FARNSWORTH. "Social Correlates of Criminal Involvement: Further Evidence on the Relationship between Social Status and Criminal Behavior." *American Sociological Review*. Vol. 47, No. 4 (August 1982):505–18.

THORNE, BARRIE, CHERIS KRAMARAE, and NANCY HENLEY, eds. *Language, Gender and Society*. Rowley, Mass.: Newbury House, 1983.

THORNTON, ARLAND. "Changing Attitudes toward Separation and Divorce: Causes and Consequences." *American Journal of Sociology*. Vol. 90, No. 4 (January 1985):856–72.

THORNTON, ARLAND, WILLIAM G. AXINN, and DANIEL H. HILL. "Reciprocal Effects of Religiosity, Cohabitation, and Marriage." *American Journal of Sociology*. Vol. 98, No. 3 (November 1992):628–51.

THUROW, LESTER C. "A Surge in Inequality." *Scientific American*. Vol. 256, No. 5 (May 1987):30–37.

TILLY, CHARLES. *From Mobilization to Revolution*. Reading, Mass.: Addison-Wesley, 1978.

———. "Does Modernization Breed Revolution?" In Jack A. Goldstone, ed., *Revolutions: Theoretical, Comparative, and Historical Studies*. New York: Harcourt Brace Jovanovich, 1986:47–57.

TIRYAKIAN, EDWARD A. "Revisiting Sociology's First Classic: The Division of Labor in Society and Its Actuality." *Sociological Forum*. Vol. 9, No. 1 (March 1994):3–16.

TITTLE, CHARLES R., and WAYNE J. VILLEMEZ. "Social Class and Criminality." *Social Forces*. Vol. 56, No. 22 (December 1977):474–502.

TITTLE, CHARLES R., WAYNE J. VILLEMEZ, and DOUGLAS A. SMITH. "The Myth of Social Class and Criminality: An Empirical Assessment of the Empirical Evidence." *American Sociological Review*. Vol. 43, No. 5 (October 1978):643–56.

TOBIN, GARY. "Suburbanization and the Development of Motor Transportation: Transportation Technology and the Suburbanization Process." In Barry Schwartz, ed., *The Changing Face of the Suburbs*. Chicago: University of Chicago Press, 1976.

TOBY, JACKSON. "Getting Serious about School Discipline." *The Public Interest*. Vol. 133 (Fall 1998):68–83.

TOCH, THOMAS. "The New Educational Bazaar." *U.S. News & World Report* (April 27, 1998):35–45.

TOCQUEVILLE, ALEXIS DE. *The Old Regime and the French Revolution*. Stuart Gilbert, trans. Garden City, N.Y.: Anchor/Doubleday Books, 1955; orig. 1856.

TOFANI, LORETTA. "AIDS Ravages a Continent, and Sweeps a Family." *Philadelphia Inquirer* (March 24, 1991):1, 15–A.

TOFFLER, ALVIN, and HEIDI TOFFLER. *War and Anti-war: Survival at the Dawn of the 21st Century*. Boston: Little, Brown, 1993.

TOLSON, JAY. "The Trouble with Elites." *The Wilson Quarterly*. Vol. XIX, No. 1 (Winter 1995):6–8.

TONER, ROBIN. "The Retirement Lobby Goes Va-Va-Boom!" *New York Times* (August 8, 1999): section 4, pp. 1, 5.

TONNIES, FERDINAND. *Community and Society (Gemeinschaft und Gesellschaft)*. New York: Harper & Row, 1963; orig. 1887.

TREAS, JUDITH. "Socialist Organization and Economic Development in China: Latent Consequences for the Aged." *The Gerontologist*. Vol. 19, No. 1 (February 1979):34–43.

———. "Older Americans in the 1990s and Beyond." *Population Bulletin*. Vol. 50, No. 2 (May 1995). Washington, D.C.: Population Reference Bureau.

TREIMAN, DONALD J. "Industrialization and Social Stratification." In Edward O. Laumann, ed., *Social Stratification: Research and Theory for the 1970s*. Indianapolis, Ind.: Bobbs-Merrill, 1970.

TRENT, KATHERINE. "Family Context and Adolescents' Expectations about Marriage, Fertility, and Nonmarital Childbearing." *Social Science Quarterly*. Vol. 75, No 2 (June 1994):319–39.

TROELTSCH, ERNST. *The Social Teaching of the Christian Churches*. New York: Macmillan, 1931.

TROIDEN, RICHARD R. *Gay and Lesbian Identity: A Sociological Analysis*. Dix Hills, N.Y.: General Hall, 1988.

TUMIN, MELVIN M. "Some Principles of Stratification: A Critical Analysis." *American Sociological Review*. Vol. 18, No. 4 (August 1953):387–94.

———. *Social Stratification: The Forms and Functions of Inequality*. 2d ed. Englewood Cliffs, N.J.: Prentice Hall, 1985.

TURNER, RALPH H., and LEWIS M. KILLIAN. *Collective Behavior*. 2d ed. Englewood Cliffs, N.J.: Prentice Hall, 1972; 3d ed., 1987; 4th ed., 1993.

TYLER, S. LYMAN. *A History of Indian Policy*. Washington, D.C.: United States Department of the Interior, Bureau of Indian Affairs, 1973.

TYREE, ANDREA, MOSHE SEMYONOV, and ROBERT W. HODGE. "Gaps and Glissandos: Inequality, Economic Development, and Social Mobility in 24 Countries." *American Sociological Review*. Vol. 44, No. 3 (June 1979):410–24.

Uggen, Christopher. "Ex-Offenders and the Conformist Alternative: A Job-Quality Model of Work and Crime." *Social Problems.* Vol. 46, No. 1 (February 1999):127–51.

United Nations Development Programme. *Human Development Report 1990.* New York: Oxford University Press, 1990.

———. *Human Development Report 1994.* New York: Oxford University Press, 1994.

———. *Human Development Report 1995.* New York: Oxford University Press, 1995.

———. *Human Development Report 1996.* New York: Oxford University Press, 1996.

———. *Human Development Report 1997.* New York: Oxford University Press, 1997.

———. *Human Development Report 1998.* New York: Oxford University Press, 1998.

———. *Human Development Report 1999.* New York: Oxford University Press, 1999.

University of Akron Research Center. *National Survey of Religion and Politics 1992.* Akron, Ohio: University of Akron Research Center, 1993.

Unnever, James D., Charles E. Frazier, and John C. Henretta. "Race Differences in Criminal Sentencing." *The Sociological Quarterly.* Vol. 21, No. 2 (Spring 1980):197–205.

Unrau, William E. *White Man's Wicked Water: The Alcohol Trade and Prohibition in Indian Country, 1802–1892.* Lawrence, Kans.: University of Kansas Press, 1996.

Unruh, John D., Jr. *The Plains Across.* Urbana: University of Illinois Press, 1979.

U.S. Bureau of Economic Analysis. *Foreign Direct Investment in the United States. Country Detail for Selected Items.* Washington, D.C.: The Bureau, 1999.

U.S. Bureau of Justice Statistics. *Violence against Women.* Washington, D.C.: U.S. Government Printing Office, 1994.

———. *Criminal Victimization 1994.* Washington, D.C.: U.S. Government Printing Office, 1996.

———. *Violence by Intimates.* Washington, D.C.: The Bureau, 1998.

———. *Criminal Victimization 1998: Changes 1997–98 with Trends 1993–98.* Washington, D.C.: The Bureau, 1999.

———. *Sourcebook of Criminal Justice Statistics 1998.* Washington, D.C.: The Bureau, 1999.

U.S. Census Bureau. *Asset Ownership of Households: 1993.* Current Population Reports, Series P-70, No. 47. Washington, D.C.: U.S. Government Printing Office, 1995.

———. *Household and Family Characteristics: March 1994.* Current Population Reports, Series P-20, No. 483, Washington, D.C.: U.S. Government Printing Office, 1995.

———. *Income, Poverty, and Valuation of Noncash Benefits: 1993.* Current Population Reports, Series P-60, No. 188. Washington, D.C.: U.S. Government Printing Office, 1995.

———. *Marital Status and Living Arrangements:* March 1995. PPL-52. Washington, D.C.: U.C. Government Printing Office, 1996.

———. *School Enrollment—Social and Economic Characteristics of Students: October 1995 (Update).* PPL-55: The Bureau, 1997.

———. "Who's Minding Our Preschoolers?" Fall 1994 (Update). P70–62. Washington, D.C.: U.S. Government Printing Office, 1997.

———. *Educational Achievement in the United States: March 1998 (Update).* Current Population Reports, P20-515. Washington, D.C.: U.S. Government Printing Office, 1998.

———. *Educational Attainment in the United States: March 1998 (Update).* Current Population Reports, P20-513. Washington, D.C.: U.S. Government Printing Office, 1998.

———. *Household and Family Characteristics: March 1998 (Update).* Current Population Reports, P20-515. Washington, D.C.: U.S. Government Printing Office, 1998.

———. *Poverty in the United States 1997.* Current Population Reports, P60-201. Washington, D.C.: U.S. Government Printing Office, 1998.

———. *Statistical Abstract of the United States 1998.* Washington, D.C.: U.S. Government Printing Office, 1998.

———. *Educational Attainment in the United States: March 1998 (Update).* Washington, D.C.: U.S. Government Printing Office, 1999.

———. *Grandchildren Living in the Home of Their Grandparents: 1970 to Present.* CH-7. Washington, D.C.: The Bureau, 1999.

———. *Health Insurance Coverage.* (P60-208) Washington, D.C.: The Bureau, 1999.

———. *Household and Family Characteristics: March 1998 (Update).* Washington, D.C.: The Bureau, 1999.

———. *Metropolitan Area Population Estimates for July 1, 1998, and Population Change for April 1, 1990, to July 1, 1998.* Washington, D.C.: The Bureau, 1999.

———. *Money Income in the United States 1998.* P60-206. Washington, D.C.: U.S. Government Printing Office, 1999.

———. *Population Estimates for Cities with Populations of 100,000 and Greater (Sorted by 1998 Population Size Rank in U.S.).* Washington, D.C.: The Bureau, 1999.

———. *Poverty in the United States 1998.* P60-207. Washington, D.C.: U.S. Government Printing Office, 1999.

———. *School Enrollment—Social and Economic Characteristics of Students: October 1998 (Update).* Current Population Report, P20-521. Washington, D.C.: The Bureau, 1999.

———. *Statistical Abstract of the United States 1999.* Washington, D.C.: U.S. Government Printing Office, 1999.

———. *Educational Attainment in the United States: March 1998 (Update).* [Online] Available http://www.census.gov/prod/3/98pubs/p20-513u.pdf, March 21, 2000.

———. Historical Income Tables—Families, Tables F-1, F-2, F-3. [Online] Available http://www.census.gov/hhes/income/histinc/f02.html, March 21, 2000.

———. *Housing Vacancies and Home Ownership: Annual Statistics: 1998.* Table 20. [Online] Available http://www.census.gov/hhes/www/housing/hvs/annual98/ann98t20.html, March 21, 2000.

———. *International Data Base.* [Online] Available http://www.census.gov/ipc/www/idbprint.html, February 24, 2000.

———. *Projections of the Total Resident Population by 5-Year Age Groups and Sex with Special Age Categories: Middle Series.* [Online] Available http://www.census.gov/population/projections/nation/summary/np-t3-?.pdf, February 24, 2000.

———. *Projections of the Total Resident Population by 5-Year Age Groups and Sex with Special Age Categories: Middle Series 2050 to 2070.* [Online] Available http://www.census.gov/population/projections/nation/summary/np-t-g.pdf, February 24, 2000.

———. *Resident Estimates of the United States by Age and Sex: April 1, 1990 to November 1, 1999.* [Online] Available http://www.census.gov/population/estimates/nation/intfile2-1.txt, February 24, 2000.

———. *Resident Population Estimates of the United States by Sex, Race, and Hispanic Origin: April 1, 1990 to November 1, 1999.* [Online] Available http://www.census.gov/population/estimates/nation/intfile3-1.txt, April 22, 2000.

———. Table F-7: Type of Family (All Races) by Median and Mean Income: 1947 to 1998. [Online] Availablehttp://www.census.gov/hhes/income/histinc/f07.html, March 21, 2000.

———. Table P-10: Age—People (Both Sexes Combined—All Races) by Median and Mean Income: 1974 to 1998. [Online] Available http://www.census.gov/hhes/income/histinc/p10.html, January 28, 2000.

U.S. Census Office. *Census of the United States (1900).* Vol. II: Population. Washington, D.C.: The Office, 1902.

U.S. Centers for Disease Control and Prevention. *Morbidity and Mortality Weekly Report.* Vol. 46, No. 51 (December 26, 1997).

———. *HIV/AIDS Surveillance Report.* Vol. 11, No. 1 (Midyear 1999).

———. *Sexually Transmitted Disease Surveillance 1998.* Atlanta, Ga.: The Centers, 1999.

U.S. Department of Labor. Bureau of Labor Statistics. *Employment and Earnings.* Vol. 46, No. 1 (January 1999).

———. Bureau of Labor Statistics. *Employment Projections.* Table 5. Civilian Labor Force by Sex, Age, Race, and Hispanic Origin, 1978, 1988, 1998, and Projected 2008. Washington, D.C.: The Bureau, 1999.

———. Bureau of Labor Statistics. *Employment and Earnings.* Vol. 47, No. 1 (January 2000).

———. *International Comparisons of Hourly Compensation Costs for Production Workers in Manufacturing, 1975–1998.* Supplementary tables for BLS News Release USDL 00–07, January 11, 2000. Washington, D.C.: The Bureau, 2000.

———. Women's Bureau. *Women Business Owners: 1999.* [Online] Available http://www.dol.gov/dol/wb/public/wb_pubs/wbo.htm, February 12, 2000.

U.S. Department of State. Bureau of Arms Control. *World Military Expenditures and Arms Transfers 1998.* Washington, D.C.: The Bureau, 1999.

———. *Patterns of Global Terrorism 1998.* Washington, D.C.: The Department, 1999.

USEEM, BERT. "Disorganization and the New Mexico Prison Riot of 1980." *American Sociological Review.* Vol. 50, No. 5 (October 1985):677–88.

U.S. EQUAL EMPLOYMENT OPPORTUNITY COMMISSION. *Job Patterns for Minorities and Women in Private Industry, 1996.* Washington, D.C.: The Commission, 1997.

———. *Job Patterns for Minorities and Women in Private Industry 1997.* Washington, D.C.: The Commission, 1998.

U.S. FEDERAL BUREAU OF INVESTIGATION. *Crime in the United States 1998.* Washington, D.C.: The Bureau, 1999.

U.S. HOUSE OF REPRESENTATIVES. "Street Children: A Global Disgrace." Hearing on November 7, 1991. Washington, D.C.: U.S. Government Printing Office, 1992.

U.S. IMMIGRATION AND NATURALIZATION SERVICE. Table 3: Immigrants Admitted by Region and Selected Country of Birth, Fiscal Years 1984–94. Fax received from INS January 1996.

———. Table 5: Immigrants Admitted by Region and Selected Country of Birth, Fiscal Years 1994–96. [Online] Available http://www.ins.doj.gov/stats/annual/fy96/1005.htm, December 5, 1997.

———. *Legal Immigration, Fiscal Year 1998.* Washington, D.C.: The Service, 1999.

U.S. NATIONAL CENTER FOR EDUCATION STATISTICS. *Digest of Education Statistics 1998.* Washington, D.C.: U.S. Government Printing Office, 1999.

———. *Dropout Rates in the United States: 1997.* Washington, D.C.: The Center, 1999.

U.S. NATIONAL CENTER FOR HEALTH STATISTICS. *National Vital Statistics Report.* Vol. 47, No. 4 (October 7, 1998).

———. *Current Estimates from the National Health Interview Survey 1996.* Series 10, No. 200. Hyattsville, Md.: The Center, 1999.

———. *National Vital Statistics Report.* Vol. 47, No. 18 (April 29, 1999).

———. *National Vital Statistics Report.* Vol. 47, No. 19 (June 30, 1999).

———. *National Vital Statistics Report.* Vol. 47, No. 21 (July 6, 1999).

———. *National Vital Statistics Report.* Vol. 47, No. 25 (October 5, 1999).

U.S. NATIONAL CLEARINGHOUSE ON CHILD ABUSE AND NEGLECT. *Child Maltreatment 1996.* Washington, D.C.: The Clearinghouse, 1998.

VALDEZ, A. "In the Hood: Street Gangs Discover White-Collar Crime." *Police.* Vol. 21, No. 5 (May 1997):49–50, 56.

VALLAS, STEPHEN P., and JOHN P. BECK. "The Transformation of Work Revisited: The Limits of Flexibility in American Manufacturing." *Social Problems.* Vol. 43, No. 3 (August 1996):339–61.

VALOCCHI, STEVE. "The Emergence of the Integrationist Ideology in the Civil Rights Movement." *Social Problems.* Vol. 43, No. 1 (February 1996):116–30.

VAN BIEMA, DAVID. "Parents Who Kill." *Time.* Vol. 144, No. 20 (November 14, 1994):50–51.

———. "Sparse at Seder?" *Time.* Vol. 149, No. 17 (April 28, 1997a):67.

———. "Buddhism in America." *Time.* Vol. 150, No. 15 (October 13, 1997b):71–81.

———. "Spiriting Prayer into School." *Time.* Vol. 152, No. 20 (April 27, 1998):38–41.

———. "A Surge of Teen Spirit." *Time.* Vol. 153, No. 20 (May 31, 1999):58–59.

VAN DEN HAAG, ERNEST, and JOHN P. CONRAD. *The Death Penalty: A Debate.* New York: Plenum Press, 1983.

VAUGHAN, MARY KAY. "Multinational Corporations: The World as a Company Town." In Ahamed Idris-Soven et al., eds., *The World as a Company Town: Multinational Corporations and Social Change.* The Hague: Mouton Publishers, 1978:15–35.

VAYDA, EUGENE, and RAISA B. DEBER. "The Canadian Health Care System: An Overview." *Social Science and Medicine.* Vol. 18, No. 3 (1984):191–97.

VEBLEN, THORSTEIN. *The Theory of the Leisure Class.* New York: The New American Library, 1953; orig. 1899.

VEDDER, RICHARD, and LOWELL GALLAWAY. "Declining Black Employment." *Society.* Vol. 30, No. 5 (July–August 1993):56–63.

VINOVSKIS, MARIS A. "Have Social Historians Lost the Civil War? Some Preliminary Demographic Speculations." *Journal of American History.* Vol. 76, No. 1 (June 1989):34–58.

VOGEL, EZRA F. *The Four Little Dragons: The Spread of Industrialization in East Asia.* Cambridge, Mass.: Harvard University Press, 1991.

VOGEL, LISE. *Marxism and the Oppression of Women: Toward a Unitary Theory.* New Brunswick, N.J.: Rutgers University Press, 1983.

VOLD, GEORGE B., and THOMAS J. BERNARD. *Theoretical Criminology.* 3d ed. New York: Oxford University Press, 1986.

VON HIRSH, ANDREW. *Past or Future Crimes: Deservedness and Dangerousness in the Sentencing of Criminals.* New Brunswick, N.J.: Rutgers University Press, 1986.

VONNEGUT, KURT, JR. "Harrison Bergeron." In *Welcome to the Monkey House.* New York: Delacorte Press/Seymour Lawrence, 1968:7–13; orig. 1961.

VOYDANOFF, PATRICIA., and BRENDA W. DONNELLY. *Adolescent Sexuality and Pregnancy.* Newbury Park, Calif.: Sage, 1990.

WAITE, LINDA J., GUS W. HAGGSTROM, and DAVID I. KANOUSE. "The Consequences of Parenthood for the Marital Stability of Young Adults." *American Sociological Review.* Vol. 50, No. 6 (December 1985):850–57.

WALDER, ANDREW G. "Career Mobility and the Communist Political Order." *American Sociological Review.* Vol. 60, No. 3 (June 1995):309–28.

WALDFOGEL, JANE. "The Effect of Children on Women's Wages." *American Sociological Review.* Vol. 62, No. 2 (April 1997):209–17.

WALDMAN, STEVEN. "Deadbeat Dads." *Newsweek* (May 4, 1992):46–52.

WALDROP, JUDITH. "Live Long and Prosper." *American Demographics.* Vol. 14 (October 1992):40–45.

WALKER, KAREN. "'Always There For Me': Friendship Patterns and Expectations among Middle- and Working-Class Men and Women." *Sociological Forum.* Vol. 10, No. 2 (June 1995):273–96.

WALL, THOMAS F. *Medical Ethics: Basic Moral Issues.* Washington, D.C.: University Press of America, 1980.

WALLER, DOUGLAS. "Onward Cyber Soldiers." *Time.* Vol. 146, No. 8 (August 21, 1995):38–44.

WALLERSTEIN, IMMANUEL. *The Modern World-System: Capitalist Agriculture and the Origins of the European World-Economy in the Sixteenth Century.* New York: Academic Press, 1974.

———. *The Capitalist World-Economy.* New York: Cambridge University Press, 1979.

———. "Crises: The World Economy, the Movements, and the Ideologies." In Albert Bergesen, ed., *Crises in the World-System.* Beverly Hills, Calif.: Sage, 1983:21–36.

———. *The Politics of the World Economy: The States, the Movements, and the Civilizations.* Cambridge: Cambridge University Press, 1984.

WALLERSTEIN, JUDITH S., and SANDRA BLAKESLEE. *Second Chances: Men, Women, and Children a Decade after Divorce.* New York: Ticknor & Fields, 1989.

WALLIS, DAVID. "After Cyberoverkill Comes Cyberburnout." *New York Times* (August 4, 1996):43, 46.

WALTERS, LAUREL SHAPER. "World Educators Compare Notes." *The Christian Science Monitor: Global Report* (September 7, 1994):8.

WALTON, JOHN, and CHARLES RAGIN. "Global and National Sources of Political Protest: Third World Responses to the Debt Crisis." *American Sociological Review.* Vol. 55, No. 6 (December 1990):876–90.

WARNER, R. STEPHEN. "Work in Progress toward a New Paradigm for the Sociological Study of Religion in the United States." *American Journal of Sociology.* Vol. 98, No. 5 (March 1993):1044–93.

WARNER, W. LLOYD, and PAUL S. LUNT. *The Social Life of a Modern Community.* New Haven, Conn.: Yale University Press, 1941.

WARREN, JOHN ROBERT, and ROBERT M. HAUSER. "Social Stratification across Three Generations: New Evidence from the Wisconsin Longitudinal Study." *American Sociological Review.* Vol. 62 (August 1997):561–72.

WASKUL, DENNIS. "Selfhood in the Age of Computer Mediated Symbolic Interaction." Paper presented to the annual meeting of the Southwest Social Science Association, New Orleans, La., March, 1997.

WATERS, MELISSA S., WILL CARRINGTON HEATH, and JOHN KEITH WATSON. "A Positive Model of the Determination of Religious Affiliation." *Social Science Quarterly.* Vol. 76, No. 1 (March 1995):105–23.

WATSON, RUSSELL. "Milosevic in His Bunker." *Newsweek* (June 7, 1999):49–51.

WATTENBERG, BEN J. "The Attitudes behind American Exceptionalism." *U.S. News & World Report.* Vol. 107, No. 6 (August 7, 1989):25.

———. "The Population Explosion Is Over." *New York Times Magazine* (November 23, 1997):60–63.

WEBER, ADNA FERRIN. *The Growth of Cities.* New York: Columbia University Press, 1963; orig. 1899.

WEBER, MAX. *The Protestant Ethic and the Spirit of Capitalism.* New York: Charles Scribner's Sons, 1958; orig. 1904–5.

———. *Economy and Society.* G. Roth and C. Wittich, eds. Berkeley: University of California Press, 1978.

WEBSTER, ANDREW. *Introduction to the Sociology of Development.* London: Macmillan, 1984.
WEBSTER, MURRAY, JR., and STUART J. HYSOM. "Creating Status Characteristics." *American Sociological Review.* Vol. 63, No. 3 (June 1998):351–78.
WEBSTER, PAMELA S., TERRI ORBUCH, and JAMES S. HOUSE. "Effects of Childhood Family Background on Adult Marital Quality and Perceived Stability." *American Journal of Sociology.* Vol. 101, No. 2 (September 1995):404–32.
WEEKS, JOHN R. "The Demography of Islamic Nations." *Population Bulletin.* Vol. 43, No. 4 (December 1988). Washington, D.C.: Population Reference Bureau.
WEICHER, JOHN C. "Getting Richer (at Different Rates)." *Wall Street Journal* (June 14, 1995):A18.
WEIDENBAUM, MURRAY. "Beyond Handouts." *Across the Board* (April 1991). In Kurt Finsterbusch and George McKenna, eds., *Taking Sides: Clashing Views on Controversial Social Issues.* 8th ed. Guilford, Conn.: Dushkin Publishing Group, 1994.
———. "The Evolving Corporate Board." *Society.* Vol. 32, No. 3 (March/April 1995):9–20.
WEINBERG, GEORGE. *Society and the Healthy Homosexual.* Garden City, N.Y.: Anchor Books, 1973.
WEINER, TIM. "Head of C.I.A. Plans Center to Protect U.S. Cyberspace." *New York Times* (June 26, 1996):B7.
WEINRICH, JAMES D. *Sexual Landscapes: Why We Are What We Are, Why We Love Whom We Love.* New York: Charles Scribner's Sons, 1987.
WEISBERG, D. KELLY. *Children of the Night: A Study of Adolescent Prostitution.* Lexington, Mass.: D.C. Heath, 1985.
WEISBURD, DAVID, STANTON WHEELER, ELIN WARING, and NANCY BODE. *Crimes of the Middle Class: White Collar Defenders in the Courts.* New Haven, Conn.: Yale University Press, 1991.
WEISNER, THOMAS S., and BERNICE T. EIDUSON. "The Children of the '60s as Parents." *Psychology Today* (January 1986):60–66.
WEITZMAN, LENORE J. *The Divorce Revolution: The Unexpected Social and Economic Consequences for Women and Children in America.* New York: Free Press, 1985.
———. "The Economic Consequences of Divorce Are Still Unequal: Comment on Peterson." *American Sociological Review.* Vol. 61, No. 3 (June 1996):537–38.
WELLER, JACK M., and E. L. QUARANTELLI. "Neglected Characteristics of Collective Behavior." *American Journal of Sociology.* Vol. 79, No. 3 (November 1973):665–85.
WELLFORD, CHARLES. "Labeling Theory and Criminology: An Assessment." In Delos H. Kelly, ed., *Criminal Behavior: Readings in Criminology.* New York: St. Martin's Press, 1980:234–47.
WERTHEIMER, BARBARA MAYER. "The Factory Bell." In Linda K. Kerber and Jane De Hart Mathews, eds., *Women's America: Refocusing the Past.* New York: Oxford University Press, 1982:130–40.
WESOLOWSKI, WLODZIMIERZ. "Transition from Authoritarianism to Democracy." *Social Research.* Vol. 57, No. 2 (Summer 1990):435–61.
WESTERN, BRUCE. "Postwar Unionization in Eighteen Advanced Capitalist Countries." *American Sociological Review.* Vol. 58, No. 2 (April 1993):266–82.
———. "A Comparative Study of Working-Class Disorganization: Union Decline in Eighteen Advanced Capitalist Countries." *American Sociological Review.* Vol. 60, No. 2 (April 1995):179–201.
WESTERN, MARK, and ERIK OLIN WRIGHT. "The Permeability of Class Boundaries to Intergenerational Mobility among Men in the United States, Canada, Norway and Sweden." *American Sociological Review.* Vol. 59, No. 4 (August 1994):606–29.
WHALEN, JACK, and RICHARD FLACKS. *Beyond the Barricades: The Sixties Generation Grows Up.* Philadelphia: Temple University Press, 1989.
WHEELIS, ALLEN. *The Quest for Identity.* New York: Norton, 1958.
WHELAN, CHRISTINE B. "No Honeymoon for Covenant Marriage." *Wall Street Journal* (August 17, 1998):A14.
WHITAKER, MARK. "Ten Ways to Fight Terrorism." *Newsweek* (July 1, 1985):26–29.
WHITE, JACK E. "I'm Just Who I Am." *Time.* Vol. 149, No. 18 (May 5, 1997):32–36.
WHITE, RALPH, and RONALD LIPPITT. "Leader Behavior and Member Reaction in Three 'Social Climates.'" In Dorwin Cartwright and Alvin Zander, eds., *Group Dynamics.* Evanston, Ill.: Row, Peterson, 1953:586–611.
WHITE, WALTER. *Rope and Faggot.* New York: Arno Press and *New York Times,* 1969; orig. 1929.
WHITMAN, DAVID. "Shattering Myths about the Homeless." *U.S. News & World Report* (March 20, 1989):26, 28.
WHORF, BENJAMIN LEE. "The Relation of Habitual Thought and Behavior to Language." In *Language, Thought, and Reality.* Cambridge, Mass.: The Technology Press of MIT/New York: Wiley, 1956:134–59; orig. 1941.
WHYTE, WILLIAM FOOTE. *Street Corner Society.* 3d ed. Chicago: University of Chicago Press, 1981; orig. 1943.
WHYTE, WILLIAM H., JR. *The Organization Man.* Garden City, N.Y.: Anchor Books, 1957.
WIARDA, HOWARD J. "Ethnocentrism and Third World Development." *Society.* Vol. 24, No. 6 (September-October 1987):55–64.
WIATROWSKI, MICHAEL A., DAVID B. GRISWOLD, and MARY K. ROBERTS. "Social Control Theory and Delinquency." *American Sociological Review.* Vol. 46, No. 5 (October 1981):525–41.
WIDOM, CATHY SPATZ. "Childhood Sexual Abuse and Its Criminal Consequences." *Society.* Vol. 33, No. 4 (May/June 1996):47–53.
WILCOX, CLYDE. "Race, Gender, and Support for Women in the Military." *Social Science Quarterly.* Vol. 73, No. 2 (June 1992):310–23.
WILES, P. J. D. *Economic Institutions Compared.* New York: Halsted Press, 1977.
WILKINSON, DORIS. "Transforming the Social Order: The Role of the University in Social Change." *Sociological Forum.* Vol. 9, No. 3 (September 1994):325–41.
WILLIAMS, RHYS H., and N. J. DEMERATH, III. "Religion and Political Process in an American City." *American Sociological Review.* Vol. 56, No. 4 (August 1991):417–31.
WILLIAMS, ROBIN M., JR. *American Society: A Sociological Interpretation.* 3d ed. New York: Alfred A. Knopf, 1970.
WILLIAMSON, JEFFREY G., and PETER H. LINDERT. *American Inequality: A Macroeconomic History.* New York: Academic Press, 1980.
WILSON, BARBARA. "National Television Violence Study." Reported by Julia Duin, "Study Finds Cartoon Heroes Initiate Too Much Violence." *Washington Times* (April 17, 1998):A4.
WILSON, BRYAN. *Religion in Sociological Perspective.* New York: Oxford University Press, 1982.
WILSON, EDWARD O. "Biodiversity, Prosperity, and Value." In F. Herbert Bormann and Stephen R. Kellert, eds., *Ecology, Economics, and Ethics: The Broken Circle.* New Haven, Conn.: Yale University Press, 1991:3–10.
WILSON, JAMES Q. *Bureaucracy: What Government Agencies Do and Why They Do It.* New York: Basic Books, 1991.
———. "Crime, Race, and Values." *Society.* Vol. 30, No. 1 (November-December 1992):90–93.
WILSON, JAMES Q., and RICHARD J. HERRNSTEIN. *Crime and Human Nature.* New York: Simon and Schuster, 1985.
WILSON, LOGAN. *American Academics Then and Now.* New York: Oxford University Press, 1979.
WILSON, THOMAS C. "Urbanism and Tolerance: A Test of Some Hypotheses Drawn from Wirth and Stouffer." *American Sociological Review.* Vol. 50, No. 1 (February 1985):117–23.
———. "Urbanism and Unconventionality: The Case of Sexual Behavior." *Social Science Quarterly.* Vol. 76, No. 2 (June 1995):346–63.
WILSON, WILLIAM JULIUS. *The Declining Significance of Race.* Chicago: University of Chicago Press, 1978.
———. *When Work Disappears: The World of the New Urban Poor.* New York: Alfred A. Knopf, 1996a.
———. "Work." *New York Times Magazine* (August 18, 1996b):26–31, 40, 48, 52, 54.
WINKLER, KAREN J. "Scholar Whose Ideas of Female Psychology Stir Debate Modifies Theories, Extends Studies to Young Girls." *Chronicle of Higher Education.* Vol. XXXVI, No. 36 (May 23, 1990):A6–A8.
WINNICK, LOUIS. "America's 'Model Minority'." *Commentary.* Vol. 90, No. 2 (August 1990):22–29.
WINTERS, REBECCA. "Who Needs an M.B.A.?" *Time Select: Business.* Vol. 153, No. 19 (May 17, 1999).
WIRTH, LOUIS. "Urbanism as a Way of Life." *American Journal of Sociology.* Vol. 44, No. 1 (July 1938):1–24.
WITKIN, GORDON. "The Crime Bust." *U.S. News & World Report.* Vol. 124, No. 20 (May 25, 1998):28–40.
WITKIN-LANOIL, GEORGIA. *The Female Stress Syndrome: How to Recognize and Live with It.* New York: Newmarket Press, 1984.

WITT, G. EVANS. "Say What You Mean." *American Demographics*. Vol. 21, No. 2 (February 1999):23.

WOLF, DIANE L., ed. *Feminist Dilemma of Fieldwork*. Boulder, Colo.: Westview Press, 1996.

WOLF, NAOMI. *The Beauty Myth: How Images of Beauty Are Used against Women*. New York: William Morrow, 1990.

WOLFE, DAVID B. "Targeting the Mature Mind." *American Demographics*. Vol. 16, No. 3 (March 1994):32–36.

WOLFE, TOM. *Radical Chic*. New York: Bantam, 1970.

WOLFGANG, MARVIN E., ROBERT M. FIGLIO, and THORSTEN SELLIN. *Delinquency in a Birth Cohort*. Chicago: University of Chicago Press, 1972.

WOLFGANG, MARVIN E., TERRENCE P. THORNBERRY, and ROBERT M. FIGLIO. *From Boy to Man, From Delinquency to Crime*. Chicago: University of Chicago Press, 1987.

WOLFINGER, RAYMOND E., and STEVEN J. ROSENSTONE. *Who Votes?* New Haven, Conn.: Yale University Press, 1980.

WOLFSON, ADAM. "Killing Off the Dying?" *The Public Interest*. No. 131 (Spring 1998):50–70.

WONG, BUCK. "Need for Awareness: An Essay on Chinatown, San Francisco." In Amy Tachiki et al., eds., *Roots: An Asian American Reader*. Los Angeles: UCLA Asian American Studies Center, 1971:265–73.

WOOD, PETER B., and MICHELE CHESSER. "Black Stereotyping in a University Population." *Sociological Focus*. Vol. 27, No. 1 (February 1994):17–34.

WOODBERRY, ROBERT D. "When Surveys Lie and People Tell the Truth: Church Attenders." *American Sociological Review*. Vol. 63, No. 1 (February 1998):119–22.

WOODWARD, KENNETH L. "Feminism and the Churches." *Newsweek*. Vol. 13, No. 7 (February 13, 1989):58–61.

———. "Talking to God." *Newsweek*. Vol. 119, No. 1 (January 6, 1992a):38–44.

———. "The Elite, and How to Avoid It." *Newsweek* (July 20, 1992b):55.

WOOLEY, ORLAND W., SUSAN C. WOOLEY, and SUE R. DYRENFORTH. "Obesity and Women—II: A Neglected Feminist Topic." *Women's Studies International Quarterly*. Vol. 2 (1979):81–92.

THE WORLD BANK. *World Development Report 1993*. New York: Oxford University Press, 1993.

———. *World Development Report 1995: Workers in an Integrating World*. New York: Oxford University Press, 1995.

———. *World Development Report 1997: The State in a Changing World*. New York: Oxford University Press, 1997.

———. *World Development Report: Knowledge for Development*. New York: Oxford University Press, 1999.

———. *1999 World Bank Atlas*. Washington, D.C.: The World Bank, 1999.

———. *1999 World Development Indicators*. Washington, D.C.: The World Bank, 1999.

———. *Entering the 21st Century: World Development Report 1999/2000*. New York: Oxford University Press, 2000.

WORLD HEALTH ORGANIZATION. *Constitution of the World Health Organization*. New York: World Health Organization Interim Commission, 1946.

World Values Survey, 1990–1993. Ann Arbor, Mich.: Inter-university Consortium for Political and Social Research, 1994.

WORSLEY, PETER. "Models of the World System." In Mike Featherstone, ed., *Global Culture: Nationalism, Globalization, and Modernity*. Newbury Park, Calif.: Sage, 1990:83–95.

WREN, CHRISTOPHER S. "In Soweto-by-the-Sea, Misery Lives on as Apartheid Fades." *New York Times* (June 9, 1991):1, 7.

WRIGHT, ERIK OLIN, and BILL MARTIN. "The Transformation of the American Class Structure, 1960–1980." *American Journal of Sociology*. Vol. 93, No. 1 (July 1987):1–29.

WRIGHT, ERIC R. "Personal Networks and Anomie: Exploring the Sources and Significance of Gender Composition." *Sociological Focus*. Vol. 28, No. 3 (August 1995):261–82.

WRIGHT, JAMES D. "Address Unknown: Homelessness in Contemporary America." *Society*. Vol. 26, No. 6 (September-October 1989):45–53.

———. "Ten Essential Observations On Guns in America." *Society*. Vol. 32, No. 3 (March-April 1995):63–68.

WRIGHT, QUINCY. "Causes of War in the Atomic Age." In William M. Evan and Stephen Hilgartner, eds., *The Arms Race and Nuclear War*. Englewood Cliffs, N.J.: Prentice Hall, 1987:7–10.

WRIGHT, RICHARD A. "Curing Doonesbury's Disease—A Prescription for Dialogue in the Classroom." *Quarterly Journal of Ideology*. Vol. 9, No. 4 (1985):3–8.

———. *In Defense of Prisons*. Westport, Conn.: Greenwood Press, 1994.

WRIGHT, ROBERT. "Hyperdemocracy." *Time*. Vol. 145, No. 3 (January 23, 1995):15–21.

———. "Sin in the Global Village." *Time*. Vol. 152, No. 16 (October 19, 1998):130.

WRIGHT, STUART A., and ELIZABETH S. PIPER. "Families and Cults: Familial Factors Related to Youth Leaving or Remaining in Deviant Religious Groups." *Journal of Marriage and the Family*. Vol. 48, No. 1 (February 1986):15–25.

WU, LAWRENCE L. "Effects of Family Instability, Income, and Income Instability on the Risk of a Premarital Birth." *American Sociological Review*. Vol. 61, No. 3 (June 1996):386–406.

WYNTER, LEON E. "Business and Race." *Wall Street Journal* (May 10, 1995):B1.

YAMAGATA, HISASHI, KUANG S. YEH, SHELBY STEWMAN, and HIROKO DODGE. "Sex Segregation and Glass Ceilings: A Comparative Static Model of Women's Career Opportunities in the Federal Government over a Quarter Century." *American Journal of Sociology*. Vol. 103, No. 3 (November 1997):566–632.

YANKELOVICH, DANIEL. "How Changes in the Economy Are Reshaping American Values." In Henry J. Aaron, Thomas E. Mann, and Timothy Taylor, eds., *Values and Public Policy*. Washington, D.C.: The Brookings Institution, 1994:20.

YATES, RONALD E. "Growing Old in Japan; They Ask Gods for a Way Out." *Philadelphia Inquirer* (August 14, 1986):3A.

YEATTS, DALE E. "Self-Managed Work Teams: Innovation in Progress." *Business and Economic Quarterly* (Fall-Winter 1991):2–6.

———. "Creating the High Performance Self-Managed Work Team: A Review of Theoretical Perspectives." Paper presented at the annual meeting of the Southwest Social Science Association, Dallas, February 1994.

YODER, JAN D., and ROBERT C. NICHOLS. "A Life Perspective: Comparison of Married and Divorced Persons." *Journal of Marriage and the Family*. Vol. 42, No. 2 (May 1980):413–19.

YOELS, WILLIAM C., and JEFFREY MICHAEL CLAIR. "Laughter in the Clinic: Humor in Social Organization." *Symbolic Interaction*. Vol. 18, No. 1 (1995):39–58.

ZACHARY, G. PASCAL. "Not So Fast: Neo-Luddites Say an Unexamined Cyberlife Is a Dangerous One." *Wall Street Journal* (June 16, 1997):R18.

ZALMAN, MARVIN, and STEVEN STACK. "The Relationship between Euthanasia and Suicide in the Netherlands: A Time Series Analysis, 1950–1990." *Social Science Quarterly*. Vol. 77, No. 3 (September 1996):576–93.

ZANGWILL, ISRAEL. *The Melting Pot*. Macmillan, 1921; orig. 1909.

ZBOROWSKI, MARK. *People in Pain*. San Francisco: Jossey-Bass, 1969.

ZEITLIN, IRVING M. *The Social Condition of Humanity*. New York: Oxford University Press, 1981.

ZHAO, DINGXIN. "Ecologies of Social Movements: Student Mobilization during the 1989 Prodemocracy Movement in Beijing." *American Journal of Sociology*. Vol. 103, No. 6 (May 1998):1493–1529.

ZHOU, MIN, and JOHN R. LOGAN. "Returns of Human Capital in Ethnic Enclaves: New York City's Chinatown." *American Sociological Review*. Vol. 54, No. 5 (October 1989):809–20.

ZHOU, XUEGUANG, and LIREN HOU. "Children of the Cultural Revolution: The State and the Life Course in the People's Republic of China." *American Sociological Review*. Vol. 64, No. 1 (February 1999):12–36.

ZICKLIN, G. "Re-Biologizing Sexual Orientation: A Critique." Paper presented at the Annual Meeting of the Society for the Study of Social Problems, Pittsburgh, Penn., 1992.

ZIMBARDO, PHILIP G. "Pathology of Imprisonment." *Society*. Vol. 9 (April 1972):4–8.

ZIPP, JOHN F. "Perceived Representativeness and Voting: An Assessment of the Impact of 'Choices' vs. 'Echoes'." *The American Political Science Review*. Vol. 79, No. 1 (March 1985):50–61.

ZIPP, JOHN F., and JOEL SMITH. "A Structural Analysis of Class Voting." *Social Forces*. Vol. 60, No. 3 (March 1982):738–59.

ZUBOFF, SHOSHANA. "New Worlds of Computer-Mediated Work." *Harvard Business Review*. Vol. 60, No. 5 (September-October 1982):142–52.

ZURCHER, LOUIS A., and DAVID A. SNOW. "Collective Behavior and Social Movements." In Morris Rosenberg and Ralph Turner, eds., *Social Psychology: Sociological Perspectives*. New York: Basic Books, 1981:447–82.

PHOTO CREDITS

Kevin Bubriski/The Film Study Center, Harvard University, ii; Dan Laskin, xxxiii.

CHAPTER 1: Jonathan Green, *The Spirit*, 1994, oil on canvas, 72 in. × 55 in. © Jonathan Green, Naples, Florida, collection of Jill Farwell, photograph by Tim Stamm, *xxxiv;* Rick Friedman/Black Star, *1* (*right*); Jim Harrison/Stock Boston, *1* (*left*); Caroline Penn/Corbis, *2* (*top, left*); Paul W. Liebhardt, *2* (*top, center; bottom, left; bottom, center; bottom, right*); Minh-Thu Pham, *2* (*top, right*); Paul W. Liebhardt, *3;* Luc Delahaye/Magnum Photos, Inc., *7;* Archive Photos, *11* (*left*); Simon Benning, *April: Farmyard with woman milking cow*, from *Da Costa Book of Hours*, Bruges, c. 1515, © The Pierpont Morgan Library, New York. M.399, F.5V / Art Resource, NY, *11* (*right*); The Stapleton Collection/The Bridgeman Art Library International, *12;* Corbis, *13* (*left*); Brown Brothers, *13* (*right*); Amy Jones, *St. Regis Indian Reservation*, 1937, photo courtesy Janet Marqusee Fine Arts Ltd., *15;* © Paul Marcus, *Furnishings*, oil painting on canvas, 64 in. × 48 in. Studio SPM Inc., *16;* Brown Brothers, *17;* Emil Bisttram, American (1895–1976), *Domingo Chorus*, 1936, gouache and pencil on paper, 57.8 × 43.5 cm. Christie's Images/The Bridgeman Art Library, *18*.

CHAPTER 2: Alex Colville (1920–), *To Prince Edward Island*, 1965, acrylic emulsion on masonite, 61.9 × 92.5 cm, National Gallery of Canada, Ottowa, © NGC/MBAC, *24;* Photo by Ruben Burrell, Courtesy of Hampton University, *25;* Diego Rivera, Mexican (1886–1957), *The Creation of the Earth*, page from *Popol Vuh*, watercolor on paper, Museo Casa Diego Rivera (INBA), Guanajuanto, Mexico, Index/The Bridgeman Art Library, © 2001 Banco de Mexico Diego Rivera Museum Trust, *27;* John Eastcott/Yva Momatiuk/The Image Works, *28;* Bob Daemmrich/Stock Boston, *30;* Doranne Jacobson/International Images, *32;* Steve McCurry / Magnum Photos, Inc., *33* (*left*); Argas/Liaison Agency, Inc., *33* (*right*); Mark Richards/PhotoEdit, *34;* Tony Freeman/PhotoEdit, *37;* Philip G. Zimbardo, Inc., Department of Psychology, Stanford University, *38;* Bob Daemmrich/Stock Boston, *40;* Michael Elazier, Congressional Black Caucus, June 1999, *41;* David Bradnum/Robert Estall Photo Agency, *44* (*left*); Carol Beckwith and Angela Fisher/Robert Estall Photo Agency, *44* (*right*).

CYBER.SCOPE PART I: Eugene Fisher, *54;* General Electric Company, *55*.

CHAPTER 3: Jonathan Green, *Decoration Day*, 1992, oil on canvas, 48 in. × 78 in., © Jonathan Green, Naples, FL, collection of Chuma Nwokike, *58;* Joe Giron/Corbis, *59;* Paul W. Liebhardt, *60* (*top, left; middle, left*); Carlos Humberto/TDC/Contact/The Stock Market, *60* (*top, center*); Doranne Jacobson/International Images, *60* (*top, right*); David Austen/Stock Boston, *60* (*middle, center*); J. Du Boisberran/The Image Bank, *60* (*middle, right*); Doranne Jacobson/International Images, *60* (*bottom, left*); Jack Fields/Photo Researchers, Inc., *60* (*bottom, center*); Tomas Friedmann/Photo Researchers, Inc., *61;* G. Humer/Liaison Agency, Inc., *62;* Dimitri Lovetsky/AP/Wide World Photos, *64;* Jeff Greenberg/Index Stock Imagery, Inc., *65* (*left*); Pedrick/Image Works, *65* (*center*); CLEO Photo/Jeroboam, Inc., *65* (*right*); *Mrs. Picasso Dusts the Mantlepiece*, from *Great Housewives of Art* by Sally Swain, copyright © 1988 by Sally Swain, used by permission of Viking Penguin, a division of Penguin Putnam, Inc., *67;* Jeff Greenberg/PhotoEdit, *68;* Margaret Courtney-Clarke/Tom Keller and Associates LLC, *69;* John Marshall Mantel/Corbis, *71; Wine by Lask*, 1985, photo © Henry Chalfant. from *Spraycan Art* by Henry Chalfant and James Prigoff, Thames and Hudson Ltd. 1987, London, *74;* Catherine Karnow/Corbis, *76;* J. P. Laffont/Corbis Sygma, *79;* Inge Morath/Magnum Photos, Inc., *80;* Photographer Bill Coleman, www.amish-photo.com, (814) 238-8495 #174, *One Day's Work*, *81;* Copyright 1952, 1980, Ruth Orkin, *83*.

CHAPTER 4: Marc Chagall (1887–1985), *Le cirque au village*, Christie's Images, © Artists Rights Society (ARS), New York/ADAGP, Paris, *88;* © 1996, *The Washington Post*, photo by Carol Guzy, reprinted with permission, *89;* Patrick Bordes/Photo Researchers, Inc., *90;* Victor Englebert/Photo Researchers, Inc., *91;* Robert Frerck/Woodfin Camp & Associates, *92;* Archive Photos, *95* (*left*); Universal Studios and Amblin/Foto Fantasies, *95* (*right*); Corbis, *99;* Norbert Goeneutte, *The Paupers' Meal on a Winter Day in Paris*, Waterhouse and Dodd, London, Fine Art Photographic Library, London/Art Resource, NY, *100;* Charles Steiner/The Image Works, 102; The Granger Collection, *104;* George Tooker, *Landscape with Figures*, 1963, egg tempera on gesso panel, 26 × 30 inches, *106;* Elliot Landy/Magnum Photos, Inc., *107* (*left three photos*); Robert Sorbo/AP/Wide World Photography, *107* (*right*); Paul W. Liebhardt, *109* (*left*); Librado Romero/New York Times Pictures, *109* (*right*).

CHAPTER 5: Andrew Macara (English), *Footballers, Kos*, 1993, oil on canvas, 63.5 × 76.2 cm, private collection/The Bridgeman Art Gallery, *114;* Blair Seitz/Photo Researchers, Inc., *115;* Ted Horowitz/The Stock Market, *116* (*left*); Henley & Savage/The Stock Market, *116* (*center*); Tom Pollak/Monkmeyer Press, *116* (*right*); Bettmann/Corbis, *117;* A. Ramey/Woodfin Camp & Associates, *118;* Reuters Newmedia Inc./Corbis, *119;* Elizabeth Crews/Elizabeth Crews Photography, *120;* Keith Carter/Photographer, Inc., *121;* Rimma Gerlovina and Valeriy Gerlovin, *Manyness*, 1990, © the artists, New City, NY, *122;* Henry Ossawa Tanner, *The Banjo Lesson*, 1893, oil on canvas, Hampton University Museum, Hampton, Virginia, *125;* Everett Collection, Inc., *129;* Bernstein/Spooner/Liaison Agency, Inc., *131;* G. G. Kopliak (b.1942), *Still Life*, private collection, SuperStock, Inc., *132;* Shana Raab/New York Times Pictures, *133;* Eastcott/Momatiuk/Woodfin Camp & Associates, *134*.

CHAPTER 6: Bernard Stanley Hoyes, *Card Players Revelling*, oil on paper 11 × 12 in., painted at Desert Hot Springs Studio, 1994, original oil on paper in the collection of the artist, © Caribbean Arts, Inc., *138;* John Macionis, *139;* Jim Anderson/Woodfin Camp & Associates, *140;* AP/Wide World Photography, *141;* Richard Lord Enterprises, Inc., *142;* Dimaggio/Kalish/The Stock Market, *144;* Paul Cadmus (b. 1904), *Mask with False Noses: An Allegory on Promiscuity*, 1955, pen and ink and egg tempera on paper, 19 1/4 × 12 inches, private collection, courtesy DC Moore Gallery, New York, © Estate of Paul Cadmus, photo © Christie's Images, *147;* David Cooper/Liaison Agency, Inc., *149* (*top, left*); Alan Weiner/Liaison Agency, Inc., *149* (*top, center*); Lynn McLaren/Index Stock Imagery, Inc., *149* (*top, right*); Guido Rossi/The Image Bank, *149* (*bottom, left*); Richard Pan, *149* (*bottom, center*); Costa Manos/Magnum Photos, Inc, *149* (*bottom, right*); Paul Ekman, Ph.D., Professor of Psychology, University of California, San Francisco, *150;* Duke University Hartman Center for Sales Advertising and Marketing History, with permission of Pepsi-Cola Company, *151;* Paul W. Liebhardt, *153;* Tony Freeman / PhotoEdit, *154;* Angela Maynard/PhotoDisc, Inc., *155;* Kevork Djansezian/AP/Wide World Photos, *157;* Myrleen Ferguson/PhotoEdit, *158*.

CHAPTER 7: Pablo Picasso (1881–1973), *The Three Dancers*, 1925, Tate Gallery, London/Art Resource, NY, © 2001 Estate of Pablo Picasso/Artists Rights Society (ARS), New York, *162;* Nik Wheeler/Corbis, *163;* Jean-Marc Giboux/Liaison Agency, Inc., *164;* Jonathan Green, *Friends*, 1992, oil on masonite, 14 in. × 11 in. © Jonathan Green, Naples, FL, collection of Patric McCoy, *169;* Dan Habib/Impact Visuals Photo & Graphics, Inc., *170;* Cliche Bibliotheque nationale de France, Paris, from *The Horizon History of China* by the editors of Horizon Magazine, The Horizon Publishing Co., Inc., 551 5th Avenue, New York, NY 10017, © 1969, *174;* Paul Liebhardt, *176;* George Tooker, *Government Bureau*, 1956, egg tempera on gesso panel, 19 5/8 × 29 5/8 inches, The Metropolitan Museum of Art, George A. Hearn Fund, 1956 (56.78), photograph © The Metropolitan Museum of Art, *177;* Gerhard Steiner/The Stock Market, *179;* Michael S. Yamashita/Corbis, *180;* Ed Lallo/Liaison Agency, Inc., *181;* Gabe Palmer/The Stock Market, *183;* Pablo Bartholomew/Liaison Agency, Inc., *184*.

CHAPTER 8: Emil Kazaz, *Saratoga*, 1998, oil on linen, 60 in. × 72 in., collection of Rafael and Marina Akopian, courtesy of Noah's Ark Fine Art, *190;* John Chiasson/Liaison Agency, Inc., *191;* SIPA Press, *192;* Cliff Owen/UPI/Corbis, *194;* North Wind Picture Archives, *195;* Paul W. Liebhardt, *197;* Edward Gargan/New York Times Pictures, *198;* Jon Levy/Liaison Agency, Inc., *199;* Frank Romero, *Freeway Wars*, 1990, serigraph, 31 1/2 × 38 inches, ©Frank Romero, Nicholas and Cristina Hernandez Trust Collection, Pasadena, California, *202;* Danny Hellman, *204;* Residents near the site of Ricky Byrdsong's home, originally published in the July 8 *Pioneer Press/Skokie Review*, reprinted with special permission from the Pioneer Press, Inc., © 2000, *207;* Campbell/Corbis, *208;* © Paul Marcus, *Cracked-Up*, oil on panel, 24 in. × 30 in. Studio SPM Inc., *210;* Benali/Liaison Agency, 213.

CHAPTER 9: Andy Warhol, *Marilyn*, 1967, © 2001 Andy Warhol Foundation for the Visual Arts/Artists Rights Society (ARS), New York, Tate Gallery, London, Art Resource, NY, *220;* Doranne Jacobson/International Images, *221;* Andre Gallant/The Image Bank, *222* (*top, left*); Pete Turner/The Image Bank, *222* (*top, center*); Brun/Photo Researchers, Inc., *222* (*top, right*); Bruno Hadjih/Liaison Agency, Inc., *222* (*bottom, left*); Elliot Erwitt/Magnum Photos, Inc., *222* (*bottom, center*); George Holton/Photo Researchers, Inc., *222* (*bottom, right*); Bryan Patrick/The Sacramento Bee, *223* (*left*); Kim D. Johnson/The Sacramento Bee, *223* (*right*); Reproduced by special permission of Playboy magazine, copyright © 1953, © 1981 by Playboy, all rights reserved, *224;* Arnie Sachs/CNP/ Archive Photos, *225;* Robert Noonan/Photo Researchers, Inc., *227*(*a*); Biophoto Associates/Science Source/Photo Researchers, Inc., *227*(*b*); SIU/Photo Researchers, Inc., *227*(*c*); Ray Ellis/Science Source/Photo Researchers, Inc., *227*(*d*); SIU/Photo Researchers, Inc., *227*(*e*); Scott Camazine/Sue Trainor/Photo Researchers, Inc., *227*(*f, g*); John Marshall Mantel/Corbis, *229;* Charlesworth/SABA Press Photos, Inc., *235;* Mark Peterson/SABA Press Photos, Inc., *237;* Jean-Baptiste Greuze (1725–1805), *The Broken Jug*, 1772–1773 (*Le cruche cassee*), rococo painting, canvas, 85 × 86.5 cm, Louvre, Dpt. des Peintures, Paris, France, © photograph by Erich Lessing/Art Resource, NY, *238;* Richard Lord Enterprises, Inc., *239*.

CYBER.SCOPE PART II: T. Crosby/Liaison Agency, Inc., *244;* © The New Yorker Collection 1993, Peter Steiner from cartoonbank.com. all rights reserved, *245*.

CHAPTER 10: © Paul Marcus, *The New Nanny*, oil painting on wood, 48 × 72 in. Studio SPM Inc., *246;* Illustration by Ken Marschall © 1992 from *Titanic: An Illustrated History*, a Viking/Madison Press Book, *247;* Sebastiao Salgado/Contact Press Images Inc., *248;* Doranne Jacobson/International Images, *249;* Per-Anders Pettersson/Black Star, *251;* John Launois/Black Star, *253;* Francisco Conde/Impact Visuals Photo & Graphics, Inc., *254; September: Harvesting Grapes* by the Limbourg Brothers, *Tres riches heures du duc de Berry* (early 15th century), Victoria & Albert Museum, London, UK, The Bridgeman Art Library, *256;* Mitchell Gerber/Corbis, *259;* The Granger Collection, *260;* Doranne Jacobson/International Images, *262;* Ford Maddox Brown (1821–93), *Work*, Superstock, Inc., *265*.

CHAPTER 11: Jacob Lawrence (b. 1917), *New Jersey*, 1946, watercolor wash and pencil on paper, 61.2 × 50.9 cm, National Museum of American Art, Smithsonian Institution, Washington, D.C./Art Resource, NY, © Jacob Lawrence, by permission of DC Moore Gallery, New York, *270;* Index Stock Imagery, Inc., *271* (*left*); Beryl Goldberg, *271* (*right*); Bachmann/The Image Works, *277;* Kenneth Meyer/Pearson Education/PH College, *278;* Grapes/Michaud/Photo Researchers, Inc., *279* (*left*); Burt Glinn/Magnum Photos, Inc., *279* (*right*); Camilo Jose Vergara, *280*); Russell Lee/Corbis, *281;* Bob Krist/Corbis, *282;* George Tooker (b. 1920), *Laundress*, 1952, oil on masonite, 23 1/2 × 24 in. (59.7 × 61 cm.) Christie's Images, NY, © George Tooker, *287;* William Julius Wilson, *291;* Phil Schermeister/Corbis, *292;* Bob Daemmrich Photography, Inc., *293;* Brooks Kraft/Corbis Sygma, *294*.

CHAPTER 12: Juan O'Gorman (1905–1982), *The March of Loyalty* (*La marcha de la lealdad*), detail, mural, Museo Nacional de Historia, Castillo de Chapultepec, Mexico

City, Mexico. Schalkwij/Art Resource, NY, © Juan O'Gorman, kindly lent by Americo Arte Editores, *298;* Tony Arruza/Corbis, *301 (left);* Reuters/Juan Carlos Ulate/Archive Photos, *301 (right);* Martin Benjamin/The Image Works, *302 (top, left);* Peter Turnley/Black Star, *302 (top, right);* Pablo Bartholomew/Liaison Agency, Inc., *302 (bottom, left);* David Stewart-Smith/SABA Press Photos, Inc., *303;* Claus Meyer/Black Star, *307;* Malcolm Linton/Liaison Agency, Inc., *309;* Steve Maines/Stock Boston, *310;* Joe McDonald/Corbis, *311 (left);* Robert van der Hilst/Corbis, *311 (center);* Wolfgang Kaehler/Corbis, *311 (right);* Sean Sprague/Impact Visuals Photo and Graphics, Inc., *313;* Diego Rivera, *Colonial Domination,* The Granger Collection © Banco de Mexico Diego Rivera Museums Trust, *315;* Steve McCurry/Magnum Photos, Inc., *317.*

CHAPTER 13: Ernst Ludwig Kirchner (1880-1938), *Self-Portrait with a Model,* 1907, oil on canvas, 150.5 × 100 cm, Kunsthalie, Hamburg, Germany, The Bridgeman Art Library International Ltd., *324;* Archive Photos, *325;* Jon Feingersh/The Stock Market, *326;* Aspect Picture Library /The Stock Market, *328;* Explorer/Y. Layma/Photo Researchers, Inc., *324;* Ed Malitsky/Index Stock Imagery, Inc., *332;* R.W. Jones/Corbis, *341;* Catherine Leroy/Sipa Press, *342;* Bettmann/Corbis, *345 (left);* APA/Archive Photos, *345 (center);* Hulton-Deutsch Collection/Corbis, *345 (right);* UNICEF/HQ96-1041/Tapas Barua, *347.*

CHAPTER 14: © Paul Marcus, *Dreaming of Fred and Ginger,* oil painting on wood, 24 × 28 in. Studio SPM Inc., *352;* AP/Wide World Photos, *353;* Joel Gordon/Joel Gordon Photography, *354 (top, left);* Leong Ka Tai/Material World, *354 (top, center);* Owen Franen/Corbis, *354 (top, right);* Charles O'Rear/Corbis, *354 (bottom, left);* Paul W. Liebhardt, *354 (bottom, center);* Lisi Dennis/The Image Bank, *354 (bottom, right);* Tony Freeman/PhotoEdit, *355;* Bob Daemmrich Photography, Inc., *358;* Peter Turnley/Corbis, *359;* Archive Photos, *363 (left);* Robbie Robinson/Photo by Robbie Robinson. © 1995 Paramount Pitures. All Rights Reserved. Courtesy Foto Fantasies, *363 (right);* UPI/Corbis, *364;* Photo by Sheldon Preston. From *The Native Americans* by Turner Publishing, Inc. Atlanta. *365;* Corbis, *370 (far left);* Culver Pictures, Inc., *370 (left);* Photographs and Prints Division,Schomburg Center for Research in Black Culture The New York Public Library/Astor, Lenox and Tilden Foundation,. *370 (right);* UPI/Corbis, *370 (far right);* UPI/Corbis, *372;* Jeff Greenberg / Stock Boston, *373;* © Nick Quijano 1997, *La vida en Broma, 1988: Streetlife in Old San Juan, 376;* Bob Daemmrich Photography, Inc., *378.*

CYBER.SCOPE PART III: Beth Krieser/AP/Wide World Photos, *406.*

CHAPTER 15: *Gifts,* © Deidre Scherer, 1996, from the collection of St. Mary's Foundation, Rochester, NY, *382;* Reuters Newmedia Inc./Corbis, *383;* Elliot Erwitt/Magnum Photos, Inc., *388 (left);* AP/Wide World Media, *388 (right);* Eve Arnold/Magnum Photos, Inc., *391;* Bob Daemmerich Photography, Inc., *394;* Laima Druskis/Pearson Education/PH College, *395;* Alese and Mort Pechter/The Stock Market, *396;* A. Ramsey/PhotoEdit, *397;* Chris Rainier/Corbis, *399;* Ira Wyman/Corbis Sygma, *400;* Reuters/Dutch TV/Archive Photos, *401;* Alan Oddie/PhotoEdit, *403.*

CHAPTER 16: Rene Magritte (1898–1967), *Le modele rouge,* © 2000 C. Herscovici, Brussels/Artists Rights Society (ARS), New York, private collection, Art Resource, NY, *408;* Bob Daemmrich Photography, Inc., *409;* Underwood & Underwood/Library of Congress, *411;* Bob Daemmrich Photography, Inc., *412;* Bellavia/REA/SABA Press Photos Inc., *415 (left);* John Bryson/Corbis Sygma, *415 (right);* Robert Nickelsberg/Liaison Agency, Inc., *416;* Patrick Ward/Stock Boston, *417;* Scott Cunningham/Merrill Education, *421 (left);* Jeff Maloney/PhotoDisc, Inc., *421;* Jose Clemente Orozco, *The Unemployed,* photograph © Christie's Images. © Fundacion Jose Clemente Orozco. Reproduction authorized by the Instituto Nacional de Bellas Artes and Literature, *422;* Z. Bzdak/The Image Works, *425;* Bob Daemmrich Photography, Inc., *426;* Hulton Getty/Liaison Agency, Inc., *428;* UPI/Corbis, *429.*

CHAPTER 17: Pablo Picasso (1881–1973), *Massacre in Coree,* 1951, oil on canvas, Musee Picasso, Paris, France, Peter Willi/The Bridgeman Art Library, © 2000 Estate of Pablo Picasso/Artists Rights Society (ARS), New York, *134;* Tomas Muscionico/Contact Press Images, Inc., *435;* Durand/SIPA Press, *437;* David Ball/Index Stock Imagery, Inc., *441;* A. Ramey/Woodfin Camp & Associates, *444 (left);* Joel Gordon/Joel Gordon Photography, *444 (right); A Versailles, A Versailles (March of the Women on Versailles),* Paris, October 5, 1789, engraving by French School (18th century), Musee Carnavalet, Paris, France, Bulloz/The Bridgeman Art Library, *449;* David Hoffman Photo Library, *450;* Srdjan Ilic/AP/Wide World Photos, *452;* Leonard Rosoman (b. 1913), *A House Collapsing on Two Fireman, Shoe Lane, London,* 1940, Imperial War Museum, London/The Bridgeman Art Library, *453;* Joe McNally, Life Magazine © Time Inc., *454.*

CHAPTER 18: John Falter (1910–1982), *July 4th — The Family Portrait,* oil on canvas, 26 × 24 in. (66 × 61 cm.), Christie's Images, NY, © 1952 The Curtis Publishing Company, *460;* Index Stock Imagery, Inc., *461;* Carmen Lomas Garza, *The Blessing on Wedding Day / La Bendicion en el dia de la boda,* alkyds on canvas, 24 × 32 inches, © 1993 Carmen Lomas Garza (reg. 1994), photo credit: M. Lee Fatherree, collection of Smith College Museum, Northampton, Mass., *463;* Bo Zaunders/The Stock Market, *464;* Marc Chagall (1887–1985), *To My Wife,* 1933–44, Georges Pompidou Centre, Paris, The Bridgeman Art Library, London, © 2001 Artists Rights Society (ARS), New York/ADAGP, Paris, *467;* Christian Pierre, b. 1962, *I Do,* American Private Collection. Superstock, Inc., *468;* Barbara Walton/AP/Wide World Images, *469;* Carmen Lomas Garza, *Una tarde (An afternoon),* gouache painting, 18 × 25 inches, © 1990 Carmen Lomas Garza, photo credit: Judy Reed, collection of Sophie and Daniel Share, Birmingham, MI, *473;* © Susan Pyzow, *Bridal Bouquet,* watercolor on paper, 10 × 13.5 in. Studio SPM, Inc., *475;* Edward Hopper (1882–1967), *Room in New York,* 1932, oil on canvas, 29 × 36 in. UNL-Sheldon Memorial Art Gallery & Sculpture Garden, F.M. Hall Collection. 1932.H-166, *477:* Stern (Ullah)/Black Star, *482.*

CHAPTER 19: Castera Bazile (1923–1965), *Ceremonie sous mapou,* 1962, oil on masonite, photo © Christie's Images, *488;* David H. Wells/Corbis, *489;* Michael Freeman/Corbis, *490;* Owen Franken/Corbis, *491;* Mathieu Polak/Corbis Sygma, *493;* Doranne Jacobson/International Images, *495;* Craig Lovell/Corbis, *496;* Annie Griffiths Belt/NGS Image Collection, *498;* Reuters/Yun Sukbong/Archive Photos, *501;* Hans Kemp/Corbis Sygma, *502;* James L. Amos/Corbis, *507;* Stephanus Garsia, Page with *Flood, Commentary on the Apocalypse,* by Beatus of Leibana, made for the Abbey of Saint-Sever, Gascony, France, 1028–72, ink and tempera on vellum, 14 1/2 × 11 in. (35.5 × 28 cm), Bibliotheque Nationale, Paris, MS lat. 8878 fol. 85r, *508;* Nick Kelsh/Kelsh Wilson Design Inc., *509.*

CHAPTER 20: Jacob Lawrence, *The Libraries Are Appreciated,* 1943, gouache and watercolor on paper, 14 1/4 × 21 1/4 in., Louis E. Stern Collection, Philadelphia Museum of Art, Philadelphia, PA, 63-181-40, © Philadelphia Museum of Art/Corbis, © Jacob Lawrence, by permission of DC Moore Gallery, New York, *514;* Don Hebib/Concord Monitor/Impact Visuals Photo & Graphics, Inc., *515;* Doranne Jacobson/International Images, *516;* Bob Daemmrich Photography, Inc., *521;* Susan Lemer/Design Conceptions, *523 (left);* Beryl Goldberg, *523 (right);* Tom and Dee Ann McCarthy/The Stock Market, *528;* Bob Daemmrich Photography, Inc., *530;* Peter Hamblin/Edison Schools, Inc., *533.*

CHAPTER 21: Jacob Lawrence (b. 1917) *Harlem Surgery* 1953 tempera on masonite, 20 x 24 in., signed and dated. Courtesy of Michael Rosenfeld Gallery, New York © Jacob Lawrence. By permission of DC Moore Gallery, New York, *538;* Reuters/Fred Prouser/Archive Photos, *539;* Lucas van Leyden, *The Surgeon and the Peasant,* Rijksmuseum, Amsterdam, *540;* W. Campbell/Corbis Sygma, *541 (left);* Steve Lehman/SABA Press Photos, Inc., *541 (right);* Tony Freeman/PhotoEdit, *545;* John Coletti/Index Stock Imagery, Inc., *548;* A.F. Seligmann, *Allgemeines Krankenhaus (General Hospital),* 19th century painting, canvas, *Professor Theodor Billroth lectures at the General Hospital, Vienna. 1880,* Erich Lessing/Art Resource, NY, *551;* Galen Rowell/Mountain Light Photography, Inc., *553;* John Cancalosi/Stock Boston, *554;* Joseph Nettles/Stock Boston, *556;* ABC Television/Globe Pictures, Inc., *557 (left);* NBC/Everett Collection, Inc., *557 (right);* Al Diaz, *559;* Steve Murez/Black Star, *561.*

CYBER.SCOPE PART IV: Courtesy of L.L. Bean, reprinted by permission, *564;* Tara Sosrowardoyo/Indo-pix, *565.*

CHAPTER 22: Millard Sheets, *Tenement Flats (Family Flats),* ca. 1934, National Museum of American Art, Washington D.C./Art Resource, NY, *566;* Alan S. Weiner, *567;* Shawn G. Henry/Material World, *574 (left);* Jose Manuel Navia/Material World, *574 (right);* Lauren Goodsmith/The Image Works, *575;* Valley Forge Historical Society, *579;* Ernest Fiene (1894–1965), *Nocturne,* photograph © Christie's Images, *580 (left);* Pieter Breughel the Elder (c. 1525/30-1569), *Peasant Dance,* c. 1565, Kunsthistorisches Museum, Vienna/Superstock, Inc., *580 (right);* John Wang/PhotoDisc, Inc., *582;* Chip Simons/FPG International LLC, *583;* Culver Pictures, Inc., *587;* Paul W. Liebhardt, *589;* Tony Freeman/PhotoEdit, *590 (left);* Gregory G. Dimijian/Photo Researchers, Inc., *590 (right);* Eric Pasquier/Corbis Sygma, *591;* Rick Gerharter/Impact Visuals Photo & Graphics, Inc., *592.*

CHAPTER 23: G. Pellizza da Volpedo, *The Fourth Estate,* Milano, Galleria Civica D'Art Moderna, © Canali Photobank, *598;* George Hall/Corbis, *599;* Alexis Duclos/Liaison Agency, Inc., *601;* Culver Pictures, Inc., *602;* Christopher Morris/Black Star, *603;* Sabina Dowell, *605;* Tom Kelly/FPG International LLC, *608 (top, left);* Inge Morath/Magnum Photos, Inc., *608 (top, center);* Owen Franken/Stock Boston, *608 (top, right);* Willie L. Hill, Jr./Stock Boston, *608 (bottom, left);* Michael Grecco/Stock Boston, *608 (bottom, center);* Charles Krupa/AP/Wide World Photos, *609;* Michael Schumann/SABA Press Photos, Inc., *612;* J.L. Atlan/Corbis Sygma, *613;* Reuters/Blake Sell/Archive Photos, *614;* Hans Edinger/AP/Wide World Photos, *615.*

CHAPTER 24: Joan Truckenbrod, *Seize Steering,* 1995, iris ink jet, 22 × 38 in., © Joan Truckenbrod 1995, represented by The Williams Gallery of Fine Art, Princeton, NJ, *622;* Corbis, *623;* Mark Peters, *625;* Paul Gauguin (1848–1903), *Les trois huttes Tahiti,* photo © Christie's Images, *627;* George Tooker, *The Subway,* 1950, egg tempera on gesso panel, 18 1/8 × 36 1/8 in., Whitney Museum of American Art, New York, purchased with funds from the Juliana Force Purchase Award, 50.23, Photograph ©2000 Whitney Museum of American Art, *628;* Pearson Education/PH College, *630;* Mirta Cerra (1904-1986), *Trabajadores,* oil on canvas laid down on panel, 46 × 62 in. (107.3 × 157.5 cm), © Christie's Images, *633;* Edvard Munch, *The Scream,* Oslo, National Gallery, Scala/Art Resource, NY, © 1998 Artists Rights Society (ARS), New York/ADAGP, Paris, *635 (left);* © Paul Marcus, *Crossing the Rio Grande,* 1999, oil painting on canvas, 63 × 72 in., Studio SPM Inc., *635 (right);* Mauri Rautkari/WWF UK (World Wide Fund For Nature), *636;* John Launois/Black Star, *639;* Corbis, *643.*

CYBER.SCOPE PART V: Peter Charlesworth/SABA Press Photos, Inc., *647.*

NAME INDEX

SUBJECT INDEX

USE TECHNOLOGY
to enhance your learning experience . . .
www.prenhall.com/macionis

Chapter Overview: Focuses your learning on the most important sociological points made in that chapter.

Study Guide: Offers multiple-choice, true-false, essay questions, and line art essays that can be graded immediately and e-mailed to your instructor.

Applications & Exercises: Brings to life the exercises from the end of each chapter by linking you directly to Internet sites.

Boxed Material: Links to relevant Internet sites so you can delve more deeply into topics covered in the text's boxed features.

Key Word Search: Lets you search the Internet using the key words from each chapter.

Communication Tools: Communicate easily with instructors and other students using our Message Board and i-Chat.

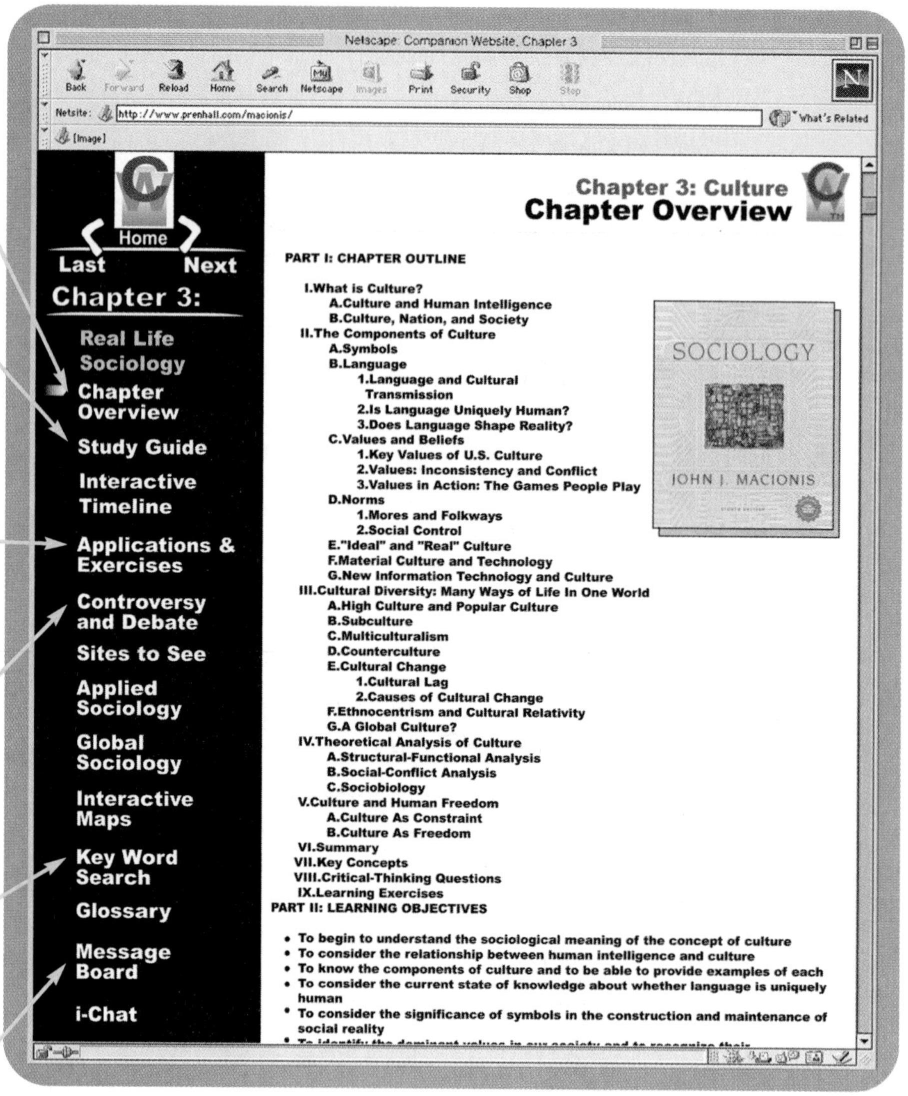

The Macionis **Companion Website™** provides you with review and assessment tools for each chapter of the text while offering a direct gateway to the wealth of resources available on the World Wide Web. Through quizzes and links to related sites on the Internet, this site will reinforce what you are learning in the classroom and in the textbook. So if you are looking for the easiest way to improve your grade in this course, your solution is to make use of this innovative tool in your studies throughout the semester.

and improve your grade in the process!!

SOCIOLOGY: INTERACTIVE EDITION

This exciting new **CD-ROM** serves as a true resource to help you master the material in this course with or without an Internet connection. It provides multiple tools for review and reinforcement of the chapter material while offering multimedia-rich content to enrich, engage, and enlighten your study of sociology. The features include chapter-opening author tip videos, multimedia chapter introductions, real-life sociology applications, interactive maps, learning objectives, interactive study quizzes and essays, Web links, Internet activities, and an interactive glossary, as well as substantial portions of the text itself.

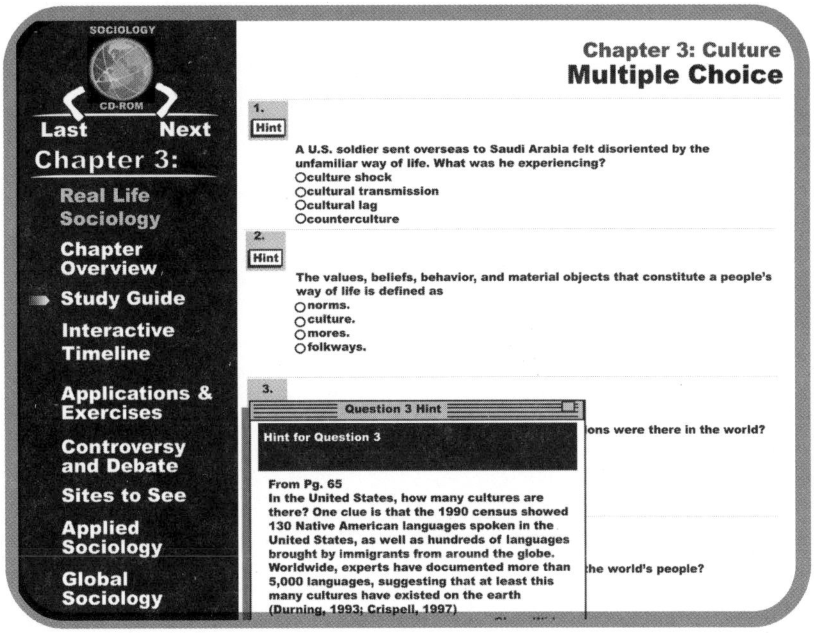

The study guide modules require a Netscape 4.x browser to function—a live Internet connection is not needed. If you are already using a 4.x version of Netscape, you do not need to install any additional software.

If you would like to install Netscape 4.7, a copy has been provided on this CD. Double-click on the icon labeled "Netscape.exe" (PC) or "Netscape Installer" (MAC) to begin installation.

Note: If you choose to use another browser to view *Sociology: Interactive Edition,* please be aware that the study guide quizzes may not function without a live Internet connection.

Using **Real Life Sociology applications**, each chapter begins by showing you how the material to be covered helps you to look at everyday life in a sociological way.

For each chapter, the **Chapter Overview** includes:

- an Author Tip videoclip featuring John J. Macionis.
- a multimedia chapter-opening vignette.
- a chapter outline and chapter learning objectives.
- a chapter summary for easy student review, with each point linked to the corresponding page in the text for deeper review.

The **Study Guide** offers multiple choice, true-false, essay questions, and line art essays that can be graded immediately and e-mailed to your instructor.

Boxed material is brought to life through sections that include the full box contents as well as relevant links to the Internet.

The **Seeing Ourselves national maps** and **Window on the World global maps** become interactive on the CD as you roll your cursor over the key for each map.

And much, much more....

How to Install:

Windows 95/98/00/NT

Insert CD
Double-click "My Computer"
Double-click CD-ROM icon for "Sociology"
Double-click "index.html" (or open this file from within your Internet browser)

Macintosh:

Insert CD
Double-click CD-ROM icon for "Sociology"
Double-click "index.html" (or open this file from within your Internet browser)

SINGLE PC LICENSE AGREEMENT AND LIMITED WARRANTY

READ THIS LICENSE CAREFULLY BEFORE OPENING THIS PACKAGE. BY OPENING THIS PACKAGE, YOU ARE AGREEING TO THE TERMS AND CONDITIONS OF THIS LICENSE. IF YOU DO NOT AGREE, DO NOT OPEN THE PACKAGE. PROMPTLY RETURN THE UNOPENED PACKAGE AND ALL ACCOMPANYING ITEMS TO THE PLACE YOU OBTAINED THEM.

1. GRANT OF LICENSE and OWNERSHIP: The enclosed computer programs ("Software") are licensed, not sold, to you by Prentice-Hall, Inc. ("We" or the "Company") and in consideration of your purchase or adoption of the accompanying Company textbooks and/or other materials, and your agreement to these terms. We reserve any rights not granted to you. You own only the disk(s) but we and/or our licensors own the Software itself. This license allows you to use and display your copy of the Software on a single computer (i.e., with a single CPU) at a single location for academic use only, so long as you comply with the terms of this Agreement. You may make one copy for backup, or transfer your copy to another CPU, provided that the Software is usable on only one computer.

2. RESTRICTIONS: You may not transfer or distribute the Software or documentation to anyone else. Except for backup, you may not copy the documentation or the Software. You may not network the Software or otherwise use it on more than one computer or computer terminal at the same time. You may not reverse engineer, disassemble, decompile, modify, adapt, translate, or create derivative works based on the Software or the Documentation. You may be held legally responsible for any copying or copyright infringement which is caused by your failure to abide by the terms of these restrictions.

3. TERMINATION: This license is effective until terminated. This license will terminate automatically without notice from the Company if you fail to comply with any provisions or limitations of this license. Upon termination, you shall destroy the Documentation and all copies of the Software. All provisions of this Agreement as to limitation and disclaimer of warranties, limitation of liability, remedies or damages, and our ownership rights shall survive termination.

4. LIMITED WARRANTY AND DISCLAIMER OF WARRANTY: Company warrants that for a period of 60 days from the date you purchase this SOFTWARE (or purchase or adopt the accompanying textbook), the Software, when properly installed and used in accordance with the Documentation, will operate in substantial conformity with the description of the Software set forth in the Documentation, and that for a period of 30 days the disk(s) on which the Software is delivered shall be free from defects in materials and workmanship under normal use. The Company does not warrant that the Software will meet your requirements or that the operation of the Software will be uninterrupted or error-free. Your only remedy and the Company's only obligation under these limited warranties is, at the Company's option, return of the disk for a refund of any amounts paid for it by you or replacement of the disk. THIS LIMITED WARRANTY IS THE ONLY WARRANTY PROVIDED BY THE COMPANY AND ITS LICENSORS, AND THE COMPANY AND ITS LICENSORS DISCLAIM ALL OTHER WARRANTIES, EXPRESSED OR IMPLIED, INCLUDING WITHOUT LIMITATION, THE IMPLIED WARRANTIES OF MERCHANTABILITY AND FITNESS FOR A PARTICULAR PURPOSE. THE COMPANY DOES NOT WARRANT, GUARANTEE, OR MAKE ANY REPRESENTATION REGARDING THE ACCURACY, RELIABILITY, CURRENTNESS, USE, OR RESULTS OF USE, OF THE SOFTWARE.

5. LIMITATION OF REMEDIES AND DAMAGES: IN NO EVENT, SHALL THE COMPANY OR ITS EMPLOYEES, AGENTS, LICENSORS, OR CONTRACTORS BE LIABLE FOR ANY INCIDENTAL, INDIRECT, SPECIAL, OR CONSEQUENTIAL DAMAGES ARISING OUT OF OR IN CONNECTION WITH THIS LICENSE OR THE SOFTWARE, INCLUDING LOSS OF USE, LOSS OF DATA, LOSS OF INCOME OR PROFIT, OR OTHER LOSSES, SUSTAINED AS A RESULT OF INJURY TO ANY PERSON, OR LOSS OF OR DAMAGE TO PROPERTY, OR CLAIMS OF THIRD PARTIES, EVEN IF THE COMPANY OR AN AUTHORIZED REPRESENTATIVE OF THE COMPANY HAS BEEN ADVISED OF THE POSSIBILITY OF SUCH DAMAGES. IN NO EVENT SHALL THE LIABILITY OF THE COMPANY FOR DAMAGES WITH RESPECT TO THE SOFTWARE EXCEED THE AMOUNTS ACTUALLY PAID BY YOU, IF ANY, FOR THE SOFTWARE OR THE ACCOMPANYING TEXTBOOK. BECAUSE SOME JURISDICTIONS DO NOT ALLOW THE LIMITATION OF LIABILITY IN CERTAIN CIRCUMSTANCES, THE ABOVE LIMITATIONS MAY NOT ALWAYS APPLY TO YOU.

6. GENERAL: THIS AGREEMENT SHALL BE CONSTRUED IN ACCORDANCE WITH THE LAWS OF THE UNITED STATES OF AMERICA AND THE STATE OF NEW YORK, APPLICABLE TO CONTRACTS MADE IN NEW YORK, AND SHALL BENEFIT THE COMPANY, ITS AFFILIATES AND ASSIGNEES. THIS AGREEMENT IS THE COMPLETE AND EXCLUSIVE STATEMENT OF THE AGREEMENT BETWEEN YOU AND THE COMPANY AND SUPERSEDES ALL PROPOSALS OR PRIOR AGREEMENTS, ORAL, OR WRITTEN, AND ANY OTHER COMMUNICATIONS BETWEEN YOU AND THE COMPANY OR ANY REPRESENTATIVE OF THE COMPANY RELATING TO THE SUBJECT MATTER OF THIS AGREEMENT. If you are a U.S. Government user, this Software is licensed with "restricted rights" as set forth in subparagraphs (a)-(d) of the Commercial Computer-Restricted Rights clause at FAR 52.227-19 or in subparagraphs (c)(1)(ii) of the Rights in Technical Data and Computer Software clause at DFARS 252.227-7013, and similar clauses, as applicable.

Should you have any questions concerning this agreement or if you wish to contact the Company for any reason, please contact in writing: Senior Media Editor, Social Sciences, HSS, Prentice Hall, One Lake Street, Upper Saddle River, NJ 07458.

SYSTEM REQUIREMENTS

MACINTOSH: minimum 68040/33MHz, System 7.5 or above, 12mb RAM (16mb recommended), 1mb free HD space, 2x CD-ROM, 640X480 screen resolution, color monitor (thousands of colors required). QuickTime 4.0 installed from CD.

PC: minimum 486/DX25, Windows 95/98 (minimum 16mb RAM), 1mb free HD space, 2X CD-ROM, SVGA monitor, thousands of colors, sound and video cards required. QuickTime 4.0 installed from CD.

THAT LIBERTY SHALL NOT
PERISH FROM THE EARTH
BUY LIBERTY BONDS
FOURTH LIBERTY LOAN
First Call
I Need You in the Navy this Minute!
Our Country will always
be proudest of those who
answered the FIRST CALL
Navy Recruiting Stations:
34 East 23rd Street
New York
115 Flatbush Ave.
Brooklyn

Heroes and Weaponry
Progressivism in War Time
Propaganda and Civil Liberties
Vigilantes
Espionage and Sedition Acts
The Lost Peace
Spanish Flu Pandemic

World War I

Europe Before the War

Prior to World War I, the major powers of Europe were divided into two great military alliances. The "Triple Entente" united Britain, France, and Russia. If any of the three were attacked, the attacking country possibly risked war with all three. The purpose of the alliance was to deter other countries from attacking any of the three—thus supposedly preserving the peace. The Central European powers of Germany, the Austro-Hungarian Empire, and Italy were allied in a similar arrangement known as the "Triple Alliance."

Each country had its own security concerns, and several had expansionist desires that could be expected to be resisted by other countries. England had been the dominant power in the nineteenth century and still had the world's largest colonial empire from which to draw resources and the most powerful navy. To enhance its advantage, England converted its navy from coal to oil in 1913, a move that made their ships faster and more efficient, while oil-deficient Germany retained its inferior coal-driven navy.

The French navy was inferior to Britain's, but France had maintained the largest army in Western Europe until the rise of Germany in 1870. Germany unified as a country from a collection of some thirty principalities in 1870 and experienced forty years of rapid industrial growth. By 1914, Germany had surpassed England to become the leading industrial power in Europe; and its army, constructed under Kaiser Wilhelm II, was larger than that of France.

At the time of its unification in 1870, Germany had defeated France in a war and taken the coal rich area of Alsace-Lorraine from France. Germany also humiliated the French by forcing them to pay $50 million in gold bullion in reparations. The French desired revenge for that debacle of 1870 and the return of Alsace-Lorraine.

The Austro-Hungarian Empire was a conglomeration in decline at the time of the outbreak of the war and was primarily controlled by the Austrians. The empire included not only Austria and Hungary, but also most of what is now Poland, Czech Republic, Slovakia, Slovenia, Bosnia, and Croatia. Austria, though German in ethnicity, had been left out of German unification due to their ambitions to the east since Austria's principal commercial river, the Danube, flowed east into the Black Sea; hence, Austria's principal trade partners were to the east along the Danube. German Chancellor Otto Von Bismarck distained the land to the east, most of which was populated by Slavic people instead of Germans; consequently he opposed Austria's unification with Germany in spite of the fact that the Austrians were German in ethnicity and spoke German. In the words of Bismarck, "The entire Balkans are not worth the hair on the head of one Pomeranian Grenadier."

Though Bismarck clearly underestimated the value of the land and people to the east, he did not underestimate the potential for trouble. In 1906, Austria-Hungary defeated Serbia in a war and annexed the territory of Bosnia from Serbia. Bosnia was an area of many competing factions, but it included both factions that favored Bosnian nationalism and those that desired a return of Bosnia to Serbian control. These sentiments would fester in Bosnia for eight years until a spark in Sarajevo ignited World War I.

▶ Giuseppe Garibaldi

Elsewhere, Italy was unified as a country in 1870 from a collection of city states through a "Revolution from above" led by Giuseppe Garibaldi and Giuseppe Mazzini; but an area of the Alps with a large Italian-speaking population remained under the control of Austria. Italians that wanted all Italians united under one flag argued for the annexation of this Austrian Tyrol.

Ever since Peter the Great, Russia had considered itself the "Defenders of the Slavs" and was essentially sworn to come to the aid of any slavic country, if that country were attacked, in what was essentially the Russian version of the Monroe Doctrine. Thus, any problems in the slavic Balkans were likely to bring Russia into a war.

Finally, Belgium, a small defenseless country of low relief on the Western European Coast, was internationally recognized as a "neutral" country by virtue of a treaty signed by all the great European powers. Violation of Belgian neutrality would also end up playing a role in World War I.

Outbreak of Hostilities

On June 28, 1914, in Sarajevo, Bosnia, an obscure Serbian nationalist named Gavrilo Princep shot the heir to the Austro-Hungarian throne, Archduke Francis Ferdinand, and his wife. The resultant crisis between Austria-Hungary and Serbia might have been localized if Europe had not been organized into a network of alliances that reflected deep divisions of militant nationalism, and if the Russian and Austrian governments had not been spurred to reckless action by dangers of national revolt.

After Ferdinand's assassination, Germany guaranteed Austria-Hungary its full support and guaranteed victory if the Austrians would attack Serbia in retaliation for the assassination. Germany feared the breakup of the Austro-Hungarian Empire, their friends to the east whom they viewed as a buffer between themselves and Russia; and they urged the Austrians to make an example of the Serbs so as to dissuade anyone else in the Austro-Hungarian Empire who may have similar nationalist intentions. After Serbia rejected impossible demands by Austria, the Austrians opened hostilities against the Serbs. Russia then came to the aid of Serbia; and when Russia mobilized its army to defend Serbia out of its role as "Defenders of the Slavs," Germany declared war on Russia, prompting France to enter the war on the side of Russia, both to honor the Entente, but also to regain Alsace Lorraine and exact revenge for 1870. When German troops pushed through neutral Belgium in a vain effort to knock out France immediately, Great Britain declared war against Germany—ostensibly to defend Belgian neutrality and honor the Entente. The British action prompted Germany's Chancellor Theobald von Bethmann Hollweg to remark that the English were "going to war over a scrap of paper." In reality, the British were merely playing the "balance of power" game and making a move to prevent Germany from becoming the dominant power in Europe.

The Ottoman Empire (Turkey) decided to seize the opportunity against its traditional enemy Russia and entered the war on the side of Germany both out of fear of Russian dominance in Eastern Europe and a desire to gain territory in Southwestern Russia where Muslims of Turkish ethnicity resided.

Japan entered the war on the side of the Allies desiring to gain Germany's possessions in the Pacific. Bulgaria entered the war on the side of Germany out of ethnic hatred and a desire to gain territory held by Serbia. Italy eventually broke with the Triple Alliance and entered the war in 1915 on the side of the Triple Entente for the purpose of gaining the Tyrol from Austria. Four years and three months later, a generation of Europeans—almost 8.5 million—lay dead.

President Wilson believed, at first, that geography would save the United States from the holocaust. He issued a proclamation of neutrality and then adjured the American people to be "impartial in thought as well as in action." But despite an initial resolve to avoid military involvement, the American public was never disposed to be neutral in thought. The dominant British and French bias was compounded by ethnic, business, and cultural ties and was intensified by a vaguely formed feeling that a German victory would adversely affect American interests by putting an aggressive military regime in control of Europe and possibly of the high seas. Key foreign policy spokesmen, also, believed that the preservation of the European balance of power by Britain had long served American interests and that, as Senator Henry Cabot Lodge phrased it on September 23, if "Germany conquers France, England and Russia, she will dominate Europe, and will subsequently extend that domination, if she can, to the rest of the world." "The principle of Anglo-Saxon liberty seems to have met the irreconcilable conception of the German State," wrote Elihu Root at the time, "and the two ideas are battling for control of the world."

In these circumstances, Germany's violation of Belgian neutrality and later resort to indiscriminate submarine warfare simply solidified standing fears. Similarly, British propaganda served mainly to sharpen perceptions and inflame passions already present. The British cut the Atlantic Cable, making communication with Germany difficult and creating a situation where the only war news received in America was biased coverage from Britain. American newspapers then simply published the biased British versions of what was going on so that many more Americans supported the British.

These sentiments were far from unanimous. The great majority of the country's eight million Germans and German-Americans were strongly attached to the fatherland. The spokesmen of the nation's 4.5 million Irish-Americans were almost universally anti-British, and several million Poles and Jews were almost fanatically anti-Russian. From the outset, these groups fed on German propaganda in their foreign-language or diocesan newspapers, and neither the pro-Allied cast of the regular press nor German actions changed their sympathies during the period of 1914–1916. Because most of these groups were lower or lower-middle class, however, they never exercised an influence proportionate to their numbers.

The divisions among the American people were accentuated by the impossibility of genuine neutrality. German might was based on dominance of the land mass of central Europe, and Great Britain's on control of the seas. To impose an embargo, as the pro-Germans and many pacifists demanded, would be to deal Britain a paralyzing blow. To supply the Allies, as the United States soon did, was to strengthen them in relation to Germany—hence the difficulty of substantive, as distinct from formalistic, neutrality.

President Wilson's decision to accept Britain's control of the seas seems to have been based on two factors: his desire to adhere to traditional rules of neutrality and his fear of a German victory. As he said to his Cabinet in 1915, "The Allies are standing with their backs to the wall fighting wild beasts. I will permit nothing to be done by our country to hinder or embarrass them ... unless admitted rights are grossly violated." In short, Wilson's own democratic ideals were at stake. As an admirer of the British Parliamentary system, he was loath to see it put asunder by what he viewed as an undemocratic government of Kaiser Wilhelm. In Wilson's words, "Everything I love is at stake. A German victory would be fatal to our form of government and American ideals." Assuredly, he protested Britain's expansion of the contraband list (goods which they could intercept under international law) to include even food, but at no time did Wilson consider military action against Britain to uphold his shifting and, in some cases, historically untenable construction of neutral rights.

As the war progressed, the president authorized positive action to assure the flow of supplies to the Allies. Anticipating a strain on American gold reserves in the summer of 1914, he had permitted Secretary of State Bryan to declare that the administration disapproved of loans to the Allies because they violated the spirit of neutrality. He modified this policy in March 1915, by allowing the Morgan banking house to extend a $50 million credit to the French government. He rejected a German-American proposal to prohibit the export of all war materials. Then, in the summer of 1915, he completely lifted Bryan's ban on loans. By 1917, Allied debt to the United States exceeded $2 billion, which the United States banks stood to lose if the Allies lost. An Allied loss, therefore, could have crumbled the whole American banking and monetary system.

The president's realization that war orders had boosted American prosperity undoubtedly influenced these decisions. By 1916 exports to the Allies exceeded $3 billion in value, four times their 1914 level. "To maintain our prosperity, we must finance it," Secretary of the Treasury McAdoo warned Wilson in August 1915. "Otherwise it may stop and that would be disastrous."

German Submarine Warfare

Very quickly, World War I bogged down into a stalemated trench warfare that neither side could win on the battlefield. However, neither Britain nor Germany were self-sufficient in food and fuel; consequently, if either power could cut off the food and fuel supplies to the other, they would ultimately win the war by starving the other side. Britain, with a superior navy, instituted a blockade of Europe with the intention of starving Germany and cutting off their fuel supplies.

Germany's navy was inferior and could not challenge the British blockade, however, the Germans had invented the "undersea boat" (commonly referred to as the "U-boat") or submarine, which Germany could use to prevent England from getting its supplies by sinking cargo ships bound for England. On February 4, 1915, the German admiralty marked out a broad war zone around the British Isles in which neutral vessels would run the risk of being sunk without warning by German submarines.

▶The "undersea boat" or "U-boat" was used by Germany to sink merchant ships during World War I.

Technically, the British blockade violated international law since under international law neutral countries, such as the United States, had the right to sell nonmilitary goods to belligerents (warring nations). In other words, international law allowed the United States to sell nonmilitary goods to Germany as well as England; but the English blockade prevented the United States from selling anything to Germany, thus violating American rights as a neutral under international law and provoking a protest by American President Woodrow Wilson. International law also required, however, that military ships provide fair warning to ships before sinking them by firing shots over their bows. The ship under attack would be then given time to evacuate and paddle off in lifeboats before the attacking ship shelled it to the bottom of the ocean. International law in this case, however, was antiquated in that it was written before the invention of the submarine. The German U-boats were very vulnerable on the surface, even to small arms fire, and could not surface and give fair warning without risk of being sunk or damaged themselves. Consequently, in order to be effective, the German submarines had no recourse but to fire torpedoes at merchant ships without warning, thus violating international law. Six days after Germany's announcement that they would sink ships without warning, Wilson replied that Germany would be held to "strict accountability" for illegal destruction of American ships and American lives.

The issue was first addressed in March when an American was lost on a British liner torpedoed without warning. Arguing passionately that the United States should not indulge the technical right of its citizens to sail through war zones on belligerent ships, Bryan proposed that the government warn them against it; but before a decision was reached, an event of tragic proportions virtually destroyed all hopes of such a solution. On May 7, off the coast of Ireland, the British liner *Lusitania*, the largest passenger liner in the world at the time with a length of over seven hundred feet, was sunk by German submarines without warning, with a loss of 1,198 lives, 124 of them American. The sinking of the luxury liner could be seen from the coast of Ireland. With the water's temperature at only 43 degrees, people died of hypothermia in approximately ten minutes, and it was impossible for anyone to save the passengers of the *Lusitania*. Germany argued that it had published warnings in the United States newspapers imploring people not to travel on the *Lusitania* due to the fact that they intended to sink it, because they believed it to be carrying four million rounds of ammunition.

The immensity of the disaster appalled the nation and violated the American collective conscience, but few voices called out for war. From all over the country, in fact, came fervent appeals for peace, and from Democratic leaders in Congress came a warning that Wilson probably could not obtain passage of a war resolution. As a Kansas progressive leader informed Roosevelt, the Midwest's sense of outrage "died down as suddenly as it had risen." When President Wilson soon afterward declared, "There is such a thing as a man being too proud to fight," Roosevelt was almost alone in denouncing him.

Determined to find a peaceful solution, Wilson called on the German government to renew its allegiance to "the rights of humanity" by conforming to the traditional rules of war. The second of his three notes was so stern that Bryan, who feared that it would provoke Germany into hostilities, resigned in protest. Bryan also denounced Wilson's policies of shipping military goods on passenger ships as "tantamount to protecting an army with women and children at the front." The president was prepared, at the most, to sever relations, but fearing war, the Germans proved unwilling to gamble on his intent. On June 6, the Admiralty ordered U-boats to spare large liners. Wilson demanded that the Germans make reparations and apologize for the *Lusitania*, but Germany argued that they had given fair warning in the American newspapers and that the *Lusitania* was aiding the enemy; therefore, Germany owed neither reparations nor apology.

When a German submarine commander provoked a more severe crisis by violating orders and sinking the British liner *Arabic* on August 19, 1915, killing two Americans, the

▶The British ship *Lusitania,* sunk in 1915 by a German U-boat, was the largest passenger liner in the world at that time.

German government avoided a break with America only by pledging that liners would not be sunk "without warning and without safety of the lives of noncombatants," providing they did not offer resistance or try to escape. Following the torpedoing of the French steamer *Sussex,* injuring a number of Americans, in March 1916, Wilson sent the Imperial Government an even stronger ultimatum, demanding reparations and the cessation of Germany's "sink all ships" policy. The Germans again pledged restraint, subject to British observance of international law. Germany pledged to stop sinking merchant ships without warning and agreed to pay reparations for the *Lusitania*. Essentially, Germany decided that the advantage gained from sinking merchant ships bound for England was not worth the disadvantage of bringing the United States into the war. Germany, however, refused to admit to any wrongdoing in the *Lusitania* incident. Wilson accepted the German pledge but not the qualification; and the crisis was temporarily resolved.

Steps Toward United States Preparedness

Meanwhile, Wilson began to prepare the nation for the hazards of an uncertain future. He was reluctant to do so, believing that a military buildup by the United States would violate American neutrality and be viewed as provocative by the Germans. However, under the hammering of a bellicose former president Roosevelt and a substantial element of the Republican Party, however, he finally faced the implications of his "strict accountability" policy. He took the first tentative steps in the summer of 1915, came out for major increases in the navy and army in December, and then toured the Midwest in January and February 1916 to whip up support for his new preparedness program. Despite his proposed half billion dollar military buildup, the Democratic Party's slogan in the campaign of 1916 became, "He kept us out of the war."

No other issue of the period proved to be so revealing of the configuration of isolationist sentiment. Progressives of all three parties, including the secondary leadership of the disintegrating Bull Moose organization, opposed preparedness as a movement of munitions makers, in particular, and capitalists, in general. Farmers in upstate New York, in California, on the Carolina Piedmont, and in the valley of Virginia, no less than on the plains of Kansas and Nebraska, charged that preparedness would lead to war. Organized labor all over the country—in New York and San Francisco as well as in Chicago, Milwaukee, and St. Louis—agreed.

Conversely, conservatives from every section of the nation supported preparedness enthusiastically. The Chamber of Commerce in almost every state endorsed it overwhelmingly. Bankers' and manufacturers' associations in the Midwest and South also came out militantly for preparedness.

The main opposition in Congress came from Bryan Democrats and a few Republican progressives. Attributing the movement to conservative Republicans, they resolved to make them bear its cost. "I am persuaded to think that when the income tax will have to pay for the increase in the army and navy," wrote Claude Kitchin of North Carolina to Bryan, "they will not be one-half so frightened over the future invasion by Germany." Not until Wilson agreed to accept their inheritance, munitions-profits, and progressive income tax program did they relax their opposition. Even then, it was to approve a severely compromised program as the defense legislation of 1916 provided for only moderate increases in the army.

The Election of 1916

Prewar progressivism had reached full flower by the spring and summer of 1916. In the convention at St. Louis in mid-June, the progressive-agrarian Democrats ignored the president's orders to make "Americanism" their keynote and indulged, instead, in one long and tremendous demand for peace. "He kept us out of war" became their campaign theme, and Wilson had little recourse but to accept it. Compared to the extreme measures advocated by the Roosevelt and Old Guard wings of the reunited Republican Party—the so-called jingoes—Wilson's was, in fact, the policy of moderation. This was widely recognized at the time; and along with the Democrats' remarkable legislative record, it exerted a powerful pull on independents and ex-Bull Moosers.

Divisions within the Republican Party also worked to Wilson's advantage. Although the G.O.P. platform criticized the Democratic preparedness program as inadequate, and virtually called for war against Mexico, it deferred to the sensibilities of the more than one hundred German-American delegates at the Republican convention by equivocating on neutral rights. As a result, the Republican campaign lacked consistency. The Republican presidential candidate, former Justice Charles Evans Hughes, was forced, on the one hand, to call for a hard policy toward Germany and to contend, on the other hand, that such a policy would assure peace. Graphically, the *St. Louis Post-Dispatch* described his dilemma:

> To satisfy the pro-Germans he must quarrel with the pro-British, who demand war with Germany. To satisfy Wall Street, he must quarrel with the western radicals. To satisfy the jingoes and the Munitions Trust, he must quarrel with most of the country. To satisfy privilege and plutocracy, he must quarrel with the people. Even as a candidate Mr. Hughes dare not have a policy, because to have a policy is to antagonize one element or another of his followers.

▶ Charles Evans Hughes.

Wilson squeezed through by a narrow, half-million plurality and just twenty-three electoral votes. On election night it appeared that Wilson had lost, but Wilson won every state west of the central time zone except Oregon and was declared the winner the next day. The resentment of Irish-, German-, Jewish-, and Polish-American voters possibly cost him much of the East and such Midwestern states as Illinois and Wisconsin, though some recent scholars dispute this. At any rate, he swept most states where isolationism reflected agrarian rather than ethnocentric views and where the progressive impulse was strong. He also carried most of the Western states in which women could vote.

The Failure of Mediation

Hardly were the election returns counted than the president sought to end the war. At the time of his electoral victory, Wilson was perhaps as neutral as he had been at any time since 1914. The Germans had stopped sinking merchant ships without warning, and the British had elevated his irritation by their restrictions on neutral trade with their blockade. For almost two years he had been striving to persuade the belligerents to accept a negotiated peace. His efforts had failed because both the Allies and the Central Powers still aspired to victory in the field. Taking new hope in a German peace overture of December 12, 1916, six days later Wilson called on the belligerents to define their war aims. The British replied privately that they would negotiate on liberal terms (even though the Allies had returned a belligerent public answer); but the Germans answered evasively—and understandably so, for the real terms included control of Belgium and a strip of the French coast.

The president, thereupon, appealed to world opinion in a speech before the Senate on January 22, 1917. He asserted the right of the United States to share in laying the foundations for a lasting peace, set forth his plan for a League of Nations, and added the noblest of all his perorations: "It must be a peace without victory. Victory would mean peace forced upon the loser, a victor's terms imposed upon the vanquished. ... Only a peace between equals can last." Wilson also called for the principle that all states are equal and the principle of self-determination. Wilson called for international disarmament and "freedom of the seas," an American principle dating back almost to the American Revolution.

People of good will the world over were intoxicated by Wilson's great vision, but realists knew that it was hopeless to expect the German military party to will its own destruction. On January 31, the German government submitted terms that would have assured its hegemony in Europe. It also announced resumption of unrestricted submarine warfare as it launched a major offensive in France—a dramatic gamble to win the war before the United States could join the war effort and arrive in significant numbers. The Germans were low on food and fuel, and they knew they needed to win the war quickly. Consequently, they hoped to cut off supplies to the British through the renewed "sink all ships" policy and then defeat their enemies before American help could arrive. The president responded by severing diplomatic relations with Germany after German U-boats sunk the U.S.S. *Housatonic* on February 3rd.

Although Wilson still hoped to avert war, the onrush of events soon overtook him. From British intelligence on February 25, he received a transcript of the "Zimmermann note," a diplomatic message from German Foreign Secretary Arthur Zimmermann, proposing to Mexico that in the event of war between the United States and Germany, Mexico should join Germany against the United States. As a reward, Mexico should recover "the lost territory in Texas, New Mexico, and Arizona." The same day, German U-boats sunk the passenger liner *Laconia,* killing two Americans.

The next day the president asked Congress for authority to arm American ships for defense and to employ other measures to protect American commerce on the high seas, but the bill died by filibuster in the Senate. Bolstered by the public's militant reaction to the Zimmermann note, he castigated progressive senators who prevented adoption of the armed-ship bill as "a little group of willful men representing no opinion but their own." He then ordered, by Executive Order on March 9, that merchant ships be armed.

Events now moved swiftly to a climax. On March 19, three American ships went down with heavy losses. That same week a liberal revolution in Russia overthrew the czar. This softened the pro-German stance of Russian-American Jews and made progressives everywhere more willing to support the Allies. Great throngs of people in mass meetings in New York and other cities now called for war. Meanwhile, the White House received reports from London that the Allies were in such desperate straits that only American intervention could save them.

Weighed down by these pressures, the president sorrowfully decided for full-scale war. As his biographer, Arthur S. Link, concludes, he did so mainly for two reasons. First, he believed that the war was already in its final stages and that American participation would bring it to a quick conclusion. Second, and much more important, he believed that Allied war aims posed such a threat to enduring peace that only a decisive American presence at the peace conference could assure a rational reconstruction of the world order. For this reason, the United States became an Associate power rather than an Ally.

At eight-thirty in the evening on April 2, 1917, Wilson asked a joint session of Congress to recognize that Germany was at war against the United States and mankind. "The world must be made safe for democracy," he said, ". . . for the right of those who submit to authority to have a voice in their own Governments, for the rights and liberties of small nations, for a universal domination of right by such a concert of free peoples as shall bring peace and safety to all nations and make the world itself at last free."

Four days later, on April 6, 1917, the Senate voted for a war resolution 82 to 6, the House 373 to 50. How much this vote reflected Congress' acceptance of Wilson's concept of a world democratic mission, how much a purely nationalistic reaction against the loss of American shipping, and how much a conviction that British naval supremacy in the Atlantic was in the United States' continuing interest, is impossible to say. All that is clear is that many Republican interventionists conceived the war as a power struggle involving American interests and disparaged the proposed League of Nations from the outset. "I am an American," expostulated Congressman Augustus P. Gardner of Massachusetts. "I want no internationalism. I want no conglomerate flag of all nations, with a streak of yellow down the middle." Among the fifty who voted against the war was Jeannette Rankin of Montana, who not only voted against the War Declaration in 1917, but also would be the only member of the House to vote against the War Declaration that marked the American entry into World War II.

The Carnage and Stalemate of World War I

At the time of the United States entry into the war, the German offensive had again failed; the war continued its stalemated trench warfare into its third year. Almost the entire war on the Western Front had been fought along a 500-mile front at essentially the same place after the original German offensive had failed outside Paris in 1914. In 1914, the German army made it to the outskirts of Paris in six weeks with well-planned precision; but the inexperienced German troops panicked and retreated when they saw the French army advance to meet them from Paris in a barrage of civilian vehicles, which made the French army appear

▶ Almost the entire war on the Western Front had been fought along a five-hundred-mile front ("trench warfare") at essentially the same place.

larger than it was. The Germans fell back, the war stalemated, and three years of bloody trench warfare followed.

The development of military machinery had outpaced battle tactics, and both sides were able to kill the enemy faster with machine guns and new heavy artillery than anyone could advance. Generals ordered their men to hurl themselves into machine gun fire across open fields, wasting literally millions of lives in the process. A million men died in the battle of Verdun, and another six hundred thousand died at the Somme; yet nothing was settled. It was into this lunacy that President Wilson was sending the United States Army.

A People at War

The president and his advisers soon learned that disaster loomed on almost every side. On the Western Front a French offensive had been stopped, and ten French divisions had already mutinied. In the Balkans the Allies were being pushed back. In Italy the Austrians, reinforced by the Germans, were soon to win a great victory at Caporetto. In the East the Russian armies were withdrawn from the war after the Bolshevik Revolution in November 1917, where V. I. Lenin and the Bolsheviks took over the government of Russia with the promise of "bread, land, and peace" to the Russian people. While ending famine would prove more difficult for Lenin, he quickly signed a separate peace with Germany, withdrawing Russia from the war. That allowed the Germans to shift six hundred thousand troops from the Eastern front to the Western front and thus tip the balance in their favor. On all fronts the Allies were running out of reserves. More ominous still, the Germans were destroying three times as many ships each month as the Allies were building. Britain faced starvation unless something could be done.

The Washington administration responded boldly. At once the navy began to patrol the Western Hemisphere and to give assistance to the antisubmarine campaign around the British Isles. By July 1917, thirty-five American destroyers were based at Queenstown, Ireland. By the end of the war, almost four hundred American ships were overseas. Meanwhile, the American navy virtually coerced the British into adopting the convoy system. The results of this critical decision were spectacular. Shipping losses fell from 881,027 tons in April 1917 to half that figure in December. By May 1918, they dropped to two hundred thousand tons per month, thus destroying the calculations on which the Germans had based their decision to risk hostilities with the United States.

Mobilization for Victory

President Wilson rejected the idea of an all-volunteer army, and Congress passed the Selective Service Act in May 1917, which eventually provided over three million United

MAP 22.1 World War I

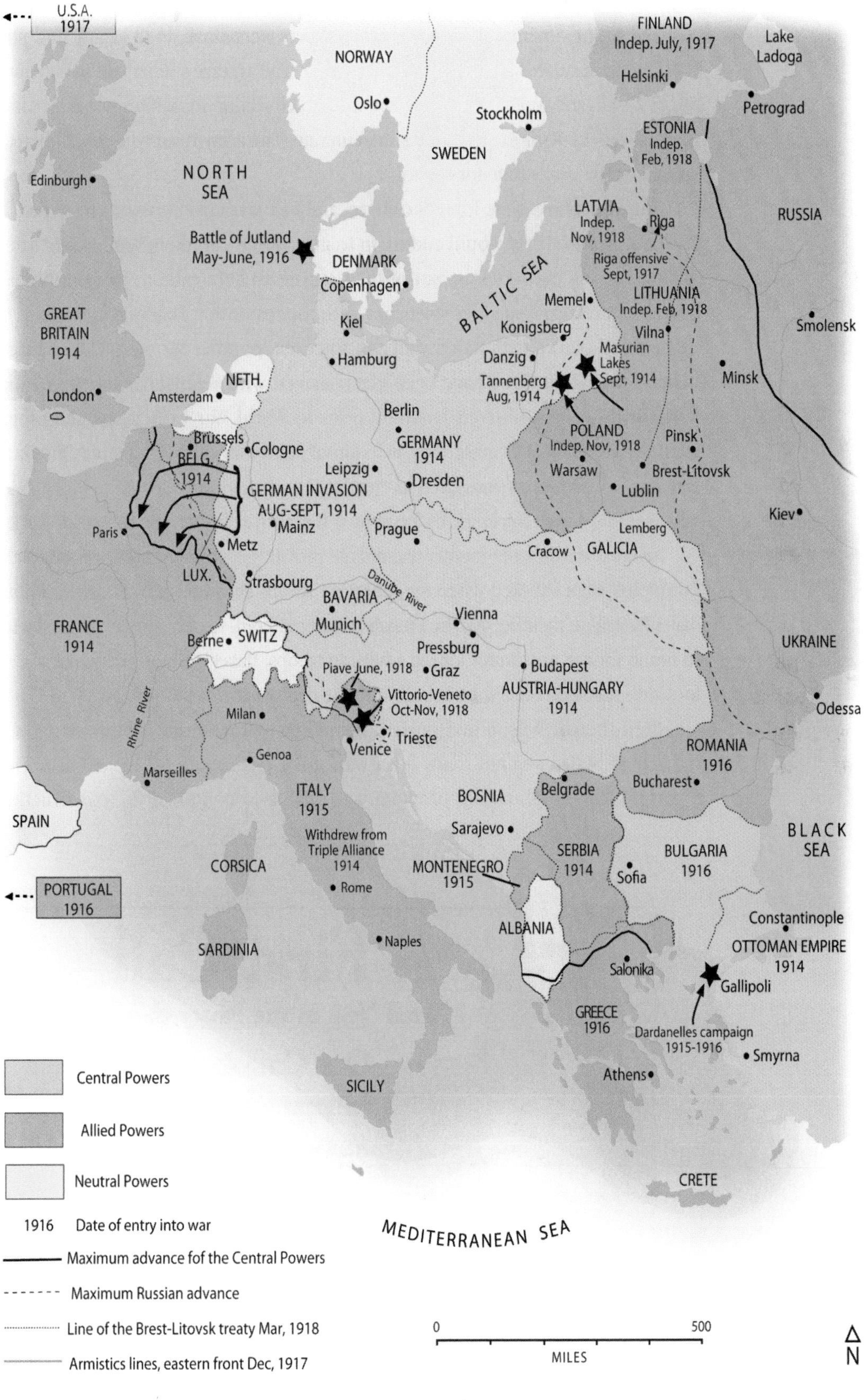
U.S.A. 1917
NORWAY
Oslo
SWEDEN
Stockholm
FINLAND Indep. July, 1917
Helsinki
Lake Ladoga
Petrograd
ESTONIA Indep. Feb, 1918
NORTH SEA
Edinburgh
LATVIA Indep. Nov, 1918
Riga
RUSSIA
Battle of Jutland May-June, 1916
DENMARK
Copenhagen
Riga offensive Sept, 1917
BALTIC SEA
Memel
LITHUANIA Indep. Feb, 1918
GREAT BRITAIN 1914
Kiel
Konigsberg
Vilna
Smolensk
Hamburg
Danzig
Masurian Lakes Sept, 1914
Tannenberg Aug, 1914
Minsk
NETH.
London
Amsterdam
Berlin
POLAND Indep. Nov, 1918
Pinsk
Brussels
Cologne
GERMANY 1914
BELG. 1914
Leipzig
Warsaw
Brest-Litovsk
Dresden
GERMAN INVASION AUG-SEPT, 1914
Lublin
Mainz
Kiev
Paris
Metz
Prague
Lemberg
Cracow
GALICIA
LUX.
Strasbourg
Danube River
BAVARIA
Vienna
Munich
FRANCE 1914
Berne
SWITZ
Pressburg
UKRAINE
Piave June, 1918
Graz
Budapest
Vittorio-Veneto Oct-Nov, 1918
AUSTRIA-HUNGARY 1914
Rhine River
Milan
Odessa
Trieste
Venice
ROMANIA 1916
Genoa
Marseilles
Bucharest
ITALY 1915
BOSNIA
Belgrade
SPAIN
Sarajevo
BLACK SEA
Withdrew from Triple Alliance 1914
SERBIA 1914
BULGARIA 1916
CORSICA
MONTENEGRO 1915
Sofia
Rome
PORTUGAL 1916
Constantinople
ALBANIA
Naples
OTTOMAN EMPIRE 1914
SARDINIA
Salonika
Gallipoli
GREECE 1916
Dardanelles campaign 1915-1916
Smyrna
Central Powers
Athens
SICILY
Allied Powers
Neutral Powers
CRETE
1916 Date of entry into war
MEDITERRANEAN SEA
Maximum advance fof the Central Powers
Maximum Russian advance
Line of the Brest-Litovsk treaty Mar, 1918
0 500
MILES
N
Armistics lines, eastern front Dec, 1917

States soldiers. Another two million Americans volunteered for service. Over two million Americans eventually made the voyage to Europe virtually unmolested as the German high command made the decision to sink supply ships instead of troop carriers, believing the British supplies to be of greater value.

The typical American "doughboys" or soldiers were small, in ill health, and poorly educated by the standards of the twenty-first century. The average soldier was twenty-two years of age, 5'7" tall, and weighed 141 lbs. The median education for whites was 6.9 years, and 2.6 years for blacks, with 31 percent testing illiterate. The army rejected a full 29 percent of the recruits as physically unfit for service.

The doughboys were forced to shave, and hair was cut short so as to reduce head lice and body lice that they would endure in trench warfare. Soldiers were issued safety razors and were given cigarettes as part of their rations to help calm nerves on the battlefield. Soldiers were also issued wristwatches with the result that fashions in America changed. Being clean-shaven with hair styled short became popular for men. (All American presidents since World War I have been clean-shaven with relatively short hair.) Cigarettes, which had been considered feminine prior to World War I (men smoked pipes and cigars), have been just as masculine as feminine, if not more so, ever since. Similarly, wristwatches, which were considered as "jewelry" and "feminine" prior to World War I, have been standard male accessories for almost the entire century since World War I.

America was the only country that did not provide government prostitutes for their troops. Europeans were shocked when the American troops showed up in Europe without any females to tend to their needs. The French Premier offered, to Secretary of State Newton Baker, to supply French prostitutes for the American troops. Baker's famous response was, "Yes, but for God's sake don't tell Wilson; he'll stop the damn war."

Even though Wilson had pushed his military preparedness bill through Congress, the United States was not ready for a war of the magnitude of World War I. The United States military shipbuilding program was unable to complete the construction of any

First Call
I Need You in the Navy this Minute!
Our Country will always be proudest of those who answered the FIRST CALL
Navy Recruiting Stations:
34 East 23rd Street
New York
115 Flatbush Ave.
Brooklyn

▶The typical American "doughboy" was twenty-two years old, small, and in ill health. 31 percent of soldiers were found to be illiterate. Hair was cut short so as to avoid lice which was easily contracted in trench warfare, and cigarettes were offered in rations so as to calm soldiers' nerves on the battlefield.

major new vessels until after the war ended. Similarly, the American army supplied only eight thousand of 8.8 million artillery shells fired by the United States army during the war. Congress authorized the production of twenty thousand airplanes, but less than fifty were actually completed, shipped to Europe, and used in the war. Instead, American pilots flew British and French-made planes.

Three months after American intervention, the administration created the War Industries Board (WIB) to coordinate purchases, allocate (ration) raw materials, control production, set prices (prices were set high in an effort to boost production and companies made record profits), and supervise labor relations. The WIB made rapid progress in some areas but failed to control military purchases. "The Military Establishment ... has fallen down," a Democratic senator exclaimed in January 1918. "It has almost stopped functioning ... because of inefficiency in every bureau and in every department of the Government." Rejecting a Republican demand for a coalition cabinet, Wilson boldly conferred such sweeping authority on the WIB's new head, Bernard Baruch, that the industrial machine was soon hammered into shape.

Meanwhile, Herbert Hoover, director of the War Food Administration, stimulated dramatic agricultural increases by pegging prices. Food exports to the Allies doubled in 1917–1918 and tripled in 1918–1919. The War Food Administration encouraged conservation through "Wheatless Monday" and "Meatless Tuesday" campaigns. The War Fuel Administration was not so spectacularly successful, but it too performed effectively. The War Fuel Administration rationed coal and other fuels, including "coal holidays" where citizens were forced to go without fuel on certain days.

Conversely, the shipbuilding program proved a failure, less than a half-million new tons being afloat by the end of the war. Only by commandeering three million tons already under construction in private yards and by seizing a million tons of German and Dutch shipping did the United States acquire the fleet that saved the Allies.

For a while the railroad situation was even worse. The eastern freight system nearly collapsed in December 1917, but conditions rapidly improved after the president put all railroad

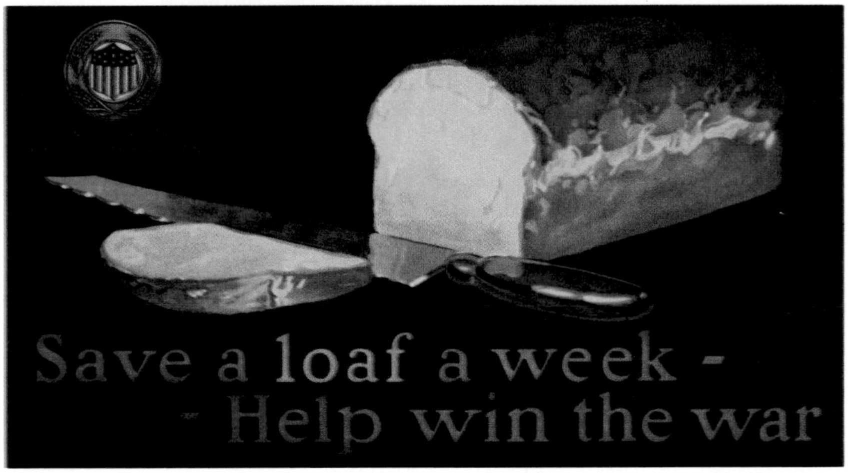

▶The War Food Administration, encouraged conservation through "Wheatless Monday" and "Meatless Tuesday" campaigns during the war. Coal, fuels, and other materials were rationed for the war effort as well.

transportation under the control of William G. McAdoo. The demands of the great military effort of 1918 were fully met.

Conservatives objected to Wilson's wholesale economic intervention. However, since prices were typically set artificially high to encourage production, big business complaints were minimized. Furthermore, vehement condemnation of Wilson's policies placed one at risk of being labeled unpatriotic.

The War on Land

Six weeks after adoption of the war resolution, a selective service law that applied to rich and poor alike was enacted; and by the summer of 1917 a great army was being formed. The following winter a small American expeditionary force held a quiet sector of the front and served generally to bolster sagging Allied morale. The first American troops reached the Western Front in October 1917, a full six months before the Germans had anticipated.

Meanwhile the American commander, General John J. Pershing, systematically prepared a major offensive. The Americans fought as separate units from the Allies, and the United States was never formally "allied" with the Allies, but merely "associates." Appalled by the defense-mindedness of Allied generals, Pershing was determined "to draw the best

MAP 22.2 World War I: The Western Front

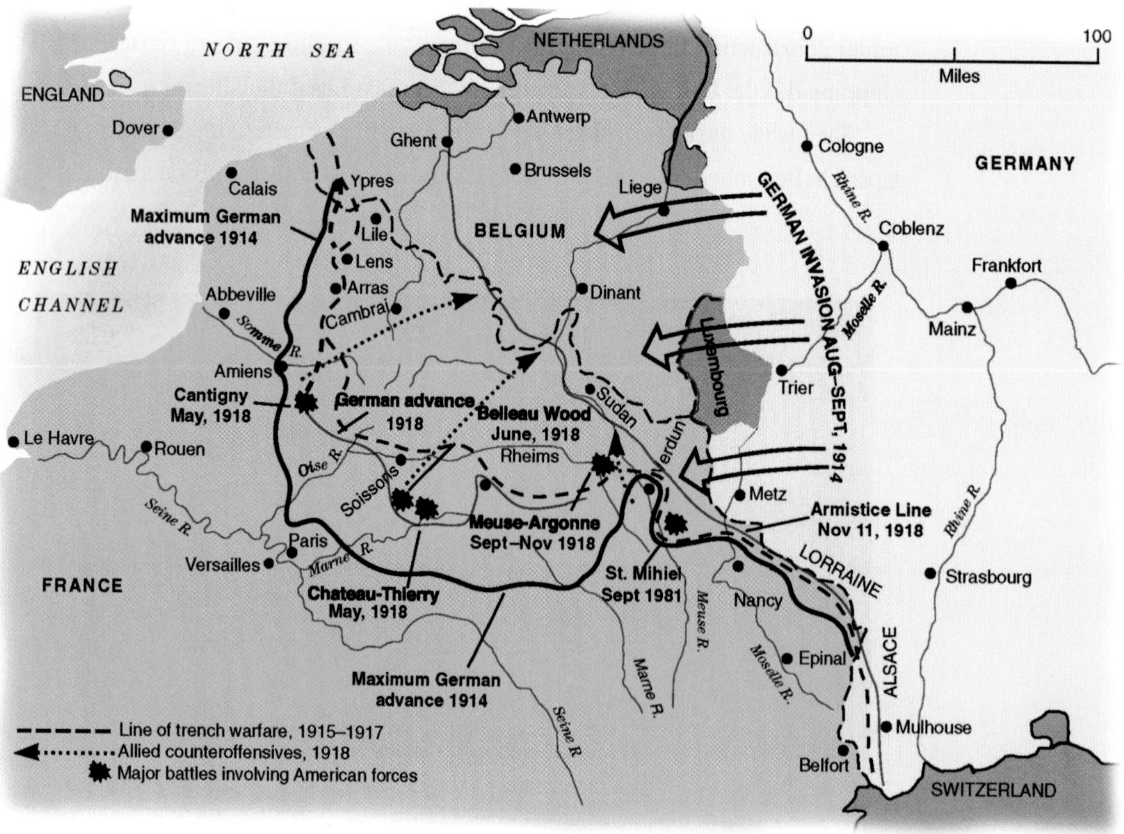

German divisions to our front and consume them." Before he could do so, he had to throw two divisions into Chateau-Thierry to support the French in May 1918. Two months later, eighty-five Americans helped the Allies turn back the last great German drive to break through the Marne pocket and take Paris.

Finally, in mid-September Pershing's army, now greatly reinforced, took the offensive at Saint-Mihiel in its first independent action. It attained its objective after a two-day battle that cost six thousand in dead and wounded. More than half a million strong, the Americans turned west and won a fiercely fought battle in the Meuse-Argonne area. Nevertheless, it was British and French successes in the central and northern sectors, not the American offensive, brought Germany to its knees. Only in the sense that American involvement convinced the Germans that they could not win and would eventually lose did the United States' military contribution prove crucial. By November of 1918, Germany was out of food and out of fuel, and its leaders knew that they could not continue through the winter. Hence, Germany surrendered, and an armistice was signed on November 11, 1918. The Armistice went into effect at 11:00 a.m. on the 11th day of the 11th month of 1918. Although the two sides had agreed on the ending time eight hours earlier, both sides continued fighting in full force until 11:00 a.m., resulting in thousands of senseless deaths and wounds.

Though the Armistice had been signed, the German army had not been defeated on the battlefield, and the Allies were not on German soil at the war's end. Instead, the British blockade had created food and fuel shortages so acute that at war's end house cats in Germany had become known as "roof rabbits." The starving nation had little choice but to surrender as the German people were facing winter with neither food nor fuel. The Armistice came as a shock both to the German people, who had been told for four years by the German Press that they were winning the war, and to the soldiers in the trenches, who well understood that they were not defeated militarily.

Heroes and Weaponry

The Great War (as it was called prior to World War II) produced new weaponry and heroes on both sides in the greatest struggle the world had ever known. It was during World War I that airplanes were first introduced into warfare. In the beginning, airplanes were used only for reconnaissance and opposing armies were known to wave at the pilots in the enemy planes. Later, planes were armed with bombs and machine guns and used in battle, but their contribution was not significant, though celebrated in the press.

Planes in World War I were primitive structures of light wood frames and canvas. They tended to put off toxic carbon monoxide fumes that poisoned pilots so quickly that flights had to be limited to one to two hours. Planes also often crashed from mechanical failures and were generally inaccurate in bombing missions. On occasion, poorly synchronized machine guns even shot off the planes' own propellers. Nevertheless, Baron Manfred Von Richtoven, the "Red Baron," became the toast of Germany for shooting down eighty Allied planes. Similarly, American Ace Eddie Rickenbacker was credited with twenty-seven kills and shot down enemy planes at a rate even faster than the Red Baron.

The greatest hero of World War I, however, was Sergeant Alvin York, a Tennessee sharpshooter who single-handedly captured 132 Germans and thirty-five machine guns after killing

▶ Pictured is an Airco DH.2 which was used by the United Kingdom in World War I. It was during World War I that airplanes were first introduced into warfare.

seventeen Germans (who dared to raise their heads out of a trench) with seventeen bullets. York explained his incredible feat with humility, stating, "Of course, it weren't no trouble no how for me to hit them big army targets. They were so much bigger than turkey's heads."

The war also produced other new weapons; tanks, which would make trench warfare obsolete in the next war; Zeppelins, which were ominous, but obviously too slow and too easy to shoot down; and poison gas, which was so horrible that no army used it in World War II. Some gasses were heavier than air; consequently, persons had the choice during gas attacks of staying in the trench and being killed by gas, or coming out of the trench and being killed by bullets. Mustard gas burned the lungs of those who breathed it, while nerve gasses not only killed people but also left others crippled with disorders of the central nervous system. It was these horrible lung and nervous system injuries that, in part, prompted the United States government to fund the Veteran's Administration (VA) and the chain of VA hospitals across the country as a way of meeting the health care needs of the returning doughboys.

Progressivism in War Time

Over the bitter protests of conservatives, almost a third of the $32 billion total war bill was raised by war profits, income, corporate, and luxury taxes. In total, new taxation produced over $9 billion in government revenue. Borrowing essentially financed the rest of the war. The United States government also introduced "liberty bonds," which were purchased by private citizens. Through an aggressive campaign, the bonds eventually raised $23 billion.

The National War Labor Board was placed in charge of labor relations and promoted harmony between labor and management. In return for a guarantee of no strikes, the National War Labor Board pressured companies to provide eight-hour work days, equal pay for women, and the recognition of the right of collective bargaining, and to set wages high so as to attract workers. For example, wages in the steel mills doubled during World War I. As a result, the AFL increased its membership from 2,072,702 to 3,260,168. Hours of labor declined from 53.5 per week in 1914 to

THAT LIBERTY SHALL NOT
PERISH FROM THE EARTH
BUY LIBERTY BONDS
FOURTH LIBERTY LOAN

50.4 in 1920, and addition, real wages rose sharply—14 percent above the prewar level in 1917 and 20 percent in 1918. Unfortunately, many of the gains proved temporary. The administration failed to devise and implement a viable economic reconversion plan, and upon the end of hostilities management resumed its old practices. After a series of long and bitter strikes, labor failed to organize steel and other industries.

Women and blacks were also recruited to the workforce to perform jobs previously occupied by the five million men who went off to war. Southern blacks moved to Northern cities and established their own enclaves within the Northern cities themselves. Most famously, the Harlem area of New York City became a complex African-American city within a city complete with black business entrepreneurs, intellectuals, artists, and entertainers along with factory workers. The migration, which received a boost with the increased demand for labor that accompanied World War I, would continue throughout the 1920s.

Propaganda and Civil Liberties

The record on civil liberties proved far less exemplary, partly because of Wilson's belief in the need to create a solid front. In some respects, World War I whipped the American public into a frenzy of hyper-patriotism, which was perhaps unparalleled in American history. On the other hand, millions of Americans believed on April 6, 1917, that the United States should not have entered the war. In 1917 mayoral candidates of the antiwar Socialist Party polled close to half the vote in Dayton, Ohio, more than a third in Chicago, and nearly a quarter in New York and Buffalo—impressive evidence of both the magnitude and the geographic spread of antiwar sentiments.

The administration struck back with a vast propaganda program and legislation to discourage criticism of the war. Fanning the flames of this pro-war frenzy, President Wilson created the Committee on Public Information (CPI), essentially a federal war propaganda agency, and endowed it with the responsibility for selling the war to the American public. The CPI, under George Creel, induced the press to accept voluntary censorship and organized some fifteen thousand writers, scholars, and businessmen into a public speaking and pamphlet-writing bureau. Under such an atmosphere, free speech and truth and accuracy in the news media became seriously compromised as the news media essentially published the CPI's accounts of the war without question or criticism. The CPI painted the war as a crusade for freedom and democracy, and the German enemies were simplistically portrayed as cruel, savage, anti-democratic thugs bent on destroying the American way and dominating the world. The CPI placed ads in magazines and newspapers asking Americans to keep watch on their neighbors and report evidence of disloyalty, pessimism, or yearning for peace.

The American people generally accepted the draft, subscribed liberally to numerous bond drives, and adjusted reasonably well to the dislocations and inconveniences wrought by mobilization. They generally came also to believe the president's reiterated assertions, echoed again and again by Creel and his speakers and writers, that Americans were fighting to make the world safe for democracy.

At the same time, however, they indulged in an orgy of intolerance and bigotry. With the urging from the CPI, persons against Wilson's war policies became subject to public ridicule and attack. School boards outlawed the teaching of the German language, and the German department at the University of Texas was closed so as to promote "purer Americanism." The University of Wisconsin censured Wisconsin progressive Senator Robert LaFollette for his antiwar views. The director of the Boston Symphony was fired, simply for being German. German books and music were removed from library and retail store shelves, and German-Americans changed their names so as to conceal their ethnicity and avoid ridicule and attack. State committees of public safety persecuted pacifists, pro-Germans, and radicals almost capriciously. One German-American was lynched. Conservatives read "Bolshevist" and "German socialist" into almost any sign of labor strife. Meanwhile, black servicemen were proscribed from full participation in the "crusade for democracy."

Vigilantes

Vigilante organizations quickly developed to enforce American patriotism. The most important of these was the American Protective League, a group whose purpose was to "mobilize respectable members of the community to root out disloyal members." The American Protective League claimed over 250,000 members at its peak in 1918. Other similar organizations—including the National Security League, American Defense Society, and Boy Spies of America—collectively claimed another 250,000 members. The organizations opened mail, tapped telephones, subjected targeted citizens to shakedowns, and engaged in lynching and violence against those suspected of being disloyal. In Cincinnati, a pacifist clergyman was pulled from his bed, dragged to a nearby hillside, and whipped—"in the name of the women and children of Belgium." In Indiana, a man was acquitted of murdering an alien who had yelled, "To hell with the United States." In Montana, one member of the Industrial Workers of the World (IWW), a left-leaning labor organization that conservatives viewed as communist and un-American, was hanged and another was dragged to death behind a truck. IWW leader Big Bill Haywood fled to the Soviet Union rather than face potential lynching at the hands of vigilantes.

Espionage and Sedition Acts

From the outset, the administration was determined to suppress opposition that might hinder the war effort. Congress then fanned the flames of hysteria with several laws that essentially criminalized political dissent. The Espionage Act of June 1917 made it a crime to "aid the enemy" or "obstruct the United States war effort." On the surface, these items do not appear to be out of the ordinary, but in practice they became launching pads for oppression and the erosion of freedom. This restrictive approach was broadened as the war progressed, partly because the labor agitation of the "Wobblies" (the Industrial Workers of the World) caused production of copper to decline precipitously. The Trading-with-the-Enemy Act of October 1917 forbade trade with Germany and its allies. In May 1918, however, Congress took things a step further with the passage of the Sedition Act, which declared it illegal to utter, print, write, or publish, any disloyal, profane, scurrilous, or abusive language about the government, Constitution, or armed forces. Furthermore, "saying anything" to discourage the purchase of war bonds was declared to be criminal activity. In effect, the Sedition Act of 1918 imposed virtual closure on free speech in the United States. By war's end, some fifteen hundred people had been convicted for violating the provisions of either these measures or the Espionage Act. The similarities between the Alien and Sedition Acts of 1798 and the Congressional actions of World War I are uncanny, and the results of the twentieth century laws were just as oppressive as those in the eighteenth century, if not more so. Under the Sedition Act of 1918, communist and socialist parties (who criticized the United States government effort during the War) were effectively silenced and over five hundred communists were deported. The Justice Department initiated over two thousand prosecutions under the acts resulting in the incarceration of nine hundred persons during the nineteen months of American involvement in World War I. Many of the famous radicals—Eugene Debs and Emma Goldman, for example—were imprisoned or deported.

The oppressive rampage was not limited to the socialists and communists, however. Anarchist Ricardo Flores Magon was sentenced to twenty years in prison for publishing a statement criticizing Wilson's policies in Mexico (where there was much to criticize, but space limits us from elaborating here) that were completely separate from the issue of United States involvement in the

▶ Under the Sedition Act of 1918 authorities gained the right to arrest and incarcerate people suspected of being communists or socialists. Many of the famous radicals such as Emma Goldman (left) were imprisoned or deported.

Great War. One woman, Sarah Parker, received a five-year prison sentence for writing, "I am for the people, and the government is for the profiteers." Movie producer Robert Goldstein, who had made a film about the American Revolution entitled *Spirit of '76*, was sentenced to ten years in prison because his film's depiction of atrocities committed by the British during the American Revolution was deemed by a judge to be a violation of the Espionage Act under the pretense that it might lead the public to "question the good faith of our ally, Great Britain."

The Lost Peace

As early as the spring of 1916, President Wilson had committed himself both to a liberal peace and to American participation in a postwar league of nations. He had amplified this program in his "Peace without Victory" speech of January 22, 1917, and had spelled out its details in the memorable "Fourteen Points" address a year later.[1] Wilson, in the first week of December 1918, departed for the peace conference in Paris where a crowd of over one million people greeted him to a hero's welcome. Wilson was less of a hero both to the Republicans in the United States Senate and to the European diplomats, however. The Republican-controlled Senate was miffed that Wilson had ignored the "advice" portion of the Constitutional "advice and consent of the Senate" provision of the United States Constitution. This was in spite of the fact that no president had sought Senate advice in making a treaty since George Washington. When Washington had done so, he became so frustrated at the Senate's bickering that he remarked, "I'll be damned if I ever go in there again;" and he never did. European leaders, Georges Clemenceau of France and David Lloyd George of England, favored punitive measures against Germany in direct contradiction of Wilson's "peace without victory" principle. Nevertheless, Wilson remained determined to impose this program on the Allies in spite of their secret treaties for the division of the German, Austro-Hungarian, and Turkish empires.

The president faced imposing obstacles. A narrow Republican victory in the congressional elections, in November 1918, had weakened his moral authority. Many Republicans had already expressed opposition to his program; and Roosevelt and Lodge would soon write Prime

---

1 Wilson's "Fourteen Points," pronounced on January 8, 1918, may be paraphrased as follows:

I. "Open covenants openly arrived at"

II. Freedom of the seas in peace and in war alike

III. The removal of all economic barriers and the establishment of an equality of trade conditions among all nations

IV. Reduction of national armaments

V. A readjustment of all colonial claims, giving the interests of the population concerned equal weight with the claims of the ruling government

VI. The evacuation of foreign troops from Russian territory and the independent determination by Russia of its own political development and national policy

VII. The evacuation of foreign troops and restoration of Belgium

VIII. The evacuation of foreign troops and restoration of France and the return of Alsace-Lorraine

IX. A readjustment of the frontiers of Italy along national lines

X. Self-determination for the peoples of Austria-Hungary

XI. Evacuation of foreign troops from Rumania, Serbia, and Montenegro and access to the sea for Serbia

XII. Self-determination for the peoples under Turkish rule and freedom of the Dardanelles under international guarantee

XIII. The independence of Poland, with free access to the sea guaranteed by international covenant

XIV. The formation of a general association of nations (i.e. the League of Nations) under specific covenants for the purpose of affording mutual guarantees of political independence and territorial integrity to great and small states alike

Minister David Lloyd George of Great Britain and Premier Georges Clemenceau of France that Wilson did not speak for the American people. Undoubtedly, Wilson did not speak for England or France. Clemenceau perhaps best summed the European attitude when he proclaimed that, "God has given us 10 Commandments and we have been unable to keep them. Wilson has given us 14 points. We shall see."

The president reached France convinced, nevertheless, that he might well deliver all Europe from the tyranny of history. Triumphal tours of Paris, London, and Rome confirmed his sense of mission. "Wilson heard from his carriage, something different, inhuman or super human," wrote a correspondent who had seen other leaders of the age on parade. Hardly conscious of the fear, lust, and vindictiveness that would shatter his hopes, he sat down with Lloyd George, Clemenceau, and Vittono Orlando of Italy to forge a lasting peace.

The president first rejected a proposal by the French, who were obsessed with the need for security against Germany, to convert the west bank of the Rhine into buffer states under French control; but he did agree that the west bank should be permanently demilitarized and occupied by the Allies for fifteen years. He also acquiesced in the return of Alsace-Lorraine to France, the reduction of the German army and navy to cadre strength, and the mandating of Germany's colonies to victor nations under the League of Nations. Finally, he won Clemenceau's acceptance of the League idea by agreeing to join Britain and France in a defense treaty against Germany.

At Paris, Wilson also opposed expansion of Allied intervention in Siberia, where the British, Americans, French, and Japanese had sent troops in the summer of 1919. Point VI of the Fourteen Points had called for the evacuation of foreign troops from Russia in order to give Russia "an unhampered and unembarrassed opportunity for the independent determination of her own political development and national policy." Though Wilson had reluctantly supported the anti-Bolshevik campaign in Siberia with American troops, he feared that the intervention would backfire by strengthening the Russian people's support of the Bolsheviks.

Actually, he hoped that the Bolshevik government would be supplanted by a liberal-democratic-capitalist regime such as he envisioned for the entire world, including Japan and China. To that end, he instituted a policy of non-recognition of Soviet Russia that persisted until 1933.

More victories and more concessions followed. A new Poland was created without violating unduly the principle of self-determination. Italy gained control of the Brenner Pass for security reasons, but not a long strip of the Dalmatian coast, including Fiume, which it had requested; and the Covenant of the League of Nations was firmly embedded in the peace treaty. On the other hand, though Wilson desired "peace without victory," England and France demanded—and achieved—a settlement of, $56 billion in war reparations against Germany. Germany, therefore, faced a potentially astronomical reparations bill and was compelled to admit war guilt. German Pacific colonies were given to Japan, who had taken them in the war and refused to relinquish them to the League of Nations. More important still, economic barriers within Europe and throughout the world remained intact.

Wilson did get, however, his League of Nations; and he prevented the Allies from splitting up Germany into several smaller states. The Versailles Treaty created new states of Yugoslavia, Poland, Austria, Hungary, and Czechoslovakia, based on Wilson's principle of

▶ President Wilson had committed himself both to a liberal peace and to American participation in a postwar league of nations. He also prevented the Allies from splitting up Germany into several smaller states. The Versailles Treaty created new states of Yugoslavia, Poland, Austria, Hungary, and Czechoslovakia.

self-determination, and the League of Nations would manage the German and Ottoman possessions until they were ready for self-rule. Thus, Wilson had won considerably more than his critics later conceded, though a great deal less than he had hoped.

The president returned to the United States on July 8, 1919, and threw down the gauntlet two days later. "Our isolation was ended twenty years ago," he warned the Senate. "There can be no question of our ceasing to be a world power. The only question is whether we can refuse the moral leadership that is offered, whether we shall accept or reject the confidence of the world."

Wilson's words fell on a divided country. The German-Americans and their powerful journalistic ally, the Hearst press, opposed the treaty's harshness toward Germany. Italian-Americans were unhappy over Wilson's refusal to allow Italy to take Fiume. Irish-Americans mounted a virulent opposition because of President Wilson's failure to support the movement for Ireland's independence. Furthermore, a small group of sincere and irreconcilable isolationists in the Senate pledged themselves to the complete defeat of the treaty because of the provision for the League of Nations. Many intellectuals and idealists also revolted. "The European politicians who with American complicity have hatched this inhuman monster," said the New Republic, "have acted either cynically, hypocritically or vindictively." Opponents argued that the treaty ignored freedom of the seas, a major principle that had brought the United States into the war in the first place. Conservatives opposed the idea of disarmament as a violation of sovereignty and a naïve measure that sacrificed America's security. In the words of Senator Albert Beverage of Indiana: "The League of Nations is the work of amiable old grannies, who over their afternoon tea, are planning to denationalize America's manhood." Conversely, some progressives argued that the League of Nations could not possibly work if it excluded Bolshevik Russia.

Nevertheless, Wilson might still have won the fight for ratification had he not been so uncompromising. Wilson revealed his attitude in the matter by stating, "Anyone who opposes me I'll crush. The Senate must take its medicine." The Republican Senators, however, had no inten-

MAP 22.3 Europe After Versailles

tion of taking their "medicine." Senator Henry Cabot Lodge and a small group of pro-war Republican nationalists feared that the League, by raising false hopes, would compromise the balance-of-power foreign policy that they had always deemed essential to the nation's security. William Borah of Idaho perhaps best summed up the feelings of the opposition when he stated, "I would vote against the League if Jesus Christ returned to the earth to argue in its behalf."

More than two thirds of the Senate approved the League Covenant in broad principle; and the president received a tremendous response as he traveled through the American West in September of 1919. Wilson believed that the fight for the Versailles Treaty and the League of Nations was one that he must win. "My clients are the children; my clients are the next generation," he exclaimed with tears in his eyes to a cheering throng in Pueblo, Colorado. "I intend to redeem my pledges to the children; they shall not be sent [to France]." Seven days after this memorable peroration, the president suffered a devastating stroke that paralyzed his left side. Wilson lost most of his ability to speak and other cognitive abilities and would remain bed-ridden for the rest of his presidency. Edith Wilson tightly controlled access to the president and other close aids, and the country essentially went on without its president for the next year and a half.

While Wilson battled with the health catastrophe that would eventually take his life, the political battle over the Versailles Treaty now ground slowly to its tragic end. Lodge, as chairman of the foreign relations committee, presented the treaty to the Senate on November 6 for approval, subject to Fourteen Reservations to match Wilson's Fourteen Points. Lodge's reservations essentially allowed the United States to opt out of the treaty's provisions in cases where American sovereignty was compromised. Elihu Root had suggested the most important one earlier. It asserted that the United States assumed no obligations under Article X of the League Covenant to preserve the territorial integrity or political independence of any country, to interfere in controversies between nations, or to use its armed forces to uphold any of the articles of the treaty for any purpose, unless Congress by joint resolution so provided.

The ailing president refused to accept the Lodge reservations on the grounds that they crippled the Covenant. From his bedside, Wilson urged the Democrats in the Senate to reject the Versailles Treaty with Lodge's reservations. Democrats, on November 19, dutifully followed his command and voted against the treaty with reservations. Their vote was sufficient to prevent approval.

Pro-League sentiment throughout the country proved so strong that the Treaty was brought to a second vote on March 19, 1920. By this time Wilson had recovered sufficiently to take an active part in the controversy. "Either we should enter the League fearlessly," he wrote in a public letter, "accepting the responsibility and not fearing the role of leadership which we now enjoy … or we should retire as gracefully as possible from the great concert of powers by which the world was saved." If the Senate failed to ratify without crippling reservations, he concluded, the election of 1920 should then be a "great and solemn referendum" on the issue. In spite of—perhaps because of—Wilson's last stand, the Senate again refused to approve ratification of the Versailles Treaty. Republicans voted down the Treaty without Reservations, and Democrats voted against the Treaty with Reservations; the Treaty was never ratified by the Senate, and the United States never joined the League of Nations.

Most historians doubt that American participation in the League of Nations would have altered more than the tone of postwar foreign affairs. The division between Wilsonian internationalists and conservative isolationists would rage throughout the interwar period. The punitive measures in the Versailles Treaty against Germany and the chaotic economic and political situation in Germany following World War I, which led to the rise of the right-wing Nazi Party, may have occurred regardless of American participation in the League of Nations; given the course of events over the next quarter-century, however, it is clear that the failure to forge a lasting peace at the end of the Great War was an opportunity lost.

Spanish Flu Pandemic

As if to add insult to injury, the death and destruction that was the Great War was followed by an influenza pandemic in 1918–1919 that resulted in more deaths than the Great War, with estimates ranging between twenty and forty million people. As such, the Spanish Flu

▶ U.S. soldiers returning from World War I parade through a Minneapolis street.

pandemic of 1918–1919 has been cited as the most devastating epidemic in recorded world history. In the two years that the pandemic raged, it is estimated that the flu infected up to 20 percent of the world's population; and it infected an estimated 28 percent of all Americans, causing 675,000 American deaths. Of the U.S. soldiers who died in Europe, it is estimated that up to 50 percent died from the influenza virus. Although the cause of the pandemic cannot be determined with certainty, it is reasonable to conclude that the Great War, with its mass movements of men in armies and aboard ships, along with the conditions of trench warfare, probably aided in the flu's rapid diffusion and attack. In the final analysis, it is possible that the Great War was so devastating and destructive that it disturbed nature itself, with disastrous consequences for humans. Thus, the Spanish Flu became one more reminder to many Americans and others throughout the world that such a war should be avoided at all costs as the twentieth century's tumultuous second decade passed into the history books.

▶ ▶ ▶

Chapter Review

Summary

At the time of the outbreak of World War I in 1914, Europe was divided into two great alliances, the Triple Alliance consisting of Germany, Austria-Hungary, and Italy, and the Triple Entente, consisting of England, France, and Russia. The purpose of both alliances ostensibly was to keep the peace, and the idea of both alliances was that an armed attack on one was an armed attack on all. There were circumstances in Europe at the time that threatened to undermine the peace as each great power on the continent had either territorial or security ambitions that threatened one or several of the others. Perhaps, most importantly, Germany feared the breakup of its neighbor to the east, the Austro-Hungarian Empire, whom the Germans viewed as a friendly "buffer" between themselves and their enemies, the Russians, to the east. When Archduke Ferdinand and his wife were assassinated on June 28, 1914, in Sarajevo by a Serbian nationalist, the Germans offered their full support to Austria in an invasion of Serbia in an effort to ensure the preservation of the Austro-Hungarian Empire. Russia, however, in its traditional role as "defenders of the slavs" mobilized its army to defend Serbia. In a chain reaction of events at the beginning of August 1914, all of the great powers of Europe were suddenly at war, each for its own territorial ambitions or security concerns.

The war quickly stalemated into bloody trench warfare, and the war became a war of attrition. Both Germany and England lacked self-sufficiency in food and fuel; consequently, the first to run out of food or fuel would lose. Britain, with the most powerful navy, blockaded Europe in an effort to cut off German food and fuel and violated American rights as a neutral to trade with the rest of Europe. Germany, with an inferior navy but with the invention of the submarine, announced that it would sink all ships bound for Britain in an effort to cut off British food and fuel. German submarine warfare (especially the sinking of the *Lusitania*), however, violated international law (formulated before the invention of the submarine) and shocked the American conscience.

Although Wilson had proclaimed that America would be neutral in thought as well as deed, America was neutral in neither as Wilson favored the English for his own prejudices. American loans and war orders to the Allies threw the United States into the Allies' camp from the start. When Germany, short on food and fuel, resumed sinking all ships in February 1917 in the hopes of defeating the French and British before the Americans arrived, it was a calculated gamble that the Germans lost. Not only were England and France not defeated but also the U.S. arrived in Europe six months before the Germans anticipated. The Germans were then forced to accept an Armistice on November 11, 1918, knowing that they could not win, only lose.

Unfortunately, while the U.S. was making the world safe for democracy abroad, democracy was compromised at home as the Espionage Act and Sedition Act squelched American democratic freedoms at home. vigilantes preyed on citizens that they deemed to be disloyal. The American government under Wilson autocratically took over the economy and converted it to war production while Wilson's Committee on Public Information sold the war to the American public with slanted information.

President Woodrow Wilson had introduced his 14 Points in January 1917, outlining his vision for the postwar order, but his 14 Points generally failed at Versailles, where France and England demanded punitive measures against Germany. Although Wilson did get his League of Nations, the Allies imposed $56 billion in reparations on Germany that Germany could not pay. Furthermore, Republicans in the Senate opposed the League of Nations as an infringement on American sovereignty and attached 14 Reservations to the Versailles Treaty, thus allowing America to opt out of the Treaty in cases where it eroded American sovereignty. Wilson, who suffered a massive stroke in September 1919, opposed the Versailles Treaty with the Reservations. Republicans, however, voted down the treaty without Reservations. Thus the U.S. did not ratify the Versailles Treaty and never joined the League of Nations. In perhaps the final saga of World War I, a Spanish Flu pandemic of 1918–1919 killed approximately 675,000 Americans and twenty to forty million people worldwide.

Chronological Time Line

1870 Germany unified as one country, but Austria was left out of the union.

1870 Germany defeated France in a war and took Alsace Loraine.

1870 Italy unified as a country, but the Tyrol remained in Austria.

1906 Austria took Bosnia from Serbia in a war in the Balkans.

1913 England switched its navy from coal to oil power.

1914 June 28: Austrian heir to the throne Archduke Ferdinand and his wife were assassinated in Sarajevo by a Serbian nationalist.

1914 July 28: Austria-Hungary invaded Serbia, beginning World War I.

1914 July 30: Germany mobilized its army.

1914 August 1: France mobilized its army against Germany.

1914 August 1: Germany declared war on Russia.

1914 August 4: Britain declared war on Germany.

1915 February 4: Germany announced its intention to sink all ships in a war zone around England.

Chapter Review (cont'd)

Time Line (cont'd)

1915	March: Wilson allowed the Morgan banking house to extend $50 million in credit to the French government, beginning American loans to the Allies.
1915	April 26: Italy entered the war on the side of Triple Entente.
1915	May 7: Germany sank the Lusitania killing 1,198 people, including 124 Americans.
1915	August 19: Germany sank the British liner *Arabic*.
1916	Germany sank the French steamer *Sussex*.
1916	November: Woodrow Wilson won reelection on a peace platform.
1916	December: Wilson asked the Europeans on what terms they would accept peace.
1917	January: Wilson outlined his vision for the post-war world.
1917	January 31: Germany resumed sinking all ships and launched a new offensive against France in an effort to win before America could arrive.
1917	February 3: Germany sink USS *Housatonic.*
1917	February 25: British delivered the Zimmerman Telegram to the U.S.
1917	Wilson armed merchant ships by Executive Order.
1917	March 15: Democratic reformers led by Alexander Kerensky deposed Czar Nicholas II in Russia.
1917	March 19: Three U.S. ships were sunk.
1917	April 2: Wilson asked Congress for a Declaration of War to "make the world safe for democracy."
1917	April 6: Congress declared war on Germany.
1917	April 13: Lenin arrived in Russia.

Time Line (cont'd)

1917 May: Congress passed Selective Service.

1917 June: Congress passed the Espionage Act making it a crime to aid the enemy or obstruct the U.S. war effort.

1917 October: The first American troops arrived on the Western Front in Europe.

1917 October: Congress passed the "Trading with the Enemy Act" prohibiting trade with Germany or its Allies.

1917 November 7: Bolshevik Revolution in Russia ousted the Kerensky government.

1917 December: Bolsheviks signed the Armistice with Germany.

1918–1919 Spanish Flu Pandemic killed 675,000 Americans and twenty to forty million people worldwide.

1918 Wilson announced his Fourteen Points.

1918 May: Congress passed the Sedition Act declaring it illegal to utter, print, write, or publish, any disloyal, profane, scurrilous, or abusive language about the government, Constitution, or armed forces.

1918 November 11: Armistice was signed, ending hostilities in World War I.

1918 December: Wilson departed for France to negotiate the Versailles Treaty.

1919 September: Wilson had a massive stroke.

1919 November 19: Democrats in the Senate rejected the Versailles Treaty with Republican Reservations attached.

1920 March 19: Republicans in the Senate rejected the Versailles Treaty without their Reservations attached.

Chapter Review (cont'd)

Key Terms

Triple Alliance: Security alliance between Germany, Italy, and the Austro-Hungarian Empire

Triple Entente: Security alliance between England, France, and Russia

Kaiser Wilhelm II: Monarch of Germany during World War I

Alsace-Loraine: Coal rich region on the French/German border taken by Germany militarily in 1870

Austro-Hungarian Empire: Loose conglomeration in Central Europe including what is now Austria, Hungary, Poland, Czech Republic, Slovakia, Slovenia, and Bosnia

Otto Von Bismarck: Chancellor of Germany after its unification in 1870

Balkans: The states on the Balkan Peninsula including Serbia and Bosnia where World War I began

Serbia: Balkan state attacked by Austria in retaliation for the assassination of Archduke Ferdinand

Revolution from Above: Italy's revolution of 1912 that was instigated by the upper classes

Tyrol: Border area between Austria and Italy that was coveted by Italy prior to World War I

Defenders of the Slavs: Russia's foreign policy approach that committed Russia to the defense of any Slavic country that is attacked

Archduke Francis Ferdinand: Heir to the throne of Austria whose assassination was the spark that ignited World War I

Belgian Neutrality: Pre-war international agreement among the powers of Europe that Belgium would be neutral in any war

Ottoman Empire: What is present-day Turkey that entered World War I on the side of Germany out of desire for territory in Russia

Lusitania: Luxury passenger liner that was sunk by Germany in May 1915, killing 1198 people including 124 Americans

Preparedness: Wilson's military buildup prior to World War I

Election of 1916: Wilson defeated Charles Evans Hughes on a peace platform five months before leading the U.S. into World War I.

Zimmerman Note: Note from German foreign minister Arthur Zimmerman to Venustiano Carranza promising land in the Southwestern U.S. to Mexico if Mexico will join World War I against the U.S.

Selective Service: Wilson's military draft begun in May 1917 that provided three million of the five million Americans that served in World War I

Jeannette Rankin: The only member of Congress that voted against both the Declaration of War in 1917 and the Declaration of War in 1941

Trench Warfare: The fighting method on the Western Front in World War I that led to stalemate and slaughter

Verdun: Battle in France from February-December 1916 that resulted in one million combined casualties

The Somme: Battle in France from July–November 1916 that resulted in a combined six hundred thousand deaths

V. I. Lenin: Leader of Bolshevik Russia that pulled Russia out of World War I

Key Terms (cont'd)

Bolshevik Revolution: Communist revolution in November 1917 that ousted the Democratic government of Alexander Kerensky and installed Communist rule

Doughboys: American soldiers in World War I

War Industries Board: World War I agency that was established by Woodrow Wilson and put in charge of converting American industry to war production

Manfred Von Richtoven: Also known as "The Red Baron," he was World War I's greatest ace who is credited with shooting down eighty Allied planes.

Eddie Rickenbacker: America's greatest World War I ace who shot down twenty-seven German planes

Alvin York: America's greatest hero of World War I who killed seventeen Germans with seventeen bullets and captured 132 Germans single-handedly

Zeppelins: Giant hydrogen air ships used by Germany to bomb England

Poison Gas: Chemical weapons of several types, including mustard gas and nerve gas used by both sides in World War I

Veteran's Administration: Bureaucratic agency in charge of health care needs of World War I veterans

Liberty Bonds: Sold by the U.S. government to U.S. citizens to finance World War I

Committee on Public Information: Propaganda Agency created by Woodrow Wilson to sell the war to the American people

Vigilantes: Groups and individuals that harassed their fellow citizens that they believed to be disloyal

Espionage Act: Passed in June 1917, making it a crime to aid the enemy or obstruct the U.S. war effort

Sedition Act: Passed in May 1918, declaring it illegal to utter, print, write, or publish, any disloyal, profane, scurrilous, or abusive language about the government, Constitution, or armed forces

Fourteen Points: Wilson's points that explained his vision for the postwar world in January 1918

Versailles Treaty: Treaty officially ending World War I and creating the League of Nations, but never ratified by the U.S.

Reparations: The $56 billion burden the Allies placed on Germany in the Versailles Treaty, forcing Germany to pay for the damage caused by World War I.

Self-Determination: The idea that people living in any particular location should be able to decide for themselves who should be sovereign over them

League of Nations: International organization established by the Versailles Treaty to manage international relations and keep the peace

Henry Cabot Lodge: Republican Senator that attached 14 Reservations to the Versailles Treaty

Fourteen Reservations: Republican attachments to the Versailles Treaty allowing the U.S. to opt out of its provisions

Spanish Flu: Pandemic of 1918–1919 that led to the deaths of 675,000 Americans and twenty to forty million people worldwide

Pandemic: Global epidemic

Pop Quiz

Chapter 22

1. Prior to the Great War, Europe was divided into two military alliances, the Triple Alliance and the __________.
   a. Triple Entente
   b. Triple Conference
   c. Pact of Steel
   d. Triple Axis

2. Whid did German Chancellor Otto Von Bismarck leave the Austrians out of German unification in 1870?
   a. The Austrians had ambitions in the Balkans.
   b. He predicted that an evil dictator would someday arise out of Austria.
   c. The Austrians were not Germans.
   d. He predicted that the Austrians would follow the treasonous rebellion of Captain Von Trapp and his former nun wife, Maria.

3. Russia mobilized its army to defend Serbia under Peter the Great's definition of Russia as __________.
   a. "Defenders of the Slavs"
   b. the "Containers" of German aggression
   c. the "Vanguard of the Proletariat"
   d. the "Evil Empire"

4. The British strategy to win the war included which of the following?
   a. daily bombing raids of Berlin
   b. the development of nuclear weapons
   c. a blockade of Europe to cut off German supplies of food and fuel
   d. staging an attack on the U.S. and blaming Germany

5. Why did Secretary of State William Jennings Bryan resign in 1915?
   a. He realized that Wilson would get a second term, and he himself would be too old to run for president if he had to wait until 1920.
   b. He favored an immediate war declaration after the sinking of the *Lusitania*.
   c. He opposed Wilson's policy of shipping military goods on passenger liners.
   d. He believed that Germany should be able to sink all the ships they wanted to during wartime.

6. Wilson requested a declaration of war from Congress to __________.
   a. eliminate weapons of mass destruction in Germany
   b. bring freedom to the German people

Pop Quiz (cont'd)

c. make the world safe for Democracy
d. create regime change in Germany

7. What was the importance of the Bolshevik Revolution for the Germans in World War I?
   a. It allowed them to sign a separate peace with Russia and shift six hundred thousand troops to the Western front.
   b. It meant that East Germany would be communist and controlled by Russia.
   c. Germany had to shift six hundred thousand troops to the Eastern front to fight communists.
   d. Kaiser Wilhelm's government was no longer the stupidest in Europe.

8. Herbert Hoover, the director of the War Food Administration, stimulated production by ___________.
   a. pegging prices
   b. letting the free market work
   c. lowering agricultural prices
   d. asking people to voluntarily pay more for agricultural products

9. The greatest American "ace" of the war was ___________.
   a. Manfred Von Richtoven
   b. Alvin York
   c. Eddie Rickenbacker
   d. Wrong-Way Feldman

10. Which of the following occurred during World War I?
    a. The German department at University of Texas was closed to promote "purer Americanism."
    b. Free speech protections were expanded and cherished.
    c. Vigilante groups were essentially wiped out by the U.S. government.
    d. Blacks achieved full citizenship rights thanks to their participation in the war.

11. What was one problem that Wilson faced at the Versailles Conference?
    a. The representative from Bolshevik Russia opposed most of his proposals.
    b. France and England desired to spend too much money rebuilding Germany.
    c. His negotiations were undermined by opposition from American Republican Party leaders.
    d. Mexico demanded the return of the territory it lost in 1848.

Chapter Review (cont'd)

Pop Quiz (cont'd)

12. Which of the following is true of the conclusion of the Senate debates over the Versailles Treaty?
    a. The Senate approved the Treaty with Reservations.
    b. The Senate approved the Treaty without Reservations.
    c. Pro-League sentiment in the country was so strong that the Treaty was brought to a second vote, on March 19, 1920.
    d. The U.S. joined the League of Nations.

13. Wilson decided to go to war in 1917 hoping that American troops would bring a quick end to the conflict. T F

14. The American economy came under almost complete government control during the war. T F

15. After the sinking of the *Lusitania,* Secretary of State William Jennings Bryan resigned because Wilson refused to ask for a declaration of war. T F

1. A	5. C	9. C	13. T
2. A	6. C	10. A	14. T
3. A	7. A	11. C	15. F
4. C	8. A	12. C	

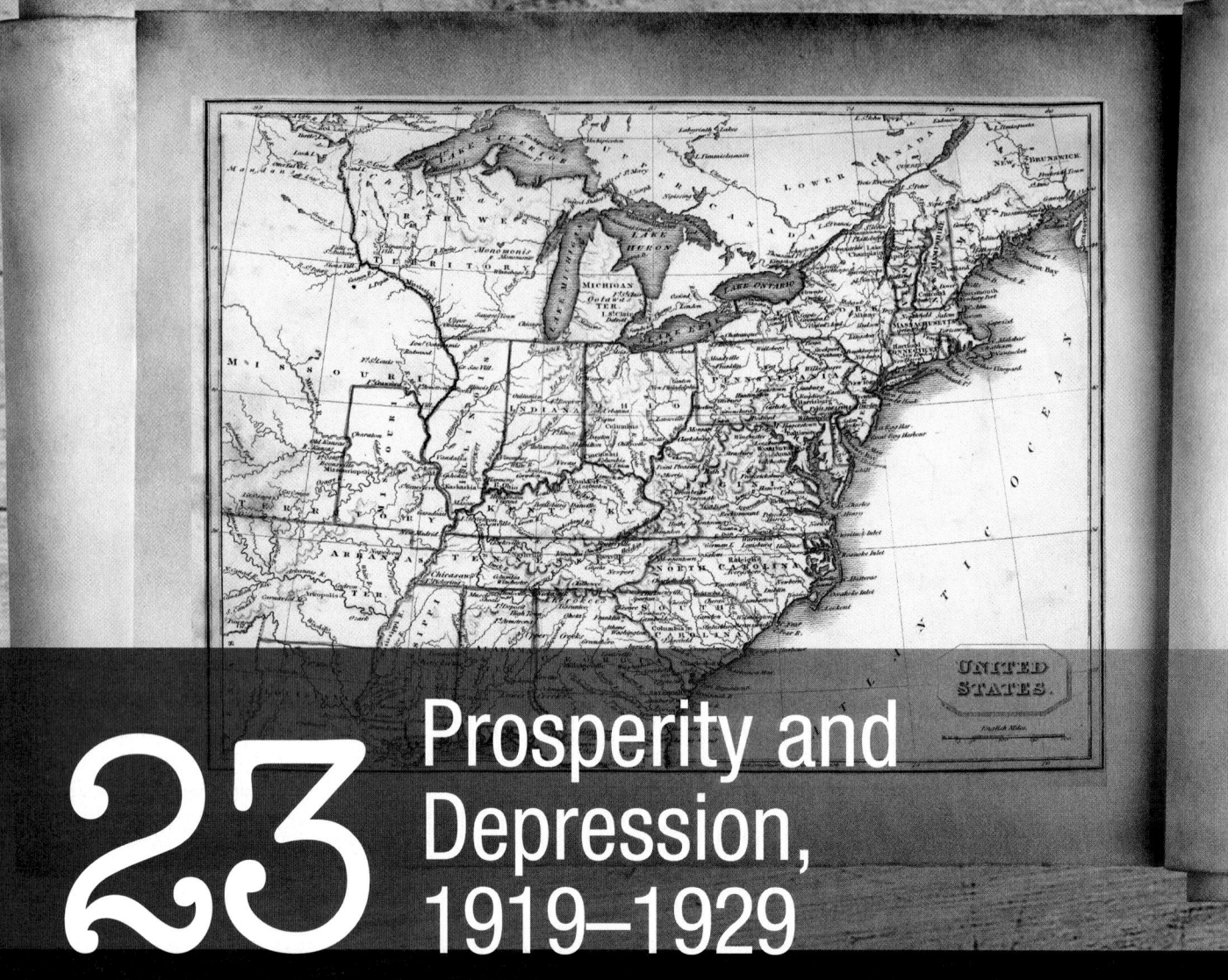

23 Prosperity and Depression, 1919–1929

Chapter Objectives

The Swing Toward Conservatism

- Demobilization
- The Red Scare
- Repression of African Americans
- The Klan
- Immigration Quotas
- Triumph of the Conservatives
- Warren G. Harding
- Harding and the Ohio Gang
- Republican National Policy

Expansion of Government

- Federal, State, and Local Change
- Security in the Pacific
- High Tariffs
- War Debts
- Republican Leadership Reaffirmed
- Calvin Coolidge

High Hopes for a Prosperous Nation

Postwar Economic Change

The Decline of Craft Unionism

Industrial Distress

Agricultural Depression

A Slower Rate of Growth

Technological Advance

The New Era in Business

Managerial Enterprise

Shaping Public Opinion

Stock Market Boom and Bust

The Swing Toward Conservatism

Nineteen-nineteen was a year of disillusionment in America. During the war progressives, once satisfied with social legislation and national regulation of trusts, had raised their hopes for such fundamental changes as federal control of railroads, shipping, prices, and employment. John Dewey, America's most famous philosopher, had predicted in 1918, "no matter how many among the special agencies for public control decay with the disappearance of war stress, the movement will never go backward." In spite of Dewey's bold pronouncement, during 1919, however, the Progressive movement toward a publicly regulated economy not only receded but also was lost altogether in a wave of reaction.

Like all sweeping changes in opinion, the swing to conservatism between early 1919 and 1920 had many causes. The unsatisfactory peace in Europe, publicized in the worst light by opponents of the League of Nations, cooled the popular enthusiasm that President Wilson had temporarily aroused. The result appears to have been apathy about America's role in world affairs that carried over into domestic issues as well.

Along with this indifference to further reform was, undoubtedly, a real fear on the part of middle-class Americans that revolution on the Russian model might spread. Socialism had ceased to be a utopian goal, safe to discuss at social club meetings, and had instead become a gray, alien world of commissars and secret police. As a result, the unprecedented series of strikes used by labor in 1919 to keep wages abreast of soaring prices was widely regarded as a dangerous indication of revolutionary sentiment, inspired by the subversive activities of a foreign power. In some cases, management publicly condemned the strikers as Reds, and demagogic politicians manipulated public fears to their advantage.

Demobilization

At the close of the Great War, the war boards that Wilson had hastily put together—to convert the economy to wartime production—quickly relinquished control of the economy to the free market with predictable harsh dislocations. Wilson had naively assumed that the economy would adjust itself without complications; however, World War I had brought high wages and record profits, which along with a shortage of consumer goods produced record personal savings. When the free market was unleashed, the buying public was all too eager to unleash their savings in the form of consumption with the result that there were too many dollars chasing too few goods in the marketplace, thus creating rapid inflation. The American cost of living increased 50 percent from the end of the war to 1921; wages were unable to keep pace, thereby precipitating a wave of strikes. Over four million American workers, some 20 percent of the workforce, were on strike at one time or another during 1919, and in some cases paralyzed American industry and international trade.

In spite of the fact that the primary reason for the strikes was that wages had not kept up with inflation, American business managers generally argued, the media reported, and the public believed that the strikes were the result of communist agitation. Perhaps the most famouns strike of all in 1919 was the strike of the Boston police force. Massachusetts' Governor, Calvin Coolidge,became a hero among conservatives during the strike by putting down the strike with a force of Harvard University students and United States Army veterans. Coolidge dismissed the striking policemen and refused to reinstate them, proclaiming, "there is no right to strike against the public safety by anybody, anywhere, any time."

The Red Scare

Though communist agitation was not the precipitant for the strikes in 1919, it is true that communist activity in the United States at the time was perhaps greater in scope that at any time in American history, even though it was greatly overblown by the media and a paranoid public on the heels of the Bolshevik Revolution in Russia and World War I. Of course, political demagogues were ready to ride to power by playing upon such fears.

The political violence, which precipitated the conservative reactionary backlash that became known as the "Red Scare," began during an international shipping strike in 1919 when a bomb was sent to the home of the mayor of Seattle, who had opposed the labor union activity in Seattle shipyards. Although the Seattle bomb did not detonate, it provided more evidence for the American people that dangerous left-wing radicals dominated the labor unions. Labor Unions had been connected with bombs, political radicalism, communism, and anarchism in the minds of American conservatives ever since the Chicago Haymarket riot of 1886, where four anarchist labor leaders were executed for a bomb that killed seven policemen at a labor rally. The Haymarket affair combined with other violence-filled strikes, such as the American Railway Union sympathetic strike against the Pullman Palace Car Company and the Homestead Steel strike (both in 1892), to indelibly etch into the minds of Americans the connection between labor unions and left-wing political violence.

In 1919, the conservative perception of labor unions as organizations of communist and anarchist "bomb-throwing radicals" was greatly reinforced, not only by the Seattle bomb, but also by the discovery by the United States Post Office of sixteen bombs that were not delivered due to insufficient postage. A subsequent examination revealed that each was addressed to prominent persons such as John D. Rockefeller, Oliver Wendell Holmes, and Attorney General A. Mitchell Palmer. In April 1919, a bomb was delivered and detonated that blew the hands off of the maid of a former Georgia senator, Thomas Hardwick, who was known to be anti-union. In June, a bomb destroyed the front of the home of United States Attorney General A. Mitchell Palmer. The damage to Palmer's home could have been much worse; but the bomber's plan went awry when he apparently tripped on Palmer's porch, dropped the bomb, and blew himself to pieces. The bombing of Palmer's house was followed by several other bombings, suggesting to many that the terror activity was widespread. In all, seven bombs were detonated in five states.

Congress and the American public demanded that something be done about the terror, and the United States Senate passed a motion of censure against Attorney General Palmer for his inaction. After the bombing of his home, however, Palmer launched an unparalleled crusade against the terrorists and organized an anti-radical division within the Justice Department.

Palmer then put J. Edgar Hoover in charge of coordinating the anti-radical division's activities and ensuring that safeguarding the Constitutional rights of the terror suspects received a low priority. In November 1919, the Justice Department rounded up and detained 250 members of the Union of Russian Workers. Thirty-three of the Russian workers were severely beaten by Justice Department officers, suggesting gross rights violations, but the raids were popular with the public. The next month, 249 aliens were deported for being "threats to the government," including the famed left-wing feminist, Emma Goldman. Palmer's raids were a tremendous success with the American people and the American press who applauded Palmer's actions. The *Washington Post* perhaps summed up the views of many Americans well when it argued, "there is no time to waste on hairsplitting over infringement of liberty."

On January 2, 1920, Palmer ordered hundreds of federal agents to thirty-three American cities to destroy the imagined Bolshevik conspiracy. In all, Palmer and Hoover's agents arrested six thousand individuals on charges of conspiracy to overthrow the United States government. In furtherance of his crusade, Palmer attempted to alter basic criminal rights protections, a clear sacrifice of principles in the service of a desired end in a manner consistent with the arguments of the *Washington Post*. Specifically, Palmer attempted to persuade Secretary of Labor William B. Wilson to amend a portion of the deportation law that allowed suspects to secure counsel. He also requested a blanket deportation warrant to cover any aliens discovered once a raid had commenced. President Wilson refused these abuses of individual liberties; but while Wilson was on sick leave, one of his underlings, John W. Abercrombie, provided the changes that Palmer requested. Rights to counsel and habeas corpus, along with the rule that suspects had to be informed of the charges against them, were suspended for those arrested by Palmer's men.

Armed with the blanket suspensions of civil liberties, Palmer's abuses were legion. In Detroit, carrying with them three thousand blank mimeographed warrants (with the names to be filled in later), Palmer's men arrested and jailed eight hundred people. It is certain that the experience was at least uncomfortable for those arrested since eight hundred detainees were allowed access to only one toilet for the entire group. In Boston, similar raids jailed another eight hundred people. In New Jersey, one man was arrested simply because he "looked like an alien," and the practice of arresting people simply because of how they looked was essentially encouraged by the Attorney General himself. In the words of Palmer:

> "Out of the sly and crafty eyes of many of them leap cupidity, cruelty, insanity, and crime; from their lopsided faces, sloping brows, and misshapen features may be recognized the unmistakable criminal type."

In all, six thousand people were arrested, and 556 were deported by the end of 1920; and Palmer had lists with over two hundred thousand names as suspects. In spite of his gross abuses, Palmer briefly became a national hero for "ferreting out communists." Many Americans agreed with Christian evangelist Billy Sunday, who argued, "The best solution is to shoot aliens rather than deport them."

Regardless, all of the activity from Palmer's Justice Department was carried out without any supporting or enabling legislation from Congress. Palmer appeared before a congressional committee and asked for legislation authorizing the suppression of sedition during

▶ Those determined to be aliens during the "Red Scare" were deported for being "threats to the government." Many Americans agreed with popular, Christian evangelist Billy Sunday, (far left) who argued, "The best solution is to shoot aliens rather than deport them."

peacetime. Seventy bills were pending in Congress within five months of his request; but none of the measures passed. Palmer's paranoid zeal, however, would eventually become his own undoing as his over-reactive brutal raids began to stir the public conscience. In the words of William Preston:

> "The net was so wide and bureau detectives were so careless that some ten thousand persons were arrested including many citizens and many individuals not members of either party. Abuse of due process characterized the early stages of the drive. This ill-treatment proceeded from the official decision to protect undercover informers. Indiscriminate arrests of the innocent with the guilty, unlawful searches and seizures by federal detectives, intimidating preliminary interrogation of aliens held incommunicado, high-handed levying of excessive bail, and denial of counsel were the government's response to stiffening alien radical resistance to deportation."

Additionally, less than ten percent of arrests led to deportation, suggesting that the threat was overblown. Palmer's raids uncovered no explosives and confiscated only three pistols in six thousand arrests.

Finally, Palmer discredited himself by making the mistake of playing the role of false prophet in predicting the day of the apocalypse. Palmer announced, in April 1920, that the communists were going to launch a major revolt on May Day (May 1), 1920. In New York and other major U.S. cities the police were put on round-the-clock alert, and National Guards were called out to head off the crisis. May Day passed without a single incident, however; Palmer's actions made him appear paranoid and ridiculous. As a consequence, public support for his reactionary tactics evaporated, and the Red Scare dissipated as the economy adjusted to the end of the War. The American public came to realize that the communist threat had been greatly overstated.

Nevertheless, seventeen states passed "criminal syndicalist" laws providing for the arrest of agitators proposing other forms of government. The New York state legislature carried out a lengthy investigation of revolutionary radicalism and refused to seat Socialist representatives from New York City. Meanwhile, Congress refused to admit Victor Berger from Wisconsin until his Milwaukee constituents had again elected that very moderate Socialist.

One final tragedy did result from the "Red Scare," however, in the form of the arrest and conviction of two alien anarchists, Nicola Sacco and Bartolomeo Vanzetti, for the murder of a factory paymaster and guard during a robbery in South Braintree, Massachusetts. The Sacco and Vanzetti cases turned out to be the *cause célèbre* of the 1920s. Eyewitnesses were unable to positively identify Sacco and Vanzetti, and most of the evidence against the two men was circumstantial. Because of the alleged bias of the judge, Webster Thayer, who had privately referred to the two defendants as "those anarchist bastards" and the prejudicial tactics of the prosecuting attorney at the trial, many progressives protested that the men had been convicted for their radicalism rather than for the stated crime. In the six years following their conviction in 1921, protest meetings took place all over the world; and people of international prominence, like Albert Einstein and novelist Anatole France, gave their support to petitions urging clemency or a retrial. In Massachusetts, however, public opinion remained hostile. A special commission headed by the president of Harvard found that the trial had been fair and that the defendants were guilty. On August 23, 1927, Sacco and Vanzetti were electrocuted in an atmosphere of martyrdom. Supporters of the prosecution were vindicated in 1960 when ballistics ex-

▶ Italian anarchists Nicola Sacco and Bartolomeo Vanzetti were incarcerated for crime in which there was no hard evidence tying them to the deed. In the six years following their conviction in 1921, protest meetings took place all over the world; and people of international prominence, like Albert Einstein and novelist Anatole France, gave their support to petitions urging clemency or a retrial.

perts with more advanced crime technology concluded that Sacco's revolver was, indeed, the murder weapon. Supporters of the defendants, however, were also vindicated in that the same ballistics experts concluded that Vanzetti's revolver did not fire the fatal shots. In any case, most historians agree that the two men were executed as much for their political views (anarchism) as the evidence against them.

Perhaps the most alarming aspect of the wave of anti-Red hysteria in the 1920s, however, was not the injustices visited upon a few hundred leftists and aliens, though those people themselves may beg to differ, but the general suppression of free thought that accompanied the unrelenting efforts of the Attorney General and certain "patriotic" societies. Teachers became afraid to impart normal, necessary criticisms of American leaders and American society. Business employees were afraid to be associated with people or organizations branded by the super-patriots as subversive. Liberal journals were called revolutionary, and people were afraid to be seen reading them. Compared to the second Red Scare that would occur during the Cold War of the 1950s, that of the early 1920s was less serious in its impact on government but probably more repressive in its effect on ordinary citizens.

Repression of African Americans

Over four hundred thousand black Americans had served in World War I, half of whom served in Europe, and forty thousand served in combat roles. Additionally, an estimated half million African Americans migrated from the South to the northern cities during the war to engage in factory employment traditionally held by whites and contribute to the home front war effort. Blacks hoped that the war experience would secure for them greater citizenship rights; but after the war, there were mass layoffs of blacks in both the North and South as whites returned from the war to occupy the jobs they previously held.

Blacks in both the North and South were subjected to a new round of racial oppression as whites pressed to "keep them in their place." In 1919 alone, some seventy African Americans were lynched and killed by whites in the South. Urban centers, both north and south, experienced a new round of violent racial unrest. In East St. Louis in 1917, forty-nine people were killed in a race riot, including thirty-nine blacks and ten whites. In Chicago in 1919, a race riot killed fifteen whites and twenty-three blacks in a week of rioting that destroyed over one thousand homes and injured over five hundred people. The Chicago riot was precipitated by an incident on Lake Michigan in which a young black swimmer swam too near a white beach, resulting in whites pelting him with rocks until he was rendered unconscious by the stoning and drowned. Race riots also occurred in Houston and in Philadelphia in 1919, with the result that one hundred twenty people died during 1919 as a result of urban racial unrest. Two years later in Tulsa, Oklahoma, whites dropped dynamite from airplanes on the black section of town, killing seventy-five people and destroying one thousand homes.

The Klan

With the defeat of the "evil" Huns secured sooner than anticipated, the end of World War I found the American people essentially whipped into an emotional patriotic and moral fer-

▶ In Chicago in 1919, a race riot killed fifteen whites and twenty-three blacks in a week of rioting that destroyed over 1,000 homes and injured over 500 people.

vor that was suddenly without direction. In the words of Life magazine Editor Robert Coughlan, the American political mindset was essentially in a state of "coitus interruptus." The general emotion among the American people at the time was one of continued chauvinistic patriotism and hatred for the devil they had been fighting; but the evil entity had essentially cheated them by surrendering before it could be obliterated. Into this void would step the KKK to provide substitute devils to slay in place of the old ones and provide different means by which to slay them.

William J. Simmons, a Methodist minister from Georgia, and fifteen like-minded followers, reorganized the KKK on Thanksgiving night, 1915. At first, Simmons experienced difficulties in recruiting members, although he claimed over fifteen hundred recruits by the end of World War I; but in 1920, he enlisted the help of wealthy Atlanta widow Elizabeth Tyler and former newspaperman and solicitor for the Woodmen of the World, Edward Young Clarke. The KKK fortunes would abruptly change.

With Simmons as the front man, Clarke as the organizer, and Tyler as the financier, the KKK quickly rose to prominence, playing on American moralism, nativism, religion, patriotism, greed, and the social energy and inertia that followed World War I. Simmons and Clarke developed what they termed as the "four major tenets of the Klan philosophy" or "character" of the Klan: a white man's organization, a gentile organization, an American organization, and a Protestant organization. Anything that the Klansmen did not view as "white gentile" and American Protestant in character would become a Klan target.

The Klan was modeled, loosely, after religious organizations, with much attention was given to titles, symbolism, and ceremony. Any room could serve as a Klan meeting place; however, all meetings would have an altar—upon which there would be an American flag, a Bible open at Romans chapter 12, an unsheathed sword, and a container of initiation water that was sprinkled over new members to ceremonially cleanse them of any "alien" defilement.

The Klan's rapid growth in the 1920s is, at least partially, explained by its financial aspects in that it was essentially an early twentieth century political version of a multi-level marketing scheme. New members were required to pay a $10 initiation fee, of which $4 went to the Klansman that recruited the new member. The cyclops (local leader) of the klavern (local group) joined by the new member received $.50. The Imperial Kleagle, Edward Clarke, received $3, and the remaining $1.50 went to the Imperial Wizard, William J. Simmons. Klansmen also had to purchase the official robes for $6.50, a figure that included a minimum profit of $3.50 for the Klan. Initiation water had to be purchased at $10 per quart from the Imperial Wizard, who admittedly drew the water straight from the Chattahoochee River in Georgia. Other Klan profits were made from the robes for the Klansmen's horses, carrying cases for the costumes, pocketknives, and other "official" Klan paraphernalia. Given that the Klan estimated its membership, before a Congressional investigation in 1921, at seven hundred thousand, it is not difficult to determine that Simmons and Clarke (as well as others) reaped tremendous windfalls. A postal inspector testified before Congress that Clarke's department alone received $860,393.50 from June 1920 to September 1921.

This, however, was only the beginning. In 1921, publicity, caused by an undercover investigation of the Klan by the *New York World,* and a Congressional investigation that followed the *New York World* piece, provided a boost to Klan membership as nativists that had not known about the organization prior to the publicity rushed to join. The Klan was essentially swamped with 1.2 million applications for membership in the year following the Congressional investigations. In 1922, Simmons boasted that the Klan's membership increased daily by 3,500 new members, and the Klan's average daily income was $45,000 at a time when GNP per capita was under $1,000. The Klan also claimed membership in all forty-eight states, Alaska, and the Panama Canal Zone.

The stated goals of the Klan were to "return America to its Godly heritage and purge America of un-American and un-Godly influences." The Klan also claimed that it existed "to enforce law at a time of lawlessness." Hence, the Klan's appeal had as much to do with conservative reactions to the "immorality" of the roaring twenties, with its excesses of alcohol, up-tempo dancing, and shorter skirts and shorter hair for women—along with perceived greater sexual promiscuity—as it did with bigotry. Similar to other nativist groups, the KKK integrated elements of conspiracy theory into their teachings. In the words of Emerson Loucks:

> "The belief in the minds of the nativists that there was a serious plot against American ideals and institutions, the success of which only immediate organization and united action could prevent, was as important for the growth of the Ku Klux Klan as the belief in the Devil and his angels was for the growth of the medieval Christian Church. It was the sine qua non of its existence."

For example, D. C. Stephenson, a prominent northern Klan leader, argued that World War I was the result of a conspiracy by Jewish bankers and part of a systematic plan designed to limit Christianity. Other Klan arguments included the contention that Jews had organized the Bolshevik Revolution in Russia and were the driving force behind international communism. The KKK also espoused conspiracy theories concerning the death of Warren G. Harding and the assassinations of Presidents Garfield and McKinley, essentially arguing that Harding's death was in reality a Catholic assassination plot, as were the assassinations of Lincoln, Garfield, and McKinley. In *Searchlight,* the national publication of the Klan, it was proposed that a secret Catholic army of a million Knights of Columbus were secretly arming themselves for a takeover of the country.

Another consistent Klan theme that conforms to the conservative extremist pattern was anti-intellectualism. In particular, the Klan accused college professors of encouraging communism. In the words of one Klan leader:

> "In a nation toleration becomes a vice when fundamentals are in danger ... The American liberals ... have extended their liberality til they are willing to help the aliens tear at the foundations of the nation. They have become one of the chief menaces of the country, instead of the sane intellectual leaders they should be ... They give an almost joyous welcome to alien criticism of everything American. The unopposed attack on the Puritan conscience is only one illustration; our liberals today seem ashamed of having any conscience at all. Tolerance is more prized by them than conviction."

This Klan leader's message contains one further theme: that is consistent among conservative extremists, and that is, they (Klan members) that are being somehow persecuted. In the words of Lipset and Raab (1970, 140):

> "Most successful spokesmen found that the best way to appeal to prospective followers was by casting 'the native white Protestant—not as belonging to the predominant and controlling group ... but as the oppressed poor, oppressed sufferer, plundered by foreigners, tricked by Jesuits, and robbed of his birthright by scheming descendants of Abraham.'"

In doing so, the Klan appealed to the sympathy that the American masses tend to have for the "underdog." Hence, the Klan was able to link itself to anti-elitist and egalitarian populist traditions while simultaneously fostering bigotry and hate (Lipset and Raab, 1970, 140).

Selling bigotry and hate is much easier if it is cloaked in morality and patriotism. As a consequence, the KKK advocated specific curriculum for school children—including the Golden Rule, the Ten Commandments, opposition to Charles Darwin's theory of evolution, and opposition to the evils of alcohol—as part of their stated goal of fostering "morality" (Mecklin, 1924, 13, 28). The Klan was not the first group, nor would they be the last conservative group, to cloak their bigotry under the guise of "morality." In the 1920s, however, they were perhaps the most successful. It is worth of note, however, that in these Klan positions, as well as in their persecution syndrome and anti-intellectualism, the Klan's views, goals, and platform of the 1920s are almost indistinguishable from that of the Christian Coalition of the early twenty-first century, with the exception that the Christian Coalition is much less noteworthy for racial bigotry.

The targets of KKK activities in the 1920s were not exclusively racial, and certainly included blacks; but they also included everything and everyone else that conservative extremists at the time viewed as unchristian, un-American, or immoral. The list of targets, therefore, also included

▶Selling bigotry and hate is much easier if it is cloaked in morality and patriotism; Ku Klux Klan members appealed to the sympathy of the American masses to gain support; painting themselves not as belonging to the predominant and controlling group but as the oppressed poor, oppressed sufferer, plundered by foreigners (the blacks).

Catholics, Jews, Mexicans, immigration in general, short skirts, abortions, all forms of sexual immorality, adultery, divorce, "demon rum," dance halls, movie theaters, businessmen charged with corrupting young women, husbands who abandoned their wives, divorcees who set "immoral" examples, pimps, prostitutes, gamblers, thieves, bootleggers, and doctors who performed abortions. The KKK also identified paintings and books that they considered to be immoral and argued for their censorship. Among other things, the Klan opposed beauty contests, carnivals, and jazz clubs as activities that led to immorality.

The KKK (along with other Protestant fundamentalist groups) also led the fight for State laws that required the closing of businesses on Sundays. Municipal laws were passed against "public flirting," women smoking in public, and the playing of jazz after midnight. Other municipal laws imposed restrictions on the brevity of bathing suits. In the Texas legislature, a bill was introduced, but not passed, banning women's heels to no more than one inch.

The fact that the KKK and Protestant fundamentalism were intertwined in the 1920s is testified to by the fact that two thirds of the national Klan lecturers were Protestant ministers. The Klan's tirades against evolution and immorality were attractive to fundamentalist Protestant ministers, who regularly filled their sermons with similar messages. One of the Klan's most effective tactics for enlisting the support of Protestant ministers was to have its members appear unannounced at Sunday church services in full regalia. Klansmen would march solemnly and silently down the aisles, hand the minister envelopes full of cash, and then silently march out of the church as quickly as they had arrived. The tactics were evidently effective. In Knoxville, Tennessee, for example, Klan files of membership applications showed that 71.2 percent were Baptist and 24.4 percent were Methodist.

The Klan's solicitation of ministers was part of an overall effort to recruit members from the "top" of society down. The strategy was to recruit the leaders of communities, including political and religious leaders—as well as the prominent businessmen of the communities, and then enlist their help in getting others to fall in line. As a result, Klan leadership in any town often mirrored the leadership of the community. The Klan also recruited the police in every town, an obvious advantage for a group that engages in illegal activities. It is estimated that 10 percent of the policemen in California, including the police chiefs in Los Angeles and Bakersfield, and the sheriff of Los Angeles County, belonged to the Klan in the 1920s. The rank and file of the Klan, however, were predominantly the blue collar, uneducated, working class. Hiram Evans, the Grand Wizard in 1926 described the Klan thusly:

▶ A strategy of the KKK was to recruit the political, religious, and other prominent leaders in communities, and then enlist their help in getting others to fall in line. In the 1920s, two thirds of the national Klan lecturers were Protestant ministers.

> "We are a movement of the plain people, very weak in the matter of culture, intellectual support, and trained leadership. We are demanding, and we expect to win, a return of power into the hands of everyday, not highly cultured, not overly intellectualized, but unspoiled and not de-Americanized, average citizen of the old stock ... This is undoubtedly a weakness. It lays us open to the charge of being hicks and rubes and drivers of second hand Fords. We admit it."

Whether "hicks and rubes" or not, with money and numbers comes political influence; and by the 1920s, the Klan had accumulated its fair share. Retail merchants were told to display a TWK (Trade With Klansmen) sticker in their window or expect to suffer a boycott by the Klan, and Klansmen were instructed to frequent businesses owned by other Klansmen. By economic boycott, the Klan could (and did) bankrupt merchants that opposed it. The Klan became so economically powerful at one point that it purchased its own college, Lanier University in Atlanta. It attempted to purchase Valparaiso University in Indiana, as well, for the purpose of providing a place where one could receive a "proper" education.

The Klan also used its economic might to provide political backing for electoral candidates, and numerous Klansmen were elected to political office throughout the South. In Georgia, United States Senator William J. Harris won a bid for re-election after his opponent produced a letter signed by Elizabeth Tyler to Harris in which she addressed him as "Hon. W. J. Harris, A.K.I.A." (A Klansman Am I). Clifford Walker, the governor of Georgia in 1924, admitted that he was a Klansman and addressed the Second Imperial Klonvokation of the Klan in 1924. In Alabama, in 1926, a United States Senate seat was won by future United States Supreme Court Justice Hugo Black, who had resigned from the Klan just prior to the election. The other Alabama Senator was another Klansman, the rabidly anti-Catholic Tom Heflin. In Texas in 1922, Earle Mayfield, an admitted Klansman, won a United States Senate seat. Two years later, Klan candidate Felix Robertson, who claimed he stood for the "God-given right and supremacy of white Christian men," almost won the governorship of Texas; but on the day of the primary election, a white-sheeted crowd threw rocks at the home of his female gubernatorial opponent (Ma Ferguson). Unfortunately for Robertson, the attack backfired since conservatives in Texas viewed the attack as an unmanly attack on a woman. Robertson garnered more votes than Ferguson in the primary that day, but the KKK rock-throwing incident helped Ferguson gain enough votes to force a runoff and defeat Robertson in November 1924 by 98,000 votes.

Perhaps the apex of Klan political strength was at the 1924 Democratic Convention where it is estimated that three hundred Klan members were present as delegates. The Klan proved that it essentially controlled the convention when William H. Pattengall of Maine introduced an anti-Klan plank in the Democratic platform. Chaos ensued following Pattengall's proposal, and Madison Square Garden was filled with the hissing and booing of Klansmen along with fistfights, chair tossing, and destruction of convention decorations. Among the notables that came out opposed to the anti-Klan plank was the old populist warrior from Nebraska, William Jennings Bryan. The anti-Klan plank was defeated along with the presidential nomination bid of Al Smith of New York, whom the Klan opposed due to his Roman Catholicism and anti-prohibition stance. Smith would win the Democratic nomination four years later only after the Klan had begun to subside.

In August 1925, the Klan further demonstrated its political strength when it held a national parade in Washington, D.C. where over fifty thousand Klansmen participated in a four-hour march down Pennsylvania Avenue. Although the march was peaceful, the sight of fifty thousand robed Klansmen filing past the White House provided an ominous symbol less than a decade before the National Socialists of Adolph Hitler took power in Germany.

After 1925, however, the KKK began to decline, with the result that the organization would become a shadow of its former self by World War II. There are numerous reasons why the Klan in the United States, in spite of its comparatively superior strength in 1925, was unable to take over power completely as did their German Nazi counterparts in Europe. The fact that the United States was on the winning, rather than losing side in World War I (World War I being the primary precipitant for the right-wing backlash in both the United States and Europe) was certainly one reason that the Klan failed in the United States while Hitler's Nazis succeeded. However, Klan violence also clearly violated the sensibilities of millions of Americans who clamored for their government to act against Klan threats to stability. In response, states began ushering "Anti-Mask" bills through their legislatures that prevented Klan members from wearing their hoods in public, with the result that the "undedicated" members of the KKK quickly abandoned the organization in an overt sense. The Klan was also certainly guilty of over-reach. Put simply, if all of the people and all of the activities that the Klan were supposedly against were combined, (all minorities, immigrants, all non-Protestants, consumers of alcohol, anyone who had sex outside of marriage, etc.), it clearly represented the majority of Americans. It should be a fairly safe assumption that persons who were potential Klan targets would be less inclined to support the Klan.

Some of the decline of the Klan, however, is perhaps best explained by the fact that the Klan did experience some successes and achieve some of its goals. In fact, major political parties and other groups—religious fundamentalists, in general—took up as part of their platforms, many of the issues that concerned the Klan. In 1924, for example, the passage of strict immigration restrictions limiting immigration to a total number of one hundred fifty thousand persons should be considered a Klan victory, but it also in part diffused the anti-immigration elements that were drawn to the Klan. Similarly, numerous Southern states passed laws outlawing the teaching of evolution, and prohibition was firmly embedded. In these instances, the Klan's demise falls into the pattern of other interest groups, such as the anti-nuclear protesters of the 1980s, whose demise is at least partially due to their own success. Finally, as the decade of the 1920s came to a close, the passage of time allowed the nation to distance itself from the hyper-patriotism and "100 percent pure Americanism" that had accompanied World War I. As they had before, however, these patterns of nativism, moralism, and bigotry would resurface again during the next political crisis.

Against the ominous rise of lower-middle-class reaction, the stuff of which the Klan was made in the American South, and fascism was to be made in Germany, must be placed the continuation of liberal and even radical farmer movements in the upper Midwest and the Northwest. Led by the old Non-Partisan League, a Farmer-Labor Party ran second to the victorious Republicans in the election of 1920 in Minnesota, South Dakota, and Washington. Thus, the decentralized character of American politics sustained minority movements while making it difficult for them to win national power.

Immigration Quotas

A major change in American political policy in the early 1920s was the regulation of immigration on a quota basis. While the law had excluded the Chinese in 1882, and diplomatic agreements had excluded the Japanese, other Asian and African people had not attempted to immigrate in any large numbers. Meanwhile the door had been held open for most Europeans although organized labor and "old stock" Americans had long tried to restrict the vast flood of newcomers, which in peaceful and prosperous years comprised more than a million annually. Finally, a combination of factors—resumption of heavy immigration from Eastern Europe, unemployment at home, and the Red Scare—led Congress to establish quotas based on the number of foreign-born residents in the United States in 1910. Opposed vigorously in Congress only by Catholics, the bill met a veto by Wilson. Passed again in the special session of 1921, it was signed by Harding. During the first year of operation the restrictions reduced yearly immigration from around one million to three hundred thousand.

To organized labor, nativists, and those who feared communism, the number of "undesirable" or "unassimilable" immigrants from Eastern Europe still seemed too large. The National Origins Act of 1924 set up a temporary quota of two percent of the foreign-born residents in 1890 (a time when immigrants were still largely of British, German, or Scandinavian origin) and established a commission to work out quotas by a formula based on numbers of foreign-born over the whole range of the United States on the basis of census data. The bill excluded "Orientals."

Japan, which had been voluntarily restricting emigration to the United States, regarded this as an affront to its national dignity and declared a "National Humiliation Day" in response; but the Japanese protest was brushed aside by Congress. Enacted into law in 1929, the final report of the Commission on National Origins reduced southern and eastern European quotas to negligible size and held the total of restricted immigrants to about one hundred fifty thousand annually. Citizens of countries in the Western Hemisphere were exempted from restriction. During periods of high employment, like the 1920s, the diminished pool of immigrant labor led to the hiring of more blacks and poor whites in the growing industrial centers.

Triumph of the Conservatives

In the middle of the confusing year 1920, the Republican and Democratic conventions met to nominate candidates for the presidency. The leading Republican contenders—Governor Frank O. Lowden of Illinois and General Leonard Wood—fought each other to a deadlock. The compromise candidate supported by a group of business representatives and conservative congressional leaders was Senator Warren G. Harding of Ohio, a man virtually unknown to the American public but one who had the gracious, commanding look of a president.

Although Harding was nobody's first choice for president and he essentially received the Republican nomination when the Republican Convention became gridlocked between warring factions, and Harding seemed an inoffensive "second choice." Harding was amiable and able to unite the Party. Harding himself perhaps best summed up the situation when he exclaimed, "We drew a pair of deuces and filled."

▶ Senator Warren G. Harding of Ohio essentially received the Republican nomination when the Republican Convention became gridlocked between warring factions. Harding was amiable and able to unite the Party.

In 1920, Harding's nomination made sense to the Republicans because his candidacy seemed to offend no one; and he was, in the words of Ohio boss Harry Daugherty, "a handsome devil . . . and women could vote." In other words, Harding received the Republican nomination at least partially because he "looked like a president," rather than because of immense talent. Harding and his successor Calvin Coolidge would essentially be a return to the precedent set in the Gilded Age—that of choosing mediocre presidents of average talent, but men who possessed the correct conservative ideological leanings.

Harding's campaign promised what Harding referred to as a "return to normalcy." The "normalcy" campaign resonated with Americans in the upheaval following World War I, complete with economic and labor unrest along with the excesses of the Red Scare. Furthermore, Americans had experienced twenty years of progressivism that had brought prohibition, women's suffrage, and government economic and social regulation. By 1920, perhaps progressivism had merely run its course, and Americans were ready to return to conservatism. In the words of progressive journalist William Allen White, Americans in 1920 were "tired of issues, sick at heart of ideals, and weary of being noble." At any rate, the election of Harding would signal that the Progressive Era was over.

Harding took a non-controversial approach to the 1920 campaign and straddled the fence on divisive issues so as not to alienate progressives. For example, Harding avoided the issue of segregation and neither attacked nor endorsed the KKK.

The Democrats had even greater difficulty in choosing a candidate. During thirty-seven indecisive ballots, Attorney General Palmer, the anti-Red champion, fought William G. McAdoo, the liberal ex-Secretary of the Treasury and son-in-law of Woodrow Wilson. Then the convention jettisoned both and compromised on a progressive who had been twice elected governor of Ohio, James M. Cox. While Cox was as little known to the general public as Harding, the Democratic ticket was strengthened by the vice-presidential nomination of Assistant Secretary of the Navy Franklin D. Roosevelt.

The election of 1920 also marked the last hurrah for Socialist leader, Eugene V. Debs, a particularly remarkable candidacy in that Debs ran for president from prison and obtained about one million votes. A strong critic of American participation in World War I, Debs had attempted to confine his remarks in speeches to those that would not be illegal under the Espionage Act of 1917. He was, however, arrested for saying that the master classes declared war while the lower classes fought it—and he was subsequently convicted. In 1921, President Warren Harding would pardon him. This was the last of Debs's five presidential runs.

Partly in deference to President Wilson, the two major-party candidates Cox and Roosevelt made entry into the League of Nations a major issue of the campaign. The Republicans avoided commitment on the League question and, instead, advocated higher tariffs and tax reduction. Reading the popular temper correctly, they were extremely confident. During the campaign Harding stayed on his front porch in Marion, Ohio. His speeches, according to McAdoo, were "an army of pompous phrases moving across the landscape in search of an idea." In spite of—or perhaps because of—the assurance of victory, the Republicans were aided by a campaign fund of $8 million.

▶ Running against Warren Harding in the election of 1920 was the Democratic candidate James M. Cox. Assistant Secretary of the Navy Franklin D. Roosevelt was nominated as his vice-president.

The Republican landslide was the greatest since the second election of James Monroe. Harding carried every state outside the "solid South," and there he carried Tennessee. He received 61 percent of the popular vote, as much as Franklin D. Roosevelt was to poll in his greatest victory. In Congress, the Republican majority was one hundred sixty-seven in the House and twenty-two in the Senate. Although this was the first election following women's suffrage, no significant changes were apparent as a result of women's vote.

Warren G. Harding

Warren Harding as president would be an abrupt change from his predecessor Woodrow Wilson. Unlike Wilson, Harding had few strong convictions, was open to compromise, and could be easily persuaded to change his position on most issues. Harding was also non-confrontational and indecisive by nature; therefore, he did not enjoy the presidency, an office that epitomizes confrontation and decision-making.

Harding is perhaps unique among presidents in that he possessed an overwhelming awareness of his own incompetence. For example, Harding once stated, "I am not fit for this office and never should have been here." Similarly, to Judge John Barton Payne, Harding once exclaimed, "I don't think I'm big enough for the presidency." In a similar vein, to Calvin Coolidge, Harding once offered, "I am a man of limited talents from a small town. … I don't seem to grasp that I am president." To compound matters, Harding was generally ignorant of policy issues and realized the situation as such. For instance, he once stated his frustration on a tax issue by proclaiming, "I don't know what to do or where to turn on this taxation matter." Although generally ignorant in most policy areas, Harding was particularly ignorant on foreign affairs. When asked once by a reporter about European affairs at the time, Harding replied, "I don't know anything about this European stuff."

Harding's doubts about his own abilities were widely shared by contemporary intellectuals and astute politicians. Harding frequently butchered the English language in his speech and made frequent misstatements. Republican Senator Bose Penrose of Philadelphia perhaps best summed up the Republican Party's position on Harding when he argued that the Republicans should:

> "Keep Warren at home. Don't let him make any speeches. If he goes out on a tour, somebody's sure to ask him questions, and Warren's just the sort of damn fool to try to answer them."

Due to these shortcomings, Harding did not enjoy being president. In the words of Harding, "the White House is a prison and I cannot get away from the men who dog my footsteps." As a counter balance, Harding focused on the positive input from the public in the way of letters he received from his adoring fans; and he spent much of his time writing letters to citizens and greeting ordinary people at the White House. When one White House aide questioned the amount of time Harding spent in his letter-writing and small-talking with the public, Harding responded with, "I love to meet people. It's the most pleasant thing I do; it is really the only fun I have. It does not tax me, and it seems to be a very great pleasure to them."

Harding and the Ohio Gang

While Harding enjoyed the public support from Protestant fundamentalists and the prohibitionist KKK, a few blocks from the White House at the "House on K Street," Harding and the "Ohio Gang" drank mass quantities of bootleg liquor during Prohibition while they gambled, entertained women, sold government favors, and bribed Congressmen. Alice Roosevelt (Theodore's daughter) once came into the White House study and found the air "heavy with tobacco smoke and its tables cluttered with bottles containing every imaginable brand of whiskey and cards and poker chips at hand." The Ohio Gang plundered the government, private business, and taxpayers in almost every way imaginable. Jesse Smith, a top aide to Daugherty in the Attorney General's office, used his office to sell pardons, government contracts, and government access. As a result of his misdeeds, Smith was accused of influence peddling and committed suicide in 1923. After the incident, Harding is reported to have stated:

> "My God, this is a hell of a job. I have no trouble with my enemies. I can take care of my enemies all right. But my damn friends, my God-damn friends, they're the ones that keep me walking the floor nights".

Similarly, Charles R. Forbes, head of the Veterans Bureau, pocketed millions of dollars appropriated for construction of veterans hospitals. Forbes fled to Europe, later eventually returned, and was sentenced to two years in prison. Forbes, however, fared much better than his assistant, Charles F. Cramer, who escaped the prosecution by committing suicide. Thomas W. Miller, the Alien Property Custodian, who was in charge of seized German assets from World War I, was sentenced to prison for accepting bribes in exchange for the release of assets to their original owners. Attorney General Harry Daugherty was implicated in the scandals, but he took the Fifth Amendment on the stand and was not convicted.

▶ President Warren G. Harding and Vice President Calvin Coolidge.

The most celebrated of the scandals during the Harding administration, however, was the Teapot Dome Scandal involving Secretary of the Interior Albert Fall. Fall arranged with Navy Secretary Edwin Denby for the transfer to the Department of the Interior of Navy oil reserves in Elk Hills, California, and Teapot Dome, Wyoming. Fall then leased the reserves to Edward L. Doheny's Pan-American Petroleum and Harry F. Sinclair's Mammoth Oil Company. Doheny "loaned" Fall $100,000 in cash (handed over in a "little black bag") while Sinclair gave Fall $300,000 in cash and securities. Sinclair was given nine months in jail for tampering with a jury, but acquitted of defrauding the United States government. Fall was fined $100,000 and given one year in prison for accepting a bribe, while Doheny went unpunished. President Harding evidently knew nothing of the scandal, and it did not become public until after his death; hence, the scandal did not harm Harding's reputation during his lifetime.

Also in 1927 (some four years after Harding's death), it became publicly known that Harding had had an extramarital affair with Nan Britton, a young woman thirty years his younger. She began seeing Harding in 1917 after she wrote him from her home in Harding's hometown of Marion, Ohio, asking him for a job. Harding was able to secure employment for Britton in a clerical position at U.S. Steel in Washington. They then commenced with their affair, which continued until Harding's death. Britton gave birth to Harding's daughter, Elizabeth Ann, in 1919, and Harding made child support payments, which were hand-delivered by the U.S. Secret Service from the White House to Britton. After Harding's death, Britton sued his estate to gain a trust fund for her daughter. Britton then wrote a book entitled *The President's Daughter,* which she dedicated to "all unwed mothers and their innocent children whose fathers are usually not known to the world." Britton recounted details of the affair in the book, including accounts of trysts with Harding, not only in the Oval Office, but also in a White House closet.

Harding also had a fifteen-year relationship with Carrie Phillips, the wife of his longtime friend, James Phillips. The affair began in Marion, Ohio, in 1905 and continued until Harding was running for president of the United States. This is in spite of the fact that in 1917 Phillips, a German sympathizer who had lived in Berlin, tried to blackmail then Senator Harding into voting against a Declaration of War on Germany. In 1920, the Republican National Committee, so as to avoid any possible embarrassment of their presidential candidate, removed Ms. Phillips, by paying Mr. and Mrs. Phillips $20,000 in cash and providing them with a free, slow, trip to Japan, along with monthly hush money.

By the summer of 1923, there was a rumor that the House, now controlled by Democrats and Progressives, might try to impeach the president. However, on August 2, in the midst of the increasing revelations of corruption, Harding died of an apoplectic stroke. With Vice-President Calvin Coolidge now succeeding to the presidency, the Republican Party had a man superbly qualified to make amends for the laxity of the Harding administration. Coolidge, a slight, dry-looking, diffident Vermonter who after graduation from Amherst had won success in Massachusetts law and politics, seemed to personify the traditional virtues of thrift and frugality. His intimate friends would not betray him because he had none. At a time when business and most of the middle class seemed satisfied with the status quo, Coolidge could be relied upon not to rock the boat.

Republican National Policy

Led for eight years either by Harding, who had been installed by the right wing of the Party, or by Coolidge, whom Hoover called a "real conservative," the Republican administration tried to lessen or remove controls over business activity. In this policy the president was often at odds with Democratic-progressive coalitions in the House and the Senate, but the presidential powers of appointment and veto proved effective weapons in cutting down federal activities.

The Republican presidents appointed conservative, business-minded members to federal regulatory commissions. This led to such a relaxation in vigilance that, in the words of a famous authority, the Federal Trade Commission "tried to commit *hara-kiri*"—to cease functioning as a regulatory agency. The antitrust division of the Justice Department seldom prosecuted mergers. The Federal Power Commission, established in 1920 to regulate interstate electric power, did little to justify its existence; and the efforts of the Interstate Commerce Commission to bring about railroad consolidation and recapture excess earnings were without significant effect.

Ocean shipping in the 1920s presented special problems. At the end of the war, the government owned some two million deadweight tons of hastily constructed freighters which were slow and inefficient in comparison with new turbine or diesel electric vessels coming from British and Continental yards. In addition, United States wages and manning requirements made it impossible for American ship owners to compete on an equal basis with foreign operators. To keep some of the ships at sea, for a decade the Shipping Board pursued a policy of selling the freighters for $5 to $10 a ton and granting mail subsidies for operation on strategically important routes.

One of the first conflicts between the conservative Presidents Harding and Coolidge and the less conservative Congress was over the soldiers' bonus bill. This proposed legislation provided a twenty year endowment policy totaling $1 for each day a veteran had served in the United States and $1.25 for each day overseas. President Harding, in 1921, and President Coolidge, in 1924, vetoed the bill. The Harding veto was sustained, but a more generous Congress overrode that of Coolidge.

Freed from fear of federal regulation, businessmen also were gradually relieved of the higher taxes of the war period, as Harding was essentially a standard laissez-faire and pro-business conservative. Harding perhaps well summed up the mood of the times when he stated,"what we need is less government in business and more business in government." In 1921, Harding exhibited his conservative pro-business and anti-labor stripes when he called in the National Guard to put down a United Mine Workers' Strike in West Virginia and Pennsylvania. As a result of the federal government's tilt back toward management, Union membership nationwide dropped from five million in 1921 to three million in 1929.

Harding proved to be a "compassionate conservative," however, in that he pardoned radical dissidents imprisoned during the Wilson years, including Eugene V. Debs, the Socialist Party leader imprisoned for his anti-war stance against World War I. Harding also denounced lynching in a message to Congress in 1921, but did not follow up with initiative for an anti-lynching bill. In most cases, however, Harding personally was able to provide little in the way of policy direction, with the result that leadership flowed to Congress and Harding's executive appointees.

Harding concentrated on appointing what he believed were capable aides and cabinet members and delegating most of his authority. Harding rewarded Party leaders who had helped him gain the nomination with important positions, and Harding's trust in what eventually came to be known as the "Ohio Gang" turned out to be partially misguided as Harding's appointees plundered the government for personal gain. Among Harding's most important appointees was Treasury Secretary Andrew Mellon, whose laissez-faire economic policies became those that guided the nation.

Mellon, formerly head of the Aluminum Company of America and one of the richest men in the world, believed sincerely that high income taxes retarded economic growth. As Secretary of the Treasury he immediately sponsored a tax bill that repealed the excess profits tax and sharply reduced the surtaxes on personal income. After amendments by the Republican farm bloc and by Democrats in the Senate, the Revenue Act of 1921 repealed the excess profits tax but cut the maximum surtax on personal income only from 65 to 50 percent. Nevertheless, since federal revenues steadily exceeded expenses, there was increasing pressure for tax reduction. By 1929 four subsequent revenue acts had reduced the maximum surtax to 20 percent and the effective initial rate to less than half of one percent. The tax on corporate income was slightly reduced, to 11 percent.

These tax reductions, which retarded repayment of the national debt and left it at $16 billion at the beginning of the Great Depression, have been vigorously criticized; yet Republican administrations faced a real economic dilemma. To have repaid the debt more rapidly would have released to the money markets as much cash as came from the untaxed savings of high incomes, if not more. Only if the government could have found a way to use the money so as to increase lower incomes or to pay it to some of the two million unemployed could the surplus have been kept from feeding the inflation in stocks and mortgage bonds. Such a fiscal policy would have been directly contrary to the firmly held beliefs of the conservative majority, and as an explicit policy, probably beyond the imagination of most of the more liberal minority.

One proposed use for federal funds that would not have involved the government in new types of business or competed with private industry was the support of farm incomes. Farmers had been led by the demands of World War I to expand wheat acreage, which in view of long-run trends was already excessive in 1914. After the collapse of the reconstruction boom in 1920, farm prices fell more than those of things the farmer had to buy, and both foreign and domestic markets for such staples as wheat and cotton declined. As a result, America's farmers were not participating in the general prosperity that visited most of the nation in the 1920's.

A plan put forward by two farm machinery manufacturers in 1922 did not involve federal subsidy but merely required a federal marketing agency that could maintain a domestic price in excess of the world price. Written into the McNary-Haugen Bill and endorsed by practically all farmer organizations, the proposal was resisted by conservative Republicans as a dangerous extension of federal power. The bill was passed in 1926 and again in 1927, but killed both times by a Coolidge veto.

Although by the late 1930s the Farm Bureau Federation, the chief agricultural pressure group, was to seem conservative, in the 1920s it formed a rallying point for liberals. In spite of the conservative presidential leadership, progressives of both parties maintained their strength in Congress. The greatest obstacle to liberal victories during the decade was probably not the relatively small group of conservatives with substantial incomes but rather the general political apathy bred by prosperity from 1923 to 1929. Presidential elections drew only a little more than half the voters to the polls. Coolidge was sustained in the 1924 presidential election by a mere 28 percent of the possible electorate.

Expansion of Government

Federal, State, and Local Change

Even within the administration, men like Charles E. Hughes and Herbert Hoover did not share the Coolidge stand-pat type of conservatism. Hoover, as Secretary of Commerce, tried to bring more efficiency into business operations. To avoid destructive competition, he urged small companies to have trade associations administer their mutual concerns, and he invited them to post their prices with the Commerce Department and to refrain from secret rebates. To lower production costs, he put his influence behind the movement for standard sizes. The number of shapes of bottles and the various sizes of bricks, for example, were both cut 90 percent. After unsuccessfully preaching self-regulation to the young air transport and radio industries, his department established regulatory agencies in 1926 and 1927, respectively. He and Andrew Mellon also took leading parts in introducing federal budgeting of income and expenses. In these directions Hoover was a planner; as he saw it, he was using the power of government primarily to suggest better voluntary planning to private industry.

State and local authorities, still the most important forms of government, were led to expand their operations greatly. Increasing high-school attendance, in particular, demanded new buildings and bigger school budgets. Skyscrapers concentrated so many workers in the centers of the largest cities that new public transportation was required. On the other hand, automobiles moved so many families to the open areas of the cities or suburbs that new streets and sewers were continually needed. New York and some other states increased the scope and size of their expenditures for welfare. New laws or municipal ordinances, regulating business practices, sanitation, and housing, required new bureaus and squads of inspectors. From all these needs of a growing industrial society, the expenses of government soared. Between 1922 and 1927 the annual cost of state and local government rose nearly 40 percent, and the rise had undoubtedly passed 50 percent by 1929. The debts of these governments increased even faster, up nearly 50 percent from 1922 to 1927 and perhaps by two thirds, had figures been collected, by 1929.

It is also worth remembering that in 1929 state and local governments cost about two and a half times as much to run as the federal government and had about twice as many civilian employees, exclusive of schoolteachers. Thus what appears on the federal level to have been a period of low government expenditure and reduction of debt was *in toto* one of rapid increase in government expenditure and dangerous accumulation of local indebtedness.

Security in the Pacific

While there was a vigorous movement for the League of Nations and world peace, most of the minority of Americans who thought about foreign relations probably wanted to avoid being involved in either European or Far Eastern affairs. The war against Germany was officially ended by a resolution of Congress on July 2, 1921; and separate treaties were negotiated with the new governments of Germany, Austria, and Hungary. However, Far Eastern problems were far from settled.

Meanwhile, as World War I had proven that naval power was the most important military power, the Navy Department had plans for building the world's largest battle fleet. In spite of congressional refusal to pass the "big-navy" bills, England and Japan were deeply worried over the possibility of having to compete with the United States in naval construction. Therefore, they readily accepted Secretary of State Hughes' invitation to meet in Washington in 1921 to discuss naval disarmament. Since a naval agreement would have to be linked with treaties establishing and guaranteeing Far Eastern arrangements, France, Italy, Belgium, the Netherlands, and Portugal (nations with Asian territories) were invited to the conference together with China.

Early in 1922, Secretary Hughes led the way to a naval agreement known as the Five Power Treaty whereby the United States, England, Japan, France, and Italy scrapped hundreds of thousands of tons of battleships afloat or in construction and agreed to a 5–5–3 ratio for capital ships, with Britain and the United States at equal strength and Japan held to 60 percent of that tonnage. To secure Japan's interests in the western Pacific, each party agreed not to fortify new bases or enlarge old ones. Japan acquiesced to the treaty because it was concerned primarily with the Pacific and it allowed Japan to be equal to, if not superior to, England and the U.S. in the Pacific. A major flaw in the Five Power Treaty, however, was that it set no limits on the building of smaller ships, including submarines, destroyers, and small cruisers. Within a year after signing, all nations violated the spirit of the treaty by embarking on the construction programs for these smaller ships.

After some argument, France and Italy were persuaded to sign the treaty, each limiting the tonnage of its capital ships to 35 percent of the Anglo-American maximum. A new Four-Power Pact (United States, British Empire, France, Japan) replaced the Anglo-Japanese Alliance and pledged those powers to respect each other's possessions and rights in the Pacific. A Nine-Power Pact, also concluded during the Washington Conference, affirmed the sovereignty, independence, and administrative and territorial integrity of China. The American policy of an "open door" for Chinese trade was reaffirmed and essentially agreed to by the European powers. The Washington treaties established a system of security for Asia such as the Treaty of Versailles was presumed to have provided for Europe. The treaty had a major flaw, however, in that it permitted intervention by any of the signatories in China if China did not develop and maintain an effective and stable government. There was also no provision for enforcement or sanctions on the violators of the treaty.

High Tariffs

High tariffs continued to be a major Republican policy throughout the 1920s. Ironically, the Midwestern farmers who feared Canadian, Irish, and Argentine competition led the protectionist group opposed to the Republicans in Congress in the early 1920s. Wilson vetoed their first bill for increased agricultural duties on the grounds that American farmers also needed foreign markets.

The Harding administration favored higher duties, but the increases in the Fordney-McCumber Tariff of 1922 were generally moderate. Although agricultural products gained protection, the principle of a tariff that would equalize prices of domestic and foreign products was generally maintained. The farm bloc managed to get manufactures like shoes and wagons on the free list, but some industries received very high protection. The Tariff Commission still had the right to recommend changes, and the president had the power to alter the rates by 50 percent. Neither Harding nor Coolidge made important use of this power.

War Debts

The Treaty of Versailles had a number of major weaknesses, but perhaps paramount among them was an unrealistic structure of reparations and war debts. In 1921 Germany was forced to accept a reparations commission bill for $33 billion, but no such sum could be transferred in a few decades from one European country to the others without severely disrupting the economies involved. Germany attempted to meet its obligations by issuing massive amounts of paper money, which had the impact of devaluing the German currency. By 1923, Germany experienced inflation rates of 26 billion percent, and their economy suffered an economic meltdown. Prices were altered in German stores by the hour, and people were paid hourly in piles of cash. It was said that Germany was the only country where a wheelbarrow full of money could buy a wallet full of goods. As a consequence, the Allied European powers were unable to collect their full reparations from Germany.

Similarly the United States tried to collect war debts of $4.6 billion from England, $4 billion from France, and $2 billion from Italy. The European states, arguing that they had paid for World War I with their lives while Americans were only out money, advised a cancellation of all international payments that would endanger normal economic growth; however, presidents from Wilson to Roosevelt insisted on the principle of collection. Calvin Coolidge, in particular, refused the European request to forgive the debt, quipping, "They hired the money, didn't they?"

Since such sums could be paid only in goods and since Mellon's high United States tariffs limited European exports to the United States, thus further hindering the European ability to pay, debt payments were regularly more than balanced by new American lending and investment abroad. Throughout the decade, bankers sold annually about $1 billion worth of foreign government, municipal, and corporate bonds to American investors. This was a profitable system for the bankers; and by giving foreigners dollars to spend, it allowed United States manufacturers to maintain large exports. It meant, however, that world financial stability depended on continued prosperity and an easy money market in the United States.

Congress, however, was not completely deaf to the global economic problems and took several measures in the 1920s to try to alleviate the global currency crisis. In 1921, Congress lowered the interest rates on the debt and extended the terms, but the European nations remained unable to meet their obligations. In 1924 the so-called Dawes Plan, devised by Owen D. Young and Charles G. Dawes of the United States, cut reparations to what seemed like a manageable level. In 1925, the United States Foreign Debt Commission cancelled 80 percent of the Italian debt, 60 percent of the French debt, and reduced interest rates even further. By this time, the $33 billion bill had shrunk to about $2 billion. During the 1920s the Allies paid the United States about $2.6 billion in war debts, and the Americans loaned Germany some $2.5 billion, 80 percent of which was paid to the Allies.

Therefore, there was nearly a mutual balancing. The Allies paid the United States, which loaned to Germany, which paid reparations to Allies, and the cycle continued; but the American investors and banks that had advanced the money, however, were left with foreign bonds that soon defaulted on their interest payments. This untenable system could be maintained during the economic good times of the 1920s; but after the onset of the Crash of '29 and the onset of the Great Depression, the system collapsed, causing President Herbert Hoover to suspend debt payments for one year in December 1931. In 1932, the European nations collectively cancelled 90 percent of Germany's reparations, hoping that the United States would then cancel the debt. Hoover refused to do so, with the result that when the moratorium on European debt payments ended in December 1932, the Europeans could not pay and all but Finland defaulted by 1934.

Meanwhile, the United States pursued a rather uncertain course of international cooperation. Secretary of State Hughes started the practice of sending "unofficial observers" to League of Nations sessions and to meetings of the principal League committees, but isolationists in the Senate prevented the United States from joining the World Court. This, however, did not prevent Americans, as individuals, from serving as justices.

In 1921, the United States, Britain, France, Italy, and Japan signed the Five-Power Treaty that placed a 10-year moratorium on the construction of battleships and other large naval ships. Maximum "tonnage" of large naval ships was set for each nation with the United States and Great Britain receiving limits of five hundred twenty-five thousand tons, Japan three hundred twenty-five thousand, and France and Italy each one hundred twenty-five thousand tons. The United States and Great Britain agreed to prevent any further fortifications of their Pacific possessions; and this, along with the fact that Japan's Pacific fleet would actually be the largest of the three, induced Japan to sign the treaty. A major flaw in the treaty, however, was that it set no limits on the building of smaller ships—including submarines, destroyers, and small cruisers. Within a year after signing, all nations violated the spirit of the Five-Party Treaty by embarking on the construction programs for these smaller ships.

The next year, the United States, Japan, and seven European powers signed the Nine-Power Treaty where all agreed to respect the Open Door in China. The treaty had a major flaw, however, in that it permitted intervention by any of the signatories in China if China did not develop and maintain an effective and stable government. There was also no provision for enforcement or sanctions on the violators of the treaty.

In 1925, the United States and other world powers signed the Geneva Convention of 1925 that established the rules for war, including the rights and treatment of POWs during wartime. In 1928, French Foreign Minister Aristide Briand invited the United States to join France in a bilateral treaty renouncing war. The French were considering occupation of parts of Germany near the French border and wanted to prevent the United States from intervening on the side of Germany if hostilities erupted. Secretary of State Frank B. Kellogg thought that the proposal was folly; but a pact outlawing war had popular support in the United States and refusal would make America appear belligerent. Consequently, Kellogg declared that Briand's proposal was so laudable that the United States would invite all nations to join America and France in outlawing war. Kellogg then took the lead in negotiating a general agreement to outlaw war as an instrument of national policy. The Pact of Paris, or Kellogg-Briand Pact, was signed ultimately by sixty-three nations, including all the great powers, but Kellogg regarded the pledge as more valuable for appeasing peace sentiment at home than for influencing foreign nations. Providing no means of applying collective sanctions against an aggressor, the pact was an idealistic but empty gesture, much pressure for which had been generated by the activism of women's organizations.

Paradoxically, the idealistic foreign policy of Woodrow Wilson had left the United States deeply involved in the affairs of Caribbean countries. United States troops were in Haiti, Nicaragua, and the Dominican Republic, and diplomatic relations with Mexico had been suspended. On the South American mainland, hostility toward these United States occupations interfered with both trade and investment.

Republican Leadership Reaffirmed

In the depression year of 1922, discontented agrarian and labor elements met at the Conference for Progressive Political Action. Continuing its meetings into 1924, the conference agreed to support the presidential nomination of Senator Robert M. La Follette at the Republican convention and, if defeated there, to organize a third party with La Follette as its candidate.

Obviously the progressive minority had no chance of winning the Republican nomination, but it might have swung over to the Democrats if that party had supported an advanced liberal ticket. The Democratic Party, however, was disastrously split over such issues as prohibition, the Ku Klux Klan, Catholicism, and immigration restriction. Hampered additionally by a rule requiring a two-thirds majority for nomination, its convention took 103 ballots to select a relatively unknown, New York corporation lawyer, John W. Davis, who failed to inspire enthusiasm in any faction.

When the Republican convention met and nominated Coolidge on the first ballot, the Progressives held their own convention and put forward La Follette. Supported by the American Federation of Labor, many Western farm organizations, and the Socialist Party, La Follette ran on a platform advocating the type of action that Europeans called social-democratic nationalization. Under La Follette's platform, injunctions in labor disputes were to be effectively forbidden, and Congress was to be given power to overrule the Supreme Court.

Coolidge swept the election with 15,718,000 popular votes to 8,385,000 for Davis and 4,831,000 for La Follette. Davis won only the solid South, and La Follette carried only Wisconsin. The Progressive Party had failed to develop the strength necessary for survival and would not be a major factor in the election of 1928.

▶ Calvin Coolidge, a conversative Protestant differed greatly with Harding in that he was quiet, detached, sober, endowed with a Puritan moral ethic, and considered to be honest beyond reproach.

Calvin Coolidge

Calvin Coolidge was a standard conservative clone of Harding in regard to economic and social policy, but a great contrast on a personal level. Coolidge's conservative laissez-faire ideology was perhaps best summed up by Coolidge himself when he stated, "The chief business of the American people is business. The man who builds a factory builds a temple. The man who works there, worships there."

On the personal level, however, Coolidge differed greatly with Harding in that he was quiet, detached, sober, endowed with a Puritan moral ethic, and considered to be honest beyond reproach. In these things, unlike Harding, Coolidge was at least consistent with the ideals of his conservative Protestant fundamentalist supporters. Coolidge's ethical standards, however, proved to be much more than window dressing; consequently, he quickly forced the resignation of Attorney General Daugherty and others tainted by scandal during the Harding administration.

Coolidge would be less quick to action in other areas, however, since his stated goal was "to become the least president that the country ever had." Coolidge's statement is a reference to his Hobbesian conservative laissez-faire philosophy of government, but he may have achieved his goal in more ways than one. Coolidge was non-energetic, both in policy and in his personal life, and generally chose to confront crises by taking long naps in the White House. Those around Coolidge described his disposition as "eternally tired." Coolidge's "Silent Cal" nickname was earned by keeping appointments and meetings to a minimum, engaging in as little conversation as possible. Coolidge himself acknowledged his own preference for "silence" and once remarked to reporters, "I don't recall any candidate for president that ever injured himself very much by not talking." Comedian and political commentator Will Rogers perhaps summed it up best when he observed of Coolidge: "Silent Cal. He don't say much, but when he does say something, he don't say much."

When Coolidge did choose to speak, he sometimes revealed that he was actually better off remaining silent. A good example of this is Coolidge's assessment of the economy in 1928, prior to the onset of the Depression when he stated, "The future may be better or worse. ... I am certain of one thing, however, when people are thrown out of work, unemployment results." On another occasion, Coolidge astutely observed that "the final solution for unemployment is work."

▶ Calvin Coolidge's decision not to run for president in 1928, left the enthusiastic Republican Herbert Hoover in the running.

Few American presidents have enjoyed four such prosperous, peaceful, and generally pleasant years as those from 1924 to 1928. Coolidge could easily have been re-nominated and elected again had he chosen to run for a second elected term in 1928; but after keeping the bosses in doubt long enough to preserve his influence in the convention, Coolidge announced simply that he chose not to run. With this announcement, the energetic Commerce Secretary Herbert Hoover became the obvious Republican choice for president. Hoover won the Republican nomination at the Republican National Convention on the first ballot despite a stinging rebuke from Coolidge, who labeled the more progressive Hoover as a "spendthrift" with "bad ideas." Coolidge further exclaimed concerning Hoover, "that man has offered me unsolicited advice for six years, all of it bad."

Hoover was supported both by big business and by conservative moralists, who favored his "dry" position on Prohibition. Quickly nominated, Hoover ran on a platform of continuing the Harding-Coolidge policies. With these, he said, "We shall soon, with the help of God, be in sight of the day when poverty shall be banished from this nation."

The Democratic managers probably had little hope of defeating a strong Republican, but they thought that an unusual candidate might bring new voters to the polls. Such reasoning may explain the swing to Governor Alfred E. Smith of New York, a Catholic of Irish immigrant parentage who emphasized his origins by wearing a brown derby. Other than prohibition, the Democratic platform scarcely differed from the Republican, and on economic questions in particular, Smith differed little from Hoover. Smith made John J. Raskob, a fellow Catholic and chairman of the Finance Committee of General Motors, manager of the Democratic campaign. Raskob gave the utmost assurance to business that there would be no upsetting changes.

▶ Democrats were doubtful they could defeat a strong Republican, but they thought that an unusual candidate might bring change. Such reasoning may explain the swing to Governor Alfred E. Smith of New York, a Catholic of Irish immigrant parentage.

Aside from the immense support given the Republicans by the boom prosperity, the issues came to be Catholicism and prohibition. Smith could do nothing about the former except give assurances of his independence from Rome and his religious tolerance, and these apparently had little effect in the strongly Protestant back country. In the belief that labor and many businessmen were now in favor of repeal of the Eighteenth Amendment, Smith departed from the plank in the Party's platform that had been inserted to win the support of the dry South and campaigned strongly against prohibition.

While probably no candidate could have defeated Hoover in the year 1928, Smith lost or miscalculated on all fronts save one. His "me-tooism" in support of business probably changed few votes. His Catholicism and anti-prohibition sentiments lost seven Southern states and, at the most, gained only two Northern ones. Smith even lost his home state of New York and lost the electoral vote 444 to 87. Smith did, however, have an appeal for the urban masses. This urban swing, scarcely noticeable in the Hoover landslide, was a portent of the basic change in party strength that was to come from the increase in urban Democrats in the decades ahead.

High Hopes for a Prosperous Nation

In his inaugural address Hoover said, "I have no fears for the future of our country; it is bright with hope." His memoirs also show the high hopes with which he started his administration: "Mr. Coolidge was reluctant to undertake much that was either new or cost money, and by 1929 many things were already fourteen years overdue." Hoover had a number of plans for bringing more efficiency into government activity, but his first major act, calling a special congressional session to redeem Republican promises to farmers, unfortunately misfired. The president sponsored the Smoot-Hawley Tariff bill to raise the rates on agricultural products; but when the bill finally passed the Senate in June 1930, it carried higher rates on numerous manufactured products, as well, and raised the general level of rates on dutiable articles about 25 percent. Although this was not what the president had intended, he signed the bill to give assurance to business. Meanwhile, other nations had been raising their tariffs—some in retaliation for the United States' action—and the outlook for world trade and repayment of international obligations steadily grew darker.

In place of the McNary-Haugen scheme, passed twice by Congress but vetoed both times by Coolidge, the administration planned to help the farmer by the Agricultural Marketing Act of 1929. This originally provided for loans to aid cooperative selling, but progressives added a provision for the use of federal money to stabilize the market price of grain. For these purposes, a Federal Farm Board was given a revolving fund of $500 million, the largest single appropriation up to that time for nonmilitary purposes. The plan for buying grain to raise domestic prices and reselling when the market could absorb the surplus might have worked for a time had there been rapid worldwide recovery in 1930; but since the trend toward oversupply in wheat already seemed clear, however, this cure through manipulating the market was, at best, a makeshift expedient.

After the onset of the depression in 1929, most of President Hoover's plans for efficiency and mild reform were abandoned in the effort to bring back prosperity. "Instead of being able to devote my four years wholly to these purposes," he lamented, "I was overtaken by the economic hurricane.... Then the first need was economic recovery and employment." Fearing that reform would upset business and deepen the depression, the president became as conservative as his predecessors.

Postwar Economic Change

The Decline of Craft Unionism

World War I and the postwar boom, along with the failure of wages to keep pace with prices after the Great War, brought union membership to a peak of 5 million workers in 1920, about 12 percent of the total labor force. While this was a record for the United States, the level of organization was low in comparison with Western Europe. A major reason was that American labor organizations were limited largely to the skilled crafts and older types of industrial activity, thus excluding millions of workers, not only white men with poor skills but also people of color and white women. The new mass production industries of the twentieth century, such as automobiles, chemicals, and electrical equipment, had successfully resisted efforts at organization.

The union situation of 1920, however, was essentially unstable. Many union members in war industries and postwar construction soon had to seek other jobs as the country made the transition from the war economy to a peace economy. Employer organizations, held back since 1917 by government policy and competition for workers, were now ready to marshal business-minded people against organized labor. Furthermore, during the Red Scare it was easy to convince the middle class that unions had radical intentions. The Supreme Court dealt unions a major blow in 1921 when they ruled that "Dangerous strike activity" was illegal. Furthermore, the court defined picket lines as "dangerous strike activity" when they declared that any picket placed within 50 feet of another to be "dangerous activity" and, therefore, illegal. Under this definition, all picket lines, in the traditional sense, were illegal; and strikers could not block the entrance of scab workers into the workplace without being arrested. The same year, President Harding called in the National Guard to put down a United Mine Workers' Strike in West Virginia and Pennsylvania.

Unions also faced political pressure from big business. The National Association of Manufacturers, representing small and medium-sized business, sponsored the American Plan, which various trade and employer organizations vigorously pursued. It called for the open shop—a shop in which workers could be hired without joining a union. Some of the organizations associated with the movement insisted that their members should not enter into any union contracts. Advertisements, denouncing the closed shop (one restricted to union members) as un-American were placed in newspapers. Labor spies were hired by management in larger numbers than before in order to detect union organizers.

One important "welfare" device for preventing national unions from organizing workers was the employee representation plan, or company union. The government demand that contractors in World War I enter into collective bargaining with their employees led 125 of the largest companies to organize their own unions with some four hundred thousand members. Since these unions and their officers were controlled and supported financially by the companies, they were not generally regarded as true representatives of labor. Yet in the 1920s, they constituted the one growing area of labor organization. By 1928 it was estimated that company union membership had grown to 1.5 million, half that of the AFL.

In addition to the American Plan and competing company unions, independent unions may also have been weakened by reforms in employee relations. In some big companies, the personnel departments that had been established during the war sought to decrease turnover and increase productivity by improving working conditions and proposing various measures to bolster workers' morale. It may still be argued, however, that the independent unions declined because of the depression of 1920 to 1922 and because business was growing away from the old skilled crafts. The immediate drop in union membership during those two years of depression was 1.4 million. Another two hundred thousand members were lost during the prosperous years from 1923 to 1929. As a consequence, by 1930 less than seven percent of the labor force was organized in independent unions.

Only in coal and textiles were white labor leaders engaged in vigorous campaigns during the mid-20s. Both industries had the same basic problems: Southern areas were not unionized, and Communists were undermining the existing union leadership. Although John L. Lewis was able to preserve the United Mine Workers' bargaining position in the older areas, he had to agree to wage cuts during the years of high national prosperity. Neither the United Textile Workers nor its Communist-led rival, the National Textile Workers' Union, was able successfully to invade the South and unionize the new mills. With lower wages in that region, the industry continued to drift away from New England and the Middle Atlantic states.

As militancy declined in the ranks of labor in the 1920s, there was a trend toward cooperation with employers. Where an employer had a small business and was often poorly informed, as in the garment industry, unions could help to improve shop practices and overall efficiency. Even some of the large railroads found that union-management cooperation increased productivity in their shops. When one looked at the labor scene as a whole, however, the areas of advancing cooperation were small.

Another trend during this period was toward surrender of union leadership to racketeers. In unions where the complacency of the mid-20s made the members careless about attending meetings, dishonest local officials, supported by so-called gorillas, built up machines that the rank and file dared not oppose. Often these labor racketeers dealt secretly with employers, taking payments from them to prevent the union members from demanding wage increases. The 20s were not a decade of pleasant prosperity for organized labor.

Industrial Distress

In the twenties, reformers increasingly criticized that symbol of modern mass production, the automated assembly line. The speed of the line was set by management; and with no independent unions to protect the workers, those who could not maintain the pace were summarily fired. In addition, such plants generally had many workers under a single supervisor or foreman, who consequently had little contact with the workers as individuals. While such big-plant assembly-line jobs involved only a small fraction of the labor force, to many artists and intellectuals they dramatized the plight of the individual in an impersonal, mechanized society.

Blacks who had come to industrial centers during the war and the postwar boom faced problems of a special type. Many companies would not hire them for anything but menial service jobs, and AFL unions would not accept them in the skilled crafts. This discrimination made many blacks quite ready to act as strike breakers against organized white labor. A. Philip Randolph, one of the few influential black labor leaders, organized a union of Pullman Company maids and porters in 1925; but in spite of the all-black personnel on the cars, the Brotherhood of Sleeping Car Porters was unable, at that time, to displace a company union and force collective bargaining. Other efforts by Randolph to create a national organization of black unions were even less successful.

Agricultural Depression

The poorer and the less efficient farmers also failed to share in the prosperity of the 1920s. Those who had been encouraged by the government to borrow money in order to bring more land under cultivation to meet the wartime demand now found themselves with heavy debts and a declining market. The hardest hit were wheat farmers in the western prairie and plains states and cotton growers in the South. Mortgage foreclosures forced owners to become tenants, and losses on farm loans led to the closing of thousands of small banks in country towns. In the South, thousands of black sharecroppers, particularly, were forced off the land and had to seek jobs in the growing cities.

During the decade, advances in soil biology and chemistry made diversification of crops much safer than they formerly had been. Hybrid seeds were developed which could increase the yield and resistance to unfavorable weather of both corn and wheat, and all-purpose tractors were reduced in cost. Since few farmers had extra capital and the overly competitive situation failed to interest other investors, the new agricultural knowledge and new agricultural technologies were little used until World War II again brought high prices, rural prosperity, and a shortage of labor. Nevertheless, the development of the internal combustion engine-driven tractor increased American agricultural production at the same time that European demand for American farm products diminished, as Europe recovered from the devastation of World War I. The development of synthetic fibers further depressed prices of cotton and wool; by the end of the 1920s, when GNP per capita was $873, farm GNP per capita was only $223.

A Slower Rate of Growth

In the long run, economic growth depended upon the making of more and more capital goods such as buildings, factories, roads, and machines. For the decade 1919 to 1928, net capital formation (that is, the creation of new capital goods) in relation to national income was 14 percent less than in the previous decade and nearly 18 percent less than two decades earlier. During the years 1924 to 1929, the annual investment in new capital goods was actually falling. On the other hand, lower taxes were increasing the net income of the wealthiest classes, and their savings were rising. These savings of funds for investment were, by 1924, beginning to run ahead of the needs of industry and business for capital for physical expansion. In other words, the upper-income groups had more savings each year than there were productive new securities to be bought. As a result, investors were competing for the available securities, and the price of securities went up. A large part of the nation's savings was being used for speculation, while rising interest rates in 1929 were attracting unneeded billions in bank loans from Europe.

Why should the rate of creation of capital goods slow down when there was plenty of saved money to pay for them? Two explanations can be offered. One is that since there was little change in real wages or salaries from 1924 to 1929, consumer demand did not rise rapidly enough to encourage industrial expansion. The other explanation is more speculative in that changes in technology occur in incalculable ways. Some that promise substantial profits require large new investments, as in the case of railroads, while others do not, as in the case of the phonograph. A series of technological innovations requiring large investment absorb savings and labor and produce an expanding economy, but in the 1920s few major capital-absorbing innovations in technology occurred. While some older developments—such as electrification, roads for automobiles, and improvements in steel production—were still going forward, there was a slowing down of the combined rate of growth after 1927.

Technological Advance

Although the new technological developments of the 1920s did not actually increase the rate of capital investment, new devices were sought more vigorously than ever before. By 1929 about a thousand large firms were all supporting some type of research. Better control of industrial products through careful cost accounting, spot testing, and laboratory analysis (collectively referred to as "quality control") also led to higher efficiency and productivity.

Radio broadcasting and air travel first reached the general public in this decade, and automobiles and electricity also came into general use. Until 1919, the federal government forbade private use of radio, but broadcasts by Westinghouse's station KDKA of the results of the presidential election of 1920 demonstrated the great public possibilities of the new medium of communication. Within the next few years, the industry assumed the general pattern that was to remain for decades: Competing national networks would subsist on substantial revenue from large advertisers, and high-priced performers would offer a variety of programs. By 1930, 12 million American families, about 40 percent of the total, could tune in stars like Rudy Vallee and Eddie Cantor, and sports announcer Graham McNamee on their radio sets.

The airplane, invented before World War I, had never attracted much interest in America. During the war, the government made an effort to catch up with European development but produced few planes before the Armistice led to cancellation of contracts. The Post Office started an experimental airmail route between New York and Washington in 1918, and after six years extended service to Chicago and San Francisco. Meanwhile, commercial plane production was negligible, and flying was limited to selling rides at airfields and local fairs. In 1925 the government first made an effort to build commercial transport by allowing the Post Office to grant airmail contracts to private firms. The following year Congress gave general regulatory authority to the Commerce Department.

The regular use of air service in Europe and a series of spectacular overseas flights, culminating in Charles A. Lindbergh's solo crossing of the Atlantic in 1927, gave some Americans confidence enough to travel by plane. Between 1928 and 1930 passengers increased from fourteen hundred to thirty-two thousand, and revenue miles flown multiplied about thirty times to a total of 4.3 million. Although the young industry continued to grow during the Depression, the 100 million passenger miles flown in 1940 were almost negligible compared to the 24 billion passenger miles by rail and the incalculable travel by private cars.

In the automotive industry, however, even in the prosperous years of the 1920s, the smaller assemblers of cars had been dropping out. The early years of the Depression reduced the number of competitors to fewer than a dozen, all producing similar cars within four or five price ranges. Ford finally had to give up his famous Model T in 1927 and bring out the Model A, a car similar to those of his chief competitors. This episode temporarily convinced American manufacturers that the public wanted size and luxury in new cars rather than cheapness. No one was more easily convinced than Walter P. Chrysler, who had a passion for fine cars. (See *Walter P. Chrysler: Lover of Fine Cars.*)

Both homes with electricity and total consumption of electrical energy doubled from 1920 to 1930. In urban and suburban areas five-sixths of all residences came to have electricity, but farm electrification was only beginning. In 1920 1.4 percent of farms had electricity and by 1930 only 10 percent.

The New Era in Business

Managerial Enterprise

As usual in times of business prosperity, the number of firms grew faster than the population as a whole. In 1920 there were probably fewer than 2.5 million firms, but in 1929 there were over 3 million. About two-thirds of all firms were in trade and service, and very few of these had more than two or three employees. The overall growth figures, however, conceal a great deal of routine change. Every year of the 1920s, thirty to fifty thousand new firms started, and every year a slightly smaller number left the business scene. While adequately capitalized small companies that were started by people who knew the business they were entering had good chances of success, a large percentage of entrepreneurs lacked both qualifications. At the top, a few medium-sized or large firms disappeared each year through mergers, but these equaled only one or two percent of the new firms starting up.

The American business structure appeared to have reached a plateau of stability. Big companies continued to dominate highly capitalized manufacturing industries, railroads, and utilities; but antitrust laws checked the rise of true monopoly. In industries dominated by a few companies, competition in price was avoided; however, competition in quality and marketing was generally vigorous.

By the 1920s, the stock of most very large companies was widely held. Neither the officers nor the directors of the company owned any considerable percentage of the shares. The chief officers were chosen from among men who had made successful careers in management and were professional executives, rather than either relatives of an owner or large personal investors. The connection of such men with profit was indirect. Profit for the company was a mark of success, a guarantee of security, and a fund from which larger salaries could be drawn, but it did not directly enrich the professional manager. These men were interested in building strong organizations capable of weathering bad times, rather than in reaping quick profits in the market. They favored spending earnings for research, expert advice, and improvement of company morale, rather than using them to pay extra dividends to the stockholders. As a result, the common stock dividends of the biggest companies tended to move toward moderate, stable rates rather than to fluctuate with profits.

While scarcely a thousand companies were big enough to have professional, bureaucratic management remote from control by owners, the thousands of top executives of these big companies were leaders of business opinion. Executives commanded specialized knowledge and expert staff work. They hired the best lawyers, lobbyists, accountants, and engineers. Their assistants wrote for them speeches and articles analyzing business problems. Hence, America on the surface seemed much more a land of big business than was the case statistically.

Shaping Public Opinion

George Creel's Committee on Public Information, similar to European agencies for propaganda during World War I, provided a new emphasis on creating favorable opinion. About 1920, Edward Bernays and Ivy Lee began to call themselves public relations counselors. Soon the major advertising agencies also had public relations departments. The usual techniques were to publicize events that showed the client in a good light and to plant favorable stories in magazines. Much of the content of newspapers in the peaceful years of the 20s originated in public relations offices.

The value of the stockholder as a public relations resource was also exploited. By lowering the price of shares through splitting them two or more ways, and by aggressive selling to small investors, often through agents of the company, it was possible for a big corporation to acquire tens of thousands of new stockholders. American Telephone and Telegraph, which took a leading part in this movement, increased the number of its owners from 50,000 in 1920 to 210,000 in 1930. Stockholders were sent attractive annual reports and letters from the president designed to make them feel that they were an important part of the organization. In return, many stockholders undoubtedly used their votes and influence for government policies favorable to the company.

Whether as a result of the new public relations or prosperity, or for other less obvious causes, the American public seemed to have given up much of its traditional hostility to big corporations. Articles in praise of business signed by corporate leaders made popular reading in mass-circulation magazines, and business periodicals boasted of the dominance of the businessman and his values. Advertising executive Bruce Barton even pictured Christ as a businessman. In this friendly atmosphere, business was bold in the use of direct influence in legislatures, in community pressures through business clubs, and in the use of advertising contracts to influence editors. A basic danger, as illustrated in the 30s, was that business developed few new progressive policies to go with its added power.

Stock Market Boom and Bust

Besides lacking a suitable social philosophy, businessmen and their economic advisers lacked understanding of relationships in the economy. Consequently, the stock market boom from

▶ Walter P. Chrysler: Lover of Fine Cars

▶ Walter P. Chrysler

Early in the century Henry Ford had first supplied sturdy, homely, reliable automobiles at moderate prices. By the 1920s Walter P. Chrysler had brought luxury cars within the financial reach of the middle class. In the long view, the high performance of Chryslers from 1924 to after World War II typifies the trend of American automobile design much more than the stark, bare Model T's. Chrysler's role in setting the pattern for the principal American industry of the twentieth century makes him one of the most important men of his time.

When Chrysler was born in 1875, his father was a locomotive engineer living in Wamego, Kansas. Even such aristocrats of labor, however, couldn't afford to send their children to engineering school. After high school Chrysler went into the railroad shops to learn by doing. His rise was rapid, and his devoted wife and young children moved often as he climbed up the ladder of railroad shop positions to a top rung as Superintendent of Motive Power for the Chicago Great Western.

Chrysler was a big, broad-faced, genial man with an emotional power that often controlled his own decisions, as well as impressing those around him. Fortunately his intuitive reactions usually turned out to be right. In 1908 he saw a white Locomobile with red upholstery, four cylinders, and chain drive at the Chicago automobile show. It shared, with half a dozen other makes, the highest prestige in the luxury part of the market. Chrysler promptly fell in love with fine cars. For a man making $4,200 a year to buy a $5,000 automobile was madness. Yet Chrysler, with the help of a banker friend, managed to do it. He didn't want the car to drive, and it was weeks before his family even had a ride. Instead, he wanted to take the car apart. He wanted to learn everything about it, which he proceeded to do during nights and weekends.

Meanwhile, to learn more about the problems of production, still unconsciously driven, no doubt, by his dreams of creating motorcars, he quit his railroad job in 1910 and took one in manufacturing with the American Locomotive Company in Pittsburgh at 20 percent less salary. Within two years the chance came to make automobiles. Although American Locomotive wanted to keep him at $12,000 a year—real wealth in the last year before federal income taxes—he became Works Manager for the Buick division of General Motors at $6,000.

Now he was on the main track of his career in a prodigiously expanding industry. Buick, a medium-price car, was the most popular of the General Motors lines. An offshoot of William C. Durant's wagon works, Buick construction was still being supervised by men who had originally been craftsmen in wood. Chrysler quickly introduced the techniques of large-scale metalworking he had learned at American Locomotive and actually had part of the works on an assembly line earlier than the Ford Plant.

Chrysler was so successful in both making and marketing cars that in 1915 Durant, the founder of General Motors, who had regained control of the company with help from the du Ponts, made Chrysler president of Buick at a salary of $500,000, payable largely in GM stock. By 1919, his division was forging ahead of the others at General Motors, and Chrysler was one of the key men in the industry. He had come to be respected for his great ability at selling and finance, as well as in production; and he had enough money in GM stock to be independent. Consequently, when Chrysler thought Durant was overexpanding early in the inflationary years of 1919, he decided to leave the company and dispose of his stock. Selling out near the peak of the boom, he put the cash in trust for his wife and children and prepared to retire.

General Motors was not the only major automobile company to be caught with too much inventory and too little cash in the rapid market decline of the spring and summer of 1920. Chrysler was soon drawn back into industry affairs, first as a "doctor" for Willys-Overland at an incredible $1 million-a-year salary, and two years later as Chairman of the Reorganization Committee for the ailing Maxwell Motor Company. Meanwhile, in talking with design engineers Fred M. Zeder, Owen Skelton, and Carl Breer, Chrysler succumbed to the overwhelming urge to bring out a new car with its own name and design, using the Maxwell facilities.

Over numerous difficulties, chiefly financial, Chryslers were displayed to large crowds at the Commodore Hotel in New York during the 1924 annual automobile show at nearby Grand Central Palace. Besides being attractive and well made, the Chryslers were the first to combine high-compression engines (which meant higher speed), four-wheel hydraulic brakes, and a shorter wheelbase—a majority of the most important engineering innovations that would be made during the next fifteen years. And the cars sold for no more than Buicks of comparable size.

As young people, particularly, swung toward Chryslers, the company quickly took steps to move beyond medium-priced cars sold to hundreds of customers to cheap cars sold to millions. To compete with Ford and Chevrolet, which dominated this market, Chrysler purchased Dodge Brothers in 1927 in one of the largest financial deals in American automotive history. This marked the formation of the "big three" in the American automobile market, with Chrysler for many of the early years ahead of Ford in sales.

Chrysler's emphasis on engineering and performance permanently shifted sales efforts toward attractive new models offered at relatively uniform, noncompetitive prices. Chrysler's new ideas created the American automobile market, whose features were to last with little change until the advent of the compact in the late 1950s, and in many respects without much alteration until the gasoline crisis of the 1970s. Few other twentieth-century Americans have been so responsible for shaping the everyday utilities of life.

1927 to 1929, though not reflected in any corresponding upswing in real capital formation, was not regarded as dangerous. Confidence that the severe business cycle was a thing of the past pervaded American finance.

The wealthiest class (about 5 percent of the population) received about a third of all income and was taxed at very low rates. Thus, their savings were tremendous. Low corporate taxes allowed big companies to accumulate unprecedented cash surpluses. Both personal savings and corporate surpluses were used for speculation. Moreover, brokers, by means of loans, made it easy for investors of even modest income to purchase securities beyond their means. Investors could buy "on margin"—that is, deposit only a small percentage of the total price of a block of securities, with the broker advancing the rest of the money. The hope was, of course, that the price of the securities would rise and enable the investor to make a large profit on his small equity. Often brokerage houses and banks would lend three quarters of the cost of new securities, the customer depositing only a 25 percent margin. In practice, margins often were allowed to go down to 10 percent or less. Not only were both domestic and European banks happy to lend on this type of "demand" or "call" loan, but big business companies also employed unused reserves for stock market loans.

Since investors would readily buy the shares of railroad and public utility holding companies, ambitious entrepreneurs like the Van Sweringen brothers in Cleveland, Samuel Insull in Chicago, and S. Z. Mitchell in New York set up pyramids of one holding company on top of another. By selling stock in these companies to the public, the empire builders got the money to buy dozens of operating companies while keeping personal control of the organization through the top holding company. In theory, economies were being achieved through removal of wasteful competition, but in fact the savings were often consumed by greater managerial costs.

High-pressure selling by the agents of bankers and brokers led investors into buying many other questionable securities. Mortgages on the new urban hotels, apartments, and office buildings that were rising all over the nation were divided into small bonds for sale to investors. Ultimately these buildings would be needed, but in 1929 construction was already outrunning the demand for such space. United States investment firms literally coaxed foreign governments into issuing bonds that could be marketed to the American public. In spite of all this manufacture of new securities, the demand exceeded the supply and boosted the price of existing stocks higher and higher.

By the summer of 1929, many insiders, convinced that stock prices were too high in relation to earnings, started to sell; but thousands of speculators could only cling to the limb they were on and hope for some miraculous support. Late in October of 1929, the limb broke. In a series of panic days on the New York Stock Exchange, stocks sank so fast that holders on margin were generally wiped out. Efforts by J. P. Morgan and Company to stabilize the market failed, and European banks began withdrawing the $2 billion they had loaned on call. On October 29, the day of most extreme panic, 16 million shares were traded, and at times stocks could not be sold for want of buyers at any reasonable price. By November 1929, stocks had lost 40 percent of their September value.

Stunned by this disaster in what appeared to be stabilized prosperity, business and political leaders insisted that the economy was sound and that the market break would not affect industry. Only about half a million people had margin accounts, and only a million and a half had brokerage accounts of any kind; however, since this small group included most of the chief accumulators and users of capital, their importance was not to be measured in numbers. Furthermore, the whole economy had become more closely geared to the stock market than ever before. In the collapse of values, corporations lost their surpluses. Brokerage houses were unable to sell fast enough to cover their loans. Banks, in turn, were left with demand loans that could be liquidated only at a fraction of their value, and foreign governments were no longer able to borrow on Wall Street.

Chapter Review

23

Summary

The abrupt end of World War I found America leaning toward conservatism after twenty years of Progressivism and a world war. Demobilization of the war economy was immediate, leading to a rush of consumer spending in an economy short of consumer goods and rapid inflation. When wages did not keep up with price increases, a series of major strikes paralyzed the economy. The strike activity resulted in a few celebrated terrorist bombings, including the house of American Attorney General A. Mitchell Palmer. The country became gripped in fear of a communist takeover, just two years after the Bolshevik Revolution in Russia. Palmer led the crusade against communism with an overbroad sweep that led to six thousand arrests and six hundred deportations, trampling on civil rights. Palmer's raids, however, uncovered no bomb materials or vast communist conspiracy. Palmer discredited himself by predicting a communist uprising on May Day 1920, but not before the Red Scare resulted in the trial and execution of two Italian immigrant anarchists, Sacco and Vanzetti, based more on their political beliefs than the evidence against them.

The years 1917–1921 were years of major race riots in a number of American cities with 120 people dying in riots in 1919 alone. In Tulsa, in 1921, whites even resorted to dropping dynamite from airplanes on black neighborhoods. Amidst this atmosphere of racial tension, the Ku Klux Klan made a major comeback after being re-formed by Methodist minister William J. Simmons from Georgia. The Klan was a money making organization as well as a nativist terror organization and political movement. Simmons and his top partners reaped huge profits while the Klan terrorized blacks and others that the Klan deemed immoral and took over politics in many states and municipalities. Eventually, the Klan over-reached and dissipated as its list of targets was extremely long, but not before hundreds of lives were lost in Klan violence with seventy people lynched in 1919 alone. The Klan was also successful in passing the National Origins Act in 1924 that greatly reduced immigration and eliminated it for "Orientals" altogether.

In 1920, the affable but ignorant Republican Warren G. Harding was elected president. Harding was a laissez-faire conservative who delegated most of his authority to his cabinet members while he escaped the White House to party at "The House on K Street" with other top aides, Congressmen, women, and illegal alcohol during Prohibition. Harding had multiple long-running affairs and is believed to have fathered an illegitimate child with Nan Britton. Meanwhile, members of his administration were involved in a series of scandals that resulted in prison for some and suicide for others. Harding himself was not involved in the scandals and died of a heart attack in 1923 before the scandals could sully his reputation.

With Harding's death, the quiet and sober Calvin Coolidge became president and continued Harding's conservative laissez-faire policies. Harding and Coolidge, with authority delegated to Treasury Secretary Andrew Mellon, imposed high tariffs and cut taxes and kept balanced budgets. Secretary of State Charles Evans Hughes took the lead in foreign policy and negotiated the Five Power Treaty that called for a moratorium on production of large capital ships, the Nine Power Treaty that recognized the Open Door in China, and the Geneva Convention of 1925 that established rules for war and POWs.

There were problems in the global economy, however, that were obscured by the prosperity of the 1920s. The war debts from World War I were reduced, but never paid off completely; and by 1934 all countries defaulted except Finland. American agriculture overproduced, leading to low prices and an agricultural depression. Labor Unions declined in power after President Harding sent the National Guard to put down a United Mine Workers Strike and the Supreme Court declared "dangerous strike activity" to be illegal. Finally, an overvalued stock market crashed in October–November 1929, and the economy slid into the Great Depression just six months after Herbert Hoover assumed the presidency.

Chronological Time Line

1915 November: William J. Simmons re-formed the Ku Klux Klan in Georgia.

1917 July: East St. Louis Race Riot resulted in deaths of thirty-nine blacks and ten whites.

1919 Red Scare

1919 April: A bomb blew the hands off of the maid of former Senator Thomas Harwick of Georgia, who had been anti-union.

1919 June: A bomb blew the porch off the home of Attorney General A. Mitchell Palmer.

1919 The Boston Police Force Strike was put down by Governor Calvin Coolidge.

1919 Seventy African-Americans are lynched in the South.

1919 From July 27–August 3, in Chicago, a race riot killed fifteen whites and twenty-three blacks in a week of rioting that destroyed over one thousand homes and injured over five hundred people.

1919 November: the Justice Department detained 250 members of the Union of Russian Workers.

1920 Palmer and J. Edgar Hoover arrested six thousand persons for conspiracy to overthrow the U.S. government; however, no bomb materials and only three revolvers were confiscated.

1920 April: Palmer announced his anticipation of a communist revolt on May 1, which passed without incident.

Chapter Review (cont'd)

Time Line (cont'd)

1920 November: Republican Warren G. Harding defeated Democrat James Cox for the presidency on a "return to normalcy" platform.

1921 Italian immigrants and anarchists Sacco and Vanzetti were accused of murder.

1921 From May 31–June 1, whites in Tulsa dropped dynamite from airplanes on the predominantly black section of town, killing seventy-five people and destroying over one thousand homes.

1921 On September 2, President Harding uses federal troops to put down a United Mine Workers' Strike.

1922 The Five Power Treaty limited the building of capital naval ships.

1923 Jesse Smith, an official in the Office of the Attorney General, was accused of influence-peddling and committed suicide.

1923 On August 2, Warren G. Harding died of a heart attack, and Calvin Coolidge assumed the presidency.

1923 Germany experienced hyperinflation of 26 billion percent.

1924 The National Origins Act limited the total number of immigrants to 150,000 annually and excluded "Orientals."

1924 Congress passed the Soldiers' Bonus Bill.

1924 In the Dawes Plan, the U.S. cancels 80 percent of the Italian Debt and 60 percent of the French debt from World War I.

1924 November: Calvin Coolidge was elected president over Democrat John Davis and Progressive Party candidate Robert La Follette.

1925 The Geneva Convention established rules for war and POWs.

1925 On August 25, fifty thousand Klansmen parade down Pennsylvania Avenue in Washington.

1927 Ford introduced the Model A.

Time Line (cont'd)

1927 On April 23, Sacco and Vanzetti were executed.

1927 On May 20–21, Charles Lindbergh made the first solo flight over the Atlantic.

1928 Kellogg-Briand Pact was signed by sixty-three countries outlaws war.

1928 November: Herbert Hoover defeated Al Smith for the U. S. presidency.

1929 The stock market crash in October–November signaled the beginning of the Great Depression.

1930 June: Congress passed the Smoot-Hawley Tariff.

1931 December: President Herbert Hoover suspended European debt payments for one year.

1933 Europeans defaulted on debt to the United States.

Key Terms

Demobilization: The abrupt change from the tightly controlled wartime economy and war production to a free market and consumer production

Calvin Coolidge: Governor of Massachusetts that put down the Boston police strike and later became president

Red Scare: Panic of 1919–1920 precipitated by demobilization, strikes, and a few terrorist bombings that resulted in the arrest of six thousand Americans and deportation of six hundred others

A. Mitchell Palmer: Overzealous U. S. Attorney General during the Red Scare that fanned the flames of panic and trampled on Constitutional rights

Palmer Raids: Palmer's overbroad sweep to ferret out communists that resulted in six thousand arrests and six hundred deportations, violating Constitutional rights protections

Emma Goldman: Anarchist and suffragette that was deported as a result of the Red Scare

Sacco and Vanzetti: Anarchists and Italian immigrants that were executed for murder in 1927, perhaps as much for their political views as for the evidence against them

Ku Klux Klan: Ultra-right nativist organization that gained control of politics in a number of states in the 1920s and terrorized blacks and others it deemed as un-American or immoral

Chapter Review (cont'd)

Key Terms (cont'd)

William J. Simmons: Methodist minister from Georgia that re-formed the Ku Klux Klan in 1915.

Searchlight: National publication of the Ku Klux Klan

TWK: "Trade with Klansmen" stickers that were required in Klan-controlled areas to prevent Klan boycotts and vandalism

A.K.I.A.: Klan abbreviation for "A Klansman Am I"

Earle Mayfield: Texas Klansman that won a U.S. Senate seat in 1922

Felix Robertson: Texas judge and Klansman that narrowly lost the Texas governor's race in 1924 after Klansmen pelted his opponent's house with rocks

Immigration restriction: The National Origins Act established immigration quotas, limiting immigration to 150,000 annually and excluded "Orientals."

Harry Daugherty: U. S. Attorney General under Warren G. Harding that was implicated in scandals, but pleaded the Fifth Amendment and was not convicted

Warren G. Harding: Republican president elected in 1920 that was known for his ignorance of issues, laissez-faire, delegation of authority, and undisciplined personal conduct

"Ohio Gang": Top assistants to President Harding that were involved in scandals

"House on K Street": House where President Harding and his top advisors partied with women and members of Congress during Prohibition

Charles Forbes: Head of the Veterans' Bureau that served two years in prison stemming from profits he made from construction of Veteran's hospitals

Thomas Miller: Alien property custodian that was sentenced to prison for accepting bribes

Teapot Dome Scandal: This scandal involved Navy oil reserves in Teapot Dome, Wyoming, where Interior Secretary Albert Fall arranged with Navy Secretary Edwin Denby for the transfer to the Department of the Interior of Navy oil reserves. They then leased the reserves to Edward L. Doheny's Pan-American Petroleum and Harry F. Sinclair's Mammoth Oil Company in exchange for cash and securities.

Albert Fall: Interior Secretary that was fined $100,000 and given one year in prison for accepting a bribe in the Teapot Dome Scandal

Edward Doheny: Head of Pan-American Oil Company that loaned Interior Secretary Albert Fall $100,000 in the Teapot Dome Scandal

Harry Sinclair: Head of Mammoth Oil Company that gave Interior Secretary Albert Fall $300,000 in cash and securities in the Teapot Dome Scandal and served nine months for witness tampering

Nan Britton: Woman that claimed to have had a child with President Warren G. Harding

Carrie Phillips: Senator's wife that was paid by the Republicans to take a world cruise to keep her away from Warren G. Harding during the campaign of 1920.

Andrew Mellon: U. S. Treasury Secretary under Harding and Coolidge that was influential in American economic policy in the 1920s

Key Terms (cont'd)

Charles Evans Hughes: U. S. Secretary of State under Harding and Coolidge that was influential in foreign policy in the 1920s

Five Power Treaty: U.S., England, France, Italy, and Japan agreed to limits on the construction of capital naval ships.

Nine Power Treaty: The U.S. and other great powers agreed to the Open Door principle in China.

Geneva Convention of 1925: Established rules of conduct for war and treatment of POWs

"Silent Cal": President Calvin Coolidge's nickname in the press due to his quiet nature

Will Rogers: Radio personality, comedian, and political commentator in the 1920s

Al Smith: Irish-Catholic Democratic Party candidate for president in 1928

Herbert Hoover: Republican Commerce Secretary under Calvin Coolidge that won the presidency in 1928

Kellogg-Briand Pact: 1928 agreement signed by sixty-three countries that outlawed war

Walter B. Chrysler: Head of Chrysler Corporation, one of America's "Big Three" auto manufacturers

Crash of '29: The stock market crash of October–November 1929

Pop Quiz ▶ ▶ ▶

23

Chapter 16

1. Factors that led to the "swing to conservatism" after World War I included which of the following?
   a. the happiness with the peace in Europe that Americans wanted to conserve.
   b. fear that communist revolution along the Russian model might spread.
   c. a wave of strikes that followed World War I as workers tried to increase their wages along with inflation.
   d. both b and c.

2. What did Calvin Coolidge state during the Boston Policemen's strike?
   a. Firemen could strike, but police could not.
   b. Policemen could strike, but firemen could not.
   c. There is no right for public employees to strike—anytime, anywhere.
   d. Public employees may strike as long as they give the government proper notice.

Chapter Review (cont'd)

Pop Quiz (cont'd)

3. Which of the following was of the problems with the Sacco and Vanzetti trial?
   a. Judge Webster Thayer was clearly biased against the defendants.
   b. Judge Webster Thayer was clearly biased in favor of the defendants.
   c. They were not tried by a judge, but by a military tribunal.
   d. Their confessions were extracted by torture.

4. Why did *Life* magazine editor Robert Coughlan describe the post-World War I political mindset as "Coitus Interruptus"?
   a. World War I had provided a sobering interruption of the free love mentality in America.
   b. World War I proved that freedom isn't free.
   c. The general emotion of the people at the time was one of hatred for the devil they had been fighting, but the evil entity had cheated them by surrendering before it could be obliterated
   d. The general emotion of the people was hatred of the devil and love for Jesus.

5. Which of the following is true of the KKK in the 1920s?
   a. It was a nonprofit organization.
   b. Klan leaders reaped tremendous economic benefits.
   c. Klan leaders expended their entire fortunes to keep the Klan afloat.
   d. The Klan rejected Jesus and adopted Satanism.

6. KKK recruiting efforts in their "top down" strategy included __________.
   a. business leaders
   b. civic leaders
   c. church leaders
   d. all of the above

7. TWK stickers in the windows of businesses stood for __________.
   a. "trade with Klansmen"
   b. "trade without the Klan"
   c. "typical witless Klansman"
   d. "time to whip the Klan"

Pop Quiz (cont'd)

8. Which of the following is true of Warren G. Harding?
   a. scholar-president
   b. strong political beliefs and convictions
   c. uncompromising
   d. received the Republican nomination partially because he was described as a "handsome devil" and women could vote

9. Economic policies under the Harding Administration included __________.
   a. tax cuts
   b. a government health care plan
   c. old age pensions
   d. the establishment of the right to collective bargaining

10. Which of the following is a characteristic of Calvin Coolidge?
    a. energetic
    b. known as a "party animal"
    c. overly verbose
    d. none of the above

11. In 1921, with which of the following did the U.S. Supreme Court deal labor unions a blow?
    a. "Dangerous strike activity" was illegal.
    b. Immigrants could not be in unions.
    c. Communists could not be in unions.
    d. Members of the mafia could not be in unions.

12. Which of the following was included as an explanation for the slowdown in the creation of capital goods?
    a. Since there was little change in real wages 1924–29, consumer demand did not rise.
    b. There were too many new capital-absorbing innovations that left the economy capital short.
    c. There was too much government economic regulation.
    d. There was too much government deficit spending.

Chapter Review (cont'd)

Pop Quiz (cont'd)

13. When Ford finally discontinued the Model T for the Model A, it convinced auto manufacturers of which of the following?
    a. The public wanted cheap cars.
    b. The public wanted black cars.
    c. The public wanted size and luxury in cars.
    d. The public was unconcerned with safety and reliability.

14. After the stock market crash of 1929, what did political and business leaders argue?
    a. The nation had slid into an economic recession.
    b. The economy had fallen into a Great Depression.
    c. The economy was sound, and the market break would not affect industry.
    d. The economy needed a massive government bailout.

15. Al Smith was the first Catholic to win the presidency. T F

1. D	5. B	9. A	13. C
2. C	6. D	10. D	14. C
3. A	7. A	11. A	15. F
4. C	8. D	12. A	

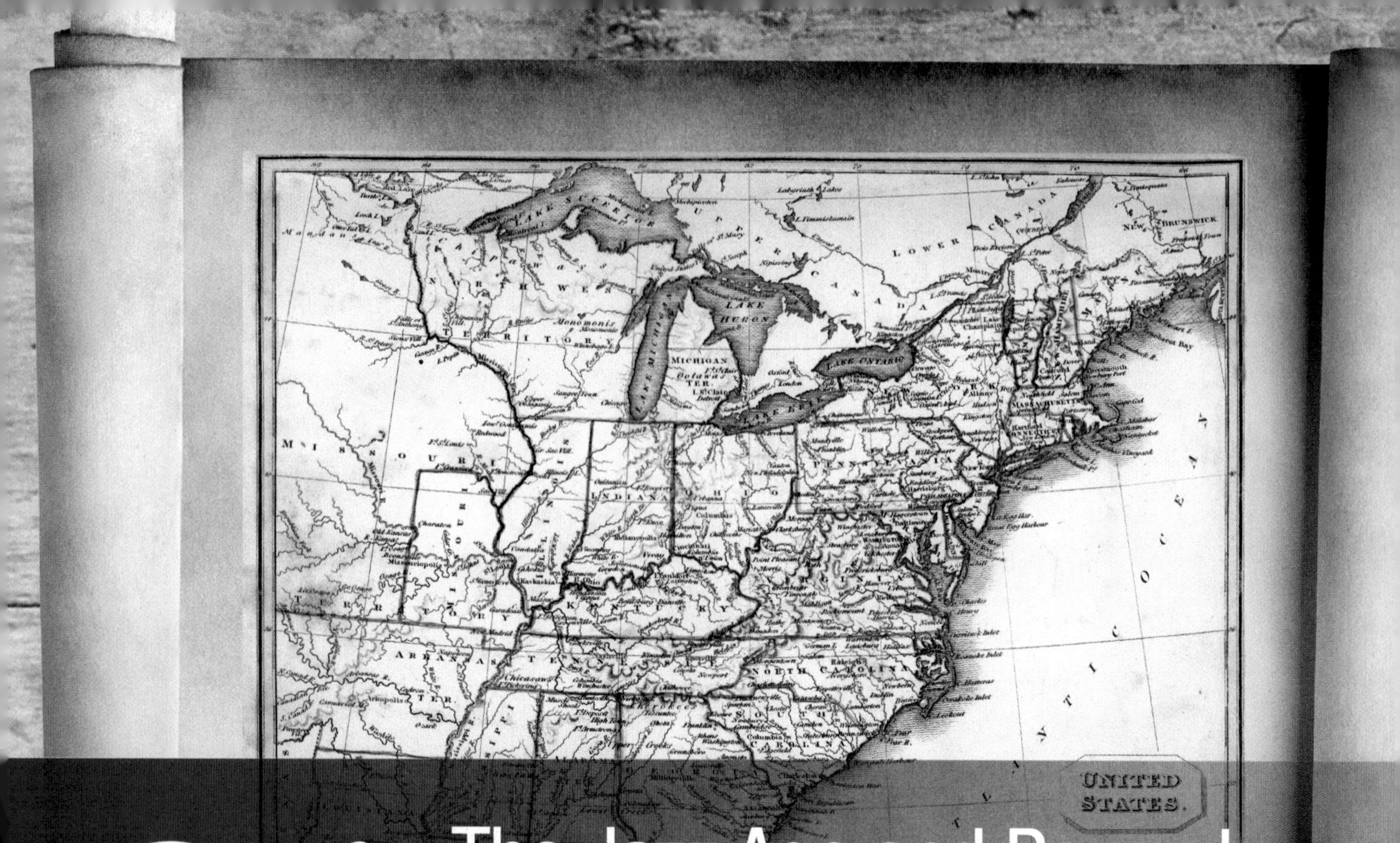

24 The Jazz Age and Beyond; American Culture in Prosperity and Depression

Chapter Objectives

The Inner Revolution

Living in Good Times and Bad

A New World of Uncertainty

Psychological Theories

Changes in Education

Physical and Social Theory

Keynesian Economics

Religion

Religious Fundamentalism in the 1920s and the Scopes "Monkey" Trial

Scopes Monkey Trials

Ethnic Churches in Urban Centers

Mass Communication

Newspapers

Magazines

Radio

Painting

Photography

Music

Literature and Drama

Motion Pictures

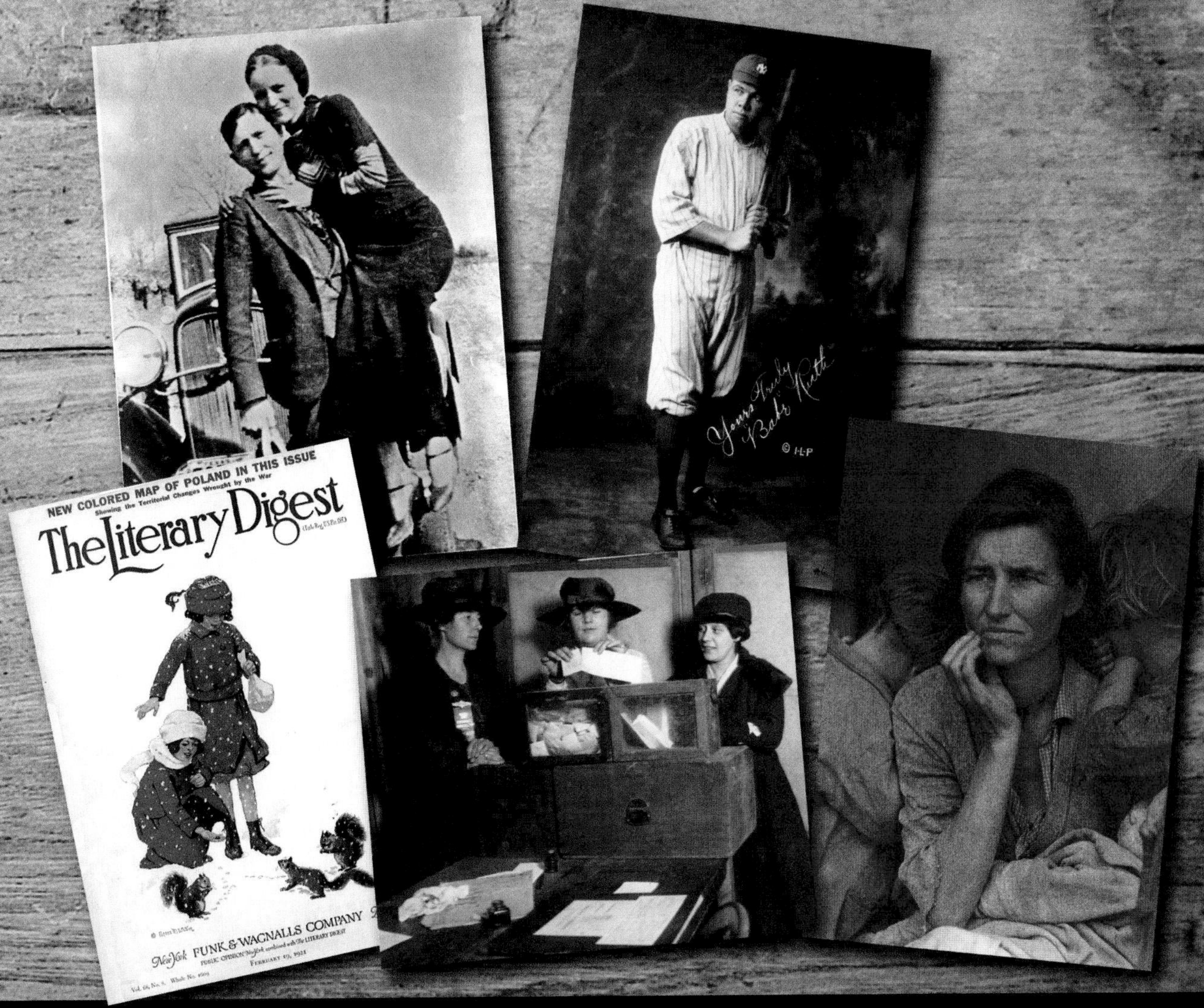

Architecture

Social Change

Motorization and Urbanization

The "Automotive Social Ladder"

The Emancipated Woman

An Urban Black Society

Prohibition

Gangster Wars

Interwar Transition

The interwar years provided two, quite different, challenges for Americans. The decade of the 1920s was generally, if not universally, prosperous, with people having to adjust to a whole new world of communication, of transport, of technology in general. Often called "the Jazz Age," the era saw a new plenitude of consumer products, as well as a flowering of the new media of mass culture. Then the stock market crashed in 1929; and as the country slid into its worst-ever depression, most Americans began to focus on saving, rather than spending—except when it came to movie attendance as this form of escape was proving steadily popular despite the hard times.

The Inner Revolution

Living in Good Times and Bad

If there was such a thing as the "normal" or "ordinary" American family during the interwar period, it lived in or near a small town—even as late as the 1920s. In the 20s people's lives expanded in movement and variety as families acquired an automobile and a radio, and towns acquired a movie house. Real incomes advanced somewhat; and manufactured items like vacuum cleaners, washing machines, and ready-made clothes lightened the household chores that wives had been expected to perform throughout recorded history. Yet this new world of material things probably had little effect on people's ideas. In general, newspapers, radio, and movies were conservative forces, reinforcing the pro-business traditions of American culture. If nothing else, votes cast in the presidential election of 1928 suggested that most people were reasonably contented with things as they were.

The period has been called the Jazz Age, characterized by wild parties, tobacco, free wheeling women, and heavy drinking during Prohibition. These aspects of the time period, however, were limited largely to the upper middle class of the largest metropolitan areas and to young people on certain college campuses—among whom "flappers" and "jazz babies" flourished. While easier, less formal manners spread across the nation and automobiles provided young couples with an opportunity to escape supervision, the change in customs in most parts of the country was gradual and moderate. The real revolution in the manners of youth was still more than a generation away, and deliberate flouting of the liquor laws occurred chiefly in urban industrial communities where public opinion was opposed to prohibition.

In contrast with the 1920s, the Depression of the 1930s had very unequal effects on the world of "mid-America." If the workers of a small town had been employed in manufacturing, they were likely to suffer unemployment and lack of money during much of the thirties; but in trade, employment kept up. In many areas local buying and selling of food, even on a barter basis, declined by only a moderate percentage. Conditions were worse in rural regions where crops were grown for export and not for home consumption. Many cotton farmers, for example, had to try their hand at growing food crops, with mixed results. The middle-class belief (and President Hoover) that a "dole" would undermine self-reliance delayed a general system of relief payments during Hoover's administration. The worst period was over by 1933, when federal funds under Franklin Roosevelt's New Deal lifted the burden of unemployment

▶ The Jazz Age was characterized by wild parties, tobacco, free wheeling women, and heavy drinking during Prohibition. However, entertainment was limited largely to the upper middle class of the largest metropolitan areas and to young people on certain college campuses—among whom "flappers" and "jazz babies" flourished.

relief from the bankrupt states and communities. License statistics from the 1930s and gasoline sales indicate that most families living outside of towns kept their automobiles in service, even at the sacrifice of food or clothing. Inadequate diet, however, was a more difficult problem with which to cope. In an abstract, theoretical view, the American standard of living was high enough in the 1920s that a decline of a quarter to a third could be handled. Unfortunately, the burden was not uniformly distributed, and Americans did die from malnutrition in the early thirties.

A New World of Uncertainty

In the late nineteenth century, middle- and upper class Americans subscribed to well-defined values of Christian morality and the doctrine of self-improvement through the use of reason and will. They viewed the physical universe as a coherent, understandable system regulated by simple laws. As a result of their certainties, parents and teachers tended to be authoritative, and political and economic leaders tended to be dogmatic.

During the first two decades of the twentieth century, however, several areas of advanced learning attacked this orderly system of beliefs. Historical analysis in seminaries and Darwin's theory of evolution cast increasing doubt upon the literal truth of the Bible, while psychology questioned older theories of learning and mental discipline. With the discovery that only mathematics provided a reliable guide to the behavior of matter, understanding the nature of matter seemed lost to all but scientists. One could argue that none of these new ideas were satisfactory substitutes for the old "truths," especially since the new sciences were based on uncertainty and a continual search for answers that could be, at best, only tentative.

The new scientific theories of the period, which were difficult for most to comprehend, entered the popular culture only partially and imperfectly. Nevertheless, ideas that three-quarters of the people never understood might, still, subtly influence all of society. Leaders in America come chiefly from the group with higher education and upper-middle-class family backgrounds; and these favored people tend to set the standards, shape the customs, and wield the ultimate power in society. Consequently, what is a far-out idea in one generation can become the guide for social action in the next. By the 1920s, in fact, the impact of the new scientific ideas was being felt in urban middle-class child rearing practices, education, and popular thought.

Psychological Theories

Of great impact were the psychological theories that questioned the human ability to reason objectively and the importance of reason as a basis for action. In the first place, the founder of behaviorism, John B. Watson, regarded consciousness itself as only a byproduct of physical processes and having no role in causing behavior. He insisted that both human and animal learning occurred simply through "conditioned reflexes." Significantly different ideas of Sigmund Freud, a Viennese physician and neurologist, also had a lasting social impact.

Freud popularized the idea that people were impelled to think and act in certain ways by unconscious pressures rather than by logical reasoning. He further held that these irrational, unconscious urges were of a "sexual" nature, although he used the term sex broadly to include many cravings for gratification not normally thought of as sexual. Thus when people thought they were behaving rationally, their behavior might be merely a disguise for a mixture of erotic urges and cravings based upon unmet childhood needs that, though unrecognized by the individuals, influenced their behavior in many ways.

One of the great appeals of Freudianism was that it offered help to people who were emotionally disturbed. Through a patient's free association of ideas in the presence of a psychoanalyst, together with the analyst's scientific interpretation of the patient's dreams, it might be possible to bring the disturbing elements to conscious recognition and thus to lessen or end the patient's feelings of conflict or anxiety.

The Freudian emphasis on the *libido*—the instinctive sexual drive in humans—as well as the Freudian denial of the validity of religious feelings had a profound effect upon the thinking of well-educated people all over the Western world. By placing no emphasis on abstinence and little on reason, and by offering salvation through indulgent secular "confession," Freudianism turned older theological doctrine upside down. People who sought Freudian therapy did not necessarily discard their religious faith, and a few clergymen managed to reach a compromise with the new doctrine. Again, however, the scientific approach weakened, or contradicted, the values of the nineteenth century.

In social life, Freudianism provided an excellent weapon for attacking Victorian formalities, rural Protestant virtues, and older educational ideas. Leading intellectuals like Walter Lippmann, Harold Lasswell, and Jerome Frank applied it to politics, public opinion, and the law, with the general effect of further weakening respect for rationality and traditional standards. Magazines and books were full of the new language of psychiatry, and many well-educated people enjoyed being amateur Freudian analysts. Well-informed parents now worried about the danger of suppressing their children's urges, and the child-centered home joined the child-centered school in relaxing discipline.

Changes in Education

The mid-nineteenth century American view was that education should be directed primarily toward moral or religious rather than intellectual ends. The philosophy of Horace Mann was a "blend of natural law, faith in progress, capitalistic morality, and liberal Protestantism." The teacher's role was to see that the pupils memorized passages that inculcated abstract truths.

John Dewey was, however, advancing a radically progressive approach to education based on the new psychology. In the 1920s, his principles became dominant in the major teachers' colleges and spread throughout the urban public school system as theory, if not as practice. Dewey's *Democracy and Education*, written in 1916, was the most influential guide, and the Progressive Education Association, formed in 1919, was the major pressure group. The Teachers' College of Columbia University was the chief training center for progressive educators. In estimating the total influence of progressive education on pupils, however, it should be noted that in 1930 a majority of the nation's students were still in rural schools.

Often allied with progressivism were new movements for efficiency and utility in education. School superintendents applied business methods of "job-analysis" to their schools. Teachers were rated by their efficiency in performing the "housekeeping" necessities of the school while their intellectual worth was often ignored. The idea of preparing students for daily life, rather than requiring them to master a body of knowledge, led a writer in 1922 to divide school activities into four major categories: health, fundamental processes, civic and social relations, and recreation. Of these, only the second embraced conventional learning.

From the emphasis on utility came more practically oriented curricula on the secondary level. The Smith-Hughes Act of 1917, granting federal aid to vocational education, started a rapid spread of special high schools and manual or trade departments in older schools. An increasing distinction was made between the minority in high school who expected to go to college and the majority who should substitute the development of practical skills for "book learning."

▶An early twentieth century home-economics class. The idea of preparing students for daily life, rather than requiring them to master a body of knowledge, led a writer in 1922 to divide school activities into four major categories: health, fundamental processes, civic and social relations, and recreation.

In the 1930s, the extreme child-centered philosophy was superseded by a community-centered approach. No doubt the depression put emphasis on social and community duties; but, in addition, child-centeredness had been pushed to such chaotic extremes in a few schools that even Dewey had become critical of the results. The newer view stressed good group relations among students and teachers, plus the responsiveness of schools to the needs and problems of the community. Although it partially restored discipline, this approach did not necessarily place more emphasis on academic learning.

In 1920 the average teacher's salary was $871 a year, and the usual school was a small rural building with one or two teachers. The average teacher did not have a college education, might never have heard of John Dewey, and was not paid enough to support a family. As a result, most teachers were young, single women teaching school until they married or found a more promising job. By 1930 the situation had improved somewhat. The average salary had risen to $1,400—still inadequate for a middle-class family—and buses were introducing the consolidated school. By 1940 consolidated schools, where different teachers taught different grades and with a greater degree of specialization among teachers, were becoming the rule in the more populous areas; and a majority of the children were in urban schools. Because of the fall in prices that accompanied the onset of the Great Depression, teachers' salaries had risen about 25 percent in purchasing power between 1920 and 1930.

During the 1920s and 1930s, college education followed many of these same trends. There was a decided shift away from the traditional classical program. Schools of education, in which physical education could be a major subject, multiplied. Women were offered courses in home economics, and most major universities started schools of commerce or business. For students who wanted a mixture of liberal arts and "useful" subjects, junior colleges offered two-year certificates. In 1920 there were only 52 such colleges, but by 1930 there were ten times that number.

Although many regarded these developments as a lowering of the standards of college education, colleges and universities showed substantial development as centers of learning and research. The 1920s was the first full decade in which general research was supported by massive endowments such as those of the Carnegie and Rockefeller Foundations. Increasing private donations and state grants enabled American universities to rival those of Europe as centers of research. At the same time, more and more Americans were going to college. In 1920, 8 percent of young people aged eighteen to twenty-one were in college, while by 1930 it was over 12 percent and in 1940, nearly 16 percent. While some of the 1930–1940 increase was due to lack of employment opportunities and government assistance, college degrees were becoming increasingly important in securing jobs and gaining social prestige.

Physical and Social Theory

University departments of science continued an attack on the nineteenth-century belief that human intelligence was on the verge of understanding the nature of things. Over the half century before 1920 a brilliant group of European physicists and mathematicians demonstrated that a human mind could not perceive the nature of physical reality or picture its workings by the ordinary three-dimensional images. Only mathematics had a logic that could handle the four or more dimensions of physical problems. Furthermore, they discovered that matter was not solid substance but rather a system of particles held together by electrical energy, and the only guides to this reality were mathematical equations and readings of complicated recording devices. Discoveries in the infinitesimal world inside the atom and the infinite world of outer space made reflective observers uncertain whether reality is precise and orderly or, at least, whether the human imagination is capable of grasping its order if there is one. The most famous atomic scientist of the time, who not only developed the theory of relativity but also became a well-known celebrity in his own time—a rare accomplishment for a scientist—was Albert Einstein.

Basic philosophical uncertainty, however, did not prevent progress in sub-atomic physics. By the 1930s, it was known that tremendous energy in the form of heat could be released by splitting atoms to form new elements. While Germans were in the lead in theory, large investments by the United States government, aided by German émigrés, would produce a bomb from massive atomic fission as the World War II came to a close in 1945. Wartime needs would also speed the development of electronic devices such as radar and digital computers. All these scientific innovations were pragmatic, based on experimentation to find what worked rather than on a complete understanding of electricity or of the inner structure of the atom.

Some popularizers predicted that the scientific uncertainty that was revealed to the reading public in the late 1920s would lead to a new age of faith; but actually such writing had little immediate effect. Instead, the immediate reaction seemed to be a move in the opposite direction. Like the earlier evolutionary theory, the new science undermined theology without offering anything understandable to the average person to replace it. The highly abstract characterizations of God that seemed consistent with the physical theories were without much appeal to Americans.

The academic world, of course, was required to pay heed, and the changes reported in physics were upsetting to the social sciences and philosophy. Society no longer seemed so simple as it had at the beginning of the century. If general social laws were to be discovered, it would only be by highly complex and sophisticated means. As a result, American social scientists turned

▶ The most famous atomic scientist of the time, Albert Einstein, developed the theory of relativity and became a well-known celebrity for his accomplishments.

to improving their methods and trying them out on limited, carefully defined problems rather than elaborating general systems. Philosophers, also discouraged by the mysterious character of reality, turned to studies of method. "How can any kind of truth be established?" became their major question. The testing of various systems of logic and representation consumed their time. The main body of philosophers lost interest in general systems of thought and, consequently, all contact with the public.

Keynesian Economics

While the social sciences as a whole continued their pursuit of more sophisticated methods, the economic collapse of the 1930s brought the pressure of immediate, practical problems to bear on economic thinking. A few academic social scientists embraced Marxism and gave up hope for the capitalist system, but their number was surprisingly small. The majority turned to solutions of the type that were given a rounded theoretical formulation by the British economist John Maynard Keynes.

Keynes' ideas brought about the first major revision of economic theory in the twentieth century, and they offered a more realistic view of the operation of the entire economy than had existed before. His major work, *The General Theory of Employment, Interest and Money*, published in 1936, shifted the main theoretical emphasis from supply and demand to income and investment, or from the mechanics of the market to the distribution of income. Keynes' most important conclusions were (1) that increasing the income of the poor stimulated demand, while increasing the income of the rich promoted saving; (2) that increased demand, not increased saving, led to new business investment (his major revision of older theory); (3) that total income could increase only from such investment; (4) that if the functioning of the undisturbed free market did not provide adequate business investment to maintain a sufficient flow of income, government was the only agency with sufficient spending power to see that this result was achieved.

Obviously these doctrines implied the need for higher wages and government investment and were hence resisted by conservatives. Yet by the time Keynes' work was published, the theory was already partially being applied by President Franklin Roosevelt's New Deal, which included government deficit spending to boost demand and create employment. By the end of World War II, the prosperity induced by government spending and massive redistribution of income downward was so obvious that politicians of both major parties implicitly acted on the Keynesian assumptions; and most academic economists gradually made some of Keynes' ideas the starting point for their new theoretical models. In short, Keynes supplied the rationale for the capitalist revolution that emerged from the disaster of the Great Depression.

Religion

While the pressures of clergymen for sweeping social reform lessened in the prosperous 1920s, religious groups became increasingly concerned with secular matters. Urban churches, in particular, acquired game rooms, gymnasiums, and lecture halls and seemed to be shifting their emphasis from worship to social service and recreation. By the end of the decade, the Federal

Council of Churches of Christ, the liberal Protestant organization, had commissions for such diverse matters as international justice, social service, race relations, and Christian education. The National Catholic Welfare Conference, formed to help carry out social obligations of the Catholic Church, became a powerful force with a large staff of experts on legislative matters. Missionary activities also were increasingly secularized. By 1920 effectively organized Protestant and Catholic missions in non-Christian areas of the world were emphasizing "civilizing" education, medical care, and other services.

The Great Depression brought liberal Catholic, Jewish, and Protestant organizations closer together. In 1931 the National Catholic Welfare Conference, the General Conference of Rabbis, and the Federal Council of Churches of Christ joined in a conference on "Permanent Preventatives of Unemployment." An interfaith Committee on Religious Welfare Activity continued such efforts. Despite vocal opposition from conservatives, who wanted their churches to refrain from raising political and social questions, liberal religious journals became increasingly secular in content and more concerned with economic problems. Nevertheless, parish churches and their ministers tended to remain quite conservative. World War II also shifted religious leaders away from social reform.

▶Charles Darwin proposed his theory of evolution through natural selection in his book *Origin of the Species*. In this publication Darwin questioned the creation story from the Bible's *Genesis*, and sparked further criticism and debate regarding its factuality.

Religious Fundamentalism in the 1920s and the Scopes "Monkey" Trial

The increasingly social orientation of the leading Protestant churches was resisted by fundamentalists—Protestants who believed in the literal interpretation of the Bible as a historical record and prophecy, as well as a guide to faith and morality. The conflict between fundamentalism and current scientific views, either religious or secular, was dramatized by the Scopes trial in 1925.

In the minds of many, the publication of Charles Darwin's *Origin of the Species* in 1859 and his theory of evolution called into question the literal creation story contained in the Bible's, book of Genesis. This combined with growing scholarly historical criticism of the Bible in the late nineteenth century that presented challenges to the literalist interpretations of the Bible espoused by religious fundamentalists. These "attacks" on fundamentalism then combined with the anti-communism, nativism, and hyper-patriotism of the Red Scare era to form the foundation of a Protestant fundamentalist political movement that would continue in ebbs and flows through the rest of the twentieth century.

At the turn of the century, most American biology texts supported the concepts of organic evolution and Darwin's theory of natural selection. One botany text in 1912 even went so far as to infer the rejection of the Bible creation story by stating that:

> "... evolution has been accepted because it appeals to the mind of man as being more reasonable that species should be created according to natural laws rather than by an arbitrary and special creation."

The inclusion of these types of statements in textbooks did not create much of a furor prior to World War I, at least in part because so many rural Protestant fundamentalists received so little formal education prior to World War I. In the first three decades of the twentieth century, however, states required an ever growing number of students to attend public schools, with the result that rural fundamentalists were suddenly exposed in far greater numbers to ideas apparently in contradiction with their literal interpretations of the creation story in Genesis.

William Jennings Bryan, perhaps, well-captured the sentiments of the Protestant fundamentalists in 1924 (a year before the Scopes trial) when he argued:

> "a scientific soviet is attempting to dictate what shall be taught in our schools, and, in doing so, is attempting to mold the religion of the nation."

Bryan's statement obviously infers a connection between Darwin's scientific theory and Bolshevism. Throughout the remainder of the twentieth century, religious fundamentalists would repeatedly charge the scientific community with being influenced by the radical political left. In the minds of the fundamentalists, the science itself had to be false because it conflicted with "God's Word;" and the false doctrines must, therefore, be the work of the Godless political left, who had somehow taken over the scientific community and were using it to further their atheistic "soviet" political agenda. Many religious fundamentalists agreed with William Jennings Bryan who not only believed that evolution was a false doctrine, in conflict with "God's Word" and therefore evil, but also believed that Christians had a right, if not a duty, to suppress that evil if they were able. Bryan argued that when science and religion come into conflict, the issue should be decided by the will of the "common people" rather than by scientific scholars. Bryan echoed the sentiments of thousands of fundamentalists when he declared that he could not understand "why should the Bible, which the centuries have been unable to shake, be discarded for scientific works that have to be corrected and revised every few years." Bryan further declared:

▶ William Jennings Bryan summed up the sentiments of the Protestant fundamentalists in expressing that he believed, in regards to Charles Darwin, one person was attempting to decide for all what should be in taught in schools, and in doing so, was attempting to establish the religion of the nation itself.

> "all the ills from which America suffers can be traced back to the teaching of evolution. It would be better to destroy every other book ever written, and save just the first three verses of Genesis."

Similar to Bryan in his analysis of the evolution question, a popular evangelist of the 1920s, Billy Sunday, summed up his attitudes toward the scientific revolution by stating, "When the Word of God says one thing and scholarship says another, scholarship can go to hell."

All Americans, however, did not sympathize with Sunday; William Jennings Bryan and the fundamentalists and the nation became somewhat divided between the secular and scientific left and the fundamentalist Protestant right. Columnist Walter Lippmann, perhaps, well summed up the rebuttal of the scientific community when he stated:

> "the religious doctrine that all men will at last stand equal before the throne of God was somehow transmuted in Bryan's mind into the idea that all men were equally good biologists before the ballot box."

In addition to their disdain for science and evolution, Protestant fundamentalists, in general, were decidedly patriotic and blended their patriotism with their religion. Billy Sunday epitomized this direction of Protestant fundamentalism in his assertion, "there can be no religion that does not express itself in patriotism." As a consequence, during World War I, Reverend Sunday taught children to hiss at the German flag, advocated incarceration for those who criticized Wilson's War policies, and encouraged men to volunteer for the army (although Sunday himself, who was only twenty-six at the time of the American entry into the war, did not). Concerning economics, Sunday espoused laissez-faire pro-business capitalism. Sunday denounced the use of government to help alleviate social ills, such as poverty, as "godless social service nonsense."

Protestant fundamentalists of the 1920s viewed the "once-moral" America as in decay, adrift from its founding principles and addicted to alcohol and sin. Consequently, the Protestant fundamentalists were staunch proponents of prohibition. When prohibition became enforced on January 16, 1920, Billy Sunday celebrated by holding a mock funeral for John Barleycorn.

Religious conservatives reacted to what they viewed as an attack on their religious beliefs and American society at large by proposing laws outlawing the teaching of evolution in the public schools. Such bills were introduced into the legislatures in half of the states and enacted in a number of states in the South, including Mississippi, Arkansas, Florida, Oklahoma, and Tennessee. Several bills banning evolution failed in the Texas legislature, so Texas Governor Ma Ferguson directed that state's textbook commission to adopt a policy of selecting textbooks that did not mention evolution. In issuing the directive, Ferguson proclaimed, "I am a Christian mother ... and I am not going to let that kind of rot go into Texas textbooks." The stupidity surrounding these and other laws extolling the Bible as a science book can hardly be overstated. For instance, in Kentucky in 1922, a teacher was brought to trial for teaching that the earth was round. The teacher was fired when his opponents were able to prove in court, through the use of Bible scriptures, that the earth was indeed flat.

Scopes Monkey Trials

The fundamentalists were dealt a major blow in 1925 in the famous "Scopes Monkey Trial" where twenty-five-year-old biology teacher John Scopes defied Tennessee law by teaching evolution. In this celebrated case that received national media attention, the American Civil Liberties Union (ACLU) provided free legal defense for Scopes in the persons of Maynard Shipley and the renowned and agnostic defense lawyer Clarence Darrow. The old Protestant fundamentalist, William Jennings Bryan, volunteered his services to aid the prosecution.

The national media descended on Dayton, Tennessee, and covered the trial in a manner that made the religious fundamentalists appear backward and foolish. Bryan ended up taking the stand as a Bible expert and subsequently embarrassed himself by declaring that the earth was only five thousand years old and the earth was created in six days, and then by revealing some confusion with how "Cain took a wife." Bryan was forced to concede, however, that the earth moved around the sun, which led to his admission that the Bible is filled with metaphors that need not be interpreted literally. Bryan also conceded that each of the "six days" of creation might actually stand for millions of years. Scopes was convicted and fined $100, but the fundamentalists were thoroughly embarrassed in the national press. There were no additional anti-evolution laws passed in any states.

▶ Concerning the Scopes trial in 1925, the majority of the media and press presumed John Scopes (above) would be found guilty and published illustrations mocking the defendant. *Life* magazine ran a cartoon depicting monkeys reading books and proclaimed, "the whole matter is something to laugh about."

Nevertheless, the Scopes trial did not result in a complete defeat for the anti-evolutionists. Allyn and Bacon Publishing of Boston admitted to the *New York Times* that their books were "tactfully" written so as to prevent disturbing the sensibilities of the religious fundamentalists. Other publishers followed a similar strategy so that the very word "evolution" vanished from most textbooks written after 1925. Generally, the word "development" was inserted into texts any place that the word "evolution" might have been used. In short, publishers made economic decisions not to lose the book sales in the South that might be lost from the inclusion of the word "evolution." In the end, the mighty dollar would accomplish for the fundamentalists what their political efforts in state legislatures could not.

Ethnic Churches in Urban Centers

Equally fundamentalist in their way, but with a quite different mission and influence, were the ethnic churches in the urban centers. Each immigrant group in America's urban centers, such as New York, Boston, and Chicago, had quickly established its own congregations upon arrival in the United States. These ethnic churches, most of which were Catholic, were centers of neighborhood social life and forces for the preservation of national customs and ceremonies. Wise Catholic bishops usually appointed priests of the same nationality as the parishioners in any particular urban church. Second- and third-generation immigrants often supported their churches and church schools more to preserve their national cultures than to show commitment to a particular denominational faith.

As the old-stock, white middle class deserted the cities, more and more urban Protestant churches became black. The original Southern Baptist denomination spawned numerous sects whose small churches provided centers where the members, often from the same areas of the South, could rejoice in the promise of a better life to come after death. This emphasis on the hereafter rather than the here and now made the black churches, as a whole, a conservative influence, tending to reconcile parishioners to their earthly lot.

Except in the South, mainly the urban middle class had supported the Protestant churches in America. Neither farmers in remote areas nor working-class city dwellers generally made the effort to participate in the activities of a Protestant church; yet for the increasingly mobile members of the middle class, particularly in suburban areas, the church had a definite social value. It was a place to meet leading citizens and develop friendships through cooperation in religious endeavors. Consequently, the great growth of the urban and suburban middle class and the spread of the automobile to outlying areas helped precipitate a steady increase in church membership up to 1929. By 1926, church members constituted 46 percent of the population.

These reasons for growth go far to explain why the Great Depression reversed the trend in membership. People with only shabby clothes and no money for the collection plate did not want to appear before their more prosperous neighbors. The Depression may actually have increased religious feeling, but between 1930 and 1934 the income of Protestant churches declined 50 percent. For the decade as a whole, church membership fell about 6 percent. That the decline was caused, at least partly, by financial hardships is indicated by the rapid growth in membership in the prosperous years that followed World War II.

Mass Communication

Newspapers

The newspaper continued to be the principal reading matter of adult Americans during the interwar period. Indeed, the transition from prosperity to depression gave most people more time to read and increased the size and circulation of newspapers. Where personal interests were concerned, as in attitudes toward the New Deal, readers were obviously prepared to disagree with their newspapers, most of which were strongly anti-Roosevelt. Publishers and editors, however, by subtle selection and handling of news and comment, undoubtedly influenced readers to accept many of their ideas.

The major trend in the whole period between the wars was toward papers that were less competitive in opinion and more elaborate in format. While newspaper chains stopped

▶ The newspaper was the principal reading matter of adult Americans during the interwar period. The transition from prosperity to depression gave people more time to read. With subtle selection and handling of news and comment, publishers and editors succeeded in influencing readers politically.

growing in the 1930s, another ultimately more important limitation on competition came from the merger of competing papers within the same city. In 1930, nine-tenths of the cities with a population of more than one hundred thousand had two or more directly competing papers, but of the smaller cities only a fifth had such morning or evening competition.

In the larger cities, an all-day tabloid competing against full-sized morning and evening papers often maintained competition of a sort. The first American tabloid newspaper was the *New York Daily News,* started by Joseph M. Patterson in 1919. Easy to read on subways and buses, the tabloid also digested news into short, simple stories—illustrated, as never before, by photographs. In 1924 the *News* had the largest circulation in New York City. Other publishers quickly copied Patterson's innovation, and by 1940 there were nearly 50 tabloids.

Another form of potential competition, whose effects on the full-sized daily were hard to measure, was the radio newscast. To protect themselves against competition from the new medium, many papers—250 by 1940—bought control of radio stations. In spite of the obvious fact that radio could deliver news more quickly, intimately, and dramatically, the effect of news broadcasts on newspaper circulation was not severe. As people received increasing amounts of news, they appeared to become more interested in local, national, and international events and to spend more time learning about them.

Improvements in technology and press services produced better-quality newspaper illustration, more detailed last-minute news, and an increase in special departments and columns. The humorous column by a writer like Will Rogers, who should perhaps be considered the 1920s successor to "Mr. Dooley," was an old feature, but the column of serious general comment was an innovation in the 1920s. People bought papers just to read some favorite columnist like H. L. Mencken, Heywood Broun or Walter Lippmann; and writers with such opposing views could appear in the same paper without menacing an "objective" editorial policy. Press syndicates distributed the more popular columns and comics to newspapers all over the United States.

Magazines

The increasing public appetite for current events was fed by the rise of weekly news magazines. In 1920 only the *Literary Digest,* which took its material on current events largely from the newspapers, was important in this weekly field. In 1923 *Time,* smartly written under the direction of editors Briton Hadden and Henry Luce, made an immediate hit; and in 1936 the Luce organization launched the weekly picture magazine *Life*. Both magazines then inspired imitators.

Magazine circulation survived the depression quite well, probably because the readers of most magazines were middle class or above—the groups less affected by depression than the lower half of the income scale. Throughout the 1920s the aged *Saturday Evening Post* was supreme among general weekly magazines. Closely mirroring middle-class interests and attitudes, it mixed good popular fiction with inspirational articles about business leaders and the virtues of the American way of doing things. During the 1930s the *Post,* by turning more liberal, managed to hold much of its circulation, but competition was weakening its position.

Most of the leading "serious" writers of the time, including William Faulkner, F. Scott Fitzgerald, and Earnest Hemingway, wrote for magazines. Faulkner, having only a limited audience for his novels, needed the magazine revenue to support his family. Consequently, a magazine reader could sample a wide range of American literature and thought without ever buying a bound book.

For the reader of the early 1920s that felt unable to keep up with all that was being published, Mr. and Mrs. De Witt Wallace started *The Reader's Digest,* a collection of condensed versions of what they considered the most important magazine articles of the preceding month. As the popularity of their digest grew, they also commissioned articles and condensed books for quick reading. Like the *Post,* the *Digest* appealed to middle-class values and celebrated rugged individualism and business success. Ultimately it became the most widely read magazine in the world.

There also began to be movie magazines, a means by which primarily women readers could keep up with the latest doings of their favorite stars—or at least what publicity agents wanted the public to know about the stars. For men, there were sports magazines. The *Sporting News* was actually founded as early as 1886 and featured the exploits of the era's especially thrilling star athletes, men and a few women who would assume a legendary status—such as Babe Ruth, who hit sixty home runs for the New York Yankees in 1927; tennis player Helen Wills, who dominated the women's game in the 1920s; and Notre Dame's "Four Horsemen of the Apocalypse," a famed football backfield.

That the movie stars and the sports stars loomed so large in the public imagination—indeed, one might argue that the modern phenomenon of celebrity was created in the 1920s—owed much to the new tabloid newspapers, to the magazines, and to the new medium of radio.

▶Babe Ruth achieved legendary status and became a beloved sports celebrity to Americans when he hit sixty home runs for the New York Yankees in 1927.

Of all the era's celebrities, none loomed larger than Charles Lindbergh, known affectionately to the American people as "Lucky Lindy." The public was already excited about the burgeoning possibilities of flight when on May 20, 1927, Lindbergh flew solo in the small plane *The Spirit of St. Louis* from New York to Paris, proving that airplanes could be viable transportation. When he returned home, he was a hero on a scale seldom seen before or since. Indeed, he would make headlines in newspapers when he merely flew over a city; and when he actually landed in one, he was feted on a vast scale. He seemed at the time to embody the best American values and to epitomize the spirit of the new century.

Radio

In August 1920, Station WWJ of the Detroit News initiated commercial broadcasting. The mass development of radio was retarded by many problems, including the control of necessary patents by American Telephone and Telegraph, General Electric, and Westinghouse, and the unwillingness of Associated Press (AP), the largest news service, to have its releases broadcast. In 1926, AT&T agreed to permit network broadcasting by renting its wires; and the same year AP, pressed by Hearst's International News Service and other competitors, amended its rules to allow broadcast of important news. Between 1926 and 1929, three national radio networks were created. Advertising agencies now brought their big clients to the networks, and radio quickly achieved the form that was to characterize it during the next generation.

During the depression decade, systematic polls of public opinion commenced; hence, we had the first reasonably reliable estimates of how people spent their time. By 1940, four-fifths of American households had radios, and these were turned on nearly five hours a day. Radio listeners heard Hoover, Roosevelt, and other political leaders put forth their views. Franklin Roosevelt, in particular, capitalized on his charming radio personality and on the pseudo-intimacy of home reception in his "fireside chats." Roosevelt's use of the radio helped to counterbalance the generally unfavorable newspaper opinion of him.

Since advertisers dictated what was to be performed, programs during the prime evening hours were directed at what were assumed to be the tastes of mass audiences. The leading stars of screen and stage appeared on radio, but usually as special attractions in the middle of variety shows that alternated with situation comedy. On less valuable time, however, the networks presented more serious programs. Starting in 1930, CBS broadcast the New York Philharmonic Orchestra on Saturday afternoons. This led NBC to compete the following year with Saturday Opera from New York's Metropolitan and in 1937 to start a series of Sunday performances by Arturo Toscanini conducting his own symphony orchestra. It was estimated that as many as 10 million listeners heard some of these musical programs.

As international tensions mounted in the 1930s, commentators such as H. V. Kaltenborn, Lowell Thomas, and Gabriel Heatter attracted large radio audiences during prime advertising time. In the daytime hours radio listeners were entertained by soap operas, baseball, and college football. Professional football had its successful radio debut in 1935, and important sporting events, like the heavyweight title bouts of Joe Louis, were followed by the American public on tens of millions of sets.

Painting

A number of major American artists continued to work in one or another of the modes of abstract painting launched earlier in Europe. During the reaction of the 1920s against prewar enthusiasms, however, nonrepresentational painting failed to attract young artists. It diminished in popularity during the Depression. A group that included Charles Sheeler and Georgia O'Keefe, whose works were better received by the public, emphasized the abstract esthetic form in machinery, architecture, and nature. Their craftsmanship was exacting, their themes recognizable, and their forms sharply bounded and precise.

The main body of important American painting during the interwar period was of a more conventional type that had close enough contact with reality to permit social commentary. Thomas Hart Benton, Grant Wood, and John Stuart Curry dealt with characters and characteristics of the rural Midwest, both pleasant and unpleasant. Another group of painters also concentrated on the American scene but explored the problems of urban life. Lois Jones, Ben Shahn, William Gropper, and Philip Evergood were among those stimulated by a strong sense of social justice, engendered primarily by the Depression. They sought to use art as a "social weapon," protesting in their paintings against mob violence, political corruption, slums, and strike breaking. Whereas the Ashcan School of the early twentieth century had seen poverty as picturesque or pathetic, these angry painters of the 1930s saw it as an inexcusable result of capitalism.

▶Aboard the S.S *de Grasse* in 1930, Arturo Toscanini, the Maestro, led the Philharmonic group on a European tour that gained international fame for the Orchestra.

The subsidized painters in the Federal Arts Project (one of Franklin Roosevelt's New Deal programs) did many community murals and other public pictures. Perhaps because of this, and perhaps because there was a general return in the late 30s to an appreciation of things American, their art tended to embrace the national past and to remain as the last strong surge of popular, realistic painting. It cannot be said with assurance that American painters executed any great masterpieces during the interwar period, but the total product of the abler artists was larger and more impressive than in previous generations.

Photography

By the interwar years, photography truly achieved the status of an art form, and American photographers were creating some of the most memorable pictures in the world's trove of photographic images. In fact, there had been great American practitioners going back to the mid-nineteenth century including the depictions of the Civil War by Matthew Brady and his staff, as well as the stunning photographs of Yosemite taken by Carleton Watkins, also from the 1860s. Around the turn of the century a number of photographers, most memorably Lewis Hine, captured the plight of immigrants and the urban poor. Then in the early 1900s, American photography took a giant leap forward with the life and work of Alfred Stieglitz, one of the country's most significant modern artists.

Born in 1864, Stieglitz went to Germany to train in the 1880s. In 1905, with fellow photographer Edward Steichen, he founded the Little Galleries of the Photo-Secession that became known simply as *291,* owing to the address on Fifth Avenue in New York City. At first a pictorialist, he went on to work in a strongly realist mode. Determined to elevate photography's status, he influenced generations of photographers, both with his high-quality images and with his mentoring—though he could also be difficult. Among his best-known pictures are the nude photos he took of his wife, the artist Georgia O'Keeffe.

By the time the Great Depression fastened its grip on the nation, there was a group of highly-trained and proficient photographers ready to document the plight of those who were its victims. It is impossible to discuss all of the important names, so we will focus on two of the most accomplished, Walker Evans and Dorothea Lange, both of whom were hired by the federal government's Farm Security Administration (FSA) to record rural suffering.

Born in 1903 in St. Louis, Evans moved to New York and entertained literary ambitions there before becoming a photographer. He developed his pictorial skills by collaborating on a book about Cuba for which he provided photographs. Then, in 1935, Roy Stryker of the FSA hired him for what was the most ambitious photographic project in the nation's history to that date. Evans's best-known images are those in the 1941 work *Let Us Now Praise Famous Men,* a collaboration with the writer James Agee that grew out of the FSA work. Evans took extensive pictures of three families of Alabama sharecroppers, and these images stand as a haunting record of the decade's poverty. Today those images are controversial because the descendants of the families argue that Evans played up the poverty for his own artistic and political purposes.

It was Dorothea Lange, however, who was responsible for the most famous picture of depression-era suffering, *Migrant Mother*, taken in 1936. Born in New Jersey in 1895, Lange

▶Dorothea Lange's photograph Migrant Mother, taken in 1936. The image was the most famous picture of the Depression era as it realistically captured the essence of depression-era suffering. Many Americans at the time could strongly identify and empathize with what the young mother was experiencing, as was conveyed in the photo.

moved to California in 1918 and soon set up a studio in San Francisco where she specialized in portraits of an affluent clientele. The Depression changed her priorities. She began to portray those in need and in 1935 began a collaboration with University of California economist Paul Taylor, who was studying the lives of rural migrants to California. Parenthetically, in the course of their collaboration they fell in love, divorced their respective spouses, and married one another. Lange worked for the FSA from 1935 to 1940 and in the process created a memorable and eloquent body of work.

In 1936 came the founding of *Life* magazine, a publication devoted to high-quality photojournalism. Of the many distinguished photographers whose work appeared on its pages, we can mention first Margaret Bourke-White with her striking depictions of factories, images reflecting a machine aesthetic, and then her subsequent war photos. Two other revered photojournalists were Robert Capa and W. Eugene Smith, both of whom created vivid images of the fighting in World War II. In short, American photography as an art form had come of age.

Music

The development of the phonograph and the radio gave composers and performers of serious music a vastly expanded audience. By the 1920s, phonographs and records had achieved an accuracy of reproduction that made them acceptable to the best musicians. Undoubtedly many more people than ever before became acquainted with operas, symphonies, and other classical works.

Like other artists in the years before World War I, composers had been attracted by the new scientific attitude of experimentalism and had produced dissonant, multi-tonal, non-rhythmic compositions; however, this group had few representatives in the United States. Instead, an upsurge in musical composition drawing on native materials produced works ranging from popular songs through more sophisticated show tunes and the jazz-based dance music of Duke Ellington to concertos and symphonies. Jazz—which has been called both the major African-American contribution to American culture and the only purely American contribution to the arts—was already popular in 1920. (See *Jazz in the Jazz Age: A Group Portrait*). Built on these American traditions, the musical comedies of American composers Irving Berlin, Richard Rodgers, George Gershwin, Jerome Kern, and Cole Porter captivated the Western world.

The 1930s was the decade of the dance bands, both "sweet" (Lombardo, Duchin, Whiteman, Wayne King) and "swing" (Bennie Goodman, Tommy and Jimmy Dorsey, and Glen Miller).

▶ Jazz in the Jazz Age: A Group Portrait

After World War I, jazz—a mixture of Southern folk music filtered through black combos and overlaid with a changeable, free-swinging rhythm—began to replace American ragtime and the sweet European-inspired melodies of the age by Victor Herbert and Rudolf Friml, both composers of operettas. The inspired jazz improvisers, from W. C. Handy before World War I to King Oliver, Louis Armstrong, Jelly Roll Morton, and Bessie Smith in the 1920s, played or sang melodies and rhythms that were both new and challenging to the classical traditions of Europe. Although not measurable in dollars, the principal export from the United States to Western Europe during the period between the wars was music. It traveled in the forms of sheet music, records, and visits by performers; and it was consumed in nightclubs, restaurants, and homes. America was having a flowering of native melody.

A recent book, *Jazz on the River*, by William Howland Kenney describes the way in which the music traveled from New Orleans up river on excursion boats, boats that journeyed hundreds of miles along the Mississippi and its tributaries. Over time, the music changed in response to all of the new influences encountered along the way—and in response to the new musicians who joined in. As one example of this phenomenon, a trio of saxophonists—Norman Mason, Eugene "Honey Bear" Sedric, and Walter Thomas—began playing together in tours of New Orleans harbor and thus introduced a choir of saxes to black jazz for the first time. Later, they introduced the concept up river in St. Louis, and the saxophone went on to become one of the premier jazz instruments.

By all accounts, the greatest of the jazz musicians was Louis Armstrong. Born in 1901 in New Orleans, the fatherless boy had trouble with the law and spent time in the city's Municipal Boys' Home. While there he obtained access to a cornet and some instruction, and left the Home with the intent to be a musician. Within a short time, he was playing his horn in Storyville, the famed red-light district. There he met the city's most celebrated musicians such as trumpeter Joe "King" Oliver and trombonist Kid Ory, both of whom took a kindly interest in the young man. Oliver left for Chicago in 1918, and Armstrong joined him a couple of years later—after he had had a stint playing on the riverboats.

In Chicago, Armstrong, by now playing the trumpet, began to come into his own. Performing with Oliver's Creole Jazz band, he attracted attention from the first with his virtuosity, innovativeness, and joyous personality. His recording debut came in 1923 when he appeared in a studio with Oliver's group. From then on, until his death in 1971 of a heart attack, Armstrong was continuously in the public eye, beloved for his singing as well as his trumpet playing. After World War II, he traveled the globe as a musical ambassador for the United States.

Also born in New Orleans, in 1890, Ferdinand "Jelly Roll" Morton was another of the great jazz innovators, in his case as a pianist. Like the slightly younger Armstrong, Morton had a difficult childhood; he, too, played in Storyville; and he, too, made his way to Chicago after World War I. Either as a soloist or with the Red Hot Peppers, Morton took ragtime in a different direction than had Scott Joplin, "jazzing it up" to be more free-wheeling. He pioneered techniques that would later be part of orchestral jazz, but he saw his star decline in the 1930s. Shortly before his death in 1941, the musicologist Alan Lomax directed renewed attention to Morton's immense contributions to the development of jazz.

As for women, singer Bessie Smith was a creative dynamo. Born in 1894 in Chattanooga, Tennessee, Smith was one of the most talented and innovative blues singers—indeed, one of the most influential women—in American musical history. She was born in extreme poverty and began performing on the streets of Chattanooga while still a child. Smith exerted a profound influence on Armstrong (the trumpeter on nine of her albums) and on other vocalists, who were inspired by her sharp phrasing and full, self-assured delivery. Another great blues singer, Ma Rainey, heard her sing and taught her the style of country blues. Smith then began to tour the South, performing in a great variety of venues. She enjoyed her greatest success in the 1920s, when her records for Columbia sold briskly. The Great Depression was to reduce the size of her audience and exacerbate her drinking problem. She died in an automobile accident in 1937.

Another of the great jazz names was that of Edward "Duke" Ellington, now recognized not only as a jazz performer, but also as one of the most significant American composers of the twentieth century. Born in Washington, D.C., in 1899, Ellington was raised in a relatively well-off black family. As a young man he started a sign-painting business, but he preferred to spend time in clubs. Before long, the music he heard in the clubs wooed him away from signs. A pianist, he formed his own band, the Washingtonians, a band that took off when it was joined by two jazz artists formed in the crucible of New Orleans—trumpeter James "Bubber" Miley and saxophonist Sidney Bechet (another of the all-time greats). Moving to New York, Ellington conducted the band at Harlem's Cotton Club, thereby developing his skills. By the 1940s, he was composing such classics as "Mood Indigo" or "Take the A Train." Eventually he composed music that married elements of classical music with jazz. By the end of his life Ellington had played the White House and, like Armstrong, he had been a traveling ambassador on behalf of American culture.

We have been discussing the supreme African American jazz artists, but there were also white musicians who rose to greatness—none more so than the legendary Bix Beiderbecke. Born in Iowa in 1903, Beiderbecke discovered jazz early, and it turned his life around. His parents disapproved of his newfound passion, even going so far as to send him to a military academy to break the spell. It did not work. He was expelled from the academy in 1922, and by 1924 was leading his own band for which he played cornet. With a "cool" sound that anticipated the kind of jazz that would become popular in the 1950s, Beiderbecke has inspired generations of musicians—despite the fact that he died at the tragically young age of twenty-eight.

Finally, another towering figure in twentieth-century American music, George Gershwin, was also profoundly influenced by jazz. Born in New York City, in 1898, to Russian-Jewish parents, Gershwin was an indifferent student. At the age of fifteen, he dropped out of school and went to work in Tin Pan Alley, the center of the music publishing business. When he was only twenty-one, his first show, "La La Lucille," opened on Broadway. He went on to

Jazz in the Jazz Age: A Group Portrait

(Continued)

write for both shows and films. His lasting fame, however, came because he introduced the spirit of jazz into formal music. A major effect of jazz is from improvised "blue notes" (flatted notes), and Gershwin would use this effect in his 1924 concerto, "Rhapsody in Blue"—which some critics at the time dismissed as "Negro music." Sadly, Gershwin died of brain cancer in 1938, but he left an extraordinary body of work.

Jazz soloists attracted music enthusiasts as well as dancers. Esthetes as well as "hepcats" attended "Jam sessions" given over to improvisation. Perhaps swing, or perhaps just the quest for novelty by millions of the unemployed young, brought back open dancing in such dances as the Big Apple, the Suzie-Q, and other types of "jitterbugging" away from one's partner. George Gershwin made use of jazz motifs and rhythms in *Rhapsody in Blue* (1924), *An American in Paris* (1928), and the opera *Porgy and Bess* (1935)—all of which won world acclaim. Aaron Copland, Roy Harris, Charles Ives, William Grant Still, and other Americans also wrote ballet scores and symphonies giving classic form to American rhythms and melodies.

Literature and Drama

Writers of the 1920s experienced a growing dissatisfaction with, and alienation from, American society and twentieth-century values. In particular, they were disillusioned by the ease with which Woodrow Wilson and other world leaders had converted moral idealism into a zeal for war. They were alienated by the triumph of materialism and business values in the postwar period and exasperated by the smug self-satisfaction of the American upper classes. "The younger generation," wrote Harold Stearns, "is in revolt; it does dislike almost to the point of hatred and certainly to the point of contempt the type of people dominant in our present civilization."

In *This Side of Paradise,* F. Scott Fitzgerald complained that the young writers "had grown up to find all Gods dead, all wars fought, all faiths in men shaken." They deplored American materialism, prosperity, Puritanism, and conformity—in short, much of the national heritage. Unlike confident prewar novelists, such as Winston Churchill (the American novelist and not the British statesman of the same name) and Upton Sinclair, the new writers did not preach reform, for they saw no immediate way of correcting the situation. The leading drama critic, George Jean Nathan, sweepingly expressed this prevailing nonsocial attitude: "What concerns me alone is myself and a few close friends. For all I care the rest of the world can go to hell at today's sunset."

To escape, America writers moved to the relative isolation of Greenwich Village in New York City or to the more complete separation of Paris. Critic H. L. Mencken's pungent attacks on American values were widely read both in his *American Mercury* magazine and in book form, revealing the desire of many intellectuals to divorce themselves from most traditional American attitudes.

Yet from this alienated generation of writers came as much good drama, poetry, and fiction as the United States had ever seen. Novelists denounced the world in vigorous new prose, used new literary techniques, and wrote with frankness and sincerity. Ernest Hemingway, who gave currency to the phrase "the lost generation," brilliantly pictured its disillusioned, cynical, expatriate society in *The Sun Also Rises* (1925) and traced the causes of that disillusionment and cynicism in his novel of World War I, *A Farewell to Arms* (1929). By 1940, in *For Whom the Bell Tolls,* Hemingway moved gradually to a more positive position of affirming the need for the social solidarity of free peoples against totalitarianism.

Other writers exposed the contradictions and hypocrisies of American culture. *An American Tragedy* (1925), which portrayed a young American hopelessly confused by the false social and religious values of his environment, marked the summit of Theodore Dreiser's career. Similarly, Sinclair Lewis wrote all of his important attacks on American society during the 1920s. *Main Street* (1920) satirized the small town of the Middle West, where "dullness made God." *Babbitt* (1922) parodied the self-satisfied, conformist, materialistic American businessman so successfully that "Babbitt" and "Babittry" were added to the dictionary. *Arrowsmith* (1925) depicted an America that placed frustrating impediments in the path of a doctor devoted to medical research. *Dodsworth* (1929) satirized the upper-middle-class American woman, picturing Fran Dodsworth as a pampered, selfish, superficial, and pretentious snob. Sherwood Anderson, in *Winesburg, Ohio* (1919) and in subsequent books, showed from a Freudian viewpoint how small-town morals and customs produced a neurotic society. Perhaps, however, the most brilliant literary attacks on the lack of proper values in the American upper class, to which he personally aspired, were in F. Scott Fitzgerald's *This Side of Paradise* (1920) and *The Great Gatsby* (1925).

▶Ernest Hemingway believed in the concept of "the lost generation," and its disillusioned, cynical, expatriate society. He expressed his opinions for the causes of that disillusionment and cynicism in his novel of World War I, *A Farewell to Arms* (1929)

A particularly exciting literary phenomenon of the era was the Harlem Renaissance. Urban communities of educated blacks had, from the beginning of the century, produced an increasing volume of prose and poetry. The discovery of this literature, around 1925, by Sherwood Anderson, Carl Van Vechten, and other white novelists and critics, called the attention of their readers in a wider public to this flowering. While recognition and attendant pride undoubtedly stimulated black creativity, the sudden flood of

▶ Zora Neale Hurston

publicity produced the false impression that the black literary movement was a new, brief phenomenon. In fact, James Weldon Johnson's novel, *The Autobiography of an Ex-Coloured Man,* was first published in 1912, and Langston Hughes' remarkable output of prose and poetry, fiction and nonfiction, extended into the 1960s. Other writers of the Harlem Renaissance, like Countee Cullen, Alain Locke, Claude McKay, and Jean Toomer, were by no means limited to the last half of the 1920s. As a group, their great achievement was to portray the world of the American black men and women as they knew it.

One of the most interesting writers of the Renaissance and one whose best-known works were, in fact, published in the 1930s, was Zora Neale Hurston. Born in an all-black town, Eatonville, Florida, Hurston went north to study anthropology with the great Franz Boas at Columbia University. When she wrote her best-known work, *Their Eyes Were Watching God* (1937), she brought to the task of writing her novel both an immersion in black folk culture and the tools of someone trained to analyze folklore. Controversial within the black community when it was first published because some critics saw it as painting too rosy a view of the culture at the expense of a depiction of the suffering, the novel has been rediscovered in recent years. Indeed, another African American woman novelist, Alice Walker, dedicated much effort to restoring Hurston and her work to the literary canon.

In contrast to the preoccupation of writers in the 20s with individual emotional adjustment in the light of new psychological views of personal problems, the Great Depression inevitably brought a return to social issues. Poverty amidst plenty was the writer's lot as well as that of the masses. John Dos Passos, an alienated member of the upper middle class who had begun an attack on American capitalism in *Three Soldiers* (1921), achieved his best work in this genre in a trilogy, *U.S.A.,* published between 1930 and 1935.

John Steinbeck's *The Grapes of Wrath* (1939), which chronicles the misery of a family of Oklahoma tenant farmers who migrated to California in search of work, is a graphic description of the contrast between the migratory unemployed and prosperous, propertied Americans, protected by the machinery of government. Accounts of suffering based on experience rather than observation include Henry Roth's *Call It Sleep* (1934), an autobiographical account of childhood in the slums of New York; James T. Farrell's three-volume *Studs Lonigan* (1932–1935), showing the failure of the accepted social institutions to prevent the moral ruin of a young Irish-American in Chicago; and Richard Wright's *Native Son* (1940), picturing the destructive pressures of the same city on a young black American. The strength of all three writers springs from deep emotional understanding of their subjects. Writing in the same semi-autobiographic genre, but accepting rather than damning his environment, Thomas Wolfe produced four novels between 1929 and his death in 1938. Characterized by an obsession with his own emotional responses, his long, loose-jointed books were unique in a decade largely given over to novels of social analysis.

▶John Steinbeck's *The Grapes of Wrath* (1939), chronicles the misery of a family of Oklahoma tenant farmers who migrated to California in search of work during the Great Depression. The novel was later made into a motion picture (at left).

The work of one writer, judged by critics in later decades to be the greatest of this period, virtually ignored the passing environments of war, prosperity, and depression. William Faulkner was concerned with the ultimate meaning of human existence; and while he found it in the individual's inescapable relation to nature and the land, his immediate focus was the problem faced by the traditional South in adjusting to the twentieth century. More daring as a writer than his contemporaries, he did not hesitate to depict the world through the eyes of an idiot, to manipulate time, and to imply emotional meanings beyond the range of rational communication. His great period, which ultimately won him a Nobel Prize for Literature, was from *The Sound and the Fury* in 1929 through *Light in August* (1932) and other books in the first half of the 1930s.

American poets of the 1920s—also trying to deal with ultimate or existential problems—achieved substantial world acclaim. In 1922 T. S. Eliot, expatriate but still an American citizen, published *The Waste Land,* a poem of despair with modern civilization that exerted tremendous influence. Hart Crane's major work, *The Bridge,* a difficult-to-decipher commentary on time, appeared in 1930. In addition to some of the older poets, Wallace Stevens, William Carlos Williams, Robinson Jeffers, Robert Frost, E. E. Cummings, and Marianne Moore were all writing poetry of the first rank.

In drama, the postwar rebellion against the world, in general, and America, in particular, also produced important work. The eleven plays of Eugene O'Neill, from *Beyond the Horizon* (1920) to *Mourning Becomes Electra* (1931)—all strongly influenced by Freudian psychology—marked the first major American contribution to serious theater. A number of other dramatists, including Sidney Howard, Maxwell Anderson, Elmer Rice, and Robert Sherwood, joined in this remarkable upsurge. Meanwhile, a new playwright, Clifford Odets, wrote a strong drama, *Waiting for Lefty* (1935), in praise of collective action and the labor movement. Another talented playwright of the times was Lillian Hellman, a severe critic of much in American life. Late in the decade there was a shift from anti-capitalist plays to antifascist and antiwar themes.

Motion Pictures

D. W. Griffith's silent movie *Broken Blossoms* (1919), starring Lillian Gish, was widely acclaimed by critics as marking the emergence of a new art form, said by the *Literary Digest* to be as important as music or poetry. Unfortunately, technological success and the work of this one middle-aged pioneer were not followed by a great burst of high-quality motion picture composition, directing, and acting.

▶ Scene from the Silent Film *Broken Blossoms*. The film was widely acclaimed by critics as marking the emergence of a new art form, as important as music or poetry.

The motion picture as an art medium was subordinated to the business interests that marketed the films. The major production studios owned chains of theaters and controlled the circulation of pictures. By 1930, with an investment by the owners of $2 billion to protect, the managers of the companies were unwilling to risk financing films that might not appeal to a major segment of the American public. Consequently, motion pictures of the 20s were massive spectacles of courts and armies directed by Cecil B. De Mille, sentimental melodramas starring Mary Pickford, breathtaking exploits by Douglas Fairbanks, Sr., or romantic seductions by Rudolph Valentino. Comedy, however, remained as one genre that could reconcile profit-oriented producers and talented actors. Most famous of the comedians of the silent film era was Charlie Chaplin who, producing and directing his own pictures, continued in his comedies of the underdog to protest against many of the values of American society.

Whether or not they were art, movies began to enjoy an extraordinary influence, especially on the young. What girl could escape wanting to be as glamorous, as sexy, as vivacious for example, as Clara Bow, the "It Girl"? What boy did not gaze in envy at the suave way with women that Rudolph Valentino exhibited?

In the last three years of the 1920s, sound began to make the motion picture potentially the equal of the stage. As a result, stock companies and vaudeville practically disappeared, and the professional stage became restricted to a few of the largest cities. From the 1920s to the 1950s, the motion picture was the standard form of visual dramatic entertainment for the great majority of Americans.

In the thirties the Hollywood production line turned out a steady stream of highly polished, star-laden escapist films—glittering musicals, gangster stories, westerns, heroic costume dramas, and comedies from slapstick to sophisticated. Snubbed by most highbrows, they were embraced by millions of ordinary Americans, for whom the movies—at prices as low as 10 cents—provided a warm, dark refuge from reality. The grimmer aspects of the Depression were treated in a few commercial films and in some excellent documentary films produced by the federal government. The films of the 1930s—the social commentary comedies of Frank Capra, the westerns (and *The Grapes of Wrath*) of John Ford, the screwball comedies, especially those directed by Howard Hawks—are often seen by film scholars and critics as some of the most significant American art of the twentieth century. The great stars—Fred Astaire and Ginger Rogers, Marlene Dietrich, Clark Gable, Greta Garbo, Cary Grant, Katherine Hepburn, and Jimmy Stewart, to name only a few—all are still iconic figures in American culture.

Architecture

The towering American skyscraper, created in part because of the narrow confines of the Chicago Loop and downtown Manhattan, was regarded as an architectural innovation of worldwide importance. It was a monument to American ideas of marketing. As land values rose in all U.S. cities, it became economical to increase the height of buildings in the most valuable locations; but the altitudes achieved in the 1920s far exceeded the economic need. The advertising value that accrued to the company that built a towering building and the extra amount that tenants were willing to pay for the prestige and convenience of such lofty offices led to a race for height that culminated for that era in the 1,200-foot Empire State Building.

▶ The great stars from the age of classic movie stars, such as Greta Garbo, all are still iconic figures in American culture.

The architectural design that was dominant in skyscraper architecture by the late 1920s resulted partly from the New York Zoning Act of 1916, which forced setbacks in buildings rising above certain heights. The plan of the Finnish-born architect Eliel Saarinen, which called for a series of blocks diminishing in size as the building rose and with windows set in vertical panels between continuous strips of stone or concrete, became a general model for skyscraper design.

During both prosperity and depression, older styles of architecture dominated in most public buildings and homes. The Capitol, in Washington, D.C., was rebuilt by the Hoover and Roosevelt administrations in the classical Greco-Roman style, the style also chosen for most post offices and state buildings. During the 1920s, hundreds of thousands of new residences were built by the well to do, but they or their architects and builders generally preferred to adopt or adapt some style from the past rather than experiment with the unfamiliar problems of "modern" design. Needless to say, the builders of small homes, many without architects, avoided experimentation.

Social Change

Motorization and Urbanization

While the advent of radio and progress in electronics promised great future changes, immediate changes in American society centered on the automobile. Until World War I, automobiles had been used chiefly for the recreation of the upper middle class. In 1917, fewer than one farm family in six had an automobile, and in the nation as a whole, there were fewer than five million cars. As forms of transport, trucks and buses were negligible economically and socially.

By 1930 two-thirds of America's farms—probably all the prosperous commercial farms—had automobiles, and the nation had about 23 million passenger cars. Since there were only about 26 million households, and many families in big cities did not need private automobiles, the United States was approaching the goal of a car in the garage of every family that wanted one. Even more spectacular than the fivefold increase in passenger cars was a nine-fold rise in the number of trucks. Nearly 4 million commercial vehicles, of which forty thousand were buses, signaled the beginning of the change to a society built around motor transport.

In the new geography, main highway intersections would replace villages as shopping centers, cities would be within easy reach of farms, factories would move from congested cities to the country, and consolidated grammar and high schools would collect children by bus from miles around. Few places would remain remote from the pressures, advantages, and disadvantages of an urbanized culture.

While the spread of slums had shown the inadequacy of American municipal planning for nearly a century, the automobile, more than the slum, was behind the rapid rise of city planning commissions and authorities. Although zoning was initiated in New York, in 1916, without particular regard to motor transport, that transport—by potentially opening all areas to all types of use—led to the rapid spread of zoning to other cities. The steady migration to major metropolitan areas during the 20s also forced planning on reluctant municipal authorities. By 1930, some 37 percent of the city population of the United States lived in zoned communities.

Automobiles and trucks required new bridges, tunnels, and thoroughfares into central city business districts. The Port of New York Authority, established by a "treaty" between New York and New Jersey in 1921, initiated interstate agencies to plan transportation. Generally, however, urban efforts to alleviate both traffic problems and slum congestion in the prosperous 20s could be characterized as too little and too late.

The "Automotive Social Ladder"

One of the cultural pressures directly connected with the automobile was its rise as a sign of social status. The American automobile, to be sure, depreciated rather rapidly; and for reliable service, replacement was desirable in about five to seven years. Yet social considerations worked for even briefer ownership. A new car was a symbol of success and prosperity, and the bigger and more expensive the car, the higher the presumed status of the owner. For urban and suburban apartment dwellers, the automobile took the place of an elaborate house as a mark of social standing. Only farmers and the very rich seem to have been relatively immune to such pressures.

Quickly observing this "automotive social ladder," automobile manufacturers began to differentiate each year's model and to carry on the most intensive advertising of any makers of durable goods. While there were real physical and psychological satisfactions to be gained from a swift, smooth ride in a heavy, powerful car, the lure of social approval was perhaps the strongest force behind the continuous demand for new and bigger machines. Since buyers seldom had saved the money to pay cash, the automobile became the most important item in a rapid growth of installment buying.

The Emancipated Woman

At the time that the Nineteenth Amendment of 1920 gave women the right to vote, upper-middle- and upper-class women in and around the largest urban centers were shaking off the decorum of Victorian customs. They were smoking in public, drinking illegally in speakeasies, talking freely about sex, and—in general—creating the appearance of demanding equal social rights and privileges. The publicity accorded the suffrage movement and the "emancipated woman" was in many respects highly misleading, however. Failing to establish a bloc of voters that could be used to influence legislation, as the Anti-Saloon League had done in the prohibition movement, women soon found that their influence on party politics was minimal.

By the mid 1920s, the Women's Joint Congressional Committee was losing power, and the appropriation for the new Women's and Children's Bureau was cut. The mere right to vote in

▶ Women voting. At the time that the Nineteenth Amendment of 1920 gave women the right to vote, upper-middle- and upperclass women in and around the largest urban centers were shaking off the decorum of Victorian customs.

federal elections did not seem to have given substantial new power to the women's movement. In fact, political victory and a decade of general prosperity may have lessened the drive for other forms of equality.

The emancipated upper class women were too few in number, particularly among the mature and influential, to have an effect beyond journalistic publicity. World War I produced no significant change in the definition or status of "women's work." Although the percentage of women engaged in professional life rose almost 20 percent from 1920 to 1930, women were still substantially excluded from professorships in major universities, from the medical profession, and from the most prestigious law schools.

The proportion of women in the labor force was about the same in 1930 as it was in 1910. In the latter year, 57 percent of working women were blacks or immigrants, which is equivalent to saying they were in low-paying occupations. The percentage of women in clerical jobs remained about the same during the prosperous 20s. Women continued to be paid less than men for doing the same job. There was, in effect, an openly expressed intention by most political, trade union, and business leaders to keep women in their traditional roles, which would avoid difficult adjustments and limit female competition with men. Although it lessened their militancy, the very fact of lower pay, however, helped many women keep their jobs in the Depression.

For the middle-class women who were homemakers, the trend to smaller houses and apartments and the availability of electrical housekeeping aids such as vacuum cleaners and refrigerators lessened the drudgery of housework. For the few married women who could secure good jobs, there was less social stigma attached to working than in earlier decades, but strong economic and cultural barriers still blocked the road to equality with men.

An Urban Black Society

Since the beginning of the century there had been a steady migration of rural blacks to the cities, but World War I so increased the movement that the largest Northern cities—New York, Chicago, Philadelphia—became America's major centers of black population. Although frequently able to earn more money than they ever had before, the occupants of these black urban communities soon realized that they had not achieved the Promised Land. Usually they had to move into overcrowded, run-down tenements where they replaced the most recent, poorest immigrants. Although urban blacks were usually of old-American stock, they found themselves looked down on by the foreign-born whites just as the native whites had always looked down on them. For a time in the 1920s, the singers, dancers, and musicians of black Harlem, and some of its writers and artists, as well, were "taken up" by white sophisticates and bohemians. This fad did not last, however, nor did it touch the average black person.

There had never been much feeling of labor solidarity in the United States; and black workers in industrial centers were often resented, just as women were, as intruders who threatened white male employment and wage standards. Similar resentment led to attacks on blacks as the ghettos overflowed into white neighborhoods. In 1919, racial violence broke out in a score of cities all over the nation, and blacks learned that they could not rely on either police protection or justice in the courts.

In the early 1920s, black activist organizations reacted by moving in two directions. With the support of white middle-class liberals, the National Urban League and the National Association for the Advancement of Colored People (NAACP) sought to establish for blacks the civil and political rights guaranteed by the Constitution. On this front, temporary legal victories were won in the *Sweet* case (1925) that upheld the right of blacks to defend themselves against violence, and in the *First Texas Primary* case (1927) that declared exclusion of black voters at the primary election stage in the democratic process to be unconstitutional. The organization that represented the hopes and dreams of many working-class blacks was the Universal Negro Improvement Association, founded by the charismatic Jamaican, Marcus Garvey. Garvey called on black people to take pride in their race and its history, to turn their backs on white America, and to return to their African homeland. The practical NAACP worked for integration, the romantic Garvey for black unity. The same twin stream has run throughout African Americans' long history in the decades before and since.

Prohibition

Superimposed on this society that was undergoing or resisting confusing changes was America's greatest experiment in more government control over personal habits. Few nations have had a history of more consistent attachment to the consumption of alcohol than the United States. In the decades prior to 1918, however, there had been a trend toward more drinking of beer and wine and less recorded consumption of hard liquor, as well as a trend toward various types of state prohibition. It seems possible that banning the purchase of hard liquor or making it difficult to obtain might have produced a more temperate nation without much public resistance, but this experiment was never tried. Instead, the combination of war hysteria over a shortage of grain, anti-German sentiment against the brewers, and the financing of temperance organizations by important businessmen opposed to beer for workers, led to an effort to ban all alcoholic drinks.

The Eighteenth Amendment left interpretation of what was an "intoxicating" beverage to Congress. The Volstead Act of 1919, vetoed by Wilson and then passed again by the necessary two-thirds majority, set the limit of alcoholic content at .5 percent. While farmers would continue to make wine and other drinks at home, as they always had, city dwellers were now denied the opportunity of legally buying even the weakest form of beer. As a result, the big urban areas that had opposed the prohibition movement now refused to abide by the law. As is usual under such circumstances, there was no difficulty in finding entrepreneurs ready to supply illicit demand.

It is an interesting paradox of the triumph of the prohibitionists in Congress that, having passed the amendment and the Volstead Act, they settled back and made no great effort to see that the law was enforced. The number of federal agents began at about 1,500 and rose to only a little over 2,800 at the peak. With a top salary of around $3,000, it was not surprising that these men were often corruptible. Yet even had they been entirely diligent, they were too few even to check the imports of liquor. Furthermore, the local authorities in wet areas gave them little or no help. In 1923, New York State repealed its law for local enforcement, and politicians in other big metropolitan areas connived, almost openly, with those supplying the liquor.

As a result, an illegal traffic in whiskey, wine, and beer, worth hundreds of millions of dollars annually, fell into the hands of underworld leaders. The terms "racket" and

▶ Illegal traffic in whiskey, wine, and beer, worth hundreds of millions of dollars annually, fell into the hands of underworld leaders.

"racketeer" came into use; and the newly powerful gangsters quickly branched out into other criminal activities—including bribery, extortion, arson, and murder.

"Where were the police?" one would logically ask. The answer often was "in the pay of racketeers." Al Capone, head of the liquor racket in Chicago, was as powerful politically as anyone in the municipal government of that metropolis and was the undisputed ruler of the suburban city of Cicero. In the suburbs of New York and other great cities, the liquor interests often controlled county or municipal politics. The sheriffs and police chiefs received a portion of the weekly collections from speakeasies and worked against the occasional federal agent who sought to get evidence of violation of the law.

The national picture was confusing. In dry areas prohibition appeared to work at least as well as it had before the amendment. In wet urban areas, relatively less well represented in Congress, prohibition seemed to be undermining the moral values of both the young elite and honest government. Some manufacturers thought there was less drinking among their employees, while others were sure there was more. The Republican administration continued vaguely to sponsor "the noble experiment." The Wickersham Commission, appointed by Hoover, gave an unfavorable report in January 1931, but it illogically concluded that prohibition should be continued.

In the end, it was not moral or temperance issues but the Great Depression and need for government revenue in the desperate year of 1932 that apparently tipped the balance in favor of legalizing the liquor business. There was no serious effort to substitute a new law permitting beer and wine for the unworkable Volstead Act. In 1933, the Eighteenth Amendment was quickly repealed by the Twenty-first, and the temperance problem was returned to the states.

Gangster Wars

In 1924, Calvin Coolidge appointed the iron-fisted J. Edgar Hoover as Director of the Bureau of Investigation. Hoover was a gifted criminologist and master of media relations who made the Bureau, renamed the Federal Bureau of Investigation (FBI) in 1935, famous for its efficiency. Hoover's FBI captured the imagination of Americans, during the 1930s, when city and state law enforcement agencies implored the FBI to assist in the apprehension of a growing number of gangs across the Midwest that were responsible for a string of armed bank robberies and the deaths of dozens of lawmen and innocent bystanders. The combination of automobiles, which provided fast getaways, and automatic weapons, which provided deadly firepower, allowed the gangs to successfully rob banks and retail businesses almost at will. Some Americans, nearly helpless against forces they didn't understand during the Great Depression, made heroes of outlaws who took what they wanted at gunpoint. The famed gangsters, pursued by the FBI and played up in the press, included Baby Face Nelson, Machine Gun Kelly, Pretty Boy Floyd, and of course, the man designated by the FBI as Public Enemy #1, John Dillinger. The Bureau was able to step in and pursue the gangs whose crimes normally would have been under state jurisdictions, under the Motor Vehicle Theft Act, which makes it a federal offense to take a stolen vehicle across state lines.

The criminal whose pursuit received the most attention was John Dillinger, From September 1933 until July 1934, he and his violent gang terrorized the Midwest, killing ten men, wounding seven others, robbing banks and police arsenals, and staging three jail breaks—killing a sheriff during one and wounding two guards in another. As the Dillinger cat and mouse game continued, the notoriety of both Dillinger and Hoover, as well as the FBI's "G-Men," especially Melvin Purvis who headed the Dillinger investigation, grew. A tip from a Dillinger insider Anna Sage, a Romanian immigrant who cut a deal to provide information in

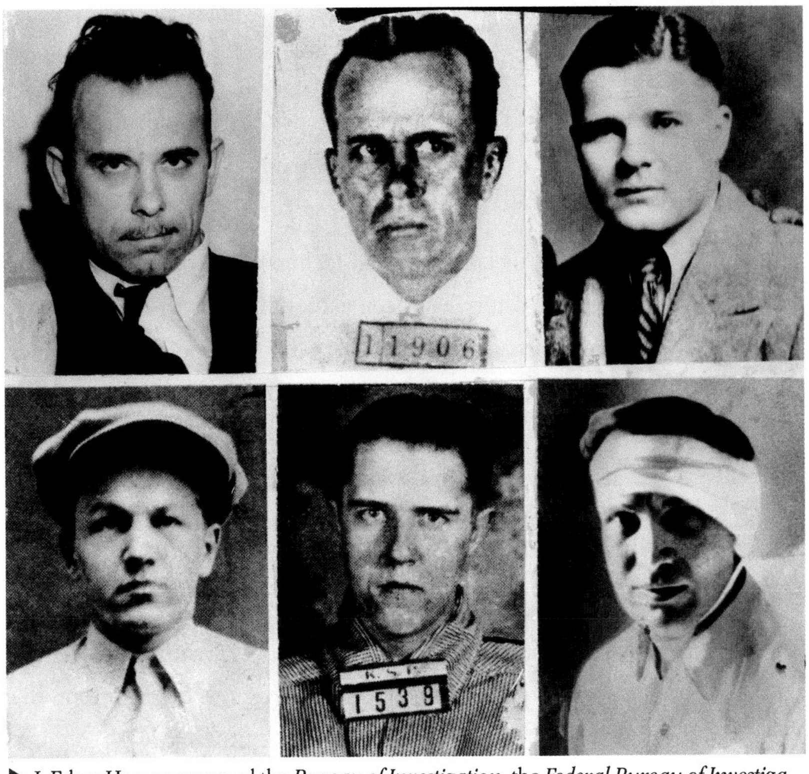

▶ J. Edgar Hoover renamed the *Bureau of Investigation*, the *Federal Bureau of Investigation* (FBI). Soon state law enforcement agencies implored the FBI to assist in the apprehension of a growing number of gangs across the Midwest that were responsible for armed bank robberies, the deaths of dozens of lawmen and innocent bystanders.

return for protection against deportation for prostitution, eventually led to the shooting death of John Dillinger by special agents outside the Biograph Theater in Chicago. Dillinger's demise, along with the capture and shootings of other famous gangsters of the era, brought a greater power to the Bureau and Hoover, who would rule it until his death in 1972.

▶Notorious gangsters, Clyde Barrow and Bonnie Parker, "Bonnie and Clyde."

Perhaps the other most celebrated group of bank robbers of the time period were the notorious gang headed by Clyde Barrow and Bonnie Parker, known more simply in American lore as "Bonnie and Clyde." Bonnie and Clyde met in Texas in January 1930. At the time, Bonnie was nineteen and married to an imprisoned murderer; Clyde was twenty-one and unmarried. Soon after they met, he was arrested for a burglary and sent to jail. He escaped, using a gun Bonnie had smuggled to him, was recaptured and sent back to prison. Clyde was paroled in February 1932, rejoined Bonnie, and resumed a life of crime. At the time they were killed in 1934, they were believed to have committed thirteen murders and several robberies and burglaries. Before dawn on May 23, 1934, a posse composed of police officers from Louisiana and Texas, including Texas Ranger Frank Hamer, concealed themselves in bushes along the highway near Sailes, Louisiana. In the early daylight, Bonnie and Clyde appeared in an automobile and died in a hail of gunfire from lawmen.

Interwar Transition

By 1940 the scientific and technological base for the highest level of consumption in the world's history had been achieved, but corresponding institutional adjustments had not taken place. The two decades following World War I were merely an interlude in a much longer period of change from the relatively stable commercial society of Western European nations in the eighteenth century to some new stage that may also have its periods of relative stability. In this transition, the 1920s in the United States marked the world's highest peak of material well being up to that time and the 1930s the greatest depth of politico-economic failure to make use of existing facilities. It was hardly surprising that each decade produced unusual problems and unique reactions.

Depression inevitably upset most Americans more than any problems caused by prosperity. In 1932, they felt the deep sense of frustration that must come from seeing people starving while crops are being burned for lack of a market; but basic rebellion against capitalism or traditional American values was rare. To a remarkable degree people suffered deprivation in silence, comforting themselves with whatever was left. The majority warmly supported Franklin Roosevelt in his programs to provide greater material security; and the protest that feebly sprouted in the dark days from 1931 to 1934 was smothered under a reaffirmation of belief in traditional American values.

There was, however, a fundamental change: it would no longer be expected that individual citizens, or at least individual families, were solely responsible for their own welfare. A new tradition of public responsibility for the welfare of private citizens was in the process of creation, a tradition that would last for many decades. We now turn to a closer look at the politics of the time period, with special attention to the New Deal.

▶ ▶ ▶

Chapter Review 24

Summary

The "Jazz Age" was a period of good times in the 1920s and followed by hard times in the 1930s. The period witnessed an explosion of consumer goods and new technologies as America moved into the automobile and aviation age, and also the age of motion pictures, radio and mass communication, and household conveniences. It was also an age of prohibition of alcohol, which led to illegal consumption and organized crime. It was an age of the relaxing of sexual mores in the 1920s, of dance halls, and of jazz, often written and performed by African-Americans.

The Jazz Age was also a time of challenges to traditional thought that were resisted by Protestant fundamentalists. Psychological theories questioned the ability of humans to reason objectively and Sigmund Freud argued that subconscious impulses, including libido, influenced human behavior and thought processes. Education was altered with the ideas of John Dewey that reflected the new psychology. The idea of preparing students for daily life, rather than requiring them to master a body of knowledge, divided school activities into four major categories: health, fundamental processes, civic and social relations, and recreation. Of these, only fundamental processes embraced conventional learning. From the emphasis on utility came more practically oriented curricula on the secondary level, including vocational education. Simultaneously, advances in physics included Einstein's theory of relativity and the discovery that atoms were all composed of identical subatomic particles.

Meanwhile, the discipline of economics became dominated by the ideas of John Maynard Keynes. His major work, *The General Theory of Employment, Interest and Money* (1936), concluded that (1) increasing the income of the poor stimulated demand, while increasing the income of the rich promoted saving; (2) increased demand, not increased saving, led to new business investment (his major revision of older theory); (3) total income could increase only from such investment; and (4) if the functioning of the undisturbed free market did not provide adequate business investment to maintain a sufficient flow of income, government was the only agency with sufficient spending power to see that this result was achieved.

The advances in science and philosophy provoked a Protestant fundamentalist backlash and the passage, especially in Southern states, of laws banning evolution. In 1925, the ACLU offered legal council to anyone that would challenge such laws; and John T. Scopes of Dayton, Tennessee, challenged Tennessee state law by teaching evolution. Clarence Darrow volunteered to represent Scopes, and William Jennings Bryan volunteered to assist the prosecution. Although Bryan and the Protestant fundamentalists were generally embarrassed in the trial, and the national media, led by H. L. Mencken, made "monkeys" out of Bryan and the fundamentalists, the Scopes laws stayed on the books. Publishers voluntarily pulled Darwin from the textbooks so as to retain their textbook sales in the South.

The national media, newspapers, radio, and magazines exploded in the Jazz Age led by three major radio networks and *Time* magazine. Music on the radio was dominated by jazz, swing, and the big band sound of Tommy and Jimmy Dorsey and Glenn Miller. Photography also came into its own, and *Life* magazine was born in 1936, dedicated to depicting American life in pictures.

In literature and drama, the Jazz Age produced American icons George Gershwin, William Falkner, Ernest Hemingway, and F. Scott Fitzgerald. In addition, American movies came of age, and the automobile dominated American life.

With Prohibition, the Jazz Age was also the age of bootleg alcohol, the growth of both the FBI and organized crime, and the era of celebrated gangsters. The most famous and notorious gangsters of all were "Public Enemy #1" John Dillinger and "Bonnie and Clyde" who were killed by lawmen within two months of each other in 1934. While the government was stamping out organized crime, the culture was changing during the Great Depression from a hyper-individualist one to one that was more holistic in character and where collective responsibilities received greater attention.

Chronological Time Line

1859 Charles Darwin published *Origin of the Species.*

1886 *The Sporting News* began publication.

1916 John Dewey published *Democracy and Education.*

1916 The New York Zoning Act forced setbacks in buildings that were to be built above certain heights.

1919 The Progressive Education Association was formed.

1919 D. W. Griffith's silent movie, *Broken Blossoms* debuted.

1919 The first American tabloid newspaper, the *New York Daily News* founded by Joseph M. Patterson, began publication.

1920 On January 16, Billy Sunday celebrated Prohibition with a mock funeral for John Barleycorn.

1920 August: Station WWJ of the Detroit News initiated commercial broadcasting.

1921 The Port of New York Authority, established by a "treaty" between New York and New Jersey, initiated interstate agencies to plan transportation.

1922 Sinclair Lewis published *Babbitt.*

Chapter Review (cont'd)

Time Line (cont'd)

1922 A teacher in Kentucky was brought to trial for teaching that the earth was round. The teacher was fired when opponents proved in court, through the Bible, that the earth was flat.

1923 *Time* magazine began publication.

1924 George Gershwin composed his first classical work, *Rhapsody in Blue.*

1924 William Jennings Bryan argued that a "scientific soviet" was attempting to dictate what is taught in schools and attempting to mold the religion of the nation.

1924 J. Edgar Hoover was appointed head of the FBI.

1925 F. Scott Fitzgerald published *The Great Gatsby*.

1925 The Scopes "Monkey" Trial was conducted in Dayton, Tennessee.

1925 Ernest Hemingway published *The Sun Also Rises*.

1925 Theodore Dreiser published *An American Tragedy*.

1925 The Sweet case upheld the right of blacks to defend themselves against violence.

1926 The Associated Press (AP) allowed radio broadcasts of its news.

1927 Babe Ruth hits sixty home runs for the New York Yankees.

1927 May 20–21: Charles Lindbergh flew solo in the small plane *The Spirit of St. Louis* from New York to Paris.

1927 The First Texas Primary case declared exclusion of black voters at the primary election stage in the democratic process to be unconstitutional.

1929 William Faulkner published *The Sound and the Fury*.

Time Line (cont'd)

1929 Ernest Hemingway published *A Farewell to Arms.*

1930 CBS began broadcast of the New York Philharmonic Orchestra on Saturday afternoons.

1930 John Dos Passos published *U.S.A.*

1931 Wickersham Commission gave an unfavorable report on Prohibition.

1931 The interdenominational conference on "Permanent Preventatives of Unemployment" was held.

1932 William Faulkner published *Light in August.*

1934 On May 23, Bonnie Parker and Clyde Barrow perished in a hail of gunfire from lawmen outside Sailes, Louisiana.

1934 On July 22, John Dillinger was gunned down at the Biograph Theater in Chicago.

1935 Professional football began radio broadcasts.

1935 George Gershwin composed the folk opera, *Porgy and Bess.*

1936 Dorothy Lange published the photo, *Migrant Mother*.

1936 *Life* magazine began publication.

1936 John Maynard Keynes published *The General Theory of Employment, Interest and Money.*

1939 John Steinbeck published *The Grapes of Wrath*.

1940 Ernest Hemingway published *For Whom the Bell Tolls.*

1941 Walker Evans published *Let Us Now Praise Famous Men*.

Chapter Review (cont'd)

Key Terms

Uncertainty: During the first two decades of the twentieth century, the previous orderly system of beliefs was attacked by several areas of advanced learning. Historical analysis in seminaries and Darwin's theory of evolution cast increasing doubt upon the literal truth of the Bible, while psychology questioned older theories of learning and mental discipline. People argued that none of these new ideas were satisfactory substitutes for the old "truths," especially since the new sciences were based on uncertainty and a continual search for answers that could be, at best, only tentative.

Behaviorism: Of great impact were the psychological theories that questioned the human ability to reason objectively and the importance of reason as a basis for action. The founder of behaviorism, John B. Watson, regarded consciousness itself as only a byproduct of physical processes, having no role in causing behavior. He insisted that both human and animal learning occurred simply through "conditioned reflexes."

Sigmund Freud: Freud popularized the ideas that people were impelled to think and act in certain ways by unconscious pressures rather than by logical reasoning. He further held that these irrational, unconscious urges were of a "sexual" nature; thus when people thought they were behaving rationally, their behavior might be merely a disguise for a mixture of erotic urges and cravings based upon unmet childhood needs which, though unrecognized by the individuals, influenced their behavior in many ways.

Social Theory: This theory promoted the idea that society no longer seemed simple as it had at the beginning of the twentieth century. If general social laws were to be discovered, it would only be by highly complex and sophisticated means.

Albert Einstein: Einstein was the most famous atomic scientist of the time, who not only developed the theory of relativity, but became a well-known celebrity in his own time—a rare accomplishment for a scientist.

Keynesian Economics: Based on the ideas of John Maynard Keynes, the most important ideas included the following: (1) increasing the income of the poor stimulated demand, while increasing the income of the rich promoted saving; (2) increased demand, not increased saving, led to new business investment; (3) total income could increase only from such investment; and (4) if the functioning of the undisturbed free market did not provide adequate business investment to maintain a sufficient flow of income, government was the only agency with sufficient spending power to see that this result was achieved.

Charles Darwin: Author of *Origin of the Species*, in which he argued that species evolved through a process of natural selection

William Jennings Bryan: Famous orator, populist, three-time Democratic candidate for president, and Protestant fundamentalist that aided the Tennessee prosecution in *Scopes v. State of Tennessee* in 1925

Clarence Darrow: Famous attorney and agnostic that offered his services to John T. Scopes and the ACLU, for free, to defend Scopes and debunk the literalist interpretation of the Bible

Scopes "Monkey" Trial: The *Scopes v. State of Tennessee* case in 1925 in Dayton, Tennessee, that received national media coverage during which the literalist interpretation of the Bible was debated in a Tennessee court

Key Terms (cont'd)

Billy Sunday: Famous evangelist of the Jazz Age who preached a literal interpretation of the Bible, denounced Darwin's theory of evolution, and combined Christianity with American patriotism

Liberal churches: Those that did not require their members to adopt a literal, inerrant interpretation of the Bible and generally supported social gospel ideas

Fundamentalists: Those that believed in a literal, inerrant interpretation of the Bible

Realist painters: Depicted realistic and often patriotic scenes of American history

Urban painters: A group of painters that concentrated on the American scene but explored the problems of urban life, these artists were generally stimulated by a strong sense of social justice engendered primarily by the Depression. They sought to use art as a "social weapon," protesting in their paintings against mob violence, political corruption, slums, and strike breaking.

Walker Evans: A photographer hired by the federal government to record images of suffering during the Depression. Evans focused on Alabama sharecroppers.

Dorothea Lange: Photographer hired by the federal government to record images of suffering during the Depression, Lange was responsible for the most famous picture of depression-era suffering, *Migrant Mother,* taken in 1936.

Jazz: The popular music of the young generation of the 1920s and 1930s generally viewed as an African-American contribution to American music, arts, and culture, that was also associated with loose morals, violations of conservative cultural mores, and a free-wheeling lifestyle.

Alienation: With growing dissatisfaction with and alienation from American society and twentieth-century values, primarily among young, Americans were disillusioned by the ease with which Woodrow Wilson and other world leaders had converted moral idealism into a zeal for war. They were alienated by the triumph of materialism and business values in the postwar period and exasperated by the smug self-satisfaction of the American upper classes.

The "Lost Generation": This disillusioned, cynical, expatriate society of the younger generation during the Jazz Age exposed the contradictions and hypocrisies of American culture.

The Harlem Renaissance: An explosion of writings, many of which contained social commentary, by educated African-American writers in the 1920s

Eugene O'Neill: Produced eleven plays from *Beyond the Horizon* (1920) to *Mourning Becomes Electra* (1931)—all strongly influenced by Freudian psychology—that marked the first major American contribution to serious theater

Charlie Chaplin: Most famous of the comedians of the silent film era, Chaplin produced and directed his own pictures that were often comedies representing underdog protest against many of the values of American society.

The Sweet case: 1925 case that upheld the right of blacks to defend themselves against violence

Chapter Review (cont'd)

Key Terms (cont'd)

Texas Primary case: 1927 case that declared exclusion of black voters at the primary election stage in the democratic process to be unconstitutional

Marcus Garvey: Flamboyant Jamaican-born founder of the Universal Negro Improvement Association, Garvey called on black people to take pride in their race and its history, to turn their backs on white America, and to return to their African homeland.

Twenty-first Amendment: Repealed the prohibition of alcohol

J. Edgar Hoover: Director of the Federal Bureau of Investigation (FBI) that led the FBI in the fight against notorious criminals of the Jazz Age including John Dillinger, Pretty Boy Floyd, Baby Face Nelson, and Bonnie and Clyde.

John Dillinger: Bank robber designated by the FBI as "Public Enemy #1" and gunned down by the FBI in Chicago in 1934

G-Men: Nickname for FBI men assigned to the cases involving the country's most notorious bank robbers such as John Dillinger and Bonnie and Clyde

Bonnie and Clyde: Clyde Barrow and Bonnie Parker, two young notorious bank robbers gunned down by the FBI and local lawmen outside Sailes, Louisiana, in 1934

Pop Quiz

Chapter 24

1. The Smith-Hughes Act of 1917 granted federal aid to __________.
   a. vocational education
   b. women's education
   c. education for blacks
   d. higher education

2. Which of the following is included in the arguments of John Maynard Keynes?
   a. Increasing the income of the poor stimulated demand.
   b. Increased demand, not increased savings, led to new investment.
   c. Total income could only increase from new investment that comes from increased demand.
   d. All of the above

Pop Quiz (cont'd)

3. What spawned the Protestant fundamentalist political movement?
   a. the view of many that Darwin's theory of evolution conflicted with the creation story in the Bible
   b. growing scholarly historical criticism of the Bible
   c. the anti-communism, hyperpatriotism, and nativism of the Red Scare
   d. all of the above

4. The Scopes Trial in Tennessee dramatized the debate between __________.
   a. fundamentalists and liberals
   b. liberals and nationalists
   c. nationalists and fundamentalists
   d. liberals and fundamentalists

5. Which of the following is true of culture in the Jazz Age?
   a. The vast majority of the population adopted the lifestyle of wild parties, free-wheeling women, and heavy drinking.
   b. While flappers and jazz babies existed, the cultural changes in most parts of the country were moderate and gradual.
   c. While flappers and jazz babies existed, the cultural changes in most parts of the country were even more radical with communism and atheism.
   d. Jazz, wild parties, free-wheeling women, and heavy drinking were characteristics only of the low income black community.

6. By 1940, the item that 80 percent of American owned and turned on five times a day was the ________.
   a. radio
   b. television
   c. still
   d. washing machine

7. The writer who gave currency to the phrase "the lost generation" was __________.
   a. Ernest Hemingway
   b. F. Scott Fitzgerald
   c. H. L. Mencken
   d. Arthur Conan Doyle

Chapter Review (cont'd) ▶▶▶

Pop Quiz (cont'd)

8. The author of *The Waste Land* was __________.
   a. Hart Crane
   b. Lillian Hellman
   c. T. S. Eliot
   d. Clifford Odets

9. The "emancipated women" of the 1920s were doing all of the following except __________.
   a. smoking in public
   b. drinking illegally in speakeasies
   c. talking freely about sex
   d. exerting tremendous influence on political parties through their new right to vote

10. The man that was appointed to head the Bureau of Investigation in 1924 (later FBI) and headed that agency until his death in 1972 was __________.
    a. J. Edgar Hoover
    b. Herbert Hoover
    c. Melvin Purvis
    d. Frank Hamer

11. Keynesian economics emphasized the laws of supply and demand. T F

12. The scientific discoveries in physics and psychology made truth less certain. T F

13. John Maynard Keynes taught that prosperity depended on high __________ and investment by __________.

14. In early radio, __________ dictated what would be broadcast.

15. Marcus Garvey founded the __________ __________ __________ Association.

1. A	7. A	13. Wages; Government
2. D	8. C	14. Advertisers
3. D	9. D	15. United Negro Improvement
4. A	10. A	
5. B	11. F	
6. A	12. T	

25 The Great Depression, 1929–1939

Chapter Objectives

The Great Depression

- Increasing Force of the Depression
- Hoover's Active Conservatism
- Initiation of the Welfare State
- Effects of the Depression
- Farm Holiday Association
- Bonus Army
- The Election of 1932
- Bottom of the Depression

FDR: The First Term

- The Honeymoon
- The Spirit of the New Deal
- Farm Relief
- Mortgage Refinancing
- Regional Development
- Industrial Recovery
- Devaluing the Dollar
- Rise of Conservative Opposition
- Reliance upon the Masses
- Public Works
- Social Security
- The Supreme Court: Challenge and Response

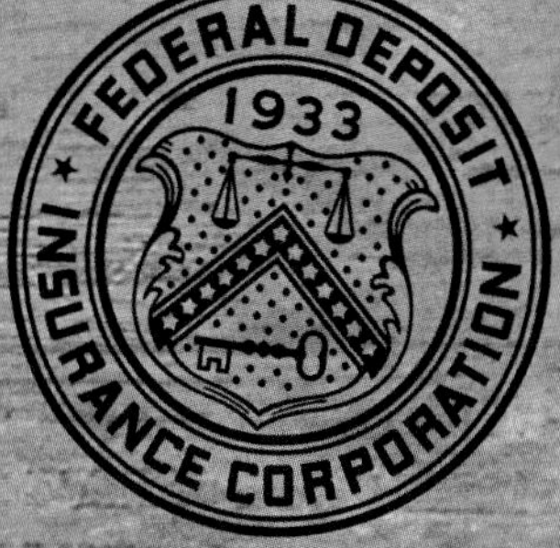

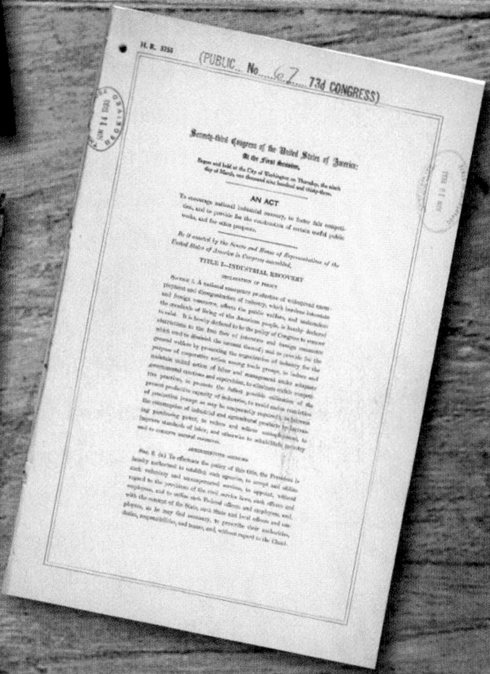

The Election of 1936

Last Phase of the New Deal

Battle over the Court

A Government-Protected Labor Movement

Women in the Depression

The Survival of the Indian

Black America

Mexican Americans

The Dust Bowl Migration

Return to Depression

New Policies

Assessing the New Deal

Lasting Effects of the New Deal

The Great Depression

Increasing Force of the Depression

In August 1928, Herbert Hoover campaigned for the presidency proclaiming, "We in America today are nearer to the final triumph over poverty than ever in the history of any land. The poor house is vanishing from among us." Hoover, as it turned out, had only six months in which to apply his management skills to the American economy before the Stock Market Crash of 1929 that signaled the beginning of the Great Depression.

Prior to the crash, however, numerous economic problems had been ignored due to the robust overall economic growth of the 1920s. For instance, as previously mentioned, the international debt situation from World War I was never fully resolved, and farming had suffered from low prices due to overproduction. Simultaneously, coal mining had been depressed due to the global switch to petroleum as the primary fuel source. The economy had become oligopolistic and automobile driven, with just a few companies controlling numerous major industries and Ford, General Motors, and Chrysler dominant in the automobile industry. The two hundred largest corporations in America controlled 50 percent of American GNP. The automobile industry, the engine of American growth, was particularly subject to recession since any household could often put off the purchase of a new automobile by simply repairing the existing car. The 1920s were also a time of great income inequality: the wealthiest twenty-seven thousand Americans held the same assets as the poorest eleven million. When the depression did hit, in such a scenario, consumption would be difficult to jumpstart. Moreover, the stock market was greatly overvalued, increasing 450 percent from 1925–1929, and was due for a major adjustment. The credit structure was also overburdened, with small banks overextended due to difficulties in the agricultural sector and large banks overextended due to foreign debt and investments in the stock market. To top it all off, demand for United States goods abroad was softening as Europe recovered from World War I, yet the foreign debt situation contributed to an American currency crisis. Over nine thousand American banks failed between 1930 and 1933, resulting in $2.5 billion in losses to depositors. As a result, economists estimate that the total United States money supply diminished by as much as a third from 1930–1933. The Federal Reserve, failing to grasp the consequences of their actions and the causes of the monetary collapse, raised interest rates in 1931, further diminishing an already shrinking money supply.

Though the Stock Market Panic of October 1929 that signaled the beginning of the Great Depression was abrupt and severe, the complete economic meltdown that became the Great Depression itself began more gradually. At the end of 1929 and the beginning of 1930, employment declined only slightly more than was seasonally normal. One Wall Street economist thought the collapse of inflated security values "a favorable development from the point of view of general business." Similarly, Secretary of the Treasury Andrew Mellon saw nothing "in the present situation that is either menacing or warrants pessimism. All evidence indicates that the worst effects of the crash on unemployment will have passed within the next sixty days." Mellon believed that the economy should be allowed to slide unchecked until it hit bottom in what he viewed as a normal business cycle occurrence. Mellon argued, "let the slump liquidate itself, liquidate labor, liquidate stocks, liquidate farmers. People will work harder, live a more moral life, values will be adjusted, and enterprising people will pick up the wrecks from less competent people."

President Herbert Hoover, initially, concurred with Mellon's optimism and laissez-faire approach due to his own ideological belief in the free market and a patriotic confidence in America itself. Hoover regarded individualism as the most important element in the development of American economic and social life, and he tenaciously believed in the power of voluntarism. In general, Hoover was ideologically opposed to federal involvement in welfare programs because he believed that they would erode individual and community responsibility and encourage a "dole mentality." As late as April 1931, Hoover argued in his memoirs that the country was recovering from a "normal recession due to domestic causes." Hoover's ideological leanings are reflected in his statement of November 15, 1929, (after two devastating months of stock market crash) when Hoover argued, "any lack of confidence in the economic future or basic strength of business in the United States is foolish."

Influenced by the prevailing expressions of optimism, Hoover sought to end the mild recession by encouraging appropriate business action and by implementing government policies favorable to business. In conferences with business leaders he urged them to maintain wages, prices, and plans for expansion. In return he promised to continue a normal program of public works, to raise tariffs, and to lower the Federal Reserve System's rediscount rate (the rate of interest at which banks could exchange customers' notes for currency at Federal Reserve Banks) in order to stimulate business activity by making credit more readily available. Unfortunately, the magnitude of the economic crisis quickly made voluntary efforts by the business sector untenable, and Hoover was soon forced to abandon the conservative principles of laissez-faire in favor of government economic intervention.

Hoover's Active Conservatism

First, Hoover attempted to jump-start the economy with a tax cut; but the volume of dollars returned to consumers for consumption through a tax cut was insufficient to remedy the cash shortage in the economy. In June 1930, Hoover attempted to attack the Depression from another traditionally conservative direction and reverted to the nineteenth century Republican Party posture of economic prosperity through tariffs. Despite a petition signed by a thousand economists warning Hoover against increasing tariffs, Hoover signed the Smoot-Hawley bill that drastically increased tariffs on imports to the United States. The tariff, of course, led to retaliatory tariffs by European nations and contributed to a precipitous decline in international trade. The Smoot-Hawley tariff would later become notorious among most free market economists as a factor that contributed further to the economic malaise by depressing trade and, therefore, hindering international debt repayment.

Hoover also adhered to the nineteenth century Republican monetary position of remaining on the gold standard, thus putting the United States at a trade disadvantage with the Europeans that abandoned the gold standard in late 1931. When the Bank of England defaulted on gold payments in September 1931, the American Federal Reserve Board responded by raising interest rates in an effort to prevent a drain on American gold reserves. In turn, the raising of interest rates further hindered the American economy by discouraging borrowing and

▶ President Herbert Hoover

thus further reducing the money supply. Hoover exacerbated the capital shortage even more by stressing the traditional conservative belief in the importance of a balanced federal budget, his reason being that since citizens had to live within their means, the government should lead through the example with fiscal responsibility. Hoover also vetoed the Bonus Act of 1931 that was slated to give almost $1 billion to veterans; but Congress passed the measure over his veto. In Hoover's conception, economic crisis was not reason enough to abandon the conservative economic principles of the balanced budget and fiscal responsibility.

Hoover did not, however, strictly adhere to all conservative economic budgetary principles. By June 1931, Hoover's federal budget was $500 million in the red since the economic decline had also produced declining federal revenue. Hoover supported increased public works programs; favored federal loans to banks, businesses, farmers, and homeowners; and called for expansion of state and local relief programs—though he continued to oppose federal involvement in direct relief. In addition, Hoover created the Federal Farm Board (created under the Agricultural Marketing Act of 1929) to establish semipublic stabilizing corporations with the authority to purchase excess farm products and thus prop up prices. The Federal Farm Board was expected to support agricultural prices by lending funds to marketing cooperatives, or to corporations set up by the cooperatives, to stabilize the market. The loan funds would be used to purchase basic farm crops and livestock at marketing time so that markets would not be glutted.

Such a program was consistent with the principles of the Agricultural Adjustment Act of 1933, a major part of Franklin Roosevelt's New Deal, championed by the liberal Democrats and opposed by conservative Republicans after Hoover was voted out of office. The Federal Farm Board efforts, however, failed to stop the collapse of agricultural prices because farmers continued to overproduce.

The president, however, refused to face realistically the condition of the unemployed and continued to manipulate figures to encourage a false optimism, probably unaware of the real weakness of the banks. In the spring of 1930, just before business unemployment climbed sharply, he assured the nation, "The worst effects of the crash upon unemployment will have passed during the next sixty days."

Hoover justified federal loan programs on the premise that such loans eventually would be repaid; hence, to Hoover, loans were not the same thing as a government dole. Direct grants or relief, however, were anathema to Hoover. By 1932, Hoover's federal government spending was a very "New Dealish" $500 million per year on public works; but because of the coincidental decline in state and local spending on public works, total public outlays on public works in 1932 were almost $1 billion below the levels of 1929. Hoover also refused to allow the federal government to become involved in local relief efforts due to his belief that welfare was a state, rather than federal, responsibility under the U.S. Constitution. Hoover's refusal to initiate direct federal relief programs was viewed by many Americans as evidence that Hoover neither understood nor cared about the plight of the common person. Furthermore, Hoover's offhand remarks that "no one is actually starving" and that "the hoboes are better fed now than they've ever been" were proof enough to many that Hoover lacked compassion; consequently, many Americans came to identify the calamities of the Great Depression personally with Hoover. Makeshift shantytowns outside of cities became known as "Hoovervilles" and an empty pocket turned inside out became known as a "Hoover Flag."

In the final analysis, historians John Garraty and Robert McCaughey argue that Hoover's policies to combat the Depression failed due to the limitations of his conservative ideology. In the words of Garraty and McCaughey:

> "Hoover was too rigidly wedded to a particular theory of government to cope effectively with the problems of the day . . . flexibility and a willingness to experiment were essential to any program aimed at restoring prosperity. Hoover lacked these qualities."

In other words, the chief barrier to effective action in dealing with the advancing Depression was that President Hoover, most economists, and practically all businessmen adhered to the traditional laissez-faire view that government should not interfere with business. Thus they considered voluntary private investment the only road to national economic recovery. They did not regard public works projects or other government programs as means of recreating prosperity through increasing demand for workers, goods, and services. Furthermore, allied to the general political failure to appreciate the possibilities of artificially increased employment and

▶ Due to President Hoover's lack of compassion, many Americans came to identify the calamities of the Great Depression personally with Hoover. Makeshift shantytowns outside of cities became known as "Hoovervilles".

demand was the traditional attitude that helping individuals by federal food or relief payments would undermine the initiative of the American people.

A slight upturn in early 1931 seemed to reinforce President Hoover's "wait-and-see" policy. Yet the business indexes soon started down again, and the international financial structure began to disintegrate. In June 1931, banks on the European continent failed. Reparations and debt payments soon stopped, and by September England went off the gold standard (refused to pay its foreign obligations in gold). In July, President Hoover, with the agreement of England, France, and Germany, declared a one-year moratorium on European debt and reparation payments. He hoped that such a temporary lifting of the burden of intergovernmental debts would promote world trade and stimulate economic recovery. Nevertheless, the European crisis resulted in continued gold withdrawals from banks in the United States, European sale of American securities, and the freezing of most foreign short-term loans owed to banks in the United States. These events forced a further contraction of bank loans in the United States and an end to the possibility of a quick return to prosperity. While the collapse of 1929 was initiated in the United States, descent into the deep trough from 1931 to 1933 was, as President Hoover claimed, precipitated by European events.

Initiation of the Welfare State

Those in "the business world," wrote President Hoover, "threw up their hands and asked for government action." As voluntary action proved inadequate to counteract the deepening depression, Hoover moved step by step toward federal legislation. In December 1931 and January 1932, the president cooperated with leaders of the politically divided Senate and the Democratic House in creating the Reconstruction Finance Corporation (RFC). This conservatively managed agency, with resources of $2 billion, was to make loans to companies such as banks and railroads to prevent bankruptcy and forced liquidation, and provide funds to state and local governments for public works. Aid was given to some five thousand medium to large sized businesses to help them meet their pressing obligations, such as bond and mortgage interest or short-term debts.

▶ President Herbert Hoover and members of the Reconstruction Finance Corporation gather for a conference. The philosophy of aid that was to be provided was to preserve those institutions whose operation was essential to the public and to other businesses.

The philosophy of aid was to preserve those institutions whose operation was essential to the public and to other businesses. Consequently, banks and railroads received the most aid while small business, in general, was not initially helped. Critics argued that the RFC helped only those businesses that needed it the least and ignored those that needed it most. Critics therefore dubbed the RFC as the "Breadline for Big Business."

Nevertheless, the RFC only provided loans; it did not provide grants to business and could not purchase stock or provide no-strings capital to businesses or financial institutions. The RFC also provided money only for those public works programs that could be shown to eventually pay for themselves such as a toll road or public housing. Furthermore, the RFC was stingy in allocating the resources under its control. For example, Congress appropriated $300 million for support of local relief efforts, but the RFC had spent only $30 million by the end of 1932.

Until this time, the "general welfare" clause of the Constitution had never been interpreted to mean maintenance of the economic system by congressional action. While later Democratic acts continuing the RFC and extending aid to agriculture and individuals were to push the doctrine much further, the nonpartisan RFC Act can be considered the beginning of the federal "welfare state" or "social capitalism." It demonstrated, in the sphere of big business, that an advanced industrial economy was so complexly interrelated that government could not stand by and see any essential parts break down.

Other recovery measures enacted in the spring of 1932 included the Glass-Steagall Act, which made government bonds and additional types of commercial paper acceptable as collateral for Federal Reserve notes—thus liberalizing the lending powers of banks—and made available to business about $750 million of the government gold supply. In July, the Federal Home Loan Bank Act created twelve regional Federal Home Loan Banks to extend federal financial assistance to building and loan associations, savings banks, and insurance companies that were in trouble because of falling prices. Democratic congressional efforts at direct aid to individuals, however, were defeated by presidential vetoes. Hoover continued to view relief as a function of state and local governments; consequently relief limped along on the basis of small RFC loans to the states.

Effects of the Depression

By the spring of 1932, conditions in the United States reached what seemed to be an intolerable impasse. Then, after remaining relatively unchanged for some nine months, the situation grew even worse. Historians essentially agree that American capitalism had failed in 1932 with thousands roaming both the countryside and the city streets searching for food. Food prices were so low that farmers in Iowa and Nebraska burned their corn for fuel while millions had not enough to eat. In Birmingham, Alabama, landlords ceased evictions to prevent people from burning their abandoned dwellings for fuel. Federal immigration officials in the Southwest began deporting all Mexican aliens in an attempt to reduce the labor force and create jobs for the whites that remained. An estimated half million Mexicans left the United States for Mexico from 1931–1933.

Yet in this year of material, social, and moral prostration, there wasn't any threat of revolution, or even any important rise of radicalism in American politics, at least not initially. The

American cultural traditions of self-help and individual responsibility seemed, for the most part, to make the sufferers feel guilty, and perhaps sullen and resentful, but not ready to fight for a new order. By the end of the decade, however, a small but significant minority of Americans had moved in a more radical direction, either joining the Communist Party or becoming what was called a "fellow traveler," though actual Communist Party membership may never have eclipsed one hundred thousand people during its peak in 1934. Nevertheless, Communist Party parades on May Day between 1932 and 1934 drew an estimated fifty thousand people in New York. The radicals were disproportionately located in certain sectors, such as among artists and intellectuals or among those active in the labor movement.

Beginning in 1935, however, the American Communist Party shifted its strategy away from the goal of communist revolution and ceased to work independently from other organizations. Instead, the Communists worked through the labor unions with a focus on increasing wages and improving working conditions. The efforts of the Communists and the labor unions paid off in 1938 when the Supreme Court upheld the right, in *NLRB v. Jones and Laughlin Steel,* to bargain collectively. As a result of this success and the fusion with the labor unions, the Communist parades in New York in 1938 drew only two thousand people.

The overall statement that unemployment rose somewhere to one-fourth and one-third of the labor force gives too optimistic a picture of the effects of the Depression on human beings. To begin with, total man hours worked in mid-1932 were only about 40 percent those in 1929, and many experienced workers were being paid only five to ten cents per hour. Furthermore, destitute farmers were not considered unemployed; and people who had given up seeking work and students who stayed in school or college solely because they had no hope of finding jobs were not part of the "labor force." In general, the most easily replaceable workers, such as the unskilled, lost their jobs first; and work that remained was apportioned between management and skilled labor. Both managers and women office employees kept their jobs more often than workers in plants.

One-industry towns could be paralyzed by the failure of two or three local companies. By early 1932, the entire county of Williamson in southern Illinois had almost no employment. Some Appalachian mining cities had two hundred or three hundred employed out of many thousands. If a community depended on industries that made goods for other industries, it usually suffered mass unemployment.

Without income or housing to hold them together, many families disintegrated. A father without a job—who washed dishes, made beds, sat around, and failed to provide food—lost status in his family. Sometimes his position became intolerable, and he was driven to suicide. Many more unemployed fathers and older children started drifting around the country, presumably looking for work but perhaps really seeking escape through activity. The drift of a million or more of these "migrants of despair" was aimless but generally toward warm areas, where each city tried to keep the wayfarers moving to somewhere else. In many cities they could get a meal but could not stay.

In the larger cities the major burden of relief fell first on private donors and then on voluntary organizations—like the Red Cross, Salvation Army, Community Chest—and as these exhausted their resources, on small local and state appropriations. Before the end of 1930, people who administered relief recognized that these resources were inadequate.

"Local organizations," said C. A. Dykstra of Cleveland in 1932, "have tried to make $400 million play substitute for $20 or more billion, formerly paid in wages." In small cities, conditions were often worse than in the major centers. A survey of fifty-nine cities of upstate New York during the winter of 1930–1931 revealed that most of them had no relief programs. "By the fall of 1931," says Professor Irving Bernstein, "municipal relief—private and public—was bankrupt in virtually every city in the United States," and it is estimated that unemployment rose 50 percent in the next eighteen months.

Recipes developed and circulated on the best way to cook violet tops, various weeds, flowers, and dandelions. Some municipalities planted municipal gardens in attempts to feed people. Communities in west Texas sponsored rabbit hunts and snake hunts with the kills distributed to the poor as food. Crowds often developed around garbage cans, behind groceries and restaurants as people searched for food. Despite the despair, an estimated 50 percent of the jobless declined any sort of state aid because of pride.

The Depression altered family structures by forcing extended families to move in together. Young couples put off marriage for lack of a way to support themselves; and marriage rates, divorce rates, and college attendance—all declined 20–30 percent as people could not afford changes to their living arrangements. The American birthrate was 27.7 per one thousand in 1920, but dropped to 18.4 per one thousand in 1930's United States.

Virtually every economic indicator reflected a similar decline. American GNP was $104 billion in 1929, but declined to $76 billion in 1932—a 25 percent decline. In 1929, $16.2 billion was spent on capital investment, but by 1933 the aggregate of all capital investment was a paltry $330 million. Wholesale prices fell 43 percent from 1929–1933, and by 1932 unemployment is estimated to have been over 20 percent with an estimated thirteen million unemployed.

The farming country presented the most outrageous paradox of all. With no effective means of controlling prices or production, farmers literally ruined each other. To keep his income up when prices were falling, each farmer tried to produce more and more, thus driving prices down still further until the value of some crops and animals was too low to justify taking them to market. Because gifts of food would potentially compete with sales, no permissible way was found to distribute and use agricultural surpluses. As a result, a sheep raiser cut the throats of young lambs and threw them into a canyon because he could not afford to feed them while the families on so-called "bread lines" had watered-down soup. Southern share croppers fared worst of all. Owners unable to finance new crops left former tenants without food, and these rural areas generally lacked charitable or other relief organizations.

Farm Holiday Association

With the economy in shambles, especially in agricultural areas, a certain level of political unrest perhaps should have been expected; and while there was some political unrest in the Great Depression, the degree of political unrest given the economic circumstances should be considered mild at best. Nevertheless, Midwest farmers in the summer of 1932 became politically active with the creation of the Farm Holiday Association. The association endorsed the idea of withholding farm products from the market—in effect, a farm strike—in an effort to increase agricultural prices. The strike began in August 1932, in Iowa, and spread to the surrounding areas. Over the short term, the strike was effective in keeping some farm products from reaching the market; however, the scope of the strike was too small to impact farm prices as a whole, and most farmers did not comply with the strike. Consequently, some farmers turned to violence in efforts to enforce their strike. Rail lines were blocked, and trucks carrying farm products were attacked and overturned in efforts to enforce the strike. These activities, however, were too little and too isolated to impact prices, and the strike dissolved by the end of 1932.

Bonus Army

World War I veterans were scheduled to receive a bonus, in 1945, for their services in the Great War. In 1932, a group of veterans organized and demanded that the government pay the bonus immediately, rather than delay until 1945. President Hoover was opposed to early payment because he believed it would prevent the government from running a balanced budget.

In June 1932, twenty thousand veterans, calling themselves the "Bonus Army," marched into Washington, built a crude camp, and announced their intention to stay until the bonus was paid. In July, Hoover ordered the D.C. police to remove the protesters from some abandoned buildings where they had been staying with the result that the veterans threw rocks at the police when they attempted to evict them from the empty dwellings. The police then retaliated with gunfire, which killed two.

Hoover, convinced that the veterans were radical and dangerous, called in the army to help the police. General Douglas MacArthur, army Chief of Staff, carried out the operation himself. In full battle dress, MacArthur led the Third Cavalry (under the command of General George S. Patton), two infantry regiments, six tanks, and a machine gun unit down Pennsylvania Avenue to disperse the

▶ Twenty thousand veterans, calling themselves the "Bonus Army," marched into Washington, built a crude camp, and announced their intention to stay until their promised bonus was paid to them early.

▶ General George S. Patton

"Bonus" army, which fled in terror under a barrage of tear gas and bayoneted, rifle-carrying troops. MacArthur followed the protesters across the Anacostia River and burned their camp. At least one hundred demonstrators were injured, and one infant was trampled to death by the fleeing protesters.

The majority of United States newspapers supported Hoover's use of troops, but the photos of the United States Army chasing unarmed veterans with tanks and tear gas were not well received by the American public. The entire affair was proof to many Americans that Hoover was insensitive to their plight. Hoover further damaged his reputation with a series of insensitive and inaccurate statements, such as, "Nobody is actually starving," and "The hoboes are better fed than they have ever been."

By the summer of 1932, the patience of various groups throughout the nation was nearing exhaustion. In addition to the Farm Holiday Association and the Bonus Army, police had killed numbers of unemployed men in riots around Detroit, and some conservative editors were calling for a dictatorship to preserve the state. A majority of the leaders of both major parties, however, conservatively opposed any substantial change in policy. Of the Democratic leaders only Governor Franklin D. Roosevelt of New York seemed to lean toward a more progressive approach, favoring the use of government power to whatever extent necessary, and in whatever ways necessary, to reverse the trend of economic events.

The Election of 1932

Franklin Delano Roosevelt (FDR), the son of a wealthy railroad tycoon and a fifth cousin of Theodore, had been brought up on a country estate above Poughkeepsie, New York, and educated at Harvard and at Columbia Law School. In 1910, he entered politics and was elected to the New York State assembly, where he stood for progressivism and reform and was an ardent supporter of Woodrow Wilson. President Wilson, aware of the personal charm of the big, strong-jawed, smiling young man, appointed Roosevelt Assistant Secretary of the Navy, the same post that had been occupied by his cousin Teddy in 1898. The 1920 Democratic convention, needing the magic of the Roosevelt name, nominated him for the vice-presidency. Meanwhile, Teddy's children, Ted and Alice, were offended that their distant relative was running on the family name and campaigned against FDR believing that it was Ted, not Franklin, that should be the torchbearer of the Roosevelt name in politics.

Shortly after his defeat as Cox's running mate in 1920, Roosevelt contracted infantile paralysis (polio), losing forever his ability to walk; but by 1924 he had recovered sufficiently to appear, supported by crutches, at the Democratic convention and make the nominating speech for Alfred E. Smith. As much as possible, Roosevelt would do his best to shield the public from his infirmity, however, under the premise that many Americans at the time would hesitate to vote for a "cripple."

While he was recovering, his wife Eleanor (niece of Theodore Roosevelt) maintained the visibility of the Roosevelt name through her own hard work in the Democratic Party of New York. Franklin had married Eleanor in 1904, and the couple had four children together before Eleanor discovered a briefcase full of love letters between Franklin and Lucy Mercer in 1918. Eleanor was heartbroken, but she agreed to remain by his side because of their mutual political ambitions. Eleanor would later become, perhaps, the most political and influential First Lady in American history.

Eleanor also had to deal with Franklin's overbearing mother, Sarah, who meddled in the couple's lives and attempted to drive a wedge not only between Eleanor and Franklin but also between Eleanor and her own children. Sarah built a house in New York for Franklin and Eleanor, next to her own, with the two houses open to one another on all four floors. To the children, Sarah reportedly stated, "I am your real mother; Eleanor merely bore you."

In spite of the challenges at home, in 1928, at Al Smith's insistence, Roosevelt ran for governor of New York. Carrying the state by 25,000 votes, while Smith lost it for the presidency, marked Roosevelt as one of the coming men in the Democratic Party. As governor of New York, Roosevelt gained a reputation for using government to solve social problems. Under Roosevelt's tutelage, New York enacted unemployment insurance, old age pensions, and public works projects. In 1930, after one term as a rather easygoing, liberal governor, he was reelected governor of New York by a record-breaking 725,000 votes.

These repeated victories made him the party's logical candidate for the presidency in 1932; Roosevelt, fearful of a strong undercurrent of conservative opposition, left nothing to chance, however. His able secretary, Louis M. Howe, planned and advised, and New York State Democratic chairman James A. Farley toured the country and talked to politicians. At the Democratic convention, Farley skillfully negotiated with William Randolph Hearst and William C. McAdoo for California's support on the fourth ballot—in return for the nomination of conservative House Speaker John Nance Garner for vice-president. This shift swung Garner's state of Texas and other Southern states to the Roosevelt bandwagon, but Al Smith held on to his delegates and left Chicago without congratulating the nominee.

The Republicans had no recourse but to renominate Hoover, and in truth, the prosperous people who financed and ran the national machinery in both parties probably thought that Hoover had done all that could be expected. Yet everyone knew he would not be a strong candidate with the public.

▶ First Lady Eleanor Roosevelt on a coal train about to enter the Willow Grove Mine, 1935. She went below the surface and visited the mines to gain first hand information concerning mine conditions.

Alice Roosevelt openly campaigned for Hoover and publicly made fun of Eleanor's poorly aligned teeth. Later, Alice would publicly state in reference to Franklin, "I would rather vote for Hitler." Not to be outdone, Eleanor followed Ted Roosevelt at campaign stops with a teapot, representative of Ted's involvement in the Teapot Dome scandal.

The campaign mirrored the complete confusion in both parties regarding acceptable economic policy. The two platforms were nearly the same, and both candidates talked of public works and relieving misery while reducing spending and balancing the budget; but Garner was no doubt right when he told Roosevelt that to win "all you have to do is to stay alive until election day." FDR was not a miracle worker in New York, and the state suffered from the Great Depression along with the rest of America. However, FDR appeared to most Americans to be more energetic and open to different approaches than Hoover, who probably gained no votes with his weary and often bitter campaign. FDR lacked any concrete plan for attacking the Depression, but he won over Americans with his "Try Something" approach. FDR explained to Americans, "The country needs bold, persistent, experimentation. It is common sense to take a method and try it. If it fails, admit it frankly and try another, but above all, try something." FDR and the "Try Something" approach carried all but six states and 57.4 percent of the popular vote, and Hoover polled only 15,759,000 votes to Roosevelt's 22,800,000.

While many middle-class voters supported Socialist Party candidate Norman Thomas as the only candidate with a constructive program, Thomas failed utterly to attract the masses. His 881,951 Socialist votes were fewer than in 1920—when Eugene Debs had campaigned from prison—and relatively less than half the Socialist vote in 1912. Some artists and intellectuals desiring a stronger protest supported William Z. Foster, the Communist; but his meager 102,785 votes indicated that few workers had supported him, and there was no real Red Scare underway in America in spite of the almost complete collapse of communism.

Bottom of the Depression

The Great Depression reached its lowest ebb in the four months between the election and Roosevelt's inauguration. During this critical period there was little constructive leadership. Hoover thought that everything justifiable had been done in the domestic field and was interested in stimulating foreign trade. Roosevelt could not accept Hoover's analysis of the domestic situation and was not prepared to work for return to an international gold standard, the keynote of Hoover's plans. When FDR had accepted the nomination at the Democratic convention in the summer of 1932, he offered Americans a "New Deal" in his acceptance speech. "I pledge you, I pledge myself, to a New Deal for the American people." "The New Deal was a vague reference to government economic and social intervention; but before FDR could even take office, the depression worsened with a major bank panic and a rash of runs on banks and bank failures. In Michigan, its governor temporarily closed all banks for eight days. Other states followed. By the March 4 inauguration, forty states had ceased all banking operations, and all but one had imposed some type of banking restriction. Hoover wrote to FDR insisting that the panic was the result of a lack of confidence in the policies of the incoming administration, and Hoover asked FDR to announce that his new administration would stay on the gold standard and balanced budget. FDR intended to do neither and refused. The result was a rift between the two men that all could see during their famous ride down Pennsylvania Avenue on the way to the inauguration—as a gleeful Roosevelt waved to the crowd while a sulking Hoover looked the other direction.

The final breakdown of commercial banking was responsible for bringing the economy to its lowest ebb. Of the sixteen thousand state banks in 1929 that were not members of the Federal Reserve System, nearly half had closed their doors by 1933. These banks had no system to save them, and many of their officers, in truth, knew little about banking. Furthermore, of the seventy-five hundred members of the Federal Reserve, about fourteen hundred disappeared during the depression, demonstrating that even these banks were too small and poorly connected to stand the strain. Banks that failed drew away deposits kept in the banks of the larger cities. The first major metropolitan area to buckle under the pressure was New Orleans. Early in February 1933, the governor of Louisiana declared a temporary "bank holiday," freezing loans and deposits.

Meanwhile, a Senate committee investigating banking practices had uncovered dishonesty and evasion of responsibility in the highest circles. Major banks had lent money to their officers on no proper security, and bad securities had been sold to banks to save investment subsidiaries or affiliates from disaster. Federal examiners had overlooked these and other questionable practices. Faced with such uncertainties, depositors began to withdraw their surplus cash from the banks and stuff it into safe deposit boxes.

Following Louisiana's financial collapse, the governor of Michigan temporarily closed all banks in Michigan for eight days. Other states followed; and by Inauguration Day, forty states had ceased all banking operations, and all but one had imposed some type of banking restriction. The closing of the banks in Louisiana and Michigan started a chain reaction that did not end until March 4, 1933—the day of Roosevelt's inauguration—when Governor Lehman of New York and other governors joined in declaring a "bank holiday" to stop destructive runs as depositors rushed to withdraw savings. The banking crisis had, in turn, hurt business, driving unemployment up to somewhere between fourteen and seventeen million, perhaps as much as a third of the labor force. The economy was producing at about half the rate of 1929, and the trend was downward.

As the nation drifted without leadership, the silver shirts, white shirts, khaki shirts, and other fascist organizations strove unsuccessfully for mass support. "Technocracy," a vaguely defined plan for placing control of the nation's means of production in the hands of technicians in order to realize the full efficiency of industrial equipment, created a midwinter furor; but it died quickly from lack of immediate, practical proposals. In general, the people waited patiently, putting their hopes in the new administration.

FDR: The First Term

The Honeymoon

When FDR took office, the mood of the people, Congress, and even big business, was generally in favor of drastic government action. The first change was in February 1933, when Congress passed the Twenty-first Amendment repealing Prohibition. The necessary three-fourths of the states ratified the amendment by the end of 1933; Prohibition, on the nationwide scale, was ended.

▶ Franklin Delano Roosevelt

Roosevelt's inaugural address on March 4, 1933, struck a note of hope. The nation was strong, he said, and would recover from this crippling depression. "The only thing we have to fear is fear itself—nameless, unreasoning, unjustified terror which paralyzes needed efforts to convert retreat into advance." Roosevelt gave an indication as to his direction by stating, "This nation asks for action, and action now." He closed by affirming, "The people of the United States ... have asked for discipline and direction under leadership. They have made me the present instrument of their wishes. In the spirit of the gift I take it." The nation and Congress, which Roosevelt immediately called into emergency session, responded to his appeal; and quickly the pattern of the "New Deal" began to reveal itself.

"Our greatest primary task," Roosevelt declared in his inaugural address, "is to put people to work." Preferably Roosevelt thought that employment should be in private firms; but if necessary, he thought, the federal government should use its resources to provide employment on the most useful work projects that could be quickly devised. Second, Roosevelt thought that the abuses that aggravated the Depression must be corrected. Anyone guilty of criminal acts of financial or corporate manipulation must be punished, banking laws should be made more stringent, controls over the stock exchanges and the commodity markets should be tightened, and abuse of the holding-company device should be corrected by closer control of its use, especially in public utilities. After these emergency corrective measures had been taken, Roosevelt proposed a series of permanent steps to bring about a fuller development of the country and to make the lives of most Americans more secure and prosperous. Roosevelt referred to these three objectives of the New Deal as "Relief, Recovery, and Reform."

On March 6, before Congress met in special session, the president proclaimed a four-day national bank holiday and a four-day embargo on the export of gold, silver, and currency. Congress, convening on March 9, began what perhaps should be considered the most productive one hundred days in the history of the United States Congress. With a Democrat majority, FDR essentially faced no opposition in Congress, and there was almost complete unanimity in favor of greater federal economic intervention. First, Congress provided for the reopening of banks to relieve the financial emergency. The Emergency Banking Relief Act (EBRA)—enacted that day—confirmed the president's earlier actions and provided for Treasury Department inspection of all banks before they could reopen. The EBRA also provided federal assistance to unstable banks in the form of loans and the absorption of bad loans by the federal government. At the same time, Congress prohibited the use of gold, except under license, for export.

FDR then restored the American confidence in the banking system through his radio "fireside chats" where he declared to the American public that the banks would be safe when they reopened. FDR explained to Americans over the radio, "It is safer to keep your money in a reopened bank than under the mattress." Though no major substantive changes had been made to the banks, Americans believed the president; and by April 10, 1933, over $1 billion in hoarded currency returned to the banks. Importantly, the banks had not been nationalized because FDR had chosen reform rather than revolutionary change.

The special session of Congress, subsequently, was fed a stream of recovery measures drawn up by various groups in the administration, often with differing philosophies; however, with the force of the president behind them, sweeping bipartisan majorities. The Economy Act, in March 1933, cut federal salaries 15 percent and cut veteran's pensions 15 percent in an effort designed to help balance the budget since the government faced a $1 billion deficit without the cuts. FDR was trying to convince both the public and the business community that the economy was in safe, responsible hands. The Economy Act was problematic, however, in that it also had the effect of shrinking the money supply even further in a cash-short economy and, therefore, worsening the depression.

Congress established the Federal Deposit Insurance Corporation (FDIC) to ensure bank deposits and guard against further runs on banks. The Federal Securities Act required full public information on new stock issues and appointed the newly created Securities and Exchange Commission (SEC) to regulate securities transactions.

By the time this famous "Hundred Days" or political "honeymoon" ended in June 1933, the basic emergency legislation was complete. The Federal Emergency Relief Administration (FERA) was created with $500 million in funds to be granted to states for direct relief. A Civilian Conservation Corps (CCC) was set up to put unemployed young men into camps to carry out various reforestation and erosion-control projects. The demand for relief in the states was so great that the FERA had already spent the majority of the $500 million by the end of 1933.

The Spirit of the New Deal

It did not take long for the new administration to reveal an utterly unprecedented approach to governing—and not only because of the legislation it pushed through Congress. Appointments to major positions drew in an unusual mix of college professors and former settlement house workers—such as Secretary of Labor Frances Perkins, the first woman to be appointed to a cabinet position—as well as career politicians and bureaucrats. Indeed, more women were appointed to influential governmental positions than ever before in the nation's history. Moreover, FDR was eager to encourage new ideas although he did not necessarily always decide to employ them. Nothing embodied the new spirit more than the character of First Lady Eleanor Roosevelt. Born to privilege, she had been a neglected and underloved child with a mother that died young and a father that suffered from alcohol abuse. Scholars have suggested that this phenomenon helped give her the capacity to identify with the many victims of the Depression to the extent that she did. With her husband still suffering from the effects of polio, she traveled the country in his stead and became, in effect, his eyes and ears. She descended into coal mines or visited the rural poor. When she would return to Washington from one of these trips, she would bring with her the conviction that government could do something to help. Further, she reached out to African Americans in a way no other White House resident ever had. Many people called her "the conscience of the New Deal."

Farm Relief

From the standpoint of loss in money income, farmers were the hardest hit of any occupational group. From 1925 on, they were in a vicious circle of increasing overproduction of staple crops and declining prices. Earnings were so low that grain and cotton farmers could not afford the investment needed to shift to other produce for which there was a better market. The Depression, unfortunately, turned hardship into disaster. Total cash income for farmers fell from an average of nearly $11 billion per year in the late 1920s to $4.7 billion in 1932. Even these figures fail to suggest however, the desperate straits of marginal cotton, corn, and wheat growers that were even worse than national farm averages.

By May 1933, FDR was perhaps more concerned about the plight of the farmers than any other segment of society. The Agricultural Adjustment Act created the Agricultural Adjustment Administration (AAA), which was charged with reducing agricultural production in order to increase prices. The AAA controlled seven base commodities (wheat, cotton, corn, hogs, rice, tobacco, and dairy products) and would decide production limits for each crop. Then, the AAA would allocate to each farmer how much he could plant, paying subsidies to farmers to leave some of their land idle in an effort to curb production and increase prices.

The Agricultural Adjustment Act of June 1933 contained the basic principle of subsequent farm legislation. The government should pay staple crop farmers to plant fewer acres, thus reducing output and raising the prices on farm products. Money to subsidize the farmers was to come from a tax on millers and other processors of the staple products. In this way, the law would be self-supporting. To get the program going quickly, the Secretary of Agriculture arranged for the plowing under of millions of acres of cotton and the slaughter of six million pigs of less than usual market weights, with the pigs to be put to uses other than providing human food. Although many Americans considered the destruction of food and cotton positively sinful when millions were hungry and poorly clothed, farm prices and income did improve in 1934 and 1935.

There were multiple problems with the AAA, however, as it led to sharecropper unemployment as landowners would remove land from production (in effect laying off sharecroppers that had been working the land) and accept government subsidies. With less land to tend, wage-earning field hands also suffered layoffs. The drops in agricultural production hurt other areas of the economy, such as the railroads that carried fewer products to market. Finally, the Supreme Court struck down the AAA in 1936, as unconstitutional and argued that Congress had no authority to limit production.

In February 1936, Congress responded by passing the Soil Conservation and Domestic Allotment Act, which permitted the government to pay farmers to "conserve soil" and prevent erosion. Although the final result was much the same as that of the AAA, the Soil Conservation Act survived Court challenges.

Mortgage Refinancing

The government had to try not only to revive farm income but also to take care of hundreds of thousands of defaulted mortgages, both farm and non-farm. In two initial acts creating the Federal Farm Mortgage Corporation and the Home Owners Loan Corporation, the government offered to refinance mortgages on longer terms and at lower interest.

In addition, the Federal Housing Administration Act of 1934 introduced the guaranteed packaged mortgage—one that could be repaid, principal and interest, by uniform monthly payments. This government guarantee of loans for a high percentage of the total cost of homes in the low-price range constituted the most important change in the history of American home ownership. Now people with steady jobs could afford to build or buy, where they had had to rent before; and payment was much easier. This new system also marked an important step in the development of less expensive homes and long-term installment buying.

Regional Development

One of the most revolutionary of the acts passed by Congress during Roosevelt's first Hundred Days initiated the redevelopment of an entire region—the economically ailing seven-state Tennessee valley area. The Muscle Shoals–Tennessee Valley Development Act of May 1933 created an independent public corporation, the Tennessee Valley Authority, which was given control of the government property at Muscle Shoals, Alabama, and the power to build and operate other dams and power plants on the Tennessee River and its branches wherever the authority thought advisable. In addition to generation and distribution of electric power, TVA was charged with controlling the floodwaters of the Tennessee River and improving its navigation facilities, promoting the conservation of soil in the valley, aiding reforestation, and producing nitrates and other fertilizers for the improvement of the valley's agriculture. Government-financed improvements in the valley continued over the next generation, leading ultimately to industrial development as well as greatly increasing animal husbandry. The TVA eventually built twenty new dams and improved five others. Flooding was controlled on the Tennessee River, and the TVA became the largest and cheapest producer of electricity in the United States. Other power companies were forced to lower their rates to compete with the TVA.

The power dams, plants, and distribution systems of the TVA, however, were criticized by private power companies as unfair competition, since the public facilities were not required to pay the same taxes as private companies and received other government subsidies. The Supreme Court upheld the constitutionality of the TVA, however, in 1936. The

▶President Roosevelt signing the Tennessee Valley Development Act, 1933. The act would give the Tennessee Valley Authority, control of the property at Muscle Shoals, Alabama, and authority to build dams and power plants on the Tennessee River.

following year, President Roosevelt asked Congress to set up six additional regional river valley authorities, but Congress declined. The areas in which they were to be located were not quite such distinct units as the Tennessee valley, nor were the people of these other areas in such a distressed condition as those in the Tennessee valley had been in 1933. The general business outlook was brighter in early 1937, and the business community supported the widespread contention that private capital could develop these valleys as effectively as the federal government.

Partially thwarted in his larger conservation and development plans, the president succeeded in having the Civilian Conservation Corps (CCC) plant a tree belt across the Great Plains, while the Department of Agriculture checked soil erosion by urging farmers to plow furrows at right angles to the slope of the land, a practice called contour plowing. Thus the New Deal period may be looked upon as the beginning of a heightened federal consciousness of ecological problems.

Industrial Recovery

While banking, currency, mortgages, and agriculture had occupied the president's attention during the first weeks of his administration, he learned in, April 1933, that unless he acted quickly, Congress would pass a uniform thirty hour-a-week law governing all industry. Because he regarded such a law as impractical, the president had his advisers prepare a substitute. The resulting National Industrial Recovery Act (NIRA), though hastily improvised, actually was the outgrowth of much thought by business, labor, and government about how to reconcile "free" private enterprise with effective governmental control of wages and competition.

In many industries, excess industrial capacity, unemployed labor, and nearly bankrupt firms had reduced the market to chaos. With women receiving as little as $5 for a full week's

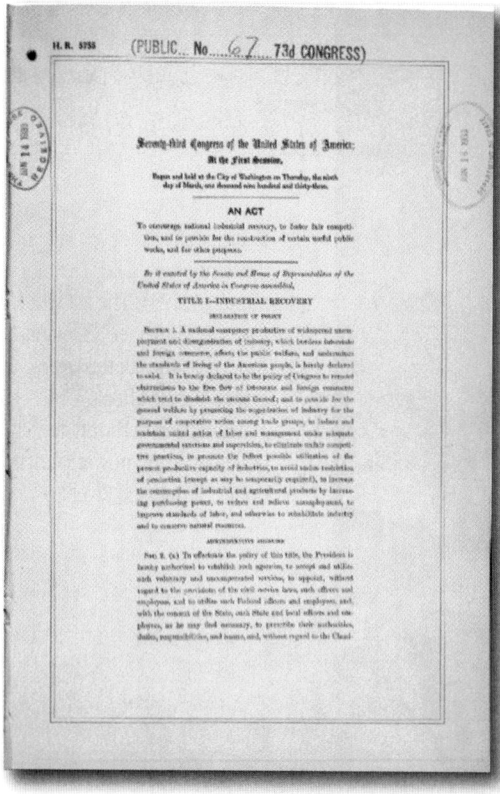
H.R. 5755 (PUBLIC No. 67 73d CONGRESS)

Seventy-third Congress of the United States of America;
At the First Session,

AN ACT

TITLE I—INDUSTRIAL RECOVERY

▶ The solution that was the NIRA was to have each industry agree to a code of "fair competition" defining wages, hours, and minimum prices. Industries were encouraged to set minimum wages at $.30 per hour, maximum hours at forty per week, and place severe restrictions on child labor.

work, companies that tried to maintain fair labor standards found themselves undersold. The solution proposed in the act was to have each industry, probably through its trade association, agree to a code of "fair competition" defining wages, hours, and minimum prices. Industries were encouraged to set minimum wages at $.30 per hour, maximum hours at forty per week, and place severe restrictions on child labor. Labor would be represented in the making of such industry agreements by representatives of its own choosing without any pressure from the employer. The NIRA guaranteed workers the right to bargain collectively through representatives of their own choosing. The public would also be represented so that the interests of consumers would not be ignored. When all three parties were represented in the determination of policies for an industry, the government could overlook the fact that a price agreement would appear to be a clear "conspiracy to restrain trade" under the terms of the Sherman Antitrust Act. The National Recovery Administration (NRA) was set up to administer this section of the law.

The second section of NIRA set up the Public Works Administration (PWA) and authorized the expenditure of $3.3 billion for public works projects, designed both to provide work for relief and to stimulate recovery. The bill became law in June 1933, and the president appointed retired General Hugh S. Johnson as administrator of the first section. The negotiation of codes proved difficult and time consuming. In July 1933, President Roosevelt, in an attempt to speed matters, announced a blanket President's Reemployment Agreement (PRA) governing wages and hours for those industries that could not agree upon a code. A blue eagle was adopted as the symbol of the cooperating firms. Those that signed codes or the PRA were allowed to display it on their stores, plants, or merchandise, and the public was strongly urged not to patronize those who didn't have the symbol. Within months, millions of Americans were working under the blue eagle. The original idea of cooperation between the employer, organized labor, and consumer representatives, however, was all but lost in the difficulties of reaching agreements. Furthermore, consumers were unorganized and unable to protect their interests as management and government drew up a flood of codes. As time passed, thousands of cases of noncompliance with codes were reported. Labor was extremely restive because the union organization as authorized by NIRA was often opposed by industry. Furthermore, the country was plagued by strikes. The dominant corporations in each industry often wrote codes under the NIRA; and, therefore, the codes were criticized for helping big businesses more than small businesses. Employers began to fear that they had made a mistake in agreeing to negotiate with labor in drawing up the codes. The public also began to feel that it was being fleeced by prices that were rising faster than income.

Although the NRA contributed to the raising of wages from the low levels of 1932, did away with child labor, and in some industries helped small business stay alive, the NIRA experiment illustrated the difficulty of suddenly regulating a complex economy. More important, it failed to bring back prosperity. Limiting production had a negative effect on employment, and higher prices had a negative impact on consumption. Industrial production declined 30 percent in the third quarter of 1933, in spite of higher prices. By the spring of 1935, there was widespread cheating by firms who could no longer financially abide by the codes. Businesses cut wages and cut prices to reduce costs and gain market share.

To make matters worse, the PWA was slow to act and had not spent the majority of its appropriations after five years. Blacks complained that the PWA was discriminatory as it prohibited blacks from public works programs and the PWA constructed segregated housing. Blacks mocked the NRA by joking that the acronym really stood for "niggers rarely allowed." Nevertheless, the United States Chamber of Commerce and labor leaders as diverse as William Green, John L. Lewis, and Sidney Hillman continued to support the NRA until the Supreme Court ruled, in *Schechter Poultry v. United States,* that the act (along with collective bargaining) was unconstitutional. Roosevelt himself denounced what he termed as the "sick chicken" decision by the Court and denounced the Court for their "horse and buggy" interpretation of the United States Constitution. FDR would have to seek another direction in trying to combat the Depression since the NIRA and its programs were no more.

Devaluing the Dollar

Controllable inflation, the president hoped, would raise farm prices and, in general lighten, the burden of debts in relation to income. The administration felt that such inflation could be stimulated either by heavy government spending or by altering the value of the dollar. Of the two possibilities, devaluing the dollar had the immediate advantages of not adding to government costs and of stimulating exports.

While the president was supporting the inflationist group in Congress, the United States, Japan, and European nations were meeting, in June and July 1933, in London to attack the worldwide depression by attempting to agree on stabilizing national currencies and restoring the international gold standard. Contrary to this spirit, however, an amendment to the Agricultural Adjustment Act of May 1933 gave the president the right to inflate U.S. currency by issuing $3 billion in paper currency, freely coining silver, and devaluing the gold content of the dollar up to 50 percent. For the time being he did none of these things, waiting to see whether the AAA and the NRA would do the inflationary job, but neither would he enter into any international agreement fixing the value of the dollar. European delegates at the Economic Conference in London angrily accused Roosevelt of undermining the conference. As a result, the London Economic Conference quickly failed. The conference had been further undermined by the behavior of American delegate Key Pittman of Nevada, the Chairman of the United States Senate Foreign Relations Committee. While Belgium, Italy, and France were seeking stabilization of currency through the gold standard, Pittman—from a silver mining state—called for the international monetization of silver. Pittman also went on a drinking binge in London (during prohibition in the United States) and on one occasion shot out streetlights in London with a pistol. On another occasion, he was seen naked in the halls of a posh London hotel with a whiskey bottle in one hand and a bowie knife in the other as he chased terrified delegates through the halls and screaming about the silver standard.

▶ Key Pittman

Although there was a sharp increase in manufacturing production, employment, and prices between March and July 1933—in part, the result of an effort to produce before the restrictive NRA codes went into effect—by the autumn of 1933, manufacturing and employment were declining, and wholesale prices had again leveled off. At this point the president decided to use his power to devalue the dollar in the expectation that the resulting inflation would lead to higher prices. The Treasury Department began purchasing gold on the open market in July in an attempt to drive up the price of gold and thus devalue the currency. The efforts failed to significantly alter gold prices, so Congress passed the Gold Reserve Act in January 1934. The Gold Reserve Act allowed the president to arbitrarily set the price of gold. Once endowed with this power, FDR increased the price of gold from $25 an oz. to $35—an increase of 40 percent. Thus the currency was devalued, and the degree of devaluation was calculated to restore the price level of 1926. Prices rose slightly, but not nearly so much as the administration had expected.

Rise of Conservative Opposition

Early criticism of the New Deal had come primarily from advanced liberals and labor leaders. Some of the most progressive members of Congress, for instance, would have nationalized banking and railroads. They and the moderate liberals, even more so, regarded the restoration of the banking system in relatively unchanged form as the loss of a great opportunity for progress toward a more stable economy. Organized labor was particularly dissatisfied with its treatment by the NRA, which in labor circles came to be called the "national run-around."

On the other hand, monetary manipulation during the last half of 1933 lost the president the support of many conservative Democratic leaders, who opposed any tinkering with the monetary system. Efforts at permanent reform of financial operations, as distinct from mere recovery, widened the rift between liberals and conservatives.

The reform program really began with the Federal Securities Act of 1933, by which the Federal Trade Commission was given the power to see that underwriters fully disclosed to investors all essential details pertaining to new securities issues. A further reform was enacted with the Banking Act of June 1933, which divorced investment banking from commercial banking on the premise that the promoting and selling of new securities by commercial banks gave them an improper amount of power over other businesses and was inconsistent with the policy of caution and prudence which banks should follow. The Banking Act also created the Federal Deposit Insurance Corporation (FDIC) to insure bank deposits up to established limits and prevent losses to depositors. Because it involved more governmental regulation, leading bankers vigorously opposed deposit insurance; increase in general business opposition was aroused by the stricter regulation of the securities markets.

The battle between liberals and conservatives was intensified when the Securities Exchange bill was before Congress in the spring of 1934. This bill called for the establishment of a three-member Securities and Exchange Commission (SEC) to regulate the practices of stock exchanges, including the size of margins; to require full disclosure of details about all securities; and to enforce other parts of the Federal Securities Act of 1933. Stockbrokers and investment bankers complained strongly about the restrictions this legislation would place on them. Despite bitter debate in Congress, the bill was passed in June 1934; and the die-hard opponents of all governmental regulation of the financial community were decisively defeated.

Another development in the spring of 1934 that alarmed some businessmen was adoption of the Reciprocal Trade Agreements Act, which gave the president power to make separate agreements with foreign nations and to alter U.S. tariff rates by 50 percent in either direction. Even moderate Republicans denounced it as a surrender of power to the president. The Democrats, however, with strong Southern support, held firm and enacted this change in American tariff policy.

In the course of debates over the Securities Act and the tariff, business arguments against the New Deal took their permanent shape. The government was condemned for creating a vast and irresponsible bureaucracy, for depriving individuals of their freedom and initiative, and for increasing the national debt. Direct relief, in particular, was condemned as running contrary to the deeply ingrained tradition that self-help was the basis of American greatness.

In August 1934, a group of wealthy Republicans and conservative Democrats formed the Liberty League to defend the rights and liberty of the individual against the New Deal. Backed by Du Pont and General Motors executives, the League won the support of previous Democratic presidential candidates John W. Davis and Alfred E. Smith and many other conservative political leaders in both parties. The Liberty League and other opponents of the New Deal were bolstered by the big city daily newspapers, which were moving in the same direction. Within a year, at least two-thirds of the metropolitan dailies were strongly in opposition to the New Deal, and their influential columnists were attacking the "third-rate college professors" and other "impractical intellectuals" of the "Brain Trust" that was held to be guiding the policies of the administration. Moreover, the activist First Lady Eleanor Roosevelt became a lightning rod for criticism.

Reliance upon the Masses

The business attack on the New Deal, though backed by adequate finances and the support of major newspapers, had the fatal weakness of lacking a positive philosophy. Business leaders could only ask the public again to put its faith in the self-regulating economy. That, in fact, the public would not trust self-regulation was shown in the election of 1934. Normally the presidential administration's party loses strength in Congress in the mid-term elections. Instead, in 1934, the Democrats gained nine seats in the House and nine in the Senate, with nearly 57 percent of the popular vote—an off-year administration victory unmatched since before the Civil War.

What had built the Democratic majority? The answer of a number of presidential advisers was that it was the voters' desire for security—for assurance that when unemployed or old they would be cared for. At this point, therefore, the New Deal became more egalitarian and humanitarian than any of the previous progressive movements.

Public Works

In November 1933, Congress created the Civil Works Administration (CWA), which provided public works employment. By January 1934, four million were employed for the CWA. Congress spent one billion dollars in five months of operation of the CWA. However, FDR was afraid of running massive deficits prior to the Congressional elections of 1934, and he cancelled the program due to costs. In the spring of 1935 Congress created the Works Progress Administration (WPA), which essentially took over where the CWA left off. Jobs ranging from mixing concrete to painting murals were to be created from an appropriation of nearly $5 billion. Pay would be at rates above relief but lower than approved for private employment. The Works Progress Administration lasted until World War II and spent some $11 billion from 1935–1943. Although it could employ only from two to three million workers, it kept those with the more valuable skills from deteriorating through idleness. Congress also created the National Youth Administration, which employed over two million persons between the ages of sixteen and twenty-one in public works projects. Other minor forms of aid were instituted to help students stay in school and to provide potential farmers with subsistence homesteads.

Disliked by the conservative opponents of the New Deal, the various arts projects supported by the public works programs, however, left a remarkable legacy for the nation. Many public buildings were adorned with murals; and such distinguished artists as Jackson Pollock, Alice Neel, Willem de Kooning, and Louise Nevelson received support from the WPA. Aaron Copland wrote his two ballets, *Billy the Kid* (1938) and *Rodeo* (1942) for the WPA. The Federal Writers' Project sponsored guidebooks to each of the then forty-eight states, books rich with

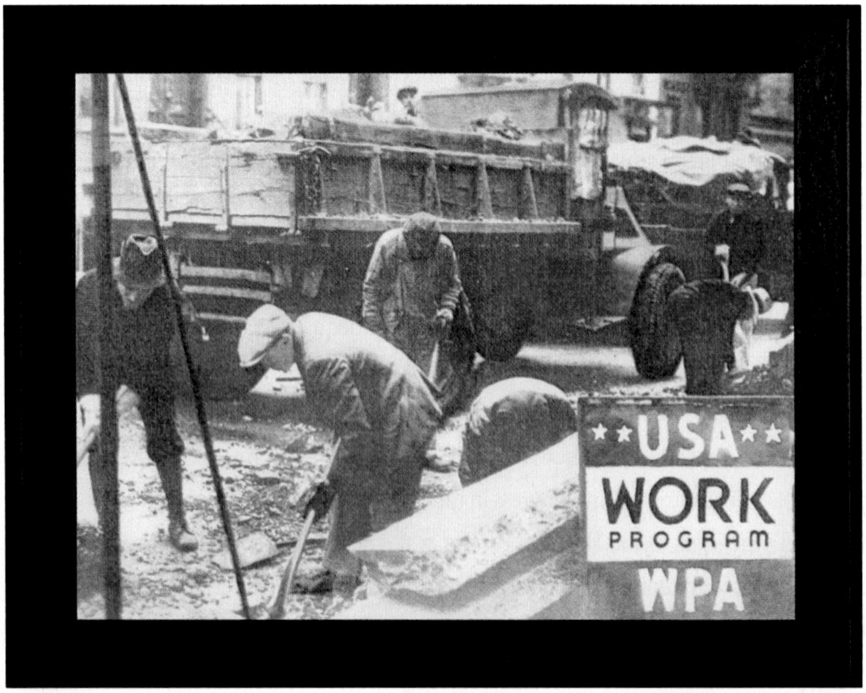

▶ Works Progress Administration (WPA), created by Congress in 1935, took over where the Civil Works Administration had left off when it had been cancelled. The program provided public works employment.

material that might have otherwise gone unrecorded. African Americans with memories of slavery and the southern poor were interviewed. Hundreds of American folk songs were catalogued, and the creative lifeblood of the country was kept in circulation.

Social Security

In the president's mind, the most important legislation of his administration was the Social Security Act of 1935. This act created a Social Security Board to administer unemployment compensation, old-age security, and various social services. Payroll taxes of 1 percent were levied on both employers and employees to finance old-age pensions from $10 to $85 per month for retired workers. Pensions under the new system would not begin until 1942, but meanwhile the federal government would assist the states in paying small pensions. In the beginning, many groups, including farm and educational workers, were not eligible for pensions; however, in succeeding years coverage was broadened and rates increased to compensate for inflation. The Social Security Act also extended federal-state unemployment insurance to 28 million workers and authorized money grants to states to assist them in relief of the blind, the crippled, delinquent children, and other dependents. Suddenly, the power of Congress to legislate for the general welfare had a new meaning.

The Supreme Court: Challenge and Response

Early in 1935, with the Social Security bill on its way through Congress, the president regarded his program as virtually complete. Had the Supreme Court upheld the legislation of 1933 and 1934, the Roosevelt administration, like that of Woodrow Wilson, might have turned its attention to matters other than domestic reform. However, Supreme Court had four justices unalterably opposed to the New Deal, and two others, Owen J. Roberts and Chief Justice Charles E. Hughes, who were very doubtful about the constitutionality of delegating congressional power to administrative agencies and using the commerce power to regulate conditions of production and trade within the states.

The crucial tests came in the spring of 1935, when the Court declared the NIRA and a number of other basic acts of the New Deal unconstitutional. There was little hope that those still to be tested, such as the Agricultural Adjustment Act, would fare any better. Indeed the Supreme Court invalidated the first AAA in January 1936.)

The Court's failure to interpret the Constitution flexibly and to support the type of laws planned in cooperation with business leaders, pushed the president toward further regulation. The influence of the administration was already behind Senator Robert F. Wagner's National Labor Relations Act to replace the labor provisions of the outlawed NIRA. The Wagner Act created a new National Labor Relations Board (NLRB) for administrative purposes and upheld the right of employees to join labor organizations and to bargain collectively through representatives of their own choosing.

This support of labor accompanied other New Deal measures that antagonized conservatives. A new tax bill, introduced in June 1935, had the announced purpose of shifting the tax burden from the poor to the rich. The "Soak the Rich Act" of 1935 actually made few changes in taxes on income under $50,000 a year. The graduated, corporation income tax stopped at 15 percent; but high taxes on big incomes and on inheritance of estates further alarmed the wealthy over the "communistic" trend of the New Deal.

The widespread attack on the New Deal by the rich probably strengthened support for the president. More politically dangerous, however, was the attack on his policies by radical reformers. In his weekly radio broadcasts, Father Charles F. Coughlin, a demagogic right-wing Catholic priest, first criticized the president for failure to take care of the rural poor; then he progressed to a fascist type of attack on Jews and international bankers. Coughlin had supported the New Deal at first, but then turned against it with a vengeance, viewing it as part of an international communist conspiracy. Contending that Adam Weishaupt, the founder of the Illuminati, was the inspirer of Karl Marx, Coughlin essentially tied the global communist threat to an Illuminati conspiracy. Also in cahoots with the communists, in Coughlin's conception, were international bankers, Jews, and Masons, especially Jewish Masons. Coughlin was decidedly anti-Semitic and denounced those with whom he disagreed politically as being Jews. Coughlin even went so far as to argue that Alexander Hamilton, a founding father who had favored national government economic intervention, was actually Jewish and that his original name was Alexander Levine. Coughlin also published a newspaper, *Social Justice,* where he denounced FDR as "stupid," referred to him as "Franklin Double-crossing Roosevelt," and called for his impeachment. Coughlin wielded tremendous influence with conservatives in the 1930s and used his radio show to organize a political lobby of five million members. In 1934, his lobby group was responsible for sending two hundred thousand letters to Congress in protest of the establishment of the World Court. In 1934, Coughlin received more mail than any person in the world, and he took in over $500,000 in donations at the height of the Great Depression.

In a more constructive vein, Dr. Francis Townsend of California advocated pensions of $200 a month for the elderly, but the most comprehensive political and economic appeal of the day came from Senator Huey P. Long of Louisiana. A mixture of machine politician and shrewd administrator who believed the Depression could be cured by government spending, Senator Long advocated a guaranteed minimum income and a capital levy on the rich to provide every family with a home, a car, and a radio. His simple country-boy manner and his slogan, "Every man a king," made him a real threat to Roosevelt's control of the Democratic Party. Long was killed by a personal enemy in September 1935. Coughlin and other unorthodox reformers continued to keep the administration under fire, but without Long they lacked a strong political leader.

The Election of 1936

The election of 1936 was clearly a national referendum on the New Deal. Republicans were deeply divided over the New Deal. The more staunch conservatives violently opposed all aspects of it, and a more moderate faction that supported the New Deal, for the most part, but rejected its deficit spending. Many Republicans felt that with Alfred M. Landon, ex-governor of Kansas, they would defeat Roosevelt in 1936. The *Literary Digest's* poll of telephone subscribers, which indicated a Landon presidential victory, helped sustain this view. (Overlooked was the fact that Roosevelt supporters were not adequately represented among telephone subscribers.) Landon promised to do everything that the New Deal was doing for the common man, but to do it in ways more satisfactory to business. The president responded with a more advanced liberalism than in earlier campaigns. In his speech accepting re-nomination, he denounced the "economic royalists" and said that Americans, in their achievement of economic and social democracy, had a "rendezvous with destiny." The result was the greatest landslide since 1920. Landon carried only Maine and Vermont with 16.7 million votes (36 percent) to the president's 27.8 million (61 percent). The Democrats increased their majority in both houses while the fascist Coughlin group, supporting a radical farm leader, polled less than a million votes. The Socialists' and Communists' votes were negligible. No president since Monroe had received such strong second-term support from the people.

Last Phase of the New Deal

Battle over the Court

In a surprise move after the election of 1936, Roosevelt boldly attempted to use his great political strength and national popularity to alter the composition of the ultraconservative Supreme Court—and thus, liberalize the Court's attitude toward New Deal legislation. In eight of ten major New Deal cases from 1933–1936, the Court struck down New Deal legislation as unconstitutional. The New Deal programs consistently lost on the Supreme Court by a 6-to-3 vote. Roosevelt had good reason to believe that in 1937 the Court would strike down a number of major provisions of his New Deal. In fact, lawyers were so confident that the Courts would rule against the New Deal that they were advising corporations to ignore the Social Security Act. In reaction, the president presented Congress, in February 1937 with a bill to reorganize the federal judiciary by adding up to fifty judges to the federal court system as a whole. The bill further proposed to increase the membership of the Supreme Court from nine to a maximum of fifteen by permitting the president to appoint one new justice for each justice over seventy who refused to retire. The number of justices on the Supreme Court was not set by the U.S. Constitution and the Court had increased in members from its original six to the nine that sat on the Court in 1937. Roosevelt's ostensible argument for the bill was that federal judges were overworked and decisions too long delayed because the judiciary was "handicapped by insufficient personnel." Furthermore, the president contended that the aging judges were antiquated in outlook—"little by little, new facts become blurred through old glasses fitted, as it were, for the needs of another generation." For the lower courts, Roosevelt's argument was valid; but the highest tribunal was not far behind in its casework, and the justices over seventy included some of the most vigorous and liberal members of the Court.

The magnitude of the change from nine to fifteen justices when no previous Congress had ever altered the size of the Court so drastically, and the doubtful sincerity of Roosevelt's argument for the major provision of the bill, created unexpected Congressional opposition to the administration. Liberal Democrats and progressive Republicans joined conservatives in opposing the measure. The press was violent in its denunciation, and public opinion polls showed popular distaste for so arbitrary an action by the president.

While Congress debated the president's "Court-packing" bill, the Court itself removed much of Roosevelt's reason for the bill by voluntarily liberalizing its stand on New Deal legislation. Justice Roberts and Chief Justice Hughes abandoned the conservative camp and joined Justices Brandeis, Cardozo, and Stone in reversing the legal doctrines of 1935 and 1936. In March 1937, the Court, by a 5-to-4 decision, upheld a Washington state minimum wage law for women, whereas the previous year it had declared unconstitutional a similar law of the state of New York. In April, the Court declared the National Labor Relations Act constitutional, and the next month it upheld the Social Security Act. Furthermore, Justice Van Devanter's resignation from the Court in May 1937 gave Roosevelt a chance to appoint a justice who would convert the liberal minority of the Court to a majority in future decisions. To succeed Van Devanter, Roosevelt appointed Senator Hugo L. Black of Alabama, an enthusiastic supporter of the New Deal.

In June 1937, the Senate Judiciary Committee reported the court reform bill unfavorably. The Senate, after bitter debate, subsequently rejected the proposal by voting seventy to twenty to return it to the Judiciary Committee. Congress did, however, pass a Supreme Court Retirement Act permitting Supreme Court justices to retire, with full pay, at age seventy. It also passed a Judicial Procedure Reform Act that established reforms in the lower courts.

New Dealers found consolation for the defeat of the administration bill in the fact that the few years after defeat of the "Court-packing" plan saw a radical change in the complexion of the Supreme Court. A succession of deaths and resignations enabled Roosevelt to make eight new appointments to the Court and gave him the liberal tribunal that Congress had denied him.

▶ Senator and Associate Supreme Court Justice, Hugo L. Black

A Government-Protected Labor Movement

Early in 1933 the total independent union membership in the United States had fallen to less than 2.7 million, including about two million in the AFL. Unemployment had reduced company union membership to less than a million. As a consequence, the morale of union leaders was at low ebb, and in general their proposals for recovery were no more imaginative than Hoover's.

Section 7(a) of NIRA (granting to organized labor the right of collective bargaining through representatives of their own choosing) and the subsequent upswing in employment gave unions a chance to expand. Organizational drives and some help from the National Labor Board of the NRA raised total union membership to 3.6 million in 1935. Meanwhile, faced with the threat of being forced by code authorities to bargain collectively, the larger employers were setting up new company unions. By 1935 this type of membership had passed 2.5 million.

In the same year, a group within the AFL, led by John L. Lewis of the United Mine Workers, was urging the organization of all workers in a given industry—skilled or unskilled—into a single union. The AFL as a whole, however, was dominated by craft unions and continued to be officially opposed to all moves toward unionization by industries.

The Wagner Act of 1935 gave industrial organizers new, and potentially effective, weapons. The powerful National Labor Relations Board created by the act could hold a plant election at the request of a union but not of an employer. If the union received the vote of a majority of workers, it became the bargaining agent for all. Furthermore, the Board could determine the unit—plants, companies, or industries—for election purposes; and it could also prevent employers from interfering in any way with organizers or trying to influence the election. If the winning union was able to negotiate a closed-shop agreement, the employer was required to deduct union dues from the pay of all workers. In view of the decisions of the Supreme Court in 1935 and 1936, however, even labor leaders regarded the law as probably unconstitutional.

Encouraged somewhat by the opportunities the new law might offer and much more by the sweeping reelection of a friendly president, the leaders of eight AFL unions defied the parent body and formed a Committee for Industrial Organization. Led by John L. Lewis, the CIO refused to compromise with the crafts, and the AFL expelled the unions involved in 1937. The following year, the committee became the Congress of Industrial Organizations with Lewis as president and a membership roughly equal to that of the AFL.

While Lewis in 1936 wanted to use the government-supported power of labor to organize steel workers, the local unions in the automotive industries initiated action on their own front. Late in the year, when General Motors refused to recognize and bargain with the United Automobile Workers, union members in Flint, Michigan, occupied their plants. The sit-down strike left the workers in possession of valuable machinery. Food was brought in by their families. Efforts by local authorities failed to dislodge the workers, and the newly elected Democratic governor, Frank Murphy, refused to enforce court orders to remove them by using the state militia. Meanwhile, orders for cars increased as the motor industry enjoyed a return to prosperity, and President Roosevelt kept a steady pressure on General Motors to bargain with Lewis. As a result of both factors, a settlement was reached that established a pattern of collective bargaining with the UAW. During the prosperous spring of 1937, similar agreements were worked out with the other motor companies, except for Ford.

In April, the Supreme Court, under pressure from the judicial "reform" bill in Congress, reversed its previous attitude and declared the Wagner Act constitutional. Even before this, the two major steel companies, also anxious to avoid a costly and perhaps useless strike, had signed agreements with the CIO. While Ford and the smaller steel companies violently resisted organization for some years more, by World War II they had all been forced into line by government action.

In spite of the sharp downswing of business and employment from mid-1937 to 1939, union strength continued to increase. Enthusiastic young organizers, government protection of the processes of organization and election, and compulsory bargaining were building a labor movement of unprecedented strength. In self-defense, the AFL was forced to adopt the principle of industrial unionism and compete vigorously with the CIO. That led to the AFL successfully organizing, for example, a union among the female-dominant canning industry in northern California, just the kind of work force that the AFL had previously ignored. In 1940 there were nearly 9 million organized workers: over 4 million in the AFL, 3.5 million in the CIO, and 1 million in independent unions. Although substantially less than the 28 percent organized in Great Britain, the 30 percent in France, and the 50 percent in Australia and Denmark, the total of nonagricultural unionized employees was at a peak for the United States.

Women in the Depression

The AFL would not accept women members into most of its unions, but the new CIO would. Therefore, division in the ranks of labor worked in favor of women's rights. The fact that women worked for lower wages than men also kept a few more of them at their jobs during the worst years of the depression, but with partial recovery, the situation returned to about that of 1930.

The inevitable effect of hard times was to move feminist activity from direct efforts to compete more equally with men in the job market, which could scarcely succeed in the face of high unemployment, to national legislative reforms. Eleanor Roosevelt took her place as leader in this movement. She encouraged Mary Dewson, head of a Women's Division of the Democratic Party, to work hard for FDR and his reform legislation. She also recruited women to run for Congress.

In spite of making Frances Perkins Secretary of Labor, it seems doubtful that FDR personally was a strong advocate of women's rights. His pressure on the Supreme Court seems partly responsible for the decision in 1936 upholding state minimum wage laws for women, and another decision in 1941 validating the equal pay provisions of the Fair Labor Standards Act of 1938. Yet even by 1940, in many states women had not become the legal equals of men. Twenty states still prohibited women from serving on juries, sixteen denied a wife the right to make contracts, and eleven forbade a wife to retain earnings without her husband's consent. Thus women entered the war period with few realized gains from the previous decade, but with a potential in both the labor movement and the job market to make some lasting progress.

The Survival of the Indian

In 1924 Congress passed the Indian Citizenship Act, granting citizenship to Native Americans on a systematic basis. Before this time, Native Americans had become United States citizens on a piecemeal basis and by a variety of means—such as military service and marriage, or by receiving allotments under the Dawes Act of 1887. This reform notwithstanding, by the mid-20s it was obvious that, in general, government policy concerning the three hundred twenty-five thousand Indians scattered across the nation had failed. The Dawes Act, providing for individual ownership of tribal land, had reduced tribal land acreage by some 60 percent through subsequent white fraud, high-pressure sales, and a variety of illegal schemes to steal more land from the Indians. Indians had been given the land individually, without the equipment to farm it, or the schooling on how to use it for grazing, farming, or timber cutting. They were an impoverished people financially, but psychologically they may have been in worse shape.

Indian health was a national disgrace. The plains Indians, for example, were forced to cease their nomadic way of life, yet were not taught to handle the sanitation problems of sedentary living. Indians were made to depend on a government diet that was lacking in vitamin C, proteins, and roughage. Often if they were "unruly," local administrators withheld food. They were given a very few doctors and nurses when, in fact, they needed many more than the average white population. The doctors they did have were quite often incompetent. Consequently Indians suffered from rampant diseases, high infant mortality, and rates of suicide and alcoholism much higher than those for the rest of the population. Nevertheless, they responded to the army volunteer drive of World War I with enthusiasm and were conspicuous for their bravery in battle. It is believed this war record sparked another reform drive on behalf of the Indians.

Reform was a complex problem. Generally speaking, legislators from states with many Indians fought against giving extra federal funds earmarked for their states to a largely nonvoting minority that, even if they did vote, did not have the numbers to elect anyone. The rest of Congress was generally lacking in knowledge about the variety of problems each of the two hundred fifty to three hundred tribes faced.

The Bureau of Indian Affairs, run by the Executive branch of the government also had an extremely poor reputation among the Indians because its policies, usually administered by patronage employees, changed with every new president. These administrators naturally knew or cared, very little about Indian cultures. Boarding school education, promoted by the Bureau of Indian Affairs, alienated many children from their hereditary culture, while it equipped them for participation in white society that, in most states, did not want them.

To reformers such as John Collier and the American Indian Defense Association, the best hope for the future appeared to be in strengthening tribal organization and restoring communal landholding. Collier was influential in getting the Wheeler-Howard Indian Reorganization Act through Congress in 1934. For those tribes who voted to accept it, this act ended further individual allotments and restored all remaining lands to tribal ownership. The government was to purchase more land to resettle landless Indians. Tribes were to be set up as corporations, able to draw on a $10 million revolving fund for new economic enterprises. Each cooperating tribe was also to draw up and ratify a constitution that would restore government by tribal council.

Although education improved, the policies pursued by the Bureau over the next generation were, on the whole, unsuccessful. By congressional mandate, the Reorganization Act was not applied in Oklahoma, where the "Five Civilized Tribes" lived and enjoyed some unevenly distributed wealth from oil. The Navajo tribe, suspicious of white benevolence—with good historic reasons—numbered about a quarter of all Indians and refused to join. Applying the act to most of the remaining tribes, who were given over 7 million acres of poor land, led to no considerable gain in their prosperity; it did lead, however, to a great deal of trouble between the Indians, the paternalistic local agents, and the remote Bureau. In all, this well-intentioned policy came too late in the history of Indian-government relations to alter the results of decades of neglect and abuse in both policies and administration. By the mid-twentieth century, Indian grazing culture and white industrial society were so far apart that any assimilation could only be slow and difficult. Reconstitution of tribal society, on the other hand, was both artificial and—given the great differences among the Indian peoples—extremely difficult.

Black America

The depression decade was nearly spanned by coverage of a particularly well-publicized and flagrant denial of justice to nine young blacks. On March 25, 1931, on the railroad line from Chattanooga to Memphis, a fight developed between white and black youths on one of the boxcars. The fight resulted in the white boys being expelled from the train, and they then alerted local authorities.When police arrested the black youths at the next stop for assault, two white women, who had also been in the rail car, accused nine black young men, ranging in age from twelve to nineteen, of rape. The black youths were charged with rape and held in a jailhouse in Scottsboro, Alabama. An all white jury found all nine guilty and eight were sentenced to death. One woman later recanted her charge, and a new trial was held in 1937. Four of the Scottsboro Boys were released in 1937, four more in 1944, and the final man escaped in 1944. During the thirties, the case achieved worldwide notoriety, thanks in part to the action of the legal bureau of the Communist Party. Yet the case had pointed out the kind of "justice" blacks often received.

President Roosevelt appointed white race-relations counselors in many government departments. From 1932 on, as the urban black vote shifted dramatically from Republican to Democratic. Mary M. Bethune became Director of Negro Affairs in the National Youth Administration, and Robert C. Weaver became adviser to the Department of the Interior—the highest federal posts held by blacks since World War I. In *United States v. Classic* (1941), the Supreme Court made the state governments responsible for the conduct of party primaries and hence for the enforcement of constitutional rights in these contests, which were in fact the real elections in the solidly Democratic South. On the whole, however, the president was not prepared to battle Southern congressmen over enforcement of the rights of blacks, and New Deal housing policies actually increased segregation. The successful struggle of the poor black—and of the impoverished and neglected Indian—continued as before, but with growing spiritual strength. As a result, that spirit won allies such as the president's remarkable wife Eleanor.

▶ The nine young black men accused of rape by two white women. The black youths were charged and held in a jailhouse in Scottsboro, Alabama. Fearing a mob lynching, the National Guard was called in to protect the accused.

Toward the mid-forties, some progress was made toward equality of economic opportunity. The NAACP, directing its energy toward winning equal pay for black schoolteachers, had little immediate success. Then, in 1941, the federal district court for Virginia, at least, ordered equality in pay by 1943. The CIO, in principle, admitted blacks to all its unions, though in the South they were often put into separate locals and denied true job equality. The growth of the new labor movement brought black workers into the mass production industries, and in a few cases to minor administrative positions in big white companies. Although still largely impoverished, blacks were making new efforts to improve their condition.

Mexican Americans

Owing to the political instability in Mexico, the Mexican American population in the United States grew substantially during the early twentieth century. Mostly concentrated in the Southwest, immigrants and their families typically made their living as agricultural workers. Given that the agricultural sector was hit so hard by the Great Depression, it is not surprising that farm workers were among the groups to suffer the greatest problems. In addition to such market-driven difficulties as falling wages and deteriorating working conditions, the Mexican workers also faced the wrath of those who blamed them for stealing jobs that might have gone to others. As a consequence, some five hundred thousand Mexicans and Mexican Americans were repatriated to Mexico during the 1930s. Some—but not all—left voluntarily. It is important to note that among those who were sent back to the mother country, there were a good many American citizens, some of whom had been born in the United States—which was, in fact, their true mother country.

The Dust Bowl Migration

During the mid and late 1930s, nature added to the woes of farmers in a swath of states in the Midwest and Southwest as severe drought, compounded by summer heat waves, farm bankruptcies, and poor agricultural practices, laid waste their land and created the conditions for what became known as the Dust Bowl. The drought essentially continued on the Great Plains for an entire decade, converting once fertile farmland into desert. To make matters worse, three-fifths of farmers on the Great Plains went bankrupt. Consequently, millions of acres went uncultivated; and without crops to keep the soil in place, the topsoil left with the wind. The combination of these factors, along with plagues of locusts, resulted in interstate dust storms that carried millions of tons of topsoil into the atmosphere. During the Dust Bowl, dust from the Great Plains was carried by prevailing winds all the way to the Atlantic Ocean, dropping dust on the coastal cities of New York and Washington as well as on ships over three hundred miles off shore in the Atlantic Ocean. Dust storms on the Great Plains during the Dust Bowl were so intense that the sky would be dark at noon, and people could not see their hands in front of their faces in some cases.

Faced with the impossibility of farming their land profitably, some three hundred thousand people migrated to California, where they were categorized as "Okies" and treated harshly. Indeed, for a brief time the city of Los Angeles posted guards (illegally) at the state line to turn

▶ The characteristic dust storms on the Great Plains were so intense that the sky would be dark and in some cases people could not see their hands in front of their faces. The devastation of the Dust Bowl came under control in 1941 when demand for agricultural products rose, rains returned and the land was cultivated again.

away indigent migrants. Scholars estimate that during this period about one-third of the farms in the Dust Bowl states of Kansas, Missouri, Arkansas, Oklahoma, and Texas were abandoned.

This tragic movement of people—tragic because what they encountered in the Golden State was often little better or even worse than what they had left behind—inspired some of the greatest and most profound of American art: John Steinbeck's novel *The Grapes of Wrath*, John Ford's film based on the same novel, songs by the folksinger Woody Guthrie (himself an Oklahoman), and the photographs of Dorothea Lange. The historian James Gregory wrote *American Exodus: The Dust Bowl Migration and Okie Culture in California,* a prize-winning account of the Okies' travail. It would take at least a generation before the Okies and their descendants began to fit into their new home and be accepted as Californians.

Regardless, the Dust Bowl would not come under control until 1941, during World War II, when demand for agricultural products increased, the rains returned, and a much greater percentage of the land became cultivated again, thus reducing, but not eliminating, the volume of dust.

Return to Depression

Aided by increased federal spending for the WPA, more state spending for public works, and payment of the remainder of the World War I soldier's bonus certificates (over the president's veto), 1936 and early 1937 saw returning prosperity. However, at this point, the lack of any clear economic policy by either the administration or most of its critics was disastrously illustrated. To suit the conservatives in Congress, whose votes were needed to pass the Supreme Court bill, the president promised a balanced budget for 1937–1938. His own fear of running large federal deficits, even though 6 million were still unemployed, was displayed when the Federal Reserve System took steps to tighten the money market.

National income, which was $82 billion in 1929, dropped to $40 billion in 1932, and then rebounded to $72 billion in 1937. The economic improvements convinced FDR that it was time for a retreat from his government spending programs, and time to attempt to balance the federal budget. FDR feared the mounting deficits, and leading economists, at the time, were now more concerned about inflation than with unemployment (which was still over 10 percent). Consequently, FDR pushed the Federal Reserve to raise interest rates in an effort to curb inflation. In doing so, the money supply would diminish, and the economy would slow. FDR attempted to balance the budget by instituting sweeping budget cuts in New Deal Public Works and Relief programs. As a result, the index of industrial production was 117 in August 1937, but dropped to 76 by May 1938; and 4 million more Americans were added to the lists of unemployed. As a result of this drastic reversal in federal policies, the sharpest business decline in American history began in July 1937 and reached bottom about mid-1938. Not until the beginning of 1940, when the European war and American rearmament had become important economic factors, was there a return to the business volume of 1937. The severity of the depression was about equal to that of late 1931. Unemployment rose above 10 million—a fifth of the labor force. Even with the return toward prosperity in 1940, over 8 million people were still looking for jobs.

FDR was certain that his actions had produced the new recession. In April 1938, he asked Congress for an additional $5 billion for public works and relief, and Congress complied. By 1940, unemployment returned to the level of 1937, and GNP returned to the level of 1937 by 1939.

New Policies

The renewal of the Depression forced the government to institute new policies to promote recovery. Agricultural production had been sharply cut by the severe drought in 1934 that had created the "dust bowl." It had been stalled again by a more moderate drought in 1936. In the latter year, Congress had passed a soil-conservation act to check the planting of soil-depleting crops and to encourage planting of soil-restoring crops. As a result of these developments, agricultural income, including government payments, withstood the renewed depression better than did the income of some other sectors; and in 1938, the well-organized farmers won substantial new support in the Agricultural Adjustment Act.

Soil conservation was to be encouraged by payments to staple crop producers who agreed to acreage allotments. Marketing quotas could also be imposed by the vote of two-thirds of the growers of a staple crop. Whenever actual prices fell below "parity prices," government-determined prices intended to keep the farmer's purchasing power in relation to nonfarm commodities at the 1909–1919 level, farmers conforming to these regulations would be given "parity payments" if Congress appropriated the money.

Crop loans were also available to all farmers of crops with marketing quotas, but those who did not accept the quota could borrow only 60 percent as much as could the cooperators. In spite of many loopholes and much subsequent criticism, this law remained the basic plan of agricultural support.

Wage and hour guarantees, attempted in the NIRA, were now incorporated in the Fair Labor Standards Act. The labor of children under sixteen was prohibited, the minimum wage was set at twenty-five cents an hour, and overtime was to be paid for work beyond forty-four hours a week. The Housing Act of 1937, now in operation, began the great task of slum clearance. With increases in other parts of the federal budget, including public works and defense, federal expenditures in 1939 were more than 25 percent above 1938, the highest of any peacetime year in previous American history.

Assessing the New Deal

While the New Deal had greatly improved stability and security in the national economy, it had not brought satisfactory recovery. For the first time the gross national product per capita had failed to achieve a level higher than in the previous decade. What had been wrong? Several different answers were possible, depending upon different economic theories.

It was possible, first of all, to emphasize the fact that from beginning to end President Roosevelt, either from conviction or for political expediency, held down spending and tried to balance the budget. Prior to the renewed depression of 1938, only 1934 and 1936 showed substantial increases in government spending in relation to receipts; and in both cases, the level of spending dropped the following year. The failure of the New Deal to end the depression was largely because the economy needed a larger infusion of capital than was supplied by the New Deal. The depression was instead halted by World War II, which provided that capital infusion in the form of massive deficit spending and increased demand. In short, the New Deal failed because it was too conservative and its balanced budget constraints hindered its effectiveness. Put another way, the administration failed to make a clean break with the idea of the self-regulating economy and failed to develop a philosophy of where and how to spend. Yet while failing to spend at the level necessary to promote expansion, the government did not announce policies that encouraged expansion through investment by business.

Another line of reasoning pointed to the failure of NIRA, and other legislation, to redistribute income enough to create sharply increased consumer demand. Still another was that by chance too few technological innovations had occurred that would offer profits in return for large capital investment.

Whatever approach one took, the disturbing question remained: How could a healthy economy be assured in time of peace?

Lasting Effects of the New Deal

Nevertheless, the New Deal produced lasting effects on the American political system. The New Deal and the Great Depression created a precedent for federal government intervention in the economy that has never been abandoned. For example, when the economy slipped into recession in 2008, Republican President George W. Bush and the Democratic Congress responded with a tax rebate in an effort to stimulate the economy. The New Deal also permanently established the right to collective bargaining, which still benefits labor unions through the present. In addition, the New Deal increased the regulatory functions and the scope of the federal government, responsibilities that have never been relinquished. Moreover, the New Deal created the beginnings of the federal welfare state and increased the general welfare responsibilities of the United States government. Even under conservative President George W. Bush in the twenty-first century, federal entitlements (Medicare) have been expanded. The New Deal also altered the state-federal relationship from "dual federalism" or "separate spheres of influence" to "cooperative federalism" with shared state and federal responsibilities. Furthermore, Democrats were propelled to dominance in American politics, especially in the United States House of Representatives, until 1994 when Newt Gingrich and the Republicans took over the House in a conservative "revolution." Finally, the New Deal elevated the president to a position as the nation's foremost policy leader, a position that has never been relinquished. In terms of the presidency, only Eisenhower's eight years would interrupt the Democratic dominance of the White House that lasted from 1933–1969 when Democratic candidates won seven of nine presidential elections, four by Franklin Roosevelt.

Chapter Review 25

Summary

Herbert Hoover had only been in office six months when the stock market crash of October–November 1929 signaled the beginning of the worst economic depression in American history. The optimistic Hoover and his administration did not immediately recognize the magnitude of the problem, and therefore used government to intervene only too little and too late. Hoover's attempts to remedy the economic collapse were limited by his preference for loans rather than direct grants to combat the problems and his beliefs in limited government and balanced budgets. Hence, in spite of the Reconstruction Finance Corporation, the Depression reached its lowest depths in 1932 when Hoover was defeated in his reelection attempt by Democrat, Franklin Delano Roosevelt.

Roosevelt offered a "New Deal" to the American people and a "try something" approach to combating the Great Depression. Before Roosevelt could take office, however, America was gripped in the midst of a bank panic. Roosevelt and Congress quickly went to work after his inauguration and produced perhaps the most productive hundred days of legislation in American history. FDR assured Americans that the banks were safe during his fireside radio chats, and over $1 billion was returned to the banks. The dizzying array of programs that were passed by FDR and Congress included public works programs, such as the WPA, CCC, and CWA, banking and securities regulations with the creation of the FDIC and SEC, limits on agricultural production with the AAA, efforts at soil conservation to both put people to work and combat the Dust Bowl, Codes of Fair Business Practices with the NIRA, the reestablishment of the right of workers to bargain collectively, and the beginning of federal entitlement state with the Social Security Act.

The Depression had a drastic impact on America with falling prices, falling wages, massive unemployment, falling birth rates, marriage rates, divorce rates, and declining college attendance. Evictions and homelessness led to the development of shantytowns outside American urban centers. Vagrants wandered the roads and rail yards, and migrants left the Great Plains for low-paying agricultural work in California. Farm bankruptcies, poor soil conservation, a heat wave, drought, and locusts all contributed to the development of the Dust Bowl—a series of dust storms that covered the Great Plains for much of the decade and contributed to the migration from the Plains.

Roosevelt's New Deal engendered stiff competition from conservatives who viewed it as "communistic" and a group of elite conservatives created the Liberty League to combat the New Deal. Simultaneously, the most popular radio host in the country was Father Charles Coughlin, a conservative Catholic priest that sympathized with Adolph Hitler and the Nazis in Germany. He opposed the New Deal, and referred to FDR as "Franklin Double-crossing Roosevelt." Roosevelt and the New Deal also had enemies on the Supreme Court who struck down New Deal programs in eight of ten major New Deal cases prior to 1937. Finally, Roosevelt fought back against the Court with a plan to increase the number of justices to fifteen so that he could pack the Court with New Deal supporters. Although FDR's bill died in Congress, one justice retired and another changed his mind. The Court began upholding the New Deal with *NRLB v. Jones and Laughlin Steel* in 1937 where the Court upheld collective bargaining.

Conservative pressure along with his own fears of massive deficits caused FDR to impose austerity measures in 1937, resulting in the economy slipping back into recession in 1937–38. This caused Roosevelt to authorize more deficit spending to jump-start the economy. In the end, Roosevelt's New Deal did not end the Depression, but it did appear to improve with virtually all economic measures being improved after the New Deal was implemented more from where they were in 1932. The essential problem was that 25 percent of the capital had simply vanished from the economy between 1929 and 1932, and the deficit spending during the 1930s was not sufficient to replace the lost capital. The Depression essentially ended by the increased demand and massive government deficit spending that accompanied World War II that finally infused the necessary capital into the economy.

The New Deal did leave, however, a lasting legacy as it changed the nature of American federalism to end the idea of separate spheres of state and national responsibility, and it set a precedent for federal intervention and federal deficit spending during economic crises. The New Deal also permanently established collective bargaining and created Social Security, the beginning of federal entitlements. The presidency was elevated to the position of the nation's foremost policy leader, and the Democrats would have the upper hand in American politics for the most part for the next four decades.

Chronological Time Line

1929 Agricultural Marketing Act of 1929 created a Federal Farm Board to establish semipublic stabilizing corporations with the authority to purchase excess farm products and thus prop up prices.

1929 October 29, Stock Market Crash signaled the beginning of the Great Depression.

1929 November 15, Hoover argued that "any lack of confidence in the economic future or basic strength of business in the United States is foolish."

1930–1933 Nine thousand banks failed and the money supply diminished by one-third.

1931–1933 Five hundred thousand Mexican aliens living in the United States returned to Mexico.

1931 Congress passed the Bonus Act over Hoover's veto.

1931 March, two women accused "Scottsboro boys" of rape in a boxcar.

1931 June, European banks failed and European debt payments ceased.

Chapter Review (cont'd)

Time Line (cont'd)

1931	July: Hoover declared a one-year moratorium on European debt payments.
1931	September: Federal Reserve Board raised interest rates.
1931	September: England abandoned the gold standard.
1932	Congress created the Reconstruction Finance Corporation to provide loans to businesses and funds to states for public works.
1932	February: Glass-Steagall Act liberalized the lending powers of banks and made available to business about $750 million of the government gold.
1932	May 1: fifty thousand communists paraded in New York City.
1932	June: Bonus Army marched on Washington, but was dispersed by the U.S. Army.
1932	July: Federal Home Loan Bank Act created twelve regional Federal Home Loan Banks to extend federal financial assistance to building and loan associations, savings banks, and insurance companies.
1932	August: Farm Holiday Association Farm had a strike.
1932	November: Franklin Roosevelt was elected president.
1933	February: Congress passed the 21st Amendment repealing Prohibition, and was subject to ratification by the states.
1933	February–March: bank panic shut down banking in the U.S.
1933	March 4: Roosevelt announced at his inaugural that "The only thing we have to fear is fear itself."
1933	March 20: Economy Act cut Federal salaries and veterans' pensions by 15 percent.
1933	April 5: FDR created the Civilian Conservation Corp (CCC) to provide public works jobs.
1933	May: Federal Emergency Relief Administration was created to supply direct relief to the states.
1933	May: the Muscle Shoals–Tennessee Valley Development Act of May 1933 created an independent public corporation, the Tennessee Valley Authority.

Time Line (cont'd)

1933 May: Federal Securities Act granted the Federal Trade Commission the power to see that underwriters fully disclosed to investors all essential details pertaining to new securities issues.

1933 June: Agricultural Adjustment Act authorized the government to set agricultural production limits in efforts to raise agricultural prices.

1933 June: National Industrial Recovery Act attempted to establish Codes of Fair Business Practices in an effort to boost wages and prices.

1933 June: Banking Act divorced investment banking from commercial banking and created the Federal Deposit Insurance Corporation (FDIC).

1933 November: Congress created the Civil Works Administration to provide public works employment.

1934 January: Gold Reserve Act allowed the president to arbitrarily set the price of gold, and FDR increased gold prices 40 percent.

1934 Federal Housing Administration Act of 1934 introduced the guaranteed packaged mortgage—one that could be paid, principal and interest, by uniform monthly payments.

1934 June: Securities Exchange Bill created the Securities and Exchange Commission.

1934 June: Wheeler-Howard Indian Reorganization Act ended individual land allotments and allots land to tribes.

1934 August: Liberty League was formed by wealthy conservatives to combat the New Deal.

1935 April: Congress created the Works Progress Administration to create employment in public works projects.

1935 May: *Schechter Poultry v. U. S.* struck down NIRA.

1935 "Soak the Rich" Act increased income taxes on the wealthy.

1935 August: Social Security Act began federal entitlements.

1936 February: Soil Conservation and Domestic Allotment Act permitted the government to pay farmers to "conserve soil" and prevent erosion.

Chapter Review (cont'd)

Time Line (cont'd)

1936 November: FDR defeated Alfred Landon for reelection.

1937 February: Roosevelt's court-packing bill was passed.

1937 April: *NLRB v. Jones and Laughlin Steel* upheld the right of collective bargaining.

1937–1938 FDR's austerity measures were followed by a recession.

Key Terms

Crash of '29: Stock market crash in October–November 1929 that signaled the onset of the Great Depression

Andrew Mellon: Treasury Secretary that opposed intervention in the economic free fall.

Herbert Hoover: Republican president at the onset of the Great Depression whose policies failed to prevent economic collapse

Great Depression: A decade of economic downturn beginning with the stock market crash of October 1929 and lasting until World War II

Smoot-Hawley Tariff: Tariff increase in 1930 that had the impact of reducing trade and hindering European debt repayment

Reconstruction Finance Corporation: Agency established to combat the Depression with loans to businesses and relief for states under the Hoover administration

Glass-Steagall Act of 1932: Liberalized the lending policies of banks and made available to business $750 million in government gold

NLRB v. Jones and Laughlin Steel: Upheld the right of workers to bargain collectively.

Farm Holiday Association: Midwestern farm group that staged an ineffective farm strike in 1932.

Bonus March: A group of twenty thousand unemployed World War I veterans that marched on Washington in 1932 demanding early payment of a bonus, but were dispersed by the U.S. Army on the orders of President Hoover

Eleanor Roosevelt: Politically active First Lady of the United states 1933–1945

Franklin Delano Roosevelt: Democratic president of the United States elected to four terms, beginning in 1933

New Deal programs: A host of federal government programs intervening into the economy in the 1930s in efforts to correct the economic malaise

Bank Holiday: The temporary closing of the banks in 1933 so that consumer confidence could be restored

Key Terms (cont'd)

Economy Act: 15 percent cuts in federal employee salaries and veterans' pensions was designed to help alleviate the budget deficit.

FDIC: The Federal Deposit Insurance Corporation insured bank deposits.

CCC: Civilian Conservation Corp, a public works agency designed to create employment and help with soil conservation.

AAA: Agricultural Adjustment Act placed limits on agricultural production in an effort to boost prices.

Federal Housing Administration Act: Introduced the guaranteed packaged mortgage—one that could be paid, principal and interest, by uniform monthly payments

TVA: Tennessee Valley Authority, constructed dams and power plants on the Tennessee River and became the largest and cheapest producer of electricity in the U.S.

NIRA: National Industrial Recovery Act sought to establish codes of fair business practices in order to boost wages and prices.

PWA: Public Works Administration was created under the NIRA to provide public works employment.

Schechter Poultry v. U. S.: 1935 ruling that struck down the National Industrial Recovery Act, which allowed the president to arbitrarily set the price of gold.

Federal Securities Act: Required full public information on new stock issues and appointed the newly created Securities and Exchange Commission to regulate securities transactions

Liberty League: The group formed by wealthy conservatives in opposition to the New Deal.

CWA: Civil Works Administration was created in 1933 to create public works employment.

National Youth Administration: Public works agency for people aged sixteen to twenty-one

WPA: Works Progress Administration, the largest of the New Deal public works programs.

Social Security Act: Provided limited old age pensions and began federal entitlement programs

Roosevelt's Court Packing Plan: Roosevelt's failed proposal to increase the size of the Supreme Court to fifteen members so that he could change the philosophy of the Court

Father Charles Coughlin: Ultra-conservative radio host that was sympathetic to the Nazis in Germany and opposed the New Deal

Alfred Landon: Republican presidential candidate in 1936

Huey Long: The governor of Louisiana that proposed "sharing the wealth" and income redistribution.

AFL: American Federation of Labor

CIO: Congress of Industrial Organizations

John Collier: Supporter of reform for Native Americans

Scottsboro Trial: Nine black men were convicted of rape and sentenced to death, but one of their accusers changed her story and all were eventually freed or escaped.

Dust Bowl: A series of massive dust storms that devastated the Great Plains during the Great Depression due to a heat wave, drought, locusts, farm bankruptcies, and poor soil conservation practices

Pop Quiz

Chapter 25

1. Hoover's policies exacerbated the capital shortage by ___________.
   a. remaining on the gold standard
   b. lowering interest rates
   c. deficit spending
   d. all of the above

2. President Hoover vetoed which of the following?
   a. high tariffs
   b. federal loans to businesses
   c. the Glass-Steagall Act
   d. federal direct relief to the poor

3. Which of the following is true of the Depression between 1929 and 1932?
   a. GNP declined as much as 25 percent.
   b. Man-hours worked declined as much as 60 percent.
   c. Wholesale prices fell as much as 43 percent.
   d. All of the above

4. The Farm Holiday Association unsuccessfully attempted ___________.
   a. to overthrow of the U.S. government
   b. a communist revolution
   c. a farm strike
   d. all of the above

5. Which of the following is true of Eleanor Roosevelt?
   a. no relation to Theodore
   b. a favorite of Franklin's mother, Sarah Roosevelt
   c. endured Franklin's extramarital affairs for mutual political ambitions
   d. known for her beauty and high fashion

6. FDR restored confidence in the bank with ___________.
   a. a massive government bailout
   b. a commitment to the gold standard
   c. a commitment to a balanced budget
   d. fireside chats on the radio

Pop Quiz (cont'd)

7. What was the reason for the creation of the Federal Housing Administration?
    a. It was the first step toward a federal takeover of the housing industry.
    b. It was an important step in the development of less expensive housing and long term installment buying.
    c. It was the first step toward European socialism in America.
    d. It was the brainchild of the American Communist Party.

8. Senator Key Pittman of Nevada disrupted the 1933 economic conference in London by ____________.
    a. calling for a "silver standard"
    b. shooting out streetlights in London with a pistol
    c. drunken and erratic behavior
    d. all of the above

9. The Gold Reserve Act of 1934 allowed the president to ____________.
    a. store up American gold in reserve at Fort Knox
    b. release American gold reserves on the free market
    c. arbitrarily set the price of gold
    d. declare a government monopoly on gold ownership

10. In what is known as Roosevelt's "Court-Packing Plan," FDR called for what?
    a. Americans to pack the halls of the Supreme Court in protest
    b. increasing the size of the Court from nine justices to fifteen
    c. closing the court and packing their belongings for shipment to Nazi Germany where its members would be more comfortable
    d. packing the Court with Illuminati, communists, Jews, and Masons

11. The Wheeler-Howard Indian Reorganization Act did which of the following for the tribes that accepted the act?
    a. It ended the policy of granting land to tribes instead of individuals.
    b. It restored all remaining tribal lands to tribal ownership.
    c. It declared that the five remaining Indian tribes were "civilized."
    d. It declared that Indians could open gambling casinos on their reservations.

Chapter Review (cont'd)

Pop Quiz (cont'd)

12. Lasting effects of the New Deal included which of the following?
    a. the beginnings of federal economic regulation and the welfare state
    b. Congressional dominance
    c. Republican dominance
    d. the restoration of laissez-faire as the guiding ideology

13. Roosevelt's plan to change the Supreme Court was defeated in Congress. T F

14. The Indians on reservations were generally prosperous and healthy. T F

15. The New Deal did not bring any recovery to the economy. T F

1 A	5. C	9. C	13. T
2. D	6. D	10. B	14. F
3. D	7. B	11. B	15. F
4. C	8. D	12. A	

26 World War II

Chapter Objectives

The Road to War

Breakdown of the Security System

Growing Dangers in Europe

Mein Kampf

Isolation and Neutrality

Rise of the Axis

Panay Incident

Anschluss and Lebensraum

Blitzkrieg

The American Quandary

Battle for Britain

A Year of Decision

America First Committee

Lend-Lease

Roosevelt's Dilemma

Hemispheric Defense

Undeclared War

The End of Hesitation

Japanese-American Relations, 1940–1941

Pearl Harbor

War in Two Hemispheres

Creation of the Grand Alliance
Holding the Line
Island Hopping
European Theater
Allied War Strategies/Divisions
The Turning Point
Eastern Front
Italy
Setting the Goals of War

Support at Home

The Battle for Production
Controlling Inflation
Civil Liberties
Seeds of a More Just Society
The Election of 1944

Pushing Toward Victory

Island Hopping in the Pacific
The Invasion of Europe
The Big Three at Yalta
The End of the Third Reich
Holocaust
The United Nations and Potsdam
The End of the War with Japan
Atomic Bomb and Surrender

The Road to War

Breakdown of the Security System

In the aftermath of the Great War, during the 1920s and the Great Depression, Americans had become decidedly isolationist in their foreign policy outlook. Many Americans, including among them the famous American hero Charles Lindbergh, viewed World War I as a mistake and were determined to remain out of any future European squabbles. Despite the prevailing isolationist sentiment in the 1920s, however, the United States was part of a system of international security: the Washington Treaties of 1922, governing Far Eastern relations; the structure of international debt and reparations payments worked out in the agreements after World War I; and the ability of the League of Nations—or its leading members, England and France—to police the settlement of Versailles. Between 1931 and 1935, this entire security structure was demolished, leaving the world perennially on the verge of war.

Partly because Russia had not been invited to take part in the Washington Conference, the treaties of 1922 did not bring peace to China. During the next decade, Russia and China first combined to reunify China by defeating local warlords and then fought each other in an undeclared war. When peace was restored with Russia, the Chinese Nationalist leader Chiang Kai-shek tried to assert his power in southern Manchuria, long within the Japanese sphere of influence. This gave the strongly imperialist Japanese army the excuse to overthrow the liberal ministry in Tokyo and to wage a war for complete control of Manchuria with a full-scale invasion of the province in 1931.

▶ Chiang Kai-shek, the leader of China when Japan used its imperialist Japanese army to invade Manchuria and wage a war for complete control of the province in 1931.

The islands of Japan are volcanic and poor in natural resources. The Japanese sought to remedy their deficiencies in food, fuel, and the precious metals needed for a developed industrial economy through control of foreign territory. The League of Nations, as well as individual countries like Britain and the United States, condemned the Japanese aggression in the Far East, but it did not impose economic sanctions. Japan ignored the protests and established a puppet government in Manchuria known as Manchuko. The United States and the League of Nations responded with American Secretary of State Henry L. Stimson's "Doctrine of Nonrecognition," whereby the United States and the League of Nations would not recognize governments established by force. In response, Japan completed its conquest of Manchuria and withdrew from the League in 1933. This demonstration that a great power could embark on aggression without meeting effective opposition from the strong League members marked the beginning of the disintegration of the League of Nations, exposing the fatal flaw in the peacekeeping treaties that had been signed after the Great War—the West lacked the will to enforce those treaties. It also marked the beginning of the Japanese view of the United States as the central obstacle to its ambitions in Asia. Japan's foreign minister Yosuke Matsuoka summed up the Japanese view by stating, "The United States taught Japan the game, and now wants to take up contract bridge."

International debt and reparation payments depended upon continuing loans from the United States. With the collapse of the Wall Street security market in 1929, it was only a question of time before payments would end. President Hoover's moratorium in 1931 temporarily eased the debt burden on European nations; however, neither the Hoover nor the Roosevelt administration was ready to profit from the inevitable by canceling the war debts. As the international economic Depression worsened and destroyed the ability of the European nations to service their debts, all defaulted by 1934, except Finland. With the defaults, another part of the World War I settlement had come to an end.

Growing Dangers in Europe

▶ Adolf Hitler must bear the most responsibility for the end of world peace in the 1930s. Elected Chancellor in 1933, and shortly thereafter, the Bundestag passed an Enabling Act that allowed Hitler to rule Germany by decree.

A single man, Adolf Hitler, however, must bear the most responsibility for the end of world peace in the 1930s. By 1933, the German democracy—centered in Weimar, Germany, and imposed by the Allies after World War I—was weakened by economic and political chaos that followed the Great War and stark internal political conflicts between conservatives, liberals, Socialists, and Communists in Germany, including multiple coup attempts by competing groups, invited the rise of a man who could impose order and bring prosperity back to Germany. Supported by many—much of labor, patriots who wanted to undo the hated Versailles Treaty, the military, patriotic nationalists, rural religious conservatives, and business conservatives who viewed Hitler as a check against communism—Hitler's Party won a plurality of the vote in the German Parliament (Bundestag). Thus, Hitler became Chancellor in 1933. Shortly thereafter, the Bundestag voted to dissolve and passed an Enabling Act that allowed Hitler to rule Germany by decree. The German experiment in democracy during the interwar period came to an end.

Hitler began an industrialization and militarization program backed through massive government deficits. The government spending boosted the economy and softened the harshness of the depression in Germany, thus increasing Hitler's popularity. Hitler also imposed rigid discipline on Germany, bringing order to the chaos that had permeated Germany's political landscape after the Great War, while brutally murdering his political enemies in the process. In foreign affairs, Hitler pulled Germany out of the League of Nations and the Geneva Disarmament Conference in October 1933.

Mein Kampf

In a book he wrote while serving time in prison for treason in 1924 for his role in what is known as the Beer Hall Putsch—a failed attempt at government overthrow, Adolph Hitler outlined his plans for creating a superior German State. In his autobiographical work entitled *Mein Kampf*, Hitler explains that the German loss in World War I was the result of German insufficiencies in food and energy supplies, as well as the treasonous acts by Jews. As a consequence, Hitler argued that Germany must secure land with agricultural production to ensure that it is self-sufficient in food (the wheat fields of Poland and the Ukraine) and must, also, secure access to energy (the oil fields of the Caucuses in the Southwestern Soviet Union). Hitler viewed the German people as racially superior and also viewed the fact that all persons of German ethnicity were not united within the borders of Germany as a problem. Hitler, therefore, called for the unification of all the German people (Anschluss), which included the absorption, by Germany, of areas in France, Austria, Czechoslovakia, and Poland that were predominantly German in ethnicity. Hitler also argued that the expansion of Germany's borders was necessary to give the German people needed "Lebensraum" (living space) and secure their food and energy supplies. Furthermore, Hitler argued that Germany was never defeated on the battlefield in World War I, and the war was never fought on German soil. Hence, Hitler perpetuated the Dolchstoss myth (backstab myth): Germany had not actually lost the Great War, but was, instead, sold out by traitorous Jews.

Although his aim, set forth in *Mein Kampf*, was to gain control of Europe by war, British and French leaders chose to regard his statements as mere political slogans. Even by 1938, when Hitler had already annexed unresisting neighboring territories and commenced his deadly Jewish pogroms, the conservative leaders of Western Europe valued him as a defense against communism. Furthermore, President Roosevelt—hindered by the depression and isolationism in America—took no decisive action.

Meanwhile, Italy followed Japan's lead in aggressive expansion. In October 1935, the Italian fascist dictator Mussolini launched a wholesale invasion of the African kingdom of Ethiopia (Abyssinia) in an attempt to unite all Italians behind him in a foreign war. The League of Nations, under British pressure, condemned Italy as an aggressor and imposed economic sanctions. But because Britain and France were afraid of driving Germany and Italy into an alliance, the embargo did not include coal and oil. Furthermore, the League had little machinery for enforcing economic sanctions, and non-members like Germany and the United States largely ignored the prohibitions. As a result, the conquest of Ethiopia was quickly completed, and the authority of the League was totally undermined.

Why had the major military and naval powers of the world failed to enforce the peace? In the first place, Russia, the nation most feared in the long run by Great Britain, was not a party to the Western agreements. (The Soviet Union was not even recognized by the United States until 1933.) The fact that Hitler was a professed enemy of Russia made it difficult for British governments, particularly the Conservative ones, to decide where the ultimate national interest lay. Yet even if the British decided to let Hitler gain strength, they did not want him too strong; and this weakened them in dealing with Italy. In France, many conservatives in the army and the government feared communism much more than they feared Hitler's fascism.

Another factor faced by Britain, France, and the United States was the strength of pacifist and neutralist movements in their own countries. It had been less than a generation since 6 million Frenchmen and 2 million British had died in the Great War; few were interested in a path that could lead to such carnage again. Therefore, a government embarking on vigorous policies that risked war might find itself lacking in the necessary legislative support.

Isolation and Neutrality

The breakdown of the world order led the United States to strict isolationist legislation and to an effort to weld the Western Hemisphere into a self-sufficient defense system. The latter presented many difficulties. Aside from Canada, the nations of the Western Hemisphere were further removed from the United States by tradition and national culture than were the nations of western Europe. The capitals of the three largest South American powers—Argentina, Brazil, and Chile—were also farther removed geographically. Economically, as well, the United States had more ties with Europe, as did each of the major South American nations.

Upon his becoming president, FDR's initial concerns were in producing reciprocal trade agreements that would boost the economy. President Roosevelt's inaugural address in 1933 dedicated the United States to "the policy of the good neighbor"—nonaggression, nonintervention, and friendly cooperation to solve mutual problems in the Western Hemisphere. His first attempt was at the International Conference of American States, in 1933, in Montevideo, Uruguay. In order to create better relations in Latin America, Secretary of State Cordell Hull signed a convention that stated, "no state has the right to intervene in the external affairs of another." The initiative was designed to eliminate interventionist fears in Latin America and produce attitudes more receptive to trade with the United States. Congress followed with the Reciprocal Trade Act of 1934 that authorized the president to take the initiative in lowering tariffs on a reciprocal basis, up to 50 percent, with any country. As a result, United States trade with Latin America increased—from 30 percent to 50 percent of all of Latin American trade by 1940. Nevertheless, the attitude of the United States toward social democratic governments in the Caribbean area remained ambiguous. In the same year that the new pact was adopted, Washington withheld recognition of a liberal government in Cuba that was opposed by the island's land and business interests; and American warships surrounded the island. These actions, engineered by conservative State Department officials rather than by President Roosevelt, led eventually to the overthrow of the liberal government by the military dictator Fulgencio Batista.

The president's long-range policy was reaffirmed the next year by abrogation of the Platt Amendment authorizing intervention in Cuba and by withdrawal of marines from Haiti. In 1936 the United States ratified a treaty restoring sovereign powers to Panama. Reciprocal trade agreements negotiated with six Latin American nations strengthened economic ties. While the bonds between "good neighbors" five thousand miles apart remained somewhat tenuous, the Roosevelt administration policy marked a great improvement over inter-American relations of the previous thirty years.

Though Americans in the mid-30s were fully cognizant of the onrush of fascism in Europe, most of them were confident that the United States could remain a neutral bystander in that impending conflict. As Europe's crises deepened, determination mounted in the United States to "sit this one out." At the time of the Nazi takeover of Germany, Roosevelt's Republican opposition was divided over what should be the proper American role. For the conservative "nationalist" wing of the party, sound foreign policy was based on isolationism with regard to European affairs and unilateralism, protectionism, anti-communism, and the Monroe Doctrine in the Western Hemisphere. In the words of historian Lewis Gould:

> "Disillusion with the outcome of World War I, antipathy toward Great Britain, some degree of anti-Semitism, and sympathy for Germany moved together in various degrees to feed the argument on behalf of continued isolation. Senators such as William Borah of Idaho and Gerald Nye of North Dakota led the block of Republicans in the upper house who wanted to stay out of European disputes."

▶ General Fulgencio Batista of Cuba

In furtherance of these foreign policy guides, Republicans had generally opposed Roosevelt's recognition of the Soviet Union in 1933 (which Roosevelt did as much to boost American grain exports as to counterbalance the emergence of Nazi Germany in Europe), regardless of whatever benefits trade with the Soviets might bring to the American economy. While conservatives typically supported the free market, they did not extend that to doing business with communists. Rural Republicans, in particular, tended to support isolationism and opposed alliances and any encroachments on sovereignty embodied in international organizations such as the League of Nations. In 1935, Republicans had thwarted Roosevelt's effort to secure American participation in the World Court under the premise that it would erode American sovereignty. Similarly, rural Republicans tended to view foreign aid and loans to foreign countries as idealistic utopian fantasies and outside the parameters of American national interests.

The hastily improvised Neutrality Act of 1935, prompted by Italy's invasion of Ethiopia and reluctantly signed by Roosevelt, prohibited the export of arms or ammunition to belligerents. It also led the president to forbid American citizens to travel on the ships of belligerents except at their own risk. A "permanent" Neutrality Act in 1937 retained the earlier restrictions on loans and munitions in time of war and declared travel on belligerent vessels unlawful for American citizens. In addition, it provided that, for a period of two years, belligerent nations could purchase goods, other than munitions, from the United States only on a "cash-and-carry" basis. The intent of these two acts was to prevent the recurrence of the events that had led to the American entry into the Great War—debts incurred by belligerent nations and the deaths of American civilians on the high seas.

During the Spanish Civil War of 1936–1939, in which Germany and Italy lent aid to the forces of the right-wing Generalissimo Francisco Franco (the Nationalists) and the Soviet Union supported the opposite side (the Republicans), the United States remained resolutely neutral. Americans generally had sympathy for the Spanish government in their struggle against Franco's fascist rebels, but since the Soviet Union supported the Spanish government, the United States could not become involved in the struggle on the same side as the communists.

Rise of the Axis

In 1936, the last safeguards of the World War I diplomatic structure were finally swept away. In October and November, Germany, Italy, and Japan entered into an anticommunist pact that became known as the Rome-Berlin-Tokyo Axis. Though the Alliance was never as strong as the Allies believed and Hitler's war machine had not yet been built to its full capacity, Hitler worked a diplomatic revolution that made defeated and penalized Germany the strongest nation in Europe in the middle of the Great Depression.

▶ An Italian bomber during a raid in the Spanish Civil War. The United States remained resolutely neutral in regards to this conflict as Americans did not want to become involved in the struggle on the same side as the communists.

Why did this happen? Causes may be traced far back, but three were abundantly clear in 1936. First, mutual distrust between England and France on one side and Russia on the other prevented revival of the old World War I alliance against the central powers. Second, the isolationist United States could not be relied upon for active support. Third, England and France had not kept up with military development. To make their plight worse, England and France guaranteed the independence of Czechoslovakia and, in 1939, of Poland, which they could not possibly defend against Germany. Faced with the choice of arming for possible war or muddling along in the hope that some change would occur in the German situation, the conservative leaders of the Western powers chose the latter course.

Tension in the Pacific also increased in the summer of 1937 when Japan expanded its six-year-old war in China and attacked five other Chinese provinces. The Japanese invasion was full scale and brutal, and over one hundred thousand Chinese were killed in 1937 alone. The large-scale Japanese inroads in northern China led President Roosevelt, in a speech of October 1937, to test American sentiment by advocating a "quarantine" of aggressor nations. The term "quarantine" had no official meaning in international law, but rather was a general reference by FDR to a severing of diplomatic relations and a trade embargo. He quickly found that Congress was two to one against cooperation with the League of Nations in bringing effective sanctions against Japan. Additionally, public reaction to FDR's quarantine speech was so overwhelmingly negative in an America dominated by isolationism that FDR decided that he could not proceed with any further action. Underlying much of this isolationist attitude was a belief that problems in Asia should not concern Americans, and an implicit confidence that England and France were still capable of controlling the situation in Europe. From 1938 on, however, as Germany continued to build up its mechanized army, the European situation spun beyond the control of England and France. Hitler was ready to embark on a daring program of expansion, and his territorial demands were to prove limitless. All the while, the Japanese continued their belligerence in Asia unabated.

Panay Incident

On December 12, 1937, Japanese planes bombed and sunk the United States gunboat *Panay* on the Yangtze River in China. The attack occurred in broad daylight, with clear visibility and a large United States flag painted on the deck of the boat. The only logical conclusion was that the attack was deliberate. Three Standard Oil tankers, which were under the *Panay's* escort, were also sunk. Two Americans died and thirty were wounded, some by the planes' machine guns as the planes made a second pass while their victims attempted to swim to safety.

Japan claimed that the attack was accidental, formally apologized, and agreed to more than $2 million in reparations. Approximately two-thirds of the American public, according to opinion polls, was satisfied with Japan's apology. In July 1938, FDR had Secretary of State Cordell Hull send letters to United States manufacturers urging a voluntary "moral embargo" on Japan. To this, Japan responded with the announcement that there was a "New Order" in Asia: the Open Door in China was no longer in effect.

▶ The American gunboat *Panay* was attacked along with three Standard Oil tankers on the Yangtze River in China by Japanese bombers. Japan insisted that the attack was accidental and agreed to over $2 million in reparations to the United States in order to maintain peaceful relations.

Anschluss and Lebensraum

Beginning in 1936, Adolph Hitler began the implementation of his plans, as outlined in *Mein Kampf*, for Anschluss, which involved the annexation of the ethnically German areas outside Germany's political borders and the expansion of Germany's Lebensraum or living space. In 1936, Hitler informed foreign ambassadors in Berlin that he would no longer abide by the Locarno Agreement of 1925 that set Germany's western borders. Hitler then moved his army into a demilitarized zone of western Germany known as the Rhineland, without first consulting the Reichstag (Parliament). The Rhineland had been in German hands prior to World War I, but in French hands before 1870 and in French hands after World War I. Hitler's bold move defied both the Versailles Treaty, which had required the area to be demilitarized, and the Locarno Agreement of 1925 that had the security of the borders to the countries to Germany's west. Yet international reaction was somewhat ho-hum since a large percentage of the population of the area was German in ethnicity, and people could justify the Nazi control of the area as "natural."

Hitler turned his attention to the annexation of entire countries. Hitler's first victim was his neighbor Austria. First Hitler demanded that Austrian Chancellor Kurt von Schuschnigg award positions in his government's cabinet to members of the Austrian Nazi Party. Schuschnigg did so, but he also called for a plebiscite that he expected to be a public rejection of the German annexation of Austria. Hitler then mobilized his army along the Austrian border and called for Schuschnigg's resignation. Facing a Nazi invasion, Schusschnigg resigned on March 11, so as to prevent the destruction of Austria by Hitler's war machine. The following day his successor,

Arthur Seyss-Inquart of the Austrian Nazi Party, invited Hitler's army into his country, ostensibly, to keep order. Next, Germany announced the Anschluss (annexation) of Austria on March 14, 1938. Less than a month later, Austrian voters approved of the annexation by 99.75 percent in an obviously fraudulent election controlled by the Nazis.

After the Austrian coup, Hitler moved on to his next objective—the annexation of the Sudetenland, a German-speaking portion of Czechoslovakia. Czechoslovakia favored war instead of submission, if it could secure help from France and England, because Czechoslovakia realized that resistance was futile against the German war machine without outside help. Hitler bluntly informed English Prime Minister Neville Chamberlain that he was determined to secure self-determination for the Sudeten Germans. Chamberlain, in turn, persuaded Édouard Daladier, the French premier, that a sacrifice on the part of Czechoslovakia would save the peace. In September 1938, Hitler, Mussolini, Daladier, and Chamberlain met in Munich—without any representative from Czechoslovakia involved in the negotiations. They worked out the details of the surrender of the Sudetenland in return for Hitler's promise that he had no further territorial ambitions. Neville Chamberlain returned to England to a hero's welcome and rode down the streets of London in an open car to cheering crowds, waving the agreement and declaring that it had secured "peace in our time." Chamberlain's conservative opponent in Parliament, Winston Churchill, however, denounced the agreement as "appeasement" and argued, "Tyrants should not be appeased, but thwarted at the outset." After the onset of World War II in Europe, the Munich accords became known as representing the policy of "appeasement" and have been condemned by scholars and politicians worldwide ever since.

While the Munich Pact gave Britain precious time to build up its air force, British and French hopes that the agreement would appease Hitler's expansionistic cravings were shattered, just six months later, when, in March 1939, the German army invaded and seized the remainder of the Czech nation. Mussolini seized Albania, the poorest and weakest country in Europe, the following month; and the two dictators celebrated by signing a military alliance, the "Pact of Steel." France and England reacted by assuring Romania and Greece that the Allies would come to their aid if Mussolini attacked them next. Albania, however, would be the only country during World War II that Mussolini's Italy would be able to attack and conquer without assistance from the German army.

The shock of Hitler's callous violation of the solemn pledge made at Munich ended the appeasement policy of France and Great Britain. Britain launched a tremendous arms program, and in Paris Daladier obtained special emergency powers to push forward national defense.

It was Germany's aggression against Poland, however, that finally precipitated the Second World War in Europe. During the summer of 1939, Hitler had made increasingly insistent territorial demands upon Poland. Poland refused the cession and appealed to France and England for help. France and England assured the Poles that they would come to the aid of Poland if Hitler attacked. Chamberlain, with the French government concurring, also warned the Nazi government that "in the event of any action which clearly threatened Polish independence" the British would "at once lend the Polish government all support in their power." Hitler viewed the area of northwestern Poland, which had been formerly known as East Prussia, as no different than the Rhineland, Austria, or the Sudetenland because it had a large, ethnic German population and sections of it had actually been part of Germany prior to the Great War. Hitler did not believe that the French or the English really cared about Poland; and if the annexation of the Rhineland had been viewed as "natural," why not Poland?

As German threats against Poland increased, Britain and France sought an alliance with the Soviet Union but refused to assent to its reannexation of the Baltic states. Meanwhile, the Nazi and Soviet foreign secretaries were secretly working out an agreement of their own. On August 23, 1939, Russia and Germany signed a nonaggression pact. Stalin, perhaps, correctly surmised that he could not count on the Western powers to come to the aid of the communist Soviet Union if the Nazi belligerents turned their war machine to the east. Stalin knew that his military status, as of the summer of 1939, was greatly inferior to that of the Germans and reasoned that an agreement with his traditional and ideological enemy would provide him the best chance at security. Furthermore, a conflict in Western Europe after Germany invaded Poland would give the Soviet Union time to build up its armaments. Hitler understood well the traditional Russian position as "defenders of the slavs" from the German experience in World War I and sought to avoid conflict with the Soviet Union in 1939 if he sent the German army into Slavic Poland. The Soviet Union also secured German recognition of Soviet claims in eastern Poland and the Baltic states, thus securing Hitler's recognition of long-standing Soviet foreign policy in the process. In essence, Hitler had agreed to recognition of Stalin's Slavic interests, but Stalin and Hitler had agreed to divide Poland between them.

Now Hitler could attack Poland without fear of intervention by his great rival to the east, but he also had to legitimate his planned invasion of Poland with the German people. In order to do so, Hitler dressed German soldiers in Polish uniforms and had them stage an attack on a radio station in Germany near the Polish border. Hitler denounced the Polish aggression to the German people. Without a declaration of war, Nazi troops crossed the Polish frontier on the morning of September 1, 1939, and the *Luftwaffe* began to bomb Polish cities. Hitler hoped that the appeasing governments of France and Great Britain would wring their hands and do nothing, but he had miscalculated. In September 1939, Hitler was in the process of building his war machine to be the most formidable and technologically advanced force the world had ever known, but his war machine was not on schedule to be fully constructed until some time in 1942 or 1943. With the Polish invasion, the two Western democracies, knowing that their own time would come sooner or later, declared war on Germany on September 3. The Second World War in Europe had begun. Hitler had begun World War II in Europe with his invasion of Poland, but that had not been his intention. Instead, he had merely intended to take Poland—as he had the Rhineland, Austria, and Czechoslovakia then he would cease his expansion until his military buildup was fully completed. Beginning World War II three to four years ahead of his own schedule was perhaps the first of Hitler's many major miscalculations that would eventually lead to his own demise, but not before six years of the most devastating war in human history would be waged against him.

Blitzkrieg

Germany unveiled its new type of war strategy in the Polish invasion that became known as Blitzkrieg or "lightning war." Essentially, Blitzkrieg was rapid armored advance accompanied by massive air support, an approach to warfare that has been employed by advanced armies ever since. In World War I, neither planes nor tanks were well developed as military tools, but they proved in Poland to be the most important weapons of modern warfare in 1939. Poland's air force was small and vastly inferior, and the Poles lacked anything that proved effective at stopping the advanced German tanks.

The Poles had known before the war that help from France and England would be required if the Poles were to successfully halt a Nazi invasion. The French and English, however, were not ready and help would, therefore, not arrive quickly. Thus, Germany subdued Poland in six weeks (with help from the Soviets who invaded Poland from the East) before the Allies could provide any significant assistance to Poland. Hitler then ceased any further attack.

The American Quandary

Beginning with Germany's invasion of Poland, the political debate in the United States over intervention into the war in Europe dominated foreign policy discussions. American public opinion quickly shifted in favor of support for Britain and France—short of war—thus leaving conservative isolationism at odds with the opinion of the majority. Congress quickly voted to repeal the arms embargo portion of the Neutrality Acts and allowed belligerents to purchase military goods from the United States, but the "cash and carry" limitation that had been imposed under the Neutrality Acts remained. The United States would not extend credit to the warring nations, and belligerents would have to pick up the military goods in United States ports using their own ships. In Congress, Republicans opposed the end of the arms embargo and other subsequent aid to the Allies by an average of 85 percent on the key votes. Conservative Southern Democrats, however, broke with the isolationist conservative Republicans and favored war intervention, thus helping to shore up support for Roosevelt, in 1940, for his record third term.

▶A propaganda postcard of German tanks. Tanks were not well developed as military tools during World War I, but they proved to be the most important weapons of modern warfare in 1939.

While the Western powers were preoccupied with Germany, Stalin used the opportunity in the fall of 1939 to overrun Latvia, Estonia, Lithuania, and Finland. Stalin's invasion of Lithuania violated his Non-Aggression pact with Hitler where they had secretly divided Europe into spheres of influence. Since Lithuanians are Germanic in language and ethnicity, Hitler had planned to put them under his sphere of influence.

In retaliation against Soviet aggression, the United States placed a "moral embargo" on the shipment of arms to Russia. The moral embargo was completely ineffective, and the Soviets secured Finland and the Baltic States by March of 1940. Furthermore, United States exports to the U.S.S.R. actually doubled during the Soviet campaign against Finland.

After the rapid conquest of Poland, Germany remained virtually inactive during the winter of 1939–1940. This "Phony War" ended abruptly on April 9, 1940, when Germany simultaneously invaded Denmark and Norway. A month later, Nazi armies invaded Belgium, France, and Holland; in six weeks all had surrendered. The French had staked their security on the Maginot Line, a complicated series of trenches, tunnels, bunkers, stationary guns, and subterranean rails along the German border. Essentially constructing defenses in anticipation of an advanced version of the trench warfare of World War I, the French had invested in a defense for the war of yesteryear. The French did not, however, build fortifications along the border with Belgium; and the German army simply went around the Maginot Line and invaded France through Belgium as they had in World War I. Without the Maginot Line to protect them, the outmoded French army was overwhelmed by the German Blitzkrieg and lost one hundred ten thousand men in a month. France surrendered on June 22, 1940, and Hitler's Nazi army goose-stepped through Paris.

After the fall of France, the British rescued over three hundred thousand of their troops from the beach at Dunkirk through a heroic civilian flotilla, called for by Winston Churchill via radio, as England lacked the necessary means to evacuate their army before the Nazis overran them. Unfortunately, the British had to abandon practically all their equipment at Dunkirk as the civilian flotilla could carry soliders, but little else. Thus, the British army returned to an island without land defense against armored columns. On June 10, when the defeat of France was certain, Italy came into the war on the side of Germany. As of June 22, Britain stood alone against German and Italian aggression.

▶Winston Churchill, Prime Minister of the United Kingdom during World War II.

FDR reacted by freezing the assets of conquered countries to keep them out of Hitler's control. FDR was also concerned that the colonial possessions in Latin America of conquered countries could fall into German hands. As a result, Congress passed the "no transfer resolution," whereby the United States opposed "the transfer of territory in the Americas from one non-American to another non-American power," thus denying Germany control over the colonial possessions of the conquered powers of Western Europe.

Battle for Britain

In August 1940, Germany launched an air war against the British, attacking English air bases in preparation for an invasion. At one point, it appeared that the German strategy might be successful as the British were losing planes and pilots faster than they could be replaced. FDR cancelled a previous American purchase of three hundred fifty planes from Britain, which had already been delivered and paid for, and sent them back to England to help the British replenish the Royal Air Force (RAF). FDR also traded the British fifty outdated American destroyers for American naval bases on British territory in the Caribbean, Bermuda, and Newfoundland.

As fate would have it, the character of the battle for Britain would change. On one raid, German pilots got lost over cloudy English skies and accidentally bombed a residential section of London. In retaliation, Churchill launched a daring five hundred-plane raid, bombing Berlin and shocking the Germans. The bombing of Berlin provided a morale boost to the British and proved to the British people that Germany was not invincible. Hitler was enraged and let his rage get in the way of good military sense, and he retaliated by shifting his air strategy away from targeting air bases and toward punishing the British by bombing residential London. Although the German raids on British cities were devastating, the British minimized civilian deaths through the employment of underground bomb shelters. Meanwhile, the shift in German strategy allowed the British to rebuild their air force and airfields. The BBC kept British spirits high through a propaganda campaign full of erroneous information and exaggerated claims. BBC reports of British "kills" of German aircraft were typically triple American estimates. The British perpetuated the myth of the superiority of the British spitfire fighter plane as a German killer due to its unique-shaped wings; but, in actuality, more German planes were shot down by the more conventional looking British hurricane. The British accuracy in anticipating and intercepting German raids was also greatly enhanced due to the new invention of radar. RAF pilots remained on 24-hour alerts for months, prompting Churchill to proclaim that "never has so much been owed by so many to so few." Against odds that seemed to many to be impossible at the time, Britain did not fall.

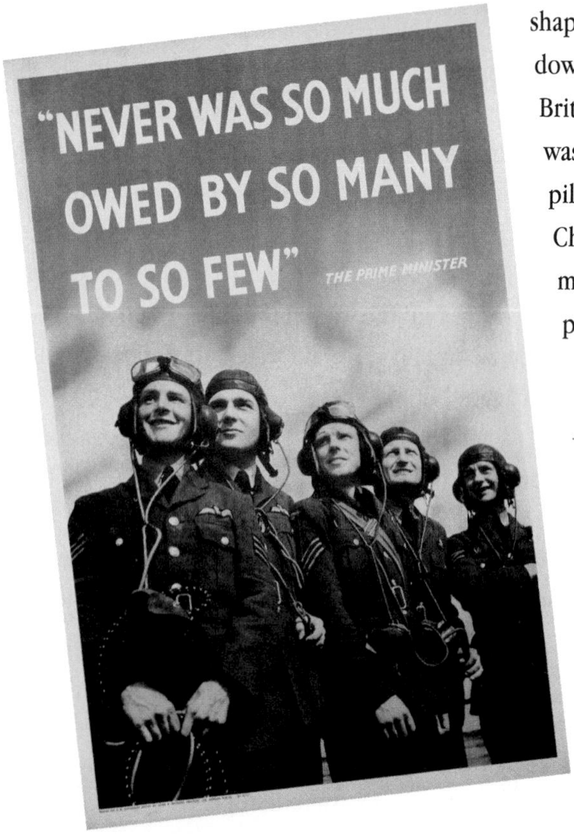

A Year of Decision

What should American policy be now that Hitler and his ally, Italy, controlled Western Europe, and military men regarded the conquest of England as likely? The joint planners of the War and Navy Departments thought that the United States should husband its resources at home to prepare for attack. Isolationists, including many leading citizens and scholars, opposed any action that went beyond defense preparations.

The leader of the Nationalist Republican faction, Senator Robert Taft, for example, continued to oppose intervention in the European war even after the fall of France in June 1940. Nationalist Republicans argued that United States intervention in the war would increase the power and scope of the national government, as it had in World War I, and thus institute a form of "national socialism" in the United States and destroy American freedom, the supposed purpose for intervention in the war in the first place. Furthermore, the Nationalist Republicans argued that the expansion of Nazi Germany posed no threat to the security or economic well being of the United States. Nationalist Conservatives also argued that Britain and France had made a mistake in declaring war on Germany after the Nazi invasion of Poland. The argument was that the Allies should have allowed Hitler to take Eastern Europe—with the result that the totalitarian dictators, Hitler and Stalin, would eventually come to blows between themselves to the benefit of the free world. Hitler's army then would bog down in the Soviet Union, thus preventing an invasion of western Europe and eliminating any necessity of another war between Germany and the powers of western Europe. Furthermore, intervention in the European war would be unlikely to advance the causes of freedom and democracy any more than did World War I. Instead, World War I had created the chaos and destruction that led to the germination and growth of Communism and Fascism, the current scourges of international politics. Why would another war be expected to do anything different?

Robert Taft echoed the sentiments of leftist war protestors in the conflicts of later decades in Southeast Asia (1960s) and Iraq (2000s) when he argued that the Republican Party:

> "... should be opposed to risking the lives of 5 million American boys in an imperialistic war for the domination of Europe, Asia, and Africa, and the supposed 'manifest destiny' of America."

Taft argued that it was the eastern Wall Street wing of the Republican Party that favored intervention while the farmers, working men, and small businessmen opposed the war. In Taft's words:

> "The war party is made up of the business community of the cities, the newspaper and magazine writers, the radio and movie commentators, the Communists and the University intelligentsia."

America First Committee

In the summer of 1940, Nationalist Republicans organized the America First Committee to lobby and produce propaganda against war intervention. Backed by the financing of Robert E. Wood, Chairman of the Board of Sears, and William H. Regnery, president of the Western Shade Cloth Company, the America First Committee had over eight hundred thousand members by the end of 1941, including Charles Lindbergh, a bonafide American hero and the first man to fly nonstop across the Atlantic in 1927. Lindbergh himself was an isolationist that viewed the interventionists' position as part of a grand conspiracy, the primary forces behind which were "the British, the Jewish, and the Roosevelt Administration."

It is clear from the arguments of the America First Committee and others that conservatives generally preferred Nazi Germany to the communist Soviet Union and were essentially comfortable with, and unthreatened by, the Nazi presence. Nationalist Conservatives argued that the entry of the Soviet Union into the war against Germany in 1941 took the pressure off Britain and eliminated the need for United States intervention. Furthermore, entrance into the war on the side of Britain would now aid the communists in Russia; hence, the war could not be a war to end totalitarianism. In essence, the policy that the nationalist/isolationist conservatives pursued is the policy that would later be condemned by American conservatives, in general, as "appeasement."

Republicans did, however, typically support the British in principle against Nazi Germany and believed that there was a need for military preparedness. The America First Committee argued that military preparedness would prevent war because, with an impregnable defense, no foreign power could dare attack the United States. Similarly, Herbert Hoover in 1940 argued, "We are determined to be armed to the teeth to defend ourselves and the Western Hemisphere."

Military preparedness, in turn, did not necessitate aid to the British, and it most certainly did not necessitate aid to the Soviet Union. The America First Committee argued that "aid short of war" weakened military preparedness at home by siphoning off resources. Furthermore, "aid short of war" was likely to cause the United States to cross paths with Nazi Germany and thus drag the United States into the war. Aid to the communist Soviet Union, on the other hand, was complete anathema. On August 5, 1941, a group of Republican leaders—including Herbert Hoover, 1936 presidential nominee Alf Landon, former Vice President Charles Dawes, and former RNC Chairman Henry P. Fletcher—issued a statement criticizing what they viewed as "unauthorized aid to Russia" and arguing that American aid should be "utilized only to protect the independence of 'democracies.'"

The president was for as much aid to Britain as he could arrange without being overridden by the antiwar majority in Congress. The president's decision to take a chance on British survival through all-out United States aid was probably the most fateful one of the entire period. He could have pursued a more isolationist policy without alienating his political support, and the policy he elected to pursue led almost inevitably to war. In the decisions of both Roosevelt and Wilson, the overriding fact appears to have been an unwillingness to permit a Europe in which a militaristic Germany was the dominant power. FDR's neutrality, however, was overtly different than Wilson's: FDR from the beginning told Americans that he could not ask them to be neutral in thought.

In a contest over policy involving military action the president has a great advantage over Congress. He can act and then seek support for his action later, whereas Congress, as a non-administrative body, is always behind a rapid march of events. This is, in effect, what happened from June 1940 forward. The president went ahead administratively to give England as much aid as possible. In so doing, he educated the public toward his point of view, and Congress was usually presented with actions that had already been taken and would be hard to reverse.

In June, for example, Congress thought to restrict the president by passing a law forbidding him to give away military equipment unless the Army Chief of Staff and the Chief of Naval Operations certified it as not essential to the national defense. On September 2, an executive agreement was signed with England transferring fifty overage American destroyers in return for British bases in Newfoundland, Bermuda, and the Caribbean. Since the bases theoretically increased American security, this action was technically not a violation of the law; yet it tied the United States to the defense of the British Empire and marked the end of any pretext of neutrality. Germany did not declare war at this time because it did not want the United States in the war; but later in the same month, however, Germany, Italy, and Japan formed their "Pact of Steel" military alliance, obviously aimed at the United States.

These critical strokes of foreign policy took place during the presidential campaign of 1940. Four days before the Republican Convention met in June, the president appointed Republican leaders Henry L. Stimson and Frank Knox to his cabinet as Secretaries of War and of the Navy. Two days before the convention, France surrendered. In the general confusion that followed, the political climate favored the internationalists. As none of the leading Republican contenders developed decisive strength, Wendell L. Willkie, a businessman who sympathized with Roosevelt's foreign policy, was skillfully maneuvered to become the Republican challenger to Roosevelt. As in 1936, the Republicans had gone far away from the principles of their right wing base to attract marginal Democratic votes.

The international emergency led the president to seek a third term. Through the manipulations of Harry Hopkins, representing the president, the Democratic bosses were reluctantly forced to accept Henry A. Wallace, the liberal Secretary of Agriculture, for the vice-presidency.

During the campaign, both those favoring all-out aid to Britain and those opposed to risks that might lead to war were nationally organized. The journalist William Allen White of Kansas headed a Committee to Defend America by Aiding the Allies, in direct opposition to Robert F. Wood's isolationist America First Committee. The effect of the controversy on the campaign, however, was not immediately clear since both candidates were internationalists.

By October, however, as Great Britain withstood Germany's bombing attacks and was not invaded, the argument that aid to Britain was more important than keeping out of war lost its immediate urgency. When public opinion pollsters found that the number of those favoring foreign aid had declined to less than half the voters, Willkie shifted his ground. Having failed to gain support on the issues of the third term and mismanaged defense, Willkie now attacked Roosevelt as a warmonger. Alarmed by the apparent success of the Willkie strategy, the president was pushed further and further away from his true beliefs. Just before election he told his listeners, "I have said this before, but I shall say it again and again and again. Your boys are not going to be sent into any foreign wars." In his mind, conflict resulting from an attack on the United States would not be a "foreign" war.

The Democratic vote was slightly below that of 1936, and the Republican 5.5 million larger; but Willkie won only eighty-two electoral votes to Roosevelt's four hundred forty-nine. The total minor party vote fell below two hundred thousand. It was hard to call the result a referendum on any policy since there had been no substantial disagreement; but it could be read as a vote of confidence in Roosevelt personally or, as Republicans saw it, as proof of the strength of habitual patterns of voting and the Democratic political machine. To the president, it was support for more vigorous foreign aid and military preparation.

Characteristically, the president had put political and foreign problems ahead of domestic ones. By August, Congress had appropriated some $16 billion for defense—enough, if it could be used, to move toward a war footing. The following month Congress agreed on a bipartisan basis to a selective service (draft) act, but the economic organization essential for defense preparedness faltered. Production, the president felt, could be called into existence later when needed.

This was, of course, far from true. Coordination of production was in the hands of a nearly powerless National Defense Advisory Commission. In the words of Donald Nelson, its coordinator for procurement, the commission "began to stagger in the late summer and early autumn of 1940. In November it was punch drunk. It did not fall flat on its face until five days before Christmas." Its successor, the Office of Production Management, had little more success.

The basic difficulty was that private industry did not want to be regimented in time of peace; and for fear of strengthening the isolationists, the president was reluctant to ask Congress for the necessary power. Fortunately, however, the United States had great capacity for manufacturing the automotive and other steel equipment needed for this war. Incentives such as quick tax write-offs and long-term contracts stimulated big business to undertake much of the new construction that had to precede mass production of military equipment.

Lend-Lease

By December 1940 the opinion polls indicated that around 60 percent of the American people were in favor of helping Great Britain, even at the risk of war. Thus, when Churchill told Roosevelt that British credit for the purchase of war supplies was nearing exhaustion, Roosevelt believed he had popular support for extending more liberal, outright aid. Polls suggested that public opinion in America was approximately two thirds in favor of aid to England. A bill was quickly drawn up and introduced in Congress calling for "munitions of war and supplies of many kinds to be turned over to those nations which are now in actual war with aggressor nations," to be paid back in goods and services at the end of the war. In support of the bill, FDR argued, "When your neighbor's house is on fire, you loan him a hose." Senator Robert Taft quipped that it was actually "More like loaning someone your chewing gum. After it is used, you don't want it back." Others, such as America's Irish-American Ambassador to London, Joseph Kennedy, opposed aid to England as a waste of America's resources on the British lost cause. Though opposed by Republican leaders in Congress, the Lend-Lease bill had the compulsion of the situation behind it. On March 11, "Lend-Lease" became law, and the next day the president asked Congress for an initial $7 billion to implement the policy.

The United States had already broken, beyond repair, the laws of neutrality by aiding only one side and keeping the vessels of the other out of the western Atlantic. Lend-Lease marked the point of no return on the road to war. The bill committed American industrial power, nearly equal to that of all the rest of the world, to the defeat of Germany.

Roosevelt's Dilemma

The Lend-Lease Act of March 1941 was only the first step that President Roosevelt was prepared to take in a broader effort to help Britain resist German aggression. Although he probably overestimated the strength of the vocal isolationist minority, he estimated correctly the great reluctance of most Americans to become directly involved in a war. As a result, in his pursuit of what he thought was the defense of American interests, he was not always open and candid. Sometimes he acted secretly, as he did in late April 1941, when he ordered a naval patrol of the North Atlantic to help the British detect German submarines. Other times he acted as boldly as he thought the majority of the people would permit, as in July 1941, when American troops were ordered to Iceland to relieve the British in protecting it from German invasion.

When Hitler, in a surprise move, invaded the Soviet Union on June 22, 1941, Roosevelt followed Churchill in welcoming a new fighting force in the war against Germany, even though few military advisers believed the Russians could hold out more than three months against the German blitz. Acutely aware of the weakness of British and Russian defenses, Roosevelt, in early July, asked Congress for an extension of the draft law and repeal of the prohibition on overseas service for draftees. Isolationists branded the request as yet another of the president's covert efforts to get the United States into war, but after acrimonious debate, the draft extension passed by a single vote in the House of Representatives.

Hemispheric Defense

Despite Lend-Lease, FDR had further problems in getting arms to the British in that German U-boats were sinking British shipping at a rate of five hundred thousand tons per month—faster than England could build ships. Much of the Lend-Lease shipments would be going to the ocean floor unless British shipping could be protected. Consequently, in July 1941, FDR declared that the Western Atlantic was a "neutral zone" and the collective responsibility of the "American Nations" under what he termed as "Hemispheric Defense." Under the policy of "Hemispheric Defense," United States ships patrolled the Atlantic as far east as Iceland and reported to the British the location of German submarines.

One month prior to FDR's implementation of "Hemispheric Defense" (June, 1941), Hitler made perhaps his greatest error of the war and invaded Russia without first defeating England. In doing so, Hitler opened the war on two fronts. Hitler expected to overwhelm Russia within six weeks, but the massive operation over a four thousand-mile front overwhelmed his ability to supply his army. Consequently, the advance slowed, and Russia did not fall as Hitler had planned. FDR reacted to the German invasion of Russia by extending Lend-Lease to the U.S.S.R. in the beginning of what would, eventually, grow to become a formal alliance.

From August 9–12, Roosevelt and Prime Minister Churchill met secretly on the *U.S.S. Augusta* in Placentia Bay, Newfoundland. The result was the Atlantic Charter, which set forth the aims of the war: No territorial changes would be made in favor of the victors, and all nations would be protected in their right to choose their own governments, without fear of aggressive threats. FDR and Churchill also agreed that their mutual goals included the final destruction of Nazi Germany. When announced on August 15, this meeting between a technically neutral country and an active belligerent brought loud protests from isolationists in the United States. Nevertheless, upon his return home Roosevelt asked for increased appropriations for aid to Britain and the Soviet Union.

Undeclared War

In September, when a German U-boat attacked the American destroyer Greer, which unbeknown to the American public was sending the British navy information about German submarines, Roosevelt seized the opportunity to issue a "shoot German submarines on sight" order to the navy and asked Congress for authority to arm American merchant ships. With American naval vessels shooting without even waiting to be attacked, it was only a matter of time before a serious incident would occur. On October 17, the American destroyer *Kearny* was torpedoed and damaged off Iceland, and eleven Americans were killed. Less than three weeks later a German U-boat sank the *Reuben James,* with a loss of 115 lives. Yet most Americans seemed to support the president's policy, and in early November Congress authorized Roosevelt to arm merchant vessels and permit their entry into the war zone. Congress also authorized American ships to escort Allied cargo ships all the way to their homeports. Although the fight in Congress had been bitter, the House victory was 212 to 94, far greater than the single-vote margin of the previous summer. With the approval of these actions by Congress coupled with FDR's orders for American ships to shoot German submarines on sight, the result was essentially an undeclared naval war on Germany.

By the end of November 1941, Hitler's armies were deep inside the Soviet Union, seemingly on their way to an early victory; and Japan was obviously readying itself for an offensive against the British and Dutch colonies in Southeast Asia. The president's dilemma was acute. He could not dispel the nagging fear that the Germans might yet overwhelm Russia and Britain, despite American aid, an event that would leave the United States alone to face Germany. At the same time, he knew that Americans were so divided over the struggle in Europe that he dared not try to lead them immediately into full-scale war against Hitler.

The End of Hesitation

Japanese-American Relations, 1940–1941

Ever since the early 1930s, Japanese expansionism on the Asian mainland had met gradual but increasing American opposition. Finally, in 1939, the United States began to restrict the flow to Japan of some strategic war materials, including oil and scrap iron; but Roosevelt would not embargo all war materials as some of his advisers urged. He believed some measures were necessary to warn Japan of American opposition to aggression, but he feared that too strong a stand would push the Japanese into an adventure against the oil-rich and defenseless Dutch East Indies. The Japanese response was to move into northern Indochina in the summer of 1940 and to join the Tripartite Pact with Germany and Italy in September 1940.

By early 1941 the Japanese and American positions in Asia were irreconcilable. Japan's minimum demand was that the United States cease its aid to Chiang Kai-shek, while the United States insisted that Japan end its war against China. The Japanese refused to do so because a pullout from China would not only deny Japan the resources it needed for self-sufficiency but would also cause the Japanese to lose face. Japanese soldiers had been dying in China for a decade. Culturally, the

Japanese leaders viewed a pullout of China as meaning that all of those soldiers had died in vain. Therefore, during 1941 diplomatic efforts aimed at softening the two positions proved to be equally unsuccessful. Japanese militarists believed that war was the only answer to America's interference with Japanese ambitions in Asia; the military's hand was strengthened in April 1941 when the Soviet Union promised to remain neutral in the event of a Japanese-American war. Japan's fear of a two-front war was thus reduced while Hitler's earlier promise to support Japan in a war against the United States made it clear that the United States would be the one forced to fight on two fronts.

Japanese ambitions became clearer and more alarming in July, when Japanese military units invaded southern Indochina in obvious preparation for an attack upon the Dutch East Indies. Indeed, American code breakers had broken the Japanese codes and knew that the Japanese planned an invasion of the Dutch East Indies. In retaliation, the United States and Britain cut off all vital supplies to Japan, including oil. Given that the United States produced three-fourths of the world's oil at the time, Japan had no viable alternative source for the commodities it needed to continue its war efforts in China. To make matters worse for the Japanese war effort in China, American aid was flowing to China.

On September 6, 1941, Japan's Supreme War Council voted for war if American aid to China did not cease within six weeks. The Japanese hoped that an impressive attack on the United States, followed by a series of military victories, would force the United States to end the embargoes of oil and other materials needed by Japan for their military campaign in China. Japanese military leaders argued that the United States was unprepared for war and that, for six months, Japan could deal the United States serious military setbacks in the Pacific. After six months, however, Japanese military experts cautioned their leaders that Japan would fail to win a protracted struggle with the United States. Consequently, Japan's political leaders would have six months to negotiate open trade with the United States after the beginning of the war, after which Japan would only lose.

President Roosevelt refused to meet with the liberal Japanese Prime Minister in the fall of 1941; and before the six weeks elapsed after the Japanese Supreme War Council meeting of September 6, the militant General Hideki Tojo became premier. Though now convinced that war was inevitable, Tojo sent a personal representative, Saburo Kurusu, to Washington in early November for further fruitless talks with the Americans. By the end of the month Americans knew from their breaking of the Japanese codes that war was coming; but they did not know where in the Pacific it would start.

On November 24, American naval authorities sent out warnings of war with Japan to commanders at Pearl Harbor and Manila. On November 27, these bases were warned again—this time with "an aggressive move by Japan is expected within the next few days." Unfortunately, the authorities at Pearl Harbor had not been aware of military code changes in Washington, and the message sent to Pearl Harbor that was intended to warn of an impending air raid was misinterpreted as a warning to prepare for sabotage attacks. Consequently, planes were lined up on the runways, in the open, where they could be easily watched, making them very good targets for an air raid.

On December 1, the Japanese emperor gave his consent to war. Already a Japanese task force was steaming across the northern Pacific for a surprise attack on Pearl Harbor. In Washington, the two Japanese envoys, Kurusu and Ambassador Nomura, continued their inconclusive talks with Secretary of State Cordell Hull.

Pearl Harbor

Two new technologies would play roles in the American disaster at Pearl Harbor. First, American military intelligence believed that American ships in Pearl Harbor were safe from attack by aerial torpedoes because the torpedoes would hit the bottom of the shallow harbor, only forty-five feet deep, before they could correct their paths and hit their targets. The Japanese, however, had discovered that the attachment of wooden stabilizers to the torpedoes' fins would allow them to be dropped in depths of less than forty feet and not hit the bottom. Second, early on Sunday morning, December 7, 1941, two young radar operators noted an unusually large number of blips on their radar screen about one hundred thirty miles north of Oahu. The radar operators' superiors misinterpreted those blips as American B-17s, due to arrive that morning. No warning was issued.

The time was 7:50 on Sunday morning, December 7, 1941. In the sky over the island of Oahu, Captain Nakaya of the Japanese navy wrote in his log:

> Pearl Harbor is still asleep in the morning mist. The orderly groups of barracks, the wriggling white line of the automobile road climbing up to the mountaintop; fine objectives in all directions.... Inside the harbor were important ships of the Pacific fleet, strung out and anchored two ships side by side in an orderly manner.

Ten minutes later the first wave of Japanese planes struck the great American base. The surprise was complete. Some American sailors thought the first bombs were accidentally dropped from American planes. Although the Americans fought back fiercely, the losses sustained were enormous—all eight battleships, the main object of the attack, were put out of

▶ The first wave of Japanese planes struck the American base on Oahu in the morning of December 7, 1941, without warning. More than twenty-four hundred Americans were killed and twelve hundred wounded.

▶The devastating Japanese attack on Pearl Harbor was recreated on the big screen in 2001 starring American actors Ben Affleck and Josh Hartnett.

action. Two never saw action again. Except for three aircraft carriers, which happened to be at sea, the whole Pacific fleet was damaged or destroyed. Almost all the aircraft, most of which did not even get off the ground, were knocked out. More than twenty-four hundred Americans were killed and twelve hundred wounded. The Japanese lost twenty-nine airplanes, five midget submarines, and one fleet submarine. Considering the extensive damage, the attack on Pearl Harbor was one of the cheapest victories in the history of warfare.

For the Americans, it could have been even worse. The Japanese attacked for two hours and then stopped. They could have refueled and attacked again, but they did not. America's four aircraft carriers under William F. "Bull" Halsey were not in the harbor at the time of the attack, and Japan's Vice-Admiral Chuichi Nagumo did not order any attempt to find them. Some of Nagumo's decision was evidently influenced by Japanese cultural factors. Given that Japan was attacking without a Declaration of War, many Japanese viewed the idea of a surprise attack as dishonorable and akin to a sucker punch. Those who opposed such action forced a compromise—the Japanese military would hit the United States hard in one, lightning-surprise attack and then cease the attack until war could be declared later in the day. The aversion to the idea of a surprise attack was so strong among the Japanese pilots, believing that they had committed acts of cowardice, that some were found weeping in shame after the attack at Pearl Harbor. Hence, despite the devastating success of the raid, the decision to attack Pearl Harbor was a colossal blunder. First, the Japanese had allowed America's most important ships stationed at Pearl Harbor, the aircraft carriers, to escape—a factor that would come back to haunt the Japanese the next year at the Battle of Midway. Second, the idea that Japan could attack the United States and somehow force trade concessions by launching a devastating war is perhaps the greatest cultural misunderstanding of the twentieth century. For some time Roosevelt had feared that if the Japanese attacked British and Dutch possessions in Asia without involving the United States, it would be impossible to unify America behind a war to halt their aggression. After December 7, however, Americans were not only united in their opposition but also in the goal of the unconditional surrender of Japan.

The strike against Pearl Harbor was only one part of an audacious grand plan to destroy British, Dutch, and American power in the western Pacific. Soon after the bombing of Pearl Harbor, Japanese planes attacked the Philippines. Though this time there had been specific warning, the Americans—because of bureaucratic tie-ups—were again caught unready. On December 8, the Japanese attacked Hong Kong, Borneo, the Malay Peninsula, and the American island outpost of Guam.

The boldness and power of the Japanese advance were brought home on December 10, when Japanese land-based bombers sank the British battleship *Prince of Wales* and the battle cruiser *Repulse* off the coast of Malaya. Never before had air power destroyed a free-moving battleship. The age of the airplane in naval warfare had arrived. Successful amphibious landings in the Philippines and elsewhere also attested to the Japanese' command of the most advanced methods of offensive warfare.

The day after the attack on Pearl Harbor, Congress, at the president's request, voted for war with Japan with a unanimous vote in the Senate and only one dissenting vote in the House, Jeannette Ranking of Montana. On December 11, Hitler made another of his ill-fated decisions and fulfilled his promise to the Japanese by declaring war on the United States. Italy followed soon thereafter. Hitler's reasoning was that war with the United States would allow him to attack British and Soviet shipping without restraint and thus cut off American supplies to England. Without American supplies, Hitler believed that Britain would quickly be defeated; then he could negotiate peace with the United States. Any dilemma FDR might have had over whether the United States should go to war with Germany after the attack on Pearl Harbor was resolved by Hitler himself; and the United States was now in a position to use to the fullest its great power against aggressor nations in both Asia and Europe.

After the initial shock had passed, many Americans grew suspicious that the astonishing success of the Japanese assault must have resulted from traitorous acts; and staunch isolationists blamed Roosevelt for somehow selling out America to the Japanese. However, exhaustive investigations on the part of both the navy and Congress produced no evidence to support such allegations. The fact is that most military experts seriously underestimated Japan's ability to mount the kind of elaborate, multi-pronged assault, of which Pearl Harbor was but a part. The commanders at Pearl Harbor were lax in taking precautions after the war warnings of November, but these defects add up to nothing more sinister than inefficiency and carelessness.

War in Two Hemispheres

Creation of the Grand Alliance

Within two weeks after Pearl Harbor, Winston Churchill and his chief military advisers arrived in Washington for extended discussions with the president and American military leaders about the long-range strategy of the two-front war in which both countries were now engaged. The basic decision of the conference, as General Marshall later reported, was that "Germany is still the prime enemy and her defeat is the key to victory. Once Germany is defeated the collapse of Italy and the defeat of Japan must follow." Roosevelt, despite pressure to do otherwise, never deviated from this decision, even though Japan appeared to be the greater immediate menace to the United States. The two allies also agreed to pool their resources and military equipment for the duration of the struggle.

Finally, the conference created a Combined Chiefs of Staff in Washington to plan and coordinate global strategy. As a public manifestation of the new association, Churchill, Roosevelt, Maxim Litvinov (representing Stalin), and the representatives of twenty-three other nations at war with one or more Axis powers signed the Declaration of the United Nations on New Year's Day 1942.

As the arsenal of the alliance, the United States in subsequent months worked out new lend-lease agreements with the principal allies. According to these agreements, the costs of the war were to be borne in proportion to ability to pay. By the end of the war in 1945, the United States had contributed over $50 billion in Lend-Lease, the bulk of which went to Great Britain. In return, the Allies provided $8 billion in goods or services to the United States.

Holding the Line

UNITED
THE UNITED NATIONS FIGHT FOR FREEDOM

The first months of 1942 were filled with one Japanese success after another. (As a gesture of defiance, in April the United States dispatched General James Doolittle to lead a small, carrier-borne air strike against Tokyo, which did boost morale, but its military value was nil.) In a matter of months the Japanese overran all of Southeast Asia. In February, they took the great British naval base of Singapore and in March took Java, the main island of the Dutch East Indies. Another Japanese army, meanwhile, had overrun Siam (now Thailand) and Burma and stood poised on the borders of India.

By the end of March 1942, the Japanese controlled the western half of the Pacific from the Kuriles in the North to the Solomons in the South, as well as the islands and mainland of Southeast Asia from Indochina to India. Japan captured American outposts on Guam and Wake Island and launched a major offensive against Americans in the Philippines in January 1942. American forces under General Douglas MacArthur retreated first to the Bataan Peninsula and then to the Island of Corregidor before all resistance in the Philippines ceased on May 6. The Japanese then marched the American army and their Filipino allies sixty miles across the Bataan Peninsula, abusing them en route in what became known as the Bataan "death march." Of the eleven thousand Americans taken prisoner on the Philippines, only one thousand would survive the war. As many as twenty-six thousand Filipinos would also die during the death march and the brutal months afterward when they were subjected to malnutrition and brutality in Japanese prison camps. Living to fight another day, however, was American General Douglas MacArthur, who issued the famous personal vow, "I shall return," upon his departure from the Philippines.

The Japanese had to hold off the United States until they could develop the iron and oil in the Dutch East Indies. Not knowing that Americans had broken their naval code, the Japanese made the fatal error of trying to expand their defensive perimeter. In May 1942, in the Battle of the Coral Sea off the Southeast Coast of New Guinea, United States aircraft carriers turned back the Japanese Navy. A new kind of warfare was unveiled: Japanese and American ships attacked each other by airplane, while the ships themselves remained out of sight and out of range from each other. The United States lost the carrier *Lexington,* causing the Japanese to be "encouraged" and consider the engagement a victory; the United States also considered the battle an American victory because it had, for the first time, halted the Japanese advance.

On June 3, 1942, the Japanese launched a major naval offensive aimed at taking the Midway Islands northwest of Hawaii. The Midway Islands were imminently important because they were close enough to the United States that Japan could use them as a base from which to bomb the U.S. mainland. The United States knew of the Japanese plan from interceptions of coded transmissions and rushed every available ship and plane into the area.

Both sides suffered enormous losses. The United States lost all but one pilot from its aircraft carriers at Midway, and that one pilot was also shot down and watched the entire battle floating in the ocean. On the plus side, however, the United States sank four Japanese aircraft carriers while the Japanese only sank one of the United States. Hence, despite the heavy American losses, the Battle of Midway was a major American victory since the Japanese did not accomplish their objective: taking the Midway Islands. The battle also proved to be the turning point in the Pacific. Prior to Midway, the Japanese had won all the battles in the Pacific theater. After Midway, Japan would lose all battles. Midway also displayed the importance of the American aircraft carriers surviving the attack on Pearl Harbor—the United States surely would have lost at Midway if the aircraft carriers stationed at Pearl Harbor had not been present at Midway. Finally, Japanese losses at the Battle of Midway were so critical that, thereafter, the Imperial Navy was on the defensive and would remain so throughout the rest of the war.

▶ The United States lost the carrier *Lexington*, (at left) causing the Japanese to be "encouraged" and consider the engagement a victory; the United States also considered the battle an American victory because it had, for the first time, halted the Japanese advance.

Island Hopping

With General MacArthur pushing northward and westward from Australia and Admiral Chester Nimitz pushing west from Hawaii, the United States planned to advance toward Japan by capturing Japanese strategic outposts in each Pacific island chain that had come under Japanese control. Instead of attacking every island with Japanese soldiers on it, American military strategists decided to attack only the most important supply islands and the air bases of each island chain, effectively leaving the rest of the Japanese forces on other islands to live off the land without supplies. Each island to be invaded was to undergo an amphibious assault with massive air support, a method that the United States would use repeatedly through D-day.

The first test of the amphibious assault, island-hopping strategy was at Guadalcanal in the Solomon Islands. The first precarious American landing on Guadalcanal took place on August 7, 1942. It was not until the fifth major sea and air encounter on November 13–14, 1942, however, that the southern Solomons rested securely in American hands. Superior American air power was the deciding factor in the battle; but American deaths totaled over three thousand, and the struggle for the island took much longer than expected. Over twenty thousand Japanese were killed on the island. The Japanese fought, essentially, to the last man as the United States took only 156 prisoners, many who were wounded.

On Guadalcanal, the Americans quickly discovered that all of the fallen Japanese soldiers on the battlefield were not necessarily dead. Some were merely "playing possum" and would shoot Americans from the ground as they passed the positions of the "possum" Japanese. Americans then assigned "Possum Squads" of men to make the rounds of bodies lying on the battlefield and shoot them in the head or engulf them with flamethrowers. Some quickly battle-hardened Americans made personal items from the skulls and bones of Japanese soldiers. The gruesome pattern of Guadalcanal would be repeated throughout the Pacific in 1943, 1944,

▶ Admiral Chester Nimitz

MAP 26.1 The War in the Pacific

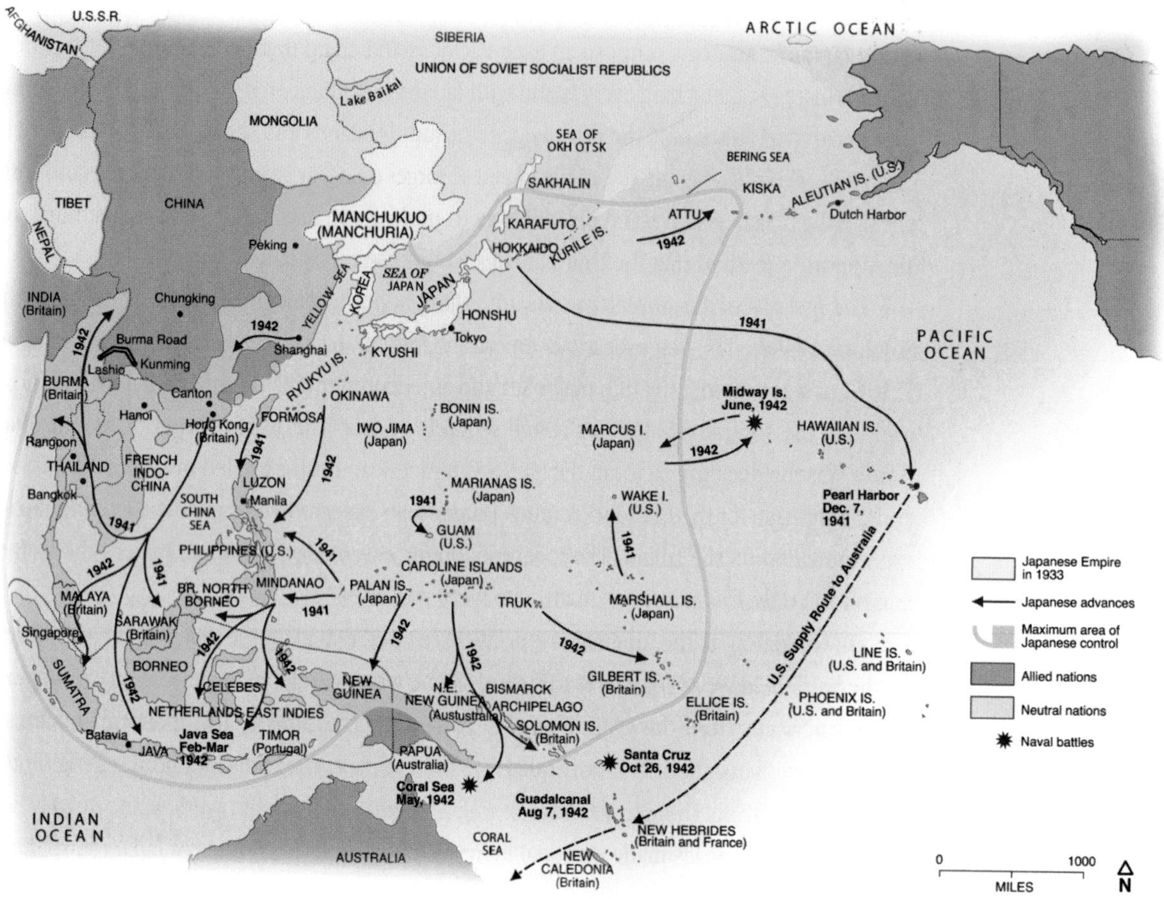

and 1945—on the islands of Tulagia, Gavutu, Tarawa, Makin, Kwajalein, Eniwetok, the Philippines, Iwo Jima, and Okinawa. For instance, on Tarawa, a tiny coral cay of less than three square miles, three thousand Japanese and one thousand Americans were killed in three days. Two thousand more Americans were wounded and only seventeen thousand Japanese survived, a survival rate of barely more than half of one percent.

European Theater

Unlike the war in the Pacific, the first year of war in Europe brought almost uninterrupted setbacks for the Allies on both land and sea. That spring and summer German submarines sank Allied tankers and merchantmen before the eyes of civilians on the shores of New Jersey and Florida. By the middle of 1942, shipping losses reached a new peak of 4.5 million tons, more than in all of 1941. Yet in the same six months only twenty-one U-boats were sunk. At the conclusion of eleven months of war and after a furious program of shipbuilding, Allied tonnage was still less than it had been on the day Pearl Harbor was bombed. Although losses were gradually reduced, the submarine menace hung over Allied preparations for counteraction until the middle of 1943. In North Africa, Nazi forces under General Erwin Rommel (The Desert Fox) took Libya and most of North Africa from the English and were within one hundred miles of Cairo and the Suez Canal. Meanwhile, the Germans had advanced deep into Russia, taking the wheat fields of the Ukraine and nearing the oil fields of the Caucuses. By the fall of 1941, German troops were within forty miles of Moscow, and the city was within eyesight.

From December 1941, when America entered the war, until the summer of 1943, the army of the Soviet Union was the only army fighting the Germans on the European continent. The Soviet Union might have been over-run in the fall of 1941 had it not been for the onset of the brutal Russian winter that stopped the advance of the German army in its tracks. The Germany army had left Germany for the assault on the Soviet Union, in the spring of 1941, with no winter coats, and expected the Soviets to be defeated by mid-summer. By October, the German army was engulfed in a winter cold front that plunged temperatures as low as forty degrees below zero. German tanks, trucks, and other military vehicles would not start, fuel in some cases turned to jelly, and horses brought by the German army to pull heavy equipment froze to death along with humans. Some German soldiers perished when the metal helmets on top of their heads froze the blood on the top of their skulls.

The Russian winter bought the Soviets time to build their army. As the Germans advanced, entire factories in the western Soviet Union were dismantled and shipped east to the Ural Mountains for reassembly. By the time the weather relented in the spring of 1942, the Soviet army would be sufficient to resist the German advance.

In contrast, the United States army would not engage the Germans on the ground anywhere until November 1942, almost a year after Pearl Harbor. This lack of a second front would be a bone of contention between the Allies until "D-day" on June 6, 1944. During these two and a half years, Stalin would repeatedly complain that his allies were leaving him to fight the Germans himself. The Americans and British argued that if they tried to invade Europe before they were ready, they would suffer unacceptable casualty rates and were doomed to failure. Stalin, however, was unimpressed with the Allies' complaints since an estimated 28 million people would perish in the Soviet Union during the war compared to three hundred twenty-one thousand Americans.

Allied War Strategies/Divisions

Though formally allies, the Soviets rarely shared military strategies with their American and British Allies because Stalin feared, throughout the war, that the British and Americans might settle for a separate peace with Germany. The United States and Britain also failed to share their nuclear weapons research with the U.S.S.R.

Despite the fact that FDR had told Soviet Foreign Commissar Vyacheslav Molotov that a second front in Europe was possible in 1942, FDR and Churchill believed that no such invasion could be launched with success until the spring of 1943, since the United States would need a full year to achieve the necessary military readiness. Churchill wanted to avoid the catastrophic British casualties of World War I; otherwise, he feared that the British people might lose heart and surrender. United States General Eisenhower believed that a lack of a second front would doom the U.S.S.R.

In the spring of 1942, the German army began to move again and make progress on the Russian front. In May, Soviet Foreign Commissar Vyacheslav Molotov visited Washington and

MAP 26.2 The European Theatre (1939–1942)

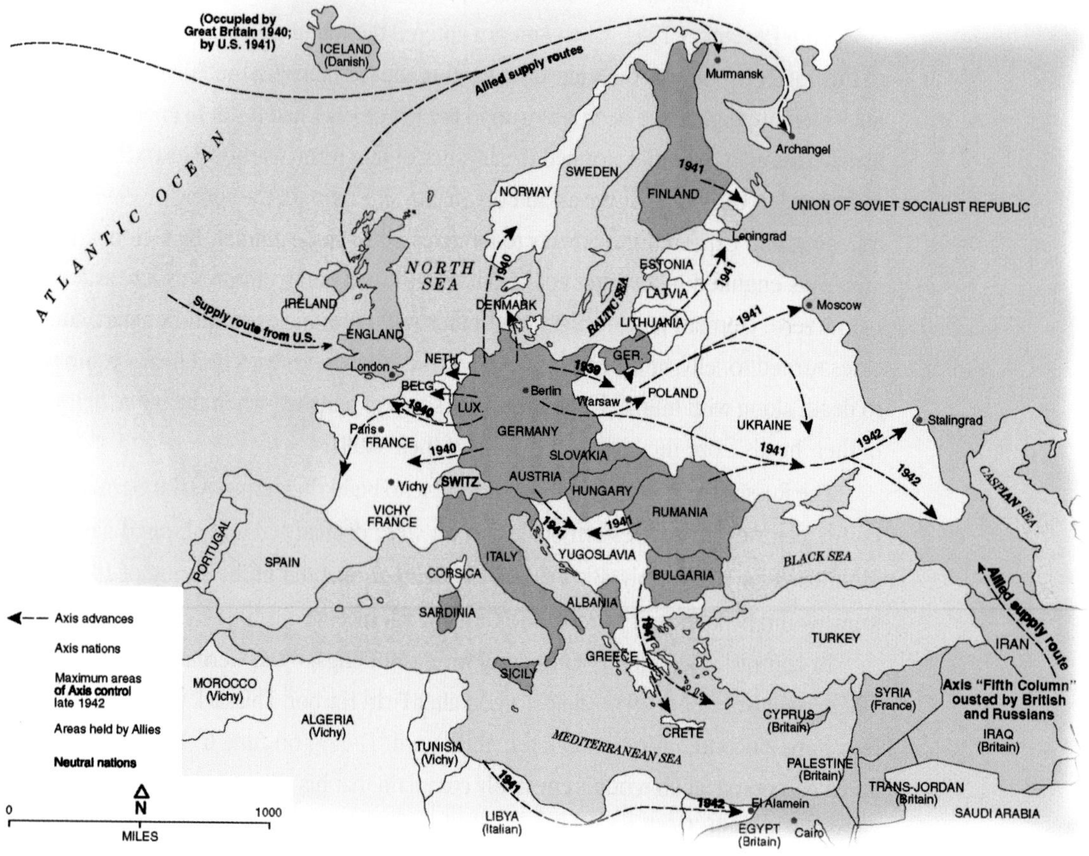

warned the Americans that unless at least forty German divisions could be diverted, the Soviet effort suffered imminent collapse. Molotov again urged the Allies to open a Western Front in Europe, and Stalin again criticized the Allies for allowing him to fight the war by himself. In response, Churchill met with FDR in Washington in June and urged an invasion of North Africa instead of Europe. FDR reasoned that the United States was not ready for an invasion of Europe, and ordered the U.S. forces to join the British in defending North Africa.

The Turning Point

Near the end of 1942, Allied forces around the globe assumed the offensive, which they never lost thereafter. November witnessed the victory on Guadalcanal. At about the same time the Russians, after a heroic defense of Stalingrad on the Volga, seized the offensive against the Germans. On November 8, 1942, eleven months after Pearl Harbor, American forces commanded by General Dwight D. Eisenhower invaded the French colonies of Morocco and Algeria with surprise landings from a giant armada of five hundred warships and three hundred fifty transports and cargo ships. United States forces landed at Casablanca, Port Lyamtey, Safi in Morocco, and Algiers. The Germans, before Eisenhower's landing, had gained control of the North African coast, east as far as Egypt. The immediate purpose of the North African landings was to catch the German armies, under General Erwin Rommel in a giant squeeze. Only a week before, General Bernard L. Montgomery's British Eighth Army had begun an offensive at El Alamein in Egypt. As Rommel's forces retreated westward before Montgomery along the North African coast in December and January, they backed up against the now well-established American forces in Algeria and Tunisia.

An agreement was signed with fascist Spain, which stated that Spain would not interfere in the Allied invasion of Spanish Morocco. In return, the United States supplied Spain with oil and purchased Spanish metal ores at a price above that of the free market. Churchill explained the Allied strategy by arguing, "My children, you are permitted in time of great danger to walk with the Devil until you have crossed the bridge."

For the first three months of the invasion, the Americans fought Vichy French troops who were in great disarray. The German-controlled Vichy French offered only scattered resistance, and total Allied casualties amounted to fewer than two thousand. The Americans made an agreement with Vichy France for it to withhold naval assistance from the Axis in exchange for United States shipments of coal, sugar, and cotton. The Americans also made an agreement with Vichy French Admiral Jean Darlan whereby the United States would recognize Darlan as the leader of Vichy France in Africa if Darlan would help with the Allied invasion. Darlan ordered his men to cease firing on the Allies as they approached the shore during the invasion of the North African coast. A supporter of the Free French Government of Charles De Gaulle, who had not known of Darlan's secret collaboration with the Allies, assassinated Darlan a few weeks later.

Simultaneously, while the Americans were invading in Morocco and Algeria, the British under Field Marshall Montgomery launched a counteroffensive against the Germans from Egypt. In their first major engagement with the Germans, however, the Americans were defeated and retreated from Kasserine Pass in Tunisia during February 14–22, 1943. The defeat at the hands of the Germans proved that the American troops were inexperienced and that American tanks were not superior to those of the Germans.

General George S. Patton was given command and regrouped the United States troops and together with the British, under Montgomery, drove the Germans from North Africa in May 1943. Rommel's once invincible Afrika Korps was no more, and German losses in Africa reached three hundred fifty thousand.

Though eventually successful, the North Africa campaign had been more costly than anticipated and had taken six months. This combined with the continued sinking, in the Atlantic, of Allied shipping caused FDR to delay his planned invasion of France that had been tentatively scheduled for May 1943.

In April 1943, the Germans unearthed and made public ten thousand Polish soldiers in a mass grave in the Katyn Forest of Poland. They had been killed by Stalin's troops in 1940. Stalin denied the atrocity, and the Americans chose to believe him, even though he refused to approve a request by the Poles to have the international Red Cross investigate. Stalin then broke relations with the Polish government in exile in London.

Eastern Front

While the United States and British were driving the Germans from North Africa, Stalin's army turned the tide against the Nazis in the winter of 1942–43. Hitler was within reach of his goal—the oil fields of the Caucuses—but ordered his army to destroy a Russian army that was dug in at Stalingrad. After three months of intense, costly, house-to-house fighting, six hundred thousand members of the cold and starving German army surrendered in February 1943. Hitler's army on the

Eastern Front would never recover. After the defeat at Stalingrad, the German army would lose all major battles on the Eastern Front.

The German army lost another five hundred thousand troops in another urban siege at Leningrad. The siege of Leningrad began in January 1941 and lasted 872 days until January 1944. During that time, the city witnessed the starvation of 1.2 million civilians in Leningrad; the evacuation of another estimated 1.4 million; and the bombing of the children of Leningrad by the Luftwaffe, as the children were evacuated on sleighs across the frozen Lake Ladoga. The undersupplied Russians at Leningrad ate frozen human bodies, both German and Russian, drank human blood, and ate wallpaper paste after pealing the wallpaper off walls. In spite of the unspeakable suffering, the Soviet city never fell to the Germans. By the time the siege ended, the German effort on the Eastern Front was all but lost.

Italy

Throughout 1943, even though the Red Army had turned the tide in the East, Stalin continued to clamor for a Western Front; but the Allies delayed a planned invasion of France in favor of an invasion of Italy. The United States and British armies landed at Sicily on July 9, 1943, and secured the island on August 16. On September 3, British and United States forces attacked the Italian mainland. Mussolini's government quickly collapsed, and the dictator attempted to flee to Germany. Mussolini was eventually captured and executed by his own people, and his body was put on public display in Milan where thousands of Italians could pass by daily to spit upon his remains.

Mussolini's successor, Marshall Pietro Badoglio, surrendered to the United States and Great Britain and signed a "separate peace" without the participation of the U.S.S.R. The United States and Britain had set a precedent in Italy that Stalin could use later. Essentially, the armies that liberated a country from the Germans would determine its postwar status.

Mussolini's empire had been a paper tiger built on show and bravado but with little real substance. Mussolini had once boasted that the Italian army would have a "million bayonets." His army, however, was never larger than six hundred thousand, and the Sec-

▶ The siege of Leningrad lasted 872 days. Russians dying of starvation at Leningrad ate frozen human bodies, both German and Russian, drank human blood, and ate wallpaper paste after pealing the wallpaper off walls. In spite of the unspeakable suffering, the Soviet city never fell to the Germans.

ond World War would not be won with bayonets. Italy's armor and air force also proved insufficient to the task, and opposing forces repeatedly repelled the Italians when not accompanied by the German army.

After the fall of Italy, Germany immediately shifted eight divisions to Italy and continued the fight on the rugged Italian peninsula. Due to the mountainous terrain in Italy, the American and British advance quickly ground to a halt. Rome would not fall to the Allies until June 4, 1944, two days before D-day, and the Germans would not be totally pushed out of Italy until 1945. The Italy invasion was so costly that it caused Churchill to urge FDR to delay the invasion of France for a year—a delay that angered Stalin, who again believed that the Allies were evading the true war and leaving the real battle up to the Russians.

Setting the Goals of War

In January 1943, soon after the consolidation of the Allied landings in North Africa, Roosevelt and Churchill met in the Moroccan city of Casablanca to discuss war aims. It was at this meeting that Roosevelt, after consulting with Churchill, announced that only unconditional surrender of Germany and Italy would be acceptable to the Allies. Later critics would argue that such uncompromising terms stiffened German resistance and prolonged the war. Certainly the Nazi propaganda machine played upon the argument that victory for the Allies spelled annihilation for the Germans. However, at the time, Roosevelt was careful to say that unconditional surrender "does not mean the destruction of the population of Germany, Italy, and Japan, but it does mean the destruction of the philosophies of those countries which are based on conquest and the subjugation of other people." Actually, it appears doubtful that the statement influenced German resistance very much. Certainly it produced exactly the opposite effect upon the Italians, who surrendered with alacrity nine months later.

Late 1943 saw several meetings of the Big Three powers. At the end of October the foreign ministers of the United States, Great Britain, and the Soviet Union met for the first time in Moscow. There it was agreed that the three nations would consult on "all matters relating to the surrender and disarmament" of their common enemies. They also recognized a need for setting "the earliest possible date" for the planning of an international organization of the "peace-loving states." Victory, in short, was already being anticipated.

En route to a meeting with Stalin in Teheran, Iran, Churchill and Roosevelt stopped at Cairo from November 22–26, 1943, to confer with the Nationalist Chinese leader Chiang Kai-shek. The three allies agreed to prosecute the Pacific war until Japan was forced into unconditional surrender. They also agreed that Manchuria, Formosa, and the Pescadore Islands, earlier seized by Japan, should be returned to China after the war.

The Teheran Conference of November 28 through December 1, 1943—the first personal encounter between Stalin, Churchill, and Roosevelt—resulted in few final decisions, although Roosevelt did secure from Stalin, as Hull had from Molotov a month earlier, a promise of Russian help against Japan soon after the end of the war against Germany. Stalin wanted Germany cut up into pieces after the war; FDR wanted Germany to be ruled by the "Four Policemen"—the United States, Britain, Russia, and China—each with a sphere of influence. The "Four Policemen" idea was agreed upon in principle. The Big Three also agreed on a spring 1944 invasion of France.

▶ Stalin, Roosevelt, and Churchill on the portico of the Russian Embassy in Teheran, during a conference between November 28–December 1, 1943.

Convinced of the need to have Stalin's friendship in the postwar world, Roosevelt did his best to charm the dictator and to dissipate Stalin's obvious suspicion of the two English-speaking allies. Stalin, on his part, was eager to get along well enough with his allies so that they would open up a second front in northern Europe, thereby relieving pressure on the Soviet Union, which was paying a fearsome price in civilian casualties because of the German invasion. Afterwards, FDR announced that he "got along fine" with Stalin and that the United States would "get along very well with him and the Russian people." At one point in the conference, Stalin suggested that after the war, the Allies should exterminate fifty thousand German officers. Churchill was horrified, and FDR said that Americans could not accept such a figure; but the president added, "forty-nine thousand would be fine."

Support at Home

The Battle for Production

In a very real sense the turning of the tide of war from constant defeat to persistent victory was attributable to the astounding production that flooded from American factories and farms. At Teheran even Stalin acknowledged that without American production the Allies would not be winning the war.

Conversion of the economy to full wartime production did not really begin until after Pearl Harbor. During 1940 and 1941, Roosevelt had created several agencies, headed by businessmen and labor leaders, to speed up and coordinate production; but when the Japanese struck, the level was still far from satisfactory. In January 1942, Roosevelt set up the War Production Board with Donald M. Nelson as chief; and though this more centralized control was the best arrangement yet, the organization of production did not achieve optimum efficiency until the creation of the Office of War Mobilization, in May 1943, under James F. Byrnes, former Democratic senator from South Carolina.

While building up an armed force of some 15 million men and women, the United States undertook to expand its productive capacity to feed, clothe, supply, house, and transport this army, as well as make sizable support contributions to the British and Russian armies spread around the globe. To meet this gargantuan assignment required not only the expenditure of billions of dollars but also the execution of a host of plans and arrangements. Priorities for materials had to be established, raw materials gathered, labor recruited to replace the men and women serving in the armed services, and civilian industries converted to war work. The automobile industry, for example, was given over entirely to the manufacture of tanks, trucks, and other military vehicles,

The aviation industry expanded its work force from 49,000 in 1939 to a peak of 2.1 million in November 1943, when it employed over 12 percent of the total number of workers in manufacturing. To keep supplies moving, the total tonnage of American shipping increased over five times between 1939 and May 1945. Whole new industries sometimes had to be created. The production of synthetic rubber was inaugurated when the Japanese cut off the major source of natural rubber from Southeast Asia. The volume of industrial production increased so rapidly that by October 1943 some cutbacks were made to prevent surpluses.

Between 1939 and 1946, agricultural production increased some 30 percent, even though the labor force on farms fell more than five percent. As a result, not only was the United States able to keep the armed forces well supplied with food but the nation as a whole ate better than ever before, and the Allies were able to draw upon the American larder during the war and after.

In order to gear up for this level of productivity, the federal government took several steps; one of which, in particular, was to have long-term consequences. In the first place, the government suspended antitrust prosecutions, which had been in abeyance during the NRA period but then had been reinvigorated during the late 1930s. Secondly, it instituted cost-plus contracts, whereby firms with defense contracts were guaranteed a profit—their costs plus a profit—in order to offer incentives to firms to convert to production for the military. Both of these decisions meant that big business grew bigger during the war, and during the Vietnam era critics of United States foreign policy pointed to the cost-plus contracts as a key element in launching the military-industrial complex.

Controlling Inflation

Simply because there was so much money and so few consumer goods, the control of prices was a major problem. Essentially, prices were kept under control by two methods—increased taxes and a price freeze. The Office of Price Administration, which was in charge of controlling inflation, failed to put a tight lid on prices until late in 1942; thus some prices, notably those of foods, rose alarmingly through most of that year. Thereafter, however, controls were more effective.

Because Congress would not follow through on legislation, taxation was not so steep as the administration had hoped. Only the Revenue Act of 1942, which increased corporate, private income, and excise taxes, took much of a bite out of civilian purchasing power. In that act, for the first time, the income tax reached into the pockets of the average citizen. About 50 million income-tax payers were recorded in 1943 as compared with 13 million in 1941.

Congress refused to heed Roosevelt's demand for a further increase in taxes in 1943. Yet in spite of government spending at a rate as high as $100 million a year, about 40 percent of the ongoing cost of the war was paid for out of taxes, a proportion which had never been achieved in any previous American war.

Civil Liberties

Unfortunately, panic gripped much of the country, but especially the west coast after the bombing of Pearl Harbor. Rumors circulated about a force of Japanese gathering for an invasion from Baja Mexico. Other rumors spread fear of Japanese fishermen mining American harbors and even poisoning America's water supply. Blackouts were imposed on the Western coastal cities so that Japanese planes would be unable to find them at night. Tragically, in Seattle fellow citizens beat a restaurant owner to death when he forgot to turn off his neon sign. Evidently gripped by some of the same panic, early in 1942 President Roosevelt issued Executive Order 9066, which authorized the rounding up of some one hundred thousand Japanese living on the West Coast, even though some two-thirds of them were American citizens. Although no specific acts of sabotage could be charged against them, these people were held in "relocation centers" in the interior for most of the war. The camps were essentially prisoner-of-war quality, and people were housed together in buildings that contained little besides bunks. One six-year-old Japanese-American boy probably summed up the situation best when he repeatedly asked his mother, "Mother, when are we going back to America?"

Meanwhile, the property of those interned was placed in the hands of often incompetent or unfriendly custodians. This action of the government, though generally supported at the time and subsequently upheld by the Supreme Court, was later condemned as an indefensible act of racism since mere Japanese ancestry was the basis for the internment. Ironically, the Japanese in Hawaii, who made up a much larger proportion of the population, were not affected by the order.

The best-known resister to the executive order was Fred Korematsu, who lived until 2005, long enough to receive the Presidential Medal of Freedom in 1998 from President Bill Clinton and to become a civil rights icon. Sent to Camp Topaz, in the Utah desert, Korematsu began a legal case against internment, *Korematsu v. United States*, a case that made it all the way to the United States Supreme Court where he lost. Over time, however, American public opinion swung around to the position that internment had been a grave injustice. Korematsu became a hero.

It should also be noted that despite the pain of internment one of the most decorated units in the war, the 442nd Battalion, was comprised of Japanese Americans. Fighting in the European theater, the battalion established a distinguished record of courage under fire.

No comparable interference with civil liberty was taken against Americans of German or Italian ancestry, nor did the population at large indulge in irrational attacks on Germans like those that had marred the domestic record during the First World War; but *Native* minorities, however, did suffer. Large numbers of whites attacked blacks in Detroit in 1943, and whites in other cities resorted to violence against blacks. During the last two years of the war, white servicemen and civilians also harassed young Mexican-Americans in the Los Angeles area in what

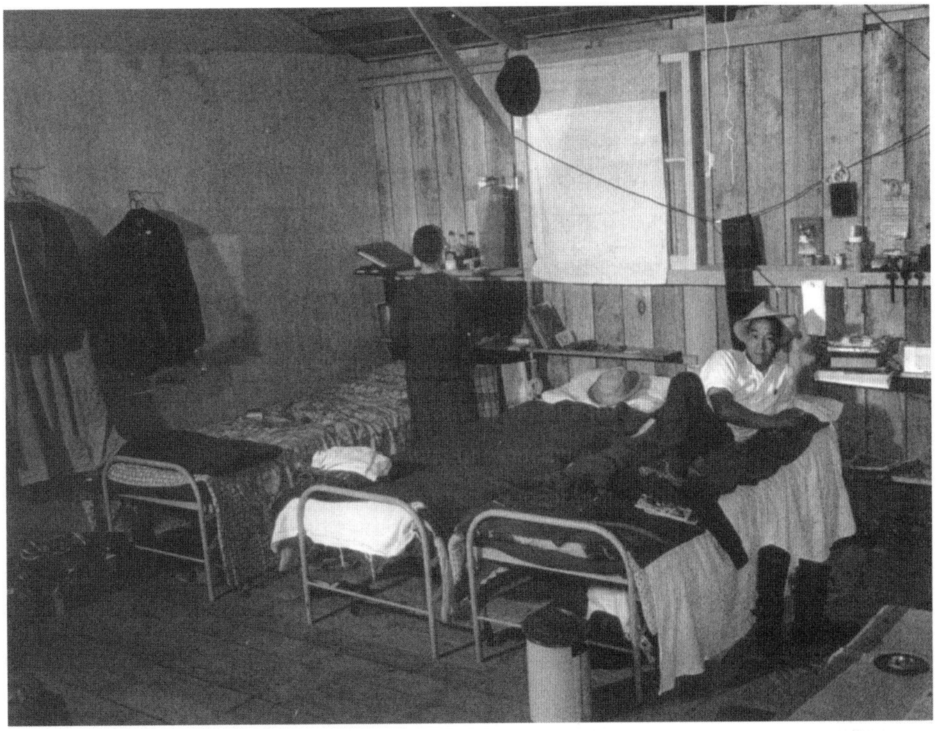

▶ Japanese-American World War II relocation center

came to be called the "zoot-suit riots," after the flamboyant styles worn by many Mexican-American youths. Later, these incidents were seen to mark the beginning of overt Mexican-American self-consciousness, which by the late 1960s became the Chicano movement.

Seeds of a More Just Society

For all the suffering and death the war brought about and the violations of the civil liberties of thousands of loyal Japanese Americans, the war also created substantial new opportunity for other disadvantaged groups. To cite two brief examples: Chinese Americans in San Francisco, heretofore almost invariably confined to employment in Chinatown itself, began to be able to get defense work. Unmarried Mexican American women in Los Angeles, hitherto closely chaperoned by their families, obtained gainful employment and more freedom. That both of these examples come from California is not a coincidence. The Golden State, more than any other state in the country, was transformed by its defense industries, aircraft in southern California and ship-building in northern California.

The two groups for whom the gains were the most significant were women—both white women and women of color—and African Americans. We begin with women. Because so many millions of men served in the armed forces, an enormous manpower shortage was created. To meet the need, some 6.5 million women went to work, including 3 million that were married. Until this point there had been a strong taboo against the employment of married women, but the taboo never had the same force after the war. Moreover, the women who already had jobs were often able to move up to better jobs, due to the demand for more workers. This was especially beneficial for black women, many of whom had been employable only as maids. During the war, they could move into factory jobs. The United States government encouraged the employment of women in the defense industry with "Rosie the Riveter" propaganda. Not only were millions of women employed outside the home, but also and for the first time in American history on this scale, tens of thousands joined the military. There were one hundred forty in the Women's Army Corps (WAC), one hundred thousand in the navy unit called WAVES (Women Assigned for Volunteer Emergency Service), and twenty-three thousand in the Marine Corps Women's Reserve.

Though the war gave so many women a taste of gainful employment and greater opportunity, it also created many difficulties. Housewives had a hard time feeding their families the food to which those families were accustomed because of the rationing of food, for example. Child-care was often nearly impossible to obtain. Schools in areas with defense plants were usually overcrowded, even sometimes operating on triple shifts. Although the war led to a great increase in the number of women in unions, the male-led unions often treated their new female members less than fairly. On balance, however, most historians believe that World War II was truly transformative for American women.

Transformative is also a good word to describe the impact on African Americans. After World War I, even though black troops had fought bravely in their segregated units, they came home to race riots in several American cities—Chicago, East St. Louis, and Tulsa saw the worst—and to a general lack of appreciation for their sacrifices. As war seemed increasingly likely in the months before Pearl Harbor, African American leaders were determined not to repeat the mistakes of an earlier generation by rallying around the flag and then having nothing to show for the patriotic effort by their people. Led by A. Philip Randolph of the Sleeping Car Porters, African Americans threatened to march on Washington on July 1, 1941, to demand redress of their grievances. When attempts to persuade them to call off the march failed, President Roosevelt yielded to the pressure and issued Executive Order 8802 forbidding racial discrimination by recipients of federal contracts, setting up the Fair Employment Practices Commission to monitor hiring practices. Nevertheless, armed forces remained segregated, however.

As was the case for white women, there were abundant new employment opportunities for black men and women. In this case, however, the discrimination by unions was even more flagrant than it was for white women. Unions took the dues of black people, for example, but sometimes relegated them to a separate category in which they received fewer benefits from union membership than did whites. In spite of these problems, overall, the war against Adolf Hitler, the arch racist, created a powerful momentum for social change. Almost as soon as the war ended, President Harry Truman issued an order desegregating the armed forces; and in the 1950s, as we shall soon learn, a civil rights revolution took place.

The Election of 1944

In the midst of the Second World War, as in the Civil War, the nation conducted a presidential election. The Republicans, who after Pearl Harbor strongly supported the war effort, now entertained high hopes for victory. In the congressional elections of 1942, they had gained forty-seven seats in the House and nine in the Senate, dropping the Democratic majority in the House to its lowest level since Roosevelt first took office. Prominently considered for the Republican nomination was Thomas E. Dewey, who had gained national renown as the first Republican since 1920 to be elected governor of New York State. Dewey spoke for the same internationalist wing of the party that had supported Wendell L. Willkie in 1940, but he did not suffer from Willkie's close identification with the administration. Moreover, Dewey, unlike Willkie, enjoyed the support of the professionals in the party.

As a result, the convention nominated Dewey on the first ballot—with only a single dissenting vote. John A. Bricker of Ohio, who as a Midwesterner and an isolationist brought balance to the ticket, received the vice-presidential nomination. The party platform was internationalist in content, but the convention's enthusiasm for Bricker betrayed the persistence of isolationism in Republican ranks.

In July, Roosevelt waited until just a week before the Democratic convention met before he indicated his willingness to seek the nomination for a fourth term. The real battle in the convention then raged around the choice of his running mate. Roosevelt's own choice, though not a strong one, was incumbent Vice-President Henry Wallace, who was unacceptable to conservatives within the party. The president's second choice was James F. Byrnes, the efficient and capable Director of the Office of War Mobilization. Labor leaders and liberals, in general, opposed Byrnes as anti-black and perhaps anti-labor. As a consequence, before the convention actually voted, Party leaders and the president had decided upon Harry S Truman as a compromise candidate. Truman, a senator from Missouri, was chairman of a Senate investigating committee that had gained national acclaim for its honest and efficient policing of government war contracts.

His head filled with plans for the postwar settlement, Roosevelt's heart was not in the political maneuvering. Nevertheless, early in the campaign he made one of the most effective political speeches of his career, and by the vigor of his few campaign speeches effectively countered Republican charges that he was physically incapable of enduring another term of office. Roosevelt won, though by a smaller margin in the popular vote than ever before, receiving 25.6 million votes to Dewey's 22 million. The Democrats retained control of both houses, gaining twenty-four new seats in the House of Representatives.

Pushing Toward Victory

Island Hopping in the Pacific

When the last Japanese resistance ended on Guadalcanal in February 1943, the United States began the long push northward toward Japan. The task was essentially one for the navy and the marines since the Japanese were dug in on a multitude of small islands scattered throughout the western Pacific. One by one through 1943, Japanese island fortresses—the central Solomons in the summer, eastern New Guinea in the fall, and the Gilbert Islands in the late fall—fell to air and amphibious attack, often only after terrible loss of life. As the great naval task forces of the United States moved northward, other Japanese outposts were bypassed with their garrisons still intact. Cut off from supplies, they would eventually have to surrender without bloodshed. By the end of June 1944, the capture of Saipan in the Marianas placed the air force's giant new B-29 bomber within easy striking distance of Tokyo itself. Systematic bombing of Japan's home islands from Saipan began in November 1944.

The Invasion of Europe

Meanwhile, preparations were well under way for the long-awaited frontal assault upon Hitler's "Fortress Europe." Ever since the middle of 1942 Stalin had been urging the Western allies to open a second front in Western Europe; but aside from the invasion of Italy, which was obviously peripheral, their response had been confined to bombings of the Third Reich. Nevertheless, by the middle of 1943 these air attacks were formidable. In one week in July 1943, for example, the combined British and American air forces dropped eight thousand tons of bombs on Hamburg, devastating three quarters of the city. Later, fifty other large German cities each received a similar pounding. More than three hundred thousand Germans died in these uninterrupted raids, which by 1944 were deliberately aimed at workers' homes, as well as factories, in an effort to destroy German morale as well as German industrial capacity. In one raid, Allied bombers killed an estimated one hundred thirty-five thousand German civilians in the incendiary bombing of the German city of Dresden. Though the air campaign was devastating for Germany, the raids also cost the Anglo-American air forces thousands of bombers and their crews.

On December 6, 1943, in appointing Dwight D. Eisenhower Supreme Allied Commander of the West, the Combined Chiefs of Staff told him, "You will enter the continent of Europe and, in conjunction with other Allied Nations, undertake operations aimed at the heart of Germany and the destruction of her armed forces." For months before the actual invasion began and while supplies, shipping, and men were being accumulated in England, Allied planes bombed and strafed German positions along the Channel coast. The Nazis could not help but know in general what was impending; but thanks to superb Allied counterintelligence, they misjudged the exact point of the attack on D-day, June 6, 1944. On June 5, three divisions of American paratroopers were dropped behind the German lines where they disrupted German communications and caused some general confusion. On June 6, four thousand ships landed troops and supplies on the beaches of Normandy, France, in the largest invasion in history. The main concentration of Allied troops was north of the Cotentin Peninsula in Normandy, where the massive invasion force quickly established five connected beachheads. Within two weeks, a million troops landed and moved inland. The United States suffered heavier casualties than anticipated because thousands of troops drowned in the rough seas. Furthermore, United States intelligence had missed German defenses at Omaha Beach where most of the United States casualties occurred; consequently, Eisenhower and the Allied commanders were sharply criticized for attempting the invasion in bad weather and for the intelligence failures. Nevertheless, by the end of July both the British and the American armies had broken out of their coastal positions and were striking north and west. On August 15, a new American army invaded southern France, and on August 25 Paris fell to French and American troops. Parisians greeted their American liberators with sweets and flowers in one of the greatest civilian celebrations of the war.

▶ United States intelligence didn't predict German defenses at Omaha Beach, and consequently most of the United States casualties occurred there with thousands of troops drowned in the rough seas when landing at the beaches.

Concomitantly with the Allied invasion of June 6, the Russians launched a broad offensive on the eastern front, bringing their armies to the Baltic, and into Poland and Romania by the end of the summer. By late autumn of 1944, the armies of the Grand Alliance were poised to strike into Germany from both east and west.

After the liberation of Paris, however, the Allied advance slowed due to the size of the operation that stretched from Switzerland to the Netherlands. British Field Marshall Montgomery argued for a massive assault and "Spearhead" drive to Berlin that could rapidly end the war. Eisenhower, however, felt that such a move was too risky and could leave thousands of Allied troops cut off and lost if it failed. Instead, Ike opted for a general advance along the entire five hundred-mile front.

Although the Allied and German armies on the western front were roughly equal in size in late 1944, the Allies had twenty times as many tanks and almost total control of the air. To compound matters further for the Germans, since they were retreating on the eastern front at the same time, they could not transfer resources from the east to the west. The Allied victory was merely a matter of time.

Despite the overwhelming land and air power being brought against it, Germany made two desperate attempts to forestall the inevitable. The first was a new secret weapon, a fast-flying rocket bomb, the V-2. (The V-1 or "buzz bomb," used somewhat earlier, was a jet-driven aerial bomb and not a rocket.) The first V-2s landed in England in August. Traveling faster than the speed of sound, the V-2 was impossible to intercept, and it hit without warning. Before Allied bombers could destroy the launching bases, the murderous V-2 attacks killed some eight thousand Britons.

The other desperate German effort was a great counteroffensive mounted on December 16, 1944, against the American forces in the Ardennes Forest of Belgium. In the fall and winter of 1944, bad weather slowed the Allied advance, and cloud cover rendered Allied air superiority almost useless on the battlefield. The adverse weather conditions provided Germany an opportunity to launch one last counteroffensive. The Battle of the Bulge, as it came to be called,

MAP 26.3 The European Theatre (1944–1945)

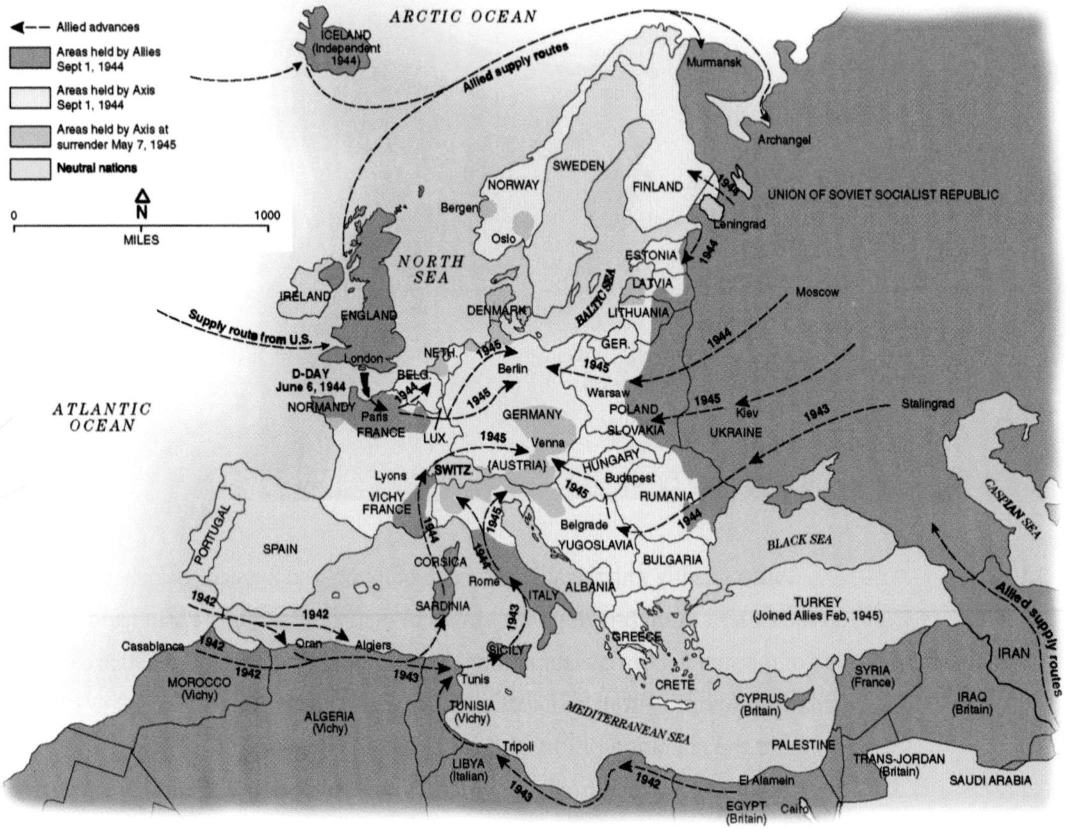

caught the Americans by surprise and forced them to retreat. The offensive was planned by Hitler himself and was directed at the center of the Allied lines on the western front. The offensive was designed to divide the allied forces in two and capture the Allied fuel depot at Antwerp in Northern Belgium.

The Germans advanced rapidly using newly constructed tanks without fear of Allied aircraft because of the cloud cover. The United States suffered seventy-seven thousand casualties in the Battle of the Bulge, their largest losses in the European theater. Despite the casualties, the Allies prevented the Germans from taking the massive Allied fuel depot at Antwerp before the weather cleared just enough for Allied aircraft to bomb the German advance. Without the Allied fuel depot at Antwerp, the Germans did not have enough fuel to continue the offensive; and many of the Germans were forced to abandon their tanks and walk back to Germany.

During the battle, German morale suffered a setback at Bastogne, Belgium, where the heavily armored German Army surrounded a company of Americans. The Germans demanded surrender, but the Allied commander at Bastogne, General Tony McAuliffe, sent back a one word reply scrawled on a piece of paper—"Nuts." The Germans did not know how to interpret the response and were demoralized that the Americans did not give up when faced with certain death. The troops at Bastogne were saved by Patton's troops three days later. After the end of the German advance in the Battle of the Bulge on January 16, 1945, Germany would only retreat.

▶ American soldiers of the 290th Infantry Regiment in the forested Ardennes Mountains region in Belgium. The Battle of the Bulge, as it came to be called, was an offensive launched by the Germans towards the end of World War II. The attack caught the Americans by surprise and forced them to retreat.

As a result of the Battle of the Bulge, however, the whole Allied timetable in the west was set back over six weeks. The first Allied troops did not cross the Rhine until March 7, 1945, when soldiers of the American Ninth Armored Division unexpectedly took the bridge of Remagen, one of the few remaining Rhine bridges. By that time the Russians stood on the banks of the Oder River, less than forty-five miles from Berlin.

The Big Three at Yalta

As the coils of Allied power tightened around Germany, Roosevelt, Stalin, and Churchill met from February 4 through 11, 1945, at Yalta, a resort town in the Crimea. Desirous of securing Russian aid against the Japanese and of bringing the Soviet Union into a new world organization, Roosevelt did his best to assure Stalin that the United States recognized Russia's special interests in Europe. It was agreed that the new government of Poland would be the one established at Lublin by the Russians and not the one in exile in London; but it was also agreed that final recognition of the Lublin government would await "free and unfettered elections." Also, pending the signing of a German peace, Poland would receive German territory to compensate for portions of eastern Poland taken by Russia in 1939.

The Americans also favorably received Russian insistence upon a large figure for German reparations, although no final commitment was made. Stalin asked for and received cession of the Kurile Islands from Japan and concessions and bases in China. In return, Stalin agreed to participate in the new world organization and to enter the war against Japan within three months after the defeat of Germany.

Despite later criticism, the so-called concessions by Roosevelt do not seem excessive in the context of February 1945. Poland, after all, was in Russian hands, and Russian military assistance against Japan then seemed eminently desirable and worth the granting of Japanese ter-

▶ Roosevelt, Stalin, and Churchill met from February 4 through 11, 1945, at Yalta, a resort town in the Crimea, Russia.

ritory to the Soviet Union. Furthermore, Chiang Kai-shek later consented to the concessions Roosevelt agreed to support in Stalin's behalf. It is also worthy of mentioning again that the Soviet Union lost an estimated total of 28 million lives, both military and civilian deaths. Hence Stalin could negotiate on the basis of widespread knowledge of his country's terrible price paid for the Allied victory.

The End of the Third Reich

Soon after the Yalta Conference, on April 12, 1945, Franklin D. Roosevelt died of a cerebral hemorrhage at Warm Springs, Georgia. A surprised and shaken Harry S Truman, who had only been Vice president for one month and had not been involved in any of the war strategy sessions, assumed the presidency the same day. Roosevelt's death plunged the nation and the peoples of the Allied world into sorrow, but the military machine he had helped to forge drove on to total victory over Germany and Italy.

On April 30, with the Russians already fighting in flaming, bombed-out Berlin, Adolf Hitler committed suicide with a gunshot to the temple in his underground bunker beneath the Reich's chancellery. Faithful guards burned his body. Nazi Germany, however, outlasted its founder by no more than a week. On May 2, Admiral Karl Doenitz, whom Hitler had named as his successor, tried to surrender to the British while continuing the war against the Russians; but Field Marshal Bernard L. Montgomery contemptuously rejected this last attempt to divide the Western and Eastern allies. Germany surrendered, unconditionally, to all the Allied powers on the morning of May 7, 1945.

American forces under Patton advanced rapidly and could have beaten the Soviets to Berlin, but the Americans were halted by Eisenhower at the Elbe River. Eisenhower reasoned that the taking of Berlin would entail house-to-house fighting that would needlessly take thousands of American lives. Consequently, Ike left Berlin to the Russians. Estimated casualty figures from the Red Army's assault on Berlin proved Eisenhower correct. An estimated three hundred thousand Soviet troops died in the assault on Berlin, almost equivalent to the number lost by the United States in the entire war. Afterwards, Berlin devolved into chaos as Stalin allowed his troops three days of plunder, with the result that there were one hundred thousand reported rapes, countless murders of civilians, and a rampage of looting and mayhem in the Soviet sack of Berlin.

Holocaust

As Allied troops overran Germany, they uncovered the Nazi death camps and confirmed the rumors that had reached the United States as early as 1942. As many as 14 million people (6 million Jews) died during the Holocaust, including an estimated 90 percent of Europe's Jewish population. FDR had dismissed the intelligence reports on the death camps as exaggerated propaganda from the Jewish Lobby. As early as 1943, the Jewish Lobby in the United States had pushed for the bombing of the Nazi death camps; but FDR refused, however, on the grounds that bombing the camps took men, planes, ammunition, and resources away from the defeat of the German Army, which took precedent. In FDR's view, the U.S. simply could not spare the planes for nonmilitary targets. To make matters worse, during the war both the United States and England had denied immigration to most Jewish refugees fleeing Europe because the U.S. Department of State feared that German spies could hide among the Jewish refugees.

Upon uncovering the death camps, however, even the most hardened American soldiers were aghast at what they encountered. The camps were teeming with unfed human skeletons packed into crowded housing in inhuman conditions, awaiting execution. By the end of the war, the Nazis had made killing people in the camps into a scientific study of efficiency. Humans were brought into the camps in crowded railroad boxcars, jammed into the camps to await execution, stripped of all their possessions, and herded into buildings where they were killed with poison gas. The bodies were then burned in massive ovens. The Nazi death camp at Auschwitz accomplished the record for efficiency by exterminating nine thousand people in just one day and 1.5 million over all.

The Nazis had adopted the death camp strategy after simply machine-gunning people proved to be too labor intensive: The bodies had to be buried, some people had to be chased down as they ran from machine gun fire, and German soldiers suffered from resulting mental problems. The Nazis attempted to remedy part of the problem, in conquered territories, by forcing non-Jewish townspeople to be the triggermen. The excessive labor problem remained, however, thus leading to the death camp as the "final solution."

Evidently, it had been Hitler's intent to kill every Jewish person in Europe, if not the world. The crime was so heinous that Allied troops could hardly believe their eyes when they encountered the Holocaust operation. General Eisenhower ordered media and cameras to the death camps to document the atrocities and ordered that German townspeople be forced to tour the death camps to see what their country had done. Eisenhower remarked that such measures were necessary because the crime was so great that the world would later be unable to believe it if it were not well documented. Unfortunately, his words have proven prophetic.

The United Nations and Potsdam

With Roosevelt's death, President Truman was left to complete the task his predecessor had considered preeminent—the convocation of the representatives of the Allied and other na-

▶In order to reach the death camp Germans packed people into crowded railroad boxcars like cattle. Sometimes they rode for days in horrifying conditions to reach the camp, many died before reaching their destination.

tions at San Francisco to draw up a charter for a new world security organization. All fifty countries signed the completed Charter of the United Nations on June 26, 1945. Despite America's long history of isolationism and its rejection of the League of Nations after World War I, the Senate agreed to American membership in the United Nations after only six days of debate and with only two dissenting votes.

President Truman was also called upon to represent the United States at the last conference of the Big Three powers. Since no final decisions on Germany had been made at Yalta and since the United States still wanted Russia's support against Japan, Truman, Stalin, and Churchill (later replaced by Clement Attlee, representing the newly elected Labour government in Britain) met at Potsdam, outside ruined Berlin, on July 17, 1945.

Differences between East and West were more evident than before. Wrangling frequently occurred over details and the meaning of previous agreements. The two Western allies were deeply suspicious of Russian policy in Poland, which Stalin seemed intent upon making a Russian satellite despite agreement on its independence at Yalta. Stalin also insisted that the new border between Germany and Poland was final although at Yalta the border had been considered only temporary. Furthermore, Stalin now insisted that the tentative agreements on reparations were final.

All three powers agreed that Germany should remain united; however, for purposes of temporary military administration, each of the three powers (later France was added) would occupy a separate zone. Berlin itself was to be occupied jointly by the victors. Even though Russia had not yet entered the war in the Pacific, the conference issued a demand for Japan's unconditional surrender. The Allies also agreed that after the war the leading Nazis would be tried as war criminals by an international tribunal.

Truman had attended the conference with the intention of dictating terms to the Soviets. Unknown to Stalin, the United States had performed its first successful nuclear test just one day prior to the Potsdam conference; and armed with the knowledge of the bomb, Truman entered the negotiations with confidence. Truman quickly discovered, however, that Stalin was not so easily manipulated. After the conference, Truman remarked that Stalin was "one smart as hell S.O.B."

The End of the War with Japan

As the European war reached its climax in the summer and fall of 1944, the United States Air Force and Navy moved ever closer to the Japanese home islands. Admiral Chester Nimitz, in command of the Pacific Fleet, wanted to use all available military strength to reach Iwo Jima, an island near enough to mainland Japan so that fighter escorts could protect bombers. He reasoned that with the conquest of the mainland, all other Japanese-held areas would have to surrender.

General Douglas MacArthur, the commanding general of the Pacific area, however, wanted to divert planes and ships to reconquer the Philippines and make good on his promise from 1942 of "I shall return." He convinced the Joint Chiefs of Staff to divide American forces so as to pursue both policies simultaneously, and necessarily, more slowly. In February 1945, the reconquest of the Philippines was completed; the island of Iwo Jima, five hundred miles from Japan, was conquered in a bloody assault. On Iwo Jima the Japanese continued their policy of fighting to the last man, with the result that fifty thousand Japanese soldiers were killed. American casualties were also heavy, with an estimated twenty thousand killed or wounded. The action on Iwo Jima provided the most reproduced image in the history of photography, the raising of the American flag on Mt. Suribachi, a picture taken by Associated Press photographer Joe Rosenthal. In the Philippines, the Americans witnessed the first Japanese use of kamikaze attacks (suicide bombers) at Leyte Gulf. There is no Japanese tactic that would be more damaging to the United States Navy for the rest of the war than the kamikaze attacks, both in terms of lives lost and ships sunk. Kamikaze attacks were also damaging to American morale since it provided a vivid illustration of the Japanese dedication to defending their homeland. Ultimately, the Japanese would lose thirty-five hundred pilots of planes and small submarines to kamikaze attacks.

On March 9, B-29s from Saipan dropped a record load of firebombs on Tokyo, igniting the wooden and paper houses of the city. The resulting holocaust was rivaled only by that at Hiroshima five months later. The Japanese had dispersed their manufacturing into private homes in residential neighborhoods so as to avoid detection. Not knowing where to bomb in order to target Japanese industrial capacity, the United States made the decision to destroy entire Japanese cities with firebombing. In the Tokyo bombing, sixteen square miles of densely populated Tokyo were destroyed, resulting in the deaths of two hundred fifty thousand Japanese citizens in one night. The deaths in the firebombing of Tokyo would exceed those produced by either atomic bomb. Another two hundred fifty thousand Japanese citizens would die in American firebombing of other Japanese cities, so that a total of over half a million Japanese would die in the incendiary bombings. Some historians later condemned the attacks as atrocities, but there was little protest in the United States at the time. From Pearl Harbor to the Japanese surrender, the dominant view of the Japanese in America was one that considered the Japanese to be

▶ The United States made the decision to destroy entire Japanese cities with firebombing. In the Tokyo bombing, sixteen square miles of densely populated Tokyo were destroyed, resulting in the deaths of two hundred fifty thousand Japanese citizens in one night.

treacherous vermin, almost subhuman, and certainly deranged and evil. The image was reinforced by the surprise attack at Pearl Harbor while Japanese diplomats were pretending to negotiate in Washington, the fighting to the last man mentality in the island-hopping campaign, the Bataan Death March, deplorable Japanese treatment of POWs, and the kamikaze attacks. Therefore, there was little remorse over the killing of such enemy civilians.

Even as fierce fighting continued in the Philippines, the Americans invaded Okinawa, close to the home islands. Once again, as at Tarawa in the Gilberts and Iwo Jima in the Bonins, the Japanese dug in and fought virtually to the last man, while Kamikaze hurled their planes at the Americans, sinking thirty-four ships of the invading fleet. By the end of the campaign in June 1945, some one hundred ten thousand Japanese had died on Okinawa. Fewer than eight thousand had been taken prisoner. The forty-nine thousand American casualties were the heaviest of any engagement in the Pacific theater and a grisly prefiguring of the costs to be expected from the contemplated assault on the Japanese home islands.

Atomic Bomb and Surrender

That dreaded encounter, however, never came. At 8:15 A.M. on August 6, 1945, a lone B-29, the Enola Gay, dropped a single atomic bomb ("Little Boy") on the industrial city of Hiroshima. Hiroshima was chosen because it was one of the few major Japanese cities that had not yet been fire bombed by the United States. The tremendous blast waves, fire waves, and radiation leveled sixty percent of the city and killed over seventy thousand people outright; ten thousand more were never found. Another one hundred thousand people would die over the next year due to excessive exposure to radiation. Because the bewildered Japanese did not surrender immediately, a second nuclear bomb ("Fat Man") was dropped on Nagasaki on August 9, also with equally devastating consequences. Nagasaki was chosen actually as the bomber's fourth alternate target on August 9 because the first three cities on the pilot's list could not be found due to heavy cloud cover. Just before the pilot had to turn back due to low fuel supplies, he spotted Nagasaki through a hole in the clouds and released his deadly cargo. The bomb landed on the edge of town and was, therefore, less effective than the Hiroshima bomb. However, twenty-five thousand people died instantly, and another sixty thousand would eventually die of radiation and other injuries from the Nagasaki bomb. A day before, on August 8, the Soviet Union had fulfilled its promise by declaring war on Japan and invading Manchuria.

Japan's leaders, recognizing that their country faced certain destruction, convened their Diet and debated surrender. Given that the United States had dropped two atomic bombs in three days, and the Japanese had no way of knowing that the United States could not drop another bomb every three days (the United States expected another bomb to be ready in six weeks), the choice faced by the government was one of either surrender or suicide. Conservative hawks in the Japanese government favored continuation of the fight to the last man mentality under which the Japanese military had been operating throughout the war. Their opposition, however, reasoned that there was nothing honorable in continuing the fight since the United States had proven that they could kill every man, woman, and child in Japan with no casualties of their own. The Japanese government was deadlocked over the surrender decision, and Emperor Hirohito was asked to intervene and break the deadlock. The Emperor mournfully favored surrender; the Japanese government, heeding the emperor's pleas that no more lives be sacrificed, unconditionally surrendered on August 14 on the condition that Hirohito would nominally remain Emperor. The official surrender took place on September 2, aboard the battleship *Missouri* anchored in Tokyo Bay.

The story of the development of the nuclear bomb began in August 1939 when President Roosevelt received a letter from Albert Einstein informing him that the splitting (fission) of the nucleus of an atom of uranium seemed possible. The consequent release of energy, Ein-

▶ The atomic bombing of Nagasaki, Japan, on August 9, 1945, where twenty-five thousand people died instantly, and another sixty thousand would eventually die of radiation and other injuries.

stein wrote, would be enormous. In 1940, fearful that Nazi scientists might develop such a bomb, the administration began the Manhattan Project, under the direction of Robert Oppenheimer, to try to beat the Germans to it. Working secretly in a squash court under the stands of the football stadium at the University of Chicago, a team of scientists under the direction of Leo Szilard, successfully constructed the first atomic pile in December 1942. Once it had been shown that a nuclear reaction could be controlled, the engineers took over—constructing plants at Oak Ridge, Tennessee, and Hanford, Washington, for the manufacture of materials needed for assembling a bomb. After more than $2 billion had been invested in the great gamble, the first test of the bomb took place successfully on July 16, 1945, in the desert outside Alamogordo, New Mexico.

In the "Trinity Test," as it was called, no one knew exactly what to expect. Physicist Enrico Fermi was taking bets that the bomb would create a chain reaction that would incinerate the atmosphere, a bet that would have been difficult to collect had he been correct. Fermi also estimated that the blast would be ten kilotons (equal to ten thousand tons of TNT); but after the blast, Fermi determined from measurements of blown scraps of paper he had placed on the ground that the blast was twenty kilotons. The blast turned much of the gypsum New Mexico sand near the epicenter into transparent glass-like crystals. Generals on the site had soldiers collect the crystals to make necklaces for their wives, not knowing that the crystals would be radioactive and deadly (Manhattan Project scientists quickly put a stop to this folly).

In spite of the size of the project, and the fact that literally thousands of people had been involved in the making of the bomb in one way or another, the secret of the project had been kept so well that Harry Truman did not learn of it until he became president upon Roosevelt's untimely death. At that point, Secretary of War Henry L. Stimson informed the former Missouri Senator of the Manhattan Project.

The job of building the bomb was so complicated and time-consuming that the two bombs used against Japan were the total world supply. Later it was learned that the Germans had lagged far behind the United States and Great Britain in the development of nuclear fission and probably would not have been able to construct a bomb for months or perhaps years. Not only had Hitler's racist policies driven brilliant Jewish scientists out of Germany, but Hitler had also diverted scientists from his nuclear and missile programs into less productive efforts. One was to develop a giant lens that could be used to incinerate England, as one would burn insects with a magnifying glass, and the other—a sophisticated bell that could be used to kill the British with sound. The bell project did make enough progress that the Germans could use it to kill mice in a bathtub; but in retrospect, it appears that Hitler should have diverted these scientists to his nuclear project. No matter who made the first bomb, however, once its devastating power had been released, the world could not be the same again. Thus, simultaneously with the coming of peace, the world entered the age of nuclear power—an age that would be at once an era of promise and of fear.

In the more than half century since the dropping of the bomb, historians and other American citizens have debated whether President Truman made the right decision when he authorized its use. It clearly ended the war with Japan sooner than might otherwise have been the case, thus saving an estimated one million American lives and perhaps five million Japanese—but at a fearful cost. Even some of the scientists who had developed it, most notably Leo

Szilard, were queasy about its use, urging that a bomb be dropped as a demonstration before being employed against human beings. Furthermore, many critics have questioned the necessity for the second bomb dropped on Nagasaki. Why not wait a little longer for the Japanese to respond? Others pointed out that the Japanese had sent peace delegations to Sweden and Moscow and argued that the United States might not have been able to negotiate surrender with Japan, if the Japanese had known about the bomb. These are issues of more than academic interest, especially in the early twenty-first century when the question of nuclear proliferation is so consequential.

Truman, who ultimately had the final decision on the bomb, decided against any such demonstration because such a demonstration would remove the element of surprise; and Truman believed "surprise" was necessary for maximum psychological impact. Furthermore, Truman believed that it would be embarrassing to the United States if the bomb used in any such demonstration were a dud; such a disaster could only prolong the war. Truman also believed that the damage to the Japanese caused by the bomb would provide better leverage against the Russians in post-war negotiations. As to whether or not the bomb should be used at all, Truman never seriously considered that. Truman believed that the bomb could and should be used just like any other weapon that had been developed. The use of the bomb, Truman believed, could shorten the war and ultimately save lives, both American and Japanese.

Although it is true that the Japanese had already sent peace delegations to Sweden and Moscow before the atomic bombs were dropped, the fact that the Japanese Diet was deadlocked over the decision to surrender after the United States dropped the bombs suggests that the Japanese were not going to be persuaded by a nonmilitary demonstration. Those that favored peace in Japan were not the majority as of August 6. After the surrender decision, there was a rash of suicides in Japan among the hawkish members of the government and the top Japanese military leaders. For these men, incineration by atomic bomb may have been preferable to the disembowelment they ultimately experienced at their own hands.

Chapter Review 26

Summary

Americans generally favored isolationism during the interwar period; however, this would gradually change throughout the 1930s as Japan, Italy, and Germany became expansionist under right-wing dictators. Japan began World War II in the Pacific with an invasion of Manchuria in 1931 designed to remedy Japan's deficiencies in food, fuel, and precious metals. The U.S. and the League of Nations denounced the aggression but did little immediately. President Roosevelt would gradually steer the U.S. on a collision course with Japan by aiding China in its war against Japan and imposing a trade "quarantine" and eventual embargo on Japan. To end the embargo, FDR demanded that Japan pull out of China, which Japan could not do without losing face.

Simultaneously, Italy invaded Abyssinia in 1935; and the United States responded with two Neutrality Acts that prevented the sale of military goods to belligerents, warned Americans not to travel abroad, and established a cash and carry policy on the trade of nonmilitary goods with belligerents. The U.S. did, however, continue to sell oil, a nonmilitary good, to Italy while they were at war in Abyssinia.

The larger threat on the European continent, however, was in Germany where Adolf Hitler's far-right National Socialist Party, or "Nazis," won a plurality in elections to the German Bundestag in 1933. Hitler was named chancellor. Hitler quickly began rearming Germany and acting on the goals he had outlined in *Mein Kampf*. Hitler sought to make Germany self-sufficient in food and fuel, unite all the German people, give the German people more territory or "living space," and purge Germany of Jewish traitors.

Beginning in 1936 when Hitler moved his army into the Rhineland, he was able to annex most of the areas of Europe with predominantly German populations, including Austria and the Sudetenland, and then the rest of Czechoslovakia. Hitler coveted, also, Northwestern Poland. When it was not handed to him diplomatically, he invaded, thus bringing war declarations from France and England against Germany.

The U.S. was neutral, but anti-Nazi, and aided the British with supplies and what eventually became an undeclared naval war on Germany by the summer of 1941. Germany would declare war on the U.S. on December 11, 1941, four days after Japan bombed Pearl Harbor to drag the U.S. into the war in the Pacific. Germany had over-run Western Europe between April 9 and June 22, 1940, and Britain stood alone for a year in Europe against Germany. Hitler, however, was unable to defeat Britain and in June 1941 opened the war on two fronts with an invasion of the Soviet Union.

The German army in the east would be stopped in October 1941 by the brutal Russian winter and then lose six hundred thousand troops the next year in a siege of Stalingrad, from which they would never recover.

In the Pacific, Japan won all of the battles the first six months of 1942 including conquest of eleven thousand American troops on the Philippines who were then subjected to a sixty-mile death march across the Bataan Peninsula. The Japanese advance was stopped, however, in May 1942 at the Coral Sea, and Japan's navy was so devastated a month later at Midway that Japan would lose all remaining major battles of World War II. The U.S. would island-hop its way across the Pacific with amphibious assaults on strategic Japanese islands until the United States took Saipan (from which it could bomb Japan daily). Essentially, the Japanese fought to the last man in every encounter, making the Pacific theater a very bloody one.

In the European theater, although Stalin clamored for a Western front immediately in 1942, the U.S. did not engage the enemy on the ground for almost a year when it invaded North Africa in November 1942. The campaign was more difficult than expected, taking six months, and caused a delay in the opening of a Western front. Meanwhile, the Allies landed on the Italian mainland on September 3, 1943; and Italy surrendered, though the country was not secured by the Allies until 1945, due to a large contingent of German troops in Italy.

Finally, the Allies invaded Normandy, France, on June 6, 1944, in the largest military invasion in history. The Allies advanced along a general front and were slowed by Hitler's counterattack in the Battle of the Bulge. However, control of the air was decisive. Eisenhower stopped the U.S. advance at the Elbe River to allow the Soviets to take Berlin and avoid high casualties. Hitler committed suicide April 30, 1945, and Germany surrendered May 8. Meanwhile, the Allies uncovered Hitler's attempt to systematically kill all of Europe's Jews.

With Germany defeated, the U.S. firebombed Japan daily in preparation for an invasion while Japan fought back with deadly kamikaze attacks. The leaders of the Big Three met at Potsdam on July 16; they outlined how the postwar world would be managed and agreed to try high-ranking Nazis as war criminals. On August 6 and August 9, 1945, the U.S. dropped atomic bombs on Hiroshima and Nagasaki. The Japanese Diet was deadlocked in a debate over surrender; Emperor Hirohito broke the deadlock, choosing surrender. Japan surrendered September 2 aboard the USS *Missouri;* but Japan was allowed to keep Hirohito as a symbolic emperor. The deadliest war in human history was over.

Chronological Time Line

1924 Hitler worte *Mein Kampf* while serving time in prison for his role in a failed Putsch.

1931 September 19, Japan invaded Manchuria.

1933 Adolph Hitler's National Socialists won a plurality in elections to Germany's Parliament, and on January 30, Hitler became chancellor.

1933 The U.S. recognized the Soviet Union.

1933 International Conference of American States in Montevideo, Uruguay

1933 Japan withdrew from the League of Nations.

Chapter Review (cont'd)

Time Line (cont'd)

1933 October, Hitler withdraws Germany from the League of Nations and the Geneva Disarmament Conference.

1934 Reciprocal Trade Act of 1934 that authorized the president to take the initiative in lowering tariffs on a reciprocal basis up to 50 percent with any country.

1935 October, Mussolini's Italy invades Abyssinia (Ethiopia).

1935 Neutrality Act of 1935 prohibits the sale of military goods to belligerents and warns American citizens to travel at their own risk.

1936–1939 Spanish Civil War eventually won by the fascist forces of Francisco Franco.

1936 In November, Germany, Italy, and Japan formed the Rome-Berlin-Tokyo Axis.

1936 On March 7, Hitler militarily occupied the Rhineland.

1937 In May, the Neutrality Act of 1937 imposed arms embargoes against belligerents, forbade the use of U.S. ships in trade with belligerents, and required that belligerents pay cash for U.S. goods.

1937 Japan invaded five more Chinese provinces.

1937 October, FDR announced a quarantine of Japan.

1937 On December 12, Japanese planes bombed the U.S. gunboat *Panay* and three Standard Oil tankers in China, killing two Americans and wounding thirty.

1938 In March, Hitler annexed Austria.

1938 Munich Conference: Edouard Dalodier of France and Neville Chamberlain of England awarded Hitler the Sudetenland with Hitler's promise of no further expansion.

1939 March: Hitler moved his army into the rest of Czechoslovakia.

1939 April: Mussolini invaded Albania.

1939 August: Non-Aggression Pact was signed between the Soviet Union and Nazi Germany.

Time Line (cont'd)

1939	On September 1, Germany invaded Poland, beginning World War II in Western Europe.
1940	March: the Soviet Union completed its military operations in taking over Finland, Latvia, Estonia, and Lithuania.
1940	On April 9, Germany invaded Denmark and Norway.
1940	On June 22, France fell to Nazi Germany.
1940	August: Germany launched an air war on Britain.
1940	On September 2, FDR traded fifty overage destroyers to England for bases in the Western Hemisphere.
1940	September: Germany, Italy, and Japan formed a military alliance.
1940	November: FDR was reelected over Republican Wendell Willkie.
1941	On March 11, U.S. began lend-lease with England.
1941	April: FDR ordered the navy to help the British locate German submarines.
1941	On June 22, Hitler launched his invasion of the Soviet Union.
1941	July: American troops were ordered to Iceland to protect it against a possible German invasion.
1941	July: U.S. imposed an oil embargo on Japan.
1941	On August 15, Roosevelt and Churchill agreed, in the Atlantic Charter, that their mutual goals included the final destruction of Nazi Germany.
1941	September: FDR issued orders to shoot German submarines on sight.
1941	On September 6, Japan decided on war with the U.S. if U.S. aid to China did not end in six weeks.
1941	October: German Army was halted on the Eastern Front by severe winter weather.

Chapter Review (cont'd)

Time Line (cont'd)

1941 On December 7, Japanese torpedo planes bombed Pearl Harbor.

1941 On December 8, the U.S. declared war on Japan.

1941 On December 8, Japan attacked Hong Kong, Guam, Borneo, and the Maylay Peninsula.

1941 On December 11, Germany declared war on the U.S.

1942 April 18: Doolittle's raid dropped bombs on Tokyo.

1942 May 6: U.S. forces surrendered in the Philippines.

1942 May 4–8: Japanese advance was halted in the Battle of the Coral Sea.

1942 June 4–7: Japanese were defeated at the Battle of Midway.

1942 August 7–November 14: Battle of Guadalcanal.

1942 November 8: American forces invaded North Africa.

1943 January: Roosevelt and Churchill met at Casablanca.

1943 On February 2, six hundred thousand German troops surrendered at Stalingrad.

1943 May: German troops in North Africa were defeated.

1943 July 9–August 17: Allied invasion of Sicily

1943 On September 3, Allies invaded Italian mainland and Italy's government surrendered.

1943 November 28–December 1: Teheran, first face-to-face meeting between Churchill, Stalin, and Roosevelt

1944 January 27: Siege at Leningrad was lifted after 872 days.

1944 June 4: Allies took Rome.

Time Line (cont'd)

1944	June 6: D-Day invasion of Normandy, France
1944	August 25: Paris was liberated by Allied troops.
1944	October 23–26: Battle of Leyte Gulf, Philippines, was the largest naval battle in history and the first use of kamikazes.
1944	November: Roosevelt defeated Thomas Dewey to win his fourth presidential term.
1944	On November 17, the U.S. began bombings of Japan from Saipan.
1944	On December 16, Germans launched the offensive known as the Battle of the Bulge.
1944	December 20–27: German siege of Bastogne
1945	February 4–11: Conference of the Big 3 at Yalta
1945	On March 26, Iwo Jima fell to the United States.
1945	On April 30, Hitler committed suicide in his bunker.
1945	On May 8, Germany surrendered (V-E Day).
1945	On June 21, Okinawa fell to the U.S. after an 81-day battle.
1945	July 16–August 2: Potsdam Conference
1945	July 16: Trinity Test at Alamogordo, New Mexico, first atomic explosion.
1945	On August 6, B-29 *Enola Gay* dropped the atomic bomb on Hiroshima.
1945	On August 9, B-29 dropped the atomic bomb on Nagasaki.
1945	On September 2, Japan surrendered on USS *Missouri.*

Chapter Review (cont'd)

Key Terms

Manchuria: Northeastern Chinese province was invaded by Japan in 1931.
Stimson Nonrecognition Doctrine: The U.S. would not recognize governments established by force.
Manchuko: Puppet government established by Japan in Manchuria.
Mein Kampf: Hitler's book in which he outlines his plans for Germany and World War II
Anschluss: Hitler's annexation of all of the areas of Europe that were German in ethnicity
Lebensraum: "Living Space" that Hitler planned to acquire militarily for the German people
Dolchstoss Myth: The "backstab myth" that Germany was not really defeated in World War I, but betrayed by treacherous Jews
Montevideo Conference: 1933 conference of American states in Uruguay where the U.S. agreed not to interfere in the affairs of other states
Isolation: The idea that the United States should not get involved in foreign affairs
Neutrality Acts: Acts of Congress in 1935 and 1937 that prevented the U.S. from selling arms to belligerents, warned Americans to travel abroad at their own risk, and established a "cash and carry" policy for the trade of nonmilitary goods with belligerents
Francisco Franco: The fascist general that became the dictator of Spain in 1939 after a three-year civil war
Rome-Berlin-Tokyo Axis: Alliance between Italy, Germany, and Japan
Quarantine of Japan: Effectively, an embargo, but FDR used the word quarantine since it is not recognized under International Law.
Panay Incident: Japanese planes bombed an American gunboat and three Standard Oil tankers in China, killing two and wounding thirty.
Munich Conference: Later condemned as "appeasement," Hitler was granted the Sudetenland by Chamberlain and Dalodier in return for a promise of no further expansion.
Nazi-Soviet Pact: Non-Aggression Pact between Hitler and Stalin in August 1939 that allowed the two dictators to divide Poland between them
Blitzkrieg: "Lightning War" that consisted of rapid armored advance with massive air support
The "Phony War": The period that consisted of little fighting between the fall of Poland in October 1939 and April 9, 1940 when Hitler attacked Western Europe
Maginot Line: French defenses on the German border consisting of underground bunkers, stationary guns, and underground railroads
Dunkirk: Site where the British army was saved by a civilian flotilla in June, 1940
"No Transfer" Resolution: The American resolution that colonies owned by fallen countries would not be transferred to the conquering powers
America First Committee: Isolationist conservatives in the U.S. that opposed the U.S. entry into World War II
Wendell Willkie: Republican presidential candidate in 1940
Lend-Lease: Policy under which the U.S. would lend or lease arms to any nation vital to the defense of the U.S.

Key Terms (cont'd)

Atlantic Charter: Roosevelt and Churchill agreed that their ultimate goal was the destruction of Nazi Germany.

Hemispheric Defense: An undeclared naval war on Germany in 1941

Hideki Tojo: Japan's militaristic head of government during World War II

Pearl Harbor: Site of the Japanese surprise attack on America on December 7, 1941

Bataan Death March: Sixty mile march across the Bataan Peninsula by captured American soldiers who were abused and tortured by the Japanese

Island Hopping: The American Pacific strategy that included a series of amphibious invasions of strategic Pacific islands

Battle of Midway: Generally considered the turning point in the Pacific in June 1942, after which Japan would lose all of the battles

Erwin Rommel: Germany's "Desert Fox" that commanded Germany's campaign in North Africa

General George S. Patton: American general in command in the North Africa campaign and Sicily and who also rescued American troops at Bastogne

Stalingrad: The turning point on the Eastern Front where Germany lost six hundred thousand soldiers after a six month siege of the city

Vichy France: The French state under occupation and control by the Nazis

Teheran: Site of the first Big 3 Conference

Casablanca: January 1943 meeting between Churchill and Roosevelt where they agreed that their war aims included the unconditional surrender of Germany.

James F. Byrnes: Secretary of State under Harry Truman that favored using the atomic bomb to bully the Soviet Union

Fred Korematsu: Japanese-American that filed a lawsuit challenging his internment.

Executive Order 8802: FDR's 1942 order interning the Japanese-Americans on the West Coast into concentration camps in the interior

D-Day: Allied invasion of France on June 6, 1944, the largest military invasion in history

Battle of the Bulge: Hitler's offensive of December 1944 that broke through the American lines in a push toward the Allied fuel depot at Antwerp, Belgium

Holocaust: The attempted genocide by Adolph Hitler of Europe's Jewish population that led to the death of 14 million people and 90 percent of Europe's Jews.

Yalta Conference: Conference of the Big 3 in the Crimean Peninsula where the fate of postwar Europe was discussed and Stalin agreed to join the war against Japan ninety days after the defeat of Germany

May 8, 1945: Germany surrendered (VE Day).

United Nations: New organization that was established by fifty nations to manage international affairs and maintain the peace.

Chapter Review (cont'd)

Key Terms (cont'd)

Potsdam: Site of Big 3 Conference in the summer of 1945 where Germany and Berlin were to be divided into four zones to be administered by the conquering powers and high ranking Nazis were to be tried as war criminals.

Trinity Test: First successful detonation of an atomic bomb at Alamogordo, New Mexico, on July 16, 1945

Hiroshima: City devastated by the first atomic bomb attack on August 6, 1945

Nagasaki: City devastated by the second atomic bomb attack on August 9, 1945

Pop Quiz

Chapter 26

1. What did Hitler argue in *Mein Kampf*?
   a. The cause of instability in the world was the evil regime in Iraq.
   b. Germany could invade Iraq and bring about regime change.
   c. A new regime in Iraq after a German invasion could bring democracy and peace to the entire Middle East.
   d. None of the above

2. Nationalist Republicans opposed which of the following?
   a. recognition of the Soviet Union
   b. the World Court
   c. free trade
   d. all of the above

3. Which of the following occurred under Hitler's policy of Anschluss?
   a. Germany annexed Austria.
   b. Germany demilitarized.
   c. Germany passed a law granting equal rights to all.
   d. Germany withdrew from East Prussia.

Pop Quiz (cont'd)

4. Congress passed the ___________ ___________ program in 1941 that allowed Britain to buy war equipment and pay for it after the war.
   a. Cash-and-carry
   b. Atlantic Charter
   c. Munich
   d. Lend-Lease

5. The war aims of the Allies were established in the ___________.
   a. Pact of Steel
   b. Atlantic Charter
   c. Munich Pact
   d. Charter of the United Nations

6. Why did Hitler declare war on the U.S. on December 11, 1941?
   a. He was secretly working with the Japanese in the Pearl Harbor attack.
   b. He was obligated under the Pact of Steel he signed with Japan.
   c. He hated American freedom and democracy.
   d. He believed it would allow him to attack British shipping without restraint, cut off British supplies, and thus defeat England.

7. What did American soldiers discover on Guadalcanal?
   a. Japanese soldiers lacked the will to fight.
   b. Japanese soldiers refused to surrender and essentially fought to the last man.
   c. The U.S. would need housing for thousands of Japanese prisoners.
   d. The war would be very one-sided since the Japanese fought with swords instead of guns.

8. The largest invasion in history was on D-Day (June 6, 1944) at __________.
   a. Sicily
   b. Casablanca
   c. Normandy, France
   d. Okinawa

Chapter Review (cont'd)

Pop Quiz (cont'd)

9. At the Yalta Conference all of the following were agreed to EXCEPT:
   a. The Soviets would declare war on Japan.
   b. Stalin agreed to join the United Nations.
   c. The U.S. would recognize Russia's "special interest" in Eastern Europe.
   d. The U.S. would share atomic bomb information with the Soviets.

10. Which of the following is true of the Japanese surrender?
    a. Japan surrendered immediately after the U.S. dropped two atomic bombs on Japan.
    b. The Japanese cabinet was deadlocked over the decision to continue or surrender after the U.S. dropped two atomic bombs.
    c. Emperor Hirohito was asked to break the deadlock and decided on surrender.
    d. Both b and c

11. Franklin Roosevelt apparently knew in advance of the Japanese attack on Pearl Harbor. T F

12. One consequence of World War II was the growth of women in the workforce. T F

13. The Soviet Union lost more than __________ million people during the war.

14. The two Japanese cities hit by atomic bombs in 1945 were __________ and __________.

15. In a 1937 speech Franklin Roosevelt called for a __________ of aggressor nations.

1. D	6. D	11. F	14. Hiroshima
2. D	7. B	12. T	Nagasaki
3. A	8. C	13. 28	15. Quarantine
4. A	9. D		
5. B	10. D		

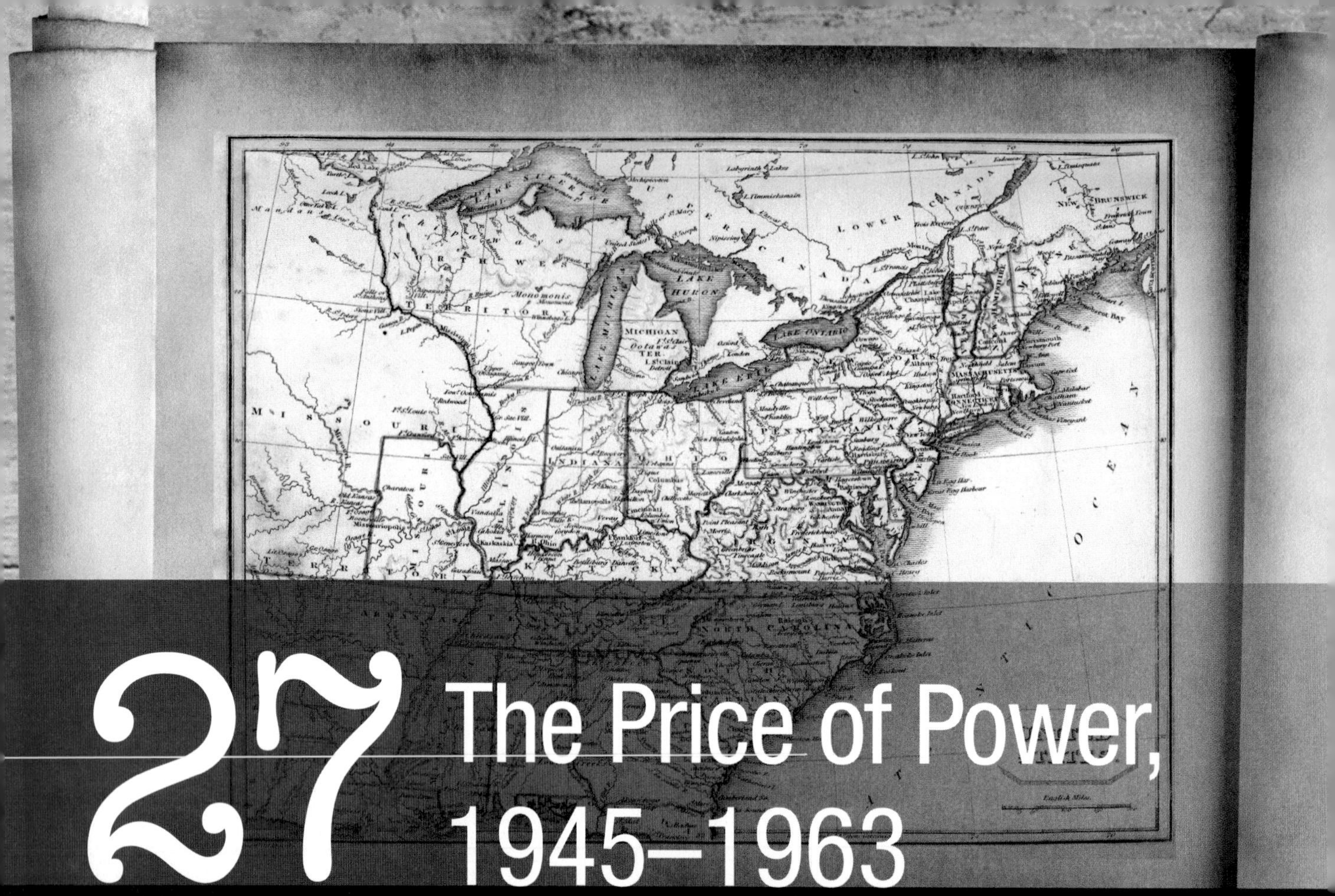

27 The Price of Power, 1945–1963

Chapter Objectives

From Peace to Cold War

The Economic Problems of Reconversion

Truman Versus a Republican Congress

Soviet Expansionism

The Problem of Germany

The Containment Policy

The Truman Doctrine

The Marshall Plan

NATO

The Asian Revolution

The Overthrow of Colonialism

The Victory of Chinese Communism

The Democrats Stay In

The Miracle of 1948

The Fair Deal

The Outbreak of the Korean War

The Effects of the Korean War

The End of the Korean Fighting

The Great Fear

The Rise and Fall of McCarthy

A Republican Interlude

The Election of 1952

The First Eisenhower Administration

The Election of 1956

Working with Democrats

Sputnik and the Race to Catch Up

America's Space Program

The Military Impact of Sputnik

A New ERA in Foreign Affairs

The Death of Stalin

Middle East: Israel

Iranian Crisis

Crisis in the Middle East:

The Hungarian Revolt

Latin America

Guatemala and the Overthrow of Arbenz

The U-2 Incident

Troubles with Castro

The Election of 1960

The Kennedy Administration

Limited Success with Congress

Losses and Gains in Foreign Affairs

Operation Mongoose

Cuban Missile Crisis

The Assassination of President Kennedy

The Legacy of the Kennedy Administration

From Peace to Cold War

The surrender of Japan, soon after the dropping of the two nuclear bombs in August 1945, caught most Americans, in and out of government, by surprise. Since the Nazi defeat in April, the army and the navy had been readying the great military machine for the final assault upon the Japanese home islands. Yet within weeks after the Japanese surrender, the dismantling of the military establishment, built up over four years of war, had begun. Public clamor to "bring the boys home" was insistent throughout the remainder of 1945. By January 1946, the government was discharging members of the armed forces at the rate of thirty-five thousand a day. By the end of 1946, the military establishment was down to one-fifth of wartime strength.

Simultaneously with the discharge of soldiers, the government began the cancellation of war contracts; and within a month after the surrender of Japan, $35 billion worth were dropped. The end of war contracts and the glutting of the labor market with discharged veterans seemed, to many, to presage a severe depression, but billions of dollars of personal savings and the rapid transition from war needs to peacetime production made things turn out otherwise. Inflation, instead, became the principal problem in the ensuing years as American manufacturing struggled to keep up with consumer demand.

The Economic Problems of Reconversion

The ending of overtime work at war plants and the upward movement of prices provoked organized labor into a wave of strikes in 1945 and 1946. In October 1945, for example, the number of worker days lost through strikes doubled over that of September. Lost workdays continued to rise; all told, about 4.5 million workers went out on strike in 1946. Since the strikes were usually for increased wages, the federal government ran into difficulties trying to hold the line on prices. Demands by Congress and the public for tax reductions also increased pressure on prices. In November 1945, Congress cut income taxes by some $9 billion and repealed the wartime excess-profits tax as an inducement to increased production.

Nevertheless, the big issues of 1946 were prices and labor unrest. The Truman administration tried to hold the line on prices by continuing wartime price controls; but businessmen, most Republicans, and other large sectors of the population were anxious to remove all wartime restrictions. The results were inadequate price-control legislation and a steadily rising price curve. Americans attempted to spend their wartime savings in a marketplace that had experienced shortages of consumer goods during the war, and their demands for consumer goods outstripped the capacity of American industry to produce them.

With the election of a Republican Congress in November 1946, the Truman administration gave up and abolished virtually all controls over prices. Nevertheless, shortages of all kinds of goods persisted with the result that prices in 1947 continued to reach new heights almost every month. Despite the high prices, or perhaps because of them, employment remained high and business activity good. Undoubtedly many workers, especially unorganized labor and white-collar workers, suffered from the steady increase in the cost of living; but the country as a whole enjoyed a post-war boom.

▶ Harry S. Truman

In February 1946, before it was clear that a boom would shape the postwar era, Congress passed the Employment Act, which placed responsibility upon the federal government for the prevention of mass unemployment and economic depression in the aftermath of the war. Although no specific measures were spelled out in that act (because of the need to win conservative support), it did create the Council of Economic Advisors to the president. In a sense, the Employment Act was a reflex from the days of the Great Depression and demonstrated the continuing effect of the New Deal revolution.

Truman Versus a Republican Congress

Opposition to price controls, support of labor control bills, and demand for tax reductions marked a rising conservative tide across the country and in the Congress. This conservatism was clearly reflected in the congressional elections of 1946. Brandishing the slogan "Had Enough?" the Republicans elected majorities in both houses for the first time since 1928. First on the agenda of the new Eightieth Congress was legislation to control labor unions, which since the end of the war had been disrupting the economy with nationwide strikes. Earlier in 1946 Truman had vetoed a severe anti-labor law, even though he had threatened to draft rail workers into the army when beset by a national railroad strike in May 1946. In June 1947, the new Republican Congress under the leadership of conservative Senator Robert A. Taft passed the Labor-Management Relations, or Taft-Hartley Act. Truman returned the bill with a stinging veto message, but Congress quickly overrode his veto.

The Taft-Hartley Act attempted to meet two public complaints against labor. In an effort to deal with nationwide strikes that disrupted the economy, the act empowered the president to force a union to accept a sixty-day "cooling-off period" before striking. If at the end of the cooling-off period the dispute was not settled, the employer's last offer would have to be presented to the workers for a secret vote. The act was also intended to reverse the alleged favoritism of New Deal legislation toward labor by listing a number of unfair union practices. It banned the closed shop (the requirement that employees join unions), permitted employers to sue unions for broken contracts or strike damages, required unions to make their financial statements public, forbade union contributions to political campaigns, limited the "check off" system whereby employers collected union dues, and required union leaders to take oaths that they were not Communists. Despite the opposition of labor organizations and of many liberal Democrats, the Taft-Hartley Act has remained unchanged, a measure of the American people's conviction in the postwar era that national labor unions, like business, need some kind of public control.

Although Truman and the Republican Eightieth Congress rarely agreed on domestic policies, they often did agree on defense and foreign policies. Both Truman and the Republican Congress were staunchly anti-communist and would quickly begin waging a war against communism with vigor. Truman and Congress also agreed to reorganize the armed forces. The army, navy, and air force were merged into the Department of Defense under the National Security Act of July 1947. James V. Forrestal, former Secretary of the Navy, was named the first Secretary of Defense.

Soviet Expansionism

Even before the Potsdam Conference in July 1945, there had been signs that the Allied unity displayed at Yalta was superficial. Before his death, for example, Roosevelt had warned Stalin that the Yalta agreements concerning Poland must not be ignored. Stalin's initial refusal to send Foreign Minister Molotov to the United Nations conference in April 1945 also aroused Western suspicions of Russian intentions about the postwar world. Meanwhile, the abrupt end of Lend-Lease in early May (after the fall of Germany) raised doubts in Russian minds about Western friendship, even though Truman reinstated a scaled-down version of Lend-Lease to placate the Soviets after their vehement protests. At Potsdam Stalin insisted on having his way in Poland and with German reparations, which the Russians considered imperative for the rebuilding of their devastated country. In Poland, Stalin refused to allow free elections because he knew that they would have resulted in the election of the Polish government-in-exile, in London, which would oppose Stalin's control. Stalin was also determined to render Germany powerless since they had twice invaded the Soviet Union in less than a quarter century. The British, in contrast, wanted a strong Germany allied with the West as a check on Soviet expansionism.

During the last half of 1945 and most of 1946, at the United Nations and at meetings of the Council of Foreign Ministers to draw up peace treaties with the lesser enemy states, the West and the Soviet Union clashed repeatedly; each viewed the other as increasingly threatening or uncooperative. Obviously the two sides had different security concerns and differing views of the future of Europe—especially of Germany. The Soviets also protested unilateral United States control of Japan and favored Soviet involvement through the United Nations. The matter was essentially solved when Secretary of State Byrnes agreed to recognize Soviet control in Romania and Bulgaria, in return for Russian acceptance of the United States role in Japan.

Particularly ominous for the peace of the postwar world was the Soviet Union's refusal to withdraw its troops from Iran, which the Russians and the British had jointly occupied during the war. Only vigorous protests by the United States and the United Nations impelled a Russian withdrawal in late May 1946. To the Russians the important point was that they had withdrawn under pressure. To the West, and particularly the Americans, it was the necessity to threaten the Russians that was significant. Two months later, in early August, the Soviets demanded slices of Turkish territory and a share in the control of the Dardanelles. To many Western observers Russian behavior announced a resurgence of historic czarist ambitions.

Actually, Soviet conquests already far exceeded any dreams of the czars. Russian armies stood as far west as Berlin and central Germany, and all of Eastern Europe lay under their control. Indeed, throughout the 40s and early 50s it was the presence of large Russian armies in central Europe, at a time when the West had long since demobilized its wartime forces, that sustained the suspicions and aroused the fears of Western leaders. Today the likelihood of a Russian military advance against Western Europe seems nonexistent, but to a generation that had seen Russian power move west against Hitler, that likelihood was ever present.

Moreover, although Yugoslavia was not occupied by Russian troops, it had become firmly Communist under the leadership of Marshal Tito. Indeed, in 1946 Tito was more truculent in his dealings with the West than was Stalin himself. The same month that the Soviets served their demands upon Turkey, Tito's planes on two different occasions shot down unarmed American transport planes which had accidentally crossed the Yugoslav frontier. It was Yugoslavia, not Russia, which was supplying Communist-led guerrillas fighting the British-dominated Greek Monarchy in a civil war that erupted in Greece following World War II.

Churchill, now out of office because of a Labour Party victory, gave voice to the concern of the Western nations. At Fulton, Missouri, on March 5, 1946, with President Truman sitting conspicuously on the platform, Churchill called attention to the "iron curtain" which "has descended across the continent" from "Stettin in the Baltic to Trieste in the Adriatic." Moreover, he went on, "Nobody knows what Soviet Russia and its Communist international organization intends to do in the immediate future, or what are the limits, if any, to their expansive and proselytizing tendencies."

Meanwhile, the Soviets in the United Nations turned down the American plan for international control of nuclear energy. Since under the plan the United States would have voluntarily surrendered its monopoly of nuclear power, Americans took the Soviet rejection as another sign that the Soviets were not interested in peace and order in the world. The Russians, apparently, saw the American plan as a way of denying them their own nuclear bomb. On both sides, suspicions grew.

The Problem of Germany

The major European dispute between East and West concerned the future of Germany. In the view of the Western powers, particularly the United States, the revival of a united Germany had been agreed upon at Yalta and reaffirmed at Potsdam. Russian insistence upon large German reparations could only mean that Stalin intended to keep Germany weak and without hope of recovery for the foreseeable future. As a result, the Russians obtained very little in the way of reparations from the Western occupation zones, though in their own zone they carted eastward everything they could.

By the fall of 1946 Secretary of State James F. Byrnes was convinced that the Russians did not really want a reunited and independent Germany and were using the continued division of Germany as a means of impeding German recovery. He, therefore, persuaded the British to merge their zone with that of the Americans (The French, as skeptical of German unification as the Russians, did not join the other Western allies until 1949); however, in merging the Western zones, Byrnes was helping to divide Germany ever more decisively between East and West. Thus, in Germany as in the United Nations, the Cold War had obviously come into being by the end of 1946. Increasingly in the years ahead, West Germany (which became independent as the German Federal Republic in 1954) would be viewed by the West as the chief bulwark against Russian expansion into Western Europe, while the Soviet Union would see it as the chief threat to Russian hegemony in Eastern Europe.

The Containment Policy

In 1946, Stalin publicly asserted his confidence in the eventual triumph of the communist system. Stalin argued that communism and capitalism were on a collision course and that capitalism would be torn apart. Stalin further stated that the U.S.S.R. would do without consumer goods, if it needed to do so, in order to strengthen its military and ensure its own survival. In response, United States Supreme Court Justice William O. Douglas referred to Stalin's speech as the "Declaration of World War III." Meanwhile, Churchill reacted to the Stalin speech by arguing in his Fulton Missouri Speech that the United States and England must work together to "contain Soviet aggression."

For a time after World War II, it seemed that the Russians might well be in a position to extend their influence into Western as well as Eastern Europe. Economically and militarily prostrate from their struggles, the nations of Western Europe were in poor position to defend themselves against Soviet military force and subversion. In France and Italy, strong Communist parties seemed on the verge of taking power either through the ballot box or by force.

In Greece, Communist-led guerrillas fought pro-Western government forces for control of the country. Even Great Britain, presumably one of the principal victors of the war, was on the verge of bankruptcy. Economically bled, Britain could no longer sustain its traditional role as guardian of Greek independence. In February 1947, the British announced the imminent withdrawal of aid. In Turkey, too, an unstable government was being pressured by the Soviets for territorial grants and administrative concessions in the Dardanelles.

In Asia and Africa the steady drive for independence had already begun. With their lack of experience in democratic procedures and the difficulties of maintaining stability in the midst of poverty and strife, the new nations seemed ripe for Communist revolution or subversion—either of which, American leaders anticipated, would make them allies of the Russians.

The American response to this global Communist threat was the establishment and gradual implementation of the policy of "containment." As publicly announced in July 1947 in an article by State Department aide George F. Kennan, "The main element of any U.S. policy toward the Soviet Union must be that of a long-term, patient but firm and vigilant containment of Russian expansive tendencies." While accepting—though not happily—the accomplished fact of Soviet control over Eastern Europe, the policy of containment sought to hold the line against the further extension of Soviet power, military or political.

Kennan, in a document known as his "Long Telegram" and in his article "The Sources of Soviet Conduct," argued that the U.S.S.R. contained internal political and economic contradictions that it could not stand over the long haul. Consequently, if the United States would merely contain the U.S.S.R., it would eventually crumble from within due to the internal contradictions. Kennan argued that the U.S.S.R. was not a legitimate government to the people of the U.S.S.R. and, therefore, could only rule by massive coercion, which would take tremendous energy and be very expensive. The Soviet Union would, therefore, eventually burn itself out. Furthermore, Kennan argued that the Soviet economy was untenable, partially due to the command nature of the economy that ignored the demand-driven principle, and partially because the allocation of 15 percent of its resources to military purposes would cause serious consumer shortages and eventual economic collapse. Kennan expected containment to last no longer than twenty years, but he warned that the policy would be very expensive and that Americans would tire of the policy before it was over.

The same month that Kennan's article was published, Congress passed the National Security Act, which created the National Security Council to advise the president on domestic and foreign policy related to national security. The National Security Act also created the Central Intelligence Agency to gather and analyze intelligence. CIA activities were to include covert operations outside the country, including sabotage and subversion, as well as spreading untrue propaganda that would further American interests and undermine the interests of its enemies—primarily the Soviet Union.

The Truman Doctrine

Even before the containment policy was officially enunciated, the Truman administration had taken steps to stem the Communist advance. After much soul-searching and consultation with congressional leaders of both parties, President Truman urged the United States to take up the burden of aid to Greece and Turkey. In a historic address to Congress and the nation on March 12, 1947, he called for $400 million in economic and military aid for the two beleaguered countries to save them from "aggressive movements that seek to impose upon them totalitarian regimes." Liberals and left-wingers, who denounced his proposal as warmongering, and conservatives that protested its cost opposed Truman's proposal. All recognized that this "Truman Doctrine," pledging aid to nations resisting aggression or subversion, signaled a sharp departure from the entire previous practice of American foreign policy. For the first time in peace, the United States was being asked to commit its military might (though that part of the proposal was underplayed by the president) and economic power to the defense of countries outside the Western Hemisphere. George Kennan, the father of the containment policy, argued that the Truman Doctrine was "grandiose" and "sweeping" and might lead to a worldwide crusade that the United States was neither militarily nor economically prepared to support.

Nevertheless, Secretary of State Dean Acheson met with Congressional leaders and argued for United States aid to the imperiled Greek monarchy. Acheson argued that: "Like apples in a barrel infected by one rotten one, the corruption of Greece would infect Iran and all to the East." Although Acheson did not mention the word "domino," his speech was essentially the beginning of the "domino theory," which held that if one country fell to communism, others would also fall to communism, like "dominoes." Acheson argued that a communist victory in Greece would "open three continents to Soviet penetration." Acheson—"The major powers are now at Armageddon as the Soviet Union presses for advantage. Only the U.S. has the power to resist."

By votes of 67 to 23 in the Senate in April and 287 to 107 in the House in May, the Republican Congress sanctioned the new turn in foreign policy by voting the funds. Three hundred United States military and civilian advisors were sent to Greece to help the monarchy against the leftist rebels. Yugoslavia's Marshall Tito had aided the rebels, but Tito cut off aid to the Greek rebels in July of 1948. United States Navy planes dropped napalm on areas where the guerrillas were hiding in the Grecan Mountains; and the rebels were defeated. The Greek Monarchy upheld, and the first test of the policy of containment was a success.

The Marshall Plan

An immediate Soviet military invasion was not the greatest threat to Western Europe in the first postwar years. It was the legacy of war—persistent poverty, widespread misery, and mass unemployment—in which communism found its greatest ally, especially in countries like Italy and France, where economic and political instability was an open invitation to subversion. A strong possibility existed in both countries that Communist parties would be voted into power. Many in both countries viewed the Communists as the true patriots because the Communists, unlike the French and Italian right-wing elements, had never collaborated with the Nazis. If the capitalist economies failed, the Communists stood poised to seize power. Therefore, to stimulate European recovery and stave off communism, the Truman administration began plans for extending massive economic assistance. The idea—first suggested in a speech by Under Secretary of State Dean Acheson—was brought to the attention of the world, and Europe in particular, in a Harvard commencement address delivered by Secretary of State George C. Marshall on June 5, 1947.

Marshall's speech offered American economic aid to any European nation seriously interested in restoring the shattered economy of Europe, including those nations closely associated with Soviet Russia. The nations of Western Europe accepted with enthusiasm; however, Russia, after some preliminary exploration, compelled its allies to stay out of the scheme, suggesting that the Marshall Plan was a cover-up for American imperialistic designs. The proposal also evoked widespread opposition in the United States, from both the right and the left; but leading Republicans, notably Senator Arthur H. Vandenberg, championed it from the outset. Calling the idea a "calculated risk" to "help stop World War III before it starts," Vandenberg countered assertions that it was a gigantic "international WPA" or a "Socialist blueprint." As presented to Congress in December, the measure envisioned the expenditure of $17 billion over a four-year period, with $6.8 billion to be spent in the fifteen months following April 1, 1948.

During the fall and winter of 1947, the continued decline of the European economy and the many stories of starvation and misery in Western Europe gave substance to the argument for United States assistance. Equally influential, however, were the continued signs of Soviet pressure. For example, in February 1948 a Communist workers' coup thrust democratic Czechoslovakia behind the Iron Curtain, and in March reports of a Russian advance to the

West circulated among government officials. Furthermore, a Communist victory appeared to be a real possibility in the Italian elections coming up in April. Responding to these pressures and to others from an anxious administration, Congress, on April 2, 1948, passed the European Recovery Act, or Marshall Plan, granting to the president about 90 percent of the funds he had requested for the first year. Though Congress refused to commit the United States to anything thereafter, subsequent grants were made on an annual basis.

The full four-year plan was never carried out, however, because the Korean War intervened. However, the $12.5 billion extended to 16 western European countries achieved the purpose of reviving the European economy. Between 1948 and 1951 production in all the countries rose about 37 percent. With a more prosperous economy and resultant political stability, the internal threat of communism receded noticeably. The Marshall Plan also had the impact of boosting American exports since much of the money returned to the United States as Europeans purchased American consumer goods while their own manufacturing infrastructure was rebuilding. Moreover, the international cooperation fostered by the plan afforded the European nations a new insight into the advantages of closer economic union. That insight bore fruit in the 1950s with the formation of the European Coal and Steel Community and, later, the Common Market, or European Economic Community—leading eventually to the European Union.

NATO

In June 1948, the West established the West German Republic and introduced a new West German mark to curb the rapid inflation in Germany due to the flooding of the German market with Russian-made currency in East Germany. Stalin retaliated by cutting off land access to West Berlin from West Germany. Without outside aid, West Berlin would starve. Stalin also cut off electric power to West Berlin from power plants in East Berlin. Stalin issued the Warsaw Declaration, which demanded a return to the four-power division of Germany stipulated at Potsdam.

President Truman was influenced by the arguments of Presidential Counsel Clark Clifford, in what was known as the Clifford Memorandum, in which he argued that the United States must prepare for imminent atomic and biological warfare from the U.S.S.R. and that Soviet aggressions could be stopped only from counter-pressure from the United States. Consequently, Truman desired to implement "counter-pressure" against the Soviet action at Berlin. In considering courses of action, United States General Omar Bradley warned against a truck convoy of supplies to Berlin because the Soviet military in the region outnumbered NATO forces 3–1. Therefore, Bradley and the United States military commanders considered any such ground campaign to supply Berlin as unnecessarily risky. The dominant view was perhaps best expressed by Colonel Frank Howley, who argued, "We would have got our derrieres shot off." Faced with the prospect of a perhaps disastrous war if they forced their way overland to Berlin, the Western Allies instead instituted a gigantic airlift to fly in supplies and food. Over 2 million tons of supplies—over thirteen thousand tons a day—were airlifted to Berlin. Planes left for Berlin every three minutes and provided three times the amount of supplies needed to sustain the city. The food and supplies were flown to Berlin daily for over one year until May 1949, when Stalin lifted the blockade.

MAP 27.1 NATO and Eastern Europe

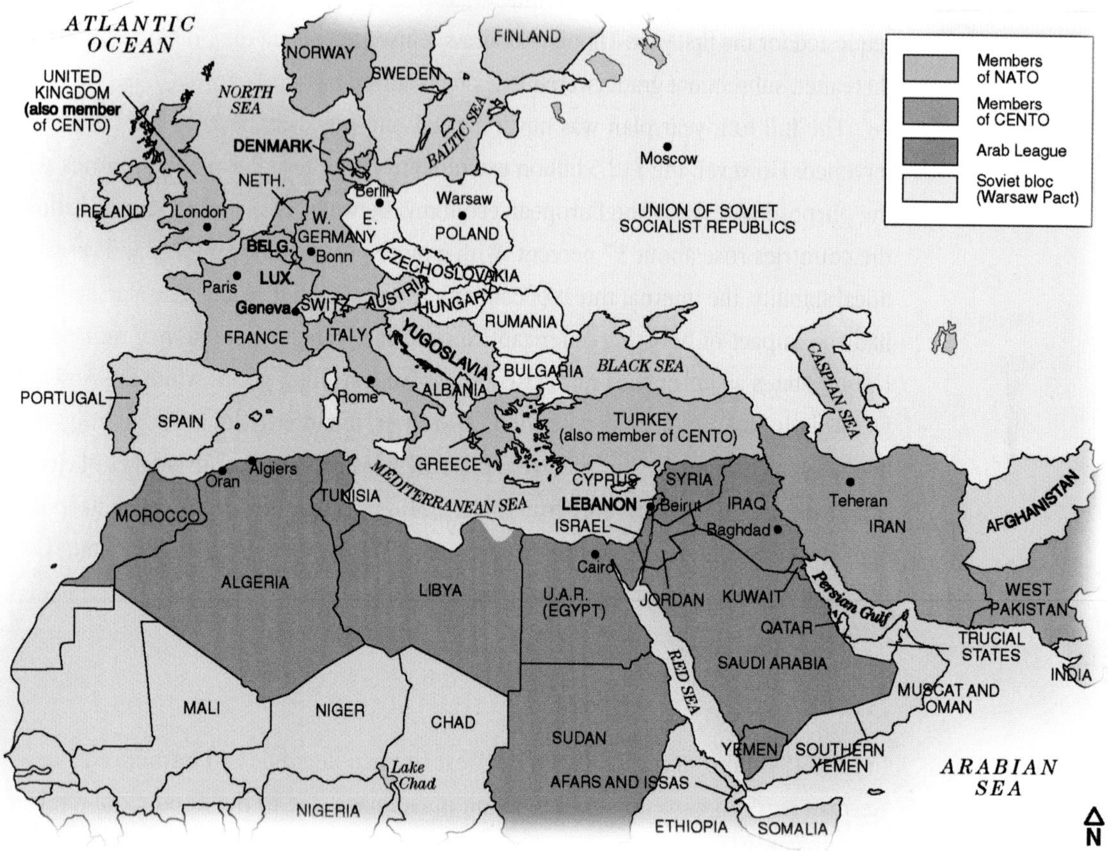

In the event that the airlift failed, Truman appeared prepared to resort to the atomic bomb. Truman secured Britain's permission to accept sixty B-29 bombers and declared to the press that they were "atomic capable" (they really weren't, and the United States did not even have sixty atomic bombs at the time). Although the Russians did not molest the airlift, they did not agree to end the blockade until May 1949. Meanwhile the airlift had proved its ability to both sustain the West Berliners and maintain the Western right of access to Berlin.

The Berlin blockade reinforced the American belief in the need for closer military cooperation among the western European nations. The Brussels Pact of March 1948 had already created a defensive alliance among Great Britain, France, Belgium, Luxembourg, and the Netherlands. Toward the end of 1948 the United States encouraged widening the Brussels Pact alliance to include other nations rimming the North Atlantic. In the spring of 1949, twelve countries, including Canada and the United States in the New World, joined the North Atlantic Treaty Organization, which in 1952 expanded to include Turkey and Greece and in 1955 West Germany.

With the signing of the treaty in April 1949, the United States obligated itself to come to the aid of the Europeans—the strongest commitment yet assumed in the course of the diplomatic revolution that had begun only four years earlier with the ratification of the United Nations Charter. The NATO treaty encountered only slight opposition in the Senate, which ratified it on July 21, 1949. Under the treaty, "an armed attack against one was considered an armed attack against all." The stated purpose of NATO was to maintain a ground

▶A C-54; During the Berlin Blockade it hauled coal and food supplies to West Berlin. Western Allies began using gigantic aircraft to airlift supplies and food to Western Germany when Stalin instituted the Berlin Blockade.The food and supplies—over thirteen thousand tons a day— were flown to Berlin daily for over a year until 1949, when Stalin lifted the blockade.

force in Europe large enough to hold off Soviet attack until the United States could engage the Strategic Air Command—in other words, nuclear bombers. In early 1951, General Dwight D. Eisenhower was appointed Supreme Commander of the new integrated NATO defense force to be fashioned out of the national armies of the twelve signatories.

Since the Soviet decision to blockade Berlin had been calculated to break the Western alliance, but had only made the alliance stronger, the Soviets called off their blockade in May 1949. The U.S.S.R. then countered NATO with the creation of the Warsaw Pact, a similar alliance between the U.S.S.R. and the states under its control in Eastern Europe. As it had been prior to World War I, Europe was again divided into two great opposing alliances.

The Asian Revolution

The Overthrow of Colonialism

If the results of the war in Europe dropped unexpected problems into the laps of Americans, the consequences of the war in Asia constituted a revolution. The great colonial powers, though victors in the war, lost virtually all their Asian possessions within five years after the defeat of the Japanese. (It should be mentioned that an end to colonialism might well have been seen as implicit in the Atlantic Charter of 1941). When the British returned to Malaya and Burma, the Dutch to the East Indies, and the French to Indochina, they were greeted with demands for independence and sometimes by open military rebellion.

One by one the European nations made the only reasonable response—granting independence to the former colonies and removing themselves from Asia. The United States, acting on a prewar promise, led the movement by granting final independence to the Philippines on July 4, 1946. Britain followed, finally reducing its once vast empire in Asia to a few pinpoints on the map, the most important of which was Hong Kong. Not all the European powers, however, recognized the shape of the future as clearly as Britain. The Dutch did not transfer power to the new nationalist government of the United States of Indonesia until 1949, and until 1954, the French sacrificed the flower of their officer corps and thousands of young men in a futile struggle to suppress the nationalist movement of the Viet Minh under their leader Ho Chi Minh in Indochina. The liquidation of colonialism was the first part of the Asian revolution.

The Transformation of Japan

The second part of the revolution in Asia was the American occupation of Japan. Although ostensibly representing all the Allied powers, General Douglas MacArthur, the American occupation commander, in reality was the supreme authority in that country, with his policy dictated by the United States. Aside from stripping Japan of all its colonies, including Formosa and Korea, the United States deliberately undertook to destroy the old Japan. Thoroughgoing land reform, which spread land ownership more widely than ever before, improved the lot of the peasantry. A new democratic constitution, in which the emperor was reduced from a god to a mere symbol of national unity, also removed the army from politics. In fact, Article IX of the Japanese Constitution eliminated the Japanese military for all purposes whatsoever, forever. Simultaneously, Japan signed a security treaty with the United States where the security of Japan became the exclusive responsibility of the United States. Women were enfranchised for the first time and given greater freedom in society and within the family. As Edwin O. Reischauer, an authority on Japanese history and ambassador to Japan under the Kennedy administration, once wrote: “During the early postwar years in Japan, MacArthur played the role not only of the most radical American revolutionary of modern times but also of the most successful.”

When the Korean War broke out in 1950, the United States and its non-Communist allies in the war against Japan hastened to conclude peace with the Japanese, despite the objections of the Soviet Union. MacArthur ordered the Japanese to construct a seventy-thousand-man security force for self-defense, an apparent contradiction with Article IX of the Japanese Constitution. The final peace treaty between the U.S. and Japan was signed in September 1951, and in a separate agreement the United States was permitted to retain military bases in Japan.

The Victory of Chinese Communism

The third prong of the Asian revolution was the Communist conquest of China. When World War II ended, China was accorded the status of a great power, receiving, for example, a permanent seat in the Security Council of the United Nations. With the Japanese defeat, most people assumed that Generalissimo Chiang Kai-shek’s Nationalists would reinforce their rule over all China. Even Stalin at the close of the war recognized Chiang’s Nationalist government, not Communist leader Mao Tse-tung’s (Mao Ze Dong), as the rightful regime.

The Chinese Communists, however, had a sizable army and a government in northwestern China and were stronger than many observers thought. The Communists had gained a reputation in China as true Chinese patriots for their efforts in World War II against the Japanese invaders, and they gained more popular support by promising and carrying out land redistribution to the peasants.

At first the United States helped Chiang in his effort to spread his military authority over all of China. When that failed, the United States attempted, through most of 1946 and 1947, to find a basis for agreement between Chiang and Mao Tse-tung. In December 1945, President Truman had dispatched General George C. Marshall to China where he worked for over a year on such a mission, but without success. By late 1947 the two sides were fighting it out in open civil war, during which Chiang's lack of support from the masses of the Chinese people became increasingly evident.

By the close of 1949, the Nationalists had been forced to flee to the island of Formosa (Taiwan), some one hundred miles off the coast. In October 1949 the Soviet Union extended diplomatic recognition to the new People's Republic of China, and in February 1950 the two Communist powers signed a mutual assistance agreement and pact of alliance. Thus, just as the end of the Berlin blockade and the creation of NATO marked the ebbing of the Communist danger in Western Europe, the Cold War came to Asia.

At almost the same time in 1949, the Soviets shocked Americans by detonating their own Atomic bomb, twenty years prior to American expectations. In response, the United States formulated NSC-68 in 1947, and the National Security Council adopted it in 1950. NSC-68 contained several arguments that would guide American foreign policy for the coming years. First, the document stated that conflict between East and West is unavoidable and that amoral Soviet objectives were counter to United States aims. Furthermore, negotiations were considered useless because the U.S.S.R. could not be trusted to bargain in good faith; consequently, the United States must increase its military spending 40 percent.

The Democrats Stay In

The Miracle of 1948

By 1948 Harry Truman had warmed up well to the role of president, which had been thrust upon him so suddenly three years before; and he was eager to try himself before the electorate. Although opposed by many Democrats who thought he lacked popular appeal (according to opinion polls, his presidency was approved by only 36 percent of the people in April 1948), the president controlled the July Democratic convention, which dutifully nominated him on the first ballot. Truman named Senator Alben W. Barkley of Kentucky as his running mate. When the Republican Congress was called into special session by Truman that summer and refused to enact his program, Truman went into the campaign talking about the "do-nothing" Eightieth Congress.

In the election, Truman faced a serious loss of votes from both the right and left wings of his own party. Because the Democratic convention adopted a strong civil rights plank (following both the desegregation of the Armed Forces in 1946 and that of major league baseball by Jackie Robinson in 1947), several Southern states bolted from the Democratic Party and put forth their own States' Rights segregationist "Dixiecrat" Party candidate, Governor J. Strom Thurmond of South Carolina. Thurmond, it was expected, would cut deeply into Truman's support in the Deep South. The candidacy of Henry A. Wallace, who favored negotiations with the Soviets rather than resistance, on the newly formed Progressive Party ticket promised to draw away left-wing and liberal votes. Wallace campaigned vigorously against the administration's containment policy, contending that it was anti-Russian and would lead to war instead of peace.

The Republicans, more confident of victory than at any time since the Great Depression, nominated for president their 1944 standard bearer, Governor Thomas E. Dewey of New York, with Governor Earl Warren of California as the vice-presidential nominee. Dewey's campaign was a model of caution. Sure of victory, he preached unity and the need for efficiency. Accepting all of the New Deal reforms, even though they were also Truman's stock in trade, Dewey simply said he would administer them better. Even commentators opposed to Dewey conceded, along with the public opinion polls, that a Republican victory was foreordained. Harry Truman, though, was not convinced. He barnstormed around the country, attacking the Republican Congress for being against the people's interests. Republicans, he said, were "old moss backs ... gluttons of privilege ... all set to do a hatchet job on the New Deal." He traveled some thirty-two thousand miles and made 356 speeches, far exceeding the campaign effort of Dewey, his overly confident and much younger opponent.

Truman deflected charges from the right that he was soft on communism with the creation of the Loyalty Review Board that investigated and fired federal employees for supposed communist ties. Truman's anti-communist credentials were also boosted with the Berlin Air Lift as a response to Stalin's blockade of West Berlin. The Berlin crisis also created a "rally around the flag" effect that was beneficial to Truman and his administration. Furthermore, Truman's continuation of the New Deal was a political winner among both agricultural interests and the urban working class.

Election night brought the big surprise, as Truman never lost the slight lead he gained in the early returns. By the next morning the miracle had occurred—Truman swept the late-reporting western states and was re-elected by a 2-million-vote margin. Some newspapers that had gone to press on election night ran headlines the next morning entitled, "Dewey Defeats Truman," but it was not to be so. Truman was elected by 2 million votes. Truman's vigorous appeals to popular memories of the Great Depression and his uncompromising defense of the New Deal had apparently struck fire in millions of voters (though seven hundred thousand who cast votes for state candidates did not even bother to vote for president). Moreover, by emphasizing the decline in farm prices under Republican farm legislation, Truman actually recaptured the farm vote, which Roosevelt had lost in 1940 and 1944. Dewey, however, fared better than Republican congressional candidates, probably because of Truman's vigorous attacks on the Eightieth Congress.

Not surprisingly, the Democrats gained seventy-five new seats in the House and nine in the Senate. Although Truman lost four Southern states (thirty-nine electoral votes) to Thurmond, he had shown that a united South was not necessary for a Democratic victory, especially since his Southern losses were more than made up for in the North by urban black votes. Henry Wallace's candidacy, which at one time had been viewed as a threat to Democratic strength in Northern cities, affected Truman's total hardly at all.

The Fair Deal

In his inaugural speech in January 1949, Truman spoke of his program as the "Fair Deal." In effect, it was a continuation and extension of the New Deal that called for civil rights legislation, a national health program, aid for public education, and support for low-income housing. Truman also asked for repeal of the Taft-Hartley Act and enactment of a new farm subsidy program (the Brannan Plan); but the Congress, despite its Democratic complexion, would agree to neither. A coalition of Republicans and conservative Southern Democrats killed off not only civil rights legislation but also most of the other measures of the Fair Deal. On the other hand, in 1949 Truman did succeed in obtaining a housing act and a minimum-wage increase to seventy-five cents an hour. In 1950 Congress also agreed to broaden Social Security coverage to cover dependents, largely due to the widows and orphans problem that resulted from World War II, placing some 10 million more persons under the benefits of the system. At the time, with only a 1 percent payroll tax, Social Security had accumulated a $9 billion surplus.

After 1949, Truman was increasingly plagued by revelations of corruption in his administration. Although none of the disclosures compared with the Teapot Dome scandals of the 1920s, many officials, especially in the Internal Revenue Service, were proved in court to be corrupt. Moreover, some White House officials turned out to have rather casual standards of proper behavior for government officers. In short, the Republican charge that the Democrats had been too long in control of the executive branch of government seemed to have some validity. An issue of foreign policy, however, was to supersede corruption as a Republican weapon against the administration. Truman himself would eventually leave office essentially broke, suggesting that he, himself, at the very least, did not use his position for personal enrichment.

The Outbreak of the Korean War

When in 1945 the United States and the Soviet Union occupied the former Japanese colony of Korea, they arbitrarily divided the country between them along the 38th line of latitude. Originally

▶ In his inaugural speech in January 1949, Truman spoke of his program as the "Fair Deal." It was a continuation and extension of the previous "New Deal" that called for civil rights legislation, a national health program, aid for public education, and support for low-income housing.

MAP 27.2 The Election of 1948

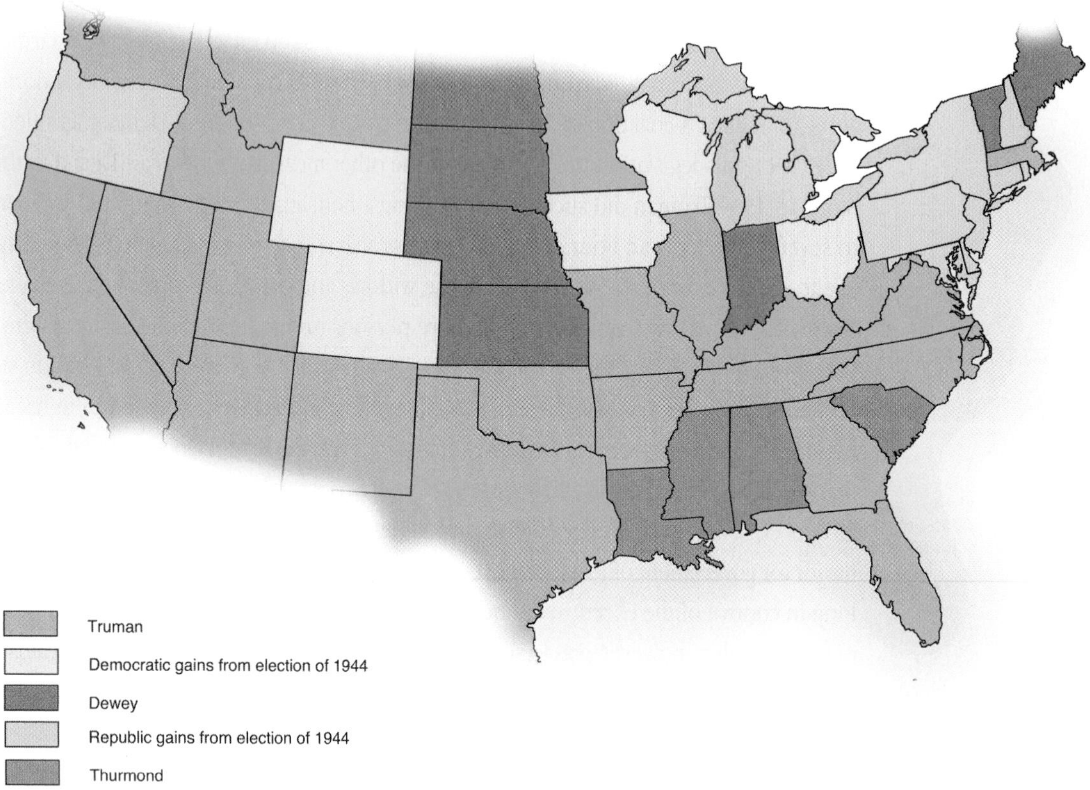

intended to be temporary, the line, in the suspicious atmosphere of the Cold War, hardened into a border between two Korean regimes—the communist North under Russian tutelage and the capitalist South under American. Because each of the Korean regimes wanted to unite the peninsula under its own rule, border clashes were frequent. When the Americans withdrew their troops from South Korea in 1949, they carefully refrained from leaving behind any offensive weapons, such as tanks or heavy artillery, for fear that the strongly nationalist president of South Korea, Syngman Rhee, would attempt to conquer North Korea by force of arms.

The Russians, withdrawing at about the same time, left a well-trained and heavily equipped North Korean army behind, complete with Soviet T-34 tanks. After the withdrawal of American troops, low intensity conflict and border raids between North and South Korea increased in intensity. Over one hundred thousand Koreans died between 1946 and 1950 in border clashes and raids. Then on June 24, 1950, Communist North Korea, armed with Soviet weapons, attacked capitalist South Korea. Stalin denied any involvement in the North Korean action and even pulled his troops near Korea away from the borders to display his non-involvement. Instead, Stalin announced that North Korea was acting on its own. Nevertheless, the United States viewed the attack as "Soviet aggression" and responded through the UN.

The North Korean army stormed across the 38th parallel, quickly overwhelming the thin South Korean defenses. Before the rapidly advancing invaders, Rhee's government fled the capital of Seoul. The UN unanimously denounced North Korea as the aggressor and passed a resolution to militarily aid South Korea. The U.S.S.R. could have vetoed the measure had their

▶ The T-34, a Soviet medium tank was one of the most effective, efficient, and influential tank designs of World War II.

representative been present, but the Soviet minister was absent that day in protest of the failure of the UN to admit Communist China to the UN. China had fallen to the Communist rebels of Mao Tse Tung the previous year, but the UN had recognized "Nationalist" China on the island of Formosa instead. The fact that the Soviets were absent at the UN the day of the vote on the use of force in Korea suggests that either the Soviets fumbled or that North Korea, indeed, was acting on its own. If the Soviets had known of the attack in advance, surely the Soviet representative in the UN would have ended the Soviet boycott of the UN and registered a veto of the resolution to aid South Korea.

Thereupon, the Truman administration, faced with a naked act of military aggression, decided to commit the United States to South Korea's defense, even though the American army then comprised no more than ten and one-half infantry divisions and one armored division. On June 30, when it became evident that American air and naval support alone could not save the South Koreans, the first United States ground troops landed in Korea. On June 27, the United Nations, prodded by the United States, branded the North Koreans as aggressors and called upon all member states to "furnish such assistance to the Republic of Korea as may be necessary to repel the armed attack and to restore international peace and security to the area." On July 7, General Douglas MacArthur was designated United Nations commander-in-chief. Although all during the fighting in Korea, American and South Korean troops made up the great preponderance of UN forces, some twenty nations had sent some kind of support by the end of 1950. Truman did not ask Congress for a Declaration of War because he described the situation as a "police action." Truman recognized that Korea had no strategic importance, but had great symbolic importance in showing the Soviets that the United States would not allow the spread of communism.

The North Korean troops, using Soviet tanks, rolled through South Korea with ease before help could arrive in sufficient number—since the South Koreans had no weapons that could penetrate the armor on the Soviet tanks. Seoul fell on June 28, 1950, and Truman responded with United States air strikes against targets in North Korea. General Douglas MacArthur recommended that the United States send an invasion force, blockade the coast, and launch air strikes wherever militarily necessary. For over two months the American and South Korean forces suffered uninterrupted defeats as the powerful North Korean armies pushed them down the peninsula into a small pocket around the port city of Pusan. Then on September 15, 1950, in a surprise maneuver, General MacArthur led a successful amphibious landing at Inchon on the west coast, far behind the North Korean lines. MacArthur's subordinates had argued against the Inchon landing because of high tides and rocky cliffs, but MacArthur believed that those same conditions gained him the element of surprise. A simultaneous drive from the Pusan area caught the Communists in a giant pincer movement. By the end of September, the United Nations forces were on the verge of crossing the 38th parallel into North Korea. When they did, a new phase of the war in Asia opened.

President Truman altered his war strategy from containment to "liberation" and began what was known as "Operation Rollback." The American military purpose was no longer merely "containment" of the spread of communism but became one to liberate all of Korea from communism. Truman consequently approved the advance of MacArthur's troops north of the 38th parallel. George Kennan warned that the Soviets would resist such a move; and the People's Republic of China warned the United States that they would intervene if the United States approached the Chinese border.

MAP 27.3 The Korean War

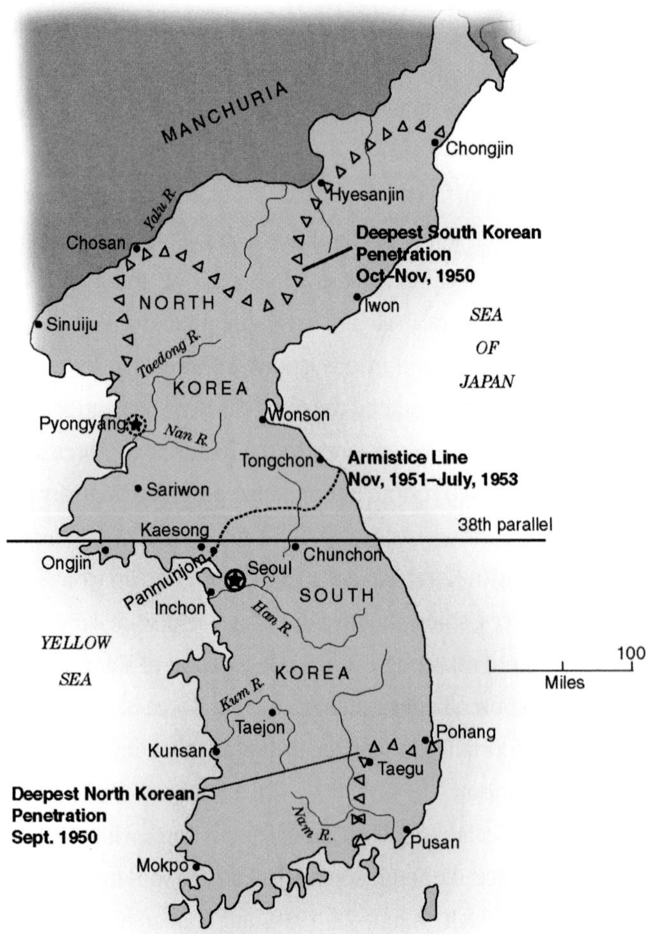

The United States believed that the Chinese warning was merely bluster and that China was too weak to intervene. Dean Acheson, in particular, argued that Chinese intervention would be "sheer madness." Similarly, General MacArthur believed that the Chinese would not intervene because they had no air force and would, therefore, be completely vulnerable to the advanced United States air power, resulting in massive casualties. On September 29, Secretary of Defense George Marshall gave MacArthur the authority to cross the 38th parallel. On October 9, 1950, two United States jets mistakenly strafed a Soviet airstrip near Vladivostok, Russia. The Soviets protested, and the United States apologized as the two superpowers attempted to avoid direct confrontation. Also on October 9, the United Nations General Assembly passed a resolution calling for a unified democratic Korea, thus authorizing MacArthur to invade North Korea and providing UN support for Truman's new goal of eliminating communism in all of Korea.

MacArthur's invasion forces pushed the North Koreans back across the 38th Parallel and into North Korea, but China's Communist leader Mao Tse Tung retaliated against the invasion by sending a group of "Chinese Volunteers" to attack the UN forces on October 26, 1950. The attack by Mao's "volunteers" was a warning from Mao that he would not tolerate the proposed UN takeover of communist North Korea. In response, on November 24 MacArthur called for an all-out offensive in North Korea, declaring that his men would drive the communists out by Christmas.

On November 26, as units of the United Nations forces approached the Yalu River—the border between Korea and Communist China—large contingents of Chinese "volunteers," perhaps as many as six hundred thousand in number ambushed the twenty thousand American troops, compelling the UN troops to retreat. In temperatures as low as thirty degrees below zero, the American troops were simply overwhelmed by superior numbers. Thereafter, increasing numbers of Chinese poured across the Yalu, and the UN troops were once again pushed far south of the 38th parallel. In January 1951, the Chinese invasion force pushed all the way to Seoul and retook the South Korean capitol. The UN denounced the Chinese invasion and called for their withdrawal; but the Chinese demanded the withdrawal of UN troops, the cessation of United States aid to Taiwan, and admission of the People's Republic of China to the UN. MacArthur then regrouped his forces and launched a counter-offensive that pushed the Chinese back to the 38th Parallel in March 1951. The war stalemated.

Thus deprived of total victory, General MacArthur asked for permission to bomb the Chinese in what he called their "sanctuary" across the Yalu. The Truman administration turned down his request on the ground that such action might well invoke the Sino-Soviet mutual assistance pact and thus bring on a war with the two chief Communist powers. Furthermore, Truman authorized UN forces to bomb only the southern half of bridges on the Yalu River (the North Korean border with China), provoking MacArthur to reply sarcastically that he did not know how to bomb "half a bridge."

Truman favored a negotiated peace, but General MacArthur favored a military victory. MacArthur called for a blockade of the Chinese coast, bombings of Manchuria and China's major industrial centers, a Nationalist/American invasion of the Chinese mainland from Taiwan, and the dropping of a field of radioactive cobalt along the Chinese-North Korean border. MacArthur also favored the use of atomic bombs on the North Koreans. Truman feared that MacArthur's strategies would lead to Soviet intervention, and possibly World War III. Furthermore, United States allies were not in favor of expanding the war. The Nationalists in Taiwan had already proven incapable of defeating the communists on the Mainland, and MacArthur's bombings would most likely not stop the Chinese intervention in North Korea.

If through Truman's strategy the nation was spared another world war, however positive that may be, a limited war far from American shores produced frustrations that made the Korean struggle immensely unpopular. Public opinion polls indicated that after January 1951 Truman never again received the support of a majority of the American people. Many spoke bitterly of "Truman's War." A draft board in Montana went so far as to refuse to draft any more men until General MacArthur was authorized to bomb as he saw fit in China.

As the leading advocate of striking directly against China, MacArthur inevitably came into fatal clash with the administration. When a letter written by MacArthur to the House Republican minority leader was released to the press—a letter in which MacArthur charged administration "diplomats" with fighting the Asian war "with words" rather than "with arms" and declared that "there is no substitute for victory"—President Truman on April 11, 1951, summarily removed the general from his commands in Korea and Japan on the grounds of insubordination. It should be noted, however, that MacArthur did emphasize in his address to Congress, "No man in his right mind would advocate sending our ground forces into continental China." Therefore, MacArthur was also, like Truman, actually advocating a limited war, but with a victory over communism in Korea. The nation was surprised and shocked that Truman would fire one of the great American heroes of World War II. The president was widely attacked, and MacArthur accorded a hero's welcome when he returned to the United States.

After an address by the dismissed general before Congress, a Senate investigation exhaustively inquired into the removal. At the end of several weeks of hearings, during which the pitch of emotionalism gradually declined, the Senate committee agreed with General Omar Bradley when he said that MacArthur's policy would have extended the fighting to the mainland of Asia, which would "involve us in the wrong war, at the wrong place, at the wrong time, and with the wrong enemy." There was brief talk in Republican circles in 1952 of drafting MacArthur for a run at the presidency, but Republican attention quickly shifted to another World War II general—General Dwight Eisenhower.

The Effects of the Korean War

By demonstrating that aggression could be halted if the nations of the world were determined to do so, the Korean War stimulated the expansion of America's armed forces and put life into the recently created NATO. Domestically the Korean "police action," as Truman once called the war, forced the administration to institute economic controls, but not to the extent of World War II. Although both income and excise taxes went up in 1950 and a new, excess profits tax became law in 1951, there was enough military production by the end of 1952 to permit the easing of many of the economic controls. Indeed, the war had pushed the nation into a new boom, quickly ending the recession of 1948–1949. Thus, conditions of life in the United States were such that many Americans, who had no relatives in Korea, hardly knew there was a war at all. That such was the case only made the war more unpopular among those who did have sons fighting overseas.

▶ World War II General, Dwight Eisenhower

The End of the Korean Fighting

Once the Chinese intervention demonstrated that the whole peninsula could not be united under Syngman Rhee, the Truman administration sought to end the fighting as soon as possible. By the end of 1952, strengthened UN forces had pushed the Chinese northward again to the region of the 38th parallel. Although the United States was prepared to strike a truce at that point, the Communists held off. Although the American "kill ratio" against the

Communists approximated twenty to one, the war stalemated near the 38th parallel into a "you take this hill and I'll take that hill" war by mid-1951. Peace talks had begun between the United States and the communists in the summer of 1951, but they went nowhere over the issue of repatriation of prisoners. The Communists demanded that all prisoners be returned, but the UN refused to repatriate those who did not want to go home. In a stinging indictment of the North Korean communist regime, some eighty thousand of the UN's one hundred seventy thousand North Korean prisoners opposed repatriation.

Dwight Eisenhower was elected president in 1952 and assumed office in 1953. Eisenhower opposed the repatriation of prisoners. The new president secretly offered the communists a cease-fire, but simultaneously threatened the use of nuclear weapons to win the war. The communists then agreed to armistice that returned the border to the "status quo antebellum."

The cost, however, was great, with fifty-four thousand American deaths and two million Korean and Chinese (one million on each side).

The Great Fear

Between 1949 and 1954, the nation was gripped by a pervasive fear that communism was about to subvert the Republic, and any program or any idea remotely traceable to Communist ideology became suspect. Even an unproved accusation of having been a Communist was sometimes enough to condemn an individual to lose job or friends. A veritable witch-hunt for traitors and disloyal citizens was carried out by government and by private groups. Actually, throughout the whole period the number of disloyal persons discovered in positions of trust was insignificant, especially in proportion to the hysteria that had been engendered.

The "Great Fear" grew out of the deteriorating international situation of 1946 and 1947, when some Communists in the United States, Canada, and Britain showed that regardless of their formal citizenship, they owed first loyalty to the Soviet Union. In 1947 the federal government instituted a program to check on the loyalty of government employees, and many public educational institutions, like the University of California, demanded oaths of loyalty from their faculties. Congressional investigations in 1947 and 1948 revealed evidence of spying in government by Communists during the 1930s. During those investigative hearings of the House Un-American Activities Committee (HUAC), Elizabeth Bentley, a former courier for Soviet espionage, testified that Lauchlin Currie, a White House assistant during the Roosevelt Administration and former Lend-Lease Administrator for China, and Harry Dexter White, formerly Assistant Secretary of the Treasury and architect of the World Bank and IMF, had been involved in the transfer of government documents to Soviet agents. In the same hearings, Whittaker Chambers, editor of *Time* magazine and a former Communist, testified that he knew former State Department employee and president of the Carnegie Endowment for International Peace, Alger Hiss, to be a Communist. While in the State Department, Hiss had played a role in organizing the United Nations, was in attendance at Yalta, and was a friend of Secretary of State Dean Acheson, whom conservatives vilified for "losing China." In essence, Hiss perfectly fit the profile for the belief that communists, in some sort of grand plot against America, had infiltrated the United States government, especially the State Department.

In spite of these "discoveries" of Communist infiltration, Truman won the election of 1948, partially by beating his own anti-Communist drum. After the election was over, the anti-communist machinery set in place continued its onslaught against the imagined demons. In October 1949, the Department of Justice obtained the conviction of the leaders of the American Communist Party under the Smith Act of 1940 that had made teaching or advocating overthrow of the United States government illegal. In 1950, the Congress of Industrial Organizations expelled Communist-led unions from its organization. In essence, the Communist Party in the United States, which had never been a major force in American politics even during the worst years of the Great Depression, was at low ebb.

In 1949, however, Whittaker Chambers launched new fears by introducing new evidence to HUAC that Alger Hiss had actually passed State Department documents to him back in the 1930s. Chambers produced his so-called "pumpkin papers" (so named because he had supposedly kept them buried in his pumpkin patch), which included some State Department documents copied in Hiss' handwriting and some typed on Hiss' typewriter. Hiss could not be indicted for espionage due to the statute of limitations, but he was charged with perjury. After one mistrial resulting from a hung jury, Hiss was convicted and given a five-year jail sentence in January 1950.

Hiss' trial and conviction, like other revelations about Communists in government, concerned espionage prior to 1945; however, in 1950, the FBI revealed that American spies had transmitted secret A-bomb data to the Russians in 1945 and 1946. In February 1950, more "proof" emerged that the nation had been infiltrated by Communists when British physicist Klaus Fuchs, who had worked at Los Alamos, was arrested in Britain on charges of passing nuclear secrets to the Soviets. The apprehension of Fuchs then led to the arrest of Americans Harry Gold and Julius and Ethel Rosenberg on the charge of conspiracy to commit espionage. Although the information transferred to the Soviets was not the information that led to the Soviet development of the atomic bomb, the Rosenbergs, whose cause the Communists tried vainly to make into a new Sacco-Vanzetti case, were executed in 1953. For many, the discovery of espionage by nuclear scientists not only proved, once again, that there was Communist infiltration but that it was also gravely dangerous.

To these and other sensational revelations of Communist activity in the United States, the Congress responded with the Internal Security (or McCarran) Act of 1951, passing it over Truman's veto. The new law required Communist and Communist-front organizations to register with the government and to identify as Communist all their mail and literature. It also forbade employment of Communists in defense work and barred anyone who had belonged to a Communist or fascist organization from entering the country. The most drastic of all provisions, and the one that measured the extremity of congressional concern, was the authorization for the government to place Communists, citizens and aliens alike, in concentration camps whenever a national emergency occurred. This provision was not repealed until 1970.

The Rise and Fall of McCarthy

The person who more than any other intensified the Great Fear during these years was Joseph McCarthy, a Republican senator from Wisconsin. McCarthy first came into national prominence in February 1950, when he charged in a speech at Wheeling, West Virginia, that fifty-seven or more Communists were then working in the State Department. "In my opinion," he said, "the State Department, which is one of the most important government departments, is thoroughly infested with Communists," and it was all the fault of Secretary of State Dean Acheson,

▶ Joseph McCarthy, a Republican senator from Wisconsin, claimed in a speech that fifty-seven or more Communists were then working in the State Department.

that "pompous diplomat in striped pants, with a phony British accent."

On February 20, McCarthy followed up his Wheeling performance with a speech in the Senate where he presented what he said were some eighty cases drawn from the loyalty files of the State Department compiled by Robert E. Lee, an investigator for HUAC. McCarthy ignored the fact that the FBI already had cleared forty of the cases and not all of the "loyalty" files had anything to do with Communism in the first place. Republican minority leader Kenneth Wherry demanded a Senate investigation of McCarthy's charges, and a subcommittee of the Senate Foreign Relations Committee, under Democratic Senator Millard Tydings of Maryland, was given authority over the investigations. Tydings' lack of zeal for McCarthy's witch-hunt would give McCarthy reason to later target Tydings.

The anti-Communist right, however, rallied to McCarthy's aid. Reporters for the Hearst and McCormick media empires provided McCarthy with information and gave him favorable coverage. McCarthy did not bring forth any new information; instead he unearthed the names of twenty-two thousand presumed communist sympathizers from a report, which had been compiled by the Dies Committee staff in 1944, but then withdrawn by the full committee. McCarthy also used material from previous investigations by HUAC that had gone nowhere.

In March 1950, McCarthy recklessly named Owen Lattimore, a Johns Hopkins professor, as the "top Russian espionage agent" in the United States. Louis Budenz, the former managing editor of *The Daily Worker* (the newspaper of the Communist Party), stepped forward to identify Lattimore as a Communist. Lattimore was anathema to Republicans because he was associated with the Institute of Pacific Relations, had been an adviser to Chiang Kai-shek, and had accompanied Henry Wallace on a trip to China in 1944. Unfortunately for McCarthy, Budenz' testimony directly contradicted statements he had given to the State Department in 1947—that he knew nothing to implicate Lattimore with the Communist Party.

The Tydings subcommittee also again investigated the Amerasia incident. Former Office of Strategic Services (OSS) employee Frank Bielaski testified that he had noticed a document in the Amerasia office that was marked "A-bomb." However, none of the other OSS officers who had accompanied him on the raid could remember such a document, and the term "A-bomb" had not come into use yet at the time of the OSS raid of the Amerasia offices. In the end, the Tydings subcommittee found McCarthy's charges to be groundless and, therefore, refused to conduct an independent investigation of the State Department as McCarthy wished. In July, the subcommittee issued a majority report, which described McCarthy's claims as "a fraud and a hoax."

During the election campaign of 1952, Senator McCarthy "invaded Maryland" and campaigned for John Marshall Butler against his nemesis Millard Tydings. The McCormick publishing empire, which provided Butler with the *Chicago Times-Herald*'s printing services at cut-rate prices, thus aiding him. McCarthy's staff worked with *Times-Herald* employees to produce a faked photograph of Tydings conversing with Communist Party leader Earl Browder, with the result that Tydings was defeated in his Senate re-election bid. Tydings filed a complaint with the Senate's Subcommittee on Privileges and Elections, but the damage had been done and McCarthy had been vindicated.

McCarthy's attacks on government officials showed no limits other than his targets tended to be Democrats. McCarthy's allies even accused Truman's Secretary of Defense George Marshall of links to communism. Republican Senator William E. Jenner of Indiana exemplified the McCarthyist position when he referred to Marshall specifically as a "front man for traitors." Jenner denounced Marshall in apocalyptic language, arguing:

> "The day of reckoning had arrived concerning how the Democratic Party has been captured from within and used to hasten our destruction, both from within and without, during these tragic years."

Jenner then denounced and blamed Marshall for the Pearl Harbor defeat, for his role in helping FDR "trick America into a war," the extension of Lend-Lease to the Communist Soviet Union, the "selling out" of Eastern Europe at Yalta, the loss of China, and the inclusion of an offer of aid to the Soviet Union under the Marshall Plan.

Joseph McCarthy emerged in June 1950 to also denounce Marshall on the floor of the Senate. McCarthy claimed that since World War II, the free world had been losing 100 million people per year to international communism. This might technically have been true since it had been only five years since World War II and the Communist People's Republic of China had a population of 500 million. If China and Eastern Europe were removed from the picture, however, the "advance" of Communism appeared much less bleak.

Conservatives followed up McCarthy's tirade by accusing Acheson of "inviting" the North Korean invasion by excluding South Korea from the During the election campaign of 1952, defense perimeter. Conservatives further suggested that communist spies who had infiltrated the government under the direction of Moscow were manipulating the State Department. Senator Styles Bridges argued that there was a Soviet "Master Spy" in the State Department and demanded that Acheson be thoroughly questioned by the Tydings subcommittee. In December 1950, The Republicans passed a resolution at the Republican Conference in Congress demanding Acheson's resignation, but the Democrats blocked any such move.

Republican Dwight Eisenhower won the presidential election of 1952, but McCarthy's attacks on the State Department and other agencies of the executive branch continued even under Eisenhower's Republican administration. Indeed, during the 1952 campaign Eisenhower hesitated to criticize the senator publicly even though it was widely known that Eisenhower deeply resented the scurrilous attacks that McCarthy had made upon General George C. Marshall, a man Eisenhower greatly admired. As late as January 1954, a Gallup public opinion poll showed that 50 percent of the American people favored McCarthy's activities and only 29 percent opposed him, although by then the senator had driven from the State Department almost all its experts on China on the grounds that they had "lost" China to the Communists.

(For the story of another able American sacrificed on the altar of McCarthy's anti-communism, see *J Robert Oppenheimer: The Destroyer Destroyed.*)

A Senate investigating committee later exonerated the State Department, but McCarthy continued to make similar unsubstantiated charges of Communists in government, in his deep, bass, Lone Ranger-type voice, occasionally naming a name but citing numbers by the score.

In the context of the Great Fear, his spectacular, headline-making accusations often gained credence. Occasionally he was courageously repudiated and criticized, but most government officials, including his fellow senators, feared to gainsay him—to do so would have laid his accusers open to charges of being "soft" on communism. Furthermore, Eisenhower's inaction and silence on the matter had the impact of legitimizing McCarthy.

Nevertheless, some Republicans were apprehensive about McCarthy, and Vice President-Elect Richard Nixon was dispatched from the White House to the McCarthyists to discuss the directions of McCarthy's attacks. At a meeting at Key Biscayne, Florida, on December 30, 1952, Nixon pressed McCarthy to agree that he would direct his venom only at the Democrats.

In spite of McCarthy's assurances to Nixon, McCarthy pressed forward in an effort to obtain the loyalty/security files of the United States Army. McCarthy's primary attack-dog, Roy Cohn, however, had his own personal reasons for going after the army. The United States Army had drafted Cohn's assistant and homosexual lover, G. David Schine. Cohn pressed the army for special release privileges for Schine, but the Army refused to grant his requests. In retaliation, Cohn launched his ill-fated crusade against the United States Army. In taking on the Army, however, Cohn and McCarthy had taken on a formidable foe with near unlimited resources and legions of allies.

McCarthy's power to frighten came to an abrupt end in 1954 when he obliquely attacked President Eisenhower and directly assailed Secretary of the Army Robert Stevens as an "awful dupe" of the Communists. McCarthy's now-apparent demagoguery caused his popularity to plummet. McCarthy's hearings on the Army dragged on for two months and were televised to the nation, but there was little doubt as to who won the encounter. At the end of the hearings, McCarthy's approval rating had dropped to 35 percent. While Cohn ranted and raved, Army counsel Joseph Welch calmly revealed how McCarthy had introduced altered photographs as evidence in an attempt to smear Army personnel. Cohn resigned as McCarthy's chief counsel, and the Senate Select Committee recommended censure of McCarthy on two counts of contempt of the Senate. Specifically, the Select Committee cited McCarthy's refusal to appear before the Subcommittee on Privileges and Elections in 1952 and the abuse of Brigadier General Zwicker before the Permanent Investigations Subcommittee. The Democrats voted unanimously for Censure, forty-five to zero, with only Senator John F. Kennedy of Massachusetts abstaining; and the Republicans were split evenly, twenty-two for and against, although a mere twelve months before only one senator had been willing to stand out against an appropriation for McCarthy's Committee on Government Operations. The senator's influence abruptly collapsed. Soon thereafter he went into a physical decline, dying in May 1957 of cirrhosis of the liver, and thus ending the most reactionary wave that followed World War II. McCarthy's fall marked the end of the Great Fear. A product of that fear and not a cause of it, McCarthyism could last only so long as Americans believed that the internal menace of communism was greater than the external threat; and by 1954 they no longer thought so.

▶ J. Robert Oppenheimer: The Destroyer Destroyed

▶ Dr. J. Robert Oppenheimer

To win the Second World War quickly, science and government linked, as they had never been before. The incredible result was the invention of the nuclear bomb. Its detonation over Hiroshima and Nagasaki in August 1945, made the stakes of the later Cold War the highest imaginable: literally, the destruction of the world. At the center of this new relation between science and government stood J. Robert Oppenheimer, often called the father of the atomic bomb. He was also one of the most illustrious victims of the Cold War.

Born in New York City in 1904, Oppenheimer, the son of a well-to-do businessman, was educated at the private Ethical Culture School in New York City and at Harvard. After graduating from college in only three years, he spent almost four years more in Europe, earning a Ph.D. at Cambridge in England and studying theoretical physics in Germany, Holland, and Switzerland. Upon his return to the United States in 1929, he accepted posts at the University of California and the California Institute of Technology.

At Berkeley, Oppenheimer at first had only one graduate student, a young man no other professor would accept. Oppenheimer's exciting and lucid teaching, his mastery of the latest in theoretical physics, and his broad cultural interests soon changed that. Within four years the best young minds in physics were seeking him out. At that time, Oppenheimer had no interest in public affairs. Outside of physics, his greatest pleasure was studying Hindu scriptures in Sanskrit and reading English Renaissance poetry. He had no telephone or radio. Indeed, it was only in 1930, on a long walk with a fellow physicist, that he first learned of the stock market crash the year before!

This detachment from public affairs began to change in the middle 1930s. Through a love affair, he became caught up, as many idealistic young Americans of the time did, in the cause of the Spanish Republic, which was fighting for its life against a military coup headed by General Francisco Franco and aided by the troops of Hitler and Mussolini. In 1940, Oppenheimer married a young widow whose husband had been a Communist party official, killed in Spain. For a while his new wife was a party member and so were his brother and sister-in-law. These Communist associations, however, did not stand in the way of Oppenheimer becoming involved in the biggest, secret undertaking ever initiated by any government.

The secret was the construction of the first nuclear weapon. Oppenheimer was made the director of the most important—and most secret—part of the Manhattan District Project: the design of the bomb at the isolated mesa in New Mexico called Los Alamos. Without the incentive of a war, the government probably would not have gambled on the project; and without Oppenheimer, there probably would not have been a bomb before the war ended. Oppenheimer brought the necessary scientists together in a totally isolated community of several thousand people and kept them working amicably and productively to solve the myriad design problems. So intense was the secrecy that even the babies born at Los Alamos were given false birth certificates. During this period, Oppenheimer's weight fell from one hundred thirty to one hundred sixteen pounds. His gangling frame, clothed in an unpressed suit and surmounted by his famous broad-brimmed porkpie hat, seemed never to be still. He was the heart as well as the brain of Los Alamos.

On that July dawn in 1945 when the bomb was tested at Alamagordo, in southern New Mexico, Oppenheimer was so nervous that the military commander had to take him for a walk in the desert to calm him. When the bomb exploded with a silent burst of light brighter than the sun itself, illuminating even distant mountains, a line from Hindu scriptures leaped into Oppenheimer's mind: "I am become Death, Destroyer of Worlds." Outwardly, though, he smiled with relief; his three-year mission was accomplished. This man who believed in "ahisma"—the Hindu principle of nonviolence—had built the most devastating weapon the world had ever known.

The success of the Los Alamos enterprise catapulted Oppenheimer into public, as well as scientific, prominence around the world. He acted as scientific adviser to several government agencies and to the president himself, but his great prestige was not enough to protect him against the fears spawned by the new weapon he had worked so hard to create.

In 1949, before any American political leader had thought possible, the Soviet Union exploded a nuclear device. With the United States no longer in possession of a nuclear monopoly and the Cold War in full swing, pressure mounted for new military weapons. For some, the answer was the thermonuclear or fusion bomb, many times more powerful than the nuclear bomb, but then little more than a theory; and for a while, the practical difficulties seemed to rule it out.

By 1953, though, when Oppenheimer's term in government ended, work on a hydrogen bomb had been moving ahead for some time. Still, the new chairman of the Atomic Energy Commission, Lewis Strauss, was convinced the work was not proceeding fast enough. He persuaded President Eisenhower that Oppenheimer had delayed progress because of his Communist sympathies. By that time, however, Oppenheimer no longer had any connection with the government, and even his advice had not been sought for months. Eisenhower, in March 1954, ordered that "a blank wall be placed between Dr. Oppenheimer and any secret data," pending a hearing.

At the hearings, all the old information about Oppenheimer's communist associations in the 1930s was again brought forward. Especially damning, though, was the testimony of his old Los Alamos associate (and strong anti-Communist) Edward Teller, who pronounced Oppenheimer unreliable. No one ever accused Oppenheimer of giving away secrets. Nevertheless, the Atomic Energy Commission decided by a four-to-one vote to deny him security clearance. The sole dissenter, significantly, was the single scientist on the Commission.

Only with the moderating of the Cold War in the 1960s did Oppenheimer regain any of the recognition he had earned so laboriously during the war. In 1963 President Lyndon Johnson presented him with the Commission's prestigious Fermi Award for contributions to physics. At the White House ceremony an ill and emaciated Oppenheimer hobbled to the rostrum. In his

People that Made a Difference

J. Robert Oppenheimer: The Destroyer Destroyed

(Continued)

brief, almost private words to the president, he succinctly described the special new relation between science and politics, which had lain at the root of his own public humiliation. Thomas Jefferson, he recalled, often wrote of " 'the brotherly spirit of science which unites into a family all of its votaries.' " But, Oppenheimer continued, "we have not always given evidence of that brotherly spirit in science. This is ... because we are engaged in this great enterprise of our time, testing whether men can live without war as the great arbiter of history." Though Oppenheimer died in 1967, that testing continues. The figure of Oppenheimer continues to fascinate his fellow Americans. In 2006, a book on the father of atomic bomb, *American Prometheus* by Kai Bird and Martin Sherwin, won the Pulitzer Prize for biography.

A Republican Interlude

The Election of 1952

As early as 1950, leading Republicans, especially those of an internationalist persuasion, had been talking of Dwight D. Eisenhower as the ideal candidate for the party in 1952. Still incredibly popular because of his war record, Eisenhower also possessed political appeal because his rise from poor boy in Kansas to international renown seemed to epitomize the American dream. When his name was first suggested for the nomination, Eisenhower announced he was not interested; however, in July 1952, after much public and private pressure, he resigned his command of the NATO forces and agreed to try for the nomination.

His most formidable opponent was Senator Robert A. Taft of Ohio, a conservative in domestic affairs and neo-isolationist. Twice Taft had been turned down in favor of Dewey. Now the senator's supporters, who were legion, felt Taft's chance had come; but the convention nominated Eisenhower on the first ballot with Senator Richard M. Nixon of California as his running mate. As a congressman a few years earlier, Nixon had gained national renown as a member of the House Un-American Activities Committee that unmasked Alger Hiss.

After Harry Truman took himself out of the race, the Democrats centered their attention upon new prospects, notably Adlai E. Stevenson, governor of Illinois. Although Stevenson was not sure he wanted to run, the July convention "drafted" him on the third ballot. In an effort to heal the wounds from the party split over civil rights in 1948, the convention nominated a Southerner, Senator John J. Sparkman of Alabama, for vice-president.

From the outset Eisenhower was the favorite. While Stevenson was compelled to defend the Truman administration, the Republicans fiercely attacked it for alleged corruption, for coddling Communists in government, and, above all, for the Korean War. Late in the campaign Stevenson's manager, referring to the Republican barrage of criticism, remarked, "We are suffering from a new kind of KKK—Korea, Communism, and corruption."

Stevenson, however, proved to be an admirable candidate. His speeches were undoubtedly the most sophisticated addresses heard from a presidential candidate since the days of Woodrow Wilson. His ratings on the public opinion polls steadily rose during the campaign, but never to the level of Eisenhower's.

Toward the end of October, Eisenhower capitalized on the pervasive discontent over Korea by promising that, if elected, he would personally make a trip to the battlefront in an effort to bring the fighting to an end. Even the prosperous times, which ordinarily would have worked to the advantage of the incumbent party, could not overcome the force of the Korean issue.

Eisenhower scored a sweeping personal victory with 442 electoral votes to Stevenson's 89 and almost 34 million popular votes to Stevenson's 27 million. Eisenhower's popular vote ran 15 percent ahead of his party's vote for Congress, for the Republicans captured both houses by only slim majorities (and, in fact, lost that control to the Democrats in the mid-term elections two years later). Another measure of Eisenhower's victory was that he broke into the Democratic South, capturing not only border states like Maryland and Missouri, and Tennessee and Virginia, but also Texas and Florida as well. Even in the traditionally isolationist mid-West Eisenhower won easily despite his record as an internationalist.

Blacks, rural Southerners, and the big city voters in the North remained loyal to the Democrats; but close post-election analyses showed that Eisenhower won support from all classes and income levels. A striking measure of his popularity was that perhaps as much as a quarter of his popular vote came from people who had voted for Truman.

The First Eisenhower Administration

Many Americans, knowing Eisenhower's long record as a military man, anticipated a stern and exacting leader of Congress and the nation. In fact, Eisenhower turned out quite the opposite. Basically he conceived the president's functions to be quite distinct from those of Congress. He generally refused even to comment upon legislation while it was passing through the legislative mill.

The first administration was intended to be a businessman's government, in the best sense of the phrase: It would not be subservient to business, but it would do its best to encourage business. Thus all economic controls left over from the Korean War were abolished early in February 1953. Similarly, government enterprises that competed with private business were dropped. A balanced budget became the guiding aim of the administration under the leadership of Secretary of the Treasury George C. Humphrey. When he took office, Eisenhower cut over a billion dollars from Truman's foreign aid budget; but in the main he would not let the drive for economy endanger the national security. When there was any choice, the administration generally gave preference to business over government; thus, it awarded an electric power contract to a private utility instead of to the Tennessee Valley Authority. Furthermore, and in 1956 the Atomic Energy Commission authorized the private development of electric power through nuclear energy.

In at least two respects the Republicans carried on New Deal-Fair Deal policies without question. One was in showing a willingness to use federal authority to counteract the recession of 1954, and the other was in expanding the coverage of the Social Security system in 1953.

Eisenhower also tried to overcome the isolationism that still persisted among many Republicans. Indeed, it was to advance the cause of internationalism that he had run in the first place; but it required all of Eisenhower's prestige to prevent the passage in 1954 of the so-called Bricker Amendment, which would have limited the treaty-making power of the government and enlarged congressional control over foreign relations. Although advanced as a means of preventing the treaty-making power from being abused, this proposed amendment to the Constitution would have seriously handicapped the president's handling of foreign affairs.

The Election of 1956

Normally, in view of Eisenhower's immense popularity, his nomination again, in 1956, would have been unquestioned; however, in September 1955, the president suffered a severe heart attack that incapacitated him for two months. Although his steady recovery emboldened the party leaders to call once again for his nomination, the president himself withheld his consent until February 1956. That summer he was nominated, once again, along with Richard M. Nixon, and the Democrats also nominated Adlai Stevenson, who this time had eagerly sought the nomination.

Eisenhower would win again as the Republican campaign capitalized on "peace and prosperity," but the victory is better explained by the character of a man who could inspire millions of voters to display campaign buttons reading "I like Ike." Eisenhower's personal popularity won him 457 electoral votes to Stevenson's 73. That it was a personal victory was attested by the fact that Eisenhower failed to bring a Republican Congress into office with him, and the Democrats continued to control the Senate and the House. Ike ran 6.5 million votes ahead of Republican congressional candidates. Not since 1848 had a president failed to carry with him at least one house, and for a popular president such a failure was unprecedented.

Working with Democrats

Throughout his second term, Eisenhower was confronted with Democratic majorities in both houses. (In the elections of 1958 these majorities reached numbers not seen since the mid-1930s.) Seeing his presidential role as one of resisting a "wasteful" Democratic Congress, Eisenhower regularly vetoed government salary increases and demands for tax cuts during the 1958 recession. Despite the Democratic majorities, all save one of Eisenhower's vetoes of antirecession measures held.

One of the three principal pieces of legislation of Eisenhower's second term was the Labor-Management Reporting and Disclosure Act (1959), growing out of Senate committee hearings on racketeering, corruption, and extortion in labor unions. (The others were the Civil Rights Act of 1957 and the National Defense Education Act of 1958, the latter discussed in the preceding chapter.) The labor act followed the thinking of the Taft-Hartley Act, assuming a divergence of interest between union members and leaders. Since Senator John L. McClellan, whose committee held the hearings, and Representative Philip M. Landrum, who sponsored the bill in the House, were both Southern Democrats, the bill also symbolized the Republican-Southern Democratic alliance that usually supported the president on labor and financial measures. The Landrum-Griffin Act, as it was also called, set up a "bill of rights" to protect union members against assessments and coercion by labor leaders; required unions to make public, largely for the benefit of their members, all expenditures and all payments made to officers; and provided that unions must hold regular elections of officers.

Sputnik and the Race to Catch Up

The Russians' successful launch of the first Sputnik into orbit around the earth on October 4, 1957, shook both the administration and the American people, used to thinking of themselves as second to none in science and technology. Its effects on American space capability and on our military hardware were even more dramatic.

America's Space Program

After the launching of Sputnik I, it took four months for the United States to be ready to put a far smaller vehicle into space. By then the Russians had put into orbit a second satellite large enough to carry a dog. With the prestige of both countries now hinging upon successfully orbiting hardware, satellites were hurled into the skies in profusion during 1958 and in subsequent years. By 1961 the most obvious consequence of the first Sputnik was that the United States had mounted six separate series of rocket probes, each more ambitious and scientifically sophisticated than the preceding one. In 1959, the United States initiated Project Mercury aimed at placing a human in orbit around the earth. Although the Soviet Union would put the first man in space, the first American in space, Alan Shepard, made his flight in a Mercury capsule in May 1961. John Glenn became the first man to orbit the earth in outer space in February 1962; suddenly, the U.S. appeared to have caught up with the Soviet Union in the "space race."

In 1961 President John F. Kennedy announced the beginning of the most dramatic of all the rocket series, Project Apollo, which was designed to land a man on the moon by 1970. Between Mercury and Apollo was Project Gemini, which developed techniques for longer space flights that would be necessary for the success of Project Apollo. Despite some cutbacks in funds during the middle 1960s and the death of three astronauts in a tragic fire in the capsule while still on the launch pad, American successes in orbiting man-carrying satellites around the earth and in spacewalks and docking vehicles in space quickly put the United States on a par with, if not ahead of, the U.S.S.R. and on course to land men on the moon before 1970.

The Military Impact of Sputnik

A factor in the dismay of most Americans over the initial Russian successes in space rocketry was the fear that the United States was vulnerable to a new kind of military attack. In 1949, the Soviets had shocked the Americans by developing their own atomic bomb, twenty years ahead of American expectations. Similarly, the United States developed the hydrogen bomb in 1952, only to find that the Soviets developed their own thermonuclear bomb in 1953.

Prior to the orbiting of Sputnik I, the Eisenhower administration had deprecated Russian boasts of being able to shoot nuclear-tipped missiles that could reach the United States from bases in the Soviet Union. At that time, American military missile capability was unable to reach more than five hundred miles. With the orbiting of Sputnik I, the Russians proved their claim, and the immediate American response was a congressional and public clamor for a crash program to catch up with the Russians. In early 1958, Congress and the administration responded with a $1.27 billion program for accelerating missile development. In the budget of 1958–1959, President Eisenhower proposed the largest peacetime military expenditures in American history.

As a result of the new and feverish interest in military rocketry, the United States developed a whole new spectrum of weapons that included short- and medium-range rockets. These could be used against planes, troop formations, and ships, and giant intercontinental ballistic missiles (ICBM) that could span oceans at speeds in excess of fifteen thousand miles per hour and devastate cities with their nuclear warheads. Perhaps the closest to an invulnerable weapon was the fifteen-hundred-mile-range Polaris missile, designed to be fired from a submerged nuclear-powered submarine. Such a submarine could remain submerged for months at a time without refueling and would present an almost impossible target for an enemy to locate and destroy.

One measure of the character of the missile race between the two superpowers was that in the late 1960s the more powerful and longer-range Poseidon missile was replacing even the Polaris missile. By the early 1970s, the more sophisticated Trident, in turn, replaced the Poseidon.

▶ Trident I first launch on in 1977. The more sophisticated Trident I replaced the Poseidon missile.

Behind the missile race was the recognition that an all-out attack by nuclear-tipped missiles could devastate the whole country in a matter of an hour or so. The principal defense against nuclear attack became the threat of retaliation from secure bases, as invulnerable to surprise attack as engineers and scientists could make them. Once the first attack had been launched, there would be no time for mobilization. So in addition to the submarine missiles, the United States also placed ICBMs in great protective concrete emplacements in the ground in order to have them operational even after a direct enemy strike.

Meanwhile, military authorities on both sides developed an antiballistic missile (ABM)—a projectile to knock an enemy missile out of the sky before it could reach its target. By 1970 Moscow was ringed by ABMs, and the United States had ABMs around some of its missile sites. Both sides were also beginning to arm their missiles with multiple warheads that could be independently targeted in order to complicate the work of the ABMs.

As weapons of nuclear power became ever more complicated—and more expensive—Congress and a sizable portion of the public began to have doubts that so much power was actually necessary to maintain the balance of terror. By the end of the 1960s there were fewer than three thousand cities in the world with populations over one hundred thousand. These numbers alone suggested to many that there is a limit as to how many nuclear warheads are actually expedient. It was in the context of astronomical, escalating costs for the new missile systems that the beginnings of a movement against the arms race began to stir.

A New Era in Foreign Affairs

The Death of Stalin

In January 1953, a Republican administration took office in Washington. On March 5 Joseph Stalin died in Moscow, and in July, the Korean War came to a halt. These events, coming so close together, marked a new era in the Cold War. Although no single Soviet leader emerged immediately to inherit Stalin's enormous personal power, the new Russian leaders demonstrated more flexibility and resourcefulness in foreign policy than Stalin had shown. Georgi Malenkov, who focused more on Soviet domestic problems than Cold War conflict, formally replaced Stalin. Malenkov resigned in 1955 and was replaced by Nikolai Bulgamin as Premier, but power gravitated to Nakita Khrushchev, the General Secretary of the Communist Party. Under Khrushchev, the Cold War began to soften a bit as the new Soviet regime approved visits by United States tourists and the United States, in turn, allowed visits by Soviet journalists and agriculturalists. Khrushchev stated at the Geneva Conference in 1955, however, that the Soviets would forget about Marx and Lenin "when shrimps learn to whistle."

In February 1956, Khrushchev shocked the world by denouncing Stalin and calling for peaceful coexistence between the U.S. and the Soviet Union before the 20th Communist Party Congress in Moscow. Khrushchev abandoned Lenin's thesis that war between capitalism and communism was inevitable and argued that communism could defeat capitalism by peaceful means. Stalin icons were destroyed all over the U.S.S.R., Stalin's body was removed from Red Square, and Russian history was rewritten to eliminate all of the false claims and self-aggrandizement by Stalin in the history books. In 1959 Khrushchev even visited the United States.

Simultaneously, the Eisenhower administration sought to alter foreign policy by taking a new approach. Despite his overall commitment to the major policies of the Truman administration, John Foster Dulles, the new Secretary of State, hoped to do more than merely contain communism. Toward the end of 1953, for example, he tried unsuccessfully to badger the European nations into a new defense community that would include a rearmed Germany. A looser grouping, agreed upon in 1954, did provide for a revived German army to be included in NATO.

On the other side of the world in Asia, soon after Communist-led Vietnamese guerrillas drove the French from Indochina in 1954, Secretary Dulles moved to counter further Communist expansion by the formation of the Southeast Asia Treaty Organization (SEATO). It was modeled after NATO but was conspicuously weaker on at least two counts. First the signatories were required only to consult, not to take action, in the event of attack. Second, the organization failed to include the chief powers of the region. Composed of Thailand, Australia, New Zealand, the Philippines, Pakistan, Britain, France, and the United States, SEATO did not include India, Indonesia, Ceylon, and Burma—all of which refused invitations to join.

Dulles also hoped to use the threat of American nuclear capability as a means of countering the superior manpower of the Communist bloc; but his threat of "massive retaliation" in the event of aggression was weakened by the fact that the Soviet Union also possessed the new weapons of war. The acquisition of nuclear weapons by the Soviet Union spurred arrangements for a meeting of the heads of government of the United States, Great Britain, France, and the Soviet Union. A meeting at the summit, as Winston Churchill called it, took place in the summer of 1955 at Geneva, Switzerland. There was little concrete achievement, but Eisenhower's suggestions that the United States and the U.S.S.R. exchange plans for their military establishments and permit aerial photography of each other's bases seemed, for a while, like promising ideas. Even though the Russians saw little merit in Eisenhower's "open skies" proposal, the suggestion made evident the American president's sincere and anxious search for a way out of the terrible nuclear impasse between the two giant powers.

Middle East: Israel

In 1948, there were some 250,000 Jewish refugees in Europe that had survived the Holocaust. Many of these refugees wanted to leave Europe, but major political factions in the United States and Britain opposed the immigration of large numbers of European Jews to Britain and the United States. The major Zionist movement that had been gathering strength since the late nineteenth century, however, suddenly found the political winds shifting in its direction. With support from Britain and the United States, United Nations partitioned Palestine into an Arab state (Lebanon) and a Jewish state (Israel). Both the United Nations and Zionists viewed this partition as the final solution to the Jewish refugee problem. American President Harry Truman recognized Israel fifteen minutes after the new State of Israel was proclaimed by the United Nations.

Unfortunately, no one had asked the Palestinian Arab residents, who made up the majority of the population in Palestine, what they thought. Almost immediately, Egypt, Syria, Jordan, Lebanon, and Iraq attacked the new Jewish state of Israel. Israel's army, outnumbered six to one, but armed with superior United States and British weapons along with arms purchased through communist Czechoslovakia, quickly routed their attackers. An estimated 1 million Arab Palestinians fled Israel with the retreating Arab armies, most to Jordan, the poorest country in the Middle East. Jordan and the other Arab countries were ill equipped to handle the flow of refugees, leading to widespread death, disease, and suffering. American support of the State of Israel produced widespread animosity toward the United States in the Arab Muslim world.

Iranian Crisis

In 1950, Shah (King) Mohammed Reza Pahlavi was displaced by democratic and leftist forces within Iran and fled the country. The Iranians attempted to create a Parliamentary government; but the leftists within Parliament wanted a complete socialist revolution, and the coalition government was in chaos. The British convinced the CIA that the only hope for stability in Iran was to return the deposed Shah. In 1953, the CIA aided the twenty-two-year-old Shah of Iran in an overthrow of the Parliamentary government of Prime Minister Mohammed Mossadegh, who had nationalized the Iranian oil fields and seized millions in assets from United States oil companies.

Mossadegh was an eccentric, who normally did not get dressed and walked around in his house in pink pajamas all day. Mossadegh was also a "crier" who would burst into emotional floods of tears at seemingly any occasion, and United States Secretary of State John Foster Dulles despised Mossadegh. Upon reviewing the CIA plan to oust Mossadegh in a coup, Dulles exclaimed, "Finally, a way to get rid of that madman!"

After the Shah's takeover, American oil companies regained control of their possessions. The United States government immediately provided massive aid to the Shah, including military aid to prop up his government, in spite of CIA intelligence that suggested that the Iranian people supported Mossadegh rather than the Shah. Given that he had little legitimacy with the Iranian people, the Shah ruled with an iron fist and used a secret police network, the SAVAK, which used torture, arbitrary imprisonment, and other repressive measures to ensure loyalty to the Shah.

Crisis in the Middle East: The Hungarian Revolt

The foreign policies of both the United States and Russia were tested more severely in November 1956. Early that month Israeli, French, and British military forces invaded Egypt without the support of the United States. All three countries had deep grievances against Colonel Gamal Nasser's nationalistic regime in Egypt. Nasser had long been a champion of Arab opposition to Israel, refusing to recognize that new country and constantly threatening invasion. Nasser had desired to build a series of dams on the Nile River and had asked the United States for aid. When Eisenhower would not sell arms to Egypt and would not help build a dam, Nasser turned to the Soviet Union for assistance. The U.S.S.R. was willing to both build the Aswan Dam and supply military aid. When Nasser established relations with communist China in 1956, Secretary of State John Foster Dulles withdrew the offer of aid for the Aswan project and the building of the dam was left to the U.S.S.R. In retaliation, Nasser militarily seized and nationalized the British-controlled Suez Canal in July 1956 and then closed the canal to Israeli ships.

Without informing the United States, their ally, Britain and France dropped paratroopers on the Suez area ten days after Israel invaded Egypt, quickly overwhelming the inefficient Egyptian army. Eisenhower was irate that he was not consulted and feared that the invasion would push Egypt into the Soviet orbit. The United States then sponsored a United Nations resolution that condemned the invasion and cut off Middle East oil from France and England. Nakita Khrushchev threatened to send Soviet "volunteers" to Egypt and to launch nuclear missiles against France and England, if they did not withdraw. Nasser then declared the canal open but, in actuality, closed the canal by sinking ships in it and blocking the passageway. Under such immense international pressure and without the support of the United States, on November 6, 1956, England and Israel announced a cease-fire and withdrawal from Egypt.

At almost the same time, the Soviet Union ruthlessly suppressed a widespread and heroic revolt of the Hungarians against Communist rule. The Hungarians had set up their own anti-Soviet government and asked the United States for aid. When the Soviets dispatched the Red Army to put down the rebellion, the Hungarian people staged a guerrilla war that became famous for civilian street participation and the "Molotov Cocktail" bomb. The Soviet forces quickly squelched the rebellion. The Soviets executed the leaders of the revolt, and thirty thousand Hungarians died in the repressive backlash. Once again, the United States denounced the Soviet action but did nothing else. The clear inference that could be drawn was that the United States was not going to come to the aid of people that were already living within the Soviet orbit.

Both the Suez and Hungarian invasions took the United States by surprise. The administration opposed both, but its power over the Soviets was nil. The opposition of the United States to the Suez adventure was more successful, both because the United States was an ally of Britain and France and because world opinion and the United Nations vehemently condemned it.

The immediate consequence of the Suez crisis, however, was that Egypt drew closer to the Soviet Union, and Communist penetration of the Middle East seemed imminent. Reacting to this development and in response to a request from the president, in March 1957 Congress passed a resolution affirming America's intention to aid any country in the Middle East that seemed to be threatened by a Communist coup, internal or external. The first test of what came to be called the Eisenhower Doctrine occurred in July 1958, when American marines landed in Lebanon to forestall a possible invasion from neighboring Syria, then a satellite of Nasser's and judged to be overly friendly toward the Soviet Union. The pro-Western regime in Lebanon was not overthrown, and by the end of October 1958 all American troops had withdrawn.

"Molotov Cocktail" bomb used by the Hungarian people during the guerrilla war against the Red Army.

The Middle East crisis of 1956–1958 brought the Eisenhower administration full circle. Once hopeful of avoiding "brush-fire wars," it found itself dispatching troops to trouble spots much as Truman had done in Korea. It was also evident after 1956 that Moscow was not the only source of instability in the world. Rising nationalism in Asia, Africa, and even the Americas presented new problems and dangers. Khrushchev was adept at winning friends in the new regions, and he consciously identified his country with the fierce opposition of the former colonial peoples to their old rulers. In part to offset Khrushchev's successful international salesmanship, the president, in December 1959 and through the first half of 1960, embarked upon extensive good-will tours of the Middle East, Southeast Asia, Latin America, and eastern Asia. Although the first two tours were eminently successful, the reception in Latin America was less enthusiastic, and anti-American riots in Japan prevented the president from visiting that country at all.

Latin America

After World War II, the United States sought a mutual defense treaty against communism in the Western Hemisphere. In pursuit of that end, in September 1947, a Western Hemisphere defense alliance was signed at Rio De Janeiro between the United States and the Latin American states, and the Organization of American States or OAS came into being. Under the OAS Charter, the United States increased aid to Latin America for economic purposes, the primary United States purpose for economic aid being to prop up the Latin American political and economic systems against communism. At the International Conference of American States at Bogotá the next year, however, Latin Americans rioted and disrupted the conference, and over one thousand people died in street violence. The Latin Americans were protesting the American offer of five hundred million in aid, because it was only about 3 percent of what went to Europe under the Marshall Plan.

Guatemala and the Overthrow of Arbenz

In 1954 in Guatemala, the elected government of Jacobo Arbenz Guzman introduced Socialist reforms and imported Soviet weapons. American Secretary of State John Foster Dulles ordered the CIA to stage a coup—even though fifty-four of the fifty-six members in the Guatemalan Congress were not Communists and neither was Arbenz, although he did lean to the left. Dulles himself admitted that he could not prove a link between Arbenz and the Kremlin. Arbenz called for land redistribution in a country where 2 percent of the people owned 70 percent of the land, and the largest landholder was the United Fruit Company of Boston. In furtherance of his goals of land reform, Arbenz expropriated four hundred thousand acres from United Fruit that were not at that time in use by United Fruit. Arbenz also provided compensation, but not at the price demanded by United Fruit.

United Fruit pressured Dulles to intervene in Guatemala to regain for the company its assets. United States Ambassador John Peurifoy told his superiors in Washington, "Arbenz thought like a Communist and talked like a Communist and if not actually one, would do until one came along." The United States cut off aid to Guatemala, and then the CIA coordinated with a mercenary army led by exiled Guatemalan military officer Carlos Castillo Armas in Honduras to stage a coup. CIA pilots in United States planes provided air support for the rebels and bombed Guatemala City. The rebels under Armas overthrew the Arbenz government in 1954.

Armas installed a right-wing military dictatorship that ruled Guatemala for the next thirty years, and the repressive government killed over one hundred thousand people over the next three decades. The U.S. involvement was well known in Latin America, and the American actions engendered Latin American resentment of the United States. Eisenhower ignored the repression and hailed the demise of Arbenz as a "victory over communism." Four years later, in 1958, Vice President Nixon toured Venezuela and was met with hostile crowds. Nixon's car was attacked by angry demonstrators with rocks and almost tipped over by the crowd before Nixon's driver abandoned the procession and sped away down back streets.

The U-2 Incident

Even before the Tokyo riots of June 1960, other events seriously tarnished the American image abroad and further impaired Soviet-American relations. Early in 1960 the president, still hopeful of being able to arrange some kind of disarmament agreement with Khrushchev, had agreed to another summit meeting in Paris. Just before the conference opened, however, the Russians announced the shooting down of a high-flying American espionage plane deep inside the Soviet Union. At first the American officials denied the accusation, claiming that the Russians had downed a weather plane. But after the Russians triumphantly produced the plane and its pilot, Francis Gary Powers, who was still alive, and published spy photos of Soviet military installations taken by the plane, the United States shamefacedly admitted undertaking this and other flights over the Soviet Union. Outraged, Khrushchev called off the summit meeting, deliberately insulting Eisenhower in the process. In their propaganda around the world the Russians made the most of the American admission. The incident of the U-2, as the special plane was called, dealt a heavy blow to American prestige and honor. Not only was the flight contrary to standard usages under international law, but the United States had also been caught in an official lie that undermined its credibility before the world. The capture of the plane and pilot also revealed that Soviet technology was more advanced than Americans had believed and gave the American people a sense of insecurity. President Eisenhower promised Khrushchev that there would be no more American U-2 flights over the Soviet Union during his presidency.

Troubles with Castro

American relations with Cuba also deteriorated seriously in 1960. On January 1, 1959, a young revolutionary, Fidel Castro, aided by Argentine revolutionary Che Guevara, succeeded in overthrowing the corrupt dictatorship of General Fulgencio Batista. At first the new government enjoyed the support of the American people, who welcomed Castro when he visited the United States soon after assuming power. When it became evident that the social revolution Castro proclaimed also included the confiscation of American property and the wholesale execution of the "enemies of the revolution," the attitude of the American people and their government cooled noticeably.

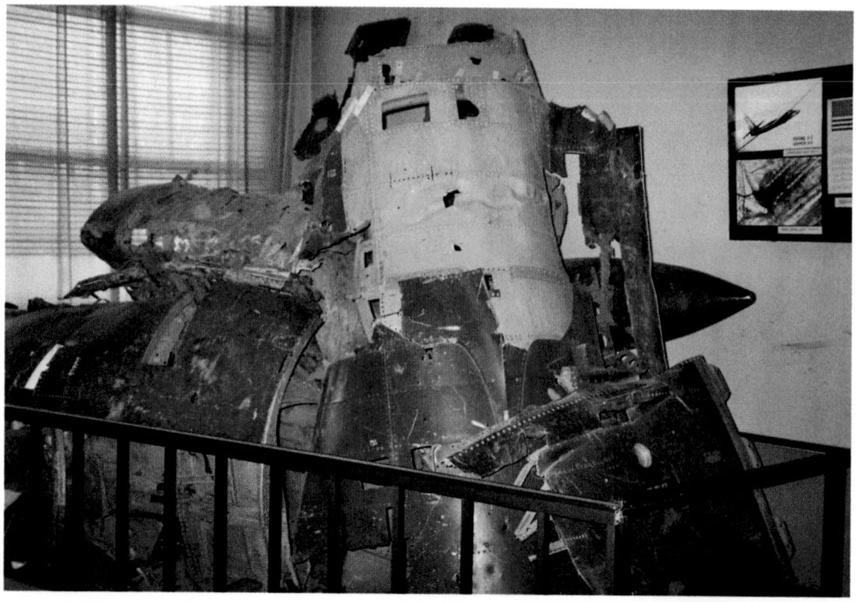

▶ Remains on display of the U-2 aircraft. In the 1960s, the Russians shot down a high-flying American espionage plane deep inside the Soviet Union airspace. The United States government at first denied the plane's purpose and mission, but then was forced to admit its role as a covert surveillance aircraft when the Soviet government produced its remains (largely intact) and surviving pilot.

▶ Fidel Castro, communist revolutionary, in 1974.

By early 1960 over a billion dollars worth of American property had been confiscated without compensation, and a steady stream of refugees from Cuba entered Miami. Furthermore, in January 1960, Castro completed an agreement to sell sugar to the U.S.S.R., and Cuba resumed diplomatic relations with the U.S.S.R. in May. Also in May, Castro demanded that American oil refineries in Cuba process crude oil purchased from the U.S.S.R. The American companies refused at the urging of the Eisenhower administration, and Castro expropriated the refineries. In retaliation, late in May 1960, the United States ended all economic aid to Cuba; and in July, at the recommendation of an angry Congress, the president cut imports of Cuban sugar by 95 percent. Since the United States was Cuba's principal customer, and sugar the island's chief export, this action harmed the Cuban economy. Castro then retaliated by expropriating more American-owned properties. In October, Eisenhower banned all United States exports to Cuba, an embargo that remains through the present. The Castro regime, subsequently, became increasingly anti-American and looked to the Soviet Union for aid and assistance.

The Election of 1960

Because the recently ratified Twenty-second Amendment limited presidents to two terms, the Republicans in 1960 did not have to wait to learn whether Eisenhower would run for a third term. Vice-President Richard M. Nixon was the choice of most party leaders, including the president. Nixon was nominated on the first ballot; Henry Cabot Lodge, the United States ambassador to the United Nations, was chosen as his running mate.

The front-runner at the Democratic Convention was Massachusetts Senator John F. Kennedy, who had shown strength in a number of state primaries. Thanks to a well-prepared campaign and a highly organized staff, Kennedy was nominated on the first ballot. Astutely, he urged the nomination of his erstwhile opponent, Senator Lyndon Johnson of Texas, for second place on the ticket because Kennedy, an Irish-Catholic from Massachusetts, lacked support in the South. Kennedy had expected Johnson, with whom he shared mutual animosity, to decline the offer and remain Majority leader in the Senate. Johnson, however, viewed the vice presidency as a good springboard to the presidency itself and surprised Kennedy by accepting the nomination. The Democrats wrote a deliberately liberal platform, including support of the Supreme Court decision on desegregation.

Since both candidates were in their youthful forties, the campaigning was strenuous, despite extensive use of television and jet travel. Nixon personally visited all fifty states, and Kennedy appeared in forty-four. The candidates also inaugurated a series of four joint appearances on television, which helped Kennedy since he had enjoyed less national recognition than Nixon and because he appeared better able to take advantage of the new medium. Kennedy made use of Hollywood makeup for his on-camera debates, while Nixon did not, with the result that the public witnessed a cool-looking Kennedy juxtaposed with a "sweating" Nixon with facial stubble. Though no one can say how much the television debates aided Kennedy, most historians argue that they did work to his advantage.

Kennedy also stole some of the conservatives' thunder by campaigning on a Cold War platform and arguing that the Eisenhower administration had allowed a "missile gap" to develop between the United States and the Soviet Union. Kennedy argued that the United States was behind the U.S.S.R. both in missile technology (as proven by Sputnik) and in numbers of missiles. The American "inferiority" in these areas that Kennedy spoke of was primarily fiction, but Sputnik provided all of the political ammunition Kennedy needed in order to make his point. After all, many conservatives had voiced the same criticisms of the Eisenhower administration for years; thus, the casting of America as "behind" the Soviet Union in missile technology was an easy sell.

Kennedy also ran under the handicap of being a Roman Catholic. Although the Republicans officially did not allude to his religion or use it against him, a number of private persons and organizations did question the fitness of a Catholic for the presidency. Kennedy met the prejudice head-on, candidly and without rancor. "I am not the Catholic candidate for president," he said at one point in the campaign. "I do not speak for the Catholic Church on issues of public policy, and none in that Church speaks for me. . . . Are we to say that a Jew can be elected Mayor of Dublin, a Protestant be named foreign minister of France . . . but a Catholic cannot be president of the United States?" Subsequent analyses showed that Kennedy's religion was the central issue for most voters.

The election turned out to be one of the closest in American history, with Kennedy winning by fewer than 113,000 votes out of a record 68.6 million votes cast. At least 4.5 million Protestants who had voted for Stevenson voted for Nixon, it has been estimated; but Kennedy's Catholicism brought out new Catholic voters, and he won support from some Eisenhower Protestants. Few Republican Catholics shifted. Lyndon Johnson was essential in helping to stem the Southern Protestant opposition to a Catholic president. Kennedy's election finally disproved the political platitude that a Catholic could not be elected president.

Although a shift of merely twelve thousand votes in five states would have given Nixon an Electoral College majority, the congressional elections were one-sidedly Democratic. At that level, at least, it was clear that the country was still strongly Democratic.

The Kennedy Administration

Limited Success with Congress

In keeping with the youthful, vigorous image he had projected during the campaign, John Fitzgerald Kennedy called his program "The New Frontier." More eloquent than any president since Woodrow Wilson, more concerned with elevating and educating the people than any president since Theodore Roosevelt, Kennedy entered office surrounded by driving intellectuals and men of high purpose. He soon found, however, that the conservative—albeit Democratic—Congress was decidedly cool, if not hostile, to his program. Twice during 1961 and 1962 Congress rejected his bills

▶John Fitzgerald Kennedy motorcade, 1963. John F. Kennedy maintained the youthful, vigorous tenacity he had projected during the campaign, in his duties as president.

for medical care for the aged and federal aid to education. Congress also voted down his recommendation for a new cabinet post of urban affairs. In the first two years of his administration, Congress gave the president only a part of his requests for tax reforms. In 1963 it refused to act on his request for an income tax cut of $11 billion, which Kennedy had strongly urged as a necessary stimulus to the economy.

Like Roosevelt and Truman before him, Kennedy discovered that a heavily Democratic Congress was no guarantee that a Democratic president's program would be enacted. Most of the slowness or hostility of Congress centered in the House of Representatives, which was dominated by conservative Southern Democrats and Republicans, often working in coalition. In the congressional elections of 1962, the president vigorously campaigned for a Democratic Congress; and, contrary to the usual results of mid-term elections, the Democrats lost very few seats in the House and actually gained some in the Senate. Yet the result for the president's program was largely negative. At the time of Kennedy's death by assassination on November 22, 1963, Congress had failed to pass a single major piece of the legislative program he had enunciated the previous January.

The administration's principal legislative success had come in the previous year. The Trade Expansion Act of 1962 was important because it marked an even more significant departure from protectionism than the Reciprocal Trade Act of 1934. It gave the president new and unprecedented wide powers to cut tariff rates although for decades Congress had jealously guarded its prerogatives in this field. The act also provided for federal aid to business firms and workers adversely affected by the resulting increased competition from abroad. Kennedy correctly hailed the Reciprocal Trade Act because it provided means for increasing the rate of American economic growth through the expansion of American exports. By permitting the importation of certain foreign goods, especially those from the booming European Common

Market (composed of France, Italy, West Germany, and the Benelux countries) and from Japan, the administration hoped to secure important and wider markets for American goods abroad, while increasing, through competition, the efficiency of industry at home.

Several times Kennedy publicly denied that his administration harbored any of that hostility toward business usually associated with the Democratic regimes of Roosevelt and Truman. The business community, however, clearly felt uneasy about Kennedy's leadership—particularly after he used threats of government intervention and harassment to force United States Steel to rescind its price increases in the spring of 1962.

Losses and Gains in Foreign Affairs

The Kennedy administration's foreign policy record was mixed. At his death, the long-term problems of the Cold War were still unresolved and some new ones had been added. Germany and Berlin were still divided, and the several thousand advisers and support troops that Kennedy had sent to South Vietnam to help its anti-Communist government fight Communist rebels constituted the beginning of a much larger involvement to come.

During the early days of his administration, Kennedy launched the Alliance for Progress in Latin America, a long-range economic aid program designed to combat the conditions of poverty that contributed to the spread of communism and denied a decent living to millions. Through technical advice, loans, and grants, the Alliance endeavored to help Latin Americans help themselves in effecting land reform, improving farming techniques, and accelerating industrial development.

Unfortunately, the Alliance's laudable aim of not permitting United States funds to be used to bolster undemocratic or unpopular regimes was not easily put into practice. Military juntas in Argentina, Brazil, and Peru in 1962 and in the Dominican Republic in 1963 interfered with or actually overthrew constitutional governments, thereby bringing into serious question the political stability and commitment to constitutional and democratic procedures of those nations. It could be said, though, that the Alliance at least ended the long neglect of Latin America, whose leaders and intellectuals had both resented United States' indifference and feared its power and its intentions.

In 1965, President Johnson admitted that the program would have to continue for twenty years, instead of the original ten, before it could be properly evaluated. By 1970 the rate of economic growth among members of the Alliance was higher than it had been in the early years of the program, but the average still fell below the planned-for 2.5 percent growth per year. An enduring problem was the unwillingness of governments in Catholic Latin America to encourage birth control, although birth rates in most of these countries were among the highest in the world.

During the Kennedy administration, however, the storm center of Latin American affairs proved to be Cuba. In April 1961, Kennedy ill advisedly lent token naval support to an invasion of Cuba at a place called Bay of Pigs by a small group of anti-Castro Cuban refugees; but the effort to overthrow Castro's avowedly Communist regime ended in fiasco when the fifteen hundred-man invasion force was easily defeated and its members killed or captured. Kennedy had mistakenly believed that the people of Cuba would come to the aid of the invading exiles, but the Cuban peasants, at that point, sided with Castro. The Bay of Pigs invasion was easily thwarted. Kennedy had also promised American air support to the invasion, but then withdrew the support on the day of the invasion in an effort to mask American involvement in the entire affair. The

United States' prestige suffered grievously because the U.S. had once again, as in the U-2 incident, contravened the normal procedures of international law and had broken its own agreements under the inter-American security system. The immediate result was the strengthening of the Castro regime and the tightening of Cuba's connection with the Soviet Union. One month after the Bay of Pigs, Castro announced the allegiance of the Cuban revolution to socialism. Two days prior to the invasion, United States Ambassador to the United Nations Adlai Stevenson had announced to the UN that the United States planned no such invasion; consequently, American prestige and credibility in the world was once again damaged.

Operation Mongoose

After the Bay of Pigs fiasco, President Kennedy remained committed to ousting Castro by any means possible and approved "Operation Mongoose," a CIA covert operation to bring down Castro. The CIA sponsored anti-Castro propaganda and violence in Cuba, including burning cane fields and blowing up factories, department stores, and oil storage tanks. The CIA even contaminated Cuban sugar headed for the U.S.S.R. Five times, the CIA attempted to work through the American Mafia to have Castro assassinated, essentially granting immunity to organized crime bosses in America in return for their cooperation in eliminating Castro. CIA plans to assassinate Castro included poisoning Castro's pens, pills, and cigars, implanting explosives in Castro's cigars, and placing a chemical in his shoes that would make his beard fall out. All attempts failed. CIA propaganda specialist Edward Lansdale even launched a campaign to convince the Cuban peasants of the imminent return of Christ, by lighting up the Cuban night sky with incendiaries launched by submarines while driving home the allegation that the Lord was unhappy with Castro and wanted the people to overthrow him. In spite of all these efforts, Castro remained.

Cuban Missile Crisis

How close that Russo-Cuban tie actually was became painfully clear in the summer and fall of 1962, when the Soviet Union began supplying the island nation with large amounts of economic and military aid. Then, in early October, American reconnaissance planes photographed Soviet medium-range missile sites under construction on Cuban soil. Kennedy privately admitted to his brother, Attorney General Robert Kennedy, that he couldn't make heads or tails of the photos; but if the intelligence people were convinced they were missile sites, he found them unacceptable and would have to take action. In spite of the fact that some of Kennedy's advisors explained to him that the missiles did not actually alter the military equation, since the Soviets had proven that they could hit the United States with nuclear missiles with the launch of Sputnik, Kennedy remained alarmed at what he termed the upsetting of the "nuclear status quo" in the world. Consequently, on October 22, 1962, Kennedy declared a naval quarantine of Cuba, broadcasting to the world, and particularly to the Soviet Union, the American intention to risk war rather than to permit a buildup of Soviet missile power in Cuba, only ninety miles from the United States. Adlai Stevenson presented the American case at the United Nations where the Soviets denied the presence of any missiles in Cuba. Stevenson then embarrassed Soviet Ambassador Valerian Zorin with pictures of the missile sites and declared he was prepared to wait until "hell freezes over" for the Soviet minister's response.

Soviet ships stopped dead in the water rather than attempt to run what amounted to an American naval blockade, thus avoiding a direct military confrontation. Though the crisis had brought the world to the very brink of nuclear war, but within three days the Russians agreed to withdraw their missiles in exchange for an American agreement not to support any future invasion of Cuba. Although Soviet technicians and support troops remained on the island, the extension of Soviet missiles to the Western Hemisphere had been stopped. The United States then withdrew its intermediate range missiles from Turkey.

Then, and later, Kennedy was criticized for risking a world holocaust in order to show the Russians how determined he was, but most observers in the United States and Western Europe praised his coolness and his success in dealing with the crisis. In any event, he did not gloat over the Soviet retreat. Instead, he continued to seek ways of breaking the circle of mutual suspicion that perpetuated the Cold War. His success in making some accommodations with the Russians suggests that the ordeal of the missile crisis of 1962 marked a significant shift in Soviet-American relations.

Kennedy's most concrete accommodation was the orchestration of a limited test-ban treaty with the Soviet Union during the summer of 1963. The treaty, which was ratified overwhelmingly by the Senate in October 1963, prohibited any testing of nuclear weapons in the atmosphere, in outer space, or under water. Although the stockpiles of nuclear weapons on both sides continued to grow, the test-ban treaty promised to reduce the contamination of the atmosphere and showed that careful and limited negotiations with the Russians could bear fruit.

The United States and the Soviet Union also agreed to establish a "hot line," or direct teletype circuit, between the Kremlin and the White House for instant communication between the two superpowers should an international emergency arise that made it crucial for them to know each other's intentions. The hot line proved valuable at the outbreak of the Arab-Israeli war of June 1967, and again in the war of 1973, when the leaders of the U.S.S.R. and the United States used it to assure each other of their intentions to refrain from direct intervention.

The Assassination of President Kennedy

On November 22, 1963, in Dallas, Texas, to the horror of a stunned nation and a shocked world on both sides of the Iron Curtain, an assassin's bullet turned to ashes the shining but unfulfilled promise of John Fitzgerald Kennedy. Lee Harvey Oswald was arrested for the crime, and police concluded that he had fired the fatal shots, using a high-powered rifle, from the sixth floor of the Book Depository building. Two days later, while law enforcement authorities were transporting him, Oswald was shot and killed by Dallas nightclub owner Jack Ruby. The new President Lyndon Johnson appointed a commission headed by Chief Justice Earl Warren to investigate the crime, and the Warren Commission concluded that both Oswald and Ruby acted alone. Unfortunately, the Warren Commission has been criticized in the years since for being less than thorough, and conspiracy theories persist.

In the short time that John F. Kennedy had been before the world, his youthful vigor, self-deprecating wit, and incisive intellect had won favor among Americans of all political persuasions. Young adults, especially, were deeply affected by this novel political figure that spoke inimitably to and for their generation. Foreign nations, from leaders to ordinary citizens, responded to his image of the United States as a nation compassionate toward the weak, imaginative in confronting old problems, and firm in leadership. His eloquence and bright intelligence moved people in all walks of life, from affluent suburbanites to the inner-city poor. His death seemed horrifying even to an age hardened to violence and inured to irrationality.

In later years, the reputation of John F. Kennedy would tarnish somewhat as less admirable sides of his personality, most notably his sexual indiscretions with Hollywood starlets would become public knowledge. Nevertheless, his assassination left unanswered forever the question of what John F. Kennedy might have been and done, given his potentialities and great popular appeal.

The Legacy of the Kennedy Administration

In assessing the larger meaning of JFK's presidency, we can begin with his unique wife, Jacqueline Bouvier Kennedy. Though a traditional woman in many respects—she did not enjoy a significant career before her marriage and she kept her silence about her husband's many infidelities—she was also a First Lady who foreshadowed a new and more accomplished type of American woman. Her beauty and her glamour gave her a position on the world stage that no other woman of the twentieth century would occupy, with the possible later exception of Princess Diana. Jackie Kennedy was more than a pretty face; she was a cultivated, multi-lingual woman as well as a devoted mother. For young women, she served as a role model. The preceding decade had featured blonde icons, Marilyn Monroe being the most famous, whose personae were often passive and unambitious, unlike the iconic female film stars of the 1930s, for example, Jackie suggested that being brainy did not rule out being attractive, a potent message to the young women of America.

Together the Kennedys seemed to embody a decisive break with the past and that included the realm of gender roles, despite what we now know about the president's womanizing. How much they had to do with inspiring later developments of the 1960s is an open question; but there is no doubt that one of the most important steps in fostering women's rights was set in motion by President Kennedy—the Kennedy Commission on the Status of Women. In 1961, faced with a dilemma about what stance to take with respect to the controversial Equal Rights Amendment, Kennedy decided to form the first-ever presidential commission to study women's issues. The aging Eleanor Roosevelt—who had supported Adlai Stevenson for the presidential nomination in 1960—agreed to chair the commission; and with that a number of high-powered men and women accepted appointment to the commission, also. We cannot single out a particular piece of legislation that came out of this effort, but the group served as a catalyst for focusing attention on the shortfalls in women's access to educational and employment opportunities. Moreover, it inspired the creation of state commissions, also, and thereby created a network of activists for the legislative changes of the succeeding era.

Another important element in inspiring young people was the creation of the Peace Corps in 1961. Established by executive order, the Corps was later formalized by Congress

MAP 27.4 Postwar Alliances

as a means of sending American volunteers abroad to help with educational and humanitarian projects in poor countries. Critics have pointed out that the Peace Corps gave the United States the ability to go into Third World countries so as to combat Soviet influence "on the ground;" but the Peace Corps also called on the idealism of many thousands of those who wanted to help solve the world's problems in a direct way.

As for civil rights, critics have pointed out that JFK was very cautious—as had been Eisenhower—because he did not want to alienate Southern Democrats. Nonetheless, there were moments of great symbolic import in which the power of the presidency seemed to be ranged on the side of the movement. Perhaps most dramatic was an episode that occurred even before JFK occupied the White House. Martin Luther King had been arrested and sentenced to jail on a technicality in Georgia in October 1960. Mrs. King was pregnant, and she was distraught about the situation. Kennedy phoned her to express sympathy, and the following day his brother Robert (soon to be Attorney General in the new administration) called a local judge to try to help. Over the next few years, King and his followers would not always find the president to be so cooperative. Yet in the end events forced Kennedy's hand. He sent federal marshals to protect James Meredith in 1962. The following year he addressed a national television audience to proclaim that the time had come for the nation to deal with civil rights.

One of the most consequential aspects of the JFK legacy, however, lay in the realm of culture. The Great Fear of the 1950s had tended to produce a somnolent and complacent popular culture. In the mid-1950s there began to be young, white male icons of rebellion, such as James Dean and Elvis Presley, but the rebellion they expressed was diffuse and apolitical. By the early 1960s, however, Bob Dylan was singing protest songs that were expressly political—including 1964's "The Times They Are A' Changing." Indeed, they were.

Chapter Review 27

Summary

The abrupt end of World War II brought with it some economic adjustment as the economy had to absorb the return of all the troops and transition to a peacetime economy. This transcended into some labor unrest and the Republican Congress countered with the Taft-Hartley Act that eliminated closed union shops. Simultaneously, antagonism began between the U.S. and the Soviet Union as the Soviets did not allow free elections in Eastern Europe, which caused Winston Churchill to proclaim in 1946 that an "Iron Curtain" had descended on Europe. That same year Stalin gave a speech in which he proclaimed that communism and capitalism were on a collision course and capitalism would be torn apart. Supreme Court Justice William O. Douglas termed the speech as the Declaration of World War III.

The U.S. countered what it viewed as Soviet expansion with a policy of containment, which was outlined by George Kennan. In the first test of containment in 1947, the U.S. aided the Greek monarchy against communist rebels, and the monarchy survived. In what became known as the "Truman Doctrine," Truman announced that the U.S. would aid any country that was being threatened by communism. In furtherance of the Truman Doctrine and containment, the U.S. passed the Marshall Plan to prop up the European capitalist governments against the threat of communism.

In 1948, Stalin blockaded Berlin and the U.S. countered with the Berlin Airlift, which supplied the city of Berlin for over a year. Stalin lifted the blockade because he reasoned that it had only brought the West closer together and he had meant to divide the Western powers. Instead, the U.S. and other Western powers created NATO in 1949 as a defense alliance against the Soviet Union. Stalin countered with the Warsaw Pact, a defense alliance between the Soviet Union and its satellite countries of Eastern Europe.

On the other side of the globe, Chiang Kai-shek's Nationalist Chinese government was ousted by communist rebels under Mao Zedong in 1949, and Mao quickly leaned toward the Soviet Union. Communist North Korea invaded South Korea in June 1950, and the U.S. responded through the United Nations, which sent troops to South Korea to repel the communist invasion. The communists were almost pushed out of Korea five months later when China sent six hundred thousand troops into the fray on November 26. The communists pushed the Americans out of North Korea, and then the war stalemated until an armistice was signed in 1953 on the principle of status quo antebellum. Communism had not been ended in all Korea, but it had been contained. Meanwhile, an eight year communist revolt in Vietnam resulted in the defeat of the French in 1954. The U.S. countered with SEATO and aid to South Vietnam.

Amidst the containment focus on the foreign policy front was anti-communist hysteria on the home front. A Loyalty Review Board was assembled to investigate federal employees for possible communist ties. The House Un-American Activities Committee investigated suspected communist activities, and Senator Joseph McCarthy launched a communist witch hunt using fabricated evidence. Alger Hiss received five years for perjury for his denial that he passed State Department documents to *Time* editor Whittaker Chambers, a reformed communist. Julius and Ethel Rosenberg were executed for passing atomic secrets to the Soviet Union. McCarthy went too far, however, when he accused the U.S. Army of communist infiltration, and

Army lawyer Joseph Welch exposed McCarthy's altered photographs. McCarthy was censured by the Senate, and the hysteria diminished somewhat, but the Cold War continued.

In domestic politics, Harry Truman pulled an electoral "miracle" in 1948 when he defeated Republican Thomas Dewey in spite of the fact that the Democratic Party was divided between Truman, the segregationist "Dixiecrat" candidate Strom Thurmond, and liberal Democrat Henry Wallace. General Dwight David Eisenhower won the next two presidential elections in 1952 and 1956 defeating Democrat Adlai Stevenson. Eisenhower did not, however, dismantle the New Deal and charted a centrist course in domestic politics.

On October 4, 1957, the Soviet Union shocked the United States by launching Sputnik, the first satellite in space. The U.S. quickly countered with its own space program and launched its first man into space, Alan Shepard, in 1961, and John Glenn became the first man to orbit the earth the next year. Eisenhower also launched a massive military build-up including the stockpiling of nuclear missiles.

In 1953 Stalin died and power eventually gravitated to Nakita Khrushchev. In 1956, Khrushchev denounced Stalin and announced a policy of "peaceful coexistence" with the United States. Khrushchev, however, would brutally put down a Hungarian revolt that same year.

In the Middle East, Israel was created in 1948 and immediately had to fight for its survival against its Arab neighbors. The U.S. backed Israel. Across the Persian Gulf, the U.S. sponsored a coup in 1953 against Iranian Prime Minister Mohammed Mossadegh after Mossadegh nationalized Iran's oil fields. The U.S. helped install Shah Reza Pahlavi who would rule Iran until 1979. In 1956, Israel, France, and England invaded Egypt, but the U.S. did not support the invasion because of fears that it would push Egypt further into the Soviet camp.

In Latin America, the U.S. created the Organization of American States (OAS) with the Latin American states in 1947, but created ill will in Latin America due to a paltry aid package and the overthrow of Guatemalan leader Jacobo Arbenz in 1954—he had expropriated property from United Fruit Company of Boston.

On the other side of the world, the U.S. was embarrassed in May 1960 when the Soviet Union shot down an American U-2 spy plane. The U.S. at first claimed the Soviets shot down a weather balloon, but had to recant when the Soviets produced the pilot, Francis Gary Powers.

The overthrow of Cuban dictator Fulgencio Batista in a coup led by Fidel Castro had installed him as leader in Latin America that the U.S. felt leaned too far toward the Soviet Union, which resulted in an embargo on American exports to Cuba. In October 1962, the U.S. discovered that the Soviet Union had placed offensive missiles in Cuba. President Kennedy, who had narrowly defeated Republican Richard Nixon in the presidential election of 1960, had tried to oust the Cuban dictator with an invasion by exiles at the Bay of Pigs and ordered a series of assassination plots. Finally he ordered a quarantine of Cuba. Soviet ships stopped dead in the water and did not try to run the American blockade, and war with the Soviet Union was averted. The U.S. removed its missiles from Turkey, and the Soviet Union removed it missiles from Cuba. A year later, the young president would be assassinated on November 22, 1963 by Lee Harvey Oswald in Dallas, and it seemed that America had reached the end of an era.

Chapter Review (cont'd)

Chronological Time Line

1946 Stalin declared capitalism and communism on a collision course and capitalism will be "torn apart."

1946 March 5: Churchill declared that an "Iron Curtain" had descended on Europe.

1946 November: Republicans won control of both Houses of Congress for the first time since 1928.

1947 March 12: Truman pledged aid to Greece and Turkey and issued the "Truman Doctrine."

1947 June: The Taft-Hartley Act banned the closed shop.

1947 July: The National Security Act was created by the Department of Defense.

1947 July: George Kennan called for a policy of "containment" of the Soviet Union.

1947 Organization of American States (OAS) was formed.

1948 The nation of Israel was created.

1948 April 2: Congress passed the Marshall Plan, a massive aid package for Europe.

1948 November: Harry Truman was reelected president in the "Miracle of '48."

1948–1949 Soviet Berlin Blockade and Berlin Airlift

1949 Soviets detonated an atomic bomb twenty years ahead of U.S. estimates.

1949 April: U.S. and European powers formed NATO.

1949 October: The Soviet Union recognized the communist People's Republic of China.

1949–1954 The Great Fear of communism gripped the country.

1950 NSC-68 was adopted by the National Security Council.

1950 January: Alger Hiss was convicted of perjury and sentenced to five years in prison.

Time Line (cont'd)

1950 February: Senator Joseph McCarthy claimed in Wheeling, West Virginia, that he had a list of communists working in the State Department.

1950 On June 24, North Korea launched an invasion of South Korea.

1950 On June 27, the UN branded North Korea as the aggressor and called on other states to supply military force to repel the North Korean invasion.

1950 On June 30, the first U.S. troops arrive in Korea.

1950 On September 15, MacArthur made his daring landing at Inchon.

1950 On October 9, the UN authorized MacArthur to invade North Korea.

1950 On November 26, six hundred thousand communist Chinese troops invaded North Korea.

1951 On April 11, Truman fired MacArthur for insubordination.

1952 November: Dwight Eisenhower was elected president.

1953 The U.S. backed Shah Reza Pahlavi in a coup against democratically elected Iranian leader Mohammed Mossadegh.

1953 On March 5, Stalin died.

1953 June: Julius and Ethel Rosenberg executed for espionage.

1953 On July 27, armistice ended the Korean War on principle of status quo antebellum.

1954 American CIA overthrew Guatemalan leader Jacobo Arbenz.

1954 April–June: Army-McCarthy hearings

1954 May: French were defeated in Vietnam at Dien Bien Phu.

1954 On December 2, the Senate voted to censure McCarthy.

Chapter Review (cont'd)

Time Line (cont'd)

1956 Dwight Eisenhower wins his second term as president, defeating Adlai Stevenson for the second time.

1956 February: Khrushchev denounced Stalin.

1956 Suez Crisis: France, England, and Israel invaded Egypt.

1956 Hungarians revolted against the Soviet Union.

1957 On October 4, the Soviet Union launched Sputnik, the first satellite in space.

1958 July–October: U.S. troops were dispatched to Lebanon to prevent a possible takeover by Syria.

1959 On January 1, Fidel Castro led a successful coup in Cuba against the government of Fugencio Batista.

1959 The U.S. initiated "Project Mercury" to put men in orbit around the earth.

1960 On May 1,the American U-2 spy plane with pilot Francis Gary Powers was shot down over the Soviet Union.

1960 June: Riots in Tokyo prevented President Eisenhower from touring the country.

1960 October: President Eisenhower banned all U.S. exports to Cuba.

1960 November: John F. Kennedy narrowly defeated Republican Vice President Richard Nixon for the presidency.

1961 April: President Kennedy backed a failed invasion by a group of CIA-trained Cuban exiles at the Bay of Pigs in Cuba, but did not give the exiles air support.

1961 May: Alan Shepard became the first American in space.

1962 February: John Glenn was the first man to orbit the earth in space.

Time Line (cont'd)

1962 October: Cuban Missile Crisis took place.

1963 October: Senate ratified the Nuclear Test-ban Treaty.

1963 On November 22, John F. Kennedy was assassinated by Lee Harvey Oswald in Dallas, and Lyndon Baines Johnson became president.

Key Terms

Taft-Hartley Act: Anti-union legislation that eliminated the "closed shop"

Harry Truman: Senator from Missouri and vice president under Franklin Roosevelt that became president during World War II upon Roosevelt's death

The Cold War: International tension between the United States and communism throughout the world, most importantly the Soviet Union

Joseph Stalin: General Secretary of the Communist Party and dictator of the Soviet Union from 1925–1953

The Truman Doctrine: The U.S. would aid any country that was threatened by communism.

The Marshall Plan: $17 billion aid plan for Europe designed to rebuild capitalist Europe after World War II as a measure against communism.

Containment policy: American policy to prevent the spread of Soviet-backed communism all over the world

Stalin's "Declaration of World War III": Stalin's 1946 speech where he declared that capitalism and communism were on a collision course and that capitalism would be torn apart.

George Kennan: U.S. ambassador to the Soviet Union that provided the intellectual justification for containment.

Clifford Memorandum: A memorandum from Truman's Presidential Counsel Clark Clifford where he argued that the U.S. must prepare for imminent atomic and biological warfare from the USSR and that Soviet aggressions could be stopped only from counter-pressure from the U.S.

Berlin Airlift: American airlift of supplies to the city of Berlin in 1948–1949 in response to Stalin's blockade of the city

NATO: The North Atlantic Treaty Organization was a military alliance between the U.S. and the Western European powers formed as a defense alliance against the Soviet Union.

Chapter Review (cont'd)

Key Terms (cont'd)

Warsaw Pact: Defense alliance between the Soviet Union and its satellite states of Eastern Europe organized as a counter-measure against NATO

Japan's Article IX: Provision of the Japanese constitution that prevented Japan from having a military for any purpose whatsoever, forever.

NSC-68: National Security Council document was adopted in 1950 that called for containment of the Soviet Union and a defense build-up.

Strom Thurmond: South Carolina senator that ran for president in 1948 as a "Dixiecrat" on a segregation platform.

Loyalty Review Board: The board established by President Truman in 1947 that investigated federal employees for disloyalty or communist leanings.

Miracle of '48: Truman's surprising electoral victory in 1948 over Republican Thomas Dewey when the Democratic Party was divided by Segregationist Strom Thurmond and Liberal Democratic Candidate Henry Wallace

Dixiecrats: Segregationist Democrats that supported Strom Thurmond for president in 1948 on a segregation platform

Mao Zedong: Communist leader of the People's Republic of China 1949–1976

Korean War: 1950-53: U.S. and UN forces repelled the invasion of South Korea by communist North Korea.

Operation Rollback: Truman's alteration of goals in October 1953 from preventing the spread of communism into South Korea to the elimination of communism from all Korea

Douglas MacArthur: Famous General in the Pacific Theater of World War II that was fired for insubordination by President Truman during the Korean War

Whittaker Chambers: Editor of *Time* magazine and a former communist, who testified in 1948 that he knew former State Department employee and president of the Carnegie Endowment for International Peace, Alger Hiss, to be a communist.

Alger Hiss: The State Department employee accused of being a communist in 1948 that was convicted of perjury and sentenced to five years in prison.

Pumpkin Papers: The State Department documents which were supposedly kept buried in a pumpkin patch by Whittaker Chambers that were given to Chambers by Hiss, some copied in Hiss' handwriting and some typed on Hiss' typewriter.

Julius and Ethel Rosenberg: Convicted of espionage for passing nuclear secrets to the Soviet Union and executed in 1953

Joseph McCarthy: Wisconsin Senator that led an anti-communist crusade in the early 1950s based at least in part on false and misleading evidence. McCarthy was censured by the Senate in 1954

Key Terms (cont'd)

Millard Tydings: Maryland Senator that opposed McCarthy and was voted out of office after being smeared by McCarthy using doctored photographs

Roy Cohn: McCarthy's Chief Counsel who was exposed using altered photographs as evidence during the McCarthy hearings on the army in 1954

G. David Schine: Roy Cohn's homosexual lover that was drafted into the army and for whom Cohn attempted to get special favors from the army

Joseph Welch: Army lawyer that exposed Cohn's altered photographs in the McCarthy hearings of 1954

Dwight Eisenhower: Supreme Allied Commander in World War II elected president as a Republican in 1952 and 1956

1952 election: Republican Dwight Eisenhower defeated Democrat Adlai Stevenson.

Nakita Khrushchev: General Secretary of the Communist Party that denounced Stalin in 1956

Iran 1953: Iran nationalized its oil fields in 1953, which prompted the United States to sponsor a coup and installed Shah Reza Pahlavi as leader of Iran.

Mohammed Mossadegh: Iranian Prime Minister deposed by the U.S. in the 1953 coup

Gamal Nasser: Leader of Egypt during the Suez Crisis of 1956 that contracted with the Soviet Union to build the Aswan Dam

John Foster Dulles: Anti-communist Secretary of State under Eisenhower

Hungarian Revolt: Uprising by the Hungarian people in 1956 that was brutally squashed by the Soviet Union

Guatemala, 1954: Guatemalan leader Jacobo Arbenz expropriated property from United Fruit Company of Boston and was ousted in a coup.

U-2 Incident: May 1, 1960, Francis Gary Powers and his U2 were shot down over the Soviet Union. The U.S. first denied the incident, but was embarrassed when the Soviets produced Powers, the plane, and photographs.

Francis Gary Powers: Pilot of the U-2 shot down over the Soviet Union on May 1, 1960

Che Guevara: Argentine communist revolutionary and assistant to Castro in the Cuban revolt against Fulgencio Batista.

Fidel Castro: Leader of the overthrow of Fulgencio Batista in 1959 that leaned toward the Soviet Union and faced an American embargo

1960 election: John F. Kennedy narrowly defeated Republican Richard Nixon to become the first Catholic president of the United States.

Richard Nixon: Vice president under Dwight Eisenhower who narrowly lost the presidential election of 1960 to John F. Kennedy

The New Frontier: John F. Kennedy's proposed program of 1961 that included tax cuts, government health insurance for seniors, and federal aid to education

Chapter Review (cont'd)

Key Terms (cont'd)

Bay of Pigs Invasion: John F. Kennedy's failed attempt to overthrow Fidel Castro in Cuba using an invasion force of Cuban exiles

Operation Mongoose: John F. Kennedy's planned to kill Fidel Castro that included the use of the American mafia and multiple other plots, all unsuccessful

Cuban Missile Crisis: The discovery by the United States in October 1962 that the Soviet Union was placing offensive Missiles in Cuba—Kennedy announced a "quarantine" of Cuba and Soviet ships bound for Cuba stopped rather than confront the U.S. Navy. The Soviets withdrew missiles from Cuba and the U.S. withdrew missiles from Turkey.

Kennedy's assassination: Kennedy was assassinated in Dallas on November 22, 1963, by Lee Harvey Oswald with two shots from a high powered rifle from the sixth floor of the Book Depository building.

Pop Quiz

Chapter 27

1. The Soviets agreed to unilateral American control of Japan when the U.S. agreed to __________.
   a. allow the performance of the *Nutcracker* in the U.S. at Christmas time
   b. recognize Soviet control in Romania and Bulgaria
   c. build a wall in Berlin
   d. only fly over the Soviet Union in high-flying U-2 aircraft

2. Dean Acheson's speech about the dangers of communism in Greece was __________.
   a. the beginning of the domino theory
   b. the beginning of detente
   c. the beginning of the American policy of preemption
   d. the beginning of the American policy of Armageddon

3. The United States assisted in what way during the Berlin Airlift?
   a. The U.S. evacuated pro-democracy citizens from Berlin.
   b. The U.S. flew food and other supplies in to citizens of Berlin for over a year.
   c. The U.S. flew weapons and explosives to the people of Berlin.
   d. The U.S. flew shovels and other digging tools to the people of Berlin.

Pop Quiz (cont'd)

4. Arguments contained in NSC-68 included which of the following?
   a. The U.S. can avoid conflict with the Soviet Union.
   b. American and Soviet aims are greatly congruent.
   c. The Soviets can be trusted to bargain in good faith.
   d. The U.S. must increase its military spending 40 percent.

5. Which of the following is true of the North Korean invasion of South Korea in 1950?
   a. Stalin forced the North Koreans to invade South Korea.
   b. Stalin denied any involvement and announced that North Korea was acting on its own.
   c. Stalin sent six hundred thousand Soviet troops to North Korea.
   d. Stalin induced the Chinese to send six hundred thousand troops to North Korea.

6. President Truman relieved General MacArthur of command due to __________.
   a. insubordination in the form of a letter from MacArthur to the House minority leader undermining Truman's policies.
   b. treason for secretly helping the communists
   c. incompetence for not knowing how to bomb half a bridge
   d. Alzheimer's disease symptoms

7. Persons accused by Senator Joseph McCarthy of communist activity included __________.
   a. Senator Millard Tydings
   b. Johns Hopkins Professor Owen Lattimore
   c. Secretary of Defense George Marshall
   d. all of the above

8. Which of the following is true of Robert Oppenheimer?
   a. He believed in ahisma, the Hindu principle of nonviolence.
   b. He was known for his calm demeanor.
   c. He was known for his finely tailored suits.
   d. He was known for his tremendous physical size and strength.

9. Soviet leader Nakita Khrushchev did which of the following?
   a. He denounced Stalin.
   b. He called for peaceful coexistence between the U.S. and Soviet Union.
   c. He argued that communism could defeat capitalism by peaceful means.
   d. All of the above.

Chapter Review (cont'd)

Pop Quiz (cont'd)

10. The primary purpose of American aid to Latin America under the OAS was __________.
    a. to improve nutrition, literacy, and medicine in Latin America
    b. to prop up the Latin American political and economic systems against communism
    c. to combat the growing illegal drug trade
    d. to combat the growing illegal arms trade

11. Operation Mongoose is best described as __________.
    a. John F. Kennedy's plan to eliminate snakes in Ireland
    b. a covert CIA operation to eliminate Fidel Castro in Cuba
    c. covert CIA plans to undermine the Soviet Union
    d. Soviet plans to place offensive missiles in Cuba

12. In 1952, the Rosenberg's were executed for selling atomic bomb secrets to China. T F

13. Joseph McCarthy had very little public support—less than 29 percent—for his anticommunist crusade. T F

14. The United States sent troops into Hungary in 1956 to save the lives of thousands of "freedom fighters." T F

15. John Kennedy was cautious on civil rights because he needed the support of Southern Democrats in Congress. T F

1. B	5. B	9. D	13. F
2. A	6. A	10. B	14. F
3. B	7. D	11. B	15. T
4. D	8. A	12. F	

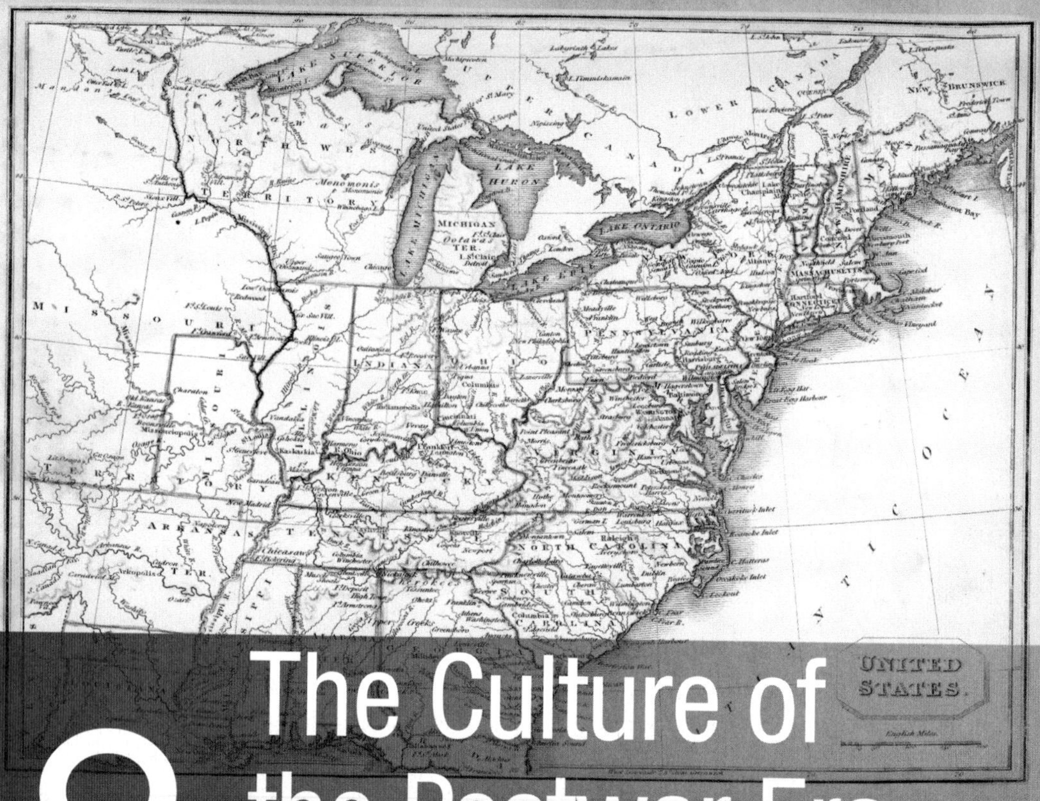

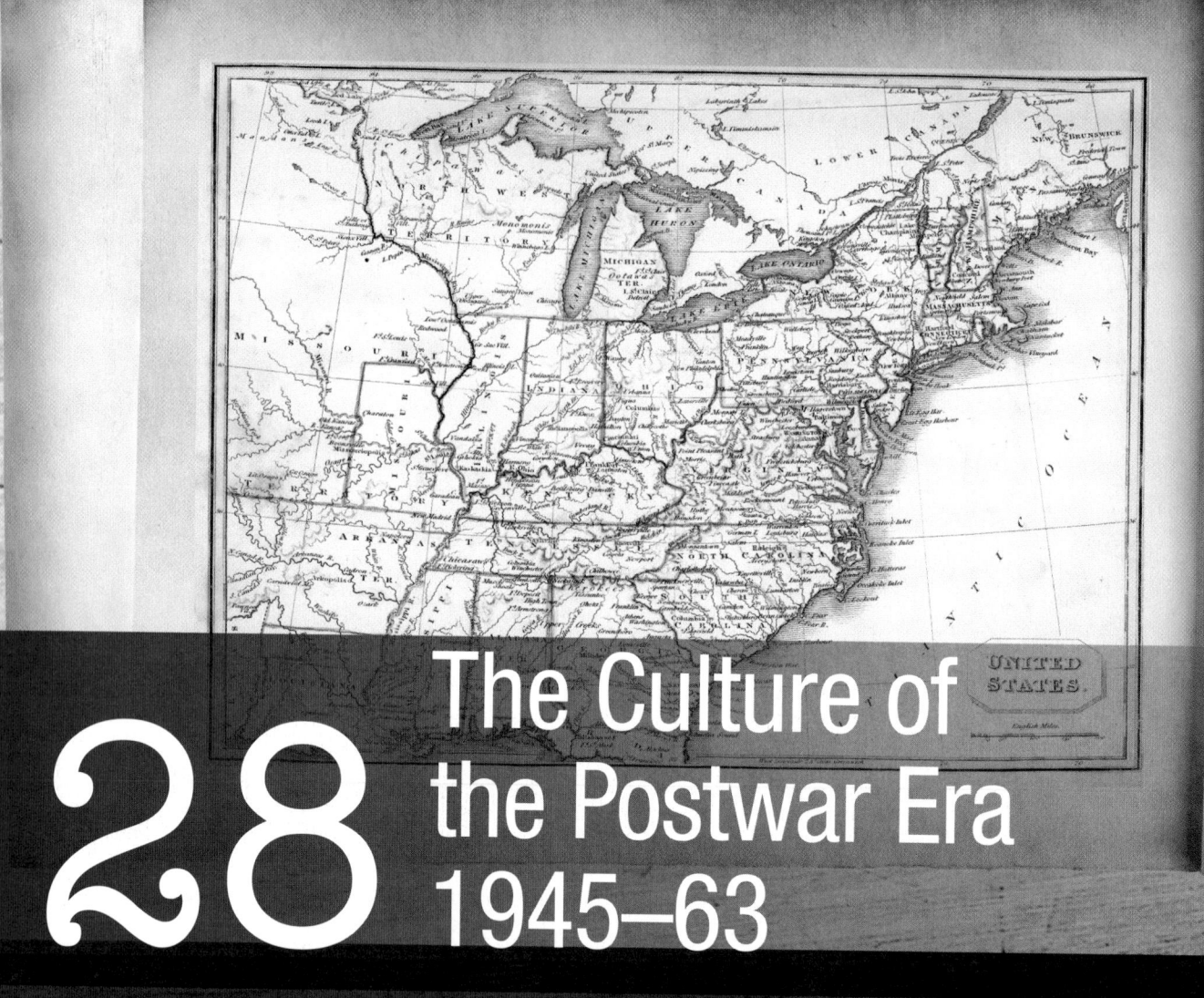

28 The Culture of the Postwar Era 1945–63

Chapter Objectives

The Rise of the Consumer Society

The Prosperous American

An Affluent Society

The Toy Boom

The Corporate Economy

Rise of the White-Collar Class

The Growth of the High-Tech Industry

A Revolution in Agriculture

Advances in Chemistry

Literary and Dramatic Expression

The Novel

Television and the Movies

The Dark Side and the Beginnings of Change

Sources of Anxiety

The Transformation of the City

A New Ethnic and Racial Self-Consciousness

THE SECOND RECONSTRUCTION

The 1954 Decision

Southern Resistance

A New Civil Rights Movement

THE NEW ACTIVIST SUPREME COURT

The Youth Culture

A Resurgence of Religion

The Rise of the Consumer Society

The Prosperous American

The hallmark of life in the United States during most of the generation after 1945 was the expanding prosperity of the ordinary citizen. The Great Depression had not ended immediately nor had it ended uniformly for all Americans. Even at the conclusion of the period in the 1960s, millions of Americans, particularly those with dark skin, remained poor and disadvantaged. Yet, measured against any previous period, the economic pattern of life for most Americans distinctly improved during the first two decades years after World War II. The economic abundance of these years calls for some understanding and explanation, for it was abundance that shaped the life of the ordinary American.

Who was this American? What was his life like? The first point to note is that the average American, in a statistical sense, was not a "he" at all. For the first time in the history of the country, the majority of Americans in the years after 1945 were female. The "average" American was white, married, and probably a mother. Although 80 percent of adult male Americans worked, most women during these years did not, meaning that most Americans did not.

Furthermore, neither the average American, if she worked outside the home, or her husband, worked with their hands at a machine in a factory. Both were likely to be white-collar workers in an office or performing some personal service for others. If she had been born before 1940, it was likely that her children would be attending college.

The recreation of the average American centered on her family, with a heavy dependence upon watching TV by the early 1960s. Movies, which had once been a major form of popular entertainment, had become principally an entertainment of young people by the late 1950s. Some spectator sports, particularly professional football, had burgeoned into a major popular entertainment. Professional football came into its own with the first nationally televised game, the NFL championship game between the Baltimore Colts and New York Giants, won by Baltimore in overtime. Over the next decade, professional football would supplant baseball as America's favorite sport.

▶ In the early 1960s the common recreation of the average American consisted of watching TV with family.

As the figures for dollars spent on appliances, possessions, and recreation imply, the United States of the 1950s and 1960s was a consumer society of the highest order. The production and acquisition of goods and services became almost an obsession. The very diversity of goods available as compared to the Depression and World War II years was at once tantalizing and bewildering. Consumption threatened to outrun production as Americans sought to increase their material possessions and leisure, and reduce their work. Although millions of Americans still lived outside the urban environment, they did not escape city values or materialistic temptations, if only because they had a direct line to the city in their televisions. Few farmhouses were without the thrusting TV aerial to link them to the wider world.

In the summer America became a nation on wheels, and one reason Americans could do so is that World War II had brought advancements in automotive technology. Automobiles in the postwar era were much faster, more powerful, and generally more comfortable than those that had existed prior to World War II. Additionally, vacations for American workers had become longer. Before 1940 the average annual vacation was one week. After the war, the average doubled; and for increasing numbers of Americans, vacation time stretched to three and four weeks. Tourism in America boomed. America's summer highways and national parks were suddenly clogged with automobiles, many of which pulled recreational campers, another booming post-war business. Similarly, motels and service areas sprang up along America's highways to provide needed services to the automobile travelers.

How was it possible for average Americans to have improved their standard of living so dramatically in the years following World War II? To understand that story, let us look at the various segments of the economy and the society.

An Affluent Society

After 1940 and through 1963, high productivity and prosperity were the dominant social facts in America. Goods spilled from American factories and farms in ever-increasing volume and variety. Between 1940 and 1960, the gross national product (GNP), after price changes are discounted, rose 114 percent, although the population grew less than 36 percent. As rates of economic growth go among industrial nations, this was not spectacular; measured in quantity of goods, however, American production dwarfed that of any economy in the world.

Other periods in American history—the 1920s, for example—had been notable for productive capacity and prosperity; but the novelty of the years between 1945 and 1963 was that lower-income groups, as well as upper-income groups, shared in the prosperity. Millions of American families moved up the income ladder. One sign of this rise is that the weekly wage of workers in manufacturing between 1947 and 1957 rose 16 percent—even after the rise in the cost of living is taken into consideration.

Another striking fact about the 1950s and 1960s—in contrast with the 1930s and 1940s—was that unemployment, which as late as 1939 was running at 17 percent of the labor force, did not go above 8 percent at any time in the following thirty years. This was true even though there were at least three rather severe recessions during those years. In these post war years, economists and government policymakers at least understood the workings of the economy well enough to help prevent these recessions from returning to the massive unemployment of the Great Depression, which had been the great fear in the years immediately following World War II. The principal single agency responsible for that achievement was the federal government.

That the prosperity was as widespread as it was, and that millions of Americans achieved middle-class status, owed much to one unprecedented piece of federal legislation, the G.I. Bill

MAP 28.1 United States Population (1950–1960)

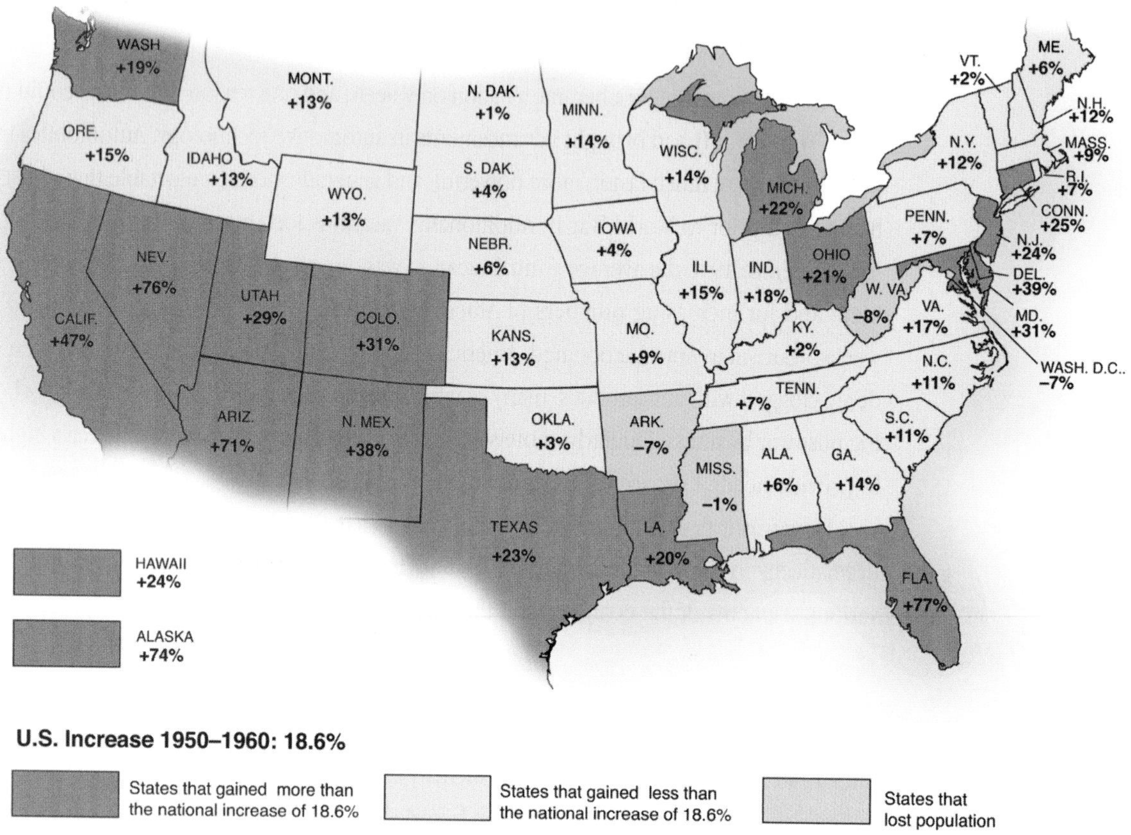

of Rights, passed in the spring of 1944. Thanks to the G.I. Bill, returning servicemen, of whom there were 16 million, were entitled to help with a college education, help in purchasing a home, and unemployment benefits—should these be needed. Before the war, a college education had been reserved for the sons and daughters of relatively affluent families. With G.I. Bill benefits, about one half of the returning veterans were able to achieve at least some higher education. Thus, the bill had a powerful impact in democratizing access to college, and thus in helping millions of families into the middle class. When coupled with relatively high, albeit regionally specific, levels of investment in public education, the Baby Boom generation (those born between 1945 and 1960 when record numbers of babies were born following fifteen years of depressed birth rates during the Great Depression and World War II)—and the economy as a whole—received a tremendous boost.

Some of the economic boost came from the babies, who stimulated demand for goods and services. The babies had to be fed and clothed, needed medical care, and then later needed to be educated. The economic effects of this extra large birth cohort have rippled through the American economy in the decades since, as the Baby Boomers reached different stages of development. That the country devolved into political unrest when they reached young adulthood in the late 1960s may not be coincidental.

The Toy Boom

The immense birth cohort of the Baby Boom generation created a boom in the manufacture of toys in the 1950s and 1960s as American toy manufacturers, such as Mattel, Marx, Wham-O, and Hasbro, competed to introduce thousands of new innovative toys, leading to toy fads and countless new activities for children. The toy boom was made possible, in part, by the new innovations in molded plastics and advancements in electronics that were spawned by World War II. Toy makers moved beyond yo-yo's and tops, which remained popular, and invented Hula Hoops, Frisbees, and Superballs. The militarism of the American society that had just experienced two world wars was reflected in a plethora of militaristic toys for boys including toy guns, toy army helmets, walkie-talkies, and plastic army men. Hasbro converted the male gender to dolls (previously the domain only of females) with the introduction of GI Joe, and Marx followed with its own successful set of action figures led by the all-American cowboy, Johnny West. Bicycle sales boomed, as did those of electric trains, Lincoln Logs, and electric racetracks. For girls, dolls of all shapes and sizes dominated the market, but the most important doll that every girl possessed was Barbie, a beautiful young blonde with an unbelievable figure. Girls were also treated to toy ovens where they could bake miniature cookies and toy versions of other household appliances. The toy boom spawned by the Baby Boomers would continue through the 1960s; and some of the most successful toys, including Barbie and the Frisbee, remained popular in the subsequent decades.

The Corporate Economy

The rapidly expanding economy of the 1950s and 1960s was highly institutionalized. Most people in the labor force worked for someone else, usually a corporation. In 1900, 36 percent of all members of the work force had been self-employed. By 1958 that figure was down to 15 percent. There were still millions of small businesses, but measured by income and production they constituted only a small proportion of the economy.

Government, too, with its large outlays of funds, encouraged the corporations and stimulated the economy. Defense expenditures alone reached $50 billion a year in the early 1960s. In fact, after the Second World War the federal government moved far beyond its largely regulatory role under the New Deal. It was now, with its huge budget, a significant participant in the marketplace as well.

The federal government was also one of the principal forces in sustaining the housing boom of the 1950s and 1960s, a major stimulus of the prosperity of those years. Through agencies like the Federal Housing Administration and the Veterans Administration, the government helped finance mortgages for the construction of millions of homes and poured money as well into the housing industry through its support of low-income public housing. Since residential construction makes up between 20 and 25 percent of all private investment, the significance of government aid to construction can hardly be exaggerated in explaining the economic growth of the postwar years.

At the root of economic growth, of course, was the increase in the productivity of the labor force. Generally this gain was achieved through a greater use of machines and power. As machines became more sophisticated and versatile, workers became primarily feeders, supervisors, and operators. The machines did almost all the labor. Even in primary work like digging ditches, machines were used. Forklifts, cranes, and other types of equipment greatly reduced the heavy lifting by workers, which as recently as the 1930s was common in foundries, mills, and warehouses. New integration processes, whereby interruptions in the manufacture of goods were eliminated, further enhanced efficiency. In the so-called continuous-flow processes, a sequence of operations now became a single operation. A result was that whereas in 1947 it took 310.5 hours to make an automobile, by 1962 the time had been cut in half.

One consequence of the growth of industry and big business was the expansion of American enterprises abroad in the form of the multinational corporation. Industrial giants like Ford and IBM opened plants in foreign countries in order to more easily tap foreign markets and cheaper labor. Sometimes the products of these American-owned companies in foreign countries competed with American exports, thus arousing the ire of organized labor in the United States. At other times multinational corporations, not all of which were American by any means, encountered opposition from the host countries because they dominated or threatened to stifle local enterprises.

Some of the multinational corporations became enormous. The incomes of the largest corporations dwarfed the national economies of two-thirds of the countries of the world. Seen in historical perspective, the multinational corporation imposed a new stability and order on the international economy, not unlike that which the trusts and giant corporations of the nineteenth century had imposed on the national economy of the United States. Like the nineteenth-century trusts, they were great aggregations of economic power—but on an international rather than a national scale, and consequently even more difficult to regulate or monitor. The size of the multinational corporations measured, too, how the technological advances of the affluent postwar era had tied together the United States and the rest of the world in a global economy.

Rise of the White-Collar Class

As the emphasis upon machine production implies, the work performed in the United States in the postwar years was quite different from the industrial labor of previous years. During most of America's history the majority of workers had been farmers, miners, fishermen, and factory workers—that is, blue-collar workers. Ever since the opening of the twentieth century, however, an increasing proportion of the labor force has comprised white-collar workers—managers, clerks, professionals, government employees, and self-employed proprietors. Beginning in the 1950s more than half of American workers were white-collar and service workers rather than blue-collar workers.

The growth of a white-collar class meant that an increasing number of people were being supplied with goods by an ever-smaller proportion of agricultural and manufacturing employees. It also was a measure of the maturity of the economy, since only a highly mechanized and skilled society could achieve such a division of labor.

White-collar predominance also testified to the consumer nature of the economy. Whereas in previous history most paid labor was employed in making new goods, by the end of the

1950s, most working people were consuming goods, helping others consume goods, or performing a service.

The growth in the white-collar class thus seemed to explain, at least partly, the stagnation in labor organizing in the 1950s. A large part of the white-collar class was composed of women, who after 1940 entered the labor force in ever increasing numbers.Women entering the labor force, however, were frequently compelled to accept jobs that paid less or were otherwise less rewarding than their education or training warranted. This was especially true of college-educated women that, proportionately, returned to work in larger numbers than their non-college sisters. Furthermore, the needs of the economy apparently did not encourage women to develop their powers. In the 1950s women made up a smaller proportion of all college students than they had in the 1920s; and fewer women, proportionately, were entering graduate schools.

The Growth of the High-Tech Industry

Much as in the early nineteenth century Yankee ingenuity in New England spurred regional growth there, the big news in the early twentieth century was the development of the automotive industry in and around Detroit; and in the mid-twentieth century the action lay in a former agricultural and fruit processing region in California—which happened to be adjacent to Stanford University. The growth of the high-tech industry in what was known as the "Silicon Valley" (geographically, the Santa Clara Valley) of California in the postwar years was one of those remarkable regional spurts of creativity and economic dynamism that has periodically characterized the U. S.'s economic development.

As we have already learned, the military necessities created by World War II transformed California's economy, with a huge aircraft industry in southern California and a concentration of shipbuilding in the San Francisco Bay Area. Not too long after the war ended, the military necessities created by the Cold War ensured that the defense sector would continue to be a significant factor in the state's economic health. For example, Lockheed Aircraft created its Missiles and Space Division in the mid-1950s and located it in the former cannery town of Sunnyvale, about twelve miles south of Stanford. That, in turn, provided a market for the nascent electronics industry that was famously launched in a garage in Palo Alto (the town where Stanford is located) in 1938 when David Packard and William Hewlett started a firm, Hewlett Packard, that would become another one of the giants. Many scholars have pointed out that this juxtaposition of a great research university supplying the brainpower and a market for what their brainpower produced was a winning combination.

The next truly consequential development occurred when William Shockley, who had been in on the invention of that essential building block of the electronics revolution, the transistor, decided to forsake Bell Laboratories in New York and set up his own firm in his home town of Palo Alto. Shockley, however, was an immensely difficult man in some estimations, and before long a group of his most talented employees—"the traitorous eight" in his eyes—left to found their own firm, Fairchild. It was spin-offs from Fairchild that would create Silicon Valley as the center of the high-tech industry in America, but first, research teams at

Fairchild and at Texas Instruments independently developed the integrated circuit between 1959 and 1961. An integrated circuit contains several transistors (essentially tiny switches that "semi-conduct" electrons), plus resistors, capacitors, and diodes on one small portion of a silicon wafer, the portion being known as a "chip." The integrated circuit and the concept of the "chip" would drive economic development in the Silicon Valley and in America, in general, for decades to come.

A Revolution in Agriculture

Like industry, farming experienced a revolution in productivity during the 1950s and 1960s as tractors and other farm implements became larger, more powerful, and capable of more work with the same amount of human labor. The increased ability to produce food was an important impetus to the prosperity and the high standard of living of those years. In 1960, for example, an hour of employment in manufacturing bought 2.2 pounds of round steak. In 1929 the same amount of labor had bought only 1.2 pounds.

If, as these figures suggest, American farming overall had become much more productive, it was also in some areas backward, inefficient, and a cause of poverty for hundreds of thousands of people who could not afford the costly machines and costly methods that produced the agricultural revolution of the postwar years. Even though the number of farmers had been steadily declining ever since the 1920s, as late as 1961 some 1.6 million farm-families, or 44 percent of the total, earned so little from agriculture that they had to engage in other kinds of employment to make ends meet. These people—black and white sharecroppers in the South and farmers on marginal lands in Appalachia and the Middle West—actually were as hard up as the poor of the central cities.

It was the highly efficient farms that produced the great bulk of food, thanks to more advanced mechanization and the encouragement of high government price supports during the 1950s.

The most important consequence of the changes in agriculture after 1945, however, is that the family farm, at least in the form as it has been known in the United States since the beginning, has almost disappeared. Between 1949 and 1959 some 1.2 million farm-families simply left agriculture because fewer people were needed to operate the ever-larger farm machinery and chemical herbicides replaced human laborers ridding the fields of weeds with hand tools.

Advances in Chemistry

A large part of the enormous increase in agricultural productivity derived from advances in chemistry. New hybrid seeds were developed that produced better yields, pesticides were developed that wiped out insect infestations, and herbicides were developed that killed weeds but not the agricultural crops themselves. The new chemistry, however, also had a profound effect in areas outside of agriculture. The breakthrough came just before World War II when artificial fibers, such as nylon, which had been created in the laboratory, began to replace cotton, linen, and silk in the manufacture of cloth. Then during the war, when the supply of natural rubber in Asia was cut off by the war with Japan, chemists were able to develop a new synthetic rubber industry. The discovery of how to create giant molecules called polymers allowed chemists to lay the foundation, after the war, of the plastics industry.

Plastics, it was found, could be used in place of wood, rubber, and metals, and had the decided advantage of being moldable. As a result, the shaping of objects made out of plastics did not incur high labor costs. Moreover, plastics were lightweight, resistant to corrosion, and good at insulating. Consequently, plastics came to be used in a myriad of ways, some of which were quite central to the economy. The average automobile, for example, now contains about one hundred pounds of plastics. Since almost all plastics are made from petroleum waste products, the dependence of the American economy on foreign oil derives from more than simply the American love affair with the automobile and the burning of gasoline.

Chemistry also reshaped the field of medicine, and a whole range of new drugs and medicines have been developed for the relief of pain and the treatment of many diseases, including mental illness. In 1954, Jonas Salk developed a vaccine that virtually wiped out polio, the deadly and crippling disease that had afflicted millions of Americans including President Franklin Roosevelt. Antibiotics provided defense against infections, such as pneumonia, that had been the leading causes of death prior to the development of antibiotics. Tranquilizers, sleeping aids, birth control pills, fertility pills, and many other kinds of drugs and chemicals not only are new since the Second World War but also are now a part of the everyday lives of millions of Americans. It has been estimated that at least half of the current products of the current chemical industry were unknown before 1950. In the drug branch of the industry, specifically, no more than 10 percent were known before 1955.

Literary and Dramatic Expression

The Novel

Not surprisingly, World War II fostered a number of novels by important American writers. Among them were John Hersey's *A Bell for Adano* (1944), which depicts the struggle of an American major in World War II to rebuild an Italian town where the town's bell had been melted down to make bullets, and Irwin Shaw's *The Young Lions* (1948), which portrays the experiences of ordinary American soldiers during World War II. Norman Mailer published his first, and many think best, novel with *The Naked and the Dead* (1949), which follows an army platoon of foot soldiers fighting the Japanese in the Pacific and includes insight into the fears, real and imagined, in the soldiers' thoughts. James Jones in *From Here to Eternity* (1951) depicts the courage, violence, and passions of young men serving in the United States military and—ten years later, for another generation—Joseph Heller's *Catch-22*, where his main character, World War II flier John Yossarian decides that his real mission, above all else, is to survive.

By 1960 the final works of a number of novelists of the first and second rank—Faulkner, Hemingway, Dos Passos, Steinbeck, and O'Hara—had appeared. Some of the best of the new writers carried on in the realistic tradition: Saul Bellow (*The Adventures of Augie Mach*, 1953), for example, and Bernard Malamud (*The Assistant*, 1957; *A New Life*, 1961). Meanwhile, John Updike, a virtuoso performer, moved in and out of the realistic tradition with *Rabbit Run* (1960) and *The Centaur* (1963).

The best-known African American writers in the opening years of the period were Ralph Ellison, whose *Invisible Man* (1952) became a classic, and James Baldwin (*Go Tell It on the Mountain*, 1953; *Another Country*, 1962).

Though William Faulkner was in decline, the tradition of splendid writing emanating from the American South continued. Georgia-born Flannery O'Connor wrote short stories in a Gothic mode. Mississippian Eudora Welty also wrote highly-regarded short stories. From Alabama came Harper Lee, whose 1960 novel *To Kill a Mockingbird,* which depicted racial injustice in the segregated South through the eyes of a young girl, became one of the best-loved books of the twentieth century.

Television and the Movies

By the early 1950s, there was a new form of entertainment that captivated most Americans, television. As previously noted, more households had a TV set than dishwashers and washing machines combined. Very soon patterns of family behavior began to change to accommodate the new medium: people gathered around the set to watch such beloved favorites as *I Love Lucy*—a cultural phenomenon in itself—or *The Ed Sullivan Show*. In those early decades, families typically had only one set, and the programming tended to appeal to people across a broad span of ages and interests. The Sullivan show provided a good example of this. There were animal acts for the children, Elvis or the Beatles for teenagers, and stars of classical music for those of more highbrow tastes. By contrast, in the early twenty-first century, television sets abound in the typical household; and programming tends to reflect that pattern with cartoon networks for kids, MTV for teenagers, and so on.

As early as 1954, television began to demonstrate its potential for providing riveting, real-time programming that documented actual events, a demonstration that occurred when networks televised the Army-McCarthy hearings. In 1960, the networks followed the presidential election and shortly thereafter, the early space flights. In 1963, a heartbroken nation followed the events surrounding the assassination of President John Kennedy, including the murder of the assassin, Lee Harvey Oswald, on live television.

The initial impact of television, when it burst upon the entertainment scene, was to cause a decline in public interest in movies. Hundreds of movie theaters closed down during the 1950s and 1960s, and the Hollywood studios either went unused or were turned over to making movies for TV. In 1948 there were 18,600 movie houses in the country, but by 1963 the number was a mere 9,200.

The Dark Side and the Beginnings of Change

Sources of Anxiety

The unusual prosperity of the post-war years obscured a number of nagging fears and broad dissatisfactions. These, too, however, were a part of the postwar social scene. The end of World War II unfortunately did not mean the end of international suspicions or even of war for the United States. This was the time of the Cold War when the immense military power and broadened aspirations of the Soviet Union seemed to threaten first Europe and then Asia. Fear of Communist ideology during part of the 1950s so undermined the self-confidence of Americans that a "witch-hunt" was mounted for Communist spies and sympathizers. Hostilities between nations not only threatened but also brought death to thousands of Americans, first in Korea and then in Vietnam. Fear of nuclear war was sufficiently high in those years to put schoolchildren through bomb drills, and for many citizens to build home bomb shelters. Over one million private bomb shelters were constructed nationwide, and *Architectural Digest* reported that the bomb shelter would become as much a part of the American home as the garage.

The Transformation of the City

The bright and dark sides of the years after 1945 were summarized in the achievements and the problems of the nation's cities, then undergoing important changes. The trend toward urbanization had begun early in the nineteenth century and accelerated after World War II as advancements in the automobile made society more mobile. By 1960, two-thirds of all Americans lived in urban areas, and the trend appeared irreversible with each census reporting a further decline in the rural population. During the 50s and 60s, however, the kinds of urban areas in which Americans chose to live began to change. Central metropolitan districts did not keep up with the general urban growth. Between 1950 and 1960, for example, the aggregate total population of cities over one hundred thousand increased only 9.3 percent, and four out of five of the giant cities of over a million actually decreased in population. America was becoming more urban, but people were actually leaving the central cities.

Increasingly, people moving from the country or small towns settled in the suburbs of the big cities rather than the cities themselves. Simultaneously, many people residing in the cities were also deserting the central cities for the suburbs. This movement had begun in earnest in the 1920s, but by the 50s it was a mass exodus. In 1953 the editors of *Fortune* compared the suburban migration to the great immigration from Europe in the early years of the twentieth century. About as many people—1.2 million—moved to the suburbs that year as had entered the United States in 1907.

A New Ethnic and Racial Self-Consciousness

Almost from its inception in 1776, the United States has been a broad mixture of peoples. Yet for most of those two hundred years, the national emphasis has been upon denying or suppressing that diversity in order to create a unified American people. The irony was often recognized in the observation that there were more Irish in Boston than in Dublin or more Germans in Milwaukee than in Heidelberg.

During the years after World War II, the ethnic and racial diversity of America began to receive its proper due. Political scientists and historians—as well as movies, TV shows, and novels—began to emphasize the sense of loyalty, community, and identity that people felt toward their national, racial, or religious kin, while simultaneously retaining their American identity. Jewish humor, Italian families, and Irish political activity became the subjects of studies, novels, and entertainment. Young people took a new pride in their European roots and found no serious conflict, as once their parents had been warned, between their Americanism and their ancestry.

A large part of the reason for the new pride in ethnic and racial identity was the emergence into political and economic prominence of these once-submerged groups. The Irish, it is true, were prominent in urban politics in the late nineteenth century; but the Jews, Poles, and Italians, African Americans, Mexican Americans, Japanese, and Chinese came forward to push for full participation only in the twentieth century and principally after World War II. This is partially due to changes in demographics that occurred after 1950, however, as at mid-century, nonwhites still made up only 10 percent of the American population. This would change greatly over the next several decades, however, due to increases in immigration from Asia and Latin America.

The Second Reconstruction

The 1954 Decision

On May 17, 1954, in handing down a decision in *Brown v. Board of Education of Topeka*, the Supreme Court of the United States unanimously concluded "that in the field of public education the doctrine of 'separate but equal' has no place." In the middle of the twentieth century, the Court concluded, "separate education facilities are inherently unequal." In thus overturning the decision in *Plessey v. Ferguson* (1896), on which all Southern states rested the validity of their segregated public facilities, the Court opened a new chapter in the history of African Americans in the United States.

For over a decade the Supreme Court had been invalidating state laws that discriminated on grounds of race, but the school decision shocked the South. Although a few border-state communities like Baltimore and Washington, D.C., began desegregation of schools in 1954, in most of the South the decision met stiff and determined resistance. By the middle of 1956 only some three hundred fifty school districts out of sixty-three hundred were desegregated in the South, and none of these desegregated districts was located in the middle or Deep South.

Southern Resistance

In 1957 Southern opposition to school desegregation reached the point of clashes with federal military power, and Little Rock, Arkansas, became the flash point. Under a plan of gradual desegregation worked out by the local school board and the federal district court, nine black students were scheduled to enter Central High School in Little Rock, Arkansas, in the fall of 1957; but Arkansas' Governor Orville Faubus used state troops to bar their entrance. Faced with state defiance of federal authority, President Eisenhower sent in United States paratroopers to enforce the orders of the federal court. For several weeks, soldiers with fixed bayonets escorted the black students to classes. Later, federalized Arkansas troops remained to patrol the school grounds for the entire school year.

If the breakdown of orderly processes of law in Arkansas shocked the nation and the world, the use of federal troops temporarily stiffened resistance in the South. "Massive resistance" statutes, as they were called, were hastily enacted in a number of states, resulting in the closing of schools in Little Rock and in three communities in Virginia. Southern states repealed mandatory attendance laws and allowed parents to keep their children at home if their local schools integrated. Other laws were passed preventing school boards from integrating unless it was approved by popular vote. Other states allowed school districts to use safety and "morality" as valid reasons to delay federal orders to integrate.

By 1959, though, the more moderate people in Arkansas and Virginia accepted at least token desegregation in preference to no public schools at all. In 1960 and 1961, token desegregation came to the Deep Southern states of Louisiana and Georgia, particularly in the big cities of New Orleans and Atlanta. It should be noted that white churchwomen in several cities organized to uphold the rule of law and the continuance of public education.

The determined opposition of segregationist leaders and White Citizens Councils in the Deep South was not to be broken so easily, however. In September and October 1962, a transfixed nation watched as the state of Mississippi, through its elected officials, defied a federal court order requiring the University of Mississippi to permit a black man, James Meredith, to enroll as a student. The federal authorities tried their best to avoid the use of armed force by working behind the scenes to secure compliance with the court; but Governor Ross Barnett's public statements of defiance encouraged thousands of segregationists, including many students, to attack physically the federal marshals assigned to protect Meredith upon his arrival at the university.

▶ In 1957 nine black students were scheduled to integrate into Central High School in Little Rock, Arkansas, but state troopers were ordered to block their entrance. President Eisenhower sent in United States paratroopers to enforce the orders of the federal court. For several weeks, soldiers with fixed bayonets escorted the black students to classes.

As a result of the vehemence of the attack, President John F. Kennedy (elected in 1960) dispatched thousands of federalized Mississippi national guardsmen and regular army troops to the university town of Oxford to restore peace and to ensure the execution of the court's orders. Meredith entered the university as its first known African American student.

A New Civil Rights Movement

The decline of segregation in the South during the 1950s and 1960s was hastened by a rising assertiveness among Southern African Americans in opposing segregation. One of the most influential efforts, as well as most successful, was the boycott of local buses in Montgomery, Alabama. The fifty thousand black residents opposed the requirement that blacks must sit on the back of the bus and give up their seat to a white person, if there are not enough seats for whites in the front half of the bus. The boycott against segregation on the buses began in December 1955, when an African American seamstress named Rosa Parks refused to surrender her seat on a bus to a white person and was subsequently arrested. Parks had not intended to start a civil rights movement, but stated that she was merely tired and wanted to sit down. Although the subsequent bus boycott by Montgomery's black community brought hardship to the blacks who ordinarily depended upon public transportation to get to work, it was sustained for almost a year through carpooling and the joint efforts of the black community. When Rosa Parks died in October 2005, her body lay in state in the Capitol rotunda in Washington, making her the first woman to be so honored.

▶ Rosa Parks refused to surrender her seat on a bus to a white person and was consequentially arrested for her small act of defiance.

One of the leaders of this boycott was the Reverend Martin Luther King, Jr., a young African American clergyman who became nationally known for his remarkably effective oratory and his moral leadership, based upon the principle of nonviolence. His successes at Montgomery and later in other causes on behalf of equality and justice, in the North as well as in the South, brought him worldwide recognition and, in 1964, the Nobel Peace Prize. In the short term, the Supreme Court declared segregation of bus passengers unconstitutional in November 1956. In the long term, King went on to offer leadership in the battle for voting rights, in worker struggles, and in the antiwar movement. After his death, King won recognition as one of the great Americans of the twentieth century. When Rosa Parks died in October 2005, her body lay in state in the Capitol rotunda in Washington, making her the first woman to be so honored.

In the late 1950s the slow pace of desegregation, despite the efforts of the civil rights movement, provoked the federal government to take action against discrimination. In August 1957 Congress, after much debate, passed the first Civil Rights Act since the days of Reconstruction. Its purpose was to protect the voting rights of blacks. Though the provisions were weaker than those originally advocated by the Eisenhower administration, they empowered federal judges to jail for contempt anyone—including state officials—who prevented a qualified person from voting. The law also created a temporary Civil Rights Commission to investigate violations of civil rights and to make recommendations for new legislation. (The Commission was continued into the 1970s.)

A second Civil Rights Act, against which Southerners filibustered unsuccessfully, was passed in 1960 to further protect the voting rights of blacks. That act, however, lacked sufficient federal enforcement to make it effective; and it was not until the Johnson administration in 1965 that a voting rights bill was passed that was successful in substantially increasing voting by blacks in the South.

From 1960 on, however, African Americans themselves undertook new ways of attacking segregation in the South. There were "sit-ins" at segregated lunch counters and bus depots, "wade-ins" at segregated beaches, and even "pray-ins" at segregated churches—all aimed at nonviolent achievement of integration and equal rights. From the lunch counter sit-ins in Greensboro, North Carolina, in April 1960, where young black men sat down and waited to be served at lunch counters in whites-only establishments, came another of the major civil rights organizations, the Student Nonviolent Coordinating Committee or SNCC. Founded by one of the legendary civil rights leaders, Ella Baker, SNCC played an important role in the subsequent sit-ins and in Freedom Rides, where blacks rode whites-only buses and thus challenged segregated interstate bus travel, and many other campaigns.

The New Activist Supreme Court

If in the 1930s the Supreme Court was the center of controversy because of its conservatism, in the 1950s and 1960s it was the object of both criticism and praise because of its willingness to innovate in a number of different legal areas. One of the most visible areas of this activism was that of civil rights and individual liberties. Perhaps the most striking instance was the 1954 decision already mentioned in which the Court struck down segregated education, but there were other examples as well.

After the appointment of Chief Justice Earl Warren in 1952, the Court spoke out clearly in defense of individual rights even when the accused were Communists. In the case of *Yates v. U.S.* (1957), the Court seriously modified the *Dennis v. U.S.* decision of 1951 that had upheld the conviction of eleven Communist leaders for conspiring to over-throw the government by force in violation of the Smith Act, which made teaching or advocating overthrow of the U.S. government illegal. Chief Justice Vinson had stated in his 1951 decision that government could act if "a highly organized conspiracy" to overthrow in the future were established. The *Yates* decision distinguished between "advocacy of forcible overthrow as mere abstract doctrine" (which is within the free speech protection of the First Amendment) and "advocacy that incites to illegal action" (proscribed by the Smith Act). Thus mere advocacy of a theoretical desirability of violence was now not sufficient for conviction. Moreover, "mere membership or the holding of office in the Communist party" was held not to be sufficient proof of specific intent to "incite" persons to overthrow the government. That being the case, the eleven communists that had been imprisoned under the Smith Act were released.

The Youth Culture

Society's apparent indifference to the injustices being dramatized by civil rights leaders in the South, along with Cold War tensions and the immense birth cohort of the baby boom, led to an increasing self-consciousness among affluent college youth by the 1960s. In increasing numbers they began to challenge the older generation's failure to live up to its professed moral and religious values and, by implication, to examine their own justification for existence. In 1962 Tom Hayden, who would become one of the best-known student leaders in the country, wrote "the Port Huron Statement" for presentation to the evolving Students for a Democratic Society. In the statement, one of the founding documents of the "New Left" that represented so much vitality and activism during the period, Hayden criticized the combined affluence and injustice of American society. In 1958, William Lederer and Eugene Burdick published *The Ugly American*, a fictional portrayal of American misbehavior in Southeast Asia based on real characters with the names changed. Lederer and Burdick's perspective was a precursor to the Vietnam protests that would occur in the next decade.

Also in the late 1950s there arose the Beat Culture whose adherents became known as Beatniks. The Beatniks celebrated hedonism, nonconformity, and spontaneous creativity, along with abandonment of the clean-cut and clean-shaven appearance. As such, the Beatniks were essentially the precursor to the counterculture that emerged in the 1960s. In 1956, Beat writer Allen Ginsberg published *Howl,* a work that contained graphic sexual language that led to an obscenity trial and increased its fame. Three years later, William S. Burroughs published *The Naked Lunch*, a novel with even more graphic sexual language than *Howl*. Burroughs also faced an obscenity trial with the result that if anything was deemed to have literary value, it was not to be considered obscene.

The novel that personified the Beat Generation, however, was Jack Kerouac's *On the Road* (1957), which chronicled Kerouac's years traveling North America with a friend in a quest for self-knowledge and experience. Kerouac's love of unrestrained freedom and sense of longing essentially defined what it meant to be a member of the Beat Generation. In fact, it was Kerouac himself who coined the term "Beat Generation."

A Resurgence of Religion

In the early 1800s the French visitor Alexis de Tocqueville noted the importance of religion in the lives of Americans. Because of the long-standing importance of religion to Americans, their

MAP 28.2 Population Density of the United States (1900 and 1960)

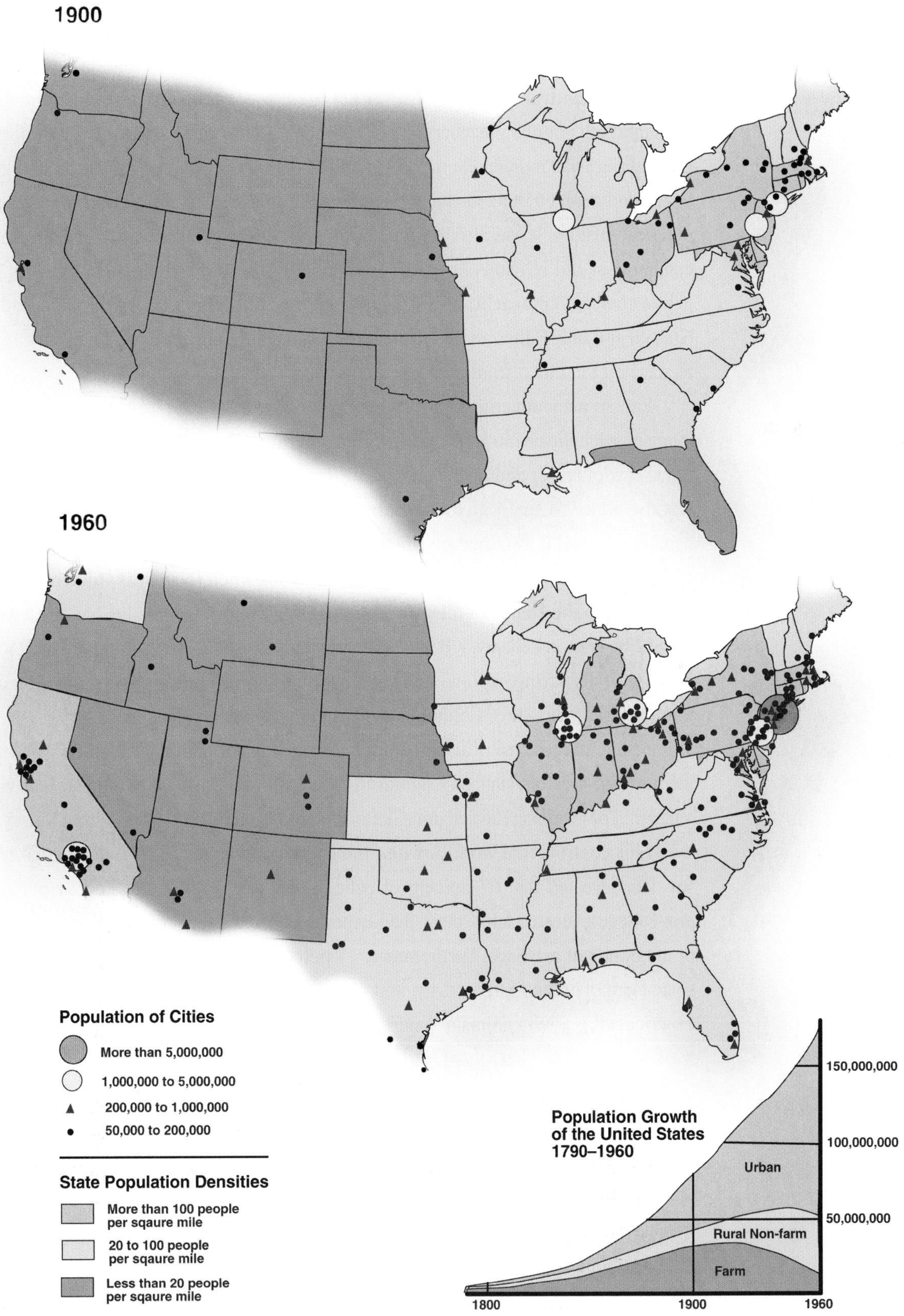

ways of worship have reflected—often quite closely—the social, as well as the spiritual, changes in their society. Therefore, it is not surprising that alterations in religious outlook and practices in the decades after World War II reflected both the prosperity and the anxiety that so strikingly characterized those years. It is also perhaps unsurprising that after fifteen years that were permeated by economic depression and global war, followed by a boom in family life, that Americans would turn to religion.

Consequently, during the postwar era there was a religious revival among Protestants in which popular preachers like Billy Graham and Norman Vincent Peale extolled traditional Christian morality. Some 95 percent of Americans claimed some form of religious belief, and a full 60 percent claimed to attend church weekly, the highest percentages in American history. It was also the time of the Cold War when contrasts between atheistic communism and religious America served political as well as religious purposes. Evangelists combined evangelical Christianity with the anticommunism of the Cold War. Billy Graham and Billy Hargis argued that Americans must be converted to Christianity in order to stave off the threat from godless communism.

With so many Americans displaying their religious beliefs, Congress reacted with a string of symbolic resolutions that reflected American religiosity. Congress declared a National Day of Prayer and made "In God We Trust" the national motto. "In God We Trust" was also added to American folded currency (It had been on coins since 1863 when Abraham Lincoln had it inscribed on Union coins to show the faith of the Union in juxtaposition with the Confederacy). It was also in the 1950s when the words "under God" were first added to the Pledge of Allegiance to the Flag. The original pledge had been written in 1892 by Francis Bellamy, a Baptist minister and Christian socialist, in the 1890s for the purpose of displaying national unity in a nation of immigrants and in recognition of the four hundred years since Columbus' arrival in the Western Hemisphere.

In spite of these overt displays of religiosity, it is not entirely evident, however, that the move to greater religiosity significantly altered other aspects of human behavior in America. For instance, the religious nation was stunned in 1948 when Alfred Kinsey published his controversial work, *Sex and the Human Male,* where his much-criticized survey data revealed that 67 percent of college-educated adult males and 84 percent of non-college educated adult males had experienced some form of sexual activity outside of the bonds of marriage. Furthermore, 37 percent reported that they had experienced some form of homosexual activity, and 18 percent of rural males reported that they had experienced sex with animals. America had become more religious, but clearly human weaknesses had not been eradicated.

Nevertheless, there had been significant cultural, social, and economic changes in the United States in the postwar years. Those changes owed much to the advances in technology that accompanied World War II, the economic boost provided by World War II, and the altered position of the United States in the world as a result of its total victory over its enemies in World War II. That victory helped to shape not only how Americans thought about their responsibilities in the world but also what they believed about themselves as a people. In some ways the victory gave Americans a sense of mission and a sense of power that encouraged them to transform their society for the better and to assume a positive role in the preservation of freedom abroad. That same self-confidence and sense of mission, however, led them to undertake policies and actions that many would later deplore and regret—policies that not only imposed excessive burdens, but also threatened the life of the Republic, repudiated its ideals, and brought destruction upon thousands of people living far beyond the borders of the United States. Though the postwar era was in many ways a shining time in American history, the problems and contradictions below the surface, obscured by the political and economic success, would arise to the surface in the coming decades.

Chapter Review 28

Summary

The postwar period from 1945–1963 was characterized by expanding prosperity for most Americans, even though ethnic minorities still suffered from poverty and legal and cultural discrimination. Women, for the first time were the majority of the American population, though the percentage of women attending college and entering the workforce was not yet on the upswing. Instead, more women were staying at home with their children, who composed the largest birth cohort in American history. Women that did work, along with men, were more likely to be white collar workers working for corporations and less likely to be self-employed. Meanwhile, the G.I. Bill helped the sixteen million men who had served in World War II purchase houses and get a college education, which contributed to a housing boom and an upswing in college enrollment.

The corporate economy included a high-tech boom that began in the Silicon Valley of California with the independent development of the integrated circuit by Fairchild and Texas Instruments. Meanwhile, farming became more efficient and food less expensive due to advancements in farm mechanization and the development of herbicides and pesticides. The chemical industry also experienced a boom that included not only agricultural products, but an explosion in the use of plastics as well as new medicines, such as the Salk vaccine, which prevented polio. It has been estimated that at least half of the current products of the current chemical industry were unknown before 1950. In the drug branch of the industry, no more than 10 percent were known before 1955.

The American prosperity brought a boom not only in household appliances and other items for the home, but also in leisure activities, including spectator sports, such as football, vacationing,travel and a boom in the manufacturing of toys, including Barbie, G.I. Joe, Frisbees, and Hula Hoops.

In literature, the Second World War fostered a number of novels by important American writers that depicted the experiences and struggles of ordinary soldiers in World War II. Among them were John Hersey's *A Bell for Adano* (1944), Irwin Shaw's *The Young Lions* (1948), Norman Mailer's *The Naked and the Dead* (1949), James Jones' *From Here to Eternity* (1951), and Joseph Heller's *Catch-22.* In other literature, African-American Ralph Ellison's *Invisible Man* (1952) became a classic as did Harper Lee's *To Kill a Mockingbird* (1960).

By the early 1950s television had begun to captivate most Americans. Patterns of family behavior began to change as people gathered around the set to watch such beloved favorites as *I Love Lucy* or *The Ed Sullivan Show*. As early as 1954 television began to demonstrate its potential for providing riveting, real-time programming that documented actual events when networks televised the Army-McCarthy hearings. In 1960, the networks followed the presidential election, and in 1963 television covered the events surrounding the assassination of President John Kennedy, including the murder of the assassin, Lee Harvey Oswald, on live television. Meanwhile, hundreds of movie theaters closed down during the 1950s and 1960s, supplanted by television.

The post-war era also witnessed the Second Reconstruction as African-Americans and other minorities struggled for full citizenship rights. Congress passed Civil Rights Acts in 1957, 1960, and 1964 and a Voting Rights

Act in 1965 while the Supreme Court ordered the integration of the schools and struck down the Separate but Equal Doctrine in *Brown v. Board of Education* in 1954. African-Americans themselves took the initiative in organizing a spontaneous bus boycott in Montgomery, Alabama after Rosa Parks refused to give up her seat on a bus to a white person in December of 1955. The bus boycotts would propel Martin Luther King into a leadership role in the movement for the first time. In 1960, young African-Americans associated with the Student Nonviolence Coordinating Committee staged lunch counter sit-ins beginning in Greensboro, North Carolina. Blacks also challenged the segregated interstate bus lines with the Freedom Rides on the interstate bus system. In 1963, Martin Luther King gave his "I have a dream" speech in Washington, D.C.

The Southern reaction to the new racial consciousness was "massive resistance," or the use of state and local government power to block integration. Due to this resistance, President Eisenhower sent federal troops to enforce school integration in Little Rock, Arkansas, in 1957; and John F. Kennedy sent federal troops to assist James Meredith in integrating the University of Mississippi in 1962.

Simultaneously, a new youth culture began to challenge the older generation's failure to live up to its professed moral and religious values and, by implication, to examine their own justification for existence. In 1962 Tom Hayden wrote "the Port Huron Statement" that criticized the combined affluence and injustice of American society. In 1958, William Lederer and Eugene Burdick published *The Ugly American*, a fictional portrayal of American misbehavior in Southeast Asia based on real characters with the names changed. Also in the late 1950s there arose the Beat Culture whose adherents became known as Beatniks. The Beatniks celebrated hedonism, nonconformity, and spontaneous creativity, along with abandonment of the clean-cut and clean-shaven appearance. In 1956, Beat writers Allen Ginsberg and William S. Burroughs respectively published *Howl*, and *The Naked Lunch*—works that contained graphic sexual language. This led to obscenity trials with the result that if anything was deemed to have literary value, it was not to be considered obscene. The novel that personified the Beat Generation, however, was Jack Kerouac's *On the Road* (1957), which chronicled Kerouac's years traveling North America with a friend in a quest for self-knowledge and experience. Kerouac's love of unrestrained freedom and sense of longing essentially defined what it meant to be a member of the Beat Generation. In fact, it was Kerouac himself who coined the term, "Beat Generation."

Coterminous with the rise of the new youth culture was a religious renaissance that sprang from the highest religiosity in American history. Approximately 60 percent attended religious services weekly and 95 percent claimed religious belief. The high religiosity translated into symbolic Acts of Congress that included a National Day of Prayer, "In God We Trust" enshrined as the National Motto, and "Under God" added to the flag salute. Additionally, religion became intertwined with the anti-communist politics of the time. Nevertheless, Alfred Kinsey's study of sexual behavior in the human male suggested that the religiosity had not necessarily translated into a change in sexual behavior.

Chapter Review (cont'd)

Chronological Time Line

1938 David Packard and William Hewlett founded Hewlett-Packard.

1944 John Hersey published *Bell for Adano*.

1944 Congress passed the G.I. Bill of Rights.

1945–1960 The "Baby Boom" era had a record number of births in the United States.

1945 Majority of Americans for the first time were female.

1948 Alfred Kinsey published *Sex and the Human Male*.

1948 On June 20, *Ed Sullivan Show* debuted on television.

1948 Irwin Shaw published *The Young Lions*.

1949 Norman Mailer published *The Naked and the Dead*.

1950 White collar workers became the largest segment of the work force.

1951 James Jones published *From Here to Eternity*.

1951 On October 15, *I Love Lucy* debuted on television.

1952 Ralph Ellison published *The Invisible Man*.

1952 Congress established a National Day of Prayer.

1953 Editors of *Fortune* magazine compared the migration to the suburbs with the Great Immigration of the early twentieth century.

1953 Saul Bellow published *The Adventures of Augie Mach*.

1954 Jonas Salk developed a vaccine against polio.

Time Line (cont'd)

1954 April–June: Army-McCarthy hearings were shown on television.

1954 On May 17, *Brown v. Board of Education* struck down the "separate but equal" doctrine and mandated school integration.

1955 December: Rosa Parks refused to give up her seat on a bus and provided the spark for the Montgomery bus boycotts.

1955 "Under God" was added to the flag salute.

1956 "In God We Trust" became the National Motto.

1956 Beat writer, Allen Ginsberg, published *Howl*.

1957 "In God We Trust" was placed on paper currency.

1957 Jack Kerouac published *On the Road*.

1957 President Dwight Eisenhower sent Federal troops to Little Rock, Arkansas, to enforce school integration.

1957 Wham-O introduced the Hula Hoop.

1957 Civil Rights Act of 1957 empowered federal judges to jail for contempt anyone that interfered with voting rights.

1957 *Yates v. U.S.* released communists imprisoned for advocating the overthrow of the U.S. government.

1958 First National Football League game was nationally televised.

1958 William Lederer and Eugene Burdick published *The Ugly American*.

1959 William S. Burroughs published *The Naked Lunch*.

Chapter Review (cont'd)

Time Line (cont'd)

1959 Mattel launched Barbie.

1959–1961 Fairchild and Texas Instruments independently developed the integrated circuit.

1960 The Lunch-Counter sit-in protested against segregation in Greensboro, North Carolina.

1960 Television networks followed the presidential election, including televised debates.

1960 Harper Lee published *To Kill a Mockingbird*.

1961 May: Freedom Rides commenced in which blacks challenged segregation by riding buses interstate.

1961 Joseph Heller published *Catch-22*.

1962 Tom Hayden wrote the *Port Huron Statement* against injustice.

1962 Duncan marketed the Duncan "Butterfly" Yo-Yo using television advertisement.

1962 October: John F. Kennedy sent federal troops to Oxford, Mississippi, to protect James Meredith, the first black student at the University of Mississippi.

1963 Martin Luther King gave his "I have a dream" speech in Washington.

1963 November: Kennedy's assassination received extensive television coverage.

1964 Hasbro marketed the G.I. Joe.

1964 Wham-O marketed its "professional" Frisbee using television advertisements.

1964 Martin Luther King won the Nobel Peace Prize.

1965 Voting Rights Act provide federal enforcement of voting rights.

Key Terms

G.I. Bill of Rights: Military veterans were entitled to federal help with a college education, help in purchasing a home, and unemployment benefits.

Baby Boom Generation: The generation of people born between 1945 and 1960, the largest birth cohort in American history

Hula Hoop: Plastic toy hoop that became a pop sensation when introduced by Wham-O in 1957

Frisbee: Plastic flying disk that became a pop sensation when Wham-O introduced its "professional model" in 1964

GI Joe: "Action figure" introduced by Hasbro in 1964 that became a pop sensation

Barbie: Doll introduced by Mattel in 1959 that becomes the most popular doll in history

Federal Housing Administration: Federal administration established to help finance long-term mortgages.

Multinational Corporations: Corporations that operate in multiple countries

Silicon Valley: The Santa Clara Valley of California that experienced a high-tech boom

Jonas Salk: Developed a vaccine for polio in 1954

White collar class: Workers in the professional and service sectors

Norman Mailer: Author of *The Naked and the Dead*, which follows an army platoon of foot soldiers fighting the Japanese in the Pacific, including insight into the fears, real and imagined, in the soldiers' thoughts

Joseph Heller: The author of *Catch-22,* a novel in which his main character, World War II flier John Yossarian decides that his real mission above all else is to survive

Harper Lee: The author of *To Kill a Mockingbird*, which exposes the injustices of racial prejudice in the American South through the eyes of a young girl

I Love Lucy: Popular television show from 1951–57 starring Lucille Ball

Ed Sullivan Show: Popular television variety show from 1948–1971 hosted by Ed Sullivan that introduced numerous performing artists to America, including The Beatles

Brown v. Board of Education: 1954 Supreme Court ruling that struck down the "Separate but Equal" doctrine and mandated integration of the schools

Orville Faubus: Arkansas Governor that resisted school integration in Arkansas in 1957 with the result that President Eisenhower sent federal troops to Little Rock to enforce integration

Massive Resistance: The efforts of Southern legislatures, municipalities, and school districts to resist federally mandated integration

James Meredith: First African-American admitted to the University of Mississippi that had to be protected by federal troops

Chapter Review (cont'd)

Key Terms (cont'd)

Ross Barnett: Mississippi Governor that resisted integration and opposed the admission of James Meredith to the University of Mississippi

Rosa Parks: Woman that sparked the 1956 Montgomery, Alabama, bus boycotts when she refused to give up her seat to a white person

Bus Boycotts: 1956 boycotts of the bus system in Montgomery, Alabama, that resulted in integration of the Montgomery municipal bus system and the entrance of Martin Luther King as a civil rights leader

Lunch Counter Protests: Sit-in protests at segregated lunch counters by African Americans, beginning in Greensboro, North Carolina, in 1960, in protest of segregation

SNCC: Student Nonviolence Coordinating Committee organized by Ella Baker that led the lunch counter demonstrations

Ella Baker: Civil rights leader and founder of the Student Nonviolent Coordinating Committee

Freedom Rides: African-American protests against segregated busing and bus facilities where blacks rode on interstate buses and suffered violent attacks by whites

Earl Warren: Chief Justice of the United States that wrote the opinion in *Brown v. Board of Education*

Yates v. U.S.: Court ruled that communist party leaders imprisoned for advocating overthrow of the U.S. government must be released from prison as they did not represent a clear and present danger.

***The Ugly American*:** William Lederer and Eugene Burdick's 1958 fictional portrayal of American misbehavior in Southeast Asia based on real characters with the names changed

The Beat Generation: Reference to young people in the late 1950s and early 1960s that rejected conformity in a quest for self-knowledge and experience—the Beat Generation valued unrestrained freedom and was associated with sexual promiscuity and illegal drug use.

Jack Kerouac: Author of *On the Road* that coined the phrase "Beat Generation" and essentially provided its definition

Billy Hargis: Evangelist that combined anti-communism with evangelism

Billy Graham: Evangelist that combined anti-communism with evangelism and effective use of the radio

Alfred Kinsey: Author of *Sex and the Human Male* that shocked America with his survey data that conflicted with the ideals of American sexual behavior

Pop Quiz

Chapter 28

1. After World War II, the majority of American workers were __________.
   a. working in agriculture
   b. working in manufacturing
   c. white collar workers
   d. working in the computer industry

2. The novelty of the American economy in the post war era was that __________.
   a. the government stayed completely out of the economy
   b. only America was capitalist while all of Europe had gone socialist
   c. most Americans worked in agriculture
   d. lower income groups, as well as upper income groups, shared in the prosperity

3. What percent of the workforce was self-employed in 1958?
   a. 36%
   b. 51%
   c. 1%
   d. 15%

4. The high-tech boom in the Silicon Valley was made possible by the invention of __________.
   a. potato chip
   b. silicon
   c. integrated circuit
   d. dilithium crystals

5. It has been estimated that the percentage of products available in the current chemical industry that were not available in 1950 is __________.
   a. 5%
   b. 10%
   c. 17%
   d. 90%

6. The author of *The Naked and the Dead* was __________.
   a. Norman Mailer
   b. Joseph Heller
   c. Jack Kerouac
   d. Hugh Heffner

Chapter Review (cont'd)

Pop Quiz (cont'd)

7. Which of the following is true concerning the urban areas in the postwar era?
   a. Most Americans still lived in rural areas.
   b. Most of Americans now lived in the cities.
   c. The trend toward urbanization accelerated in the postwar era.
   d. Both b and c

8. The laws passed by Southern states in attempts to prevent school integration were called ___________.
   a. "Massive Resistance"
   b. Jim Crow Laws
   c. Black Codes
   d. Compassionate Conservatism

9. The African-American seamstress that refused to surrender her seat on a bus to a white person in Montgomery, Alabama, in 1955 was ___________.
   a. Martin Luther King
   b. Shirley Chisholm
   c. Rosa Parks
   d. Malcolm X

10. The activist Chief Justice that presided over the *Brown v. Board of Education* decision was ___________.
    a. Earl Warren
    b. Thurgood Marshall
    c. Roger Taney
    d. Earl Baron Duke

11. In *On the Road*, Jack Kerouac defined what it meant to be a member of the Beat Generation with ___________.
    a. his incessant questions to his older brother Wally
    b. his love of unrestrained freedom and sense of longing
    c. his love of marijuana and hatred of hygiene
    d. his homosexuality and hatred of war

Pop Quiz (cont'd)

12. What did Alfred Kinsey discover while writing *Sex and the Human Male?*
    a. Illicit sexual behavior had greatly declined since the nation's church attendance had risen.
    b. Very few American men had sex outside of marriage.
    c. Most of the people having sex outside of marriage were communists.
    d. The vast majority of American men had experienced some form of sex outside of the bonds of marriage.

13. The Federal Government played no role in the prosperity of the 1950s. T F

14. The 1957 Civil Rights Bill was the first such legislation passed since Reconstruction. T F

15. The beatniks were known mostly for their high religiosity. T F

1. C	5. D	9. C	13. F
2. D	6. A	10. A	14. T
3. D	7. D	11. B	15. F
4. C	8. A	12. D	

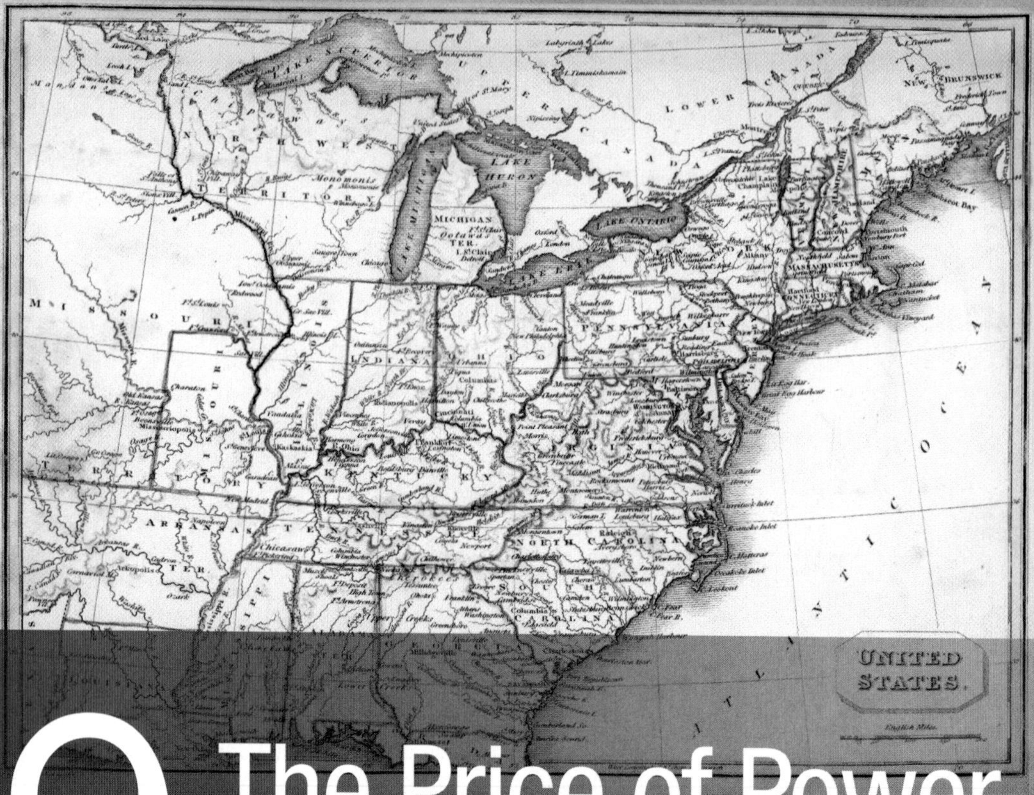

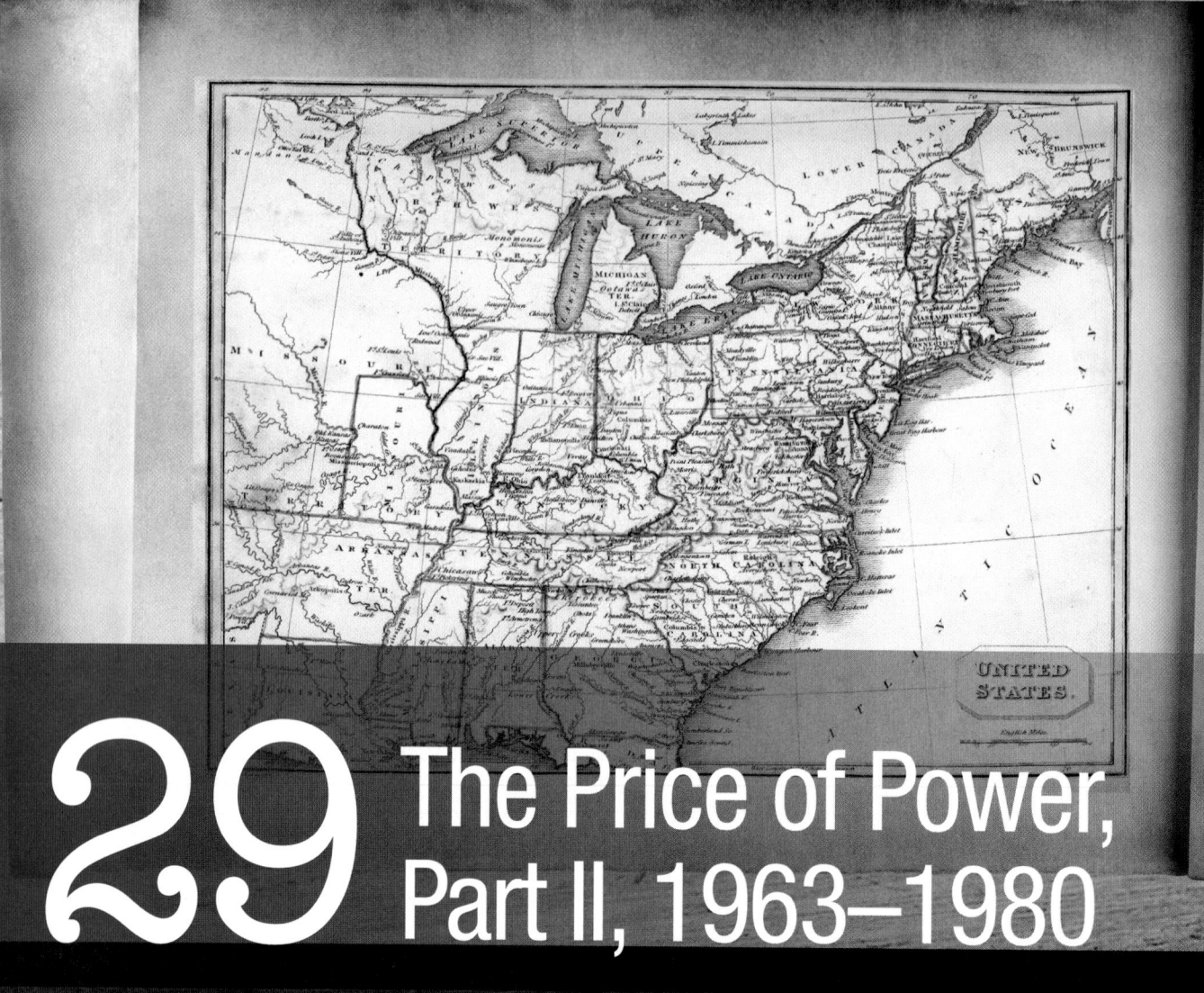

29 The Price of Power, Part II, 1963–1980

Chapter Objectives

Johnson and Domestic Reform

"The Great Society"

President in His Own Right

Constructing the Great Society

The Education President

"Let Us Continue"

Johnson and Vietnam

Gulf of Tonkin

Rolling Thunder

Escalation

Monkeying with the Numbers

Growing Discontent at Home

Tet Offensive

The Nixon Years

The Election of 1968

Men on the Moon

Nixon and the War

Diplomatic Breakthroughs

Paris Agreement

A Costly War

Nixon in Domestic Affairs

The Avalanche of 1972

The Departure of Richard Nixon

Watergate

An Abortive Administration

The Elections of 1974

The Ford Administration

The New President

A Changing World Scene

New Era, New President

The Arrival of Jimmy Carter

A New Administration

Restoring Government to the People

Carter's Retrenchment

A Promising Start in Foreign Affairs

The Canal Treaty

Middle East Accord

The Election of 1978

A Political Paradox

Lowering Expectations

The Election of 1980

Johnson and Domestic Reform

Within ninety minutes of Kennedy's assassination, Vice President Lyndon Baines Johnson, who was also in Dallas that day, was sworn in as president of the United States and was immediately flown back to Washington to evade any other possible attacks on high officials. The smell of conspiracy was strong in Dallas that November day.

The new president was quite a different man from the wealthy, Eastern-born Kennedy. Born in Texas in modest circumstances in 1908, Lyndon Johnson had spent most of his adult years in the swirling politics of Texas and Washington. He served first as an aide to a Texas congressman, then as a member of the House of Representatives during the Roosevelt era, and finally as a senator and Senate Majority Leader during the Eisenhower years.

Privately, Johnson was known for his direct mannerisms, folksy sayings and humor, unrelenting energy, and hard-nosed bullying tactics when he thought it necessary. If there were ever a president that understood how to get legislation through Congress and had the energy to do it, it was Johnson. The Johnson years would be the most active in terms of policy production in American history, and early in his term Johnson would be the most successful president in getting his legislation through Congress that the nation had ever witnessed. Johnson also had big ideas and hoped to forge for himself a legacy similar to that of Franklin Roosevelt. Like FDR, Johnson liked to be referenced by his three initials, "LBJ." Roosevelt had his New Deal, and Johnson would introduce his "Great Society." Unfortunately for Johnson, like Roosevelt, Johnson would also serve as Commander-in-Chief while America was at war. Unlike Roosevelt, Johnson's War would not result in a decisive American victory.

▶ President Lyndon Johnson

"The Great Society"

In his State of the Union message in January 1964, President Johnson called for "a war against poverty" as the central goal of his administration. The Economic Opportunity Act, passed in August 1964, was only the first of the legislative steps to be taken in that war. The act recognized that most of the poverty in the nation resulted from lack of education and training among the unemployed rather than from a dearth of jobs or lack of individual initiative. The law appropriated almost $1 billion for agencies and programs designed to train or retrain the workless in order to prepare them for the more highly skilled jobs available in an advanced society. President Johnson named his program the Great Society, and he defined it as "a place where men are more concerned with the quality of their goals than the quantity of their goods."

Johnson's long and distinguished career in the legislative branch gave him an understanding of Congress that enabled him to push through legislation that had been stalled for half a year under Kennedy. Within Johnson's first year in office, Congress passed the first reduction in income taxes in thirty years, the already mentioned Economic Opportunity Act; the long-pending foreign-aid bill; the Higher Education Facilities Act; and the strongest, most far-reaching civil rights act ever put into law. Not all the measures that were put forward for the Great Society were enacted that first year; however, the record made clear that in his dealings with Congress Johnson was highly successful, despite the handicap of following a martyred president. In fact, many historians have argued that Congress was willing to pass civil rights legislation as a tribute to the fallen Kennedy, although it was Johnson that got it done.

President in His Own Right

Inasmuch as Johnson was advocating the same kind of a liberal program advanced by Democratic presidents since Franklin Roosevelt, conservatives in the Republican Party were convinced that, to win the presidency in 1964, the GOP had to put forward a candidate with a political philosophy diverse from that of Eisenhower and Dewey—someone who did not represent the Eastern, liberal wing of the party. For too long, conservative Republicans contended, the Republican Party had been merely an echo of the Democrats. Victory would come, they believed, only if the voters were presented with a real choice.

The man the conservatives selected as their standard-bearer was Barry Goldwater, a senator from Arizona who ever since his election to the Senate in 1958, had been publicly opposing the liberal point of view and the liberal programs that had long dominated both parties. In 1963, for example, he said that Social Security should be voluntary and that the TVA should be sold. As a result of careful organization and arduous preconvention campaigning, the Goldwater forces won the Republican nomination for their candidate. The platform of the party reflected his philosophy. It called for an end to deficit spending; further tax reduction; and a more militant foreign policy, which it characterized as a "dynamic strategy aimed at victory," a reference to the increasingly frustrating American involvement in Vietnam.

There was no doubt, of course, that Lyndon Johnson would be the Democratic candidate although his selection of Hubert Humphrey as his running mate came as something of a surprise. Humphrey had long been associated with the more liberal wing of the Democratic Party, toward which Johnson was not thought to be favorably disposed. The platform was as liberal as Humphrey ever was, stressing civil rights for blacks, medical insurance for the aged, full employment, and aid to education. In addition, it denounced not only the Communist Party but also such super-nationalistic organizations as the John Birch Society and the Ku Klux Klan. The contest between the Republican and Democratic parties, in short, was unusually ideological for an American presidential campaign and was devoid of the usual balancing of philosophies in candidates and platforms.

Johnson proved to be not only the more relaxed and experienced campaigner but also the more popular. His margin of votes was the largest in United States history, topping even Franklin Roosevelt's in 1936. He won 61 percent of the popular vote, carried forty-four states and won two hundred ninety-five seats in the House of Representatives and sixty-eight of the one hundred seats in the Senate. Goldwater's record as a believer in military solutions to problems of foreign policy, such as that in Vietnam, and his repudiation of the social gains of the New Deal lost him many votes among moderate Republicans, the poor, the aged, and ethnic minorities. Democrats successfully painted Goldwater as a reckless warmonger and were helped, in part, by Goldwater's refusal to rule out the use of nuclear weapons in Vietnam. The Democrats countered with a highly controversial negative campaign ad, considered the first of its kind on television, where a young girl plucked petals off of a flower while a nuclear bomb detonated. Meanwhile, Johnson essentially campaigned against expanding the war in Vietnam, stating, "... We are not sending American boys ten thousand miles around the world to do what Asian boys ought to be doing." While Johnson's approach won big with the liberal "peaceniks," and unsurprisingly, Johnson's proportion of the black vote in the big cities of the North and in several Southern states reached as high as 90 and 95 percent due to his stance on civil rights.

Farmers, too, voted Democratic because they feared that Goldwater's laissez-faire views would jeopardize the government support program for agriculture. Four of the six states Goldwater carried were in the Deep South where it was believed that his position on the rights of black Americans (he had voted against the Civil Rights Act of 1964) was less dangerous to white supremacy than that of Johnson. While Goldwater was no bigot, he also endeared himself to the white South by his emphasis upon states' rights and his steady denunciations of centralization of power in Washington. The strategy of the Goldwater Republicans became known as the "Southern strategy," whereby the Republicans would play on the racial fears of white conservatives in the South in order to lure them away from the Democratic Party. Northeastern Republicans led by Nelson Rockefeller, however, condemned the strategy as immoral, racist, and exclusive in character. In the words of Rockefeller:

> "Completely incredible as it is to me, it is now being seriously proposed to the Republican Party that as a strategy for victory in 1964, that it write off the Negro and other minority groups, that it deliberately write off the great industrial states of the North (representing nearly 50 percent of the country's population), that it write off the big cities, and that it direct its appeal primarily to the electoral votes of the South, plus the West and a scattering of other states. The transparent purpose behind this plan is to erect political power on the outlawed and immoral base of segregation and to transform the Republican Party from a national party of all the people to a sectional party for some of the people."

What Rockefeller saw in the Goldwater supporters clearly contained elements of truth; but the white South, motivated by bigotry, would begin to abandon the Democratic Party in 1964, even though Goldwater himself was a landslide election loser. The landslide victory for Democratic candidate Lyndon Johnson over Goldwater owed more, perhaps, to the complex emotional reactions of the public to the Kennedy assassination than to any coherent, grand strategy by the opposition. In essence, the groundwork for the future success of the conservative Republicans had been laid—even if the immediate battle had ended in miserable failure. The debacle that the Republicans suffered in 1964 was somewhat repaired in the November elections of 1966, when the Party was able to win 47 new seats in the House of Representatives and eight new governorships. That almost all the Republican winners had either opposed Goldwater's nomination in 1964 or simply ignored his conservative ideology in 1966 indicated once again how damaging the party's shift to the right two years before had been. Two years later Richard Nixon would be able to ride the "Southern strategy" to the White House.

Constructing the Great Society

Thanks to his overwhelming victory at the polls in 1964, Johnson found that the new Congress quickly passed the legislation he wanted. To continue the war against poverty, the legislators appropriated $1.1 billion to alleviate rural poverty in Appalachia and $3.3 billion for the economic development of depressed urban areas. By the end of 1968 some one hundred sixty-two thousand new housing units had been constructed through federal aid, as compared with thirty-four thousand five years before. A high of four hundred thousand units was reached in 1970.

At the president's urging, in 1965, Congress also authorized rent subsidies to the poor living in privately owned housing. The program was designed to help low-income people living outside public housing. Johnson called the program "the single most important breakthrough" in housing legislation. That same year Johnson secured the passage of the Medicare bill, which provided for federal government health insurance aid for persons over sixty-five through the Social Security system, a measure that Kennedy had advocated earlier, but had twice failed to get through Congress.

Johnson also redeemed Kennedy's 1960 pledge to revise the immigration laws in order to remove the discrimination against immigrants from eastern and southern Europe that had been a part of national policy since the 1920s. The Immigration Act of 1965 provided for the elimination, by 1968, of quotas based on national origin, but it maintained a ceiling on the total number of immigrants admitted each year and introduced the first ceiling on immigrants from the Western Hemisphere. No one, at the time, realized how profound an impact this law would have in transforming American society. With the refugees coming from Southeast Asia after decades of war in that part of the world and others coming owing to the poverty in their homelands, immigration rates would skyrocket. By 2000 the country would have more foreign-born than at any time since the 1930s.

The Education President

One of Johnson's most dramatic and path-breaking contributions was in education. For years the role of the federal government in supporting education had been vehemently

▶ President Lyndon Johnson signing the Immigration Act of 1965 on Liberty Island. This act made a profound impact in transforming American society in years to come.

debated, without either side able to prevail. Under Johnson, the question was settled positively. From now on it would be a question only of how much support the federal government ought to provide. The National Defense Education Act of 1964, for example, offered federal support for the teaching of the humanities, as well as the sciences, in college. Federal support of education no longer needed to be confined to subjects useful in repelling foreign threats, as it had at the passage of the first NDEA under Eisenhower in 1958.

The Elementary and Secondary Education Act of 1965 was also a landmark measure. It provided for the expenditure of over $1 billion for improving education in schools below the college level and, also for the first time, permitted federal money to be granted to private church-supported schools. For thirty years the major stumbling block in the path of federal aid to education had been the demand of such schools—principally Roman Catholic—for funds and the refusal of many people to countenance such aid on the ground that it would violate the traditional separation of church and state. These obstacles were transcended in the act by confining the federal funds to nonreligious expenditures, while justifying such grants as aid to pupils rather than as aid to religious institutions.

In the Higher Education Act of 1965, the federal government, for the first time, provided scholarships for college students in an effort to realize President Johnson's goal of making it financially possible for any young American to attend college. The act also constituted a continuation of the long-term trend toward popularization of higher education that had begun in the 1920s and had been continued by measures such as the G.I. Bill, which had offered financial aid to World War II veterans wishing to attend college.

"Let Us Continue"

With these words Lyndon Johnson announced his support of John F. Kennedy's policies after the assassination in Dallas. The same words might be used to sum up the deeper springs of Johnson's policies, for the new president was also following in the path of

Franklin Roosevelt's New Deal during which he had first entered national politics. Indeed, Johnson's programs in education and civil rights went beyond anything done under the New Deal. The Housing and Urban Development Act of 1968, providing $5.3 billion over a three-year period for new housing, especially for low-income families, made New Deal housing expenditures seem paltry. Lyndon Johnson's Great Society, however, never went beyond the New Deal in concept; it simply moved forward in the direction the New Deal had pointed.

It was not, however, the limited imagination of the architects of the Great Society that diminished it in the eyes of the American people and brought it to an unexpected close. Instead, it was the inability of the president to end the Vietnam War. Dissatisfaction was already evident in the elections of 1966, when the Republicans picked up forty-seven seats in the House and three in the Senate. By the end of November 1967, according to a Gallup poll, only 38 percent of the American people were satisfied with Johnson's handling of his office, though three years before he had been elected in a historic landslide. To understand what one historian has called "the tragedy of Lyndon Johnson," we have to look at foreign affairs—an area of presidential activity where Johnson was neither expert nor happy.

Johnson and Vietnam

If Johnson was responsible for the enactment of much of the liberal legislation that Kennedy could not get through, he benefited, in turn, from his predecessor's superior handling of foreign affairs. Indeed, looking back on their administrations, it appears that Kennedy's successes lay principally in foreign affairs while Johnson's enduring monuments are probably found in his domestic programs. One advantage that Johnson inherited from Kennedy was a more relaxed and understanding relationship with the Soviet Union. The Cold War still remained, but it had obviously been moderated as a result of Kennedy's resistance to Russian pressures (as in Cuba). At the same time Kennedy had been working out accommodations to lessen tensions, like the test ban treaty, an agreement to sell wheat to Russia, and his conversations with the Russians to limit the spread of nuclear weapons.

It was in Southeast Asia that Kennedy's cold war containment policies ill-served his successor. What Kennedy, and later Johnson, viewed as containment of the spread of communism is probably better termed as an indigenous struggle for independence. After World War II, the Vietnamese people clamored for their independence and the end of French colonial rule; but President Truman desired French friendship in the Cold War against the Soviet Union and, thus, supported the return of Vietnam to France. As a consequence, the Viet Minh under Ho Chi Minh, who had fought on the American side in World War II against the Japanese, sought aid from the Soviet Union for a communist revolution in Vietnam. The Soviets complied. The Viet Minh then launched an eight-year guerrilla war to oust the French colonialists. The French were eventually forced to surrender and withdraw, but not before asking the United States to intervene. President

▶ President John F. Kennedy is shown here signing the Nuclear Test Ban Treaty. Kennedy had been working out accommodations to lessen tensions between the Soviet Union and the United States.

Eisenhower opposed intervention with ground troops due to expected high casualties, and he opposed intervention with air strikes as "against sound military judgment" and "just silly." Eisenhower believed that it would be impossible to defeat a guerrilla enemy dispersed in the jungle by using air strikes.

Without American intervention, a French army of twenty thousand was surrounded at Dienbienphu and surrendered on May 7, 1954. A conference was held in Geneva to decide the country's fate. The nineteen countries in attendance decided that the country would be divided into two parts, North and South, divided temporarily along the northern 17th parallel as a demarcation line that was not intended to be a permanent border. The northern half of Vietnam was openly Communist under Ho Chi Minh, while the southern half of the country, led by the Emperor Bao Dai, was strongly anti-Communist and supported by the United States. The Geneva agreement of 1954, which established the division, also called for unification of Vietnam within two years on the basis of free elections. However, since it appeared that the elections would result in the triumph of Ho Chi Minh in both sections of the country, the Eisenhower administration encouraged the establishment of an independent republic in South Vietnam, as part of its global strategy to prevent the spread of communism. The United States installed Ngo Dinh Diem, a French-speaking Catholic in a country that was 98 percent Buddhist, as Premier. Diem was a fervent anti-communist who had lived in exile in the United States. Eisenhower increased aid to the Diem government and in 1954 sent 675 military advisors, who stayed throughout the decade.

The American policy of aid to Vietnam as part of the effort to contain communism would continue and expand under President Kennedy. After the Bay of Pigs fiasco, Kennedy decided to increase aid to Vietnam, both military and economic, and also to increase the number of military advisors, which stood at thirty-two hundred at the end of 1961. Expansion continued throughout Kennedy's presidency. The number of American advisors in Vietnam was at sixteen thousand by the time of Kennedy's assassination, and 120 United States soldiers had been killed. These sixteen thousand people were only advisors, however; Kennedy balked at sending combat troops. Kennedy once remarked, "Sending troops

MAP 29.1 The Two Vietnams

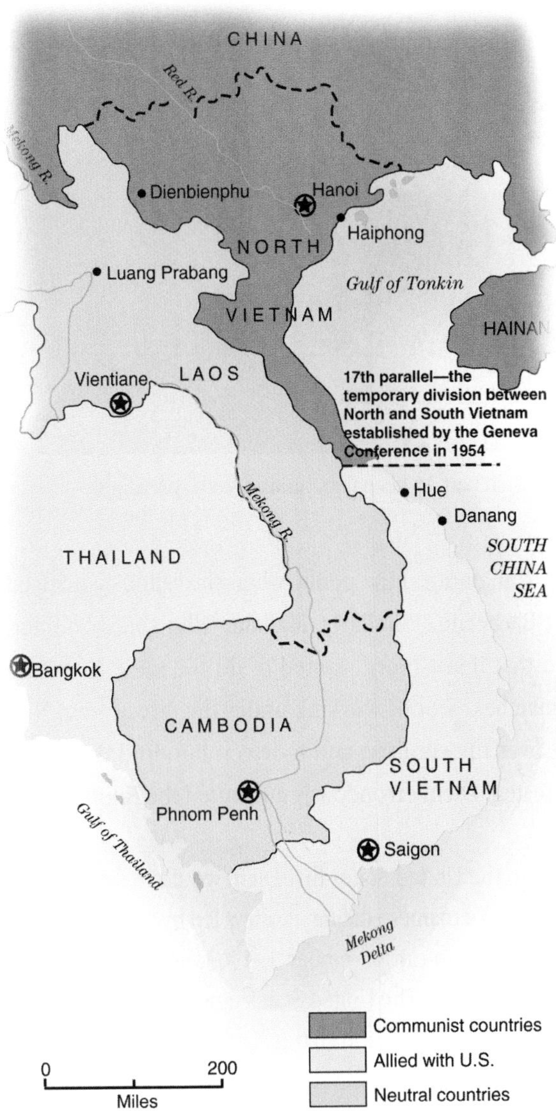

is like taking a drink. The effect wears off and you have to take another."

Kennedy's reasoning in escalating the American involvement was that the problems in Vietnam were part of the American strategy to contain the spread of communism on a global basis, an effort that Kennedy believed was vital to America's long-term security. In retrospect, however, the American commitment to resist the spread of Communist power everywhere was based upon an overly simple analysis and, in the case of Vietnam, misguided. Events would show that not all Communist governments were under the control or discipline of Moscow, as many United States officials in the 1950s and even into the 1960s had insisted they were. Nor was it evident that a world order of peace depended, as Secretary of State Dean Rusk asserted during the Johnson years, upon resistance at any cost to any form of aggression by Communists. Nor was it accurate to see the war in Vietnam as simply a replay of the Korean conflict. The war in Vietnam began as a war of independence against the French and transformed into a civil war in the South—directed largely against the tyrannical rule of the U.S.-backed South Vietnamese government of Ngo Dinh Diem, who lacked the support of the Vietnamese people.

One of Diem's problems was that his communist opposition was waging a guerrilla effort against his government. It was impossible for Diem to know who among the population were the enemy since they gave the appearance of being law-abiding citizens, but would then covertly launch attacks on Diem's government. The United States, therefore, urged Diem to adopt a "strategic hamlet" program whereby peasants in problem areas, both communist and noncommunist since it was not known who among the populace were enemies, would be relocated to concentration camps—thus denying the Viet Cong (Vietnamese Communists or "VC") any recruits.

Unsurprisingly, the "strategic hamlet" strategy stirred up political unrest since innocents were concentrated into camps as well as insurgents. The unrest became much more agitated in the spring of 1963, when the Catholic Diem prohibited Buddhists from flying their religious flags to commemorate Buddha's birth. Buddhists staged a protest in the city of Hue that was put down when government troops fired into the crowd and killed nine protesters.

A month later, an elderly Buddhist monk protested the government actions against Buddhists by dousing himself in gasoline and burning himself to death in the streets of

▶ The American policy of aid to Vietnam was, in part, to keep communism from spreading.

Saigon. Diem's sister-in-law, Madame Nhu, enraged the public when she callously referred to the protest action as a "Buddhist Barbecue." Similarly, Madame Nhu's husband and Diem advisor, Ngo Dinh Nhu, stated that if any more wanted to do the same he would gladly furnish the gasoline and the matches. Troops working under the direction of Nhu then destroyed Buddhist shrines all over the country, and fourteen hundred Buddhists who tried to stop the attacks were arrested. Diem erroneously attributed the Buddhist unrest to the Communists.

By the end of 1963, it became clear to the United States that Diem would never have the support of the Vietnamese population. South Vietnamese military leaders led by General Duong Van Minh, encouraged by the CIA, staged a coup on November 1, 1963, assassinated Diem and his top aid Nhu, and took over the government. The United States quickly extended recognition to the new government, thus giving the impression that it had backed the assassination. The North Vietnamese proposed negotiations with the new government for a cease-fire and free general elections to unify the country, but the United States rejected the offer fearing a communist electoral victory.

Johnson, in the campaign of 1964, promised to keep the United States free from a land war in Asia while continuing to support South Vietnam's resistance to the local guerrillas of the Viet Cong, or National Liberation Front; and the Communist troops sent from the North. The fall of General Minh's government in another military coup in January 1964, however, ushered in more political uncertainty in Vietnam and intensification of the civil war. President Johnson and his advisors believed that the unrest was caused by the communist threat from Hanoi and ignored the possibility that the revolt was merely a populist uprising against an illegitimate government by people who simply wanted to rule themselves.

Gulf of Tonkin

In early August, however, when North Vietnamese ships in the Gulf of Tonkin allegedly attacked two American warships, President Johnson seized the opportunity to broaden his powers. On August 2 and 4, 1964, North Vietnamese torpedo boats in the Gulf of Tonkin off the coast of North Vietnam attacked two American surveillance destroyers. The North Vietnamese torpedoes missed both boats. There is some speculation that there were never any torpedoes at all, and the United States Navy was merely shooting at "flying fish." Johnson had been looking for a reason to justify escalation of the United States presence in the Vietnamese fracas, however; and the Gulf of Tonkin incident provided an opportunity. Johnson called the attacks "unprovoked" and "North Vietnamese aggression on the high seas." In truth, however, the destroyers had been providing radar and reconnaissance for South Vietnamese raids against military installations on two North Vietnamese islands. Nevertheless, Johnson asked Congress to authorize him to take whatever measures might be necessary to resist aggression. On August 7, 1964, Congress passed the "Gulf of Tonkin Resolution," which authorized Johnson to "take all necessary measures to repel any armed attack against the forces of the United States and to prevent further aggression." The Gulf of Tonkin Resolution eventually became known as Johnson's "Blank Check" from Congress to do whatever he wanted in Vietnam. In Johnson's words, "It was like Grandma's nightshirt—it covered everything." The resolution passed almost without opposition, 416–0 in the House and 88–2 in the Senate, and asserted that peace and security in Southeast Asia were vital to the national security of the United States. The Gulf of Tonkin Resolution thus became the president's authority for an almost unlimited expansion of the American involvement.

After the Gulf of Tonkin Resolution, the North Vietnamese government in Hanoi offered negotiations; but Johnson refused, believing the communist threat could only be thwarted by force. Johnson also feared being viewed as "soft" on communism and subject to charges of "appeasement" in Vietnam. With negotiations failing, the North Vietnamese responded by sending forty-five hundred troops to South Vietnam.

▶In the summer of 1964, North Vietnamese ships in the Gulf of Tonkin allegedly attacked two American warships. Following the Gulf of Tonkin incident, which may or may not have been accurately reported, President Johnson seized this opportunity to engage the North Vietnamese. Congress finally authorized retaliation and the war began between North Vietnam and the United States.

Rolling Thunder

By early 1965, the likelihood of military and, therefore, political defeat in the South became so great that President Johnson sharply increased the American commitment to contain communism in Asia. On February 5, 1965, Viet Cong guerrillas killed eight and wounded 126 Americans in an attack on a United States base at Pleiku. Johnson responded with Operation "Rolling Thunder," which was a retaliatory bombing campaign of North Vietnam aimed at cutting off the supply lines to the Communists in the South. Undersecretary of State George Ball warned that such action was likely to unite all of Vietnam against the fire from the sky, but his warnings went unheeded. Six months later, military intelligence concluded that the bombing had little effect on supply lines because supplies to the Viet Cong in the South had moved outside of Vietnam to what was known as the Ho Chi Minh Trail in Laos and Cambodia. Furthermore, the bombing destroyed no strategic targets, but killed innocents, thus alienating the United States from the population it was trying to support. Despite being informed of this information, Johnson continued the bombing campaign, believing that the United States military could handle any situation in any "piddly little piss-ant country." Operation Rolling Thunder continued with a few interruptions until 1973. Four times the amount of bombs used in World War II were dropped on Vietnam, with the result that one thousand Vietnamese civilians per week died in the bombings. After the bombing began, the North Vietnamese deployed another sixty-five hundred troops to South Vietnam, thus increasing, rather than decreasing, the number of armed communists in South Vietnam.

▶ Operation "Rolling Thunder," was a retaliatory bombing campaign of North Vietnam aimed at cutting off the supply lines to the Communists in the South.

Escalation

Later that year Johnson not only increased the number of American military personnel in the South but also authorized, for the first time, the direct engagement of the enemy by American ground troops. This new turn in American involvement in the war had several consequences. For one thing, by 1966 the military presence of some four hundred thousand United States troops removed the possibility that the Communist-led guerrillas could take over the South as long as the Americans remained. It also meant that the war was now being fought largely by Americans, though some five hundred thousand South Vietnamese troops were also mobilized.

Since Rolling Thunder required American air bases in South Vietnam, the Viet Cong quickly began launching sabotage raids on United States air bases. In March 1965, General William C. Westmoreland requested more combat troops to defend the United States airfields. President Johnson responded by sending thirty-five hundred troops to Danang on March 8, 1965, to protect United States air bases. Colin Powell described the circular reasoning that permeated the entire operation: "When I arrived in Vietnam at an air field, I asked General Cho why the air field was there. He said that it was to service the supply depot. When I asked him why the supply depot was there, he said that it was to service the air field." Nevertheless, once Americans were "defending" the airfields, they quickly began roaming the countryside to ferret out saboteurs. Westmoreland called for more troops, and Johnson began to escalate the war rapidly. By the end of 1965, 184,000 American troops were in Vietnam; by the end of 1968, the number was 538,000.

Despite this escalation, the United States had no plans for "winning the war" or destroying the enemy. It was feared that an American invasion of North Vietnam might bring Chinese or Soviet involvement, as the invasion of North Korea had done in 1950. The goal was simply to prevent Communists from taking over South Vietnam, and this meant that the United States would maintain a military presence as long as the enemy retained the will to fight. Since the Vietnamese had been fighting for independence since the Japanese invasion in 1942, they had already proven their resolve. Fighting in their homeland, the Vietnamese people possessed a national will that the United States underestimated. Ho Chi Minh once stated, "You can kill ten of my men for every one I kill of yours, but even at those odds, you will lose and I will win." Ho proved to be prophetic since the American kill ratio was ten to one, but the communists would eventually win the war.

The Vietnamese, both North and South, generally viewed the United States as an unwanted invader in the "People's War." Essentially, the United States was primarily at war not only against the North Vietnamese Army but also almost the entire population. Most of American casualties, including the wound to the foot of Colin Powell, for which he received a Purple Heart, were caused by booby traps rather than engagement.

In general, American soldiers noted that children would spend the day picking up sticks and bamboo shoots. The children took their sticks home to the women, who would sharpen the sticks; and then the men would go out at night, dig pits, and put the sharpened sticks in the bottom. Fecal material or rotten food was often put on the shoots to cause infection. The pits would be covered with leaves and brush so that unsuspecting soldiers on patrol would fall in. The lucky ones would have their feet impaled and quickly be out of action, while the unlucky ones fell headfirst.

Because it was obvious that the villages and countryside were replete with Viet Cong, the United States Army began the policy of "Securing Sectors," which entailed removing the population of entire villages from their huts and then burning the villages so that they could not return. Those who resisted were removed by force. In such a situation, exactly who was the enemy became completely muddled. In the words of American serviceman Thomas Slate, "We were taught that our objective was to kill gooks. There was no distinction between a North gook and South gook; a gook is a gook and you shoot it."

In May 1965, the United States called off bombings to encourage negotiations; but the North Vietnamese demanded a United States withdrawal before negotiations could begin, and talks went nowhere. In June 1965, South Vietnam became under the control of General Nguyen Cao Ky and General Nguyen Van Thieu. Nguyen Cao Ky imprisoned thousands of political enemies after another Buddhist upheaval, and South Vietnam became flooded with refugees.

In 1967, the head of the CIA in Vietnam, William Colby, created what was known as the "Phoenix Program," the goal of which was to promote "pacification" in South Vietnam through mass arrests and trials of civilians accused of helping the enemy. The Phoenix Program quickly became associated with assassinations where thousands of suspected Viet Cong (VC) and their sympathizers were "neutralized." The results of the bombings and pacification programs were that by 1968, four million people—25 percent of South Vietnam's population—were refugees.

Monkeying with the Numbers

United States military analysts argued that at least 3-to-1 strength was needed to win a guerrilla war. The British argued that their experience in the Boer War proved that 10-to-1 strength was necessary. In order to win the war then, military analysts needed to estimate the size of the enemy and then send at least triple that if the United States were to have any chance at victory. In 1964, the official "Order of Battle" set the number of the enemy forces at two hundred and seventy thousand. Between 1964 and 1968, the United States military claimed to have killed two hundred fifty thousand of the enemy. Based on these numbers, unless the enemy had gained many new recruits, the war was supposed to be winding down by 1968. Unfortunately, such was not to be the case.

CIA intelligence officer Sam Adams investigated the Order of Battle in 1968, expecting to find that the Viet Cong had been almost wiped out. Using captured Vietnamese documents, Adams instead estimated the total number of VC at six hundred thousand. Adams informed his superiors and top military officials; but the military rejected Adams' numbers. The official Order of Battle remained at two hundred and seventy thousand, the exact figure from 1964. President Johnson did not want to send more troops since already a half-million men were in Vietnam; nor did he want to increases taxes to pay for the war because such measures were likely to make the war unpopular. Consequently, the United States pretended that there were fewer enemy troops than there were and could then justify limiting the troop strength to somewhere near five hundred thousand—although Johnson never imposed an official cap on American troop strength.

Growing Discontent at Home

Nevertheless, within the United States, the Johnson policy of gradually, but relentlessly, escalating the war had divided the American people. Few Americans wanted a full-scale war against China or the Soviet Union, yet it seemed that the escalation policy in Vietnam might lead in that direction. Also, many Americans had voted for Johnson in preference to Goldwater in 1964 on the pretense that the war would not be expanded if Johnson were elected; they now felt that he had misled them. Others found Johnson's policy faulty on moral grounds, contending that the regime the United States was keeping in power in South Vietnam was representative of neither its people nor their national aspirations. Still others opposed his policy on the more pragmatic level that the United States was overextended in commitments and power in Vietnam. Furthermore, others argued the question of whether or not Vietnam fell to the Communists did not impact national security and, therefore, was not an American concern.

Advocates of American abandonment of the long involvement in Vietnam grew in number as the war dragged on. Most Americans, to be sure, supported the general policy of containing Communism in Asia, just as they had supported it in Europe; but as the cost of that containment mounted and the connection between the interests and safety of the United States and the interminable war became less and less clear, however, many Americans began to think that the price was too high. Even those who accepted the administration's claim that the war was primarily a defense against aggression from the North could not help but recognize that, even in 1968, with over a half million American troops in Vietnam, victory was still not in sight. Although President Johnson insisted that American withdrawal could mean national ignominy and national danger, the direct interest of the United States in the war was never spelled out. The administration relied more and more upon the argument that the war involved the prestige of the United States and the "credibility" of its word among its allies.

The effect of the war on American foreign relations elsewhere was evident when Johnson dispatched several thousand marines in 1965 to prevent an alleged Communist coup from overturning the government of the Dominican Republic in the Caribbean. Although the troops were withdrawn within a year, the United States had once again violated its pledge not to intervene in the affairs of Latin American nations.

The consensus was that Johnson had intervened in the Dominican Republic out of fear of having another Cuba near American shores. Though the evidence of Communist power in Santo Domingo was slight, Johnson was not willing to take the chance that the non-Communists could remain in control without help from the United States. In the context of the frustrating war in Vietnam and the continued existence of a Communist regime in Cuba, even the slightest threat of yet another Communist regime in the Western Hemisphere seemed too risky to contemplate.

On the other hand, when war between Egypt and Israel became imminent in May and June of 1967, the United States hesitated to get involved, despite moral and perhaps legal obligations to support Israel (a nation the U.S. helped create) against a military threat to its survival. Undoubtedly the heavy involvement in Vietnam played an important part in the hesitation. The United States was unable to prevent the brief "Six Day War" in the Middle East, which began in early June 1967.

At home it was also evident that the rising cost of the war—at least $20 billion a year—was stiffening resistance in Congress and across the country to further expenditures on behalf of the Great Society. In November 1967, Senator Eugene McCarthy, a liberal Democratic senator from Minnesota, announced that he would run in the upcoming primaries against

Johnson in order to provide an alternative on the question of the war. By this time the high cost of the war in money and personnel, as well as its persistence, had aroused much public hostility, even within the president's own party. Yet few thought McCarthy's challenge would seriously affect the president or the continuance of the war.

Tet Offensive

On January 29, 1968, at the beginning of Tet, the Vietnamese lunar New Year, the Viet Cong (VC) and the North Vietnamese launched a major offensive against thirty provincial capitals held by South Vietnamese forces. The power of the attack took the Americans and their Vietnamese allies by surprise. At one point, fighting was going on within the American Embassy in Saigon. Although a shaken administration bravely called the Tet Offensive a complete failure, few believed it.

Two weeks prior to Tet, President Johnson had stated that South Vietnam was "nearly all secure" in his State of the Union address. The scope of the Tet offensive quickly proved otherwise, as perhaps one hundred thousand VC and VC sympathizers were involved in the offensive. Communist losses in the offensive were huge, and the United States claimed a 10-to-1 kill ratio. Tet proved that the war was not near over, and the VC were not close to being wiped out as a fighting force. The American public turned against the war as a consequence. In February, NBC news showed footage of Saigon's police chief executing a handcuffed VC prisoner with a pistol shot to the head. In the provincial capital of Ben Tre, American and South Vietnamese troops killed one thousand civilians while rooting out VC, further shocking the American conscience.

That March, Senator Eugene McCarthy, campaigning on his anti-war platform, received almost as many votes in the New Hampshire Democratic primary as the president of the United States. For months Johnson had been unable to appear in public without insulting harassment and even danger to his person from the opponents of the war, and this new measure of public repudiation put unendurable pressure upon him. He could either abandon the war—a policy he had resolutely refused to consider—or abandon the presidency. In a surprise television announcement at the end of March, Johnson removed himself from consideration for renomination, at the same time announcing a partial cessation of the bombing of North Vietnam.

Yet Johnson's withdrawal from political life was only the first of the shocks that preceded the election of 1968. Five days later, Martin Luther King, Jr. was assassinated in Memphis, Tennessee—an event that, as we have already noted, caused violence to erupt in over a hundred cities. Then two months later, Senator Robert Kennedy of New York, brother of the assassinated president, was shot and killed by a fanatical anti-Zionist, Sirhan Sirhan—just after Robert Kennedy won California's Democratic primary at the conclusion of a furious primary campaign for the Democratic nomination that Johnson's retirement had begun. With President Johnson's withdrawal from the race, the charismatic Robert Kennedy, almost as widely idolized as his brother, had been well on his way to the Democratic presidential nomination; the victory in California appeared to be only the first big step. The tragedy of his assassination in Los Angeles, however, robbed the nation of what might have been.

By the summer of 1968, antiwar protests had spread to many cities. Students, in particular the male students among them facing a possible draft, became increasingly vociferous in their demonstrations. A favorite chant was "Hey, hey, LBJ. How many kids did you kill today?" Mass graves uncovered at Hue after the Tet Offensive revealed over three thousand bodies of civilians, many buried alive by the Viet Cong. American citizens were treated to television news footage of U.S. soldiers setting fire to the houses of Vietnamese citizens. Television newsmen accompanied the infantry on raids on the Viet Cong, recording the American futility, deaths by friendly fire, drug usage among the American troops, and gruesome civilian deaths and injuries from napalm.

The most important event, perhaps, was the My Lai incident of 1968 that was made public in 1970. American troops at My Lai, a small Vietnamese village, killed over two hundred people in cold blood under the direction of Lt. William L. Calley. The testimony of Paul Meadlo was particularly chilling:

> Calley's orders were "round everybody up and take care of them." "We huddled them up. We made them squat down. I poured about four clips into the group. The mothers was hugging their children … well, we kept right on firing. They was waving their arms and begging."

Calley was court-martialed and sentenced to life in prison. The sentence was reduced to ten years, and Calley was released in six months on parole.

The Nixon Years

The Election of 1968

Robert Kennedy's death assured the nomination of Vice-President Hubert Humphrey as the Democratic presidential candidate, but not until after the passions stirred up by Vietnam had disrupted the Democratic Party convention in Chicago. Thousands of disenchanted young people—both moderates who had worked in Senator McCarthy's primary campaign and radicals out to "confront" the Establishment—demonstrated in the streets until they were brutally dispersed by the police in full view of television news cameras. The sight of the bloody clashes between overzealous police and protesters shocked the American people. Similarly, the video footage of Chicago's mayor Richard Daley, pulling his hand across his neck horizontally in a "cut it" gesture that led to the silencing of the microphones of several people at the Democratic Convention, contributed to the image of cronyism and corruption by "the Establishment." Young CBS correspondent Dan Rather found himself silenced by Daily's strongmen at the Convention while CBS' Walter Cronkite narrated, "It looks like we've got some thugs here, Dan." Amid all of the unrest, neither the Democratic platform, which offered no significant alternative to the Johnson war policies, nor the candidate, who was identified with those policies, provided a rallying point for opponents of the war.

MAP 29.2 The Election of 1968

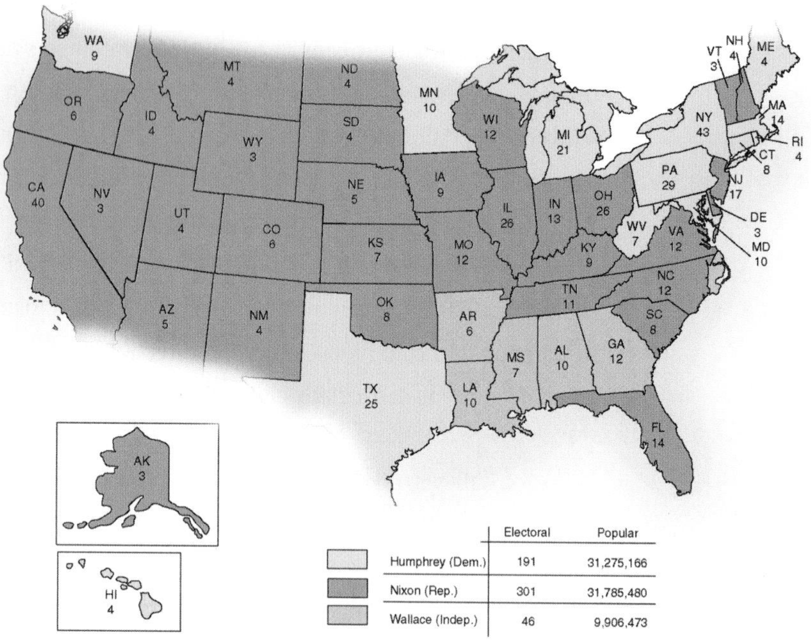

Meanwhile, the Republican convention had nominated Richard Nixon. He had survived not only his defeat by John Kennedy in 1960 but also the subsequent loss of a race for the governorship of California, after which he briefly retired from politics, stating that the media would not have "Nixon to kick around any more." Since then, however, he had worked hard to build support within the party and keep himself in the public eye through meetings with world leaders. Recognizing that he must win a substantial number of Southern votes, Nixon chose Spiro Agnew, governor of the border state of Maryland, as his running mate.

The campaign was complicated by the candidacy of George Wallace of Alabama, who ran on the new American Independent Party ticket and its platform of a return to segregation and a premium on law and order. No one expected him to win, but he clearly threatened Humphrey in the traditionally Democratic South; and the enthusiasm he stirred in some Northern states reflected the opposition of many blue-collar workers to the Democratic stand on civil rights. There was a possibility that he could prevent either major candidate from winning a majority of the electoral vote and, thereby, throw the election into the House of Representatives.

The campaign revolved around the war overseas and the social problems at home. Nixon stressed the alarming increase of violence in the cities, which he attributed to the leniency of the Democratic administration toward demonstrators and rioters and of the Supreme Court toward criminals. Playing upon the public's fears, he promised to end the "permissiveness" that, he insisted, fostered lawlessness. Although he had supported the aims of the war against communism in Southeast Asia since his own vice-presidency, he promised to bring the conflict in Vietnam to an end—though he declined to say how. In the television appearances on which he chiefly relied, he shunned the issue of integration, which was unpopular among many whites, and concentrated on "law and order," about which there could be little controversy. Generally, he portrayed himself as a leader dedicated to national unity and peace.

Burdened with the Johnson record on Vietnam, Humphrey finally announced that, if elected, he would stop the bombing of the North. As Election Day approached, his popular support rose steadily, bolstered by the efforts of his powerful allies in organized labor to win working-class voters back from George Wallace. Just before the election, President Johnson announced the cessation of American bombing in North Vietnam.

Given the shambles at the Democratic convention, the election was remarkably close as George Wallace siphoned conservative segregationists in the South away from the Republican Party. Nixon won by only a half million votes out of 73 million cast. He carried thirty-two states, however, to Humphrey's fourteen. Nixon won seven Southern states, Wallace five, and Humphrey one—Texas. While the outcome indicated that the Democrats could no longer count on even a majority of Southern states in a presidential election, the vote for Congress showed that most Americans still voted Democratic. Both House and Senate remained comfortably in Democratic hands.

Men on the Moon

On July 20, 1969, well ahead of the deadline President Kennedy had set, two American astronauts landed on the moon. Americans watched on television as Neil Armstrong, when he took the first human step onto the moon, called it "One small step for a man, one giant leap for mankind." Five other Apollo missions landed men on the moon over the next three years, the last flight occurring in 1972. During the three years of American moon landings, astronauts put American flags on the moon, brought back rock samples, hit golf balls on the moon, and drove around the lunar surface in a four-wheeled vehicle. The third mission to the moon by Apollo 13, however, had to be aborted due to an explosion of an oxygen tank aboard the Command Module. NASA engineers and the astronauts improvised and used the Lunar Lander for propulsion from space back to earth and what appeared to be almost certain tragedy for the astronauts was narrowly averted.

▶In 1969, Americans watched on television as Neil Armstrong took the first human step onto the moon.

Nixon and the War

The political destruction of Lyndon Johnson and the mood of the country during the campaign made it clear to the newly elected President Nixon that the public would no longer stand for the emotional and financial drain of an endless Asian war. Within six months after taking office, Nixon announced that he would withdraw twenty-five thousand troops from Vietnam over the next ninety days. Thus began the policy of gradual withdrawal that was to continue for the next four years. Meanwhile, the South Vietnamese army was further trained and equipped to carry on the war by itself through an increase in American aid to the government of South Vietnam, most of it in the form of military hardware. This policy President Nixon labeled Vietnamization.

Nixon's willingness to use American power to ensure the success of his policy marked a new high in brinkmanship. In the spring of 1970, he ordered American forces to support a South Vietnamese invasion of neighboring Cambodia (and eventually of neighboring Laos), in order to destroy enemy supplies and troop buildups. This action, taken at a time when the war was supposedly "winding down," outraged Americans who saw it as expanding the conflict. That same week, the killing of four students (two of whom were merely walking to class) at Kent State University in Ohio by national guardsmen during an antiwar demonstration and the killing of two students by police at Jackson State University in Mississippi triggered student strikes at almost three hundred colleges and universities. Furthermore, withdrawal of American troops from Cambodia and Laos did not end, as Nixon would order bombing wherever he saw fit, either inside or outside of Vietnam.

As he continued to remove American ground troops from Vietnam, Nixon also continued the negotiations in Paris that President Johnson had agreed to in 1968. Neither side would accept the other's demands. In the early spring of 1972, North Vietnamese troops launched a powerful assault across the demilitarized zone in the North and the Cambodian border in the West. To support the reeling South Vietnamese forces, President Nixon widened the war once again. He ordered increased bombing raids against North Vietnam, including the capital, Hanoi, and the major port, Haiphong, neither of which had been bombed since 1968, and the rail lines from China. He also ordered the navy, for the first time, to mine Haiphong harbor. His intention was to cut off the military supplies from the Soviet Union and China that made such offensives possible. China and Russia denounced the American "aggression" but took no other action.

President Nixon was gambling for high stakes, since in November he would be up for reelection. If the war were still going on at that time, his Democratic opponent would have an enormous advantage with an electorate that was clearly sick of the war. Yet if he withdrew all American power from Southeast Asia and the Saigon regime collapsed under Communist pressure, he would be held responsible for "losing" Vietnam to communism. Thus he needed to continue to withdraw the troops, but he also needed some assurance that Saigon could survive. As a consequence, Nixon increased the bombing of North Vietnam.

To critics of his policy, it seemed that Nixon was following the tactics of the Johnson administration and trying to bomb the North Vietnamese into an acceptable settlement. By 1970 more tons of bombs had been dropped on the small country of Vietnam than had been dropped on Germany and Japan in all of World War II, and the raids of 1972 were setting new records in sheer destructiveness. Yet after all the punishment, the Viet Cong and the North Vietnamese continued to fight and continued to score successes in the South. To make matters worse, in what was known as the "Christmas bombing" campaign of 1972, the United States was losing 10 percent of its B-52 bombers on each bombing mission, an unsustainable casualty rate.

Diplomatic Breakthroughs

In the summer of 1971, the president made the dramatic announcement that he had accepted an invitation to visit the People's Republic of China. Henry Kissinger, a former Harvard professor of political science, had secretly arranged the visit. Kissinger was President Nixon's trusted adviser on foreign policy, and his influence on the Nixon clearly exceeded that of the Secretary of State, though Nixon at times exhibited jealousy of Kissinger's status with the media. The implications of the trip, which took place in February 1972, were far-reaching: it ended twenty years of frigid enmity between the two powers. Soon after the trip was announced, United States opposition to seating Mao's China in the United Nations ended. Communist China took the place of Chiang Kai-shek's China on the United Nations Security Council and in the United Nations General Assembly in the fall of 1971. Nixon's visit ended China's long isolation (although it should be noted that Prime Minister Pierre Trudeau of Canada had visited China prior to Nixon.) By 1973, following Nixon's visit, Japan, too, had established commercial and diplomatic relations with the People's Republic of China.

Nixon's visit did not convert China and the United States into instant allies. Diplomatic recognition did not immediately follow, and the United States pledged itself to maintain its treaty obligations to Chiang Kai-shek's regime on Taiwan, even though Communist China claimed the island. A new era in the relations between the United States and the Communist powers seemed to have begun, however. This was confirmed when the White House announced that, within two months after his visit to Beijing, President Nixon would visit Moscow as well. (He also became the first president to visit Communist Yugoslavia, Romania, and Poland.)

Behind this about-face by the long-time anti-Communist Richard Nixon and the leaders of the two largest Communist states was the hostility between the Russians and the Chinese. China, as the weaker of the two Communist giants, wanted a counterweight in the form of better relations with the United States. Russia, on the other hand, feared that the United States and China might combine against it. As a result, President Nixon was welcomed in both capitals, even as his bombers unloaded unprecedented tons of explosives on his hosts' ally, North Vietnam.

Nixon's primary goal in his diplomacy with China and the U.S.S.R. was to get them to agree to stop spreading Communism abroad; and Nixon, evidently, believed that he had done that. If China and the Soviet Union were no longer going to spread Communism abroad, then the United States no longer needed to contain it in Southeast Asia and Nixon could, then, pull the United States army out of the unpopular war in Vietnam. Furthermore, the new relationships with both China and the Soviet Union gave Nixon an opportunity to appeal privately to them both to put pressure on North Vietnam to conclude the war on terms the United States could accept. Since American troops were steadily being removed (the last ground combat forces were withdrawn in August 1972), Nixon's desire for an end to hostilities was clear. At the same time, the continued bombing of North Vietnam and the massing of naval power off the Vietnam coast and air power in neighboring Thailand made it equally clear that he intended to keep up the pressure until his minimum conditions were met.

Even after Kissinger had negotiated for months with the North Vietnamese in Paris for a cease-fire, the war had not been brought to a close. Just before Christmas 1972, Nixon increased the pressure further with massive bombings of the North, including Hanoi and Haiphong. Later he would contend (although not all historians agree) that it was these B-52 bombings that brought the cease-fire agreement, which was announced in January 1973. Soon thereafter, all remaining United States combat troops were withdrawn.

Paris Agreement

Under the Paris Agreement that ended American involvement in the Vietnam War, North Vietnam was allowed to keep troops in South Vietnam. The United States agreed to pull out, and its last troops left Vietnam on March 29, 1973. North Vietnam agreed to release United States POWs and released them March 29, though the United States contended that the North Vietnamese release of POWs was not complete. The U.S. was to pay North Vietnam $5 billion in "reconstruction assistance." For their role in bringing about the agreement, Henry Kissinger and Le Duc Tho of North Vietnam won the Nobel Peace Prize, but Le Duc Tho rejected the prize, however, because he explained that the war was not over. The only change was that the United States went home.

For Americans the fighting was over, but for the Vietnamese it continued until April 30, 1975, when the South surrendered to Northern troops after the communists had launched a major offensive that spring and overwhelmed the South Vietnamese government. All of Vietnam was finally united, but under communism, and President Ford did not send the United States military to intervene. Earlier that same month rebels friendly to the Communists succeeded in defeating the pro-American government forces in Cambodia, which had gained power as a result of the American and South Vietnamese invasion in May 1970. Later, in 1975, Communist rebels also took over Laos. Thus, after more than ten years of active American involvement in Southeast Asia to prevent Communist control, three of the four countries of the Indochinese peninsula were under rule friendly to communism.

On the other hand, for facing up to the changed international realities of the 1970s, the first Nixon administration was likely to go down in history as among the important influences in moderating the Cold War. After the Moscow meetings in the spring of 1972, the Soviet Union and the United States agreed to new limitations on missiles and submarines, as well as on joint explorations of space. By 1972 few Americans continued to look on China as the Great Red Menace that a whole generation of Americans had been taught to fear. To have been instrumental in bringing about such an alteration in the world scene was no meager achievement.

A Costly War

Although fought far from American shores, the Vietnam struggle had been the longest in American history. Its cost in American lives (58,000) ranked behind only that of the Civil War and the First and Second World Wars. Over the fifteen years the United States had spent $141 billion on behalf of South Vietnam, or $7,000 for each of the 20 million people in that country. Even those astronomical figures were dwarfed by the cost to the Vietnamese themselves. Between February 1965 and August 1972, the United States dropped three and one half times as many bombs and shells on Vietnam, both the North and South, as all the allies had dumped on Germany and Japan during the Second World War. Perhaps as many as 10 million Vietnamese in the South alone became refugees, while civilian deaths there reached almost half a million. Moreover, thirty years of civil war and the corrupting intrusion of American money and power placed severe strains on the social and cultural fabric of the rural, traditional society of Vietnam.

Nixon in Domestic Affairs

Nixon's flexibility in dealing with China and Russia was repeated in some aspects of his approach to domestic matters. As he did in foreign affairs, Nixon surprised friend and foe alike in domestic matters with his ability to abandon or drastically modify attitudes and principles for which he had stood during his lifetime in public affairs.

When President Nixon took office, he proclaimed an end to federal deficits; and for two years he insisted that he would never impose economic controls. In 1969 Congress went along with his recommendations for a tax cut in an effort to stimulate the economy. However, in 1970, for the first time in nine years, inflation wiped out the gain in median income for a family of four; and since the economy was sluggish as well as inflationary, government tax receipts fell below expectations. Furthermore, unemployment was up from 3 million in 1968 to over 5 million in 1971. In August 1971 the president ordered a freeze on prices, wages, and rents; three months later he set up agencies to police observance of federal economic guidelines.

Thus, having for years pronounced himself an opponent of the "New Economics," Nixon ended up embracing Keynesian theory and the familiar Democratic belief that government has a responsibility to regulate the economy. With the spiraling cost of the Vietnam War, his administration, by 1972, had run up not only the largest budgetary deficit since the Second World War but also two of the largest in American history.

Nixon also showed his flexibility by recommending that the federal government provide a minimum income of $1,600 for every family of four on welfare. Since liberals had advocated the idea years earlier, many Democrats could support it in principle; however, liberal senators rejected the $1,600 figure as inadequate. No agreement was reached, and no new welfare program was enacted then or later.

Another Democratic idea that Nixon sought to make a part of what he called his "New American Revolution" was that of sharing federal revenues with the states and cities. A revenue-sharing bill was finally passed in September 1972. Congress also accepted presidential proposals for making the Postal Service an independent agency and for establishing the National Rail Passenger Corporation (Amtrak) to reorganize and run the nation's passenger rail service.

Congress, however, went far beyond Nixon's lukewarm recommendations on the improvement of the environment. At the end of the 1972 session, it passed a $24.6 billion sewage treatment bill that was vetoed by Nixon on the grounds that such expenditure was inflationary. Nixon had recommended only $6 billion. Congress, in a rare exhibition of independence, quickly overrode the veto.

In June 1972 the president signed a landmark bill providing, for the first time, that nearly every college and university would receive some federal money. It also provided that, as a matter of policy, any student needing money to attend college could obtain a loan of up to $1,400 a year. Public colleges and graduate schools were prohibited from discriminating against women students on pain of loss of federal funds.

The bill also marked the first interference by Congress in the school desegregation issue. It prohibited, until June 1974, any new court-ordered school busing for purposes of racial balance. President Nixon angrily denounced the provision for not prohibiting present as well as future court-ordered busing on any grounds and promised to carry the busing issue—merely a new form of the old segregated school issue—into the presidential campaign. In fact, busing became an issue in the 1972 campaign even when candidates avoided it.

Especially in some Northern cities, busing continued to be a hotly contested public issue long after Nixon was gone. At the end of the 1970s, despite its continued acceptance of busing, the Supreme Court was taking cognizance of the widely expressed complaint that the defense of minority rights was going too far. In the *Bakke* case in 1978, the Supreme Court struck down the quota system that a state of California medical school had set up to keep a certain number of places for minority applicants. A white student, Allan Bakke, who had been denied admission, contended that his civil rights had been violated because of the policy.

However, the opinion of the majority of the court, while rejecting the medical school's quota system, did not rule out some kind of preference for minority students in admission to state educational institutions. The intention was to provide some way of compensating minorities for damage done through past discrimination. In *U.S. Steelworkers v. Weber* (1979), the Court upheld a private company's policy of affirmative action, which gave some preference to blacks over whites in training programs. In short, the Court was not prepared to countenance rigid quotas for minorities but it was willing to uphold the idea of opening preferential opportunities for minorities through special arrangements.

On balance, despite the liberal character of some of Nixon's policies, both foreign and domestic, his administration frankly repudiated the liberalism of the Kennedy and Johnson years in other areas, particularly civil rights. The conservatism was manifested most ideologically in the speeches of Vice-President Spiro Agnew, who went out of his way to castigate liberals—especially reporters and commentators critical of the administration—as dangerous to America and to condemn youthful protestors and demonstrators for their lack of discipline and lack of respect. The president himself spoke out against laws making abortion easier to obtain, and he vetoed a bill that would have provided federally supported child-care centers for working mothers, arguing that such measures weakened traditional family ties.

Nixon's first attorney general, John Mitchell (who had been his campaign manager in 1968), considered the Supreme Court decisions protecting the rights of accused persons to be too lenient and sought to slow down school integration in the South. His efforts in this direction were rejected by the federal courts, as was his use of wiretapping without court orders in the name of national security.

Nixon appointed a new chief justice in 1969, but his next two nominees for the Supreme Court—Southern "strict constructionists," to use Nixon's description—were rejected by the Senate as inadequately qualified. Before his first term was completed, however, he appointed three more justices, all with records that revealed conservative legal philosophies. They soon began to make their views felt. In June 1972, for example, the Court for the first time in eighteen years was unable to render a unanimous decision on school desegregation because two of the new justices voted against the majority.

The Avalanche of 1972

For a long time, Richard Nixon had made clear that he intended to run again for president. Before the Republican convention met in August he had also made evident that he wanted Vice-President Spiro Agnew again as his running mate. The Democrats, however, could not settle as easily upon Nixon's opponent. Hubert Humphrey, who had been only narrowly defeated by Nixon in 1968, was eager to try again. But before the Democratic convention met in July, George McGovern—senator from South Dakota, Doctor of Philosophy, and long an outspoken opponent of the war in Vietnam—showed that he was a favorite in the various state primaries where the Democratic base was making its voice heard. Those victories won him the nomination on the first ballot. The Democratic convention itself was unusual that year since a new process that guaranteed representation to ethnic minorities, women, and young people had selected its members. This new kind of party convention—more serious and dedicated to the question of political issues than any convention since the Progressives' in 1912—enthusiastically supported McGovern's liberal posture. The platform promised a quick end to the war, a deep reduction in military expenditures, tax revisions, and increased expenditures on social services.

The vice-presidential candidate that the convention named, Senator Thomas Eagleton from Missouri, however, was soon compelled to resign because he admitted to having undergone psychological treatment in recent years. Sargent Shriver, a brother-in-law of John F. Kennedy, was named in Eagleton's place. This unexpected change gave a setback to the hitherto highly successful McGovern organization from which it never recovered.

As the weeks of the campaign passed, it became clear that McGovern was really the nominee of only a minority of his party and that his very liberal positions on tax reform, welfare, and particularly on reductions in military spending were frightening many traditional Democrats into the Nixon camp. Roman Catholics, workingmen, Southerners, and ethnic groups were especially unhappy about McGovern. Rather than putting Nixon on the defensive for failing to end the war after four years in office, McGovern found himself on the defensive for being less than candid in his handling of the resignation of Eagleton and for being less than informed in proposing welfare and tax reform programs that he later had to withdraw. Although McGovern publicized what later became known as the Watergate break-in, the connection to the White House was not known and the country did not seem to think that McGovern's charges were worth taking seriously.

Moreover, when a gun-wielding assassin definitively removed George Wallace from the campaign in May because of permanent paralysis after an attempt upon his life, the Wallace supporters moved to Nixon, not McGovern. Nixon's stand against busing in school integration and a "hard line" on both urban crime and welfare won the support of many white Southerners and traditional Democrats in the cities of the North. Together they made up what Nixon termed as the "silent majority"—in contrast to the very loud and violent Vietnam War protestors.

The enormous lead that the polls showed for Nixon over McGovern early in the campaign continued until Election Day. As a result, the president left the actual campaigning to Vice President Agnew and other subordinates. Nixon probably made fewer campaign speeches than Franklin Roosevelt did in 1944 in the midst of the Second World War. Although President Nixon and his foreign policy adviser Henry Kissinger worked hard to arrange an agreement with North Vietnam to end the war before the election, the foot-dragging of South Vietnam prevented that feather from being added to the president's cap.

The results of the election made clear that he did not need an end to the war in order to win one of the biggest victories in American history with Electoral College victories in forty-nine states and 61 percent of the popular vote. McGovern, winning only Massachusetts and the District of Columbia, was as badly defeated as Alf Landon had been in 1936. Those who had contended that McGovern would be the "Democratic Goldwater"—too far out of the mainstream of either party to be able to win—proved to be right. Nixon completed the breakup of the Democratic solid South, which Harding had begun in 1920. He captured, with large majorities, every one of the former states of the Confederacy, a feat never before achieved by a Republican president. Significant for the future politics of the South was the election of three Republican congressmen from Mississippi and Louisiana for the first time since Reconstruction.

Yet it would be a mistake to see Nixon's victory as a complete Republican resurgence. Indeed, Nixon's campaign had concentrated on "reelecting the president," rather than on winning a Republican majority. In his few campaign speeches Nixon rarely mentioned his party, and in some Southern states his campaigners refused to help Republican candidates who were running against conservative Democrats. The result was that the Democrats continued to control both houses of Congress by substantial majorities, as they had done since 1957. Most Americans, it would seem, were still Democrats; but they apparently did not see George McGovern as their type of Democratic president.

The Departure of Richard Nixon

The intention of the first Nixon administration had been to increase the power and autonomy of the president at the expense of Congress. Its overwhelming victory at the polls in 1972 encouraged the administration to reorganize the government so that the presidential office would be free from Congress on the one hand and from the federal bureaucracy on the other. By enormously increasing the White House staff, it would be possible to bypass the permanent staff of the government. Since, as assistants to the president, none of the White House staff would have to be confirmed by the Senate, the office of the president would escape control, or even influence, from Congress; and none of his staff would be a part of the permanent bureaucracy. In effect, the executive would now be accountable only to the voters once every four years.

This move toward plebiscitary government, which was to be put into operation through a reorganization of the executive branch in the first months of the second administration, was stopped in its tracks by the unraveling of the Watergate affair in early 1973. Watergate was a dramatic example of the great danger to constitutional government that could result when a few people, whose first loyalty was to a person and not to the office he or she occupied, were free to exercise power without accounting to anyone except themselves and the person they served.

Watergate

In the spring of 1969, the *New York Times* reported that the Nixon administration had secretly bombed communist sanctuaries in Cambodia, a neutral country during the Vietnam conflict that Nixon had no Congressional authorization to attack. The unauthorized bombings, therefore, exceeded Nixon's Constitutional powers as commander-in-chief since the president may only perform his commander-in-chief powers at the pleasure of Congress. The bombings also violated the president's Constitutional authority to keep Congress "fully and faithfully" informed. Nixon was infuriated at the "leaks" that led to the *New York Times* article and viewed the story as part of the liberal media conspiracy against his administration. Nixon also viewed the article as proof that there were those within his administration that were not only disloyal but also co-conspirators bent on destroying his administration and undermining his authority. Consequently, Nixon fought back in a paranoid rage and asked the FBI for seventeen wiretaps of newsmen and strategically placed White House staff, particularly members of Henry Kissinger's National Security Council staff. Nixon decided that power must be centralized in the White House so as to fend off those in the bureaucracy that were plotting against him. Displaying excessive vindictiveness and paranoia, Nixon demanded the resignation of all non-career officials the day after his reelection victory in 1972.

During the presidential election campaign of 1972, Nixon felt that he needed political intelligence on his opponents and, to that end, assigned G. Gordon Liddy the job of Director of Political Intelligence for the Committee to Re-elect the President. During spring and summer 1972, Liddy's political intelligence operatives made four attempts, only one successful, to burglarize the offices of the Democratic National Committee and install a wiretap. On their fourth attempt on June 17, 1972, five burglars were caught and arrested by Washington, D.C. police. Reflecting their own plot mentality and paranoia,

Liddy and E. Howard Hunt had ordered their intelligence burglars to search for evidence of ties to Communist Cuba and other left-wing organizations within the United States.

Although the Democrats naturally tried to make political capital out of what the White House immediately dismissed as a "third-rate burglary," the Democrats' effort had no impact on the campaign. The trial and subsequent conviction of the five burglars, however, soon started newspapermen, and then Senate investigators, along a trail of evidence that led to the White House.

Unbeknownst to Americans at the time of the Watergate break-in, but part of the revelations that came out in the course of various investigations, was the fact that, in the summer of 1971, the White House had set up an extra-legal unit known informally as the "plumbers." The "plumbers" included David Young, an assistant to Henry Kissinger; Egil Krogh, an assistant to John Ehrlichman; Walter Minnick of the Cabinet Committee on International Narcotics Control; White House consultant E. Howard Hunt; and G. Gordon Liddy, Assistant to the Secretary of the Treasury. The plumbers' task was to stop leaks to the media—whether by legal or dubious means. The plumbers came up with plans to discredit Daniel Ellsberg, a defense intellectual that had leaked the *Pentagon Papers* to the *New York Times* earlier that summer. In 1969 Ellsberg had prepared a detailed and top-secret study of United States decision-making in Vietnam, a study about which he came to believe the public had a right to know. Hence, Ellsberg leaked documents to the press. The *Pentagon Papers* revealed to the American public details of American involvement in Vietnam that were outside of that which Congress had been fully and faithfully informed about by the White House.

Though the study did not concern the Nixon administration per se, its disclosure horrified the White House, which went to court in an unsuccessful attempt to prevent its release. In addition to this open effort, it also set up the plumbers and began a process whereby the presidents' men justified illegal acts to themselves. Through discrediting Ellsberg, the plumbers hoped that they could also discredit other important members of the political opposition as well: Lesli Gelb, Director of the Vietnam History Task Force that produced the *Pentagon Papers*; Paul Warnke, who had served as an Assistant Secretary of Defense; Morton Halperin, who had been Warnke's deputy; and Clark Clifford, the former Secretary of Defense in the Johnson Administration. Collectively, the men were viewed as the "doves" of the Johnson administration that opposed and undermined Nixon's Vietnam War strategy. Thus even before the Watergate break-in there had been discreditable episodes, most particularly a similar break-in to the office of Daniel Ellsberg's psychiatrist in an effort to discredit Ellsberg. The office of Ellsberg's psychiatrist was burglarized and vandalized by a group led personally by Liddy although the burglars were unable to find any evidence of value against Ellsberg in their raid.

In spite of this failure, the efforts of the plumbers continued unabated. The plumbers formulated a plan to disrupt the Democratic opposition—including a plan to harass and burglarize the Brookings Institution, a liberal-leaning Washington "think tank." The plumbers also came up with a plan for "hush money" with which to prevent Nixon aides from providing evidence to federal investigators. G. Gordon Liddy submitted a separate plan to discredit the liberal opposition to Attorney General John Mitchell. The Liddy plan included infiltration of the Democratic Party leadership with spies and electronic surveillance, "demonstration squads" or "street-fighting teams" that could break up Vietnam war protests, "kidnapping teams" that could kidnap members of the demonstrating opposition, and prostitutes trained to extract information from the Democratic Party leadership via sexual relationships.

By spring 1973, Nixon's cover-up of the Watergate burglary began to unravel through a combination of the United States Senate investigation into the case and reporting by *Washington Post* correspondents Bob Woodward and Carl Bernstein, based on their un-named source in the case, "Deep Throat." On March 19, 1973, a major break in the case occurred when convicted Watergate burglar and former CIA Agent James McCord handed a letter to Judge John J. Sirica, asserting that there had been political pressure applied on the defendants to plead guilty and remain silent and that perjury had occurred during the trial. Furthermore, McCord charged that others involved in the Watergate operation not been identified during the trial. Finally, McCord exclaimed that the Watergate burglary was not a CIA operation as had been alleged. Judge Sirica, hoping to elicit previously withheld information from the defendants, reacted by handing down harsh "provisional sentences" to the other defendants with the provision that they were to be reexamined in ninety days.

Throughout the spring and early summer of 1973, in the course of several weeks of public, televised hearings before the Select Committee of the Senate, presided over by Senator Sam Ervin of North Carolina, the public heard some of the evidence linking the illegal act at the Watergate building with the president's office. It became clear not only that the men closest to President Nixon, H. R. Haldeman and John D. Ehrlichman, had been instrumental in bringing about the break-in but also that they had conspired with other White House and campaign officials to cover up the involvement of the president's staff in those activities. Eventually, three White House aides were convicted of crimes as a result of the break-in, and top Nixon aide John Ehrlichman was convicted of violating the civil rights of Ellsberg's psychiatrist, Lewis Fielding, and of lying to a grand jury. Ellsberg, however, had to defend himself against indictment for theft of government property and unauthorized possession of documents related to the national defense, as a result of his role in procuring the *Pentagon Papers*.

The president denied knowing anything about the matter, insisting instead that he sought only to uncover the extent and nature of the involvement. In seeking to maintain this claim, Nixon was forced eventually to ask for the resignations of Haldeman and Ehrlichman. Soon thereafter Attorney General Richard Kleindienst and Nixon's former attorney general, John Mitchell, were indicted and later convicted for their involvement in the cover-up and other incidents.

By 1975 some thirty-three former members of the White House staff or cabinet had been indicted, convicted, or pleaded guilty to various criminal acts. Moreover, the administration had used the FBI, the Internal Revenue Service, and the CIA for purposes that were illegal or unethical. (Still later investigations would show that previous presidents had also misused these agencies in ways similar to those employed by Nixon, although not in cover-ups of criminal acts.)

In April, White House aide John Dean, seeing the writing on the wall, retained a lawyer and began negotiating with prosecutors for immunity. On April 30 Richard Nixon formally fired Dean, but the cover-up continued to unravel. Dean, who was a direct point of contact with the president, became the chief witness for the prosecution in implicating Nixon in the Watergate cover-up. Undoubtedly the most sensational revelation that came out of the Senate investigations and hearings was that in 1970 President Nixon had had hidden microphones installed in his own office, thus preserving on tape every conversation in the Oval Office. On July 16, White House aide Alexander Butterfield revealed the existence of a tape recording system in the Oval Office that could verify the allegations of Watergate witnesses. Special Prosecutor Archibald Cox subpoenaed several of the tapes, thus making them evidence in the case and their destruction illegal.

The news was earthshaking since it promised that the question of Nixon's involvement in the burglary could be answered, provided that the tape recordings could be obtained. President Nixon, however, refused to permit the tapes to be examined by the Senate Committee or the Watergate trial court on the grounds of the constitutional separation of powers and executive privilege. Even when a special prosecutor was named to probe into the scandal, the president continued his adamant refusal, citing executive privilege. On October 19, 1973, Special Prosecutor Archibald Cox pressed too hard for the tapes, and Nixon reacted by ordering Attorney General Elliot Richardson to fire Special Prosecutor Cox. Richardson refused, and Nixon then accepted Richardson's resignation. Nixon then turned to Richardson's deputy, William Ruckleshaus and ordered him to fire Cox; Ruckleshaus also refused and resigned. Finally, Nixon turned to Solicitor General Robert Bork, who dutifully fired Cox in what became known as the "Saturday Night Massacre".

This effort by Nixon to blunt the investigation backfired. On the following day the White House was deluged with letters and telegrams expressing the public's outrage over the self-serving dismissal. With public opinion beginning to turn against the president, so did the Republicans in Congress. Republican Senator Howard Baker of Tennessee asked the famous question, "What did the president know, and when did he know it?" For the first time Congress seriously considered impeachment of Nixon as the sole remedy still open for getting to the bottom of the matter. Nixon then retreated, agreeing to appoint a new prosecutor who would be free from presidential control or interference. The new prosecutor, however, found the president no more cooperative than before.

Meanwhile, Nixon continued to assert his innocence, announcing at one press conference, for example, "The people have to know whether their president is a crook. Well, I am not a crook. I have earned everything I've got." Until then, no one had argued that the president had profited financially from the Watergate incident. Indeed, a sinister aspect of the whole affair was that Watergate was not a financial scandal along the lines of those of the Grant and Harding administrations, in which defrauding the government of money was the principal crime. Watergate, rather, was a scandal involving misuse of government power and authority, thus striking at the underlying assumptions of a democratic society. Even in his denial of financial gain, Nixon was not being completely honest. Later investigations would show that he had, in fact, padded his income-tax deductions while president, thus reducing his personal taxes by almost $450,000.

If Nixon misgauged what the public would stand for when he fired Cox in October, he repeated his misjudgment in April of 1974. By publishing selected excerpts from the tapes, Nixon sought to quiet the ceaseless public and investigatory clamor for free access to that invaluable evidence. His enemies discounted the usefulness or even the validity of these carefully culled documents; but when the verbatim transcripts were printed, they placed the inner councils of the Nixon administration in a devastatingly ugly light. The level of discourse was shockingly low and was pushed several levels lower by frequent use of the phrase "expletive deleted." Instead of improving Nixon's image, this device left entirely to one's imagination the degree of obscenity that had actually been used in the Oval Office.

More important was the petty, selfish, and often amoral content of the conversations, even though they had been selected for the purpose of putting the best face on the evidence. Even hardened politicians were amazed. Some of the president's staunchest supporters now called for impeachment.

Thereafter, events moved swiftly. In July, the Supreme Court ordered President Nixon to turn over all the tapes to the special prosecutor, who had been seeking them for half a year. A few weeks later, the Judiciary Committee of the House, which for months had been considering in closed session the evidence for impeachment, began to hold public, televised hearings. Not surprisingly, the Democratic majority on the Committee was unanimously in favor of impeachment. More threatening to President Nixon were the seven of seventeen Republicans who also voted for two of the three charges and the two Republicans who went along with the Democrats on the third. The first charge cited Nixon for obstruction of justice, the second for abuse of power, and the third for contempt of Congress. Unlike the impeachment proceedings against Andrew Johnson over a hundred years before, these were carefully and fairly conducted. Not even Republican partisans could sustain allegations that procedures had been improper or that the president was being "railroaded."

Before the Committee's recommendations could be sent to the full House for a vote, the situation changed dramatically. When the president complied with the Supreme Court's order to hand over the tapes, those long-sought-for pieces of evidence fully exposed Nixon's involvement in the Watergate cover-up. In June 1972, the FBI had begun investigating the source of funding for the Watergate burglary that had been routed through Mexico by the Committee to Re-elect the President. A week later on June 23, 1972, Nixon had approved a plan to have the CIA intervene into the FBI Mexico investigation. The CIA was to provide the FBI with information that would throw them off-track so as to conceal the relationship of the Watergate burglars to the Committee to Re-elect the President. In furtherance of this plan, Deputy Director of the CIA Vernon Walters told FBI Director L. Patrick Gray that the FBI investigation into Mexico jeopardized CIA operations. Eventually, the taped recording of Nixon's involvement in this ploy to cover up the connection would become the "smoking gun" that the House of Representatives would use to construct an "Obstruction of Justice" case against the president. No longer could there be any doubt that the president had lied from the beginning about his complicity in crime. Nixon's public approval rating dropped to 27 percent.

On August 9, 1973, before the House could respond to the recommendation of impeachment, Richard Nixon resigned his office, becoming the first president in history to do so. Characteristically, his emotion-filled farewell statement made no mention of his complicity or guilt. It merely referred to his loss of "a strong enough political base in the Congress" to allow him to remain in office.

President Nixon also argued that when national security is threatened, presidents might operate above the law. The Supreme Court had visited that argument and rejected it after the Civil War in *Ex parte Milligan* (1866). If such emergency powers were rejected by the Court during the Civil War, obviously, it is a bit of a stretch to argue that "national security" had been so threatened by the Democratic National Committee that it justified emergency powers of the Executive Branch outside the powers granted in the Constitution or thus justifying the president's aides in ordering a burglary of DNC headquarters. The fact that Nixon and those that aided him in his attempts to thwart his political enemies appear to have viewed it this way is a testimony to his personal paranoia. In the end, Nixon's downfall had, perhaps, more to do with his paranoia than anything else. Had Nixon not felt the need to illegally keep tabs on his political opposition due to his paranoia, there might not have been a Watergate break-in in the first place. Furthermore, if Nixon had trusted the entire sordid operation to his security apparatus, he would have been free to deny explicit authorization of the actions and, most likely, would not have had to resign. Nixon, however, was suspicious of both the FBI and CIA, believing that they had a globally liberal bias; therefore, he felt the need to create his own intelligence capabilities in the Committee to Re-elect the President.

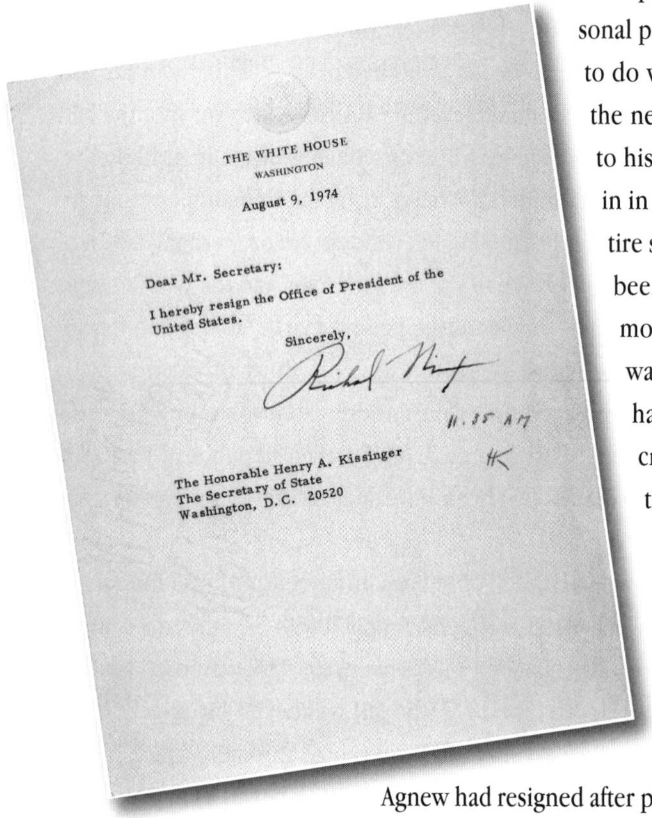
THE WHITE HOUSE
WASHINGTON

August 9, 1974

Dear Mr. Secretary:

I hereby resign the Office of President of the United States.

Sincerely,

11.35 AM

HK

The Honorable Henry A. Kissinger
The Secretary of State
Washington, D.C. 20520

The resignation brought into office Gerald R. Ford, the former Republican leader in the House, who had been appointed vice president under the Twenty-fifth Amendment the previous year. Former Vice President Spiro Agnew had been compelled to resign because of revelations of financial wrongdoing while governor of Maryland. Agnew had resigned after pleading no contest to tax evasion in a case in which he was accused of taking kickbacks from Maryland contractors. When he was vice president, Ford had been almost a last-ditch defender of the president's integrity. In assuming the presidency, however, he publicly emphasized the need to recognize that "truth is the glue that holds governments together." Nixon had chosen Ford, at least partially, because he believed that Ford offered an insurance policy against his own impeachment, given that Congress surely would not want to risk replacing Nixon with such an unproven commodity as Ford. Unfortunately for Nixon, Ford also had a reputation for honesty. Consequently, the prospects of a Ford presidency, regardless of any other shortcomings, appeared refreshing to many members of Congress, both Republican and Democrat, after the revelations of Watergate. Similarly, the American public was undoubtedly relieved to have a chance to restore some of the faith in government that the Nixon years had severely eroded.

While in the White House, Ford proved to be straightforward, relaxed, and low-keyed where Nixon had been devious, tense, and pretentious. Ironically, one of the first acts of the new president was also his least popular. In September, within a month after taking office, President Ford pardoned Nixon for any possible crimes he might have committed in office.

A pardon implicitly acknowledges guilt, but Nixon, in accepting the pardon, neither alluded to nor admitted any wrongdoing. For some months he remained secluded in his mansion overlooking the Pacific Ocean in southern California, nursing his health, which had deteriorated seriously during the long ordeal of Watergate.

An Abortive Administration

Although Nixon tried to govern during 1973–1974 as if Watergate were not a major public issue, the forced and voluntary resignations of key administration officials because of the scandal weakened and distracted his government. At the same time, the federal bureaucracy was increasingly alienated and presidential relations with Congress were blighted by the impeachment proceedings. As a consequence, little effective action could be taken against inflation. By June 1974, prices rose above an annual rate of 10 percent—a level not reached since World War I. A marked slowing down of the economy compounded the effects of inflation. This combination of economic burdens aroused more dissatisfaction with the administration and the Republican Party than even the revelations about Watergate.

The Nixon administration received further criticism for failing to anticipate the crisis in energy that the Arab-Israeli war of 1973, and which the rise in the price for oil imposed by the Arab oil-producing countries forcefully underlined. President Nixon countered by committing the United States to a policy of self-sufficiency in energy by the end of the 1970s. Although the United States, as an industrialized nation, was second only to the Soviet Union in its ability to meet domestically a large share of its energy needs, the goal of self-sufficiency was unlikely to be achieved by a society as dependent on petroleum as the United States.

If domestically the Nixon administration seemed able only to mark time because of Watergate, in foreign policy, also, there was not much movement. Although not personally tainted by Watergate, Henry Kissinger, who had become secretary of state in the fall of 1973, was not able to obtain congressional authorization for the president to revise the tariff so that the Soviet Union could obtain the trade status of a "most favored nation." Kissinger sought this authority as part of his policy of détente with the Soviet Union. That the Russians, too, had doubts about the survival of the Nixon presidency was suggested by the rapidity with which they concluded agreements on strategic missiles and other military equipment with President Ford in November 1974, after months of dragging their feet during negotiations with the Nixon administration.

The Elections of 1974

The resignation of Nixon did not have the restorative effect upon Republicans in the congressional elections in the fall of 1974 that some members of the party had hoped for. Ford's unpopular pardoning of Nixon, however compassionate the intention, probably lost votes for the Republicans. Clearly, the country still held the party responsible for Watergate and the cover-up. Democrats captured three-quarters of the seats in the House—enough in theory, if not in fact, to make the body "veto-proof." They also won three-fifths of the Senate seats and almost three-quarters of the governors' chairs.

For the first time since the Johnson landslide of 1964, the suburbs voted heavily Democratic. Even Ford's old, sure seat in Michigan went to a Democrat. That Watergate had been an issue in the election was shown by the fact that four of the Republicans who had defended the president until his complicity was fully revealed went down to defeat. On the other hand, only one Republican who had supported impeachment before the final revelations failed to be reelected.

The election appeared to be a repudiation of Nixon's conservatism as well as his criminality. Many of the newly elected members of Congress were not only young but also known for their liberal views on public issues. Another measure of the voters' rejection of conservatism was the widespread success of black candidates, even in the South. Almost one hundred state or national offices were now held by blacks, among them lieutenant governorships in Colorado and California.

Despite their numbers, however, the liberals did not run the new Congress, as the first year of the Ford administration would show. While Ford may not always have gotten his way, the liberals, despite their numbers, not only failed to get their way but showed themselves unable to agree on what their "way" was.

A further analysis of the election statistics provided a clue as to why the apparent liberal revival was less significant than it seemed. For one thing, it was probably unrepresentative of the electorate. Only 38 percent of the eligible voters had bothered to go to the polls in 1974, as compared with 45 percent in the previous off-year election. The declining interest in voting undoubtedly stemmed from disenchantment with government, the cause of which extended back beyond Watergate and Nixon, at least to the Vietnam War.

The Ford Administration

The New President

Born in Nebraska in 1913 as Leslie King, Jr., but raised in Michigan after his parents were divorced and his mother remarried, Gerald Ford became a star football player in high school and college. Deciding against a promising career in pro football, he went to Yale Law School, then into legal practice, and finally into politics. In 1948 he was elected from Michigan to the House of Representatives, where he served for twenty-five years, eventually becoming Republican leader. Never known for anything but his conservative, rather combative Republicanism, Ford was a natural successor to Vice-President Agnew, who had also been known for his outspokenly conservative views.

As the first appointed vice president and then president by the first resignation of a Chief Executive in history, Ford entered the White House with no popular mandate at all. His energetic personality and his willingness to laugh at himself and to recognize his limitations brought him instant appreciation. As he said at the time of his nomination for the vice-presidency, "I am a Ford, not a Lincoln."

▶ President Gerald Ford's down to earth, outgoing personality was greatly appreciated by Americans. His openness to the press and the public was a refreshing change from previous presidents.

In the White House, Ford removed many of the ceremonial, almost monarchical trappings of office that Nixon had insisted upon. Ford's relations with the press were friendly and open, a refreshing change after the secretiveness of Lyndon Johnson and the suspicious hostility of Richard Nixon.

The new First Lady, Betty Ford, was also in striking contrast to Pat Nixon and to most other presidents' wives. Though a somewhat retiring person, Betty Ford was so open and liberal in her aspirations for women that she quickly became a public personality in her own right. Not since Eleanor Roosevelt, had a First Lady cast herself so forthrightly in the role of a champion of policies. Betty Ford made no secret of her efforts to persuade her husband to appoint a woman cabinet officer (which he did in 1975) and a woman Supreme Court justice.

Unlike Nixon, Ford loved meeting people, and in his first two years in office he indulged himself to the fullest. In fact, he was frequently criticized in the press for traveling too much, not only to foreign countries but around the United States as well. Observers wondered how he could find time to think about large national and international issues while on such an incessantly active schedule. When he announced in early 1975 that he would indeed be a candidate to succeed himself, his travels and speechmaking acquired a political as well as a personal explanation. As the *New York Times* sternly noted at the end of 1975, President Ford "gives every appearance of having effectively abdicated the presidency today in favor of his candidacy for the nomination next year." Two attempts on his life in California, in September 1975, brought the president's propensity for "pressing the flesh" under more serious criticism.

True to his conservative career in the House, Ford as president followed along the Nixon path in minimizing or deploring the government's intervention in the economy. "A government big enough to give you everything you want," he said several times in his first year in the White House, "is big enough to take from you everything you have." Not surprisingly, during his first year in office he kept almost all of the Nixon cabinet officers. Equating large government expenditures with "self-indulgence," President Ford vetoed several welfare measures on the ground that they were extravagant. In July of 1975, for example, he vetoed a $7.9 billion aid-to-education bill because he thought it inflationary. It was his 35th veto. The Democrats accused him of being niggardly with the poor, in the name of cutting back on government costs while permitting increased expenditures for the military and higher prices for petroleum products in the campaign to reduce U.S. dependence on foreign oil. Ford denied that the country needed another Democratic New Deal. More to the point, he insisted, was "a fresh start." It is time, he said, "for us to declare our independence from governmental bureaucracies grown too large, too powerful, too costly, too remote, and yet too deeply involved in our day-to-day lives."

He sought, also, to reduce the regulatory activities of the federal government. Thus, in late 1975, the administration submitted a bill removing some governmental controls over the bus and trucking industry in order to stimulate competition. Some of Ford's appointments to vacancies on the regulatory agencies were so favorable to business that in one month alone the Senate turned down four of them almost as soon as the names were submitted. Ford's conservatism, however, did not cause him to follow Nixon in trying to place a conservative Southerner and strict constructionist on the Supreme Court when liberal Justice William O. Douglas resigned. The new appointee was John Paul Stevens, a moderately conservative federal judge from Chicago.

The administration's assessment of the economic problems of the country also reflected conservative Republican principles. Early in the Ford administration unemployment began to climb until in the spring of 1975 when it reached its highest level (over 9 percent of the labor force) since the Great Depression. Simultaneously, inflation spurted to an annual rate of 12 percent. At first the administration concentrated its attention almost entirely on controlling inflation. Ford warned Congress against excessive expenditures of any kind, including efforts to put people to work. To back up his warning, Ford vetoed a bill to spend $5.3 billion to create jobs for the unemployed, and another that would have raised farm prices. He also vetoed several environmental bills, notably a stiff anti-strip-mining measure in December 1974, because they would have increased the cost of business operation, thus adding to inflation and reducing the incentive to increase the sources of energy. As unemployment mounted and the economy remained sluggish, however, he came to recognize that inflation was not the only menace.

In March 1975 he signed the biggest tax cut in American history as a stimulus to the economy. Even after being pruned by Congress, the cut amounted to $22 billion. Again the president was careful to warn Congress against excessive expenditures that would increase the federal deficit beyond the current (more than $50 billion) figure. As it was, the Ford and Nixon administrations, for all their Republican character and emphasis on fiscal responsibility, had recorded the highest deficits in American history. By the end of 1975 Ford's efforts to deal with economic problems were showing mixed results at best. The rate of unemployment barely declined at all, going from slightly more than 9 percent in early 1975 to about 8 percent in early 1976. Inflation did slow down from a high of 12 percent a year to a low at the end of 1975 of 6 percent although the economy, as a whole, was still not working at capacity.

Having spent his political life in the House, the president showed himself adept in countering the lopsided Democratic majority in Congress. Although the Democrats promised to come up with energy and economic policies of their own, the administration's policies prevailed—if only because the legislature could not agree on what it wanted. In the contests with the White House, the legislators provided no match for someone who had long known the ways of the House. Congress, even the allegedly liberal House with its extraordinary majority of Democrats, sustained all but seven of Ford's forty-one vetoes in his first sixteen months in office. Even Ford's veto of the jobs bill to combat unemployment could not be overturned.

At the beginning of his second year, in the fall of 1975, Ford demonstrated his political authority and self-confidence, if not his political shrewdness. He summarily fired Secretary of Defense James Schlesinger and William Colby, the head of the CIA. Ford dropped Colby because he had been too cooperative with congressional investigations of past undercover operations by the CIA. Schlesinger's removal stemmed from his long conflict with Henry Kissinger over the proper relation between the United States and Russia. Schlesinger thought Kissinger's policy of détente was too trusting of Soviet intentions and aspirations in the world.

A Changing World Scene

Ford, still depending upon Nixon's Secretary of State, Henry Kissinger, tried to implement the breakthrough that his predecessor had made in 1972 in visits of his own to Communist China (the People's Republic of China) and the Soviet Union. Ford met with Leonid Brezhnev in Vladivostok, Soviet Siberia, in November 1974, to discuss missile reduction and again in Helsinki, in August 1975, along with some thirty other heads of government, to recognize formally Soviet and Western boundaries in Europe. Then in December 1975, he traveled to Beijing to show the Chinese, who were still fearful of Soviet military intentions, that he continued to be interested in expanding friendly relations with them.

One consequence of the détente with the Communist powers, as well as a measure of it, was a five-year agreement between the Soviet Union and the United States on the sale of American grain to Russia. This action assured a ready market for American farmers while avoiding a sudden, inflationary push on domestic American grain prices, as had occurred the year before when the Russians suddenly began to buy grain.

An effort to get the Russians to swap grain for oil and thus help the United States reduce its dependence on Arabian oil did not come off. Despite that failure, the Ford administration pressed toward the goal, also inherited from Nixon, that the United States would become independent of outside sources of energy by the 1980s. Few observers thought the achievement of the goal was possible, and not many more thought it necessary. No one, however, was optimistic about the future since oil supplies were entangled in the always-smoldering conflict between Israel and the Arab states.

The elusiveness of a firm and enduring settlement in the Middle East threatened to produce a confrontation between the two nuclear superpowers, which were ranged on opposite sides in the controversy over Israel. Alone among the industrial nations of the world, the United States championed Israel. However much the other industrial nations might be mindful of the Nazi horror against the Jews, which had been the justification for the establishment of Israel in 1948, they could not ignore the central importance of Arab oil in their economies. Russia viewed Israel as an outpost of American imperialism and supported the Arab states in their hostility toward Israel.

It was this antagonism that threatened to shatter the peace that the ending of the Vietnam War had finally brought to the United States. For almost the first time since the end of World War II no large-scale war was being waged anywhere. Guerrilla fighters in the Philippines, Thailand, the Middle East, and Africa continued to operate; but no national army actively confronted a national enemy. In fact, the anti-colonialism that had lain at the root of most of the wars since 1945, including the Vietnam War, had come to a final close in 1975 when Portugal surrendered its last colony, Angola, to the contending independence forces in that African territory. The colonial dependencies now left in the world were mostly small islands or bits of territory, which neither desired nor seemed likely to profit from independence.

The Ford administration, then, coincided with the close of an era. The postwar world could now be said to have come to an end. Those social, economic, and political forces that the Second World War had set loose upon the world had run their course. Traditional colonialism had been ended. Even though the relation between the two extra-European victors in the war, the Soviet Union and the United States, was not entirely amicable, the Cold War as it had been known for a quarter of a century had thawed. Europe was not united, but it was entirely recovered from the war and once again carrying weight in the world. In Asia, Japan was not only the dominant economic power but also the most stable democratic ally of the West. China was no longer hostile to either the West, in general, or the United States, in particular; but it was fearful of its Communist neighbor, the USSR. Economically, too, the world passed over a watershed in the middle 70s when it became clear that the price of energy, thanks to the cartel formed by the oil-producing countries of the Third World, was not only going to rise but would also inevitably diminish that amazing prosperity that had dominated the economies of the industrial countries of the world for the preceding quarter of a century.

Domestically, 1976 was a dividing line because by then the social changes and upheavals associated with the 1960s and the early 1970s were clearly over. The Ford Administration had put the trauma of Watergate, like the nightmare of Vietnam, behind the nation, at least in part.

New Era, New President

The Arrival of Jimmy Carter

Just about the time that Gerald Ford assumed office after the resignation of Richard M. Nixon, Governor James Earl Carter, Jr. of Georgia decided to run for the presidency. He was still in his first term as governor, not yet fifty years of age, and virtually unknown outside his own state. In fact, he had never tried for public office before 1962, having been defeated then. Yet, in January 1977, Jimmy Carter was inaugurated president of the United States, just as he had said all along he would be.

▶ President Jimmy Carter was unusual, in that he was a white Southerner that, as governor, made explicit his belief in equality of opportunity for white and black people.

Jimmy Carter, as he insisted upon being known officially as well as unofficially, was unusual in other ways. He was the first candidate from the Deep South since Zachary Taylor in 1848. He was a businessman-farmer rather than a lawyer, and he was the first graduate of the Naval Academy at Annapolis to be president. He actually served in the regular Navy for eight years before returning to his birthplace in the tiny village of Plains, Georgia, where he soon made himself a millionaire by raising peanuts. Carter was unusual for a white Southerner in that as governor he made explicit his belief in equality of opportunity for white and black people.

Nevertheless, Jimmy Carter was a Southern Baptist from a small town—the epitome of the conservative family values espoused by the emerging Christian right in the Republican Party. Carter, however, did not overstress his religious faith and believed in church-state separation as well; consequently, he was palatable to the secular left as well as the Christian right and quickly emerged as a serious challenger to now incumbent Republican Gerald Ford for the presidency.

Carter also echoed a number of other conservative preferences on several important issues. For one, Carter expressed his disdain for the welfare system, always a conservative whipping post, and argued that the system needed to be reformed so that it "encourages work and encourages family life." In addition, Carter also promised to reform the tax system in a way that would help families stay together, encourage a program of family planning that would prevent the need for abortion, and require that federal programs all present "family impact statements" that show their impact on American families. Also, Carter favored federal aid to parochial schools, a position that both fundamentalist Protestants and Catholics embraced.

Thanks to a persistent and energetic campaign of almost two years, in the course of which he traveled around the country, often staying at private homes and talking to no more than handfuls of people, Carter captured most of the Democratic primaries in the spring of 1976. He was nominated on the first ballot at the Democratic convention that summer in New York.

Carter's choice of Senator Walter Mondale of Minnesota to be his running mate, however, suggested that he was also comfortable with a more liberal, activist Democrat in the Roosevelt and Kennedy mold. Indeed, Mondale's professional, effective campaigning helped

Carter overcome some of his own limitations as a campaigner, especially against the incumbent and more experienced Gerald Ford. On the other hand, Ford's selection of the strongly conservative and acerbic Senator Robert Dole from Kansas as his candidate for vice president weakened the president's appeal. Even so, the folksy and energetic Ford came from far behind in the public opinion polls in the late summer to almost win in November.

Ford had provided Jimmy Carter and the Democrats with a favor one month into his presidency: he pardoned Richard Nixon for any and all crimes connected with Watergate. Ford believed that losing the presidency and the public disgrace associated with it were enough punishment for Nixon, and he also viewed the pardon as necessary for political healing. To a large segment of the American public, however, the pardon appeared to reflect a corrupt bargain between Ford and Nixon whereby Nixon appointed Ford as vice president (and later president) with the understanding that Ford would pardon Nixon of all crimes if and when the time came. Though there is no record of such a bargain between Ford and Nixon, Ford's approval rating, nevertheless, dropped from 71 percent to 50 percent inside of a week after the pardon. Ford's own press secretary, who had advised against the pardon, resigned in disgust. Ford would never regain the popularity he lost with the pardon, and voters would punish Ford at the polls two years later in the general election.

To make matters worse for Ford and the Republicans, the double-digit inflation and high unemployment that Ford had inherited from the Nixon administration continued unabated. Presidents Kennedy, Johnson, and Nixon, had spent a decade of deficit spending to support the Vietnam War and Johnson's Great Society welfare programs. In addition, oil prices remained high, and the manufacturing sector experienced major problems due to international free market competition. The economic problems were decades in the making and simply too large for any president to solve in such a short period of time; and the electorate, both right and left, would not be so patient. Ford also alienated the right wing of the Republican Party with his nomination of their old nemesis, Nelson Rockefeller, for vice president.

Finally, Ford had public relations problems that were related to his rather vanilla personality and an inaccurate public perception of his intellectual capabilities. Though a graduate of Yale law school, Ford was also an ex-collegiate football player from the University of Michigan and not a dynamic speaker; consequently, Ford somehow became portrayed in the media as an ex-athlete who was a bit dull-minded. The fact that he stumbled to the ground on occasion in front of the TV cameras only contributed to this reputation, in spite of the fact that the link between sure-footedness and intellect is a dubious one at best. Ex-President Lyndon Johnson perhaps exemplified the inaccurate, general consensus with his assessment that Ford "can't fart and chew gum at the same time." Ford would be unable to ever completely shake the "dumb" label with which he became associated. To make matters even worse for Ford, he suffered through the traumatic experience of two assassination attempts, both by women in California. In Sacramento, a member of Charles Manson's Cult, Lynette "Squeaky" Fromme, tried to shoot the president; in San Francisco, Sara Jane Moore shot over President Ford's head outside the St. Francis Hotel.

Ironically, among those that thought Ford lacked the intellectual prowess to be president was Ronald Reagan. This is in spite of the fact that Reagan, himself, had been an average student

▶ September 22, 1975, Sara Jane Moore, using a .38 caliber revolver, shot over President Ford's head outside the St. Francis Hotel in San Fransisco. Moore's assassination attempt was one of two the president survived during his term.

at Eureka College, was not known as an avid reader, had much less impressive governmental credentials than Ford, and was also not known as a deep thinker. Instead, Reagan was a Hollywood actor that previously had been a Democrat and had supported both Franklin Roosevelt and Hubert Humphrey in the 1940s.

Ford would win the Republican nomination, but only after a serious challenge from Reagan produced deep divisions within the Republican Party. In order to placate the conservative Reagan faction, Ford was compelled to dump Nelson Rockefeller as his running mate and replace him with the more conservative Kansas Senator, Bob Dole. Ford's victory was secured only after Ronald Reagan lost the Florida primary when senior citizens reacted negatively to his plan to invest the Social Security Trust Fund in the stock market. Ford was also forced to make major concessions to the right at the 1976 Republican convention, adding an anti-abortion plank and, essentially, abandoning Nixon's détente in foreign policy.

Nevertheless, the Reagan challenge in the primaries had weakened the Republican Party, and the economic malaise Ford had inherited from the Nixon administration continued. The Democrats gained mileage from the economic "misery index," that combined an inflation rate of over 6 percent with an unemployment rate of 8 percent. Ford then fumbled the second of his presidential debates with Carter when he inexplicably asserted that the Soviet Union did not dominate Eastern Europe and stated, "I don't believe that the Poles consider themselves dominated by the Soviet Union." The episode reinforced for the American public that Ford was a bit slow-minded. That view—combined with the economic malaise, the bloodletting within the Republican party, and the inability of the public to disassociate Ford from his pardon of Richard Nixon—created the situation where the inexperienced Jimmy Carter could win.

On Election Day, Carter surpassed Ford by fewer than 2 million votes, and the tally in the Electoral College was so close that a shift in ten thousand votes in two states would have given Ford the victory. Jimmy Carter had won the presidency with the backing of Southern Christian fundamentalists due to his own Baptist religious beliefs and the moral outrage of Americans over the Watergate affair, coupled with Ford's pardon of Nixon. Carter also played the "regular guy" well to the American people, with his humble origins as a peanut farmer from the small town of Plains, Georgia. Carter held town meetings and call-in talk sessions and asked callers, in good Southern fashion, if they were kin to someone of the same name that he knew in Georgia. Carter wore a cardigan sweater while in front of the television cameras in the White House, mended his own clothes in front of reporters on an airplane, and carried his own luggage, thus proving to many Americans, conservative and liberal alike, that he was "just like them." Both houses of Congress, however, went overwhelmingly Democratic, as they had in 1972 and 1974. To this political inconsistency we will return later in this chapter.

A New Administration

In line with his promise during the campaign, Carter brought two women, one of whom was black, into his Cabinet, and named a black fellow Georgian, Andrew Young, to be the Ambassador to the United Nations. This was not as high a representation of minorities and women as had been anticipated, but it was greater than in any previous administration.

Carter's desire to signal the novelty of his administration was evident immediately after his inauguration when he eschewed the usual ride in a large black Cadillac down Pennsylvania Avenue. Instead he and his wife Rosalyn walked hand-in-hand down the avenue to the White House, waving and smiling broadly to the pleasantly surprised crowds along the way. Another novel act, within a month of taking office, was his pardoning of some ten thousand draft evaders from the days of the Vietnam War, something none of his immediate predecessors had wanted to do. (Even Carter, however, did not pardon the sixty-nine thousand military deserters.)

Carter tried, also early in his administration, to break new ground in foreign policy. He publicly encouraged Soviet dissidents who were seeking greater freedom within the Soviet Union, a gesture Henry Kissinger, the previous secretary of state, had refused to make on the ground that it would interfere with impending agreements with the Soviet state on larger matters. The Carter administration, however, contended that international agreements were achieved because of self-interest on both sides, not because an American president refrained from criticizing the denials of free speech and press in the Soviet Union. Therefore, early in his administration, Carter dispatched his new secretary of state, Cyrus Vance, to Moscow with a series of proposals to restrict the number and kinds of missiles that the two superpowers could maintain.

Contrary to his expectations, the Russians coolly turned down the proposals. One interpretation was that Carter had been too quick in his diplomacy. Some feared that Carter's insistence upon denouncing denial of human rights might revive the Cold War.

In subsequent months, as Carter continued to speak out in behalf of human rights, he seemed to be less than consistent in his denouncements. Violations of human rights among our allies were rarely noted. Yet there was no question that Carter's emphasis on human rights was consonant with America's long history of freedom and concern over the denial of freedom in other countries. Some highly placed cynics in capitals around the world made fun of Carter's addition of human rights concerns to foreign policy, especially when the selectivity of application became evident. Yet the prominence the issue achieved thereafter at international conferences and at the United Nations suggested that Carter's initiative had made human rights a concern among nations such as it had not been since the 1930s.

Restoring Government to the People

During his campaign Carter had promised to bring government back to the people. Some politicians had complained that he had "campaigned against Washington while trying his best to get there." Early in his administration, Carter emphasized two policies that he thought would give Americans a sense of controlling their future.

One was his promise to balance the federal budget by 1980, though that had not been accomplished under Republican or Democratic presidents since the beginning of American involvement in the Vietnam War. Only reducing government expenditures could do it. Although Congress is rarely happy about cutting expenditures, it did stay within the guidelines set by the administration during the first year, though not without the help of some presidential vetoes. A public works appropriation and a plan to build a nuclear carrier were both killed by the president for a saving of some $2 billion. Carter demonstrated some willingness to cut down on military spending in his decision not to develop the B-1 superbomber, which many powerful congressmen were supporting.

Carter's second effort to give Americans a sense of control over their future was his call, in March 1977, for a "moral equivalent of war" on the energy shortage, particularly on the dependence of the United States on foreign oil. This was a subject that both presidents Ford and Nixon had addressed, but oil imports had been continuing to rise. Essentially, Carter's program called for a reduction in consumption and provided for a series of incentives to industry and private citizens to use alternative sources of energy, such as coal, which was plentiful in the United States, and solar energy.

Despite the overwhelming majority his party held in both houses of Congress, Carter did not by any means obtain all that he asked for that first year. In fact, the energy program was bogged down for almost eighteen months in Congress, as various groups debated the details of the program. All that the president received that year from Congress in regard to energy was agreement to create a new cabinet post, the Department of Energy. Former Secretary of Defense James Schlesinger, fired by Ford, was named its first secretary. During the Vietnam War, Congress had been overawed by Johnson and Nixon and had followed their leads without much questioning. When the war was over, revelations about Congress' conduct and about Watergate were evidence that Congress had been negligent. As a result, Congress under Carter became highly independent on both domestic and foreign affairs. Moreover, even Democrats became more conservative in their social outlook. As a result, even though the labor unions had supported Carter and the Democrats in the recent election, the unions' bill to revise the Labor Relations Act in order to control obstructionist employers was killed in the Senate after passing the House. Also, Carter's effort to get a new Department of Education, in order to bring the wide range of federal educational programs under one roof, died in committee.

Carter's Retrenchment

Congress approved of Carter's plan to streamline the federal bureaucracy through new hiring and firing procedures and salary incentives. Carter suffered a deep wound officially, as well as personally, however, when his trusted friend and adviser, Bert Lance, the Director of the government's Office of Management and Budget was compelled to resign in September 1977 for questionable banking practices in Georgia. Carter's reluctance during several weeks of public hearings to admit his friend's defects spoke well for his sense of personal loyalty but seemed to undercut the high moral claims of his campaign.

Carter entered office with the image of an activist, and during that first year many in Congress were heard to complain of too many proposals coming from the White House in too short a time. By the second year, however, things had changed if only because so little had been achieved in the first year. President Carter's first State of the Union message reflected the change; retrenchment and caution now seemed to be the watchwords. "Government cannot solve our problems," he warned. "Government cannot eliminate poverty, or provide a bountiful economy, or reduce inflation, or save our cities, or cure illiteracy, or provide energy, or mandate goodness." Only people cooperating with government can accomplish anything, he asserted.

In his budget message he did present his long-awaited proposal for tax reform and reduction, but it did not stir hearts or bring much that was new. The cuts were designed primarily to relieve the burdens on low- and middle-income Americans, who increasingly were feeling the effects of rising prices.

Although prices had been rising ominously throughout his first eighteen months as president, Carter had hesitated to make a fight against inflation his first priority. He feared that slowing down the economy would produce unemployment. The most he ventured was to set guidelines on prices and wages, but they were only voluntary for business and labor. That half-hearted tactic did not work. By early 1979 the annual rate of inflation was over 10 percent and still rising. That fact probably explained why in early 1979 only 18 percent of Americans thought Carter's handling of the economy was satisfactory.

In Carter's mind, a more crucial test of his leadership than the issue of inflation was the question of energy. He had begun his administration by calling for a "moral equivalent of war" on the energy problem, but the measure Congress finally passed was at best a compromise and at worst only an excuse for an energy policy. It cut in half the figure by which importations of oil were to be reduced in the next five years and offered only financial incentives for oil users to shift to coal or solar sources of energy. Obviously the question of energy would have to come before the administration and the nation again, for the nation had not yet faced up to the problem of American dependence on foreign oil and finite global oil reserves.

A Promising Start in Foreign Affairs

Just as his personally democratic ways and high intelligence had won President Carter many admirers domestically, these qualities, at least at first, also won him friends abroad. On an official visit to London in May 1977, to meet with the heads of government of the principal western European nations, Carter was an immediate hit with the British public and the leaders of government. At conferences, his command of the issues was quickly evident.

On a two-week tour of Latin America, his wife Rosalyn also impressed governmental officials there with her solid preparation and skillful diplomacy, as well as her clear authority to speak for the president. No other American president, including Franklin Roosevelt, had relied so heavily and drawn so much support from his wife as Carter. Rosalyn Carter frequently attended Cabinet meetings, as well as accompanying him on virtually every trip abroad.

In fact, trips abroad were so successful for the Carters that in December the president embarked upon another one to Poland, Iran, India, Saudi Arabia, France, and Belgium, covering a distance of 18,500 miles in only nine days. Just when some observers were becoming concerned that travel might turn out to be the only diplomatic achievement of the new president, Carter managed to score two significant gains.

The Canal Treaty

The first significant gain was winning the Senate's acceptance of a new treaty with Panama regarding the Panama Canal. Ever since the early years of the Johnson administration, Panamanians had been demanding that they be given a more equal role in the management of the

The Misery Index: Inflation and Recession

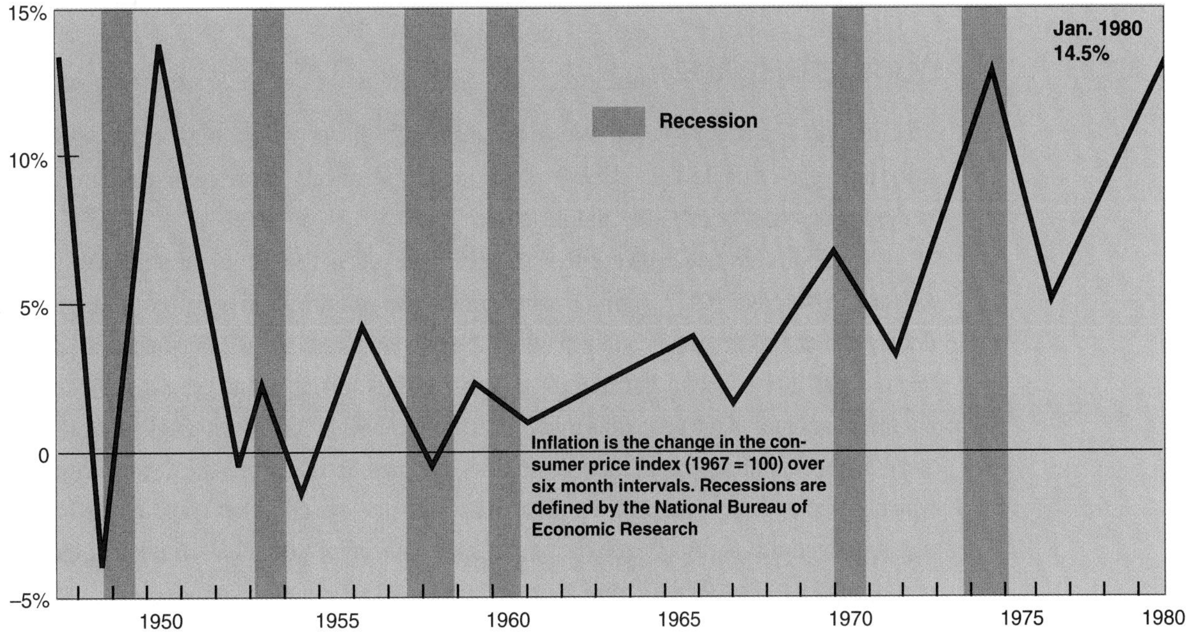

canal, but the Vietnam War and then the defeat of the United States in Asia made it difficult to bring the issue before the country. Finally, in August 1977, the American negotiators concluded a treaty that would turn the canal over to Panama by the year 2000.

Although leading foreign policy experts on the Republican side, like Henry Kissinger, supported the treaty, Republican opposition was vocal and adamant. When conservative Democratic opponents joined the criticism, the treaty seemed likely to be defeated in the Senate. After lengthy hearings and the sometimes-acrimonious public debate, the Senate gave its approval in April 1978, but with only one vote to spare. To achieve even that narrow victory, certain reservations had to be added. Fortunately, Panama was prepared to accept them so that the treaty could be ratified without renegotiation.

Carter's close victory demonstrated that in foreign policy, as in domestic affairs, his influence over Congress was severely limited for a leader with a party majority in both houses. Thanks to the passage of the Canal Treaty, Carter's standing in the opinion polls rose from 37 percent to 42 percent of Americans approving his administration. Those who approved, however, were still significantly less than a majority.

Carter and the two thirds of the senators that ratified the Canal Treaty recognized that the Panama Canal no longer had the strategic or commercial importance that it once had. Commercially, the most important ships, the oil supertankers, could not use the canal because they were simply too large. Strategically, the canal had been reduced in importance since the largest and most important military surface ships, the latest aircraft carriers, were also too large. The canal was also useless to American nuclear submarines since use of the canal would reveal their positions (which were kept secret as much as possible as a check on the Soviet Union). Given these factors, Carter and the Senators calculated that the advantage in good will with Latin America gained by the Canal Treaty would outweigh any strategic or commercial negatives associated with the return of the canal to Panama. The opposition simply ignored such analysis and viewed the Canal Treaty as an agreement that sold out American interests and weakened America.

Middle East Accord

That minority approval, however, swelled to a majority by the end of the summer as Carter had made the biggest gamble of his career by deliberately undertaking to bring about an agreement between Egypt and Israel in the Middle East.

The opportunity had been created by the surprise visit of President Anwar Sadat of Egypt to Israel, in November 1977, just four years after the two countries had been at war. This melodramatic break in the long hostility between the two countries seemed pregnant with possibilities for an end to conflict in that war-torn region. Israel and Egypt had been at war with one another four times in the preceding thirty years. Prime Minister Menachem Begin of Israel and Sadat met several times again, their lieutenants met, and Secretary of State Cyrus Vance met with both sides. Yet it seemed the differences between the two countries could not be ironed out. It seemed that Sadat's courageous act of rapprochement would be wasted, and the opportunities he had opened up were about to be lost. At that juncture Carter acted.

Undoubtedly worried about his low standing in the polls and his inability to move Congress on energy and other domestic issues, and aware that Congressional elections would be coming up in the fall, Carter invited the two Middle Eastern leaders to come to Camp David, the private presidential retreat in the Maryland mountains, for a confidential conference. Obviously the risk was enormous. If nothing came of the meeting, Carter's prestige would sink still lower and he would be seen as acting impetuously and presumptuously. When before had a president presumed to act as a mediator in a situation so charged with animosity and bad history? Not even Theodore Roosevelt had been intimately involved in the actual negotiations at the Portsmouth Conference that ended the Russo-Japanese War in 1905. Besides, that conference had taken place after a war in which one side had been roundly defeated.

For over ten days the three leaders were secluded at Camp David, a length of time none had expected. Yet Carter was insistent. The intransigence of Begin almost caused Sadat at one point to leave for Cairo. In fact, Carter found that he often could not even have Sadat and Begin in the same room together and spoke with them individually in separate rooms. Then, on the ninth day, Carter convinced Begin to change his mind on one of the major obstacles to agreement. On September 17, a triumphant Carter presented the two leaders to a hastily assembled audience in the East Room of the White House to witness the signing of a framework for peace between the two longtime enemies.

Although the Camp David Accords were hailed as a major breakthrough in the progression toward peace in the Middle East, the delicacy and dangers surrounding the issues of the Mideast animosities were so great, in fact, that even after the agreement at Camp David, Israel was slow to put into practice the principles that had been agreed upon. Ever fearful for its security after four wars, Israel could not easily give up territory it thought essential to its safety. Nevertheless, after months of further discussion in Cairo and Jerusalem and Washington, a treaty of peace was signed between Israel and Egypt at the White House on March 26, 1979. It not only ended the state of war between the two countries but also, among other things,

▶ Camp David is the private country retreat of the president of the United States. It is not open to the public and its exact location is not indicated on any park maps so as to maintain the privacy and security of the president and his visitors.

specified the withdrawal of Israel from the Sinai Peninsula, which Israel had conquered in the 1967 war and had occupied ever since. The United States was to supply massive aid to both countries. The treaty was undoubtedly the most hopeful sign for future peace in the region since the creation of Israel thirty years before. That it should have been brought about by the twentieth-century president least informed or experienced in politics and foreign affairs was at once ironic and a tribute to the intelligence and educability of Jimmy Carter.

Thanks to his successful handling of the Middle East summit, Carter's standing in the polls shot up in September and his ability to convince Congress to go along with foreign policy recommendations improved. He managed, for example, to obtain Congressional approval to sell modern fighter aircraft to Egypt and Saudi Arabia as well as Israel, despite strong objections from pro-Israel members of Congress. Congress also approved his lifting of the arms embargo against Turkey, even though friends of Greece opposed it.

From a certain point of view, there ought not to have been any reason to emphasize his successes with Congress. After all, his own party dominated both houses as well as running all the committees of Congress, yet it was just that lack of party loyalty to the president and lack of party discipline that was one of the striking aspects of American politics increasingly evident in the middle 1970s. This situation was particularly noticeable in the results of the Congressional elections of 1978.

The Election of 1978

One of the clichés of off-year elections is that the incumbent party usually loses seats in Congress, and the first off-year elections of Carter's presidency were no exception. Republicans gained three seats in the Senate, twelve seats in the House of Representatives, and three gubernatorial chairs in the state capitals. The tally of state legislatures controlled by Republicans, however, revealed the lack of real significance for these gains. The number went from four to a mere twelve! Even after adding the off-year gains, the Republicans still remained a decided minority in most of the states and in Congress.

This disparity between Republicans and Democrats was not new to 1978. Between 1960 and 1974 the proportion of seats in the House of Representatives held by Democrats had rarely gone below 60 percent. Though it went over that figure at times, it had never fallen as low as 55 percent; except for four years (1966–1970) a majority of the governors of the states during that same span of years had also been Democrats. In 1977 only 32 percent of all state legislators were Republicans—as compared with 53 percent in 1948 and 44 percent in 1956.

It was figures like those that caused political commentators in the late 1970s to refer to the American polity as no longer a two-party system, but rather a "one-and-a-half" party system. When public opinion polls were examined in a similar light, it was evident that the Democrats were the "everyone party." The polls showed that virtually every social group was well represented in the party. Even wealthy people were Democrats, two to one.

At one time in American history it could have been assumed that college graduates would tend to be Republicans; however, by the late 1970s, 42 percent of them were listing themselves as Democrats while only 31 percent identified themselves as Republicans.

Since the poor, the blacks, and most of the middle class had been captured by the New Deal, if not before, and securely held ever since, no significant social groups were absent from the Democratic coalition. In the South where conservative ideology dominated the social structure, the Democrats still dominated politics due to the legacy of the Civil War, in which the Republican Party had been the Party of the Union. This meant, however, that the Democratic Party was not united ideologically and liberal resolutions were likely to be opposed by the conservative Southern members of the Democratic Party who voted with the Republicans on many issues.

A Political Paradox

Despite this overwhelming preference of American voters for the Democrats, that party could never be sure of winning the White House. Between 1948 and 1976 the Democrats won only half of the presidential elections, and even then the Republicans won 51 percent of the popular vote for the two parties! In short, a two-tier political system seemed to be emerging in the country: presidential and legislative levels. Voters apparently made little connection between their votes for Congress and their votes for president; changes occurring in the South provided some of the explanation for the development of the two-tiered politics.

One of the consequences of World War II was that the South finally began to catch up with the rest of the nation in industrial and urban development. As a result, its politics began to change, too. It was certainly significant that Republican Eisenhower had chalked up much of his unusually strong support for a Republican in the South between city and suburban dwellers, and in the 1960s Southern support for Republican presidents continued to be notable in the cities of the region. Moreover, the Second Reconstruction of the South during the 1960s was associated in the minds of many white Southerners with Democratic presidents, an association that split off many old-line Southern Democrats from support of their party's presidential candidates. Segregationist whites could not support Democratic presidential candidates that favored Civil Rights for blacks.

Beginning in 1960, the South began to give its votes to Republican presidential candidates, even when Jimmy Carter was elected, even though he was himself a son of the South. At the same time, white Southerners continued to support Democratic Congressional candidates because they were local people, untainted by support for pro-black programs.

Outside the South, the tendency for voters to split their party preferences between Congress and the president developed more slowly. As late as 1952, only one-fifth of voters in the country cast ballots for congressional and presidential candidates from different parties. By 1968 the proportion was up to a third, and by 1972 it was over two-fifths. (During the nineteenth century it has been estimated that probably less than 10 percent of voters split their tickets.)

Another phenomenon of these years was the rise in the independent or nonparty vote. At the end of the 1960s pollsters began to find a significant number of voters who said they had no allegiance to any party. By 1974 one-third of Americans claimed to be independents; in the 1950s only one-fifth had made that self-designation. Among college-educated people in 1973 the proportion that labeled themselves Independent (38 percent) outnumbered those who designated themselves as either Republicans or Democrats.

A further measure of this decline in Americans' belief in their country's historical political system was underscored by the results of the 1978 elections when most Americans chose not to vote at all. The turnout in November 1978 was the lowest in recent history. Only 38 percent of eligible voters bothered to cast their ballots, and 96 million people stayed away. As recently as 1962, some 48 percent of voters turned out even for an off-year election. Moreover, in presidential elections, Americans have one of the lowest turnouts of any modern democracy. In short, there was not only a disquieting turning away from political parties but also a disturbing alienation from the whole political process as well.

Part of the explanation is quite properly sought in events of the 1960s and 1970s when government leaders of both parties, from the president on down, misused their authority to defend the Vietnam War and to cover up the Watergate crimes. During this period a deep sense of cynicism regarding authority and its abuse of power spread among many Americans, particularly college-age people. By the end of the 1970s they were a large and influential part of the electorate. The shift can also be seen in a decline in trust of authority generally. In 1966, for example, 72 percent of Americans had said they had a "great deal of confidence" in the leadership of American medicine. By 1977 only 43 percent expressed that degree of confidence. For leaders of higher education, the slide was from 61 percent to 37 percent. For the military, as one might expect, the decline was precipitous: from 62 percent in 1966 to 27 percent in 1977.

It was on a promise of restoring confidence in government that Carter campaigned in 1976; and presumably his victory was attributable, at least in part, to the voters' hope that he could do just that. In several ways Carter was in tune with the new mood. He was not authoritarian in his dealings with his family or his subordinates. He probably spent more time as a candidate and as president visiting the homes of ordinary citizens than any president in history. In fact, his thirst for the opinion of the average American was so strong that some observers thought it counterproductive. His effort to maintain an "open presidency" was clearly in response to the popular hostility to the Nixon administration's "bunker mentality," which had produced so many mistakes and abuses of power.

More was involved in the distrust of government, however, than particular evils committed by past presidents and governments. Also at work were the profound social and cultural changes of the 1960s, among which was a new emphasis upon the dignity of all people—black, brown, and red, poor as well as rich, both female and male. The social order that emerged in America from the turbulent 60s and early 70s was less rigid, less deferential, and more democratic than had been true before. As one commentator expressed it, "ordinary people in this country now have a higher estimation of their endowments and broader conceptions of their entitlements than ever before."

The upshot was that the country was probably more difficult to govern than at any time in American history. Americans in the era of Jackson, for example, may have been more turbulent and even harder to discipline or guide, but they also expected less of government. Even with its social diversity, what the nation demanded was less dependence upon the federal government.

It was with these changes, long germinating, that the Carter administration had to contend in the closing years of the 1970s. It was soon evident that the encounter and its resolution were not going to be easy. Without a strong sense of party loyalty in Congress and without a strong belief among the people in the virtues of parties, elections, and even the benevolence of government itself, solutions to the difficult problems of inflation, recession, and energy would be difficult for any president to carry out. That seemed to be the meaning of Carter's many problems as he entered upon the second half of his presidency in January 1979.

Lowering Expectations

In his State of the Union message in January 1979, President Carter stressed good management and efficiency in the federal government, rather than new programs. He talked about laying a "New Foundation," reminiscent of the New Deal and the New Frontier. Yet he was concerned, primarily, to steer a path between the continuing inflation and the threat of recession. As a result, established programs received no increases in his new budget and even the military received only a three percent increase. The national health insurance program he had promised the country at the beginning of his administration was clearly shaped by fears of fueling inflation. It was limited in scope to keep governmental spending down.

Worrisome and potentially dangerous as the long siege of mounting prices was, the sharpest crisis for Carter came from a different though not unrelated source. In the spring of 1979, the enduring problem of what to do about American dependence upon foreign oil in the face of growing domestic demand leaped into dramatic prominence. The overthrow of the government of the Shah of Iran by internal revolutionaries abruptly reduced the world's supply of oil, causing new upward pressures on the cost of energy. In May and June, motorists panicked—first in California, and later on the east coast. Thinking gasoline would be impossible to obtain, they began to buy it in inordinate amounts that so strained the allocation system of the country that suddenly it was hard to find gas. Prices began to shoot up. Long lines of cars appeared outside gasoline stations, depressingly reminiscent of the days of the Arab oil embargo in 1973.

This time, however, when the lines finally disappeared not only was the price of gasoline considerably higher but also the sense of urgency about the energy shortage remained. For the first time in their history, Americans paid a dollar a gallon for gasoline; and the price promised to increase considerably more in short order. (Europeans had been paying a dollar a gallon or more for decades and in June 1979 they were paying twice what Americans were.) The day of cheap gasoline was now definitely over, but American adjustment to the new situation was only beginning.

The gasoline lines, which caught everyone by surprise, concretely revealed the weakness of the president's grip on the problem and on the political process. Earlier that spring Carter had asked Congress to give him power to set up a "standby" gasoline rationing plan for just such an emergency as occurred in June. Congress refused, reflecting the reluctance of most Americans to admit that cheap energy was no longer a given. Once the gas lines materialized, however, the public clamor energized Congress. Within days, several bills setting up machinery for rationing gasoline in an emergency, along the lines advocated by the president only a few weeks before, went into the legislative mill. Congress suddenly became interested in the development of synthetic fuels, too. Meanwhile, Carter's standings in the polls plummeted to a level similar to that of Nixon at the time of his forced resignation. Only 29 percent of the American people approved of his administration, while a whopping 56 percent said they disapproved. (In May 2006, according to some polls, President George W. Bush's approval ratings plunged to the same level).

A feeling that no one in Washington was in charge of the country reached the president himself in early July, soon after he returned from a meeting with European and Japanese heads of government convened to coordinate responses to the world energy shortage. Carter canceled a television address to the people scheduled for July 5 and went instead into seclusion at Camp David. Over the ensuing ten days he invited scores of people from a wide range of professions to discuss the crisis of leadership he, as well as the country, now felt so deeply. In an unprecedented display of presidential self-criticism, Carter pleaded with his visitors and with the ordinary Americans he visited privately at their homes to advise him as to what he might do. At the conclusion of the extraordinary discussions and almost public self-examination, Carter appeared on national television. The address he gave was almost devoid of policy statements. It called upon Americans to have faith, and to use the energy crisis as a way of uniting the country and freeing the nation from dependence upon foreign sources of oil. In a second speech the next day he outlined a new program to reduce consumption of oil and to expand the production of energy. The new proposal was monumental in its conception and cost, dwarfing the giant Manhattan District Project during the Second World War that developed the atomic bomb. Carter's new moral equivalent of war was expected to cost $142 billion over the next ten years and was to be financed largely by a tax on the so-called windfall profits of oil companies.

The immediate public response was positive. Carter's standing in the polls improved considerably, although those who approved his actions constituted still less than half of the voters. For all of the rhetoric of sacrifice in the president's speeches, however, little specific sacrifice was actually demanded. Some of his advisers had hoped that he would take the hard but necessary road, of asking for a sharp increase in the price of gasoline in order to compel Americans to use less. Instead, his plan to reduce consumption relied primarily on exhortations to be patriotic and to conserve.

Some hoped he would abandon reliance upon nuclear energy, which in the light of a serious and totally unanticipated accident at a nuclear reactor at Three Mile Island, Pennsylvania, shortly before, seemed increasingly dubious, if not dangerous. Yet Carter apparently contemplated no changes in his past policy of including nuclear energy as a substantial part of the national solution to the shortage.

Later in July, presumably in an effort to strengthen his administration internally and to give an impression externally of being in direct control, Carter fired five of his cabinet officers. The replacements, however, did not suggest that there would be much change in policy.

The wholesale firing aroused a furor among many leaders of the Democratic Party and in Congress, and puzzled—even alarmed—many observers abroad who were already beginning to view Carter as indecisive or lacking in steadfastness. Nor did the summary dismissals encourage the Senate to act on the second SALT (Strategic Arms Limitation Talks) Treaty with the Soviet Union, which Carter had submitted just when the gas lines were capturing the attention of Americans in the spring of 1979. SALT had been in the works a long time, yet it constituted only a small step in the direction of limiting the largest nuclear weapons of the two superpowers. It placed ceilings on numbers of submarine- and land-based missiles and on bombers capable of carrying nuclear bombs and limited each side to the development of one new weapon system. Many Republicans and some Democrats thought such acceptance of virtual nuclear equality with the Soviet Union was dangerous and so opposed the treaty, but even those who may have favored it soon were distracted by two significant events in the late fall of 1979.

One was the sudden capturing of the American Embassy in Teheran, Iran, with all its occupants, by a group of armed student supporters of the new religious and secular leader of the Iranian revolution, the Ayatollah Khomeini. They demanded the exchange of the American hostages for the former Shah, who, for a while, was in the United States seeking medical treatment for cancer. When the Administration refused to return the Shah, who was in the country legally, the militants continued to hold the hostages, threatening to put them on trial as spies. The Iranians would hold fifty-two Americans hostage in Iran for 444 days, releasing them only on the day of Ronald Reagan's inauguration in 1981. The anti-Americanism in Iran was not new, but had been virtually unknown to the American public who knew only the face of the friendly Shah. In fact, however, from 1953 onward there had been simmering anti-Americanism in Iran. That year the CIA had helped overthrow a political leader, Mohammed Mossadegh, who had wanted to nationalize foreign oil interests. Once the Shah was gone, the anti-American sentiment came to the surface—and was actively fomented by Iranian politicians loyal to the Ayatollah and Islamic Revolution.

The second event that virtually killed the SALT discussions in the Senate was the invasion of Afghanistan by Soviet troops in late December 1979, in order to shore up a faltering Communist regime on its southern border and prevent the takeover of Afghanistan by Islamic extremists. President Carter reacted strongly—even exaggeratedly—by calling the Soviet intrusion a most serious threat to peace and comity among nations. He sought to arouse other nations to condemn the Soviet action, though not with great success, as most European nations understood the security concerns of the Soviets who desired to avoid a hostile government on their border. At home, by contrast, the Senate and the country viewed the Soviet measures as inconsistent with SALT, and so the agreement did not even come before the Senate in 1980.

As the 1980 election primaries began, Carter was hardly in good political shape. He was burdened with the problem of the American hostages in Teheran and with a rate of inflation that was close to 20 percent on an annual basis. Moreover, all indications were that unemployment, too, would increase as the economy slowed down in response to the high interest rates and other measures aimed at combating inflation. Despite these handicaps, however, the president emerged from most of his primaries as the favored Democratic candidate, easily winning over his once highly favored opponent, Senator Edward Kennedy. Many Democrats, leaders as well as rank and file, were not pleased with Carter; however, Kennedy was apparently viewed as even less attractive due to the death of a woman with him in an automobile accident at Chappaquiddick more than a decade earlier. Despite Kennedy's vigorous campaign and magical name, the Democrats again nominated Jimmy Carter. Meanwhile, Ronald Reagan, the aging former governor of California, an acknowledged conservative on both domestic and foreign policy issues, easily captured enough delegates in the Republican primaries to win the nomination on the first ballot at the Republican convention.

The Election of 1980

Once the campaign began, it was apparent that voters were unhappy about the options. Although Republican Congressman John Anderson offered himself as an alternative, his candidacy soon faded as Americans clung to their historic distrust of third party candidates. Carter and Reagan's campaigning was intensive and vigorous, but neither said much specifically about how he would handle inflation—a concern of anxious voters—or any other problem. Neither was able to arouse voter enthusiasm, and throughout the fall polls showed a large proportion of voters stubbornly undecided.

For his running mate, after a brief flirtation with former President Gerald Ford, who indicated that he would decline any such invitation, Reagan chose George H. W. Bush, who had been his strongest challenger for the nomination in the Republican primaries. In spite of Bush's resume as a Republican Congressional leader, Ambassador to China, Ambassador to the United Nations, and Director of the CIA, there were reservations in some Republican corners concerning Bush. In specific, Bush had vocally criticized the central feature of Reagan's "supply-side" economic plan as "voodoo economics," correctly arguing that the tax cuts and proposed defense spending increases espoused by candidate Reagan could only produce massive deficits. Furthermore, Bush had been a supporter of the Equal Rights Amendment and had a history of a pro-choice stance on abortion. In fact, Bush had been such an ardent supporter of population control in the 1960s that he had earned the nickname "Rubbers" in Congress.

Up until Election Day, the polls had been predicting a cliffhanger. The disappointing campaign, however, culminated in a stunning surprise when Reagan won by a landslide. Carter won only four states and the District of Columbia for forty-nine electoral votes. Surprising, too, was the Republican capture of the Senate for the first time in twenty-five years. Democrats lost in both the South and the North. The Democratic stronghold in the South crumbled with the victories of four new Republican senators and eleven new Republican congressmen. In the North, Republicans defeated three liberal Democratic senators and two congressmen.

These victories seemed to assure Reagan's ability to reshape the judiciary along more conservative lines and to take a harder line in foreign policy. The Republican triumphs also forecast a strong turn to the right in domestic policy, in line with the Republican platform. Among other things, the platform opposed the Equal Rights Amendment and abortion, while favoring higher military spending and a substantial tax cut. Also promised was a greater role for the states in domestic matters and a cutback in Federal spending and social programs.

Yet, some old patterns persisted. Democrats still controlled the House, as they had done since 1930 with only two interruptions. More important, voter turnout continued to decline, as it had been doing for a third of a century. The election seemed more a criticism of the Carter administration's inadequacies in dealing with a weakening economy, the Iranian Hostage Crisis, and declining prestige abroad than a sign of support for Reagan and the Republicans.

When Carter left office, he was a highly unpopular figure. Yet, it should be noted, he has restored his prestige as few other unpopular presidents have ever done. Writing some twenty books—including a novel—as of 2006, he has, in addition, dedicated his post-presidential years to furthering democracy and human rights around the world, as well as to Habitat for Humanity in the United States. In 2002 he won the Nobel Peace Prize.

Chapter Review 29

Summary

The death of John F. Kennedy passed the presidency to Lyndon Johnson, a hard-nosed Texan with an understanding of the legislative process and the ability to get things accomplished in Congress. Johnson would almost immediately launch his "Great Society," which included a government's "war on poverty," federal housing programs, urban renewal, government health insurance for senior citizens and the indigent, federal aid to education, and civil rights and voting rights for African-Americans. Never had any American president accomplished so much in so little time. Amidst it all, Johnson defeated Republican Barry Goldwater, an uncompromising Republican senator from Arizona, in an electoral landslide with 61 percent of the popular vote.

Very quickly, however, Johnson's political fortunes would turn sour as he used an uneventful incident in the Gulf of Tonkin to extract authorization from Congress to expand American involvement in Vietnam. Johnson was determined not to "lose" Vietnam to communism and was confident that the U.S. military could accomplish the task. Johnson launched Operation Rolling Thunder, a bombing campaign designed to cut off supplies to communist insurgents in South Vietnam. The bombing proved ineffective as the communists simply moved their supply routes through Laos and Cambodia, but the bombing killed one thousand civilians weekly and left others homeless so that the country became flooded with refugees.

An attack on an American air base at Pleiku prompted Johnson to send ground troops to defend the American bases and as General William C. Westmoreland requested more and more soldiers, American involvement in Vietnam increased from sixteen thousand men in Vietnam when Johnson took office to five hundred thousand by 1968. The American news media reported the war up close and personal, and Americans were treated to a concentration camp program known as "Strategic Hamlets," summary executions known as the "Phoenix program," and massacres of innocent civilians by American troops, most notoriously at My Lai in 1968. As the public turned against the war, Johnson in his inaugural address of 1968 announced to the American people that the war was winding down and that the Viet Cong were almost wiped out. Two weeks later, the communists launched the Tet Offensive involving up to five hundred thousand Viet Cong and proven that CIA agent Sam Adams' contention—the military had under-counted the enemy by more than half was correct. Johnson's popularity plummeted and the country erupted in violent protests, both against the Vietnam War and racial unrest. Consequently, Johnson announced on March 31, 1968, that he would not seek reelection. On April 4, 1968, Martin Luther King was assassinated in Memphis, and on June 5th, Johnson's heir apparent, Robert F. Kennedy, was assassinated hours after winning the California Democratic primary.

Democrats nominated Vice President Hubert Humphrey at the Democratic Convention in Chicago amidst riots outside and the thuggish behavior by Chicago Mayor Richard Daley inside. Republicans nominated former Vice President Richard Nixon, who narrowly defeated Humphrey as segregationist Third Party candidate George Wallace siphoned off conservative votes in the South and winning five Southern states.

Nixon implemented a three-pronged strategy to end the Vietnam War: increasing bombing, providing aid to South Vietnam while gradually withdrawing troops and seeking peace at the negotiating table. The Paris agreement in 1973 ended American involvement in the war, but left a communist army in South Vietnam. Two years after the U.S. withdrawal, the Communists launched a full scale assault on South Vietnam and took over the country.

Nixon also made headlines by visiting both China and the Soviet Union in 1972, which led to a thaw in the Cold War known as détente. On the domestic front, Nixon repudiated the liberal policies of Kennedy and Johnson while simultaneously using the powers of government to combat inflation, ensure women's rights, and protect the environment. Nixon easily defeated 1972 Democratic challenger George McGovern, but was almost immediately embroiled in the Watergate scandal that would destroy his presidency. Nixon's Committee to Re-Elect the president had broken into the Democratic headquarters in the Watergate building in Washington. Nixon's efforts to cover up his administration's involvement in the burglary led to a string of revelations about shady dealings in the Nixon Administration. When it appeared that Nixon would be impeached for obstructing justice in the summer of 1974, Nixon became the first president to resign the office.

Gerald Ford, appointed by Nixon as Vice President when Spiro Agnew had been forced to resign due to tax evasion, assumed the presidency and at first seemed a breath of fresh air with his "I'm a Ford, not a Lincoln" approach, but saw his popularity drop almost immediately when he pardoned Nixon on September 8, 1974. Ford suffered negative media coverage that portrayed him as a stumbler and a bumbler. Ford himself contributed to that image when he asserted in the 1976 presidential debates that the Soviet Union did not control Eastern Europe.

Ford would survive a primary challenge from Ronald Reagan only to go down to defeat in November to Georgia Governor Jimmy Carter. Carter, however, would be faced with an economic malaise that included stagflation and the second oil crisis of the 1970s that catapulted gasoline prices over $1.00 per gallon for the first time. In spite of Carter's foreign policy success with the Camp David Accords in 1976 that established peace between Israel and Egypt, Carter's foreign policy would also plague his presidency. Carter's Panama Canal Treaty that returned control of the Canal to Panama was unpopular, and when Iranian militants stormed the U.S. Embassy and took fifty-two Americans hostage, Carter appeared inept and his popularity plummeted. The hostages would be held in Iran until the inauguration of Ronald Reagan, who defeated Carter in a landslide election in 1980.

Chapter Review (cont'd)

Chronological Time Line

1954 On May 7, the French surrendered to Viet Minh in Vietnam.

1954 Geneva Agreement divided Vietnam between a communist North and capitalist South.

1954 Eisenhower sent 675 advisors to South Vietnam, which began the U.S. involvement.

1963 On June 11, a Buddhist monk burned himself to death in Vietnam in protest of the policies of the South Vietnamese government.

1963 On November 1, General Duong Van Minh, encouraged by the CIA, staged a coup and assassinated Diem and took over the government of South Vietnam.

1963 December: Higher Education Facilities Act authorized the federal government to fund construction of facilities for higher education.

1964 January: Johnson called for a "war on poverty."

1964 August 2–4: Two American surveillance destroyers were allegedly attacked by North Vietnamese torpedo boats in the gulf of Tonkin.

1964 August 7: Congress passed the Gulf of Tonkin Resolution.

1964 August: Economic Opportunity Act appropriated almost $1 billion for agencies and programs designed to train or retrain the jobless.

1964 Congress appropriated $1.1 billion for economic development in Appalachia and $3.3 billion for urban renewal.

1964 National Defense Education Act of 1964 offered federal support for the teaching of the humanities as well as the sciences in college.

1964 Lyndon Johnson defeated Republican Barry Goldwater for the presidency with a record 61 percent of the popular vote.

Time Line (cont'd)

1965 On February 5, Viet Cong guerrillas killed eight and wounded 126 Americans in an attack on a U.S. base at Pleiku.

1965 March: General Westmoreland requested more troops in Vietnam.

1965 April: The Elementary and Secondary Education Act provided federal funds to education.

1965 May: The U.S. temporarily halted bombings in Vietnam to encourage a negotiated settlement.

1965 On July 30, Social Security Act of 1965 created Medicare, a government health insurance for those over sixty-five, and Medicaid, a government health insurance for the indigent.

1965 The Immigration Act of 1965 provided for the elimination by 1968 of quotas based on national origin.

1965 Higher Education Act provided federal funding for scholarships.

1965 Voting Rights Act provided federal enforcement of voting rights.

1966 November: Republicans won forty-seven House seats in the mid-term elections.

1967 CIA Chief William Colby implemented the Phoenix Program in South Vietnam.

1968 Housing and Urban Development Act of 1968, provided $5.3 billion over a three-year period for new housing, especially for low-income families.

1968 CIA agent Sam Adams in Vietnam discovered that there were far more Viet Cong than had been previously believed.

1968 On January 29, communists in Vietnam launched the Tet Offensive.

1968 On March 16, a massacre at My Lai in Vietnam took place.

1968 On March 31, Lyndon Johnson withdrew from the presidential race knowing that he could not win.

Chapter Review (cont'd)

Time Line (cont'd)

1968 On April 4, Martin Luther King was assassinated in Memphis by James Earl Ray.

1968 On June 5, Robert F. Kennedy was assassinated in Los Angeles after winning the California Democratic Primary.

1968 November: Republican Richard Nixon narrowly defeated Democrat Hubert Humphrey and segregationist George Wallace, who won five Southern states, for the presidency.

1969 Congress passed a tax cut to stimulate the economy.

1969 On July 20, Neil Armstrong became the first human to walk on the moon.

1970 Kent State massacre led to the death of four college students in Ohio.

1971 On June 13, the *New York Times* published the "Pentagon Papers" that revealed American involvement in Southeast Asia had expanded to Cambodia and Laos without congressional knowledge.

1971 Nixon established the "Plumbers" to stop leaks of information from the White House.

1972 February: Nixon visited China.

1972 May: Nixon visited the Soviet Union.

1972 June: Nixon and Congress provided federal money for colleges and loans to college students, and schools could not discriminate against women.

1972 On June 17, five burglars working for the Committee to Re-Elect the President were arrested in the Watergate building in Washington, D.C.

1972 On June 23, Nixon had the CIA give false information to the FBI concerning the source of funding for the Watergate burglary.

1972 August: Last ground combat forces were withdrawn from Vietnam.

1972 September: Congress passed President Nixon's Revenue Sharing bill.

Time Line (cont'd)

1972	November: Richard Nixon defeated Democrat George McGovern in a landslide election where McGovern won only one state.
1972	On December 18–29, the "Christmas Bombing" occurred in Vietnam.
1973	On January 27, the Paris Agreement called for the end of U.S. involvement in Vietnam.
1973	On March 19, convicted Watergate burglar, James McCord, handed a letter to Judge John J. Sirica asserting that there had been pressure applied on the defendants to plead guilty and that perjury had occurred.
1973	On March 29, U.S. troops were withdrawn from Vietnam and POWs exchanged.
1973	On April 30, John Dean was fired by Richard Nixon for cooperating with the Watergate prosecutors.
1973	On June 13, Nixon instituted a ninety-day freeze on wages and prices.
1973	On July 16, White House aide, Alexander Butterfield, revealed the existence of a tape recording system in the Oval Office that could verify the allegations of Watergate witnesses.
1973	On October 19, "Saturday Night Massacre" led to the firing of Watergate Prosecutor, Archibald Cox, by Richard Nixon.
1974	April: Nixon published selected excerpts from the Watergate tapes.
1974	June: Price inflation reached 10 percent.
1974	July: The Supreme Court ordered Nixon to turn over all of the tapes to the special prosecutor.
1974	On August 9, Nixon became the first president to resign the Office of the presidency.
1974	On September 8, Ford pardoned Nixon.
1974	November: Democrats won the mid-term elections.
1975	March: Congress passed the largest tax cut in American history ($22 billion).

Chapter Review (cont'd)

Time Line (cont'd)

1975 On April 30, South Vietnam surrendered to the communists.

1976 November: Jimmy Carter defeated Gerald Ford in the presidential election.

1977 September: OMB Director, Burt Lance, resigned due to questionable banking practices in Georgia.

1978 April: Senate approved the Panama Canal Treaty.

1978 November: Only 38 percent voted in congressional elections, a record low.

1978 On June 28, University of *California v. Bakke* struck down Affirmative Action quota systems but ruled that race may be used as an admission criterion.

1978 On September 17, Israel and Egypt signed the Camp David Accords.

1979 May: Lines to purchase gasoline developed in California.

1979 June: gasoline prices reach $1 per gallon for the first time.

1979 On November 4, Iranian students took over the U.S. Embassy in Teheran and held fifty-two Americans hostage, a crisis that would last 444 days.

1979 December: Soviet Union invaded Afghanistan.

1980 Republican Ronald Reagan defeated Jimmy Carter in a landslide in the presidential election.

Key Terms

The Great Society: Lyndon Johnson's domestic program that included a "war on poverty," civil rights, and government health insurance for senior citizens

Barry Goldwater: Arizona Senator and Republican presidential candidate in 1964 who lost in a landslide to Lyndon Johnson, but was viewed as the instigator of a long-term conservative movement

"Southern Strategy": The Republican strategy to exploit the racist sentiments of white voters in the South

Key Terms (cont'd)

The War on Poverty: A host of programs, including welfare, public housing, government health insurance, and job training programs designed for low income Americans

Ho Chi Minh: Leader of the Vietnamese communists that struggled for independence against the Japanese, French, and then the United States

Viet Minh: Vietnamese nationalist group led by Ho Chi Minh

Dienbienphu: Site of the decisive battle in 1954 that resulted in a Vietnamese victory and French withdrawal from Vietnam

Bao Dai: Chief of State in Vietnam in the 1950s until ousted in an election by Ngo Dinh Diem in 1955

Ngo Dinh Diem: Catholic, French-speaking president of South Vietnam 1955-1963 until ousted in a CIA-backed coup in November, 1963

Strategic Hamlet: American and South Vietnamese strategy in South Vietnam that included removing the population in guerrilla-ridden sectors to concentration camps

Madame Nhu: Wife of the South Vietnamese president's brother, Ngo Dinh Nhu, who helped fuel a revolt with her callous remarks in reference to immolation protests by Buddhist monks

Ngo Dinh Nhu: Brother and top advisor of South Vietnamese President Ngo Diem Dinh

Duong Van Minh: South Vietnamese general that became president after leading the coup and assassination of Ngo Dinh Diem in 1963

Robert C. Weaver: First African-American to hold a cabinet position as head of Housing and Urban Development in 1966

Thurgood Marshall: First African-American Supreme Court justice

George Wallace: Alabama governor and segregationist that won five Southern states as a third party candidate in 1968

Martin Luther King, Jr.: Most famous civil rights leader of the 1960s who was assassinated in Memphis in 1968

The War in Vietnam: War for Vietnamese independence that raged from 1946-1975 with varying degrees of U.S. involvement

National Liberation Front: Known to most Americans as the "Viet Cong," a communist rebel group in South Vietnam that opposed the U.S.-backed government of South Vietnam and favored a United Vietnam under communism

Gulf of Tonkin Resolution: The Resolution of Congress on August 7, 1964 granting the president the authority to "take all necessary measures" to ensure American interests in Southeast Asia—known by historians as Johnson's "Blank Check" in Vietnam

Johnson's "Blank Check": The broadly written Gulf of Tonkin Resolution that gave the president wide latitude in Vietnam

Rolling Thunder: Lyndon Johnson's unsuccessful bombing campaign aimed at communist rebel supply lines in South Vietnam

Chapter Review (cont'd)

Key Terms (cont'd)

William C. Westmoreland: Commander of the American forces in Vietnam most famous for requesting more troops

Nguyen Cao Ky: South Vietnamese Air Force General that participated in the coup against Ngo Dinh Diem in 1963. Ky became South Vietnamese Prime Minister 1965-67 and Vice president under Nguyen Van Thieu 1967–71.

Nguyen Van Thieu: South Vietnamese Army General that became president of South Vietnam 1965–75 after the overthrow of the government of Ngo Dinh Diem in 1963

William Colby: Head of the CIA during the Vietnam War

Phoenix Program: Program instigated by William Colby and the CIA that included summary executions of suspected Viet Cong

Viet Cong: Formally known as the National Liberation Front, a communist rebel group in South Vietnam that opposed the U.S.-backed government of South Vietnam and favored a United Vietnam under communism

Sam Adams: CIA agent that investigated the Order of Battle in 1968 and found that the U.S. military had grossly undercounted the Viet Cong with the implication that the U.S. did not have enough troops in South Vietnam to win the war

Ben Tre: Provincial Capital in South Vietnam where American and South Vietnamese troops killed one thousand civilians while rooting out VC, further shocking the American conscience. AP correspondent Peter Arnett quoted an American officer as saying "We had to destroy the town to save it."

Dominican intervention: The landing of American Troops in the Dominican Republic in 1965 to restore order.

Eugene McCarthy: Democratic Senator that campaigned unsuccessfully for president in 1968 on a platform against the Vietnam War

Tet Offensive: Massive communist offensive beginning on January 29, 1968 that proved to Americans that the war was not near over and the Viet Cong were not near wiped out

Election of 1968: Republican Richard Nixon defeated Democrat Hubert H. Humphrey and Segregationist third-party candidate George Wallace, who won five Southern states, for the presidency

Robert F. Kennedy: Former Attorney General and younger brother of John F. Kennedy who won the Democratic Primary in the presidential election in California in 1968, but was assassinated the same night by Sirhan Sirhan

Sirhan Sirhan: Robert F. Kennedy's assassin who opposed Kennedy's views on Israel and Palestine

My Lai: The site of a 1968 massacre in Vietnam led by Lt. William L. Calley where U.S. troops killed two hundred Vietnamese villagers, including unarmed women and children. Calley was sentenced to life in prison, but was released in six months on parole.

William L. Calley: U.S. lieutenant that ordered the My Lai massacre

Key Terms (cont'd)

Richard Daley: Strong-armed mayor of Chicago that silenced his political opponents at the 1968 Democratic convention in Chicago

Richard Nixon: Republican former vice president and governor of California who won the presidential elections of 1968 and 1972, but resigned under threat of impeachment during the Watergate scandal in 1974

Hubert Humphrey: Democratic Party vice president under Lyndon Johnson and failed as the Democratic Party presidential candidate of 1968

Vietnamization: Nixon's plan to increase aid to South Vietnam while the U.S. gradually withdrew its troops and left the war to the South Vietnamese

Henry Kissinger: National Security Advisor and then Secretary of State under Nixon and Ford who won the Nobel Prize for negotiating peace in Vietnam in 1973

Le Duc Tho: He was the North Vietnamese diplomat that also won the Nobel Prize for negotiating peace in Vietnam in 1973, but returned his Nobel Prize because he believed that the war was not over and the only change was that America had gone home.

"New Economics": Essentially, the Keynesian idea that government intervention into the economy, including some deficit spending in down times, can be good for the economy

Revenue-sharing: Nixon's idea that federal transfers to the states could be granted with much greater discretion for the states

Amtrak: The American public rail transportation system

School busing: Forced integration of the schools through forced busing of children out of their neighborhood districts

Alan Bakke: Sued the University of California for denying him admission in favor of an ethnic minority when he had better test scores

Affirmative Action: The idea that government should give preferences to ethnic minorities in hiring and in school admissions

Spiro Agnew: Nixon's vice president that was forced to resign due to tax evasion

George McGovern: South Dakota Senator and liberal Democratic candidate for president in 1972 that lost a landslide election to Richard Nixon

Election of 1972: Richard Nixon soundly defeated Democrat George McGovern, who won only Massachusetts and the District of Columbia

Watergate: The building in Washington that was home to the Democratic Party headquarters in 1972 that was burglarized by the Committee to Re-elect the President under Richard Nixon. ("Watergate" became not only the name of the building, but the name of the scandal itself.)

G. Gordon Liddy: Top aide to Richard Nixon who was in charge of the "Plumbers." Liddy favored outlandish schemes to discredit democrats that included prostitutes and thugs.

CREEP: Committee to Re-Elect President Nixon that was responsible for the Watergate burglary

The "Plumbers": Groups organized by Richard Nixon to stop leaks from the Executive Branch

Chapter Review (cont'd)

Key Terms (cont'd)

Daniel Ellsberg: Defense intellectual that leaked the Pentagon Papers to the *New York Times*

John Dean: Top aide to Nixon that cooperated with the prosecution

Bob Woodward: *Washington Post* reporter who along with Carl Bernstein, worked with a confidential government employee, "Deep Throat," to expose the wrongdoing in the White House during the Watergate scandal

Carl Bernstein: *Washington Post* reporter who along with Bob Woodward, worked with a confidential government employee, "Deep Throat," to expose the wrongdoing in the White House during the Watergate scandal

John J. Sirica: Chief judge for the United States District Court of the District of Columbia that ordered Nixon to turn over the Watergate tapes

John Ehrlichman: Counsel and Assistant for Domestic Affairs to President Nixon who was sentenced to prison for his role in the Watergate scandal

Archibald Cox: Special prosecutor in the Watergate Scandal fired in the "Saturday Night Massacre"

Robert Bork: Solicitor general who fired Special Prosecutor Archibald Cox after the attorney general and assistant attorney general had declined to do so

Saturday Night Massacre: October 19, 1973, when Nixon ordered Attorney General Elliot Richardson to fire Special Prosecutor Cox. Richardson refused, and Nixon then accepted his resignation. Nixon then turned to Richardson's deputy, William Ruckleshaus and ordered him to fire Cox, but Ruckleshaus also refused and resigned. Finally, Nixon turned to Solicitor General Robert Bork, who dutifully fired Cox.

Howard Baker: Republican senator who asked the question concerning Nixon in the Watergate affair, "What did the president know and when did he know it?"

Gerald Ford: Republican House minority leader appointed vice president, and then president by Richard Nixon, but failed to win re-election after pardoning Nixon.

Lynette "Squeaky" Fromme: Member of serial killer Charles Manson's "family" that waved a gun at President Ford in Sacramento on September 5, 1975, and was sentenced to life in prison for attempted assassination of a president.

Sara Jane Moore: Attempted to assassinate President Ford outside the St. Francis Hotel in San Francisco on September 22, 1975, firing a shot that missed the president's head by six inches with a .38 caliber pistol.

Misery Index: The combination of high unemployment and high inflation that plagued the 1970s

Jimmy Carter: One-term governor of Georgia, peanut farmer, and graduate of Annapolis that defeated Republican Gerald Ford for the presidency in 1976

Human Rights: The focus of Jimmy Carter's foreign policy

Panama Canal Treaty: 1978 treaty that relinquished sovereignty of the Panama Canal Zone to Panama, but was unpopular in the United States

Camp David Accords: 1978 peace agreement negotiated by Jimmy Carter between Israel and Egypt

Iran Hostage Crisis: The capture of the U.S. Embassy in Teheran by militant Iranian students in 1979 and the holding of fifty-two Americans hostage for 444 days

Key Terms (cont'd)

The Election of 1980: Republican Ronald Reagan's landslide victory against incumbent Democrat Jimmy Carter

George Bush: Ronald Reagan's Republican opponent in the Republican Primary that became vice president under Ronald Reagan

Supply-Side Economics: The idea that tax cuts would boost the economy so much that the government would not run deficits in spite of the cuts

John Anderson: Third party candidate that won 1 percent of the vote in 1980

Ronald Reagan: Former actor and governor of California that won the election of 1980 on a platform of less government and stronger military

Pop Quiz ▶ ▶ ▶

Chapter 29

1. Who said he wanted to build a society where "men are more concerned with the quality of their goals than the quantity of their goods"?
   a. John Kennedy
   b. Lyndon Johnson
   c. Richard Nixon
   d. Jimmy Carter

2. The Republicans' "Southern Strategy" was predicated on __________.
   a. the promise of a fully integrated society
   b. playing on the racial fears of white Southern conservatives
   c. the promise of equal rights for women
   d. the promise of immigration from Mexico

3. What did the Immigration Act of 1965 provide?
   a. provided for the elimination of quotas for immigration based on national origin
   b. prohibited the immigration of Europeans in favor of Latin Americans and Asians
   c. granted citizenship to illegal immigrants that had been in the country ten years
   d. provided for free immigration of Latin Americans and Asians provided that they open restaurants

Chapter Review (cont'd)

Pop Quiz (cont'd)

4. Martin Luther King was assassinated in 1968 by __________.
   a. Lee Harvey Oswald
   b. Jack Ruby
   c. James Earl Ray
   d. John Wilkes Booth

5. American-backed South Vietnamese Premier Ngo Dinh Diem __________.
   a. had lived in exile in the United States
   b. was a staunch Buddhist
   c. opposed the use of the French language in Vietnam
   d. was strongly supported by the people of South Vietnam

6. Why did the U.S. reject the North Vietnamese proposal for an election to unify the country in 1963?
   a. U.S. leaders were afraid the communists would win.
   b. U.S. leaders feared that the communists would kill people that were trying to vote.
   c. U.S. leaders did not think that any country should have election while there was a war going on.
   d. The sixteen thousand American advisors in Vietnam had not had sufficient time to explain voting and democracy to the Vietnamese.

7. Operation Rolling Thunder was the U.S. bombing campaign that was directed at __________.
   a. communist supply lines
   b. killing Ho Chi Minh
   c. killing as many civilians as possible
   d. preventing communism in Cambodia

8. The "Phoenix Program" was a CIA program designed to pacify the communists through __________.
   a. mass arrests and trials of civilians accused of aiding the enemy
   b. democratic education programs
   c. humanitarian aid
   d. Bible lessons stressing pacifism

9. Robert F. Kennedy was assassinated in 1968 by fanatical anti-zionist __________.
   a. Theodore Herzl
   b. Sirhan Sirhan
   c. Lee Harvey Oswald
   d. Mary Hartman Mary Hartman

Pop Quiz (cont'd)

10. What was guaranteed under the Paris Agreement?
    a. North Vietnam could leave its troops in South Vietnam.
    b. The U.S. would withdraw from South Vietnam.
    c. Both sides agreed to release POWs.
    d. All of the above

11. Richard Nixon was indicted by the House of Representatives for all of the following reasons EXCEPT __________.
    a. ordering the secret bombing of Cambodia
    b. obstructing justice
    c. abuse of power
    d. contempt of Congress

12. One factor that harmed Jimmy Carter's presidency was __________.
    a. his inability to release fifty-two hostages held by Iran for 444 days
    b. his inability to relate to common people
    c. his image as a city slicker
    d. his atheism

13. Democrats controlled Congress when Richard Nixon was president. T F

14. Republicans controlled Congress when Jimmy Carter was president. T F

15. A majority of Americans expressed great confidence in their leaders in a 1977 poll. T F

1. B	5. A	9. B	13. T
2. B	6. A	10 D	14. F
3. D	7. A	11. A	15. F
4. C	8. A	12. A	

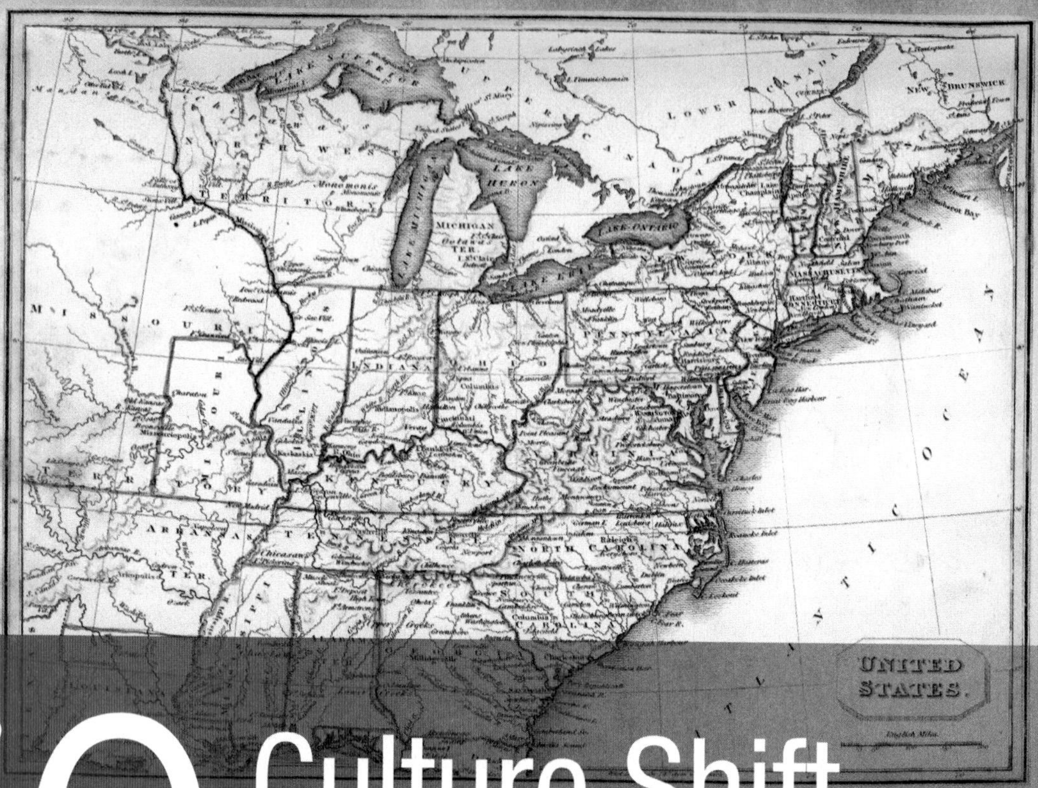

30 Culture Shift, 1963–1980

Chapter Objectives

The Consumer Society Continued

The Prosperous American of the 1960s and 70s

Sports and Leisure

Diet and Health

Productivity and Poverty

The Agricultural Sector 1963–1980

Components of Economic Growth

The Decline of Labor Unions

Stagflation

Literary and Dramatic Expression

The Novel

Television and the Movies

The Dark Side and the Beginnings of Change

Sources of Anxiety

The Transformation of the City

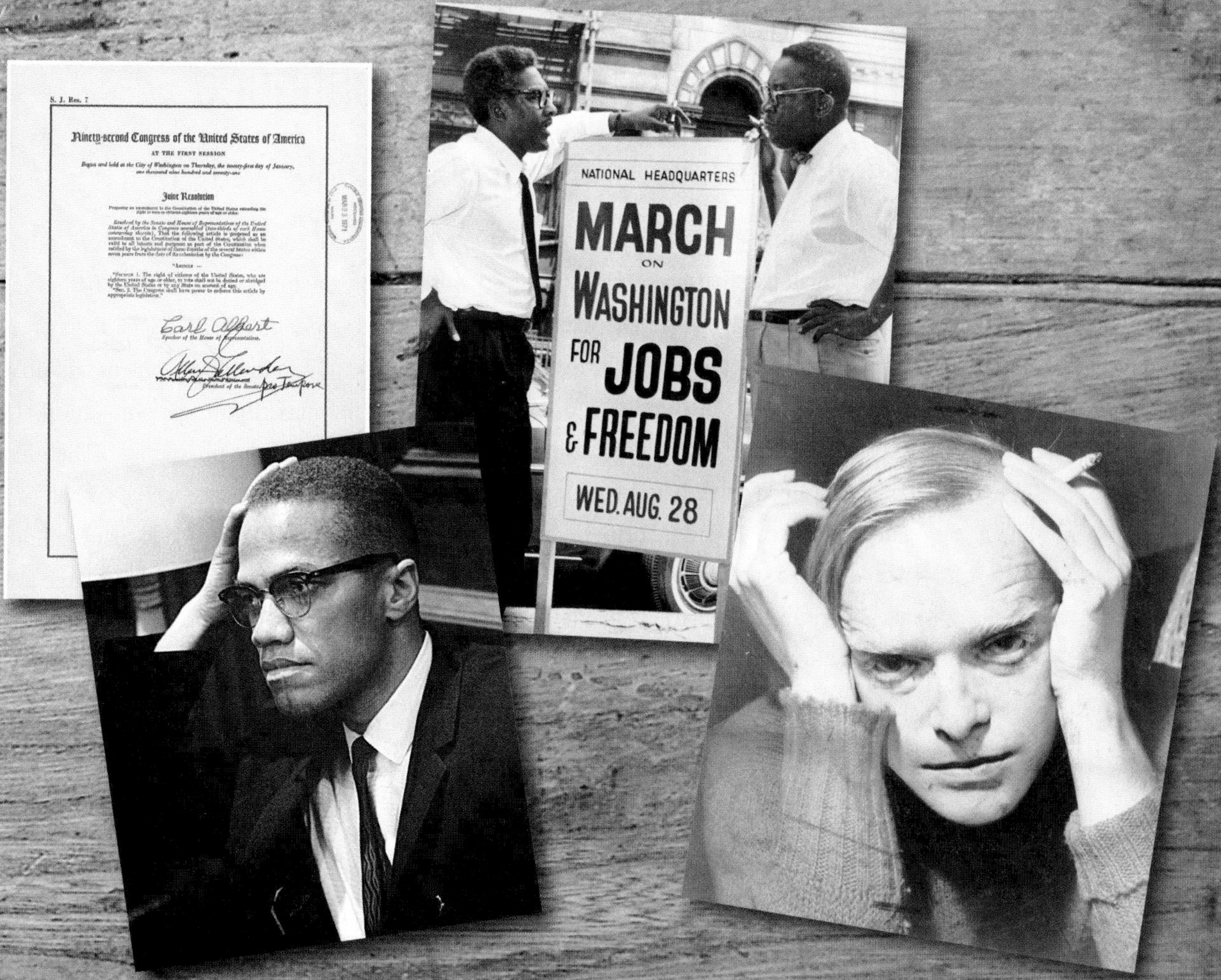

A New Ethnic and Racial Self-Consciousness

The Second Reconstruction Continued

A New Civil Rights Movement
The Rights of Urban Dwellers
Black Power
A Southern President and Black America
Two Steps Forward, One Backward
The Mexican-American Movement
The American Indian Movement
The Decline of the Civil Rights Movement
Challenges to the Educational System
The Youth Culture
The Women's Movement
The New Right
Right to Privacy and Abortion Rights.
The Religious Right and Republicanism
Criminal Rights
Gay Liberation

The Consumer Society Continued

The Prosperous American of the 1960s and 70s

The prosperity of the post-war era of the 1950s continued through the 1960s. By 1971, however, to maintain that prosperity, a majority of married women worked outside the home at least part of the time. That same year, over half of married workingwomen were mothers of children under eighteen, though birth rates were in decline due to the development and proliferation of birth control pills; and females remained the majority of the population. The possessions of the average American and her husband reflected the prosperity of the times. They typically owned their own home, most likely in an urban area since well over half of all Americans lived in cities. Furthermore, by the end of the period it was likely that the house would be in a suburb rather than a metropolitan city. Regardless of where she lived, the average American would have a car, a telephone, and a television set.

So popular was television in the lives of Americans that more owned TV sets than owned washing machines and dishwashers together. Televisions and refrigerators were the only major appliances the ownership of which did not vary significantly by income. In 1974, almost two thirds of American homes contained a color TV, and 45 percent of them had two or more television sets. Thus 94.4 per cent of families with incomes under $5,000 in 1974 had a TV and a refrigerator, but only 55 per cent of them owned a washing machine.

College opportunities were present for most, although even in the 1970s when about half the young people continued their education after high school, only about a third of college-age people actually graduated from college. Educational opportunities for women continued to expand, with home economics departments, degrees in secretarial science, and nursing and elementary education were still the chosen educational paths for most of America's university women.

Sports and Leisure

Spectator sports continued to expand and attendance figures at the National Football League (NFL) games jumped almost 500 percent between 1950 and 1973. The NFL, which had had only twelve teams in 1950, merged with the upstart American Football League (AFL) in 1970 to create one league with twenty-six teams. The first Super Bowl was played after the 1966 season between the Green Bay Packers of the NFL and the AFL's Kansas City Chiefs. Two years later, the New York Jets of the AFL, led by a flamboyant quarterback named Joe Namath, shocked the football world by defeating the NFL's Baltimore Colts and in doing so catapulted professional football and the Super Bowl into a new era of popularity. Additionally, in 1970 some 30 million people attended college football games. The University of Texas defeated Notre Dame in the Cotton Bowl on January 1, 1969, with the NCAA's last all-white national championship team. By the end of the 1970s, African-Americans would dominate the game on both the college and professional level. Similarly, Texas Western University (now University of Texas at El Paso) would win the NCAA national championship in basketball in 1966 with five black starting players. Meanwhile, UCLA under legendary coach John Wooden would win eight NCAA basketball titles in ten years, and the Boston Celtics would win eleven NBA titles in thirteen years. The Green Bay Packers, under coach Vince Lombardi, won five NFL titles between 1961 and 1967, and Denny McClain won thirty-one games pitching for the Detroit Tigers in 1968.

While spectator sports boomed, participatory sports—that is, those that cost money to participate in, such as bowling, golfing, riding, or swimming—also surged. In fact, in 1976 Americans spent more on such sports than on movies or on spectator sports. An equal amount ($3.9 billion) was spent on flowers, plants, and seeds, suggesting that gardening was another significant leisure activity.

Although never avid book readers, Americans once supported a large number of newspapers, but in the years between 1950 and 1970 the numbers of newspapers declined in the face of rising costs and declining revenues. During the 1970s, however, the number began to rise again, and the number of periodicals increased throughout the period as well. Magazines catered increasingly to the specialized interests and hobbies of Americans—sports, woodworking, sailing, gardening, hunting, sewing, and cooking—as well as prurient interests, with the rise of "men's" magazines such as *Playboy* and *Penthouse* that thrived in the 1960s and 1970s by offering photos of nude and semi-nude women, articles with sexual subject matter, and monthly centerfolds.

The pursuit of recreation in a period of prosperity can be measured by the fact that 16 million Americans rode horses, 10 million played golf, and 7 million owned motorboats. Between 1950 and 1975, the number of people who took out hunting licenses doubled, and fishing licenses also more than doubled, reaching 35 million in 1975.

Although more and more Americans traveled outside the United States—the number increased tenfold between 1950 and 1970—the average American spent her vacations with her family inside the United States, usually at the seashore, at lakes, in the mountains, or visiting the national parks in the West. In 1973 there were more visits to the national parks than there were people in the country, reflecting the visits of many people to more than one park or monument. Simultaneously, attendance at amusement parks reached unprecedented levels. Although the rising price of gasoline began to curtail that kind of

▶ The pursuit of recreation in a period of prosperity can be measured by the fact that 16 million Americans rode horses, 7 million owned motorboats, and 10 million played golf.

vacationing in the late 1970s, the quarter century after the Second World War witnessed an ever-growing dependence upon the automobile for pleasure. Families used the automobiles to take family vacations, but young college and high school age students drove their cars back and forth on selected streets in towns throughout America in an activity known throughout America as "cruising" or "dragging."

Diet and Health

During the years of prosperity, Americans also ate differently. The near-full employment that prevailed during these years encouraged people to buy more prepared foods like TV dinners, pastry and other mixes, frozen vegetables and juices, and more costly kinds and cuts of meat. Per capita consumption of frozen foods jumped 300 percent between 1950 and 1973, while per capita purchases of beef went up 150 percent and those of chicken and turkey more than doubled. Simultaneously, the per capita intake of hard liquors rose almost 90 percent after 1950, and that of wine, 74 percent. The increase in wine consumption over twenty-five years reflected not only an increase in alcoholic intake but also a broadening of tastes.

Despite the increasing richness of the diet and the rise in the consumption of alcohol and tobacco, the life expectancy of the average American significantly improved due to better hygiene, antibiotics, and improved medical practices. In 1940, the average life expectancy at birth was 62.9 years, but by 1976 it was up to 72.5; by 1977, it was 73.2. An even more significant measure of improvement was the increase in the life expectancy of black males—from 53 years in 1940 to 68.3 years in 1976. A large part of the improvement stemmed from the lowering of infant mortality rates during those years. A 70 percent drop in infant mortality for whites and 67 percent for blacks reflected not only improvements in medical care but also general prosperity. It also reflected the rise in urbanization as far fewer babies were being born on rural kitchen tables.

Although the federal government and private medical organizations mounted extensive campaigns against cigarette smoking during the 1950s and 1960s because of the clear linkage between smoking and cancer, the per capita consumption of cigarettes actually increased from 175 packs a year in 1950 to 210 packs in 1973. It declined then, however, to 203 per capita in 1977.

Productivity and Poverty

In 1971 the GNP for the first time passed $1 trillion when as recently as 1960 it had been "only" half that. Even when the growth is measured in constant dollars—that is, taking inflation into account—the GNP increased 150 percent between 1950 and 1977. Only Sweden and Switzerland equaled the per capita production of the American economy at the beginning of the 1970s when Americans had buying power that exceeded any they had ever had before. By 1969 an hour's work in a factory bought 2.4 pounds of round steak, and even at the height of inflation in 1974, an hour of factory work still bought 2.3 pounds of round steak. In 1969, less than five minutes of factory work would buy a quart of milk.

Another measure of the American prosperity of the time period is that between 1950 and 1970, the average income of the bottom tenth of the population had risen about 55 percent, after discounting price changes. Similarly, in 1940 fewer than 44 percent of American families, including farmers, lived in homes they purchased; by 1973 the proportion was up to 65 percent. Moreover, the proportion of Americans who lived below the poverty line steadily declined from 22 percent in 1959, when the statistics were first compiled, to 11.4 percent sixteen years later. This latter figure was clearly a measure not only of America's prosperity but also of the fact that the U.S. government launched numerous programs aimed at combating poverty in the 1960s.

When Lyndon Johnson assumed the presidency in 1963, millions of Americans still lived "in want" in spite of America's robust economic growth. As a result, Johnson initiated his "Great Society" and federal outlays for welfare rose rapidly. In 1966 federal expenditures on behalf of low-income people amounted to $11.3 billion. By 1971, under the first Nixon administration, the figure had more than doubled to $25.5 billion.

Despite these aids to the poor and the move up the income ladder of millions of lower-class and middle-class Americans, not to mention the decline in the number of Americans living in poverty, the distribution of income barely changed in these years. In 1950 the top 5 percent of families received 17 percent of aggregate income, while the lowest 20 percent received 4.5 percent. Twenty-five years later the proportion of total aggregate income received by the top 5 percent was down to 15.5 percent, but the proportion received by the lowest 20 percent was up only to 5.4 percent. Furthermore, the top 20 percent of income receivers got about the same share in 1975 that they had in 1950—that is, about 40 percent. As might be expected in a competitive society, income distribution remained far from equal; yet it was greatly improved from the Gilded Age and was much better than it would be after the Reagan Revolution of the 1980s moved America away from the social welfare state model that was developed in the 1960s, toward a model that favored greater reliance on the free market.

The Agricultural Sector 1963–1980

One labor group that did not share economically in the good times was the laborers in the agricultural sector. Indeed, in 1968 it was estimated that 23 percent of the farm population lived below the poverty line, as compared with 12 percent of the urban population. By 1960 less than 8 percent of the American population lived on farms, and by 1970 that proportion was down to less than 5 percent. Yet the value of total farm production rose about 20 percent in the same ten-year period. Thus, a farmer either was a large-scale operator with a large capital investment or would soon be compelled to withdraw from farming.

Capital per farm in 1974 was about 6.6 times in constant dollars what it had been in 1950. Put another way, in the 1960s the amount of capital per farm work was about $5,000 more than the amount of capital per worker in manufacturing. It was this high capitalization that explained the enormous increase in farm productivity. In 1969 over 4.5 million tractors were in use on American farms; and thousands of mechanical cotton pickers had displaced hundreds of thousands of Southern black workers, who had left agriculture to seek wider opportunities in Northern cities. New seeds, new machines, and new chemicals of all kinds also gave impetus to a farm revolution in the postwar years that increased production, but required less human labor.

The chemical revolution had a massive impact on agricultural employment. Chemicals were used not only to kill harmful insects but also to hasten crop maturity, to kill weeds, to defoliate plants in order to facilitate harvesting, or to inhibit growth in crops—like tobacco, where only certain kinds of leaves are desired. The chemical industry also developed new feeds for chickens, which sped up growth and made it possible to raise broilers from egg to maturity in eight to nine weeks. The disastrous effects of some of these chemicals upon nature have posed a serious dilemma for a society wanting cheap and abundant food and protection for wildlife at the same time. Perhaps the most notorious of these was DDT, a pesticide that proved to have a deleterious effect on the reproductive capacity of bald eagles and reduced the American National Bird to the status of an endangered species before DDT was banned by the federal government.

Components of Economic Growth

Numerous factors contributed to economic growth of the 1960s and 1970s, but among the most important were the large multinational corporations. In 1968, less than 3 percent of all corporations earned almost four-fifths of the total income of corporations. Corporate enterprises, with their large capital resources and heavy expenditures on research and development, were at once both a cause and a consequence of the prosperity of the 1960s.

▶ In pursuit of increasing agricultural productivity and profit, chemicals were introduced in order to hasten the process of maturing for livestock as well as crops. These chemicals soon proved to be dangerous to nature and were banned by the federal government.

Simultaneously, federal defense spending surged to over $80 billion at the height of the Vietnam War. By 1970, the federal government alone spent a quarter of the nation's money and, when combined with state and local governments, hired almost a fifth of the labor force.

The housing boom of the 1950s continued into the 1960s as the federal government helped facilitate low interest loans to American citizens. The extent of the housing boom of the 1950s and 1960s can be measured by the simple fact that in 1971 two-fifths of all the houses and apartments occupied in the country had been built in the preceding twenty years.

Technology also continued to fuel economic growth and changes in the American economic structure. A single invention, like the digital computer and, later, the microchip, made a whole range of clerical and arithmetical activities amazingly rapid, thus releasing labor and money for other tasks. In 1970, white-collar workers constituted 50.8 percent of the nonagricultural labor force, blue-collars 34.5 percent, and service workers (policemen, bank tellers, domestics, and others) 10.5 percent. By 1970 less than 5 percent of the work force was in agriculture, compared with 18 percent employed by government—in a society that prided itself on being the antithesis of socialistic! (In officially Communist Yugoslavia in 1972, 20 percent of the work force was employed by the government.)

The Decline of Labor Unions

One segment of the American economic infrastructure that was suddenly in decline, however, was organized labor. Traditionally, white-collar workers have resisted joining unions, even though white-collar pay is often inferior to industrial wages. In 1972, for example, only 16.5 percent of all unionized workers were employed in white-collar occupations. Despite its organizing drives and its power, organized labor in the 1960s barely kept pace with the growing size of the labor force. In 1964, for example, about 30 percent of nonagricultural workers were in unions. Eight years later the proportion was down to 26.7 percent.

While unions were struggling, women joined the workforce in record peacetime numbers. Indeed, between 1950 and 1970 some 13.2 million women joined the labor force, as compared with only 9.5 million men; and among these workingwomen were growing numbers of wives and mothers. By 1970 over two-fifths of all married women were employed in paying jobs. Almost a third of women with children under six were working, counting only married women whose husbands were present. In short, women now constituted the largest source of new workers in the economy. By the 1970s, the percentage of women enrolling in colleges and universities began to rise significantly.

Silicon Valley and the High Tech Industry

In 1968 defectors from William Shockley's Fairchild Corporation founded Intel in Santa Clara, which neighbors Sunnyvale, CA, and the stage was set for the next breakthrough, the microprocessor, a more sophisticated cousin of the integrated circuit. What was so exciting about the microprocessor was that it permitted memory to be electronically embedded and thus was essential to the development of the personal computer. Having developed this, Intel would become yet another of the giants; and the Santa Clara Valley would become America's high-tech center. In 1971, a journalist gave the Santa Clara Valley the nickname of Silicon Valley. Between 1959 and 1976, in fact, forty-five semiconductor firms were established in the country, forty of which were in the Santa Clara Valley. With the invention of the microprocessor came a turn away from the military market to a burgeoning consumer market.

In 1977 Steve Jobs and Steve Wozniak founded another of the pioneering firms in the Valley, Apple Computers. Jobs and Wozniak were very young, and at that early stage they looked like quintessential hackers. Though they may have resembled hippies, their firm's rise from zero to Fortune 500 within five years was a phenomenon in American business history. Soon there were several manufacturers of personal computers, and Bill Gates and Paul Allen and Microsoft, in the Seattle region, were well on their way as well.

Though Silicon Valley is no longer quite so dominant as it was at its height—and the dot.com bust of the early twenty-first century would take a terrible toll—it is noteworthy that as the Internet has developed its success, Silicon Valley firms continue to be innovators in the early twenty-first century, with Google and eBay being two of the most famous.

Stagflation

Economically, perhaps no situation can be expected to last forever, and this is also true of America's postwar boom. By the early 1970s, a number of economic factors combined to send the economy into an economic malaise that would essentially last into the mid-1980s, when the economy would finally be rescued by an information-processing high-tech boom. In the 1960s and early 1970s, however, the United States spent approximately $647 billion (unsupported by taxes) on the Vietnam War. Simultaneously, the federal government funded Lyndon Johnson's Great Society programs, also, without raising taxes. President Johnson announced that the nation could have both "guns and butter" and ignored the need to tax for the war and the Great Society because he surmised that taxing for the War or the Great Society would cause them to become unpopular. As a result, the billions in federal spending dumped on the economy, unsupported by taxes, meant that the money supply increased faster than economic growth, thus resulting in both debt and inflation by the 1970s.

To make matters worse, an energy crisis in 1973 and another one in 1978 would cause oil prices to rise from $3 per barrel in 1973 to $34 in 1981. The rising costs of fuel would trickle through the rest of the economy and cause rising prices in everything else as well. Simultaneously, multinational corporations were in the process of moving manufacturing to developing countries to take advantage of lower labor costs. The result was the collapse of the American manufacturing sector and an accompanying spike in unemployment. Some manufacturing cities, such as Detroit, would never recover.

The rise in prices, or inflation, accompanied by high unemployment was an economic situation termed as "stagflation" that had been unexpected by economists. Unfortunately, politicians and economists alike seemed clueless as to how to return the nation to its postwar prosperity.

Literary and Dramatic Expression

The Novel

Not surprisingly, the 1960s and 1970s fostered a number of novels by important American writers. Kurt Vonnegut's macabre *Slaughterhouse Five* (1969), combined science fiction with a historical fiction about the bombing of Dresden in World War II. Through his main character, Billy

Pilgrim, Vonnegut explores the concepts of fate, free will, and the irrational nature of human beings. Norman Mailer, in a reflection of the spirit of protest of the late 1960s, produced *Armies in the Night* (1968), his remarkable account of his own participation in an antiwar demonstration at the Pentagon.

Saul Bellow carried on the realistic literary tradition in *Herzog* (1964), and *Humboldt's Gift* (1975). In 1976 Bellow won the Nobel Prize for Literature. (That bicentennial year, in fact, Americans won all five Nobel Prizes.)

Meanwhile, Philip Roth abandoned the realistic tradition and swerved to the wild sexual excess of *Portnoy's Complaint* (1969) and the vitriolic political satire of *Our Gang* (1971), which was about President Nixon. His interest in outrageous fantasy continued with *The Breast* (1972) and *The Professor of Desire* (1977).

John Updike continued to move in and out of the realistic tradition with *Rabbit Redux* (1971), and his rising interest in Africa was reflected in his *The Coup* (1978). Of a much more traditional character was the work of Isaac Bashevis Singer, written in Yiddish though Singer lived in the United States. He recounted in compelling narrative and wry humor the joys and sorrows of Jewish life. His remarkably diverse body of work was recognized internationally in 1978 with the Nobel Prize. Truman Capote, a childhood friend of Harper Lee, wrote his 1966 classic work of non-fiction, *In Cold Blood*, about the murder of the Clutter family in Kansas. Capote and the book became the subjects of an Oscar-winning film in 2005, *Capote*.

The most striking black literary talent in the second half of the twentieth century was female: Toni Morrison, whose *The Bluest Eye* (1970) captured attention immediately, would go on to win a Nobel Prize in 1993; and Maya Angelou, whose autobiography *I Know Why the Caged Bird Sings* (1970), was both popular and significant.

Finally, in 1973 Erica Jong published *Fear of Flying*, which heralded a new voice in American literature with a frank account of female sexuality. That it appeared when it did was no coincidence. The novel was both cause and effect of the feminist revolution then taking shape.

▶ Truman Capote, American author and comedian, wrote his "non-fiction novel" *In Cold Blood* in 1966 about the murder of the Clutter family in Kansas. Capote and his book became the subjects of an Oscar-winning film in 2005, *Capote*.

Television and the Movies

Due to the advent of television, the movie industry had been in decline in the 1950s. By the mid-1960s, however, a revival began as independent producers and moviemakers came upon the scene. By 1967 there were some twelve thousand movie houses (up from nine thousand two hundred in 1963), and by 1977 the figure was seventeen thousand. Moreover, by 1976 more money was being spent on movie tickets than for all spectator sport events, theater, and opera admissions put together.

By the late 1960s, it was evident that a sizable segment of the population did not want to stay home nights and stare at the TV set. Reared on television, the young were ready to leave the "tube" to their parents. Many members of the new movie audience were college students or recent graduates, for during the 1960s there was also a great increase in college attendance. To reach this expanding potential audience, the movies had to grow up, and the best of them did. As in the theater and the novel, censorship was virtually dead—a development that conservatives blamed on the "permissive liberalism" of the Supreme Court, but which permitted a new realism and a new frankness of both theme and treatment. More significant, perhaps, was the new sophistication the audience demanded. Westerns would still succeed, but movies that laughed at the clichés (*Cat Ballou, True Grit*) or depicted three-dimensional characters instead of cardboard cutouts (*Butch Cassidy and the Sundance Kid*) did best. War, long the subject of romantic or chauvinistic epics, came in for ironic attacks in movies like *Dr. Strangelove*, *Catch-22*, and *M*A*S*H*. The Vietnam War was treated seriously—and critically—in the poignant *Coming Home*, starring, appropriately enough, the antiwar actress Jane Fonda, and in *The Deerhunter*, which unblinkingly depicted the cost of the war to those who supported it. *The Deerhunter* was also one of several movies dealing realistically with working-class life in America. Another was *Norma Rae*, for which Sally Field won an Academy Award.

Some of the best of the new movies were addressed directly to the young. *The Graduate* came to be considered a classic statement of what young people held against their parents and what they thought of themselves. *Easy Rider* offered a sympathetic view of the drug culture in idyllic settings, and *One Flew Over the Cuckoo's Nest* expressed many a young person's sense of the insanity of the conventional world and its institutions. If some older fans were troubled by the moral ambiguities in the new films and wondered whether there was, in fact, anything particularly grown up or sophisticated about clinical studies of loveless sex (*Deep Throat*) or celebrations of mindless violence (*Straw Dogs*, *Clockwork Orange*), by the 1970s the movies were an important emotional and intellectual experience for a great many young Americans. In *Saturday Night Fever* and *Grease* the importance of rock music and dancing in the lives of millions of young people was brought home to all who saw those films.

Older Americans also found certain films in the 1970s attractive, perhaps because they stirred remembrances of things past (*The Great Gatsby*, *The Sting*) or sentimental ethnicity (*The Godfather*) or the love of being frightened (*Jaws* and *The Exorcist*). Science fiction movies, the groundbreaker of which was the highly creative *2001: A Space Odyssey*, proved inordinately attractive to young as well as old. *The Man Who Fell to Earth* was not a great success in 1976, but in the next two years three science fiction movies each challenged all money-making records: *Star Wars*, *Close Encounters of the Third Kind*, and *Superman*, the last based upon the old comic strip and TV serial. Was this new interest in science fiction a delayed reaction to the success of the 1960s in putting a man on the moon—or merely escape?

By the 1970s movies made about blacks and for blacks began to appear (*Shaft*, *Super Fly*, and *Sounder*). Blacks were increasingly a part of the mainstream of America and were recognized as such in the social mirror of the movies. Some blacks as well as whites deplored the separatism and racial chauvinism sometimes depicted in these movies, but others cheered the fact that there were beginning to be some black heroes and heroines with whom black fans could identify. Situation comedies on TV also began to feature blacks with some of the top shows, such as *Sanford and Son*, *The Jeffersons*, and *Good Times*, being primarily black in cast and outlook, though generally written by whites.

The most spectacular success in all of television production during the time period dealt with African Americans. *Roots*, a series running eight consecutive evenings, told the story of a black family from its beginnings in Africa, through the darkness of slavery in America, and finally into freedom. Written by African American author Alex Haley, *Roots* was seen in January 1977 by almost three-quarters of the owners of television sets in the country—in itself a powerful comment on the impact of the black experience on the consciousness of Americans, white as well as black.

The Dark Side and the Beginnings of Change

Sources of Anxiety

The unusual prosperity of the 1960s was itself a source of anxiety and confusion of values. It encouraged many Americans to choose buying goods to "keep up with the Joneses" over reaching goals. Many adults who had grown up during the Great Depression sacrificed to give their children material advantages they themselves never enjoyed. In doing so, they laid the groundwork for the anti-materialism of the 1960s counterculture, which, in turn, alienated many children from their parents. Since even poor people had television, they knew first-hand of the goods they were denied by their poverty. The resentment of many erupted into violence in dozens of cities. For others, the resentment was kept hidden, but it was no less alienating and divisive.

The highly organized corporate economy and its burgeoning bureaucracy, which was in large part responsible for the prosperity, reduced the individual's feelings of significance and effectiveness. The efficient organization of work, on which the prosperity depended, made the work place for millions of Americans monotonous, impersonal, and dispiriting.

New sources of anxiety appeared on a global scale: rapid population growth, impending world shortages of food and irreplaceable resources like oil and gas, the deadly effects of pollution and toxic wastes, and the growing gap between the rich and poor nations because of the latter's increasing insistence upon a fairer share of the world's production. Behind all these threats stood the most immediate and ominous danger of all: the possibility of a nuclear war that might obliterate half the world. The arms race between the United States and the Soviet Union was still uncontrolled, and nuclear weapons by the 1970s were in the hands of at least four other nations, including communist China.

The Transformation of the City

By 1970, three-fourths of all Americans lived in urban areas, but the flight from the cities to the suburbs continued. According to the census of 1970, between 1960 and 1970, sixty-one of the

153 cities of one hundred thousand or more lost population. For many it was the first loss of population since the beginning of the urbanizing movement. In comparison, in 1920, 19 percent of Americans had lived in New York City alone.

In 1970 less than a third of Americans lived in central cities, while more than two-fifths lived in surrounding suburbs, which were now becoming places of work as well as residence. By 1970 the suburbs were providing only slightly fewer jobs than the central cities. They were no longer simply "bedroom communities," although 85 percent of American workers used their cars to get to work, especially in the West, where cities had developed after the invention of the automobile.

For the central city, commuters and their automobiles presented a growing problem. The demand for parking facilities alone—not to mention the multiplying demands for new expressways and freeways—ate significantly into the prime real estate of the great cities, and cut into the tax base that was needed for increased urban expenditures. Moreover, commuter trains, forced to compete with the automobile, found it more and more difficult to make a profit or even to survive; many were forced to reduce or discontinue their service. Yet much of the metropolitan labor force still depended on the commuter lines for daily transportation. As a consequence, a number of state and local governments faced pressures to subsidize the commuter lines in one way or another.

The Urban Mass Transportation Assistance Act of 1970 brought some federal money for mass transportation to the beleaguered cities, but the need far outran the remedy. The automobile was still a formidable competitor—as San Francisco's computerized light rail Bay Area Rapid Transportation (BART) discovered soon after it opened in 1972. In spite of an impressive multimillion-dollar engineering feat that included building a train tunnel under San Francisco Bay, seven years later it had not yet fulfilled the promise either to reduce auto traffic significantly or to pay for itself. Nevertheless, the need for mass transit was reflected in the new subways that opened in the late 1970s in New Orleans, Atlanta, and Washington, D.C.—the last pronounced a practical and visual success from the outset—and in the plans for a Texas version of San Francisco's BART in Houston and later in Dallas.

The flight to the suburbs was both a symptom and a cause of the decline of the central city as a place of human habitation. As middle-class families fled the overcrowded schools, substandard housing, and polluted air, the city became the home of the poor. Metropolitan areas deteriorated still more. High land prices, caused in part by land speculation and by rapid, unplanned growth in the new areas, created a major obstacle to the construction of adequate low- and middle-income housing in the suburbs. Consequently, low-income urban dwellers could not move to the suburbs along with their more affluent neighbors. Nonexistent or poorly enforced building and housing codes, haphazard zoning laws, and the profits to be made from slum real estate, further contributed to the continual rotting of the core cities in America's metropolitan areas.

When the Housing Act of 1968 authorized the building of 1.7 million units—mainly low- and moderate-income—over the next three years, it was estimated that at least 6 million were needed. After the units were built, both the government efforts and the residents of these "projects" came under criticism for poor maintenance and vandalism in the government-built housing. In addition to the problems of adequate urban housing, urban

▶The Urban Mass Transportation Assistance Act of 1970 approved federal funds for providing mass transportation. The Bay Area Rapid Transportation (BART) in San Francisco opened in 1972. Subways soon were developed in other major cities across the country.

schools were often overcrowded; and understaffed and large areas of modern cities were generating increasing rates of crime, including juvenile delinquency.

These perplexing urban problems stimulated attempts to restore the nation's cities to economic and social health. Under the generic term "urban renewal," many cities attempted to rehabilitate run-down neighborhoods by land clearance and new construction or by renovating existing structures and bringing such areas into conformity with zoning, housing, health, and safety standards.

Despite the success of urban renewal projects in several of America's metropolitan areas, progress was slow. Land clearance ran into vexing legal delays, and the relocation of former tenants was a continuing source of irritation for all concerned. Renewal critics attacked everything from spiraling costs to the esthetic and social drawbacks of the new construction. They charged that the billions already spent to rejuvenate America's cities had helped only to destroy their individuality. They called the new middle-income housing "a marvel of dullness and regimentation." Furthermore, some correctly predicted that new, low-income projects would themselves be slums by the 1970s. Moreover, urban renewal, as it was then practiced, gave scant attention to the wishes of slum dwellers themselves and hence was labeled by some critics, "Negro removal."

In 1966 one device by which the Johnson administration pushed better housing for the poor was to provide rent subsidies that permitted people to live in nongovernment housing, even if rents were higher than they could afford. Another was to provide federal funds for the renovation of older houses and tenements in established neighborhood, allowing residents to escape the often starkly unattractive housing projects. These efforts, too, often resulted in ownership of still more slums by the federal government when the private owners defaulted.

Since coordination of the many efforts to deal with the problems of the decaying city was a paramount need, Congress, in 1965, created one new cabinet post for urban development and another for transportation in 1966. The latter was designed to encourage and coordinate efforts in behalf of better intra- and interurban transportation since the automobile had itself become a problem of urban living.

A New Ethnic and Racial Self-Consciousness

A significant piece of the new cultural attitudes that emerged in the 1960s was a reflection of the recognition by the dominant majority that racial and ethnic prejudice had no place in a society that prided itself on equality of opportunity. Undoubtedly the most conspicuous and immediate impetus to the belated recognition of religious, national, or racial identities in American life was the Black Revolution of the 1960s, which started as a nonviolent civil rights movement and was led by Martin Luther King, Jr. until his assassination in 1968. That movement, simply because of its power and its influence on politics, was a catalyst, if not a model, for the rise in ethnic self-consciousness of other groups in the 1960s and after. Ironically, the success of the blacks' demands for recognition and a share in the national pie of prosperity caused some ethnic groups to react against black aspirations. In the 1970s, for example, the Irish in Boston and the Poles in Detroit were conspicuous in the demonstrations against forced busing to integrate public schools.

The Second Reconstruction Continued

In spite of the *Brown v. Board of Education* decision in 1954 ordering the integration of schools, primary and secondary schools in the South had little more than token integration until 1965. The Elementary and Secondary Education Act of 1965, however, which for the first time authorized $3 billion in federal funds to aid school districts, allocated dollars based on the number of poor children that the districts educated and provided equipment and supplies to schools to be used for poor children. Many school districts, therefore, integrated to ensure that they could tap into the federal funding by teaching poor black children. Between then and 1971, the proportion of black children doubled in Southern schools heretofore wholly white, reaching 39 percent. This was a greater increase and a larger proportion than that for the nation as a whole. As early as 1971, only 14 percent of black children in the South were still in schools that were entirely black. In short, the movement toward integration in the South had proceeded further than it had elsewhere in the country, and federal grants had accomplished what federal coercion could not. Even so, resistance continued. The principal evidence was the growing number of private, often religious, all-white schools in the South. In 1971 it was estimated that about 4 percent of school age children attended such schools.

A New Civil Rights Movement

In August 1963 occurred one of the most significant of the protests, the March on Washington. Some two hundred fifty thousand Americans, black and white alike, converged on the nation's capital to call for more progress in achieving racial justice. The highlight of the event was Reverend King's "I Have a Dream" speech, one of the rhetorical high points in American history.

▶ In the March on Washington protest, two hundred and fifty thousand Americans, black and white alike, converged on the nation's capital to call for more progress in achieving racial justice. The highlight of the event was Reverend King's "I Have a Dream" speech.

Coterminous with the anti-segregation movement in the South, Northern blacks in cities like New York and Chicago campaigned against segregated public schools. Northern segregation resulted primarily from residential patterns rather than from laws, but the effects were often similar. Blacks demanded, with some success, that their children be accepted in white schools outside their local districts, where the schools were often crowded and run-down or underfinanced.

In the early 1970s, however, when the federal courts used compulsory busing to bring about racial mixture in Northern schools, as it had done in the South, strong white opposition exploded. In some Northern cities, including San Francisco, Pontiac, Michigan, and Brooklyn, New York, parents who opposed forced busing kept their children out of school for weeks. In Boston during 1974–1975, the resistance to busing was as vehement—and violent—as resistance to integration had been at Little Rock in 1957. In 1971, a Gallup poll found that 76 percent of Americans opposed busing as a means of bringing about desegregation. Opponents argued that busing children to different sections of town could add hours to their day. Furthermore, it was argued that high-minded members of Congress that favored busing sent their own children to private schools. Nevertheless, the courts continued to uphold busing as a constitutional means of breaking segregation. In 1979, the Supreme Court reaffirmed the principle, though by a divided vote.

By the close of the 1970s, school segregation was clearly less pronounced in the once completely segregated South than in the North. Only 12 percent of Southern black children were in predominantly black schools as compared to 31 percent of Midwestern and Northeastern children. Nevertheless, progress had been made. As recently as 1968, the proportion of black children in segregated schools throughout the nation had been 53 percent.

The Rights of Urban Dwellers

The Supreme Court's decisions in *Baker v. Carr*, handed down in March 1962, and in *Reynolds v. Sims* two years later, were freighted with almost as much significance for the future as the *Brown* decision on segregation in 1954. The *Baker* case concerned the refusal of Tennessee to reapportion its legislative seats in accordance with changes in the distribution of population. The Court decreed that districts of markedly unequal populations constituted an inequity for which the courts could rightly be expected to provide a remedy.

For a number of years, as population flowed from the rural areas to the cities, urban dwellers had smarted under the failure of their growing numbers to be reflected in increased representation in the state legislatures. It was well known that rural-dominated legislatures simply refused, as in the case of Tennessee, to reapportion seats; to do so might mean loss of rural conservative control. Until the *Baker* decision the courts had held that such inequity was a "political" question beyond their jurisdiction.

The *Reynolds* decision extended the reasoning of the *Baker* decision to include the upper as well as the lower houses of the state legislatures. These decisions opened up the possibility that with equitable apportionment of representation the cities would be able to get a better hearing in the state legislatures for their many and worsening problems.

The effects of the *Baker* decision were soon apparent. In a number of states where rural dominance in politics had long depended upon underweighting urban populations, the redistricting that the *Baker* and *Reynolds* decisions required translated into new political strength of cities in the state legislatures. Atlanta, for example, suddenly gained new strength in the Georgia legislature. In 1967, a reapportioned Tennessee legislature succeeded in repealing the anti-evolution statute passed in 1925 (during the heyday of rural domination of the legislature). By 1971, more than half the states had reapportioned their legislatures, though the courts had thrown some of the new plans out as inadequate.

Black Power

The new emphasis upon equality and group identity, as well as impatience at the slow rate of progress from nonviolent methods, caused new Black Nationalist or separatist groups to come to the fore during the latter sixties. The Black Muslims, a religious society founded by Elijah Muhammad during the 1930s, attracted national attention in the mid-1950s when the articulate and dynamic Malcolm X became head of the Muslims in Harlem. The Black Muslims preached a form of Islam in religion and black separatism in social policy. After he had turned away from the narrow nationalism of Elijah Muhammad, Malcolm X died at the hands of an assassin in 1965.

The most militant of the nationalist groups, however, was the Black Panther party, which began in Oakland, California in 1966. The best-known spokesman of the party was Eldridge Cleaver, a former convict of some literary talent. His book *Soul on Ice* is one of the classics of the Black Revolution, along with *The Autobiography of Malcolm X*. Cleaver argued that blacks should return racist violence from whites with violence of their own. Cleaver fled to Algeria in 1968 after a series of confrontations between police and the Panthers. By 1972, however, the Panthers were less involved in shoot-outs with the police and more concerned with educational and breakfast programs for black children in the urban ghettos. In 1975 Cleaver returned to the United States, prepared to stand trial on the criminal charges against him.

A third figure of prominence in the new black nationalism of the 1960s was Stokely Carmichael, who in 1966, at twenty-four, became head of the Student Nonviolent Coordinating Committee (SNCC). His slogan "Black Power" aroused a new sense of self-awareness and pride among young blacks and a sense of identification and cohesion among blacks of all ages. The idea that "black is beautiful" rather than a badge of shame would catch on and

▶ Malcolm X, radical human rights activist for African Americans.

endure. As a leader, Carmichael did not last into the 1970s, nor did the idea of Black Power; however, both left a sense of positive identity among dark-skinned Americans in regard to their blackness and their African origins. Thenceforth, most African-Americans preferred to refer to themselves as black rather than Negro. (See *Muhammad Ali: Float Like a Butterfly, Sting Like a Bee.*)

A Southern President and Black America

John F. Kennedy's moving television appeal to all Americans in 1963 to accept the moral challenge of full equality for blacks justly earned him the distinction of being the first president in the twentieth century to attack the question of discrimination against black Americans in clearly moral terms. To Lyndon Johnson, however, must go the credit for the most sweeping attack on the unequal treatment of black people mounted by any president at any time. The Civil Rights Act of 1964 originated under the Kennedy administration, but it remained for Johnson to push it through a three-month filibuster in the Senate. The Act prohibited racial discrimination in public places, in employment, and in labor unions. As a sanction of compliance, it provided for the withholding of federal funds from any state that practiced racial discrimination. Since much federal money went to support schools, hospitals, and other state services, this provision gave bite to the law.

The Act also sought to get around the literacy requirements for voting, which were often used in the South as a means of disenfranchising blacks. It provided that any adult with a sixth-grade education was presumed to be literate. The immediate effect was to open public accommodations to blacks in many cities of the South for the first time in the twentieth century—though not much was changed in the rural and small-town South—and to increase voting by blacks in many communities.

It is also worth noting that the Civil Rights Act of 1964 was the broadest statement of American belief in equality ever enacted. It outlawed not only racial discrimination but also discrimination in employment for reasons of sex, nationality, and religion as well, and thus became fundamental to progress for the budding women's movement. The federal government was committed to enforcing equality of treatment for two of the most visible groups in the United States—blacks and women. Within a very short time after its passage, women activists, who had become acquainted through their work on various commissions on the status of women, formed the National Organization for Women (NOW) as an advocacy group to push for greater equality.

The Johnson administration also pushed through a new voting bill in 1965. Despite protections for black voters in the acts of 1957, 1960, and 1964, blacks were still being kept

▶ Muhammed Ali: "Float Like a Butterfly, Sting Like a Bee"

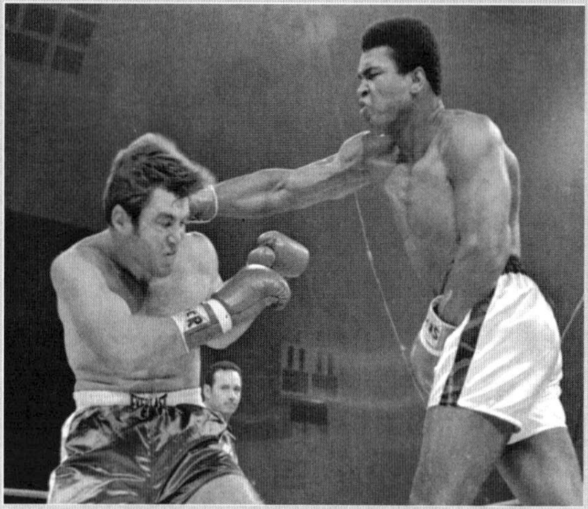

Besides being enormously popular, spectator sports in America have become a big business and a source of cultural idols. In the turbulent sixties, sports figures became political figures as well. No figure in modern sports has been more successful, more popular, or more controversial than boxer Muhammad Ali.

Ali was born Cassius Marcellus Clay, Jr., in Louisville, Kentucky, on January 17, 1942, the son of a black sign painter. The Clays were proud of their lineage, claiming descent from the South's most famous white opponent of slavery, Cassius Marcellus Clay, a relative of the statesman Henry Clay. At the age of twelve, Clay began amateur boxing when Joe Martin, a local policeman, offered to train him. Later Martin would say Clay had been a model student—never smoking, drinking, or using foul language, and always working hard at the gym. After more than a hundred amateur fights, Clay won the competition to represent the United States at the 1960 Olympic games in Rome.

Clay early on exhibited a trait that would make him notorious: he talked incessantly, almost always boasting about himself. As a form of psychological warfare, he would predict the round in which he would defeat his opponent and often he made the prediction come true. Even before he went to the Olympics, fans booed him for his unabashed egotism. After he won an Olympic gold medal for boxing, he ostentatiously wore it around his neck for weeks. His triumphant return to Louisville brought out the whole town, and a group of local wealthy white men agreed to back him as a professional fighter. Clay had just completed high school.

That same year he teamed up with Angelo Dundee, who became both trainer and friend. Clay later summed up their relation with a piece of doggerel: "He's got the connection and the complexion to get me the right protection which leads to good affection."

One of the reasons Clay worked so hard at making himself controversial was that it bettered his chance at a heavyweight championship bout. Fight promoters look for boxers who can attract great numbers of paying spectators. In 1964, when Clay was just twenty-two, he got his chance to fight the champion, Sonny Liston. After six rounds, a battered and stunned Liston could not respond to the bell. Clay was the new champ. In his dressing room a shouting, exuberant Clay taunted the reporters, who had long resented his boasting. "Who is the greatest?" Clay demanded. "You are," they reluctantly answered.

Soon thereafter he went on a tour of Africa and was received by the presidents of Ghana and Egypt. Clay used the trip to announce that he was a member of the Black Muslims, a religious sect known for its hostility toward whites and its belief in black separatism. Suddenly Clay was no longer the All-American black but a critic, even an opponent, of the white establishment. He dropped his name, contending that white slave masters had given it, for one from his new religion: Muhammad Ali. Openly he associated himself with the rising civil rights movement and the new interest among blacks in Africa. Although his wife divorced him and his parents disapproved, he did not waver. Floyd Patterson's 1965 challenge to Ali's title seemed a defense of the establishment when Patterson proclaimed that he intended to bring "the championship back to America." Ali, however, kept the crown easily.

The most severe test of Ali's convictions came later over his induction into the Army. When first called up in 1962, Ali failed the achievement test and was deferred. His critics, particularly in the white South, were outraged; nor did Ali soften their wrath by quipping, "I only said I was the greatest, not the smartest."

The consequence was that in 1966 he was reclassified as eligible. By then over one hundred fifty thousand Americans were fighting in Vietnam. In that context, Ali's remark, "I ain't got nothing against those Vietcongs," set off a barrage of protests. In early 1967, when he refused induction on religious grounds, the boxing authorities stripped him of his title. Within another two months he was indicted and convicted of draft evasion by a Texas jury. An indignant judge levied the maximum sentence: five years in prison and a $10,000 fine.

Although he did not go to jail while appealing the conviction, Ali could not obtain matches. Between 1968 and 1970 no promoter could find an opponent, and no state would let him fight. By taking away his passport, the federal government prevented him from going abroad to seek matches. He earned what he could by speaking at antiwar rallies and on college campuses where he was a hero to the opponents of the war. Ultimately, in 1971, the U.S. Supreme Court unanimously upheld Ali's contention that he should have been exempt from the draft because of his religious convictions.

Even before this, the barriers to his fighting had begun to come down. He was still a heavy drawing card—the best known as well as the most-hated boxer of the century. In 1971 he was matched against Joe Frazier, the official champion. Because Frazier had never fought, much less defeated Ali, most boxing fans did not consider him the true world's champion. The fight was a sellout, with the contestants each promised $2.5 million. After fifteen rounds of hard slugging, Ali lost by the decision of the judges.

Ali was then determined to do what only one other American had done before—to win back the championship. He accomplished this in 1974, against George Foreman, an American, in Kinshasa, Zaire, the first time a heavyweight fight had been set in Africa. Although Foreman was also black, the sixty thousand fans that came to watch rooted for the best-known challenger. "Ali, bombaye," they chanted. "Ali, kill him." Ali's victory was not only a spectacular comeback but also an unprecedented one for a fighter over thirty.

Ali said he would soon retire as undefeated champion, but he could not resist the popular acclaim or the money that always came with being on top. The inevitable occurred. In February 1978, he lost his title to Leon Spinks, a man twelve years his junior. The urge to be the best would not die. Later that same year in a match televised around the world, Ali defeated Spinks to become the only man to win the world heavyweight championship three times—and at age 36, to boot! In 1979 he announced his "final" retirement while still champion.

from the polls in the South by subterfuge, intimidation, or outright refusal by state officials. In response, Congress passed The Voting Rights Act of 1965 that provided for federal officers to register black voters in any county in which the Justice Department found less than 50 percent of the eligible voters actually participating in presidential elections. State voter qualifications that discriminated against blacks, such as literacy tests and poll taxes, were struck down; any new state electoral changes had to be approved by the U.S. Department of Justice. Federal examiners would oversee state elections to ensure compliance and federal marshals would provide enforcement if necessary. A striking measure of how far the country had come on the question of federal power, as well as on the rights of blacks, was that in 1890 a similar bill by Representative Henry Cabot Lodge had been denounced and killed in the Senate for being a "Force Bill." In 1965, such a bill seemed a mild and necessary measure to most Americans.

As a result of the protection and support provided by the law, registration drives over the subsequent years brought millions of black voters into the political process. By 1970 about two-thirds of the eligible black adults in the South were registered, a proportion that had not been achieved since the days of Reconstruction. Black voter registration in the South doubled in the five years following passage of the Voting Rights Act. As a result, by 1970 Alabama counted 105 black elected officials—the second highest number in the nation.

The new interest in black voting, in fact, led in the following years to the election of a large number of black elected officials throughout the country. In 1977, over forty-three hundred blacks held elective office, an increase of 150 percent since 1970. By mid-decade scores of cities, including Los Angeles, New Orleans, Atlanta, Detroit, Gary, and Newark, were headed by black mayors.

President Johnson also took pride in appointing the first black to the cabinet (Robert C. Weaver as Secretary of Housing and Urban Development) and the first African-American to the Supreme Court, Thurgood Marshall.

The path-breaking civil rights legislation of the 1960s, which opened the gates to progress for African-Americans, came about not only as a result of President Johnson's leadership but also as a result of the pressure coming from grass-roots activism by African Americans, especially the non-violent protests spearheaded by Martin Luther King and his Southern Christian Leadership Conference. These were met all too often by brutality, a spectacle that unfolded on national television and helped create popular support for the new policies. To summarize the events of those years is, in effect, to recite a litany of civil rights martyrs: civil rights leader Medger Evers, gunned down the very night that President Kennedy made his television address to the nation in 1963; the four school girls killed in the bombing of a church in Birmingham that same year; and then the martyrs during Freedom Summer in 1964, when young people of both races went south to register voters and challenge the racial caste system. Those young men, killed by a Klan mob in Mississippi, were James Cheney, a local black activist, and two white volunteers, Michael Schwerner and Andrew Goodman. The following year, as a consequence of the protests to achieve the voting rights legislation, three people lost their lives: Jimmy Lee Jackson, a young black man; James Reeb, a white Unitarian minister; and Viola Liuzzo, a white Detroit housewife. In addition to the killings, civil rights workers were frequently beaten, jailed, and generally intimidated by those who opposed the coming changes.

Two Steps Forward, One Backward

In 1966, Congress failed to pass an open housing bill—the first civil rights bill to fail in almost ten years. Despite the Johnson administration's commitment to civil rights and the passage of four civil rights acts since 1954, resistance to acceptance of blacks as equals was persisting. White violence against black demonstrators in Alabama in the spring of 1965 had caused President Johnson to send federal troops into his native South to provide the protection that George C. Wallace, Alabama's segregationist governor, would not. In the elections of 1966, strong segregationists won the governorships in Alabama and Georgia.

Another factor in the changing racial equation was an upsurge in riots, an onset that began in Harlem in 1964 following an episode in which a white policeman shot a black teenager. The next summer there was a riot in Watts, a predominantly black area of Los Angeles, which lasted five days and cost thirty-four lives. In the spring and summer of 1967, riots in varying degrees of severity occurred in more than thirty cities. In Detroit and Newark alone, sixty-eight persons lost their lives, about fourteen hundred others were injured, and almost seven thousand were arrested. Property damages from looting and burning were estimated in hundreds of millions of dollars.

President Johnson again asked Congress to enact a civil rights bill that would end discrimination in the sale and rental of housing, one of the bases for all-black schools in the North as well as a major handicap to blacks in achieving equal opportunity. Congress was slow to move on the measure until the assassination of Martin Luther King, Jr., on April 4, 1968, impelled it to action. King was undoubtedly the leading African American in the nation, uncompromising in the commitment to the achievement of equality through nonviolence. He was shot by a white racist, James Earl Ray, in Memphis where King had been participating in a protest movement on behalf of striking black garbage collectors.

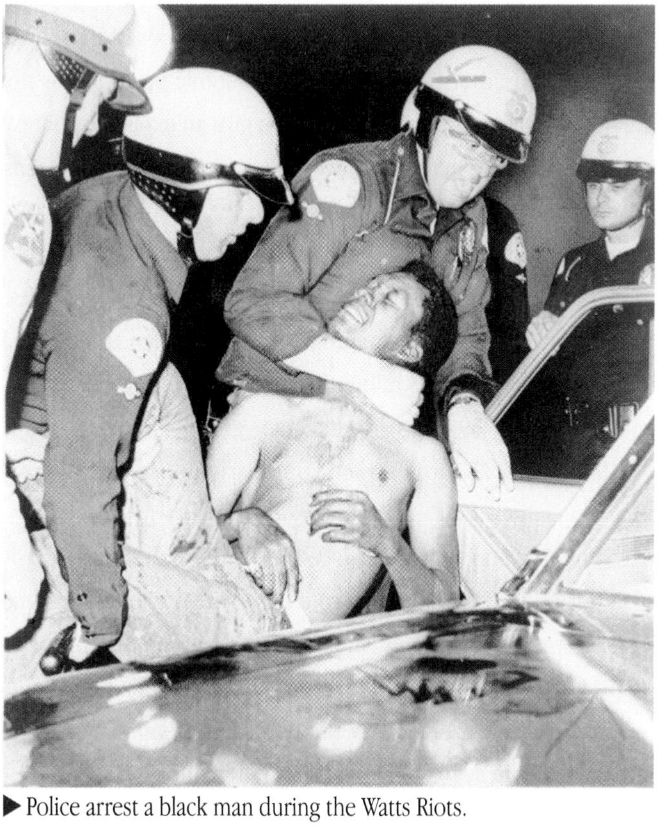

▶ Police arrest a black man during the Watts Riots.

Following King's death, there were outbursts of black rage in some 125 cities across the country. This time, Washington, Baltimore, Chicago, and Kansas City were conspicuous for the level of damage and violence. All told, 46 persons were killed, more than twenty-six hundred injured, and some twenty-two thousand arrested in unrest throughout the country. Total property losses were put at $45 million. The civil rights bill that King's death hastened to the president's desk outlawed discrimination on racial grounds in the sale and rental of about 80 percent of the housing in the country.

During the late 1960s and early 1970s, however, there were many signs in various Northern cities that as the movement for racial equality sought to break down housing barriers and to desegregate schools with enrollments based on segregated housing patterns, white resistance would become stronger rather than weaker. The failure of the 1966 open housing bill was one sign. Another was the approval that greeted the Nixon administration's slowdown on implementing school integration in 1969 and afterward.

Yet in spite of these setbacks, progress had been made. More blacks were voting in the South than had voted in almost a century. The whole legal basis of segregation in the South was gone, and by 1972 school integration throughout the region had moved far beyond mere tokenism. Although blacks still experienced a higher rate of unemployment than whites, that disparity in 1970, for the first time, was less than 100 percent. Between 1960 and 1970 the proportion of blacks that had purchasing power equivalent to $10,000 in 1969 dollars rose from 9 percent to 24 percent. That increase was considerably greater than the doubling that took place over the same period for whites. Yet it was still true that blacks, constituting only 11 percent of the population, made up 30 percent of those who were below the official government poverty line.

Toward the end of the Johnson administration it was recognized that equality of opportunity would involve more than removing legal barriers. Instead, it would require efforts to eliminate a century of accumulated discrimination in housing, education, and jobs and the deep prejudices underlying it. Unfortunately, neither most whites nor the Nixon and Ford administrations, as would be shown by subsequent events, were prepared to do what was needed to achieve that goal.

The Mexican-American Movement

The Black Revolution, by its example, spurred into visibility a large minority heretofore almost unknown to most Americans: the Mexican-Americans, who then numbered as many as 10 million. Although they were concentrated principally in the Southwest, hundreds of thousands lived in the Detroit-Chicago area; their disadvantaged social and economic position was not simply a regional concern. The new Chicano (as they were called to give an explicitly political self definition) organizations were most active in the Southwest, however. In Texas, for example, the Raza Unida party was sometimes successful in local politics.

Cesar Chavez of California was perhaps the best known of the Chicano leaders, principally because of his successful organizing of the California grape pickers, most of whom were Mexican-Americans. Chavez, like King, based his movement on principles of nonviolence and aimed at ultimate reconciliation with the dominant majority rather than victory of one group over another. His grape boycott in the years 1965–1969 compelled the grape growers to recognize the union and to bargain with it. In 1975, Chavez' 'Farm Workers' Union triumphed over the rival unions in gaining recognition among largely Chicano farm workers in California.

More Mexican-Americans were now entering the universities and politics, particularly in the Southwest, suggesting that soon they would play a role in the life of the region commensurate with their numbers. Both Texas and New Mexico sent Mexican-Americans to Congress. In addition, President Carter appointed a Mexican-American to head the Immigration Service Bureau, an agency now confronting the issue of large numbers of Mexicans entering the United States illegally in search of jobs and a better life.

Another, but socially quite different, Spanish-speaking minority in the United States had already made an impact on its region. That was the Cuban-American community of southern Florida, which grew out of the large number of refugees from Castro's Communist dictatorship in the early 1960s. These largely middle-class refugees soon came to dominate large parts of Dade County (Miami) culturally, economically, and even politically. In 1980, for example, the mayor of Miami was a Cuban-American,

Then, by June 1980, more than one hundred ten thousand refugees from Castro's Cuba entered the United States on a flotilla of small boats, the operation being largely financed by Florida's Cuban community. The freedom and economic opportunities available in the United States were still acting as a social magnet—this time for poor Mexicans and Cubans of all classes.

The American Indian Movement

The newest minority group to assert itself in the late 1960s was also the oldest—the Native Americans. Books by militant friends of the Indian, like Alvin Josephy's *Red Power* (1971), or by Native Americans themselves, like Vine Deloria, Jr.'s *Custer Died for Your Sins* (1969) brought the Native Americans' outlook to a wider public; and the federal government took some steps to recognize the just claims of Native Americans for fairer treatment. Native Americans organized and formed the American Indian Movement under the leadership of Russell Means. Key incidents demonstrated that some thought the government was moving too slowly: the occupation of Alcatraz Island in San Francisco Bay by a group of Native Americans in 1971; the occupation and vandalism of the Bureau of Indian Affairs building in Washington, causing over $1 million in damage; and a shoot-out between Native Americans and federal authorities at Wounded Knee, South Dakota, in 1973. These violent demonstrations occurred in spite of the fact that under President Johnson, a Native American headed the Bureau of Indian Affairs for the first time.

In June 1970 President Nixon proclaimed, "The historic relationship between the Federal Government and the Indian communities cannot be abridged without the consent of the Indians." His announcement ended the policy, begun under the Eisenhower administration, of turning the Indians off the reservations into society. That same year, in recognition of past injustices to the Indian, the Nixon administration returned to the Taos Pueblo Indians forty-eight thousand acres of land around Blue Lake, New Mexico, which they had long held sacred. Native Americans were still often caught between two cultures, without much preparation or opportunity to move into the mainstream of American economic life—if that was even what they wished to do. However, at least more recognition was being given to their situation as a separate culture than at any time since the Indian Reorganization Act under the New Deal.

The Decline of the Civil Rights Movement

One of the purposes of the new ethnic and racial consciousness of the 1960s and 1970s had been the expansion of opportunities for minorities in American society. By the opening of the 1980s, however, minority appeals to the remainder of the society were considerably less effective, especially those made by blacks. Segregation had been officially ended with the Civil Rights Act of 1964, voting rights had been federalized and enforced by the Voting Rights Act of

1965, and numerous federal government programs put in place by the Johnson and Nixon administrations were designed to help the poor, many of whom were black. Consequently, believing they had done enough, the white majority was no longer finding Black Power or Black Nationalism of interest. The consequence was that many of the sources of funds on behalf of black advancement were shrinking or drying up.

Even moderate organizations like the NAACP learned that indifference to the cause of racial equality presented serious problems in raising funds and support. In Ronald Reagan's America of the 1980s, few government programs for minority rights would be championed. Affirmative action on behalf of ethnic and racial minorities and women would also come under attack. By 1980, gains had certainly been made in the direction of greater equality under law, voting rights, and equality of opportunity, thanks to the new sense of racial and ethnic identification; but the day when color or race or ethnic origin would not matter in getting a job, making friends, or being accepted into a neighborhood was still far in the future. Furthermore, many ethnic and racial groups were doubtful whether they wanted to see the day when such distinctions did not count.

Challenges to the Educational System

As the Baby Boom generation grew to young adulthood, their large birth cohort would strain America's higher educational system. In 1970, 2.9 million students graduated from high school, and 2 million enrolled in some institution of higher learning, reflecting the fact that many older Americans were also signing up for college courses. This included many military veterans that returned from service in Vietnam. Between 1960 and 1976, the number of full-time students in four-year colleges increased 150 percent to 6.8 million. Never before had a college education seemed so necessary to the average American. In itself, this drive to college was at once both a sign of the affluence of American society and a measure of the need for highly trained personnel in an advanced economy. In the late 1960s, the Vietnam War also had the effect of increasing college enrollment as men eligible for the military draft chose college as a way to avoid military service in Vietnam. This situation would change, however, when President Nixon altered the draft deferment to eliminate college attendance as a way to evade military service.

To meet the rising demand of those attending college, existing facilities were expanded and new institutions were founded across the nation. For example, by 1967 New York State had surpassed California with the largest state system of higher education, with two hundred thousand students enrolled in the several branches of its state university system, which had only begun in 1947. It was reported, moreover, that each week in 1967 (during the Vietnam War escalation) saw a new institution of higher learning being founded in the United States. The expansion of state systems—with junior colleges, liberal arts colleges, and graduate and professional schools—posed a new and serious threat to even the best of the long-established private institutions as they all competed fiercely for high-quality students and faculty.

Undoubtedly, higher education by the middle 1960s was one of the great "growth" industries of the economy. By the early 1970s, however, that growth had slackened considerably, thanks in part, at least, to some of the unforeseen consequences of the unprecedented expansion. Also contributing to the decrease in enrollments were the smaller numbers of the baby boom birth cohort in the late 1950s that matured to college age in the late 1970s and the end of the Vietnam War.

Before the decline, however, the state systems became so large that students began to protest that they were being lost in the rush to "greatness." The first of several spectacular manifestations of student concern was a series of student protests on the Berkeley campus of the University of California in 1964, known as the Free Speech Movement, which brought classes at that huge educational complex to a halt for several days. The immediate cause was the fact that the administration had denied space for political activity on campus. This outraged students, some of whom had recently returned from civil rights organizing in the South. Though the upheavals at Berkeley and other institutions caused administrators and faculty to think afresh about their enterprise, these demonstrations did not prevent even more massive disruptions at Columbia University in 1968 and at Harvard in 1969, to mention only two of the more prominent Universities that witnessed major student protests. Indeed, between January and June 1968, the National Student Association counted 221 major demonstrations at 101 colleges and universities, involving some forty thousand students. By this time the protests were against not only the impersonality of the large educational institution and the alleged irrelevance of higher education but also the continuation of the Vietnam War. Suddenly, the American college student, long known for docility and lack of interest in social protest, was aroused. That the phenomenon was not simply related to the Vietnam War was evident from the riots and disturbances on many campuses in foreign countries in 1968 and 1969. For several days, for example, the whole university system of Paris was brought to a halt by student rebellion.

The Paris Protests, known as the "May Movement" began as a protest against the quality of food on campus and shabby conditions at the dormitories, but it was indicative of the larger factors that underlay the student protests. The baby boom of the 1950s resulted in a birth cohort that was so large that it simply overwhelmed the societal infrastructure that was in place to handle it. Furthermore, the Depression followed by World War II created a situation where social changes that might have occurred earlier were delayed until the 1960s when the baby boomers could force change by their sheer numbers.

Among the complaints of these young adults, some of who were returning from their military service in Vietnam, was that they were treated like children, rather than adults. For instance, it was standard practice at dormitories to require all residents to be in the dormitory by 10:00 PM on weekdays, with mandatory "lights out" by 11:00 PM. Some universities had dress codes that prevented women from wearing slacks instead of skirts. Some universities had limitations on the length of skirts, while others banned black leather jackets as dangerous attire linked to gang activity. The students could be drafted into the military at age eighteen, but the drinking age was twenty-one and alcohol was generally banned on campuses across the country. Furthermore, the legal voting age was generally twenty-one, so students could not even vote.

The student demonstrations in the United States, which had started as nonviolent protests, became more militant and reached a peak in September 1970, with the bombing of a computer center at the University of Wisconsin in which a researcher was killed. Thereafter, the demonstrations, as well as the violence subsided sharply. During the academic year 1972, most college campuses were undisturbed by the interruptions of classes and academic routine that had been almost standard at dozens of campuses for half a decade. The reasons for the decline of the demonstrations are not clear, though administrative and curricular changes along the lines demanded by student protesters undoubtedly helped. Certainly the growing violence and the repeated interruptions of classes made many students increasingly intolerant of them. University administrations and faculty also became more adept at defusing or countering demonstrations than had been the case in the beginning. Moreover, the fact that the U.S. was withdrawing troops from Vietnam in 1972, rather than sending more, and the termination of the draft in 1973 removed a good deal of the force behind the student rebellion.

One consequence of the student demonstrations was a more fundamental rethinking of the goals and nature of university education than even Sputnik had spurred. Some educational authorities, as well as lay citizens, began to question seriously the value of a liberal arts education for all the high-school students who were going on to college each year. Despite the escalating tuition charges and the termination of many of the student amenities, scholarships, and curriculum programs initiated by student activism, enrollments remained high. In the face of the rising competition for jobs in a weakening economy, however, the less-well-endowed institutions responded more than ever to student demands for practical education. Furthermore, university rules regarding bedtime in dormitories, dress codes, and such were generally relaxed.

▶ In 1970 the University of Wisconsin, Sterling Hall was bombed by four students protesting against the research lab's connections to the U.S. Military. A physics professor, working late in his lab, was killed.

The Youth Culture

If any one date could be selected for the start of the increasing self-consciousness among young people who found American society hypocritical and misdirected, it was the summer of 1964. That was the time when hundreds of white students, predominantly from Northern and Western colleges and universities, descended on Mississippi and other parts of the South to work for the black civil rights movement. Although some were disillusioned by that foray against injustice, many went on to other causes, particularly the movement to end the war in Vietnam. It was this cause that most affected their generation, through the draft, the casualty lists, the emigrations to Canada, and the desertions to Sweden. It was this cause that mobilized their forces. In October 1967, a confrontation at the Pentagon involved some thirty-five thousand people, most of them young. Later, several antiwar demonstrations attracted over one hundred thousand participants.

It would be a mistake, however, to see the rise of a socially conscious youth movement as simply a consequence of political events or as a political event in itself. At bottom, it was a criticism of American society; not infrequently it went beyond criticism to outright rejection of the values of that society and the embracing of a new "counterculture." For a tiny revolutionary minority, rejection came to mean destruction by bombing.

The most visible manifestation of the rejection of society was the revolution in dress and hairstyle. The dress that many young people assumed—pseudoproletarian blue jeans, denim shirts, and work boots; fringed jackets and Indian headbands; flamboyant colors and designs—set them apart from the "straight" world, even as it created a new uniformity. An even bolder rejection of contemporary mores by young men was the wearing of long hair, a practice that developed in the mid-sixties. Fashion designers and the straight society—including in many cases the parental generation—first fought the revolution in dress and hair styling, then adapted it to their own uses. Whether this was victory or a defeat for the young, it undeniably showed their influence and their ability to provide alternatives in lifestyle.

Behind the casual dress, however, lay a greater significance: an emphasis upon equality and a denial of deference, rank, and hierarchy. People, many of the young insisted, should be recognized for their individual human dignity and not for what society said they were. The new equality was evident in the impatience of most college-age students with the traditional distinctions of race and sex. Even in many Southern universities young people were much less racially prejudiced than their elders.

Establishment spokesmen like President Nixon and Vice President Agnew often stigmatized the decline in deference as a result of "permissiveness." Yet it was clearly part of a broader world movement toward equal rights and empowerment of the powerless and disadvantaged everywhere. An important facet was the insistence that people have a voice in the making of decisions that would affect them, whether they lived in "third-world" countries emerging from colonialism or in the inner cities of America. This outlook was seen in organizations among welfare recipients as well as in demands on behalf of various other minority groups, including homosexuals seeking respect and freedom from harassment and people with disabilities seeking societal support for better access on a variety of fronts.

▶ A 1967 antiwar confrontation at the Pentagon. These protests could draw up to one hundred thousand participants mostly young people.

Perhaps the most significant difference between the young people of the counterculture and their elders was the emphasis the young now placed upon feeling and emotion. It appeared most obviously in the interest among college students in mysticism, Zen Buddhism, and the works of radical psychologist R. D. Laing. It was also to be seen in the spreading use of hallucinatory drugs, particularly marijuana, which enhances feelings and imagination while dulling reason and rational thought. It is true that the consumption of alcohol—the most "successful" drug of all time—continued to exceed, by far, the use of all other drugs; however, the rise in the use of marijuana and later cocaine among both old and young was yet another measure of youth's influence.

The new emphasis upon feeling was also indicated by the enormous popularity during the 1960s—and after—of the loud, rhythmic rock music and the vigorous, often explicitly erotic dancing that accompanied it, These dances were out of a different culture from the ballroom dancing of the previous generation, (as many young people in the early 1980s well recognized when ballroom dancing began to come back onto college campuses.)

The new emphasis on feeling and emotion also helps to explain the new freedom between the sexes that came to be called the *sexual revolution*. In 1960, the contraceptive pill began to be widely available; within a decade there had been a change in many Americans' attitudes toward abortion, a "birth-control" measure that had traditionally been seen as immoral. Given the new reproductive rights, many young people saw no reason to deny their feelings by postponing sexual relations until marriage. The traditional emphasis on female virginity before marriage was widely abandoned; and living together out of wedlock was accepted in many areas of the country and on levels of society that, only a decade before, had uniformly viewed premarital sexual relations, especially for women, as immoral. Indeed, the whole society in the course of the 1960s and early 1970s came to accept a freedom of expression on sexual matters, on nudity, and in language that was striking, especially considering the great scope of the change and the rapidity with which it had been achieved. Even in small towns in the so-called Bible-belt states, pornographic literature and movies were readily available.

A less enduring side of the youth culture was the attitude toward careers and work. Since personal experience was deemed of primary importance, many young people in the 1960s saw little reason to put off traveling or experimenting with vocations or simply enjoying themselves. To many of the young, the good life was not represented by making and saving money or by working hard for a home in the suburbs. It was more likely to be found, they thought, in doing what interested them, rather than in choosing what paid well, and in having satisfying relations with people rather than in competing with each other.

To many adults, particularly those with still-sharp memories of the Great Depression, this attitude seemed shockingly impractical. The onset of the recession in the 1970s made it evident that the prosperity of the 1950s and 1960s had been an important precondition for the youth culture. When faced with the need to confront a competitive world, many young people in the 1970s began to take those courses in high school or college that would prepare them for careers and would promise some economic security in a world no longer running at full employment. Moreover, the cessation of the draft and the ending of the American involvement in Vietnam cooled down the political and social concern of many young people.

The upsurge of the young in the 1960s left enduring marks on the country, however. In 1971, the essential seriousness and responsibility of young people were acknowledged, for example, when in record time the voting age was lowered to eighteen by the passage of the Twenty-sixth Amendment. Even more significant was the fact that by 1972 over half the states, including California and New York, had also lowered the age of maturity from twenty-one to eighteen in all, or almost all, legal matters, Young people played a vigorous role in the primary campaigns of Eugene McCarthy and George McGovern, but political activity by the young in the election of 1972 was less evident than it had been in 1968. Despite the lowering of the voting age, young people did not exercise the franchise in the same proportion as older people in subsequent elections.

Although the youth culture embraced a large number of people in the 1960s and early 1970s, the majority of youth had not participated in the criticism of American society, values, and standards. Most had not demonstrated against the war in Vietnam or campaigned for Eugene McCarthy, Robert Kennedy, or George McGovern. The majority of those who went to college did so in order to get ahead and to do better than their parents. In fact, many young people worked for the reelection of Nixon and Agnew. By 1975 some of the most radical of the young leaders of the 1960s, like Tom Hayden, a founder of Students for a Democratic Society (SDS), were engaging in conventional politics. They were usually found within the Democratic Party, although they had derided the conventional parties in the 1960s.

The Women's Movement

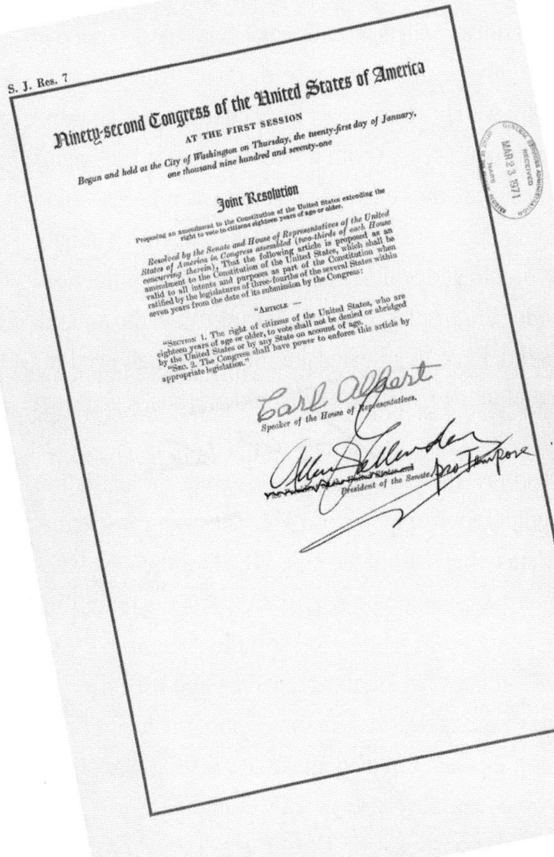
S. J. Res. 7

Ninety-second Congress of the United States of America

AT THE FIRST SESSION

Begun and held at the City of Washington on Thursday, the twenty-first day of January, one thousand nine hundred and seventy-one

Joint Resolution

Proposing an amendment to the Constitution of the United States extending the right to vote to citizens eighteen years of age or older.

Resolved by the Senate and House of Representatives of the United States of America in Congress assembled (two-thirds of each House concurring therein), That the following article is proposed as an amendment to the Constitution of the United States, which shall be valid to all intents and purposes as part of the Constitution when ratified by the legislatures of three-fourths of the several States within seven years from the date of its submission by the Congress:

"ARTICLE —

"SECTION 1. The right of citizens of the United States, who are eighteen years of age or older, to vote shall not be denied or abridged by the United States or by any State on account of age.

"SEC. 2. The Congress shall have power to enforce this article by appropriate legislation."

Carl Albert

Speaker of the House of Representatives.

President of the Senate pro Tempore

Like Chicanos, Native Americans, and young people, women also responded to the example of the Black Revolution. Although they constituted a majority of the population, women were similar to the racial and ethnic minorities in that their opportunities for jobs and prestige were arbitrarily limited. They resembled minorities, too, in that they often did not assert themselves. These were among the arguments in Betty Friedan's *Feminine Mystique* (1963) that helped spark the new feminist movement of the late 1960s and early 1970s. Beginning as only a weak voice in a society largely complacent about the denial of women's rights and opportunities, by the mid-1970s the movement was compelling a new recognition of women's quest for equality and was fueled by women getting together amongst themselves to air their grievances, a process known as "consciousness-raising." Even older women, observers pointed out, began to call for equal occupational opportunities for persons of their sex, as well as equal pay. The spreading interest produced a wide range of organizations, some highly militant or politically radical; however, the moderate National Organization for Women (NOW), which Betty Friedan founded in 1966, counted the most members.

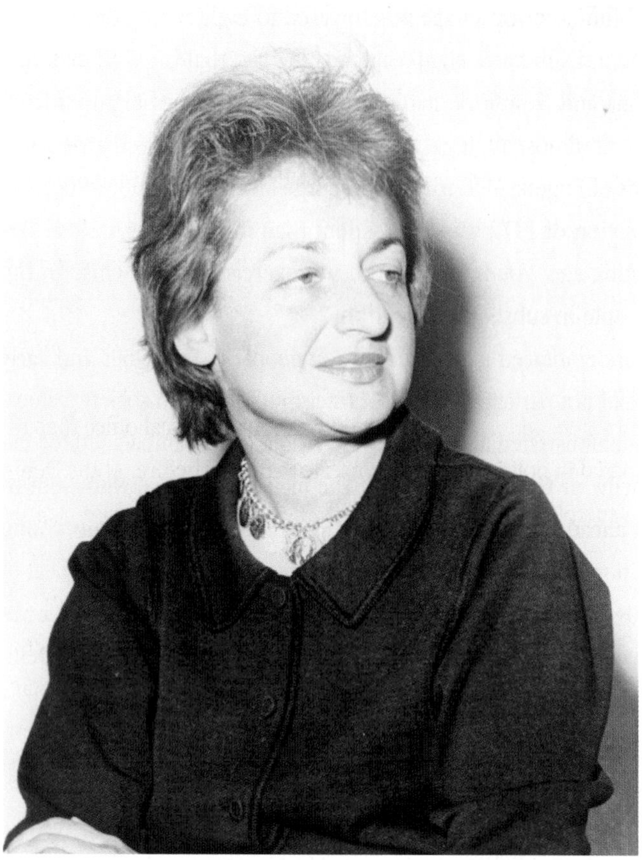

▶ Betty Friedan founded the National Organization for Women (NOW) in 1966. Friedan's 1963 book, *Feminine Mystique* helped spark the new feminist movement of the late 1960s and early 1970s.

In 1972, the women's movement helped push through Congress a women's equal-rights amendment to the federal Constitution, designed to ensure that women could not be denied the same rights as men, subject to ratification by three-fourths of the states. The Equal Rights Amendment had been originally introduced in the 1960s with Republican support. It passed both houses of Congress in 1972 under the Nixon administration.

Conservatives, led by social conservative activist Phyllis Schlafly, would turn against ERA after its passage in Congress, however, and oppose its ratification by the states. Early on, it appeared that the Amendment would sail easily through the ratification process. ERA had been allotted seven years to achieve ratification by three-fourths of the states, but twenty-two states ratified it the very first year. Phyllis Schlafly, however, founded the Eagle Forum, a conservative women's organization opposed to the ratification of ERA. Schlafly and her followers depicted the Equal Rights Amendment as leading to unisex toilets, homosexual marriages, women in combat, and the release of males from their responsibility to support their children. Schlafly and the Eagle Forum were also able to successfully confuse ERA with homosexuality and gay rights (never the intention of the Amendment's sponsors), thus ensuring that the Amendment would not be supported by the religious right, and therefore ensuring that the Amendment would not be ratified in the Protestant fundamentalist-dominated Southern States or Mormon-influenced Utah and Idaho. Consequently, the window for ERA's ratification would expire, and the Amendment would not be resurrected. Congress did agree to an extension of the time allowed for the ratification, as President Carter had recommended, but the ERA would eventually go down to defeat regardless.

In spite of ERA's failure, these years also saw the passage of much significant legislation on behalf of women, such as the Equal Credit Opportunity Act of 1974. The political scientist Ethel Klein has argued that it is no coincidence that, except for Title VII, all of the new legislation followed a huge, national demonstration by women on August 26, 1970, the fiftieth anniversary of women's suffrage. Politicians pay attention to this kind of mobilization.

Thanks to the afore-mentioned Title VII of the Civil Rights Act of 1964 and executive orders prohibiting discrimination on grounds of sex as well as race or religion, the federal government forced open new jobs for women in private employment while insisting that public institutions increase their proportion of women employees, especially in high-level jobs.

Another highly significant piece of legislation was Title IX of the Education Amendments Act of 1972, which prohibited sex discrimination in educational programs receiving federal funding. This law has remade the nature of athletics for women, creating scholarships and other opportunities that were unheard of in earlier generations. The new drive to expand women's opportunities saw traditionally male occupations—like those of army general, telephone lineman, jockey, air-traffic controller, and FBI agent—being filled by women either for the first time or in unprecedented numbers. The new women's organizations also mounted a successful campaign to change state laws to make abortions and birth control information easier to obtain. They aroused a new popular demand for, and in some instances succeeded in gaining government support for, child-care centers and thus gave mothers a true choice as to whether or not to seek employment. These social changes have remade the demographic make-up of certain professions that had been nearly entirely male, such as medicine, law, and academia.

Although not many more women were actually elected to national political office than in previous years, women participated in politics on a greater scale than ever before. At the Democratic convention in 1972, for example, about 35 percent of the delegates were women—a proportion previously unheard of—and a black woman, Representative Shirley Chisholm of New York, was placed in nomination for president. Even at the Republican convention, which had no minimum quota for women delegates, women made up almost 30 percent of the membership. In 1974, Ella Grasso was elected governor of Connecticut. She was the first woman to reach that level of government unaided by a husband's political prestige or power. Women were also elected to a number of mayoralties, including those of San Jose, California, a city of half a million, and Chicago, the nation's second largest city.

The 1960s and 1970s also brought monumental changes for women in the area of jurisprudence. It may be recalled that immediately after the Civil War, certain suffragists had tried to use the Fourteenth Amendment as the basis for voting—but to no avail. In 1971, for the first time in American history, the U.S. Supreme Court employed the equal-protection clause of the amendment to strike down legislation on the grounds that it discriminated on the basis of sex. The case was *Reed v. Reed*, and it revolved around an Idaho statute that had given the preference to males in administering estates. This case then legitimated a whole new field of law, whereby women could now bring suit to overturn discriminatory laws or hiring practices.

Although female workers were still concentrated in low-paying and low-prestige jobs, the new interest among women and throughout the society in equality of opportunities of all kinds provided broader horizons for women than had previously been the case in the United States. Whether all women wanted to compete with men in the world was still an open question, if antifeminist women's groups were to be believed; that many women welcomed the widening of their horizons, no one could deny.

The New Right

Though Barry Goldwater lost badly in 1964, from that campaign forward there was a dedicated—and growing—group of conservative activists in the spirit of Goldwater. Some lived in places like California's Orange County, where "suburban warriors," to use the title of Lisa McGirr's book about the rise of the New Right in Orange County, planned political strategies. Others were in the midwestern heartland, many were in the states that had once belonged to the Confederacy, and a sprinkling (but an influential sprinkling) were in such big cities as New York or Washington. They raised money. They created think tanks, and they did grass roots organizing. By 1980, when conservative Republican Ronald Reagan won the presidency, it was clear that all of the effort was paying off.

Taking nothing away from the remarkable energy and resources devoted to a restructuring of the American political landscape that occurred in the 1960s and early 1970s, it is also true that the rapid social change of the period was bound to stir a backlash. In the space of two decades, racial mores in the South had been both challenged and changed, gender norms remade, abortion rights protected in the first trimester by a decision of the U.S. Supreme Court, and there was the beginning of a new norm where sexual orientation was concerned. All of this change was clearly destined to be more popular on the coasts and in big cities than in regions that were still closely linked to the rural past.

To examine the career of one of the early activists, Phyllis Schlafly, is to gain insight into how the New Right could be so successful. Schlafly first came to public attention with the campaign biography she published about Barry Goldwater, *A Choice Not an Echo*. She then began to write a monthly newsletter for her conservative constituency, the *Phyllis Schlafly Report*, in which she focused principally on the dangers of communism. Within a few years, she began to be alarmed about the changes set in motion by the birth of modern feminism, especially the looming possibility of ratification of the Equal Rights Amendment. (It will be recalled that Congress sent the ERA to the states in 1972). Rather than placing her faith in an amendment, Schlafly believed that women needed to be protected by the men in their lives. Hence, she organized the single most effective organization opposed to ratification, STOP-ERA, and is widely credited with having been instrumental in the amendment's defeat, with its time running out in 1982. This defeat was all the more remarkable in that the ERA began its journey through the ratification process with widespread public support, according to polling data.

▶American conservative publicist, Phyllis Schlafly, opposed modern feministic ideas. She organized the single most effective organization opposed to ratification of the Equal Rights amendment, STOP-ERA.

Schlafly's own life story both confirms and transcends her anti-feminist ideology. On the one hand, she was the stay-at-home mother of six children. On the other, she obtained a law degree from Washington University as a re-entry woman. Never practicing law, she used the legal training to help shape her testimony before various Congressional Committees.

In its earliest manifestation, the New Right was held together more by fervent anti-communism than by the fundamentalist religion that was so important a factor in the constituency of President George W. Bush in the early twenty-first century. The New Right in the 1970s (as well as ever since) was decidedly anti-gay; and, as previously mentioned, the linkage of gay rights to ERA was most certainly a contributor to the demise of ERA. However, the religious right did not limit their opposition to homosexuality exclusively to the battle over ERA.

According to the Reverend Jerry Falwell, homosexuality was an evil sin in the same category with rape, adultery, and incest. Consequently, when San Francisco Mayor George Moscone and City Supervisor Harvey Milk, the city's first openly gay elected official, were assassinated, Falwell stated that the murders, which were committed by a fundamentalist Christian who admitted that his belief in God had prompted his action, were a judgment from God.

All conservatives, however, were not comfortable with the positions of the New Right, including "Mr. Conservative" Barry Goldwater, himself, who criticized it after 1981, stating, "That Christian bunch is crazy." Yet by the time of Reagan's administration, the religious right had begun increasingly to make its presence felt. Indeed, Jerry Falwell had founded the Moral Majority in 1975, and this date can be taken as among the first truly significant flexings of this set of muscles. In the ensuing decades, the growing clout of Southern white Protestants would make a profound impact on American politics.

Right to Privacy and Abortion Rights

Another landmark related to women's rights in these years was a case in Connecticut involving contraceptives and the right to privacy. As of 1965, a number of states still had statutes limiting access to contraception. In *Griswold v. Connecticut* in 1965, the Supreme Court struck down a Connecticut law that limited access to birth control devices, even for married people. With a 7–2 decision, the Court established, in essence, a constitutional right to marital privacy that ensured access to birth-control information and devices. This decision was an important precedent for the following decade's *Roe v. Wade*.

The Supreme Court's most controversial assertion of individual rights since *Brown v. Board of Education* in 1954 was, in fact, the case of *Roe v. Wade*, decided in 1973 by a 7–2 division among the justices. In this decision, the Court invalidated all state laws prohibiting abortion in the first trimester on the ground that there was no compelling health/safety interest in the mother in the first trimester because more women were likely to die carrying the fetus to full term than through having first trimester abortions. Furthermore, there was no state health/safety interest in the fetus in the first trimester because it would be unable to live outside the womb, and therefore was not yet "viable" life. During the second trimester, however, states could regulate abortions because there was, at that time, a state health/safety interest in the life of the mother because it was more dangerous to abort in the second trimester than to continue the pregnancy to full term. In the third trimester, the Court's decision struck down all abortions because the fetus was considered to be "viable" life and therefore received state health/safety protections.

The decision was welcomed by the women's movement, but opposed by many conservatives and by some religious groups, notably the Roman Catholic Church, due to the long-standing Catholic Church prohibition against any form of birth control. At the time, protestant fundamentalists were essentially unconcerned with the abortion issue; and in 1971, the Southern Baptist convention even voted in support of a resolution affirming a woman's right to have an abortion, if the health of the mother were threatened. In fact, evangelist Jerry Falwell, who later made opposition to abortion a central focus of the Moral Majority, did not preach his first sermon against abortion until 1978, five years after the *Roe v. Wade* decision. Instead, Falwell and his allies chose to focus on abortion as a calculated strategy to convert pro-life Catholics, who traditionally voted Democrat, to the Republican Party.

Prior to Falwell's focus on abortion, others were already carrying the torch. In 1975, fundamentalist Protestant evangelists Billy Graham and Francis Schaeffer, along with Christianity Today editor Harold O.J. Brown and pediatrician C. Everett Koop, formed the Christian Action Council that lobbied Congress for measures to curb abortions. Koop and Schaeffer produced a five-segment film and companion book entitled *Whatever Happened to the Human Race?* They taught that abortion was both a cause and the result of the loss of appreciation for human life in American society and that acceptance of abortion would eventually lead to acceptance of infanticide and euthanasia. That same year, Jerry Falwell, along with Paul Weyrich of the Heritage Foundation, founded the Moral Majority and made opposition to abortion a focus.

In subsequent years, the question of abortion has become a highly charged political issue. Some anti-abortion organizations have sought to overturn the decision in *Roe v. Wade* by constitutional amendment. The necessary public support, however, has so far not been forthcoming. In 1980, though, the Republican Party platform called for such an amendment, even though no such Amendment would materialize after Ronald Reagan's landslide election.

The Religious Right and Republicanism

Nevertheless, Falwell's Moral Majority would quickly catapult the Religious Right to a position of major importance in American politics in support of the Republican Party and ideologically conservative politics, a positioning that would remain fundamentally unaltered for the next three decades. Falwell himself characterized the Moral Majority as "pro-life, pro-family, pro-moral, pro-American, pro-Israel, and against abortion, divorce, and secular humanism." Falwell argued that the Moral Majority's goals would be to,

> "exert a significant influence on the spiritual and moral direction of the nation by: (a) mobilizing the grassroots of moral Americans in one clear and effective voice; (b) informing the moral majority what is going on behind their backs in Washington and in state legislatures across the country; (c) lobbying intensively in Congress to defeat left-wing, social-welfare bills that will further erode our precious freedom; (d) pushing for positive legislation such as that to establish the Family Protection Agency, which will ensure a strong, enduring America; and (e) helping the moral majority in local communities to fight pornography, homosexuality, the

> advocacy of immorality in school textbooks, and other issues facing each and every one of us."

Falwell's exhortation to the religious right to become involved in politics was a reversal of his position in the 1960s, when he had urged Christians to stay out of the Civil Rights movement. By 1979, however, religious fundamentalists who had supported Jimmy Carter in 1976 because of Carter's religious faith were becoming disenchanted with President Carter due to his failure to adopt anything resembling the Moral Majority's platform. As Bill Godsey, a member of Jerry Falwell's Thomas Road Baptist Church put it, "Carter practiced a version of Christianity that, if you used the term 'liberal,' you would probably be close to what he was, and that was not popular with evangelicals and fundamentalists." Similarly, editorial columnist Bob Novak stated in 1979 that he knew that Carter was going to lose in 1980:

> "Minister after minister stood up and said, 'I was part of Carter's team in 1976. I delivered my congregation for Carter. I urged them all to vote for Carter because I thought he was a moral individual. I found out otherwise and I'm angry.' "

Falwell and his followers were drawn into politics due to what they viewed as attacks on the family and moral social issues, but they quickly adopted conservative positions on non-values issues as well. Both the Moral Majority and the Christian Voice (another Christian political organization) opposed, for example, American economic sanctions against Uganda for the human rights abuses by Idi Amin, abrogation of the U.S. military treaty with Taiwan, and the "giving away" of the Panama Canal.

Criminal Rights

During the 1960s, the Court also reached out to offer constitutional protection to citizens charged with crimes. In a series of cases beginning with *Gideon v. Wainwright* (1962) and culminating in *Miranda v. Arizona* (1966), the Court held that the police must not infringe in any way on an individual's right to be presumed innocent until proved guilty. The *Gideon* decision, overturning a twenty-year rule, concluded that paupers had the right to a lawyer even if the court had to pay the lawyer's fee. In the *Miranda* decision the court ruled that police could not question an accused person unless his or her lawyer was present and that persons must be informed of certain basic rights upon their arrest. Although many police officials contended that these decisions hindered the conviction of known criminals, defenders of civil liberties hailed the decisions as landmarks in the protection of the individual against arbitrary power.

In 1972, a continuation of this line of reasoning in a case was of particular significance because by then four members of the court were appointees of the Nixon administration, which had been among the prominent critics of the Court's liberal view of individual rights in criminal cases. In a 7–2 decision, the Court held that in all cases in which jail sentences resulted, including cases involving minor crimes (misdemeanors), a defendant must be provided with counsel if too poor to pay a lawyer. Only forty years before, anyone convicted of a capital crime could be executed, even though deprived of legal defense because of lack of funds. Now a defendant could not be sent to jail for drunken driving except after a trial with adequate legal representation.

In 1972 the Court extended its protection of individual rights when it ruled in the *Furman v. Georgia* case that capital punishment violated the Fourteenth Amendment equal protection clause because black men were nine times more likely to be executed for premeditated murder than whites. In 1976, however, the Court modified that position, somewhat, by deciding that the death penalty was not unconstitutional so long as it was not arbitrarily or unreasonably applied. In *Coker v. Georgia*, the next year, however, a divided court held that exacting the death penalty for rape was unconstitutional because it was cruel and unusual punishment.

Despite the Court's concern for individual rights, some other government officials had been less than protective of them. In 1976 the head of the Federal Bureau of Investigation, Clarence Kelley, publicly apologized for the illegalities perpetrated by his agency while under the leadership of the best-known G-man of them all, J. Edgar Hoover. Among the violations were persecution and harassment of citizens and radical groups, and the illegal tapping of telephone wires. Among those on whom the FBI had conducted illegal wiretaps was the Reverend Martin Luther King.

Gay Liberation

On June 28, 1969, there took place an event that has been seen as the symbolic launching of the gay rights movement, the Stonewall riot in New York City. On that date, police raided a bar with a reputation of being frequented by gay people, the Stonewall Tavern. At that time, in fact, such a bar constituted an illegal assembly of homosexuals under New York law. On this occasion, the patrons fought back, and there was soon a new slogan: "Gay Power."

It must be pointed out that there had long been gay communities in major American cities—and even gay activism. That activism was, of necessity, discreet; and the communities' residents had remained closeted, fearful of losing their jobs—or of other forms of harassment. This did not represent paranoia on their part, inasmuch as consensual sex between adults of the same gender was illegal in most states. Moreover, until 1973 the American Psychiatric Association labeled homosexuality a mental disease. After Stonewall, and no doubt inspired by the civil rights activism of so many other groups, there began to be Gay Pride parades and flourishing, uncloseted gay and lesbian communities in big cities or bohemian smaller cities. The new attitude was perhaps best expressed by gay artist Andy Warhol, who stated, "I didn't think I should want to change.... Others should change their attitudes but not me."

A Resurgence of Religion

The turn toward popularizing traditional Christianity in the 1950s proved to be short-lived in the face of the drive for social reform during the 1960s. Most of the established churches

▶ In 1969 police raided Stonewall Tavern, which had a reputation of being frequented by gay people. The patrons fought back, and there was soon a new slogan: "Gay Power."

became caught up in the great civil rights movement and in the opposition to the war in Vietnam. The heavy involvement of Roman Catholics, both clerical and laypersons, was especially notable inasmuch as the Church had long been recognized as conservative in its outlook on both religion and social change. Efforts to democratize the Church internally were encouraged by liberal Pope John XXIII, whose two Vatican Councils marked a turning point in broadening the Church's outlook on the world. For the American Catholic Church, though, the effect of the changes seemed to be divisive, a sign of which was a drop of one third in the rate of church attendance among Catholics from 75 percent in 1957—among the highest for Americans—to 54 percent in 1975.

This substantial drift away from Church among Catholics was experienced by many traditional Protestant denominations as well. One of the consequences of the churches' emphasis on social issues during the 1960s was that many Americans began to fear that the spiritual message of religion was being forgotten in the process. Moreover, the materialism of the consumer society apparently aroused in many a yearning for a spiritual balance.

As a result, by the 1970s those Christian churches that emphasized personal salvation and individual fulfillment rather than social action grew rapidly. Sometimes they were old denominations, like the Southern Baptists; but more often they were new evangelical churches like the Assembly of God, the Churches of God, or what came to be called the Pentecostals. All of them emphasized forceful, emotional preaching, Christian fellowship, and personal conversion—that is, "being born again." At the same time, they minimized theological doctrines and encouraged outpourings of emotion and a literal interpretation of the Bible. In 1976 a Gallup poll reported that a third of all Americans considered themselves as having been "born again."

The new stress on the search for personal spiritual meaning in an anxious, if affluent society, also showed itself outside conventional religious groups. It could be seen in the 6 million people who took up Transcendental Meditation (TM) and in the 3 million who practiced yoga during the 1960s. The thirst for personal commitment was noticeable, too, among the young people who joined the studious Jesus Movement, the chanting, begowned Hare Krishnas, or the aggressively proselytizing Unification Church of the Reverend Moon.

This concern for personal religious commitment was making itself felt in secular politics. President Carter proudly announced that he was a "born-again" Christian, and John Anderson, one of Carter's rivals in the 1980 campaign, made a similar statement. The increasing attractiveness of the conservative politics even drew Republican candidate Ronald Reagan to the new evangelical churches of the South and Southwest, whose members traditionally had been Democratic.

By 1980 religion was still clearly important to many Americans. Surveys showed that, of all the industrial nations of the world, the United States was the most religious. Yet, it should be observed that it was precisely because Americans continued to place a high value on religion that they put pressure on the churches and synagogues to respond to social change. In July 1978, for example, the authoritarian Mormon Church for the first time permitted black men to become full-fledged members of the priesthood, and several Protestant denominations and Jewish synagogues in the late 1970s granted pastoral roles to women in response to demands from their members and the women's movement in general. The times were not just changing as songwriter Bob Dylan had proclaimed in the 1960s; instead they, in fact, had changed.

Chapter Review

30

Summary

The prosperity of the postwar era continued through the 1960s and 1970s though by the 1970s it was maintained by women entering the workplace in record numbers. Leisure and recreational activities expanded, including spectator sports, participatory sports, hobbies, and television. Life expectancy increased, infant mortality decreased, and economic productivity continued to increase. Employment in agriculture and manufacturing declined, while white-collar jobs dominated employment and service sector jobs were on the rise. By the mid-1970s, a high-tech boom was beginning to take shape in California's "Silicon Valley" as Steve Jobs and Steve Wozniak founded Apple Computers in 1977. Two years earlier, Bill Gates and Paul Allen from Seattle founded Microsoft Corporation. In spite of this, the 1970s witnessed an economic "malaise" as "stagflation," the combination of rising prices and high unemployment, and two energy crises dominated the economics of the decade.

Artistically, the era witnessed some fine novels including Kurt Vonnegut's *Slaughterhouse Five,* Norman Mailer's *Armies in the Night,* and Saul Bellow's *Humbolt's Gift*. Alex Haley's *Roots* was made into a television miniseries that became a smashing success. In movies, the time period is known for a series of classics that include *The Sound of Music, Dr. Zhivago, The Graduate, The Godfather, Patton, The Exorcist, Jaws, One Flew Over the Cuckoo's Nest, The Sting, Rocky, Star Wars, The Deer Hunter, and Close Encounters of the Third Kind,* and *Grease*.

The "Second Reconstruction" in America continued throughout the 1960s and into the 1970s as Congress, the Supreme Court, and a grass roots movement all worked to bring equal rights for African-Americans. Congress passed the Civil Rights Act of 1964 eliminating racial discrimination in public accommodations, the Voting Rights Act of 1965 making it a federal crime to hinder voting rights and providing federal enforcement, built public housing and required "Affirmative Action" in hiring practices. Congress also forced busing of school children when necessary to ensure the integration of the schools. The Supreme Court upheld congressional actions and African-Americans took to the streets with marches, protests, and unfortunately, eventually violence.

By the mid-1960s the country erupted into race riots resulting in hundreds of deaths and hundreds of millions of dollars in property damage. Simultaneously, Malcolm X, Martin Luther King, and Robert F. Kennedy were all assassinated as were dozens of lesser-known civil rights workers. At the same time that the race riots and civil rights demonstrations were occurring, student protests and Vietnam war protests occurred all over the country resulting in more violence and deaths, most famously the death of four students at Kent State, shot to death by the Ohio National Guard.

By the late 1960s, a significant women's movement had begun, spurred on by Betty Friedan's *Feminine Mystique* and the founding of the National Organization for Women. In 1969, the Gay Rights movement had its beginning with a riot at the Stonewall Inn in New York City. Cesar Chavez organized Hispanic migrant workers in California into a successful union, creating the beginnings of a Hispanic political movement in the United States. Native Americans became politically active as well, taking over Alcatraz Island in San Francisco

Chapter Review (cont'd)

Summary (cont'd)

Bay, and also occupying the Bureau of Indian Affairs building in Washington D.C., where they caused over $1.5 million in damage, and engaging in a standoff gun battle with federal Marshals at Wounded Knee. Amid all of the movements and protests, a youth counterculture emerged advocating peace, free love, illegal drug use, rock and roll music, long hair, and communal living.

Unsurprisingly, a New Right emerged in opposition to all of the changes. Phyllis Schlafly organized the Eagle Forum to oppose the Equal Rights Amendment, and Jerry Falwell founded the Moral Majority to oppose abortions and unite Protestants and Catholics together in the Republican Party. Simultaneously, however, there was a liberal movement working within religion as Protestant denominations began to recognize female clergy, Catholicism slowly liberalized after the Vatican II council, and the Mormon Church allowed black men to serve as priests. Undoubtedly, even in religion, the times had changed.

Chronological Time Line

1962 *Baker v. Carr* required equal size legislative districts.

1962 *Gideon v. Wainwright* extended the right to state-supported council to all felonies on the state level.

1963 On June 12, Medgar Evers was assassinated in his own driveway in Jackson, Mississippi.

1963 August: March on Washington and Martin Luther King's "I Have a Dream" speech.

1963 On September 15, four young black girls were killed in the bombing of 16th Street Baptist Church in Birmingham, Alabama.

1963 Betty Friedan published *The Feminine Mystique*.

1964 Civil Rights Act struck down racial discrimination in public accommodations.

1964 On June 21, James Cheney, Michael Schwerner, and Andrew Goodman were killed by the KKK in Philadelphia, Mississippi.

1964 October–December: Free Speech Movement at University of California Berkeley led to eight hundred arrests.

1965 On February 21, Malcolm X was assassinated.

Time Line (cont'd)

1965 On March 25, Jimmy Lee Jackson, James Reeb, and Viola Liuzzo were shot to death after the Selma to Montgomery March in Alabama.

1965 On June 7, in *Griswold v. Connecticut*, the Supreme Court created the Right to Privacy and struck down state prohibitions of contraceptives.

1965 August: Thirty-four died in Watts Riots in Los Angeles.

1965 Elementary and Secondary Education Act provided $3 billion in federal funding to schools, but only to those that were integrated.

1965 Voting Rights Act provided federal enforcement of voting rights.

1965 Congress created the Department of Housing and Urban Development.

1966 Texas Western University won the NCAA national championship with five black starting players.

1966 Black Panther Party was founded in Oakland.

1966 Truman Capote published *In Cold Blood*.

1966 Betty Friedan founded the National Organization for Women.

1966 Congress created the Department of Transportation.

1966 *Miranda v. Arizona* created "Miranda Rights" that must be read to persons upon arrest.

1967 On January 15, the Green Bay Packers defeated the Kansas City Chiefs in the first Super Bowl (then called the AFL-NFL Championship game).

1967 Race riots in thirty cities led to the deaths of sixty-eight people.

1967 October: Anti-war demonstration at the Pentagon drew thirty-five.

1968 Housing Act authorized the building of 1.7 million housing units with federal funding.

Chapter Review (cont'd)

Time Line (cont'd)

1968 January–June: Two hundred twenty-one student demonstrations occurred at 101 colleges and universities.

1968 On April 4, Martin Luther King was assassinated in Memphis.

1968 Denny McClain won thirty-one games for the Detroit Tigers.

1968 Intel was founded in Santa Clara.

1968 Norman Mailer published *Armies in the Night.*

1968 Black Panther leader Eldridge Cleaver fled to Algeria.

1969 On January 12, the New York Jets shocked the football world by defeating the heavily favored Baltimore Colts in Super Bowl III.

1969 On June 28, Stonewall Riot in New York City marked the beginning of the Gay Rights movement.

1969 Kurt Vonnegut published *Slaughterhouse Five*.

1970 On January 1, University of Texas defeated Notre Dame in the Cotton Bowl to be the last all-white team to win the NCAA football championship

1970 September: The bombing of a computer center at the University of Wisconsin in which a researcher was killed.

1970 The AFL and NFL merged to form one twenty-six-team professional football league.

1970 Federal spending reached 25 percent of GDP

1970 Urban Mass Transportation Assistance Act provided federal funds to cities for mass transportation.

1971 The Southern Baptist convention voted in support of a resolution affirming a woman's right to have an abortion if the health of the mother was threatened.

1971 The majority of married women were employed outside the home.

Time Line (cont'd)

1971 American GNP exceeded $1 trillion.

1971 A group of Native Americans occupied Alcatraz prison in San Francisco Bay.

1971 Twenty-sixth Amendment lowered the voting age to eighteen.

1972 San Francisco opened its Bay Area Rapid Transit (BART) system of light rail.

1972 Unionized percentage of the workforce dropped to 26.7 percent

1972 Congress passed the Equal Rights Amendment.

1972 Congress passed Title IX of the Education Amendments Act of 1972, which prohibited sex discrimination in educational programs receiving federal funding.

1972 *Furman v. Georgia* struck down the death penalty as a violation of the Fourteenth Amendment equal protection clause.

1972 On December 31, the Environmental Protection Agency banned DDT.

1973 Military draft was ended.

1973 American Psychiatric Association no longer labeled homosexuality as a "disease."

1973 First Energy Crisis tripled oil prices and doubles the price of gasoline.

1973 On January 22, *Roe v. Wade* struck down state restrictions on abortions in the first trimester as violations of right to privacy.

1973 February–May: a group of Native Americans took over Wounded Knee, South Dakota, and held it for seventy-one days. Shootouts with federal authorities led to the deaths of two natives, and one marshal was paralyzed from the waist down.

1974 Ella Grasso was elected governor of Connecticut.

1975 Poverty rate dropped to 11.4 percent from 22 percent in 1959.

Chapter Review (cont'd) ▶▶▶

Time Line (cont'd)

1975 On April 4, Bill Gates and Paul Allen founded Microsoft.

1975 Jerry Falwell founded the Moral Majority.

1976 Saul Bellow won the Nobel Prize for literature the year after publishing *Humbolt's Gift*.

1976 Supreme Court reinstated the death penalty in the death penalty cases as long as it was not arbitrarily and capriciously applied.

1977 January: *Roots* television miniseries reached three-quarters of American homes.

1977 Life expectancy at birth reached 73.2 years.

1977 Steve Jobs and Steve Wozniak founded Apple Computers.

1978 Church of Jesus Christ of Latter Day Saints allowed black men to enter into the priesthood.

1978 Jerry Falwell preached his first sermon against abortion.

1980 June: More than one hundred ten thousand refugees from Castro's Cuba entered the United States in a flotilla of small boats.

1982 ERA failed to be ratified by three-quarters of the states.

Key Terms

Playboy: Popular magazine for men in the 1960s and 1970s that featured photography of nude women
Inflation: Rising prices that plagued the 1970s
DDT: Pesticide that was banned by the EPA after it led to the classification of the bald eagle as an endangered species
Intel: The inventor of x86 microprocessors, the computer chips found in most personal computers
Steve Jobs and Steve Wozniak: Founders of Apple Computers
Bill Gates and Paul Allen: Founders of Microsoft Corporation
Stagflation: Economic situation where unemployment and inflation are both high
Norman Mailer: Author of *Armies in the Night*
Harper Lee: Author of *To Kill a Mockingbird*

Key Terms (cont'd)

Kurt Vonnegut: Author of *Slaughterhouse Five*

Saul Bellow: Winner of the 1976 Nobel Prize for literature and author of *Humbolt's Choice*

Philip Roth: Author of *Portnoy's Complaint* and *Our Gang*

John Updike: Author of *Rabbit Redux* and *The Coup*

Truman Capote: Author of *In Cold Blood*

The Deer Hunter: 1978 movie about the Vietnam War and its impact on the lives of those who fought in it

One Flew Over the Cuckoo's Nest: 1975 film that won five Academy Awards for its look inside an Oregon State mental facility

Roots: Television miniseries based on the book by Alex Haley that chronicled the generations of a slave family was the most successful television event in history

BART: San Francisco's Bay Area Rapid Transit light rail system

Housing Act of 1968: Authorized the building of 1.7 million housing units with federal funding

Elementary and Secondary Education Act of 1965: Appropriated $3 billion to schools that educated low income children, thus forcing schools to integrate in order to get the money available to schools with low-income children

"I Have A Dream": Martin Luther King's most famous speech on the steps of the Lincoln Memorial at the March on Washington in 1963

"Busing": The transportation of children to schools outside their neighborhoods in the interest of ending school segregation

Baker v. Carr: 1962 case that required State legislatures to have equal sized electoral districts

Civil Rights Act of 1964: Ended racial discrimination in public accommodations

Voting Rights Act 1965: Made it a federal crime to hinder voting rights, required preclearance of any electoral changes by the Justice Department, and provided federal enforcement

Black Power: Controversial slogan coined by Stokely Carmichael of SNCC

Malcolm X: Leading spokesman for the Nation of Islam and the black separatist movement until his assassination in 1965

Eldridge Cleaver: Leader of the Black Panther Party that fled to Algeria in 1968

Stokely Carmichael: SNCC leader that coined the slogan, "Black Power"

Thurgood Marshall: NAACP lawyer that became the first African-American Supreme Court Justice

Medgar Evers: Civil rights advocate that was assassinated on his own driveway in Jackson, Mississippi, in 1963

Freedom Summer: A campaign in the summer of 1964 to register black voters that resulted in the deaths of James Cheney, Michael Schwerner, and Andrew Goodman on June 21, gunned down by the KKK

George C. Wallace: Governor of Alabama that exploited segregationist sentiments for political gain and attempted to prevent the integration of the University of Alabama

Watts Riot: Race riot in Los Angeles in the summer of 1965 that led to the deaths of thirty-four people

James Earl Ray: Assassinated Martin Luther King on April 4, 1968 in Memphis

Cesar Chavez: Leader of the California migrant workers

Chapter Review (cont'd)

Key Terms (cont'd)

American Indian Movement: Pressure group that took over Alcatraz Island in 1968 and vandalized the Bureau of Indian Affairs

Wounded Knee "shoot-out": 1973 seventy-one-day standoff between the AIM and federal Marshals at Wounded Knee, South Dakota, that led to the death of two AIM members, and one marshal was paralyzed by a gunshot

May Movement: Student movement in Paris in 1968 that virtually paralyzed the country

Counterculture: Youth culture in the 1960s that advocated peace, free love, rock music, and illegal drug use

Sexual revolution: With the introduction of the birth control pill, more young people argued that sex was not just for married people.

Twenty-Sixth Amendment: Extended the right to vote to age eighteen

Eugene McCarthy: Democratic Senator that ran for president on a peace platform in 1968

Robert F. Kennedy: Younger brother of John F. Kennedy, Attorney General of the United States, Democratic Senator from New York, and presidential Candidate in 1968 who was assassinated hours after he won the California Democratic Primary on June 5

Betty Friedan: Author of *The Feminine Mystique* and founder of the National Organization for Women

NOW: National Organization for Women, a political pressure group advocating equal rights for women

Title VII: Provision of the Civil Rights Act of 1964 that prohibits discrimination based on sex

Title IX: Provision of the Education Amendments Act of 1972 that prohibited sex discrimination in educational programs receiving federal funding

Free Speech Movement: 1964 student movement at the University of California at Berkeley in 1964

Barry Goldwater: Uncompromising Republican Arizona senator that unsuccessfully ran for president in 1964, but helped spawn a conservative movement

Andy Warhol: Gay modern artist who stated that "I didn't think I should want to change. . . .others should change their attitudes but not me"

Equal Rights Amendment: Proposed Amendment to the Constitution passed by Congress in 1972, but never ratified by the required three-quarters of the states

Phyllis Schlafly: Founder of Eagle Forum, a conservative group opposed to the Equal Rights Amendment

Eagle Forum: A conservative group opposed to the Equal Rights Amendment founded by Phyllis Schlafly

Griswold v. Connecticut: 1965 Supreme Court ruling striking down state prohibitions on contraceptives as violations of rights to privacy

Roe v. Wade: 1973 case where the Supreme Court struck down state restrictions on abortions in the first trimester as violations of the right to privacy

Jerry Falwell: Virginia evangelist that founded the Moral Majority and made abortion a Protestant Christian issue in an effort to unite Protestants and Catholics in the Republican Party

Moral Majority: Conservative Christian pressure group founded by Jerry Falwell

Harvey Milk: First openly gay official elected to office in the United States when he won a seat as a City Supervisor in San Francisco in 1977—Milk was assassinated on November 27, 1978.

Key Terms (cont'd)

C. Everett Koop: Pediatrician that formed the Christian Action Council with *Christianity Today* Editor Harold O. J. Brown that lobbied Congress for measures to curb abortions

Christian Action Council: Pressure group formed by Pediatrician C. Everett Koop and *Christianity Today* Editor Harold J. Brown to lobby Congress for restrictions on abortions

Paul Weyrich: Co-founder of the conservative Washington Think Tank, The Heritage Foundation, and co-founder of the Moral Majority with Jerry Falwell

Gideon v. Wainwright: 1963 Supreme Court case that established the right to state-supported counsel for the indigent in all felony cases on the state level

Miranda v. Arizona: 1966 Supreme Court case that required that persons be informed of their Constitutional rights upon arrest or interrogation

Furman v. Georgia: 1972 Supreme Court case that struck down the death penalty as a violation of the Fourteenth Amendment Equal Protection Clause because it was arbitrary and capricious in its application

J. Edgar Hoover: First director of the FBI who remained the director until his death in 1972

Stonewall Riot: Riot at the Stonewall Inn in New York City in 1969 that marks the beginning of the Gay Rights movement

Pop Quiz ▶ ▶ ▶

30

Chapter 30

1. By 1974, 94.4 percent of American households had __________.
   a. a washing machine
   b. a dishwasher
   c. a television and a refrigerator
   d. a car

2. Between 1950 and 1973, per capita consumption of which of the following significantly increased?
   a. frozen foods
   b. beef, chicken, and turkey
   c. hard liquor and wine
   d. all of the above

Chapter Review (cont'd)

Pop Quiz (cont'd)

3. What percent of income belonged to the poorest 20 percent of Americans in 1950?
   a. 20%
   b. 17%
   c. 14%
   d. less than 5%

4. By 1972, the percentage of the nonagricultural workforce involved in organized labor was __________.
   a. 5%
   b. 10%
   c. 26.7%
   d. 50%

5. The movie that offered a sympathetic view of the drug culture was __________.
   a. *Roots*
   b. *The Exorcist*
   c. *Easy Rider*
   d. *A Clockwork Orange*

6. The Elementary and Secondary Education Act of 1965 induced many school districts to integrate by __________.
   a. providing money to school districts based on the number of poor children they educated
   b. threatening to send paratroopers to school districts that did not integrate
   c. providing money for classes in cultural diversity
   d. all of the above

7. Native Americans asserted themselves in the late 60s and early 1970s by __________.
   a. taking over Alcatraz Island in San Francisco Bay
   b. engaging in a shoot-out with federal authorities at Wounded Knee, South Dakota
   c. writing books like Vine Deloria's *Custer Died for Your Sins*.
   d. all of the above

8. The most visible manifestation of the counterculture's rejection of traditional society was __________.
   a. a revolution in dress and hair style (long hair and denim)
   b. the counterculture's overt racism
   c. the counterculture's preference for nostalgia
   d. the counterculture's preference for luxury cars

Pop Quiz (cont'd)

9. During the 1960s, a sea of change occurred in the attitudes of many Americans toward __________.
   a. communism
   b. sexual relations
   c. football
   d. the purpose of a college education

10. Women gathering in groups to air their grievances among themselves was known as __________.
    a. consciousness-raising
    b. issue avoidance
    c. mellowing out
    d. gripe sessions

11. One religious group that suffered a significant decline in attendance in America between 1957 and 1975 was __________.
    a. the Catholic Church
    b. nondenominational Christianity
    c. American Muslims
    d. the Church of Scientology

12. Reverend Jerry Falwell viewed homosexuality as __________.
    a. an alternative lifestyle
    b. an evil sin on the level with murder and rape
    c. a genetic predisposition
    d. a mental illness

13. Many of the gains made by women in employment and education came about because of government action. T F

14. *Baker v. Carr* increased the strength of urban areas in state legislatures. T F

15. Church attendance declined when churches became more active in fighting social problems. T F

1. C	5. A	9. B	13. T
2. D	6. A	10. A	14. T
3. D	7. D	11. A	15. T
4. C	8. A	12. B	

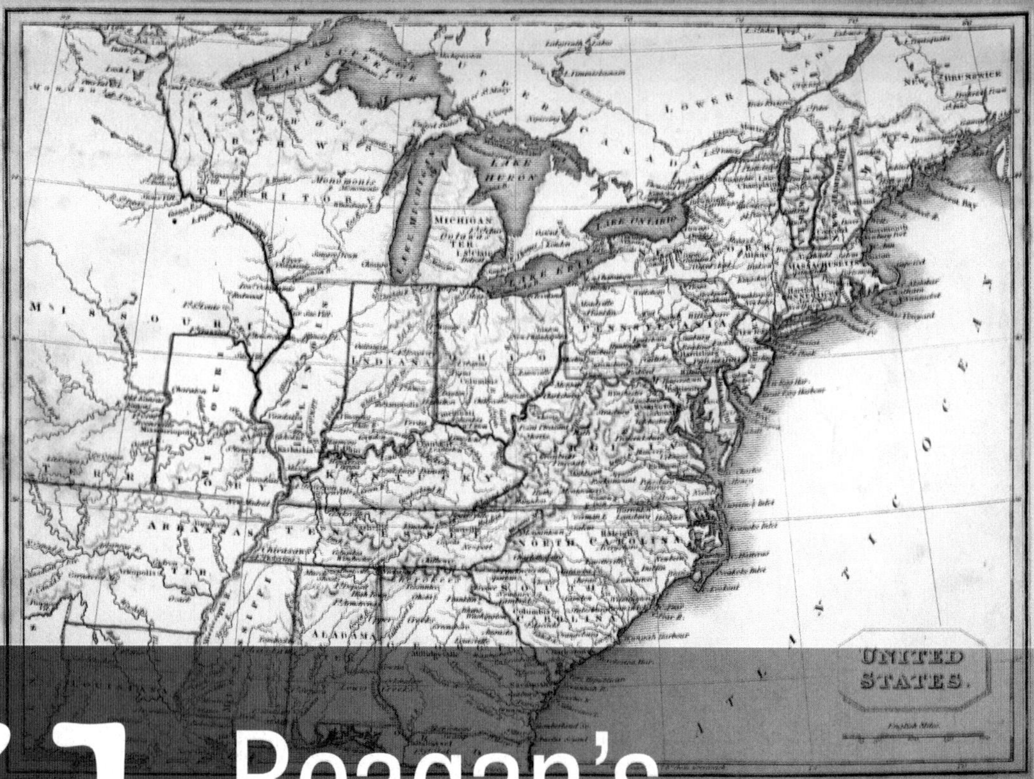

31 Reagan's America

Chapter Objectives

The First Couple

Domestic Issues

Reaganomics

The Air Traffic Controllers' Strike

Shaping the Supreme Court

Robert Bork Appointment

The Great Crash

Economic Inequality

Deregulation and its Consequences

A New Cold War?

The Middle East

The Americas

America in the 80s

The High-Tech Revolution

AIDS

The Election of 1984

Challenges of the Second Term

Reagan and Gorbachev

Immigration Reform

Reagan's Legacy

The Election of 1988

The Bush Presidency

Foreign Policy

The Fall of Communism in Eastern Europe

The Collapse of the U.S.S.R.

Operation Just Cause

Persian Gulf War

Domestic Issues

The Americans with Disabilities Act

An Eruption of Rage in Los Angeles

The Clarence Thomas Nomination

The Year of the Woman

Elements of a One-Term Presidency

The First Couple

When Ronald and Nancy Reagan moved into the White House in January 1981, they were a most unusual presidential couple. Each had been a movie star, though Nancy on a lesser scale. Each was more familiar with the halls of power in Hollywood than those in Washington, and each had a personal style at odds with the usual expectations of the American people for White House occupants. Indeed, not since the Kennedys had so much glamour been injected into politics. This would have consequences beyond the surface glitter because the president, in particular, deployed his celebrity status to excellent advantage in advancing his conservative political agenda. Another important piece of information about the couple is that their marriage was so close and trusting that Mrs. Reagan had the clout very few First Ladies have enjoyed. Finally, Ronald Reagan, born in February 1911 and thus nearly seventy when he took the oath of allegiance, was older than most American presidents have been upon inauguration; and when he completed his second term, he set a record as the oldest person to serve in the office.

Ronald Reagan was born in Tampico, Illinois, and spent the rest of his life celebrating the virtues of small-town America. In fact, his own childhood, which included the necessity of dealing with an alcoholic father, was not an easy or uncomplicated one. His ability to rise above such memories typified not only his approach to life in general but also his approach to political life. Having graduated from Eureka College in Illinois, where he majored in economics, he went on to work as a sports broadcaster before being invited

▶Ronald Reagan and Nancy Reagan waving to the crowds during the Inaugural Parade, Washington, D.C. on Inauguration Day, 1981.

to Hollywood for a screen test. The screen test secured him employment in front of the cameras; and he enjoyed success but not overwhelming success, which is to say that he was a leading man but not an icon, as were some of his contemporaries. In the 1940s he was the president of the Screen Actors Guild, where he became active in "ferreting out communists" during the McCarthy era. In the 1950s, he hosted a television series for General Electric and began to give motivational speeches for business groups, an activity that completed his conversion from New Deal Democrat to Republican. By the time of Barry Goldwater's nomination for the presidency in 1964, Reagan had become one of the most visible spokespeople for the conservative cause and one whose geniality softened his sometimes harsh message.

His political rise coincided with a turbulent period of student activism on college campuses in California. When he competed for governor of that state in 1966 against Pat Brown, an effective incumbent, he was able to run against "out-of-control activists" as well as his actual opponent, a strategy that served him well. Once in office, he governed more as a pragmatist than as an ideologue—contrary to what his rhetoric might have suggested—and served two terms. He followed his success in California by running a surprisingly close race against Gerald Ford for the Republican presidential nomination in 1976 and then winning the Republican nomination for president in 1980. Reagan went to defeat an unpopular incumbent, Jimmy Carter.

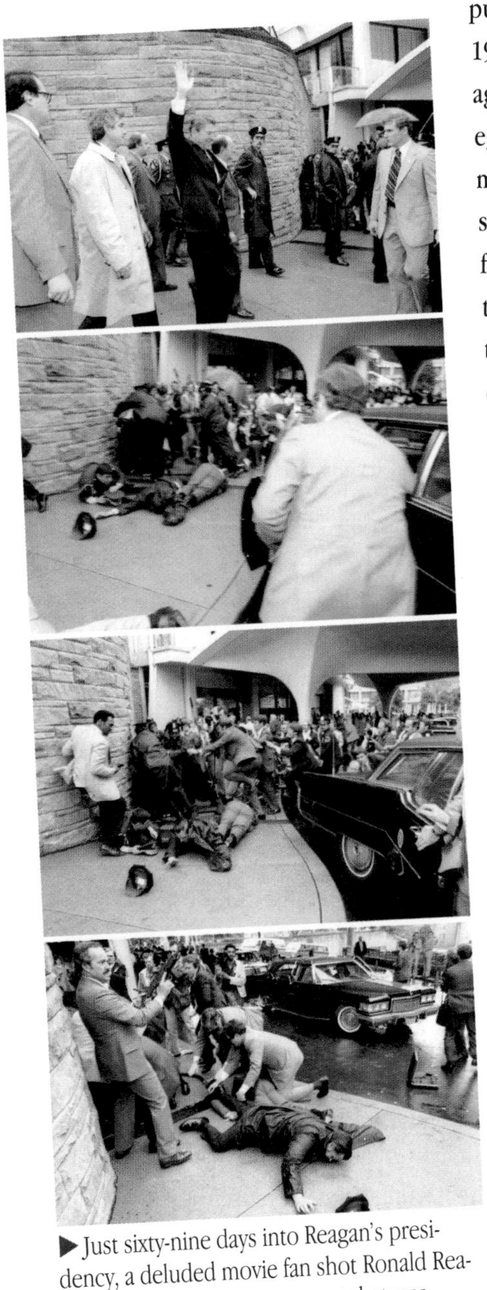
▶ Just sixty-nine days into Reagan's presidency, a deluded movie fan shot Ronald Reagan in an assassination attempt that was nearly successful.

His partner in life as well as in politics Nancy Reagan, was born in 1921, the child of a stage actress that had remarried a neurosurgeon, Dr. Loyal Davis, when Nancy was six. The girl had a fine education, eventually graduating from Smith College as a theater major and then pursuing her own acting dream. That dream carried her to Hollywood by the early 1950s, where she met Ronald Reagan. The two were married in 1952, her first marriage and his second; hence, Ronald Reagan became America's first "divorced" president. As his political career advanced, Mrs. Reagan became known as a political wife of exemplary devotion and able to fix a rapt gaze on her husband, even when he was delivering a stump speech that she may well have heard many times before.

Just sixty-nine days into Reagan's presidency, a deluded movie fan shot Ronald Reagan in an assassination attempt that had many important repercussions, although the public did not know of the severity of the wounds at the time or that it was, in fact, nearly a successful attempt. What the public did know was that their president showed remarkable courage and gallantry, even walking into the hospital unaided. Polls soon revealed how much more admiration he garnered after the episode, even from Democrats, and he became a far more formidable political figure, despite having to deal with a House of Representatives controlled by the opposition party.

Thereafter, Mrs. Reagan became ever more anxious about her husband's well being. It was at this point that she began to consult a San Francisco astrologer about the president's schedule, a practice that continued throughout the Reagan administration and that was revealed in a tell-all book by Mrs. Reagan's adversary (she had worked to get him fired) former chief-of-staff, Donald Regan, and corroborated by her own daughter, Patti Davis.

Domestic Issues

Reaganomics

Ronald Reagan signaled his intentions with respect to the economy by appointing a Cabinet filled with businessmen and conservatives, a move consonant with the pro-business speeches he had been giving for many years. Reagan favored "supply-side economics." This policy was predicated on the belief that tax cuts would produce such a boost to the economy that the government would not run budget deficits. It had been labeled "voodoo economics" by his adversary during the run-up to the 1980 nomination, George H. W. Bush—the man whom Reagan then chose as his vice president in an effort to unite the Party.

In essence, supply-side economics promised that it would be possible to cut taxes rigorously and thereby attract the productive investment of capital, all without damaging the fundamental soundness of the economy. Cutting taxes was dogma to conservatives, not merely to enhance their own pocketbooks but also because they viewed it as an effective means of reducing big government, a highly desired goal in their eyes. Reagan went so far as to announce in his first inaugural, "In the present crisis, government is not the solution to our problem; government is the problem."

In fact, when Reagan took office, the economy was still suffering the after-effects of the Vietnam War, the decline of America's manufacturing base, and the second oil crisis of the 1970s. The late 1970s had also featured an unprecedented, and unwelcome, phenomenon known as "stagflation," where double-digit inflation was accompanied by double-digit unemployment. Presidents Johnson and Nixon, during the previous decade, had paid for the Vietnam War without the support of increased taxes, thus leading to deficits and eventually devaluation of the currency. The new president argued that an excess of regulation, taxation, and spending had created the problem—all of which had put a damper on business activity—had created the problem. Congress listened to him and passed the Economic Recovery Tax Act in 1981, reducing income tax rates by 25 percent over three years, in spite of the fact that the federal government was already operating at a deficit. The cuts were supposed to be linked to cuts in spending, but it proved easier to indulge in rhetoric about runaway spending than to find politically palatable ways to cut it. Furthermore, Reagan believed that the United States was behind the Soviet Union in the cold war arms race; and he, therefore, effectively doubled military spending. As a consequence, Reagan's legacy included a tripling of the national debt during the eight years of his administration and the worst economic recession since the Great Depression in 1982, but by 1983, the

▶ President Reagan signing the Economic Recovery Tax Act, 1981. The Act reduced income tax rates by 25 percent over three years.

economy began to improve. Many scholars would argue the dominant factors in the recovery were that world oil prices declined (from $40 a barrel in 1981 to $9 in 1986) and Bill Gates' DOS operating system created an information processing revolution. Another factor many credit in reviving the economy is the aggressive action of the Federal Reserve Board in tightening the money supply and thereby limiting inflation and that the economic recovery was not attributable to Reagan's supply-side economic policies. Yet the improvement itself is unarguable.

The Air Traffic Controllers' Strike

Another episode of great historical significance involved one of the few unions to support Ronald Reagan in 1980, the Professional Air Traffic Controllers Organization or PATCO. PATCO'S president, Robert Poli, wanted wage increases of up to 40 percent for his members, as well as a reduction in their workweek. Reagan's Director of the Budget, David Stockman, who was trying to hold the line against increased federal spending and deficits, opposed this step. In August 1981, PATCO's membership rejected a lesser offer from the government; nearly twelve thousand controllers went on strike, and in so doing, violated a no-strike clause in their contract. Poli and his members were gambling on support from the public and perhaps from President Reagan, himself a former labor leader. They made a fatal miscalculation.

The president's response was swift and decisive. He fired all the striking controllers, saying that they had broken the law by going on strike as public employees, and stipulated that they could never be rehired. He then ordered military personnel into the control towers. Except for those who were close to the labor movement, the public overwhelmingly approved of the president's action; and so, no doubt, did some union members. Most historians now agree that over the long haul Reagan's breaking the PATCO union did more to intimidate and weaken the labor movement than any other single episode since the 1940s. In concert with his pro-business appointments to the National Labor Relations Board, the PATCO debacle intensified the hemorrhaging of union membership since the 1950s.

Shaping the Supreme Court

One of Ronald Reagan's most popular decisions was his appointment of the first woman to the Supreme Court, Sandra Day O'Connor, in 1981. Reagan and his advisers felt that he needed to do something to reach out to women voters after a statistically significant "gender gap" in voting showed up for the first time in American history in the election of 1980, with women favoring Jimmy Carter disproportionately over the male vote for him. From the time that women had gotten the vote in 1920, activists had been waiting for a "women's bloc" to materialize; but they waited in vain—that is until 1980. Once aware of the phenomenon, Republican operatives were eager to counter it immediately. Hence the general concurrence among Reagan's top advisors that the time was right to put a woman on the nation's highest bench.

Sandra Day O'Connor, a conservative who would become Reagan's choice, enjoyed a career that is a case study in victory against sexism. After a distinguished law school career, in 1952, Sandra Day graduated from Stanford Law School and was offered only secretarial jobs, at first, in spite of her law degree from one of America's elite institutions. After marrying a law school classmate, John O'Connor, she returned to her native Arizona, began to practice law, and became involved in Republican politics. From 1965 to 1969, she served as Arizona's assistant attorney general. In 1969 she was appointed to the Arizona Senate, winning reelection twice. In 1973 she was chosen as the state's senate majority leader. Resigning from the legislature, she was elected to be a superior court judge in Phoenix in 1974 and then was chosen to be a judge on the Arizona Court of Appeals in 1979; thus she had an unusual combination of legislative and judicial experience. What's more, during her interview with President Reagan, it was soon apparent that Reagan liked her. With these factors in her favor, the stage was set for her nomination, a selection confirmed by the Senate by a vote of 99 to 0.

The O'Connor appointment proved to be a decision that would only grow in stature over the years as Justice O'Connor garnered the reputation of being one of the truly outstanding justices in American history by reason of her ability to "count to five." This expression means that she was especially shrewd in staking out a centrist position and then shaping a majority to support it. O'Connor would essentially act as the swing vote on the Court for over two decades as her colleagues were normally divided 4–4 between the solidly liberal and conservative factions. Though the conservative William Rehnquist was Chief Justice for most of those years, it was O'Connor's vote that more often decided which direction the Court would rule.

Reagan would eventually also chose two other members of the Supreme Court: the very conservative devout Catholic, Antonin Scalia, and the more moderately conservative Anthony Kennedy. Moreover, in 1986 Reagan elevated Associate Justice William Rehnquist to the position of Chief Justice. All told, Reagan's many appointments at various levels of the judiciary during his eight years in office had a powerful impact, this despite the Senate's refusal to confirm his nomination of the ultra-conservative Robert Bork to the Supreme Court in 1987.

Robert Bork Appointment

In June 1987, Justice Lewis Powell resigned his position on the Supreme Court, leaving President Reagan the task of appointing a successor. Reagan chose Yale law professor and United States Court of Appeals judge Robert Bork, a staunch conservative who had opposed the 1964 Civil Rights Act for "intruding on the rights of citizens." Bork also disagreed with the Supreme Court's "Judicial Activism" and the "creation of new rights," such as the Right to Privacy that had been the basis of the *Roe v. Wade* decision. Provoking further anger from the left, Bork had been the Solicitor General in the Watergate "Saturday Night Massacre" and had fired Special Prosecutor Archibald Cox at the behest of Richard Nixon during the Watergate scandal. As a result, therefore, of what Democrats viewed as his extreme conservative views, coupled with his actions in the Watergate affair, Bork was voted down in the Senate by a vote of 58 to 42.

Reagan followed up the Bork appointment with the nomination of Douglas Ginsburg, a Harvard Law professor; but the Ginsburg nomination unraveled when it was revealed that Ginsburg had used marijuana while working as a professor at Harvard. Finally, Reagan appointed Appeals Court Justice Anthony Kennedy, who was confirmed unanimously by the Senate in 1988.

The Bork affair, however, had long-term consequences. Republicans charged that the Democrats had voted down Bork for his political views rather than for his legal qualifications. After the Bork affair, Senate confirmation of judicial appointees became highly politicized, and a series of similar affairs would rage on in cases of appointees to lower courts for the next decade and a half. Those who would fail to be confirmed were often said to be "Borked."

The reasons for the political firestorm over Bork were ideologically based and reflected the political realities of the new ideological bitterness that had developed in American politics in the late twentieth century. Members of the opposing political parties in Congress tended to socialize with each other less than they had in the past due to the increased emphasis on social, cultural, and moral issues that forced a premium on ideological consistency within parties and constituencies. Demonization of the political opposition became more common and tended to produce more campaign contributions and political support for the "demonizers." Southern conservatives had largely exited the Democratic Party, leaving the Democrats, by subtraction, more liberal. The loss of their conservative faction rendered the Democratic Party more ideological and less flexible in dealing with their Republican counterparts. Simultaneously, religiosity in the United States had not only become more intense but the makeup of American religion had also shifted away from the more liberal, old-line Protestant churches and toward religious fundamentalist sects. Although members of religious fundamentalist Protestant churches were only approximately a fourth of the American population, fundamentalist Protestants had become a majority of the Republican Party. Both parties recognized the negatives of the development of ideological polarization; but religious conservatives that now had power in the Republican Party were not open to compromise. Neither party was able to make any headway in reducing the partisan and ideological strife that would continue into the twenty-first century.

The Great Crash

On October 19, 1987, known as "Black Monday," the New York Stock Exchange dropped 22.6 percent, almost doubling the record 12.8 percent drop of the 1929 crash that had signaled the dawning of the Great Depression of the 1930s. Although the market rallied to recoup 40 percent of its losses by the end of the week, economic prognosticators and the general public feared that another Great Depression might follow, thus causing a drop in consumer confidence and further depressing the economy. Many economic observers blamed the crash on the reckless deficit spending by the Reagan administration. Chrysler chairman Lee Iacocca summed up the views of many when he stated, "I don't know what they're on down in Washington. It's wacko time." The stock market would eventually recover; but the crash and fears that ensued suggested to many that "deregulation" of the financial markets might not be quite so wise after all, and thus allowed a political opening for the Democrats in 1988.

Economic Inequality

As could have, perhaps, been expected with the move toward a more free market-oriented economy during the Reagan years, economic inequality increased significantly during the 1980s. In 1979, the poorest 40 percent of Americans held 18 percent of the total income in America, and the wealthiest 5 percent held 15.6 percent of the total income. After eight years of Reaganomics, however, the wealthiest 5 percent of Americans produced 21 percent of all income while the poorest 40 percent of Americans earned only 14 percent of all income. Unfortunately for America's working class and poor, Adam Smith's "rising tide" did not lift all boats equally. Personal income for the wealthiest 20 percent of Americans increased, while it actually decreased 9.8 percent for the poorest 20 percent of Americans. No longer could all Americans expect, as they had in the previous decades following World War II, that their children would live better than they had. Similarly, between 1980 and 1988, the number of individuals living below the poverty line increased from 11.7 percent of the population to 13.5 percent, the highest poverty rate among industrialized democracies of the world.

Deregulation and its Consequences

In *Reckoning with Reagan*, Michael Schaller entitled one of his chapters "Prophets (Profits) of Deregulation." This play on words highlights the extent to which many of those who advocated the dismantling of the regulatory state, regulations put in place during the Progressive period and the New Deal years, managed to do well during the years of the Reagan administration. In no area was this truer than that of the savings-and-loan (S & L) industry.

Deregulation had begun during the Carter years, but the pace greatly accelerated under Ronald Reagan. In some industries—telecommunications, for example—deregulation may have had a benign effect by encouraging competition—to the ultimate benefit of the consumer. The impact was to encourage high-risk investments between the S & Ls, however, because government oversight of investment practices was terminated. By the time the dust settled in the

1990s, some thirteen hundred financial institutions had failed; but no one lost money because the S & L's deposits were federally insured. On the other hand, American taxpayers were left with a bill of $160 billion to cover the losses incurred by the S & L industry.

The best-known instance of corruption in the thrift industry lay in the case of Charles Keating and the California-based Lincoln Federal Savings and Loan. As an instance of illegal behavior, Lincoln's tellers sold "junk bonds"—not guaranteed like regular savings accounts—to thousands of gullible, mostly elderly customers, while misleading these customers into thinking that this was a safe investment. When Keating's shady practices came to light, it became known that he had contributed some $3 million dollars in campaign contributions to a bi-partisan group of five United States Senators, one of whom was 2008 Republican presidential nominee John McCain. In return, the Keating Five had apparently tried to offer Keating help with his problems.

In a book about the Reagan years published in 1991, Haynes Johnson offered the following count: by that point 138 Reagan administration officials had been convicted, indicted, or officially investigated, including several cabinet officers up to Edwin Meese, the Attorney General, and Caspar Weinberger, the Secretary of Defense. Not personally corrupt, Reagan presided over an administration steeped in ethical problems. His desire to deregulate was based on an optimistic faith that business leaders and people in power would behave with integrity—all too often, it seems, a misplaced faith. Perhaps James Madison said it best when he stated, "If men were angels, no government would be necessary." Unfortunately, men are not. The Reagan years demonstrated that at least some government regulation is an essential part of the mix, both to protect the public safety and to maintain the consumer confidence necessary to a vibrant economy.

▶Caspar Weinberger, Secretary of Defense, was one of over one hundred administrative officials who were officially investigated during Reagan's term.

Foreign Policy

A New Cold War?

When he took office, Reagan arrived with as much baggage from prior speeches about the Soviet Union and the threat of international communism as those he possessed about deregulating the economy. In 1980, at a time that America seemed, to many, impotent in foreign policy (largely due to the Iranian hostage crisis and the Soviet invasion of Afghanistan), Ronald Reagan had campaigned against Jimmy Carter, promising to "make America strong again" and arguing for a foreign policy of

"Peace through strength." Reagan talked of a "missile gap" between the United States and the Soviet Union; and he argued that the Soviet "Evil Empire" was the basis of all of the world's unrest and, therefore, had to be contained. Reagan also termed the Vietnam War as a "noble cause" to prevent the spread of communism. Reagan essentially reversed Nixon's détente by referring to the U.S.S.R. as the "focus of evil in the modern world." Reagan was not only anti-Soviet but also determined to fight communism anywhere and everywhere in the world, through military means if necessary.

George Kennan, the original architect of the containment doctrine, was unimpressed with Reagan's new cold warrior attitude and termed the president's views as "intellectual primitivism." However, Reagan's views played well with the American public, just as they had for Kennedy in 1960. In 1981, Reagan began a defense buildup that amounted to a 40 percent defense spending increase in his first three years in office. The defense spending increases were so immense that Reagan's defense budget exceeded Vietnam War spending as a percentage of the economy.

Adding to his massive buildup, in 1983, Reagan introduced the Strategic Defense Initiative (SDI) in his State of the Union Address. Without first consulting scientists, Reagan proposed to spend $24 billion on a space laser system designed to shoot down Soviet Intercontinental Ballistic Missiles (ICBMs). Despite almost unanimous proclamations from the scientific community that such a system was infeasible, Congress appropriated the funding for the program. By 2004, over $60 billion had been spent on the program with essentially marginal results. Reagan also installed new cruise missiles in Europe and doubled the size of the American nuclear arsenal in an attempt to gain "parity" with the Soviet Union. Reagan's claims that the United States had fallen behind in the nuclear race were true, however, only if one merely counted land based missiles and ignored the fact that the

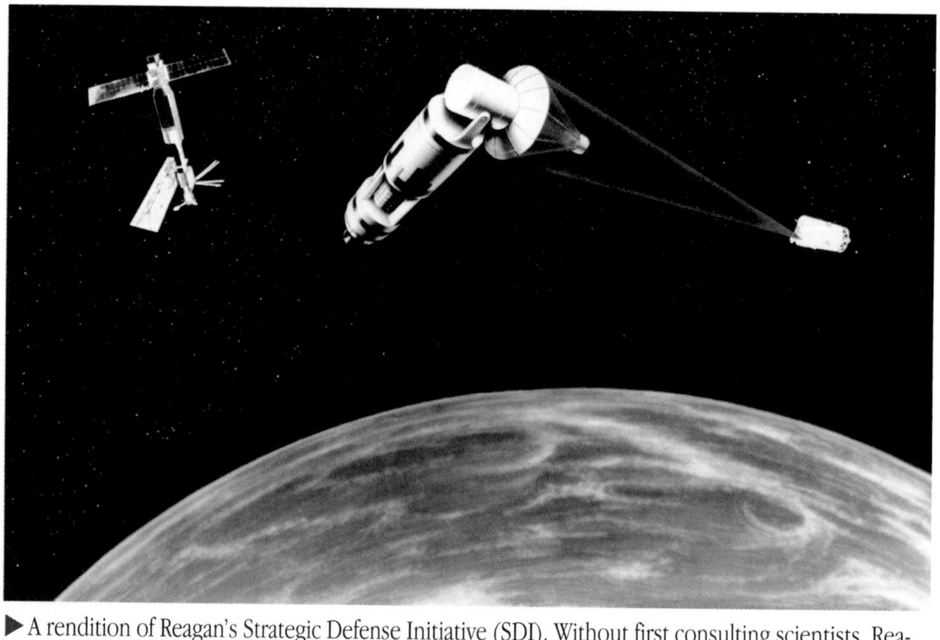

▶ A rendition of Reagan's Strategic Defense Initiative (SDI). Without first consulting scientists, Reagan proposed to spend $24 billion on a space laser system designed to shoot down Soviet Intercontinental Ballistic Missiles (ICBMs).

United States had a 2-to-1 advantage over the Soviets in submarine-launched missiles in 1982, counterbalancing the disadvantage in land based systems.

Before the U.S. and the Soviet Union could reach comity, there were many rocky periods in the relationship, but none more so than following the Soviet downing of Korean Air Lines Flight #007 in September 1983. In a flight from Alaska to Seoul, the Korean 747 civilian jetliner had wandered off course and had flown over Soviet territory. A Soviet fighter plane shot it down, killing all 269 people on board, a group that included a member of the United States Congress. The exact facts of this incident have never been fully determined, but Reagan denounced it as an "act of barbarism." For this and other reasons, there was a massive build-up in United States military might, with the consequent impact of increasing the deficit spending by the administration, an avowed opponent of Keynesian economics.

Reagan also proclaimed the "Reagan Doctrine" whereby the United States would provide aid to "freedom fighters" resisting communism in Third World countries. As a practical matter, this often meant making dubious allies, as in Afghanistan, where Reagan continued Jimmy Carter's policy of aiding the Mujahedin who were fighting against the Soviets. Twenty years later many of these men comprised the Taliban forces. Some would become known as al Qaeda, against which the United States would launch an invasion of Afghanistan following the terrorist attack of September 11, 2001, orchestrated by al Qaeda.

The Middle East

President Reagan inherited an ongoing set of difficulties in this troubled region, difficulties that were compounded by the outbreak of a war between Iran and Iraq in 1980 that lasted till 1988 and claimed some two million lives. In addition to dealing with this, Reagan's administration

▶ The Deep Drone deploying from the fleet tug, during search operations for Korean Airlines Flight 007. The Korean 747 civilian jetliner had wandered off course and had flown over Soviet territory. A Soviet fighter plane shot it down, killing all 269 people on board.

faced the recurring tensions between Israel and the Palestinians, as well as the outbreak of civil strife in Lebanon and Afghanistan.

In 1982, a civil war broke out in Lebanon between Maronite Christians, several groups of Lebanese Muslims, and the Palestinian Liberation Organization (PLO). In an attempt to remedy the chaos on their border due to the bloody Lebanese civil war, Syria subsequently invaded Lebanon with a "peacekeeping force." Israel retaliated against the Syrian invasion with an invasion of their own, and the Israeli "peacekeeping force" then pushed Syrian and PLO forces from near the Israeli border all the way back to Beirut. Israel then shelled the city of Beirut, and the United States sent Ambassador Philip Habib to the Middle East to attempt to negotiate a cease-fire. The next year, the combatants signed an agreement to allow United States, French, and Italian troops to supervise the PLO withdrawal of Beirut, and the Syrian and Israeli withdrawals of Lebanon. Many Lebanese Muslims resented this intrusion; and on April 18, 1983, a suicide squad attacked the American Embassy in Beirut, with a death toll of sixty-three lives lost.

In response, the battleship *New Jersey,* off the Lebanese shore, shelled Muslim positions. American troops were deployed to Lebanon pursuant to the agreement. On October 23, 1983, an Islamic suicide bomber, working for the Iranian terrorist organization Hezbollah, drove a truck full of explosives into the United States marine headquarters at the Beirut airport and killed 241 United States marines. Congress failed to pass a resolution authorizing the placement of American troops in a combat zone as required by the War Powers Act of 1973, so President Reagan was forced to redeploy the marines to ships offshore in the Mediterranean.

▶ The battleship *New Jersey* shelled Muslim positions in response to a suicide squad attack on the American Embassy in Beirut. The attack had claimed sixty-three Americans lives.

Liberals in the press criticized the Reagan administration for recklessly placing American troops in harm's way. Two days later, Reagan diverted attention from the Lebanon disaster by ordering a United States invasion of Grenada, a small island in the Caribbean that had been taken over by a Marxist group. Almost six thousand American troops were involved in the operation, which quickly overwhelmed the Grenadian leftists and Cuban construction workers; however, eighteen Americans were killed and 134 were wounded in the fighting. In addition, 396 Grenadians and Cubans were killed, but the invasion had the desired effect for the Reagan administration since the focus of the American media and the public shifted from the tragedy and defeat of Lebanon to the "victory" in Grenada. Furthermore, Reagan could boast that he had ended the "communist threat" on the tiny Caribbean Island. As for the Iran-Iraq war, though it raged for the entire first Reagan administration, it was destined to play a large role in the second Reagan administration, as the U.S. increased its involvement on the side of Saddam Hussein's Iraq.

The Americas

Because Reagan was so concerned about the specter of international communism, he gave an enormous amount of attention to its possible spread in Central America, a region where poverty and social injustice were widespread. Cuba—where Fidel Castro had overthrown the dictator Fulgencio Batista in 1959, installed a Marxist state, and then engaged in what American policymakers perceived as anti-American activities—was not a model that Reagan wanted to see emulated. The problem for him was that even he, to whom the media referred as the Great Communicator, had a hard time convincing other world leaders, Congress, and the American people, to take the threat as seriously as he did. Pierre Trudeau of Canada and Francois Mitterrand of France, for instance, considered Reagan's views to be an overreaction to a communist threat that was more imagined than real.

In his December 1985 State of the Union Address, Reagan announced what became known as the "Reagan Doctrine," proclaiming his administration's support for anti-communist "freedom fighters" as part of American "self-defense." The announcement was essentially a reversal of the policies of Nixon and Carter, where foreign countries would be held responsible for their own defense against communism. Instead, the Reagan Doctrine represented a return to the Cold War Truman and Eisenhower Doctrines that had been largely discredited since they had led to the disastrous war in Vietnam. Reagan's critics argued that the United States had been extracted from Vietnam for barely over a decade, but evidently the "lessons" of Vietnam already had been forgotten.

For Reagan, however, there were two countries in Latin America of particular concern. In one, El Salvador, a savage civil war was raging. Despite the presence of a nominally in charge civilian regime, in fact, the right-wing military held the actual power. Left-wing insurgents were fighting against this military, and in response the army waged a fierce campaign of repression. Reagan armed the government of the unpopular right-wing dictator, Jose Napoleon Duarte, against the leftist rebels. Aid to El Salvador was $6 million under Carter—and $82 million in Reagan's first budget. Critics charged that American aid to

Duarte's government was partially to blame for the escalation of the Salvadoran conflict and for the fact that fifty-three thousand El Salvadorans were killed in the civil war, along with a small number of American church workers. In advocating aid to the Salvadorian government, Reagan was tacitly accepting the price of supporting a bloodstained regime; hence the controversy attached to this policy.

Nicaragua, however, presented a different set of issues. There, the legitimate government was led by the Marxist Sandinistas, who had finally succeeded in defeating the dictatorial right-wing authoritarian Somoza regime in 1979 after decades of struggle. The Sandinistas confirmed their legitimacy by winning Nicaragua's first free election in 1984. Those opposed to the Sandinistas formed a guerrilla group known as the "Contras." The Contras were a natural focus for President Reagan, every fiber of whose being was clearly horrified by the presence of another Marxist regime, on good terms with both Cuba and the Soviet Union, so close to the United States. From time to time, Congress permitted American aid to go to the Contras, but at other times, it turned off the spigot. In fact, as Richard Reeves points out, the Sandinista government was often its own worst enemy, making it difficult for Congressional Democrats to oppose aid to the Contras by reason of the Sandinista leader, Daniel Ortega, who showed up in Moscow around the time of a key vote. In furtherance of the Reagan Doctrine, Reagan armed the Contra rebels against the communist government of the Sandinistas in Nicaragua at a cost of $19 million. Reagan also mined the harbors of Nicaragua, an action that is considered an act of war under international law. In the end, the Marxist Sandinista regime, strangled by American sanctions, lasted until 1990, when it was defeated in an election.

America in the 80s

The High-Tech Revolution

By the 1980s the power of a new and much smaller computer—and all that power would entail in the lives of ordinary Americans—was beginning to be manifested. Computers were not new—IBM was already a giant corporation—but personal computers were introduced into the middle-class household in the mid-80s. Meanwhile, other types of consumer electronics, such as video games, fueled a strong growth in this arena as well. No region would have more to do with this revolution than California's Silicon Valley, as the Santa Clara Valley (about an hour's drive south of San Francisco) became known.

AIDS

Early in Reagan's presidency there appeared a new scourge, Acquired Immune Deficiency Syndrome (AIDS). Because it is spread through the exchange of blood or bodily fluids, the disease has been linked in the public mind primarily with sexual intercourse, the likeliest mode of transmission, though it can also be transmitted by needle sharing among intravenous drug users, and in the early days, by the transfusion of infected blood.

AIDS was devastating, especially early on, when a diagnosis was an automatic death sentence. Because it has disproportionately, although by no means exclusively, affected male homosexuals and/or those who are sexually promiscuous, everything about it, from transmission to prevention to treatment, has been controversial. Certain fundamentalist clergymen, such as Reverend Jerry Falwell, have gone so far as to suggest that its toll on gay men has been God's punishment for the sin of their sexual orientation. Deferring to his New Right constituency, Ronald Reagan refused to even use the term AIDS in public until 1985, several years into the epidemic.

Congress mandates that the Surgeon General of the United States inform the American people about the prevention of disease and the promotion of health, but the Reagan Administration instructed Surgeon General C. Everett Koop not to make any statements about AIDS because any federal AIDS education plan was likely to alienate Reagan's support from the religious right. Consequently, the media were told at Reagan's press conferences by Reagan officials that AIDS questions were not on the agenda.

With silence on the issue coming from the Reagan Administration, AIDS hysteria began to unravel in the media. Reverend Donald Wildmon of the American Family Association called for a quarantine of "all homosexual establishments." In Nevada, a newspaper ran a full page "AIDS Alert" advertisement posted by a fundamentalist minister who stated, "I think we should do what the Bible says and cut their throats." In 1988, a *Los Angeles Times* poll revealed that 57 percent of religious fundamentalists favored a quarantine of people with AIDS. *National Review* editor William F. Buckley added his contribution to the paranoia when he suggested that those afflicted with AIDS should be given an identifiable tattoo so that others could recognize them and thus avoid contact.

Congress, as the official representative of the people in the United States, was not immune to the hysteria. California Republican Congressman William Dannemeyer stated that if it were possible to identify every HIV positive person in the country, he would "wipe them off the face of the earth" if he were able to do so. The response of the Reagan administration reflected similar thinking. Dr. James O. Mason, Director of the Center for Disease Control, acknowledged that quarantine was being considered as an option as late as 1985.

With the AIDS hysteria in full swing, in July 1985, Surgeon General C. Everett Koop told his superiors that he could no longer remain silent about AIDS. Koop was then given the permission to say whatever he felt was necessary about AIDS, along with the authority to appoint a task force to study the problem. In February 1986, President Reagan asked Koop to prepare a special report on AIDS, and the report was finally released in October the same year. That year, Reagan's friend and fellow movie star Rock Hudson succumbed to the disease, a tragedy that began to change public attitudes. (Another important turning point in public attitudes came in 1991 when basketball star Earvin "Magic" Johnson announced that he was HIV-positive, the predecessor condition to full-blown AIDS. As of this writing, Magic Johnson is still alive and still vigorous although the condition did end his basketball career prematurely.) Reagan planned to mention AIDS in his 1986 State of the Union Address, but plans changed owing to other developments. In 1987, he gave his first speech on the subject, telling the College of Physicians in Philadelphia that he considered AIDS to be "Public Health Enemy No. 1." By the end of his presidency, it should

▶ An important turning point in public attitudes toward Acquired Immune Deficiency Syndrome came in 1991 when basketball star Earvin "Magic" Johnson announced that he was HIV-positive, the predecessor condition to full-blown AIDS.

be noted, the federal government had begun to make a real commitment to a disease that would infect 65 million people worldwide by 2006.

The problem has been that to discuss effective prevention means to discuss "safe sex," a subject that is anathema to conservatives. Prevention might also involve the wide dissemination of condoms, another controversial plan because it seemed to condone free-and-easy sex. Finally, as the past decade has shown, issues having to do with homosexuality have been a sure-fire way of engendering passion among members of the religious right.

The Election of 1984

By 1984, the economy had made a comeback that would continue throughout the decade, due largely to the boom in the information-processing sector. In this election year, campaigning on the issueless theme of "It's Morning in America," Ronald Reagan was decisively re-elected over his opponent Walter Mondale, Jimmy Carter's vice president. The election was noteworthy for a reason other than Reagan's success, however. Mondale chose Geraldine Ferraro as his running mate. For the first time in American history, a woman appeared on a national ticket for one of the major parties.

Geraldine Ferraro was a congresswoman from New York when she was tapped to be the vice presidential nominee, and in general, she was an effective campaigner. However, Reagan was a tough man to beat, especially when Mondale, the man at the top of the Democratic ticket, said that he would need to raise taxes, a bow to reality given the growing deficit but not popular with voters. Despite the fact that Reagan seemed confused during some of the debates—with people for the first time beginning to express public doubts about his failing cognitive ability—his optimism was still popular with voters. He captured 58.8 percent of the popular vote, with Mondale winning 40.6 percent. On Election Day, Reagan won every state except Mondale's home state of Minnesota and the District of Columbia. The Democrats even lost Geraldine Ferraro's home state of New York. In the Electoral College, the vote was 525 to 13. The Democrats, however, were able to maintain control of the House and would go on to recapture the Senate in 1986.

Challenges of the Second Term

The Iran-Contra Scandal

Shortly after Ronald Reagan's second inauguration, events began to unfold that would lead to the worst scandal of his presidency, the Iran-Contra affair. The background to the scandal, however, developed during his first term when a few American hostages were taken prisoners in Lebanon, and when Reagan became frustrated with the limits Congress placed on his ability to supply as much help to the anti-Sandinista forces in Nicaragua as he would have liked. Reagan had termed the contra rebels in Nicaragua as "freedom fighters" without seriously investigating what kind of group they actually were. They were opposed to the communist Sandinista government of Nicaragua, and that was all that the president needed to know. In Reagan's view, any group that was anti-communist was worthy of support. In 1984, however, Congress cut off Contra aid because the Sandinista government had been elected democratically in 1984; and many felt that it was questionable whether or not the contras, regardless of their anti-communism, were "good guys."

Between 1984 and 1986, however, Reagan's National Security Council kept aid to the Contras flowing secretly contrary to the Congressional ban; in doing so, he violated a host of federal laws, as well as Reagan's Oath of Office where he pledged to "faithfully execute the laws of Congress," rather than circumvent them. The covert Contra aid was secretly funded through a scheme developed by Lieutenant Colonel Oliver North, who ran the operation out of the White House basement. According to the Congressional report that was eventually compiled about the operation, Lieutenant North was running his operation openly within the Reagan administration; it would have been difficult for Reagan and his senior aides not to know what was going on.

In July 1985 an Israeli official suggested to National Security Advisor Robert McFarlane that providing arms to Iran (then engaged in hostilities with Iraq, which the United States was aiding in its war with Iran) could lead to the release of some of the American hostages. Despite maintaining a public profile of making no deals with terrorists to secure the release of any hostages—and Washington had labeled Iran as a terrorist regime—the administration decided to go along. The money provided by Iran to pay for the armaments was then channeled to a fund to aid the contras. It should be noted that at no point did the deal lead, unequivocally, to the release of all the hostages. Nor, for that matter, did the contras succeed in overthrowing the Sandinistas.

The arms sales to Iran violated a Congressional Embargo on Iran, which not only had held Americans hostage for 444 days during the Carter administration but also was heavily engaged in an effort to spread Shiite Islamic revolution throughout the globe. In addition, it was involved in the 1983 truck bombing of the United States marine compound in Lebanon. The Reagan Administration Iran-Contra operation also made use of planes owned by South American drug lords, who flew cocaine into the United States with their planes under CIA protection and flew arms from the U.S. to the contras for the American government. South American cocaine trafficker George Morales admitted that he donated $3 million in cash and some aircraft, as well as his top pilots, at the request of the CIA, to the arms-to-the-Contras effort. Also involved in aiding the arms-to-the-Contras scheme with planes was Panamanian President Manuel Noriega, who would later be indicted in Florida for drug trafficking during the same arms-to-Contras covert operation.

To help the contra operation, mercenaries were recruited in the United States, trained in Central America, and then sent to the contra camps to fight. Americans were involved in operating two of the training camps and using Miami Cubans as contras, and thus also violating the Neutrality Act.

Since Congress would not fund the Contra operation, the Reagan administration also solicited private funds to support the Contra rebels and was successful in gaining support from American right-wing groups and individuals. The largest single private donor among these was Pat Robertson's Christian Broadcast Network (CBN), which contributed between three and seven million dollars in contra aid.

Between November 21 and 25, 1987, Attorney General Ed Meese launched an inquiry into the Iran-Contra scandal at the request of the president. Meese then informed senior White House officials a day in advance of the impending document review. Immediately thereafter, Lieutenant Colonel Oliver North, who was in charge of the Iran-Contra arms dealings, and his subordinates shredded most of the documents connected to the Iran-Contra affair. As a consequence of the headstart given by the Attorney General to those involved, the full scope of the scandal could never be completely known. North's actions (and Meese's) were essentially acts of Obstruction of Justice, one of the same charges that led to Richard Nixon's resignation in the previous decade and President Bill Clinton's impeachment in the following decade.

Reagan first admitted on November 13, 1987, that he had ordered the covert Iran-Contra operation under John Poindexter and Lt. Colonel Oliver North, although he denied that the United States had sold arms to Iran in exchange for hostages. Furthermore, on May 15, 1988, Reagan stated that the arms-to-the-Contras covert scheme was "my idea to begin with." Reagan later changed his story, however, and said that he couldn't remember whether he had known about the operation or not. This was despite the possession by Congress of taped phone conversations of Reagan asking Poindexter if the arms did, in fact, get to the contras.

Upon reading the Congressional Report on the Iran-Contra scandal, CBS and National Public Radio correspondent Daniel Schorr stated,

> "What really emerges from this report is a picture of a president who doesn't want to know all the details of the things that he has ordered. He sits there and dreams. He dreams about freedom fighters. He dreams that in Nicaragua—and in Angola and in Afghanistan—there are these people, anti-communist freedom fighters. Boy, you could make a really great movie about these guerrilas who selflessly fight for freedom against the Soviet horror. And he says, 'I think Congress is wrong to say we can't arm them. I want them kept alive.' "

In late 1986, the public began to learn some of the details of the scandal, and Reagan's immense popularity suffered a decline. Robert McFarlane unsuccessfully attempted suicide, and many of the other architects of the policy encountered serious legal problems. Yet the president, whose defense before a congressional committee of investigation substantially consisted of "I don't remember," managed to regain his equilibrium. Indeed, it was during this troubled time in his presidency that the First Lady showed her mettle as she threw her influence behind a massive overhaul of the personnel in the administration—a move that most scholars credit for having helped him rescue the balance of his term.

The Congressional Committee that was constructed to investigate the Iran-Contra scandal included twenty-six persons, seventeen of whom had favored Contra aid and were considered loyal to the president. As a consequence, the Committee essentially ignored the damning evidence against Reagan and chose to do nothing. By that time, Reagan was near the end of his term anyway, so the idea of impeachment and removal was, in a sense, pointless. President George H. W. Bush later pardoned Oliver North and John Poindexter, and a scandal that some view as a greater Constitutional breach than Watergate was essentially swept under the rug.

Reagan and Gorbachev

Richard Nixon, who was an ardent Cold War warrior early in his career, was responsible for normalizing U.S. relations with Communist China. Another ardent Cold War warrior, Ronald Reagan, built a warm camaraderie with his Soviet counterpart, Mikhail Gorbachev. This led not only to improved relations between the United States and the U.S.S.R., while the Soviet leader implemented reforms that would lead to the collapse of the Soviet empire not long after Reagan left office.

In June 1987, President Reagan had given a speech in West Berlin—then a divided city in a divided country—in which he had memorably proclaimed, "Mr. Gorbachev, tear down this wall!" The wall in question was the Berlin Wall, which then separated east and west, preventing those living under communist rule from leaving. Six months later, Gorbachev made a trip to Washington on terms sufficiently friendly so that at one point he plunged into a crowd of Washingtonians and greeted them in the style of an American politician. How did the change come about?

In the first place, Mikhail Gorbachev, chosen to lead his country in 1985, was a new-style Soviet leader, with a keen sense of urgency about repairing his country's economy. Gorbachev was so eager to achieve that goal that he was willing to contemplate bold new initiatives, including a scaling-down of the arms race so that the Soviet Union could invest its resources in non-military ways. Although Gorbachev had intended to maintain some form of socialism and argued that he remained a communist, he implemented twin reforms: *perestroika*, which was essentially capitalist restructuring of the Soviet economy, and *glasnost*, which was a policy of openness and democratization. With the goal of relieving cold war tensions, Gorbachev made numerous unilateral moves: putting a stop to nuclear testing, calling for on-site verification, and unilaterally halting the ongoing installation of Soviet intermediate-range missiles aimed at Europe. Gorbachev removed Andrei Gromyko, a Cold War hard-liner, from his position as foreign minister that Gromyko had held for almost three decades and replaced him with a more accommodating Eduard Shevardnadze. Gorbachev also reached out to the rest of the world, seeking technological assistance from Japan and West Germany.

Secondly, Mrs. Reagan, who had an ever-vigilant eye for burnishing her husband's image, believed that his legacy should be a peaceful one; and, by all accounts, she lobbied her husband to that end. Further, President Reagan had the imagination to meet Gorbachev halfway, although Gorbachev's changes were initially met with great skepticism in the United States. Finally, given the political difficulties engendered by Iran-Contra, Reagan needed the good publicity brought about by the friendly meetings with a former foe.

In any event, the two world leaders met for the first time in Geneva in November 1985. On this occasion they concluded no agreements, but came away with the dawning of a personal connection (although their wives found each other to be insufferable). Raisa Gorbachev was a highly educated woman with a doctorate in philosophy and a broad knowledge of global political issues. Nancy, on the other hand, was an ex-actress with little in-depth political knowledge and a person who consulted astrologers. Consequently, the women found little common ground. Similarly, Mikhail Gorbachev proved to have superior knowledge of global affairs and familiarity with details that caused President Reagan some embarrassment; however, the two experienced a remarkable absence of hostilities.

Their next encounter, a dramatic one, took place in Reykjavik, Iceland in 1986. They came very close to a major reduction in lethal weaponry. Here the sticking point was Reagan's devotion to "Star Wars," or the Strategic Defense Initiative (SDI), an extremely costly and ambitious missile defense program that, the Soviets argued, would destabilize the balance of power. Gorbachev offered what became known as the "grand compromise"—a halt in American research toward "Star Wars" in exchange for major Soviet reductions in nuclear weapons. Reagan, however, refused to consider any proposal that endangered the development of SDI since the entire idea had been his brainchild in 1983. In 1987, however, the breakthrough came. According to Richard Reeves, the Soviets had concluded that Star Wars was never going to work. The two former adversaries agreed to ban all land-based intermediate-range nuclear missiles in Europe in what became known as the Intermediate-Range Nuclear Forces Treaty (INF Treaty). Gorbachev also continued with more changes, agreeing to a United Nations mediation proposal calling for a Soviet troop withdrawal from Afghanistan. Gorbachev then visited the United States in December 1988, and he became the first Soviet Premier since Khrushchev (in 1960) to speak before the United Nations General Assembly. Whereas Khrushchev's speech had included a Cold War shoe-pounding tirade, Gorbachev's included an announcement of huge reductions in Soviet conventional military capabilities. The cold war was over. Reagan and Gorbachev, whatever else might belong to their respective legacies, earned glowing mention in the media in this regard. In retrospect, it is clear that most of the movement came unilaterally from Gorbachev.

Immigration Reform

As we have already learned, the Immigration Act of 1965 brought in many millions of newcomers, far more than Congress had anticipated when it originally passed the law. By the mid-80s, there was growing concern about the influx of undocumented workers. In 1986, Congress passed the Immigration Reform and Control Act. Aimed at slowing down the flow of illegal immigrants, the act imposed sanctions on employers who knowingly hired those without documents. It also offered amnesty to millions of people who had arrived before 1982. What it did not do, however, was "fix" the problem, a problem that occurs in many parts of the world when desperately poor people seek access to a relatively well-off country.

Reagan's Legacy

Even his most severe critics would concede that Ronald Reagan had a profound impact on the nation. Though he spoke warmly of Franklin Delano Roosevelt, Reagan's policies did more to unravel the various safeguards created by the New Deal, in fact, than did those of any president since 1945. Beyond the specifics of policy, Reagan used the bully pulpit of the presidency to convince a goodly proportion of his fellow Americans that "government is the problem." When it comes to tampering with Social Security and reducing the size of the federal government, however, neither he nor any of his successors to date has had much luck. Reagan introduced deregulation into the economy; but the results were mixed. The 1980s witnessed more bank failures than any decade since the Great Depression, and the taxpayers were stuck with a multi-billion dollar bailout of the failed Savings and Loan industry. Reagan also doubled American military spending, but he did so while cutting taxes, thus tripling the national debt from $700 billion in 1981 to over $2 trillion by the time he left office.

Tellingly, Reagan's personal hero among his predecessors was Calvin Coolidge, a choice made on the basis of Coolidge's laissez-faire, pro-business approach to governance. Coolidge, however, presided over balanced budgets in the 1920s due to a high tariff policy—in contrast to the free trading Ronald Reagan. Similar to Coolidge, Reagan's White House years followed a period of rapid social change, change alienating to conservative voters in what are now known as the "red states" owing to their seemingly reliable Republican voting habits. Much as the changes of the progressive era helped set the stage for the success of Republican conservatives in the 1920s, the rapid social changes of the 1960s and 1970s no doubt helped create the constituency for the Reagan Revolution.

Though slightly tainted by the Iran-Contra Scandal, President Reagan largely upheld his reputation as the "Teflon President" (nothing politically negative seemed to stick to him) and has perhaps become even more popular in the years after he left office. As president, Reagan typically charted a general course—whether it was tax cuts, less government, or a stronger military—and delegated authority to others to carry out the larger policy. President Reagan was America's oldest president, falling asleep in Cabinet meetings, taking regular afternoon naps, and, some say, showing the early signs of the Alzheimer's that would eventually take his life. Reagan spent more of his presidency on vacation than any previous president and generally did not arrive for work before 9:00 a.m, after which he first stopped to feed the squirrels before moving on to other business. Chief of Staff James Baker relays a story of how he once chastised the president for not reading a briefing book that Baker had given him the night before in preparation for an important meeting the next day. President Reagan's response was, "Well, Jim, the *Sound of Music* was on last night." If anything, Reagan proved that one could be considered a successful president without being involved in many of the details of public policy.

The Election of 1988

Would Reaganism survive the end of Reagan's presidency? With President Reagan unable to run again in 1988 because of term limits, Vice President George H. W. Bush quickly emerged as the best candidate to continue the Reagan legacy, although he first had to withstand primary election challenges from Senator Bob Dole of Kansas and televangelist Pat Robertson. Bush was visibly irritated at his Republican challengers. There was a general sense in the Bush camp that it was simply "his turn," since he had waited patiently for eight years as a loyal vice president to Reagan during Reagan's presidency. Nevertheless, the Bush camp would be forced to prove their mettle against more formidable Republican opponents than they had hoped. To make matters worse, Bush was not generally viewed as a dynamic personality type and was even referenced frequently in the media as a "wimp." For most Republicans, however, Bush was essentially viewed as "Reagan without the charm," and Bush was expected to continue the low tax, strong defense policies that Reagan had earlier initiated.

Polls, however, suggested that Bush lacked Reagan's popularity among women voters, however, so Bush chose Dan Quayle, a youthful Congressman from Indiana as his running mate in an attempt to appeal to women voters. For their part, the Democrats chose as their nominee the well-respected governor of Massachusetts, Michael Dukakis, a political moderate and son of Greek immigrants and who personified the "self-made man" story that sells so well to the American electorate. The Democrats added Lloyd Bentsen of Texas as the vice presidential nominee to balance the ticket geographically. Indeed, Bush, Dukakis, and Bentsen all had impressive resumes; and even Quayle had served in Congress for several terms. Bush, in particular had been a Congressman, Nixon's Ambassador to the United Nations, Ambassador to China, and the head of the CIA, among other things.

▶Bush chose Dan Quayle, a young Congressman from Indiana as his running mate in an attempt to appeal to women voters. However, Quayle's shortcomings as a public speaker soon established him as the subject of public ridicule and the polls dropped for the Republicans.

The Quayle selection, however, quickly turned against George H.W. Bush. Democrats criticized Quayle for ducking out of the Vietnam War by serving in the Indiana National Guard. Quayle further hurt Bush's campaign with repeated verbal gaffes that essentially became known as "Qualyespeak." Quayle quickly proved himself to be a less than adept public speaker, appearing nervous (even frightened) in front of television cameras, often fumbling his way through prepared speeches, and his extemporaneous comments frequently defied comprehension. For example, Quayle once exclaimed, "It isn't pollution that's harming the environment. It's the impurities in the air and water that are doing it." Quayle also stated in a manner most humorous to Democrats, "I am not part of the problem. I am a Republican." Finally, Quayle defended himself against the critics of his gaffes by stating, "I stand by all the misstatements that I've made."

Quayle and his gaffes soon became the butt of numerous jokes from late-night comedians; and the public and the media characterized Quayle as "stupid"—a label that would prove impossible for the Republicans to remove once it had been affixed.

The Democrats also painted the Republican candidate as the son of privilege, his father Prescott Bush having been both a partner in a top Wall Street firm and a United States Senator. At first, George Bush badly trailed Dukakis in the polls, with critics suggesting that he lacked the common touch required of a good campaigner. Given that Republicans expected their candidate to continue the Reagan legacy, Bush offered no real changes for the future, instead arguing, "We don't need radical new directions."

Subsequently, Bush's staff decided to go negative; and through his negative campaign propaganda, Bush was successfully able to tie Dukakis to most of the libertine social and cultural stances that conservatives had come to identify with "liberals."Without any new and exciting program to promote, Bush instead concentrated on attacking Michael Dukakis' record as governor of Massachusetts. In particular, the Republicans made mileage from their criticism of a furlough program for convicted felons in Massachusetts' state prison system. The Massachusetts furlough program that the Republicans so disparaged was actually initiated by Dukakis' Republican predecessor and simply inherited and continued by Dukakis, a fact that the Republicans neglected to mention. Furthermore, Ronald Reagan had favored a similar policy as governor of California in the 1960s. Nevertheless, the Republicans found and used the case of William Horton, an African-American, who had been serving a life sentence in Massachusetts for murder. Horton was released by the Governor on a weekend furlough—only to assault a couple in Maryland and rape the woman in the process. The Republicans referred to William Horton as "Willie Horton," while pro-Bush groups, not directly affiliated with the Republican Party or the candidate, created commercials featuring Horton's unflattering mug shot that explained how Dukakis favored the furlough program that allowed convicted murderers to be released, only to commit crimes again. Dukakis then did the Republicans a favor with an ill-conceived publicity stunt where he donned a military helmet and rode around in a tank. Dukakis' tank episode backfired since he essentially, to many, looked like a *Saturday Night Live* parody of a military leader in a comedy sketch, and Dukakis quickly dropped in the polls.

By November, the name of Willie Horton was as familiar to American voters as the names of the candidates, owing to a television blitz linking Dukakis to Willie Horton and masterminded by Republican campaign operative Lee Atwater—although Bush himself retained his distance from the attacks. The tactics worked, with Bush winning the popular vote by 53.4 percent to 45.6 percent for Dukakis and winning the Electoral College by 426 to 112. It should also be said that Dukakis, himself, must bear his share of responsibility for his loss because he proved to be a lackluster candidate. The Democrats did retain control of both houses of Congress. Interestingly, shortly before Lee Atwater died of a brain tumor in 1991, he expressed regret about the Willie Horton ads.

The Bush Presidency

Foreign Policy

Within less than a year of Bush's moving into the White House, the world order had begun to change in profound ways, ways unimaginable just a few short years earlier. In June 1989, world attention was focused on China as thousands of Chinese students held pro-democracy demonstrations in Tiananmen Square in Beijing. The visual images of the unarmed students standing up to the Communist government roused feelings of patriotism and sympathy in the United States, but on June 3, Chinese leader Deng Xiao Peng put down the demonstrations with the Chinese military in brutal fashion. Bush responded with an embargo on military goods to China and announced that the United States would not consider reestablishment of good relations with China until the leadership acknowledged the "validity of the pro-democracy movement." On June 20, Bush then halted all contact with the Chinese government.

Bush's "get tough with China" stance, however, turned out to be little more than show and political posturing. One month later, Bush secretly directed National Security Adviser Brent Scowcroft to restore relations. Before the end of the year, Bush lifted the ban on weapons sales to China and approved loans to businesses dealing with China. In December, NSA Brent Scowcroft officially visited Beijing, thus restoring relations, and China retained its Most Favored Nation Trade status.

The Fall of Communism in Eastern Europe

In 1989, the Communist regimes that had dominated political life in Eastern Europe since 1945 collapsed after Soviet leader Mikhail Gorbachev, in July 1989, renounced the right of any nation to interfere with the sovereignty of another, thus Gorbachev's statement essentially let the Eastern European nations know that if they peacefully overthrew their Soviet-imposed communist governments, Gorbachev would not intervene. The Soviet Union was in dire financial straits after seven decades of their inefficient command economy, combined with the excessive Cold War military spending that had essentially bankrupted the country. Consequently, the Soviets no longer had the energy or resources to militarily control Eastern Europe. Without the Soviet tanks to prop up the illegitimate communist governments, the entire Soviet system in Eastern Europe collapsed like a house of cards.

In Poland, the Solidarity Union forced negotiations with the Communists through strikes and demonstrations. The Polish Communists granted free elections, in which some seats were reserved for Communists. When the elections were held, the anti-communist Solidarity Union won an overwhelming majority. Further negotiations between Solidarity and the Communists led to the Communists peacefully giving up power in August 1989. The other governments of Eastern Europe would quickly follow the Polish footsteps in a series of bloodless revolutions (although the Romanian Revolution was not "bloodless" since the Romanian rebels assassinated Communist leader Nikolai Ceaucescu). Communists allowed the destruction of the

Berlin Wall, one of the Cold War's most vivid symbols, on November 9, 1989; and free elections were held in East Germany in the spring of 1990, with the anti-communist Democratic opposition winning easily. The two Germanys united soon after, although German unification was initially opposed by the Bush administration.

Meanwhile, another repressive government, the apartheid regime of South Africa, changed its profile in February 1990. F. W. De Klerk, the white leader, legalized all political parties, including the black-led African National Congress, and ordered the release of the revered black leader Nelson Mandela after his prison stay of twenty-seven years. The pace of the change and the global march toward democratic government was breathtaking.

The Collapse of the U.S.S.R.

In the U.S.S.R., in 1990, new political organizations were forming everywhere, and nationalist groups emerged in all fourteen Republics. Concurrently, street violence erupted all over the U.S.S.R. In the summer of 1990, Boris Yeltsin led radical reformers in a split with the Communist Party. Gorbachev reacted by increasingly turning to the communist hard-liners for support. In April 1991, Lithuania, Estonia, and Latvia all declared independence from the Soviet Union; and Gorbachev did not put down the revolts militarily. Realizing that the breakup of the U.S.S.R. was imminent, Soviet military leaders staged a coup against Gorbachev in August of 1991, and placed Gorbachev under arrest. Gorbachev and his wife were held hostage for four days until Boris Yeltsin led the people in the streets to overthrow the coup and free Gorbachev. The main arms of the Soviet Military turned from their military leaders and supported Yeltsin; communism in Russia was essentially finished.

▶ Communists allowed the destruction of the Berlin Wall, one of the Cold War's most vivid symbols, on November 9, 1989.

On August 22, Gorbachev returned to power in Moscow, but by December 31, 1991, all fourteen of the Soviet Republics had declared their independence. In December, the new leaders of each republic met and agreed to form a new Commonwealth of Independent States. Gorbachev resigned as the president of the U.S.S.R., which ceased to exist on December 31, 1991. With the new governments in Eastern Europe, the Warsaw Pact, the formidable alliance formed in 1955 among eastern European nations, was no longer; and the Russian Federation took the place of the Soviet Union in the United Nations.

As these monumental events of the twentieth century occurred across the waters, George

Bush's approach was to adopt what he called a "status quo plus" approach to these developments. Bush used as his road map Secretary of Defense Dick Cheney's "Forward Defense Policy," where the now-defunct Soviet Union was still viewed as a threat that should be contained. Furthermore, Cheney's Forward Defense Policy called for the continuation of a forward American military presence throughout the globe. Bush essentially accepted the Cheney view that the defunct Soviet Union should still be viewed as a threat. Instead of immediately assisting the Eastern Europeans in their transition to capitalist democracies, Bush was cautious and hesitant to alter the American approach to eastern Europe. Bush, at first, even opposed the reunification of Germany, fearing that a reunited Germany posed another "threat." Bush changed his position on German reunification only after it became clear that reunification was inevitable. It also became clear very quickly that the old Soviet Union and communist threat were clearly gone. Yet Cheney's "Forward Defense Policy," premised on containing the Soviet Union, would remain in place throughout the Bush presidency.

Some scholars argue that such a forward defense policy was no longer necessary due to the end of the Cold War. Many other scholars, however, argue that the United States and the rest of the world had still not quite figured out what the new international system would look like, and that because, for all of its terrors, the Cold War did create a kind of stability. What had, for the moment, replaced the bipolar world divided between the Soviet and the American superpowers—with a scattering of non-aligned states—was the unquestioned hegemony of only one superpower, the United States. That situation caused misgivings, even among countries traditionally friendly to the United States.

Important treaties to reduce arms followed the collapse of the traditional adversary, but the U.S. continued to have an immense defense budget, now justified on the basis of the war on terror. Thus the hoped for "peace dividend" whereby domestic needs might benefit from the cooling-off of the decades-long competition with the Soviet Union has never materialized.

Operation Just Cause

In Central America, President Bush took a more hands-off approach than had Reagan. Indeed, Reagan's foreign policy there had been a notable failure, not having produced any concrete positive results. Despite the greater restraint, however, in December 1989 American troops invaded Panama to capture the Panamanian leader, Manuel Noriega, a longtime drug trafficker, for trial (and conviction) in Florida.

In 1983, Noriega had been the head of the Panamanian military, and he became the Head of State in Panama in 1984, with American CIA help. Noriega had also cooperated with the CIA against the Sandinistas in Nicaragua in the 1980s and was confident that the United States government was a friend who supported his regime, especially since Bush had been so heavily involved in the Iran-Contra affair. In 1988, however, Noriega was indicted by a grand jury in Miami and Tampa, Florida, for drug trafficking, gun running, and money laundering, some of which was associated with his role in the Iran-Contra operation. Noriega's troubles were compounded in November 1989, when he lost the Panamanian election and then followed the defeat at the polls with a refusal to vacate office. Noriega then had his electoral opponents severely beaten, and their battered and bloody images were shown on international television. Given this gross violation of the democratic process and human rights, coupled with his status as a wanted fugitive in Florida, the Bush administration denounced the Noriega government and asked him to step down.

On December 15, 1989, Panama's National Assembly named Noriega Head of Government and proclaimed that Panama was in a "State of War" with the United States. The next day, Panamanian police beat four, off-duty United States servicemen, one of which was shot and killed. The Panamanian police also roughed up one of the officer's wives. That officer and his wife turned out to be personal friends of President George H. W. Bush, who was incensed that the Panamanians had put their hands all over his friend's wife. According to Colin Powell, the attack was very personal to the president, and Bush believed that retribution against Noriega would be a "just cause."

Bush responded with "Operation Just Cause," an American invasion of Panama on December 20, 1989. Twelve thousand American troops landed and combined with the twelve thousand United States troops already present in Panama for the invasion. Noriega attempted to flee from the invading force and hide in the Vatican Embassy, but he surrendered to the United States on December 31. The invasion was considered a smashing success, but twenty-three United States soldiers were killed, as were four thousand Panamanians, many of whom were civilians. Noriega was taken to Miami where he was imprisoned and convicted on drug charges stemming from his 1989 indictment.

▶"Operation Just Cause," was an American invasion of Panama on December 20, 1989. Twelve thousand American troops landed and combined with the twelve thousand United States troops already present in Panama for invasion.

Persian Gulf War

In 1990 came Bush's greatest foreign policy challenge when Iraq invaded the neighboring Kuwait, with Iraq's leader, Saddam Hussein, having made the miscalculation that the United States would look the other way. Iraq had recently concluded its war with Iran, with a loss of some four hundred thousand lives. In the aftermath of the Iran-Iraq war, when Saudi Arabia and Kuwait had flooded the world market with oil, Kuwait continued to produce oil at a rate of 40 percent over OPEC quotas and demanded payment of the $14 billion that Iraq owed to Kuwait (stemming from Kuwaiti loans to Iraq during the Iran-Iraq War). Kuwait's continued production over the OPEC quotas, while it simultaneously demanded debt payments, angered Saddam Hussein of Iraq, who viewed the cheating on OPEC quotas as damaging to Iraq's economy and a hindrance to his ability to pay his international debts of $98 billion. Saddam Hussein was also unenthusiastic about repaying the loans to Kuwait because he believed that his war with Iran had saved Kuwait from imminent takeover by Iranian Shiite revolutionaries. While Kuwait had supported the Iraqi war against Iran with billions in oil money, the Iraqis had paid with their lives; and Saddam Hussein viewed Kuwaiti aid during the war as insufficient and insignificant in comparison with the shedding of Iraqi blood during the War. To make matters worse, Kuwait announced another increase in oil production one day after the Iran-Iraq truce—further angering Saddam Hussein. Saddam declared that he considered cheating on OPEC quotas to be "war on Iraq" and threatened retaliation. Saddam revealed that for every dollar that oil declined, Iraq would lose $1 billion annually. Saddam also, probably accurately, accused Kuwait of horizontal drilling near the Kuwait-Iraq border.

Facing war debts and a disgruntled population, Saddam hoped that access to Kuwaiti oil would shore up his rule. Because of ships sunk in the Shatt al-Arab Waterway during the Iran-Iraq war, Iraq had also lost the use of the waterway, its most important access waterway to the Persian Gulf. Kuwait possessed a fine port and coastline on the Gulf that Saddam Hussein coveted. Thus, Saddam Hussein had a number of motives for an invasion and takeover of Kuwait. A takeover of Kuwait would not only solve some of his debt problems but also would gain him better Gulf access, thus allowing him to shut down Kuwaiti overproduction of oil and force an increase in oil prices.

On June 25, 1990, U.S. Ambassador to Iraq April Glaspie assured Saddam Hussein that the United States would not get involved in a dispute between two Arab neighbors. Glaspie testified before Congress, "I told him we would defend our vital interests, support our friends in the Gulf, and defend their sovereignty and integrity. My main mistake was that I did not realize he was stupid." With what he evidently believed was assurance from Glaspie, Saddam Hussein apparently believed that he could invade his neighbor and the United States would not intervene. On August 2, 1990, Saddam Hussein's Iraqi army invaded Kuwait, and the conquest and occupation was completed in only eight hours. The United Nations Security Council reacted to the Iraqi aggression by condemning the invasion and voting 14 to 0 to demand withdrawal. The United States and the U.S.S.R. issued a Joint Statement of Condemnation, and the United Nations Security Council unanimously imposed trade sanctions. Saddam countered with an attempt to gain sympathy from his other Arab neighbors by announcing a peace proposal that involved the withdrawal of Israel from the occupied territories while Saddam withdrew from Kuwait.

In response to the invasion, President Bush and the members of his administration engaged in skillful diplomacy to convince not only traditional American allies but also most of the Arab and Islamic world to support his call for an economic boycott of Iraq. George Bush denounced Saddam Hussein's peace proposal, arguing that there could be no "linkage" between the Iraqi invasion of Kuwait and the Israeli/Palestinian issue. Meanwhile, *Amnesty International* published a report portraying widespread arrests, torture, and summary executions in Kuwait. Bush demanded that Iraq withdraw from Kuwait; and when Iraq did not do so, he immediately began "Operation Desert Shield," building United States troop strength in Saudi Arabia to 580,000 in preparation for an invasion.

The war in the Persian Gulf, however, was a tough sell in Congress, even though the Iraqis had made an unprovoked attack on Kuwait. Memories of Vietnam were still quite fresh, and the vote revealed how divided Congress was. Bush's request for authorization of help for Kuwait passed the House by 250 to 183 and the Senate by 52 to 47. When war came, the assault on Iraq was of overwhelming force; and the hostilities only lasted until March 1.

On January 16, 1991, after Iraq had failed to meet the American deadline for the withdrawal of Kuwait, the United States began a forty-two-day bombing operation in Iraq and Kuwait. On January 18, Saddam fired twelve SCUD missiles at Israel. He fired three more on January 22, in an attempt to goad Israel into the war and, thereby, divide the Arab coalition that had joined the United States against him. Israel denounced the attacks, but realizing that

▶ When Iraq refused to withdraw from Kuwait, President Bush immediately began "Operation Desert Shield," building United States troop strength in Saudi Arabia to 580,000 in preparation for an invasion. Shown at left, M1A1 Abrams main battle tanks move out on a mission during Operation Desert Storm.

any Israeli action against Iraq could unite all Arab nations against them, stayed out of the war so as not to divide the coalition that Bush had forged.

In an attempt to stave off the imminent destruction of Saddam's army, at 12:00 Greenwich mean time (GMT) on February 23, Iraq announced the acceptance of a Soviet peace plan that called for immediate and unconditional withdrawal from Kuwait. In spite of his knowledge of this development, at 18:00 GMT, George Bush ordered General Norman Schwarzkopf to expel the Iraqis from Kuwait. The ground war to expel the Iraqi military from Kuwait followed on February 24 and took one hundred hours. At 10:00 GMT February 24, the United States launched its ground war. At 21:30 GMT February 24, Saddam ordered a withdrawal from Kuwait. Retreating Iraqis then set over six hundred Kuwaiti oil wells ablaze in one of the worst environmental disasters in human history. The black petroleum cloud that developed over Kuwait was clearly visible from satellites in outer space. By noon on February 26, the Iraqi troops had withdrawn from Kuwait City and its suburbs, and a long convoy of Iraqi vehicles was on its way to Basra along a six-lane highway north of Kuwait City. As it approached Mitla Ridge, twenty miles north of Kuwait City, the Iraqi convoy was hit in a massive attack by U.S. ground-attack aircraft. U.S. planes would attack the convoy for the next forty hours until the truce at 08:00, local time, on February 28.

The end came all the more quickly because President Bush and his advisors decided to stop short of trying to topple Saddam Hussein. They felt, it seems, that they could not carry the coalition along with them, had they attempted regime change; and they also wondered who might replace Saddam. The toll of the war was disproportionate with some forty thousand Iraqis dying as opposed to 240 members of the allied troops. The Security Council of the United Nations then demanded that Iraq provide information about its various weapons systems, pursuant to Resolution 687. Most Iraqis died in the bombings (thirty

▶After the United States launched its ground war, Saddam ordered a withdrawal from Kuwait. Retreating Iraqis then set over six hundred Kuwaiti oil wells ablaze in one of the worst environmental disasters in human history. The black petroleum cloud that developed over Kuwait was clearly visible from satellites in outer space.

thousand in the convoy alone), but some were buried in their bunkers by United States bulldozers when the Iraqis were given orders to surrender or suffocate. The American public generally approved of the attack on the retreating convoy, but many Arabs did not; and the event was reported in the Arab media as "the most terrible harassment of a retreating army from the air in the history of warfare."

Before the Iraqis fled Kuwait, Iraqi soldiers had looted virtually everything of value, even eating most of the animals at the Kuwaiti National Zoo and thus further justifying the war to the American people. Although many conservatives, such as future Undersecretary of State Paul Wolfowitz, argued that the United States military should go all the way into Iraq and remove Saddam Hussein from power, Bush would not do so because the United Nations Resolution did not call for ousting Hussein. For Bush to do so would surely destroy the international coalition. Bush also recognized that an impotent Iraq would make Iran the most powerful military nation in the region without a chief rival; hence, leaving Saddam Hussein in power made sense in the Persian Gulf balance of power. Ousting Hussein, as George W. Bush would discover in the next decade, would also mean a costly long-term occupation army with many more potential casualties and "another Vietnam" that the elder Bush was determined not to repeat. Finally, Bush had hoped that Saddam's own military officers would overthrow him, but after the war Saddam carried out an internal purge on all of his political opposition within Iraq. Gruesome videotape was also circulated throughout Iraq and the Middle East that showed Saddam's executed military officers hanging on meat hooks, thus discouraging others from coup attempts. The Security Council of the United Nations then demanded that Iraq provide information about its various weapons systems, pursuant to Resolution 687.

Immediately after the war, Saddam Hussein also faced a Shiite uprising in the south of Iraq that was aided by Iran. Iran sent not only supplies and weapons but also thousands of "volunteers" that crossed the border into Iraq. On March 9, 1991, Saddam sent his Republican Guard into the South to put down the Shiite rebellion. The United States did not intervene because the Bush administration favored Saddam Hussein over the Shiite revolutionaries. After all, the United States had aided Saddam Hussein in his war with Iran in the 1980s, specifically to prevent a takeover by Shiite revolutionaries. An estimated thirty thousand people died in Saddam's crushing defeat of the Shiite rebellion, and seventy thousand Shiites fled to Iran. The rebellion was over in a week. National Security adviser Brent Scowcroft told ABC News:

> "I frankly wish the uprising hadn't happened. I envisioned a post-war government being a military government … It's the colonel with the brigade patrolling his palace that's going to get Saddam if someone gets him."

Similarly, Richard Haas, then director for Near East Affairs on the NSC stated, "Our policy is to get rid of Saddam, not his regime." Obviously, Democracy (or the lack of it) in Iraq was not the highest American priority in 1992.

Simultaneous with the Iraqi Shiite rebellion in 1991, Kurdish nationalists rebelled in northern Iraq as a one hundred thousand-man Kurdish Auxiliary force in Saddam's army changed sides and turned on Saddam. Turkey feared that an independent Kurdistan in Iraq might lead Kurds in Turkey to also revolt and demand that part of Turkey be united with a new Kurdistan. Consequently, Turkey urged President Bush not to intervene in the Iraqi Kurdish rebellion. Bush viewed the rebellion as an Iraqi civil war with potential as another Vietnam that should be avoided. The United States again remained on the sidelines while Saddam's army quickly put down the rebellion, with the result that an estimated 1.5 million Kurds were forced to flee to Turkey.

In 1992, President George H. W. Bush was voted out of office, and Iraq began challenging the no-fly zones imposed by the United States. The lame-duck President Bush, however, continued his resolve to keep Saddam subdued. In December 1992, the United States shot down an Iraqi MIG fighter. On January 10, 1993, Iraq refused to allow United Nations inspectors to use airspace south of the 32nd parallel as demanded by the United States. The United States responded on January 13 by bombing five Iraqi air bases; on January 17, the United States hit an Iraqi factory with a cruise missile. The next day, United States' jets hit seventy-five Iraqi targets south of the 32nd parallel of southern Iraq. On January 21, Baghdad announced acceptance of United Nations inspections so that the new American president could "study the no-fly zone." Thus was the status of the American-Iraqi situation upon the inauguration of Bill Clinton in January 1993.

Domestic Issues

Early in George H. W. Bush's presidency, the new Republican Executive quickly revealed that he was not genuinely the flag bearer for the Reagan legacy. Although Bush had well-played the part of the vice presidential loyalist during Reagan's tenure in office, Bush demonstrated his private disdain for his presidential predecessor when he quietly instituted a purge of Reagan loyalists from the federal executive branch. In the words of one close friend of Ronald Reagan, there was a "systematic purge" ... of anyone with any association with the Reagan-Nixon-Goldwater wing of the Party. Bush did not, however, favor a complete abandonment of the conservative "less government" mantra; and he used the veto thirty-six times during his tenure in office to block Congressional bills that would have lifted abortion restrictions, extended unemployment benefits, raised taxes, mandated family and medical leave for workers, and reformed campaign financing. The veto of such measures was not only consistent with Reaganism, but also was perhaps to be expected, given "divided government" with Democratic control of Congress and Republican control of the presidency.

Bush, however, quickly embarked on a more activist approach to governing and implemented a much more hands-on management approach than Reagan. For example, billing himself as the "Environmental President," Bush signed the Clean Air Act of 1990, perhaps the strongest, most comprehensive environmental law in history. The Clean Air Act required power plants to cut sulfur dioxide emissions by more than 50 percent by the year 2000, and oil companies were required to develop cleaner-burning gasoline. Clearly, the Clean Air Act was hardly consistent with the deregulatory push of the Reagan administration and was, instead, the same type of federal government regulation of industry that conservatives had been fighting against for decades.

The Americans with Disabilities Act

On July 26, 1990, President Bush signed into law the Americans with Disabilities Act, a law that drew upon and completed earlier civil rights activism by members of other disadvantaged groups. For decades, the disabled had organized and protested, and this law was the result of their years of effort. Not only did it prohibit discrimination against the handicapped in employment, it also mandated that many types of buildings and facilities contain provisions for disabled access. Americans have now become used to the sight of curb cuts, for example, which facilitate the movement of those in wheelchairs. It should be noted that the law, particularly as it relates to issues of employment, has generated litigation, as courts struggle to refine the meaning of terms such as "reasonable" accommodation or "essential" tasks of the job. Conservative opponents argued that ADA constituted a massive unfunded federal mandate to the states that forced states and local governments to spend billions in order to ensure that public accommodations were handicapped-accessible. The measure was, therefore, not only a violation of conservative laissez-faire ideology and a reversal of Reagan's "deregulation," it also eroded state sovereignty by removing state discretion concerning the handicapped and thus violated the traditional conservative preference for the preservation of states' rights in juxtaposition with national power.

An Eruption of Rage in Los Angeles

In March 1991 police in a tough neighborhood in the San Fernando Valley section of Los Angeles gave chase to a speeding car. When they succeeded in stopping its African American occupant, Rodney King, he resisted arrest and appeared to be intoxicated. The police subdued him with great use of force, force that looked like a police beating as captured on

▶ On July 26, 1990, President Bush signed into law the Americans with Disabilities Act. The law not only prohibited discrimination against the handicapped in employment, it also mandated that many types of buildings and facilities contain provisions for disabled access.

video by a nearby resident. The video was widely aired, and as a result four policemen were charged with the beatings. The trial, however, was then moved to nearby Simi Valley in Ventura County, a largely white enclave. Testimony during the televised trial revealed many less than flattering facts about the Los Angeles Police Department (LAPD). For example, more than one white chief of police, who had been insensitive about race and thus perpetuated a culture inappropriate to a multiethnic city, had led the LAPD. Moreover, police training was revealed to be woefully inadequate.

In April 1992, three of the four policemen were found not guilty of using excessive force, and the all-white jury deadlocked on the fourth decision. At that point the city's black neighborhoods, particularly South Central Los Angeles, erupted in several days of fighting, looting, and destruction. Such neighborhoods had long been breeding grounds for despair, it should be noted, with high unemployment and other indicators of social distress. Rodney King himself ultimately appeared on television to appeal for calm, saying, "Can we all get along?" When the rioting finally ended, fifty-five people had lost their lives, and twenty-three hundred had been injured. With some eight hundred buildings destroyed, there had been an estimated $1 billion worth of property damage. During the fighting, the racial fissures of Los Angeles manifested themselves in ugly ways, such as blacks against the Korean Americans who owned small shops, for example.

On the third night of the riots, President Bush addressed a national television audience and virtually promised that there would be subsequent federal prosecution based on civil rights issues, prosecution which did ensue. In April 1993, a trial on federal charges of civil rights violations ended with two of the four officers having been found guilty. The media were careful not to sensationalize this trial, and the city remained calm when the verdict was announced.

▶ The trial of the fourth police officer involved in the Rodney King arrest was deadlocked. At that point South Central Los Angeles, erupted in several days of fighting, looting, and destruction.

The Clarence Thomas Nomination

The well-respected civil rights lawyer Thurgood Marshall, the first African American to serve on the nation's highest court, had been appointed to the United States Supreme Court by Lyndon Johnson in 1967. By 1991, at the age of eighty-three, he was ready to step down. He would be difficult to replace, however, for many reasons. President Bush, whose choice of David Souter for the court in 1990 had sailed through, opted to nominate an African American conservative with little judicial experience, Clarence Thomas, to replace Marshall. Democrats on the Senate Judiciary Committee found themselves in a quandary during the hearings about Thomas's nomination. They did not want to appear racist in going after Thomas's relatively slim resume (he had only been a federal judge for eighteen months); but, on the other hand, they were leery of Bush's choice because Thomas had spoken out against affirmative action and was suspected of being opposed to *Roe v. Wade*. To make matters worse for Bush, the National Association for the Advancement of Colored People (NAACP), the leading organization for the championing of African-American causes, opposed Thomas' confirmation.

Just as the hearings appeared to be drawing to a close, a new witness came before the committee: Professor Anita Hill of the University of Oklahoma Law School, also African American. She testified that when she had worked for Thomas in the 1980s, first as his assistant in the U.S. Department of Education and then in the Equal Employment Opportunities Commission, he had repeatedly used crudely sexual language in speaking to her, language that had been unpleasant and unwelcome to her. Specifically, Hill alleged that Thomas asked her to view pornographic movies with him and once handed her a soft drink can with a pubic hair on the top. When testifying on his own behalf, Thomas alleged that he was the victim of a "high-tech lynching," thus bringing up the racial issue that Democrats had been so eager to avoid.

▶ Professor Anita Hill testfying against the Clarence Thomas Supreme Court nomination.

The country was riveted by the controversy, with both Hill and Thomas having their proponents. Certain Republicans went on the attack. "She's a little bit nutty, and a little bit slutty," said one. Polls at the time showed that Thomas had the majority of public opinion on his side. The Senate Judiciary Committee investigated the hearings, but dismissed Hill's charges after three days of nationally televised hearings in which other women who came forward with similar allegations were not allowed to testify. In the end, the Senate narrowly confirmed his nomination by a vote of 52 to 48.

Though Hill appeared to have lost in the court of public opinion, in fact, the controversy galvanized the women who were on her side, many of whom had themselves been the victims of sexual harassment. What was particularly troubling to the women, by all accounts, was the fact that the Senate Judiciary Committee was all-male, not surprising given the breakdown in the Senate of ninety-eight men and two women. In 1992, a number of women set out to rectify that imbalance.

The Year of the Woman

If 1980 was the year in which a gender gap showed up in election returns for the first time, then 1992 was the year in which the promise of having a female voting bloc became fully manifest. An unprecedented number of women ran for office—chiefly as Democrats, though that has begun to change in the early twenty-first century—and an unprecedented number won.

In 1916 Republican Jeannette Rankin of Montana had been elected to the House of Representatives, the first woman in the world to be elected to a national legislature. In 1922 Georgia's Rebecca Latimer Felton served one day in the Senate, appointed to the position as a token by the governor of Georgia in a tricky maneuver to gain favor with newly enfranchised women en route to the accession of the "real" male senator. Progress for women office-holders was slow, both in achieving election and—in the unusual event that they did—in feeling free to articulate issues of concern to other women. Not only did women not vote as a bloc but also a smaller percentage of them voted at all compared with male voters, a pattern that did not change until the 1960s. In 1990, former Senator Margaret Chase Smith told an interviewer: "I never was a woman candidate," as she reflected on her congressional career of more than thirty years, a career that began in the 1940s. "Had I been a woman candidate I never would have been elected."

The birth of modern feminism would begin to induce more women to run than in the past, a few for major office. In 1974 Ella Grasso of Connecticut became the first woman to be elected as governor of a state in her own right—that is, not following the death of a husband or acting as a surrogate for a husband unable to run himself. In 1990 Ann Richards of Texas was elected as governor, a particularly noteworthy race because she had "run as a woman," even going so far as to pose with her hairdresser for campaign literature.

The year 1992, however, was different. That year women raised money for women candidates in unprecedented amounts, drawing on a well of grass-roots anger about the treatment of Anita Hill. The election in November produced tremendous progress and many firsts. Women in the House of Representatives had gone from twenty-nine to forty-eight, while the number of female senators had gone from two to six. Carol Moseley-Braun of Illinois became the first African American woman to be elected to the Senate. California became the first state to be represented by two women in the Senate, Dianne Feinstein and Barbara Boxer. Nydia Velasquez of New York became the first Puerto Rican woman elected to the House, and Lucille Roybal-Allard of California the first Mexican American woman. Women were also elected to state legislatures in unprecedented numbers, with the state of Washington leading the pack with a legislature that was almost 40 percent female. When the new Congress convened in 1993, both Moseley-Braun and Feinstein were appointed to serve on the Senate Judiciary Committee.

Though the pace of change has slowed, women have continued to make progress. As of mid-2006 there were fourteen women in the Senate and sixty-seven in the House. Even more impressive is the fact that there are eight women governors, impressive because there have only been twenty-six women governors in all of American history.

Elements of a One-Term Presidency

During the short Gulf War President Bush was enormously popular, achieving a 91 percent approval rating, at the time, according to one poll. Despite effective leadership on several fronts, he seemed as unable to cope with the economy as had Jimmy Carter. With the nation entering a full-fledged recession following the Persian Gulf War, with real estate prices and sales stagnating, with unemployment climbing to eight percent, and saddled with a growing deficit, Bush effected a compromise budget with congressional Democrats that called for tax increases. Because he had pledged in 1988, "Read my lips; no new taxes," his pragmatism once in office left him vulnerable to enemies in both parties. The sagging economy was the issue that Democrat Bill Clinton would ride to victory in 1992. The era of Reaganism and Republican dominance was seemingly over.

Chapter Review 31

Summary

As a couple of Hollywood movie personalities, Ronald Reagan and his wife Nancy infused glamour into the White House that had been missing since the Kennedy administration. Once in office, Ronald Reagan attempted to construct a pro-business government, instituting tax cuts in spite of the fact that the government was already running deficits. Reagan also believed the United States had fallen behind the Soviet Union in the arms race, so he doubled the defense budget with the result that the national debt tripled during Reagan's eight years in the White House, but ironically, the economic recovery followed the nation's worst recession since the Great Depression in 1982.

In 1981, President Reagan showed his resolve when he fired the striking air traffic controllers in the PATCO strike for violating their contracts. That same year, Reagan appointed the first woman to the Supreme Court in Sandra Day O'Connor.

In foreign policy, Reagan renewed the Cold War, denouncing the Soviet Union as the "Evil Empire" and doubling spending on defense. In January, 1983, Reagan antagonized the Soviet Union with his Strategic Defense Initiative, a proposal to build an anti-ballistic missile system based on space-based lasers. That same year, Reagan faced foreign policy challenges elsewhere as Islamic extremists blew up the U.S. Embassy in Lebanon, killing sixty-three, and Hezbollah suicide bombers blew up the American marine compound in Lebanon with a truck bomb that killed 241 U.S. marines. Two days later, Reagan made Americans feel good again with a military invasion of Grenada in the Caribbean to oust a communist group that had taken over the island.

Under the Reagan Doctrine, the United States was to support "freedom fighters" against communism everywhere. When the communist Sandinistas won the elections in Nicaragua in 1984, Congress banned aid to the Contra rebel group. President Reagan and his administration then continued to aid the Contras covertly in violation of the congressional ban. Aid to the Contras was in part funded by arms sales to Iran (also banned by Congress) in exchange for the release of American hostages. Reagan's popularity prevented Congress from fully prosecuting the president and other members of his administration, but the president had clearly committed impeachable offenses.

Meanwhile, communism was crumbling in Eastern Europe as Soviet Premier Mikhail Gorbachev instituted glasnost and Perestroika. Gorbachev also signed the INF Treaty with the U.S. agreeing to arms limitations on intermediate range nuclear weapons. In 1989, Gorbachev announced that no country had the right to interfere in the sovereignty of another and the people of Eastern Europe then overthrew their communist governments knowing that the Red Army would not intervene. In the Soviet Union two years later, Gorbachev was ousted in a military coup only to be saved two days later when Boris Yeltsin led a rebel faction of the Soviet Army and the Soviet people to free Gorbachev. On December 31, 1991, the Soviet Union dissolved and communist rule in Russia was no more.

In 1988, Reagan's vice president, George H.W. Bush, defeated Michael Dukakis for the presidency and continued the Reagan Revolution. Bush, however, would also pass the Clean Air Act and Americans with Disabilities Act that were contradictory with the Reagan idea of limited government.

In 1989 when Manuel Noriega in Panama refused to step down and had his opponents beaten after losing an election, Bush launched Operation Just Cause and ousted the Panamanian leader. Two years later when Saddam Hussein's Iraq invaded Kuwait, Bush responded with Operation Desert Shield, an American military buildup in the Persian Gulf followed by Operation Desert Storm, a forty-two-day bombing campaign and one hundred hour ground campaign to oust the Iraqi army from Kuwait. Afterward, Bush allowed Saddam Hussein to brutally repress Shiite uprisings in the South and Kurdish uprisings in the North in the interest of stability in Iraq.

Domestically, the conscience of the nation was shaken in March 1991 when a video of the beating of African-American Rodney King by Los Angeles Police was released in the media. The next year, when four policemen involved were acquitted on charges of excessive force, Los Angeles erupted into violent rioting that led to the deaths of fifty-three people and did not stop before the National Guard was called in to restore order.

Earlier, in October, 1991 the U.S. Senate confirmed Clarence Thomas as George H.W. Bush's appointee to the Supreme Court after University of Oklahoma Law Professor Anita Hill had accused Thomas of sexual harassment during the confirmation hearings. The Thomas confirmation preceded the "Year of the Woman" in 1992 when Carol Moseley Braun became the first African-American woman to serve in the U.S. Senate and forty-eight women were elected to seats in the U.S. House of Representatives. Women would also figure prominently in the election of Bill Clinton as president in November, 1992 and the era of Republican dominance seemed at an end.

Chronological Time Line

1911 Ronald Reagan was born in Tampico, Illinois.

1932 Ronald Reagan graduated from Eureka College.

1941 Ronald Reagan was president of the Screen Actors Guild and supplied names of suspected communists to the FBI.

1949 Ronald Reagan and Jane Wyman divorced.

1949 Ronald Reagan met Nancy Davis, and helped remove her name from the list of blacklisted communist actors.

1952 Reagan married Nancy Davis.

1962 Ronald Reagan switched political parties from the Democrats to the Republicans.

Chapter Review (cont'd)

Time Line (cont'd)

1966 Ronald Reagan was elected governor of California.

1976 Ronald Reagan lost to Gerald Ford in the Republican Primary.

1979 Communist Sandinistas overthrew the Samoza regime in Nicaragua.

1980 November: Ronald Reagan defeated Jimmy Carter in a landslide to become president of the United States.

1981 Economic Recovery Tax Act in 1981 reduced income tax rates by 25 percent over three years.

1981 August: Nearly twelve thousand PATCO air traffic controllers went on strike and were quickly fired by Ronald Reagan.

1981 Reagan appointed Sandra Day O'Connor to the Supreme Court.

1981 Reagan began a defense buildup that exceeded Vietnam War spending as a percentage of the economy.

1982 Deepest economic recession since the Great Depression.

1983 January: Ronald Reagan introduced the Strategic Defense Initiative (SDI) or "Star Wars."

1983 On April 18, a suicide truck bomber destroyed the U.S. Embassy in Beirut, killing sixty-three people.

1983 September: Korean Air Lines flight #007 was shot down by a Soviet fighter plane over Soviet air space, killing all 269 people on board.

1983 On October 23, a suicide truck bomber blew up the U.S. marine compound at the Beirut airport, killing 241 U.S. marines.

1983 On October 25, U.S. forces invaded Grenada to eliminate communist presence on the Island, killing nineteen Americans and sixty Cubans and Grenada natives.

1984 Communist Sandinistas won election in Nicaragua and Congress cut off aid to the Contras.

1984–1986 President Reagan covertly continued aid to the Contras in violation of Congressional mandate.

1984 November: Ronald Reagan won reelection against Walter Mondale and Geraldine Ferraro in a landslide with over 58 percent of the popular vote.

Time Line (cont'd)

1985	On March 11, Mikhail Gorbachev became General Secretary of the Communist Party in the Soviet Union.
1985	July: Reagan Administration began a secret program to trade arms to Iran for the release of American hostages.
1985	November: First meeting occurred between Reagan and Mikhail Gorbachev in Geneva.
1985	December: Reagan announced the "Reagan Doctrine" or U.S. government support of "Freedom fighters" against communism.
1986	Reagan appointed William Rehnquist Chief Justice of the Supreme Court.
1986	Reagan appointed Antonin Scalia, a devout Catholic, to the Supreme Court.
1986	October: Summit between Reagan and Gorbachev at Reykjavik, Iceland
1986	On November 6, Congress passed the Immigration Reform and Control Act.
1987	Senate rejected Reagan's appointment to the Supreme Court, Robert Bork.
1986	October: Surgeon General C. Everett Coop released the government's first public report on AIDS.
1987	June: Reagan's "Tear Down this Wall" speech
1987	On October 19, was "Black Monday," the stock market crash.
1987	On November 13, Reagan publicly admitted that he had ordered the covert Iran-Contra operation under John Poindexter and Lt. Colonel Oliver North, though he denied that the U.S. had sold arms to Iran in exchange for hostages.
1987	On November 21, Attorney General Ed Meese launched an investigation of the Iran-Contra Scandal.
1987	On December 8, Reagan and Gorbachev signed the Intermediate-Range Nuclear Forces (INF) Treaty.
1988	Senate confirmed Reagan's Supreme Court appointee, Anthony Kennedy.

Chapter Review (cont'd)

Time Line (cont'd)

1988 The *Los Angeles Times* poll revealed that 57 percent of religious fundamentalists favored a quarantine of people with AIDS.

1988 On May 15, Reagan stated that the arms-to-the-Contras covert scheme was "my idea to begin with."

1988 November: George H.W. Bush defeated Michael Dukakis in the presidential election.

1988 December: Mikhail Gorbachev visited the U.S. and spoke at the UN General Assembly.

1989 On June 3, the Chinese government put down Democracy demonstrations in Tiananmen Square.

1989 July: Mikhail Gorbachev renounced the right of any nation to interfere with the sovereignty of another.

1989 August: Communists peacefully gave up power in Poland.

1989 On November 9, Communists allowed the destruction of the Berlin Wall.

1989 On December 20, the U.S. began Operation "Just Cause" to oust Panamanian leader Manuel Noriega.

1990 February: White South African leader F.W. De Klerk legalized all political parties and released Nelson Mandela after twenty-seven years in prison.

1990 On July 26, Congress passed the Americans with Disabilities Act.

1990 On August 2, Saddam Hussein's Iraqi army invaded Kuwait.

1990 Sandinistas were voted out in Nicaragua.

1991 On January 16, the U.S. began forty-two days of bombing operations in Iraq and Kuwait.

1991 On February 24, George H.W. Bush ordered the commencement of the ground war against Iraq.

1991 On February 28, truce ended the Persian Gulf War.

1991 On March 3, a private video was taken of Los Angeles police beating Rodney King.

1991 On March 9, Saddam Hussein sent his Republican Guard into southern Iraq to quell a Shiite rebellion.

Time Line (cont'd)

1991 April: Latvia, Estonia, and Lithuania all declared independence from the Soviet Union.

1991 On August 19, Soviet military leaders staged a coup and placed Mikhail Gorbachev under arrest.

1991 On August 22, Gorbachev was returned to power after Boris Yeltsin led factions of the Soviet army to reverse the coup.

1991 On October 15, 1991, the U.S. Senate confirmed Clarence Thomas' nomination to the Supreme Court.

1991 On November 7, basketball star Earvin "Magic" Johnson announced he was HIV positive.

1991 All fourteen Soviet republics declared their independence, and the Soviet Union no longer existed.

1992 On April 29, police were acquitted of using excessive force in the Rodney King beating, sparking riots in Los Angeles that resulted in fifty-three deaths.

1992 November: Carol Moseley Braun became the first African-American woman elected to the U.S. Senate.

1992 November: Bill Clinton defeated George W. Bush and Ross Perot to become the 42nd president of the United States.

Key Terms

Nancy Reagan: Second wife of Ronald Reagan, actress, and First Lady of the United States 1981–1989

PATCO: Professional Air Traffic Controllers Association that went on strike in August of 1981 and were fired for breach of contract by President Reagan

Sandra Day O'Connor: First female Supreme Court Justice appointed by Ronald Reagan in 1981

Robert Bork: Conservative judge appointed to the Supreme Court by Ronald Reagan that was not confirmed by the Senate

The Great Crash: Stock market crash of October 19, 1987, when the New York Stock Exchange dropped 22.6 percent in one day

Deregulation: Ronald Reagan's program of deregulation of banking and other segments of the economy

Savings-and-Loan collapse: The failure of over seven hundred Savings and Loans between 1985 and 1995 that cost taxpayers over $160 billion due to federally insured deposits

"Evil Empire": Ronald Reagan's reference to the Soviet Union

Chapter Review (cont'd)

Key Terms (cont'd)

SDI: Strategic Defense Initiative or "Star Wars," Ronald Reagan's plan to create a laser weapons anti-ballistic missile system

Reagan Doctrine: Reagan's assertion that the United States would support "freedom fighters" anywhere in the world fighting against communism

PLO: The Palestinian Liberation Organization that sought the expulsion of Jews from Palestine and the establishment of an Arab state in Palestine

Menachem Begin: Israeli leader that signed the Camp David Accords

Hezbollah: Iranian-backed Shiite revolutionary group that was responsible for the truck bombing of the U.S. marine compound in Lebanon in 1983

Grenada: Island off the coast of Venezuela taken over by communists in 1983 and liberated by the U.S. military on the orders of Ronald Reagan

"Freedom Fighters": Ronald Reagan's term to describe an group fighting against communism anywhere

Jose Napoleon Duarte: Right-wing dictator of El Salvador in the 1980s aided by the Reagan Adminstration

Contras: Rebels in Nicaragua and Honduras in the 1980s aided by the U.S. government of Ronald Reagan against the communist Sandinista government in Nicaragua

Sandinistas: Communist group that ruled Nicaragua during the years of the Reagan Administration

C. Everett Koop: Reagan's Surgeon General that informed the nation of the dangers of AIDS

Iran-Contra Affair: Late 1980s scandal where the Reagan administration violated Congressional bans with arms shipments to Contra rebels in Nicaragua and Arms sales to Iran in exchange for the release of American hostages

Oliver North: Marine Corp Lieutenant Colonel that ran much of the Iran-Contra operations from the White House basement

John Poindexter: Deputy National Security Advisor in the Reagan Administration in charge of the Arms-to-Contras operation

Pat Robertson: Televangelist and Republican candidate for president in 1988

Robert McFarlane: National Security Advisor in the Reagan Administration during the Iran-Contra operation

Mikhail Gorbachev: Premier of the Soviet Union that instituted glasnost, perestroika, and the principle that one state cannot violate the sovereignty of another, thus leading to the end of communism in Eastern Europe

Raisa Gorbachev: Wife of Mikhail Gorbachev and scholar of international politics

Teflon President: Label given to Ronald Reagan in the media because the scandals that rocked his presidency never completely destroyed his popularity as Watergate had with Richard Nixon

Glasnost: Mikhail Gorbachev's program of "openness" or free speech in the Soviet Union

Perestroika: Mikhail Gorbachev's program of capitalist economic restructuring in the Soviet Union

Michael Dukakis: Greek immigrant, governor of Massachusetts, and Democratic candidate for president in 1988

Key Terms (cont'd)

Keating 5: Senators that took campaign contributions from junk-bond dealer Charles Keating in return for promises to help Keating with his legal battles against the U.S. government

Dan Quayle: Congressman from Indiana and vice presidential running mate of George H.W. Bush in 1988 (eventually vice president of the United States) that was prone to verbal gaffes

Willie Horton: Subject of a Republican smear campaign in the 1988 election, Horton was an African-American who had been serving a life sentence in Massachusetts for murder, but was released by the Governor on a weekend furlough, only to assault a couple in Maryland and rape the woman in the process.

Solidarity: Polish workers' union that pushed for democracy in Poland

Tiananmen Square: Square in Beijing, China, where young Democracy demonstrators defied the Chinese government in 1989

Boris Yeltsin: Popular Russian leader that led the Army and the people in the streets in August 1991 to free Mikhail Gorbachev, who had been arrested by the Soviet military

Dick Cheney: George H.W. Bush's Secretary of Defense that argued for a Forward Defense Policy and containment of the Soviet Union even though it no longer existed

Forward Defense Policy: The view of Defense Secretary Dick Cheney that the now-defunct Soviet Union still should be viewed as a threat that should be contained. Cheney also called for the continuation of a forward American military presence throughout the globe

Manuel Noriega: Leader of Panama that was ousted by Operation Just Cause in 1989

Operation Just Cause: George H.W. Bush's name for the operation to oust Panamanian President Manuel Noriega in 1989

Saddam Hussein: Leader of Iraq during the Persian Gulf War

Persian Gulf War: 1991 American war to expel the Iraqi army from Kuwait after Saddam Hussein's Iraqi army had invaded Kuwait in 1990

April Glaspie: American Ambassador to Iraq that informed Saddam Hussein that the U.S. would not get involved in a dispute between Arab states

Operation Desert Shield: George H.W. Bush's military buildup in Saudi Arabia prior to the Persian Gulf War.

SCUD: Missiles fired by Iraq against Israel during the Persian Gulf War

Shiite Rebellion: 1991 insurrection by Shiites in Iraq against the government of Saddam Hussein put down by Saddam Hussein's Iraqi military after the U.S. allowed Saddam to fly attack helicopters in the "No Fly Zone"

Brent Scowcroft: National Security Advisor under George H.W. Bush

Kurdish Rebellion: 1991 insurrection by Kurds in Northern Iraq put down by the Iraqi army under Saddam Hussein

Clean Air Act: 1990 Act of Congress that set new Clean Air standards

Americans with Disabilities Act: 1990 Act of Congress that required states to ensure access to public accommodations for those with disabilities

Chapter Review (cont'd)

Key Terms (cont'd)

Rodney King: African-American man whose beating by Los Angeles police in 1990 sparked a riot in 1991 that killed fifty-three people when the police were acquitted in King's beating

Anita Hill: University of Oklahoma Law Professor that claimed sexual harassment by Supreme Court nominee Clarence Thomas in 1991

Clarence Thomas: George H.W. Bush's nominee to the Supreme Court in 1991 that was accused of sexual harassment by University of Oklahoma Law Professor Anita Hill

Pop Quiz

Chapter 31

1. George W. Bush denounced supply-side economics as ________.
   a. voo doo economics
   b. economics for people that can't add
   c. Keynesian economics by another name
   d. free lunch economics

2. What happened on October 19, 1987, known as "Black Monday"?
   a. Ronald Reagan was shot by John Hinkley Jr.
   b. The Space Shuttle Challenger exploded shortly after liftoff.
   c. The stock market fell 22.6 percent.
   d. Rodney King was beaten by Los Angeles police.

3. According to Haynes Johnson, the number of officials in the Reagan Administration that were officially investigated, convicted, or indicted was ________.
   a. none
   b. one
   c. two
   d. 138

4. What was one of the reasons that Saddam Hussein apparently believed he could invade Kuwait?
   a. He understood U.S. Ambassador April Glaspie to say that the U.S. would not get involved.
   b. He understood U.S. Ambassador April Glaspie to say that the U.S. preferred Iraq to Kuwait.

Pop Quiz (cont'd)

c. He understood U.S. Ambassador April Glaspie to say that the U.S. wanted him to invade for higher oil prices.
d. He understood U.S. Ambassador April Glaspie to say that Iraq should always have controlled Kuwait.

5. One driving force of the American economy in the 1980s was ________.
   a. agricultural expansion
   b. a manufacturing boom
   c. a high tech boom
   d. a Savings and Loan boom

6. The first woman to win the vice presidential nomination from a major Party was ________.
   a. Geraldine Ferraro
   b. Hillary Clinton
   c. Nancy Pelosi
   d. Sandra Day O'Connor

7. What was provided under the Immigration Reform and Control Act of 1986?
   a. Sanctions were imposed on employers who knowingly hired illegal aliens.
   b. Two million people who had arrived illegally in the U.S. after 1982 were deported.
   c. A series of fences was constructed on the Mexican border.
   d. All of the above

8. What caused the communist governments of Eastern Europe to fall in 1989?
   a. Ronald Reagan implored Gorbachev to "tear down this wall."
   b. Gorbachev renounced the right of any nation to interfere in the sovereignty of another.
   c. Ronald Reagan announced that the U.S. army would back any democratic revolutions against communism.
   d. Ronald Reagan announced that the U.S. could destroy the Soviet Union with space lasers.

9. Between Saddam Hussein's invasion of Kuwait and his expulsion by the U.S. military, Saddam attempted to link his removal from Kuwait to ________.
   a. American removal of troops from the Holy Land
   b. the withdrawal of Israel from the occupied territories
   c. the end of American support of Shiite and Kurdish rebels in Iraq
   d. all of the above

Chapter Review (cont'd)

Pop Quiz (cont'd)

10. The American president that billed himself as the "Environmental President" was __________.
    a. Ronald Reagan
    b. George H. W. Bush
    c. Bill Clinton
    d. Jimmy Carter

11. A major cause of the savings-and-loan industry collapse was __________.

12. In 1983 American Marines were sent to __________ and in October of that year __________ of them were killed by a suicide bomber.

13. The Iran-Contra Affair involved the sale of missiles to __________ and the profits from that sale were used to support rebels in __________.

14. The Tiananmen Square Massacre cost the lives of five thousand __________ students.

15. The most expensive riot in American history took place after four police officers were acquitted of brutalizing __________ __________.

1. A	6. A	11. Corruption	15. Rodney King
2. C	7. A	12. Beirut; 24	
3. D	8. B	13. Iran; Nicaragua	
4. A	9. B		
5. C	10. B	14. Chinese	

32 America at the Turn of the Millennium

Chapter Objectives

The Clinton Years

The Election of 1992

Clinton Takes Charge

Setbacks for the Clinton Agenda

The "Gingrich Revolution" and Clinton's Comeback

Election of 1996

Clinton and the World

Clinton's Iraq Policy

Terrorism: At Home and Abroad

Computers and the Internet

The "Trial of the Century"

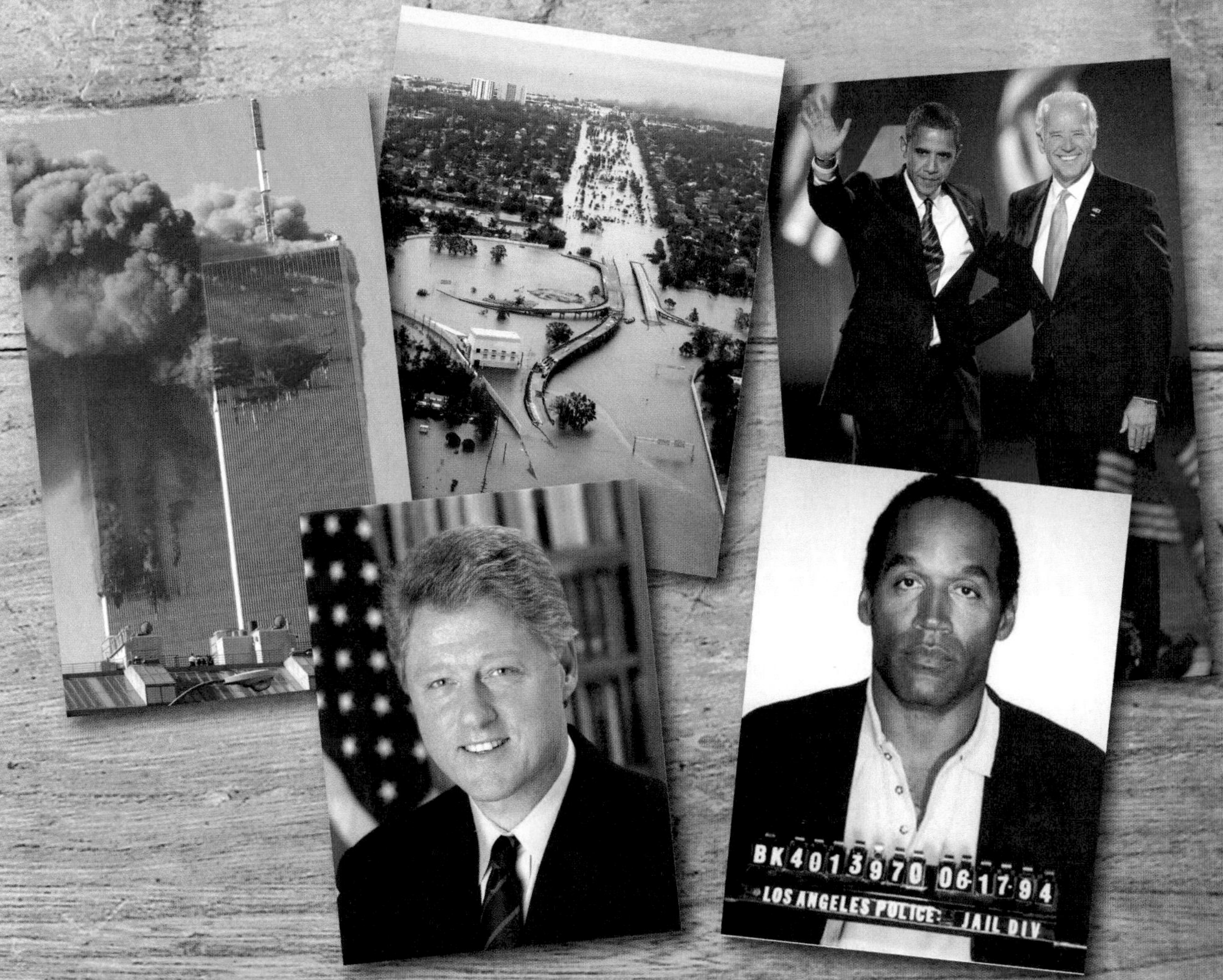

A White House Besieged

Hillary Rodham Clinton as First Lady

A Second Bush Presidency

The Election of 2000

The Bush Domestic Agenda

9/11 and the American Response

War in Iraq

The Election of 2004

Second-Term Blues

The Unfinished American Journey

Election 2008

Obama in the White House

In his 1961 inaugural address, the youngest man ever elected president of the United States announced, "the torch has been passed to a new generation of Americans." When John F. Kennedy spoke those words, he meant that America would be led by those shaped in their young adult years by World War II and the early Cold War. In 1993, Kennedy's generation of leaders, embodied by World War II Navy flier George H. W. Bush, handed the torch of White House leadership to yet another generation, the postwar Baby Boomers in the person of William Jefferson Clinton. Eight years later, Bush's own son, George W. Bush, became the second Baby Boomer president.

The nation Bill Clinton and the younger George Bush led during the last decade of the twentieth century and the first decade of the twenty-first differed from that served by World War II veteran-presidents from John Kennedy through the first George Bush. Most crucially, of course, the Cold War was no more. Although many foreign policy challenges existed—from the security of the former Soviet Union's nuclear arsenal to environmental destruction and global warming—most Americans had domestic issues on their minds as they pulled the levers for Clinton in 1992 and 1996 and Bush in 2000. By 2004, needless to say, the domestic focus would have changed dramatically.

The first two Baby Boomer presidents had much in common. Both born in 1946, they had attended prestigious eastern universities—Georgetown and Yale Law School in Clinton's case, Yale and Harvard Business School in Bush's. Neither had served in Vietnam, their generation's war, although Bush joined the Texas Air National Guard in the late 1960s and early 1970s. Through their thirties, both men had lacked the discipline to control destructive impulses. Clinton's extramarital relationships and Bush's drinking caused them, and their families, great pain. Rumors of illegal drug use in their youth persisted about both. Indeed, Clinton had not entirely vanquished his demons before entering the White House, with unhappy results for his presidential legacy.

Despite their similarities, their routes through life to the White House greatly differed. Clinton came from very humble beginnings. His father died before he was born, and the future president spent his childhood either with his storekeeper-grandparents in the small town of Hope, Arkansas, or with his mother and abusive stepfather. Bright and fascinated by politics—as a delegate to a national youth conference in 1962, he met President Kennedy—Clinton received a Rhodes Scholarship to Oxford University. After law school at Yale, he went home to Arkansas to teach and enter politics. Just shy of thirty, he became the state's attorney general. Two years later he was inaugurated as the nation's youngest governor. While serving as governor for twelve years, Clinton established a reputation as a centrist who sought ways of using government to help people.

Bush was born into a prominent political family. His great grandfather, Sam Bush, had been a Wall Street banker, as had his grandfather, Prescott Bush, who served Connecticut in the U.S. Senate. His father made a fortune in the Texas oil business before beginning a distinguished career that culminated in the presidency. Not known for academic excellence, the younger Bush was rejected by the University of Texas law school and scored in the 25th percentile on his Air National Guard exam, although he was accepted at Yale and received his MBA at Harvard. After his experience at Harvard, Bush worked for and had ownership in several oil companies in Midland, Texas. He lost a congressional race in 1978 in a west Texas district. With assistance from his family's well-connected friends and relatively little money down, Bush became co-owner of the Texas Rangers baseball team in 1986. Several years later, after convincing the city of Arlington to build the Rangers a showcase stadium, Bush sold his interest (for which he had paid slightly more than $600,000) for over $14 million. In 1994, Texans elected him governor, his first public office, defeating popular moderate Democrat and long time veteran of Texas politics, Ann Richards. As the state's chief executive, he received good marks for his ability to work in a bipartisan way with conservative Democrats in the Texas Legislature to achieve his goals, which included reductions in the state's property taxes.

Both Clinton and Bush came to the White House with agendas to pursue; yet they found that changing events and surprising turns—the stuff of history—forced them to alter their plans.

The Clinton Years

The Election of 1992

In the wake of the Gulf War in February 1991, 89 percent of Americans in a Gallup poll approved of President George H. W. Bush's handling of his job. His poll numbers remained elevated for some time, discouraging high-profile Democrats such as Governor Mario Cuomo of New York from entering the presidential race. Instead, a group of lesser-known Democrats, whom the press dubbed the "Seven Dwarves," competed for the right to take on Bush. The next year and a half, however, would see the country slide into a prolonged economic recession, and Bush's own ideological preference for laissez-faire would make him appear inattentive and uncaring about the plight of the average American. As unemployment rose to over 7 percent in 1992, a large segment of the electorate began to call for bold action against the recession. Bush would not deliver. Instead, Bush clung to his position that the economy was improving and that others should simply stop saying that it was not. In his contention that the economy was improving, Bush was actually correct. When the third quarter economic numbers were released that fall, they did, indeed, indicate that the economy was on the upswing. The economic recovery, however, would be too little and too late to save the Bush presidency.

▶ President George H. W. Bush's official 1989 portrait.

As Bush's popularity slid in the winter of 1991, Bush fired the unpopular White House Chief of Staff John Sununu, thus separating himself from one of his top advisers. To further complicate things for Bush, former Republican National Committee (RNC) chief Lee Atwater had died of a brain tumor earlier in the year. Without these advisers, the Bush campaign was unable to articulate a message for his campaign. In the words of one Bush friend, "If you asked him why he wanted to be reelected, he'd have to look at his note cards. That's the fundamental problem at the core."

Arkansas Governor Bill Clinton emerged from the Democratic Party pack to claim his party's nomination, despite questions the press and opponents raised about his marital fidelity, his alleged countercultural past, and his participation in a failed real estate venture in the 1980s. Clinton succeeded largely because of his formidable skills as a campaigner and his moderate stance as a "pro-business" Democrat. A leader of the centrist Democratic Leadership Council, Clinton positioned himself as a "New Democrat" who abandoned the 60s liberalism of many of his primary opponents. He sought to persuade white middle-class and working-class voters, including those known in the 1980s as Reagan Democrats, that he could be trusted on issues of importance to them. He supported new government spending—a traditional Democratic approach—to combat the recession that had wounded Bush's popularity by early 1992. (The recession made "It's the Economy, Stupid" the Clinton campaign's internal slogan.) At the same time, Clinton signaled his support for more conservative social policies than those advocated by many Democrats, such as that of 1988 nominee Michael Dukakis. For instance, Clinton favored the death penalty and distanced himself from black activist Jesse Jackson, who had run a strong, but ultimately unsuccessful, campaign for the Democratic presidential nomination in 1988. Clinton also chose a fellow southern moderate, U.S. Senator Albert Gore, Jr., of Tennessee, as his running mate.

▶ William (Bill) Jefferson Clinton, 42nd president of the United States.

Before he could take on Clinton, President Bush faced a primary challenge from Patrick Buchanan, a conservative television commentator and former aide to presidents Nixon and Reagan. Buchanan ran a spirited but low budget campaign that appealed chiefly to blue-collar Republicans concerned about the recession, strongly pro-life social conservatives, gun advocates, libertarians, and isolationists uncomfortable with Bush's "new world order." Buchanan referred to President Bush as "King George" and denounced what he termed as Bush's "moderate" policies that failed to put

America first. Buchanan then embarrassed the president by gaining 37 percent of the vote in the New Hampshire Primary. Buchanan, however, never posed a serious threat to Bush; he won no primaries (his best showing was in New Hampshire where he lost to Bush, 53 percent to 37 percent) and only received eighteen votes to Bush's 2,166 at the Republican convention. Still, Buchanan raised questions about the president's leadership. As a consequence, Bush was forced to move somewhat to the right so as to prevent alienation of the Buchanan voters, but a rightward move would hinder Bush in his effort to pick up Democratic middle voters in the November general election. Some argue, however, that Buchanan did the most damage to Bush with his performance at the party's Houston convention. There, while endorsing the president, Buchanan turned some centrist voters away from the GOP with a right-wing speech warning of "a religious war going on in our country for the soul of America."

As the Republican nominee, President Bush ran a lackluster campaign that reflected his inability to define his presidency. He had trouble with, as he put it, "the vision thing." Comfortable and generally successful with foreign policy, he seemed ill at ease dealing with domestic issues such as the fallout from the Los Angeles riots in the spring of 1992. In a series of presidential debates, he seemed detached and unable to connect with audiences as the empathetic Clinton did. During one debate, he glanced at his wristwatch as though wondering when his torment would end. In contrast to Bush's lackluster campaign, Democratic candidate and Arkansas governor Bill Clinton articulated a more dynamic campaign and better-defined message. Clinton stole some of the Republican thunder by denouncing welfare and calling for tax cuts to the middle class, as well as advocating the use of the powers of the federal government to combat the recession. However, because of problems in Clinton's personal life that included marital infidelity, the Bush camp mistakenly did not view Clinton as a serious threat in the spring of 1992. A Bush aide even wrote Bush in April 1992, telling him, "The swing voters have dismissed Bill Clinton as a serious alternative to President Bush."

A third candidate, billionaire businessman Ross Perot, entered, then left, and then re-entered the presidential race as an Independent during 1992. Perot popularized concern about the expansive federal budget deficits of the Reagan-Bush years and presented himself as a can-do, problem-solving executive. Although Perot appealed to many Americans weary of excessive partisan bickering, his behavior struck others as too mercurial—perhaps too unstable—for the White House. Many wondered about Perot's suitability for office when he alleged that the Bush administration had sought to disrupt his (Perot's) daughter's wedding.

In the end, Perot captured an impressive 18.9 percent of the popular vote, a higher percentage than any third-party candidate had received since Theodore Roosevelt ran as a Progressive in 1912. Polling of Perot supporters, however, revealed that one-third would have supported Bush had Perot not been in the race, one-third would have supported Clinton, and one-third would not have voted at all. Consequently, it is unclear whether or not Perot's candidacy impacted the election's outcome. Clinton would essentially defeat both Bush and Perot in the presidential debates, thus harming Bush's popularity. The approval ratings of the president fell even further just five days before the election when it was revealed by Lawrence Walsh, the independent counsel investigating the Iran-Contra affair, that while he was Reagan's vice president Bush had known about the effort to exchange arms for hostages with Iran, an allegation that Bush had long denied. To make matters worse, former Secretary of Defense Caspar Weinberger was indicted for his role in the affair, further suggesting that Bush was guilty by association. Compounding Bush's electoral problems, the economy was still in recession. In spite of Bush's tax hike, the debt situation inherited from the Reagan administration continued to spiral out of control, producing a crowding out of credit, rising interest rates, and sluggish economic growth. As a consequence, Bush would suffer the worst loss of any sitting president since William Howard Taft in 1912. Bush won only 37 percent of the popular vote as compared to 43 percent for Clinton and 18 percent for Ross Perot. The twelve years of Republican dominance of the White House that had been initiated by Ronald Reagan had come to an abrupt end.

Clinton Takes Charge

As he came into office, the youthful Clinton (the second youngest man ever elected president) brought a renewed vigor to the White House. He liked policy "bull sessions" that often lasted into the wee hours of the morning. A self-confessed "policy wonk," he impressed observers with his keen mind. Yet he displayed a surprising lack of personal discipline and allowed an inexperienced White House staff to behave in ways that bothered even Clinton boosters. Summing him up, historian Arthur Schlesinger, Jr., would once say Clinton was "a rare combination of talents and infirmities."

Stressing ethnic and gender diversity in government, Clinton promised "an administration that looks like America." His initial cabinet included more African Americans (four) and women (four) than any other president's first cabinet; the number of Hispanics (two) tied the

▶ Clinton, the second youngest man ever elected president, takes the oath of office during his inauguration, 1993. The Democratic president promised "an administration that looks like America."

number appointed by President Bush in 1989. In Clinton's second term, former Congressman Norman Mineta became the first Asian American in the cabinet when he took over the Department of Commerce. In addition, an assistant secretary of housing and urban development, Roberta Achtenberg, was the first openly gay person appointed by a president and confirmed by the Senate. In putting together a cabinet that drew on the talents of Americans from various backgrounds, Clinton hit a few snags in addition to criticism for playing into "identity politics." Two of his nominees for attorney general, both women, were forced to withdraw when it was revealed each had failed to pay Social Security taxes for her children's nannies. Finally, a third nominee, Janet Reno, a candidate favored by the president's political wife, Hillary, became the first woman to head the Justice Department.

Very early, Clinton realized that his lack of a strong electoral mandate—he had won only 43 percent of the popular vote—limited his policy options. In part to appeal to Perot voters, Clinton concentrated, initially, more on bringing down the deficit than on stimulating the economy with new spending programs. The president chafed at the prospect of supporting tax and spending policies that made him, as he fumed, such a good Eisenhower Republican. Still, his fiscal and spending proposals, which passed on party-line votes, helped insulate him from conservative charges that he was a "tax and spend" liberal. With the exception of a small increase in gasoline taxes and some higher taxes for the best-off Social Security recipients, the Clinton plan raised taxes only on the wealthiest 1.2 percent of Americans while reducing them for the working poor and small businesses. Moreover, the plan helped cut the deficit by $50 billion from 1993 to 1994 and another $40 billion the next year.

Setbacks for the Clinton Agenda

Clinton suffered political damage when he took on explosive issues at the outset of his administration. He stirred controversy when he sought to fulfill a campaign pledge to end the ban on homosexuals in the military. Congressional opposition, even from key Democrats, and a recalcitrant Joint Chiefs of Staff forced Clinton to accept a compromise policy. Under "don't ask, don't tell," military officials were not to seek out homosexuals for expulsion from the ranks, while gays were to be silent about their sexuality. The policy, which gay civil rights groups initially greeted with guarded optimism, actually led to increased numbers of discharges. "Don't ask, don't tell" ultimately satisfied few on either side of the issue, and this first major public policy battle weakened the new president.

Clinton's unsuccessful struggle to enact new national health care legislation damaged him even more. The 1992 Democratic platform pledged "universal access to quality, affordable health care" for Americans, and polls showed it a popular idea. Clinton appointed a task force in 1993, chaired by First Lady Hillary Rodham Clinton, to devise a plan. The task force's proposals, submitted to Congress in 1994, envisioned a system of federally regulated private health insurance plans to cover all Americans. Some to Clinton's political left attacked this rather complex "managed competition" idea. They preferred to replace private insurance companies with the government as the "single payer" for health care costs.

Opponents on the political right proved more effective in stopping the Clinton plan. Many Republicans charged, incorrectly, that it amounted to "socialized medicine," complete with a

▶ Personal portrait of Hilary Rodham Clinton, 1992. The First Lady of the Clinton administration would play an influential roll in her husband's presidential term, and in later years, leave a prominent political legacy for herself in the minds of Americans.

new bureaucracy and lack of patient choice in the selection of physicians. They also criticized the leadership of the first lady, who enjoyed little popularity with conservatives, in drafting the plan. A trade association of private health insurance companies fueled opposition to the measure by spending millions on a television advertising campaign featuring a middle-class couple, known only as Harry and Louise, expressing theirs fears about the Clinton measure. These conservative attacks turned the public against the administration's plan, and in the summer of 1994, the Senate let it die. This failure of the centerpiece of Clinton's domestic agenda represented a severe blow to the administration.

The "Gingrich Revolution" and Clinton's Comeback

In November 1994, Republicans capitalized on Clinton's perceived weakness and swept to power in both houses of Congress. Republicans gained an impressive fifty-two seats in the House and eight in the Senate (within months, two Democratic senators switched parties to add to the Republican margin). The 104th Congress, which took office in January 1995, was the first controlled by the GOP since the 83rd Congress of 1953–1955. The Republican victory extended to all levels of government; numerous well-known incumbent Democrats lost state races, including Governor Mario Cuomo of New York. Another prominent Democrat, Governor Ann Richards of Texas, lost her re-election bid to former President Bush's oldest son, baseball team co-owner George W. Bush.

Conservative talk radio hosts, led by Rush Limbaugh, contributed significantly to the Republican victory. Limbaugh spent three hours on the national airwaves each weekday blasting Bill and Hillary Clinton as radicals. New Republican members of the 104th Congress recognized Limbaugh's efforts by naming him an honorary member of their freshman class.

A brilliant, "nationalized" campaign also helped Republicans win Congress. GOP congressional candidates signed onto a set of ten poll-tested items known as the Contract with America. Among other things, the Contract pledged Republicans to reform welfare, reduce crime, and pass constitutional amendments to balance the federal budget and limit the number of terms members of Congress could serve—all popular with the Republican public. However, polls suggested that the majority of Americans actually disagreed with the majority of the specific items in the Republican Contract with America.

Republicans chose as the new Speaker of the House Georgia's Newton Leroy (Newt) Gingrich, an energetic and visionary leader who had spearheaded the Contract with America.

Buoyed by his party's victory and his own high approval ratings, the colorful Gingrich quickly became the apparent center of power in Washington. As promised, he brought the ten items of the Contract with America up for votes within the first one hundred days of the new Congress. Few of the Contract items actually became law, and Congress failed to pass the balanced budget or term limits constitutional amendments. Moreover, in 1996, the Supreme Court struck down as unconstitutional one part of the Contract, the line item veto law. Still, Gingrich and his Republican colleagues were setting the national agenda and certainly turning national policy in a more conservative direction.

Republican control of Congress and Gingrich's place in the media spotlight (*Time* magazine named the Speaker its 1995 "Man of the Year") appeared to diminish Clinton's importance. The president even found himself protesting his relevance to national politics in an April 1995 press conference. Smelling presidential blood in the water, numerous Republicans prepared to take on the hemorrhaging Clinton in 1996.

Then Clinton's excellent political survival instincts kicked in. Aided by sometime Republican political advisor, Dick Morris, and much to the dismay of liberal Democrats, the president responded to the Republicans by tacking to the right. "The era of big government is over," declared Clinton in his 1996 State of the Union Address, and later that year he signed welfare reform legislation formulated largely by Republicans. Under it, the number of welfare recipients dropped and the entitlement to welfare for impoverished children ended. Liberals complained that, for the first time since the Great Depression, children from poor families were not guaranteed financial assistance. Angering gay rights' supporters, the president also signed the Defense of Marriage Act, which permitted any state to refuse to recognize same-sex marriages contracted in another state. No state actually allowed same-sex marriages in 1996, although Hawaii seemed on the verge of doing so. In 2000, Vermont became the first state to allow something like marriage—a "civil union"—for partners of the same sex. On the economic front, Clinton also pushed to lower the budget deficit even more.

While agreeing to cuts in programs for the poor, Clinton shrewdly set himself up as the protector of popular middle-class entitlement programs such as Social Security and Medicare. When Republicans insisted on making cuts in Medicare, Clinton refused to go along. In resulting showdowns with Congress, Clinton even allowed all but the most important functions of the federal government to cease for a few days rather than agree to GOP budget demands. As national parks closed and Social Security checks stopped, the public overwhelmingly blamed congressional Republicans for the impasse. Gingrich and his allies caved to Clinton, whose approval ratings rose while those of congressional Republican leaders sank.

Election of 1996

No less than eight Republicans announced their candidacy for the presidency in 1996, including Phil Gramm, Pat Buchanan, Bob Dole, publishing magnate Steve Forbes, California Governor Pete Wilson, and Lamar Alexander of Tennessee. Dole was the big money favorite, but his campaign essentially stumbled out of the gate in the 1996 primary season. Forbes stole some of Dole's thunder with a proposal to eliminate the graduated tax structure and replace

▶ President Clinton speaks at the opening of the White House Conference on Social Security, 1998. Clinton told lawmakers and policy advocates, "Our ears and our minds must remain open to any good idea and to any person of good will."

it with a flat tax, and Pat Buchanan, a perpetual darling of the far right, defeated Dole in the New Hampshire primary. Dole regrouped, and in spite of the presence of Southerners Gramm and Alexander, did well in the Southern primaries and essentially locked up the Republican nomination prior to the convention. At the Republican Convention in July, Dole abandoned his history of support for fiscal responsibility and announced his support for tax cuts and reform of the tax code to produce a "fairer, flatter tax." Democrats charged that Dole's tax cuts would create massive deficits; but Dole, echoing Ronald Reagan, promised that he would offset the tax cuts with unnamed spending cuts. Dole then tabbed supply-side enthusiast Senator Jack Kemp of New York as his running mate.

Ross Perot once again ran as a third party candidate; but Perot met with much less success this time around since during his previous run, he had developed for him a reputation as an eccentric, which he could not overcome. Furthermore, Perot offered little that voters could latch on to as a real difference between the conservative platform of Dole and Kemp. The Democrats, however, were able to paint Dole as a "mean spirited" man, and voters were generally turned off by Dole's age at 72. Clinton had helped himself by following a more moderate path since the failure of his health care proposal, and the Republicans had hurt themselves with the gridlock and shutdown of the government. Clinton led the race from beginning to end and won almost 50 percent of the popular vote to Dole's 41 percent. Clinton also won the largest gender gap in history, with 54 percent of American women casting votes for Clinton and only 38 percent for Bob Dole.

Clinton, however, failed again to capture a majority of the popular vote. This time, Perot, calling his the Reform Party, captured 8.4 percent of the popular vote, less than half his 1992 level but still significant for a third party candidate. Republicans maintained control of both houses of Congress, though, and continued to cause Clinton trouble. For instance, despite calls by Chief Justice William Rehnquist and others to fill numerous vacant federal judgeships, Senate Republicans confirmed very few of Clinton's judicial appointments. In the last year of his presidency, the Republican-controlled Senate approved only thirty-nine judges while a Democratic-controlled Senate had approved sixty-six in the final year of his Republican predecessor's term.

Clinton began his second term in the midst of a booming economy and soaring stock market that increased federal tax revenues. The tax windfall from the economic good fortune allowed Clinton and the Republicans to compromise on a budget in 1997 that actually balanced for the first time in three decades. It was difficult to conclude anything other than the fact that Clinton's 1993 tax increase, which the Republicans had fought against, had produced long-term benefits for the fiscal health of the nation. Republican attempts to claim responsibility for the balanced budget success rang hollow after Bob Dole's presidential campaign based on tax cuts. Clinton's strong position was aided by Republican infighting in the House as a rebellious group of Republicans, unhappy with the Republican failures in the government shutdown and the 1996 election, attempted to oust Newt Gingrich as Speaker in the summer of 1997. Gingrich survived the attempted coup, but the Republicans were left in disarray.

Clinton and the World

Clinton came into office with very little interest in or knowledge of the complexities of international relations. By and large, he and his first secretary of state, experienced diplomat and lawyer Warren Christopher, continued Bush administration policies.

During the 1992 campaign, Clinton endorsed the North American Free Trade Agreement (NAFTA) negotiated by the Bush administration. Many traditionally Democratic groups strongly objected to the treaty, which lowered trade barriers with Canada and Mexico. Organized labor officials charged that NAFTA would accelerate the loss of jobs to Mexico while environmentalists pointed to dangers posed by heavily polluting Mexican factories. Although sensitive to these concerns, Clinton and "New Democrats" favored freer trade. President Clinton pressed ahead and achieved ratification of NAFTA, but with special side accords to allay the fears about the treaty's effect on labor and the environment. Economists differed as to whether NAFTA resulted in positive changes for the U.S. economy.

Even with the end of the Cold War, Russia remained a major focus of American foreign policy. Like Bush, Clinton supported the efforts of President Boris Yeltsin—who replaced Mikhail Gorbachev, to move his country towards democracy and a market economy. Clinton received praise from former Republican foreign policy specialists as well as Democrats when he stood by Yeltsin during the Russian president's 1993 power struggle with parliamentary opponents. Clinton and Yeltsin did not always see eye-to-eye, as for instance when the Russians used strong force against secessionists in Chechnya; but the American president had little choice but to back Yeltsin, given the alternatives of the right-wing Russian nationalism of Vladimir Zhirinovsky or a resurgent Communist party. Elsewhere in Eastern Europe, Clinton pushed for the extension of NATO to include former Soviet bloc states. In 1998, the Czech Republic, Hungary, and Poland became the first of these to assume full membership in the western defense alliance. NATO softened this potential affront to Russia in its sphere of influence by including Moscow in some of its defense consultations.

Clinton also played the role of peacemaker in several international disputes, with mixed results. The president helped broker the 1995 Dayton Accords, which brought peace to Bosnia-Herzegovina, one of the former Yugoslavian republics wracked by civil war since 1991.

When the communist system collapsed all across Eastern Europe, individual "republics" within Yugoslavia quickly declared their independence; and the European Union quickly accorded official recognition to the new states. Minorities within the new states of Croatia and Bosnia, however, rose up against those who advocated independence from Yugoslavia. Croatia and Bosnia quickly devolved into civil war and "ethnic cleansing," complete with mass executions and the depopulation of entire areas, causing a massive refugee problem and over two hundred fifty thousands deaths.

The government of Yugoslavia, located in the "republic" of Serbia and dominated by ethnic Serbs that wished to halt the disintegration of Yugoslavia, aided the minority rebels. In Croatia, the Serbian minority refused to recognize Croatian authority, and the Yugoslav army bombed the Croatian Capitol of Zagreb. In retaliation, the Croatians forcibly ousted thousands of Serbs from their country.

In Bosnia, which was 50 percent Muslim, 30 percent Serb, and 17 percent Croat, the Muslim-dominated government declared independence in 1992, resulting in a Serbian rebellion that was supported by neighboring Serbia. This civil war created over two million refugees over the next three years. The United States government, under Bill Clinton, held talks in Dayton, Ohio in 1995, negotiating a truce that partitioned Bosnia into two sectors and was signed by all parties involved. The Dayton Accords required an international peacekeeping force to occupy Bosnia to enforce the cease-fire. Under the Dayton Accords, the Serbs, who were 30 percent of the population, received 48 percent of the territory, while Muslims, who were 50 percent of the population, received only 27 percent of the territory with the rest allotted to the Croats. One narrow, three-mile-wide zone along the river port city of Brcko was not assigned under the Dayton Accords, but placed under joint jurisdiction. The area was under Muslim control before the civil war, but the Serbs also claimed the area as "vital."

As part of the peace package, Clinton committed American troops as peacekeepers there for a year. Yet conditions required their continuing presence into the next administration. The president also took a great interest in Northern Ireland where Protestant and Roman Catholic factions had long been at loggerheads. Clinton's mediator, former Senate Majority Leader George Mitchell, brokered the Good Friday Agreement in 1998 that called for the disarming of sectarian paramilitary organizations and greater autonomy for Northern Ireland within Great Britain. Although snags lay ahead, the agreement brought a historic opportunity for peace.

The Israeli-Palestinian conflict, however, occupied much of Clinton's time and energy. In October 1993, he hosted Israeli Prime Minister Yitzhak Rabin and Palestinian leader Yasser Arafat at the White House for the signing of an historic agreement. The accord, made possible by years of secret negotiations in Oslo, Norway, transferred Gaza and Jericho from Israeli occupation to control by a new Palestinian Authority. It also urged more bilateral talks between Israel and its Arab neighbors. Soon, Jordan and Israel made an agreement; and during Clinton's terms in office, this Oslo peace process reached several crisis points, including just after the assassination of Rabin by a militant Israeli opponent of land cessions to the Palestinians. To break the impasses that developed, Clinton pursued personal diplomacy, not all of which resulted in progress, although the Wye River meetings of October 1998 did push the process along. There the Palestine Liberation Organization agreed to delete anti-Israel language from its founding charter, and Israel agreed to transfer more occupied territory to Palestinian control. However, Clinton's efforts in the fall of 2000 to seek a comprehensive settlement, including finalizing the status of Jerusalem, failed, largely because of Arafat's intransigence; and many loose ends remained as the Clinton administration came to a close. For a president famous for his opposition to the Vietnam War as a student—opponents delighted in calling him a draft-dodger, which he was not (Clinton faced the draft along with other young American males, but his number did not come up)—Clinton supported military intervention in a surprising number of global hotspots. He continued to enforce President Bush's no-fly zones in Iraq and authorized bombing of that country on several occasions.

Clinton's Iraq Policy

In April 1993, two years after the Persian Gulf War and three months after Bill Clinton's inauguration, Kuwaiti security services uncovered an Iraqi plot to kill former President George H. W. Bush with a car bomb during his visit to Kuwait. Kuwaiti officials arrested eleven Iraqis for the attempt on Bush's life, and four were executed. The next month President Clinton unveiled his policy of "dual containment" under which the United States was committed to containing not only Iran, but also Iraq. Clinton included in the policy a call for "regime change" in Iraq.

On June 26, 1993, the United States launched twenty-three Tomahawk cruise missiles at Baghdad, destroying the headquarters of Iraqi intelligence. It was the first time the Clinton administration used military force and the first such United States retaliation since the bombing of Moamar Qaddafi in Libya in 1986. Of the twenty-three Tomahawks fired by the United States, three unfortunately went astray, hitting residential neighborhoods and killing eight people—including Leila Attar, a leading Iraqi painter. The Tomahawk missile attack by the United States technically violated the United Nations charter since Iraq had not launched an armed attack on the United States.

Clinton continued the American sanctions on Iraq. In April 1994, Clinton's Secretary of State Warren Christopher stated, "The United States does not believe that Iraq's compliance with United Nations Resolutions is enough to justify lifting the embargo." In other words, whether Saddam complied with disarmament or not, Clinton was dead set on regime change. In doing so, the Clinton policy was unilateral in character and ignored the United Nations.

On September 3, 1996, Clinton fired forty-four cruise missiles at Iraq's military command posts and air defense centers near the southern no-fly zone. In September 1997, the World Health Organization (WHO) published a report that claimed that over five hundred thousand Iraqi children under age five had died since 1991 as the result of malnutrition and lack of medicine caused by the United Nations embargo. By October 1997, the United Nations had dispatched 373 inspection teams to Iraq at a cost of $120 million—paid for from Iraq's frozen assets. On October 29, Iraq demanded the end of American "spies" on inspection teams, and six American inspectors were expelled the next month. Clinton responded to the expulsion of

United nations inspectors by stating, "Saddam has ensured that the sanctions will be there until the end of time or as long as he lasts." Clinton then ordered a military buildup in the Persian Gulf. Arab states, however, unanimously opposed United States military action.

To educate the American public, Clinton had the National Security Council arrange a worldwide "town hall" meeting at Ohio State University with Secretary of State Madeleine Albright, National Security Advisor Sandy Berger, and Defense Secretary William Cohen to discuss Iraq's Weapons of Mass Destruction (WMDs). The audience of six thousand in the town hall meeting was unconvinced that Saddam's WMDs posed any real threat, and a February 22, 1998 *Newsweek* poll showed backing for military action against Iraq at only 18 percent. Clinton's options were further limited by the conclusions of the United States military as Chairman of the Joint Chiefs Henry Shelton argued that the United States would not be able to destroy Saddam's well-hidden weapons from the air.

In October 1998, Congress passed the Iraq Liberation Act that entitled the president to spend up to $97 million for military aid to train, equip, and finance an Iraqi opposition army and authorized the Department of Defense to train insurgents. General Anthony Zinni, commander of the United States Central Command, however, argued against the plan. Zinni argued, "I know of no viable opposition to Saddam in Iraq. Under such conditions any attempt to remove the Iraqi leader by force could dangerously fragment Iraq and destabilize the entire region. A weakened, fragmented, chaotic Iraq—which could happen if this isn't done carefully—is more dangerous in the long run than a contained Saddam now." This was perhaps especially true since the primary opposition group in Iraq at the time was the Supreme Assembly of Islamic Revolution in Iraq (SAIRI) that is funded by Iran.

Madeline Albright took a tour of the Persian Gulf states and was told by Middle-East rulers that change imposed on Iraq from outside would lead to rifts and civil war, and no Middle-Eastern leader stated that they would comply with a United States plan to oust Saddam. Instead, Middle-Eastern leaders warned Albright that United States support of insurgents undermined their credibility because it made them appear that they were American agents.

On October 31, 1998, Iraq ceased compliance with United Nations inspectors and demanded a review of its compliance linked to a timetable for ending sanctions. In response, President Clinton sent a fleet of B-52s armed with cruise missiles to bomb Iraq on November 14, 1998; but one hour before the planes released their missiles, Iraq announced that the inspectors could return. On November 18, 1998, the inspectors returned but found themselves obstructed by Iraqi officials. The next month, Clinton ordered the evacuation of United Nations' weapons inspectors so that he could launch a one hundred-hour bombing campaign aimed at ousting Saddam Hussein. On Wednesday, December 16, two days before the impeachment hearings began in the House, Clinton ordered the bombing to begin. The U.S. dropped 415 cruise missiles (ninety more than were fired during the Gulf War) and six hundred laser-guided bombs on Iraq. Saddam survived, and weapons inspectors were no longer in Iraq. Essentially, it was Clinton, not Saddam, who ousted the inspectors.

In the months of January to August 1999, Clinton stepped up strikes against Iraq's air defenses in the no-fly zones. Over eleven hundred missiles were fired at 359 targets in all. In August 1999, Clinton ordered the bombing of Iraqi air defense targets outside the United

States-imposed no-fly zones. This would be the situation in Iraq that would be inherited by Clinton's successor, George W. Bush.

Aside from Iraq, Clinton inherited from George H. W. Bush an obligation to provide military support to a U.N. humanitarian effort in war-torn Somalia. United States soldiers sought to create a secure environment for the delivery of food to famine victims, but this operation soon became hampered by armed struggles among various Somali factions. Forces loyal to warlord Mohammed Aideed killed some and captured others of the United States soldiers seeking those responsible for the deaths of a Pakistani U.N. contingent. In October 1993, in one instance recorded by television cameras, Aideed's men dragged the body of a Marine through the streets of the capital city, Mogadishu. Negotiations led to the release of captured Americans and the withdrawal of United States personnel. The operation saved thousands of Somalis from starvation, but it made Americans less willing to intervene for humanitarian reasons in unstable situations. In 1994, for instance, the Clinton administration did nothing to stop violence in Rwanda where members of one ethnic group, the Hutu, engaged in mass slaughter of another group, the Tutsi. During a four-month period in 1994, between five hundred thousand and 1 million Rwandans died. After the killings, U.S. troops moved in to provide limited humanitarian assistance.

The Clinton administration did intervene militarily for humanitarian-linked missions in countries or regions where the United States traditionally had important interests. For instance, in 1994, the United States announced the dispatch of troops to Haiti to support the winner of a recent presidential election, Jean-Bertrand Aristide, against a dictator who refused to yield power. Just before troops were to go in, the dictator agreed to leave the country in a plan brokered by former President Carter with Clinton's blessing; and American troops entered Haiti as peacekeepers. Then, in 1999 Serbian troops began forcing the evacuation—as well as slaughtering—of residents of Kosovo, a district within Serbia dominated by ethnic Albanians. Kosovo was a "republic" on the southwestern corner of Albania with a Muslim majority of two million people and a Serbian population of about 200,000. Kosovo had enjoyed local autonomy under Serbian rule since the Serbs captured it in 1912. Muslims had taken the area from the Serbs in 1389 and ruled it themselves for the next five centuries.

In 1989, Serbian President Slobodan Milosevic revoked Kosovo's local autonomy and began a campaign to suppress Kosovo's Muslim culture. Kosovars formed armed resistance groups that attacked the Serbian government officials and installations, as well as Serbian civilians in Kosovo. Milosevic responded with an armed invasion by Serbian troops aimed at expelling the Muslims from Kosovo. Thousands of Kosovars became refugees and five hundred thousand crossed the border into Albania. President Clinton attempted negotiations with the Serbs and Kosovars to reach an agreement that would return Kosovo to its autonomy and cease the ethnic cleansing. The Kosovars signed the agreement, but the Serbs refused.

Clinton and NATO responded with the first military action in Europe by NATO since its creation in 1949. In March 1999, the United States and NATO launched a massive bombing campaign that destroyed much of Serbia's infrastructure and military capability. Finally, Milosevic capitulated under NATO pressure, and U.N. peacekeeping forces were dispatched to prevent further bloodshed. Kosovo remained technically part of Serbia, but the Serbian population in Kosovo was less than half of what it had been prior to the unrest.

The next October (2000) elections were held in Serbia, and President Milosevic was defeated. Milosevic refused to abdicate his position, and Belgrade erupted in violent protests. Angry mobs stormed the Federal Parliament building in Belgrade and set fire to offices. Milosevic then announced that he would step down under both domestic and international pressure.

One of Clinton's great strengths as president lay in his ability to connect with people abroad as well as voters at home. During the course of his presidency he made a number of trips that must be accounted as successes, particularly the trips to several African countries and to the People's Republic of China. During the latter he even addressed the Chinese public directly on television. In short, his foreign policy decisions may be judged to have been only partially successful, but he made friends for the United States around the world when he traveled.

Terrorism: At Home and Abroad

With the end of the Cold War, the United States no longer faced major security threats from another superpower. A new peril became apparent, though: terrorism. Carried out by individuals or small groups (sometimes associated with a foreign nation) attempting to make a political point, terrorism involves violence inflicted on civilian populations usually without warning. Until the 1990s, terrorist attacks had been rare in the twentieth century United States; yet during the Clinton years, Americans experienced several major attacks, both at home and abroad, and began to feel vulnerable as never before.

On April 19, 1995, twenty-six-year-old Timothy McVeigh blew up a federal office building in Oklahoma City. The explosion killed 168 men, women, and children (one person died later of injuries sustained in the blast) and demolished the nine-story building. It was the worst act of domestic terrorism yet recorded in the United States.

McVeigh's terrorist actions brought to the forefront of the nation's consciousness the phenomenon of self-described "patriot" groups. Extremely right-wing in their politics and devoted to conspiracy theories, the members often formed paramilitary groups—militias—to defend American sovereignty against world government, of which they considered Bush's "new world order" the harbinger. They considered any gun control legislation, such as that Clinton advocated, an attempt to disarm Americans in preparation for a takeover of the country by a powerful United Nations. Primarily white (and often white supremacist and anti-Semitic) as well as lower middle class or blue collar, these "patriots" likely joined these groups to compensate for what they considered their loss of power and status in American society. They tended to live in relatively economically depressed areas, untouched by the expanding economy. Moreover, the white membership took umbrage at what they saw as preferential treatment for non-whites in the more multicultural America Bill Clinton celebrated.

McVeigh shared the ideology of these "patriots." A part-time gun dealer, he acted to strike back at the federal government for what he considered its anti-gun policies. In addition, he

▶ On April 19, 1995, twenty-six-year-old Timothy McVeigh blew up a federal office building in Oklahoma City. It was the worst act of domestic terrorism yet recorded in the United States.

sought retribution for the deaths two years before of some eighty members of a millennialist religious group called the Branch Davidians. In that incident, federal agents had sought to serve an arrest warrant to the group's leader, David Koresh (born Vernon Howell), for the possession of illegal weapons. When Koresh and his followers rebuffed the federal agents by shooting four of them to death, a fifty-one-day standoff ensued between the agents and the well-armed Branch Davidians barricaded inside their compound near Waco, Texas. Then, on April 19, 1993, agents moved in against Koresh. Shooting began, with reports differing as to who fired first. In the resulting struggle, most of the compound's residents—including some children—died in a fire. It is clear the blaze began within the compound—and conspicuously no Branch Davidians attempted to flee from the burning building, suggesting mass suicide. However, McVeigh and other conspiracy theorists asserted the federal government had purposely set the fire to massacre Koresh and his followers.

In addition to domestic terrorists such as McVeigh, foreign terrorists also targeted the United States. In February 1993. Radical Islamic terrorists led by Sheik Omar Abdul Rahman set off a bomb in a parking garage at the World Trade Center in New York. Rahman's group also placed a barrel full of poisonous chemicals in the vicinity of the car bomb they detonated in the parking garage underneath the building. Fortunately, the heat from the bomb destroyed the chemicals before they could be dispersed or perhaps thousands could have died. As it was, the blast resulted in six deaths and nearly one thousand injuries.

Because of United States support for Israel or U.S. military presence in Arab countries, other terrorist attacks by Islamic groups took place abroad. For instance, in June 1996, a militant group killed nineteen United States soldiers in a bomb-blast at a military base in Saudi Arabia. This bombing eventually proved to be linked to several Islamic terrorist groups, most notably an international terrorist group known as al Qaeda (Arabic for "the base"), formed by Saudi millionaire and Islamic radical Osama bin Laden in the late 1980s. During the Soviet war in Afghanistan, al Qaeda organized Arabs to go to Afghanistan to fight what they viewed as a global jihad or holy war against the Russians. This put Osama bin Laden on the same side as the United States in that struggle. The United States under presidents Jimmy Carter and Ronald Reagan supplied massive aid to the Afghan resistance groups known collectively as the Mujahadeen. Famously, the American aid to the

Mujahadeen included shoulder-fired missiles that were effective at bringing down Soviet attack helicopters. Much of the American money and aid was funneled to the Mujahadeen through Pakistani intelligence, which was concerned not only with preventing a communist takeover of Afghanistan but also with ensuring that Afghanistan would be dominated by Sunni Muslims rather than Shiites. As a consequence, Pakistani Intelligence funneled American aid to radical Sunni Muslim groups, including al Qaeda. President Reagan praised the Mujahadeen as "freedom fighters," but American policy makers ignored the fact that the Mujahadeen were as anti-Western as they were anti-communist. Later, during the first Gulf War, bin Laden resented the reliance of Saudi Arabia on American troops for its defense. He preferred that a pan-Arab army, such as that he had deployed in Afghanistan, protect his home country, site of Islamic holy places. He also detested the United States because of its support for Israel. Consequently, bin Laden offered the services of his Mujahadeen, conquerors of the Soviet Red Army in Afghanistan, to the Kingdom of Saudi Arabia for the purpose of ousting Saddam Hussein's Iraqi army from Kuwait. In February 1998, bin Laden called for a jihad or holy war against Americans and issued a fatwa (religious ruling) that called for the killing of any American anywhere. Later that year, bin Laden associates killed at least 301 persons in attacks on United States embassies in Kenya and Tanzania. In the Nairobi bomb, at least forty-five hundred people, many of whom were Muslims, were also wounded. FBI task forces investigated the scene of both bombings. In subsequent investigations, two arrests were made and warrants were issued for the arrest of Osama bin Laden and other members of al Qaeda. President Clinton also ordered cruise missile attacks on selected al Qaeda targets in the Sudan and on six al Qaeda bases in Afghanistan. Numerous members of al Qaeda were killed in the attacks, but bin Laden escaped before the missiles hit their targets. The United States also linked al Qaeda to the October 2000 assault in Yemen that damaged the U.S.S. *Cole*, killed seventeen sailors, and injured thirty-nine others.

Although American intelligence services and law enforcement officers headed off several potential terrorist attacks—including a plan to blow up the Los Angeles airport in early 2000—the government found it difficult to deal with all terrorist threats. American retaliation against al Qaeda following the attacks in Africa failed to damage the group significantly. Indeed, the Clinton administration suffered embarrassment when U.S. forces destroyed a suspected al Qaeda nerve gas production facility in the Sudan with approximately thirteen Tomahawk cruise missiles. Evidence soon indicated that the facility was a legitimate pharmaceutical plant rather than an al Qaeda factory. Missile strikes against an al Qaeda training camp in Afghanistan also proved ineffective.

Computers and the Internet

As previously discussed, the high-tech industry began to achieve many breakthroughs in the 1960s, perhaps most significantly, the invention of the microprocessor. In the 1970s, new companies such as Apple began using microprocessors to manufacture early versions of microcomputers, and in the early 1980s industry giant IBM introduced its personal computer (PC). Macintoshes (Apple's microcomputers), IBM PCs, and PC clones produced by a variety of companies soon became common features in offices as well as in ordinary American homes.

In the 1980s, someone with a home computer might use it to write a letter, process financial records, or play a game. In the 1990s, however, a computer owner's world expanded with the introduction of the Internet. The Internet's origins lie in the 1960s, when Pentagon-funded researchers developed a way to link networks of computers at various universities. They called this an "internetwork," or "internet" for short. A European computer scientist, Tim Berners-Lee, then developed a simple way to find information on the new Internet. Called the World Wide Web (www), Berners-Lee's system debuted to the public in 1991. After that, anyone with a computer and access to the Internet could tap into a truly global information system.

Americans enthusiastically took to the web not only for information but also for entertainment, communication, and commerce. Universities, museums, and libraries created web sites for the dispersion of knowledge, as did enthusiasts of all sorts. Electronic mail (e-mail) and on-line "chatting" transformed the way many Americans interacted with one another. On-line businesses popped up to offer consumers everything from pet supplies to books to clothing. Anyone with Internet access and a credit card could shop late at night from home by the glow of a monitor.

The commercial potential of the Internet raised the interest of Wall Street as well as of eager entrepreneurs. The success of Microsoft, which developed the disk operating system (DOS) for IBM as well as other computer software, showed everyone the fortunes that could be made in computers. Indeed, in the 1990s, Bill Gates and Paul Allen, the company's founders, were the first and third richest persons, respectively, in the world. With the introduction of the user-friendly World Wide Web, pioneers in electronic commerce (e-commerce) rushed to spin their business ideas into Internet gold. Jerry Yang, co-founder of the Web browser company Yahoo, and Jeff Bezos, who created Internet bookseller Amazon.com, provided the models of success as the value of their stock made them into millionaires, if not billionaires, practically overnight.

Investors willingly paid top dollar to get in on the ground floor of an Internet company. On the day in 1999 that Priceline.com—a seller of airline tickets—premiered on the

▶The success of Microsoft, which developed the disk operating system (DOS) for IBM showed everyone the fortunes that could be made in computers. In the 1990s, Bill Gates (at left) and Paul Allen, the company's founders, were the first and third richest persons, respectively, in the world.

stock market, the price of one of its shares rose from $16 to as high as $85 before closing at $68. The company's value as measured by its stock price reached nearly $10 billion that day—more than the net worth of several major airlines combined. Some questioned the rationality of such valuation in the new Internet economy. After all, Priceline had lost more than $114 million in 1998, the year before it went public. In early 2000, the skeptics were proven to be right. Too many new Internet startups simply found themselves losing too much money, investor confidence plummeted, and the "dot-com" bubble burst. To be sure, e-commerce was not dead; consumers apparently had taken to Internet shopping, and better-established companies lived on. Indeed, Amazon.com, founded in 1995, finally showed its first profit in the fourth quarter of 2001 and had expanded beyond books to include other merchandise. Similarly, eBay would become an enormous success and revolutionize the buying and selling of used goods.

The "Trial of the Century"

▶O. J. Simpson's mug shot, taken 17 June 1994 at the time of his arrest.

For over a year, from June 1994 to October 1995, the public attention was fixated on O. J. Simpson. Simpson had long been in the limelight—first as a football star, then as a television sports announcer, a commercial spokesman, and a movie actor. An African American, he enjoyed great popularity with audiences of all ethnic backgrounds. A poor boy who made good through hard work and talent, Simpson in 1994 lived the American Dream in the affluent Brentwood section of Los Angeles. In June of that year, however, the dream turned nightmarish: authorities arrested Simpson for the brutal murder of his ex-wife, Nicole Brown Simpson, and her friend, Ronald Goldman.

The televised events of the Simpson case—from arrest through jury verdict—captivated viewers, as the case seemed tailor-made for America's obsessions with celebrity and sensationalism. The trial helped the careers of various commentators, particularly on cable television outlets, who dispensed their analysis to a public with an apparently limitless fascination with the horrific details of the case. The seriousness of the crime often became lost in all the media attention, particularly in attempts at humor such as the *Tonight Show's* skits featuring dancers modeled on the trial judge.

Race also played a significant role in the trial. Simpson's attorneys sought to portray Simpson as a black man wronged by the system. (Ironically, many blacks before the trial thought Simpson culturally "too white"—which in their eyes his marriage to the white

▶ Despite overwhelming evidence, O. J. Simpson was acquitted of the brutal murder of his ex-wife, Nicole Brown Simpson, and her friend, Ronald Goldman.

Nicole Brown had confirmed.) The lawyers wished to persuade the jury—nine African Americans, two whites, and one Hispanic—as well as the public that the police had planted evidence to frame Simpson. (Testimony did indicate that the detectives' work was sometimes shoddy.) During the trial, it became apparent that, in the aggregate, African Americans and whites thought differently about the trial based on their preexisting conceptions about the fairness of the justice system. When the verdict—not guilty—came down in October 1995, blacks and whites reacted in quite opposite ways. According to a Gallup poll, 89 percent of African Americans believed the jury made the right decision. Many blacks suspected the police had framed Simpson or that enough reasonable doubt existed. Others simply considered the verdict payback for all the times innocent blacks had been lynched by white mobs or treated unfairly by American courts. On the other hand, only 36 percent of whites endorsed the jury's verdict; indeed, a clear majority (53 percent) of whites deemed it wrong. Many noted that the jury only took three hours to deliberate following a trial lasting 133 days, hardly enough time to consider all the testimony thoroughly. Although a key piece of evidence, a "bloody glove" found on Simpson's property turned out to be beneficial to Simpson since it did not fit his hand, and one of the Los Angeles policemen, Mark Furman, was on tape making racial slurs against blacks, there was a lot of other evidence that many viewed as condemning of Simpson. Simpson had written a letter to his friend Al Cowlings that appeared to many to be a suicide note that while not admitting guilt, at least inferred it. Furthermore, Simpson and Al Cowlings led Los Angeles police down the freeway in a slow-speed chase toward Simpson's house in a white Ford Bronco before Simpson gave himself up to police. To many, this did not seem to be the action of an innocent man. The victims were killed with a knife, and Simpson had a cut on his hand and an instructional video in his house on the subject of how to kill someone with a knife. In addition, footprints at the scene matched Simpson's rare Bruno Mali shoes, samples of the victims' blood were found on Simpson's socks, and blood with DNA matching Simpson's was found at the scene. Television audiences also heard a frantic 911 call from a previous domestic disturbance at the Simpson home in which Simpson appeared to be very threatening to his wife. Finally, Mark Furman had been the eighteenth policeman to arrive at the scene; thus, even if he did harbor ill will toward Simpson due to his racial attitudes, the idea that he could have rearranged the evidence at that point appeared suspect to many.

Later, in more conservative Orange County, California, the parents of Nicole Brown Simpson and of Ronald Goldman sued Simpson in a civil court, arguing that Simpson was responsible for the losses they had suffered as a result of the wrongful death of their loved ones. In February 1997, a heavily white jury found him responsible for the wrongful death and ordered him to pay $33.5 million in compensatory and punitive damages. Although O. J. was free, he had spent fifteen months in jail and spent millions on legal fees. His celebrity career was over, and eventually he faded from the headlines.

Little serious discussion ensued about what the country might have learned from the Simpson trial about curbing police misconduct, bridging racial differences on the courts, or reforming the jury system. Instead, Americans looked for other scandals to fill their television viewing hours.

A White House Besieged

Another American obsession, as measured by the number of stories in the news media, involved the scandals surrounding the first family. During the 1992 presidential campaign, questions arose concerning an investment Bill and Hillary Clinton had made in the late 1970s in an Arkansas real estate venture called Whitewater Development Corporation. Whitewater was a reference to property in which the Clintons invested during the 1980s in

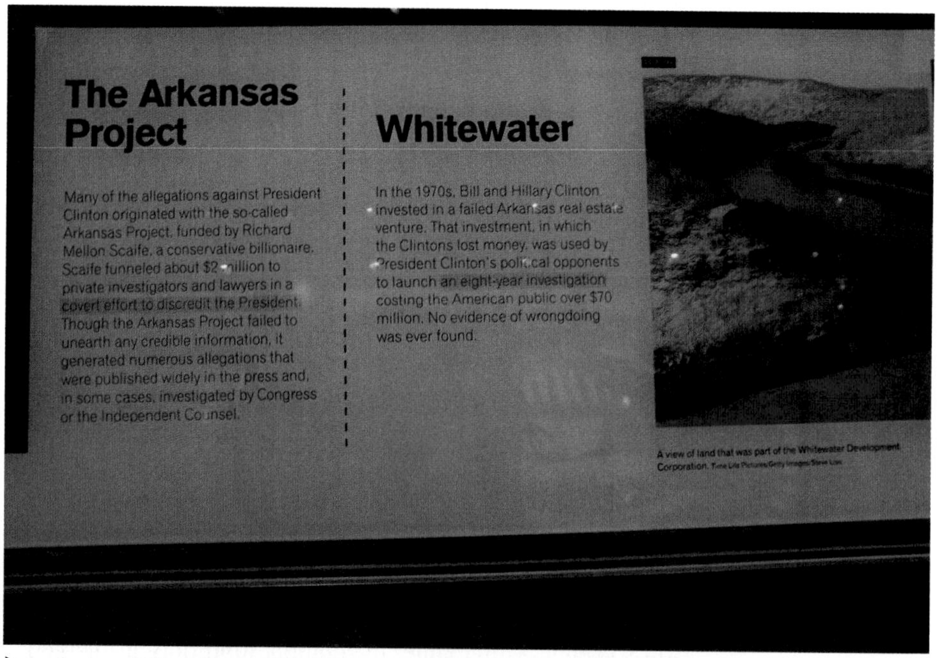

▶ In the late 1970s, Bill and Hillary Clinton had made in an investment in an Arkansas real estate venture called Whitewater Development Corporation. The small real estate venture failed, and from its humble beginnings came a major scandal that threatened Clinton's presidency.

a small, failed, Arkansas real estate venture. The Clintons' total investment, together with their partner's, in the Whitewater property in the Ozark Mountains was only $200,000. If the deal had worked as well as they had anticipated, their total profit would have been $45,000. However, James McDougal, the Clintons' partner in the Whitewater venture, turned out to be less than honest in his business dealings and less than mentally stable in his personal life. McDougal was indicted in 1990 for fraud in a check-kiting scheme, but the FBI and the United States Attorney concluded that there was insufficient evidence to suggest that the Clintons had knowledge of McDougal's illegal activity. The venture lost money for the Clintons, but from that humble beginning came a major scandal that threatened Clinton's presidency. A year into his first term, the political pressure to look into the matter built to the point that Clinton authorized the appointment of a special prosecutor, Robert Fiske, to investigate. Later in 1994, after Congress passed a new independent counsel statute, a panel of federal judges selected Kenneth Starr, solicitor general in the Bush Justice Department, to head up the investigation of Clinton.

When the Republicans gained control of Congress in 1995, House Speaker Newt Gingrich, who had stated during the 1994 election campaign that he would use "subpoena power" to wage political war with the White House, pressed forward anew with investigations of Whitewater, in particular, and the White House, in general. Gingrich referred to Clinton as "the enemy of normal Americans" and stated that he envisioned as many as "twenty Congressional committees simultaneously investigating the White House." Thus, the House Banking Committee under James Leach of Iowa and the Senate Banking Committee under new chairman Alfonse D'Amato revived the Whitewater probe with renewed vigor. Other probes were launched investigating the White House for firing of White House travel office employees, alleged misuse of FBI files, and, of course, the failed Madison Guaranty Savings and Loan in Arkansas that was connected to Whitewater.

Witnesses that could dispute accusations against the Clintons were not allowed to testify, and exculpatory evidence was repeatedly ignored. On June 26, 1995, the *Wall Street Journal* published details of a report prepared for the Resolution Trust Corporation (RTC) by the San Francisco Law firm of Pillsbury, Madison, and Sutro, concerning the Whitewater affair. The report showed that the Clintons were passive investors in Whitewater. They weren't involved in its financial transactions until 1986, and therefore could not have played a role in the collapse of the Madison Guaranty Savings and Loan that transferred $43,000 to Whitewater prior to 1986. Furthermore, the report concluded that the Clinton's partner, James McDougal had, without their knowledge, taken money from their investment and transferred money between entities he owned (essentially a check kiting scheme)—including Whitewater.

After ten weeks of hearings, some of it even occurring during the government shutdown, the Senate Banking Committee finally concluded, without proving any of the Republicans' initial accusations. In spite of all of the allegations of perjury and obstruction of justice, not a single witness was ever charged with any offense. As Whitewater dragged on and on, even some of the most rabid Republicans began to give up on it. In February 1997, Independent Counsel Kenneth Starr, with essentially no more leads and all of his roads toward anything substantial exhausted, temporarily resigned his post as Independent Counsel in the Whitewater case in favor of a position as Dean of the Law School at Pepperdine University. In April 1997, even Republican Senator Alfonse D'Amato confessed that the entire affair needed to end.

During his brief tenure in 1994, Robert Fiske also examined the circumstances of the suicide of Clinton aide Vincent Foster, deputy White House counsel and close friend of the Clintons. Starr later re-investigated the Foster suicide. In both cases the conclusion was that Foster was suffering from depression, and in that state decided to take his own life. Nevertheless, "rumors" that the Clintons had something to do with Foster's death persisted.

The investigation into these matters yielded the indictment and conviction of several persons, including Clinton's successor as governor, Jim Guy Tucker. Never did evidence of criminal wrongdoing by the president or first lady emerge. Starr's inquiry seemed to be at a standstill in late 1997 when suddenly it took a new direction because of a civil law suit originally filed against Clinton in 1994.

On May 27, 1997, the Republicans were handed a break in the case when the United States Supreme Court ruled that Paula Jones' sexual harassment civil suit against President Clinton should go forward while he remained in office. Paula Jones had been a clerical employee of the Arkansas Industrial Development Commission in 1991, and had helped staff a state-sponsored "quality management" conference at Little Rock's Excelsior Hotel. Jones claimed that Clinton had invited her to a room at the hotel, made sexually aggressive advances, asked her for "a type of sex," and exposed himself to her in the hotel room. Jones' claims appeared dubious, however, since she claimed that she met Clinton on the afternoon of May 8, 1991, at 2:30. Yet Clinton had given a breakfast speech at the hotel that morning and left the hotel not long afterward. That afternoon, a function at the governor's mansion precluded any secret return by Clinton to the Excelsior unless he could be in two places at once. Jones later changed her story and claimed that Clinton had ducked out of the reception at the governor's mansion and "walked three blocks" back to the Ex-

▶ Grave of Vincent Foster, White House counsel and close friend of the Clintons. Later investigation of the suicide, concluded that Foster was suffering from depression, and in that state decided to take his own life. However, this was just one more scandal for the Clinton administration to address.

celsior to meet with her. However, the governor's mansion and the Excelsior are at opposite ends of downtown Little Rock, over a mile apart and separated by a six-lane freeway. Seeking to establish a pattern of similar sexual advances, Jones's attorneys pursued information that Clinton had been involved for some time with a young White House intern, Monica Lewinsky, beginning in 1995. Fuel was added to the sex-scandal fire later that year when Kathleen Willey, a financially strapped widow and former White House worker, claimed that Clinton had groped her in the Oval Office in 1993. Ironically, Monica Lewinsky confidant Linda Tripp, who testified before a grand jury that there was "no harassment whatsoever" in the Willey case, unraveled Willey's story. Tripp testified that instead of Clinton chasing Willey, Willey had been chasing Clinton because her husband had died and she was in dire financial straits. Nevertheless, in a deposition with Jones's attorneys, Clinton denied having had a sexual relationship with Lewinsky.

In January 1998, however, the Republicans received another break when Linda Tripp, a friend of former presidential intern Monica Lewinsky, brought evidence of an extramarital affair between Lewinsky and Clinton to the attention of the independent counsel. Tripp had secretly taped conversations between herself and Lewinsky, in which Lewinsky discussed details of the affair, including her possession of a dress with stains left by the president's semen. Starr investigated the Lewinsky affair in conjunction with the Paula Jones case (a loose connection at best). The Jones case, of course, Starr had been investigating due to its purported connection to Whitewater. Then in early 1998 Starr received permission from Attorney General Reno to expand his investigation to include the Lewinsky matter. (Interestingly, before his appointment as independent counsel, Starr had provided legal advice to the Jones attorneys in their case against the president.) After some months, he struck a deal with Lewinsky under which she provided his office details about her sexual relationship with Clinton. The president agreed to testify before a grand jury. There a prosecutor questioned him at length about Lewinsky. President Clinton, unaware that Lewinsky had kept the stained dress, would lie under oath to cover up his affair with Lewinsky, thus committing perjury and giving the Republicans the "crime" they needed to commence with impeachment (though Clinton and the prosecutors differed on the definition of "sexual relations"). Based on Lewinsky's information and the DNA evidence from her dress, the prosecutors now accused Clinton of lying to the grand jury.

In September 1998, Starr sent Congress a 445-page report on the Lewinsky matter outlining what he considered impeachable offenses. This impeachment referral went into graphic detail about Clinton's encounters with Lewinsky. This was necessary, Starr maintained, to demonstrate the falseness of Clinton's statements to the grand jury. Very soon, before members of Congress could review it, the House leadership authorized the report's posting on the Internet where anyone could read about the president's alleged sexual indiscretions.

Despite widespread and often prurient public interest in and overwhelming disapproval of the Clinton-Lewinsky relationship, most Americans opposed impeachment. Generally, they gave Clinton's job performance high marks (especially with the economy doing well) and considered his extramarital affairs a matter for his wife and him. Observers sympathetic to Clinton argued that his shading of the truth about the Lewinsky matter, even before a grand jury, did not constitute the "high crimes and misdemeanors" that the Constitution requires as a basis for impeachment.

Congressional Republicans pressed ahead toward impeachment, nonetheless, even when the November 1998 congressional elections might have given them pause. Normally, the party that controls the White House loses a few seats in non-presidential election years. Amazingly, even with the Clinton scandal, his party picked up—and the Republicans lost—five seats in the House. In the Senate, where Republicans had believed they would gain several seats, there was no net change in party numbers. Still, two Republican senators who had emphasized the Clinton scandals—Alfonse D'Amato of New York and Lauch Faircloth of North Carolina—went down in defeat. The congressional defeats for his party shocked Newt Gingrich, who had expected to increase the GOP majority in the House by twenty seats or more. Many Republicans blamed Gingrich for the party's poor showing; and within days he announced that he would not seek re-election as Speaker and would, in fact, resign from Congress. That Gingrich had had widely publicized sexual improprieties in his life may have also been part of the equation.

After the election, the House Judiciary Committee moved forward and reported four articles of impeachment. Meanwhile Democrats—and some Republicans such as former President Gerald Ford—urged that Congress censure the president, a less severe punishment. At the same time, numerous Clinton opponents and newspaper editorial pages called for Clinton's resignation; but congressional Republicans, however, refused to pursue anything less than impeachment and removal from office. The president steadfastly declined to step down. On December 19, 1998, the full House approved two of the articles—largely on party line votes. One article alleged Clinton perjured himself before the federal grand jury in August 1998, while the other charged him with obstructing justice by seeking to influence potential witnesses in the case.

For only the second time in American history, the Senate conducted an impeachment trial for a president. The trial, which took five weeks beginning in early January 1999, ended with the president's acquittal on February 12. Forty-five senators supported, and fifty-five opposed conviction on the perjury matter. On obstruction of justice, senators split 50–50. These results were not unexpected; it had been unlikely that enough Democrats would join the majority of Republicans to reach the constitutionally required two-thirds of senators needed to convict Clinton. Moreover, polls indicated that most Americans disapproved of conviction.

Although Clinton finished his term, the Lewinsky matter would certainly tarnish his legacy. Just before leaving office in 2001, Clinton agreed, in a deal with the independent counsel, to admit that he gave "misleading and evasive" testimony in the Jones case. The final report of the last Whitewater independent counsel appeared in March 2002, eight years and $70 million after the probe began. It cleared Bill and Hillary Clinton of any wrongdoing in the various matters pursued by the investigators.

Hillary Rodham Clinton as First Lady

As the wife of a man whose infidelities were better documented than perhaps any other errant husband in history, Hillary Rodham Clinton had to endure considerable humiliation as an occupant of the White House. Painful though that experience must have been, it also seems to have garnered her more sympathy from the American people than she had enjoyed when she was seen primarily as the unsuccessful advocate of a failed health care reform package.

A brilliant woman and graduate of Wellesley College and Yale Law School, Mrs. Clinton had had her own legal career before moving into 1600 Pennsylvania Ave. Though she was the devoted mother of one child, she raised hackles among those for whom the social changes of the 1960s had been experienced as a coup d'état. Her enemies depicted her as a power-mad feminist who undervalued the traditional female virtues and values. Not since Eleanor Roosevelt had a first lady been so polarizing. Yet after the Monica Lewinsky episode and the new public sympathy that the affair engendered, she was able to win election to the United States Senate from New York with she and her family establishing residence there in time for the fall campaign in 2000.

Like her husband, Mrs. Clinton made a number of well-publicized trips abroad, especially to Third World countries, where she tried to call attention to women's issues and concerns. These trips constitute, perhaps, her most valuable legacy.

A Second Bush Presidency

The Election of 2000

In 2000, Republicans nominated Texas Governor George W. Bush, son of the 41st president, as their presidential candidate. Bush enjoyed the support of key insiders from the administrations of Reagan and his father. Moreover, financing proved crucial to his victory. Refusing to accept federal matching funds for his campaign so that he would be free from spending limits imposed by law, he overwhelmed his less well-financed competition in the primaries. On

▶ Mrs. Clinton made a number of well-publicized trips abroad, especially to Third World countries, where she tried to call attention to women's issues and concerns.

policy matters, Bush touted a program of "compassionate conservatism" that stressed cutting taxes, reforming education, and seeking non-governmental solutions to social ills. He selected the politically experienced Richard Cheney to run for vice president. A former Wyoming congressman, Cheney had also served as chief of staff to President Ford and secretary of defense under President George H. W. Bush, before taking over as chief executive officer of the world's largest oil field services company, Halliburton.

In the general election, Governor Bush faced Vice President Albert Gore, Jr., who had defeated former New Jersey Senator (and New York Knicks basketball star) Bill Bradley to win the Democratic nomination. He chose as his running mate Senator Joseph Lieberman of Connecticut, the first Jew ever nominated by a major party for vice president. Although most pundits considered Gore more conversant with public policy issues than Bush, voters seemed to find the Texas governor's folksier style more appealing. In a series of televised debates, Bush generally exceeded expectations and was deemed by pundits to have bested Gore.

Although not included in the debates, two other key candidates also sought the presidency in 2000. Ralph Nader, pioneering consumer advocate and environmentalist, ran on the Green Party ticket, while Patrick Buchanan served as the candidate of Ross Perot's Reform Party. In what was expected to be a close contest, many observers believed Nader might siphon voters from Gore and Buchanan from Bush.

▶ Vice President Albert Gore, Jr. official portrait, 1994

Election night, November 7, 2000, proved to be one of the most exciting in a generation. Although early returns indicated Bush victories throughout most of the South and lower Midwest, they also pointed to wins for Gore in swing states rich in electoral votes, such as Pennsylvania and Michigan. Just before 8:00 p.m. (EST), the networks predicted that Gore would win Florida, a sobering loss for Bush whose brother, Jeb, served as that state's governor. Later in the evening, networks retracted their call, and after midnight awarded Florida to Bush. Doubt remained, however, because of the extreme closeness of the vote there.

As the sun rose on November 8, the electoral votes of three states—not only Florida but also New Mexico and Oregon—remained in question. Gore needed all three to win, whereas Florida alone would put Bush over the top. Oregon and New Mexico both shortly went to Gore, but uncertainty about Florida's returns persisted for five weeks. During this period, Americans received a national civics lesson about the meaning of voting in a democracy and the intricacies of the Electoral College system.

Bush led Gore by a narrow margin in Florida's popular vote; initial estimates ranged from around three hundred fifty to one thousand votes out of nearly 6 million cast. However, irregularities muddied the result. In liberal Palm Beach County, a confusing arrangement of names on the ballot almost certainly led some Gore supporters to cast votes inadvertently for the conservative Buchanan. Six thousand ballots in West Palm Beach County were double-punched for both Gore and Pat Buchanan and another three thousand were double-punched for Gore and Socialist candidate David McReynolds. In all, Gore's name was included in forty-six thousand such "over-votes" while Bush's name was included in only seventeen thousand. This unfortunate confusion, along with the ninety thousand far-left votes in Florida that were siphoned from the Democrats by Ralph Nader, would essentially give Bush the presidency. In addition, there were other unsavory elements that surfaced as well.

In the summer of 1999, Florida Republican Secretary of State Katherine Harris arranged for the State of Florida to pay $4 million to a company called Database Technologies to go through Florida's voter rolls and remove any felons from the approved voter lists. Unfortunately, thousands of eligible voters with similar names to convicted felons, mostly minorities who typically vote Democrat, were also purged from the voter lists. Among the one hundred eighty-one thousand citizens that were purged from the voter lists were eight thousand individuals on a list supplied by the State of Texas (where candidate Bush was governor at the time) of suspected felons from Texas that had moved to Florida. The Gore campaign also alleged that voting machine problems in several other counties affected the outcome, and it called for a recount of those ballots. In the first count, Bush was declared the winner by 537 votes, but Florida law called for a recount in an election so close. The Democrats asked for a hand recount this time since machine errors had left hundreds of votes unrecorded in several heavily Democratic counties. The Bush team then sued to stop the recount, in spite of the fact that Bush himself had signed a similar law in Texas in 1997 that required hand recounts in such cases and required that election officials accept various degrees of punching or indentation that "show a clearly ascertainable intent of the voter to vote." Partisan politics apparently intruded as Florida Republican Secretary of State Katherine Harris, the state's chief election official and the Bush campaign's Florida co-chair, supported Bush's position in several key procedural decisions, while the state's Democratic attorney general, Robert Butterworth, filed a friend of the court brief on behalf of Gore.

After a series of legal maneuvers by both campaigns and conflicting rulings by state and federal courts, the United States Supreme Court delivered its final opinion in the case of *Bush v. Gore* on December 12. By a five-to-four majority, the Republican-dominated Court barred any further recounts (which the Democratic majority on the Florida Supreme Court had previously authorized). The Court majority declared that recounting ballots in certain counties and not in others violated the voters' right to equal protection of the laws. With no recount possible and Bush slightly ahead in Florida's popular vote tally, Gore conceded the race on December 13. Nationwide, Gore received approximately five hundred forty thousand more votes than his Republican opponent. However, with Florida's electoral vote secured, George W. Bush became the 43rd president of the United States.

For only the second time in American history, the son of a president took office as president. (John Quincy Adams was the other presidential offspring to be chief executive.) It should further be noted about the election of 2000 and the role played by the Florida outcome that it was subsequently documented that Republicans in that state had attempted

▶ With the results in for the election of 2000, George W. Bush (center) became the 43rd president of the United States.

various means of suppressing the African American vote. Thus the Florida outcome has continued to trouble not only partisan Democrats but also scholars who study political processes because of all the irregularities there were during the election and its aftermath.

The election left Republicans with a slim majority in the U.S. House and the Senate split evenly between the two parties. Officially, Democrats held the Senate majority from the time Congress convened on January 3 until January 20 because until then Democratic Vice President Gore could cast tie-breaking votes as the Senate's presiding officer. After Bush's inauguration, Vice President Cheney took over from Gore so that the Senate became Republican again. In June, however, the control of the Senate shifted again when Republican James Jeffords of Vermont left his party to become an Independent. The departure of the moderate Jeffords, upset over the power of social conservatives within the GOP, meant Democrats now outnumbered Republicans, 50 to 49, and thus controlled the Senate.

The Bush Domestic Agenda

Some observers believed the new President Bush would be forced to seek consensus with Democrats and not stake out very conservative positions once he took office. After all, he had been elected in an unusual fashion and was the first president since Benjamin Harrison in 1888 to have received fewer popular votes than his major opponent. However, it soon became apparent as he made his Cabinet nominations that Bush's administration would bear his stamp and no one else's. Some of his choices received wide bipartisan approval, most notably, Colin Powell for Secretary of State. Powell, former chairman of the Joint Chiefs of Staff, became the first African American to hold the top cabinet post.

Other Bush cabinet picks proved more controversial. He chose for attorney general the very conservative John Ashcroft (a man defeated the previous November in his Senate re-election bid by a dead candidate) and for interior secretary, Gale Norton, whom environmentalists disliked because of her work with former Reagan interior head, James Watt. Many of Bush's appointees came from big business, and several had worked in the petroleum industry—as had both he and the vice president had. The pro-business tilt of the new administration concerned labor, consumer, and environmental groups. Only one of his nominees, though, faced serious opposition. His labor secretary-designee, Linda Chavez, a prominent conservative commentator, withdrew her name when the press revealed she had employed an illegal alien to work in her home. Bush replaced Chavez with Elaine Chao, the first Asian American woman in the Cabinet. In the end, he selected only one Democrat for his cabinet, Norman Mineta, Clinton's last commerce secretary, whom Bush tapped for the transportation department.

In the first months of his administration, Bush moved ahead on his domestic agenda, including tax cuts, education, energy, and "faith-based" initiatives. True to his campaign pledge, Bush proposed and signed into law a significant income tax cut. The measure reduced tax revenues by an estimated $1.35 trillion over ten years. It trimmed tax rates for all income groups, lowered the so-called "marriage penalty," and provided for doubling child credits over time. Supporters lauded the cut as necessary for stimulating economic growth and for giving Americans greater control over their paychecks. Opponents argued it would result in the return of deficit spending rather than providing continued surpluses to shore up the Social Security system. Indeed, by the next year, the federal budget again ran a deficit. Tax cut foes also noted that the law favored wealthier Americans. Those with incomes in the top 1 percent received better than 37 percent of the tax cut; by comparison, taxpayers in the bottom 20 percent pocketed just 0.9 percent of the cut. Moreover, the cuts raised the after-tax income for the top 1 percent by 6.3 percent, while no other group received more than a 2.8 percent income boost. The law also would eliminate the estate (or "death") tax by 2010. This provision also favored the wealthiest Americans because they were the only ones subject to it.

Bush redeemed another campaign promise with the passage of new education reforms. The No Child Left Behind Act, signed into law in January 2002, tied increased federal funding for education to student scores on standardized tests. Ironically, this president who talked about reducing the role of the federal government signed this law that actually increased federal oversight of elementary and secondary education, traditionally a state responsibility.

On two issues, however, energy and faith-based initiatives, the administration experienced less success than on taxes and education reform. The fact that both Bush and Cheney were former oil industry executives primed Democrats and environmentalists to oppose the Bush energy plan unveiled in the summer of 2001. The plan's most controversial element involved its proposal to drill for oil in Alaska's environmentally sensitive Arctic National Wildlife Refuge (ANWR). Other controversy surrounded the plan. The task force that wrote the plan was chaired by Cheney and apparently included representatives of major energy firms, some of which had made large financial contributions to the Bush campaign. Cheney refused to divulge details about the composition or deliberations of his energy task force, so Congress's investigative arm, the General Accounting Office, sued the White House to obtain the information. The Republican-controlled House passed an energy bill very close to Bush's plan, while Democrats in the Senate insisted on eliminating drilling in ANWR. Because Bush demanded the ANWR provision, the plan stalled.

Faith-based initiatives formed a central pillar of Bush's campaign theme of "compassionate conservatism." Bush wanted to permit faith-based groups such as churches, synagogues, and other religious organizations to compete with secular groups to receive federal funding to administer social services. He established offices in the White House and five executive departments to promote the plan. Proponents argued that faith-based social programs had a higher degree of success than many secular ones, while opponents suggested that the plan violated church-state separation. Even some conservative religious organizations that generally supported Bush feared that government regulations would inevitably accompany federal funds. Again, the administration made little progress on this plan in 2001, especially with the August resignation of the White House aide heading up the faith-based effort.

Despite some successes, Bush did not enjoy very strong job approval ratings in the first few months of his presidency. The Harris polling organization found that Bush's positive rating—49 percent in March 2001—was lower than that of all recent presidents (going back to Lyndon Johnson) at comparable points in their administrations. His positive ratings improved later that spring following the shooting down of an American spy plane in China—they stood at 62 percent in early May according to Gallup—but declined steadily to the low 50s by early September. One liberal opinion journal placed a picture of a diminutive Bush on its mid-August 2001 cover under the title, "The Incredible Shrinking Presidency." Shortly, however, as the United States faced a major new crisis, the country rallied behind George W. Bush.

9/11 and the American Response

September 11, 2001, began as a beautiful late summer day in New York City. Then, at 8:45 a.m., a commercial airliner flew across the city's famed skyline and slammed into the 110-story north tower of the World Trade Center. Seventeen minutes later, a second plane crashed into the Center's south tower. The planes acted as enormous missiles—each carrying about sixty thousand pounds of jet fuel and traveling at three hundred miles per hour. As stunned on-lookers below raced for cover from falling debris, balls of fire engulfed the upper floors. Shocked Americans realized that the crashes were no accidents, but that terrorists had attacked the United States. At 9:43 a.m., a third plane rammed into the Pentagon just across the Potomac River from Washington, D.C., while less than half an hour later in western Pennsylvania, a fourth plane heading from Newark to San Francisco came down in rural Somerset County. Later reports indicated that passengers on board that fourth flight, aware of the New York attacks, struggled with hijackers, and foiled hijacker plans to destroy another Washington-area building, possibly the Capitol or the White House.

The extent of the devastation was incomprehensible. More than three thousand persons died in the attacks, including many New York City firefighters and police officers attempting to help victims in the burning buildings. The two World Trade Center towers collapsed, as did

▶ The extent of the devastation was incomprehensible. More than three thousand persons died in the attacks, including many New York City firefighters and police officers. September 11, 2001 can be considered the single worst day of domestic terrorism in American history.

several surrounding buildings. Reports estimated the property damage from the attacks that day at $25 billion. September 11, 2001, replaced April 19, 1995, as the single worst day of domestic terrorism in American history. Unfortunately, more terror followed in the ensuing days and weeks as several news organizations and two Democratic United States senators received letters laced with the deadly anthrax virus. Investigators believed that a domestic terrorist, trying to piggyback on the airline crashes, most likely sent the letters. In any event, the attacks left many Americans feeling helpless.

U.S. authorities traced the nineteen men responsible for hijacking the jets. They belonged to al Qaeda, the terrorist organization linked to the attacks on the United States embassies in Africa in 1998 and on the U.S.S. Cole in 2000. Headquartered since 1996 in Afghanistan where it enjoyed the protection of the fundamentalist Islamic Taliban regime, al Qaeda had cells in American and European cities. Several of the nineteen men had lived for a number of years in the United States where they took flying lessons to prepare for their deadly mission.

"Make no mistake," President Bush declared on September 11, "the United States will hunt down and punish those responsible for these cowardly acts." In the days that followed the attacks, Bush called for a new war against terror. He demanded that Afghanistan hand over bin Laden and his key associates. After the Taliban leadership refused, the United States and allied forces initiated aerial bombing of suspected al Qaeda targets on October 7. They also joined anti-Taliban groups (the Northern Alliance) within Afghanistan to overthrow the regime militarily. The first United States commandoes parachuted in on October 19 and took over a key airfield. Within weeks, Taliban and al Qaeda forces began surrendering in droves, although many remained in fortified, remote mountain hideouts in eastern Afghanistan. After allied bombings and some cave-to-cave operations by American and British forces, the United States in mid-December declared the Taliban defeated. Meanwhile, Afghani factional and tribal leaders opposed to the Taliban agreed on a new interim government headed by Hamid Karzai. In January 2002, the Taliban leaders officially gave up, although pockets of resistance remained in isolated spots. Polls indicated Americans overwhelmingly supported Bush and the war on terror. The president's job approval rating soared to 90 percent in the aftermath of September 11, and it

▶ As a result of the attacks in New York City, the two World Trade Center towers collapsed, as did several surrounding buildings.

remained above 70 percent well into the following year. Americans of all backgrounds—men and women, white and non-white, Republicans and Democrats—gave the president and his administration high marks.

Still, voices of dissent spoke out. A particularly vexing set of questions concerned the treatment of prisoners and detainees in the war on terror. The United States established a special detention center, Camp X-Ray, for Taliban and al Qaeda prisoners at the U.S. navy's base at Guantanamo Bay, Cuba, but refused to treat them as prisoners of war under international law. In addition, in the United States itself, the federal government rounded up and detained for months more than eleven hundred persons of Middle Eastern or Islamic background suspected of violating immigration laws (and of potentially being terrorists) or because they could be material witnesses in terrorist investigations. Civil liberties groups objected to these detentions because the government denied detainees basic constitutional rights, such as access to legal counsel. In addition, the government did not charge these alleged terrorists with any crime, a violation of the right to habeas corpus.

For its part, Congress gave strong approval to broader governmental powers to wage the war on terrorism at home by passing the USA PATRIOT Act in October 2001. This law weakened civil liberties guarantees by, among other things, expanding the government's ability to tap telephones, track e-mail, and conduct searches without warning. Supporters of privacy on both the political right and left raised concerns about how an open, democratic society based on individual liberties could permit such a law. In late 2001, however, security appeared more crucial than civil liberties to most members of Congress as they sought ways to prevent further terrorist attacks within the United States.

War in Iraq

Alarmed by the ongoing threat of terrorism that might be unleashed by Muslim fundamentalists in the aftermath of September 11, the American people and the Congress both overwhelmingly supported the American military action in Afghanistan—and much of the world concurred. Operation Enduring Freedom, to overthrow the extremist Taliban regime, was carried out in conjunction with NATO troops and in conjunction, also, with the homegrown Afghan Northern Alliance, long opposed to the Taliban. The campaign, which began in October 2001, resulted by

November of that year in the allies' capture of the capital, Kabul. The elusive Osama bin Laden, however, remained at large.

By early 2002, it was becoming apparent that the Bush administration had its eyes on other foes besides the Taliban. Having already proclaimed a "war on terror," in his State of the Union speech in late January, President Bush identified a so-called "axis of evil" consisting of the countries of North Korea, Iraq, and Iran. Using bellicose rhetoric, he made clear his administration's unwillingness to stand by while these states might be engaged in acquiring weapons of mass destruction or in sponsoring terror. During the course of 2002, it emerged that Iraq and its unsavory dictator, Saddam Hussein, were the chief targets of the administration's wrath, and President Bush foreshadowed his intentions by enunciating an American right to use preemptive force. Bush and others in the administration also began to issue stern warnings about the danger posed by the presence of alleged weapons of mass destruction in the hands of Saddam, the man whose invasion of Kuwait in 1990 had been responsible for the Persian Gulf War of 1991. In fact, it has subsequently emerged that certain members of the Bush team, above all, Vice President Cheney, had been eager to go after Saddam ever since the first President Bush had opted not to pursue this goal. The horror engendered by 9/11 then provided them with an excuse to do so: they were able to imply, if not outright assert, that Saddam was somehow connected with 9/11—an allegation since proven to have no substance. Cynics have suggested that the former oilman Cheney may have had oil-related motives that underlay his fixation with oil-rich Iraq.

While world opinion largely supported the action against the Taliban, the prospect of an American invasion of Iraq was another matter. America's French and German allies were strongly opposed; and while Prime Minister Tony Blair of the United Kingdom would send troops when the invasion took place, his government's action flew in the face of a British public opinion opposed to this stance. Trying to make its case, the Bush administration made

▶ The invasion of Iraq took place with a coalition consisting of American troops with a smaller number of troops from supporting countries. Within a few weeks Saddam had fled, Baghdad had fallen, and the real work of subduing an unruly and divided populace had begun.

ever-stronger claims about Saddam's weapons of mass destruction, culminating with a speech by the widely respected American Secretary of State Colin Powell to the United Nations in February 2003. Secretary Powell provided detailed "evidence" of the weapons in question, evidence that has subsequently been proven to be either flimsy or fallacious. The speech failed to persuade the U.N.; but the administration's case did persuade the majority of the American public, many Democrats in Congress—and members of the president's own party—to authorize the use of force in Iraq in a vote taken in the fall of 2002. (It should be noted that some of the Democrats voting for the use of force might have been not so much persuaded by the administration's case as afraid to be painted as unpatriotic in the wake of 9/11 should they oppose the administration).

The invasion took place with a coalition consisting overwhelmingly of American troops with a smaller number of British troops, and a smattering of troops from Italy, Spain, Japan (those from Japan in Iraq only for humanitarian purposes), and a few other countries. The U.N., whose inspectors felt that their ongoing effort to determine the state of Iraqi weapons programs was working, refused to endorse the invasion, as did NATO. Within a few weeks of the opening salvos in March 2003, Saddam had fled, Baghdad had fallen, and the real work of subduing an unruly and divided populace had begun.

Before the invasion, many military officials had tried to convince Secretary of Defense Donald Rumsfeld that this war could not be fought on the cheap. Most prominent among those making this argument was General Eric Shinseki, Army Chief of Staff, who warned in February 2003 that the Iraq action would require several hundred thousand troops (the number used in the less ambitious Gulf War of 1991). When Rumsfeld refused to provide him with the troops that he required, Shinseki resigned shortly thereafter, his warning having been ignored. As events unfolded, it was clear that the one hundred thirty thousand to one hundred fifty thousand troops on the ground had an extraordinarily tough assignment, especially as an Iraqi insurgency gathered steam. The troops' assignment was rendered even more difficult because the military found it challenging to maintain an adequate supply of the kind of armor necessary for the brutal conditions created by frequent roadside bombings (this according to widely-reported accounts). Indeed, reports of parents who themselves sent armor to sons and daughters appeared in the press. The Bush administration had not anticipated that there would be an insurgency at all and, therefore, had not sent the American soldiers to Iraq with the appropriate protection.

▶ In December 2003 Saddam was brought to trial under the Iraqi interim government and convicted of charges related to the 1982 killing of 148 Iraqi Shi'ites and was sentenced to death by hanging. He was executed on 30 December 2006.

There had been a certain amount of good news for the Bush administration coming out of Iraq. Saddam Hussein had been captured, brought to trial, and executed. Elections had been held, and an Iraqi government had come into power. As of mid-2008, however, the government was far from being able to maintain order on its own, and even the foreign troops had been unable to pacify the country fully. Not only are there still jihadi eager to kill Americans and those who cooperate with Americans, there has also been strife between the two strands of Islam in Iraq, the majority Shia and the Sunnis, long in control under the Sunni, Saddam Hussein. Further, the Kurdish population also constitutes a significant element of the population, one often at odds with the Shia and the Sunnis. Experts differ on whether there is an actual civil war or merely the preamble to one, but polls have shown that most Americans have been growing increasingly uneasy about a war that has cost the lives of at least four thousand Americans and tens of thousands of Iraqis—with no end in sight. Worst of all, no weapons of mass destruction have ever been discovered, and, belatedly, the administration has finally ceased to use this rationale for its Iraqi adventure.

Other unfortunate byproducts of the war have included a decline in the world's favorable opinion of the United States a phenomenon well documented by polling data collected by the Pew Research Center. Respect for the United States suffered an especially serious blow with revelations, in May 2004, about the widespread abuse of prisoners at Abu Ghraib, a facility built by Saddam Hussein but used by the Americans to house suspected troublemakers. Shocking pictures of American soldiers engaged in humiliating the inmates—or worse—backed up the revelations. At least one Iraqi inmate is known to have died from the abuse. To date, only low-level members of the military have been punished for the abuses at Abu Ghraib, in spite of the testimony of Private Lyndie England that she was only following "standard operating procedures."

Secondly, the war in Iraq has led to a diversion of attention and resources away from Afghanistan. Osama bin Laden remains at large as of mid-2008, and the Taliban has been resurgent, despite many hopeful signs of budding democracy in the beleaguered country. The respected Pakistani journalist, Ahmed Rashid, reported that as of late May 2006, "a revived

▶ Americans have been growing increasingly uneasy about a war that has cost the lives of at least four thousand Americans and tens of thousands of Iraqis.

Taliban movement has made one third of the country ungovernable." By late summer of 2008, more American soldiers were dying in Afghanistan on a monthly basis than in Iraq.

Thus five years after an exultant President Bush stood on the deck of an aircraft carrier near a sign proclaiming "Mission Accomplished" and three years after Vice President Cheney announced that the insurgency was in its last throes, the bloodshed was continuing. In fairness to the administration, it must be said that, as of mid-2008 there have been no new terrorist attacks on American soil since 9/11—though whether that is due to the Bush policies is an open question. After all, it was also eight years between the first bombing of the World Trade Center in 1993 and the second attack on 9/11. It must also be said that the administration has faced hitherto unknown challenges in trying to protect the American people from terrorism.

The Election of 2004

With politics still revolving around 9/11 and its consequences, the Republicans found that pitching themselves as the party best-suited to wage the war on terror worked well for them. Indeed, in the mid-term Congressional elections of 2002 they were able to pick up two seats in the Senate and three in the House, contrary to the usual pattern of mid-term losses for the party occupying the White House. Most galling for the Democrats, perhaps, was the defeat of incumbent Democratic Senator Max Cleland of Georgia, a wheelchair-bound Vietnam veteran. His successful opponent, Saxby Chambliss, ran ads that questioned the patriotism of this profoundly disabled man, disabled because of having fought for his country.

President Bush also had to withstand a significant challenge in the primaries from Senator John McCain of Arizona, a decorated Vietnam Veteran who was famously shot down in Vietnam and spent the war in a North Vietnamese prison camp known as the Hanoi Hilton. There, McCain underwent torture and suffered from multiple injuries, such as broken bones, to which the North Vietnamese did not attend. Bush proved that it was his intention to win at all costs when Bush supporters conducted anonymous telephone polls in South Carolina in which voters were asked whether they would be more or less likely to vote for McCain knowing he had fathered an illegitimate black child. What McCain and his wife, Cindy, had actually done was adopt a girl from Bangladesh whom they had originally brought to the United States for medical care. When complaints about the "poll" were aired by the McCain campaign, Bush's campaign manager Karl Rove's response was that no one had ever produced evidence that he or anyone in the Bush campaign had sponsored a poll about an out-of-wedlock child. For his part, Bush did not disavow the underhanded tactics, which were evidently carried out by Bush supporters at Bob Jones University.

With the certain knowledge that Republicans would play up their strengths as the party best able to protect the country in the terrifying new post-9/11 world, the Democrats chose to nominate a war hero in 2004, Massachusetts Senator John Kerry. Kerry had wrestled the nomination away from early leader Howard Dean after Dean had frightened voters with a speech where he intentionally threw a demonstrative emotional fit on stage to

▶ Massachusetts Senator John Kerry

show his passion. However, the emotional tactic backfired; and Dean, who had grabbed the early lead due to his consistent opposition to the Iraq war and adept use of the Internet, quickly faded. Kerry emerged from the pack of Democratic challengers that had included at one time nine candidates, including Dick Gephart and Al Sharpton.

Kerry, however, was an unusual type of war hero. After being wounded in Vietnam, he came home and took a leadership role in the Vietnam Veterans Against the War, testifying before Congress on the alleged war crimes he had witnessed. In so doing, he made enemies that would haunt him more than thirty years later. In the short term, however, his outspoken opposition to the war in Vietnam gave him visibility and made him a public figure—a platform that led to a political career.

At the Democratic convention in 2004, Senator Kerry gave a speech that was long on his military credentials and short on his ultimate opposition to Vietnam, thus signaling his intention to position himself as a potentially effective commander-in-chief in the war on terror. If he thought that such credentials might afford him immunity from the type of attack suffered by Max Cleland (especially in the light of George W. Bush's own ambiguous military record), he would soon learn otherwise. A group of Vietnam veterans, long disgruntled about Kerry's critique of Vietnam, launched an initiative known as the Swift Boat Veterans for Truth. Obviously very well funded, these men disputed Kerry's valor, his account of his wounds, and much else. In just nine months in Vietnam, Kerry had earned a Bronze Star and a Silver Star for valor, and three purple hearts. Yet in the Swift Boat ads, he was portrayed as a coward who lacked leadership skills and was awarded medals he did not deserve. In spite of the fact that the ads were entirely bogus (the United States military does not hand out medals to those who do not earn them), in the view of most pundits, the Swift Boat campaign played a role in Kerry's defeat. President Bush was not directly responsible for the Swift Boat ad, and it is true that it was not directly funded by his campaign. However, he did not denounce it either. Supporters of Kerry did not retaliate with a similar smear campaign of their own.

Most pundits further contended that the Republicans' adroit use of social issues also helped lead them to victory. Bush campaign strategist Matthew Dowd reviewed the 2000 election data and determined that the percentage of voters who could be persuaded to cross party lines had declined from 22 percent of the electorate in 1980 to just 7 percent in 2000. Conventional wisdom in presidential election strategy for decades had been that the party that wins the middle wins the election. Dowd's analysis, however, suggested that the persuadable middle had become so small and politics so polarized that the party that would win would be not the one that won the swing voters but rather the one that did the best job at getting its own partisans to the polls. Consequently, their strategy was to do a superb job of turning out their conservative base by evoking the threat of gay marriage, for example. Whether the Republican success owed primarily to this strategy, to the Swift Boat campaign, to the lingering effects of 9/11, or to Kerry's own shortcomings as a candidate, in fact, Bush did better than he had in 2000. Bush captured 50.7 percent of the popular vote to Kerry's 48.3 percent, with voter turnout at 61 percent, the highest since the late nineteenth century. John Kerry actually received more votes than Al Gore had in winning the popular vote in 2000, but George W. Bush received more votes, over 59 million, than any candidate in history. The vote in the Electoral College stood at 286 for Bush and 251 for Kerry. The Republicans also did well in the Congressional races, picking up three seats in the House and four in the Senate. Bush only won Ohio by 118,000 votes, however. If 60,000 of those voters had voted for John Kerry instead, Kerry would have won Ohio's 20 electoral votes and, thus, the election.

Second-Term Blues

Claiming that he had "won political capital" and intended to "spend it," George W. Bush announced at the beginning of his second term that he would seek to reform the Social Security system, in effect, privatizing it. He made many trips around the country to reach out to voters and convince them that this change would be in their interest, but his efforts were to no avail; and the projected change went nowhere as Bush's popularity diminished as the Iraq war dragged on. Unfortunately for Bush, the failure to mobilize public support for privatizing Social Security was only the beginning of his headaches as the year 2005 unfolded.

Bush's problems, and those of his party, deepened in 2005 when House Majority Leader Tom DeLay began to run into legal difficulties. Elected to the House in 1984 from a Houston district, DeLay had risen quickly through the ranks, becoming known as "the Hammer" because of his capacity to enforce party discipline. Within the halls of Congress, Delay's other nickname was "Hot Tub Tom" due to his proclivity for hot tubs and young women, while his supporters in Texas knew him as a Congressman who supported conservative Christian causes and referred to the occupied territories in Palestine as "Judea and Samaria." After the Republicans took control of the House in 1995, DeLay became Majority Whip. In 2002 he became House Majority Leader. Fiercely partisan, DeLay was known to be the driving force behind the impeachment of Bill Clinton. He also bore the credit—or blame, depending on one's point of view—for the K Street project, an initiative to reach out to lobbying firms (whose offices tended to be on K Street in Washington) and encourage them to hire only Republicans for leadership positions. What landed DeLay in trouble initially was his highly successful, from a partisan point of view, attempt to coordinate redistricting efforts in Texas so as to create "safer" Republican seats in the House. In 2005, this attempt led to a Texas grand jury indicting him on criminal charges of conspiring to violate Texas campaign finance laws. DeLay fought back by asserting that the charges were partisan in nature—but he did step down as Majority Leader. Over the next year he gradually surrendered more of his power until he resigned altogether from the House in June 2006.

That DeLay was driven from office owed also to the legal problems of one Jack Abramoff, a Washington wheeler-dealer and lobbyist—as well as an alleged DeLay crony—who ran into a legal buzz-saw of his own. In January 2006, Abramoff pleaded guilty to three felony counts of conspiracy, fraud, and tax evasion in conjunction with his dealings with certain clients. Soon thereafter, two former DeLay aides were convicted on charges related to the Abramoff scandal. Connections to Abramoff became so politically poisonous that the Bush administration classified the White House visitors' log, and critics charged that the motivation was to prevent the public from seeing that Abramoff had visited the White House.

Regardless, the reason why DeLay's fall was so problematic for his party and his president is that after his departure there was no other Republican in the House with his ability to deliver the votes for the Bush legislative program. On the other hand, since Ronald Reagan took office in 1981, the GOP has proven itself to be more than adept at political strategy and political recovery. Hence, even with this set of problems, it will no doubt continue to be a match for the sometimes-hapless Democrats.

▶Katrina first formed on August 23, and as it gathered strength it would become the third-strongest hurricane ever to reach land in the United States.

If Bush and his administration had shown themselves able to engage in successful combat with their political foes, they found Mother Nature to be a truly formidable foe when Hurricane Katrina hit the Gulf Coast in late August 2005. As Douglas Brinkley documents in *The Great Deluge*, the whole coast, including its largest city, New Orleans, constituted a disaster waiting to happen: an area of coastal erosion owing to natural causes and human alteration of the Mississippi River itself; the fact that much of New Orleans, situated next to America's largest river, is actually below sea level; and a situation further compounded by engineering mistakes. Moreover, oil companies had installed miles of pipelines in fragile terrain, and shipping companies had pressured the government to install channels. For all of these reasons, the natural defenses that had prevented New Orleans at the mouth of the Mississippi River, and other coastal cities from being repeatedly swamped by big storms had been undermined. When added to the ineptitude of government at every level, the result was a human catastrophe of nearly unimaginable proportions.

Katrina first formed on August 23, and as it gathered strength it would become the third-strongest hurricane ever to reach land in the United States. It touched southern Florida as a category 1 storm; but by the time it made its second landfall along the Gulf Coast on August 29, it had morphed into a category 3. At first New Orleans itself seemed to have escaped truly major consequences. Before very long, however, word came that the storm surge created by Katrina had breached the levees, leaving large sections of the city vulnerable to flooding—flooding that would eventually engulf some five hundred thousand homes. Thousands of New Orleans residents had either been unable or unwilling to evacuate the city; hence there arose an urgent need for rescue operations, operations that seemed to be feeble and ineffective. In the end, between the damage in New Orleans and in the rest of the devastated area, Katrina was estimated to have cost at least $75 billion in damages and nearly two thousand lives.

As these events unfolded, a horrified nation watched television images of mostly African American storm victims, huddling in the New Orleans Superdome or the Convention Center and lacking basic sanitation—with the authorities seemingly dithering about how to alleviate their problems. Brinkley forcefully delineates the failure of leadership at many levels. In New Orleans itself, for example, Mayor Ray Nagin failed to use all of his powers to ensure the evacuation of as many people as humanly possible before it was too late. President Bush, on vacation in Crawford, Texas (where he had similarly been—and stayed—in August 2001 when then-National Security Adviser Condoleezza Rice had warned him about a possible al Qaeda attack) stayed put until the disaster was well underway. Michael D. Brown, head of the Federal Emergency Management Agency, received a briefing about the expected severity of the storm and then let a whole day go by before taking action. Finally, when Brown did mobilize for action, his e-mails reveal him to have been extremely preoccupied with how he would look on television.

▶ In the end, between the damage in New Orleans and in the rest of the devastated area, Katrina was estimated to have cost at least $75 billion in damages and nearly two thousand lives.

At first President Bush praised Brown, saying to him publicly "Brownie, you're doing a heckuva job"; but within less than two weeks Brown had lost his job, a job for which he had no obvious qualifications (his most noteworthy previous job having been as head of a trade association for owners of Arabian horses). Trying to make amends, the president made a series of trips to the Gulf Coast to demonstrate his commitment to the region. As of mid-2006, however, there was still an overwhelming amount of work to be done, so overwhelming an amount that the *New York Times* reported an enormous surge in suicides and other mental health problems in New Orleans in the wake of Katrina.

Another casualty of Katrina had been President Bush's standing in the polls. Between the inadequate response to the hurricane and the increasingly unpopular war in Iraq, Bush's ratings plummeted, going as low as 27 percent approval at one point. That Vice President Cheney accidentally shot a friend in the face in February 2006, thereby becoming fodder for comics on late-night TV, did not help the administration's standing with the public. To make matters worse, his administration ended with the worst financial collapse since the Great Depression. The situation in Iraq showed improvement as Bush departed, but American involvement in Iraq appears to be long-term. Meanwhile, President Obama sent another thirty thousand American troops to Afghanistan in an attempt to accomplish American objectives there. Like Iraq, America's involvement in Afghanistan appears to be long term.

The Unfinished American Journey

To take the long view of how far the nation had traveled by the first decade of the new millennium we have only to think about the first national census in 1790, which counted just fewer than 4 million Americans, nearly seven hundred thousand of them enslaved persons of African descent. They primarily lived in cities, towns, and farms hugging the Atlantic Coast; the mean center of population lay twenty-three miles east of Baltimore. In 2000, the census recorded 281,421,906 Americans—all legally free—spread out in states stretching from the Atlantic to the Pacific, and even in the Pacific. By 2000 the mean center of population lay in south central Missouri's Phelps County, reflecting the continuing westward and southward movement of the population. Moreover, the population of nearly 300 million United States citizens included persons who came (or whose ancestors came) from every country on earth. People have come to these shores because they have believed in their chances to better themselves, and many barriers based on race and gender have crumbled. To cite just one example of positive change in breaking down barriers, leading Americans of Thomas Jefferson's day would have found it unimaginable that in 2006 an African American woman, Condoleezza Rice, would hold his old job as secretary of state. Though the country is far from being a full embodiment of the American Dream of justice and opportunity for all, it is far closer to realizing the dream than it was one hundred years earlier, let alone at the country's founding. Perhaps no one personifies the realization of this American dream more than the 44th president of the United States, Barack Obama.

Election 2008

The election of 2008 was historic in many ways, but perhaps most notably in the fact that the charismatic Democratic candidate Barack Obama became the first African-American

Democratic president, defeating Republican candidate John McCain 52 percent to 46 percent, and 364 to 174 in the electoral college. The election campaign should be, perhaps, considered the longest in American history as well as the most expensive. It began with a hard-fought primary contest on the Democratic side, with former First Lady and Democratic Senator Hillary Clinton amassing almost as many primary votes as Barack Obama and staying in the race until the Democratic Convention. But on November 4 the result was clear: Obama beat John McCain by six points in the popular vote (52 percent to 46 percent) and 190 votes in the Electoral College (364 votes to 174). Obama was the first Democrat since Jimmy Carter to win more than 50 percent of the vote (President Carter won 50.1 percent).

▶The election of 2008 was historic in that the Democratic candidate Barack Obama became the first African-American Democratic president.

In all likelihood, the moment when Mr. Obama won the campaign was in mid-September, when the bankruptcy of Lehman Brothers triggered the worst global financial crisis since the Great Depression. Undecided voters concluded that Obama's calm and cerebral style was exactly what Americans needed in difficult times, and they worried about Mr. McCain's temperament and judgment—especially his proclamation that "the fundamentals of our economy are strong." Additionally, by the fall of 2008 the Republicans had become a "tainted brand" due to a series of missteps by the Bush administration. Obama therefore benefited simply by being not Bush and not a Republican.

In August, however, McCain contributed the largest political surprise of the campaign when he nominated Alaska Governor Sarah Palin as his running mate. Palin was an unknown commodity at the time to most Americans and just two years earlier had been the mayor of the small town of Wasilla, Alaska. However, Palin, a former beauty pageant contestant and communication major, delivered one of the most effective convention speeches in American history at the Republican National Convention. A mother of five and a Protestant fundamentalist and social conservative, Palin appealed to the Republican base in a way that McCain did not. Suddenly, McCain drew virtually even with Obama in the polls as late as September 2008. Unfortunately for McCain and Palin, the economic meltdown tainted the Republican brand and Palin stumbled badly, revealing a lack of command of the issues in an interview with Katie Couric. Obama regained the lead.

Obama in the White House

In his first twelve months in office, Barack Obama managed the stabilizing of the American economy and pushed an overhaul of the American health care system designed to provide health insurance to the almost 50 million Americans without health insurance coverage (which eventually passed). Under his administration the controversial policy that included enhanced interrogation techniques (denounced by critics as torture) of suspected terrorists ended, and the American commitment to the war in Afghanistan increased, while gradually disengaging from Iraq. American foreign policy changed from the unilateralism that had characterized the Bush administration to a more internationally cooperative strategy.

On the down side, the president's economic stimulus package contributed over $700 billion to the burgeoning federal deficit; and though the country avoided another Great Depression, the economic recession that began in the fall of 2008 lingered into 2010 with unemployment levels remaining near 10 percent. Hope remained that America would climb out of its economic malaise and return to economic prosperity; but if it did not, President Obama's political future was in doubt at the end of his first year in office, as the country remained sharply and bitterly divided between conservative Republicans and liberal Democrats. Obama's approval rating fell even further in the summer of 2010 when a deep water oil rig explosion in the Gulf of Mexico spewed millions of barrels of crude oil into the Gulf. Though many Americans blamed British Petroleum oil company (BP) for negligence in the disaster, many also viewed President Obama's response to the crisis as inadequate.

In August 2010, President Obama declined even further in the polls when he announced his support for the building of a Muslim cultural center in New York City—just two blocks from

▶ In his first year in office, Obama pushed for an overhaul of the American health care system designed to provide health insurance to the almost 50 million Americans without health insurance coverage.

the site of the 9/11 attacks. Republicans opposed the construction of the Muslim cultural center as insensitive and disrespectful to the victims of 9/11, while Obama cited the separation of Church and State guarantees of the First Amendment. Republicans contended that the site was "hallowed ground," even though the site where the Muslim cultural center was to be built was the former site of a retail store for the Burlington Coat Factory retail clothing chain. Regardless of one's views on the controversy, Republicans were poised for victory in the mid-term election of 2010, just two years after being labeled as a "tainted brand." Perhaps the most exciting part of the Republican resurgence is that it demonstrates, again, that regardless of whether or not economic prosperity shortly returns or whether or not President Obama's presidency could survive the political storms, the American struggle with the difficult task of self-rule and the American experiment with Democracy can be expected to continue.

Bin Laden's Death

The Obama administration and the collective American psyche received a boost on May 1, 2011 when 9/11 financier, leader of Al Qaeda, and the world's most notorious international terrorist, Osama bin Laden, was gunned down in the dead of night in a raid on his private compound in Abbottabad, Pakistan carried out by American Joint Special Operations Command working within the CIA. Bin Laden's death came after some fifteen years of pursuit by three American presidents and an American war in Afghanistan that was still being waged almost a decade after the 9/11 attacks.

A poll by the Pew Research Center and the Washington Post shortly after the raid found that 56 percent of Americans approved of the way Obama was handling his job, up from 47 percent the previous month. Furthermore, more than 70 percent of Americans polled said that they felt "relieved" that bin Laden was dead and 60 percent of Americans reported that they felt "proud" that American forces killed bin Laden. President Obama announced the results of the raid to the nation and proclaimed that "justice has been done."

There was little outcry in the Muslim world in protest of the American raid and Obama ordered that photographs of bin Laden's dead body would not be released to the press so as to prevent stirring emotions in the Islamic realm. Bin Laden was quickly buried at sea so as to prevent any sort of issue arising over bin Laden's body.

Although Americans were generally pleased with the death of bin Laden, and later videos released by the Obama administration revealed bin Laden at the time of his death to be aging rather ungracefully and living in general isolation with his family, the war on terror continued with no real end in sight and the fact that bin Laden was found in Pakistan reinforced the fact that Radical Islam, with which America had been waging war since 9/11, was not limited to Afghanistan and Iraq, and the struggle would continue.

Chapter Review

Summary

The last decade of the twentieth century and the first decade of the twenty-first would be led by two baby boomer presidents: Bill Clinton, a Democrat with humble roots, and George W. Bush, from a wealthy, politically connected family where his father was the 41st president of the United States. In fact, Clinton would defeat the elder Bush and Independent candidate Ross Perot in the presidential election of 1992 as the economy slid into recession. Clinton, however, essentially stumbled out of the gate, introducing a controversial "don't ask, don't tell" policy for gays in the military and placing First Lady Hillary Clinton in charge of a task force forging a plan to reform health care. Republicans were able to defeat the proposed health care changes with an effective propaganda campaign and then used the health care debate against Clinton to sweep to victory in the mid-term elections of 1994, winning fifty-two seats in the House.

Led by House Speaker Newt Gingrich and his "Contract with America," the Republicans suddenly became fiscal hawks and demanded spending cuts in government. Clinton resisted Republican cuts to Medicare, resulting in a budget impasse and a government shutdown. The government shutdown backfired on the Republicans because the public blamed them for it. Republican approval ratings dropped and Clinton's rose before the 1996 election year. Republicans nominated long-time Senator Bob Dole of Kansas, and Ross Perot again ran as an Independent candidate. Clinton defeated Dole in November amidst a robust economy and booming stock market.

In foreign policy, Clinton largely continued the policies set in place by the Bush administration. Clinton ushered the North American Free Trade Agreement (NAFTA) through Congress and pushed for the expansion of NATO to the new capitalist democracies in Eastern Europe. Yugoslavia disintegrated in 1992, and a civil war between Muslims and Serbs ensued in Bosnia. In 1995, Clinton negotiated the Dayton Accords, a peace agreement in Bosnia. In the Middle East, Clinton negotiated the Oslo Accords in October, Israel relinquished control of Jericho and the Gaza strip to a new Palestinian authority. In 1998, the Wye River Agreements took things a step further as the PLO deleted anti-Israel language from its charter, and Israel agreed to give up more territory to the Palestinians. In Iraq, Clinton continued the no-fly zones in Iraq, including bombings and missile launches against Saddam Hussein's weapons capabilities and the continuation of economic sanctions against Iraq. Clinton also funded Kurdish rebellions and other plots against Saddam Hussein in a general policy of "regime change" in Iraq that followed Saddam's attempt to assassinate former President Bush in Kuwait in 1993.

Clinton inherited an American effort to provide relief to starving people in the war-torn country of Somalia, but the effort was thwarted when an American helicopter was shot down and the body of a U.S. soldier was dragged through the streets. The U.S. not only withdrew from Somalia, but it also did not get involved in the 1994 genocide in Rwanda where an estimated five hundred thousand to one million people died in ethnic cleansing. When Serbia commenced ethnic cleansing in Kosovo in 1998, however, Clinton ordered the bombing of Serbia until the policy was halted.

During the Clinton years, the world was rocked by terrorism at home and abroad. In February 1993, a radical Islamist group led by Sheikh Omar Abdul Rahman set off a bomb in a parking garage at the World Trade Center in New York, resulting in six deaths and nearly one thousand injuries. On February 28, 1993, Branch

Chapter Review (cont'd)

Summary (cont'd)

Davidians in Waco, Texas, fired on federal agents that were attempting to serve them with search warrants, killing four federal agents. Federal authorities surrounded the Branch Davidian compound until April 19 when the Branch Davidians committed mass suicide by burning down their own compound. Seventy-six people, including their leader, David Koresh. One year later, Christian soldier Timothy McVeigh, himself a member of another separatist sect on the Oklahoma-Arkansas border, blew up the Federal building in Oklahoma City with a truck loaded with fuel oil and fertilizer, killing 168 people.

On the foreign front, nineteen Americans died in a 1996 blast of a housing complex at Khobar Towers in Saudi Arabia. This was the first attack on Americans that involved a new terror group known as Al Qaeda. Two years later, Al Qaeda would blow up U.S. embassies in Nairobi, Kenya, and Dar es Salaam, Tanzania, resulting in the deaths of over two hundred people and injuring forty-five hundred. In 2000, Al Qaeda operatives bombed the USS *Cole* in the Port of Aden, Yemen, killing seventeen U.S. sailors and wounding thirty-nine others. Clinton retaliated against Al Qaeda with cruise missile attacks, but the attacks missed Al Qaeda leader Osama bin Laden. The terror attacks all occurred during a high-tech boom in America fueled by the introduction of the internet.

In spite of the spectacular terrorist attacks, the news story that gained the most attention in the first term of the Clinton administration was the O. J. Simpson murder trial. Simpson, an ex-NFL football star, Hollywood actor and sports commentator, was accused of killing his ex-wife, Nicole Brown Simpson, and her companion, Ronald Goldman with a knife. America watched as Simpson led Los Angeles police down the freeway in a seemingly endless low-speed chase of his white Ford Bronco. Then America stayed tuned for the next fifteen months, watching his televised trial. Although most Americans believed O. J. to be guilty, the jurors, many of whom were African-American, had reasonable doubt in part due to racial slurs spoken by Los Angeles policeman Mark Furman. Simpson was found not guilty by the jury, but his celebrity career was wrecked for good.

By the time the Simpson trial was over, media attention shifted to a White House besieged by Congressional investigations. The Republican-led Congress hired an independent counsel to investigate a real estate venture entered into by the Clintons while Bill Clinton was governor of Arkansas. The Clintons lost money on their "Whitewater" investment, and investigators found no wrongdoing by the Clintons. However, a federal judge allowed Independent Counsel Kenneth Starr to investigate the Paula Jones sexual harassment lawsuit against the president as part of the Whitewater investigation. When Monica Lewinsky's friend Linda Tripp informed the office of the independent counsel that Lewinsky had admitted having oral sex with the president to her in confidence, a federal judge allowed Starr to investigate the Lewinsky affair with the president as part of the Paula Jones lawsuit in conjunction with the Whitewater investigation. Clinton committed perjury in his deposition in the case and attempted to conspire with Lewinsky to mislead the investigators. As a result, Clinton was impeached by the House of Representatives for perjury and obstruction of justice, but the

Summary (cont'd)

Senate did not convict the president because Democrats in the Senate did not think the offenses were ones for which presidents should be impeached, convicted, and removed from office.

In the election of 2000, Texas Governor George W. Bush, the son of former President George H.W. Bush, defeated Democratic Vice President Al Gore in one of the closest and most disputed elections in American history. Gore won the popular vote by over five hundred thousand, but the winner of the electoral vote was in dispute for thirty-six days due to several electoral irregularities. Florida law called for a recount when the vote was that close, and George W. Bush sued in federal court to stop the recount. The Supreme Court ruled on the side of Bush and stopped the Florida recount, thus giving the election to Governor Bush.

Bush quickly moved on his reformation of America: pushing tax cuts, a reform of education with the No Child Left Behind Act, and for drilling for oil in the Arctic National Wildlife Refuge (ANWR). Although Bush was thwarted by environmentalists in his effort to drill for oil in the ANWR, the rest of his program would be smooth sailing, especially after the terrorist attacks of 9/11, the worst terror attacks in American history These were carried out by Al Qaeda operatives against the World Trade Center in New York City and the Pentagon. A fourth plane was crashed in a Pennsylvania field after passengers thwarted the terrorist attempt by the hijackers.

Bush retaliated with an invasion of Afghanistan in October aimed at apprehending Osama bin Laden and destroying Al Qaeda. Bush, however, made no distinctions between the terrorists and the governments that "harbor them." He took down the government of the Taliban in Afghanistan, leaving America with the responsibility of nation-building in Afghanistan, which continues a decade later. The next year, Bush told the nation that America was threatened by Saddam Hussein's weapons of mass destruction and ordered an invasion of Iraq to oust Saddam Hussein. The invasion in March 1993 went well. Saddam was ousted, and Bush proclaimed military combat operations to be at an end on May 1, 1993. Unfortunately, Bush's post-war plans for Iraq were sketchy at best and did not include plans for an insurgency and civil unrest. Iraq erupted into looting followed by insurgency and civil unrest that occupied the U.S. military in varying degrees for the rest of Bush's presidency. Americans were guilty of prisoner abuse of Iraqis at Abu Ghraib prison, and no weapons of mass destruction were ever found.

Nevertheless, Bush defeated Republican challenger John McCain in the primaries, with the aid of some unscrupulous campaign tactics in South Carolina, and narrowly defeated Democratic Senator John Kerry of Massachusetts in the general election of 2004 with the aid of the unscrupulous Swift Boat Veterans for Truth ads that questioned John Kerry's courage and patriotism. The second term, however, would be difficult for Bush. His approval rating dropped steadily after what the public viewed as an inadequate government response to Hurricane Katrina, which flooded New Orleans and the Gulf Coast leading to the deaths of over eighteen hundred Americans. In 2008, a financial crisis led to further disenchantment of the Republicans by the public, and Democratic Senator from Illinois, Barack Obama, defeated Republican Arizona Senator John McCain to be the first African-American president of the United States.

Chapter Review (cont'd)

Chronological Time Line

1991 Tim Berners-Lee's World Wide Web (www) system debuted to the public in 1991.

1992 Arkansas Democratic Governor Bill Clinton defeated incumbent Republican George H.W. Bush and Independent candidate Ross Perot for the presidency.

1993 President Clinton appointed a task force headed by First Lady Hillary Clinton to formulate a plan for the reform of the nation's health care system.

1993 Clinton's first budget raised taxes on the wealthiest 1.2 percent of Americans and cut the budget deficit $50 billion.

1993 On February 26, radical Islamic terrorists led by Sheik Omar Abdul Rahman set off a bomb in a parking garage at the World Trade Center in New York, resulting in six deaths and nearly one thousand injuries.

1993 On February 28, the siege at Waco began when Branch Davidians fired on federal agents serving search warrant. Four were killed and sixteen wounded.

1993 April: Kuwaiti security services uncovered a plot by Iraq's Saddam Hussein to kill former President George H.W. Bush with a car bomb.

1993 On April 19, the siege at Waco ended when Branch Davidians burned their own compound, killing seventy-six people, including Branch Davidian leader David Koresh.

1993 On June 26, the U.S. launched twenty-three Tomahawk cruise missiles at Baghdad, destroying the headquarters of Iraqi intelligence.

1993 October: Oslo Agreement transferred Gaza and Jericho from Israeli occupation to control by a new Palestinian authority. It also urged more bilateral talks between Israel and its Arab neighbors.

1993 October: recorded by television cameras, Somali warlord Mohammed Aideed's men dragged the body of a U.S. Marine through the streets of the capital city, Mogadishu.

1993 December: Clinton signed the North American Free Trade Agreement (NAFTA) that created free trade between the U.S. and Mexico.

1993 December: President Clinton instituted the "don't ask, don't tell" policy concerning gays in the military.

Time Line (cont'd)

1994 Up to a million people died in ethnic cleansing in Rwanda, and the U. S. did not intervene.

1994 Clinton's health care reforms failed to pass in Congress.

1994 April: Clinton's Secretary of State Warren Christopher stated, "The U. S. does not believe that Iraq's compliance with UN Resolutions is enough to justify lifting the embargo."

1994 June: The O. J. Simpson murder case hit the media and stayed there until its conclusion in October 1995.

1994 On September 19, President Clinton sent troops to Haiti to restore Jean Bertrand Aristide to the presidency after he was ousted in a military coup.

1994 November: Republicans won the Congressional mid-term elections, picking up fifty-two seats in the House of Representatives.

1994 November: Republican George W. Bush defeated incumbent Democrat Ann Richards to become governor of Texas.

1995 On April 19, Timothy McVeigh blew up the Federal building in Oklahoma City with a truck full of fuel oil and fertilizer, killing 168 people.

1995 Republican House Speaker Newt Gingrich was *Time* magazine's "Man of the Year."

1995 On June 26, 1995, the *Wall Street Journal* published details of a report prepared for the Resolution Trust Corporation (RTC) showing that the Clintons were passive investors in Whitewater, weren't involved in its financial transactions until 1986, and therefore could not have played a role in the collapse of the Madison Guaranty Savings and Loan.

1995 November 14–19: A federal government shutdown resulted from the budget impasse between the Republican Congress and President Clinton.

1995 December: Dayton Accords bring peace to Bosnia-Herzegovina.

1995 December 16–January 6: A second federal government shutdown resulted from budget impasse.

Chapter Review (cont'd)

Time Line (cont'd)

1996 January: Clinton declared "The era of big government is over."

1996 Congress passed the Line Item Veto Act granting the president the Line Item Veto.

1996 June: Nineteen U.S. soldiers are killed at the Khobar Towers bombing in Saudi Arabia orchestrated by Al Qaeda.

1996 August: Clinton signed the Personal Responsibility and Work Opportunity Act that dropped welfare rolls by 40 percent over the next two years.

1996 September: Clinton signed the Defense of Marriage Act that released states from Full Faith and Credit Clause obligations in cases of same sex marriage and defined marriage as between one man and one woman.

1996 On September 3, Clinton ordered the launch of forty-four cruise missiles at Iraq's military command posts and air defense centers near the southern no-fly zone.

1996 November: Bill Clinton defeated Republican Senator Bob Dole of Kansas and Independent candidate Ross Perot for a second term in the White House.

1997 President Clinton and Congress agreed on a balanced budget for the first time since the 1960s.

1997 In February, a heavily white jury found O. J. Simpson responsible for the wrongful death of Nicole Brown Simpson and Ronald Goldman and ordered him to pay $33.5 million in compensatory and punitive damages. Pleading that he was broke, Simpson never paid any of the damages.

1997 February: Kenneth Starr temporarily resigned as independent counsel in the White Water case due to lack of evidence.

1997 On May 27, the U.S. Supreme Court ruled that Paula Jones' sexual harassment civil suit against President Clinton should go forward while he remained in office.

1997 September: the World Health Organization (WHO) published a report that claimed that over five hundred thousand Iraqi children under age five had died since 1991 as the result of malnutrition and lack of medicine caused by the UN embargo.

Time Line (cont'd)

1997 On October 29, Iraq demanded the end of American "spies" on inspection teams, and six American inspectors were expelled the next month.

1998 January: Linda Tripp, a friend of former presidential intern Monica Lewinsky, brought evidence of an extramarital affair between Lewinsky and Clinton to the attention of the independent counsel.

1998 February: Osama bin Laden called for holy war on America and the killing of any American, anywhere.

1998 On April 10, the "Good Friday Agreement" or "Belfast Agreement" called for the disarming of sectarian paramilitary organizations and greater autonomy for Northern Ireland within Great Britain.

1998 On June 25, the Supreme Court struck down the Line Item Veto as unconstitutional in *Clinton v. New York City*.

1998 On August 7, Al Qaeda orchestrated bombings in Nairobi, Kenya, and Dar Es Salaam, Tanzania, that kill or injure over five thousand people, many of whom were Muslims.

1998 On October 23, in the Wye River Agreements, the Palestine Liberation Organization agreed to delete anti-Israel language from its founding charter, and Israel agreed to transfer more occupied territory to Palestinian control.

1998 On October 31, Congress passed the Iraq Liberation Act that entitled the president to spend up to $97 million for military aid to train, equip, and finance an Iraqi opposition army and authorized the Department of Defense to train insurgents.

1998 On October 31, Iraq ceased compliance with UN inspectors and demanded a review of its compliance linked to a timetable for ending sanctions.

1998 On November 18, UN weapons inspectors returned to Iraq, but found themselves obstructed by Iraqi officials.

1998 On December 16, Clinton ordered 415 cruise missiles (ninety more than were fired during the Gulf War) and six hundred laser-guided bombs to be dropped on Iraq. Saddam survived and weapons inspectors were no longer in Iraq.

Chapter Review (cont'd)

Time Line (cont'd)

1998 On December 19, the House of Representatives impeached Bill Clinton for perjury and obstruction of justice in the Monica Lewinsky case.

1999 January–August: Over eleven hundred missiles were fired at 359 targets in Iraq. In August Clinton ordered the bombing of Iraqi air defense targets outside the U.S.-imposed no-fly zones.

1999 On February 12, the U.S. Senate failed to convict President Clinton on impeachment for perjury and obstruction of justice.

1999 March: President Clinton ordered the bombing of Serbia to halt ethnic cleansing in Kosovo.

2000 October: Slobodan Milosevic is voted out in Serbia.

2000 On October 12, the USS *Cole* is blown up by suicide bombers in the Port of Aden, Yemen, killing seventeen U.S. sailors and wounding thirty-nine.

2000 On December 12, the U.S. Supreme Court stopped the Florida recount and awarded the presidency to Republican George W. Bush over Democratic Vice President Al Gore.

2001 On September 11, Al Qaeda terrorists flew jetliners into the World Trade Center, Pentagon, and a field in Pennsylvania, killing over three thousand people in the worst terrorist attack in American history.

2001 On October 7, the U.S. began bombing Al Qaeda positions in Afghanistan.

2001 October: Congress passed the USA PATRIOT ACT, granting extraordinary powers to the U.S. government and compromising individual liberties in the interest of fighting terrorism.

2002 January: Congress passed the No Child Left Behind Act.

2002 January: The Taliban government was toppled in Afghanistan by U.S. forces and the "Northern Alliance."

2003 On March 20, the U.S. invaded Iraq

2003 On May 1, President Bush declared major combat operations to be over in Iraq.

Time Line (cont'd)

2004 May: Information surfaced in the media about American abuse of Iraqi prisoners at Abu Ghraib prison in Iraq.

2004 November: George W. Bush won reelection, defeating Democratic Senator from Massachusetts, John Kerry.

2005 August: Hurricane Katrina flooded New Orleans.

2006 June: Republican House Majority Leader Tom DeLay resigned due to ethics violations.

2008 September: News that Lehman Brothers was insolvent led to a collapse of the financial industry and recession.

2008 November: Barack Obama defeated Republican Arizona Senator John McCain to become the first African-American president of the United States.

Key Terms

Pat Buchanan: Former speechwriter for Richard Nixon that won 37 percent of the vote in the New Hampshire primary on an essentially populist right-wing platform

Ross Perot: Texas billionaire that ran for president as an Independent candidate in 1992 and 1996 and won over 18 percent of the vote in 1992, but no electoral votes

Bill Clinton: Arkansas governor that defeated George H.W. Bush in 1992 to become the 42nd president of the United States

Hillary Clinton: First Lady of the United States that was assigned a substantive policy role in the attempt to reform health care in 1993–1994

Janet Reno: First female Attorney General of the United States that was criticized for her handling of the siege at Waco

Don't Ask, Don't Tell: President Clinton's policy regarding gay people in the U.S. military

Gingrich Revolution: The 1994 mid-term Congressional elections where the Republicans won fifty-two seats and elected Newt Gingrich Speaker of the House

Rush Limbaugh: Conservative radio talk show host that was made an "honorary member" of Congress by the new Republican majority in 1995

Chapter Review (cont'd)

Key Terms (cont'd)

Contract With America: Newt Gingrich's Republican Platform in the House of Representatives in 1995

Defense of Marriage Act: 1996 act that defined marriage as between one man and one woman and released states from Full Faith and Credit Clause Responsibilities in cases of same sex marriage

Bob Dole: Republican Senate Majority Leader and presidential candidate in 1996 that lost the presidential election to Bill Clinton

Jack Kemp: Republican Senator from New York, supply-side advocate, and ex-NFL quarterback that ran for Vice president in 1996 as Bob Dole's running mate

NAFTA: North American Free Trade Agreement that established free trade between the U.S., Mexico, and Canada

Chechnya: Muslim enclave in the Soviet Union fraught with political unrest due to separatism and Islamist terrorism

Bosnia: A majority Muslim province of the former Yugoslavia that gained its independence after a civil war in 1995

Dayton Accords: Bosnian peace agreement of 1995

WMDs: Weapons of Mass Destruction

Anthony Zinni: U.S. general that warned that a stable Iraq under Saddam Hussein was less dangerous than an unstable Iraq without Saddam Hussein

Rwanda: African country where up to 1 million people died in ethnic cleansing in 1994

Kosovo: Serbian province where Serbian ethnic cleansing in 1999 provoked American air strikes against Serbia to halt the ethnic cleansing.

Slobodan Milosevic: Serbian leader during the crisis in Kosovo in 1999

Timothy McVeigh: American ultranationalist and Christian extremist that killed 168 people with a truck loaded with fuel oil and fertilizer in Oklahoma City in 1994

Branch Davidians: Narrow Christian sect at Waco, Texas, that fired on federal agents and committed mass suicide in a 1993 siege at Waco

David Koresh: Leader of the Branch Davidians who died in the 1993 siege at Waco

Sheikh Omar Abdul Rahman: Also known as "The Blind Sheikh," and was ringleader of the 1993 World Trade Center bombing plot

Mujahadeen: Islamic Jihadists aided by the U.S., Saudi Arabia, and Osama bin Laden in Afghanistan against the Soviet Union in the 1980s, some of whom turned their jihad against the United States in the 1990s

Al Qaeda: Osama bin Laden's global terrorist organization that was responsible for the 9/11 attacks on the United States

Osama bin Laden: Son of a wealthy Saudi Arabian construction magnate that financed Al Qaeda's global jihad, including the 9/11 attacks on the United States

Nairobi bombing: 1998 suicide bombing of the U.S. Embassy orchestrated by Al Qaeda in Nairobi, Kenya that killed over two hundred people and injured over four thousand, some of whom were Muslims

Key Terms (cont'd)

USS *Cole*: U.S. destroyer that was blown up by Al Qaeda in the Port of Aden in Yemen in 2000 killing seventeen U.S. sailors and wounding thirty-nine

O.J. Simpson: Ex-NFL football star and Heisman Trophy winner, Hollywood actor, and sports commentator that was accused of murder in the death of his ex-wife, Nicole Brown Simpson, and her companion Ronald Goldman

Mark Furman: Los Angeles policeman whose use of racial slurs may have placed reasonable doubt in the minds of the jurors in the O.J. Simpson case

Whitewater: This was the name for both the scandal and Independent Counsel investigation that plagued the Clinton administration. Although no evidence of wrongdoing by the Clintons was discovered in the Whitewater affair itself, the investigation led to investigation of the Paula Jones' sexual harassment allegations and eventually to the investigation of Clinton's affair with Monica Lewinsky.

James McDougal: A financial partner with the Clintons in the Whitewater real estate venture and operator of the failed Madison Guaranty Savings and Loan, McDougal was convicted on eighteen counts of fraud having to do with bad loans made by his failed Madison Guaranty Savings and Loan.

Kenneth Starr: Independent counsel that headed the Whitewater investigation that eventually led to the impeachment of President Clinton

Paula Jones: Little Rock, Arkansas, woman that accused President Clinton of exposing himself to her when he had been governor of Arkansas (Kenneth Starr investigated the Jones case as part of the Whitewater investigation)

Kathleen Willey: Financially strapped widow and White House worker that claimed she was groped by President Clinton in the Oval Office in 1993 and whose allegations were contradicted by Linda Tripp

Linda Tripp: Federal Employee and friend of Monica Lewinsky that contacted the Whitewater investigators concerning the affair between President Clinton and Monica Lewinsky

Monika Lewinsky: Twenty-five-year-old White House intern that admitted to performing oral sex on President Clinton in the Oval Office

West Palm Beach County: In this Florida county in the 2000 election, a confusing butterfly ballot resulted in six thousand ballots in West Palm Beach county being double-punched for both Gore and Pat Buchanan, and another three thousand for Gore and Socialist candidate David McReynolds. In all, Gore's name was included in forty-six thousand such "over-votes" while Bush's name was included in only seventeen thousand.

Katherine Harris: This Florida secretary of state and Bush campaign worker arranged for the state of Florida to pay $4 million to a company called Database Technologies to go through Florida's voter rolls and remove any felons from the approved voter lists. Unfortunately, thousands of eligible voters with similar names to convicted felons, mostly minorities who typically vote Democrat, were also purged from the voter lists.

Chapter Review (cont'd)

Key Terms (cont'd)

Bush v. Gore: The lawsuit filed by George W. Bush to stop the Florida recounts ultimately gave him the electoral victory in 2000.

James Jeffords: Republican Senator from Vermont that abandoned the Republicans to become an Independent in January 2000 and give the Democrats a 50–49 majority in the Senate

John Ashcroft: George W. Bush's controversial Protestant fundamentalist attorney general that had lost his previous U.S. Senate reelection to an opponent who had died before the election

No Child Left Behind Act: George W. Bush's education reforms that focused on standardized testing to ensure accountability in the public schools

ANWR: Alaskan National Wildlife Reserve where President Bush, Vice President Cheney, and the Republicans favored drilling for oil and the Democrats opposed

Compassionate conservatism: Bush's campaign theme of 2000

9/11: Date of the worst terrorist attack in American history, orchestrated by Al Qaeda where nineteen Muslim men hijacked four jetliners, crashing two into the World Trade Center in New York, one into the Pentagon, and one into a field in Pennsylvania, with over three thousand people dying as a result

USA PATRIOT Act: Controversial act passed by Congress giving the president broad powers in the War on Terror, essentially eroding many of the criminal rights protections of the Bill of Rights

Taliban: Radical Islamist group in Afghanistan that controlled the government of Afghanistan at the time of the 9/11 attacks and was accused by the Bush administration of harboring terrorists, including Osama bin Laden.

Axis of Evil: President George W. Bush's reference to Iraq, Iran, and North Korea

Donald Rumsfeld: Defense Secretary that was in charge of the occupation of Iraq, but had no plans for an insurgency

Abu Ghraib: Notorious prison in Iraq, under Saddam Hussein, where American soldiers abused Iraqi prisoners

Max Cleland: U.S. Senator from Georgia, Vietnam War veteran and triple amputee who lost his Senate seat after Republican opponent Saxby Chambliss ran attack ads questioning his patriotism

Karl Rove: George W. Bush's political advisor and campaign manager, known for attack ads, smear campaigns, relentless propaganda, "dirty tricks," and winning

John McCain: U.S. Senator from Arizona, Vietnam veteran and former POW, who ran as the Republican presidential candidate in 2008, losing to Democrat Barack Obama

John Kerry: U.S. Senator from Massachusetts and Vietnam war veteran that became the Democratic presidential nominee in 2004 and narrowly lost to Republican George W. Bush

Howard Dean: Former governor of Vermont that ran for the Democratic presidential nomination in 2004, Dean was one of the first candidates to successfully use the internet for fundraising. Dean later became Chair of the Democratic National Committee.

Swift Boat Veterans for Truth: Attack ad financed by supporters of George W. Bush that questioned the patriotism of John Kerry, who served in Vietnam and was awarded three Purple Hearts, a Bronze Star, and a Silver Star

Key Terms (cont'd)

Matthew Dowd: Republican political analyst that argued in 2004 that the number of persuadable voters in America was only 3 percent–7 percent, and, consequently, a better Republican strategy would be to fire up the Republican base and ensure greater Republican voter turnout

Tom DeLay: Republican House Majority leader that resigned while under investigation for ethics violations

Jack Abramoff: Washington lobbyist with extensive access to the Bush administration and House Speaker Tom DeLay that was convicted of fraud in his representation of American Indian tribes

Hurricane Katrina: This devastating hurricane hit the Gulf Coast in August 2005 and flooded 80 percent of New Orleans. Over eighteen hundred people died in the hurricane, over 1500 of whom lived in Louisiana.

FEMA: Federal Emergency Management Agency whose response to Hurricane Katrina was viewed as inadequate by the public

Michael Brown: Head of FEMA when Hurricane Katrina hit the Gulf Coast and who was originally lauded by President Bush but then later fired when FEMA's response was viewed by the public as inadequate

Condoleeza Rice: National Security Advisor and then Secretary of State under George W. Bush, Rice is the first African American female to hold either position.

Barack Obama: First African-American president of the United States

Sarah Palin: Alaska governor and mother of five that was John McCain's running mate in the presidential election of 2008

Pop Quiz ▶ ▶ ▶

Chapter 32

1. Which of the following did Bill Clinton and George W. Bush have in common?
   a. Both of the "Baby boom" generation
   b. Rumors persisted of drug use in their youth
   c. Neither served in Vietnam
   d. All of the above

2. Which of the following do some historians believe harmed Bush's reelection efforts?
   a. The attacks and convention speech of Republican Pat Buchanan
   b. The crystal clarity of Bush's note cards
   c. Bush's illegal drug use
   d. Bush's marital indiscretions

Chapter Review (cont'd)

Pop Quiz (cont'd)

3. Which of the following is true of Clinton's fiscal policy in his first two years?
   a. Clinton's tax increases only affected the wealthiest 1.2 percent of Americans.
   b. Clinton's tax plan reduced taxes for the working poor and small businesses.
   c. Clinton's tax plan helped cut the federal deficit by $50 billion the first year and $40 billion the second year.
   d. All of the above

4. Clinton's political opponents were able to prevent his health care reforms by incorrectly labeling it as ___________.
   a. unconstitutional
   b. socialized medicine
   c. political corruption
   d. a whitewater fall

5. Which of the following is true of the "Contract with America?"
   a. The majority of Americans signed the contract.
   b. The majority of Americans supported the contract.
   c. The majority of Americans opposed the majority of the contract.
   d. The majority of Americans believed the contract to be a communist plot.

6. For what purpose was the North American Free Trade Agreement designed?
   a. create free trade between the U.S., Canada, and Mexico
   b. increase immigration from Mexico to the U.S.
   c. legalize medical marijuana in the U.S.
   d. stop illegal immigration from Mexico to the U.S.

7. Clinton's policy in Iraq included which of the following?
   a. a call for "regime change" in Iraq
   b. numerous cruise missile and bombing attacks
   c. support for Iraqi rebel groups aimed at deposing Saddam
   d. all of the above

Pop Quiz (cont'd)

8. In March 1999, President Clinton launched a bombing campaign against Serbia to halt the ethnic cleansing in __________.
   a. Bosnia
   b. Kosovo
   c. Chechnya
   d. Somalia

9. Why did the federal authorities lay siege to the Branch Davidian compound in 1993?
   a. Branch Davidians shot federal agents that attempted to serve them with a warrant.
   b. President Clinton was an atheist that hated Christians.
   c. President Clinton was trying to confiscate all the guns in America.
   d. They thought Timothy McVeigh was hiding there.

10. President Clinton responded to the Al Qaeda bombings in Kenya and Tanzania with __________.
    a. a strong statement of rebuke for terrorists
    b. a UN Resolution
    c. cruise missile attacks at Al Qaeda installations in the Sudan and Afghanistan
    d. all of the above

11. Independent Counsel Kenneth Starr investigated the Monica Lewinsky scandal as a component of which of the following?
    a. the Paula Jones case, which he was investigating as a component of the Whitewater case
    b. the Vince Foster murder case
    c. the Branch Davidian case
    d. the Gennifer Flowers case

12. George W. Bush's domestic policies included __________.
    a. tax cuts
    b. separation of church and state
    c. the removal of the federal government from education due to states' rights
    d. all of the above

Chapter Review (cont'd)

Pop Quiz (cont'd)

13. Which of the following were included in the problems with the Iraq invasion?
    a. The Bush administration did not prepare for an insurgency.
    b. No weapons of mass destruction were found.
    c. Although Bush declared the war over in May 2003, over one hundred thousand American troops remained in Iraq at the end of his presidency.
    d. All of the above

14. Which of the following did the Bush campaign do in the election of 2004?
    a. adopt the polarizing strategy of Matthew Dowd
    b. use "push-polling" tactics of questionable ethics against John McCain
    c. slander John Kerry's honorable military record with the Swift Boat Veteran's for Truth ad
    d. all of the above

15. The accomplishments of the Obama presidency included _________.
    a. the passage of an economic stimulus package
    b. the passage of health care reform
    c. the end of enhanced interrogation techniques
    d. all of the above

1. D	5. C	9. D	13. B
2. D	6. A	10. D	14. C
3. B	7. A	11. A	15. A
4. A	8. D	12. D	

The Declaration of Independence

When in the course of human events, it becomes necessary for one people to dissolve the political bands which have connected them with another, and to assume among the Powers of the earth, the separate and equal station to which the Laws of Nature and of Nature's God entitle them, a decent respect to the opinions of mankind requires that they should declare the causes which impel them to the separation.

We hold these truths to be self-evident, that all men are created equal, that they are endowed by their Creator with certain unalienable Rights, that among these are Life, Liberty and the pursuit of Happiness. That to secure these rights, Governments are instituted among Men, deriving their just Powers from the consent of the governed, That whenever any Form of Government becomes destructive of these ends, it is the Right of the People to alter or to abolish it, and to institute new Government, laying its foundation on such principles and organizing its Powers in such form, as to them shall seem most likely to effect their Safety and Happiness. Prudence, indeed, will dictate that Governments long established should not be changed for light and transient causes; and accordingly all experience hath shewn, that mankind are more disposed to suffer, while evils are sufferable, than to right themselves by abolishing the forms to which they are accustomed. But when a long train of abuses and usurpations, pursuing invariably the same object evinces a design to reduce them under absolute Despotism, it is their right, it is their duty, to throw off such Government, and to provide new Guards for their future security. Such has been the patient sufferance of these Colonies: and such is now the necessity which constrains them to alter their former Systems of Government. The history of the present King of Great Britain is a history of repeated injuries and usurpations, all having in direct object the Establishment of an absolute Tyranny over these States. To prove this, let Facts be submitted to a candid World:

He has refused his Assent to Laws, the most wholesome and necessary for the public good.

He has forbidden his Governors to pass Laws of immediate and pressing importance, unless suspended in their operation till his Assent should be obtained; and when so suspended, he has utterly neglected to attend to them.

He has refused to pass other Laws for the accommodation of large districts of people, unless those people would relinquish the right of Representation in the Legislature, a right inestimable to them and formidable to tyrants only.

He has called together legislative bodies at places unusual, uncomfortable, and distant from the depository of their Public Records, for the sole purpose of fatiguing them into compliance with his measures.

He has dissolved Representative Houses repeatedly, for opposing with manly firmness his invasions on the rights of the people.

He has refused for a long time, after such dissolutions, to cause others to be elected; whereby the Legislative Powers, incapable of the Annihilation, have returned to the People at large for their exercise; the State remaining in the mean time exposed to all the dangers of invasion from without, and the convulsions within.

He has endeavored to prevent the population of these States; for that purpose obstructing the Laws of Naturalization of Foreigners; refusing to pass others to encourage their migrations hither, and raising the conditions of new Appropriations of Lands.

He has obstructed the Administration of justice, by refusing his Assent to Laws for establishing Judiciary Powers.

He has made judges dependent on his Will alone, for the tenure of their offices, and the amount and payment of their salaries.

He has erected a multitude of New Offices, and sent hither swarms of Officers to harass our People, and eat out their substance.

He has kept among us, in times of peace, Standing Armies, without the consent of our legislature.

He has affected to render the Military independent of and superior to the Civil Power.

He has combined with others to subject us to a jurisdiction foreign to our constitution, and unacknowledged by our laws; giving his Assent to their acts of pretended legislation—

For quartering large bodies of armed troops among us;

For protecting them, by a mock Trial, from Punishment for any Murders which they should commit on the Inhabitants of these States;

For cutting off our Trade with all parts of the world;

For imposing Taxes on us without our Consent;

For depriving us in many cases, of the benefits of Trial by Jury;

For transporting us beyond Seas to be tried for pretended offences;

For abolishing the free System of English Laws in a neighboring Province, establishing therein an Arbitrary government, and enlarging its Boundaries so as to render it at once an example and fit instrument for introducing the same absolute rule into these Colonies;

For taking away our Charters, abolishing our most valuable Laws, and altering fundamentally the Forms of our Governments;

For suspending our own Legislatures, and declaring themselves invested with Power to legislate for us in all cases whatsoever.

He has abdicated Government here, by declaring us out of his Protection, and waging War against us.

He has plundered our seas, ravaged our Coasts, burnt our towns, and destroyed the lives of our people.

He is at this time transporting large armies of foreign mercenaries to compleat the works of death, desolation and tyranny, already begun with circumstances of Cruelty & perfidy, scarcely paralleled in the most barbarous ages, and totally unworthy the Head of a civilized nation.

He has constrained our fellow Citizens taken Captive on the high Seas to bear Arms against their Country, to become the executioners of their friends and Brethren, or to fall themselves by their Hands.

He has excited domestic insurrections amongst us, and has endeavoured to bring on the inhabitants of our frontiers, the merciless Indian Savages, whose known rule of warfare, is an undistinguished destruction of all ages, sexes and conditions.

In every stage of these Oppressions We have Petitioned for Redress in the most humble terms: Our repeated Petitions have been answered only by repeated injury. A Prince, whose character is thus marked by every act which may define a Tyrant, is unfit to be the ruler of a free People.

Nor have We been wanting in attentions to our British brethren. We have warned them from time to time of attempts by their legislature to extend an unwarrantable jurisdiction over us. We have reminded them of the circumstances of our emigration and settlement here. We have appealed to their native justice and magnanimity, and we have conjured them by the ties of our common kindred to disavow these usurpations, which, would inevitably interrupt our connections and correspondence. They too have been deaf to the voice of justice and of consanguinity. We must, therefore, acquiesce in the necessity, which denounces our Separation, and hold them, as we hold the rest of mankind, Enemies in War, in Peace, Friends.

We, therefore, the Representatives of the United States of America, in General Congress, Assembled, appealing to the Supreme judge of the world for the rectitude of our intentions, do, in the Name, and by Authority of the good People of these Colonies, solemnly publish and declare, That these United Colonies are, and of Right ought to be Free and Independent States; that they are Absolved from all Allegiance to the British Crown, and that all political connection between them and the State of Great Britain, is and ought to be totally dissolved; and that, as Free and Independent States, they have full Power to levy War, conclude Peace, contract Alliances, establish Commerce, and to do all other Acts and Things which independent States may of right do. And for the support of this Declaration, with a firm reliance on the Protection of Divine Providence, we mutually pledge to each other our Lives, our Fortunes and our sacred Honor.

The Constitution of the United States

We the people of the United States, in Order to form a more perfect Union, establish justice, insure domestic Tranquility, provide for the common defense, promote the general Welfare, and secure the Blessings of Liberty to ourselves and our Posterity, do ordain and establish this Constitution for the United States of America.

Article I

Section 1. All legislative Powers herein granted shall be vested in a Congress of the United States, which shall consist of a Senate and House of Representatives.

Section 2. 1. The House of Representatives shall be composed of Members chosen every second Year by the People of the several States, and the Electors in each State shall have the Qualifications requisite for Electors of the most numerous Branch of the State Legislature.

2. No person shall be a Representative who shall not have attained to the Age of twenty-five Years, and been seven Years a Citizen of the United States, and who shall not, when elected, be an Inhabitant of that State in which he shall be chosen.

3. Representatives and direct Taxes[1] shall be apportioned among the several States which may be included within this Union, according to their respective Numbers, which shall be determined by adding to the whole Number of free Persons, including those bound to Service for a Term of Years, and excluding Indians not taxed, three fifths of all other Persons.[2] The actual Enumeration shall be made within three Years after the first Meeting of the Congress of the United States, and within every subsequent Term of ten Years, in such Manner as they shall by Law direct. The Number of Representatives shall not exceed one for every thirty Thousand, but each State shall have at Least one Representative; and until such enumeration shall be made, the State of New Hampshire shall be entitled to chuse three, Massachusetts eight, Rhode Island and Providence Plantations one, Connecticut five, New York six, New Jersey four, Pennsylvania eight, Delaware one, Maryland six, Virginia ten, North Carolina five, South Carolina five, and Georgia three.

4. When vacancies happen in the Representation from any State, the Executive Authority thereof shall issue Writs of Election to fill such Vacancies.

5. The House of Representatives shall chuse their Speaker and other officers; and shall have the sole Power of Impeachment.

Section 3. 1. The Senate of the United States shall be composed of two Senators from each State, chosen by the Legislature thereof,[3] for six Years; and each Senator shall have one Vote.

2. Immediately after they shall be assembled in Consequence of the first Election, they shall be divided as equally as may be into three Classes. The Seats of the Senators of the first Class shall be vacated at the Expiration of the second Year, of the second Class at the Expiration of the fourth Year, and of the third Class at the Expiration of the sixth Year, so that one third may be chosen every second Year; and if Vacancies happen by Resignation, or otherwise, during the Recess of the Legislature of any State, the Executive thereof may make temporary Appointments until the next Meeting of the Legislature, which shall then fill such Vacancies.[4]

3. No Person shall be a Senator who shall not have attained to the Age of thirty Years, and been nine Years a Citizen of the United States, and who shall not, when elected, be an Inhabitant of that State for which he shall be chosen.

4. The Vice President of the United States shall be President of the Senate, but shall have no vote, unless they be equally divided.

5. The Senate shall chuse their other Officers, and also a President pro tempore, in the absence of the Vice President, or when he shall exercise the Office of President of the United States.

6. The Senate shall have the sole Power to try all Impeachments. When sitting for that purpose, they shall be on Oath or Affirmation. When the President of the United States is tried, the Chief justice shall preside: And no person shall be convicted without the Concurrence of two thirds of the Members present.

7. Judgment in Cases of impeachment shall not extend further than to removal from Office, and disqualification to hold and enjoy any Office of honor, Trust, or Profit under the United States: but the Party convicted shall nevertheless be liable and subject to Indictment, Trial, judgment and Punishment, according to Law.

Section 4. 1. The Times, Places and Manner of holding Elections for Senators and Representatives, shall be prescribed in each state by the Legislature thereof; but the Congress may at any time by Law make or alter such Regulations, except as to the Places of Chusing Senators.

2. The Congress shall assemble at least once in every Year, and such Meeting shall be on the first Monday in December, unless they shall by Law appoint a different Day.

Section 5. 1. Each House shall be the judge of the Elections, Returns and Qualifications of its own Members, and a Majority of each shall constitute a Quorum to do Business; but a smaller number may adjourn from day to day, and may be authorized to compel the Attendance of absent Members, in such manner, and under such Penalties, as each House may provide.

2. Each House may determine the Rules of its Proceedings, punish its Members for disorderly Behavior, and, with the Concurrence of two thirds, expel a Member.

3. Each House shall keep a journal of its Proceedings, and from time to time publish the same, excepting such Parts as may in their judgment require Secrecy; and the Yeas and Nays of the Members of either House on any question shall, at the Desire of one fifth of those Present, be entered on the journal.

4. Neither House, during the Session of Congress, shall, without the Consent of the other, adjourn for more than three days, nor to any other Place than that in which the two Houses shall be sitting.

Section 6. 1. The Senators and Representatives shall receive a Compensation for their Services, to be ascertained by Law, and paid out of the Treasury of the United States. They shall in all Cases, except Treason, Felony, and Breach of the Peace, be privileged from arrest during their Attendance at the Session of their respective Houses, and in going to and returning from the same; and for any Speech or Debate in either House, they shall not be questioned in any other Place.

2. No Senator or Representative shall, during the Time for which he was elected, be appointed to any civil office under the Authority of the United States, which shall have been created, or the Emoluments whereof shall have been increased, during such time; and no Person holding any Office under the United States shall be a Member of either House during his continuance in Office.

Section 7. 1. All Bills for raising Revenue shall originate in the House of Representatives; but the Senate may propose or concur with Amendments as on other bills.

2. Every Bill which shall have passed the House of Representatives and the Senate, shall, before it become a Law, be presented to the President of the United States; If he approve he shall sign it, but if not he shall return it, with his Objections, to that House in which it shall have originated, who shall enter the Objections at large on their journal, and proceed to reconsider it. If after such Reconsideration two thirds of that House shall agree to pass the bill, it shall be sent, together with the objections, to the other House, by which it shall likewise be reconsidered, and if approved by two thirds of that House, it shall become a Law. But in all such Cases the Votes of both Houses shall be determined by Yeas and Nays, and the Names of the Persons voting for and against the Bill shall be entered on the journal of each House respectively. If any Bill shall not be returned by the President within ten

[1] See the Sixteenth Amendment.

[2] See the Fourteenth Amendment.

Days (Sundays excepted) after it shall have been presented to him, the Same shall be a Law, in like Manner as if he had signed it, unless the Congress by their Adjournment prevent its Return, in which Case it shall not be a Law.

3. Every Order, Resolution, or Vote to which the Concurrence of the Senate and House of Representatives may be necessary (except on a question of Adjournment) shall be presented to the President of the United States; and before the Same shall take Effect, shall be approved by him, or being disapproved by him, shall be repassed by two thirds of the Senate and House of Representatives, according to the Rules and Limitations prescribed in the Case of a Bill.

Section 8. The Congress shall have Power

1. To lay and collect Taxes, Duties, Imposts and Excises, to pay the Debts and provide for the common Defense and general Welfare of the United States; but all Duties, Imposts and Excises shall be uniform throughout the United States;
2. To borrow money on the credit of the United States;
3. To regulate Commerce with foreign Nations, and among the several States, and with the Indian Tribes;
4. To establish an uniform Rule of Naturalization, and uniform Laws on the subject of Bankruptcies throughout the United States;
5. To coin Money, regulate the Value thereof, and of foreign Coin, and fix the Standard of Weights and Measures;
6. To provide for the Punishment of counterfeiting the Securities and current Coin of the United States;
7. To establish Post offices and post Roads;
8. To promote the Progress of Science and useful Arts, by securing for limited Times to Authors and inventors the exclusive Right to their respective Writings and Discoveries;
9. To constitute Tribunals inferior to the Supreme Court;
10. To define and punish Piracies and Felonies committed on the high Seas, and Offences against the Law of Nations;
11. To declare War, grant Letters of Marque and Reprisal, and make Rules concerning Captures on Land and Water;
12. To raise and support Armies, but no Appropriation of Money to that Use shall be for a longer Term than two Years;
13. To provide and maintain a Navy;
14. To make Rules for the Government and Regulation of the land and naval forces;
15. To provide for calling forth the Militia to execute the Laws of the Union, suppress Insurrections and repel invasions;
16. To provide for organizing, arming, and disciplining the Militia, and for governing such Part of them as may be employed in the Service of the United States, reserving to the States respectively, the Appointment of the Officers, and the Authority of training the Militia according to the discipline prescribed by Congress;
17. To exercise exclusive Legislation in all Cases whatsoever, over such District (not exceeding ten Miles square) as may, by Cession of particular States, and the acceptance of Congress, become the Seat of Government of the United States, and to exercise like Authority over all Places purchased by the Consent of the Legislature of the State in which the Same shall be, for the Erection of Forts, Magazines, Arsenals, dock Yards, and other needful Buildings; And
18. To make all Laws which shall be necessary and proper for carrying into Execution the foregoing Powers, and all other Powers vested by this Constitution in the government of the United States, or in any Department or Officer thereof.

Section 9. 1. The Migration or Importation of such Persons as any of the States now existing shall think proper to admit, shall not be prohibited by the Congress prior to the Year one thousand eight hundred and eight, but a tax or duty may be imposed on such Importation, not exceeding ten dollars for each Person.

2. The Privilege of the Writ of Habeas Corpus shall not be suspended, unless when in Cases of Rebellion or Invasion the public Safety may require it.

3. No Bill of Attainder or ex post facto Law shall be passed.

4. No capitation, or other direct, Tax shall be laid unless in Proportion to the Census or Enumeration herein before directed to be taken.[5]

[3] See the Seventeenth Amendment.

[4] See the Seventeenth Amendment.

5. No Tax or Duty shall be laid on Articles exported from any State.
6. No Preference shall be given by any Regulation of commerce or Revenue to the Ports of one State over those of another: nor shall Vessels bound to, or from, one state, be obliged to enter, clear, or pay Duties in another.
7. No Money shall be drawn from the Treasury, but in Consequence of Appropriations made by Law; and a regular Statement and Account of the Receipts and Expenditures of all public Money shall be published from time to time.
8. No Title of Nobility shall be granted by the United States: And no Person holding any Office of Profit or Trust under them, shall, without the Consent of the Congress, accept of any present, Emolument, Office, or Title, of any kind whatever, from any King, Prince, or Foreign State.
Section 10. 1. No State shall enter into any Treaty, Alliance, or Confederation; grant Letters of Marque and Reprisal; coin Money; emit Bills of Credit; make any Thing but gold and silver Coin a Tender in Payment of Debts; pass any Bill of Attainder, ex post facto Law, or Law impairing the obligation of Contracts, or grant any Title of Nobility.
2. No State shall, without the Consent of the Congress, lay any Imposts or Duties on Imports or Exports, except what may be absolutely necessary for executing its inspection Laws: and the net Produce of all Duties and Imposts, laid by any State on Imports or Exports, shall be for the Use of the Treasury of the United States; and all such Laws shall be subject to the Revision and Control of the Congress.
3. No State shall, without the Consent of Congress, lay any duty of Tonnage, keep Troops, or Ships of War in time of peace, enter into any Agreement or Compact with another State, or with a foreign Power, or engage in War, unless actually invaded, or in such imminent Danger as will not admit of delay.

Article II

Section 1. 1. The executive Power shall be vested in a President of the United States of America. He shall hold his Office during the Term of four Years, and, together with the Vice President, chosen for the same Term, be elected, as follows:
2. Each State shall appoint, in such Manner as the Legislature thereof may direct, a Number of Electors, equal to the whole Number of Senators and Representatives to which the State may be entitled in the Congress; but no Senator or Representative, or Person holding an Office of Trust or Profit under the United States, shall be appointed an Elector.
The Electors shall meet in their respective States, and vote by Ballot for two persons, of whom one at least shall not be an Inhabitant of the same State with themselves. And they shall make a List of all the Persons voted for, and of the Number of Votes for each; which List they shall sign and certify, and transmit sealed to the Seat of the Government of the United States, directed to the President of the Senate. The President of the Senate shall, in the Presence of the Senate and House of Representatives, open all the Certificates, and the Votes shall then be counted. The Person having the greatest Number of Votes shall be the President, if such Number be a Majority of the whole Number of Electors appointed; and if there be more than one who have such Majority, and have an equal Number of Votes, then the House of Representatives shall immediately chuse by Ballot one of them for President; and if no Person have a Majority, then from the five highest on the List the said House shall in like Manner chuse the President. But in chusing the President, the votes shall be taken by States, the Representation from each State having one Vote; a quorum for this Purpose shall consist of a Member or Members from two thirds of the States, and a Majority of all the States shall be necessary to a Choice. In every Case, after the Choice of the President, the Person having the greatest Number of Votes of the Electors shall be the Vice President. But if there should remain two or more who have equal votes, the Senate shall chuse from them by Ballot the Vice President.[6]
3. The Congress may determine the time of chusing the Electors, and the Day on which they shall give their Votes; which Day shall be the same throughout the United States.
4. No person except a natural born Citizen, or a Citizen of the United States, at the time of the Adoption of this Constitution, shall be eligible to the Office of President; neither shall any Person be eligible to that office who shall not have attained to the Age of thirty-five Years, and been fourteen Years a Resident within the United States.
5. In Case of the Removal of the President from Office, or

of his Death, Resignation, or Inability to discharge the Powers and Duties of the said Office, the same shall devolve on the Vice President, and the Congress may by Law provide for the Case of Removal, Death, Resignation, or Inability, both of the President and Vice President, declaring what Officer shall then act as President, and such Officer shall act accordingly, until the Disability be removed, or a President shall be elected.

6. The President shall, at stated Times, receive for his Services a Compensation, which shall neither be increased nor diminished during the Period for which he shall have been elected, and he shall not receive within that Period any other Emolument from the United States, or any of them.

7. Before he enter on the execution of his Office, he shall take the following Oath or Affirmation: "I do solemnly swear (or affirm) that I will faithfully execute the Office of President of the United States, and will, to the best of my Ability, preserve, protect, and defend the Constitution of the United States."

Section 2. 1. The President shall be Commander in Chief of the Army and Navy of the United States, and of the Militia of the several States, when called into the actual Service of the United States; he may require the Opinion, in writing, of the principal Officer in each of the executive Departments, upon any subject relating to the Duties of their respective Offices, and he shall have Power to Grant Reprieves and Pardons for Offences against the United States, except in Cases of Impeachment.

2. He shall have Power, by and with the Advice and Consent of the Senate, to make Treaties, provided two thirds of the Senators present concur; and he shall nominate, and by and with the Advice and Consent of the Senate, shall appoint Ambassadors, other public Ministers and Consuls, judges of the supreme Court, and all other Officers of the United States, whose Appointments are not herein otherwise provided for, and which shall be established by Law: but the Congress may by Law vest the Appointment of such inferior Officers, as they think proper, in the President alone, in the Courts of Law, or in the Heads of Departments.

3. The President shall have Power to fill up all Vacancies that may happen during the Recess of the Senate, by granting Commissions which shall expire at the End of their next Session.

Section 3. He shall from time to time give to the Congress Information of the State of the Union, and recommend to their Consideration such Measures as he shall judge necessary and expedient; he may, on extraordinary occasions, convene both Houses, or either of them, and in Case of Disagreement between them, with respect to the Time of Adjournment, he may adjourn them to such Time as he shall think proper; he shall receive Ambassadors and other public Ministers; he shall take Care that the Laws be faithfully executed, and shall Commission all the officers of the United States.

Section 4. The President, Vice President and all civil Officers of the United States, shall be removed from Office on Impeachment for, and Conviction of, Treason, Bribery, or other high Crimes and Misdemeanors.

Article III

Section 1. The judicial Power of the United States, shall be vested in one supreme Court, and in such inferior Courts as the Congress may from time to time ordain and establish. The judges, both of the supreme and inferior Courts, shall hold their Offices during good Behaviour, and shall, at stated Times, receive for their Services, a Compensation, which shall not be diminished during their Continuance in Office.

Section 2. 1. The judicial Power shall extend to all Cases, in Law and Equity, arising under this Constitution, the Laws of the United States, and treaties made, or which shall be made, under their Authority;—to all Cases affecting Ambassadors, other public ministers and consuls; to all cases of admiralty and maritime jurisdiction;—to Controversies to which the United States shall be a party;[7]—to Controversies between two or more States; between a State and citizens of another States;—between Citizens of different States;—between Citizens of the same State claiming Lands under Grants of different States, and between a State, or the Citizens thereof, and foreign States, Citizens or Subjects.

2. In all Cases affecting Ambassadors, other public Ministers and Consuls, and those in which a State shall be Party, the supreme Court shall have original Jurisdiction. In all the other Cases before mentioned, the supreme Court shall have appel-

late jurisdiction, both as to Law and Fact, with such Exceptions, and under such Regulations as the Congress shall make.
3. The trial of all Crimes, except in Cases of Impeachment, shall be by jury; and such Trial shall be held in the State where the said Crimes shall have been committed; but when not committed within any State, the trial shall be at such Place or Places as the Congress may by Law have directed.
Section 3. 1. Treason against the United States, shall consist only in levying War against them, or in adhering to their Enemies, giving them Aid and Comfort. No Person shall be convicted of Treason unless on the testimony of two Witnesses to the same overt Act, or on Confession in open Court.
2. The Congress shall have power to declare the Punishment of Treason, but no Attainder of Treason shall work Corruption of Blood, or Forfeiture except during the Life of the Person attainted.

Article IV

Section 1. Full Faith and Credit shall be given in each State to the public Acts, Records, and judicial Proceedings of every other State. And the Congress may by general Laws prescribe the Manner in which such Acts, Records and Proceedings shall be proved, and the Effect thereof.
Section 2. 1. The Citizens of each State shall be entitled to all Privileges and Immunities of Citizens in the several States.[8]
2. A Person charged in any State with Treason, Felony, or other Crime, who shall flee from justice, and be found in another State, shall on demand of the executive Authority of the State from which he fled, be delivered up, to be removed to the State having jurisdiction of the crime.
3. No Person held to Service or Labour in one State, under the Laws thereof, escaping into another, shall, in Consequence of any Law or Regulation therein, be discharged from such Service or Labour, but shall be delivered up on Claim of the Party to whom such Service or Labour may be due.[9]
Section 3. 1. New States may be admitted by the Congress into this Union; but no new State shall be formed or erected within the Jurisdiction of any other State, nor any State be formed by the junction of two or more States, or parts of States, without the Consent of the Legislatures of the States concerned as well as of the Congress.
2. The Congress shall have Power to dispose of and make all needful Rules and Regulations respecting the Territory or other Property belonging to the United States; and nothing in this Constitution shall be so construed as to Prejudice any Claims of the United States, or of any particular State.
Section 4. The United States shall guarantee to every State in this Union a Republican Form of Government, and shall protect each of them against Invasion; and on Application of the Legislature, or of the Executive (when the Legislature cannot be convened) against domestic Violence.

Article V

The Congress, whenever two-thirds of both Houses shall deem it necessary, shall propose Amendments to this Constitution, or, on the Application of the Legislatures of two-thirds of the several States, shall call a Convention for proposing Amendments, which, in either Case, shall be valid to all Intents and Purposes, as part of this Constitution, when ratified by the Legislatures of three-fourths of the several States, or by Conventions in three-fourths thereof, as the one or the other Mode of Ratification may be proposed by the Congress; Provided that no Amendment which may be made prior to the Year One thousand eight hundred and eight shall in any Manner affect the first and fourth Clauses in the Ninth Section of the first Article; and that no State, without its Consent, shall be deprived of its equal Suffrage in the Senate.

Article VI

1. All Debts contracted and Engagements entered into, before the Adoption of this Constitution, shall be as valid against the United States under this Constitution, as under the Confederation.[10]
2. This Constitution, and the Laws of the United States which shall be made in Pursuance thereof; and all Treaties made, or which shall be made, under the Authority of the United States, shall be the supreme Law of the Land; and the judges in every State shall be bound thereby, any Thing in the Constitution or Laws of any State to the Contrary notwithstanding.

[5] See the Sixteenth Amendment.

3. The Senators and Representatives before mentioned, and the Members of the several State Legislatures and all executive and judicial Officers, both of the United States and of the several States, shall be bound by Oath or Affirmation, to support this Constitution; but no religious Test shall ever be required as a qualification to any Office or public Trust under the United States.

Article VII

The Ratification of the Conventions of nine States, shall be sufficient for the Establishment of this Constitution between the States so ratifying the same.

Done in Convention by the Unanimous Consent of the States present the Seventeenth Day of September in the Year of our Lord one thousand seven hundred and Eighty seven, and of the independence of the United States of America the Twelfth. In Witness whereof We have hereunto subscribed our Names.

[Names omitted]

* * *

Articles in addition to, and amendment of, the Constitution of the United States of America, proposed by Congress, and ratified by the legislatures of the several States, pursuant to the fifth article of the original Constitution.

Amendment I

[December 15, 1791]

Congress shall make no law respecting an establishment of religion, or prohibiting the free exercise thereof, or abridging the freedom of speech, or of the press; or the right of the people peaceably to assemble, and to petition the Government for a redress of grievances.

Amendment II

[December 15, 1791]

A well regulated Militia, being necessary to the security of a free State, the right of the people to keep and bear Arms shall not be infringed.

Amendment III

[December 15, 1791]

No Soldier shall, in time of peace, be quartered in any house, without the consent of the owner, nor in time of war, but in a manner to be prescribed by law.

Amendment IV

[December 15, 1791]

The right of the people to be secure in their persons, houses, papers, and effects, against unreasonable searches and seizures, shall not be violated, and no Warrants shall issue, but upon probable cause, supported by Oath or affirmation, and particularly describing the place to be searched, and the persons or things to be seized.

Amendment V

[December 15, 1791]

No person shall be held to answer for a capital or otherwise infamous crime, unless on a presentment or indictment of a Grand jury, except in cases arising in the land or naval forces, or in the Militia, when in actual service in time of War or public danger; nor shall any person be subject for the same offence to be twice put in jeopardy of life or limb; nor shall be compelled in any criminal case to be a witness against himself, nor be deprived of life, liberty, or property, without due process of law; nor shall private property be taken for public use, without just compensation.

Amendment VI

[December 15, 1791]

In all criminal prosecutions, the accused shall enjoy the right to a speedy and public trial, by an impartial jury of the State and district wherein the crime shall have been committed, which district shall have been previously ascertained by law, and to be informed of the nature and cause of the accusation; to be confronted with the witnesses against him; to have compulsory

[6] Superseded by the Twelfth Amendment.

process for obtaining witnesses in his favor, and to have the Assistance of Counsel for his defense.

Amendment VII

[December 15, 1791]

In suits at common law, where the value in controversy shall exceed twenty dollars, the right of trial by jury shall be preserved, and no fact tried by a jury, shall be otherwise reexamined in any Court of the United States, than according to the rules of the common law.

Amendment VIII

[December 15, 1791]

Excessive bail shall not be required, nor excessive fines imposed, nor cruel and unusual punishments inflicted.

Amendment IX

[December 15, 1791]

The enumeration in the Constitution, of certain rights, shall not be construed to deny or disparage others retained by the people.

Amendment X

[December 15, 1791]

The powers not delegated to the United States by the Constitution, nor prohibited by it to the States, are reserved to the States respectively, or to the people.

Amendment XI

[January 8, 1798]

The judicial power of the United States shall not be construed to extend to any suit in law or equity, commenced or prosecuted against one of the United States by Citizens of another State, or by Citizens or Subjects of any Foreign State.

Amendment XII

[September 25, 1804]

The Electors shall meet in their respective States and vote by ballot for President and Vice-President, one of whom, at least, shall not be an inhabitant of the same State with themselves; they shall name in their ballots the person voted for as President, and in distinct ballots the person voted for as Vice-President, and they shall make distinct lists of all persons voted for as President, and of all persons voted for as Vice-President, and of the number of votes for each, which lists they shall sign and certify, and transmit sealed to the seat of the government of the United States, directed to the President of the Senate; The President of the Senate shall, in the presence of the Senate and House of Representatives, open all the certificates and the votes shall then be counted; The person having the greatest number of votes for President, shall be the President, if such number be a majority of the whole number of Electors appointed; and if no person have such majority, then from the persons having the highest numbers not exceeding three on the list of those voted for as President, the House of Representatives shall choose immediately, by ballot, the President. But in choosing the President, the votes shall be taken by states, the representation from each state having one vote; a quorum for this purpose shall consist of a member or members from two-thirds of the states, and a majority of all the states shall be necessary to a choice. And if the House of Representatives shall not choose a President whenever the right of choice shall devolve upon them, before the fourth day of March next following, then the Vice-President shall act as President, as in the case of the death or other constitutional disability of the President. The person having the greatest number of votes as Vice President, shall be the Vice-President, if such number be a majority of the whole number of Electors appointed, and if no person have a majority, then from the two highest numbers on the list, the Senate shall choose the Vice-President; a quorum for the purpose shall consist of two-thirds of the whole number of Senators, and a majority of the whole number shall be necessary to a choice. But no person constitutionally ineligible to the office of President shall be eligible to that of Vice-President of the United States.

Amendment XIII

[December 18, 1865]

Section 1. Neither slavery nor involuntary servitude, except as a punishment for crime whereof the party shall have been duly convicted, shall exist within the United States, or any place subject to their jurisdiction.

Section 2. Congress shall have power to enforce this article by appropriate legislation.

Amendment XIV

[July 28, 1868]

Section 1. All persons born or naturalized in the United States, and subject to the jurisdiction thereof, are citizens of the United States and of the State wherein they reside. No State shall make or enforce any law which shall abridge the privileges or immunities of citizens of the United States; nor shall any State deprive any person of life, liberty, or property, without due process of law; nor deny to any person within its jurisdiction the equal protection of the laws.

Section 2. Representatives shall be apportioned among the several States according to their respective numbers, counting the whole number of persons in each State, excluding Indians not taxed. But when the right to vote at any election for the choice of electors for President and Vice-President of the United States, Representatives in Congress, the Executive and Judicial officers of a State, or the members of the Legislature thereof, is denied to any of the male inhabitants of such State, being twenty-one years of age, and citizens of the United States, or in any way abridged, except for participation in rebellion, or other crime, the basis of representation therein shall be reduced in the proportion which the number of such male citizens shall bear to the whole number of male citizens twenty-one years of age in such State.

Section 3. No person shall be a Senator or Representative in Congress, or elector of President and Vice-President, or hold any office, civil or military, under the United States, or under any State, who, having previously taken an oath, as a member of Congress, or as an officer of the United States, or as a member of any State legislature, or as an executive or judicial officer of any State, to support the Constitution of the United States, shall have engaged in insurrection or rebellion against the same, or given aid or comfort to the enemies thereof. But Congress may by a vote of two-thirds of each House, remove such disability.

Section 4. The validity of the public debt of the United States, authorized by law, including debts incurred for payment of pensions and bounties for services in suppressing insurrection or rebellion, shall not be questioned. But neither the United States nor any State shall assume or pay any debt or obligation incurred in aid of insurrection or rebellion against the United States, or any claim for the loss or emancipation of any slave; but all such debts, obligations, and claims shall be held illegal and void.

Section 5. The Congress shall have the power to enforce, by appropriate legislation, the provisions of this article.

Amendment XV

[March 30, 1870]

Section 1. The right of citizens of the United States to vote shall not be denied or abridged by the United States or by any State on account of race, color, or previous condition of servitude

Section 2. The Congress shall have power to enforce this article by appropriate legislation.

Amendment XVI

[February 25, 1913]

The Congress shall have power to lay and collect taxes on incomes, from whatever source derived, without apportionment among the several States, and without regard to any census or enumeration.

[7] See the Eleventh Amendment.

[8] See the Fourteenth Amendment, Section 1.

Amendment XVII

[May 31, 1913]

The Senate of the United States shall be composed of two Senators from each State, elected by the people thereof, for six years; and each Senator shall have one vote. The electors in each State shall have the qualifications requisite for electors of the most numerous branch of the State legislatures.

When vacancies happen in the representation of any State in the Senate, the executive authority of such State shall issue writs of election to fill such vacancies: Provided, That the legislature of any State may empower the executive thereof to make temporary appointments until the people fill the vacancies by election as the legislature may direct.

This amendment shall not be so construed as to affect the election or term of any Senator chosen before it becomes valid as part of the Constitution.

Amendment XVIII

[January 29, 1919]

Section 1. After one year from the ratification of this article the manufacture, sale, or transportation of intoxicating liquors within, the importation thereof into, or the exportation thereof from the United States and all territory subject to the jurisdiction thereof for beverage purposes is hereby prohibited.

Section 2. The Congress and the several States shall have concurrent power to enforce this article by appropriate legislation.

Section 3. This article shall be inoperative unless it shall have been ratified as an amendment to the Constitution by the legislatures of the several States, as provided in the Constitution, within seven years from the date of the submission hereof to the States by the Congress.

Amendment XIX

[August 26, 1920]

The right of citizens of the United States to vote shall not be denied or abridged by the United States or by any State on account of sex.

Congress shall have power to enforce this article by appropriate legislation.

Amendment XX

[January 23, 1933]

Section 1. The terms of the President and Vice-President shall end at noon on the 20th day of January, and the terms of Senators and Representatives at noon on the 3d day of January, of the years in which such terms would have ended if this article had not been ratified; and the terms of their successors shall then begin.

Section 2. The Congress shall assemble at least once in every year, and such meeting shall begin at noon on the 3rd day of January, unless they shall by law appoint a different day.

Section 3. If, at the time fixed for the beginning of the term of the President, the President elect shall have died, the Vice-President elect shall become President. If a President shall not have been chosen before the time fixed for the beginning of his term, or if the President elect shall have failed to qualify, then the Vice-President elect shall act as President until a President shall have qualified; and the Congress may by law provide for the case wherein neither a President elect nor a Vice-President elect shall have qualified, declaring who shall then act as President, or the manner in which one who is to act shall be selected, and such person shall act accordingly until a President or Vice-President shall have qualified.

Section 4. The Congress may by law provide for the case of the death of any of the persons from whom the House of Representatives may choose a President whenever the right of choice shall have devolved upon them, and for the case of the death of any of the persons from whom the Senate may choose a Vice-President whenever the right of choice shall have devolved upon them.

Section 5. Sections 1 and 2 shall take effect on the 15th day of October following the ratification of this article.

Section 6. This article shall be inoperative unless it shall have been ratified as an amendment to the Constitution by the legislatures of three-fourths of the several States within seven years from the date of its submission.

[9] See the Thirteenth Amendment

[10] See the Fourteenth Amendment, Sec. 4..

Amendment XXI

[December 5, 1933]

Section 1. The eighteenth article of amendment to the Constitution of the United States is hereby repealed.

Section 2. The transportation or importation into any State, Territory, or possession of the United States for delivery or use therein of intoxicating liquors, in violation of the laws thereof, is hereby prohibited.

Section 3. This article shall be inoperative unless it shall have been ratified as an amendment to the Constitution by conventions in the several States, as provided in the Constitution, within seven years from the date of the submission hereof to the States by the Congress.

Amendment XXII

[March 1, 1951]

Section 1. No person shall be elected to the office of the President more than twice, and no person who has held the office of President, or acted as President, for more than two years of a term to which some other person was elected President shall be elected to the office of the President more than once.

But this Article shall not apply to any person holding the office of President when this Article was proposed by the Congress, and shall not prevent any person who may be holding the office of President or acting as President, during the term within which this Article becomes operative from holding the office of President or acting as President during the remainder of such term.

Section 2. This article shall be inoperative unless it shall have been ratified as an amendment to the Constitution by the legislatures of three-fourths of the several states within seven years from the date of its submission to the states by Congress.

Amendment XXIII

[March 29, 1961]

Section 1. The District constituting the seat of Government of the United States shall appoint in such manner as the Congress may direct:

A number of electors of President and Vice President equal to the whole number of Senators and Representatives in Congress to which the District would be entitled if it were a State, but in no event more than the least populous State; they shall be in addition to those appointed by the States, but they shall be considered, for the purposes of the election of President and Vice President, to be electors appointed by a State; and they shall meet in the District and perform such duties as provided by the twelfth article of amendment.

Section 2. The Congress shall have power to enforce this article by appropriate legislation.

Amendment XXIV

[January 23, 1964]

Section 1. The right of citizens of the United States to vote in any primary or other election for President or Vice President, for electors for President or Vice President, or for Senator or Representative in Congress, shall not be denied or abridged by the United States or any State by reason of failure to pay any poll tax or other tax.

Section 2. The Congress shall have the power to enforce this article by appropriate legislation.

Amendment XXV

[February 10, 1967]

Section 1. In case of the removal of the President from office or of his death or resignation, the Vice President shall become President.

Section 2. Whenever there is a vacancy in the office of the Vice President, the President shall nominate a Vice President who shall take office upon confirmation by a majority vote of both houses of Congress.

Section 3. Whenever the President transmits to the President pro tempore of the Senate and the Speaker of the House of Representatives his written declaration that he is unable to discharge the powers and duties of his office, and until he transmits to them a written declaration to the contrary, such powers and duties shall be discharged by the Vice President as Acting President.

Section 4. Whenever the Vice President and a majority of either the principal officers of the executive departments, or of such other body as Congress may by law provide, transmit to the President pro tempore of the Senate and the Speaker of the House of Representatives their written declaration that the President is unable to discharge the powers and duties of his office, the Vice President shall immediately assume the powers and duties of the office as Acting President.

Thereafter, when the President transmits to the President pro tempore of the Senate and the Speaker of the House of Representatives his written declaration that no inability exists, he shall resume the powers and duties of his office unless the Vice President and a majority of either the principal officers of the executive departments, or of such other body as Congress may by law provide, transmit within four days to the President pro tempore of the Senate and the Speaker of the House of Representatives their written declaration that the President is unable to discharge the powers and duties of his office. Thereupon Congress shall decide the issue, assembling within forty-eight hours for that purpose if not in session. If the Congress, within twenty-one days after receipt of the latter written declaration, or, if Congress is not in session, within twenty-one days after Congress is required to assemble, determines by two-thirds vote of both houses that the President is unable to discharge the powers and duties of his office, the Vice President shall continue to discharge the same as Acting President; otherwise, the President shall resume the powers and duties of his office.

Amendment XXVI

[June 30, 1971]

Section 1. The right of citizens of the United States, who are eighteen years of age or older, to vote shall not be denied or abridged by the United States or by any state on account of age.

Section 2. The Congress shall have power to enforce this article by appropriate legislation.

Amendent XXVII

[May 7, 1992]

No law varying the compensation for the services of the Senators and Representatives shall take effect, until an election of Representatives shall have intervened.

PRESIDENTIAL ELECTIONS

YEAR	NUMBER OF STATES	CANDIDATES	PARTY	POPULAR VOTE*	ELECTORAL VOTE**	PERCENTAGE OF POPULAR VOTE
1789	11	GEORGE WASHINGTON	No party designations		69	
		John Adams			34	
		Other Candidates			35	
1792	15	GEORGE WASHINGTON	No party designations		132	
		John Adams			77	
		George Clinton			50	
		Other Candidates			5	
1796	16	JOHN ADAMS	Federalist		71	
		Thomas Jefferson	Democratic-Republican		68	
		Thomas Pinckney	Federalist		59	
		Aaron Burr	Democratic-Republican		30	
		Other Candidates			48	
1800	16	THOMAS JEFFERSON	Democratic-Republican		73	
		Aaron Burr	Democratic-Republican		73	
		John Adams	Federalist		65	
		Charles C. Pinckney	Federalist		64	
		John Jay	Federalist			
1804	17	THOMAS JEFFERSON	Democratic-Republican		162	
		Charles C. Pinckney	Federalist		14	
1808	17	JAMES MADISON	Democratic-Republican		122	
		Charles C. Pinckney	Federalist		47	
		George Clinton	Democratic-Republican		6	
1812	18	JAMES MADISON	Democratic-Republican		128	
		DeWitt Clinton	Federalist		89	
1816	19	JAMES MONROE	Democratic-Republican		183	
		Rufus King	Federalist		34	
1820	24	JAMES MONROE	Democratic-Republican		231	
		John Quincy Adams	Independent Republican		1	
1824	24	JOHN QUINCY ADAMS		108,740	84	30.5
		Andrew Jackson		153,544	99	43.1
		William H. Crawford		46,618	41	13.1
		Henry Clay		47,136	37	13.2
1828	24	ANDREW JACKSON	Democrat	647,286	178	56.0
		John Ouincy Adams	National Republican	508,064	83	44.0
1832	24	ANDREW JACKSON	Democrat	687,502	219	55.0
		Henry Clay	National Republican	530,189	49	42.4
		William Wirt	Anti-Masonic	33,108	7	2.6
		John Floyd	National Republican		11	
1836	26	MARTIN VAN BUREN	Democrat	765,483	170	50.9
		William H. Harrison	Whig		73	
		Hugh L. White	Whig	739,795	26	49.1
		Daniel Webster	Whig		14	
		W. P. Mangum	Whig		11	
1840	26	WILLIAM H. HARRISON	Whig	1,274,624	234	53.1
		Martin Van Buren	Democrat	1,127,781	60	46.9
1844	26	JAMES K. POLK	Democrat	1,338,464	170	49.6
		Henry Clay	Whig	1,300,097	105	48.1
		James G. Birney	Liberty	62,300		2.3
1848	30	ZACHARY TAYLOR	Whig	1,360,967	163	47.4
		Lewis Cass	Democrat	1,222,342	127	42.5
		Martin Van Buren	Free Soil	291,263		10.1
1852	31	FRANKLIN PIERCE	Democrat	1,601,117	254	50.9
		Winfield Scott	Whig	1,385,453	42	44.1
		John P. Hale	Free Soil	155,825		5.0

* Percentage of popular vote given for any election year may not total 100 percent because candidates receiving less than 1 percent of the popular vote have been omitted.

** Prior to the passage of the Twelfth Amendment in 1904, the electoral college voted for two presidential candidates; the runner-up became Vice President. Data from *Historical Statistics of the United States, Colonial Times to 1957* (1961), pp. 682–883, and *The World Almanac*.

PRESIDENTIAL ELECTIONS *(continued)*

YEAR	NUMBER OF STATES	CANDIDATES	PARTY	POPULAR VOTE*	ELECTORAL VOTE**	PERCENTAGE OF POPULAR VOTE
1856	31	JAMES BUCHANAN	Democrat	1,832,955	174	45.3
		John C. Frémont	Republican	1,339,932	114	33.1
		Millard Fillmore	American	871,731	8	21.6
1860	33	ABRAHAM LINCOLN	Republican	1,865,593	180	39.8
		Stephen A. Douglas	Democrat	1,382,713	12	29.5
		John C. Breckinridge	Democrat	848,356	72	18.1
		John Bell	Constitutional Union	592,906	39	12.6
1864	36	ABRAHAM LINCOLN	Republican	2,206,938	212	55.0
		George B. McClellan	Democrat	1,803,787	21	45.0
1868	37	ULYSSES S. GRANT	Republican	3,013,421	214	52.7
		Horatio Seymour	Democrat	2,706,829	80	47.3
1872	37	ULYSSES S. GRANT	Republican	3,596,745	286	55.6
		Horace Greeley	Democrat	2,843,446	*	43.9
1876	38	RUTHERFORD B. HAYES	Republican	4,036,572	185	48.0
		Samuel J. Tilden	Democrat	4,284,020	184	51.0
1880	38	JAMES A. GARFIELD	Republican	4,453,295	214	48.5
		Winfield S. Hancock	Democrat	4,414,082	155	48.1
		James B. Weaver	Greenback-Labor	308,578		3.4
1884	38	GROVER CLEVELAND	Democrat	4,879,507	219	48.5
		James G. Blaine	Republican	4,850,293	182	48.2
		Benjamin F. Butler	Greenback-Labor	175,370		1.8
		John P. St. John	Prohibition	150,369		1.5.
1888	38	BENJAMIN HARRISON	Republican	5,447,129	233	47.9
		Grover Cleveland	Democrat	5,537,857	168	48.6
		Clinton B. Fisk	Prohibition	249,506		2.2
		Anson J. Streeter	Union Labor	146,935		1.3
1892	44	GROVER CLEVELAND	Democrat	5,555,426	277	46.1
		Benjamin Harrison	Republican	5,182,690	145	43.0
		James B. Weaver	People's	1,029,846	22	8.5
		John Bidwell	Prohibition	264,133		2.2
1896	45	WILLIAM MCKINLEY	Republican	7,102,246	271	51.1
		William J. Bryan	Democrat	6,492,559	176	47.7
1900	45	WILLIAM MCKINLEY	Republican	7,218,491	292	51.7
		William J. Bryan	Democrat; Populist	6,356,734	155	45.5
		John C. Woolley	Prohibition	208,914		1.5
1904	45	THEODORE ROOSEVELT	Republican	7,628,461	336	57.4
		Alton B. Parker	Democrat	5,084,223	140	37.6
		Eugene V. Debs	Socialist	402,283		3.0
		Silas C. Swallow	Prohibition	258,536		1.9
1908	46	WILLIAM H. TAFT	Republican	7,675,320	321	51.6
		William J. Bryan	Democrat	6,412,294	162	43.1
		Eugene V. Debs	Socialist	420,793		2.8
		Eugene W. Chafin	Prohibition	253,840		1.7
1912	48	WOODROW WILSON	Democrat	6,296,547	435	41.9
		Theodore Roosevelt	Progressive	4,118,571	88	27.4
		William H. Taft	Republican	3,486,720	8	23.2
		Eugene V. Debs	Socialist	900,672		6.0
		Eugene W. Chafin	Prohibition	206,275		1.4
1916	48	WOODROW WILSON	Democrat	9,127,695	277	49.4
		Charles E. Hughes	Republican	8,533,507	254	46.2
		A. L. Benson	Socialist	585,113		3.2
		J. Frank Hanly	Prohibition	220,506		1.2
1920	48	WARREN G. HARDING	Republican	16,143,407	404	60.4
		James M. Cox	Democrat	9,130,328	127	34.2
		Eugene V. Debs	Socialist	919,799		3.4
		P. P. Christensen	Farmer-Labor	265,411		1.0

*Because of the death of Greeley, Democratic electors scattered their votes.

PRESIDENTIAL ELECTIONS *(CONTINUED)*

YEAR	NUMBER OF STATES	CANDIDATES	PARTY	POPULAR VOTE*	ELECTORAL VOTE**	PERCENTAGE OF POPULAR VOTE
1924	48	CALVIN COOLIDGE	Republican	15,718,211	382	54.0
		John W. Davis	Democrat	8,385,283	136	28.8
		Robert M. La Follette	Progressive	4,831,289	13	16.6
1928	48	HERBERT C. HOOVER	Republican	21,391,993	444	58.2
		Alfred E. Smith	Democrat	15,016,169	87	40.9
1932	48	FRANKLIN D. ROOSEVELT	Democrat	22,809,638	472	57.4
		Herbert C. Hoover	Republican	15,758,901	59	39.7
		Norman Thomas	Socialist	881,951		2.2
1936	48	FRANKLIN D. ROOSEVELT	Democrat	27,752,869	523	60.8
		Alfred M. Landon	Republican	16,674,665	8	36.5
		William Lemke	Union	882,479		1.9
1940	48	FRANKLIN D. ROOSEVELT	Democrat	27,307,819	449	54.8
		Wendell L. Wilkie	Republican	22,321,018	82	44.8
1944	48	FRANKLIN D. ROOSEVELT	Democrat	25,606,585	432	53.5
		Thomas E. Dewey	Republican	22,014,745	99	46.0
1948	48	HARRY S. TRUMAN	Democrat	24,105,812	303	49.5
		Thomas E. Dewey	Republican	21,970,065	189	45.1
		J. Strom Thurmond	States' Rights	1,169,063	39	2.4
		Henry A. Wallace	Progressive	1,157,172		2.4
1952	48	DWIGHT D. EISENHOWER	Republican	33,936,234	442	55.1
		Adlai E. Stevenson	Democrat	27,314,992	89	44.4
1956	48	DWIGHT D. EISENHOWER	Republican	35,590,472	457*	57.6
		Adlai E. Stevenson	Democrat	26,022,752	73	42.1
1960	50	JOHN F. KENNEDY	Democrat	34,227,096	303**	49.9
		Richard M. Nixon	Republican	34,108,546	219	49.6
1964	50	LYNDON B. JOHNSON	Democrat	42,676,220	486	61.3
		Barry M. Goldwater	Republican	26,860,314	52	38.5
1968	50	RICHARD M. NIXON	Republican	31,785,480	301	43.4
		Hubert H. Humphrey	Democrat	31,275,165	191	42.7
		George C. Wallace	American Independent	9,906,473	46	13.5
1972	50	RICHARD M. NIXON***	Republican	47,165,234	520	60.6
		George S. McGovern	Democrat	29,168,110	17	37.5
1976	50	JIMMY CARTER	Democrat	40,828,929	297	50.1
		Gerald R. Ford	Republican	39,148,940	240	47.9
		Eugene McCarthy	Independent	739,256		
1980	50	RONALD REAGAN	Republican	43,201,220	489	50.9
		Jimmy Carter	Democrat	34,913,332	49	41.2
		John B. Anderson	Independent	5,581,379		
1984	50	RONALD REAGAN	Republican	53,428,357	525	59.0
		Walter F. Mondale	Democrat	36,930,923	13	41.0
1988	50	GEORGE BUSH	Republican	48,901,046	426	53.4
		Michael Dukakis	Democrat	41,809,030	111	45.6
1992	50	WILLIAM J. CLINTON	Democrat	44,909,806	370	43.0
		George Bush	Republican	39,104,550	168	37.5
		H. Ross Perot	Independent	19,742,240		18.9
		Andre Marrau	Libertarian	291,631		0.3
1996	50	WILLIAM J. CLINTON	Democrat	47,402,357	379	49.2
		Robert Dole	Republican	39,198,755	159	40.7
		H. Ross Perot	Reform	8,085,402		8.4
		Ralph Nader	Green	685,128		0.7
		Harry Browne	Libertarian	485,798		0.5

*Walter B. Jones received 1 electoral vote.
**Harry F. Byrd received 15 electoral votes.
***Resigned August 9,1974; Vice President Gerald R. Ford became President.

PRESIDENTIAL ELECTIONS *(continued)*

YEAR	NUMBER OF STATES	CANDIDATES	PARTY	POPULAR VOTE*	ELECTORAL VOTE**	PERCENTAGE OF POPULAR VOTE
2000	50	GEORGE W. BUSH	Republican	50,459,624	271	47.9
		Albert Gore, Jr.	Democrat	51,003,238	266	48.4
		Ralph Nader	Green	2,882,985		2.7
		Patrick Buchanan	Reform	449,120		0.4
		Harry Browne	Libertarian	384,440		0.4
2004	50	GEORGE W. BUSH	Republican	62,040,610	286	58.9
		John F. Kerry	Democrat	59,028,111	251	56.1
		Ralph Nader	Independent/Reform	463,653		0.0
2008	50	BARACK OBAMA	Democrat	69,456,898	365	52.9
		John McCain	Republican	59,934,814	173	45.6
		Ralph Nader	Independent	738,771		0.6
		Bob Barr	Libertarian	523,686		0.4

Photo Credits

Chapter 15: iStockphoto, 1; iStockphoto, 1; iStockphoto, 1; Library of Congress, 2; Corbis Images, 2; Wikipedia photo, 2, Corbis Images, 2; Wikipedia photo, 3; Wikipedia photo, 4; Corbis Images, 5; Corbis Images, 9; Library of Congress, 10; Wikipedia photo, 11; Corbis Images, 12; Wikipedia photo, 13; Wikipedia photo, 14; Wikipedia photo, 15 (left); Library of Congress, 15 (right); Wikipedia photo, 16; Library of Congress, 17; Wikipedia photo, 21; Wikipedia photo, 22

Chapter 16: iStockphoto, 29; iStockphoto, 29; iStockphoto, 29; Library of Congress, 30; Wikipedia photo, 30; Library of Congress, 30; Wikipedia photo, 30; Wikipedia photo, 30; Wikipedia photo, 34; Library of Congress, 36; Wikipedia photo, 37; Library of Congress, 38; Wikipedia photo, 41; Wikipedia photo, 42; Wikipedia photo, 48; Wikipedia photo, 52; Wikipedia photo, 53; Wikipedia photo, 54; Wikipedia photo, 55; Corbis, 58; Wikipedia photo, 61; Wikipedia photo, 63; Corbis Images, 64; Wikipedia photo, 66; Wikipedia photo, 70; Corbis Images, 73; Wikipedia photo, 74; Wikipedia photo, 75; Wikipedia photo, 77; Corbis Images, 78

Chapter 17: iStockphoto, 89; iStockphoto, 89; iStockphoto, 89; Library of Congress, 90; Wikipedia photo, 90; Wikipedia photo, 90; Corbis Images, 90; Library of Congress, 90; Wikipedia photo, 93; Wikipedia photo, 95; Library of Congress, 96; Wikipedia photo, 97; Corbis Images, 98; Library of Congress, 100; Wikipedia photo, 102; Wikipedia photo, 105; Wikipedia photo, 109; Wikipedia photo, 110; Library of Congress, 111; Library of Congress, 115; Corbis Images, 117; Corbis Images, 118

Chapter 18: iStockphoto, 127; iStockphoto, 127; iStockphoto, 127; Library of Congress, 128; Wikipedia photo, 128; Corbis Images, 128; Wikipedia photo, 128; Wikipedia photo, 128; Wikipedia photo, 128; Library of Congress, 130; Wikipedia photo, 133; Wikipedia photo, 134; Corbis Images, 141; Wikipedia photo, 143; Library of Congress, 144; Wikipedia photo, 145; Corbis Images, 146; Library of Congress, 147; Wikipedia photo, 150; Corbis Images, 151; Wikipedia photo, 152; Wikipedia photo, 155; Wikipedia photo, 156; Wikipedia photo, 157; Library of Congress, 160; Wikipedia photo, 162; Wikipedia photo, 165; Corbis Images, 171; Library of Congress (both), 174; Wikipedia photo, 175; Wikipedia photo, 178

Chapter 19: iStockphoto, 191; iStockphoto, 191; iStockphoto, 191; Library of Congress, 192; Corbis Images, 192; Wikipedia photo, 192; Wikipedia photo, 192; Corbis Images, 192; Library of Congress, 192; Corbis Images, 193; Wikipedia photo, 194; Wikipedia photo, 195; Library of Congress, 198; Corbis Images, 200; Wikipedia photo, 201; Wikipedia photo, 202; Library of Congress, 203; Wikipedia photo, 205; Wikipedia photo, 207; Library of Congress, 208; Library of Congress, 209; Corbis Images, 211; Wikipedia photo, 214; Wikipedia photo, 215; Corbis Images, 217; Wikipedia photo, 218; Library of Congress, 220; Wikipedia photo, 224

Chapter 20: iStockphoto, 239; iStockphoto, 239; iStockphoto, 239; iStockphoto, 240; Wikipedia photo, 240; Wikipedia photo, 240; Wikipedia photo, 240; Wikipedia photo, 240; Corbis Images, 240; Wikipedia photo, 241; Corbis Images, 243; Wikipedia photo, 246; Wikipedia photo, 250; Wikipedia photo, 252; Wikipedia photo, 253; Wikipedia photo, 255; Library of Congress, 257; Wikipedia photo, 258; Library of Congress, 260; Library of Congress, 265; Wikipedia photo, 266; Library of Congress, 268; Library of Congress, 269; Corbis Images, 270, Library of Congress, 271

Chapter 21: iStockphoto, 285; iStockphoto, 285; iStockphoto, 285; iStockphoto, 286; Wikipedia photo, 286; Corbis Images (inset), 286; Library of Congress, 286; Wikipeda photo, 286; Corbis Images, 286; Corbis Images, 289; Library of Congress, 291; Library of Congress, 292; Corbis Images, 293; Wikipedia photo, 295; Wikipedia photo, 298; Corbis Images, 300; Library of Congress, 302; Corbis Images, 303; Wikipedia photo, 305; Library of Congress, 307; Wikipedia photo, 310; Library of Congress, 312

Chapter 22: iStockphoto, 325; iStockphoto, 325; iStockphoto, 325; iStockphoto, 326; Library of Congress, 326; Corbis Images, 326; Wikipedia photo, 326; Wikipedia photo, 326; Corbis Images, 328; Library of Congress, 331; Library of Congress, 332; Library of Congress, 334; Wikipedia photo, 337; Corbis Images, 339; Corbis Images, 340; Wikipedia photo, 343; Wikipedia photo, 344; Wikipedia photo, 346; Corbis Images, 349; Wikipedia, 351

Chapter 23: iStockphoto, 363; iStockphoto, 363; iStockphoto, 363; iStockphoto, 364; Library of Congress, 364; Wikipedia photo, 364; Corbis Images, 364; Library of Congress, 364; Corbis Images, 368; Wikipedia photo, 369; Corbis Images, 371; Wikipedia photo, 374; Corbis Images, 375; Wikipedia photo, 378; Corbis Images, 379; Library of Congress, 381; Wikipedia photo, 389; Library of Congress, 390; Wikipedia photo, 391; Corbis, 399

Chapter 24: iStockphoto, 413; iStockphoto, 413; iStockphoto, 413; iStockphoto, 414; Wikipedia photo, 414; Wikipedia photo, 414; Wikipedia photo, 414; Library of Congress, 414; Wikipedia photo, 414; Wikipedia photo, 416; Library of Congress, 418; Wikipedia photo, 420; Library of Congress, 422; Wikipedia photo, 423; Wikipedia photo, 425; Corbis Images, 427; Wikipedia photo, 428; Wikipedia photo, 429; Wikipedia photo, 430; Wikipedia photo, 432; Corbis Images, 436; Library of Congress, 437; Corbis Images, 438; Corbis Images, 439; Wikipedia photo, 440; Library of Congress, 442; Library of Congress, 445; Corbis Images, 446; Wikipedia photo, 447

Chapter 25: iStockphoto, 459; iStockphoto, 459; iStockphoto, 459; iStockphoto, 460; iStockphoto, 460; Corbis Images, 460; Wikipedia photo, 460; Wikipedia photo, 463; Corbis Images, 464; Corbis Images, 465; Corbis Images, 469; Wikipedia photo, 470; Corbis Images, 471; Library of Congress, 474; Wikipedia photo, 475; Corbis Images, 478; Wikipedia photo, 479; Library of Congress, 481; iStockphoto, 483; Library of Congress, 487; Corbis Images, 491; Wikipedia photo, 493

Chapter 26: iStockphoto, 507; iStockphoto, 507; iStockphoto, 507; iStockphoto, 508; Wikipedia photo, 508; Wikipedia photo, 508; Wikipedia photo, 508; Corbis Images, 508; AP Photo, 508; ; Wikipedia photo, 509; Wikipedia photo, 510; Wikipedia photo, 511; Library of Congress, 513; Wikipedia photo, 514; Library of Congress, 516; Corbis Images, 519; Wikipedia photo, 520; Corbis Images, 521; Corbis Images, 529; Corbis Images, 530; Wikipedia photo, 532; Wikipedia photo, 533; Library of Congress, 534; Wikipedia photo, 539; AP Photo, 541; Library of Congress, 544; Wikipedia photo, 545; Wikipedia photo, 548; Wikipedia photo, 550; Library of Congress, 551; Wikipedia photo, 553; Wikipedia photo, 555; Wikipedia photo, 556

Chapter 27: iStockphoto, 571; iStockphoto, 571; iStockphoto, 571; iStockphoto, 572; Wikipedia photo, 572; Wikipedia photo, 572; Wikipedia photo, 572; Wikipedia photo, 572; Library of Congress, 574; Wikipedia photo, 575; Wikipedia photo, 578; Wikipedia photo, 582; Wikipedia photo, 586; Wikipedia photo, 588; Wikipedia photo, 591; Wikipedia photo, 594; Library of Congress, 597; Wikipedia photo, 603; Wikipedia photo, 606; Wikipedia photo, 609; Wikipedia photo, 610; Wikipedia photo, 612

Chapter 28: iStockphoto, 631; iStockphoto, 631; iStockphoto, 631; iStockphoto, 632; Wikipedia Photo, 632; Wikipedia Photo, 632; Wikipedia Photo, 632; Wikipedia Photo, 633; Wikipedia Photo, 644; Wikipedia Photo, 645

Chapter 29: iStockphoto, 661; iStockphoto, 661; iStockphoto, 661; iStockphoto, 662; Wikipedia Photo, 662; Wikipedia Photo, 662; Wikipedia Photo, 662; Wikipedia Photo, 663; Wikipedia Photo, 667; Wikipedia Photo, 669; Wikipedia Photo, 671; Wikipedia Photo, 672; Wikipedia Photo, 673; Wikipedia Photo, 680; Wikipedia Photo, 693; Wikipedia Photo, 696; Wikipedia Photo, 700; Wikipedia Photo, 702; Wikipedia Photo, 708

Chapter 30: iStockphoto, 731; iStockphoto, 731; iStockphoto, 731; iStockphoto, 732; Wikipedia Photo, 732; Wikipedia Photo, 732; Wikipedia Photo, 732; Wikipedia Photo, 732; Wikipedia Photo, 734; Wikipedia Photo, 737; Wikipedia Photo, 739; Wikipedia Photo, 740; Wikipedia Photo, 744; Wikipedia Photo, 746; Wikipedia Photo, 748; Library of Congress, 749; Wikipedia Photo, 752; Wikipedia Photo, 757; Wikipedia Photo, 758; Wikipedia Photo, 760; Wikipedia Photo, 761; Wikipedia Photo, 763; Wikipedia Photo, 768

Chapter 31: iStockphoto, 781; iStockphoto, 781; iStockphoto, 781; iStockphoto, 782; Wikipedia photo, 782; Wikipedia photo, 782; Wikipedia photo, 782; Wikipedia photo,; 782; Wikipedia photo, 783; Wikipedia photo, 784; Wikipedia photo, 786; Wikipedia photo, 790; Wikipedia photo, 791; Wikipedia photo, 792; Wikipedia photo, 793; AP Photo, 797; Wikipedia photo, 803; AP Photo, 806; Wikipedia photo, 808; Wikipedia photo, 810; Wikipedia photo, 811; Wikipedia photo, 814; AP Photo, 815; AP Photo, 816

Chapter 32: iStockphoto, 831; iStockphoto, 831; iStockphoto, 831; iStockphoto, 832; AP Photo, 832; Wikipedia Photo, 832; AP Photo, 832; Wikipedia Photo, 832; Wikipedia Photo, 832; Wikipedia Photo, 834; Wikipedia Photo, 835; Wikipedia Photo, 837; Wikipedia Photo, 839; AP Photo, 841; Wikipedia Photo, 848; AP Photo, 850; Wikipedia Photo, 851; AP Photo, 852; Wikipedia Photo, 853; Wikipedia Photo, 855; AP Photo, 858; Wikipedia Photo, 859; AP Photo, 861; Wikipedia Photo, 864; AP Photo, 865; Wikipedia Photo, 866; Wikipedia Photo, 867; Wikipedia Photo, 868; Wikipedia Photo, 870; Wikipedia Photo, 872; Wikipedia Photo, 873; AP Photo, 875; Wikipedia Photo, 876

Index

C

D

E

F

M

N

O

P

Q

R

Y